# Random House
# English-Spanish
# English-Spanish
# Dictionary

## Second Edition

Margaret H. Raventós, M.A.
*Special Lecturer in Spanish at the*
*University of Manchester*

*Revised and Updated by*
David L. Gold
*Doctor in Romance Philology*
*University of Barcelona*

RANDOM HOUSE
NEW YORK

**Library of Congress Cataloging-in-Publication Data**
Raventós, Margaret H. (Margaret Hambleton)
    Random House Spanish–English, English–Spanish dictionary / Margaret H. Raventós; revised and updated by David L. Gold.—2nd ed.
        p. cm.
    ISBN 0-375-40483-X (hc).—ISBN 0-375-70436-1 (pbk.)
    1. Spanish language—Dictionaries—English. 2. English language—Dictionaries—Spanish. I. Gold, David L. II. Title.
    PC4640.R32 1999
    463´.21—dc21                                                                99-10228
                                                                                    CIP

Visit the Random House Reference Web site at www.randomwords.com

Typeset and printed in the United States of America.

Second Edition

April 2001
ISBN: 0-375-40483-X (Hardcover)
9 8 7 6 5 4

ISBN: 0-375-70436-1 (Paperback)
9 8 7 6 5 4 3

New York Toronto London Sydney Auckland

# Contents

# Preface

## New Second Edition

This is a revised Second Edition of *Random House Spanish–English English–Spanish Dictionary,* first published in 1995. New to this edition are pronunciations for all Spanish and English main entries, using IPA (International Phonetic Alphabet) symbols. The IPA symbols are explained in the pronunciation key for English on page viii and for Spanish on page xiv. Also included in this dictionary are detailed guides to the pronunciation of both languages.

## Selection of Vocabulary

The aim of this dictionary is to cover as much current vocabulary as possible, as well as certain terms found in standard works of modern Spanish and English literature.

This dictionary includes items often omitted in other bilingual dictionaries—road and street signs, for example—though few things could be as frustrating (and, sometimes, as dangerous) as seeing such signs but not knowing what they mean (in this dictionary, all kinds of public notices are enclosed by the symbols << >> in Spanish and by quotation marks in English). Also, many vocabulary items consisting of more than one word have been covered here (see for instance **do** in the English–Spanish section).

## Spanish Spelling and Alphabetization

On January 1, 1959, the Spanish language academies changed certain spelling rules and on April 27, 1994, they eliminated **ch** and **ll** as separate letters of the alphabet. Thus, whereas words like **chico** and **chocolate** were formerly alphabetized under their own letter (**ch,** which came between **c** and **d**) and words like **llamar** and **llegar** were formerly alphabetized under their own letter (**ll,** which came between **l** and **m**), words containing **ch** or **ll,** in whatever part of the word they may appear, are now alphabetized as they would be in English (**chico** therefore now appears under **c** and **llegar** under **l**).

## Field Labels

Only essential field labels are given in this dictionary. For example, the label *medicine* or *pathology* is unnecessary at **flebitis** "phlebitis" (in the Spanish–English section) because both the Spanish and English words refer only to the medical condition so called in those languages.

In contrast to that entry, we do need a label at **foca** "seal" (in the Spanish–English section) because English **seal** has several meanings and only the zoological one is intended here. English speakers looking up **foca** thus need the label *zoology* (Spanish speakers need no label because they know that **foca** is the name of an animal, and so they will correctly assume that **seal** is intended only in its zoological sense).

## Regional Labels for Spanish

Regional labels are given in this dictionary when a less than universal usage is found in a certain region or country. A regional label should be interpreted as meaning that the usage so labeled is found in that particular place, but it may also be found elsewhere. For instance, the regional label *Mexican* means that the usage so labeled is found in Mexico, but further research would be necessary to determine whether the usage is present or absent in other countries. The label *West. Hem.* is used for Spanish terms that are in general use throughout the Western Hemisphere.

## Subentries

If a main entry head is repeated in a subentry in exactly the same form, it is abbreviated to its first letter (for instance, at **fin** in the Spanish–English section we find **a f. de,** which stands for **a fin de**). If the main entry head appears in any other form, the full form is given in the subentry (thus, at **fin,** the subentry head **a fines de** is spelled without abbreviation).

## Irregular Spanish Verbs and the Direction "See . . ."

If a Spanish verb is irregular, it has been treated in one of two ways: either its principal parts are shown (see for example the end of the entry for **caber**) or you are referred to an analogous irregular verb for guidance (see for example the end of the entry for **comparecer,** where you are directed to **conocer**). Thus, since the irregular form **conozco** is shown at **conocer** (it being irregular in the sense that it has a **z**), you may infer that **comparecer** has the irregular form **comparezco.**

One of the consequences of the changes in Spanish spelling is that a new kind of orthographically irregular verb has come into existence (for example, **ahijar, ahincar, ahitar, ahuchar, ahumar, ahusar, cohibir, desahuciar, prohibir, prohijar, rehilar, rehusar, sahumar, sobrehilar,** and **trashumar**).

If "See . . ." is all you find at an entry, you are being directed to a synonym. Thus, "**descompasarse** See **descomedirse**" means that the translations of **descomedirse** are those of **descompasarse** too.

## Spanish Equivalents of "you"

Today's Spanish, when taken as a whole, has at least six equivalents of "you": **tú, vos, usted** (abbreviated to **Vd.**), **su merced** (all of which are used in addressing one person), **ustedes** (abbreviated to **Vds.**), **vosotros, vosotras,** and **sus mercedes** (all used in addressing more than one person).

When **you** occurs in this dictionary, usually only one of those words has been chosen to translate it, though three are never used here: **su merced, sus mercedes,** because they are now limited to only a small area of the Spanish-speaking world (the Cundinamarca Savanna, in Colombia) and even there they are now obsolescent, and **vos,** because the verb forms corresponding to this pronoun often vary from country to country.

Usually, the selection of one pronoun or another in this dictionary has been arbitrary, in which case any of the others could just as easily have been chosen. For example, for **How are you?** the translation "¿Cómo está Vd.?" is offered, yet any of the other pronouns could appear instead (with, in certain cases, a different verb form, for instance "¿Cómo están Vds.?").

In certain cases, however, not all pronouns (whether actually used or just implicit) would be appropriate. For example, among the translations of **please** . . . are imperative forms of **servirse.** . . . Because **servirse** in this sense is a formal usage (found mostly in impersonal writing like application blanks), it is not found in any familiar form of the imperative. The dictionary therefore gives ¡**sírvase** . . . ! (where the understood subject is **usted,** a formal pronoun). It could also have given ¡**sírvanse** . . . ! (where the understood subject is **ustedes,** likewise a formal pronoun), but not any form in which the subject were an informal pronoun.

## Masculine and Feminine, Male and Female

As women engage in more and more activities once the domain of men, a growing number of Spanish nouns formerly used only in the masculine gender are being used in the feminine too. This dictionary thus labels **nauta, paracaidista, púgil, pugilista, recluta, reservista,** and **seminarista,** for example, as both masculine and feminine (the gender to be chosen depending on the gender of the person in question). For the user's convenience, the gender of Spanish nouns is indicated not only in the Spanish–English section but also in the English–Spanish one.

Many sample Spanish phrases and sentences in this dictionary can refer to people of either gender. For example, under **wish** in the English–Spanish section the sample sentence **I wished him a Merry Christmas** is translated "Le deseé unas Pascuas muy felices" and "Le felicité las Pascuas." Since they both also mean "I wished her a Merry Christmas," the sentence could as easily have contained **her** rather than **him.** In this dictionary, male and female references have been chosen randomly, hopefully in about equal number.

In other cases, a slight change is needed to turn a male reference into a female one or vice versa. For instance, **He was within an inch of being killed** (under **within,** in the English–Spanish section) is rendered by "Por poco le matan." Changing **he** to **she** and **le** to **la** will yield a correct equivalence referring to a female. With just an elementary knowledge of both languages, users of this dictionary will be able to make the necessary changes and thus have at their disposal many more sample phrases and sentences than it supplies.

# Símbolos de Pronunciacíon por los Sonidos del inglés

# Pronunciation Symbols for the Sounds of English

| Símbolos del AFI / IPA Symbols | Ejemplos / Key Words |
|---|---|
| /æ/ | *Eng.* hat |
| /ei/ | *Eng.* stay; *Fr.* cité; *Ger.* bequem; *It.* fréccia; *Sp.* reina |
| /ɛə/ [followed by /r/] | *Eng.* hair; *Fr.* frère; *Ger.* mehr; *It.* mercante; *Sp.* ver |
| /ɑ/ | *Eng.* father; *Fr.* tasse; *Ger.* Vater; *It.* pasta; *Sp.* casa |
| /ɛ/ | *Eng.* bet; *Fr.* gazelle; *Ger.* Bett; *It.* freschezza; *Sp.* entre |
| /i/ | *Eng.* bee; *Fr.* difficile; *Ger.* Wiegen; *It.* limone; *Sp.* vida |
| /ɪə/ [followed by /r/] | *Eng.* hear; *Fr.* rire; *Ger.* hier |
| /ɪ/ | *Eng.* sit; *Ger.* ist |
| /ai/ | *Eng.* try; *Ger.* zeigen; *It.* operaio; *Sp.* ay |
| /ɒ/ | *Eng.* hot |
| /o/ | *Eng.* boat; *Fr.* chapeau; *Ger.* Mond |
| /ɔ/ | *Eng.* saw; *Fr.* donner; *Ger.* doch; *It.* oglio; *Sp.* nota |
| /ɔi/ | *Eng.* toy; *Ger.* Deutsch; *Sp.* hoy |
| /ʊ/ | *Eng.* book |
| /u/ | *Eng.* too; *Fr.* tout; *Ger.* tun; *It.* inutile; *Sp.* luna |
| /au/ | *Eng.* cow; *Ger.* aus; *Sp.* pausa |
| /ʌ/ | *Eng.* up |
| /ɜ/ [followed by /r/] | *Eng.* burn; *Fr.* fleur; *Ger.* böse |
| /ə/ | *Eng.* alone; *Fr.* demain; *Ger.* stehen |
| /ᵊ/ | *Eng.* fire (fiᵊr); *Fr.* bastille |
| /æ̃/, /ɔ̃/, /ɛ̃/, /ɑ̃/ [A tilde over a vowel shows that it is nasalized] | As in *Fr.* un bon vin blanc |
| /b/ | *Eng.* boy; *Fr.* bête; *Ger.* backen; *It.* buio; *Sp.* boca |
| /tʃ/ | *Eng.* child; *It.* cibo; *Sp.* mucho |
| /d/ | *Eng.* dad; *Fr.* danse; *Ger.* dieser; *It.* destra; *Sp.* doy |
| /f/ | *Eng.* for; *Fr.* fête; *Ger.* fahren; *It.* fretta; *Sp.* fecha |
| /g/ | *Eng.* give; *Fr.* garde; *Ger.* gut; *It.* seguito; *Sp.* gato |

| Símbolos del AFI<br>IPA Symbols | Ejemplos<br>Key Words |
|---|---|
| /h/ | *Eng.* happy; *Ger.* heben; *It.* hascisc |
| /dʒ/ | *Eng.* just; *It.* giugno |
| /k/ | *Eng.* kick; *Fr.* capable; *Ger.* Kirche; *It.* amichevole; *Sp.* kilogramo |
| /l/ | *Eng.* love; *Fr.* lait; *Ger.* lieben; *It.* lira; *Sp.* libro |
| /m/ | *Eng.* mother; *Fr.* manger; *Ger.* Mann; *It.* meandro; *Sp.* limbo |
| /n/ | *Eng.* now; *Fr.* noble; *Ger.* nach; *It.* nulla; *Sp.* noche |
| /ŋ/ | *Eng.* sing; *Ger.* singen; *It.* vengo |
| /p/ | *Eng.* pot; *Fr.* parfum; *Ger.* Post; *It.* pace; *Sp.* papa |
| /r/ | *Eng.* read; *Fr.* rouge; *Ger.* Rat; *It.* ricco; *Sp.* para |
| /s/ | *Eng.* see; *Fr.* santé; *Ger.* essen; *It.* sérpo; *Sp.* hasta |
| /ʃ/ | *Eng.* shop; *Fr.* chercher; *Ger.* Schlaf; *It.* scelto |
| /t/ | *Eng.* ten; *Fr.* tête; *Ger.* Teil; *It.* topo; *Sp.* tomar |
| /θ/ | *Eng.* thing; *Sp.* (in Spain) cerdo |
| /ð/ | *Eng.* father; *Sp.* codo |
| /v/ | *Eng.* victory; *Fr.* vie; *Ger.* was; *It.* voi; *Sp.* verdad |
| /w/ | *Eng.* witch; *Fr.* oui; *It.* guardare |
| /y/ | *Eng.* yes; *Fr.* yeux; *Ger.* jung; *Sp.* yacer |
| /z/ | *Eng.* zipper; *Fr.* zéro; *Ger.* Sieg |
| /ʒ/ | *Eng.* pleasure; *Fr.* jeune |

# Los sonidos del inglés americano

## Vocales y diptongos

**a**  Cuando representa el sonido /æ/, se pronuncia más cerrada que la *a* de *paro* (por ejemplo: **act, at, bat, hat, marry**); también se encuentra este sonido en palabras deletreadas con: -ah- (d*ah*lia), -ai- (pl*ai*d), -al- (h*al*f), -au- (l*au*gh), -ua- (g*ua*rantee).

**a**  Cuando representa el sonido /ei/, se pronuncia más cerrada que la *e* de *hablé* y como si fuera seguido de *i* (por ejemplo: **age, gate, rate**); también se encuentra este sonido en palabras deletreadas con: -ai- (r*ai*n, *ai*r), -aigh- (str*aigh*t), -au- (g*au*ge), -ay- (s*ay*), -ea- (st*ea*k), -ei- (v*ei*l, w*ei*gh), -ey- (ob*ey*).

**a** /ɑ/  Equivale aproximadamente a la *a* de *sentado* y *bajo* (por ejemplo: **ah, father, part**); también se encuentra este sonido en palabras deletreadas con: -al- (c*al*m), -e(r)- (s*er*geant), -ea(r)- (h*ear*t), -ua- (g*ua*rd).

**a** /ə/  Equivale aproximadamente a la *e* de las palabras francesas *de* y *le* (por ejemplo: **alone, about**); también se encuentra este sonido en palabras deletreadas con: -e- (syst*e*m), -i- (eas*i*ly), -o- (gallop), -u- (circ*u*s), -y- (mart*y*r).

**e** /ɛ/  Equivale aproximadamente a la *e* de *templo* y *perro* (por ejemplo: **edge, set, merry**); también se encuentra este sonido en palabras deletreadas con: a-, -a- (*a*ny, m*a*ny), -ai- (s*ai*d), -ay- (s*ay*s), -ea- (l*ea*ther), -ei- (h*ei*fer), -eo- (j*eo*pardy), -ie- (fr*ie*nd).

**e** /i/  Equivale aproximadamente a la *i* de *Chile* (por ejemplo: **be, equal, secret**); también se encuentra este sonido en palabras deletreadas con: ea- *(ea*ch, t*ea*), -ee- (f*ee*, k*ee*p), -ei- (rec*ei*ve), -eo- (p*eo*ple), -ey- (k*ey*), -ie- (f*ie*ld), -y (cit*y*).

**i** /ɪ/  Se pronuncia menos cerrada que la *i* de *Chile* (por ejemplo: **if, big, fit, mirror**); también se encuentra este sonido en palabras deletreadas con: e- (*E*ngland), -ee- (b*ee*n), -ei- (counterf*ei*t), -ia- (carr*ia*ge), -ie- (s*ie*ve), -o- (w*o*man), (b)u(s)- (b*u*siness), -y- (s*y*mpathetic).

**i** /ai/  Equivale aproximadamente a la *ai* de *aire, baile* (por ejemplo: **bite, ice, pirate**); también se encuentra este sonido en palabras deletreadas con: ais- (*ai*sle), -ei- (h*ei*ght, st*ei*n), -eye- *(eye)*, -ie (p*ie*), -igh (h*igh*), is- (*i*sland), -uy (b*uy*), -y (cycle, sk*y*), -ye (l*ye*).

**o** /ou/  Se pronuncia más cerrada que la *o* de *supo* (por ejemplo: **hope, go, oh, over**); también se encuentra este sonido en palabras deletreadas con: -au- (m*au*ve), -aux (f*au*x pas), -eau (b*eau*), -ew (s*ew*), -oa- (r*oa*d), -oe (t*oe*), -oo- (br*oo*ch), -ot (dep*o*t), -ou- (s*ou*l), -ow (fl*ow*), -owe- *(owe)*.

**o** /ɔ/  Se pronuncia más cerrada que la *o* de *corre* (por ejemplo: **alcohol, order, raw**); también se encuentra este sonido en palabras deletreadas con: -a- (t*a*ll), -al- (w*a*lk), au- (*au*thor, v*au*lt), -augh- (c*augh*t), -oa- (br*oa*d), -oo- (fl*oo*r), -ough- (s*ough*t).

**oi** /oi/  Equivqale aproximadamente a la *oy* de *doy* (por ejemplo: **oil, joint, voice**); también se encuentra este sonido en palabras deletreadas con: -awy- (l*aw*yer), -oy- (b*oy*).

**oo** /ʊ/  Se pronuncia menos cerrada que la *u* de *insulto* (por ejemplo: **book, foot**); también se encuentra este sonido en palabras deletreadas con: -o- (w*o*lf), -ou- (t*ou*r), -u- (p*u*ll).

**oo** /u/   Se pronuncia más larga que la *u* de *susto* (por ejemplo: **too, ooze, fool**); también se encuentra este sonido en palabras deletreadas con: -eu- (man*eu*ver), -ew (gr*ew*), -o (wh*o*), -o...e (m*o*ve), -oe (can*oe*), -ou- (tr*ou*pe), -u...e (r*u*le), -ue (fl*ue*), -ui- (s*ui*t).

**ou** /au/   Equivale aproximadamente a la *au* de *aurora* (por ejemplo: **loud, out**); también se encuentra este sonido en palabras deletreadas con -ow (br*ow*, c*ow*, pl*ow*).

**u** /iu/   Equivale aproximadamente a la *iu* de *ciudad* (por ejemplo: **cue, use, utility**); también se encuentra este sonido en palabras deletreadas con: -eau- (b*eau*ty), -eu- (f*eu*d), -ew (f*ew*), (h)u- (h*u*man), (h)u...e (h*u*ge), -iew (v*iew*), you (*you*), yu...e (*yu*le).

**u** /ʌ/   Es sonido intermedio entre la *o* de *borro* y la *a* de *barro*, algo parecido a la pronunciación de la *eu* francesa de *peur;* (por ejemplo: **up, sun, mud**); también se encuentra este sonido en palabras deletreadas con: o- (*o*ther), -o- (s*o*n), -oe- (d*oe*s), o...e (l*o*ve), -oo- (bl*oo*d), -ou (tr*ou*ble).

## Consonantes

**b**   Se pronuncia igual que la *p* española salvo que en la pronunciación de la *b* suenan las cuerdas vocales. La *b* inglesa es más fuerte (más aspirada) que la española. Se encuentra en palabras escritas con *b* (**bed, amber, rub**) y también en palabras deletreadas con -bb- (ho*bb*y).

**c**   Como la *c* española, lleva dos sonidos, /s/ y /k/. La /s/ se pronuncia igual que la *s* española y se encuentra en palabras deletreadas con ce- (**center**) y ci- (**city**). La /k/ es semejante a la *c* española cuando aparece delante de -a, -o, y -u *(católica, cómo, cuándo)* pero se pronuncia más fuerte (más aspirada). La /k/ se encuentra en palabras deletreadas con ca-, co-, y cu- (**cat, account, cut**).

**ch**   Equivale aproximadamente a la *ch* española (por ejemplo: **chief, beach**); también se encuentra en palabras deletreadas con: -tch- (ca*tch*, bu*tch*er), -te- (righ*te*ous), -ti- (ques*ti*on), -tu- (na*tu*ral). A veces equivale a la /š/ de la palabra francese *chèrie* (**chef**), o a la /k/ de *cómo* (**character**).

**d**   Equivale aproximadamente a la *d* de *onda* (por ejemplo: **do, odor, red**); también se encuentra en palabras deletreadas con -dd- (la*dd*er) y -de- (fa*de*). La *d* inglesa es siempre más fuerte (más aspirada) que la española y no se pronuncia nunca /dʒ/ como la *d* de *padre* o las *d*'s de *Madrid*.

**f**   Equivale aproximadamente a la *f* española (por ejemplo: **feed, safe**); también se encuentra en palabras deletreadas con -ff- (mu*ff*in) y -fe (li*fe*).

**g**   Equivale aproximadamente a la *g* de *globo* (por ejemplo: **give, fog**); también se encuentra en palabras deletreadas con -gg- (e*gg*), gh- (*gh*ost), y -gue (pla*gue*). La *g* cuando cae delante de -i y -e se pronuncia /dʒ/ (**George, gem, legitimate**). El sonido /dʒ/ es semejante a, pero más fuerte que, la *y* y la *ll* españolas de *yo* y *llevar*. Véase *j*.

**h**   Se pronuncia más aspirada pero menos áspera que la *j* española en *jabón* (por ejemplo: **hit, hope**); también se encuentra en palabras deletreadas con wh- (*wh*o).

**j**  Equivale aproximadamente a la *y* de *yo* en su pronunciación enfática (p.ej. . . . *yo, y yo sólo soy el dueño aquí!*) o como la *y* de *cónyuge* en ciertas modalidades del español (por ejemplo: **just, joke**); también se encuentra en palabras deletreadas con: -dg- (ju*dg*e), -di- (sol*di*er), -ge (sa*ge*), -gg- (exa*gg*erate), gi- (*gi*n). La pronunciación de la *j* y de la *g* delante de -i y -e /dʒ/ es igual que la de la *ch* española, salvo que suenan las cuerdas vocales en la pronunciación del sonido /dʒ/.

**k**  (Por ejemplo: **keep, make, token**) equivale a la *qui-* y *que* españolas pero se pronuncia más fuerte (más aspirada). La *k* inglesa no se pronuncia cuando cae delante de una *n* (**knife, knight, knee**).

**l**  Se pronuncia aproximadamente como la *l* de *lago* (por ejemplo: **leap, sail**); también se encuentra en palabras deletreadas con -le (mi*le*) y -ll (ca*ll*).

**m**  Equivale aproximadamente a la *m* española (por ejemplo: **more, drum, him, summer**). Tengan cuidado de pronunciar la *m* al final de una palabra igual que se pronuncia en medio de la palabra y de no convertir el sonido en *n*.

**n**  Equivale aproximadamente a la *n* de *bueno* (por ejemplo: **now, sunny**); tambièn se encuentra en palabras deletreadas con gn- (*gn*at) y kn- (*kn*ife).

**ng**  (Por ejemplo: **sing, Washington**) equivale aproximadamente a la *n* de *blanco*.

**p**  (Por ejemplo: **pool, spool, supper, stop**) tras consonante equivale aproximadamente a la *p* española, pero lleva más aspiración. La *p* delante de una *s* (**psychologist, psyche**) no se pronuncia.

**r**  Se pronuncia con la punta de la lengua elevada hacia el paladar (sin tocarlo) y doblada para atrás (por ejemplo: **red, hurry, near**); también se encuentra en palabras deletreadas con: -re (pu*re*), rh- (*rh*ythm), y wr- (*wr*ong).

**s**  Equivale aproximadamente a la *s* de *salir*, pero algo más tensa y larga (por ejemplo: **see, kiss**).

**sh**  Equivale aproximadamente a la *ch* de las palabras francesas *changer* and *chapeau* (por ejemplo: **ship, wash**); también se encuentra en palabras deletreadas con: -ce- (o*ce*an), -ch- (ma*ch*ine), -ci- (spe*ci*al), s(u)- (*s*ugar), -sci- (con*sci*ence), -si- (man*si*on), -ss- (ti*ss*ue, mi*ss*ion), -ti- (cap*ti*on).

**t**  (Por ejemplo: **team, ten, steam, bit**) tras consonante equivale aproximadamente a la *t* española salvo con más aspiración; también se encuentra en palabras deletreadas con: -bt (dou*bt*), -cht (ya*cht*), -ed (talk*ed*), -ght (bou*ght*), -te (bi*te*), th- (*th*yme), -tt- (bo*tt*om), tw- (*tw*o).

**th**  (Por ejemplo: **thin, ether, path**) equivale aproximadamente a la *z* española en el norte de España.

**th**  (Por ejemplo: **that, the, either, smooth**) equivale aproximadamente a la *d* de *adoptar*.

**v**  (Por ejemplo: **voice, river, live**) equivale aproximadamente a la *b* de *haba* pero es labiodental en vez de bilabial. La pronunciación de la *v* inglesa es igual que la de la *f*, salvo que suenan las cuerdas vocales en la pronunción de la *v*.

**w**  (Por ejemplo: **west, witch, away**) equivale aproximadamente a la *u* de *puesto*.

**y** (Por ejemplo: **yes, beyond**) equivale aproximadamente a la *i* de *bien;* también se encuentra en palabras deletreadas con -i- (on*i*on, un*i*on), -j- (hallelu*j*ah), y -ll- (torti*ll*a).

**z** Tiene dos sonidos: /z/ y /zh/. La /z/, la más común (por ejemplo: **zoo, lazy, zone**), equivale aproximadamente a la *s* de *isla* y *mismo* en ciertas modalidades del español, pero con más sonoridad. Este sonido se pronuncia igual que la *s* española, salvo que en la pronunciación de la /z/ suenan las cuerdas vocales. Se encuentra el sonido /z/ en algunas palabras deletreadas con: -s- (ha*s*), -se (ri*se*), x- (*x*ylophone), y -zz- (bu*zz*ard, fu*zz*). El sonido /zh/ que se encuentra en **azure** y **brazier** equivale aproximadamente a la *ll* del español de la gente mayor de la cuidad de Buenos Aires (o sea, como la *j* de la palabra francesa *bonjour*). El sonido /zh/ también se encuentra en ciertas palabras deletreadas con -ge (gara*ge*, mira*ge*), -si- (vi*si*on), y su- (plea*su*re).

# Pronunciation Symbols for the Sounds of Spanish
## Símbolos de Pronunciacíon por los Sonidos del español

| IPA Symbols Símbolos del AFI | Key Words Ejemplos | Key Words Ejemplos |
|---|---|---|
| a | albo, banco, cera | father, depart |
| e | esto, del, parte | rain, eight |
| i | ir, fino, adiós, muy | beet, conceive |
| o | oler, flor, grano | telephone, goal |
| u | un, luna, cuento | fool, group |
| b | bajo, vaca | by, abet |
| β | hablar, escribir, lavar | |
| d | dar, desde, dos, dueña | deal, adept |
| ð | pedir, Pedro, verdad | that, gather |
| f | fecha, afectar, golf | fan, after |
| g | gato, grave, gusto, largo | garden, ugly |
| h | gemir, giro, junta, bajo, relojes | horse, loch |
| k | cacao, claro, cura, cuenta, que, quinto | kind, actor |
| l | lado, lente, habla, papel | lot, altar |
| ʎ | llamar, calle, olla | million, civilian |
| m | mal, amor | more, commit |
| n | nada, nuevo, mano, bien | not, enter |
| ɲ | ñaques, año | canyon, companion |
| ŋ | angosto, aunque | ring, anchor |
| p | peso, guapo | pill, applaud |
| r | real, faro, deber | rice, carpet |
| s | sala, espejo, mas | say, clasp |
| θ | cena, hacer, cierto, cine, zarzuela, lazo, vez | thin, myth |
| t | tocar, estado, cenit | table, attract |
| y | ya, ayer | you, voyage |
| tʃ | chica, mucho | chill, batch |

## Diphthongs

| | | |
|---|---|---|
| ai, ay | baile, hay | high, rye |
| au | auditor, laudar | out, round |
| ei | veinte, seis | aim, ray |
| eu | euscaro, deuda | |
| oi, oy | roido, hoy | coin, loyal |
| ue | buena, suerte | sway, quaint |
| ie | miel, tambien | fiesta, pieta |

# The Basics of Standard Spanish Pronunciation

Whereas the fit between English spelling and pronunciation has for centuries been less than ideal (think, for example, of the various pronunciations of -**ough**, as in **although, bough, cough,** and **slough**), the fit between today's Spanish spelling and pronunciation is quite good, thanks to the regulatory efforts of the Spanish academies.

The following instructions thus take spelling as their starting point. Pronunciation is described in two ways: with phonetic symbols (enclosed in slashes) and by way of approximate comparisons with English. A wavy line separates variants (like **esnob ~ snob**). A stress mark (') means that the syllable following it is stressed (as in /re'lo/). An asterisk indicates a nonexistent form (like English *****llion**). A right-facing "arrow" ( > ), or "greater than" sign, means "became in Spanish" (as in English **rum** and French **rhum** > **ron ~ romo**).

As may be expected of a language that has been used for many centuries, over a vast area, and by many diverse people, Spanish is now pronounced in various ways. Of the many current pronunciations, two are offered as most suitable for speakers of Spanish as a second language. The two standards are identical to a large extent, differing chiefly with respect to the pronunciation of **c** before **e**; **c** before **i**; **z** in any position; and, optionally, **ll, g,** and **j.**

To the extent that the two standards differ, features belonging to just one of them are labeled either *Standard 1* or *Standard 2* below.

Features labeled *Standard 1* are accepted as standard in Spain but not in the Western Hemisphere. Features labeled *Standard 2* are accepted as standard in the Western Hemisphere but not in Spain. If you speak Spanish mostly with Spaniards or mostly with people from the Western Hemisphere, your choice of standard will thus be straightforward. If you speak with people from both areas, you can either try to master both standards or, if you want to follow just one of them no matter to whom you speak, pick Standard 2.

**a** is pronounced /a/, which is similar to the second vowel of the English interjection **aha!** and the vowel of the English interjection **ah,** although much shorter in duration. See also "Diphthongs and Triphthongs" below.

**b** has three pronunciations. At the beginning of an utterance, after /m/ (whether represented by **m** or by **n**), or after /n/ (whether represented by **n** or by **m**), the letter **b** is pronounced /b/, which is similar to the pronunciation of the first consonant of English **beach, broth, pebble,** etc. For example, in the sentence **Bulgaria envió a ambos embajadores en un barco japonés,** each of the four instances of **b** (and the one instance of **v**) is pronounced in this way.

At the end of a word, more than one pronunciation of **b** may be heard. For example, **club** may be /klub/, /kluβ/, or /klu/. Its plural, **clubs,** may be /klups/, /klus/, and possibly /kluβs/, unless the plural **clubes** is used, whose universal pronunciation is /kluβes/ (see the next paragraph for interpreting /β/, and **e** for interpreting /ε/). All of the foregoing holds for compounds of **club,** like **aeroclub.** In **esnob ~ snob,** the final **b** is pronounced /b/.

In all other positions (for example, **hablas, hablar,** and **habré**), **b** is pronounced /β/, a sound absent in English, which is made by bringing the lips close together without letting them touch each other (as if you were blowing dust away or blowing out a match or candle), expelling air through the mouth, and vibrating the vocal cords. This sound is thus similar to /v/ (as in English **very** and **vowel**), except that the latter is made by making the lower lip touch the upper teeth. English-speakers should not mistake Spanish /β/ for English /v/.

It follows from the foregoing that if the position of **b** in the utterance changes, its pronunciation may change. For example, when the word **baba** is pronounced in isolation, the first **b** is rendered /b/ and the second one /β/, but in the phrase **la baba,** the first **b** is no longer at the beginning of an utterance (nor is it preceded by the sounds /m/ or /n/), hence the phrase is pronounced /laβaβa/.

These rules of pronunciation also hold true for the letter **v,** which is pronounced /b/ at the beginning of words, and /β/ in the middle. See also **v.**

**c** has several pronunciations. If it is followed by **e** or **i,** the letter **c** is pronounced /θ/ in Standard 1 and /s/ in Standard 2. The pronunciation of /θ/ in Spanish is similar to that of **th** in English **thatch, think,** etc., but made with somewhat more protrusion of the tongue. The sound /s/ is similar to the pronunciation of **s** in English **say, simple,** etc.

Although Standard 1 has /θ/ for **c** before **e** or **i,** people who use that pronunciation will not be put off if they hear you pronounce the **c** as /s/, because the latter is widespread (though not standard) in Spain. In the Western Hemisphere, **c** before **e** or **i** is always pronounced /s/ and never /θ/. Speakers of Western Hemispheric Spanish will react to /θ/ either as "the correct pronunciation" ("though we don't use it") or as a pretentious pronunciation (unless it comes from people to the manner born, i.e., many Spaniards). Thus, whereas it is desirable though not obligatory that you use Standard 1 in Spain, you would be well advised to use only Standard 2 in the Western Hemisphere, where /θ/ is bound to elicit a sharp reaction of one kind or another (as sharp as British **drawing pin, lorry,** or **trunk call** instead of **thumbtack, truck,** and **long-distance call** would probably elicit in the United States).

**ch,** wherever it is found, is always pronounced as /tʃ/, which is similar to the pronunciation of **ch** in English **church, child,** etc.

If **c** ends a syllable (for instance, **accionista, facsimíl,** and **técnico**), **c** is pronounced as /k/. Spanish /k/ is similar to the pronunciation of **c** in English **escape, scandal,** etc. To achieve a good rendition of Spanish /k/, hold your open palm in front of your mouth and pronounce first **cape** and **coop,** then **escape** and **scandal.** When pronouncing the first two words, you felt a noticeable puff of air on your palm, but in the last two words you felt almost no puff at all. A noticeable puff of air accompanying a speech sound is called *aspiration;* sounds pronounced with aspiration are *aspirated,* and those pronounced without it are *unaspirated.* Spanish /k/ (like Spanish /p/ and /t/) is always unaspirated, wherever it occurs. Thus, you should have no trouble with Spanish **escapar** and **escandalo** because here /k/ occurs after /s/, and as an English speaker you will automatically pronounce it as unaspirated, just as you would the **c** of the English cognates of those words: **escape** and **scandal.** It is in other positions that you have to be careful not to aspirate: **claro, crear,** etc. (contrast them with their English cognates, both of which have an aspirated /k/: **clear, create**).

See also **k, ll** (under **l**), **q, s,** and **z.**

**d** has several pronunciations. At the beginning of an utterance, after /n/, or after /l/, this letter is pronounced /d/, which is similar to the pronunciation of **d** in English **dear, dust,** etc., with this difference: in the production of Spanish /d/, the tongue touches the lower edge of the upper front incisors.

When between two vowels, when preceded by a vowel and followed by **r,** or when at the end of a word and not preceded by **r** (as in **pedir, Pedro,** and

**libertad**), the letter **d** is pronounced /ð/, which is similar to the pronunciation of **th** in English **that, there,** etc., but less interdental than English /ð/ (in the production of the Spanish sound, the tip of the tongue gently touches the lower edge of the upper incisors).

It follows from the foregoing that if the position of **d** in the utterance changes, its pronunciation may change. Contrast, for example, these three utterances: (1) **Dinamarca mandó embajadores a doce países,** (2) **En Dinamarca viven unos cuantos americanos,** and (3) **Iremos a Dinamarca.** In (1), the **d** of **Dinamarca** is pronounced /d/ because it comes at the beginning of an utterance; in (2) the same **d** is also pronounced /d/ because it comes after /n/; but in (3) the same **d** is pronounced /ð/ because none of the conditions for pronouncing it /d/ is met. Similarly, when the word **dedo** is pronounced in isolation, the first **d** is rendered /d/ (and the second one /ð/), but in the phrase **mi dedo,** the first **d** is no longer at the beginning of an utterance (nor is it preceded by /n/ or /l/); hence the phrase is pronounced /miðeðo/.

**e** has two pronunciations. The instruction given in some books that **e** is pronounced /e/ when stressed and /ɛ/ when unstressed does not hold true for today's Spanish and may never have been an accurate description of its pronunciation in any variety of the language.

Here are better guidelines for **e** (except when it is part of a diphthong or triphthong):

If **e** is found in a syllable ending in a consonant (see "Syllabification" below), it is pronounced /ɛ/, which is similar to the pronunciation of **è** in French or to the vowel of **bet, let, met,** etc., as pronounced in Standard English, that is, with considerable lowering of the jaw, for example, **embaldosar, fresco, hablen,** and **mestizo.**

If **e** ends a syllable and the next one begins with **r, rr,** or **t,** it is pronounced /ɛ/, for instance, **pero, caballete** (the first **e**), **cerrar,** and **jinete.**

Otherwise, **e** is pronounced /e/, which is similar to the pronunciation of **é** in French, that is, the jaw is lowered only minimally (the closest English comes to having a sound like /e/ is the vowel of **ache, rake, stake,** etc.), for example, **caballete** (the second **e**), **hablé,** and **mesa.** In this dictionary, the sounds /e/ and /ɛ/ are both represented by /e/.

See also "Diphthongs and Triphthongs" below.

**f** is pronounced /f/, which is similar to the pronunciation of **f** in English **fate, feet,** etc., for example, **afectar, fecha, golf, golfo, ¡uf!.**

**g** has several pronunciations. At the beginning of an utterance and when followed by **a, o, u,** or a consonant letter except **n** (as in **gato, goma, gusto,** or **glaciar**), **g** is pronounced /g/, which is similar to the pronunciation of **g** in English **get, go, gumption,** etc.

At the beginning of a word and when followed by **n,** the letter **g** is silent (as in **gnomo**). That pronunciation is in fact so widespread and reputable that a **g**-less spelling is now acceptable and is in fact preferred in this dictionary (see "Miscellaneous" below).

When **g** occurs at the end of a syllable and is preceded by **n,** it is silent, as in **búmerang.** In older borrowings from other languages, that **g** was systematically or sometimes omitted, as in **sterling > esterlina, pudding > pudín.**

Before **e** or **i** (as in **gemir** and **gigante**), except if it comes at the end of a word, the letter **g** is pronounced /x/, which is absent in most varieties of current English. This sound is similar to the pronunciation of **ch** in German **Bach,** that of **ch** in Israeli Hebrew **zecher,** and that of **ch** in Scots English **loch, Lochaber,** etc. Press the back of the tongue against the soft palate, expel air (as if coughing), and do not vibrate the vocal chords. **g** before **e** or **i** can also be pronounced /h/, as in English **"house,"** which is common in Latin America and in southern Spain. In this dictionary, both /x/ and /h/ are represented by /h/.

If **g** ends a syllable that is not the last syllable of the word (as in **dogma** and the first syllable of **zigzag**), this letter is pronounced /g/. In such cases, the next syllable always begins with a consonant.

Otherwise, **g** is pronounced /ɣ/, a sound absent in English, which is made by bringing the back of the tongue close to the soft palate (without letting them touch), expelling air through the mouth, and vibrating the vocal chords. Examples are **hago** and **hígado.** In this dictionary, both sounds, /g/ and /ɣ/, are represented by /g/.

**h** is silent.

**i** is pronounced /i/, which is similar to the vowel of English **beet, feet, sheen,** etc., but shorter (for instance, **dicho, isla,** and **cursi**).

See also **y.**

**j** is almost always pronounced /x/, although a pronunciation as /h/ is also acceptable in parts of Latin America and southern Spain (see **g** for interpreting these symbols). A notable exception is **reloj,** which many speakers pronounce /re'lo/. That pronunciation of **reloj** is so widespread that **reló** is an alternate spelling of the singular form, but only in informal writing. In the plural, everyone pronounces /x/ or /h/ and therefore writes the **j: relojes.**

See **x.**

**k,** which is now found only in recent borrowings from other languages, is pronounced /k/ (see **c** for interpreting that symbol). The letter combination **ck** (as in **crack, flashback, shock, snack, stock**) is pronounced /k/.

**l** when not doubled is pronounced /l/, which is formed by putting the tip of the tongue against the sockets of the upper incisors, the remainder of the tongue lying flat. Spanish /l/ thus does not have the hollow sound of English /l/, in whose formation the back of the tongue rises toward the palate.

**ll** has two pronunciations, /ʎ/ and /y/, which vary by region and class rather than by placement within a word. /ʎ/, a sound similar to the Italian **gli,** has no real equivalent in English, although the **lli** of **million** comes close. While /λ/ is held to be the "correct" pronunciation by Spanish radio and television guidelines, it is almost never used in Latin America, except among some academics and the very wealthy. In Spain it is only heard in the northern regions of Castile. Much more common, and almost universally accepted today, is the pronunciation /y/, which is similar to our **y** in **yes** or **yam.**

In the Southern Cone of Latin America, a third pronunciation, /ʒ/ (like the French **Geneviève**), is also used.

**m** is pronounced /m/, which is similar to the pronunciation of **m** in English **make, might,** etc.

Traditionally, Spanish does not have /m/ at the end of a word when it is pronounced in isolation. However, a few words (all learned borrowings from other languages) end in **m** (for example, **álbum, factótum, ídem, médium, memorándum, ultimátum,** and **vademécum**), and that letter always appears in the Spanish names of many places outside Spanish-speaking areas, like **Bírmingham, Búckingham, Siam,** and **Vietnam.** Both /m/ and /n/ are heard in such words, depending on people's ability to pronounce /m/ at the end of a word (as more and more Spanish-speakers study other languages, they find it easier to produce that sound in that position) and their interest in maintaining the supposedly "correct" (i.e., non-Spanish) pronunciation of that letter.

**n** has several pronunciations. If immediately followed by a labial consonant (represented by **b, f, m, p,** or **v**) whether in the same word or in the next one, it is pronounced /m/ (as in the words **anfitrión, inmediato, anverso,** or the sentences **insiste en bucear, insiste en pelear,** and **en muchos casos hay más**). Since /m/ + /m/ is reduced to a single /m/, **en muchos casos** actually has just one /m/.

However, /m/ + /n/ (as in **insomne**) is not reduced.

Before /k/ or /g/ (as in **aunque** and **angosto**), **n** is pronounced /ŋ/, which is similar to the final consonant of **sing, long,** and **song** as pronounced in English.

In all other positions (as in **Anatolia, andan,** and **nombrar**), **n** is pronounced /n/, which is similar to the pronunciation of **n** in English **hand, near,** etc.

See also **m,** "Stress," and, "Miscellaneous" below.

**ñ** is pronounced /ɲ/, which is similar to the pronunciation of **ny** in English **canyon** or **ni** in English **onion.**

**o** is pronounced similarly to the **o** in the English words **tote** and **gloat.** English speakers, however, must be careful not to end the pronunciation of this vowel with an "off-glide" (an "off-glide," in this case, would close the **o** into a **u** sound at the end of the vowel). Thus, the Spanish **no** and the English **no** are not exactly alike, as the Spanish ends in a pure /o/ sound, while the English "off-glides" into a /u/, producing /nou/.

**p,** where it is pronounced, stands for /p/, which is similar to the pronunciation of **p** in English **space, spare, spook,** etc., but different from that of **p** in English **pike, peak, poke,** etc., in that it is not aspirated (see **c** for definitions of aspirated and unaspirated sounds).

Spanish **ps** at the beginning of a word is pronounced /s/.

**q** is always followed by **ue** or **ui.** The sequence **que** is pronounced /ke/ and **qui** is pronounced /ki/ (for example, **quince**).

To represent the sound sequences /kue/ and /kui/, Spanish has **cue** and **cui** respectively (as in **cueva** and **cuidar**).

Because **q** is always followed by **u,** if Spanish-speakers borrow words containing just **q** from other languages, that letter is changed to **k.** Thus, the Spanish names of Iraq and Qatar, for example, are **Irak** and **Katar.**

**r** has two pronunciations. At the beginning of a word or when it comes after **l, n,** or **s** (for example, **reir, alrededor, enrojecer,** and **Israel**), this letter has the same pronunciation as **rr** (see below).

In all other positions, **r** is pronounced with one flip of the upper part of the tongue against the sockets of the upper incisors (for instance, **leer, para, pera, pero, tercero,** and **treinta**).

**rr** is pronounced with a trill (several flips) of the upper front part of the tongue against the sockets of the upper incisors (for instance, **parra, perra, perro,** and **sierra**). Thus, **para** and **parra** are different words, with different meanings. The same applies to **caro** and **carro, pera** and **perra, pero** and **perro, torero** and **torrero,** and other pairs of words.

**s** has several pronunciations. When it represents the plural ending of nouns recently borrowed from other languages, it is silent in certain words, like **cabarets, carnets, complots, conforts, superávits, tíckets, trusts, vermuts.**

Before the letters **b, v, d, g** (but only when the letter is not followed by **e** or **i**), **l, m, n,** or **r** (whether any of those eight letters appear in the same word as **s** or they appear in the next word), you have an alternative in both standards if **s** is not the last letter of the word: it may be pronounced /z/ (a sound similar to the pronunciation of **z** in English **zebra, zoo,** etc.) or /s/ (see **c** for interpreting that symbol): **esbelto, esdrújulo, esgrimir, isla, esmalte, Israel, los baúles, los varones, los dedos, los guantes, los lagos, los maestros, los nervios, los ratones,** etc. If **s** is the last letter, only /s/ is found (for instance, in the family name **Pons**).

If **s** is followed by **r** (whether in the same word or in the next one), besides the two pronunciations suggested above, /s/ or /z/, a third possibility is not to pronounce the **s** at all and, as compensation, trill the **r** more. The word **Israel** (and its derivatives) thus has three pronunciations: /isrrael/, /izrrael/, and /irrrael/.

Otherwise, **s** is pronounced /s/ (as in **ese, especial, hablas, hasta, insistir, seco**).

If **s** is followed by **h,** the foregoing paragraph applies, except in the case of Spanish words recently borrowed from other languages or words modeled on such recently borrowed words, in which **sh** constitutes a unit, to be pronounced /ʃ/ (a sound similar to the pronunciation of **sh** in English **shall, sheet, should,** etc.). Thus, in **deshacer,** an old Spanish word not recently borrowed from another language, the instructions about **s** apply and the **h** is silent (hence the first two syllables of that word are /desa/), whereas in **riksha, sh** is pronounced /ʃ/.

See also **b, c, t, z,** and "Syllabification" below.

**t** is pronounced /t/, which is similar to the pronunciation of **t** in English **stoop, stake, steer,** etc., but different from that of **t** in English **take, teak, took,** etc., in that it is less aspirated (see **c**).

The Spanish /t/ is made by touching the tip of the tongue against the upper incisors (in contrast to English /t/, in whose production the tongue touches the gums). In two positions, **t** may not be pronounced as described above. First, before **l** or **m** in the same word (as in **atleta, aritmético,** and **ritmo**) you have an alternative: **t** may be pronounced as described or it may be pronounced /ð/ (see **d** for interpreting that symbol).

Second, the **t** at the end of a word may be silent. Probably many, most, or all Spanish-speakers pronounce it in **cenit, déficit, fagot, mamut, superavít,** and **el Tíbet ~ el Tibet,** whereas in other words the **t** is silent, for instance **cabaret, carnet, complot, tícket, trust,** and **vermut,** which are pronounced as if written \*cabaré, \*carné, \*compló, \*tique, \*trus, and \*vermú (the plurals are pronounced identically to their singulars). In still other words you have an alternative: **confort** is pronounced either /kom'for/ or /kom'fort/ (the plural **conforts** has both variants too).

**u** has two pronunciations. In the combinations **gue, gui, que,** and **qui,** the letter **u** is silent, for example, **guedeja** /geðeha/, **quedar** /keðar/, and **quien** /kien/ (see **q** and **e** on the pronunciation of those letters).

In all other cases, it is pronounced /u/, which is similar to the vowel sound of English **who** and **cool.** Thus, **puesto** and **seudonónimo,** for example, are pronounced /puesto/ and /seuðonónimo/.

**v** has two pronunciations. At the beginning of an utterance or after **n** (which in this position is pronounced /m/), the letter **v** is pronounced /b/, which is similar to the first consonant of English **beach, broth,** etc. In all other positions, this letter is pronounced /β/ (see **b** for interpreting that symbol). For example, in the sentence **¿Es verdad que en el anverso de la medalla se ve un pavo real?,** the second and sixth words have /b/ and the eleventh and thirteenth have /β/.

The instructions for pronouncing **b** and those for pronouncing **v** are identical (depending on the position of those letters in the utterance), as a consequence of which pairs of words like **baca** and **vaca** or **hube** and **uve** are homophones in today's Spanish and, as a further consequence of which, if you hear /b/ or /β/, you cannot tell whether it is to be represented by **b** or by **v** unless you know how to spell the word.

See also **b.**

**w,** which is found only in borrowings from Germanic languages and French, has several pronunciations. In several words, it is pronounced as if it were **b** or **v** and in such cases alternate spellings with **v** are found too: **wagneriano ~ vagneriano, Westfalia ~ Vestfalia.** The forms with **v** are preferable.

In at least a few words, **w** is pronounced /w/ (a sound similar to the first sound of English **win** and **won**), and for one of them an alternate spelling with **u** exists: **Malawi, Taiwán, Zimbabwe.**

In **whisky,** the letter combination **wh** is pronounced /w/ by those who want to show off their knowledge of English or, alternatively, /gw/.

**x** has several pronunciations. If **x** occurs before a consonant (as in **experiencia, extremidad,** and **mixto**), pronounce it /ks/. That pronunciation is probably the most frequent in words beginning with the prefix **ex-** followed by a consonant, for example **excelente,** widely pronounced /eksselente/ in Latin America, or /eksθelente/ in Castile.

If **x** occurs between vowels, you have an alternative in certain words (**examen** and **exiguo,** for example, may be pronounced with /ks/ or /gz/, but not in others (for instance, all Spanish-speakers, it seems, now pronounce **sexo** with /ks/).

At the end of a word, the pronunciation of **x** is in flux. In **ántrax, Benelux, dux, fénix, látex,** and **tórax,** /ks/ seems to be the most frequent if not universal pronunciation today, although /s/ is also heard.

At least some exceptions to those pronunciations are heard in words of Native American origin: for example, in **México** and **mexicano,** the **x** is now always pronounced /x/ (those are the spellings official and universal in Mexico; elsewhere, **Méjico** and **mejicano** are used); in **Xochimilco** (a Mexican place name), the **x** is always pronounced /s/.

Further exceptions are certain given and family names, which are found in two variants: one preserving a now archaic spelling with **x** (like **Xavier** and **Ximénez**) and the other spelled in modern fashion with **j** (**Javier** and **Jiménez**). Here, **x** is pronounced /h/, that is, just like **j.**

**y** has several pronunciations. In the word **y,** it is pronounced /i/ (see **i** for interpreting that symbol).

When it represents the first or last segment of a diphthong or triphthong (see "Diphthongs and Triphthongs" below), as in **ya, yegua, yunque, ley, rey, soy,** and **Paraguay,** the letter **y** is pronounced /y/ (see **ll** for interpreting that symbol).

In certain varieties of Spanish, **y** is pronounced with more occlusion, so that it has come to be close to /ʒ/ if not actually that sound (see **ll** for interpreting the latter symbol); and in still other varieties it is pronounced with so much occlusion that is has come to be close to /dʒ/ if not actually that (/dʒ/ is similar to the first consonant of English **Jacob, Jerusalem, Jew,** etc.)

Certain family names have two spelling variants, an archaic one with **y** and one spelled in modern fashion with **i** (like **Yglesias ~ Iglesias**). Here, **y** is pronounced /i/, that is, just like **i.**

**z** has several pronunciations. In Standard 1, you have an alternative: (1) In all positions, pronounce it /θ/ (see **c** for interpreting that symbol). Or, (2) Before the letters **b, v, d, g, l, m, n,** or **r** (whether in the same word or in the next one), pronounce it /ð/ (see **d** for interpreting that symbol), and in all other positions pronounce it /θ/.

In Standard 2, you have an alternative: (3) In all positions, pronounce it /s/ (see **c** for interpreting that symbol). Or, (4) Before the letters **b, v, d, g, l, m, n,** or **r** (whether in the same word or in the next one), pronounce it /z/, and in all other positions pronounce it /s/.

## Diphthongs and Triphthongs

Spanish has fifteen diphthongs and eight triphthongs.

Eight of the diphthongs begin with a semivowel:

**ia** /ia/ is spelled **ya** at the beginning of a word, e.g., **desahuciar, yámbico.**

**ua** /ua/, e.g., **guardar.**

**ie** /ie/ is spelled **ye** at the beginning of a word, e.g., **agüero, bien, higiene, siete, yema.**

**ue** /ue/ is spelled **üe** after **g** that is not pronounced /h/, e.g., **huelga, hueste, huevo, vergüenza.**

**io** /io/ e.g., **biombo, piojo.** The spelling **io** at the beginning of a word is an imitation of Greek.

**uo** /uo/, e.g., **arduo.**

**iu** /iu/ is spelled **yu** at the beginning of a word, e.g., **yuca, yugo, triunfo.**

**ui** /ui/ (spelled **uy** in **muy**), e.g., **cuidar, muy.** For **uy** representing /uy/, see **uy** in the next section.

Take care to pronounce diphthongs beginning with a semivowel as diphthongs and not as two syllables. Thus, whereas English **barrio** has three syllables, Spanish **barrio** has two (**ba-rrio**), pronounced /barrio/.

Seven of the diphthongs end in a semivowel:

**ai** /ai/ is spelled **ay** at the end of most words; rarely, **ay** is found in the middle of a word, e.g., **aimará ~ aymará, hay, Raimundo, Seychelles.** If **ay** occurs before a vowel in the same word, it represents not a diphthong but /a/ + /y/, and each of those sounds belongs to a different syllable (thus, **aya** and **haya** for example are syllabified **a-ya** and **ha-ya).**

**au** /au/, e.g., **caudillo.**

**ei** is almost always pronounced /ey/ and is almost always spelled **ey** at the end of a word, e.g., **reina, rey.** A pronunciation exception is **reir,** which is pronounced as if it is spelled *reír. If **ey** occurs before a vowel in the same word, it represents not a diphthong but /e/ + /y/, and each of those sounds belongs to a different syllable (thus, **reyes** and **leyenda** for instance are syllabified **reyes** and **le-yen-da).**

**eu** /eu/, e.g., **seudonónimo.**

**oi** is almost always pronounced /oi/ and is spelled **oy** at the end of a word, e.g., **hoy,** and in certain family names in other positions too (like **Goytisolo).** A pronunciation exception is **oir,** which is pronounced as if spelled *oír. If **oy** occurs before a vowel in the same word, it represents not a diphthong but /o/ + /y/ and each of those sounds belongs to a different syllable (thus, **Goya** is syllabified **Go-ya).**

**uy,** which always occurs at the end of a word, is almost always pronounced /ui/ (as in ¡**huy!, Jujuy**). The exception is **muy,** whose pronunciation is given in the previous section. If **uy** occurs before a vowel in the same word, it represents not a diphthong but /u/ + /y/ and each of those sounds belongs to a different syllable (thus, **cuyo** and **tuyas** are syllabified **cu-yo** and **tu-yas).**

The triphthongs are:

**iai** /iai/ e.g., **despreciáis**.

**iau** /iau/ e.g., **miau**.

**iei** /iei/ e.g., **desprecieís**.

**uai** /uai/ (spelled **uay** at the end of a word), e.g., **evaluáis, Uruguay.**

**uau** /uau/ e.g., **guau**.

**uei** /uei/ (spelled **uey** at the end of a word), e.g., **evaluéis, buey.**

## Syllabification

Spanish is a consonant-vowel language, that is, syllables preferably end in a vowel (though many exceptions are found). Therefore, a single consonant and the vowel following it usually form a syllable or, expressed otherwise, a single consonant between two vowels usually goes with the following vowel (thus, **ba-jo, ad-he-sión**). Since **ch, ll, ñ,** and **rr** represent a single consonant, the syllabification is, for example, **mu-cha-cho, ha-llar, ni-ño, ba-rrio,** and **haz-me-rreír.**

The consonant clusters **bl, cl, dl, fl, gl, pl, tl, br, cr, dr, fr, gr, pr,** and **tr** form a syllable with the following vowel, for instance, **ha-blar, a-cla-rar, a-flo-jar, a-glo-me-rar, a-pla-zar, a-tle-ta, a-bra-zar, a-cre-di-tar, a-dre-de, a-fran-ce-sar, a-gre-gar,** and **a-pren-der.**

When representing /ʃ/, **sh** is not divided, whereas if a consonant letter + **h** is found in the middle of a word and the **h** is silent, the **h** begins a new syllable: **al-ha-ra-ca, clor-hi-dra-to, des-hi-dra-tar, in-hu-ma-ción.**

All other clusters of two consonants between vowels (including diphthongs and triphthongs) are usually divided, so that the first consonant belongs to the preceding syllable and the second consonant to the following syllable, for example, **a-cos-tar-se, ac-tuar, cuer-do, en-car-gar, es-la-vo, fras-co, Is-ra-el, llan-ta, per-di-ción, sol-da-du-ra,** and **der-vi-che.** Subject to that rule are also instances of double **c** or **n,** as in **per-fec-ción** and **en-ne-gre-cer.**

If a cluster of three or more consonants stands between vowels, the last two consonants are usually **bl, cl, fl, gl, pl, tl, br, cr, dr, fr, gr, pr,** or **tr** and they go with the following syllable, for instance, **tem-blar, ten-dré, ex-plo-tar, tem-pra-no.**

If a cluster of three or more consonants stands between vowels and if the second consonant is **s,** the **s** goes with the preceding syllable, for example **ins-tan-te** and **pers-pec-ti-va.**

If one vowel follows another and they do not constitute a diphthong (see above), they belong to separate syllables, for instance, **ma-es-tro, cre-o, le-er, to-a-lla.** Accordingly, if **i** or **u** (which represent respectively /i/ or /u/ in diphthongs and triphthongs) represents a vowel, it belongs in a separate syllable and that fact is indicated by a stress mark. Thus, **ahínco** (three syllables: **a-hín-co**), **búho** (two syllables: **bú-ho**), **desahúcio** (four syllables: **de-sa-hú-cio**), **traído** (three syllables: **tra-í-do**), **prohíbo** (three syllables: **pro-hí-bo**), **Raúl** (two syllables: **Ra-úl**), **haría** (three syllables: **ha-rí-a**), **haríais** (three syllables: **ha-rí-ais**), etc.

If **y** is preceded and followed by a vowel, it forms a diphthong with the following one and therefore belongs in the following syllable, for instance **ca-yó, tu-yo, cre-yó.** In fact, all diphthongs and triphthongs (see the list above) form syllables of their own. In contrast, identical contiguous vowels (as in **creer**) and vowels that do not form diphthongs or triphthongs (as in **leal**), as well as diphthongs or triphthongs dissolved by the stress mark (see the examples from **ahinco** to **haríais** in the previous paragraph), form separate syllables (thus, **cre-er, le-al,** etc.).

It is permissible but not obligatory to set aside the foregoing rules in the case of prefixes, which one may consider as forming syllables of their own (whether or not such would be the case if the rules were followed) or which one may subject to the rules. For example, **ab-ro-ga-ción** or **a-bro** . . ., **des-a-bro-char** or **de-sa** . . ., **ex-a-cer-ba-ción** or **e-xa** . . ., **sub-li-mar** or **su-bli** . . . (in each pair, the first variant reflects treatment of the prefix as a syllable in its own right, no matter what the rules should require, and the second variant shows syllabification when the rules are applied). The same applies to solid compounds: **no-so-tros, vos-o-tras** or **vo-so-tras,** etc.

The foregoing paragraph notwithstanding, the rules must be followed with respect to a succession of three consonant letters, the second of which is **s,** in which case **s** belongs with the preceding, not the following letter (thus, as already noted, **ins-tan-te, pers-pect-ti-va,** not **in-st** . . ., **per-sp** . . .) and with respect to prefixes if the first letter immediately following them is **h** (thus, **des-ha-cer** and **des-hi-dra-tar,** not **de-sha** . . . or **de-shi** . . .).

## Stress

Most Spanish words have only one primary stress, which can be determined from the spelling according to these rules:

(1) If a word is spelled with a stress mark, stress the syllable in which it is found (like **águila, bíceps, fórceps, hablarán, Martínez**).

(2) If a word contains no stress mark:

[2.A] Stress the last syllable if the word ends in:

[2.A.i] a vowel letter + **y** (like **convoy, Uruguay, virrey**),

[2.A.ii] a consonant letter other than **n** or **s** (like **consentir, David, lateral**),

[2.A.iii] **n** not preceded by a vowel letter (like **Isern**),

[2.A.iv] **s** not preceded by a vowel letter (like **Fontanals, Casals**).

[2.B] Stress the next-to-last syllable if the word ends in:

[2.B.i] a vowel letter other than **y** (like **casi, habla, hable, hablo, fatuo, patria, sitio**),

[2.B.ii] a vowel letter + **n** (like **consienten, hablan**),

[2.B.iii] a vowel letter + **s** (like **consientes, hablas**).

The triplets **árbitro, arbitro, arbitró; público, publico, publicó; término, termino, terminó; tráfago, trafago, trafagó;** and **válido, valido, validó** illustrate several possibilities.

## Miscellaneous

It is noted above that /m/ + /m/, /n/ + /n/, /p/ + /p/, and /s/ + /s/ are respectively reduced to one /m/, /p/, and /s/. Since the number of instances of /s/ + /s/ is not the same in all varieties of Spanish, the number of reductions to /s/ varies accordingly. For example, **absceso** is pronounced /apseso/ only where **c** before **e** (or **i**) is pronounced /s/ (otherwise it is rendered /apθeso/); see also **excelente** in the remarks on **x.**

Reduction of identical contiguous sounds (whether vowels or consonants) is widespread in Spanish, whether within a word or between two words. Thus, /a/ + /a/ is reduced to /a/ both in the word **portaaviones** and in a phrase like **a ambos;** or, /e/ + /e/ is reduced to /e/ in the word **sobreexcitar.** The spellings **guardagujas, guardalmacén, remplazar, sobrentender,** etc., are in fact used too and they are preferable. In many cases, only spellings reflecting a reduction are now found, for example, **aprensión, prensil,** and **reprensible** (contrast those forms with their English cognates: **apprehension, prehensile,** and **reprehensible**).

English, especially British English, is a stress-timed language (it has a rhythm in which stressed syllables tend to occur at regular intervals of time, regardless of the number of intervening unstressed syllables) whereas Spanish is a syllable-timed language (with rhythm in which syllables are approximately equal in duration and thus tend to follow one another at regular intervals). Consequently, speakers of English, especially British English, tend to reduce unstressed syllables (as in the British pronunciation of **momentary, pattern, secretary**), whereas Spanish-speakers tend to pronounce each syllable distinctly and do not often slur over any of them. Spanish-speakers thus often react to English-accented Spanish as one in which **se comen las vocales** 'the vowels are swallowed up' and speakers of English (especially British English) tend to react to Spanish-accented English as "overly precise." To get an idea of the difference between stress- and syllable-timed languages, contrast American and British pronunciations of **momentary** and **secretary:** Americans pronounce each syllable of those words with more or less the same degree of distinctiveness, whereas the British pronounce only the first syllable distinctly and slur over the others; thus, American English is more syllable-timed and British English more stress-timed. To pronounce Spanish correctly, English-speakers should therefore give each vowel its full value.

Formerly, in the Spanish-speaking world, the pronunciation and spelling of words borrowed from other languages were routinely changed so that they conformed to Spanish norms. Thus for example, **bowline > bolina, coolie > culi, goal > gol,** and **kerosene > kerosen.**

Now, however, the trend is to retain non-Spanish spellings, though not necessarily non-Spanish pronunciations, with the result that the good fit between the Spanish spelling and pronunciation is in certain words absent.

# List of Abbreviations Used in This Dictionary

*a* adjective
*Abbr.* abbreviation
*acc* accusative
*adv* adverb
*Aer.* aeronautics
*Agr.* agriculture
*Anat.* anatomy
*Archit.* architecture
*Archeol.* archeology
*art.* article
*art* art
*Astron.* astronomy
*Astrol.* astrology
*Auto.* automobiles
*aux* auxiliary
*Biol.* biology
*Bot.* botany
*Cards.* card games
*Chem.* chemistry
*Com.* commerce
*Compar.* comparative
*condit* conditional
*conjunc* conjunction
*Culin.* culinary
*Dance.* dancing
*dat* dative
*dim* diminutive
*Eccl.* ecclesiastical
*Educ.* education
*Elec.* electricity
*Engin.* engineering
*Ent.* entomology
*Euph.* euphemism
*f* feminine
*Fig.* figurative
*Fig. Inf.* used
  figuratively in
  informal speech
  or writing
*fut* future
*gen* generally; genitive

*Geog.* geography
*Geol.* geology
*Geom.* geometry
*Gram.* grammar
*Gym.* gymnastics
*Herald.* heraldry
*Hist.* history
*Ichth.* ichthyology
*imperf* imperfect
*impers* impersonal
*indic* indicative
*indef art* indefinite
  article
*Inf.* informal
*infin* infinitive
*insep* inseparable
*interj* interjection,
  exclamation
*interr* interrogative
*Ironic.* ironical
*irr* irregular
*Law.* law
*Ling.* linguistics
*Lit.* literature
*m* masculine
*Mas.* masonry
*Math.* mathematics
*Mech.* mechanics
*Med.* medical
*Metall.* metallurgy
*mf* masculine or femi-
  nine
*Mil.* military
*Mineral.* mineralogy
*Mus.* music
*Myth.* mythology
*n* noun
*Naut.* nautical
*Nav.* naval
*neut* neuter
*Obs* obsolete

*Opt.* optics
*Ornith.* ornithology
*part* participle
*Pers.* personal; person
*Pharm.* pharmacy
*Philos.* philosophy
*Phonet.* phonetics
*Photo.* photography
*Phys.* physics
*Physiol.* physiology
*pl* plural
*Poet.* poetic
*Polit.* political
*Polit. Econ.* political
  economy
*poss* possessive
*prep* preposition
*pres* present
*Print.* printing
*pron* pronoun
*Psychol.* psychology
*Radio.* radio
*Rail.* railway
*Sew.* sewing
*sing* singular
*Spirit.* spiritualism
*Sports.* sports
*subjunc* subjunctive
*Superl* superlative
*Surg.* surgery
*Surv.* surveying
*Tan.* tanning
*Theat.* theater
*Theol.* theology
*v aux* auxiliary verb
*vi* intransitive verb
*vr* reflexive verb
*vt* transitive verb
*West. Hem.* Western
  Hemispheric Spanish
*Zool.* zoology

# Spanish-English
# Dictionary

# A

**a** /a/ *f*, name of the letter A

**a** /a/ *prep* to; at; on; by; in, into; up to; according to; if, etc. 1. Denotes the direct complement of verb before objects representing specified persons or animals, personified nouns, pronouns referring to specific persons (**alguien, entrambos, cualquiera,** etc.), demonstrative or relative pronouns, collective nouns representing persons (**el público, la muchedumbre,** etc.), names of countries, cities, rivers, etc., except where these invariably take the def. art., e.g. *Dejé a Varsovia,* I left Warsaw, *but Dejé el Perú,* I left Peru. 2. Introduces indirect obj. when this is a noun governed by a verb implying motion, or an emphatic pers. pron., e.g. *Nos conviene a ti y a mí,* It suits both you and me. It is also used before indirect obj. to avoid ambiguity when there is both an indirect and direct obj. 3. Denotes the complement of verb when this is an infin., e.g. *Enseñó a pintar a María,* He taught Mary to paint. 4. Indicates direction or destination, e.g. *Vamos a Edimburgo,* We are going to Edinburgh. 5. Signifies location, or point of time when action takes place, e.g. *Vinieron a las doce.* They came at twelve o'clock. 6. Describes position of persons or things, e.g. *Se sentaron a la puerta,* They sat down at the door. *La casa queda a la derecha,* The house is on the right. 7. Denotes interval of time or place between one thing and another, e.g. *de tres a cinco de la tarde,* from three to five in the afternoon, *de calle a calle,* from street to street. 8. Expresses manner of action, e.g. *a la francesa,* in the French way, *bordado a mano,* embroidered by hand. 9. Indicates rate or price, e.g. *a cuatro pesetas la libra,* at four pesetas the lb. 10. Indicates difference or comparison, e.g. *Va mucho de querer a hacer,* There's a difference between wishing and doing. 11. Sometimes is synonymous with *hasta, según, hacia* and governs almost all parts of speech. Has many idiomatic uses. 12. Before infin. sometimes has conditional sense, e.g. *A haber sabido las noticias no lo hubiéramos hecho,* If we had heard the news we would not have done it. 13. With nouns and adjectives forms adverbial phrases, e.g. *poco a poco,* little by little, *a veces,* sometimes, *a ciegas,* blindly, etc. *A + el* becomes *al,* e.g. *al rey,* to the king. *Al + infin.* means when or on, e.g. *al marcharme yo,* when I left (on my leaving)

**abacería** /aβaθe'ria; aβase'ria/ *f*, grocery shop

**abacero** /aβa'θero; aβa'sero/ **(-ra)** *n* grocer

**ábaco** /'aβako/ *m, Archit.* abacus; counting frame

**abad** /a'βaδ/ *m,* abbot

**abadesa** /aβa'δesa/ *f,* abbess

**abadía** /aβa'δia/ *f,* abbacy; abbey

**abajamiento** /a¡βaha'miento/ *m,* lowering; letting down

**abajar** /aβa'har/ *vt* to lower

**abajo** /a'βaho/ *adv* under; underneath; below; down. Used immediately after noun in adverbial phrases, e.g. *cuesta a., escalera a.,* downhill, downstairs —*interj* Down with! e.g., *¡A. el rey!* Down with the king! *venirse a.,* to fall down; *Fig.* collapse

**abalanzamiento** /aβa¡lanθa'miento; aβa¡lansa-'miento/ *m,* balancing; rushing upon; dashing

**abalanzar** /aβalan'θar; aβalan'sar/ *vt* to balance; impel violently; —*vr* throw oneself upon; attack, rush upon; *(with prep a)* rush into, risk. **Se abalanzó hacia ellos,** He rushed toward them

**abalorio** /aβa'lorio/ *m,* glass bead; bead work

**abanderado** /aβande'raδo/ *m,* standardbearer; *(Argentina)* valedictorian

**abanderar** /aβande'rar/ *vt* to register (a ship)

**abanderizar** /aβanderi'θar; aβanderi'sar/ *vt* to organize in groups; —*vr* band together

**abandonado** /aβando'naδo/ *a* deserted; forlorn; helpless; indolent, careless; slovenly

**abandonamiento** /a¡βandona'miento/ *m,* desertion; forlornness; helplessness; carelessness; slovenliness

**abandonar** /aβando'nar/ *vt* to forsake, desert; neglect; leave; give up; renounce; —*vr* neglect oneself; grow discouraged; *(with prep a)* give oneself over to

**abandono** /aβan'dono/ *m,* abandonment; defenselessness; forlornness; dilapidation; renunciation; neglect; slovenliness; debauchery

**abanicar** /aβani'kar/ *vt* to fan

**abanico** /aβa'niko/ *m,* fan; anything fan-shaped; *Inf.* sword; railway signal; *Naut.* derrick. **en a.,** fanshaped

**abaniqueo** /aβani'keo/ *m,* fanning; swinging, oscillation; gesticulation

**abaratar** /aβara'tar/ *vt* to cheapen, make less expensive; —*vr* fall in price

**abarca** /a'βarka/ *f,* leather sandal, worn chiefly in the Basque provinces

**abarcador** /aβarka'δor/ **(-ra)** *n* one who clasps or embraces; monopolist

**abarcadura** /aβarka'δura/ *f,* **abarcamiento** /aβarka-'miento/ *m,* inclusion; scope

**abarcar** /aβar'kar/ *vt* to clasp, encircle; include, comprise; undertake, attempt; monopolize

**abarquillar** /aβarki'ʎar; aβarki'yar/ *vt* to shape into a roll; roll; curl

**abarracar** **(se)** *vi* and *vr Mil.* to go into barracks

**abarrancadero** /aβarranka'δero/ *m,* rough road; ravine, precipice; *Fig.* difficult situation

**abarrancar** /aβarran'kar/ *vt* to ditch; make a ravine; —*vr* fall into a pit; stick (in the mud, etc.); get into difficulties; *Naut.* run aground

**abastar** /aβas'tar/ see **abastecer**

**abastecedor** /aβasteθe'δor; aβastese'δor/ **(-ra)** *a* provisioning, supplying —*n* provider; purveyor, supplier; caterer

**abastecer** /aβaste'θer; aβaste'ser/ *vt irr* to supply, provide; purvey. See **conocer**

**abastecimiento** /aβasteθi'miento; aβastesi'miento/ *m,* providing; supply, provision; catering; supplies

**abasto** /a'βasto/ *m,* provisions, food; *Com.* supply —*adv* plentifully, abundantly

**abatanar** /aβata'nar/ *vt* to full (cloth)

**abate** /a'βate/ *m,* abbé

**abatido** /aβa'tiδo/ *a* dejected, depressed; spiritless; discouraged; crushed, humbled; *Com.* depreciated

**abatimiento** /aβati'miento/ *m,* dejection, depression; humiliation; discouragement; falling; lowering; *(Aer. Naut.)* drift

**abatir** /aβa'tir/ *vt* to knock down; overthrow; demolish; lower, take down; droop; humiliate; discourage; *Naut.* dismantle; —*vi (Naut. Aer.)* drift; —*vr* be despondent, despair; humble oneself; swoop down (of birds). **a. el vuelo,** to fly down

**ABC** /aβe'θe; aβe'se/ *m,* ABCs (e.g. *el ABC de la física,* the ABCs of physics)

**abdicación** /aβδika'θion; aβδika'sion/ *f,* abdication

**abdicar** /aβδi'kar/ *vt* to abdicate; revoke, cancel; give up (rights, opinions)

**abdomen** /aβ'δomen/ *m,* abdomen

**abdominal** /aβδomi'nal/ *a* abdominal

**abecé** /aβe'θe; aβe'se/ *m,* ABCs

**abecedario** /aβeθe'δario; aβese'δario/ *m,* ABC, alphabet; reading book, primer

**abedul** /aβe'δul/ *m,* birch tree; birch wood

**abeja** /a'βeha/ *f,* bee. **a. maestra,** queen bee. **a. obrera,** worker

**abejar** /aβe'har/ *m,* beehive

**abejero** /aβe'hero/ **(-ra)** *n* beekeeper

**abejón** /aβe'hon/ *m,* drone; hornet

**abejorro** /aβe'horro/ *m,* bumblebee

**abellacar** /aβeʎa'kar; aβeya'kar/ *vt* to make a rogue of; —*vr* become a rogue

**aberración** /aβerra'θion; aβerra'sion/ *f,* deviation; error, lapse; *(Astron. Phys. Biol.)* aberration

**abertura** /aβer'tura/ *f,* opening; aperture, gap, hole; fissure, cleft; mountain pass; naturalness, frankness

**abeto** /a'βeto/ *m,* yew-leaved fir

**abetunado** /aβetu'naðo/ *a* bituminous

**abiertamente** /aβierta'mente/ *adv* openly; frankly.

**abierto** /a'βierto/ *a* free, unobstructed; open, not enclosed; open, full-blown (flowers); frank, sincere —*adv* openly

**abigarrado** /aβiga'rraðo/ *a* variegated; varied; speckled

**abigarrar** /aβiga'rrar/ *vt* to variegate; vary; speckle; fleck; spot; dapple

**abigotado** /aβigo'taðo/ *a* having a thick moustache

**abintestato** /aβintes'tato/ *a Law.* intestate

**abiselar** /aβisel'ar/ *vt* to bevel

**abismal** /aβis'mal/ *a* abysmal

**abismar** /aβis'mar/ *vt* to plunge into an abyss; depress, sadden; —*vr* despair; be plunged in thought, be abstracted; be amazed

**abismo** /a'βismo/ *m,* chasm, abyss, gulf; hell

**abjuración** /aβhura'θion; aβhura'sion/ *f,* abjuration

**abjurar** /aβhu'rar/ *vt* to forswear, retract

**ablactar** /aβlak'tar/ *vt* to wean

**ablandamiento** /aβlanda'miento/ *m,* softening; placating

**ablandante** /aβlan'dante/ *a* softening; placatory

**ablandar** /aβlan'dar/ *vt* to soften; appease, placate; loosen; relax; —*vi* and *vr* be softened; be appeased; grow less stormy; (elements) decrease in force

**ablandecer** /aβlande'θer; aβlande'ser/ *vt irr* to soften. See **conocer**

**ablución** /aβlu'θion; aβlu'sion/ *f,* ablution

**abnegación** /aβnega'θion; aβnega'sion/ *f,* abnegation, self-sacrifice

**abnegado** /aβne'gaðo/ *a* self-sacrificing

**abnegarse** /aβne'garse/ *vr irr* to deprive oneself, sacrifice oneself. See **cegar**

**abobado** /aβo'βaðo/ *a* bewildered; foolish-looking, silly

**abobar** /aβo'βar/ *vt* to daze, bewilder; make stupid

**abocado** /aβo'kaðo/ *a* full-flavored, pleasant (of wine)

**abocar** /aβo'kar/ *vt* to seize with the mouth; bring nearer; transfer (contents of one jug to another); —*vr* meet, assemble; —*vi Naut.* enter (a channel, port, etc.). **abocarse (con...),** to contact (...), get in touch (with...)

**abocetado** /aβoθe'taðo; aβose'taðo/ *a Art.* unfinished; sketchy

**abochornado** /aβotʃor'naðo/ *a* flushed (of the face); ashamed; embarrassed

**abochornar** /aβotʃor'nar/ *vt* to overheat, make flushed; shame; embarrass; —*vr* (plants) dry up

**abofetear** /aβofete'ar/ *vt* to slap, hit; buffet

**abogacía** /aβoga'θia; aβoga'sia/ *f,* legal profession; practice of law; advocacy

**abogado** /aβo'gaðo/ **(-da)** *n* lawyer

**abogar** /aβo'gar/ *vi* to defend at law; intercede for; advocate, champion

**abolengo** /aβo'leŋgo/ *m,* lineage, descent, family; inheritance

**abolición** /aβoli'θion; aβoli'sion/ *f,* abolition

**abolir** /aβo'lir/ *vt* to abolish; cancel; annul

**abolladura** /aβoʎa'ðura; aβoya'ðura/ *f,* bruise; dent; embossment

**abollar** /aβo'ʎar; aβo'yar/ *vt* to bruise; dent

**abollonar** /aβoʎo'nar; aβoyo'nar/ *vt* to emboss, do raised work on; —*vr* (vines) sprout

**abombado** /aβom'baðo/ *a* convex; domed

**abombar** /aβom'bar/ *vt* to make convex; *Inf.* deafen, bewilder; —*vr* begin to putrefy; get intoxicated

**abominable** /aβomi'naβle/ *a* abominable

**abominación** /aβomina'θion; aβomina'sion/ *f,* abomination; loathing, detestation

**abominar** /aβomi'nar/ *vt* to abominate, loathe, detest

**abonable** /aβo'naβle/ *a* subscribable; payable

**abonado** /aβo'naðo/ **(-da)** *a* trustworthy, reliable; ready, prepared, inclined —*n* subscriber; season ticket holder (for concerts, etc.)

**abonanzar** /aβonan'θar; aβonan'sar/ *vi impers* to clear up, be fine (weather)

**abonar** /aβo'nar/ *vt* to guarantee; go surety for; improve, better; manure; ratify, confirm; pay; *Com.* place to the credit of; —*vr* subscribe, become a subscriber; take out (season tickets, etc.)

**abonaré** /aβona're/ *m, Com.* due bill; promissory note, I.O.U.

**abono** /a'βono/ *m,* subscription; voucher; guarantee; manure. **a. verde,** leaf mold. **en a. de,** in payment of; in support of

**aboquillado** /aβoki'ʎaðo; aβoki'yaðo/ *a* tipped (of cigarettes)

**abordaje** /aβor'ðahe/ *m, Naut.* boarding of a ship

**abordar** /aβor'ðar/ *vt Naut.* to board a ship; *Naut.* collide, run into; accost, tackle; undertake; —*vi Naut.* put into port

**aborigen** /aβor'ihen/ *a* aboriginal

**aborígenes** /aβo'rihenes/ *m pl,* aborigines

**aborrachado** /aβorra'tʃaðo/ *a* bright red; highly colored; flushed

**aborrascarse** /aβorras'karse/ *vr* to grow stormy

**aborrecedor** /aβorreθe'ðor; aβorrese'ðor/ **(-ra)** *a* hateful —*n* hater, loather

**aborrecer** /aβorre'θer; aβorre'ser/ *vt irr* to hate, loathe; desert offspring (animals, birds). See **conocer**

**aborrecible** /aβorre'θiβle; aβorre'siβle/ *a* hateful, detestable

**aborrecimiento** /aβorreθi'miento; aβorresi'miento/ *m,* hate, detestation; dislike

**abortar** /aβor'tar/ *vt* to abort; foil (a plot); —*vi Med.* miscarry; fail, go awry

**abortivo** /aβor'tiβo/ *a* abortive

**aborto** /a'βorto/ *m,* abortion; miscarriage; monster; failure

**abotagarse** /aβota'garse/ *vr* to swell up, become bloated

**abotonador** /aβotona'ðor/ *m,* button-hook

**abotonar** /aβoto'nar/ *vt* to button; —*vi* bud, sprout

**abozalar** /aβoθa'lar; aβosa'lar/ *vt* to muzzle

**abra** /'aβra/ *f,* cove, small bay; narrow gorge; fissure, cleft

**abrasador** /aβrasa'ðor/ *a* burning, flaming

**abrasamiento** /aβrasa'miento/ *m,* burning; ardor, heat

**abrasar** /aβra'sar/ *vt* to burn; dry up, parch (plants); squander, waste; shame; —*vi* burn; —*vr* be very hot, glow; burn with passion

**abrasión** /aβra'sion/ *f,* abrasion

**abrasivo** /aβra'siβo/ *a* and *m,* abrasive

**abrazadera** /aβraθa'ðera; aβrasa'ðera/ *f,* clasp; clamp

**abrazamiento** /aβraθa'miento; aβrasa'miento/ *m,* embracing

**abrazar** /aβra'θar; aβra'sar/ *vt* to embrace, clasp in one's arms; follow, adopt; engage in; seize, take advantage of; comprise, include; surround; take in hand; clamp; clasp. **abrazarse a,** to clutch, hang on to

**abrazo** /a'βraθo; a'βraso/ *m,* embrace

**abrelatas** /aβre'latas/ *m,* can opener

**abrevadero** /aβreβa'ðero/ *m,* watering place (for cattle)

**abrevar** /aβre'βar/ *vt* to water cattle; irrigate, water

**abreviación** /aβreβia'θion; aβreβia'sion/ *f,* abbreviation, shortening; summary; hastening

**abreviador** /aβreβia'ðor/ *m,* abridger, condenser

**abreviar** /aβre'βiar/ *vt* to abbreviate, shorten; hasten, accelerate; condense, abridge. **a. tiempo,** to save time. **Y para a....,** And, to cut a long story short...

**abreviatura** /aβreβia'tura/ *f,* abbreviation, contraction; shorthand

**abridor** /aβri'ðor/ *m,* opener; ear-ring (for keeping holes in ears open). **a. de guantes,** glove-stretcher. **a. de láminas,** engraving needle. **a. de latas,** can opener

**abridura** /aβri'ðura/ *f,* (act of) opening (e.g. of a trunk)

**abrigada** /aβri'gaða/ *f,* **abrigadero** *m,* sheltered place

**abrigar** /aβri'gar/ *vt* to shelter, protect (against the cold, etc.); defend, help; hold (opinions); nurse (a hope, etc.); cover; —*vr* take shelter; wrap oneself up

**abrigo** /a'βrigo/ *m,* shelter; defense; protection; help; sheltered place; wrap, coat; *Naut.* haven

**abril** /a'βril/ *m,* April; youth; *pl Poet.* years

**abrillantar** /aβriʎan'tar; aβriyan'tar/ *vt* to cut in

facets like a diamond; polish, burnish; cause to shine; *Fig.* improve, add luster to

**abrir** /a'βrir/ *vt* to open; reveal; unlock; slide the bolt of; extend, spread out; cleave; engrave; clear (the way, etc.); begin; head, lead; separate; dig; inaugurate —*vi* unfold (flowers); expand; **en un abrir y cerrar de ojos,** in the twinkling of an eye, in the wink of an eye; —*vr* open; expand; (*with con*) confide in. **a. el camino (a...),** to pave the way (for...). **abrirse camino,** to make one's way; **abrirse paso a codazos,** to elbow one's way out, (or through)

**abrochador** /aβrotʃa'ðor/ *m,* button-hook

**abrochamiento** /aβrotʃa'miento/ *m,* buttoning; fastening

**abrochar** /aβro'tʃar/ *vt* to button; fasten, clasp; hook up (a dress, etc.); buckle

**abrogación** /aβroga'θion; aβroga'sion/ *f,* repeal, annulment

**abrogar** /aβro'gar/ *vt* to repeal, annul

**abrojo** /a'βroho/ *m,* thistle; *Bot.* caltrops; thorn, prickle; *pl* submerged rocks in sea

**abroncar** /aβron'kar/ *vt Inf.* to bore, annoy

**abrumador** /aβruma'ðor/ *a* burdensome, crushing, oppressive; troublesome, tiresome; exhausting

**abrumar** /aβru'mar/ *vt* to weigh down; overwhelm, oppress; weary, exhaust; —*vr* grow misty

**abrupto** /a'βrupto/ *a* steep; rough, broken (ground); rugged

**absceso** /aβs'θeso; aβ'sseso/ *m,* abscess

**absentismo** /aβsen'tismo/ *m,* absenteeism

**ábside** /'aβsiðe/ *mf, Archit.* apse. *m, Astron.* apsis

**absolución** /aβsolu'θion; aβsolu'sion/ *f,* (*Eccl.* and *Law.*) absolution; remission, pardon

**absoluta** /aβso'luta/ *f, Mil.* discharge

**absolutismo** /aβsolu'tismo/ *m,* absolutism

**absolutista** /aβsolu'tista/ *mf* absolutist

**absoluto** /aβso'luto/ *a* absolute; categorical; *Inf.* despotic. **en a.,** absolutely

**absolver** /aβsol'βer/ *vt irr* to absolve; acquit (of a charge). *Law.* **a. de la instancia,** to dismiss the case. See **mover**

**absorbente** /aβsor'βente/ *a* and *m,* absorbent

**absorber** /aβsor'βer/ *vt* to absorb; consume, use up; attract, hold (the attention, etc.); imbibe

**absorción** /aβsor'θion; aβsor'sion/ *f,* absorption

**absortar** /aβsor'tar/ *vt* to amaze, dumbfound

**absorto** /aβ'sorto/ *a* amazed, astounded; abstracted, lost in thought

**abstemio** /aβs'temio/ *a* abstemious

**abstención** /aβsten'θion; aβsten'sion/ *f,* abstention

**abstenerse** /aβste'nerse/ *vr irr* to refrain; abstain. See **tener**

**abstinencia** /aβsti'nenθia; aβsti'nensia/ *f,* abstinence; fasting

**abstinente** /aβsti'nente/ *a* abstemious; temperate

**abstracción** /aβstrak'θion; aβstrak'sion/ *f,* abstraction; preoccupation; absent-mindedness

**abstracto** /aβs'trakto/ *a* abstract. **en a.,** in the abstract

**abstraer** /aβstra'er/ *vt irr* to abstract; consider separately; —*vi* (*with de*) do without, exclude; —*vr* be preoccupied; let one's thoughts wander. See **traer**

**abstraído** /aβstra'iðo/ *a* retired, recluse; preoccupied; absent-minded

**abstruso** /aβ'struso/ *a* abstruse

**absurdidad** /aβsurði'ðað/ *f,* absurdity; folly, nonsense

**absurdo** /aβ'surðo/ *a* ridiculous, absurd. *m,* piece of folly, nonsense

**abuchear** /aβutʃe'ar/ *vt vi* to boo, hoot, jeer

**abuela** /a'βuela/ *f,* grandmother; old woman, dame

**abuelo** /a'βuelo/ *m,* grandfather; ancestor (gen. *pl*); old man; *pl* grandparents

**abulia** /a'βulia/ *f,* lack of will-power, abulia

**abúlico** /a'βuliko/ *a* abulic, lacking will-power

**abultado** /aβul'taðo/ *a* bulky, large; voluminous; exaggerated

**abultamiento** /aβulta'miento/ *m,* bulkiness; enlargement, increase; mound; exaggeration

**abultar** /aβul'tar/ *vt* to enlarge, increase; exaggerate; model in rough (sculpture); —*vi* be bulky; be large

**abundancia** /aβun'danθia; aβun'dansia/ *f,* abundance, plenty

**abundante** /aβun'dante/ *a* abundant, plentiful; abounding (in)

**abundar** /aβun'dar/ *vi* to be plentiful, abound

**abundoso** /aβun'doso/ *a* See **abundante**

**aburrido** /aβu'rriðo/ *a* boring, tedious, dull; tired, weary

**aburrimiento** /aβurri'miento/ *m,* boredom, dullness; wearisomeness, tediousness

**aburrir** /aβu'rrir/ *vt* to bore; *Inf.* spend (time, money); (birds) desert the nest; —*vr* grow bored; be weary

**abusar** /aβu'sar/ *vi* to abuse; exceed one's rights, go too far; (*with de*) take advantage of

**abusivo** /aβu'siβo/ *a* abusive

**abuso** /a'βuso/ *m,* abuse. **a. de confianza,** abuse of trust

**abyección** /aβyek'θion; aβyek'sion/ *f,* degradation, misery; abjectness, servility

**abyecto** /aβ'yekto/ *a* abject, wretched; servile

**acá** /a'ka/ *adv* hither, here; at this time, now. **a. y acullá,** hither and thither. **desde ayer a.,** from yesterday until now

**acabable** /aka'βaβle/ *a* terminable, finishable; achievable

**acabado** /aka'βaðo/ *a* complete; perfect; expert, consummate; old, worn out; ill, infirm. *m,* finish

**acabamiento** /akaβa'miento/ *m,* finishing, completion; end; death, decease

**acabar** /aka'βar/ *vt* to end, terminate; finish; complete, perfect; kill; (*with con*) destroy, finish off; suppress; squander; —*vi* end; die; be destroyed; (*with de* + *infin*) to have just (e.g. *Acaba de salir,* He has just gone out); —*vr* end, be exhausted, run out of (e.g. *Se le acabó el dinero,* His money ran out); fade, grow weak; be destroyed. **Se les acabaron las dudas,** Their doubts were cleared up. **a. de desconcertar,** to nonplus completely; **a. de decidirse,** to come to a decision; **a. de saber,** to finally learn

**acacia** /a'kaθia; a'kasia/ *f, Bot.* acacia

**academia** /aka'ðemia/ *f,* academy

**academicismo** /akaðemi'θismo; akaðemi'sismo/ *m,* academicism, academism

**académico** /aka'ðemiko/ (**-ca**) *a* academic —*n* academician. **a. de la lengua,** member of the Royal Spanish Academy

**acaecer** /akae'θer; akae'ser/ *vi irr* to happen, occur. See **conocer**

**acaecimiento** /akaeθi'miento; akaesi'miento/ *m,* happening, occurrence, event

**acalambrarse** /akalam'brarse/ (muscle) to contract with cramps. **Estar acalambrado,** to have cramps

**acalenturarse** /akalentu'rarse/ *vr* to grow feverish

**acallar** /aka'ʎar; aka'yar/ *vt* to quieten, hush; soothe, appease

**acalorado** /akalo'raðo/ *a* hot; fervent; *Fig.* heated

**acaloramiento** /akalora'miento/ *m,* excitement, agitation, vehemence; ardor

**acalorar** /akalo'rar/ *vt* to warm; aid, encourage; excite, stimulate; stir, move (to enthusiasm); inflame, rouse; tire (by exercise); —*vr* grow hot; become agitated or excited; become heated (arguments)

**acamar** /aka'mar/ *vt* to lay flat (plants by the wind); —*vr* be flattened (plants); lie down (animals); go rotten (fruit)

**acampar** /akam'par/ *vi* and *vt* to encamp

**acanalar** /akana'lar/ *vt* to groove; striate, flute; corrugate; furrow, channel

**acantilado** /akanti'laðo/ *a* steep, precipitous; shelving (ocean-bed). *m,* cliff

**acanto** /a'kanto/ *m,* (*Archit. Bot.*) acanthus

**acantonamiento** /akantona'miento/ *m,* billeting; cantonment

**acantonar** /akanto'nar/ *vt* to billet or quarter troops

**acaparador** /akapara'ðor/ (**-ra**) *n* monopolist

**acaparar** /akapa'rar/ *vt Com.* to monopolize, corner; seize, take possession of

**acápite** /a'kapite/ *m, West. Hem.* new paragraph

**acaracolado** /akarako'laðo/ *a* spiral, winding, twisting

**acardenalar** /akarðena'lar/ *vt* to bruise; —*vr* be bruised; be covered with livid marks

**acarear** /akare'ar/ *vt* to face; face up to, meet with courage

**acariciador** /akariθia'ðor; akarisia'ðor/ **(-ra)** *a* caressing, loving —*n* fondler

**acariciar** /akari'θiar; akari'siar/ *vt* to caress; brush, touch lightly; cherish, treat affectionately; toy with (a suggestion)

**acarreador** /akarrea'ðor/ **(-ra)** *n* carrier, carter

**acarreamiento, acarreo** /akarrea'miento, aka'reo/ *m*, cartage, carting; transport, carriage; occasioning

**acarrear** /akarre'ar/ *vt* to cart, transport; occasion, bring (gen. evil). **La guerra acarreó la carestía,** The war brought scarcity

**acartonado** /akarto'naðo/ *a* shriveled; shrunken; of cardboard; *Fig.* forced (dialogue)

**acaso** /a'kaso/ *m*, chance —*adv* by chance; perhaps, perchance. **por si a.,** in case (e.g. *Por si a. venga,* In case he comes)

**acatable** /aka'taβle/ *a* venerable, worthy

**acatadamente** /akataða'mente/ *adv* with respect, humbly

**acatamiento** /akata'miento/ *m*, respect; reverence; observance

**acatar** /aka'tar/ *vt* to treat with respect, honor, revere; observe

**acatarrarse** /akata'rrarse/ *vr* to catch a cold

**acaudalado** /akauða'laðo/ *a* wealthy, well-to-do

**acaudalar** /akauða'lar/ *vt* to make money; hoard up wealth; acquire (learning, etc.)

**acaudillar** /akauði'ʎar; akauði'yar/ *vt* *Mil.* to command, lead; head (a party, etc.)

**acceder** /akθe'ðer; akse'ðer/ *vi* (*with prep a*) to concede, grant; accede to, agree to

**accesibilidad** /ak,θesiβili'ðað; ak,sesiβili'ðað/ *f*, accessibility; approachableness

**accesible** /akθe'siβle; akse'siβle/ *a* accessible; approachable

**accesión** /akθe'sion; akse'sion/ *f*, agreement, acquiescence; accession; accessory; feverish attack

**acceso** /ak'θeso; ak'seso/ *m*, access; paroxysm, outburst; *Med.* attack

**accesorio** /akθe'sorio; akse'sorio/ *a* accessory

**accesorios** /akθe'sorios; akse'sorios/ *m pl*, accessories; *Theat.* properties

**accidentado** /akθiðen'taðo; aksiðen'taðo/ *a* rough, uneven; stormy, troubled (life, etc.)

**accidental** /akθiðen'tal; aksiðen'tal/ *a* accidental; *m*, *Mus.* accidental

**accidentar** /akθiðen'tar; aksiðen'tar/ *vt* to cause (someone) an accident; —*vr* be the victim of an accident; be seized by a fit

**accidente** /akθi'ðente; aksi'ðente/ *m*, chance; accident, mishap; illness, indisposition; *Med.* fit; *Gram.* accidence; *Mus.* accidental. **a. del trabajo,** accident at work. **por a.,** by chance, accidentally

**acción** /ak'θion; ak'sion/ *f*, action; battle; skirmish; *Mech.* drive; *Com.* share; gesture; lawsuit; *Lit.* action (of play, etc.); *Art.* posture, pose. **a. de gracias,** thanksgiving; *Com.* **a. liberada,** paid-up share. **a. privilegiada,** preference share

**accionar** /akθio'nar; aksio'nar/ *vi* to gesture, gesticulate

**accionista** /akθio'nista; aksio'nista/ *mf Com.* shareholder

**acechar** /aθe'tʃar; ase'tʃar/ *vt* to spy upon, watch; lie in ambush for

**acecho** /a'θetʃo; a'setʃo/ *m*, spying upon, watch; waylaying, ambush. **al a.,** in ambush; on the watch

**acechona** /aθe'tʃona; ase'tʃona/ *f*, waylaying; ambush

**acecinar** /aθeθi'nar; asesi'nar/ *vt* to salt and dry (meat); —*vr* (persons) wither, dry up

**acedar** /aθe'ðar; ase'ðar/ *vt* to make bitter, sour; embitter, displease; —*vr* turn sour; wither (plants)

**acefalía** /aθefa'lia; asefa'lia/ *f*, acephalia, headlessness

**acéfalo** /a'θefalo; a'sefalo/ *a* acephalous

**aceitar** /aθei'tar; asei'tar/ *vt* to oil, lubricate; rub with oil

**aceite** /a'θeite; a'seite/ *m*, olive oil; oil. **a. de hígado**
**de bacalao,** cod-liver oil. **a. de linaza,** linseed oil. **a. de ricino,** castor-oil. **a. de trementina,** oil of turpentine

**aceitera** /aθei'tera; asei'tera/ *f*, woman who sells oil; oil can; oil bottle; *pl* cruet

**aceitero** /aθei'tero; asei'tero/ *m*, oil seller —*a* oil

**aceitoso** /aθei'toso; asei'toso/ *a* oily

**aceituna** /aθei'tuna; asei'tuna/ *f*, *Bot.* olive

**aceitunado** /aθeitu'naðo; aseitu'naðo/ *a* olive-colored

**aceitunero** /aθeitu'nero; aseitu'nero/ **(-ra)** *n* olive picker; olive seller. *m*, warehouse for storing olives

**aceituno** /aθei'tuno; asei'tuno/ *m*, olive tree

**aceleración** /aθelera'θion; aselera'sion/ *f*, speed, haste; acceleration

**aceleradamente** /aθele,raða'mente; asele,raða'mente/ *adv* hastily, swiftly

**acelerador** /aθelera'ðor; aselera'ðor/ *a* accelerating. *m*, hastener; *Auto.* accelerator

**acelerar** /aθele'rar; asele'rar/ *vt* to hasten, speed up; accelerate

**acémila** /a'θemila; a'semila/ *f*, beast of burden, mule

**acendrado** /aθen'draðo; asen'draðo/ *a* pure, unblemished, spotless

**acendrar** /aθen'drar; asen'drar/ *vt* to refine (metals); purify, make spotless

**acento** /a'θento; a'sento/ *m*, accent; tone, inflection; *Poet.* voice, words. **a. agudo,** acute accent. **a. circunflejo,** circumflex accent. **a. grave,** grave accent. **a. ortográfico,** graphic accent, written accent. **a. tónico,** tonic accent

**acentuación** /aθentua'θion; asentua'sion/ *f*, accentuation, stress; emphasis

**acentuar** /aθen'tuar; asen'tuar/ *vt* to accent; stress, emphasize; —*vr* become evident, become marked, be noticeable

**aceña** /a'θeɲa; a'seɲa/ *f*, water-mill; irrigation waterwheel; chain-well

**acepción** /aθep'θion; asep'sion/ *f*, meaning, significance, acceptation. **a. de personas,** partiality, preference

**acepilladura** /aθe,piʎa'ðura; ase,piya'ðura/ *f*, sweeping, brushing; planing; wood-shaving

**acepillar** /aθepi'ʎar; asepi'yar/ *vt* to sweep, brush; plane; *Inf.* brush up, polish up

**aceptabilidad** /a,θeptaβili'ðað; a,septaβili'ðað/ *f*, acceptability

**aceptable** /aθep'taβle; asep'taβle/ *a* acceptable

**aceptación** /aθepta'θion; asepta'sion/ *f*, acceptance; popularity; approval

**aceptador** /aθepta'ðor; asepta'ðor/ **(-ra)** *a* accepting —*n* acceptor

**aceptar** /aθep'tar; asep'tar/ *vt* to accept; approve; accept a challenge; *Com.* honor

**acequia** /a'θe'kia; ase'kia/ *f*, ditch, trench; irrigation channel

**acequiero** /aθe'kiero; ase'kiero/ *m*, keeper of irrigation ditches

**acera** /a'θera; a'sera/ *f*, sidewalk, pavement. **a. del sol,** sunny side of the street

**acerado** /aθe'raðo; ase'raðo/ *a* steel; steel-like; strong, tough; mordant, incisive

**acerar** /aθe'rar; ase'rar/ *vt* to steel; treat (liquids) with steel; harden, make obdurate

**acerbidad** /aθerβi'ðað; aserβi'ðað/ *f*, bitterness, acerbity, sourness; harshness, cruelty

**acerbo** /a'θerβo; a'serβo/ *a* sour, tart, bitter; cruel, harsh

**acerca de** /a'θerka de; a'serka de/ *adv* about, concerning

**acercamiento** /aθerka'miento; aserka'miento/ *m*, approach

**acercar** /aθer'kar; aser'kar/ *vt* to bring nearer; —*vr* be near at hand, draw near; (*with prep a*) approach

**acerico** /aθe'riko; ase'riko/ *m*, small cushion; pincushion

**acero** /a'θero; a'sero/ *m*, steel; blade, sword; *pl* bravery, spirit; *Inf.* good appetite. **a. inoxidable,** stainless steel

**acérrimo** /a'θerrimo; a'serrimo/ *a superl* extremely strong, mighty; most harsh; most resolute, unflinching; very strong (taste, smell)

**acerrojar** /aθerro'har; aserro'har/ *vt* to lock, padlock; bolt

**acertado** /aθer'taðo; aser'taðo/ *a* well-aimed; fitting, suitable; wise; successful

**acertar** /aθer'tar; aser'tar/ *vt irr* to hit the mark; find, come across; succeed (in), achieve; guess, find out; **No acertaba a explicármelo**, I couldn't quite understand it. **a. por chambra**, to make a lucky guess —*vi* be successful; thrive (of plants); (*with prep a + infin*) happen, occur, come to pass —*Pres. Indic.* **acierto, aciertas, acierta, aciertan.** *Pres. Subjunc.* **acierte, aciertes, acierte, acierten**

**acertijo** /aθer'tiho; aser'tiho/ *m*, riddle

**acervo** /a'θerβo; a'serβo/ *m*, pile, heap; *Fig.* storehouse, wealth (e.g. of words)

**acetato** /aθe'tato; ase'tato/ *m*, acetate

**acético** /a'θetiko; a'setiko/ *a* acetic

**acetileno** /aθeti'leno; aseti'leno/ *m*, acetylene

**achacar** /atʃa'kar/ *vt* to attribute, impute, assign. **achacable a**, imputable to

**achacoso** /atʃa'koso/ *a* ailing, ill, sickly

**achantarse** /atʃan'tarse/ *vr Inf.* to hide from danger; put up with, bear

**achaparrado** /atʃapa'rraðo/ *a* stocky

**achaque** /a'tʃake/ *m*, ailment, illness (permanent); *Inf.* period, menstruation; pregnancy; matter, affair; pretext; failing, bad habit. **En a. de...**, Re..., concerning...

**achatamiento** /atʃata'miento/ *m*, flattening

**achatar** /atʃa'tar/ *vt* to flatten, make flat

**achicado** /atʃi'kaðo/ *a* childish

**achicar** /atʃi'kar/ *vt* to make smaller, diminish; drain, bail out; depreciate, belittle

**achicarse** /atʃi'karse/ *Inf.* to sing small

**achicharrar** /atʃitʃa'rrar/ *vt Cul.* to overcook; overheat; annoy, importune

**achicoria** /atʃi'koria/ *f*, chicory

**achique** /a'tʃike/ *m*, bailing, draining

**achispado** /atʃis'paðo/ *a Inf.* tipsy

**achubascarse** /atʃuβas'karse/ *vr* to become overcast, grow stormy

**achuchar** /atʃu'tʃar/ *vt Inf.* to squeeze, hug; jostle, push against

**achuchón** /atʃu'tʃon/ *m*, *Inf.* shove, push; hug, squeeze

**achulado** /atʃu'laðo/ *a Inf.* brazen, tough

**aciago** /a'θiago; a'siago/ *a* unhappy, ill-omened; fateful

**acíbar** /a'θiβar; a'siβar/ *m*, aloe tree; bitter aloes; sorrow, bitterness

**acibarar** /aθiβa'rar; asiβa'rar/ *vt* to add bitter aloes to; embitter, sadden

**acicalado** /aθika'laðo; asika'laðo/ *a* polished; neat; well-groomed. *m*, polishing, burnishing (of weapons)

**acicalador** /aθikala'ðor; asikala'ðor/ **(-ra)** *a* polishing —*n* polisher. *m*, burnisher (machine)

**acicalar** /aθika'lar; asika'lar/ *vt* to burnish (weapons); adorn, deck; —*vr* dress oneself with care

**acicate** /aθi'kate; asi'kate/ *m*, Moorish spur; incitement, stimulus

**acicatear** /aθikate'ar; asikate'ar/ *vt* to induce, spur on. **a. la curiosidad**, arouse curiosity

**acidez** /aθi'ðeθ; asi'ðes/ *f*, acidity, bitterness

**acidia** /a'θiðia; a'siðia/ *f*, indolence; sluggishness

**ácido** /a'θiðo; 'asiðo/ *a* acid; sour; harsh. *m*, acid. **a. fénico**, carbolic acid. **a. graso**, fatty acid

**acidular** /aθiðu'lar; asiðu'lar/ *vt Chem.* to acidulate

**acídulo** /a'θiðulo; a'siðulo/ *a Chem.* acidulous

**acierto** /a'θierto; a'sierto/ *m*, good hit, bull's-eye; success; achievement; cleverness; dexterity, skill; wisdom, sense; tact

**acimut** /aθi'mut; asi'mut/ *m*, *Astron.* azimuth

**aclamación** /aklama'θion; aklama'sion/ *f*, acclamation; shout of acclamation. **por a.**, unanimously

**aclamador** /aklama'ðor/ **(-ra)** *a* acclaiming —*n* applauder, acclaimer

**aclamar** /akla'mar/ *vt* to acclaim; applaud

**aclaración** /aklara'θion; aklara'sion/ *f*, explanation; elucidation

**aclarado** /akla'raðo/ *m*, rinse; rinsing

**aclarador, aclaratorio** /aklara'ðor, aklara'torio/ *a* explanatory

**aclarar** /akla'rar/ *vt* to clarify, purify; clear; rinse (clothes); explain; thin; —*vi* clear; (sky) clear up; dawn

**aclimatación** /aklimata'θion; aklimata'sion/ *f*, acclimatization

**aclimatar** /aklima'tar/ *vt* to acclimatize

**acné** /ak'ne/ *m*, acne

**acobardar** /akoβar'ðar/ *vt* to intimidate, frighten

**acocear** /akoθe'ar; akose'ar/ *vt* to kick; *Inf.* insult, humiliate

**acocharse** /ako'tʃarse/ *vr* to squat, crouch

**acodalar** /akoða'lar/ *vt* to prop

**acodiciar** /akoði'θiar; akoði'siar/ *vt* to yearn for, covet, desire

**acogedizo** /akohe'ðiθo; akohe'ðiso/ *a* gathered haphazardly

**acogedor** /akohe'ðor/ **(-ra)** *a* welcoming, friendly; inviting (e.g. a chair or room); —*n* protector

**acoger** /ako'her/ *vt* to receive, welcome, admit; protect, harbor; —*vr* take refuge; (*with prep a*) make use of, resort to; **acogerse a sagrado**, seek sanctuary

**acogida** /ako'hiða/ *f*, reception, welcome; protection, shelter; meeting place; confluence (of waters). **tener buena a.**, to be well received

**acogollar** /akogo'ʎar; akogo'yar/ *vt* to protect, cover (plants); —*vi* sprout, shoot

**acogotar** /akogo'tar/ *vt* to fell by a blow on the neck; *Inf.* knock out

**acolada** /ako'laða/ *f*, accolade

**acolitar** /akoli'tar/ *vi* to serve as an altar boy, serve as an altar girl

**acólito** /a'kolito/ *m*, acolyte

**acometedor** /akomete'ðor/ **(-ra)** *a* capable, enterprising; aggressive —*n* aggressor, attacker

**acometer** /akome'ter/ *vt* to attack furiously; undertake; take in hand; overcome (of sleep, etc.)

**acometida** /akome'tiða/ *f*, **acometimiento** *m*, assault, onrush; undertaking

**acometividad** /akometiβi'ðað/ *f*, aggressiveness

**acomodable** /akomo'ðaβle/ *a* easily arranged

**acomodación** /akomoða'θion; akomoða'sion/ *f*, adjustment; adaptation; accommodation

**acomodadizo** /akomoða'ðiθo; akomoða'ðiso/ *a* accommodating, easy-going

**acomodado** /akomo'ðaðo/ *a* suitable; convenient; wealthy, well-off; comfort-loving; moderate, low (of price)

**acomodador** /akomoða'ðor/ **(-ra)** *n* theater attendant, usher

**acomodamiento** /akomoða'miento/ *m*, agreement, transaction; accommodation

**acomodar** /akomo'ðar/ *vt* to arrange, adjust, accommodate; adapt; appoint; place; reconcile; employ, take on; equip, provide; lodge; —*vi* suit, be convenient; —*vr* compromise, agree

**acomodaticio** /akomoða'tiθio; akomoða'tisio/ *a* accommodating

**acomodo** /ako'moðo/ *m*, post, employment; arrangement; settlement

**acompañamiento** /akompaɲa'miento/ *m*, accompaniment; following, retinue; *Mus.* accompaniment; *Theat.* crowd, chorus

**acompañanta** /akompa'ɲanta/ *f*, chaperon; maid, servant

**acompañante** /akompa'ɲante/ *m*, *Mus.* accompanist

**acompañar** /akompa'ɲar/ *vt* to accompany; follow, escort; enclose (a letter, etc.); *Mus.* accompany

**acompasado** /akompa'saðo/ *a* rhythmic; deliberate, slow

**acondicionado** /akondiθio'naðo; akondisio'naðo/ *a* conditioned; (*with bien or mal*) in good or bad condition; of good or bad quality; good- or ill-natured. **reflejo acondicionado** *Med.* conditioned reflex

**acondicionar** /akondiθio'nar; akondisio'nar/ *vt* to prepare; mend, repair; —*vr* condition oneself

**acongojar** /akongo'har/ *vt* to sadden, grieve; oppress

**aconsejable** /akonse'haβle/ *a* advisable

**aconsejar** /akonse'har/ *vt* to advise; —*vr* (*with con*) consult, ask advice of

**aconsonantar** /akonsonan'tar/ vt and vi to rhyme

**acontecedero** /akonteθe'ðero; akontese'ðero/ a possible

**acontecer** /akonte'θer; akonte'ser/ vi irr impers to happen. See **conocer**

**acontecimiento** /akonteθi'miento; akontesi'miento/ m, event, occurrence

**acopiar** /ako'piar/ vt to collect, amass, gather

**acopio** /a'kopio/ m, collection, store; accumulation, gathering

**acopladura** /akopla'ðura/ f, **acoplamiento** m, (Mech.) joint; coupling; yoking; mating (of animals)

**acoplar** /ako'plar/ vt to join, couple; yoke; mate (animals); reconcile (opinions); —vr Inf. fall in love

**acoquinar** /akoki'nar/ vt Inf. to intimidate, terrify

**acorazado** /akora'θaðo; akora'saðo/ a (Nav. Mil.) armored, iron-clad. m, iron-clad, battleship

**acorazar** /akora'θar; akora'sar/ vt (Nav. Mil.) to armor

**acorcharse** /akor'tʃarse/ vr to dry up, shrivel; go numb (limbs)

**acordadamente** /akor,ðaða'mente/ adv by common consent, unanimously; deliberately, after due thought

**acordar** /akor'ðar/ vt irr to decide unanimously; resolve; remind; tune; harmonize (colors); —vi agree; —vr remember; come to an agreement. **Si mal no me acuerdo,** If memory serves me right —Pres. Indic. **acuerdo, acuerdas, acuerda, acuerdan.** Pres. Subjunc. **acuerde, acuerdes, acuerde, acuerden**

**acorde** /a'korðe/ a agreed; in harmony; in agreement. m, Mus. chord; harmony

**acordeón** /akorðe'on/ m, accordion; (slang) crib sheet

**acordonar** /akorðo'nar/ vt to lace; cordon off, surround; mill (coins)

**acornear** /akorne'ar/ vt to butt, toss (bulls)

**acorralado** /akorra'laðo/ a at bay, intimidated

**acorralamiento** /akorrala'miento/ m, corralling, penning

**acorralar** /akorra'lar/ vt to corral, pen; confine; corner, silence (in argument); frighten; harass

**acorrer** /ako'rrer/ vt to aid, assist; —vi run, hasten; —vr take refuge

**acortamiento** /akorta'miento/ m, shortening

**acortar** /akor'tar/ vt to shorten; —vr be speechless, be shy. **a. las velas,** to take in sail

**acosador** /akosa'ðor/ **(-ra)** a persecuting —n persecutor

**acosamiento** /akosa'miento/ m, persecution

**acosar** /ako'sar/ vt to persecute relentlessly; annoy, harass

**acostado** /ako'staðo/ a in bed; stretched out; Herald. couchant

**acostar** /ako'star/ vt irr to lay down, stretch out; put to bed; —vi lean, tilt; —vr lie down; go to bed; Naut. come alongside. See **contar**

**acostumbrado** /akostum'braðo/ a accustomed, usual

**acostumbrar** /akostum'brar/ vt to habituate, accustom; —vi be in the habit of (e.g. Acostumbramos ir a la playa en el verano, We generally go to the seashore in summer); —vr (with prep a) become used to

**acotación** /akota'θion; akota'sion/ f, noting; marginal note; stage direction; ordnance survey number

**acotar** /ako'tar/ vt to annotate; mark out boundaries; fix, establish; accept; Inf. choose; testify; fill in elevation figures (on a map); —vr seek refuge

**acotillo** /ako'tiʎo; ako'tiyo/ m, sledgehammer

**acre** /'akre/ a bitter, sour; harsh; biting, mordant. m, acre (land measure)

**acrecencia** /akre'θenθia; akre'sensia/ f, **acrecentamiento** m, increase; addition

**acrecentar** /akreθen'tar; akresen'tar/ vt irr to increase; augment; promote, prefer. See **acertar**

**acrecer** /akre'θer; akre'ser/ vt irr to increase; augment. See **conocer**

**acreción** /akre'θion; akre'sion/ f, accretion

**acreditado** /akreði'taðo/ a accredited, well-reputed; respected

**acreditar** /akreði'tar/ vt to prove; verify; accredit; recommend; sanction, authorize; vouch for, guarantee; Com. credit

**acreedor** /akree'ðor/ **(-ra)** n creditor; claimant —a deserving. **a. hipotecario,** mortgagee

**acreencia** /akre'enθia; akre'ensia/ f, debt; Com. claim

**acribillar** /akriβi'ʎar; akriβi'yar/ vt to riddle with holes; wound repeatedly; pelt; torment; Inf. pester, harass

**acriminación** /akrimina'θion; akrimina'sion/ f, accusation

**acriminador** /akrimina'ðor/ **(-ra)** a incriminating —n accuser

**acriminar** /akrimi'nar/ vt to accuse, charge

**acrimonia** /akri'monia/ f, acrimony

**acrisolar** /akriso'lar/ vt to refine, purify (metals); perfect; clarify, elucidate

**acrobacia** /akro'βaθia; akro'βasia/ f, acrobatics

**acróbata** /a'kroβata/ mf acrobat

**acrobático** /akro'βatiko/ a acrobatic

**acromatópsico** /akroma'topsiko/ a color-blind

**acrópolis** /a'kropolis/ f, acropolis

**acróstico** /a'krostiko/ a and m, acrostic

**acta** /'akta/ f, minutes, record; certificate of election (as deputy to Cortes, etc.); pl deeds (of a martyr). **a. matrimonial,** marriage register

**actitud** /akti'tuð/ f, attitude

**activar** /akti'βar/ vt to stimulate, make active; accelerate, hasten

**actividad** /aktiβi'ðað/ f, activity; movement, bustle. **en a.,** in action; at work

**activo** /ak'tiβo/ a active. m, Com. assets

**acto** /'akto/ m, act, deed, action; act, law; act (of a play); public ceremony; pl minutes (of a meeting), proceedings (of a conference). **a. continuo** or **a. seguido,** immediately afterwards. **a. vandálico,** act of vandalism. **los Actos de los Apóstoles,** Acts of the Apostles. **en a.,** in the act (of doing). **en el a.,** in the act; immediately

**actor** /ak'tor/ m, actor; Law. plaintiff

**actriz** /ak'triθ; ak'tris/ f, actress

**actuación** /aktua'θion; aktua'sion/ f, operation, functioning; action; pl legal functions, judicial acts

**actual** /ak'tual/ a present; contemporary

**actualidad** /aktuali'ðað/ f, present, present time; topic of interest. **actualidades,** current events. **en la a.,** at the present time

**actuar** /ak'tuar/ vt to operate, set in motion; —vi act; exercise legal functions

**actuario** /ak'tuario/ **(de seguros)** m, actuary

**acuarela** /akua'rela/ f, water-color painting

**acuarelista** /akuare'lista/ mf water-colorist

**acuario** /a'kuario/ m, aquarium; Aquarius

**acuartelamiento** /a,kuartela'miento/ m, billeting (of troops); billet, quarters

**acuartelar** /akuarte'lar/ vt to billet

**acuático, acuátil** /a'kuatiko, a'kuatil/ a aquatic

**acuatinta** /akua'tinta/ f, aquatint

**acuchillado** /akutʃi'ʎaðo; akutʃi'yaðo/ a taught by experience, schooled

**acuchillar** /akutʃi'ʎar; akutʃi'yar/ vt to hack, cut about; stab, put to the sword; slash (sleeves, etc.); —vr fight with swords, daggers

**acucia** /a'kuθia; a'kusia/ f, fervor, zeal; yearning, longing

**acuciar** /aku'θiar; aku'siar/ vt to incite; goad; stimulate; encourage

**acuciosidad** /akuθiosi'ðað; akusiosi'ðað/ f, eagerness, fervor, zeal

**acucioso** /aku'θioso; aku'sioso/ a eager, fervent, keen, zealous

**acuclillarse** /akukli'ʎarse; akukli'yarse/ vr to squat, crouch

**acudir** /aku'ðir/ vi to go, repair (to); come; go or come to the aid of; attend, be present; **No me acude ningún ejemplo a la memoria,** No example comes to mind; resort (to), seek protection; reply, respond

**acueducto** /akue'ðukto/ m, aqueduct

**acuerdo** /a'kuerðo/ m, motion, resolution; decision; harmony, agreement; opinion, belief; remembrance; report; meeting (of members of a tribunal); Art. harmony (of colors). **de a.,** in agreement, in conformity; unanimously. **estar de a. (con),** to agree (with). **es-**

**tar de acuerdo en** (+ inf.), to agree to (+ inf.) **ponerse de a.**, to come to an understanding
**acuitar** /aku'tar/ vt to distress, trouble; grieve
**acullá** /aku'ʎa; aku'ya/ adv afar, yonder, in the distance
**acumulación** /akumula'θion; akumula'sion/ f, accumulation, collection
**acumulador** /akumula'ðor/ (-ra) a accumulative. m, accumulator, storage battery —n collector, accumulator
**acumulamiento** /akumula'miento/ m, accumulation (act)
**acumular** /akumu'lar/ vt to accumulate, amass, collect; accuse, charge with
**acuñación** /akuɲa'θion; akuɲa'sion/ f, minting, coining; wedging
**acuñador** /akuɲa'ðor/ (-ra) n coiner, stamper; wedge. m, coining machine
**acuñar** /aku'ɲar/ vt to mint, stamp, coin; wedge
**acuosidad** /akuosi'ðað/ f, wateriness
**acuoso** /a'kuoso/ a aqueous, watery
**acurrucarse** /akurru'karse/ vr to huddle; curl up; crouch
**acusación** /akusa'θion; akusa'sion/ f, accusation; Law. charge; Law. prosecution
**acusado** /aku'saðo/ (-da) a accused; prominent; well-defined; —n accused; Law. defendant
**acusador** /akusa'ðor/ (-ra) a accusing —n accuser; Law. prosecutor
**acusar** /aku'sar/ vt to accuse; blame; denounce; Com. acknowledge receipt; Law. prosecute; Law. charge. **acusarle a uno las cuarenta**, Inf. to give someone a piece of one's mind
**acusatorio** /akusa'torio/ a accusatory
**acusón** /aku'son/ (-ona) n Inf. telltale, sneak, informer
**acústica** /a'kustika/ f, acoustics
**acústico** /a'kustiko/ a acoustic
**adagio** /a'ðahio; also for 2 a'dadʒio/ m, adage; Mus. adagio
**adalid** /aða'lið/ m, chieftain; head, leader
**adamado** /aða'maðo/ a effeminate; refined; genteel
**adamantino** /aðaman'tino/ a adamantine
**adaptabilidad** /aðaptaβili'ðað/ f, adaptability
**adaptación** /aðapta'θion; aðapta'sion/ f, adaptation
**adaptar** /aðap'tar/ vt to adapt, make suitable; —vr adapt oneself
**adarme** /a'ðarme/ m, tittle, jot. **por adarmes**, in bits and pieces, in drabs and driblets
**adecentar** /aðeθen'tar; aðesen'tar/ vt to make decent; tidy up; —vr tidy oneself
**adecuación** /aðekua'θion; aðekua'sion/ f, adequacy; suitability
**adecuado** /aðe'kuaðo/ a adequate; suitable
**adecuar** /aðe'kuar/ vt to proportion, fit; Fig. tailor
**adefesio** /aðe'fesio/ m, Inf. folly, absurdity (gen. pl); extravagant attire; guy, sight
**adelantado** /aðelan'taðo/ a precocious; forward, pert; fast (clocks); early (of fruit); excellent; capable, proficient. m, Obs. provincial governor or chief justice or captain-general (Spanish history). **por a.**, in advance
**adelantamiento** /aðelanta'miento/ m, promotion, furtherance; progress, advancement; betterment, improvement; Obs. office of **adelantado**; anticipation
**adelantar** /aðelan'tar/ vt to advance, move on; hasten; forestall; overtake; put on (the hands of clocks); improve, better; beat, excel; place in front; —vi progress, advance; be fast (clocks); grow, develop; —vr come forward
**adelante** /aðe'lante/ adv on, forward; further on; straight ahead. **¡A.!** Onward!; Come in! **de hoy en a.**, henceforth, from today
**adelanto** /aðe'lanto/ m, anticipation; progress; Com. payment in advance. **el a. de la hora**, moving the clock forward
**adelfa** /a'ðelfa/ f, Bot. rose-bay, oleander
**adelgazamiento** /aðel̩ɡaθa'miento; aðel̩ɡasa-'miento/ m, loss of weight; slenderness; thinness
**adelgazar** /aðel̩ɡa'θar; aðel̩ɡa'sar/ vt to make slender or thin; Fig. split hairs; whittle, taper; —vi grow slender or thin

**ademán** /aðe'man/ m, posture, attitude; gesture; pl behavior, manners
**además** /aðe'mas/ adv besides, in addition; moreover. **a. de**, as well as
**adentellar** /aðente'ʎar; aðente'yar/ vt to bite, sink the teeth into
**adentro** /a'ðentro/ adv inside, within
**adentros** /a'ðentros/ m pl, private thoughts (e.g. Pensé para mis adentros, I thought to myself) —interj **¡Adentro!** Come in!; Go in!
**adepto** /a'ðepto/ a affiliated; adept, proficient
**aderezamiento** /aðe̩reθa'miento; aðe̩resa'miento/ m, dressing; seasoning; embellishment
**aderezar** /aðere'θar; aðere'sar/ vt to deck, embellish; cook; Cul. season; Cul. dress; prepare; repair, mend; guide, direct; dress (cloth)
**aderezo** /aðe'reθo; aðe'reso/ m, dressing, adornment; beautifying; finery, ornament; preparation; seasoning; set of jewels; horse's trappings; gum starch (for dressing cloth); equipment
**adeudar** /aðeu'ðar/ vt to owe; be dutiable (goods); Com. debit; —vi become related (by marriage); —vr run into debt
**adeudo** /a'ðeuðo/ m, debt; customs duty; Com. debit
**adherencia** /aðe'renθia; aðe'rensia/ f, adherence; adhesion
**adherente** /aðe'rente/ a adhesive; connected, attached. mf adherent, follower; m pl. **adherentes**, accessories, requisites
**adherirse** /aðe'rirse/ vr irr to adhere, stick; follow; believe (in). See **herir**
**adhesión** /aðe'sion/ f, adhesion; adherence
**adhesivo** /aðe'siβo/ a adhesive
**adición** /aði'θion; aði'sion/ f, addition
**adicional** /aðiθio'nal; aðisio'nal/ a additional, extra
**adicionar** /aðiθio'nar; aðisio'nar/ vt to add up; add to
**adicto** /a'ðikto/ (-ta) a addicted, fond; joint —n addict; follower, disciple
**adiestrador** /aðiestra'ðor/ (-ra) n trainer, coach; guide, teacher
**adiestrar** /aðies'trar/ vt to train, coach; guide, teach; lead; —vr practice, perfect oneself
**adieta** /aðie'tar/ vt Med. to put on a diet
**adinerado** /aðine'raðo/ a wealthy, well-off, rich
**adiós** /a'ðios/ interj Good-bye!; Hello, God be with you! (used as greeting). m, farewell
**adiposo** /aði'poso/ a adipose
**aditamento** /aðita'mento/ m, addition
**adive** /a'ðiβe/ m, jackal
**adivinación** /aðiβina'θion; aðiβina'sion/ f, divination; guess
**adivinador** /aðiβina'ðor/ (-ra) a prophesying, divining —n soothsayer
**adivinanza** /aðiβi'nanθa; aðiβi'nansa/ f, divination; riddle; puzzle. **adivinanzas**, guessing games. **no estar para jugar a las a.**, to be in no mood for guessing games
**adivinar** /aðiβi'nar/ vt to prophesy, foretell; divine, guess; solve, guess (riddles, etc.)
**adivino** /aði'βino/ (-na) n soothsayer, prophet
**adjetivo** /aðhe'tiβo/ a adjectival. m, adjective
**adjudicación** /aðhuðika'θion; aðhuðika'sion/ f, adjudication, award
**adjudicador** /aðhuðika'ðor/ (-ra) n adjudicator
**adjudicar** /aðhuði'kar/ vt to adjudge; award; —vr appropriate
**adjudicatario** /aðhuðika'tario/ (-ia) n recipient (of a prize, etc.); grantee
**adjuntar** /aðhun'tar/ vt to enclose (with a letter, etc.)
**adjunto** /að'hunto/ a attached; enclosed, accompanying; assistant, deputy; adjectival. m, addition, supplement
**administración** /aðministra'θion; aðministra'sion/ f, administration; direction, control; administratorship
**administrador** /aðministra'ðor/ (-ra) a administrative —n administrator. **a. de correos**, postmaster
**administrar** /aðminis'trar/ vt to control, manage; provide, supply; administer. **administrarse el tiempo**, to budget one's time

administrativo 10

**administrativo** /aðministra'tiβo/ *a* administrative, executive
**admirable** /aðmi'raβle/ *a* admirable
**admirablemente** /aðmi,raβle'mente/ *adv* admirably, excellently
**admiración** /aðmira'θion; aðmira'sion/ *f,* amazement; admiration; wonder; exclamation mark
**admirador** /aðmira'ðor/ **(-ra)** *a* admiring —*n* admirer
**admirar** /aðmi'rar/ *vt* to admire; surprise, amaze (e.g. *Me admira su acción,* His action surprises me); to see (e.g. *Desde la colina se pueden admirar varios edificios de la ciudad,* From the hill several buildings in the city can be seen); —*vr* (*with de*) be surprised at or by
**admirativo** /aðmira'tiβo/ *a* admiring; admirable, excellent
**admisibilidad** /aðmisiβili'ðað/ *f,* allowability, permissibility
**admisible** /aðmi'siβle/ *a* admissible; permissible
**admisión** /aðmi'sion/ *f,* admission; acceptance; allowance
**admitir** /aðmi'tir/ *vt* to admit; receive, accept; tolerate, brook; allow, permit
**admonición** /aðmoni'θion; aðmoni'sion/ *f,* admonition, warning; reprimand
**adobar** /aðo'βar/ *vt* to prepare; *Cul.* garnish; pickle (meat); cook; dress (hides)
**adobo** /a'ðoβo/ *m,* repairing; dressing (for cloth, leather); *Cul.* savory sauce; pickling sauce; make-up, cosmetic
**adocenado** /aðoθe'naðo; aðose'naðo/ *a* ordinary; narrow-minded
**adoctrinar** /aðoktri'nar/ *vt* to instruct
**adolecer** /aðole'θer; aðole'ser/ *vi irr* to fall ill; (*with de*) suffer from (diseases, defects); —*vr* be sorry for, regret. See **conocer**
**adolescencia** /aðoles'θenθia; aðoles'sensia/ *f,* adolescence
**adolescente** /aðoles'θente; aðoles'sente/ *a* and *mf* adolescent
**adonde** /a'ðonde/ *adv* (*interr* a **dónde**) where to, whither (e.g. *¿A dónde fuiste?* Where did you go to?)
**adondequiera** /a,ðonde'kiera/ *adv* wherever
**adopción** /aðop'θion; aðop'sion/ *f,* adoption
**adoptador** /aðopta'ðor/ **(-ra)** *a* adopting —*n* adopter
**adoptar** /aðop'tar/ *vt* to adopt (children); make one's own, embrace (opinions); take (decisions)
**adoptivo** /aðop'tiβo/ *a* adoptive
**adoquín** /aðo'kin/ *m,* cobble-stone; *Fig.* blockhead
**adoquinado** /aðoki'naðo/ *m,* cobbling, paving. *m,* cobbled pavement
**adoquinar** /aðoki'nar/ *vt* to pave with cobble-stones
**adorable** /aðo'raβle/ *a* adorable
**adoración** /aðora'θion; aðora'sion/ *f,* worship, adoration. **A. de los Reyes,** Adoration of the Magi; Epiphany
**adorador** /aðora'ðor/ **(-ra)** *a* adoring —*n* adorer
**adorar** /aðo'rar/ *vt* to adore; worship; (*with en*) dote on; —*vi* pray
**adormecedor** /aðormeθe'ðor; aðormese'ðor/ *a* soporific, drowsy
**adormecer** /aðorme'θer; aðorme'ser/ *vt irr* to make drowsy; soothe, lull; hush to sleep; —*vr* go to sleep; (limbs); fall asleep; (*with en*) persist in. See **conocer**
**adormecimiento** /aðormeθi'miento; aðormesi'miento/ *m,* sleepiness; lulling asleep; numbness
**adormitarse** /aðormi'tarse/ *vr* to doze, take a nap, snooze
**adornamiento** /aðorna'miento/ *m,* adornment, decoration
**adornar** /aðor'nar/ *vt* to deck, beautify; decorate; trim, embellish; adorn (of virtues, etc.)
**adorno** /a'ðorno/ *m,* decoration, adornment; ornament; trimming. **de a.,** ornamental; flowering (shrubs)
**adquiridor** /aðkiri'ðor/ **(-ra)** *a* acquiring —*n* acquirer
**adquirir** /aðki'rir/ *vt irr* to acquire, get; achieve, obtain —*Pres. Indic.* **adquiero, adquieres, adquiere, adquieren.** *Pres. Subjunc.* **adquiera, adquieras, adquiera, adquieran**
**adquisición** /aðkisi'θion; aðkisi'sion/ *f,* acquirement; acquisition. **poder de a.,** purchasing power

**adquisidor** /aðkisi'ðor/ **(-ra)** *a* acquiring —*n* acquirer, obtainer
**adquisitivo** /aðkisi'tiβo/ *a* acquisitive
**adquisividad** /aðkisiβi'ðað/ *f,* acquisitiveness
**adrazo** /a'ðraθo; a'ðraso/ *m,* salt-water still
**adrede** /a'ðreðe/ *adv* on purpose, intentionally
**adrenalina** /aðrena'lina/ *f,* adrenaline
**adriático** /a'ðriatiko/ *a* Adriatic
**adscribir** /aðskri'βir/ *vt* to ascribe, attribute; appoint (to a post, etc.)
**adscripción** /aðskrip'θion; aðskrip'sion/ *f,* ascription, attribution; appointment
**aduana** /a'ðuana/ *f,* customs house, customs. **pasar por la a.,** to go through customs
**aduanero** /aðua'nero/ *a* customs. *m,* customs officer
**aducir** /aðu'θir; aðu'sir/ *vt irr* to adduce, allege, cite; add. See **conducir**
**adueñarse** /aðue'parse/ **(-de)** *vr* to appropriate, take possession (of)
**adulación** /aðula'θion; aðula'sion/ *f,* adulation, flattery
**adulador** /aðula'ðor/ **(-ra)** *a* fawning —*n* flatterer
**adular** /aðu'lar/ *vt* to flatter, fawn upon, adulate
**adulteración** /aðultera'θion; aðultera'sion/ *f,* adulteration; falsification
**adulterador** /aðultera'ðor/ **(-ra)** *a* adulterant —*n* adulterator; falsifier; coiner
**adulterar** /aðulte'rar/ *vi* to commit adultery; —*vt* adulterate; falsify
**adulterino** /aðulte'rino/ *a* adulterous; false
**adulterio** /aðul'terio/ *m,* adultery
**adúltero** /a'ðultero/ **(-ra)** *a* adulterous; corrupt —*n* adulterer
**adulto** /a'ðulto/ **(-ta)** *a* and *n* adult
**adunar** /aðu'nar/ *vt* to join, unite; unify, combine
**adusto** /a'ðusto/ *a* extremely hot (of climate); grave, austere; standoffish, reserved
**advenedizo** /aðβene'ðiθo; aðβene'ðiso/ *a* foreign, alien; strange, unknown; upstart; newly rich
**advenimiento** /aðβeni'miento/ *m,* advent, arrival; ascension (to the throne)
**advenir** /aðβe'nir/ *vi irr* to come, arrive; happen, befall. See **venir**
**adventicio** /aðβen'tiθio; aðβen'tisio/ *a* casual, accidental; *Bot.* adventitious
**adverbio** /að'βerβio/ *m,* adverb
**adversario** /aðβer'sario/ **(-ia)** *n* adversary, rival; opponent
**adversidad** /aðβersi'ðað/ *f,* adversity, misfortune, sorrow
**adverso** /að'βerso/ *a* unfavorable, contrary, adverse; opposite
**advertencia** /aðβer'tenθia; aðβer'tensia/ *f,* warning; introduction, preface; remark
**advertido** /aðβer'tiðo/ *a* capable, clever; experienced; expert
**advertir** /aðβer'tir/ *vt irr* to observe, notice; warn; advise; feel, be conscious of; point out, indicate; inform; discover. See **sentir**
**Adviento** /að'βiento/ *m, Eccl.* Advent
**adyacente** /aðya'θente; aðya'sente/ *a* adjacent, near-by, neighboring
**aedo** /a'eðo/ *m, Poet.* poet
**aeración** /aera'θion; aera'sion/ *f,* aeration
**aéreo** /'aereo/ *a* aerial; airborne; airy; air; aeronautic; unsubstantial, fantastic. **correo a.,** airmail. **linea aérea** airline
**aerobismo** /aero'βismo/ *m,* aerobics
**aerodinámica** /aeroði'namika/ *f,* aerodynamics
**aeronauta** /aero'nauta/ *mf* aeronaut, balloonist
**aeronáutica** /aero'nautika/ *f,* aeronautics
**aeronáutico** /aero'nautiko/ *a* aeronautic
**aeropuerto** /aero'puerto/ *m,* airport
**aeróstato** /ae'rostato/ *m,* dirigible
**afabilidad** /afaβili'ðað/ *f,* affability, geniality, friendliness
**afable** /a'faβle/ *a* affable, genial, pleasant
**afamado** /afa'maðo/ *a* famous, well-known
**afamar** /afa'mar/ *vt* to make famous
**afán** /a'fan/ *m,* effort; manual labor; desire, anxiety. **a. de mando,** thirst for power

**afanar** /afa'nar/ *vt* to press, urge on; filch; —*vr* toil, labor; (*with por*) work hard to, try to

**afanoso** /afa'noso/ *a* hard, laborious; hard-working, painstaking; eager, anxious

**afasia** /a'fasia/ *f, Med.* aphasia

**afear** /afe'ar/ *vt* to make ugly; distort, deform; blame; criticize

**afección** /afek'θion; afek'sion/ *f,* fondness, affection; complaint, ailment, trouble

**afectación** /afekta'θion; afekta'sion/ *f,* affectation

**afectado** /afek'taðo/ *a* affected

**afectar** /afek'tar/ *vt* to feign, assume; affect; move, touch; *Law.* encumber

**afectivo** /afek'tiβo/ *a* affective

**afecto** /a'fekto/ *a* fond, affectionate; *Law.* encumbered; (*with prep a*) addicted to. *m,* emotion, sentiment; affection

**afectuosidad** /afektuosi'ðað/ *f,* affectionateness

**afectuoso** /afek'tuoso/ *a* affectionate, fond

**afeitada** /afei'taða/ *f,* shave, shaving

**afeitar** /afei'tar/ *vt* to shave; make up (one's face); adorn, beautify

**afeite** /a'feite/ *m,* cosmetic; make-up (for the complexion)

**afelpado** /afel'paðo/ *a* velvet-like, plushy

**afeminación** /afemina'θion; afemina'sion/ *f,* effeminacy; weakness, languor

**afeminado** /afemi'naðo/ *a* effeminate

**afeminar** /afemi'nar/ *vt* to make effeminate; weaken; —*vr* grow effeminate

**aferradamente** /aferraða'mente/ *adv* tenaciously, persistently, obstinately

**aferramiento** /aferra'miento/ *m,* seizing, clutching; *Naut.* furling; *Naut.* grappling; mooring, anchoring; obstinacy

**aferrar** /afe'rrar/ *vt* to seize, clutch; *Naut.* take in, furl; *Naut.* grapple; —*vi Naut.* anchor; —*vr* (*with con, en, a*) persist in, insist on

**afestonado** /afesto'naðo/ *a* festooned

**Afganistán** /afganis'tan/ Afghanistan

**afgano** /af'gano/ (**-na**) *a* and *n* Afghan

**afianzamiento** /afianθa'miento; afiansa'miento/ *m,* fastening, fixing; propping; grasping; guarantee, security

**afianzar** /afian'θar; afian'sar/ *vt* to fasten, fix; prop; consolidate (e.g. one's power); guarantee, be security for; grasp

**afición** /afi'θion; afi'sion/ *f,* propensity, inclination; fondness. **tomar a. (a),** to take a liking to

**aficionado** /afiθio'naðo; afisio'naðo/ (**-da**) *a* amateur —*n* amateur, fan, enthusiast. **ser a a.,** to be fond of, have a liking for

**aficionar** /afiθio'nar; afisio'nar/ *vt* to inspire liking or affection; —*vr* (*with prep a*) take a liking to, grow fond of; become an enthusiast of

**afijo** /a'fiho/ *m, Gram.* affix

**afiladera** /afila'ðera/ *f,* whetstone, grindstone

**afilado** /afi'laðo/ *a* sharp, keen (of edges)

**afilador** /afila'ðor/ *m,* grinder (of scissors, etc.); razor strop

**afilalápices** /afila'lapiθes; afila'lapises/ *m,* pencil sharpener

**afilar** /afi'lar/ *vt* to sharpen; grind, whet; taper; —*vr* grow thin; taper

**afiliación** /afilia'θion; afilia'sion/ *f,* affiliation

**afiliar** /afi'liar/ *vt* (*with prep a*) to affiliate with; —*vr* (*with prep a*) become affiliated with; join, become a member of

**afiligranado** /afiligra'naðo/ *a* filigree; delicate, fine; slender

**afilón** /afi'lon/ *m,* steel, knife sharpener; razor-strop

**afín** /a'fin/ *a* nearby, contiguous; similar, related. *mf* relative by marriage

**afinador** /afina'ðor/ *m,* tuning key; tuner (of pianos, etc.)

**afinar** /afi'nar/ *vt* to finish, perfect; *Fig.* polish, refine; tune (musical instruments); refine (metals); —*vi* sing in tune; —*vr* grow refined

**afinidad** /afini'ðað/ *f,* affinity, analogy; relationship (by marriage); *Chem.* affinity

**afirmación** /afirma'θion; afirma'sion/ *f,* affirmation, statement

**afirmadamente** /afir,maða'mente/ *adv* firmly

**afirmar** /afir'mar/ *vt* to make firm; fix, fasten; affirm; —*vr* steady oneself; hold on to

**afirmativa** /afirma'tiβa/ *f,* affirmative

**afirmativo** /afirma'tiβo/ *a* affirmative

**aflicción** /aflik'θion; aflik'sion/ *f,* affliction, grief

**aflictivo** /aflik'tiβo/ *a* sorrowful, grievous

**afligidamente** /afli,hiða'mente/ *adv* sorrowfully

**afligir** /afli'hir/ *vt* to sadden; afflict, trouble; —*vr* lament, mourn

**aflojamiento** /afloha'miento/ *m,* slackening; loosening; diminution

**aflojar** /aflo'har/ *vt* to slacken; loosen; —*vi* relax, weaken; abate, diminish. **a. el paso,** to slow down

**afluencia** /a'fluenθia; a'fluensia/ *f,* crowd, concourse; eloquence, fluency

**afluente** /a'fluente/ *a* fluent, eloquent. *m,* tributary (river)

**afluir** /aflu'ir/ *vi irr* to crowd, swarm; flow (into). See **huir**

**afonía** /afo'nia/ *f, Med.* aphonia, loss of voice; hoarseness

**afónico** /a'foniko/ *a* hoarse

**aforismo** /afo'rismo/ *m,* aphorism

**aforrador** /aforra'ðor/ (**-ra**) *n* one who lines jackets, etc.

**aforrar** /afo'rrar/ *vt* to line (clothes, etc.); —*vr* wrap oneself up; *Inf.* gormandize

**afortunadamente** /afortu,naða'mente/ *adv* luckily, fortunately

**afortunado** /afortu'naðo/ *a* lucky, fortunate; happy; stormy

**afortunar** /afortu'nar/ *vt* to bring luck to, make happy

**afrancesado** /afranθe'saðo; afranse'saðo/ (**-da**) *a* Francophile; Frenchified —*n* Francophile

**afrancesamiento** /afranθesa'miento; afransesa'miento/ *m,* adoption of the French way of life; servile imitation of everything French

**afrancesar** /afranθe'sar; afranse'sar/ *vt* to make French, gallicize; Frenchify; —*vr* become a Francophile

**afrenta** /a'frenta/ *f,* insult, affront; disgrace

**afrentar** /afren'tar/ *vt* to insult; —*vr* be ashamed

**afrentoso** /afren'toso/ *a* insulting, outrageous; disgraceful

**África** /'afrika/ Africa

**africanismo** /,afrikan'ismo/ *m,* Africanism

**africano** /afri'kano/ **-na** *a* and *n* African

**afrodisíaco** /afroði'siako/ *a* and *m,* aphrodisiac

**afrontar** /afron'tar/ *vt* to place opposite; confront; face (danger, etc.)

**afuera** /a'fuera/ *adv* outside, out.

**afueras** /a'fueras/ *f pl,* suburbs, outskirts

**agachada** /aga'tʃaða/ *f,* crouch, duck; jerk

**agachar** /aga'tʃar/ *vt Inf.* bend, bow; —*vr Inf.* crouch down; lie low, hide

**agalla** /a'gaʎa; a'gaya/ *f,* oak-apple; tonsil (gen. *pl*); *Zool.* gill; *Inf.* gall, cheek

**ágape** /'agape/ *m,* agape; banquet, feast

**Agar** /a'gar/ Hagar

**agárico** /a'gariko/ *m, Bot.* agaric

**agarrada** /aga'rraða/ *f, Inf.* brawl, scuffle

**agarradero** /agarra'ðero/ *m,* handle; heft; *Inf.* influence, pull

**agarrado** /aga'rraðo/ *a Inf.* tight-fisted, mean

**agarrar** /aga'rrar/ *vt* to grip, grasp; seize, take; *Inf.* nab (jobs); —*vr* grip, hold on

**agarro** /a'garro/ *m,* hold; grip, grasp

**agarrotar** /agarro'tar/ *vt* to garrotte; tighten (ropes, etc.); press, squeeze; —*vr* (limbs) go numb

**agasajar** /agasa'har/ *vt* to indulge, spoil, pet; receive kindly; entertain; caress

**agasajo** /aga'saho/ *m,* indulgence, kindness; affability, geniality; entertainment; gift, offering

**ágata** /'agata/ *f, Mineral.* agate

**agauchado** /agau'tʃaðo/ *a* gaucho-like

**agazapar** /agaθa'par; agasa'par/ *vt Inf.* to nab, catch; —*vr Inf.* squat, crouch

**agencia** /a'henθia; a'hensia/ f, influence, agency
**agenciar** /ahen'θiar; ahen'siar/ vt to negotiate, arrange; procure, manage
**agenda** /a'henda/ f, notebook; agenda
**agente** /a'hente/ m, agent. **a. de bolsa** or **a. de cambio,** bill broker. **a. de negocios,** business agent. **a. de policia,** police officer. **a. fiscal,** revenue officer
**agerasia** /ahe'rasia/ f, sickness-free old age
**agestado** /ahes'taðo/ a used generally with advs. **bien** or **mal,** well or ill-featured
**agigantado** /ahigan'taðo/ a enormous, gigantic; outstanding, extraordinary
**ágil** /'ahil/ a agile, nimble; easy to use (e.g. un libro ágil, a book easy to use)
**agilidad** /ahili'ðað/ f, agility, nimbleness
**agilizar** /ahili'θar; ahili'sar/ vt to make agile, limber; refresh one's knowledge of (e.g. Quiero agilizar mi español, I want to refresh my knowledge of Spanish); to enable; —vr limber up
**agitación** /ahita'θion; ahita'sion/ f, shaking; agitation, excitement
**agitador** /ahita'ðor/ **(-ra)** a stirring; agitating —n agitator. m, stirrer, stirring rod
**agitar** /ahi'tar/ vt to stir; shake; agitate, excite **a. una cuestión,** raise a question; discuss a question
**aglomeración** /aglomera'θion; aglomera'sion/ f, agglomeration
**aglomerado** /aglome'raðo/ m, briquette
**aglomerar** /aglome'rar/ vt to agglomerate, amass
**aglutinación** /aglutina'θion; aglutina'sion/ f, agglutination
**aglutinar(se)** /agluti'nar/ vt and vr to stick, agglutinate
**agnosticismo** /agnosti'θismo; agnosti'sismo/ m, agnosticism
**agnóstico** /ag'nostiko/ **(-ca)** a and n agnostic
**agobiar** /ago'βiar/ vt to bow, bend down; Fig. weigh down, oppress; —vr bend (beneath a weight)
**agobio** /a'goβio/ m, bowing, bending down; oppression, burden, weight
**agolparse** /agol'parse/ vr to rush, crowd, swarm
**agonía** /ago'nia/ f, agony, anguish
**agónico** /a'goniko/ a dying; agonizing
**agonizante** /agoni'θante; agoni'sante/ a dying
**agonizar** /agoni'θar; agoni'sar/ vt to attend a dying person; Inf. pester, annoy; —vi be dying (gen. **estar agonizando)**
**agorar** /ago'rar/ vt to prophesy, foretell
**agorero** /ago'rero/ **(-ra)** a prophetic; ill-boding —n seer, augur
**agostarse** /agos'tarse/ vt and vr to dry up, shrivel
**agosto** /a'gosto/ m, August; harvest. Inf. **hacer su a.,** to make hay while the sun shines
**agotable** /ago'taβle/ a exhaustible
**agotado** /ago'taðo/ a exhausted; out of print (of books)
**agotador** /agota'ðor/ a exhausting; exhaustive
**agotamiento** /a„gota'miento/ m, exhaustion
**agotar** /ago'tar/ vt to drain off (water); empty (a glass); exhaust; run through (money); study thoroughly, examine closely (a subject)
**agraciado** /agra'θiaðo; agra'siaðo/ a graceful; pretty
**agraciar** /agra'θiar; agra'siar/ vt to lend grace to; make pretty; favor
**agradable** /agra'ðaβle/ a agreeable, pleasant
**agradar** /agra'ðar/ vi to be pleasing, like, please (e.g. Me agrada su sinceridad, I like his sincerity)
**agradecer** /agraðe'θer; agraðe'ser/ vt irr to be grateful for; thank for; Fig. repay, requite. See **conocer**
**agradecido** /agraðe'θiðo; agraðe'siðo/ a grateful; thankful
**agradecimiento** /agraðeθi'miento; agraðesi'miento/ m, gratitude; thankfulness
**agrado** /a'graðo/ m, pleasure; desire, liking; amiability, affability
**agrandar** /agran'dar/ vt to enlarge
**agrario** /a'grario/ a agrarian
**agravación** /agraβa'θion; agraβa'sion/ f, **agravamiento** m, aggravation, worsening
**agravador** /agraβa'ðor/ a aggravating; worsening; increasing

**agravar** /agra'βar/ vt to aggravate, increase; oppress (taxes, responsibilities); make worse; exaggerate; —vr grow worse
**agraviador** /agraβia'ðor/ **-ra** a offensive —n offender
**agraviar** /agra'βiar/ vt to offend; wrong; —vr take offense, be insulted
**agravio** /a'graβio/ m, offense, insult; wrong, injury
**agraz** /a'graθ; a'gras/ m, unripened grape; verjuice; Fig. bitterness
**agredir** /agre'ðir/ vt to attack
**agregación** /agrega'θion; agrega'sion/ f, association, aggregation; total, collection, aggregate
**agregado** /agre'gaðo/ m, aggregate; assistant; attaché
**agregar** /agre'gar/ vt to add; collect, amass; appoint (to a post). **agregarse a...,** to join... (e.g. an association)
**agresión** /agre'sion/ f, aggression
**agresivo** /agre'siβo/ a aggressive
**agresor** /agre'sor/ **(-ra)** a and n aggressor
**agreste** /a'greste/ a rural, rustic; wild; uncouth, rude
**agriar** /a'griar/ vt to make bitter or sour; exasperate, provoke
**agrícola** /a'grikola/ a agricultural; mf agriculturalist, farmer
**agricultura** /agrikul'tura/ f, agriculture
**agridulce** /agri'ðulθe; agri'ðulse/ a bitter-sweet
**agrietarse** /agrie'tarse/ vr to crack, split
**agrimensor** /agrimen'sor/ m, surveyor
**agrimensura** /agrimen'sura/ f, surveying
**agrio** /'agrio/ a bitter, sour; rough, uneven (ground); brittle; sharp (of color contrast); unsociable; disagreeable
**agrisetado** /agrise'taðo/ a flowered (of materials)
**agronomía** /agrono'mia/ f, agronomy
**agrónomo** /a'gronomo/ a agronomic. m, agronomist
**agrupación** /agrupa'θion; agrupa'sion/ f, congregation, assembly; group; crowd; crowding, grouping
**agrupar** /agru'par/ vt to assemble, group; —vr crowd, cluster
**agrura** /a'grura/ f, bitterness; sourness; asperity
**agua** /'agua/ f, water; rain; slope of a roof; pl shot or watered effect on silks, etc.; medicinal waters; waves; water (of precious stones). **a. abajo,** down-stream. **a. arriba,** upstream. **a. bendita,** holy water. **a. cruda,** hard water. **a. de colonia,** eau de Cologne. **a. dulce,** fresh water. **a. fresca,** cold water. **a. nieve,** sleet. **a. oxigenada,** hydrogen peroxide. Fig. Inf. **estar con el a. al cuello,** to be in low water. Fig. Inf. **estar entre dos aguas,** to be between two fires. Naut. **hacer a.,** to leak. **Todo eso es ya a. pasada,** That's all water under the bridge
**aguacero** /agua'θero; agua'sero/ m, heavy rainfall, shower
**aguada** /a'guaða/ f, water supply on board ship; flood (in mines); watering station; Art. water color
**aguadero** /agua'ðero/ m, (animals') watering place
**aguado** /a'guaðo/ a watery; abstemious; watered
**aguador** /agua'ðor/ **(-ra)** m water carrier, water seller; drawer (of water)
**aguafiestas** /„agua'fiestas/ mf Fig. Inf. wet blanket
**aguafuerte** /„agua'fuerte/ f, etching
**aguaje** /a'guahe/ m, tide, waves; sea current; water supply (on board ship); wake (of a ship)
**aguamanil** /aguama'nil/ m, washstand; pitcher, ewer
**aguamanos** /agua'manos/ m, water for washing hands; pitcher
**aguamarina** /aguama'rina/ f, aquamarine
**aguamiel** /agua'miel/ f, honey and water, hydromel
**aguantable** /aguan'taβle/ a tolerable, bearable
**aguantar** /aguan'tar/ vt to bear, tolerate, endure; restrain, resist, oppose; —vr bear in silence, keep quiet
**aguante** /a'guante/ m, patience, endurance; resistance
**aguar** /a'guar/ vt to water down (wine, etc.); spoil (fun, etc.); —vr be filled with water; be flooded; become watery or thin
**aguardar** /aguar'ðar/ vt to await; expect; allow time to (debtors)
**aguardentería** /aguar„ðente'ria/ f, liquor shop

**aguardentoso** /aguarðen'toso/ *a* spirituous, containing; **aguardiente** hoarse, husky (of the voice)

**aguardiente** /aguar'ðiente/ *m*, liquor. **a. de caña,** rum

**aguardo** /a'guarðo/ *m*, ambush (for a hunter)

**aguarrás** /agua'rras/ *m*, oil of turpentine

**aguatinta** /agua'tinta/ *f*, aquatint

**aguatocha** /agua'totʃa/ *f*, pump (for water, etc.)

**aguaturma** /agua'turma/ *f*, Jerusalem artichoke

**agudeza** /agu'ðeθa; agu'ðesa/ *f*, sharpness; keenness; distinctness; alertness, cleverness; witty sally, repartee; wit; swiftness

**agudo** /a'guðo/ *a* sharp; alert, clever; (*Geom. Med.*) acute; fine, keen; rapid; high-pitched; strong (of scents, etc.)

**agüero** /a'guero/ *m*, omen, sign; prophecy, prediction

**aguerrido** /age'rriðo/ *a* veteran, war-hardened

**aguerrir** /age'rrir/ *vt defective* to harden to war; toughen

**aguijada** /agi'haða/ *f*, goad, spur

**aguijar** /agi'har/ *vt* to prick (with a goad); urge on, encourage (animals); incite, instigate; spur on; —*vi* walk swiftly

**aguijón** /agi'hon/ *m*, goad; sting; thorn, prickle; spur; incitement, stimulus. **tener aguijones,** to be on pins and needles

**aguijonazo** /agiho'naθo; agiho'naso/ *m*, prick (with a goad)

**águila** /'agila/ *f*, eagle; master mind. **a. caudal** *or* **a. real,** royal eagle. **á. o sol,** heads or tails (Mexico)

**aguileña** /agi'leɲa/ *f*, *Bot.* columbine

**aguileño** /agi'leɲo/ *a* aquiline

**aguilón** /agi'lon/ *m*, *Archit.* gable; boom (of a crane)

**aguinaldo** /agi'naldo/ *m*, Christmas present; New Year's gift

**aguja** /a'guha/ *f*, needle; hand, pointer; hatpin; engraver's burin; switch; *Rail.* point; *Rail.* rail; obelisk; spire; bodkin; knitting needle; crochet hook; (compass) needle *pl Bot.* plumelet. **a. capotera, a. de zurcir,** darning needle. **a. de marear** *Naut.,* binnacle; mariner's compass. **a. de media,** knitting needle. **a. espartera,** packing needle

**agujerear** /aguhere'ar/ *vt* to perforate, make holes in

**agujero** /agu'hero/ *m*, hole, aperture; needle maker or seller; needle case

**agujeta** /agu'heta/ *f*, lace (for shoes, etc.); *pl* muscular pains, aches; tip, gratuity

**agusanarse** /agusa'narse/ *vr* to become worminfested

**aguzadura** /aguθa'ðura; agusa'ðura/ *f*, sharpening, grinding, whetting

**aguzar** /agu'θar; agu'sar/ *vt* to sharpen; grind, whet; stimulate, encourage; urge on, incite

**ahechadura** /aetʃa'ðura/ *f*, chaff (of grain)

**ahembrado** /aem'braðo/ *a* effeminate

**aherrojar** /aerro'har/ *vt* to put (a prisoner) in irons; oppress

**aherrumbrar** /aerrum'brar/ *vt* to give the color or taste of iron to; —*vr* taste or look like iron; go rusty

**ahí** /a'i/ *adv* there; over there. **de a.,** thus, so. **por a.,** somewhere about, near at hand.

**ahidalgado** /aiðal'gaðo/ *a* gentlemanly; noble, generous

**ahijado** /ai'haðo/ **(-da)** *n* godchild; protégé

**ahijar** /ai'har/ *vt* to adopt (children); mother (animals); attribute, impute; —*vi* bring forth offspring; *Bot.* sprout. See **prohibir**

**ahincado** /ain'kaðo/ *a* earnest, eager

**ahincar** /ain'kar/ *vt* to urge, press; —*vr* hurry, hasten. See **prohibir**

**ahínco** /a'inko/ *m*, earnestness, eagerness

**ahitar** /ai'tar/ *vt* to stuff with food; bore, disgust. See **prohibir**

**ahíto** /a'ito/ *a* full of food; *Fig.* fed up. *m*, indigestion

**ahogado** /ao'gaðo/ **(-da)** *a* drowned; suffocated; stuffy, unventilated; stifling —*n* drowned person; victim of suffocation

**ahogamiento** /aoga'miento/ *m*, drowning; suffocation

**ahogar** /ao'gar/ *vt* to drown; suffocate; put out (the fire); stifle (yawns, etc.); suppress, extinguish; tire; overwater (plants); —*vr Naut.* sink, founder; drown; suffocate

**ahogo** /a'ogo/ *m*, anxiety, grief; difficulty in breathing, oppression; asthma; embarrassment; suffocation; straitened circumstances

**ahondamiento** /aonda'miento/ *m*, in-depth treatment (e.g. *el a. de un problema*, in-depth treatment of a problem)

**ahondar** /aon'dar/ *vt* to deepen; excavate, dig; go into thoroughly; go deep into, penetrate; —*vr* (earth) subside

**ahora** /a'ora/ *adv* now; very soon; just now, a short time ago —*conjunc* whether; now. **a. bien,** well now, given that. **a. mismo,** immediately, at once. **por a.,** for the present

**ahorcado** /aor'kaðo/ **(-da)** *n* hanged man

**ahorcar** /aor'kar/ *vt* to execute by hanging, hang. *Inf.* **a. los hábitos,** to leave the priesthood, cease to be an ecclesiastic

**ahormar** /aor'mar/ *vt* to adjust, shape; break in (new shoes); make (a person) see reason

**ahorquillar** /aorki'ʎar; aorki'yar/ *vt* to prop up (trees) with forks; —*vr* grow forked

**ahorrar** /ao'rrar/ *vt* to free (slaves); save, economize; avoid, eschew; —*vr* avoid; remove clothing

**ahorro** /a'orro/ *m*, economy, thrift; *pl* savings

**ahuchar** /au'tʃar/ *vt* to hoard; expel, drive away. See **desahuciar**

**ahuciar** /au'θiar; au'siar/ *vt* take possession of (a house)

**ahuecar** /aue'kar/ *vt* to hollow out; loosen; shake out; puff out, inflate; put on a solemn voice; hoe, dig; *Inf. vr* puff oneself out; put on airs

**ahumada** /au'maða/ *f*, smoke signal

**ahumado** /au'maðo/ *a* smoked; smoky

**ahumar** /au'mar/ *vt* to smoke (herrings, etc.); fill with smoke; —*vi* smoke, burn; —*vr* be full of smoke; taste smoked; *Inf.* get drunk. See **desahuciar**

**ahusado** /au'saðo/ *a* spindle-shaped

**ahuyentar** /auyen'tar/ *vt* to frighten off; drive away; dismiss, banish (anxiety, etc.); —*vr* flee

**airadamente** /airaða'mente/ *adv* wrathfully, angrily

**airado** /ai'raðo/ *a* angry

**airar** /ai'rar/ *vt* to annoy, anger; —*vr* grow annoyed

**aire** /'aire/ *m*, air; atmosphere (sometimes *pl*); breeze, wind; bearing, appearance; vanity; (horse's) gait; futility, frivolity; grace, charm; gracefulness; *Mus.* air; *Mus.* tempo. **a. popular,** popular tune. **al a. libre,** in the open air, outdoors. *Inf.* **beber los aires (por),** to yearn (for)

**aireación** /airea'θion; airea'sion/ *f*, airing; ventilation

**airear** /aire'ar/ *vt* to air; ventilate; aerate; —*vr* take the air; catch a chill

**airosidad** /airosi'ðað/ *f*, gracefulness; jauntiness

**airoso** /ai'roso/ *a* airy, open; windy, breezy, fresh; graceful; handsome; jaunty; victorious, successful

**aislacionamismo** /aislaθiona'mismo; aislasiona'mismo/ *m*, *Polit.* isolationism

**aislacionista** /aislaθion'ista; aislasion'ista/ *mf Polit.* isolationist

**aislado** /ais'laðo/ *a* isolated; remote; individual; single; *Elec.* insulated

**aislador** /aisla'ðor/ *m*, *Phys.* insulator

**aislamiento** /aisla'miento/ *m*, isolation; *Phys.* insulation

**aislante** /ais'lante/ *a* isolating; insulating

**aislar** /ais'lar/ *vt* to isolate; *Elec.* insulate; —*vr* become a recluse; become isolated

**¡ajá!** /a'ha/ *interj Inf.* Aha! Good!

**ajaquecarse** /ahake'karse/ *vr* to have a headache

**ajar** /a'har/ *vt* to crease, crumple, spoil; humiliate; —*vr* fade, wither (flowers)

**ajear** /ahe'ar/ *vi* (partridge) to squawk (when cornered)

**ajedrecista** /aheðre'θista; aheðre'sista/ *mf* chess player

**ajedrez** /ahe'ðreθ; ahe'ðres/ *m*, chess

**ajenjo** /a'henho/ *m*, *Bot.* wormwood; absinthe

**ajeno** /a'heno/ *a* alien; belonging to another; various, diverse; free, exempt; unsuitable; irrelevant

**ajetrear** /ahetre'ar/ *vt* to tire out, exhaust; —*vr* be overtired

**ajetreo** /ahe'treo/ *m*, exhaustion, fatigue

**ajo** /'aho/ *m*, garlic; *Inf.* make up, paint; disreputable affair, shady business; curse, oath. *Inf.* **revolver el a.**, to stir up trouble

**ajorca** /a'horka/ *f*, bracelet; slave bangle

**ajornalar** /ahorna'lar/ *vt* to hire by the day

**ajuar** /ahu'ar/ *m*, trousseau; household equipment

**ajustado** /ahus'taðo/ *a* exact; tight-fitting; trim

**ajustador** /ahusta'ðor/ **(-ra)** *a* adjusting —*n* adjuster. *m*, tight-fitting jacket

**ajustamiento** /ahusta'miento/ *m*, adjustment; agreement

**ajustar** /ahus'tar/ *vt* to adjust; fit; arrange; make an agreement about; reconcile; settle (accounts); engage, employ; retain (a barrister); regulate; tune up (a motor); —*vi* fit; —*vr* adapt oneself. *Inf.* **a. cuentas viejas,** to settle old accounts

**ajuste** /a'huste/ *m*, fitting; adjustment; agreement; arrangement; *Print.* make-up. reconciliation; settlement; regulation; engagement, appointment

**ajusticiado** /ahusti'θiaðo; ahusti'siaðo/ **(-da)** *n* executed person

**ajusticiar** /ahusti'θiar; ahusti'siar/ *vt* to put to death

**al** /al/ (contraction of *a* + *el*). I —*prep a* + *m. def. art.,* to the, e.g. *Han ido al mar,* They have gone to the sea. 2 —*prep a* + *el* used as *dem. pron* to that, to the one, e.g. *Mi sombrero se parece mucho al que tiene Vd.,* My hat is very similar to the one you have. *al* + *infin.* means when, as, at the same time as, e.g. *Al llamar a la puerta la vi en el jardín,* As I was knocking at the door, I saw her in the garden

**ala** /'ala/ *f*, *Zool.* wing; row, line; brim (of a hat); eaves; (*Archit. Aer. Mil. Bot.*) wing; blade (of propeller); fin (of fish); *pl* courage. **a. del corazón,** *Anat.* auricle. **arrastrar el a.,** to woo, flirt with. *Fig.* **cortar** (*or* **quebrar) las alas (a),** to clip a person's wings

**Alá** /a'la/ *m*, Allah

**alabador** /alaβa'ðor/ **(-ra)** *n* praiser, extoller

**alabanza** /ala'βanθa; ala'βansa/ *f*, praise; eulogy

**alabar** /ala'βar/ *vt* to praise; —*vr* brag, boast

**alabarda** /ala'βarða/ *f*, halberd

**alabardero** /alaβar'ðero/ *m*, halberdier; *Theat.* claque, clapper

**alabastrino** /alaβas'trino/ *a* alabastrine, alabaster

**alabastro** /ala'βastro/ *m*, alabaster

**alacena** /ala'θena; ala'sena/ *f*, cupboard; recess; closet; safe (for food)

**alacrán** /ala'kran/ *m*, scorpion

**alacridad** /alakri'ðað/ *f*, alacrity, eagerness

**alado** /a'laðo/ *a* winged; feathered; *Fig.* soaring

**alambicado** /alambi'kaðo/ *a* sparing, frugal; subtle; euphuistic

**alambicar** /alambi'kar/ *vt* to distil; examine carefully, scrutinize; make over-subtle or euphuistic (of style)

**alambique** /alam'bike/ *m*, still

**alambrada** /alam'braða/ *f*, *Mil.* wire-entanglement

**alambrado** /alam'braðo/ *m*, wire-netting; *Mil.* wire-entanglement; wire cover

**alambrar** /alam'brar/ *vt* to wire (fence)

**alambre** /a'lambre/ *m*, wire; sheep bells. **a. espinoso,** barbed wire

**alambrera** /alam'brera/ *f*, wire fence; wire-netting; wire cover

**alambrista** /alam'brista/ *mf* tight-rope walker; (Mexico) wetback

**alameda** /ala'meða/ *f*, poplar wood or grove; avenue of poplars

**álamo** /'alamo/ *m*, poplar. **a. temblón,** aspen tree

**alano** /a'lano/ *m*, mastiff

**alarde** /a'larðe/ *m*, *Mil.* parade; display, ostentation. **hacer a. de,** to brag about

**alargamiento** /alarga'miento/ *m*, lengthening; stretching

**alargar** /alar'gar/ *vt* to lengthen; prolong; pass, hand (things); pay out (ropes, etc.); increase; —*vr* go away, depart; be wordy, spread oneself; lengthen

**alarido** /ala'riðo/ *m*, yell, shout; shriek, scream; howl; yelp; cry (of a seagull)

**alarma** /a'larma/ *f*, alarm. **a. aérea,** air-raid warning

**alarmante** /alar'mante/ *a* alarming

**alarmar** /alar'mar/ *vt* to give the alarm; frighten; —*vr* be alarmed

**alarmista** /alar'mista/ *mf* alarmist

**alazán** /ala'θan; ala'san/ *a* sorrel-colored. *m*, sorrel horse

**alazo** /a'laθo; a'laso/ *m*, flap or stroke of the wings

**alba** /'alβa/ *f*, dawn; *Eccl.* alb, vestment. **al a.,** at dawn

**albacea** /alβa'θea; alβa'sea/ *mf* executor, executrix; testator

**albanés** /alβa'nes/ **(-esa)** *a* and *n* Albanian. *m*, Albanian language

**albañil** /alβa'ɲil/ *m*, mason, bricklayer

**albañilería** /alβaɲile'ria/ *f*, masonry; bricklaying

**albarda** /al'βarða/ *f*, pack-saddle

**albardilla** /alβar'ðiʎa; alβar'ðiya/ *f*, small saddle; pad; small pillow; *Archit.* coping

**albaricoque** /alβari'koke/ *m*, apricot

**albaricoquero** /alβariko'kero/ *m*, apricot tree

**albarrada** /alβa'rraða/ *f*, stone wall; mud fence

**albatros** /alβa'tros/ *m*, albatross

**albear** /alβe'ar/ *vi* to become white, whiten

**albedrío** /alβe'ðrio/ *m*, free will; fancy, caprice

**albéitar** /al'βeitar/ *m*, veterinary surgeon; farrier

**alberca** /al'βerka/ *f*, reservoir, tank; vat; artificial lake

**albergar** /alβer'gar/ *vt* to shelter; nourish, harbor; —*vi* and *vr* take refuge or shelter; lodge

**albergue** /al'βerge/ *m*, shelter, refuge; den, lair; hospitality; lodging; asylum

**albo** /'alβo/ *a* pure white

**albóndiga** /al'βondiga/ *f*, forced meat ball, rissole

**albor** /al'βor/ *m*, whiteness; dawnlight, dawn. **a. de la vida,** life's dawning; childhood

**alborada** /alβo'raða/ *f*, dawn; reveille; *Mil.* dawn attack; *Mus.* aubade

**alborear** /alβore'ar/ *vi* to grow light, dawn

**albornoz** /alβor'noθ; alβor'nos/ *m*, burnouse

**alborotado** /alβoro'taðo/ *a* impulsive; turbulent; noisy; excitable

**alborotar** /alβoro'tar/ *vt* to disturb; —*vi* make a noise; be gay; —*vr* riot; grow rough (sea)

**alboroto** /alβo'roto/ *m*, noise; confusion; tumult; riot; rejoicing, gaiety; *pl* popcorn

**alborozar** /alβoro'θar; alβoro'sar/ *vt* to overjoy, gladden; —*vr* rejoice, be glad

**alborozo** /alβo'roθo; alβo'roso/ *m*, gladness, rejoicing, joy

**albricias** /al'βriθias; al'βrisias/ *f pl*, reward for bringer of good tidings —*interj* **¡A.!** Joy! Congratulations!

**álbum** /'alβum/ *m*, album

**albúmina** /al'βumina/ *f*, albumin

**albur** /al'βur/ *m*, *Ichth.* dace; chance, risk. **al a. de,** at the risk of

**alcachofa** /alka'tʃofa/ *f*, artichoke

**alcahueta** /alka'ueta/ *f*, procuress, go-between

**alcahuete** /alka'uete/ *m*, procurer, go-between, pimp, pander; *Fig. Inf.* protector, screen; *Inf.* scandalmonger

**alcahuetear** /alkauete'ar/ *vt* to procure, act as a go-between for; —*vi* be a pimp or a procuress

**alcaide** /al'kaiðe/ *m*, governor of a fortress *Obs.*; governor of a prison

**alcalde** /al'kalde/ *m*, mayor; magistrate. *Inf.* **tener el padre a.,** to have a friend at court

**alcaldesa** /alkal'desa/ *f*, mayoress

**alcaldía** /alkal'dia/ *f*, office or authority of an alcalde

**álcali** /'alkali/ *m*, *Chem.* alkali

**alcalino** /alka'lino/ *a* alkaline

**alcaloide** /alka'loiðe/ *m*, *Chem.* alkaloid

**alcance** /al'kanθe; al'kanse/ *m*, reaching, attainment; range (of firearms, etc.); scope; arm's length or reach; pursuit; stop press *or* extra edition (newspapers); *Com.* deficit; importance; *pl* talent; capacity. **al a. de la voz,** within call. **hombre de cortos alcances,** a limited, dull man. **poner al a. de,** to make available to; make intelligible to

**alcancía** /alkan'θia; alkan'sia/ *f*, money-box; coin bank, piggy bank

**alcanfor** /alkan'for/ *m*, camphor

**alcanforado** /alkanfo'raðo/ *a* camphorated

**alcantarilla** /alkanta'riʎa; alkanta'riya/ f, little bridge; sewer; culvert; bed for electric cable

**alcantarillado** /alkantari'ʎaðo; alkantari'yaðo/ m, sewage system; main sewer

**alcanzable** /alkan'θaβle; alkan'saβle/ a obtainable; attainable

**alcanzadizo** /alkanθa'ðiθo; alkansa'ðiso/ a attainable, easily reached

**alcanzar** /alkan'θar; alkan'sar/ vt to overtake; reach; range (of guns, etc.); attain, achieve; understand; Fig. equal (in attainments); live at the same time as, be contemporaneous with; be capable of, be able; —vi reach; share, participate in; be enough

**alcaparra** /alka'parra/ f, Bot. caper; caper bush

**alcaucil** /alkau'θil; alkau'sil/ m, (in most places) wild artichoke; (in some places) cultivated artichoke

**alcazaba** /alka'θaβa; alka'saβa/ f, fortress (within a walled town or city), casbah

**alcázar** /al'kaθar; al'kasar/ m, fortress; royal residence, castle; Naut. quarterdeck

**alción** /al'θion; al'sion/ m, Ornith. kingfisher

**alcista** /al'θista; al'sista/ mf speculator (on Stock Exchange)

**alcoba** /al'koβa/ f, bedroom; alcove, recess; Moorish flute

**alcohol** /al'kool/ m, alcohol; galena; eye black (cosmetic); spirits of wine. **a. desnaturalizado,** industrial alcohol, methylated spirit. **a. metílico,** wood alcohol

**alcohólico** /alko'oliko/ a alcoholic

**alcoholismo** /alkool'ismo/ m, alcoholism

**alcor** /al'kor/ m, hill; slope

**Alcorán** /alko'ran/ m, Koran

**alcornoque** /alkor'noke/ m, cork tree; dunderhead, dolt

**alcorza** /al'korθa; al'korsa/ f, Cul. icing, sugar-paste

**alcorzar** /alkor'θar; alkor'sar/ vt Cul. to ice, cover with sugar; decorate, adorn

**alcurnia** /al'kurnia/ f, lineage, family, descent

**alcuza** /al'kuθa; al'kusa/ f, oil-bottle; oil-can; cruet

**aldaba** /al'daβa/ f, door knocker; bolt, latch; pl protectors, influential helpers. Inf. **tener buenas aldabas,** to have plenty of pull

**aldabada** /alda'βaða/ f, rap with the knocker; sudden shock

**aldabeo** /alda'βeo/ m, knocking

**aldea** /al'dea/ f, village

**aldeano** /alde'ano/ **(-na)** a village; country, ignorant —n villager; countryman, peasant

**aldehído** /alde'iðo/ m, Chem. aldehyde

**aleación** /alea'θion; alea'sion/ f, alloy

**alear** /ale'ar/ vi to flutter, beat the wings; flap one's arms; recuperate, grow well; —vt alloy

**aleatorio** /alea'torio/ a accidental, fortuitous

**aleccionamiento** /alekθiona'miento; aleksiona'miento/ m, teaching, training, coaching

**aleccionar** /alekθio'nar; aleksio'nar/ vt to teach, train, coach

**aledaño** /ale'ðaɲo/ a adjoining; border. m, boundary, border

**alegación** /alega'θion; alega'sion/ f, allegation, statement

**alegar** /ale'gar/ vt to allege, state; cite; —vi Law. bring forward, adduce

**alegato** /ale'gato/ m, Law. speech (for the prosecution or defense)

**alegoría** /alego'ria/ f, allegory

**alegórico** /ale'goriko/ a allegorical

**alegorizar** /alegori'θar; alegori'sar/ vt to interpret allegorically, treat as an allegory

**alegrar** /ale'grar/ vt to make happy, gladden, rejoice; adorn, beautify; stir (fires); —vr be glad, rejoice; Inf. be merry (tipsy)

**alegre** /a'legre/ a joyful, glad; cheerful, gay; bright (colors, etc.); pretty, attractive; Inf. risqué; Inf. flirtatious, light

**alegría** /ale'gria/ f, joy, gladness; cheerfulness, gaiety; pl public rejoicings

**alegrón** /ale'gron/ m, sudden unexpected joy; Inf. flash of light —a Inf. flirtatious

**alejamiento** /aleha'miento/ m, placing at a distance, removal; withdrawal

**Alejandría** /alehan'dria/ Alexandria

**alejar** /ale'har/ vt to place at a distance, remove; withdraw; ward off (dangers, etc.); —vr depart, go away; withdraw. **alejarse de,** to abandon (a belief, custom, superstition, etc.)

**alelar** /ale'lar/ vt to make silly or stupid

**aleluya** /ale'luya/ mf, alleluia. m, Eastertide. f, small Easter cake; Inf. daub, poor painting; Inf. doggerel; joy, rejoicing

**alemán** /ale'man/ **(-ana)** a and n German. m, German language.

**Alemania** /ale'mania/ Germany

**alentada** /alen'taða/ f, deep breath

**alentado** /alen'taðo/ a valiant, spirited; proud

**alentador** /alenta'ðor/ a encouraging, inspiring, stimulating

**alentar** /alen'tar/ vi irr to breathe; —vt encourage, inspire; —vr be encouraged. See **sentar**

**alerce** /a'lerθe; a'lerse/ m, larch tree and wood

**alergia** /aler'hia/ f, allergy

**alergólogo** /aler'gologo/ m, allergist

**alero** /a'lero/ m, projecting roof; splashboard (of carriages); eaves; gable end

**alerón** /ale'ron/ m, Aer. aileron

**alerta** /a'lerta/ adv watchfully —interj Take care! Look out! **estar ojo a.,** to be on the watch

**alerto** /a'lerto/ a watchful, alert

**aleta** /a'leta/ f, dim small wing; fin

**aletargado** /aletar'gaðo/ a lethargic; comatose

**aletargamiento** /aletarga'miento/ m, lethargy

**aletargar** /aletar'gar/ vt to cause lethargy; —vr become lethargic

**aletazo** /ale'taθo; ale'taso/ m, flapping, beating (of wings); Inf. theft

**aletear** /alete'ar/ vi to flap the wings, flutter; move the arms up and down; become convalescent

**aleteo** /ale'teo/ m, fluttering, flapping of wings; beating, palpitation (of heart)

**aleve** /a'leβe/ a See **alevoso**

**alevosía** /aleβo'sia/ f, Law. malice; treachery

**alevoso** /aleβo'βoso/ a Law. malicious; treacherous

**alfabético** /alfa'βetiko/ a alphabetical

**alfabetización** /alfaβetiθa'θion; alfaβetisa'sion/ f, literacy work

**alfabetizador** /alfaβetiθa'ðor; alfaβetisa'ðor/ m, literacy worker

**alfabeto** /alfa'βeto/ m, alphabet. **a. manual,** sign language

**alfalfa** /al'falfa/ f, Bot. lucerne

**alfar** /al'far/ m, potter's workshop; pottery, earthenware

**alfarería** /alfare'ria/ f, pottery shop; potter's workshop; potter's craft

**alfarero** /alfa'rero/ m, potter

**alfeñique** /alfe'ɲike/ m, Cul. icing, sugarpaste; Inf. affectation

**alférez** /al'fereθ; al'feres/ m, Mil. ensign; second lieutenant; lieutenant. Nav. **a. de fragata,** sub-lieutenant. Nav. **a. de navío,** lieutenant

**alfil** /al'fil/ m, bishop (in chess)

**alfiler** /alfi'ler/ m, pin; brooch with a pin; tiepin; pl pin-money, dress-allowance; Fig. Inf. **no estar uno con sus alfileres,** to have a slate loose. Inf. **vestido de veinticinco alfileres,** dressed to the nines

**alfiletero** /alfile'tero/ m, needle-case

**alfombra** /al'fombra/ f, carpet; rug

**alfombrado** /alfom'braðo/ m, carpeting

**alfombrar** /alfom'brar/ vt to carpet

**alfombrilla eléctrica** /alfom'briʎa e'lektrika; alfom'briya e'lektrika/ f, electric pad or blanket

**alfombrista** /alfom'brista/ m, carpet merchant; layer of carpets

**alforja** /al'forha/ f, saddle-bag; Mil. knapsack

**alforza** /al'forθa; al'forsa/ f, Sew. tuck; Inf. scar

**alforzar** /alfor'θar; alfor'sar/ vt Sew. to tuck

**alga** /'alga/ f, alga, seaweed

**algalia** /al'galia/ f, civet

**algarabía** /algara'βia/ f, Arabic; Inf. gibberish; din of voices, uproar

**algarada** /alga'raða/ f, troop of horse; uproar, hubbub; outcry

**algarroba** /alɣa'rroβa/ *f*, *Bot.* carob bean

**algazara** /alɣa'θara; alɣa'sara/ *f*, Moorish war cry; rejoicing, merriment; noise, clamor

**álgebra** /'alheβra/ *f*, algebra; art of bone setting

**algebraico** /alhe'βraiko/ *a* algebraic

**algebrista** /alhe'βrista/ *mf* bonesetter; algebraist

**álgido** /'alhiðo/ *a* icy cold

**algo** /'alɣo/ *indef pron* some, something (e.g. *Se ve que hay a. que le molesta*, You can see that something is irritating him) —*adv* somewhat, a bit. **en a.,** in some way

**algodón** /alɣo'ðon/ *m*, cotton plant; cotton flower; cotton fabric; candy floss (UK), cotton candy (USA). **a. en rama,** cotton-wool. **a. hidró-filo,** absorbent cotton wool. **a. pólvora,** nitrocellulose

**algodonal** /alɣoðo'nal/ *m*, cotton plantation

**algodonero** /alɣoðo'nero/ **(-ra)** *a* cotton —*n* cotton merchant

**alguacil** /alɣwa'θil; alɣwa'sil/ *m*, policeman, constable; *Obs.* city governor; short-legged spider

**alguien** /'alɣien/ *indef pron* someone, somebody, e.g. *Dime si viene a.*, Tell me if anyone comes

**algún** /al'ɣun/ *Abbr.* of **alguno** bef. *m sing* noun, e.g. *a. libro*

**alguno** /al'ɣuno/ *a* (*Abbr.* **algún** bef. *m*, *sing*) some, any —*indef pron* someone, somebody; *pl* some, some people. **alguno que otro,** a few

**alhaja** /al'aha/ *f*, jewel; ornament; treasure; precious object; *Inf.* gem, excellent person (also ironic, e.g. *Es una a.*, He's a fine fellow)

**alhajar** /ala'har/ *vt* to adorn with jewels, bejewel; furnish, equip

**alharaca** /alar'aka/ *f*, vehemence, demonstration, fuss (gen. *pl*)

**alheña** /al'eɲa/ *f*, *Bot.* privet; henna

**alhóndiga** /al'ondiɣa/ *f*, corn exchange; public granary

**aliado** /a'liaðo/ **(-da)** *a* allied —*n* ally

**alianza** /a'lianθa; a'liansa/ *f*, alliance; pact, agreement; relationship (by marriage); sum total, whole (of factors, etc.); wedding-ring

**aliarse** /a'liarse/ *vr* to join together, become allies; be associated

**alicaído** /alika'iðo/ *a* drooping; *Inf.* weak, exhausted; discouraged, downhearted; come down in the world

**alicates** /ali'kates/ *m pl*, pincers, pliers

**aliciente** /ali'θiente; ali'siente/ *m*, attraction, inducement

**alícuota** /a'likuota/ *f*, *a* aliquot; proportional. **partes alícuotas,** aliquot parts

**alienación** /aliena'θion; aliena'sion/ *f*, alienation

**alienado** /alie'naðo/ *a* insane, mad

**alienar** /alie'nar/ *vt* See **enajenar**

**alienista** /alie'nista/ *mf Med.* alienist

**aliento** /a'liento/ *m*, breathing; breath; courage, spirit; encouragement. **el posterior a.,** one's last breath. **cobrar a.,** to regain one's breath; take heart. **de un a.,** in one breath; without stopping

**alifafe** /ali'fafe/ *m*, *Inf.* ailment; tumor on horse's hock

**aligación** /aliɣa'θion; aliɣa'sion/ *f*, binding together, alligation

**aligeramiento** /aˌlihera'miento/ *m*, lightening, reduction in weight

**aligerar** /alihe'rar/ *vt* to lighten, make less heavy; quicken, hasten; ease, alleviate; moderate; shorten, abbreviate

**alígero** /a'lihero/ *a Poet.* winged; fleet, swift

**alimaña** /ali'maɲa/ *f*, destructive animal

**alimentación** /alimenta'θion; alimenta'sion/ *f*, nourishment; feeding

**alimentar** /alimen'tar/ *vt* to feed; nourish; encourage, foment; assist, aid; keep, support

**alimenticio** /alimen'tiθio; alimen'tisio/ *a* nourishing; feeding

**alimento** /ali'mento/ *m*, food, nourishment; stimulus, encouragement; *pl* allowance

**alindar** /alin'dar/ *vt* to mark the boundary of; beautify, adorn; —*vi* border, be contiguous

**alineación** /alinea'θion; alinea'sion/ *f*, alignment

**alinear** /aline'ar/ *vt* to align, range in line; dress (troops); —*vr* fall into line

**aliñar** /ali'ɲar/ *vt* to decorate, adorn; *Cul.* season; prepare; set (bones)

**aliño** /a'liɲo/ *m*, decoration, ornament; preparation; condiment, seasoning; setting (bones)

**aliquebrado** /alike'βraðo/ *a* broken-winged; *Inf.* down in the mouth

**alisador** /alisa'ðor/ **(-ra)** *a* smoothing; polishing —*n* polisher

**alisar** /ali'sar/ *vt* to smooth; polish; sleek; plane; comb lightly

**alisios** /a'lisios/ *m pl*, trade winds

**aliso** /a'liso/ *m*, alder tree and wood

**alistador** /alista'ðor/ *m*, enroller

**alistamiento** /alista'miento/ *m*, enlistment; conscription; enrolment

**alistar** /alis'tar/ *vt* to enroll, list; enlist; conscript; prepare, get ready; —*vr* enroll; *Mil.* enlist; get ready

**aliviar** /ali'βiar/ *vt* to lighten; alleviate, mitigate; relieve; ease; quicken (one's step); hasten, speed up; steal

**alivio** /a'liβio/ *m*, lightening; relief; alleviation; ease

**aljaba** /al'haβa/ *f*, quiver (for arrows)

**aljibe** /al'hiβe/ *m*, tank, cistern; watership or tanker

**aljófar** /al'hofar/ *m*, small irregular shaped pearl; dew-drop, raindrop, tear drop

**aljofifa** /alho'fifa/ *f*, floorcloth

**allá** /a'ʎa; a'ya/ *adv* there; to that place. **más a.,** farther on, beyond. Used in conjunction with phrases of time, indicates remoteness, e.g. *a. en tiempos de los Reyes Católicos*, long ago in the time of the Catholic Monarchs. *a. por 1900*, way back in 1900

**allanamiento** /aʎana'miento; ayana'miento/ *m*, leveling, flattening; condescension, affability; (police) raid, (police) search acceptance of a judicial finding

**allanar** /aʎa'nar; aya'nar/ *vt* to level, flatten; overcome (difficulties); soothe; break into (a house, etc.); give entrance to the police; —*vr* collapse (buildings, etc.); abide by, adapt oneself (to); condescend, be affable. **a. el camino (a...),** to pave the way (for...)

**allegado** /aʎe'ɣaðo; aye'ɣaðo/ **(-da)** *a* near, allied; related —*n* follower, ally

**allegar** /aʎe'ɣar; aye'ɣar/ *vt* to gather, collect; draw nearer; *Agr.* reap; add; —*vi* arrive

**allende** /a'ʎende; a'yende/ *adv* beyond; besides. **de a. el mar,** from beyond the sea

**allí** /a'ʎi; a'yi/ *adv* there; to that place, thereto; thereupon, then. **por a.,** through there; that way

**alma** /'alma/ *f*, soul; living person; essence, core; vivacity, animation; energy, vitality; spirit, ghost; core (of a rope). **a. de cántaro,** fool, ninny. **a. de Dios,** simple soul, kind person. **a. en pena,** soul in purgatory. **¡A. mía!** My darling! **con todo el a.,** with all my heart. **Lo siento en el a.,** I feel it deeply

**almacén** /alma'θen; alma'sen/ *m*, warehouse; store, shop

**almacenaje** /almaθe'nahe; almase'nahe/ *m*, cost of storage

**almacenar** /almaθe'nar; almase'nar/ *vt* to store; put in store; hoard

**almacenero** /almaθe'nero; almase'nero/ *m*, warehouseman, storekeeper

**almacenista** /almaθe'nista; almase'nista/ *mf* owner of a store; assistant, salesman (saleswoman)

**almáciga** /al'maθiɣa; al'masiɣa/ *f*, mastic; tree plantation or nursery

**almagre** /al'maɣre/ *m*, *Mineral.* red ocher; stain, mark

**almanaque** /alma'nake/ *m*, calendar, almanac

**almeja** /al'meha/ *f*, *Ichth.* clam

**almenara** /alme'nara/ *f*, beacon fire

**almendra** /al'mendra/ *f*, almond; kernel; crystal drop (of chandeliers, etc.); cocoon; bean (of cocoa tree, etc.). **a. garapiñada,** sugar almond

**almendro** /al'mendro/ *m*, almond tree

**almendruco** /almen'druko/ *m*, green almond

**almete** /al'mete/ *m*, casque, helmet; helmeted soldier

**almiar** /al'miar/ *m*, haystack, hayrick

**almíbar** /al'miβar/ *m*, sugar syrup; nectar

**almibarado** /almiβa'raðo/ *a* syrupy; *Inf.* sugary

**almibarar** /almiβa'rar/ *vt* to coat with sugar; preserve (fruit) in syrup; flatter with sweet words

**almidón** /almi'ðon/ *m*, starch

**almidonado** /almiðo'naðo/ *a* starched; *Fig. Inf.* stiff, unbending; prim, starchy

**almidonar** /almiðo'nar/ *vt* to starch

**alminar** /almi'nar/ *m*, minaret (of mosque)

**almiranta** /almi'ranta/ *f*, admiral's wife; flagship

**almirantazgo** /almiran'taθgo; almiran'tasgo/ *m*, Admiralty; admiralship; Admiralty Court

**almirante** /almi'rante/ *m*, admiral

**almizcle** /al'miθkle; al'miskle/ *m*, musk

**almizcleño** /almiθ'kleɲo; almis'kleɲo/ *a* musk (of scents)

**almizclero** /almiθ'klero; almis'klero/ *a* musky. *m, Zool.* musk-deer

**almocafre** /almo'kafre/ *m, Agr.* hoe; trowel, dibble

**almohada** /almo'aða/ *f*, pillow; pillowcase; cushion. *Inf.* **aconsejarse** *or* **consultar con la a.,** to think over (a matter) carefully, sleep on it

**almohadilla** /almoa'ðiʎa; almoa'ðiya/ *f, dim* small cushion; lace or sewing cushion; pin cushion

**almohadillado** /almoaði'ʎaðo; almoaði'yaðo/ *a* cushioned; padded

**almoneda** /almo'neða/ *f*, auction; furniture sale

**almonedear** /almoneðe'ar/ *vt* to auction; sell off (furniture)

**almorranas** /almo'rranas/ *f pl*, hemorrhoids

**almorzar** /almor'θar; almor'sar/ *vi irr* to lunch; breakfast. See **forzar**

**almuecín, almuédano** /almue'θin, al'mueðano; almue'sin, al'mueðano/ *m*, muezzin

**almuerzo** /al'muerθo; al'muerso/ *m*, luncheon; breakfast (not so usual)

**alocado** /alo'kaðo/ *a* feather-brained, reckless, crazy, wild

**alocución** /aloku'θion; aloku'sion/ *f*, allocution, address, harangue

**áloe** /'aloe/ *m, Bot.* aloe

**alojado** /alo'haðo/ **(-da)** *m*, billeted soldier —*n* lodger

**alojamiento** /aloha'miento/ *m*, lodging; dwelling; *Mil.* billeting; *Naut.* steerage; camp, encampment

**alojar** /alo'har/ *vt* to lodge; billet, quarter (troops); insert, introduce; —*vi* and *vr* lodge; live, dwell

**alondra** /a'londra/ *f, Ornith.* lark

**alopatía** /alopa'tia/ *f, Med.* allopathy

**alpaca** /al'paka/ *f*, alpaca (animal and fabric); nickel silver

**alpargata** /alpar'gata/ *f*, sandal with hemp sole

**alpargatero** /alparga'tero/ **(-ra)** *n* manufacturer or seller of alpargatas

**Alpes, los** /'alpes, los/ the Alps

**alpestre** /al'pestre/ *a* Alpine; rock (of plants); mountainous, lofty

**alpinismo** /alpi'nismo/ *m*, mountaineering

**alpinista** /alpi'nista/ *mf* mountaineer, climber

**alpino** /al'pino/ *a* Alpine

**alpiste** /al'piste/ *m*, bird seed

**alpro** /'alpro/ *f*, (Alianza para el Progreso)

**alquería** /alke'ria/ *f*, farmstead

**alquiladizo** /alkila'ðiðo; alkila'ðiso/ *a* rentable, hirable

**alquilador** /alkila'ðor/ **(-ra)** *n* hirer

**alquilamiento** /alkila'miento/ *m*, See **alquiler**

**alquilar** /alki'lar/ *vt* to rent; hire out; hire; —*vr* hire oneself out, serve on a wage basis

**alquiler** /alki'ler/ *m*, hiring out; renting; rental; hire; wages. **de a.,** for hire, on hire

**alquimia** /al'kimia/ *f*, alchemy

**alquímico** /al'kimiko/ *a* alchemic

**alquimista** /alki'mista/ *mf* alchemist

**alquitrán** /alki'tran/ *m*, tar, pitch. **a. mineral,** coal tar

**alquitranado** /alkitra'naðo/ *a* tarred. *m, Naut.* tarpaulin

**alrededor** /alreðe'ðor/ *adv* around, round about. **a. de,** around; approximately, about (e.g. *a. de cinco dólares,* about $5)

**alrededores** /alreðe'ðores/ *m pl*, environs, surrounding country

**Alsacia** /al'saθia; al'sasia/ Alsace

**alsaciano** /alsa'θiano; alsa'siano/ **(-na)** *a* and *n* Alsatian

**alta** /'alta/ *f*, certificate of discharge from hospital

**altanería** /altane'ria/ *f*, hawking; haughtiness, disdain; superciliousness

**altanero** /alta'nero/ *a* soaring, high-flying (of birds); supercilious; haughty, disdainful

**altar** /al'tar/ *m*, altar. **a. mayor,** high altar

**altavoz** /,alta'βoθ; ,alta'βos/ *m*, loudspeaker; megaphone

**altearse** /alte'arse/ *vr* to rise, grow steep (of land)

**alterabilidad** /alteraβili'ðað/ *f*, alterability, changeability

**alteración** /altera'θion; altera'sion/ *f*, alteration, change; debasement (of coinage); agitation

**alterar** /alte'rar/ *vt* to change, alter; debase (coinage); disturb, agitate; —*vr* grow angry; become excited

**altercación** /alterka'θion; alterka'sion/ *f.* **altercado** *m*, altercation, quarrel

**altercar** /alter'kar/ **(se)** *vi* and *vr* to quarrel, dispute, altercate

**alternación** /alterna'θion; alterna'sion/ *f*, alternation

**alternado** /alter'naðo/ *a* alternate

**alternador** /alterna'ðor/ *a* alternating. *m, Elec.* alternator

**alternante** /alter'nante/ *a* alternating

**alternar** /alter'nar/ *vt* to alternate; make one's debut as a **matador;** —*vi* alternate; (*with con*) have dealings with, know

**alternativa** /alterna'tiβa/ *f*, alternative, option; service performed by turns; alternation

**alternativo** /alterna'tiβo/ *a* alternative

**alterno** /al'terno/ *a* alternative; *Bot.* alternate

**alteza** /al'teθa; al'tesa/ *f*, altitude, height; sublimity, perfection; **(A.)** Highness (title)

**altibajo** /alti'βaho/ *m*, embossed velvet; *pl Inf.* rough ground; *Inf.* vicissitudes of fortune

**altillo** /al'tiʎo; al'tiyo/ *m*, hillock, eminence; garret, attic

**altímetro** /al'timetro/ *m*, *Aer.* altimeter

**altiplanicie** /altipla'niθie; altipla'nisie/ *f*, plateau; highland

**altisonante** /altiso'nante/ *a* sonorous; sublime; high-flown, pompous

**altitud** /alti'tuð/ *f*, altitude, height

**altivez** /alti'βeθ; alti'βes/ *f*, arrogance, haughtiness

**altivo** /al'tiβo/ *a* arrogant, haughty

**alto** /'alto/ *a* high; tall; difficult, arduous; sublime; deep; most serious (of crimes, etc.); dear (of price); small, early (hours). *m*, height; eminence, hill; story, floor; *Mil.* halt; red light (traffic light) —*adv* up, above, on high; loudly —*interj* ¡**A.!** *Mil.* Halt! *Mil.* **A. Mando,** High Command. **las altas horas de la noche,** the small (or early) hours. **en alta voz,** in a loud voice. **en alto,** on high; up above. **hacer alto,** to halt, stop

**altoparlante** /,altopar'lante/ *m, Radio.* loudspeaker

**altozano** /alto'θano; alto'sano/ *m*, mound, hillock; viewpoint, open space

**altruismo** /altru'ismo/ *m*, altruism

**altruista** /altru'ista/ *a* altruistic. *mf* altruist

**altura** /al'tura/ *f*, height; altitude; *Geom.* altitude or height; top, peak; sublimity; tallness

**alucinación** /aluθina'θion; alusina'sion/ *f,* **alucinamiento,** *m*, hallucination

**alucinado** /aluθi'naðo; alusi'naðo/ *m*, person suffering from hallucinations

**alucinador** /aluθina'ðor; alusina'ðor/ *a* hallucinatory, deceptive

**alucinar** /aluθi'nar; alusi'nar/ *vt* to dazzle, fascinate; deceive

**alud** /a'luð/ *m*, avalanche

**aludir** /alu'ðir/ *vi* to allude (to); refer (to), cite

**alumbrado** /alum'braðo/ *m*, lighting; *pl* illuminati

**alumbramiento** /alumbra'miento/ *m*, lighting, supply of light; childbirth

**alumbrar** /alum'brar/ *vt* to light, illuminate; give sight to the blind; instruct, teach; inflict (blows); hoe vine roots; —*vi* give birth to a child; —*vr Inf.* grow tipsy

**alumbre** /a'lumbre/ *m*, alum
**aluminio** /alu'minio/ *m*, aluminum
**alumno** /a'lumno/ **(-na)** *n* ward, adopted child; pupil. **a. externo,** day pupil. **a. interno,** boarder
**alunizaje** /aluni'θahe; aluni'sahe/ *m*, landing on the moon, moon-landing
**alunizar** /aluni'θar; aluni'sar/ *vi* to land on the moon
**alusión** /alu'sion/ *f*, allusion
**alusivo** /alu'siβo/ *a* allusive, suggestive; hinting
**aluvial** /alu'βial/ *a* alluvial
**aluvión** /alu'βion/ *m*, alluvium. **de a.,** alluvial
**alza** /'alθa; 'alsa/ *f*, rise (of temperature, etc.); increase (in price); front sight (of guns)
**alzacuello** /alθa'kueʎo; alsa'kueyo/ *m*, high collar, clerical collar; neck stock
**alzada** /al'θaða; al'saða/ *f*, horse's stature; mountain pasture; *Law.* appeal
**alzado** /al'θaðo; al'saðo/ *a* fraudulent (of bankruptcy); fixed (of price). *m*, theft; *Archit.* front elevation
**alzamiento** /alθa'miento; alsa'miento/ *m*, raising, lifting; higher bid (at auction); rising, rebellion; fraudulent bankruptcy
**alzaprima** /alθa'prima; alsa'prima/ *f*, lever; wedge; bridge (of string instruments)
**alzar** /al'θar; al'sar/ *vt* to raise; lift up; elevate (the Host); steal, remove; hide; gather in the harvest; build, construct; *Naut.* heave; —*vr* rise (of temperature, mercury, price, etc.); make a fraudulent bankruptcy; *Law.* appeal; (*with con*) run off with, steal. *Naut.* **a. la vela,** to set sail
**ama** /'ama/ *f*, mistress of the house; owner; housekeeper; wet nurse. **a. de casa,** homemaker, housewife. **a. de leche,** foster-mother. **a. de llaves** *or* **a. de gobierno,** housekeeper. **a. seca,** children's nurse
**amabilidad** /amaβili'ðað/ *f*, lovableness; kindness; niceness, goodness, helpfulness
**amable** /a'maβle/ *a* lovable; kind; nice, good, helpful
**amador** /ama'ðor/ **(-ra)** *a* loving —*n* lover, admirer
**amadrigar** /amaðri'gar/ *vt* to welcome, receive well; —*vr* go into a burrow or lair; go into seclusion
**amaestrar** /amaes'trar/ *vt* to train, instruct; tame; break in (horses)
**amagar** /ama'gar/ *vt* and *vi* to threaten; —*vt* show signs of (diseases, etc.); —*vr Inf.* hide
**amago (contra...),** /a'mago/ threat (to...), menace (to...)
**amainar** /amai'nar/ *vt Naut.* to take in the sails; —*vi* drop (of the wind); —*vi* and *vt* relax (efforts, etc.)
**amaine** /a'maine/ *m*, dropping, abatement (of the wind)
**amalgama** /amal'gama/ *f, Chem.* amalgam
**amalgamación** /amalgama'θion; amalgama'sion/ *f*, amalgamation
**amalgamar** /amalga'mar/ *vt* to amalgamate; —*vr* be amalgamated
**amamantamiento** /amamanta'miento/ *m*, suckling, nursling
**amamantar** /amaman'tar/ *vt* to suckle
**amancebado** /amanθe'βaðo; amanse'βaðo/ *m*, concubine
**amancillar** /amanθi'ʎar; amansi'yar/ *vt* to discredit, dishonor; tarnish; stain
**amanecer** /amane'θer; amane'ser/ *vi irr* to dawn; arrive *or* be somewhere *or* be doing, at dawn (e.g. *Amanecimos en el barco,* Dawn came while we were on the ship. *Amanecimos escribiendo la carta,* The day broke as we were writing the letter); appear at daybreak; begin to appear. *m*, dawn, daybreak. See **conocer**
**amanerado** /amane'raðo/ *a* mannered; affected
**amaneramiento** /amanera'miento/ *m*, manneredness; mannerism
**amanerarse** /amane'rarse/ *vr* to acquire mannerisms or tricks of style; become affected
**amansador** /amansa'ðor/ **(-ra)** *a* soothing, calming —*n* appeaser
**amansamiento** /amansa'miento/ *m*, taming; appeasement; soothing; breaking in (horses)
**amansar** /aman'sar/ *vt* to tame; appease, moderate; soothe, pacify; break in (horses)
**amante** /a'mante/ *a* loving. *mf* lover

**amanuense** /ama'nuense/ *mf* amanuensis, secretary, clerk
**amanzanar** /amanθa'nar; amansa'nar/ to lay out the streets of
**amañar** /ama'ɲar/ *vt* to execute with skill; —*vr* grow skillful
**amaño** /a'maɲo/ *m*, skill, dexterity; *pl* schemes, intrigues; tools, equipment
**amapola** /ama'pola/ *f*, poppy
**amar** /a'mar/ *vt* to love
**amaranto** /ama'ranto/ *m, Bot.* amaranth
**amarar** /ama'rar/ *vi* to alight on the water (of hydroplanes)
**amargar** /amar'gar/ *vi* to taste or be bitter; —*vt* make bitter; embitter
**amargo** /a'margo/ *a* bitter; embittered; grievous, sad. *m*, bitterness; *pl* bitters
**amargor** /amar'gor/ *m*, **amargura,** /amar'gura/ *f*, bitter taste, bitterness; trouble, affliction, pain
**amaricado** /amari'kaðo/ *a Inf.* effeminate
**amarilis** /ama'rilis/ *f, Bot.* amaryllis; *Poet.* shepherdess
**amarillear** /amariʎe'ar; amariye'ar/ *vi* to look yellow; turn yellow; tend to yellow
**amarillento** /amari'ʎento; amari'yento/ *a* yellowish, turning yellow
**amarilleo** /amari'ʎeo; amari'yeo/ *m*, yellowing
**amarillez** /amari'ʎeθ; amari'yes/ *f*, yellowness
**amarillo** /ama'riʎo; ama'riyo/ *a* and *m*, yellow
**amarra** /a'marra/ *f*, cable, thick rope
**amarradero** /amarra'ðero/ *m, Naut.* mooring berth; mooring-post; hitchingpost or ring
**amarraje** /ama'rrahe/ *m, Naut.* mooring charge
**amarrar** /ama'rrar/ *vt* to tie up, hitch; moor
**amarre** /a'marre/ *m*, mooring; hitching
**amartelar** /amarte'lar/ *vt* to make jealous; court, woo, make love to; —*vr* be jealous; fall madly in love
**amartillar** /amarti'ʎar; amarti'yar/ *vt* to hammer, knock; cock (firearms)
**amasadera** /amasa'ðera/ *f*, kneading-trough
**amasador** /amasa'ðor/ **(-ra)** *a* kneading —*n* kneader
**amasar** /ama'sar/ *vt* to knead; massage; scheme, plot
**amasia** /a'masia/ *f*, concubine
**amasiato** /ama'siato/ *m*, concubinage
**amasijo** /ama'siho/ *m, Cul.* dough; kneading; portion of plaster or mortar; *Inf.* hotchpotch, mixture; scheme, plot
**amatista** /ama'tista/ *f*, amethyst
**amatorio** /ama'torio/ *a* amatory
**amazacotado** /a,maθako'taðo; a,masako'taðo/ *a* heavy, dense; *Fig.* stodgy (of writings, etc.)
**amazona** /ama'θona; ama'sona/ *f*, Amazon; independent woman; woman rider; woman's riding habit
**ambages** /am'bahes/ *m pl*, maze, intricate paths; circumlocutions
**ámbar** /'ambar/ *m*, amber. **a. gris,** ambergris
**ambarino** /amba'rino/ *a* amber
**Amberes** /am'beres/ Antwerp
**ambición** /ambi'θion; ambi'sion/ *f*, ambition
**ambicionar** /ambiθio'nar; ambisio'nar/ *vt* to long for; desire eagerly; be ambitious to
**ambicioso** /ambi'θioso; ambi'sioso/ *a* ambitious; eager, desirous
**ambidextro** /ambi'ðekstro/ *a* ambidextrous
**ambiente** /am'biente/ *a* ambient, surrounding. *m*, air, atmosphere; environment
**ambigú** /ambi'gu/ *m*, cold buffet; buffet (in theaters, etc.)
**ambigüedad** /ambigue'ðað/ *f*, ambiguity
**ambiguo** /am'biguo/ *a* ambiguous
**ámbito** /'ambito/ *m*, precincts; boundary, limit; compass, scope
**amblar** /am'blar/ *vi* to pace (of a horse)
**ambos,** /'ambos,/ *a* and *m pl*, **ambas** *a f pl*, both, e.g. *ambas casas,* both houses
**ambulancia** /ambu'lanθia; ambu'lansia/ *f*, ambulance. **a. de correos,** railway post office. **a. fija,** field-hospital
**ambulante** /ambu'lante/ *a* walking; traveling, wandering

**amedrentador** /ameðrenta'ðor/ *a* frightening; terrible; intimidating

**amedrentar** /ameðren'tar/ *vt* to frighten, scare; intimidate

**ameliorar** /amelio'rar/ *vt* to better, improve

**amelonado** /amelo'naðo/ *a* melon-shaped; *Inf.* madly in love

**amén** /a'men/ *m*, amen, so be it. **a. de,** besides, in addition to. *Inf.* **en un decir a.,** in a trice

**amenaza** /ame'naθa; ame'nasa/ *f*, threat

**amenazador, amenazante** /amenaθa'ðor, amena-'θante; amenasa'ðor, amena'sante/ *a* menacing, threatening

**amenazar** /amena'θar; amena'sar/ *vt* to threaten; —*vt* and *vi* presage, be pending

**amenguamiento** /amengua'miento/ *m*, lessening, diminution; discredit; loss of prestige

**amenguar** /amen'guar/ *vt* to lessen, decrease; dishonor, discredit

**amenidad** /ameni'ðað/ *f*, amenity; agreeableness

**amenizar** /ameni'θar; ameni'sar/ *vt* to make pleasant or attractive

**ameno** /a'meno/ *a* pleasant; entertaining; agreeable, delightful

**América** /a'merika/ America

**América del Norte** /a'merika del 'norte/ North America

**América del Sur** /a'merika del sur/ South America

**americana** /ameri'kana/ *f*, (man's) jacket

**americanismo** /amerika'nismo/ *m*, usage typical of Western-Hemisphere Spanish

**americano** /ameri'kano/ *a* American

**ameritar** /ameri'tar/ *vt West. Hem.* to deserve, merit

**ametrallador** /ametraʎa'ðor; ametraya'ðor/ *m*, machine-gunner

**ametralladora** /ametraʎa'ðora; ametraya'ðora/ *f*, machine-gun

**amianto** /a'mianto/ *m*, *Mineral.* amianthus, asbestos

**amiba** /a'miβa/ *f*, *Zool.* ameba

**amicísimo** /ami'θisimo; ami'sisimo/ *a superl* **amigo,** most friendly

**amiga** /a'miga/ *f*, woman friend; mistress, lover; dame, schoolmistress; dame school

**amigabilidad** /amigaβili'ðað/ *f*, friendliness, amicability

**amigable** /ami'gaβle/ *a* friendly, amicable; harmonious; suitable

**amígdala** /a'migðala/ *f*, tonsil

**amigdalitis** /amigða'litis/ *f*, tonsillitis

**amigo** /a'migo/ **(-ga)** *a* friendly; fond, addicted —*n* friend. *m*, lover. *Inf.* **ser muy a. de,** to be very friendly with; be very keen on or fond of

**amilanado** /amila'naðo/ *a* cowed, spiritless

**amilanar** /amila'nar/ *vt* to terrify, intimidate; —*vr* grow discouraged

**aminorar** /amino'rar/ *vt* to diminish, lessen

**amir** /a'mir/ *m*, emir, Arab prince or chief

**amistad** /amis'tað/ *f*, friendship; liaison; favor; *pl* acquaintances, friends

**amistar** /amis'tar/ *vt* to introduce, make known to each other; bring about a reconciliation between or with

**amistoso** /amis'toso/ *a* friendly

**amnesia** /am'nesia/ *f*, amnesia

**amnistía** /amnis'tia/ *f*, amnesty

**amnistiar** /amnisti'ar/ *vt* to concede an amnesty, pardon

**amo** /'amo/ *m*, head of the house; master; owner; overlord; overseer. **a. de huéspedes,** keeper of a boarding house. **Nuestro A.** Our Lord. *Inf.* **ser el a. del cotarro,** to rule the roost

**amodorramiento** /amoðorra'miento/ *m*, stupor, deep sleep

**amodorrarse** /amoðo'rrarse/ *vr* to fall into a stupor; fall into a heavy sleep

**amoladera** /amola'ðera/ *f*, whetstone

**amolador** /amola'ðor/ *m*, scissors grinder; knife grinder; sharpener

**amoladura** /amola'ðura/ *f*, grinding, whetting, sharpening

**amolar** /amo'lar/ *vt irr* to grind, sharpen; *Inf.* pester, annoy. See **colar**

**amoldar** /amol'dar/ *vt* to mold; adjust; —*vr* adapt oneself

**amonedación** /amoneða'θion; amoneða'sion/ *f*, coinage, minting

**amonedar** /amone'ðar/ *vt* to coin, mint

**amonestación** /amonesta'θion; amonesta'sion/ *f*, warning; advice. **correr las amonestaciones,** to publish bans of marriage

**amonestador** /amonesta'ðor/ **(-ra)** *a* warning, admonitory —*n* admonisher

**amonestar** /amones'tar/ *vt* to warn; advise; rebuke; *Eccl.* publish bans of marriage

**amoníaco** /amo'niako/ *m*, ammonia

**amontillado** /amonti'ʎaðo; amonti'yaðo/ *m*, kind of pale, dry sherry

**amontonamiento** /amontona'miento/ *m*, accumulation; gathering, collection; piling up, heaping

**amontonar** /amonto'nar/ *vt* to pile up, heap; gather; collect; accumulate; —*vr Inf.* fly into a rage

**amor** /a'mor/ *m*, love; beloved; willingness, pleasure; *pl* love affairs; caresses. **a. propio,** self-esteem; vanity. *Inf.* **con mil amores,** with great pleasure. **por a. de,** for love of; for the sake of

**amoral** /amo'ral/ *a* amoral

**amoralidad** /amorali'ðað/ *f*, amorality

**amoratado** /amora'taðo/ *a* livid, bluish

**amorcillo** /amor'θiʎo; amor'siyo/ *m*, *dim* little love; unimportant love affair; Cupid

**amordazamiento** /amorðaθa'miento; amorðasa-'miento/ *m*, muzzling; gagging

**amordazar** /amorða'θar; amorða'sar/ *vt* to muzzle; gag; prevent speaking

**amorfo** /a'morfo/ *a* amorphous

**amorío** /amo'rio/ *m*, *Inf.* wooing, love making; *pl* love affairs

**amoroso** /amo'roso/ *a* loving; gentle; mild, balmy

**amorrar** /amo'rrar/ *vi Inf.* to hang one's head; sulk, be sullen

**amortajar** /amorta'har/ *vt* to wrap in a shroud; enshroud

**amortiguador** /amortigua'ðor/ *m*, *Mech.* shock absorber. *Auto.* **a. de los muelles,** shock-absorber

**amortiguamiento** /amortigua'miento/ *m*, softening, deadening; mitigation, lessening

**amortiguar** /amorti'guar/ *vt* to soften, deaden; absorb (shocks); moderate, mitigate; soften (colors)

**amortización** /amortiθa'θion; amortisa'sion/ *f*, amortization

**amortizar** /amorti'θar; amorti'sar/ *vt* to amortize; recover, redeem; suppress, abolish (posts)

**amoscarse** /amos'karse/ *vr Inf.* to be piqued or annoyed; become agitated

**amostazar** /amosta'θar; amosta'sar/ *vt Inf.* to annoy; —*vi* become peeved

**amotinador** /amotina'ðor/ **(-ra)** *a* mutinous, rebellious —*n* rebel, mutineer; rioter

**amotinar** /amoti'nar/ *vt* to incite to rebellion; unbalance, unhinge (mind); —*vr* rebel; riot; *Fig.* be unhinged

**amovible** /amo'βiβle/ *a* movable, removable; removable (of officials, etc.)

**amovilidad** /amoβili'ðað/ *f*, movability, removability; liability to discharge or dismissal

**amparador** /ampara'ðor/ **(-ra)** *a* protective; sheltering —*n* protector, defender, helper; shelterer

**amparar** /ampa'rar/ *vt* to protect, favor, help; shelter; —*vr* take refuge, take shelter; defend oneself

**amparo** /am'paro/ *m*, shelter, refuge; protection, favor, help; defense

**amper** /am'per/ *m*, *Elec.* ampere

**amperímetro** /ampe'rimetro/ *m*, *Elec.* ammeter

**amperio** /am'perio/ *m*, *Elec.* ampere

**ampliable** /am'pliaβle/ *a* amplifiable

**ampliación** /amplia'θion; amplia'sion/ *f*, enlargement, increase, extension; *Photo.* enlargement

**ampliador** /amplia'ðor/ **(-ra)** *a* enlarging —*n* enlarger

**ampliadora** /amplia'ðora/ *f*, *Photo.* enlarger

**ampliar** /am'pliar/ *vt* to extend, enlarge, increase; *Photo.* enlarge

**amplificación** /amplifika'θion; amplifika'sion/ f, extension, amplification; *Photo.* enlargement

**amplificar** /amplifi'kar/ vt to enlarge; extend; increase; amplify, expatiate upon

**amplio** /'amplio/ a wide; extensive; roomy, ample; prolix

**amplitud** /ampli'tuð/ f, extension; width; spaciousness, amplitude

**ampolla** /am'poʎa; am'poya/ f, blister; ampoule; bubble; *Elec.* bulb

**ampulosidad** /ampulosi'ðað/ f, pomposity, redundancy (of style)

**ampuloso** /ampu'loso/ a pompous, high-flown (style)

**amputación** /amputa'θion; amputa'sion/ f, amputation

**amputar** /ampu'tar/ vt to amputate

**amuchachado** /amutʃa'tʃaðo/ a boyish

**amueblar** /amue'βlar/ vt to furnish; provide with furniture

**amuleto** /amu'leto/ m, amulet, charm

**amurallar** /amura'ʎar; amura'yar/ vt to surround with a wall, wall

**amusgar** /amus'gar/ vt and vi to flatten the ears (animals); —vt screw up the eyes (to see better)

**ana** /'ana/ f, ell (measure)

**anabaptismo** /anaβap'tismo/ m, Anabaptism

**anabaptista** /anaβap'tista/ mf Anabaptist

**anacardo** /ana'karðo/ m, cashew (nut)

**anacoreta** /anako'reta/ mf anchorite, hermit

**anacreóntico** /anakre'ontiko/ a Anacreontic

**anacrónico** /ana'kroniko/ a anachronous

**anacronismo** /anakro'nismo/ m, anachronism

**ánade** /'anaðe/ mf duck

**anadear** /anaðe'ar/ vi to waddle (like a duck)

**anadeo** /ana'ðeo/ m, waddle

**anadino** /ana'ðino/ (-na) n duckling

**anadón** /ana'ðon/ m, drake

**anáfora** /a'nafora/ f, anaphora

**anafrodisíaco** /anafroði'siako/ a anaphrodisiac

**anagrama** /ana'grama/ m, anagram

**analectas** /ana'lektas/ f, pl analects

**anales** /a'nales/ m, pl annals

**analfabetismo** /analfaβe'tismo/ m, illiteracy

**analfabeto** /analfa'βeto/ (-ta) a and n illiterate

**analgesia** /anal'hesia/ f, analgesia

**analgésico** /anal'hesiko/ a and m, *Med.* analgesic

**análisis** /a'nalisis/ m, analysis; *Gram.* parsing

**analista** /ana'lista/ mf analyst

**analizar** /anali'θar; anali'sar/ vt to analyse

**analogía** /analo'hia/ f, analogy

**analógico, análogo** /ana'lohiko, a'nalogo/ a analogous

**ananás** /ana'nas/ m, pineapple

**anaquel** /ana'kel/ m, shelf, ledge

**anaranjado** /anaran'haðo/ a and m, orange (color)

**anarquía** /anar'kia/ f, anarchy

**anárquico** /a'narkiko/ a anarchical

**anarquismo** /anar'kismo/ m, anarchism

**anarquista** /anar'kista/ mf anarchist

**anatema** /ana'tema/ mf. anathema

**anatematizar** /anatemati'θar; anatemati'sar/ vt to anathematize, denounce

**anatomía** /anato'mia/ f, anatomy

**anatómico** /ana'tomiko/ a anatomical

**anatomista** /anato'mista/ mf anatomist

**anca** /'anka/ f, croup, hindquarters of a horse

**ancho** /'antʃo/ a wide, broad. m, width, breadth. *Inf.* **a mis** (**tus, sus,** etc.) **anchas** or **anchos,** at my (your, his, etc.) ease, with complete freedom

**anchoa** /an'tʃoa/ f, anchovy

**anchura** /an'tʃura/ f, width, breadth; ease, freedom; extent

**anchuroso** /antʃu'roso/ a very wide; extensive; spacious

**ancianidad** /anθiani'ðað; ansiani'ðað/ f, old age; seniority; oldness

**anciano** /an'θiano; an'siano/ (-na) a old; ancient —n old person

**ancla** /'ankla/ f, anchor. **a. de la esperanza,** sheet anchor. **echar anclas,** to anchor

**ancladero, anclaje** /ankla'ðero, an'klahe/ m, anchorage

**anclar** /an'klar/ vi to anchor

**áncora** /'ankora/ f, anchor; refuge, haven

**andada** /an'daða/ f, wandering, roving; hard bread roll; pasture; pl trail, tracks. *Fig. Inf.* **volver a las andadas,** to return to one's old tricks

**andaderas** /anda'ðeras/ f pl, go-cart (for learning to walk)

**andadoba** /anda'ðoβa/ f, lansquenet (card game)

**andador** /anda'ðor/ a walking; swift walking; wandering. m, walker; garden path; pl leading-strings, reins

**andadura** /anda'ðura/ f, walk, gait; pace, step

**Andalucía** /andalu'θia; andalu'sia/ Andalusia

**andaluz** /anda'luθ; anda'lus/ (-za) a and n Andalusian

**andaluzada** /andalu'θaða; andalu'saða/ f, *Inf.* exaggeration, tall story

**andamio** /an'damio/ m, scaffolding; stand, platform

**andanada** /anda'naða/ f, *Naut.* broadside; cheapest priced seat in a bullring; *Inf.* dressing-down, scolding

**andante** /an'dante/ a walking, strolling; errant (of knights) —a and m, *Mus.* andante

**andanza** /an'danθa; an'dansa/ f, happening, occurrence; pl doings, deeds. **buena a.,** good fortune

**andar** /an'dar/ vi irr to walk; move; work, operate, run (machines, etc.); progress, get along (negotiations, etc.); be, feel; elapse (of time); be occupied; behave; (*with prep a*) administer (blows, etc.); (*with en*) upset, turn over (papers, etc.); ride in or on (cars, bicycles, etc.); be engaged in; (*with con*) use, handle; —vt traverse. m, gait, walk. **a. por los cuarenta,** to be in one's forties. **a. con paños tibios,** not to be firm. **a. con pies de plomo,** to be extremely cautious. **a. tras,** to follow, go after; persecute; desire ardently (things). **andarse a la flor del berro,** to sow one's wild oats. *Fig. Inf.* **andarse por las ramas,** to beat about the bush. **¡Anda!** Get along with you!; Hurry up!; You don't say so! **¡Andando!** Let's get going!, Let's get a move on it! *Preterite* **anduve,** etc —*imperf subjunc* **anduviese,** etc.

**andariego** /anda'riego/ a swift walking; wandering, vagrant

**andarín (-ina)** /anda'rin/ n good walker; professional walker

**andas** /'andas/ f pl, kind of stretcher; bier

**andén** /an'den/ m, railway platform

**andero** /an'dero/ m, bearer (of a bier)

**andino** /an'dino/ a Andean

**andorrano (-na)** /ando'rrano/ a and n Andorran

**andrajo** /an'draho/ m, rag, wisp of cloth, tatter

**andrajoso** /andra'hoso/ a ragged, tattered

**andurriales** /andu'rriales/ m pl, byways, unfrequented paths; remote places

**anécdota** /a'nekðota/ f, anecdote

**anecdótico** /anek'ðotiko/ a anecdotal

**anegación** /anega'θion; anega'sion/ f, drowning, flooding, inundation

**anegar** /ane'gar/ vt to drown; inundate; shipwreck; —vr drown; be flooded

**anejo** /a'neho/ a attached, annexed. m, annexed borough

**anemia** /a'nemia/ f, anemia

**anémico** /a'nemiko/ a anemic

**anémona, anémone** /a'nemona, a'nemone/ f, anemone. **anémona de mar,** sea-anemone

**anestesia** /anes'tesia/ f, anesthesia

**anestesiador (-ra)** /anestesia'ðor/ n anesthetist

**anestesiar** /aneste'siar/ vt to anesthetize

**anestésico** /anes'tesiko/ a and m, anesthetic

**aneurisma** /aneu'risma/ mf *Med.* aneurism

**anexar** /anek'sar/ vt to annex

**anexión** /anek'sion/ f, annexation

**anexo** /a'nekso/ a attached, joined. m, annex

**anfibio** /an'fiβio/ a amphibious. m, amphibian

**anfiteatro** /anfite'atro/ m, amphitheater; operating theater; dissecting room; morgue; *Theat.* dress-circle

**anfitrión** /anfitri'on/ m, *Inf.* host, one who entertains guests

**ánfora** /'anfora/ f, amphora

**angarillas** /aŋga'riʎas; aŋga'riyas/ *f pl*, hand barrow; table cruet; yoke and panniers

**ángel** /'anhel/ *m*, angel. **á. de la guarda,** guardian angel. **estar con los ángeles,** to be in Heaven (euphem. for "to be dead")

**angelical, angélico** /anheli'kal, an'heliko/ *a* angelic; divine, excellent

**angina** /an'hina/ *f*, *Med*. angina, tonsillitis. **a. de pecho,** angina pectoris

**anglicanismo** /aŋglika'nismo/ *m*, Anglicanism

**anglicano (-na)** /aŋgli'kano/ *a* and *n* Anglican

**anglicismo** /aŋgli'θismo; aŋgli'sismo/ *m*, anglicism

**anglo (-la)** /'aŋglo/ *a* and *n* Angle —*a* Anglo-

**angloamericano (-na)** /ˌaŋgloameri'kano/ *a* and *n* Anglo-American

**anglófilo (-la)** /aŋ'glofilo/ *n* Anglophile

**anglosajón (-ona)** /aŋglosa'hon/ *a* and *n* Anglo-Saxon. *m*, Anglo-Saxon language

**angostar** /aŋgos'tar/ *vi* and *vt* to narrow; tighten

**angosto** /aŋ'gosto/ *a* narrow; tight

**angostura** /aŋgos'tura/ *f*, narrowness; tightness; narrow pass; strait; *Fig*. tight corner, fix

**anguila** /aŋ'gila/ *f*, *Ichth*. eel; *pl Naut*. slipway, slips

**angula** /aŋ'gula/ *f*, *Ichth*. elver (young eel)

**angular** /aŋgu'lar/ *a* angular

**ángulo** /'aŋgulo/ *m*, angle. **á. inferior izquierdo,** lower lefthand corner. **á. inferior derecho,** lower righthand corner. **á. superior izquierdo,** upper lefthand corner. **á. superior derecho,** upper righthand corner. **á. recto,** right angle

**anguloso** /aŋgu'loso/ *a* angulate; angular, gaunt; cornered

**angustia** /aŋ'gustia/ *f*, anguish, grief

**angustiante** /aŋgus'tiante/ *a* distressing

**angustiar** /aŋgus'tiar/ *vt* to grieve; afflict; —*vr* be full of anguish

**anhelación** /anela'θion; anela'sion/ *f*, panting, hard breathing; yearning, longing

**anhelar** /ane'lar/ *vi* to pant, breathe with difficulty; —*vi* and *vt* long for, yearn for, desire

**anhélito** /a'nelito/ *m*, pant, hard breathing

**anhelo (de)** /a'nelo/ *m*, longing (for), desire (for), yearning (for)

**anheloso** /ane'loso/ *a* difficult, labored (of breathing); anxious, longing

**anidar** /ani'ðar/ *vi* to nest (birds); swell; —*vt* shelter, protect; —*vr* nest; dwell; nestle

**anilla** /a'niʎa; a'niya/ *f*, curtain ring; *pl* gymnastic rings

**anillo** /a'niʎo; a'niyo/ *m*, finger ring; small ring; coil (of serpents and ropes). *Inf*. **venir como a. al dedo,** to fit like a glove; come just at the right moment

**ánima** /'anima/ *f*, soul, spirit; soul in purgatory; bore (of firearms); *pl* prayer bell for the souls of the departed

**animación** /anima'θion; anima'sion/ *f*, liveliness, gaiety; animation, vivacity; bustle, movement

**animal** /ani'mal/ *m*, animal; *Inf*. dolt, brute —*a* animal; *Inf*. brutish, doltish

**animalada** /anima'laða/ *f*, *Inf*. stupidity, foolishness

**animalidad** /animali'ðað/ *f*, animalism

**animar** /ani'mar/ *vt* to animate; encourage, incite; invigorate, enliven; make gay, cheer up; make attractive, adorn; —*vr* take heart; make up one's mind; cheer up; grow gay

**animismo** /ani'mismo/ *m*, animism

**ánimo** /'animo/ *m*, soul, spirit; courage; endurance, fortitude; will, intention; mind. **con ánimo de + inf.,** with the intention of + *ger*. **¡Á.!** Courage!

**animosidad** /animosi'ðað/ *f*, hatred, animosity, dislike

**animoso** /ani'moso/ *a* spirited, lively; valiant

**aniñado** /ani'naðo/ *a* childlike, childish

**aniquilable** /aniki'laβle/ *a* destructible

**aniquilación** /anikila'θion; anikila'sion/ *f*, destruction, annihilation; suppression; decay

**aniquilador (-ra)** /anikila'ðor/ *a* destructive, annihilating —*n* destroyer

**aniquilamiento** /anikila'miento/ *m*, See **aniquilación**

**aniquilar** /aniki'lar/ *vt* to annihilate, destroy completely; —*vr* waste away, decay

**anís** /a'nis/ *m*, aniseed, anise; anisette (liqueur)

**anisar** /ani'sar/ *vt* to flavor with aniseed

**anisete** /ani'sete/ *m*, anisette

**aniversario** /aniβer'sario/ *a* annual. *m*, anniversary

**Anjeo** /an'heo/ Anjou

**ano** /'ano/ *m*, anus

**anoche** /a'notʃe/ *adv* last night; the previous night

**anochecer** /anotʃe'θer; anotʃe'ser/ *vi irr* to grow night; become dark; be in a place *or* be doing something at nightfall (e.g. *Anochecimos en Lérida,* We were in Lerida at nightfall) —*vr Poet*. be obscured or darkened. *m*, nightfall, dusk. See **conocer**

**anochecida** /anotʃe'θiða; anotʃe'siða/ *f*, dusk, late twilight

**anodino** /ano'ðino/ *a Med*. anodyne; ineffective, useless; inoffensive. *m*, anodyne

**anomalía** /anoma'lia/ *f*, anomaly, inconstancy, irregularity; *Astron*. anomaly

**anómalo** /a'nomalo/ *a* anomalous, abnormal, unusual

**anonadar** /anona'ðar/ *vt* to destroy, annihilate; suppress; *Fig*. overwhelm, depress; humble

**anónimo** /a'nonimo/ *a* anonymous. *m*, anonymity; anonymous letter; unsigned literary work

**anormal** /anor'mal/ *a* abnormal; irregular, unusual. *mf* abnormal person

**anormalidad** /anormali'ðað/ *f*, abnormality; irregularity, inconsistency

**anotación** /anota'θion; anota'sion/ *f*, annotation

**anotador (-ra)** /anota'ðor/ *(-ra)* *n* annotator

**anotar** /ano'tar/ *vt* to annotate; note down

**anquilostoma** /ankilos'toma/ *m*, *Med*. hookworm

**ánsar** /an'sar/ *m*, goose; drake

**ansarino** /ansa'rino/ *a* goose. *m*, gosling

**anseático** /anse'atiko/ *a* Hanseatic

**ansia (de)** /'ansia/ *f*, anxiety, trouble; grief; longing (for), yearning (for); greed

**ansiar** /an'siar/ *vt* to long for, yearn for; covet, desire

**ansiedad** /ansie'ðað/ *f*, anxiety, anguish, worry

**ansión** /an'sion/ *f*, intense desire

**ansioso** /an'sioso/ *a* anxious; grievous, painful; eager, desirous; greedy

**anta** /'anta/ *f*, *Zool*. elk; obelisk

**antagónico** /anta'goniko/ *a* antagonistic

**antagonismo** /antago'nismo/ *m*, antagonism

**antagonista** /antago'nista/ *mf* antagonist, adversary

**antaño** /an'tano/ *adv* last year, yesteryear; long ago

**antártico** /an'tartiko/ *a* antarctic

**ante** /'ante/ *m*, *Zool*. elk; suede; buffalo

**ante** /'ante/ *prep* in the presence of, before; regarding, in the face of (e.g. *a. deber tan alto,* in the face of so noble a duty)

**anteado** /ante'aðo/ *a* beige, buff-colored, fawn

**anteanoche** /antea'notʃe/ *adv* the night before last

**anteayer** /antea'yer/ *adv* the day before yesterday

**antebrazo** /ante'βraθo; ante'βraso/ *m*, forearm

**antecámara** /ante'kamara/ *f*, antechamber

**antecedente** /anteθe'ðente; antese'ðente/ *m*, antecedent. **antecedentes** *m pl* background (of a case, situation, etc.)

**antecedentemente** /anteθe,ðente'mente; antese,ðente'mente/ *adv* previously

**anteceder** /anteθe'ðer; antese'ðer/ *vt* to precede

**antecesor** /anteθe'sor; antese'sor/ **(-ra)** *a* previous —*n* predecessor. *m*, forebear, ancestor

**antecoger** /anteko'her/ *vt* to carry in front, lead before; pick too soon

**antecomedor** /antekome'ðor/ *m*, breakfast nook, breakfast room

**antedata** /ante'ðata/ *f*, antedate

**antedatar** /anteða'tar/ *vt* to antedate

**antedicho** /ante'ðitʃo/ *a* aforementioned, aforesaid

**antediluviano** /anteðilu'βiano/ *a* antediluvian

**antelación** /antela'θion; antela'sion/ *f*, advance, anticipation

**antemano, de** /ante'mano, de/ *adv* in advance, beforehand

**antemeridiano** /antemeri'ðiano/ *a* antemeridian, forenoon

**antena** /an'tena/ *f*, antenna; *Radio*. aerial

**antenacido** /antena'θiðo; antena'siðo/ *a* born prematurely
**antenombre** /ante'nombre/ *m*, title (placed before name)
**anteojera** /anteo'hera/ *f*, horse's blinker; eyeglass case
**anteojo** /ante'oho/ *m*, spy-glass, small telescope; *pl* horse's blinkers; eyeglasses, glasses; spectacles; goggles
**antepagar** /antepa'gar/ *vt* to pay in advance
**antepalco** /ante'palko/ *m*, vestibule of a box in a theater
**antepasado** /antepa'saðo/ *a* previous, past. *m*, ancestor (gen. *pl*)
**antepecho** /ante'petʃo/ *m*, parapet; windowsill; railing, balustrade; front (of a theater box, etc.); *Naut.* bulwark
**antepenúltimo** /antepe'nultimo/ *a* antepenultimate, second from the last
**anteponer** /antepo'ner/ *vt irr* to place before; prefer, favor. See **poner**
**anteproyecto** /antepro'yekto/ *m*, first sketch, preliminary work or plan
**antepuerta** /ante'puerta/ *f*, door-curtain, portiere; *Mil.* anteport
**anterior** /ante'rior/ *a* previous, former; anterior; aforementioned, preceding
**anteriormente** /anterior'mente/ *adv* beforehand, previously
**antes** /'antes/ *adv* before; rather, on the contrary; previously. **a. bien**, rather, sooner. **a. con a.** *or* **cuanto a.**, as soon as possible
**antesala** /ante'sala/ *f*, antechamber
**antevíspera** /ante'βispera/ *f*, two days previously
**antiaéreo** /anti'aereo/ *a* antiaircraft. *m pl*. **(cañones) antiaéreos**, A.A. guns
**anticiclón** /antiθi'klon; antisi'klon/ *m*, anticyclone
**anticipación** /antiθipa'θion; antisipa'sion/ *f*, anticipation; advance
**anticipada** /antiθi'paða; antisi'paða/ *f*, foul thrust (in fencing, etc.)
**anticipadamente** /antiθi,paða'mente; antisi,paða'mente/ *adv* in advance; prematurely
**anticipado** /antiθi'paðo; antisi'paðo/ *a* in advance; premature
**anticipador** /antiθipa'ðor; antisipa'ðor/ *a* anticipatory
**anticipar** /antiθi'par; antisi'par/ *vt* to anticipate; foresee; forestall; advance (money); lend; —*vr* happen before time; (*with prep a*) act in advance of, anticipate; get ahead of oneself
**anticipo** /anti'θipo; anti'sipo/ *m*, anticipation, advance; advance payment; sum of money lent
**anticlerical** /antikleri'kal/ *a* anticlerical
**anticlímax** /anti'klimaks/ *m*, anticlimax
**anticonstitucional** /antikonstituθio'nal; antikonstitusio'nal/ *a* unconstitutional
**Anticristo** /anti'kristo/ *m*, Antichrist
**anticuado** /anti'kuaðo/ *a* antiquated, ancient
**anticuario** /anti'kuario/ *m*, antiquarian, antique dealer
**antídoto** /an'tiðoto/ *m*, antidote
**antiesclavista** /antieskla'βista/ *a* antislavery. *mf* antislavist
**antiespasmódico** /antiespas'moðiko/ *a* and *m*, *Med.* antispasmodic
**antiestético** /anties'tetiko/ *a* unesthetic
**antietimológico** /antietimo'lohiko/ *a* nonetymological, unetymological
**antifaz** /anti'faθ; anti'fas/ *m*, mask; face-covering
**antiflogístico** /antiflo'histiko/ *a* and *m*, *Med.* antiphlogistic
**antigramatical** /antigramati'kal/ *a* ungrammatical
**antigualla** /anti'guaʎa; anti'guaya/ *f*, antique; ancient custom; anything out-of-date
**antiguamente** /antigua'mente/ *adv* in time past, formerly
**antiguamiento** /antigua'miento/ *m*, seniority
**antigüedad** /antigue'ðað/ *f*, antiquity; ancients; length of service (in an employment); *pl* antiquities
**antiguo** /an'tiguo/ *a* ancient, very old; antique; sen-

ior (in an employment); former. *m*, senior member (of a community, etc.). *m pl*, ancients. **A. Testamento**, Old Testament. **de a.**, from ancient times. **en lo antiguo**, in ancient times; in former times, in days of yore
**antillano** /anti'ʎano; anti'yano/ **(-na)** *a* and *n* of or from the Antilles
**Antillas, las** /an'tiʎas, las; an'tiyas, las/ the Antilles
**antílope** /an'tilope/ *m*, antelope
**antimacasar** /antimaka'sar/ *m*, antimacassar
**antimilitarismo** /antimilita'rismo/ *m*, antimilitarism
**antimilitarista** /antimilita'rista/ *a* antimilitaristic
**antimonárquico** /antimo'narkiko/ *a* antimonarchical
**antimonio** /anti'monio/ *m*, *Metall.* antimony
**antipalúdico** /antipa'luðiko/ *a* antimalarial
**antipapa** /anti'papa/ *m*, antipope
**antipara** /anti'para/ *f*, screen, shield
**antiparras** /anti'parras/ *f pl*, *Inf.* spectacles, eyeglasses, glasses
**antipatía** /antipa'tia/ *f*, antipathy
**antipático** /anti'patiko/ *a* disagreeable; unattractive
**antipatriótico** /antipa'triotiko/ *a* unpatriotic
**antípoda** /an'tipoða/ *a* and *m*, or *f*, antipode
**antiquísimo** /anti'kisimo/ *a superl*, **antiguo**, most ancient
**antirrepublicano** /antirrepuβli'kano/ *a* antirepublican
**antisemita** /antise'mita/ *a* anti-Semitic. *mf* anti-Semite
**antisemitismo** /antisemi'tismo/ *m*, anti-Semitism
**antiséptico** /anti'septiko/ *a* and *m*, antiseptic
**antisifilítico** /antisifi'litiko/ *a Med.* anti-syphilitic
**antisocial** /antiso'θial; antiso'sial/ *a* antisocial
**antítesis** /an'titesis/ *f*, antithesis
**antitético** /anti'tetiko/ *a* antithetic, contrasted
**antófago** /an'tofago/ *a* anthophagous, flower-eating
**antojadizo** /antoha'ðiθo; antoha'ðiso/ *a* capricious, fanciful, whimsical
**antojarse** /anto'harse/ *vr* to have a fancy for, want (e.g. *Se me antoja marcharme al campo*, I have a yen to go to the country); suspect, imagine
**antojo** /an'toho/ *m*, caprice, fancy, whim; desire, will; *pl* birthmark
**antología** /antolo'hia/ *f*, anthology
**antólogo** /an'tologo/ *m*, anthologist
**antonomasia** /antono'masia/ *f*, antonomasia. **por a.**, by analogy, by transference
**antorcha** /an'tortʃa/ *f*, torch, flambeau
**antracita** /antra'θita; antra'sita/ *f*, anthracite
**ántrax** /'antraks/ *m*, *Med.* anthrax
**antro** /'antro/ *m*, cave, cavern; *Anat.* antrum
**antropofagia** /antropo'fahia/ *f*, cannibalism, anthropophagy
**antropófago** /antro'pofago/ **(-ga)** *a* cannibalistic —*n* cannibal
**antropología** /antropolo'hia/ *f*, anthropology
**antropológico** /antropo'lohiko/ *a* anthropological
**antropólogo** /antro'pologo/ *m*, anthropologist
**antropometría** /antropome'tria/ *f*, anthropometry
**antropomorfo** /antropo'morfo/ *a* anthropomorphous
**antroposofía** /antroposo'fia/ *f*, anthroposophy
**antruejo** /antru'eho/ *m*, three days of carnival before Lent
**anual** /a'nual/ *a* yearly, annual
**anualidad** /anuali'ðað/ *f*, annuity
**anuario** /a'nuario/ *m*, directory, yearbook, handbook
**anubarrado** /anuβa'rraðo/ *a*, covered with clouds, cloudy
**anublado** /anu'βlaðo/ *a* lowering, overcast; clouded
**anublar** /anu'βlar/ *vt* to cloud; darken, obscure; blight (plants); —*vr* cloud over; become blighted or mildewed
**anudar** /anu'ðar/ *vt* to knot; tie, fasten; join; continue; **a. amistad de,** to strike up a friendship with. **a. la corbata,** to put on one's tie, tie one's tie; —*vr* grow stunted
**anulable** /anu'laβle/ *a* annulable, voidable
**anulación** /anula'θion; anula'sion/ *f*, annulment, abrogation
**anular** /anu'lar/ *a* annular, ring-shaped —*vt* to annul; *Math.* cancel out

**anuloso** /anu'loso/ *a* annulate, formed of rings

**anunciación** /anunθia'θion; anunsia'sion/ *f, Eccl.* Annunciation; announcement

**anunciador** /anunθia'ðor; anunsia'ðor/ **(-ra)**, *n* announcer; advertiser

**anunciante** /anun'θiante; anun'siante/ *mf* announcer; advertiser

**anunciar** /anun'θiar; anun'siar/ *vt* to announce; publish, proclaim; advertise; foretell, presage. **Anuncian lluvia,** The forecast calls for rain

**anuncio** /a'nunθio; a'nunsio/ *m,* announcement; publication, proclamation; advertisement; presage, omen. **a. luminoso,** sky-sign

**anverso** /am'berso/ *m,* obverse, face

**anzuelo** /an'θuelo; an'suelo/ *m,* fish-hook; *Cul.* fritter; *Inf.* attraction, inducement

**añadido** /aɲa'ðiðo/ *m,* hair-switch; make-weight

**añadidura** /aɲaði'ðura/ *f,* addition; make-weight, extra

**añadir** /aɲa'ðir/ *vt* to add; increase

**añagaza** /aɲa'gaθa; aɲa'gasa/ *f,* decoy bird; enticement, lure

**añejo** /a'ɲeho/ *a* very old

**añicos** /a'ɲikos/ *m pl,* fragments, small pieces. **hacer a.,** to break into fragments

**añil** /a'ɲil/ *m,* indigo; indigo blue

**año** /'aɲo/ *m,* year; *pl* birthday. **a. bisiesto,** leap-year. **a. económico,** fiscal year. **A. Nuevo,** New Year. **tener (siete) años,** to be (seven) years old. **los Años Bobos,** the period from 1874 to 1898 in Spain

**añoranza** /aɲo'ranθa; aɲo'ransa/ *f,* homesickness, loneliness; nostalgia

**añorar** /aɲo'rar/ *vi* to be homesick or lonely

**añoso** /a'ɲoso/ *a* very old, full of years

**añublo** /a'ɲuβlo/ *m,* mildew

**aojamiento** /aoha'miento/ *m,* evil eye, wicked spell

**aojar** /ao'har/ *vt* to bewitch, place under a spell; spoil, frustrate

**aojo** /a'oho/ *m,* evil eye; magic spell

**aorta** /a'orta/ *f, Anat.* aorta

**aovillarse** /aoβi'ʎarse; aoβi'yarse/ *vr* to roll oneself into a ball; curl up

**apabullante** /apaβu'ʎante; apaβu'yante/ *a* crushing, flattening

**apacentadero** /apaθenta'ðero; apasenta'ðero/ *m,* grazing land, pasture

**apacentamiento** /apaθenta'miento; apasenta'miento/ *m,* pasturage; grazing

**apacentar** /apaθen'tar; apasen'tar/ *vt irr* to put out to grass; teach, instruct; satisfy (one's desires); —*vr* graze (cattle). See **acertar**

**apacibilidad** /apaθiβili'ðað; apasiβili'ðað/ *f,* agreeableness; mildness; peaceableness

**apacible** /apa'θiβle; apa'siβle/ *a* agreeable; mild; peaceable; calm, peaceful

**apaciguamiento** /a,paθigua'miento; a,pasigua'miento/ *m,* appeasement, soothing, pacification

**apaciguar** /apaθi'guar; apasi'guar/ *vt* to appease, pacify; calm

**apadrinar** /apaðri'nar/ *vt* to act as godfather to; be best man to (at a wedding); act as a second for (in a duel); sponsor; favor

**apagable** /apa'gaβle/ *a* extinguishable

**apagado** /apa'gaðo/ *a* timid, nervous; pale (of colors); dull, lusterless

**apagador** /apaga'ðor/ **(-ra)** *a* quenching —*n* extinguisher. *m,* candle-snuffer; damper (of a piano)

**apagaincendios** /apa,pagain'θendios; a,pagain'sendios/ *m,* ship's fire-extinguisher

**apagamiento** /apaga'miento/ *m,* quenching, extinguishment

**apagar** /apa'gar/ *vt* to extinguish, put out; *Fig.* quench, moderate; slake (lime); *Art.* tone down (colors); shut off (engines)

**apagarrisas** /apaga'rrisas/ *mf* crapehanger, killjoy, wet blanket

**apagavelas** /apaga'βelas/ *m,* candle-snuffer

**apalabrar** /apala'βrar/ *vt* to make an appointment with; discuss, consider

**apaleamiento** /apalea'miento/ *m,* beating, thrashing

**apalear** /apale'ar/ *vt* to beat, thrash; knock down with a stick

**apandillarse** /apandi'ʎarse; apandi'yarse/ *vr* to form a gang or group

**apañar** /apa'ɲar/ *vt* to take away, remove; seize; steal; dress, get ready; *Inf.* wrap up; patch, repair; —*vr Inf.* grow skillful

**apaño** /a'paɲo/ *m,* dexterity, skill; craft, guile

**aparador** /apara'ðor/ *m,* shop window; sideboard; workshop; *Eccl.* credence (table)

**aparato** /apa'rato/ *m,* apparatus; equipment, utensils; pomp, ostentation; symptoms; sign, circumstance, token. **a. digestivo,** digestive system; digestive tract. **a. fonador,** speech apparatus

**aparatoso** /apara'toso/ *a* showy, ostentatious. **incendio. a.,** conflagration, large fire

**aparcería** /aparθe'ria; aparse'ria/ *f,* partnership (in a farm)

**aparear** /apare'ar/ *vt* to match, make equal; pair; mate (animals); —*vr* form up in pairs

**aparecer** /apare'θer; apare'ser/ **(se)** *vi* and *vr irr* to appear; seem; be. See **conocer**

**aparecido** /apare'θiðo; apare'siðo/ *m,* apparition, specter

**aparejador** /apareha'ðor/ *m,* overseer, foreman; *Naut.* rigger

**aparejar** /apare'har/ *vt* to prepare, make ready; saddle (horses); prime, size; rig (a ship)

**aparejo** /apa'reho/ *m,* preparation, arrangement; harness, trappings; *Naut.* rigging; *Naut.* gear; priming, sizing; *Mech.* tackle; *pl* equipment

**aparentar** /aparen'tar/ *vt* to pretend, simulate

**aparente** /apa'rente/ *a* seeming, apparent; obvious, visible; suitable, proper

**aparición** /apari'θion; apari'sion/ *f,* appearance, arrival; apparition, phantom

**apariencia** /apa'rienθia; apa'riensia/ *f,* appearance, looks, probability, likelihood; outward semblance; *pl Theat.* scenery

**apartadamente** /apartaða'mente/ *adv* apart, in private; secretly

**apartadero** /aparta'ðero/ *m,* passing place for cars; railway siding; grass verge. **a. ferroviario,** railway marshaling yard

**apartado** /apar'taðo/ *a* distant, far off; secluded; different. *m,* post-office box; secluded room; smelting house; sorting of cattle; selection of bulls for a bull-fight

**apartamiento** /aparta'miento/ *m,* separation; withdrawal, retiral; seclusion; apartment, flat; *Law.* withdrawal of an action

**apartar** /apar'tar/ *vt* to separate; remove (e.g. an obstacle), take away; *Rail.* shunt; dissuade; sort; —*vr* obtain a divorce; *Law.* withdraw an action. **apartarse de la tradición,** to depart from tradition

**aparte** /a'parte/ *adv* aside, on one side; separately; *Theat.* aside; besides; beyond. *m, Theat.* aside; paragraph; space between words. **¡Aparte!** Move to one side!

**apartidario** /aparti'ðario/ *a* non-partisan

**apasionado** /apasio'naðo/ **(-da)** *a* impassioned; fervent, devoted; passionate; enthusiastic —*n* admirer, lover; enthusiast

**apasionamiento** /apasiona'miento/ *m,* passion

**apasionar** /apasio'nar/ *vt* to arouse to passion; pain; —*vr* (*with por*) grow passionately fond of; become enthusiastic for

**apatía** /apa'tia/ *f,* apathy

**apático** /a'patiko/ *a* apathetic

**apeadero** /apea'ðero/ *m,* mounting-block; halt, stopping place; wayside railway station; pied-à-terre, occasional dwelling

**apear** /ape'ar/ *vt* to dismount, hobble (horse); survey, map out; fell a tree; *Fig.* overcome (difficulties); *Inf.* dissuade; prop; remove, bring down; scotch (a wheel); —*vr* dismount; alight, step off

**apechugar** /apetʃu'gar/ *vi* to push with the breast; *Inf.* put up with reluctantly

**apedazar** /apeða'θar; apeða'sar/ *vt* to tear; break; mend, repair

**apedrear** /apeðre'ar/ *vt* to stone; stone to death; —*vi impers.* hail; —*vr* be damaged by hail (crops)

**apegarse** /ape'garse/ *vr* to grow fond (of), become attached (to)

**apego** /a'pego/ *m*, fondness, inclination; affection, attachment

**apelación** /apela'θion; apela'sion/ *f*, *Law*. appeal; *Inf*. doctor's consultation

**apelante** /ape'lante/ *a* and *mf Law*. appellant

**apelar** /ape'lar/ *vi Law*. to appeal; (*with prep a*) have recourse to; —*vi* be of the same color (horses)

**apellidar** /apeʎi'ðar; apeyi'ðar/ *vt* to name, call; acclaim; call to arms; —*vr* be named

**apellido** /ape'ʎiðo; ape'yiðo/ *m*, surname; nickname; call to arms; clamor; name

**apenar** /ape'nar/ *vt* to grieve, afflict; cause sorrow

**apenas** /a'penas/ *adv* scarcely; immediately, as soon as; with trouble or difficulty

**apéndice** /a'pendiθe; a'pendise/ *m*, appendix, supplement; *Anat*. appendix

**apendicitis** /apendi'θitis; apendi'sitis/ *f*, appendicitis

**Apeninos, los** /ape'ninos, los/ the Apennines

**apeo** /a'peo/ *m*, survey; scaffolding; prop, support

**apercibimiento** /aperθiβi'miento; apersiβi'miento/ *m*, preparation; provision; warning; *Law*. summons

**apercibir** /aperθi'βir; apersi'βir/ *vt* to prepare, furnish; warn; *Law*. summon

**apergaminado** /apergami'naðo/ *a* parchment; parchment-like

**apergaminarse** /apergami'narse/ *vr Inf*. to shrivel, dry up (with old age, etc.)

**aperitivo** /aperi'tiβo/ *a* aperitive. *m*, aperient; aperitive, appetizer

**apertura** /aper'tura/ *f*, opening; inauguration; reading (of a will)

**apesadumbrar** /apesaðum'brar/ *vt* to sadden, afflict, grieve

**apestar** /apes'tar/ *vt* to infect with the plague; catch the plague; *Fig*. corrupt; *Inf*. pester, annoy; —*vi* stink

**apestoso** /apes'toso/ *a* stinking, putrid

**apetecer** /apete'θer; apete'ser/ *vt irr* to want, desire; attract. See **conocer**

**apetecible** /apete'θiβle; apete'siβle/ *a* attractive, desirable

**apetencia** /ape'tenθia; ape'tensia/ *f*, appetite; desire

**apetito** /ape'tito/ *m*, appetite

**apetitoso** /apeti'toso/ *a* appetising; tasty, savory; attractive

**apiadarse** /apia'ðarse/ *vr* (*with de*) to have compassion on, be sorry for

**ápice** /'apiθe; 'apise/ *m*, apex; peak, summit, top; orthographic accent; iota, tittle; crux (of a problem)

**apicultor** /apikul'tor/ (**-ra**) *n* apiarist, beekeeper

**apicultura** /apikul'tura/ *f*, apiculture, beekeeping

**apilar** /api'lar/ *vt* to pile, heap

**apiñado** /api'ɲaðo/ *a* crowded, serried

**apiñamiento** /apiɲa'miento/ *m*, crowding; congestion

**apiñar** /api'ɲar/ *vt* to group together, crowd; —*vr* crowd

**apio** /'apio/ *m*, celery

**apisonadora** /apisona'ðora/ *f*, steam-roller; roller

**apisonar** /apiso'nar/ *vt* to roll, stamp, flatten, ram down; tamp, pack down (e.g. tobacco in a pipe)

**apizarrado** /apiθa'rraðo; apisa'rraðo/ *a* slate-colored

**aplacable** /apla'kaβle/ *a* appeasable, placable

**aplacamiento** /aplaka'miento/ *m*, appeasement

**aplacar** /apla'kar/ *vt* to appease, calm; moderate, mitigate

**aplacible** /apla'θiβle; apla'siβle/ *a* agreeable, pleasant

**aplanar** /apla'nar/ *vt* to flatten, level; toll (pastry); *Inf*. dumbfound, overwhelm; —*vr* collapse (buildings); lose heart

**aplastar** /aplas'tar/ *vt* to flatten, squash, crush; *Inf*. squash flat, floor

**aplaudir** /aplau'ðir/ *vt* to applaud, clap; praise, commend, approve

**aplauso** /a'plauso/ *m*, applause; clapping, plaudit; approbation, commendation

**aplazamiento** /aplaθa'miento; aplasa'miento/ *m*, postponement; appointment, summons

**aplazar** /apla'θar; apla'sar/ *vt* to summon, arrange a meeting; postpone; adjourn

**aplicabilidad** /aplikaβili'ðað/ *f*, applicability

**aplicable** /apli'kaβle/ *a* applicable

**aplicación** /aplika'θion; aplika'sion/ *f*, application; diligence, assiduity; appliqué, ornamentation

**aplicado** /apli'kaðo/ *a* diligent, hardworking; appliqué

**aplicar** /apli'kar/ *vt* to apply; impute; intend, destine (for processions); *Law*. adjudge; —*vr* engage in; apply oneself. **a. el oído,** to listen intently. **a. sanciones,** *Polit*. to impose sanctions

**aplomado** /aplo'maðo/ *a* self-possessed, dignified; leaden, lead-colored

**aplomar** /aplo'mar/ *vt* and *vi* to plumb, test with a plumb-line; —*vr* collapse, fall down

**aplomo** /a'plomo/ *m*, self-possession, dignity; sang-froid

**apocado** /apo'kaðo/ *a* spiritless, timid; base, mean

**Apocalipsis** /apoka'lipsis/ *m*, Apocalypse

**apocalíptico** /apoka'liptiko/ *a* apocalyptic

**apocamiento** /apoka'miento/ *m*, timidity, pusillanimity; depression, discouragement; shyness; baseness, meanness

**apocar** /apo'kar/ *vt* to diminish, reduce; humiliate, scorn

**apócrifo** /a'pokrifo/ *a* fictitious, false; apocryphal. **Apócrifos,** Apocrypha

**apodar** /apo'ðar/ *vt* to nickname

**apoderado** /apoðe'raðo/ *a* authorized. *m*, attorney; deputy; proxy

**apoderar** /apoðe'rar/ *vt* to authorize; grant powers of attorney to; —*vr* (*with de*) seize, take possession of

**apodo** /a'poðo/ *m*, nickname

**apogeo** /apo'heo/ *m*, *Astron*. apogee; *Fig*. zenith, peak (of fame, etc.)

**apolillar** /apoli'ʎar; apoli'yar/ *vt* to eat clothes (moths); —*vr* be moth-eaten

**apolíneo** /apo'lineo/ *a* Apollo-like

**apologético** /apolo'hetiko/ *a* apologetic

**apologista** /apolo'hista/ *mf* apologist

**apólogo** /a'pologo/ *m*, apologue, moral fable

**apoltronarse** /apoltro'narse/ *vr* to grow idle

**apoplejía** /apople'hia/ *f*, apoplexy

**apoplético** /apo'pletiko/ (**-ca**) *a* and *n* apoplectic

**aporrear** /aporre'ar/ *vt* to beat, cudgel; —*vr* work hard, slog away

**aportación** /aporta'θion; aporta'sion/ *f*, contribution; occasionnard

**aportar** /apor'tar/ *vt* to cause, occasion; contribute; —*vi Naut*. reach port; **El buque aportó a Nueva York,** The ship reached New York, The ship sailed into New York harbor; arrive at an unexpected place

**aposentador** /aposenta'ðor/ *m*, usher; *Mil*. billeting officer

**aposentar** /aposen'tar/ *vt* to lodge, give hospitality to; —*vr* lodge, settle down

**aposento** /apo'sento/ *m*, room; suite, apartments; lodging, accommodation; *Theat*. box

**aposición** /aposi'θion; aposi'sion/ *f*, *Gram*. apposition

**apósito** /a'posito/ *m*, poultice, external application; (medical) dressing

**apostadero** /aposta'ðero/ *m*, *Naut*. naval station; placing or stationing (of soldiers)

**apostar** /apos'tar/ *vt irr* to bet; station (soldiers); —*vi* compete, rival. See **contar**

**apostasía** /aposta'sia/ *f*, apostasy

**apóstata** /a'postata/ *mf* apostate

**apostilla** /apos'tiʎa; apos'tiya/ *f*, marginal note, gloss

**apóstol** /a'postol/ *m*, apostle

**apostólico** /apos'toliko/ *a* apostolic

**apóstrofe** /a'postrofe/ *m*, or *f*, apostrophe, hortatory exclamation

**apóstrofo** /a'postrofo/ *m*, *Gram*. apostrophe

**apostura** /apos'tura/ *f*, neatness, spruceness

**apotegma** /apo'tegma/ *m*, apothegm, maxim

**apoteosis** /apote'osis/ *f*, apotheosis

**apoyar** /apo'yar/ *vt* (*with en*) to lean against; rest upon; —*vt* uphold, favor; confirm, bear out; droop the head (horses); second (a motion); —*vi* (*with en*) rest on; lean against; —*vr* (*with en*) rest on; lean against; **apoyarse de codos,** to lean on one's elbows; be upheld by; *Fig*. be founded on; *Fig*. depend on, lean on

**apoyo** /a'poyo/ *m,* support, prop; windowsill, sill; assistance; backing, support

**apreciable** /apreθia'βle; apresia'βle/ *a* appreciable; estimable; important

**apreciación** /apreθia'θion; apresia'sion/ *f,* appreciation; valuation, estimate

**apreciador** /apreθia'ðor; apresia'ðor/ **(-ra)** *a* appreciatory —*n* appreciator

**apreciar** /apre'θiar; apre'siar/ *vt* to estimate (values); appreciate; like, esteem, have a regard for

**apreciativo** /apreθia'tiβo; apresia'tiβo/ *a* appreciative

**aprecio** /a'preθio; a'presio/ *m,* valuation; appreciation, regard

**aprehender** /apreen'der/ *vt* to apprehend, catch; seize (contraband); understand, grasp

**aprehensión** /apreen'sion/ *f,* seizure, apprehension

**apremiador, apremiante** /apremia'ðor, apre'miante/ *a* urgent, pressing

**apremiar** /apre'miar/ *vt* to hurry; urge, press; force, oblige; burden, oppress (with taxes)

**apremio** /a'premio/ *m,* insistence, pressure; compulsion; demand note

**aprendedor** /aprende'ðor/ **(-ra)** *n* learner

**aprender** /apren'der/ *vt* to learn. **a. de memoria,** to learn by heart

**aprendiz** /apren'diθ; apren'dis/ **(-za)** *n* apprentice

**aprendizaje** /aprendi'θahe; aprendi'sahe/ *m,* apprenticeship. **hacer el a.,** to serve an apprenticeship

**aprensión** /apren'sion/ *f,* capture; fear, apprehension; suspicion, fancy; prejudice, scruple

**aprensivo** /apren'siβo/ *a* apprehensive, nervous, fearful

**apresar** /apre'sar/ *vt* to nab, catch; capture (a ship); imprison; fetter

**aprestar** /apres'tar/ *vt* to prepare, arrange; dress (fabrics)

**apresto** /a'presto/ *m,* preparation, arrangement; dressing (for cloth)

**apresurar** /apresu'rar/ *vt* to quicken; —*vr* hasten, be quick

**apretado** /apre'taðo/ *a* difficult, dangerous; tight; crabbed (of handwriting); clustered (e.g. *casas apretadas alrededor de la sinagoga,* houses clustered around the synagogue). *Inf.* mean, close-fisted. *m,* small close handwriting

**apretadura** /apreta'ðura/ *f,* tightening, compression

**apretar** /apre'tar/ *vt irr* to tighten; compress; urge on, press; harass, vex; trouble, worry; speed up; squeeze; press (bells, gun triggers, etc.); —*vi* increase, grow worse (storms, heat, etc.); pinch, hurt (shoes). **a. los pasos,** to quicken one's pace. *Inf.* **a. a correr,** to take to one's heels. **¡Aprieta!** *Inf.* Nonsense! It can't be! See **acertar**

**apretón** /apre'ton/ *m,* squeeze, grip, pressure; *Inf.* sprint, spurt; *Inf.* fix, pickle. **a. de manos,** handshake

**apretujamiento** /apretuha'miento/ *m,* squeezing together

**apretujar** /apretu'har/ *vt Inf.* to squeeze, hug

**aprieto** /a'prieto/ *m,* crowd, crush; urgency; *Inf.* jam, trouble, fix

**aprisa** /a'prisa/ *adv* quickly, in a hurry

**aprisco** /a'prisko/ *m,* cattle-shed; sheepfold

**aprisionar** /aprisio'nar/ *vt* to imprison; bind, fetter; tie

**aprobación** /aproβa'θion; aproβa'sion/ *f,* approbation, approval, commendation; ratification (of a bill); pass (in an examination)

**aprobado** /apro'βaðo/ *m,* pass certificate (in examinations)

**aprobar** /apro'βar/ *vt irr* to approve; pass (in an examination). See **contar**

**apropiación** /apropia'θion; apropia'sion/ *f,* appropriation; application; adaptation

**apropiado** /apro'piaðo/ *a* appropriate, suitable, proper

**apropiar** /apro'piar/ *vt* to appropriate; adapt, fit; —*vr* appropriate, take possession

**aprovechable** /aproβe'tʃaβle/ *a* usable, available

**aprovechado** /aproβe'tʃaðo/ *a* advantageous; assiduous, conscientious; capable; thrifty

**aprovechador** /aproβetʃa'ðor/ *a* self-seeking

**aprovechamiento** /aproβetʃa'miento/ *m,* utilization, employment; exploitation; profitable use

**aprovechar** /aproβe'tʃar/ *vi* to be advantageous or useful; be beneficial; make progress (in studies, etc.); —*vt* use; profit by; —*vr* take advantage of, make use of. **¡Que aproveche!** May it do you good! (said to anyone eating)

**aprovisionar** /aproβi'sionar/ *vt* to provision, supply

**aproximación** /aproksima'θion; aproksima'sion/ *f,* approximation; consolation prize (in a lottery)

**aproximadamente** /aproksimaða'mente/ *adv* approximately; nearly, almost

**aproximar** /aproksi'mar/ *vt* to bring or draw nearer; —*vr* approach; be almost, be approximately; draw closer

**aptitud** /apti'tuð/ *f,* aptitude, ability; fitness; propensity

**apto** /'apto/ *a* suitable, fitting; competent. **no apta para menores,** not suitable for children (of films, etc.)

**apuesta** /a'puesta/ *f,* bet, wager; competition

**apuestas benéficas de fútbol** /a'puestas be'nefikas de 'futβol/ football pools

**apuesto** /a'puesto/ *a* elegant; handsome, well set-up

**apuntación** /apunta'θion; apunta'sion/ *f,* noting down; note; *Mus.* notation

**apuntador** /apunta'ðor/ **(-ra)** *n* note-taker; observer. *m, Theat.* prompter; *Theat.* stage-manager

**apuntalar** /apunta'lar/ *vt* to prop, prop up, underpin, bolster

**apuntamiento** /apunta'miento/ *m,* summary; *Law.* indictment, minute

**apuntar** /apun'tar/ *vt* to aim (a gun, etc.); point to, indicate; note down; mark; sketch; sharpen; bet (at cards); fasten temporarily; *Inf.* mend; *Theat.* prompt; suggest, hint (e.g. *La fecha está apuntada en vanos manuscritos,* The date is hinted at in various manuscripts); —*vi* begin to appear. *Inf.* **a. y no dar,** to promise and do nothing

**apunte** /a'punte/ *m,* abstract; note; annotation; sketch; *Theat.* prompt or prompter or prompt book or cue; stake in a card game

**apuñalado** /apuɲa'laðo/ *a* dagger-shaped

**apuñalar** /apuɲa'lar/ *vt* to stab, attack with a dagger

**apurado** /apu'raðo/ *a* poor, needy; dangerous; difficult; accurate, exact; hurried

**apurar** /apu'rar/ *vt* to purify; drain; exhaust; finish, conclude; examine closely, scrutinize (e.g. *apurar una materia,* to exhaust a subject, examine a subject thoroughly); irritate, make impatient; urge on, hasten; —*vr* be anxious, fret

**apuro** /a'puro/ *m,* difficulty, fix; poverty, want; anxiety, worry. **pasar apuros,** to have a hard time

**aquejar** /ake'har/ *vt* to afflict; weary, beset, harass; —*vr* complain; hurry

**aquel, aquella, aquellos, aquellas** /a'kel,/ *a m* **aquella,** *a f* **aquellos,** *a m pl* *a f pl,* that, those; that or those over there (farther off than **ese**)

**aquel** /a'kel/ *m,* charm, attraction, it

**aquél, aquélla, aquéllos, aquéllas** /a'kel, a'keʎa, a'keʎos, a'keʎas; a'kel, a'keya, a'keyos, a'keyas/ *dem pron m, f,* sing. and pl., that, the one, those, those ones; the former. e.g. *La casa que ve usted a lo lejos aquélla es la vivienda de mi tío,* The house that you see in the distance, that is my uncle's dwelling. *Éste no me gusta pero aquél sí,* I do not like the latter, but I like the former

**aquello** /a'keʎo; a'keyo/ *dem pron neut* that; the fact; the matter, the affair, the former (remark, idea, etc.). e.g. *Todo a. por fin acabó,* All that came to an end at last. *a. de,* the fact that

**aquende** /a'kende/ *adv* on this side (rarely used)

**aquí** /a'ki/ *adv* here. **de a.,** hence the fact that. **¡He a.!** Behold!

**aquiescencia** /akies'θenθia; akies'sensia/ *f,* consent, acquiescence

**aquietar** /akie'tar/ *vt* to calm, soothe

**aquilatar** /akila'tar/ *vt* to assay; scrutinize; examine, weigh up (persons)

**aquistar** /akis'tar/ *vt* to attain, acquire

**ara** /'ara/ *f*, altar; **en aras de,** in honor of; for the sake of

**árabe** /'araβe/ *a* Arab, Arabic. *mf* Arab. *m*, Arabic (language)

**arabesco** /ara'βesko/ *a* Arabic. *m*, *Art*. arabesque

**Arabia Saudita** /a'raβia sau'ðita/ Saudi Arabia

**arábigo** /a'raβigo/ *a* Arabic. *m*, Arabic (language)

**arácnido** /a'rakniðo/ *m*, *Zool*. arachnid

**arado** /a'raðo/ *m*, plow

**arador** /ara'ðor/ *a* plowing. *m*, plowman. **a. de la sarna,** *Ent*. scabies mite

**aragonés** /arago'nes/ **(-esa)** *a* and *n* Aragonese

**arahuaco** /ara'uako/ *a* and *n* Arawak, Arawakian

**arancel** /aran'θel; aran'sel/ *m*, tariff, duty, tax

**arancelar** /aranθe'lar; aranse'lar/ *to* charge tuition for (e.g. *a. la universidad,* charge tuition for college studies)

**arancelario** /aranθe'lario; aranse'lario/ *a* tariff, tax; customs

**arándano** /a'randano/ *m*, *Bot*. bilberry

**arandela** /aran'dela/ *f*, candle-dripper; *Mech*. washer; wall candelabrum

**araña** /a'rana/ *f*, spider; chandelier

**arañacielos** /a,rana'θielos; a,rana'sielos/ *m*, skyscraper

**arañar** /ara'nar/ *vt* to scratch; *Inf*. scrape together, hoard

**arañazo** /ara'naθo; ara'naso/ *m*, scratch

**arar** /a'rar/ *vt* to plough. **a. en el mar,** to labor in vain

**arbitrador** /arβitra'ðor/ **(-ra)** *n* arbitrator

**arbitraje** /arβi'trahe/ *m*, arbitration; arbitrament, decision

**arbitrar** /arβi'trar/ *vt* to judge freely; *Law*. arbitrate, mediate; devise; invent; marshal (money, resources, etc.); draft (a law) *vr* make shift, contrive

**arbitrariedad** /arβitrarie'ðað/ *f*, arbitrariness

**arbitrario** /arβi'trario/ *a* arbitral, mediatory; arbitrary, capricious

**arbitrio** /ar'βitrio/ *m*, free will; arbitration; means, way; discretion; arbitrament, judgment; *pl* rates, municipal taxes

**árbitro** /'arβitro/ **(-ra)** *a* arbitrary —*n* arbiter. *m*, *Sports*. umpire; referee

**árbol** /'arβol/ *m*, tree; *Mech*. shaft; *Naut*. mast; axis of a winding shaft. **a. de amor** *or* **a. de Judas,** Judas tree. **a. de la ciencia** ( **del bien y del mal),** Tree of Knowledge (of good and evil). **a. de levas,** *Mech*. camshaft. **a. del pan,** breadfruit tree. *Naut*. **a. mayor,** mainmast. **a. motor** *Mech*., drivingshaft

**arbolado** /arβo'laðo/ *a* tree-covered, wooded. *m*, copse, woodland

**arboladura** /arβola'ðura/ *f*, *Naut*. masts and spars

**arbolar** /arβo'lar/ *vt* to hoist (flags); *Naut*. fit with masts; place upright; —*vr* rear, prance (horses)

**arboleda** /arβo'leða/ *f*, copse, grove, spinney

**arbotante** /arβo'tante/ *m*, flying buttress

**arbusto** /ar'βusto/ *m*, shrub, woody plant

**arca** /'arka/ *f*, chest; money-box, coffer; ark; *pl* (treasury) vaults. **a. caudal,** strong box. **a. de agua,** water-tower. **a. de la alianza.** *or* **a. del testamento,** Ark of the Covenant (Bible). **a. de Noé,** Noah's Ark; lumber box

**arcabucero** /arkaβu'θero; arkaβu'sero/ *m*, arquebusier; maker of arquebuses

**arcabuz** /arka'βuθ; arka'βus/ *m*, arquebus

**arcada** /ar'kaða/ *f*, arcade; series of arches; *pl* sickness, nausea

**árcade** /ar'kaðe/ *a* and *mf* Arcadian

**arcaico** /ar'kaiko/ *a* archaic

**arcaísmo** /arka'ismo/ *m*, archaism

**arcángel** /ar'kanhel/ *m*, archangel

**arcano** /ar'kano/ *a* secret. *m*, mystery, arcanum

**arce** /'arθe; 'arse/ *m*, *Bot*. maple tree

**archifeliz** /artʃife'liθ; artʃife'lis/ *a* extremely happy, in bliss

**archimandrita** /artʃiman'drita/ *m*, archimandrite

**archimillonario** /artʃimiʎo'nario; artʃimiyo'nario/ **(-ia)** *a* and *n* multimillionaire

**archipiélago** /artʃi'pielago/ *m*, archipelago

**Archipiélago de Colón** /artʃi'pielago de ko'lon/ *m*, Galapagos Islands

**archivar** /artʃi'βar/ *vt* to place in an archive; file (papers)

**archivero** /artʃi'βero/ *m*, archivist, keeper of the archives; librarian; registrar; (Mexico) file cabinet, filing cabinet

**archivista** /artʃi'βista/ *mf* archivist; file clerk, filing clerk

**archivo** /ar'tʃiβo/ *m*, archives

**arcilla** /ar'θiʎa; ar'siya/ *f*, clay

**arcilloso** /arθi'ʎoso; arsi'yoso/ *a* clayey, like or full of clay

**arcipreste** /arθi'preste; arsi'preste/ *m*, archpriest

**arco** /'arko/ *m*, *Geom*. arc; *Mil*. bow; bow (of a stringed instrument); hoop (of casks, etc.); *Archit*. arch. **a. del cielo** *or* **a. de San Martín** *or* **a. iris,** rainbow. **a. voltaico,** electric arc. *Mus*. **para a.,** for strings

**arder** /ar'ðer/ *vi* to burn; shine, gleam; *Fig*. burn (with passion, etc.); —*vt* to set alight, burn

**ardid** /ar'ðið/ *a* crafty. *m*, trick, stratagem

**ardiente** /ar'ðiente/ *a* burning; ardent, passionate; vehement; enthusiastic; flame-colored; fiery-red

**ardilla** /ar'ðiʎa; ar'ðiya/ *f*, squirrel

**ardite** /ar'ðite/ *m*, ancient Spanish coin of little value; *Fig*. farthing, fig, straw. **no valer un a.,** to be not worth a straw

**ardor** /ar'ðor/ *m*, great heat; zeal, earnestness; passion, ardor; courage

**ardoroso** /arðo'roso/ *a* ardorous

**arduo** /'arðuo/ *a* arduous

**área** /'area/ *f*, area; small plot of ground; common threshing floor; arc (surface measure)

**arena** /a'rena/ *f*, sand; arena; grit, gravel. **a. movediza,** quicksand

**arenal** /are'nal/ *m*, quicksand; sand pit; sandy place

**arenero** /are'nero/ **(-ra)** *n* sand merchant. *m*, sandbox (carried by railway engines)

**arenga** /a'renga/ *f*, harangue, discourse

**arenilla** /are'niʎa; are'niya/ *f*, sand (for drying writing)

**arenisca** /are'niska/ *f*, sandstone

**arenisco** /are'nisko/ *a* sandy

**arenque** /a'renke/ *m*, herring

**arete** /a'rete/ *m*, earring

**argamasa** /arga'masa/ *f*, mortar

**argayo** /ar'gayo/ *m*, landslide; (Asturias) **a. de nieve,** avalanche

**Árgel** /'arhel/ Algiers

**Argelia** /ar'helia/ Algeria

**argelino** /arhe'lino/ **(-na)** *a* and *n* Algerian

**argentado** /arhen'taðo/ *a* silvered; silvery

**argénteo** /ar'henteo/ *a* silver; silvery

**argentífero** /arhen'tifero/ *a* silver-yielding

**argentino** /arhen'tino/ **(-na)** *a* silvery —*a* and *n* Argentinian. *m*, Argentinian gold coin

**argento** /ar'hento/ *m*, silver. **a. vivo,** mercury

**argolla** /ar'goʎa; ar'goya/ *f*, thick metal ring (for hitching, etc.); croquet (game); stocks, pillory; hoop, iron arch

**argonauta** /argo'nauta/ *m*, *Myth*. Argonaut; *Zool*. paper nautilus, argonaut

**argucia** /ar'guθia; ar'gusia/ *f*, sophism, quibble; subtlety

**argüir** /ar'guir/ *vt irr* to deduce, imply; prove; reveal, manifest; accuse; —*vi* argue, debate; dispute, oppose. See **huir**

**argumentador** /argumenta'ðor/ **(-ra)** *a* argumentative —*n* arguer

**argumentar** /argumen'tar/ *vi* to argue; dispute; oppose

**argumento** /argu'mento/ *m*, contention, case; theme (of a book, etc.); argument, discussion

**aridez** /ari'ðeθ; ari'ðes/ *f*, aridity, dryness; drought; sterility, barrenness; dullness, lack of interest

**árido** /'ariðo/ *a* dry, arid; sterile, barren; uninteresting, dull

**ariete** /a'riete/ *m*, *Mil*. battering ram

**ario** /'ario/ **(-ia)** *a* and *n* Aryan

**arisco** /a'risko/ *a* unsociable, surly; wild, shy (animals)

**arista** /a'rista/ *f, Bot.* arista, awn, beard; pebble; edge, side

**aristocracia** /aristo'kraθia; aristo'krasia/ *f,* aristocracy

**aristócrata** /aris'tokrata/ *mf* aristocrat

**aristocrático** /aristo'kratiko/ *a* aristocratic

**aristotélico** /aristo'teliko/ *a* Aristotelian

**aristotelismo** /aristote'lismo/ *m,* Aristotelianism

**aritmética** /arit'metika/ *f,* arithmetic

**aritmético** /arit'metiko/ **(-ca)** *a* arithmetical —*n* arithmetician

**arlequín** /arle'kin/ *m,* harlequin; *Inf.* fool, buffoon; Neapolitan ice-cream

**arlequinada** /arleki'naða/ *f,* harlequinade; buffoonery

**arma** /'arma/ *f,* weapon; *Mil.* arm, branch; bull's horn; *pl* troops, army; means, way; arms, coat of arms. **a. arrojadiza,** missile. **a. blanca,** steel weapon. **a. de fuego,** fire-arm. **¡Armas al hombro!** Shoulder Arms! **armas portátiles,** small arms. *Inf.* **de armas tomar,** belligerent; resolute. **pasar por las armas,** *Mil.* to shoot. **presentar las armas,** *Mil.* to present arms. **ser a. de dos filos,** *Fig.* to cut both ways

**armada** /ar'maða/ *f,* navy, armada; fleet, squadron

**armadía** /arma'ðia/ *f,* raft, pontoon

**armador** /arma'ðor/ **(-ra)** *n* supplier, outfitter. *m,* shipowner; pirate, privateer; jacket; assembler, fitter

**armadura** /arma'ðura/ *f,* armature, armor; frame, framework; skeleton (of a building); skeleton (of vertebrates); *Phys.* armature; plate armor (of persons)

**armamento** /arma'mento/ *m, Mil.* armament; arms, military equipment

**armar** /ar'mar/ *vt* to arm; *Mech.* mount; man (guns); put together, assemble; roll (a cigarette); reinforce (concrete); *Inf.* arrange, prepare; *Inf.* occasion (quarrels); *Inf.* outfit; *Naut.* equip; commission (a ship); —*vr* prepare oneself, arm oneself. **a. caballero,** to knight. **a. los remos,** to ship the oars. *Inf.* **armarla,** to cause a row or quarrel

**armario** /ar'mario/ *m,* cupboard; wardrobe. **a. de luna,** wardrobe with a mirror

**armatoste** /arma'toste/ *m,* unwieldy piece of furniture; *Fig. Inf.* dead weight, clumsy person; snare

**armazón** /arma'θon; arma'son/ *f,* frame, framework; ship's hulk. *m, Anat.* skeleton

**armenio** /ar'menio/ **(-ia)** *a* and *n* Armenian. *m,* Armenian language

**armería** /arme'ria/ *f,* armory; heraldry; gunsmith's craft or shop

**armero** /ar'mero/ *m,* gunsmith, armorer; stand for weapons. **a. mayor,** Royal Armorer

**armiño** /ar'miɲo/ *m,* ermine

**armisticio** /armis'tiθio; armis'tisio/ *m,* armistice

**armón de artillería** /ar'mon de artiʎe'ria; ar'mon de artiye'ria/ *m,* gun-carriage

**armonía** /armo'nia/ *f,* harmony; friendship, concord; *Mus.* harmony

**armónica** /ar'monika/ **(de boca)** *f,* mouth-organ

**armónico** /ar'moniko/ *a* harmonious —*a* and *m, Mus.* harmonic

**armonio** /ar'monio/ *m,* harmonium

**armonioso** /armo'nioso/ *a* harmonious

**armonización** /armoniθa'θion; armonisa'sion/ *f, Mus.* harmonization

**armonizar** /armoni'θar; armoni'sar/ *vt* to bring into harmony; *Mus.* harmonize

**arnés** /ar'nes/ *m,* armor; harness; *pl* horse trappings; *Inf.* equipment, tools

**aro** /'aro/ *m,* hoop; rim (of wheel, etc.); napkin-ring; croquet hoop; *Bot.* wild arum; child's hoop. **a. de empaquetadura,** *Mech.* gasket

**aroma** /a'roma/ *m,* aroma, fragrance; balsam; sweet-smelling herb

**aromático** /aro'matiko/ *a* aromatic

**arpa** /'arpa/ *f,* harp. **a. eolia,** Eolian harp

**arpar** /ar'par/ *vt* to scratch, claw; tear, rend

**arpegio** /ar'pehio/ *m, Mus.* arpeggio

**arpía** /ar'pia/ *f,* harpy

**arpicordio** /arpi'korðio/ *m,* harpsichord

**arpista** /ar'pista/ *mf* harpist, harp player

**arpón** /ar'pon/ *m,* harpoon

**arponear** /arpone'ar/ *vt* to harpoon

**arponero** /arpo'nero/ *m,* harpooner; harpoon maker

**arquear** /arke'ar/ *vt* to arch; bend; beat (wool); gauge (ship's capacity); —*vi* retch

**arqueo** /ar'keo/ *m,* arching; bending, curving; *Naut.* tonnage; gauging (of ship's capacity); *Com.* examination of deposits and contents of safe

**arqueología** /arkeolo'hia/ *f,* archeology

**arqueológico** /arkeo'lohiko/ *a* archeological

**arqueólogo** /arke'ologo/ *m,* archeologist

**arquero** /ar'kero/ *m, Com.* cashier; treasurer; *Mil.* archer

**arquitecto** /arki'tekto/ *m,* architect. **a. de jardines,** landscape gardener

**arquitectónico** /arkitek'toniko/ *a* architectural

**arquitectura** /arkitek'tura/ *f,* architecture

**arquitrabe** /arki'traβe/ *m,* architrave

**arrabal** /arra'βal/ *m,* suburb, district; *pl* outskirts

**arracada** /arra'kaða/ *f,* pendant-earring

**arracimarse** /arraθi'marse; arrasi'marse/ *vr* to cluster; group

**arraigadamente** /arrai,gaða'mente/ *adv* deeply, firmly

**arraigado** /arrai'gaðo/ *a* deep-rooted; firm; convinced

**arraigar** /arrai'gar/ *vi* to take root; —*vi* and *vr Fig.* become established, take hold; —*vr* settle; take up residence

**arraigo** /a'rraigo/ *m,* rooting; settlement, establishment; landed property

**arrancaclavos** /a,rranka'klaβos/ *m,* nail-puller

**arrancadero** /a,rranka'ðero/ *m, Sports.* starting-point

**arrancar** /arran'kar/ *vt* to uproot; pull out; wrench; tear off; extirpate; obtain by threats; clear one's throat; —*vt* and *vi Naut.* put on speed; —*vi* start (a race); *Inf.* leave, quit; derive, originate **¡Arrancan!** And they're off! (races)

**arranque** /a'rranke/ *m,* uprooting; extirpation; wrenching, pulling, seizing; stimulus (of passion); sudden impulse; *Mech.* start; *Mech.* starter. **a. automático,** self-starter

**arras** /'arras/ *f pl,* dowry; coins given by bridegroom to his bride; earnest money, token

**arrasamiento** /arrasa'miento/ *m,* demolition, destruction; leveling

**arrasar** /arra'sar/ *vt* to demolish, destroy; level; fill to the brim; —*vi* and *vr* clear up (sky). **ojos arrasados de lágrimas,** eyes brimming with tears

**arrastrado** /arras'traðo/ *a Inf.* poverty-stricken, wretched; *Inf.* knavish; unhappy, unfortunate

**arrastrar** /arras'trar/ *vt* to drag; trail; convince; haul; —*vi* trail along or touch the ground; trump (at cards); —*vr* crawl, creep; shuffle along; humble oneself

**arrastre** /a'rrastre/ *m,* dragging, trailing; haulage; trumping (at cards)

**¡arre!** /'arre/ *interj* Gee up! Get along!

**arrear** /arre'ar/ *vt* to spur on, whip up (horses, etc.); —*interj Inf.* **¡Arrea!** Hurry up! Get on!

**arrebañar** /arreβa'ɲar/ *vt* to pick clean, clear; eat or drink up

**arrebatado** /arreβa'taðo/ *a* precipitate, headlong; rash; flushed, red

**arrebatador** /arreβata'ðor/ *a* overwhelming; violent; bewitching, captivating; delightful

**arrebatamiento** /arreβata'miento/ *m,* abduction; seizure; fury; ecstasy

**arrebatar** /arreβa'tar/ *vt* to abduct, carry off; seize, grab; attract, charm; grip (the attention); —*vr* be overcome with rage

**arrebatiña** /arreβa'tiɲa/ *f,* grab; scuffle, scrimmage

**arrebato** /arre'βato/ *m,* fit (gen. of anger); ecstasy, rapture

**arrebol** /arre'βol/ *m,* red flush in the sky; rouge; *pl* red clouds

**arrebozar** /arreβo'θar; arreβo'sar/ *vt* to muffle; envelop

**arrebujarse** /arreβu'harse/ *vr* to huddle; wrap oneself up

**arrechucho** /arre'tʃutʃo/ *m, Inf.* fit of rage; sudden slight ailment

**arreciar** /arre'θiar; arre'siar/ *vi* to increase in intensity; —*vr* grow strong

**arrecife** /arre'θife; arre'sife/ *m*, reef (in the sea); stone-paved road

**arredrar** /arre'ðrar/ *vt* to separate, remove; force back, repel; terrify

**arregazar** /arrega'θar; arrega'sar/ **(se)** *vt* and *vr* to tuck up one's skirts

**arreglado** /arre'glaðo/ *a* regular; regulated; ordered; methodical

**arreglar** /arre'glar/ *vt* to regulate; arrange; adjust, put right; tidy; make up (the face); —*vr* (*with prep a*) conform to; (*with con*) reach an agreement with. **Me voy a a.,** I am going to make myself presentable. *Inf.* **arreglárselas,** to shift for oneself

**arreglo** /a'rreglo/ *m,* arrangement; rule; regulation; method, order; agreement; adjustment; compromise

**arrellanarse** /arreʎa'narse; arreya'narse/ *vr* to settle comfortably in one's chair; be happy in one's work

**arremangar** /arremaŋ'gar/ *vt* to roll up (sleeves, trousers, etc.); —*vr Inf.* make a decision

**arremango** /arre'maŋgo/ *m,* rolling or tucking up (of sleeve, etc.)

**arremetedor** /arremete'ðor/ **(-ra)** *n* attacker, assailant

**arremeter** /arreme'ter/ *vt* to attack, assail; —*vi* launch oneself (at); *Fig.* spoil the view, shock the eye

**arremetida** /arreme'tiða/ *f,* attack, assault

**arremolinarse** /arremoli'narse/ *vr* to crowd, cluster, group

**arrendador** /arrenda'ðor/ **(-ra)** *n* landlord; renter; hirer; tenant

**arrendamiento** /arrenda'miento/ *m,* letting, renting; hiring; rental; agreement, lease

**arrendar** /arren'dar/ *vt irr* to let, lease; hire; rent (as a tenant); train (horses); tie up (horses); restrain; mimic, imitate. See **recomendar**

**arrendatario** /arrenda'tario/ **(-ia)** *a* rent, lease —*n* tenant; lessee; hirer. **a. de contribuciones,** tax farmer

**arreo** /a'rreo/ *m,* ornament; apparel; *pl* horse trappings; appurtenances, equipment

**¡Arrepa!** /a'rrepa/ But look!, Hold on!, Hold your horses!, Not so fast!

**arrepentimiento** /arrepenti'miento/ *m,* repentance

**arrepentirse** /arrepen'tirse/ *vr irr* to repent. See **sentir**

**arrestado** /arres'taðo/ *a* courageous, audacious, bold

**arrestar** /arres'tar/ *vt* to arrest, detain; —*vr* be bold, dare

**arresto** /a'rresto/ *m,* arrest; detention; imprisonment; audacity, boldness

**arriada** /a'rriaða/ *f,* lowering (of a boat); taking in (of sail)

**arriar** /a'rriar/ *vt Naut.* to strike (colors); take in (sail); pay out (ropes, etc.); lower (boats); flood, inundate

**arriate** /a'rriate/ *m,* garden border; avenue, walk; trellis (for plants)

**arriba** /a'rriβa/ *adv* up, above; overhead; upstairs; earlier, before; upwards (with prices) —*interj* **¡A.!** Up with!; Long live! **de a. abajo,** from head to foot, from one end to the other; completely, wholly

**arribada** /arri'βaða/ *f, Naut.* arrival. **de a.,** emergency (port)

**arribar** /arri'βar/ *vi Naut.* to arrive; put into an emergency port; reach, arrive at; *Inf.* convalesce; attain; *Naut.* drift

**arribista** /arri'βista/ *mf* social climber

**arribo** /a'rriβo/ *m,* arrival

**arriero** /a'rriero/ *m,* farrier; muleteer

**arriesgado** /arries'gaðo/ *a* dangerous, risky; rash, daring

**arriesgar** /arries'gar/ *vt* to risk; —*vr* run into danger; dare, risk

**arrimar** /arri'mar/ *vt* to bring or draw near; abandon (professions, etc.); lay aside, discard; *Inf.* administer (blows); *Naut.* stow (cargo); —*vr* (*with prep a*) lean against, rest on; join, go with; seek the protection of. **Cada cual se arrima a su cada cual,** Birds of a feather flock together

**arrimo** /a'rrimo/ *m,* bringing or placing near; leaning

or resting against; abandonment, giving up; protection; staff, support

**arrinconado** /arrinko'naðo/ *a* remote, secluded; forgotten, neglected

**arrinconar** /arrinko'nar/ *vt* to discard, lay aside; corner, besiege; set aside, dismiss; forsake; —*vr* go into retirement, withdraw

**arriscado** /arris'kaðo/ *a* craggy, rugged; bold, resolute; sprightly, handsome

**arro, arro, arro** /'arro, 'arro, 'arro/ purrrr (echoic of a cat's purr)

**arroba** /a'rroβa/ *f,* weight of 25 lb.; variable liquid measure

**arrobamiento** /arroβa'miento/ *m,* ecstasy, rapture; trance

**arrobar** /arro'βar/ *vt* to charm, entrance; —*vr* be enraptured; be in ecstasy

**arrodillar** /arroði'ʎar; arroði'yar/ *vt* to cause to kneel down; —*vi* and *vr* kneel down

**arrogancia** /arro'ganθia; arro'gansia/ *f,* arrogance; courage; majesty, pride

**arrogante** /arro'gante/ *a* arrogant, haughty; courageous; proud, majestic

**arrogar** /arro'gar/ *vt* to adopt (as a son); —*vr* usurp, appropriate

**arrojadizo** /arroha'ðiθo; arroha'ðiso/ *a* easily cast or hurled; projectile

**arrojado** /arro'haðo/ *a* bold, determined; rash

**arrojar** /arro'har/ *vt* to throw, hurl, cast; shed (light, etc.; e.g. *La cuenta arroja un total de cien dólares,* The bill shows a total of a hundred dollars); *Com.* show (a balance, etc.); put out (sprouts); dismiss, send away; —*vr* cast oneself; (*with prep a*) hurl oneself against or upon; undertake, venture upon. **a. de sí ( a),** to get rid of, dismiss

**arrojo** /a'rroho/ *m,* daring, intrepidity; boldness

**arrollar** /arro'ʎar; arro'yar/ *vt* to roll; make into a roll, roll up; defeat (the enemy); silence, confound; rock to sleep; bear along, carry off

**arromar** /arro'mar/ *vt* to blunt; flatten

**arropamiento** /arropa'miento/ *m,* wrapping up, covering, muffling

**arropar** /arro'par/ *vt* to wrap up, cover

**arrostrar** /arros'trar/ *vt* to confront, defy, face up to; —*vr* fight hand to hand. **a. las consecuencias,** *Fig.* to face the music

**arroyada** /arro'yaða/ *f,* gorge, gully; course, channel; flood

**arroyo** /a'rroyo/ *m,* stream, brook; street gutter; road, street; *Fig.* flood, plenty

**arroz** /a'rroθ; a'rros/ *m,* rice

**arrozal** /arro'θal; arro'sal/ *m,* rice field

**arruga** /a'rruga/ *f,* wrinkle; fold, pleat; crease

**arrugamiento** /arruga'miento/ *m,* wrinkling; fold, pleating; crumpling, creasing; corrugation

**arrugar** /arru'gar/ *vt* to wrinkle; pleat; corrugate; crumple, crease. **a. el ceño,** to knit one's brow, scowl

**arruinamiento** /arruina'miento/ *m,* ruin, decay, decline

**arruinar** /arrui'nar/ *vt* to ruin; destroy, damage severely

**arrullar** /arru'ʎar; arru'yar/ *vt* to bill and coo (doves); lull to sleep; *Inf.* whisper sweet words to, make love to

**arrullo** /a'rruʎo; a'rruyo/ *m,* cooing of doves; lullaby

**arrumaco** /arru'mako/ *m, Inf.* embrace, caress (gen. *pl*); ornament in bad taste

**arrumaje** /arru'mahe/ *m, Naut.* stowage; clouds on the horizon

**arrurruz** /arru'rruθ; arru'rrus/ *m,* arrowroot

**arsenal** /arse'nal/ *m,* dockyard; arsenal; *Fig.* store (of information, etc.)

**arsénico** /ar'seniko/ *m,* arsenic

**arte** /'arte/ *mf, art;* skill; ability, talent, guile; craftiness. **las bellas artes,** fine arts. *Inf.* **no tener a. ni parte en,** to have nothing to do with, have no part in

**artefacto** /arte'fakto/ *m,* machine, mechanism, apparatus; device, appliance. **a. atómico,** atomic bomb

**arteria** /ar'teria/ *f, Med.* artery; main line of (communication)

**artería** /arte'ria/ *f,* craftiness, guile

**arterial** /arte'rial/ *a* arterial

**artesa** /ar'tesa/ f, wooden trough; kneading bowl

**artesano** /arte'sano/ **(-na)** n artisan; mechanic

**artesiano** /arte'siano/ a artesian

**artesón** /arte'son/ m, bucket, pail; *Archit.* curved ceiling-panel; paneled ceiling

**artesonado** /arteso'naðo/ a *Archit.* paneled (ceiling). m, paneled ceiling

**ártico** /'artiko/ a Arctic

**articulación** /artikula'θion; artikula'sion/ f, joint, articulation; jointing; enunciation, pronunciation

**articular** /artiku'lar/ vt to joint, articulate; enunciate, pronounce clearly

**articulista** /artiku'lista/ mf article writer

**artículo** /ar'tikulo/ m, finger knuckle; heading; article; *Anat.* joint; *Gram.* article; pl goods, things. **a. de fondo,** leading article (in a newspaper). **a. de primera necesidad,** prime necessity, essential

**artífice** /ar'tifiθe; ar'tifise/ mf craftsman, artificer; author, creator; forger

**artificial** /artifi'θial; artifi'sial/ a artificial

**artificio** /arti'fiθio; arti'fiçsio/ m, skill, art; appliance, contraption, mechanism; trick, cunning device; guile, craftiness

**artificioso** /artifi'θioso; artifi'sioso/ a skilful; artificial; crafty, cunning

**artillería** /artiʎe'ria; artiye'ria/ f, artillery. **a. de costa,** coastal guns. **a. ligera, a. montada, a. rodada** or **a. volante,** field artillery

**artillero** /arti'ʎero; arti'yero/ m, gunner

**artimaña** /arti'maɲa/ f, trick, ruse, stratagem

**artista** /ar'tista/ mf artist; performer

**artístico** /ar'tistiko/ a artistic

**artrítico** /ar'tritiko/ a *Med.* arthritic

**artritis** /ar'tritis/ f, *Med.* arthritis

**arveja** /ar'βeha/ f, *Bot.* vetch

**arzobispado** /arθoβis'paðo; arsoβis'paðo/ m, archbishopric

**arzobispo** /arθo'βispo; arso'βispo/ m, archbishop

**as** /as/ m, Roman copper coin; ace (*Aer.* cards, etc.)

**asa** /'asa/ f, handle; pretext, excuse

**asado** /a'saðo/ m, *Cul.* roast

**asador** /asa'ðor/ m, *Cul.* roasting-spit; roaster

**asadura** /asa'ðura/ f, *Cul.* chitterlings; offal

**asalariar** /asala'riar/ vt to fix a salary for

**asaltador** /asalta'ðor/ **(-ra)** a attacking —n assailant, attacker

**asaltar** /asal'tar/ vt to storm, besiege; assault, attack; occur to (ideas); come on suddenly (illness)

**asalto** /a'salto/ m, storming, besieging; assault, attack; bout (in fencing, boxing, wrestling); round (in a fight)

**asamblea** /asam'βlea/ f, congregation, assembly; meeting; legislative assembly; *Mil.* assembly (bugle call)

**asambleísta** /asamble'ista/ mf member of an assembly

**asar** /a'sar/ vt *Cul.* to roast; grill; —vr be burning-hot; *Fig.* burn (with enthusiasm)

**asaz** /a'saθ; a'sas/ adv sufficiently, enough; very; in abundance —a sufficient; many

**asbesto** /as'βesto/ m, asbestos

**ascalonia** /aska'lonia/ f, *Bot.* shallot

**ascendencia** /asθen'denθia; assen'densia/ f, lineage, ancestry, origin

**ascendente** /asθen'dente; assen'dente/ a ascending

**ascender** /asθen'der; assen'der/ vi irr to ascend, climb; be promoted; (*with prep* a) amount to (bills, etc.); —vt promote. See **entender**

**ascendiente** /asθen'diente; assen'diente/ mf ancestor, forbear. m, influence, ascendancy

**ascensión** /asθen'sion; assen'sion/ f, ascension; promotion; *Astron.* exaltation

**ascenso** /as'θenso; as'senso/ m, ascent; promotion; preferment

**ascensor** /asθen'sor; assen'sor/ m, lift, elevator

**ascensorista** /asθenso'rista; assenso'rista/ mf elevator operator

**asceta** /as'θeta; as'seta/ mf ascetic

**ascético** /as'θetiko; as'setiko/ a ascetic

**ascetismo** /asθe'tismo; asse'tismo/ m, asceticism

**asco** /'asko/ m, nausea; repugnance, loathing; revolting thing. *Inf.* **Me da a.,** It sickens me

**ascua** /'askua/ f, live coal, ember. **estar como una a. de oro,** to be as bright as a new pin. **estar en ascuas,** *Fig.* to be on pins

**aseado** /ase'aðo/ a clean, tidy

**asear** /ase'ar/ vt to tidy, make neat; clean up; decorate, adorn

**asechanza** /ase'tʃanθa; ase'tʃansa/ f, ambush; trick, snare, stratagem

**asechar** /ase'tʃar/ vt to ambush, waylay; *Fig.* lay snares for

**asediador** /aseðia'ðor/ **(-ra)** n besieger

**asediar** /ase'ðiar/ vt to besiege; pester, importune

**asedio** /a'seðio/ m, siege; importunity

**asegurado** /asegu'raðo/ **(-da)** a insured —n insured person

**asegurador** /asegura'ðor/ **(-ra)** a insuring —n insurer

**asegurar** /asegu'rar/ vt to fasten, make secure; pinion, grip; reassure, soothe; assert, state; *Com.* insure; guarantee; ensure, secure; —vr *Com.* insure oneself; (*with de*) make sure of

**asemejar** /aseme'har/ vt to imitate, copy; make similar to; —vr (*with prep* a) be like, be similar to

**asenderear** /asendere'ar/ vt to make a pathway through; persecute, harass

**asenso** /a'senso/ m, assent. **dar a.,** to believe, give credence (to)

**asentaderas** /asenta'ðeras/ f pl, *Inf.* buttocks, seat

**asentado** /asen'taðo/ a prudent, circumspect; permanent, stable

**asentamiento** /asenta'miento/ m, seating; settlement, residence; prudence, judgment

**asentar** /asen'tar/ vt irr to seat; place; fasten, fix; found; plant (flags); pitch (a tent); establish, make firm; smooth; hone (razors); estimate, budget, arrange, set forth; note down; affirm, believe; *Com.* enter (in an account); —vi fit (clothes); —vr seat oneself; alight (birds); settle (liquids); *Archit.* settle, subside; to be located (e.g. *El edificio se asienta en una esquina,* The building is located on a corner). **a. la mano en,** to strike hard. See **acertar**

**asentimiento** /asenti'miento/ m, assent; consent, approval

**asentir** /asen'tir/ vi irr to assent, agree; (*with en*) consent to. See **sentir**

**aseñorado** /aseɲo'raðo/ a refined, gentlemanly; ladylike; presumptuous

**aseo** /a'seo/ m, cleanliness, neatness

**asepsia** /a'sepsia/ f, asepsis

**asequible** /ase'kiβle/ a attainable; obtainable

**aserción** /aser'θion; aser'sion/ f, assertion

**aserradero** /aserra'ðero/ m, sawmill; saw-pit

**aserrador** /aserra'ðor/ **(-ra)** n sawyer

**aserrar** /ase'rrar/ vt irr to saw. See **acertar**

**aserrín** /ase'rrin/ m, sawdust

**asertivo** /aser'tiβo/ a assertive

**aserto** /a'serto/ m, assertion

**asesinar** /asesi'nar/ vt to assassinate, murder

**asesinato** /asesi'nato/ m, assassination, murder

**asesino** /ase'sino/ mf assassin, murderer; murderess

**asesor** /ase'sor/ **(-ra)** n assessor

**asesorar** /aseso'rar/ vt to give advice; —vr take legal advice; seek advice

**asestar** /ases'tar/ vt to aim (firearms); fire; deal (a blow)

**aseveración** /aseβera'θion; aseβera'sion/ f, assertion, statement

**aseveradamente** /aseβeraða'mente/ adv affirmatively

**aseverar** /aseβe'rar/ vt to affirm, assert

**asfaltado** /asfal'taðo/ m, asphalting; asphalt pavement

**asfaltar** /asfal'tar/ vt to asphalt

**asfalto** /as'falto/ m, asphalt

**asfixia** /as'fiksia/ f, *Med.* asphyxia

**asfixiante** /asfik'siante/ a asphyxiating

**asfixiar** /asfik'siar/ vt to asphyxiate

**asfódelo** /as'foðelo/ m, *Bot.* asphodel

**así** /a'si/ adv thus, so, in this way; like this (e.g. *en días a.,* on days like this); even if; so that, therefore. **a. a.,** middling, so-so. **a. como a.,** as well as; as soon

**as. a. las cosas,** that being the case, **a. que,** as soon as, immediately; consequently, thus
**Asia Menor** /'asia me'nor/ Asia Minor
**asiático** /a'siatiko/ **(-ca)** a and n Asiatic
**asidero** /asi'ðero/ m, hold, grasp; handle, haft; pretext, excuse
**asido a** /a'siðo a/ wedded to (e.g. a belief)
**asiduidad** /asiðui'ðað/ f, assiduity
**asiduo** /a'siðuo/ a assiduous
**asiento** /a'siento/ m, seat; place, position; site; base (of a vase, etc.); lees, sediment; indigestion; *Archit.* subsidence, settling; treaty, pact; contract; note, reminder; *Com.* entry; permanence, stability; prudence; bit (of a bridle); pl buttocks, seat. **estar de a.,** to be established (in a place)
**asignación** /asigna'θion; asigna'sion/ f, assignation; appropriation (of money); salary; portion, share
**asignar** /asig'nar/ vt to assign; apportion; destine, intend; appoint
**asignatura** /asigna'tura/ f, subject (of study in schools, etc.)
**asilar** /asi'lar/ vt to give shelter to, receive; put into an institution
**asilo** /a'silo/ m, shelter, refuge; sanctuary, asylum; *Fig.* protection, defense; home, institution
**asimetría** /asime'tria/ f, asymmetry
**asimétrico** /asi'metriko/ a asymmetrical
**asimiento** /asi'miento/ m, hold, grasp; attachment, affection
**asimilable** /asimi'laβle/ a assimilable
**asimilación** /asimila'θion; asimila'sion/ f, assimilation
**asimilar** /asimi'lar/ vt to compare, liken; (*Bot. Zool. Gram.*) assimilate; —vi resemble, be like; *Fig.* assimilate, digest (ideas)
**asimismo** /asi'mismo/ adv similarly, likewise
**asir** /a'sir/ vt irr to grasp, take hold of; seize; —vi take root (plants); —vr (with de) lay hold of; take advantage of; make an excuse to —*Pres. Indic.* **asgo,** **ases,** etc —*Pres. Subjunc.* **asga,** etc.
**asirio** /a'sirio/ **(-ia)** a and n Assyrian. m, Assyrian language
**asistencia** /asis'tenθia; asistensia/ f, presence, attendance; minimal attendance required (e.g. *Los alumnos tienen que completar una a.,* Pupils must attend a certain number of classes) assistance, help; service, attendance; medical treatment; remuneration; pl allowance. **a. pública,** Public Assistance. **a. social,** social work
**asistenta** /asis'tenta/ f, daily maid; waiting-maid
**asistente** /asis'tente/ m, assistant; *Mil.* orderly
**asistir** /asis'tir/ vt to accompany; assist, help; attend, treat; (with de) act as; —vi (with prep a) be present at, attend; follow suit (in cards)
**asma** /'asma/ f, asthma
**asmático** /as'matiko/ **(-ca)** a asthmatic —n asthma sufferer
**asnal** /as'nal/ a asinine; brutish, stupid
**asno** /'asno/ m, ass
**asociación** /asoθia'θion; asosia'sion/ f, association; company, partnership; society, fellowship
**asociado** /aso'θiaðo; aso'siaðo/ **(-da)** n associate; member; partner
**asociar** /aso'θiar; aso'siar/ vt to associate; —vr associate oneself; join together; form a partnership
**asolar** /aso'lar/ vt irr to destroy, devastate, lay flat; —vr wither; settle (liquids). See **contar**
**asoldar** /asol'dar/ vt irr to employ, engage, hire. See **contar**
**asolear** /asole'ar/ vt to expose to the sun; —vr sun oneself; become sunburnt
**asomada** /aso'maða/ f, brief appearance; vantage point
**asomar** /aso'mar/ vt to show, allow to appear, put forth; —vi begin to show; —vr show oneself, appear; *Inf.* be flushed (with wine); (with prep a, por) look out of. **asomarse a la ventana,** to show oneself at, or look out of, the window
**asombrar** /asom'βrar/ vt to shade, shadow; darken (a color); terrify; amaze
**asombro** /a'sombro/ m, fright, terror; amazement; wonder, marvel

**asombroso** /asom'βroso/ a amazing; marvelous, wonderful
**asonancia** /aso'nanθia; aso'nansia/ f, assonance; congruity, harmony
**asonante** /aso'nante/ a and m, assonant
**asordar** /asor'ðar/ vt to deafen
**aspa** /'aspa/ f, cross; sail of a windmill
**aspaviento** /aspa'βiento/ m, exaggerated display of emotion; gesture (of horror, etc.); **hacer aspavientos,** to make a fuss
**aspecto** /as'pekto/ m, look, appearance; aspect, outlook
**aspereza** /aspe'reθa; aspe'resa/ f, roughness, harshness; ruggedness, rockiness; severity, asperity
**áspero** /'aspero/ a rough, harsh; uneven, rocky; jarring, grating; hard, severe
**aspersión** /asper'sion/ f, *Eccl.* aspersion; sprinkling
**áspid** /'aspið/ m, asp, viper
**aspiración** /aspira'θion; aspira'sion/ f, breath; breathing; aspiration, desire; *Mus.* pause
**aspirador** /aspira'ðor/ **(de polvo)** m, vacuum cleaner
**aspirante** /aspi'rante/ m, aspirant, novice; office-seeker; applicant
**aspirar** /aspi'rar/ vt to breathe in, inhale; *Gram.* aspirate; (with prep a) aspire to, desire
**aspirina** /aspi'rina/ f, aspirin
**asquear** /aske'ar/ vi and vt to hate, loathe
**asquerosidad** /askerosi'ðað/ f, filthiness, loathsomeness; vileness, hatefulness
**asqueroso** /aske'roso/ a nauseating; loathsome, revolting; vile, hateful
**asta** /'asta/ f, lance, spear, pike; horn (of bull); antler; flagstaff; shaft. **a media a.,** at half-mast
**asterisco** /aste'risko/ m, asterisk
**astigmático** /astig'matiko/ a astigmatic
**astigmatismo** /astigma'tismo/ m, astigmatism
**astil** /as'til/ m, handle, pole, shaft; bar of a balance; beam feather
**astilla** /as'tiʎa; as'tiya/ f, splinter
**astillar** /asti'ʎar; asti'yar/ vt to splinter, chip
**astillero** /asti'ʎero; asti'yero/ m, shipyard; rack for lances and pikes
**astilloso** /asti'ʎoso; asti'yoso/ a splintery, fragile
**astracán** /astra'kan/ m, astrakhan
**astringente** /astrin'hente/ a astringent
**astringir** /astrin'hir/ vt to tighten up; compress; constrain
**astro** /'astro/ m, heavenly body
**astrolatría** /astrola'tria/ f, astrolatry, star worship
**astrología** /astrolo'hia/ f, astrology
**astrológico** /astro'lohiko/ a astrological
**astrólogo** /as'trologo/ **(-ga)** n astrologist
**astronauta** /astro'nauta/ m, astronaut
**astronomía** /astrono'mia/ f, astronomy
**astronómico** /astro'nomiko/ a astronomical
**astrónomo** /as'tronomo/ m, astronomer
**astucia** /as'tuθia; as'tusia/ f, astuteness, guile, craftiness
**asturiano** /astu'riano/ **(-na)** a and n Asturian
**astuto** /as'tuto/ a guileful, crafty, astute
**Asuero** /a'suero/ Ahasuerus
**asueto** /a'sueto/ m, day's holiday
**asumir** /asu'mir/ vt to assume; adopt, appropriate
**asunción** /asun'θion; asun'sion/ f, assumption
**asunto** /a'sunto/ m, matter, theme, subject; business, affair
**asustadizo** /asusta'ðiθo; asusta'ðiso/ a timid, nervous, easily frightened
**asustar** /asus'tar/ vt to frighten; **que asusta,** terribly (e.g. *Es de una ñoñería que asusta,* It's a terribly timid thing to do) vr be frightened
**atablar** /ata'βlar/ vt to roll, flatten (earth)
**atacado** /ata'kaðo/ a *Inf.* hesitant; mean, stingy
**atacador** /ataka'ðor/ **(-ra)** a attacking —n aggressor, attacker
**atacar** /ata'kar/ vt to attack; fasten, button; fit (clothes); ram (guns); *Fig.* press hard, corner (persons). **a. a los nervios,** to jar on the nerves
**atadero** /ata'ðero/ m, rope, tie, cord; hook, ring, etc. (for hitching); hindrance, impediment; hitching or fastening point

**atado** /a'taðo/ *m*, bundle, roll

**atadura** /ata'ðura/ *f*, tying, stringing, fastening, tie; knot; connection

**atajar** /ata'har/ *vi* to take a short cut; —*vt* intercept, cut off; screen off, divide; impede, stop; interrupt (people); **atajarle la palabra a uno,** to cut somebody off, interrupt *vr* be overcome (by fear, shame, etc.)

**atajo** /a'taho/ *m*, short cut, quick way; cutting, abbreviation; division. *Inf.* **echar por el a.,** to go to the root of (a matter)

**atalaya** /ata'laya/ *f*, look out, watch tower; observation point. *m*, lookout

**atalayar** /atala'yar/ *vt* to scan, watch; spy upon

**atalón** /ata'lon/ *m*, atoll, coral island

**atañadero: en lo atañadero a** /ataɲa'ðero en lo ataɲa'ðero a/ with regard to, with respect to

**atañer** /ata'ɲer/ *vi impers* to concern, affect; belong, pertain

**ataque** /a'take/ *m*, (*Mil. Med.*) attack; quarrel, fight

**atar** /a'tar/ *vt* to tie; fasten; lace; stop, paralyse; —*vr* get in a fix; confine oneself. **a. cabos,** to put two and two together

**atardecer** /atarðe'θer; atarðe'ser/ *vi irr impers* to grow dusk. See **conocer**

**atardecer** /atarðe'θer; atarðe'ser/ *m*, dusk, evening

**atarear** /atare'ar/ *vt* to set to work, assign work to; —*vr* work hard

**atarugar** /ataru'gar/ *vt* to wedge; stop up; plug; block; *Inf.* silence, shut up; stuff, cram; —*vr Fig. Inf.* lose one's head

**atasajar** /atasa'har/ *vt* to cut up, jerk (beef, etc.)

**atascadero** /ataska'ðero/ *m*, deep rut, boggy place; impediment, obstacle

**atascar** /atas'kar/ *vt* to plug; block up; stop (a leak); hinder, obstruct; —*vr* stick in the mud; be held up or delayed; *Inf.* get stuck in a speech

**atasco** /a'tasko/ *m*, obstruction, block

**ataúd** /ata'uð/ *m*, coffin

**Ataulfo** /a'taulfo/ Ataulf

**ataviar** /ata'βiar/ *vt* to deck, apparel, adorn

**atavío** /ata'βio/ *m*, get-up, dress, apparel; *pl* ornaments

**atavismo** /ata'βismo/ *m*, atavism

**ate** /'ate/ *m*, (Mexico) kind of Turkish delight

**ateísmo** /ate'ismo/ *m*, atheism

**atelaje** /ate'lahe/ *m*, team, yoke (of horses); trappings, harness; *Inf.* trousseau

**atemperación** /atempera'θion; atempera'sion/ *f*, moderation, mitigation; tempering

**atemperar** /atempe'rar/ *vt* to moderate, mitigate; adapt, adjust; temper, cool. **atemperarse a la realidad,** to adjust to reality

**Atenas** /a'tenas/ Athens

**atenazar** /atena'θar; atena'sar/ *vt* to grip, grasp; torture

**atención** /aten'θion; aten'sion/ *f*, attention; solicitude, kindness; courtesy, civility; *pl* business affairs —*interj* **¡A.!** Take care! Look out!; *Mil.* Attention! **en a.** ( **a),** taking into consideration. **estar en a.,** (patient) to be under treatment

**atender** /aten'der/ *vt irr* to await, expect; take care of, look after; —*vi* (*with prep a*) attend to, listen to; —*vi* remember. See **entender**

**ateneo** /ate'neo/ *m*, atheneum —*a* Athenian

**atenerse** /ate'nerse/ *vr irr* (*with prep a*) to abide by; resort to, rely on. See **tener**

**ateniense** /ate'niense/ *a* and *mf* Athenian

**atentado** /aten'taðo/ *a* prudent, sensible; secret, silent. *m*, infringement, violation; attempt (on a person's life); crime

**atentar** /aten'tar/ *vt irr* to do illegally; attempt a crime; —*vr* proceed cautiously; restrain oneself. See **acertar**

**atento** /a'tento/ *a* attentive; courteous, civil —*adv* taking into consideration. **su atenta** ( **atta),** *Com.* your favor

**atenuación** /atenua'θion; atenua'sion/ *f*, attenuation, diminution

**atenuante** /ate'nuante/ *a* attenuating; extenuating (of circumstances)

**atenuar** /ate'nuar/ *vt* to attenuate, diminish; extenuate

**ateo** /a'teo/ **(-ea)** *a* atheistic —*n* atheist

**aterciopelado** /aterθiope'laðo; atersiope'laðo/ *a* velvety

**aterirse** /ate'rirse/ *vr defective* to grow stiff with cold

**aterrador** /aterra'ðor/ *a* terrifying, dreadful

**aterraje** /ate'rrahe/ *m*, (*Aer. Naut.*) landing

**aterramiento** /aterra'miento/ *m*, horror, terror; terrorization; *Naut.* landing; ruin, demolition

**aterrar** /ate'rrar/ *vt irr* to demolish; discourage; cover with earth; —*vi* land; —*vr Naut.* draw near to land. See **acertar**

**aterrizaje** /aterri'θahe; aterri'sahe/ *m*, *Aer.* landing. **a. forzoso,** forced landing. **campo de a.,** landing field

**aterrizar** /aterri'θar; aterri'sar/ *vi Aer.* to land, touch down

**aterrorizar** /aterrori'θar; aterrori'sar/ *vt* to terrify; terrorize

**atesorar** /ateso'rar/ *vt* to hoard, treasure up

**atestación** /atesta'θion; atesta'sion/ *f*, attestation, affidavit

**atestar** /ates'tar/ *vt irr* to stuff, cram; insert; *Inf.* stuff with food; crowd, fill with people. See **acertar**

**atestar** /ates'tar/ *vt* to attest, testify

**atestiguación** /atestigua'θion; atestigua'sion/ *f*, deposition, testimony

**atestiguar** /atesti'guar/ *vt* to testify, attest

**atetar** /ate'tar/ *vt* to suckle; —*vi* suck

**atezado** /ate'θaðo; ate'saðo/ *a* bronzed, sunburnt; black

**ático** /'atiko/ *a* Attic; *m*, penthouse

**atiesar** /atie'sar/ *vt* to stiffen

**atildar** /atil'dar/ *vt* to place a tilde over; blame, criticize; decorate, ornament

**atimia** /a'timia/ *f*, loss of status

**atinado** /ati'naðo/ *a* pertinent, relevant

**atinar** /ati'nar/ *vi* to find by touch; discover by chance; guess; hit the mark

**atinente a...** /ati'nente a / concerning...

**atisbadura** /atisβa'ðura/ *f*, watching, spying, prying

**atisbar** /atis'βar/ *vt* to spy upon, watch

**atisbo** /a'tisβo/ *m*, prying, watching; suspicion, hint

**atisbón** /atis'βon/ *a* penetrating (mind, vision)

**atizador** /atiθa'ðor; atisa'ðor/ *m*, poker (for the fire)

**atizar** /ati'θar; ati'sar/ *vt* to poke (the fire); dowse, snuff; trim (lamps); excite, rouse; *Inf.* slap, wallop

**atlántico** /at'lantiko/ *a* Atlantic. *m*, Atlantic Ocean

**Atlántida** /at'lantiða/ Atlantis

**atleta** /at'leta/ *m*, athlete

**atlético** /at'letiko/ *a* athletic

**atletismo** /atle'tismo/ *m*, athletics

**atmósfera** /at'mosfera/ *f*, atmosphere

**atmosférico** /atmos'feriko/ *a* atmospheric

**atolladero** /atoʎa'ðero; atoya'ðero/ *m*, rut; mud; bog

**atolón** /ato'lon/ *m*, atoll, coral island

**atolondrado** /atolon'draðo/ *a* scatter-brained, flighty

**atolondramiento** /atolondra'miento/ *m*, rashness, recklessness; bewilderment

**atolondrar** /atolon'drar/ *vt* to bewilder, confuse

**atómico** /a'tomiko/ *a* atomic

**atomización** /atomiθa'θion; atomisa'sion/ *f*, atomization

**átomo** /'atomo/ *m*, atom; speck, particle

**atónito** /a'tonito/ *a* amazed, astounded

**atontar** /aton'tar/ *vt* to confuse, daze; make stupid; stun

**atormentador** /atormenta'ðor/ **(-ra)** *a* torturing —*n* tormentor; torturer

**atormentar** /atormen'tar/ *vt* to torment; torture; grieve, harass

**atorrante** /ato'rrante/ *a* and *mf* (Argentina) good-for-nothing

**atracadero** /atraka'ðero/ *m*, jetty, landingstage

**atracar** /atra'kar/ *vt Inf.* to stuff with food; *Naut.* tie up, moor; hold up, rob; —*vi Naut.* moor, stop; —*vr Inf.* guzzle, gorge

**atracción** /atrak'θion; atrak'sion/ *f*, attraction

**atraco** /a'trako/ **(a)** *m*, hold up (of), ambush (of)

**atracón** /atra'kon/ *m*, *Inf.* gorge, fill; surfeit. **darse atracones de,** to gorge oneself on

**atractivo** /atrak'tiβo/ *a* attractive. *m*, attraction, charm

**atractriz** /atrak'triθ; atrak'tris/ *a* attracting; *f*, force of attraction; (fig.) lure

**atraer** /atra'er/ *vt irr* to attract; charm, enchant. See **traer**

**atragantarse** /atragan'tarse/ *vr* to choke; *Inf.* be at a loss, dry up (in conversation)

**atraíble** /atra'iβle/ *a* attractable, able to be attracted

**atrancar** /atran'kar/ *vt* to bar the door; obstruct, block; hinder; —*vi Inf.* stride; skip (in reading)

**atrapar** /atra'par/ *vt Inf.* grab, seize, catch; net, obtain; deceive

**atrás** /a'tras/ *adv* behind, back; past; previously. **¡A.!** Back! **años a.**, years ago

**atrasado** /atra'saðo/ *a* slow (of clocks); backward; old-fashioned; hard-up, poor. **a. mental**, retarded person

**atrasar** /atra'sar/ *vt* to delay, retard; fix a later date than the true one; put back (clocks) —*vi* be slow (clocks); —*vr* be late; be left behind

**atraso** /a'traso/ *m*, delay; backwardness, dullness; slowness (clocks); lateness; *pl* arrears. **El reloj lleva cinco minutos de a.**, The watch is five minutes slow

**atravesado** /atraβe'saðo/ *a* slightly squint-eyed; mongrel, crossbreed; half-caste; ill-intentioned

**atravesar** /atraβe'sar/ *vt irr* to lay across, put athwart; cross, traverse; pierce; obstruct; *Naut.* lie to; —*vr* be among, mingle (with); interrupt; interfere, take part; quarrel; occur, arise. See **confesar**

**atrayente** /atra'yente/ *a* attractive

**atreverse** /atre'βerse/ *vr* to dare, risk, venture; be overbold or insolvent

**atrevido** /atre'βiðo/ *a* bold, audacious; hazardous, dangerous; brazen, impudent

**atribución** /atriβu'θion; atriβu'sion/ *f*, attribution; perquisite, attribute

**atribuible** /atri'βuiβle/ *a* attributable

**atribuir** /atri'βuir/ *vt irr* to impute, attribute; assign, turn over to; —*vr* take upon oneself, assume. See **huir**

**atributo** /atri'βuto/ *m*, attribute, quality

**atril** /a'tril/ *m*, lectern, reading desk; music stand

**atrincherar** /atrintʃe'rar/ *vt* to protect with entrenchments; —*vr* entrench oneself

**atrio** /'atrio/ *m*, atrium; hall, vestibule; *Archit.* parvis

**atrocidad** /atroθi'ðað; atrosi'ðað/ *f*, atrocity, cruelty; *Inf.* terrific amount; enormity, crime

**atrofia** /a'trofia/ *f*, atrophy

**atrofiarse** /atro'fiarse/ *vr* to atrophy

**atronado** /atro'naðo/ *a* harebrained, foolish

**atronar** /atro'nar/ *vt irr* to deafen, stun with noise; confuse, daze. See **tronar**

**atropelladamente** /atropeʎaða'mente; atropeyaða'mente/ *adv* in disorder, helter-skelter

**atropellado** /atrope'ʎaðo; atrope'yaðo/ *a* rash, foolhardy

**atropellar** /atrope'ʎar; atrope'yar/ *vt* to trample upon; thrust out of the way; knock down; disregard, violate (feelings); insult, abuse; transgress; do hastily; —*vr* act rashly

**atropello** /atro'peʎo; atro'peyo/ *m*, trampling; road accident; knocking over; upsetting; violation; outrage

**atroz** /a'troθ; a'ntros/ *a* atrocious, savage; monstrous, outrageous; *Inf.* terrific, enormous

**atufar** /atu'far/ *vt* to irritate, vex; —*vr* grow irritated; turn sour (wine, etc.)

**atún** /a'tun/ *m*, tuna

**aturdido** /atur'ðiðo/ *a* reckless, scatterbrained, silly; thoughtless; stunned

**aturdimiento** /aturði'miento/ *m*, daze; confusion; bewilderment

**aturdir** /atur'ðir/ *vt* to daze; confuse, bewilder; amaze; stun

**atusar** /atu'sar/ *vt* to trim (hair, beard); *Agr.* prune; smooth down (hair); —*vr* dress over-carefully

**audacia** /au'ðaθia; au'ðasia/ *f*, audacity

**audaz** /au'ðaθ; au'ðas/ *a* audacious, daring

**audibilidad** /auðiβili'ðað/ *f*, audibility

**audición** /auði'θion; auði'sion/ *f*, audition

**audiencia** /au'ðienθia; au'ðiensia/ *f*, audience, hearing; *Law.* audience; audience chamber

**audifono** /au'ðifono/ *m*, hearing aid

**audioteca** /auðio'teka/ *f*, audio library

**auditivo** /auði'tiβo/ *a* auditory

**auditor** /auði'tor/ *m*, magistrate, judge

**auditorio** /auði'torio/ *a* auditory. *m*, audience

**auge** /'auhe/ *m*, *Fig.* zenith, height; *Astron.* apogee

**augusto** /au'gusto/ *a* august, awesome

**aula** /'aula/ *f*, lecture or class room; *Poet.* palace

**aullador** /auʎa'ðor; auya'ðor/ *a* howling

**aullar** /au'ʎar; au'yar/ *vi* to howl; bay

**aullido** /au'ʎiðo; au'yiðo/ *m*, howl; baying

**aumentar** /aumen'tar/ **(se)** *vt vi vr* to increase, augment

**aumentativo** /aumenta'tiβo/ *a Gram.* augmentative

**aumento** /au'mento/ *m*, increase; progress; enlargement. **ir en a.**, to increase; advance, progress; prosper

**aun** /a'un/ *adv* even. **A. los que viven lejos han de oíros**, Even those who live far must hear you. **a. así** *or* **a. siendo así**, even so. **a. ayer**, only yesterday. **a. cuando**, even if. **más a.**, even more. **ni a. si**, not even if.

**aún** /a'un/ *adv* still, yet. **A. no te creen** *or* **No te creen a.**, They still don't believe you **¿A. se lo darás?** *or* **¿Se lo darás a.?** Will you still give it to her?

**aunque** /'aunke/ *conjunc* although, even if, even though. It takes the Indicative referring to statement of fact and Subjunctive referring to a hypothesis, e.g. *A. vino, no lo hizo*, Although he came, he did not do it. *A. él cantase yo no iría allí*, Even though he sang (were to sing), I should not go there

**aura** /'aura/ *f*, zephyr, gentle breeze; popularity, approbation; aura. **a. epiléptica**, *Med.* epileptic aura

**áureo** /'aureo/ *a* gold, gilt; golden

**auricular** /auriku'lar/ *a* auricular. *m*, little finger; receiver, ear-piece (of a telephone); earphone (radio)

**aurífero** /au'rifero/ *a* gold-yielding, auriferous

**auriga** /au'riga/ *m*, charioteer

**aurora** /au'rora/ *f*, dawn; genesis, beginnings. **a. boreal**, aurora borealis, Northern Lights

**auscultación** /auskulta'θion; auskulta'sion/ *f*, *Med.* auscultation

**auscultar** /auskul'tar/ *vt Med.* to auscultate

**ausencia** /au'senθia; au'sensia/ *f*, absence. **en ausencia de**, in the absence of

**ausentar** /ausen'tar/ *vt* to send away; —*vr* absent oneself

**ausente** /au'sente/ *a* absent. *mf* absent person

**auspicio** /aus'piθio; aus'pisio/ *m*, augury, prediction; favor, patronage; *pl* auspices

**austeridad** /austeri'ðað/ *f*, austerity; mortification of the flesh

**austero** /aus'tero/ *a* austere, ascetic; severe, harsh; honest, upright

**austral** /aus'tral/ *a* southerly, austral

**australiano** /austra'liano/ **(-na)** *a* and *n* Australian

**austríaco** /aus'triako/ **(-ca)** *a* and *n* Austrian

**Austrias, los** /'austrias, los/ the Hapsburgs (ruling house of Spain, 1516–1700)

**austrófilo** /aus'trofilo/ *a n* Austrophile

**autenticación** /autentika'θion; autentika'sion/ *f*, authentication

**autenticar** /autenti'kar/ *vt* to authenticate, attest; prove genuine

**autenticidad** /autentiθi'ðað; autentisi'ðað/ *f*, authenticity

**auténtico** /au'tentiko/ *a* authentic

**auto** /'auto/ *m*, *Law.* sentence, decision; *Theat.* one-act allegory (gen. religious); *pl* proceedings. **a. de fe**, auto-da-fé. **a. de reconocimiento**, search-warrant. **a. sacramental**, one-act religious drama on theme of mystery of the Eucharist. **hacer a. de fe de**, to burn

**autobiografía** /autoβiogra'fia/ *f*, autobiography

**autobús** /auto'βus/ *m*, motor bus, bus

**autocitarse** /autoθi'tarse; autosi'tarse/ *vr* to quote from one's own works

**autoclave** /auto'klaβe/ *m*, pressure cooker

**autocracia** /auto'kraθia; auto'krasia/ *f*, autocracy

**autócrata** /au'tokrata/ *mf* autocrat

**autocrático** /auto'kratiko/ *a* autocratic

**autocrueldad** /autokruel'dað/ *f*, self-inflicted pain

                                                            **avión**

**autodescubrimiento** /autoðeskuβri'miento/ *m*, self-discovery

**autodidacto** /autoði'ðakto/ *a* autodidactic; self-educated, self-taught

**autódromo** /au'toðromo/ *m*, speedway

**autógeno** /au'toheno/ *a* autogenous, self-generating

**autogiro** /auto'hiro/ *m*, *Aer*. autogyro

**autografía** /autogra'fia/ *f*, autography

**autográfico** /auto'grafiko/ *a* autographic, in lithographic reproduction

**autógrafo** /au'tografo/ *a* autographical. *m*, autograph

**autoinducción** /autoinduk'θion; autoinduk'sion/ *f*, self-induction

**autómata** /au'tomata/ *m*, automaton

**automático** /auto'matiko/ *a* automatic. *m*, *Sew*. press stud

**automatismo** /automa'tismo/ *m*, automatism

**automejoramiento** /autome,hora'miento/ *m*, self-improvement

**automóvil** /auto'moβil/ *m*, automobile, motor car —*a* automatic

**automovilismo** /automoβi'lismo/ *m*, motoring

**automovilista** /automoβi'lista/ *mf* motorist

**autonombrarse** /autonom'βrarse/ *vr* to call oneself, go by the name of

**autonomía** /autono'mia/ *f*, autonomy

**autónomo** /au'tonomo/ *a* autonomous

**autopista** /auto'pista/ *f*, motor road

**autopsia** /au'topsia/ *f*, *Med*. autopsy, post-mortem

**autor** /au'tor/ **(-ra)** *n* agent, originator; author; inventor; *Law*. perpetrator

**autoridad** /autori'ðað/ *f*, authority; pomp, show

**autoritario** /autori'tario/ *a* authoritarian; authoritative

**autorización** /autoriθa'θion; autorisa'sion/ *f*, authorization

**autorizado** /autori'θaðo; autori'saðo/ *a* approved, authorized, responsible

**autorizar** /autori'θar; autori'sar/ *vt* to authorize; *Law*. attest, testify; cite, prove by reference; approve; exalt

**autorretratarse** /autorretra'tarse/ *vr* to have one's portrait painted, sit for one's portrait

**autorretrato** /autorre'trato/ *m*, self-portrait

**autostopista** /autosto'pista/ *mf* hitchhiker (Spain)

**autosugestión** /autosuhes'tion/ *f*, autosuggestion

**auxiliador** /auksilia'ðor/ **(-ra)** *a* assistant; helpful —*n* helper, assistant

**auxiliar** /auksi'liar/ *vt* to help, aid; attend (the dying). *m*, *Educ*. lecturer —*a* assisting

**auxiliaría** /auksilia'ria/ *f*, *Educ*. lectureship

**auxilio** /auk'silio/ *m*, help, aid, assistance

**aval** /a'βal/ *m*, *Com*. endorsement; voucher

**avalar** /aβa'lar/ *vt* to enhance. **avalado por la tradición,** hallowed by tradition

**avalentado** /aβalen'taðo/ *a* boastful, bragging

**avalorar** /aβalo'rar/ *vt* to value, estimate; put spirit into, encourage

**avance** /a'βanθe; a'βanse/ *m*, advance; advance payment; balance sheet; attack

**avanzada** /aβan'θaða; aβan'saða/ *f*, *Mil*. advance guard

**avanzado** /aβan'θaðo; aβan'saðo/ *a* advanced, progressive

**avanzar** /aβan'θar; aβan'sar/ *vt* to advance; promote; —*vi* advance; attack; grow late (time)

**avanzo** /a'βanθo; a'βanso/ *m*, balance sheet; price estimate

**avaricia** /aβa'riθia; aβa'risia/ *f*, greed, avarice

**avaricioso, avariento** /aβari'θioso, aβa'riento; aβari'sioso, aβa'riento/ *a* avaricious, greedy

**avaro** /a'βaro/ **(-ra)** *a* miserly; greedy —*n* miser

**avasallador** /aβasaʎa'ðor; aβasaya'ðor/ *a* dominating; *Fig*. overwhelming; enslaving

**avasallar** /aβasa'ʎar; aβasa'yar/ *vt* to subdue, dominate; —*vr* become a vassal; surrender, yield

**ave** /'aβe/ *f*, bird. **a. de paso,** migratory bird; *Fig*. bird of passage. **a. de rapiña,** bird of prey. **a. fría,** *Ornith*. plover. **ave cantora,** songbird

**avecinarse** /aβeθi'narse; aβesi'narse/ *vr* to be approaching (e.g. *el año que avecina,* the coming year)

**avellana** /aβe'ʎana; aβe'yana/ *f*, hazel nut

**avellanarse** /aβeʎa'narse; aβeya'narse/ *vr* to shrivel

**avellano** /aβe'ʎano; aβe'yano/ *m*, *Bot*. hazel

**avemaría** /aβema'ria/ *f*, Hail Mary (prayer); Angelus; rosary bead. *Inf*. **en un a.,** in a trice

**avena** /a'βena/ *f*, oats; *Poet*. oaten pipe. **a. loca,** wild oats

**avenal** /aβe'nal/ *m*, oatfield

**avenar** /aβe'nar/ *vt* to drain (land); drain off (liquids)

**avenencia** /aβe'nenθia; aβe'nensia/ *f*, agreement, arrangement; transaction; conformity, harmony

**avenida** /aβe'niða/ *f*, flood, spate; avenue; abundance; way, approach (to a place)

**avenido** /aβe'niðo/ *a* (*with bien or mal*) well *or* ill-suited

**avenidor** /aβeni'ðor/ **(-ra)** *n* arbitrator, mediator

**avenir** /aβe'nir/ *vt irr* to reconcile; —*vi* happen (used in infinitive and third singular and plural); —*vr* be reconciled; agree; compromise, give way; harmonize (things); (*with con*) get on with, agree with. See **venir**

**aventador** /aβenta'ðor/ *m*, *Agr*. winnower; pitchfork

**aventajado** /aβenta'haðo/ *a* outstanding, talented; advantageous. *m*, *Mil*. private who enjoys extra pay

**aventajar** /aβenta'har/ *vt* to improve, better; promote, prefer; excel; —*vr* (*with prep a*) surpass, excel. **Te aventajo en diez años,** I'm ten years older than you

**aventamiento** /aβenta'miento/ *m*, winnowing

**aventar** /aβen'tar/ *vt irr* to fan; air, ventilate; winnow; *Inf*. drive away, expel; —*vr* be inflated; *Inf*. flee; smell (bad meat). See **sentar**

**aventura** /aβen'tura/ *f*, adventure; chance, luck; risk, danger

**aventurar** /aβentu'rar/ *vt* to risk, hazard

**aventurero** /aβentu'rero/ **(-ra)** *a* adventurous; unscrupulous, intriguing; undisciplined (of troops) —*n* adventurer

**avergonzar** /aβergon'θar; aβergon'sar/ *vt irr* to shame; make shy, abash; —*vr* be ashamed; be shy or sheepish —*Pres. Indic*. **avergüenzo, avergüenzas, avergüenza, avergüenzan.** *Pres. Subjunc*. **avergüence, avergüences, avergüence, avergüencen**

**avería** /aβe'ria/ *f*, aviary; damage (to merchandise); loss, harm; *Elec*. fault; breakdown. **a. gruesa,** general average (marine insurance)

**averiarse** /aβe'riarse/ *vr* to be damaged; deteriorate; break down

**averiguable** /aβeri'guaβle/ *a* examinable, investigable; discoverable

**averiguación** /aβerigua'θion; aβerigua'sion/ *f*, inquiry, investigation; discovery

**averiguar** /aβeri'guar/ *vt* to investigate, inquire into; discover, ascertain. **¡averigüelo Vargas!** Beats me!, Search me!

**averío** /aβe'rio/ *m*, flock of birds

**Averno** /a'βerno/ *m*, *Poet*. Avernus, Hades

**aversión** /aβer'sion/ *f*, aversion, repugnance

**avestruz** /aβes'truθ; aβes'trus/ *m*, ostrich

**avetado** /aβe'taðo/ *a* veined, mottled, streaked

**avezar** /aβe'θar; aβe'sar/ *vt* to accustom; —*vr* grow accustomed (to)

**aviación** /aβia'θion; aβia'sion/ *f*, aviation

**aviador** /aβia'ðor/ *m*, aviator

**aviar** /a'βiar/ *vt* to outfit, equip; prepare, make ready; *Inf*. speed up; caulk (ship). *Fig. Inf*. **estar aviado,** to be in a mess

**avidez** /aβi'ðeθ; aβi'ðes/ *f*, avidity, greed; longing, desire

**ávido** /'aβiðo/ *a* avid, greedy

**avieso** /a'βieso/ *a* twisted, crooked; ill-natured; sinister

**avillanado** /aβiʎa'naðo; aβiya'naðo/ *a* countrified; gross, vulgar; boorish

**avinagrado** /aβina'graðo/ *a Inf*. crabbed, sour, testy

**avío** /a'βio/ *m*, preparation, provision; picnic lunch; money advanced (to miners or laborers); *pl Inf*. equipment, tools. **avíos de pesca,** fishing tackle

**avión** /a'βion/ *m*, airplane; *Ornith*. martin or swift. **a. de bombardeo,** bomber. **a. de caza,** fighter plane. **a. de combate nocturno,** night fighter. **a. de hostigamiento,** interceptor. **a. de reacción,** jet airplane. **a. de transporte,** *Aer*. transport. **a. en picado,** dive-bomber. **a. taxi,** air taxi. **por a.,** by airmail **«Avión»** "Airmail"

**avioneta** /aβio'neta/ *f,* light airplane, small airplane

**avisado** /aβi'saðo/ *a* shrewd, sensible. **mal a.,** ill-advised, imprudent

**avisar** /aβi'sar/ *vt* to inform, acquaint; warn; advise

**aviso** /a'βiso/ *m,* notice, announcement; warning; advice; care, caution; attention; shrewdness, prudence. **estar sobre a.,** to be on call; be on the alert

**avispa** /a'βispa/ *f,* wasp

**avispado** /aβis'paðo/ *a Inf.* smart, clever, quick; wide-awake

**avispar** /aβis'par/ *vt* to goad, prick; *Inf.* rouse, incite; —*vr* be uneasy, fret

**avispero** /aβis'pero/ *m,* wasp's nest; swarm of wasps; *Fig. Inf.* hornet's nest

**avispón** /aβis'pon/ *m,* hornet

**avistamiento** /aβista'miento/ *m,* sighting, spotting (e.g. of a ship)

**avistar** /aβis'tar/ *vt* to descry, sight, spot; —*vr* **avistarse con,** to interview

**avituallar** /aβitua'ʎar/ aβitua'yar/ *vt* to victual, supply with food

**avivar** /aβi'βar/ *vt* to enliven; stimulate, encourage; stir (fire); trim (wicks); brighten (colors); inflame; vivify, invigorate; —*vi* revive, recover

**avizor** /aβi'θor; aβi'sor/ *m,* watcher, spy —*a* watchful, vigilant

**avizorar** /aβiθo'rar; aβiso'rar/ *vt* to watch, spy upon

**avutarda** /aβu'tarða/ *f,* bustard

**axila** /ak'sila/ *f, Bot.* axil; *Anat.* axilla, armpit

**axioma** /ak'sioma/ *m,* axiom

**axiomático** /aksio'matiko/ *a* axiomatic

**¡ay!** /ai/ *interj* Alas! Woe is me! *m,* complaint, sigh

**aya** /'aya/ *f,* governess

**ayer** /a'yer/ *adv* yesterday; a short while ago; in the past. *m,* past

**ayo** /'ayo/ *m,* tutor

**ayuda** /a'yuða/ *f,* help, assistance; enema; clyster; watch dog. *m,* **a. de cámara,** valet

**ayudador** /ayuða'ðor/ **(-ra)** *a* helping, assisting —*n* helper

**ayudante** /ayu'ðante/ *m,* assistant; teaching assistant; *Mil.* adjutant. **a. a cátedra,** *Educ.* assistant lecturer. **a. de plaza,** post adjutant

**ayudar** /ayu'ðar/ *vt* to assist; help, aid; —*vr* make an effort; avail oneself of another's help

**ayunador** /ayuna'ðor/ **(-ra)** *a* fasting —*n* faster; abstainer

**ayunar** /ayu'nar/ *vi* to fast

**ayuno** /a'yuno/ *m,* fast —*a* fasting; ignorant, unaware. **en a.** *or* **en ayunas,** before breakfast, fasting; *Inf.* ignorant, unaware

**ayuntamiento** /ayunta'miento/ *m,* meeting, assembly; municipal government; town hall; sexual union

**azabache** /aθa'βatʃe; asaβatʃe/ *m, Mineral.* jet

**azada** /a'θaða; a'saða/ *f, Agr.* spade; hoe

**azadón** /aθa'ðon; asa'ðon/ *m, Agr.* hoe

**azafata** /aθa'fata; asa'fata/ *f,* queen's waiting-maid *Obs.*; flight attendant

**azafate** /aθa'fate; asa'fate/ *m,* flat basket; small tray

**azafrán** /aθa'fran; asa'fran/ *m, Bot.* saffron; crocus

**azafranado** /aθafra'naðo; asafra'naðo/ *a* saffron-colored

**azahar** /a'θaar; a'saar/ *m,* flower of orange, lemon or sweet lime tree

**azar** /a'θar; a'sar/ *m,* chance, hazard; unexpected misfortune; losing card or throw of dice

**azararse** /aθa'rarse; asa'rarse/ *vr* to go wrong, fail (negotiations, etc.); grow nervous; become confused; blush

**azaroso** /aθa'roso; asa'roso/ *a* unlucky, ill-omened; hazardous

**ázimo** /'aθimo; 'asimo/ *a* unleavened (bread)

**ázoe** /'aθoe; 'asoe/ *m,* nitrogen

**azogar** /aθo'gar; aso'gar/ *vt* to silver (mirrors, etc.); slake lime; —*vr* suffer from mercury poisoning; *Inf.* grow uneasy, be agitated

**azogue** /a'θoge; a'soge/ *m, Mineral.* mercury, quicksilver; market-place

**azolve** /a'θolβe; a'solβe/ *m,* silt

**azoramiento** /aθora'miento; asora'miento/ *m,* alarm, terror; confusion, stupefaction; incitement

**azorar** /aθo'rar; aso'rar/ *vt* to alarm, terrify; confuse, stun, dumbfound; excite, stimulate; encourage

**azotacalles** /aθota'kaʎes; asota'kayes/ *mf Inf.* idler, street loafer

**azotaina** /aθo'taina; aso'taina/ *f, Inf.* whipping, spanking

**azotamiento** /aθota'miento; asota'miento/ *m,* flogging, beating, whipping

**azotar** /aθo'tar; aso'tar/ *vt* to whip, beat, flog; scourge, ravage; knock against or strike repeatedly

**azotazo** /aθo'taθo; aso'taso/ *m,* spank

**azote** /a'θote; a'sote/ *m,* whip; scourge; lash, blow with a whip; spank, slap; misfortune, disaster. *Inf.* **azotes y galeras,** monotonous diet

**azotea** /aθo'tea; aso'tea/ *f,* flat terrace roof

**azozador** /aθoθa'ðor; asosa'ðor/ *m,* party whip, whip

**azteca** /aθ'teka; as'teka/ *a* and *mf* Aztec

**azúcar** /a'θukar; a'sukar/ *m,* sugar. **a. blanco** *or* **a. de flor,** white sugar. **a. de pilón,** loaf sugar. **a. moreno,** brown sugar. **a. quebrado,** brown sugar. **a. y canela,** sorrel gray (of horses)

**azucarado** /aθuka'raðo; asuka'raðo/ *a* sugary; sugared, sugar-coated; *Inf.* honeyed, flattering

**azucarar** /aθuka'rar; asuka'rar/ *vt* to coat with sugar; sweeten; *Inf.* soften, mitigate; —*vr* crystallize; go sugary (jam)

**azucarera** /aθuka'rera; asuka'rera/ *f,* sugar-basin

**azucarero** /aθuka'rero; asuka'rero/ *a* sugar-producing (e.g. province)

**azucarillo** /aθuka'riʎo; asuka'riyo/ *m, Cul.* bar made of white of egg and sugar for sweetening water

**azucena** /aθu'θena; asu'sena/ *f,* white lily. **a. de agua,** water-lily

**azuela** /a'θuela; a'suela/ *f,* adze

**azufrar** /aθu'frar; asu'frar/ *vt* to sulphurate

**azufre** /a'θufre; a'sufre/ *m,* sulphur

**azufroso** /aθu'froso; asu'froso/ *a* sulphurous

**azul** /a'θul; a'sul/ *a* and *m,* blue. **a. celeste,** sky blue, azure. **a. de mar** *or* **a. marino,** navy blue. **a. de ultramar,** ultramarine. **a. turquí,** indigo

**azulado** /aθu'laðo; asu'laðo/ *a* bluish, blue

**azulear** /aθule'ar; asule'ar/ *vi* to look bluish, have a blue tint

**azulejo** /aθu'leho; asu'leho/ *m,* ornamental glazed tile

**azumbre** /a'θumbre; a'sumbre/ *f,* liquid measure (just over 2 liters)

**azuzar** /aθu'θar; asu'sar/ *vt* to set on (dogs); irritate, provoke; incite, urge

# B

**baba** /'baβa/ *f*, saliva; secretion (of snails, etc.); viscous fluid (of plants). *Inf.* **caérsele ( a uno) la b.,** to ooze satisfaction; be dumbfounded

**babador, babero** /baβa'ðor, ba'βero/ *m*, bib, feeder

**babear** /baβe'ar/ *vi* to dribble, slaver; *Fig. Inf.* slobber over, be sloppy

**babel** /ba'βel/ *m*, babel

**babélico** /ba'βeliko/ *a* Babelian, Babel-like confusion; unintelligible

**Babia, estar en** /'baβia, es'tar en/ to be daydreaming

**babieca** /ba'βieka/ *mf Inf.* stupid person. **Babieca** *f*, the Cid's horse

**Babilonia** /baβi'lonia/ Babylon

**babilónico** /baβi'loniko/ *a* Babylonian

**bable** /'baβle/ *m*, Asturian (language)

**babor** /ba'βor/ *m*, *Naut.* larboard, port

**babosa** /ba'βosa/ *f*, slug; young onion

**baboso** /ba'βoso/ *a* slavering; *Fig. Inf.* "sloppy"; *Inf.* incompetent, useless

**babucha** /ba'βutʃa/ *f*, heelless slipper, babouche

**babuino** /ba'βuino/ *m*, *Zool.* baboon

**baca** /'baka/ *f*, luggage carrier (on roof of bus, etc.)

**bacalao** /baka'lao/ *m*, codfish

**bacanales** /baka'nales/ *f pl*, Bacchanalia

**bacante** /ba'kante/ *f*, Bacchante

**bacará** /baka'ra/ *m*, baccarat (card game)

**baceta** /ba'θeta; ba'seta/ *f*, pool (in card games)

**bache** /'batʃe/ *m*, rut (in road); pothole

**bacheo** /ba'tʃeo/ *m*, repairing of streets

**bachiller** /batʃi'ʎer; batʃi'yer/ *mf* high-school graduate *m*, *Inf.* babbler. *f*, **bachillera,** *Inf.* blue-stocking; garrulous woman

**bachillerarse** /batʃiʎe'rarse; batʃiye'rarse/ *vr* to graduate as a bachelor

**bachillerato** /batʃiʎe'rato; batʃiye'rato/ *m*, baccalaureate, bachelor's degree

**bacía** /ba'θia; ba'sia/ *f*, bowl; barber's circular shaving-dish; barber's trade sign

**bacilar** /baθi'lar; basi'lar/ *a* bacillary

**bacilo** /ba'θilo; ba'silo/ *m*, bacillus

**bacterial, bacteriano** /bakte'rial, bakte'riano/ *a* bacterial

**bactericida** /bakteri'θiða; bakteri'siða/ *m*, bactericide

**bacteriología** /bakteriolo'hia/ *f*, bacteriology

**bacteriológico** /bakterio'lohiko/ *a* bacteriological

**bacteriólogo** /bakte'riologo/ *m*, bacteriologist

**báculo** /'bakulo/ *m*, staff; walking-stick; *Fig.* support. **b. episcopal,** bishop's crozier

**badajo** /ba'ðaho/ *m*, clapper (of a bell); chatterbox, gossip

**badana** /ba'ðana/ *f*, cured sheepskin, chamois leather, washleather; sweat band; *Inf.* **zurrar** (*a uno*) **la b.,** to take the hide off; insult

**badén** /ba'ðen/ *m*, channel made by rain, furrow; conduit

**badil** /ba'ðil/ *m*, fire-shovel

**badulaque** /baðu'lake/ *m*, *Inf.* good-for-nothing

**bagaje** /ba'gahe/ *m*, *Mil.* baggage; beast of burden, transport animal; luggage

**bagatela** /baga'tela/ *f*, trifle, oddment, bagatelle

**bagazo** /ba'gaθo; ba'gaso/ *m*, oilcake, bagasse

**bagual** /ba'gual/ *a West. Hem.* untamed, wild; doltish, dull. *m*, untamed horse, wild horse

**bahía** /ba'ia/ *f*, bay, harbor

**bailable** /bai'laβle/ *a* dance (of music). *m*, *Theat.* dance number

**bailador** /baila'ðor/ **(-ra)** *n* dancer

**bailar** /bai'lar/ *vi* to dance; spin around. **b. al son que le toca,** to adapt oneself to circumstances

**bailarín** /baila'rin/ *a* dancing. *m*, professional dancer. **b. de cuerda, bailarín de la cuerda floja,** tightrope dancer

**bailarina** /baila'rina/ *f*, ballerina

**baile** /'baile/ *m*, dance; ball; ballet. **b. de máscaras, b. de trajes,** fancy-dress ball. **b. de San Vito,** St. Vitus' dance. **b. ruso,** ballet

**bailotear** /bailote'ar/ *vi* to jig about; dance

**baja** /'baha/ *f*, drop, diminution; fall (in price, etc.); *Mil.* casualty; discharge. *Inf.* **darse de b.,** to leave an employment

**bajada** /ba'haða/ *f*, descent, fall; slope, incline; hollow, depression. **b. de aguas,** roof gutter

**bajalato** /baha'lato/ *m*, pashalik

**bajamar** /baha'mar/ *f*, low tide

**bajamente** /baha'mente/ *adv* basely, abjectly

**bajar** /ba'har/ *vi* to descend; go down; get off; drop; fall, decrease; —*vt* lower, take down, bring down; let down; dismount, alight, bend, droop; drop; reduce (price); *Fig.* lower (voices); humiliate, humble; **b. a tierra,** to step ashore; **b. la cabeza ante,** to submit to (e.g. a judgment) *vr* alight, dismount; humble oneself

**bajel** /ba'hel/ *m*, *Naut.* galley, ship

**bajeza** /ba'heθa; ba'hesa/ *f*, base action; meanness; *Fig.* humble estate, lowliness. **b. de ánimo,** timorousness

**bajío** /ba'hio/ *m*, *Naut.* shallows, shoal; depression, hollow

**bajista** /ba'hista/ *mf* speculator, bear (Stock Exchange)

**bajo** /'baho/ *a* low; short, not tall; downcast; under; subordinate; pale (of colors); humble (origin); base; coarse, vulgar; cheap (price); low (sounds). *m*, depth; shoal, sand bank; *Mus.* bass; *pl* petticoats, skirts; horses' hoofs —*adv* beneath, below —*prep* under, beneath. **b. juramento,** upon oath. **bajo relieve,** bas relief. **en voz baja,** in a low voice. **planta baja,** ground floor. **por lo b.,** in a whisper; in secret, on the sly

**bajolatino** /bahola'tino/ *a* Low Latin

**bajón** /ba'hon/ *m*, *Mus.* bassoon; bassoon player; *Fig. Inf.* downfall

**bajonista** /baho'nista/ *mf* bassoon player

**bala** /'bala/ *f*, bullet, ball; bale. **b. fría,** spent bullet. **b. luminosa,** tracer bullet. **b. perdida,** stray bullet. *Inf.* **como una b.,** like a shot

**balada** /ba'laða/ *f*, ballad, song

**baladí** /bala'ði/ *a* worthless, insignificant

**baladro** /ba'laðro/ *m*, yell, outcry, shout

**baladrón** /bala'ðron/ *a* braggart

**baladronada** /balaðro'naða/ *f*, bravado, bragging

**balagar** /bala'gar/ *m*, straw rick

**bálago** /'balago/ *m*, straw; soap-ball; straw rick

**balance** /ba'lanθe; ba'lanse/ *m*, balance; swinging; oscillation; rolling, rocking (of a ship, etc.); doubt, insecurity, *Com.* balance; *Com.* balance sheet

**balancear** /balanθe'ar; balanse'ar/ *vi* to swing; oscillate; vacillate, hesitate; —*vt* balance; —*vr* balance oneself; rock or swing oneself

**balanceo** /balan'θeo; balan'seo/ *m*, balancing; rocking; swinging; rolling (of a ship, etc.)

**balancín** /balan'θin; balan'sin/ *m*, swing-bar; whipple-tree; balance beam; tight-rope dancer's pole; minting-mill; yoke (for carrying pails); *pl Naut.* lifts

**balandra** /ba'landra/ *f*, *Naut.* sloop, cutter

**balanza** /ba'lanθa; ba'lansa/ *f*, balance; scale; judgment; comparison. **b. de comercio,** balance of trade. **en balanzas,** in doubt or danger, in the balance

**balar** /ba'lar/ *vi* to bleat (sheep)

**balasto** /ba'lasto/ *m*, *Rail.* ballast

**balaustrada** /balaus'traða/ *f*, balustrade

**balaustre** /bala'ustre/ *m*, baluster

**balazo** /ba'laθo; ba'laso/ *m*, shot; bullet wound

**balbuceo** /balβu'θeo; balβu'seo/ *m*, stammering; babbling; lisping; **balbuceos** *Fig.* beginnings, early stages (e.g. *los b. de la literatura yídica,* the beginnings of Yiddish literature)

**balbuciente** /balβu'θiente; balβu'siente/ *a* stammering; babbling; lisping

**balbucir** /balβu'θir; balβu'sir/ *vi irr defective* to stammer; lisp; babble; read hesitantly. See **lucir**

**Balcanes, los** /bal'kanes, los/ the Balkans

**balcánico** /bal'kaniko/ *a* Balkan

**balcón** /bal'kon/ *m*, balcony

**baldaquin** /balda'kin/ *m*, canopy, baldachin

**baldar** /bal'dar/ *vt* to cripple; impede, obstruct

**balde** /'balde/ *m*, bucket

**balde** /'balde/ **(en)** *adv* in vain. **de b.,** gratis, free of charge

**baldear** /balde'ar/ *vt Naut.* to wash the decks

**baldío** /bal'dio/ *a* untilled; fallow; useless, worthless; vagrant

**baldón** /bal'don/ *m*, insult; dishonor

**baldonar** /baldo'nar/ *vt* to insult

**baldosa** /bal'dosa/ *f*, paving stone; tile

**baldrufa** /bal'drufa/ *f*, top, spinning top

**balduque** /bal'duke/ *m*, red tape

**Baleares, las Islas** /bale'ares, las 'islas/ the Balearic Islands

**baleárico** /bale'ariko/ *a* Balearic

**balido** /ba'liðo/ *m*, bleat, bleating

**balística** /ba'listika/ *f*, ballistics

**baliza** /ba'liθa; ba'lisa/ *f*, *Naut.* buoy, beacon

**balizamiento** /baliθa'miento; balisa'miento/ *m*, marking with beacons, marking with buoys; traffic signs and signals

**ballena** /ba'ʎena; ba'yena/ *f*, whale; whalebone

**ballenero** /baʎe'nero; baye'nero/ *a* whaling. *m*, whaler

**ballesta** /ba'ʎesta; ba'yesta/ *f*, crossbow; spring (of carriages)

**ballestería** /baʎeste'ria; bayeste'ria/ *f*, archery; crossbowmen

**ballestero** /baʎes'tero; bayes'tero/ *m*, archer; crossbowman; crossbow maker

**balneario** /balne'ario/ *a* pertaining to public baths; bathing; holiday; spa. *m*, watering place, spa

**balompié** /balom'pie/ *m*, football (game)

**balón** /ba'lon/ *m*, large ball; football; *Chem.* balloon; bundle; bale. **b. de ensayo,** *Fig.* feeler

**baloncesto** /balon'θesto; balon'sesto/ *m*, *Sports.* basketball

**balota** /ba'lota/ *f*, ballot

**balotaje** /balo'tahe/ *m*, balloting; run-off election

**balotar** /balo'tar/ *vi* to ballot

**balsa** /'balsa/ *f*, pond; raft

**balsadera** /balsa'ðera/ *f*, ferry

**balsámico** /bal'samiko/ *a* balmy

**bálsamo** /'balsamo/ *m*, balm

**balsero** /bal'sero/ *m*, ferryman; rafter (person fleeing a country by raft, rowboat, etc.)

**balso** /'balso/ *m*, *Naut.* sling

**báltico** /'baltiko/ *a* Baltic. **el Mar Báltico** the Baltic Sea

**baluarte** /ba'luarte/ *m*, bulwark; bastion; protection, defense

**bambalina** /bamba'lina/ *f*, fly (theatrical scenery)

**bamboleante** /bambole'ante/ *a* swaying, swinging; *Fig.* tottering (e.g. empire)

**bambolearse** /bambole'arse/ *vr* to sway; swing; totter; be shaky; stagger

**bamboleo** /bambo'leo/ *m*, rocking; swinging; tottering; staggering; reeling

**bambolla** /bam'βoʎa; bam'βoya/ *f*, *Inf.* ostentation, swank

**bambú** /bam'βu/ *m*, bamboo

**banal** /ba'nal/ *a* banal, commonplace

**banana** /ba'nana/ *f*, banana

**banasta** /ba'nasta/ *f*, big basket

**banastero** /banas'tero/ **(-ra)** *n* basket maker or dealer

**banasto** /ba'nasto/ *m*, big round basket

**banca** /'banka/ *f*, bench; card game; stall; *Com.* banking

**bancada** /ban'kaða/ *f*, rowing seat

**bancal** /ban'kal/ *m*, oblong garden plot; terrace

**bancario** /ban'kario/ *a* banking, bank

**bancarrota** /banka'rrota/ *f*, bankruptcy. **hacer b.,** to go bankrupt

**banco** /'banko/ *m*, form, bench; rowing seat; settle; seat; bench; *Com.* bank; *Naut.* bar, shoal; school (of fish). **b. azul,** government benches in Spanish Parliament. **b. de arena,** sand-bank. **b. de descuento,** discount bank. **b. de emisión, banco emisor,** bank of issue. **b. de hielo,** iceberg. **b. de nivel,** benchmark

**banda** /'banda/ *f*, wide ribbon; sash; ribbon, insignia; strip; border; party, group; gang; flock (of birds); zone, belt; side (of ship); *Mus.* band; cushion (billiards); *Herald.* bar, bend. **b. elástica,** rubber band. *Naut.* **dar a la b.,** to lie along

**bandada** /ban'daða/ *f*, flock (of birds)

**bandeja** /ban'deha/ *f*, tray, salver

**bandera** /ban'dera/ *f*, banner, flag; colors, standard. **b. de popa,** ensign. **jurar la b.,** (*Mil. Nav.*) to take the oath of allegiance

**banderilla** /bande'riʎa; bande'riya/ *f*, banderilla (bullfighting)

**banderillear** /banderiʎe'ar; banderiye'ar/ *vt* to put banderillas on bulls

**banderillero** /banderi'ʎero; banderi'yero/ *m*, man who puts banderillas on bulls

**banderín** /bande'rin/ *m*, *dim* small flag; recruiting post

**banderizo** /bande'riθo; bande'riso/ *a* factious; vehement, excitable

**banderola** /bande'rola/ *f*, banderole, pennon; bannerole

**bandido** /ban'diðo/ **(-da)** *a* and *n* outlaw, fugitive. *m*, bandit; highwayman; rogue, desperado

**bando** /'bando/ *m*, proclamation, order; faction, group, party

**bandola** /ban'dola/ *f*, *Mus.* pandora, pandore

**bandolerismo** /bandole'rismo/ *m*, brigandage

**bandolero** /bando'lero/ *m*, robber, footpad, brigand

**bandolín** /bando'lin/ *m*, mandolin

**bandurria** /ban'durria/ *f*, *Mus.* mandolin

**banjo** /'banho/ *m*, banjo

**banquero** /ban'kero/ *m*, banker

**banqueta** /ban'keta/ *f*, three-legged stool; seat; footstool

**banquete** /ban'kete/ *m*, banquet, feast

**banquetear** /bankete'ar/ *vt* and *vi* to banquet

**banqueteo** /banke'teo/ *m*, banqueting, feasting

**bañado** /ba'ɲaðo/ *m*, chamber pot; *West. Hem.* marshy land, marsh; **bañados** *pl* marsh

**bañador** /baɲa'ðor/ **(-ra)** *a* bathing —*n* bather. *m*, bathing dress; bath, vat

**bañar** /ba'ɲar/ *vt* to bathe; coat, cover; dip; lave, wash; *Fig.* bathe (of sunlight, etc.) —*vr* take a bath; bathe

**bañera** /ba'ɲera/ *f*, bath attendant; bathtub

**bañista** /ba'ɲista/ *mf* bather; one who takes spa waters

**baño** /'baɲo/ *m*, bathing; bath; bathroom; bathtub; bagnio, Turkish prison; covering, coat; *pl* mineral baths, spa. **b. de mar,** sea bath. **b. de María,** double saucepan. **b. de sol,** sunbath. **casa de baños,** public baths. **cuarto de b.,** bathroom

**bao** /'bao/ *m*, *Naut.* beam

**baptisterio** /baptis'terio/ *m*, baptistery; *Eccl.* font

**baquelita** /bake'lita/ *f*, bakelite

**baqueta** /ba'keta/ *f*, ramrod; *pl* drumsticks; *Mil.* gauntlet

**bar** /bar/ *m*, bar; café

**barahúnda** /bara'unda/ *f*, See **baraúnda**

**baraja** /ba'raha/ *f*, pack (of cards); game of cards

**barajar** /bara'har/ *vt* to shuffle (cards); jumble, mix; —*vi* quarrel

**baranda** /ba'randa/ *f*, handrail, banister; cushion (of billiard table)

**barandilla** /baran'diʎa; baran'diya/ *f*, *dim* railing

**baratija** /bara'tiha/ *f*, (gen. *pl*) trifle, oddment

**baratillo** /bara'tiʎo; bara'tiyo/ *m*, second-hand article, frippery; second-hand shop or stall; bargain counter

**barato** /ba'rato/ *a* cheap; easy. *m*, bargain sale —*adv* cheaply

**baratura** /bara'tura/ *f*, cheapness

**baraúnda** /bara'unda/ *f*, uproar, confusion

**barba** /'barβa/ *f*, chin; beard; whiskers; fin; barb (of a feather); *m*, actor who plays old men. *f pl*, fibers of plants. **b. bien poblada,** a thick beard. **barbas de ballena,** whalebone. *Fig. Inf.* **echar a las barbas,** to throw in a person's face. **en la barba, en las barbas,** to ones face (e.g. *Me lo dijeron en las barbas. They* told me so to my face). **hacer la b.,** to shave; *Inf.* annoy

**barbacoa** /barβa'koa/ *f, West Hem.* barbecue; trellis (for climbing plants)

**barbado** /bar'βaðo/ *a* bearded. *m,* shoot; sucker; transplanted plant

**barbárico** /bar'βariko/ *a* barbarian; barbaric

**barbaridad** /barβari'ðað/ *f,* barbarity; blunder; atrocity; outrage; *Inf.* huge amount. **¡Qué b.!** How awful! You don't say so!

**barbarie** /bar'βarie/ *f,* barbarism; barbarity, cruelty

**barbarismo** /barβa'rismo/ *m,* barbarism; cruelty; barbarians

**bárbaro** /'barβaro/ **(-ra)** *a* and *n* barbarian —*a* fierce; headstrong; uncivilized. **como un b.,** like crazy (e.g. *estudiar como un b.,* to study like crazy)

**barbechar** /barβe'tʃar/ *vt* to plow; leave fallow

**barbecho** /bar'βetʃo/ *m, Agr.* fallow; first plowing

**barbería** /barβe'ria/ *f,* barber shop

**barbero** /bar'βero/ *m,* barber

**barbihecho** /barβi'etʃo/ *a* fresh-shaved

**barbilampiño** /barβilam'piɲo/ *a* smooth-faced, beardless, clean-shaven

**barbilindo** /barβi'lindo/ *a* dandified, dappy; *m,* dandy

**barbilla** /bar'βiʎa; bar'βiya/ *f,* point of the chin; chin. **acariciar la b.** ( **de**), to chuck under the chin

**barbiquejo** /barβi'keho/ *m, Naut.* bobstay; hat-guard

**barbudo** /bar'βuðo/ *a* heavily bearded

**barbulla** /bar'βuʎa; bar'βuya/ *f, Inf.* babble, chatter, murmur of voices

**barca** /'barka/ *f,* small boat, bark; barge. **b. de pasaje,** ferryboat. **b. plantaminas** minelayer

**barcada** /bar'kaða/ *f,* boat-load; ferry crossing

**barcaza** /bar'kaθa; bar'kasa/ *f, Naut.* lighter; barge. **b. de desembarco,** landingcraft

**barcelonés** /barθelo'nes; barselo'nes/ **(-esa)** *a* and *n* of or from Barcelona

**barcino** /bar'θino; bar'sino/ *a* ruddy (of animals); fawn and white; *Inf.* turncoat (of politicians)

**barco** /'barko/ *m,* boat; ship; hollow, rut. **b. barredero,** trawler. **b. siembraminas,** minelayer

**barda** /'barða/ *f,* horse armor; thatch; shingle; (Mexico) cement fence, cement wall

**bardal** /bar'ðal/ *m,* thatched wall; mud wall

**bardar** /bar'ðar/ *vt* to thatch

**bardo** /'barðo/ *m,* poet, bard

**bario** /'bario/ *m,* barium

**barítono** /ba'ritono/ *m,* baritone

**barloventear** /barloβente'ar/ *vi Naut.* to tack; ply to windward; *Inf.* wander about

**barlovento** /barlo'βento/ *m, Naut.* windward

**barnacla** /bar'nakla/ *m,* barnacle

**barniz** /bar'niθ; bar'nis/ *m,* varnish; glaze; smattering, veneer

**barnizar** /barni'θar; barni'sar/ *vt* to varnish; glaze

**barométrico** /baro'metriko/ *a* barometric

**barómetro** /ba'rometro/ *m,* barometer

**barón** /ba'ron/ *m,* baron

**baronesa** /baro'nesa/ *f,* baroness

**baronía** /baro'nia/ *f,* barony

**barquero** /bar'kero/ *m,* boatman; bargee; *Ent.* waterboatman

**barquillero** /barki'ʎero; barki'yero/ *m,* seller of wafers; waffle-iron

**barquillo** /bar'kiʎo; bar'kiyo/ *m,* wafer, cornet

**barquín** /bar'kin/ *m,* furnace bellows

**barra** /'barra/ *f,* bar; ingot; railing (in courtroom); sandbank; fault (in cloth); lever, crossbar; (in cricket) bail; *Mus.* bar. **b. de jabón de afeitar,** shaving-stick. **a barras derechas,** without deceit

**barrabasada** /barraβa'saða/ *f, Inf.* wilfulness, escapade

**barraca** /ba'rraka/ *f,* cabin, hut; stall; sideshow. **b. de tiro,** shooting gallery

**barracón** /barra'kon/ *m,* side-show; stall

**barragana** /barra'gana/ *f,* concubine, mistress

**barranca,** /ba'rranka,/ *f,* **barranco** *m,* furrow, channel, rut; gorge; difficulty, fix

**barrancoso** /barran'koso/ *a* rutty, uneven

**barredor** /barre'ðor/ **(-ra)** *n* sweeper

**barredura** /barre'ðura/ *f,* sweeping; *pl* sweepings; rubbish

**barrena** /ba'rrena/ *f,* borer, gimlet, drill, auger. *Aer.* **b. de cola,** tail-spin

**barrenar** /barre'nar/ *vt* to drill, bore; blast (in quarries)

**barrendero** /barren'dero/ **(-ra)** *n* sweeper, scavenger

**barrenero** /barre'nero/ *m,* driller; blaster

**barreno** /ba'rreno/ *m,* blast hole; bore, drill; vanity

**barreño** /ba'rreɲo/ *m,* earthenware bowl (for dish washing, etc.)

**barrer** /ba'rrer/ *vt* to sweep; *Fig.* clear, make a clean sweep

**barrera** /ba'rrera/ *f,* barrier; barricade; *Fig.* obstacle. **b. de golpe,** automatic gate (at level crossings, etc.). **b. de minas,** minefield

**barriada** /ba'rriaða/ *f,* district; quarter (of a city)

**barrica** /ba'rrika/ *f,* cask; barrel

**barricada** /barri'kaða/ *f,* barricade

**barriga** /ba'rriga/ *f, Inf.* belly

**barrigón, barrigudo** /barri'gon, barri'guðo/ *a* potbellied

**barril** /ba'rril/ *m,* barrel; cask; water-butt

**barrilero** /barri'lero/ *m,* cooper

**barrilete** /barri'lete/ *m, dim* keg; clamp; *Naut.* mouse

**barrio** /'barrio/ *m,* district, quarter; suburb. **barrios bajos,** slums, back streets. **el otro b.,** the other world, Eternity

**barrizal** /barri'θal; barri'sal/ *m,* muddy place; claypit

**barro** /'barro/ *m,* mud; clay; earthenware drinking vessel; *Inf.* money

**barroco** /ba'rroko/ *a* baroque

**barroso** /ba'rroso/ *a* muddy; pimpled; mud-colored

**barrote** /ba'rrote/ *m,* thick iron bar; stave, bond

**barruntar** /barrun'tar/ *vt* to conjecture; suspect

**barrunto** /ba'rrunto/ *m,* conjecture; indication, sign

**bártulos** /'bartulos/ *m pl,* household goods; *Fig.* means, wherewithal

**barullo** /ba'ruʎo; ba'ruyo/ *m, Inf.* confusion, disorder; mob

**basa** /'basa/ *f,* base; *Archit.* pedestal; foundation, basis

**basalto** /ba'salto/ *m,* basalt

**basar** /ba'sar/ *vt* to base, place on a base; *Fig.* found, base; —*vr* (*with en*) rely upon, base oneself on

**basca** /'baska/ *f,* (gen. *pl*) nausea; retching; wave of anger

**báscula** /'baskula/ *f,* weighing-machine, platformscale; weigh-bridge

**base** /'base/ *f,* base; (*Chem. Geom. Mil.*) base; basis; *Archit.* pedestal; *Mus.* root. **sin b.,** baseless

**básico** /'basiko/ *a* basic

**Basilea** /basi'lea/ Basel, Basle

**basílica** /ba'silika/ *f,* palace; church, basilica

**basilisco** /basi'lisko/ *m,* basilisk; antique cannon

**basquear** /baske'ar/ *vi* to retch; feel squeamish

**bastante** /bas'tante/ *a* sufficient, enough —*adv* sufficiently; enough; fairly; a good deal; somewhat. **Hace b. calor,** It is quite hot. **Tengo b.,** I have enough. **Tenemos b. tiempo,** We have sufficient time

**bastar** /bas'tar/ *vi* to suffice. **¡Basta!** Enough! No more! Stop! **¡Basta de...!** Enough of...! **Basta decir que...,** Suffice it to say that...

**bastardía** /bastar'ðia/ *f,* bastardy, illegitimacy; baseness, meanness

**bastardilla** /bastar'ðiʎa; bastar'ðiya/ *f, Print.* italics

**bastardo** /bas'tarðo/ **(-da)** *a* bastard; spurious —*n* bastard

**bastear** /baste'ar/ *vt Sew.* to baste

**bastidor** /basti'ðor/ *m,* embroidery frame; *Art.* stretcher (for canvas); *Theat.* wing; *Mech.* underframe; chassis, carriage; frame (of a window). *Fig.* **entre bastidores,** behind the scenes

**bastilla** /bas'tiʎa; bas'tiya/ *f, Sew.* hem; bastille

**bastimentar** /bastimen'tar/ *vt* to provision; supply

**bastimento** /basti'mento/ *m,* supplies; provisioning

**bastión** /bas'tion/ *m,* bastion

**basto** /'basto/ *m,* pack-saddle; ace of clubs; clubs (cards) —*a* rude; tough; *Fig.* unpolished, rough

**bastón** /bas'ton/ *m,* cane, walking-stick; rod (of office); truncheon. **b. de junquillo,** Malacca cane. **empuñar el b.,** to take control, take over. **meter el b.,** to mediate

**bastonear** /bastoneˈar/ *vt* to cane; stir with a stick

**basura** /baˈsura/ *f,* rubbish, refuse; dung; sweepings

**basurero** /basuˈrero/ *m,* dustman; dunghill, rubbish dump; kitchen middens; dust-bin

**bata** /ˈbata/ *f,* dressing-gown; smoking-jacket; old-fashioned dress; overall, smock

**batacazo** /bataˈkaθo; bataˈkaso/ *m,* bump, noise of a fall; *Polit.* dark horse

**batahola** /bataˈola/ *f, Inf.* hurly-burly, hubbub

**batalla** /baˈtaʎa; baˈtaya/ *f,* battle; *Fig.* struggle, conflict; tournament; *Art.* battle-piece. **b. campal,** pitched battle

**batallador** /bataʎaˈðor; batayaˈðor/ *a* fighting, warlike

**batallar** /bataˈʎar; bataˈyar/ *vi* to battle, fight; dispute, argue; hesitate

**batallón** /bataˈʎon; bataˈyon/ *m,* battalion

**batanero** /bataˈnero/ *m,* fuller

**batata** /baˈtata/ *f,* sweet potato

**batayola** /bataˈyola/ *f, Naut.* rail

**batea** /baˈtea/ *f,* wooden tray; punt

**batería** /bateˈria/ *f, (Mil. Elec. Naut.)* battery. **b. de cocina,** kitchen utensils. **b. de pilas secas,** dry battery. **b. de teatro,** stage lights. **b. eléctrica,** electric battery

**baticola** /batiˈkola/ *f,* crupper

**batida** /baˈtiða/ *f,* game drive; attack; *Metall.* beating

**batido** /baˈtiðo/ *a* beaten (of metals); shot (of silk); trodden, worn (roads, etc.). *m, Cul.* batter; hunting party

**batidor** /batiˈðor/ *m,* beater; scout; outrider; hair comb; *Cul.* whisk. **b. de oro** ( *or* **de plata**), gold (*or* silver) beater

**batiente** /baˈtiente/ *m,* jamb (of door, etc.); damper (piano); leaf (of door); place where sea beats against cliffs, etc.

**batihoja** /batiˈoha/ *m,* gold beater; metal worker

**batimiento** /batiˈmiento/ *m,* beating

**batín** /baˈtin/ *m,* smoking-jacket; man's dressing-gown

**batintín** /batinˈtin/ *m,* Chinese gong

**batir** /baˈtir/ *vt* to beat, slap; demolish; dismantle, take down (stall, etc.); hammer, flatten; batter; *Fig.* beat (of sun, etc.); stir; pound; churn; comb (hair); vanquish, defeat; coin; reconnoiter, beat; throw down or drop; —*vr* fight; swoop (birds of prey). **b. palmas,** to clap, applaud

**batista** /baˈtista/ *f,* cambric, batiste

**baturrillo** /batuˈrriʎo; batuˈrriyo/ *m,* hotchpotch (gen. food); *Inf.* farrago, medley

**batuta** /baˈtuta/ *f,* baton, conductor's wand. **llevar la b.,** *Inf.* boss the show, call the music, be in charge, to rule the roost

**baúl** /baˈul/ *m,* trunk; *Inf.* belly. **b. escaparate** *or* **b. mundo,** wardrobe trunk

**bauprés** /bauˈpres/ *m, Naut.* bowsprit

**bausán** /bauˈsan/ **(-ana)** *n* guy, strawman; puppet; fool, idiot; lazybones

**bautismo** /bauˈtismo/ *m,* baptism

**bautista** /bauˈtista/ *m,* baptizer, baptist. **San Juan B.,** St. John the Baptist

**bautisterio** /bautisˈterio/ *m,* baptistery

**bautizar** /bautiˈθar; bautiˈsar/ *vt* to baptize, christen; *Inf.* nickname; *Inf.* water (wine); accidentally shower with water

**bautizo** /bauˈtiθo; bauˈtiso/ *m,* baptism; christening party

**bávaro** /ˈbaβaro/ **(-ra)** *a* and *n* Bavarian

**baya** /ˈbaia/ *f,* berry

**bayadera** /bayaˈðera/ *f,* Indian dancing girl

**bayeta** /baˈyeta/ *f,* baize; flannel

**bayo** /ˈbayo/ **(-ya)** *a* bay (of horses)

**Bayona** /baˈyona/ Bayonne

**bayoneta** /bayoˈneta/ *f,* bayonet. **b. calada,** fixed bayonet

**bayonetazo** /bayoneˈtaθo; bayoneˈtaso/ *m,* bayonet thrust

**baza** /ˈbaθa; ˈbasa/ *f,* tricks taken (playing cards). *Fig. Inf.* **meter b.,** to stick one's oar in

**bazar** /baˈθar; baˈsar/ *m,* bazaar; shop, store; department store

**bazo** /ˈbaθo; ˈbaso/ *m, Anat.* spleen —*a* yellow-brown

**bazucar, bazuquear** /baθuˈkar, baθukeˈar; basuˈkar, basukeˈar/ *vt* to shake or stir (liquids)

**bazuqueo** /baθuˈkeo; basuˈkeo/ *m,* shaking or stirring of liquids

**be** /be/ *f,* letter B. *m,* baa

**beata** /beˈata/ *f,* devout woman; *Inf.* pious hypocrite, prude; Sister of Mercy; over-religious woman

**beatería** /beateˈria/ *f,* sanctimoniousness; bigotry

**beatificación** /beatifikaˈθion; beatifikaˈsion/ *f,* beatification

**beatificar** /beatifiˈkar/ *vt* to make happy; sanctify; beatify

**beatífico** /beaˈtifiko/ *a* beatific

**beatitud** /beatiˈtuð/ *f,* blessedness, beatitude; happiness

**beato** /beˈato/ **(-ta)** *a* happy; blessed, beatified; devout; prudish —*n* devout person; over-pious person

**bebé** /beˈβe/ *m,* baby

**bebedero** /beβeˈðero/ *a* drinkable. *m,* drinking trough or place

**bebedizo** /beβeˈðiθo; beβeˈðiso/ *a* drinkable. *m,* draught of medicine; love-potion; poisonous drink

**bebedor** /beβeˈðor/ **(-ra)** *a* drinkable —*n* drinker; toper

**beber** /beˈβer/ *vt* to drink; absorb; —*vi* toast, drink to the health (of); tipple. *m,* drinking; drink

**bebida** /beˈβiða/ *f,* drink; beverage; alcoholic liquor

**beca** /ˈbeka/ *f,* academic scarf or sash; scholarship, exhibition

**becado, becario** /beˈkaðo, beˈkario/ *m,* exhibitioner, scholarship holder

**becerra** /beˈθerra; beˈserra/ *f,* calf; *Bot.* snapdragon

**becerro** /beˈθerro; beˈserro/ *m,* bullock; bull calf; calf-skin. **b. marino,** *Zool.* seal

**Beda el Venerable** /ˈbeða el beneˈraβle/ the Venerable Bede

**bedel** /beˈðel/ *m,* beadle; servitor, university porter

**beduino** /beˈðuino/ **(-na)** *a* and *n* Bedouin. *m,* savage, bloodthirsty man

**befar** /beˈfar/ *vt* to mock, ridicule

**befo** /ˈbefo/ *a* thick-lipped; knock-kneed. *m,* animal's lip

**begonia** /beˈgonia/ *f, Bot.* begonia

**bejín** /beˈhin/ *m, Bot.* puff-ball; spoiled child

**bejuco** /beˈhuko/ *m,* rattan

**beldad** /belˈdað/ *f,* beauty; belle

**beldar** /belˈdar/ *vt Agr.* to winnow

**Belén** /beˈlen/ Bethlehem

**belén** /beˈlen/ *m,* nativity, manger; *Inf.* bedlam; *Inf.* gossip

**belfo** /ˈbelfo/ *a* thick-lipped

**belga** /ˈbelga/ *a* and *mf* Belgian

**Bélgica** /ˈbelhika/ Belgium

**bélgico** /ˈbelhiko/ *a* Belgian

**Belgrado** /belˈgraðo/ Belgrade

**Belice** /beˈliθe; beˈlise/ Belize

**belicista** /beliˈθista; beliˈsista/ *adj* war, militaristic; *mf* warmonger

**bélico** /ˈbeliko/ *a* warlike, military

**belicosidad** /belikosiˈðað/ *f,* bellicosity

**belicoso** /beliˈkoso/ *a* bellicose, aggressive; warlike

**beligerancia** /beliheˈranθia; beliheˈransia/ *f,* belligerency

**beligerante** /beliheˈrante/ *a* and *mf* belligerent

**belitre** /beˈlitre/ *a Inf.* knavish, cunning

**bellaco** /beˈʎako; beˈyako/ **(-ca)** *a* artful, cunning —*n* knave

**belladona** /beʎaˈðona; beyaˈðona/ *f,* belladonna

**bellaquería** /beʎakeˈria; beyakeˈria/ *f,* roguery, knavery, cunning

**bellasombra** /beʎaˈsombra; beyaˈsombra/ *f,* umbra tree

**belleza** /beˈʎeθa; beˈyesa/ *f,* beauty, loveliness, fairness

**bello** /ˈbeʎo; ˈbeyo/ *a* beautiful

**bellota** /be'ʎota; be'yota/ *f*, acorn; carnation bud; ornamental button, knob

**bellote** /be'ʎote; be'yote/ *m*, round-headed nail

**bemol** /be'mol/ *a* and *m*, *Mus.* flat. *Inf.* **tener bemoles,** to be thorny, be difficult

**bencina** /ben'θina; ben'sina/ *f*, benzine; gasoline

**bendecir** /bende'θir; bende'sir/ *vt irr* to praise, extol; bless; dedicate, consecrate. See **decir**

**bendición** /bendi'θion; bendi'sion/ *f*, benediction; blessing; consecration; *pl* marriage ceremony. **b. de la mesa,** grace before meals

**bendito** /ben'dito/ *a* holy, blessed; fortunate; simple. **ser un b.,** to be a simpleton; be a good soul. **¡Benditos los ojos que te ven!** It's so nice to see you!

**benedictino** /beneði'ktino/ **(-na)** *a* and *n* Benedictine. *m*, Benedictine liqueur

**beneficencia** /benefi'θenθia; benefi'sensia/ *f*, beneficence; charitable institutions

**beneficiación** /benefiθia'θion; benefisia'sion/ *f*, benefaction

**beneficiado** /benefi'θiaðo; benefi'siaðo/ **(-da)** *n* beneficiary. *m*, incumbent of a benefice

**beneficiador** /benefiθia'ðor; benefisia'ðor/ **(-ra)** *n* benefactor

**beneficiar** /benefi'θiar; benefi'siar/ *vt* to benefit; improve; cultivate (land); exploit (mine); purchase (directorship, etc.); sell at a loss (bonds, etc.)

**beneficiario** /benefi'θiario; benefi'siario/ **(-ia)** *n* beneficiary

**beneficiencia** /benefi'θienθia; benefi'siensia/ *f*, beneficence, charity

**beneficio** /bene'fiθio; bene'fisio/ *m*, benefit; profit; cultivation (land, etc.); working (mine); *Eccl.* benefice; *Theat.* benefit

**beneficioso** /benefi'θioso; benefi'sioso/ *a* beneficial; useful

**benéfico** /be'nefiko/ *a* beneficent; kind, helpful; charitable

**benemérito** /bene'merito/ *a* benemeritus, worthy, meritorious

**beneplácito** /bene'plaθito; bene'plasito/ *m*, approbation; consent

**benevolencia** /beneβo'lenθia; beneβo'lensia/ *f*, benevolence, goodwill

**benévolo** /be'neβolo/ *a* benevolent, kind

**Bengala** /beŋ'gala/ Bengal

**bengalí** /beŋga'li/ *a* and *mf* Bengali

**benignidad** /benigni'ðað/ *f*, kindness; mildness (of the weather, etc.)

**benigno** /be'nigno/ *a* kind; benign; mild; balmy

**beodo** /be'oðo/ **(-da)** *a* drunk, intoxicated —*n* drunkard

**Berbería** /berβe'ria/ Barbary

**bereber** /bere'βer/ *a* and *mf* Berber

**berenjena** /beren'hena/ *f*, eggplant

**bergante** /ber'gante/ *m*, rascal, rogue

**bergantín** /bergan'tin/ *m*, *Naut.* brig, brigantine

**berilo** /be'rilo/ *m*, beryl

**Berlín** /ber'lin/ Berlin

**berlinés** /ber'lines/ **(-esa)** *a* and *n* of or from Berlin

**bermejear** /bermehe'ar/ *vi* to be or look reddish

**bermejo** /ber'meho/ *a* reddish; red; redgold; carroty (of hair)

**bermellón** /berme'ʎon; berme'yon/ *m*, vermilion

**Berna** /'berna/ Berne

**bernardina** /bernar'ðina/ *f*, lie; boast; gibberish

**bernardo** /ber'narðo/ **(-da)** *a* and *n* *Eccl.* Bernardine (Order of St. Bernard)

**berquelio** /ber'kelio/ *m*, berkelium

**berrear** /berre'ar/ *vi* to low, bellow; yell, squall; shriek; —*vr* reveal, confess

**berrido** /be'rriðo/ *m*, lowing, bellowing; *Inf.* yell

**berrinche** /be'rrintʃe/ *m*, *Inf.* tantrum, fit, fit of sulks

**berro** /'berro/ *m*, watercress

**berroqueña** /berro'keɲa/ *f*, granite

**berza** /'berθa; 'bersa/ *f*, cabbage

**besamanos** /besa'manos/ *m*, ceremony of kissing royal hand, levee; kissing fingers (in salute)

**besar** /be'sar/ *vt* to kiss; *Inf.* brush against, touch (of things); —*vr* kiss one another; *Inf.* bang into, knock against one another

**beso** /'beso/ *m*, kiss; knock, collision

**bestia** /'bestia/ *f*, quadruped (especially horses or mules); beast. *mf Inf.* nasty piece of work. **b. de carga,** beast of burden. **como una b.,** like a dog (e.g. *Trabajo como una b.* I work like a dog)

**bestial** /bes'tial/ *a* bestial; brutal; beastly

**bestialidad** /bestiali'ðað/ *f*, brutality; bestiality; beastliness

**bestialismo** /bestia'lismo/ *m*, bestiality (sexual orientation)

**besuquear** /besuke'ar/ *vt Inf.* to cover with kisses; —*vr Inf.* spoon, make love

**besuqueo** /besu'keo/ *m*, *Inf.* kissing and spooning

**bético** /'betiko/ *a* Andalusian

**betún** /be'tun/ *m*, bitumen; shoe blacking; kind of cement. **b. de Judea** *or* **b. judaico,** asphalt

**bey** /bei/ *m*, bey

**bezo** /'beθo; 'beso/ *m*, blubber lip; proud flesh (of a wound)

**bezudo** /be'θuðo; be'suðo/ *a* thick-lipped

**biberón** /biβe'ron/ *m*, feeding bottle

**Biblia** /'biβlia/ *f*, Bible

**bíblico** /'biβliko/ *a* biblical

**bibliófilo** /biβli'ofilo/ *m*, bibliophile

**bibliografía** /biβliogra'fia/ *f*, bibliography

**bibliográfico** /biβlio'grafiko/ *a* bibliographical

**biblioteca** /biβlio'teka/ *f*, library; book series. **b. por subscripción,** circulating library

**bibliotecario** /biβliote'kario/ **(-ia)** *n* librarian

**bibliotecnia,** **bibliotecología,** **biblioteconomía** /biβlio'teknia, biβlioteko'lohia, biβliotekono'mia/ *f*, library science

**bicarbonato** /bikarβo'nato/ *m*, bicarbonate

**bíceps** /'biθeps; 'biseps/ *m*, biceps

**bicho** /'bitʃo/ *m*, any small animal or reptile; quadruped; fighting bull; scarecrow, sight. **b. viviente,** *Inf.* living soul. **mal b.,** rogue

**bicicleta** /biθi'kleta; bisi'kleta/ *f*, bicycle, bike. **ir** ( *or* **andar** *or* **montar**) **en b.,** to bicycle, bike, go by bicycle, go bike

**bicoca** /bi'koka/ *f*, *Inf.* trifle, bagatelle

**bicolor** /biko'lor/ *a* bicolored

**bidé** /bi'ðe/ *m*, bidet

**biela** /'biela/ *f*, axle-tree; connecting-rod; big-end

**bielda** /'bielda/ *f*, pitchfork; *Agr.* winnowing

**bien** /bien/ *m*, ideal goodness, perfection; benefit, advantage; welfare; *pl* property, wealth —*adv* well; willingly; happily; perfectly; easily; enough, sufficient; all right! very well! **b. que,** although. **b. de equipo,** capital good. **bienes muebles,** movables, goods and chattels. **bienes raíces,** real estate. **el B. y el Mal,** Good and Evil. **¡Está b.!** All right! **no b.,** scarcely, as soon as. **si b.,** although, even if. **¿Y b.?** And so what? Well, then; What next?

**bienal** /bie'nal/ *a* biennial

**bienamado** /biena'maðo/ *a* dearly beloved

**bienandante** /bienan'dante/ *a* prosperous; happy

**bienandanza** /bienan'danθa; bienan'dansa/ *f*, happiness, welfare; prosperity

**bienaventurado** /bienaβentu'raðo/ *a* blessed, holy; happy; *Inf.* over-simple, innocent, foolish

**bienaventuranza** /bienaβentu'ranθa; bienaβentu'ransa/ *f*, blessedness

**bienestar** /bienes'tar/ *m*, wellbeing; ease; comfort

**bienhablado** /biena'βlaðo/ *a* well-spoken; civil, polite

**bienhadado** /biena'ðaðo/ *a* fortunate, happy

**bienhechor** /biene'tʃor/ **(-ra)** *a* kind, helpful —*n* benefactor

**bienintencionado** /bieninten θio'naðo; bieninten sio'naðo/ *a* well-meaning

**bienio** /'bienio/ *m*, biennium, space of two years, period of two years

**bienquisto** /bien'kisto/ *a* respected; generally esteemed

**bienvenida** /biembe'niða/ *f*, safe or happy arrival; welcome. **dar la b.,** to welcome

**bienvivir** /biembi'βir/ *vi* to live comfortably; live decently or uprightly

**bies** /bies/ *m*, bias, cross; slant

**biftec** /bif'tek/ *m*, beefsteak

**bifurcación** /bifurka'θion; bifurka'sion/ f, bifurcation; fork, branch, junction

**bifurcarse** /bifur'karse/ vr to fork, branch

**bigamia** /bi'gamia/ f, bigamy

**bígamo** /'bigamo/ **(-ma)** a bigamous —n bigamist

**bigornia** /bi'gornia/ f, anvil

**bigote** /bi'gote/ m, moustache; pl whiskers

**bigotudo** /bigo'tuðo/ a moustached, whiskered

**bikini** /bi'kini/ m, bikini

**bilateral** /bilate'ral/ a bilateral

**bilbaíno** /bilβa'ino/ a pertaining to or native of Bilbao

**bilingüe** /bi'liŋgue/ a bilingual

**bilioso** /bi'lioso/ a bilious

**bilis** /'bilis/ f, bile

**billar** /bi'ʎar; bi'yar/ m, billiards; billiard table

**billete** /bi'ʎete; bi'yete/ m, note, short letter; ticket; banknote. **b. circular,** excursion ticket. **b. de abono,** season ticket. **b. de andén,** platform ticket. **b. de banco,** banknote. **b. de favor,** free ticket. **b. de ida y vuelta,** round trip ticket. **b. entero,** full fare. **b. kilométrico,** tourist ticket. **b. sencillo,** one-way. **medio b.,** half-fare

**billón** /bi'ʎon; bi'yon/ m, billion

**bimestral** /bimes'tral/ a bimonthly

**bimestre** /bi'mestre/ a bimonthly. m, two months' duration; money paid or received at two-monthly intervals

**bimotor** /bimo'tor/ a two-motor. m, twin-engined aircraft

**binario** /bi'nario/ a binary

**binóculo** /bi'nokulo/ m, opera glasses

**binomio** /bi'nomio/ a and m, binomial

**biodiversidad** f, biodiversity

**biofísica** /bio'fisika/ f, biophysics

**biografía** /biogra'fia/ f, biography

**biográfico** /bio'grafiko/ a biographical

**biógrafo** /'biografo/ **(-fa)** n biographer; (Chile) movie theater (e.g. ¡Vamos al biógrafo! Let's go to the movies!)

**biología** /biolo'hia/ f, biology

**biológico** /bio'lohiko/ a biological

**biólogo** /'biologo/ m, biologist

**biombo** /'biombo/ m, screen

**bioquímica** /bio'kimika/ f, biochemistry

**bioquímico** /bio'kimiko/ m, biochemist

**bipartido** /bipar'tiðo/ a bipartite

**bípedo** /'bipeðo/ a and m, biped

**biplano** /bi'plano/ m, biplane

**biplaza** /bi'plaθa; biplasa/ a two-seater

**birla** /'birla/ f, skittle

**birlar** /bir'lar/ vt to bowl from where the bowl stopped; Inf. knock down; snatch away; Inf. rob

**birlocha** /bir'lotʃa/ f, child's kite

**birlocho** /bir'lotʃo/ m, barouche

**Birmania** /bir'mania/ Burma

**birmano** /bir'mano/ **(-na)** a and n Burmese

**birreta** /bi'rreta/ f, biretta

**birrete** /bi'rrete/ m, biretta; university cap; cap

**bis** /bis/ adv twice; repeat; encore —a duplicate; **B** (in addresses, e.g., Calle de Alcalá 18bis, 18b Alcalá St.)

**bisabuela** /bisa'βuela/ f, great-grandmother

**bisabuelo** /bisa'βuelo/ m, great-grandfather

**bisagra** /bi'sagra/ f, hinge; shoemaker's polisher

**bisbís** /bis'βis/ m, game of chance

**bisbisar** /bisβi'sar/ vt Inf. to mutter; whisper

**bisbiseo** /bisβi'seo/ m, Inf. muttering; murmuring; whispering

**bisecar** /bise'kar/ vt to bisect

**bisección** /bisek'θion; bisek'sion/ f, Geom. bisection

**bisectriz** /bisek'triθ; bisek'tris/ f, bisector

**bisel** /bi'sel/ m, bevel, chamfer

**bisiesto** /bi'siesto/ a leap and m, leap (year)

**bisílabo** /bi'silaβo/ a two-syllabled

**bismuto** /bis'muto/ m, bismuth

**bisnieto** /bis'nieto/ **(-ta)** n great-grandchild

**bisonte** /bi'sonte/ m, bison

**bisoño** /bi'soɲo/ **(-ña)** a inexperienced, raw —n recruit; Inf. greenhorn

**bistec** /bis'tek/ m, beef steak

**bisturí** /bistu'ri/ m, surgical knife

**bisunto** /bi'sunto/ a grubby, greasy

**bisutería** /bisute'ria/ f, imitation jewelry

**bituminoso** /bitumi'noso/ a bituminous

**bivalvo** /bi'βalβo/ a bivalve

**Bizancio** /bi'θanθio; bi'sansio/ Byzantium

**bizantinismo** /biθanti'nismo; bisanti'nismo/ m, Byzantinism

**bizantino** /biθan'tino; bisan'tino/ a Byzantine

**bizarría** /biθa'rria; bisa'rria/ f, handsomeness; dash; verve; gallantry, courage; magnificence; liberality; whim, caprice

**bizarro** /bi'θarro; bi'sarro/ a handsome; dashing; gallant, courageous; liberal; splendid, magnificent

**bizcaitarrismo** /biθkaita'rrismo; biskaita'rrismo/ m, doctrine of Basque autonomy; Basque autonomy movement

**bizco** /'biθko; 'bisko/ a squint-eyed, cross-eyed

**bizcocho** /biθ'kotʃo; bis'kotʃo/ m, biscuit; sponge-cake; bisque

**bizma** /'biθma; 'bisma/ f, poultice. **poner bizmas,** to poultice

**biznieto** /biθ'nieto; bis'nieto/ n See **bisnieto**

**blanca** /'blanka/ f, old Spanish coin; Inf. penny; Mus. minim. **sin b.,** penniless

**blanco** /'blanko/ a white; fair-skinned; blank, vacant; Inf. cowardly. m, target; blank left in writing; white person; interval. **b. de España,** whiting. **b. de la uña,** half-moon of the nail. **dar en el b.,** to hit the mark. **en b.,** blank, unused; Inf. in vain; uncomprehendingly; (of nights) sleepless

**blancor,** /blan'kor,/ m. **blancura** f, whiteness; fairness (of skin)

**blandear** /blande'ar/ vt to moderate, soothe; brandish; —vi Fig. give way, yield

**blandir** /blan'dir/ vt to brandish, wield, flourish

**blando** /'blando/ a soft; mild (weather); delicate; kind; peaceable; delicate, effeminate; Inf. cowardly

**blandón** /blan'don/ m, wax taper

**blandura** /blan'dura/ f, softness; poultice; blandishment, compliment; mildness (of weather); gentleness, affability; luxury

**blanquear** /blanke'ar/ vt to bleach; whitewash; whiten; —vi appear white; show white

**blanquecino** /blanke'θino; blanke'sino/ a whitish

**blanqueo** /blan'keo/ m, whitening; whitewashing; bleaching

**blanquizal** /blanki'θal; blanki'sal/ m, pipe-clay

**blasfemador** /blasfema'ðor/ **(-ra)** a blaspheming —n blasphemer

**blasfemar** /blasfe'mar/ vi to blaspheme; curse, swear

**blasfemia** /blas'femia/ f, blasphemy; insult

**blasfemo** /blas'femo/ **(-ma)** n blasphemer —a blasphemous

**blasón** /bla'son/ m, heraldry; escutcheon; glory, honor. **una familia con antiguos blasones,** a family of ancient lineage

**blasonar** /blaso'nar/ vt to blazon; —vi boast, brag, blazon abroad

**bledo** /'bleðo/ m, blade, leaf. **no importar un b.,** not to matter a straw

**blenda** /'blenda/ f, Mineral. blende

**blindado** /blin'daðo/ a Nav. armored, ironclad

**blindaje** /blin'dahe/ m, Nav. armor-plating; Mil. blindage

**blindar** /blin'dar/ vt to plate with armor, to case with steel

**blocao** /blo'kao/ m, Mil. blockhouse

**blonda** /'blonda/ f, blonde (of lace)

**blondo** /'blondo/ a fair, blond, flaxen-haired

**bloque** /'bloke/ m, block, slab

**bloquear** /bloke'ar/ vt to blockade; besiege

**bloqueo** /blo'keo/ m, blockade; siege; blocking; freezing (of assets). **violar el b.,** to run the blockade

**blusa** /'blusa/ f, blouse

**boa** /'boa/ f, boa, large snake. m, boa (fur)

**boato** /bo'ato/ m, outward show, ostentation

**bobería** /boβe'ria/ f, foolishness, stupidity

**bóbilis, bóbilis** /'boβilis, 'boβilis/ **(de)** adv Inf. free of charge; without effort

**bobina** /bo'βina/ *f*, bobbin, spool, reel; *Elec.* coil; spool (of fishing rod)

**bobo** /'boβo/ **(-ba)** *a* stupid, idiotic; simple, innocent —*n* fool. *m*, clown, jester

**boca** /'boka/ *f*, mouth; pincers (of crustaceans); entrance or exit; mouth (of a river), gulf, inlet; orifice, opening; muzzle (of guns); cutting edge (of tools); taste (of wine, etc.). **b. abajo,** face down, prone. **b. arriba,** on one's back, face up, supine. **b. del estómago,** pit of the stomach. **b. rasgada,** large mouth. **a b.,** verbally. **a b. de jarro,** point-blank. **a pedir de b.,** just as one would wish. **de b.,** by word of mouth. *Inf.* **sin decir esta b. es mía,** without a word, in silence

**bocacalle** /boka'kaʎe; boka'kaye/ *f*, entrance (to a street); street junction

**Bocacio** /bo'kaθio; bo'kasio/ Bocaccio

**bocadillo** /boka'ðiʎo; boka'ðiyo/ *m*, narrow ribbon; sandwich

**bocado** /bo'kaðo/ *m*, mouthful. **b. de reyes,** delicacy, exquisite dish (of food); snack; bite; (horse's) bit; bridle; *pl* preserved fruit cut up

**bocamanga** /boka'manga/ *f*, wrist (of sleeve)

**bocanada** /boka'naða/ *f*, mouthful (of liquid); cloud (of smoke). **b. de aire,** gust of wind

**boceto** /bo'θeto; bo'seto/ *m*, sketch; outline; roughcast model

**bocha** /'botʃa/ *f*, *Sports.* bowl; *pl* bowls

**bochorno** /bo'tʃorno/ *m*, sultry weather; heat, stuffiness; blush, hot flush; shame

**bochornoso** /botʃor'noso/ *a* sultry; shameful

**bocina** /bo'θina; bo'sina/ *f*, trumpet; megaphone; foghorn; hooter; *Auto.* horn; horn (of gramophone); *Astron.* Ursa Minor

**bocio** /'boθio; 'bosio/ *m*, *Med.* goiter

**bocoy** /bo'koi/ *m*, hogshead; large cask

**boda** /'boða/ *f*, wedding, marriage. **bodas de oro,** fiftieth (golden) anniversary. **bodas de plata,** silver wedding anniversary

**bodega** /bo'ðega/ *f*, wine-cellar; storeroom; stockroom; granary; *West Hem.* grocery store; *Naut.* hold (of ship)

**bodegón** /boðe'gon/ *m*, eating-house; tavern; *Art.* still-life; genre picture

**bóer** /'boer/ *a* and *mf* Boer

**bofes** /'bofes/ *m pl*, lungs, lights. *Inf.* **echar los b.,** to work oneself to death

**bofetada** /bofe'taða/ *f*. **bofetón** *m*, blow, slap; box on the ear

**boga** /'boga/ *f*, rowing; fashion, vogue; *Mech.* bogie. *mf* oarsman, rower. **estar en b.,** to be fashionable

**bogador** /boga'ðor/ **(-ra)** *n* rower, oarsman

**bogar** /bo'gar/ *vi* to row

**bogavante** /boga'βante/ *m*, lobster

**bogotano** /bogo'tano/ **(-na)** *a* and *n* of or from Bogotá

**bohemio** /bo'emio/ **(-ia)** *a* and *n* gipsy; bohemian; Bohemian. *m*, archer's short cloak

**boicot, boicoteo** /boi'kot, boiko'teo/ *m*, boycott

**boicotear** /boikote'ar/ *vt* to boycott

**boina** /'boina/ *f*, Basque cap; beret

**boj** /boh/ *m*, box tree; boxwood; box oak; shoemaker's tool

**bola** /'bola/ *f*, globe; ball; *Sports.* bowl; *Archit.* balloon; *Inf.* trick, lie; (Cuba) rumor. **b. de nieves,** snowball. *Inf.* **dejar rodar la b.,** to let things slide

**bolardo** /bo'larðo/ *m*, bollard

**bolchevique** /boltʃe'βike/ *a* and *mf* bolshevist

**bolchevismo** /boltʃe'βismo/ *m*, Bolshevism

**bolchevista** /boltʃe'βista/ *mf* bolshevist

**bolea** /bo'lea/ *f*, (tennis) volley; throw

**bolera** /bo'lera/ *f*, bowling alley

**bolero** /bo'lero/ *m*, bolero; dancer; *Inf.* top hat

**boleta** /bo'leta/ *f*, admission ticket; billet ticket; warrant, voucher; summons, ticket, traffic ticket

**boletín** /bole'tin/ *m*, bulletin; admission ticket; pay warrant; *Com.* price list; learned periodical. **b. de noticias,** news bulletin. **b. meteorológico,** weather report

**boliche** /bo'litʃe/ *m*, jack (in bowls); cup-and-ball

toy; small oven (for charcoal); dragnet. **juego de b.,** bowls

**bólido** /'boliðo/ *m*, *Astron.* bolide, meteor

**bolígrafo** /bo'ligrafo/ *f*, ballpoint pen

**bolillo** /bo'liʎo; bo'liyo/ *m*, bobbin (lace making)

**bolina** /bo'lina/ *f*, *Naut.* bowline; *Naut.* sounder; *Inf.* uproar, tumult

**bolita** /bo'lita/ *f*, pellet

**boliviano** /boli'βiano/ **(-na)** *a* and *n* Bolivian. *m*, silver coin

**bollo** /'boʎo; 'boyo/ *m*, bread roll; bun; bulge, bruise (in metal); *Med.* lump

**bollón** /bo'ʎon; bo'yon/ *m*, round-headed or brassheaded nail; *Bot.* bud (especially vines)

**bolo** /'bolo/ *m*, skittle, ninepin; pillow (for lace making); Cuban coin; *Med.* large pill; *Fig. Inf.* blockhead; *pl* skittles (game of)

**boloñés** /bolo'nes/ **(-esa)** *a* and *n* Bolognese

**bolsa** /'bolsa/ *f*, purse; bag; footmuff; fold, pucker; pouch; exchange, stock exchange, capital, money; prize money; *Med.* sac; *Mineral.* pocket. **b. de estudio,** scholarship grant. **b. de trabajo,** labor exchange. **b. de valores,** stock exchange. **bajar** ( *or* **subir**) **la b.,** to fall (or rise) (of stock exchange quotations). **jugar a la b.,** to speculate on the stock exchange

**bolsillo** /bol'siʎo; bol'siyo/ *m*, pocket; purse; money

**bolsista** /bol'sista/ *mf* stock-broker; speculator (on the stock exchange)

**bomba** /'bomba/ *f*, *Mech.* pump; pumping engine; bomb; *Mil.* shell; lamp globe; *Inf.* improvised verses; *Inf.* drinking bout. **¡B.!** Listen! Here goes! **b. de incendios,** fire-engine. **b. marina,** waterspout. **b. de mecha atrasada,** time bomb. **b. volante,** flying-bomb. **a prueba de b.,** bombproof. **arrojar bombas,** to bomb. *Inf.* **caer como una b.,** to be a bombshell

**bombachos** /bom'βatʃos/ *a* baggy, loose-fitting; *m pl*, plus fours

**bombardear** /bombarðe'ar/ *vt* to bombard; bomb; shell

**bombardeo** /bombar'ðeo/ *m*, bombardment, bombing; shelling

**bombardero** /bombar'ðero/ *m*, gunner, bombardier; *Aer.* bomber. **b. pesado,** *Aer.* heavy bomber. **Servicio de b.,** Bomber Command

**bombástico** /bom'βastiko/ *a* bombastic, high sounding

**bombazo** /bom'βaθo; bom'βaso/ *m*, bombshell; bomb crater; noise of an exploding bomb

**bombear** /bombe'ar/ *vt* to pump; bombard, shell; praise

**bombero** /bom'βero/ *m*, worker of a pressure pump; fireman; mortar, howitzer

**bombilla** /bom'βiʎa; bom'βiya/ *f*, *Naut.* lantern; (*Elec. Phys.*) bulb; small pump; straw for drinking maté *West Hem.*

**bombillo** /bom'βiʎo; bom'βiyo/ *m*, w.c. siphon; handpump

**bombo** /'bombo/ *m*, big drum or player of it; *Naut.* barge, ferry; ballot box; exaggerated praise

**bombón** /bom'βon/ *m*, bonbon, sweet

**bombonera** /bombo'nera/ *f*, box for toffee, etc.

**Bona** /'bona/ Bonn

**bonachón** /bona'tʃon/ *a Inf.* genial, good-natured

**bonaerense** /bonae'rense/ *a* and *mf* of or from the Province of Buenos Aires

**Bonaira** /bo'naira/ Bonaire

**bonancible** /bonan'θiβle; bonan'siβle/ *a* calm (of weather, sea)

**bonanza** /bo'nanθa; bo'nansa/ *f*, fair weather; prosperity

**bondad** /bon'dað/ *f*, goodness; kindness, helpfulness. **Tenga la b. de...,** Be good enough to..., Please...

**bondadoso** /bonda'ðoso/ *a* good, kind

**bonete** /bo'nete/ *m*, academic cap; *Zool.* reticulum (ruminants); *Eccl.* biretta. **gran b.,** important person. *Inf.* **a tente b.,** insistently

**bonetero** /bone'tero/ **(-ra)** *n* seller or maker of caps and birettas

**bonificación** /bonifika'θion; bonifika'sion/ *f*, bonus; allowance, discount

**bonito** /bo'nito/ *a* pretty; graceful; (ironical) fine. *m*, *Ichth.* bonito

**bono** /'bono/ *m*, voucher; *Com*. bond, certificate. **b. postal,** postal money order. **bono del gobierno,** government bond

**boñiga** /bo'ɲiga/ *f*, cow-dung, animal manure

**boqueada** /boke'aða/ *f*, gasp, opening of the mouth. **dar las boqueadas, estar en las últimas boqueadas,** to be at the last gasp

**boquear** /boke'ar/ *vi* to gasp; be dying; *Inf*. be at last gasp (of things); —*vt* say, utter

**boquera** /bo'kera/ *f*, sluice (in irrigation canal)

**boquerón** /boke'ron/ *m*, large opening; *Ichth*. anchovy (fish); whitebait

**boquete** /bo'kete/ *m*, narrow entrance, aperture; gap, breach; hole

**boquiabierto** /bokia'βierto/ *a* open-mouthed; amazed

**boquiancho** /bo'kiantʃo/ *a* wide-mouthed

**boquiasombrado** /bokiasom'βraðo/ *a* gaping

**boquilla** /bo'kiʎa; bo'kiya/ *f*, *dim* small mouth; mouthpiece (of wind instruments, etc.); cigar- or cigarette-holder; gas-burner; nozzle; tip (of cigarettes)

**boquirroto** /boki'rroto/ *a Inf*. loquacious, indiscreet

**borbollar** /borβo'ʎar; borβo'yar/ *vi* to bubble, foam, froth

**borbollón, borbotón** /borβo'ʎon, borβo'ton; borβo'yon, borβo'ton/ *m*, gushing, bubbling, welling up. **a borbollones,** in a torrent; hastily, impetuously

**borbónico** /bor'βoniko/ *a* Bourbon

**borbotar** /borβo'tar/ *vi* to gush out, well up

**borceguí** /borθe'gi; borse'gi/ *m*, buskin, boot

**borda** /'borða/ *f*, hut, cabin; *Naut*. gunwale

**bordado** /bor'ðaðo/ *m*, embroidery

**bordador** /borða'nðor/ **(-ra)** *n* embroiderer

**bordar** /bor'ðar/ *vt* to embroider; *Fig*. perform perfectly

**borde** /'borðe/ *m*, edge; fringe; verge; rim; mount (of a picture); brim (of a hat); side (of ship) —*a* wild (of plants); illegitimate. **estar lleno hasta los bordes,** to be full to the brim

**bordear** /borðe'ar/ *vt* to border, trim with a bordear; line (a street, e.g. *Diez mil personas bordearon las calles durante el desfile,* Ten thousand people lined the streets during the parade)

**bordelés** /bor'ðeles/ **(-esa)** *a* and *n* of or from Bordeaux

**bordillo** /bor'ðiʎo; bor'ðiyo/ *m*, curbstone, curb.

**bordo** /'borðo/ *m*, side (of ships); border, edge. **a b.,** on board

**bordón** /bor'ðon/ *m*, pilgrim's staff; monotonous repetition; refrain; *Mus*. bass string; *Fig*. guide, stay

**borgoña** /bor'goɲa/ *m*, Burgundy wine

**borgoñón** /borgo'ɲon/ **(-ona)** *a* and *n* Burgundian

**bórico** /'boriko/ *a* boric

**borla** /'borla/ *f*, tassel; puff (for powder). *Fig*. **tomar la b.,** to take one's doctorate, graduate

**borne** /'borne/ *m*, tip (of lance); *Elec*. terminal

**bornear** /borne'ar/ *vt* to bend, twist; *Archit*. hoist into position; —*vr* warp (wood)

**borra** /'borra/ *f*, yearling ewe; thickest wool; wadstuffing; lees, sediment; fluff, dust; *Inf*. trash. **b. de algodón,** cotton-waste

**borrachera** /borra'tʃera/ *f*, drunkenness; orgy, carousal; *Inf*. blunder

**borrachín** /borra'tʃin/ **(-ina)** *n* tippler, toper

**borrachito** /borra'tʃito/ *a* high (on liquor), tipsy

**borracho** /bo'rratʃo/ **(de)** *a* drunk (on), intoxicated (with); *Inf*. blind (with rage, etc.) —*n* tippler, drunkard

**borrador** /borra'ðor/ *m*, rough draft. **en borrador,** in the works (e.g. *Tiene dos ensayos en borrador,* She has two essays in the works). **estar en borrador,** to be in the works

**borradura** /borra'ðura/ *f*, erasure

**borrajear** /borrahe'ar/ *vt* to scribble

**borrar** /bo'rrar/ *vt* to erase; cross out; blot out; *Fig*. obliterate

**borrasca** /bo'rraska/ *f*, storm, tempest; peril, danger; *Inf*. orgy

**borrascosidad** /borraskosi'ðað/ *f*, storminess

**borrascoso** /borras'koso/ *a* stormy; disordered, turbulent

**borrego** /bo'rrego/ **(-ga)** *n* lamb; *Inf*. nincompoop, simpleton; *m pl*, fleecy clouds; white horses (waves)

**borrico** /bo'rriko/ **(-ca)** *n* donkey; fool. *m*, sawing-horse

**borrón** /bo'rron/ *m*, blot; rough draft; defect; *Fig*. stigma

**borroso** /bo'rroso/ *a* blurred, indistinct; full of dregs, muddy

**boscaje** /bos'kahe/ *m*, grove, group of trees, thicket

**Bósforo, el** /'bosforo, el/ the Bosporus

**bosque** /'boske/ *m*, wood, forest

**bosquejar** /boske'har/ *vt Art*. to sketch; sketch out, draft; model in rough (sculpture); outline

**bosquejo** /bos'keho/ *m*, outline, sketch; rough plan or idea; unfinished work. **en bosquejo,** grosso modo

**bostar** /bos'tar/ *m*, ox barn

**bostezar** /boste'θar; boste'sar/ *vi* to yawn

**bostezo** /bos'teθo; bos'teso/ *m*, yawning; yawn

**bota** /'bota/ *f*, small wineskin; barrel, butt; boot. **b. de montar,** riding boot. **botas de campaña,** topboots. **botas de vadear,** waders

**botada, botadura** /bo'taða, bota'ðura/ *f*, launching (of a ship)

**botador** /bota'ðor/ *m*, thrower; boating-pole; nailpuller

**botafuego** /bota'fuego/ *m*, *Mil*. linstock; *Inf*. quick-tempered, irascible person

**botalón** /bota'lon/ *m*, *Naut*. boom. **b. de foque,** jib-boom

**botánica** /bo'tanika/ *f*, botany

**botánico** /bo'taniko/ **(-ca)** *a* botanical —*n* botanist

**botar** /bo'tar/ *vt* to fling; launch (boat); *Naut*. shift the helm; —*vi* jump; bounce, rebound; rear, prance (horses)

**botarate** /bota'rate/ *m*, *Inf*. madcap, devil-may-care

**botarel, botarete** /bota'rel, bota'rete/ *m*, *Archit*. abutment, buttress, flying buttress

**botarga** /bo'targa/ *f*, motley; harlequin

**bote** /'bote/ *m*, thrust (with lance, etc.); rearing (of horse); rebound; *Aer*. bump; open boat; small bottle, jar. **b. salvavidas,** lifeboat. *Inf*. **de b. en b.,** chockfull

**botella** /bo'teʎa; bo'teya/ *f*, bottle; bottleful; flask

**botica** /bo'tika/ *f*, chemist's shop; medicines, remedies; physic; store, shop; medicine chest

**boticario** /boti'kario/ *m*, apothecary, chemist

**botija** /bo'tiha/ *f*, earthen jug; *Slang* chunky person

**botijo** /bo'tiho/ *m*, earthenware jar with spout and handle

**botillería** /botiʎe'ria; botiye'ria/ *f*, ice-cream bar

**botín** /bo'tin/ *m*, gaiter; buskin; booty

**botiquín** /boti'kin/ *m*, first-aid kit; medicine chest

**botón** /bo'ton/ *m*, bud; button; knob, handle; switch (electric); press button (bell); *Bot*. center; button (on a foil); *Mech*. stud

**botonero** /boto'nero/ **(-ra)** *n* button maker or seller

**bóveda** /b'oβeða/ *f*, *Archit*. vault, arch; crypt; cavern. **b. celeste,** sky

**bovino** /bo'βino/ *a* bovine

**boxeador** /boksea'ðor/ *m*, boxer

**boxear** /bokse'ar/ *vi Sports*. to box

**boxeo** /bok'seo/ *m*, *Sports*. boxing

**boya** /'boya/ *f*, *Naut*. buoy; float

**boyante** /bo'yante/ *a* floating; light, buoyant; prosperous

**boyar** /bo'yar/ *vi Naut*. to float

**boyera** /bo'yera/ *f*, ox-stall

**boyero** /bo'yero/ *m*, cowherd

**boza** /'boθa; 'bosa/ *f*, painter (of a boat)

**bozal** /bo'θal; bo'sal/ *m*, muzzle; nosebag; harness bells. *mf Inf*. greenhorn; —*a* wild, untamed (horses)

**bozo** /'boθo; 'boso/ *m*, down which precedes beard; muzzle; headstall; lips, snout

**bracero** /bra'θero; bra'sero/ *m*, one who offers his arm (to a lady); day laborer; strong man. **de b.,** arm-in-arm

**bracete** /bra'θete; bra'sete/ *m*, small arm. **de b.,** arm-in-arm

**bracmán** /brak'man/ *m*, Brahmin

**braga** /'braga/ *f*, (gen. *pl*) breeches; knickerbockers; hoist or pulley rope

**bragazas** /bra'gaθas; bra'gasas/ *m, Inf.* weak-willed, fellow, soft specimen

**braguero** /bra'gero/ *m, Med.* truss

**bragueta** /bra'geta/ *f*, fly (of breeches)

**brahmanismo** /brama'nismo/ *m*, Brahmanism

**bramante** /bra'mante/ *a* roaring. *m*, twine, pack-thread

**bramar** /bra'mar/ *vi* to roar; rage; *Fig.* howl (of the wind, etc.)

**bramido** /bra'miðo/ *m*, bellowing; roaring; yell of rage; *Fig.* howling (wind, sea, etc.)

**brancada** /bran'kaða/ *f*, drag net

**branquia** /'brankia/ *f*, (gen. *pl*) *Ichth.* gill

**branquial** /bran'kial/ *a* branchiate

**braquicefalia** /bra,kiθe'falia; bra,kise'falia/ *f*, brachy-cephaly

**braquiotomía** /brakioto'mia/ *f, Surg.* brachiotomy, amputation of the arms

**brasa** /'brasa/ *f*, live coal. **estar como en brasas,** to be like a cat on hot bricks

**brasero** /bra'sero/ *m*, brazier

**Brasil** /bra'sil/ Brazil

**brasileño** /brasi'leɲo/ **(-ña)** *a* and *n* Brazilian

**bravata** /bra'βata/ *f*, bravado; threat

**braveza** /bra'βeθa; bra'βesa/ *f*, ferocity, savageness; valor; violence, fury (of elements)

**bravío** /bra'βio/ *a* savage, untamed; wild (plants); uncultured

**bravo** /'braβo/ *a* valiant; surly, rude; independent, strong-minded, good, excellent; savage (animals); stormy (sea); rough, rugged; violent, angry; *Inf.* sumptuous, magnificent.

**bravura** /bra'βura/ *f*, ferocity (animals); courage (persons); boastful threat

**braza** /'braθa; 'brasa/ *f, Naut.* fathom; stroke (in swimming)

**brazado** /bra'θaðo; bra'saðo/ *m*, armful

**brazal** /bra'θal; bra'sal/ *m*, armlet, brassard

**brazalete** /braθa'lete; brasa'lete/ *m*, bracelet; brassard

**brazo** /'braθo; 'braso/ *m*, arm; upper arm; front paw; *Mech.* arm; branch (of chandelier, etc.); bough; arm (of chair); power, courage; *pl* protectors; workmen, hands. **b. de mar,** firth, arm of the sea. **a b. partido,** in unarmed fight, man to man. **con los brazos abiertos,** welcomingly; willingly, gladly. **dar los brazos(a),** to embrace. *Inf.* **hecho un b. de mar,** dressed up to the nines

**brea** /'brea/ *f*, pitch, tar; sacking, canvas

**brebaje** /bre'βahe/ *m*, beverage; unpleasant drink; *Naut.* draft (of beer, grog, etc.)

**brecha** /'bretʃa/ *f, Mil.* breach; opening; *Fig.* impression (on mind). **morir en la b.,** to fight to the last ditch; die in harness

**brécol** /'brekol/ *m, Bot.* broccoli

**brega** /'breɡa/ *f*, fight; quarrel; disappointment, trick. **andar a la b.,** to work hard. **dar b.,** to play a trick

**bregar** /bre'ɡar/ *vi* to fight; work hard; *Fig.* struggle; **bregarse con,** to tackle (a problem)

**Brema** /'brema/ Bremen

**breña** /'breɲa/ *f*, rough ground, bramble patch

**breñal** /bre'ɲal/ *m*, scrub, brushwood

**breñoso** /bre'ɲoso/ *a* rugged, rocky

**Bretaña** /bre'taɲa/ Brittany

**brete** /'brete/ *m*, fetters, shackles; *Fig.* fix, squeeze, tight spot, tight squeeze (e.g. *Estoy en un brete.* I'm in a tight spot)

**bretón** /bre'ton/ **(-ona)** *a* and *n* Breton. *m*, Breton (language)

**breva** /'breβa/ *f*, early fig; early acorn; *Fig.* advantage, "plum"; *Inf.* peach (girl); *Inf.* windfall, piece of luck; Havana cigar

**breve** /'breβe/ *a* brief; concise. *m*, papal brief. *f, Mus.* breve. **en b.,** shortly, concisely; in a short while, soon

**brevedad** /breβe'ðað/ *f*, brevity

**breviario** /bre'βiario/ *m*, breviary

**brezal** /bre'θal; bre'sal/ *m*, heath, moor

**brezo** /'breθo; 'breso/ *m, Bot.* heath

**bribón** /bri'βon/ **(-ona)** *n* rogue, ruffian —*a* knavish, dishonest; lazy

**bribonada** /briβo'naða/ *f*, knavery, mischievous trick

**bribonear** /briβone'ar/ *vi* to idle; play tricks, be a rogue

**bribonería** /briβone'ria/ *f*, rascality, vagrant life

**brida** /'briða/ *f*, bridle

**brigada** /bri'ɡaða/ *f, Mil.* brigade; *Naut.* division of fleet; beasts of burden. **brigada millonaria,** (Castroist Cuba) team of thirty sugarcane cutters who cut a million or more arrobas in one harvest

**brigadier** /briɡa'ðier/ *m*, brigadier-general

**brillante** /bri'ʎante; bri'yante/ *a* sparkling, brilliant; *Fig.* outstanding. *m*, diamond

**brillantez** /briʎan'teθ; briyan'tes/ *f*, brightness, luster; fame; *Fig.* brilliance

**brillantina** /briʎan'tina; briyan'tina/ *f*, brilliantine

**brillar** /bri'ʎar; bri'yar/ *vi* to shine, sparkle, gleam, glisten; *Fig.* be brilliant or outstanding

**brillo** /'briʎo; 'briyo/ *m*, brilliancy, brightness, shine; fame, glory; distinction, brilliance, splendor

**brincar** /brin'kar/ *vi* to spring, leap, skip, frisk; *Fig. Inf.* skip, omit; *Inf.* grow angry; —*vt* jump a child up and down

**brinco** /'brinko/ *m*, leap, spring; skip, frolicking

**brindar** /brin'dar/ *vi* to invite, provoke (of things); (with prep *a* or *por*) drink the health of, toast; —*vt* and *vi* give, present; offer; —*vr* offer one's services

**brindis** /'brindis/ *m*, toast (drink)

**brío** /'brio/ *m*, vigor; spirit, courage; gusto, verve

**brioso** /'brioso/ *a* vigorous, enterprising; spirited, courageous; dashing, lively

**briqueta** /bri'keta/ *f*, briquette

**brisa** /'brisa/ *f*, breeze; grape pressings

**británico** /bri'taniko/ *a* British

**brizna** /'briθna; 'brisna/ *f*, shred, paring; blade (grass); filament, fiber; string (of bean-pod, etc.); splinter, chip

**broca** /'broka/ *f*, reel; tack (shoemaker's); *Mech.* drill, bit

**brocado** /bro'kaðo/ *m*, brocade —*a* brocade or embroidered like brocade

**brocal** /bro'kal/ *m*, puteal (of a well); mouthpiece (of wineskin); metal ring (of sword-sheath)

**brocamantón** /brokaman'ton/ *m*, large jeweled brooch

**brocatel** /broka'tel/ *m*, imitation brocade

**brocha** /'brotʃa/ *f*, brush. **b. de afeitar,** shaving brush. **de b. gorda,** crudely painted. **pintor de b. gorda,** decorator

**brochada** /bro'tʃaða/ *f*, stroke (of the brush)

**brochado** /bro'tʃaðo/ *a* brocaded, embossed

**brochadura** /brotʃa'ðura/ *f*, fastening, set of hooks and eyes

**broche** /'brotʃe/ *m*, clasp, fastening; brooch; hooks and eyes

**brochón** /bro'tʃon/ *m*, whitewash brush

**broma** /'broma/ *f*, merriment; joke, jest; ship-worm. **b. literaria,** literary hoax

**bromear** /brome'ar/ **(se)** *vi* and *vr* to joke, make fun

**bromista** /bro'mista/ *a* joking, jesting; mischievous. *mf* genial person; prankster, tease

**bromo** /'bromo/ *m*, bromine

**bromuro** /bro'muro/ *m*, bromide

**bronca** /'bronka/ *f*, Inf. shindy

**bronce** /'bronθe; 'bronse/ *m*, bronze; brass; *Poet.* gun, bell, trumpet; bronze statue; sunburn

**bronceado** /bronθe'aðo; bronse'aðo/ *a* bronzed; sunburned. *m*, sunburn

**broncear** /bronθe'ar; bronse'ar/ *vt* to bronze; sunburn

**bronco** /'bronko/ *a* rough, coarse; brittle; (of metals); harsh (voice, musical instruments); rigid, stiff; surly

**bronconeumonía** /,bronkoneumo'nia/ *f*, broncho-pneumonia

**bronquial** /bron'kial/ *a* bronchial

**bronquio** /'bronkio/ *m*, (gen. *pl*) bronchi

**bronquitis** /bron'kitis/ *f*, bronchitis

**broquel** /bro'kel/ *m*, shield; *Fig.* protection

**broquelero** /broke'lero/ *m*, shield maker; quarrel-some man

**broqueta** /bro'keta/ *f*, skewer

**brotadura** /brota'ðura/ f, budding

**brotar** /bro'tar/ vi to germinate, sprout; gush forth (water); issue forth, burst out; Fig. appear (of rash); Fig. begin to appear; —vt to bring forth; produce (of earth)

**brote** /'brote/ m, bud, sprout; Fig. germ, genesis; iota, jot, atom

**broza** /'broθa; 'brosa/ f, garden rubbish; debris; thicket

**bruces** /'bruθes; 'bruses/ (a or de) adv face downwards. **caer de b.,** to fall flat. Also with other verbs: **dar, echarse,** etc.

**bruja** /'bruha/ f, witch; owl; Inf. hag

**Brujas** /'bruhas/ Bruges

**brujear** /bruhe'ar/ vi to practice witchcraft

**brujería** /bruhe'ria/ f, witchcraft

**brujo** /'bruho/ m, magician, wizard

**brújula** /'bruhula/ f, magnetic needle; compass; mariner's compass. **b. de bolsillo,** pocket compass. **b. giroscópica,** gyrocompass

**bruma** /'bruma/ f, haze; sea-mist

**brumoso** /bru'moso/ a misty, hazy

**bruno** /'bruno/ a dark brown

**bruñido** /bru'ɲiðo/ m, polishing; burnish

**bruñidor** /bruɲi'ðor/ (-ra) a polishing —n burnisher. m, polisher (instrument)

**bruñir** /bru'ɲir/ vt to polish, burnish; Inf. apply make up

**brusco** /'brusko/ a brusque, rude; blunt; sudden, unexpected; sharp (of bends)

**Bruselas** /bru'selas/ Brussels

**bruselense** /bruse'lense/ a and mf of or from Brussels

**brusquedad** /bruske'ðað/ f, brusquerie, rudeness; bluntness; suddenness, unexpectedness; sharpness (of a bend)

**brutal** /bru'tal/ a brutal

**brutalidad** /brutali'ðað/ f, brutality; Fig. brutishness; viciousness

**bruto** /'bruto/ a stupid, unreasonable; vicious; unpolished, rough. m, animal (gen. quadruped). **en b.,** in the rough; Com. in bulk. **diamante en b.,** an uncut diamond

**bruza** /'bruθa; 'brusa/ f, strong brush; scrubbing brush

**Bs. As.** /,buenos 'aires/ abbrev. of Buenos Aires

**bu** /bu/ m, Inf. bogey man

**buba** /'buβa/ f, pustule; pl buboes

**bubónico** /bu'βoniko/ a bubonic

**bucal** /bu'kal/ a buccal

**bucanero** /buka'nero/ m, buccaneer

**Bucarest** /buka'rest/ Bucharest

**búcaro** /'bukaro/ m, arsenical clay; jar made of arsenican clay

**buceador** /buθea'ðor; busea'ðor/ m, diver

**bucear** /buθe'ar; buse'ar/ vi to work as a diver; swim under water; Fig. investigate

**bucéfalo** /bu'θefalo; bu'sefalo/ m, bucephalus; Inf. fool, blockhead

**buceo** /bu'θeo; bu'seo/ m, diving; dive; Fig. investigation

**buche** /'butʃe/ m, craw or crop; mouthful; wrinkle, pleat; Inf. stomach, belly. Fig. Inf. inmost heart

**bucle** /'bukle/ m, ringlet, curl

**bucólico** /bu'koliko/ a bucolic

**búdico** /'buðiko/ a Buddhist

**budín** /bu'ðin/ m, pudding

**budismo** /bu'ðismo/ m, Buddhism

**budista** /bu'ðista/ a and mf Buddhist

**buen** /buen/ a Abbr. of **bueno,** good. Used before m, singular nouns and infinitives used as nouns, e.g. un b. libro, a good book. el b. cantar, good singing

**buenamente** /buena'mente/ adv easily; comfortably, conveniently; willingly

**buenaventura** /buenaβen'tura/ f, good luck; fortune told from hand

**bueno** /'bueno/ (see **buen**) a good; kind; useful; convenient; pleasant; healthy; large (drink, etc.); simple, innocent; suitable; sufficient; opportune. ¡**B.!** Good!; Enough!; All right! **a buenas,** willingly. **de**

**buenas a primeras,** at first sight, from the beginning. **hacer bueno,** to prove, justify (a claim)

**buey** /buei/ m, ox. **b. suelto,** Inf. freelance; bachelor

**búfalo** /'bufalo/ (-la) n buffalo

**bufanda** /bu'fanda/ f, scarf

**bufar** /bu'far/ vi to bellow; snort; Inf. snort with rage

**bufete** /bu'fete/ m, desk, writing table; lawyer's office or practice; sideboard

**bufido** /bu'fiðo/ m, snort; bellow

**bufo** /'bufo/ a comic. m, clown, buffoon

**bufón** /bu'fon/ m, buffoon, clown; jester —a comical, clownish

**bufonada** /bufo'naða/ f, buffoonery, clowning; raillery, taunt

**bufonear** /bufone'ar/ (se) vr and vi to joke, jest, parody

**bufonería.** /bufone'ria/ See **bufonada**

**buhardilla** /buar'ðiʎa; buar'ðiya/ f, garret; skylight

**búho** /'buo/ m, owl; Inf. hermit, unsociable person

**buhonería** /buone'ria/ f, peddling, hawking; peddler's wares

**buhonero** /buo'nero/ m, pedler

**buido** /'buiðo/ a sharp-pointed; sharp

**buitre** /'buitre/ m, vulture

**bujía** /bu'hia/ f, candle; candlestick; Elec. candle-power; Auto. sparking plug

**bula** /'bula/ f, (Papal) bull

**bulbo** /'bulβo/ m, Bot. bulb. **b. dentario,** pulp (of teeth)

**bulboso** /bul'βoso/ a bulbous

**bulevar** /bule'βar/ m, boulevard, promenade

**búlgaro** /'bulgaro/ (-ra) a and n Bulgarian

**bulla** /'buʎa; 'buya/ f, noise; bustle; confusion; fuss. Inf. **meter a b.,** to throw into great confusion

**bullebulle** /buʎe'βuʎe; buye'βuye/ mf busybody; madcap

**bullente** /bu'ʎente; bu'yente/ adj boiling, bubbling; frothy (beer); swarming, teeming. **b. de sol,** drenched in sunlight, sun-drenched

**bullicio** /bu'ʎiθio; bu'yisio/ m, noise, bustle; rioting; uproar

**bullicioso** /buʎi'θioso; buyi'sioso/ a noisy, merry, boisterous; rebellious; lively, restless

**bullir** /bu'ʎir; bu'yir/ vi to boil; foam, bubble; Fig. seethe; Fig. swarm (insects); bustle; —vt move, stir; —vr stir, give signs of life

**bulto** /'bulto/ m, bulk, mass, size; form of person, etc., seen indistinctly; swelling; bust, statue; bundle, package, piece of luggage; pillowcase. Fig. Inf. **poner de b.,** to put clearly, emphasize. **ser de b.,** to be obvious

**bumerang** /bume'raŋ/ m, boomerang

**buñolería** /buɲole'ria/ f, bun or waffle shop

**buñuelo** /bu'ɲuelo/ m, bun; waffle, fritter; Fig. botch

**buque** /'buke/ m, ship, vessel; capacity of ship; ship's hull. **b. barreminas,** minesweeper. **b. de guerra,** battleship, man-of-war. **b. de vapor,** steamer. **b. de vela,** sailing ship. **b. escuela,** trainingship. **b. mercante,** merchant vessel. **b. submarino,** submarine. **b. transbordador,** train-ferry

**burbuja** /bur'βuha/ f, bubble

**burbujear** /burβuhe'ar/ vi to bubble

**burdel** /bur'ðel/ m, brothel; Inf. untidy, noisy place —a lascivious

**burdo** /'burðo/ a coarse, tough

**burgalés** /burga'les/ (-esa) a and n of or from Burgos

**burgo** /'burgo/ m, borough, burgh

**burgomaestre** /burgoma'estre/ m, burgomaster

**burgués** /bur'ges/ (-esa) a and n bourgeois

**burguesía** /burge'sia/ f, bourgeoisie

**buriel** /bu'riel/ a dark red

**buril** /bu'ril/ m, burin, engraver's tool

**burla** /'burla/ f, mockery; joke, jest; trick. **b. burlando,** without effort; negligently. **de burlas,** in fun. **entre burlas y veras,** half-jokingly

**burlador** /burla'ðor/ a mocking. m, libertine, rake; deceiver

**burlar** /bur'lar/ vt to play a trick on; deceive; disappoint; —vr and vi (with de) make fun of, laugh at, ridicule

**burlesco** /bur'lesko/ a jocular, comic, burlesque

**burlón** /bur'lon/ **(-ona)** *a* joking; mocking, scoffing —*n* joker; scoffer

**buró** /bu'ro/ *m,* bureau, writing-desk

**burocracia** /buro'kraθia; buro'krasia/ *f,* bureaucracy

**burócrata** /bu'rokrata/ *mf* bureaucrat

**burocrático** /buro'kratiko/ *a* bureaucratic

**burocratismo** /burokra'tismo/ *m,* bureaucracy, red tape

**burra** /'burra/ *f,* she-ass; foolish, unteachable woman; painstaking, patient woman

**burrajo** /bu'rraho/ *m,* dry stable dung used as fuel

**burro** /'burro/ *m,* ass, donkey; sawing-horse; card game

**bursátil** /bur'satil/ *a Com.* relating to the stock exchange; financial

**busca** /'buska/ *f,* search; hunting party; research; pursuit

**buscado** /bus'kaðo/ *adj* deliberate, intentional (negligence, etc.)

**buscador** /buska'ðor/ **(-ra)** *n* searcher; investigator. *m,* finder (of a camera, etc.)

**buscapié** /buska'pie/ *m,* hint or suggestion; *Fig.* feeler

**buscapiés** /buska'pies/ *m,* squib, cracker

**buscar** /bus'kar/ *vt* to search, look for; pursue. **ir a b.,** to go to look for, go and get; bring, fetch

**buscarruidos** /buska'rruiðos/ *mf Inf.* quarrel maker

**buscavidas** /buska'βiðas/ *mf Inf.* busybody; *Inf.* gogetter

**buscón** /bus'kon/ **(-ona)** *n* searcher; pickpocket, thief, swindler, rogue

**buscona** /bus'kona/ *f,* prostitute

**busilis** /bu'silis/ *m, Inf.* knotty problem, snag; **ahí está el b.,** there's the rub; core, main point

**búsqueda** /'buskeða/ **(de)** *f,* search (for)

**busto** /'busto/ *m, Art.* bust, head and shoulders

**butaca** /bu'taka/ *f,* armchair; *Theat.* orchestra stall; seat (in movies, etc.)

**butifarra** /bu'tifarra/ *f,* sausage made principally in Catalonia and the Balearic Islands; *Inf.* badly fitting stocking

**buz** /buθ/ *m,* respectful kiss

**buzo** /'buθo; 'buso/ *m,* diver

**buzón** /bu'θon; bu'son/ *m,* mailbox; letter-box; canal, channel; sluice

# C

**C.** /k/ abbrev. of ciudadano

**¡ca!** /ka/ *interj* Fancy! Oh no!

**cabal** /ka'βal/ *a* just, exact; perfect; complete; faultless —*interj* Exactly! **por sus cabales,** according to plan; perfectly

**cábala** /'kaβala/ *f,* cabala; divination; *Inf.* intrigue. **hacer cábalas,** to venture a guess

**cabalgada** /kaβal'gaða/ *f,* cavalcade; foray, raid

**cabalgador** /kaβalga'ðor/ **(-ra)** *n* rider, horseman

**cabalgadura** /kaβalga'ðura/ *f,* riding horse; beast of burden

**cabalgar** /kaβal'gar/ *vi* to ride a horse; ride in procession

**cabalgata** /kaβal'gata/ *f,* cavalcade; troop of horse

**cabalístico** /kaβa'listiko/ *a* cabalistic; mysterious

**caballa** /ka'βaʎa; ka'βaya/ *f,* mackerel

**caballada** /kaβa'ʎaða; kaβa'yaða/ *f,* pack of horses; stud (of horses)

**caballeresco** /kaβaʎe'resko; kaβaye'resko/ *a* gentlemanly; knightly; chivalrous

**caballerete** /kaβaʎe'rete; kaβaye'rete/ *m, dim Inf.* foppish young man, dandy

**caballería** /kaβaʎe'ria; kaβaye'ria/ *f,* riding animal; cavalry; knightly deed or quest; any of Spanish Military Orders; knight-errantry; knighthood; chivalry; share of the spoils of war; horsemanship. **c. andante,** knight-errantry. **c. ligera,** *Mil.* light horse. **c. mayor,** horses, mares, mules. **c. menor,** asses, donkeys

**caballeriza** /kaβaʎe'riθa; kaβaye'risa/ *f,* stable; stud of horses; staff of a stable

**caballerizo** /kaβaʎe'riθo; kaβaye'riso/ *m,* head stable-groom. **c. mayor del rey,** Master of the King's Horse

**caballero** /kaβa'ʎero; kaβa'yero/ *m,* gentleman; cavalier; knight. **c. andante,** knight-errant. *Inf.* **c. de industria,** adventurer, sharper. **el C. de la Mancha,** the Knight of La Mancha. **el C. Sin Miedo y Sin Tacha,** the Seigneur de Bayart. **c. del hábito,** knight of one of the Spanish Military Orders. **c. novel,** untried knight. **armar c.,** to dub a knight

**caballerosidad** /kaβaʎerosi'ðað; kaβayerosi'ðað/ *f,* gentlemanliness; nobility; generosity; chivalry

**caballeroso** /kaβaʎe'roso; kaβaye'roso/ *a* gentlemanly; noble; generous; chivalrous

**caballete** /kaβa'ʎete; kaβa'yete/ *m,* ridge (of a roof); *Mil.* wooden horse; brake (for flax and hemp); *Agr.* furrow; easel; sawing-frame; trestle; bridge (of the nose)

**caballito** /kaβa'ʎito; kaβa'yito/ *m, dim* little horse; *pl* merry-go-round; automatic horse gambling game; circus equestrian act. **c. del diablo,** dragonfly

**caballo** /ka'βaʎo; ka'βayo/ *m,* horse; (chess) knight; (Spanish cards) queen; sawing-frame; *pl* cavalry. **c. balancín,** rocking horse. **c. de batalla,** war-horse; *Fig.* hobby-horse; forte; crux. **c. de cartón,** hobby-horse; rocking horse. **c. de carrera,** racehorse. **c. de tiro,** draft-horse. **c. de vapor,** horsepower. **c. marino,** sea-horse. **a c.,** on horseback. **A c. regalado no le mires el diente,** Never look a gift horse in the mouth. **caer bien a c.,** to have a good seat (on a horse). **ser un c. loco en una cacharrería,** to be like a bull in a china shop

**cabaña** /ka'βaɲa/ *f,* hut, cabin, cottage; flock (of sheep); drove (of mules); *Art.* pastoral scene; balk (billiards)

**cabaret** /kaβa'ret/ *m,* cabaret, nightclub

**cabaretero** /kaβare'tero/ *m,* nightclub owner

**cabecear** /kaβeθe'ar; kaβese'ar/ *vi* to nod; shake the head in disapproval; move the head from side to side; toss the head (horses); (*Aer. Naut.*) pitch; sway (of a carriage); lean; —*vt* refoot (socks); head (wine)

**cabeceo** /kaβe'θeo; kaβe'seo/ *m,* nod, shake (of head); (*Naut. Aer.*) pitching; lurching (of a carriage, etc.); bight (of river)

**cabecera** /kaβe'θera; kaβe'sera/ *f,* top, upper portion, head; seat of honor; bed-head; river source; capital

(country or county); illustrated chapter heading; pillow; inscription, heading

**cabecilla** /kaβe'θiʎa; kaβe'siya/ *dim f,* small head. *mf Inf.* hothead. *m,* rebel leader

**cabellera** /kaβe'ʎera; kaβe'yera/ *f,* head of long hair; hair-switch; tail (of comet)

**cabello** /ka'βeʎo; ka'βeyo/ *m,* hair; head of hair; silk (of maize). *Fig. Inf.* **asirse de un c.,** to clutch at a straw

**cabelludo** /kaβe'ʎuðo; kaβe'yuðo/ *a* hairy; *Bot.* fibrous

**caber** /ka'βer/ *vi irr* to room for, contain; fit into, go into (e.g. *No cabemos todos en este coche,* There isn't room for all of us in this car); happen, befall, have (e.g. *No les cupo tal suerte,* They did not have such luck--Such luck did not befall them); be possible (e.g. *Todo cabe en Dios,* All things are possible with God). **No cabe más,** There's no room for anything else; *Fig.* That's the limit. *Fig.* **no c. en sí,** to be beyond oneself (with joy, pride, etc.). **No cabe duda de que,** There's no doubt that —*Pres. Indic.* **quepo, cabes,** etc —*Fut.* **cabré,** etc —*Conditional* **cabría,** etc —*Preterite* **cupe, cupiste,** etc —*Pres. Subjunc.* **quepa, quepas,** etc —*Imperf. Subjunc.* **cupiese,** etc.

**cabestrar** /kaβes'trar/ *vt* to halter

**cabestrillo** /kaβes'triʎo; kaβes'triyo/ *m,* sling; thin chain (for ornament). **en c.,** in a sling (e.g. *Tenía el brazo en c.,* His arm was in a sling)

**cabestro** /ka'βestro/ *m,* halter; sling; leading ox

**cabeza** /ka'βeθa; ka'βesa/ *f,* head; top, upper end; nail-head; brain; mind; judgment; self-control; edge (of book); peak, summit; source, origin; individual, person; head of cattle; capital city. *m,* leader, chief, head. *Mech.* **c. de biela,** big-end. *Inf.* **c. de chorlito,** scatterbrain (person). **c. de hierro,** blockhead. *Mil.* **c. de puente,** bridgehead. **c. de partido,** principal town of a region. **c. de turco,** scapegoat. **irse la c.** ( **a alguien),** to feel giddy. *Fig. Inf.* **meter a uno en la c.,** to put into someone's head. *Inf.* **quebrarse la c.,** to rack one's brains. *Inf.* **quitar a uno de la c.** ( **una cosa),** to dissuade; get an idea out of someone's head

**cabezada** /kaβe'θaða; kaβe'saða/ *f,* blow with or on the head; nod; headshake; headstall; *Naut.* pitching. **dar cabezadas,** to nod, go to sleep

**cabezal** /kaβe'θal; kaβe'sal/ *m,* small head pillow; *Surg.* pad; bolster; narrow mattress; *Mech.* head

**cabezo** /ka'βeθo; ka'βeso/ *m,* summit (of mountain); hill; *Naut.* reef

**cabezón** /kaβe'θon; kaβe'son/ *m,* tax-register; collar-band; head-opening (of a garment)

**cabezudo** /kaβe'θuðo; kaβe'suðo/ *a* large-headed; *Inf.* obstinate; *Inf.* heady (of wine). *m,* carnival grotesque

**cabida** /ka'βiða/ *f,* space, capacity; extent, area

**cabildear** /kaβilde'ar/ *vi* to canvass votes, lobby

**cabildo** /ka'βildo/ *m, Eccl.* chapter; municipal council; meeting, or meeting place of council. **c. abierto,** town meeting

**cabina** /ka'βina/ *f,* cabin. **c. telefónica** phone booth

**cabizbajo** /kaβiθ'βaho; kaβis'βaho/ *a* crestfallen; pensive, melancholy

**cable** /'kaβle/ *m,* cable; string (of bridge); cable's length; **c. aéreo,** overhead cable. **c. alimentario,** feed line. **c. eléctrico,** electric cable

**cabo** /'kaβo/ *m,* end, extremity; stump, stub; handle, shaft, haft; leader; *Geog.* cape; end, conclusion; *Naut.* rope; ply (of wool, etc.); *Mil.* corporal; *pl* accessories (clothes); horse's tail and mane. **c. de maestranza,** foreman. **c. de mar,** naval quartermaster. **c. furriel,** *Mil.* quartermaster. **al c.,** in the end. **llevar a c.,** to finish

**Cabo de Buena Esperanza** /'kaβo de 'buena espe'ranθa; 'kaβo de 'buena espe'ransa/ Cape of Good Hope

**Cabo de Hornos** /'kaβo de 'ornos/ Cape Horn

**cabotaje** /kaβo'tahe/ *m, Naut.* coasting trade

**cabra** /'kaβra/ f, nanny-goat; goat. **c. montesa,** wild goat

**cabrahigo** /kaβra'igo/ m, wild fig; wild fig tree

**cabrerizo** /kaβre'riθo; kaβreriso/ **(-za)** a goatish. m, goatherd

**cabrero** /ka'βrero/ **(-ra)** m, goatherd

**cabrestante** /kaβres'tante/ m, Naut. capstan

**cabria** /'kaβria/ f, winch, hoist

**cabrilla** /ka'βriʎa; ka'βriya/ f, saw-horse; pl Astron. Pleiades; burn marks on legs from sitting too near fire; white crests (of waves)

**cabrillear** /kaβriʎe'ar; kaβriye'ar/ vi to foam, froth (the sea)

**cabrío** /ka'βrio/ a goatish. m, herd of goats. **macho c.,** male goat, he-goat

**cabriola** /ka'βriola/ f, fouetté (in dancing); spin in the air (acrobats); curvet (horses); caper

**cabriolar** /kaβrio'lar/ vi to curvet; caper, skip

**cabriolé** /kaβrio'le/ m, cabriolet; short cape with or without sleeves

**cabritilla** /kaβri'tiʎa; kaβri'tiya/ f, dressed kid; lambskin, etc.

**cabrito** /ka'βrito/ m, Zool. kid; pl toasted maize, popcorn

**cabrón** /ka'βron/ m, billy goat, buck, he-goat; Inf. complaisant husband, cuckhold; Chile owner or operator of a brothel

**cabrona** /ka'βrona/ f, Chile bawd, madam

**cabruno** /ka'βruno/ a goatish

**cabujón** /kaβu'hon/ m, Mineral. uncut gem; unpolished ruby; pl vignettes

**cacahual** /kaka'ual/ m, cacao plantation

**cacahuete** /kaka'uete/ m, Bot. peanut, monkey nut

**cacao** /ka'kao/ m, Bot. cacao tree; cacaonut

**cacarear** /kakare'ar/ vi to crow, cackle; —vt Inf. boast

**cacareo** /kaka'reo/ m, crowing, cackling; Inf. boast

**cacatúa** /kaka'tua/ f, cockatoo

**cacera** /ka'θera; ka'sera/ f, irrigation channel

**cacería** /kaθe'ria; kase'ria/ f, hunting party; hunting bag, booty; Art. hunting scene

**cacerola** /kaθe'rola; kase'rola/ f, stew-pot, casserole

**cachalote** /katʃa'lote/ m, sperm whale

**cachano** /ka'tʃano/ m, Old Nick

**cachar** /ka'tʃar/ vt to break in fragments; split (wood)

**Cachemira** /katʃe'mira/ Kashmir

**cachemira** /katʃe'mira/ f, cashmere

**cacheo** /ka'tʃeo/ m, search (of persons) for weapons

**cachete** /ka'tʃete/ m, blow on the head or face with one's fist; cheek (especially fat one)

**cachetero** /katʃe'tero/ m, dagger

**cachetina** /katʃe'tina/ f, hand-to-hand fight

**cachiporra** /katʃi'porra/ f, club, bludgeon

**cachivache** /katʃi'βatʃe/ m, Inf. (gen. pl) trash; pots, pans, utensils

**cacho** /'katʃo/ m, small slice (gen. of bread or fruit)

**cachón** /ka'tʃon/ m, breaker, wave; small waterfall

**cachorro** /ka'tʃorro/ **(-rra)** n puppy; cub. m, small pistol

**cachuela** /ka'tʃuela/ f, Extremaduran pork stew

**cacillo** /ka'θiʎo; ka'siyo/ m, ladle; basting spoon

**cacique** /ka'θike; ka'sike/ m, Indian chief, cacique; Inf. political "boss"

**caciquismo** /kaθi'kismo; kasi'kismo/ m, political "bossism"

**caco** /'kako/ m, pickpocket, thief; Inf. poltroon

**cacofonía** /kakofo'nia/ f, cacophony

**cacografía** /kakogra'fia/ f, cacography

**cacto** /'kakto/ m, cactus

**cacumen** /ka'kumen/ m, Inf. brains, acumen

**cada** /'kaða/ a every, each. **c. cual,** each. **c. que,** whenever; every time that. **c. y cuando que,** whenever

**cadalso** /ka'ðalso/ m, scaffold; platform, stand

**cadáver** /ka'ðaβer/ m, corpse

**cadavérico** /kaða'βeriko/ a cadaverous, ghastly

**cadena** /ka'ðena/ f, chain; link, tie; Fig. bond; Fig. sequence (of events); Law. imprisonment; Archit. buttress; grand chain (dancing); **c. de montañas,** range of mountains. **c. perpetua,** life imprisonment

**cadencia** /ka'ðenθia; ka'ðensia/ f, cadence; rhythm; Mus. measure, time; Mus. cadenza

**cadencioso** /kaðen'θioso; kaðen'sioso/ a rhythmic

**cadente** /ka'ðente/ a falling, declining; decaying, dying; rhythmic

**cadera** /ka'ðera/ f, hip; flank

**caderillas** /kaðe'riʎas; kaðe'riyas/ f pl, bustle, panniers

**cadete** /ka'ðete/ m, Mil. cadet

**cadi** /'kaði/ mf caddy

**Cádiz** /'kaðiθ; 'kaðis/ Cadiz

**caducar** /kaðu'kar/ vi to become senile; become invalid, be annulled; expire, lapse; Fig. be worn out

**caduceo** /kaðu'θeo; kaðu'seo/ m, Mercury's wand

**caducidad** /kaðuθi'ðað; kaðusi'ðað/ f, decrepitude; lapse, expiry

**caduco** /ka'ðuko/ a senile; decrepit; perishable; lapsed; obsolete

**caduquez** /kaðu'keθ; kaðu'kes/ f, senility

**caedizo** /kae'ðiθo; kae'ðiso/ a ready to fall; timid, cowardly, weak

**caer** /ka'er/ vi irr to fall, drop; drop out or off; suit, fit, become; fail; fade (colors); Fig. drop (voice); (with sobre) attack, fall upon; (with en) fall in or on to; decay, collapse; understand; (with preps. a, hacia) Fig. look on to, face; (with por, en) Fig. fall on, occur on; —vr Aer. crash; fly off (buttons, etc.). **c. de cabeza,** to fall head foremost. **c. en conflicto (con),** to come into conflict (with) **c. en las manos de uno,** to come into somebody's possession (come to be owned by somebody). **c. en gracia,** to make a good impression, arouse affection. **caerse de suyo,** to be selfevident. **c. por tierra,** (plan, etc.) to fall through. Cayó enfermo, He was taken ill. **cayendo y levantado,** dying Pres. Indic. **caigo, caes,** etc —Pres. Part. **cayendo.** Preterite **cayó cayeron.** Pres. Subjunc. **caiga.**

**café** /ka'fe/ m, coffee (tree, berry, drink); café, coffeehouse. **c. con leche,** café au lait

**cafeína** /kafe'ina/ f, caffeine

**cafetal** /kafe'tal/ m, coffee plantation

**cafetera** /kafe'tera/ f, coffeepot; Peru cab, taxi

**cafeto** /ka'feto/ m, coffee tree

**cafiche** /ka'fitʃe/ m, Argentina, Chile pimp

**caficultor** /kafikul'tor/ m, coffee-grower

**caficultura** /kafikul'tura/ f, coffee-growing

**cafúa** /ka'fua/ f, Argentina clink, slammer

**cagadas** /ka'gaðas/ f pl, droppings, dung

**cagar** /ka'gar/ **(se)** vi vt vr to evacuate (bowels); —vt Inf. spoil, make a botch of

**cagarruta** /kaga'rruta/ f, dung of sheep, deer, rabbits, etc.

**caída** /ka'iða/ f, falling; fall; ruin; failure; close (of day); Fig. falling off; hanging (curtains, etc.); diminution; incline; pl coarse wool; Inf. repartee. **a la c. de la tarde,** at the end of the afternoon. **a la c. del sol,** at sunset

**caído** /ka'iðo/ **(-da)** a debilitated, languid; lapsed; (of a shoulder) sloping. **los caídos,** the fallen, the dead (in war, etc.)

**caimán** /kai'man/ m, alligator; Inf. shark, astute person

**caja** /'kaha/ f, box; safe, cash box; coffin; (of a vehicle) body; Mus. drum; case (of piano, watch, etc.); cavity; well (of a stair); Com. cash; cash-desk; cashier's office; Bot. sheath. **c. de ahorros,** savings bank. **c. de caudales,** strong-box. Print. **c. de imprenta,** type case. **c. de música,** musical box. **c. de reclutamiento,** recruiting office. **c. de velocidades,** gearbox. **c. registradora,** cash register. **c. torácica,** rib cage, thoracic cage

**cajero** /ka'hero/ **(-ra)** m, boxmaker; —n Com. cashier; pedler **c. automático,** automatic teller, automatic teller machine, bank machine, money machine

**cajetilla** /kahe'tiʎa; kahe'tiya/ f, packet (cigarettes, etc.)

**cajista** /ka'hista/ mf Print. compositor

**cajón** /ka'hon/ *m*, chest, locker, case; drawer. **c. de municiones,** ammunition-box
**cajonera** /kaho'nera/ *f*, *Eccl.* chest of drawers in sacristy; *Agr.* frame
**cal** /kal/ *f*, lime. **c. muerta,** slaked lime. **c. viva,** quicklime. *Fig. Inf.* **de c. y canto,** tough, strong
**cala** /'kala/ *f*, sample slice (of fruit); *Naut.* hold; *Surg.* probe; cove, small bay; *Bot.* iris
**calabacera** /kalaβa'θera; kalaβa'sera/ *f*, *Bot.* pumpkin or gourd plant
**calabacín** /kalaβa'θin; kalaβa'sin/ *m*, kind of vegetable marrow; *Inf.* dolt
**calabaza** /kala'βaθa; kala'βasa/ *f*, *Bot.* pumpkin (plant and fruit); gourd; *Inf.* dolt. **dar calabazas,** to refuse (suitor); flunk (an examinee). *Inf.* **llevar calabazas,** to get the sack; be jilted
**calabobos** /kala'βoβos/ *m*, *Inf.* drizzle
**calabocero** /kalaβo'θero; kalaβo'sero/ *m*, jailer
**calabozo** /kala'βoθo; kala'βoso/ *m*, dungeon; prison cell; pruning knife
**calabrés** /kala'βres/ **(-esa)** *a* and *n* Calabrian
**calada** /ka'laða/ *f*, soaking, wetting through; flight of bird of prey; swoop. **dar una c.,** *Fig. Inf.* to dress down
**calado** /ka'laðo/ *a* soaked, wet through. *m*, *Sew.* open-work; fretwork; *Naut.* draft of a ship; water level; *pl* lace. **c. hasta los huesos,** soaked to the skin; madly in love
**calador** /kala'ðor/ *m*, one who does open or fretwork; caulking iron; borer; *Surg.* probe
**calafate** /kala'fate/ *m*, caulker
**calafatear** /kalafate'ar/ *vt* *Naut.* to caulk
**calamar** /kala'mar/ *m*, *Zool.* squid, calamary
**calambre** /ka'lambre/ *m*, cramp. **c. del escribiente,** writer's cramp
**calamidad** /kalami'ðað/ *f*, misfortune, calamity
**calamina** /kala'mina/ *f*, *Mineral.* calamine
**calamitoso** /kalami'toso/ *a* calamitous; unfortunate, unhappy
**cálamo** /'kalamo/ *m*, ancient flute; stalk (of grass); *Poet.* pen
**calamocano** /kalamo'kano/ *a* maudlin, tipsy
**calandria** /ka'landria/ *f*, *Ornith.* calender, lark; *Mech.* calender; treadmill. *mf Inf.* malingerer
**calaña** /ka'laɲa/ *f*, sample; model; pattern; kind, quality; temperament; cheap fan
**calar** /ka'lar/ *vt* to permeate, soak through; pierce; do openwork (in cloth, paper, metal); cut a sample slice from fruit; pull (hat, etc.) well down on head; put down (an eyeshade or visor); fix (bayonets, etc.); *Inf.* understand (persons); *Inf.* guess, realize; *Naut.* let down; —*vi Naut.* draw (water); —*vr* be drenched, wet through; swoop (birds of prey); *Inf.* sneak in —*a* calcareous
**calar** /ka'lar/ *m*, limestone deposit or region
**calavera** /kala'βera/ *f*, skull. *m*, dare-devil, madcap; roué
**calaverada** /kalaβe'raða/ *f*, *Inf.* dare-devilment, foolishness; escapade
**calcañar** /kalka'ɲar/ *m*, heel (of foot)
**calcar** /kal'kar/ *vt* to trace (drawing); press with foot; copy servilely, imitate
**calcáreo** /kal'kareo/ *a* calcareous
**calce** /'kalθe; 'kalse/ *m*, rim of a wheel; wedge; tire
**calcés** /kal'θes; kal'ses/ *m*, *Naut.* masthead
**calceta** /kal'θeta; kal'seta/ *f*, stocking; fetter. *Inf.* **hacer c.,** to knit
**calcetería** /kalθete'ria; kalsete'ria/ *f*, hosiery shop; hosiery trade
**calcetero** /kalθe'tero; kalse'tero/ **(-ra)** *n* hosier; hose maker or darner
**calcetín** /kalθe'tin; kalse'tin/ *m*, sock
**calcificación** /kalθifika'θion; kalsifika'sion/ *f*, *Med.* calcification
**calcinación** /kalθina'θion; kalsina'sion/ *f*, calcination
**calcinar** /kalθi'nar; kalsi'nar/ *vt* to calcine
**calcio** /'kalθio; 'kalsio/ *m*, calcium
**calco** /'kalko/ *m*, tracing (drawing)
**calcografía** /kalkogra'fia/ *f*, chalcography
**calcografiar** /kalkogra'fiar/ *vt* to transfer; make chalcographies of

**calcomanía** /kalkoma'nia/ *f*, transfer
**calculación** /kalkula'θion; kalkula'sion/ *f*, calculation
**calculadamente** /kalkulaða'mente/ *adv* calculatedly
**calculado** /kalku'laðo/ *a* calculated
**calculador** /kalkula'ðor/ *a* calculating. *m*, calculating machine, comptometer
**calcular** /kalku'lar/ *vt* to calculate
**cálculo** /'kalkulo/ *m*, calculation; *Math.* estimate; investigation; conjecture; *(Math Med.)* calculus. **c. hepático,** *Med.* gallstone
**Calcuta** /kal'kuta/ Calcutta
**calda** /'kalda/ *f*, heating; *pl* hot mineral baths
**Caldea** /kal'dea/ Chaldea
**caldear** /kalde'ar/ *vt* to heat
**caldeo** /kal'deo/ **(-ea)** *a* and *n* Chaldean
**caldeo** /kal'deo/ *m*, heating
**caldera** /kal'dera/ *f*, cauldron; cauldron full; *West Hem.* teapot; *Engin.* boiler. **c. de vapor,** steam-boiler
**calderería** /kaldere'ria/ *f*, coppersmith's trade and shop
**calderero** /kalde'rero/ *m*, boiler maker; coppersmith; tinker
**calderilla** /kalde'riʎa; kalde'riya/ *f*, holy water stoup; any copper coin
**caldero** /kal'dero/ *m*, small cauldron; casserole; kettle
**calderón** /kalde'ron/ *m*, large cauldron; *Mus.* rest; *Mus.* trill; pause
**caldo** /'kaldo/ *m*, broth; salad dressing; *pl Agr.* oil, wine, vegetable juices
**calefacción** /kalefak'θion; kalefak'sion/ *f*, heating. **c. central,** central heating
**calendario** /kalen'dario/ *m*, calendar. **c. deportivo,** fixture card. **c. gregoriano,** Gregorian calendar
**calendas** /ka'lendas/ *f pl*, calends. **en las c. griegas,** at the Greek calends
**caléndula** /ka'lendula/ *f*, marigold
**calentador** /kalenta'ðor/ *a* heating, warming. *m*, heater; warming-pan
**calentamiento** /kalenta'miento/ *m*, heating, warming
**calentar** /kalen'tar/ *vt irr* to heat, warm; rev-up (an engine); hasten; *Inf.* spank; —*vr* warm oneself; be in heat (animals); grow excited. See **acertar**
**calentura** /kalen'tura/ *f*, fever
**calenturiento** /kalentu'riento/ *a* feverish
**calera** /ka'lera/ *f*, lime-pit; lime-kiln; fishing smack
**calesa** /ka'lesa/ *f*, calash, calèche, chaise (two-wheeled carriage)
**caleta** /ka'leta/ *f*, cove, creek
**caletre** /ka'letre/ *m*, *Inf.* discernment, head, sense
**calibrar** /kali'βrar/ *vt* to calibrate; gauge
**calibre** /ka'liβre/ *m*, *Mech.* gauge; bore, caliber; diameter (tubes, pipes, etc.)
**calidad** /kali'ðað/ *f*, quality; role; character, temperament; condition, requisite; importance, gravity; personal particulars; nobility; *pl* qualities of the mind. **c. originaria,** rank and birth. **c. de oficio,** justification for action. **en c. de,** in the capacity of
**cálido** /'kaliðo/ *a* warm, hot; warming, heating; vehement, ardent; *Art.* warm
**calidoscópico** /kaliðos'kopiko/ *a* kaleidoscopic
**calidoscopio** /kaliðos'kopio/ *m*, kaleidoscope
**calientalibros** /kalienta'liβros/ *m*, bookworm (person)
**calientapiés** /kalienta'pies/ *m*, footwarmer
**calientaplatos** /kalienta'platos/ *m*, hot plate, plate-warmer
**caliente** /ka'liente/ *a* warm, hot; excited; *Art.* warm
**calientito** /kalien'tito/ *a* piping hot
**califa** /ka'lifa/ *m*, caliph
**califal** /kali'fal/ *a* caliphal
**califato** /kali'fato/ *m*, caliphate
**calificable** /kalifi'kaβle/ *a* classifiable; qualifiable
**calificación** /kalifika'θion; kalifika'sion/ *f*, classification; qualification; judgment; mark, place (examinations)
**calificar** /kalifi'kar/ *vt* to class; authorize; judge (qualities); *Fig.* ennoble; —*vr* prove noble descent
**calificativo** /kalifi'tiβo/ *a* *Gram.* qualifying. *m*, epithet

**californio** /kali'fornio/ (-ia) *a* and *n* Californian

**caliginoso** /kalihi'noso/ *a* murky, dark

**caligrafía** /kaligra'fia/ *f,* calligraphy

**calígrafo** /ka'ligrafo/ *m,* calligraphist

**calinoso** /kali'noso/ *a* hazy

**caliqueño** /kali'keɲo/ *m,* cheroot

**calistenia** /kalis'tenia/ *f,* callisthenics

**cáliz** /'kaliθ; 'kalis/ *m,* chalice; *Poet.* cup; *Bot.* calyx

**caliza** /ka'liθa; ka'lisa/ *f,* limestone

**calizo** /ka'liθo; ka'liso/ *a* calcareous

**callado** /ka'ʎaðo; ka'yaðo/ *a* silent; reserved; secret

**callar** /ka'ʎar; ka'yar/ (se) *vi* and *vr* to say nothing, keep silent; stop speaking; stop making any sound (persons, animals, things); —*vt* conceal, keep secret; omit, leave out; *Inf. interj* ¡**Calle!** You don't say so! **Quien calla otorga,** Silence gives consent

**calle** /'kaʎe; 'kaye/ *f,* street. *Inf.* **abrir c.,** to clear the way. *Inf.* **dejar en la c.,** to leave destitute. *Inf.* **echar a la c.,** put out of the house, to throw out of the house; make known, publish. **ponerse en la c.,** to go out

**calleja, callejuela** /ka'ʎeha, kaʎe'huela; ka'yeha, kaye'huela/ *f,* small street, alley, side street

**callejear** /kaʎehe'ar; kayehe'ar/ *vi* to walk the streets, wander about the streets, loaf around the streets

**callejero** /kaʎe'hero; kaye'hero/ *a* fond of gadding. *m,* street directory

**callejón** /kaʎe'hon; kaye'hon/ *m,* alley, lane. **c. sin salida,** cul-de-sac; *Fig.* impasse

**callicida** /kaʎi'θiða; kayi'siða/ *m,* corn cure

**callista** /ka'ʎista; ka'yista/ *mf* chiropodist

**callo** /'kaʎo; 'kayo/ *m,* corn, callosity; *Med.* callus; *pl* tripe

**calloso** /ka'ʎoso; ka'yoso/ *a* callous, horny

**calma** /'kalma/ *f,* calm, airlessness; serenity, composure; quiet, tranquillity, peace. **c. chicha,** dead calm. **en c.,** at peace; tranquil; calm (of the sea)

**calmante** /kal'mante/ *a* calming, soothing. *Med. a* and *m,* sedative, tranquilizer

**calmar** /kal'mar/ *vt* to soothe, calm; moderate, mitigate; pacify; quench (thirst); —*vi* grow calm; moderate; be becalmed

**calmoso** /kal'moso/ *a* calm, tranquil; *Inf.* sluggish, lazy; imperturbable

**calor** /ka'lor/ *m,* heat; ardor, vehemence; cordiality; *Fig.* heat (of battle); excitement

**caloría** /kalo'ria/ *f, Phys.* calorie

**calórico** /ka'loriko/ *a Phys.* caloric, thermic

**calorífero** /kalo'rifero/ *a* heat-giving. *m,* heater, radiator

**calorífico** /kalo'rifiko/ *a* calorific

**calumnia** /ka'lumnia/ *f,* calumny; *Law.* slander

**calumniador** /kalumnia'ðor/ (-ra) *a* slandering —*n* calumniator, slanderer

**calumniar** /kalumni'ar/ *vt* to calumniate; *Law.* slander

**calumnioso** /kalum'nioso/ *a* calumnious, slanderous

**caluroso** /kalu'roso/ *a* hot, warm; cordial, friendly; enthusiastic; ardent, impassioned; excited

**calva** /'kalβa/ *f,* bald patch on head; worn place (cloth, etc.); bare spot, clearing (trees, etc.)

**Calvario** /kal'βario/ *m,* Calvary; *Inf.* series of disasters; *Inf.* debts

**calvero** /kal'βero/ *m,* clearing (in a wood); chalk or marl pit

**calvicie** /kal'βiθie; kalβisie/ *f,* baldness

**calvinismo** /kalβi'nismo/ *m,* Calvinism

**calvinista** /kalβi'nista/ *mf* Calvinist —*a* Calvinistic

**calvo** /'kalβo/ *a* bald; bare, barren (land); worn (cloth, etc.)

**calza** /'kalθa; 'kalsa/ *f,* breeches (gen. *pl*); wedge; *Inf.* stocking. *Inf.* **tomar calzas,** to beat it

**calzada** /kal'θaða; kal'saða/ *f,* roadway. **c. romana,** Roman road

**calzado** /kal'θaðo; kal'saðo/ *m,* footwear, shoes

**calzador** /kalθa'ðor; kalsa'ðor/ *m,* shoehorn

**calzadura** /kalθa'ðura; kalsa'ðura/ *f,* wedging (of a wheel); act of putting on shoes; felloe of a wheel

**calzar** /kal'θar; kal'sar/ *vt* to put on shoes; wear (spurs, gloves, etc.); wedge, block (wheel); scotch (a

wheel). *Fig. Inf.* **c. el coturno,** don the buskin; write in the sublime style; write a tragedy, write tragedies.

**calzarse a una persona,** to have a person in one's pocket

**calzón** /kal'θon; kal'son/ *m,* breeches (gen. *pl*). *Fig. Inf.* **ponerse los calzones,** to wear the breeches (of a woman)

**calzonazos** /kalθo'naθos; kalso'nasos/ *m, Inf.* weak-willed, easily led fellow

**calzoncillos** /kalθon'θiʎos; kalson'siyos/ *m pl,* drawers, pants

**cama** /'kama/ *f,* bed; bedstead; bedhanging; lair, form; floor (of a cart); check (of bridle) (gen. *pl*). **c. de campaña,** camp bed. **c. de matrimonio,** double bed. **c. de monja,** single bed. **c. de operaciones,** operating table. **c. turca,** settee-bed. **guardar c.,** to stay in bed

**camada** /ka'maða/ *f,* brood, litter; *Inf.* gang

**camafeo** /kama'feo/ *m,* cameo

**camaleón** /kamale'on/ *m,* chameleon; *Inf.* changeable person

**cámara** /'kamara/ *f,* chamber; hall; house (of deputies); granary; *Naut.* state room; chamber (firearms, mines); *Phys.* camera; human excrement; *Auto.* inner tube. **c. acorazada,** strong-room. **c. alta,** Upper House, **c. baja** *or* **c. de los comunes,** lower house, house of commons. **c. de comercio,** chamber of commerce. **c. oscura,** (optics) dark room

**camarada** /kama'raða/ *mf* pal, companion, comrade

**camaradería** /kamaraðe'ria/ *f,* comradeship, companionship

**camarera** /kama'rera/ *f,* waiting-maid; waitress; chambermaid; stewardess

**camarero** /kama'rero/ *m,* waiter; papal chamberlain; chamberlain; steward; valet. **c. mayor,** lord chamberlain

**camarilla** /kama'riʎa; kama'riya/ *f,* palace or other clique, coterie; *Inf.* back-scratch

**camarín** /kama'rin/ *m, Theat.* dressing-room; closet; boudoir; cage (of a lift); niche

**camarón** /kama'ron/ *m,* prawn, shrimp; tip, reward

**camarote** /kama'rote/ *m,* cabin; berth

**cambalachear** /kambalatʃe'ar/ *vt Inf.* to barter

**cámbaro** /'kambaro/ *m,* sea-crab

**cambiable** /kam'βiaβle/ *a* exchangeable; changeable

**cambiante** /kam'βiante/ *a* exchanging; changing. *m,* sheen, luster (gen. *pl*); money changer

**cambiar** /kam'βiar/ *vt* to exchange; convert —*vt* and *vi* change, alter; —*vi* and *vr* to veer (wind). **c. de aguas,** *Poet.* to move (change one's residence). **c. de aire,** get a change of scenery. **c. de frente,** to face about; *Fig.* change front

**cambio** /'kambio/ *m,* exchange; change; *Com.* rate of exchange; money change; *Com.* premium on bills of exchange. **a c. de, en c. de,** in exchange for; instead of. **en c.,** instead, on the other hand. **c. de velocidad,** *Auto.* gear-changing. **letra de c.,** bill of exchange. **libre c.,** free trade

**cambista** /kam'βista/ *mf* money changer. *m,* banker

**Camboya** /kam'βoia/ Cambodia

**Cambrige** /kam'βrihe/ Cambridge

**camelar** /kame'lar/ *vt Inf.* to woo; seduce

**camelia** /ka'melia/ *f,* camelia. **c. japonesa,** japonica

**camellero** /kame'ʎero; kame'yero/ *m,* camel keeper or driver

**camello** /ka'meʎo; ka'meyo/ *m,* camel. **c. pardal,** giraffe

**camellón** /kame'ʎon; kame'yon/ *m,* furrow; drinking trough; *Mexico* island, traffic island, median strip

**camelo** /ka'melo/ *m, Inf.* eyewash

**Camerún** /kame'run/ Cameroon

**camilla** /ka'miʎa; ka'miya/ *f,* couch; small round skirted table with brazier underneath; stretcher, litter

**camillero** /kami'ʎero; kami'yero/ *m, Mil.* stretcher-bearer

**caminador** /kamina'ðor/ *a* in the habit of walking a great deal

**caminante** /kami'nante/ *mf* walker, traveler

**caminar** /kami'nar/ *vi* to travel; walk; *Fig.* move on, go (inanimate things). *Fig. Inf.* **c. derecho,** to walk uprightly

**caminata** /kami'nata/ *f,* long, tiring walk; excursion

**caminejo** /kami'neho/ *m*, worn path

**camino** /ka'mino/ *m*, road; route; journey; way, means; **c. de hierro,** railway. **c. de mesa,** table-runner. **c. de sirga,** towpath. **c. real,** highway, main road. **de c.,** on the way, in passing. **ponerse en c.,** to set out

**camión** /ka'mion/ *m*, truck. **c. de volteo, c. volquete** dump truck; *Mexico* bus

**camioneta** /kamio'neta/ *f*, light truck, pick-up truck; *West. Hem.* station wagon

**camisa** /ka'misa/ *f*, shirt, stiff shirt; thin skin (of fruit); sloughed skin of snakes; coat (of whitewash, etc.); *Mech.* jacket; mantle (gas). **c. de fuerza,** strait-jacket. **dejar sin c.,** *Inf.* to leave penniless

**camisería** /kamise'ria/ *f*, shirt shop or factory

**camisero** /kami'sero/ **(-ra)** *n* shirt maker or seller

**camiseta** /kami'seta/ *f*, vest, T-shirt. **c. de fútbol,** soccer player's jersey

**camisola** /kami'sola/ *f*, stiff shirt; ruffled shirt

**camisón** /kami'son/ *m*, large wide shirt; night shirt

**camomila** /kamo'mila/ *f*, chamomile

**camorra** /ka'morra/ *f*, *Inf.* brawl, shindy. **armar c.,** to start a row

**campal** /kam'pal/ *a* field, country

**campamento** /kampa'mento/ *m*, camping; *Mil.* encampment; camp; jamboree

**campana** /kam'pana/ *f*, bell; anything bell-shaped; church, parish. **c. de chimenea,** mantelpiece. **c. de hogar,** hood, shutter (of a fireplace)

**campanada** /kampa'naða/ *f*, peal of a bell; scandal

**campanario** /kampa'nario/ *m*, belfry, bell tower

**campanear** /kampane'ar/ *vi* to ring bells frequently

**campaneo** /kampa'neo/ *m*, bell-ringing; chime

**campanero** /kampa'nero/ *m*, bell-founder; bell ringer

**campanil** /kampa'nil/ *m*, small belfry, campanile

**campanilla** /kampa'niʎa; kampa'niya/ *f*, hand-bell; bubble; any bell-shaped flower

**campanillazo** /kampani'ʎaθo; kampani'yaso/ *m*, loud peal of a bell

**campante** /kam'pante/ *a* outstanding; *Inf.* proud, satisfied

**campanudo** /kampa'nuðo/ *a* bell-shaped; sonorous (of words); pompous (of speech)

**campaña** /kam'paɲa/ *f*, level country; campaign. *Naut.* voyage, cruise. **correr la c.,** to reconnoiter. **la C. del Desierto,** the War against the Gauchos (in Argentina)

**campar** /kam'par/ *vi* to camp. *Inf.* **c. por sus respetos,** to stand on one's own feet

**campeador** /kampea'ðor/ *a* mighty in battle

**campear** /kampe'ar/ *vi* to go out to graze; grow green (crops); excel; *Mil.* be engaged in a campaign, reconnoiter

**campechano** /kampe'tʃano/ *a Inf.* hearty; frank; cheerful; generous

**campeche** /kam'petʃe/ *m*, *Bot.* logwood

**campeón** /kampe'on/ *m*, champion; advocate, defender

**campeonato** /kampeo'nato/ *m*, championship

**campesinado** /kampesi'naðo/ *m*, peasantry

**campesino** /kampe'sino/ **(-na)** *a* rural, rustic —*n* country dweller

**campestre** /kam'pestre/ *a* rural

**campiña** /kam'piɲa/ *f*, expanse of cultivated land; countryside, landscape

**campo** /'kampo/ *m*, country (as opposed to urban areas); field; *Fig.* sphere, province; (*Phys. Herald. Mil.*) field; *Art.* ground; *Mil.* camp, army; plain ground (of silks, etc.). **«C. Abierto»,** "Miscellaneous" (e.g. as the title of a section in a book catalog). **c. de aterrizaje,** *Aer.* landing-field. **c. de batalla,** battlefield. **c. de concentración,** concentration camp. **c. de experimentación,** testing ground. **c. de golf,** golf course. **c. de prisioneros** *Mil.* prison camp. **c. de tiro,** rifle-range. **c. santo,** graveyard. **c. visual,** field of vision. **a c. abierto,** in the open air. **a c. travieso,** cross-country

**camuflaje** /kamu'flahe/ *m*, camouflage

**camuflar** /kamu'flar/ *vt* to camouflage

**can** /kan/ *m*, dog; trigger; *Archit.* modillion; *Astron.* Dog Star

**cana** /'kana/ *f*, gray hair

**Canadá** /kana'ða/ Canada

**canadiense** /kana'ðiense/ *a* and *mf* Canadian

**canal** /ka'nal/ *m*, canal. *mf*, *Geol.* subterranean waterway; channel; *Anat.* canal, duct; defile, narrow valley; gutter; drinking trough; animal carcass. **abrir en c.,** to open up, split open

**Canal de la Mancha** /ka'nal de la 'mantʃa/ English Channel

**canalera** /kana'lera/ *f*, roof gutter

**canaleta** /kana'leta/ *f*, (wooden) trough; gutter (on roof)

**canalete** /kana'lete/ *m*, paddle

**canalización** /kanaliθa'θion; kanalisa'sion/ *f*, canalization; *Elec.* main, mains; piping; tubing

**canalizar** /kanali'θar; kanali'sar/ *vt* to make canals or channels; regulate waters of rivers, etc.; canalize

**canalla** /ka'naʎa; ka'naya/ *f*, *Inf.* mob, rabble. *m*, *Inf.* scoundrel

**canallesco** /kana'ʎesko; kana'yesko/ *a* scoundrelly, knavish; despicable

**canalón** /kana'lon/ *m*, gutter, spout; shovel hat; pantile

**canana** /ka'nana/ *f*, cartridge belt

**canapé** /kana'pe/ *m*, sofa

**Canarias, las Islas** /ka'narias, las 'islas/ the Canary Islands

**canario** /ka'nario/ **(-ia)** *m*, canary —*a* and *n* pertaining to or native of the Canary Islands.

**canasta** /ka'nasta/ *f*, hamper, basket; card game

**canastilla** /kanas'tiʎa; kanas'tiya/ *f*, small basket; layette

**canastillo** /kanas'tiʎo; kanas'tiyo/ *m*, basket-work tray

**cáncamo** /'kankamo/ *m*, ring-bolt

**cancamusa** /kanka'musa/ *f*, *Inf.* trick, deception

**cancel** /kan'θel; kan'sel/ *m*, draftscreen; *Eccl.* screen

**cancela** /kan'θela; kan'sela/ *f*, wrought-iron door

**cancelación** /kanθela'θion; kansela'sion/ *f*, cancellation; expunging

**cancelar** /kanθe'lar; kanse'lar/ *vt* to cancel; expunge, annul; abolish, blot out; pay off, clear (a mortgage)

**cancelaría** /kanθe'laria; kanse'laria/ *f*, papal chancery

**cancelario** /kanθe'lario; kanse'lario/ *m*, chancellor (universities)

**cáncer** /'kanθer; 'kanser/ *m*, cancer

**cancerar** /kanθe'rar; kanse'rar/ *vt* to consume; weaken; mortify; —*vr* suffer from cancer; become cancerous

**cancerbero** /kanθer'βero; kanser'βero/ *m*, *Myth.* Cerberus; *Fig.* unbribable guard

**canceroso** /kanθe'roso; kanse'roso/ *a* cancerous

**cancha** /'kantʃa/ *f*, *Sports.* fronton; (tennis) court; cockpit; yard; hippodrome; widest part of a river; road; toasted maize

**canciller** /kanθi'ʎer; kansi'yer/ *m*, chancellor; foreign minister; assistant vice-consul

**cancillería** /kanθiʎe'ria; kansiye'ria/ *f*, chancellorship; chancellery; foreign ministry

**canción** /kan'θion; kan'sion/ *f*, song; lyric poem; musical accompaniment; old name for any regional composition. **volver a la misma c.,** *Fig.* to be always harping on the same theme

**cancionero** /kanθio'nero; kansio'nero/ *m*, collection of songs and verses; songbook

**cancionista** /kanθio'nista; kansio'nista/ *mf* singer; song writer

**candado** /kan'daðo/ *m*, padlock; earring

**candeal** /kande'al/ *a* white (of bread)

**candela** /kan'dela/ *f*, candle; horse-chestnut flower; candlestick; *Inf.* fire. **en c.,** *Naut.* vertical (of masts, etc.)

**candelabro** /kande'laβro/ *m*, candelabrum

**candelaria** /kande'laria/ *f*, Candlemas

**candelero** /kande'lero/ *m*, candlestick; lamp; candle maker or seller; *Naut.* stanchion

**candente** /kan'dente/ *a* candescent, red-hot

**candidatear** /kandiðate'ar/ *vi* to run (for office)

**candidato** /kandi'ðato/ **(-ta)** *n* candidate

**candidatura** /kandiða'tura/ *f*, candidature

**candidez** /kandi'ðeθ; kandi'ðes/ *f*, simplicity, ingenuousness; candidness

**cándido** /'kandiðo/ a white; simple, ingenuous; candid, frank

**candil** /kan'dil/ m, oil lamp; Greek lamp; tips of stag's horns; Inf. cock of a hat

**candileja** /kandi'leha/ f, oil reservoir of lamp; pl footlights, floats

**candor** /kan'dor/ m, extreme whiteness; sincerity, candor; simplicity, innocence

**candoroso** /kando'roso/ a candid, open; simple, honest

**canela** /ka'nela/ f, Bot. cinnamon; Fig. anything exquisitely perfect

**canelo** /ka'nelo/ m, cinnamon tree —a cinnamon-colored

**cangilón** /kanhi'lon/ m, pitcher, jar; bucket (for water); dredging bucket

**cangreja** /kaŋ'greha/ f, Naut. gaffsail. **c. de mesana,** Naut. jigger

**cangrejo** /kaŋ'greho/ m, crab. **c. de mar,** sea-crab. **c. ermitaño,** hermit crab

**canguro** /kaŋ'guro/ m, kangaroo

**caníbal** /ka'niβal/ a and mf cannibal

**canibalismo** /kaniβa'lismo/ m, cannibalism

**canica** /ka'nika/ f, marble (for playing with)

**canícula** /ka'nikula/ f, dog days; Astron. Dog star

**caniculares** /kaniku'lares/ m pl dog days

**canijo** /ka'niho/ a Inf. delicate, sickly; anemic, stunted

**canilla** /ka'niʎa; ka'niya/ f, long bone of leg or arm; any principal bones in bird's wing; tap, faucet; spool, reel; fault (in cloth)

**canino** /ka'nino/ a canine

**canje** /'kanhe/ m, (diplomacy, Mil., Com.) exchange, substitution. **c. de prisioneros,** exchange of prisoners

**canjear** /kanhe'ar/ vt to exchange

**cano** /'kano/ a white-haired, hoary; ancient; Poet. white

**canoa** /ka'noa/ f, canoe; launch. **c. automóvil,** motor launch

**canódromo** /ka'noðromo/ m, dog-race track

**canoero** /kano'ero/ **(-ra)** n canoeist

**canon** /'kanon/ m, rule; (Eccl. Print.) canon; catalog; part of the Mass; Mus. canon, catch; tax pl canon law

**canonesa** /kano'nesa/ f, canoness

**canónico** /ka'noniko/ a canonic, canonical

**canónigo** /ka'nonigo/ m, canon; prebendary

**canonización** /kanoniθa'θion; kanonisa'sion/ f, canonization

**canonizar** /kanoni'θar; kanoni'sar/ vt to canonize; extol, exalt; approve, acclaim

**canonjía** /kanon'hia/ f, canonry, canonship; Inf. sinecure

**canoso** /ka'noso/ a white-haired, hoary

**cansado** /kan'saðo/ **(-da)** a tired; weary; exhausted; decadent; tiresome; Inf. fed up —n bore, tedious person

**cansancio** /kan'sanθio; kan'sansio/ m, fatigue, weariness

**cansar** /kan'sar/ vt to tire, weary; Agr. exhaust soil; bore; badger, annoy; —vr be tired; grow weary

**cansino** /kan'sino/ a worn-out (of horses, etc.)

**cantable** /kan'taβle/ a singable; Mus. cantabile

**cantábrico** /kan'taβriko/ **(-ca)** a and n Cantabrian

**cantante** /kan'tante/ a singing. mf professional singer

**cantar** /kan'tar/ vi to sing; twitter, chirp; extol; Inf. squeak, creak; Fig. call (cards); Inf. squeal, confess. m, song. **C. de los Cantares,** Song of Songs. **cantarlas claras,** to call a spade a spade

**cántara** /'kantara/ f, pitcher, jug

**cantárida** /kan'tariða/ f, Spanish fly

**cántaro** /'kantaro/ m, pitcher, jug; jugful; varying wine measure; ballot box; tax on spirits and oil

**cantata** /kan'tata/ f, cantata

**cantatriz** /kanta'triθ; kanta'tris/ f, singer, prima donna

**cante** /'kante/ m, song; singing

**cantera** /kan'tera/ f, Mineral. quarry; capacity, talent

**cantería** /kante'ria/ f, stone-cutting; quarrying; building made of hewn stone

**cantero** /kan'tero/ m, stone-cutter; quarryman

**cántico** /'kantiko/ m, Eccl. canticle; Poet. poem

**cantidad** /kanti'ðað/ f, quantity; large part; portion; sum of money; quantity (prosody). **c. llovida,** rainfall

**cantiga** /kan'tiga/ or **cántiga** /'kantiga/ f, old poetic form designed to be sung

**cantil** /kan'til/ m, cliff; steep rock

**cantimplora** /kantim'plora/ f, water cooler; canteen (of water); siphon

**cantina** /kan'tina/ f, wine cellar; canteen; refreshment room

**cantinero** /kanti'nero/ m, sutler; owner of a canteen

**canto** /'kanto/ m, singing; song; canto; epic or other poem; end, rim, edge; non-cutting edge (knives, swords); pebble, stone; angle (of a building). Mus. **c. llano,** plain-song. **al c. del gallo,** at cockcrow. **de c.,** on edge

**cantón** /kan'ton/ m, province, region; corner (of a street); cantonment; Herald. canton, quartering

**cantonera** /kanto'nera/ f, corner-piece (books, furniture, etc., as ornament); angle-iron; bracket, small shelf

**cantor** /kan'tor/ **(-ra)** a singing —n singer; song-bird

**Cantórbery** /kan'torβeri/ Canterbury

**canturía** /kantu'ria/ f, singing exercise; vocal music; monotonous song; droning; Mus. execution, technique

**canturreo,** /kantu'rreo,/ m, **canturria** f, humming, droning

**canturriar** /kantu'rriar/ vi Inf. to hum, sing under one's breath

**caña** /'kaɲa/ f, stalk; reed; bone of arm or leg; leg (of a trouser, stocking, boot, etc.); marrow; Bot. cane; tumbler, glass; wine measure; gallery (of mine); pl mock joust on horseback using **cañas** as spears. **c. de azúcar,** sugar-cane. **c. de pescar,** fishing rod. **c. del timón,** tiller Naut.

**cañada** /ka'ɲaða/ f, glen, gulch, gully, hollow, ravine, vale, cattle path; West. Hem. brook, cattle track

**cañal** /ka'ɲal/ m, cane-break; weir (for fish)

**cañamazo** /kaɲa'maθo; kaɲa'maso/ m, hempen canvas; embroidery canvas; embroidered canvas

**cañamelar** /kaɲame'lar/ m, sugar-cane plantation

**cáñamo** /'kaɲamo/ m, hemp

**cañamón** /kaɲa'mon/ m, hemp-seed

**cañar** /ka'ɲar/ m, canebrake; growth of reeds; fishgarth made of reeds

**cañavalera** /kaɲaβa'lera/ f, canefield

**cañaveral** /kaɲaβe'ral/ m, cane-brake; West Hem. bamboo field

**cañazo** /ka'ɲaθo; ka'ɲaso/ m, blow with a cane

**cañería** /kaɲe'ria/ f, conduit; pipe; piping

**cañero** /ka'ɲero/ m, pipe layer

**caño** /'kaɲo/ m, pipe, tube, sewer; organ pipe; jet (of water); mine gallery

**cañón** /ka'ɲon/ m, pipe, cylindrical tube; flue; quill (of birds); cannon; soft down; Archit. shaft (of column); stack (of a chimney). **c. antiaéreo,** A.A. gun. **c. antitanque,** anti-tank gun. **c. de escalera,** well of a staircase; Slang. terrific-looking, absolutely gorgeous (e.g. mujer cañón)

**cañonazo** /kaɲo'naθo; kaɲo'naso/ m, cannon shot; roar of a cannon

**cañonear** /kaɲone'ar/ vt to bombard

**cañoneo** /kaɲo'neo/ m, cannonade; bombardment

**cañonera** /kaɲo'nera/ f, embrasure (for cannon)

**cañonería** /kaɲone'ria/ f, Mil. group of cannon; Mus. set of organ pipes

**cañonero** /kaɲo'nero/ m, gunboat

**cañuto** /ka'ɲuto/ m, Bot. internode; small pipe or tube; Inf. tale-bearer

**caoba** /ka'oβa/ f, Bot. mahogany

**caos** /'kaos/ m, chaos; confusion

**caótico** /ka'otiko/ a chaotic

**capa** /'kapa/ f, cloak; cape; Eccl. cope; coating; layer; cover; coat (animals); Fig. cloak, disguise; Geol. stratum. **la c. del cielo,** the canopy of heaven. Fig. Inf. **echar la c. al toro,** to throw one's cap over the windmill. Naut. **estarse ( or ponerse) a la c.,** to lie to

**capacete** /kapa'θete; kapa'sete/ m, helmet

**capacidad** /kapaθi'ðað; kapasi'ðað/ f, capacity; extension, space; mental capacity; talent; opportunity, means; *Law.* capacity. **c. de compra,** buying power, purchasing power. **c. de producción,** output

**capacitación** /kapaθita'θion; kapasita'sion/ *f*, qualification, (act of) qualifying; (act of) training

**capacitar** /kapaθi'tar; kapasi'tar/ *vt* to capacitate, qualify, enable

**capadura** /kapa'ðura/ *f*, castration

**capar** /ka'par/ *vt* to castrate, geld; *Inf.* diminish, reduce

**caparazón** /kapara'θon; kapara'son/ *m*, caparison, horse blanket; waterproof cover; hood (of carriages); nosebag; shell (insects, crustaceans)

**capataz** /kapa'taθ; kapa'tas/ *m*, foreman; steward; overseer

**capaz** /ka'paθ; ka'pas/ *a* capacious; large, spacious; capable, competent; *Law.* able

**capcioso** /kap'θioso; kap'sioso/ *a* deceitful, artful; captious, carping

**capear** /kape'ar/ *vt* to steal a cape; play the bull with a cape (bullfighting); *Inf.* put off with excuses, deceive; *Naut.* lie to

**capellán** /kape'ʎan; kape'yan/ *m*, chaplain; any ecclesiastic

**capellanía** /kapeʎa'nia; kapeya'nia/ *f*, chaplaincy

**capelo** /ka'pelo/ *m*, cardinal's hat; cardinalate

**capeo** /ka'peo/ *m*, playing the bull with a cape (bullfighting)

**caperuza** /kape'ruθa; kape'rusa/ *f*, hood, pointed cap; *Archit.* coping-stone

**capigorrón** /kapigo'rron/ *a Inf.* loafing. *m*, loafer, idler

**capilar** /kapi'lar/ *a* capillary

**capilaridad** /kapilari'ðað/ *f*, capillarity

**capilla** /ka'piʎa; ka'piya/ *f*, cowl, hood; chapel; *Eccl.* chapter; *Eccl.* choir. **c. ardiente,** chapelle ardente. **estar en c.,** to await execution (criminals); *Inf.* be in suspense, await anxiously

**capillero** /kapi'ʎero; kapi'yero/ *m*, sexton; churchwarden

**capillo** /ka'piʎo; ka'piyo/ *m*, baby's bonnet; cocoon of silkworm; flowerbud

**capirotazo** /kapiro'taθo; kapiro'taso/ *m*, box on the ear; fillip

**capirote** /kapi'rote/ *m*, academic hood and cap; hood (falconry); tall pointed cap. **ser tonto de c.,** *Inf.* to be a complete fool

**capitación** /kapita'θion; kapita'sion/ *f*, poll-tax, capitation

**capital** /kapi'tal/ *a* relating to the head; capital (sins, etc.); main, principal. *m*, capital, patrimony; *Com.* capital stock. *f*, capital (city). **c. pagado,** paid-in capital stock

**capitalismo** /kapita'lismo/ *m*, capitalism

**capitalista** /kapita'lista/ *a* capitalistic. *mf* capitalist

**capitalización** /kapitaliθa'θion; kapitalisa'sion/ *f*, capitalization

**capitalizar** /kapitali'θar; kapitali'sar/ *vt* to capitalize

**capitán** /kapi'tan/ *m*, captain, skipper; chief, leader; ringleader. *Aer.* **c. de aviación,** group captain. **c. de fragata,** *Nav.* commander. **c. de puerto,** harbor master. **c. general de ejército,** field-marshal

**capitana** /kapi'tana/ *f*, admiral's ship; *Inf.* captain's wife

**capitanear** /kapitane'ar/ *vt* to captain, command; *Fig.* guide, lead

**capitanía** /kapita'nia/ *f*, captaincy; captainship

**capitel** /kapi'tel/ *m*, *Archit.* capital

**capitolio** /kapi'tolio/ *m*, dignified building; *Archit.* acropolis; Capitol

**capitulación** /kapitula'θion; kapitula'sion/ *f*, agreement, pact; capitulation; *pl* marriage articles

**capitular** /kapitu'lar/ *a* capitulary, belonging to a Chapter. *m*, capitular, member of a Chapter —*vi* to make an agreement; capitulate; sing prayers; arrange order

**capítulo** /ka'pitulo/ *m*, *Eccl.* Chapter; meeting of town council, etc.; chapter (of book); item (in a budget); determination, decision

**capó** /ka'po/ *m*, *Auto.* hood

**capón** /ka'pon/ *a* castrated; gelded. *m*, capon; bundle of firewood or vines

**caponera** /kapo'nera/ *f*, coop for fattening capons;

*Inf.* gaol; *Inf.* place where one lives well free of charge

**capota** /ka'pota/ *f*, *Bot.* head of teasel; bonnet; hood (of vehicles)

**capote** /ka'pote/ *m*, short, brightly colored cape (used by bullfighters); cape coat; (cards) slam; *Inf.* scowl

**capricho** /ka'pritʃo/ *m*, caprice, fancy; strong desire

**caprichoso** /kapri'tʃoso/ *a* capricious; whimsical

**caprichudo** /kapri'tʃuðo/ *a* headstrong; capricious

**Capricornio** /kapri'kornio/ *m*, Capricorn

**cápsula** /'kapsula/ *f*, cartridge-case; bottlecap; (*Bot. Med. Chem. Zool.*) capsule

**captar** /kap'tar/ *vt* gain, attract (goodwill, attention, etc.); *Mech.* collect; monitor (foreign broadcasts)

**captor** /kap'tor/ *m*, capturer

**captura** /kap'tura/ *f*, *Law.* capture; seizing, arrest

**capturar** /kaptu'rar/ *vt* to capture; arrest, apprehend

**capucha** /ka'putʃa/ *f*, hood; cowl; *Print.* circumflex accent

**capuchina** /kapu'tʃina/ *f*, Capuchin nun; *Bot.* nasturtium; table-lamp with an extinguisher

**capuchino** /kapu'tʃino/ **(-na)** *a* and *n* Capuchin

**capucho** /ka'putʃo/ *m*, cowl

**capullo** /ka'puʎo; ka'puyo/ *m*, cocoon; flower bud; acorn cup; *Anat.* prepuce

**caqui** /'kaki/ *m*, khaki; khaki color

**cara** /'kara/ *f*, face; likeness, aspect; façade, front; surface; side (of metal, etc.); mien. **c. a c.,** face to face; frankly; openly. *Inf.* **c. de juez,** severe face. *Inf.* **c. de pascua,** smiling face. *Inf.* **c. de vinagre,** sour face. **c. o cruz,** heads or tails. **de c.,** opposite. **hacer a dos caras,** to be deceitful, be two-faced. **hacer c.(a),** to stand up to

**caraba** /ka'raβa/ *f*, *Slang.* 25-centimo coin

**cárabe** /'karaβe/ *m*, amber

**carabina** /kara'βina/ *f*, carbine; rifle

**carabinazo** /karaβi'naθo; karaβi'naso/ *m*, report of a carbine

**carabinero** /karaβi'nero/ *m*, carabineer; customs' guard, revenue guard; customs officer, customs official

**caracol** /kara'kol/ *m*, snail; snail's shell; cure; *Zool.* cochlea; winding stair. **c. marino,** periwinkle. **¡Caracoles!** Fancy!

**caracola** /kara'kola/ *f*, conch shell used as a horn

**caracolear** /karakole'ar/ *vi* to prance from side to side (horses)

**carácter** /ka'rakter/ *m*, sign, mark; character, writing (gen. *pl*); style of writing; brand (animals); nature, temperament; character, individuality, strong-mindedness, energy, firmness; condition, state, capacity. **comedia de c.,** psychological play. **en su c. de,** as in one's capacity as. **caracteres de imprenta,** printing types

**característica** /karakte'ristika/ *f*, quality, characteristic; *Math.* characteristic; actress who plays the part of an old woman

**característico** /karakte'ristiko/ *a* characteristic, distinctive. *m*, actor who plays roles of old men

**caracterización** /karakteriθa'θion; karakterisa'sion/ *f*, characterization; *Theat.* make-up

**caracterizar** /karakteri'θar; karakteri'sar/ *vt* to characterize; confer an office, honor, dignity, on; *Theat.* create a character; —*vr Theat.* to make up, dress as, a character

**caraísmo** /kara'ismo/ *m*, Karaism

**caraíta** /kara'ita/ *a* and *mf* Karaite

**¡caramba!** /ka'ramba/ *interj* gosh!; blast!

**carámbano** /ka'rambano/ *m*, icicle

**carambola** /karam'βola/ *f*, cannon (billiards); *Inf.* double effect; *Inf.* trick, deception

**caramelo** /kara'melo/ *m*, caramel; toffee

**caramillo** /kara'miʎo; kara'miyo/ *m*, flageolet; small flute, pipe; gossip, intrigue

**carantamaula** /karanta'maula/ *f*, *Inf.* hideous mask; ugly person

**carapacho** /kara'patʃo/ *m*, carapace, shell

**carátula** /ka'ratula/ *f*, mask; *Fig.* dramatic art, the theater

**caravana** /kara'βana/ *f*, caravan, group of traders, pilgrims, etc. (especially in East); *Inf.* crowd of excursionists, picnickers, etc.

**¡caray!** /ka'rai/ *interj* blast!; gosh!

**carbólico** /kar'βoliko/ *a* carbolic

**carbón** /kar'βon/ *m,* coal; charcoal; black chalk, crayon. **c. bituminoso,** soft coal. **c. de coque,** coke. **c. de leña,** charcoal. **c. mineral,** coal, anthracite. **mina de c.,** coal-mine

**carboncillo** /karβon'θiʎo; karβon'siyo/ *m,* charcoal crayon

**carbonear** /karβone'ar/ *vt* to turn into charcoal; *Naut.* coal

**carboneo** /karβo'neo/ *m,* coaling

**carbonera** /karβo'nera/ *f,* coal-cellar, coal-house, etc.; coal-scuttle; woman who sells charcoal or coal; charcoal burner

**carbonería** /karβone'ria/ *f,* coal or charcoal merchant's office

**carbonero** /karβo'nero/ *a* relating to coal or charcoal. *m,* collier; charcoal maker; coal merchant; *Naut.* coal-ship

**carbónico** /kar'βoniko/ *a Chem.* carbonic

**carbonífero** /karβo'nifero/ *a* carboniferous

**carbonizar** /karβoni'θar; karβoni'sar/ *vt* to carbonize

**carbono** /kar'βono/ *m, Chem.* carbon

**carbonoso** /karβo'noso/ *a* carbonaceous; coaly

**carbunco** /kar'βunko/ *m, Med.* carbuncle

**carbúnculo** /kar'βunkulo/ *m,* carbuncle, ruby

**carburador** /karβura'ðor/ *m,* carburetor

**carcaj** /kar'kah/ *m,* quiver (for arrows)

**carcajada** /karka'haða/ *f,* burst of laughter, guffaw. **reírse a carcajadas,** to roar with laughter

**carcajearse** /karkahe'arse/ *vi* to guffaw

**carcamal** /karka'mal/ *m, Inf.* dotard

**cárcel** /'karθel; 'karsel/ *f,* prison, jail

**carcelario** /karθe'lario; karse'lario/ *a* prison, jail

**carcelero** /karθe'lero; karse'lero/ **(-ra)** *a* jail —*n* jailer

**cárcola** /'karkola/ *f,* treadle (of a loom)

**carcoma** /kar'koma/ *f,* wood-worm; dry rot; *Fig.* gnawing care; spendthrift

**carcomer** /karko'mer/ *vt* to gnaw wood (worms); *Fig.* undermine (health, etc.); —*vr* be worm-eaten

**carda** /'karða/ *f,* card, carding; teasel head; card brush; *Inf.* reprimand

**cardador** /karða'ðor/ **(-ra)** *n* carder, comber

**cardadura** /karða'ðura/ *f,* carding; carding frame

**cardar** /kar'ðar/ *vt* to card, tease; brush up (felt, etc.)

**cardenal** /karðe'nal/ *m,* cardinal; cardinal bird; bruise

**cardenalato** /karðena'lato/ *m,* cardinalate, cardinalship

**cardenillo** /karðe'niʎo; karðe'niyo/ *m,* verdigris; *Art.* verditer

**cárdeno** /'karðeno/ *a* livid

**cardíaco** /kar'ðiako/ *a Med.* cardiac

**cardinal** /karði'nal/ *a* principal; cardinal (point); *Gram.* cardinal (number)

**cardiógrafo** /kar'ðiografo/ *m, Med.* cardiograph

**cardiograma** /karðio'grama/ *m, Med.* cardiogram

**cardizal** /karði'θal; karði'sal/ *m,* waste land covered with thistles and weeds

**cardo** /'karðo/ *m, Bot.* thistle

**carear** /kare'ar/ *vt* to confront; compare; —*vi* turn towards, face; —*vr* meet; come together

**carecer** /kare'θer; kare'ser/ *vi irr* to be short; lack, need (e.g. *Carece de las condiciones necesarias,* It lacks the necessary conditions). See **conocer**

**carena** /ka'rena/ *f, Naut.* bottom; careening

**carenar** /kare'nar/ *vt* to careen

**carencia** /ka'renθia; ka'rensia/ *f,* shortage, lack

**carestía** /kares'tia/ *f,* shortage, scarcity; famine; dearness, high price

**careta** /ka'reta/ *f,* mask; beekeeper's veil; fencing mask. *Fig.* **quitar la c.** ( a), to unmask

**carey** /ka'rei/ *m, Zool.* shell turtle; tortoise-shell

**carga** /'karga/ *f,* loading; *Elec.* charging, charge; load; burden, weight; cargo; explosive charge; *Fig.* imposition; tax; duty, obligation. *Naut.* **c. de profundidad,** depth charge

**cargadero** /karga'ðero/ *m,* place where goods are loaded or unloaded

**cargado** /kar'gaðo/ *a* loaded; heavy, sultry; strong (tea, coffee). **c. de cadenas,** (prisoner, etc.) in chains. **c. de espaldas,** round-shouldered

**cargador** /karga'ðor/ *m,* loader; porter; dockhand; pitchfork; rammer; *Mech.* stoker; *Elec.* charger

**cargamento** /karga'mento/ *m, Naut.* cargo, freight, shipload

**cargar** /kar'gar/ *vt* to load; charge (guns, etc.); stoke; overburden; tax, impose; blame for, charge with; *Inf.* annoy, bore; *Argentina Inf.* to kid, tease; *Com.* charge, book; *Mil.* attack; (football) tackle; —*vi* tip, slope; (*with con*) carry away; be loaded with (fruit); assume responsibility; (*with sobre*) importune, urge; lean against; —*vr* turn (head, etc.); lower, grow darker (sky); (*with de*) be abundant (in or with); load oneself with

**cargazón** /karga'θon; karga'son/ *f,* cargo; loading; heaviness; darkness (of the sky)

**cargo** /'kargo/ *m,* loading; load, weight; post, office; duty, obligation; management, charge; care; *Com.* debit; accusation. *Com.* **el c. y la data,** debit and credit. **hacerse c. de,** to take charge of; understand; consider carefully. **ser en c.** ( a), to be debtor (to)

**cariacontecido** /kariakonte'θiðo; kariakonte'siðo/ *a* crestfallen, disappointed; glum

**cariancho** /kari'antʃo/ *a Inf.* broadfaced

**cariarse** /ka'riarse/ *vr* to become carious

**cariátide** /kari'atiðe/ *f, Archit.* caryatid

**caribe** /ka'riβe/ *a* Caribbean. *mf* cannibal, savage

**caricatura** /karika'tura/ *f,* caricature

**caricaturesco** /karikatu'resko/ *a* caricaturish

**caricaturista** /karikatu'rista/ *mf* caricaturist

**caricaturizar** /karikaturi'θar; karikaturi'sar/ *vt* to caricature

**caricia** /ka'riθia; ka'risia/ *f,* caress

**caridad** /kari'ðað/ *f,* charity; charitableness; alms

**caries** /'karies/ *f,* caries

**carilargo** /kari'largo/ *a Inf.* long-faced

**carilla** /ka'riʎa; ka'riya/ *f, dim* small face; mask; page (of a book)

**carilleno** /kari'ʎeno; kari'yeno/ *a Inf.* plump-faced, round-faced

**carillón** /kari'ʎon; kari'yon/ *m,* peal (of bells)

**cariño** /ka'riɲo/ *m,* affection; love; caress affectionately (gen. *pl*); fondness, inclination. **con c.,** affectionately

**cariñoso** /kari'ɲoso/ *a* affectionate; loving; kind

**carirredondo** /karirre'ðondo/ *a Inf.* roundfaced

**carismático** /karis'matiko/ *a* charismatic

**caritativo** /karita'tiβo/ *a* charitable

**cariz** /ka'riθ; ka'ris/ *m,* appearance of the sky; look, face; aspect; *Inf.* outlook (for a business deal, etc.)

**carlista** /kar'lista/ *a* and *mf* Carlist

**carmelita** /karme'lita/ *a* and *mf* Carmelite

**carmen** /'karmen/ *m,* country house and garden (Granada); song; poem

**carmesí** /karme'si/ *a* crimson. *m,* crimson color; cramoisy

**carmín** /kar'min/ *m,* red, carmine color; red wild rose-tree and flower

**carnada** /kar'naða/ *f,* bait

**carnaje** /kar'nahe/ *m,* salted meat

**carnal** /kar'nal/ *a* carnal; lascivious; materialistic, worldly; related by blood

**carnalidad** /karnali'ðað/ *f,* carnality

**carnaval** /karna'βal/ *m,* carnival. **martes de c.,** Shrove Tuesday

**carnavalesco** /karnaβa'lesko/ *a* carnival

**carne** /'karne/ *f,* flesh; meat; pulpy part of fruit; carnality, **c. concentrada,** meat extract. **c. congelada,** frozen meat. **c. de gallina** *Fig.* gooseflesh. **c. de membrillo,** quince cheese or conserve. **c. y hueso,** *Fig.* flesh and blood. *Inf.* **cobrar carnes,** to put on weight. **poner toda la c. en el asador,** *Inf.* to put all one's eggs in one basket

**carnerada** /karne'raða/ *f,* flock of sheep

**carnerero** /karne'rero/ **(-ra)** *n* shepherd

**carnero** /kar'nero/ *m,* sheep; mutton; mortuary; charnel-house; family burial vault. **c. marino,** *Zool.* seal

**carnestolendas** /karnesto'lendas/ *f pl* three days of carnival before Ash Wednesday

**carnet** /kar'net/ *m,* notebook, diary; identity card; membership card, pass. **c. de chófer,** driving license

**carnicería** /karniθe'ria; karnise'ria/ *f,* butcher's shop; carnage, slaughter

**carnicero** /karni'θero; karni'sero/ *a* carnivorous; inhuman, cruel. *m,* butcher

**carnívoro** /kar'niβoro/ *a* carnivorous. *m,* carnivore

**carnosidad** /karnosi'ðað/ *f,* proud flesh; local fat; fatness

**carnoso** /kar'noso/ *a* meaty; fleshy; full of marrow; *Bot.* pulpy, juicy

**caro** /'karo/ *a* beloved; expensive; dear —*adv* expensively; dear

**carolingio** /karo'linhio/ **(-ia)** *a* and *n* Carolingian

**carótida** /ka'rotiða/ *f,* carotid artery

**carpa** /'karpa/ *f, Ichth.* carp. **c. dorada,** goldfish

**carpanta** /kar'panta/ *f, Inf.* violent hunger

**Cárpatos, los Montes** /'karpatos, los 'montes/ the Carpathian Mountains

**carpeta** /kar'peta/ *f,* table or chest cover, doily; writing case; portfolio; docket, letter file

**carpetazo, dar** /karpe'taθo, dar; karpe'taso, dar/ *vt* to shelve (a project, etc.)

**carpintear** /karpinte'ar/ *vi* to carpenter

**carpintería** /karpinte'ria/ *f,* carpenter's shop; carpentry

**carpinteril** /karpinte'ril/ *a* carpentering

**carpintero** /karpin'tero/ *m,* carpenter, joiner; *Theat.* scene-shifter. **c. de carretas,** wheelwright. **c. de ribera,** shipwright

**carraca** /ka'rraka/ *f,* rattle; ratchet-drill

**Carrapempe** /karra'pempe/ *m,* Old Nick

**carrascal** /karras'kal/ *m,* field of pinoaks

**carraspear** /karraspe'ar/ *vi* to clear one's throat, cough

**carraspera** /karras'pera/ *f, Inf.* hoarseness

**carraspique** /karras'pike/ *m, Bot.* candytuft

**carrera** /ka'rrera/ *f,* run; race; racing; racecourse; *Astron.* course; high road; route; *Mas.* layer, course; line, row; *Fig.* ladder (in stockings, etc.); course; duration (of life); career, profession; conduct; girder. **c. de fondo,** long-distance race. **c. de relevos, c. de equipos,** relay race. **a c. abierta, a c. tendida,** at full speed

**carrerista** /karre'rista/ *mf* racing enthusiast; professional racer

**carreta** /ka'rreta/ *f,* long, narrow two-wheeled cart; wagon; tumbril

**carretada** /karre'taða/ *f,* cart-load; *Inf.* great deal, mass

**carretaje** /karre'tahe/ *m,* cartage; carriage; transport

**carrete** /ka'rrete/ *m,* spool, reel, bobbin; fishing reel; *Elec.* coil; *Photo.* film spool

**carretear** /karrete'ar/ *vt* to cart; drive a cart

**carretela** /karre'tela/ *f,* calash

**carretera** /karre'tera/ *f,* high road

**carretería** /karrete'ria/ *f,* number of carts; carting trade; cartwright's yard

**carretero** /karre'tero/ *m,* cartwright; carter, driver

**carretilla** /karre'tiλa; karre'tiya/ *f,* wheelbarrow; hand cart; railway truck; squib. **de c.,** *Inf.* mechanically, without thought; (*with saber, repetir,* etc.) by rote

**carretón** /karre'ton/ *m,* truck, trolley; hand cart

**carril** /ka'rril/ *m,* wheel mark; furrow, rut; cart road, narrow road; rail (railways, etc.)

**carrillera** /karri'λera; karri'yera/ *f,* jaw (of some animals); chin strap; *pl* bonnet strings, etc.

**carrillo** /ka'rriλo; ka'rriyo/ *m,* cheek; jowl

**carriola** /ka'rriola/ *f,* truckle bed; curricle

**carro** /'karro/ *m,* cart; cartload; car, chariot; carriage (of a typewriter, etc.); chassis; *Astron.* Plow, Great Bear. *Mil.* **c. blindado,** armored car. *Mil.* **c. de asalto,** tank. **c. de mudanzas,** moving van. **c. de regar,** watercart

**carrocería** /karroθe'ria; karrose'ria/ *f,* place where carriages are made, sold, repaired; *Auto.* coachwork, body shop

**carrocha** /ka'rrotʃa/ *f,* eggs (of insects)

**carrochar** /karro'tʃar/ *vi* to lay eggs (insects)

**carromato** /karro'mato/ *m,* road wagon; covered wagon

**carroña** /ka'rroɲa/ *f,* putrid flesh, carrion

**carroza** /ka'rroθa; ka'rrosa/ *f,* elegant coach; state coach; carriage; float (for tableaux, etc.); *Naut.* awning

**carruaje** /ka'rruahe/ *m,* carriage; any vehicle

**carta** /'karta/ *f,* letter; charter; royal order; playing card; chart, map. **c. certificada,** registered letter. **c. de amparo,** safe-conduct. **c. de crédito,** *Com.* letter of credit. **c. de marear,** sea chart. **c. de naturaleza,** naturalization papers. **c. de pésame,** letter of condolence. **c. de venta,** *Com.* bill of sale. **c. ejecutoria de hidalguía,** letters patent of nobility. **carta-poder,** letter of proxy, proxy. **cartas rusas,** (game of) consequences. **poner las cartas boca arriba,** *Fig.* to lay one's cards on the table

**cartabón** /karta'βon/ *m,* set-square; shoemaker's slide; quadrant

**cartaginés** /kartahi'nes/ **(-esa)** *a* and *n* Carthaginian

**Cartago** /'kartago/ Carthage

**cartapacio** /karta'paθio; karta'pasio/ *m,* note-book; schoolbag, satchel; file, batch of papers

**cartear** /karte'ar/ *vi Cards.* to play low; —*vr* to correspond by letter

**cartel** /kar'tel/ *m,* placard, poster; cartel; pasquinade, lampoon. **fijar carteles,** to placard

**cartela** /kar'tela/ *f,* tablet (for writing); slip (of paper, etc.); *Archit.* console, bracket

**cartelera** /karte'lera/ *f,* billboard

**cartelero** /karte'lero/ *m,* billpaster, billsticker

**carteo** /kar'teo/ *m,* correspondence (by letter)

**cartera** /kar'tera/ *f,* pocketbook; wallet; dispatch-case; portfolio; notebook; pocket flap; office of a cabinet minister; *Com.* shares

**cartería** /karte'ria/ *f,* sorting room (in a post-office)

**carterista** /karte'rista/ *mf* pickpocket

**cartero** /kar'tero/ *m,* mail carrier, postman

**cartesiano** /karte'siano/ **(-na)** *a* and *n* Cartesian

**Cartesio** /kar'tesio/ Descartes

**carteta** /kar'teta/ *f,* lansquenet (card game)

**cartilaginoso** /kartilahi'noso/ *a* cartilaginous

**cartílago** /kar'tilago/ *m,* cartilage

**cartilla** /kar'tiλa; kar'tiya/ *f,* first reading book; primer; certificate of ordination; note-book; liturgical calendar. **c. de racionamiento,** ration book

**cartografía** /kartogra'fia/ *f,* cartography

**cartógrafo** /kar'tografo/ *m,* map maker

**cartón** /kar'ton/ *m,* pasteboard, cardboard; *Archit.* bracket; *Art.* cartoon, design

**cartuchera** /kartu'tʃera/ *f,* cartridge-pouch; cartridge-belt

**cartucho** /kar'tutʃo/ *m,* cartridge; paper cone

**cartuja** /kar'tuha/ *f,* Carthusian Order or monastery

**cartujano** /kartu'hano/ *a* Carthusian

**cartujo** /kar'tuho/ *m,* Carthusian monk; *Inf.* taciturn, reserved man

**cartulina** /kartu'lina/ *f,* Bristol board, oaktag, pasteboard, card

**carúncula** /ka'runkula/ *f,* caruncle, comb of cock, etc.

**casa** /'kasa/ *f,* house; home; household; residence, dwelling; family house; *Com.* firm. **c. consistorial,** town hall. **c. cuna,** crèche. **c. de campo,** country-house. **c. de empeño,** pawnshop. **c. de huéspedes,** boarding house, lodging-house. **c. de los sustos,** haunted house (at amusement park). **c. de moneda,** mint. **c. de socorro,** First Aid Post. **c. de vecindad,** tenement. **c. mala,** house of ill repute. **c. solar** or **c. solariega,** family seat. **en c.,** at home (also sport usage). **poner c.,** to set up house

**casaca** /ka'saka/ *f,* dress coat. **volver la c.,** to become a turncoat, change one's allegiance

**casación** /kasa'θion; kasa'sion/ *f, Law.* cassation

**casadero** /kasa'ðero/ *a* marriageable

**casadoro** /kasa'ðoro/ *m, Costa Rica* bus

**casamata** /kasa'mata/ *f, Mil.* casemate

**casamiento** /kasa'miento/ *m,* marriage; wedding

**casar** /ka'sar/ *vt* to marry (of a priest); *Law.* repeal; *Inf.* marry off; join; match, harmonize; —*vi* and *vr* (*with con*) to get married

**casar** /ka'sar/ *m*, group of houses

**casca** /'kaska/ *f*, grape skin; tan (bark); shell, peel, rind

**cascabel** /kaska'βel/ *m*, small bell (for harness, etc.). **serpiente de c.,** rattlesnake. *Inf.* **ser un c.,** to be feather-brained

**cascabeleo** /kaska'βeleo/ *m*, jingling of bells

**cascabillo** /kaska'βiʎo; kaska'βiyo/ *m*, husk (of cereals)

**cascada** /kas'kaða/ *f*, cascade; waterfall

**cascadura** /kaska'ðura/ *f*, cracking, crack

**cascajo** /kas'kaho/ *m*, gravel, shingle; *Inf.* broken, old things, junk; nuts

**cascanueces** /kaska'nueθes; kaska'nueses/ *m*, nut-crackers

**cascar** /kas'kar/ *vt* to crack, split, break; *Inf.* beat; *Fig. Inf.* break down (of health); —*vi Inf.* talk, chatter

**cáscara** /'kaskara/ *f*, shell; peel, rind; bark. *Med.* **c. sagrada,** cascara

**cascarón** /kaska'ron/ *m*, eggshell; *Archit.* vault

**cascarrabias** /kaska'rraβias/ *mf Inf.* spitfire

**casco** /'kasko/ *m*, cranium; broken fragment of china, glass, etc.; crown of hat; helmet; tree of saddle; bottle; tank; pipe; barrel; *Naut.* hull; hoof; quarter (of fruit); *pl Inf.* head. **c. colonial,** sun-helmet. **c. respiratorio,** smoke-helmet

**cascote** /kas'kote/ *m*, rubble, ruins

**caseoso** /kase'oso/ *a* cheesy

**caserío** /kase'rio/ *m*, group of houses; country house

**casero** /ka'sero/ *a* home made; home bred; familiar; informa; *Inf.* domesticated, home-loving; domestic. *m*, *landlord*; caretaker; tenant

**caserón** /kase'ron/ *m*, large tumbledown house, mansion, hall

**caseta** /ka'seta/ *f*, hut; cottage; booth, stall. **c. de baños,** bathing van

**casi** /'kasi/ *adv* almost, nearly. **c. c.,** very nearly

**casilla** /ka'siʎa; ka'siya/ *f*, hut; cabin; lodge; ticket office; pigeon-hole. *Aer.* **c. del piloto,** cockpit

**casillero** /kasi'ʎero; kasi'yero/ *m*, file cabinet, filing cabinet; locker (as in a locker room); set of pigeon-holes; *Sports.* scoreboard; *Rail.* crossing guard

**casino** /ka'sino/ *m*, casino; club

**caso** /'kaso/ *m*, happening, event; chance, hazard; occasion, opportunity; case, matter; (*Med. Gram.*) case. **en el c. de,** in a position to (e.g. *No estamos en el c. de pagar tanto dinero.* We are in no position to pay so much money). **en tal c.,** in such a case. **en todo c.,** in any case. **no hacer c. de,** to take no notice of. **venir al c.,** to be opportune

**caspa** /'kaspa/ *f*, dandruff; scab

**caspio** /'kaspio/ *a* Caspian

**¡cáspita!** /'kaspita/ *interj* Amazing! Wonderful!

**casquete** /kas'kete/ *m*, helmet; skullcap; half wig

**casquijo** /kas'kiho/ *m*, gravel

**casquillo** /kas'kiʎo; kas'kiyo/ *m*, tip, cap, ferrule; socket; arrow-head; metal cartridge-case

**casquivano** /kaski'βano/ *a Inf.* giddy, feather-brained

**casta** /'kasta/ *f*, race; caste; breed (animals); kind, species, quality. **de buena c.,** pedigree (e.g. *perros de buena c.,* pedigree dogs)

**castaña** /kas'taɲa/ *f*, *Bot.* chestnut; knot, bun (of hair)

**castañar** /kasta'ɲar/ *m*, chestnut plantation or grove

**castañetear** /kastaɲete'ar/ *vi* to play the castanets; snap one's fingers; chatter (of teeth); knock together (of knees)

**castaño** /kas'taɲo/ *a* chestnut-colored. *m*, chestnut tree; chestnut wood. **c. de Indias,** horse-chestnut tree

**castañuela** /kasta'ɲuela/ *f*, castanet. **tocar las castañuelas,** to play the castanets

**castellano** /kaste'ʎano; kaste'yano/ *m*, castellan

**castellano** /kaste'ʎano; kaste'yano/ **(-na)** *n* Castilian; Spaniard. *m*, Spanish (language); castellan —*a* Castilian; Spanish

**casticismo** /kasti'θismo; kasti'sismo/ *m*, purity (of language); Spanish spirit; traditionalism

**castidad** /kasti'ðað/ *f*, chastity

**castigador** /kastiga'ðor/ *a* punishing. *m*, punisher; *Inf.* lady-killer

**castigadora** /kastiga'ðora/ *f*, *Inf.* man-hunter

**castigar** /kasti'gar/ *vt* to punish; chastise; chasten, advise; pain, grieve; correct, edit; decrease (expenses); *Com.* allow a discount

**castigo** /kas'tigo/ *m*, punishment; emendation, correction

**Castilla** /kas'tiʎa; kas'tiya/ Castile

**castillo** /kas'tiʎo; kas'tiyo/ *m*, castle; howdah. **c. de naipes,** house of cards. **c. de proa,** *Naut.* forecastle. **c. fuerte,** fortified castle. *Inf.* **hacer castillos en el aire,** to build castles in the air or in Spain

**castizo** /kas'tiθo; kas'tiso/ *a* pure-blooded; prolific; pure (of language); typically Spanish; traditional

**casto** /'kasto/ *a* chaste; pure, unsullied

**castor** /kas'tor/ *m*, *Zool.* beaver (animal and fur); soft, woollen cloth

**castración** /kastra'θion; kastra'sion/ *f*, castration, gelding

**castrado** /kas'traðo/ *a* castrated. *m*, *Inf.* eunuch

**castrador** /kastra'ðor/ *m*, castrator, gelder

**castrapo** /kas'trapo/ *m*, mixed Spanish and Galician spoken in Galicia, Spain

**castrar** /kas'trar/ *vt* to castrate, geld; prune; remove honeycomb from hives; weaken

**castrense** /kas'trense/ *a* military

**castrista** /kas'trista/ *v* and *mf* Castroite

**casual** /ka'sual/ *a* accidental, casual

**casualidad** /kasuali'ðað/ *f*, chance, coincidence. **por c.,** by chance. **ser mucha c. que...,** to be too much of a coincidence that...

**casucha** /ka'sutʃa/ *f*, *Inf.* tumbledown hut

**casuista** /ka'suista/ *a* casuistic. *mf* casuist

**casuística** /ka'suistika/ *f*, casuistry

**casulla** /ka'suʎa; ka'suya/ *f*, chasuble

**cata** /'kata/ *f*, tasting; taste, sample

**catabolismo** /kataβo'lismo/ *m*, catabolism

**cataclismo** /kata'klismo/ *m*, cataclysm

**catacumbas** /kata'kumbas/ *f pl*, catacombs

**catador** /kata'ðor/ *m*, taster, sampler

**catadura** /kata'ðura/ *f*, tasting; look, countenance (gen. qualified)

**catafalco** /kata'falko/ *m*, catafalque

**catalán** /kata'lan/ **(-ana)** *a* and *n* Catalan, Catalonian. *m*, Catalan (language)

**catalejo** /kata'leho/ *m*, telescope

**cataléptico** /kata'leptiko/ *a* cataleptic

**catálisis** /ka'talisis/ *f*, *Chem.* catalysis

**catalítico** /kata'litiko/ *a* catalytic

**catalogar** /katalo'gar/ *vt* to catalog, list

**catálogo** /ka'talogo/ *m*, catalog, list

**Cataluña** /kata'luɲa/ Catalonia

**cataplasma** /kata'plasma/ *f*, cataplasm

**catapulta** /kata'pulta/ *f*, catapult

**catar** /ka'tar/ *vt* to taste, sample; see, examine; inspect; regard

**catarata** /kata'rata/ *f*, cataract, waterfall; *Med.* cataract (of the eyes)

**catarral** /kata'rral/ *a* catarrhal

**catarro** /ka'tarro/ *m*, catarrh; common cold

**catástrofe** /ka'tastrofe/ *f*, *Lit.* tragic climax; catastrophe

**catastrófico** /katas'trofiko/ *a* catastrophic

**catavino** /kata'βino/ *m*, taster (cup)

**catavinos** /kata'βinos/ *m*, professional wine taster; *Inf.* tippler, tavern haunter

**cate** /'kate/ *m*, *Slang* flunk (failure in a course at school)

**catecismo** /kate'θismo; kate'sismo/ *m*, catechism

**catecúmeno** /kate'kumeno/ **(-na)** *n* catechumen

**cátedra** /'kateðra/ *f*, university chair; chair in a Spanish **instituto;** professorship; university lecture room; subject taught by professor; reading desk, lectern; *Eccl.* throne; *Eccl.* see. **c. del espíritu santo,** pulpit. **c. de San Pedro,** Holy See

**catedral** /kate'ðral/ *f*, and *a* cathedral

**catedrático** /kate'ðratiko/ **(-ca)** *n* professor

**categoría** /katego'ria/ *f*, *Philos.* category; class, rank

**categórico** /kate'goriko/ *a* categorical, downright

**cateo** /ka'teo/ *m*, *West. Hem.* sampling; prospecting; house search (by the police)

**catequismo** /kate'kismo/ *m*, catechism; question and answer method of teaching

**catequista** /kate'kista/ *mf* catechist

**catequizar** /kateki'θar; kateki'sar/ *vt* to catechize; persuade, induce

**caterva** /ka'terβa/ *f*, crowd, throng; jumble, collection

**catéter** /ka'teter/ *m*, *Surg*. probe; catheter

**catódico** /ka'toðiko/ *a Elec*. cathodic

**cátodo** /'katoðo/ *m*, cathode

**catolicidad** /katoliθi'ðað; katolisi'ðað/ *f*, catholicity; catholic world

**catolicismo** /katoli'θismo; katoli'sismo/ *m*, Catholicism

**católico** /ka'toliko/ **(-ca)** *a* universal, catholic; infallible —*a* and *n* Catholic (by religion)

**catorce** /ka'torθe; ka'torse/ *a* fourteen; fourteenth. *m*, number fourteen; fourteenth (of days of month)

**catorzavo** /kator'θaβo; kator'saβo/ *a* fourteenth

**catre** /'katre/ *m*, camp-bed; truckle-bed; cot

**caucáseo** /kau'kaseo/ **(-ea)** *a* and *n* Caucasian

**Cáucaso, el** /'kaukaso, el/ the Caucasus

**cauce** /'kauθe; 'kause/ *m*, river or stream bed; ditch, irrigation canal

**cauchal** /kau'tʃal/ *m*, rubber plantation

**cauchera** /kau'tʃera/ *f*, rubber tree

**cauchero** /kau'tʃero/ *m*, rubber planter

**caucho** /'kautʃo/ *m*, caoutchouc, rubber

**caución** /kau'θion; kau'sion/ *f*, caution, precaution; surety; security

**caucional** /kauθio'nal; kausio'nal/ *a* See **libertad**

**caudal** /kau'ðal/ *m*, wealth, capital; flow, volume (of water); plenty, abundance (e.g. *un c. de conocimientos*, a wealth of knowledge)

**caudaloso** /kauða'loso/ *a* carrying much water; wealthy; abundant

**caudillo** /kau'ðiʎo; kau'ðiyo/ *m*, head, leader; chieftain. **el C.,** (title of Francisco Franco)

**causa** /'kausa/ *f*, cause; reason, motive; lawsuit; *Law*. trial. **c. final,** *Philos*. final cause. **c. pública,** public welfare. **ser c. bastante para...,** to be reason enough to...

**causador** /kausa'ðor/ **(-ra)** *a* motivating —*n* occasioner, originator

**causalidad** /kausali'ðað/ *f*, causality

**causante** /kau'sante/ *a* causative, causing. *m*, *Law*. principal; *Mexico* taxpayer

**causar** /kau'sar/ *vt* to cause; occasion

**causticidad** /kaustiθi'ðað; kaustisi'ðað/ *f*, causticity; mordacity

**cáustico** /'kaustiko/ *a* burning, caustic; scathing; mordant; *Surg*. caustic

**cautela** /kau'tela/ *f*, caution; astuteness, cunning

**cauteloso** /kaute'loso/ *a* cautious; cunning

**cauterio** /kau'terio/ *m*, cautery

**cauterización** /kauteriθa'θion; kauterisa'sion/ *f*, cauterization

**cauterizar** /kauteri'θar; kauteri'sar/ *vt* to cauterize

**cautivar** /kauti'βar/ *vt* to capture; captivate, charm; attract; —*vi* become a prisoner

**cautiverio** /kauti'βerio/ *m*, captivity

**cautivo** /kau'tiβo/ **(-va)** *a* and *n* captive

**cauto** /'kauto/ *a* cautious; prudent; sly

**cava** /'kaβa/ *f*, digging (especially vines); wine cellar in royal palaces

**cavador** /kaβa'ðor/ **(-ra)** *n* digger, hoer

**cavadura** /kaβa'ðura/ *f*, digging, hoeing; sinking (wells)

**cavar** /ka'βar/ *vt* to dig, hoe; sink (wells); —*vi* hollow; *Fig*. go deeply into a thing

**caverna** /ka'βerna/ *f*, cavern, cave; *Med*. cavity (generally in the lung)

**cavernícola** /kaβer'nikola/ *a* cave. **hombre c.,** caveman

**cavernoso** /kaβer'noso/ *a* cavernous; caverned; *Fig*. hollow (cough, etc.); deaf

**cavidad** /kaβi'ðað/ *f*, cavity; sinus; cell

**cavilación** /kaβila'θion; kaβila'sion/ *f*, caviling

**cavilar** /kaβi'lar/ *vt* to cavil; criticize

**caviloso** /kaβi'loso/ *a* captious

**cayado** /ka'yaðo/ *m*, crook; bishop's crozier

**caz** /kaθ; kas/ *m*, channel, canal; head-race, flume

**caza** /'kaθa; 'kasa/ *f*, hunting; hunt, chase; game. *m*, *Aer*. fighter. *Aer*. **c. lanzacohetes,** rocket-launching

aircraft. **c. nocturno,** night fighter. *Naut*. **dar c.,** to pursue

**cazaautógrafos** /ˌkaθaau'tografos; ˌkasaau'tografos/ *m*, autograph hunter

**cazabombardero** /ˌkaθaβombar'ðero; ˌkasaβombar-'ðero/ *m*, *Aer*. fighter bomber

**cazadero** /kaθa'ðero; kasa'ðero/ *m*, hunting ground

**cazador** /kaθa'ðor; kasa'ðor/ *a* hunting. *m*, *Mil*. chasseur; huntsman

**cazadora** /kaθa'ðora; kasa'ðora/ *f*, huntress; jacket; forage cap

**cazadotes** /kaθa'ðotes; kasa'ðotes/ *m*, dowry hunter

**cazafortunas** /kaθafor'tunas; kasafor'tunas/ *mf* fortune hunter

**cazar** /ka'θar; ka'sar/ *vt* to hunt, chase; *Fig. Inf*. run to earth; *Fig. Inf*. catch out; *Inf*. overcome by flattery

**cazasubmarino** /kaθasuβma'rino; kasasuβma'rino/ *m*, submarine chaser

**cazatorpedero** /kaθatorpe'ðero; kasatorpe'ðero/ *m*, *Naut*. torpedo-boat destroyer

**cazo** /'kaθo; 'kaso/ *m*, ladle; dipper

**cazolada** /kaθo'laða; kaso'laða/ *f*, panful

**cazoleta** /kaθo'leta; kaso'leta/ *f*, small pan; bowl (of pipe, etc.); sword guard; boss of a shield; pan (of a firelock)

**cazuela** /ka'θuela; ka'suela/ *f*, earthenware cooking dish; stew-pot; part of theater formerly reserved for women; *Theat*. gallery

**cazumbrón** /kaθum'βron; kasum'βron/ *m*, cooper

**cazurro** /ka'θurro; ka'surro/ *a Inf*. unsociable; surly, boorish

**c.c.p.** /θeθe'pe; sese'pe/ abbrev. of **con copia para**

**ce** /θe; se/ *f*, name of the letter C —*interj* Look! Chist! **ce por be,** in detail

**cebada** /θe'βaða; se'βaða/ *f*, barley (plant and grain). **c. perlada,** pearl barley

**cebadal** /θeβa'ðal; seβa'ðal/ *m*, barley field

**cebadera** /θeβa'ðera; seβa'ðera/ *f*, nose-bag; barley bin

**cebadero** /θeβa'ðero; seβa'ðero/ *m*, barley dealer

**cebado** /θe'βaðo; se'βaðo/ *a* on the prowl; having tasted human flesh (animal)

**cebar** /θe'βar; se'βar/ *vt* to feed or fatten (animals); fuel, feed (furnace, etc.); prime, charge (firearms, etc.); start up (machines); bait (fish hook); stimulate (passion, etc.); —*vi* stick in, penetrate (nails, screws, etc.); —*vr* put one's mind to; grow angry. **cebarse en vanas esperanzas,** to nurture vain hopes

**cebo** /'θeβo; 'seβo/ *m*, fodder; detonator; encouragement, food; bait

**cebolla** /θe'βoʎa; se'βoya/ *f*, onion; onion bulb; any bulbous stem; oil bulb (of lamp). **c. escalonia,** shallot

**cebollana** /θeβo'ʎana; seβo'yana/ *f*, chive

**cebollero** /θeβo'ʎero; seβo'yero/ **(-ra)** *n* onion seller

**cebolleta** /θeβo'ʎeta; seβo'yeta/ *f*, leek; young onion

**cebollino** /θeβo'ʎino; seβo'yino/ *m*, onion seed; onion bed; chive

**cebra** /'θeβra; 'seβra/ *f*, zebra

**ceca** /'θeka; 'seka/ *f*, mint (for coining money); name of mosque in Cordova. **de C. en Meca,** from pillar to post, hither and thither

**cecear** /θeθe'ar; sese'ar/ *vi* to lisp

**ceceo** /θe'θeo; se'seo/ *m*, lisping

**ceceoso** /θeθe'oso; sese'oso/ *a* lisping

**cecial** /θe'θial; se'sial/ *m*, dried fish

**cecina** /θe'θina; se'sina/ *f*, dried salt meat

**cedazo** /θe'ðaθo; se'ðaso/ *m*, sieve, strainer

**ceder** /θe'ðer; se'ðer/ *vt* to cede, give up; transfer; —*vi* give in, yield; diminish, decrease (fever, storm, etc.); fail, end; happen, turn out; sag, give, stretch. **No c. la fama a,** to be no less famous than

**cedro** /'θeðro; 'seðro/ *m*, cedar tree; cedar wood. **c. dulce,** red cedar

**cédula** /'θeðula; 'seðula/ *f*, document, certificate, card. *Eccl*. **c. de comunión,** Communion card. **c. personal,** identity card. **c. real,** royal letters patent

**céfiro** /'θefiro; 'sefiro/ *m*, west wind; *Poet*. zephyr

**cegajoso** /θega'hoso; sega'hoso/ *a* blear-eyed

**cegar** /θe'gar; se'gar/ *vi irr* to become blind; —*vt* to put out the eyes; *Fig*. blind; wall up, close up, stop up; infatuate —*Pres. Indic.* **ciego, ciegas, ciega, ciegan.** *Pres. Subjunc.* **ciegue, ciegues, ciegue, cieguen**

**cegato** /θe'gato; se'gato/ *a Inf.* short-sighted

**ceguedad, ceguera** /θege'ðað, θe'gera; sege'ðað, se'gera/ *f,* blindness; delusion; ignorance

**Ceilán** /θei'lan; sei'lan/ Ceylon

**ceja** /'θeha; 'seha/ *f,* eyebrow; cloud cap; mountain peak; *Mus.* bridge (of stringed instruments). *Fig.* **quemarse las cejas,** to burn the midnight oil

**cejar** /θe'har; se'har/ *vi* to go backwards; give way, hesitate

**cejijunto** /θehi'hunto; sehi'hunto/ *a* having eyebrows that almost meet, beetle-browed

**cejo** /'θeho; 'seho/ *m,* river mist

**cejudo** /θe'huðo; se'huðo/ *a* having long thick eyebrows

**celada** /θe'laða; se'laða/ *f,* helmet; ambush; fraud, trick

**celador** /θela'ðor; sela'ðor/ **(-ra)** *a* watchful, zealous —*n* supervisor; caretaker; guard (at a museum, etc.)

**celaje** /θe'lahe; se'lahe/ *m,* sky with scudding clouds (gen. *pl*); skylight, window; promising sign, presage

**celar** /θe'lar; se'lar/ *vt* to be zealous in discharge of duties; spy upon; watch; oversee, superintend; conceal; engrave

**celda** /'θelda; 'selda/ *f,* cell

**celdilla** /θel'diʎa; sel'diya/ *f,* cell (bees, wasps, etc.); (*Zool. Bot.*) cell; *Bot.* capsule

**celebérrimo,** /θele'βerrimo; sele'βerrimo,/ *a superl* **célebre** most celebrated

**celebración** /θeleβra'θion; seleβra'sion/ *f,* celebration; applause

**celebrador** /θeleβra'ðor; seleβra'ðor/ **(-ra)** *n* celebrator; applauder

**celebrante** /θele'βrante; sele'βrante/ *a* celebrating. *m, Eccl.* celebrant

**celebrar** /θele'βrar; sele'βrar/ *vt* to celebrate; applaud; praise; venerate; hold, conduct; **c. que** + *subj,* to be happy that, be glad that —*vt* and *vi Eccl.* officiate; —*vr* take place

**célebre** /'θeleβre; 'seleβre/ *a* famous

**celebridad** /θeleβri'ðað; seleβri'ðað/ *f,* fame, celebrity; magnificence, show, pomp

**celeridad** /θeleri'ðað; seleri'ðað/ *f,* celerity

**celeste** /θe'leste; se'leste/ *a* celestial, heavenly

**celestial** /θeles'tial; seles'tial/ *a* celestial, heavenly; perfect, delightful; *Inf.* foolish (ironical)

**celestina** /θeles'tina; seles'tina/ *f,* procuress (allusion to *Tragicomedia de Calixto y Melibea*)

**celestinaje** /θelesti'nahe; selesti'nahe/ *m,* pandering, procuring

**celibato** /θeli'βato; seli'βato/ *m,* celibacy; *Inf.* bachelor

**célibe** /'θeliβe; 'seliβe/ *a* celibate, unmarried. *mf* unmarried person

**celo** /'θelo; 'selo/ *m,* enthusiasm, ardor; religious zeal; devotion; jealousy; heat, rut; *pl* jealousy, suspicion. **dar celos (a),** to make jealous

**celosía** /θelo'sia; selo'sia/ *f,* lattice; Venetian blind

**celoso** /θe'loso; se'loso/ *a* zealous; jealous; suspicious

**celta** /'θelta; 'selta/ *a* Celtic. *mf* Celt

**célula** /'θelula; 'selula/ *f,* cell

**celular** /θelu'lar; selu'lar/ *a* cellular —*m,* cellular phone.

**celuloide** /θelu'loiðe; selu'loiðe/ *f,* celluloid

**celulosa** /θelu'losa; selu'losa/ *f,* cellulose

**celuloso** /θelu'loso; selu'loso/ *a* cellular

**cementación** /θementa'θion; sementa'sion/ *f,* cementation

**cementar** /θemen'tar; semen'tar/ *vt* to cement

**cementerio** /θemen'terio; semen'terio/ *m,* cemetery

**cemento** /θe'mento; se'mento/ *m,* cement

**cena** /'θena; 'sena/ *f,* evening meal; supper; Last Supper

**cenacho** /θe'natʃo; se'natʃo/ *m,* marketing bag

**cenáculo** /θe'nakulo; se'nakulo/ *m,* cenacle

**cenador** /θena'ðor; sena'ðor/ *m,* diner out; arbor, pergola

**cenagal** /θena'gal; sena'gal/ *m,* quagmire; *Fig.* impasse

**cenagoso** /θena'goso; sena'goso/ *a* miry, muddy

**cenar** /θe'nar; se'nar/ *vi* to dine, sup; —*vt* eat for evening meal, sup off

**cenceño** /θen'θeɲo; sen'seɲo/ *a* slim, thin

**cencerrada** /θenθe'rraða; sense'rraða/ *f,* noisy mock serenade given to widows or widowers on the first night of their new marriage

**cencerrear** /θenθerre'ar; senserre'ar/ *vi* to jingle; *Inf.* play out of tune; bang in the wind, rattle; squeak

**cencerreo** /θenθe'rreo; sense'rreo/ *m,* jingling; jangle; rattling; squeaking

**cencerro** /θen'θerro; sen'serro/ *m,* cow-bell

**cendal** /θen'dal; sen'dal/ *m,* gauze; *Eccl.* stole; barbs of a feather

**cenefa** /θe'nefa; se'nefa/ *f,* border; valance, flounce; edging

**cenicero** /θeni'θero; seni'sero/ *m,* ash-pan; ash-pit; ash-tray

**ceniciento** /θeni'θiento; seni'siento/ *a* ash colored, ashen. **la Cenicienta,** Cinderella

**cenit** /'θenit; 'senit/ *m, Astron.* zenith; *Fig.* peak, summit

**ceniza** /θe'niθa; se'nisa/ *f,* ash, cinders

**cenotafio** /θeno'tafio; seno'tafio/ *m,* cenotaph

**censo** /'θenso; 'senso/ *m,* census; agreement for settlement of an annuity; annual ground rent; leasehold

**censor** /θen'sor; sen'sor/ *m,* censor; censorious person; *Educ.* proctor

**censual** /θen'sual; sen'sual/ *a* pertaining to census, annuity, rents

**censualista** /θensua'lista; sensua'lista/ *mf* annuitant

**censura** /θen'sura; sen'sura/ *f,* censorship; criticism; blame, reproach; scandal, gossip; *Psychol.* censorship

**censurable** /θensu'raβle; sensu'raβle/ *a* reprehensible; censorable

**censurar** /θensu'rar; sensu'rar/ *vt* to judge; censure; criticize

**centauro** /θen'tauro; sen'tauro/ *m, Myth.* centaur

**centavo** /θen'taβo; sen'taβo/ *m,* hundredth part; cent

**centella** /θen'teʎa; sen'teya/ *f,* lightning; spark; flash; *Fig.* spark (of anger, affection, etc.)

**centellador** /θenteʎa'ðor; senteya'ðor/ *a* flashing

**centellear** /θenteʎe'ar; senteye'ar/ *vi* to flash; twinkle; sparkle

**centelleo** /θente'ʎeo; sente'yeo/ *m,* scintillation; sparkle; flash

**centén** /θen'ten; sen'ten/ *m,* Spanish gold coin once worth 100 reals and later 25 pesetas

**centena** /θen'tena; sen'tena/ *f,* hundred

**centenal, centenar** /θente'nal, θente'nar; sente'nal, sente'nar/ *m,* hundred; centenary; rye field. **a centenares,** by the hundred, in crowds

**centenario** /θente'nario; sente'nario/ **(-ia)** *a* centenary —*n* centenarian. *m,* centenary

**centeno** /θen'teno; sen'teno/ *m, Bot.* rye

**centésimo** /θen'tesimo; sen'tesimo/ *a* and *m,* hundredth

**centigrado** /θen'tigraðo; sen'tigraðo/ *a* centigrade

**centigramo** /θenti'gramo; senti'gramo/ *m,* centigram

**centilitro** /θenti'litro; senti'litro/ *m,* centiliter

**centímetro** /θenti'metro; senti'metro/ *m,* centimeter. **c. cúbico,** cubic centimeter, milliliter

**céntimo** /'θentimo; 'sentimo/ *a* hundredth. *m,* centime (coin)

**centinela** /θenti'nela; senti'nela/ *mf Mil.* sentry, sentinel; person on watch. **estar de c.,** to be on sentry duty; be on guard

**centolla** /θen'toʎa; sen'toya/ *f,* marine crab

**centón** /θen'ton; sen'ton/ *m,* patchwork quilt

**central** /θen'tral; sen'tral/ *a* central; centric. *f,* head office; central depot; mother house. **c. de fuerza,** power-house. **c. telefónica,** telephone exchange

**centralilla, centralita** /θentra'liʎa, θentra'lita; sentra'liya, sentra'lita/ *f,* local exchange, private exchange

**centralismo** /θentra'lismo; sentra'lismo/ *m,* centralism

**centralista** /θentra'lista; sentra'lista/ *a* centralistic. *mf* centralist

**centralización** /θentrali̱θa'θion; sentralisa'sion/ f, centralization

**centralizador** /θentrali̱θa'ðor; sentralisa'ðor/ a centralizing

**centralizar** /θentrali'θar; sentrali'sar/ vt to centralize

**centrar** /θen'trar; sen'trar/ vt to center

**céntrico** /'θentriko; 'sentriko/ a central, centric; centrally located; downtown

**centrifugo** /θen'trifugo; sen'trifugo/ a centrifugal

**centrípeto** /θen'tripeto; sen'tripeto/ a centripetal

**centro** /'θentro; 'sentro/ m, center; headquarters, meeting place, club; center, hub; middle; core (of a rope); Fig. focus. Phys. **c. de gravedad,** center of gravity. **c. de mesa,** table center-piece. Anat. **centro nervioso,** nerve center

**centroamericano** /θentroameri'kano; sentroameri'kano/ (**-na**) a and n Central American

**céntuplo** /'θentuplo; 'sentuplo/ a centuple

**centuria** /θen'turia; sen'turia/ f, century

**centurión** /θentu'rion; sentu'rion/ m, centurion

**ceñidamente** /θeɲiða'mente; seɲiða'mente/ tightly (e.g. un argumento c. organizado, a tightly organized plot)

**ceñido** /θe'ɲiðo; se'ɲiðo/ a thrifty; wasp-waisted, slender waisted; fitting (of garments)

**ceñidor** /θeɲi'ðor; seɲi'ðor/ m, girdle, belt

**ceñir** /θe'ɲir; se'ɲir/ vt irr to girdle; surround; shorten, abbreviate; —vr be moderate (speech, expenditure, etc.); conform, confine oneself (to). **ceñirse a las reglas,** to abide by the rules —Pres. Indic. **ciño, ciñes, ciñen.** Pres. Part. **ciñendo.** Preterite **ciñó, ciñeron.** Pres. Subjunc. **ciña,** etc —Imperf. Subjunc. **ciñese,** etc.

**ceño** /'θeɲo; 'seɲo/ m, band, hoop; frown; Fig. dark outlook

**ceñudo** /θe'ɲuðo; se'ɲuðo/ a frowning

**cepa** /'θepa; 'sepa/ f, stump; vine-stock; root (tails, antlers, etc.); Fig. origin, trunk (of a family); Biol. strain. **de la más pura c.,** of the best quality

**cepillar** /θepi'ʎar; sepi'yar/ vt to brush; plane; smooth

**cepillo** /θe'piʎo; se'piyo/ m, brush; plane; poor-box, offertory-box. **c. para los dientes,** toothbrush. **c. para ropa,** clothes-brush. **c. para el suelo,** scrubbing-brush. **c. para las uñas,** nail-brush

**cepo** /'θepo; 'sepo/ m, bough; wooden stocks; snare; trap; poor-box; collecting-box

**cera** /'θera; 'sera/ f, beeswax; wax; wax candles, etc., used at a function. Inf. **ser como una c.,** to be like wax (in the hands of)

**cerador** /θera'ðor; sera'ðor/ m, floor waxer (person)

**ceradora** /θera'ðora; sera'ðora/ f, floor waxer (machine)

**cerámica** /θe'ramika; se'ramika/ f, ceramics; ceramic art, pottery

**cerámico** /θe'ramiko; se'ramiko/ a ceramic

**cerbatana** /θerβa'tana; serβa'tana/ f, blow-pipe, pop-gun; pea-shooter; ear-trumpet

**cerca** /'θerka; 'serka/ f, fence, wall

**cerca** /'θerka; 'serka/ adv near. **c. de,** near to; almost, nearly (e.g. c. de las once, nearly eleven o'clock)

**cercado** /θer'kaðo; ser'kaðo/ m, enclosure, fenced in place; fence

**cercanía** /θerka'nia; serka'nia/ f, nearness, proximity; (gen. pl) outskirts, surroundings

**cercano** /θer'kano; ser'kano/ a near, neighboring; impending, early

**cercar** /θer'kar; ser'kar/ vt to enclose; build a wall or fence round; to lay siege to; crowd round; Mil. surround

**cercenamiento** /θerθena'miento; sersena'miento/ (**a**) m, curtailment (of)

**cercenar** /θerθe'nar; serse'nar/ vt to lop off the ends, clip; curtail, diminish; abridge; whittle

**cerciorar** /θerθio'rar; sersio'rar/ vt to assure, confirm; —vr make sure

**cerco** /'θerko; 'serko/ m, ring, hoop; fence; siege; small conversational circle; spin, circling; halo (sun, moon); frame; sash (of a window). **poner c. ( a),** to lay siege to, blockade

**cerda** /'θerða; 'serða/ f, sow; bristle

**Cerdeña** /θer'ðeɲa; ser'ðeɲa/ Sardinia

**cerdo** /'θerðo; 'serðo/ m, pig, hog

**cerdoso** /θer'ðoso; ser'ðoso/ a bristly

**cereal** /θere'al; sere'al/ a and m, cereal

**cerebelo** /θere'βelo; sere'βelo/ m, Anat. cerebellum

**cerebral** /θere'βral; sere'βral/ a cerebral

**cerebro** /θe'reβro; se'reβro/ m, cerebrum; brain; intelligence

**cerebro-espinal** /θe'reβro-espi'nal; se'reβro-espi'nal/ a cerebrospinal

**ceremonia** /θere'monia; sere'monia/ f, ceremony; function, display; formality. **de c.,** ceremonial; formally. **por c.,** for politeness' sake

**ceremonial** /θeremo'nial; seremo'nial/ a ceremonial. m, ceremony; rite; protocol (rules of behavior)

**ceremonioso** /θeremo'nioso; seremo'nioso/ a ceremonious; formal, over-courteous

**cerero** /θe'rero; se'rero/ m, wax-chandler

**cereza** /θe'reθa; se'resa/ f, cherry

**cerezal** /θere'θal; sere'sal/ m, cherry orchard

**cerezo** /θe'reθo; se'reso/ m, cherry tree; cherry wood

**cerilla** /θe'riʎa; se'riya/ f, wax taper; match; ear wax

**cerner** /θer'ner; ser'ner/ vt irr to sieve; watch, observe; Fig. sift, clarify; —vi bolt (of plants); drizzle; —vr waddle; hover; threaten (of evil, etc.) —Pres. Indic. **cierno, ciernes, cierne, ciernen.** Pres. Subjunc. **cierna, ciernas, cierna, ciernan**

**cernícalo** /θer'nikalo; ser'nikalo/ m, Ornith. kestrel; Inf. lout

**cernidillo** /θerni'ðiʎo; serni'ðiyo/ m, drizzle; teetering walk

**cernido** /θer'niðo; ser'niðo/ m, sifting, sieving; sifted flour

**cerniduras** /θerni'ðuras; serni'ðuras/ f pl, siftings

**cero** /'θero; 'sero/ m, Math. zero; naught; (tennis) love. Fig. Inf. **ser un c.,** to be a mere cipher

**cerote** /θe'rote; se'rote/ m, cobbler's wax. Inf. fear

**cerquillo** /θer'kiʎo; ser'kiyo/ m, tonsure; welt (of a shoe)

**cerquita** /θer'kita; ser'kita/ adv very near, hard by

**cerradero** /θerra'ðero; serra'ðero/, m, **cerradera** f, bolt staple; catch of a lock; clasp or strings of a purse

**cerradizo** /θerra'ðiθo; serra'ðiso/ a closable, lockable

**cerrado** /θer'raðo; ser'raðo/ a closed; compact; incomprehensible, obscure; overcast, cloudy; Inf. taciturn; secretive. m, enclosure

**cerradura** /θerra'ðura; serra'ðura/ f, fastening, lock; closing, locking

**cerraja** /θer'raha; ser'raha/ f, lock (of a door); bolt

**cerrajería** /θerrahe'ria; serrahe'ria/ f, locksmith's craft; locksmith's workshop or shop

**cerrajero** /θerra'hero; serra'hero/ m, locksmith

**cerramiento** /θerra'miento; serra'miento/ m, closing, locking up; fence; enclosure, shooting preserve; partition wall

**cerrar** /θer'rar; ser'rar/ vt irr to close; lock, fasten, bolt; shut up; Mech. shut off, turn off; fold up; block or stop up; seal (letters, etc.); close down; terminate; obstruct; (with con) attack; —vi close; close in (of night, etc.); —vr heal up (wounds); close (flowers); Radio. close down; crowd together; Fig. stand firm. Inf. **cerrarse la espuela,** to take a nightcap, have a last drink. **c. la marcha,** to bring up the rear. **al c. la edición,** stop press. See **acertar**

**cerrazón** /θerra'θon; serra'son/ f, dark, overcast sky heralding a storm

**cerril** /θe'rril; se'rril/ a rough, rocky; wild, untamed (cattle, horses); Inf. boorish

**cerrillar** /θerri'ʎar; serri'yar/ vt to mill coins

**cerro** /'θerro; 'serro/ m, neck of an animal; spine, backbone; hill. Fig. **irse por los cerros de Úbeda,** to go off the track, indulge in irrelevancies

**cerrojo** /θe'rroho; se'rroho/ m, bolt (of a door, etc.); lock (of a door, gun, etc.)

**certamen** /θer'tamen; ser'tamen/ m, contest; competition; match

**certero** /θer'tero; ser'tero/ a well-aimed; sure, well-timed; knowledgeable, sure

**certeza** /θer'teθa; ser'tesa/, **certidumbre** /θer'teθa, θerti'ðumbre; ser'tesa, serti'ðumbre/ f, certitude, assurance

**certificación** /θertifika'θion; sertifika'sion/ f, certification; certificate; affidavit

**certificado** /θertifi'kaðo; sertifi'kaðo/ *a* certified; registered. *m*, registered letter; certificate

**certificar** /θertifi'kar; sertifi'kar/ *vt* to certify; register (letter, etc.)

**certificatorio** /θertifika'torio; sertifika'torio/ *a* certifying or serving to certify

**certísimo** /θer'tisimo; ser'tisimo/ *a* a learned form of the superlative of **cierto** (see **certísimo**)

**certitud** /θerti'tuð; serti'tuð/ *f*, certitude

**cervantino** /θerβan'tino; serβan'tino/ *a* Cervantine

**cervato** /θer'βato; ser'βato/ *m*, fawn

**cervecería** /θerβeθe'ria; serβese'ria/ *f*, brewery; alehouse

**cervecero** /θerβe'θero; serβe'sero/ **(-ra)** *n* brewer; beer seller

**cerveza** /θer'βeθa; ser'βesa/ *f*, beer, ale. **c. negra,** stout

**cerviz** /θer'βiθ; ser'βis/ *f*, cervix, nape (of neck). **doblar** ( *or* **bajar**) **la c.,** to humble oneself

**cesación** /θesa'θion; sesa'sion/ *f*, cessation, stopping

**cesante** /θe'sante; se'sante/ *a* dismissed; pensioned off. **declarar c.** ( **a),** to dismiss (a person from a post). **estar c.,** to be out of a job

**cesantía** /θesan'tia; sesan'tia/ *f*, status of dismissed or retired official; retirement pension

**cesar** /θe'sar; se'sar/ *vi* to cease, stop, end; leave an employment; desist; retire

**cesáreo** /θe'sareo; se'sareo/ *a* Cesarean; imperial

**cese** /'θese; 'sese/ *m*, stopping of payment for an employment

**cesión** /θe'sion; se'sion/ *f*, cession; transfer; resignation; *Law.* release

**cesionario** /θesio'nario; sesio'nario/ **(-ia)** *n* cessionary, transferee

**cesionista** /θesio'nista; sesio'nista/ *mf* grantor, transferer

**césped** /'θespeð; 'sespeð/ *m*, grass, sward; sod, lawn

**cesta** /'θesta; 'sesta/ *f*, basket, hamper; *Sports.* racket; cradle (for a wine bottle)

**cestada** /θes'taða; ses'taða/ *f*, basketful

**cestería** /θeste'ria; seste'ria/ *f*, basketmaking, basketweaving; basket factory; basket shop; basketwork

**cestero** /θes'tero; ses'tero/ **(-ra)** *n* basket maker or seller

**cesto** /'θesto; 'sesto/ *m*, basket, hamper, skip

**cesura** /θe'sura; se'sura/ *f*, cesura

**cetáceo** /θe'taθeo; se'taseo/ *a* and *m*, *Zool.* cetacean

**cetorrino** /θeto'rrino; seto'rrino/ *m*, basking shark

**cetrería** /θetre'ria; setre'ria/ *f*, falconry

**cetrino** /θe'trino; se'trino/ *a* greenish-yellow; sallow; citrine; melancholy; reserved, aloof

**cetro** /'θetro; 'setro/ *m*, scepter; verge; reign

**Cevenes, los** /θe'βenes, los; se'βenes, los/ the Cevennes

**chabacanería** /tʃaβakane'ria/ *f*, bad taste; vulgarity

**chabacano** /tʃaβa'kano/ *a* vulgar, common; rude, uncouth

**chacal** /tʃa'kal/ *m*, *Zool.* jackal

**cháchara** /'tʃatʃara/ *f*, *Inf.* empty chatter; verbiage

**chacharear** /tʃatʃare'ar/ *vi* to chatter; gabble, cackle

**chacharero** /tʃatʃa'rero/ *a* *Inf.* chattering; talkative

**chacolotear** /tʃakolote'ar/ *vi* to clatter, clink (loose horseshoe)

**chacota** /tʃa'kota/ *f*, merriment, mirth

**chacotear** /tʃakote'ar/ *vi* *Inf.* to be merry, have fun

**chacotón** /tʃako'ton/ *a* of a boisterous humor

**chafado** /tʃa'faðo/ *a* taken aback; disappointed

**chafallar** /tʃafa'ʎar; tʃafa'yar/ *vt* *Inf.* to mend carelessly, botch

**chafandín** /tʃafan'din/ *m*, vain fool

**chafar** /tʃa'far/ *vt* to flatten; crumple, crease (clothes); *Inf.* heckle

**chafarrinar** /tʃafarri'nar/ *vt* to stain, mark, blot

**chaflán** /tʃa'flan/ *m*, bevel edge, chamfer

**chagrén** /tʃa'gren/ *m*, shagreen leather

**chal** /tʃal/ *m*, shawl

**chalán** /tʃa'lan/ *m*, horse-dealer

**chalana** /tʃa'lana/ *f*, *Naut.* wherry, lighter

**chalanear** /tʃalane'ar/ *vt* to bargain; indulge in sharp practice

**chalar** /tʃa'lar/ *vt* to drive mad; enamor

**chaleco** /tʃa'leko/ *m*, waistcoat; cardigan

**chalina** /tʃa'lina/ *f*, flowing scarf, artist's bow

**Chalo** /'tʃalo/ pet form of the male given name *Carlos* "Charles', hence = English *Chuck; Bud, Mac* (in direct address to a male whose name one does not know)

**chalote** /tʃa'lote/ *m*, shallot

**chalupa** /tʃa'lupa/ *f*, shallop; launch; canoe; long boat, ship's boat

**chamar** /tʃa'mar/ *vt* *Inf.* to palm off, barter

**chamarasca** /tʃama'raska/ *f*, brushwood, tinder

**chamarilero** /tʃamari'lero/ **(-ra)** *n* secondhand dealer

**chamarreta** /tʃama'rreta/ *f*, sheepskin jacket; *Mexico* jacket

**chambelán** /tʃambe'lan/ *m*, court chamberlain

**chambergo** /tʃam'βergo/ *a* pertaining to the Chambergo regiment. *m*, broad-brimmed hat

**chambón** /tʃam'βon/ *a* *Inf.* awkward, clumsy; lucky

**chambonada** /tʃambo'naða/ *f*, *Inf.* blunder; fluke, chance

**chambra** /'tʃambra/ *f*, dressing-jacket, peignoir, negligee

**chamicera** /tʃami'θera; tʃami'sera/ *f*, piece of scorched earth (woodland, etc.)

**chamorro** /tʃa'morro/ *a* close-cropped, shorn (hair)

**champán** /tʃam'pan/ *m*, champagne. **c. obrero,** humorous cider

**champaña** /tʃam'paɲa/ *m*, champagne

**champar** /tʃam'par/ *vt* *Inf.* to cast in a person's face, remind

**champú** /tʃam'pu/ *m*, shampoo

**chamuscar** /tʃamus'kar/ *vt* to scorch; singe

**chamusquina** /tʃamus'kina/ *f*, scorching; singeing; *Inf.* brawl

**chanada** /tʃa'naða/ *f*, *Inf.* trick, mischievous act

**chancearse** /tʃanθe'arse; tʃanse'arse/ *vr* to joke

**chancero** /tʃan'θero; tʃan'sero/ *a* joking, facetious

**chanchollada** /tʃantʃo'ʎaða; tʃantʃo'yaða/ *f*, dirty trick, foul play, trick

**chanchullo** /tʃan'tʃuʎo; tʃan'tʃuyo/ *m*, *Inf.* fraud

**chanciller** /tʃanθi'ʎer; tʃansi'yer/ *m*, chancellor

**chancillería** /tʃanθiʎe'ria; tʃansiye'ria/ *f*, chancery

**chancla** /'tʃankla/ *f*, down at heel shoe; heelless slipper

**chancleta** /tʃan'kleta/ *f*, heelless slipper, babouche. *mf Inf.* ninny

**chancleteo** /tʃankle'teo/ *m*, clicking of heelless slippers

**chanclo** /'tʃanklo/ *m*, overshoe; Wellington

**chanfaina** /tʃan'faina/ *f*, *Cul.* savory fricassee

**chanflón** /tʃan'flon/ *a* tough, coarse; ungainly

**chantaje** /tʃan'tahe/ *m*, blackmail

**chantajista** /tʃanta'hista/ *mf* blackmailer

**chantar** /tʃan'tar/ *vt* to put on, clothe; *Inf.* tell plainly. *Inf.* **c. sus verdades,** to tell hometruths

**chanza** /'tʃanθa; 'tʃansa/ *f*, joke, jest

**chanzoneta** /tʃanθo'neta; tʃanso'neta/ *f*, canzonetta; *Inf.* joke

**chapa** /'tʃapa/ *f*, plate, sheet; veneer; clasp; *Inf.* prudence, common sense; rouge. **c. de hierro,** sheet-iron. **c. de identidad,** number plate

**chapado a la antigua** /tʃa'paðo a la an'tigua/ *a* old-fashioned

**chapalear** /tʃapale'ar/ *vi* to dabble in water; splash; clatter (of a horseshoe)

**chapaleo** /tʃapa'leo/ *m*, dabbling, paddling; splash; clattering, clink (of a horseshoe)

**chapaleteo** /tʃapale'teo/ *m*, lapping of water; splashing (of rain)

**chaparrear** /tʃaparre'ar/ *vi* to pour with rain

**chaparrón** /tʃapa'rron/ *m*, heavy shower of rain, downpour

**chapear** /tʃape'ar/ *vt* to veneer; —*vi* clatter (loose horseshoe)

**chapeo** /tʃa'peo/ *m*, hat

**chaperón** /tʃape'ron/ *m*, hood

**chapeta** /tʃa'peta/ *f*, *dim* clasp; red flush or spot on cheek

**chapetón** /tʃape'ton/ **(-ona)** *n* *West Hem.* recently arrived European, especially Spaniard

**chapín** /tʃa'pin/ *m,* cork-soled leather overshoe (for women) *Obs.*

**chapino** /tʃa'pino/ *a* and *m, Mexico contemptuous* Guatemalan

**chapitel** /tʃapi'tel/ *m, Archit.* capital; spire

**chapodar** /tʃapo'ðar/ *vt* to prune, lop off branches; cut down, reduce

**chapotear** /tʃapote'ar/ *vt* to sponge, moisten, damp; —*vi* paddle, splash; dabble or trail the hands (in water)

**chapoteo** /tʃapo'teo/ *m,* moistening, sponging; paddling, splashing; dabbling

**chapucear** /tʃapuθe'ar; tʃapuse'ar/ *vt* to botch, do badly; bungle

**chapuceramente** /tʃapuθera'mente; tʃapusera'mente/ *adv* awkwardly. **hablar el japonés c.,** to speak broken Japanese

**chapucería** /tʃapuθe'ria; tʃapuse'ria/ *f,* roughness, poor workmanship; botch

**chapucero** /tʃapu'θero; tʃapu'sero/ *a* rough, badly finished; bungling, clumsy, awkward

**chapurrado** /tʃapu'rraðo/ *a* broken (e.g. *hablar un italiano c.,* to speak broken Italian)

**chapurrar, chapurrear** /tʃapu'rrar, tʃapurre'ar/ *vt* to speak badly (a language); jabber; *Inf.* mix (drinks)

**chapuz** /tʃa'puθ/ *m,* ducking, submerging; plunge; unimportant job; clumsiness

**chapuzar** /tʃapu'θar; tʃapu'sar/ *vt* to duck, submerge; plunge

**chaqué** /tʃa'ke/ *m,* morning coat; morning suit

**chaqueta** /tʃa'keta/ *f,* jacket; *Mech.* casing

**chaquete** /tʃa'kete/ *m,* backgammon

**chaquetilla** /tʃake'tiʎa; tʃake'tiya/ *f,* short jacket; coatee; blazer

**chaquetón** /tʃake'ton/ *m,* short coat. **c. de piloto,** *Aer.* pea-jacket

**charabán** /tʃara'βan/ *m,* charabanc

**charada** /tʃa'raða/ *f,* charade

**charanguero** /tʃaraŋ'guero/ *a* rough, badly finished; clumsy. *m,* Andalusian boat

**charca** /tʃarka/ *f,* pond, pool; reservoir

**charco** /tʃarko/ *m,* puddle; *Inf.* sea

**charla** /tʃarla/ *f, Inf.* chatter; conversation; talk, informal lecture

**charlar** /tʃarlar/ *vi Inf.* to prattle, chatter; chat, converse; give a talk (on)

**charlatán** /tʃarla'tan/ **(-ana)** *a* loquacious, garrulous; indiscreet; fraudulent, false —*n* charlatan; chatterer

**charlatanería** /tʃarlatane'ria/ *f,* loquacity, garrulity; quackery

**charlatanismo** /tʃarlata'nismo/ *m,* charlatanism, quackery

**charnela** /tʃar'nela/ *f,* hinge; hinged joint

**charol** /tʃa'rol/ *m,* japan, varnish; patent leather

**charolar** /tʃaro'lar/ *vt* to japan, varnish

**charolista** /tʃaro'lista/ *m,* varnisher

**charpa** /tʃarpa/ *f,* pistol-belt; sling

**charrán** /tʃa'rran/ **(-ana)** *n* rogue, trickster

**charranada** /tʃarra'naða/ *f,* roguery, knavery

**charrería** /tʃarre'ria/ *f,* tawdriness; gaudiness

**charretera** /tʃarre'tera/ *f, Mil.* epaulet; garter

**charro** /tʃarro/ *a* churlish, coarse; flashy, tawdry

**chasca** /tʃaska/ *f,* brushwood, firewood

**chascar** /tʃas'kar/ *vi* to creak, crack; clack (the tongue); swallow

**chascarrillo** /tʃaska'rriʎo; tʃaska'rriyo/ *m, Inf.* amusing anecdote, good story

**chasco** /tʃasko/ *m,* trick, practical joke; disappointment. **llevarse un c.,** to meet with a disappointment

**chasis** /tʃasis/ *m, Auto.* chassis; *Photo.* plate-holder; *Mech.* underframe

**chasquear** /tʃaske'ar/ *vt* to play a trick on; wag (one's tongue); crack (a whip, one's knuckles); break a promise, disappoint; —*vi* creak, crack; meet with a disappointment

**chasquido** /tʃas'kiðo/ *m,* crack (of whip); creaking (of wood); click (of the tongue)

**chatarra** /tʃa'tarra/ *f,* scrap iron; junk

**chato** /tʃato/ *a* flat-nosed; flat

**chauvinismo** /tʃauβi'nismo/ *m,* chauvinism

**chaval** /tʃa'βal/ *a Inf.* young. *m,* lad

**chaveta** /tʃa'βeta/ *f, Mech.* bolt, pin, peg, cotter, key

**che** /tʃe/ *f,* name of the letter *ch*

**checo** /tʃeko/ **(-ca)** *a* and *n* Czech. Czech (language)

**checoslovaco** /tʃekoslo'βako/ **(-ca)** *a* Czechoslovakian —*n* Czechoslovak

**Checoslovaquia** /tʃekoslo'βakia/ Czechoslovakia

**Chejov** /tʃe'hoβ/ Chekov

**chelín** /tʃe'lin/ *m,* shilling

**Chengis-Jan** /tʃenhis-'han/ Genghis Khan

**chepa** /tʃepa/ *f, Inf.* hunch (back); hump

**cheque** /tʃeke/ *m,* check. **c. cruzado,** crossed check

**chica** /tʃika/ *f,* girl; *Inf.* dear

**chicana** /tʃi'kana/ *f,* chicanery

**chicano** /tʃi'kano/ **(-na)** *a* and *n* Chicano, American of Mexican ancestry

**chícharo** /tʃitʃaro/ *m,* pea

**chicharrón** /tʃitʃa'rron/ *m, Cul.* crackling; burnt meat; *Inf.* sunburnt person

**chichón** /tʃi'tʃon/ *m,* bruise, bump

**chichonera** /tʃitʃo'nera/ *f,* child's protective hat (something like a straw crash-helmet)

**chicle** /tʃikle/ *m,* chewing gum

**chiclero** /tʃi'klero/ *m,* chicle-gatherer

**chico** /tʃiko/ *a* little, small; young. *m,* little boy; youth; *Inf.* old boy, dear. **Es un buen c.,** He's a good fellow

**chicoleo** /tʃiko'leo/ *m, Inf.* compliment

**chicote** /tʃi'kote/ *mf* sturdy child. *m, Inf.* cigar

**chifla** /tʃifla/ *f,* whistling, whistle; tanner's paring knife

**chiflado** /tʃi'flaðo/ *a Inf.* cracked, daft; crack-brained

**chifladura** /tʃifla'ðura/ *f,* whistling; *Inf.* whim, mania, hobby

**chiflar** /tʃi'flar/ *vi* to whistle; —*vt* to make fun of, hiss; pare or scrape leather; *Inf.* swill, tipple; —*vr Inf.* have a slate loose; be slightly mad; *Inf.* lose one's head over, adore

**chifle** /tʃifle/ *m,* whistle, whistling; decoy call (birds)

**chile** /tʃile/ *m, Bot.* red pepper, chilli

**chileno** /tʃi'leno/ **(-na)** *a* and *n* Chilean

**chillador** /tʃiʎa'ðor; tʃiya'ðor/ *a* screaming, shrieking

**chillar** /tʃi'ʎar; tʃi'yar/ *vi* to scream, shriek; creak; squeak; jabber (monkeys, etc.); *Art.* be strident (of colors)

**chillería** /tʃiʎe'ria; tʃiye'ria/ *f,* shrieking, screaming

**chillido** /tʃi'ʎiðo; tʃi'yiðo/ *m,* scream, shriek; squeak (of mice, etc.); jabber (of monkeys, etc.)

**chillón** /tʃi'ʎon; tʃi'yon/ *a Inf.* screaming, yelling; strident, piercing; crude, loud (colors)

**chimenea** /tʃime'nea/ *f,* chimney; funnel; fireplace; kitchen range

**chimpancé** /tʃimpan'θe; tʃimpan'se/ *m,* chimpanzee

**china** /tʃina/ *f,* pebble; porcelain, china; Chinese silk

**chinche** /tʃintʃe/ *f,* bedbug; thumbtack, drawing-pin. *mf Inf.* bore

**chinchona** /tʃin'tʃona/ *f,* quinine

**chinchorrería** /tʃintʃorre'ria/ *f, Inf.* impertinence, tediousness; gossip

**chinela** /tʃi'nela/ *f,* mule, slipper; overshoe, patten *Obs.*

**chinero** /tʃi'nero/ *m,* china cupboard

**chinesco** /tʃi'nesko/ *a* Chinese. **a la chinesca,** in Chinese fashion

**chino** /tʃino/ **(-na)** *a* and *n* Chinese. *m,* Chinese (language)

**Chipre** /tʃipre/ Cyprus

**chipriota** /tʃi'priota/ *a* and *mf* Cypriot

**chiquero** /tʃi'kero/ *m,* pigsty; stable for bulls

**chiquillada** /tʃiki'ʎaða; tʃiki'yaða/ *f,* childishness, puerility

**chiquillería** /tʃikiʎe'ria; tʃikiye'ria/ *f, Inf.* crowd of children

**chiquillo** /tʃi'kiʎo; tʃi'kiyo/ **(-lla)** *n* small boy

**chiquito** /tʃi'kito/ **(-ta)** *a dim* **chico,** tiny, very small —*n* little one, small boy

**chirimía** /tʃiri'mia/ *f,* flageolet. *m,* flageolet player

**chiripa** /tʃi'ripa/ *f,* (billiards) fluke; *Inf.* happy coincidence, stroke of luck; lucky guess

**chirivía** /tʃiri'βia/ *f, Bot.* parsnip; *Ornith.* wagtail

**chirlar** /tʃir'lar/ *vi Inf.* to gabble, talk loudly

**chirlo** /tʃirlo/ *m,* knife wound, sabre cut; knife scar

**ciempiés**

**chirona** /tʃiˈrona/ f, Inf. jail

**chirriador** /tʃirriaˈðor/ a sizzling, crackling; creaking, squeaking

**chirriar** /tʃiˈrriar/ vi to sizzle, crackle; creak, squeak; squawk; Inf. croak, sing out of tune

**chirrido** /tʃiˈrriðo/ m, squawk; croaking; noise of grasshoppers; squeaking; creaking, creak

**¡chis!** /tʃis/ interj Shh! Silence!

**chisme** /ˈtʃisme/ m, gossip, tale; Inf. small household utensil, trifle

**chismear** /tʃismeˈar/ vt to tell tales, gossip

**chismero** /tʃisˈmero/ (-ra), **chismoso (-sa)** a gossiping, talebearing —n gossip, tale bearer

**chispa** /ˈtʃispa/ f, spark; ember; Elec. spark; tiny diamond; small particle; wit; quickwittedness; Inf. drunkenness. **c. del encendido,** ignition spark

**chispazo** /tʃisˈpaθo/ tʃisˈpaso/ m, flying out of a spark, sparking; damage done by spark; Inf. gossip, rumor

**chispeante** /tʃispeˈante/ a sparking; sparkling; Fig. scintillating (with wit etc.)

**chispear** /tʃispeˈar/ vi to throw out sparks, spark; sparkle, gleam; Fig. scintillate; drizzle gently

**chisporrotear** /tʃisporroteˈar/ vi Inf. to sputter; fizz

**chisporroteo** /tʃisporroˈteo/ m, Inf. sputtering; fizz

**chisposo** /tʃisˈposo/ a sputtering, throwing out sparks

**chistar** /tʃisˈtar/ vi to speak, break silence (gen. used negatively)

**chiste** /ˈtʃiste/ m, witticism, bon mot; amusing incident; joke

**chistera** /tʃisˈtera/ f, creel (for fish); Inf. top-hat, tile

**chistoso** /tʃisˈtoso/ a joking; amusing, funny

**chiticallando** /tʃitikaˈʎando/ tʃitikaˈyando/ adv quietly, stealthily; Inf. on the quiet, in secret

**¡chito! ¡chitón!** /ˈtʃito/ tʃiˈton/ interj Hush! Sh!

**chiva** /ˈtʃiβa/ f, Panama bus

**chivo** /ˈtʃiβo/ m Zool. kid. **c. expiatorio,** scapegoat

**chocante** /tʃoˈkante/ a colliding; provoking; shocking; surprising

**chocar** /tʃoˈkar/ vi to collide; strike (against); run into; fight, clash; —vt clink (glasses); provoke, annoy; surprise, shock. **¡Choca cinco!** Clasp five!, Gimme five!, Put it there!, Give some skin! (invitation to shake hands)

**chocarrería** /tʃokarreˈria/ f, coarse joke

**chochear** /tʃotʃeˈar/ vi to be senile; Fig. Inf. dote (on)

**chocho** /ˈtʃotʃo/ a senile; Fig. Inf. doting

**choco** /ˈtʃoko/ m, small hump, hunchback

**chocolate** /tʃokoˈlate/ m, chocolate; drinking chocolate. **c. a la española,** thick chocolate. **c. a la francesa,** French drinking chocolate

**chocolatería** /tʃokolateˈria/ f, chocolate factory or shop

**chocolatero** /tʃokolaˈtero/ (-ra) a fond of chocolate —n chocolate maker or seller

**chófer** /ˈtʃofer/ m, chauffeur; driver

**chopera** /tʃoˈpera/ f, grove or plantation of black poplar trees

**chopo** /ˈtʃopo/ m, Bot. black poplar; Inf. gun

**choque** /ˈtʃoke/ m, collision; shock; jar; Med. concussion; fight; clink (of glasses); clash; Mil. skirmish

**choricera** /tʃoriˈθera/ tʃoriˈsera/ f, sausage-making machine

**choricero** /tʃoriˈθero/ tʃoriˈsero/ (-ra) n sausage maker

**chorizo** /tʃoˈriθo/ tʃoˈriso/ m, kind of pork sausage; counterweight

**chorrear** /tʃorreˈar/ vi to spout, jet; drip; Fig. Inf. trickle, arrive slowly

**chorreo** /tʃoˈrreo/ m, drip, dripping; spouting, gushing

**chorrera** /tʃoˈrrera/ f, spout; drip; jabot, lace front

**chorro** /ˈtʃorro/ m, jet; stream (of water, etc.); Fig. shower. **a chorros,** in a stream; in abundance, plentifully

**chova** /ˈtʃoβa/ f, rook; carrion crow; jackdaw

**choza** /ˈtʃoθa/ tʃosa/ f, hut, cabin; cottage

**chubasco** /tʃuˈβasko/ m, squall, downpour; storm; transitory misfortune

**chuchería** /tʃutʃeˈria/ f, gewgaw, trinket; savory titbit; snaring, trapping

**chucruta** /tʃuˈkruta/ f, sauerkraut

**chueca** /ˈtʃueka/ f, round head of a bone; small ball; game like shinty; Inf. practical joke

**chufa** /ˈtʃufa/ f, Bot. chufa; Inf. joke, trick

**chufería** /tʃufeˈria/ f, place where drink made of **chufas** is sold

**chufla** /ˈtʃufla/ f, flippant remark

**chufleta** /tʃuˈfleta/ f, Inf. joke; taunt

**chulada** /tʃuˈlaða/ f, mean trick, base action; drollery

**chulería** /tʃuleˈria/ f, drollness; attractive personality

**chuleta** /tʃuˈleta/ f, Cul. cutlet, chop; mutton-chop; Inf. slap

**chulo** /ˈtʃulo/ a droll, amusing; attractive. m, slaughterhouse worker; bullfighter's assistant; pimp; rogue

**chumbera** /tʃumˈβera/ f, prickly pear; Indian fig

**chunga** /ˈtʃuŋga/ f, Inf. banter, teasing

**chupada** /tʃuˈpaða/ f, sucking; suck; suction

**chupado de cara, c. de mofletes** /tʃuˈpaðo de ˈkara; mofˈletes/ a lantern-jawed

**chupador** /tʃupaˈðor/ a sucking. m, baby's comforter or dummy

**chupar** /tʃuˈpar/ vt to suck; absorb (of plants); Fig. Inf. drain, rob; —vr grow thin. **chuparse los dedos,** Inf. to lick one's lips; be delighted

**chupatintas** /tʃupaˈtintas/ m, Inf. scrivener, clerk (scornful)

**churdón** /tʃurˈðon/ m, raspberry cane; raspberry; raspberry vinegar

**churrería** /tʃurreˈria/ f, place where **churros** are made or sold

**churrero** /tʃuˈrrero/ (-ra) n maker or seller of **churros**

**churrigueresco** /tʃurrigeˈresko/ a Churrigueresque

**churro** /ˈtʃurro/ a coarse (of wool). m, Cul. a kind of fritter eaten with chocolate, coffee, etc.

**churumbela** /tʃurumˈβela/ f, Mus. pipe; reed for drinking mate West Hem.

**chusco** /ˈtʃusko/ a droll, witty, amusing

**chusma** /ˈtʃusma/ f, galley hands, crew; rabble, mob

**chutar** /tʃuˈtar/ vt Sports. to shoot (a goal)

**chuzo** /ˈtʃuθo/ tʃuso/ m, Mil. pike

**chuzón** /tʃuˈθon/ tʃuˈson/ a wily, suspicious, cunning

**cianuro** /θiaˈnuro/ sia'nuro/ m, cyanide

**ciar** /θiar/ siar/ vi to go backwards; Naut. row backwards; Fig. make no headway (negotiations)

**ciática** /ˈθiatika/ ˈsiatika/ f, sciatica

**ciático** /ˈθiatiko/ ˈsiatiko/ a sciatic

**ciberespacio** m, cyberspace

**ciborio** /θiˈβorio/ siˈβorio/ m, ciborium

**cicatería** /θikateˈria/ sikateˈria/ f, niggardliness, avarice

**cicatero** /θikaˈtero/ sikaˈtero/ a avaricious, niggardly, mean

**cicatriz** /θikaˈtriθ/ sikaˈtris/ f, cicatrice; Fig. scar, mark, impression

**cicatrización** /θikatriθaˈθion/ sikatrisaˈsion/ f, cicatrization

**cicatrizar** /θikatriˈθar/ sikatriˈsar/ vt to cicatrize, heal; —vr scar over

**ciclamino** /θiklaˈmino/ siklaˈmino/ m, cyclamen

**cíclico** /ˈθikliko/ ˈsikliko/ a cyclic, cyclical

**ciclismo** /θiˈklismo/ siˈklismo/ m, bicycling

**ciclista** /θiˈklista/ siˈklista/ mf cyclist

**ciclo** /ˈθiklo/ ˈsiklo/ m, cycle (of time). **c. artúrico, c. de Artús,** Arthurian Cycle. **c. de conferencias,** series of lectures

**ciclón** /θiˈklon/ siˈklon/ m, cyclone

**ciclópeo** /θiˈklopeo/ siˈklopeo/ a cyclopean

**ciclostilo** /θiklosˈtilo/ siklosˈtilo/ m, cyclostyle

**cicuta** /θiˈkuta/ siˈkuta/ f, hemlock

**cid** /θið/ sið/ m, great warrior, chief. **el Cid,** national hero of Spanish wars against the Moors

**cidra** /ˈθiðra/ ˈsiðra/ f, citron

**cidro** /ˈθiðro/ ˈsiðro/ m, citron tree

**ciego** /ˈθiego/ ˈsiego/ a blind; dazed, blinded; choked up. m, blind man; Anat. cæcum. **a ciegas,** blindly; heedlessly

**cielo** /ˈθielo/ ˈsielo/ m, sky, firmament; atmosphere; climate; paradise; Providence; bliss, glory; roof, canopy; Inf. darling. **a c. abierto,** in the open air. **parecer un c.,** to be heavenly

**ciempiés** /θiemˈpies/ siemˈpies/ m, centipede

**cien** /θien; sien/ *a* abb. **ciento,** hundred. Used always before substantives (e.g. *c. hombres,* 100 men)

**ciénaga** /'θienaga; 'sienaga/ *f,* swamp; morass

**ciencia** /'θienθia; 'siensia/ *f,* science; knowledge; erudition, ability. **ciencias naturales,** natural science. **a c. cierta,** for certain, without doubt (gen. with *saber*)

**cienmilésimo** /θiemi'lesimo; siemi'lesimo/ *a* hundred-thousandth

**cieno** /'θieno; 'sieno/ *m,* slime, mud; silt

**científico** /θien'tifiko; sien'tifiko/ *a* scientific. *m,* scientist

**ciento** /'θiento; 'siento/ (cf. **cien**) *a* hundred; hundredth. *m,* hundred. **por c.,** per cent.

**cierne, en** /'θierne, en; 'sierne, en/ in flower; *Fig.* in the early stages, in embryo

**cierre** /'θierre; 'sierre/ *m,* closing, shutting; closing time of shops, etc.; fastening; fastener; clasp (of a necklace, handbag, etc.). **c. cremallera,** zip fastener. **c. metálico,** doorshutter

**ciertamente** /θierta'mente; sierta'mente/ *adv* certainly; undoubtedly; indeed

**ciertísimo** /θier'tisimo; sier'tisimo/ *a* everyday form of the superlative of **cierto** (see **certísimo**)

**cierto** /'θierto; 'sierto/ *a* certain, sure; true; particular (e.g. *c. hombre,* a certain man (note no *def. art.*)). **un c. sabor,** a special flavor. **una cosa cierta,** something certain. **no, por c.,** no, certainly not. **por c.,** truly, indeed

**cierva** /'θierβa; 'sierβa/ *f,* hind

**ciervo** /'θierβo; 'sierβo/ *m,* stag. **c. volante,** stag-beetle

**cierzo** /'θierθo; 'sierso/ *m,* northerly wind

**cifra** /'θifra; 'sifra/ *f,* number; figure; sum total; cipher, code; monogram; abbreviation

**cifrar** /θi'frar; si'frar/ *vt* to write in cipher; summarize, abridge; (*with en*) be dependent on; depend on

**cigarra** /θi'garra; si'garra/ *f, Ent.* cicada, harvest fly

**cigarral** /θiga'rral; siga'rral/ *m,* (Toledo) country-house and garden or orchard

**cigarrera** /θiga'rrera; siga'rrera/ *f,* woman who makes or sells cigars; cigar-cabinet; cigar-case

**cigarrillo** /θiga'rriλo; siga'rriyo/ *m,* cigarette

**cigarro** /θi'garro; si'garro/ *m,* cigar

**cigüeña** /θi'gueɲa; si'gueɲa/ *f, Ornith.* stork; *Mech.* crank

**ciliar** /θi'liar; si'liar/ *a* ciliary

**cilicio** /θi'liθio; si'lisio/ *m,* hairshirt

**cilindrar** /θilin'drar; silin'drar/ *vt* to roll; calendar; bore

**cilindrero** /θilin'drero; silin'drero/ *m,* organ grinder

**cilíndrico** /θi'lindriko; si'lindriko/ *a* cylindrical

**cilindro** /θi'lindro; si'lindro/ *m,* cylinder; roller

**cima** /'θima; 'sima/ *f,* summit; top of trees; apex; *Archit.* coping; head (thistle, etc.); *Fig.* aim, goal, end

**cimbalero** /θimba'lero; simba'lero/ **(-ra)** *n* cymbalist

**cimbalo** /'θimbalo; 'simbalo/ *m,* cymbal

**cimborrio** /θim'βorrio; sim'βorrio/ *m, Archit.* cupola; cimborium

**cimbrar, cimbrear** /θim'βrar, θimbre'ar; sim'βrar, simbre'ar/ *vt* to bend; brandish; —*vr* sway (in walking)

**cimbreño** /θim'βreɲo; sim'βreɲo/ *a* graceful, lithe, willowy

**cimbreo** /θim'βreo; sim'βreo/ *m,* swaying, bending

**cimentar** /θimen'tar; simen'tar/ *vt irr* to lay foundations; refine (gold, metals, etc.); found; *Fig.* ground (in virtue, etc.). See **acertar**

**cimera** /θi'mera; si'mera/ *f,* crest of helmet

**cimiento** /θi'miento; si'miento/ *m,* foundation (of a building); bottom; groundwork; origin, base. **abrir los cimientos,** to lay the foundations

**cimitarra** /θimi'tarra; simi'tarra/ *f,* scimitar

**cinabrio** /θi'naβrio; si'naβrio/ *m,* cinnabar; vermilion

**cinc** /θink; sink/ *m,* zinc

**cincel** /θin'θel; sin'sel/ *m,* chisel; burin, engraver

**cincelador** /θinθela'ðor; sinsela'ðor/ **(-ra)** *n* engraver; chiseler

**cincelar** /θinθe'lar; sinse'lar/ *vt* to chisel; carve; engrave

**cincha** /'θintʃa; 'sintʃa/ *f,* girth of a saddle

**cinchar** /θin'tʃar; sin'tʃar/ *vt* to tighten the saddle girths

**cincho** /'θintʃo; 'sintʃo/ *m,* belt, girdle; iron hoop

**cinco** /'θinko; 'sinko/ *a* and *m,* five; fifth. **a las c.,** at five o'clock

**cincuenta** /θin'kuenta; sin'kuenta/ *a* and *m,* fifty; fiftieth

**cincuentavo** /θinkuen'taβo; sinkuen'taβo/ *a* fiftieth

**cincuentenario** /θinkuente'nario; sinkuente'nario/ *m,* fiftieth anniversary

**cincuentón** /θinkuen'ton; sinkuen'ton/ **(-ona)** *a* and *n* fifty years old (person)

**cine, cinema** /'θine, θi'nema; 'sine, si'nema/ *m,* cinema, movies. **c. sonoro,** sound film

**cinemática** /θine'matika; sine'matika/ *f, Phys.* kinematics

**cinematografía** /θinematogra'fia; sinematogra'fia/ *f,* cinematography

**cinematografiar** /θinematogra'fiar; sinematogra'fiar/ *vt* to film

**cinematográfico** /θinemato'grafiko; sinemato'grafiko/ *a* cinematographic

**cinematógrafo** /θinema'tografo; sinema'tografo/ *m,* motion-picture camera; cinema

**cínico** /'θiniko; 'siniko/ *a* cynical; impudent; untidy. *m,* cynic

**cinismo** /θi'nismo; si'nismo/ *m,* cynicism

**cinta** /'θinta; 'sinta/ *f,* ribbon; tape; strip; film (cinematograph). **c. métrica,** tape-measure

**cintillo** /θin'tiλo; sin'tiyo/ *m,* hatband; small ring set with gems

**cinto** /'θinto; 'sinto/ *m,* belt, girdle. **c. de pistolas,** pistol-belt

**cintoteca** /θinto'teka; sinto'teka/ *f,* tape library

**cintura** /θin'tura; sin'tura/ *f,* waist; belt, girdle

**cinturón** /θintu'ron; sintu'ron/ *m,* large waist; belt girdle; sword-belt; that which encircles or surrounds. **c. de seguridad,** seat belt

**ciprés** /θi'pres; si'pres/ *m, Bot.* cypress tree or wood

**cipresal** /θipre'sal; sipre'sal/ *m,* cypress grove

**cipresino** /θipre'sino; sipre'sino/ *a* cypress; cypress-like

**circasiano** /θirka'siano; sirka'siano/ **(-na)** *a* and *n* Circassian

**circo** /'θirko; 'sirko/ *m,* circus; amphitheater

**circón** /θir'kon; sir'kon/ *m,* zircon

**circuir** /θir'kuir; sir'kuir/ *vt. irr* to surround, encircle. See **huir**

**circuito** /θir'kuito; sir'kuito/ *m,* periphery; contour; (*Elec. Phys.*) circuit. **corto c.,** short circuit

**circulación** /θirkula'θion; sirkula'sion/ *f,* circulation; traffic. **c. de la sangre,** circulation of the blood. **calle de gran c.,** busy street

**circular** /θirku'lar; sirku'lar/ *a* circular. *f,* circular —*vt* to pass round; —*vi* circle; circulate; move in a circle; move about; run, travel (traffic)

**circulatorio** /θirkula'torio; sirkula'torio/ *a* circulatory

**círculo** /'θirkulo; 'sirkulo/ *m,* circle; circumference; circuit; casino, social club

**circuncidar** /θirkunθi'ðar; sirkunsi'ðar/ *vt* to circumcise; modify, reduce

**circuncisión** /θirkunθi'sion; sirkunsi'sion/ *f,* circumcision

**circunciso** /θirkun'θiso; sirkun'siso/ *a* circumcised

**circundar** /θirkun'dar; sirkun'dar/ *vt* to surround

**circunferencia** /θirkunfe'renθia; sirkunfe'rensia/ *f,* circumference

**circunflejo** /θirkun'fleho; sirkun'fleho/ *a* circumflex. **acento c.,** circumflex accent

**circunlocución** /θirkunloku'θion; sirkunloku'sion/ *f,* circumlocution

**circunnavegación** /θirkunnaβega'θion; sirkunnaβega'sion/ *f,* circumnavigation

**circunnavegar** /θirkunnaβe'gar; sirkunnaβe'gar/ *vt* to circumnavigate

**circunscribir** /θirkunskri'βir; sirkunskri'βir/ *vt* to circumscribe —*Past Part.* **circunscrito**

**circunscripción** /θirkunskrip'θion; sirkunskrip'sion/ *f,* circumscription

**circunspección** /θirkunspek'θion; sirkunspek'sion/ *f,* circumspection; seriousness, dignity

**circunspecto** /θirkuns'pekto; sirkuns'pekto/ *a* circumspect; serious, dignified

**circunstancia** /θirkuns'tanθia; sirkuns'tansia/ *f*, circumstance; incident, detail; condition. **c. agravante,** aggravating circumstance. **c. atenuante,** extenuating circumstance. **bajo las circunstancias,** in the circumstances. **de circunstancias,** occasional (e.g. *poesías de circunstancias,* occasional verse). **estar al nivel de las circunstancias,** to rise to the occasion

**circunstanciado** /θirkunstan'θiaðo; sirkunstan'siaðo/ *a* circumstantiated, detailed

**circunstancial** /θirkunstan'θial; sirkunstan'sial/ *a* circumstantial; occasional (e.g. *poesías circunstanciales,* occasional verse)

**circunstante** /θirkuns'tante; sirkuns'tante/ *a* surrounding; present. *mf* person present, bystander

**circunvecino** /θirkumbe'θino; sirkumbe'sino/ *a* adjacent, neighboring

**circunvolución** /θirkumbolu'θion; sirkumbolu'sion/ *f*, circumvolution

**cirial** /θi'rial; si'rial/ *m*, processional candlestick

**cirio** /'θirio; 'sirio/ *m*, wax candle

**cirro** /'θirro; 'sirro/ *m*, *Med.* scirrhus; *Bot.* tendril; *Zool.* cirrus

**cirrosis** /θi'rrosis; si'rrosis/ *f*, cirrhosis

**cirroso** /θi'rroso; si'rroso/ *a Med.* scirrhous; (*Zool. Bot.*) cirrose

**ciruela** /θi'ruela; si'ruela/ *f*, plum; prune. **c. claudia, c. veidal,** greengage. **c. damascena,** damson

**ciruelo** /θi'ruelo; si'ruelo/ *m*, plum tree

**cirugía** /θiru'hia; siru'hia/ *f*, surgery

**cirujano** /θiru'hano; siru'hano/ *m*, surgeon

**cisco** /'θisko; 'sisko/ *m*, coal dust, slack coal; *Inf.* hubbub, quarrel

**cisma** /'θisma; 'sisma/ *m*, or *f*, schism; disagreement, discord. **el C. de Occidente,** the Western Schism

**cismático** /θis'matiko; sis'matiko/ *a* schismatic; discordant, inharmonious

**cisne** /'θisne; 'sisne/ *m*, swan

**cisterciense** /θister'θiense; sister'siense/ *a* Cistercian

**cisterna** /θis'terna; sis'terna/ *f*, water-tank, cistern

**cístico** /'θistiko; 'sistiko/ *a* cystic

**cistitis** /θis'titis; sis'titis/ *f*, cystitis

**cita** /'θita; 'sita/ *f*, appointment; quotation, citation

**citable** /θi'taβle; si'taβle/ *a* quotable

**citación** /θita'θion; sita'sion/ *f*, quotation; *Law.* summons

**citar** /θi'tar; si'tar/ *vt* to make an appointment; cite, quote; *Law.* summon. **c. en comparecencia,** to summon to appear in court

**cítara** /'θitara; 'sitara/ *f*, *Mus.* zither

**citatorio** /θita'torio; sita'torio/ *m*, summons

**citerior** /θite'rior; site'rior/ *a* hither, nearer

**citrato** /θi'trato; si'trato/ *m*, *Chem.* citrate

**cítrico** /'θitriko; 'sitriko/ *a* citric

**ciudad** /θiu'ðað; siu'ðað/ *f*, city; municipal body. **la c. señorial,** the Aristocratic City (Ponce, Puerto Rico)

**ciudadanía** /θiuðaða'nia; siuðaða'nia/ *f*, citizenship

**ciudadano** /θiuða'ðano; siuða'ðano/ **(-na)** *a* city; civic, born in or belonging to a city —*n* citizen; burgess; bourgeois. **c. de honor,** freeman (of a city)

**ciudadela** /θiuða'ðela; siuða'ðela/ *f*, citadel

**cívico** /'θiβiko; 'siβiko/ *a* civic; patriotic

**civicultura** /θiβikul'tura; siβikul'tura/ *f*, raising of civets

**civil** /θi'βil; si'βil/ *a* civil; civilian; polite

**civilidad** /θiβili'ðað; siβili'ðað/ *f*, politeness, civility

**civilización** /θiβiliθa'θion; siβilisa'sion/ *f*, civilization

**civilizador** /θiβiliθa'ðor; siβilisa'ðor/ *a* civilizing

**civilizar** /θiβili'θar; siβili'sar/ *vt* to civilize; educate; —*vr* grow civilized; be educated

**civismo** /θi'βismo; si'βismo/ *m*, civism; patriotism; civics

**cizalla** /θi'θaʎa; si'saya/ *f*, shears, shearing machine; metal filings

**cizaña** /θi'θaɲa; si'saɲa/ *f*, *Bot.* darnel, tare; vice, evil; dissension, discord (gen. with *meter* and *sembrar*)

**clac** /klak/ *m*, opera-hat; tricorne

**clamar** /kla'mar/ *vi* to cry out; *Fig.* demand (of inanimate things); vociferate; speak solemnly

**clamor** /kla'mor/ *m*, outcry, shouting; shriek, complaint; knell, tolling of bells

**clamorear** /klamore'ar/ *vt* to implore, clamor (for); —*vi* toll (of bells)

**clamoroso** /klamo'roso/ *a* noisy, clamorous

**clandestino** /klandes'tino/ *a* clandestine, secret

**clangor** /klaŋ'gor/ *m*, *Poet.* blare, bray (of trumpet)

**claqué** /kla'ke/ *m*, tap-dance

**clara** /'klara/ *f*, white of egg; bald patch (in fur); *Inf.* fair interval on a rainy day

**claraboya** /klara'βoya/ *f*, skylight; *Archit.* clerestory

**claramente** /klara'mente/ *adv* clearly, evidently

**clarear** /klare'ar/ *vt* to clear; give light to; —*vi* to dawn; grow light; —*vr* be transparent; *Inf.* reveal secrets unwittingly

**clarete** /kla'rete/ *m*, claret (wine); claret color —*a* claret; claret-colored

**claridad** /klari'ðað/ *f*, clearness; transparency; lightness, brightness; distinctness; clarity; good reputation, renown; plain truth, home truth (gen. *pl*)

**clarificación** /klarifika'θion; klarifika'sion/ *f*, clarification; purifying, refining

**clarificar** /klarifi'kar/ *vt* to illuminate; clarify, purify; refine (sugar, etc.)

**clarín** /kla'rin/ *m*, bugle; clarion; organ stop; bugler

**clarinete** /klari'nete/ *m*, clarinet; clarinet player

**clarión** /kla'rion/ *m*, white chalk, crayon

**clarividencia** /klariβi'ðenθia; klariβi'ðensia/ *f*, perspicuity, clear-sightedness

**clarividente** /klariβi'ðente/ *a* perspicacious, clear-sighted

**claro** /'klaro/ *a* clear; light, bright; distinct; pure, clean; transparent, translucent; light (of colors); easily understood; evident, obvious; frank; cloudless; shrewd, quick-thinking; famous. *m*, skylight; space between words; break in a speech; space in procession, etc.; *Art.* (gen. *pl*) high lights —*interj* ¡**C.!** or ¡**C. está!** Of course! **a las claras,** openly, frankly

**claroscuro** /klaros'kuro/ *m*, chiaroscuro; monochrome

**clase** /'klase/ *f*, class, group; kind, sort, quality; class (school, university); lecture room; lecture, lesson; order, family. **c. dirigente,** ruling class. **c. media,** middle class. **c. social,** social class

**clasicismo** /klasi'θismo; klasi'sismo/ *m*, classicism

**clasicista** /klasi'θista; klasi'sista/ *a* and *mf* classicist

**clásico** /'klasiko/ *a* classic; notable; classical. *m*, classic

**clasificación** /klasifika'θion; klasifika'sion/ *f*, classification

**clasificador** /klasifika'ðor/ **(-ra)** *n* classifier. **c. de billetes,** ticket-punch

**clasificar** /klasifi'kar/ *vt* to classify, arrange. **c. correspondencia,** to file letters

**claudicación** /klauðika'θion; klauðika'sion/ *f*, limping; negligence; hesitancy, weakness; backing down

**claudicar** /klauði'kar/ *vi* to limp; be negligent; hesitate, give way

**claustral** /klaus'tral/ *a* cloistral

**claustro** /'klaustro/ *m*, cloister; council, faculty, senate (of university); monastic rule

**claustrofobia** /klaustro'foβia/ *f*, claustrophobia

**cláusula** /'klausula/ *f*, clause. **c. de negación implícita,** contrary-to-fact clause. **c. principal,** main clause. **c. subordinada,** dependent clause, subordinate clause. **c. sustantiva,** noun clause

**clausura** /klau'sura/ *f*, sanctum of convent; claustration; solemn ending ceremony of tribunal, etc. **la vida de c.,** monastic or conventual life

**clava** /'klaβa/ *f*, club, truncheon; *Naut.* scupper

**clavadizo** /klaβa'ðiθo; klaβa'ðiso/ *a* nail-studded (doors, etc.)

**clavar** /kla'βar/ *vt* to nail; fasten with nails; pierce, prick; set gems (jeweler); spike (cannon, gun); *Fig.* fix (eyes, attention, etc.); *Inf.* cheat

**clave** /'klaβe/ *m*, clavichord; *f*, code, key; *Mus.* clef; *Archit.* keystone; plug (telephones); **c. (de),** key to. *Mus.* **c. de sol,** treble clef

**clavel** /kla'βel/ *m*, *Bot.* carnation plant and flower

**clavelito** /klaβe'lito/ *m*, *Bot.* pink plant and flower

**clavero** /kla'βero/ **(-ra)** *n* keeper of the keys. *m*, clove tree

**clavetear** /klaβete'ar/ *vt* to stud with nails; *Fig.* round off (business affairs)

**clavicordio** /klaβi'korðio/ *m,* clavichord

**clavícula** /kla'βikula/ *f,* clavicle

**clavija** /kla'βiha/ *f,* peg, pin; plug; peg of stringed instrument; axle-pin

**clavo** /'klaβo/ *m,* nail, spike, peg; corn (on foot); anguish. **c. de especia,** clove. **c. de herradura,** hob-nail

**claymore** /klai'more/ *f,* claymore

**clemátide** /kle'matiðe/ *f, Bot.* clematis

**clemencia** /kle'menθia; kle'mensia/ *f,* mildness; clemency; mercy

**clemente** /kle'mente/ *a* mild; clement; merciful

**cleptomanía** /kleptoma'nia/ *f,* kleptomania

**cleptómano** /klep'tomano/ **(-na)** *a* and *n* kleptomaniac

**clerecía** /klere'θia; klere'sia/ *f,* clergy

**clerical** /kleri'kal/ *a* belonging to the clergy; clerical

**clericalismo** /klerika'lismo/ *m,* clericalism

**clerigalla** /kleri'gaʎa; kleri'gaya/ *f,* (*contemptuous*) dog-collar men

**clérigo** /'klerigo/ *m,* cleric, clergyman; clerk (in Middle Ages)

**clero** /'klero/ *m,* clergy

**cliente** /'kliente/ *mf* client, customer; protégé; ward

**clientela** /klien'tela/ *f,* patronage, protection; clientele

**clima** /'klima/ *m,* climate, clime

**climatérico** /klima'teriko/ *a* climacteric

**climático** /kli'matiko/ *a* climatic

**climatología** /klimatolo'hia/ *f,* climatology

**clímax** /'klimaks/ *m,* climax

**clínica** /'klinika/ *f,* clinic, nursing home; department of medicine or surgery

**clínico** /'kliniko/ *a* clinical

**clíper** /'kliper/ *m,* (*Aer.* and *Naut.*) clipper

**clisar** /kli'sar/ *vt Print.* to cast from a mold, stereotype

**clisé** /kli'se/ *m, Print.* stereotype plate

**cloaca** /klo'aka/ *f,* sewer, drain; *Zool.* cloaca

**cloquear** /kloke'ar/ *vi* to go broody (hen); cluck

**cloqueo** /klo'keo/ *m,* cluck, clucking

**cloquera** /klo'kera/ *f,* broodiness (hens)

**clorato** /klo'rato/ *m,* chlorate

**clorhidrato** /klori'ðrato/ *m,* hydrochloride

**clorhídrico** /klor'iðriko/ *a* hydrochloric

**cloro** /'kloro/ *m,* chlorine

**clorofila** /kloro'fila/ *f,* chlorophyll

**cloroformizar** /kloroformi'θar; kloroformi'sar/ *vt* to chloroform

**cloroformo** /kloro'formo/ *m,* chloroform

**clorosis** /klo'rosis/ *f,* chlorosis

**cloruro** /klo'ruro/ *m,* chloride

**club** /kluβ/ *m,* club

**clueca** /'klueka/ *f,* broody hen

**clueco** /'klueko/ *a* broody (hens); *Inf.* doddering

**C.N.T.** /knt/ initialism of Confederación Nacional de Trabajo

**coacción** /koak'θion; koak'sion/ *f,* coercion

**coactivo** /koak'tiβo/ *a* coercive

**coadjutor** /koaðhu'tor/ *m,* co-worker, assistant

**coadunar** /koaðu'nar/ *vt* to join or mingle together

**coadyuvar** /koaðyu'βar/ *vt* to assist

**coagulación** /koagula'θion; koagula'sion/ *f,* coagulation

**coagular** /koagu'lar/ *vt* to coagulate; clot; curdle

**coágulo** /ko'agulo/ *m,* clot; coagulation; congealed blood

**coalición** /koali'θion; koali'sion/ *f,* coalition

**coartada** /koar'taða/ *f,* alibi. **probar la c.,** to prove an alibi

**coartar** /koar'tar/ *vt* to limit, restrict

**coautor** /koau'tor/ **(-ra)** *n* co-author

**cobalto** /ko'βalto/ *m,* cobalt

**cobarde** /ko'βarðe/ *a* cowardly; irresolute. *m,* coward

**cobardía** /koβar'ðia/ *f,* cowardice

**cobayo** /ko'βayo/ *m,* guinea-pig

**cobertera** /koβer'tera/ *f,* lid, cover

**cobertizo** /koβer'tiθo; koβer'tiso/ *m,* overhanging roof; shack, shed, hut. **c. de aeroplanos,** *Aer.* hangar

**cobertura** /koβer'tura/ *f,* covering; coverlet; wrapping

**cobija** /ko'βiha/ *f,* imbrex tile; cover

**cobijar** /koβi'har/ *vt* to cover; shelter

**cobra** /'koβra/ *f, Zool.* cobra; rope or thong for yoking oxen; retrieval (of game)

**cobradero** /koβra'ðero/ *a* that which can be collected, recoverable

**cobrador** /koβra'ðor/ *m,* collector, receiver —*a* collecting. **c. de tranvía,** tram conductor

**cobranza** /ko'βranθa; ko'βransa/ *f,* receiving, collecting; collection of fruit or money

**cobrar** /ko'βrar/ *vt* to collect (what is owed); charge; earn; regain, recover; feel, experience (emotions); wind, pull in (ropes, etc.); gain, acquire; retrieve (game); —*vr* recuperate. **c. ánimo,** to take courage. **c. cariño (a),** to grow fond of. **c. fuerzas,** to gather strength. **c. importancia,** to gain importance. **¿Cuánto cobra Vd.?** How much do you charge?; How much do you earn?

**cobre** /'koβre/ *m, Mineral.* copper; copper kitchen utensils; *pl Mus.* brass

**cobrizo** /ko'βriθo; ko'βriso/ *a* containing copper; copper-colored

**cocacolismo** /kokako'lismo/ *n Inf.* economic dependence on the United States and adoption of its pop culture

**cocacolonización** /kokakoloniθa'θion; kokakolonisa'sion/ *f,* economic domination by the United States and introduction of its pop culture

**cocacolonizar** /kokakoloni'θar; kokakoloni'sar/ *vt* (United States) to gain economic control of... and introduce into its pop culture

**cocaína** /koka'ina/ *f,* cocaine

**cocción** /kok'θion; kok'sion/ *f,* coction

**coceador** /koθea'ðor; kosea'ðor/ *a* inclined to kick; kicking (animals)

**coceadura** /koθea'ðura; kosea'ðura/ *f,* kicking

**cocear** /koθe'ar; kose'ar/ *vi* to kick; *Inf.* kick against, oppose

**cocedero** /koθe'ðero; kose'ðero/ *a* easily cooked

**cocer** /ko'θer; ko'ser/ *vt. irr* to boil; cook; bake (bricks, etc.); digest; *Surg.* suppurate; —*vi* boil (of a liquid); ferment; —*vr* suffer pain or inconvenience over a long period —*Pres. Indic.* **cuezo, cueces, cuece, cuecen.** *Pres. Subjunc.* **cueza, cuezas, cueza, cuezan**

**coche** /'kotʃe/ *m,* carriage, car. **c. camas,** sleeping car. **c. -camioneta,** station wagon. **c. cerrado,** *Auto.* sedan. **c. de muchos caballos,** high-powered car. **c. de plaza,** hackney-carriage. **c. fúnebre,** hearse. **c. -línea,** intercity bus. *f, Ecuador* puddle

**cochera** /ko'tʃera/ *f,* coach house; tramway depot

**cochero** /ko'tʃero/ *m,* coachman; driver —*a* easily cooked

**¡cochi!** /'kotʃi/ (call to pigs)

**cochina** /ko'tʃina/ *f,* sow

**cochinería** /kotʃine'ria/ *f, Inf.* filthiness; mean trick

**cochinilla** /kotʃi'niʎa; kotʃi'niya/ *f,* wood louse; cochineal insect; cochineal

**cochinillo** /kotʃi'niʎo; kotʃi'niyo/ *m,* sucking-pig. **c. de Indias,** guinea-pig

**cochino** /ko'tʃino/ *m,* pig; *Inf.* filthy person —*a* filthy

**cocido** /ko'θiðo; ko'siðo/ *a* boiled, cooked, baked. *m,* dish of stewed meat, pork, chicken, with peas, etc.

**cociente** /ko'θiente; ko'siente/ *m,* quotient

**cocimiento** /koθi'miento; kosi'miento/ *m,* cooking; decoction

**cocina** /ko'θina; ko'sina/ *f,* kitchen; pottage; broth; cookery. **c. de campaña,** field-kitchen. **c. económica,** cooking range

**cocinar** /koθi'nar; kosi'nar/ *vt* to cook; —*vi Inf.* meddle, interfere

**cocinería** /koθine'ria; kosine'ria/ *f, Naut.* galley

**cocinero** /koθi'nero; kosi'nero/ *n* cook, chef

**cocinilla** /koθi'niʎa; kosi'niya/ *f,* spirit-stove

**coco** /'koko/ *m, Bot.* coconut tree and fruit; coconut shell; grub, maggot; bogeyman; hobgoblin; *Inf.* grimace. *Inf.* **ser un c.,** to be hideously ugly

**cocodrilo** /koko'ðrilo/ *m,* crocodile

**cócora** /'kokora/ *mf Inf.* bore, nosy Parker

**cocotal** /koko'tal/ *m,* grove of coconut palms

**cocotero** /koko'tero/ *m,* coconut palm

**coctel** /kok'tel/ *m,* cocktail

**cocuyo** /ko'kuyo/ *m*, firefly

**codal** /ko'ðal/ *a* cubital. *m*, shoot of a vine; prop, strut; frame of a hand-saw

**codazo** /ko'ðaθo; ko'ðaso/ *m*, blow or nudge of the elbow. **dar codazos,** to elbow, shoulder out of the way

**codear** /koðe'ar/ *vi* to jostle; elbow, nudge; —*vr* be on terms of equality with

**codeína** /koðe'ina/ *f*, codeine

**codelincuente** /koðelin'kuente/ *mf* partner in crime, accomplice

**codera** /ko'ðera/ *f*, elbow rash; elbow-piece or patch

**codeso** /ko'ðeso/ *m*, laburnum

**códice** /'koðiθe; 'koðise/ *m*, codex

**codicia** /ko'ðiθia; ko'ðisia/ *f*, covetousness; greed

**codiciar** /koðiθi'ar; koðisi'ar/ *vt* to covet

**codicilo** /koði'θilo; koði'silo/ *m*, codicil

**codicioso** /koðiθi'oso; koðisi'oso/ **(-sa)** *a* covetous; *Inf.* hardworking —*n* covetous person

**codificación** /koðifika'θion; koðifika'sion/ *f*, codification

**codificar** /koðifi'kar/ *vt* to codify, compile

**código** /'koðigo/ *m*, code of laws. **c. civil,** civil laws. **c. de la circulación, c. de la vía pública,** highway code, traffic code. *Naut.* **c. de señales,** signal code. **c. penal,** criminal laws. **c. postal,** zip code

**codillo** /ko'ðiʎo; ko'ðiyo/ *m*, knee (of quadrupeds); shaft (of branch); bend (pipe, tube); stirrup

**codo** /'koðo/ *m*, elbow; angle, bend (pipe, tube); cubit. *Inf.* **hablar por los codos,** to chatter

**codorniz** /koðor'niθ; koðor'nis/ *f*, *Ornith.* quail

**coeducación** /koeðuka'θion; koeðuka'sion/ *f*, co-education

**coeficiente** /koefi'θiente; koefi'siente/ *m*, coefficient

**coercer** /koer'θer; koer'ser/ *vt* to restrain, coerce

**coerción** /koer'θion; koer'sion/ *f*, *Law.* coercion

**coercitivo** /koerθi'tiβo; koersi'tiβo/ *a* coercive

**coetáneo** /koe'taneo/ **(-ea)** *a* contemporaneous —*n* contemporary

**coevo** /ko'eβo/ *a* coeval

**coexistencia** /koeksis'tenθia; koeksis'tensia/ *f*, co-existence

**coexistir** /koeksis'tir/ *vi* to co-exist

**cofia** /'kofia/ *f*, hairnet; coif

**cofín** /ko'fin/ *m*, basket

**cofradía** /kofra'ðia/ *f*, confraternity, brotherhood or sisterhood **c. de gastronomía,** eating club (US), dining society (UK)

**cofre** /'kofre/ *m*, trunk, chest (for clothes); coffer

**cogedor** /kohe'ðor/ *m*, collector, gatherer; dustpan; coal-shovel

**coger** /ko'her/ *vt* to seize, hold; catch; take, collect, gather; have room for; take up or occupy space; find; catch in the act; attack, surprise; reach; **c. una berrinche,** have a fit, have a tantrum —*vi* have room, fit

**cogida** /ko'hiða/ *f*, gathering, picking; *Inf.* fruit harvest; toss (bullfighting)

**cogido** /ko'hiðo/ *m*, pleat, fold; crease. **estar c. de tiempo** to be pressed for time.

**cogitabundo** /kohita'βundo/ *a* very pensive

**cognación** /kogna'θion; kogna'sion/ *f*, cognation; kinship

**cognoscitivo** /kognosθi'tiβo; kognossi'tiβo/ *a* cognitive

**cogollo** /ko'goʎo; ko'goyo/ *m*, heart (of lettuce, etc.); shoot; topmost branches of pine tree

**cogote** /ko'gote/ *m*, nape (of neck)

**cogulla** /ko'guʎa; ko'guya/ *f*, monk's habit

**cohabitación** /koaβita'θion; koaβita'sion/ *f*, cohabitation

**cohabitar** /koaβi'tar/ *vt* to cohabit

**cohechador** /koetʃa'ðor/ **(-ra)** *a* bribing —*n* briber

**cohechar** /koe'tʃar/ *vt* to bribe, corrupt, suborn

**cohecho** /ko'etʃo/ *m*, bribing; bribe

**coheredero** /koere'ðero/ **(-ra)** *n* co-heir

**coherencia** /koe'renθia; koe'rensia/ *f*, coherence, connection

**coherente** /koe'rente/ *a* coherent

**cohesión** /koe'sion/ *f*, cohesion

**cohesivo** /koe'siβo/ *a* cohesive

**cohete** /ko'ete/ *m*, rocket

**cohetero** /koe'tero/ *m*, firework manufacturer

**cohibir** /koi'βir/ *vt* to restrain; repress. See **Prohibir.**

**cohombrillo** /koom'briʎo; koom'briyo/ *m*, *dim* gherkin

**cohombro** /ko'ombro/ *m*, cucumber

**cohonestar** /koones'tar/ *vt Fig.* to gloss over, cover up; make appear decent (actions, etc.)

**cohorte** /ko'orte/ *f*, cohort

**coincidencia** /koinθi'ðenθia; koinsi'ðensia/ *f*, coincidence

**coincidir** /koinθi'ðir; koinsi'ðir/ *vt* to coincide; (two or more people) be in the same place at the same time. **c. con que...** to agree that...

**coito** /'koito/ *m*, coitus

**cojear** /kohe'ar/ *vi* to limp; wobble, be unsteady (of furniture); *Fig. Inf.* go wrong or astray; *Inf.* suffer from (vice, bad habit)

**cojera** /ko'hera/ *f*, lameness, limp

**cojijoso** /kohi'hoso/ *a* peevish

**cojín** /ko'hin/ *m*, cushion; pad; pillow (for lace-making)

**cojinete** /kohi'nete/ *m*, small cushion; *Mech.* bearing. **c. de bolas,** ball-bearing

**cojo** /'koho/ *a* lame; unsteady, wobbly (of furniture, etc.)

**col** /kol/ *f*, cabbage. **c. de Bruselas,** Brussels sprouts

**cola** /'kola/ *f*, tail; train (of gown); shank (of a button); queue; tailpiece (of a violin, etc.); appendage; glue. **c. de milano,** dovetail. **c. de pescado,** isinglass. **formar c.,** to line up, queue up

**colaboración** /kolaβora'θion; kolaβora'sion/ *f*, collaboration. **en c.,** joint (e.g. *obra en colaboración,* joint work)

**colaboracionista** /kolaβoraθio'nista; kolaβorasio'nista/ *mf* collaborationist

**colaborador** /kolaβora'ðor/ **(-ra)** *n* collaborator

**colaborar** /kolaβo'rar/ *vt* to collaborate

**colación** /kola'θion; kola'sion/ *f*, conferment of a degree; collation (of texts); light repast; cold supper; area of a parish

**colada** /ko'laða/ *f*, wash; bleaching; mountain path; *Metall.* casting; *Inf.* trusty sword (allusion to name of one of the Cid's swords)

**coladero** /kola'ðero/ *m*, colander, sieve, strainer; narrow path

**colador** /kola'ðor/ *m*, colander

**coladura** /kola'ðura/ *f*, straining, filtration; *Inf.* untruth; *Inf.* howler, mistake

**colapso** /ko'lapso/ *m*, *Med.* prostration, collapse

**colar** /ko'lar/ *vt ir* to filter, strain; bleach; *Metall.* cast; —*vi* go through a narrow place; *Inf.* drink wine; —*vr* thread one's way; *Inf.* enter by stealth, steal in; *Inf.* tell untruths —*Pres. Indic.* **cuelo, cuelas, cuela, cuelan.** *Pres. Subjunc.* **cuele, cueles, cuele, cuelen**

**colateral** /kolate'ral/ *a* collateral

**colcha** /'koltʃa/ *f*, bedspread, counterpane, quilt

**colchadura** /koltʃa'ðura/ *f*, quilting

**colchero** /kol'tʃero/ *m*, quilt maker

**colchón** /kol'tʃon/ *m*, mattress. **c. de muelles,** spring-mattress. **c. de viento,** air-bed

**colchonero** /koltʃo'nero/ *m*, mattress maker or seller

**colchoneta** /koltʃo'neta/ *f*, pad, thin mattress

**coleada** /kole'aða/ *f*, wag of the tail

**colear** /kole'ar/ *vi* to wag the tail

**colección** /kolek'θion; kolek'sion/ *f*, collection

**coleccionador** /kolekθiona'ðor; koleksiona'ðor/ **(-ra)** *n* collector

**coleccionar** /kolekθio'nar; koleksio'nar/ *vt* to collect

**coleccionista** /kolekθio'nista; koleksio'nista/ *mf* collector

**colecta** /ko'lekta/ *f*, assessment; collection (of donations); *Eccl.* collect; voluntary offering

**colectivero** /kolekti'βero/ *m*, bus driver

**colectividad** /kolektiβi'ðað/ *f*, collectivity; body of people

**colectivismo** /kolekti'βismo/ *m*, collectivism

**colectivista** /kolekti'βista/ *a* collectivist

**colectivo** /kolek'tiβo/ *a* collective; *Argentina* (local) bus

**colector** /kolek'tor/ *m*, gatherer; collector; tax-collector; water-pipe; water-conduit; *Elec.* commutator, collector

**colega** /ko'lega/ *m,* colleague

**colegiado** /kole'hiaðo/ *a* collegiate

**colegial** /kole'hial/ **(-la)** *a* college, collegiate —*n* student; pupil; *Fig. Inf.* novice.

**colegiarse** /kole'hiarse/ *vr* to meet as an association (professional, etc.)

**colegiata** /kole'hiata/ *f,* college church

**colegiatura** /kolehia'tura/ *f,* scholarship, fellowship (money granted a student); tuition (fee paid by a student), tuition fee, tuition fees

**colegio** /ko'lehio/ *m,* college; school; academy; association (professional); council, convocation; college or school buildings. **c. de abogados,** bar association. **c. de cardenales,** College of Cardinals. **c. electoral,** polling-booth. **c. militar,** military academy

**colegir** /kole'hir/ *vt irr* to collect, gather; deduce, infer. See **elegir**

**cólera** /'kolera/ *f,* bile, anger. *m,* cholera. **montar en c.,** to fly into a rage

**colérico** /ko'leriko/ *a* angry; choleric; suffering from cholera

**colesterina** /koleste'rina/ *f, Chem.* cholesterol

**coleta** /ko'leta/ *f,* pigtail; queue; *Inf.* postscript

**coletazo** /kole'taθo; kole'taso/ *m,* blow with one's tail, lash with one's tail; lash of a dying fish; *Fig.* last hurrah

**coleto** /ko'leto/ *m,* leather jerkin; *Inf.* body of a man

**colgadero** /kolga'ðero/ *a* able to be hung up. *m,* coat-hanger, hook

**colgadizo** /kolga'ðiθo; kolga'ðiso/ *a* hanging. *m,* overhanging roof

**colgadura** /kolga'ðura/ *f,* hangings, drapery, tapestries. **c. de cama,** bedhangings

**colgajo** /kol'gaho/ *m,* tatter; bunch (of grapes, etc.); *Surg.* skin lap

**colgar** /kol'gar/ *vt irr* to hang up; decorate with hangings; *Inf.* hang, kill; —*vi* hang, be suspended; *Fig.* be dependent. See **contar**

**colibrí** /koli'βri/ *m,* hummingbird

**cólico** /'koliko/ *m,* colic

**colicuar** /koli'kuar/ *vt* to dissolve

**coliflor** /koli'flor/ *f,* cauliflower

**coligarse** /koli'garse/ *vr* to confederate, unite

**colilla** /ko'liʎa; ko'liya/ *f,* stub (of a cigar or cigarette)

**colina** /ko'lina/ *f,* hill; cabbage seed; *Chem.* choline

**colindante** /kolin'dante/ *a* adjacent, contiguous

**coliseo** /koli'seo/ *m,* coliseum; theater

**colisión** /koli'sion/ *f,* collision; abrasion, bruise; *Fig.* clash (of ideas)

**colitis** /ko'litis/ *f,* colitis

**collado** /ko'ʎaðo; ko'yaðo/ *m,* hill, hillock

**collar** /ko'ʎar; ko'yar/ *m,* necklace; chain of office or honor; collar (dogs, etc.)

**collera** /ko'ʎera; ko'yera/ *f,* **collerón,** *m,* horse collar

**colmado** /kol'maðo/ *a* abundant. *m,* provision shop

**colmar** /kol'mar/ *vt* to fill to overflowing; bestow generously, heap upon

**colmena** /kol'mena/ *f,* beehive

**colmenero** /kolme'nero/ **(-ra)** *n* beekeeper

**colmillo** /kol'miʎo; kol'miyo/ *m,* canine tooth; tusk; fang

**colmilludo** /kolmi'ʎuðo; kolmi'yuðo/ *a* having large canine teeth; tusked; fanged; sagacious

**colmo** /'kolmo/ *m,* overflow; highest point; completion, limit, end. **ser el c.,** *Inf.* to be the last straw. **el c. de los colmos,** the absolute limit

**colocación** /koloka'θion; koloka'sion/ *f,* placing, putting; situation, place; employment; *Sports.* placing; order, arrangement; *Ling.* collocation

**colocar** /kolo'kar/ *vt* to place, put, arrange; place in employment. **c. bajo banderas,** to draft (into the armed forces) —*vr* place oneself

**colofón** /kolo'fon/ *m, Print.* colophon

**colofonia** /kolo'fonia/ *f,* solid resin (for bows of stringed instruments, etc.)

**coloide** /ko'loiðe/ *a* and *m,* colloid

**colombiano** /kolom'biano/ **(-na)** *a* and *n* Colombian

**colombina** /kolom'bina/ *f,* columbine

**colombofilia** /kolombo'filia/ *f,* pigeon fancying

**colonia** /ko'lonia/ *f,* colony; plantation

**colonial** /kolo'nial/ *a* colonial

**colonización** /koloniθa'θion; kolonisa'sion/ *f,* colonization

**colonizador** /koloniθa'ðor; kolonisa'ðor/ **(-ra)** *a* colonizing —*n* colonizer

**colonizar** /koloni'θar; koloni'sar/ *vt* to colonize; settle

**colono** /ko'lono/ *m,* settler, colonist; farmer

**coloquio** /ko'lokio/ *m,* colloquy, conversation, talk; colloquium

**color** /ko'lor/ *m,* color; dye; paint; rouge; coloring; pretext, excuse; character, individuality; *pl* natural colors. **c. estable, c. sólido,** fast color. **mudar de c.,** to change color. **de c.,** colored. **so c.,** under the pretext. **ver las cosas c. de rosa,** to see things through rose-colored glasses

**coloración** /kolora'θion; kolora'sion/ *f,* coloration, painting

**colorado** /kolo'raðo/ *a* colored. *West Hem.* red, reddish; *Inf.* blue, obscene; specious

**colorante** /kolo'rante/ *a* coloring. *m,* dyestuff; coloring (substance)

**colorar** /kolo'rar/ *vt* to color; dye

**colorear** /kolore'ar/ *vt* to color; pretext; *Fig.* whitewash, excuse; —*vi* show color; be reddish; grow red, ripe (tomatoes, cherries, etc.)

**colorero** /kolo'rero/ *m,* dyer

**colorete** /kolo'rete/ *m,* rouge

**colorido** /kolo'riðo/ *m,* coloring, color

**colorín** /kolo'rin/ *m,* goldfinch; bright color

**colorista** /kolo'rista/ *a* and *mf* colorist

**colosal** /kolo'sal/ *a* colossal, enormous; extraordinary, excellent

**coloso** /ko'loso/ *m,* colossus; *Fig.* outstanding person or thing, giant; **el C. del Norte, el Gran C. del Norte,** (contemptuous epithet for the United States of America)

**columbino** /kolum'bino/ *a* pertaining to a dove; dovelike; candid, innocent; purply-red

**columbrar** /kolum'brar/ *vt* to discern in the distance, glimpse; conjecture, guess

**columna** /ko'lumna/ *f, Mil. Archit. Print.* column; *Fig.* protection, shelter; *Naut.* stanchion. **c. cerrada,** *Mil.* etc. mass formation. **c. de los suspiros,** agony column (in a newspaper)

**columnata** /kolum'nata/ *f,* colonnade

**columpiar** /kolum'piar/ *vt* to swing; dangle (one's feet); —*vr Inf.* sway in walking; swing

**columpio** /ko'lumpio/ *m,* swing

**colusión** /kolu'sion/ *f,* collusion

**colusorio** /kolu'sorio/ *a* collusive

**coma** /'koma/ *f, Gram.* comma. *m, Med.* coma

**comadre** /ko'maðre/ *f,* midwife; *Inf.* procuress, gobetween; *Inf.* pal, gossip

**comadrear** /komaðre'ar/ *vi Inf.* to gossip

**comadreja** /koma'ðreha/ *f, Zool.* weasel

**comadrón** /koma'ðron/ *m,* accoucheur

**comadrona** /koma'ðrona/ *f,* midwife

**comandancia** /koman'danθia; koman'dansia/ *f, Mil.* command; commandant's H.Q.

**comandante** /koman'dante/ *m,* commandant; commander; major; squadron-leader —*a Mil.* commanding. **c. en jefe,** commanding officer

**comandar** /koman'dar/ *vt Mil.* to command

**comandita** /koman'dita/ *f, Com.* sleeping partnership; private company

**comando** /ko'mando/ *m, Mil.* commando

**comarca** /ko'marka/ *f,* district, region

**comatoso** /koma'toso/ *a* comatose

**comba** /'komba/ *f,* bend, warping; jump rope, skipping-rope; camber (of road)

**combadura** /komba'ðura/ *f,* curvature; warping; camber (of a road)

**combar** /kom'bar/ *vt* to bend; twist; warp; camber

**combate** /kom'bate/ *m,* fight, combat; mental strife; contradiction, opposition. **c. judicial,** trial by combat. **dejar fuera de c.,** (a) (boxing) to knock out

**combatiente** /komba'tiente/ *m,* combatant, soldier

**combatir** /komba'tir/ *vi* to fight; —*vt* attack; struggle against (winds, water, etc.); contradict, oppose; *Fig.* disturb, trouble (emotions)

**combinación** /kombina'θion; kombina'sion/ *f*, combination; list of words beginning with same letter; project; concurrence; underskirt, petticoat. **estar en c.** ( **con**), to be in cahoots (with), connive (with)

**combinar** /kombi'nar/ *vt* to combine; (*Mil. Nav.*) join forces; arrange, plan; *Chem.* combine; **combinar para + inf.** (two or more people) to make arrangements to + inf.

**combustible** /kombus'tiβle/ *a* combustible. *m*, fuel

**combustión** /kombus'tion/ *f*, combustion. **c. activa**, rapid combustion. **c. espontánea**, spontaneous combustion

**comedero** /kome'ðero/ *a* edible. *m*, feeding-trough; dining-room

**comedia** /ko'meðia/ *f*, comedy; play; theater; comic incident; *Fig.* play-acting, theatricalism. **c. alta**, art theater. **c. de costumbres**, comedy of manners. **c. de enredo**, play with very involved plot. *Inf.* **hacer la c.**, to play-act, pretend

**comedianta** /kome'ðianta/ *f*, actress

**comediante** /kome'ðiante/ *m*, actor; *Inf.* dissembler.

**comedido** /kome'ðiðo/ *a* courteous; prudent; moderate

**comedimiento** /komeði'miento/ *m*, courtesy; moderation; prudence

**comedir** /kome'ðir/ *vt irr* to prepare, premeditate; —*vr* restrain oneself, be moderate; offer one's services. See **pedir**

**comedor** /kome'ðor/ *a* voracious. *m*, dining-room

**comendador** /komenda'ðor/ *m*, knight commander

**comendatorio** /komenda'torio/ *a* commendatory (of letters)

**Comenio** /ko'menio/ Comenius

**comensal** /komen'sal/ *mf* table companion

**comentador** /komenta'ðor/ **(-ra)** *n* commentator

**comentar** /komen'tar/ *vt* explain (document); *Inf.* comment

**comentario** /komen'taric/ **(a)** *m*, commentary (on)

**comentarista** /komenta'rista/ *mf* commentator

**comento** /ko'mento/ *m*, comment; (of) commentary

**comenzante** /komen'θante; komen'sante/ *mf* beginner, novice —*a* initial

**comenzar** /komen'θar; komen'sar/ *vt vi irr* to begin, commence. See **empezar**

**comer** /ko'mer/ *m*, eating; food —*vi* to eat; feed; dine —*vt* eat; *Inf.* enjoy an income; waste (patrimony); consume, exhaust; fade (of colors); —*vr* be troubled, uneasy, remorseful. **ser de buen c.**, to have a good appetite; taste good. **tener que c.**, to be obliged to eat; have to eat; have enough to eat

**comerciable** /komer'θiaβle; komer'siaβle/ *a* marketable; sociable, pleasant (of persons)

**comercial** /komer'θial; komer'sial/ *a* commercial

**comerciante** /komer'θiante; komer'siante/ *a* trading. *mf* merchant, trader

**comerciar** /komer'θiar; komer'siar/ *vt* to trade; have dealings (with)

**comercio** /ko'merθio; ko'mersio/ *m*, trade, commerce; intercourse, traffic; illicit sexual intercourse; shop, store; tradesmen; commercial quarter of town

**comestible** /komes'tiβle/ *a* edible, eatable. *m*, (gen. *pl*) provisions

**cometa** /ko'meta/ *m*, *Astron.* comet. *f*, kite (toy). **c. celular**, box-kite

**cometedor** /komete'ðor/ **(-ra)** *n* perpetrator

**cometer** /kome'ter/ *vt* to entrust, hand over to; commit (crime, sins, etc.); *Com.* order

**cometido** /kome'tiðo/ *m*, charge, commission; moral obligation; function

**comezón** /kome'θon; kome'son/ *f*, itching, irritation; hankering, longing

**comicidad** /komiθi'ðað; komisi'ðað/ *f*, comic element; comic spirit

**cómico** /'komiko/ *a* comic; funny, comical. *m*, actor; comedian. **c. de la legua**, strolling player

**comida** /ko'miða/ *f*, food; meal; dinner; eating. **c. de gala**, state banquet. **c. de prueba**, *Med.* test meal

**comienzo** /ko'mienθo; ko'mienso/ *m*, beginning, origin

**comillas** /ko'miʎas; ko'miyas/ *f pl*, *Gram.* inverted commas

**comilón** /komi'lon/ **(-ona)** *a* *Inf.* gluttonous —*n* glutton

**comino** /ko'mino/ *m*, *Bot.* cumin. **no valer un c.**, to be not worth a jot

**comisar** /komi'sar/ *vt* to confiscate, sequestrate

**comisaría** /komisa'ria/ *f*, commissaryship; commissariat. **c. de policía**, police station

**comisario** /komi'sario/ *m*, deputy, agent; commissary, head of police; commissioner. **alto c.**, high commissioner. **c. propietario**, stockholders' representative

**comisión** /komi'sion/ *f*, perpetration, committal; commission; committee; *Com.* commission

**comisionado** /komisio'naðo/ **(-da)** *a* commissioned. *m*, commissary

**comisionar** /komisio'nar/ *vt* to commission

**comisionista** /komisio'nista/ *mf* *Com.* commission agent

**comiso** /ko'miso/ *m*, *Law.* confiscation, sequestration; contraband

**comité** /komi'te/ *m*, committee

**comitiva** /komi'tiβa/ *f*, retinue, following

**como** /'komo/ *adv* like, as; in the same way; thus, accordingly; in the capacity of; so that; since —*conjunc* if (*followed by subjunc.*); because. **c. no**, unless. **¿Cómo?** How? In what way? Why? Pardon? What did you say? *interj* **¡Cómo!** What! You don't say! **¡Cómo no!** Why not! Of course! Surely! **¿Cómo que...?** What do you mean that...?

**cómo** /'komo/ *m*, the wherefore. **no saber el porqué ni el c.**, not to know the why or wherefore

**cómoda** /'komoða/ *f*, chest of drawers

**comodidad** /komoði'ðað/ *f*, comfort; convenience; advantage; utility, interest

**comodín** /komo'ðin/ *m*, (in cards) joker

**cómodo** /'komoðo/ *a* comfortable; convenient; opportune

**comodón** /komo'ðon/ *a* *Inf.* comfort-loving; easygoing; egoistical

**comodoro** /komo'ðoro/ *m*, *Naut.* commodore

**comoquiera que** /komo'kiera ke/ *adv* by any means that, anyway; whereas; given that

**compacidad** /kompaθi'ðað; kompasi'ðað/ *f*, compactness

**compacto** /kom'pakto/ *a* compact, dense; close (type)

**compadecer** /kompaðe'θer; kompaðe'ser/ *vt irr* to pity; —*vr* (*with* **de**) sympathize with; pity; harmonize, agree with. See **conocer**

**compadre** /kom'paðre/ *m*, *Inf.* pal

**compaginación** /kompahina'θion; kompahina'sion/ *f*, joining, fixing; *Print.* making-up

**compaginar** /kompahi'nar/ *vt* to fit together; join, put in order; harmonize, square (e.g. *compaginé una cuenta con la otra*, I squared one account with the other); *Print.* make up

**compañero** /kompa'ɲero/ **(-ra)** *n* companion, comrade; fellow-member; partner (games); *Fig.* pair, fellow, mate (things). **c. de armas**, brother-in-arms, companion-at-arms. **c. de cabina**, boothmate. **c. de exilio**, companion in exile, fellow exile. **c. de generación**, contemporary, person of the same generation. **c. de viaje**, traveling companion; *Polit.* fellow traveler (communist sympathizer)

**compañía** /kompa'ɲia/ *f*, company; society, association; theatrical company; (*Com. Mil.*) company. **C. de Jesús**, Order of Jesus. **c. de la zarza**, guild of guards and woodcutters for autos de fe. **c. de navegación**, shipping company. **c. por acciones**, joint stock company

**comparable** /kompa'raβle/ *a* comparable

**comparación** /kompara'θion; kompara'sion/ *f*, comparison

**comparar** /kompa'rar/ *vt* to compare; collate

**comparativo** /kompara'tiβo/ *a* comparative

**comparecencia** /kompare'θenθia; kompare'sensia/ *f*, (gen. *Law.*) appearance

**comparecer** /kompare'θer; kompare'ser/ *vi irr* *Law.* to appear (before tribunal, etc.); present oneself. See **conocer**

**comparendo** /kompa'rendo/ *m*, *Law.* summons

**comparsa** /kom'parsa/ *f,* retinue; *Theat.* chorus; troop of carnival revelers dressed alike. *mf Theat.* supernumerary actor

**comparte** /kom'parte/ *mf Law.* partner; accomplice

**compartimiento** /komparti'miento/ *m,* share, division; railway carriage. *Naut.* **c. estanco,** compartment

**compartir** /kompar'tir/ *vt* to share out, divide; participate

**compás** /kom'pas/ *m,* compasses; callipers; size; compass, time; range of voice; (*Naut. Mineral.*) compass; *Mus.* time, rhythm, bar, marking time. **c. de mar,** mariner's compass. **c. de puntas,** dividers, callipers. **fuera de c.,** *Mus.* out of time; out of joint (of the times). *Mus.* **llevar el c.,** to beat time

**compasar** /kompa'sar/ *vt* to measure with compasses; arrange or apportion accurately; *Mus.* put into bars

**compasillo** /kompa'siʎo; kompa'siyo/ *m, Mus.* $\frac{4}{4}$ measure

**compasivo** /kompa'siβo/ *a* compassionate; tenderhearted

**compatibilidad** /kompatiβili'ðað/ *f,* compatibility

**compatible** /kompa'tiβle/ *a* compatible

**compatriota** /kompa'triota/ *mf* compatriot

**compeler** /kompe'ler/ *vt* to compel, force

**compendiar** /kompen'diar/ *vt* to abridge, summarize

**compendio** /kom'pendio/ *m,* compendium. **en c.,** briefly

**compendioso** /kompen'dioso/ *a* summary, condensed; compendious

**compenetración** /kompenetra'θion; kompenetra'sion/ *f,* co-penetration; intermingling

**compenetrado** /kompene'traðo/ **(de)** *a* thoroughly convinced (of)

**compenetrarse** /kompene'trarse/ *vr* to co-penetrate; intermingle

**compensación** /kompensa'θion; kompensa'sion/ *f,* compensating; compensation

**compensar** /kompen'sar/ *vt* to equalize, counterbalance; compensate

**compensatorio** /kompensa'torio/ *a* compensatory; equalizing

**competencia** /kompe'tenθia; kompe'tensia/ *f,* competition, contest; rivalry; competence; aptitude; *Law.* jurisdiction

**competente** /kompe'tente/ *a* adequate, opportune; rightful, correct; apt, suitable; learned, competent

**competer** /kompe'ter/ *vi irr* to belong to; devolve on; concern. See **pedir**

**competición** /kompeti'θion; kompeti'sion/ *f,* competition

**competidor** /kompeti'ðor/ **(-ra)** *n* competitor

**competir** /kompe'tir/ *vi irr* to compete, contest; be equal (to), vie (with). See **pedir**

**compilación** /kompila'θion; kompila'sion/ *f,* compilation

**compilador** /kompila'ðor/ **(-ra)** *n* compiler —*a* compiling

**compilar** /kompi'lar/ *vt* to compile

**compinche** /kom'pintʃe/ *mf Inf.* pal, chum

**complacencia** /kompla'θenθia; kompla'sensia/ *f,* satisfaction, pleasure

**complacer** /kompla'θer; kompla'ser/ *vt irr* to oblige, humor; —*vr* (*with en*) be pleased or satisfied with; delight in, like to. See **nacer**

**complaciente** /kompla'θiente; kompla'siente/ *a* pleasing; obliging, helpful

**complejidad** /komplehi'ðað/ *f,* complexity

**complejo** /kom'pleho/ *a* complex; intricate. *m,* complex. **c. de inferioridad,** inferiority complex

**complementario** /komplemen'tario/ *a* complementary

**complemento** /komple'mento/ *m,* complement (all meanings)

**completar** /komple'tar/ *vt* to complete; perfect

**completo** /kom'pleto/ *a* full; finished; perfect

**complexión** /komplek'sion/ *f,* physical constitution

**complexo** /kom'plekso/ *a* complex; intricate

**complicación** /komplika'θion; komplika'sion/ *f,* complication

**complicar** /kompli'kar/ *vt* to complicate; muddle,

confuse; —*vr* be complicated; be muddled or confused

**cómplice** /'kompliθe; 'komplise/ *mf* accomplice

**complicidad** /kompliθi'ðað; komplisi'ðað/ *f,* complicity

**complot** /kom'plot/ *m, Inf.* conspiracy, plot, intrigue

**complutense** /komplu'tense/ *a* native of, or belonging to, Alcalá de Henares

**componedor** /kompone'ðor/ **(-ra)** *n* repairer; arbitrator; bone-setter; *Mus.* composer; writer, author, compiler; *Print.* compositor

**componenda** /kompo'nenda/ *f,* mending, repair; *Inf.* settlement; compromise, arbitration; *Inf.* shady business

**componente** /kompo'nente/ *a* and *m,* component

**componer** /kompo'ner/ *vt irr* to construct, form; *Mech.* resolve; compose, create; *Print.* compose; prepare, concoct, mend, repair; settle (differences); remedy; trim; correct, adjust; *Lit. Mus.* compose; add up to, amount to; —*vi* write (verses); *Mus.* compose; —*vr* dress oneself up. **c. el semblante,** to compose one's features; *Inf.* **componérselas,** to fix matters, use one's wits. See **poner**

**componible** /kompo'niβle/ *a* reparable, mendable; able to be arranged or adjusted

**comportamiento** /komporta'miento/ *m,* conduct; deportment

**comportar** /kompor'tar/ *vt* to tolerate; —*vr* behave, comport oneself

**composición** /komposi'θion; komposi'sion/ *f,* composition; repair; arrangement, compromise; *Print.* composition; *Gram.* compound; *Chem.* constitution; *Mech.* resolution

**compositor** /komposi'tor/ **(-ra)** *n Mus.* composer; *Print.* compositor

**Compostela** /kompos'tela/ Compostella

**compostura** /kompos'tura/ *f,* composition, structure; repair; neatness (of person); adulteration; arrangement, agreement; discretion, modesty

**compota** /kom'pota/ *f,* fruit preserve, compote; thick sauce

**compotera** /kompo'tera/ *f,* jam or preserve dish

**compra** /'kompra/ *f,* buying; marketing, shopping; purchase. **estar de compras,** *Euph.* to be in the family way. **ir de compras,** to go shopping

**comprable** /kom'praβle/ *a* purchasable

**comprador** /kompra'ðor/ **(-ra)** *a* purchasing —*n* purchaser; buyer; shopper

**comprar** /kom'prar/ *vt* to buy; bribe

**comprender** /kompren'der/ *vt* to encircle, surround; include, comprise, contain; understand

**comprensible** /kompren'siβle/ *a* comprehensible

**comprensión** /kompren'sion/ *f,* comprehension, understanding

**comprensivo** /kompren'siβo/ *a* understanding; comprehensive

**compresa** /kom'presa/ *f, Med.* compress, swab; pack (for the face, etc.)

**compresión** /kompre'sion/ *f,* compression; squeeze

**compresivo** /kompre'siβo/ *a* compressive

**compresor** /kompre'sor/ *m,* compressor; *Auto. Aer.* supercharger

**comprimido** /kompri'miðo/ *m,* tablet, pill

**comprimir** /kompri'mir/ *vt* to compress; squeeze; restrain; —*vr* restrain oneself

**comprobación** /komproβa'θion; komproβa'sion/ *f,* verification; checking; proof

**comprobante** /kompro'βante/ *a* verifying; confirmatory

**comprobar** /kompro'βar/ *vt irr* to verify, check; confirm, prove. See **probar**

**comprobatorio** /komproβa'torio/ *a* confirmatory; verifying; testing

**comprometedor** /kompromete'ðor/ *a Inf.* compromising; jeopardizing

**comprometer** /komprome'ter/ *vt* to submit to arbitration; compromise; imperil, jeopardize; —*vr* pledge oneself; *Inf.* compromise oneself

**comprometido** /komprome'tiðo/ *a* awkward, embarrassing; (e.g. literature of a writer) committed, engagé

**compromiso** /kompro'miso/ *m,* compromise, agreement, arbitration, commitment, obligation; appointment, engagement; jeopardy; difficulty

**compuerta** /kom'puerta/ *f,* half-door, wicket, hatch; floodgate, sluice. **c. flotante,** floating dam

**compuesto** /kom'puesto/ *a* and *past part* made-up, built-up; composite; circumspect; *Bot. Gram.* compound. *m,* composite; preparation, compound

**compulsar** /kompul'sar/ *vt* to collate; *Law.* make a transcript of

**compulsivo** /kompul'siβo/ *a* compelling

**compunción** /kompun'θion; kompun'sion/ *f,* compunction

**compungir** /kompun'hir/ *vt* to cause remorse or pity; —*vr* repent; sympathize with, pity

**computable** /kompu'taβle/ *a* computable

**computación** /komputa'θion; komputa'sion/ *f,* **cómputo** *m,* calculation, computation

**computador** /komputa'ðor/ **(-ra)** *n* computer

**computar** /kompu'tar/ *vt* to compute

**computista** /kompu'tista/ *mf* computer

**cómputo** /'komputo/ *m,* computation; estimate

**comulgar** /komul'gar/ *vt* to administer Holy Communion; —*vi* receive Holy Communion

**comulgatorio** /komulga'torio/ *m,* communion rail, altar rail

**común** /ko'mun/ *a* general, customary, ordinary; public, communal; universal, common; vulgar, low. *m,* community, population; water-closet. **en c.,** in common; generally. **por lo c.,** generally. **sentido c.,** common sense

**comunal** /komu'nal/ *a* communal; common. *m,* commonalty

**comunero** /komu'nero/ *a* popular, affable, democratic. *m,* joint owner; commoner; *Hist.* commune

**comunicable** /komuni'kaβle/ *a* communicable; communicative, sociable

**comunicación** /komunika'θion; komunika'sion/ *f,* communication; (telephone) call, message; letter (to the press); *Mil.* communiqué; *pl* lines of communication, transport

**comunicado** /komuni'kaðo/ *m,* official communication, communiqué; letter (to the press)

**comunicante** /komuni'kante/ *a* communicating

**comunicar** /komuni'kar/ *vt* to communicate; transmit; impart, share; —*vr* **comunicarse con,** (door) to open onto (e.g. *Esta puerta se comunica con el jardín.* This door opens onto the garden); communicate, converse, correspond with each other

**comunicativo** /komunika'tiβo/ *a* communicative; talkative, not reserved

**comunidad** /komuni'ðað/ *f,* the common people; community; generality, majority; *pl Hist.* Commune

**comunión** /komu'nion/ *f,* communion; intercourse, fellowship; *Eccl.* Communion

**comunismo** /komu'nismo/ *m,* communism

**comunista** /komu'nista/ *a* and *mf* communist

**comunistófilo, comunistoide** /komunis'tofilo, komunis'toiðe/ *a* fellow-traveling; —*n* fellow traveler

**comúnmente** /komu'mente/ *adv* commonly, generally; frequently

**con** /kon/ *prep* with; by means of; in the company of; towards, to; although (followed by *infin.*, but generally translated by an inflected verb, e.g. *C. ser almirante, no le gusta el mar,* Although he is an admiral, he doesn't like the sea); by (followed by *infin.* and generally translated by a gerund, e.g. *c. hacer todo esto,* by doing all this). **c. bien,** safe and sound, safely (e.g. *Llegamos con bien.* We arrived safely.) **c. cuentagotas,** sparingly; stingily. **c. que,** so, then. **c. tal que,** provided that, on condition that. **c. todo,** nevertheless. **¿Con...?** Is this...? (on the telephone, e.g. *¿Con el Sr. Piñangos?* Is this Mr. Piñangos?)

**conato** /ko'nato/ *m,* effort, endeavor; tendency; *Law.* attempted crime

**concatenación** /konkatena'θion; konkatena'sion/ *f,* concatenation

**concavidad** /konkaβi'ðað/ *f,* concavity; hollow

**cóncavo** /'konkaβo/ *a* concave. *m,* concavity; hollow

**concebible** /konθe'βiβle; konse'βiβle/ *a* conceivable

**concebimiento** /konθeβi'miento; konseβi'miento/ *m.* See **concepción**

**concebir** /konθe'βir; konse'βir/ *vi irr* to become preg-

nant; conceive, imagine; understand; —*vt* conceive, acquire (affection, etc.). See **pedir**

**concedente** /konθe'ðente; konse'ðente/ *a* conceding

**conceder** /konθe'ðer; konse'ðer/ *vt* to confer, grant; concede; agree to

**concejal** /konθe'hal; konse'hal/ *m,* councillor; alderman

**concejil** /konθe'hil; konse'hil/ *a* pertaining to a municipal council; public

**concejo** /kon'θeho; kon'seho/ *m,* town council; town hall; council meeting

**concentración** /konθentra'θion; konsentra'sion/ *f,* concentration

**concentrado** /konθen'traðo; konsen'traðo/ *a* concentrated; (of persons) reserved

**concentrar** /konθen'trar; konsen'trar/ *vt* to concentrate

**concéntrico** /kon'θentriko; kon'sentriko/ *a* concentric

**concepción** /konθep'θion; konsep'sion/ *f,* conception; idea, concept; *Eccl.* Immaculate Conception

**conceptismo** /konθep'tismo; konsep'tismo/ *m, Lit.* Concetism (cf. **Euphuism**)

**conceptista** /konθep'tista; konsep'tista/ *a* and *mf* concettist

**concepto** /kon'θepto; kon'septo/ *m,* idea, concept; epigram; opinion. **en mi c.,** in my opinion; judgment. **por c. de,** in payment of

**conceptualismo** /konθeptua'lismo; konseptua'lismo/ *m,* conceptualism

**conceptuar** /konθep'tuar; konsep'tuar/ *vt* to judge, take to be; believe; imagine

**conceptuoso** /konθep'tuoso; konsep'tuoso/ *a* witty, ingenious

**concernencia** /konθer'nenθia; konser'nensia/ *f,* respect, relation

**concerniente** /konθer'niente; konser'niente/ *a* concerning

**concernir** /konθer'nir; konser'nir/ *vi irr defective* to concern. See **discernir**

**concertadamente** /konθertaða'mente; konsertaða'mente/ *adv* methodically, orderly; by arrangement, or agreement

**concertar** /konθer'tar; konser'tar/ *vt irr* to arrange, settle, adjust; bargain; conclude (business deal); harmonize; compare, correlate; tune instruments; —*vi* reach an agreement. See **acertar**

**concertina** /konθer'tina; konser'tina/ *f,* concertina

**concertista** /konθer'tista; konser'tista/ *mf Mus.* performer, soloist; *Mus.* manager. **c. de piano,** concert pianist

**concesión** /konθe'sion; konse'sion/ *f,* conceding, grant; concession; lease

**concesionario** /konθesio'nario; konsesio'nario/ *m, Law.* concessionaire, leaseholder

**concha** /'kontʃa/ *f,* shell; turtle-shell; prompter's box; cove, creek; anything shell-shaped. *Fig.* **meterse en su c.,** to retire into one's shell. *Inf.* **tener más conchas que un galápago,** to be very cunning

**conchado** /kon'tʃaðo/ *a* scaly, having a shell

**conciencia** /kon'θienθia; kon'siensia/ *f,* consciousness; conscience; conscientiousness. **c. doble,** dual personality. **ancho de c.,** broad-minded. **a c.,** conscientiously

**concienzudo** /konθien'θuðo; konsien'suðo/ *a* of a delicate conscience, scrupulous; conscientious

**concierto** /kon'θierto; kon'sierto/ *m,* methodical arrangement; agreement; *Mus.* concert; *Mus.* concerto. **de c.,** by common consent

**conciliable** /konθi'liaβle; konsi'liaβle/ *a* reconcilable, compatible

**conciliábulo** /konθi'liaβulo; konsi'liaβulo/ *m,* conclave, private meeting; secret meeting

**conciliación** /konθilia'θion; konsilia'sion/ *f,* conciliation; similarity, affinity; protection, favor

**conciliador** /konθilia'ðor; konsilia'ðor/ *a* conciliatory

**conciliar** /konθi'liar; konsi'liar/ *m,* councilor —*vt* to conciliate; *Fig.* reconcile (opposing theories, etc.). **c. el sueño,** to induce sleep, woo sleep —*vr* win liking (or sometimes dislike)

**concilio** /kon'θilio; kon'silio/ *m,* council; *Eccl.* assembly; conciliary decree; findings of council

**concinidad** /konθini'ðað; konsini'ðað/ f, concinnity

**concino** /kon'θino; kon'sino/ a concinnous

**concisión** /konθi'sion; konsi'sion/ f, conciseness, brevity

**conciso** /kon'θiso; kon'siso/ a concise

**concitar** /konθi'tar; konsi'tar/ vt to stir up, foment

**conciudadano** /konθiuða'ðano; konsiuða'ðano/ **(-na)** n fellow citizen; fellow countryman

**cónclave** /'konklaβe/ m, conclave; meeting

**concluir** /kon'kluir/ vt irr to conclude, finish; come to a conclusion, decide; infer, deduce; convince by reasoning; Law. close legal proceedings; —vr expire, terminate. **c. con,** to put an end to. See **huir**

**conclusión** /konklu'sion/ f, finish, end; decision; close, denouement; theory, proposition (gen. pl); deduction, inference; Law. close. **en c.,** in conclusion

**conclusivo** /konklu'siβo/ a final; conclusive

**concluyente** /konklu'yente/ a concluding; convincing; conclusive

**concomer** /konko'mer/ vi Inf. to give a shrug, shrug one's shoulders; fidget with an itch. **c. de placer,** to itch with pleasure

**concomitancia** /konkomi'tanθia; konkomi'tansia/ f, concomitance

**concomitante** /konkomi'tante/ a and m, concomitant

**concordable** /konkor'ðaβle/ a conformable

**concordador** /konkorða'ðor/ **(-ra)** a peacemaking —n peacemaker

**concordancia** /konkor'ðanθia; konkor'ðansia/ f, harmony, agreement; (Mus. Gram.) concord; pl concordance

**concordar** /konkor'ðar/ vt irr to bring to agreement; —vi agree. See **acordar**

**concordato** /konkor'ðato/ m, concordat

**concorde** /kon'korðe/ a agreeing; harmonious

**concordia** /kon'korðia/ f, concord, agreement, harmony; written agreement

**concreción** /konkre'θion; konkre'sion/ f, concretion

**concretar** /konkre'tar/ vt to combine, bring together; make concise; resume; —vr Fig. confine oneself (to a subject) to hammer out, work out (an agreement)

**concreto** /kon'kreto/ a concrete, real, not abstract. **en c.,** in definite terms; finally, to sum up

**concubina** /konku'βina/ f, concubine, mistress

**concubinato** /konkuβi'nato/ m, concubinage

**conculcación** /konkulka'θion; konkulka'sion/ f, trampling, treading; violation

**conculcador** /konkulka'ðor/ m, violator

**conculcar** /konkul'kar/ vt to trample under foot, tread on; break, violate

**concupiscencia** /konkupis'θenθia; konkupis'sensia/ f, concupiscence, lust; greed

**concupiscente** /konkupis'θente; konkupis'sente/ a concupiscent, lustful; greedy

**concurrencia** /konku'rrenθia; konku'rrensia/ f, assembly; coincidence; attendance; help, influence

**concurrido** /konku'rriðo/ a crowded; busy; frequented

**concurrir** /konku'rrir/ vi to coincide; contribute; meet together; agree, be of same opinion; compete (in an examination, etc.)

**concurso** /kon'kurso/ m, crowd, concourse; conjunction, coincidence; help; competition; (tennis) tournament; competitive examination; invitation to offer tenders. **c. de acreedores,** creditors' meeting. **c. interno,** competitive examination for a position open to staff members only

**concusión** /konku'sion/ f, concussion; shock; extortion

**condado** /kon'daðo/ m, earldom; county

**condal** /kon'dal/ a of an earl, earl's; of a count, count's; of Barcelona

**conde** /'konde/ m, earl; king of the gypsies

**condecir** /konde'θir; konde'sir/ **(con)** vi to agree (with)

**condecoración** /kondekora'θion; kondekora'sion/ f, conferment of an honor, decoration; medal

**condecorar** /kondeko'rar/ vt to confer a decoration or medal

**condena** /kon'dena/ f, Law. sentence; punishment; penalty

**condenable** /konde'naβle/ a culpable, guilty; worthy of damnation

**condenado** /konde'naðo/ **(-da)** a damned; wicked, harmful —n Law. convicted criminal

**condenador** /kondena'ðor/ a condemning; incriminating; blaming

**condenar** /konde'nar/ vt Law. to pronounce sentence (on), convict; condemn; disapprove; wall or block or close up. **c. a galeras,** to condemn to the gallies —vr blame oneself; be eternally damned

**condenatorio** /kondena'torio/ a condemnatory; incriminating

**condensación** /kondensa'θion; kondensa'sion/ f, condensation

**condensador** /kondensa'ðor/ a condensing. m, (Elec. Mech. Chem.) condenser

**condensante** /konden'sante/ a condensing

**condensar** /konden'sar/ vt to condense; thicken; abridge

**condesa** /kon'desa/ f, countess

**condescendencia** /kondesθen'denθia; kondessen'densia/ f, affability, graciousness

**condescender** /kondesθen'der; kondessen'der/ vi irr to be obliging, helpful, agreeable. See **entender**

**condescendiente** /kondesθen'diente; kondessen'diente/ a affable, gracious

**condestable** /kondes'taβle/ m, Hist. constable, commander-in-chief

**condición** /kondi'θion; kondi'sion/ f, condition; quality; temperament; character; (social) position; rank, family; nobility, circumstance; stipulation, condition, requirement. **estar en condiciones de,** to be in a position to. **no estar en condiciones de,** to be in no condition to

**condicional** /kondiθio'nal; kondisio'nal/ a conditional

**condicionar** /kondiθio'nar; kondisio'nar/ vi to come to an agreement, arrange; —vt impose conditions

**condigno** /kon'digno/ a condign

**condimentación** /kondimenta'θion; kondimenta'sion/ f, Cul. seasoning

**condimentar** /kondimen'tar/ vt to flavor, season (food)

**condimento** /kondi'mento/ m, condiment, flavoring

**condiscípulo** /kondis'θipulo; kondis'sipulo/ m, schoolfellow

**condolencia** /kondo'lenθia; kondo'lensia/ f, compassion; condolence

**condolerse** /kondo'lerse/ vr (with de) to sympathize with, be sorry for. See **doler**

**condonar** /kondo'nar/ vt to condone

**conducción** /konduk'θion; konduk'sion/ f. **conducencia,** f, transport, conveyance, carriage; guiding; direction, management; Phys. conduction; Mech. control-gear. Auto. **c. a izquierda,** left-hand drive

**conducente** /kondu'θente; kondu'sente/ a conducting, conducive

**conducir** /kondu'θir; kondu'sir/ vt irr to transport, convey, carry; Phys. conduct; guide, lead; manage, direct; Auto. drive; conduce; —vi be suitable; —vr behave, conduct oneself —Pres. Indic. **conduzco, conduces,** etc —Preterite **conduje, condujiste,** etc —Pres. Subjunc. **conduzca, conduzcas,** etc —Imperf. Subjunc. **condujese,** etc.

**conducta** /kon'dukta/ f, transport, conveyance; management, conduct, direction; behavior

**conductibilidad** /konduktiβili'ðað/ f, Phys. conductivity

**conductivo** /konduk'tiβo/ a conductive

**conducto** /kon'dukto/ m, pipe, conduit, drain, duct; Fig. channel, means; Anat. tube

**conductor** /konduk'tor/ **(-ra)** n guide; leader; driver (vehicles); m, Phys. conductor. **c. de caballos,** teamster. **c. de entrada,** Radio. lead-in. **c. del calor,** heat-conductor. **c. eléctrico,** electric wire or cable

**conectar** /konek'tar/ vt Elec. to connect, switch on; couple; attach, join

**conectivo** /konek'tiβo/ a connective; (Elec. Mech.) connecting

**conejera** /kone'hera/ f, rabbit-warren; *Inf.* low dive or haunt

**conejillo de Indias** /kone'hiʎo de 'indias; kone'hiyo de 'indias/ m, guineapig

**conejo** /ko'neho/ m, rabbit

**conejuna** /kone'huna/ f, rabbit fur, coney

**conejuno** /kone'huno/ a rabbit, rabbit-like

**conexión** /konek'sion/ f, connection; *Elec.* switching on, connection; joint; joining; pl friends, connections; *Elec.* wiring

**conexo** /ko'nekso/ a connected

**confabulación** /konfaβula'θion; konfaβula'sion/ f, confabulation, conspiracy

**confabular** /konfaβu'lar/ vi to confer; —vr scheme, plot

**confalón** /konfa'lon/ m, standard, banner

**confección** /konfek'θion; konfek'sion/ f, making; confection; making-up; concoction, remedy; ready-made garment

**confeccionador** /konfekθiona'ðor; konfeksiona'ðor/ (-ra) n maker (of clothes, etc.)

**confeccionar** /konfekθio'nar; konfeksio'nar/ vt to make; prepare; make up (pharmaceuticals)

**confederación** /konfeðera'θion; konfeðera'sion/ f, alliance, pact; confederacy, federation

**confederarse** /konfeðe'rarse/ vr to confederate, be allied

**conferencia** /konfe'renθia; konfe'rensia/ f, conference, meeting; lecture; (telephone) long-distance call (US), trunk call (UK)

**conferenciante** /konferen'θiante; konferen'siante/ mf lecturer

**conferenciar** /konferen'θiar; konferen'siar/ vi to confer

**conferir** /konfe'rir/ vt irr to grant, concede; consider, discuss; compare, correlate. See **herir**

**confesable** /konfe'saβle/ a acknowledgeable, avowable

**confesar** /konfe'sar/ vt irr to avow, declare; acknowledge, admit; *Eccl.* hear confession; —vr *Eccl.* confess —*Pres. Indic.* **confieso, confiesas, confiesa, confiesan.** *Pres. Subjunc.* **confiese, confieses, confiese, confiesen**

**confesión** /konfe'sion/ f, confession

**confesional** /konfesio'nal/ a confessional

**confesionario, confesonario, confesorio** /konfesio'nario, konfeso'nario, konfe'sorio/ m, *Eccl.* confessional

**confeso** /kon'feso/ a confessed; converted (of Jews). m, *Eccl.* lay brother

**confesor** /konfe'sor/ m, confessor

**confeti** /kon'feti/ m, confetti

**confianza** /kon'fianθa; kon'fiansa/ f, confidence, trust; assurance, courage; over-confidence, conceit; intimacy; familiarity. **de c.,** reliable (e.g. *persona de c.*, reliable person); informal (e.g. *reunión de c.*, informal meeting). **en c.,** in confidence, confidentially

**confianzudo** /konfian'θuðo; konfian'suðo/ a *Inf.* overconfident

**confiar** /kon'fiar/ vi (with en) to trust in, hope; —vt (with prep a or en) entrust, commit to the care of; confide in

**confidencia** /konfi'ðenθia; konfi'ðensia/ f, trust; confidence; confidential information

**confidencial** /konfi'ðen'θial; konfiðen'sial/ a confidential

**confidente** /konfi'ðente/ (-ta) a trustworthy, true. m, seat for two —n confidant(e); spy

**configuración** /konfigura'θion; konfigura'sion/ f, configuration, form, lie

**configurar** /konfigu'rar/ vt to shape

**confín** /kon'fin/ m, boundary, frontier; limit —a boundary

**confinado** /konfi'naðo/ a banished. m, *Law.* prisoner

**confinar** /konfi'nar/ vi (with con) to be bounded by, contiguous to; —vt banish; place in confinement

**confirmación** /konfirma'θion; konfirma'sion/ f, corroboration; *Eccl.* confirmation

**confirmar** /konfir'mar/ vt to corroborate; uphold; *Eccl.* confirm

**confirmatorio** /konfirma'torio/ a confirmatory

**confiscación** /konfiska'θion; konfiska'sion/ f, confiscation

**confiscar** /konfis'kar/ vt to confiscate

**confitar** /konfi'tar/ vt to candy, crystallize or preserve (fruit, etc.); *Fig.* sweeten

**confite** /kon'fite/ m, bonbon, sugared almond, etc.

**confitería** /konfite'ria/ f, confectionery

**confitero** /konfi'tero/ (-ra) n confectioner

**confitura** /konfi'tura/ f, preserve, jam

**conflagración** /konflagra'θion; konflagra'sion/ f, conflagration, blaze; uprising, rebellion

**conflicto** /kon'flikto/ m, strife, struggle; spiritual conflict; *Fig.* difficult situation

**confluencia** /kon'fluenθia; kon'fluensia/ f, confluence; crowd

**confluir** /kon'fluir/ vi irr to meet, flow together (rivers); run together (roads); crowd. See **huir**

**conformación** /konforma'θion; konforma'sion/ f, conformation; make-up, structure (e.g. of an organization)

**conformar** /konfor'mar/ vt to fit, adjust; —vr agree, be of the same opinion; submit, comply; to make up (e.g. *los grupos sociales que conforman este país,* the social groups who make up this country)

**conforme** /kon'forme/ a similar, alike; consistent; in agreement; long-suffering, resigned —adv according (to), in proportion (to)

**conformidad** /konformi'ðað/ f, conformity; similarity; resignation; agreement, harmony; proportion, symmetry. **de c.,** by common consent. **en c.,** according to

**confort** /kon'fort/ m, comfort

**confortante** /konfor'tante/ a comforting; consoling; strengthening (of beverages)

**confortar** /konfor'tar/ vt to comfort, reassure; encourage; console

**confortativo** /konforta'tiβo/ a comforting; comfortable; strengthening, warming (of beverages); encouraging, cheering

**confrontación** /konfronta'θion; konfronta'sion/ f, confrontment; comparison (of texts, etc.)

**confrontar** /konfron'tar/ vt to bring face to face; compare, correlate; —vi face; (with con) be contiguous to, border on

**confucianismo** /konfuθia'nismo; konfusia'nismo/ m, Confucianism

**confundible** /konfun'diβle/ a mistakable, liable to be confused

**confundimiento** /konfundi'miento/ m, confounding; mistaking; confusion

**confundir** /konfun'dir/ vt to mix, confuse; jumble together; mistake; *Fig.* confound (in argument); humble; bewilder, perplex; —vr be mixed together; mistake, confuse; be ashamed; be bewildered

**confusión** /konfu'sion/ f, confusion; perplexity; shame; jumble

**confuso** /kon'fuso/ a mixed, upset; jumbled; obscure; indistinct; blurred; bewildered

**confutación** /konfuta'θion; konfuta'sion/ f, confutation

**confutar** /konfu'tar/ vt to confute

**conga** /'konga/ f, conga (dance; drum)

**congelación** /konhela'θion; konhela'sion/ f, freezing; congealment. **punto de c.,** freezing point

**congelar** /konhe'lar/ vt to congeal; freeze

**congeniar** /konhe'niar/ vi to be congenial

**congénito** /kon'henito/ a congenital

**congestión** /konhes'tion/ f, *Med.* congestion

**congestionar** /konhestio'nar/ vt to congest; —vr *Med.* be overcharged (with blood)

**conglomeración** /konglomera'θion; konglomera'sion/ f, conglomeration

**conglomerar** /konglome'rar/ vt to conglomerate

**congoja** /kon'goha/ f, anguish, anxiety, grief

**congraciarse** /kongra'θiarse; kongra'siarse/ (con), vr to ingratiate oneself (with), get into the good graces (of)

**congratulación** /kongratula'θion; kongratula'sion/ f, congratulation

**congratular** /kongratu'lar/ vt to congratulate; —vr congratulate oneself

**congratulatorio** /koŋgratula'torio/ a congratulatory

**congregación** /koŋgrega'θion; koŋgrega'sion/ f, gathering, meeting, congregation; brotherhood, guild

**congregar** /koŋgre'gar/ **(se)** vt and vr to meet, assemble

**congresista** /koŋgre'sista/ mf member of a congress

**congreso** /koŋ'greso/ m, congress; conference, meeting; sexual intercourse

**congrio** /'koŋgrio/ m, conger eel

**congruencia** /koŋ'gruenθia; koŋ'gruensia/ f, suitability, convenience; Math. congruence

**congruente** /koŋ'gruente/ a convenient, opportune; Math. congruent

**cónico** /'koniko/ a conical, tapering Math. conic

**conifera** /ko'nifera/ f, conifer

**conifero** /ko'nifero/ a coniferous

**conjetura** /konhe'tura/ f, conjecture

**conjetural** /konhetu'ral/ a conjectural

**conjeturar** /konhetu'rar/ vt to conjecture, surmise

**conjugación** /konhuga'θion; konhuga'sion/ f, conjugation

**conjugar** /konhu'gar/ vt to conjugate

**conjunción** /konhun'θion; konhun'sion/ f, connection, union association; (Astron. Gram.) conjunction

**conjuntivitis** /konhunti'βitis/ f, conjunctivitis

**conjunto** /kon'hunto/ a united, associated adjoining; mingled, mixed (with) bound, affiliated. m, whole; combo, ensemble (of musicians). **c. habitacional,** housing complex, housing project

**conjura, conjuración** /kon'hura, konhura'θion; kon'hura, konhura'sion/ f, conspiracy, plot

**conjurador** /konhura'ðor/ **(-ra)** n conspirator, plotter; exorcist

**conjurar** /konhu'rar/ vi to conspire, plot vt swear, take an oath; exorcise; implore, beg; ward off (danger)

**conjuro** /kon'huro/ m, plot, conspiracy, spell, incantation; entreaty

**conllevar** /konʎe'βar; konye'βar/ vt to share (troubles) bear, put up with; endure

**conmemoración** /komemora'θion; komemora'sion/ f, commemoration

**conmemorar** /komemo'rar/ vt to commemorate

**conmemorativo** /komemora'tiβo/ a commemorative

**conmensurable** /komensu'raβle/ a commensurable

**conmigo** /ko'migo/ pers pron 1st pers. sing. mf with myself, with me

**conminar** /komi'nar/ vt to threaten

**conminatorio** /komina'torio/ a threatening

**conmiseración** /komisera'θion; komisera'sion/ f, commiseration, compassion, pity

**conmoción** /komo'θion; komo'sion/ f, disturbance (mind or body); upheaval, commotion. **c. eléctrica,** electric shock

**conmovedor** /komoβe'ðor/ a moving, pitiful; stirring, thrilling

**conmover** /komo'βer/ vt irr to perturb, stir; move to pity. **c. los cimientos de,** to shake the foundations of; —vr be emotionally moved. See **mover**

**conmutable** /komu'taβle/ a commutable

**conmutación** /komuta'θion; komuta'sion/ f, mutation

**conmutador** /komuta'ðor/ m, Elec. commutator; change-over switch

**conmutar** /komu'tar/ vt to commute; Elec. switch, convert

**conmutatriz** /komuta'triθ; komuta'tris/ f, Elec. converter

**connato** /kon'nato/ a contemporary

**connatural** /konnatu'ral/ a innate, inborn

**connaturalizar** /konnaturali'θar; konnaturali'sar/ vt to connaturalize

**connaturalizarse** /konnaturali'θarse; konnaturali'sarse/ **(con)** vr to become accustomed (to), become acclimated (to)

**connivencia** /konni'βenθia; konni'βensia/ f, connivance

**connotación** /konnota'θion; konnota'sion/ f, connotation

**connotar** /konno'tar/ vt to connote

**cono** /'kono/ m, (Geom. Bot.) cone. **el C. Sur,** the Southern Cone

**conocedor** /konoθe'ðor; konose'ðor/ **(-ra)** n one who knows; connoisseur; expert

**conocer** /kono'θer; kono'ser/ vt irr to know; understand; observe, perceive; be acquainted (with); conjecture; confess, acknowledge; know carnally; —vr know oneself; know one another. **conocerle a uno la voz,** to recognize somebody's voice (e.g. Le conozco la voz. I recognize her by her voice.) **conocerle a uno en su manera de andar,** to recognize somebody by his gait, recognize somebody by his walk —Pres. Indic. **conozco, conoces,** etc —Pres. Subjunc. **conozca,** etc.

**conocido** /kono'θiðo; kono'siðo/ **(-da)** a illustrious, distinguished —n acquaintance

**conocimiento** /konoθi'miento; konosi'miento/ m, knowledge; understanding; intelligence; acquaintance (not friend); consciousness; Com. bill of lading; pl knowledge, learning

**conque** /'konke/ conjunc so, so that (e.g. ¿C. Juan se va? So John's going away?)

**conquista** /kon'kista/ f, conquest

**conquistador** /konkista'ðor/ **(-ra)** a conquering —n conqueror

**conquistar** /konkis'tar/ vt to conquer; Fig. captivate, win

**consabido** /konsa'βiðo/ a aforesaid, beforementioned

**consagración** /konsagra'θion; konsagra'sion/ f, consecration; dedication

**consagrar** /konsa'grar/ vt to consecrate; dedicate, devote; deify; —vr (with prep a) dedicate oneself to, engage in

**consanguíneo** /konsaŋ'guineo/ a consanguineous

**consanguinidad** /konsaŋguini'ðað/ f, consanguinity

**consciente** /kons'θiente; kons'siente/ a conscious; aware; sane. m, Psychol. conscious

**conscripción** /konskrip'θion; konskrip'sion/ f, conscription

**conscripto** /kons'kripto/ m, conscript

**consecución** /konseku'θion; konseku'sion/ f, obtainment; attainment

**consecuencia** /konse'kuenθia; konse'kuensia/ f, consequence, outcome; logical consequence, conclusion; importance; consistence (of people)

**consecuente** /konse'kuente/ a consequent, resultant; consistent. **c. consigo mismo,** self-consistent m, consequence; Math. consequent

**consecutivo** /konseku'tiβo/ a consecutive, successive

**conseguir** /konse'gir/ vt irr to obtain, achieve. See **seguir**

**conseja** /kon'seha/ f, story, fairy-tale; old wives' tale

**consejero** /konse'hero/ **(-ra)** n adviser; member of council. m. **c. de estado,** counselor of state

**consejo** /kon'seho/ m, advice; council, commission, board; council chamber or building. **c. de administración,** board of directors. **c. de guerra,** council of war. **c. del reino,** council of the realm. **c. privado,** privy council

**consenso** /kon'senso/ m, consensus of opinion, unanimity

**consentido** /konsen'tiðo/ a complaisant (of husband); spoiled, over-indulged

**consentimiento** /konsenti'miento/ m, consent; assent

**consentir** /konsen'tir/ vt irr to permit, allow; believe; tolerate, put up with; over-indulge, spoil; —vr crack, give way (furniture, etc.). **c. en,** to consent to; to agree to. See **sentir**

**conserje** /kon'serhe/ m, concierge, porter; warden or keeper (of castle, etc.)

**conserjería** /konserhe'ria/ f, conciergerie, porter's lodge; warden's dwelling (in castles, etc.)

**conserva** /kon'serβa/ f, jam; preserve; pickles; Naut. convoy. **en c.,** preserved, tinned

**conservación** /konserβa'θion; konserβa'sion/ f, upkeep; preservation, maintenance; Cul. preserving; conservation. **c. refrigerada,** cold storage

**conservador** /konserβa'ðor/ **(-ra)** a keeping, preserving —a and n preserver; Polit. conservative; traditionalist. m, curator

**conservadurismo** /konserβaðu'rismo/ *m*, conservatism

**conservar** /konser'βar/ *vt* to keep, maintain, preserve; keep up (custom, etc.); guard; *Cul.* preserve. **c. en buen estado,** to keep in repair

**conservatorio** /konserβa'torio/ *m*, conservatoire; academy. **c. de música,** academy of music, conservatoire

**considerable** /konsiðe'raβle/ *a* considerable; worthy of consideration, powerful; numerous; large; important

**consideración** /konsiðera'θion; konsiðera'sion/ *f*, consideration, attention; reflection, thought; civility; importance. **en c. de,** considering

**considerado** /konsiðe'raðo/ *a* considerate; prudent; distinguished; important

**considerar** /konsiðe'rar/ *vt* to consider, reflect upon; treat with consideration (persons); judge, estimate, feel (e.g. *Considero que...* I feel that...)

**consigna** /kon'signa/ *f*, *Mil.* watchword; left luggage office

**consignador** /konsigna'ðor/ **(-ra)** *n Com.* consigner, sender

**consignar** /konsig'nar/ *vt* to assign, lay aside; deposit; *Com.* consign; entrust, commit; put in writing; *Law.* deposit in trust; book (a suspect)

**consignatario** /konsigna'tario/ *m*, *Law.* trustee; mortgagee; *Com.* consignee. **c. de buques,** shipping agent

**consigo** /kon'sigo/ *pers pron* 3rd sing. and pl. *mf* with himself, herself, oneself, yourself, yourselves, themselves

**consiguiente** /konsi'giente/ *a* consequent, resulting. *m*, consequence. **por c.,** in consequence

**consistencia** /konsis'tenθia; konsis'tensia/ *f*, solidity; consistence, density; consistency, congruity, relevance

**consistente** /konsis'tente/ *a* of a certain consistency; solid

**consistir** /konsis'tir/ *vi* (*with en*) to consist in; be comprised of; be the result of

**consistorio** /konsis'torio/ *m*, consistory; municipal council (in some Spanish towns); town hall

**consola** /kon'sola/ *f*, console table; piertable; *Mech.* bracket

**cónsola** /'konsola/ *f*, radio cabinet

**consolable** /konso'laβle/ *a* consolable

**consolación** /konsola'θion; konsola'sion/ *f*, consolation

**consolador** /konsola'ðor/ **(-ra)** *n* comforter, consoler

**consolar** /konso'lar/ *vt irr* to comfort, console. **consolarse de + inf.,** to console oneself for + *pp.* See **contar**

**consolidación** /konsoliða'θion; konsoliða'sion/ *f*, consolidation; stiffening

**consolidar** /konsoli'ðar/ *vt* to consolidate; strengthen; combine, unite; —*vr Law.* unite

**consomé** /konso'me/ *m*, consommé

**consonancia** /konso'nanθianb; konso'nansia/ *f*, harmony; agreement

**consonante** /konso'nante/ *a* consonant, consistent. *m*, rhyme. *f*, *Gram.* consonant

**consonantismo** /konsonan'tismo/ *m*, consonantism, consonant system

**consorcio** /kon'sorθio; kon'sorsio/ *m*, partnership; trust; intimacy, common life

**consorte** /kon'sorte/ *mf* consort; companion, associate, partner; spouse

**conspicuo** /kons'pikuo/ *a* outstanding, distinguished; conspicuous

**conspiración** /konspira'θion; konspira'sion/ *f*, conspiracy

**conspirador** /konspira'ðor/ **(-ra)** *n* conspirator

**conspirar** /konspi'rar/ *vi* to conspire; plot, scheme; tend, combine

**constancia** /kons'tanθia; kons'tansia/ *f*, constancy, steadfastness; stability, steadiness; transcript (of grades). **c. de estudios,** transcript (of grades)

**constante** /kons'tante/ *a* constant; durable; *Mech.* steady, non-oscillating. *m*, constant

**Constantinopla** /konstanti'nopla/ Constantinople

**Constanza** /kons'tanθa; kons'tansa/ Constance (female given name and lake)

**constar** /kons'tar/ *vi* to be evident, be clear; (*with de*) be composed of, consist of, comprise

**constelación** /konstela'θion; konstela'sion/ *f*, *Astron.* constellation; climate

**consternación** /konsterna'θion; konsterna'sion/ *f*, dismay, alarm

**consternarse** /konster'narse/ *vr* to be dismayed or alarmed

**constipado** /konsti'paðo/ *m*, *Med.* cold; chill

**constiparse** /konsti'parse/ *vr* to catch a cold or chill

**constitución** /konstitu'θion; konstitu'sion/ *f*, constitution; composition, make-up (e.g. *la c. del suelo,* the make-up of the soil)

**constitucional** /konstituθio'nal; konstitusio'nal/ *a* constitutional

**constituir** /konsti'tuir/ *vt irr* to constitute, form; found, establish; (*with en*) appoint, nominate; *Fig.* place in (a difficult situation, etc.); —*vr* (*with en* or *por*) be appointed or authorized; be under (an obligation). See **huir**

**constituyente, constitutivo** /konstitu'yente, konsti-tu'tiβo/ *a* and *m*, constituent

**constreñir** /konstre'ɲir/ *vt irr* to constrain, oblige; constrict; constipate. See **ceñir**

**constricción** /konstrik'θion; konstrik'sion/ *f*, constriction; contraction, shrinkage

**construcción** /konstruk'θion; konstruk'sion/ *f*, construction; art or process of construction; fabric, structure; *Gram.* construction; building, erection. **c. de caminos,** road making. **c. naval,** shipbuilding

**constructor** /konstruk'tor/ **(-ra)** *a* building, constructive —*n* builder; constructor

**construir** /kons'truir/ *vt irr* to construct; build, make; *Gram.* construct. See **huir**

**consuelo** /kon'suelo/ *m*, consolation; comfort, solace; joy, delight

**cónsul** /'konsul/ *m*, consul

**consulado** /konsu'laðo/ *m*, consulate. **c. general,** consulate general

**consulta** /kon'sulta/ *f*, deliberation, consideration; advice; reference; conference, consultation

**consultar** /konsul'tar/ *vt* to discuss, consider; seek advice, consult. **consultarlo con la almohada,** *Fig.* to sleep on it, think it over, mull it over

**consultor** /konsul'tor/ **(-ra)** *a* consultative, advisory; consulting —*n* consultant; adviser. **c. externo,** outside consultant

**consultorio** /konsul'torio/ *m*, *Med.* consulting rooms; surgery; technical information bureau

**consumación** /konsuma'θion; konsuma'sion/ *f*, consummation; completion, attainment; extinction, end

**consumado** /konsu'maðo/ *a* consummate; *Inf.* thorough, perfect

**consumar** /konsu'mar/ *vt* to consummate; complete, accomplish, perfect

**consumido** /konsu'miðo/ *a Inf.* emaciated, wasted away; timid, spiritless

**consumidor** /konsumi'ðor/ **(-ra)** *a* consuming —*n* consumer, user

**consumir** /konsu'mir/ *vt* to destroy; consume, use; waste away, wear away; *Eccl.* take communion; *Inf.* grieve; —*vr* be destroyed; *Inf.* be consumed with grief

**consumo** /kon'sumo/ *m*, consumption; demand. **c. de combustible,** fuel consumption

**contabilidad** /kontaβili'ðað/ *f*, bookkeeping; accounts; accounting

**contable** /kon'taβle/ *m*, bookkeeper

**contacto** /kon'takto/ *m*, contact (also *Elec. Mil.*). **en c.,** in common (e.g. *Los dos libros tienen mucho en c.* The two books have much in common.)

**contado** /kon'taðo/ *a* few; infrequent; rare. **al c.,** *Com.* cash down. **por de c.,** presumably; of course, naturally

**contador** /konta'ðor/ *a* counting. *m*, accountant; *Law.* auditor; counter (in banks); *Elec.* meter, counter; *Naut.* purser. **c. oficial,** *Argentina* certified public accountant. **c. público titulado,** certified public accountant

**contaduría** /kontaðu'ria/ *f*, accountancy; counting house; accountant's office; auditorship; *Theat.* box-office; *Naut.* purser's office

**contagiar** /konta'hiar/ *vt* to infect; corrupt, pervert; —*vr* (*with* con, de *or* por) be infected by or through

**contagio** /kon'tahio/ *m*, infection; contagious disease; *Fig.* contagion, perversion, corruption

**contagioso** /konta'hioso/ *a* infectious; *Fig.* catching, contagious

**contaminación** /kontamina'θion; kontamina'sion/ *f*, contamination, pollution

**contaminar** /kontami'nar/ *vt* to pollute, contaminate; infect; *Fig.* corrupt

**contante** /kon'tante/ *a* ready (of money)

**contar** /kon'tar/ *vt irr* to count; recount, tell; place to account; include, count among; —*vi* calculate, compute. **contarle a uno las cuarenta,** *Inf.* to give someone a piece of one's mind. **c. con,** to rely upon; reckon upon —*Pres. Indic.* **cuento, cuentas, cuenta, cuentan.** *Pres. Subjunc.* **cuente, cuentes, cuente, cuenten**

**contemplación** /kontempla'θion; kontempla'sion/ *f*, meditation, contemplation; consideration

**contemplar** /kontem'plar/ *vt* to consider, reflect upon; look at, contemplate; indulge, please

**contemplativo** /kontempla'tiβo/ *a Eccl.* contemplative; reflective, thoughtful; kind, indulgent

**contemporáneo** /kontempo'raneo/ **(de)** *a* contemporaneous (to *or* with) *n* contemporary

**contemporizar** /kontempori'θar; kontempori'sar/ *vi* to temporize, gain time

**contencioso** /konten'θioso; konten'sioso/ *a* contentious, argumentative; *Law.* litigious

**contender** /konten'der/ *vi irr* to contain; restrain, hold back; comprise; —*vr* control oneself. See **entender**

**contendiente** /konten'diente/ *mf* contestant

**contener** /konte'ner/ *vt irr* to contain; include; comprise; hold back; restrain; check, repress; hold down, subdue; suppress, put down; —*vr* contain oneself; keep one's temper; keep quiet; refrain. See **tener**

**contenido** /konte'niðo/ *m*, contents —*a* contained; *Fig.* restrained; reserved (of persons)

**contentamiento** /kontenta'miento/ *m*, contentment

**contentar** /konten'tar/ *vt* to satisfy, please; *Com.* endorse; —*vr* be pleased or satisfied

**contento** /kon'tento/ *a* happy; content; satisfied; pleased. *m*, pleasure; contentment. **no caber de c.,** to be overjoyed

**contestación** /kontesta'θion; kontesta'sion/ *f*, reply, answer; discussion, argument, dispute

**contestar** /kontes'tar/ *vt* to reply, answer; confirm, attest; —*vi* accord, harmonize

**contexto** /kon'teksto/ *m*, context

**contextura** /konteks'tura/ *f*, structure; context; physique, frame

**contienda** /kon'tienda/ *f*, struggle, fight; quarrel, dispute; discussion

**contigo** /kon'tigo/ *pers pron* 2nd *sing. mf* with thee, with you

**contigüidad** /kontigui'ðað/ *f*, proximity, nearness

**contiguo** /kon'tiguo/ *a* adjacent, near

**continencia** /konti'nenθia; konti'nensia/ *f*, moderation, self-restraint; continence; chastity; containing

**continental** /konti'nental/ *a* continental. *m*, express messenger service; *Puerto Rico* person from the mainland United States

**continente** /konti'nente/ *a* continent. *m*, container; demeanor, bearing; *Geog.* continent; mainland

**contingencia** /kontin'henθia; kontin'hensia/ *f*, contingency; risk, danger

**contingente** /kontin'hente/ *a* incidental; fortuitous; dependent; *m*, *Mil.* taskforce, contingent

**continuación** /kontinua'θion; kontinua'sion/ *f*, continuation; prolongation; sequel (of a story, etc.)

**continuador** /kontinua'ðor/ **(-ra)** *n* continuer

**continuar** /konti'nuar/ *vt* to continue; —*vi* continue; last, remain, go on; —*vr* be prolonged

**continuidad** /kontinui'ðað/ *f*, continuity

**continuo** /kon'tinuo/ *a* continuous, steady, uninterrupted; persevering, tenacious; persistent, lasting, unremitting. *m*, a united whole. **de c.,** continuously

**contonearse** /kontone'arse/ *vr* to swing the hips (in walking); strut

**contorno** /kon'torno/ *m*, contour, outline; (gen. *pl*) environs, surrounding district

**contorsión** /kontor'sion/ *f*, contortion

**contorsionista** /kontorsio'nista/ *mf* contortionist

**contra** /'kontra/ *prep* against, counter, athwart; opposed to, hostile to; in front of, opposite; towards. *m*, opposite view or opinion. *f*, *Inf.* difficulty, trouble. **c. la corriente,** upstream. **el pro y el c.,** the pros and cons. **en c.,** in opposition, against

**contraalmirante** /kontraalmi'rante/ *m*, rear admiral

**contraataque** /kontraa'take/ *m*, counterattack

**contraaviso** /kontraa'βiso/ *m*, countermand

**contrabajo** /kontra'βaho/ *m*, doublebass; player of this instrument; deep bass voice

**contrabalancear** /kontraβalanθe'ar; kontraβalanse'ar/ *vt* to counterbalance; *Fig.* compensate

**contrabandista** /kontraβan'dista/ *a* smuggling. *mf* smuggler

**contrabando** /kontra'βando/ *m*, contraband; smuggling

**contracción** /kontrak'θion; kontrak'sion/ *f*, contraction; shrinkage; abridgment; abbreviation

**contracubierta** /kontraku'βierta/ *f*, book jacket, jacket

**contradanza** /kontra'ðanθa; kontra'ðansa/ *f*, square dance

**contradecir** /kontraðe'θir; kontraðe'sir/ *vt irr* to contradict; —*vr* contradict oneself. See **decir**

**contradicción** /kontraðik'θion; kontraðik'sion/ *f*, contradiction

**contradictorio** /kontraðik'torio/ *a* contradictory

**contraer** /kontra'er/ *vt irr* to shrink, reduce in size, shorten; abridge; contract (matrimony, obligations); *Fig.* acquire (diseases, habits); —*vr* shorten, contract, shrink. See **traer**

**contrafuerte** /kontra'fuerte/ *m*, buttress, counterfort, abutment; *Geog.* spur

**contrahacer** /kontraa'θer; kontraa'ser/ *vt irr* to forge, counterfeit; mimic; imitate. See **hacer**

**contrahecho** /kontra'etʃo/ *a* deformed

**contralor** /kontra'lor/ *m*, comptroller

**contraloría** /kontralo'ria/ *f*, comptrollership, office of comptroller (position); comptroller's office (place)

**contralto** /kon'tralto/ *m*, contralto (voice)

**contraluz** /kontra'luθ; kontra'lus/ *f*, counterlight

**contramaestre** /kontrama'estre/ *m*, *Naut.* boatswain; overseer, superintendent, foreman

**contramarcha** /kontra'martʃa/ *f*, retrogression; *Mil.* countermarch

**contramedida** /kontrame'ðiða/ *f*, counter-measure

**contraorden** /kontra'orðen/ *f*, countermand

**contrapedalear** /kontrapeðale'ar/ *vi* to backpedal

**contrapelo** /kontra'pelo/ *a adv* the wrong way of the hair, against the grain; *Inf.* reluctantly, distastefully

**contrapeso** /kontra'peso/ *m*, counterpoise, counterweight; balancing-pole (acrobats); *Fig.* counterbalance; makeweight

**contraponer** /kontrapo'ner/ *vt irr* to compare; place opposite; oppose. See **poner**

**contraproducente** /kontraproðu'θente; kontraproðu'sente/ *a* counteractive, counterproductive, unproductive, self-deceiving; self-defeating

**contrapuesto** /kontra'puesto/ *a* opposing, divergent

**contrapunto** /kontra'punto/ *m*, counterpoint

**contrariar** /kontra'riar/ *vt* to counter, oppose; impede; vex, annoy

**contrariedad** /kontrarie'ðað/ *f*, contrariety, opposition; obstacle; vexation, trouble

**contrario** /kon'trario/ **(-ia)** *a* opposite; hostile, opposed; harmful; adverse, contrary —*m* adversary; opponent. *m*, obstacle. *f*. **contraria,** contrary, opposite. **al contrario,** on the contrary. **llevar la contraria (a),** to oppose; contradict

**contrarreforma** /kontrarre'forma/ *f*, counter-Reformation

**contrasentido** /kontrasen'tiðo/ *m*, wrong sense, opposite sense (of words); contradiction of initial premise; self-contradiction; nonsense

**contraseña** /kontra'seɲa/ *f*, countersign; *Mil.* password

**contrastar** /kontras'tar/ *vt* to contrast; oppose, resist;

check (weights and measures); assay; *Mech.* calibrate, gauge; —*vi* contrast

**contraste** /kon'traste/ *m*, contrast; opposition, difference; weights and measures inspector; dispute, clash. **en c. a,** in contrast to

**contrata** /kon'trata/ *f*, **contrato,** *m*, contract. **contrato de arrendamiento,** lease

**contratación** /kontrata'θion; kontrata'sion/ *f*, hiring; *Com.* transaction; commerce, trade

**contratapa** /kontra'tapa/ *f*, back cover (of a periodical, etc.)

**contratar** /kontra'tar/ *vt* to contract, enter into an agreement; make a bargain (with), deal (with); hire, contract

**contratiempo** /kontra'tiempo/ *m*, mishap, accident

**contratista** /kontra'tista/ *mf* contractor

**contratorpedero** /kontratorpe'ðero/ *m*, torpedoboat destroyer

**contravención** /kontraβen'θion; kontraβen'sion/ *f*, contravention; violation. **en c. a,** in violation of

**contraveneno** /kontraβe'neno/ *m*, *Med.* antidote; remedy, precaution

**contravenir** /kontraβe'nir/ *vt irr* to infringe, contravene. See **venir**

**contraventana** /kontraβen'tana/ *f*, shutter (for windows)

**contravidriera** /kontraβið'riera/ *f*, storm window

**contrayente** /kontra'yente/ *a* contracting. *mf* contracting party (used of matrimony)

**contribución** /kontriβu'θion; kontriβu'sion/ *f*, contribution; tax. **c. sobre la propiedad,** property tax

**contribuir** /kontri'βuir/ *vt irr* to pay (taxes); contribute. See **huir**

**contribuyente** /kontriβu'yente/ *a* contributing; contributory. *mf* contributor; taxpayer

**contrición** /kontri'θion; kontri'sion/ *f*, contrition

**contrincante** /kontrin'kante/ *m*, competitor, candidate (public examinations); rival, opponent

**contrito** /kon'trito/ *a* contrite

**control** /kon'trol/ *m*, control; checking. **c. de precios,** price control

**controlar** /kontro'lar/ *vt* to control

**controversia** /kontro'βersia/ *f*, controversy

**controvertir** /kontroβer'tir/ *vi* and *vt irr* to dispute, argue against, deny. See **sentir**

**contumacia** /kontu'maθia; kontu'masia/ *f*, obstinacy; *Law.* contumacy

**contumaz** /kontu'maθ; kontu'mas/ *a* stubborn; impenitent; *Law.* contumacious; *Med.* obstinate, resistant (to cure)

**contumelia** /kontu'melia/ *f*, contumely

**conturbar** /kontur'βar/ *vt* to perturb, make anxious, disturb; —*vr* be perturbed

**contuso** /kon'tuso/ *a* contused, bruised

**convalecencia** /kombale'θenθia; kombale'sensia/ *f*, convalescence; convalescent home

**convalecer** /kombale'θer; kombale'ser/ *vi irr* to convalesce, get better; *Fig.* recover, regain (influence, etc.). See **conocer**

**convaleciente** /kombale'θiente; kombale'siente/ *a* and *mf* convalescent

**convalidar** /kombali'ðar/ *vt* to ratify, confirm

**convecino** /kombe'θino; kombe'sino/ *a* nearby; neighboring

**convencedor** /kombenθe'ðor; kombense'ðor/ *a* convincing

**convencer** /komben'θer; komben'ser/ *vt* to convince; prove beyond doubt, demonstrate to (persons); be convincing (e.g. *No convence*, It's not convincing; He's not convincing.) *vr* be convinced

**convencimiento** /kombenθi'miento; kombensi'miento/ *m*, conviction, belief, assurance

**convención** /komben'θion; komben'sion/ *f*, pact, formal agreement; harmony, conformity; convention

**convencional** /kombenθio'nal; kombensio'nal/ *a* conventional (all meanings)

**convencionalismo** /kombenθiona'lismo; kombensiona'lismo/ *m*, conventionality

**convenido** /kombe'niðo/ *a* agreed

**conveniencia** /kombe'nienθia; kombe'niensia/ *f*, conformity, harmony, adjustment; experience, suita-

bility, convenience; advantage; agreement, pact; post as domestic; ease, comfort; *pl* income; social conventions

**conveniente** /kombe'niente/ *a* convenient, opportune; suitable, fitting; profitable; useful; decorous. **tener por c. + inf,** to think it fitting to + *inf,* find it appropriate to + *Inf.*

**convenio** /kom'benio/ *m*, pact, treaty; *Com.* agreement, contract

**convenir** /kombe'nir/ *vi irr* to agree; assemble, congregate; belong; be suitable; —*vr* agree; suit oneself. **No me conviene salir esta tarde,** It does not suit me to go out this afternoon. **Me convendría pasar un mes allí,** It would be a good idea (or a wise thing) for me to spend a month there. See **venir**

**convento** /kom'bento/ *m*, convent; monastery; religious community

**conventual** /komben'tual/ *a* conventual; monastic. *m*, *Eccl.* conventual

**convergencia** /komber'henθia; komber'hensia/ *f*, convergence

**convergir** /komber'hir/ *vi* to converge; *Fig.* coincide (views, etc.)

**conversación** /kombersa'θion; kombersa'sion/ *f*, conversation; intercourse, company; *Law.* criminal conversation

**conversar** /komber'sar/ *vi* to converse; chat; live with others; know socially

**conversión** /komber'sion/ *f*, conversion; change, transformation; *Com.* conversion; *Mil.* wheel; wheeling

**converso** /kom'berso/ **(-sa)** *n* convert

**convertible** /komber'tiβle/ *a* convertible

**convertir** /komber'tir/ *vt irr* to change, transform; convert; reform; —*vr* be transformed; be converted; be reformed. See **sentir**

**convexidad** /kombeksi'ðað/ *f*, convexity

**convexo** /kom'bekso/ *a* convex

**convicción** /kombik'θion; kombik'sion/ *f*, conviction; certitude; *Law.* conviction

**convicto** /kom'bikto/ **(-ta)** *a* and *n Law.* convict

**convidado** /kombi'ðaðo/ **(-da)** *n* guest

**convidar** /kombi'ðar/ *vt* to invite (persons); encourage, provoke; entice, attract; —*vr* invite oneself; offer one's services

**convincente** /kombin'θente; kombin'sente/ *a* convincing

**convite** /kom'bite/ *m*, invitation; banquet; party

**convivencia** /kombi'βenθia; kombi'βensia/ *f*, coexistence, common life, life together. **c. pacífica,** peaceful coexistence

**convivial** /kombi'βial/ *a* convivial

**convivir** /kombi'βir/ *vi* to live together, live under the same roof

**convocación** /komboka'θion; komboka'sion/ *f*, convocation

**convocar** /kombo'kar/ *vt* to convene, convoke

**convoy** /kom'boi/ *m*, convoy; escort; following; cruet-stand

**convoyar** /kombo'yar/ *vt* to convoy, escort

**convulsión** /kombul'sion/ *f*, convulsion

**convulsivo** /kombul'siβo/ *a* convulsive

**conyugal** /konyu'gal/ *a* conjugal

**cónyuge** /'konyuhe/ *mf* husband or (and) wife (used gen. in *pl*)

**coñac** /ko'nak/ *m*, brandy

**cooperación** /koopera'θion; koopera'sion/ *f*, cooperation

**cooperador** /koopera'ðor/ **(-ra)** *a* cooperative —*n* cooperator, collaborator

**cooperar** /koope'rar/ *vt* to cooperate

**cooperativa** /koopera'tiβa/ *f*, cooperative society

**cooperativo** /koopera'tiβo/ *a* cooperative

**coordenada** /koorðe'naða/ *f*, coordinate

**coordinación** /koorðina'θion; koorðina'sion/ *f*, coordination

**coordinar** /koorði'nar/ *vt* to coordinate, classify

**copa** /'kopa/ *f*, wineglass, goblet; glassful; top branches (of trees); crown (of hat); *Cards.* heart; gill (liquid measure); *Inf.* drink, glass; *pl Cards.* hearts (in Spanish pack, goblets)

**copartícipe** /kopar'tiθipe; kopar'tisipe/ *mf* co-partner, partaker, participant

**copec** /'kopek/ *m*, kopeck

**Copenhague** /kope'nage/ Copenhagen

**copernicano** /koperni'kano/ *a* Copernican

**copero** /ko'pero/ *m*, cupbearer; sideboard; cocktail cabinet

**copete** /ko'pete/ *m*, lock, tress (hair); tuft, crest; forelock (horses); head, top (ice-cream, drinks); *Inf.* **de alto c.**, aristocratic; socially prominent

**copia** /'kopia/ *f*, abundance, plenty; copy, reproduction; transcript; imitation

**copiador** /kopia'ðor/ **(-ra)** *a* copying —*n* copier; transcriber. *m*, copybook

**copiar** /ko'piar/ *vt* to copy

**copioso** /ko'pioso/ *a* abundant, plentiful

**copla** /'kopla/ *f*, couplet; popular four-line poem; couple, pair; *pl Inf.* verses

**coplero** /kop'lero/ **(-ra)** *n* balladmonger; poetaster

**copo** /'kopo/ *m*, cop (of a spindle); snowflake

**copón** /ko'pon/ *m*, large goblet; *Eccl.* ciborium, chalice

**coprófago** /ko'profago/ *a* coprophagous

**copropietario** /kopropie'tario/ **(-ia)** *n* coproprietor, coowner

**cóptico** /'koptiko/ *a* Coptic. *m*, Coptic (language)

**copto** /'kopto/ **(-ta)** *n* Copt

**cópula** /'kopula/ *f*, connection; coupling; joining; copulation

**copularse** /kopu'larse/ *vr* to copulate

**coque** /'koke/ *m*, coke

**coqueluche** /koke'lutʃe/ *f*, whooping cough

**coqueta** /ko'keta/ *f*, coquette, flirt

**coquetear** /kokete'ar/ *vi* to flirt

**coqueteo** /koke'teo/ *m*, coquetry; flirtation

**coquetería** /kokete'ria/ *f*, coquetry

**coquetón** /koke'ton/ *a* coquettish

**coracero** /kora'θero; kora'sero/ *m*, cuirassier

**coraje** /ko'rahe/ *m*, courage, valor; anger

**coral** /ko'ral/ *m*, coral. *f*, coral snake. *m*, *Bot.* coral tree; *pl* coral beads

**coral** /ko'ral/ *a* choral

**coralina** /kora'lina/ *f*, coral (polyp).

**coraza** /ko'raθa; ko'rasa/ *f*, cuirass; shell (of tortoise); armor-plate, armor (ships, etc.)

**corazón** /kora'θon; kora'son/ *m*, heart; courage, spirit; love, tenderness; goodwill, benevolence; core (of a fruit); *Fig.* pith. **de c.**, sincerely. **tener el c. en la mano,** to wear one's heart on one's sleeve

**corazonada** /koraθo'naða; koraso'naða/ *f*, feeling, instinct; presentiment, apprehension

**corbata** /kor'βata/ *f*, necktie; scarf; ribbon (insignia)

**corbatería** /korβate'ria/ *f*, necktie shop

**corbatero** /korβa'tero/ *m*, necktie maker; necktie dealer; tie rack

**corbeta** /kor'βeta/ *f*, corvette

**Córcega** /'korθega; 'korsega/ Corsica

**corcel** /kor'θel; kor'sel/ *m*, charger or battle horse

**corchea** /kor'tʃea/ *f*, *Mus.* quaver

**corchete** /kor'tʃete/ *m*, *Sew.* hook and eye; hook

**corcho** /'kortʃo/ *m*, *Bot.* cork, cork bark; stopper, cork; cork mat; bee hive

**corcova** /kor'koβa/ *f*, hump, abnormal protuberance

**corcovado** /korko'βaðo/ **(-da)** *a* hunchbacked, crooked —*n* hunchback

**corcovear** /korkoβe'ar/ *vi* to curvet, caper

**cordaje** /kor'ðahe/ *m*, *Naut.* cordage, tackling, rope

**cordel** /kor'ðel/ *m*, cord; *Naut.* line. **a c.,** in a straight line

**cordelería** /korðele'ria/ *f*, rope making; ropeyard; cordage

**cordelero** /korðe'lero/ **(-ra)** *n* rope maker

**cordera** /kor'ðera/ *f*, ewe lamb; sweet, gentle woman

**cordero** /kor'ðero/ *m*, lamb; dressed lambskin; peaceable, mild man; Jesus (gen. **Divino C.**)

**cordial** /kor'ðial/ *a* warming, invigorating; affectionate, loving, friendly. *m*, *Med.* cordial

**cordialidad** /korðiali'ðað/ *f*, cordiality, friendliness

**cordillera** /korði'ʎera; korði'yera/ *f*, mountain range

**Córdoba** /'korðoβa/ Cordova

**cordobán** /korðo'βan/ *m*, cured goatskin; Cordovan leather, Spanish leather

**cordobés** /korðo'βes/ **(-esa)** *a* and *n* Cordovan

**cordón** /kor'ðon/ *m*, cord; cordon; *Eccl.* rope girdle; *Archit.* string-course

**cordoncillo** /korðon'θiʎo; korðon'siyo/ *m*, rib (in cloth); ridge, milling (of coins); *Sew.* piping

**cordura** /kor'ðura/ *f*, good sense, prudence

**Corea** /ko'rea/ Korea

**corego, corega** /ko'rego, ko'rega/ *m*, choragus

**coreografía** /koreogra'fia/ *f*, choreography; art of dancing

**coreográfico** /koreo'grafiko/ *a* choreographic

**coreógrafo** /kore'ografo/ *m*, choreographer

**corintio** /ko'rintio/ **(-ia)** *a* and *n* Corinthian

**Corinto** /ko'rinto/ Corinth

**corista** /ko'rista/ *m*, *Eccl.* chorister. *mf Theat.* member of the chorus

**cornada** /kor'naða/ *f*, horn thrust or wound (bulls, etc.)

**cornalina** /korna'lina/ *f*, *Mineral.* cornelian

**cornamenta** /korna'menta/ *f*, horns (bulls, deer, etc.)

**córnea** /'kornea/ *f*, cornea

**corneja** /kor'neha/ *f*, carrion or black crow

**córneo** /'korneo/ *a* horny, corneous

**corneta** /kor'neta/ *f*, *Mus.* bugle; *Mus.* cornet; swineherd's horn; *Mil.* pennon. *m*, bugler; *Mil.* cornet. **c. de monte,** hunting horn

**cornetín** /korne'tin/ *m*, *dim* **corneta**, *Mus.* cornet; cornet player

**cornezuelo** /korne'θuelo; korne'suelo/ *m*, *dim* little horn; *Med.* ergot; *Bot.* variety of olive

**cornisa** /kor'nisa/ *f*, cornice

**cornucopia** /kornu'kopia/ *f*, cornucopia, horn of plenty; sconce; mirror

**cornudo** /kor'nuðo/ *a* horned. *m*, cuckold. **el C.,** the Devil

**coro** /'koro/ *m*, choir; chorus; *Archit.* choir. **hacer c. ( a),** to listen to, support. **saber de c.,** to know by heart

**corolario** /koro'lario/ *m*, corollary

**corona** /ko'rona/ *f*, garland, wreath; halo; (*Astron. Archit.*) corona; crown (of tooth); crown (of head); tonsure; crown (coin); royal power; kingdom; triumph; reward; summit, height, peak; circlet (for candles)

**coronación** /korona'θion; korona'sion/ *f*, coronation; coping stone

**coronamiento** /korona'miento/ *m*, coronation; coping stone; *Fig.* crowning touch; *Naut.* taffrail

**coronar** /koro'nar/ *vt* to crown; crown (in draughts); complete, round off; —*vr* be crowned; crown oneself; be tipped or capped

**coronel** /koro'nel/ *m*, colonel

**coronela** /koro'nela/ *f*, *Inf.* colonel's wife

**coronelía** /korone'lia/ *f*, colonelcy

**coronilla** /koro'niʎa; koro'niya/ *f*, *dim* small crown; crown of head; *Fig. Inf.* **estar hasta la c.,** to be fed up

**coroza** /ko'roθa; ko'rosa/ *f*, dunce's cap

**corpiño** /kor'piɲo/ *m*, bodice

**corporación** /korpora'θion; korpora'sion/ *f*, corporation, body, association

**corporal** /korpo'ral/ *a* and *m*, *Eccl.* corporal

**corporativo** /korpora'tiβo/ *a* corporate, corporative

**corpóreo** /kor'poreo/ *a* corporeal

**corporizar** /korpori'θar; korpori'sar/ *vt* to embody

**corpulento** /korpu'lento/ *a* corpulent, stout

**Corpus** /'korpus/ *m*, Corpus Christi

**corpúsculo** /kor'puskulo/ *m*, corpuscle

**corral** /ko'rral/ *m*, yard; pen, enclosure, corral; old-time theater. **c. de madera,** timber yard. *Inf.* **hacer corrales,** to play truant

**correa** /ko'rrea/ *f*, leather strap or thong; flexibility; *Mech.* belt, band

**corrección** /korrek'θion; korrek'sion/ *f*, correction; correctness; punishment; emendation. **c. de pruebas,** proofreading, proofing, reading proof

**correcional** /korre'θional; korre'sional/ *a* correctional. *m*, reformatory

**correctivo** /korrek'tiβo/ *a* and *m*, corrective

**correcto** /ko'rrekto/ *a* correct; well-bred; unexceptionable, irreproachable; regular (of features)

**corredera** /korre'ðera/ *f*, link (engines); *Mech.* slide; *Naut.* log; racecourse; *Inf.* procuress

**corredizo** /korre'ðiθo; korre'ðiso/ *a* easy to untie; running (of knots); sliding

**corredor** /korre'ðor/ *n* runner. *m*, *Com.* broker; corridor; *Inf.* meddler; *Inf.* procurer, pimp —*a* running. **c. de bolsa,** stockbroker

**corregible** /korre'hiβle/ *a* corrigible

**corregidor** /korrehi'ðor/ *m*, Spanish magistrate; *Obs.* mayor

**corregidora** /korrehi'ðora/ *f*, wife of corregidor; mayoress

**corregir** /korre'hir/ *vt irr* to correct; scold, punish; moderate, counteract; *Mech.* adjust; —*vr* mend one's ways. **c. pruebas,** to read proof —*Pres. Indic.* **corrijo, corriges, corrige, corrigen.** *Pres. Part.* **corrigiendo.** *Pres. Subjunc.* **corrija, corrijas,** etc —*Imperf. Subjunc.* **corrigiese,** etc.

**correlación** /korrela'θion; korrela'sion/ *f*, correlation

**correligionario** /korrelihio'nario/ **(-ia)** *n* coreligionist; fellow-supporter or believer

**correo** /ko'rreo/ *m*, courier; mail; post-office; letters. **c. aéreo,** air-mail. **c. certificado,** registered mail. **c. electrónico,** e-mail. **a vuelta de c.,** by return of mail. **tren c.,** mail train

**correr** /ko'rrer/ *vi* to run; race; sail, steam; flow; blow; flood; extend, stretch; pass (of time); fall due (salary, etc.); be current or general; (*with con*) be in charge of or responsible for; —*vt* run (a horse); fasten, slide (bolts, etc.); draw (curtains); undergo, suffer; sell, auction; *Inf.* steal; *Fig.* embarrass; spread (a rumor, etc.); catch, make (bus, train, etc.); —*vr* slide, glide, slip; run (of colors); *Inf.* spread oneself, talk too much. **c. cañas,** to participate in a mock joust using reeds as spears

**correría** /korre'ria/ *f*, raid, foray; excursion, trip

**correspondencia** /korrespon'denθia; korrespon'densia/ *f*, relationship, connection; intercourse, communication; correspondence, letters; equivalence, exact translation

**corresponder** /korrespon'der/ *vi* to requite, repay; be grateful; belong to, concern; devolve upon, fall to; suit, harmonize (with); fit; —*vr* correspond by letters; like or love each other

**correspondiente** /korrespon'diente/ *a* suitable; proportionate; corresponding. *mf* correspondent

**corresponsal** /korrespon'sal/ *mf* correspondent (especially professional); *Com.* agent

**corretear** /korrete'ar/ *vi* to wander about the streets; gad

**correveidile** /korreβei'ðile/ *mf Inf.* tale-bearer, gossip

**corrida** /ko'rriða/ *f*, race, run; *Aer.* taxying; bull fight (abb. for **c. de toros**)

**corrido** /ko'rriðo/ *a* extra, over (of weight); embarrassed; experienced

**corriente** /ko'rriente/ *a* current, present; well-known; usual, customary; fluent (style); ordinary, average; easy. *f*, flow, stream; *Fig.* course (of events, etc.); *Elec.* current —*adv* quite, exactly. *Elec.* **c. alterna,** alternating current. **c. continua,** direct current. **c. de aire,** draft. **estar al c.,** to be informed (of something)

**Corriente del Golfo** /ko'rriente del 'golfo/ Gulf Stream

**corrillo** /ko'rriʎo; ko'rriyo/ *m*, knot, group, huddle (of people)

**corro** /'korro/ *m*, circle, group; ring (for children's games)

**corroboración** /korroβora'θion; korroβora'sion/ *f*, corroboration, confirmation

**corroborar** /korroβo'rar/ *vt* to fortify; corroborate, support

**corroborativo** /korroβora'tiβo/ *a* corroborative

**corroer** /korro'er/ *vt irr* to corrode, waste away; *Fig.* gnaw. See **roer**

**corromper** /korrom'per/ *vt* to rot; mar; spoil, ruin; seduce, corrupt (texts); bribe; *Fig.* contaminate, corrupt; —*vi* stink; —*vr* putrefy, rot; be spoiled; *Fig.* be corrupted

**corrosión** /korro'sion/ *f*, corrosion

**corrosivo** /korro'siβo/ *a* corrosive

**corrugación** /korruga'θion; korruga'sion/ *f*, corrugation, wrinkling

**corrupción** /korrup'θion; korrup'sion/ *f*, rot, putrefaction; corruption, depravity; decay; stink; bribery; falsification (of texts); corruption (of language, etc.)

**corrupto** /ko'rrupto/ *a* corrupt

**corruptor** /korrup'tor/ **(-ra)** *n* corrupter

**corsario** /kor'sario/ *m*, pirate; privateer

**corsé** /kor'se/ *m*, corset

**corsetería** /korsete'ria/ *f*, corset shop or manufactory

**corso** /'korso/ **(-sa)** *a* and *n* Corsican

**corta** /'korta/ *f*, felling, cutting

**cortacircuitos** /kortaθir'kuitos; kortasir'kuitos/ *m*, *Elec.* circuit breaker, cut-out; disconnecting switch

**cortado** /kor'taðo/ *a* fitting, proportioned; disjointed (style); confused, shamefaced

**cortador** /korta'ðor/ *m*, cutter; cutter-out (dresses, etc.); butcher

**cortadura** /korta'ðura/ *f*, cut, wound; cutting (from periodicals); defile; *pl* clippings, cuttings

**cortafrío** /korta'frio/ *m*, cold chisel; hammer-head chisel

**cortalápices** /korta'lapiθes; korta'lapises/ *m*, pencil sharpener

**cortante** /kor'tante/ *a* cutting; sharp; piercing (of wind, etc.); trenchant

**cortapapel** /kortapa'pel/ *m*, paper-knife

**cortapisa** /korta'pisa/ *f*, condition, stipulation

**cortaplumas** /korta'plumas/ *m*, penknife

**cortapuros** /korta'puros/ *m*, cigar cutter

**cortar** /kor'tar/ *vt* to cut; cut out (dresses, etc.); switch off, shut off (water, electricity, etc.); cleave, divide; cut (cards); pierce (wind, etc.); interrupt, impede; omit, cut; *Fig.* interrupt (conversation); decide, determine; —*vr* be confused or shamefaced; curdle, turn sour (e.g. *Se cortó la leche,* The milk turned sour); split, fray; chap

**cortavidrios** /korta'βiðrios/ *m*, diamond, glasscutter

**cortaviento** /korta'βiento/ *m*, windscreen

**corte** /'korte/ *f*, court (royal); retinue; yard; *pl* Spanish parliament. *m*, cutting, cut; blade, cutting edge; cutting out, dressmaking; length, material required for garment, shoes, etc.; cut, fit; style; book edge; *Archit.* section; means, expedient; counting of money (in a till). **c. de caja,** counting of money (in a till). **c. trasversal,** side view

**cortedad** /korte'ðað/ *f*, shortness, brevity; smallness; stupidity, dullness; timidity, shyness. **c. de fuerzas,** lack of strength

**cortejar** /korte'har/ *vt* to accompany, escort; woo, court

**cortejo** /kor'teho/ *m*, courtship, wooing; suite, accompaniment; gift, present; homage, attention; *Inf.* lover, beau

**cortés** /kor'tes/ *a* polite, attentive, courteous, civil

**cortesana** /korte'sana/ *f*, courtesan

**cortesano** /korte'sano/ *a* court; courtly. *m*, courtier

**cortesía** /korte'sia/ *f*, politeness, courtesy; attentiveness; civility; gift, present; favor. **c. internacional,** courtesy of nations. **c. de boca mucho vale y poco cuesta.** Courtesy is worth much and costs little

**corteza** /kor'teθa; kor'tesa/ *f*, *Bot.* bark; *Anat.* cortex; skin, peel, crust; aspect, appearance; roughness. **c. terrestre,** Earth's crust, crust of the Earth. **de c.,** superficial (e.g. explanation)

**cortijo** /kor'tiho/ *m*, farmhouse and land

**cortina** /kor'tina/ *f*, curtain; *Fig.* veil; *Inf.* heel taps; *Mil.* curtain, screen. **c. de fuego de artillería,** antiaircraft barrage. **c. de globos de intercepción,** balloon barrage. **c. de humo,** smoke screen. **c. metálica,** metal shutter

**cortinaje** /korti'nahe/ *m*, curtains, hangings

**corto** /'korto/ *a* short, brief; timid, bashful; concise; defective; stupid, dull; tongue-tied, inarticulate. **c. circuito,** *Elec.* short-circuit. **c. de alcances,** dull-witted. **c. de vista,** short-sighted

**coruscar** /korus'kar/ *vi* to glitter, shine

**corvadura** /korβa'ðura/ *f*, bend; curvature

**corvea** /kor'βea/ *f*, corvée

**corveta** /kor'βeta/ *f*, curvet, prancing

**corvetear** /korβete'ar/ *vi* to curvet

**corzo** /'korθo; 'korso/ *m*, roe-deer, fallow-deer

**cosa** /'kosa/ *f*, thing. **c. rara,** strange to relate; an extraordinary thing. **como si tal c.,** as though nothing had happened. *Inf.* **poquita c.,** a person of no account

**cosaco** /ko'sako/ **(-ca)** *a* and *n* Cossack

**coscorrón** /kosko'rron/ *m*, blow on the head, cuff

**cosecha** /ko'setʃa/ *f*, harvest; harvest time; reaping, gathering, lifting; yield, produce; crop, shower (of honors, etc.). **c. de vino,** vintage

**cosechar** /kose'tʃar/ *vt* and *vt* to harvest, reap

**coseno** /ko'seno/ *m*, cosine

**coser** /ko'ser/ *vt* to sew, stitch; join, unite; press together (lips, etc.). **c. a puñaladas,** to stab repeatedly

**Cosme** /'kosme/ Cosmo

**cosmético** /kos'metiko/ *a* and *m*, cosmetic

**cósmico** /'kosmiko/ *a* cosmic

**cosmografía** /kosmogra'fia/ *f*, cosmography

**cosmógrafo** /kos'mografo/ *m*, cosmographer

**cosmonave** /kosmo'naβe/ *f*, spaceship

**cosmopolita** /kosmopo'lita/ *a* and *mf* cosmopolitan

**cosmopolitismo** /kosmopoli'tismo/ *m*, cosmopolitanism

**cosmos** /'kosmos/ *m*, cosmos

**cospel** /kos'pel/ *m*, blank (from which to stamp coins); to ken; subway to ken

**cosquillas** /kos'kiʎas; kos'kiyas/ *f pl*, tickling. **hacer c.** ( **a),** to tickle

**cosquillear** /koskiʎe'ar; koskiye'ar/ *vt* to tickle

**cosquilleo** /koski'ʎeo; koski'yeo/ *m*, tickle, tickling

**cosquilloso** /koski'ʎoso; koski'yoso/ *a* ticklish; hypersensitive, touchy

**costa** /'kosta/ *f*, cost; expense; coast; *pl Law.* costs. **a c. de,** by dint of; at the cost of. **a toda c.,** at all costs

**Costa del Oro, la** /'kosta del 'oro, la/ the Gold Coast

**Costa de Marfil** /'kosta de mar'fil/ Ivory Coast

**costado** /kos'taðo/ *m*, *Anat.* side; *Mil.* flank; side; *pl* line of descent, genealogy. *Naut.* **dar el c.,** to be broadside on

**costal** /kos'tal/ *m*, sack, bag

**costanero** /kosta'nero/ *a* sloping; coast, coastal

**costar** /kos'tar/ *vi irr* to cost; cause. See **contar**

**costarriqueño** /kostarri'keɲo/ **(-ña)** *a* and *n* Costa Rican

**coste** /'koste/ *m*, cost, price

**costear** /koste'ar/ *vt* to pay for, defray the expense of; *Naut.* coast; —*vr* pay (for itself)

**costilla** /kos'tiʎa; kos'tiya/ *f*, (*Anat. Aer. Naut. Archit.*) rib; *Fig. Inf.* better half, wife; *pl Inf.* back, behind

**costillaje, costillar** /kosti'ʎahe, kosti'ʎar; kosti'yahe, kosti'yar/ *m*, *Anat.* ribs; *Naut.* ship's frame

**costoso** /kos'toso/ *a* expensive, costly; valuable; dear, costly, difficult

**costra** /'kostra/ *f*, crust; scab; rind (of cheese)

**costumbre** /kos'tumbre/ *f*, habit; custom

**costumbrista** /kostum'brista/ *mf* writer on everyday life and customs —*a* (of literary work) dealing with life and customs

**costura** /kos'tura/ *f*, sewing; seam; needlework; joint; riveting

**costurera** /kostu'rera/ *f*, seamstress

**costurero** /kostu'rero/ *m*, work-box, sewing bag

**cota** /'kota/ *f*, *Surv.* elevation, height; coat (of mail); quota. **c. de malla,** chain-mail

**cotangente** /kotan'hente/ *f*, cotangent

**cotejar** /kote'har/ *vt* to compare; collate

**cotejo** /ko'teho/ *m*, comparison; collation

**cótel** /'kotel/ *m*, cocktail, drink

**cotelera** /kote'lera/ *f*, cocktail shaker

**coti** /ko'ti/ *m*, ticking (cloth)

**cotidiano** /koti'ðiano/ *a* daily

**cotillón** /koti'ʎon; koti'yon/ *m*, cotillion

**cotizable** /koti'θaβle; koti'saβle/ *a* valued at; (of prices, shares) quoted

**cotización** /kotiθa'θion; kotisa'sion/ *f*, *Com.* quotation; *Com.* rate. **boletín de c.,** price list (of shares, etc.)

**cotizar** /koti'θar; koti'sar/ *vt Com.* to quote (prices, rates)

**coto** /'koto/ *m*, enclosed ground; boundary stone;

preserve, covert; hand's breadth; end, stop, limit. **c. de caza,** game preserve

**cotorra** /ko'torra/ *f*, small green parrot; magpie; *Inf.* chatterbox

**cotufa** /ko'tufa/ *f*, earthnut; titbit; *Inf.* **pedir cotufas en el golfo,** to ask for the moon

**coturno** /ko'turno/ *m*, buskin

**coyote** /ko'yote/ *m*, coyote, prairie wolf; *Mexico* fixer (anyone who can pull strings to cut red tape or achieve something illegally); smuggler (of goods or people)

**coyuntura** /koyun'tura/ *f*, *Anat.* joint; juncture, occasion

**coz** /koθ; kos/ *f*, kick, recoil (of gun); butt (of a rifle); *Inf.* slap in the face, unprovoked rudeness. **dar coces,** to kick

**craneal** /krane'al/ *a* cranial

**cráneo** /'kraneo/ *m*, cranium, skull

**crápula** /'krapula/ *f*, drunkenness; depravity, immorality, debauchery

**craquear** /krake'ar/ *vt* to crack (petroleum)

**crasitud** /krasi'tuð/ *f*, greasiness; fatness; crassness

**craso** /'kraso/ *a* fat, greasy; thick; unpardonable, crass (often with *ignorancia*). *m*, fatness; ignorance

**creación** /krea'θion; krea'sion/ *f*, creation; universe, world; foundation, establishment; appointment (dignitaries)

**creador** /krea'ðor/ **(-ra)** *n* creator, originator. *m*, God —*a* creative

**crear** /kre'ar/ *vt* to create; found, institute, establish; make, appoint

**crecer** /kre'θer; kre'ser/ *vi irr* to grow; grow up; increase in size; grow longer; wax (moon); come in (of the tide); increase in value (money); —*vr* become more sure of oneself; swell with pride; grow in authority. See **nacer**

**creces** /'kreθes; 'kreses/ *f pl*, increase, interest. **con c.,** fully, amply. **pagar con c.,** *Fig.* to pay with interest

**crecida** /kre'θiða; kre'siða/ *f*, swollen river or stream; food; rising (of the tide)

**crecido** /kre'θiðo; kre'siðo/ *a* grown up; considerable; abundant, plentiful; large; full; serious, important

**crecidos** /kre'θiðos; kre'siðos/ *m pl*, widening stitches (knitting)

**creciente** /kre'θiente; kre'siente/ *a* growing; rising (of the tide); crescent (moon). *m*, *Herald.* crescent. *f*, rising of the tide; crescent moon

**crecimiento** /kreθi'miento; kresi'miento/ *m*, growing; growth, development; increase (in value, money); waxing (of moon)

**credencial** /kreðen'θial; kreðen'sial/ *a* accrediting

**credenciales** /kreðen'θiales; kreðen'siales/ *f pl*, credentials

**credibilidad** /kreðiβili'ðað/ *f*, credibility

**crédito** /'kreðito/ *m*, belief, credence; assent, acquiescence; reputation, name; favor, popularity, acceptance; *Com.* credit; *Com.* letter of credit. **créditos activos,** assets. **créditos pasivos,** liabilities. **a c.,** on credit

**credo** /'kreðo/ *m*, creed. *Inf.* **en un c.,** in a jiffy

**credulidad** /kreðuli'ðað/ *f*, credulity

**crédulo** /'kreðulo/ *a* credulous

**creencia** /kre'enθia; kre'ensia/ *f*, belief; religion, sect, faith

**creer** /kre'er/ *vt irr* to believe; think, consider, opine; think likely or probable. **¡Ya lo creo!** I should just think so! Rather! **creerse la divina garza,** *Mexico* to think one is God's gift to the world. **creerse descender del sobaco de Jesucristo,** to think one is God's gift to the world —*Pres. Part.* **creyendo.** *Preterite* **creyó, creyeron.** *Imperf. Subjunc.* **creyese,** etc.

**creíble** /kre'iβle/ *a* credible

**crema** /'krema/ *f*, cream (off milk); custard mold, cream, shape; face cream; cold cream; elect, flower (of society, etc.)

**cremación** /krema'θion; krema'sion/ *f*, cremation; burning, incineration

**cremallera** /krema'ʎera; krema'yera/ *f*, *Mech.* rack, ratch; zip fastener. **colgar la c.,** to give a house-warming

**crematístico** /krema'tistiko/ *a* economic, financial

**crematorio** /krema'torio/ *m,* crematorium —*a* burning; cremating

**cremor** /kre'mor/ *m, Chem.* cream of tartar

**cremoso** /kre'moso/ *a* creamy

**crencha** /'krentʃa/ *f,* parting (of the hair); each side of parting

**creosota** /kreo'sota/ *f,* creosote

**crepitación** /krepita'θion; krepita'sion/ *f,* crackling, sputtering; hissing; roar (of a fire); *Med.* crepitation

**crepitar** /krepi'tar/ *vi* to crackle; sputter; hiss; roar (of a fire); *Med.* crepitate

**crepuscular** /krepusku'lar/ *a* twilight

**crepúsculo** /kre'puskulo/ *m,* twilight, half light

**cresa** /'kresa/ *f,* maggot; cheese-mite; fly's egg

**Creso** /'kreso/ Croesus

**crespo** /'krespo/ *a* curly, frizzy (hair); rough (of animal's fur); curled (leaves); artificial, involved (style)

**crespón** /kres'pon/ *m,* crape

**cresta** /'kresta/ *f,* comb (of cock, etc.); tuft, topknot (birds); plume; summit, top (of mountains); crest (of a wave); *Herald.* crest

**crestado** /kres'taðo/ *a* crested

**Creta** /'kreta/ Crete

**creta** /'kreta/ *f,* chalk

**cretense** /kre'tense/ *a* Cretan

**cretinismo** /kreti'nismo/ *m,* cretinism

**cretino** /kre'tino/ **(-na)** *a* and *n* cretin

**creyente** /kre'yente/ *a* believing; religious. *mf* believer

**cría** /'kria/ *f,* rearing; bringing up; nursing; suckling; breeding; brood; litter

**criada** /kri'aða/ *f,* servant, maid

**criadero** /kria'ðero/ *m, Mineral.* vein, deposit; tree nursery, plantation; breeding farm or place —*a* prolific

**criado** /kri'aðo/ *m,* servant —*a* bred, brought up (used with *bien* or *mal,* well *or* badly brought up)

**criador** /kria'ðor/ **(-ra)** *m* breeder, keeper, raiser —*a* creating; rearing; creative; fertile, rich

**crianza** /kri'anθa; kri'ansa/ *f,* feeding, suckling; lactation; manners. **buena** (or **mala**) **c.,** good (or bad) breeding or upbringing

**criar** /kri'ar/ *vt* to create; procreate; rear, educate, bring up; feed, nurse, suckle; raise (birds, animals); inspire, give rise to. **Me crié raquítico,** I grew up delicate

**criatura** /kria'tura/ *f,* being, creature; man, human being; infant; small child; fetus; *Fig.* puppet, tool

**criba** /'kriβa/ *f,* sieve, cribble

**cribar** /kri'βar/ *vt* to sieve; riddle (earth, etc.)

**crimen** /'krimen/ *m,* crime. **c. pasional,** crime of passion

**criminal** /krimi'nal/ *a* and *m,* criminal

**criminalidad** /kriminali'ðað/ *f,* guilt; crime ratio; delinquency

**criminalista** /krimina'lista/ *mf* criminal lawyer; criminologist

**criminología** /kriminolo'hia/ *f,* criminology

**crin** /krin/ *f,* horsehair; (gen. *pl*) mane

**crinolina** /krino'lina/ *f,* crinoline

**crío** /'krio/ *m, Inf.* kid, brat

**criollo** /'krioʎo; 'krioyo/ **(-lla)** *a* and *n* creole —*a* indigenous, native

**cripta** /'kripta/ *f,* crypt

**criptografía** /kriptogra'fia/ *f,* cryptography

**criquet** /kri'ket/ *m, Sports.* cricket

**crisálida** /kri'saliða/ *f,* chrysalis

**crisantemo** /krisan'temo/ *m,* chrysanthemum

**crisis** /'krisis/ *f,* crisis. **c. de desarrollo,** growing pains. **c. de vivienda,** housing shortage

**crisma** /'krisma/ *m,* or *f,* chrism

**crisol** /kri'sol/ *m,* crucible; melting pot

**crispado** /kris'paðo/ *a* stiffened

**crispar** /kris'par/ *vt* to cause to contract or twitch; —*vr* twitch. *Inf.* **Se me crispan los nervios,** My nerves are all on edge

**cristal** /kris'tal/ *m,* crystal; glass; windowpane; mirror; water. **c. tallado,** cut glass

**cristalería** /kristale'ria/ *f,* glassware; glass manufacture; glass panes; glass and china shop

**cristalino** /krista'lino/ *a* crystalline. *m,* lens (of the eye)

**cristalización** /kristaliθa'θion; kristalisa'sion/ *f,* crystallization

**cristalizar** /kristali'θar; kristali'sar/ *vi* to crystallize; *Fig.* take shape; —*vt* cause to crystallize

**cristalografía** /kristalogra'fia/ *f,* crystallography

**cristiandad** /kristian'dað/ *f,* Christendom

**cristianismo** /kristia'nismo/ *m,* Christianity; Christendom

**cristianizar** /kristiani'θar; kristiani'sar/ *vt* to convert to Christianity, christianize

**cristiano** /kris'tiano/ **(-na)** *a* and *n* Christian —*a Inf.* watered (of wine). *m, Inf.* Spanish (contrasted with other languages); *Inf.* soul, person

**cristino** /kris'tino/ **(-na)** *a* and *n* supporting, or follower of, Queen Regent Maria Cristina during Carlist wars

**cristo** /'kristo/ *m,* Christ; crucifix. *Inf.* **donde C. dio las tres voces,** in the middle of nowhere

**cristus** /'kristus/ *m,* Christ-cross; alphabet. **no saber el c.,** to be extremely ignorant

**criterio** /kri'terio/ *m,* criterion, standard; judgment, discernment; opinion. **a c. de,** in the opinion of. **según mi c.,** in my opinion

**crítica** /'kritika/ **(a)** *f,* criticism (of)

**criticar** /kriti'kar/ *vt* to criticize; censure, find fault with, blame

**crítico** /'kritiko/ *a* critical; censorious; dangerous, difficult; *Med.* critical. *m,* critic; fault-finder

**criticón** /kriti'kon/ **(-ona)** *a* censorious, hyper-critical —*n* fault-finder

**Croacia** /kro'aθia; kro'asia/ Croatia

**croar** /kro'ar/ *vi* (of frog) to croak

**croata** /kro'ata/ *a* and *mf* Croatian

**croché** /kro'tʃe/ *m,* crochet work

**crol** /krol/ *m,* crawl (swimming)

**cromado** /kro'maðo/ *a* chromium-plated

**cromático** /kro'matiko/ *a* chromatic

**cromato** /kro'mato/ *m,* chromate

**crómico** /'kromiko/ *a* chromic

**cromo** /'kromo/ *m,* chrome; chromium; chromolithograph

**crónica** /'kronika/ *f,* chronicle; diary of events

**crónico** /'kroniko/ *a* chronic; inveterate

**cronista** /kro'nista/ *mf* chronicler

**cronología** /kronolo'hia/ *f,* chronology

**cronológico** /krono'lohiko/ *a* chronological

**cronómetro** /kro'nometro/ *m,* stop-watch

**croqueta** /kro'keta/ *f,* croquette

**croquis** /'krokis/ *m,* sketch, outline, drawing. **c. de nivel,** (optical) foresight

**crótalo** /'krotalo/ *m,* rattlesnake; snapper (kind of castanet)

**cruce** /'kruθe; 'kruse/ *m,* crossing; point of intersection; crossroads

**crucero** /kru'θero; kru'sero/ *m, Eccl.* cross-bearer; crossroads; *Archit.* transept; *Astron.* Cross; *Naut.* cruiser

**crucificar** /kruθifi'kar; krusifi'kar/ *vt* to crucify; *Fig. Inf.* torment, torture

**crucifijo** /kruθi'fiho; krusi'fiho/ *m,* crucifix

**crucifixión** /kruθifik'sion; krusifik'sion/ *f,* crucifixion

**cruciforme** /kruθi'forme; krusi'forme/ *a* cruciform

**crucigrama** /kruθi'grama; krusi'grama/ *m,* crossword puzzle

**cruda** /'kruða/ *f, Mexico* hangover

**crudelísimo** /kruðe'lisimo/ *a superl* **cruel,** most cruel, exceedingly cruel

**crudeza** /kru'ðeθa; kru'ðesa/ *f,* rawness, uncookedness; unripeness; rawness (silk, etc.); crudeness; harshness; *Inf.* boasting

**crudo** /'kruðo/ *a* uncooked, raw; green, unripe; indigestible; raw, natural, unbleached; harsh, cruel; cold, raw; *Inf.* boastful. **crudos de petróleo,** *m pl* crude oil

**crueldad** /kruel'dað/ *f,* cruelty; harshness

**cruento** /'kruento/ *a* bloody

**crujía** /kru'hia/ *f,* passage, corridor; *Naut.* midship gangway

**crujidero** /kruhi'ðero/ *a* crackling; creaking; crispy; clattering; rustling; chattering

**crujido** /kru'hiðo/ *m*, creak, crack, crackling, rustle

**crujir** /kru'hir/ *vi* to creak, crackle, rustle

**crup** /krup/ *m*, croup

**crupié** /kru'pie/ *m*, croupier

**crustáceo** /krus'taθeo; krus'taseo/ *a* and *m*, crustacean

**crux** /kruks/ *f*, cross; tails (of coin); withers (of animals); insignia, decoration; affliction, trouble; *Astron.* Southern Cross; *Print.* dagger, obelisk, obelus. **c. doble**, diesis, double dagger. **c. de mayo**, May cross. **c. gamada**, swastika. *Inf.* **¡c. y raya!** An end to this! **en c.**, in the shape of a cross. *Inf.* **hacerse cruces**, to be left speechless, be dumbfounded

**cruzada** /kru'θaða; kru'saða/ *f*, crusade; crossroads; campaign

**cruzado** /kru'θaðo; kru'saðo/ *a* cross; double-breasted (of coats). *m*, crusader; member of military order

**cruzamiento** /kruθa'miento; krusa'miento/ *m*, crossing; intersection

**cruzar** /kru'θar; kru'sar/ *vt* to cross; intersect; interbreed; bestow a cross upon; *Naut.* cruise; —*vr* take part in a crusade; cross one another; coincide; *Geom.* intersect

**cu** /ku/ *f*, name of the letter Q

**cuacuac** /kua'kuak/ *m*, quack (of a duck)

**cuaderna** /kua'ðerna/ *f*, *Naut.* ship's frame, timber; double fours (backgammon)

**cuaderno** /kua'ðerno/ *m*, notebook, jotter, account book; *Inf.* card pack. *Naut.* **c. de bitácora**, logbook

**cuadra** /'kuaðra/ *f*, stable; ward, dormitory; hall, large room; quarter of a mile

**cuadrado** /kua'ðraðo/ *a* square; perfect, exact. *m*, square; (*Mil. Math.*) square; window-frame; clock (of a stocking)

**cuadragenario** /kuaðrahe'nario/ *a* forty years old

**cuadragésima** /kuaðra'hesima/ *f*, Quadragesima

**cuadragésimo** /kuaðra'hesimo/ *a* fortieth

**cuadrángulo** /kua'ðrangulo/ *m*, quadrangle

**cuadrante** /kua'ðrante/ *m*, quadrant; dial, face

**cuadrar** /kua'ðrar/ *vt* (*Math.*) to square; make square; —*vi* correspond, tally; fit, be appropriate —*vr Mil.* stand at attention; *Fig. Inf.* dig one's heels in

**cuadrática** /kua'ðratika/ *f*, quadratic equation

**cuadrático** /kua'ðratiko/ *a* quadratic

**cuadratura** /kuaðra'tura/ *f*, squareness; (*Math. Astron.*) quadrature

**cuadrienio** /kua'ðrienio/ *m*, space of four years

**cuadriga** /kua'ðriga/ *f*, quadriga

**cuadrilátero** /kuaðri'latero/ *m*, quadrilateral; boxing ring —*a* quadrilateral

**cuadrilla** /kua'ðriʎa; kua'ðriya/ *f*, gang; company, band, group; police patrol; quadrille (dance); matadors and their assistants (at a bull fight). **c. carrillana**, track gang

**cuadrilongo** /kuaðri'longo/ *a* and *m*, oblong

**cuadrimotor** /kuaðrimo'tor/ *a Aer.* four-engined

**cuadrivio** /kua'ðriβio/ *m*, quadrivium

**cuadro** /'kuaðro/ *m*, square; picture-frame; frame (of bicycle); flowerbed; *Theat.* tableau, scene; spectacle, sight; board (of instruments); description (in novel, etc.); *Mil.* command, officers; square (of troops). **c. de distribución**, *Elec.* main switchboard. **c. enrejado**, play pen. **cuadro de costumbres**, word-picture of everyday life and customs. **cuadro vivo**, tableau vivant. **a cuadros**, checked, in squares

**cuadrúpedo** /kua'ðrupeðo/ **(-da)** *a* and *n* quadruped

**cuádruple** /kua'ðruple/ *a* quadruple

**cuadruplicar** /kuaðrupli'kar/ *vt* to quadruple

**cuajada** /kua'haða/ *f*, curd (of milk)

**cuajar** /kua'har/ *m*, maw (of a ruminant)

**cuajar** /kua'har/ *vt* to coagulate; curdle; —*vi Inf.* achieve, get away with; —*vr* be coagulated or curdled; *Inf.* be packed or chock full; get stuck (e.g. a piece of food in one's throat)

**cuajarón** /kuaha'ron/ *m*, clot (of blood, etc.)

**cuajo** /'kuaho/ *m*, rennet; coagulation; curdling; *Anat.* abomasum

**cual** /kual/ *rel pron* sing. *mf* and *neut pl* **cuales**, which; who; such as (e.g. *Le detuvieron sucesos cuales suelen ocurrir*, He was detained by events such as usually happen). **a c. mas**, vying (with) (e.g. *Los dos canónigos a c. más grueso*, The two canons each fatter (vying in fatness) than the other). **c.** is used with *def art* **el (la, lo, los, las) cual(es)**, who; which, when the antecedent is a noun (e.g. *Juan saltó en el barco, el c. zarpó en seguida*, John jumped into the boat which sailed at once). **por lo c.**, for which reason —*adv* like (gen. literary or poet.). **¿cuál?** *interr. pron* (no article) which? what? e.g. *Aquí tienes dos cuadros, ¿cuál de ellos te gusta?* Here are two pictures, which one do you like? Also expresses an implicit question, e.g. *No sé cuál te guste*, I don't know which you will like. **¡cuál!** *adv interj* how! **c.... c.** *indef pron* some... some

**cualesquier** /kuales'kier/ *a pl* of **cualquier**

**cualesquiera** /kuales'kiera/ *a pl* of **cualquiera**

**cualidad** /kuali'ðað/ *f*, quality; characteristic; talent

**cualitativo** /kualita'tiβo/ *a* qualitative

**cualquier** /kual'kier/ *Abbr.* **of cualquiera**, any; *pl* **cualesquier**. Only used as abb. *before* noun

**cualquiera** /kual'kiera/ *a mf* any, e.g. *una canción c.*, any song —*pron* anybody, each, anyone whatsoever, whoever (e.g. *¡C. diría que no te gusta!* Anyone would say you don't like it!) *Inf.* **un c.**, a nobody

**cuán** /ku'an/ *adv* how (e.g. *¡C. bello es!* How beautiful it is). Used only before *a* or *adv.* Abb. of **cuándo**

**cuando** /'kuando/ *adv* when; if —*interr* **¿cuándo?** *conjunc* although; since; sometimes; —*prep* during (e.g. *c. la guerra*, during the war) **c. más**, at most, at best. **c. menos**, at the least. **c. no**, if not (e.g. *Es agnóstica cuando no atea*, She's an agnostic, if not an atheist) **de c. en c.**, from time to time

**cuandoquiera** /kuando'kiera/ *adv* whenever

**cuanta, teoría de la** /'kuanta, teo'ria de la/ *f*, quantum theory

**cuantía** /kuan'tia/ *f*, quantity, amount; importance, rank, distinction

**cuantiar** /kuan'tiar/ *vt* to value, estimate; tax

**cuantidad** /kuanti'ðað/ *f*, quantity

**cuantioso** /kuan'tioso/ *a* large, considerable; numerous; plentiful, abundant

**cuantitativo** /kuantita'tiβo/ *a* quantitative

**cuanto** /'kuanto/ *a* as much as, all the; *pl* as many as, all the (e.g. *Te daré cuantas muñecas veas allí*, I'll give you all the dolls you see there) —*a* correlative the... the, as... as (e.g. *C. más tanto, mejor*, The more the better). **cuánto**, *a* and *pron interr* and *interj* how much; *pl* how many (e.g. *¡Cuánto tiempo sin verla!* How long without seeing her!) *pron neut* **cuanto**, as much as, all that (e.g. *Te daré c. quieras*, I shall give you all that you wish) —*adv* quanto, as much as. **c. antes**, as soon as possible. **c. a** *or* **en c. a**, concerning —*adv* and *conjunc* **c. más**, all the more (e.g. *Se lo diré c. más que tenía esa intención*, I shall tell him all the more because I meant to do so) —*adv* **en c.**, as soon as, immediately (e.g. *Lo haré en c. venga*, I shall do it immediately he comes). **en c. a**, with regard to. **por c.**, inasmuch, for this reason —*adv interr* **¿Cuánto?** How much? How long? *adv interj* How! How much! (e.g. *¡Cuánto me gustaría ir!* How much I should like to go!)

**cuaquerismo** /kuake'rismo/ *m*, Quakerism

**cuáquero** /'kuakero/ **(-ra)** *n* Quaker

**cuarenta** /kua'renta/ *a* and *m*, forty; fortieth

**cuarentena** /kuaren'tena/ *f*, fortieth; period of forty days, months or years; Lent; quarantine

**cuarentón** /kuaren'ton/ **(-ona)** *n* person forty years old

**cuaresma** /kua'resma/ *f*, Lent

**cuaresmal** /kuares'mal/ *a* Lenten

**cuarta** /'kuarta/ *f*, quarter, fourth; hand's breadth; *Mus.* fourth; *Astron.* quadrant

**cuartana** /kuar'tana/ *f*, quartan (fever)

**cuarteadura** /kuartea'ðura/ *f*, crack

**cuartear** /kuarte'ar/ *vt* to quarter, divide into quarters; cut or divide into pieces

**cuartel** /kuar'tel/ *m*, barracks; *Naut.* hatch; quarter, fourth; *Herald.* quarter; district, ward; flowerbed; *Inf.* house, accommodation; *Mil.* quarter, mercy; *Mil.* billet, station. *Mil.* **c. general**, general headquarters

**cuartelada** /kuarte'laða/ *f*, *Naut.* quarter; military rebellion, military uprising, mutiny

**cuartelar** /kuarte'lar/ *vt Herald.* to quarter

**cuartelazo** /kuarte'laθo; kuarte'laso/ *m*, military rebellion, military uprising, mutiny

**cuarterón** /kuarte'ron/ **(-ona)** *n* quadroon

**cuarteta** /kuar'teta/ *f*, quatrain

**cuarteto** /kuar'teto/ *m*, *Mus.* quartet; *Poet.* quatrain

**cuartilla** /kuar'tiʎa; kuar'tiya/ *f*, sheet of paper; liquid measure; quarter of an arroba; pastern (horses)

**cuarto** /'kuarto/ *m*, room; quarter, fourth; point of compass); watch (on battleships); *Astron.* quarter, phase; portion, quarter; joint (of meat); *pl* quarters (of animals); *Inf.* penny, farthing —*a* quarter, fourth. **c. creciente,** first phase (of moon). **c. de hora,** quarter of an hour. **en c.,** *Print.* in quarto. *Inf.* **no tener un c.,** to be broke

**cuarzo** /'kuarθo; 'kuarso/ *m*, quartz

**cuasi** /'kuasi/ *adv* almost, nearly, quasi

**cuasidelito** /kuasiðe'lito/ *m*, *Law.* technical offense

**cuasimodo** /kuasi'moðo/ *m*, *Eccl.* Low Sunday, Quasimodo

**cuaterna** /kua'terna/ *f*, quaternion

**cuatrillón** /kuatri'ʎon; kuatri'yon/ *m*, quadrillion

**cuatrimestre** /kuatri'mestre/ *a* of four months' duration. *m*, space of four months

**cuatrimotor** /kuatrimo'tor/ *m*, *Aer.* four-engine airplane

**cuatrisílabo** /kuatri'silaβo/ *a* quadrisyllabic

**cuatro** /'kuatro/ *a* four; fourth. *m*, figure four; fourth (of days of months); playing-card with four spots; *Mus.* quartet. **el c. de mayo,** the fourth of May. **Son las c.,** It is four o'clock

**cuatrocientos** /kuatro'θientos; kuatro'sientos/ *a* four hundred; four hundredth.

**cuba** /'kuβa/ *f*, barrel, cask; tub, vat; *Inf.* pot-bellied person; *Inf.* drunkard, toper

**cubano** /ku'βano/ **(-na)** *a* and *n* Cuban

**cubería** /kuβe'ria/ *f*, cooperage

**cubeta** /ku'βeta/ *f*, *dim* keg, small cask; bucket, pail; *Photo.* developing dish

**cubicar** /kuβi'kar/ *vt* *Math.* to cube; *Geom.* measure the volume of

**cúbico** /'kuβiko/ *a* cubic

**cubículo** /ku'βikulo/ *m*, cubicle

**cubierta** /ku'βierta/ *f*, cover; envelope; casing; deck (of ship); tire cover; book-jacket; pretext, excuse. **c. de escotilla,** *Naut.* companion-hatch. **c. de paseo,** promenade deck

**cubierto** /ku'βierto/ *m*, cover, place at table; course (of a meal); table d'hôte, complete meal; roof. **un c. de doscientas pesetas,** a two hundred peseta meal

**cubil** /ku'βil/ *m*, lair, den (of animals)

**cubilete** /kuβi'lete/ *m*, *Cul.* mold; dice box; conjurer's cup

**cubismo** /ku'βismo/ *m*, cubism

**cubista** /ku'βista/ *mf* cubist —*a* cubistic

**cubo** /'kuβo/ *m*, bucket, pail; *Mech.* socket; *Math.* cube; hub (of a wheel); mill-pond

**cubrecama** /kuβre'kama/ *m*, bedspread

**cubrecorsé** /kuβrekor'se/ *m*, camisole

**cubrimiento** /kuβri'miento/ *m*, covering

**cubrir** /ku'βrir/ *vt* to cover; *Mil.* defend; spread over, extend over; conceal, hide; *Com.* dissemble; *Archit.* roof; —*vr* cover one's head; pay, meet (debts, etc.); cover or protect oneself (by insurance, etc.) —*Past Part.* **cubierto**

**cucaña** /ku'kaɲa/ *f*, greasy pole; *Inf.* snip, cinch, bargain

**cucaracha** /kuka'ratʃa/ *f*, cockroach

**cuchara** /ku'tʃara/ *f*, spoon; ladle; *Naut.* boat scoop; scoop, dipper. *Fig.* **meter c.,** to stick one's oar in

**cucharada** /kutʃa'raða/ *f*, spoonful; ladleful

**cuchicheador** /kutʃitʃea'ðor/ **(-ra)** *n* whisperer

**cuchichear** /kutʃitʃe'ar/ *vi* to whisper

**cuchicheo** /kutʃi'tʃeo/ *m*, whisper; whispering; murmur

**cuchillada** /kutʃi'ʎaða; kutʃi'yaða/ *f*, knife thrust or wound; *pl* (in sleeves, etc.) slashes; fight, blows

**cuchillería** /kutʃiʎe'ria; kutʃiye'ria/ *f*, cutlery; cutler's shop

**cuchillero** /kutʃi'ʎero; kutʃi'yero/ *m*, cutler

**cuchillo-** /ku'tʃiʎo; ku'tʃiyo/ *m*, knife; *Sew.* gore, gus-

set (gen. *pl*); authority, power; anything triangular in shape. **pasar a c.,** to put to the sword

**cuclillas, en** /ku'kliʎas, en; ku'kliyas, en/ *adv* in a squatting position

**cuclillo** /ku'kliʎo; ku'kliyo/ *m*, *Ornith.* cuckoo; *Inf.* cuckold

**cuco** /'kuko/ *a* *Inf.* pretty, cute; crafty, smart

**cucú** /ku'ku/ *m*, cry of the cuckoo

**Cucufo** /ku'kufo/ *m*, the Devil

**cuculla** /ku'kuʎa; ku'kuya/ *f*, cowl, hood

**cucurucho** /kuku'rutʃo/ *m*, paper cornet

**cuello** /'kueʎo; 'kueyo/ *m*, *Anat.* neck; neck (of bottle, etc.); *Sew.* neck; collar; necklet (of fur, etc.)

**cuenca** /'kuenka/ *f*, socket (of eye); *Geog.* catchment-basin; gorge, deep valley. **c. de un río,** river-basin

**cuenta** /'kuenta/ *f*, count, counting; calculation; account; bead; charge, responsibility; reckoning; explanation, reason; *Com.* bill. **c. a cero, c. a la inversa, c. atrás,** countdown. **c. corriente,** current account. **cuentas alegres, cuentas galanas,** *Inf.* idle dreams, illusions. **c. pendiente,** outstanding account. *Geom.* **caer en la c.,** to tumble to, realize. **llevar la c.,** to reckon, keep account. **sin c.,** countless. **tener en c.,** to bear in mind

**cuentacorrentista** /kuentakorren'tista/ *mf* one who has a bank account

**cuentagotas** /kuenta'gotas/ *m*, dropper, dropping tube

**cuentakilómetros** /kuentaki'lometros/ *m*, speedometer

**cuentapasos** /kuenta'pasos/ *m*, pedometer

**cuentista** /kuen'tista/ *mf* storyteller; *Inf.* gossip

**cuento** /'kuento/ *m*, story, tale; narrative; calculation; *Inf.* gossip, fairytale; *Math.* million. **c. de viejas,** old wives' tale. *Fig. Inf.* **dejarse de cuentos,** to go straight to the point. *Inf.* **Va de c.,** It is told, they say

**cuerda** /'kuerða/ *f*, rope; cord; string; *Geom.* chord; *Mus.* string; catgut; chain (of clock); *Mus.* chord; vocal range. **dar c. ( a),** to wind up (a watch); lead on, make talk. **de cuerdas cruzadas,** overstrung (of a piano)

**cuerdo** /'kuerðo/ *a* sane; prudent; levelheaded

**cuerno** /'kuerno/ *m*, *Anat.* horn; feeler, antenna; *Mus.* horn; horn (of the moon). **c. de abundancia,** horn of plenty. *Inf.* **poner en los cuernos de la luna,** to praise to the skies

**cuero** /'kuero/ *m*, hide, pelt; leather. **c. charolado,** patent leather. **en cueros,** stark naked

**cuerpo** /'kuerpo/ *m*, *Anat.* body or trunk; flesh (as opposed to spirit); bodice; volume, book; main portion; collection; size, volume; physical appearance; corpse; group, assembly; corporation, association; *Geom.* solid; *Chem.* element; thickness, density; *Mil.* corps. **c. de bomberos,** fire brigade. **c. de guardia,** guardhouse. **c. de la vida,** staff of life; *Inf.* **dar con el c. en tierra,** to fall flat. **de c. entero,** *Art.* full-length (portrait). **en c.,** without a coat, lightly clad. **un c. a c.,** a clinch (in wrestling)

**cuervo** /'kuerβo/ *m*, raven; crow

**cuesco** /'kuesko/ *m*, stone, seed, pip

**cuesta** /'kuesta/ *f*, slope, incline, gradient. **c. abajo (arriba),** down (up) hill. **a cuestas,** on one's back; having the responsibility of

**cuestión** /kues'tion/ *f*, problem, question; quarrel; disagreement; affair, matter; torture

**cuestionable** /kuestio'naβle/ *a* doubtful, questionable

**cuestionar** /kuestio'nar/ *vt* to discuss, debate

**cuestionario** /kuestio'nario/ *m*, questionnaire

**cueva** /'kueβa/ *f*, cave, cavern; basement, cellar. *Fig.* **c. de ladrones,** den of thieves

**cuévano** /'kueβano/ *m*, hamper, basket

**cuidado** /kui'ðaðo/ *m*, carefulness, pains; attention; charge, care, responsibility; anxiety, fear —*interj* ¡**C.**! Careful! Look out! **Me tiene sin c. su opinión,** I am not interested in his (your) opinion. *Inf.* **estar al c. de,** to be under the direction of. **estar de c.,** to be dangerously ill

**cuidadoso** /kuiða'ðoso/ **(de)** *a* careful (about or with); anxious (about); concerned (with); watchful; conscientious

**cuidar** /kui'ðar/ *vt* to care for; tend; take care of, look after; mind, be careful of; —*vr* look after oneself

**cuita** /'kuita/ *f*, misfortune, anxiety, trouble

**cuitado** /kui'taðo/ *a* unfortunate, worried; timid, bashful, humble

**culata** /ku'lata/ *f*, *Anat*. haunch; butt (of fire-arms); back, rear; *Auto*. sump

**culatazo** /kula'taθo; kula'taso/ *m*, recoil (of fire-arms)

**culebra** /ku'leβra/ *f*, snake; *Inf*. trick, joke; *Inf*. sudden uproar. **hacer c.,** to stagger along

**culebrear** /kuleβre'ar/ *vi* to wriggle; grovel; meander, wind

**culebreo** /kule'βreo/ *m*, wriggling; meandering, winding

**culí** /ku'li/ *m*, coolie

**culinario** /kuli'nario/ *a* culinary

**culminación** /kulmina'θion; kulmina'sion/ *f*, culmination, peak; *Astron*. zenith

**culminante** /kulmi'nante/ *a* culminating; *Fig*. outstanding

**culminar** /kulmi'nar/ *vi* to culminate (in)

**culo** /'kulo/ *m*, buttocks, seat; rump; anus; base, bottom. **c. de lámpara,** *Archit*. pendant; *Print*. tail-piece

**culpa** /'kulpa/ *f*, fault; blame. **echar la c.** ( **a**), to blame. **por c. de,** through the fault of. **tener la c.,** to be to blame

**culpabilidad** /kulpaβili'ðað/ *f*, guilt

**culpable** /kul'paβle/ *a* culpable

**culpado** /kul'paðo/ **(-da)** *n* culprit

**culpar** /kul'par/ *vt* to blame, accuse; criticize, censure

**culteranismo, cultismo** /kultera'nismo, kul'tismo/ *m*, involved literary style (cf. **Euphuism**)

**cultígeno** /kul'tiheno/ *m*, cultigen

**cultismo** /kul'tismo/ *m*, cultism (Gongorism); learned form, learnedism, learned word

**cultivable** /kulti'βaβle/ *a* cultivable

**cultivación** /kultiβa'θion; kultiβa'sion/ *f*, cultivation; culture

**cultivador** /kultiβa'ðor/ **(-ra)** *n* cultivator; planter

**cultivar** /kulti'βar/ *vt* to cultivate; develop; exercise, practice (professions); culture (bacteriology)

**cultivo** /kul'tiβo/ *m*, cultivation; farming; culture (bacteriological)

**culto** /'kulto/ *a* cultivated; educated; cultured; elegant, artificial (style). *m*, worship; cult; religion, creed; homage

**cultura** /kul'tura/ *f*, cultivation; culture. **de c. universitaria,** college-educated

**cultural** /kultu'ral/ *a* cultural

**cumbre** /'kumbre/ *f*, peak, crest, summit; *Fig*. zenith, acme

**cumpleaños** /kumple'aɲos/ *m*, birthday

**cumplidamente** /kumpliða'mente/ *adv* fully, completely

**cumplido** /kum'pliðo/ *a* complete; thorough; long; plentiful; courteous, punctilious; fulfilled. *m*, courtesy, attention; formality. **gastar cumplidos,** to stand on ceremony; be formal

**cumplimentar** /kumplimen'tar/ *vt* to congratulate; perform, carry out

**cumplimentero** /kumplimen'tero/ *a* overcomplimentary; *Inf*. gushing

**cumplimiento** /kumpli'miento/ *m*, fulfillment, performance; courtesy, formality; completion; complement

**cumplir** /kum'plir/ *vt* to perform, carry into effect; reach (of age); keep (promises). **c. su palabra,** to keep one's word; —*vi* complete a duty; expire, fall due; serve the required term of military service; be necessary, behove; —*vr* be fulfilled, come true. **por c.,** as a matter of form

**cumulativo** /kumula'tiβo/ *a* cumulative

**cúmulo** /'kumulo/ *m*, heap, pile; great many, host, mass, myriad; (cloud) cumulus, thunderhead

**cuna** /'kuna/ *f*, cradle; foundling hospital; birthplace; origin, genesis; *pl* cat's cradle (game)

**cundir** /kun'dir/ *vi* to extend, spread (gen. liquids); be diffused (news); expand, grow

**cuneiforme** /kunei'forme/ *a* wedge-shaped, cuneiform

**cunero** /ku'nero/ **(-ra)** *n* foundling, orphan

**cuña** /'kuɲa/ *f*, wedge; *Mech*. quoin. *Mil*. **practicar una c.,** to make a wedge

**cuñada** /ku'ɲaða/ *f*, sister-in-law

**cuñado** /ku'ɲaðo/ *m*, brother-in-law

**cuño** /'kuɲo/ *m*, die, stamp; *Fig*. impression; mark on silver, hallmark. **de viejo c.,** old-guard (e.g. socialites)

**cuota** /'kuota/ *f*, quota; share; subscription; fee

**cupé** /ku'pe/ *m*, coupé

**Cupido** /ku'piðo/ *m*, Cupid; philanderer

**cuplé** /ku'ple/ *m*, couplet; song

**cupo** /'kupo/ *m*, quota; share; tax rate; *Mil*. contingent

**cupón** /ku'pon/ *m*, coupon

**cúpula** /'kupula/ *f*, *Archit*. dome, cupola; *Bot*. cup

**cuquería** /kuke'ria/ *f*, craftiness, smartness; cuteness, prettiness

**cura** /'kura/ *m*, parish priest; *Inf*. Roman Catholic priest. *f*, cure (e.g. *La enfermedad tiene c.,* The illness can be cured); healing; remedy. **c. de almas,** cure of souls. **primera c.,** first aid. *Inf*. **c. de misa y olla,** ignorant priest

**curable** /ku'raβle/ *a* curable

**curación** /kura'θion; kura'sion/ *f*, cure, remedy; healing

**curador** /kura'ðor/ **(-ra)** *n* curer, salter. *m*, (*Scots law*) curator —*a* curing; healing

**curaduría** /kuraðu'ria/ *f*, *Law*. guardianship

**curanderismo** /kurande'rismo/ *m*, quackery, charlatanism; quack medicine

**curandero** /kuran'dero/ **(-ra)** *n* quack doctor; charlatan

**curar** /ku'rar/ *vi* to heal, cure; (*with de*) take care of; care about, mind; —*vt* cure; salt; treat medically (bandage, give medicines, etc.); cure (leather); bleach (cloth); season (timber); *Fig*. remedy (an evil)

**curasao** /kura'sao/ *m*, curaçao (drink)

**curativo** /kura'tiβo/ *a* curative

**curato** /ku'rato/ *m*, *Eccl*. parish, cure

**Curazao** /kura'θao; kura'sao/ Curaçao

**cúrcuma** /'kurkuma/ *f*, turmeric

**curdo** /'kurðo/ **(-da)** *a* Kurdish —*n* Kurd

**cureña** /ku'reɲa/ *f*, gun-carriage

**curia** /'kuria/ *f*, *Law*. bar; tribunal; *Eccl*. curia; care, attention

**curiana** /ku'riana/ *f*, cockroach

**curiche** /ku'ritʃe/ *m*, swamp

**curiosamente** /kuriosa'mente/ *adv* curiously; carefully, attentively; neatly

**curiosear** /kuriose'ar/ *vi* to pry; be curious (about); meddle, be a busybody

**curiosidad** /kuriosi'ðað/ *f*, curiosity; inquisitiveness, meddlesomeness; neatness; carefulness, conscientiousness; curio

**curioso** /ku'rioso/ *a* curious; inquisitive; interesting, odd; neat, clean; conscientious, careful

**Curita** /ku'rita/ *f*, *trademark* Band-Aid

**cursado** /kur'saðo/ *a* experienced, versed

**cursante** /kur'sante/ *m*, student

**cursar** /kur'sar/ *vt* to frequent, visit; do repeatedly; study, attend classes, take courses (e.g. *¿En qué escuela cursan?* At what school are you studying?); expedite (public admin.)

**cursi** /'kursi/ *a Inf*. vulgar, in bad taste; loud, crude

**cursilería** /kursile'ria/ *f*, *Inf*. vulgarity, bad taste

**cursillo** /kur'siʎo; kursiyo/ *m*, minicourse, short course; short series of lectures

**cursiva** /kur'siβa/ *f*, italics. **en c.,** in italics, italicized

**cursivo** /kur'siβo/ *a* cursive

**curso** /'kurso/ *m*, course, direction; duration, passage (time); progress; route; course of study; academic year; succession, series; *Com*. tender

**curtido** /kur'tiðo/ *m*, tanning; leather; tanned leather (gen. *pl*)

**curtidor** /kurti'ðor/ *m*, tanner

**curtiduría** /kurtiðu'ria/ *f*, tannery

**curtimiento** /kurti'miento/ *m*, tanning; effect of weather on the complexion; toughening-up; hardening

**curtir** /kur'tir/ *vt* to tan; *Fig*. bronze (complexions); make hardy, harden up; —*vr* be weatherbeaten; be hardy. *Inf.* **estar curtido en,** to be experienced in; be expert at

**curul** /ku'rul/ *a* **curule** *m,* seat (in parliament)

**curva** /'kurβa/ *f,* curve; bend. *Surv.* **c. de nivel,** contour line

**curvatura, curvidad** /kurβa'tura, kurβi'ðað/ *f,* curvature

**curvilíneo** /kurβi'lineo/ *a* curvilinear

**curvo** /'kurβo/ *a* curved; bent. *m,* curve

**cúspide** /'kuspiðe/ *f,* peak, summit; (*Geom. Archit.*) cusp

**custodia** /kus'toðia/ *f,* custody; guardianship, care; *Eccl.* monstrance; custodian, keeper; guardian; guard

**custodiar** /kusto'ðiar/ *vt* to watch, guard; look after, care for; *Naut.* convoy

**custodio** /kus'toðio/ *a* guardian; guarding; custodial. *m,* custodian; guard. **angel c.,** guardian angel

**cutáneo** /ku'taneo/ *a* cutaneous, skin

**cúter** /'kuter/ *m, Naut.* cutter

**cutícula** /ku'tikula/ *f,* cuticle

**cutis** /'kutis/ *m,* complexion; skin (sometimes *f*)

**cuyo** /'kuyo/ (**cuya, cuyos, cuyas**) *rel pron poss* whose, of which (e.g. *el viejo cuya barba era más blanca que la nieve,* the old man whose beard was whiter than snow) —*interr* ¿**Cúyo?** Whose? (e.g. *¿Cúyos son estos lápices?* Whose pencils are these?) (gen. **de quién** or **de quiénes** is used rather than **cuyo**). *m,* beau, lover

# D

**dable** /'daβle/ *a* practicable, possible
**daca** /'daka/ Give me!
**dactilografía** /daktilogra'fia/ *f*, typewriting
**dactilógrafo** /dakti'lografo/ **(-fa)** *n* typist
**dactilología** /daktilolo'hia/ *f*, dactylology
**dádiva** /'daðiβa/ *f*, gift, present
**dadivosidad** /daðiβosi'ðað/ *f*, generosity
**dadivoso** /daðiˈβoso/ *a* generous, liberal
**dado** /'daðo/ *m*, die; *Archit.* dado —*conjunc* **d. que,** given that, supposing that. **cargar los dados,** to load the dice
**dador** /da'ðor/ **(-ra)** *n* giver, donor. *m*, *Com.* bearer; *Com.* drawer (of a bill of exchange)
**daga** /'daga/ *f*, dagger
**daguerrotipo** /dagerro'tipo/ *m*, daguerreotype
**daifa** /'daifa/ *f*, concubine
**¡dale!** /'dale/ *interj* Stop! No more about...!
**dalia** /'dalia/ *f*, *Bot.* dahlia
**dallar** /da'ʎar; da'yar/ *vt* to scythe (grass)
**dalle** /'daʎe; 'daye/ *m*, scythe
**dálmata** /'dalmata/ *a* and *mf* Dalmatian
**dalmática** /dal'matika/ *f*, dalmatic, loose tunic or vestment
**dalmático** /dal'matiko/ **(-ca)** *a* and *n* Dalmatian
**daltoniano** /dalto'niano/ *a* color-blind
**daltonismo** /dalto'nismo/ *m*, color-blindness
**dama** /'dama/ *f*, lady; noblewoman; lady-in-waiting; lady-love; mistress, concubine; queen (chess); king (checkers); *Theat.* **d. primera,** leading lady
**damajuana** /dama'huana/ *f*, demijohn
**damas** /'damas/ *f pl*, checkers (game)
**damasceno** /damas'θeno; damas'seno/ **(-na)** *a* and *n* Damascene
**Damasco** /da'masko/ Damascus
**damasco** /da'masko/ *m*, damask
**damasquino** /damas'kino/ *a* damascened (swords, etc.)
**damería** /dame'ria/ *f*, prudery, affectation
**damisela** /dami'sela/ *f*, damsel; *Inf.* woman of the town
**damnificar** /damnifi'kar/ *vt* to injure
**dandi** /'dandi/ *m*, dandy
**dandismo** /dan'dismo/ *m*, dandyism
**danés** /da'nes/ **(-esa)** *a* Danish —*n* Dane. *m*, Danish (language)
**danta** /'danta/ *f*, *Zool.* tapir
**dantesco** /dan'tesko/ *a* Dantesque
**Danubio, el** /da'nuβio, el/ the Danube
**danza** /'danθa; 'dansa/ *f*, dance; set (of dancers); *Fig. Inf.* dirty business. **d. de arcos,** dance of the arches. **d. de cintas,** maypole dance. **d. de monos,** amusing spectacle
**danzador** /danθa'ðor; dansa'ðor/ **(-ra)** *n* dancer; —*a* dancing
**danzante** /dan'θante; dan'sante/ **(-ta)** *n* dancer; *Fig. Inf.* live wire; *Inf.* busybody
**danzar** /dan'θar; dan'sar/ *vt* and *vi* to dance; —*vi* jump up and down, rattle; *Inf.* interfere, meddle
**danzarín** /danθa'rin; dansa'rin/ **(-ina)** *n* good dancer; *Inf.* meddler; *Inf.* playboy
**danzón** /dan'θon; dan'son/ *m*, Cuban dance
**dañable** /da'ɲaβle/ *a* harmful; worthy of condemnation
**dañado** /da'ɲaðo/ *a* evil, perverse; damned; spoiled, damaged
**dañador** /daɲa'ðor/ **(-ra)** *a* harmful —*n* injurer, offender
**dañar** /da'ɲar/ *vt* to hurt, harm; damage, spoil; —*vr* spoil, deteriorate
**dañino** /da'ɲino/ *a* destructive (often of animals); hurtful, harmful. **animales dañinos,** vermin, pests
**daño** /'daɲo/ *m*, hurt; damage; loss. *Law.* **daños y perjuicios,** damages. **hacerse d.,** to hurt oneself
**dañoso** /da'ɲoso/ *a* hurtful, harmful
**dar** /dar/ *vt irr* to give; wish, express

(congratulations, etc.); hand over; concede, grant; inspire; produce, yield; cause, create; sacrifice; propose, put forward; take (a walk); believe, consider; deliver (blows, etc.); administer (medicine); provide with; apply, coat with; occasion; perform (plays); propose (a toast); give forth, emit; set (norms), render (thanks, etc.); hold (banquets, etc.); proffer, hold out; —*vi* to strike (clocks); (*with prep a*) overlook, look on to (e.g. *Su ventana da a la calle,* His window looks on to the street); (*with con*) find, meet (things, persons); (*with de*) fall on, fall down (e.g. *Dio de cabeza,* He fell head first. *Dio de espaldas,* He fell on his back); (*with en*) fall into, incur; insist on or persist in (doing something); acquire the habit of (e.g. *Dieron en no venir a vernos,* They took to not coming to see us); solve, guess (riddles, etc.); strike, wound, hurt (e.g. *La bala le dio en el brazo,* The bullet struck him in the arm); (*with por*) decide on (e.g. *Di por no hacerlo,* I decided not to do it) —*vr* to yield, give in; (*with prep a*) engage in, devote oneself to; (*with por*) think or consider oneself (e.g. *Me di por muerto,* I gave myself up for dead). **d. alas a,** to propagate, spread (a belief). **darse a la vela,** to set sail. **darse la mano,** to shake hands. **darse por buenos,** to make up a quarrel, be friends. **darse prisa,** to hurry up, make haste. **darse uno a conocer,** to make oneself known. **darse uno por entendido,** to show that one understands; be grateful. **No se me da un bledo,** I don't care a straw. **d. abajo,** to fall down. **d. bien por mal,** to return good for evil. **d. a conocer,** to make known. **d. a entender,** to suggest, hint. **d. a luz,** to give birth; publish, issue. **d. cuenta de,** to give an account of. **d. de baja,** *Mil.* to muster out, discharge. **d. de comer,** to feed. **d. de sí,** to stretch, expand; produce, yield; give of itself (oneself, himself, themselves) (either in good or bad sense). **d. diente con diente,** to chatter (of teeth), shiver. **d. el pésame,** to tender condolences. **d. en cara,** *Fig. Inf.* to throw in one's face. **d. en el clavo,** *Fig.* to hit the mark. **d. en qué pensar,** to make suspicious, cause to think. **d. fe,** to certify, attest. **d. fiado,** to give on credit. **d. fianza,** to give security. **d. fin a,** to finish. **d. licencia,** to permit, allow. **d. los buenos días,** to wish good day or good morning. **d. mal,** to have bad luck at cards. **d. parte de,** to announce; issue a communiqué about (e.g. *Dieron parte de la pérdida del buque,* They announced the loss of the ship). **d. prestado,** to lend. **d. qué decir,** to cause a scandal. **d. qué hacer,** to cause trouble. **d. razón de,** to give an account of. **d. sobre uno,** to assault a person. **d. un abrazo,** to embrace. **d. voces,** to shriek; call out. *Inf.* **Donde las dan las toman,** It's only tit-for-tat. *Inf.* **No me da la real gana,** I darn well don't want to —*Pres. Indic.* **doy, das,** etc —*Preterite* **di, diste,** etc —*Pres. Subjunc.* **dé,** etc —*Imperf. Subjunc.* **diese,** etc.
**Dardanelos, los** /darða'nelos, los/ the Dardanelles
**dardo** /'darðo/ *m*, (*Mil. Sports.*) dart; *Ichth.* dace; lampoon
**dares y tomares** /dares i tomares/ *m, pl* give and take; *Inf.* back-chat. Generally used with *andar, haber* or *tener*
**dársena** /'darsena/ *f*, *Naut.* dock
**darviniano** /darβi'niano/ *a* Darwinian
**darvinismo** /darβi'nismo/ *m*, Darwinism
**darvinista** /darβi'nista/ *mf* Darwinian
**data** /'data/ *f*, date (calendar); *Com.* credit
**datar** /'datar/ *vt* to date; —*vi* (*with de*) date from; —*vr Com.* credit
**dátil** /'datil/ *m*, *Bot.* date
**datilado** /dati'laðo/ *a* date-like or date-colored
**datilera** /dati'lera/ *f*, *Bot.* date-palm
**dativo** /da'tiβo/ *m*, *Gram.* dative
**dato** /'dato/ *m*, datum; basis, fact
**davídico** /da'βiðiko/ *a* Davidic
**de** /de/ *f*, name of letter D —*prep* of (possessive) (e.g. *Este cuadro es de Vd.,* This picture is yours); from (place and time) (e.g. *Vengo de Madrid,* I come from

Madrid. *de vez en cuando,* from time to time); with, of, from, as the result of (e.g. *Lloraban de miedo,* They were crying with fright. *Murió de un ataque del corazón,* He died from a heart attack); for, to (e.g. *Es hora de marchar,* It is time to leave); with (of characteristics) (e.g. *el señor de los lentes,* the gentleman with the eyeglasses. *el cuarto de la alfombra azul,* the room with the blue carpet); when, as (e.g. *De niños nos gustaban los juguetes,* When we were children we liked toys); by (e.g. *Es un ensayo del mismo autor,* It is an essay by the same author. *Fue amado de todos,* He was loved by all. *Es hidalgo de nacimiento,* He is a gentleman by birth). Indicates the material of which a thing is made (e.g. *La mesa es de mármol,* The table is marble). Indicates contents of a thing (e.g. *un vaso de leche,* a glass of milk). Shows manner in which an action is performed (e.g. *Lo hizo de prisa,* He did it hurriedly). Shows the use to which an article is put (e.g. *una mesa de escribir,* a writing-table. *una máquina de coser,* a sewing-machine. *un caballo de batalla,* a war-horse). Sometimes used for emphasis (e.g. *El tonto de tu secretario,* That fool of a secretary of yours). Used by Spanish married women before husband's family name (e.g. *Señora Martínez de Cabra,* Mrs. Cabra (née Martínez)). Used after many adverbs (generally of time or place) to form prepositional phrases (e.g. *detrás de,* behind. *enfrente de,* opposite to; in front of. *de acá para allá,* here and there. *de allí a poco,* shortly afterward. *de allí a pocos días,* a few days later. *de bamba,* by chance. *de cabo a rabo,* from cover to cover. *además de,* besides, etc.). Used at beginning of various adverbial phrases (e.g. *de noche,* at night. *de día,* by day. *de antemano,* previously, *la persona de mi derecha* the person at my right, etc.). Used partitively before nouns, pronouns, adjectives (e.g. *Estas historias tienen algo de verdad,* These stories have some truth in them. *¿Qué hay de nuevo?* What's the news?) Forms many compound words (e.g. *deponer, denegar,* etc.). With **"uno"** means "at" (e.g. *Lo cogió de un salto,* He caught it at one bound). **de a** is used before expressions of price, weight, etc. (e.g. *un libro de a cinco pesetas,* a five-peseta book)

**dea** /dea/ *f, Poet.* goddess
**deán** /de'an/ *m,* dean
**debajo** /de'βaho/ *adv* underneath; below
**debate** /de'βate/ *m,* discussion, debate; dispute
**debatible** /deβa'tiβle/ *a* debatable
**debatir** /deβa'tir/ *vt* to discuss, debate, argue
**debe** /'deβe/ *m, Com.* debtor
**debelación** /deβela'θion; deβela'sion/ *f,* conquest
**debelador** /deβela'ðor/ **(-ra)** *a* conquering —*m* conqueror
**debelar** /deβe'lar/ *vt* to conquer, overthrow
**deber** /de'βer/ *vt* to owe (e.g. *Le debo mil pesetas,* I owe him one thousand pesetas). Used as auxiliary verb followed by infinitive, ought to, be obliged to (e.g. *Debía haberlo hecho,* I ought to have done it. *Deberá hacerlo,* He will have to do it); be destined to (e.g. *La princesa que más tarde debió ser reina,* The princess who later was destined to be queen); be essential, must (e.g. *La cuestión debe ser resuelta,* The question must be settled); (*with de + infin.*) be probable (indicates supposition) (e.g. *Debe de tener cincuenta años,* He is probably about fifty. *Debía de sufrir del corazón,* He probably suffered from heart trouble); (preceded by a negative *with de + infin.*) be impossible (e.g. *No debe de ser verdad,* It can't be true)
**deber** /de'βer/ *m,* duty, obligation; debt. **hacer su d.,** to do one's duty
**debidamente** /deβiða'mente/ *adv* justly, rightly; duly
**debido** /de'βiðo/ *a* correct, due. **d. a,** owing to, because of
**débil** /'deβil/ *a* weak; *Fig.* spineless; frail
**debilidad** /deβili'ðað/ *f,* weakness; feebleness
**debilitación** /deβilita'θion; deβilitasion/ *f,* debilitation
**debilitante** /deβili'tante/ *a* weakening
**debilitar** /deβili'tar/ *vt* to weaken; —*vr* become weak
**débito** /'deβito/ *m,* debit, debt; duty

**debutar** /deβu'tar/ *vi* to appear for the first time, make one's début
**década** /'dekaða/ *f,* decade
**decadencia** /deka'ðenθia; dekaðensia/ *f,* decadence, decline
**decadente** /deka'ðente/ *a* decadent, decaying
**decaer** /deka'er/ *vi irr* to fail (persons); decay, decline. See **caer**
**decagramo** /deka'gramo/ *m,* decagram
**decaimiento** /dekai'miento/ *m,* decadence; *Med.* prostration
**decalaje** /deka'lahe/ *m, Aer.* stagger
**decalitro** /deka'litro/ *m,* decaliter
**decálogo** /de'kalogo/ *m,* decalogue, the Ten Commandments
**decámetro** /de'kametro/ *m,* decameter
**decampar** /dekam'par/ *vi Mil.* to decamp
**decanato** /dekan'ato/ *m,* deanery; *Educ.* dean's rooms
**decano** /de'kano/ *m,* senior member; *Educ.* dean
**decantación** /dekanta'θion; dekantasion/ *f,* decantation
**decantar** /dekan'tar/ *vt* to decant (wines); praise
**decapitación** /dekapita'θion; dekapitasion/ *f,* decapitation
**decapitar** /dekapi'tar/ *vt* to decapitate, behead
**decena** /de'θena; de'sena/ *f,* ten; *Mus.* tenth
**decenal** /de'θenal; de'senal/ *a* decennial
**decenario** /deθe'nario; dese'nario/ *m,* decade
**decencia** /de'θenθia; de'sensia/ *f,* propriety, decency; decorum, modesty
**decenio** /de'θenio; de'senio/ *m,* decade
**deceno** /de'θeno; de'seno/ *a* tenth
**decentar** /deθen'tar; desen'tar/ *vt irr* to begin, cut (loaves, etc.); *Fig.* undermine (health, etc.); —*vr* suffer from bedsores. See **acertar**
**decente** /de'θente; de'sente/ *a* decent, honest; respectable; suitable; tidy
**decepción** /deθep'θion; desep'sion/ *f,* disillusionment, disappointment
**dechado** /de'tʃaðo/ *m,* model, ideal; *Sew.* sampler; exemplar, ideal
**decible** /de'θiβle; de'siβle/ *a* expressible
**decidero** /de'θiðero; de'siðero/ *a* that which can be safely said
**decidido** /deθi'ðiðo; desi'ðiðo/ *a* decided; resolute, determined
**decidir** /deθi'ðir; desi'ðir/ *vt* to resolve, decide; —*vr* make up one's mind
**decidor** /deθi'ðor; desi'ðor/ **(-ra)** *a* talkative, fluent, eloquent —*n* good talker
**decigramo** /deθi'gramo; desi'gramo/ *m,* decigram
**décima** /'deθima; 'desima/ *f,* tenth; tithe; ten-line stanza of eight-syllable verse
**decimal** /deθi'mal; desi'mal/ *a* decimal; pertaining to tithes. **sistema d.,** metric system
**decímetro** /de'θimetro; de'simetro/ *m,* decimeter
**décimo** /'deθimo; 'desimo/ *a* tenth. *m,* tenth part; tenth of a lottery ticket
**decimoctavo** /deθimok'taβo; desimok'taβo/ *a* eighteenth
**decimocuarto** /deθimo'kuarto; desimo'kuarto/ *a* fourteenth
**decimonono** /deθimo'nono; desimo'nono/ *a* nineteenth
**decimoquinto** /deθimo'kinto; desimo'kinto/ *a* fifteenth
**decimoséptimo** /deθimo'septimo; desimo'septimo/ *a and m,* seventeenth
**decimosexto** /deθimo'seksto; desimo'seksto/ *a* sixteenth
**decimotercio** /deθimoter'θio; desimoter'sio/ *a* thirteenth
**decir** /de'θir; de'sir/ *vt irr* to say; name; indicate; show; tell. **d. bien,** to go with, suit; speak the truth; be eloquent. **d. entre** (or **para**) **sí,** to say to oneself. *Inf.* **d. nones,** to refuse. **¡Diga!** Hello! (telephone). *Inf.* **el que dirán,** public opinion (what will people say!). **Es d.,** That is to say. **Se dice,** It is said, people say —*Pres. Ind.* **digo, dices,** etc —*Pres. Part.* **diciendo.** *Past Part.* **dicho.** *Fut.* **diré,** etc —*Condit.*

**diría,** etc —*Preterite* **dije,** etc —*Pres. Subjunc.* **diga,** etc —*Imperf. Subjunc.* **dijese,** etc.

**decir** /de'θir; de'sir/ *m,* saying, saw; maxim, witticism (often *pl.*)

**decisión** /deθi'sion; desi'sion/ *f,* decision, resolution; *Law.* judgment; firmness, strength (of character)

**decisivo** /deθi'siβo; desi'siβo/ *a* decisive

**declamación** /deklama'θion; deklama'sion/ *f,* declamation, oration; *Theat.* delivery; recitation

**declamador** /deklama'ðor/ **(-ra)** *a* declamatory —*n* reciter; orator

**declamar** /dekla'mar/ *vi* to make a speech, declaim; recite

**declamatorio** /deklama'torio/ *a* declamatory, rhetorical

**declaración** /deklara'θion; deklara'sion/ *f,* declaration; exposition, explanation; confession; statement; *Law.* deposition. **d. jurada,** affidavit, sworn statement

**declaradamente** /deklaraða'mente/ *adv* avowedly

**declarante** /dekla'rante/ *a* declaring. *mf Law.* deponent

**declarar** /dekla'rar/ *vt* to declare; make clear, explain; *Law.* find; —*vi Law.* give evidence; —*vr* avow, confess (one's sentiments, etc.); show, reveal itself

**declarativo, declaratorio** /deklara'tiβo, deklara'torio/ *a* explanatory, declarative.

**declinación** /deklina'θion; deklina'sion/ *f,* fall, descent; decadence, decay; *Astron.* declination; *Gram.* declension. *Inf.* **no saber las declinaciones,** not to know one's ABC, be very ignorant

**declinante** /dekli'nante/ *a* declining; sloping

**declinar** /dekli'nar/ *vi* to slope; diminish, fall; decline, deteriorate; *Fig.* near the end; —*vt Gram.* decline

**declive,** /de'kliβe,/ *m.* **declividad** *f,* slope, incline; gradient

**decocción** /dekok'θion; dekok'sion/ *f,* decoction

**decoloración** /dekolora'θion; dekolora'sion/ *f,* decoloration; decolorization

**decomisar** /dekomi'sar/ *vt* to confiscate, seize

**decoración** /dekora'θion; dekora'sion/ *f,* decoration; ornament, embellishment; *Theat.* scenery

**decorado** /deko'raðo/ *m, Theat.* scenery, décor

**decorador** /dekora'ðor/ *m,* decorator

**decorar** /deko'rar/ *vt* to adorn, ornament; *Poet.* decorate, honor

**decorativo** /dekora'tiβo/ *a* decorative

**decoro** /de'koro/ *m,* respect, reverence; prudence, circumspection; decorum, propriety; integrity, decency; *Archit.* decoration

**decoroso** /deko'roso/ *a* decorous, honorable, decent

**decrecer** /dekre'θer; dekre'ser/ *vi irr* to decrease, grow less. See **conocer**

**decreciente** /dekre'θiente; dekre'siente/ *a* decreasing

**decrepitación** /dekrepita'θion; dekrepita'sion/ *f, Chem.* decrepitation, crackling

**decrepitar** /dekrepi'tar/ *vi Chem.* to decrepitate, crackle

**decrépito** /de'krepito/ *a* decrepit

**decrepitud** /dekrepi'tuð/ *f,* decrepitude

**decretar** /dekre'tar/ *vt* to decree, decide; *Law.* give a judgment (in a suit)

**decreto** /de'kreto/ *m,* decree, order; judicial decree

**decuplar, decuplicar** /dekup'lar, dekupli'kar/ *vt* to multiply by ten

**décuplo** /'dekuplo/ *a* tenfold

**decurso** /de'kurso/ *m,* course, lapse (of time)

**dedada** /de'ðaða/ *f,* thimbleful, finger; pinch

**dedal** /de'ðal/ *m,* thimble; finger-stall

**dédalo** /'deðalo/ *m,* labyrinth

**dedeo** /de'ðeo/ *m, Mus.* touch

**dedicación** /deðika'θion; deðika'sion/ *f,* dedication (all meanings)

**dedicar** /deði'kar/ *vt* to dedicate; devote; consecrate; —*vr* (*with prep a*) dedicate oneself to, engage in

**dedicatoria** /deðika'toria/ *f,* dedication (of a book, etc.)

**dedicatorio** /deðika'torio/ *a* dedicatory

**dedil** /'deðil/ *m,* finger-stall

**dedillo, saber al** /de'ðiʎo, saβer al; de'ðiyo, saβer al/ *Fig.* to have at one's fingertips, know perfectly

**dedo** /'deðo/ *m,* finger; toe; finger's breadth. **d. anular,** third (ring) finger. **d. de en medio** *or* **del corazón,** middle finger. **d. índice,** forefinger. **d. meñique,** little finger. **d. pulgar,** thumb or big toe. *Fig. Inf.* **a dos dedos de,** within an inch of. *Fig. Inf.* **chuparse los dedos,** to smack one's lips over. *Inf.* **estar unidos como los dedos de la mano,** to be as thick as thieves

**deducción** /deðuk'θion; deðuk'sion/ *f,* inference, deduction; derivation; (*Mus. Math.*) progression

**deduciente** /deðu'θiente; deðu'siente/ *a* deductive

**deducir** /deðu'θir; deðu'sir/ *vt irr* to deduce, infer; deduct, subtract; *Law.* plead, allege in pleading. See **conducir**

**deductivo** /deðuk'tiβo/ *a* deductive

**defecación** /defeka'θion; defeka'sion/ *f,* purification; defecation

**defecar** /defe'kar/ *vt* to clarify, purify; defecate

**defección** /defek'θion; defek'sion/ *f,* defection

**defectible** /defek'tiβle/ *a* deficient; imperfect

**defecto** /de'fekto/ *m,* defect, fault; imperfection

**defectuoso** /defek'tuoso/ *a* imperfect, defective

**defender** /defen'der/ *vt irr* to defend, protect; maintain, uphold; forbid; hinder; —*vr* defend oneself. See **entender**

**defendible** /defen'diβle/ *a* defensible

**defensa** /de'fensa/ *f,* defence; protection; (hockey) pad; *Law.* defense; *Sports.* back; *pl Mil.* defenses; *Naut.* fenders. **d. química,** chemical warfare. *Mil.* **defensas costeras,** coastal defenses

**defensiva** /defen'siβa/ *f,* defensive

**defensivo** /defen'siβo/ *a* defensive. *m,* safeguard

**defensor** /defen'sor/ **(-ra)** *n* defender. *m, Law.* counsel for the defense

**deferencia** /defe'renθia; deferensia/ *f,* deference

**deferente** /defe'rente/ *a* deferential

**deferir** /defe'rir/ *vi irr* to defer, yield; —*vt* delegate —*Pres. Indic.* **defiero, defieres, defiere, defieren.** *Pres. Part.* **defiriendo.** *Preterite* **defirió, defirieron.** *Pres. Subjunc.* **defiera,** etc —*Imperf. Subjunc.* **defiriese,** etc.

**deficiencia** /defi'θienθia; defi'siensia/ *f,* defect, deficiency

**deficiente** /defi'θiente; defi'siente/ *a* faulty, deficient

**déficit** /'defiθit; 'defisit/ *m,* deficit

**definible** /defi'niβle/ *a* definable

**definición** /defini'θion; defini'sion/ *f,* definition; decision

**definido** /defi'niðo/ *a* definite

**definir** /defi'nir/ *vt* to define; decide

**definitivo** /defini'tiβo/ *a* definitive. **en definitiva,** definitely; in short

**deflagración** /deflagra'θion; deflagra'sion/ *f,* sudden blaze, deflagration

**deflagrador** /deflagra'ðor/ *m, Elec.* deflagrator

**deflagrar** /defla'grar/ *vi* to go up in flames

**deformación** /deforma'θion; deforma'sion/ *f,* deformation; *Radio.* distortion

**deformado** /defor'maðo/ *a* deformed; misshapen

**deformador** /deforma'ðor/ **(-ra)** *a* disfiguring, deforming —*n* disfigurer

**deformar** /defor'mar/ *vt* to deform; —*vr* become deformed or misshapen

**deformidad** /deformi'ðað/ *f,* deformity; gross error; vice, lapse

**defraudación** /defrauða'θion; defrauða'sion/ *f,* defrauding; deceit

**defraudador** /defrauða'ðor/ **(-ra)** *n* defrauder

**defraudar** /defrau'ðar/ *vt* to defraud; usurp; frustrate, disappoint; impede

**defuera** /de'fuera/ *adv* outwardly, externally

**defunción** /defun'θion; defun'sion/ *f,* decease, death

**degeneración** /dehenera'θion; dehenera'sion/ *f,* degeneration. **d. grasienta,** fatty degeneration

**degenerado** /dehene'raðo/ **(-da)** *a* and *n* degenerate

**degenerar** /dehene'rar/ *vi* to degenerate

**deglución** /deglu'θion; deglu'sion/ *f,* swallowing, deglutition

**deglutir** /deglu'tir/ *vi* and *vt* to swallow

**degollación** /degoʎa'θion; degoya'sion/ *f,* decollation, throat slitting

**degolladero** /dego&#x28E;a'&#x00F0;ero; degoya'&#x00F0;ero/ *m,* slaughterhouse; execution block

**degollador** /dego&#x28E;a'a&#x00F0;or; degoya'&#x00F0;or/ *m,* executioner

**degolladura** /dego&#x28E;a'&#x00F0;ura; degoya'&#x00F0;ura/ *f,* slitting of the throat

**degollar** /dego'&#x28E;ar; dego'yar/ *vt irr* to behead; slit the throat; *Fig.* destroy; (*Fig. Theat.*) murder; *Inf.* annoy, bore —*Pres. Indic.* **degüello, degüellas, degüella, degüellan.** *Pres. Subjunc.* **degüelle, degüelles, degüelle, degüellen**

**degollina** /dego'&#x28E;ina; dego'yina/ *f, Inf.* massacre

**degradación** /degra&#x00F0;a'&#x03B8;ion; degra&#x00F0;a'sion/ *f,* degradation; humiliation, debasement; *Art.* gradation, shading (colors, light)

**degradante** /degra'&#x00F0;ante/ *a* degrading, humiliating

**degradar** /degra'&#x00F0;ar/ *vt* to degrade; humiliate; *Art.* grade, blend; —*vr* degrade oneself

**degüello** /de'gue&#x28E;o; de'gueyo/ *m,* decollation; havoc, destruction; haft (of swords, etc.)

**degustación** /degusta'&#x03B8;ion; degusta'sion/ *f,* act of tasting or sampling

**dehesa** /de'esa/ *f,* pasture, meadow

**deicida** /dei'&#x03B8;i&#x00F0;a; dei'si&#x00F0;a/ *mf* deicide (person)

**deicidio** /dei'&#x03B8;i&#x00F0;io; dei'si&#x00F0;io/ *m,* deicide (act)

**deidad** /dei'&#x00F0;a&#x00F0;/ *f,* divinity; deity, idol

**deificación** /deifika'&#x03B8;ion; deifika'sion/ *f,* deification

**deificar** /deifi'kar/ *vt* to deify; overpraise

**deífico** /de'ifiko/ *a* deific, divine

**deísmo** /de'ismo/ *m,* Deism

**deísta** /de'ista/ *mf* deist —*a* deistic

**dejación** /deha'&#x03B8;ion; deha'sion/ *f,* relinquishment, abandonment

**dejadez** /deha'&#x00F0;e&#x03B8;; deha'&#x00F0;es/ *f,* slovenliness; neglect; laziness; carelessness

**dejado** /de'ha&#x00F0;o/ *a* lazy; neglectful; slovenly; discouraged, depressed

**dejamiento** /deha'miento/ *m,* relinquishment; negligence; lowness of spirits; indifference

**dejar** /de'har/ *vt* to leave; omit, forget, allow, permit (e.g. *Déjame salir,* Let me go out); yield, produce, entrust, leave in charge; believe, consider; intend, appoint; cease, stop; forsake, desert; renounce, relinquish; bequeath; give away; —*vr* neglect oneself; engage (in); lay oneself open to, allow oneself; abandon oneself (to), fling oneself (into); *Fig.* be depressed or languid; (*with de* + *infin.*) cease to (e.g. *Se dejó de hacerlo,* He stopped doing it); —*vi* (*with de* + *adjective*) be none the less, be rather (e.g. *No deja de ser sorprendente,* It isn't any the less surprising). **d. aparte,** to omit, leave out. **d. atrás,** to overtake; *Fig.* leave behind, beat. **d. caer,** to let fall. **dejarse caer,** to let oneself fall; *Fig. Inf.* to let fall, utter; appear suddenly. **dejarse vencer,** to give way, allow oneself to be persuaded

**dejo** /'deho/ *m,* relinquishment; end; accent (of persons); savor, after-taste; negligence; *Fig.* touch, flavor

**del** /del/ contraction of **de + el,** (*def. art. m.*) of the (e.g. *del perro,* of the dog)

**delación** /dela'&#x03B8;ion; dela'sion/ *f,* accusation, denunciation

**delantal** /delan'tal/ *m,* apron

**delante** /de'lante/ *adv* before, in front, in the presence (of)

**delantera** /delan'tera/ *f,* front, front portion; *Theat.* orchestra stall, front seat; front (of garment). **tomar la d.,** to take the lead; *Inf.* steal a march on

**delantero** /delan'tero/ *a* fore, front. *m,* postilion; *Sports.* forward. **d. centro,** *Sports.* centerforward

**delatable** /dela'ta&#x03B2;le/ *a* impeachable; blameworthy

**delatar** /dela'tar/ *vt* to inform against, accuse; impeach

**delator** /dela'tor/ **(-ra)** *a* denunciatory, accusing —*n* denouncer, informer

**delectación** /delekta'&#x03B8;ion; delekta'sion/ *f,* delectation, pleasure

**delegación** /delega'&#x03B8;ion; delega'sion/ *f,* delegation; proxy

**delegado** /dele'ga&#x00F0;o/ **(-da)** *n* delegate; proxy

**delegar** /dele'gar/ *vt* to delegate

**deleitable** /delei'ta&#x03B2;le/ *a* delightful

**deleitar** /delei'tar/ *vt* to delight, charm, please; —*vr* delight (in)

**deleite** /de'leite/ *m,* delight; pleasure

**deleitoso** /delei'toso/ *a* delightful, pleasant

**deletéreo** /dele'tereo/ *a* deleterious; poisonous

**deletrear** /deletre'ar/ *vi* to spell; *Fig.* decipher

**deletreo** /dele'treo/ *m,* spelling; *Fig.* decipherment

**deleznable** /dele&#x03B8;'na&#x03B2;le; deles'na&#x03B2;le/ *a* fragile, brittle; slippery; brief, fugitive, transitory

**délfico** /'delfiko/ *a* Delphic

**delfín** /del'fin/ *m,* (*Ichth. Astron.*) dolphin; dauphin

**delfina** /del'fina/ *f,* dauphiness

**Delfos** /'delfos/ Delphi

**delgadez** /delga'&#x00F0;e&#x03B8;; delga&#x00F0;es/ *f,* thinness; slenderness, leanness

**delgado** /del'ga&#x00F0;o/ *a* slim; thin; scanty; poor (of land); sharp, perspicacious

**delgaducho** /delga'&#x00F0;ut&#x0283;o/ *a* slenderish, somewhat thin

**deliberación** /deli&#x03B2;era'&#x03B8;ion; deli&#x03B2;era'sion/ *f,* deliberation; consideration; discussion

**deliberadamente** /deli&#x03B2;era&#x00F0;a'mente/ *adv* deliberately

**deliberante** /deli&#x03B2;e'rante/ *a* deliberative, considering

**deliberar** /deli&#x03B2;e'rar/ *vi* to deliberate, consider; —*vt* decide after reflection; discuss

**delicadez** /delika'&#x00F0;e&#x03B8;; delika'&#x00F0;es/ *f,* weakness; delicacy; hypersensitiveness; amiability

**delicadeza** /delika'&#x00F0;e&#x03B8;a; delika'&#x00F0;esa/ *f,* delicacy; fastidiousness; refinement, subtlety; sensitiveness; consideration, tact; scrupulosity

**delicado** /deli'ka&#x00F0;o/ *a* courteous; tactful; fastidious; weak, delicate; fragile, perishable; delicious, tasty; exquisite; difficult, embarrassing; refined, discriminating, sensitive; scrupulous; subtle; hypersensitive, suspicious. **d. de salud,** in poor health

**delicia** /deli'&#x03B8;ia; deli'sia/ *f,* pleasure, delight; sensual pleasure

**delicioso** /deli'&#x03B8;ioso; deli'sioso/ *a* delightful, agreeable, pleasant

**delimitar** /delimi'tar/ *vt* to delimit

**delincuencia** /delin'kuen&#x03B8;ia; delin'kuensia/ *f,* delinquency

**delincuente** /delin'kuente/ *a* and *mf* delinquent

**delineación** /delinea'&#x03B8;ion; delinea'sion/ *f,* delineation; diagram, design, plan

**delineador** /delinea'&#x00F0;or/ **(-ra),** *n* **delineante** *m,* draftsman, designer

**delineamiento** /delinea'miento/ *m,* delineation

**delinear** /deline'ar/ *vt* to delineate; sketch; describe

**delinquimiento** /delinki'miento/ *m,* delinquency; crime

**delinquir** /delin'kir/ *vi irr* to commit a crime —*Pres. Indic.* **delinco.** *Pres. Subjunc.* **delinca**

**deliquio** /deli'kio/ *m,* faint, swoon

**delirante** /deli'rante/ *a* delirious

**delirar** /deli'rar/ *vi* to be delirious; act or speak foolishly

**delirio** /de'lirio/ *m,* delirium; frenzy; foolishness, nonsense. **d. de grandezas,** illusions of grandeur

**delito** /de'lito/ *m,* delict, offense against the law, crime

**delta** /'delta/ *f,* fourth letter of Greek alphabet. *m,* delta (of a river)

**delusorio** /delu'sorio/ *a* deceptive

**demacración** /demakra'&#x03B8;ion; demakrasion/ *f,* emaciation

**demacrado** /dema'kra&#x00F0;o/ *a* emaciated

**demacrarse** /dema'krarse/ *vr* to become emaciated

**demagogia** /dema'gohia/ *f,* demagogy

**demagógico** /dema'gohiko/ *a* demagogic

**demagogo** /dema'gogo/ **(-ga)** *n* demagogue

**demanda** /de'manda/ *f,* petition, request; collecting (for charity); collecting box; want ad; question; search; undertaking; *Com.* order or demand; *Law.* claim

**demandadero** /demanda'&#x00F0;ero/ **(-ra)** *n* convent or prison messenger; errandboy

**demandado** /deman'da&#x00F0;o/ **(-da)** *n Law.* defendant; *Law.* respondent

**demandante** /deman'dante/ *mf Law.* plaintiff

**demandar** /deman'dar/ *vt* to ask, request; desire, yearn for; question; *Law.* claim

**demarcación** /demarka'θion; demarka'sion/ *f,* demarcation, limit

**demarcar** /demar'kar/ *vt* to fix boundaries, demarcate

**demás** /de'mas/ *a* other —*adv* besides. **lo d.,** the rest. **los ( las) d.,** the others. **por d.,** useless; superfluous. **por lo d.,** otherwise; for the rest

**demasía** /dema'sia/ *f,* excess; daring; insolence; guilt, crime. **en d.,** excessively

**demasiado** /dema'siaðo/ *a* too; too many; too much —*adv* excessively

**demencia** /de'menθia; de'mensia/ *f,* madness, insanity

**demencial** /demen'θial; demen'sial/ *a* insane

**dementar** /demen'tar/ *vt* to render insane; —*vr* become insane

**demente** /de'mente/ *a* insane, mad. *mf* lunatic

**demérito** /de'merito/ *m,* demerit, fault

**demeritorio** /demeri'torio/ *a* undeserving, without merit

**demisión** /demi'sion/ *f,* submission, acquiescence

**democracia** /demo'kraθia; demo'krasia/ *f,* democracy

**demócrata** /de'mokrata/ *mf* democrat

**democrático** /demo'kratiko/ *a* democratic

**democratizar** /demokrati'θar; demokrati'sar/ *vt* to make democratic

**demoledor** /demole'ðor/ **(-ra)** *a* demolition —*n* demolisher

**demoler** /demo'ler/ *vt irr* to demolish, destroy, dismantle. See **moler**

**demolición** /demoli'θion; demoli'sion/ *f,* demolition, destruction, dismantling

**demoníaco** /demo'niako/ *a* devilish; possessed by a demon

**demonio** /de'monio/ *m,* devil; evil spirit —*interj* **¡Demonios!** Deuce take it! *Inf.* **tener el d. en el cuerpo,** to be always on the move, be very energetic

**demontre** /de'montre/ *m, Inf.* devil

**demora** /de'mora/ *f,* delay; *Naut.* bearing; *Com.* demurrage

**demorar** /demo'rar/ *vt* to delay; —*vi* stay, remain, tarry; *Naut.* bear

**demostrable** /demos'traβle/ *a* demonstrable

**demostración** /demostra'θion; demostra'sion/ *f,* demonstration; proof

**demostrador** /demostra'ðor/ **(-ra)** *a* demonstrating —*n* demonstrator

**demostrar** /demos'trar/ *vt irr* to demonstrate, explain; prove; teach. See **mostrar**

**demostrativo** /demostra'tiβo/ *a* demonstrative. *Gram.* **pronombre d.,** demonstrative pronoun

**demudación** /demuða'θion; demuða'sion/ *f,* change; alteration

**demudar** /demu'ðar/ *vt* to change, vary; alter, transform; —*vr* change suddenly (color, facial expression, etc.); grow angry

**denario** /de'nario/ *a* denary. *m,* denarius

**denegación** /denega'θion; denega'sion/ *f,* denial; refusal

**denegar** /dene'gar/ *vt irr* to deny, refuse. See **acertar**

**dengoso** /deŋ'goso/ *a* fastidious, finicky

**dengue** /'deŋgue/ *m,* affectation, faddiness, fastidiousness

**denigrable** /deni'graβle/ *a* odious

**denigración** /denigra'θion; denigra'sion/ *f,* slander, defamation (of character)

**denigrante** /deni'grante/ *a* slanderous

**denigrar** /deni'grar/ *vt* to slander; insult

**denodado** /deno'ðaðo/ *a* valiant, daring

**denominación** /denomina'θion; denomina'sion/ *f,* denomination

**denominador** /denomina'ðor/ *a* denominating *m, Math.* denominator

**denominar** /denomi'nar/ *vt* to name, designate

**denostada** /denos'taða/ *f,* insult

**denostar** /denos'tar/ *vt irr* to revile, insult. See **acordar**

**denotar** /deno'tar/ *vt* to denote, indicate

**densidad** /densi'ðað/ *f,* density; closeness, denseness; *Phys.* specific gravity; obscurity

**denso** /'denso/ *a* compact, close; thick, dense; crowded; dark, confused

**dentado** /den'taðo/ *a* toothed; pronged; dentate

**dentadura** /denta'ðura/ *f,* set of teeth (real or false). **d. de rumiante,** teeth like an ox. **d. postiza,** false teeth

**dental** /den'tal/ *a* dental

**dentar** /den'tar/ *vt irr* to provide with teeth, prongs, etc.; —*vi* cut teeth. See **sentar**

**dentellada** /dente'ʎaða; dente'yaða/ *f,* gnashing or chattering of teeth; bite; toothmark

**dentellar** /dente'ʎar; dente'yar/ *vt* to chatter, grind, gnash (teeth)

**dentellear** /denteʎe'ar; denteye'ar/ *vt* to bite, sink the teeth into

**dentera** /den'tera/ *f,* (**dar**) to set one's teeth on edge; *Fig. Inf.* make one's mouth water

**dentición** /denti'θion; denti'sion/ *f,* teething, dentition

**dentífrico** /den'tifriko/ *m,* toothpaste

**dentista** /den'tista/ *mf* dentist

**dentro** /'dentro/ *adv* within, inside. **d. de poco,** soon, shortly. **por d.,** from the inside; on the inside

**dentudo** /den'tuðo/ *a* having large teeth

**denudación** /denuða'θion; denuða'sion/ *f,* denudation; *Geol.* erosion

**denudar** /denu'ðar/ *vt* to denude

**denuedo** /de'nueðo/ *m,* courage, daring

**denuesto** /de'nuesto/ *m,* insult

**denuncia** /de'nunθia; de'nunsia/ *f,* denunciation, accusation

**denunciante** /denun'θiante; denun'siante/ *a* accusing. *mf Law.* denouncer

**denunciar** /denun'θiar; denun'siar/ *vt* to give notice, inform; herald, presage; declare, proclaim; denounce; *Law.* accuse

**denunciatorio** /denunθia'torio; denunsia'torio/ *a* denunciatory

**deparar** /depa'rar/ *vt* to furnish, offer, present

**departamental** /departamen'tal/ *a* departmental

**departamento** /departa'mento/ *m,* department; compartment (railway); branch, section. **d. de lactantes,** nursery (in a hospital)

**departir** /depar'tir/ *vi* to converse

**depauperación** /depaupera'θion; depaupera'sion/ *f,* impoverishment; *Med.* emaciation

**depauperar** /depaupe'rar/ *vt* to impoverish; —*vr Med.* grow weak, become emaciated

**dependencia** /depen'denθia; depen'densia/ *f,* dependence; subordination; dependency; *Com.* branch; firm, agency; business affair; kinship or affinity; *pl Archit.* offices; *Com.* staff; accessories

**depender** /depen'der/ *vi* (*with de*) to be subordinate to; depend on; be dependent on, need

**dependiente** /depen'diente/ **(-ta)** *a* and *n* dependent, subordinate. *m,* employee; shop assistant

**depilación** /depila'θion; depila'sion/ *f,* depilation

**depilar** /depi'lar/ *vt* to depilate

**depilatorio** /depila'torio/ *m,* depilatory

**deplorar** /deplo'rar/ *vt* to deplore, lament

**deponente** /depo'nente/ *a* deposing; affirming. *mf* deponent. *Gram.* **verbo d.,** deponent verb

**deponer** /depo'ner/ *vt irr* to lay aside; depose, oust; affirm, testify; remove, take from its place; *Law.* depose. See **poner**

**deportación** /deporta'θion; deporta'sion/ *f,* deportation

**deportar** /depor'tar/ *vt* to exile; deport

**deporte** /de'porte/ *m,* sport; *pl* games. **d. de vela,** sailing; boating

**deportismo** /depor'tismo/ *m,* sport

**deportista** /depor'tista/ *a* sporting. *mf* sportsman (sportswoman)

**deportivo** /depor'tiβo/ *a* sporting

**deposición** /deposi'θion; deposi'sion/ *f,* affirmation, statement; *Law.* deposition; degradation, removal (from office, etc.)

**depositador** /deposita'ðor/ **(-ra)** *a* depositing —*n* depositor

**depositar** /deposi'tar/ *vt* to deposit; place in safety; entrust; lay aside, put away; —*vr Chem.* settle

**depositaría** /deposita'ria/ f, depository; trusteeship; accounts office

**depositario** /deposi'tario/ **(-ia)** a pertaining to a depository —n depositary, trustee

**depósito** /de'posito/ m, deposit; depository; Com. depot, warehouse; Chem. deposit, sediment; tank, reservoir; Mil. depot. **d. de bencina, d. de gasolina,** gas tank; service station. **d. de municiones,** munitions dump. Com. **en d.,** in bond. **Queda hecho el d. que marca la ley,** Copyright reserved

**depravación** /depraβa'θion; depraβa'sion/ f, depravity

**depravar** /depra'βar/ vt to deprave, corrupt; —vr become depraved

**deprecación** /depreka'θion; depreka'sion/ f, supplication, petition; deprecation

**deprecar** /depre'kar/ vt to supplicate, petition; deprecate

**depreciación** /depreθia'θion; depresia'sion/ f, depreciation, fall in value

**depreciar** /depre'θiar; depre'siar/ vt to depreciate, reduce the value (of)

**depredación** /depreða'θion; depreða'sion/ f, depredation, robbery

**depredar** /depre'ðar/ vt to pillage

**depresión** /depre'sion/ f, depression. **d. nerviosa,** nervous breakdown

**depresivo** /depre'siβo/ a depressive; humiliating

**deprimir** /depri'mir/ vt to depress, compress, press down; depreciate, belittle; —vr be compressed

**depuración** /depura'θion; depura'sion/ f, cleansing, purification; Polit. purge

**depurar** /depu'rar/ vt to cleanse, purify; Polit. purge

**derecha** /de'retʃa/ f, right hand; Polit. (gen. pl) Right. Mil. **¡D.!** Right Turn! **a la d.,** on the right

**derechamente** /deretʃa'mente/ adv straight, directly; prudently, justly; openly, frankly

**derechera** /dere'tʃera/ f, direct road

**derechista** /dere'tʃista/ mf Polit. rightist

**derecho** /de'retʃo/ a straight; upright; right (not left); just, reasonable; Sports. forehand —adv straightaway. m, right; law; just claim; privilege; justice, reason; exemption; right side (cloth, etc.); pl dues, taxes; fees. **d. a la vía,** right of way. **d. de apelación,** right to appeal. **d. de visita,** (international law) right of search. **derechos de aduana,** customhouse duties. **derechos de entrada,** import duties. **según d.,** according to law. **usar de su d.,** to exercise one's right

**derechura** /dere'tʃura/ f, directness, straightness; uprightness

**deriva** /de'riβa/ f, (Naut. Aer.) drift, leeway

**derivación** /deriβa'θion; deriβa'sion/ f, origin, derivation; inference, consequence; Gram. derivation

**derivar** /deri'βar/ vt to originate; Naut. drift; —vt conduct, lead; Gram. derive; Elec. tap

**derivativo** /deriβa'tiβo/ a derivative

**dermatitis** /derma'titis/ f, dermatitis

**dermatología** /dermatolo'hia/ f, dermatology

**dermatólogo** /derma'tologo/ m, dermatologist

**derogación** /deroga'θion; deroga'sion/ f, repeal, annulment; deterioration

**derogar** /dero'gar/ vt to annul, repeal; destroy, suppress

**derogatorio** /deroga'torio/ a Law. repealing

**derrama** /de'rrama/ f, apportionment of tax

**derramado** /derra'maðo/ a extravagant, wasteful

**derramamiento** /derrama'miento/ m, pouring out; spilling; scattering

**derramar** /derra'mar/ vt to pour out; spill; scatter; apportion (taxes); publish abroad, spread; —vr be scattered; overflow

**derrame** /de'rrame/ m, spilling; leakage; overflow; scattering; slope

**derredor** /derre'ðor/ m, circumference. **al** ( or **en**) **d.,** round about

**derrelicto** /derre'likto/ a abandoned; derelict. m, Naut. derelict

**derrengado** /derreŋ'gaðo/ a crooked; crippled

**derretimiento** /derreti'miento/ m, melting; thaw; liquefaction; Inf. burning passion

**derretir** /derre'tir/ vt irr to melt, liquefy; waste, dissi-

pate; —vr be very much in love; Inf. be susceptible (to love); Inf. long, be impatient. See **pedir**

**derribar** /derri'βar/ vt to demolish; knock down; fell; throw down; Aer. shoot down; throw (in wrestling); Fig. overthrow; demolish, explode (a myth); control (emotions); —vr fall down; prostrate oneself; throw oneself down. **d. el chapeo,** humorous to doff one's hat

**derribo** /de'rriβo/ m, demolition; debris, rubble; throw (in wrestling)

**derrocadero** /derroka'ðero/ m, rocky precipice

**derrocar** /derro'kar/ vt to throw down from a rock; demolish (buildings); overthrow, oust

**derrochador** /derrotʃa'ðor/ **(-ra)** a wasteful, extravagant —n spendthrift

**derrochar** /derro'tʃar/ vt to waste, squander

**derroche** /de'rrotʃe/ m, squandering

**derrota** /de'rrota/ f, road; route, path; Naut. course; Mil. defeat

**derrotar** /derro'tar/ vt to squander; destroy, harm; Mil. defeat; —vr Naut. drift, lose course

**derrotero** /derro'tero/ m, Naut. course; Naut. ship's itinerary; number of sea charts; means to an end, course of action

**derrotismo** /derro'tismo/ m, defeatism

**derrotista** /derro'tista/ mf defeatist

**derruir** /de'rruir/ vt irr to demolish (a building). See **huir**

**derrumbadero** /derrumba'ðero/ m, precipice; risk, danger

**derrumbamiento** /derrumba'miento/ m, landslide; collapse, downfall

**derrumbar** /derrum'bar/ vt to precipitate; —vr throw oneself down, collapse, tumble down (buildings, etc.)

**derrumbe** /de'rrumbe/ m, collapse; subsidence

**derviche** /der'βitʃe/ m, dervish

**desabarrancar** /desaβarran'kar/ vt to pull out of a ditch or rut; extricate (from a difficulty)

**desabillé** /desaβi'ʎe; desaβi'ye/ m, deshabille

**desabor** /desa'βor/ m, insipidity

**desabotonar** /desaβoto'nar/ vt to unbutton; —vi open (flowers)

**desabrido** /desa'βriðo/ a insipid, poor-tasting; inclement (weather); disagreeable; unsociable; homely, plain (woman)

**desabrigar** /desaβri'gar/ vt to uncover; leave without shelter

**desabrigo** /desa'βrigo/ m, want of clothing or shelter; poverty, destitution

**desabrimiento** /desaβri'miento/ m, insipidity; harshness, disagreeableness; melancholy, depression

**desabrir** /desa'βrir/ vt to give a bad taste (to food); annoy, trouble

**desabrochar** /desaβro'tʃar/ vt to unbutton, untie; open; —vr Inf. confide, open up

**desacatar** /desaka'tar/ vt to behave disrespectfully (towards); lack reverence

**desacato** /desa'kato/ m, irreverence; disrespect

**desacertado** /desaθer'taðo; desaser'taðo/ a wrong, erroneous; imprudent

**desacertar** /desaθer'tar; desaser'tar/ vi irr to be wrong; act imprudently. See **acertar**

**desacierto** /desa'θierto; desa'sierto/ m, mistake, miscalculation, blunder

**desacomodado** /desakomo'ðaðo/ a lacking means of subsistence; poor; unemployed (servants); troublesome

**desacomodar** /desakomo'ðar/ vt to incommode, make uncomfortable, inconvenience; dismiss, discharge

**desaconsejado** /desakonse'haðo/ a ill-advised

**desaconsejar** /desakonse'har/ vt to advise against, dissuade

**desacoplar** /desakop'lar/ vt to disconnect

**desacordar** /desakor'ðar/ vt irr Mus. to put out of tune; —vr (with de) forget. See **acordar**

**desacorde** /desa'korðe/ a discordant, inharmonious; Mus. out of tune

**desacostumbrado** /desakostum'braðo/ a unaccustomed; unusual

**desacostumbrar** /desakostum'brar/ *vt* to break of a habit

**desacotar** /desako'tar/ *vt* to remove (fences); refuse, deny; —*vi* withdraw (from agreement, etc.)

**desacreditar** /desakreði'tar/ *vt* to discredit

**desacuerdo** /desa'kuerðo/ *m*, disagreement, discord; mistake; forgetfulness; swoon, loss of consciousness

**desadeudar** /desaðeu'ðar/ *vt* to free from debt

**desadornar** /desaðor'nar/ *vt* to denude of ornaments

**desadorno** /desa'ðorno/ *m*, lack of ornaments; bareness

**desafecto** /desa'fekto/ *a* disaffected; hostile. *m*, disaffection

**desaferrar** /desafe'rrar/ *vt irr* to untie, unfasten; *Fig.* wean from; *Naut.* weigh anchor. See **acertar**

**desafiador** /desafia'ðor/ **(-ra)** *a* challenging —*n* challenger. *m*, duelist

**desafiar** /desa'fiar/ *vt* to challenge; compete with; oppose

**desafinar** /desafi'nar/ *vi Mus.* to go out of tune; *Fig. Inf.* speak out of turn

**desafío** /desa'fio/ *m*, challenge; competition; duel

**desaforado** /desafo'raðo/ *a* lawless; outrageous; enormous

**desaforar** /desafo'rar/ *vt* to infringe (laws, etc.); —*vr* be disorderly

**desaforrar** /desafo'rrar/ *vt* to remove the lining of or from

**desafortunado** /desafortu'naðo/ *a* unfortunate

**desafuero** /desa'fuero/ *m*, act of injustice; outrage, excess

**desagarrar** /desaga'rrar/ *vt Inf.* to release, loosen; unhook

**desagraciado** /desagra'θiaðo; desagra'siaðo/ *a* ugly, unsightly

**desagraciar** /desagra'θiar; desagra'siar/ *vt* to disfigure, make ugly

**desagradable** /desagra'ðaβle/ *a* disagreeable; unpleasant

**desagradar** /desagra'ðar/ *vi* to be disagreeable, displease (e.g. *Me desagrada su voz,* I find his voice unpleasant)

**desagradecer** /desagraðe'θer; desagraðe'ser/ *vt irr* to be ungrateful (for). See **conocer**

**desagradecido** /desagraðe'θiðo; desagraðe'siðo/ *a* ungrateful

**desagradecimiento** /desagraðeθi'miento; desagraðesimiento/ *m*, ingratitude

**desagrado** /desa'graðo/ *m*, displeasure, dislike, dissatisfaction

**desagraviar** /desagra'βiar/ *vt* to make amends, apologize; indemnify

**desagravio** /desa'graβio/ *m*, satisfaction, reparation; compensation

**desagregar** /desagre'gar/ **(se)** *vt* and *vr* to separate

**desaguadero** /desagua'ðero/ *m*, drain, waste pipe

**desaguar** /desa'guar/ *vt* to drain off; dissipate; —*vi* flow (into sea, etc.)

**desagüe** /de'sague/ *m*, drainage; outlet, drain; catchment

**desaguisado** /desagi'saðo/ *a* outrageous, lawless. *m*, offense, insult

**desahogado** /desao'gaðo/ *a* brazen, insolent; clear, unencumbered; in comfortable circumstances

**desahogar** /desao'gar/ *vt* to ease, relieve; —*vr* unburden oneself; recover (from illness, heat, etc.); get out of debt; speak one's mind

**desahogo** /desa'ogo/ *m*, relief, alleviation; ease; comfort, convenience; freedom, frankness; unburdening (of one's mind). *Inf.* **vivir con d.,** to be comfortably off

**desahuciar** /desau'θiar; desau'siar/ *vt* to banish all hope; give up, despair of the life of; put out (tenants). When the third syllable of this verb is stressed, it is spelled with **ú:** *Pres. Indic.* **desahúcio, desahúcias, desahúcia, desahúcian.** *Pres. Subj.* **desahúcie, desahúcies, desahúcie, desahúcien.** *Imperf.* **desahúcia, desahúcie, desahúcien**

**desahúcio** /desa'uθio; desa'usio/ *m*, ejection, dispossession (of tenants)

**desahumar** /desau'mar/ *vt* to clear of smoke

**desairado** /desai'raðo/ *a* unattractive, graceless, ugly; unsuccessful, crestfallen; slighted

**desairar** /desai'rar/ *vt* to disdain, slight, disregard; underrate (things)

**desaire** /des'aire/ *m*, gracelessness, ugliness; insult, slight

**desalabanza** /desala'βanθa; desala'βansa/ *f*, disparagement; criticism

**desalabar** /desala'βar/ *vt* to censure, disparage

**desalación** /desala'θion; desala'sion/ *f*, desalinization

**desalado** /desa'laðo/ *a* anxious, precipitate, hasty

**desalar** /desa'lar/ *vt* to remove the salt from; take off wings; —*vr* walk or run at great speed; long for, yearn

**desalentar** /desalen'tar/ *vt irr* to make breathing difficult (work, fatigue); discourage; —*vr* be depressed or sad. See **sentar**

**desaliento** /desa'liento/ *m*, depression, discouragement, dismay

**desalinear** /desaline'ar/ *vt* to throw out of the straight

**desaliñado** /desali'ɲaðo/ *a* slovenly; slipshod

**desaliñar** /desali'ɲar/ *vt* to disarrange, make untidy, crumple

**desaliño** /desa'liɲo/ *m*, untidiness, slovenliness; negligence, carelessness

**desalmado** /desal'maðo/ *a* soulless, conscienceless; cruel

**desalmamiento** /desalma'miento/ *m*, inhumanity, consciencelessness; cruelty

**desalmidonar** /desalmiðo'nar/ *vt* to remove starch from

**desalojamiento** /desaloha'miento/ *m*, dislodgement, ejection

**desalojar** /desalo'har/ *vt* to dislodge, remove, eject; —*vi* move out, remove

**desalquilado** /desalki'laðo/ *a* untenanted, vacant

**desalquilar** /desalki'lar/ *vt* to leave, or cause to leave, rented premises

**desalterar** /desalte'rar/ *vt* to soothe, calm

**desamar** /desa'mar/ *vt* to cease to love; hate

**desamarrar** /desama'rrar/ *vt* to untie; separate; *Naut.* unmoor

**desamor** /desa'mor/ *m*, indifference; lack of sentiment or affection; hatred

**desamotinarse** /desamoti'narse/ *vr* to cease from rebellion; submit

**desamparar** /desampa'rar/ *vt* to abandon, forsake; leave (a place)

**desamparo** /desam'paro/ *m*, desertion; need

**desamueblado** /desamue'βlaðo/ *a* unfurnished

**desamueblar** /desamue'βlar/ *vt* to empty of furniture

**desandar lo andado** /desan'dar lo an'daðo/ *vt irr* to retrace one's steps. See **andar**

**desangrar** /desaŋ'grar/ *vt Med.* to bleed; drain (lake, etc.); impoverish, bleed; —*vr* lose much blood

**desanidar** /desani'ðar/ *vi* to leave the nest; —*vt* eject, expel

**desanimado** /desani'maðo/ *a* downhearted; (of places) dull, quiet

**desanimar** /desani'mar/ *vt* to discourage, depress

**desanublar,** /desanu'βlar,/ *vt* **desanublarse** *vr* to clear up (weather)

**desanudar** /desanu'ðar/ *vt* to untie; disentangle

**desaojar** /desao'har/ *vt* to cure of the evil eye

**desapacibilidad** /desapaθiβili'ðað; desapasiβili'ðað/ *f*, disagreeableness, unpleasantness

**desapacible** /desapa'θiβle; desapa'siβle/ *a* disagreeable; unpleasant; unsociable

**desaparecer** /desapare'θer; desapare'ser/ *vt irr* to cause to disappear; —*vi* and *vr* disappear. See **conocer**

**desaparecido** /desapare'θiðo; desapare'siðo/ *a* late (deceased); *Mil.* missing

**desaparejar** /desapare'har/ *vt* to unharness

**desaparición** /desapari'θion; desapari'sion/ *f*, disappearance

**desapegar** /desape'gar/ *vt* to unstick, undo; —*vr* be indifferent, cast off a love or affection

**desapego** /desa'pego/ *m*, lack of affection or interest, coolness

**desapercibido** /desaperθi'βiðo; desapersi'βiðo/ a unnoticed; unprovided, unprepared

**desapercibimiento** /desaperθiβi'miento; desapersiβi'miento/ m, unpreparedness

**desapestar** /desapes'tar/ vt to disinfect

**desapiadado** /desapia'ðaðo/ a merciless

**desaplicación** /desaplika'θion; desaplika'sion/ f, laziness, lack of application; carelessness, negligence

**desaplicado** /desapli'kaðo/ a lazy; careless

**desapoderado** /desapoðe'raðo/ a precipitate, uncontrolled; furious, violent

**desapoderar** /desapoðe'rar/ vt to dispossess, rob; remove from office

**desapolillar** /desapoli'ʎar; desapoli'yar/ vt to free from moths; —vr Inf. take an airing

**desaposentar** /desaposen'tar/ vt to evict; drive away

**desapreciar** /desapre'θiar; desapre'siar/ vt to scorn

**desaprender** /desapren'der/ vt to unlearn

**desaprensivo** /desapren'siβo/ a unscrupulous

**desapretar** /desapre'tar/ (se) vt and vr irr to slacken. See **acertar**

**desaprisionar** /desaprisio'nar/ vt to release from prison

**desaprobación** /desaproβa'θion; desaproβa'sion/ f, disapproval

**desaprobar** /desapro'βar/ vt irr to disapprove; disagree with. See **probar**

**desapropiamiento** /desapropia'miento/ m, renunciation or transfer of property

**desapropiarse** /desapropi'arse/ vr to renounce or transfer (property)

**desaprovechado** /desaproβe'tʃaðo/ a unprofitable; backward; unintelligent

**desaprovechar** /desaproβe'tʃar/ vt to take no advantage of, waste; —vi Fig. lose ground, lose what one has gained

**desapuntar** /desapun'tar/ vt to unstitch; lose one's aim

**desarbolar** /desarβo'lar/ vt Naut. to unmast

**desarenar** /desare'nar/ vt to clear of sand

**desarmar** /desar'mar/ vt to disarm; dismantle, dismount; appease

**desarme** /de'sarme/ m, disarming; disarmament

**desarraigar** /desarrai'gar/ vt to pull up by root (plants); extirpate, suppress; eradicate (opinion, etc.); exile

**desarraigo** /desa'rraigo/ m, uprooting; extirpation; eradication; exile

**desarrebujar** /desarreβu'har/ vt to disentangle, uncover; explain

**desarreglado** /desarre'glaðo/ a disarranged; untidy; intemperate, immoderate

**desarreglar** /desarre'glar/ vt to disarrange

**desarreglo** /desa'rreglo/ m, disorder; disarrangement; irregularity

**desarrendar** /desarren'dar/ vt irr to unbridle a horse; end a tenancy or lease. See **recomendar**

**desarrollar** /desarro'ʎar; desarro'yar/ vt to unroll; increase, develop, grow, unfold; explain (theory); —vr develop, grow

**desarrollo** /desa'rroʎo; des'arroyo/ m, unrolling; development, growth; explanation

**desarropar** /desarro'par/ vt to uncover, remove the covers, etc. from

**desarrugar** /desarru'gar/ vt to take out wrinkles or creases

**desarticulación** /desartikula'θion; desartikula'sion/ f, disarticulation

**desarticular** /desartiku'lar/ vt to disarticulate; Mech. disconnect

**desaseado** /desase'aðo/ a dirty; unkempt, slovenly

**desaseo** /desa'seo/ m, dirtiness; slovenliness

**desasimiento** /desasi'miento/ m, loosening; liberality; disinterestedness; indifference, coldness

**desasir** /desa'sir/ vt irr to loosen, undo —vr disengage oneself. See **asir**

**desasnar** /desas'nar/ vt Inf. to instruct, educate, polish

**desasosegar** /desasose'gar/ vt irr to disturb, make anxious. See **cegar**

**desasosiego** /desaso'siego/ m, uneasiness, disquiet

**desastre** /de'sastre/ m, disaster, calamity

**desastroso** /desas'troso/ a unfortunate, calamitous

**desatacar** /desata'kar/ vt to unfasten, undo, unbutton

**desatadura** /desata'ðura/ f, untying

**desatar** /desa'tar/ vt to untie; melt, dissolve; elucidate, explain; —vr loosen the tongue; lose self control; lose all reserve; unbosom oneself

**desatascar** /desatas'kar/ vt to pull out of the mud; free from obstruction; extricate from difficulties

**desataviar** /desata'βiar/ vt to strip of ornaments

**desatavío** /desata'βio/ m, carelessness in dress, slovenliness

**desatención** /desaten'θion; desaten'sion/ f, inattention, abstraction; incivility

**desatender** /desaten'der/ vt irr to pay no attention to; disregard, ignore. See **entender**

**desatentado** /desaten'taðo/ a imprudent, ill-advised; excessive, immoderate

**desatento** /desa'tento/ a inattentive, abstracted; discourteous

**desatinado** /desati'naðo/ a foolish, imprudent, wild

**desatinar** /desati'nar/ vt to bewilder; —vi behave foolishly; lose one's bearings

**desatino** /desa'tino/ m, folly, foolishness, imprudence, rashness; blunder, faux pas, mistake

**desatracar** /desatra'kar/ vi Naut. to push off

**desatrancar** /desatran'kar/ vt to unbar the door; remove obstacles

**desaturdir** /desatur'ðir/ vt to rouse (from torpor, etc.)

**desautorizar** /desautori'θar; desautori'sar/ vt to remove from authority; discredit

**desavenencia** /desaβe'nenθia; desaβe'nensia/ f, disharmony, disagreement

**desavenido** /desaβe'niðo/ a disagreeing, discordant

**desavenir** /desaβe'nir/ vt irr to upset. See **venir**

**desaventajado** /desaβenta'haðo/ a disadvantageous; unfavorable, inferior

**desaviar** /desa'βiar/ vt to lead astray; deprive of a necessity; —vr lose one's way

**desavisado** /desaβi'saðo/ a unaware, unprepared

**desavisar** /desaβi'sar/ vt to take back one's previous advice

**desayunador** /desayuna'ðor/ m, breakfast nook

**desayunarse** /desayu'narse/ vr to have breakfast, eat breakfast

**desayuno** /desa'yuno/ m, breakfast

**desazón** /desa'θon; desa'son/ f, insipidity, lack of flavor; poorness (soil); anxiety, trouble; vexation

**desazonar** /desaθo'nar; desaso'nar/ vt to make insipid; make anxious, worry, vex; —vr feel out of sorts

**desbancar** /desβan'kar/ vt to break the bank (gambling); supplant

**desbandada** /desβan'daða/ f, dispersal, rout. **a la d.,** in confusion or disorder

**desbandarse** /desβan'darse/ vr to disband, retreat in disorder; Mil. desert

**desbaratado** /desβara'taðo/ a Inf. corrupt, vicious

**desbaratar** /desβara'tar/ vt to spoil, destroy; dissipate, waste; foil, thwart (a plot); Mil. rout; —vi talk foolishly; —vr go too far, behave badly

**desbarbado** /desβar'βaðo/ a beardless

**desbastar** /desβas'tar/ vt to plane, dress; polish, refine, civilize

**desbocado** /desβo'kaðo/ a (of tools) blunt; runaway (of a horse); Inf. foul-tongued

**desbocar** /desβo'kar/ vt to break the spout or neck (of jars, etc.); —vi run (into) (of streets, etc.); —vr bolt (horses); curse, swear

**desboquillar** /desβoki'ʎar; desβoki'yar/ vt to remove or break a stem or mouthpiece

**desbordamiento** /desβorða'miento/ m, overflowing, flood

**desbordarse** /desβor'ðarse/ vr to overflow; lose self-control. **d. en alabanzas para,** to heap praise on

**desbravar** /desβra'βar/ vt to break in (horses, etc.); —vi grow less savage; lose force, decrease

**desbrozar** /desβro'θar; desβro'sar/ vt to free of rubbish, clear up

**descabalgadura** /deskaβalga'ðura/ f, alighting (from horses, etc.)

**descabalgar** /deskaβal'gar/ *vi* to alight (from horse); —*vt* dismantle (gun)

**descabellado** /deskaβe'ʎaðo; deskaβe'yaðo/ *a* disheveled; ridiculous, foolish

**descabellar** /deskaβe'ʎar; deskaβe'yar/ *vt* to disarrange, ruffle (hair)

**descabezado** /deskaβe'θaðo; deskaβe'saðo/ *a* headless; rash, impetuous

**descabezar** /deskaβe'θar; deskaβe'sar/ *vt* to behead; cut the top off (trees, etc.); *Fig. Inf.* break the back of (work); —*vi* abut, join; —*vr* (*with con* or *en*) rack one's brains about

**descalabazarse** /deskalaβa'θarse; deskalaβa'sarse/ *vr Inf.* to rack one's brains

**descalabradura** /deskalaβra'ðura/ *f*, head wound or scar

**descalabrar** /deskala'βrar/ *vt* to wound in the head; wound; harm

**descalabro** /deska'laβro/ *m*, misfortune, mishap

**descalzar** /deskal'θar; deskal'sar/ *vt* to remove the shoes and stockings; undermine; —*vr* remove one's shoes and stockings; lose a shoe (horses)

**descalzo** /des'kalθo; des'kalso/ *a* barefoot

**descaminar** /deskami'nar/ *vt* to lead astray; pervert, corrupt

**descamisado** /deskami'saðo/ **(-da)** *a Inf.* shirtless; ragged, poor —*n Inf.* down and out, outcast; vagabond

**descansadero** /deskansa'ðero/ *m*, resting place

**descansado** /deskan'saðo/ *a* rested, refreshed; tranquil

**descansar** /deskan'sar/ *vi* to rest, repose oneself; have relief (from anxiety, etc.); sleep; *Agr.* lie fallow; sleep in death; (*with en*) trust, have confidence in; (*with sobre*) lean on or upon; —*vt* (*with sobre*) rest (a thing) on another. **¡Que en paz descanse!** May he rest in peace!

**descanso** /des'kanso/ *m*, rest, repose; relief (from care); landing of stairs; *Mech.* bench, support; *Mil.* stand easy

**descarado** /deska'raðo/ *a* impudent, brazen

**descararse** /deska'rarse/ *vr* to behave impudently

**descarbonizar** /deskarβoni'θar; deskarβoni'sar/ *vt* to decarbonize

**descarburación** /deskarβura'θion; deskarβura'sion/ *f*, decarbonization

**descarga** /des'karga/ *f*, unloading; *Naut.* discharge of cargo; *Elec.* discharge; *Mil.* volley. **d. cerrada**, dense volley, fusillade

**descargadero** /deskarga'ðero/ *m*, wharf

**descargador** /deskarga'ðor/ *m*, unloader, docker; *Elec.* discharger

**descargar** /deskar'gar/ *vt* to unload; *Mil.* fire; unload (fire-arms); *Elec.* discharge; rain (blows) upon; *Fig.* free, exonerate; —*vi* disembogue (of rivers); burst (clouds); —*vr* relinquish (employment); shirk responsibility; *Law.* clear oneself

**descargo** /des'kargo/ *m*, unloading; *Com.* acquittance; *Law.* answer to an impeachment

**descargue** /des'karge/ *m*, unloading

**descarnado** /deskar'naðo/ *a* fleshless; scraggy; spare, lean

**descarnador** /deskarna'ðor/ *m*, dental scraper; tanner's scraper

**descarnar** /deskar'nar/ *vt* to scrape off flesh; corrode; inspire indifference to earthly things

**descaro** /des'karo/ *m*, impudence

**descarriar** /deska'rriar/ *vt* to lead astray; —*vr* be lost, be separated (from others); *Fig.* go astray

**descarrilamiento** /deskarrila'miento/ *m*, derailment

**descarrilar** /deskarri'lar/ *vi* to run off the track, be derailed

**descarrío** /deska'rrio/ *m*, losing one's way

**descartar** /deskar'tar/ *vt* to put aside; —*vr* discard (cards); shirk, make excuses

**descarte** /des'karte/ *m*, discard (cards); excuse, pretext

**descascarar** /deskaska'rar/ *vt* to peel; shell; —*vr* peel off

**descendencia** /desθen'denθia; dessen'densia/ *f*, descendants, offspring; lineage, descent

**descender** /desθen'der; dessen'der/ *vi irr* to descend;

flow (liquids); (*with de*) descend from, derive from; —*vt* lower, let down. See **entender**

**descendiente** /desθen'diente; dessen'diente/ *mf* descendant, offspring —*a* descending

**descendimiento** /desθendi'miento; dessendi'miento/ *m*, descent

**descenso** /des'θenso; des'senso/ *m*, descent; lowering, letting down; degradation

**descentralización** /desθentraliθa'θion; dessentralisa'sion/ *f*, decentralization

**descentralizar** /desθentrali'θar; dessentrali'sar/ *vt* to decentralize

**desceñir** /desθe'ɲir; desse'ɲir/ **(se)** *vt* and *vr irr* to ungird, remove a girdle, etc. See **ceñir**

**descepar** /desθe'par; desse'par/ *vt* to tear up by the roots; *Fig.* extirpate

**descercado** /desθer'kaðo; desser'kaðo/ *a* unfenced, open

**descercar** /desθer'kar; desser'kar/ *vt* to pull down a wall or fence; *Mil.* raise a siege

**descerrajar** /desθerra'har; desserra'har/ *vt* to remove the locks (of doors, etc.)

**descifrable** /desθi'fraβle; dessi'fraβle/ *a* decipherable

**descifrador** /desθifra'ðor; dessifra'ðor/ *m*, decipherer, decoder

**descifrar** /desθi'frar; dessi'frar/ *vt* to decipher; decode

**descinchar** /desθin'tʃar; dessin'tʃar/ *vt* to loosen or remove girths (of horse)

**desclavar** /deskla'βar/ *vt* to remove nails; unnail, unfasten

**descoagular** /deskoagu'lar/ *vt* to liquefy, dissolve, melt

**descobijar** /deskoβi'har/ *vt* to uncover; undress

**descocado** /desko'kaðo/ *a Inf.* brazen, saucy

**descoco** /des'koko/ *m*, *Inf.* impudence

**descogollar** /deskogo'ʎar; deskogo'yar/ *vt* to prune a tree of shoots; remove hearts (of lettuces, etc.)

**descolar** /desko'lar/ *vt irr* to cut off or dock an animal's tail. See **colar**

**descolgar** /deskol'gar/ *vt irr* to unhang; lower; —*vr* lower oneself (by rope, etc.); come down, descend; *Inf.* come out (with), utter. See **volcar**

**descollar** /desko'ʎar; desko'yar/ *vi irr* to excel, be outstanding. See **degollar**

**descoloramiento** /deskolora'miento/ *m*, discoloration

**descolorar** /deskolo'rar/ *vt* to discolor; —*vr* be discolored

**descolorido** /deskolo'riðo/ *a* discolored; pale-colored; pallid

**descomedido** /deskome'ðiðo/ *a* excessive, disproportionate; rude

**descomedimiento** /deskomeði'miento/ *m*, disrespect, lack of moderation, rudeness

**descomedirse** /deskome'ðirse/ *vr irr* to be disrespectful or rude. See **pedir**

**descompasarse** /deskompa'sarse/ *vr* See **descomedirse**

**descomponer** /deskompo'ner/ *vt irr* to disorder, disarrange; *Chem.* decompose; unsettle; —*vr* go out of order; rot, putrefy; be ailing; lose one's temper. See **poner**

**descomposición** /deskomposi'θion; deskomposi'sion/ *f*, disorder, confusion; discomposure; *Chem.* decomposition; putrefaction

**descompostura** /deskompos'tura/ *f*, decomposition; slovenliness, dirtiness, untidiness; impudence, rudeness

**descompuesto** /deskom'puesto/ *a* rude, impudent

**descomunal** /deskomu'nal/ *a* enormous, extraordinary

**desconcertar** /deskonθer'tar; deskonser'tar/ *vt irr* to disorder, disarrange; dislocate (bones); disconcert, embarrass; —*vr* disagree; be impudent. See **acertar**

**desconcharse** /deskon'tʃarse/ *vr* to flake off, peel

**desconcierto** /deskon'θierto; deskon'sierto/ *m*, disorder, disarrangement; dislocation; embarrassment; disagreement; impudence

**desconectar** /deskonek'tar/ *vt* to disconnect; switch off

**desconfianza** /deskon'fianθa; deskon'fiansa/ *f,* lack of confidence

**desconfiar** /deskon'fiar/ *vi* to lack confidence

**desconformidad** /deskonformi'ðað/ *f,* See **disconformidad**

**desconformismo** /deskonfor'mismo/ *m,* nonconformism

**desconocer** /deskono'θer; deskono'ser/ *vt irr* to forget; be unaware of; deny, disown; pretend ignorance; not to understand (persons, etc.). See **conocer**

**desconocido** /deskono'θiðo; deskonos'iðo/ **(-da)** *a* unknown; ungrateful —*n* stranger; ingrate

**desconocimiento** /deskonoθi'miento; deskonosi'miento/ *m,* unawareness; ignorance; ingratitude

**desconsiderado** /deskonsiðe'raðo/ *a* inconsiderate; discourteous; rash

**desconsolación** /deskonsola'θion; deskonsola'sion/ *f,* affliction, trouble

**desconsolar** /deskonso'lar/ *vt irr* to afflict, make disconsolate; —*vr* grieve, despair. See **colar**

**desconsuelo** /deskon'suelo/ *m,* anguish, affliction, despair

**descontar** /deskon'tar/ *vt irr Com.* to make a discount; ignore, discount; take for granted, leave aside. See **contar**

**descontentadizo** /deskontenta'ðiθo; deskontenta'ðiso/ *a* discontented, difficult to please; fastidious, finicky

**descontentar** /deskonten'tar/ *vt* to displease; —*vr* be dissatisfied

**descontento** /deskon'tento/ *m,* discontent, dissatisfaction

**descontextualizar** /deskontekstuali'θar; deskontekstuali'sar/ *vt* to take out of context

**descontrolarse** /deskontro'larse/ *vr* to lose control, lose control of oneself.

**desconveniencia** /deskombe'nienθia; deskombe'niensia/ *f,* inconvenience, unsuitability, disagreement

**desconvenir** /deskombe'nir/ *vi irr* to disagree; be unsuitable, unsightly or odd (things). See **venir**

**descorazonamiento** /deskoraθona'miento; deskorasona'miento/ *m,* depression, despair

**descorazonar** /deskoraθo'nar; deskoraso'nar/ *vt* to tear out the heart; depress, discourage

**descorchar** /deskor'tʃar/ *vt* to take the cork from cork tree; draw a cork (bottles); force, break into (safes)

**descorrer** /desko'rrer/ *vt* to re-run (race, etc.); draw back (curtains, etc.); —*vi* run, flow (liquids)

**descorrimiento** /deskorri'miento/ *m,* overflow (liquids)

**descortés** /deskor'tes/ *a* impolite

**descortesía** /deskorte'sia/ *f,* impoliteness, discourtesy

**descortezadura** /deskorteθa'ðura; deskortesa'ðura/ *f,* peeling (of bark)

**descortezar** /deskorte'θar; deskorte'sar/ *vt* to decorticate; remove crust (bread, etc.); polish, civilize

**descoser** /desko'ser/ *vt Sew.* to unpick; —*vr* be unpicked; be indiscreet or tactless

**descosido** /desko'siðo/ *a* tactless, talkative; *Fig.* disjointed; desultory; unsewn. *m, Sew.* rent, hole

**descoyuntamiento** /deskoyunta'miento/ *m,* dislocation (bones); irritation, bore; ache, pain

**descoyuntar** /deskoyun'tar/ *vt* to dislocate (bones); bore, annoy; —*vr* be dislocated

**descrédito** /des'kreðito/ *m,* fall in value (things); discredit (persons)

**descreer** /deskre'er/ *vt irr* to disbelieve; depreciate, disparage (persons). See **creer**

**descreído** /deskre'iðo/ **(-da)** *a* unbelieving —*n* unbeliever; infidel

**describir** /deskri'βir/ *vt* to describe; outline, sketch —*Past Part.* **descrito**

**descripción** /deskrip'θion; deskrip'sion/ *f,* description; *Law.* inventory

**descriptible** /deskrip'tiβle/ *a* describable

**descriptivo** /deskrip'tiβo/ *a* descriptive

**descuajar** /deskua'har/ *vt* to liquefy; *Inf.* discourage; *Agr.* pull up by the root

**descuartizar** /deskuarti'θar; deskuarti'sar/ *vt* to quarter; joint (meat); *Inf.* carve, cut into pieces, break up

**descubierto** /desku'βierto/ *a* bareheaded; exposed.

*m,* deficit. **al d.,** openly; in the open, without shelter. **girar en d.,** to overdraw (a bank account)

**descubridero** /deskuβri'ðero/ *m,* viewpoint, lookout

**descubridor** /deskuβri'ðor/ **(-ra)** *n* discoverer; inventor; explorer. *m, Mil.* scout

**descubrimiento** /deskuβri'miento/ *m,* find; discovery; revelation; newly discovered territory

**descubrir** /desku'βrir/ *vt* to reveal; show; discover; learn; unveil (memorials, etc.); —*vr* remove one's hat; show oneself, reveal one's whereabouts —*Past Part.* **descubierto**

**descuello** /des'kueʎo; des'kueyo/ *m,* extra height; *Fig.* pre-eminence; arrogance

**descuento** /des'kuento/ *m,* reduction; *Com.* rebate, discount

**descuidado** /deskui'ðaðo/ *a* negligent; careless; untidy; unprepared

**descuidar** /deskui'ðar/ *vt* to relieve (of responsibility, etc.); distract, occupy (attention, etc.); —*vi* and *vr* be careless; —*vr* (*with de* or *en*) neglect

**descuido** /des'kuiðo/ *m,* carelessness, negligence; oversight, mistake; incivility; forgetfulness; shameful act

**desde** /'desðe/ *prep* since, from (time or space); after (e.g. *d. hoy,* from today). **d. la ventana,** from the window. **d. allá,** from the other world. **d. aquella época,** since that time

**desdecir** /desðe'θir; desðe'sir/ *vi irr* (*with de*) to degenerate, be less good than; be discordant, clash; be unworthy of; —*vr* unsay one's words, retract. See **decir**

**desdén** /des'ðen/ *m,* indifference, coldness; disdain, scorn

**desdentado** /desðen'taðo/ *a* toothless; *Zool.* edentate

**desdentar** /desðen'tar/ *vt* to remove teeth

**desdeñar** /desðe'ɲar/ *vt* to scorn; —*vr* (*with de*) dislike, be reluctant

**desdeñoso** /desðe'ɲoso/ *a* disdainful, scornful

**desdevanar** /desðeβa'nar/ *vt* to unwind thread, etc.

**desdibujado** /desðiβu'haðo/ *a* badly drawn; blurred, confused

**desdicha** /des'ðitʃa/ *f,* misfortune; extreme poverty, misery. **por d.,** unfortunately

**desdichado** /desði'tʃaðo/ *a* unfortunate; *Inf.* timid, weak-kneed

**desdicharse** /desði'tʃarse/ *vr* to bewail one's fate

**desdinerarse una fortuna** /desðine'rarse 'una for'tuna/ *vr* to spend a fortune

**desdoblar** /desðo'βlar/ *vt* to unfold

**desdorar** /desðo'rar/ *vt* to remove the gilt; *Fig.* tarnish, sully

**desdoro** /des'ðoro/ *m,* discredit, dishonor

**deseable** /dese'aβle/ *a* desirable

**desear** /dese'ar/ *vt* to desire; yearn or long for

**desecar** /dese'kar/ *vt* to dry; —*vr* be desiccated

**desechar** /dese'tʃar/ *vt* to reject, refuse; scorn; cast out, expel; put away (thoughts, etc.); cast off (old clothes); turn (key); give up

**desecho** /de'setʃo/ *m,* residue, rest, remains; cast-off; scorn

**desembalar** /desemba'lar/ *vt* to unpack

**desembanastar** /desembana'star/ *vt* to take out of a basket; *Inf.* unsheath (sword); —*vr* break loose (animals); *Inf.* get out, alight

**desembarazar** /desembara'θar; desembara'sar/ *vt* to clear of obstruction; disembarrass, free; vacate; —*vr* *Fig.* rid oneself of obstacles

**desembarazo** /desemba'raθo; desemba'raso/ *m,* freedom, insouciance, naturalness

**desembarcadero** /desembarka'ðero/ *m,* landing-stage

**desembarcar** /desembar'kar/ *vt* to unload; —*vi* disembark; alight from vehicle

**desembarco** /desem'barko/ *m,* disembarkation, landing; staircase landing

**desembargar** /desembar'gar/ *vt* to free of obstacles or impediments; *Law.* remove an embargo

**desembargo** /desem'bargo/ *m, Law.* removal of an embargo

**desembarque** /desem'barke/ *m,* disembarkation, landing

**desembarrancar** /desembarran'kar/ *vt* and *vi Naut.* to refloat

**desembaular** /desembau'lar/ *vt* to unpack from a trunk; disinter, empty; *Inf.* unbosom oneself

**desembocadero** /desemboka'ðero/ *m,* exit, way out; mouth (rivers, etc.)

**desembocadura** /desemboka'ðura/ *f,* mouth (rivers, etc.); street opening

**desembocar** /desembo'kar/ *vi* (*with en*) to lead to, end in; flow into (rivers)

**desembolsar** /desembol'sar/ *vt* to take out of a purse; pay, spend

**desembolso** /desem'bolso/ *m,* disbursement; expenditure

**desemboscarse** /desembos'karse/ *vr* to get out of the wood; extricate oneself from an ambush

**desembozar** /desembo'θar; desembo'sar/ *vt* to unmuffle

**desembozo** /desem'boθo; desem'boso/ *m,* uncovering of the face

**desembragar** /desembra'gar/ *vt Mech.* to disengage (the clutch, etc.)

**desembravecer** /desembraβe'θer; desembraβe'ser/ *vt irr* to tame, domesticate. See **conocer**

**desembriagar** /desembria'gar/ (**se**) *vt* and *vr* to sober up (after a drinking bout)

**desembrollar** /desembro'ʎar; desembro'yar/ *vt Inf.* to disentangle, unravel

**desemejanza** /deseme'hanθa; deseme'hansa/ *f,* unlikeness

**desemejar** /deseme'har/ *vi* to be unlike; —*vt* disfigure, deform

**desempacar** /desempa'kar/ *vt* to unpack

**desempapelar** /desempape'lar/ *vt* to unwrap, remove the paper from; remove wallpaper

**desempaquetar** /desempake'tar/ *vt* to unpack

**desemparejar** /desempare'har/ *vt* to split (a pair); make unequal

**desemparentado** /desemparen'taðo/ *a* without relatives

**desempedrar** /desempe'ðrar/ *vt irr* to take up the flags (of a pavement). See **acertar**

**desempeñar** /desempe'ɲar/ *vt* to redeem (pledges); free from debt; fulfil (obligations, etc.); take out of pawn; hold, fill (an office); extricate (from difficulties, etc.); perform, carry out; *Theat.* act

**desempeño** /desempe'ɲo/ *m,* redemption of a pledge; fulfillment (of an obligation, etc.); performance, accomplishment; *Theat.* acting of a part

**desempolvar** /desempol'βar/ *vt* to free from dust, dust

**desenamorar** /desenamo'rar/ *vt* to kill the affection of; —*vr* fall out of love

**desencadenar** /desenkaðe'nar/ *vt* to unchain, unfetter; *Fig.* unleash, let loose; —*vr Fig.* break loose

**desencajamiento** /desenkaha'miento/ *m,* disjointedness, dislocation; ricketiness, broken-down appearance

**desencajar** /desenka'har/ *vt* to disconnect, disjoint; dislocate; —*vr* be out of joint; be contorted (of the face); be tired looking

**desencaje** /desen'kahe/ *m,* See **desencajamiento**

**desencallar** /desenka'ʎar; desenka'yar/ *vt Naut.* to float a grounded ship

**desencantar** /desenkan'tar/ *vt* to disenchant

**desencanto** /desen'kanto/ *m,* disenchantment; disillusionment

**desencerrar** /desenθe'rrar; desense'rrar/ *vt irr* to set at liberty; unlock; disclose, reveal. See **acertar**

**desenchufar** /desentʃu'far/ *vt* to disconnect, unplug (electric plugs, etc.)

**desenclavijar** /desenklaβi'har/ *vt* to remove the pegs or pins; disconnect, disjoint

**desencoger** /desenko'her/ *vt* to unfold, spread out; —*vr* grow bold

**desencolerizar** /desenkoleri'θar; desenkoleri'sar/ *vt* to placate; —*vr* lose one's anger, grow calm

**desenconar** /desenko'nar/ *vt* to reduce (inflammation); appease (anger, etc.); —*vr* become calm

**desencono** /desen'kono/ *m,* reduction of inflammation; appeasement (of anger, etc.)

**desencordelar** /desenkorðe'lar/ *vt* to untie the ropes (of), unstring

**desencorvar** /desenkor'βar/ *vt* to straighten (curves, etc.)

**desenfadado** /desenfa'ðaðo/ *a* expeditious; natural, at ease; gay; forward, bold; wide, spacious

**desenfadar** /desenfa'ðar/ *vt* to appease, make anger disappear

**desenfado** /desen'faðo/ *m,* freedom; ease; unconcern, frankness

**desenfardar** /desenfar'ðar/ *vt* to unpack bales

**desenfrailar** /desenfrai'lar/ *vi* to leave the cloister, become secularized; *Inf.* emancipate oneself

**desenfrenar** /desenfre'nar/ *vt* to unbridle (horses); —*vr* give rein to one's passions, etc.; break loose (storms, etc.)

**desenfreno** /desen'freno/ *m,* license, lasciviousness; complete freedom from restraint

**desengalanar** /deseŋgala'nar/ *vt* to strip of ornaments

**desenganchar** /deseŋgan'tʃar/ *vt* to unhook; uncouple; unfasten; unharness

**desengañador** /deseŋgaɲa'ðor/ *a* undeceiving

**desengañar** /deseŋga'ɲar/ *vt* to undeceive, disillusion

**desengaño** /deseŋ'gaɲo/ *m,* undeceiving, disabuse; disillusionment

**desengarzar** /deseŋgar'θar; deseŋgar'sar/ *vt* to loosen from its setting; unlink, unhook, unclasp

**desengastar** /deseŋgas'tar/ *vt* to remove from its setting (jewelry, etc.)

**desengrasar** /deseŋgra'sar/ *vt* to remove the grease from, clean; —*vi Inf.* grow thin

**desenlace** /desen'laθe; desen'lase/ *m,* loosening, untying; *Lit.* denouement, climax (of play, etc.)

**desenlazar** /desenla'θar; desenla'sar/ *vt* to untie, unloose; *Lit.* unravel (a plot)

**desenlosar** /desenlo'sar/ *vt* to remove flagstones

**desenmarañar** /desemara'ɲar/ *vt* to disentangle; *Fig.* straighten out

**desenmascarar** /desemaska'rar/ *vt* to remove the mask from; *Fig.* unmask

**desenmudecer** /desemuðe'θer; desemuðe'ser/ *vi irr* to be freed of a speech impediment; break silence, speak. See **conocer**

**desenojar** /deseno'har/ *vt* to soothe, appease; —*vr* distract oneself, amuse oneself

**desenojo** /dese'noho/ *m,* relenting, abatement of anger

**desenredar** /desenre'ðar/ *vt* to disentangle; *Fig.* set right; straighten out; —*vr* extricate oneself, get out of a difficulty

**desenredo** /desen'reðo/ *m,* disentanglement; *Lit.* climax

**desentablar** /desenta'βlar/ *vt* to tear up planks or boards; disorder, disrupt

**desentenderse** /desenten'derse/ *vr irr* (*with de*) to pretend to be ignorant of; take no part in. See **entender**

**desenterrador** /desenterra'ðor/ *m,* disinterrer, unearther

**desenterramiento** /desenterra'miento/ *m,* disinterment; *Fig.* unearthing, recollection

**desenterrar** /desente'rrar/ *vt irr* to unbury, disinter; rummage out; *Fig.* unearth, bring up, recall. See **acertar**

**desentoldar** /desentol'dar/ *vt* to take away an awning; *Fig.* strip of ornament

**desentonar** /desento'nar/ *vt* to humiliate; —*vi Mus.* be out of tune; speak rudely; —*vr* be inharmonious; raise the voice (anger, etc.), behave badly

**desentono** /desen'tono/ *m,* bad behavior, rudeness; *Mus.* discord; grating quality or harshness (of voice)

**desentorpecer** /desentorpe'θer; desentorpe'ser/ *vt irr* to restore feeling to (numbed limbs); free from torpor; —*vr* become bright and intelligent. See **conocer**

**desentramparse** /desentram'parse/ *vr Inf.* free oneself from debt

**desentrañar** /desentra'ɲar/ *vt* to disembowel; *Fig.* unravel, penetrate; —*vr* give away one's all

**desentronizar** /desentroni'θar; desentroni'sar/ *vt* to dethrone; dismiss from office

**desentumecer** /desentume'θer; desentume'ser/ *vt irr*

to free from numbness (limbs); —*vr* be restored to feeling (numb limbs). See **conocer**

**desenvainar** /desembai'nar/ *vt* to unsheath; *Inf.* reveal, bring into the open

**desenvoltura** /desembol'tura/ *f,* naturalness, ease, freedom; eloquence, facility (of speech); effrontery, audacity, shamelessness (especially in women)

**desenvolver** /desembol'βer/ *vt irr* to unroll; unfold; *Fig.* unravel, explain; *Fig.* develop, work out (theories, etc.); —*vr* unroll; unfold; lose one's timidity, blossom out; be over-bold; extricate oneself (from a difficulty). See **resolver**

**desenvuelto** /desem'buelto/ *a* natural, easy; impudent, bold

**deseo** /de'seo/ *m,* desire, will, wish

**deseoso** /dese'oso/ *a* desirous, wishful

**desequilibrar** /desekili'βrar/ **(se)** *vt* and *vr* to unbalance

**desequilibrio** /deseki'lβrio/ *m,* lack of balance; confusion, disorder; mental instability

**deserción** /deser'θion; deser'sion/ *f, Mil.* desertion. **d. estudiantil,** school dropout

**desertar** /deser'tar/ *vt Mil.* to desert; *Inf.* quit

**desertor** /deser'tor/ *m, Mil.* deserter; *Inf.* quitter

**deservicio** /deser'βiθio; deserβisio/ *m,* disservice

**desesperación** /desespera'θion; desespera'sion/ *f,* desperation, despair; frenzy, violence

**desesperado** /desespe'raðo/ *a* desperate, hopeless; frenzied

**desesperanza** /desespe'ranθa; desespe'ransa/ *f,* despair; hopelessness

**desesperanzar** /desesperan'θar; desesperan'sar/ *vt* to render hopeless; —*vr* despair, lose hope

**desesperar** /desespe'rar/ *vt* to make hopeless; *Inf.* annoy, make furious; —*vr* lose hope, despair; be frenzied

**desestañar** /desesta'ɲar/ *vt* to unsolder

**desestimación** /desestima'θion; desestima'sion/ *f,* disrespect, lack of esteem; rejection

**desestimar** /desesti'mar/ *vt* to scorn; reject

**desfachatado** /desfatʃa'taðo/ *a Inf.* impudent, brazen

**desfachatez** /desfatʃa'teθ; desfatʃa'tes/ *f, Inf.* effrontery, cheek

**desfalcador** /desfalka'ðor/ **(-ra)** *a* embezzling —*n* embezzler

**desfalcar** /desfal'kar/ *vt* to remove a part of; embezzle

**desfalco** /des'falko/ *m,* diminution, reduction; embezzlement

**desfallecer** /desfaλe'θer; desfaye'ser/ *vt irr* to weaken; —*vi* grow weak; faint, swoon. See **conocer**

**desfallecimiento** /desfaλeθi'miento; desfayesi'miento/ *m,* weakness, languor; depression, discouragement; faint, swoon

**desfavorable** /desfaβo'raβle/ *a* unfavorable; hostile, contrary

**desfavorecer** /desfaβore'θer; desfaβore'ser/ *vt irr* to withdraw one's favor, scorn; disfavor; oppose. See **conocer**

**desfiguración** /desfigura'θion; desfigura'sion/ *f,* deformation; disfigurement

**desfigurar** /desfigu'rar/ *vt* to deform, misshape; disfigure; *Fig.* disguise, mask; obscure, darken, distort, misrepresent; —*vr* be disfigured (by rage, etc.)

**desfijar** /desfi'har/ *vt* to unfix, pull off, remove

**desfiladero** /desfila'ðero/ *m,* defile, gully

**desfilar** /desfi'lar/ *vi* to walk in file; *Inf.* file out; *Mil.* file or march past

**desfile** /des'file/ *m, Mil.* march past; parade; walk past; procession

**desflecarse** /desfle'karse/ **(en)** *vr* to disintegrate (into)

**desfloración** /desflora'θion; desflora'sion/ *f,* defloration

**desflorar** /desflo'rar/ *vt* to tarnish, stain; deflower, violate; *Fig.* touch upon, deal lightly with

**desfortalecer** /desfortale'θer; desfortale'ser/ *vt irr Mil.* to dismantle a fortress. See **conocer**

**desfruncir** /desfrun'θir; desfrun'sir/ *vt* to unfold, shake out

**desgaire** /des'gaire/ *m,* untidiness, slovenliness; affectation of carelessness (in dress); scornful gesture. **al d.,** with an affectation of carelessness, negligently

**desgajar** /desga'har/ *vt* to tear off a tree branch; break; —*vr* break off; dissociate oneself (from)

**desgalgar** /desgal'gar/ *vt* to throw headlong

**desgana** /des'gana/ *f,* lack of appetite; lack of interest, indifference; reluctance

**desganar** /desga'nar/ *vt* to dissuade; —*vr* lose one's appetite; become bored or indifferent, lose interest

**desgarbado** /desgar'βaðo/ *a* slovenly, slatternly; gawky, graceless

**desgarrado** /desga'rraðo/ *a* dissolute, vicious; impudent, brazen

**desgarrador** /desgarra'ðor/ *a* tearing; heart-rending

**desgarrar** /desga'rrar/ *vt* to tear; —*vr* leave, tear oneself away

**desgarro** /des'garro/ *m,* tearing; rent, breach; boastfulness, impudence, effrontery

**desgastar** /desgas'tar/ *vt* to corrode, wear away; spoil, corrupt; —*vr* lose one's vigor, grow weak; wear away

**desgaste** /des'gaste/ *m,* attrition; wearing down or away; corrosion; wear and tear

**desgobernado** /desgoβer'naðo/ *a* uncontrolled (of persons)

**desgobernar** /desgoβer'nar/ *vt irr* to upset or rise against the government; dislocate (bones); *Naut.* neglect the tiller; —*vr* affect exaggerated movements in dancing. See **recomendar**

**desgobierno** /desgo'βierno/ *m,* misgovernment; mismanagement; maladministration; disorder, tumult

**desgomar** /desgo'mar/ *vt* to ungum (fabrics)

**desgorrarse** /desgo'rrarse/ *vr* to doff one's cap, doff one's hat

**desgoznar** /desgoθ'nar; desgos'nar/ *vt* to unhinge; —*vr Fig.* lose one's self-control

**desgracia** /des'graθia; des'grasia/ *f,* misfortune, adversity; mishap, piece of bad luck; disgrace, disfavor; disagreeableness, brusqueness; ungraciousness. **por d.,** unhappily, unfortunately

**desgraciado** /desgra'θiaðo; desgra'siaðo/ *a* unfortunate, unhappy; unlucky; dull, boring; disagreeable

**desgraciar** /desgra'θiar; desgra'siar/ *vt* to displease; spoil the development (of), destroy; maim; —*vr* fall out of friendship; be out of favor; turn out badly, fail; be destroyed or spoiled; be maimed

**desgranar** /desgra'nar/ *vt Agr.* to thresh, flail; —*vr* break (string of beads, etc.)

**desgrasante** /desgra'sante/ *m,* grease remover

**desgreñar** /desgre'ɲar/ *vt* to dishevel the hair; —*vr Inf.* pull each other's hair, come to blows

**desguarnecer** /desguarne'θer; desguarne'ser/ *vt irr* to strip of trimming; *Mil.* demilitarize; *Mil.* disarm; dismantle; unharness. See **conocer**

**desguazar** /desgua'θar; desgua'sar/ *vt* to break up (ships)

**deshabitado** /desaβi'taðo/ *a* uninhabited, empty

**deshabitar** /desaβi'tar/ *vt* to desert, quit, leave (a place)

**deshabituar** /desaβi'tuar/ *vt* to disaccustom; —*vr* lose the habit, become unaccustomed

**deshacer** /desa'θer; desa'ser/ *vt irr* to undo; destroy; *Mil.* rout, defeat; take to pieces; melt; pulp (paper); untie (knots, etc.); open (parcels); diminish, decrease; break in pieces, smash; *Fig.* obstruct, spoil; —*vr* be wasted or spoiled; be full of anxiety; vanish; try or work very hard; injure oneself; be emaciated, grow extremely thin; (*with de*) part with. **d. agravios,** to right wrongs. See **hacer**

**desharrapado** /desarra'paðo/ *a* tattered, shabby

**deshebillar** /deseβi'λar; deseβi'yar/ *vt* to unbuckle

**deshebrar** /dese'βrar/ *vt* to unravel; shred

**deshecha** /des'etʃa/ *f,* pretense, evasion; courteous farewell; obligatory departure

**deshechizar** /desetʃi'θar; desetʃi'sar/ *vt* to disenchant

**deshelar** /dese'lar/ *vt irr* to thaw, melt. See **acertar**

**desherbar** /deser'βar/ *vt irr* to pull up weeds. See **acertar**

**desheredación** /desereða'θion; desereða'sion/ *f,* disinheritance

**desheredar** /desere'ðar/ *vt* disinherit; —*vr Fig.* lower oneself

**desherrar** /dese'rrar/ *vt irr* to unfetter, unchain; strike off horseshoes; —*vr* lose a shoe (horses). See **acertar**

**desherrumbrar** /deserrum'brar/ *vt* to remove the rust from; clean off rust from

**deshidratación** /desiðrata'θion; desiðrata'sion/ *f*, dehydration

**deshidratar** /desiðra'tar/ *vt* to dehydrate

**deshielo** /des'ielo/ *m*, thaw

**deshilado** /desi'laðo/ *a* in single file. *m*, *Sew*. drawn-thread work (gen. *pl*). **a la deshilada**, *Mil*. in file formation; secretly

**deshiladura** /desila'ðura/ *f*, unraveling

**deshilar** /desi'lar/ *vt* to unravel; *Sew*. draw threads; *Cul*. shred, grate

**deshilvanado** /desilβa'naðo/ *a Fig*. disjointed, disconnected

**deshilvanar** /desilβa'nar/ *vt Sew*. to remove the tacking threads

**deshincar** /desin'kar/ *vt* to pull out, remove, draw out

**deshinchar** /desin'tʃar/ *vt* to remove a swelling; deflate; lessen the anger of; —*vr* decrease, subside (swellings); deflate; *Inf*. grow humble

**deshojar** /deso'har/ *vt* to strip off leaves or petals

**deshollejar** /desoʎe'har; desoye'har/ *vt* to skin, peel (fruit); shell (peas, etc.)

**deshollinador** /desoʎina'ðor; desoyina'ðor/ *m*, chimney-sweep; wall-brush; chemical chimney cleaner

**deshollinar** /desoʎi'nar; desoyi'nar/ *vt* to sweep chimneys; clean down walls; *Inf*. examine closely

**deshonestidad** /desonesti'ðað/ *f*, immodesty, shamelessness; indecency

**deshonesto** /deso'nesto/ *a* shameless, immodest; dissolute, vicious; indecent

**deshonor** /deso'nor/ *m*, dishonor; disgrace, insult

**deshonra** /de'sonra/ *f*, dishonor

**deshonrabuenos** /desonra'βuenos/ *mf Inf*. slanderer; degenerate

**deshonrador** /desonra'ðor/ **(-ra)** *a* dishonorable —*n* dishonorer

**deshonrar** /deson'rar/ *vt* to dishonor; insult; seduce (women)

**deshonroso** /deson'roso/ *a* dishonorable, insulting, indecent

**deshora** /de'sora/ *f*, inconvenient time. **a d.**, *or* **a deshoras**, at an inconvenient time, unseasonably; extempore

**deshuesar** /desue'sar/ *vt* to bone, remove the bone (from meat); stone (fruit)

**deshumedecer** /desumeðe'θer; desumeðe'ser/ *vt irr* to dry; —*vr* become dry. See **conocer**

**desidia** /de'siðia/ *f*, negligence; laziness

**desidioso** /desi'ðioso/ *a* negligent; lazy

**desierto** /de'sierto/ *a* deserted, uninhabited, solitary. *m*, desert; wilderness

**designación** /designa'θion; designa'sion/ *f*, designation; appointment

**designar** /desig'nar/ *vt* to plan, intend; designate; appoint

**designio** /de'signio/ *m*, intention, idea

**desigual** /desi'gual/ *a* unequal; uneven (ground); rough; arduous, difficult; changeable

**desigualar** /desigua'lar/ *vt* to make unequal; —*vr* prosper

**desigualdad** /desigual'dað/ *f*, inequality; unevenness, rockiness; *Fig*. changeability; variability

**desilusión** /desilu'sion/ *f*, disillusionment; disappointment

**desilusionar** /desilusio'nar/ *vt* to disillusion; —*vr* become disillusioned; be undeceived

**desinclinar** /desinkli'nar/ *vt* to dissuade

**desinfección** /desinfek'θion; desinfek'sion/ *f*, disinfection

**desinfectante** /desinfek'tante/ *a* and *m*, disinfectant

**desinfectar** /desinfek'tar/ *vt* to disinfect

**desinflación** /desinfla'θion; desinfla'sion/ *f*, deflation

**desinflar** /desin'flar/ *vt* to deflate

**desinterés** /desinte'res/ *m*, disinterestedness

**desinteresado** /desintere'saðo/ *a* disinterested; generous

**desinteresarse** /desintere'sarse/ *vr* to lose interest, grow indifferent

**desistencia,** /desis'tenθia,; desis'tensia,/ *f*, **desistimiento** *m*, desistance, ceasing

**desistir** /desis'tir/ *vi* to desist; cease; *Law*. renounce

**desjuntamiento** /deshunta'miento/ *m*, separation; division

**desjuntar** /deshun'tar/ **(se)** *vt* and *vr* to separate; divide

**deslavado** /desla'βaðo/ *a* brazen, impudent

**deslavar** /desla'βar/ *vt* to wash superficially; spoil by washing, take away the body of (cloth, etc.)

**desleal** /desle'al/ *a* disloyal, treacherous

**deslealtad** /desleal'tað/ *f*, disloyalty

**desleír** /desle'ir/ *vt irr* to dissolve; dilute. See **reír**

**deslenguado** /desleŋ'guaðo/ *a* shameless, foulmouthed

**deslenguar** /desleŋ'guar/ *vt* to remove the tongue; —*vr Inf*. be insolent

**desliar** /des'liar/ *vt* to untie, undo, unloose

**desligadura** /desliga'ðura/ *f*, untying, loosening

**desligar** /desli'gar/ *vt* to unfasten, unbind; *Fig*. solve, unravel; relieve of an obligation; *Mus*. play staccato; —*vr* come unfastened, grow loose. **desligarse de,** to weasel out of, wiggle out of (a promise)

**deslindador** /deslinda'ðor/ *m*, one who fixes boundaries or limits

**deslindar** /deslin'dar/ *vt* to fix the boundaries (of); limit, circumscribe

**deslinde** /des'linde/ *m*, demarcation, boundary

**desliz** /des'liθ; des'lis/ *m*, slipping, slip, slide; skid; indiscretion, slip; peccadillo, trifling fault

**deslizadero** /desliθa'ðero; deslisa'ðero/ *m*, slippery place; chute

**deslizadizo** /desliθa'ðiθo; deslisa'ðiso/ *a* slippery

**deslizar** /desli'θar; desli'sar/ *vt* to slip, slide; skid; —*vr* commit an indiscretion; speak or act unwisely; escape, slip away; slip; skid

**deslucido** /des'luθiðo; des'lusiðo/ *a* fruitless, vain; stupid, clumsy, awkward; discolored; tarnished, dull; unsuccessful

**deslucimiento** /desluθi'miento; deslusi'miento/ *m*, clumsiness, gracelessness; failure, lack of success

**deslucir** /deslu'θir; deslu'sir/ *vt irr* to fade; discolor; stain; tarnish; spoil; sully the reputation of; —*vr* do a thing badly, fail at. See **lucir**

**deslumbrador** /deslumbra'ðor/ *a* dazzling

**deslumbramiento** /deslumbra'miento/ *m*, brilliant light, glare, dazzle; bewilderment, confusion

**deslumbrar** /deslumb'rar/ *vt* to dazzle; confuse, bewilder; *Fig*. daze (with magnificence)

**deslustrar** /deslus'trar/ *vt* to dull, dim, tarnish; frost (glass); discredit, sully (reputation)

**deslustre** /des'lustre/ *m*, dullness, tarnish; frosting (of glass); disgrace, stigma

**deslustroso** /deslus'troso/ *a* ugly, unsuitable, unbecoming

**desmadejar** /desmaðe'har/ *vt* to debilitate, enervate

**desmán** /des'man/ *m*, outrageous behavior; disaster, misfortune

**desmandado** /desman'daðo/ *a* disobedient

**desmandar** /desman'dar/ *vt* to cancel, revoke (orders); withdraw (an offer) —*vr* behave badly; stray

**desmantelado** /desmante'laðo/ *a* dismantled, dilapidated

**desmantelamiento** /desmantela'miento/ *m*, dismantling; dilapidation

**desmantelar** /desmante'lar/ *vt* to dismantle; abandon, forsake

**desmaña** /des'maɲa/ *f*, lack of dexterity, clumsiness, awkwardness

**desmañado** /desma'ɲaðo/ *a* clumsy, awkward, unhandy

**desmayado** /desma'yaðo/ *a* pale, faint (of colors); weak (of a voice)

**desmayar** /desma'yar/ *vt* to cause to faint; —*vi* grow discouraged, lose heart; —*vr* swoon, faint

**desmayo** /des'mayo/ *m*, depression, discouragement; faint, swoon

**desmedido** /desme'ðiðo/ *a* disproportionate; excessive

**desmedirse** /desme'ðirse/ *vr* to misbehave, go too far

**desmedrado** /desme'ðraðo/ *a* thin, emaciated; deteriorated, spoiled

**desmedrar** /desme'ðrar/ *vt* to spoil, ruin; —*vi* deteriorate; decline

**desmedro** /des''meðro/ *m*, impairment; decline, deterioration. **en d. de,** to the detriment of

**desmejora** /desme'hora/ *f*, deterioration

**desmejorar** /desmeho'rar/ *vt* to spoil, impair, cause to deteriorate; —*vr* deteriorate; —*vi* and *vr* decline in health; lose one's beauty

**desmelenar** /desmele'nar/ *vt* to ruffle or dishevel the hair

**desmembración** /desmembra'θion; desmembrasion/ *f*, dismemberment

**desmembrar** /desmem'brar/ *vt* to dismember; separate, divide

**desmemoriarse** /desmemo'riarse/ *vr* to forget, lose one's memory

**desmenguar** /desmeŋ'guar/ *vt* to reduce, decrease; *Fig.* diminish

**desmentida** /desmen'tiða/ *f*, action of giving the lie to

**desmentir** /desmen'tir/ *vt irr* to give the lie to; contradict, deny; lower oneself; behave unworthily; —*vi* deviate (from right direction, etc.). See **sentir**

**desmenuzar** /desmenu'θar; desmenu'sar/ *vt* to crumble, break into small pieces; *Fig.* examine in detail; —*vr* be broken up

**desmeollar** /desmeo'ʎar; desmeo'yar/ *vt* to remove the marrow of

**desmerecedor** /desmereθe'ðor; desmerese'ðor/ *a* unworthy

**desmerecer** /desmere'θer; desmere'ser/ *vt irr* to become undeserving of; —*vi* deteriorate; be inferior to. See **conocer**

**desmesura** /desme'sura/ *f*, insolence; disproportion; excess

**desmesurado** /desmesu'raðo/ *a* disproportionate; excessive, enormous; insolent, uncivil

**desmesurar** /desmesu'rar/ *vt* to disarrange, disorder; —*vr* be insolent

**desmigajar** /desmiga'har/ **(se)** *vt* and *vr* to crumble

**desmigar** /desmi'gar/ *vt Cul.* to make breadcrumbs

**desmilitarizar** /desmilitari'θar; desmilitari'sar/ *vt* to demilitarize

**desmochar** /desmo'tʃar/ *vt* to lop off the top; pollard (trees)

**desmonetización** /desmoneti θa'θion; desmonetisa'sion/ *f*, demonetization; conversion of coin into bullion

**desmonetizar** /desmoneti'θar; desmoneti'sar/ *vt* to convert money into bullion; demonetize; —*vr* depreciate (shares, etc.)

**desmontable** /desmon'taβle/ *a* movable; sectional

**desmontadura** /desmonta'ðura/ *f*, clearing; deforestation; leveling; demounting, dismounting

**desmontar** /desmon'tar/ *vt* to clear wholly or partly of trees or shrubs; clear up (rubbish); level (ground); dismantle; dismount; uncock (firearms); —*vi* and *vr* dismount (from horse, etc.)

**desmonte** /des'monte/ *m*, clearing of trees and shrubs; clearing, cleared ground; timber remaining

**desmoralización** /desmoraliθa'θion; desmoralisa'sion/ *f*, demoralization, corruption

**desmoralizador** /desmoraliθa'ðor; desmoralisa'ðor/ *a* demoralizing

**desmoralizar** /desmorali'θar; desmorali'sar/ *vt* to demoralize, corrupt

**desmoronamiento** /desmorona'miento/ *m*, crumbling; decay, ruin

**desmoronar** /desmoro'nar/ *vt* to destroy, decay; crumble; —*vr* crumble away, fall into ruin; decline, decay; wane, fade (power, etc.)

**desmovilización** /desmoβiliθa'θion; desmoβilisa'sion/ *f*, demobilization

**desmovilizar** /desmoβili'θar; desmoβili'sar/ *vt* to demobilize

**desnacificación** /desnaθifika'θion; desnasifika'sion/ *f*, denazification

**desnatar** /desna'tar/ *vt* to skim; *Fig.* take the cream or best

**desnaturalización** /desnaturaliθa'θion; desnaturalisa'sion/ *f*, denaturalization

**desnaturalizar** /desnaturali'θar; desnaturali'sar/ *vt* to denaturalize; exile; deform, disfigure, pervert; —*vr* give up one's country

**desnivel** /desni'βel/ *m*, unevenness; slope, drop

**desnivelar** /desniβe'lar/ **(se)** *vi* and *vr* to become uneven

**desnudar** /desnu'ðar/ *vt* to undress; *Fig.* despoil, strip, denude; —*vr* undress oneself; deprive oneself

**desnudez** /desnu'ðeθ; desnu'ðes/ *f*, nudity; nakedness; bareness; plainness

**desnudo** /des'nuðo/ *a* nude; ill-clad; bare, naked; clear, patent; *Fig.* destitute (of grace, etc.). *m*, *Art.* nude

**desnutrición** /desnutri'θion; desnutri'sion/ *f*, malnutrition

**desobedecer** /desoβeðe'θer; desoβeðe'ser/ *vt irr* to disobey. See **conocer**

**desobediencia** /desoβeðien'θia; desoβeðien'sia/ *f*, disobedience

**desobediente** /desoβe'ðiente/ *a* disobedient

**desobligar** /desoβli'gar/ *vt* to free from obligation; offend, hurt

**desocupación** /desokupa'θion; desokupa'sion/ *f*, lack of occupation; leisure

**desocupado** /desoku'paðo/ *a* idle; vacant, unoccupied

**desocupar** /desoku'par/ *vt* to empty; vacate; —*vr* give up an employment or occupation

**desodorante** /desoðo'rante/ *a* and *m*, deodorant

**desoír** /deso'ir/ *vt irr* to pay no attention, pretend not to hear. See **oír**

**desojar** /deso'har/ *vt* to break the eye of (needles, etc.); —*vr* gaze intently

**desolación** /desola'θion; desola'sion/ *f*, destruction, desolation; affliction

**desolador** /desola'ðor/ *a* desolate; grievous

**desolar** /deso'lar/ *vt irr* to lay waste, destroy; —*vr* grieve, be disconsolate. See **contar**

**desoldar** /desol'dar/ *vt* to unsolder; —*vr* become unsoldered

**desolladero** /desoʎa'ðero; desoya'ðero/ *m*, slaughterhouse

**desollado** /deso'ʎaðo; deso'yaðo/ *a Inf.* impertinent, barefaced. *m*, carcass

**desolladura** /desoʎa'ðura; desoya'ðura/ *f*, flaying, skinning; *Inf.* slander

**desollar** /deso'ʎar; deso'yar/ *vt irr* to flay, skin; harm, discredit. **d. vivo,** *Inf.* to extort an exorbitant price; slander. See **contar**

**desopinado** /desopi'naðo/ *a* discredited

**desopinar** /desopi'nar/ *vt* to discredit, defame

**desorden** /de'sorðen/ *m*, disorder, disarray; confusion; excess

**desordenado** /desorðe'naðo/ *a* disordered; vicious; licentious

**desordenar** /desorðe'nar/ *vt* to disorder; confuse; —*vr* go beyond the just limits; behave badly; be impertinent

**desorganización** /desorganiθa'θion; desorganisa'sion/ *f*, disorganization

**desorganizador** /desorganiθa'ðor; desorganisa'ðor/ *a* disorganizing

**desorganizar** /desorgani'θar; desorgani'sar/ *vt* to disorganize; disband

**desorientación** /desorienta'θion; desorienta'sion/ *f*, disorientation, loss of bearings; lack of method, confusion

**desorientar** /desorien'tar/ *vt* to disorient; perplex, confuse; —*vr* lose one's way; be disoriented

**desovar** /deso'βar/ *vi* to spawn

**desove** /de'soβe/ *m*, spawning; spawning season

**desovillar** /desoβi'ʎar; desoβi'yar/ *vt* to unwind; uncoil; uncurl; explain, clarify

**despabiladeras** /despaβila'ðeras/ *f pl,* snuffers

**despabilado** /despaβi'laðo/ a alert, wide-awake; watchful, vigilant

**despabiladura** /despaβila'ðura/ f, snuff of a candle, lamp, etc.

**despabilar** /despaβi'lar/ vt to snuff (a candle); trim (lamps); hasten, expedite; finish quickly; steal, rob; Fig. quicken (intelligence, etc.); Inf. kill; —vr rouse oneself, wake up

**despachador** /despatʃa'ðor/ (-ra) n dispatcher, sender

**despachar** /despa'tʃar/ vt to expedite; dispatch, conclude; forward, send; attend to correspondence; sell; dismiss; Inf. serve in a shop; Inf. kill; —vi hasten; carry letters to be signed (in offices, etc.); —vr get rid of

**despacho** /despa'tʃo/ m, transaction, execution; study; office, room; department; booking-office; dispatch, shipment; expedient; commission, warrant; dispatch (diplomatic); telegram; telephone message.
**d. particular,** private office

**despachurrar** /despa'tʃurrar/ vt Inf. to crush, squash; recount in a muddled fashion; Fig. squash flat, confound

**despacio** /des'paθio; des'pasio/ adv slowly, little by little; deliberately, leisurely —interj Careful! Gently now!

**despacito** /despa'θito; despa'sito/ adv Inf. very slowly

**despalmador** /despalma'ðor/ m, dockyard

**despalmar** /despal'mar/ vt Naut. to careen, caulk

**despampanar** /despampa'nar/ vt Agr. to prune vines; Inf. amaze, stun, astound; —vi Inf. relieve one's feelings; —vr Inf. receive a serious injury (through falling)

**desparpajar** /desparpa'har/ vt to spoil; —vi Inf. chatter

**desparpajo** /despar'paho/ m, Inf. loquaciousness, pertness; disorder, muddle

**desparramar** /desparra'mar/ vt to disperse, scatter; squander, waste (money, etc.); —vr amuse oneself; be dissipated

**despavorido** /despaβo'riðo/ a terrified, panicstricken

**despechar** /despe'tʃar/ vt to anger; make despair; Inf. wean; —vr be angry; be in despair

**despecho** /des'petʃo/ m, rancor, malice; despair. **a d. de,** in spite of

**despechugar** /despetʃu'gar/ vt to cut off the breast (fowls); —vr Inf. show the bosom

**despectivo** /despek'tiβo/ a contemptuous, depreciatory

**despedazar** /despeða'θar; despeða'sar/ vt to cut or break into pieces; Fig. break (heart, etc.)

**despedida** /despe'ðiða/ f, dismissal, discharge; seeing off (a visitor, etc.); farewell, good-by

**despedir** /despe'ðir/ vt irr to throw out, emit, cast up; dismiss, discharge; see off (on a journey or after a visit); banish (from the mind); get rid of; —vr say good-by; leave (employment). See **pedir**

**despedregar** /despeðre'gar/ vt to clear of stones

**despegadamente** /despegaða'mente/ adv uninterestedly, unconcernedly, indifferently

**despegado** /despe'gaðo/ a Inf. indifferent, unconcerned, cold

**despegar** /despe'gar/ vt to unstick; unglue; separate, detach; —vr become estranged; come apart or unstuck; —vi Aer. take off. **sin d. los labios,** without saying a word

**despegue** /des'pege/ m, Aer. take-off

**despeinar** /despei'nar/ vt to disarrange the hair; undo the coiffure

**despejado** /despe'haðo/ a lively, sprightly; logical, clear-cut; cloudless; spacious, unobstructed, clear

**despejar** /despe'har/ vt to clear, free of obstacles; **d. el camino de,** to clear the way for; Fig. elucidate, solve; Math. find the value of; —vr smarten up, grow gay; amuse oneself; clear up (weather, sky, etc.); improve (a patient)

**despejo** /des'peho/ m, freeing of obstacles; smartness, gaiety; grace, elegance; perkiness; clearsightedness, intelligence

**despellejar** /despe'ʎehar; despe'yehar/ vt to flay, skin; slander

**despeluzar** /despelu'θar; despelu'sar/ vt to disorder the hair; cause the hair to stand on end; horrify; —vr stand on end (hair); be horrified or terrified

**despeluznante** /despeluθ'nante; despelus'nante/ a hair-raising, terrifying

**dependedor** /despende'ðor/ (-ra) n spendthrift, waster

**despender** /despen'der/ vt to spend; waste

**despensa** /des'pensa/ f, larder, pantry; store (of food); Naut. steward's room; stewardship

**despensero** /despen'sero/ (-ra) n steward; caterer; victualler; Naut. steward

**despeñadero** /despeɲa'ðero/ m, precipice, crag; dangerous undertaking, risk —a steep, precipitous

**despeñar** /despe'ɲar/ vt to precipitate, fling down from a height, hurl down; —vr fling oneself headlong; throw oneself into (vices, etc.)

**despeño** /des'peɲo/ m, precipitation; headlong fall; Fig. collapse, ruin

**despepitar** /despepi'tar/ vt to remove seeds or pips; —vr vociferate; act wildly; Inf. desire, long (for)

**desperdiciador** /desperði'θiaðor; desperði'siaðor/ (-ra) a squandering, wasting —n squanderer

**desperdiciar** /desperði'θiar; desperði'siar/ vt to squander; Fig. misspend, waste

**desperdicio** /desper'ðiθio; desper'ðisio/ m, waste; remains, leftovers (gen. pl)

**desperdigar** /desperði'gar/ vt to separate, sever; scatter

**desperecerse** /despere'θerse; despere'serse/ vr irr to crave, yearn (for). See **conocer**

**desperezarse** /despere'θarse; despere'sarse/ vr to stretch oneself

**desperfecto** /desper'fekto/ m, imperfection, flaw; slight deterioration

**despernado** /desper'naðo/ a weary, footsore

**despertador** /desperta'ðor/ (-ra) a awakening —n awakener. m, alarm clock; incentive, stimulus

**despertar** /desper'tar/ vt irr to awaken; bring to mind, recall; incite, stimulate; —vi waken; Fig. wake up, become more intelligent. See **acertar**

**despiadado** /despia'ðaðo/ a cruel, merciless

**despicar** /despi'kar/ vt to satisfy, content; —vr revenge oneself

**despierto** /des'pierto/ a wide-awake, clever

**despilfarrado** /despilfa'rraðo/ a ragged, shabby; wasteful; spendthrift

**despilfarrar** /despilfa'rrar/ vt to squander, waste

**despilfarro** /despil'farro/ m, slovenliness; waste, extravagance; mismanagement, maladministration

**despintar** /despin'tar/ vt to paint out; wash off the paint; efface, blot out; disfigure, deform; —vi be unlike or unworthy (of); —vr fade (colors); forget

**despiojar** /despio'har/ vt to remove lice, delouse; Inf. rescue from misery

**despique** /des'pike/ m, vengeance, revenge

**despistar** /despis'tar/ vt to throw off the scent; mislead

**desplacer** /despla'θer; despla'ser/ vt irr to displease. m, disgust, displeasure, sorrow. See **placer**

**desplantar** /desplan'tar/ (se) vt and vr to deviate from the vertical

**desplazamiento** /desplaθa'miento; desplasa'miento/ m, Naut. displacement

**desplegadura** /desplega'ðura/ f, unfolding

**desplegar** /desple'gar/ vt irr to unfold; spread open; Fig. reveal, disclose, explain; evince, display; Mil. deploy troops; —vr unfold, open (flowers, etc.); Mil. deploy. See **cegar**

**despliegue** /des'pliege/ m, unfolding; spreading out; evincing, demonstration; Mil. deployment

**desplomar** /desplo'mar/ vt to put out of the straight, cause to lean (walls, buildings); —vr lean, tilt (buildings); topple, fall down (walls, etc.); collapse (people); be ruined

**desplome** /des'plome/ m, collapse

**desplomo** /des'plomo/ m, tilt, cant, deviation from vertical

**desplumar** /desplu'mar/ vt to remove feathers, pluck; rob, despoil

**despoblación** /despoβla'θion; despoβla'sion/ f, depopulation. **d. forestal,** deforestation

**despoblado** /despo'βlaðo/ *m,* wilderness; deserted place

**despoblar** /despo'βlar/ *vt* to depopulate; despoil, rob; —*vr* become depopulated

**despojador** /despoha'ðor/ **(-ra)** *a* robbing, despoiling —*n* despoiler

**despojar** /despo'har/ *vt* to plunder, despoil; dispossess; —*vr* (with de) remove (garments, etc.); relinquish, give up

**despojo** /des'poho/ *m,* pillaging, spoliation; booty, plunder; butcher's offal; *pl* remains, leavings; debris, rubble; corpse

**despolvorear** /despolβore'ar/ *vt* to remove dust; *Fig.* shake off

**desposado** /despo'saðo/ *a* recently married; fettered, handcuffed. **los desposados,** the newlyweds

**desposar** /despo'sar/ *vt* to perform the marriage ceremony; —*vr* become betrothed; marry

**desposeer** /despose'er/ *vt* to dispossess; —*vr* renounce one's possessions. See **creer**

**desposeimiento** /desposei'miento/ *m,* dispossession

**desposorio** /despo'sorio/ *m,* betrothal, promise of marriage; (gen. *pl*) wedding, marriage

**déspota** /'despota/ *m,* despot, tyrant

**despótico** /des'potiko/ *a* tyrannical

**despotismo** /despo'tismo/ *m,* despotism

**despotricarse** /despotri'karse/ *vr* to rave (against), rail (against)

**despreciable** /despre'θiaβle; despre'siaβle/ *a* worthless, contemptible

**despreciar** /despre'θiar; despre'siar/ *vt* to scorn, despise; —*vr* despise oneself

**despreciativo** /despreθia'tiβo; despresia'tiβo/ *a* contemptuous, scornful

**desprecio** /des'preθio; des'presio/ *m,* contempt, scorn

**desprender** /despren'der/ *vt* to loosen, remove, unfix; give off (gases, etc.); —*vr* work loose, give way; deduce, infer; give away, deprive oneself (of)

**desprendido** /despren'diðo/ *a* disinterested; generous

**desprendimiento** /desprendi'miento/ *m,* loosening; removal, separation; emission; indifference, lack of interest; generosity; impartiality

**despreocupación** /despreokupa'θion; despreokupa'sion/ *f,* fair mindedness, impartiality; lack of interest

**despreocupado** /despreoku'paðo/ *a* unprejudiced, broadminded; indifferent, uninterested

**despreocuparse** /despreoku'parse/ *vr* to shake off prejudice; (with de) pay no attention to; set aside

**desprestigiar** /despresti'hiar/ *vt* to discredit; —*vr* lose prestige; lose caste

**desprestigio** /despres'tihio/ *m,* loss of prestige, discredit

**desprevenido** /despreβe'niðo/ *a* unprepared, improvident

**desproporción** /despropor'θion; despropor'sion/ *f,* disproportion

**desproporcionado** /desproporθio'naðo; desproporsio'naðo/ *a* disproportionate; out of proportion

**despropósito** /despro'posito/ *m,* nonsense, absurdity

**desproveer** /desproβe'er/ *vt irr* to deprive of necessities. See **creer**

**despueble** /des'pueβle/ *m,* depopulation

**después** /des'pues/ *adv* afterwards, after, next (of time and place) (e.g. *Vendrá d. de Pascua,* He will come after Easter. *Zaragoza viene d. de Madrid,* Saragossa comes after Madrid)

**despuntar** /despun'tar/ *vt* to blunt the point; *Naut.* double, sail round; —*vi* show green, sprout; appear (the dawn); grow clever; *Fig.* stand out, excel

**desquiciamiento** /deskiθia'miento; deskisia'miento/ *m,* unhinging; disconnecting; *Fig.* upsetting, throwing out of gear; downfall, fall from favor

**desquiciar** /deski'θiar; deski'siar/ *vt* to unhinge; disconnect; *Fig.* throw out of gear, upset; banish from favor; —*vr* become unhinged; *Fig.* be disordered; upset

**desquitar** /deski'tar/ **(se)** *vt* and *vr* to retrieve a loss; take revenge, retaliate

**desquite** /des'kite/ *m,* compensation; revenge

**destacamento** /destaka'mento/ *m, Mil.* detachment

**destacar** /desta'kar/ *vt Mil.* to detach; —*vr* excel; be prominent; be conspicuous; *Art.* stand out

**destajador** /destaha'ðor/ *m,* smith's hammer

**destajar** /desta'har/ *vt* to cut (cards); set forth conditions, stipulate, contract

**destajista** /desta'hista/ *mf* pieceworker; jobber (worker)

**destajo** /des'taho/ *m,* piecework; job. **a d.,** quickly and diligently. *Inf.* **hablar a d.,** to chatter, talk too much

**destapar** /desta'par/ *vt* to remove the cover or lid; reveal, uncover; —*vr* be uncovered; reveal oneself. **no destaparse,** to keep quiet, be mum

**destartalado** /destarta'laðo/ *a* tumble-down, rickety; poverty-stricken

**destechado** /deste'tʃaðo/ *a* roofless

**destejar** /deste'har/ *vt* to remove tiles or slates; leave unprotected

**destejer** /deste'her/ *vt* to unweave, unravel; *Fig.* undo, spoil

**destello** /des'teʎo; deste'yo/ *m,* gleam, sparkle, brilliance; flash, beam, ray; *Fig.* gleam (of talent)

**destemplado** /destem'plaðo/ *a* out of tune; inharmonious; intemperate; *Art.* inharmonious; *Inf.* out of sorts, indisposed

**destemplanza** /destem'planθa; destem'plansa/ *f,* inclemency, rigor (weather); intemperance, excess, abuse; *Inf.* indisposition; lack of moderation (actions, speech)

**destemplar** /destem'plar/ *vt* to disturb, upset, alter; *Mus.* put out of tune; put to confusion; —*vr* be unwell; *Fig.* go too far, behave badly; lose temper (metals)

**destemple** /des'temple/ *m, Mus.* being out of tune; *Med.* indisposition; uncertainty (weather); lack of temper (metals); disturbance, disorder; intemperance, excess, confusion

**desternillarse de risa** /desterni'ʎarse de 'rrisa; desterni'yarse de 'rrisa/ *vr* to shake with laughter

**desterrado** /deste'rraðo/ **(-da)** *a* exiled —*n* exile

**desterrar** /deste'rrar/ *vt irr* to exile; shake off the soil; *Fig.* discard, lay aside; extirpate (an error). See **recomendar**

**destetar** /deste'tar/ *vt* to wean

**destete** /des'tete/ *m,* weaning

**destiempo, a** /des'tiempo, a/ *adv* untimely, inopportunely

**destierro** /des'tierro/ *m,* banishment, exile; place of exile; remote place

**destilación** /destila'θion; destila'sion/ *f,* distillation

**destilador** /destila'ðor/ **(-ra)** *n* distiller. *m,* still

**destilar** /desti'lar/ *vt* to distill; filter; —*vi* to drip

**destilatorio** /destila'torio/ *a* distilling. *m,* distillery; still

**destilería** /destile'ria/ *f,* distillery

**destinación** /destina'θion; destina'sion/ *f,* destination

**destinar** /desti'nar/ *vt* to destine; appoint; assign

**destino** /des'tino/ *m,* fate, destiny; post, appointment; destination. **con d. a,** going to, bound for

**destitución** /destitu'θion; destitu'sion/ *f,* destitution; discharge, dismissal

**destituir** /destitu'ir/ *vt irr* (with de) to dismiss or discharge from (employment); deprive of. See **huir**

**destorcer** /destor'θer; destor'ser/ *vt irr* to untwist; straighten out; —*vr Naut.* drift. See **torcer**

**destornillado** /destorni'ʎaðo; destorni'yaðo/ *a* reckless; *Fig. Inf.* with a screw loose

**destornillador** /destorni'ʎaðor; destorni'yaðor/ *m,* screwdriver

**destornillamiento** /destorniʎa'miento; destorniya'miento/ *m,* unscrewing

**destornillar** /destorni'ʎar; destorni'yar/ *vt* to unscrew; —*vr* act rashly

**destrenzar** /destren'θar; destren'sar/ *vt* to unplait. **destrenzarse las cintas,** to unlace one's shoes

**destreza** /des'treθa; des'tresa/ *f,* dexterity; agility

**destrón** /des'tron/ *m,* blind person's guide

**destronamiento** /destrona'miento/ *m,* dethronement

**destronar** /destro'nar/ *vt* to dethrone, depose; oust

**destroncamiento** /destronka'miento/ m, detruncation

**destroncar** /destron'kar/ vt to lop, detruncate (trees); dislocate, disjoint; mutilate; Fig. ruin, seriously harm; tire out; —vr be exhausted or tired

**destrozar** /destro'θar; destro'sar/ vt to destroy; break in pieces, shatter; Mil. wipe out, annihilate; squander, dissipate

**destrozo** /des'troθo; des'troso/ m, destruction, ruin; shattering; Mil. rout; dissipation, waste

**destrozón** /destro'θon; destro'son/ a hard on wearing apparel, shoes, etc.

**destrucción** /destruk'θion; destruk'sion/ f, destruction; ruin, irreparable loss

**destructible** /destruk'tiβle/ a destructible

**destructivo** /destruk'tiβo/ a destructive

**destructor** /destruk'tor/ (-ra) a destructive —n destroyer. m, Nav. destroyer

**destruible** /destrui'βle/ a destructible

**des'truir** /destruir/ vt irr to destroy, ruin, annihilate; frustrate, blast, disappoint; deprive of means of subsistence; squander, waste; —vr Math. cancel. See **huir**

**desuello** /desue'ʎo; desue'yo/ m, flaying, skinning; forwardness, impertinence; extortion, fleecing. Fig. Inf. **¡Es un d.!** It's highway robbery!

**desu'nión** /desu'nion/ f, disunion, separation; Fig. discord, disharmony

**desunir** /desu'nir/ vt to disunite, separate; Fig. cause discord or disharmony

**desusarse** /desu'sarse/ vr to fall into disuse, become obsolete

**desuso** /de'suso/ m, disuse

**desvaído** /desβa'iðo/ a gaunt, lanky; pale, faded, dull (of colors)

**desvainar** /desβai'nar/ vt to shell (peas, beans)

**desvalido** /desβa'liðo/ a unprotected, helpless

**desvalijar** /desβali'har/ vt to rifle (a suitcase, etc.); swindle

**desvalimiento** /desβali'miento/ m, defenselessness, lack of protection; lack of favor; desertion, abandonment

**desvalorización** /desβaloriθa'θion; desβalorisa'sion/ f, devaluation

**desván** /des'βan/ m, garret

**desvanecer** /desβane'θer; desβane'ser/ vt irr to cause to disappear; disintegrate; make vain; remove; —vr evaporate, faint, swoon; grow vain or conceited. See **conocer**

**desvanecimiento** /desβaneθi'miento; desβanesi'miento/ m, faintness, loss of consciousness; vanity, conceit

**desvarar** /desβa'rar/ vt to slip, slide; Naut. refloat

**desvariar** /desβa'riar/ vi to be delirious; rave, talk wildly

**desvarío** /desβa'rio/ m, foolish action, absurdity; delirium; monstrosity; whim, caprice

**desvedar** /desβe'ðar/ vt to raise a ban or prohibition

**desvelar** /desβe'lar/ vt to keep awake; —vr be sleepless; (with por) take great care over

**desvelo** /des'βelo/ m, sleeplessness, vigil; care, attention, vigilance; anxiety. **con d.,** watchfully

**desvencijar** /desβenθi'har; desβensi'har/ vt to loosen, disconnect, disjoint; —vr work loose, become disjointed

**desventaja** /desβen'taha/ f, disadvantage. **estar en d.,** to be at a disadvantage

**desventajoso** /desβenta'hoso/ a disadvantageous

**desventura** /desβen'tura/ f, misfortune

**desventurado** /desβentu'raðo/ a unfortunate; timid, faint-hearted; miserly

**desvergonzado** /desβergon'θaðo; desβergonsaðo/ a shameless, brazen, impudent

**desvergonzarse** /desβergon'θarse; desβergon'sarse/ vr irr to be brazen, be impudent. See **avergonzar**

**desvergüenza** /desβer'guenθa; desβer'guensa/ f, insolence; shamelessness

**desvestir** /desβes'tir/ (se) vt and vr irr to undress. See **pedir**

**desviación** /desβia'θion; desβia'sion/ f, deviation, deflection

**desviadero** /desβia'ðero/ m, diversion, Rail. siding

**desviar** /des'βiar/ vt to divert, deflect; dissuade

**desvío** /des'βio/ m, deviation; indifference, coldness; repugnance

**desvirgar** /desβir'gar/ vt to deflower

**desvirtuar** /desβir'tuar/ vt to decrease in strength or merit

**desvivirse** /desβi'βirse/ vr (with por) to adore, love dearly; yearn for, be dying to; do one's best to please; (e.g. Juan se desvive por servirme, John does his best to help me)

**detallar** /deta'ʎar; deta'yar/ vt to tell in detail; relate

**detalle** /de'taʎe; de'taye/ m, detailed account; detail, particular

**detallismo** /deta'ʎismo; deta'yismo/ m, meticulous attention to details

**detective** /de'tektiβe/ mf detective

**detector** /detek'tor/ m, detector; Radio. catwhisker

**detención** /deten'θion; deten'sion/ f, stop, halt; delay; prolixity; arrest, detention. **con d.,** carefully, meticulously

**detener** /dete'ner/ vt irr to detain, stop; arrest; retain, keep; —vr go slowly; tarry; halt, stop; (with en) pause over, stop at. See **tener**

**detenido** /dete'niðo/ a timid, irresolute; miserable, mean

**deterioración** /deteriora'θion; deteriora'sion/ f, deterioration

**deteriorar** /deterio'rar/ (se) vt and vr to deteriorate

**determinación** /determina'θion; determina'sion/ f, determination; daring; decision

**determinado** /determi'naðo/ a resolute, determined

**determinar** /determi'nar/ vt to determine, limit; discern, distinguish; specify, appoint; decide, resolve; Law. define, judge; —vr make up one's mind

**determinativo** /determina'tiβo/ a determining

**determinismo** /determi'nismo/ m, determinism

**determinista** /determi'nista/ mf determinist —a deterministic

**detersorio** /deter'sorio/ a and m, detergent

**detestable** /detes'taβle/ a detestable

**detestación** /detesta'θion; detesta'sion/ f, detestation

**detestar** /detes'tar/ vt to abominate, detest

**detonación** /detona'θion; detona'sion/ f, detonation

**detonador** /detona'ðor/ m, detonator

**detonar** /deto'nar/ vi to detonate

**detracción** /detrak'θion; detrak'sion/ f, detraction

**detractor** /detrak'tor/ (-ra) a slandering n detractor, slanderer

**detraer** /detra'er/ vt irr to detract, take away; separate; slander. See **traer**

**detrás** /de'tras/ adv behind, after (place). **por d.,** in the rear; Fig. behind one's back

**detrimento** /detri'mento/ m, detriment; moral harm. **en d. de,** to the detriment of

**deuda** /'deuða/ f, debt; fault, offense; sin. **d. exterior,** foreign debt. **estar en d. con,** to be indebted to. **Perdónanos nuestras deudas,** Forgive us our trespasses

**deudo** /'deuðo/ m, relative, kinsman; kinship, relationship

**deudor** /deu'ðor/ (-ra) a indebted —n debtor. **d. hipotecario,** mortgagor

**devanadera** /deβana'ðera/ f, bobbin, reel, spool; winder (machine)

**devanador** /deβana'ðor/ (-ra) n winder (person). m, spool, bobbin

**devanar** /deβa'nar/ vt to reel, wind. Inf. **devanarse los sesos,** to rack one's brains

**devanear** /deβane'ar/ vi to rave, talk nonsense

**devaneo** /deβa'neo/ m, delirium; foolishness, nonsense; dissipation; love affair

**devastación** /deβasta'θion; deβasta'sion/ f, devastation

**devastar** /deβas'tar/ vt to devastate, lay waste; Fig. destroy, ruin

**develador** /deβela'ðor/ m, betrayer

**devengar** /deβeŋ'gar/ vt to have a right to, earn (salary, interest, etc.)

**devoción** /deβo'θion; deβo'sion/ f, piety; affection; love; pious custom; prayer

**devocionario** /deβoθio'nario; deβosio'nario/ *m,* prayer book

**devolución** /deβolu'θion; deβolu'sion/ *f,* restitution, return; its devolution

**devolutivo** /deβolu'tiβo/ *a Law.* returnable

**devolver** /deβol'βer/ *vt irr* to restore to original state; return, give back; repay. See **resolver**

**devorador** /deβora'ðor/ **(-ra)** *a* devouring —*n* devourer

**devorar** /deβo'rar/ *vt* to devour; destroy, consume

**devoto** /de'βoto/ **(-ta)** *a* devout, pious; devoted, fond —*n* devotee. *m,* object of devotion

**día** /dia/ *m,* day; daylight; *pl* name or saint's day; birthday (e.g. *Hoy son los días de María,* This is Mary's saint's day (or birthday)). **d. de Año Nuevo,** New Year's Day. **d. de asueto,** day off. **d. de ayuno** or **de vigilia,** fast day. **d. del cura,** *humorous* wedding day. **d. del juicio,** Day of Judgment. **d. de los difuntos,** All Souls' Day. **d. de recibo,** at home day. **d. de Reyes,** Epiphany (when Spanish children receive their Christmas presents). **d. de trabajo** or **d. laborable,** working day. **d. por medio,** every other day. **días caniculares,** dog days. **d. por d.,** day by day. **al d.,** up to date; per day. **al otro d.,** next day. **¡Buenos días!** Good morning! Good day! **de d.,** by day. **de d. en d.,** from day to day. **de un d. a otro,** any time now, very soon. **el d. de mañana,** tomorrow, the near future. **un d. sí y otro no,** every other day. **vivir al d.,** to live up to one's income

**diabético** /dia'βetiko/ *a* diabetic

**diablillo** /dia'βliʎo; dia'βliyo/ *m, dim* devilkin, imp; *Inf.* madcap

**diablo** /'diaβlo/ *m,* devil; Satan; *Fig.* fiend. *Inf.* **d. cojuelo,** mischievous devil; *Fig. Inf.* imp. *Inf.* **Anda el d. suelto,** The Devil's abroad, there's trouble. *Inf.* **tener el d. en el cuerpo,** to be as clever as the Devil; be mischievous

**diablura** /dia'βlura/ *f,* mischief, prank; devilry

**diabólico** /dia'βoliko/ *a* diabolical, devilish; *Inf.* fiendish, iniquitous

**diaconisa** /diako'nisa/ *f,* deaconess

**diácono** /'diakono/ *m,* deacon

**diadema** /dia'ðema/ *f,* diadem; crown; tiara

**diafanidad** /diafani'ðað/ *f,* transparency

**diáfano** /'diafano/ *a* transparent, diaphanous

**diafragma** /dia'fragma/ *m, Anat. Mech.* diaphragm; sound-box (of a phonograph)

**diagnosticar** /diagnosti'kar/ *vt Med.* to diagnose

**diagnóstico** /diag'nostiko/ *a* diagnostic. *m,* diagnosis. **d. precoz,** early diagnosis

**diagonal** /diago'nal/ *a* diagonal; oblique

**diagrama** /dia'grama/ *m,* diagram

**diagramación** /diagrama'θion; diagrama'sion/ *f,* layout (of a publication)

**dialectal** /dialek'tal/ *a* dialect

**dialéctica** /dia'lektika/ *f,* dialectic

**dialéctico** /dia'lektiko/ *a* dialectic. *m,* logician

**dialecto** /dia'lekto/ *m,* dialect

**dialogar** /dialo'gar/ *vi* to hold dialogue, converse; —*vt* write dialogue

**diálogo** /'dialogo/ *m,* dialogue

**diamante** /dia'mante/ *m,* diamond; miner's lamp; glass-cutting diamond. **d. bruto,** rough diamond

**diamantífero** /diaman'tifero/ *a* diamond-bearing

**diamantino** /diaman'tino/ *a* diamantine; *Poet.* adamant

**diamantista** /diaman'tista/ *mf* diamond-cutter; diamond merchant

**diametral** /diame'tral/ *a* diametrical

**diámetro** /'diametro/ *m,* diameter

**diana** /'diana/ *f, Mil.* reveille; bull's-eye (of a target); the moon

**¡diantre!** /'diantre/ *interj Inf.* the deuce!

**diapasón** /diapa'son/ *m, Mus.* tuning fork; diapason; neck (of violins, etc.). **d. normal,** tuning fork. **d. vocal,** pitch-pipe

**diapositiva** /diaposi'tiβa/ *f, Photo.* diapositive; (lantern) slide

**diario** /'diario/ *a* daily. *m,* diary; daily paper; daily expenses. **d. de navegación,** ship's log. **d. de viaje,** travel diary, trip journal

**diarista** /dia'rista/ *mf* journalist, diarist

**diarrea** /dia'rrea/ *f,* diarrhea

**diatónico** /dia'toniko/ *a Mus.* diatonic

**diatriba** /dia'triβa/ *f,* diatribe

**diávolo** /'diaβolo/ *m,* diabolo (game)

**dibujante** /diβu'hante/ *m,* sketcher; draftsman; designer

**dibujar** /diβu'har/ *vt Art.* to draw; describe, depict; —*vr* appear, be revealed; be outlined, stand out

**dibujo** /di'βuho/ *m,* drawing; sketch, design, pattern; depiction, description. **d. a la pluma,** pen-and-ink drawing. **d. a pulso,** freehand drawing. **d. del natural,** drawing from life

**dicción** /dik'θion; dik'sion/ *f,* word; diction, language, style

**diccionario** /dikθio'nario; diksio'nario/ *m,* dictionary

**díceres** /'diθeres; 'diseres/ *m pl West. Hem.* news

**dicha** /'ditʃa/ *f,* happiness; good fortune. **por d.,** by chance; fortunately

**dicharacho** /ditʃa'ratʃo/ *m, Inf.* vulgar expression, slangy expression

**dicho** /'ditʃo/ *m,* saying, phrase, expression; witty remark; *Law.* declaration; *Inf.* insult —*a* said, aforementioned —*past part* decir, "said." **D. y hecho,** No sooner said than done. **Del d. al hecho hay muy gran trecho,** There's many a slip 'twixt the cup and the lip. **Lo d. d.,** The agreement stands

**dichoso** /di'tʃoso/ *a* happy; lucky; *Inf.* blessed, wretched, darn

**diciembre** /di'θiembre; di'siembre/ *m,* December

**dictado** /dik'taðo/ *m,* title of honor; dictation; *pl* promptings (of heart, etc.). **escribir al d.,** to write to dictation

**dictador** /dikta'ðor/ *m,* dictator

**dictadura** /dikta'ðura/ *f,* dictatorship

**dictáfono** /dik'tafono/ *m,* dictaphone

**dictamen** /dik'tamen/ *m,* judgment, opinion

**dictaminar** /diktami'nar/ *vi* to give judgment or opinion

**dictar** /dik'tar/ *vt* to dictate; suggest, inspire. **dictar fallo,** to hand down a decision, render judgment

**dictatorial, dictatorio** /diktato'rial, dikta'torio/ *a* dictatorial

**dicterio** /dik'terio/ *m,* taunt, insult

**didáctica** /di'ðaktika/ *f,* didactics

**didáctico** /di'ðaktiko/ *a* didactic

**diecinueve** /dieθi'nueβe; diesi'nueβe/ *a* and *m,* nineteen

**diecinueveavo** /dieθinueβe'aβo; diesinueβe'aβo/ *a* and *m,* nineteenth

**dieciochavo** /dieθio'tʃaβo; diesio'tʃaβo/ *a* and *m,* eighteenth

**dieciocheno** /dieθio'tʃeno; diesio'tʃeno/ *a* See **décimoctavo**

**dieciocho** /die'θiotʃo; die'siotʃo/ *a* and *m,* eighteen

**dieciséis** /dieθi'seis; diesi'seis/ *a* and *m,* sixteen

**dieciseisavo** /dieθisei'saβo; diesisei'saβo/ *a* and *m,* sixteenth

**dieciseiseno** /dieθisei'seno; diesisei'seno/ *a* See **décimosexto**

**diecisiete** /dieθi'siete; diesi'siete/ *a* and *m,* seventeen

**diecisieteavo** /dieθisiete'aβo; diesisiete'aβo/ *a* and *m,* seventeenth

**diente** /diente/ *m,* tooth; tooth (of saw, etc.); tusk; cog (of wheel); prong (of fork); tongue (of a buckle). **d. de leche,** milk-tooth. *Bot.* **d. de león,** dandelion. **d. de perro,** *Sew.* feather-stitch. *Inf.* **dar d. con d.,** to chatter (teeth). *Fig. Inf.* **enseñar** ( *or* mostrar) **los dientes,** to show one's teeth; threaten. *Inf.* **estar a d.,** to be famished. **hablar entre dientes,** to mutter; fume, grumble. *Inf.* **tener buen d.,** to have a good appetite. **traer a uno entre dientes,** to loathe someone; speak scandal of

**Diepa** /'diepa/ Dieppe

**diestra** /'diestra/ *f,* right hand; protection

**diestro** /'diestro/ *a* right (hand); skillful, dextrous; shrewd; astute, cunning; favorable, happy. *m,* expert fencer; bullfighter; halter; bridle

**dieta** /'dieta/ *f, Med.* diet; *Inf.* fast, abstinence; legislative assembly; travel allowance (gen. *pl*); day's journey of ten leagues; daily fee (gen. *pl*)

**dietario** /die'tario/ *m,* household accounts' book

**dietética** /die'tetika/ *f*, dietetics
**dietético** /die'tetiko/ *a* dietetic
**dietista** /die'tista/ *mf* dietician
**diez** /dieθ; dies/ *a* ten; tenth. *m*, ten; decade of rosary
**diezmar** /dieθ'mar; dies'mar/ *vt* to tithe; decimate; punish every tenth person
**diezmero** /dieθ'mero; dies'mero/ **(-ra)** *n* tax-gatherer
**diezmesino** /dieθme'sino; diesme'sino/ *a* ten months old
**diezmilésimo** /dieθmi'lesimo; diesmi'lesimo/ *a* ten-thousandth
**diezmo** /'dieθmo; 'diesmo/ *m*, ten per cent tax; tithe
**difamación** /difama'θion; difama'sion/ *f*, defamation, libel
**difamador** /difama'ðor/ **(-ra)** *a* libeling —*n* libeler
**difamar** /difa'mar/ *vt* to libel; denigrate
**difamatorio** /difama'torio/ *a* libelous, defamatory
**diferencia** /dife'renθia; dife'rensia/ *f*, unlikeness, dissimilarity; *Math.* difference; dissension, disagreement. **a d. de,** unlike; in contrast to
**diferenciación** /diferenθia'θion; diferensia'sion/ *f*, differentiation. **d. del trabajo,** division of labor
**diferencial** /diferen'θial; diferen'sial/ *a* differential
**diferenciar** /diferen'θiar; diferen'siar/ *vt* to differentiate; change the function (of); —*vi* dissent, disagree; —*vr* be different, differ; distinguish oneself
**diferente** /dife'rente/ *a* different, various
**diferir** /dife'rir/ *vt irr* to delay, retard; postpone; suspend, interrupt; —*vi* be different. See **discernir**
**difícil** /di'fiθil; di'fisil/ *a* difficult
**dificultad** /difikul'taθ/ *f*, difficulty; impediment, obstacle; objection
**dificultar** /difikul'tar/ *vt* to raise difficulties; put obstacles in the way; —*vi* think difficult (of achievements)
**dificultoso** /difikul'toso/ *a* difficult; *Inf.* ugly (face, figure, etc.)
**difidencia** /difi'ðenθia; difi'ðensia/ *f*, mistrust; lack of faith, doubt
**difidente** /difi'ðente/ *a* mistrustful
**difracción** /difrak'θion; difrak'sion/ *f*, diffraction
**difractar** /difrak'tar/ *vt* to diffract
**difteria** /dif'teria/ *f*, diphtheria
**difundir** /difun'dir/ *vt* to diffuse (fluids); spread, publish, divulge; *Radio.* broadcast
**difunto** /di'funto/ **(-ta)** *a* and *n* deceased. *m*, corpse
**difusión** /difu'sion/ *f*, diffusion; prolixity; *Radio.* broadcasting
**difusivo** /difu'siβo/ *a* diffusive
**difuso** /di'fuso/ *a* widespread, diffuse; prolix, wordy
**digerible** /dihe'riβle/ *a* digestible
**digerir** /dihe'rir/ *vt irr* to digest; bear patiently; consider carefully; *Chem.* digest. See **sentir**
**digestible** /dihes'tiβle/ *a* easily digested
**digestivo** /dihes'tiβo/ *a* digestive
**digesto** /di'hesto/ *m*, *Law.* digest
**digitación** /dihita'θion; dihita'sion/ *f*, *Mus.* fingering
**digital** /dihi'tal/ *a* digital. *f*, *Bot.* foxglove, digitalis
**dígito** /'dihito/ *a* digital. *m*, (*Astron. Math.*) digit
**dignación** /digna'θion; digna'sion/ *f*, condescension
**dignarse** /dig'narse/ *vr* to deign, condescend
**dignatario** /digna'tario/ *m*, dignitary
**dignidad** /digni'ðaθ/ *f*, dignity, stateliness; serenity, loftiness; high office or rank; high repute, honor; *Eccl.* dignitary
**dignificar** /dignifi'kar/ *vt* to dignify
**digno** /'digno/ *a* worthy, deserving; upright, honorable; fitting, suitable, appropriate
**digresión** /digre'sion/ *f*, digression
**dije** /'dihe/ *m*, charm; trinket, any small piece of jewelry; *Inf.* person of excellent qualities, jewel
**dilacerar** /dilaθe'rar; dilase'rar/ *vt* to lacerate, tear flesh; *Fig.* discredit
**dilación** /dila'θion; dila'sion/ *f*, delay
**dilapidación** /dilapiða'θion; dilapi'ðasion/ *f*, waste, dissipation, squandering
**dilapidar** /dilapi'ðar/ *vt* to waste, squander
**dilatación** /dilata'θion; dilata'sion/ *f*, expansion; enlargement, widening; prolongation; *Surg.* dilatation; respite (in trouble)

**dilatador** /dilata'ðor/ *a* dilating. *m*, *Surg.* dilater
**dilatar** /dila'tar/ *vt* to dilate, enlarge; expand; delay, postpone; spread, publish abroad; prolong; —*vr* expand; be prolix, spread oneself
**dilatorio** /dila'torio/ *a* procrastinating, dilatory
**dilección** /dilek'θion; dilek'sion/ *f*, affection, love
**dilema** /di'lema/ *m*, dilemma
**diletantismo** /diletan'tismo/ *m*, dilettantism
**diligencia** /dili'henθia; dili'hensia/ *f*, care, conscientiousness, industry; haste, briskness; diligence (coach); *Inf.* business, occupation. **hacer sus diligencias,** to try one's best
**diligenciar** /dilihen'θiar; dilihen'siar/ *vt* to set on foot, put into motion
**diligente** /dili'hente/ *a* diligent, conscientious, industrious; speedy, prompt
**dilucidación** /diluθiða'θion; dilusiða'sion/ *f*, elucidation, clarification
**dilucidar** /diluθi'ðar; dilusi'ðar/ *vt* to elucidate, clarify
**dilución** /dilu'θion; dilu'sion/ *f*, dilution
**diluir** /di'luir/ *vt irr* to dilute. See **huir**
**diluviano** /dilu'βiano/ *a* diluvian
**diluviar** /dilu'βiar/ *vi* to teem with rain
**diluvio** /di'luβio/ *m*, flood, inundation; *Inf.* very heavy rain, deluge; overabundance
**dimanación** /dimana'θion; dimana'sion/ *f*, emanation, source
**dimanar** /dima'nar/ *vi* (*with de*) to rise in (rivers); proceed from, originate in
**dimensión** /dimen'sion/ *f*, dimension; size, extent
**dimes y diretes** /'dimes i di'retes/ *m pl*, *Inf.* backchat
**diminutivo** /diminu'tiβo/ *a* diminutive; diminishing; *Gram.* diminutive
**diminuto** /dimi'nuto/ *a* defective, incomplete; minute, very small
**dimisión** /dimi'sion/ *f*, resignation (of office, etc.)
**dimisorias** /dimi'sorias/ *f pl*, *Eccl.* letter dimissory. *Inf.* **dar d. a uno,** to give a person his marching orders, dismiss
**dimitente** /dimi'tente/ *a* resigning; retiring. *mf* resigner (of a post)
**dimitir** /dimi'tir/ *vt* to resign (office, post, etc.)
**Dinamarca** /dina'marka/ Denmark
**dinamarqués** /dinamar'kes/ **(-esa)** *a* Danish —*n* Dane
**dinámica** /di'namika/ *f*, dynamics
**dinámico** /di'namiko/ *a* dynamic
**dinamita** /dina'mita/ *f*, dynamite
**dinamo** /'dinamo/ *f*, dynamo
**dinasta** /di'nasta/ *mf* dynast
**dinastía** /dinas'tia/ *f*, dynasty
**dinástico** /di'nastiko/ *a* dynastic
**dineral** /dine'ral/ *m*, large amount of money, fortune
**dinero** /di'nero/ *m*, money; Peruvian coin; wealth, fortune; currency. **d. contante, d. junto,** ready cash, **Poderoso caballero es Don D.,** Money talks
**dinosauro** /dino'sauro/ *m*, dinosaur
**dintel** /'dintel/ *m*, lintel
**diocesano** /dioθe'sano; diose'sano/ *a* diocesan
**diócesis** /'dioθesis; 'diosesis/ *f*, diocese
**Dios** /dios/ *m*, God; deity. **¡D. le guarde!** God keep you! **¡D. lo quiera!** God grant it! **D. mediante,** God willing (D.V.). **¡D. mío!** Good gracious! **De menos nos hizo D.,** Nothing is impossible, Never say die. *Inf.* **haber** ( *or* **armarse**) **la de D. es Cristo,** to be the deuce of a row. **¡No lo quiera D.!** God forbid! **¡Plegue a D.!** Please God! **¡Por D.!** For goodness sake! Heavens! **¡Válgame D.!** Bless me! **¡Vaya Vd. con D.!** Goodbye! Off with you! Depart! **¡Vive D.!** By God!
**diosa** /'diosa/ *f*, goddess
**diploma** /di'ploma/ *m*, license, bull; diploma. **d. de suficiencia,** general diploma
**diplomacia** /diplo'maθia; diplo'masia/ *f*, diplomacy; tactfulness; *Inf.* astuteness
**diplomático** /diplo'matiko/ *a* diplomatic; tactful; *Inf.* astute. *m*, diplomat. **cuerpo d.,** diplomatic corps
**dipsomanía** /dipsoma'nia/ *f*, dipsomania
**dipsómano** /dip'somano/ **(-na)** *n* dipsomaniac

**diptongo** /dip'toŋgo/ *m,* diphthong

**diputación** /diputa'θion; diputa'sion/ *f,* deputation; mission

**diputado** /dipu'taðo/ **(-da)** *n* deputy, delegate. **d. a Cortes,** member of the Spanish Parliament, congressman

**diputar** /dipu'tar/ *vt* to appoint, depute; delegate; empower

**dique** /'dike/ *m,* dike; dam; dry dock; *Fig.* bulwark, check; **d. flotante,** floating dock

**dirección** /direk'θion; direk'sion/ *f,* direction; management, control, guidance; directorate; instruction; information; order, wish, command; editorial board; directorship, managership; (postal) address; managerial office. **d. cablegráfica,** cable address. **d. particular,** home address

**directiva** /direk'tiβa/ *f,* board, governing body

**directivo** /direk'tiβo/ *a* directive, control, ling, guiding, managing

**directo** /di'rekto/ *a* direct; straight

**director** /direk'tor/ **(-ra)** *a* directing, controlling —*n* director; manager; principal, head (schools, etc.); editor. **d. del ceremonial,** chief of protocol. **d. de escena,** stagemanager. **d. espiritual,** *Eccl.* father confessor. **d. gerente,** managing director

**directorio** /direk'torio/ *a* directory, advising. *m,* directory; directorate, board of directors

**dirigible** /diri'hiβle/ *m,* airship

**dirigir** /diri'hir/ *vt* to direct; regulate; govern; supervise; guide; *Mus.* conduct; address (an envelope, etc.); keep (a shop, etc.); edit; put (a question); point (a gun); cast (a glance); —*vr* go; wend one's way. **d. la palabra** ( **a**), to speak to, address. **d. la vista a,** to look towards, look in the direction of, turn towards, turn in the direction of. **dirigirse a,** to go towards; make one's way to

**dirimir** /diri'mir/ *vt* to annul, make void; break, dissolve; settle (disputes, etc.)

**discernidor** /disθerni'ðor; disserni'ðor/ **(-ra)** *n* discerner —*a* discerning

**discernimiento** /disθerni'miento; disserni'miento/ *m,* discernment; judgment; discrimination

**discernir** /disθer'nir; disser'nir/ *vt irr* to discern, distinguish —*Pres. Indic.* **discierno, disciernes, discierne, disciernen.** *Pres. Subjunc.* **discierna, disciernas, discierna, disciernan**

**disciplina** /disθi'plina; dissi'plina/ *f,* discipline; system, philosophy, education; submission, obedience; subject (arts or science); *pl* scourge

**disciplinante** /disθipli'nante; dissipli'nante/ *a* disciplinary. *m,* scourge

**disciplinar** /disθipli'nar; dissipli'nar/ *vt* to train; educate; scourge, beat; discipline; —*vr* scourge oneself

**disciplinario** /disθipli'nario; dissipli'nario/ *a* disciplinary

**discipulado** /disθipu'laðo; dissipu'laðo/ *m,* pupilship, studentship; education, teaching; discipleship; body of pupils (of a school, etc.)

**discípulo** /dis'θipulo; dis'sipulo/ **(-la)** *n* pupil, student; disciple, follower

**disco** /'disko/ *m,* discus; disk; phonograph record; *Astron.* disk. **d. compacto,** compact disc. **d. de señales,** railway signal. **d. giratorio,** turntable (of a phonograph)

**discóbolo** /dis'koβolo/ *m,* discus thrower

**díscolo** /'diskolo/ *a* willful, unmanageable

**disconformidad** /diskonformi'ðað/ *f,* disagreement; disconformity

**discontinuo** /diskon'tinuo/ *a* intermittent, discontinuous

**discordancia** /diskor'ðanθia; diskor'ðansia/ *f,* discord, disagreement

**discordar** /diskor'ðar/ *vi* to be discordant; disagree; *Mus.* be out of tune

**discorde** /dis'korðe/ *a* discordant; *Mus.* dissonant

**discordia** /dis'korðia/ *f,* discord, disagreement

**discreción** /diskre'θion; diskre'sion/ *f,* discretion; circumspection; prudence, good sense; shrewdness; pithy or clever saying. **a d.,** at discretion; at will; voluntarily. *Mil.* **darse** ( *or* **entregarse**) **a d.,** to surrender unconditionally

**discrecional** /diskreθio'nal; diskresio'nal/ *a* optional, voluntary

**discrepancia** /diskre'panθia; diskre'pansia/ *f,* discrepancy; disagreement

**discrepar** /diskre'par/ *vi* to be discrepant; differ; disagree

**discreto** /dis'kreto/ *a* discreet; ingenious, witty

**disculpa** /dis'kulpa/ *f,* excuse

**disculpabilidad** /diskulpaβili'ðað/ *f,* pardonableness

**disculpable** /diskul'paβle/ *a* excusable

**disculpar** /diskul'par/ *vt* to excuse; forgive, pardon; —*vr* apologize; excuse oneself

**discurrir** /disku'rrir/ *vi* to wander, roam; flow, run (rivers, etc.); (*with en*) consider, think about; (*with sobre*) discourse on; —*vt* invent; conjecture

**discursivo** /diskur'siβo/ *a* discursive; thoughtful, reflective

**discurso** /dis'kurso/ *m,* reasoning power; oration, discourse; consideration, reflection; speech, conversation; dissertation. **d. aceptatorio,** acceptance speech

**discusión** /disku'sion/ *f,* discussion

**discutible** /disku'tiβle/ *a* debatable; disputable

**discutir** /disku'tir/ *vt* to discuss, debate, consider

**disecar** /dise'kar/ *vt Anat.* to dissect; stuff animals; mount plants

**disección** /disek'θion; disek'sion/ *f,* dissection

**disector** /disek'tor/ *m,* dissector, anatomist

**diseminación** /disemina'θion; disemina'sion/ *f,* dissemination

**diseminar** /disemi'nar/ *vt* to disseminate; spread

**disensión** /disen'sion/ *f,* dissension

**disentería** /disente'ria/ *f,* dysentery

**disentimiento** /disenti'miento/ *m,* dissent

**disentir** /disen'tir/ *vi irr* to dissent; disagree. See **sentir**

**diseñador** /diseɲa'ðor/ *m,* delineator, drawer

**diseñar** /dise'ɲar/ *vt* to outline, sketch

**diseño** /di'seɲo/ *m,* outline, sketch; plan; description

**disertación** /diserta'θion; diserta'sion/ *f,* dissertation

**disertar** /diser'tar/ *vi* (*with sobre*) to discourse on, discuss, treat of

**diserto** /di'serto/ *a* eloquent

**disfavor** /disfa'βor/ *m,* disfavor, discourtesy, slight

**disforme** /dis'forme/ *a* deformed; ugly; enormous

**disfraz** /dis'fraθ; dis'fras/ *m,* disguise; mask; fancy dress; pretense

**disfrazar** /disfra'θar; disfra'sar/ *vt* to disguise; dissemble, misrepresent; —*vr* disguise oneself; wear fancy dress

**disfrutar** /disfru'tar/ *vt* to enjoy (health, comfort, friendship, etc.); reap the benefit of; —*vi* take pleasure in, enjoy

**disfrute** /dis'frute/ *m,* enjoyment, use, benefit

**disgregación** /disgrega'θion; disgrega'sion/ *f,* separation, disjunction

**disgregar** /disgre'gar/ *vt* to separate, disjoin

**disgustado** /disgus'taðo/ *a* annoyed; discontented, dissatisfied; melancholy, depressed

**disgustar** /disgus'tar/ *vt* to displease, dissatisfy; annoy; *Fig.* depress; —*vr* quarrel, fall out. **Me disgusta la idea de marcharme,** I don't like the idea of going away

**disgusto** /dis'gusto/ *m,* displeasure, dissatisfaction; discontent; annoyance; affliction, sorrow, trouble; quarrel; boredom; repugnance

**disidente** /disi'ðente/ *a* dissenting. *mf* dissenter, nonconformist

**disidir** /disi'ðir/ *vi* to dissent

**disímil** /di'simil/ *a* dissimilar, different, unlike

**disimulación** /disimula'θion; disimula'sion/ *f,* dissimulation, pretense

**disimulado** /disimu'laðo/ *a* feigned, pretended

**disimular** /disimu'lar/ *vt* to dissemble; pretend, feign; put up with, tolerate; misrepresent, misinterpret

**disimulo** /di'simulo/ *m,* pretense, dissimulation; tolerance, patience

**disipación** /disipa'θion; disipa'sion/ *f,* dispersion; dissipation, frivolity; immorality

**disipado** /disi'paðo/ *a* spendthrift; dissipated, frivolous

**disipar** /disi'par/ *vt* to disperse; squander; —*vr* evaporate; vanish, fade, disappear

**dislate** /di'slate/ *m*, absurdity, nonsense

**dislocación** /disloka'θion; disloka'sion/ *f*, dislocation

**dislocar** /dislo'kar/ *vt* to dislocate; —*vr* dislocate; sprain

**disminución** /disminu'θion; disminu'sion/ *f*, diminution. **ir ( una cosa) en d.,** to diminish, decrease; taper, grow to a point

**disminuido físico** /dismi'nuiðo 'fisiko/ *m*, physically impaired person, physically handicapped person

**disminuir** /dismi'nuir/ *vt* and *vi irr* to diminish, decrease. See **huir**

**disociación** /disoθia'θion; disosia'sion/ *f*, dissociation. **d. nuclear,** nuclear fission

**disociar** /diso'θiar; diso'siar/ *vt* to dissociate, separate; *Chem.* dissociate

**disoluble** /diso'luβle/ *a* dissoluble

**disolución** /disolu'θion; disolu'sion/ *f*, dissolution; immorality, laxity; disintegration; loosening, relaxation

**disolutivo** /disolu'tiβo/ *a* dissolvent, solvent

**disoluto** /diso'luto/ *a* dissolute, vicious

**disolvente** /disol'βente/ *m*, dissolvent, solvent

**disolver** /disol'βer/ *vt* and *irr* to loosen, undo; *Chem.* dissolve; separate, disintegrate; annul. See **resolver**

**disonancia** /diso'nanθia; diso'nansia/ *f*, dissonance; disagreement; *Mus.* dissonant

**disonante** /diso'nante/ *a* dissonant; discordant, inharmonious

**disonar** /diso'nar/ *vi irr* to be inharmonious; disagree. See **sonar**

**dísono** /di'sono/ *a* dissonant

**dispar** /dis'par/ *a* unequal; unlike, different

**disparadero** /dispara'ðero/ *m*, trigger of a firearm

**disparador** /dispara'ðor/ *m*, shooter, firer; trigger (of firearms); ratchet (of watch)

**disparar** /dispa'rar/ *vt* to shoot, fire; throw or discharge with violence; —*vr* run precipitately; rush (towards); bolt (horses); race (of a machine); explode, go off; *Inf.* go too far, misbehave

**disparatado** /dispara'taðo/ *a* foolish; absurd, unreasonable

**disparatar** /dispara'tar/ *vi* to act or speak foolishly

**disparate** /dispa'rate/ *m*, foolishness, nonsense

**disparidad** /dispari'ðað/ *f*, disparity, dissimilarity

**disparo** /dis'paro/ *m*, shooting; explosion; racing (of an engine); discharge; foolishness

**dispendio** /dis'pendio/ *m*, squandering, extravagance

**dispendioso** /dispen'dioso/ *a* costly, expensive

**dispensa** /dis'pensa/ *f*, dispensation; privilege

**dispensable** /dispen'saβle/ *a* dispensable; excusable

**dispensación** /dispensa'θion; dispensa'sion/ *f*, dispensation; exemption

**dispensar** /dispen'sar/ *vt* to grant, concede, distribute; exempt; excuse, forgive

**dispensario** /dispen'sario/ *m*, dispensary

**dispepsia** /dis'pepsia/ *f*, dyspepsia

**dispéptico** /dis'peptiko/ **(-ca)** *a* and *n* dyspeptic

**dispersar** /disper'sar/ *vt* to disperse, scatter, separate; *Mil.* rout

**dispersión** /disper'sion/ *f*, dispersion

**disperso** /dis'perso/ *a* dispersed, scattered; *Mil.* separated from regiment

**displicencia** /displi'θenθia; displi'sensia/ *f*, disagreeableness, coldness; hesitation, lack of enthusiasm

**displicente** /displi'θente; displi'sente/ *a* unpleasant, disagreeable; difficult, peevish

**disponer** /dispo'ner/ *vt irr* to arrange, dispose; direct, order; decide; prepare, get ready; —*vi* (*with de*) dispose of, make free with; possess; have at one's disposal; —*vr* prepare oneself to die; make one's will; get ready. See **poner**

**disponible** /dispo'niβle/ *a* disposable; available

**disposición** /disposi'θion; disposi'sion/ *f*, arrangement; order, instruction; decision; preparation; aptitude, talent; disposal; condition of health; temperament; grace of bearing; promptitude, competence; measure, step, preliminary; *Archit.* plan; proviso, stipulation; symmetry. **A la d. de Vd,** I (we, he, it, etc.) am at your disposal. **hallarse en d. de hacer**

**una cosa,** to be ready to do something. **última d.,** last will and testament

**dispositivo** /disposi'tiβo/ *a* directory, advisory

**dispuesto** /dis'puesto/ *a* ready, prepared; handsome, gallant; clever, wide-awake. **bien d.,** well-disposed; well, healthy. **mal d.,** ill-disposed; disinclined; out of sorts, indisposed

**disputa** /dis'puta/ *f*, dispute. **sin d.,** undoubtedly

**disputar** /dispu'tar/ *vt* to argue, debate; dispute, question; *Fig.* fight for

**disquisición** /diskisi'θion; diskisi'sion/ *f*, disquisition

**distancia** /dis'tanθia; dis'tansia/ *f*, distance; interval of time; difference, dissimilarity; unfriendliness, coolness

**distanciar** /distan'θiar; distan'siar/ *vt* to separate, place farther apart

**distante** /dis'tante/ *a* separated; distant; far off

**distar** /dis'tar/ *vi* to be distant (time and place); be different, unlike

**distender** /disten'der/ **(se)** *vt* and *vr Med.* to distend, swell

**distinción** /distin'θion; distin'sion/ *f*, distinction, differentiation; difference, individuality; privilege, honor; clarity, order; distinction (of bearing or mind). **a d. de,** unlike, different from

**distinguible** /distin'guiβle/ *a* distinguishable

**distinguido** /distin'guiðo/ *a* distinguished, illustrious

**distinguir** /distin'guir/ *vt* to distinguish, discern; differentiate; characterize; esteem, honor, respect; discriminate; see with difficulty; make out; —*vr* be different; excel, distinguish oneself

**distintivo** /distin'tiβo/ *a* distinguishing; distinctive. *m*, distinguishing mark

**distinto** /dis'tinto/ *a* different; distinct; clear

**distracción** /distrak'θion; distrak'sion/ *f*, distraction; abstraction, heedlessness, absentmindedness; pleasure, amusement; licentiousness

**distraer** /distra'er/ *vt irr* to lead astray; distract (attention); influence for bad; amuse —*vr* be absentminded; amuse oneself. See **traer**

**distraído** /distra'iðo/ *a* abstracted, absentminded; inattentive; licentious

**distribución** /distriβu'θion; distriβu'sion/ *f*, distribution; (gen. *pl*) share

**distribuidor** /distriβui'ðor/ **(-ra)** *a* distributing —*n* distributor

**distribuir** /distri'βuir/ *vt irr* to distribute; share out, divide. See **huir**

**distributivo** /distriβu'tiβo/ *a* distributive

**distrito** /dis'trito/ *m*, district

**disturbio** /dis'turβio/ *m*, disturbance

**disuadir** /disua'ðir/ *vt* to dissuade

**disuasión** /disua'sion/ *f*, dissuasion

**disuasivo** /disua'siβo/ *a* dissuasive

**disyunción** /disyun'θion; disyun'sion/ *f*, disjunction

**ditirambo** /diti'rambo/ *m*, dithyramb; excessive praise

**diurético** /diu'retiko/ *a* diuretic

**diurno** /'diurno/ *a* diurnal

**diva** /'diβa/ *f*, prima donna; woman singer

**divagación** /diβaga'θion; diβaga'sion/ *f*, wandering, roaming; digression

**divagar** /diβa'gar/ *vi* to wander, roam; digress

**diván** /di'βan/ *m*, divan (Turkish supreme council); divan, sofa; collection of Arabic, Persian or Turkish poems

**divergencia** /diβer'henθia; diβer'hensia/ *f*, divergence; disagreement

**divergente** /diβer'hente/ *a* divergent; conflicting, dissentient

**divergir** /diβer'hir/ *vi* to diverge; dissent

**diversidad** /diβersi'ðað/ *f*, diversity, unlikeness, difference; variety

**diversificar** /diβersifi'kar/ *vt* to differentiate; vary

**diversión** /diβer'sion/ *f*, pastime, amusement; *Mil.* diversion

**diverso** /di'βerso/ *a* diverse, unlike; *pl* various, many

**divertido** /diβer'tiðo/ *a* amusing, funny, entertaining

**divertir** /diβer'tir/ *vt irr* to lead astray, turn aside; entertain; *Mil.* create a diversion —*vr* amuse oneself. See **sentir**

**dividendo** /diβi'ðendo/ *m*, dividend. *Com.* **d. activo**, dividend

**dividir** /diβi'ðir/ *vt* to divide; distribute; stir up discord; —*vr* (*with de*) part company with, leave

**divieso** /di'βieso/ *m*, *Med.* boil

**divinamente** /diβina'mente/ *adv* divinely; excellently, admirably, perfectly

**divinidad** /diβini'ðað/ *f*, divinity, Godhead; person or thing of great beauty

**divinizar** /diβini'θar; diβini'sar/ *vt* to deify; sanctify; extol

**divino** /di'βino/ *a* divine; excellent, admirable, superb

**divisa** /di'βisa/ *f*, badge, emblem; *Herald.* motto

**divisar** /diβi'sar/ *vt* to glimpse, descry

**divisibilidad** /diβisiβili'ðað/ *f*, divisibility

**divisible** /diβi'siβle/ *a* divisible

**división** /diβi'sion/ *f*, division, partition; discord; (*Math. Mil.*) division; hyphen; apportionment; district, ward

**divisor** /diβi'sor/ (**-ra**) *a* dividing, separating. *m*, *Math.* divisor —*n* divider, separator

**divisoria** /diβi'soria/ *f*, dividing line

**divisorio** /diβi'sorio/ *a* dividing

**divorciar** /diβor'θiar; diβor'siar/ *vt* to divorce; separate; —*vr* be divorced, be separated

**divorcio** /di'βorθio; di'βorsio/ *m*, divorce

**divulgación** /diβulga'θion; diβulga'sion/ *f*, spreading, publication, propagation

**divulgar** /diβul'gar/ (**se**) *vt* and *vr* to spread abroad, publish

**do** /do/ *m*, *Mus.* doh, C. *Poet.* where

**dobladillo** /doβla'ðiʎo; doβla'ðiyo/ *m*, *Sew.* hem; turn-up (of a trouser)

**doblado** /do'βlaðo/ *a* stocky, thickset, sturdy; rocky, rough, uneven; dissembling. *m*, garret

**dobladura** /doβla'ðura/ *f*, fold, crease; crease mark

**doblamiento** /doβla'miento/ *m*, doubling; folding

**doblar** /do'βlar/ *vt* to double, multiply by two; fold, double; bend; persuade, induce; *Naut.* double, sail round; turn, walk round; —*vi Eccl.* ring the passing bell; *Theat.* double a role; —*vr* fold, double; bend; bow; stoop; allow oneself to be persuaded

**doble** /'doβle/ *a* double, twofold; duplicate; insincere, false; thick (cloth); *Bot.* double (flowers); hardy, robust. *m*, fold, crease; *Eccl.* passing-bell; Spanish dance step —*adv* double, twice. *Eccl.* **rito d.**, full rites

**doblegar** /doβle'gar/ *vt* to fold; bend; brandish; dissuade in favor of another proposition; —*vr* submit, give way, acquiesce

**doblete** /do'βlete/ *a* of medium thickness. *m*, imitation jewel

**doblez** /do'βleθ; do'βles/ *m*, fold, crease; fold mark. *mf*, double dealing, treachery

**doblilla** /do'βliʎa; do'βliya/ *f*, twenty-real coin

**doblón** /do'βlon/ *m*, doubloon

**doce** /'doθe; 'dose/ *a* twelve. *m*, twelve; twelfth (of the month). **las d.**, twelve o'clock

**docena** /do'θena; do'sena/ *f*, dozen. **la d. del fraile**, baker's dozen

**docente** /do'θente; do'sente/ *a* teaching

**dócil** /'doθil; 'dosil/ *a* docile; obedient; flexible, easily worked (metals, etc.)

**docilidad** /doθili'ðað; dosili'ðað/ *f*, docility; obedience; flexibility

**docto** /'dokto/ *a* learned, erudite

**doctor** /dok'tor/ (**-ra**) *n* doctor; physician; teacher. *f*, *Inf.* blue-stocking

**doctorado** /dokto'raðo/ *m*, doctorate

**doctorarse** /dokto'rarse/ *vr* to get one's doctorate

**doctrina** /dok'trina/ *f*, doctrine; instruction, teaching; theory, conception; *Eccl.* sermon

**doctrinar** /doktri'nar/ *vt* to teach, instruct

**documentación** /dokumenta'θion; dokumenta'sion/ *f*, documentation; collection of documents, papers

**documental** /dokumen'tal/ *a* documental. *m*, documentary film

**documentar** /dokumen'tar/ *vt* to document

**Dodecaneso, el** /doðeka'neso, el/ the Dodecanese

**dogal** /do'gal/ *m*, halter; noose; slipknot. *Fig.* **estar con el d. a la garganta**, to be in a fix

**dogma** /'dogma/ *m*, dogma

**dogmático** /dog'matiko/ *a* dogmatic

**dogmatizar** /dogmati'θar; dogmati'sar/ *vt* to teach heretical doctrines; dogmatize

**dólar** /'dolar/ *m*, dollar

**dolencia** /do'lenθia; do'lensia/ *f*, ailment; pain; ache

**doler** /do'ler/ *vi* irr to be in pain; be reluctant; —*vr* be sorry, regretful; grieve; sympathize, be compassionate; complain —*Pres. Indic.* **duelo, dueles, duele, duelen.** *Pres. Subjunc.* **duela, duelas, duela, duelan**

**doliente** /do'liente/ *a* suffering; ill; afflicted, sad. *mf* sufferer, ill person. *m*, chief mourner

**dolo** /'dolo/ *m*, fraud; deception; deceit; *Law.* premeditation

**dolor** /do'lor/ *m*, pain, ache; mental suffering. **d. sordo**, dull pain

**dolorido** /dolo'riðo/ *a* painful; afflicted, sad

**doloroso** /dolo'roso/ *a* sad, regrettable; mournful, sorrowful; pitiful; painful

**doloso** /do'loso/ *a* deceitful, fraudulent

**domable** /do'maβle/ *a* tamable; controllable

**domador** /doma'ðor/ (**-ra**) *n* subduer, controller; wild animal tamer; horsebreaker

**domadura** /doma'ðura/ *f*, taming, breaking in; controlling (emotions)

**domar** /do'mar/ *vt* to tame, break in; control, repress (emotions)

**domesticable** /domesti'kaβle/ *a* tamable; domesticable

**domesticar** /domesti'kar/ *vt* to tame; domesticate; —*vr* grow tame; become domesticated

**domesticidad** /domestiθi'ðað; domestisi'ðað/ *f*, domesticity

**doméstico** /do'mestiko/ (**-ca**) *a* domestic, domesticated; tame —*n* domestic worker

**domiciliar** /domiθi'liar; domisi'liar/ *vt* to domicile; —*vr* become domiciled, settle down

**domiciliario** /domiθi'liario; domisi'liario/ *a* domiciliary

**domicilio** /domi'θilio; domi'silio/ *m*, domicile; house

**dominación** /domina'θion; domina'sion/ *f*, domination; power, authority; command (of a military position, etc.); *Mil.* high ground; *pl* dominions, angels

**dominador** /domina'ðor/ *a* dominating; overbearing

**dominante** /domi'nante/ *a* dominating; overbearing, domineering; dominant. *f*, *Mus.* dominant

**dominar** /domi'nar/ *vt* to dominate; repress, subdue; *Fig.* master (branch of knowledge); —*vi* stand out; —*vr* control oneself

**dómine** /'domine/ *m*, *Inf.* teacher; pedant, know-all

**domingo** /do'miŋgo/ *m*, Sunday. **d. de Cuasimodo**, Low Sunday. **d. de Pentecostés**, Whitsuntide Sunday. **d. de Ramos**, Palm Sunday. **d. de Resurrección**, Easter Sunday

**dominguero** /domiŋ'guero/ *a* *Inf.* Sunday; special; excursion (trains)

**dominicano** /domini'kano/ (**-na**) *a* and *n* Dominican; native of Santo Domingo

**dominio** /do'minio/ *m*, authority, power; rule, sovereignty; dominion (country); domain

**dominó** /domi'no/ *m*, domino; game of dominoes

**don** /don/ *m*, gift; quality, characteristic; talent. **d. de gentes**, the human touch; charm

**don** /don/ *m*, title of respect equivalent to English Mr. or Esquire. Used only before given name and *not* before a family name, e.g. *don Juan Martínez*, or *don Juan*

**donación** /dona'θion; dona'sion/ *f*, donation, gift, grant

**donador** /dona'ðor/ (**-ra**) *a* donating —*n* donor

**donaire** /do'naire/ *m*, discretion; wit; witticism; gracefulness, elegance

**donar** /do'nar/ *vt* to bestow, give; transfer; grant

**donatario** /dona'tario/ *m*, recipient, grantee

**donativo** /dona'tiβo/ *m*, gift, present, donation

**doncel** /don'θel; don'sel/ *m*, squire, youth not yet armed; knight; male virgin; king's page

**doncella** /don'θeʎa; don'seya/ *f,* virgin, maid; maid-servant; lady's maid

**doncellez** /donθe'ʎeθ; donse'yes/ *f,* virginity; maidenhood

**donde** /'donde/ *adv* where, wherein. Sometimes used as relative pronoun "in which" (e.g. *La casa d. estaba,* The house in which I was) —*interr* ¿**dónde?** ¿**A dónde va Vd.?** Where are you going to? ¿**De dónde viene Vd.?** Where do you come from? ¿**Por dónde se va a Madrid?** Which is the way to Madrid?

**dondequiera** /donde'kiera/ *adv* wherever, anywhere, everywhere

**donoso** /do'noso/ *a* witty; graceful

**donostiarra** /donos'tiarra/ *a* and *mf* of or from San Sebastian (N. Spain)

**donosura** /dono'sura/ *f,* wit; grace; dash, verve

**doña** /'doɲa/ *f,* feminine equivalent of **don** (e.g. *D. Catalina Palacios*)

**dorado** /do'raðo/ *a* golden, gilded; fortunate, happy. *m,* gilding

**dorador** /dora'ðor/ *m,* gilder

**doradura** /dora'ðura/ *f,* gilding

**dorar** /do'rar/ *vt* to gild; make golden; *Fig.* gild the pill; *Cul.* toast lightly; —*vr* become golden

**dórico** /'doriko/ *a* Doric

**dormidero** /dormi'ðero/ *a* soporiferous, narcotic

**dormilón** /dormi'lon/ **(-ona)** *a Inf.* sleepy —*n* sleepyhead

**dormir** /dor'mir/ *vi irr* to sleep; spend the night; *Fig.* grow calm; sleep (tops); (*with sobre*) sleep on, consider; —*vt* put to sleep; —*vr* go to sleep; go slow over, neglect; be dormant; go numb (limbs). **d. como un lirón,** to sleep like a top. *Inf.* **d. la mona,** to sleep oneself sober. **entre duerme y vela,** half-awake —*Pres. Indic.* **duermo, duermes, duerme, duermen.** *Pres. Part.* **durmiendo.** *Preterite* **durmió, durmieron.** *Pres. Subjunc.* **duerma, duermas, duerma, duerman**

**dormitar** /dormi'tar/ *vi* to doze

**dormitivo** /dormi'tiβo/ *a,* sedative

**dormitorio** /dormi'torio/ *m,* dormitory; bedroom

**dorsal** /dor'sal/ *a* dorsal

**dorso** /'dorso/ *m,* back; dorsum

**dos** /dos/ *a* two. *m,* two; second (of the month). **las d.,** two o'clock. **d. a d.,** two against two. **de d. en d.,** two by two. *Inf.* **en un d. por tres,** in a twinkling

**doscientos** /dos'θientos; dos'sientos/ *a* and *m,* two hundred; two hundredth

**dosel** /do'sel/ *m,* canopy; dais

**dosis** /'dosis/ *f,* dose; quantity

**dotación** /dota'θion; dota'sion/ *f,* endowment; *Naut.* crew; staff, workers; equipment

**dotar** /do'tar/ *vt* to give as dowry; endow, found; *Fig.* endow (with talents, etc.); equip; apportion (salary)

**dote** /'dote/ *mf,* dowry. *f,* (gen. *pl*) gifts, talents. **dotes de mando,** capacity for leadership

**dracma** /'drakma/ *f,* drachma; dram

**draga** /'draga/ *f,* dredger

**dragado** /dra'gaðo/ *m,* dredging

**dragaminas** /draga'minas/ *m, Nav.* minesweeper

**dragar** /dra'gar/ *vt* to dredge

**dragón** /dra'gon/ *m,* dragon; *Bot.* snapdragon; *Mil.* dragoon; *Zool.* dragon, giant lizard; *Astron.* Draco

**dragona** /dra'gona/ *f,* female dragon; *Mil.* shoulderstrap

**drama** /'drama/ *m,* drama; play; drama. **d. lírico,** opera

**dramática** /dra'matika/ *f,* dramatic art

**dramático** /dra'matiko/ *a* dramatic; vivid, unexpected, moving

**dramaturgo** /drama'turgo/ *m,* dramatist, playwright

**drenaje** /dre'nahe/ *m,* drainage (of land and wounds)

**Dresde** /'dresðe/ Dresden

**dril** /dril/ *m,* drill, cotton cloth

**droga** /'droga/ *f,* drug; falsehood, deception; nuisance

**droguería** /droge'ria/ *f,* chemist's shop; drug trade

**droguero** /dro'gero/ **(-ra)** *n* chemist, druggist

**dromedario** /drome'ðario/ *m, Zool.* dromedary

**druida** /'druiða/ *m,* Druid

**dualidad** /duali'ðað/ *f,* duality

**ducado** /du'kaðo/ *m,* dukedom; duchy; ducat

**ducentésimo** /duθen'tesimo; dusen'tesimo/ *a* two hundredth

**ducha** /'dutʃa/ *f,* shower-bath; douche; stripe in cloth; furrow

**ducho** /'dutʃo/ *a* experienced, skillful

**dúctil** /'duktil/ *a* ductile (metals); adaptable, docile, flexible

**ductilidad** /duktili'ðað/ *f,* ductility; adaptability

**duda** /'duða/ *f,* doubt, hesitation; problem. **sin d.,** doubtless

**dudable** /du'ðaβle/ *a* doubtful

**dudar** /du'ðar/ *vi* to be in doubt; —*vt* doubt, disbelieve

**dudoso** /du'ðoso/ *a* doubtful; uncertain, not probable

**duela** /'duela/ *f,* hoop, stave

**duelista** /due'lista/ *mf* dueler; duelist

**duelo** /'duelo/ *m,* sorrow, grief; mourning; mourners; duel; (gen. *pl*) troubles, trials. **duelos y quebrantos,** *Cul.* fried offal. **sin d.,** in abundance

**duende** /'duende/ *m,* imp, elf, sprite, ghost

**dueña** /'dueɲa/ *f,* owner, proprietress, mistress; duenna; married lady *Obs.*

**dueño** /'dueɲo/ *m,* owner, proprietor; master (of servants). **d. de sí mismo,** self-controlled

**Duero, el** /'duero, el/ the Douro

**duetista** /due'tista/ *mf* duetist

**dula** /'dula/ *f,* common pasture ground or herds

**dulce** /'dulθe; dulse/ *a* sweet; fresh, pure; fresh, not salty; fragrant; melodious; pleasant, agreeable; tender, gentle; soft (metals). *m,* sweetmeat, bonbon. **d. de almíbar,** preserved fruit.

**dulcedumbre** /dulθe'ðumbre; dulse'ðumbre/ *f,* sweetness; softness

**dulcémele** /dulθe'mele; dulse'mele/ *m,* dulcimer

**dulcera** /dul'θera; dul'sera/ *f,* preserve dish, fruit dish

**dulcería** /dulθe'ria; dulse'ria/ *f,* See **confitería**

**dulcificar** /dulθifi'kar; dulsifi'kar/ *vt* to make sweet; alleviate, sweeten

**dulcinea** /dul'θinea; dul'sinea/ *f, Inf.* sweetheart; ideal

**dulzaina** /dul'θaina; dul'saina/ *f, Mus.* flageolet

**dulzura** /dul'θura; dul'sura/ *f,* sweetness; gentleness; pleasure; meekness; agreeableness

**duna** /'duna/ *f,* (gen. *pl*) sand dune

**Dunas, las** /'dunas, las/ the Downs

**Dunquerque** /dun'kerke/ Dunkirk

**dúo** /'duo/ *m, Mus.* duet

**duodécimo** /duo'ðeθimo; duoðesimo/ *a* twelfth

**duodeno** /duo'ðeno/ *a* twelfth. *m, Anat.* duodenum

**duplicación** /duplika'θion; duplika'sion/ *f,* duplication

**duplicado** /dupli'kaðo/ *m,* duplicate

**duplicar** /dupli'kar/ *vt* to duplicate; double

**duplicidad** /dupliθi'ðað; duplisi'ðað/ *f,* duplicity, falseness

**duplo** /'duplo/ *a* double

**duque** /'duke/ *m,* duke

**duquesa** /du'kesa/ *f,* duchess

**duración** /dura'θion; dura'sion/ *f,* duration; durability

**duradero** /dura'ðero/ *a* lasting; durable

**durante** /du'rante/ *adv* during

**durar** /du'rar/ *vi* to continue; endure, last

**dureza** /du'reθa; du'resa/ *f,* hardness; *Med.* callosity; severity, harshness

**durmiente** /dur'miente/ *a* sleeping. *mf* sleeper; *m, Archit.* dormant

**duro** /'duro/ *a* hard; firm, unyielding; vigorous, robust; severe, inclement; exacting, cruel; *Mus.* metallic, harsh; *Art.* crude, too sharply defined; miserly, avaricious; obstinate; self-opinionated; unbearable, intolerable; merciless, hard; harsh (style). *m,* Spanish coin worth five pesetas

**dux** /duks/ *m,* doge

# E

**e** /e/ *f,* letter E —*conjunc* used instead of *y* (and) before words beginning with *i* or *hi,* provided this last is not followed by a diphthong (e.g. *e invierno, e hijos,* but *y hierro*)

**¡ea!** /'ea/ *interj* Well!; Come on!; Let's see! (often used with **pues**)

**ebanista** /eβa'nista/ *mf* cabinetmaker

**ebanistería** /eβaniste'ria/ *f,* cabinetmaker's shop; cabinetmaking or work

**ébano** /'eβano/ *m,* ebony

**ebonita** /eβo'nita/ *f,* ebonite, vulcanite

**ebrio** /'eβrio/ *a* intoxicated, inebriated

**ebullición** /eβuʎi'θion; eβuyi'sion/ *f,* boiling, ebullition

**ebúrneo** /e'βurneo/ *a* eburnine, ivory-like

**echada** /e'tʃaða/ *f,* throw, cast; pitch; fling; length of a man

**echador** /etʃa'ðor/ **(-ra)** *n* thrower. *m, Inf.* chucker-out

**echadura** /etʃa'ðura/ *f,* sitting on eggs to hatch them; (gen. *pl*) gleanings

**echamiento** /etʃa'miento/ *m,* throw, fling; throwing, casting; expulsion; rejection

**echar** /e'tʃar/ *vt* to throw, fling; eject, drive away; cast out, expel; put forth, sprout; emit, give forth; cut (teeth); dismiss, discharge; couple (animals); pour (liquids); place, apply; put into, fill; turn (keys, locks); impute; attribute; impose (penalty, taxes, etc.); play (game); try one's luck; distribute; publish, make known; perform (plays); (*with por*) go in direction of; (*with prep a* + *infin.*) begin to (**e. a andar,** to begin to walk); —*vr* throw oneself down, lie down; sit on eggs (birds); abate, calm (wind); apply oneself, concentrate on; rush (towards), fling oneself (upon). **e. abajo,** to overthrow; demolish. **e. aceite al fuego,** to add fuel to the flames. **e. a perder,** to spoil, deteriorate. *Naut.* **a. a pique,** to sink. **e. a vuelo,** to ring (bells). **e. carnes,** to put on weight, grow fat. **e. cuentas,** to reckon up. **e. de menos,** to miss; mourn absence of. **e. de ver,** to notice. *Fig.* **e. en cara,** to throw in one's face, reproach. **echarla de majo,** to play the gallant. **e. las cartas al correo,** to post the letters. **e. las cartas,** to tell fortunes. **e. el pie atrás,** *Fig.* to climb down; *Fig.* back out. **e. raíces,** to take root; **e. las bases de, e. los cimientos de,** to lay the foundation of, lay the foundation for. *Fig.* become established. **e. rayos por la boca,** to fly into a rage. **e. suertes,** to draw lots. **echarlo todo a rodar,** to spoil everything. **e. una mano,** to lend a hand

**echazón** /etʃa'θon; etʃa'son/ *f,* throw, cast; jetsam

**eclecticismo** /eklekti'θismo; eklekti'sismo/ *m,* eclecticism

**ecléctico** /e'klektiko/ **(-ca)** *a* and *n* eclectic

**eclesiástico** /ekle'siastiko/ *a* ecclesiastical. *m,* ecclesiastic, clergyman; Ecclesiasticus

**eclipsar** /eklip'sar/ *vt Astron.* to eclipse; surpass, outvie; —*vr Astron.* be in eclipse; disappear

**eclipse** /e'klipse/ *m, Astron.* eclipse; retirement, withdrawal

**écloga** /'ekloga/ *f,* eclogue

**eco** /'eko/ *m,* echo; verse-echo; muffled sound; slavish imitation or imitator

**economato** /ekono'mato/ *m,* trusteeship; cooperative store

**econometría** /ekonome'tria/ *f,* econometrics

**economía** /ekono'mia/ *f,* economy, thrift; structure, organization; poverty, shortage; saving (of time, labor, etc.); *pl* savings. **e. dirigida,** planned economy. **e. doméstica,** domestic economy. **e. política,** political economy

**económico** /eko'nomiko/ *a* economic; thrifty; avaricious; cheap

**economista** /ekono'mista/ *mf* economist

**economizar** /ekonomi'θar; ekonomi'sar/ *vt* to economize; save

**ecónomo** /e'konomo/ *m,* trustee, guardian

**ecuación** /ekua'θion; ekua'sion/ *f,* (*Math.* and *Astron.*) equation. **e. personal,** personal equation

**ecuador** /ekua'ðor/ *m,* equator

**ecuánime** /ekua'nime/ *a* calm, unruffled; impartial

**ecuanimidad** /ekuanimi'ðað/ *f,* calmness, serenity; impartiality

**ecuatorial** /ekuato'rial/ *a* equatorial

**ecuatoriano** /ekuato'riano/ **(-na)** *a* and *n* Ecuadorian

**ecuestre** /e'kuestre/ *a* equestrian

**ecuménico** /eku'meniko/ *a* ecumenical

**eczema** /'ekθema; 'eksema/ *m,* eczema

**edad** /e'ðað/ *f,* age; epoch; period. **e. de piedra,** Stone Age. **e. media,** Middle Ages. **de cierta e.,** middle-aged. **ser mayor de e.,** to have attained one's majority. **ser menor de e.,** to be a minor

**edecán** /eðe'kan/ *m,* aide-de-camp

**edema** /e'ðema/ *m,* edema

**Edén** /e'ðen/ *m,* Eden; *Fig.* paradise

**edición** /eði'θion; eði'sion/ *f,* edition. **e. diamante,** miniature edition. **e. príncipe,** first edition

**edicto** /e'ðikto/ *m,* edict, decree; public notice

**edificación** /eðifika'θion; eðifika'sion/ *f,* building, construction; edification

**edificador** /eðifika'ðor/ **(-ra)** *a* uplifting, edifying; building —*n* builder

**edificante** /eðifi'kante/ *a* building, constructing; edifying

**edificar** /eðifi'kar/ *vt* to build, construct; edify

**edificio** /eði'fiθio; eði'fisio/ *m,* building, structure, fabric

**Edimburgo** /eðim'burgo/ Edinburgh

**editar** /eði'tar/ *vt* (of a publisher) to publish; edit

**editor** /eði'tor/ **(-ra)** *n* publisher; editor

**editorial** /eðito'rial/ *a* publishing; editorial. *m,* editorial, leading article

**edredón** /eðre'ðon/ *m,* down of an eiderduck; eiderdown, quilt

**eduardiano** /eðuar'ðiano/ **(-na)** *a* and *n* Edwardian

**educable** /eðu'kaβle/ *a* educable

**educación** /eðuka'θion; eðuka'sion/ *f,* upbringing; education; good breeding, good manners

**educado** /eðu'kaðo/ *a* educated. **ser mal e.,** to be badly brought up; be ill-mannered

**educador** /eðuka'ðor/ **(-ra)** *a* educating —*n* educator

**educando** /eðu'kando/ **(-da)** *n* pupil

**educar** /eðu'kar/ *vt* to educate; bring up, train, teach, develop

**educativo** /eðuka'tiβo/ *a* educational, educative

**educción** /eðuk'θion; eðuk'sion/ *f,* eduction; inference, deduction

**educir** /eðu'θir; eðu'sir/ *vt irr* to educe; infer, deduce. See **conducir**

**efe** /'efe/ *f,* name of letter F

**efectismo** /efek'tismo/ *m,* sensationalism; striving after effect

**efectista** /efek'tista/ *a* (*Art. Lit.*) striking, sensational

**efectivo** /efek'tiβo/ *a* effective; real. *m,* cash. **hacer e.,** to put into effect

**efecto** /e'fekto/ *m,* effect, result; purpose, intent; impression; *pl* assets; goods, chattels. **efectos de escritorio,** stationery. **efectos públicos,** public securities. **en e.,** in fact, actually. **llevar a e.,** to put into effect; make effective

**efectuación** /efektua'θion; efektua'sion/ *f,* accomplishment, execution

**efectuar** /efek'tuar/ *vt* to accomplish, effect; make (a payment); —*vr* be effected; happen, take place

**eferente** /efe'rente/ *a* efferent

**efervescencia** /eferβes'θenθia; eferβes'sensia/ *f,* effervescence; excitement, enthusiasm

**efervescente** /eferβes'θente; eferβes'sente/ *a* effervescent

**Éfeso** /e'feso/ Ephesus

**eficacia** /efi'kaθia; efi'kasia/ *f,* efficacy; effectiveness

**eficaz** /efi'kaθ; efi'kas/ *a* efficacious; effective

**eficiencia** /efi'θienθia; efi'siensia/ *f,* efficiency

**eficiente** /efi'θiente; efi'siente/ *a* efficient, effective

**efigie** /e'fihie/ *f*, effigy; image, representation, symbol

**efímero** /e'fimero/ *a* ephemeral; brief

**eflorescencia** /eflores'θenθia; eflores'sensia/ *f*, *Chem.* efflorescence

**efluvio** /e'fluβio/ *m*, effluvium; exhalation

**efugio** /e'fuhio/ *m*, subterfuge, evasion

**efusión** /efu'sion/ *f*, effusion; *Fig.* spate (of words, etc.)

**efusivo** /efu'siβo/ *a* effusive, expansive

**Egeo, Mar** /e'heo, mar/ Aegean Sea

**égida** /'ehiða/ *f*, shield; egis, protection

**egipcíaco** /ehip'θiako; ehip'siako/ **(-ca), egipcio (-ia)** *a* and *n* Egyptian

**Egipto** /e'hipto/ Egypt

**egiptólogo** /ehip'tologo/ **(-ga)** *n* Egyptologist

**égloga** /'egloga/ *f*, eclogue

**egoísmo** /ego'ismo/ *m*, egoism

**egoísta** /ego'ista/ *a* egoistic. *mf* egoist

**egolatría** /egola'tria/ *f*, self-love

**egotismo** /ego'tismo/ *m*, egotism

**egotista** /ego'tista/ *a* egotistical. *mf* egotist

**egregio** /e'grehio/ *a* distinguished, celebrated

**egresado** /egre'saðo/ *m*, graduate (of a certain school)

**eje** /'ehe/ *m*, axis; axle-tree; shaft; pivot, fundamental idea. **e. trasero,** rear-axle

**ejecución** /eheku'θion; eheku'sion/ *f*, accomplishment, performance; execution, technique; death penalty

**ejecutable** /eheku'taβle/ *a* feasible, practicable

**ejecutante** /eheku'tante/ *mf Mus.* executant, performer

**ejecutar** /eheku'tar/ *vt* to discharge, perform; put to death; (*Art. Mus.*) execute; serve (a warrant, etc.); *Law.* seize (property)

**ejecutivo** /eheku''tiβo/ *a* executive; urgent

**ejecutor** /eheku'tor/ *m*, executor

**ejecutoria** /eheku'toria/ *f*, letters patent of nobility; *Law.* judgment, sentence

**ejecutoría** /ehekuto'ria/ *f*, executorship

**ejemplar** /ehem'plar/ *a* exemplary. *m*, copy, specimen; precedent; example; warning

**ejemplificar** /ehemplifi'kar/ *vi* to exemplify

**ejemplo** /e'hemplo/ *m*, example, precedent; illustration, instance; specimen. **dar e.,** to set an example. **por e.,** for example

**ejercer** /eher'θer; eher'ser/ *vt* to practice (a profession); perform, fulfill; exercise, use

**ejercicio** /eher'θiθio; eher'sisio/ *m*, exercise; practice; performance; exertion, effort; *Mil.* exercises (gen. *pl*). **ejercicios espirituales,** spiritual exercises. **ejercicios físicos,** physical training

**ejercitar** /eherθi'tar; ehersi'tar/ *vt* to exercise; train, teach; —*vr* exercise; practice

**ejército** /e'herθito; e'hersito/ *m*, army

**el** /el/ *def art m, sing* the

**él** /el/ *pers pron sing m*, he; it (*f*. **ella.** *neut* **ello**) (e.g. *Lo hizo él*, He did it). Also used with prep. (e.g. *Lo hicimos por él*, We did it for him)

**elaboración** /elaβora'θion; elaβora'sion/ *f*, elaboration, working out

**elaborado** /elaβo'raðo/ *a* elaborate

**elaborar** /elaβo'rar/ *vt* to elaborate; produce, work out

**elasticidad** /elastiθi'ðað; elastisi'ðað/ *f*, elasticity; adaptability

**elástico** /e'lastiko/ *a* elastic; adaptable. *m*, elastic tape; elastic material

**ele** /'ele/ *f*, name of letter L

**elección** /elek'θion; elek'sion/ *f*, choice; election; selection; discrimination

**electivo** /elek'tiβo/ *a* elective

**electo** /e'lekto/ *m*, elect, candidate elect

**elector** /elek'tor/ **(-ra)** *n* elector, voter. *m*, German prince *Obs.*

**electorado** /elekto'raðo/ *m*, electorate

**electoral** /elekto'ral/ *a* electoral

**electricidad** /elektriθi'ðað; elektrisi'ðað/ *f*, electricity

**electricista** /elektri'θista; elektri'sista/ *mf* electrician

**eléctrico** /e'lektriko/ *a* electric; electrical

**electrificación** /elektrifika'θion; elektrifika'sion/ *f*, electrification

**electrificar** /elektrifi'kar/ *vt* to electrify

**electrizar** /elektri'θar; elektri'sar/ *vt* to electrify; startle; —*vr* be electrified

**electrocución** /elektroku'θion; elektroku'sion/ *f*, electrocution

**electrocutar** /elektroku'tar/ *vt* to electrocute

**electrodinámica** /elektroði'namika/ *f*, electrodynamics

**electrodo** /elek'troðo/ *m*, electrode

**electroimán** /elektroi'man/ *m*, electromagnet

**electrólisis** /elek'trolisis/ *f*, electrolysis

**electrólito** /elek'trolito/ *m*, electrolyte

**electrolizar** /elektroli'θar; elektroli'sar/ *vt* to electrolyze

**electromagnético** /elektromag'netiko/ *a* electromagnetic

**electromotriz** /elektro'motriθ; elektro'motris/ *a* electromotive. **fuerza e.,** electromotive force

**electrón** /elek'tron/ *m*, electron

**electroquímica** /elektro'kimika/ *f*, electrochemistry

**electroscopio** /elektro'skopio/ *m*, electroscope

**electrotecnia** /elektro'teknia/ *f*, electrical engineering

**electroterapia** /elektrote'rapia/ *f*, *Med.* electrotherapy

**elefante** /ele'fante/ **(-ta)** *n* elephant

**elefantíasis** /elefan'tiasis/ *f*, elephantiasis

**elefantino** /elefan'tino/ *a* elephantine

**elegancia** /ele'ganθia; ele'gansia/ *f*, elegance, grace; fashionableness; *Lit.* beauty of style

**elegante** /ele'gante/ *a* elegant; graceful, lovely; fashionable, stylish

**elegía** /ele'hia/ *f*, elegy

**elegíaco** /ele'hiako/ *a* elegiac

**elegibilidad** /elehiβili'ðað/ *f*, eligibility

**elegible** /ele'hiβle/ *a* eligible

**elegir** /ele'hir/ *vt irr* to select, prefer; elect —*Pres. Indic.* **elijo, eliges, elige, eligen.** *Pres. Part.* **eligiendo.** *Preterite* **eligió, eligieron.** *Pres. Subj.* **elija,** etc.

**elemental** /elemen'tal/ *a* elemental; fundamental; elementary

**elemento** /ele'mento/ *m*, element; component, constituent; *Elec.* element; *pl* rudiments. *Mil.* **elementos de choque,** shock troops

**elevación** /eleβa'θion; eleβa'sion/ *f*, lifting, raising; height, high ground; elevation; altitude; *Fig.* eminence; elevation, advancement; ecstasy; raising (of the voice)

**elevado** /ele'βaðo/ *a* sublime, lofty

**elevar** /ele'βar/ *vt* to raise, lift; *Fig.* exalt; —*vr* be in ecstasy, be transported. **elevarse de categoría,** to rise in status

**elfo** /'elfo/ *m*, elf

**elidir** /eli'ðir/ *vt* (phonetics) to elide

**eliminación** /elimina'θion; elimina'sion/ *f*, elimination

**eliminador** /elimina'ðor/ *a* eliminatory. *m*, eliminator

**eliminar** /elimi'nar/ *vt* to eliminate

**elipse** /e'lipse/ *f*, ellipse

**elipsis** /e'lipsis/ *f*, ellipsis

**elíptico** /e'liptiko/ *a* elliptic

**elíseo** /e'liseo/ *m*, Elysium —*a* Elysian. **campos elíseos,** Elysian fields

**ella** /'eʎa; 'eya/ *pers pron 3rd sing f* she; it. See **él**

**elle** /'eʎe; 'eye/ *f*, name of letter LL

**ello** /'eʎo; 'eyo/ *pers pron 3rd sing neut* that, the fact, it. **Ello es que...,** The fact is that... **No tengo tiempo para ello,** I have no time for that

**ellos, ellas** /'eʎos, 'eʎas; 'eyos, 'eyas/ *pers pron 3rd pl m* and *f*, they. See **él**

**elocución** /eloku'θion; eloku'sion/ *f*, elocution; style of speech

**elocuencia** /elo'kuenθia; elo'kuensia/ *f*, eloquence

**elocuente** /elo'kuente/ *a* eloquent

**elogiador** /elohia'ðor/ **(-ra)** *a* eulogistic —*n* eulogist

**elogiar** /elo'hiar/ *vt* to eulogize, praise

**elogio** /e'lohio/ *m*, eulogy, praise. **«Elogio de la Locura»,** "In Praise of Folly"

**elucidación** /eluθiða'θion; elusiða'sion/ *f*, elucidation, explanation

         

**elucidar** /eluθi'ðar; elusi'ðar/ *vt* to elucidate, clarify

**eludible** /elu'ðiβle/ *a* escapable, avoidable

**eludir** /elu'ðir/ *vt* to elude, avoid

**emaciación** /emaθia'θion; emasia'sion/ *f*, emaciation

**emanación** /emana'θion; emana'sion/ *f*, emanation; effluvium

**emanar** /ema'nar/ *vi* to emanate (from), originate (in)

**emancipación** /emanθipa'θion; emansipa'sion/ *f*, emancipation; enfranchisement

**emancipador** /emanθipa'ðor; emansipa'ðor/ **(-ra)** *a* emancipatory —*n* emancipator

**emancipar** /emanθi'par; emansi'par/ *vt* to emancipate, free; enfranchise; —*vr* emancipate oneself; become independent; free oneself

**emascular** /emasku'lar/ *vt* to emasculate

**embadurnar** /embaður'nar/ *vt* to smear, smudge, daub

**embajada** /emba'haða/ *f*, embassy; ambassadorship; embassy building; *Inf.* message

**embajador** /embaha'ðor/ *m*, ambassador; emissary

**embajadora** /embaha'ðora/ *f*, wife of ambassador; woman ambassador

**embalador** /embala'ðor/ *m*, packer

**embalaje** /emba'lahe/ *m*, packing; bale; wrapper; packing charge

**embalar** /emba'lar/ *vt* to pack

**embaldosado** /embaldo'saðo/ *m*, tiled pavement or floor

**embaldosar** /embaldo'sar/ *vt* to tile, pave with tiles

**embalsamador** /embalsama'ðor/ *a* embalming. *m*, embalmer

**embalsamar** /embalsa'mar/ *vt* to embalm; perfume

**embalse** /em'balse/ *m*, dam; damming, impounding (of water)

**embanastar** /embanas'tar/ *vt* to place in a basket; crowd, squeeze

**embarazada** /embara'θaða; embara'saða/ *a f*, pregnant

**embarazar** /embara'θar; embara'sar/ *vt* to impede, hinder, embarrass; —*vr* be hindered or embarrassed; be pregnant

**embarazo** /emba'raθo; emba'raso/ *m*, difficulty, impediment; pregnancy; timidity, embarrassment

**embarazoso** /embara'θoso; embara'soso/ *a* embarrassing; inconvenient; difficult, troublesome

**embarcación** /embarka'θion; embarka'sion/ *f*, ship, vessel; embarkation

**embarcadero** /embarka'ðero/ *m*, wharf, dock; quay; pier; jetty

**embarcador** /embarka'ðor/ *m*, shipper

**embarcar** /embar'kar/ *vt* to embark, ship; board (boat, train, etc.); —*vr* embark; board

**embarco** /em'barko/ *m*, embarking, embarkation

**embargar** /embar'gar/ *vt* to obstruct, impede; *Law.* seize; suspend, paralyse

**embargo** /em'bargo/ *m*, *Law.* seizure; embargo. **sin e.,** nevertheless, however

**embarque** /em'barke/ *m*, loading, embarkation (goods)

**embarrancar** /embarran'kar/ *vi Naut.* to run aground; —*vr Naut.* be stuck on a reef or in the mud

**embarrilar** /embarri'lar/ *vt* to barrel

**embarullar** /embaru'ʎar; embaru'yar/ *vt Inf.* to mix up, muddle; do hastily and badly

**embasamiento** /embasa'miento/ *m*, *Archit.* foundation

**embastar** /embas'tar/ *vt Sew.* to baste; tack

**embaste** /em'baste/ *m*, *Sew.* basting; tacking stitch

**embate** /em'bate/ *m*, beating of the waves; sudden attack; unexpected misfortune

**embaucamiento** /embauka'miento/ *m*, trick, deception

**embaucar** /embau'kar/ *vt* to deceive, hoodwink

**embaular** /embau'lar/ *vt* to pack in a trunk; *Inf.* stuff with food

**embazar** /emba'θar; emba'sar/ *vt* to dye brown; hinder; amaze; —*vr* be amazed; be tired or bored; be satiated

**embebecer** /embeβe'θer; embeβe'ser/ *vt irr* to enter-

tain, amuse; engross, fascinate; —*vr* be dumbfounded. See **conocer**

**embebecimiento** /embeβeθi'miento; embeβesi'miento/ *m*, astonishment; absorption, engrossment

**embeber** /embe'βer/ *vt* to absorb; contain; shrink, contract; saturate; insert, introduce; incorporate; —*vi* shrink; —*vr* be amazed; master or absorb (a subject). **embebido en sus pensamientos,** absorbed in thought

**embelecar** /embele'kar/ *vt* to dupe, deceive, trick

**embeleco** /embe'leko/ *m*, deception, fraud

**embelesar** /embele'sar/ *vt* to astonish; fascinate, enchant; —*vr* be astonished or fascinated

**embeleso** /embe'leso/ *m*, astonishment; fascination; charm

**embellecer** /embeʎe'θer; embeye'ser/ *vt irr* to embellish; —*vr* beautify oneself. See **conocer**

**embellecimiento** /embeʎeθi'miento; embeyesi'miento/ *m*, beautifying, embellishment

**emberizo** /embe'riθo; embe'riso/ *m*, *Ornith.* yellowhammer

**embermejecer** /embermehe'θer; embermehe'ser/ *vt irr* to dye red; shame, make blush; —*vi* turn red or reddish; —*vr* blush. See **conocer**

**embestida** /embes'tiða/ *f*, assault, attack, onrush; *Inf.* importunity

**embestir** /embes'tir/ *vt irr* to rush upon, assault; *Inf.* importune, be a nuisance to; —*vi Fig. Inf.* clash, be inharmonious. See **pedir**

**emblema** /em'blema/ *m*, emblem; symbol; badge

**emblemático** /emble'matiko/ *a* emblematic; symbolical

**embobamiento** /emboβa'miento/ *m*, stupefaction, amazement

**embobar** /embo'βar/ *vt* to entertain, fascinate; —*vr* be dumbfounded

**embobecer** /emboβe'θer; emboβe'ser/ *vt irr* to make stupid. See **conocer**

**embobecimiento** /emboβeθi'miento; emboβesi'miento/ *m*, stupefaction

**embocadero** /emboka'ðero/ *m*, narrow entrance, bottleneck; mouth of a channel

**embocadura** /emboka'ðura/ *f*, entrance by a narrow passage; *Mus.* mouthpiece; flavor (of wine); estuary, mouth of a river; *Theat.* proscenium

**embocar** /embo'kar/ *vt* to put in the mouth; go through a narrow passage; deceive; *Inf.* devour, wolf; initiate a business deal

**embolia** /em'bolia/ *f*, embolism

**émbolo** /'embolo/ *m*, *Mech.* piston, plunger

**embolsar** /embol'sar/ *vt* to place money in a purse; collect (a debt, etc.)

**emborrachar** /emborra'tʃar/ *vt* to intoxicate; daze, stupefy; —*vr* become intoxicated; run (of dyes)

**emborrascarse** /emborras'karse/ *vr* to be furious; become stormy (weather); *Fig.* go downhill (business concern)

**emborronar** /emborro'nar/ *vt* to blot; scribble, write hastily

**emboscada** /embos'kaða/ *f*, ambuscade, ambush; intrigue, spying

**emboscar** /embos'kar/ *vt Mil.* to set an ambush; —*vr* lie in ambush

**embosquecer** /emboske'θer; emboske'ser/ *vi irr* to become wooded. See **conocer**

**embotar** /embo'tar/ *vt* to blunt (cutting edge); —*vi Fig.* weaken; —*vr* become blunt

**embotellado** /embote'ʎaðo; embote'yaðo/ *m*, bottling; *Fig.* bottleneck

**embotellador** /embote'ʎaðor; embote'yaðor/ **(-ra)** *n* bottler. *f*. **embotelladora,** bottling outfit

**embotellar** /embote'ʎar; embote'yar/ *vt* to bottle; bottle up, prevent from escaping

**embotijar** /emboti'har/ *vt* to put into jars; —*vr Inf.* be enraged

**embozar** /embo'θar; embo'sar/ *vt Fig.* to cloak, dissemble; muffle; —*vr* muffle oneself up

**embozo** /em'boθo; em'boso/ *m*, anything used to cover or muffle the face; pretense, pretext; facings (gen. *pl*); yashmak

**embragar** /embra'gar/ *vt* to sling, lift; *Mech.* let in the clutch

**embrague** /em'brage/ *m*, hoisting, slinging; *Mech.* clutch

**embravecer** /embraβe'θer; embraβe'ser/ *vt irr* to infuriate; —*vr* be enraged; be boisterous (sea). See **conocer**

**embravecimiento** /embraβeθi'miento; embraβesi'miento/ *m*, fury, rage

**embrazadura** /embraθa'ðura; embrasa'ðura/ *f*, grasping, clasping; handle, clasp

**embreadura** /embrea'ðura/ *f*, tarring

**embrear** /embre'ar/ *vt* to tar, paint with pitch

**embriagador** /embriaga'ðor/ *a* intoxicating

**embriagar** /embria'gar/ *vt* to intoxicate; enrapture; —*vr* become inebriated

**embriaguez** /embria'geθ; embria'ges/ *f*, intoxication, inebriation; rapture

**embriología** /embriolo'hia/ *f*, embryology

**embrión** /em'brion/ *m*, embryo; germ, rough idea

**embrionario** /embrio'nario/ *a* embryonic

**embrocación** /embroka'θion; embroka'sion/ *f*, *Med.* embrocation

**embrollar** /embro'ʎar; embro'yar/ *vt* to entangle; embroil

**embrollo** /em'broʎo; em'broyo/ *m*, tangle; falsehood; difficult situation

**embromar** /embro'mar/ *vt* to tease, chaff; trick, deceive; waste the time of; annoy; harm

**embrujar** /embru'har/ *vt* to bewitch

**embrutecer** /embrute'θer; embrute'ser/ *vt irr* to make brutish or stupid; —*vr* become brutish. See **conocer**

**embudo** /em'buðo/ *m*, *Chem.* funnel

**embuste** /em'buste/ *m*, lie, fraud; *pl* trinkets

**embustero** /embus'tero/ **(-ra)** *a* deceitful, knavish —*n* liar, cheat, trickster

**embutido** /embu'tiðo/ *m*, inlaid work; *Cul.* sausage

**embutir** /embu'tir/ *vt* to inlay; stuff full, cram; —*vt* and *vr Inf.* stuff with food

**eme** /'eme/ *f*, name of letter M

**emergencia** /emer'henθia; emer'hensia/ *f*, emergence; accident, emergency

**emergente** /emer'hente/ *a* emergent

**emerger** /emer'her/ *vi* to emerge; have its source (rivers, etc.)

**emérito** /e'merito/ *a* emeritus

**emético** /e'metiko/ *a* and *m*, emetic

**emigración** /emigra'θion; emigra'sion/ *f*, emigration; migration; number of emigrants

**emigrado** /emi'graðo/ *m*, emigrant, emigré

**emigrante** /emi'grante/ *a* and *mf* emigrant

**emigrar** /emi'grar/ *vi* to emigrate; migrate

**emigratorio** /emigra'torio/ *a* emigration

**eminencia** /emi'nenθia; emi'nensia/ *f*, highland; importance, prominence; outstanding personality, genius; title given to cardinals

**eminente** /emi'nente/ *a* high, elevated; prominent, illustrious

**emirato** /emi'rato/ *m*, emirate

**emisario** /emi'sario/ **(-ia)** *n* emissary

**emisión** /emi'sion/ *f*, emission; *Radio.* broadcast; *Com.* issue (bonds, etc.); floating (of a loan)

**emisor** /emi'sor/ *m*, *Elec.* transmitter.

**emisora** /emi'sora/ *f*, *Radio.* broadcasting station

**emitir** /emi'tir/ *vt* to emit; *Radio.* broadcast; *Com.* issue (bonds, paper money, etc.); utter, give voice to

**emoción** /emo'θion; emo'sion/ *f*, emotion

**emocional** /emo'θional; emo'sional/ *a* emotional; emotive

**emocionante** /emoθio'nante; emosio'nante/ *a* moving, causing emotion; thrilling

**emocionar** /emoθio'nar; emosio'nar/ *vt* to cause emotion, move; —*vr* be stirred by emotion; be thrilled

**emoliente** /emo'liente/ *a* and *m*, emollient

**emolumento** /emolu'mento/ *m*, emolument (gen. *pl*)

**emotivo** /emo'tiβo/ *a* emotive

**empachado** /empa'tʃaðo/ *a* awkward, clumsy

**empachar** /empa'tʃar/ *vt* to hinder, impede; disguise, dissemble; —*vr* overeat, stuff; be bashful

**empacho** /em'patʃo/ *m*, bashfulness, timidity; embarrassment, impediment; indigestion, satiety

**empadronamiento** /empaðrona'miento/ *m*, census

**empadronar** /empaðro'nar/ *vt* to take the census

**empalagar** /empala'gar/ *vt* to cloy (of food); tire, annoy

**empalagoso** /empala'goso/ *a* sickly, oversweet; cloying; *Fig.* sugary, honeyed

**empalar** /empa'lar/ *vt* to impale

**empalizada** /empali'θaða; empali'saða/ *f*, stockade, fencing

**empalmar** /empal'mar/ *vt* to dovetail; splice (ropes); clamp; *Fig.* combine (plans, actions, etc.); —*vi* join (railroad lines); couple (railroad trains); —*vr* palm (as in conjuring)

**empalme** /em'palme/ *m*, connection; splicing; *Fig.* combination (of plans, etc.); railroad junction; continuation; palming, secreting

**empanada** /empa'naða/ *f*, savory turnover or pie; secret negotiations, intrigue

**empanar** /empa'nar/ *vt* to bread; *Cul.* cover with breadcrumbs; *Agr.* sow grain

**empantanar** /empanta'nar/ *vt* to turn into marsh; embog; delay, embarrass

**empañar** /empa'nar/ *vt* to swaddle; tarnish, dim; blur; *Fig.* sully (fame, etc.)

**empapar** /empa'par/ *vt* to saturate; absorb; impregnate; —*vr* be saturated; absorb; *Fig.* be imbued

**empapelado** /empape'laðo/ *m*, paperhanging; wallpaper

**empapelador** /empapela'ðor/ *m*, paperhanger

**empapelar** /empape'lar/ *vt* to wrap in paper; paper (a room, etc.)

**empaque** /em'pake/ *m*, packing; paneling; *Inf.* mien, air; pomposity

**empaquetador** /empaketa'ðor/ **(-ra)** *n* packer

**empaquetar** /empake'tar/ *vt* to pack; make up parcels or packages; overcrowd

**emparedado** /empare'ðaðo/ **(-da)** *a* cloistered, reclusive —*n* recluse. *m*, *Cul.* sandwich

**emparedar** /empare'ðar/ *vt* to shut up, immure; —*vr* become a recluse

**emparejar** /empare'har/ *vt* to pair, match; equalize, make level; —*vi* come abreast (of); be equal

**emparentar** /emparen'tar/ *vi irr* to become related by marriage. See **acertar**

**emparrado** /empa'rraðo/ *m*, vine arbor; vine prop; pergola

**empastadura** /empasta'ðura/ *f*, filling (of teeth)

**empastar** /empas'tar/ *vt* to cover with glue or paste; bind in boards (books); fill (teeth). **empastado en tela,** clothbound

**empaste** /em'paste/ *m*, pasting, gluing; filling (teeth)

**empatar** /empa'tar/ *vt* to equal, tie with

**empate** /em'pate/ *m*, tie, draw; dead heat

**empecatado** /empeka'taðo/ *a* willful; evil-minded, wicked; incorrigible, impenitent; extremely unlucky

**empecer** /empe'θer; empe'ser/ *vt irr* to harm, damage; —*vi* hinder. See **conocer**

**empedernido** /empeðer'niðo/ *a* stony-hearted, cruel

**empedrado** /empe'ðraðo/ *a* dappled (horses); *Fig.* flecked (with clouds). *m*, paving; pavement

**empedrador** /empeðra'ðor/ *m*, stone paver

**empedrar** /empe'ðrar/ *vt irr* to pave with stones. See **acertar**

**empegadura** /empega'ðura/ *f*, coat of pitch

**empegar** /empe'gar/ *vt* to coat with pitch; mark with pitch (sheep)

**empeine** /em'peine/ *m*, groin; instep

**empellar** /empe'ʎar; empe'yar/ *vt* to push, jostle

**empellón** /empe'ʎon; empe'yon/ *m*, hard push. *Inf.* **a empellones,** by pushing and shoving

**empenachado** /empena'tʃaðo/ *a* plumed

**empeñado** /empe'naðo/ *a* violent, heated (of disputes)

**empeñar** /empe'nar/ *vt* to pledge, leave as surety; pawn; oblige, compel; appoint as mediator; —*vr* bind oneself, be under an obligation; (*with en*) insist on; persist in; —*vr* intercede; mediate; *Mil.* begin (a battle). **empeñado en,** determined to, intent on

**empeño** /em'peno/ *m*, pledge, surety; obligation, engagement; fervent desire; purpose, intention; determination, resolve; guarantor; *Inf.* influence, favor

**empeoramiento** /empeora'miento/ *m*, worsening; deterioration

**empeorar** /empeo'rar/ *vt* to make worse; —*vi* and *vr* deteriorate, grow worse

**empequeñecer** /empekeɲe'θer; empekeɲe'ser/ *vt irr* to diminish, lessen; make smaller; belittle. See **conocer**

**emperador** /empera'ðor/ *m*, emperor

**emperatriz** /empera'triθ; empera'tris/ *f*, empress

**emperezar** /empere'θar; empere'sar/ *vt* to obstruct, hinder; —*vr* be lazy

**empernar** /emper'nar/ *vt* to peg, bolt

**empero** /em'pero/ *conjunc* but; nevertheless

**empezar** /empe'θar; empe'sar/ *vt irr* to begin, commence; initiate; —*vi* begin —*Pres. Indic.* **empiezo, empiezas, empieza, empiezan.** *Preterite* **empecé, empezaste,** etc —*Pres. Subjunc.* **empiece, empieces, empiece, empecemos, empecéis, empiecen**

**empicotar** /empiko'tar/ *vt* to pillory

**empinado** /empi'naðo/ *a* steep; lofty; arrogant; exalted

**empinar** /empi'nar/ *vt* to raise; tip, tilt (drinking vessels); —*vr* stand on tiptoe; rear, prance; tower, rise; *Aer.* zoom, climb steeply. *Inf.* **e. el codo,** to lift the elbow, tipple

**empingorotado** /empiŋgoro'taðo/ *a* important, prominent; *Inf.* stuck-up

**empíreo** /em'pireo/ *a* empyreal; heavenly, divine. *m*, empyrean

**empírico** /em'piriko/ **(-ca)** *a* empiric —*n* quack, charlatan

**empirismo** /empi'rismo/ *m*, empiricism

**empizarrado** /empiθa'rraðo; empisa'rraðo/ *m*, slate roof

**empizarrar** /empiθa'rrar; empisa'rrar/ *vt* to roof with slate

**emplastar** /emplas'tar/ *vt Med.* to apply plasters; make up; paint; *Inf.* hinder, obstruct; —*vr* be smeared

**emplasto** /em'plasto/ *m, Med.* plaster; poultice; *Inf.* put-up job, fraud

**emplazamiento** /emplaθa'miento; emplasa'miento/ *m*, placing, location; site; *Law.* summons; *Naut.* berth

**emplazar** /empla'θar; empla'sar/ *vt* to convene, arrange a meeting; *Law.* summon

**empleado** /emple'aðo/ **(-da)** *n* employee; clerk. **e. público,** civil servant

**emplear** /em'plear/ *vt* to employ; lay out, invest (money); use; —*vr* be employed or occupied

**empleo** /em'pleo/ *m*, employment; investment, laying out (of money); occupation; post, office

**emplomar** /emplo'mar/ *vt* to lead, solder or cover with lead; affix lead seals on or to; weight (a stick, etc.)

**emplumar** /emplu'mar/ *vt* to feather; decorate with feathers; tar and feather

**emplumecer** /emplume'θer; emplume'ser/ *vi irr* to fledge, grow feathers. See **conocer**

**empobrecer** /empoβre'θer; empoβre'ser/ *vt irr* to impoverish; —*vi* and *vr* become poor; decay. See **conocer**

**empobrecimiento** /empoβreθi'miento; empoβresi-'miento/ *m*, impoverishment

**empollar** /empo'ʎar; empo'yar/ *vt* to hatch; —*vi* produce a brood (of bees); *Inf.* brood on, consider; *Inf.* grind, cram, swot (of students)

**empollón** /empo'ʎon; empo'yon/ **(-ona)** *n Inf.* plodder, grind, swot

**empolvar** /empol'βar/ *vt* to cover with dust; powder

**emponzoñamiento** /emponθoɲa'miento; empon-soɲa'miento/ *m*, poisoning

**emponzoñar** /emponθo'ɲar; emponso'ɲar/ *vt* to poison; pervert, corrupt

**emporio** /em'porio/ *m*, emporium

**empotrar** /empo'trar/ *vt* to embed, implant; fix down

**emprendedor** /emprende'ðor/ *a* capable, efficient, enterprising

**emprender** /empren'der/ *vt* to undertake; (*with prep a or con*) *Inf.* accost, tackle, buttonhole

**empresa** /em'presa/ *f*, undertaking, task; motto, device; intention, design; management, firm; enterprise, deal

**empresarial** /empresa'rial/ *a* entrepreneurial

**empresario** /empre'sario/ *m*, contractor; theatrical manager

**empréstito** /em'prestito/ *m*, loan

**empujar** /empu'har/ *vt* to push; *Fig.* exert pressure, influence

**empuje** /em'puhe/ *m*, push; *Archit.* pressure; energy; power, influence

**empujón** /empu'hon/ *m*, violent thrust or push. *Inf.* **a empujones,** by pushing and shoving; intermittently

**empuñadura** /empuɲa'ðura/ *f*, hilt (of a sword); *Inf.* preamble

**empuñar** /empu'ɲar/ *vt* to grasp; grip; clutch

**emu** /'emu/ *m*, emu

**emulación** /emula'θion; emula'sion/ *f*, emulation, competition, rivalry

**emulador** /emula'ðor/ *a* emulative

**emular** /emu'lar/ *vt* to emulate, rival, compete with

**émulo** /'emulo/ **(-la)** *a* emulative, rival —*n* competitor, rival

**emulsión** /emul'sion/ *f*, emulsion

**emulsivo** /emul'siβo/ *a* emulsive

**en** /en/ *prep* in; into; on, upon; at; by. **en Madrid,** in Madrid. **en junio,** in June. **Se echó en un sillón,** He threw himself into an armchair. **Se transformó en mariposa,** It turned into a butterfly. **Hay un libro en la mesa,** There is a book on the table. **María está en casa,** Mary is at home. **en un precio muy alto,** at a very high price. **El número de candidatos ha disminuido en un treinta por ciento,** The number of candidates has decreased by thirty percent. **En** appears in a number of adverbial phrases, e.g. *en particular,* in particular, *en secreto,* in secret, *en seguida,* immediately. When it is used with a gerund, it means after, as soon as, when, e.g. *En llegando a la puerta llamó,* When he arrived at the door, he knocked. *En todas partes se cuecen habas,* That happens everywhere; It happens in the best of families

**enagua** /e'nagua/ *f*, slip, crinoline, petticoat

**enajenación** /enahena'θion; enahena'sion/ *f*, transference, alienation (property); abstraction, absentmindedness. **e. mental,** lunacy

**enajenar** /enahe'nar/ *vt* to transfer (property)

**enaltecer** /enalte'θer; enalte'ser/ *vt irr* to elevate, raise; exalt. See **conocer**

**enamoradizo** /enamora'ðiθo; enamora'ðiso/ *a* susceptible, easily enamored; fickle

**enamorado** /enamo'raðo/ *a* in love, lovesick; easily enamored

**enamorar** /enamo'rar/ *vt* to arouse love in; court, make love to; —*vr* fall in love; (with *de*) become fond of (things)

**enano** /e'nano/ **(-na)** *a* small, dwarf —*n* dwarf

**enarbolar** /enarβo'lar/ *vt* to hoist (flags); —*vr* prance (horses); become angry

**enardecer** /enarðe'θer; enarðe'ser/ *vt irr* to kindle, stimulate (passion, quarrel, etc.); —*vr* be afire (with passion); *Med.* be inflamed. See **conocer**

**encabestrar** /enkaβe'strar/ *vt* to halter; lead, dominate

**encabezamiento** /enkaβeθa'miento; enkaβesa-'miento/ *m*, census taking; tax register; tax assessment; heading, inscription, running head

**encabezar** /enkaβe'θar; enkaβe'sar/ *vt* to take the census of; put on the tax register; open a subscription list; put a heading or title to; lead, head; —*vr* compound, settle by agreement (taxes, etc.)

**encabritarse** /enkaβri'tarse/ *vr* to rear, prance (horses)

**encadenamiento** /enkaðena'miento/ *m*, fettering, chaining; connection, link, relation

**encadenar** /enkaðe'nar/ *vt* to chain, fetter; *Fig.* link up, connect; *Fig.* paralyze. **encadenar el interés de,** to capture the interest of

**encajar** /enka'har/ *vt* to insert, fit one thing inside another; force in; fit tightly; *Inf.* be opportune, fit in (often with *bien*); —*vr* squeeze or crowd in; *Inf.* butt in, interfere

**encaje** /en'kahe/ *m*, fitting, insertion; socket, groove; joining; lace; inlay, mosaic

**encajera** /enkaˈhera/ f, lace maker or seller

**encaladura** /enkalaˈðura/ f, whitewashing

**encalar** /enkaˈlar/ vt to whitewash

**encalladero** /enkaʎaˈðero; enkayaˈðero/ m, Naut. sandbank, reef, shoal

**encallar** /enkaˈʎar; enkaˈyar/ vi Naut. to run aground; Fig. be held up (negotiations, etc.)

**encalmado** /enkalˈmaðo/ a calm; Com. dull

**encalmarse** /enkalˈmarse/ vr to become calm (wind, weather)

**encalvecer** /enkalβeˈθer; enkalβeˈser/ vi irr to grow bald. See **conocer**

**encamado** /enkaˈmaðo/ a bedridden, confined to one's bed; m, person confined to his bed

**encamarse** /enkaˈmarse/ vr to go to bed (gen. illness); be laid flat (grain, etc.); crouch

**encaminadura** /enkaminaˈðura/ f, **encaminamiento** m, directing, forwarding, routing

**encaminar** /enkamiˈnar/ vt to guide; direct; regulate; manage; promote, advance; —vr (with prep a) make for, go in the direction of

**encandecer** /enkandeˈθer; enkandeˈser/ vt irr to make incandescent. See **conocer**

**encandilar** /enkandiˈlar/ vt to dazzle; mislead; Inf. poke (the fire); —vr be bloodshot (eyes)

**encanecer** /enkaneˈθer; enkaneˈser/ vi irr to grow gray- or white-haired; grow mold; grow old. See **conocer**

**encanijar** /enkaniˈhar/ vt to make weak, sickly (gen. of babies); —vr be delicate or ailing

**encantado** /enkanˈtaðo/ a Inf. daydreaming, abstracted; haunted; rambling (of houses)

**encantador** /enkantaˈðor/ a captivating, bewitching, delightful. m, sorcerer, magician. **e. de serpientes,** snake charmer

**encantamiento** /enkantaˈmiento/ m, enchantment, spell, charm

**encantar** /enkanˈtar/ vt to enchant, weave a spell; delight, captivate, charm

**encañada** /enkaˈɲaða/ f, gorge, ravine

**encañado** /enkaˈɲaðo/ m, trellis; pipeline

**encañar** /enkaˈɲar/ vt to run water through a pipe; stake plants; wind thread on a spool

**encañonar** /enkaɲoˈnar/ vt to run into pipes; pleat, fold

**encapotarse** /enkapoˈtarse/ vr to muffle oneself in a cloak; scowl; be overcast; lower (sky)

**encapricharse** /enkapriˈtʃarse/ vr to take a fancy (to); insist on having one's own way, be stubborn

**encapuchar** /enkapuˈtʃar/ vt to cover or hide with a hood

**encaramar** /enkaraˈmar/ vt to raise, lift; climb; praise, extol. **e. al poder,** to put in power (e.g. a dictator). **encaramarse por,** to climb up

**encarar** /enkaˈrar/ vt to place face to face; aim (at); —vt and vr face; come face to face

**encarcelación** /enkarθelaˈθion; enkarselaˈsion/ f, incarceration

**encarcelar** /enkarθeˈlar; enkarseˈlar/ vt to imprison, jail; clamp

**encarecer** /enkareˈθer; enkareˈser/ vt irr to raise the price; overpraise, exaggerate; recommend strongly; —vi and vr increase in price. See **conocer**

**encarecimiento** /enkareθiˈmiento; enkaresiˈmiento/ m, increase (in price); enhancement; exaggeration. **con e.,** insistently, earnestly

**encargado** /enkarˈgaðo/ m, person in charge; manager; agent, representative. **e. de negocios,** chargé d'affaires

**encargar** /enkarˈgar/ vt to enjoin; commission; recommend; advise; Com. order

**encargo** /enˈkargo/ m, charge, commission; order; office, employ; responsibility

**encariñarse** /enkariˈɲarse/ (con), vi to become fond (of)

**encarnación** /enkarnaˈθion; enkarnaˈsion/ f, incarnation

**encarnadino** /enkarnaˈðino/ a incarnadine

**encarnado** /enkarˈnaðo/ a incarnate; flesh-colored; red

**encarnar** /enkarˈnar/ vi to incarnate; pierce the flesh;

Fig. leave a strong impression; —vt symbolize, personify; —vr mingle, blend

**encarnizado** /enkarniˈθaðo; enkarniˈsaðo/ a bloodshot (eyes); flesh-colored; bloody, cruel (gen. of battles)

**encarnizamiento** /enkarniθaˈmiento; enkarnisaˈmiento/ m, cruelty, fury

**encarnizar** /enkarniˈθar; enkarniˈsar/ vt to infuriate; —vr devour flesh (animals); persecute, ill-treat

**encaro** /enˈkaro/ m, stare, gaze; aim

**encarrilar** /enkarriˈlar/ vt to set on the track or rails (vehicles); Fig. put right, set on the right track

**encartamiento** /enkartaˈmiento/ m, proscription; charter

**encartar** /enkarˈtar/ vt to proscribe, outlaw; place on the tax register; Law. summon, cite

**encartonar** /enkartoˈnar/ vt to cover with cardboard; bind in boards (books)

**encasar** /enkaˈsar/ vt Surg. to set (a bone)

**encasillado** /enkasiˈʎaðo; enkasiˈyaðo/ m, set of pigeonholes

**encasillar** /enkasiˈʎar; enkasiˈyar/ vt to pigeonhole; file, classify

**encasquetar** /enkaskeˈtar/ (se) vt and vr to pull a hat well down on the head; —vr get a fixed idea

**encastillar** /enkastiˈʎar; enkastiˈyar/ vt to fortify with castles; —vr retire to a castle; be headstrong, obstinate

**encauzamiento** /enkauθaˈmiento; enkausaˈmiento/ m, channeling; Fig. direction

**encauzar** /enkauˈθar; enkauˈsar/ vt to channel; Fig. direct, guide

**encefalitis** /enθefaˈlitis; ensefaˈlitis/ f, encephalitis. **e. letárgica,** encephalitis lethargica, sleeping sickness.

**encéfalo** /enˈθefalo; enˈsefalo/ m, Anat. brain

**encenagarse** /enθenaˈgarse; ensenaˈgarse/ vr to wallow in mire; muddy oneself; take to vice

**encendedor** /enθendeˈðor; ensendeˈðor/ a lighting. m, lighter. **e. de bolsillo,** pocket lighter

**encender** /enθenˈder; ensenˈder/ vt irr to light; switch on; set fire to, kindle; arouse (emotions); inflame, incite; —vr blush. See **entender**

**encendido** /enθenˈdiðo; ensenˈdiðo/ a high-colored; inflamed; ardent. m, Auto. ignition

**encerado** /enθeˈraðo; enseˈraðo/ a wax-colored. m, oilskin; sticking plaster; blackboard; tarpaulin

**enceramiento** /enθeraˈmiento; enseraˈmiento/ m, waxing

**encerar** /enθeˈrar; enseˈrar/ vt to wax, varnish with wax; stain with wax; inspissate (lime)

**encerotar** /enθeroˈtar; enseroˈtar/ vt to wax (thread)

**encerrar** /enθeˈrrar; enseˈrrar/ vt irr to shut up, imprison; include, contain; —vr go into seclusion. See **acertar**

**encerrona** /enθeˈrrona; enseˈrrona/ f, Inf. voluntary retreat; Fig. Inf. tight corner

**encespedar** /enθespeˈðar; ensespeˈðar/ vt to cover with sod

**enchufar** /entʃuˈfar/ vt to connect tubes; Fig. combine (jobs, etc.); Elec. plug, connect

**enchufe** /enˈtʃufe/ m, joint, fitting together (of tubes); Elec. wall socket, plug; part-time post; Inf. cushy job. **e. de reducción,** Elec. adapter

**encía** /enˈθia; enˈsia/ f, gum (of the mouth)

**encíclica** /enˈθiklika; enˈsiklika/ f, encyclical

**enciclopedia** /enθikloˈpeðia; ensikloˈpeðia/ f, encyclopedia

**enciclopédico** /enθikloˈpeðiko; ensikloˈpeðiko/ a encyclopedic

**encierro** /enˈθierro; enˈsierro/ m, act of closing or shutting up; prison; retreat, confinement

**encima** /enˈθima; enˈsima/ adv over; above; at the top; besides; (with de) on, on top of. **por e. de esto,** over and above this, besides this

**encina** /enˈθina; enˈsina/ f, Bot. evergreen or holm oak

**encinar** /enθiˈnar; ensiˈnar/ m, grove of evergreen or holm oaks

**encinta** /enˈθinta; enˈsinta/ a f, pregnant

**encintar** /enθinˈtar; ensinˈtar/ vt to decorate with ribbons

**enclavar** /enkla'βar/ vt to nail; pierce; embed; *Inf.* deceive

**enclenque** /en'klenke/ a ailing, weak; puny, anemic

**enclocar** /enklo'kar/ vi irr to begin to brood (hens). See **contar**

**encobar** /enko'βar/ vi to hatch eggs

**encoger** /enko'her/ vt to shrink, contract, recoil; discourage; —vi shrink (wood, cloth, etc.); —vr shrink from, recoil; be discouraged; be timid or bashful

**encogimiento** /enkohi'miento/ m, shrinkage; contraction; depression, discouragement; timidity; bashfulness

**encoladura** /enkola'ðura/ f. **encolamiento** m, gluing; sizing

**encolerizar** /enkoleri'θar; enkoleri'sar/ vt to anger; —vr be angry

**encomendar** /enkomen'dar/ vt irr to charge with, entrust; recommend, commend; —vr (with prep a) put one's trust in; send greetings to. See **acertar**

**encomiar** /enko'miar/ vt to eulogize, praise

**encomiástico** /enko'miastiko/ a encomiastic

**encomienda** /enko'mienda/ f, commission, charge; knight commandership; insignia of knight commander; land formerly granted in America to *conquistadores*; recommendation, commendation; protection, defense; pl greetings, compliments, messages

**encomio** /en'komio/ m, eulogy; strong recommendation

**enconar** /enko'nar/ vt to irritate, exasperate; —vr *Med.* be inflamed; be exasperated; (with en) burden one's conscience with

**encono** /en'kono/ m, rancor, resentment, ill will

**encontrado** /enkon'traðo/ a facing, opposite, in front; hostile, inimical, opposed (to)

**encontrar** /enkon'trar/ vt irr to meet; find; —vi meet; encounter unexpectedly; (with con) run into, collide with; —vr be antagonistic; find; feel, be; differ, disagree (opinions); (with con) meet, come across. **e. eco**, to strike a responsive chord. **encontrarse con el cura de su pueblo**, to find someone who knows all about, meet someone who knows all about. **¿Cómo se encuentra Vd?** How are you? *Pres. Indic.* **encuentro**, etc —*Pres. Subjunc.* **encuentre**, etc.

**encontrón** /enkon'tron/ m, collision, violent impact

**encopetado** /enkope'taðo/ a conceited, proud; of noble descent; prominent, important

**encorajar** /enkora'har/ vt to encourage, inspire, hearten; —vr be angry

**encordelar** /enkorðe'lar/ vt to cord, rope

**encorsetar** /enkorse'tar/ vt to correct

**encorvadura** /enkorβa'ðura/ f, bending, curving

**encorvar** /enkor'βar/ vt to bend, curve; —vr have a leaning toward, favor

**encostrar** /enkos'trar/ vt to cover with a crust; —vr form a crust

**encrespador** /enkrespa'ðor/ m, curling irons

**encrespar** /enkres'par/ vt to curl (hair); enrage; —vr be curly (hair); stand on end (hair, feathers, from fright); be angry; grow rough (sea); become complicated, entangled

**encrestado** /enkres'taðo/ a crested; haughty, arrogant

**encrestarse** /enkres'tarse/ vr to stiffen the comb or crest (birds)

**encrucijada** /enkruθi'haða; enkrusi'haða/ f, crossroad, intersection; ambush

**encrudecer** /enkruðe'θer; enkruðe'ser/ vt irr to make raw-looking; annoy; —vr be annoyed. See **conocer**

**encuadernación** /enkuaðerna'θion; enkuaðerna'sion/ f, bookbinding; binding (of a book); bookbinder's workshop. **e. en tela**, cloth binding

**encuadernador** /enkuaðerna'ðor/ (-ra) n bookbinder

**encuadernar** /enkuaðer'nar/ vt to bind (a book)

**encuadrar** /enkuað'rar/ vt to frame; fit one thing into another, insert; limit; *Mil.* enlist

**encubar** /enku'βar/ vt to put into casks (wine, etc.)

**encubiertamente** /enkuβierta'mente/ adv secretly; deceitfully

**encubierto** /enku'βierto/ a concealed; secret

**encubridor** /enkuβri'ðor/ (-ra) a concealing, hiding —n hider; harborer; accomplice; receiver (of stolen goods); *Law.* accessory after the fact

**encubrimiento** /enkuβri'miento/ m, hiding, concealment; *Law.* accessory before (after) the fact; receiving (of stolen goods)

**encubrir** /enkuβ'rir/ vt to conceal; receive (stolen goods); *Law.* prosecute as an accessory. *Past. Part.* **encubierto**

**encuentro** /en'kuentro/ m, collision; meeting, encounter; opposition, hostility; *Mil.* fight, skirmish; *Archit.* angle. **ir al e. de**, to go in search of. **salir al e. (de)**, to go to meet; resist

**encuesta** /en'kuesta/ f, investigation, examination

**encumbrado** /enkum'braðo/ a elevated, high

**encumbramiento** /enkumbra'miento/ m, act of elevating; height; aggrandizement; advancement

**encumbrar** /enkum'brar/ vt to raise, elevate; exalt, promote; ascend, climb to the top; —vr be proud; be lofty, tower

**encurtido** /enkur'tiðo/ m, pickle

**encurtir** /enkur'tir/ vt to pickle

**ende** /'ende/ adv *Obs.* there. **por e.,** therefore

**endeble** /en'deβle/ a weak, frail

**endeblez** /ende'βleθ; ende'βles/ f, weakness

**endecha** /en'detʃa/ f, dirge

**endémico** /en'demiko/ a *Med.* endemic

**endemoniado** /endemo'niaðo/ a devil-possessed; *Inf.* fiendish, malevolent

**endemoniar** /endemo'niar/ vt to possess with a devil; *Inf.* enrage

**endentar** /enden'tar/ vt irr *Mech.* to cut the cogs (of a wheel); engage, interlock (gears, wheels, etc.). See **regimentar**

**endentecer** /endente'θer; endente'ser/ vi irr to cut teeth. See **conocer**

**enderezamiento** /endereθa'miento; enderesa-'miento/ m, straightening; directing, guiding; putting right, correction

**enderezar** /endere'θar; endere'sar/ vt to straighten; direct, guide; put right, correct; —vi take the right road; —vr straighten oneself; prepare to

**endeudarse** /endeu'ðarse/ vr to contract debts; be under an obligation

**endiablado** /endia'βlaðo/ a ugly, monstrous; *Inf.* fiendish

**endiosar** /endio'sar/ vt to deify; —vr be puffed up with pride; be abstracted or lost in ecstasy

**endocrino** /endo'krino/ a endocrine

**endocrinología** /endokrinolo'hia/ f, endocrinology

**endomingarse** /endomiŋ'garse/ vr to put on one's Sunday best

**endosante** /endo'sante/ m, endorser

**endosar** /endo'sar/ vt *Com.* to endorse; transfer, pass on

**endoso** /en'doso/ m, *Com.* endorsement

**endrino** /en'drino/ m, sloe tree —a blue-black, sloe-colored

**endulzar** /endul'θar; endul'sar/ vt to sweeten; soften, mitigate

**endurecer** /endure'θer; endure'ser/ vt irr to harden; toughen, inure; make severe or cruel; —vr grow hard; become hardened or robust; be harsh or cruel. **endurecerse al trabajo**, to become hardened to work. See **conocer**

**endurecimiento** /endureθi'miento; enduresi-'miento/ m, hardness; obstinacy, tenacity

**ene** /'ene/ f, name of letter N

**enemiga** /ene'miga/ f, hostility, enmity

**enemigo** /ene'migo/ (-ga) a hostile —n enemy; antagonist. m, devil

**enemistad** /enemis'tað/ f, enmity, hostility

**enemistar** /enemis'tar/ vt to make enemies of; —vr (with con) become an enemy of; cease to be friendly with

**energía** /ener'hia/ f, energy, vigor

**enérgico** /e'nerhiko/ a energetic, vigorous

**energúmeno** /ener'gumeno/ (-na) n energumen

**enero** /e'nero/ m, January

**enervación** /enerβa'θion; enerβa'sion/ f, enervation

**enervar** /ener'βar/ vt to enervate, weaken; *Fig.* take the force out of (reasons, etc.)

**enfadar** /enfa'ðar/ vt to make angry; —vr become angry

**enfado** /en'faðo/ *m*, anger; annoyance; trouble, toil

**enfadoso** /enfa'ðoso/ *a* vexatious; troublesome, wearisome

**enfaldada** /enfal'daða/ *f*, skirtful

**enfaldar** /enfal'dar/ *vt* to tuck up the skirts; lop off lower branches (of trees)

**enfangarse** /enfaŋ'garse/ *vr* to cover oneself with mud; *Inf.* dirty one's hands, sully one's reputation; wallow in vice

**enfardar** /enfar'ðar/ *vt* to pack; make bales or bundles

**énfasis** /'enfasis/ *m*, or *f*, emphasis

**enfático** /en'fatiko/ *a* emphatic

**enfermar** /enfer'mar/ *vi* to fall ill; —*vt* cause illness; *Fig.* weaken. **Enfermó del corazón,** He fell ill with heart trouble.

**enfermedad** /enferme'ðað/ *f*, illness; *Fig.* malady, distemper. **e. del sueño,** sleeping sickness

**enfermera** /enfer'mera/ *f*, nurse

**enfermería** /enferme'ria/ *f*, infirmary; hospital; first-aid station

**enfermero** /enfer'mero/ *m*, nurse

**enfermizo** /enfer'miθo; enfer''miso/ *a* ailing, delicate; unhealthy, unwholesome

**enfermo** /en'fermo/ **(-ma)** *a* ill; *Fig.* corrupt, diseased; delicate, sickly —*n* patient. **e. venéreo,** person with a venereal disease

**enfilar** /enfi'lar/ *vt* to place in line; string; *Mil.* enfilade

**enflaquecer** /enflake'θer; enflake'ser/ *vt irr* to make thin; weaken, enervate; —*vi* grow thin; lose heart. See **conocer**

**enflaquecimiento** /enflakeθi'miento; enflakesi-'miento/ *m*, loss of flesh; discouragement

**enfocar** /enfo'kar/ *vt* to focus; envisage

**enfoque** /en'foke/ *m*, focus

**enfoscado** /enfos'kaðo/ *a* ill-humored; immersed in business matters

**enfrascar** /enfras'kar/ *vt* to bottle; —*vr* (*with en*) plunge into, entangle oneself in (undergrowth, etc.); become engrossed or absorbed in

**enfrenar** /enfre'nar/ *vt* to bridle; curb (a horse); restrain, repress; check

**enfrente** /en'frente/ *adv* in front, opposite, facing; in opposition

**enfriadero** /enfria'ðero/ *m*, cooling place, cold cellar, root cellar

**enfriamiento** /enfria'miento/ *m*, cooling

**enfriar** /enf'riar/ *vt* to cool; *Fig.* chill, make indifferent; —*vr* grow cold; *Fig.* grow stormy (weather)

**enfurecer** /enfure'θer; enfure'ser/ *vt irr* to enrage. See **conocer**

**enfurecimiento** /enfureθi'miento; enfuresi'miento/ *m*, fury

**enfurruñarse** /enfurru'ɲarse/ *vr Inf.* to fume, be angry; be disgruntled

**engalanar** /eŋgala'nar/ *vt* to decorate, embellish. **engalanado como nunca,** dressed to the nines, dressed to kill

**enganchar** /eŋgan't∫ar/ *vt* to hook; couple, connect; hitch, harness, yoke; *Inf.* seduce, hook; *Mil.* bribe into army; —*vr* be hooked or caught on a hook; *Mil.* enlist

**enganche** /eŋ'gant∫e/ *m*, hooking; coupling (of railroad trains, etc.); connection; yoke, harness, hook; *Inf.* enticement; *Mil.* enlistment

**engañifa** /eŋga'ɲifa/ *f, Inf.* swindle, fraud

**engañadizo** /eŋgaɲa'ðiθo; eŋgaɲaðiso/ *a* easily deceived, simple

**engañador** /eŋgaɲa'ðor/ **(-ra)** *a* deceiving; deceptive —*n* deceiver, impostor

**engañar** /eŋga'ɲar/ *vt* to deceive; defraud, cheat; beguile, while away; hoax, humbug; —*vr* be mistaken; deceive oneself. **e. como a un chino,** *Inf.* to pull the wool over a person's eyes. **Las apariencias engañan,** Appearances are deceptive

**engañifa** /eŋga'nhook;ifa/ *f, Inf.* swindle, fraud

**engaño** /eŋ'gaɲo/ *m*, deceit; deception, illusion; fraud; falsehood

**engañoso** /eŋga'ɲoso/ *a* deceitful, false; fraudulent; deceptive, misleading

**engarabatar** /eŋgaraβa'tar/ *vt Inf.* to hook; —*vr* become hooked, curved, crooked

**engarce** /eŋ'garθe/ *m*, hooking; coupling; setting (of jewels)

**engarzar** /eŋgar'θar; eŋgar'sar/ *vt* to link, couple, enchain; hook; curl; set (jewels)

**engastar** /eŋgas'tar/ *vt* to set (jewels)

**engaste** /eŋ'gaste/ *m*, setting (of jewels)

**engatusar** /eŋgatu'sar/ *vt Inf.* to wheedle, coax, flatter

**engendrador** /enhendra'ðor/ **(-ra)** *a* engendering; original —*n* begetter

**engendrar** /enhen'drar/ *vt* to procreate; engender, produce, cause

**engendro** /en'hendro/ *m*, fetus; abnormal embryo; literary monstrosity

**englobar** /eŋglo'βar/ *vt* to include, comprise, embrace

**engolfarse** /eŋgol'farse/ *vr* to sail out to sea; (*with en*) *Fig.* be absorbed in

**engomar** /eŋgo'mar/ *vt* to gum

**engordar** /eŋgor'ðar/ *vt* to fatten; —*vi* grow fat; *Inf.* prosper, grow rich

**engorde** /eŋ'gorðe/ *m*, fattening (of stock)

**engorro** /eŋ'gorro/ *m*, impediment, obstacle, difficulty

**engorroso** /eŋgo'rroso/ *a* difficult, troublesome

**engranaje** /eŋgra'nahe/ *m*, *Mech.* gearing, gear; *Fig.* connection, link

**engrandecer** /eŋgrande'θer; eŋgrande'ser/ *vt irr* to enlarge; augment; eulogize; promote, exalt. See **conocer**

**engrandecimiento** /eŋgrandeθi'miento; eŋgrandesi-'miento/ *m*, enlargement; increase; exaggeration, eulogization; advancement, promotion

**engrasado** /eŋgra'saðo/ *m*, oiling; greasing

**engrasador** /eŋgrasa'ðor/ *m*, greaser, lubricator; oiler

**engrasar** /eŋgra'sar/ *vt* to grease; lubricate, oil; manure; stain with grease

**engreimiento** /eŋgrei'miento/ *m*, conceit, vanity

**engreír** /eŋgre'ir/ *vt irr* to make conceited; —*vr* become vain or conceited. See **reír**

**engrescar** /eŋgres'kar/ **(se)** *vt* and *vr* to start a quarrel

**engrosar** /eŋgro'sar/ *vt irr* to fatten, thicken; *Fig.* increase, swell; manure; —*vi* put on weight, grow fat. See **contar**

**engrudar** /eŋgru'ðar/ *vt* to paste, glue

**engrudo** /eŋ'gruðo/ *m*, paste, glue

**enguantarse** /eŋ'guantarse/ *vr* to put on one's gloves

**enguijarrado** /eŋguiha'rraðo/ *a* pebbled. *m*, pebbled path

**engullir** /eŋgu'ʎir; eŋgu'yir/ *vt* to gobble, swallow

**enhebrar** /ene'βrar/ *vt* to thread (needles); string

**enhestar** /enes'tar/ *vt irr* to erect; set upright; —*vr* rise; rear up; straighten oneself up. See **acertar**

**enhiesto** /en'iesto/ *a* upright, erect

**enhorabuena** /enora'βuena/ *f*, congratulation —*adv* well and good. **dar la e.,** to congratulate

**enhoramala** /enora'mala/ *adv* in an evil hour. *Inf.* **¡Vete e.!** Go to the devil!

**enhorquetado** /enorke'taðo/ *a* in the saddle

**enhuerar** /enue'rar/ *vt* to addle; —*vi* become addled

**enigma** /e'nigma/ *m*, enigma

**enigmático** /enig'matiko/ *a* enigmatical

**enjabonar** /enhaβo'nar/ *vt* to soap; *Inf.* soap down, flatter

**enjaezar** /enhae'θar; enhae'sar/ *vt* to harness (a horse)

**enjalbegar** /enhalβe'gar/ *vt* to whitewash

**enjambrar** /enhamb'rar/ *vt* to hive bees; —*vi* multiply, increase

**enjambre** /en'hambre/ *m*, swarm (of bees); crowd

**enjaretado** /enhare'taðo/ *m*, latticework

**enjaular** /enhau'lar/ *vt* to cage; *Inf.* jail

**enjoyar** /enho'yar/ *vt* to adorn with jewels; beautify; set with precious stones

**enjuagadura** /enhuaga'ðura/ *f*, rinsing (the mouth); rinse water; mouthwash

**enjuagar** /enhua'gar/ *vt* to rinse; —*vr* rinse the mouth

**enjuague** /en'huaɣe/ *m,* rinse; rinsing; mouthwash; tooth mug; scheme, plan

**enjugar** /enhu'ɣar/ *vt* to dry; cancel, write off; wipe, mop (perspiration, tears, etc.); —*vr* grow lean

**enjuiciar** /enhui'θiar; enhui'siar/ *vt* to submit a matter to arbitration; *Law.* prosecute; *Law.* render judgment; *Law.* adjudicate (a case)

**enjundia** /en'hundia/ *f,* animal fat or grease; *Fig.* substance, meat; strength, vigor; constitution, temperament

**enjuto** /en'huto/ *a* dry; lean. *m pl,* brushwood; *Cul.* canapés, savories

**enlace** /en'laθe; en'lase/ *m,* connection; link; tie; *Chem.* bond; alliance, relationship; marriage

**enladrillado** /enladri'ʎado; enladri'yado/ *m,* brick floor or pavement

**enlardar** /enlar'ðar/ *vt Cul.* to baste

**enlazar** /enla'θar; enla'sar/ *vt* to tie, bind; join, link; lasso; —*vr* marry; be allied, related. **e. con,** to connect with (of trains); link up with

**enlentecerse** /enlente'θerse; enlente'serse/ *vr* to decelerate, go slow, slow down

**enlodar** /enlo'ðar/ *vt* to muddy; *Fig.* smirch, sully

**enloquecer** /enloke'θer; enloke'ser/ *vt irr* to drive insane; —*vi* go mad. See **conocer**

**enlosado** /enlo'saðo/ *m,* tile floor

**enlosar** /enlo'sar/ *vt* to pave with flags

**enlucir** /enlu'θir; enlu'sir/ *vt irr* to plaster (walls); polish (metals). See **lucir**

**enlutar** /enlu'tar/ *vt* to put in mourning, drape with crepe; darken, obscure; sadden; —*vr* go into mourning; become dark

**enmaderar** /emaðe'rar/ *vt* to panel in wood, board up

**enmarañar** /emara'ɲar/ *vt* to tangle, disorder (hair, etc.); complicate, confuse; —*vr* be tangled; be sprinkled with clouds

**enmaridar** /emari'ðar/ *vi* to become a wife

**enmarillecerse** /emariʎe'θerse; emariye'serse/ *vr irr* to grow yellow. See **conocer**

**enmascarar** /emaska'rar/ *vt* to mask; disguise, dissemble; —*vr* be masked

**enmasillar** /emasi'ʎar; emasi'yar/ *vt* to putty

**enmendar** /emen'dar/ *vt irr* to correct, improve; reform; compensate, indemnify; *Law.* repeal; —*vr* be improved or corrected; mend one's ways. See **acertar**

**enmienda** /e'mienda/ *f,* correction; reform; indemnity; compensation; amendment; *pl Agr.* fertilizers

**enmohecer** /emoe'θer; emoe'ser/ *vt irr* to rust; —*vr* become moldy. See **conocer**

**enmudecer** /emuðe'θer; emuðe'ser/ *vt irr* to silence; —*vi* become dumb; be silent. See **conocer**

**enmugrecer** /emugre'θer; emugre'ser/ *vt irr* to cover with grime; —*vr* be grimy, dirty. See **conocer**

**ennegrecer** /ennegre'θer; ennegre'ser/ *vt irr* to dye black; make black; —*vr* become black; become dark or cloudy. See **conocer**

**ennoblecer** /ennoβle'θer; ennoβle'ser/ *vt irr* to ennoble; enrich, embellish; adorn, befit. See **conocer**

**ennoblecimiento** /ennoβleθi'miento; ennoβlesi'miento/ *m,* ennoblement; enrichment

**enojadizo** /enoha'ðiθo; enoha'ðiso/ *a* irritable, peevish

**enojar** /eno'har/ *vt* to anger; annoy, irritate; —*vr* be angry; rage, be rough (wind, sea)

**enojo** /e'noho/ *m,* anger; resentment; vexations, troubles, trials (gen. *pl*). **con gran e. de,** much to the annoyance of

**enojoso** /eno'hoso/ *a* annoying; troublesome, tiresome

**enorgullecer** /enorguʎe'θer; enorguye'ser/ *vt irr* to make proud; —*vr* be proud. See **conocer**

**enorme** /e'norme/ *a* enormous, huge; monstrous, heinous

**enormidad** /enormi'ðað/ *f,* hugeness; enormity; wickedness

**enramar** /enra'mar/ *vt* to intertwine branches; embower; —*vi* branch (trees)

**enramada** /enrami'ðað/ *f,* bower; thick foliage

**enrarecer** /enrare'θer; enrare'ser/ *vt irr* to rarefy; —*vr* become rarefied; grow rare. See **conocer**

**enrarecimiento** /enrareθi'miento; enraresi'miento/ *m,* rarefaction

**enredadera** /enreða'ðera/ *f,* convolvulus —*a f,* climbing, twining (plant)

**enredador** /enreða'ðor/ **(-ra)** *a* mischievous, willful; intriguing, scheming; *Inf.* gossiping, meddlesome —*n* intriguer; *Inf.* meddler

**enredar** /enre'ðar/ *vt* to catch in a net; put down nets or snares; entangle; sow discord; compromise, involve (in difficulties); —*vi* be mischievous; —*vr* be entangled; be involved (in difficulties)

**enredo** /en'reðo/ *m,* tangle; mischief, prank; intrigue, malicious falsehood; difficult situation; plot

**enredoso** /enre'ðoso/ *a* tangled; fraught with difficulties

**enrejado** /enre'haðo/ *m,* railing, paling; trellis or latticework; *Sew.* openwork

**enrejar** /enre'har/ *vt* to fence with a railing; cover with grating

**enriquecer** /enrike'θer; enrike'ser/ *vt irr* to enrich; exalt, aggrandize; —*vi* grow rich; prosper, flourish. See **conocer**

**enriscado** /enris'kaðo/ *a* craggy, rocky

**enriscar** /enris'kar/ *vt* to raise; —*vr* hide among crags

**enristrar** /enris''trar/ *vt* to couch (a lance); string (onions, etc.); *Fig.* surmount (difficulties); go straight to (a place)

**enrojecer** /enrohe'θer; enrohe'ser/ *vt irr* to redden; make blush; —*vr* grow red; blush. See **conocer**

**enroscar** /enros'kar/ *vt* to twist, twine; —*vr* turn (screw); twist; coil

**ensaimada** /ensai'maða/ *f,* Spanish pastry cake

**ensalada** /ensa'laða/ *f,* salad; hodgepodge

**ensaladera** /ensala'ðera/ *f,* salad bowl

**ensalmar** /ensal'mar/ *vt Surg.* to set (bones); cure by spells

**ensalmo** /en'salmo/ *m,* spell, charm. **por e.,** as if by magic, rapidly

**ensalzar** /ensal'θar; ensal'sar/ *vt* to exalt, promote; praise

**ensamblador** /ensambla'ðor/ *m,* joiner, assembler

**ensambladura** /ensambla'ðura/ *f,* assemblage, joining; joining; dovetailing

**ensamblar** /ensam'blar/ *vt* to assemble; join, dovetail, mortise

**ensanchador** /ensantʃa'ðor/ *m,* glove stretcher

**ensanchar** /ensan'tʃar/ *vt* to widen, enlarge, extend; *Sew.* let out, stretch; —*vr* put on airs

**ensanche** /en'santʃe/ *m,* dilatation, widening; stretch; extension; *Sew.* turnings, letting out; (city) extension

**ensangrentar** /ensaŋgren'tar/ *vt irr* to stain with blood; —*vr* be bloodstained; be overhasty. See **regimentar**

**ensañar** /ensa'ɲar/ *vt* to irritate, infuriate; —*vr* be merciless (with vanquished)

**ensartar** /ensar'tar/ *vt* to string (beads); thread (needles); spit, pierce; tell a string (of falsehoods)

**ensayador** /ensaia'ðor/ *m,* metal assayer

**ensayar** /ensa'yar/ *vt* to try out; *Chem.* test; *Theat.* rehearse; assay

**ensaye** /en'saye/ *m,* assaying (of metals)

**ensayista** /ensa'yista/ *mf* essayist

**ensayo** /ensa'yo/ *m,* test, trial; *Lit.* essay; assay; experiment; rehearsal. **e. general,** dress rehearsal

**ensenada** /ense'naða/ *f,* cove, inlet

**enseña** /en'seɲa/ *f,* ensign, standard

**enseñanza** /ense'ɲanθa; ense'ɲansa/ *f,* teaching; education; example, experience. **e. primaria,** elementary education. **e. secundaria,** secondary education. **e. superior,** higher education

**enseñar** /ense'ɲar/ *vt* to teach, instruct; train; point out; exhibit, show; —*vr* become accustomed. **e. la oreja,** *Fig.* to show the cloven hoof

**enseñorearse** /enseɲore'arse/ *vr* to take possession (of)

**enseres** /en'seres/ *m pl,* household goods; utensils; equipment

**ensilladero** /ensiʎa'ðero; ensiya'ðero/ *m,* paddock

**ensillar** /ensi'ʎar; ensi'yar/ *vt* to saddle

**ensimismarse** /ensimis'marse/ *vr* to be lost in thought

**ensoberbecer** /ensoβerβe'θer; ensoβerβe'ser/ *vt irr* to make haughty; —*vr* become arrogant; grow rough (sea). See **conocer**

**ensordecedor** /ensorðeθe'ðor; ensorðese'ðor/ *a* deafening

**ensordecer** /ensorðe'θer; ensorðe'ser/ *vt irr* to deafen; —*vi* become deaf; keep silent, refuse to reply. See **conocer**

**ensuciar** /ensu'θiar; ensu'siar/ *vt* to soil, dirty; *Fig.* sully; —*vr* be dirty; *Inf.* accept bribes

**ensueño** /en'sueṇo/ *m*, dream; illusion, fancy

**entablado** /enta'βlaðo/ *m*, stage, dais; wooden floor; planking

**entablar** /enta'βlar/ *vt* to plank, floor with boards; board up; *Surg.* splint; undertake, initiate (negotiations, etc.); begin (conversations, etc.); —*vr* settle (winds). **e. acción judicial,** to take legal action

**entalegar** /entale'gar/ *vt* to put into sacks or bags; hoard (money)

**entalladura** /entaʎa'ðura; entaya'ðura/ *f*, carving; sculpture; mortise, notch

**entallar** /enta'ʎar; enta'yar/ *vt* to carve; sculpture; engrave; notch, groove; tap (trees); fit (well or ill) at the waist

**entallecer** /entaʎe'θer; entaye'ser/ *vi irr* to sprout (plants). See **conocer**

**entapizar** /entapi'θar; entapi'sar/ *vt* to hang with tapestry; upholster; *Fig.* cover, carpet

**entarimado** /entari'maðo/ *m*, wooden floor; dais

**ente** /'ente/ *m*, entity, being; *Inf.* object, individual

**enteco** /en'teko/ *a* sickly, ailing, delicate

**entendederas** /entende'ðeras/ *f pl*, *Inf.* understanding

**entendedor** /entende'ðor/ **(-ra)** *a* understanding, comprehending —*n* one who understands. **A buen e. pocas palabras,** A word to the wise is sufficient

**entender** /enten'der/ *vt irr* to comprehend, understand; know; deduce, infer; intend; believe; (*with de*) be familiar with or knowledgeable about; (*with en*) have as a profession or trade; be engaged in; have authority in; —*vr* understand oneself; have a reason (for behavior); understand each other; have an amatory understanding; be meant, signify; (*with con*) have an understanding with. **a mi e.,** in my opinion, as I see it —*Pres. Indic.* **entiendo, entiendes, entiende, entienden.** *Pres. Subjunc.* **entienda, entiendas, entienda, entiendan**

**entendido** /enten'diðo/ *a* learned, knowledgeable

**entendimiento** /entendi'miento/ *m*, understanding; mind, reason, intelligence

**enteramente** /entera'mente/ *adv* completely, entirely, wholly

**enterar** /ente'rar/ *vt* to inform, advise

**entereza** /ente'reθa; enteresa/ *f*, entirety; completeness; impartiality, integrity; fortitude, constancy; strictness, rigor

**enternecer** /enterne'θer; enterne'ser/ *vt irr* to soften, make tender; move to pity; —*vr* be touched by compassion. See **conocer**

**enternecimiento** /enterneθi'miento; enternesi'miento/ *m*, compassion, pity; tenderness

**entero** /en'tero/ *a* entire; whole; robust, healthy; upright, just; constant, loyal; virgin; pure; *Inf.* strong, tough (cloth); *Math.* integral

**enterrador** /enterra'ðor/ *m*, gravedigger

**enterrar** /ente'rrar/ *vt irr* to inter; outlive; bury, forget. See **acertar**

**entibiar** /enti'βiar/ *vt* to make lukewarm; *Fig.* cool, temper

**entidad** /enti'ðað/ *f*, entity; value, importance

**entierro** /en'tierro/ *m*, interment, burial; grave; funeral; buried treasure

**entoldar** /entol'dar/ *vt* to cover with an awning; hang with tapestry, tent; drape; cover (sky, clouds)

**entomología** /entomolo'hia/ *f*, entomology

**entomológico** /entomo'lohiko/ *a* entomological

**entomólogo** /ento'mologo/ *m*, entomologist

**entonación** /entona'θion; entona'sion/ *f*, intonation; modulation (voice); conceit

**entonado** /ento'naðo/ *m*, haughty, conceited

**entonar** /ento'nar/ *vt* to modulate (voice); intone; blow (organ bellows); lead (song); *Med.* tone up;

*Art.* harmonize; —*vr* become conceited; *Com.* improve, harden (stock, etc.)

**entonces** /en'tonθes; entonses/ *adv* then, at that time; in that case, that being so

**entonelar** /entone'lar/ *vt* to put in barrels or casks

**entontecer** /entonte'θer; entonteser/ *vt irr* to make stupid or foolish; —*vr* become stupid. See **conocer**

**entornar** /entor'nar/ *vt* to leave ajar; half-close; upset, turn upside down

**entorpecer** /entorpe'θer; entorpe'ser/ *vt irr* to numb, make torpid; confuse, daze; obstruct, delay; —*vr* go numb; be confused. See **conocer**

**entorpecimiento** /entorpeθi'miento; entorpesi'miento/ *m*, numbness, torpidity; stupidity, dullness; delay, obstruction

**entrada** /en'traða/ *f*, entrance; door, gate; admission; *Cul.* entree; admission ticket; *Theat.* house; takings, gate; *Mil.* entry; beginnings (of month, etc.); intimacy; right of entry. **entradas y salidas,** comings and goings; collusion; *Com.* ingoing and outgoing

**entrampar** /entram'par/ *vt* to trap (animals); swindle; *Fig. Inf.* entangle (business affairs); *Inf.* load with debts; —*vr* be bogged down; *Inf.* be in debt

**entrante** /en'trante/ *a* incoming, entrant; next, coming (month)

**entraña** /en'traṇa/ *f*, entrail; *pl* heart; *Fig.* center, core; humaneness; temperament. *Inf.* **no tener entrañas,** to be heartless, be without feeling

**entrañable** /entra'ṇaβle/ *a* intimate; dearly loved

**entrar** /en'trar/ *vi* (*with en*) to enter, go into, come in; flow into; *Fig.* have access to; join, become a member; *Fig.* be taken by (fever, panic, etc.); *Mil.* enter; be an ingredient of; (*with por, en*) penetrate, pierce; (*with de*) embrace (professions, etc.); (*with prep a + infin*) begin to; (*with en + noun*) begin to be (e.g. *e. en calor,* begin to be hot) or begin to take part in (e.g. *e. en lucha,* begin to fight); —*vt* introduce, make enter; *Mil.* (*with en*) occupy; —*vr* (*with en*) squeeze in. **e. en apetito,** to work up an appetite, get an appetite. *Inf.* **no e. ni salir en,** to take no part in. *Inf.* **No me entra,** I don't understand it

**entre** /'entre/ *prep* between; among; to. **e. joyas,** among jewels. **E. las dos se escribió la carta,** Between them, they wrote the letter. **Dije e. mí,** I said to myself. **los días de e. semana,** weekdays. **e. tanto,** in the meanwhile.

**entreabrir** /entrea'βrir/ *vt* to leave ajar; half-open —*Past Part.* **entreabierto**

**entreacto** /entre'akto/ *m*, interval, entr'acte; small cigar

**entrecano** /entre'kano/ *a* going gray, grayish (hair)

**entrecejo** /entre'θeho; entre'seho/ *m*, space between the eyebrows; frown

**entrecoger** /entreko'her/ *vt* to intercept, catch; constrain, compel

**entrecortado** /entrekor'taðo/ *a* intermittent (sounds); faltering, broken (voice)

**entrecubiertas** /entreku'βiertas/ *f pl*, *Naut.* between decks

**entredicho** /entre'ðitʃo/ *m*, prohibition; *Eccl.* interdiction

**entredós** /en'treðos/ *m*, *Sew.* insertion

**entrefino** /entre'fino/ *a* middling, fairly fine

**entrega** /en'trega/ *f*, handing over; delivery; *Lit.* part, serial; installment. **por entregas,** as a serial, serial (of stories)

**entregar** /entre'gar/ *vt* to hand over; deliver; surrender; —*vr* give oneself up; surrender; submit; (*with prep a*) engage in, be absorbed in; (*with prep a or en*) give oneself over to (vice, etc.)

**entreguista** /entre'gista/ *mf* defeatist

**entrelazar** /entrela'θar; entrela'sar/ *vt* to interlace, intertwine; interweave

**entrelistado** /entrelis'taðo/ *a* striped

**entrelucir** /entrelu'θir; entrelu'sir/ *vi irr* to show through, be glimpsed. See **lucir**

**entremedias** /entre'meðias/ *adv* in between, halfway; in the meantime

**entremés** /entre'mes/ *m*, hors d'oeuvres (gen. *pl*); interlude, one-act farce

**entremesista** /entreme'sista/ *mf* author of, or actor in, one-act farces

**entremeter** /entreme'ter/ *vt* to place between or among; —*vr* intrude; meddle, pry

**entremetido** /entreme'tiðo/ **(-da)** *a* meddlesome —*n* busybody, meddler

**entremetimiento** /entremeti'miento/ *m*, meddlesomeness

**entremezclar** /entremeθ'klar; entremes'klar/ *vt* to intermingle

**entrenador** /entrena'ðor/ **(-ra)** *n* trainer; *Sports.* coach

**entrenamiento** /entrena'miento/ *m*, training, exercise

**entrenar** /entre'nar/ **(se)** *vt* and *vr* to train; exercise; *Sports.* coach

**entreoír** /entreo'ir/ *vt* to overhear; hear imperfectly

**entrepaño** /entre'paɲo/ *m*, *Archit.* panel; pier (between windows, etc.)

**entrepiernas** /entre'piernas/ *f pl*, crotch

**entrepuente** /entre'puente/ *m*, *Naut.* between decks; steerage quarters

**entresacar** /entresa'kar/ *vt* to choose or pick out; thin out (plants); thin (hair)

**entresuelo** /entre'suelo/ *m*, mezzanine, entresol; ground floor

**entresueño** /entre'sueɲo/ *m*, daydream

**entretalladura** /entretaʎa'ðura; entretayae'th;ura/ *f*, bas-relief

**entretallar** /entreta'ʎar; entreta'yar/ *vt* to carve in bas-relief; engrave; *Sew.* do openwork; intercept; —*vr* connect, dovetail

**entretejer** /entrete'her/ *vt* to interweave; interlace; *Lit.* insert

**entretela** /entre'tela/ *f*, *Sew.* interlining

**entretener** /entrete'ner/ *vt irr* to keep waiting; make more bearable; amuse, entertain; delay, postpone; maintain, upkeep; —*vr* amuse oneself. See **tener**

**entretenido** /entrete'niðo/ *a* amusing, entertaining

**entretenimiento** /entreteni'miento/ *m*, amusement; pastime, diversion; upkeep, maintenance

**entretiempo** /entre'tiempo/ *m*, between seasons, spring or autumn

**entreventana** /entreβen'tana/ *f*, space between windows

**entreverado** /entreβe'raðo/ *a* variegated; streaky (of bacon)

**entreverar** /entreβe'rar/ *vt* to intermingle

**entrevía** /entre'βia/ *f*, railroad gauge

**entrevista** /entre'βista/ *f*, meeting, interview

**entristecer** /entriste'θer; entriste'ser/ *vt irr* to sadden; —*vr* grieve. See **conocer**

**entristecimiento** /entristeθi'miento; entristesi'miento/ *m*, sadness

**entrometer** /entrome'ter/ *vt* See **entremeter**

**entronar** /entro'nar/ *vt* See **entronizar**

**entroncar** /entron'kar/ *vt* to prove descent; —*vi* be related, or become related (by marriage)

**entronerar** /entrone'rar/ *vt* to pocket (in billiards)

**entronización** /entroniθa'θion; entronisa'sion/ *f*, enthronement

**entronizar** /entroni'θar; entroni'sar/ *vt* to enthrone; exalt

**entronque** /entron'ke/ *m*, blood relationship, cognation; junction

**entumecer** /entume'θer; entume'ser/ *vt irr* to numb; —*vr* go numb; swell, rise (sea, etc.). See **conocer**

**enturbiar** /entur'βiar/ *vt* to make turbid or cloudy; confuse, disorder; —*vr* become turbid; be in disorder

**entusiasmar** /entusias'mar/ *vt* to inspire enthusiasm; —*vr* be enthusiastic

**entusiasmo** /entu'siasmo/ *m*, enthusiasm

**entusiasta** /entu'siasta/ *a* enthusiastic. *mf* enthusiast

**enumeración** /enumera'θion; enumera'sion/ *f*, enumeration

**enumerar** /enume'rar/ *vt* to enumerate

**enunciación** /enunθia'θion; enunsia'sion/ *f*, statement, declaration, enunciation

**enunciar** /enun'θiar; enun'siar/ *vt* to state clearly, enunciate

**envainar** /embai'nar/ *vt* to sheathe

**envalentonamiento** /embalentona'miento/ *m*, boldness; braggadocio, bravado

**envalentonar** /embalento'nar/ *vt* to make bold (gen. in a bad sense); —*vr* strut, brag; take courage

**envanecer** /embane'θer; embane'ser/ *vt irr* to make vain or conceited; —*vr* be vain; be conceited

**envanecimiento** /embaneθimiento; embanesi-'miento/ *m*, conceit, vanity

**envasador** /embasa'ðor/ **(-ra)** *n* packer. *m*, funnel

**envasar** /emba'sar/ *vt* to bottle; barrel; sack (grain, etc.); pack in any container; pierce (with sword)

**envase** /em'base/ *m*, bottling; filling; container; packing

**envejecer** /embehe'θer; embehe'ser/ *vt irr* to make old, wear out; —*vi* grow old. See **conocer**

**envenenador** /embenena'ðor/ **(-ra)** *n* poisoner

**envenenamiento** /embenena'miento/ *m*, poisoning

**envenenar** /embene'nar/ *vt* to poison; corrupt, pervert; put a malicious interpretation on; embitter; —*vr* take poison

**envergadura** /emberga'ðura/ *f*, wingspan

**envés** /em'bes/ *m*, wrong side of anything; *Inf.* back. **al e.**, wrong side out

**enviado** /em'biaðo/ *m*, messenger; envoy. **e. extraordinario**, special envoy

**enviar** /em'biar/ *vt* to send, dispatch

**enviciar** /embi'θiar; embi'siar/ *vt* to corrupt, make vicious; —*vr* (*with con, en*) take to (drink, etc.)

**envidia** /em'biðia/ *f*, envy; emulation; desire (to possess)

**envidiable** /embi'ðiaβle/ *a* enviable

**envidiar** /embi'ðiar/ *vt* to envy, grudge; emulate

**envidioso** /embi'ðioso/ *a* envious

**envilecer** /embile'θer; embile'ser/ *vt irr* to debase; —*vr* degrade oneself. See **conocer**

**envío** /em'bio/ *m*, *Com.* remittance; consignment

**envite** /em'bite/ *m*, stake (at cards); offer; push, shove

**enviudar** /embiu'ðar/ *vi* to become a widow or widower

**envoltorio** /embol'torio/ *m*, bundle

**envoltura** /embol'tura/ *f*, swaddling clothes; covering; wrapping

**envolver** /embol'βer/ *vt irr* to enfold; envelop; wrap up, parcel; *Fig.* contain, enshrine; swaddle, swathe; roll into a ball; confound (in argument); *Mil.* outflank; implicate (person). See **mover**

**enyesado** /enye'saðo/ *m*, plastering; stucco

**enyesar** /enye'sar/ *vt* to plaster; *Surg.* apply a plaster bandage

**enzarzar** /enθar'θar; ensar'sar/ *vt* to fill or cover with brambles; —*vr* be caught on brambles; set one person against another; get in difficulties; quarrel

**eñe** /'eɲe/ *f*, name of letter Ñ

**eón** /e'on/ *m*, eon

**eperlano** /eper'lano/ *m*, smelt

**épica** /'epika/ *f*, epic

**épico** /'epiko/ *a* epic

**epicúreo** /epi'kureo/ **(-ea)** *a* epicurean; sensual, voluptuous —*n* epicure

**epidemia** /epi'ðemia/ *f*, epidemic

**epidémico** /epi'ðemiko/ *a* epidemic

**epifanía** /epifa'nia/ *f*, Epiphany, Twelfth Night

**epiglotis** /epi'glotis/ *f*, epiglottis

**epígrafe** /epi'grafe/ *m*, epigraph, inscription; title, motto

**epigrafía** /epigra'fia/ *f*, epigraphy

**epigrama** /epi'grama/ *m*, inscription; epigram

**epigramático** /epigra'matiko/ **(-ca)** *a* epigrammatic —*n* epigrammatist

**epilepsia** /epi'lepsia/ *f*, epilepsy

**epiléptico** /epi'leptiko/ **(-ca)** *a* and *n* epileptic

**epilogar** /epilo'gar/ *vt* to summarize, recapitulate

**epílogo** /e'pilogo/ *m*, recapitulation; summary, digest; epilogue

**episcopado** /episko'paðo/ *m*, episcopate; bishopric

**episódico** /epi'soðiko/ *a* episodic

**episodio** /epi'soðio/ *m*, episode; digression

**epístola** /e'pistola/ *f*, epistle

**epistolar** /episto'lar/ *a* epistolary

**epitafio** /epi'tafio/ *m*, epitaph

**epíteto** /e'piteto/ *m*, epithet
**epítome** /e'pitome/ *m*, epitome; summary, abstract
**época** /'epoka/ *f*, epoch, period; space of time. **é. de celo,** mating season. **é. de lluvias,** rainy season. **é. de secas,** dry season. **en aquella é.,** at that time
**épodo** /'epoðo/ *m*, *Poet.* epode
**epopeya** /epo'peya/ *f*, epic poem; *Fig.* epic
**equidad** /eki'ðað/ *f*, fairness; reasonableness; equity
**equidistancia** /ekiðis'tanθia; ekiðistansia/ *f*, equidistance
**equidistante** /ekiðis'tante/ *a* equidistant
**equilibrar** /ekili'βrar/ *vt* to balance; *Fig.* maintain in equilibrium, counterbalance
**equilibrio** /eki'liβrio/ *m*, equilibrium; equanimity; *Fig.* balance
**equilibrista** /ekili'βrista/ *mf* equilibrist, tightrope walker
**equino** /e'kino/ *a* equine. *m*, *Archit.* echinus; sea urchin
**equinoccio** /eki'nokθio; ekinoksio/ *m*, equinox
**equipaje** /eki'pahe/ *m*, luggage, baggage; *Naut.* crew
**equipar** /eki'par/ *vt* to equip, furnish
**equipo** /e'kipo/ *m*, outfitting, furnishing; equipment; team; trousseau
**equis** /'ekis/ *f*, name of letter X
**equitación** /ekita'θion; ekita'sion/ *f*, horsemanship, riding
**equitativo** /ekita'tiβo/ *a* equitable, just, fair
**equivalencia** /ekiβa'lenθia; ekiβalensia/ *f*, equivalence, equality
**equivalente** /ekiβa'lente/ *a* equivalent
**equivaler** /ekiβa'ler/ *vi irr* to be equivalent; *Geom.* be equal. See **valer**
**equivocación** /ekiβoka'θion; ekiβoka'sion/ *f*, error, mistake
**equivocadamente** /ekiβokaða'mente/ *adv* mistakenly, by mistake
**equivocar** /ekiβo''kar/ *vt* to mistake; —*vr* be mistaken or make a mistake. **equivocarse de medio a medio,** to be off by a long shot
**equívoco** /e'kiβoko/ *a* equivocal, ambiguous. *m*, equivocation
**era** /'era/ *f*, era; threshing floor; vegetable or flower bed
**erario** /e'rario/ *m*, public treasury, exchequer
**erección** /erek'θion; erek'sion/ *f*, raising; erection, elevation; foundation, institution
**eremita** /ere'mita/ *mf* hermit
**ergio** /'erhio/ *m*, erg
**erguir** /er'gir/ *vt irr* to raise; straighten; lift up; —*vr* straighten up; tower; grow proud —*Pres. Indic.* **irgo** (or **yergo**), **irgues, irguen.** *Pres. Part.* **irguiendo.** *Preterite* **irguió, irguieron.** *Pres. Subjunc.* **irga** or **yerga,** etc.
**erial** /e'rial/ *m*, uncultivated land
**erigir** /eri'hir/ *vt* to found, establish; promote, exalt. **erigirse contra,** to rise up against
**erisipela** /erisi'pela/ *f*, erysipelas
**erizado** /eri'θaðo; eri'saðo/ *a* standing on end (of hair); prickly, covered with bristles or quills. **e. de espinas,** bristling with thorns; covered with bristles or quills
**erizar** /eri'θar; eri'sar/ *vt* to set on end (hair); beset with difficulties; —*vr* stand on end, bristle (hair, quills, etc.)
**erizo** /e'riθo; e'riso/ *m*, hedgehog; husk (of some fruits); *Inf.* touch-me-not, unsociable person; *Mech.* sprocket wheel. **e. de mar,** sea urchin
**ermita** /er'mita/ *f*, hermitage
**ermitaño** /ermi'taño/ *m*, hermit
**erosión** /ero'sion/ *f*, erosion
**erótico** /e'rotiko/ *a* erotic
**errabundo** /erra'βundo/ *a* wandering, errant, vagrant
**erradamente** /erraða'mente/ *adv* erroneously
**erradicable** /erraði'kaβle/ *a* eradicable
**erradicación** /erraðika'θion; erraðika'sion/ *f*, eradication
**erradicar** /erraði'kar/ *vt* to eradicate
**errante** /e'rrante/ *a* wandering; erring; errant
**errar** /e'rrar/ *vi irr* to err, fail; rove, roam; wander (attention, etc.); —*vr* be mistaken. *Auto.* **e. el en-**cendido, to misfire —*Pres. Indic.* **yerro, yerras, yerra, yerran.** *Pres. Subjunc.* **yerre, yerres, yerre, yerren**
**errata** /e'rrata/ *f*, misprint
**errático** /e'rratiko/ *a* wandering, vagrant; *Med.* erratic
**erre** /'erre/ *f*, name of letter R
**erróneo** /e'rroneo/ *a* erroneous, mistaken
**error** /e'rror/ *m*, error. **error de más,** an overestimate. **error de menos,** an underestimate
**eructar** /eruk'tar/ *vi* to eructate, belch
**eructo** /e'rukto/ *m*, eructation, belching
**erudición** /eruði'θion; eruði'sion/ *f*, erudition
**erudito** /eru'ðito/ *a* learned, erudite. *m*, scholar. **e. a la violeta,** pseudo-learned
**erupción** /erup'θion; erup'sion/ *f*, *Med.* rash; eruption
**eruptivo** /erup'tiβo/ *a* eruptive
**es** /es/ *irr 3rd pers. sing Pres. Indic.* of ser, is
**esa** /'esa/ *f*, *dem a* that. **ésa,** *f*, *dem. pron* that one; the former; the town in which you are (e.g. *Iré a é. mañana,* I shall come to your town tomorrow). Used generally in letters. See **ése**
**esbeltez** /esβel'teθ; esβel'tes/ *f*, slenderness
**esbelto** /es'βelto/ *a* tall and slim and graceful, willowy
**esbozar** /esβo'θar; esβo'sar/ *vt* to sketch, outline
**esbozo** /es'βoθo; es'βoso/ *m*, sketch; outline, rough plan, first draft
**escabechar** /eskaβe'tʃar/ *vt* to pickle; dye (the hair, etc.); *Inf.* kill in anger; *Inf.* fail (an examination)
**escabeche** /eska'βetʃe/ *m*, *Cul.* pickle; hair dye
**escabechina** /eskaβe'tʃina/ *f*, *Inf.* heavy failure (in an examination)
**escabel** /eska'βel/ *m*, footstool; small backless chair; *Fig.* steppingstone
**escabioso** /eska'βioso/ *a* scabby, scabious
**escabro** /es'kaβro/ *m*, scab, mange
**escabroso** /eska'βroso/ *a* rough; rocky; uneven; rude, unpolished, uncivil; risqué, improper
**escabullirse** /eskaβu'ʎirse; eskaβu'yirse/ *vr irr* to escape; run away; slip out unnoticed. See **mullir**
**escafandra** /eska'fandra/ *f*, diving suit, diving outfit
**escala** /es'kala/ *f*, ladder; (*Mus. Math.*) scale; dial (of machines); proportion, ratio; stage, stopping place; measuring rule; *Naut.* port of call. **e. de toldilla,** companion ladder. *Mus.* **e. mayor,** major scale. **e. menor,** minor scale. *Naut.* **hacer e. en un puerto,** to call at a port
**escalada** /eska'laða/ *f*, escalade
**escalafón** /eskala'fon/ *m*, salary scale; roll, list
**escalamiento** /eskala'miento/ *m*, scaling, climbing, storming
**escalar** /eska'lar/ *vt* to scale; climb, ascend; storm, assail, enter or leave violently
**escaldadura** /eskalda'ðura/ *f*, scalding; scald
**escaldar** /eskal'dar/ *vt* to scald; make red-hot; —*vr* scald or burn oneself. **Gato escaldado del agua fría huye,** Once bitten, twice shy
**escalera** /eska'lera/ *f*, staircase; stair. **e. abajo,** below stairs. **e. de caracol,** spiral staircase. **e. de mano,** ladder. **e. de tijera,** stepladder. **e. móvil,** escalator
**escalfar** /eskal'far/ *vt* to poach (eggs); burn (bread)
**escalinata** /eskali'nata/ *f*, outside staircase or flight of steps, perron
**escalofrío** /eskalo'frio/ *m*, (gen. *pl*) shiver, shudder
**escalón** /eska'lon/ *m*, step, stair; rung (of a ladder); *Fig.* steppingstone; grade, rank. **en escalones,** in steps
**escalpar** /eskal'par/ *vt* to scalp
**escalpelo** /eskal'pelo/ *m*, scalpel
**escama** /es'kama/ *f*, *Zool.* scale; anything scale-shaped; flake; suspicion, resentment
**escamar** /eska'mar/ *vt* to scale (fish); make suspicious —*vr Inf.* be suspicious or disillusioned
**escamondar** /eskamon'dar/ *vt Agr.* to prune
**escamoso** /eska'moso/ *a* scaly
**escamotear** /eskamote'ar/ *vt* to make disappear; palm (in conjuring); steal
**escamoteo** /eskamo'teo/ *m*, disappearance; stealing
**escampada** /eskam'paða/ *f*, *Inf.* clear interval on a rainy day

**escampar** /eskam'par/ *vi* to cease raining; clear up (of the weather, sky); stop (work, etc.)

**escamujar** /eskamu'har/ *vt* Agr. to cut out superfluous wood (of trees, etc.)

**escanciar** /eskan'θiar; eskan'siar/ *vt* to pour out wine; —*vi* drink wine

**escandalizar** /eskandali'θar; eskandali'sar/ *vt* to shock, scandalize; disturb with noise; —*vr* be vexed or irritated

**escandallo** /eskan'daʎo; eskan'dayo/ *m*, Naut. deep-sea lead; random test

**escándalo** /es'kandalo/ *m*, scandal; commotion, uproar; bad example; viciousness; astonishment

**escandaloso** /eskanda'loso/ *a* disgraceful, scandalous; turbulent

**Escandinavia** /eskandi'naβia/ Scandinavia

**escandinavo** /eskandi'naβo/ **(-va)** *a* and *n* Scandinavian

**escandir** /eskan'dir/ *vt* to scan (verse)

**escansión** /eskan'sion/ *f*, scansion

**escantillón** /eskanti'ʎon; eskanti'yon/ *m*, template, pattern; rule

**escaño** /es'kaɲo/ *m*, bench with a back

**escapada** /eska'paða/ *f*, escape; escapade

**escapar** /eska'par/ *vt* to spur on (a horse); —*vi* escape; flee; avoid, evade; —*vr* escape; leak (gas, etc.). **Se me escapó su nombre,** His name escaped me. **e. por un pelo,** to have a narrow escape

**escaparate** /eskapa'rate/ *m*, showcase, cabinet; shop window

**escapatoria** /eskapa'toria/ *f*, escape, flight; Inf. way out, loophole

**escape** /es'kape/ *m*, flight; evasion; escape (gas, etc.); Auto. exhaust. **a e.,** at full speed

**escápula** /es'kapula/ *f*, scapula

**escaque** /es'kake/ *m*, square (chessboard or checkerboard); *pl* chess

**escaqueado** /eskake'aðo/ *a* checked, worked in squares

**escara** /es'kara/ *f*, scar

**escarabajo** /eskara'βaho/ *m*, beetle, scarab; Fig. Inf. dwarf; *pl* Inf. scrawl

**escaramuza** /eskara'muθa; eskara'musa/ *f*, skirmish

**escaramuzar** /eskaramu'θar; eskaramu'sar/ *vi* to skirmish

**escarapela** /eskara'pela/ *f*, cockade, rosette; brawl

**escarbadientes** /eskarβa'ðientes/ *m*, toothpick

**escarbar** /eskar'βar/ *vt* to scratch, scrabble (fowls); root, dig; rake out (the fire); inquire into

**escarcha** /es'kartʃa/ *f*, hoarfrost

**escarchar** /eskar'tʃar/ *vt* Cul. to frost, ice; spread with frosting; —*vi* freeze lightly

**escarda** /es'karða/ *f*, weeding; Fig. weeding out

**escardador** /eskarða'ðor/ **(-ra)** *n* weeder

**escardar** /eskar'ðar/ *vt* to weed; Fig. separate good from bad

**escarificación** /eskarifika'θion; eskarifika'sion/ *f*, scarification

**escarlata** /eskar'lata/ *f*, scarlet; scarlet cloth

**escarlatina** /eskarla'tina/ *f*, scarlet fever

**escarmentar** /eskarmen'tar/ *vt irr* to reprehend or punish severely; —*vi* learn from experience, be warned. See **acertar**

**escarmiento** /eskar'miento/ *m*, disillusionment, experience; warning; punishment, fine

**escarnecedor** /eskarneθe'ðor; eskarneseðor/ **(-ra)** *a* mocking —*n* mocker

**escarnecer** /eskarne'θer; eskarne'ser/ *vt irr* to mock. See **conocer**

**escarnio** /es'karnio/ *m*, gibe, jeer

**escarola** /eska'rola/ *f*, endive; frilled ruff

**escarpa** /es'karpa/ *f*, steep slope, declivity; escarpment

**escarpado** /eskar'paðo/ *a* steep, precipitous

**escarpín** /eskar'pin/ *m*, pump, slipper

**escasear** /eskase'ar/ *vt* to dole out, give grudgingly; save, husband; —*vi* be scarce or short; grow less

**escasez** /eska'seθ; eska'ses/ *f*, meanness, frugality; want; shortage, scarcity

**escaso** /es'kaso/ *a* scarce; short; bare; parsimonious

**escatimar** /eskati'mar/ *vt* to cut down, curtail

**escatimoso** /eskati'moso/ *a* malicious, guileful

**escayola** /eska'yola/ *f*, plaster of Paris

**escena** /es'θena; es'sena/ *f*, Theat. stage; scene; scenery; theater, drama; spectacle, sight; episode, incident. **director de e.,** producer. **poner en e.,** Theat. to produce

**escenario** /esθe'nario; esse'nario/ *m*, Theat. stage; scenario

**escénico** /es'θeniko; es'seniko/ *a* scenic

**escenografía** /esθenogra'fia; essenogra'fia/ *f*, scenography

**escenógrafo** /esθe'nografo; esse'nografo/ **(-fa)** *n* scenographer, scene painter

**escepticismo** /esθepti'θismo; essepti'sismo/ *m*, scepticism

**escéptico** /es'θeptiko; es'septiko/ **(-ca)** *a* sceptical —*n* sceptic

**escindir** /esθin'dir; essin'dir/ *vt* to split

**escisión** /esθi'sion; essi'sion/ *f*, cleavage, split; splitting; schism; disagreement

**esclarecer** /esklare'θer; esklare'ser/ *vt irr* to illuminate; ennoble, make illustrious; Fig. enlighten; elucidate; —*vi* dawn. See **conocer**

**esclarecido** /esklare'θiðo; esklare'siðo/ *a* distinguished, illustrious

**esclavina** /eskla'βina/ *f*, short cape

**esclavitud** /esklaβi'tuð/ *f*, slavery; fraternity

**esclavizar** /esklaβi'θar; esklaβi'sar/ *vt* to enslave

**esclavo** /es'klaβo/ **(-va)** *n* slave; member of a brotherhood —*a* enslaved. *f*, slave bracelet; ID bracelet

**esclerosis** /eskle'rosis/ *f*, sclerosis

**esclerótica** /eskle'rotika/ *f*, scleritic

**esclusa** /es'klusa/ *f*, lock; sluice gate; weir

**esclusero** /esklu'sero/ *m*, lock keeper

**escoba** /es'koβa/ *f*, broom, brush; Bot. yellow broom

**escobada** /esko'βaða/ *f*, sweep, stroke (of a broom)

**escobar** /esko'βar/ *vt* to sweep with a broom

**escobazo** /esko'βaθo; esko'βaso/ *m*, brush with a broom

**escobero** /esko'βero/ *m*, brush maker or seller

**escobilla** /esko'βiʎa; esko'βiya/ *f*, brush

**escobina** /esko'βina/ *f*, metal filing; woodshaving

**escocer** /esko'θer; esko'ser/ *vi irr* to smart; Fig. sear; —*vr* hurt, smart; be chafed. See **mover**

**escocés** /esko'θes; esko'ses/ **(-esa)** *a* Scots, Scottish —*n* Scot

**Escocia** /es'koθia; eskosia/ Scotland

**escoda** /es'koða/ *f*, claw hammer

**escofina** /esko'fina/ *f*, rasp, file

**escoger** /esko'her/ *vt* to choose, select

**escogido** /esko'hiðo/ *a* choice, select

**escolar** /esko'lar/ *a* school; pupil. *m*, pupil

**escolasticismo** /eskolasti'θismo; eskolasti'sismo/ *m*, scholasticism

**escolástico** /esko'lastiko/ *a* scholastic

**escollera** /esko'ʎera; esko'yera/ *f*, breakwater, sea wall, jetty

**escollo** /es'koʎo; es'koyo/ *m*, reef; danger, risk; difficulty, obstacle

**escolopendra** /eskolo'pendra/ *f*, centipede; hart's-tongue fern

**escolta** /es'kolta/ *f*, escort, guard

**escoltar** /eskol'tar/ *vt* to escort; guard, conduct

**escombrar** /eskom'brar/ *vt* to remove obstacles, free of rubbish; Fig. clean up

**escombro** /es'kombro/ *m*, debris, rubble, rubbish; mackerel

**esconder** /eskon'der/ *vt* to hide, conceal; Fig. contain, embrace; —*vr* hide

**escondidas, a** /eskon'diðas, a/ *adv* secretly

**escondite, escondrijo** /eskon'dite, eskon'driho/ *m*, hiding place. **jugar al escondite,** to play hide-and-seek

**escopeta** /esko'peta/ *f*, shotgun. **e. de aire comprimido,** air gun, popgun. **e. de pistón,** repercussion gun. **e. de viento,** air gun

**escopetazo** /eskope'taθo; eskope'taso/ *m*, gunshot; gunshot wound; Fig. bombshell

**escopetear** /eskopete'ar/ *vt* to shoot repeatedly

**escopetero** /eskope'tero/ *m*, musketeer; gunsmith; man with a gun

**escoplear** /eskople'ar/ *vt* to notch; chisel; gouge

**escoplo** /es'koplo/ *m*, chisel

**escorbuto** /eskor'βuto/ *m*, scurvy

**escoria** /es'koria/ *f*, dross, slag; scoria, volcanic ash; *Fig.* dregs

**escorial** /esko'rial/ *m*, slag heap

**escorpión** /eskor'pion/ *m*, scorpion; Scorpio

**escorzo** /es'korθo; es'korso/ *m*, *Art.* foreshortening

**escotado** /eskota'ðo/ *a* low-cut (of dresses)

**escotadura** /eskota'ðura/ *a* low neck (of a dress); piece cut out of something; *Theat.* large trapdoor; recess

**escotar** /esko'tar/ *vt* to cut low in the neck (of dresses); pay one's share (of expenses)

**escote** /es'kote/ *m*, low neck (of a dress); shortness (of sleeves); share (of expenses); lace yoke

**escotilla** /esko'tiʎa; esko'tiya/ *f*, *Naut.* hatch

**escozor** /esko'θor; esko'sor/ *m*, smart, pricking pain; irritation, prickle; heartache

**escriba** /es'kriβa/ *m*, (Jewish hist.) scribe

**escribanía** /eskriβa'nia/ *f*, secretaryship; notaryship; bureau, office; writing case; inkstand

**escribano** /eskri'βano/ *m*, notary public; secretary

**escribiente** /eskri'βiente/ *mf* clerk

**escribir** /eskri'βir/ *vt* to write; —*vr* enlist; enroll; correspond by writing —*Past Part.* **escrito**

**escrito** /es'krito/ *m*, writing, manuscript; literary or scientific work; *Law.* writ. **por e.,** in writing

**escritor** /eskri'tor/ **(-ra)** *n* writer, author

**escritorio** /eskri'torio/ *m*, escritoire; office

**escritura** /eskri'tura/ *f*, writing; handwriting; *Law.* deed; literary work. **Sagrada E.,** Holy Scripture

**escrófula** /es'krofula/ *f*, scrofula

**escrofuloso** /eskrofu'loso/ *a* scrofulous

**escroto** /es'kroto/ *m*, scrotum

**escrúpulo** /es'krupulo/ *m*, scruple, qualm; conscientiousness; scruple (pharmacy)

**escrupulosidad** /eskrupulosi'ðað/ *f*, conscientiousness, scrupulousness

**escrupuloso** /eskrupu'loso/ *a* scrupulous; exact, accurate

**escrutador** /eskruta'ðor/ **(-ra)** *n* scrutinizer —*a* examining, inspecting

**escrutar** /eskru'tar/ *vt* to scrutinize, examine; count (votes)

**escrutinio** /eskru'tinio/ *m*, scrutiny, examination; count (votes)

**escuadra** /es'kuaðra/ *f*, carpenter's square; architect's square; *Nav.* fleet; *Aer.* squadron; *Mil.* squad. **e. de agrimensor,** *Surv.* cross-staff

**escuadrar** /eskua'ðrar/ *vt* (and *Mas.*) to square

**escuadrilla** /eskua'ðriʎa; eskua'ðriya/ *f*, squadron (airplanes, small ships)

**escuadrón** /eskua'ðron/ *m*, squadron

**escualidez** /eskuali'ðeθ; eskuali'ðes/ *f*, squalor, sordidness

**escuálido** /es'kualiðo/ *a* filthy, squalid; sordid; thin

**escucha** /es'kutʃa/ *f*, listening; peephole; *Mil.* sentinel

**escuchar** /esku'tʃar/ *vt* to listen; attend to, heed; —*vr* like the sound of one's own voice

**escudar** /esku'ðar/ *vt* to shield, protect

**escudero** /esku'ðero/ *m*, squire; page; gentleman; shield maker

**escudete** /esku'ðete/ *m*, escutcheon; shield; gusset; white water lily

**escudilla** /esku'ðiʎa; esku'ðiya/ *f*, bowl

**escudo** /es'kuðo/ *m*, shield; escudo; escutcheon; protection, defense; ward (of a keyhole)

**escudriñador** /eskuðriɲa'ðor/ **(-ra)** *a* searching; curious, prying —*n* scrutinizer; pryer

**escudriñar** /eskuðri'ɲar/ *vt* to scrutinize; scan; investigate; pry into

**escuela** /es'kuela/ *f*, school; school building; style; (Lit. and Art.) school. **e. de artes y oficios,** industrial school. **e. industrial,** technical school. **e. normal,** normal school

**escueto** /es'kueto/ *a* dry, bare, unadorned; simple, exact; unencumbered

**esculpir** /eskul'pir/ *vt* to sculpture; engrave

**escultor** /eskul'tor/ **(-ra)** *n* sculptor

**escultórico** /eskul'toriko/ *a* sculptural

**escultura** /eskul'tura/ *f*, sculpture; carving; modeling

**escupidera** /eskupi'ðera/ *f*, spittoon

**escupir** /esku'pir/ *vi* to expectorate; —*vt Fig.* spit out; cast away, throw out

**escurreplatos** /eskurre'platos/ *m*, dishrack, draining rack

**escurrido** /esku'rriðo/ *a* narrow-hipped; skintight (of skirts)

**escurridor** /eskurri'ðor/ *m*, colander, sieve; dishrack; drainingboard

**escurriduras** /eskurri'ðuras/ *f pl*, lees, dregs

**escurrir** /esku'rrir/ *vt* to drain to the dregs; wring, press out, drain; —*vi* trickle, drip; slip, slide; —*vr* slip away, edge away; escape, slip out; skid

**esdrújulo** /es'ðru'hulo/ *a Gram.* of words where the accent falls on the antepenultimate syllable

**ese** /'ese/ *f*, name of letter S; S-shaped link (in a chain). *Inf.* **andar haciendo eses,** to reel about drunkenly

**ese** /'ese/ *m*, *dem a* (*f*, **esa.** *pl* **esos, esas**) that; those. **ése,** *m*, *dem pron* (*f*, **ésa.** *neut* **eso.** *pl* **ésos, ésas**) that one; the former (e.g. *Me gusta éste, pero ése no me gusta,* I like this one, but I do not like that one

**esencia** /e'senθia; e'sensia/ *f*, essence, nature, character; extract; *Chem.* essence

**esencial** /esen'θial; esen'sial/ *a* essential

**esfera** /es'fera/ *f*, *Geom.* sphere, globe, ball; sky; rank; face, dial; province, scope

**esférico** /es'feriko/ *a* spherical

**esfinge** /es'finhe/ *f*, sphinx

**esforzado** /esfor'θaðo; esfor'saðo/ *a* valiant, courageous; spirited

**esforzador** /esforθa'ðor; esforsa'ðor/ *a* encouraging

**esforzar** /esfor'θar; esfor'sar/ *vt irr* to encourage; invigorate; —*vr* make an effort. See **contar**

**esfuerzo** /es'fuerθo; es'fuerso/ *m*, effort; courage; spirit; vigor; exertion, strain; *Mech.* stress. **sin e.,** effortless

**esfumar** /esfu'mar/ *vt Art.* shade; *Art.* stump; dim; —*vr* disappear

**esfumino** /esfu'mino/ *m*, *Art.* stump

**esgrima** /es'grima/ *f*, (art of) fencing

**esgrimidor** /esgrimi'ðor/ *m*, fencer, swordsman

**esgrimir** /esgri'mir/ *vt* to fence; fend off

**esguazar** /esgua'θar; esgua'sar/ *vt* to ford (a river)

**esguince** /es'ginθe; es'ginse/ *m*, dodging, twist; expression or gesture of repugnance; *Med.* sprain

**eslabón** /esla'βon/ *m*, link (in a chain); steel for producing fire. **e. perdido,** *Fig.* missing link

**eslabonar** /eslaβo'nar/ *vt* to link; connect, unite

**eslavo** /es'laβo/ **(-va)** *a* Slavic —*n* Slav

**eslora** /es'lora/ *f*, *Naut.* length (of a ship)

**eslovaco** /eslo'βako/ **(-ca)** *a* Slovakian —*n* Slovak

**esloveno** /eslo'βeno/ **(-na)** *a* and *n* Slovene

**esmaltador** /esmalta'ðor/ **(-ra)** *n* enameler

**esmaltar** /esmal'tar/ *vt* to enamel; decorate, adorn

**esmalte** /es'malte/ *m*, enamel; enamelwork; smalt; brilliance

**esmerado** /esme'raðo/ *a* careful, painstaking

**esmeralda** /esme'ralda/ *f*, emerald

**esmerar** /esme'rar/ *vt* to polish; —*vr* (with en) take great pains with (or to)

**esmeril** /es'meril/ *m*, emery

**esmerilar** /esmeri'lar/ *vt* to polish with emery

**esmero** /es'mero/ *m*, great care, conscientiousness

**esmoladera** /esmola'ðera/ *f*, grindstone

**esnob** /es'noβ/ *a* snobbish. *mf* snob

**eso** /'eso/ *neut dem pron* that; the fact that; that idea, affair, etc.; about (of time) (e.g. *Vendrá a e. de las nueve,* He will come about nine o'clock). **Eso** refers to an abstraction, never to one definite object. **No me gusta e.,** I don't like that kind of thing. **e. es,** that's it. **por e.,** therefore, for that reason

**esófago** /e'sofago/ *m*, esophagus

**esotérico** /eso'teriko/ *a* esoteric

**espaciar** /espa'θiar; espa'siar/ *vt* to space; *Print.* lead; —*vr* spread oneself, enlarge (upon)

**espacio** /es'paθio; es'pasio/ *m*, space; capacity; interval, duration; slowness; *Print.* lead

**espaciosidad** /espaθiosi'ðað; espasiosi'ðað/ *f*, spaciousness; capacity

**espada** /es'paða/ *f*, sword; matador; swordsman; (cards) spade. **entre la e. y la pared,** *Fig*. between a rock and a hard place; between undesirable alternatives.

**espadachín** /espaða'tʃin/ *m*, good swordsman; bully, quarrelsome fellow

**espadaña** /espa'ðaɲa/ *f*, open belfry; gladiolus

**espadería** /espaðe'ria/ *f*, sword cutler's workshop or shop

**espadero** /espa'ðero/ *m*, sword cutler

**espadín** /espa'ðin/ *m*, small dress sword

**espahi** /es'pai/ *m*, spahi

**espalda** /es'palda/ *f*, *Anat*. back (often *pl*); *pl* rear, back portion; *Mil*. rear guard. **de espaldas,** with one's (its, his, etc.) back turned; on one's (its, etc.) back

**espaldar** /espal'dar/ *m*, backpiece of a cuirass; back (of chair); garden trellis, espalier

**espaldarazo** /espalda'raθo; espalda'raso/ *m*, accolade

**espaldera** /espal'dera/ *f*, espalier, trellis

**espantadizo** /espanta'ðiθo; espanta'ðiso/ *a* easily frightened

**espantapájaros** /espanta'paharos/ *m*, scarecrow

**espantar** /espan'tar/ *vt* to frighten, terrify; chase off; —*vr* be amazed; be scared

**espanto** /es'panto/ *m*, terror, panic; dismay; amazement; threat

**espantoso** /espan'toso/ *a* horrible, terrifying, awesome; amazing

**España** /es'paɲa/ Spain

**español** /espa'ɲol/ **(-la)** *a* Spanish —*n* Spaniard. *m*, Spanish (language). **a la española,** in Spanish fashion

**españolía** /espaɲo'lia/ *f*, Spanish colony, Spanish community (outside Spain)

**españolismo** /espaɲo'lismo/ *m*, love of things Spanish; Hispanism

**españolizar** /espaɲoli'θar; espaɲoli'sar/ *vt* to hispanize; —*vr* adopt Spanish customs

**esparadrapo** /espara'ðrapo/ *m*, court plaster

**esparavel** /espara'βel/ *m*, casting net

**esparcimiento** /esparθi'miento; esparsi'miento/ *m*, scattering; naturalness, frankness; geniality

**esparcir** /espar'θir; espar'sir/ *vt* to scatter, sprinkle, disperse; spread, publish abroad; entertain; —*vr* be scattered; amuse oneself

**espárrago** /es'parrago/ *m*, asparagus

**esparraguera** /esparra'gera/ *f*, asparagus plant; asparagus bed; asparagus dish

**Esparta** /es'parta/ Sparta

**espartano** /espar'tano/ **(-na)** *a* and *n* Spartan

**espartería** /esparte'ria/ *f*, esparto industry, esparto shop

**esparto** /es'parto/ *m*, esparto grass

**espasmo** /es'pasmo/ *m*, spasm

**espasmódico** /espas'moðiko/ *a* spasmodic

**espátula** /es'patula/ *f*, spatula; palette knife

**especia** /es'peθia; es'pesia/ *f*, spice. **nuez de e.,** nutmeg

**especial** /espe'θial; espe'sial/ *a* special; particular

**especialidad** /espeθiali'ðað; espesiali'ðað/ *f*, specialty; branch (of learning)

**especialista** /espeθia'lista; espesia'lista/ *mf* specialist

**especialización** /espeθialiθa'θion; espesialisa'sion/ *f*, specialization

**especializarse** /espeθiali'θarse; espesiali'sarse/ *vr* to specialize

**especie** /es'peθie; es'pesie/ *f*, class, kind; species; affair, matter, case; idea, image; news; pretext, appearance

**especiería** /espeθie'ria; espesie'ria/ *f*, spice trade; spice shop

**especiero** /espe'θiero; espe'siero/ **(-ra)** *n* spice merchant; spice rack

**especificación** /espeθifika'θion; espesifika'sion/ *f*, specification. **e. normalizada,** standard specification

**especificar** /espeθifi'kar; espesifi'kar/ *vt* to specify, particularize

**específico** /espe'θifiko; espe'sifiko/ *a* and *m*, specific patent medicine

**espécimen** /es'peθimen; es'pesimen/ *m*, specimen, sample

**especioso** /espe'θioso; espe'sioso/ *a* lovely, perfect; specious

**espectacular** /espektaku'lar/ *a* spectacular

**espectáculo** /espek'takulo/ *m*, spectacle, sight; show, display

**espectador** /espekta'ðor/ **(-ra)** *n* spectator

**espectral** /espek'tral/ *a* spectral; faint, dim

**espectro** /es'pektro/ *m*, phantom, specter; *Phys*. spectrum

**especulación** /espekula'θion; espekula'sion/ *f*, conjecture; *Com*. speculation

**especulador** /espekula'ðor/ **(-ra)** *n* speculator

**especular** /espeku'lar/ *vt* to examine, look at; (*with en*) reflect on, consider; —*vi Com*. speculate

**especulativo** /espekula'tiβo/ *a* speculative; thoughtful, meditative

**espejería** /espehe'ria/ *f*, mirror shop or factory

**espejero** /espe'hero/ *m*, mirror manufacturer or seller

**espejismo** /espe'hismo/ *m*, mirage; illusion

**espejo** /es'peho/ *m*, mirror; *Fig*. model. **e. de cuerpo entero,** full-length mirror. **e. retrovisor,** rearview mirror

**espejuelo** /espe'huelo/ *m*, small mirror; *Mineral*. selenite; *Mineral*. sheet of talc; *pl* lenses, eyeglasses

**espeluznante** /espeluθ'nante; espelus'nante/ *a* hairraising

**espeluznar** /espeluθ'nar; espelus'nar/ *vt* to dishevel, untidy (hair, etc.); —*vr* stand on end (hair)

**espera** /es'pera/ *f*, waiting; expectation; *Law*. adjournment; caution, restraint; *Law*. respite

**esperantista** /esperan'tista/ *mf* Esperantist

**esperanto** /espe'ranto/ *m*, Esperanto

**esperanza** /espe'ranθa; espe'ransa/ *f*, hope

**esperanzar** /esperan'θar; esperan'sar/ *vt* to inspire hope in

**esperar** /espe'rar/ *vt* to hope; expect; await; (*with en*) have faith in. **e. sentado,** *Fig*. *Inf*. to whistle for

**esperma** /es'perma/ *f*, sperm, semen. **e. de ballena,** spermaceti

**esperpento** /esper'pento/ *m*, *Inf*. scarecrow, grotesque; folly, madness; fantastic dramatic composition

**espesar** /espe'sar/ *vt* to thicken; make closer; tighten (fabrics); —*vr* thicken; grow denser or thicker

**espeso** /es'peso/ *a* thick; dense; greasy, dirty

**espesor** /espe'sor/ *m*, thickness; density

**espesura** /espe'sura/ *f*, thickness; density; thicket; filth

**espetar** /espe'tar/ *vt Cul*. to spit, skewer; pierce; *Inf*. utter, give; —*vr* be stiff or affected; *Inf*. push oneself in, intrude

**espetera** /espe'tera/ *f*, kitchen or pot rack

**espetón** /espe'ton/ *m*, *Cul*. spit; poker; large pin

**espía** /es'pia/ *mf* spy. *f*, *Naut*. warp

**espiar** /es'piar/ *vt* to spy upon, watch; —*vi Naut*. warp

**espiche** /es'pitʃe/ *m*, sharp-pointed weapon or instrument; spit, spike

**espiga** /es'piga/ *f*, *Bot*. spike, ear; sprig; peg; tang, shank (of sword); tenon, dowel; *Naut*. masthead; *Herald*. garb

**espigador** /espiga'ðor/ **(-ra)** *n* gleaner

**espigar** /espi'gar/ *vt* to glean; tenon; —*vi Bot*. begin to show the ear or spike; —*vr Bot*. bolt; shoot up, grow (persons)

**espigón** /espi'gon/ *m*, sting; sharp point; breakwater; bearded spike (corn, etc.)

**espigueo** /espi'geo/ *m*, gleaning

**espín** /es'pin/ *m*, porcupine

**espina** /es'pina/ *f*, thorn; prickle; splinter; fish bone; *Anat*. spine; suspicion, doubt

**espinaca** /espi'naka/ *f*, spinach

**espinal** /espi'nal/ *a* spinal

**espinar** /espi'nar/ *m*, thorn brake; *Fig*. awkward position —*vt* to prick, wound, hurt

**espinazo** /espi'naθo; espi'naso/ *m*, backbone

**espineta** /espi'neta/ *f*, spinet; virginals

**espinilla** /espi'niʎa; espi'niya/ *f*, shinbone; blackhead

**espinoso** /espi'noso/ *a* thorny; difficult, intricate

**espión** /es'pion/ *m,* See **espía**

**espionaje** /espio'nahe/ *m,* espionage; spying

**espira** /es'pira/ *f,* (*Geom. Archit.*) helix; turn, twist (of winding stairs); whorl (of a shell)

**espiración** /espira'θion; espira'sion/ *f,* expiration; respiration

**espiral** /espi'ral/ *a* spiral. *f, Geom.* spiral; spiral watchspring

**espirar** /espi'rar/ *vt* to exhale, breathe out; inspire; encourage; —*vi* breathe; breathe out; *Poet.* blow (wind)

**espiritisimo** /espiri'tisimo/ *m,* spiritualism

**espiritista** /espiri'tista/ *a* spiritualist. *mf* spiritualist

**espiritoso** /espiri'toso/ *a* lively, active, spirited; spirituous

**espíritu** /es'piritu/ *m,* spirit; apparition, specter; soul; intelligence, mind; mood, temper, outlook; underlying principle, spirit; devil (gen. *pl*) vigor, ardor, vivacity; *Chem.* essence; *Chem.* spirits; turn of mind. **E. Santo,** Holy Ghost

**espiritual** /espiri'tual/ *a* spiritual

**espiritualidad** /espirituali'ðað/ *f,* spirituality

**espiritualismo** /espiritua'lismo/ *m, Philos.* spiritualism

**espiritualizar** /espirituali'θar; espirituali'sar/ *vt* to spiritualize

**espita** /es'pita/ *f,* spigot, tap; *Inf.* tippler

**esplender** /esplen'der/ *vi Poet.* to shine

**esplendidez** /esplendi'ðeθ; esplendi'ðes/ *f,* liberality, abundance; splendor, pomp

**espléndido** /es'plendiðo/ *a* magnificent; liberal; resplendent (gen. *pl*)

**esplendor** /esplen'dor/ *m,* splendor, brilliance; distinction, nobility

**esplendoroso** /esplendo'roso/ *a* splendid, brilliant, radiant

**espliego** /es'pliego/ *m,* lavender

**esplín** /es'plin/ *m,* spleen, melancholy

**espolada** /espo'laða/ *f,* prick with the spur

**espolear** /espole'ar/ *vt* to prick with the spur; encourage, stimulate

**espoleta** /espo'leta/ *f,* fuse (of explosives); breastbone (of fowls); wishbone. **e. de tiempo, e. graduada,** time fuse. **e. de seguridad,** safety fuse

**espolón** /espo'lon/ *m,* spur (of a bird or mountain range); *Naut.* ram; breakwater; buttress; *Naut.* fender

**espolvorear** /espolβore'ar/ *vt* to sprinkle with powder

**espondeo** /espon'deo/ *m,* (metrical foot) spondee

**esponja** /es'ponha/ *f,* sponge

**esponjadura** /esponha'ðura/ *f,* sponging

**esponjar** /espon'har/ *vt* to make spongy; sponge; —*vr* swell with pride; *Inf.* bloom with health

**esponjera** /espon'hera/ *f,* sponge holder

**esponjosidad** /esponhosi'ðað/ *f,* sponginess

**esponjoso** /espon'hoso/ *a* spongy, porous

**esponsales** /espon'sales/ *m pl,* betrothal; marriage contract

**espontaneidad** /espontanei'ðað/ *f,* spontaneity

**espontáneo** /espon'taneo/ *a* spontaneous

**espora** /es'pora/ *f,* spore

**esporádico** /espo'raðiko/ *a* sporadic

**esportillo** /espor'tiʎo; espor'tiyo/ *m,* bass, frail

**esposa** /es'posa/ *f,* wife; *pl* handcuffs

**esposo** /es'poso/ *m,* husband; *pl* husband and wife

**espuela** /es'puela/ *f,* spur; stimulus; (*Ornith. Bot.*) spur. **e. de caballero,** larkspur

**espulgar** /espul'gar/ *vt* to delouse; examine carefully

**espuma** /es'puma/ *f,* froth, foam; *Cul.* scum; *Fig.* the best of anything, flower; *Fig. Inf.* **crecer como la e.,** to flourish like weeds

**espumadera** /espuma'ðera/ *f,* skimming ladle

**espumajear** /espumahe'ar/ *vi* to foam at the mouth

**espumajoso** /espuma'hoso/ *a* frothy, foaming

**espumar** /espu'mar/ *vt* to skim (soup, etc.); —*vi* foam; increase rapidly

**espumoso** /espu'moso/ *a* frothy, foaming

**espurio** /es'purio/ *a* bastard; spurious

**esputo** /es'puto/ *m,* sputum

**esqueje** /es'kehe/ *m, Agr.* cutting

**esquela** /es'kela/ *f,* note; (printed) card

**esqueleto** /eske'leto/ *m,* skeleton; *Inf.* skinny person; framework

**esquema** /es'kema/ *f,* diagram, layout sketch; scheme, plan. **e. de una máquina,** drawing of a machine

**esquemático** /eske'matiko/ *a* schematic; diagrammatic

**esquematizar** /eskemati'θar; eskemati'sar/ *vt* to plan, outline

**esquí** /es'ki/ *m,* ski, snowshoe

**esquiador** /eskia'ðor/ *m,* skier

**esquiar** /es'kiar/ *vi* to ski

**esquife** /es'kife/ *m,* skiff

**esquila** /es'kila/ *f,* cattle bell; small bell, hand bell; sheep shearing; (*Ichth. Bot.*) squill

**esquilador** /eskila'ðor/ *a* shearing. *m,* sheep shearer

**esquiladora** /eskila'ðora/ *f,* shearing machine

**esquilar** /eski'lar/ *vt* to shear, clip (sheep, etc.)

**esquileo** /eski'leo/ *m,* shearing; shearing time or place

**esquilmar** /eskil'mar/ *vt* to harvest; impoverish

**esquilmo** /es'kilmo/ *m,* harvest

**esquimal** /eski'mal/ *a* and *mf* Eskimo

**esquina** /es'kina/ *f,* corner

**esquinado** /eski'naðo/ *a* having corners; *Fig.* difficult to approach (people)

**esquirla** /es'kirla/ *f,* splinter (of a bone); shrapnel

**esquirol** /eski'rol/ *m, Inf.* strikebreaker, blackleg

**esquisto** /es'kisto/ *m, Mineral.* slate; shale

**esquivar** /eski'βar/ *vt* to avoid; —*vr* slip away, disappear; excuse oneself

**esquivez** /eski'βeθ; eski'βes/ *f,* unsociableness; unfriendliness, aloofness

**esquivo** /es'kiβo/ *a* unsociable, elusive, aloof

**esquizado** /eski'θaðo; eskisaðo/ *a* mottled (of marble)

**estabilidad** /estaβili'ðað/ *f,* stability; fastness (of colors)

**estabilizar** /estaβili'θar; estaβili'sar/ *vt* to stabilize

**estable** /es'taβle/ *a* stable; fast (of colors)

**establecer** /estaβle'θer; estaβle'ser/ *vt irr* to establish, found, institute; decree; —*vr* take up residence; open (a business firm). See **conocer**

**establecimiento** /estaβleθi'miento; estaβlesi'miento/ *m,* law, statute; foundation, institution; establishment

**establero** /estaβ'lero/ *m,* stablegroom

**establo** /es'taβlo/ *m,* stable

**estaca** /es'taka/ *f,* stake, pole; *Agr.* cutting; cudgel

**estacada** /esta'kaða/ *f,* fence; *Mil.* palisade; place fixed for a duel

**estacar** /esta'kar/ *vt* to stake; fence; tie to a stake; —*vr Fig.* be as still as a post

**estación** /esta'θion; esta'sion/ *f,* position, situation; season; station (railroad, etc.); depot; time, period; stop, halt; building, headquarters; *Bot.* habitat; (*Surv. Geom. Eccl.*) station

**estacional** /estaθio'nal; estasio'nal/ *a* seasonal; *Astron.* stationary

**estacionamiento** /estaθiona'miento; estasiona'miento/ *m,* stationariness; *Auto.* parking

**estacionar** /estaθio'nar; estasio'nar/ *vt* to station, place; *Auto.* park (a car); —*vr* remain stationary; place oneself

**estacionario** /estaθio'nario; estasio'nario/ *a* motionless; *Astron.* stationary. *m,* stationer

**estada** /es'taða/ *f,* sojourn

**estadía** /esta'ðia/ *f,* stay, sojourn; *Art.* sitting (of a model)

**estadio** /es'taðio/ *m,* racetrack; stadium; furlong

**estadista** /esta'ðista/ *mf* statistician; statesman, stateswoman

**estadística** /esta'ðistika/ *f,* statistics

**estadístico** /esta'ðistiko/ *a* statistical

**estadizo** /esta'ðiθo; estaðiso/ *a* stagnant

**estado** /es'taðo/ *m,* state; condition; rank, position; *Polit.* state; profession; status; *Com.* statement. **e. de guerra,** state of war; martial law. **e. mayor central,** (*Nav. Mil.*) general staff. **e. tapón,** *Polit.* buffer state. **tomar e.,** to marry; *Eccl.* profess; be ordained a priest

**Estados Unidos de América** /es'taðos u'niðos de a'merika/ United States of America

**estadounidense** /estaðouni'ðense/ a United States

**estafa** /es'tafa/ f, swindle

**estafador** /estafa'ðor/ **(-ra)** n swindler

**estafar** /esta'far/ vt to swindle

**estafeta** /esta'feta/ f, courier, messenger; branch post office; diplomatic pouch

**estafilococo** /estafilo'koko/ m, staphylococcus

**estagnación** /estagna'θion; estagna'sion/ f, stagnation

**estalactita** /estalak'tita/ f, stalactite

**estalagmita** /estalag'mita/ f, stalagmite

**estallar** /esta'ʎar; esta'yar/ vi to explode; burst; Fig. break out

**estallido** /esta'ʎiðo; esta'yiðo/ m, explosion, report; crash, crack; Fig. outbreak; Auto. **e. de un neumático,** blowout (of a tire)

**estambre** /es'tambre/ m, woolen yarn, worsted; stamen

**estameña** /esta'meɲa/ f, serge

**estampa** /es'tampa/ f, illustration, picture; print; aspect; printing press; track, step; Metall. boss, stud

**estampación** /estampa'θion; estampa'sion/ f, stamping; printing; imprinting. **e. en seco,** tooling (of a book)

**estampado** /estam'paðo/ a printed (of textiles). m, textile printing; printed fabric

**estampar** /estam'par/ vt to print, stamp; leave the print (of); bestow, imprint. **e. en relieve,** to emboss. **e. en seco,** to tool (a book)

**estampería** /estampe'ria/ f, print or picture shop; trade in prints

**estampero** /estam'pero/ m, print dealer, picture dealer

**estampido** /estam'piðo/ m, report, bang, detonation; crash

**estampilla** /estam'piʎa; estam'piya/ f, rubber stamp; seal

**estampillar** /estampi'ʎar; estampi'yar/ vt to stamp, imprint

**estancación** /estanka'θion; estanka'sion/ f, stagnation

**estancado** /estan'kaðo/ a stagnant; blocked, held up

**estancar** /estan'kar/ vt to check, stem; set up a monopoly; Fig. hold up (negotiations, etc.); —vr be stagnant

**estancia** /es'tanθia; es'tansia/ f, stay, residence; dwelling; lounge, livingroom; stanza; West Hem. farm

**estanciero** /estan'θiero; estan'siero/ m, West Hem. farmer

**estanco** /es'tanko/ a Naut. watertight. m, monopoly; shop selling government monopoly goods; archive

**estandarte** /estan'darte/ m, standard, flag. **e. real,** royal standard

**estanque** /es'tanke/ m, tank; pool; reservoir

**estanquero** /estan'kero/ **(-ra)** n seller of government monopoly goods (tobacco, matches, etc.)

**estante** /es'tante/ a present; extant; permanent. m, shelf; bookcase; bin (for wine)

**estantería** /estante'ria/ f, shelving; shelves, bookcase

**estantigua** /estan'tigua/ f, hobgoblin, specter; Fig. Inf. scarecrow

**estañador** /estaɲa'ðor/ m, tinsmith

**estañar** /esta'ɲar/ vt to tin; solder

**estaño** /es'taɲo/ m, tin

**estaquilla** /esta'kiʎa; esta'kiya/ f, peg, cleat

**estar** /es'tar/ vi irr to be. Indicates: 1. Position or place (e.g. Está a la puerta, He is at the door). 2. State (e.g. Las flores están marchitas, The flowers are faded). 3. Used to form the continuous or progressive tense (e.g. **Siempre está (estaba) escribiendo,** He is (was) always writing). 4. In contrast to verb ser, indicates impermanency (e.g. Está enfermo, He is ill). 5. **Estar** forms an apparent passive where no action is implied (e.g. El cuadro está pintado al óleo, The picture is painted in oils). 6. Used in some impersonal expressions (e.g. ¡Bien está! All right! ¡Claro está! Of course! etc.). **e. de,** to be in, or on, or acting as (e.g. e. de prisa, to be in a hurry. e. de capitán, to be acting as a captain). **e. para,** to be on the point of; to be

nearly; to be in the mood for. **e. para llover,** to be on the point of raining. **e. por,** to remain to be done; have a mind to (e.g. La historia está por escribir, The story remains to be written). **e. bien,** to be well (healthy). Mech. **e. bajo presión,** to have the steam up. Polit. **e. en el poder,** to be in office. **e. en una cuenca,** Dominican Republic to be broke. **¿A cómo (** or **A cuántos) estamos?** What is the date? Pres. Ind. **estoy, estás, está, estamos, estáis, están.** Preterite **estuve,** etc —Pres. Subjunc. **esté, estés, esté, estén.** Imperf. Subjunc. **estuviese,** etc.

**estarcir** /estar'θir; estar'sir/ vt to stencil

**estatal** /esta'tal/ a state

**estática** /es'tatika/ f, Mech. statics

**estático** /es'tatiko/ a static

**estatua** /es'tatua/ f, statue

**estatuaria** /esta'tuaria/ f, statuary

**estatuir** /esta'tuir/ vt irr to establish, order. See **huir**

**estatura** /esta'tura/ f, stature, height (of persons)

**estatuto** /esta'tuto/ m, statute, law

**estay** /es'tai/ m, Naut. stay. **e. mayor,** Naut. mainstay

**este** /'este/ m, east

**este** /'este/ m, dem a this (f, **esta,** pl **estos, estas,** these). **éste,** m, dem pron this one; the latter. (f, **ésta,** neut **esto,** pl **éstos, éstas,** these ones; the latter) (e.g. Aquel cuadro no es tan hermoso como éste, That picture is not as beautiful as this one)

**estela** /es'tela/ f, wake, track (of a ship)

**estenografía** /estenogra'fia/ f, shorthand

**estenográfico** /esteno'grafiko/ a shorthand

**estenógrafo** /este'nografo/ **(-fa)** n stenographer

**estenordeste** /estenor'ðeste/ m, east-northeast

**estentóreo** /esten'toreo/ a stentorian

**estepa** /es'tepa/ f, steppe, arid plain

**estera** /es'tera/ f, matting

**esterar** /este'rar/ vt to cover with matting; —vi Inf. muffle oneself up

**estercoladura** /esterkola'ðura/ f, manuring

**estercolar** /esterko'lar/ vt to manure

**estercolero** /esterko'lero/ m, manure pile; driver of a dung cart

**estereoscopio** /estereo'skopio/ m, stereoscope

**esterería** /estere'ria/ f, matting factory, matting shop

**esterero** /este'rero/ **(-ra)** n matting maker, matting seller

**estéril** /es'teril/ a sterile, barren; unfruitful, unproductive

**esterilidad** /esterili'ðað/ f, sterility; barrenness, unfruitfulness

**esterilización** /esteriliθa'θion; esterilisa'sion/ f, sterilization

**esterilizador** /esteriliθa'ðor; esterilisa'ðor/ a sterilizing. m, sterilizer

**esterilizar** /esterili'θar; esterili'sar/ vt to make barren; Med. sterilize

**esterilla** /este'riʎa; este'riya/ f, mat, matting

**esterlina** /ester'lina/ a f, sterling. **libra e.,** pound sterling

**esternón** /ester'non/ m, sternum

**estero** /es'tero/ m, salt marsh

**estertor** /ester'tor/ m, stertorous breathing, rattle

**estesudeste** /estesu'ðeste/ m, east-southeast

**estética** /es'tetika/ f, aesthetics —a aesthete

**estético** /es'tetiko/ a aesthetic m, aesthete

**estetoscopio** /esteto'skopio/ m, stethoscope

**esteva** /es'teβa/ f, plow handle

**estevado** /este'βaðo/ a bandy-legged

**estiaje** /es'tiahe/ m, low water level (of rivers)

**estibador** /estiβa'ðor/ m, stevedore, dock worker

**estibar** /esti'βar/ vt Naut. to stow

**estiércol** /es'tierkol/ m, dung; manure

**estigio** /es'tihio/ a Stygian; (Fig. Poet.) infernal

**estigma** /es'tigma/ m, stigma

**estigmatizar** /estigmati'θar; estigmati'sar/ vt to brand; stigmatize; insult

**estilar** /esti'lar/ vi to be accustomed; —vt draw up (document)

**estilete** /esti'lete/ m, stiletto, dagger; needle, hand, pointer; Med. stylet

**estilista** /esti'lista/ mf stylist

**estilística** /esti'listika/ *f*, stylism, stylistics

**estilizar** /estili'θar; estili'sar/ *vt* to stylize

**estilo** /es'tilo/ *m*, (*Art. Archit. Lit.*) style, writing instrument; gnomon, pointer; manner, way; *Bot.* style. **por el e.,** in some such way, like that

**estilográfico** /estilo'grafiko/ *a* stylographic. **pluma estilográfica,** fountain pen

**estima** /es'tima/ *f*, appreciation, esteem, consideration

**estimable** /esti'maβle/ *a* estimable

**estimación** /estima'θion; estima'sion/ *f*, valuation, estimate; regard, esteem. **e. prudente,** conservative estimate

**estimar** /esti'mar/ *vt* to value, estimate; esteem, judge

**estimulante** /estimu'lante/ *m*, *Med.* stimulant —*a* stimulating

**estimular** /estimu'lar/ *vt* to stimulate, excite; goad on, encourage, incite

**estímulo** /es'timulo/ *m*, stimulus; incitement, encouragement

**estío** /es'tio/ *m*, summer

**estipendiar** /estipen'diar/ *vt* to pay a stipend to

**estipendiario** /estipen'diario/ *m*, stipendiary

**estipendio** /esti'pendio/ *m*, stipend, pay, remuneration

**estipulación** /estipula'θion; estipula'sion/ *f*, stipulation; *Law.* clause, condition

**estipular** /estipu'lar/ *vt* to stipulate; arrange terms; *Law.* covenant

**estirado** /esti'raðo/ *a* stretched out; tight, stiff; wiredrawn (metals); stiff, pompous, parsimonious

**estirador** /estira'ðor/ *m*, wire drawer

**estirar** /esti'rar/ *vt* to stretch; iron roughly (clothes); *Metall.* wire-draw; dole out (money); *Fig.* stretch, go beyond the permissible; —*vr* stretch oneself

**estirpe** /es'tirpe/ *f*, race, stock, lineage

**estival** /esti'βal/ *a* summer

**esto** /'esto/ *dem pron neut* this, this matter, this idea, etc. Always refers to abstractions, never to a definite object. **e. de,** the matter of. **e. es,** that's it; namely. **por e.,** for this reason. **a todo e.,** meanwhile

**estocada** /esto'kaða/ *f*, sword thrust

**Estocolmo** /esto'kolmo/ Stockholm

**estofa** /es'tofa/ *f*, *Sew.* quilting; kind, quality

**estofado** /esto'faðo/ *m*, stew —*a Sew.* quilted; stewed

**estofar** /esto'far/ *vt Sew.* to quilt; make a stew

**estoicismo** /estoi'θismo; estoi'sismo/ *m*, stoicism

**estoico** /es'toiko/ (**-ca**) *n* stoic —*a* stoical

**estolidez** /estoli'ðeθ; estoli'ðes/ *f*, idiocy

**estólido** /es'toliðo/ (**-da**) *a* idiotic —*a* idiot

**estomacal** /estoma'kal/ *a* stomach

**estómago** /es'tomago/ *m*, stomach

**estomático** /esto'matiko/ *a* pertaining to the mouth, oral

**estomatitis** /estoma'titis/ *f*, stomatitis

**estonio** /es'tonio/ (**-ia**) *a* and *n* Estonian. *m*, Estonian (language)

**estopa** /es'topa/ *f*, tow; oakum

**estopilla** /esto'piʎa; esto'piya/ *f*, batiste, lawn; calico, cotton cloth

**estopín** /esto'pin/ *m*, *Mil.* quick march

**estoque** /es'toke/ *m*, rapier; narrow sword

**estoquear** /estoke'ar/ *vt* to wound or kill with a rapier

**estoqueo** /esto''keo/ *m*, swordplay

**estorbador** /estorβa'ðor/ (**-ra**) *a* obstructive —*n* obstructer

**estorbar** /estor'βar/ *vt* to obstruct, impede; hinder

**estorbo** /es'torβo/ *m*, obstruction; hindrance, nuisance

**estornino** /estor'nino/ *m*, starling

**estornudar** /estornu'ðar/ *vi* to sneeze

**estornudo** /estor'nuðo/ *m*, sneezing; sneeze

**estrabismo** /estra'βismo/ *m*, *Med.* strabismus, squint, cast

**estrada** /es'traða/ *f*, road, highway

**estrado** /es'traðo/ *m*, dais

**estrafalario** /estrafa'lario/ *a Inf.* slovenly, untidy; *Inf.* eccentric, odd

**estragar** /estra'gar/ *vt* to corrupt, spoil, vitiate; ruin, destroy

**estrago** /es'trago/ *m*, devastation, destruction, ruin, havoc

**estrambote** /estram'bote/ *m*, refrain

**estrambótico** /estram'botiko/ *a Inf.* eccentric

**estrangul** /estraŋ'gul/ *m*, *Mus.* mouthpiece

**estrangulación** /estraŋgula'θion; estraŋgula'sion/ *f*, strangulation; *Auto.* throttling

**estrangulador** /estraŋgula'ðor/ (**-ra**) *a* strangling —*n* strangler. *m*, *Auto.* throttle

**estrangular** /estraŋgu'lar/ *vt* to strangle

**estraperlista** /estraper'lista/ *mf* black marketeer

**estraperlo** /estra'perlo/ *m*, black market

**Estrasburgo** /estras'βurgo/ Strasbourg

**estratagema** /estrata'hema/ *f*, stratagem, trick

**estrategia** /estra'tehia/ *f*, strategy

**estratégico** /estra'tehiko/ *a* strategic

**estratego** /estra'tego/ *m*, strategist

**estratificación** /estratifika'θion; estratifika'sion/ *f*, stratification

**estrato** /es'trato/ *m*, *Geol.* stratum

**estratosfera** /estratos'fera/ *f*, stratosphere

**estraza** /es'traθa; es'trasa/ *f*, rag. **papel de e.,** brown paper

**estrechar** /estre'tʃar/ *vt* to make narrower, tighten; hold tightly, clasp; compel, oblige; —*vr* tighten oneself up; reduce one's expenses; *Fig.* tighten the bonds (of friendship, etc.). **e. la mano,** to shake hands

**estrechez** /estre'tʃeθ; estre'tʃes/ *f*, narrowness; tightness; scantiness; poverty, want. **e. de miras,** narrowmindedness

**estrecho** /es'tretʃo/ *a* narrow; tight; intimate, close; austere, rigid; meanspirited. *m*, *Geog.* strait

**estregadera** /estrega'ðera/ *f*, shoe scraper; scourer

**estregar** /estre'gar/ *vt irr* to rub, scour, scrub, scrape, scratch. See **cegar**

**estrella** /es'treʎa; es'treya/ *f*, star; fortune, fate; anything star-shaped; *Fig.* star. **e. de la pantalla,** movie star. **e. de mar,** starfish. **e. de rabo,** comet. **e. fugaz,** shooting star. **tener e.,** to be born under a lucky star

**estrellado** /estre'ʎaðo; estre'yaðo/ *a* star-shaped; full of stars, starry; shattered, broken; fried (eggs)

**estrellamar** /estreʎa'mar; estreya'mar/ *f*, starfish

**estrellar** /estre'ʎar; estre'yar/ *vt Inf.* to shatter, break into fragments; fry (eggs); —*vr* be starry or sprinkled with stars; be dashed against; fail in, come up against

**estrellón** /estre'ʎon; estre'yon/ *m*, large, artificial star (painted or otherwise); star-like firework

**estremecer** /estreme'θer; estreme'ser/ *vt irr* to cause to tremble; perturb; —*vr* shudder, tremble. See **conocer**

**estremecimiento** /estremeθi'miento; estremesi'miento/ *m*, shudder, trembling; agitation

**estrenar** /estre'nar/ *vt* to use or do for the first time; inaugurate; give the first performance of (plays, etc.); —*vr* do for the first time; *Com.* make the first sale of the day

**estreno** /es'treno/ *m*, commencement, inauguration; first appearance; *Theat.* first performance, opening night, premiere

**estrenque** /es'trenke/ *m*, strong esparto rope

**estrenuo** /es'trenuo/ *a* strong, energetic, agile

**estreñimiento** /estreɲi'miento/ *m*, constipation

**estreñir** /estre'ɲir/ *vt* to constipate

**estrépito** /es'trepito/ *m*, clamor, din, great noise; fuss, show

**estrepitoso** /estrepi'toso/ *a* noisy, clamorous

**estreptococo** /estrepto'koko/ *m*, streptococcus

**estreptomicina** /estreptomi'θina; estreptomi'sina/ *f*, streptomycin

**estría** /es'tria/ *f*, *Archit.* fluting, stria

**estribadero** /estriβa'ðero/ *m*, prop, support, strut

**estribar** /estri'βar/ *vi* (*with en*) to lean on, rest on, be supported by; *Fig.* be based on

**estribillo** /estri'βiʎo; estri'βiyo/ *m*, refrain

**estribo** /es'triβo/ *m*, stirrup; footboard, step, running board (of vehicles); *Archit.* buttress or pier; *Fig.* stay, support; *Anat.* stapes; *Mech.* stirrup piece. **perder los estribos,** to lose patience, forget oneself

**estribor** /estri'βor/ *m,* starboard

**estricnina** /estrik'nina/ *f,* strychnine

**estricto** /es'trikto/ *a* strict, exact; *Art.* study. **e. de,** study to be a

**estridente** /estri'ðente/ *a* strident, shrill

**estridor** /estri'ðor/ *m,* strident or harsh sound; screech; creak

**estro** /'estro/ *m,* inspiration

**estrofa** /es'trofa/ *f,* strophe; verse, stanza

**estropajo** /estro'paho/ *m,* scourer, dishcloth; worthless person or thing

**estropajoso** /estropa'hoso/ *a Inf.* indistinct, stammering; dirty and ragged; tough (meat, etc.)

**estropear** /estrope'ar/ *vt* to spoil, damage; ruin, undo, spoil (plans, effects, etc.); ill-treat, maim; —*vr* hurt oneself, be maimed; spoil, deteriorate

**estropicio** /estro'piθio; estro'pisio/ *m, Inf.* crash (of china, etc.)

**estructura** /estruk'tura/ *f,* fabric, structure; *Fig.* construction

**estructural** /estruktu'ral/ *a* structural

**estruendo** /es'truendo/ *m,* din, clatter; clamor, noise; ostentation

**estruendoso** /estruen'doso/ *a* noisy

**estrujar** /estru'har/ *vt* to squeeze, crush (fruit); hold tightly, press, squeeze, bruise; *Fig. Inf.* squeeze dry

**estrujón** /estru'hon/ *m,* squeeze, pressure; final pressing (grapes)

**estuario** /es'tuario/ *m,* estuary

**estucado** /estu'kaðo/ *m,* stucco

**estucar** /estu'kar/ *vt* to stucco

**estuche** /es'tutʃe/ *m,* case; casket, box; cover; sheath

**estuco** /es'tuko/ *m,* stucco; plaster

**estudiante** /estu'ðiante/ *mf* student

**estudiantil** /estuðian'til/ *a Inf.* student

**estudiantina** /estuðian'tina/ *f,* strolling band of students playing and singing, generally in aid of charity

**estudiantino** /estuðian'tino/ *a Inf.* student

**estudiantón** /estuðian'ton/ *m, Inf.* grind

**estudiar** /estu'ðiar/ *vt* to study. **e. de,** study to be a (e.g. *e. de rabino,* study to be a rabbi); learn; *Art.* copy

**estudio** /es'tuðio/ *m,* study; sketch; disquisition, dissertation; studio; diligence; *Art.* study; reading room, den

**estudiosidad** /estuðiosi'ðað/ *f,* studiousness

**estudioso** /estu'ðioso/ *a* studious

**estufa** /es'tufa/ *f,* heating stove; hothouse; hot room (in bathhouses); drying chamber; *Elec.* heater

**estufador** /estufa'ðor/ *m,* stewpot or casserole

**estufilla** /estu'fiʎa; estu'fiya/ *f,* muff; small brazier

**estufista** /estu'fista/ *mf* stove maker or repairer, stove seller

**estulto** /es'tulto/ *a* foolish

**estupefacción** /estupefak'θion; estupefak'sion/ *f,* stupefaction

**estupefacto** /estupe'fakto/ *a* stupefied, stunned, amazed

**estupendo** /estu'pendo/ *a* wonderful, marvelous

**estupidez** /estupi'ðeθ; estupi'ðes/ *f,* stupidity

**estúpido** /es'tupiðo/ *a* stupid

**estupor** /estu'por/ *m, Med.* stupor; astonishment

**estupro** /es'tupro/ *m, Law.* rape

**estuque** /es'tuke/ *m,* stucco

**estuquería** /estuke'ria/ *f,* stuccowork

**esturión** /estu'rion/ *m,* sturgeon

**esvástica** /es'βastika/ *f,* swastika

**etapa** /e'tapa/ *f, Mil.* field ration; *Mil.* halt, camp; stage, juncture. **a pequeñas etapas,** by easy stages (of a journey)

**etcétera** /et'θetera; et'setera/ etcetera

**éter** /'eter/ *m,* ether; *Poet.* sky

**etéreo** /e'tereo/ *a* etheric; ethereal

**eterizar** /eteri'θar; eteri'sar/ *vt* to etherize

**eternidad** /eterni'ðað/ *f,* eternity

**eternizar** /eterni'θar; eterni'sar/ *vt* to drag out, prolong; eternize, perpetuate

**eterno** /e'terno/ *a* eternal, everlasting; lasting, enduring

**ética** /'etika/ *f,* ethics

**ético** /'etiko/ *a* ethical. *m,* moralist

**etimología** /etimolo'hia/ *f,* etymology

**etimológico** /etimo'lohiko/ *a* etymological

**etimologista** /etimolo'hista/ *mf* etymologist

**etimólogo** /eti'mologo/ *m,* etymologist

**etiología** /etiolo'hia/ *f,* etiology

**etíope** /e'tiope/ *a* and *mf* Ethiopian

**Etiopía** /etio'pia/ Ethiopia

**etiqueta** /eti'keta/ *f,* etiquette; label

**etiquetero** /etike'tero/ *a* ceremonious, stiff; prim

**étnico** /'etniko/ *a* ethnic; heathen

**etnografía** /etnogra'fia/ *f,* ethnography

**etnográfico** /etno'grafiko/ *a* ethnographic

**etnología** /etnolo'hia/ *f,* ethnology

**etnólogo** /et'nologo/ *m,* ethnologist

**etrusco** /e'trusko/ **(-ca)** *a* and *n* Etruscan

**eubolia** /eu'βolia/ *f,* discretion in speech

**eucalipto** /euka'lipto/ *m,* eucalyptus

**Eucaristía** /eukaris'tia/ *f,* Eucharist

**euclídeo** /eu'klíðeo/ *a* Euclidean

**eufemismo** /eufe'mismo/ *m,* euphemism

**eufonía** /eufo'nia/ *f,* euphony

**eufónico** /eu'foniko/ *a* euphonious

**euforia** /eu'foria/ *f,* resistance to disease; buoyancy, well-being

**eufuismo** /eu'fuismo/ *m,* euphuism

**eugenesia** /euhe'nesia/ *f,* eugenics

**eugenésico** /euhe'nesiko/ *a* eugenic

**eunuco** /eu'nuko/ *m,* eunuch

**euritmia** /eu'ritmia/ *f,* eurythmics

**eurítmico** /eu'ritmiko/ *a* eurythmic

**euro** /'euro/ *m, Poet.* east wind

**Europa** /eu'ropa/ Europe

**europeizar** /europei'θar; europei'sar/ *vt* to Europeanize

**europeo** /euro'peo/ **(-ea)** *a* and *n* European

**éuscaro** /'euskaro/ *a* Basque. *m,* Basque (language)

**eutanasia** /euta'nasia/ *f,* euthanasia

**evacuación** /eβakua'θion; eβakua'sion/ *f,* evacuation

**evacuar** /eβa'kuar/ *vt* to vacate; evacuate, empty; finish, conclude (a business deal, etc.)

**evadir** /eβa'ðir/ *vt* to avoid, elude; —*vr* escape; elope

**evaluación** /eβalua'θion; eβalua'sion/ *f,* valuation; estimation

**evaluar** /eβa'luar/ *vt* to evaluate, estimate; gauge; value

**evangélico** /eβan'heliko/ *a* evangelical

**evangelio** /eβan'helio/ *m,* Gospel; Christianity; *Inf.* indisputable truth

**evangelista** /eβanhe'lista/ *m,* evangelist

**evangelizar** /eβanheli'θar; eβanheli'sar/ *vt* to evangelize

**evaporación** /eβapora'θion; eβapora'sion/ *f,* evaporation

**evaporar** /eβapo'rar/ **(se)** *vt* and *vr* to evaporate; disappear, vanish

**evasión, evasiva** /eβa'sion, eβa'siβa/ *f,* subterfuge, evasion; flight, escape

**evasivo** /eβa'siβo/ *a* evasive

**evento** /e'βento/ *m,* happening, event; contingency

**eventual** /eβen'tual/ *a* possible, fortuitous; accidental (expenses); extra (emoluments)

**eventualidad** /eβentuali'ðað/ *f,* eventuality

**evicción** /eβik'θion; eβik'sion/ *f, Law.* eviction

**evidencia** /eβi'ðenθia; eβi'ðensia/ *f,* proof, evidence. **ponerse en e.,** to put oneself forward

**evidenciar** /eβiðen'θiar; eβiðen'siar/ *vt* to show, make obvious

**evidente** /eβi'ðente/ *a* obvious, evident

**evitable** /eβi'taβle/ *a* avoidable

**evitación** /eβita'θion; eβita'sion/ *f,* avoidance

**evitar** /eβi'tar/ *vt* to avoid; shun, eschew

**evocación** /eβoka'θion; eβoka'sion/ *f,* evocation

**evocador** /eβoka'ðor/ *a* evocative

**evocar** /eβo'kar/ *vt* to evoke

**evolución** /eβolu'θion; eβolu'sion/ *f,* evolution; development; (*Mil. Nav.*) maneuver; change; *Geom.* involution

**evolucionar** /eβoluθio'nar; eβolusio'nar/ *vi* to evolve; (*Nav. Mil.*) maneuver; change, alter

**evolucionismo** /eβoluθio'nismo; eβolusio'nismo/ *m,* evolutionism

**evolutivo** /eβolu'tiβo/ *a* evolutional

**ex** /eks/ *prefix* out of; from; formerly

**exacción** /eksak'θion; eksak'sion/ *f,* exaction; tax

**exacerbación** /eksaθerβa'θion; eksaserβa'sion/ *f,* exacerbation

**exacerbar** /eksaθer'βar; eksaser'βar/ *vt* to exasperate; exacerbate

**exactitud** /eksakti'tuð/ *f,* exactitude; correctness; punctuality

**exacto** /ek'sakto/ *a* exact; correct; punctual

**exactor** /eksak'tor/ *m,* tax collector; tyrant, oppressor

**exageración** /eksahera'θion; eksahera'sion/ *f,* exaggeration

**exagerador** /eksahera'ðor/ **(-ra)** *a* given to exaggerating —*n* exaggerater

**exagerar** /eksahe'rar/ *vt* to exaggerate

**exaltación** /eksalta'θion; eksalta'sion/ *f,* exaltation

**exaltar** /eksal'tar/ *vt* to exalt, elevate; extol; —*vr* grow excited or agitated

**examen** /ek'samen/ *m,* inquiry; investigation, research; examination; *Geol.* survey. **e. parcial,** quiz (at school)

**examinador** /eksamina'ðor/ **(-ra)** *n* examiner

**examinando** /eksami'nando/ **(-da)** *n* candidate, examinee

**examinar** /eksami'nar/ *vt* to inquire into; investigate; inspect; examine; —*vr* take an examination

**exangüe** /ek'saŋgue/ *a* bloodless, pale; exhausted, weak; dead

**exánime** /eksa'nime/ *a* lifeless; spiritless, weak

**exasperación** /eksaspera'θion; eksaspera'sion/ *f,* exasperation

**exasperador, exasperante** /eksaspera'ðor, eksaspe'rante/ *a* exasperating

**exasperar** /eksaspe'rar/ *vt* to exasperate; irritate, annoy

**excarcelar** /ekskarθe'lar; ekskarse'lar/ *vt* to release from jail

**excavación** /ekskaβa'θion; ekskaβa'sion/ *f,* excavation

**excavador** /ekskaβa'ðor/ **(-ra)** *n* excavator. *f, Mech.* excavator

**excavar** /ekska'βar/ *vt* to hollow; excavate; *Agr.* hoe (roots of plants)

**excedente** /eksθe'ðente; eksse'ðente/ *a* exceeding; excessive; surplus

**exceder** /eksθe'ðer; eksse'ðer/ *vt* to exceed; —*vr* forget oneself, go too far

**excelencia** /eksθe'lenθia; eksse'lensia/ *f,* excellence, superiority; Excellency (title)

**excelente** /eksθe'lente; eksse'lente/ *a* excellent; *Inf.* first-rate

**excelso** /eks'θelso; eks'selso/ *a* lofty, high; eminent, mighty; sublime

**excentricidad** /eksθentriθi'ðað; ekssentrisi'ðað/ *f,* eccentricity

**excéntrico** /ek'θentriko; eks'sentriko/ *a* unconventional; erratic; *Geom.* eccentric

**excepción** /eksθep'θion; ekssep''sion/ *f,* exception

**excepcional** /eksθepθio'nal; ekssepsio'nal/ *a* exceptional

**exceptuar** /eksθep'tuar; ekssep'tuar/ *vt* to except

**excerpta, excerta** /eks'θerpta, eks'θerta; eks'serpta, eks'serta/ *f,* excerpt, extract

**excesivo** /eksθe'siβo; eksse'siβo/ *a* excessive

**exceso** /eks'θeso; eks'seso/ *m,* excess; *Com.* surplus; *pl* crimes, excesses. **e. de peso** *or* **e. de equipaje,** excess baggage

**excipiente** /eksθi'piente; ekssi'piente/ *m,* excipient

**excisión** /eksθi'sion; ekssi'sion/ *f,* excision

**excitabilidad** /eksθitaβili'ðað; ekssitaβili'ðað/ *f,* excitability

**excitable** /eksθi'taβle; ekssi'taβle/ *a* excitable, highstrung

**excitación** /eksθita'θion; ekssita'sion/ *f,* excitation; excitement

**excitador** /eksθita'ðor; ekssita'ðor/ *a* exciting, stimulating. *m, Phys.* exciter

**excitar** /eksθi'tar; ekssi'tar/ *vt* to excite, stimulate, provoke; *Elec.* energize; —*vr* become agitated or excited

**exclamación** /eksklama'θion; eksklama'sion/ *f,* exclamation, interjection

**exclamar** /ekskla'mar/ *vi* to exclaim

**exclamatorio** /eksklama'torio/ *a* exclamatory

**excluir** /eksk'luir/ *vt irr* to exclude, keep out; reject, bar. See **huir**

**exclusiva** /eksklu'siβa/ *f,* exclusion; special privilege, sole right

**exclusive** /eksklu'siβe/ *adv* exclusively; excluded

**exclusivismo** /eksklusi'βismo/ *m,* exclusivism

**exclusivista** /eksklusi'βista/ *a* exclusive. *mf* exclusivist

**exclusivo** /eksklu'siβo/ *a* exclusive

**excomulgado** /ekskomul'gaðo/ **(-da)** *a* and *n Eccl.* excommunicate; *Inf.* wicked (person)

**excomulgar** /ekskomul'gar/ *vt* to excommunicate

**excomunión** /ekskomu'nion/ *f,* excommunication

**excoriar** /eksko'riar/ *vt* to flay, excoriate; —*vr* graze oneself

**excrecencia** /ekskre'θenθia; ekskre'sensia/ *f,* excrescence

**excreción** /ekskre'θion; ekskre'sion/ *f,* excretion

**excremento** /ekskre'mento/ *m,* excrement

**excretar** /ekskre'tar/ *vi* to excrete

**excretorio** /ekskre'torio/ *a* excretory

**exculpación** /ekskulpa'θion; ekskulpa'sion/ *f,* exoneration

**exculpar** /ekskul'par/ **(se)** *vt* and *vr* to exonerate

**excursión** /ekskur'sion/ *f,* excursion, trip; *Mil.* incursion

**excursionismo** /ekskursio'nismo/ *m,* sightseeing; hiking

**excursionista** /ekskursio'nista/ *mf* excursionist; hiker

**excusa** /eks'kusa/ *f,* excuse

**excusabaraja** /ekskusaβa'raha/ *f,* basket with a lid

**excusado** /eksku'saðo/ *a* excused; exempt; unnecessary, superfluous; reserved, private. *m,* lavatory, toilet

**excusar** /eksku'sar/ *vt* to excuse; avoid, ward off, prevent; exempt; —*vr* excuse oneself

**execración** /eksekra'θion; eksekra'sion/ *f,* execration

**execrar** /ekse'krar/ *vt* to execrate; denounce; loathe

**exención** /eksen'θion; eksen'sion/ *f,* exemption

**exentar** /eksen'tar/ *vt* to exempt

**exento** /ek'sento/ *a* exempt; free, liberated; open (of buildings, etc.)

**exequias** /ekse'kias/ *f pl,* obsequies

**exfoliar** /eksfo'liar/ *vt* to strip off; —*vr* flake off

**exhalación** /eksala'θion; eksala'sion/ *f,* exhalation; shooting star; lightning; emanation; effluvium

**exhalar** /eksa'lar/ *vt* to exhale, give off; *Fig.* give vent to

**exhausto** /ek'sausto/ *a* exhausted

**exhibición** /eksiβi'θion; eksiβi'sion/ *f,* exhibition

**exhibicionismo** /eksiβiθio'nismo; eksiβisio'nismo/ *m,* exhibitionism

**exhibicionista** /eksiβiθio'nista; eksiβisio'nista/ *mf* exhibitionist

**exhibir** /eksi'βir/ *vt* to exhibit, show

**exhortación** /eksorta'θion; eksorta'sion/ *f,* exhortation

**exhortar** /eksor'tar/ *vt* to exhort

**exhumación** /eksuma'θion; eksuma'sion/ *f,* exhumation

**exhumar** /eksu'mar/ *vt* to exhume, disinter

**exigencia** /eksi'henθia; eksi'hensia/ *f,* exigency; demand

**exigente** /eksi'hente/ *a* exigent

**exigir** /eksi'hir/ *vt* to exact, collect; need, require; demand

**exigüidad** /eksigui'ðað/ *f,* exiguousness

**exiguo** /ek'siguo/ *a* exiguous, meager

**eximio** /ek'simio/ *a* most excellent; illustrious

**eximir** /eksi'mir/ *vt* to exempt

**existencia** /eksis'tenθia; eksis'tensia/ *f,* existence; *pl Com.* stock on hand

**existir** /eksis'tir/ *vi* to exist, be; live

**éxito** /'eksito/ *m,* success; result, conclusion

**éxodo** /'eksoðo/ *m,* Exodus; exodus, emigration. **é. rural,** rural depopulation

**exoneración** /eksonera'θion; eksonera'sion/ *f,* exoneration

**exonerar** /eksone'rar/ *vt* to exonerate; discharge (from employment)

**exorbitancia** /eksorβi'tanθia; eksorβi'tansia/ *f*, exorbitance

**exorbitante** /eksorβi'tante/ *a* exorbitant, excessive

**exorcismo** /eksor'θismo; eksor'sismo/ *m*, exorcism

**exorcista** /eksor'θista; eksor'sista/ *m*, exorcist

**exorcizar** /eksorθi'θar; eksorsi'sar/ *vt* to exorcize

**exordio** /ek'sorðio/ *m*, exordium, introduction

**exornar** /eksor'nar/ *vt* to adorn; embellish (*Lit.* style)

**exótico** /ek'sotiko/ *a* exotic, rare

**expandir** /ekspan'dir/ *vt* to expand

**expansibilidad** /ekspansiβili'ðað/ *f*, *Phys.* expansibility

**expansión** /ekspan'sion/ *f*, expansion; recreation, hobby

**expansivo** /ekspan'siβo/ *a* expansive; communicative, frank

**expatriación** /ekspatria'θion; ekspatria'sion/ *f*, expatriation

**expatriarse** /ekspa'triarse/ *vr* to emigrate, leave one's country

**expectación** /ekspekta'θion; ekspekta'sion/ *f*, expectation; expectancy

**expectante** /ekspek'tante/ *a* expectant

**expectativa** /ekspekta'tiβa/ *f*, expectancy; expectation

**expectoración** /ekspektora'θion; ekspektora'sion/ *f*, expectoration

**expectorar** /ekspekto'rar/ *vt* to expectorate

**expedición** /ekspeði'θion; ekspeði'sion/ *f*, expedition; speed, promptness; *Eccl.* bull, dispensation; excursion; forwarding, dispatch

**expediente** /ekspe'ðiente/ *m*, *Law.* proceedings; file of documents; expedient, device, means; expedition; promptness; motive, reason; provision

**expedir** /ekspe'ðir/ *vt irr* to expedite; forward, send, ship; issue, make out (checks, receipts, etc.); draw up (documents); dispatch deal with. See **pedir**

**expedito** /ekspe'ðito/ *a* expeditious, speedy

**expeler** /ekspe'ler/ *vt* to expel, discharge, emit

**expendedor** /ekspende'ðor/ **(-ra)** *a* spending —*n* spender; agent; retailer; seller; *Law.* **e. de moneda falsa,** distributor of counterfeit money

**expendeduría** /ekspendeðu'ria/ *f*, shop where government monopoly goods are sold (tobacco, stamps, etc.)

**expender** /ekspen'der/ *vt* to spend (money); *Com.* retail; *Com.* sell on commission; *Law.* distribute counterfeit money

**expensas** /ek'spensas/ *f pl*, costs, charges

**experiencia** /ekspe'rienθia; ekspe'riensia/ *f*, experience; practice, experiment

**experimentación** /eksperimenta'θion; eksperimenta-'sion/ *f*, experiencing

**experimentar** /eksperimen'tar/ *vt* to test, try; experience; feel

**experimento** /eksperi'mento/ *m*, experiment

**experto** /ek'sperto/ **(-ta)** *a* practiced, expert —*n* expert

**expiación** /ekspia'θion; ekspia'sion/ *f*, expiation

**expiar** /eks'piar/ *vt* to expiate, atone for; pay the penalty of; *Fig.* purify

**expiatorio** /ekspia'torio/ *a* expiatory

**expiración** /ekspira'θion; ekspira'sion/ *f*, expiration

**expirar** /ekspi'rar/ *vi* to die; *Fig.* expire; die down; exhale, expire

**explanación** /eksplana'θion; eksplana'sion/ *f*, leveling; explanation, elucidation

**explanada** /ekspla'naða/ *f*, esplanade; *Mil.* glacis

**explanar** /ekspla'nar/ *vt* to level; explain

**explayar** /ekspla'yar/ *vt* to extend, enlarge; —*vr* spread oneself, enlarge (upon); enjoy an outing; confide (in)

**explicación** /eksplika'θion; eksplika'sion/ *f*, explanation; elucidation

**explicar** /ekspli'kar/ *vt* to explain; expound; interpret, elucidate; —*vr* explain oneself

**explicativo** /eksplika'tiβo/ *a* explanatory

**explícito** /eks'pliθito; eksplisito/ *a* explicit, clear

**exploración** /eksplora'θion; eksplorasion/ *f*, exploration

**explorador** /eksplora'ðor/ *a* exploring. *m*, explorer; prospector; boy scout; *Mil.* scout

**explorar** /eksplo'rar/ *vt* to explore; investigate; *Med.* probe

**exploratorio** /eksplora'torio/ *a* exploratory

**explosión** /eksplo'sion/ *f*, explosion; outburst, outbreak. **hacer falsas explosiones,** *Mech.* to misfire

**explosivo** /eksplo'siβo/ *a* and *m*, explosive. **e. violento,** high explosive

**explotación** /eksplota'θion; eksplota'sion/ *f*, development, exploitation

**explotar** /eksplo'tar/ *vt* to work (mines); *Fig.* exploit

**expoliación** /ekspolia'θion; ekspolia'sion/ *f*, spoliation

**expoliar** /ekspo'liar/ *vt* to despoil

**exponente** /ekspo'nente/ *a* and *mf* exponent. *m*, *Math.* index

**exponer** /ekspo'ner/ *vt irr* to show, expose; expound, interpret; risk, jeopardize; abandon (child). See **poner**

**exportación** /eksporta'θion; eksporta'sion/ *f*, exportation; export

**exportador** /eksporta'ðor/ **(-ra)** *a* export —*n* exporter

**exportar** /ekspor'tar/ *vt* to export

**exposición** /eksposi'θion; eksposi'sion/ *f*, exposition, demonstration; petition; exhibition; *Lit.* exposition; *Photo.* exposure; orientation, position

**expósito** /eks'posito/ **(-ra)** *a* and *n* foundling

**expositor** /eksposi'tor/ **(-ra)** *a* and *n* exponent —*n* exhibitor

**expremijo** /ekspre'miho/ *m*, cheese vat

**exprés** /eks'pres/ *a* express. *m*, messenger or delivery service; express train; transport office

**expresar** /ekspre'sar/ *vt* to express (all meanings)

**expresión** /ekspre'sion/ *f*, statement, utterance; phrase, wording; expression; presentation; manifestation; gift, present; squeezing; pressing (of fruits, etc.)

**expresivo** /ekspre'siβo/ *a* expressive; affectionate

**expreso** /eks'preso/ *a* express; clear, obvious. *m*, courier, messenger

**exprimelimones** /eksprimeli'mones/ *m*, **exprimidera,** *f*, lemon squeezer

**exprimidor de la ropa** /eksprimi'ðor de la 'rropa/ *m*, wringer, mangle

**exprimir** /ekspri'mir/ *vt* to squeeze, press (fruit); press, hold tightly; express, utter

**expropiación** /ekspropia'θion; ekspropia'sion/ *f*, expropriation

**expropiar** /ekspro'piar/ *vt* to expropriate; commandeer

**expugnar** /ekspug'nar/ *vt Mil.* to take by storm

**expulsar** /ekspul'sar/ *vt* to expel, eject, dismiss

**expulsión** /ekspul'sion/ *f*, expulsion

**expurgar** /ekspur'gar/ *vt* to cleanse, purify; expurgate

**expurgatorio** /ekspurga'torio/ *a* expurgatory. *m*, *Eccl.* index

**exquisitez** /ekskisi'teθ; ekskisi'tes/ *f*, exquisiteness

**exquisito** /eks'kisito/ *a* exquisite, choice; delicate, delicious

**extasiarse** /eksta'siarse/ *vr* to fall into ecstasy; marvel (at), delight (in)

**éxtasis** /'ekstasis/ *m*, ecstasy; rapture

**extático** /eks'tatiko/ *a* ecstatic

**extemporáneo** /ekstempo'raneo/ *a* untimely; inopportune, inconvenient

**extender** /eksten'der/ *vt irr* to spread; reach, extend; elongate; enlarge, amplify; unfold, open out, stretch; draw up (documents); make out (checks, etc.); —*vr* stretch out; lie down; spread, be generalized; extend; last (of time); record; stretch, open out. **extenderse en,** to expatiate on. See **entender**

**extensión** /eksten'sion/ *f*, extension; expanse; length; extent; duration; extension (logic)

**extensivo** /eksten'siβo/ *a* extensive, spacious; extensible

**extenso** /eks'tenso/ *a* extensive, vast

**extensor** /eksten'sor/ *a* extensor. *m*, chest expander

**extenuación** /ekstenua'θion; ekstenua'sion/ *f*, emaciation, weakness; extenuation

**extenuar** /ekste'nuar/ *vt* to exhaust, weaken; —*vr* become weak

**exterior** /ekste'rior/ *a* external; foreign (trade, etc.). *m*, outside, exterior; outward appearance

**exterioridad** /eksteriori'ðað/ *f*, outward appearance; outside, externality; *pl* ceremonies, forms; ostentation

**exteriorizar** /eksteriori'θar; eksteriori'sar/ *vt* to exteriorize, reveal

**exterminador** /ekstermina'ðor/ **(-ra)** *a* exterminating —*n* exterminator

**exterminar** /ekstermi'nar/ *vt* to exterminate; devastate

**exterminio** /ekster'minio/ *m*, extermination; devastation

**externado** /ekster'naðo/ *m*, day school

**externarse** /ekster'narse/ *vr* to stand out

**externo** /eks'terno/ **(-na)** *a* external —*n* day

**extinción** /ekstin'θion; ekstin'sion/ *f*, extinction; extinguishment; abolition, cancellation

**extinguir** /ekstin'guir/ *vt* to extinguish; destroy

**extintor** /ekstin'tor/ *m*, fire extinguisher

**extirpación** /ekstirpa'θion; ekstirpa'sion/ *f*, extirpation

**extirpador** /ekstirpa'ðor/ **(-ra)** *a* extirpating —*n* extirpator

**extirpar** /ekstir'par/ *vt* to extirpate; *Fig.* eradicate

**extorsión** /ekstor'sion/ *f*, extortion

**extorsionar** /ekstorsio'nar/ *vt* to extort

**extra** /'ekstra/ *prefix* outside, without, beyond —*prep* besides —*a* extremely, most. *m*, *Inf.* extra

**extracción** /ekstrak'θion; ekstrak'sion/ *f*, extraction; drawing (lottery); origin, lineage; exportation

**extractar** /ekstrak'tar/ *vt* to abstract, summarize

**extracto** /eks'trakto/ *m*, abstract, summary; *Chem.* extract

**extractor** /ekstrak'tor/ *a* extracting. *m*, extractor

**extradición** /ekstraði'θion; ekstraði'sion/ *f*, extradition

**extraer** /ekstra'er/ *vt irr* to extract; draw out; export; *Chem.* extract. See **traer**

**extranjero** /ekstran'hero/ **(-ra)** *a* alien, foreign —*n* foreigner. *m*, abroad, foreign country

**extrañar** /ekstra'ɲar/ *vt* to exile; alienate, estrange; wonder at; miss, feel the loss of; —*vr* be exiled; be estranged; be amazed (by); refuse (to do a thing)

**extrañeza** /ekstra'ɲeθa; ekstra'ɲesa/ *f*, strangeness; estrangement; surprise

**extraño** /eks'traɲo/ *a* strange, unusual; foreign, extraneous

**extraoficial** /ekstraofi'θial; ekstraofi'sial/ *a* unofficial

**extraordinario** /ekstraorði'nario/ *a* extraordinary; special. *m*, *Cul.* extra course

**extraterritorialidad** /ekstraterritoriali'ðað/ *f*, exterritoriality

**extravagancia** /ekstraβa'ganθia; ekstraβa'gansia/ *f*, eccentricity; queerness; folly

**extravagante** /ekstraβa'gante/ *a* eccentric; queer, strange; absurd

**extravertido** /ekstraβer'tiðo/ *m*, extrovert

**extraviar** /ekstra'βiar/ *vt* to mislead; mislay; —*vr* lose one's way; be lost (of things); *Fig.* go astray

**extravío** /ekstra'βio/ *m*, deviation, divergence; error; aberration, lapse

**extremado** /ekstre'maðo/ *a* extreme

**extremar** /ekstre'mar/ *vt* to take to extremes; —*vr* do one's best

**extremaunción** /ekstremaun'θion; ekstremaun'sion/ *f*, extreme unction

**extremeño** /ekstre'meɲo/ **(-ña)** *a* and *n* Extremaduran

**extremidad** /ekstremi'ðað/ *f*, end; extremity; remotest part; edge; limit; *pl* extremities

**extremista** /ekstre'mista/ *a* and *mf* extremist

**extremo** /eks'tremo/ *a* last, ultimate; extreme; furthest; great, exceptional; utmost. *m*, end, extreme; highest degree; extreme care; *pl* excessive emotional display

**extremoso** /ekstre'moso/ *a* immoderate, exaggerated; very affectionate

**extrínseco** /ekstrin'seko/ *a* extrinsic

**exuberancia** /eksuβe'ranθia; eksuβeransia/ *f*, abundance; exuberance

**exuberante** /eksuβe'rante/ *a* abundant, copious; exuberant

**exudar** /eksu'ðar/ *vi* and *vt* to exude

**exultación** /eksulta'θion; eksulta'sion/ *f*, exultation; rejoicing

**exultante** /eksul'tante/ *a* exultant

**exultar** /eksul'tar/ *vi* to exult

**exvoto** /eks'βoto/ *m*, votive offering

**eyaculación** /eyakula'θion; eyakula'sion/ *f*, *Med.* ejaculation

**eyacular** /eyaku'lar/ *vt Med.* to ejaculate

# F

**fa** /fa/ *m, Mus.* fa, F

**fabada** /fa'βaða/ *f,* dish of broad beans with pork, sausage or bacon

**fábrica** /'faβrika/ *f,* manufacture; making; factory, works; fabric, structure, building; creation; invention. **f. de papel,** paper mill. **marca de f.,** trademark

**fabricación** /faβrika'θion; faβrika'sion/ *f,* make; making; construction. **f. en serie,** mass production

**fabricador** /faβrika'ðor/ **(-ra)** *a* creative, inventive —*n* fabricator; maker

**fabricante** /faβri'kante/ *a* manufacturing. *m,* manufacturer; maker

**fabricar** /faβri'kar/ *vt* to manufacture; make; construct, build; devise; invent, create

**fabril** /fa'βril/ *a* manufacturing

**fabriquero** /faβri'kero/ *m,* manufacturer; churchwarden; charcoal burner

**fábula** /'faβula/ *f,* rumor, gossip; fiction; fable; story, plot; mythology; myth; laughingstock; falsehood.

**fabulista** /faβu'lista/ *mf* fabulist; mythologist

**fabulosidad** /faβulosi'ðað/ *f,* fabulousness

**fabuloso** /faβu'loso/ *a* fabulous; fictitious; incredible, amazing

**faca** /'faka/ *f,* jackknife

**facción** /fak'θion; fak'sion/ *f,* rebellion; faction, party, band; feature (of the face) (gen. *pl*); military exploit; any routine military duty

**faccionario** /fakθio'nario; faksio'nario/ *a* factional

**faccioso** /fak'θioso; fak'sioso/ **(-sa)** *a* factional; factious, seditious —*n* rebel

**faceta** /fa'θeta; fa'seta/ *f,* facet (gems); aspect, view

**facha** /'fatʃa/ *f, Inf.* countenance, look, face; guy, scarecrow. *Naut.* **ponerse en f.,** to lie to

**fachada** /fa'tʃaða/ *f,* facade, front (of a building, ship, etc.); *Inf.* build, presence (of a person); frontispiece (of a book)

**fachenda** /fa'tʃenda/ *f, Inf.* boastfulness, vanity

**facial** /fa'θial; fa'sial/ *a* facial; intuitive

**fácil** /'faθil; 'fasil/ *a* easy; probable; easily led; docile; of easy virtue (women) —*adv* easy

**facilidad** /faθili'ðað; fasili'ðað/ *f,* easiness; facility, aptitude; ready compliance; opportunity

**facilitación** /faθilita'θion; fasilita'sion/ *f,* facilitation

**facilitar** /faθili'tar; fasili'tar/ *vt* to facilitate, expedite; provide, deliver

**facineroso** /faθine'roso; fasine'roso/ *a* criminal, delinquent. *m,* criminal; villain

**facistol** /faθis'tol; fasis'tol/ *m, Eccl.* lectern; chorister's stand

**facsímile** /fak'simile/ *m,* facsimile

**factibilidad** /faktiβili'ðað/ *f,* feasibility, practicability

**factible** /fak'tiβle/ *a* feasible, practicable

**facticio** /fak'tiθio; fak'tisio/ *a* factitious, artificial

**factor** /fak'tor/ *m, Com.* factor, agent; *Math.* factor; element; consideration

**factoría** /fakto'ria/ *f,* agency; factorage; factory; merchants' trading post, especially in a foreign country

**factótum** /fak'totum/ *m, Inf.* factotum, handyman; *Inf.* busybody; confidential agent or deputy

**factura** /fak'tura/ *f, Com.* invoice, bill, account; *Art.* execution; workmanship; making

**facturar** /faktu'rar/ *vt Com.* to invoice; register (luggage on a railroad)

**facultad** /fakulta'ð/ *f,* faculty; mental or physical aptitude, capability; authority, right; science, art; *Educ.* faculty; license

**facultar** /fakul'tar/ *vt* to authorize, permit

**facultativo** /fakulta'tiβo/ *a* belonging to a faculty; optional, permissive. *m,* physician

**facundia** /fa'kundia/ *f,* eloquence

**facundo** /fa'kundo/ *a* eloquent

**faena** /fa'ena/ *f,* manual labor; mental work; business affairs (gen. *pl*)

**faetón** /fae'ton/ *m,* phaeton

**fagocito** /fago'θito; fago'sito/ *m,* phagocyte

**fagot** /fa'got/ *m,* bassoon

**fagotista** /fago'tista/ *mf* bassoon player

**faisán** /fai'san/ **(-ana)** *Ornith.* cock (hen) pheasant

**faisanera** /faisa'nera/ *f,* pheasantry

**faja** /'faha/ *f,* belt; sash, scarf; corset, girdle; *Geog.* zone; newspaper wrapper; *Archit.* fascia; swathing band

**fajar** /fa'har/ *vt* to swathe; swaddle (a child)

**fajero** /fa'hero/ *m,* swaddling band

**fajín** /fa'hin/ *m,* ceremonial ribbon or sash worn by generals, etc.

**fajina** /fa'hina/ *f,* stack; brushwood; (*fort.*) fascine

**fajo** /'faho/ *m,* bundle, sheaf; *pl* swaddling clothes

**falacia** /fa'laθia; fa'lasia/ *f,* fraud, deceit; deceitfulness; fallacy

**falange** /fa'lanhe/ *f, Mil.* phalanx; *Anat.* phalange; (*Spanish pol.*) Falange

**falangista** /falan'hista/ *a* and *mf* Falangist

**falaz** /fa'laθ; fa'las/ *a* deceitful; fallacious

**falda** /'falda/ *f,* skirt; lap, flap, panel (of a dress); slope (of a hill); the lap; loin (of beef, etc.); brim of a hat; *pl Inf.* petticoats, women. **f. escocesa,** kilt. **f.-pantalón,** divided skirt, culottes

**faldellín** /falde'ʎin; falde'yin/ *m,* skirt; underskirt

**faldero** /fal'dero/ *a* lap (dog); fond of the company of women

**faldillas** /fal'diʎas; fal'diyas/ *f pl,* coattails

**faldistorio** /faldis'torio/ *m,* faldstool

**faldón** /fal'don/ *m,* long, flowing skirt; shirttail; coattail

**falibilidad** /faliβili'ðað/ *f,* fallibility

**falible** /fa'liβle/ *a* fallible

**falla** /'faʎa; faya/ *f,* deficiency, defect; failure; *Geol.* displacement; bonfire (Valencia); *Mineral.* slide

**fallar** /fa'ʎar; fa'yar/ *vt Law.* to pass sentence; —*vi* be deficient

**falleba** /fa'ʎeβa; fa'yeβa/ *f,* shutter bolt

**fallecer** /faʎe'θer; faye'ser/ *vi irr* to die; fail. See **conocer**

**fallecimiento** /faʎeθi'miento; fayesi'miento/ *m,* death, decease

**fallido** /fa'ʎiðo; fa'yiðo/ *a* frustrated; bankrupt

**fallo** /'faʎo; 'fayo/ *m, Law.* verdict; judgment

**falsario** /fal'sario/ *a* falsifying, forging, counterfeiting; deceiving, lying. *m,* falsifier, forger, counterfeiter

**falseamiento** /falsea'miento/ *m,* falsifying; forging

**falsear** /false'ar/ *vt* to falsify; forge; counterfeit; penetrate; —*vi* weaken; *Mus.* be out of tune (strings)

**falsedad** /false'ðað/ *f,* falseness; falsehood

**falsete** /fal'sete/ *m,* spigot; *Mus.* falsetto voice

**falsificación** /falsifika'θion; falsifika'sion/ *f,* falsification; forgery

**falsificador** /falsifika'ðor/ *a* falsifying; forging. *m,* falsifier; forger

**falsificar** /falsifi'kar/ *vt* to forge, counterfeit; falsify

**falso** /'falso/ *a* false; forged, counterfeit; treacherous, untrue, deceitful; incorrect; sham; vicious (horses). **de f.,** falsely; deceitfully

**falta** /'falta/ *f,* lack, shortage; defect; mistake; *Sports.* fault; shortcoming; nonappearance, absence; deficiency in legal weight of coin; *Law.* offense. **f. de éxito,** failure. **hacer f.,** to be necessary. **sin f.,** without fail

**faltar** /fal'tar/ *vi* to be lacking; fail, die; fall short; be absent from an appointment; not to fulfill one's obligations. **f. a,** to be unfaithful to, break (e.g. *Faltó a su palabra,* He broke his promise). *Inf.* **¡No faltaba más!** I should think not!; That's the limit!

**falto** /'falto/ *a* lacking, wanting; defective; wretched, mean, timid. **f. de personal,** short-handed

**faltriquera** /faltri'kera/ *f,* pocket; hip pocket

**falúa** /fa'lua/ *f, Naut.* tender; longboat

**falucho** /fa'lutʃo/ *m,* felucca

**fama** /'fama/ *f,* rumor, report; reputation; fame

**famélico** /fa'meliko/ *a* ravenous

**familia** /fa'milia/ *f,* family; household; kindred. **ser de f.,** to run in the family

**familiar** /fami'liar/ *a* family; familiar; well known; unceremonious; plain, simple; colloquial (language). *m, Eccl.* familiar; servant; intimate friend; familiar spirit

**familiaridad** /familiari'ðað/ *f,* familiarity

**familiarizar** /familiari'θar; familiari'sar/ *vt* to familiarize; —*vr* become familiar; accustom oneself

**familiarmente** /familiar'mente/ *adv* familiarly

**famoso** /fa'moso/ *a* famous; notorious; *Inf.* excellent, perfect; *Inf.* conspicuous

**fámula** /'famula/ *f, Inf.* female servant

**fámulo** /'famulo/ *m,* servant of a college; *Inf.* servant

**fanal** /fa'nal/ *m,* lantern (of a lighthouse); *Naut.* poop lantern; lantern; lamp glass

**fanático** /fa'natiko/ **(-ca)** *a* fanatical —*n* fanatic; *Inf.* fan, enthusiast

**fanatismo** /fana'tismo/ *m,* fanaticism

**fanatizar** /fanati'θar; fanati'sar/ *vt* to make fanatical; turn into a fanatic

**fandango** /fan'dango/ *m,* lively Andalusian dance

**fanega** /fa'nega/ *f,* grain measure about the weight of 1.60 bushel; land measure (about 1½ acres)

**fanfarrón** /fanfa'rron/ **(-ona)** *a Inf.* boastful; swaggering —*n* swashbuckler; boaster

**fanfarronear** /fanfarrone'ar/ *vi* to swagger; brag

**fanfarronería** /fanfarrone'ria/ *f,* bragging

**fango** /'fango/ *m,* mud, mire; degradation

**fangoso** /fan'goso/ *a* muddy, miry

**fantasear** /fantase'ar/ *vi* to let one's fancy roam; boast

**fantasía** /fanta'sia/ *f,* fancy, imagination; fantasy; caprice; fiction; *Inf.* presumption; *Mus.* fantasia

**fantasma** /fan'tasma/ *m,* ghost, phantom; vision; image, impression; presumptuous person. *f, Inf.* scarecrow; apparition

**fantasmagoría** /fantasmago'ria/ *f,* phantasmagoria

**fantasmagórico** /fantasma'goriko/ *a* phantasmagoric

**fantástico** /fan'tastiko/ *a* fanciful, imaginary; fantastic, imaginative; presumptuous, conceited

**fantoche** /fan'totʃe/ *m,* puppet; *Inf.* yes-man, mediocrity

**faquín** /fa'kin/ *m,* porter, carrier

**faquir** /fa'kir/ *m,* fakir

**faradio** /fa'raðio/ *m,* farad

**faralá** /fara'la/ *m,* flounce, frill

**farándula** /fa'randula/ *f,* profession of low comedian; troupe of strolling players; cunning trick

**farandulero** /farandu'lero/ *m,* actor, strolling player —*a Inf.* plausible

**faraón** /fara'on/ *m,* pharaoh; faro (card game)

**fardel** /far'ðel/ *m,* bag, knapsack; bundle

**fardo** /far'ðo/ *m,* bundle, bale, package

**farfulla** /far'fuʎa; far'fuya/ *f, Inf.* mumbling; gibbering. *mf Inf.* mumbler

**farfullar** /farfu'ʎar; farfu'yar/ *vt Inf.* to mumble; gibber; *Inf.* act in haste

**faringe** /fa'rinhe/ *f,* pharynx

**faríngeo** /fa'rinheo/ *a* pharyngeal

**faringitis** /farin'hitis/ *f,* pharyngitis

**farisaico** /fari'saiko/ *a* pharisaical

**fariseísmo** /farise'ismo/ *m,* cant, hypocrisy

**fariseo** /fari'seo/ *m,* Pharisee; hypocrite

**farmacéutico** /farma'θeutiko; farma'seutiko/ *a* pharmaceutical. *m,* pharmacist

**farmacia** /far'maθia; far'masia/ *f,* pharmacy

**farmacología** /farmakolo'hia/ *f,* pharmacology

**farmacológico** /farmako'lohiko/ *a* pharmacological

**farmacólogo** /farma'kologo/ *m,* pharmacologist

**faro** /'faro/ *m,* lighthouse; beacon, guide; *Auto.* headlight

**farol** /fa'rol/ *m,* lantern, lamp; streetlamp; cresset

**farola** /fa'rola/ *f,* lamppost (generally with several branches); lantern

**farolero** /faro'lero/ *m,* lantern maker; lamplighter; lamp tender —*a Inf.* swaggering, braggart

**fárrago** /'farrago/ *m,* hodgepodge

**farsa** /'farsa/ *f,* old name for a play; farce; theatrical company; poor, badly constructed play; sham, trick, deception

**farsante** /far'sante/ *m,* comedian; *Obs.* actor; *Fig. Inf.* humbug

**fascinación** /fasθina'θion; fassina'sion/ *f,* evil eye; enchantment, fascination

**fascinador** /fasθina'ðor; fassina'ðor/ **(-ra)** *a* bewitching; fascinating —*n* charmer

**fascinante** /fasθi'nante; fassi'nante/ *a* fascinating

**fascinar** /fasθi'nar; fassi'nar/ *vt* to bewitch, place under a spell; deceive, impose upon; attract, fascinate

**fascismo** /fas'θismo; fas'sismo/ *m,* fascism

**fascista** /fas'θista; fas'sista/ *a* and *mf* fascist

**fase** /'fase/ *f,* phase; aspect

**fastidiar** /fasti'ðiar/ *vt* to disgust, bore; annoy; —*vr* be bored

**fastidio** /fasti'ðio/ *m,* sickness, squeamishness; annoyance, boredom, dislike, repugnance

**fastidioso** /fasti'ðioso/ *a* disgusting, sickening; annoying; boring, tiresome

**fastuoso** /fas'tuoso/ *a* ostentatious; pompous

**fatal** /fa'tal/ *a* fatal, mortal; predetermined, inevitable; ill-fated, unhappy, disastrous; evil

**fatalidad** /fatali'ðað/ *f,* fatality; inevitability; disaster, ill-fatedness

**fatalismo** /fata'lismo/ *m,* fatalism

**fatalista** /fata'lista/ *a* fatalistic. *mf* fatalist

**fatalmente** /fatal'mente/ *adv* inevitably, unavoidably; unhappily, unfortunately; extremely badly

**fatídico** /fa'tiðiko/ *a* prophetic (gen. of evil)

**fatiga** /fa'tiga/ *f,* fatigue; toil; difficult breathing; hardship, troubles (gen. *pl*)

**fatigar** /fati'gar/ *vt* to tire; annoy; —*vr* be tired

**fatigoso** /fati'goso/ *a* tired; tiring; tiresome, annoying

**fatuidad** /fatui'ðað/ *f,* fatuousness, inanity, foolishness; conceit; priggishness

**fatuo** /fa'tuo/ *a* fatuous, foolish; conceited; priggish. *m,* self-satisfied fool. **fuego f.,** will-o'-the-wisp

**fauces** /'fauθes; 'fauses/ *f pl,* gullet

**fauna** /'fauna/ *f,* fauna

**fauno** /'fauno/ *m,* faun

**fausto** /'fausto/ *m,* pomp, magnificence, ostentation —*a* fortunate, happy

**fautor** /fau'tor/ *m,* protector, helper; accomplice. **f. de guerra,** warmonger

**favonio** /fa'βonio/ *m, Poet.* zephyr, westerly wind

**favor** /fa'βor/ *m,* aid, protection, support; favor, honor, service; love favor, sign of favor. **a f. de,** in favor of; on behalf of

**favorable** /faβo'raβle/ *a* kind, helpful; favorable

**favorecedor** /faβoreθe'ðor; faβorese'ðor/ **(-ra)** *a* favoring, helping —*n* helper; protector

**favorecer** /faβore'θer; faβore'ser/ *vt irr* to aid, protect, support; favor; do a service, grant a favor. See **conocer**

**favoritismo** /faβori'tismo/ *m,* favoritism

**favorito** /faβo'rito/ **(-ta)** *a* and *n* favorite

**fayenza** /fa'yenθa; fa'yensa/ *f,* faience

**faz** /faθ; fas/ *f,* face; external surface of a thing, side; frontage

**fe** /fe/ *f,* faith; confidence, trust, good opinion; belief; solemn promise; assertion; certificate, attestation; faithfulness. **f. de erratas,** *Print.* errata. **dar f.,** *Law.* to testify. **de buena f.,** in good faith. **en f.,** in proof

**fealdad** /feal'dað/ *f,* ugliness; base action

**febo** /'feβo/ *m, Phoebus; Poet.* sun

**febrero** /fe'βrero/ *m,* February

**febril** /fe'βril/ *a* feverish; ardent, violent; passionate

**fecal** /fe'kal/ *a* fecal

**fecha** /'fetʃa/ *f,* date. **a la f.,** at present, now. **hasta la f.,** up to the present (day)

**fechar** /fe'tʃar/ *vt* to date, write the date

**feculento** /feku'lento/ *a* starchy; dreggy

**fecundación** /fekunda'θion; fekunda'sion/ *f,* fecundation

**fecundar** /fekun'dar/ *vt* to fertilize; fecundate

**fecundidad** /fekundi'ðað/ *f,* fecundity; fertility; fruitfulness

**fecundizar** /fekundi'θar; fekundi'sar/ *vt* to fertilize; make fruitful

**fecundo** /fe'kundo/ *a* fertile, fecund, prolific; abundant

**federación** /feðera'θion; feðera'sion/ *f,* federation, league

**federal** /feðe'ral/ *a* federal. *mf* federalist

**federalismo** /feðera'lismo/ *m,* federalism

**federalista** /feðera'lista/ *a* federal, federalist. *mf* federalist

**federativo** /feðera'tiβo/ *a* federative

**fehaciente** /fea'θiente; fea'siente/ *a Law.* authentic, attested

**feldespato** /feldes'pato/ *m,* feldspar

**felicidad** /feliθi'ðað; felisi'ðað/ *f,* happiness; contentment, satisfaction; good fortune

**felicitación** /feliθita'θion; felisita'sion/ *f,* congratulation

**felicitar** /feliθi'tar; felisi'tar/ *vt* to congratulate; wish well; —*vr* congratulate oneself

**feligrés** /feli'gres/ **(-esa)** *n* parishioner

**feligresía** /feligre'sia/ *f,* parish

**felino** /fe'lino/ *a* and *m,* feline

**feliz** /fe'liθ; fe'lis/ *a* happy; fortunate; skillful, felicitous (of phrases, etc.)

**felón** /fe'lon/ **(-ona)** *n* felon

**felonía** /felo'nia/ *f,* felony

**felpa** /'felpa/ *f,* plush; *Inf.* drubbing, beating

**felpilla** /fel'piʎa; fel'piya/ *f,* chenille

**felpudo** /fel'puðo/ *a* plush

**femenino** /feme'nino/ *a* feminine; female; *Fig.* weak

**fementido** /femen'tiðo/ *a* sly, false, treacherous, unfaithful

**feminismo** /femi'nismo/ *m,* feminism

**feminista** /femi'nista/ *a* feminist. *mf* feminist

**fémur** /'femur/ *m,* femur, thigh bone

**fenecer** /fene'θer; fene'ser/ *vt irr* to conclude, finish; —*vi* die; be ended. See **conocer**

**fenecimiento** /feneθi'miento; fenesi'miento/ *m,* end; death

**fenicio** /fe'niθio; fe'nisio/ **(-ia)** *a* and *n* Phoenician

**fénico** /'feniko/ *a* phenic, carbolic

**fénix** /'feniks/ *f,* phoenix

**fenomenal** /fenome'nal/ *a* phenomenal; *Inf.* terrific

**fenómeno** /fe'nomeno/ *m,* phenomenon; *Inf.* something of great size

**feo** /'feo/ *a* ugly; alarming, horrid; evil. *m, Inf.* slight, insult

**feraz** /'feraθ; 'feras/ *a* fruitful, fertile

**féretro** /'feretro/ *m,* coffin; bier

**feria** /'feria/ *f,* fair, market; workday; holiday; rest

**feriar** /fe'riar/ *vt* to buy at a fair; bargain —*vi* cease work, take a holiday

**fermentación** /fermenta'θion; fermenta'sion/ *f,* fermentation

**fermentar** /fermen'tar/ *vi* to ferment; be agitated; —*vt* cause to ferment

**fermento** /fer'mento/ *m,* ferment; leaven; *Chem.* enzyme

**ferocidad** /feroθi'ðað; ferosi'ðað/ *f,* ferocity, cruelty

**feroz** /fe'roθ; fe'ros/ *a* ferocious, cruel

**férreo** /'ferreo/ *a* ferrous; hard, tenacious. **línea férrea,** railroad

**ferrería** /ferre'ria/ *f,* ironworks

**ferretería** /ferrete'ria/ *f,* ironworks; ironmonger's shop; ironware, hardware

**férrico** /'ferriko/ *a* ferric

**ferrífero** /fe'rrifero/ *a* iron-bearing

**ferrocarril** /ferroka'rril/ *m,* railroad, railway; railroad train. **f. de cremallera,** rack railroad. **f. funicular,** funicular railway

**ferroso** /fe'rroso/ *a* ferrous

**ferroviario** /ferro'βiario/ *a* railroad, railway. *m,* railroad employee

**fértil** /'fertil/ *a* fertile; fruitful, productive

**fertilidad** /fertili'ðað/ *f,* fertility

**fertilización** /fertiliθa'θion; fertilisa'sion/ *f,* fertilization

**fertilizar** /fertili'θar; fertili'sar/ *vt* to fertilize, make fruitful

**férula** /'ferula/ *f,* ferule; *Surg.* splint; *Fig.* yoke, rule

**fervor** /fer'βor/ *m,* intense heat; fervor, devotion; zeal

**fervoroso** /ferβo'roso/ *a* fervent, zealous, devoted

**festejar** /feste'har/ *vt* to feast, entertain; woo; celebrate; —*vr* amuse oneself

**festejo** /feste'ho/ *m,* feast, entertainment; courtship, wooing; *pl* public celebrations

**festín** /fes'tin/ *m,* private dinner or party; sumptuous banquet

**festival** /festi'βal/ *m,* musical festival; festival

**festividad** /festiβi'ðað/ *f,* festivity; *Eccl.* celebration, solemnity; witticism

**festivo** /fes'tiβo/ *a* joking, witty; happy, gay; solemn, worthy of celebration. **día f.,** holiday

**festón** /fes'ton/ *m,* garland, wreath; festoon; border; scalloped edging

**festonear** /festone'ar/ *vt* to garland, festoon; border

**fetal** /fe'tal/ *a* fetal

**fetiche** /fe'titʃe/ *m,* fetish

**fetichismo** /feti'tʃismo/ *m,* fetishism

**fetidez** /feti'ðeθ; feti'ðes/ *f,* fetidness, fetor, stink

**fétido** /'fetiðo/ *a* stinking, fetid

**feto** /'feto/ *m,* fetus

**feudal** /feu'ðal/ *a* feudal; despotic

**feudalismo** /feuða'lismo/ *m,* feudalism

**feudo** /'feuðo/ *m,* fief; fee. **f. franco,** freehold

**fez** /feθ; fes/ *m,* fez

**fiado, al** /'fiaðo, al/ *adv* on credit. **en f.,** on bail

**fiador** /fia'ðor/ **(-ra)** *n* guarantor; bail. *m,* fastener, loop (of a coat, clock, etc.); safety catch, bolt. **salir f.,** to be surety (for); post bail

**fiambre** /'fiambre/ *m,* cold meat, cold dish; *Inf.* stale, out-of-date news, etc.; *Inf.* corpse

**fiambrera** /fiam'brera/ *f,* lunchbox, lunchpail

**fianza** /'fianθa; 'fiansa/ *f,* guarantee, bail; surety; security. *Law.* **dar f.,** to guarantee; post bail

**fiar** /fi'ar/ *vt* to go surety for, post bail; sell on credit; trust; confide; —*vr* (*with de*) confide in; trust

**fibra** /'fiβra/ *f,* fiber; filament; energy, strength; *Mineral.* vein; grain (of wood)

**fibroso** /fi'βroso/ *a* fibrous; fibroid

**ficción** /fik'θion; fik'sion/ *f,* falsehood; invention; fiction, imaginative creation; pretense

**ficha** /'fitʃa/ *f,* chip, counter; domino; index card, filing card. **f. antropométrica,** personal particulars card

**fichar** /fi'tʃar/ *vt* to record personal particulars on a filing card; file, index

**fichero** /fi'tʃero/ *m,* filing cabinet; card catalog

**fichú** /fi'tʃu/ *m,* fichu, scarf

**ficticio** /fik'tiθio; fik'tisio/ *a* fictitious

**fidedigno** /fiðe'ðigno/ *a* trustworthy, bona fide

**fideicomisario** /fiðeikomi'sario/ *m, Law.* fiduciary, trustee

**fideicomiso** /fiðeiko'miso/ *m, Law.* trust

**fidelidad** /fiðeli'ðað/ *f,* fidelity, honesty; loyalty; punctiliousness

**fideos** /fi'ðeos/ *m pl,* vermicelli. *m, Inf.* scraggy person

**fiduciario** /fiðu'θiario; fiðu'siario/ *a Law.* fiduciary. *m, Law.* trustee

**fiebre** /'fieβre/ *f,* fever; great agitation, excitement. **f. de oro,** gold fever. **f. palúdica,** malarial fever. **f. puerperal,** puerperal fever. **f. tifoidea,** typhoid fever

**fiel** /fiel/ *a* faithful, loyal; true, exact. *m,* axis; pointer (of a scale or balance)

**fieltro** /'fieltro/ *m,* felt

**fiera** /'fiera/ *f,* wild beast; cruel person

**fiereza** /fie're θa; fie'resa/ *f,* savageness, wildness; cruelty, fierceness; deformity

**fiero** /'fiero/ *a* wild, savage; ugly; huge, enormous; horrible, alarming; haughty

**fiesta** /'fiesta/ *f,* merriment, gaiety; entertainment, feast; *Inf.* joke; festivity, celebration; public holiday; caress, cajolery (gen. *pl*); *pl* holidays. **f. fija** *Eccl.* immovable feast. *Inf.* **estar de f.,** to be making merry. **hacer f.,** to take a holiday. *Inf.* **Se acabó la f.,** It's all over and done with

**figón** /fi'gon/ *m,* eating house, diner

**figulino** /figu'lino/ *a* fictile, made of terra cotta

**figura** /fi'gura/ *f,* shape, form; face; *Art.* image, figure; *Law.* form; court card; *Mus.* note; *Theat.* character, role; (*Geom. Gram. Dance.*) figure. **f. de nieve,** snowman. *Naut.* **f. de proa,** figurehead. *Fig.* **f. decorativa,** figurehead. *Fig.* **hacer f.,** to cut a figure

**figurado** /fi'guraðo/ *a* figurative; rhetorical

**figurar** /figu'rar/ *vt* to shape, mold; simulate, pretend; represent; —*vi* be numbered among; cut a figure; —*vr* imagine

**figurativo** /figura'tiβo/ *a* figurative; symbolical

**figurilla** /figu'riʎa; figu'riya/ *mf Inf.* ridiculous, dwarfish figure. *f, Art.* statuette

**figurín** /figu'rin/ *m,* fashion plate or model

**fijación** /fiha'θion; fiha'sion/ *f,* fixing; nailing; sticking, posting; attention, fixity; *Chem.* fixation; firmness, stability

**fijador** /fiha'ðor/ *m,* (*Med. Photo.*) fixative; setting lotion; *Art.* varnish —*a* fixing

**fijamente** /fiha'mente/ *adv* firmly; attentively

**fijar** /fi'har/ *vt* to fix; glue, stick; nail; make firm; settle, appoint (a date); fix, concentrate (attention, gaze); (*Photo. Med.*) fix; —*vr* decide; notice (e.g. *No me había fijado,* I hadn't noticed). **f. anuncios,** to post bills

**fijeza** /fi'heθa; fi'hesa/ *f,* fixedness; firmness, stability; constancy, steadfastness

**fijo** /'fiho/ *a* firm; fixed; stable; steadfast; permanent; exact. **de f.,** certainly, without doubt

**fila** /'fila/ *f,* line, row; *Mil.* rank; antipathy, hatred. **en f.,** in a line

**filacteria** /filak'teria/ *f,* phylactery

**filamento** /fila'mento/ *m,* filament

**filantropía** /filantro'pia/ *f,* philanthropy

**filantrópico** /filan'tropiko/ *a* philanthropic

**filántropo** /fi'lantropo/ *m,* philanthropist

**filarmónico** /filar'moniko/ *a* philharmonic

**filatelia** /fila'telia/ *f,* philately, stamp collecting

**filatélico** /fila'teliko/ *a* philatelic

**filatelista** /filate'lista/ *mf* philatelist, stamp collector

**filete** /fi'lete/ *m, Archit.* filet; *Cul.* small spit; filet (of meat or fish); thread of a screw; *Sew.* hem

**filiación** /filia'θion; filia'sion/ *f,* filiation; affiliation; relationship; *Mil.* regimental register

**filial** /fi'lial/ *a* filial; affiliated

**filibustero** /filiβus'tero/ *m,* filibuster

**filiforme** /fili'forme/ *a* filamentous

**filigrana** /fili'grana/ *f,* filigree; watermark (of paper); *Fig.* delicate creation

**filípica** /fi'lipika/ *f,* philippic

**Filipinas, las** /fili'pinas, las/ the Philippines

**filipino** /fili'pino/ **(-na)** *a* and *n* Philippine

**filisteo** /filis'teo/ **(-ea)** *a* and *n* philistine

**filmar** /fil'mar/ *vt* to film

**filme** /'filme/ *m,* (cinema) film

**filo** /'filo/ *m,* cutting edge; dividing line

**filología** /filolo'hia/ *f,* philology

**filológico** /filo'lohiko/ *a* philological

**filólogo** /fi'lologo/ *m,* philologist

**filomela** /filo'mela/ *f, Poet.* nightingale

**filón** /fi'lon/ *m, Mineral.* vein, lode; *Fig.* gold mine

**filosofar** /filoso'far/ *vi* to philosophize

**filosofía** /filoso'fia/ *f,* philosophy. **f. moral,** moral philosophy. **f. natural,** natural philosophy

**filosófico** /filo'sofiko/ *a* philosophic

**filósofo** /fi'losofo/ *m,* philosopher —*a* philosophic

**filoxera** /filo'ksera/ *f,* phylloxera

**filtración** /filtra'θion; filtra'sion/ *f,* filtration

**filtrar** /fil'trar/ *vt* to filter; —*vi* filter through, percolate; —*vr Fig.* disappear (of money, etc.)

**filtro** /'filtro/ *m,* filter, strainer; love potion, philter

**fin** /fin/ *m,* finish, end, conclusion; purpose, goal, aim; limit, extent. **a f. de,** in order to, so that. **a fines de,** toward the end of (with months, years, etc.) (e.g. *a fines de octubre,* toward the end of October). **en f.,** at last; in fine; well then! **por f.,** finally

**finado** /fi'naðo/ **(-da)** *n* deceased, dead person

**final** /fi'nal/ *a* final. *m,* end, finish; *Sports.* final (gen. *pl*)

**finalidad** /finali'ðað/ *f,* finality; purpose

**finalista** /fina'lista/ *mf Sports.* finalist

**finalizar** /finali'θar; finali'sar/ *vt* to conclude, finish; —*vi* be finished; close (stock exchange)

**finalmente** /final'mente/ *adv* finally

**financiar** /finan'θiar; finan'siar/ *vt* to finance

**financiero** /finan'θiero; finan'siero/ *a* financial. *m,* financier

**finanzas** /fi'nanθas; fi'nansas/ *f pl,* finance

**finar** /fi'nar/ *vi* to die; —*vr* desire, long for a thing

**finca** /'finka/ *f,* land, real estate; house property, country house, ranch

**fineza** /fi'neθa; fi'nesa/ *f,* fineness; excellence, goodness; kindness, expression of affection; good turn, friendly act; gift; beauty, delicacy

**fingido** /fin'hiðo/ *a* pretended; assumed; feigned; sham

**fingimiento** /finhi'miento/ *m,* pretense; affectation, assumption

**fingir** /fin'hir/ *vt* to pretend, feign; imagine

**finiquitar** /finiki'tar/ *vt* to close and pay up an account; *Inf.* end

**finiquito** /fini'kito/ *m,* closing of an account; final receipt, quittance; quietus

**finito** /fi'nito/ *a* finite

**finlandés** /finlan'des/ **(-esa)** *a* Finnish —*n* Finn. *m,* Finnish (language)

**Finlandia** /fin'landia/ Finland

**fino** /'fino/ *a* fine; excellent, good; slim, slender, thin; delicate, subtle; dainty (of people); cultured, polished; constant, loving; sagacious, shrewd; *Mineral.* refined

**finta** /'finta/ *f,* feint (in fencing); menace, threat

**finura** /fi'nura/ *f,* fineness; excellence; delicacy; courtesy

**fiordo** /'fiorðo/ *m,* fjord

**firma** /'firma/ *f,* signature; act of signing; *Com.* firm name, firm

**firmamento** /firma'mento/ *m,* firmament

**firmante** /fir'mante/ *a* signing. *mf* signatory

**firmar** /fir'mar/ *vt* to sign

**firme** /'firme/ *a* firm; hard; steady, solid; constant, resolute, loyal. *m,* foundation, base. *Mil.* **¡Firmes!** Attention! **batir de f.,** to strike hard

**firmeza** /fir'meθa; fir'mesa/ *f,* stability, firmness; constancy, resoluteness, loyalty

**fiscal** /fis'kal/ *a* fiscal. *m,* attorney general; public prosecutor; meddler. **f. de quiebras,** official receiver

**fiscalizar** /fiskali'θar; fiskali'sar/ *vt* to prosecute; pry into; meddle with; censure, criticize

**fisco** /'fisko/ *m,* national treasury, exchequer, revenue

**fisgar** /fis'gar/ *vt* to harpoon; pry; —*vi* mock, make fun of

**fisgón** /fis'gon/ **(-ona)** *a* prying; mocking —*n* pryer; mocker; eavesdropper

**fisgoneo** /fisgo'neo/ *m,* prying; eavesdropping

**física** /'fisika/ *f,* physics

**físico** /'fisiko/ *a* physical. *m,* physicist; physician; physique

**fisiología** /fisiolo'hia/ *f,* physiology

**fisiológico** /fisio'lohiko/ *a* physiological

**fisiólogo** /fisi'ologo/ *m,* physiologist

**fisioterapia** /fisiote'rapia/ *f,* physiotherapy

**fisonomía** /fisono'mia/ *f,* physiognomy

**fístula** /'fistula/ *f,* pipe, conduit; *Mus.* pipe; *Surg.* fistula

**fisura** /fi'sura/ *f,* fissure

**flaccidez** /flakθi'ðeθ; flaksi'ðes/ *f,* flabbiness

**fláccido** /'flakθiðo; 'flaksiðo/ *a* flaccid, soft, flabby

**flaco** /'flako/ *a* thin; weak, feeble; *Fig.* weak-minded; dispirited. *m,* failing, weakness. *Inf.* **hacer un f. servicio,** to do an ill turn. **estar f. de memoria,** to have a weak memory

**flagelación** /flahela'θion; flahela'sion/ *f,* flagellation

**flagelante** /flahe'lante/ *m,* flagellant

**flagelar** /flahe'lar/ *vt* to scourge; *Fig.* lash

**flagelo** /fla'helo/ *m,* whip, scourge

**flagrante** /fla'grante/ *a Poet.* refulgent; present; actual. **en f.,** in the very act, flagrante delicto

**flagrar** /fla'grar/ *vi Poet.* to blaze, be refulgent

**flamante** /fla'mante/ *a* resplendent; brand-new; fresh, spick-and-span

**flamenco** /fla'menko/ **(-ca)** *m, Ornith.* flamingo —*a* and *n* Flemish —*a* Andalusian; gypsy; buxom, fresh

**flan** /flan/ *m,* baked custard, creme caramel. **estar como un f.,** to shake like a leaf, be nervous

**flanco** /'flanko/ *m,* side; *Mil.* flank

**Flandes** /'flandes/ Flanders

**flanquear** /flanke'ar/ *vt Mil.* to flank

**flanqueo** /flan'keo/ *m, Mil.* outflanking

**flaquear** /flake'ar/ *vi* to grow weak; weaken; totter (buildings, etc.); be disheartened, flag

**flaqueza** /fla'keθa; fla'kesa/ *f*, weakness; thinness; faintness, feebleness; frailty, fault; loss of zeal

**flato** /'flato/ *m*, flatulence, gas

**flatulento** /flatu'lento/ *a* flatulent, gassy

**flauta** /'flauta/ *f*, flute

**flautín** /flau'tin/ *m*, piccolo

**flautista** /flau'tista/ *mf* flutist

**flebitis** /fle'βitis/ *f*, phlebitis

**flebotomía** /fleβoto'mia/ *f*, phlebotomy, bloodletting

**flecha** /'fletʃa/ *f*, arrow, dart

**flechar** /fle'tʃar/ *vt* to shoot an arrow or dart; wound or kill with arrows; *Inf.* inspire love; —*vi* bend a bow to shoot

**flechazo** /fle'tʃaθo; fle'tʃaso/ *m*, wound with an arrow; *Inf.* love at first sight

**flechero** /fle'tʃero/ *m*, archer; arrow maker

**fleco** /'fleko/ *m*, fringe; fringe (of hair)

**fleje** /'flehe/ *m*, iron hoop (for barrels, etc.)

**flema** /'flema/ *f*, phlegm; sluggishness

**flemático** /fle'matiko/ *a* phlegmatic; sluggish

**flemón** /fle'mon/ *m*, gumboil; abscess

**flequillo** /fle'kiʎo; fle'kiyo/ *m*, fringe (of hair)

**fletamento** /fleta'mento/ *m*, chartering (a ship)

**fletar** /fle'tar/ *vt* to charter a ship; embark merchandise or people

**flete** /'flete/ *m*, freightage; cargo, freight

**flexibilidad** /fleksiβili'ðað/ *f*, flexibility; suppleness, adaptability

**flexible** /fle'ksiβle/ *a* pliant, supple; flexible, adaptable. *m*, *Elec.* flex

**flexión** /fle'ksion/ *f*, flexion; bend, bending; deflection

**flirtear** /flirte'ar/ *vi* to flirt

**flirteo** /flir'teo/ *m*, flirtation

**flojedad** /flohe'ðað/ *f*, flabbiness; weakness, feebleness; laziness, negligence

**flojo** /'floho/ *a* flabby; slack, loose; weak, feeble; lazy, slothful; poor (of a literary work, etc.)

**floqueado** /floke'aðo/ *a* fringed

**flor** /flor/ *f*, flower; best (of anything); bloom (on fruit); virginity; grain (of leather); compliment (gen. *pl*); menstruation (gen. *pl*). **f. de especia,** mace. **f. de la edad,** prime, youth. **f. del cuclillo,** mayflower. **f. del estudiante,** French marigold. **flores de mano,** artificial flowers. **flores de oblón,** hops. **a f. de,** on the surface of, level with. **andarse en flores,** *Fig.* to beat about the bush. **echar flores,** to pay compliments. **en f.,** in bloom

**flora** /'flora/ *f*, flora

**floración** /flora'θion; flora'sion/ *f*, flowering

**floral** /flo'ral/ *a* floral. **juegos florales,** poetry contest

**florear** /flore'ar/ *vt* to adorn with flowers; —*vi* execute a flourish on the guitar

**florecer** /flore'θer; flore'ser/ *vi irr* to flower, bloom; flourish, prosper; —*vr* grow mold (of cheese, etc.). See **conocer**

**floreciente** /flore'θiente; flore'siente/ *a* flowering; prosperous

**florecimiento** /floreθi'miento; floresi'miento/ *m*, flowering; prosperity

**Florencia** /flo'renθia; flo'rensia/ Florence

**florentino** /floren'tino/ **(-na)** *a* and *n* Florentine

**floreo** /flo'reo/ *m*, witty conversation; flourish (on the guitar or in fencing)

**florero** /flo'rero/ *m*, vase; flower pot; *Art.* flower piece

**florescencia** /flores'θenθia; flores'sensia/ *f*, flowering; flowering season, florescence

**floresta** /flo'resta/ *f*, grove, wooded park, woodland; *Fig.* collector of beautiful things; anthology

**florete** /flo'rete/ *m*, fencing foil

**floricultor** /florikul'tor/ **(-ra)** *n* floriculturist

**floricultura** /florikul'tura/ *f*, floriculture

**floridamente** /floriða'mente/ *adv* elegantly, with a flourish

**florido** /flo'riðo/ *a* flowery; best, most select; florid, ornate

**florilegio** /flori'lehio/ *m*, anthology, collection

**florín** /flo'rin/ *m*, florin

**florista** /flo'rista/ *mf* artificial-flower maker; florist; flower seller

**florón** /flo'ron/ *m*, large flower; *Archit.* fleuron; honorable deed

**flósculo** /'floskulo/ *m*, *Bot.* floret

**flota** /'flota/ *f*, fleet of merchant ships. **f. aérea,** air force

**flotación** /flota'θion; flota'sion/ *f*, floating. *Naut.* **línea de f.,** water line

**flotador** /flota'ðor/ *a* floating. *m*, float

**flotamiento** /flota'miento/ *m*, floating

**flotante** /flo'tante/ *a* floating

**flotar** /flo'tar/ *vi* to float on water or in air

**flote** /'flote/ *m*, floating. **a f.,** afloat; independent, solvent

**flotilla** /flo'tiʎa; flo'tiya/ *f*, flotilla; fleet of small ships. **f. aérea,** air fleet

**fluctuación** /fluktua'θion; fluktua'sion/ *f*, fluctuation; hesitation, vacillation

**fluctuante** /fluk'tuante/ *a* fluctuating

**fluctuar** /fluktu'ar/ *vi* to fluctuate; be in danger (things); vacillate, hesitate; undulate; oscillate

**fluidez** /flui'ðeθ; flui'ðes/ *f*, fluidity

**flúido** /'fluiðo/ *a* fluid; fluent. *m*, fluid; *Elec.* current

**fluir** /flu'ir/ *vi irr* to flow. See **huir**

**flujo** /'fluho/ *m*, flow, flux; rising tide. **f. de sangre,** hemorrhage

**fluorescencia** /fluores'θenθia; fluores'sensia/ *f*, fluorescence

**fluorescente** /fluores'θente; fluores'sente/ *a* fluorescent

**fluvial** /flu'βial/ *a* fluvial

**flux** /fluks/ *m*, flush (in cards)

**foca** /'foka/ *f*, *Zool.* seal

**focal** /fo'kal/ *a* focal

**foco** /'foko/ *m*, focus; center; origin; source; *Theat.* spotlight; core (of an abscess)

**fofo** /'fofo/ *a* spongy, soft; flabby

**fogata** /fo'gata/ *f*, bonfire

**fogón** /fo'gon/ *m*, fire, cooking area, kitchen range, kitchen stove; furnace of a steamboiler; vent of a firearm

**fogonazo** /fogo'naθo; fogo'naso/ *m*, powder flash

**fogonero** /fogo'nero/ *m*, stoker

**fogosidad** /fogosi'ðað/ *f*, enthusiasm; vehemence; ardor

**fogoso** /fo'goso/ *a* ardent; vehement; enthusiastic

**folclórico** /fol'kloriko/ *a* pertaining to folklore

**folclorista** /folklo'rista/ *mf* folklorist

**foliar** /fo'liar/ *vt* to number the pages of a book

**folículo** /fo'likulo/ *m*, follicle

**folio** /'folio/ *m*, leaf of a book or manuscript, folio. **en f.,** in folio

**follaje** /fo'ʎahe; fo'yahe/ *m*, foliage; leafy ornamentation; crude, unnecessary decoration; verbosity

**folletín** /foʎe'tin; foye'tin/ *m*, feuilleton, literary article; serial story; *Inf.* dime novel, potboiler

**folletinista** /foʎeti'nista; foyeti'nista/ *mf* pamphleteer

**folleto** /fo'ʎeto; fo'yeto/ *m*, pamphlet, leaflet

**follón** /fo'ʎon; fo'yon/ *a* lazy; caddish; craven

**fomentación** /fomenta'θion; fomenta'sion/ *f*, *Med.* fomentation, poultice

**fomentador** /fomenta'ðor/ *a* fomenting. *m*, fomenter

**fomentar** /fomen'tar/ *vt* to warm, foment; incite, instigate; *Med.* apply poultices

**fomento** /fo'mento/ *m*, heat, shelter; fuel; protection, encouragement; *Med.* fomentation

**fonda** /'fonda/ *f*, inn; restaurant

**fondeadero** /fondea'ðero/ *m*, anchorage, anchoring ground

**fondear** /fonde'ar/ *vt Naut.* to sound; search a ship; examine carefully; —*vi Naut.* anchor

**fondillos** /fon'diʎos; fon'diyos/ *m pl*, seat (of the trousers)

**fondista** /fon'dista/ *mf* owner of an inn or restaurant

**fondo** /'fondo/ *m*, bottom (of a well, etc.); bed (of the sea, etc.); depth; rear, portion at the back; ground (of fabrics); background; *Com.* capital; *Com.* stock; *Fig.* fund (of humor, etc.); character, nature; temperament; *Fig.* substance, core, essence; *Naut.*

bottom; *pl Com.* resources, funds. **f. de amortización,** sinking fund. **f. doble** *or* **f. secreto,** false bottom. **f. muerto, f. perdido** *or* **f. vitalicio,** life annuity. *Com.* **fondos inactivos,** idle capital. **a fondo,** completely, thoroughly. **artículo de f.,** editorial, lead article. *Sports.* **carrera de f.,** long-distance race. *Naut.* **irse a f.,** to sink, founder

**fonética** /fo'netika/ *f,* phonetics

**fonético** /fo'netiko/ *a* phonetic

**fonetista** /fone'tista/ *mf* phonetician

**fonógrafo** /fo'nografo/ *m,* phonograph

**fonología** /fonolo'hia/ *f,* phonology

**fonológico** /fono'lohiko/ *a* phonological

**fontanar** /fonta'nar/ *m,* spring, stream

**fontanería** /fontane'ria/ *f,* pipe laying, plumbing

**fontanero** /fonta'nero/ *m,* pipe layer; plumber

**forajido** /fora'hiðo/ **(-da)** *a* fugitive, outlawed —*n* robber, fugitive

**forastero** /foras'tero/ **(-ra)** *a* strange, foreign; alien, exotic —*n* stranger

**forcejear** /forθehe'ar/ forsehe'ar/ *vi* to struggle; try, strive; oppose, contradict

**forcejo** /for'θeho/ for'seho/ *m,* struggle; endeavor; opposition, hostility

**fórceps** /'forθeps/ 'forseps/ *m pl,* forceps

**forense** /fo'rense/ *a* forensic

**forestal** /fores'tal/ *a* forestal

**forillo** /fo'riʎo/ fo'riyo/ *m, Theat.* backdrop

**forja** /'forha/ *f,* forge

**forjador** /forha'ðor/ *m,* smith, ironworker

**forjar** /for'har/ *vt* to forge; fabricate; create; counterfeit

**forma** /'forma/ *f,* shape, form; arrangement; method; style; manifestation, expression; formula, formulary; ceremonial; *Print.* form; manner; means, way; mold, matrix; style of handwriting. *Law.* **en debida f.,** in due form

**formación** /forma'θion/ forma''sion/ *f,* formation; form, contour, shape; (*Mil. Geol.*) formation. **f. del censo,** census taking

**formador** /forma'ðor/ *a* forming, shaping

**formal** /for'mal/ *a* apparent, formal; serious, punctilious, steady; truthful, reliable; sedate; orderly, regular, methodical

**formaldehído** /formalde'iðo/ *m,* formaldehyde

**formalidad** /formali'ðað/ *f,* orderliness, propriety; formality; requirement, requisite; ceremony; seriousness, sedateness; punctiliousness

**formalismo** /forma'lismo/ *m,* formalism; bureaucracy, red tape

**formalizar** /formali'θar/ formali'sar/ *vt* to put into final form; legalize; formulate, enunciate; —*vr* take seriously (a joke)

**formar** /for'mar/ *vt* to shape; form; educate, mold; *Mil.* form. **formarle causa a uno,** to bring charges against someone —*vr* develop, grow

**formativo** /forma'tiβo/ *a* formative

**formato** /for'mato/ *m, Print.* format; *Chem.* formate

**formidable** /formi'ðaβle/ *a* formidable, awe-inspiring; huge, enormous

**fórmula** /'formula/ *f,* formula; prescription; mode of expression. (*Math. Chem.*) **f. clásica,** standard formula

**formular** /formu'lar/ *vt* to formulate; prescribe

**formulario** /formu'lario/ *m, Law.* formulary; handbook

**formulismo** /formu'lismo/ *m,* formulism; bureaucracy, red tape

**fornicación** /fornika'θion; fornika'sion/ *f,* fornication

**fornicador** /fornika'ðor/ **(-ra)** *a* and *n* fornicator

**fornicar** /forni'kar/ *vi* to fornicate

**fornido** /for'niðo/ *a* stalwart, muscular, strong

**foro** /'foro/ *m,* forum; law courts; law, bar, legal profession; *Theat.* back scenery; leasehold

**forraje** /fo'rrahe/ *m,* forage, fodder; foraging

**forrajeador** /forrahea'ðor/ *m,* forager

**forrajear** /forrahe'ar/ *vt* to gather forage, go foraging

**forrar** /fo'rrar/ *vt Sew.* to line; cover, encase, make a cover for

**forro** /'forro/ *m,* lining, inner covering; cover (of a book)

**fortalecedor** /fortaleθe'ðor; fortalese'ðor/ *a* fortifying

**fortalecer** /fortale'θer; fortale'ser/ *vt irr* to fortify. See **conocer**

**fortaleza** /forta'leθa; forta'lesa/ *f,* vigor; fortitude; fortress; natural defense. *Aer.* **f. volante,** flying fortress

**fortificable** /fortifi'kaβle/ *a* fortifiable

**fortificación** /fortifika'θion; fortifika'sion/ *f,* fortification

**fortificador** /fortifika'ðor/ *a* fortifying

**fortificar** /fortifi'kar/ *vt* to fortify

**fortísimo** /for'tisimo/ *a superl* **fuerte** extremely strong

**fortuito** /for'tuito/ *a* fortuitous, chance

**fortuna** /for'tuna/ *f,* fate, destiny; fortune, capital, estate; tempest. **por f.,** fortunately. **probar f.,** to try one's luck

**forzado** /for'θaðo; for'saðo/ *a* forced, obliged. *m,* convict condemned to the galleys

**forzador** /forθa'ðor; forsa'ðor/ *m,* violator, seducer

**forzar** /for'θar; for'sar/ *vt irr* to force, break open; take by force; rape, ravish; oblige, compel —*Pres. Indic.* **fuerzo, fuerzas, fuerza, fuerzan.** *Preterite* **forcé, forzaste,** etc —*Pres. Subjunc.* **fuerce, fuerces, fuerce, forcemos, forcéis, fuercen**

**forzoso** /for'θoso; for'soso/ *a* obligatory, unavoidable, necessary

**forzudo** /for'θuðo; for'suðo/ *a* brawny, stalwart

**fosa** /'fosa/ *f,* grave; socket (of a joint). **f. común,** potter's field.

**fosar** /fo'sar/ *vt* to undermine; dig a trench around

**fosfato** /fos'fato/ *m,* phosphate

**fosforecer** /fosfore'θer; fosfore'ser/ *vi irr* to phosphoresce. See **conocer**

**fosforera** /fosfo'rera/ *f,* matchbox

**fosforero** /fosfo'rero/ **(-ra)** *n* match seller

**fosforescencia** /fosfores'θenθia; fosfores'sensia/ *f,* phosphorescence

**fosforescente** /fosfores'θente; fosfores'sente/ *a* phosphorescent

**fósforo** /'fosforo/ *m,* phosphorus; match; morning star

**fósil** /'fosil/ *a* and *m,* fossil; *Inf.* antique

**fosilizarse** /fosili'θarse; fosili'sarse/ *vr* to become fossilized

**foso** /'foso/ *m,* hole, hollow, pit; trench; pit (in garages); *Theat.* room under the stage.

**foto** /'foto/ *f,* snapshot, photo

**fotocopia** /foto'kopia/ *f,* photocopy

**fotogénico** /foto'heniko/ *a* photogenic

**fotograbado** /fotogra'βaðo/ *m,* photogravure

**fotografía** /fotogra'fia/ *f,* photography; photograph

**fotografiar** /fotogra'fiar/ *vt* to photograph

**fotográfico** /foto'grafiko/ *a* photographic

**fotógrafo** /fo'tografo/ *m,* photographer

**fotograma** /foto'grama/ *m,* (cinema) shot

**fotoquímica** /foto'kimika/ *f,* photochemistry

**fotostato** /foto'stato/ *m,* photostat

**frac** /frak/ *m,* tail coat

**fracasar** /fraka'sar/ *vi* to break, crumble, be shattered; collapse (of plans, etc.); fail; be disappointed

**fracaso** /fra'kaso/ *m,* shattering; collapse (of plans, etc.); disaster; failure, disappointment, downfall

**fracción** /frak'θion; frak'sion/ *f,* division into parts; fraction. **f. impropia,** *Math.* improper fraction

**fractura** /frak'tura/ *f,* fracture. **f. conminuta,** compound fracture

**fracturar** /fraktu'rar/ *vt* to fracture

**fragancia** /fra'ganθia; fra'gansia/ *f,* fragrance, perfume; renown, good name

**fragante** /fra'gante/ *a* fragrant; perfumed; flagrant

**fragata** /fra'gata/ *f,* frigate

**frágil** /'frahil/ *a* fragile, brittle; perishable, frail; weak, sinful

**fragilidad** /frahili'ðað/ *f,* fragility; frailty; sinfulness

**fragmentario** /fragmen'tario/ *a* fragmentary

**fragmento** /frag'mento/ *m,* fragment

**fragor** /fra'gor/ *m,* noise, crash

**fragosidad** /fragosi'ðað/ *f,* roughness, rockiness, unevenness

**fragoso** /fra'goso/ *a* craggy, rocky; rough; noisy, clamorous

**fragua** /'fragua/ *f*, forge

**fraguado** /fra'guaðo/ *m*, forging; *Mas.* setting

**fraguar** /fra'guar/ *vt* to forge, work; plot, scheme; —*vi* set (concrete, etc.)

**fraile** /'fraile/ *m*, friar, monk. *Inf.* **f. de misa y olla,** ignorant friar

**frailesco** /frai'lesko/ *a Inf.* pertaining to friars, friar-like

**frambuesa** /fram'buesa/ *f*, raspberry

**francachela** /franka'tʃela/ *f*, *Inf.* binge

**francés** /fran'θes; fran'ses/ **(-esa)** *a* French —*n* Frenchman (-woman). *m*, French (language). **a la francesa,** in French fashion

**francesilla** /franθe'siʎa; franse'siya/ *f*, *Cul.* French roll

**Francia** /'franθia; 'fransia/ France

**franciscano** /franθis'kano; fransis'kano/ **(-na)** *a* and *n* Franciscan

**francmasón** /frankma'son/ **(-ona)** *n* Freemason

**francmasonería** /frankmasone'ria/ *f*, freemasonry

**franco** /'franko/ *a* generous, liberal; exempt; sincere, genuine, frank; duty-free; Frank; Franco (in compound words). *m*, franc (coin). **f. de porte,** post-free; prepaid

**Franco-Condado** /'franko-kon'daðo/ Franche-Comté

**francotirador** /frankotira'ðor/ *m*, sharpshooter, franc tireur

**franela** /fra'nela/ *f*, flannel

**frangir** /fran'hir/ *vt* to divide, quarter

**frangollar** /frango'ʎar; frango'yar/ *vt* to scamp, skimp (work); botch, bungle

**franja** /'franha/ *f*, fringe; border, trimming; stripe. *Radio.* **f. undosa,** wave band

**franjar** /fran'har/ *vt Sew.* to fringe, trim

**franqueadora** /frankea'ðora/ *f*, postage meter

**franquear** /franke'ar/ *vt* to exempt; make free, make a gift of; clear the way; stamp, prepay; free (slaves); —*vr* fall in easily with others' plans; make confidences

**franqueo** /fran'keo/ *m*, exemption; bestowal, making free; postage, stamping; enfranchisement (of slaves)

**franqueza** /fran'keθa; fran'kesa/ *f*, exemption, freedom; generosity, liberality; sincerity, frankness

**franquicia** /fran'kiθia; fran'kisia/ *f*, exemption from excise duties

**franquista** /fran'kista/ *mf* Franquist, supporter of Franco

**frasco** /'frasko/ *m*, bottle, flask; powder flask or horn. **f. cuentagotas,** drop bottle

**frase** /'frase/ *f*, sentence; phrase; epigram; idiom, style. **f. hecha,** cliché

**frasear** /frase'ar/ *vt* to phrase

**fraseología** /fraseolo'hia/ *f*, phraseology; wording

**fratás** /fra'tas/ *m*, plastering trowel

**fraternal** /frater'nal/ *a* brotherly

**fraternidad** /fraterni'ðað/ *f*, fraternity, brotherhood

**fraternizar** /fraterni'θar; fraterni'sar/ *vi* to fraternize

**fraterno** /fra'terno/ *a* fraternal

**fratricida** /fratri'θiða; fratri'siða/ *a* fratricidal. *mf* fratricide

**fratricidio** /fratri'θiðio; fratri'siðio/ *m*, fratricide (act)

**fraude** /'frauðe/ *m*, fraud, deception

**fraudulento** /frauðu'lento/ *a* fraudulent

**fray** /frai/ *m*, *Abbr.* **fraile.** Always followed by a proper name (e.g. *F. Bartolomé*, Friar Bartholomew)

**frazada** /fra'θaða; fra'saða/ *f*, blanket

**frecuencia** /fre'kuenθia; fre'kuensia/ *f*, frequency. **f. radioeléctrica,** radiofrequency

**frecuentación** /frekuenta'θion; frekuenta'sion/ *f*, frequenting, visiting

**frecuentador** /frekuenta'ðor/ **(-ra)** *n* frequenter

**frecuentar** /frekuen'tar/ *vt* to frequent

**frecuente** /fre'kuente/ *a* frequent

**fregadero** /frega'ðero/ *m*, kitchen sink

**fregado** /fre'gaðo/ *m*, scrubbing; rubbing; scouring; washing; *Inf.* murky business

**fregador** /frega'ðor/ *m*, kitchen sink; scrub brush; dishcloth. **f. mecánico de platos,** dishwasher

**fregar** /fre'gar/ *vt irr* to rub; scour; wash (dishes). See **cegar**

**fregona** /fre'gona/ *f*, kitchen maid

**fregotear** /fregote'ar/ *vt Inf.* to clean or scour inefficiently

**freiduría** /freiðu'ria/ *f*, fried-fish shop

**freír** /fre'ir/ *vt irr Cul.* to fry. See **reír**

**fréjol** /'frehol/ *m*, kidney bean

**frenar** /fre'nar/ *vt* to restrain, hold back; bridle, check; *Mech.* brake

**frenesí** /frene'si/ *m*, madness, frenzy; vehemence, exaltation

**frenético** /fre'netiko/ *a* mad, frenzied; vehement, exalted

**freno** /'freno/ *m*, bridle; *Mech.* brake; restraint, check. **f. de pedal,** foot brake. **f. neumático,** vacuum brake, pneumatic brake

**frente** /'frente/ *f*, brow, forehead; front portion; countenance; head; heading; beginning (of a letter, etc.). *m*, *Mil.* front. *mf* facade; front; obverse (of coins) —*adv* in front, opposite. **f. a f.,** face to face. **con la f. levantada,** with head held high; proudly; insolently. **de f.,** abreast

**freo** /'freo/ *m*, strait, narrow channel

**fresa** /'fresa/ *f*, strawberry plant and fruit (especially small or wild varieties); *Mech.* milling cutter, miller

**fresadora** /fresa'ðora/ *f*, milling machine

**fresal** /fre'sal/ *m*, strawberry bed

**fresca** /'freska/ *f*, cool air; fresh air; *Inf.* home truth

**fresco** /'fresko/ *a* cool; fresh, new; recent; buxom, fresh-colored; calm, serene; *Inf.* impudent, shameless, bold; thin (cloths). *m*, coolness; fresh air; *Art.* fresco. **al f.,** in the open air. **hacer f.,** to be cool or fresh

**frescote** /fres'kote/ *a Inf.* ruddy and corpulent

**frescura** /fres'kura/ *f*, coolness; freshness; pleasant verdure and fertility; *Inf.* cheek, nerve; piece of insolence; unconcern, indifference; calmness, serenity

**fresero** /fre'sero/ **(-ra)** *n* strawberry seller

**fresneda** /fres'neða/ *f*, ash grove

**fresno** /'fresno/ *m*, *Bot.* ash

**fresón** /fre'son/ *m*, strawberry (large, cultivated varieties)

**fresquera** /fres'kera/ *f*, meat locker; cool place

**fresquista** /fres'kista/ *mf* fresco painter

**friable** /'friaβle/ *a* brittle; friable, powdery

**frialdad** /frial'dað/ *f*, coldness, chilliness; *Med.* frigidity; indifference, lack of interest; foolishness; negligence

**fríamente** /fria'mente/ *adv* coldly; coolly, with indifference; dully, flatly

**fricción** /frik'θion; frik'sion/ *f*, friction

**friccionar** /frikθio'nar; friksio'nar/ *vt* to rub; give a massage

**friega** /'friega/ *f*, friction, massage

**frigidez** /frihi'ðeθ; frihi'ðes/ *f*, See **frialdad**

**frígido** /'frihiðo/ *a* frigid

**frigio** /'frihio/ *a* and *n* Phrygian

**frigorífico** /frigo'rifiko/ *a* refrigerative. *m*, refrigerator, cold-storage locker

**frío** /'frio/ *a* cold; *Med.* frigid; indifferent, uninterested; dull, uninteresting; inefficient. *m*, coldness, chill; cold

**friolera** /frio'lera/ *f*, bagatelle, trifle, mere nothing

**friolero** /frio'lero/ *a* sensitive to cold

**frisa** /'frisa/ *f*, frieze cloth

**frisar** /fri'sar/ *vt* to frizz, curl (cloth); scrub, rub; —*vi* approach, be nearly (e.g. *Frisa en los setenta años,* He's nearly seventy)

**Frisia** /'frisia/ Friesland

**friso** /'friso/ *m*, frieze; dado, border

**frisón** /fri'son/ **(-ona)** *a* and *n* Frisian

**fritada** /fri'taða/ *f*, *Cul.* fry, fried food

**frito** /'frito/ *a* fried

**fritura** /fri'tura/ *f*, frying; fried food

**frivolidad** /friβoli'ðað/ *f*, frivolity

**frivolité** /friβoli'te/ *m*, *Sew.* tatting

**frívolo** /'friβolo/ *a* frivolous, superficial; futile, unconvincing

**fronda** /'fronda/ *f*, *Bot.* leaf; frond (of ferns); *pl* foliage

**frondosidad** /frondosi'ðað/ *f*, luxuriance of foliage

**frondoso** /fron'doso/ *a* leafy

**frontera** /fron'tera/ *f,* frontier; facade

**fronterizo** /fronte'riθo; fronte'riso/ *a* frontier; facing, opposite

**frontero** /fron'tero/ *a* facing, opposite. *m,* (*Obs. Mil.*) frontier commander

**frontispicio** /frontis'piθio; frontis'pisio/ *m,* frontispiece; facade; *Fig. Inf.* face, dial

**frontón** /fron'ton/ *m,* pelota court; jai alai court; *Archit.* pediment

**frotamiento, frote** /frota'miento, 'frote/ *m,* rubbing, friction

**frotar** /fro'tar/ *vt* to rub

**frotis** /'frotis/ *m, Med.* smear

**fructífero** /fruk'tifero/ *a* fruitful, fructiferous

**fructuoso** /fruk'tuoso/ *a* fruitful, fertile; useful

**frufrú** /fru'fru/ *m,* rustle (of silk, etc.)

**frugal** /fru'gal/ *a* frugal; saving, economical

**frugalidad** /frugali'ðað/ *f,* frugality, abstemiousness, moderation

**fruición** /frui'θion; frui'sion/ *f,* enjoyment; fruition; satisfaction

**fruir** /fru'ir/ *vi irr* to enjoy what one has long desired. See **huir**

**frunce** /'frunθe; 'frunse/ *m, Sew.* shirring; gather; ruffling; tuck; pucker; wrinkle

**fruncimiento** /frunθi'miento; frunsi'miento/ *m,* wrinkling; puckering; *Sew.* shirring

**fruncir** /frun'θir; frun'sir/ *vt* to frown; purse (the lips); pucker; *Sew.* shirr, pleat, gather; reduce in size; conceal the truth; —*vr* pretend to be prudish. **f. el ceño,** to knit one's brow, scowl

**fruslería** /frusle'ria/ *f,* trifle, nothing

**frustración** /frustra'θion; frustra'sion/ *f,* frustration

**frustrar** /frus'trar/ *vt* to disappoint; frustrate, thwart

**fruta** /'fruta/ *f,* fruit; *Inf.* consequence, result. **f. de hueso,** stone fruit. *Cul.* **f. de sartén,** fritter

**frutal** /fru'tal/ *a* fruit-bearing. *m,* fruit tree

**frutar** /fru'tar/ *vi* to bear fruit

**frutería** /frute'ria/ *f,* fruit

**frutero** /fru'tero/ **(-ra)** *a* fruit —*n* fruit seller. *m,* fruit dish; *Art.* painting of fruit; basket of imitation fruit .

**frútice** /'frutiθe; frutise/ *m,* bush, shrub

**fruticultura** /frutikul'tura/ *f,* fruit farming

**fruto** /'fruto/ *m,* fruit; product, result; profit, proceeds; *Agr.* grain

**fu** /fu/ spitting (of cats) —*interj* expression of scorn. *Inf.* **ni f. ni fa,** neither one thing nor the other

**fucilazo** /fuθi'laθo; fusi'laso/ *m,* heat lightning

**fucsia** /'fuksia/ *f,* fuchsia

**fuego** /'fuego/ *m,* fire; conflagration; firing (of firearms); beacon; hearth, home; rash; ardor; heat (of an argument, etc.); —*interj* ¡F.! *Mil.* Fire! **fuegos artificiales,** fireworks. **a sangre y f.,** by fire and sword. *Mil.* **hacer f.,** to fire (a weapon). **pegar f.,** to set on fire

**fuelle** /'fueʎe; 'fueye/ *m,* bellows; bag (of a bagpipe); *Sew.* pucker, wrinkle; hood (of a carriage, etc.); wind cloud; *Inf.* talebearer. **f. de pie,** foot pump

**fuente** /'fuente/ *f,* stream, spring; fountain; meat dish; genesis, origin; source, headwaters; tap

**fuera** /'fuera/ *adv* outside, out —*interj* get out! **f. de,** besides, in addition to. **f. de alcance,** out of reach. **f. de sí,** beside oneself (with rage, etc.). **de f.,** from the outside. **por f.,** on the outside, externally

**fuero** /'fuero/ *m,* municipal charter; jurisdiction; compilation of laws; legal right or privilege; *pl Inf.* arrogance. **los fueros de León,** the laws of León

**fuerte** /'fuerte/ *a* strong, resistant; robust; spirited, vigorous; hard (of diamonds, etc.); rough, uneven; impregnable; terrible, tremendous; overweight (of coins); active; efficacious, effective; expert, knowledgeable; *Gram.* strong; intense; loud; tough. *m,* fort; talent, strong point; *Mus.* forte —*adv* strongly; excessively. **tener genio f.,** to be quick-tempered

**fuerza** /'fuerθa; 'fuersa/ *f,* strength; power, might; force; efficacy; fortress; *Sew.* stiffening; *Mech.* power; violence; toughness, durability, solidity; potency; authority; courage; vigor; *pl Fig. Inf.* livewires, influential people. **a f. de,** by means of, by dint of. **a la f.,** forcibly. **en f. de,** because of, on account of. **por f. mayor,** by main force. **ser f.,** to be necessary

**fuga** /'fuga/ *f,* flight, escape, running away; leak (gas, etc.); elopement; *Mus.* fugue; ardor, strength. **f. de cerebros,** brain drain

**fugarse** /fu'garse/ *vr* to run away; elope; escape

**fugaz** /fu'gaθ; fu'gas/ *a* fugitive; fleeting, brief

**fugitivo** /fuhi'tiβo/ **(-va)** *a* fugitive; runaway, escaping; transient —*n* fugitive

**fulano** /fu'lano/ **(-na)** *n* so-and-so, such a person **f., zutano, y mengano,** *Inf.* Tom, Dick, and Harry

**fulcro** /'fulkro/ *m,* fulcrum

**fulgente, fúlgido** /ful'hente, 'fulhiðo/ *a* brilliant, shining

**fulgor** /ful'gor/ *m,* brilliance, brightness

**fulgurar** /fulgu'rar/ *vi* to shine, be resplendent, scintillate; flare

**fulguroso** /fulgu'roso/ *a* shining, sparkling

**fúlica** /'fulika/ *f, Ornith.* coot

**fullería** /fuʎe'ria; fuye'ria/ *f,* cheating at play; craftiness, low guile

**fullero** /fu'ʎero; fu'yero/ **(-ra)** *a* cheating; crafty, astute —*n* cheat, cardsharper

**fulminante** /fulmi'nante/ *a Med.* fulminant; fulminating; thundering. *m,* percussion cap

**fulminar** /fulmi'nar/ *vt* to fulminate (all meanings)

**fulminato** /fulmi'nato/ *m, Chem.* fulminate

**fulmíneo, fulminoso** /ful'mineo, fulmi'noso/ *a* fulminous, pertaining to lightning

**fumadero** /fuma'ðero/ *m,* smoking room

**fumador** /fuma'ðor/ **(-ra)** *a* smoking —*n* smoker. **«No fumadores»,** "Nonsmoking" (area)

**fumar** /fu'mar/ *vi* to smoke; —*vr Inf.* dissipate, waste

**fumarola** /fuma'rola/ *f,* fumarole

**fumigación** /fumiga'θion; fumiga'sion/ *f,* fumigation

**fumigador** /fumiga'ðor/ **(-ra)** *n* fumigator

**fumigar** /fumi'gar/ *vt* to fumigate

**fumigatorio** /fumiga'torio/ *a* fumigatory. *m,* perfume burner

**fumista** /fu'mista/ *m,* stove maker or seller

**fumistería** /fumiste'ria/ *f,* stove factory or store

**funámbulo** /fu'nambulo/ *f,* tightrope walker, acrobat

**función** /fun'θion; fun'sion/ *f,* function; working, operation; *Theat.* performance; activity, duty; ceremony; celebration; *Math.* function; *Mil.* battle

**funcional** /funθio'nal; funsio'nal/ *a* functional

**funcionamiento** /funθiona'miento; funsiona'miento/ *m,* functioning

**funcionar** /funθio'nar; funsio'nar/ *vi* to function, work. **«No funciona»,** "Out of order"

**funcionario** /funθio'nario; funsio'nario/ *m,* functionary, official; civil servant

**funda** /'funda/ *f,* case, cover, sheath; hold-all. **f. de almohada,** pillowcase

**fundación** /funda'θion; funda'sion/ *f,* foundation

**fundamente** /fundaða'mente/ *adv* with reason, on good evidence

**fundador** /funda'ðor/ **(-ra)** *n* founder, creator; originator

**fundamental** /funda'mental/ *a* fundamental

**fundamento** /funda'mento/ *m, Mas.* foundation; basis; basic principle, reason; origin, root

**fundar** /fun'dar/ *vt* to build, erect; base; found, institute; create, establish; —*vr* (*with en*) found, base upon. **f. una compañía,** *Com.* to float a company

**fundición** /fundi'θion; fundi'sion/ *f,* foundry; smelting, founding, casting; cast iron; *Print.* font

**fundido fotográfico** /fun'diðo foto'grafiko/ *m,* composite photograph

**fundidor** /fundi'ðor/ *m,* founder, smelter.

**fundir** /fun'dir/ *vt* to melt; found, smelt; cast (metals); —*vr* join together, unite; *Elec.* blow (fuses)

**fúnebre** /'funeβre/ *a* funeral; dismal, lugubrious, mournful

**funeral** /fune'ral/ *a* funeral

**funerala** /fune'rala/ **(a la)** *adv Mil.* with reversed arms

**funerales** /fune'rales/ *m pl,* funeral; *Eccl.* memorial masses

**funeraria** /fune'raria/ *f,* funeral home, undertaker

**funerario** /fune'rario/ *a* funeral

**funéreo** /fu'nereo/ *a* funereal, mournful

**funesto** /fu'nesto/ *a* unlucky, unfortunate; mournful, melancholy, sad

**fungoso** /fuŋ'goso/ *a* spongy, fungous

**funicular** /funiku'lar/ *a* funicular

**furgón** /fur'gon/ *m,* wagon; van; guard's van, baggage car, luggage cart. **f. postal,** mail truck

**furia** /'furia/ *f, Myth.* fury; rage, wrath; fit of madness; raging, violence (of the elements); speed, haste

**furibundo** /furi'βundo/ *a* frantic, furious; raging

**fúrico** /'furiko/ *a* stark raving mad

**furioso** /fu'rioso/ *a* furious, enraged; mad, insane; violent, terrible; enormous, excessive

**furor** /fu'ror/ *m,* fury, rage; poetic frenzy; violence; furor

**furriel** /fu'rriel/ *m,* quartermaster

**furtivo** /fur'tiβo/ *a* furtive; covert, clandestine; pirate (editions)

**fusa** /'fusa/ *f,* demisemiquaver

**fusco** /'fusko/ *a* dark

**fuselado** /fuse'laðo/ *a* streamlined

**fuselaje** /fuse'lahe/ *m,* fuselage

**fusible** /fu'siβle/ *a* fusible. *m, Elec.* fuse; fuse wire

**fusil** /fu'sil/ *m,* rifle

**fusilamiento** /fusila'miento/ *m,* execution by shooting

**fusilar** /fusi'lar/ *vt* to execute by shooting; *Inf.* plagiarize

**fusilazo** /fusi'laθo; fusi'laso/ *m,* rifle shot

**fusión** /fu'sion/ *f,* melting, liquefying; fusion, blending; mixture, union; *Com.* merger, amalgamation

**fusionar** /fusio'nar/ *vt* to blend, fuse, merge; *—vr Com.* combine, form a merger

**fusta** /'fusta/ *f,* brushwood; whip

**fuste** /'fuste/ *m,* wood, timber; *Poet.* saddle; *Fig.* core, essence; importance, substance; shaft of a lance; *Archit.* shaft. **hombre de buen f.,** a man with a good (physical) constitution

**fustigar** /fusti'gar/ *vt* to whip, lash; rebuke harshly

**fútbol** /'futβol/ *m,* football; soccer

**futbolista** /futβo'lista/ *mf* football player; soccer player

**fútil** /'futil/ *a* futile, ineffectual, worthless

**futilidad** /futili'ðað/ *f,* futility, worthlessness

**futura** /fu'tura/ *f, Law.* reversion (of offices); *Inf.* fiancée

**futurismo** /futu'rismo/ *m,* futurism

**futurista** /futu'rista/ *mf* futurist

**futurístico** /futu'ristiko/ *a* futuristic

**futuro** /fu'turo/ **(-ra)** *a* future. *m,* future *—n Inf.* betrothed

# G

**gabacho** /ga'βatʃo/ **(-cha)** *a* and *n* (*Inf.* scornful) Frenchman

**gabán** /ga'βan/ *m*, overcoat; cloak

**gabardina** /gaβar'ðina/ *f*, gabardine; weatherproof coat

**gabarra** /ga'βarra/ *f*, *Naut.* lighter, gabbard, barge

**gabarro** /ga'βarro/ *m*, flaw (in cloth); knot (in stone); snag, drawback; slip, error (in accounts)

**gabela** /ga'βela/ *f*, duty, tax; imposition, burden

**gabinete** /gaβi'nete/ *m*, study, library; sitting room; den; *Polit.* cabinet; collection, museum, gallery; laboratory; boudoir; studio; display cabinet. **g. de lectura,** reading room

**gablete** /ga'βlete/ *m*, *Archit.* gable

**gaceta** /ga'θeta; ga'seta/ *f*, bulletin, review, record; newspaper; gazette (official Spanish government organ); *Inf.* newshound

**gacetero** /gaθe'tero; gase'tero/ **(-ra)** *n* newsdealer. *m*, news reporter

**gacetilla** /gaθe'tiʎa; gase'tiya/ *f*, news in brief, miscellany column, society news; gossip column; *Inf.* newshound

**gacetillero** /gaθeti'ʎero; gaseti'yero/ *m*, paragrapher, penny-a-liner; reporter

**gacha** /'gatʃa/ *f*, unglazed crock; *pl* pap; porridge

**gaché** /ga'tʃe/ *m*, (among the Romany) Andalusian; *Inf.* fellow

**gacho** /'gatʃo/ *a* drooping, bent downward; slouch (hat); (of ears) lop

**gachón** /ga'tʃon/ *a Inf.* attractive, charming

**gaditano** /gaði'tano/ **(-na)** *a* and *n* native of, or pertaining to, Cadiz

**gaélico** /ga'eliko/ *a* and *m*, Gaelic

**gafar** /ga'far/ *vt* to claw; seize with a hook; hook; mend with a bracket (pottery)

**gafas** /'gafas/ *f pl*, spectacles; goggles; spectacle earhooks; grapplehooks

**gafete** /ga'fete/ *m*, hook and eye; clasp

**gaita** /'gaita/ *f*, bagpipe; hand organ; kind of clarinet; *Inf.* neck. **g. gallega,** bagpipe

**gaitería** /gaite'ria/ *f*, crude, gaudy garment or ornament

**gaitero** /gai'tero/ *a Inf.* overmerry; loud, crude. *m*, piper

**gajes** /'gahes/ *m pl*, salary; emoluments; perquisites

**gajo** /'gaho/ *m*, branch, bough (gen. cut); little cluster (of grapes); bunch (of fruit); quarter (of oranges, etc.); prong (of forks, etc.)

**gala** /'gala/ *f*, evening or full dress; grace, wit; flower, cream, best; gala; *pl* finery; trappings; wedding presents. **de g.,** full dress. **hacer g. de,** to glory in, boast of

**galactita** /galak'tita/ *f*, fuller's earth

**galaico** /ga'laiko/ *a* See **gallego**

**galán** /ga'lan/ *m*, handsome, well-made man; lover, wooer, gallant; *Theat.* leading man or one of leading male roles

**galancete** /galan'θete; galan'sete/ *m*, handsome little man; *Theat.* male juvenile lead

**galano** /ga'lano/ *a* smart, well-dressed; agreeable, pleasing; beautiful; ornamented; *Fig.* elegant (speech, style, etc.)

**galante** /ga'lante/ *a* gallant, courtly, attentive; flirtatious (of women); licentious

**galanteador** /galantea'ðor/ *a* flirtatious. *m*, philanderer; wooer

**galantear** /galante'ar/ *vt* to court; flirt with; make love to; *Fig.* procure assiduously

**galanteo** /galan'teo/ *m*, courtship; flirtation; lovemaking; wooing

**galantería** /galante'ria/ *f*, courtesy; attention, compliment; elegance, grace; gallantry; generosity, liberality

**galanura** /gala'nura/ *f*, showiness, gorgeousness; elegance, grace; prettiness

**galápago** /ga'lapago/ *m*, freshwater tortoise; cleat

**galardón** /galar'ðon/ *m*, reward, recompense, prize

**galardonar** /galarðo'nar/ *vt* to reward, recompense

**gálata** /'galata/ *a* and *mf* Galatian

**galbana** /gal'βana/ *f*, *Inf.* laziness, inertia

**galbanoso** /galβa'noso/ *a Inf.* slothful

**galdrufa** /gal'drufa/ *f*, top, spinning top

**galeote** /gale'ote/ *m*, galley slave

**galera** /ga'lera/ *f*, van, wagon, cart; *Naut.* galley; prison for women; *Print.* galley. **echar a galeras,** to condemn to the galleys

**galerada** /gale'raða/ *f*, galley proof

**galería** /gale'ria/ *f*, gallery; corridor, passage; collection of paintings; *Mineral.* gallery, drift; *Theat.* gallery

**galerna** /ga'lerna/ *f*, tempestuous northwest wind (gen. on Spanish north coast)

**Gales** /'gales/ Wales

**galés** /ga'les/ **(-esa)** *a* Welsh —*n* Welshman. *m*, Welsh (language)

**galga** /'galga/ *f*, boulder, rolling stone; greyhound bitch

**galgo** /'galgo/ *m*, greyhound. **g. ruso,** borzoi

**Galia** /'galia/ Gaul

**gálibo** /'galiβo/ *m*, *Naut.* mold; elegance

**galicado** /gali'kaðo/ *a* gallicized

**galicismo** /gali'θismo; gali'sismo/ *m*, gallicism

**gálico** /'galiko/ *m*, syphilis —*a* gallic

**Galilea** /gali'lea/ Galilee

**galileo** /gali'leo/ **(-ea)** *a* and *n* Galilean

**galimatías** /galima'tias/ *m*, *Inf.* gibberish, nonsense

**gallardear** /gaʎarðe'ar; gayarðe'ar/ *vi* to behave with ease and grace

**gallardete** /gaʎar'ðete; gayar'ðete/ *m*, pennant; bunting

**gallardía** /gaʎar'ðia; gayar'ðia/ *f*, grace, dignity; spirit, dash; courage; liveliness

**gallardo** /ga'ʎarðo; ga'yarðo/ *a* handsome, upstanding; gallant; spirited; fine, noble; lively

**gallear** /gaʎe'ar; gaye'ar/ *vi Inf.* to put on airs; be a bully; shout, bawl (with anger, etc.); *Fig. Inf.* stand out

**gallego** /ga'ʎego; ga'yego/ **(-ga)** *a* and *n* Galician. *m*, Galician (language)

**galleta** /ga'ʎeta; ga'yeta/ *f*, biscuit; *Inf.* slap; anthracite, lump coal; small jar or vessel

**gallina** /ga'ʎina; ga'yina/ *f*, hen. *mf Inf.* coward. **g. ciega,** blindman's buff. *Inf.* **acostarse con las gallinas,** to go to bed early

**gallinaza** /gaʎi'naθa; gayi'nasa/ *f*, hen dung

**gallinero** /gaʎi'nero; gayi'nero/ **(-ra)** *n* poultry dealer. *m*, henhouse; brood of hens; *Theat.* gallery; babel, noisy place

**gallito** /ga'ʎito; ga'yito/ *m*, small cock; cock of the walk; bully

**gallo** /'gaʎo; ga'yo/ *m*, *Ornith.* cock; *Inf.* false note (in singing); *Inf.* boss, chief. **g. de viento,** weathercock. *Inf.* **alzar el g.,** to put on airs, boast. **Cada g. canta en su muladar,** Every man is boss in his own house. *Inf.* **Otro g. nos cantara,** Our lot (or fate) would have been very different

**gallofero** /gaʎo'fero; gayo'fero/ **(-ra)** *a* mendicant, vagabond —*n* beggar

**galocha** /ga'lotʃa/ *f*, patten, clog; cap with earflaps

**galón** /ga'lon/ *m*, galloon, braid; *Mil.* stripe; gallon (measure)

**galoneadura** /galonea'ðura/ *f*, braiding, trimming

**galonear** /galone'ar/ *vt* to trim with braid

**galop** /ga'lop/ *m*, galop; gallopade

**galopante** /galo'pante/ *a* galloping (of consumption, etc.)

**galopar** /galo'par/ *vi* to gallop; *Mech.* wobble

**galope** /ga'lope/ *m*, gallop. **a** or **de g.,** at the gallop; on the run, quickly. **andar a g. corto,** to canter

**galopillo** /galo'piʎo; galopiyo/ *m*, scullion

**galopín** /galo'pin/ *m*, ragamuffin, urchin; rogue, knave; *Inf.* clever rogue; *Naut.* cabin boy

**galvanización** /galβaniθa'θion; galβanisa'sion/ *f*, galvanization

**galvanizar** /galβani'θar; galβani'sar/ *vt Elec.* to galvanize; electroplate; *Fig.* shock into life

**gama** /'gama/ *f, Mus.* scale; gamut, range; doe

**gambito** /gam'bito/ *m,* gambit (in chess)

**gamella** /ga'meʎa; ga'meya/ *f,* trough (for washing, feeding animals, etc.)

**gamo** /'gamo/ *m,* buck (of the fallow deer)

**gamuza** /ga'muθa; ga'musa/ *f,* chamois; chamois leather

**gana** /'gana/ *f,* appetite; wish, desire. **de buena g.,** willingly. **de mala g.,** reluctantly. **tener g.** ( **de** ), to wish, desire, want. **no tener g.,** to have no appetite, not be hungry. **No me da la g.,** I don't want (to), I won't

**ganable** /ga'naβle/ *a* attainable; earnable

**ganadería** /ganaðe'ria/ *f,* livestock; strain (of cattle); cattle raising; stock farm; cattle dealing

**ganadero** /gana'ðero/ *m,* cattle raiser or dealer; herdsman

**ganado** /ga'naðo/ *m,* livestock, herd; flock; hive (of bees); *Inf.* mob. **g. mayor,** cattle, mules, horses. **g. menor,** sheep, goats, etc. **g. moreno,** hogs, swine. **g. vacuno,** cattle

**ganador** /gana'ðor/ **(-ra)** *a* winning —*n* winner

**ganancia** /ga'nanθia; ga'nansia/ *f,* winning; gain, profit

**ganancial, gananancioso** /ganan'θial, ganan'θioso; ganan'sial, ganan'sioso/ *a* gainful, profitable; lucrative

**ganapán** /gana'pan/ *m,* laborer; porter; *Inf.* boor

**ganar** /ga'nar/ *vt* to gain; win; conquer; arrive at; earn; surpass, beat; achieve; acquire; —*vi* prosper

**ganchero** /gan'tʃero/ *m,* lumberjack

**ganchillo** /gan'tʃiʎo; gan'tʃiyo/ *m,* crochet hook; crochet. **hacer g.,** to crochet

**gancho** /'gantʃo/ *m,* hook; stump (of a branch); shepherd's crook; crochet hook; *Inf.* trickster, pimp; *Inf.* scribble

**ganchoso** /gan'tʃoso/ *a* hooked; bent; curved

**gandujar** /gandu'har/ *vt Sew.* to pleat, tuck, shirr

**gandul** /gan'dul/ **(-la)** *a Inf.* lazy —*n* lazybones, loafer

**gandulería** /gandule'ria/ *f,* loafing, idleness

**ganga** /'ganga/ *f, Mineral.* gangue, matrix; bargain, cinch

**ganglio** /'ganglio/ *m,* ganglion

**gangoso** /gan'goso/ *a* nasal; with a twang (of speech)

**gangrena** /gan'grena/ *f,* gangrene

**gangrenarse** /gangre'narse/ *vr* to become gangrenous, mortify

**gangrenoso** /gangre'noso/ *a* gangrenous

**ganguear** /gangue'ar/ *vi* to speak nasally, or with a twang

**ganoso** /ga'noso/ *a* wishful, desirous, anxious

**gansada** /gan'saða/ *f, Inf.* impertinence, foolishness

**ganso** /'ganso/ **(-sa)** *n* goose, gander; slow-moving person; yokel, bumpkin

**Gante** /'gante/ Ghent

**ganzúa** /gan'θua; gan'sua/ *f,* skeleton key; *Inf.* picklock, burglar; *Inf.* pumper, inquisitive person

**gañán** /ga'ɲan/ *m,* farm worker; day laborer; brawny fellow

**gañido** /ga'ɲiðo/ *m,* yowl, yelp, howl

**gañir** /ga'ɲir/ *vi irr* to yowl, yelp, howl (of dogs, etc.); crow, croak; *Inf.* talk hoarsely. See **mullir**

**garabatear** /garaβate'ar/ *vi* to hook, catch with hooks; scribble; *Fig.* beat around the bush

**garabateo** /garaβa'teo/ *m,* hooking; scribbling

**garabato** /gara'βato/ *m,* hook; *Agr.* weed clearer; scrawl, scribble; *Inf.* charm, sex appeal; pothook; boat hook; *pl* gestures, movements (with the hands)

**garaje** /ga'rahe/ *m,* garage

**garambaina** /garam'baina/ *f,* tawdry finery gaudiness; *pl Inf.* grimaces of affectation; *Inf.* scribble, scrawl

**garante** /ga'rante/ *mf* guarantor; reference (person) —*a* responsible, guaranteeing

**garantía** /garan'tia/ *f,* guarantee; security; pledge; *Law.* warranty

**garantir** /garan'tir/ *vt* to guarantee; warrant, vouch for

**garapiñar** /garapi'ɲar/ *vt* to ice, freeze (drinks, syrups, etc.); *Cul.* candy, coat with sugar

**garapiñera** /garapi'ɲera/ *f,* ice-cream freezer

**garbanzo** /gar'βanθo; gar'βanso/ *m,* chickpea. **g. negro,** *Fig.* black sheep

**garbillar** /garβi'ʎar; garβi'yar/ *vt Agr.* to sift; *Mineral.* riddle

**garbo** /'garβo/ *m,* jaunty air; grace, elegance; frankness; generosity, liberality

**garboso** /gar'βoso/ *a* attractive; handsome, sprightly, gay; graceful; munificent

**garduña** /gar'ðuɲa/ *f,* weasel; marten

**garduño** /gar'ðuɲo/ **(-ña)** *n Inf.* sneak thief

**garete** /ga'rete/ **(ir** *or* **irse al)** *Naut.* to be adrift

**garfa** /'garfa/ *f,* claw (of a bird or animal)

**garfear** /garfe'ar/ *vi* to catch with a hook, hook

**garfio** /'garfio/ *m,* grappling iron, hook, drag hook, cramp; gaff

**gargajear** /gargahe'ar/ *vi* to expectorate

**gargajo** /gar'gaho/ *m,* phlegm

**garganta** /gar'ganta/ *f,* throat; gullet; instep; defile; neck, shaft, narrowest part

**gargantear** /gargante'ar/ *vi* to warble, trill

**gárgara** /'gargara/ *f,* gargling (gen. *pl*). **hacer gárgaras,** to gargle

**gargarismo** /garga'rismo/ *m,* gargling; gargle

**gárgol** /'gargol/ *a* rotten (eggs). *m,* groove, mortise

**gárgola** /'gargola/ *f, Archit.* gargoyle; linseed

**garguero** /gar'gero/ *m,* windpipe; esophagus

**garita** /ga'rita/ *f,* sentry box; porter's lodge; hut; cabin. **g. de señales,** (railroad) signal box

**garitero** /gari'tero/ *m,* gambling house keeper; gambler

**garito** /ga'rito/ *m,* gambling house; profits of a gambling house

**garra** /'garra/ *f,* paw with claws; talon; hand; *Mech.* clamp, claw. *Fig.* **caer en las garras de,** to fall into the clutches (of)

**garrafa** /ga'rrafa/ *f,* decanter, carafe; carboy

**garrapata** /garra'pata/ *f, Ent.* tick

**garrapatear** /garrapate'ar/ *vi* to scribble

**garrapato** /garra'pato/ *m,* scribble, scrawl

**garrido** /ga'rriðo/ *a* handsome; gallant; elegant; graceful

**garroba** /ga'rroβa/ *f,* carob bean

**garrocha** /ga'rrotʃa/ *f,* goad. **salto a la g.,** pole jumping

**garrotazo** /garro'taθo; garro'taso/ *m,* blow with a truncheon or cudgel. **dar garrotazos de ciego,** to lay about one

**garrote** /ga'rrote/ *m,* truncheon, club; *Med.* tourniquet; garrote. **dar g.** (a), to strangle

**garrotillo** /garro'tiʎo; garro'tiyo/ *m,* croup

**garrucha** /ga'rrutʃa/ *f,* pulley; *Mech.* gin block

**garrulidad** /garruli'ðað/ *f,* garrulity, loquaciousness

**gárrulo** /'garrulo/ *a* twittering, chirping (birds); garrulous; murmuring, babbling (wind, water, etc.)

**garza** /'garθa; 'garsa/ *f,* heron

**garzo** /'garθo; 'garso/ *a* blue (gen. of eyes)

**gas** /gas/ *m,* gas; fumes. **g. asfixiante,** poison gas. **cámara de g.,** gasbag, gas chamber

**gasa** /'gasa/ *f,* gauze. **tira de g.,** black mourning band

**gascón** /gas'kon/ **(-ona)** *a* and *n* Gascon

**gasconada** /gasko'naða/ *f,* bravado, gasconade

**gaseosa** /gase'osa/ *f,* aerated water

**gaseoso** /gase'oso/ *a* gaseous

**gasista** /ga'sista/ *mf* gas fitter; gasman

**gasolina** /gaso'lina/ *f,* gasoline, petrol

**gasómetro** /ga'sometro/ *m,* gas meter; gasometer

**gastado** /gas'taðo/ *a* worn; worn-out; exhausted

**gastador** /gasta'ðor/ **(-ra)** *a* extravagant, wasteful —*n* spendthrift. *m, Mil.* sapper; convict condemned to hard labor

**gastar** /gas'tar/ *vt* to spend (money); wear out; exhaust; ruin, destroy; display or have habitually; possess, use, wear; —*vr* wear out; run down (of a battery)

**gasto** /'gasto/ *m,* spending; expenditure; consumption (of gas, etc.); expense, cost, charge; wear (and tear). **g. suplementario,** extra charge

**gástrico** /'gastriko/ *a* gastric

**gastritis** /gas'tritis/ *f*, gastritis

**gastronomía** /gastrono'mia/ *f*, gastronomy

**gastronómico** /gastro'nomiko/ *a* gastronomic

**gastrónomo** /gas'tronomo/ **(-ma)** *n* gastronome

**gata** /'gata/ *f*, she-cat; vinegar of mist; *Inf.* Madrilenian woman. **a gatas,** on all fours

**gatada** /ga'taða/ *f*, *Inf.* sly trick

**gatear** /gate'ar/ *vi* to climb like a cat; *Inf.* crawl on all fours; —*vt Inf.* scratch (of a cat); steal, pinch

**gatera** /ga'tera/ *f*, cat hole (in a door, etc.)

**gatillo** /ga'tiʎo; ga'tiyo/ *m*, dim small cat; dental forceps; trigger (of gun); *Inf.* juvenile petty thief

**gato** /'gato/ *m*, cat; tomcat; moneybag or its contents; *Mech.* jack; mousetrap; *Inf.* cat burglar, sneak thief; *Inf.* Madrilenian; clamp. **g. atigrado,** tiger cat. **g. de algalia,** civet cat. **g. de Angora,** Persian cat. **g. montés,** wildcat. **g. romano,** tabby cat. **dar g. por liebre,** to serve cat for hare, to deceive; misrepresent. *Inf.* **Hay g. encerrado,** There's more to this than meets the eye

**gatuno** /ga'tuno/ *a* feline

**gaucho** /'gautʃo/ **(-cha)** *n* gaucho; cowboy, rider

**gaveta** /ga'βeta/ *f*, drawer (of a desk)

**gavia** /'gaβia/ *f*, main topsail; *pl* topsails; crow's-nest

**gavilán** /gaβi'lan/ *m*, sparrow hawk; thistle flower

**gavilla** /ga'βiʎa; ga'βiya/ *f*, sheaf (of corn, etc.); gang, rabble

**gaviota** /ga'βiota/ *f*, seagull

**gavota** /ga'βota/ *f*, gavotte

**gayo** /'gayo/ *a* gay, happy; showy, attractive. **gaya ciencia,** minstrelsy, art of poetry

**gazapera** /gaθa'pera; gasa'pera/ *f*, rabbit warren; *Inf.* thieves' den; *Inf.* brawl

**gazapo** /ga'θapo; ga'sapo/ *m*, young rabbit; *Inf.* cunning fellow; fib, lie; slip, blunder

**gazmoñería** /gaθmoɲe'ria; gasmoɲe'ria/ *f*, prudery, priggish affectation

**gazmoño** /gaθ'moɲo; gas'moɲo/ *a* hypocritical, prudish, priggish

**gaznápiro** /gaθ'napiro; gas'napiro/ **(-ra)** *n* ninny, simpleton

**gaznate** /gaθ'nate; gas'nate/ *m*, windpipe

**gazpacho** /gaθ'patʃo; gas'patʃo/ *m*, cold soup containing bread, onions, vinegar, olive oil, garlic, etc.

**ge** /he/ *f*, name of the letter G

**gehena** /he'ena/ *m*, gehenna, hell

**géiser** /'heiser/ *m*, geyser

**gelatina** /hela'tina/ *f*, gelatin. **g. incendiaria,** napalm. **g. seca,** cooking gelatin

**gelatinoso** /helati'noso/ *a* gelatinous

**gélido** /'heliðo/ *a Poet.* icy; very cold

**gema** /'hema/ *f*, gem; *Bot.* bud

**gemelo** /he'melo/ **(-la)** *a* and *n* twin. *m pl*, field or opera glasses, binoculars; cuff links; *Astron.* Gemini

**gemido** /he'miðo/ *m*, groan, lament, moan

**gemidor** /hemi'ðor/ *a* groaning, moaning; wailing (of the wind, etc.)

**gemir** /he'mir/ *vi irr* to moan, groan, lament; *Fig.* wail, howl. See **pedir**

**gene** /'hene/ *m*, gene

**genealogía** /henealo'hia/ *f*, genealogy

**genealógico** /henea'lohiko/ *a* genealogical

**genealogista** /henealo'hista/ *mf* genealogist

**generación** /henera'θion; henera'sion/ *f*, generation, reproduction; species; generation

**generador** /henera'ðor/ *a* generative. *m*, *Mech.* generator

**general** /hene'ral/ *a* general; universal; widespread; common, usual. *m*, (*Mil. Eccl.*) general. **g. de división,** *Mil.* major general. **en** *or* **por lo g.,** generally

**generalato** /henera'lato/ *m*, generalship

**generalidad** /henerali'ðað/ *f*, majority, bulk; generality

**generalísimo** /henera'lisimo/ *m*, generalissimo, commander in chief

**generalización** /heneraliθa'θion; heneralisa'sion/ *f*, generalization

**generalizar** /henerali'θar; henerali'sar/ *vt* to generalize; —*vr* become widespread or general

**generar** /hene'rar/ *vt* to generate

**genérico** /he'neriko/ *a* generic

**género** /'henero/ *m*, kind; class; way, mode; *Com.* goods; species, genus; *Gram.* gender; cloth, material. **g. chico,** short theatrical pieces (gen. one act). **g. humano,** humankind

**generosidad** /henerosi'ðað/ *f*, hereditary nobility; generosity, magnanimity; liberality, munificence; courage

**generoso** /hene'roso/ *a* noble (by birth); magnanimous; generous (of wine); munificent; courageous; excellent

**genésico** /he'nesiko/ *a* genetic

**génesis** /'henesis/ *m*, Genesis. *f*, beginning, origin

**genial** /he'nial/ *a* of genius; highly talented; brilliant; characteristic, individual; pleasant; cheerful

**genialidad** /heniali'ðað/ *f*, genius; talent; brilliance; eccentricity, oddity

**genio** /'henio/ *m*, nature, individuality, temperament; temper; character; talent; genius; genie, spirit. **corto de g.,** unintelligent. **mal g.,** bad temper

**genital** /heni'tal/ *a* genital. *m*, testicle (gen. *pl*)

**genitivo** /heni'tiβo/ *a* reproductive, generative. *m*, *Gram.* genitive

**Génova** /'henoβa/ Genoa

**genovés** /heno'βes/ **(-esa)** *a* and *n* Genoese

**gente** /'hente/ *f*, people, a crowd; nation; army; *Inf.* family; followers, adherents. **g. baja,** rabble. **g. de bien,** honest folk; respectable people. **g. de paz,** friends (reply to sentinel's challenge). **g. fina,** nice, cultured people. **g. menuda,** children, small fry

**gentecilla** /hente'θiʎa; hente'siya/ *f*, dim *Inf.* rabble; contemptible people

**gentil** /hen'til/ *a* pagan, idolatrous; spirited, dashing, handsome; notable, extraordinary; graceful, charming

**gentileza** /henti'leθa; henti'lesa/ *f*, grace; elegance; beauty; verve, sprightliness; courtesy; show, ostentation

**gentilhombre** /hentil'ombre/ *m*, gentleman; handsome man; kind sir! **gentileshombres de cámara,** gentlemen-in-waiting

**gentilicio** /henti'liθio; henti'lisio/ *a* national; family

**gentílico** /hen'tiliko/ *a* pagan, idolatrous

**gentilidad** /hentili'ðað/ *f*, idolatry, paganism; heathendom

**gentío** /hen'tio/ *m*, crowd, throng

**gentualla, gentuza** /hen'tuaʎa, hen'tuθa; hen'tuaya, hen'tusa/ *f*, canaille, rabble

**genuflexión** /henuflek'sion/ *f*, genuflection

**genuino** /he'nuino/ *a* pure; authentic, genuine

**geodesia** /heo'ðesia/ *f*, geodesy

**geodésico** /heo'ðesiko/ *a* geodesic

**geofísico** /heo'fisiko/ *m*, geophysicist

**geografía** /heogra'fia/ *f*, geography

**geográfico** /heo'grafiko/ *a* geographical

**geógrafo** /he'ografo/ *m*, geographer

**geología** /heolo'hia/ *f*, geology

**geológico** /heo'lohiko/ *a* geological

**geólogo** /he'ologo/ *m*, geologist

**geometría** /heome'tria/ *f*, geometry. **g. del espacio,** solid geometry

**geométrico** /heo'metriko/ *a* geometrical

**geranio** /he'ranio/ *m*, geranium

**gerencia** /he'renθia; he'rensia/ *f*, *Com.* managership; manager's office; management

**gerente** /he'rente/ *m*, *Com.* manager

**germanía** /herma'nia/ *f*, thieves' slang; association of thieves; sixteenth-century political brotherhood

**germánico** /her'maniko/ *a* germanic

**germanófilo** /herma'nofilo/ **(-la)** *a* and *n* germanophile

**germen** /'hermen/ *m*, germ, sprout; *Bot.* embryo; genesis, origin

**germinación** /hermina'θion; hermina'sion/ *f*, germination

**germinar** /hermi'nar/ *vi* to germinate, sprout; develop, grow

**germinativo** /hermina'tiβo/ *a* germinative

**gerundio** /he'rundio/ *m*, *Gram.* gerund; *Inf.* pompous ass; *Inf.* tub-thumper

**gesta** /'hesta/ *f*, heroic deed. **cantar de g.,** epic or heroic poem

**gestación** /hesta'θion; hesta'sion/ *f*, gestation
**gestear** /heste'ar/ *vi* to gesture, grimace
**gesticulación** /hestikula'θion; hestikula'sion/ *f*, gesticulation; grimace
**gesticular** /hestiku'lar/ *vi* to grimace, gesticulate —*a* gesticulatory
**gestión** /hes'tion/ *f*, negotiation; management, conduct; effort, exertion; measure
**gestionar** /hestio'nar/ *vt* to negotiate; conduct; undertake; take steps to attain
**gesto** /'hesto/ *m*, gesture; facial expression; grimace; face, visage
**gestor** /hes'tor/ **(-ra)** *n* manager; partner; promoter —*a* managing
**Getsemaní** /hetsema'ni/ Gethsemane
**giba** /'hiβa/ *f*, hump, hunchback; *Inf.* nuisance, inconvenience
**gibón** /hi'βon/ *m*, gibbon
**giboso** /hi'βoso/ *a* hunchbacked
**gibraltareño** /hiβralta'reɲo/ *a* Gibraltarian
**giganta** /hi'ganta/ *f*, giantess
**gigante** /hi'gante/ *a* gigantic. *m*, giant.
**gigantesco** /higan'tesko/ *a* giant, gigantic; *Fig.* outstanding
**gigantez** /higan'teθ; higan'tes/ *f*, gigantic size
**gigantón** /higan'ton/ **(-ona)** *n* enormous giant; carnival grotesque
**gimnasia** /him'nasia/ *f*, gymnastics
**gimnasio** /him'nasio/ *m*, gymnasium; school, academy
**gimnasta** /him'nasta/ *mf* gymnast
**gimnástico** /him'nastiko/ *a* gymnastic
**gimotear** /himote'ar/ *vi Inf.* to whine (often used scornfully)
**gimoteo** /himo'teo/ *m*, *Inf.* whining, whimpering
**ginebra** /hi'neβra/ *f*, gin (drink); confusion; babble, din
**ginebrés** /hine'βres/ **(-esa), ginebrino (-na)** *a* and *n* Genevan
**gineceo** /hine'θeo; hine'seo/ *m*, (*Bot.* and in ancient Greece) gynaecium
**ginecología** /hinekolo'hia/ *f*, gynecology
**ginecológico** /hineko'lohiko/ *a* gynecological
**ginecólogo** /hine'kologo/ **(-ga)** *n* gynecologist
**girado** /hi'raðo/ *m*, *Com.* drawee
**girador** /hira'ðor/ *m*, *Com.* drawer
**giralda** /hi'ralda/ *f*, weathercock in the shape of a person or animal; tower at Seville
**girar** /hi'rar/ *vi* to revolve; deal (with), concern; turn, branch (streets, etc.); *Com.* trade; *Mech.* turn on, revolve; —*vt* and *vi Com.* draw, cash. **g. en descubierto,** *Com.* to overdraw
**girasol** /hira'sol/ *m*, sunflower
**giratorio** /hira'torio/ *a* revolving, gyrating; swiveling
**giro** /'hiro/ *m*, revolution, turn; revolving; trend; course (of affairs); style, turn (of phrase); threat; knife gash; *Com.* draft, drawing; *Com.* line of business, specialty. **g. postal,** postal order
**giroscopio** /hiro'skopio/ *m*, gyroscope
**gitanería** /hitane'ria/ *f*, cajolery, wheedling; gypsies; gypsy saying or action
**gitanesco** /hita'nesko/ *a* gypsy, gypsy-like
**gitano** /hi'tano/ **(-na)** *a* gypsy; gypsy-like; seductive, attractive; sly —*n* gypsy
**glaciar** /gla'θiar; gla'siar/ *m*, glacier
**gladiador** /glaðia'ðor/ *m*, gladiator
**gladiatorio** /glaðia'torio/ *a* gladiatorial
**glándula** /'glandula/ *f*, gland
**glicerina** /gliθe'rina; glise'rina/ *f*, glycerin, glycerol
**globo** /'gloβo/ *m*, *Geom.* sphere; globe, world; globe (*Elec. Gas.*); balloon. **g. aerostático,** air balloon. **g. terrestre,** world; geographical globe
**globular** /gloβu'lar/ *a* globular
**glóbulo** /'gloβulo/ *m*, globule.
**globuloso** /gloβu'loso/ *a* globulous
**gloria** /'gloria/ *f*, heavenly bliss; fame, glory; delight, pleasure; magnificence, splendor; *Art.* apotheosis, glory. *m*, *Eccl.* doxology
**gloriar** /glo'riar/ *vt* to praise; —*vr* (*with de or en*) boast about; be proud of, rejoice in

**glorieta** /glo'rieta/ *f*, bower, arbor; open space in a garden; street square
**glorificación** /glorifika'θion; glorifika'sion/ *f*, glorification
**glorificador** /glorifika'ðor/ *a* glorifying
**glorificar** /glorifi'kar/ *vt* to exalt, raise up; glorify, extol; —*vr* (*with de or en*) be proud of; glory in; boast of
**glorioso** /glo'rioso/ *a* glorious; *Eccl.* blessed; boastful, bragging
**glosa** /'glosa/ *f*, gloss; explanation, note
**glosador** /glosa'ðor/ **(-ra)** *n* glossator; commentator —*a* explanatory
**glosar** /glo'sar/ *vt Lit.* to gloss
**glosario** /glo'sario/ *m*, glossary
**glosopeda** /gloso'peða/ *f*, foot-and-mouth disease
**glotón** /glo'ton/ **(-ona)** *a* greedy, gluttonous —*n* glutton
**glotonería** /glotone'ria/ *f*, gluttony, greed
**glucosa** /glu'kosa/ *f*, glucose
**glúteo** /'gluteo/ *a* gluteal
**glutinoso** /gluti'noso/ *a* glutinous
**gn-** /gn-/ For words so beginning, see spellings without **g**.
**gobernación** /goβerna'θion; goβerna'sion/ *f*, government; governor's office or building; ministry of the interior, home office (abb. for **ministerio de G.**)
**gobernador** /goβerna'ðor/ **(-ra)** *a* governing, *n* governor
**gobernalle** /goβer'naʎe; goβer'naye/ *m*, helm
**gobernante** /goβer'nante/ *a* governing. *m*, *Inf.* self-appointed director or manager
**gobernar** /goβer'nar/ *vt irr* to govern, rule; lead, conduct; manage; steer; control; —*vi* govern; *Naut.* obey the tiller. See **recomendar**
**gobierno** /go'βierno/ *m*, government (all meanings); *Naut.* helm; control (of machines, business, etc.)
**goce** /'goθe; 'gose/ *m*, enjoyment; possession
**godo** /'goðo/ **(da)** *a* Gothic; aristocratic, noble —*n* Goth; aristocrat
**gol** /gol/ *m*, *Sports.* goal
**gola** /'gola/ *f*, throat; gullet; gorget; tucker, bib
**goleta** /go'leta/ *f*, schooner
**golf** /golf/ *m*, golf. **palo de g.,** golf club
**golfear** /golfe'ar/ *vi* to loaf
**golfería** /golfe'ria/ *f*, loafing; vagabondage; loafers
**golfo** /'golfo/ **(-fa)** *m*, *Geog.* gulf; sea, ocean —*n* ragamuffin, urchin. *m*, *Inf.* loafer; lounge lizard, wastrel
**Golfo Pérsico** /'golfo 'persiko/ Persian Gulf
**golilla** /go'liʎa; go'liya/ *f*, ruff; *m*, *Inf.* magistrate
**gollería** /goʎe'ria; goye'ria/ *f*, dainty, tidbit; *Inf.* affectation, persnicketiness
**gollete** /go'ʎete; go'yete/ *m*, gullet; neck (of a bottle, etc.); *Mech.* nozzle
**golondrina** /golon'drina/ *f*, *Ornith.* swallow. **g. de mar,** tern
**golosina** /golo'sina/ *f*, tidbit, delicacy; desire, caprice; pleasant useless thing
**goloso** /go'loso/ *a* fond of sweet things; greedy, desirous; appetizing
**golpe** /'golpe/ *m*, blow, knock; pull (at the oars); ring (of a bell); *Mech.* stroke; crowd; fall (of rain, etc.); mass, torrent; misfortune; shock, collision; spring lock; beating (of the heart); flap (of a pocket); *Sew.* passementerie; surprise; point, wit; bet. **g. de estado,** coup d'état. **g. de fortuna,** stroke of fortune. **g. de mano,** rising, insurrection. **g. en vago,** blow in the air; disappointment. **g. franco,** *Sports.* free kick. **de g.,** suddenly; quickly
**golpeadura** /golpea'ðura/ *f*. **golpeo** *m*, knocking, striking; beating, throbbing
**golpear** /golpe'ar/ *vt* and *vi* to knock, strike; beat, throb
**goma** /'goma/ *f*, gum, rubber; India rubber; rubber band
**gomería** /gome'ria/ *f*, tire store
**gomero** /go'mero/ *a* gum; rubber. *m*, *West Hem.* rubber planter
**gomorresina** /gomorre'sina/ *f*, gum resin
**gomoso** /go'moso/ *a* gummy; gum

**gónada** /'gonaða/ *f,* gonad

**góndola** /'gondola/ *f,* gondola

**gondolero** /gondo'lero/ *m,* gondolier

**gongorino** /goŋgo'rino/ *a* gongoristic, euphuistic

**gonorrea** /gono'rrea/ *f,* gonorrhea

**gordo** /'gorðo/ *a* fat, stout; greasy, oily; thick (thread, etc.). *m,* animal fat, suet. *Inf.* **ganar el g.,** to win first prize (in a lottery, etc.)

**gordura** /gor'ðura/ *f,* grease, fat; stoutness, corpulence

**gorgojo** /gor'goho/ *m,* weevil; *Fig.* dwarf

**gorgoritear** /gorgorite'ar/ *vi Inf.* to trill, quaver

**gorgorito** /gorgo'rito/ *m, Inf.* quaver, tremolo, trill (gen. *pl)*

**gorgoteo** /gorgo'teo/ *m,* gurgle

**gorjear** /gorhe'ar/ *vi* to trill, warble; twitter; —*vr* crow (of a baby)

**gorjeo** /gor'heo/ *m,* trill, shake; warbling, twitter; crowing, lisping (of a child)

**gorra** /'gorra/ *f,* cap; bonnet; *Mil.* busby; hunting cap. **vivir de g.,** *Inf.* to sponge

**gorrión** /go'rrion/ *m,* sparrow

**gorrista** /go'rrista/ *mf Inf.* parasite; sponger

**gorro** /'gorro/ *m,* cap; bonnet

**gorrón** /go'rron/ *m,* smooth, round pebble; *Mech.* pivot, gudgeon; sponger, waster —*a* parasitical

**gota** /'gota/ *f,* drop (of liquid); gout

**gotear** /gote'ar/ *vi* to drop, trickle, drip; leak; drizzle; give or receive in driblets

**goteo** /go'teo/ *m,* trickling, dripping

**gotera** /go'tera/ *f,* dripping; trickle; leak; leakage; valance

**gótico** /'gotiko/ *a* Gothic; noble, illustrious

**gotoso** /go'toso/ **(-sa)** *a* gouty —*n* sufferer from gout

**goyesco** /go'yesko/ *a* Goyesque

**gozar** /go'θar; go'sar/ *vt* to enjoy, have; take pleasure (in), delight (in); know carnally; —*vi (with de)* enjoy; have, possess

**gozne** /'goθne; 'gosne/ *m,* hinge

**gozo** /'goθo; 'goso/ *m,* enjoyment, possession; gladness, joy; *pl* couplets in honor of the Virgin Mary or a saint. *Inf.* **¡Mi g. en el pozo!** I'm sunk! All is lost!

**gozoso** /go'θoso; go'soso/ *a* glad, happy —*adv* gladly; with pleasure

**grabado** /gra'βaðo/ *m,* engraver's art; engraving; illustration, picture. **g. al agua fuerte,** etching. **g. al agua tinta,** aquatint

**grabador** /graβa'ðor/ **(-ra)** *n* engraver

**grabadura** /graβa'ðura/ *f,* act of engraving

**grabar** /gra'βar/ *vt* to engrave; *Fig.* leave a deep impression

**gracejo** /gra'θeho; gra'seho/ *m,* humor, wit; cheerfulness

**gracia** /'graθia; 'grasia/ *f,* grace; attraction, grace; favor; kindness; jest, witticism; pardon, mercy; pleasant manner; obligingness, willingness; *pl* thanks, thank you. **gracias a,** thanks to. **¡Gracias a Dios!** Thank God! Thank goodness! **las Gracias,** the Three Graces

**grácil** /'graθil; 'grasil/ *a* slender; small

**graciosidad** /graθiosi'ðað; grasiosi'ðað/ *f,* beauty, perfection, grace

**gracioso** /gra'θioso; gra'sioso/ **(-sa)** *a* attractive, graceful, elegant; witty, humorous; free, gratis —*n Theat.* comic role; *m, Theat.* fool

**grada** /'graða/ *f,* step, stair; gradin, seat; stand, gallery; *Agr.* harrow; *Naut.* runway; *pl* perron, flight of stairs

**gradación** /graða'θion; graða'sion/ *f,* gradation; climax

**gradería** /graðe'ria/ *f,* flight of steps

**grado** /'graðo/ *m,* step, stair; degree (of relationship); university degree; grade, class (in schools); *(Fig. Geom. Phys.)* degree; will, desire. **de buen g.,** willingly. **en sumo g.,** in the highest degree

**graduación** /graðua'θion; graðua'sion/ *f,* graduation; *Mil.* rank; rating (of a ship's company). **g. de oficial,** *Mil.* commission

**graduado** /gra'ðuaðo/ *a* graded; *Mil.* brevet. *m,* graduate

**gradual** /gra'ðual/ *a* gradual

**graduar** /gra'ðuar/ *vt* to classify; *Mil.* grade; confer a degree on; measure; test; *Com.* standardize; *Mech.* calibrate; —*vr* graduate, receive a degree. **g. la vista,** to test the eyes. **graduarse de oficial,** *Mil.* to get one's commission

**gráfica** /'grafika/ *f,* graph

**gráfico** /'grafiko/ *a* graphic; vivid

**grafito** /gra'fito/ *m,* graphite

**grafología** /grafolo'hia/ *f,* graphology

**grajear** /grahe'ar/ *vi* to caw; gurgle, burble (of infants)

**grajo** /'graho/ *m, Ornith.* rook

**gramática** /gra'matika/ *f,* grammar. *Inf.* **g. parda,** horse sense

**gramático** /gra'matiko/ *a* grammatical. *m,* grammarian

**gramo** /'gramo/ *m,* gram

**gramófono** /gra'mofono/ *m,* phonograph

**gran** /gran/ *a Abbr.* See **grande.** Used before a singular noun. big; great; grand

**grana** /'grana/ *f,* grain, seed; seed time; cochineal; kermes; red

**granada** /gra'naða/ *f, Mil.* grenade, shell; pomegranate

**granadero** /grana'ðero/ *m,* grenadier; *Inf.* very tall person

**granadilla** /grana'ðiΛa; grana'ðiya/ *f,* passionflower

**granadina** /grana'ðina/ *f,* grenadine

**granar** /gra'nar/ *vi Agr.* to seed; run to seed

**granate** /gra'nate/ *m,* garnet; dark red

**Gran Bretaña** /gran bre'taɲa/ Great Britain

**Gran Canaria** /gran ka'naria/ Grand Canary

**grande** /'grande/ *a* big, large; great, illustrious; grand. *m,* great man; grandee. **en g.,** in a large size; as a whole; in style, lavishly

**grandeza** /gran'deθa; gran'desa/ *f,* largeness; greatness, magnificence; grandeeship; vastness, magnitude

**grandilocuencia** /grandilo'kuenθia; grandilo'kuensia/ *f,* grandiloquence

**grandílocuo** /gran'dilokuo/ *a* grandiloquent

**grandiosidad** /grandiosi'ðað/ *f,* grandeur, greatness

**grandioso** /gran'dioso/ *a* grandiose, magnificent

**grandor** /gran'dor/ *m,* size

**granear** /grane'ar/ *vt Agr.* to sow; grain (of leather)

**granero** /gra'nero/ *m,* granary; grain-producing country

**granito** /gra'nito/ *m, dim* small grain; granite; small pimple

**granizar** /grani'θar; grani'sar/ *vi* to hail, sleet; —*vi* and *vt Fig.* shower down, deluge

**granizo** /gra'niθo; gra'niso/ *m,* hail, sleet; hailstorm; *Fig.* shower, deluge

**granja** /'granha/ *f,* farm; farmhouse; dairy farm, dairy

**granjear** /granhe'ar/ *vt* to trade, profit, earn; obtain, acquire; —*vr* gain, win

**granjería** /granhe'ria/ *f,* farming; agricultural profits; earnings, profits

**granjero** /gran'hero/ **(-ra)** *n* farmer

**Gran Lago Salado, el** /gran 'lago sa'laðo, el/ the Great Salt Lake

**grano** /'grano/ *m, Agr.* grain; seed; bean (coffee, etc.); particle; markings, grain (of wood, etc.); pimple; grain (measure). *Fig. Inf.* **ir al g.,** to go to the root of the matter; come to the point

**granuja** /gra'nuha/ *f,* grape pit. *m, Inf.* urchin; scamp; knave, rogue

**granujiento** /granu'hiento/ *a* pimply

**gránulo** /'granulo/ *m,* granule

**granuloso** /granu'loso/ *a* granulous

**grapa** /'grapa/ *f,* cramp, dowel, clamp; block hook; *Elec.* cleat; staple

**grasa** /'grasa/ *f,* fat; grease; oil; dripping, suet

**grasiento** /gra'siento/ *a* greasy; grubby, dirty

**gratificación** /gratifika'θion; gratifika'sion/ *f,* monetary reward; fee, remuneration; gratuity

**gratificar** /gratifi'kar/ *vt* to recompense; please, gratify

**gratis** /'gratis/ *a* and *adv* gratis

**gratitud** /grati'tuð/ *f,* gratitude

**grato** /'grato/ *a* pleasing, agreeable; free, gratuitous

**gratuito** /gra'tuito/ *a* gratuitous, free; baseless, unfounded

**grava** /'graβa/ *f*, gravel; stone chip, pebble; metal (of a road)

**gravamen** /gra'βamen/ *m*, obligation; burden; tax

**gravar** /gra'βar/ *vt* to burden, weigh upon; tax

**grave** /'graβe/ *a* heavy; important, momentous; grave; dignified, serious; sedate; tiresome; low-pitched, low; *Gram.* grave accent

**gravedad** /graβe'ðað/ *f*, *Phys.* gravity

**gravitación** /graβita'θion; graβita'sion/ *f*, *Phys.* gravitation; seriousness; sedateness; importance; enormity, gravity

**gravitar** /graβi'tar/ *vi* to gravitate; lean or rest (upon)

**gravoso** /gra'βoso/ *a* grievous, oppressive; onerous; costly

**graznar** /graθ'nar/ *vi* to caw; cackle; quack; croak; sing stridently, screech

**graznido** /graθ'niðo; gras'niðo/ *m*, caw; cackle; croaking; quack; screech

**Grecia** /'greθia; 'gresia/ Greece

**greco** /'greko/ **(-ca)** *a* and *n* Greek

**grecorromano** /grekorro'mano/ *a* Greco-Roman

**gregario** /gre'gario/ *a* gregarious

**gregoriano** /grego'riano/ *a* Gregorian

**gregüescos** /gre'gueskos/ *m pl*, wide breeches (sixteenth and seventeenth centuries)

**gremial** /gre'mial/ *a* pertaining to a guild, union, or association. *m*, member of a guild, union, or association

**gremio** /'gremio/ *m*, guild, corporation, union; society, association; (univ.) general council

**greña** /'greɲa/ *f*, tangled lock (of hair) (gen. *pl*); tangle, confused mass

**gresca** /'greska/ *f*, uproar, tumult; fight, row

**grey** /grei/ *f*, flock, drove, herd; *Eccl.* flock, company; people, nation

**grial** /'grial/ *m*, grail

**griego** /'griego/ **(-ga)** *a* and *n* Greek. *m*, Greek (language); *Inf.* gibberish

**grieta** /'grieta/ *f*, fissure; crevice; chink; split; flaw; vein (in stone, etc.); *Mech.* leak

**grietado** /grie'taðo/ *a* fissured; cracked

**grifo** /'grifo/ *m*, griffin; tap; cock

**grillo** /'griʎo; 'griyo/ *m*, cricket; *Bot.* shoot; *pl* fetters, irons, chains; *Fig.* shackles

**grima** /'grima/ *f*, revulsion, horror

**gringo** /'gringo/ **(-ga)** *n Inf.* foreigner (scornful)

**gripe** /'gripe/ *f*, influenza; grippe

**gris** /gris/ *a* and *m*, gray

**grisú** /gri'su/ *m*, firedamp

**gritador** /grita'ðor/ **(-ra)** *a* shouting —*n* shouter

**gritar** /gri'tar/ *vi* to shout, yell, scream; howl down; hoot

**gritería** /grite'ria/ *f*, shouting, yelling, clamor

**grito** /'grito/ *m*, shout, yell, shriek, scream. *Inf.* **poner el g. en el cielo,** to cry to high heaven, complain

**groenlandés** /groenlan'des/ **(-esa)** *a* Greenland —*n* Greenlander

**Groenlandia** /groen'landia/ Greenland

**grog** /grog/ *m*, grog

**grosella** /gro'seʎa; gro'seya/ *f*, currant. **g. blanca,** gooseberry

**grosería** /grose'ria/ *f*, rudeness; roughness (of workmanship); ignorance; rusticity

**grosero** /gro'sero/ *a* coarse; rough; thick; unpolished, rude

**grotesco** /gro'tesko/ *a* grotesque, absurd

**grúa** /'grua/ *f*, *Mech.* crane, hoist, derrick. **g. de pescante,** jib crane. **g. móvil,** traveling crane

**gruesa** /'gruesa/ *f*, twelve dozen, gross

**grueso** /'grueso/ *a* stout, corpulent; large. *m*, bulk, body; major portion, majority; thick stroke (of a letter); thickness, density. **en g.,** in bulk

**grulla** /'gruʎa; 'gruya/ *f*, *Ornith.* crane

**grumete** /gru'mete/ *m*, ship's boy, cabin boy

**grumo** /'grumo/ *m*, clot; heart (of vegetables); bunch, cluster; bud

**gruñido** /gru'ɲiðo/ *m*, grunt; growl

**gruñidor** /gruɲi'ðor/ *a* grunting; growling

**gruñir** /gru'ɲir/ *vi* to grunt; growl; grumble; squeak, creak (doors, etc.) —*Pres. Part.* **gruñendo.** *Pres. Indic.* **gruño, gruñes,** etc.

**grupa** /'grupa/ *f*, croup (of a horse); pillion (of a motorcycle)

**grupera** /gru'pera/ *f*, pillion (of a horse, etc.)

**grupo** /'grupo/ *m*, knot, cluster; band, group; *Art.* group; *Mech.* set

**gruta** /'gruta/ *f*, cavern, grotto

**guacamayo** /guaka'mayo/ *m*, macaw

**guadamecí** /guaðame'θi; guaðame'si/ *m*, embossed decorated leather

**guadaña** /gua'ðaɲa/ *f*, scythe

**guagua** /'guagua/, *f Caribbean* bus

**gualdo** /'gualdo/ *a* yellow, golden

**gualdrapa** /gual'drapa/ *f*, saddlecloth, trappings; *Inf.* tatter, rag

**guante** /'guante/ *m*, glove. **g. con puño,** gauntlet glove. **g. de boxeo,** boxing glove. **g. de cabritilla,** kid glove. **arrojar el g.,** to throw down the gauntlet; challenge, defy

**guantelete** /guante'lete/ *m*, gauntlet

**guantería** /guante'ria/ *f*, glove trade, shop, or factory

**guantero** /guan'tero/ **(-ra)** *n* glove maker or seller, glover

**guapear** /guape'ar/ *vi Inf.* to make the best of a bad job; *Inf.* pride oneself on being well dressed

**guapeza** /gua'peθa; gua'pesa/ *f*, prettiness; *Inf.* resolution, courage; *Inf.* smartness or showiness of dress; boastful act or behavior

**guapo** /'guapo/ *a* pretty; handsome; *Inf.* daring, enterprising; *Inf.* smart, well-dressed, foppish; *Inf.* handsome. *m*, braggart, brawler; beau, lover; *Inf.* fine fellow, son of a gun

**guarda** /'guarða/ *mf* keeper, guard. *f*, guarding, keeping, custodianship, preservation; guardianship; observance, fulfillment; flyleaf, end page (books); warder (of locks or keys); *Mech.* guard; guard (of a fan)

**guardabarrera** /guarðaβa'rrera/ *mf* gatekeeper at a level crossing (railroad)

**guardabarro** /guarða'βarro/ *m*, mudguard

**guardabosque** /guarða'βoske/ *mf* gamekeeper

**guardabrisa** /guarða'βrisa/ *m*, *Auto.* windshield; glass candle shield

**guardacostas** /guarða'kostas/ *m*, coast guard; *Naut.* revenue cutter

**guardafrenos** /guarða'frenos/ *m*, brakeman (railroad)

**guardagujas** /guarða'guhas/ *m*, pointsman (railroad)

**guardainfante** /guarðain'fante/ *m*, farthingale, crinoline

**guardalmacén** /guarðalma'θen; guarðalma'sen/ *mf* storekeeper

**guardameta** /guarða'meta/ *mf* goalkeeper

**guardamuebles** /guarða'mueβles/ *m*, furniture warehouse

**guardapelo** /guarða'pelo/ *m*, locket

**guardapolvo** /guarða'polβo/ *m*, dustcover; light overcoat; inner case of a pocket watch

**guardar** /guar'ðar/ *vt* to keep; preserve, retain; maintain, observe; save, put aside, lay away; defend, protect; guard; —*vr* (*with de*) avoid, guard against. **g. compás con,** to be in tune with. **guardarse mucho,** to think twice before. **g. silencio,** to keep silent. **¡Guarda!** Take care! **¡Guárdate del agua mansa!** Still waters run deep!

**guardarropa** /guarða'rropa/ *m*, cloakroom. *mf* cloakroom attendant; keeper of the wardrobe. *m*, wardrobe, clothes closet

**guardarropía** /guarðarro'pia/ *f*, theatrical wardrobe

**guardavía** /guarða'βia/ *m*, signalman (railroad)

**guardería** /guarðe'ria/ *f*, day nursery, day-care center

**guardia** /'guarðia/ *f*, guard, escort; protection; (*Mil. Naut.*) watch; regiment, body (of troops); guard (fencing). *m*, guardsman; policeman. **g. de asalto,** armed police. **g. de corps,** royal bodyguard. **g. civil,** civil guard. **g. marina,** midshipman. **g. municipal,** city police. *Mil.* **montar la g.,** to mount guard

**guardián** /guar'ðian/ **(-ana)** *n* keeper; custodian; warden. *m*, watchman; jailer

**guardilla** /guar'ðiʎa; guar'ðiya/ *f*, attic, garret

**guarecer** /guare'θer; guare'ser/ vt irr to shelter, protect, aid; preserve, keep; cure; —vr take shelter. See **conocer**

**guarida** /gua'riδa/ f, lair, den; refuge, shelter; haunt, resort

**guarismo** /gua'rismo/ m, Math. figure; number, numeral

**guarnecer** /guarne'θer; guarne'ser/ vt irr to decorate, adorn; Sew. trim, face, border; Mil. garrison; Mas. plaster. See **conocer**

**guarnecido** /guarne'θiδo; guarne'siδo/ m, Mas. plastering

**guarnición** /guarni'θion; guarni'sion/ f, Sew. trimming, ornament, border, fringe; Mech. packing; Mil. garrison; setting (of jewels); guard (of a sword, etc.); pl harness; fittings

**guarnir** /guar'nir/ vt Naut. to reeve

**guasa** /'guasa/ f, Inf. dullness, boringness; joke. **de g.,** jokingly

**guasón** /gua'son/ a Inf. dull, tedious; humorous, jocose

**guatemalteco** /guatemal'teko/ **(-ca)** a and n Guatemalan

**guau** /guau/ m, bowwow, bark of a dog

**guayaba** /gua'yaβa/ f, guava; guava jelly

**Guayana** /gua'yana/ Guiana

**gubernamental** /guβernamen'tal/ a governmental

**gubernativo** /guβerna'tiβo/ a governmental; administrative

**gubia** /'guβia/ f, chisel; gouge

**guedeja** /ge'δeha/ f, long tress or lock of hair; forelock; lion's mane

**Guernesey** /gerne'sei/ Guernsey

**guerra** /'gerra/ f, war; struggle, fight; Fig. hostility. Inf. **dar g.,** to give trouble, annoy. **en g. con,** at war with. **la g. de Cuba,** the Spanish-American War

**guerrear** /gerre'ar/ vi to make war, fight; oppose

**guerrero** /ge'rrero/ **(-ra)** a war, martial; warrior; Inf. troublesome, annoying —n fighter. m, warrior, soldier

**guerrillear** /gerriʎe'ar; gerriye'ar/ vi to wage guerrilla warfare; fight as a guerrilla

**guerrillero** /gerri'ʎero; gerri'yero/ m, guerrilla fighter

**guía** /'gia/ mf guide, conductor; adviser, director. f, guide, aid; guidebook; Mech. guide, slide; directory; signpost. **g. de ferrocarriles,** train schedule, railroad timetable. **g. de teléfonos,** telephone directory

**guiar** /giar/ vt to guide; lead, conduct; Mech. work, control; Auto. drive; pilot; teach, direct, govern

**guija** /'giha/ f, pebble

**guijarro** /gi'harro/ m, smooth, round pebble; boulder; cobblestone

**guijarroso** /giha'rroso/ a pebbly, cobbled

**guijo** /'giho/ m, gravel; granite chips; pebble

**guillotina** /giʎo'tina; giyo'tina/ f, guillotine; paper-cutting machine

**guillotinar** /giʎoti'nar; giyoti'nar/ vt to guillotine, decapitate

**guinda** /'ginda/ f, mazard cherry; Naut. height of masts

**guinea** /gi'nea/ f, guinea

**guinga** /'giŋga/ f, gingham

**guiñapo** /gi'ɲapo/ m, rag, tatter; sloven, ragamuffin

**guiñar** /gi'ɲar/ vt to wink; blink; Naut. yaw; —vr wink at each other

**guiño** /'giɲo/ m, wink

**guión** /gi'on/ m, royal standard; banner; summary; leader of a dance; Gram. hyphen; subtitle (in films). **g. mayor,** Gram. dash

**guipuzcoano** /gipuθ'koano; gipus'koano/ **(-na)** a and n Guipuzcoan

**guirigay** /giri'gai/ m, Inf. gibberish; uproar, babble

**guirnalda** /gir'nalda/ f, garland, wreath

**guisa** /'gisa/ f, way, manner; will, desire. **a g. de,** in the manner or fashion of

**guisado** /gi'saδo/ m, Cul. stew; cooked dish

**guisante** /gi'sante/ m, Agr. pea; pea plant. **g. de olor,** sweetpea

**guisar** /gi'sar/ vt to cook; stew; Cul. prepare, dress; adjust, arrange

**guiso** /'giso/ m, cooked dish

**guitarra** /gi'tarra/ f, guitar

**guitarrista** /gita'rrista/ mf guitar player

**guito** /'gito/ a vicious (horses, mules)

**gula** /'gula/ f, greed, gluttony

**gusaniento** /gusa'niento/ a worm-eaten; maggoty

**gusano** /gu'sano/ m, worm; caterpillar; maggot; meek, downtrodden person. **g. de seda,** silkworm

**gusanoso** /gusa'noso/ a wormy

**gustar** /gus'tar/ vt to taste, savor; try; —vi be pleasing, give pleasure; like. **Me gusta el libro,** I like the book. **La película no me gustó,** I didn't like the film. **g. de,** to like, is used only when a person is the subject

**gusto** /'gusto/ m, taste; flavor, savor; pleasure, delight; will, desire; discrimination, taste, style, fashion, manner; whim, caprice. **a g.,** to taste; according to taste. **con mucho g.,** with great pleasure. **dar g.,** to please. **de buen g.,** in good taste

**gustoso** /gus'toso/ a savory, palatable; willingly, with pleasure; pleasant, agreeable

**gutagamba** /guta'gamba/ f, gamboge (yellow)

**gutapercha** /guta'pertʃa/ f, guttapercha

**gutural** /gutu'ral/ a guttural

# H

**haba** /'aβa/ *f*, broad bean; bean (coffee, cocoa, etc.). **h. de las Indias,** sweetpea. **Esas son habas contadas,** That's a certainty

**Habana, la** /a'βana, la/ Havana

**habanero** /aβa'nero/ **(-ra), habano (-na)** *a* and *n* Havanese, from Havana. *m*. **habano,** Havana cigar

**habar** /a'βar/ *m*, bean field

**haber** /a'βer/ *m*, estate, property (gen. *pl*); income; *Com*. credit balance. **h. monedado,** specie

**haber** /a'βer/ *vt irr* to have; catch, lay hands on (e.g. *El reo fue habido,* The criminal was caught) —*v aux* (e.g. *Hemos escrito la carta,* We have written the letter) —*v impers* to happen, take place; be —*3rd pers. sing Pres. Indic.* **ha** is replaced by **hay,** meaning there is or there are (e.g. *No hay naranjas en las tiendas,* There are no oranges in the shops). In weather expressions, **hay** means it is (e.g. *Hay luna,* It is moonlight). Used of expressions of time, **haber** means to elapse and **ha** (*3rd pers. sing Pres. Indic.*) has adverbial force of "ago" (e.g. *muchos días ha,* many days ago). **h. de,** to be necessary (less strong than **h. que**) (e.g. *Hemos de verle mañana,* We must see him tomorrow. *He de hacer el papel de Manolo,* I am to play the part of Manolo). **h. que,** to be unavoidable, be essential. With this construction the form **hay** is used (e.g. *Hay que darse prisa,* We (or one) must hurry. **No hay que enojarse,** There's no need to get annoyed). **no h., más que pedir,** to leave nothing to be desired. **no h. tal,** to be no such thing. *Inf*. **habérselas con,** to quarrel or fall out with. **Hubo una vez...,** Once upon a time... **¡No hay de qué!,** Don't mention it!; Not at all!; You're welcome! **No hay para que...,** There's no point in.... **poco tiempo ha,** a little while ago. **¿Qué hay?** What's the matter?; What's new? **¿Qué hay de nuevo?** What's new? *Pres. Indic.* **he, has, ha, hemos, habéis, han.** *Fut.* **habré,** etc —*Condit.* **habría,** etc —*Preterite* **hube, hubiste, hubo, hubimos, hubisteis, hubieron.** *Pres. Subjunc.* **haya,** etc —*Imperf. Subjunc.* **hubiese,** etc

**habichuela** /aβi'tʃuela/ *f*, kidney bean

**hábil** /'aβil/ *a* clever; skillful; able; lawful

**habilidad** /aβili'ðað/ *f*, ability; skill; accomplishment; craftsmanship, workmanship

**habilidoso** /aβili'ðoso/ *a* accomplished; able; skillful

**habilitación** /aβilita'θion; aβilita'sion/ *f*, habilitation; paymastership; equipment; furnishing

**habilitado** /aβili'taðo/ *m*, paymaster

**habilitar** /aβili'tar/ *vt* to qualify; equip; furnish; habilitate; enable; *Com*. capitalize

**habitabilidad** /aβitaβili'ðað/ *f*, habitability

**habitable** /aβi'taβle/ *a* habitable

**habitación** /aβita'θion; aβita'sion/ *f*, habitation, dwelling; room in a house; residence; (*Bot. Zool.*) habitat; caretaking

**habitante** /aβi'tante/ *m*, inhabitant

**habitar** /aβi'tar/ *vt* to inhabit, reside in

**hábito** /'aβito/ *m*, attire; *Eccl*. habit; use, custom; skill, facility; *pl* vestments; gown, robe. **tomar el h.,** to become a monk or nun

**habitual** /aβi'tual/ *a* habitual, usual

**habituar** /aβi'tuar/ *vt* to accustom; —*vr* accustom oneself; grow used (to)

**habitud** /aβi'tuð/ *f*, habit, custom; relationship

**habla** /'aβla/ *f*, speech; language; dialect; discourse. **hablado** /a'βlaðo/ *a* spoken. **bien h.,** well-spoken; courteous. **mal h.,** ill-spoken; rude

**hablador** /aβla'ðor/ **(-ra)** *a* talkative; gossipy —*n* chatterbox; gossip

**habladuría** /aβlaðu'ria/ *f*, gossip; impertinent chatter

**hablanchín** /aβlan'tʃin/ *a Inf*. chattering, gossiping

**hablar** /a'βlar/ *vi* to speak; converse; express oneself; arrange; (*with de*) speak about, discuss; gossip about, criticize; (*with por*) intercede on behalf of; —*vt* speak (a language); say, speak; —*vr* speak to one another. **no hablarse,** to not be on speaking terms. **h. a gritos,** to shout. **h. alto,** to speak loudly or in strong terms. **h. bien** ( *or* **mal**), to be well- (or ill-) spoken; be polite (or rude). **h. claro,** to speak frankly. **h. consigo** *or* **h. entre sí,** to talk to oneself. *Inf*. **h. cristiano, h. en cristiano,** to speak clearly or intelligibly; speak frankly. **hablarlo todo,** to talk too much. **h. por h.,** to talk for talking's sake. *Inf*. **h. por los codos,** to chatter. **h. sin ton ni son,** to speak foolishly

**hablilla** /a'βliʎa; a'βliya/ *f*, rumor, tittletattle, gossip

**hacecillo** /aθe'θiʎo; ase'siyo/ *m*, small sheaf; small bundle; *Bot*. fascicle; beam (of light)

**hacedero** /aθe'ðero; ase'ðero/ *a* feasible, practicable

**hacedor** /aθe'ðor; ase'ðor/ *m*, maker; steward, manager; Creator

**hacendado** /aθen'daðo; asen'daðo/ **(-da)** *a* landed —*n* landowner; *West Hem*. cattle rancher

**hacendista** /aθen'dista; asen'dista/ *mf* political economist

**hacendoso** /aθen'doso; asen'doso/ *a* diligent, hardworking

**hacer** /a'θer; a'ser/ *vt irr* to make; fashion, form, construct; do, perform; cause, effect; arrange, put right; contain; accustom, harden; pack (luggage); imagine, invent, create; improve, perfect; compel, oblige; deliver (speeches); compose; earn; *Math*. add up to; suppose, imagine (e.g. *Sus padres hacían a María en casa,* Her parents imagined that Mary was at home); put into practice, execute; play the part of or act like (e.g. *h. el gracioso,* to play the buffoon); shed, cast (e.g. *El roble hace sombra,* The oak casts a shadow); assemble, convoke (meetings, gatherings); give off, produce (e.g. *La chimenea hace humo,* The chimney is smoking); perform (plays); (*with el, la, lo, and some nouns*) pretend to be (e.g. *Se hizo el desconocido,* He pretended to be ignorant). (**h.** followed by infin. is sometimes translated by a past participle in English (e.g. *Lo hice h.,* I had it done.)) *vi* to matter, be important, signify (e.g. *Su llegada no hace nada al caso,* His arrival makes no difference to the case. *Se me hace muy poco...,* It matters to me very little...); be fitting or suitable; concern, be pertinent; match, go with; agree, be in harmony; (*with de*) act as, discharge duties of temporarily (e.g. *h. de camarero,* to be a temporary waiter); (*with por*) try to, attempt to (e.g. *Haremos por decírselo,* We shall try to tell him) —*vi impers* Used in expressions concerning: 1. the weather. 2. lapse of time. English uses the verb "to be' in both cases, e.g.:

1. *hace buen* (*or mal*) **tiempo,** it is fine (or bad) weather. **hace mucho frío,** it is very cold. **hace sol,** it is sunny. **hace viento,** it is windy. **¿Qué tiempo hace?** What is the weather like?

2. **hace** + an expression of time is followed by **que** introducing a clause (e.g. *Hace dos horas que llegamos,* It is two hours since we arrived) or **hace** + an expression of time may be followed by **desde** + an noun (e.g. *Hace dos años desde aquel día,* It is two years since that day)

When an action or state that has begun in the past is still continuing in the present, the Spanish verb is in the Pres. Ind., whereas the English verb is in the Perfect (e.g. *Hace un mes que la veo todos los días,* I have been seeing her every day for a month). This rule holds good with other tenses. English Pluperfect, Future Perfect, Conditional Perfect become in Spanish Imperfect, Future, Conditional, respectively. *Naut*. **h. agua,** to leak. **h. aguas,** to pass water, urinate. **h. alarde de,** to boast of. **h. el amor a,** to make love to, court, woo. **h. autoridad,** to be authoritative. **h. a todo,** to have many uses; be adaptable. **h. bancarrota,** to go bankrupt. **h. un berrinche, hacerse un berrinche,** to have a fit, have a tantrum. *Fig. Inf*. **h. buena,** to justify. **h. calceta,** to knit. **h. cara** or **frente a,** to face; resist. **h. caso,** to take notice, mind (e.g. *¡No hagas caso!* Never mind!). **h. causas,** to bring charges, institute proceedings. **h. cuentas,** to reckon up. **h. daño,** to harm. *Inf*. **h. de las suyas,** to behave in his usual manner or play one of his usual tricks. **h. diligencias por,** to endeavor to. **h. fiesta,** to take a holiday. **h. fuerza,** to struggle. **h. fuerza a,** *Fig.* to do violence to (e.g. *Hizo fuerza a sus creencias,* He did violence to his beliefs). **h. h.,** to cause to be made (e.g. *He hecho hacer un vestido,* I have had a dress made). **h. juego,** to make a set, match (e.g. *El sombrero hace juego con el traje,* The hat goes with the dress). **h. la corte (a),** to court, woo. *Fig. Inf.* **h. la vista gorda,** to turn a blind eye. **h. la vida del claustro,** to lead a cloistered existence. **h. mal,** to do wrong; be harmful (food, etc.). **h. pedazos,** to break. **h. pinos** (or **pinitos**) to totter; toddle; stagger. *Aer.* **h. rizos,** to loop the loop. **h. saber,** to make known; notify. **h. seguir,** to forward (letters). **h. señas,** to make signs (wave, beckon, etc.). *Inf.* **h. una que sea sonada,** to cause a big scandal. **¡Hágame el favor!** Please! *Pres. Indic.* **hago, haces,** etc —*Fut.* **haré,** etc —*Condit.* **haría,** etc —*Imperat.* **haz, haga, hagamos, haced, hagan.** *Preterite* **hice, hiciste, hizo, hicimos, hicisteis, hicieron.** *Pres. Subjunc.* **haga,** etc —*Imperf. Subjunc.* **hiciese,** etc.

**hacerse** /a'θerse; a'serse/ *vr irr* to become (e.g. *Se ha hecho muy importante,* It (or he) has become very important); grow up (e.g. *Miguel se ha hecho hombre,* Michael has grown up (become a man)); develop, mature; pass oneself off as, pretend to be; (*with prep a*) become accustomed or used to (e.g. *Me haré a este clima,* I shall grow used to this climate); withdraw or retire to (of places); (*with de or con*) provide oneself with. **h. a la vela,** to set sail. **h. a ( uno),** to seem (e.g. *Eso que me cuentas se me hace increíble,* What you tell me seems incredible). *Inf.* **h. chiquito,** to be modest. **h. tarde,** to grow late; *Fig.* be too late. See **hacer**

**hacha** /'atʃa/ *f,* large candle; torch; ax. **h. pequeña,** hatchet

**hachazo** /a'tʃaθo; a'tʃaso/ *m,* stroke of an ax

**hache** /'atʃe/ *f,* name of the letter H

**hachero** /a'tʃero/ *m,* candlestick; woodcutter; axman

**hacho** /'atʃo/ *m,* torch; beacon

**hacia** /'aθia; 'asia/ *prep* toward, near, about. **h. adelante,** forward, onward

**hacienda** /a'θienda; a'sienda/ *f,* country estate, land; property; *pl* domestic tasks; cattle. **h. pública,** public funds. **ministerio de h.,** national treasury, exchequer

**hacina** /a'θina; a'sina/ *f, Agr.* stack; heap, pile

**hacinamiento** /aθina'miento; asina'miento/ *m,* stacking, piling; accumulation

**hacinar** /aθi'nar; asi'nar/ *vt Agr.* to stack sheaves; accumulate, amass; pile up, heap

**hada** /'aða/ *f,* fairy

**hado** /'aðo/ *m,* fate; destiny

**hagiografía** /ahiogra'fia/ *f,* hagiography

**hagiógrafo** /a'hiografo/ *m,* hagiographer

**Haití** /ai'ti/ Haiti

**haitiano** /ai'tiano/ **(-na)** *a* and *n* Haitian

**halagar** /ala'gar/ *vt* to caress; flatter; coax; please, delight

**halago** /a'lago/ *m,* flattery; coaxing; caress; source of pleasure, delight

**halagüeño** /ala'gueɲo/ *a* flattering; pleasing; caressing; hopeful, promising

**halar** /a'lar/ *vt Naut.* to haul, tow

**halcón** /al'kon/ *m,* falcon

**halconero** /alko'nero/ *m,* hawker, hunter

**hálito** /'alito/ *m,* breath; vapor; *Poet.* breeze

**hallado** /a'ʎaðo; a'yaðo/ *a* and *Past Part.* found, met. **bien h.,** welcome; happy, contented. **mal h.,** unwelcome; uneasy, discontented

**hallador** /aʎa'ðor; aya'ðor/ **(-ra)** *n* finder

**hallar** /a'ʎar; a'yar/ *vt* to find; meet; observe; discover; find out; —*vr* be present; be, find oneself

**hallazgo** /a'ʎaθgo; a'yasgo/ *m,* finding; thing found; finder's reward

**halo** /'alo/ *m,* halo

**halterofilia** /altero'filia/ *f,* weightlifting

**hamaca** /a'maka/ *f,* hammock

**hamadríade** /ama'ðriaðe/ *f,* hamadryad

**hambre** /'ambre/ *f,* hunger; famine; desire, yearning. **tener h.,** to be hungry

**hambriento** /am'briento/ *a* hungry; famished; *Fig.* starved (of affection, etc.)

**Hamburgo** /am'burgo/ Hamburg

**hamo** /'amo/ *m,* fishhook

**hampa** /'ampa/ *f,* rogue's life; gang of rogues; underworld, slum

**hangar** /aŋ'gar/ *m,* hangar

**hanseático** /anse'atiko/ *a* Hanseatic

**haragán** /ara'gan/ **(-ana)** *a* lazy, idle —*n* idler, lazybones

**harapiento** /ara'piento/ *a* ragged

**harapo** /a'rapo/ *m,* tatter, rag

**haraposo** /ara'poso/ *a* ragged

**harén** /a'ren/ *m,* harem

**harina** /a'rina/ *f,* flour; powder; farina. *Inf.* **ser h. de otro costal,** to be a horse of another color

**harinero** /ari'nero/ *a* relating to flour. *m,* flour merchant; flour bin

**harinoso** /ari'noso/ *a* floury, mealy; farinaceous

**harmónica** /ar'monika/ *f,* (*Phys. Math.*) harmonic

**harmonizar** /armoni'θar; armoni'sar/ *vt* to arrange (music)

**harnero** /ar'nero/ *m,* sieve

**harón** /a'ron/ *a* slothful, slow; lazy, idle

**harpillera** /arpi'ʎera; arpi'yera/ *f,* sackcloth, sacking

**hartar** /ar'tar/ *vt* to satiate; tire, annoy; satisfy the appetite; shower (with blows, etc.)

**hartazgo** /ar'taθgo; ar'tasgo/ *m,* satiety

**harto** /'arto/ *a* satiated; tired (of), *adv* enough

**hartura** /ar'tura/ *f,* satiety; abundance

**hasta** /'asta/ *prep* until; as far as; down or up to —*conjunc* also, even. **h. la vista,** See you! Ciao! Au revoir! **h. mañana,** until tomorrow

**hastial** /as'tial/ *m,* gable, end wall; boor, lout

**hastío** /as'tio/ *m,* loathing; distaste; nausea

**hato** /'ato/ *m,* personal clothing; herd of cattle; gang (of suspicious characters); crowd, mob; *Inf.* group, party. *Inf.* **liar el h.,** to pack up

**Hawai** /'awai/ Hawaii

**hay** /ai/ there is; there are. See **haber**

**haya** /'aya/ *f,* beech tree; beechwood

**Haya, La** /'aya, la/ The Hague

**hayal** /a'yal/ *m,* wood of beech trees, beech plantation

**hayuco** /a'yuko/ *m,* beech mast

**haz** /aθ/ *as/ m,* bundle, sheaf; *Mil.* file; *pl* fasces. *f,* visage; surface, face. **h. de la tierra,** face of the earth. **h. de luz,** beam of light. *Fig.* **ser de dos haces,** to be two-faced

**haz** /aθ/ *as/ 2nd pers imperat* **hacer**

**hazaña** /a'θaɲa; a'saɲa/ *f,* exploit, prowess

**hazañoso** /aθa'ɲoso; asa'ɲoso/ *a* heroic, dauntless, courageous

**hazmerreír** /aθmerre'ir; asmerre'ir/ *m, Inf.* laughingstock

**he** /e/ *interj* and *adv* Hallo! Hist!; Behold! **¡Heme aquí!** Here I am. **he aquí,** here is...

**hebilla** /e'βiʎa; e'βiya/ *f,* buckle

**hebra** /'eβra/ *f,* thread; fiber; flesh; *Mineral.* vein, streak; filament (textiles); grain (of wood); *pl Poet.* hair. *Inf.* **pegar la h.,** to start a conversation

**hebraísmo** /eβra'ismo/ *m,* Hebraism

**hebraísta** /eβra'ista/ *n,* Hebraist

**hebreo** /e'βreo/ **(-ea)** *a* Hebraic, Jewish —*n* Jew. *m,* Hebrew (language)

**Hébridas, las** /'eβriðas, las/ the Hebrides

**hecatombe** /eka'tombe/ *f,* hecatomb; slaughter, massacre

**hechicería** /etʃiθe'ria; etʃise'ria/ *f,* sorcery; spell, enchantment

**hechicero** /etʃi'θero; etʃi'sero/ *a* bewitching, magic; charming, attractive

**hechizar** /etʃi'θar; etʃi'sar/ *vt* to bewitch; charm, attract, delight

**hechizo** /e'tʃiθo; e'tʃiso/ *m,* magic spell; fascination, charm; delight, pleasure

**hecho** /'etʃo/ *a* developed, mature; accustomed, used; perfected, finished; ready-made. **h. una furia,** like a fury, very angry. **bien h.,** well-made, well-proportioned; well or rightly done

**hecho** /etʃo/ *m,* deed, action; fact; happening, event. **los Hechos de los Apóstoles,** the Acts of the Apostles

**hechura** /e'tʃura/ *f*, making, make; creation; form; figure, statue; *Lit.* composition; build (of body); *Fig.* puppet, creature; *pl* price paid for work done. **de h. sastre,** *a* tailor-made

**hectárea** /ekta'rea/ *f*, hectare

**hectógrafo** /ek'tografo/ *m*, hectograph

**hectogramo** /ekto'gramo/ *m*, hectogram

**hectolitro** /ekto'litro/ *m*, hectoliter

**heder** /e'ðer/ *vi irr* to stink; be intolerable. See **entender**

**hediondez** /eðion'deθ; eðion'des/ *f*, stink, stench

**hediondo** /e'ðiondo/ *a* stinking; intolerable, pestilential; obscene

**hedonismo** /eðo'nismo/ *m*, hedonism

**hedonista** /eðo'nista/ *mf* hedonist

**hegeliano** /ehe'liano/ *a* Hegelian

**hegemonía** /ehemo'nia/ *f*, hegemony

**helada** /e'laða/ *f*, frost. **h. blanca,** hoarfrost

**heladera** /ela'ðera/ *f*, refrigerator

**helado** /e'laðo/ *a* frozen; ice-cold; astounded, disdainful. *m*, iced drink; sherbet, ice cream

**helamiento** /ela'miento/ *m*, icing; freezing

**helar** /e'lar/ *vt irr* to freeze; ice, chill; astound; discourage; —*vr* become iced; freeze; become ice-cold —*v impers* to freeze. See **acertar**

**helecho** /e'letʃo/ *m*, fern

**helenismo** /ele'nismo/ *m*, Hellenism

**hélice** /'eliθe; 'elise/ *f*, spiral, helical line; screw, propeller; *Geom.* helix; *Astron.* Ursa Major

**helicóptero** /eli'koptero/ *m*, *Aer.* helicopter

**helio** /'elio/ *m*, helium

**heliógrafo** /e'liografo/ *m*, heliograph

**helioscopio** /elio'skopio/ *m*, helioscope

**helióstato** /e'liostato/ *m*, heliostat

**helioterapia** /eliote'rapia/ *f*, heliotherapy

**heliotropismo** /eliotro'pismo/ *m*, heliotropism

**heliotropo** /elio'tropo/ *m*, heliotrope; agate

**helvecio** /el'βeθio; el'βesio/ **(-ia)** *a* and *n* Helvetian

**hembra** /'embra/ *f*, female; *Inf.* woman; nut of a screw; eye of a hook

**hemiciclo** /emi'θiklo; emi'siklo/ *m*, hemicycle; floor (of a legislative building)

**hemisférico** /emis'feriko/ *a* hemispherical

**hemisferio** /emis'ferio/ *m*, hemisphere

**hemofilia** /emo'filia/ *f*, hemophilia.

**hemoglobina** /emoglo'βina/ *f*, hemoglobin

**hemorragia** /emo'rrahia/ *f*, hemorrhage

**hemorroides** /emo'rroiðes/ *f*, hemorrhoids

**henchido** /en'tʃiðo/ *a* swollen

**henchimiento** /entʃi'miento/ *m*, swelling; inflation; filling

**henchir** /en'tʃir/ *vt irr* to fill; stuff; swell —*Pres. Indic.* **hincho, hinches, hinche, hinchen.** *Pres. Part.* **hinchiendo.** *Pres. Subjunc.* **hincha,** etc —*Imperf. Subjunc.* **hinchiese,** etc —*Imperat.* **hinche, hincha, hinchamos, henchid, hinchan**

**hendedura** /ende'ðura/ *f*, fissure; rift

**hender** /en'der/ *vt irr* to split, crack; *Fig.* cleave (air, water, etc.); make one's way through. See **entender**

**hendidura** /endi'ðura/ *f*, split, fissure, crack, chink

**henil** /e'nil/ *m*, hayloft

**heno** /'eno/ *m*, hay

**hepático** /e'patiko/ *a* hepatic

**heráldica** /e'raldika/ *f*, heraldry

**heráldico** /e'raldiko/ *a* heraldic

**heraldo** /e'raldo/ *m*, herald; harbinger

**herbaje** /er'βahe/ *m*, herbage; pasture, grass; thick woolen cloth

**herbario** /er'βario/ *m*, herbalist, botanist; herbarium —*a* herbal

**herbívoro** /er'βiβoro/ *a* herbivorous

**herbolaria** /erβo'laria/ *f*, herbal

**hercúleo** /er'kuleo/ *a* herculean

**heredad** /ere'ðað/ *f*, landed property; country estate

**heredar** /ere'ðar/ *vt* to inherit; make a deed of gift to; inherit characteristics, etc.; take as heir

**heredero** /ere'ðero/ **(-ra)** *m*, heir; inheritor. **h. aparente,** heir apparent. **presunto h.,** heir presumptive

**hereditario** /ereði'tario/ *a* hereditary

**hereje** /e'rehe/ *mf* heretic

**herejía** /ere'hia/ *f*, heresy

**herencia** /e'renθia; e'rensia/ *f*, inheritance; heredity; heritage

**heresiarca** /ere'siarka/ *mf* heresiarch

**herético** /e'retiko/ *a* heretical

**herida** /e'riða/ *f*, wound; insult; anguish. **h. contusa,** contusion. **h. penetrante,** deep wound

**herir** /e'rir/ *vt irr* to wound; strike, harm; *Fig.* pierce (of sun's rays); *Fig.* pluck (strings of a musical instrument); impress (the senses); affect (the emotions); offend (gen. of words) —*Pres. Part.* **hiriendo.** *Pres. Indic.* **hiero, hieres, hiere, hieren.** *Preterite* **hirió, hirieron.** *Pres. Subjunc.* **hiera, hieras, hiera, hiramos, hiráis, hieran.** *Imperf. Subjunc.* **hiriese,** etc.

**hermafrodita** /ermafro'ðita/ *a* and *mf* hermaphrodite

**hermana** /er'mana/ *f*, sister; twin, pair (of things). **h. de leche,** foster sister. **h. política,** sister-in-law

**hermanar** /erma'nar/ *vt* to join; mate; harmonize; —*vt* and *vr* be the spiritual brother of, be compatible

**hermanastra** /erma'nastra/ *f*, stepsister

**hermanastro** /erma'nastro/ *m*, stepbrother

**hermandad** /erman'dað/ *f*, brotherhood; friendship; intimacy; relationship (of one thing to another); confraternity. **Santa H.,** Spanish rural police force instituted in the fifteenth century

**hermano** /er'mano/ *m*, brother; pair, twin (of things); *Eccl.* brother. **h. de raza,** member of the same race. **h. político,** brother-in-law

**hermético** /er'metiko/ *a* hermetic

**hermosear** /ermose'ar/ *vt* to embellish, beautify, adorn

**hermoso** /er'moso/ *a* beautiful; shapely; handsome; fine, wonderful (weather, view, etc.)

**hermosura** /ermo'sura/ *f*, beauty; pleasantness, attractiveness, perfection of form; belle

**hernia** /'ernia/ *f*, hernia

**héroe** /'eroe/ *m*, hero

**heroicidad** /eroiθi'ðað; eroisi'ðað/ *f*, heroism

**heroico** /e'roiko/ *a* heroic

**heroína** /ero'ina/ *f*, heroine

**heroismo** /ero'ismo/ *m*, heroism

**herpes** /'erpes/ *m pl*, or *f pl*, herpes

**herrada** /e'rraða/ *f*, pail

**herradero** /erra'ðero/ *m*, branding of livestock

**herrador** /erra'ðor/ *m*, blacksmith

**herradura** /erra'ðura/ *f*, horseshoe

**herraje** /e'rrahe/ *m*, ironwork

**herramienta** /erra'mienta/ *f*, tool; set of tools

**herrar** /e'rrar/ *vt irr* to shoe horses; brand (cattle); decorate with iron. See **acertar**

**herrería** /erre'ria/ *f*, forge; ironworks; blacksmith's shop; clamor, tumult, confusion

**herrero** /e'rrero/ *m*, smith

**herrete** /e'rrete/ *m*, ferrule, tag

**herrumbre** /e'rrumbre/ *f*, rust; taste of iron

**herrumbroso** /errum'broso/ *a* rusty

**hervidero** /erβi'ðero/ *m*, boiling, bubbling; *Fig.* ebullition; swarm, crowd

**hervir** /er'βir/ *vi irr* to boil; foam and froth (sea); seethe (emotions); surge (crowds); (*with en*) abound in, swarm with. See **sentir**

**hervor** /er'βor/ *m*, boiling; ebullition, vigor, zest; seething, agitation

**hesitación** /esita'θion; esita'sion/ *f*, hesitation, doubt, uncertainty

**hesitar** /esi'tar/ *vi* to hesitate, vacillate

**heteo** /e'teo/ **(-ea)** *a* and *n* Hittite

**heterodina** /etero'ðina/ *a f*, *Radio.* heterodyne

**heterodoxia** /etero'ðoksia/ *f*, heterodoxy

**heterodoxo** /etero'ðokso/ *a* heterodox

**heterogeneidad** /eterohenei'ðað/ *f*, heterogeneity

**heterogéneo** /etero'heneo/ *a* heterogeneous

**hético** /'etiko/ *a* hectic, consumptive

**hexagonal** /eksago'nal/ *a* hexagonal

**hexágono** /e'ksagono/ *m*, hexagon

**hexámetro** /e'ksametro/ *m*, hexameter

**hez** /eθ; es/ *f*, (gen. *pl* **heces**) lees, dregs

**hiato** /'iato/ *m*, hiatus

**hibernal** /'iβernal/ *a* wintry

**hibernés** /iβer'nes/ *a* Hibernian

**hibisco** /i'βisko/ *m*, hibiscus

**hibridación** /iβriða'θion; iβriða'sion/ *f*, hybridization

**hibridismo** /iβri'ðismo/ *m,* hybridism
**híbrido** /'iβriðo/ *a* and *m,* hybrid
**hidalgo** /i'ðalgo/ **(-ga)** *n* noble, aristocrat —*a* noble; illustrious; generous
**hidalguía** /iðal'gia/ *f,* nobility; generosity, nobility of spirit
**hidra** /'iðra/ *f, Zool.* hydra; poisonous snake; *Astron.* Hydra
**hidratar** /iðra'tar/ *vt Chem.* to hydrate
**hidrato** /i'ðrato/ *m,* hydrate. **h. de carbono,** carbohydrate
**hidráulica** /i'ðraulika/ *f,* hydraulics
**hidráulico** /i'ðrauliko/ *a* hydraulic
**hidroavión** /iðroa'βion/ *m,* flying boat
**hidrocarburo** /iðrokar'βuro/ *m,* hydrocarbon
**hidrocéfalo** /iðro'θefalo/ *m,* and *a* hydrocephalic
**hidrodinámica** /iðroði'namika/ *f,* hydrodynamics
**hidroeléctrico** /iðroe'lektriko/ *a* hydroelectric
**hidrofobia** /iðro'foβia/ *f,* hydrophobia; rabies
**hidrógeno** /i'ðroheno/ *m,* hydrogen
**hidrografía** /iðrogra'fia/ *f,* hydrography
**hidrología** /iðrolo'hia/ *f,* hydrology
**hidropesía** /iðrope'sia/ *f,* dropsy
**hidrópico** /i'ðropiko/ *a* dropsical
**hidroplano** /iðro'plano/ *m,* seaplane
**hidroquinona** /iðroki'nona/ *f,* hydroquinone
**hidroscopio** /iðro'skopio/ *m,* hydroscope
**hidrostática** /iðro'statika/ *f,* hydrostatics
**hidroterapia** /iðrote'rapia/ *f,* hydrotherapy
**hiedra** /'ieðra/ *f,* ivy
**hiel** /iel/ *f,* gall, bile, bitterness, affliction; *pl* troubles
**hielo** /'ielo/ *m,* ice, frost; freezing, icing; stupefaction; indifference, coldness. *Inf.* **estar hecho un h.,** to be as cold as ice
**hiena** /'iena/ *f,* hyena
**hierático** /ie'ratiko/ *a* hieratical
**hierba** /'ierβa/ *f,* grass; small plant; herb. **h. cana,** groundsel. **mala h.,** weed
**hierbabuena** /ierβa'βuena/ *f, Bot.* mint
**hierofante** /iero'fante/ *m,* hierophant
**hierra** /'ierra/ *f,* branding time
**hierro** /'ierro/ *m,* iron; brand with hot iron; iron or steel head of a lance, etc.; instrument or shape made of iron; weapon of war *pl* fetters. **h. colado,** cast iron. **h. dulce,** wrought iron. **h. en planchas,** sheet iron. **h. viejo,** scrap iron
**hígado** /'igaðo/ *m,* liver; courage
**higiene** /i'hiene/ *f,* hygiene; cleanliness, neatness. **h. privada,** personal hygiene. **h. pública,** public health
**higiénico** /i'hieniko/ *a* hygienic
**higo** /'igo/ *m,* fig. **h. chumbo,** prickly pear
**higrómetro** /i'grometro/ *m,* hygrometer
**higuera** /i'gera/ *f,* fig tree
**hija** /'iha/ *f,* daughter; native of a place; offspring
**hijastro** /i'hastro/ **(-ra)** *n* stepchild
**hijo** /'iho/ *m,* son; child; native of a place; offspring; shoot, sprout; *pl* descendants. **h. de la cuna,** foundling. **h. de leche,** foster child. **h. natural,** natural child. **h. político,** son-in-law
**hijuela** /i'huela/ *f,* little daughter; small mattress; small drain; side road; accessory, subordinate thing; piece of material for widening a garment; *Law.* part of an inheritance
**hila** /'ila/ *f,* row, line; gut; *Surg.* lint (gen. *pl*)
**hilacha** /i'latʃa/ *f,* thread raveled from cloth; fiber, filament. **h. de vidrio,** spun glass
**hilado** /i'laðo/ *m,* spinning; thread, yarn
**hilandería** /ilande'ria/ *f,* spinning; spinning mill; mill. **h. de algodón,** cotton mill
**hilandero** /ilan'dero/ **(-ra)** *n* spinner
**hilar** /i'lar/ *vt* to spin; reason, infer, discourse
**hilaridad** /ilari'ðað/ *f,* hilarity; quiet happiness
**hilaza** /i'laθa; i'lasa/ *f,* yarn
**hilera** /i'lera/ *f,* line, file, row; fine yarn; *Mil.* file, rank; *Metall.* wire drawer; *Mas.* course (of bricks)
**hilo** /'ilo/ *m,* thread; linen; wire; mesh (spiders, silkworm's web, etc.); edge (of a blade); thin stream (of liquid); thread (of discourse)
**hilván** /il'βan/ *m, Sew.* basting; tack
**hilvanar** /ilβa'nar/ *vt Sew.* to baste
**himalayo** /ima'layo/ *a* Himalayan

**himen** /'imen/ *m,* hymen
**himeneo** /ime'neo/ *m,* marriage, wedding
**himnario** /im'nario/ *m,* hymnal
**himno** /'imno/ *m,* hymn
**hin** /in/ *m,* whinny, neigh
**hincapié** /inka'pie/ *m,* foothold. **hacer h.,** to insist, make a stand
**hincar** /in'kar/ *vt* to thrust in; drive in, sink; —*vr* kneel. **h. el diente,** to bite. **h. la uña,** to scratch. **hincarse de rodillas,** to kneel down
**hinchado** /in'tʃaðo/ *a* puffed up, vain; pompous, high-flown, redundant (style)
**hinchar** /in'tʃar/ *vt* to inflate; puff out (the chest); swell (of a river, etc.); exaggerate (events); —*vr* swell; grow vain, be puffed up
**hinchazón** /intʃa'θon; intʃa'son/ *f,* swelling; vanity, presumption; pomposity, euphuism (style)
**hiniesta** /i'niesta/ *f,* Spanish broom
**hinojo** /i'noho/ *m, Bot.* fennel; knee. **de hinojos,** on bended knee
**hipar** /i'par/ *vi* to hiccup; pant (of dogs); be overanxious; be overtired; sob, cry
**hipérbole** /i'perβole/ *f,* hyperbole
**hiperbólico** /iper'βoliko/ *a* hyperbolical
**hipercrítico** /iper'kritiko/ *m,* hypercritic —*a* hypercritical
**hipertrofiarse** /ipertro'fiarse/ *vr* to hypertrophy
**hípico** /'ipiko/ *a* equine
**hipnosis** /ip'nosis/ *f,* hypnosis
**hipnótico** /ip'notiko/ *a* hypnotic. *m,* hypnotic drug
**hipnotismo** /ipno'tismo/ *m,* hypnotism
**hipnotización** /ipnotiθa'θion; ipnotisa'sion/ *f,* hypnotization
**hipnotizar** /ipnoti'θar; ipnoti'sar/ *vt* to hypnotize
**hipo** /'ipo/ *m,* hiccup; sob; longing, desire; dislike, disgust
**hipocondría** /ipokon'dria/ *f,* hypochondria
**hipocondríaco** /ipokon'driako/ **(-ca)** *a* hypochondriacal —*n* hypochondriac
**hipocrático** /ipo'kratiko/ *a* Hippocratic
**hipocresía** /ipokre'sia/ *f,* hypocrisy
**hipócrita** /i'pokrita/ *a* hypocritical. *mf* hypocrite
**hipodérmico** /ipo'ðermiko/ *a* hypodermic
**hipódromo** /i'poðromo/ *m,* hippodrome, racetrack
**hipopótamo** /ipo'potamo/ *m,* hippopotamus
**hipostático** /ipo'statiko/ *a* hypostatic
**hipoteca** /ipo'teka/ *f,* mortgage
**hipotecar** /ipote'kar/ *vt* to mortgage
**hipotenusa** /ipote'nusa/ *f,* hypotenuse
**hipótesis** /i'potesis/ *f,* hypothesis
**hipotético** /ipo'tetiko/ *a* hypothetical
**hirsuto** /ir'suto/ *a* hirsute, hairy
**hirviente** /ir'βiente/ *a* boiling
**hisca** /'iska/ *f,* birdlime
**hisopear** /isope'ar/ *vt Eccl.* to sprinkle, asperse
**hisopo** /i'sopo/ *m, Bot.* hyssop; *Eccl.* hyssop, sprinkler
**hispánico** /is'paniko/ *a* Spanish
**hispanismo** /ispa'nismo/ *m,* Hispanism
**hispanista** /ispa'nista/ *mf* Hispanist
**hispanoamericano** /ispanoameri'kano/ **(-na)** *a* and *n* Spanish-American, Hispano-American
**histeria** /is'teria/ *f,* hysteria
**histérico** /is'teriko/ *a* hysterical; hysteric
**histerismo** /iste'rismo/ *m, Med.* hysteria
**histología** /istolo'hia/ *f,* histology
**histólogo** /is'tologo/ *m,* histologist
**historia** /is'toria/ *f,* history; narrative, story; tale; *Inf.* gossip (gen. *pl*); *Art.* historical piece. **h. natural,** natural history. **h. sagrada,** biblical history. *Fig. Inf.* **dejarse de historias,** to stop beating around the bush
**historiador** /istoria'ðor/ **(-ra)** *n* historian
**historiar** /isto'riar/ *vt* to narrate, relate; record, chronicle
**histórico** /is'toriko/ *a* historical; historic
**historieta** /isto'rieta/ *f,* short story; anecdote
**historiografía** /istoriogra'fia/ *f,* historiography
**historiógrafo** /isto'riografo/ *m,* historiographer
**histriónico** /ist'rioniko/ *a* histrionic
**hitlerismo** /itle'rismo/ *m,* Hitlerism

**hito** /'ito/ *m*, milestone; boundary mark; *Fig.* mark, target. **de h. en h.,** from head to foot

**hocico** /o'θiko; o'siko/ *m*, snout; *Inf.* face, mug; *Inf.* angry gesture; *Naut.* prow. **meter el h.,** to stick one's nose into other people's business

**hogaño** /o'gaɲo/ *adv Inf.* during this year; at the present time

**hogar** /o'gar/ *m*, hearth, fireplace; home, house; family life; firebox (of a locomotive)

**hoguera** /o'gera/ *f*, bonfire

**hoja** /'oha/ *f, Bot.* leaf; petal; sheet (metal, paper, etc.); page (of book); blade (sharp instruments); leaf (door, window); sword. **h. de cálculo,** spreadsheet. **h. de servicios,** service or professional record. **h. de tocino,** side of bacon. **h. extraordinaria,** extra, special edition (of a newspaper). **h. volante,** handbill, supplement. **volver la h.,** to turn over (pages); change one's opinion; turn the conversation

**hojalata** /oha'lata/ *f*, tin plate

**hojalatería** /ohalate'ria/ *f*, tinware; tin shop

**hojalatero** /ohala'tero/ *m*, tinsmith

**hojaldre** /o'haldre/ *m*, or *f*, puff pastry

**hojarasca** /oha'raska/ *f*, withered leaves; excessive foliage; rubbish, trash

**hojear** /ohe'ar/ *vt* to turn the leaves of a book; skip, skim, read quickly; —*vi* exfoliate

**hojuela** /o'huela/ *f, dim* little leaf; *Bot.* leaflet; pancake

**¡hola!** /'ola/ *interj* Hallo! Goodness!

**Holanda** /o'landa/ Holland

**holandés** /olan'des/ **(-esa)** *a* and *n* Dutchman (-woman), *m*, Dutch (language)

**holgado** /ol'gaðo/ *a* leisured, free; loose, wide; comfortable; well-off, rich

**holganza** /ol'ganθa; ol'gansa/ *f*, repose, leisure, ease; idleness; pleasure

**holgar** /ol'gar/ *vi irr* to rest; be idle; be glad; be unused or unnecessary (things) —*vr* enjoy oneself, amuse oneself; be glad. See **contar**

**holgazán** /olga'θan; olga'san/ **(-ana)** *a* idle —*n* idler

**holgazanear** /olgaθane'ar; olgasane'ar/ *vi* to idle

**holgazanería** /olgaθane'ria; olgasane'ria/ *f*, idleness, sloth

**holgorio** /ol'gorio/ *m*, rejoicing, festivity, merriment

**holgura** /ol'gura/ *f*, enjoyment, merrymaking; width; comfort, ease; *Mech.* free play

**hollar** /o'ʎar; o'yar/ *vt irr* to trample under foot; humiliate. See **degollar**

**hollejo** /o'ʎeho; o'yeho/ *m*, peel, thin skin (of fruit); *Agr.* chaff

**hollín** /o'ʎin; o'yin/ *m*, soot

**holocausto** /olo'kausto/ *m*, holocaust

**hológrafo** /o'lografo/ *m*, holograph

**hombradía** /ombra'ðia/ *f*, manliness; courage

**hombre** /'ombre/ *m*, man; adult; omber (cards) —*interj* **¡h.!** *Inf.* Old fellow! You don't say so! **¡h. al agua!** Man overboard! **h. de bien,** honest, honorable man. **h. de estado,** statesman. **h. de muchos oficios,** jack-of-all-trades. **h. de negocios,** businessman; man of affairs. **h. de pro,** worthy man; famous man. **ser muy h.,** to be a real man, be very manly

**hombrera** /om'brera/ *f*, epaulette; shoulderpad

**hombro** /'ombro/ *m*, shoulder. **echar al h.,** to shoulder; undertake, take the responsibility of. **encogerse de hombros,** to shrug one's shoulders; be indifferent or uninterested

**hombruno** /om'bruno/ *a Inf.* mannish (of a woman)

**homenaje** /ome'nahe/ *m*, allegiance; homage; veneration, respect

**homeópata** /ome'opata/ *a* homeopathic. *mf* homeopath

**homeopatía** /omeopa'tia/ *f*, homeopathy

**homérico** /o'meriko/ *a* Homeric

**homicida** /omi'θiða; omi'siða/ *a* murderous, homicidal. *mf* murderer (-ess)

**homicidio** /omi'θiðio; omi'siðio/ *m*, homicide (act)

**homilía** /omi'lia/ *f*, homily

**homogeneidad** /omohenei'ðað/ *f*, homogeneity

**homogéneo** /omo'heneo/ *a* homogeneous

**homólogo** /o'mologo/ *a* homologous

**homónimo** /o'monimo/ *a* homonymous. *m*, homonym

**homosexual** /omose'ksual/ *a* and *mf* homosexual

**honda** /'onda/ *f*, sling, catapult

**hondear** /onde'ar/ *vt Naut.* to sound, plumb; *Naut.* unload

**hondo** /'ondo/ *a* deep; low; *Fig.* profound; deep, intense (emotion). *m*, depth

**hondón** /on'don/ *m*, depth, recess

**hondonada** /ondo'naða/ *f*, hollow; glen; valley

**hondura** /on'dura/ *f*, depth

**hondureño** /ondu'reɲo/ **(-ña)** *a* and *n* Honduran

**honestidad** /onesti'ðað/ *f*, honorableness; virtue; respectability; modesty; courtesy

**honesto** /o'nesto/ *a* honorable, virtuous; modest; honest, just

**hongo** /'oŋgo/ *m*, fungus; toadstool; bowler hat

**honor** /o'nor/ *m*, honor; fame; reputation (women); modesty (women); praise; *pl* rank, position; honors

**honorable** /ono'raβle/ *a* honorable

**honorario** /ono'rario/ *a* honorary. *m*, honorarium, fee

**honorífico** /ono'rifiko/ *a* honorary; honorable

**honra** /'onra/ *f*, self-respect, honor, personal dignity; reputation; chastity and modesty (women); *pl* obsequies

**honradez** /onra'ðeθ; onra'ðes/ *f*, honesty; honorableness, integrity; respectability

**honrado** /on'raðo/ *a* honest; honorable

**honrar** /on'rar/ *vt* to respect; honor; —*vr* to be honored

**honroso** /on'roso/ *a* honor-giving, honorable

**hora** /'ora/ *f*, hour; opportune moment; *pl* book of hours. **horas hábiles,** working hours. **horas muertas,** wee hours; wasted time. **a última h.,** at the last minute. **dar la h.,** to strike the hour. **¿Qué h. es?** What time is it?

**horaciano** /ora'θiano; ora'siano/ *a* Horatian

**horadar** /ora'ðar/ *vt* to bore, pierce

**horario** /o'rario/ *a* hourly. *m*, timetable; hour hand of a clock; watch

**horca** /'orka/ *f*, gibbet, gallows; *Agr.* pitchfork; fork; prop for trees

**horcajadas** /orka'haðas/ **(a)** *adv* astride

**horcajadura** /orkaha'ðura/ *f*, crotch

**horchata** /or'tʃata/ *f*, drink made of chufas or crushed almonds

**horda** /'orða/ *f*, horde

**horizontal** /oriθon'tal; orison'tal/ *a* horizontal

**horizonte** /ori'θonte; ori'sonte/ *m*, horizon. **nuevos horizontes,** new opportunities

**horma** /'orma/ *f*, mold; cobbler's last; stone wall. *Fig. Inf.* **hallar la h. de su zapato,** to find what suits one; meet one's match

**hormiga** /or'miga/ *f*, ant

**hormigón** /ormi'gon/ *m*, concrete. **h. armado,** ferroconcrete

**hormiguear** /ormige'ar/ *vi* to itch; crowd, swarm

**hormiguero** /ormi'gero/ *m*, anthill; crowd, swarm

**hormona** /or'mona/ *f*, hormone

**hornero** /or'nero/ **(-ra)** *n* baker

**horno** /'orno/ *m*, oven; furnace; kiln; bakery. **h. alfarero,** firing oven (for pottery). **h. de cocina,** kitchen stove. **h. de cuba,** blast furnace. **h. de ladrillo,** brick kiln. **alto h.,** iron-smelting furnace

**horóscopo** /o'roskopo/ *m*, horoscope

**horquilla** /or'kiʎa; or'kiya/ *f*, forked stick; hairpin; hatpin; *Agr.* fork; hook. **viraje en h.,** hairpin turn

**horrendo** /o'rrendo/ *a* horrible, frightful

**hórreo** /'orreo/ *m*, granary, barn

**horribilidad** /orriβili'ðað/ *f*, horribleness

**horribilísimo** /orriβi'lisimo/ *a superl* most horrible, exceedingly horrible

**horrible** /o'rriβle/ *a* horrible

**horrífico** /o'rrifiko/ *a* horrific

**horripilante** /orripi'lante/ *a* hair-raising, horrifying

**horrísono** /o'rrisono/ *a Poet.* horrid-sounding, terrifying

**horror** /o'rror/ *m*, horror; horribleness; atrocity, enormity

**horrorizar** /orrori'θar; orrori'sar/ *vt* to horrify; —*vr* be horrified, be terrified

**horroroso** /orro'roso/ *a* dreadful, horrible; horrid; *Inf.* hideous, most ugly

**hortaliza** /orta'liθa; orta'lisa/ *f*, green vegetable, garden produce

**hortelano** /orte'lano/ *m*, market gardener

**hortensia** /or'tensia/ *f*, hydrangea

**horticultor** /ortikul'tor/ **(-ra)** *n* horticulturalist

**horticultura** /ortikul'tura/ *f*, horticulture

**horticultural** /ortikultu'ral/ *a* horticultural

**hosanna** /o'sanna/ *m*, hosanna

**hosco** /'osko/ *a* dark brown; unsociable, sullen; crabbed

**hospedaje** /ospe'ðahe/ *m*, lodging; board, payment

**hospedar** /ospe'ðar/ *vt* to lodge, receive as a guest; —*vr* and *vi* lodge, stay

**hospedería** /ospeðe'ria/ *f*, hostelry, inn; lodging

**hospedero** /ospe'ðero/ **(-ra)** *n* innkeeper

**hospicio** /os'piθio; os'pisio/ *m*, hospice; almshouse, workhouse; lodging; orphanage

**hospital** /ospi'tal/ *m*, hospital; hospice. **h. de sangre,** field hospital

**hospitalario** /ospita'lario/ *a* hospitable

**hospitalidad** /ospitali'ðað/ *f*, hospitality; hospitableness; hospital

**hostelero** /oste'lero/ **(-ra)** *n* innkeeper

**hostería** /oste'ria/ *f*, hostelry; inn

**hostia** /'ostia/ *f*, *Eccl.* wafer, Host; sacrificial victim

**hostigamiento** /ostiga'miento/ *m*, harassment. **h. sexual,** sexual harassment

**hostigar** /osti'gar/ *vt* to chastise; harass; tease, annoy

**hostil** /'ostil/ *a* hostile

**hostilidad** /ostili'ðað/ *f*, hostility

**hostilizar** /ostili'θar; ostili'sar/ *vt* to commit hostile acts against; antagonize

**hotel** /'otel/ *m*, hotel; villa

**hotelero** /ote'lero/ **(-ra)** *n* hotelkeeper

**hoy** /oi/ *adv* today; at present. **h. día** *or* **h. en día,** today. **h. por h.,** day by day; at the present time. **de h. en adelante,** from today forward

**hoya** /'oya/ *f*, hole; grave; valley, glen; bed (of a river)

**hoyo** /'oyo/ *m*, hole; pockmark; grave; hollow

**hoyuelo** /o'yuelo/ *m*, *dim* little hole; dimple

**hoz** /oθ; os/ *f*, sickle; defile

**hozar** /o'θar; o'sar/ *vt* to root (pigs, etc.)

**hucha** /'utʃa/ *f*, large chest; strongbox; savings

**hueco** /'ueko/ *a* empty; hollow; vain; hollow (sound); pompous (style); spongy, soft; inflated. *m*, hollow; interval of time or place; *Inf.* vacancy; gap in a wall, etc.

**huelga** /'uelga/ *f*, strike; leisure; lying fallow; merrymaking. **h. de brazos caídos,** sit-down strike. **h. patronal,** lockout strike

**huelguista** /uel'gista/ *mf* striker

**huella** /'ueʎa; 'ueya/ *f*, footprint, track; footstep; tread (of stairs); *Print.* impression; vestige, trace. **h. digital,** fingerprint

**huérfano** /'uerfano/ **(-na)** *n* orphan —*a* unprotected, uncared for

**huero** /'uero/ *a* addled; empty, hollow

**huerta** /'uerta/ *f*, kitchen garden; orchard; irrigation land

**huerto** /'uerto/ *m*, orchard; kitchen garden

**hueso** /'ueso/ *m*, bone; stone (of fruit); kernel, core; drudgery; cheap, useless thing of poor quality. *Inf.* **no dejar un h. sano,** to tear (a person) to pieces. **tener los huesos molidos,** to be tired out; be bruised

**huésped** /'uespeð/ **(-da)** *n* guest; host; innkeeper

**hueste** /'ueste/ *f*, (gen. *pl*) army on the march, host; party; supporters

**huesudo** /ue'suðo/ *a* bony

**hueva** /'ueβa/ *f*, fish roe

**huevera** /ue'βera/ *f*, egg seller; eggcup

**huevo** /'ueβo/ *m*, egg. **h. duro,** hard-boiled egg. **h. estrellado,** fried egg. **h. pasado por agua,** soft-boiled egg. **huevos revueltos,** scrambled eggs

**hugonote** /ugo'note/ **(-ta)** *a* and *n* Huguenot

**huida** /'uiða/ *f*, flight, escape; bolting (of a horse); outlet

**huir** /uir/ *vi irr* to flee; fly (of time); elope; run away, bolt; (*with de*) avoid —*Pres. Part.* **huyendo.** *Pres. Indic.* **huyo, huyes, huyen.** *Preterite* **huyó, huyeron.** *Pres. Subjunc.* **huya,** etc —*Imperf. Subjunc.* **huyese,** etc.

**hule** /'ule/ *m*, oilcloth; rubber

**hulla** /'uʎa; 'uya/ *f*, coal mine, coal, soft coal

**hullera** /u'ʎera; u'yera/ *f*, colliery, coal mine

**humanidad** /umani'ðað/ *f*, humanity; human nature; human weakness; compassion; affability; *Inf.* stoutness; *pl* study of humanities

**humanismo** /uma'nismo/ *m*, humanism

**humanista** /uma'nista/ *mf* humanist —*a* humanistic

**humanitario** /umani'tario/ *a* humanitarian

**humanizar** /umani'θar; umani'sar/ *vt* to humanize

**humano** /u'mano/ *a* human; understanding, sympathetic. *m*, human being

**humareda** /uma'reða/ *f*, cloud of smoke

**humeante** /ume'ante/ *a* smoking; smoky

**humear** /ume'ar/ *vi* to give forth smoke; give oneself airs

**humedad** /ume'ðað/ *f*, humidity; dampness; moisture

**humedecer** /umeðe'θer; umeðe'ser/ *vt irr* to moisten, wet, damp; —*vr* grow moist. See **conocer**

**húmedo** /'umeðo/ *a* humid; damp; wet

**húmero** /'umero/ *m*, humerus

**humildad** /umil'dað/ *f*, humility; lowliness; humbleness

**humilde** /u'milde/ *a* meek; lowly; humble

**humillación** /umiʎa'θion; umiya'sion/ *f*, humiliation

**humillante** /umi'ʎante; umi'yante/ *a* humiliating; debasing; mortifying

**humillar** /umi'ʎar; umi'yar/ *vt* to humble; humiliate; —*vr* humble oneself

**humo** /'umo/ *m*, smoke; vapor, fume; vanity, airs

**humor** /u'mor/ *m*, *Med.* humor; temperament, disposition; mood. **de buen h.,** good-tempered. **de mal h.,** ill-tempered

**humorada** /umo'raða/ *f*, humorous saying, extravagance, witticism

**humorismo** /umo'rismo/ *m*, humor, comic sense; humorousness

**humorista** /umo'rista/ *mf* humorist

**humorístico** /umo'ristiko/ *a* humorous

**humoso** /u'moso/ *a* smoky, reeky

**hundible** /un'diβle/ *a* sinkable

**hundido** /un'diðo/ *a* sunken (of cheeks, etc.); hollow, deep-set (of eyes)

**hundimiento** /undi'miento/ *m*, sinking; collapse; subsidence (of earth)

**hundir** /un'dir/ *vt* to sink; oppress; confound; destroy, ruin; —*vr* collapse (building); sink; *Fig. Inf.* disappear

**húngaro** /'uŋgaro/ **(-ra)** *a* and *n* Hungarian. *m*, Hungarian (language)

**Hungría** /uŋ'gria/ Hungary

**huno** /'uno/ **(-na)** *n* Hun

**huracán** /ura'kan/ *m*, hurricane

**huraña** /ura'ɲia/ *f*, shyness, unsociableness; diffidence; wildness (of animals, etc.)

**huraño** /u'raɲo/ *a* shy, unsociable; diffident; wild (of animals, etc.)

**hurgar** /ur'gar/ *vt* to stir; poke, rake; touch; rouse, incite —*vr* pick one's nose

**hurgón** /ur'gon/ *m*, fire rake, poker; *Inf.* sword

**hurgonada** /urgo'naða/ *f*, raking (of the fire, etc.)

**hurí** /u'ri/ *f*, houri

**hurón** /u'ron/ **(-ona)** *n* ferret —*a* shy, unsociable

**¡hurra!** /'urra/ *interj* Hurrah!

**hurtadillas** /urta'ðiʎas; urta'ðiyas/ **(a)** *adv* by stealth, secretly

**hurtar** /ur'tar/ *vt* to steal; encroach (sea, river); plagiarize; —*vr* hide oneself

**hurto** /'urto/ *m*, theft. **coger con el h. en las manos,** *Fig.* to catch red-handed

**husmear** /usme'ar/ *vt* to sniff out; *Inf.* pry; —*vi* smell bad (of meat)

**huso** /'uso/ *m*, spindle; bobbin

**¡huy!** /'ui/ *interj* (denoting pain or surprise) Oh!

# I

**ibérico** /i'βeriko/ *a* Iberian

**ibero** /i'βero/ **(-ra)** *a* and *n* Iberian

**íbice** /'iβiθe; 'iβise/ *m*, ibex

**icnografía** /iknogra'fia/ *f*, ichnography

**icnográfico** /ikno'grafiko/ *a* ichnographical

**icono** /i'kono/ *m*, icon

**iconoclasta** /ikono'klasta/ *a* iconoclastic. *mf* iconoclast

**iconografía** /ikonogra'fia/ *f*, iconography

**ictericia** /ikte'riθia; ikte'risia/ *f*, jaundice

**ictiología** /iktiolo'hia/ *f*, ichthyology

**ictiólogo** /ik'tiologo/ *m*, ichthyologist

**ida** /'iða/ *f*, setting out, departure, going; impetuous action; precipitancy; track, trail (of animals). **de i. y vuelta,** round trip (of tickets)

**idea** /i'ðea/ *f*, idea. *Inf.* **¡Qué ideas tienes!** What (odd) ideas you have!

**ideación** /iðea'θion; iðea'sion/ *f*, ideation

**ideal** /i'ðeal/ *a* ideal; perfect. *m*, model; ideal

**idealidad** /iðeali'ðað/ *f*, ideality

**idealismo** /iðea'lismo/ *m*, idealism

**idealista** /iðea'lista/ *a* idealistic. *mf* idealist

**idealización** /iðealiθa'θion; iðealisa'sion/ *f*, idealization

**idealizar** /iðeali'θar; iðeali'sar/ *vt* to idealize

**idealmente** /iðeal'mente/ *adv* ideally

**idear** /iðe'ar/ *vt* to imagine; devise; plan; design; draft, draw up

**ídem** /'iðem/ *adv* idem

**idéntico** /i'ðentiko/ *a* identical

**identidad** /iðenti'ðað/ *f*, identity

**identificable** /iðentifi'kaβle/ *a* identifiable

**identificación** /iðentifika'θion; iðentifika'sion/ *f*, identification

**identificar** /iðentifi'kar/ *vt* to identify; recognize; —*vr* (*with* **con**) identify oneself with

**ideografía** /iðeogra'fia/ *f*, ideography

**ideograma** /iðeo'grama/ *m*, ideogram

**ideología** /iðeolo'hia/ *f*, ideology. **i. racista,** racial ideology

**ideológico** /iðeo'lohiko/ *a* ideological

**ideólogo** /iðe'ologo/ **(-ga)** *n* ideologist; dreamer, planner

**idílico** /i'ðiliko/ *a* idyllic

**idilio** /i'ðilio/ *m*, idyll

**idioma** /i'ðioma/ *m*, language, tongue

**idiomático** /iðio'matiko/ *a* idiomatic

**idiosincrasia** /iðiosin'krasia/ *f*, idiosyncrasy

**idiosincrásico** /iðiosin'krasiko/ *a* idiosyncratic

**idiota** /i'ðiota/ *a* idiot; idiotic. *mf* idiot

**idiotez** /iðio'teθ; iðio'tes/ *f*, idiocy

**idiotismo** /iðio'tismo/ *m*, *Gram.* idiom; ignorance

**idólatra** /i'ðolatra/ *a* idolatrous; adoring. *mf* idolater, heathen

**idolatrar** /iðola'trar/ *vt* to idolize; worship, love excessively

**idolatría** /iðola'tria/ *f*, idolatry; adoration, idolization

**ídolo** /'iðolo/ *m*, idol

**idoneidad** /iðonei'ðað/ *f*, fitness, suitability; competence; capacity

**idóneo** /i'ðoneo/ *a* suitable; competent, fit

**idus** /'iðus/ *m pl*, ides

**iglesia** /i'glesia/ *f*, church. **i. colegial,** collegiate church. **cumplir con la i.,** to discharge one's religious duties. **llevar a una mujer a la i.,** to lead a woman to the altar

**ígneo** /'igneo/ *a* igneous

**ignición** /igni'θion; igni'sion/ *f*, ignition

**ignominia** /igno'minia/ *f*, ignominy, disgrace

**ignominioso** /ignomi'nioso/ *a* ignominious

**ignorancia** /igno'ranθia; igno'ransia/ *f*, ignorance. **pretender i.,** to plead ignorance

**ignorante** /igno'rante/ *a* ignorant; unaware, uninformed. *mf* ignoramus

**ignorar** /igno'rar/ *vt* to be unaware of, not to know

**ignoto** /ig'noto/ *a* unknown, undiscovered

**igual** /i'gual/ *a* equal; level; even, smooth; very similar; alike; uniform; proportionate; unchanging; constant; indifferent; same. *mf* equal. *m*, *Math.* equal sign. **al i.,** equally. **sin i.,** peerless, without equal. **Me es completamente i.,** It's all the same to me

**iguala** /i'guala/ *f*, equalizing; leveling; agreement, arrangement; cash adjustment

**igualación** /iguala'θion; iguala'sion/ *f*, equalization; leveling; arrangement, agreement; matching; *Math.* equation

**igualador** /iguala'ðor/ *a* equalizing; leveling

**igualar** /igua'lar/ *vt* to equalize, make equal; match; pair; level, flatten; smooth; adjust; arrange, agree upon; weigh, consider; *Math.* equate; —*vi* be equal

**igualdad** /igual'dað/ *f*, equality; uniformity, harmony; evenness; smoothness; identity, sameness. **i. de ánimo,** equability, equanimity

**igualitario** /iguali'tario/ *a* equalizing; egalitarian

**igualmente** /igual'mente/ *adv* equally; the same, likewise

**ijada** /i'haða/ *f*, side, flank; pain in the side

**ijadear** /ihaðe'ar/ *vt* to pant

**ijar** /i'har/ *m*, See **ijada**

**ilación** /ila'θion; ila'sion/ *f*, connection, reference

**ilegal** /ile'gal/ *a* illegal

**ilegalidad** /ilegali'ðað/ *f*, illegality

**ilegible** /ile'hiβle/ *a* illegible, unreadable

**ilegitimidad** /ilehitimi'ðað/ *f*, illegitimacy

**ilegítimo** /ile'hitimo/ *a* illegitimate; false

**íleon** /'ileon/ *m*, ilium

**ileso** /i'leso/ *a* unharmed, unhurt

**iletrado** /ile'traðo/ *a* unlettered, uncultured

**Ilíada** /i'liaða/ *f*, Iliad

**iliberal** /iliβe'ral/ *a* illiberal; narrow-minded

**iliberalidad** /iliβerali'ðað/ *f*, illiberality; narrow-mindedness

**ilícito** /i'liθito; i'lisito/ *a* illicit

**ilicitud** /iliθi'tuð; ilisi'tuð/ *f*, illicitness

**ilimitado** /ilimi'taðo/ *a* unlimited, boundless

**iliterato** /ilite'rato/ *a* illiterate, uncultured

**ilógico** /i'lohiko/ *a* illogical

**ilota** /i'lota/ *mf* helot

**iluminación** /ilumina'θion; ilumina'sion/ *f*, illumination; lighting. **i. intensiva,** floodlighting

**iluminador** /ilumina'ðor/ **(-ra)** *a* lighting; illuminating —*n Art.* illuminator

**iluminar** /ilumi'nar/ *vt* to illuminate; light; *Art.* illuminate; enlighten

**iluminativo** /ilumina'tiβo/ *a* illuminating

**ilusión** /ilu'sion/ *f*, illusion; illusoriness; hope; dream

**ilusionarse** /ilusio'narse/ *vr* to harbor illusions

**ilusivo** /ilu'siβo/ *a* deceptive, illusive

**iluso** /i'luso/ *a* deceived, deluded; dreamy; visionary

**ilusorio** /ilu'sorio/ *a* illusory; deceptive; null

**ilustración** /ilustra'θion; ilustra'sion/ *f*, illustration, picture; enlightenment; explanation; illustrated newspaper or magazine; erudition, knowledge; example, illustration

**ilustrado** /ilu'straðo/ *a* erudite, learned; knowledgeable, well-informed

**ilustrador** /ilustra'ðor/ **(-ra)** *a* illustrative —*n* illustrator

**ilustrar** /ilus'trar/ *vt* to explain, illustrate; enlighten, instruct; illustrate (books); make illustrious; inspire with divine light

**ilustrativo** /ilustra'tiβo/ *a* illustrative

**ilustre** /i'lustre/ *a* illustrious, distinguished

**ilustrísimo** /ilus'trisimo/ *a superl* most illustrious (title of bishops, etc.)

**imagen** /i'mahen/ *f*, image; effigy, statue; idea; metaphor, simile. **i. nítida,** sharp image

**imaginable** /imahi'naβle/ *a* imaginable

**imaginación** /imahina'θion; imahina'sion/ *f*, imagination

**imaginar** /imahi'nar/ *vi* to imagine; —*vt* suppose,

conjecture; discover, invent; imagine. **¡Imagínese!** Just imagine!

**imaginario** /imahi'nario/ *a* imaginary

**imaginativa** /imahina'tiβa/ *f*, imagination; common sense

**imaginativo** /imahina'tiβo/ *a* imaginative

**imaginería** /imahine'ria/ *f*, imagery

**imán** /i'man/ *m*, magnet; attraction, charm; imam

**imanación** /imana'θion; imana'sion/ *f*, magnetization

**imanar** /ima'nar/ *vt* to magnetize

**imbécil** /im'beθil; im'besil/ *a* imbecile; stupid, idiotic. *mf* imbecile

**imbecilidad** /imbeθili'ðað; imbesili'ðað/ *f*, imbecility; folly, stupidity

**imberbe** /im'berβe/ *a* beardless. *Inf.* **joven i.,** stripling

**imbibición** /imbiβi'θion; imbiβi'sion/ *f*, imbibing, absorption

**imborrable** /imbo'rraβle/ *a* ineffaceable

**imbuir** /im'buir/ *vt irr* to imbue. See **huir**

**imitable** /imi'taβle/ *a* imitable

**imitación** /imita'θion; imita'sion/ *f*, imitation; reproduction, copy

**imitado** /imi'taðo/ *a* imitation; imitated

**imitador** /imita'ðor/ **(-ra)** *a* imitation; imitative —*n* imitator

**imitar** /imi'tar/ *vt* to imitate; counterfeit

**imitativo** /imita'tiβo/ *a* imitative

**impacción** /impak'θion; impak'sion/ *f*, impact

**impaciencia** /impa'θienθia; impa'siensia/ *f*, impatience

**impacientar** /impaθien'tar; impasien'tar/ *vt* to make impatient, annoy; —*vr* grow impatient

**impaciente** /impa'θiente; impa'siente/ *a* impatient

**impacto** /im'pakto/ *m*, impact. **i. de lleno,** direct hit

**impalpabilidad** /impalpaβili'ðað/ *f*, impalpability

**impalpable** /impal'paβle/ *a* impalpable

**impar** /im'par/ *a* odd; unpaired; single, uneven. **número impar,** odd number

**imparcial** /impar'θial; impar'sial/ *a* impartial

**imparcialidad** /imparθiali'ðað; imparsiali'ðað/ *f*, impartiality

**imparisilábico** /imparisi'laβiko/ *a* imparisyllabic

**impartible** /impar'tiβle/ *a* indivisible

**impasibilidad** /impasiβili'ðað/ *f*, impassivity, indifference

**impasible** /impa'siβle/ *a* impassive

**impavidez** /impaβi'ðeθ; impaβi'ðes/ *f*, dauntlessness; serenity in the face of danger

**impávido** /im'paβiðo/ *a* dauntless; calm, composed, imperturbable

**impecabilidad** /impekaβili'ðað/ *f*, impeccability, perfection

**impecable** /impe'kaβle/ *a* impeccable, perfect

**impedido** /impe'ðiðo/ *a* disabled

**impedimento** /impeði'mento/ *m*, obstacle; hindrance; *Law.* impediment

**impedir** /impe'ðir/ *vt irr* to impede; obstruct; prevent; thwart; disable; delay; *Poet.* amaze. See **pedir**

**impeler** /impe'ler/ *vt* to push; incite; drive; urge

**impender** /impen'der/ *vt* to spend money

**impenetrabilidad** /impenetraβili'ðað/ *f*, impenetrability; imperviousness; obscurity, difficulty

**impenetrable** /impene'traβle/ *a* impenetrable, dense; impervious; *Fig.* unfathomable; obscure

**impenitencia** /impeni'tenθia; impeni'tensia/ *f*, impenitence

**impenitente** /impeni'tente/ *a* impenitent

**impensado** /impen'saðo/ *a* unexpected, unforeseen

**imperante** /impe'rante/ *a* ruling, dominant

**imperar** /impe'rar/ *vi* to rule; command

**imperativo** /impera'tiβo/ *a* commanding —*a* and *m*, *Gram.* imperative

**imperatorio** /impera'torio/ *a* imperial, imperatorial

**imperceptible** /imperθep'tiβle; impersep'tiβle/ *a* imperceptible

**imperdible** /imper'ðiβle/ *m*, safety pin

**imperdonable** /imperðo'naβle/ *a* unpardonable, inexcusable

**imperecedero** /impereθe'ðero; imperese'ðero/ *a* undying, eternal, everlasting

**imperfección** /imperfek'θion; imperfek'sion/ *f*, imperfection, inadequacy; fault, blemish; weakness

**imperfecto** /imper'fekto/ *a* imperfect; inadequate; faulty —*a* and *m*, *Gram.* imperfect

**imperial** /impe'rial/ *a* imperial. *f*, upper deck of a bus or streetcar

**imperialismo** /imperia'lismo/ *m*, imperialism

**imperialista** /imperia'lista/ *a* imperialistic. *mf* imperialist

**impericia** /impe'riθia; impe'risia/ *f*, inexpertness; unskillfulness, unhandiness

**imperio** /im'perio/ *m*, empire; rule, reign; command, sway; imperial dignity; arrogance, haughtiness. *Fig. Inf.* **valer un i.,** to be priceless

**imperioso** /impe'rioso/ *a* imperious

**imperito** /impe'rito/ *a* inexpert; clumsy, unskilled

**impermeabilidad** /impermeaβili''ðað/ *f*, watertightness; imperviousness; impermeability

**impermeabilizar** /impermeaβili'θar; impermeaβili'sar/ *vt* to waterproof

**impermeable** /imperme'aβle/ *a* watertight, impermeable; impervious. *m*, raincoat, mackintosh

**impersonal** /imperso'nal/ *a* impersonal

**impertérrito** /imper'territo/ *a* unafraid, dauntless

**impertinencia** /impertinen'θia; impertinen'sia/ *f*, impertinence, insolence; peevishness; fancy, whim; overexactness, meticulousness; interference, intrusion

**impertinente** /imperti'nente/ *a* impertinent; irrelevant; inopportune; officious, interfering

**impertinentes** /imperti'nentes/ *m pl*, lorgnettes

**imperturbabilidad** /imperturβaβili'ðað/ *f*, imperturbability

**imperturbable** /impertur'βaβle/ *a* calm, imperturbable

**impetrar** /impe'trar/ *vt* to obtain by entreaty; implore

**ímpetu** /'impetu/ *m*, impetus, momentum; speed, swiftness; violence

**impetuosidad** /impetuosi'ðað/ *f*, impetuosity

**impetuoso** /impe'tuoso/ *a* impetuous; precipitate

**impiedad** /impie'ðað/ *f*, cruelty, harshness; irreligion

**impío** /im'pio/ *a* impious, wicked; irreverent, irreligious

**implacabilidad** /implakaβili'ðað/ *f*, implacability, relentless

**implacable** /impla'kaβle/ *a* implacable

**implantación** /implanta'θion; implanta'sion/ *f*, inculcation, implantation

**implantar** /implan'tar/ *vt* to inculcate, implant (ideas, etc.)

**implicación** /implika'θion; implika'sion/ *f*, implication; contradiction (in terms); complicity

**implicar** /impli'kar/ *vt* to implicate; imply, infer; involve, entangle; —*vi* imply contradiction (gen. with negatives)

**implicatorio** /implika'torio/ *a* contradictory; implicated (in crime)

**implícito** /im'pliθito; im'plisito/ *a* implicit; implied

**implorante** /implo'rante/ *a* imploring

**implorar** /implo'rar/ *vt* to implore, entreat

**implume** /im'plume/ *a* without feathers, unfeathered

**impolítico** /impo'litiko/ *a* impolitic; unwise, inexpedient; tactless

**impoluto** /impo'luto/ *a* unpolluted, spotless, pure

**imponderabilidad** /imponderaβili'ðað/ *f*, imponderability

**imponderable** /imponde'raβle/ *a* imponderable, immeasurable; most excellent

**imponente** /impo'nente/ *a* imposing; awe-inspiring

**imponer** /impo'ner/ *vt irr* to exact; impose; malign, accuse falsely; instruct, acquaint; *Fig.* impress (with respect, etc.); invest or deposit (money); *Print.* impose; give, bestow (a name) —*vr* assert oneself. See **poner**

**imponible** /impo'niβle/ *a* taxable; ratable

**impopular** /impopu'lar/ *a* unpopular

**impopularidad** /impopulari'ðað/ *f*, unpopularity

**importable** /impor'taβle/ *a* importable

**importación** /importa'θion; importa'sion/ *f*, *Com.* importation; import

**importador** /importa'ðor/ **(-ra)** *a* import, importing —*n* importer

**importancia** /impor'tanθia; impor'tansia/ *f,* importance; magnitude

**importante** /impor'tante/ *a* important

**importar** /impor'tar/ *vi* to matter; be important; concern, interest; —*vt* amount to; import; include, comprise. **¡No importa!** It doesn't matter! Never mind!

**importe** /im'porte/ *m,* amount; value, cost. **i. bruto,** gross or total amount. **i. líquido** *or* **neto,** net amount

**importunación** /importuna'θion; importuna'sion/ *f,* importuning; importunity

**importunadamente** /importunaða'mente/ *adv* importunately

**importunar** /importu'nar/ *vt* to importune, pester

**importunidad** /importuni'ðað/ (*also* **importunación**) *f,* importunity

**importuno** /impor'tuno/ *a* importunate, inopportune, ill-timed; persistent; tedious

**imposibilidad** /imposiβili'ðað/ *f,* impossibility

**imposibilitado** /imposiβili'taðo/ *a* disabled, crippled; incapable, unable

**imposibilitar** /imposiβili'tar/ *vt* to disable; render unable; make impossible

**imposible** /impo'siβle/ *a* impossible

**imposición** /imposi'θion; imposi'sion/ *f,* imposition; exaction; tax, duty, tribute; *Print.* makeup **i. de manos,** *Eccl.* laying on of hands

**impostor** /impos'tor/ **(-ra)** *n* impostor

**impostura** /impos'tura/ *f,* swindle, imposture; aspersion, slur, imputation

**impotable** /impo'taβle/ *a* undrinkable

**impotencia** /impo'tenθia; impo'tensia/ *f,* impotence

**impotente** /impo'tente/ *a* impotent; powerless

**impracticabilidad** /impraktikaβili'ðað/ *f,* impracticability; impassability (of roads, etc.)

**impracticable** /imprakti'kaβle/ *a* impracticable; impossible; impassable (roads, etc.)

**imprecación** /impreka'θion; impreka'sion/ *f,* imprecation; curse, malediction

**imprecar** /impre'kar/ *vt* to imprecate, curse

**impregnación** /impregna'θion; impregna'sion/ *f,* impregnation, permeation, saturation

**impregnar** /impreg'nar/ *vt* impregnate; to permeate; —*vr* become impregnated

**impremeditado** /impremeði'taðo/ *a* unpremeditated

**imprenta** /im'prenta/ *f,* printing; printing house or office; print; letterpress

**impreparación** /imprepara'θion; imprepara'sion/ *f,* unpreparedness

**imprescindible** /impresθin'diβle; impressin'diβle/ *a* indispensable, essential

**impresión** /impre'sion/ *f,* printing; impression; effect; influence; imprint, stamp; *Print.* impression; print. **impresión digital,** fingerprint

**impresionable** /impresio'naβle/ *a* impressionable, susceptible

**impresionante** /impresio'nante/ *a* imposing; moving, affecting

**impresionar** /impresio'nar/ *vt* to impress; affect; fix in the mind; *Fig.* move deeply, stir; (*Radio.* cinema) record

**impresionismo** /impresio'nismo/ *m,* impressionism

**impresionista** /impresio'nista/ *mf* impressionist —*a* impressionistic

**impreso** /im'preso/ *m,* (gen. *pl*) printed matter

**impresor** /impre'sor/ *m,* printer

**imprevisión** /impreβi'sion/ *f,* lack of foresight; improvidence

**imprevisto** /impre'βisto/ *a* unforeseen, unexpected, sudden

**imprevistos** /impre'βistos/ *m pl,* incidental expenses

**imprimación** /imprima'θion; imprima'sion/ *f,* priming (of paint, etc.)

**imprimar** /impri'mar/ *vt* to prime (of paint)

**imprimir** /impri'mir/ *vt* to print; stamp; impress upon (the mind)

**improbabilidad** /improβaβili'ðað/ *f,* improbability

**improbable** /impro'βaβle/ *a* improbable

**improbo** /im'proβo/ *a* vicious, corrupt, dishonest; hard, arduous

**improductivo** /improðuk'tiβo/ *a* unproductive; unprofitable, fruitless

**impronta** /im'pronta/ *f, Art.* cast, mold

**impronunciable** /impronun'θiaβle; impronun'siaβle/ *a* unpronounceable; ineffable

**improperio** /impro'perio/ *m,* insult, affront

**impropiedad** /impropie'ðað/ *f,* inappropriateness; unsuitableness; impropriety

**impropio** /im'propio/ *a* unsuitable; inappropriate; inadequate; improper

**improporcionado** /improporθio'naðo; improporsio'naðo/ *a* disproportionate, out of proportion

**impróvido** /im'proβiðo/ *a* improvident, heedless

**improvisación** /improβisa'θion; improβisa'sion/ *f,* improvisation

**improvisador** /improβisa'ðor/ **(-ra)** *n* improviser

**improvisamente** /improβisa'mente/ *adv* unexpectedly, suddenly

**improvisar** /improβi'sar/ *vt* to improvise

**improviso, improvisto** /impro'βiso, impro'βisto/ *a* unexpected, unforeseen. **al** ( *or* **de**) **improviso,** unexpectedly

**imprudencia** /impru'ðenθia; impru'ðensia/ *f,* imprudence, rashness, indiscretion

**imprudente** /impru'ðente/ *a* imprudent, unwise, rash

**impúbero** /im'puβero/ *a* below the age of puberty

**impudencia** /impu'ðenθia; impu'ðensia/ *f,* impudence, impertinence

**impudente** /impu'ðente/ *a* brazen, impudent

**impudicia** /impu'ðiθia; impu'ðisia/ *f,* immodesty, brazenness

**impúdico** /im'puðiko/ *a* immodest, brazen

**impuesto** /im'puesto/ *m,* tax; duty. **i. de utilidades,** income tax. **i. sucesorio,** inheritance tax

**impugnable** /impug'naβle/ *a* impugnable, refutable

**impugnación** /impugna'θion; impugna'sion/ *f,* refutation; contradiction

**impugnar** /impug'nar/ *vt* to refute, contradict; oppose; criticize

**impulsar** /impul'sar/ *vt* to impel; prompt; cause; drive, operate, propel

**impulsión** /impul'sion/ *f,* impulse; impetus; *Mech.* operation, driving; propulsion

**impulsivo** /impul'siβo/ *a* impulsive; irreflexive, precipitate

**impulso** /im'pulso/ *m,* stimulus, incitement; impulse, desire; *Mech.* drive, impulse

**impulsor** /impul'sor/ **(-ra)** *a* driving, impelling —*n* driver, operator

**impune** /im'pune/ *a* unpunished

**impunemente** /impune'mente/ *adv* with impunity

**impunidad** /impuni'ðað/ *f,* impunity

**impureza** /impu'reθa; impu'resa/ *f,* impurity; lack of chastity; obscenity, indecency

**impurificar** /impurifi'kar/ *vt* to defile; make impure; adulterate

**impuro** /im'puro/ *a* impure; adulterated; polluted; immoral, unchaste

**imputable** /impu'taβle/ *a* imputable

**imputación** /imputa'θion; imputa'sion/ *f,* imputation

**imputador** /imputa'ðor/ **(-ra)** *n* imputer, attributer

**imputar** /impu'tar/ *vt* to impute; attribute

**inacabable** /inaka'βaβle/ *a* endless, interminable, ceaseless; wearisome

**inaccesibilidad** /inakθesiβili'ðað; inaksesiβili'ðað/ *f,* inaccessibility

**inaccesible** /inakθe'siβle; inakse'siβle/ *a* inaccessible; incomprehensible

**inacción** /inak'θion; inak'sion/ *f,* inaction

**inaceptable** /inaθep'taβle; inasep'taβle/ *a* unacceptable

**inactividad** /inaktiβi'ðað/ *f,* inactivity; quiescence; idleness

**inactivo** /inak'tiβo/ *a* inactive; idle; unemployed; *Naut.* laid-up

**inadaptable** /inaðap'taβle/ *a* inadaptable

**inadecuado** /inaðe'kuaðo/ *a* inadequate, insufficient

**inadmisible** /inaðmi'siβle/ *a* inadmissible

**inadvertencia** /inaðβer'tenθia; inaðβer'tensia/ *f*, inadvertence; oversight, mistake, slip

**inadvertido** /inaðβer'tiðo/ *a* unnoticed; inattentive; inadvertent, unintentional; negligent

**inafectado** /inafek'taðo/ *a* unaffected, natural

**inagotable** /inago'taβle/ *a* inexhaustible, unfailing; abundant

**inaguantable** /inaguan'taβle/ *a* unbearable, intolerable

**inajenable** /inahe'naβle/ *a* inalienable

**inalámbrica** /ina'lambrika/ *f*, radio station

**inalienable** /inalie'naβle/ *a* inalienable

**inalterable** /inalte'raβle/ *a* unalterable

**inamovibilidad** /inamoβiβili'ðað/ *f*, immovability

**inamovible** /inamo'βiβle/ *a* immovable

**inanición** /inani'θion; inani'sion/ *f*, inanition

**inanimado** /inani'maðo/ *a* inanimate

**inapagable** /inapa'gaβle/ *a* inextinguishable

**inapelable** /inape'laβle/ *a* unappealable; irremediable, inevitable

**inapetencia** /inape'tenθia; inape'tensia/ *f*, lack of appetite

**inaplazable** /inapla'θaβle; inapla'saβle/ *a* undeferable, unable to be postponed

**inaplicable** /inapli'kaβle/ *a* inapplicable

**inaplicación** /inaplika'θion; inaplika'sion/ *f*, laziness, inattention, negligence

**inaplicado** /inapli'kaðo/ *a* lazy; inattentive; careless

**inapreciable** /inapre'θiaβle; inapre'siaβle/ *a* inappreciable; invaluable

**inarmónico** /inar'moniko/ *a* unharmonious, discordant

**inarticulado** /inartiku'laðo/ *a* inarticulate

**inasequible** /inase'kiβle/ *a* unattainable; out of reach

**inaudible** /inau'ðiβle/ *a* inaudible

**inaudito** /inau'ðito/ *a* unheard of, unprecedented; extraordinary, strange

**inauguración** /inaugura'θion; inaugura'sion/ *f*, inauguration; induction; inception, commencement

**inaugural** /inaugu'ral/ *a* inaugural

**inaugurar** /inaugu'rar/ *vt* to inaugurate; induct

**inaveriguable** /inaβeri'guaβle/ *a* unascertainable

**inca** /'inka/ *mf* Inca

**incaico** /in'kaiko/ *a* Incan

**incalculable** /inkalku'laβle/ *a* incalculable; innumerable

**incalificable** /inkalifi'kaβle/ *a* indescribable, unclassable; vile

**incandescencia** /inkandes'θenθia; inkandes'sensia/ *f*, incandescence, white heat

**incandescente** /inkandes'θente; inkandes'sente/ *a* incandescent

**incansable** /inkan'saβle/ *a* indefatigable; unflagging; unwearying

**incapacidad** /inkapaθi'ðað; inkapasi'ðað/ *f*, incapacity; incompetence

**incapacitar** /inkapaθi'tar; inkapasi'tar/ *vt* to incapacitate; disable

**incapaz** /inka'paθ; inka'pas/ *a* incapable, incompetent; inefficient

**incasable** /inka'saβle/ *a* unmarriageable; antimarriage

**incautarse** /inkau'tarse/ *vr* to seize, take possession (of)

**incauto** /in'kauto/ *a* incautious; unwary

**incendiar** /inθen'diar; insen'diar/ *vt* to set on fire, set alight

**incendiario** /inθen'diario; insen'diario/ **(-ia)** *a* and *n* incendiary

**incendiarismo** /inθendia'rismo; insendia'rismo/ *m*, incendiarism

**incendio** /in'θendio; in'sendio/ *m*, conflagration, fire; consuming passion

**incensar** /inθen'sar; insen'sar/ *vt irr Eccl.* to cense, incense; flatter. See **acertar**

**incensario** /inθen'sario; insen'sario/ *m*, incense burner, incensory

**incentivo** /inθen'tiβo; insen'tiβo/ *m*, incentive; encouragement

**incertidumbre** /inθerti'ðumbre; inserti'ðumbre/ *f*, uncertainty, incertitude

**incesable, incesante** /inθe'saβle, inθe'sante; inse'saβle, inse'sante/ *a* incessant, continuous

**incesto** /in'θesto; in'sesto/ *m*, incest

**incestuoso** /inθes'tuoso; inses'tuoso/ *a* incestuous

**incidencia** /inθi'ðenθia; insi'ðensia/ *f*, incidence

**incidental** /inθiðen'tal; insiðen'tal/ *a* incidental

**incidente** /inθi'ðente; insi'ðente/ *a* incidental. *m*, incident, event, occurrence

**incidir** /inθi'ðir; insi'ðir/ *vi* (*with en*) to incur, fall into (e.g. *Incidió en el pecado*, He fell into sin)

**incienso** /in'θienso; in'sienso/ *m*, incense; flattery

**incierto** /in'θierto; in'sierto/ *a* untrue, false; uncertain; unknown

**incineración** /inθinera'θion; insinera'sion/ *f*, incineration

**incinerador** /inθinera'ðor; insinera'ðor/ *m*, incinerator

**incinerar** /inθine'rar; insine'rar/ *vt* incinerate, reduce to ashes

**incipiente** /inθi'piente; insi'piente/ *a* incipient

**incircunciso** /inθirkun'θiso; insirkun'siso/ *a* uncircumcised

**incisión** /inθi'sion; insi'sion/ *f*, incision

**incisivo** /inθi'siβo; insi'siβo/ *a* sharp, keen; incisive, sarcastic, caustic

**inciso** /in'θiso; in'siso/ *m*, clause; comma

**incitación** /inθita'θion; insita'sion/ *f*, incitement; *Fig.* spur, stimulus

**incitar** /inθi'tar; insi'tar/ *vt* to incite; stimulate, encourage

**incivil** /inθi'βil; insi'βil/ *a* rude, discourteous, uncivil

**incivilidad** /inθiβili'ðað; insiβili'ðað/ *f*, rudeness, incivility

**inclasificable** /inklasifi'kaβle/ *a* unclassifiable

**inclemencia** /inkle'menθia; inkle'mensia/ *f*, harshness, severity; inclemency (of the weather). **a la i.,** at the mercy of the elements

**inclemente** /inkle'mente/ *a* inclement

**inclinación** /inklina'θion; inklina'sion/ *f*, inclination; slope; slant; tendency, propensity; predilection, fondness; bow (in greeting); *Geom.* inclination

**inclinar** /inkli'nar/ *vt* to incline, tilt, slant; bow; bend; influence; persuade; —*vi* resemble; —*vr* lean; stoop; tilt; tend, incline (to), view favorably (e.g. *Me inclino a creerlo*, I am inclined to believe it)

**ínclito** /in'klito/ *a* famous, celebrated

**incluir** /in'kluir/ *vt irr* to comprise, embrace, contain; include, take into account. See **huir**

**inclusa** /in'klusa/ *f*, foundling home

**inclusión** /inklu'sion/ *f*, inclusion; relationship, intercourse, friendship

**inclusive** /inklu'siβe/ *adv* including

**inclusivo** /inklu'siβo/ *a* inclusive

**incluso** /in'kluso/ *adv* including, inclusive —*prep* even

**incoar** /inko'ar/ *vt* to begin (especially lawsuits)

**incoativo** /inkoa'tiβo/ *a* inceptive

**incobrable** /inko'βraβle/ *a* irrecoverable; irredeemable

**incógnita** /in'kognita/ *f*, *Math.* X; unknown quantity; secret motive; unknown lady

**incógnito** /in'kognito/ *a* unknown. *m*, incognito, assumed name, disguise

**incoherencia** /inkoe'renθia; inkoe'rensia/ *f*, incoherence

**incoherente** /inkoe'rente/ *a* incoherent, disconnected, illogical

**íncola** /in'kinkola/ *mf* resident, dweller, inhabitant

**incoloro** /inko'loro/ *a* colorless, uncolored

**incólume** /in'kolume/ *a* unharmed, unscathed; untouched, undamaged

**incombustibilidad** /inkombustiβili'ðað/ *f*, incombustibility

**incommensurabilidad** /inkommensuraβili'ðað/ *f*, incommensurability

**incommutable** /inkommu'taβle/ *a* unalterable, immutable, unchangeable

**incomodar** /inkomo'ðar/ *vt* to disturb, incommode, inconvenience; annoy; —*vr* disturb oneself, put oneself out; grow angry. **¡No se incomode!** Please don't move!; Please don't be angry!

**incomodidad** /inkomoðí'ðaðó/ f, discomfort; inconvenience; trouble, upset; annoyance

**incómodo** /in'komoðoó/ a uncomfortable; inconvenient; troublesome, tiresome. m, discomfort; inconvenience

**incomparable** /inkompa'raβle/ a incomparable

**incompartible** /inkompar'tiβle/ a indivisible

**incompasivo** /inkompa'siβo/ a unsympathetic, hard

**incompatibilidad** /inkompatiβili'ðaðó/ f, incompatibility

**incompatible** /inkompa'tiβle/ a incompatible

**incompetencia** /inkompe'tenθia; inkompe'tensia/ f, incompetence

**incompetente** /inkompe'tente/ a incompetent

**incomplejo, incomplexo** /inkom'pleho, inkom'plekso/ a noncomplex, simple

**incompleto** /inkom'pleto/ a incomplete

**incomponible** /inkompo'niβle/ a unrepairable, unmendable

**incomprensibilidad** /inkomprensiβili'ðaðó/ f, incomprehensibility

**incomprensible** /inkompren'siβle/ a incomprehensible

**incomprensión** /inkompren'sion/ f, incomprehension

**incomunicado** /inkomuni'kaðo/ a in solitary confinement (of a prisoner)

**incomunicar** /inkomuni'kar/ vt to sentence to solitary confinement; isolate, deprive of means of communication; —vr become a recluse

**inconcebible** /inkonθe'βiβle; inkonseβiβle/ a inconceivable

**inconciliable** /inkonθi'liaβle; inkonsi'liaβle/ a irreconcilable

**incondicional** /inkondiθio'nal; inkondisio'nal/ a unconditional

**inconexión** /inkone'ksion/ f, disconnectedness

**inconexo** /inkone'kso/ a unconnected; incoherent

**inconfeso** /inkon'feso/ a unconfessed

**incongruencia** /inkoŋgru'enθia; inkoŋgru'ensia/ f, incongruity

**incongruente** /inkoŋgru'ente/ a incongruous, inappropriate

**inconmovible** /inkomo'βiβle/ a immovable; unflinching, unshakable

**inconquistable** /inkonkis'taβle/ a unconquerable; Fig. resolute, inflexible

**inconsciencia** /inkon'sθienθia; inkonssiensia/ f, unconsciousness; subconscious

**inconsciente** /inkon'sθiente; inkons'siente/ a unconscious, involuntary; subconscious

**inconsecuencia** /inkonse'kuenθia; inkonse'kuensia/ f, inconsequence; inconsistency

**inconsecuente** /inkonse'kuente/ a inconsequential; inconsistent

**inconsideración** /inkonsiðera'θion; inkonsiðera-'sion/ f, thoughtlessness

**inconsiderado** /inkonsiðe'raðo/ a thoughtless; heedless, selfish

**inconsiguiente** /inkonsi'giente/ a illogical, inconsistent

**inconsistencia** /inkonsis'tenθia; inkonsis'tensia/ f, inconsistency

**inconsistente** /inkonsis'tente/ a inconsistent

**inconsolable** /inkonso'laβle/ a inconsolable

**inconstancia** /inkons'tanθia; inkons'tansia/ f, inconstancy, infidelity

**inconstante** /inkons'tante/ a inconstant, fickle

**inconstitucional** /inkonstituθio'nal; inkonstitusio'nal/ a unconstitutional

**incontaminado** /inkontami'naðo/ a uncontaminated

**incontestable** /inkontes'taβle/ a undeniable, unquestionable

**incontinencia** /inkonti'nenθia; inkonti'nensia/ f, incontinence

**incontinente** /inkonti'nente/ a incontinent

**incontrastable** /inkontras'taβle/ a insuperable, invincible; undeniable, unanswerable; Fig. unshakable, inconvincible

**incontrovertible** /inkontroβer'tiβle/ a undeniable, incontrovertible

**inconvencible** /inkomben'θiβle; inkomben'siβle/ a inconvincible

**inconveniencia** /inkombe'nienθia; inkombe'niensia/ f, discomfort; inconvenience; unsuitability

**inconveniente** /inkombe'niente/ a awkward, inconvenient; uncomfortable; inappropriate. m, inconvenience; obstacle, impediment; disadvantage

**inconvertible** /inkomber'tiβle/ a inconvertible

**incorporación** /inkorpora'θion; inkorpora'sion/ f, incorporation

**incorporar** /inkorpo'rar/ vt to incorporate; cause to sit up, lift up; —vr sit up, raise oneself; become a member, join (associations); be incorporated; blend, mix

**incorporeidad** /inkorporei'ðaðó/ f, incorporeity

**incorpóreo** /inkor'poreo/ a incorporeal; immaterial

**incorrección** /inkorrek'θion; inkorrek'sion/ f, incorrectness; indecorum, impropriety

**incorrecto** /inko'rrekto/ a incorrect; indecorous, unbecoming, improper

**incorregible** /inkorre'hiβle/ a incorrigible

**incorrupción** /inkorrup'θion; inkorrup'sion/ f, incorruption; purity; integrity; wholesomeness

**incorrupto** /inko'rrupto/ a incorrupt; pure; chaste

**incredibilidad** /inkreðiβili'ðaðó/ f, incredibility

**incredulidad** /inkreðuli'ðaðó/ f, incredulity, scepticism

**incrédulo** /in'kreðulo/ (**-la**) a incredulous; atheistic —n atheist; unbeliever, sceptic

**increíble** /inkre'iβle/ a incredible; marvelous, extraordinary

**incremento** /inkre'mento/ m, increment, increase

**increpación** /inkrepa'θion; inkrepa'sion/ f, scolding, harsh rebuke

**increpar** /inkre'par/ vt to scold, rebuke harshly

**incriminante** /inkrimi'nante/ a incriminating

**incriminar** /inkrimi'nar/ vt to incriminate, accuse; exaggerate (a charge, etc.)

**incruento** /inkru'ento/ a bloodless, unstained with blood

**incrustación** /inkrusta'θion; inkrusta'sion/ f, incrustation; Art. inlay

**incubación** /inkuβa'θion; inkuβa'sion/ f, hatching; Med. incubation

**incubadora** /inkuβa'ðora/ f, incubator (for chickens)

**incubar** /inku'βar/ vi to sit on eggs (of hens); —vt hatch; Med. incubate

**inculcación** /inkulka'θion; inkulka'sion/ f, inculcation, instillment

**inculcar** /inkul'kar/ vt to press one thing against another; instill, inculcate; —vr grow more fixed in one's views

**inculpable** /inkul'paβle/ a blameless, innocent

**inculpar** /inkul'par/ vt to blame; accuse

**incultivable** /inkulti'βaβle/ a uncultivatable; untillable

**inculto** /in'kulto/ a uncultivated, untilled; uncultured; uncivilized

**incultura** /inkul'tura/ f, lack of cultivation; lack of culture

**incumbencia** /inkum'benθia; inkumbensia/ f, obligation, moral responsibility, duty

**incumbir** /inkum'bir/ vi to be incumbent on; concern

**incumplimiento** /inkumpli'miento/ m, nonfulfilment

**incurable** /inku'raβle/ a incurable; inveterate, hopeless

**incuria** /in'kuria/ f, negligence, carelessness

**incurioso** /inku'rioso/ a incurious

**incurrir** /inku'rrir/ vi (with en) to fall into (error, etc.); incur (dislike, etc.)

**incursión** /inkur'sion/ f, incursion; inroad

**indagación** /indaga'θion; indaga'sion/ f, investigation, inquiry

**indagador** /indaga'ðor/ (**-ra**) a investigating, inquiring —n investigator

**indagar** /inda'gar/ vt to investigate, examine; inquire. **i. precios,** to inquire about prices

**indebido** /inde'βiðo/ a undue, immoderate improper; illegal, illicit

**indecencia** /inde'θenθia; inde'sensia/ f, indecency; obscenity; impropriety

**indecente** /inde'θente; inde'sente/ *a* indecent; obscene; improper

**indecible** /inde'θiβle; inde'siβle/ *a* unutterable, ineffable, unspeakable

**indeciso** /inde'θiso; inde'siso/ *a* undecided; hesitant, irresolute; vague; noncommittal

**indeclinable** /indekli'naβle/ *a* obligatory; unavoidable; *Gram.* indeclinable, uninflected

**indecoro** /inde'koro/ *m,* impropriety, indecorum

**indecoroso** /indeko'roso/ *a* indecorous, unbecoming; base, mean

**indefectible** /indefek'tiβle/ *a* unfailing; perfect

**indefectiblemente** /indefektiβle'mente/ *adv* invariably

**indefendible** /indefen'diβle/ *a* indefensible

**indefenso** /inde'fenso/ *a* unprotected, defenseless

**indefinible** /indefi'niβle/ *a* indefinable, vague; indescribable

**indefinido** /indefi'niðo/ *a* indefinite, vague; undefined; *Gram.* indefinite

**indeleble** /inde'leβle/ *a* indelible

**indeliberado** /indeliβe'raðo/ *a* unpremeditated; unconsidered

**indemme** /in'demme/ *a* unharmed, undamaged

**indemnidad** /indemni'ðað/ *f,* indemnity

**indemnización** /indemniθa'θion; indemnisa'sion/ *f,* compensation, indemnification; indemnity

**indemnizar** /indemni'θar; indemni'sar/ *vt* to indemnify, compensate

**indemostrable** /indemo'straβle/ *a* indemonstrable, incapable of demonstration

**independencia** /indepen'denθia; indepen'densia/ *f,* independence

**independiente** /indepen'diente/ *a* independent; self-contained

**indescifrable** /indesθi'fraβle; indessi'fraβle/ *a* undecipherable; illegible

**indestructible** /indestruk'tiβle/ *a* indestructible

**indeterminado** /indetermi'naðo/ *a* indeterminate; vague, doubtful, uncertain; hesitant, irresolute; *Math.* indeterminate

**indiano** /in'diano/ **(-na)** *a* and *n* Indian; East Indian; West Indian. *m,* nouveau riche, one who returns rich from the Western Hemisphere

**indicación** /indika'θion; indika'sion/ *f,* indication; sign, evidence; intimation, hint

**indicador** /indika'ðor/ *a* indicative. *m,* indicator. **i. del nivel de gasolina,** gas gauge

**indicar** /indi'kar/ *vt* to indicate; show; point out; simply, suggest; intimate

**indicativo** /indika'tiβo/ *a* indicative —*a* and *m, Gram.* indicative

**índice** /'indiθe; 'indise/ *m,* index; indication, sign; library catalog; catalog room; hand (of a clock); pointer, needle (of instruments); gnomon (of a sundial); *Math.* index; forefinger. **I. expurgatorio,** the Index

**indicio** /in'diθio; in'disio/ *m,* indication; sign; evidence. **indicios vehementes,** circumstantial evidence

**índico** /'indiko/ *a* Indian

**indiferencia** /indife'renθia; indife'rensia/ *f,* indifference

**indiferente** /indife'rente/ *a* indifferent

**indígena** /in'dihena/ *a* native, indigenous. *mf* native

**indigencia** /indi'henθia; indi'hensia/ *f,* destitution, indigence; impecuniosity

**indigente** /indi'hente/ *a* destitute, indigent; impecunious

**indigestión** /indihes'tion/ *f,* indigestion

**indigesto** /indi'hesto/ *a* indigestible; *Lit.* muddled, confused; unsociable, brusque

**indignación** /indigna'θion; indigna'sion/ *f,* indignation, anger

**indignado** /indig'naðo/ *a* indignant

**indignar** /indig'nar/ *vt* to anger, make indignant; —*vr* grow angry

**indignidad** /indigni'ðað/ *f,* unworthiness; indignity; personal affront

**indigno** /in'digno/ *a* unworthy; base, despicable

**índigo** /'indigo/ *m,* indigo

**indio** /'indio/ **(-ia)** *a* Indian; blue —*n* Indian. *m,* indium

**indirecta** /indi'rekta/ *f,* hint, covert suggestion, innuendo. *Inf.* **i. del padre Cobos,** strong hint

**indirecto** /indi'rekto/ *a* indirect

**indisciplina** /indisθi'plina; indissi'plina/ *f,* indiscipline

**indisciplinado** /indisθipli'naðo; indissipli'naðo/ *a* undisciplined

**indiscreción** /indiskre'θion; indiskre'sion/ *f,* indiscretion

**indiscreto** /indis'kreto/ *a* indiscreet

**indiscutible** /indisku'tiβle/ *a* unquestionable, undeniable

**indisoluble** /indiso'luβle/ *a* indissoluble

**indispensable** /indispen'saβle/ *a* indispensable

**indisponer** /indispo'ner/ *vt irr* to make unfit or incapable; indispose, make ill; (*with con or contra*) set against, make trouble with; —*vr* be indisposed; (*with con or contra*) quarrel with. See **poner**

**indisposición** /indisposi'θion; indisposi'sion/ *f,* reluctance, disinclination; indisposition, brief illness

**indisputable** /indispu'taβle/ *a* indisputable

**indistinguible** /indistiŋ'guiβle/ *a* undistinguishable

**indistinto** /indis'tinto/ *a* indistinct; indeterminate; vague

**individual** /indiβi'ðual/ *a* individual; peculiar, characteristic. *m,* (tennis) single

**individualidad** /indiβiðuali'ðað/ *f,* individuality

**individualismo** /indiβiðua'lismo/ *m,* individualism

**individualista** /indiβiðua'lista/ *a* individualistic. *mf* individualist

**individuo** /indi'βiðuo/ **(-ua)** *a* individual; indivisible. *m,* individual; member, associate; *Inf.* self —*n Inf.* person

**indivisibilidad** /indiβisiβili'ðað/ *f,* indivisibility

**indivisible** /indiβi'siβle/ *a* indivisible

**indiviso** /indi'βiso/ *a* undivided

**indochino** /indo'tʃino/ **(-na)** *a* and *n* Indochinese

**indócil** /in'doθil; in'dosil/ *a* unmanageable; disobedient; brittle, unpliable (of metals)

**indocilidad** /indoθili'ðað; indosili'ðað/ *f,* indocility; disobedience; brittleness (of metals)

**indoeuropeo** /indoeuro'peo/ *a* Indo-European

**indoísmo** /indo'ismo/ *m,* Hinduism

**índole** /'indole/ *f,* temperament, nature; kind, sort

**indolencia** /indo'lenθia; indo'lensia/ *f,* idleness, indolence

**indolente** /indo'lente/ *a* nonpainful; indifferent, insensible; idle, indolent

**indoloro** /indo'loro/ *a* painless

**indomable** /indo'maβle/ *a* untamable; invincible; indomitable; ungovernable, unmanageable

**indomado** /indo'maðo/ *a* untamed

**indómito** /in'domito/ *a* untamed; untamable; unmanageable, unruly; indomitable

**indonesio** /indo'nesio/ **(-ia)** *a* and *n* Indonesian

**indostanés** /indosta'nes/ *a* Hindustani

**indostani** /indos'tani/ *m,* Hindustani (language)

**indubitable** /induβi'taβle/ *a* unquestionable

**inducción** /induk'θion; induk'sion/ *f,* persuasion; *Phys.* induction

**inducir** /indu'θir; indu'sir/ *vt irr* to persuade, prevail upon; induce; infer, conclude. See **conducir**

**inductivo, inductor** /induk'tiβo, induk'tor/ *a* inductive

**indudable** /indu'ðaβle/ *a* indubitable

**indulgencia** /indul'henθia; indul'hensia/ *f,* overkindness, tenderness; *Eccl.* indulgence

**indulgente** /indul'hente/ *a* indulgent, tender; tolerant

**indultar** /indul'tar/ *vt* to pardon; exempt

**indulto** /in'dulto/ *m,* amnesty; exemption; forgiveness; *Eccl.* indult

**indumentaria** /indumen'taria/ *f,* clothing; outfit (of clothes)

**industria** /in'dustria/ *f,* assiduity, industriousness; pains, effort, ingenuity; industry. **i. pesada,** heavy industry. **i. cárnica,** meat industry. **i. extractivos,** mining industry

**industrial** /indus'trial/ *a* industrial. *m,* industrialist

**industrialismo** /industria'lismo/ *m*, industrialism
**industrialización** /industrialiθa'θion; industrialisa'sion/ *f*, industrialization
**industriar** /indus'triar/ *vt* to teach, train; —*vr* find a way, manage, succeed in
**industrioso** /indus'trioso/ *a* industrious; diligent, assiduous
**inédito** /i'neðito/ *a* unpublished; unedited
**inefable** /ine'faβle/ *a* ineffable
**ineficacia** /inefi'kaθia; inefi'kasia/ *f*, inefficiency; ineffectiveness
**ineficaz** /inefi'kaθ; inefi'kas/ *a* ineffective; inefficient
**ineludible** /inelu'ðiβle/ *a* unavoidable
**ineptitud** /inepti'tuð/ *f*, ineptitude
**inepto** /i'nepto/ *a* inept, incompetent; unfit, unsuitable
**inequívoco** /ine'kiβoko/ *a* unequivocal
**inercia** /i'nerθia; i'nersia/ *f*, inertia
**inerme** /i'nerme/ *a* defenseless, unprotected; (*Bot. Zool.*) unarmed
**inerte** /i'nerte/ *a* inert
**inescrutable** /ineskru'taβle/ *a* inscrutable, unfathomable
**inesperado** /inespe'raðo/ *a* unexpected, sudden
**inestabilidad** /inestaβili'ðað/ *f*, instability
**inestable** /ines'taβle/ *a* unstable
**inestimable** /inesti'maβle/ *a* inestimable
**inevitable** /ineβi'taβle/ *a* inevitable
**inexactitud** /ineksakti'tuð/ *f*, inexactitude, inaccuracy; error, mistake
**inexacto** /ine'ksakto/ *a* inexact, inaccurate; erroneous
**inexcusable** /inseksku'saβle/ *a* inexcusable, unforgivable; indispensable
**inexhausto** /ineks'austo/ *a* inexhaustible
**inexistente** /ineksis'tente/ *a* nonexistent
**inexorable** /inekso'raβle/ *a* inexorable
**inexperiencia** /inekspe'rienθia; inekspe'riensia/ *f*, inexperience
**inexperto** /ineks'perto/ *a* inexperienced; inexpert
**inexplicable** /inekspli'kaβle/ *a* inexplicable
**inexplorado** /ineksplo'raðo/ *a* unexplored
**inexplosible** /ineksplo'siβle/ *a* inexplosive
**inexpresivo** /inekspre'siβo/ *a* inexpressive; reticent
**inexpugnable** /inekspug'naβle/ *a* impregnable; *Fig.* unshakable, firm; obstinate
**inextinguible** /inekstiŋ'guiβle/ *a* inextinguishable; everlasting, perpetual
**infalibilidad** /infaliβili'ðað/ *f*, infallibility
**infalible** /infa'liβle/ *a* infallible
**infamación** /infama'θion; infama'sion/ *f*, defamation
**infamador** /infama'ðor/ **(-ra)** *a* slandering —*n* slanderer
**infamar** /infa'mar/ *vt* to defame, slander
**infame** /in'fame/ *a* infamous, vile
**infamia** /in'famia/ *f*, infamy; baseness, vileness
**infancia** /in'fanθia; in'fansia/ *f*, infancy, babyhood; childhood
**infanta** /in'fanta/ *f*, female child under seven years; infanta, any Spanish royal princess; wife of a Spanish royal prince
**infantado** /infan'taðo/ *m*, land belonging to an *infante* or *infanta*
**infante** /in'fante/ *m*, male child under seven years; infante, any Spanish royal prince except an heir-apparent; infantryman. **i. de coro,** choir boy
**infantería** /infante'ria/ *f*, infantry
**infanticida** /infanti'θiða; infanti'siða/ *a* infanticidal. *mf* infanticide (person)
**infanticidio** /infanti'θiðio; infanti'siðio/ *m*, infanticide (act)
**infantil** /infan'til/ *a* infantile, babyish; innocent, candid
**infatigable** /infati'gaβle/ *a* unwearying, indefatigable
**infatuación** /infatua'θion; infatua'sion/ *f*, infatuation
**infatuar** /infa'tuar/ *vt* to infatuate; —*vr* become infatuated
**infausto** /in'fausto/ *a* unlucky, unfortunate
**infección** /infek'θion; infek'sion/ *f*, infection
**infeccioso** /infek'θioso; infek'sioso/ *a* infectious

**infectar** /infek'tar/ *vt* to infect; corrupt, pervert; —*vr* become infected; be corrupted
**infecto** /in'fekto/ *a* infected; corrupt, perverted; tainted
**infecundidad** /infekundi'ðað/ *f*, sterility
**infecundo** /infe'kundo/ *a* sterile, barren
**infelice** /infe'liθe; infe'lise/ *a* *Poet.* unhappy, unfortunate
**infelicidad** /infeliθi'ðað; infelisi'ðað/ *f*, unhappiness
**infeliz** /infe'liθ; infe'lis/ *a* unhappy; unfortunate; *Inf.* simple, good-hearted
**inferencia** /infe'renθia; infe'rensia/ *f*, inference, connection
**inferior** /infe'rior/ *a* inferior; lower; second-rate; subordinate. *mf* inferior, subordinate
**inferioridad** /inferiori'ðað/ *f*, inferiority
**inferir** /infe'rir/ *vt irr* to infer, deduce; involve, imply; occasion; inflict. See **sentir**
**infernáculo** /infer'nakulo/ *m*, hopscotch
**infernal** /infer'nal/ *a* infernal; devilish, fiendish; wicked, inhuman; *Inf.* confounded
**inferno** /in'ferno/ *a* *Poet.* infernal
**infértil** /in'fertil/ *a* infertile
**infestación** /infesta'θion; infesta'sion/ *f*, infestation
**infestar** /infes'tar/ *vt* to infest, swarm in; infect; injure, damage
**infesto** /in'festo/ *a* *Poet.* harmful, dangerous
**inficionar** /infiθio'nar; infisio'nar/ *vt* to infect; pervert, corrupt
**infidelidad** /infiðeli'ðað/ *f*, faithlessness, infidelity; disbelief in Christian religion; unbelievers, infidels
**infidelísimo** /infiðe'lisimo/, *a superl* **infiel** most disloyal; most incorrect; most incredulous, faithless
**infidencia** /infi'ðenθia; infi'ðensia/ *f*, disloyalty, faithlessness
**infiel** /in'fiel/ *a* unfaithful, disloyal; inaccurate, incorrect; infidel, unbelieving. *mf* infidel, nonbeliever
**infierno** /in'fierno/ *m*, hell; hades (gen. *pl*); *Fig. Inf.* inferno. **en el quinto i.,** very far off, at the end of the world. **en los quintos infiernos,** at the end of nowhere
**infiltración** /infiltra'θion; infiltra'sion/ *f*, infiltration; inculcation, implantation
**infiltrar** /infil'trar/ *vt* to infiltrate; imbue, inculcate
**ínfimo** /'infimo/ *a* lowest; meanest, vilest, most base; cheapest, poorest (in quality)
**infinidad** /infini'ðað/ *f*, infinity; infinitude; great number
**infinitivo** /infini'tiβo/ *a and m*, *Gram.* infinitive
**infinito** /infi'nito/ *a* infinite; endless; boundless; countless. *m*, *Math.* infinite —*adv* excessively, immensely
**infinitud** /infini'tuð/ *f*, See **infinidad**
**inflación** /infla'θion; infla'sion/ *f*, inflation; distension; pride, vanity
**inflacionismo** /inflaθio'nismo; inflasio'nismo/ *m*, inflationism
**inflacionista** /inflaθio'nista; inflasio'nista/ *mf* inflationist
**inflamabilidad** /inflamaβili'ðað/ *f*, inflammability
**inflamable** /infla'maβle/ *a* inflammable
**inflamación** /inflama'θion; inflama'sion/ *f*, inflammation; *Engin.* ignition
**inflamador** /inflama'ðor/ *a* inflammatory
**inflamar** /infla'mar/ *vt* to set on fire; *Fig.* inflame, excite; —*vr* take fire; *Med.* become inflamed; grow hot or excited
**inflamatorio** /inflama'torio/ *a* *Med.* inflammatory
**inflar** /in'flar/ *vt* to inflate; blow up, distend; throw out (one's chest); exaggerate; make haughty or vain; —*vr* be swollen or inflated; be puffed up with pride
**inflexibilidad** /infleksiβili'ðað/ *f*, inflexibility; rigidity; immovability, constancy
**inflexible** /infle'ksiβle/ *a* inflexible
**inflexión** /infle'ksion/ *f*, bending, flexion; diffraction (optics); inflection
**infligir** /infli'hir/ *vt* to impose, inflict (penalties)
**influencia** /influ'enθia; influ'ensia/ *f*, influence; power, authority; *Elec.* charge
**influir** /in'fluir/ *vt irr* to influence; affect; (*with en*) cooperate in, assist with. See **huir**

**influjo** /in'fluho/ *m*, influence; flux, inflow of the tide

**influyente** /influ'yente/ *a* influential

**infolio** /in'folio/ *m*, folio

**información** /informa'θion; informa'sion/ *f*, information; legal inquiry; report; research, investigation

**informador** /informa'ðor/ **(-ra)** *a* informing, acquainting —*n* informant

**informal** /infor'mal/ *a* informal, irregular; unreliable (of persons); unconventional

**informalidad** /informali'ðað/ *f*, irregularity; unconventionality; unreliability

**informante** /infor'mante/ *mf* informant

**informar** /infor'mar/ *vt* to inform, acquaint with; —*vi Law*. plead; —*vr* (*with de, en, or sobre*) find out about, investigate

**informática** /infor'matika/ *f*, information sciences

**informativo** /informa'tiβo/ *a* informative

**informe** /in'forme/ *a* formless, shapeless. *m*, report, statement; information; *Law*. plea; *pl* data, particulars; references

**infortificable** /infortifi'kaβle/ *a* unfortifiable

**infortuna** /infor'tuna/ *f*, *Astrol*. evil influence

**infortunado** /infortu'naðo/ *a* unfortunate

**infortunio** /infor'tunio/ *m*, misfortune; unhappiness, adversity; mischance; ill luck

**infracción** /infrak'θion; infrak'sion/ *f*, transgression, infringement

**infracto** /in'frakto/ *a* imperturbable

**infractor** /infrak'tor/ **(-ra)** *a* infringing —*n* transgressor, infringer

**infrangible** /infran'hiβle/ *a* unbreakable

**infranqueable** /infranke'aβle/ *a* insuperable, unsurmountable

**infrarrojo** /infra'rroho/ *a* infrared

**infrascrito** /infras'krito/ *a* undersigned; undermentioned

**infrecuente** /infre'kuente/ *a* infrequent

**infringir** /infrin'hir/ *vt* to infringe, transgress, break

**infructífero** /infruk'tifero/ *a* unfruitful; worthless, useless

**infructuosidad** /infruktuosi'ðað/ *f*, unfruitfulness; worthlessness, uselessness

**infructuoso** /infruk'tuoso/ *a* fruitless; useless, worthless

**infumable** /infu'maβle/ *a* unsmokable (of tobacco)

**infundado** /infun'daðo/ *a* unfounded, groundless

**infundio** /in'fundio/ *m*, *Inf*. nonsense, untruth

**infundir** /infun'dir/ *vt* to infuse, imbue with

**infusión** /infu'sion/ *f*, infusion

**ingeniar** /inhe'niar/ *vt* to devise, concoct, plan; —*vr* contrive, find a way, manage

**ingeniería** /inhenie'ria/ *f*, engineering

**ingeniero** /inhe'niero/ *m*, engineer. **i. agrónomo,** agricultural engineer. **i. de caminos, canales y puertos,** civil engineer. **i. radiotelegrafista,** radio engineer. **cuerpo de ingenieros,** royal engineers

**ingenio** /in'henio/ *m*, mind; inventive capacity; imaginative talent; man of genius; talent, cleverness; ingeniousness; machine; guillotine (bookbinding)

**ingeniosidad** /inheniosi'ðað/ *f*, ingeniousness; witticism, clever remark

**ingenioso** /inhe'nioso/ *a* talented, clever; ingenious

**ingénito** /in'henito/ *a* unengendered, unconceived; innate, inborn

**ingente** /in'hente/ *a* huge, enormous

**ingenuidad** /inhenui'ðað/ *f*, ingenuousness, naiveté

**ingenuo** /in'henuo/ *a* ingenuous, naive, artless, unaffected

**Inglaterra** /ingla'terra/ England

**ingle** /'ingle/ *f*, groin

**inglés** /in'gles/ **(-esa)** *a* English; British —*n* Englishman; Briton. *m*, English (language); *Inf*. creditor. **a la inglesa,** in English fashion. **marcharse a la inglesa,** *Inf*. to take French leave

**inglesismo** /ingle'sismo/ *m*, Anglicism

**ingobernable** /ingoβer'naβle/ *a* ungovernable, unruly

**ingratitud** /ingrati'tuð/ *f*, ingratitude

**ingrato** /in'grato/ *a* ungrateful; irksome, thankless; disagreeable

**ingrávido** /in'graβiðo/ *a* light weight

**ingrediente** /ingre'ðiente/ *m*, ingredient

**ingresar** /ingre'sar/ *vi* to return, come in (money); (*with en*) join, become a member of, enter

**ingreso** /in'greso/ *m*, joining, entering, admission; *Com*. money received; opening, commencement; *pl* earnings, takings, revenue

**ingurgitación** /ingurhita'θion; ingurhita'sion/ *f*, *Med*. ingurgitation

**ingurgitar** /ingurhi'tar/ *vt* to ingurgitate, swallow

**inhábil** /in'aβil/ *a* unskillful; unpracticed; incompetent, unfit; unsuitable, ill-chosen

**inhabilidad** /inaβili'ðað/ *f*, unskillfulness; incompetence; unsuitability; inability

**inhabilitación** /inaβilita'θion; inaβilita'sion/ *f*, incapacitation; disqualification; disablement

**inhabilitar** /inaβili'tar/ *vt* to make ineligible; disqualify; incapacitate, make unfit; —*vr* become ineligible; be incapacitated

**inhabitable** /inaβi'taβle/ *a* uninhabitable

**inhabitado** /inaβi'taðo/ *a* uninhabited, deserted

**inhalación** /inala'θion; inala'sion/ *f*, inhalation

**inhalador** /inala'ðor/ *m*, *Med*. inhaler

**inhalar** /ina'lar/ *vt* to inhale

**inhallable** /ina'ʎaβle; ina'yaβle/ *a* nowhere to be found, unfindable

**inhereditable** /inereði'taβle/ *a* uninheritable

**inherencia** /ine'renθia; ine'rensia/ *f*, inherency

**inherente** /ine'rente/ *a* inherent, innate

**inhestar** /ines'tar/ *vt irr* to raise, lift up; erect. See **acertar**

**inhibición** /iniβi'θion; iniβi'sion/ *f*, inhibition

**inhibir** /ini'βir/ *vt Law*. to inhibit; —*vr* inhibit or restrain oneself. See **prohibir**

**inhibitorio** /iniβi'torio/ *a Law*. inhibitory

**inhonesto** /ino'nesto/ *a* indecent, obscene; immodest

**inhospedable, inhospitalario** /inospe'ðaβle, inospita'lario/ *a* inhospitable; bleak, uninviting; exposed

**inhospitalidad** /inospitali'ðað/ *f*, inhospitality

**inhumación** /inuma'θion; inuma'sion/ *f*, inhumation, burial

**inhumadora** /inuma'ðora/ *f*, crematory

**inhumanidad** /inumani'ðað/ *f*, inhumanity; brutality

**inhumano** /inu'mano/ *a* inhuman; brutal, barbarous

**inhumar** /inu'mar/ *vt* to bury, inter

**iniciación** /iniθia'θion; inisia'sion/ *f*, initiation

**iniciador** /iniθia'ðor; inisia'ðor/ **(-ra)** *a* initiating; —*n* initiator

**inicial** /ini'θial; ini'sial/ *a* and *f*, initial

**iniciar** /ini'θiar; ini'siar/ *vt* to initiate; admit, introduce; originate; —*vr* be initiated; *Eccl*. take minor or first orders

**iniciativa** /iniθia'tiβa; inisia'tiβa/ *f*, initiative

**inicuo** /ini'kuo/ *a* iniquitous, most unjust, wicked

**inimaginable** /inimahi'naβle/ *a* inconceivable

**inimicísimo** /inimi'θisimo; inimi'sisimo/ *a superl* **enemigo** most hostile

**inimitable** /inimi'taβle/ *a* inimitable

**ininteligible** /ininteli'hiβle/ *a* unintelligible

**iniquidad** /iniki'ðað/ *f*, iniquity, wickedness

**injerir** /inhe'rir/ *vt irr* to insert, place within, introduce; interpolate; —*vr* meddle. See **sentir**

**injertar** /inher'tar/ *vt Agr*. to graft

**injerto** /in'herto/ *m*, *Agr*. graft; grafting; grafted plant, briar, or tree

**injuria** /in'huria/ *f*, insult; slander; outrage; wrong, injustice; harm, damage

**injuriador** /inhuria'ðor/ **(-ra)** *a* insulting —*n* offender, persecutor

**injuriar** /inhu'riar/ *vt* to insult; slander; outrage; wrong, persecute; harm, damage

**injurioso** /inhu'rioso/ *a* insulting; slanderous; offensive, abusive; harmful

**injusticia** /inhus'tiθia; inhus'tisia/ *f*, injustice; lack of justice; unjust action

**injustificable** /inhustifi'kaβle/ *a* unjustifiable

**injustificado** /inhustifi'kaðo/ *a* unjustified

**injusto** /in'husto/ *a* unjust; unrighteous

**inllevable** /inʎe'βaβle; inye'βaβle/ *a* unbearable, intolerable

**inmaculado** /imaku'laðo/ *a* immaculate, pure

**inmanejable** /imane'haβle/ *a* unmanageable; uncontrollable

**inmanencia** /ima'nenθia; ima'nensia/ *f,* immanence

**inmanente** /ima'nente/ *a* immanent

**inmarcesible, inmarchitable** /imarθe'siβle, imartʃi'taβle; imarsesiβle, imartʃitaβle/ *a* unfading, imperishable

**inmaterial** /imate'rial/ *a* incorporeal; immaterial

**inmaterialidad** /imateriali'ðað/ *f,* incorporeity; immateriality

**inmaturo** /ima'turo/ *a* immature; unripe

**inmediación** /imeðia'θion; imeðia'sion/ *f,* nearness, proximity; contact; *pl* outskirts, neighborhood, environs

**inmediatamente** /imeðiata'mente/ *adv* near; immediately, at once

**inmediato** /ime'ðiato/ *a* adjoining, close, nearby; immediate, prompt

**inmejorable** /imeho'raβle/ *a* unsurpassable, unbeatable

**inmemorable, inmemorial** /imemo'raβle, imemo'rial/ *a* immemorial

**inmensidad** /imensi'ðað/ *f,* vastness, huge extent; infinity; infinite space; immensity; huge number

**inmenso** /i'menso/ *a* vast; infinite; immense; innumerable

**inmensurable** /imensu'raβle/ *a* immeasurable, incalculable

**inmerecido** /imere'θiðo; imere'siðo/ *a* undeserved, unmerited

**inmérito** /i'merito/ *a* wrongful, unjust

**inmeritorio** /imeri'torio/ *a* unmeritorious, unpraiseworthy

**inmersión** /imer'sion/ *f,* immersion; dip

**inmigración** /imigra'θion; imigra'sion/ *f,* immigration

**inmigrante** /imi'grante/ *a* and *mf* immigrant

**inmigrar** /imi'grar/ *vi* to immigrate

**inminencia** /imi'nenθia; imi'nensia/ *f,* imminence

**inminente** /imi'nente/ *a* imminent

**inmiscuir** /imis'kuir/ *vt* to mix; —*vr* meddle. May be conjugated regularly or like **huir**

**inmisión** /imi'sion/ *f,* inspiration

**inmobiliario** /imoβi'liario/ *a* concerning real estate

**inmoble** /i'moβle/ *a* immovable; motionless, immobile, stationary; *Fig.* unshakable, unflinching

**inmoderación** /imoðera'θion; imoðera'sion/ *f,* immoderateness, excess

**inmoderado** /imoðe'raðo/ *a* immoderate; unrestrained, excessive

**inmodestia** /imo'ðestia/ *f,* immodesty

**inmodesto** /imo'ðesto/ *a* immodest

**inmolación** /imola'θion; imola'sion/ *f,* immolation

**inmolador** /imola'ðor/ **(-ra)** *a* sacrificing —*n* immolator

**inmolar** /imo'lar/ *vt* to immolate; *Fig.* sacrifice, give up; —*vr Fig.* sacrifice oneself

**inmoral** /imo'ral/ *a* immoral

**inmoralidad** /imorali'ðað/ *f,* immorality

**inmortal** /imor'tal/ *a* immortal

**inmortalidad** /imortali'ðað/ *f,* immortality

**inmortalizar** /imortali'θar; imortali'sar/ *vt* to immortalize

**inmotivado** /imoti'βaðo/ *a* unfounded, without reason

**inmoto** /i'moto/ *a* motionless, stationary

**inmóvil** /i'moβil/ *a* immovable, fixed; motionless; steadfast, constant

**inmovilidad** /imoβili'ðað/ *f,* immovability; immobility; constancy, steadfastness

**inmovilizar** /imoβili'θar; imoβili'sar/ *vt* to immobilize

**inmueble** /i'mueβle/ *m, Law.* immovable estate

**inmundicia** /imun'diθia; imun'disia/ *f,* filth, nastiness; dirt; rubbish, refuse; obscenity, indecency

**inmundo** /i'mundo/ *a* dirty, filthy; obscene, indecent; unclean

**inmune** /i'mune/ *a* exempt; *Med.* immune

**inmunidad** /imuni'ðað/ *f,* exemption; immunity

**inmunizar** /imuni'θar; imuni'sar/ *vt* to immunize

**inmutabilidad** /imutaβili'ðað/ *f,* immutability, changelessness; imperturbability

**inmutable** /imu'taβle/ *a* immutable, unchangeable; imperturbable

**inmutación** /imuta'θion; imuta'sion/ *f,* change, alteration, difference

**inmutar** /imu'tar/ *vt* to change, alter, vary; —*vr* change one's expression (through fear, etc.)

**innato** /in'nato/ *a* innate; inherent; instinctive, inborn

**innatural** /innatu'ral/ *a* unnatural

**innavegable** /innaβe'gaβle/ *a* unnavigable; unseaworthy (of ships)

**innecesario** /inneθe'sario; innese'sario/ *a* unnecessary

**innegable** /inne'gaβle/ *a* undeniable; indisputable, irrefutable

**innoble** /in'noβle/ *a* plebeian; ignoble

**innocuo** /inno'kuo/ *a* harmless, innocuous

**innovación** /innoβa'θion; innoβa'sion/ *f,* innovation

**innovador** /innoβa'ðor/ **(-ra)** *a* innovatory —*n* innovator

**innovar** /inno'βar/ *vt* to introduce innovations

**innumerabilidad** /innumeraβili'ðað/ *f,* countless number, multitude

**innumerable** /innume'raβle/ *a* innumerable, countless

**innúmero** /in'numero/ *a* countless, innumerable

**inobediencia** /inoβe'ðienθia; inoβe'ðiensia/ *f,* disobedience

**inobediente** /inoβe'ðiente/ *a* disobedient

**inobservable** /inoβser'βaβle/ *a* unobservable

**inobservancia** /inoβser'βanθia; inoβser'βansia/ *f,* inobservance

**inobservante** /inoβser'βante/ *a* unobservant

**inocencia** /ino'θenθia; ino'sensia/ *f,* innocence; simplicity, candor; harmlessness

**inocentada** /inoθen'taða; inosen'taða/ *f, Inf.* naïve remark or action; fool's trap; practical joke

**inocente** /ino'θente; ino'sente/ *a* innocent; candid, simple; harmless; easily deceived

**inocentón** /inoθen'ton; inosen'ton/ *a Inf.* extremely credulous and easily taken in

**inocuidad** /inokui'ðað/ *f,* innocuousness

**inoculación** /inokula'θion; inokula'sion/ *f,* inoculation

**inoculador** /inokula'ðor/ *m,* inoculator

**inocular** /inoku'lar/ *vt* to inoculate; pervert, corrupt; contaminate

**inodoro** /ino'ðoro/ *a* odorless. *m,* toilet, lavatory

**inofensivo** /inofen'siβo/ *a* inoffensive, harmless

**inolvidable** /inolβi'ðaβle/ *a* unforgettable

**inoperable** /inope'raβle/ *a* inoperable

**inopia** /i'nopia/ *f,* poverty; scarcity

**inopinable** /inopi'naβle/ *a* indisputable, unquestionable

**inopinado** /inopi'naðo/ *a* unexpected, sudden

**inoportunidad** /inoportuni'ðað/ *f,* inopportuneness, unseasonableness; unsuitability

**inoportuno** /inopor'tuno/ *a* inopportune, untimely

**inordenado** /inorðe'naðo/ *a* inordinate, immoderate, excessive

**inorgánico** /inor'ganiko/ *a* inorganic

**inoxidable** /inoksi'ðaβle/ *a* rustless

**inquebrantable** /inkeβran'taβle/ *a* unbreakable; final, irrevocable

**inquietador** /inkieta'ðor/ **(-ra)** *a* disturbing —*n* disturber

**inquietar** /inkie'tar/ *vt* to disturb; trouble, make anxious, worry; —*vr* be disquieted, worry

**inquieto** /in'kieto/ *a* restless; unquiet; fidgety; disturbed, anxious, worried, uneasy

**inquietud** /inkie'tuð/ *f,* restlessness; uneasiness; worry; trouble, care, anxiety

**inquilinato** /inkili'nato/ *m,* tenancy; rent; *Law.* lease; (rental) rates

**inquilino** /inki'lino/ **(-na)** *n* tenant; lessee

**inquina** /in'kina/ *f,* dislike, grudge

**inquinar** /inki'nar/ *vt* to contaminate, corrupt, infect

**inquiridor** /inkiri'ðor/ **(-ra)** *a* inquiring, examining —*n* investigator

**inquirir** /inki'rir/ *vt irr* to inquire; examine, look into. See **adquirir**

**inquisición** /inkisi'θion; inkisi'sion/ *f*, inquiry, investigation; *Eccl.* Inquisition

**inquisidor** /inkisi'ðor/ **(-ra)** *a* inquiring, investigating —*n* investigator. *m, Eccl.* inquisitor; judge

**inquisitorial** /inkisito'rial/ *a* inquisitorial

**insaciabilidad** /insaθiaβili'ðað; insasiaβili'ðað/ *f*, insatiability

**insaciable** /insa'θiaβle; insa'siaβle/ *a* insatiable

**insalivación** /insaliβa'θion; insaliβa'sion/ *f*, insalivation

**insalubre** /insa'luβre/ *a* unhealthy

**insanable** /insa'naβle/ *a* incurable

**insania** /in'sania/ *f*, insanity

**insano** /in'sano/ *a* insane, mad

**inscribir** /inskri'βir/ *vt* to inscribe; record; enter (a name on a list, etc.), register, enroll; engrave; *Geom.* inscribe —*Past Part.* **inscrito**

**inscripción** /inskrip'θion; inskrip'sion/ *f*, inscription; record, enrollment; registration; government bond

**insecable** /inse'kaβle/ *a* undryable, undrying

**insecticida** /insekti'θiða; insekti'siða/ *a* insecticide

**insectívoro** /insek'tiβoro/ *a* insectivorous

**insecto** /in'sekto/ *m*, insect

**inseguridad** /inseguri'ðað/ *f*, insecurity

**inseguro** /inse'guro/ *a* insecure; unsafe; uncertain

**insensatez** /insensa'teθ; insensa'tes/ *f*, folly, foolishness

**insensato** /insen'sato/ *a* foolish, stupid, mad

**insensibilidad** /insensiβili'ðað/ *f*, insensibility; imperception; callousness, hard-heartedness

**insensibilizar** /insensiβili'θar; insensiβili'sar/ *vt* to make insensible (to sensations)

**insensible** /insen'siβle/ *a* insensible; imperceptive, insensitive; unconscious, senseless; imperceptible, inappreciable; callous

**inseparabilidad** /inseparaβili'ðað/ *f*, inseparability

**inseparable** /insepa'raβle/ *a* inseparable

**insepulto** /inse'pulto/ *a* unburied (of the dead)

**inserción** /inser'θion; inser'sion/ *f*, insertion; interpolation; grafting

**insertar** /inser'tar/ *vt* to insert; introduce; interpolate; —*vr* (*Bot. Zool.*) become attached

**inservible** /inser'βiβle/ *a* useless; unfit; unsuitable

**insidia** /in'siðia/ *f*, insidiousness; snare, ambush

**insidiador** /insiðia'ðor/ **(-ra)** *a* ensnaring —*n* schemer, ambusher

**insidiar** /insi'ðiar/ *vt* to waylay, ambush; set a trap for; scheme against

**insidioso** /insi'ðioso/ *a* insidious; treacherous; scheming, guileful

**insigne** /in'signe/ *a* illustrious, famous; distinguished

**insignia** /in'signia/ *f*, symbol; badge; token; banner, standard; *Naut.* pennant; *pl* insignia

**insignificancia** /insignifi'kanθia; insignifi'kansia/ *f*, meaninglessness; unimportance, triviality; insignificance, insufficiency

**insignificante** /insignifi'kante/ *a* meaningless; unimportant; insignificant, small

**insinuación** /insinua'θion; insinua'sion/ *f*, insinuation; hint; implication; suggestion

**insinuador** /insinua'ðor/ *a* insinuating, suggestive, implicative

**insinuar** /insi'nuar/ *vt* to insinuate; suggest, hint; —*vr* ingratiate oneself; creep in

**insinuativo** /insinua'tiβo/ *a* insinuative

**insipidez** /insipi'ðeθ; insipi'ðes/ *f*, tastelessness, insipidity; *Fig.* dullness

**insípido** /in'sipiðo/ *a* tasteless, insipid; dull, uninteresting, boring

**insistencia** /insis'tenθia; insis'tensia/ *f*, insistence

**insistente** /insis'tente/ *a* insistent

**insistir** /insis'tir/ *vi* (*with en or sobre*) to lay stress upon, insist on; persist in

**ínsito** /'insito/ *a* inherent, innate

**insociabilidad** /insoθiaβili'ðað; insosiaβili'ðað/ *f*, unsociability

**insociable** /inso'θiaβle; inso'siaβle/ *a* unsociable

**insolación** /insola'θion; insola'sion/ *f*, insolation, exposure to the sun; sunstroke

**insolar** /inso'lar/ *vt* to expose to the sun's rays; —*vr* contract sunstroke

**insoldable** /insol'daβle/ *a* unsolderable, unable to be soldered

**insolencia** /inso'lenθia; inso'lensia/ *f*, insolence; impudence, impertinence

**insolentarse** /insolen'tarse/ *vr* to grow insolent; be impudent

**insolente** /inso'lente/ *a* insolent; impudent, impertinent

**insólito** /in'solito/ *a* unaccustomed; infrequent; unusual; unexpected

**insolubilidad** /insoluβili'ðað/ *f*, insolubility

**insoluble** /inso'luβle/ *a* insoluble

**insoluto** /inso'luto/ *a* unpaid, outstanding

**insolvencia** /insol'βenθia; insol'βensia/ *f*, insolvency

**insolvente** /insol'βente/ *a* insolvent

**insomne** /in'somne/ *a* sleepless

**insomnio** /in'somnio/ *m*, insomnia

**insondable** /inson'daβle/ *a* unfathomable, bottomless; inscrutable, secret

**insoportable** /insopor'taβle/ *a* intolerable, unbearable

**insostenible** /insoste'niβle/ *a* indefensible; arbitrary, baseless

**inspección** /inspek'θion; inspek'sion/ *f*, inspection; supervision; examination; inspectorship; inspector's office

**inspeccionar** /inspekθio'nar; inspeksio'nar/ *vt* to inspect; survey, examine. **i. una casa,** to view a house

**inspector** /inspek'tor/ **(-ra)** *a* inspecting, examining —*n* supervisor. *m*, inspector; surveyor

**inspiración** /inspira'θion; inspira'sion/ *f*, inspiration; inhalation

**inspirador** /inspira'ðor/ **(-ra)** *a* inspiring —*n* inspirer

**inspirar** /inspi'rar/ *vt* to breathe in, inhale; blow (of the wind); inspire; —*vr* be inspired; (*with en*) find inspiration in, imitate

**instabilidad** /instaβili'ðað/ *f*, instability; unsteadiness; shakiness; unreliability, inconstancy

**instable** /ins'taβle/ *a* unstable

**instalación** /instala'θion; instala'sion/ *f*, plant, apparatus; erection, fitting; induction; installment, settling in

**instalador** /instala'ðor/ **(-ra)** *n* fitter; one who installs (electricity, etc.)

**instalar** /insta'lar/ *vt* to appoint, induct; erect (a plant, etc.); install, put in; lay on; *Elec.* wire; —*vr* install oneself, settle down

**instancia** /ins'tanθia; ins'tansia/ *f*, instance; argument; suggestion; supplication; request; formal petition. **de primera i.,** in the first instance, firstly

**instantánea** /instan'tanea/ *f, Photo.* snapshot

**instantáneo** /instan'taneo/ *a* instantaneous

**instante** /ins'tante/ *a* urgent. *m*, second; instant, moment. **a cada i.,** every minute; frequently. **al i.,** at once, immediately. **por instantes,** continually; immediately

**instar** /ins'tar/ *vt* to press; persuade; insist upon; —*vi* be urgent, press

**instauración** /instaura'θion; instaura'sion/ *f*, restoration; renewal; renovation

**instaurador** /instaura'ðor/ **(-ra)** *a* renovating, renewing —*n* restorer, renovator

**instaurar** /instau'rar/ *vt* to restore; repair; renovate, renew

**instaurativo** /instaura'tiβo/ *a* restorative

**instigación** /instiga'θion; instiga'sion/ *f*, instigation, incitement

**instigador** /instiga'ðor/ **(-ra)** *n* instigator

**instigar** /insti'gar/ *vt* to instigate, incite; induce

**instilación** /instila'θion; instila'sion/ *f*, instillment, pouring drop by drop; inculcation, implantation

**instilar** /insti'lar/ *vt Chem.* instill; implant, inculcate

**instintivo** /instin'tiβo/ *a* instinctive

**instinto** /ins'tinto/ *m*, instinct. **por i.,** by instinct, naturally

**institución** /institu'θion; institu'sion/ *f*, setting up, establishment; institution; teaching, instruction; *pl* institutes, digest

**institucional** /institu'θio'nal; institusio'nal/ *a* institutional

**instituir** /insti'tuir/ *vt irr* to found, establish; institute; instruct, teach. See **huir**

**instituto** /insti'tuto/ *m*, institute; secondary school. **i. de belleza**, beauty parlor, beauty salon

**institutor** /institu'tor/ *m*, founder, instituter; tutor

**institutriz** /institu'triθ; institu'tris/ *f*, governess

**instrucción** /instruk'θion; instruk'sion/ *f*, teaching, instruction; knowledge, learning; education; *pl* orders; rules; instruction. **i. primaria,** primary education. **i. pública,** public education

**instructivo** /instruk'tiβo/ *a* instructive

**instructor** /instruk'tor/ **(-ra)** *a* instructive —*n* instructor

**instruido** /ins'truiðo/ *a* cultured, well-educated; knowledgeable

**instruir** /ins'truir/ *vt irr* to teach, instruct; train; inform, acquaint with; *Law.* formulate. See **huir**

**instrumentación** /instrumenta'θion; instrumenta'sion/ *f, Mus.* instrumentation

**instrumental** /instrumen'tal/ *a* instrumental

**instrumentar** /instrumen'tar/ *vt Mus.* to score

**instrumentista** /instrumen'tista/ *mf Mus.* instrumentalist; instrument maker

**instrumento** /instru'mento/ *m*, tool, implement; machine, apparatus; *Mus.* instrument; means, medium; legal document. **i. de cuerda,** string instrument. **i. de percusión,** percussion instrument. **i. de viento,** wind instrument

**insuave** /in'"suaβe/ *a* unpleasant (to the senses); rough

**insubordinación** /insuβorðina'θion; insuβorðina'sion/ *f*, insubordination, rebellion

**insubordinado** /insuβorði'naðo/ *a* insubordinate, unruly

**insubordinar** /insuβorði'nar/ *vt* to rouse to rebellion; —*vr* become insubordinate, rebel

**insubsistencia** /insuβsis'tenθia; insuβsis'tensia/ *f*, instability

**insubsistente** /insuβsis'tente/ *a* unstable; groundless, unfounded

**insubstancial** /insuβstan'θial; insuβstan'sial/ *a* insubstantial, unreal, illusory; pointless, worthless, superficial

**insubstancialidad** /insuβstanθiali'ðað; insuβstansiali'ðað/ *f*, superficiality, worthlessness

**insuficiencia** /insufi'θienθia; insufi'siensia/ *f*, insufficiency, shortage; incompetence, inefficiency

**insuficiente** /insufi'θiente; insufi'siente/ *a* insufficient, scarce, inadequate

**insufrible** /insu'friβle/ *a* insufferable, unbearable, intolerable

**insular** /insu'lar/ *a* insular

**insulina** /insu'lina/ *f*, insulin

**insulsez** /insul'seθ; insul'ses/ *f*, insipidity, tastelessness; dullness; tediousness

**insulso** /in'sulso/ *a* insipid, tasteless; tedious; dull

**insultador** /insulta'ðor/ **(-ra)** *a* insulting —*n* insulter

**insultante** /insul'tante/ *a* insulting

**insultar** /insul'tar/ *vt* to insult; call names; —*vr* take offense

**insulto** /in'sulto/ *m*, insult; sudden attack; sudden illness, fit

**insumable** /insu'maβle/ *a* incalculable; excessive, exorbitant

**insumergible** /insumer'hiβle/ *a* unsinkable

**insumiso** /insu'miso/ *a* rebellious

**insuperable** /insupe'raβle/ *a* insuperable

**insurgente** /insur'hente/ *a* insurgent, rebellious. *m*, rebel

**insurrección** /insurrek'θion; insurrek'sion/ *f*, insurrection

**insurreccionar** /insurrekθio'nar; insurreksio'nar/ *vt* to incite to rebellion; —*vr* rise in rebellion

**insurrecto** /insu'rrekto/ **(-ta)** *n* rebel

**insustancial** /insustan'θial; insustan'sial/ *a* See **insubstancial**

**insustituible** /insusti'tuiβle/ *a* indispensable

**intachable** /inta'tʃaβle/ *a* irreproachable; impeccable, perfect

**intacto** /in'takto/ *a* untouched; intact, uninjured; whole, entire; complete; pure

**intangibilidad** /intanhiβili'ðað/ *f*, intangibility

**intangible** /intan'hiβle/ *a* intangible

**integración** /integra'θion; integra'sion/ *f*, integration

**integral** /inte'gral/ *a* integral

**integrar** /inte'grar/ *vt* to integrate; *Com.* repay

**integridad** /integri'ðað/ *f*, wholeness; completeness; integrity, probity, honesty; virginity

**íntegro** /'integro/ *a* integral, whole; upright, honest

**integumento** /integu'mento/ *m*, integument; pretense, simulation

**intelectiva** /intelek'tiβa/ *f*, understanding

**intelecto** /inte'lekto/ *m*, intellect

**intelectual** /intelek'tual/ *a* intellectual

**intelectualidad** /intelektuali'ðað/ *f*, understanding, intellectuality; intelligentsia

**intelectualismo** /intelektua'lismo/ *m*, intellectualism

**inteligencia** /inteli'henθia; inteli'hensia/ *f*, intelligence; intellect; mental alertness; mind; meaning, sense; experience, skill; understanding, secret agreement; information, knowledge; Intelligence, Secret Service

**inteligente** /inteli'hente/ *a* intelligent; clever; skillful; capable, competent

**inteligibilidad** /intelihiβili'ðað/ *f*, intelligibility

**inteligible** /inteli'hiβle/ *a* intelligible; understandable; able to be heard

**intemperancia** /intempe'ranθia; intempe'ransia/ *f*, intemperance, lack of moderation

**intemperante** /intempe'rante/ *a* intemperate

**intemperie** /intem'perie/ *f*, stormy weather. **a la i.,** at the mercy of the elements; in the open air

**intempestivo** /intempes'tiβo/ *a* inopportune, ill-timed

**intención** /inten'θion; inten'sion/ *f*, intention; determination, purpose; viciousness (of animals); caution. *Inf.* **con segunda i.,** with a double meaning, slyly

**intencionado** /intenθio'naðo; intensio'naðo/ *a* intentioned, disposed

**intencional** /intenθio'nal; intensio'nal/ *a* intentional, designed, premeditated

**intendencia** /inten'denθia; inten'densia/ *f*, management; supervision; administration; *Polit.* intendancy. *Mil.* **cuerpo de i.,** quartermaster corps, army supply corps

**intendente** /inten'dente/ *m*, director; manager; *Polit.* intendant. **i. de ejército,** quartermaster general

**intensar** /inten'sar/ *vt* to intensify

**intensidad** /intensi'ðað/ *f*, intensity; ardor; vehemence

**intensificar** /intensifi'kar/ *vt* to intensify

**intensivo** /inten'siβo/ *a* intensive

**intenso** /in'tenso/ *a* intense; ardent; fervent; vehement

**intentar** /inten'tar/ *vt* to intend, mean; propose; try, endeavor; initiate. **i. fortuna,** to try one's luck

**intento** /in'tento/ *m*, intention, determination; purpose. **de i.,** on purpose; knowingly

**intentona** /inten'tona/ *f, Inf.* foolhardy attempt

**interacción** /interak'θion; interak'sion/ *f*, interaction; reciprocal effect; *Chem.* reaction

**intercalación** /interkala'θion; interkala'sion/ *f*, interpolation; insertion

**intercalar** /interka'lar/ *vt* to intercalate; interpolate, include, insert

**intercambiable** /interkam'biaβle/ *a* interchangeable

**intercambio** /inter'kambio/ *m*, interchange

**interceder** /interθe'ðer; interse'ðer/ *vi* to intercede, plead for

**interceptación** /interθepta'θion; intersepta'sion/ *f*, interception

**interceptar** /interθep'tar; intersep'tar/ *vt* to intercept; interrupt; hinder

**intercesión** /interθe'sion; interse'sion/ *f*, intercession

**intercesor** /interθe'sor; interse'sor/ **(-ra)** *a* interceding —*n* intercessor

**intercutáneo** /interku'taneo/ *a* intercutaneous

**interdecir** /interðe'θir; inter'ðesir/ *vt irr* to forbid, prohibit. See **decir**

**interdicción** /interðik'θion; interðik'sion/ f, interdiction, prohibition

**interdicto** /inter'ðikto/ m, interdict

**interés** /inte'res/ m, interest; yield; profit; advantage; *Com.* interest; inclination, fondness; attraction, fascination; *pl* money matters. **i. compuesto,** compound interest. **intereses creados,** bonds of interest; vested interests

**interesado** /intere'saðo/ a involved, concerned; biased; selfish

**interesante** /intere'sante/ a interesting

**interesar** /intere'sar/ **(se)** vi and vr to be interested; —vt *Com.* invest; interest

**interfecto** /inter'fekto/ **(-ta)** n *Law.* victim (of murder)

**interferencia** /interfe'renθia; interfe'rensia/ f, *Phys.* interference

**interfoliar** /interfo'liar/ vt to interleave (of books)

**ínterin** /'interin/ m, interim —adv meanwhile, in the meantime

**interinamente** /interina'mente/ adv in the interim; provisionally

**interinar** /interi'nar/ vt to discharge (duties) provisionally, act temporarily as

**interino** /inte'rino/ a acting, provisional, temporary

**interior** /inte'rior/ a interior; inner; inside; indoor; inland; internal, domestic (policies, etc.); inward, spiritual. m, interior, inside; mind, soul; pl entrails

**interjección** /interhek'θion; interhek'sion/ f, *Gram.* interjection, exclamation

**interlinear** /interline'ar/ vt to write between the lines; *Print.* lead

**interlocución** /interloku'θion; interloku'sion/ f, dialogue, conversation

**interlocutorio** /interloku'torio/ a *Law.* interlocutory

**intérlope** /in'terlope/ a interloping. mf interloper

**interludio** /inter'luðio/ m, interlude

**intermediario** /interme'ðiario/ **(-ia)** a and n intermediary. m, *Com.* middleman

**intermedio** /inter'meðio/ a intermediate. m, interim; *Theat.* interval. **por i. de,** through, by the mediation of

**intermisión** /intermi'sion/ f, intermission, interval

**intermitencia** /intermi'tenθia; intermi'tensia/ f, intermittence

**intermitente** /intermi'tente/ a intermittent

**intermitir** /intermi'tir/ vt to interrupt, suspend, discontinue

**internación** /interna'θion; interna'sion/ f, going inside; penetration; taking into

**internacional** /internaθio'nal; internasio'nal/ a international

**internacionalismo** /internaθiona'lismo; internasiona'lismo/ m, internationalism

**internacionalista** /internaθiona'lista; internasiona'lista/ mf internationalist

**internacionalización** /internaθionaliθa'θion; internasionalisa'sion/ f, internationalization

**internado** /inter'naðo/ m, boarding school

**internamiento** /interna'miento/ m, internment

**internar** /inter'nar/ vt to take or send inland; —vi penetrate; —vr (with en) go into the interior of (a country); get into the confidence of; study deeply (a subject)

**Internet** m, **el,** the Internet.

**interno** /in'terno/ **(-na)** a interior; internal; inner; inside; boarding (student) —n boarding school student; *Med.* intern

**internodio** /inter'noðio/ m, internode

**internuncio** /inter'nunθio; inter'nunsio/ m, *Eccl.* internuncio; interlocutor; representative

**interoceánico** /interoθe'aniko; interose'aniko/ a interoceanic

**interpaginar** /interpahi'nar/ vt to interleave (of books)

**interpelación** /interpela'θion; interpela'sion/ f, *Law.* interpellation; appeal

**interpelar** /interpe'lar/ vt *Law.* to interpellate; appeal to, ask protection from

**interpolación** /interpola'θion; interpola'sion/ f, interpolation, insertion; interruption

**interpolador** /interpola'ðor/ **(-ra)** n interpolator; interrupter

**interpolar** /interpo'lar/ vt to interpolate; interject

**interponer** /interpo'ner/ vt irr to interpose, insert, intervene; designate as an arbitrator; —vr intervene. See **poner**

**interposición** /interposi'θion; interposi'sion/ f, interposition; intervention; mediation, arbitration

**interpresa** /inter'presa/ f, *Mil.* surprise attack

**interpretación** /interpreta'θion; interpreta'sion/ f, interpretation; translation

**interpretador** /interpreta'ðor/ **(-ra)** a interpretative —n interpreter

**interpretar** /interpre'tar/ vt to interpret; translate; attribute; expound, explain. **i. mal,** to misconstrue; translate wrongly

**interpretativo** /interpreta'tiβo/ a interpretative

**intérprete** /in'terprete/ mf interpreter

**interregno** /inte'rregno/ m, interregnum. **i. parlamentario,** parliamentary recess

**interrogación** /interroga'θion; interroga'sion/ f, interrogation, question; *Gram.* question mark

**interrogador** /interroga'ðor/ **(-ra)** n questioner

**interrogante** /interro'gante/ a interrogating. m, *Print.* question mark

**interrogar** /interro'gar/ vt to interrogate, question

**interrogativo** /interroga'tiβo/ a interrogative

**interrogatorio** /interroga'torio/ m, interrogatory

**interrumpir** /interrum'pir/ vt to interrupt; hinder, obstruct; *Elec.* break contact

**interrupción** /interrup'θion; interrup'sion/ f, interruption; stoppage (of work); *Elec.* break

**interruptor** /interrup'tor/ **(-ra)** a interrupting —n interrupter. m, *Elec.* switch, interruptor. **i. de dos direcciones,** *Elec.* two-way switch

**intersecarse** /interse'karse/ vr *Geom.* to intersect

**intersección** /intersek'θion; intersek'sion/ f, *Geom.* intersection

**intersticio** /inter'stiθio; inter'stisio/ m, interstice, crack, crevice; interval, intervening space

**intervalo** /inter'βalo/ m, interval

**intervención** /interβen'θion; interβen'sion/ f, intervention; mediation, intercession; auditing (of accounts)

**intervenir** /interβe'nir/ vi irr to take part (in); intervene, interfere; arbitrate, mediate; happen, occur; —vt *Com.* audit. See **venir**

**interventor** /interβen'tor/ **(-ra)** a intervening —n one who intervenes. m, auditor; inspector

**intervocálico** /interβo'kaliko/ a intervocalic

**intestado** /intes'taðo/ **(-da)** a and n *Law.* intestate

**intestinal** /intesti'nal/ a intestinal

**intestino** /intes'tino/ a intestinal. m, intestine

**íntima, intimación** /'intima, intima'θion; 'intima, intima'sion/ f, intimation, notification

**intimar** /inti'mar/ vt to intimate; inform, notify; —vr penetrate; —vr and vi become intimate or friendly

**intimidación** /intimiða'θion; intimiða'sion/ f, intimidation, terrorization

**intimidad** /intimi'ðað/ f, intimacy

**intimidar** /intimi'ðar/ vt to intimidate, terrorize, cow

**íntimo** /'intimo/ a intimate; deep-seated, inward; private, personal

**intitular** /intitu'lar/ vt to give a title to, entitle, call; —vr call oneself

**intolerable** /intole'raβle/ a intolerable; unbearable

**intolerancia** /intole'ranθia; intole'ransia/ f, narrow-mindedness, intolerance, bigotry

**intolerante** /intole'rante/ a narrow-minded, illiberal; *Med.* intolerant

**intonso** /in'tonso/ a long-haired, unshorn; boorish, ignorant

**intoxicación** /intoksika'θion; intoksika'sion/ f, poisoning

**intoxicar** /intoksi'kar/ vt to poison

**intraducible** /intraðu'θiβle; intraðu'siβle/ a untranslatable

**intramuros** /intra'muros/ adv within the town walls, within the city

**intranquilidad** /intrankili'ðað/ f, disquiet, restlessness; anxiety

**intranquilizador** /intrankiliθa'ðor; intrankilisa'ðor/ *a* disquieting, perturbing

**intranquilizar** /intrankili'θar; intrankili'sar/ *vt* to disquiet, make uneasy, worry

**intranquilo** /intran'kilo/ *a* uneasy, anxious

**intransferible** /intransfe'riβle/ *a* untransferable, not transferable

**intransigencia** /intransi'henθia; intransi'hensia/ *f*, intolerance, intransigence

**intransigente** /intransi'hente/ *a* intolerant, intransigent

**intransitable** /intransi'taβle/ *a* impassable; unsurmountable

**intransitivo** /intransi'tiβo/ *a* intransitive

**intratable** /intra'taβle/ *a* intractable; impassable; rough; unsociable, difficult

**intrauterino** /intraute'rino/ *a* intrauterine

**intravenoso** /intraβe'noso/ *a* intravenous

**intrepidez** /intrepi'ðeθ; intrepi'ðes/ *f*, intrepidity, dauntlessness, gallantry

**intrépido** /in'trepiðo/ *a* intrepid, dauntless, gallant

**intriga** /in'triga/ *f*, scheme, intrigue; entanglement; *Lit.* plot

**intrigante** /intri'gante/ *mf* intriguer, schemer

**intrigar** /intri'gar/ *vi* to intrigue, scheme, plot

**intrincación** /intrinka'θion; intrinka'sion/ *f*, intricacy

**intrincado** /intrin'kaðo/ *a* intricate

**intrincar** /intrin'kar/ *vt* to complicate; obscure, confuse

**intríngulis** /in'triŋgulis/ *m*, *Inf.* ulterior motive

**intrínseco** /in'trinseko/ *a* intrinsic, inherent; essential

**introducción** /introðuk'θion; introðuk'sion/ *f*, introduction

**introducir** /introðu'θir; introðu'sir/ *vt irr* to introduce; insert; fit in; drive in; present, introduce; bring into use; cause, occasion; show in, bring in; —*vr* interfere, meddle; enter. See **conducir**

**introductor** /introðuk'tor/ **(-ra)** *n* introducer

**intromisión** /intromi'sioɲ/ *f*, intromission; interference; *Geol.* intrusion

**introspección** /introspek'θion; introspek'sion/ *f*, introspection

**introverso** /intro'βerso/ *a* introvert

**intruso** /in'truso/ **(-sa)** *a* intruding, intrusive —*n* intruder

**intuición** /intui'θion; intui'sion/ *f*, intuition

**intuir** /in'tuir/ *vt irr* to know by intuition. See **huir**

**intuitivo** /intui'tiβo/ *a* intuitive

**intuito** /in'tuito/ *m*, glance, look, view

**intumescencia** /intumes'θenθia; intumes'sensia/ *f*, intumescence

**inulto** /i'nulto/ *a* *Poet.* unavenged, unpunished

**inundación** /inunda'θion; inunda'sion/ *f*, flood; flooding; excess, superabundance

**inundar** /inun'dar/ *vt* to flood; swamp; *Fig.* inundate, overwhelm

**inurbanidad** /inurβani'ðað/ *f*, discourtesy, impoliteness

**inurbano** /inur'βano/ *a* discourteous, uncivil, impolite

**inusitado** /inusi'taðo/ *a* unusual, unaccustomed; rare

**inútil** /i'nutil/ *a* useless

**inutilidad** /inutili'ðað/ *f*, uselessness

**inutilizar** /inutili'θar; inutili'sar/ *vt* to render useless; disable, incapacitate; spoil, damage

**invadeable** /imbaðe'aβle/ *a* impassable, unfordable

**invadir** /imba'ðir/ *vt* to invade

**invaginación** /imbahina'θion; imbahina'sion/ *f*, invagination

**invalidación** /imbaliða'θion; imbaliða'sion/ *f*, invalidation

**invalidar** /imbali'ðar/ *vt* to invalidate

**invalidez** /imbali'ðeθ; imbali'ðes/ *f*, invalidity; disablement; infirmity

**inválido** /im'baliðo/ **(-da)** *a* weak, infirm; invalid, null; disabled —*n* invalid; disabled soldier

**invariabilidad** /imbariaβili'ðað/ *f*, invariability

**invariable** /imba'riaβle/ *a* invariable

**invariación** /imbaria'θion; imbaria'sion/ *f*, invariableness

**invariante** /imba'riante/ *m*, invariant

**invasión** /imba'sion/ *f*, invasion, encroachment, incursion

**invasor** /imba'sor/ **(-ra)** *a* invading; *Med.* attacking —*n* invader

**invectiva** /imbek'tiβa/ *f*, invective

**invencibilidad** /imbenθiβili'ðað; imbensiβili'ðað/ *f*, invincibility

**invencible** /imben'θiβle; imben'siβle/ *a* invincible

**invención** /imben'θion; imben'sion/ *f*, invention, discovery; deception, fabrication, lie; creative imagination; finding (e.g. *i. de la Santa Cruz*, Invention of the Holy Cross)

**invencionero** /imbenθio'nero; imbensio'nero/ **(-ra)** *n* inventor; schemer, deceiver

**invendible** /imben'diβle/ *a* unsalable

**inventar** /imben'tar/ *vt* to invent; create; imagine; concoct, fabricate (lies, etc.)

**inventariar** /imbenta'riar/ *vt* to make an inventory of; *Com.* take stock of

**inventario** /imben'tario/ *m*, inventory; *Com.* stock taking

**inventiva** /imben'tiβa/ *f*, inventiveness, ingenuity; creativeness

**inventivo** /imben'tiβo/ *a* inventive

**invento** /im'bento/ *m*, See **invención**

**inventor** /imben'tor/ **(-ra)** *n* inventor, discoverer; liar, storyteller

**inverecundia** /imbere'kundia/ *f*, impertinence, impudence

**inverecundo** /imbere'kundo/ *a* shameless, brazen

**inverisímil** /imberi'simil/ *a* See **inverosímil**

**invernáculo** /imber'nakulo/ *m*, greenhouse; conservatory

**invernada** /imber'naða/ *f*, winter season; hibernation

**invernadero** /imberna'ðero/ *m*, winter quarters; greenhouse

**invernal** /imber'nal/ *a* wintry; winter

**invernar** /imber'nar/ *vi irr* to winter; hibernate; be wintertime. See **acertar**

**invernizo** /imber'niθo; imber'niso/ *a* wintry, winter

**inverosímil** /imbero'simil/ *a* unlikely, improbable

**inverosimilitud** /imberosimili'tuð/ *f*, improbability

**inversamente** /imbersa'mente/ *adv* inversely

**inverso** /im'berso/ *a* inverse; inverted

**invertebrado** /imberte'βraðo/ *a* and *m*, invertebrate

**invertir** /imber'tir/ *vt irr* to invert, transpose; reverse; *Com.* invest; spend (time). See **sentir**

**investidura** /imbesti'ðura/ *f*, investiture

**investigación** /imbestiga'θion; imbestiga'sion/ *f*, investigation, examination; research; inquiry

**investigador** /imbestiga'ðor/ **(-ra)** *a* investigating —*n* investigator; researcher

**investigar** /imbesti'gar/ *vt* to investigate, examine; research on

**investir** /imbes'tir/ *vt irr* to confer upon, decorate with; invest, appoint. See **pedir**

**inveterado** /imbete'raðo/ *a* inveterate

**inviable** /im'biaβle/ *a* unfeasible

**invicto** /im'bikto/ *a* invincible; unconquered

**invierno** /im'bierno/ *m*, winter; rainy season

**inviolabilidad** /imbiolaβili'ðað/ *f*, inviolability. **i. parlamentaria**, parliamentary immunity

**inviolable** /imbio'laβle/ *a* inviolable; infallible

**inviolado** /imbio'laðo/ *a* inviolate

**invisibilidad** /imbisiβili'ðað/ *f*, invisibility

**invisible** /imbi'siβle/ *a* invisible

**invitación** /imbita'θion; imbita'sion/ *f*, invitation

**invitado** /imbi'taðo/ **(-da)** *n* guest

**invitar** /imbi'tar/ *vt* to invite; urge, request; allure, attract

**invocación** /imboka'θion; imboka'sion/ *f*, invocation

**invocador** /imboka'ðor/ **(-ra)** *n* invoker

**invocar** /imbo'kar/ *vt* to invoke

**involucro** /imbo'lukro/ *m*, involucre

**involuntariedad** /imboluntarie'ðað/ *f*, involuntariness

**involuntario** /imbolun'tario/ *a* involuntary

**invulnerabilidad** /imbulneraβili'ðað/ *f*, invulnerability

**invulnerable** /imbulne'raβle/ *a* invulnerable

**inyección** /inyek'θion; inyek'sion/ *f*, injection
**inyectado** /inyek'taðo/ *a* bloodshot (of eyes)
**inyectar** /inyek'tar/ *vt* to inject
**ipecacuana** /ipeka'kuana/ *f*, ipecac
**iperita** /i'perita/ *f*, mustard gas
**ir** /ir/ *vi irr* to go; bet (e.g. *Van cinco pesetas que no lo hace*, I bet five pesetas he doesn't do it); be different, be changed (e.g. *¿Qué diferencia va entre esto y aquello?* What a difference there is between this and that!); suit, be becoming, fit (e.g. *El vestido no te va bien*, The dress doesn't suit you); extend; lead, go in the direction of (e.g. *Este camino va a Lérida*, This road leads to Lerida); get along, do, proceed, be (e.g. *¿Cómo te va estos días?* How are you getting along these days?); come (e.g. *Ahora voy*, I'm coming now); *Math.* carry (e.g. *siete y van cuatro*, seven, 'and four to carry); *Math.* leave (e.g. *De quince a seis van nueve*, Six from fifteen leaves nine). With a gerund, **ir** indicates the continuance of the action, or may mean to become or to grow (e.g. *Iremos andando hacia el mar*, We shall go on walking toward the sea, or *Entre tanto iba amaneciendo*, In the meanwhile it was growing light). With a past participle, **ir** means "to be' (e.g. *Voy encantado de lo que he visto*, I am delighted with what I have seen). With *prep a + infin*, **ir** means to prepare (to do) or to intend (to do) or to be on the point of doing (e.g. *Van a cantar la canción que te gusta*, They are going (or preparing) to sing the song you like). With *prep a + noun*, **ir** indicates destination (e.g. *Voy al cine*, I'm going to the cinema. *¿A dónde vamos?* Where are we going to?). **ir** + *con* means to go in the company of, or to do a thing in a certain manner (e.g. *Hemos de ir con cuidado*, We must go carefully). **ir** + *en* means to concern, interest (e.g. *¿Qué le va a él en este asunto?* What has this affair to do with him?). **ir** + *por* means to follow the career of, become (e.g. *Juan va por abogado*, John is going to be a lawyer). It also means to go and bring, or to go for (e.g. *Iré por agua*, I shall go and bring (or for) water) —*vr* to go away, leave, depart; die; leak (of liquids); evaporate; overbalance, slip (e.g. *Se le fueron los pies*, He slipped (and lost his balance)); be worn out, grow old, deteriorate; be incontinent; *Fig. Inf.* **írsele a uno una cosa**, not to notice or not to understand a thing. *Naut.* **irse a pique**, to founder, sink. **Se le fueron los ojos tras María**, He couldn't keep his eyes off Mary. **i. a caballo**, to ride, go on horseback. **i. adelante**, to go on ahead, lead; *Fig. Inf.* forge ahead, go ahead. **i. al cuartel**, to go into the army. **i. a una**, to cooperate in. **i. bien** *Fig. Inf.* to go on well; be well. **i. de brazo**, to walk arm in arm. **i. de compras**, to go shopping. **i. de juerga** *Inf.* to go on a binge. **i. de bicicleta** *or* **en coche**, to go by bicycle or to ride (in a car or carriage). **i. por**, to do things in order, take one thing at a time. *Fig. Inf.* **tirando**, to carry on, manage. **¿Cómo le va?** How are things with you? How are you getting along? *Inf.* **no irle ni venirle a uno nada en un asunto**, to be not in the least concerned in (an affair). **¡Qué va!** Rubbish! Nothing of the sort! **¿Quién va?** *Mil.* Who goes there? **Vamos**, Let's go (also used as an exclamation: Good gracious! You don't say so! Well!) **Vamos a ver...**, Let's see.... **¡Vaya!** What a...!; Come now! Never mind! **¡Vaya a paseo!** *or* **¡Vaya con su música a otra parte!** Take yourself off! Get out! **¡Vaya con Dios!** God keep you! Good-bye! *Pres. Ind.* **voy, vas, va, vamos, váis, van.** *Pres. Part.* **yendo.** *Preterite* **fui, fuiste, fue, fuimos, fuisteis, fueron.** *Imperf.* **iba,** etc —*Pres. Subjunc.* **vaya,** etc —*Imperf. Subjunc.* **fuese,** etc —*Imperat.* ** vé**
**ira** /'ira/ *f*, wrath, anger; vengeance; raging, fury (of elements); *pl* cruelties, acts of vengeance
**iracundia** /ira'kundia/ *f*, irascibility, irritability; anger
**iracundo** /ira'kundo/ *a* irascible, irritable, choleric; angry; raging, tempestuous
**Irak** /i'rak/ Iraq
**iranio** /i'ranio/ **(-ia)** *a* and *n* Iranian
**irascibilidad** /irasθiβili'ðað; irassiβili'ðað/ *f*, irascibility; petulance
**iridiscencia** /iriðis'θenθia; iriðis'sensia/ *f*, iridescence
**iridiscente** /iriðis'θente; iriðis'sente/ *a* iridescent
**iris** /'iris/ *m*, rainbow; *Anat.* iris (of the eye)

**irisación** /irisa'θion; irisa'sion/ *f*, irisation
**irisar** /iri'sar/ *vi* to be iridescent
**Irlanda** /ir'landa/ Ireland
**irlandés** /irlan'des/ **(-esa)** *a* and *n* Irishman (woman)
**ironía** /iro'nia/ *f*, irony
**irónico** /i'roniko/ *a* ironical
**iroqués** /iro'kes/ **(-esa)** *a* and *n* Iroquois
**irracional** /irraθio'nal; irrasio'nal/ *a* irrational; illogical, unreasonable; *Math.* irrational, absurd
**irracionalidad** /irraθionali'ðað; irrasionali'ðað/ *f*, irrationality, unreasonableness
**irradiación** /irraðia'θion; irraðia'sion/ *f*, radiation, irradiation
**irradiar** /irra'ðiar/ *vt* to radiate, irradiate
**irrazonable** /irraθo'naβle; irraso'naβle/ *a* unreasonable
**irreal** /irre'al/ *a* unreal
**irrealidad** /irreali'ðað/ *f*, unreality
**irrealizable** /irreali'θaβle; irreali'saβle/ *a* unachievable, unattainable
**irrebatible** /irreβa'tiβle/ *a* irrefutable, evident
**irreconciliable** /irrekonθi'liaβle; irrekonsi'liaβle/ *a* irreconcilable, intransigent
**irrecuperable** /irrekupe'raβle/ *a* irretrievable
**irredimible** /irreði'miβle/ *a* irredeemable
**irreemplazable** /irreempla'θaβle; irreempla'saβle/ *a* irreplaceable
**irreflexión** /irreflek'sion/ *f*, thoughtlessness; impetuosity
**irreflexivo** /irreflek'siβo/ *a* thoughtless; rash, impetuous
**irreformable** /irrefor'maβle/ *a* unreformable
**irrefragable** /irrefra'gaβle/ *a* indisputable, unquestionable
**irrefrenable** /irrefre'naβle/ *a* unmanageable, uncontrollable
**irrefutable** /irrefu'taβle/ *a* irrefutable
**irregular** /irregu'lar/ *a* irregular; infrequent, rare
**irregularidad** /irregulari'ðað/ *f*, irregularity; abnormality; *Inf.* moral lapse
**irreligión** /irreli'hion/ *f*, irreligion
**irreligiosidad** /irrelihiosi'ðað/ *f*, impiety, godlessness
**irreligioso** /irreli'hioso/ *a* irreligious, impious
**irremediable** /irreme'ðiaβle/ *a* irremediable
**irremediablemente** /irremeðiaβle'mente/ *adv* unavoidably; hopelessly
**irremisible** /irremi'siβle/ *a* unpardonable, inexcusable
**irremunerado** /irremune'raðo/ *a* unremunerated, gratuitous
**irreparable** /irrepa'raβle/ *a* irreparable
**irreprensible** /irrepren'siβle/ *a* blameless, unexceptionable
**irreprochable** /irrepro'tʃaβle/ *a* irreproachable
**irresistible** /irresis'tiβle/ *a* irresistible; ravishing
**irresolución** /irresolu'θion; irresolu'sion/ *f*, vacillation, indecision
**irresoluto** /irreso'luto/ *a* hesitant, irresolute
**irrespetuoso** /irrespe'tuoso/ *a* disrespectful
**irresponsabilidad** /irresponsaβili'ðað/ *f*, irresponsibility
**irresponsable** /irrespon'saβle/ *a* irresponsible
**irreverencia** /irreβe'renθia; irreβe'rensia/ *f*, irreverence
**irreverente** /irreβe'rente/ *a* irreverent
**irrevocabilidad** /irreβokaβili'ðað/ *f*, irrevocability, finality
**irrevocable** /irreβo'kaβle/ *a* irrevocable
**irrigación** /irriga'θion; irriga'sion/ *f*, irrigation
**irrigador** /irriga'ðor/ *m*, spray, sprinkler; *Med.* syringe, spray
**irrigar** /irri'gar/ *vt* (*Med. Agr.*) to irrigate
**irrisible** /irri'siβle/ *a* ridiculous, laughable, absurd
**irrisión** /irri'sion/ *f*, derision; laughingstock
**irrisorio** /irri'sorio/ *a* ridiculous; derisive
**irritabilidad** /irritaβili'ðað/ *f*, irritability, petulance, irascibility
**irritable** /irri'taβle/ *a* irritable
**irritación** /irrita'θion; irrita'sion/ *f*, *Med.* irritation; petulance, exasperation
**irritador** /irrita'ðor/ *a* irritating; exasperating. *m*, irritant

**irritante** /irri'tante/ *a* irritating; exasperating

**irritar** /irri'tar/ *vt* to exasperate, annoy; provoke, inflame; (*Med. Law.*) irritate

**írrito** /'irrito/ *a* *Law.* null, void

**irrogar** /irro'gar/ *vt* to occasion (damage, harm)

**irrompible** /irrom'piβle/ *a* unbreakable

**irrumpir** /irrum'pir/ *vi* to enter violently, break in

**irrupción** /irrup'θion; irrup'sion/ *f*, irruption, incursion, invasion

**irruptor** /irrup'tor/ *a* invading, attacking

**isabelino** /isaβe'lino/ *a* Isabelline (pertaining to Spanish Queen Isabella II (reigned 1830–68)); bay (of horses)

**isla** /'isla/ *f*, island; block (of houses)

**islámico** /is'lamiko/ *a* Islamic

**islamismo** /isla'mismo/ *m*, Islam

**islamita** /isla'mita/ *a* and *mf* Muslim

**islandés** /islan'des/ **(-esa)**, **islándico (-ca)** *a* Icelandic —*n* Icelander. *m*, Icelandic (language)

**Islandia** /is'landia/ Iceland

**isleño** /is'leɲo/ **(-ña)** *a* island —*n* islander; native of the Canary Islands

**isleta** /is'leta/ *f*, islet

**islote** /is'lote/ *m*, barren islet

**ismaelita** /ismae'lita/ *a* and *mf* Ishmaelite

**isométrico** /iso'metriko/ *a* isometric

**isomorfo** /iso'morfo/ *a* isomorphic

**isotermo** /iso'termo/ *a* isothermal

**isótope, isótopo** /i'sotope, i'sotopo/ *m*, isotope

**israelita** /israe'lita/ *mf* Israelite —*a* Israeli

**istmeño** /ist'meɲo/ **(-ña)** *n* native of an isthmus

**ístmico** /'istmiko/ *a* isthmian

**istmo** /'istmo/ *m*, isthmus

**Istmo de Suez, el** /'istmo de 'sueθ, el; 'istmo de 'sues, el/ the Suez Canal

**Ítaca** /'itaka/ Ithaca

**Italia** /i'talia/ Italy

**italianismo** /italia'nismo/ *m*, Italianism

**italianizar** /italiani'θar; italiani'sar/ *vt* to italianize

**italiano** /ita'liano/ **(-na)** *a* and *n* Italian. *m*, Italian (language)

**itálico** /i'taliko/ *a* italic

**iteración** /itera'θion; itera'sion/ *f*, iteration, repetition

**iterar** /ite'rar/ *vt* to repeat, reiterate

**iterativo** /itera'tiβo/ *a* iterative, repetitive

**itinerario** /itine'rario/ *a* and *m*, itinerary

**izar** /i'θar; i'sar/ *vt* *Naut.* to hoist

**izote** /i'θote; i'sote/ *m*, yucca

**izquierda** /iθ'kierða; is'kierða/ *f*, left, left-hand side; *Polit.* left. **¡I.!** *Mil.* Left face! **a la i.,** on the left

**izquierdo** /iθ'kierðo; is'kierðo/ *a* left, left-hand; left-handed; bent, twisted, crooked

# JK

¡**ja, ja, ja!** /ha, ha, ha/ *interj* Ha! ha! ha!

**jabalí** /haβa'li/ *m*, wild boar

**jabalina** /haβa'lina/ *f*, sow of wild boar; javelin

**jabato** /ha'βato/ *m*, young wild boar

**jabón** /ha'βon/ *m*, soap. **j. blando,** soft soap. **j. de olor** *or* **j. de tocador,** toilet soap. **j. de sastre,** French chalk, steatite

**jabonadura** /haβona'ðura/ *f*, soaping; *pl* soapsuds, lather

**jabonar** /haβo'nar/ *vt* to soap; wash; *Inf.* dress down, scold

**jaboncillo** /haβon'θiʎo; haβon'siyo/ *m*, toilet soap; steatite

**jabonera** /haβo'nera/ *f*, soapdish or box; soapwort

**jabonería** /haβone'ria/ *f*, soap factory or shop

**jabonoso** /haβo'noso/ *a* soapy

**jaca** /'haka/ *f*, pony; filly

**jácara** /'hakara/ *f*, gay, roguish ballad; song and dance

**jácena** /'haθena; 'hasena/ *f*, *Archit.* beam, girder

**jacinto** /ha'θinto; ha'sinto/ *m*, hyacinth; jacinth. **j. de ceilán,** zircon. **j. occidental,** topaz. **j. oriental,** ruby

**jaco** /'hako/ *m*, short coat of mail; hack, jade

**jacobinismo** /hakoβi'nismo/ *m*, Jacobinism

**jacobino** /hako'βino/ **(-na)** *n* Jacobin

**jactancia** /hak'tanθia; hak'tansia/ *f*, bragging, boasting

**jactancioso** /haktan'θioso; haktan'sioso/ **(-sa)** *a* boastful —*n* braggart

**jactarse** /hak'tarse/ *vr* to brag, boast

**jaculatoria** /hakula'toria/ *f*, ejaculatory prayer

**jaculatorio** /hakula'torio/ *a* ejaculatory

**jade** /'haðe/ *m*, *Mineral.* jade

**jadeante** /haðe'ante/ *a* panting

**jadear** /haðe'ar/ *vi* to pant

**jadeo** /ha'ðeo/ *m*, pant; panting; hard breathing

**jaez** /ha'eθ; ha'es/ *m*, harness (gen. *pl*); kind, sort; *pl* trappings

**jaguar** /ha'guar/ *m*, jaguar

**jalbegar** /halβe'gar/ *vt* to whitewash; make up the face

**jalbegue** /hal'βege/ *m*, whitewash

**jalde** /'halde/ *a* bright yellow

**jalea** /ha'lea/ *f*, jelly. **j. de membrillo,** quince jelly

**jalear** /hale'ar/ *vt* to encourage, urge on (by shouts, etc.)

**jaleo** /ha'leo/ *m*, act of encouraging dancers by clapping, shouting, etc.; Andalusian song and dance, *Inf.* uproar

**jalón** /ha'lon/ *m*, surveying rod

**jamaicano** /hamai'kano/ **(-na)** *a* and *n* Jamaican

**jamás** /ha'mas/ *adv* never. **nunca j.,** never. **por siempre j.,** for always, forever

**jamba** /'hamba/ *f*, jamb (of a door or window)

**jamelgo** /ha'melgo/ *m*, sorry nag, miserable hack

**jamón** /ha'mon/ *m*, ham

**jamona** /ha'mona/ *f*, *Inf.* plumpish middle-aged woman

**jansenismo** /hanse'nismo/ *m*, Jansenism

**jansenista** /hanse'nista/ *mf* and *a* Jansenist

**Japón** /ha'pon/ Japan

**japonés** /hapo'nes/ **(-esa)** *a* and *n* Japanese. *m*, Japanese (language)

**jaque** /'hake/ *m*, check (in chess); braggart. **j. mate,** checkmate. **en j.,** at bay

**jaquear** /hake'ar/ *vt* to check (in chess); *Mil.* harass the enemy

**jaqueca** /ha'keka/ *f*, migraine, sick headache. *Inf.* **dar una j.,** to annoy

**jarabe** /ha'raβe/ *m*, syrup. **j. tapatío,** Mexican hat dance

**jarana** /ha'rana/ *f*, roundhouse; *Inf.* revelry; fight, roughhouse; trick, deception

**jarcia** /'harθia; 'harsia/ *f*, equipment; *Naut.* tackle, rigging (gen. *pl*); fishing tackle; *Inf.* heap, mixture, medley

**jardín** /har'ðin/ *m*, garden

**jardinar** /harði'nar/ *vt* to landscape

**jardinera** /harði'nera/ *f*, plant stand, jardiniere; open streetcar

**jardinería** /harðine'ria/ *f*, gardening

**jardinero** /harði'nero/ **(-ra)** *n* gardener

**jareta** /ha'reta/ *f*, *Sew.* running hem; *Naut.* netting

**jarra** /'harra/ *f*, jar, jug. **en jarras,** arms akimbo

**jarrero** /ha'rrero/ *m*, jug seller or manufacturer

**jarrete** /ha'rrete/ *m*, calf (of the leg)

**jarretera** /harre'tera/ *f*, garter. **Orden de la J.,** Order of the Garter

**jarro** /'harro/ *m*, pitcher; jug; jar; vase

**jarrón** /ha'rron/ *m*, garden urn; vase

**jaspe** /'haspe/ *m*, jasper

**jaspeado** /haspe'aðo/ *a* marbled, mottled; dappled; frosted (of glass)

**jauja** /'hauha/ *f*, *Fig.* paradise, land of milk and honey

**jaula** /'haula/ *f*, cage; crate; miner's cage

**jauría** /hau'ria/ *f*, pack of hounds

**javanés** /haβa'nes/ **(-esa)** *a* and *n* Javanese

**jazmín** /haθ'min; has'min/ *m*, jasmine. **j. amarillo,** yellow jasmine. **j. de la India,** gardenia

**jefa** /'hefa/ *f*, forewoman; manager; leader, head

**jefatura** /hefa'tura/ *f*, chieftainship; managership; leadership. **j. de policía,** police station or headquarters

**jefe** /'hefe/ *m*, chief; head, leader; manager; *Mil.* commanding officer. *Mil.* **j. de estado mayor,** chief of staff. **j. del tren,** railroad guard

**jengibre** /hen'hiβre/ *m*, ginger

**jeque** /'heke/ *m*, sheik

**jerarca** /he'rarka/ *m*, hierarch

**jerarquía** /herar'kia/ *f*, hierarchy

**jerárquico** /he'rarkiko/ *a* hierarchical

**jeremiada** /here'miaða/ *f*, lamentation

**jerez** /he'reθ; he'res/ *m*, sherry

**jerga** /'herga/ *f*, thick frieze cloth; jargon

**jergón** /her'gon/ *m*, straw or hay mattress, pallet; misfit (garments); *Inf.* fat, lazy person

**Jericó** /heri'ko/ Jericho

**jerigonza** /heri'gonθa; heri'gonsa/ *f*, jargon; gibberish

**jeringa** /he'ringa/ *f*, syringe

**jeringar** /herin'gar/ *vt* to inject; syringe; *Inf.* annoy

**jeringuilla** /herin'guiʎa; herin'guiya/ *f*, small syringe; mock orange

**jeroglífico** /hero'glifiko/ *a* hieroglyphic. *m*, hieroglyph

**jersey** /her'sei/ *m*, jersey, sweater

**Jerusalén** /herusa'len/ Jerusalem

**jesuita** /he'suita/ *m*, Jesuit

**jesuita, jesuítico** /he'suita, he'suitiko/ *a* jesuitical

**Jesús** /he'sus/ *m*, Jesus —*interj* Goodness!; Bless you! (said to someone after sneezing). **¡ay J.!** Alas! *Inf.* **en un decir J.,** in a trice

**jeta** /'heta/ *f*, hog's snout; blubber lip; *Inf.* face, mug

**jibia** /'hiβia/ *f*, cuttlefish

**jícara** /'hikara/ *f*, small cup

**jifa** /'hifa/ *f*, meat offal

**jifia** /'hifia/ *f*, swordfish

**jilguero** /hil'gero/ *m*, goldfinch

**jinete** /hi'nete/ *m*, horseman, rider; horse soldier, cavalryman

**jingoísmo** /hingo'ismo/ *m*, jingoism

**jip** /hip/ *m*, jeep

**jipijapa** /hipi'hapa/ *f*, very fine straw. **sombrero de j.,** panama hat

**jira** /'hira/ *f*, strip of cloth; picnic; tour

**jirafa** /hi'rafa/ *f*, giraffe

**jirón** /hi'ron/ *m*, rag; piece of a dress, etc.; portion of a whole

**jiujitsu** /hiu'hitsu/ *m*, jujitsu

**jocosidad** /hokosi'ðað/ *f*, pleasantry, jocularity; joke

**jocoso** /ho'koso/ *a* waggish; jocose, joyous

**jocundidad** /hokundi'ðað/ *f*, jocundity

**jocundo** /ho'kundo/ *a* jocund

**jofaina** /ho'faina/ *f*, washbowl

**jónico** /'honiko/ **(-ca)** *a* Ionic —*n* Ionian. *m*, (metrics) Ionic foot

**Jordán** /hor'ðan/ Jordan (river)

**Jordania** /hor'ðania/ Jordan (country)

**jornada** /hor'naða/ *f*, day's journey; journey, trip; *Mil.* expedition; duration of a working day; opportunity; span of life; act of a drama. **a grandes jornadas,** by forced marches, rapidly

**jornal** /hor'nal/ *m*, day's wages or labor

**jornalear** /hornale'ar/ *vi* to work by the day

**jornalero** /horna'lero/ **(-ra)** *n* day laborer; wage earner

**joroba** /ho'roβa/ *f*, hump; *Inf.* impertinence, nuisance

**jorobado** /horo'βaðo/ **(-da)** *a* humpbacked —*n* hunchback

**jota** /'hota/ *f*, name of letter J; popular Spanish dance; jot, tittle (always used negatively). **no saber j.,** to be completely ignorant

**joven** /'hoβen/ *a* young. *mf* young man or woman

**jovenzuelo** /hoβen'θuelo/ hoβen'suelo/ **(-la)** *n* youngster, boy

**jovialidad** /hoβiali'ðað/ *f*, joviality, cheerfulness

**joya** /'hoia/ *f*, jewel; present; *Archit.* astragal; *Fig.* a jewel of a person

**joyería** /hoie'ria/ *f*, jeweler's shop or workshop

**joyero** /ho'iero/ *m*, jeweler; jewel box

**juanete** /hua'nete/ *m*, bunion; prominent cheekbone; *Naut.* topgallant sail

**juanetudo** /huane'tuðo/ *a* having bunions; with prominent cheekbones

**jubilación** /huβila'θion/ huβila'sion/ *f*, retirement; pensioning off; pension

**jubilado** /huβi'laðo/ *a* retired

**jubilar** /huβi'lar/ *vt* to pension off; excuse from certain duties; *Inf.* put aside as useless (things); —*vr* rejoice; retire or be pensioned off

**jubileo** /huβi'leo/ *m*, jubilee

**júbilo** /'huβilo/ *m*, rejoicing, merriment. **j. de vivir,** joie de vivre

**jubiloso** /huβi'loso/ *a* jubilant, happy

**jubón** /hu'βon/ *m*, doublet; bodice

**judaico** /hu'ðaiko/ *a* Judaic

**judaísmo** /huða'ismo/ *m*, Judaism

**judas** /'huðas/ *m*, Judas; traitor

**judería** /huðe'ria/ *f*, Jewry

**judesmo** /hu'ðesmo/ *m*, Judezmo (Romance language of Jews)

**judía** /hu'ðia/ *f*, Jew (female); Jewish quarter, Jewish neighborhood; haricot bean. **judías verdes,** string beans

**judicatura** /huðika'tura/ *f*, judicature; judgeship; judiciary

**judío** /hu'ðio/ **(-ía)** *a* Jewish —*n* Jew. **j. errante,** wandering Jew

**juego** /'huego/ *m*, play, sport; gambling; hand (of cards); set; suite; *Mech.* play, working. **j. de café,** coffee set. **j. de los cientos,** piquet. **j. de manos,** sleight of hand, conjuring. **j. de naipes,** game of cards. **j. limpio,** fair play. **j. sencillo,** single (at tennis). **j. sucio,** foul play. **juegos florales,** floral games, poetry contest. **juegos malabares,** juggling. **en j.,** in operation; at stake. **entrar en j.,** to come into play. **hacer j.,** to match. **hacer juegos malabares,** to juggle

**juerga** /'huerga/ *f*, *Inf.* spree, binge. **ir de j.,** *Inf.* to go on a binge

**jueves** /'hueβes/ *m*, Thursday. **¡No es cosa del otro j.!** *Inf.* It's no great shakes! It's nothing to write home about!

**juez** /hueθ/ hues/ *m*, judge. **j. arbitrador,** arbitrator; referee. **j. municipal,** magistrate

**jugada** /hu'gaða/ *f*, play; playing; move, throw; *Fig.* bad turn

**jugador** /huga'ðor/ **(-ra)** *a* gambling; playing —*n* gambler; player. **j. de manos,** conjurer

**jugar** /hu'gar/ *vi irr* to play; frolic; take part in a game; gamble; make a move (in a game); *Mech.* work; handle (a weapon); *Com.* intervene; —*vt* play (a match); bet; handle (a weapon); risk. **j. el lance,** *Fig.* to play one's cards well. **j. limpio,** to play fair; *Fig. Inf.* be straightforward. **j. sucio,** to play foul. **jugarse el todo por el todo,** to stake everything —*Pres. Indic.* **juego, juegas, juega, juegan.** *Pres. Subjunc.* **juegue, juegues, juegue, jueguen**

**jugarreta** /huga'rreta/ *f*, *Inf.* bad play; dirty trick

**juglar** /hug'lar/ *m*, entertainer; buffoon, juggler; minstrel

**juglaresco** /hugla'resko/ *a* pertaining to minstrels

**jugo** /'hugo/ *m*, sap; juice; *Fig.* essence. **j. de muñeca,** elbow grease

**jugosidad** /hugosi'ðað/ *f*, juiciness, succulence; *Fig.* pithiness

**jugoso** /hu'goso/ *a* juicy, succulent; *Fig.* pithy

**juguete** /hu'gete/ *m*, toy; plaything; *Fig.* puppet

**juguetear** /hugete'ar/ *vi* to frolic, gambol

**jugueteo** /huge'teo/ *m*, gamboling; play, dalliance

**juguetería** /hugete'ria/ *f*, toy trade; toy shop

**juguetón** /huge'ton/ *a* playful

**juicio** /'huiθio; 'huisio/ *m*, judgment; wisdom, prudence; sanity, right mind; opinion; horoscope. **j. final,** Last Judgment. **j. sano,** right mind. **asentar el j.,** to settle down, become sensible. **estar fuera de j.,** to be insane. **pedir en j.,** to sue at law

**juicioso** /hui'θioso; hui'sioso/ *a* judicious; prudent

**julio** /'hulio/ *m*, July; *Elec.* joule

**jumento** /hu'mento/ *m*, ass; beast of burden

**juncal** /hun'kal/ *a* reedy; rushy; *Inf.* slim, lissome

**juncar** /hun'kar/ *m*, reedy ground

**junco** /'hunko/ *m*, *Bot.* rush, reed; *Naut.* junk

**juncoso** /hun'koso/ *a* reed-like; rushy; reedy

**junio** /'hunio/ *m*, June

**junquillo** /hun'kiλo; hun'kiyo/ *m*, jonquil; *Archit.* reed molding

**junta** /'hunta/ *f*, joint; assembly, council; committee; union, association; session, sitting; entirety, whole; board, management. **j. de comercio,** board of trade. **j. directiva,** managerial board

**juntamente** /hunta'mente/ *adv* jointly; simultaneously

**juntar** /hun'tar/ *vt* to join, unite (*with prep a or con*); couple; assemble; amass; leave ajar (door); —*vr* (*with con*) frequent company of; meet; join; copulate

**junto** /'hunto/ *a* united, together —*adv* (*with prep a*) near; —*adv* together, simultaneously. **en j.,** altogether, in all

**juntura** /hun'tura/ *f*, joining; joint; seam; juncture

**jura** /'hura/ *f*, solemn oath; swearing

**jurado** /hu'raðo/ *m*, jury; jury

**juramentar** /huramen'tar/ *vt* to swear in; —*vr* take an oath

**juramento** /hura'mento/ *m*, oath; curse, imprecation. **j. falso,** perjury, **prestar j.,** to take an oath

**jurar** /hu'rar/ *vt* to swear an oath; swear allegiance; —*vi* curse, be profane

**jurídico** /hu'riðiko/ *a* juridical, legal

**jurisconsulto** /huriskon'sulto/ *m*, jurisconsult

**jurisdicción** /hurisðik'θion; hurisðik'sion/ *f*, *Law.* jurisdiction; boundary; authority

**jurisprudencia** /hurispru'ðenθia; hurispru'ðensia/ *f*, jurisprudence

**jurista** /hu'rista/ *mf* jurist

**justa** /'husta/ *f*, joust; tournament; contest

**justar** /hus'tar/ *vi* to joust

**justicia** /hus'tiθia; hus'tisia/ *f*, justice; equity; right; penalty, punishment; righteousness; court of justice; *Inf.* death penalty, execution. **administrar j.,** to dispense justice

**justiciero** /husti'θiero; husti'siero/ *a* just

**justificable** /hustifi'kaβle/ *a* justifiable

**justificación** /hustifika'θion; hustifika'sion/ *f*, justification, impartiality, fairness; convincing proof

**justificar** /hustifi'kar/ *vt* to justify, vindicate; adjust, regulate; prove innocent; —*vr* justify oneself; prove one's innocence

**justillo** /hus'tiλo; hus'tiyo/ *m*, jerkin

**justipreciar** /hustipre'θiar; hustipre'siar/ *vt* to appraise, value

**justiprecio** /husti'preθio; husti'presio/ *m*, appraisement, valuation

**justo** /'husto/ *a* just; righteous, virtuous; exact, accurate; tight-fitting, close —*adv* justly; exactly; tightly

**Jutlandia** /hut'landia/ Jutland

**juvenil** /huβe'nil/ *a* young

**juventud** /huβen'tuð/ *f*, youthfulness, youth; younger generation

**juzgado** /huθ'gaðo; hus'gaðo/ *m*, court of law; jurisdiction; judgeship

**juzgar** /huθ'gar; hus'gar/ *vt* to judge, pass sentence on; decide, consider

**ka** /ka/ *f*, name of the letter K

**káiser** /'kaiser/ *m*, kaiser

**kan** /kan/ *m*, khan

**kantiano** /kan'tiano/ *a* Kantian

**Kenia** /'kenia/ Kenya

**kermese** /ker'mese/ *f*, kermis, festival

**kerosén** /kero'sen/ *m*, kerosene

**kilo** /'kilo/ *prefix* meaning a thousand. *m*, *Abbr*. kilogram

**kilociclo** /kilo'θiklo; kilo'siklo/ *m*, *Elec*. kilocycle

**kilogramo** /kilo'gramo/ *m*, kilogram (2.17 lb.)

**kilolitro** /kilo'litro/ *m*, kiloliter

**kilometraje** /kilome'trahe/ *m*, number of kilometers; mileage

**kilométrico** /kilo'metriko/ *a* kilometric. **billete k.,** tourist ticket

**kilómetro** /ki'lometro/ *m*, kilometer (about $\frac{5}{8}$ mile)

**kilovatio** /kilo'βatio/ *m*, *Elec*. kilowatt

**kiosco** /'kiosko/ *m*, kiosk

# L

**la** /la/ *def art f, sing* the (e.g. *la mesa,* the table). **la** is replaced by el *m, sing* before feminine nouns beginning with stressed *a* or *ha* (e.g. *el hambre,* hunger). **la** is sometimes used before names of famous women (e.g. *la Juana de Arco, la Melba* (Joan of Arc, Melba)) and is generally not translated —*pers pron acc f sing* her; it (e.g. *La veo venir,* I see her coming) —*dem. pron* followed by *de,* or by *que* introducing relative clause, that of, that which, the one that, she who (e.g. *La casa está lejos de la en que escribo,* The house is far from the one in which I write). **la de** is used familiarly for Mrs. (e.g. *la de Jiménez,* Mrs. Jimenez). **la** means some, any, one, as substitution for noun already given (e.g. *Su hija lo haría si la tuviera,* Her daughter would do it if she had one)

**lábaro** /ˈlaβaro/ *m,* labarum, standard

**laberíntico** /laβeˈrintiko/ *a* labyrinthine

**laberinto** /laβeˈrinto/ *m,* labyrinth; *Fig.* tangle, complication; *Anat.* labyrinth of the ear

**labia** /ˈlaβia/ *f, Inf.* blarney, gab

**labial** /laˈβial/ *a* labial

**labihendido** /laβienˈdiðo/ *a* harelipped

**labio** /ˈlaβio/ *m,* lip; rim, edge. **l. leporino,** harelip. **cerrar los labios,** to close one's lips; keep silent

**labor** /laˈβor/ *f,* work, toil; sewing; needlework; husbandry, farming; silkworm egg; *Mineral.* working; trimming; plowing, harrowing

**laborable** /laβoˈraβle/ *a* workable; cultivable, tillable. **día l.,** workday

**laborar** /laβoˈrar/ *vt* to work; till; plow; construct; —*vi* scheme, plot, plan

**laboratorio** /laβoraˈtorio/ *m,* laboratory

**laborear** /laβoreˈar/ *vt* to work; till, cultivate; *Naut.* reeve

**laboreo** /laβoˈreo/ *m,* tilling, cultivation, working, development (of mines, etc.)

**laboriosidad** /laβoriosiˈðað/ *f,* laboriousness, diligence

**laborioso** /laβoˈrioso/ *a* industrious, diligent; laborious, tedious, hard

**laborista** /laβoˈrista/ *a* and *mf* belonging to the Labor Party

**labra** /ˈlaβra/ *f,* stonecutting; carving or working (metal, stone, or wood)

**labrada** /laˈβraða/ *f,* fallow land ready for sowing

**labradero** /laβraˈðero/ *a* workable; cultivable, tillable

**labrado** /laˈβraðo/ *a* and *past part* worked; fashioned; carved; embroidered; figured, patterned. *m,* (gen. *pl*) cultivated ground

**labrador** /laβraˈðor/ *m,* laborer, worker; farmer; peasant

**labradora** /laβraˈðora/ *f,* peasant girl; farm girl

**labradoresco, labradoril** /laβraðoˈresko, laβraðoˈril/ *a* rustic, peasant, farming

**labrandera** /laβranˈdera/ *f,* seamstress

**labrantío** /labranˈβtio/ *a* tillable, cultivable. *m,* farming

**labranza** /laˈβranθa; laˈβransa/ *f,* tillage, cultivation; farm; farmland; farming; employment, work

**labrar** /laˈβrar/ *vt* to work, do; carve; fashion, construct, make; *Agr.* cultivate, till; plow; embroider; sew; bring about, cause; —*vi Fig.* impress deeply, leave a strong impression

**labriego** /laˈβriego/ **(-ga)** *n* agricultural laborer; peasant

**laca** /ˈlaka/ *f,* lac; lacquer, varnish; *Art.* lake (pigment)

**lacayo** /laˈkaio/ *m,* groom; lackey, footman

**lacear** /laθeˈar; laseˈar/ *vt Sew.* to trim with bows; tie, lace; snare, trap

**laceración** /laθeraˈθion; laseraˈsion/ *f,* laceration

**lacerado** /laθeˈraðo; laseˈraðo/ *a* unhappy, unfortunate; leprous

**lacerar** /laθeˈrar; laseˈrar/ *vt* to lacerate, mangle, tear; distress, wound the feelings of

**lacería** /laθeˈria; laseˈria/ *f,* poverty, misery; toil, drudgery; trouble, affliction

**lacero** /laˈθero; laˈsero/ *m,* cowboy, one who uses a lasso; poacher

**lacio** /ˈlaθio; ˈlasio/ *a* drooping, limp; withered, faded; straight (hair)

**lacónico** /laˈkoniko/ *a* laconic; concise; Laconian

**lacra** /ˈlakra/ *f,* aftereffect, trace (of illness); vice; fault

**lacrar** /laˈkrar/ *vt* to impair the health; infect with an illness; injure, prejudice (the interests, etc.); seal with sealing wax

**lacre** /ˈlakre/ *m,* sealing wax —*a* red

**lacrimal** /lakriˈmal/ *a* lachrymal

**lacrimoso** /lakriˈmoso/ *a* tearful, lachrymose

**lactancia** /lakˈtanθia; lakˈtansia/ *f,* lactation

**lactar** /lakˈtar/ *vt* to suckle; feed with milk; —*vi* take or drink milk

**lácteo** /ˈlakteo/ *a* lacteal; milky

**lacustre** /laˈkustre/ *a* lacustrine, lake

**ladear** /laðeˈar/ *vt* to incline; tilt; turn aside, twist; skirt, pass close to; reach by a roundabout way, go indirectly to; —*vr* tilt; be in favor of, incline to; be equal to

**ladeo** /laˈðeo/ *m,* tilt; sloping; turning aside

**ladera** /laˈðera/ *f,* slope, incline; hillside

**ladería** /laðeˈria/ *f,* terrace on a hillside

**ladero** /laˈðero/ *a* lateral

**ladilla** /laˈðiʎa; laˈðiya/ *f,* crab louse

**ladino** /laˈðino/ *a* eloquent; versatile linguistically; wily, crafty; *m,* Ladino (variety of Judezmo)

**lado** /ˈlaðo/ *m,* side; edge, margin; slope, declivity; faction, party; side, flank; face (of a coin); *Fig.* aspect, view; line of descent; means, way; favor, protection; *pl* helpers, protectors; advisers. **al l.,** near at hand. *Inf.* **dar de l.** ( a), to cool off, fall out with. **dejar a un l.** (**una cosa**), to omit, pass over (a thing). **mirar de l.** *or* **de medio l.,** to look upon with disapproval; steal a look at

**ladrador** /laðraˈðor/ *a* barking

**ladrar** /laˈðrar/ *vi* to bark; *Inf.* threaten without hurting

**ladrido** /laˈðriðo/ *m,* bark, barking; slander, gossip

**ladrillado** /laðriˈʎaðo; laðriˈyaðo/ *m,* brick floor or pavement

**ladrillar** /laðriˈʎar; laðriˈyar/ *vt* to floor or pave with bricks. *m,* brickyard; brickkiln

**ladrillero** /laðriˈʎero; laðriˈyero/ **(-ra)** *n* brickmaker

**ladrillo** /laˈðriʎo; laˈðriyo/ *m,* brick; tile

**ladrón** /laˈðron/ **(-ona)** *a* robbing, thieving —*n* thief, robber; burglar. *m,* **l. de corazones,** ladykiller

**ladronera** /laðroˈnera/ *f,* thieves' den; thieving, pilfering; strongbox

**lagar** /laˈgar/ *m,* wine or olive press

**lagarta** /laˈgarta/ *f,* female lizard; *Inf.* she-serpent, cunning female

**lagartera** /lagarˈtera/ *f,* lizard hole

**lagartija** /lagarˈtiha/ *f,* wall lizard, small lizard

**lagarto** /laˈgarto/ *m,* lizard; *Inf.* sly, artful person, fox; *Inf.* insignia of Spanish Military Order of Santiago

**lago** /ˈlago/ *m,* lake

**lagotear** /lagoteˈar/ *vi Inf.* to wheedle, play up to

**lagotería** /lagoteˈria/ *f,* wheedling, coaxing, flattery

**lágrima** /ˈlagrima/ *f,* tear; drop (of liquid); exudation, ozzing (from trees)

**lagrimal** /lagriˈmal/ *a* lachrymal

**lagrimear** /lagrimeˈar/ *vi* to shed tears

**lagrimeo** /lagriˈmeo/ *m,* weeping, crying; watering of the eyes

**lagrimoso** /lagriˈmoso/ *a* tearful; watery (of eyes); sad, tragic

**laguna** /laˈguna/ *f,* small lake, lagoon; lacuna; gap, hiatus

**lagunoso** /laguˈnoso/ *a* boggy, marshy

**laical** /laiˈkal/ *a* lay, secular

**laicismo** /laiˈθismo; laiˈsismo/ *m,* secularism

**laico** /'laiko/ *a* lay, secular
**lama** /'lama/ *f,* ooze, slime. *m,* lama, Buddhist priest
**lamaísmo** /lama'ismo/ *m,* lamaism
**lameculos** /lame'kulos/ *mf Inf.* toady
**lamedura** /lame'ðura/ *f,* licking; lapping
**lamentable** /lamen'taβle/ *a* lamentable
**lamentación** /lamenta'θion; lamenta'sion/ *f,* lamentation; lament
**lamentador** /lamenta'ðor/ **(-ra)** *a* lamenting, wailing —*n* wailer, mourner
**lamentar** /lamen'tar/ *vt* to mourn, lament, bewail; —*vr* bemoan, bewail
**lamento** /la'mento/ *m,* lament
**lamentoso** /lamen'toso/ *a* lamenting, afflicted; lamentable
**lamer** /la'mer/ *vt* to lick; pass the tongue over; touch lightly; lap
**lámina** /'lamina/ *f,* sheet (of metal); lamina; engraving; illustration, picture; engraving plate
**laminación** /lamina'θion; lamina'sion/ *f,* lamination, rolling (of metals)
**laminado** /lami'naðo/ *a* laminate; rolled (metals). *m,* rolling (of metals)
**laminador** /lamina'ðor/ *m,* rolling mill (for metals)
**laminar** /lami'nar/ *a* laminate; laminated —*vt* to roll (metals); laminate; lick
**lámpara** /'lampara/ *f,* lamp; radiance, light, luminous body; grease spot. **l. de los mineros** *or* **l. de seguridad,** safety lamp. **l. de soldar,** blowpipe. **l. termiónica,** *Radio.* thermionic valve. **atizar la l.,** to trim the lamp; *Inf.* refill drinking glasses
**lamparería** /lampare'ria/ *f,* lamp factory; lamp shop
**lamparero** /lampa'rero/ **(-ra),** *n* **lamparista** *mf* lamplighter; lamp maker or seller
**lamparilla** /lampa'riʎa; lampa'riya/ *f,* night-light; *Bot.* aspen; small lamp
**lamparón** /lampa'ron/ *m,* scrofula, king's evil; tumor (disease of horses)
**lampiño** /lam'piɲo/ *a* beardless, clean-shaven; smooth-faced; *Bot.* nonhirsute
**lampista** /lam'pista/ *mf* See **lamparero**
**lamprea** /lam'prea/ *f,* lamprey
**lana** /'lana/ *f,* wool; fleece; woolen garments or cloth; woolen trade (gen. *pl*)
**lanar** /la'nar/ *a* wool; wool-bearing. **ganado l.,** sheep
**lance** /'lanθe; 'lanse/ *m,* throw, cast; casting a fishing line; catch of fish; crisis, difficult moment; *Lit.* episode; quarrel; move (in a game). *Fig.* **l. apretado,** difficult position, tight corner. **l. de fortuna,** chance, fate. **l. de honor,** affair of honor; duel
**lancear** /lanθe'ar; lanse'ar/ *vt* to wound with a lance; lance
**lancero** /lan'θero; lan'sero/ *m, Mil.* lancer; *pl* lancers (dance and music)
**lanceta** /lan'θeta; lan'seta/ *f,* lancet
**lancha** /'lantʃa/ *f, Naut.* launch; lighter; ship's boat; small boat; flagstone. **l. bombardera** *or* **l. cañonera,** gunboat. **l. de salvamento,** ship's lifeboat. **l. escampavía,** patrol boat
**lancinar** /lanθi'nar; lansi'nar/ *vt Med.* to lance
**landa** /'landa/ *f,* lande
**landó** /lan'do/ *m,* landau
**lanero** /la'nero/ *a* woolen. *m,* wool merchant; wool warehouse
**langosta** /laŋ'gosta/ *f,* locust; lobster. **l. migratoria,** locust
**langostín** /laŋgos'tin/ *m,* crayfish
**languidecer** /laŋguiðe'θer; laŋguiðe'ser/ *vi irr* to languish, pine. See **conocer**
**languidez** /laŋgui'ðeθ; laŋgui'ðes/ *f,* lassitude, inertia; languor
**lánguido** /'laŋguiðo/ *a* listless, weak, languid; half-hearted; languishing, languorous
**lanolina** /lano'lina/ *f,* lanolin
**lanosidad** /lanosi'ðað/ *f,* woolliness; down (on leaves, etc.)
**lanoso, lanudo** /la'noso, la'nuðo/ *a* woolly
**lanza** /'lanθa; 'lansa/ *f,* lance, spear; lancer; nozzle (of a hosepipe). **correr lanzas,** to joust (in a tournament). **estar con la l. en ristre,** to have the lance in

rest; be prepared or ready. *Inf.* **ser una l.,** to be very clever
**lanzabombas** /lanθa'βombas; lansa'βombas/ *m,* (*Aer. Nav.*) bomb release
**lanzada** /lan'θaða; lan'saða/ *f,* lance or spear thrust
**lanzadera** /lanθa'ðera; lansa'ðera/ *f,* weaver's shuttle; sewing machine shuttle. *Inf.* **parecer una l.,** to be constantly on the go
**lanzador** /lanθa'ðor; lansa'ðor/ **(-ra)** *m,* batsman —*n* thrower, caster, tosser
**lanzallamas** /lanθa'ʎamas; lansa'yamas/ *m,* flamethrower
**lanzamiento** /lanθa'miento; lansa'miento/ *m,* throwing; cast, throw; *Law.* dispossession; *Naut.* launching
**lanzaminas** /lanθa'minas; lansa'minas/ *m,* minelayer
**lanzar** /lan'θar; lan'sar/ *vt* to throw, cast, hurl; *Naut.* launch; vomit; *Law.* dispossess; *Agr.* take root; —*vr* hurl oneself, rush; take (to), embark (upon)
**lanzatorpedos** /lanθator'peðos; lansator'peðos/ **(tubo)** *m,* torpedo tube
**lañar** /la'ɲar/ *vt* to clamp; clean fish (for salting)
**lapa** /'lapa/ *f,* barnacle, limpet
**lapicero** /lapi'θero; lapi'sero/ *m,* pencil holder, pencil case; mechanical pencil
**lápida** /'lapiða/ *f,* memorial tablet; gravestone
**lapidación** /lapiða'θion; lapiða'sion/ *f,* lapidation, stoning
**lapidar** /lapi'ðar/ *vt* to stone, lapidate; throw stones at
**lapidario** /lapi'ðario/ *a* lapidary
**lapislázuli** /lapis'laθuli; lapis'lasuli/ *m,* lapis lazuli
**lápiz** /'lapiθ; 'lapis/ *m,* graphite; pencil; crayon. **l. para los labios,** lipstick
**lapizar** /lapi'θar; lapi'sar/ *m,* graphite mine —*vt* to pencil
**lapón** /la'pon/ **(-ona)** *a* Lappish —*n* Laplander. *m,* Sami (language)
**Laponia** /la'ponia/ Lapland
**lapso** /'lapso/ *m,* lapse, period, passage; slip, error, failure
**laquear** /lake'ar/ *vt* to lacquer, paint
**lar** /lar/ *m,* home; *pl* lares
**lardear** /larðe'ar/ *vt Cul.* to baste
**lardo** /'larðo/ *m,* lard; animal fat
**lardoso** /lar'ðoso/ *a* greasy; fat; oily
**larga** /'larga/ *f,* longest billiard cue; delay (gen. *pl*). **a la l.,** in the long run
**largamente** /larga'mente/ *adv* fully, at length; generously; widely, extensively; comfortably
**largar** /lar'gar/ *vt* to slacken, loosen; *Naut.* unfurl; set at liberty; *Fig. Inf.* let fly (oaths, etc.); administer (blows, etc.); —*vr Inf.* quit, leave (in a hurry or secretly); *Naut.* set sail
**largo** /'largo/ *a* long; generous, liberal; abundant, plentiful; protracted; prolonged; expeditious; *pl* many long (e.g. *por largos años,* for many long years). *m, Mus.* largo; length. *Inf.* **¡L. de aquí!** Get out! **a la larga,** in length; eventually, finally; slowly; with many digressions. **a lo l.,** lengthwise; along the length (of); in the distance, far off; along, the length (of). *Fig.* **ponerse de l.,** to make one's debut in society; come of age
**largor** /lar'gor/ *m,* **largura** *f,* length
**largueza** /lar'geθa; lar'gesa/ *f,* length; generosity, munificence
**largura** /lar'gura/ *f,* length
**laringe** /la'rinhe/ *f,* larynx
**laríngeo** /la'rinheo/ *a* laryngeal
**laringitis** /larin'hitis/ *f,* laryngitis
**larva** /'larβa/ *f,* larva; worm, grub; specter, phantom
**las** /las/ *def art. f pl,* of **la** the —*pers pron acc f pl,* of **la,** them
**lascivia** /las'θiβia; las'siβia/ *f,* lasciviousness
**lascivo** /las'θiβo; las'siβo/ *a* lascivious, lewd; wanton
**lasitud** /lasi'tuð/ *f,* lassitude, weariness, exhaustion
**laso** /'laso/ *a* weary, exhausted; weak; untwisted (of silk, etc.)
**lástima** /'lastima/ *f,* compassion, pity; pitiful sight; complaint, lamentation. **dar l.,** to cause pity. **Es l.,** It's a pity. **tener l. ( a** *or* **de)** to be sorry for (persons)

**lastimador** /lastima'ðor/ *a* harmful, injurious; painful

**lastimar** /lasti'mar/ *vt* to hurt, harm, injure; pity; *Fig.* wound, distress; —*vr* (*with de*) be sorry for or about; complain, lament

**lastimero** /lasti'mero/ *a* pitiful; mournful; injurious, harmful

**lastimoso** /lasti'moso/ *a* pitiful, heartbreaking; mournful

**lastrar** /las'trar/ *vt* to ballast

**lastre** /'lastre/ *m,* ballast; good sense, prudence

**lata** /'lata/ *f,* can, tin; tin plate; can of food. **en l.,** canned, tinned (of food). *Inf.* **Es una l.,** It's a bore, It's an awful nuisance

**latamente** /lata'mente/ *adv* extensively, at length; broadly

**latente** /la'tente/ *a* latent

**lateral** /late'ral/ *a* lateral

**látex** /'lateks/ *m,* latex

**latido** /la'tiðo/ *m,* yelp, bark; beat; throb; palpitation

**latifundios** /lati'fundios/ *m pl,* latifundia (large agricultural estates)

**latigazo** /lati'gaθo; lati'gaso/ *m,* lash; crack of a whip; sudden blow of fate; *Inf.* draft (of wine, etc.); harsh scolding; *Naut.* jerk or flapping (of sails)

**látigo** /'latigo/ *m,* whip, lash; cinch, girth of a saddle

**latín** /la'tin/ *m,* Latin. **bajo l.,** low Latin. *Inf.* **saber l.,** to know the score; be smart

**latinajo** /lati'naho/ *m, Inf.* bad Latin

**latinidad** /latini'ðað/ *f,* Latinity

**latinismo** /lati'nismo/ *m,* Latinism

**latinista** /lati'nista/ *mf* Latinist

**latinizar** /latini'θar; latini'sar/ *vt* to latinize; —*vi Inf.* use Latin phrases

**latino** /la'tino/ *a* Latin; lateen sail

**latinoamericano** /latinoameri'kano/ **(-na)** *a* and *n* Latin-American

**latir** /la'tir/ *vi* to yelp, howl; bark; throb, palpitate, beat

**latitud** /lati'tuð/ *f,* latitude; area, extent; breadth

**latitudinario** /lati,tuði'nario/ *a* latitudinarian

**lato** /'lato/ *a* extensive; large; broad (of word meanings)

**latón** /la'ton/ *m,* brass

**latonería** /latone'ria/ *f,* brassworks; brass shop

**latoso** /la'toso/ *a* boring, troublesome, annoying

**latrocinio** /latro'θinio; latro'sinio/ *m,* larceny

**latvio** /'latβio/ **(-ia)** *a* and *n* Latvian

**laúd** /la'uð/ *m,* lute

**laudable** /lau'ðaβle/ *a* praiseworthy, laudable

**láudano** /'lauðano/ *m,* laudanum

**laudatorio** /lauða'torio/ *a* laudatory

**laurear** /laure'ar/ *vt* to crown with laurel; honor, reward

**laurel** /lau'rel/ *m,* bay tree. **l. cerezo,** laurel. **l. rosa,** rosebay, oleander

**láureo** /'laureo/ *a* laurel

**lauréola** /lau'reola/ *f,* laurel wreath

**lauro** /'lauro/ *m,* bay tree; glory, triumph

**Lausana** /lau'sana/ Lausanne

**lava** /'laβa/ *f,* lava

**lavable** /la'βaβle/ *a* washable

**lavabo** /la'βaβo/ *m,* washstand; cloakroom, lavatory

**lavada** /la'βaða/ *f,* load of wash, load

**lavadedos** /laβa'ðeðos/ *m,* fingerbowl

**lavadero** /laβa'ðero/ *m,* washing place; laundry

**lavado** /la'βaðo/ *m,* washing; cleaning; wash. **l. al seco,** dry cleaning

**lavadura** /laβa'ðura/ *f,* washing

**lavamanos** /laβa'manos/ *m,* washstand; lavatory

**lavamiento** /laβa'miento/ *m,* washing, cleansing, ablution

**lavanda** /la'βanda/ *f,* lavender

**lavandera** /laβan'dera/ *f,* laundress; washerwoman

**lavandería** /laβande'ria/ *f,* laundry

**lavandero** /laβan'dero/ *m,* laundry; laundryman

**lavaplatos** /laβa'platos/ *m,* dishwasher

**lavar** /la'βar/ *vt* to wash; *Fig.* wipe out, purify; paint in watercolors. **l. al seco,** to dry-clean

**lavativa** /laβa'tiβa/ *f,* enema; syringe, clyster; *Inf.* nuisance, bore

**lavatorio** /laβa'torio/ *m,* washing, lavation; *Eccl.* lavabo; lavatory, washing place; *Eccl.* maundy

**lavazas** /la'βaθas; la'βasas/ *f pl,* dirty soapy water

**laxante** /lak'sante/ *a* and *m,* laxative

**laxar** /lak'sar/ *vt* to loosen, relax; soften

**laxitud** /laksi'tuð/ *f,* laxity

**laxo** /'lakso/ *a* lax; slack

**laya** /'laia/ *f, Agr.* spade; kind, sort, class

**layar** /la'iar/ *vt Agr.* to fork

**lazar** /la'θar; la'sar/ *vt* to lasso

**lazareto** /laθa'reto; lasa'reto/ *m,* leper hospital; quarantine hospital

**lazarillo** /laθa'riʎo; lasa'riyo/ *m,* boy who guides a blind person

**lazarino** /laθa'rino; lasa'rino/ *a* leprous

**lázaro** /'laθaro; 'lasaro/ *m,* lazar, beggar

**lazo** /'laθo; 'laso/ *m,* bow; knot of ribbons; tie; ornamental tree; figure (in dancing); lasso; rope, bond; lace (of a shoe); *Fig.* trap, snare; bond, obligation; slipknot. **l. corredizo,** running knot. *Fig. Inf.* **armar l.,** to set a trap. *Inf.* **caer en el l.,** to fall into the trap, be deceived

**le** /le/ *pers pron dat m,* or *f, 3rd pers sing* to him, to her, to it, to you (e.g. *María le dio el perro,* Mary gave him (her, you) the dog). Clarity may require the addition of **a él, a ella, a usted** (e.g. *Le dio el perro a ella,* etc.) —*pers pron acc m, 3rd pers sing* him (e.g. *Le mandé a casa,* I sent him home)

**leal** /le'al/ *a* loyal; faithful (animals)

**lealtad** /leal'tað/ *f,* loyalty; faithfulness; sincerity, truth

**lebrel** /le'βrel/ *m,* greyhound

**lección** /lek'θion; lek'sion/ *f,* reading; lesson; oral test; warning, example. **l. práctica,** object lesson. **dar l.,** to give a lesson. **tomar la l.,** to hear a lesson

**leccionista** /lekθio'nista; leksio'nista/ *mf* private teacher, coach, tutor

**lechas** /'letʃas/ *f pl,* soft roe; milt

**leche** /'letʃe/ *f,* milk; milky fluid of some plants and seeds. *Inf.* **estar con la l. en los labios,** to be young and inexperienced

**lechera** /le'tʃera/ *f,* milkmaid; milk can or jug

**lechería** /letʃe'ria/ *f,* dairy; dairy shop

**lechero** /le'tʃero/ **(-ra)** *a* dairy, milk; milky; milch, milk-giving —*n* milk seller. **industria lechera,** dairy farming

**lecho** /'letʃo/ *m,* bed; couch; animal's bed, litter; riverbed; bottom of the sea; layer; *Geol.* stratum

**lechón** /le'tʃon/ *m,* suckling pig; hog; *Inf.* slovenly man

**lechoso** /le'tʃoso/ *a* milky

**lechuga** /le'tʃuga/ *f,* lettuce; frill, flounce. *Inf.* **como una l.,** as fresh as a daisy

**lechuguero** /letʃu'gero/ **(-ra)** *n* lettuce seller

**lechuguilla** /letʃu'giʎa; letʃu'giya/ *f,* ruff; ruche

**lechuguina** /letʃu'gina/ *f, Inf.* affected, overdressed young woman

**lechuguino** /letʃu'gino/ *m,* lettuce plant; *Inf.* young blood, gallant; *Inf.* foppish young man

**lechuza** /le'tʃuθa; le'tʃusa/ *f,* barn owl

**lector** /lek'tor/ **(-ra)** *n* reader; lecturer

**lectura** /lek'tura/ *f,* reading; lecture; culture, knowledge

**ledo** /'leðo/ *a* happy, content

**leer** /le'er/ *vt irr* to read; explain, interpret; teach; take part in an oral test. See **creer**

**lega** /'lega/ *f, Eccl.* lay sister

**legación** /lega'θion; lega'sion/ *f, Eccl.* legateship; legation

**legado** /le'gaðo/ *m,* legacy; legate

**legajo** /le'gaho/ *m,* bundle, docket; file

**legal** /le'gal/ *a* legal; legitimate; upright, trustworthy

**legalidad** /legali'ðað/ *f,* legality

**legalización** /legaliθa'θion; legalisa'sion/ *f,* legalization

**legalizar** /legali'θar; legali'sar/ *vt* to legalize

**legamente** /lega'mente/ *adv* ignorantly, stupidly

**légamo** /'legamo/ *m,* mud, slime

**legamoso** /lega'moso/ *a* slimy

**legaña** /le'gaɲa/ *f,* bleariness (of the eyes)

**legañoso** /lega'ɲoso/ *a* bleary-eyed

**legar** /le'gar/ *vt* to bequeath; send as a legate

**legatario** /lega'tario/ **(-ia)** *n* legatee, one to whom a legacy is bequeathed

**legendario** /lehen'dario/ *a* legendary

**legibilidad** /lehiβili'ðað/ *f*, legibility

**legible** /le'hiβle/ *a* legible

**legión** /le'hion/ *f*, legion

**legionario** /lehio'nario/ *a* and *m*, legionary

**legislación** /lehisla'θion; lehisla'sion/ *f*, legislation

**legislador** /lehisla'ðor/ **(-ra)** *a* legislative —*n* legislator

**legislar** /lehis'lar/ *vi* to legislate

**legislativo** /lehisla'tiβo/ *a* legislative

**legislatura** /lehisla'tura/ *f*, legislature

**legista** /le'hista/ *mf* jurist; student of law

**legítima** /le'hitima/ *f*, portion of a married man's estate that cannot be willed away from his wife and children

**legitimación** /lehitima'θion; lehitima'sion/ *f*, legitimation

**legitimar** /lehiti'mar/ *vt* to legitimize

**legitimidad** /lehitimi'ðað/ *f*, legitimacy

**legítimo** /le'hitimo/ *a* legitimate; real, true

**lego** /'lego/ *a* lay, secular. *m*, layman

**legua** /'legua/ *f*, league (approximately 5.573 meters). **a la l., de cien leguas, desde media l.,** from afar

**legumbre** /le'gumbre/ *f*, pulse; vegetable

**leguminoso** /legumi'noso/ *a* leguminous

**leído** /le'iðo/ *a* well-read

**leila** /'leila/ *f*, nocturnal Moorish merrymaking or dance

**lejanía** /leha'nia/ *f*, distance

**lejano** /le'hano/ *a* distant, remote, far off

**lejía** /le'hia/ *f*, lye; bleaching solution; *Inf.* dressing-down, scolding

**lejos** /'lehos/ *adv* far off, far, distant. *m*, perspective, view from afar; *Art.* background. **a lo l.,** far off, in the distance. **de** *or* **desde l.,** from afar, from a distance

**lelo** /'lelo/ *a* stupid; fatuous, inane

**lema** /'lema/ *m*, chapter heading; argument, summary; motto; theme, subject

**lémur** /'lemur/ *m*, lemur

**lencería** /lenθe'ria; lense'ria/ *f*, linen goods; linen merchant's shop; linen closet

**lencero** /len'θero; len'sero/ *m*, linen merchant

**lene** /'lene/ *a* smooth, soft; kind, sweet, gentle; lightweight

**lengua** /'lengua/ *f*, *Anat.* tongue; mother tongue, language; clapper of a bell; information. *mf* spokes. **l. de escorpión** *or* **mala l.,** scandalmonger, backbiter. **l. de fuego,** *Eccl.* tongue of fire, flame. **l. del agua,** waterline, tidemark. **l. de oc,** langue d'oc. **l. de oil,** langue d'oil. **l. de tierra,** neck of land, promontory. **l. viva,** modern language. *Inf.* **andar en lenguas,** to be on every lip, to be famous. *Inf.* **hacerse lenguas de,** to praise to the skies. *Inf.* **irse (a uno) la l.,** to be indiscreet, talk too much. **poner l.** *or* **lenguas en,** to gossip about. *Inf.* **tener mucha l.,** to be very talkative. **tomar l.** *or* **lenguas,** to find out about, inform oneself on

**lenguado** /len'guaðo/ *m*, *Ichth.* sole

**lenguaje** /len'guahe/ *m*, language; style; speech, idiom. **l. vulgar,** common speech

**lengüeta** /len'gueta/ *f*, *dim* little tongue; *Mus.* tongue (of wind instruments); barb (of an arrow); needle (of a balance)

**lenidad** /leni'ðað/ *f*, lenience, indulgence, mercy

**Leningrado** /lenin'graðo/ Leningrad

**lenitivo** /leni'tiβo/ *a* lenitive; soothing. *m*, *Med.* lenitive; *Fig.* balm (of sorrow, etc.)

**lente** /'lente/ *m*, lens; *pl* eyeglasses. **l. de aumento,** magnifying glass

**lenteja** /len'teha/ *f*, lentil; lentil plant

**lentejuela** /lente'huela/ *f*, sequin

**lentitud** /lenti'tuð/ *f*, lentitude; slowness, deliberation

**lento** /'lento/ *a* slow, deliberate; sluggish, heavy; *Med.* glutinous, adhesive

**leña** /'leɲa/ *f*, firewood; *Inf.* beating, birching. *Fig.*

**echar l. al fuego,** to add fuel to the flame. *Fig.* **llevar l. al monte,** to carry coals to Newcastle

**leñador** /leɲa'ðor/ **(-ra)** *n* woodcutter; firewood dealer

**leñera** /le'ɲera/ *f*, woodpile; woodshed

**leño** /'leɲo/ *m*, wooden log; wood, timber; *Poet.* ship; *Inf.* blockhead

**leñoso** /le'ɲoso/ *a* woody, ligneous

**león** /le'on/ *m*, lion. *Astron.* Leo; valiant man. **l. marino,** sea lion

**leona** /le'ona/ *f*, lioness

**leonera** /leo'nera/ *f*, lion cage; lion's den; *Inf.* gambling den; *Inf.* lumber room

**leonero** /leo'nero/ **(-ra)** *n* lionkeeper; *Inf.* keeper of a gambling house

**leonés** /leo'nes/ **(-esa)** *a* and *n* Leonese

**leonino** /leo'nino/ *a* leonine

**leopardo** /leo'parðo/ *m*, leopard

**lepra** /'lepra/ *f*, leprosy

**leproso** /le'proso/ *a* leprous

**lerdo** /'lerðo/ *a* slow, lumbering (gen. horses); stupid, slow-witted, dull

**les** /les/ *pers pron dat 3rd pers pl mf*, to them (e.g. *Les dimos las flores,* We gave them flowers. *Les hablé del asunto,* I spoke to them about the matter)

**lesbio** /'lesβio/ **(-ia)** *a* and *n* lesbian

**lesión** /le'sion/ *f*, lesion, wound; *Fig.* injury

**lesionar** /lesio'nar/ *vt* to wound; *Fig.* injure

**lesna** /'lesna/ *f*, awl

**leso** /'leso/ *a* wounded, hurt; offensive, injurious; *Fig.* unbalanced, perturbed (of the mind). **crimen de lesa majestad,** crime of lèse-majesté

**letal** /le'tal/ *a* lethal; deadly

**letanía** /leta'nia/ *f*, *Eccl.* litany

**letargia** /le'tarhia/ *f*, *Med.* lethargy

**letárgico** /le'tarhiko/ *a* lethargic

**letargo** /le'targo/ *m*, lethargy; indifference, apathy

**Letonia** /le'tonia/ Latvia

**letra** /'letra/ *f*, letter (of alphabet); *Print.* type; penmanship, hand; *Fig.* letter, literal meaning; words (of a song); inscription; *Com.* bill, draft; cunning, shrewdness; *pl* learning, knowledge. **l. abierta,** *Com.* open credit. **l. de cambio,** *Com.* bill of exchange. **l. gótica,** Gothic characters. **l. itálica,** italics. **l. mayúscula,** capital letter. **l. paladial,** palatal. **facultad de letras,** faculty of arts. **La l. con sangre entra,** Learning is acquired with pain. **primeras letras,** early education, first letters

**letrado** /le'traðo/ *a* learned, educated; *Inf.* presumptuous; pedantic. *m*, lawyer

**letrero** /le'trero/ *m*, label; inscription; poster, bill; sign, indicator. **l. luminoso,** illuminated sign

**letrilla** /le'triʎa; le'triya/ *f*, short poem, often set to music

**letrina** /le'trina/ *f*, latrine

**leucocito** /leuko'θito; leuko'sito/ *m*, leucocyte

**leva** /'leβa/ *f*, *Naut.* weighing anchor; *Mil.* levy, forced enrollment; tappet; *Mech.* lever; *Mech.* cam; *Inf.* **irse a l. y a monte,** to flee, beat it, quit

**levadizo** /leβa'ðiθo; leβa'ðiso/ *a* able to be raised or lowered (bridges). **puente l.,** drawbridge

**levadura** /leβa'ðura/ *f*, leaven, yeast; rising (of bread)

**levantada** /leβan'taða/ *f*, act of rising from bed

**levantamiento** /leβanta'miento/ *m*, raising, lifting; rebellion, revolt; ennoblement, elevation; settlement of accounts

**levantar** /leβan'tar/ *vt* to raise, lift; pick up; build, construct; cancel, remove; encourage, rouse; recruit, enlist; cut (cards); leave, abandon; survey; disturb (game); produce, raise (a swelling); found, institute; increase (prices); raise (the voice); *Fig.* ennoble, elevate; cause, occasion; libel, accuse falsely; —*vr* rise; get up; stand up; stand out, be prominent; rebel; leave one's bed after an illness. **l. bandera,** to rebel. **l. el campo,** to break camp. **levantarse del izquierdo,** *Inf.* to get out of bed on the wrong side

**levante** /le'βante/ *m*, east; Levant; east wind

**levantino** /leβan'tino/ **(-na)** *a* and *n* Levantine

**levar** /le'βar/ *vt* *Naut.* to weigh anchor; —*vr* set sail

**leve** /'leβe/ *a* light (in weight); unimportant, trifling

**levedad** /leβe'ðað/ *f*, lightness (in weight); unimportance, levity, flippancy

**leviatán** /leβia'tan/ *m*, leviathan

**levita** /le'βita/ *m*, Levite; deacon. *f*, frock coat

**levitación** /leβita'θion; leβita'sion/ *f*, levitation

**levítico** /le'βitiko/ *a* Levitical. *m*, Leviticus

**levitón** /leβi'ton/ *m*, frock coat

**léxico** /'leksiko/ *m*, lexicon

**lexicografía** /leksikogra'fia/ *f*, lexicography

**lexicógrafo** /leksi'kografo/ *m*, lexicographer

**lexicólogo** /leksi'kologo/ *m*, lexicologist

**ley** /lei/ *f*, law; precept; regulation, rule; doctrine; loyalty, faithfulness; affection, love; legal standard (weights, measures, quality); ratio of gold or silver in coins, jewelry; statute, ordinance; *pl* the Law. **l. de préstamo y arriendo,** Lend-Lease Act. **ley suntuaria,** sumptuary law. *Inf.* **a la l.,** with care and decorum. **a l. de caballero,** on the word of a gentleman. **de buena l.,** *a* excellent; —*adv* genuinely; in good faith. **de mala l.,** *a* disreputable, base; —*adv* in bad faith

**leyenda** /le'ienda/ *f*, legend; inscription; story, tale

**leyente** /le'iente/ *a* reading. *mf* reader

**lezna** /'leθna; 'lesna/ *f*, awl

**lía** /'lia/ *f*, plaited esparto rope; *pl* lees, dregs

**liar** /li'ar/ *vt* to fasten or tie up; wrap up, parcel; roll (a cigarette). *Inf.* entangle, embroil; —*vr* take a lover, enter on a liaison. *Inf.* **liarlas,** to quit, sneak off; *Inf.* kick the bucket, die

**libación** /liβa'θion; liβa'sion/ *f*, libation

**Líbano, el** /'liβano, el/ Lebanon

**libar** /li'βar/ *vt* to suck; perform a libation; sip, taste; sacrifice

**libelista** /liβe'lista/ *mf* libeler

**libelo** /li'βelo/ *m*, libel; *Law.* petition

**libélula** /li'βelula/ *f*, dragonfly

**liberación** /liβera'θion; liβera'sion/ *f*, liberation, freeing; receipt, quittance; *Law.* reconveyance (of mortgages)

**liberador** /liβera'ðor/ **(-ra)** *a* liberating, freeing —*n* liberator

**liberal** /liβe'ral/ *a* generous, openhanded; liberal, tolerant; learned (of professions) —*a* and *mf Polit.* liberal

**liberalidad** /liβerali'ðað/ *f*, generosity, magnanimity

**liberalismo** /liβera'lismo/ *m*, liberalism

**liberalizar** /liβerali'θar; liβerali'sar/ *vt* to liberalize, make liberal

**liberar** /liβe'rar/ *vt* to liberate

**libérrimo** /li'βerrimo/ *a superl* extremely free, most free

**libertad** /liβer'tað/ *f*, liberty, freedom; independence; privilege, right (gen. *pl*); exemption; licentiousness; forwardness, familiarity; naturalness, ease of manner; facility, capacity; immunity. **l. caucional,** freedom on bail, release on bail. **l. de cultos,** freedom of worship; religious toleration. **l. vigilada,** *Law.* probation. **poner en l.,** to set at liberty; (*with de*) *Fig.* free from

**libertador** /liβerta'ðor/ **(-ra)** *a* liberating, freeing —*n* liberator, deliverer

**libertar** /liβer'tar/ *vt* to liberate, free; save, deliver; exempt

**libertario** /liβer'tario/ **(-ia)** *a* anarchistic —*n* anarchist

**libertinaje** /liβerti'nahe/ *m*, libertinage, licentiousness

**libertino** /liβer'tino/ **(-na)** *a* debauched, licentious. *m*, libertine —*n* child of a freed slave

**liberto** /li'βerto/ **(-ta)** *n* freed slave, freedman

**Libia** /'liβia/ Libya

**libídine** /li'βiðine/ *f*, lust

**libidinoso** /liβiði'noso/ *a* libidinous, lustful

**libio** /'liβio/ **(-ia)** *a* and *n* Libyan

**libra** /'liβra/ *f*, pound (measure, coinage); *Astron.* Libra. **l. esterlina,** pound sterling. **l. medicinal,** pound troy

**libración** /liβra'θion; liβra'sion/ *f*, oscillation; *Astron.* libration

**librador** /liβra'ðor/ **(-ra)** *a* freeing, liberating —*n* deliverer, liberator. *m*, *Com.* drawer (of bill of exchange, etc.)

**libramiento** /liβra'miento/ *m*, liberation, deliverance; *Com.* delivery; order of payment

**libranza** /li'βranθa; li'βransa/ *f*, *Com.* draft

**librar** /li'βrar/ *vt* to liberate, free; protect (from misfortune); *Com.* draw (a draft); *Com.* deliver; place confidence in; issue, enact; —*vi* bring forth children; —*vr* (*with de*) escape from; get rid of

**libre** /'liβre/ *a* free; at liberty, disengaged; unhampered, untrammeled; independent; bold, brazen; dissolute, vicious; exempt; vacant, unoccupied; unmarried; clear, free; mutinous, rebellious; isolated, remote; innocent; unharmed. **l. cambio,** free trade

**librea** /li'βrea/ *f*, livery

**librecambio** /liβre'kambio/ *m*, free trade

**librecambista** /liβrekam'βista/ *a* free trade. *mf* free trader

**librepensador** /liβrepensa'ðor/ **(-ra)** *a* freethinking —*n* freethinker

**librepensamiento** /liβrepensa'miento/ *m*, free thought

**librería** /liβre'ria/ *f*, bookshop; book trade, bookselling; bookcase

**librero** /li'βrero/ *m*, bookseller. **l. anticuario,** antiquarian bookseller; rare-book dealer

**libreta** /li'βreta/ *f*, *Cul.* 1-lb. loaf; notebook; passbook, bankbook

**libretista** /liβre'tista/ *mf* librettist

**libreto** /li'βreto/ *m*, libretto

**librillo** /li'βriʎo; li'βriyo/ *m*, *dim* small book; book of cigarette papers; tub, pail; *Zool.* omasum

**libro** /'liβro/ *m*, book; *Mus.* libretto; *Zool.* omasum. **l. copiador,** *Com.* letter book. **l. de actas,** minute book. **l. de caja,** *Com.* cash book. **l. de cheques,** checkbook. **l. de facturas,** *Com.* invoice book. **l. de reclamaciones,** complaint book. **l. de texto,** textbook. **l. diario,** *Com.* daybook. **l. mayor,** ledger. **l. talonario,** receipt book. *Fig. Inf.* **hacer l. nuevo,** to turn over a new leaf; introduce innovations

**licencia** /li'θenθia; li'sensia/ *f*, permission, license; licentiousness; boldness, insolence; *Educ.* bachelor's degree, licentiate. **l. absoluta,** *Mil.* discharge

**licenciado** /liθen'θiaðo; lisen'siaðo/ **(-da)** *a* pedantic; free, exempt; licensed —*n Educ.* bachelor; licentiate. *m*, discharged soldier

**licenciar** /liθen'θiar; lisen'siar/ *vt* to allow, permit; license; dismiss, discharge; confer degree of bachelor or licentiate; *Mil.* discharge; —*vr* become licentious; receive bachelor's degree or licentiate

**licenciatura** /liθenθia'tura; lisensia'tura/ *f*, degree of licentiate or bachelor; graduation as such; licentiate course of study

**licencioso** /liθen'θioso; lisen'sioso/ *a* licentious, dissolute

**liceo** /li'θeo; li'seo/ *m*, lyceum

**licitación** /liθita'θion; lisita'sion/ *f*, bidding (at auction)

**licitador** /liθita'ðor; lisita'ðor/ *m*, bidder (at auction)

**licitar** /liθi'tar; lisi'tar/ *vt* to bid for (at auction)

**lícito** /'liθito; 'lisito/ *a* permissible, lawful

**licor** /li'kor/ *m*, liquor, alcoholic drink; liquid

**licorera** /liko'rera/ *f*, liqueur set; decanter

**licoroso** /liko'roso/ *a* aromatic, generous (of wines)

**licuadora** /likua'ðora/ *f*, blender

**licuar** /li'kuar/ *vt* to liquefy

**licuefacción** /likuefak'θion; likuefak'sion/ *f*, liquefaction

**lid** /lið/ *f*, combat, fight; dispute, controversy. **en buena l.,** in fair fight; by fair means

**líder** /'liðer/ *m*, leader; chief

**lidia** /'liðia/ *f*, fighting; bullfight

**lidiador** /liðia'ðor/ **(-ra)** *n* combatant, fighter

**lidiar** /li'ðiar/ *vi* to fight; *Fig.* struggle; (*with contra or con*) oppose, fight against; —*vt* fight (a bull). **¡Cuánto tienen que l. con...!** *Fig.* What a struggle they have with...!

**liebre** /'lieβre/ *f*, hare

**liendre** /'liendre/ *f*, nit

**lienza** /'lienθa; liensa/ *f*, narrow strip (of cloth)

**lienzo** /'lienθo; 'lienso/ *m*, linen; cotton; cambric; hemp cloth; *Art.* canvas

**liga** /'liga/ *f*, garter; bandage; birdlime; mixture, blend; *Metall.* alloy; alliance, coalition; league (football, etc.)

**ligación** /liga'θion; liga'sion/ *f*, tying; binding; union

**ligado** /li'gaðo/ *m, Mus.* legato; *Mus.* tie

**ligadura** /liga'ðura/ *f,* bond, tie; binding, fastening; *Fig.* shackle, link; (*Surg. Mus.*) ligature; *Naut.* lashing

**ligamento** /liga'mento/ *m,* tie, bond; mixture; *Anat.* ligament

**ligar** /li'gar/ *vt* to tie, bind; *Metall.* alloy; join, connect; render impotent by sorcery; *Mus.* slur (notes); —*vr* ally, join together; *Fig.* bind oneself. **l. cabos,** to put two and two together

**ligazón** /liga'θon; liga'son/ *f,* fastening; union; bond

**ligereza** /lihe'reθa; lihe'resa/ *f,* lightness (of weight); swiftness, nimbleness; fickleness; tactless remark, indiscretion

**ligero** /li'hero/ *a* light (in weight); swift, nimble; light (sleep); unimportant, insignificant; easily digested (food); thin (fabrics, etc.); fickle, changeable. **l. de cascos,** frivolous, gay. **a la ligera,** lightly; quickly; without fuss. **de l.,** impetuously, thoughtlessly; easily, with ease

**lignito** /lig'nito/ *m,* lignite

**lija** /'liha/ *f,* dogfish; sandpaper

**lijar** /li'har/ *vt* to sandpaper

**lila** /'lila/ *f,* lilac bush and flower; lilac color —*a Inf.* foolish, vain

**liliputiense** /lilipu'tiense/ *a* and *mf* Lilliputian

**lima** /'lima/ *f,* sweet lime, citron fruit; lime tree; file (tool); filing, polishing

**limadura** /lima'ðura/ *f,* filing; polishing; *pl* filings

**limar** /li'mar/ *vt* to file, smooth with a file; *Fig.* touch up, polish

**limazo** /li'maθo; li'maso/ *m,* slime, viscosity (especially of snails, etc.)

**limbo** /'limbo/ *m,* limbo; edge, hem; (*Astron. Bot.*) limb; limb (of a quadrant, etc.). *Inf.* **estar en el l.,** to be bewildered or abstracted

**limen** /'limen/ *m, Poet.* threshold; *Psychol.* limen

**limeño** /li'meɲo/ **(-ña)** *a* and *n* native of or belonging to Lima (Peru)

**limero** /li'mero/ **(-ra)** *n* seller of sweet limes. *m,* sweet lime tree (citron)

**limitación** /limita'θion; limita'sion/ *f,* limitation; limit, extent, bound; district, area

**limitado** /limi'taðo/ *a* dull-witted, limited

**limitáneo** /limi'taneo/ *a* bordering

**limitar** /limi'tar/ *vt* to limit; curb, restrict; bound

**límite** /'limite/ *m,* limit, extent; boundary, border; end, confine

**limítrofe** /li'mitrofe/ *a* bordering, contiguous

**limo** /'limo/ *m,* mud, mire, slime

**limón** /li'mon/ *m,* lemon; lemon tree

**limonada** /limo'naða/ *f,* lemonade. **l. seca,** lemonade powder

**limonar** /limo'nar/ *m,* lemon grove

**limonero** /limo'nero/ **(-ra)** *n* lemon seller. *m,* lemon tree

**limosna** /li'mosna/ *f,* alms

**limosnear** /limosne'ar/ *vi* to beg, ask alms

**limosnero** /limos'nero/ *a* charitable, generous. *m,* almoner

**limoso** /li'moso/ *a* slimy, muddy

**limpiabarros** /limpia'βarros/ *m,* shoe scraper

**limpiabotas** /limpia'βotas/ *m,* bootblack (person)

**limpiachimeneas** /limpiat͡ʃime'neas/ *m,* chimneysweep

**limpiador** /limpia'ðor/ **(-ra)** *a* cleaning —*n* cleaner

**limpiadura** /limpia'ðura/ *f,* cleaning; *pl* rubbish

**limpiamente** /limpia'mente/ *adv* cleanly; dexterously, neatly; sincerely, candidly; generously, charitably

**limpiametales** /limpiame'tales/ *m,* metal polish

**limpiaparabrisas** /limpiapara'βrisas/ *m,* windshield wiper

**limpiapipas** /limpia'pipas/ *m,* pipe cleaner

**limpiar** /lim'piar/ *vt* to clean; *Fig.* cleanse, clear; empty, free (from); *Agr.* thin out; *Inf.* steal, pinch; *Inf.* win (gambling); —*vr* clean oneself

**limpiauñas** /limpia'uɲas/ *m,* orange stick (for fingernails)

**limpidez** /limpi'ðeθ; limpi'ðes/ *f, Poet.* limpidity

**límpido** /'limpiðo/ *a Poet.* limpid

**limpieza** /lim'pieθa; lim'piesa/ *f,* cleanliness; cleaning; chastity; purity; altruism; uprightness, integrity; neatness, tidiness; dexterity, skill, precision; fair play

**limpio** /'limpio/ *a* clean; pure, unalloyed, unmixed; neat, tidy; pure-blooded; unharmed, free. **en l.,** in substance; as a fair copy; clearly; *Com.* net

**linaje** /li'nahe/ *m,* lineage, family; offspring; kind; sort, quality

**linajudo** /lina'huðo/ **(-da)** *a* highborn —*n* noble, aristocrat; one who alleges his noble descent

**linar** /li'nar/ *m,* field of flax

**linaza** /li'naθa; li'nasa/ *f,* linseed

**lince** /'linθe; 'linse/ *m,* lynx; fox, crafty person

**linchamiento** /lint͡ʃa'miento/ *m,* lynching

**linchar** /lin't͡ʃar/ *vt* to lynch

**lindar** /lin'dar/ *vi* to run together, be contiguous

**linde** /'linde/ *mf* limit, extent; boundary

**lindero** /lin'dero/ *a* bordering, contiguous. *m,* boundary. *Inf.* **con linderos y arrabales,** with many digressions

**lindeza** /lin'deθa; lin'desa/ *f,* beauty, loveliness; witticism; *pl* (*Inf. ironical*) insults

**lindo** /'lindo/ *a* lovely, beautiful; perfect, exquisite. *m, Inf.* fop (gen. **lindo don Diego**)

**línea** /'linea/ *f,* line; kind, class; ancestry, lineage; limit, extent; *Mil.* file; equator. **l. aérea,** airline. *Naut.* **l. de flotación,** waterline. **l. de toque,** touch-line (in soccer). **l. recta,** direct line (of descent)

**lineal** /line'al/ *a* lineal

**lineamento** /linea'mento/ *m,* lineament

**linear** /line'ar/ *a* linear —*vt* to line, mark with lines; *Art.* sketch

**linfa** /'linfa/ *f, Med.* lymph; vaccine; *Poet.* water

**linfático** /lin'fatiko/ *a* lymphatic

**lingote** /liŋ'gote/ *m,* ingot; bar (of iron). **l. de fundición,** pig iron

**lingüista** /liŋ'guista/ *mf* linguist

**lingüística** /liŋ'guistika/ *f,* linguistics

**lingüístico** /liŋ'guistiko/ *a* linguistic

**linimento** /lini'mento/ *m,* liniment

**lino** /'lino/ *m, Bot.* flax; linen; *Poet.* ship's sail, canvas

**linóleo** /li'noleo/ *m,* linoleum

**linotipia** /lino'tipia/ *f,* linotype

**linterna** /lin'terna/ *f,* lantern; lighthouse; lamp. **l. sorda,** dark lantern

**lío** /'lio/ *m,* bundle; *Inf.* muddle, imbroglio; *Inf.* liaison, amour. *Inf.* **armar un l.,** to make a muddle, cause trouble. *Inf.* **hacerse un l.,** to get in a fix; get in a muddle

**liquen** /'liken/ *m,* lichen

**liquidable** /liki'ðaβle/ *a* liquefiable

**liquidación** /likiða'θion; likiða'sion/ *f,* liquefaction; *Com.* clearance, sale; *Com.* settlement

**liquidar** /liki'ðar/ *vt* to liquefy; *Com.* settle; *Com.* liquidate; finish; —*vr* liquefy

**liquidez** /liki'ðeθ; liki'ðes/ *f,* liquidity

**líquido** /'likiðo/ *a* liquid; *Com.* net. *m,* liquid; *Com.* net profit

**lira** /'lira/ *f, Mus.* lyre; *Astron.* Lyra; lira (coin)

**lírica** /'lirika/ *f,* lyrical verse, lyric

**lírico** /'liriko/ *a* lyrical

**lirio** /'lirio/ *m,* lily. **l. cárdeno,** yellow flag (iris). **l. de los valles,** lily of the valley

**lirismo** /li'rismo/ *m,* lyricism

**lirón** /li'ron/ *m, Zool.* dormouse; *Inf.* sleepyhead

**Lisboa** /lis'βoa/ Lisbon

**lisbonense** /lisβo'nense/ *a* and *mf* **lisbonés (-esa)** *a* and *n* Lisboan

**lisiado** /li'siaðo/ *a* lame, crippled

**lisiar** /li'siar/ *vt* to cripple, lame; —*vr* be disabled; be lame

**liso** /'liso/ *a* smooth; sleek; unadorned, plain; unicolored

**lisonja** /li'sonha/ *f,* flattery, adulation

**lisonjear** /lisonhe'ar/ *vt* to flatter; fawn upon; *Fig.* delight (the ear). **lisonjearse de...,** to flatter oneself on...

**lisonjero** /lison'hero/ **(-ra)** *a* flattering; sweet, pleasant (sounds) —*n* flatterer

**lista** /'lista/ *f,* strip of cloth; streak; rib; stripe; catalog, list. **l. de correos,** general delivery, poste restante. **l. de platos,** bill of fare. **pasar l.,** to call the roll; check the list

**listado** /lis'taðo/ *a* streaked; striped; ribbed

**listo** /'listo/ *a* clever; expeditious, diligent; ready, prepared

**listón** /lis'ton/ *m,* ribbon; strip (of wood)

**lisura** /li'sura/ *f,* smoothness; sleekness; flatness; sincerity

**litera** /li'tera/ *f,* litter; *Naut.* berth

**literal** /lite'ral/ *a* literal

**literario** /lite'rario/ *a* literary

**literatear** /literate'ar/ *vi* to write on literary subjects

**literato** /lite'rato/ **(-ta)** *a* literary —*n* writer, littérateur

**literatura** /litera'tura/ *f,* literature

**litigación** /litiga'θion; litiga'sion/ *f,* litigation

**litigante** /liti'gante/ *mf* litigant

**litigar** /liti'gar/ *vt* to litigate; —*vi* dispute, argue

**litigio** /li'tihio/ *m,* lawsuit; dispute, argument

**litigioso** /liti'hioso/ *a* litigious; quarrelsome, disputatious

**litisexpensas** /litiseks'pensas/ *f pl, Law.* costs of a suit; legal expenses

**litografía** /litogra'fia/ *f,* lithography

**litografiar** /litogra'fiar/ *vt* to lithograph

**litográfico** /lito'grafiko/ *a* lithographic

**litoral** /lito'ral/ *a* and *m,* littoral

**litro** /'litro/ *m,* liter

**Lituania** /li'tuania/ Lithuania

**lituano** /li'tuano/ **(-na)** *a* and *n* Lithuanian. *m,* Lithuanian (language)

**liturgia** /li'turhia/ *f,* liturgy

**litúrgico** /li'turhiko/ *a* liturgical

**liviandad** /liβian'dað/ *f,* lightness (of weight); fickleness; unimportance; frivolity; lewdness; act of folly, indiscretion

**liviano** /li'βiano/ *a* light weight; fickle; unimportant, trifling, frivolous; lascivious

**lividez** /liβi'ðeθ; liβi'ðes/ *f,* lividness

**lívido** /'liβiðo/ *a* livid

**liza** /'liθa; 'lisa/ *f,* list (at a tournament); arena

**llaga** /'ʎaga; 'yaga/ *f,* ulcer; sore; grief, affliction; *Fig.* thorn in the flesh

**llagar** /ʎa'gar; ya'gar/ *vt* to ulcerate; make or produce sores; *Fig.* wound; —*vr* be covered with sores

**llama** /'ʎama; 'yama/ *f,* flame; ardor, vehemence; marsh; *Zool.* llama

**llamada** /ʎa'maða; ya'maða/ *f,* call; *Mil.* call-to-arms, call. **l. molestosa,** annoyance call, nuisance call

**llamado** /ʎa'maðo; ya'maðo/ *a* called; so-called

**llamador** /ʎama'ðor; yama'ðor/ **(-ra)** *n* caller. *m,* door knocker; doorbell

**llamamiento** /ʎama'miento; yama'miento/ *m,* calling; call; divine summons, inspiration; invocation, appeal; summons, convocation

**llamar** /ʎa'mar; ya'mar/ *vt* to call; invoke, call upon; summon, convoke; name; attract; —*vi* knock (at a door); ring (a bell); —*vr* be named, be called; *Naut.* veer (wind). **Se llama Pedro,** His name is Peter

**llamarada** /ʎama'raða; yama'raða/ *f,* flame, flash; blaze, flare (of anger, etc.)

**llamativo** /ʎama'tiβo; yama'tiβo/ *a* striking, showy; provocative

**llamear** /ʎame'ar; yame'ar/ *vi* to throw out flames, blaze

**llana** /'ʎana; 'yana/ *f,* mason's trowel; plain; surface of a page

**llanada** /ʎa'naða; ya'naða/ *f,* plain

**llanamente** /ʎana'mente; yana'mente/ *adv* frankly, plainly; naturally, simply; candidly, sincerely

**llanero** /ʎa'nero; ya'nero/ **(-ra)** *n* plain dweller

**llaneza** /ʎa'neθa; ya'nesa/ *f,* naturalness; candor; familiarity; simplicity (of style)

**llano** /'ʎano; 'yano/ *a* flat, level; smooth, even; shallow (of receptacles); unaffected, homely, natural; plain (of dresses); manifest, evident; easy; straightforward, candid; informal; simple (of style). *m,* plain; level stretch of ground

**llanta** /'ʎanta; 'yanta/ *f, Auto.* tire; rim, felloe. **l. de rueda,** wheel, rim

**llanto** /'ʎanto; 'yanto/ *m,* weeping, flood of tears

**llanura** /ʎa'nura; ya'nura/ *f,* smoothness, evenness; levelness; plain

**llar** /ʎar; yar/ *m,* hearth

**llave** /'ʎaβe; 'yaβe/ **(de)** *f,* key (to); spigot (of), faucet (of), tap (of); spanner, wrench; *Elec.* switch; clock winder; *Mus.* key, clef; *Archit.* keystone; *Print.* brace; *Mech.* wrench; lock (of a gun); tuning key; piston (of musical instruments); lock (in wrestling); *Fig.* key (of a problem or a study). **l. de transmisión,** sender (telegraphy). **l. inglesa,** monkey-wrench, spanner. **l. maestra,** master key, skeleton key. **echar la l.,** to lock. **torcer la l.,** to turn the key

**llavero** /ʎa'βero; ya'βero/ **(-ra)** *n* keeper of the keys. *m,* key ring. **l. de cárcel,** turnkey

**llavín** /ʎa'βin; ya'βin/ *m,* yale key, latchkey

**llegada** /ʎe'gaða; ye'gaða/ *f,* arrival, advent

**llegar** /ʎe'gar; ye'gar/ *vi* to arrive; last, endure; reach; achieve a purpose; be sufficient, suffice; amount (to), make; —*vt* bring near, draw near; gather; —*vr* come near, approach; adhere. **l. a ser,** to become. **l. a un punto muerto,** to reach a deadlock. **l. hasta...,** to stretch as far as...

**llena** /'ʎena; 'yena/ *f,* spate, overflow

**llenar** /ʎe'nar; ye'nar/ *vt* to fill; occupy (a post); satisfy, please; fulfill; satiate; pervade; fill up (a form); —*vi* be full (of the moon); —*vr Inf.* stuff, overeat; *Fig. Inf.* be fed-up

**lleno** /'ʎeno; 'yeno/ *a* full; replete; abundant; complete. *m,* full moon; *Theat.* full house; *Inf.* glut, abundance; perfection. **de l., de l. en l.,** entirely, completely

**llenura** /ʎe'nura; ye'nura/ *f,* abundance, plenty

**lleva, llevada** /'ʎeβa, ʎe'βaða; 'yeβa, ye'βaða/ *f,* carrying, bearing

**llevadero** /ʎeβa'ðero; yeβa'ðero/ *a* tolerable, bearable

**llevar** /ʎe'βar; ye'βar/ *vt* to carry, transport; charge (a price); yield, produce; carry off, take away; endure, bear; persuade; guide, take; direct; wear (clothes); carry (a handbag, etc.); introduce, present; gain, achieve; manage (a horse); pass, spend (of time); (*with past part*) have (e.g. *Llevo escrita la carta,* I have written the letter); *Math.* carry; (*with prep. a*) surpass, excel. **l. a cabo,** to accomplish. **l. a cuestas,** to carry on one's back; support. **l. la correspondencia,** to look after the correspondence. **l. la delantera,** to take the lead. **l. luto,** to be in mourning. **llevarse bien,** to get on well, agree

**llorar** /ʎo'rar; yo'rar/ *vi* to weep, cry; drip; water (eyes); —*vt* lament, mourn; bewail one's troubles

**lloriquear** /ʎorike'ar; yorike'ar/ *vi* to whine, snivel

**lloriqueo** /ʎori'keo; yori'keo/ *m,* whining, sniveling

**lloro** /'ʎoro; 'yoro/ *m,* weeping, crying; flood of tears

**llorón** /ʎo'ron; yo'ron/ *a* weeping; sniveling, whining. *m,* long plume. **niño llorón,** crybaby

**lloroso** /ʎo'roso; yo'roso/ *a* tearful; grievous, sad; sorrowful

**llovedizo** /ʎoβe'ðiθo; yoβe'ðiso/ *a* leaky; rainy

**llover** /ʎo'βer; yo'βer/ *vi impers irr* to rain; come in abundance (of troubles, etc.); —*vr* leak (roofs, etc.). **l. a cántaros,** to rain in torrents, rain cats and dogs. **l. sobre mojado,** to add insult to injury. **como llovido,** unexpectedly. See **mover**

**llovido** /ʎo'βiðo; yo'βiðo/ *m,* stowaway

**llovizna** /ʎo'βiθna; yo'βisna/ *f,* drizzle, fine rain

**lloviznar** /ʎoβiθ'nar; yoβis'nar/ *vi* to drizzle

**lluvia** /'ʎuβia; 'yuβia/ *f,* rain; rainwater; *Fig.* shower; rose (of watering can)

**lluvioso** /ʎu'βioso; yu'βioso/ *a* rainy, showery

**lo** /lo/ *def art. neut* the thing, part, fact, what, that which. Used before adjectives, past participles, sometimes before nouns and adverbs (e.g. *Lo barato es caro,* Cheap things are dear (in the long run).) **Lo mío es mío, pero lo tuyo es de ambos,** What's mine is mine, but what is yours belongs to both of us. **Juan siente mucho lo ocurrido,** John is very sorry for what has happened. **a lo lejos,** in the distance). **lo... que,** how (e.g. *No sabes lo bueno que es,* You don't know how good he is) —*pers pron acc m,* or *neut* him, it; that, it (e.g. *Lo harán mañana,* They will do it tomorrow). Means some, any, one, as substitute for noun already mentioned (e.g. *Carecemos de azúcar;*

**loa** 176

no lo hay, We are short of sugar; there isn't any). **Lo cortés no quita lo valiente,** One can be courteous and still insistent

**loa** /'loa/ f, praise, eulogy; *Theat.* prologue; short dramatic piece; *Obs.*; dramatic eulogy

**loable** /lo'aβle/ a praiseworthy

**loador** /loa'ðor/ **(-ra)** a eulogizing —n eulogist

**loar** /lo'ar/ vt to praise; commend

**lobero** /lo'βero/ a wolf; wolfish

**lobezno** /lo'βeθno; lo'βesno/ m, wolf cub

**lobo** /'loβo/ **(-ba)** n wolf. m, (*Bot. Anat.*) lobe; *Inf.* drinking fit. **l. marino,** *Zool.* seal. *Inf.* **pillar un l.,** to get drunk

**lóbrego** /'loβrego/ a murky, dark; dismal; mournful, lugubrious

**lobreguez** /loβre'geθ; loβre'ges/ f, obscurity, gloom, darkness

**lóbulo** /'loβulo/ m, lobe

**lobuno** /lo'βuno/ a wolf, wolfish

**locación** /loka'θion; loka'sion/ f, *Law.* lease; agreement, contract

**local** /lo'kal/ a local. m, premises; place, spot, scene

**localidad** /lokali'ðað/ f, location; locality; place, spot; seat (in theaters, etc.)

**localización** /lokaliθa'θion; lokalisa'sion/ f, localization, placing; place

**localizar** /lokali'θar; lokali'sar/ vt to localize

**locamente** /loka'mente/ adv insanely, madly; extraordinarily, extremely

**loción** /lo'θion; lo'sion/ f, lotion

**loco** /'loko/ **(-ca)** a insane, mad; rash, foolish, crazy; excessive, enormous; amazing; extraordinary; infatuated —n lunatic; rash person. *Fig. Inf.* **Es un l. de atar,** He's completely crazy!

**locomoción** /lokomo'θion; lokomo'sion/ f, locomotion

**locomotor** /lokomo'tor/ a locomotive

**locomotora** /lokomo'tora/ f, locomotive

**locomóvil** /loko'moβil/ a and f, locomotive

**locuacidad** /lokuaθi'ðað; lokuasi'ðað/ f, loquacity

**locuaz** /lo'kuaθ; lo'kuas/ a loquacious

**locución** /loku'θion; loku'sion/ f, style of speech; phrase, idiom; *Gram.* locution

**locuelo** /lo'kuelo/ **(-la)** n madcap

**locura** /lo'kura/ f, insanity, lunacy; madness, fury; folly, foolishness

**locutor** /loku'tor/ **(-ra)** n (radio) announcer; commentator

**locutorio** /loku'torio/ m, locutory; phone booth

**lodazal, lodazar** /loða'θal, loða'θar; loða'sal, loða'sar/ m, muddy place; quagmire

**lodo** /'loðo/ m, mud

**lodoso** /lo'ðoso/ a muddy

**logarítmico** /loga'ritmiko/ a logarithmic

**logaritmo** /loga'ritmo/ m, logarithm

**logia** /'lohia/ f, (Freemason's) lodge

**lógica** /'lohika/ f, logic. *Inf.* **l. parda,** common sense

**lógico** /'lohiko/ **(-ca)** a logical —n logician

**logística** /lo'histika/ f, logistics

**lograr** /lo'grar/ vt to achieve, attain, obtain; enjoy; (*with infin*) succeed in; —vr succeed in, achieve; reach perfection

**logrear** /logre'ar/ vi to borrow or lend at interest

**logrero** /lo'grero/ **(-ra)** n moneylender; monopolist; profiteer

**logro** /'logro/ m, achievement, attainment; profit, gain; usury, money-lending

**loma** /'loma/ f, knoll, hill

**lombarda** /lom'βarða/ f, red cabbage

**Lombardía** /lombar'ðia/ Lombardy

**lombardo** /lom'βarðo/ **(-da)** a of or from Lombardy —n native of Lombardy (Italy). m, mortgage bank

**lombriz** /lom'βriθ; lom'βris/ f, earthworm, common worm. **l. intestinal,** intestinal worm. **l. solitaria,** tapeworm

**lomo** /'lomo/ m, loin, back of a book; ridge between furrows; pl ribs; loins

**lona** /'lona/ f, canvas, sailcloth

**londinense** /londi'nense/ a London. mf Londoner

**Londres** /'londres/ London

**longanimidad** /lonɡanimi'ðað/ f, longanimity, fortitude

**longaniza** /lonɡa'niθa; lonɡa'nisa/ f, *Cul.* pork sausage

**longevidad** /lonheβi'ðað/ f, longevity

**longevo** /lon'heβo/ a long-lived

**longísimo** /lon'hisimo/ a superl luengo exceedingly long

**longitud** /lonhi'tuð/ f, length; longitude. **l. de onda,** *Radio.* wavelength

**lonja** /'lonha/ f, slice, rasher; *Com.* exchange; market; grocery store; woolen warehouse

**lonjista** /lon'hista/ mf provision merchant, grocer

**lontananza** /lonta'nanθa; lonta'nansa/ f, distance (also *Art.*). **en l.,** in the distance, far off

**loor** /lo'or/ m, praise

**loquear** /loke'ar/ vi to play the fool; romp

**lord** /lorð/ m, lord; pl **lores,** lords

**loro** /'loro/ m, *Ornith.* parrot

**los** /los/ def art m pl, the (e.g. l. sombreros, the hats) —pers pron acc 3rd pers m pl, them. **Tus cigarrillos no están sobre la mesa; los tengo en mi bolsillo,** Your cigarettes are not on the table; I have them in my pocket. Means some, any, ones, as substitution for noun already stated (e.g. Los cigarros están en la caja si los hay, The cigars are in the box, if there are any). Used demonstratively followed by de or que introducing relative clause, those of; those which, those who; the ones that (who) (e.g. Estaba leyendo algunos libros de los que tienes en tu cuarto, I was reading some books from among those which you have in your room)

**losa** /'losa/ f, flagstone; slab; tombstone

**lote** /'lote/ m, lot, portion, share

**lotería** /lote'ria/ f, lottery; lotto (game); lottery office

**lotero** /lo'tero/ **(-ra)** n seller of lottery tickets

**loto** /'loto/ m, lotus; lotus flower or fruit

**loza** /'loθa; 'losa/ f, porcelain, china

**lozanía** /loθa'nia; losa'nia/ f, luxuriance (of vegetation); vigor, lustiness; arrogance

**lozano** /lo'θano; lo'sano/ a luxuriant, exuberant; vigorous, lusty; arrogant

**lubricación** /luβrika'θion; luβrika'sion/ f, lubrication

**lubricador** /luβrika'ðor/ m, lubricator

**lubricante** /luβri'kante/ a lubricant

**lubricar** /luβri'kar/ vt to lubricate

**lúbrico** /'luβriko/ a slippery, smooth; lascivious, lustful

**lucera** /lu'θera; lu'sera/ f, skylight

**Lucerna** /lu'θerna; lu'serna/ Lucerne

**lucerna** /lu'θerna; lu'serna/ f, large chandelier; skylight

**lucero** /lu'θero; lu'sero/ m, evening star; any bright star; white star (on a horse's head); brilliance, radiance; pl *Poet.* eyes, orbs. **l. del alba,** morning star

**lucha** /'lutʃa/ f, fight; struggle; wrestling match; argument, disagreement. **l. grecorromana,** wrestling. **l. igualada,** close fight. **l. libre,** catch-as-catch-can

**luchador** /lutʃa'ðor/ **(-ra)** n fighter; struggler

**luchar** /lu'tʃar/ vi to fight hand to hand; wrestle; fight; struggle; argue

**lucidez** /luθi'ðeθ; lusi'ðes/ f, brilliance, shine; lucidity, clarity

**lucido** /lu'θiðo; lu'siðo/ a splendid, brilliant; sumptuous; fine, elegant

**lúcido** /'luθiðo; 'lusiðo/ a *Poet.* brilliant; lucid; clear

**luciente** /lu'θiente; lu'siente/ a bright, shining

**luciérnaga** /lu'θiernaga; lu'siernaga/ f, glowworm

**lucimiento** /luθi'miento; lusi'miento/ m, brilliance, luster; success, triumph; elegance; display, ostentation

**lucir** /lu'θir; lu'sir/ vi irr to shine, scintillate; excel, outshine; be successful; —vt illuminate; display, show off; show; —vr dress elegantly; be successful; excel, be brilliant —*Pres. Indic.* **luzco, luces,** etc —*Pres. Subjunc.* **luzca,** etc.

**lucrativo** /lukra'tiβo/ a lucrative

**lucro** /'lukro/ m, gain, profit

**lucroso** /lu'kroso/ a profitable

**luctuoso** /luk'tuoso/ a lugubrious, mournful

**lucubración** /lukuβra'θion; lukuβra'sion/ *f*, lucubration

**ludibrio** /lu'ðiβrio/ *m*, mockery, ridicule

**luego** /'luego/ *adv* immediately; afterward, later; then; soon, presently —*conjunc* therefore. **l. que,** as soon as. **desde l.,** immediately, at once; of course, naturally; in the first place. **hasta l.,** au revoir, good-by for the present

**luengo** /'luengo/ *a* long

**lugar** /lu'gar/ *m*, place; spot; village, town, city; region, locality; office, post; passage, text; opportunity; occasion; cause, motive; place on a list; room, space; seat. **l. común,** commonplace. **en l. de,** instead of. **en primer l.,** firstly, in the first place. **hacer l.,** to make room, make way. *Law.* **No ha l.,** The petition is refused. **tener l.,** to take place; have the time or opportunity (to)

**lugarejo** /luga'reho/ *m*, hamlet

**lugareño** /luga'reɲo/ **(-ña)** *a* peasant, regional —*n* villager, peasant

**lugarteniente** /lugarte'niente/ *m*, lieutenant; substitute, deputy

**lúgubre** /'luguβre/ *a* lugubrious, dismal, mournful

**luis** /'luis/ *m*, louis (French coin)

**lujo** /'luho/ *m*, luxury; abundance, profusion. **artículos de l.,** luxury goods

**lujoso** /lu'hoso/ *a* luxurious; abundant, profuse

**lujuria** /lu'huria/ *f*, lasciviousness; excess, intemperance

**lujuriante** /luhu'riante/ *a* luxuriant, abundant, profuse

**lujurioso** /luhu'rioso/ *a* lascivious, voluptuous

**lumbago** /lum'βago/ *m*, lumbago

**lumbre** /'lumbre/ *f*, fire; light; splendor, lustre; transom window, opening, skylight; *pl* tinderbox

**lumbrera** /lum'βrera/ *f*, luminary; skylight; dormer window; eminent authority

**luminar** /lumi'nar/ *m*, luminary (also *Fig.*)

**luminaria** /lumi'naria/ *f*, illumination; fairy lamp, small light; lamp burning before the Sacrament in Catholic churches

**luminosidad** /luminosi'ðað/ *f*, luminosity

**luminoso** /lumi'noso/ *a* luminous; bright

**luna** /'luna/ *f*, moon; mirror; satellite; sheet of plate glass. **l. creciente,** new or rising moon. **l. de miel,** honeymoon. **l. llena,** full moon. **l. menguante,** waning moon. **media l.,** crescent moon

**lunado** /lu'naðo/ *a* half-moon, crescent

**lunar** /lu'nar/ *m*, beauty spot; *Fig.* stain, blot (on reputation, etc.); blemish, slight imperfection —*a* lunar

**lunático** /lu'natiko/ **(-ca)** *a* and *n* lunatic

**lunes** /'lunes/ *m*, Monday

**luneta** /lu'neta/ *f*, lens (of eyeglasses), *Theat.* orchestra stall; (*Archit. Mil.*) lunette

**lupa** /'lupa/ *f*, magnifying glass

**lupanar** /lupa'nar/ *m*, brothel

**lupino** /lu'pino/ *a* wolf-like, lupine. *m*, *Bot.* lupine

**lúpulo** /'lupulo/ *m*, *Bot.* hop

**lusitano** /lusi'tano/ **(-na)** *a* and *n* Lusitanian

**lustrador** /lustra'ðor/ *m*, polisher. **l. de piso,** floor polisher

**lustrar** /lus'trar/ *vt* to lustrate, purify; polish, burnish; roam, journey

**lustre** /'lustre/ *m*, polish, sheen, gloss; glory, luster

**lustro** /'lustro/ *m*, lustrum, period of five years; chandelier

**lustroso** /lus'troso/ *a* shining, glossy; brilliant; glorious, noble

**luteranismo** /lutera'nismo/ *m*, Lutheranism

**luterano** /lute'rano/ **(-na)** *a* and *n* Lutheran

**luto** /'luto/ *m*, mourning; grief, affliction; *pl* mourning draperies. **estar de l.,** to be in mourning

**luxación** /luksa'θion; luksa'sion/ *f*, *Surg.* luxation, dislocation

**Luxemburgo** /luksem'βurgo/ Luxembourg

**luz** /luθ; lus/ *f*, light; glow; brightness, brilliance; information, news; *Fig.* luminary; day, daylight; *pl* culture, learning; windows. **luces de estacionamiento,** parking lights. **a buena l.,** in a good light; in a favorable light; after due consideration. **a primera l.,** at dawn. **dar a l.,** to publish (a book); bring forth (children); reveal. **entre dos luces,** in the dawn light; in the twilight; *Inf.* tipsy. **media l.,** half-light, twilight

# M

**maca** /'maka/ f, bruise or blemish on fruit; defect, flaw; Inf. fraud, swindle

**macabro** /ma'kaβro/ a macabre

**macadán** /maka'ðan/ m, macadam

**macagua** /ma'kagua/ f, Ornith. macaw

**macanudo** /maka'nuðo/ a (Inf. West. Hem.) extraordinary; enormous; robust; fine, excellent

**macareno** /maka'reno/ **(-na)** n inhabitant of the Macarena district of Seville. m, Inf. braggart

**macarrones** /maka'rrones/ m pl, macaroni; Naut. stanchions

**macarrónico** /maka'rroniko/ a macaronic, recondite, stylized

**macarse** /ma'karse/ vr to go bad, rot (fruit)

**macedón** /maθe'ðon; mase'ðon/ **(-ona), macedonio (-ia)** a and n Macedonian

**maceración** /maθera'θion; masera'sion/ f, maceration; steeping, soaking; mortification of the flesh

**macerar** /maθe'rar; mase'rar/ vt to macerate; steep, soak; mortify

**macero** /ma'θero; ma'sero/ m, mace bearer

**maceta** /ma'θeta; ma'seta/ f, dim small mace; handle, haft (of tools); stonecutter's hammer; flowerpot

**macetero** /maθe'tero; mase'tero/ m, flowerpot stand

**machaca** /ma'tʃaka/ f, pestle; pulverizer. mf Inf. bore, tedious person

**machacador** /matʃaka'ðor/ **(-ra)** a crushing, pounding —n beater, crusher, pounder

**machacar** /matʃa'kar/ vt to crush, pound; —vi importune; harp on a subject

**machacón** /matʃa'kon/ a tiresome, prolix

**machado** /ma'tʃaðo/ m, hatchet, ax

**machetero** /matʃe'tero/ m, one who cuts sugarcane with a machete

**machihembrar** /matʃiem'βrar/ vt to dovetail

**machina** /ma'tʃina/ f, derrick, crane; pile driver

**macho** /'matʃo/ m, male; male animal (he-goat, stallion, etc.); male plant; hook (of hook and eye); screw; Metall. core; tap (tool); Inf. dunderhead, fool; Archit. buttress —a male; stupid, ignorant; vigorous, strong. **m. cabrío,** he-goat

**machucadura** /matʃuka'ðura/ f, **machucamiento** m, pounding, crushing; bruising

**machucar** /matʃu'kar/ vt to crush, pound; bruise

**machucho** /ma'tʃutʃo/ a prudent, sensible; adult, mature

**macicez** /maθi'θeθ; masi'ses/ f, solidity; massiveness; thickness

**macilento** /maθi'lento; masi'lento/ a thin, lean, emaciated

**macillo** /ma'θiʎo; ma'siyo/ m, dim small mace; hammer (of a piano)

**macis** /'maθis; 'masis/ f, Cul. mace

**macizar** /maθi'θar; masi'sar/ vt to block up, fill up

**macizo** /ma'θiθo; ma'siso/ a massive; compact, solid; Fig. well-founded, unassailable; thick; strong. m, solidity, compactness; bulk, volume; flowerbed; solid tire

**macrocosmo** /makro'kosmo/ m, macrocosm

**mácula** /'makula/ f, stain, spot; Fig. blot, blemish; Inf. trick, deception; Astron. macula

**macuquero** /maku'kero/ m, unauthorized worker of abandoned mines

**madeja** /ma'ðeha/ f, skein, hank; lock of hair; Inf. dummy, useless person

**madera** /ma'ðera/ f, wood; timber; Inf. kind, sort; Mus. wind instruments. **m. contrachapada,** plywood. **m. de construcción,** timber. **maderas de sierra,** lumber wood. Inf. **ser de mala m.,** to be a ne'er-do-well

**maderada** /maðe'raða/ f, lumber wood

**maderaje** /maðe'rahe/ m, woodwork, timber work

**maderero** /maðe'rero/ m, timber merchant; lumberjack; carpenter

**madería** /maðe'ria/ f, timber yard

**madero** /ma'ðero/ m, wooden beam; log, piece of lumber; ship, vessel; Inf. blockhead or insensible person

**madrastra** /ma'ðrastra/ f, stepmother; anything unpleasant

**madraza** /ma'ðraθa; ma'ðrasa/ f, Inf. overindulgent mother

**madre** /'maðre/ f, mother; matron; cause, genesis; Inf. dame, mother; riverbed; dam; womb; main sewer; chief irrigation channel. **m. de leche,** wet nurse. **m. política,** mother-in-law; stepmother. Inf. **sacar de m. (a),** to provoke, irritate (a person)

**madreperla** /maðre'perla/ f, mother-of-pearl

**madrépora** /ma'ðrepora/ f, white coral, madrepore

**madreselva** /maðre'selβa/ f, honeysuckle

**madrigado** /maðri'gaðo/ a twice-married (women); Inf. experienced, wide-awake

**madrigal** /maðri'gal/ m, madrigal

**madriguera** /maðri'gera/ f, rabbit warren; burrow, den, hole, lair; haunt of thieves, etc.

**madrileño** /maðri'leɲo/ **(-ña)** a and n Madrilenian

**madrina** /ma'ðrina/ f, godmother; matron of honor or bridesmaid; sponsor; patroness; prop; stanchion

**madroncillo** /maðron'θiʎo; maðron'siyo/ m, strawberry

**madroño** /ma'ðroɲo/ m, strawberry tree; tuft, spot; tassel

**madrugada** /maðru'gaða/ f, dawn, daybreak; early rising. **de m.,** at dawn

**madrugador** /maðruga'ðor/ **(-ra)** a early rising —n early riser

**madrugar** /maðru'gar/ vi to get up early; gain time; anticipate, be beforehand

**maduración** /maðura'θion; maðura'sion/ f, ripening; mellowing; preparation; ripeness; maturity

**madurador** /maðura'ðor/ a ripening; maturing

**maduramente** /maðura'mente/ adv maturely; sensibly

**madurar** /maðu'rar/ vt to ripen; mature; think out; —vi ripen; grow mature, learn wisdom

**madurez** /maðu'reθ; maðu'res/ f, ripeness; maturity; mellowness; wisdom

**maduro** /ma'ðuro/ a ripe; mature; mellow; adult; wise

**maestra** /ma'estra/ f, schoolmistress; teacher, instructor; queen bee; guide, model

**maestral** /maes'tral/ a referring to the grand master of one of the Spanish military orders; teaching, pedagogic. m, mistral (wind); cell of a queen bee

**maestrear** /maestre'ar/ vt to direct, control, manage; prune vines; —vi Inf. bully, domineer

**maestría** /maes'tria/ f, mastery, skill; Educ. master's degree

**maestril** /maes'tril/ m, queen cell (of bees)

**maestro** /ma'estro/ a masterly; excellent; chief, main; midship. m, master, expert; teacher; instructor; master craftsman; Educ. master; Mus. composer; Naut. mainmast. **m. de armas,** fencing master. **m. de capilla,** Eccl. choirmaster. **m. de obras,** building contractor; master builder. **El ejercicio hace m.,** Practice makes perfect

**Magallanes, Estrecho de** /maga'ʎanes, es'tretʃo de; maga'yanes, es'tretʃo de/ Straits of Magellan

**magdalena** /magða'lena/ f, madeleine (cake); magdalen, penitent. Inf. **estar hecha una M.,** to be inconsolable

**magia** /'mahia/ f, magic

**mágica** /'mahika/ f, magic; enchantress, sorceress

**mágico** /'mahiko/ a magic; marvelous, wonderful. m, magician; enchanter; wizard

**magín** /ma'hin/ m, Inf. imagination; head, mind

**magisterio** /mahis'terio/ m, teaching profession; teaching diploma; teaching post; pedantry, pompousness. **ejercer su m. en,** to be employed as a teacher in

**magistrado** /mahis'traðo/ m, magistrate; magistracy

**magistral** /mahis'tral/ *a* magistral; authoritative, magisterial; pedantic, pompous

**magistratura** /mahistra'tura/ *f,* magistracy

**magnanimidad** /magnanimi'ðað/ *f,* magnanimity; generosity, liberality

**magnánimo** /mag'nanimo/ *a* magnanimous, generous, noble

**magnate** /mag'nate/ *m,* magnate

**magnesia** /mag'nesia/ *f,* magnesia

**magnesio** /mag'nesio/ *m,* magnesium

**magnético** /mag'netiko/ *a* magnetic

**magnetismo** /magne'tismo/ *m,* magnetism

**magnetizar** /magneti'θar; magneti'sar/ *vt* to magnetize; mesmerize

**magneto** /mag'neto/ *m,* magneto

**magnificar** /magnifi'kar/ *vt* to magnify, enlarge; praise, extol

**magnificencia** /magnifi'θenθia; magnifi'sensia/ *f,* magnificence, pomp, splendor

**magnífico** /mag'nifiko/ *a* magnificent; splendid, wonderful, fine; excellent

**magnitud** /magni'tuð/ *f,* magnitude; quantity; importance

**magno** /'magno/ *a* great; famous. **Alejandro M.,** Alexander the Great

**magnolia** /mag'nolia/ *f,* magnolia

**mago** /'mago/ *m,* magician; *pl* magi

**magra** /'magra/ *f,* rasher (of bacon, ham)

**magrez, magrura** /ma'greθ, ma'grura; ma'gres, ma'grura/ *f,* leanness; scragginess

**magro** /'magro/ *a* lean; scraggy. *m, Inf.* lean pork

**magulladura** /maguʎa'ðura; maguya'ðura/ *f,* **magullamiento** *m,* bruising; bruise, contusion

**magullar** /magu'ʎar; magu'yar/ *vt* to bruise

**mahometano** /maome'tano/ **(-na)** *a* and *n* Muslim

**mahometismo** /maome'tismo/ *m,* Islam

**mahonesa** /mao'nesa/ *f,* mayonnaise

**maíz** /ma'iθ; ma'is/ *m,* corn

**maizal** /mai'θal; mai'sal/ *m,* cornfield

**maja** /'maha/ *f,* belle

**majada** /ma'haða/ *f,* sheepfold; dung

**majadería** /mahaðe'ria/ *f,* impertinence, insolence

**majadero** /maha'ðero/ *a* persistent, tedious. *m,* bobbin (for lace making); pestle —*n* fool, bore

**majador** /maha'ðor/ *m,* pestle

**majar** /ma'har/ *vt* to pound, crush; *Inf.* importune, annoy

**majestad** /mahes'tað/ *f,* majesty (title); dignity; stateliness

**majestuosidad** /mahestuosi'ðað/ *f,* majesty; dignity

**majestuoso** /mahes'tuoso/ *a* majestic; stately; dignified

**majo** /'maho/ *a* arrogant, aggressive; gaudily attired, smart; dashing, handsome; attractive, pretty; elegant, well-dressed. *m,* beau, gallant, man about town

**majuelo** /ma'huelo/ *m,* new vine; species of white hawthorn

**mal** /mal/ *a Abbr.* **malo.** Used only before *m sing* nouns (e.g. *un m. cuarto de hora,* a bad quarter of an hour). *m,* evil; damage; harm; misfortune; illness, disease; trouble (e.g. *El m. es,* The trouble is). **m. de altura,** air sickness. **m. de ojo,** evil eye. **m. de piedra,** lithiasis, stone. **m. francés,** syphilis. **el m. menor,** the lesser of two evils —*interj* **¡M. haya!** A curse upon! **echar a m.,** to scorn (things); waste, squander. **llevar a m.** ( **una cosa),** to take (a thing) badly, complain. **No hay m. que por bien no venga,** It's an ill wind that blows no one any good, Every cloud has a silver lining. **parar en m.,** to come to a bad end

**mal** /mal/ *adv* badly; unfavorably; wrongly; wickedly; with difficulty; scarcely, barely. **m. que bien,** willingly or unwillingly; rightly or wrongly. **de m. en peor,** from bad to worse

**mala** /'mala/ *f,* mail, post. **m. real,** royal mail

**malabarista** /malaβa'rista/ *mf* juggler

**malaconsejado** /malakonse'haðo/ *a* ill-advised; imprudent

**malacostumbrado** /malakostum'βraðo/ *a* badly trained, spoiled; having bad habits

**malagueña** /mala'geɲa/ *f,* popular song of lament

**malagueño** /mala'geɲo/ *a* of or from Málaga

**malandante** /malan'dante/ *a* evildoing; unfortunate, miserable; poor

**malandanza** /malan'danθa; malan'dansa/ *f,* evildoing; misfortune, misery; poverty

**malandrín** /malan'drin/ *a* wicked, ill-disposed. *m,* scoundrel, miscreant

**malaquita** /mala'kita/ *f,* malachite

**malaria** /ma'laria/ *f,* malaria

**malaventura** /malaβen'tura/ *f,* misfortune, adversity, bad luck

**malaventurado** /malaβentu'raðo/ *a* unfortunate, unlucky

**malayo** /ma'laio/ **(-ya)** *a* Malay —*n* Malayan

**malbaratador** /malβarata'ðor/ **(-ra)** *a* wasteful, spendthrift —*n* squanderer, spendthrift

**malbaratar** /malβara'tar/ *vt* to squander, waste; sell at a loss

**malcasado** /malka'saðo/ *a* adulterous, unfaithful

**malcasar** /malka'sar/ **(se)** *vt* and *vr* to marry badly

**malcomido** /malko'miðo/ *a* underfed

**malcontento** /malkon'tento/ **(-ta)** *a* dissatisfied, discontented; rebellious —*n* malcontent, rebel

**malcriado** /mal'kriaðo/ *a* badly brought up; ill-bred; spoiled, peevish

**maldad** /mal'dað/ *f,* badness; depravity, wickedness

**maldecidor** /maldeθi'ðor; maldesi'ðor/ **(-ra)** *a* slanderous —*n* scandalmonger, slanderer

**maldecir** /malde'θir; malde'sir/ *vt irr* to curse; —*vt* and *vi* slander, backbite. See **decir**

**maldiciente** /maldi'θiente; maldi'siente/ *a* defamatory, slanderous; cursing, reviling. *m,* slanderer; curser

**maldición** /maldi'θion; maldi'sion/ *f,* malediction; curse, imprecation

**maldispuesto** /maldis'puesto/ *a* indisposed, ill; reluctant

**maldita** /mal'dita/ *f, Inf.* tongue. *Inf.* **soltar la m.,** to say too much, go too far

**maldito** /mal'dito/ *a* accursed; wicked; damned; poor (of quality); *Inf.* not a...

**maleabilidad** /maleaβili'ðað/ *f,* malleability, flexibility

**maleable** /male'aβle/ *a* malleable, flexible

**maleante** /male'ante/ *a* rascally, villainous. *mf* evildoer

**malecón** /male'kon/ *m,* breakwater

**maledicencia** /maleði'θenθia; maleði'sensia/ *f,* slander, abuse, backbiting; cursing

**maleficencia** /malefi'θenθia; malefi'sensia/ *f,* wrongdoing

**maleficio** /male'fiθio; male'fisio/ *m,* (magic) curse; spell; charm

**maléfico** /ma'lefiko/ *a* malefic, harmful. *m,* sorcerer —*n* squanderer, slanderer

**malestar** /males'tar/ *m,* indisposition, slight illness; discomfort

**maleta** /ma'leta/ *f,* suitcase, valise, grip; *m, Inf.* clumsy matador; duffer (at games, etc.). **hacer la m.,** to pack a suitcase; *Inf.* prepare for a journey, get ready to leave

**maletero** /male'tero/ *m,* seller or maker of traveling bags; porter

**maletín** /male'tin/ *m,* small suitcase or valise

**malevolencia** /maleβo'lenθia; maleβo'lensia/ *f,* malevolence, hatred, malice

**malévolo** /ma'leβolo/ *a* malevolent, malicious

**maleza** /ma'leθa; ma'lesa/ *f,* weeds; undergrowth; thicket

**malgastador** /malgasta'ðor/ **(-ra)** *a* thriftless, wasteful —*n* squanderer

**malgastar** /malgas'tar/ *vt* to waste (time); squander, throw away (money)

**malhablado** /mala'βlaðo/ *a* foul-tongued, indecent

**malhadado** /mala'ðaðo/ *a* ill-fated, unhappy

**malhecho** /mal'etʃo/ *a* deformed, twisted (persons). *m,* evil deed, wrongdoing

**malhechor** /male'tʃor/ **(-ra)** *n* malefactor; evildoer

**malhumorado** /malumo'raðo/ *a* ill-humored, bad-tempered

**malicia** /ma'liθia; ma'lisia/ *f,* wickedness, evil; malice, maliciousness; acuteness, subtlety, shrewdness; craftiness, guile; *Inf.* suspicion

**maliciar** /mali'θiar; mali'siar/ *vt* to suspect; spoil, damage; hurt, harm

**malicioso** /mali'θioso; mali'sioso/ *a* malicious; vindictive; wicked; shrewd, clever; *Inf.* suspicious; artful

**malignidad** /maligni'ðað/ *f,* malignancy, spite, ill will

**maligno** /ma'ligno/ *a* malignant, spiteful; wicked; *Med.* malignant

**malintencionado** /malinten θio'naðo; malintensio'naðo/ *a* ill-intentioned, badly disposed

**malla** /'maʎa; 'maya/ *f,* mesh (of a net); coat of mail; *pl Theat.* tights. **m. de alambre,** wire netting. **cota de m.,** coat of mail

**Mallorca** /ma'ʎorka; ma'yorka/ Majorca

**mallorquín** /maʎor'kin; mayor'kin/ **(-ina)** *a* and *n* Majorcan. *m,* Majorcan (variety of Catalan or Spanish)

**malmandado** /malman'daðo/ *a* disobedient; reluctant, unwilling

**malmaridada** /malmari'ðaða/ *f,* adultress, faithless wife

**malo** /'malo/ *a* bad; wicked; evil; injurious; harmful; illicit; licentious; ill; difficult; troublesome, annoying; *Inf.* mischievous; knavish; rotten, decaying —*interj* **¡M.!** That's bad!; You shouldn't have done that!; That's a bad sign! **de malas,** unluckily, unhappily. **el M.,** the Evil One, the Devil. **estar m.,** to be ill. **Lo m. es,** The trouble is, The worst of it is. **por malas o por buenas,** willy-nilly, willingly or unwillingly. **ser m.,** to be wicked; be evil; behave badly (children)

**malograr** /malo'grar/ *vt* to lose (time); waste, throw away (opportunities); —*vr* fall through, fail; wither, fade; die early, come to an untimely end

**malogro** /ma'logro/ *m,* loss, waste (time, opportunity); frustration; decline, fading; untimely death

**malparar** /malpa'rar/ *vt* to ill-treat; damage. **quedar malparado,** to get the worst of

**malparir** /malpa'rir/ *vt Med.* to miscarry

**malparto** /mal'parto/ *m,* miscarriage; abortion

**malquerencia** /malke'renθia; malke'rensia/ *f,* ill will, aversion, dislike

**malquistar** /malkis'tar/ *vt* to stir up trouble; make unpopular; estrange; —*vr* make oneself disliked

**malquisto** /mal'kisto/ *a* unpopular, disliked

**malsano** /mal'sano/ *a* unhealthy

**malta** /'malta/ *m,* malt

**maltés** /mal'tes/ **(-esa)** *a* and *n* Maltese

**maltraer** /maltra'er/ *vt irr* to ill-treat; insult. See **traer**

**maltratamiento** /maltrata'miento/ *m,* abuse, ill usage; damage, deterioration

**maltratar** /maltra'tar/ *vt* to ill-treat; abuse, insult; misuse, spoil, damage

**maltrato** /mal'trato/ *m,* maltreatment; misuse

**maltrecho** /mal'tretʃo/ *a* ill-treated, bruised; abused, insulted; damaged

**maltusianismo** /maltusia'nismo/ *m,* Malthusianism

**maltusiano** /maltu'siano/ *a* Malthusian

**Malucas, las** /ma'lukas, las/ the Moluccas

**malucho** /ma'lutʃo/ *a Inf.* off-color, below par, not well

**malva** /'malβa/ *f,* mallow. **m. real, m. rosa,** *or* **m. loca,** hollyhock. **ser como una m.,** *Fig. Inf.* to be a clinging vine

**malvado** /mal'βaðo/ *a* evil, malevolent, fiendish —*n* villain, fiend

**malvasia** /malβa'sia/ *f, Bot.* malvasia; malmsey (wine)

**malvavisco** /malβa'βisko/ *m, Bot.* marshmallow

**malvender** /malβen'der/ *vt* to sell at a loss

**malversación** /malβersa'θion; malβersa'sion/ *f,* malversation, maladministration; misappropriation (of funds)

**malversador** /malβersa'ðor/ **(-ra)** *n* bad or corrupt administrator

**malversar** /malβer'sar/ *vt* to misappropriate (funds)

**mama** /'mama/ *f, Inf.* mamma, mommy; breast; udder

**mamá** /ma'ma/ *f,* mamma

**mamar** /ma'mar/ *vt* to suck (the breast); *Inf.* wolf, swallow; learn from an early age; enjoy, obtain unfairly; —*vr* get drunk

**mamario** /ma'mario/ *a* mammary

**mamarracho** /mama'rratʃo/ *m, Inf.* scarecrow, dummy; anything grotesque looking

**mameluco** /mame'luko/ *m,* mameluke; *Inf.* ninny, fool

**mamífero** /ma'mifero/ *a* mammalian. *m,* mammal

**mamotreto** /mamo'treto/ *m,* notebook, memorandum; *Inf.* large book or bulky file of papers

**mampara** /mam'para/ *f,* folding screen; screen; partition

**mamparo** /mam'paro/ *m,* bulkhead

**mampostería** /mamposte'ria/ *f,* masonry, stonemasonry

**mampostero** /mampos'tero/ *m,* stonemason

**mamut** /ma'mut/ *m,* mammoth

**maná** /ma'na/ *m,* manna

**manada** /ma'naða/ *f,* handful; herd, flock; group, drove, crowd

**manadero** /mana'ðero/ *m,* herdsman, drover; spring, stream

**manantial** /manan'tial/ *m,* fountain, source, spring; head (of a river)

**manar** /ma'nar/ *vi* to flow, stream; be plentiful

**manatí** /mana'ti/ *m,* sea cow, manatee

**mancar** /man'kar/ *vt* to injure, maim; —*vi* grow calm (elements)

**manceba** /man'θeβa; man'seβa/ *f,* concubine; girl

**mancebía** /manθe'βia; manse'βia/ *f,* brothel; youth, young days

**mancebo** /man'θeβo; man'seβo/ *m,* youth, stripling; bachelor; shop assistant

**mancha** /'mantʃa/ *f,* spot, smear, stain; blotch; plot of ground; patch of vegetation; stigma, disgrace

**manchar** /man'tʃar/ *vt* to stain; smear; spot; speckle; disgrace; tarnish

**manchego** /man'tʃego/ **(-ga)** *a* and *n* of or from La Mancha (Spain)

**manchuriano** /mantʃu'riano/ **(-na)** *a* and *n* Manchurian

**mancilla** /man'θiʎa; man'siya/ *f,* stain; slur

**mancillar** /manθi'ʎar; mansi'yar/ *vt* to stain; *Fig.* smirch

**manco** /'manko/ **(-ca)** *a* maimed, disabled; onehanded; one-armed; armless; handless; incomplete, faulty —*n* disabled person

**mancomunidad** /mankomuni'ðað/ *f,* association, society; community, union; commonwealth; regional legislative assembly

**manda** /'manda/ *f,* offer, suggestion, proposition; legacy

**mandadero** /manda'ðero/ **(-ra)** *n* convent or prison messenger; errand boy (girl)

**mandado** /man'daðo/ *m,* order, command; errand

**mandamiento** /manda'miento/ *m,* order, command; *Eccl.* commandment; *Law.* writ; *pl Inf.* one's five fingers

**mandar** /man'dar/ *vt* to order, command; bequeath, will; send; control, drive; promise, offer; order (e.g. *Mandó hacerse un traje,* He ordered a suit to be made); —*vr* walk unaided (convalescents, etc.); lead into one another (rooms, etc.); **¿Quién manda aquí?** Who is in charge here?

**mandarín** /manda'rin/ *m,* mandarin; *Inf.* bureaucrat

**mandarina** /manda'rina/ *f,* mandarin (classical Chinese); mandarin orange

**mandatario** /manda'tario/ *m,* mandatary

**mandato** /man'dato/ *m,* mandate; command; *Eccl.* maundy. *Polit.* mandate. **cuarto m.,** fourth term (of President, Governor, etc.)

**mandíbula** /man'diβula/ *f,* jaw; jawbone, mandible

**mandil** /man'dil/ *m,* long leather apron; apron; Freemason's apron; close-meshed fishing net

**mandilón** /mandi'lon/ *m, Inf.* coward, nincompoop

**mandioca** /man'dioka/ *f,* manioc, cassava; tapioca

**mando** /'mando/ *m,* authority, power; (*Mil. Nav.*) command; *Engin.* regulation; controls (of a machine, etc.). **m. a distancia,** remote control. *Aer.* **m. de dos pilotos,** dual-controlled. **mandos gemelos,** dual control. **al m. de,** under the command of; under the direction of

**mandolín** /mando'lin/ *m.* **mandolina** *f,* mandolin

**mandón** /man'don/ *a* domineering, bossy

**mandrágora** /man'dragora/ *f,* mandrake

**mandril** /man'dril/ *m, Mech.* mandrel, chuck; *Zool.* mandrill

**manear** /mane'ar/ *vt* to hobble (a horse); manage, control

**manecilla** /mane'θiʎa; mane'siya/ *f, dim* little hand; hand of a clock; *Print.* fist

**manejable** /mane'haβle/ *a* manageable, controllable

**manejar** /mane'har/ *vt* to handle; use, wield; control; manage, direct; ride (horses); —*vr* manage to move around (after an accident, illness)

**manejo** /ma'neho/ *m,* handling; use, wielding; control; management, direction; horsemanship; intrigue

**maneota** /mane'ota/ *f,* hobble, shackle

**manera** /ma'nera/ *f,* manner, way, means; behavior, style (gen. *pl*); class (of people); *Art.* style, manner. **a la m. de,** like, in the style of. **de esa m.,** in that way; according to that, in that case. **de m. que,** so that. **en gran m.,** to a great extent. **sobre m.,** exceedingly

**manga** /'maŋga/ *f,* sleeve; bag; grip; handle; pipe (of a hose); strainer; waterspout; body of troops; beam, breadth of a ship; *pl* profits. **m. de viento,** whirlwind. **echar de m. a,** to make use of a person. *Inf.* **estar de m.,** to be in league. **tener m. ancha,** to be broad-minded. *Fig. Inf.* **traer ( una cosa) en la m.,** to have (something) up one's sleeve

**mangana** /maŋ'gana/ *f,* lasso

**manganeso** /maŋga'neso/ *m,* manganese

**manganilla** /maŋga'niʎa; maŋga'niya/ *f,* sleight of hand; hoax, trick

**mangle** /'maŋgle/ *m,* mangrove tree

**mango** /'maŋgo/ *m,* handle, haft, stock; mango. **m. de cuchillo,** knife handle

**mangonear** /maŋgone'ar/ *vi Inf.* to loaf, roam about; interfere, meddle

**mangonero** /maŋgo'nero/ *a Inf.* meddlesome

**mangosta** /maŋ'gosta/ *f,* mongoose

**mangote** /maŋ'gote/ *m, Inf.* long, wide sleeve; black oversleeve

**manguera** /maŋ'guera/ *f,* hose; sleeve; tube; airshaft; waterspout

**manguero** /maŋ'guero/ *m,* fireman; hoseman

**manguito** /maŋ'guito/ *m,* muff; black oversleeve; wristlet, cuff; *Mech.* bush, sleeve

**manía** /ma'nia/ *f,* mania, obsession; whim, fancy

**maníaco** /ma'niako/ **(-ca)** *a* maniacal; capricious, extravagant —*n* maniac

**maniatar** /mania'tar/ *vt* to handcuff; hobble (a cow, etc.)

**maniático** /ma'niatiko/ **(-ca)** *a* maniacal; capricious; faddy, fussy —*n* crank

**manicomio** /mani'komio/ *m,* insane asylum, mental hospital

**manicura** /mani'kura/ *f,* manicure

**manicuro** /mani'kuro/ **(-ra)** *n* manicurist

**manida** /ma'niða/ *f,* lair, den; dwelling, habitation

**manifestación** /manifesta'θion; manifesta'sion/ *f,* declaration, statement; exhibition; demonstration; *Eccl.* exposition (of the Blessed Sacrament)

**manifestante** /manifes'tante/ *mf* demonstrator

**manifestar** /manifes'tar/ *vt irr* to declare, make known, state; exhibit, show; *Eccl.* to expose (the Blessed Sacrament). See **acertar**

**manifiesto** /mani'fiesto/ *a* obvious, evident. *m,* manifesto; *Naut.* manifest; *Eccl.* exposition of the Blessed Sacrament. **poner de m.,** to show; make public; reveal

**manigua** /ma'nigua/ *f,* thicket, jungle (in Cuba)

**manija** /ma'niha/ *f,* handle, stock, haft; hand lever; clamp; tether (for horses, etc.)

**manileño** /mani'leɲo/ **(ña)** *a* and *n* Manilan

**manilla** /ma'niʎa; ma'niya/ *f,* bracelet; handcuff, manacle

**maniobra** /ma'nioβra/ *f,* operation, process; *Mil.* maneuver; intrigue; tackle, gear; handling, management; *Naut.* working of a ship; *pl* shunting (trains)

**maniobrar** /manio'βrar/ *vi Mil.* to maneuver; *Naut.* handle, work (ships)

**manipulación** /manipula'θion; manipula'sion/ *f,* handling; manipulation; control, management

**manipulador** /manipula'ðor/ *a* manipulative. *m,* sending key (telegraphy)

**manipular** /manipu'lar/ *vt* to handle; manipulate; manage, direct

**manípulo** /ma'nipulo/ *m,* maniple

**maniqueo** /mani'keo/ **(-ea)** *a* Manichean *n* Manichee

**maniquete** /mani'kete/ *m,* black lace mitten

**maniquí** /mani'ki/ *m,* mannequin; dummy; *Inf.* puppet, weak person

**manirroto** /mani'rroto/ **(-ta)** *a* wasteful, extravagant —*n* spendthrift

**manivela** /mani'βela/ *f, Mech.* crank, lever

**manjar** /man'har/ *m,* dish, food; pastime, recreation, pleasure. **m. blanco,** blancmange

**mano** /'mano/ *f,* hand; coat, coating; quire (of paper); front paw (animals); elephant's trunk; side, hand; hand (of a clock); game (of cards, etc.); lead (at cards); way, means; ability; power; protection, favor; compassion; aid, help; scolding; *Mus.* scale; pestle; workers. *Inf.* editing, correction of a literary work (gen. by a person more skilled than the author). **m. de mortero,** pestle. **m. de obra,** (manual) labor. **manos muertas,** *Law.* mortmain. **m. sobre m.,** with folded hands; lazily, indolently. **a la m.,** at hand, nearby; within one's grasp. **a manos llenas,** in abundance, abundantly. **bajo m.,** in an underhand manner, secretly. **buenas manos,** cleverness, ability; dexterity. **de primera m.,** first-hand, new. **estar dejado de la m. de Dios,** to be very unlucky; be very foolish. **poner la m. en,** to ill-treat; slap, buffet. **Si a m. viene...,** If by chance... **tender la m.,** to put out one's hand, shake hands. **traer entre manos,** to have on hand, be engaged in

**manojo** /ma'noho/ *m,* bunch, handful. **a manojos,** in handfuls; plentifully, in abundance

**manolo** /ma'nolo/ **(-la)** *n* inhabitant of low quarters of Madrid noted for pride, gaiety, quarrelsomeness, and wit

**manopla** /ma'nopla/ *f,* gauntlet

**manoseado** /manose'aðo/ *a* hackneyed

**manosear** /manose'ar/ *vt* to handle; paw, touch repeatedly; finger

**manoseo** /mano'seo/ *m,* handling; fingering; *Inf.* pawing, feeling

**manotada** /mano'taða/ *f,* slap, cuff

**manotear** /manote'ar/ *vt* to slap, cuff; —*vi* gesticulate, gesture with the hands

**manoteo** /mano'teo/ *m,* gesticulation with the hands

**manquedad** /manke'ðað/ *f,* disablement of hand or arm; lack of one of these; defect; incompleteness

**mansalva** /man'salβa/ **(a)** *adv* without danger

**mansedumbre** /manse'ðumbre/ *f,* meekness; kindness; gentleness

**mansión** /man'sion/ *f,* stay, visit; dwelling, abode; mansion

**manso** /'manso/ *a* soft, gentle; meek, mild; tame; peaceable, amiable; calm

**manta** /'manta/ *f,* blanket; horse blanket; traveling rug; *Inf.* hiding, thrashing. **m. de viaje,** traveling rug. *Inf.* **a m. de Dios,** in abundance. **dar una m.,** to toss in a blanket. *Fig. Inf.* **tirar de la m.,** to let the cat out of the bag

**manteamiento** /mantea'miento/ *m,* tossing in a blanket

**mantear** /mante'ar/ *vt* to toss in a blanket

**manteca** /man'teka/ *f,* lard; cooking fat; grease; *Argentina* butter. **como m.,** as mild as milk, as soft as butter

**mantecada** /mante'kaða/ *f,* buttered toast

**mantecado** /mante'kaðo/ *m,* French ice cream

**mantecoso** /mante'koso/ *a* greasy

**mantel** /man'tel/ *m,* tablecloth; altar cloth

**mantelería** /mantele'ria/ *f,* table linen

**mantelete** /mante'lete/ *m, (Eccl. Mil.)* mantlet

**mantener** /mante'ner/ *vt irr* to maintain; keep, feed; support; continue, persevere with; uphold, affirm; keep up; —*vr* support oneself; remain in a place; (*with en*) continue to uphold (views, etc.), persevere in. **mantenerse firme,** *Fig.* to stand one's ground. See **tener**

**mantenimiento** /manteni'miento/ *m,* maintenance; support; sustenance, nourishment; affirmation; upkeep; livelihood

**manteo** /man'teo/ *m,* tossing in a blanket; long cloak

**mantequera** /mante'kera/ *f,* churn; dairymaid; butter dish

**mantequero** /mante'kero/ *m,* dairyman; butter dish

**mantequilla** /mante'kiʎa; mante'kiya/ *f,* butter

**mantero** /man'tero/ *m,* blanket seller or maker

**mantilla** /man'tiʎa; man'tiya/ *f,* mantilla; saddlecloth *pl* baby's long clothes. **estar en mantillas,** to be in swaddling clothes; *Fig.* be in early infancy

**manto** /'manto/ *m,* cloak; cover, disguise; *Zool.* mantle; *Mineral.* layer

**mantón** /man'ton/ *m,* shawl. **m. de Manila,** Manila shawl

**mantuano** /man'tuano/ **(-na)** *a* and *n* Mantuan

**manuable** /ma'nuaβle/ *a* easy to handle or use, handy

**manual** /ma'nual/ *a* manual; handy, easy to use; docile, peaceable. *m,* manual, textbook; *Eccl.* book of ritual; notebook

**manubrio** /ma'nuβrio/ *m,* handle, crank

**manuela** /ma'nuela/ *f,* open carriage (Madrid)

**manufactura** /manufak'tura/ *f,* manufacture; manufactured article; factory

**manufacturar** /manufaktu'rar/ *vt* to manufacture

**manufacturero** /manufaktu'rero/ *a* manufacturing

**manumisión** /manumi'sion/ *f,* freeing (of a slave), manumission

**manumitir** /manumi'tir/ *vt Law.* to free, enfranchise (slaves)

**manuscrito** /manus'krito/ *a* and *m,* manuscript

**manutención** /manuten'θion; manuten'sion/ *f,* maintenance; upkeep; protection

**manzana** /man'θana; man'sana/ *f,* apple; block (of houses); city square; Adam's apple

**manzanal** /manθa'nal; mansa'nal/ *m,* apple orchard; apple tree

**manzanar** /manθa'nar; mansa'nar/ *m,* apple orchard

**manzanilla** /manθa'niʎa; mansa'niya/ *f,* white sherry wine; *Bot.* chamomile; chamomile tea; knob, ball (on furniture); pad (on an animal's foot)

**manzano** /man'θano; man'sano/ *m,* apple tree

**maña** /'maɲa/ *f,* skill, dexterity; craftiness, guile; vice, bad habit (gen. *pl*). **darse m. para,** to contrive to

**mañana** /ma'ɲana/ *f,* morning; tomorrow. *m,* future, tomorrow —*adv* tomorrow; in time to come; soon. **¡M.!** Tomorrow! Another day! Not now! (generally to beggars). **de m.,** early in the morning. **muy de m.,** very early in the morning. **pasado m.,** the day after tomorrow

**mañanica** /maɲa'nika/ *f,* early morning

**mañear** /maɲe'ar/ *vt* to arrange cleverly; —*vi* behave shrewdly

**mañero** /ma'ɲero/ *a* shrewd, clever; easily worked; handy

**mañoso** /ma'ɲoso/ *a* clever, skillful; crafty; vicious, with bad habits

**mañuela** /ma'ɲuela/ *f,* low guile

**mapa** /'mapa/ *m,* map; card. **m. en relieve,** relief map. **m. del estado mayor,** ordnance map. *Inf.* **no estar en el m.,** to be off the map; be most unusual (of things)

**mapache** /ma'patʃe/ *m,* raccoon

**mapamundi** /mapa'mundi/ *m,* map of the world

**maqueta** /ma'keta/ *f,* (*Art. Archit.*) model

**maquiavélico** /makia'βeliko/ *a* Machiavellian

**maquiavelismo** /makiaβe'lismo/ *m,* Machiavellism

**maquillaje** /maki'ʎahe; maki'yahe/ *m,* makeup, cosmetics; making up (of the face)

**maquillar** /maki'ʎar; maki'yar/ **(se)** *vt* and *vr* to make up (the face, etc.)

**máquina** /'makina/ *f,* machine, mechanism; engine; apparatus; plan, scheme; machine, puppet; *Inf.* mansion, palace; plenty; locomotive; fantasy, product of the imagination. **m. de vapor,** steam engine. **m. de arrastre,** traction engine; tractor. **m. de coser,** sewing machine. **m. de escribir,** typewriter. **m. fotográfica,** camera. **m. de impresionar,** movie camera. **m. de imprimir,** printing machine. **m. herramienta,** machine tool. **m. neumática,** air pump

**maquinación** /makina'θion; makina'sion/ *f,* intrigue, machination

**maquinador** /makina'ðor/ **(-ra)** *n* intriguer, schemer

**maquinal** /maki'nal/ *a* mechanical

**maquinar** /maki'nar/ *vt* to intrigue, scheme, plot

**maquinaria** /maki'naria/ *f,* machinery; applied mechanics; mechanism

**maquinista** /maki'nista/ *mf* driver, enginer; mechanic; machinist; locomotive driver

**mar** /mar/ *mf* sea; great many, abundance. **m. bonanza** *or* **m. en calma,** calm sea. **m. de fondo** *or* **m. de leva,** swell. **alta m.,** high seas. **a mares,** plentifully. **arar en el m.,** to labor in vain. *Naut.* **hacerse a la m.,** to put out to sea. **la m. de historias,** a great number of stories

**maraña** /ma'raɲa/ *f,* undergrowth; tangle; *Fig.* difficult position; intrigue; silk waste

**marasmo** /ma'rasmo/ *m, Med.* marasmus, atrophy; inactivity, paralysis

**maravedí** /maraβe'ði/ *m,* maravedi (old Spanish coin of fluctuating value)

**maravilla** /mara'βiʎa; mara'βiya/ *f,* marvel, wonder; admiration; amazement; marigold. **a m.,** wonderfully. **a las mil maravillas,** to perfection, excellently. **por m.,** by chance; occasionally

**maravillar** /maraβi'ʎar; maraβi'yar/ *vt* to amaze, cause admiration; —*vr* (*with de*) marvel at, admire; be amazed by

**maravilloso** /maraβi'ʎoso; maraβi'yoso/ *a* marvelous, wonderful

**marbete** /mar'βete/ *m,* label, tag; edge, border

**marca** /'marka/ *f,* mark, sign; brand; frontier zone, border country; standard, norm (of size); make, brand; measuring rule; *Sports.* record. **m. de fábrica,** brand, trademark. **m. de ley,** hallmark. **m. registrada,** registered name. **de m.,** excellent, of excellent quality

**marcado** /mar'kaðo/ *a* marked; pronounced; strong (of accents)

**marcador** /marka'ðor/ *a* marking. *m,* marker; scoreboard; bookmark

**marcar** /mar'kar/ *vt* to mark; brand; embroider initials on linen; tell the time (watches); show the amount (cash register, etc.); dial (telephone); *Sports.* score (a goal); notice, observe; set aside, earmark; —*vr Naut.* check the course. **m. el compás** to beat time

**Mar Caspio** /'mar 'kaspio/ Caspian Sea

**marcha** /'martʃa/ *f,* departure; running, working; *Mil.* march; speed (of trains, ships, etc.); *Mus.* march; progress, course (of events). **m. atrás,** backing, reversing. **m. de ensayo,** trial run. **m. forzada,** *Mil.* forced march. **a largas marchas,** with all speed. **a toda m.,** at top speed; full speed ahead; by forced marches; *Mil.* **batir la m.,** to strike up a march. **en m.,** underway; working; in operation

**marchamero** /martʃa'mero/ *m,* customs official who checks and marks goods

**marchamo** /mar'tʃamo/ *m,* customs mark on checked goods

**marchar** /mar'tʃar/ *vi* to run; work; function; go; leave, depart; progress, proceed; *Mil.* march; go (clocks); —*vr* leave, go away

**marchitable** /martʃi'taβle/ *a* perishable, fragile

**marchitamiento** /martʃita'miento/ *m,* withering

**marchitar** /martʃi'tar/ *vt* to wither, fade; blight, spoil; weaken; —*vr* wither; be blighted

**marchitez** /martʃi'teθ; martʃi'tes/ *f,* witheredness; fadedness

**marchito** /mar'tʃito/ *a* withered; faded; blighted, frustrated

**marcial** /mar'θial; mar'sial/ *a* martial; courageous, militant

**marcialidad** /marθiali'ðað; marsiali'ðað/ *f,* war-like spirit, militancy

**marciano** /mar'θiano; mar'siano/ *a* Martian

**marco** /'marko/ *m,* mark (German coin); boundary

mark; frame (of a picture, etc.). **m. de ventana,** window frame

**Mar de las Indias** /'mar de las 'indias/ Indian Ocean

**Mar del Norte** /'mar del 'norte/ North Sea

**marea** /ma'rea/ f, tide; strand, water's edge; light breeze; drizzle; dew; street dirt. **m. creciente,** flood tide. **m. menguante,** ebb tide. **m. muerta,** neap tide

**mareaje** /ma'reahe/ m, seamanship; ship's course

**marear** /mare'ar/ vt to navigate; sell; sell publicly; Inf. annoy; —vr be seasick; feel faint; feel giddy; be damaged at sea (goods)

**marejada** /mare'haða/ f, surge, swell; high sea; tidal wave; commotion, uproar

**mareo** /ma'reo/ m, seasickness; nausea, dizziness; Inf. irritation, tediousness

**mareta** /ma'reta/ f, movement of the waves; sound, noise (of a crowd)

**marfil** /mar'fil/ m, ivory

**marfileño** /marfi'leɲo/ a ivory; ivory-like

**marfuz** /mar'fuθ; mar'fus/ a spurned, rejected; deceitful

**marga** /'marga/ f, loam, marl

**margarina** /marga'rina/ f, margarine

**margarita** /marga'rita/ f, pearl; marguerite, oxeye daisy; daisy; periwinkle

**margen** /'marhen/ mf edge, fringe, border, verge; margin (of a book); opportunity; marginal note. **dar m. para,** to provide an opportunity for; give rise to

**marginal** /marhi'nal/ a marginal

**margoso** /mar'goso/ a loamy, marly

**marica** /ma'rika/ f, magpie. m, (offensive) homosexual; milksop

**maricón** /mari'kon/ m, (offensive) homosexual

**maridable** /mari'ðaβle/ a marital, matrimonial

**maridaje** /mari'ðahe/ m, conjugal union and harmony; intimate relationship (between things)

**maridar** /mari'ðar/ vi to get married; mate, live as husband and wife; —vt unite, link, join together

**marido** /ma'riðo/ m, husband

**marihuana** /mari'uana/ f, marijuana

**marimacho** /mari'matʃo/ m, Inf. mannish woman

**marina** /ma'rina/ f, coast, seashore; Art. seascape; seamanship; navy, fleet. **m. de guerra,** navy. **m. mercante,** merchant navy

**marinera** /mari'nera/ f, sailor's blouse

**marinería** /marine'ria/ f, profession of a sailor; seamanship; crew of a ship; sailors (as a class)

**marinero** /mari'nero/ m, sailor, seaman. **m. de agua dulce,** freshwater sailor (a novice). **m. práctico,** able seaman. **a la marinera,** in a seaman-like fashion

**marinesco** /mari'nesko/ a seamanly

**marino** /ma'rino/ a marine, sea; seafaring; shipping. m, sailor, mariner

**marioneta** /mario'neta/ f, marionette, puppet

**mariposa** /mari'posa/ f, butterfly; night-light

**mariposear** /maripose'ar/ vi to flutter, flit, fly about; flirt, be fickle; follow about, dance attendance on

**mariquita** /mari'kita/ f, Ent. ladybird; parakeet.

**marisabidilla** /marisaβi'ðiʎa; marisaβi'ðiya/ f, Inf. blue-stocking, know-it-all

**mariscal** /maris'kal/ m, Mil. marshal; field marshal; blacksmith

**marisco** /ma'risko/ m, shellfish

**marisma** /ma'risma/ f, bog, morass, swamp

**marital** /mari'tal/ a marital

**marítimo** /ma'ritimo/ a maritime, sea

**marjal** /mar'hal/ m, marshland, fen

**marmita** /mar'mita/ f, stewpot; copper, boiler

**marmitón** /marmi'ton/ m, kitchen boy, scullion

**mármol** /'marmol/ m, marble; work executed in marble

**marmolería** /marmole'ria/ f, marble works; work executed in marble

**marmolista** /marmo'lista/ mf marble cutter; dealer in marble

**marmóreo** /mar'moreo/ a marble; Poet. marmoreal

**marmota** /mar'mota/ f, Zool. marmot; sleepyhead, dormouse

**Mar Muerto** /mar 'muerto/ Dead Sea

**maroma** /ma'roma/ f, rope, hawser

**marqués** /mar'kes/ m, marquis

**marquesa** /mar'kesa/ f, marchioness

**marquesina** /marke'sina/ f, marquee

**marquetería** /markete'ria/ f, marquetry

**marrana** /ma'rrana/ f, sow; Inf. slattern, slut

**marrano** /ma'rrano/ m, pig, hog; Marrano

**marras** /'marras/ (**de**) adv long ago, in the dim past

**marrasquino** /marras'kino/ m, maraschino liqueur

**marro** /'marro/ m, tick, tag (game)

**Mar Rojo** /mar 'rroho/ Red Sea

**marrón** /ma'rron/ a maroon; brown. m, brown color; maroon color; quoit

**marroquí** /marro'ki/ a and mf Moroccan. m, Morocco leather

**marroquín** /marro'kin/ (**-ina**), **marrueco** (**-ca**) a and n Moroccan

**Marruecos** /ma'rruekos/ Morocco

**marrullería** /marruʎe'ria; marruye'ria/ f, flattery, cajolery

**marrullero** /marru'ʎero; marru'yero/ (**-ra**) a wheedling, flattering —n wheedler, cajoler

**Marsella** /mar'seʎa; mar'seya/ Marseilles

**marsellés** /marse'ʎes; marse'yes/ (**-esa**) a and n of or from Marseilles. f, **la Marsellesa,** the Marseillaise

**marsopa** /mar'sopa/ f, porpoise

**marta** /'marta/ f, sable; marten

**Marte** /'marte/ m, Mars

**martes** /'martes/ m, Tuesday. **m. de carnaval,** mardi gras

**martillar** /marti'ʎar; marti'yar/ vt to hammer; oppress

**martillazo** /marti'ʎaθo; marti'yaso/ m, hammer blow

**martilleo** /marti'ʎeo; marti'yeo/ m, hammering; noise of the hammer; clink, clatter

**martillo** /marti'ʎo; mar'tiyo/ m, hammer; oppressor, tyrant; auction rooms. **a m.,** by hammering. **de m.,** wrought (of metals)

**martinete** /marti'nete/ m, hammer (of a pianoforte); pile driver; drop hammer. **m. de báscula,** tilt hammer

**Martinica** /marti'nika/ Martinique

**martín pescador** /mar'tin peska'ðor/ m, kingfisher

**mártir** /'martir/ mf martyr

**martirio** /mar'tirio/ m, martyrdom

**martirizar** /martiri'θar; martiri'sar/ vt to martyr; torture, torment, martyrize; tease, annoy

**martirologio** /martiro'lohio/ m, martyrology

**marxismo** /mark'sismo/ m, Marxism

**marxista** /mark'sista/ a and mf Marxist

**marzo** /'marθo; 'marso/ m, March

**mas** /mas/ conjunc but; yet

**más** /mas/ adv compar more; in addition, besides; rather, preferably. Math. plus. **el** ( **la,** etc.) **más,** adv superl the most, etc. **m. bien,** more; rather; preferably. **m. que,** only; but; more than; although, even if. **a lo m.,** at the most; at the worst. **a m.,** besides, in addition. **de m.,** superfluous, unnecessary, unwanted. **no... m. que,** only. **por m. que,** however; even if. **sin m. ni m.,** without further ado. **M. vale un mal arreglo que un buen pleito,** A bad peace is better than a good war

**masa** /'masa/ f, mass; dough; whole, aggregate; majority (of people); mortar. **en la m. de la sangre,** Fig. in the blood, in a person's nature

**masada** /ma'saða/ f, farmhouse and stock

**masadero** /masa'ðero/ m, farmer; farm laborer

**masaje** /ma'sahe/ m, massage

**masajista** /masa'hista/ mf masseur; masseuse

**mascadura** /maska'ðura/ f, chewing

**mascar** /mas'kar/ vt to chew; masticate; Inf. mumble, mutter

**máscara** /'maskara/ f, mask; fancy dress; pretext, excuse. mf masquerader, reveler; pl masquerade. **m. para gases,** gas mask

**mascarada** /maska'raða/ f, masquerade; company of revelers

**mascarero** /maska'rero/ (**-ra**) n theatrical costumer, fancy-dress dealer

**mascarilla** /maska'riʎa; maska'riya/ f, death mask

**mascarón** /maska'ron/ m, large mask; Archit. gargoyle. **m. de proa,** Naut. figurehead

**mascota** /mas'kota/ f, mascot

**masculinidad** /maskulini'ðað/ *f*, masculinity
**masculino** /masku'lino/ *a* masculine; male; manly, vigorous
**mascullar** /masku'ʎar; masku'yar/ *vt Inf*. to chew; mutter, mumble
**masera** /ma'sera/ *f*, kneading bowl; cloth for covering dough
**masilla** /ma'siʎa; ma'siya/ *f*, mastic, putty
**masón** /ma'son/ **(-ona)** *n* Freemason
**masonería** /masone'ria/ *f*, freemasonry
**masónico** /ma'soniko/ *a* masonic
**masoquismo** /maso'kismo/ *m*, masochism
**mastelero** /maste'lero/ *m*, *Naut*. topmast
**masticación** /mastika'θion; mastika'sion/ *f*, mastication
**masticar** /masti'kar/ *vt* to masticate, eat; *Inf*. chew upon, consider
**masticatorio** /mastika'torio/ *a* masticatory
**mástil** /'mastil/ *m*, *Naut*. mast; upright, stanchion; pole (of a tent); stem, trunk; neck (of a guitar, etc.)
**mastín** /mas'tin/ *m*, mastiff
**mastodonte** /masto'ðonte/ *m*, mastodon
**mastoides** /mastoi'ðes/ *a* mastoid
**mastuerzo** /mas'tuerθo; mas'tuerso/ *m*, watercress; fool, blockhead
**masturbación** /masturβa'θion; masturβa'sion/ *f*, masturbation
**masturbarse** /mastur'βarse/ *vr* to masturbate
**mata** /'mata/ *f*, plant, shrub; stalk, sprig; grove, copse. **m. de pelo,** mat of hair
**matacandelas** /matakan'delas/ *m*, candle snuffer
**matachín** /mata'tʃin/ *m*, mummer; butcher; *Inf*. swashbuckler
**matadero** /mata'ðero/ *m*, slaughterhouse, abattoir
**matadura** /mata'ðura/ *f*, sore (on animals)
**matafuego** /mata'fuego/ *m*, fire extinguisher; fireman
**matalotaje** /matalo'tahe/ *m*, ship's supplies, stores; *Inf*. hodgepodge
**matamoros** /mata'moros/ *a* swashbuckling, swaggering
**matamoscas** /mata'moskas/ *m*, fly swatter
**matanza** /ma'tanθa; ma'tansa/ *f*, killing, massacre, slaughter; butchery (animals); *Inf*. persistence, determination
**matar** /ma'tar/ *vt* to kill; quench (thirst); put out (fire, light); slake (lime); tarnish (metal); bevel (corners, etc.); pester, importune; suppress; compel; *Art*. tone down; —*vr* kill oneself; be disappointed, grieve; overwork. **estar a m.,** to be at daggers drawn. **matarse por,** to try hard to; work hard for
**matasanos** /mata'sanos/ *m*, *Inf*. quack (doctor); bad doctor
**matasellos** /mata'seʎos; mata'seyos/ *m*, cancellation, postmark
**mate** /'mate/ *a* matte, unpolished, dull. *m*, checkmate (chess); maté, Paraguayan tea; gourd; vessel made from gourd, coconut, etc.
**maté** /ma'te/ *m*, maté, Paraguayan tea
**matemáticas** /mate'matikas/ *f pl*, mathematics. **m. prácticas,** applied mathematics. **m. teóricas,** pure mathematics
**matemático** /mate'matiko/ *a* mathematical; exact. *m*, mathematician
**materia** /ma'teria/ *f*, matter; theme, subject matter; subject (of study); matter, stuff, substance; pus, matter; question, subject; reason, occasion. **m. colorante,** dye. **materias plásticas,** plastics. **materias primas,** raw materials. **en m. de,** concerning; in the matter of
**material** /mate'rial/ *a* material; dull, stupid, limited. *m*, material; ingredient; plant, factory; equipment. **m. móvil ferroviario,** rolling stock (railroads)
**materialidad** /materiali'ðað/ *f*, materiality; external appearance (of things)
**materialismo** /materia'lismo/ *m*, materialism
**materialista** /materia'lista/ *a* materialistic. *mf* materialist
**materializar** /materiali'θar; materiali'sar/ *vt* to materialize; —*vr* materialize; grow materialistic, grow less spiritual

**maternidad** /materni'ðað/ *f*, maternity, motherhood
**materno** /ma'terno/ *a* maternal
**matiz** /ma'tiθ; ma'tis/ *m*, combination of colors; tone, hue; shade (of meaning, etc.)
**matizar** /mati'θar; mati'sar/ *vt* to combine, harmonize (colors); tint, shade; tinge (words, etc.)
**matojo** /ma'toho/ *m*, shrub, bush
**matorral** /mato'rral/ *m*, thicket, bush, undergrowth
**matraca** /ma'traka/ *f*, rattle; *Inf*. scolding, dressingdown; insistence, importunity
**matraquear** /matrake'ar/ *vi* to make a noise with a rattle; *Inf*. scold
**matriarcado** /matriar'kaðo/ *m*, matriarchy
**matricida** /matri'θiða; matri'siða/ *mf* matricide (person)
**matricidio** /matri'θiðio; matri'siðio/ *m*, matricide (crime)
**matrícula** /ma'trikula/ *f*, list, register; matriculation; registration number (of a car, etc.). **m. de buques,** maritime register. **m. de mar,** mariner's register; maritime register
**matriculación** /matrikula'θion; matrikula'sion/ *f*, matriculation; registration
**matricular** /matriku'lar/ *vt* to matriculate; enrol; *Naut*. register; —*vr* matriculate; enroll, register
**matrimonial** /matrimo'nial/ *a* matrimonial
**matrimonio** /matri'monio/ *m*, marriage, matrimony; married couple. **m. a yuras,** secret marriage. **m. de la mano izquierda** *or* **m. morganático,** morganatic marriage. **contraer m.,** to get married
**matritense** /matri'tense/ *a* and *mf* Madrilenian
**matriz** /ma'triθ; ma'tris/ *f*, uterus, womb; matrix, mold; *Mineral*. matrix; nut, female screw
**matrona** /ma'trona/ *f*, married woman; matron; midwife; female customs officer
**matusalén** /matusa'len/ *m*, Methuselah, very old man
**matute** /ma'tute/ *m*, smuggling; contraband; gambling den
**matutero** /matu'tero/ **(-ra)** *n* smuggler, contrabandist
**matutino** /matu'tino/ *a* matutinal, morning
**maula** /'maula/ *f*, trash; remnant; deception, fraud, trick. *mf Inf*. good-for-nothing; lazybones. *Inf*. **ser buena m.,** to be a trickster or a fraud
**maulería** /maule'ria/ *f*, remnant stall; trickery
**maullar** /mau'ʎar; mau'yar/ *vi* to meow, mew (cats)
**maullido** /mau'ʎiðo; mau'yiðo/ *m*, meow, cry of the cat
**Mauricio, Isla de** /mau'riθio, 'isla de; mau'risio, 'isla de/ Mauritius
**mauritano** /mauri'tano/ **(-na)** *a* and *n* Mauritian
**mausoleo** /mauso'leo/ *m*, mausoleum
**maxilar** /maksi'lar/ *a* maxillary. *m*, jaw
**máxima** /'maksima/ *f*, maxim, rule, precept, principle
**máxime** /'maksime/ *adv* principally, chiefly
**máximo** /'maksimo/ *a superl* **grande** greatest, maximum, top. *m*, maximum
**maya** /'maya/ *f*, common daisy; May queen
**mayal** /ma'yal/ *m*, flail
**mayo** /'mayo/ *m*, May; maypole; bouquet, wreath of flowers; *pl* festivities on eve of May Day
**mayólica** /ma'yolika/ *f*, majolica
**mayonesa** /mayo'nesa/ *f*, mayonnaise
**mayor** /ma'yor/ *a compar* **grande** bigger; greater; elder; main, principal; older; high (mass, etc.); *Mus*. major. *mf* major (of full age) —*a superl* **grande. el, la, lo mayor, los** ( **las**) **mayores,** the biggest, greatest; eldest; chief, principal. **por m.,** in short, briefly; *Com*. wholesale
**mayor** /ma'yor/ *m*, head, director; chief clerk; *Mil*. major; *pl* ancestors
**mayoral** /mayo'ral/ *m*, head shepherd; coachman, driver; foreman, overseer, supervisor, steward
**mayorazgo** /mayo'raθgo; mayo'rasgo/ *m*, *Law*. entail; entailed estate; heir (to an entail); eldest son; right of primogeniture
**mayordoma** /mayor'ðoma/ *f*, steward's wife; housekeeper; stewardess
**mayordomo** /mayor'ðomo/ *m*, steward, superintendent; butler; major-domo, royal chief steward
**mayoría** /mayo'ria/ *f*, majority

**mayormente** /mayor'mente/ *adv* chiefly; especially
**mayúscula** /ma'yuskula/ *f*, capital letter, upper-case letter
**mayúsculo** /ma'yuskulo/ *a* large; capital (letters). **letra mayúscula,** capital letter, upper-case letter
**maza** /'maθa; 'masa/ *f*, mallet; club; bludgeon; mace; bass drum stick; pile driver; bone, stick, etc., tied to dog's tail in carnival; *Inf.* pedant, bore; important person, authority. **m. de polo,** polo mallet
**mazacote** /maθa'kote; masa'kote/ *m*, concrete; roughhewn work of art; *Inf.* stodgy overcooked dish; bore, tedious person
**mazamorra** /maθa'morra; masa'morra/ *f*, dish made of cornmeal; biscuit crumbs; broken fragments, remains
**mazapán** /maθa'pan; masa'pan/ *m*, marzipan
**mazmorra** /maθ'morra; mas'morra/ *f*, dungeon
**mazo** /'maθo; 'maso/ *m*, mallet; bundle, bunch; importunate person; clapper (of a bell)
**mazonería** /maθone'ria; masone'ria/ *f*, stonemasonry
**mazonero** /maθo'nero; maso'nero/ *m*, stonemason
**mazorca** /ma'θorka; ma'sorka/ *f*, spindleful; spike; ear (of corn); cocoa berry; camarilla, group
**mazurca** /ma'θurka; ma'surka/ *f*, mazurka
**me** /me/ *pers pron acc* or *dat 1st sing mf* me; to me
**meandro** /me'andro/ *m*, meandering, twisting, winding; wandering
**meato** /me'ato/ *m*, meatus
**Meca, la** /'meka, la/ Mecca
**mecánica** /me'kanika/ *f*, mechanics; mechanism, machinery; *Inf.* worthless thing; mean action
**mecánico** /me'kaniko/ *a* mechanical; power-operated; base, ill-bred. *m*, engineer; mechanic
**mecanismo** /meka'nismo/ *m*, mechanism; works, machinery
**mecanizar** /mekani'θar; mekani'sar/ *vt* to mechanize
**mecanografía** /mekanogra'fia/ *f*, typewriting
**mecanografiar** /mekanografi'ar/ *vt* to typewrite, type
**mecanográfico** /mekano'grafiko/ *a* typewriting, typing; typewritten, typed
**mecanografista** /mekanogra'fista/ *mf* **mecanógrafo** **(-fa)** *n* typist
**mecedor** /meθe'ðor; mese'ðor/ *a* rocking, swaying. *m*, swing
**mecedora** /meθe'ðora; mese'ðora/ *f*, rocking chair
**mecenas** /me'θenas; me'senas/ *m*, Maecenas, patron
**mecer** /me'θer; me'ser/ *vt* to stir, mix; shake; rock; swing
**mecha** /'metʃa/ *f*, wick; bit, drill; fuse (of explosives); match (for cannon, etc.); fat bacon (for basting); lock of hair; skein, twist
**mechar** /me'tʃar/ *vt Cul.* to baste, lard
**mechero** /me'tʃero/ *m*, gas burner; pocket lighter; socket of a candlestick
**mechón** /me'tʃon/ *m*, tuft, skein, bundle; lock of hair; wisp
**medalla** /me'ðaʎa; me'ðaya/ *f*, medal; medallion; plaque, round panel; *Inf.* piece of eight (coin)
**medallón** /meða'ʎon; me'ðayon/ *m*, large medal; medallion; locket
**médano** /'meðano/ *m*, sand dune
**media** /'meðia/ *f*, stocking
**mediación** /meðia'θion; meðia'sion/ *f*, mediation, arbitration; intercession
**mediado** /me'ðiaðo/ *a* half-full. **a mediados** ( **del mes,** etc.), toward the middle (of the month, etc.)
**mediador** /meðia'ðor/ **(-ra)** *n* mediator, arbitrator; intercessor
**medianamente** /meðiana'mente/ *adv* moderately; passably, fairly well
**medianero** /meðia'nero/ **(-ra)** *a* middle; intervening, intermediate; mediatory —*n* mediator. *m*, owner of a semidetached house or of one in a row
**medianía** /meðia'nia/ *f*, average; medium, mediocrity; moderate wealth or means
**mediano** /me'ðiano/ *a* medium, average; moderate; *Inf.* middling, passable, fair
**medianoche** /meðia'notʃe/ *f*, midnight
**mediante** /me'ðiante/ *a* mediatory —*adv* by means of, by, through

**mediar** /me'ðiar/ *vi* to reach the middle; get halfway; elapse half a given time; intercede, mediate; arbitrate; be in between or in the middle; intervene, take part
**medicación** /meðika'θion; meðika'sion/ *f*, medication
**medicamento** /meðika'mento/ *m*, medicament, medicine, remedy
**medicar** /meði'kar/ *vt* to medicate
**medicastro** /meði'kastro/ *m*, unskilled physician; quack, charlatan
**medicina** /meði'θina; meði'sina/ *f*, medicine; medicament
**medicinar** /meðiθi'nar; meðisi'nar/ *vt* to attend; treat (patients)
**medición** /meði'θion; meði'sion/ *f*, measuring; measurements; survey (land); scansion
**médico** /'meðiko/ **(-ca)** *a* medical —*n* doctor of medicine. **m. de cabecera,** family doctor. **m. general,** general practitioner
**medida** /me'ðiða/ *f*, measurement; measuring stick; measure, precaution (gen. with *tomar, adoptar,* etc.); gauge; judgment, wisdom; meter; standard. **a m. que,** while, at the same time as. **tomar las medidas (a),** *Fig.* to take a person's measure, sum him up. **to mar sus medidas,** to take his (their) measurements; take the necessary measures. **un traje hecho a m.,** suit made to measure
**medieval** /meðie'βal/ *a* medieval
**medio** /'meðio/ *a* half; middle; intermediate; halfway. *m*, half; middle; *Art.* medium; spiritualist medium; proceeding, measure, precaution; environment, medium; middle way, mean; *Sports.* halfback. **m. galope,** canter. **m. tiempo,** *Sports.* halftime. **a medias,** by halves; half, partly. **de por m.,** by halves; in between; in the way. **estar de por m.,** to be in the way; take part in. *Inf.* **quitar de en m.,** to get rid of. *Inf.* **quitarse de en m.,** to go away, remove oneself
**mediocre** /me'ðiokre/ *a* mediocre
**mediocridad** /meðiokri'ðað/ *f*, mediocrity; insignificance
**mediodía** /meðio'ðia/ *m*, noon, meridian; south
**medioeval** /meðioe'βal/ *a* medieval
**mediopelo** /meðio'pelo/ *m*, lower middle class
**mediquillo** /meði'kiʎo; meði'kiyo/ *m*, *Inf.* quack; medicine man (in the Philippines)
**medir** /me'ðir/ *vt irr* to measure; (metrics) scan; survey (land); compare; —*vr* measure one's words; act with restraint. See **pedir**
**meditabundo** /meðita'βundo/ *a* pensive, meditative, thoughtful
**meditación** /meðita'θion; meðita'sion/ *f*, meditation; consideration, reflection
**meditador** /meðita'ðor/ *a* meditative, thoughtful
**meditar** /meði'tar/ *vt* to meditate, consider, muse
**meditativo** /meðita'tiβo/ *a* meditative
**mediterráneo** /meðite'rraneo/ *a* mediterranean; inland, landlocked
**médium** /'meðium/ *m*, *Spirit.* medium
**medra** /'meðra/ *f*, progress; improvement, betterment; growth; prosperity
**medrar** /me'ðrar/ *vi* to flourish, grow; become prosperous or improve one's position
**medro** /'meðro/ *m*, improvement, progress. See **medra**
**medroso** /me'ðroso/ *a* timid, frightened; frightful, horrible
**médula** /'meðula/ *f*, marrow; *Bot.* pith; *Fig.* essence, core
**medusa** /me'ðusa/ *f*, jellyfish
**mefistofélico** /mefisto'feliko/ *a* Mephistophelian
**mefítico** /me'fitiko/ *a* noxious, mephitic, poisonous
**megáfono** /me'gafono/ *m*, megaphone
**megalómano** /mega'lomano/ **(-na)** *n* megalomaniac
**mejicano** /mehi'kano/ **(-na)** *a* and *n* Mexican
**Méjico** /'mehiko/ Mexico
**mejilla** /me'hiʎa; me'hiya/ *f*, *Anat.* cheek
**mejillón** /mehi'ʎon; mehi'yon/ *m*, sea mussel
**mejor** /me'hor/ *a compar* **bueno** better —*adv* better; rather; sooner; preferably —*a superl* **bueno. el, la, lo mejor; los, las mejores,** the best; most preferable. **m. que m.,** better and better. *Inf.* **a lo m.,** probably, in all probability. **tanto m.,** so much the better

**mejora** /me'hora/ f, improvement; bettering; progress; higher bid (at auctions)

**mejorable** /meho'raβle/ a improvable

**mejoramiento** /mehora'miento/ m, betterment, improvement

**mejorar** /meho'rar/ vt to improve; better; outbid; —vi grow better (in health); improve (weather); make progress; rally (of markets). **Mejorando lo presente,** Present company excepted

**mejoría** /meho'ria/ f, improvement, progress; betterment; superiority; advantage, profit

**mejunje** /me'hunhe/ m, Inf. brew, potion, cure-all, stuff

**melado** /me'laðo/ a honey-colored. m, cane syrup

**melancolía** /melanko'lia/ f, melancholia; sadness, depression, melancholy

**melancólico** /melan'koliko/ a melancholy, sad; depressing

**melaza** /me'laθa; me'lasa/ f, molasses

**melena** /me'lena/ f, long side whiskers; loose, flowing hair (in women); overlong hair (in men); lion's mane. Inf. **andar a la m.,** to start a fight or quarrel. Inf. **traer a la m.,** to drag by the hair, force

**melifluidad** /meliflui'ðað/ f, mellifluence, sweetness

**melifluo** /me'lifluo/ a mellifluous, sweet-voiced; honeyed

**melindre** /me'lindre/ m, honey fritter; affectation, scruple, fastidiousness; narrow ribbon

**melindroso** /melin'droso/ a overfastidious, affected, prudish

**mella** /'meʎa; 'meya/ f, nick, notch; dent; gap; harm, damage (to reputation, etc.). **hacer m.,** Fig. to make an impression (on the mind); Mil. breach, drive a wedge

**mellar** /me'ʎar; me'yar/ vt to nick, notch; dent; damage

**mellizo** /me'ʎiθo; me'yiso/ **(-za)** a and n twin

**melocotón** /meloko'ton/ m, peach; peach tree

**melocotonero** /melokoto'nero/ m, peach tree

**melodía** /melo'ðia/ f, melody, tune; melodiousness

**melódico** /me'loðiko/ a melodic, melodious

**melodioso** /melo'ðioso/ a melodious, tuneful, sweet-sounding

**melodrama** /melo'ðrama/ m, melodrama

**melodramático** /meloðra'matiko/ a melodramatic

**melón** /me'lon/ m, melon

**melosidad** /melosi'ðað/ f, sweetness

**meloso** /me'loso/ a honeyed; sweet; gentle; mellifluous

**membrana** /mem'brana/ f, membrane

**membrete** /mem'brete/ m, note, memorandum; note or card of invitation; superscription, heading; address (of person)

**membrillo** /mem'briʎo; mem'briyo/ m, quince tree; quince; quince jelly

**membrudo** /mem'bruðo/ a brawny, strong, muscular

**memo** /'memo/ a silly, stupid

**memorable** /memo'raβle/ a memorable

**memorándum** /memo'randum/ m, notebook, jotter; memorandum

**memorar** /memo'rar/ **(se)** vt and vr to remember, recall

**memoria** /me'moria/ f, memory; remembrance, recollection; monument; memorial; report; essay, article; codicil; memorandum; record, chronicle; pl regards, compliments, greetings; memoirs; memoranda. Inf. **m. de grillo,** poor memory. **de m.,** by heart. **flaco de m.,** forgetful. **hacer m.,** to remember

**memorial** /memo'rial/ m, notebook; memorial, petition

**memorialista** /memoria'lista/ mf secretary, amanuensis

**memorioso** /memo'rioso/ a mindful, unforgetful

**mena** /'mena/ f, Mineral. ore

**menaje** /me'nahe/ m, household or school equipment or furniture

**mención** /men'θion; men'sion/ f, mention. **m. honorífica,** honorable mention. **hacer m. de,** to mention

**mencionar** /menθio'nar; mensio'nar/ vt to mention

**mendacidad** /mendaθi'ðað; mendasi'ðað/ f, mendacity, untruthfulness

**mendaz** /men'daθ; men'das/ a mendacious, untruthful

**mendelismo** /mende'lismo/ m, Mendelism

**mendicante** /mendi'kante/ a begging; Eccl. mendicant. mf beggar

**mendicidad** /mendiθi'ðað; mendisiða'ð/ f, mendicancy, begging

**mendigar** /mendi'gar/ vt to beg for alms; entreat, supplicate

**mendigo** /men'digo/ **(-ga)** n beggar

**mendoso** /men'doso/ a mendacious, untruthful; mistaken

**mendrugo** /men'drugo/ m, crust of bread

**menear** /mene'ar/ vt to sway, move; wag; shake; manage, control, direct; —vr Inf. get a move on; sway, move; wriggle

**meneo** /me'neo/ m, swaying movement; wagging; shaking; wriggling; management, direction; Aer. bump; Inf. spanking

**menester** /menes'ter/ m, lack, shortage; necessity; occupation, employment; pl physical necessities; Inf. tools, implements, equipment. **haber m.,** to need, require. **ser m.,** to be necessary or requisite

**menesteroso** /meneste'roso/ a indigent, poverty-stricken, needy

**menestra** /me'nestra/ f, vegetable soup; dried vegetable (gen. pl)

**menestral** /menes'tral/ **(-la)** n artisan; worker; mechanic

**mengano** /meŋ'gano/ **(-na)** n so-and-so (used instead of the name of the person)

**mengua** /'meŋgua/ f, decrease; lack, shortage; waning (of the moon, etc.); dishonor, disgrace; poverty

**menguado** /meŋ'guaðo/ **(-da)** a timid, cowardly; silly, stupid; mean, avaricious —n coward; fool; skinflint. m, narrowing stitch when knitting socks

**menguante** /meŋ'guante/ a ebb; waning; decreasing. f, ebb tide; decadence, decline. **m. de la luna,** waning of the moon

**menguar** /meŋ'guar/ vi to decrease; decline, decay; wane; ebb; narrow (socks); —vt diminish; disgrace, discredit

**menina** /me'nina/ f, child attendant (on Spanish royalty)

**menino** /me'nino/ m, Spanish royal page; little dandy

**menjurje** /men'hurhe/ m, See **mejunje**

**menopausia** /meno'pausia/ f, menopause

**menor** /me'nor/ a compar less, smaller; younger, minor; Mus. minor. m, minor. f, (logic) minor —a superl **el, la, lo m.; los, las menores,** the least; smallest; youngest. **m. de edad,** minor (in age). **por m.,** at retail; in detail

**Menorca** /me'norka/ Minorca

**menoría** /meno'ria/ f, subordination, dependence; inferiority; minority (underage); childhood, youth

**menos** /'menos/ adv less; minus; least; except. **m. de** or **m. que,** less than. **al por, lo m.,** at least. **a m. que,** unless. **De m. nos hizo Dios,** Never say die, Nothing is impossible. **poco más o m.,** more or less, about

**menoscabar** /menoska'βar/ vt to lessen, diminish, decrease; deteriorate, damage; disgrace, discredit

**menoscabo** /menos'kaβo/ m, decrease, diminishment; harm, damage, loss

**menospreciable** /menospre'θiaβle; menospre'siaβle/ a despicable, contemptible

**menospreciador** /menospreθia'ðor; menospresia'ðor/ **(-ra)** a scornful —n scorner, despiser

**menospreciar** /menospre'θiar; menospre'siar/ vt to despise, scorn; underestimate, have a poor opinion of

**menospreciativo** /menospreθia'tiβo; menospresia'tiβo/ a scornful, slighting, derisive

**menosprecio** /menos'preθio; menos'presio/ m, scorn, derision; underestimation

**mensaje** /men'sahe/ m, message; official communication

**mensajería** /mensahe'ria/ f, carrier service; steamship line

**mensajero** /mensa'hero/ **(-ra)** n messenger; errand boy

**menstruación** /menstrua'θion; menstrua'sion/ *f*, menstruation
**menstruar** /menstru'ar/ *vi* to menstruate
**mensual** /men'sual/ *a* monthly
**mensualidad** /mensuali'ðað/ *f*, monthly salary, monthly payment
**mensurable** /mensu'raβle/ *a* measurable
**mensurar** /mensu'rar/ *vt* to measure
**menta** /'menta/ *f*, menthe, mint; peppermint
**mentado** /men'taðo/ *a* celebrated, distinguished, famous
**mental** /men'tal/ *a* mental
**mentalidad** /mentali'ðað/ *f*, mentality
**mentalmente** /mental'mente/ *adv* mentally
**mentar** /men'tar/ *vt irr* to mention. See **sentar**
**mente** /'mente/ *f*, mind; intelligence, understanding; will, intention
**mentecatería** /mentekate'ria/ *f*, folly, stupidity
**mentecato** /mente'kato/ (**-ta**) *a* foolish, silly; feebleminded, simple —*n* fool, idiot
**mentir** /men'tir/ *vi irr* to lie, be untruthful; deceive, mislead; falsify; *Poet.* belie; disagree, be incompatible; —*vt* break a promise, disappoint. **m. como un bellaco,** to lie like a trooper See **sentir**
**mentira** /men'tira/ *f*, lie, falsehood; error (in writing); *Inf.* white spot (on a fingernail); cracking (of fingerjoints). **m. oficiosa,** white lie. **Parece m.,** It seems incredible
**mentiroso** /menti'roso/ *a* lying, false; full of errors (literary works); deceptive
**mentís** /men'tis/ *m*, giving the lie (literally, you lie); proof, demonstration (of error)
**mentol** /'mentol/ *m*, menthol
**mentón** /men'ton/ *m*, chin
**mentonera** /mento'nera/ *f*, chin rest
**menú** /me'nu/ *m*, menu
**menudamente** /menuða'mente/ *adv* minutely; in detail, circumstantially
**menudear** /menuðe'ar/ *vt* to do frequently; do repeatedly; —*vi* happen frequently; describe in detail; *Com.* sell by retail
**menudencia** /menu'ðenθia; menu'ðensia/ *f*, minuteness, smallness; exactness, care, accuracy; trifle, worthless object; small matter; *pl* offal; pork sausages
**menudeo** /menu'ðeo/ *m*, repetition; description in detail; *Com.* retail. **al m.,** at retail
**menudillos** /menu'ðiʎos; menu'ðiyos/ *m pl*, giblets; offal
**menudo** /menu'ðo/ *a* minute, tiny; despicable; thin; small; vulgar; meticulous, exact; small (money). *m*, small coal; *m pl*, offal, entrails; small change (money). **a m.,** often, frequently. **por m.,** in detail, carefully; *Com.* in small lots
**meñique** /me'ɲike/ *a Inf.* very small. *m*, little finger (in full, **dedo m.**)
**meollo** /me'oʎo; me'oyo/ *m*, brain; *Anat.* marrow; *Fig.* essence, core, substance; understanding; *Inf.* **no tener m.** ( una cosa), to be worthless, unsubstantial (things)
**mequetrefe** /meke'trefe/ *m*, *Inf.* coxcomb, whippersnapper
**meramente** /mera'mente/ *adv* solely, simply, merely
**mercachifle** /merkat'ʃifle/ *m*, peddler; small merchant
**mercadear** /merkaðe'ar/ *vi* to trade, traffic
**mercadeo** /merka'ðeo/ *m*, marketing (study of markets)
**mercader** /merka'ðer/ *m*, dealer, merchant, trader. **m. de grueso,** wholesaler
**mercadería** /merkaðe'ria/ *f*, See **mercancía**
**mercado** /mer'kaðo/ *m*, market; marketplace
**mercancía** /merkan'θia; merkan'sia/ *f*, goods, merchandise; commerce, trade, traffic
**mercante** /mer'kante/ *a* trading; commercial. *m*, merchant, dealer, trader
**mercantil** /merkan'til/ *a* mercantile, commercial
**mercantilismo** /merkanti'lismo/ *m*, mercantilism
**merced** /mer'θeð; mer'seð/ *f*, salary, remuneration; favor, benefit, kindness; will, desire, pleasure; mercy, grace; courtesy title given to untitled person (e.g. vu-

estra *m.*, your honor. Has now become *usted* and is universally used). **m. a,** thanks to. **estar uno a m. de,** to live at someone else's expense, be dependent on
**mercenario** /merθe'nario; merse'nario/ (**-ia**) *n Eccl.* member of the Order of la Merced. *m*, *Mil.* mercenary; day laborer —*a* mercenary
**mercería** /merθe'ria; merse'ria/ *f*, haberdashery, mercery
**mercerizar** /merθeri'θar; merseri'sar/ *vt* to mercerize
**mercero** /mer'θero; mer'sero/ *m*, haberdasher, mercer
**mercurio** /mer'kurio/ *m*, mercury, quicksilver; *Astron.* Mercury
**merecedor** /mereθe'ðor; merese'ðor/ *a* deserving, worthy
**merecer** /mere'θer; mere'ser/ *vt irr* to deserve, be worthy of; attain, achieve; be worth; —*vi* deserve, be deserving. **m. bien de,** to deserve well of; have a claim on the gratitude of. See **conocer**
**merecido** /mere'θiðo; mere'siðo/ *m*, due reward
**merecimiento** /mereθi'miento; meresi'miento/ *m*, desert; merit
**merendar** /meren'dar/ *vi irr* to have lunch; pry into another's affairs; —*vt* have (a certain food) for lunch. *Inf.* **merendarse** ( una cosa), to obtain (a thing), have it in one's pocket. See **recomendar**
**merendero** /meren'dero/ *m*, lunchroom; tearoom
**merengue** /me'reŋgue/ *m*, *Cul.* meringue
**meretriz** /mere'triθ; mere'tris/ *f*, prostitute
**meridiana** /meri'ðiana/ *f*, daybed, chaise longue; siesta
**meridiano** /meri'ðiano/ *a* meridian. *m*, meridian. **a la meridiana,** at noon
**meridional** /meriðio'nal/ *a* meridional, southern
**merienda** /me'rienda/ *f*, tea, snack; lunch; *Inf.* hunchback. *Inf.* **juntar meriendas,** to join forces, combine interests
**merino** /me'rino/ *a* merino. *m*, merino wool; shepherd of merino sheep
**meritísimo** /meri'tisimo/ *a superl* most worthy, most deserving
**mérito** /'merito/ *m*, merit; desert; worth, excellence. **de m.,** excellent, notable. **hacer m. de,** to mention
**meritorio** /meri'torio/ *a* meritorious. *m*, unpaid worker, learner
**merluza** /mer'luθa; mer'lusa/ *f*, hake; *Inf.* drinking bout. *Inf.* **pescar una m.,** to get drunk
**merma** /'merma/ *f*, decrease, drop; loss, waste, reduction; leakage
**mermar** /mer'mar/ *vi* to diminish, waste away, decrease; evaporate; leak; —*vt* filch, pilfer; reduce, decrease
**mermelada** /merme'laða/ *f*, conserve, preserve; jam; marmalade
**mero** /'mero/ *a* mere; simple; plain
**merodeador** /meroðea'ðor/ *a* marauding. *m*, marauder, raider
**merodear** /meroðe'ar/ *vi* to maraud, raid
**merodeo** /mero'ðeo/ *m*, raiding, marauding
**mes** /'mes/ *m*, month; menses, menstruation
**mesa** /'mesa/ *f*, table; board, directorate; meseta, tableland; staircase landing; flat (of a sword, etc.); game of billiards. **m. de batalla,** post office sorting table. **m. de caballete,** trestle table. **m. de noche,** bedside table. **m. de tijeras,** folding table. **m. giratoria,** turntable. **alzar** ( *or* **levantar**) **la m.,** to clear the table. **cubrir** (*or* **poner**) **la m.,** to set the table
**mesada** /me'saða/ *f*, monthly wages, monthly payment
**mesadura** /mesa'ðura/ *f*, tearing of the hair or beard
**mesarse** /me'sarse/ *vr* to tear one's hair or beard
**mesenterio** /mesen'terio/ *m*, mesentery
**meseta** /me'seta/ *f*, staircase landing; plateau, tableland
**mesiánico** /me'sianiko/ *a* Messianic
**Mesías** /me'sias/ *m*, Messiah
**mesilla** /me'siʎa; me'siya/ *f*, small table; laughing admonition; landing (of a stair)
**mesmerismo** /mesme'rismo/ *m*, mesmerism
**mesnada** /mes'naða/ *f*, association, company, society

**mesocracia** /meso'kraθia; meso'krasia/ *f*, mesocracy; middle class, bourgeoisie

**mesón** /me'son/ *m*, inn, tavern

**mesonero** /meso'nero/ **(-ra)** *n* innkeeper

**mesta** /'mesta/ *f*, ancient order of sheep farmers; *pl* confluence, meeting (of rivers)

**mester** /'mester/ *m*, craft, occupation. **m. de clerecía,** learned poetic meter of the Spanish Middle Ages. **m. de juglaría,** popular poetry and troubadour songs

**mestizo** /mes'tiθo; mes'tiso/ *a* half-breed; hybrid; cross-breed

**mesura** /me'sura/ *f*, sedateness; dignity; courtesy; moderation

**mesurado** /mesu'raðo/ *a* sedate; dignified; moderate, restrained, temperate

**meta** /'meta/ *f*, goalpost *Fig.* aim, end; goal; goalkeeper

**metabolismo** /metaβo'lismo/ *m*, metabolism

**metafísica** /meta'fisika/ *f*, metaphysics

**metafísico** /meta'fisiko/ *a* metaphysical. *m*, metaphysician

**metáfora** /me'tafora/ *f*, metaphor

**metafórico** /meta'foriko/ *a* metaphorical

**metal** /me'tal/ *m*, metal; brass; timbre of the voice; state, condition; quality, substance; *Herald.* gold or silver; *Mus.* brass (instruments)

**metalario** /meta'lario/ *m*, metalworker

**metálico** /me'taliko/ *a* metallic. *m*, metalworker; coin, specie; bullion

**metalistería** /metaliste'ria/ *f*, metalwork

**metalizar** /metali'θar; metali'sar/ *vt* to metallize, make metallic; —*vr* become metallized; grow greedy for money

**metalurgia** /metalur'hia/ *f*, metallurgy

**metalúrgico** /meta'lurhiko/ *a* metallurgical. *m*, metallurgist

**metamorfosis** /metamor'fosis/ *f*, metamorphosis

**metano** /me'tano/ *m*, methane

**metatarso** /meta'tarso/ *m*, metatarsus

**metátesis** /me'tatesis/ *f*, metathesis

**metedor** /mete'ðor/ **(-ra)** *n* placer, inserter; smuggler, contrabandist

**metempsicosis** /metempsi'kosis/ *f*, metempsychosis

**metemuertos** /mete'muertos/ *Inf.* meddler, Nosy Parker

**meteórico** /mete'oriko/ *a* meteoric

**meteorito** /meteo'rito/ *m*, meteorite

**meteoro** /mete'oro/ *m*, meteor

**meteorología** /meteorolo'hia/ *f*, meteorology

**meteorológico** /meteoro'lohiko/ *a* meteorological

**meteorologista** /meteorolo'hista/ *mf* meteorologist; weather forecaster

**meter** /me'ter/ *vt* to place; put; introduce, insert; stake (gambling); smuggle; cause, occasion; place close together; persuade to take part in; *Sew.* take in fullness; deceive, humbug; cram in, pack tightly; *Naut.* take in sail; —*vr* interfere, butt in; meddle (with); take up, follow (occupations); be overfamiliar; disembogue, empty itself (rivers, etc.); attack with the sword; (*with prep a*) follow (occupations); become, turn (e.g. *meterse a predicar,* to turn preacher); (*with con*) pick a quarrel with. **meterse en precisiones,** to go into details. *Inf.* **meterse en todo,** to be very meddlesome

**metesillas y sacamuertos** /mete'siʎas i saka'muertos; mete'siyas i saka'muertos/ *m*, scene shifter, stagehand

**meticulosidad** /metikulosi'ðað/ *f*, meticulosity; timorousness

**meticuloso** /metiku'loso/ *a* meticulous, fussy; timid, nervous

**metido** /me'tiðo/ *a* tight; crowded; crabbed (of handwriting). *m*, *Sew.* material for letting out (seams). **m. en años,** quite old (person)

**metílico** /me'tiliko/ *a* methylic

**metimiento** /meti'miento/ *m*, insertion, introduction; influence, sway

**metódico** /me'toðiko/ *a* methodical

**metodismo** /meto'ðismo/ *m*, Methodism

**metodista** /meto'ðista/ *a* methodistic. *mf* Methodist

**método** /'metoðo/ *m*, method

**metodología** /metoðolo'hia/ *f*, methodology

**metralla** /me'traʎa; me'traya/ *f*, *Mil.* grapeshot, shrapnel

**métrica** /'metrika/ *f*, metrics

**métrico** /'metriko/ *a* metric; metrical

**metro** /'metro/ *m*, (verse) meter; meter (measurement); subway, underground railway

**metrónomo** /me'tronomo/ *m*, metronome

**metrópoli** /me'tropoli/ *f*, metropolis, capital; see of a metropolitan bishop; mother country

**metropolitano** /metropoli'tano/ *a* metropolitan. *m*, metropolitan bishop

**México** /'mehiko/ Mexico

**mezcla** /'meθkla; 'meskla/ *f*, mixture; blend, combination; mixed cloth, tweed; mortar

**mezclar** /meθ'klar; mes'klar/ *vt* to mix, blend, combine; —*vr* mix, mingle; take part; interfere, meddle; intermarry

**mezcolanza** /meθko'lanθa; mesko'lansa/ *f*, *Inf.* hodgepodge

**mezquindad** /meθkin'dað; meskin'dað/ *f*, poverty; indigence; miserliness; paltriness; meanness, poorness

**mezquino** /meθ'kino; mes'kino/ *a* needy, impoverished; miserly, stingy; small, diminutive; unhappy; mean, paltry

**mezquita** /meθ'kita; mes'kita/ *f*, mosque

**mi** /'mi/ *poss pron* my. *m*, *Mus.* mi, E

**mí** /'mi/ *pers pron acc gen dat 1st pers sing* me. Used only after prepositions (e.g. *Lo hicieron por mí,* They did it for me)

**miaja** /'miaha/ *f*, See **migaja**

**miasma** /'miasma/ *m*, miasma

**miasmático** /mias'matiko/ *a* miasmatic, malarious

**miau** /'miau/ *m*, meow

**mica** /'mika/ *f*, *Mineral.* mica; coquette, flirt

**micción** /mik'θion; mik'sion/ *f*, micturition

**micho** /'mitʃo/ **(-cha)** *n* *Inf.* puss, pussycat

**micología** /mikolo'hia/ *f*, mycology

**micra** /'mikra/ *f*, micron, thousandth part of a millimeter

**microbiano** /mikro'βiano/ *a* microbial, microbic

**microbio** /mi'kroβio/ *m*, microbe

**microbiología** /mikroβiolo'hia/ *f*, microbiology

**microbrigada** /mikroβri'gaða/ *f*, team of volunteer workers (Castroist Cuba)

**microcéfalo** /mikro'θefalo; mikro'sefalo/ *a* microcephalous

**microcosmo** /mikro'kosmo/ *m*, microcosm

**micrófono** /mi'krofono/ *m*, microphone

**microonda** /mikro'onda/ *f*, microwave

**microscópico** /mikros'kopiko/ *a* microscopic

**microscopio** /mikros'kopio/ *m*, microscope

**miedo** /'mieðo/ *m*, fear, apprehension, terror. **m. al público,** stagefright. **tener m.,** to be afraid

**miedoso** /mie'ðoso/ *a* *Inf.* fearful, nervous

**miel** /miel/ *f*, honey. **m. de caña,** sugarcane syrup. *Inf.* **quedarse a media m.,** to see one's pleasure snatched away. *Inf.* **ser de mieles,** to be most pleasant or agreeable

**mielitis** /mie'litis/ *f*, myelitis

**miembro** /mi'embro/ *m*, *Anat.* limb; penis; member, associate; part, portion, section; *Math.* member

**miente** /'miente/ *f*, thought, imagination, mind. **parar** *or* **poner mientes en,** to consider, think about. **venírsele a las mientes,** to occur to one's mind

**mientras** /'mientras/ *adv* while. **m. más...,** the more.... **m. que,** while (e.g. *m. que esperaba en el jardín,* while he was waiting in the garden). **m. tanto,** in the meanwhile

**miércoles** /'mierkoles/ *m*, Wednesday. **m. de ceniza,** Ash Wednesday

**mierda** /'mierða/ *f*, (*vulgar*) shit; *Inf.* filth

**mies** /'mies/ *f*, cereal plant, grain; harvest time; *pl* grain fields

**miga** /'miga/ *f*, breadcrumb; crumb; *Inf.* essence, core; substance; bit, scrap; *pl* fried breadcrumbs. *Inf.* **hacer buenas (** *or* **malas) migas,** to get on well (*or* badly) together

**migaja** /mi'gaha/ *f*, breadcrumb; bit, scrap; trifle,

mere nothing; *pl* crumbs (from the table); remains, remnants

**migajón** /miga'hon/ *m*, crumb (of a loaf): *Fig. Inf.* essence, substance, core

**migración** /migra'θion; migra'sion/ *f*, migration; emigration

**migraña** /mi'graɲa/ *f*, migraine

**migratorio** /migra'torio/ *a* migratory

**mijo** /'miho/ *m*, millet; maize

**mil** /mil/ *a* thousand; thousandth; many, large number. *m*, thousand; thousandth. *Inf.* **Son las m. y quinientas,** It's extremely late (of the hour)

**miladi** /mi'laði/ *f*, my lady

**milagrero** /mila'grero/ *a Inf.* miraculous

**milagro** /mi'lagro/ *m*, miracle; marvel, wonder. **¡M.!** Amazing! Just fancy!

**milagroso** /mila'groso/ *a* miraculous; marvelous, wonderful

**milanés** /mila'nes/ **(-esa)** *a* and *n* Milanese

**milano** /mi'lano/ *m*, *Ornith.* kite

**mildeu** /'mildeu/ *m*, mildew

**milenario** /mile'nario/ *a* millenary; millennial. *m*, millenary; millennium

**milésimo** /mi'lesimo/ *a* thousandth

**milicia** /mi'liθia; mi'lisia/ *f*, militia; military; art of war; military profession

**miliciano** /mili'θiano; mili'siano/ *a* military. *m*, militiaman

**miligramo** /mili'gramo/ *m*, milligram

**mililitro** /mili'litro/ *m*, milliliter

**milímetro** /mi'limetro/ *m*, millimeter

**militante** /mili'tante/ *a* militant

**militar** /mili'tar/ *a* military. *m*, soldier —*vi* to fight in the army; struggle (for a cause); *Fig.* militate (e.g. *Las circunstancias militan en favor de* (or *contra*) **sus ideas,** Circumstances militate against his ideas)

**militarismo** /milita'rismo/ *m*, militarism

**militarista** /milita'rista/ *a* militaristic. *mf* militarist

**militarizar** /militari'θar; militari'sar/ *vt* to militarize; make war-like

**milla** /'miʎa; 'miya/ *f*, mile

**millar** /mi'ʎar; mi'yar/ *m*, thousand; vast number (gen. *pl*)

**millón** /mi'ʎon; mi'yon/ *m*, million

**millonario** /miʎo'nario; miyo'nario/ **(-ia)** *a* and *n* millionaire

**millonésimo** /miʎo'nesimo; miyo'nesimo/ *a* millionth

**milmillonésimo** /milmiʎo'nesimo; milmiyo'nesimo/ *a* billionth

**milord** /mi'lorð/ *m*, my lord *pl* **milores,** my lords

**mimar** /mi'mar/ *vt* to spoil, overindulge; caress, fondle

**mimbre** /'mimbre/ *mf* osier; willow tree. *m*, wicker

**mimbrear** /mimbre'ar/ *vi* to sway, bend

**mimbrera** /mim'brera/ *f*, osier; osier bed; willow

**mímica** /'mimika/ *f*, mimicry; mime

**mímico** /'mimiko/ *a* mimic

**mimo** /'mimo/ *m*, mimic, buffoon; mime; caress, expression of affection, tenderness; overindulgence

**mimoso** /mi'moso/ *a* affectionate, demonstrative

**mina** /'mina/ *f*, mine; excavation, mining; underground passage; lead (in a pencil); (*Mil. Nav.*) mine; *Fig.* gold mine. *Mil.* **m. terrestre,** landmine

**minador** /mina'ðor/ *m*, excavator; *Nav.* minelayer; *Mil.* sapper

**minar** /mi'nar/ *vt* to excavate, mine; *Fig.* undermine; (*Mil. Nav.*) mine; work hard for

**minarete** /mina'rete/ *m*, minaret

**mineraje** /mine'rahe/ *m*, exploitation of a mine, mining; mineral products

**mineral** /mine'ral/ *a* and *m*, mineral

**mineralogía** /mineralo'hia/ *f*, mineralogy

**mineralógico** /minera'lohiko/ *a* mineralogical

**mineralogista** /mineralo'hista/ *mf* mineralogist

**minería** /mine'ria/ *f*, mining, mineworking; mineworkers

**minero** /mi'nero/ *a* mining. *m*, miner, mineworker; source, origin

**miniar** /mini'ar/ *vt Art.* to illuminate

**miniatura** /minia'tura/ *f*, miniature

**miniaturista** /miniatu'rista/ *mf* miniaturist

**mínima** /'minima/ *f*, *Mus.* minim; very small thing or portion

**mínimo** /'minimo/ *a superl* **pequeño** smallest; minimum; meticulous, precise. *m*, minimum; (meteorological) trough

**ministerial** /ministe'rial/ *a* ministerial

**ministerio** /minis'terio/ *m*, office, post; *Polit.* cabinet; ministry; government office; government department.

**ministrar** /minis'trar/ *vt* and *vi* to fill; administer (an office); —*vt* minister to; give, provide

**ministro** /mi'nistro/ *m*, instrument, agency; minister of state, cabinet minister; clergyman, minister; minister plenipotentiary; policeman. **m. de estado,** secretary of state. **m. de gobernación,** secretary of the interior. **m. de hacienda,** treasurer. **m. de relaciones extranjeras,** foreign secretary. **primer m.** prime minister

**minoración** /minora'θion; minora'sion/ *f*, reduction, decrease

**minorar** /mino'rar/ *vt* to diminish, decrease

**minoría** /mino'ria/ *f*, minority, smaller number; minority (of age)

**minoridad** /minori'ðað/ *f*, minority (of age)

**minucia** /minu'θia; minu'sia/ *f*, smallness; morsel, mite; *pl* details, trifles, minutiae

**minuciosidad** /minuθiosi'ðað; minusiosi'ðað/ *f*, meticulousness, minuteness, precision

**minucioso** /minu'θioso; minu'sioso/ *a* meticulous, precise, minute

**minué** /mi'nue/ *m*, minuet

**minúsculo** /mi'nuskulo/ *a* minute, very small

**minuta** /mi'nuta/ *f*, memorandum, minute; note; list, catalog

**minutario** /minu'tario/ *m*, minute book

**minutero** /minu'tero/ *m*, minute hand (of a clock)

**minuto** /mi'nuto/ *a* minute, very small. *m*, minute

**mío** /'mio/ *m*. **mía,** *f*, (*m pl.* **míos,** *f pl.* **mías**) *poss pron* mine (e.g. *Las flores son mías,* The flowers are mine). **Mi** is used before nouns, *not* **mío.** Also used with article (e.g. *Este sombrero no es el mío,* This hat is not mine (my one)). **de mío,** by myself, without help. *Inf.* **¡Esta es la mía!** This is my chance!

**miope** /mi'ope/ *a* myopic. *mf* myopic person

**miopía** /mio'pia/ *f*, shortsightedness

**miosota** /mio'sota/ *f*, myosotis, forget-me-not

**mira** /'mira/ *f*, sight (optical instruments, guns); intention, design; *Mil.* watchtower; care, precaution. **andar, estar** *or* **quedar a la m.,** to be vigilant, be on the lookout

**mirada** /mi'raða/ *f*, look; gaze. **lanzar miradas de carnero degollado** ( **a** ), to cast sheep's eyes at

**miradero** /mira'ðero/ *m*, object of attention, cynosure; observation post, lookout

**mirador** /mira'ðor/ **(-ra)** *n* spectator. *m*, *Archit.* oriel; enclosed balcony; observatory

**miramiento** /mira'miento/ *m*, observation, gazing; scruple, consideration; precaution, care; thoughtfulness

**mirar** /mi'rar/ *vt* to look at, gaze at; observe, behold; watch; consider, think; (*with prep a*) overlook, look on to; face; (*with por*) care for, protect; look after, consider. **m. contra el gobierno,** *Inf.* to be squint-eyed. **m. de hito en hito,** to look over, stare at. **mirarse en** ( **una cosa** ), to consider (a matter) carefully

**miríada** /mi'riaða/ *f*, myriad, huge number

**mirilla** /mi'riʎa; mi'riya/ *f*, peephole

**miriñaque** /miri'ɲake/ *m*, trinket, ornament; crinoline

**mirlarse** /mir'larse/ *vr Inf.* to give oneself airs

**mirlo** /'mirlo/ *m*, blackbird; *Inf.* pompous air

**mirón** /mi'ron/ *a* inquisitive, curious

**mirra** /'mirra/ *f*, myrrh

**mirto** /'mirto/ *m*, myrtle

**misa** /'misa/ *f*, (*Eccl. Mus.*) mass. **m. de difuntos,** requiem mass. **m. del gallo,** midnight mass. **m. mayor,** high mass. **m. rezada,** low mass. **como en m.,** in profound silence. **oír m.,** to attend mass

**misal** /mi'sal/ *m*, missal

**misantropía** /misantro'pia/ *f*, misanthropy

**misantrópico** /misan'tropiko/ *a* misanthropic

**misántropo** /mi'santropo/ *m*, misanthrope

**miscelánea** /misθe'lanea; misse'lanea/ *f*, medley, assortment, miscellany

**misceláneo** /misθe'laneo; misse'laneo/ *a* assorted, miscellaneous, mixed

**miscible** /mis'θiβle; mis'siβle/ *a* mixable

**miserable** /mise'raβle/ *a* miserable, unhappy; timid, pusillanimous; miserly, mean; despicable

**miseria** /mi'seria/ *f*, misery; poverty, destitution; avarice, miserliness; *Inf.* poor thing, trifle

**misericordia** /miseri'korðia/ *f*, mercy, compassion

**misericordioso** /miserikor'ðioso/ *a* merciful, compassionate

**mísero** /'misero/ *a Inf.* fond of churchgoing

**misérrimo** /mi'serrimo/ *a superl* most miserable

**misión** /mi'sion/ *f*, mission; vocation; commission, duty, errand

**misionar** /misio'nar/ *vi* to missionize, act as a missionary; *Eccl.* conduct a mission

**misionero** /misio'nero/ *m*, missioner; missionary

**Misisipi, el** /misi'sipi, el/ the Mississippi

**misiva** /mi'siβa/ *f*, missive

**mismo** /'mismo/ *a* same; similar; self (e.g. *ellos mismos*, they themselves); very, same (e.g. *Ahora m. voy*, I'm going this very minute). **Me da lo m.**, It makes no difference to me. **por lo m.**, for that self-same reason

**misógamo** /mi'sogamo/ **(-ma)** *n* misogamist

**misógino** /mi'sohino/ *m*, misogynist

**misterio** /mis'terio/ *m*, mystery

**misterioso** /miste'rioso/ *a* mysterious

**mística** /'mistika/ *f*, mysticism

**misticismo** /misti'θismo; misti'sismo/ *m*, mysticism

**místico** /'mistiko/ *a* mystic

**mistificación** /mistifika'θion; mistifika'sion/ *f*, mystification; mystery; deception

**mistificar** /mistifi'kar/ *vt* to mystify; deceive

**Misuri, el** /mi'suri, el/ the Missouri

**mitad** /mi'tað/ *f*, half; middle, center. *Fig. Inf.* **cara m.**, better half. *Inf.* **mentir por la m. de la barba**, to lie barefacedly

**mítico** /'mitiko/ *a* mythical

**mitigación** /mitiga'θion; mitiga'sion/ *f*, mitigation

**mitigador** /mitiga'ðor/ **(-ra)** *a* mitigatory —*n* mitigator

**mitigar** /miti'gar/ *vt* to mitigate, moderate, alleviate; appease

**mitin** /'mitin/ *m*, mass meeting

**mito** /'mito/ *m*, myth

**mitología** /mitolo'hia/ *f*, mythology

**mitológico** /mito'lohiko/ *a* mythological

**mitologista, mitólogo** /mitolo'hista, mi'tologo/ *m*, mythologist

**mitón** /mi'ton/ *m*, mitten

**mitra** /'mitra/ *f*, miter; bishopric; archbishopric

**mitrado** /mi'traðo/ *a* mitred

**mixto** /'miksto/ *a* mixed, blended; hybrid; composite; mongrel. *m*, mixed train (carrying freight and passengers); sulphur match

**mixtura** /miks'tura/ *f*, mixture, blend; compound; mixture (medicine)

**¡miz, miz!** /miθ, miθ; mis, mis/ puss, puss!

**moabita** /moa'βita/ *mf* Moabite

**mobiliario** /moβi'liario/ *a* movable (goods). *m*, furniture

**moblaje** /mo'βlahe/ *m*, household goods and furniture

**mocasín** /moka'sin/ *m*, moccasin

**mocedad** /moθe'ðað; mose'ðað/ *f*, youth, adolescence; mischief, prank. *Fig. Inf.* **correr sus mocedades**, to sow one's wild oats

**mochila** /mo'tʃila/ *f*, knapsack; nosebag; military rations for a march

**mocho** /'motʃo/ *a* blunted, topless, lopped; *Inf.* shorn, cropped. *m*, butt, butt end

**mochuelo** /mo'tʃuelo/ *m*, owl; *Inf.* difficult job

**moción** /mo'θion/ *f*, motion, movement; impulse, tendency; divine inspiration; motion (of a debate)

**moco** /'moko/ *m*, mucus; candle drips; snuff of a candle. *Inf.* **caérsele el m.**, to be very simple, be easily deceived

**mocoso** /mo'koso/ **(-sa)** *a* running of the nose, sniffling; unimportant, insignificant —*n* coxcomb, stripling

**moda** /'moða/ *f*, fashion. **estar** *or* **ser de m.**, to be fashionable, be in fashion. **la última m.**, the latest fashion

**modales** /mo'ðales/ *m pl*, manners, behavior

**modalidad** /moðali'ðað/ *f*, form, nature; *Mus.* modality

**modelado** /moðe'laðo/ *m*, *Art.* modeling

**modelar** /moðe'lar/ *vt Art.* to model; —*vr* model oneself (on), copy

**modelo** /mo'ðelo/ *m*, example, pattern; model. *mf Art.* life model

**módem** *m*, modem

**moderación** /moðera'θion; moðerasion/ *f*, moderation; restraint, temperance, equability

**moderado** /moðe'raðo/ *a* moderate; restrained, temperate

**moderador** /moðera'ðor/ **(-ra)** *a* moderating —*n* moderator

**moderantismo** /moðeran'tismo/ *m*, moderate opinion; moderate political party

**moderar** /moðe'rar/ *vt* to moderate; temper, restrain; —*vr* regain one's self-control; behave with moderation

**modernidad** /moðerni'ðað/ *f*, modernity

**modernismo** /moðer'nismo/ *m*, modernism

**modernista** /moðer'nista/ *a* modernistic; modern. *mf* modernist

**modernización** /moðerniθa'θion; moðernisa'sion/ *f*, modernization

**modernizar** /moðerni'θar; moðerni'sar/ *vt* to modernize

**moderno** /mo'ðerno/ *a* modern. *m*, modern. **a la moderna**, in modern fashion

**modestia** /mo'ðestia/ *f*, modesty

**modesto** /mo'ðesto/ *a* modest

**módico** /'moðiko/ *a* moderate (of prices, etc.)

**modificable** /moðifi'kaβle/ *a* modifiable

**modificación** /moðifi'kaθion; moðifika'sion/ *f*, modification

**modificador, modificante** /moðifi'kaðor, moðifi'kante/ *a* modifying, moderating

**modificar** /moðifi'kar/ *vt* to modify; moderate

**modismo** /mo'ðismo/ *m*, idiom, idiomatic expression

**modista** /mo'ðista/ *mf* dressmaker; couturier; milliner

**modo** /'moðo/ *m*, mode, method, style; manner, way; moderation, restraint; civility, politeness (often *pl*); *Mus.* mode; *Gram.* mood. **m. de ser**, nature, temperament. **de m. que**, so that. **de ningún m.**, not at all, by no means. **de todos modos**, in any case

**modorra** /mo'ðorra/ *f*, deep sleep, stupor

**modorro** /mo'ðorro/ *a* drowsy, heavy

**modoso** /mo'ðoso/ *a* demure; well-behaved

**modulación** /moðula'θion; moðula'sion/ *f*, modulation

**modulador** /moðula'ðor/ **(-ra)** *a* modulative —*n* modulator, *m*, *Mus.* modulator

**modular** /moðu'lar/ *vt* and *vi* to modulate

**mofa** /'mofa/ *f*, mockery, ridicule, jeering

**mofador** /mofa'ðor/ **(-ra)** *a* jeering —*n* scoffer, mocker

**mofarse** /mo'farse/ *vr* (*with de*) to make fun of, jeer at

**mofeta** /mo'feta/ *f*, noxious gas; damp (gas); *Zool.* skunk

**moflete** /mo'flete/ *m*, *Inf.* plump cheek

**mofletudo** /mofle'tuðo/ *a* plump-cheeked

**mogol** /'mogol/ **(-la)** *a* and *n* Mongolian.

**mogote** /mo'gote/ *m*, hill; pyre, stack

**mohicano** /moi'kano/ *a* and *n* Mohican

**mohín** /mo'in/ *m*, grimace

**mohína** /mo'ina/ *f*, grudge, rancor; sullenness; sulkiness

**mohíno** /mo'ino/ *a* depressed, gloomy; sulky; black or black-nosed (of animals)

**moho** /'moo/ *m*, mold, fungoid growth; moldiness; moss. *Inf.* **no criar m.**, to be always on the move

**mohoso** /mo'oso/ *a* mossy; moldy

**mojada** /mo'haða/ f, wetting; Inf. stab; sop of bread

**mojador** /moha'ðor/ **(-ra)** n wetter. m, stamp moistener

**mojar** /mo'har/ vt to wet; moisten; Inf. stab, wound with a dagger; —vi take part in; meddle, interfere; —vr get wet

**mojicón** /mohi'kon/ m, kind of spongecake; Inf. slap in the face

**mojiganga** /mohi'ganga/ f, masquerade, mummer's show; farce; funny sight, figure of fun

**mojigatería** /mohigate'ria/ f, hypocrisy; sanctimoniousness; prudery

**mojigato** /mohi'gato/ **(-ta)** a hypocritical; sanctimonious; prudish —n hypocrite; bigot; prude

**mojón** /mo'hon/ m, boundary marker; milestone; heap. **m. kilométrico,** milestone

**molar** /mo'lar/ a molar

**moldavo** /mol'daβo/ **(-va)** a and n Moldavian

**molde** /'molde/ m, mold, matrix; Fig. model, pattern. **de m.,** printed; suitably, conveniently; perfectly. **letra de m.,** printed letters, print

**moldeador** /moldea'ðor/ **(-ra)** n molder

**moldear** /molde'ar/ vt to mold, cast

**moldura** /mol'dura/ f, molding

**moldurar** /moldu'rar/ vt to mold

**molécula** /mo'lekula/ f, molecule

**molecular** /moleku'lar/ a molecular

**moler** /mo'ler/ vt irr to grind, crush; tire, exhaust; illtreat; pester, annoy. **m. a palos,** to beat black and blue —Pres. Indic. **muelo, mueles, muele, muelen.** Pres. Subjunc. **muela, muelas, muela, muelan.**

**molestia** /mo'lestia/ f, inconvenience, trouble; annoyance; discomfort, pain; bore, nuisance. **Es una m.,** It's a nuisance

**molesto** /mo'lesto/ a inconvenient, troublesome; annoying; painful; uncomfortable; boring, tedious

**moletón** /mole'ton/ m, flannelet

**molicie** /mo'liθie; mo'lisie/ f, softness, smoothness; effeminacy, weakness

**molienda** /mo'lienda/ f, milling; grinding; mill; portion ground at one time; Inf. exhaustion, fatigue; Inf. nuisance

**molificar** /molifi'kar/ vt to mollify, appease

**molimiento** /moli'miento/ m, milling; grinding; exhaustion, fatigue

**molinera** /moli'nera/ f, (woman) miller; miller's wife

**molinero** /moli'nero/ a mill. m, miller

**molinillo** /moli'niʎo; moli'niyo/ m, hand mill, small grinder; mincing machine; beater. **m. de café,** coffee mill

**molino** /mo'lino/ m, mill; harum-scarum, rowdy; bore, tedious person; Inf. mouth. **m. de rueda de escalones,** treadmill. **m. de viento,** windmill

**molleja** /mo'ʎeha/ f, gizzard

**mollera** /mo'ʎera/ f, crown of the head; brains, sense. Inf. **ser duro de m.,** to be obstinate; be stupid

**molusco** /mo'lusko/ m, mollusk

**momentaneidad** /momentanei'ðað/ f, momentariness

**momentáneo** /momen'taneo/ a momentary, brief; instantaneous, immediate

**momento** /mo'mento/ m, moment, minute; importance; Mech. moment. **al m.,** immediately. **a cada m.,** all the time; frequently. **por momentos,** continually; intermittently

**momería** /mome'ria/ f, mummery

**momero** /mo'mero/ **(-ra)** n mummer

**momia** /'momia/ f, mummy

**momificación** /momifika'θion; momifika'sion/ f, mummification

**momificar** /momifi'kar/ vt to mummify; —vr become mummified

**mona** /'mona/ f, female monkey; Inf. imitator; drinking bout; drunk. Inf. **Aunque la m. se vista de seda, m. se queda,** Breeding will tell. Inf. **ser la última m.,** to be of no account, be unimportant

**monacal** /mona'kal/ a monkish, monastic

**monacillo** /mona'θiʎo; mona'siyo/ m, Eccl. acolyte

**monada** /mo'naða/ f, mischievous prank; affected

gesture or grimace; small, pretty thing; childish cleverness; flattery; rash act; pl monkey shines

**monaguillo** /mona'giʎo; mona'giyo/ m, Eccl. acolyte

**monarca** /mo'narka/ mf monarch

**monarquía** /monar'kia/ f, monarchy

**monárquico** /mo'narkiko/ **(-ca)** a monarchic —n monarchist

**monarquismo** /monar'kismo/ m, monarchism

**monasterio** /mona'sterio/ m, monastery; convent

**monástico** /mo'nastiko/ a monastic

**monda** /'monda/ f, skinning, peeling; Agr. pruning; cleansing

**mondadientes** /monda'ðientes/ m, toothpick

**mondar** /mon'dar/ vt to skin, peel; Agr. prune; cut the hair; cleanse; free of rubbish; Inf. deprive of possessions; —vr pick one's teeth

**mondo** /'mondo/ a simple, plain; bare; unadulterated, pure

**moneda** /mo'neða/ f, coin, piece of money; coinage; Inf. wealth; cash. **m. corriente,** currency. **m. metálica,** specie. **pagar en buena m.,** to give entire satisfaction. **pagar en la misma m.,** to pay back in the same coin, return like for like. Inf. **ser m. corriente,** to be usual or very frequent

**monedero** /mone'ðero/ m, coiner, minter; handbag; purse

**monería** /mone'ria/ f, mischievous trick; unimportant trifle; pretty thing; childish cleverness, pretty ways

**monetario** /mone'tario/ a monetary. m, collection of coins and medals

**monetización** /monetiθa'θion; monetisa'sion/ f, monetization

**monigote** /moni'gote/ m, Inf. boor; grotesque, puppet

**monitor** /moni'tor/ m, monitor

**monitorio** /moni'torio/ a monitory

**monja** /'monha/ f, nun; pl sparks

**monje** /'monhe/ m, monk

**monjil** /mon'hil/ a nun-like. m, nun's habit

**mono** /'mono/ a Inf. pretty, attractive; amusing, funny. m, monkey; person given to grimacing; rash youth; coverall. Inf. **estar de monos,** to be on bad terms

**monocromo** /mono'kromo/ a monochrome; monochromatic

**monóculo** /mo'nokulo/ m, monocle

**monogamia** /mono'gamia/ f, monogamy

**monógamo** /mo'nogamo/ a monogamous —n monogamist

**monografía** /monogra'fia/ f, monograph

**monograma** /mono'grama/ m, monogram

**monolítico** /mono'litiko/ a monolithic

**monolito** /mono'lito/ m, monolith

**monólogo** /mo'nologo/ m, monologue

**monomanía** /monoma'nia/ f, monomania

**monomaníaco** /monoma'niako/ **(-ca)** n monomaniac

**monopatín** /monopa'tin/ m, scooter

**monoplano** /mono'plano/ m, monoplane

**monopolio** /mono'polio/ m, monopoly

**monopolista** /monopo'lista/ mf monopolist

**monopolizar** /monopoli'θar; monopoli'sar/ vt to monopolize

**monosilábico** /monosi'laβiko/ a monosyllabic

**monosílabo** /mono'silaβo/ m, monosyllable

**monoteísmo** /monote'ismo/ m, monotheism

**monoteísta** /monote'ista/ mf monotheist

**monotipia** /mono'tipia/ f, monotype

**monotonía** /monoto'nia/ f, monotony; monotone

**monótono** /mo'notono/ a monotonous

**monroísmo** /monro'ismo/ m, Monroe doctrine

**monseñor** /monse'ɲor/ m, monsignor

**monserga** /mon'serga/ f, Inf. rigmarole; jargon

**monstruo** /'monstruo/ m, monster; freak, monstrosity; cruel person; hideous person or thing

**monstruosidad** /monstruosi'ðað/ f, monstrousness, monstrosity

**monstruoso** /mon'struoso/ a monstrous, abnormal; enormous; extraordinary; atrocious, outrageous

**monta** /'monta/ f, mounting a horse; total; Mil. mounting signal; breeding station (horses)

**montacargas** /monta'kargas/ *m,* hoist, lift; freight elevator

**montador** /monta'ðor/ *m,* mounter; mounting block

**montadura** /monta'ðura/ *f,* mounting; mount, setting (of jewels)

**montaje** /mon'tahe/ *m,* assembling, setting up (machines); presentation (of a book); (cinema) montage

**montañés** /monta'ɲes/ **(-esa)** *a* mountain —*n* mountain dweller; native of Santander

**montano** /mon'tano/ *a* hilly, mountainous

**montante** /mon'tante/ *m,* upright, stanchion; tent pole

**montaña** /mon'taɲa/ *f,* mountain; mountainous country. **montañas rusas,** roller coaster (at an amusement park)

**montañés** /monta'ɲes/ **(-esa)** *a* mountain —*n* mountain dweller; native of Santander

**montañoso** /monta'ɲoso/ *a* mountainous; hilly

**montar** /mon'tar/ *vi* to ascend, climb up, get on top; mount (a horse); ride (a horse); be important; —*vt* get on top of; ride (a horse); total, amount to; set up (apparatus, machinery); *Naut.* sail around, double; set, mount (gems); cock (firearms); fine for trespassing; wind (a clock); command (a ship); *Naut.* carry, be fitted with (guns, etc.). **m. a horcajadas en,** to mount astride; straddle. **montarse en cólera,** to fly into a rage

**montaraz** /monta'raθ; monta'ras/ *a* mountain-dwelling; wild, savage; rude, uncivilized, uncouth. *m,* gamekeeper, forester

**montazgo** /mon'taθgo; mon'tasgo/ *m,* toll payable for cattle moving from one province to another

**monte** /'monte/ *m,* mount, hill; woodland; obstacle, impediment. **m. de piedad,** pawnshop. **m. pío,** savings fund

**montenegrino** /montene'grino/ **(-na)** *a* and *n* Montenegrin

**montera** /mon'tera/ *f,* cap; glass roof

**montería** /monte'ria/ *f,* hunt, chase; art of hunting

**montero** /mon'tero/ **(-ra)** *n* hunter, huntsman

**montés** /mon'tes/ *a* wild, savage, untamed

**montevideano** /monteβiðe'ano/ **(-na)** *a* and *n* Montevidean

**montículo** /mon'tikulo/ *m,* mound, hill

**montón** /mon'ton/ *m,* heap, pile; *Inf.* abundance, lot. *Inf.* **a, de** *or* **en m.,** all jumbled up together. **a montones,** in abundance

**montuoso** /mon'tuoso/ *a* mountainous

**montura** /mon'tura/ *f,* riding animal, mount; horse trappings; setting up, mounting (artillery, etc.)

**monumental** /monumen'tal/ *a* monumental

**monumento** /monu'mento/ *m,* monument; document, record; tomb

**monzón** /mon'θon; mon'son/ *mf,* monsoon

**moña** /'moɲa/ *f,* doll; dressmaker's model; bow for the hair; bullfighter's black bow; baby's bonnet; *Inf.* drinking bout

**moño** /'moɲo/ *m,* bun, chignon; topknot (birds); bunch of ribbons; *pl* tawdry trimmings

**moqueta** /mo'keta/ *f,* moquette

**moquete** /mo'kete/ *m,* slap in the face

**moquillo** /mo'kiʎo; mo'kiyo/ *m,* distemper (of animals)

**mora** /'mora/ *f,* blackberry; mulberry; bramble; Moorish girl, Moorish woman

**morada** /mo'raða/ *f,* dwelling, abode; sojourn, stay

**morado** /mo'raðo/ *a* purple

**morador** /mora'ðor/ **(-ra)** *n* dweller; sojourner

**moral** /mo'ral/ *a* moral, ethical. *f,* morality, ethics; morale. *m,* blackberry bush

**moraleja** /mora'leha/ *f,* moral, lesson

**moralidad** /morali'ðað/ *f,* morality

**moralista** /mora'lista/ *mf* moralist

**moralización** /moraliθa'θion; moralisa'sion/ *f,* moralization

**moralizador** /moraliθa'ðor; moralisa'ðor/ **(-ra)** *a* moralizing —*n* moralizer

**moralizar** /morali'θar; morali'sar/ *vt* to reform, correct; —*vi* moralize

**moratoria** /mora'toria/ *f,* moratorium

**moravo** /mo'raβo/ **(-va)** *a* and *n* Moravian

**morbidez** /mor'βiðeθ; mor'βiðes/ *f, Art.* morbidezza; softness

**mórbido** /'morβiðo/ *a* morbid, diseased; *Art.* delicate (of flesh tones); soft

**morbo** /'morβo/ *m,* illness. **m. gálico,** syphilis

**morboso** /mor'βoso/ *a* ill; morbid, unhealthy

**morcilla** /mor'θiʎa; mor'siya/ *f, Cul.* black pudding; *(Inf. Theat.)* gag

**morcillero** /morθi'ʎero; morsi'yero/ **(-ra)** *n* seller of black puddings; *(Inf. Theat.)* actor who gags

**mordacidad** /morðaθi'ðað; morðasi'ðað/ *f,* corrosiveness; mordacity, sarcasm; *Cul.* piquancy

**mordaz** /mor'ðaθ; mor'ðas/ *a* corrosive; sarcastic, caustic, mordant; *Cul.* piquant

**mordaza** /mor'ðaθa; mor'ðasa/ *f,* gag

**mordedor** /morðe'ðor/ *a* biting; scandalmongering

**mordedura** /morðe'ðura/ *f,* bite, biting

**morder** /mor'ðer/ *vt irr* to bite; nibble, nip; seize, grasp; corrode, eat away; slander; etch —*Pres. Indic.* **muerdo, muerdes, muerde, muerden.** *Pres. Subjunc.* **muerda, muerdas, muerda, muerdan**

**mordiente** /mor'ðiente/ *m,* fixative (for dyeing); mordant —*a* mordant (of acid)

**mordiscar** /morðis'kar/ *vt* to nibble, bite gently; bite

**mordisco** /mor'ðisko/ *m,* nibble; nibbling; bite; biting; piece bitten off

**morena** /mo'rena/ *f,* moraine

**moreno** /mo'reno/ **(-na)** *a* dark brown; swarthy complexioned; dark (of people) —*n Inf.* negro, mulatto

**morera** /mo'rera/ *f,* mulberry bush

**morería** /more'ria/ *f,* Moorish quarter

**morfina** /mor'fina/ *f,* morphine

**morfinómano** /morfi'nomano/ **(-na)** *n* morphine addict

**morfología** /morfolo'hia/ *f,* morphology

**morfológico** /morfo'lohiko/ *a* morphological

**morganático** /morga'natiko/ *a* morganatic

**moribundo** /mori'βundo/ **(-da)** *a* moribund, dying —*n* dying person

**morillo** /mo'riʎo; mo'riyo/ *m,* andiron, fire-dog

**morir** /mo'rir/ *vi irr* to die; fade, wither; decline, decay; disappear; yearn (for); long (to); go out (lights, fire); —*vr* die; go numb (limbs); *(with por)* adore, be mad about. *Inf.* **m. vestido,** to die a violent death. **¡Muera!** Down with! *Past Part.* **muerto.** For other tenses see **dormir**

**morisco** /mo'risko/ **(-ca)** *a* Moorish —*n* Morisco, Moor converted to Christianity

**morisma** /mo'risma/ *f,* Mohammedanism; multitude of Moors

**mormón** /mor'mon/ **(-ona)** *n* Mormon

**mormónico** /mor'moniko/ *a* Mormon

**mormonismo** /mormo'nismo/ *m,* Mormonism

**moro** /'moro/ **(-ra)** *a* Moorish —*n* Moor; Mohammedan. *Inf.* **haber moros y cristianos,** to be the deuce of a row. *Inf.* **Hay moros en la costa,** The coast is not clear; There's trouble in the offing

**morosidad** /morosi'ðað/ *f,* slowness, delay; sluggishness, sloth

**moroso** /mo'roso/ *a* slow, dilatory; sluggish, lazy

**morra** /'morra/ *f,* crown of the head

**morral** /mo'rral/ *m,* nose-bag; knapsack; game-bag; *Inf.* lout

**morriña** /mo'rriɲa/ *f,* cattle plague, murrain; *Inf.* depression, blues; homesickness

**morrión** /mo'rrion/ *m,* morion (helmet)

**morro** /'morro/ *m,* anything round; hummock, hillock; round pebble; headland, cliff

**morsa** /'morsa/ *f,* walrus

**mortaja** /mor'taha/ *f,* shroud, winding sheet

**mortal** /mor'tal/ *a* mortal; fatal, deadly; on the point of death; great, tremendous; certain, sure. *mf* mortal

**mortalidad** /mortali'ðað/ *f,* humanity, human race; mortality, death-rate

**mortandad** /mortan'dað/ *f,* mortality, number of deaths

**mortecino** /morte'θino; morte'sino/ *a* dead from natural causes (animals); weak; fading; dull, dead (of eyes); flickering; on the point of death or extinction

**mortero** /mor'tero/ *m,* mortar (for building); *Mil.* mortar; pounding mortar

**mortífero** /mor'tifero/ *a* deadly, mortal

**mortificación** /mortifika'θion; mortifika'sion/ *f,* *Med.* gangrene; humiliation; wounding; mortification (of the flesh)

**mortificar** /mortifi'kar/ *vt Med.* to mortify; humiliate, wound, hurt; mortify (the flesh); —*vr* become gangrenous

**mortuorio** /mor'tuorio/ *a* mortuary. *m,* funeral, obsequies

**mosaico** /mo'saiko/ *a* and *m,* mosaic

**mosca** /'moska/ *f,* fly; *Inf.* nuisance; bore, pest; cash; *pl* sparks. *Inf.* **m. muerta,** underhanded person. *Inf.* **papar moscas,** to gape, be dumbfounded. *Inf.* **soltar la m.,** to give or spend money unwillingly

**moscardón** /moskar'ðon/ *m,* gadfly

**moscatel** /moska'tel/ *a* muscatel. *m,* muscatel (grapes and wine); *Inf.* pest, tedious person

**moscovita** /mosko'βita/ *a* and *mf* Muscovite

**Moscú** /mos'ku/ Moscow

**mosquear** /moske'ar/ *vt* to drive off flies; reply crossly; whip; —*vr* be exasperated; brush aside obstacles

**mosquero** /mos'kero/ *m,* flypaper

**mosquete** /mos'kete/ *m,* musket

**mosquetería** /moskete'ria/ *f,* musketry; (*Obs. Theat.*) male members of the audience who stood at the back of the pit

**mosquetero** /moske'tero/ *m,* musketeer; (Spanish theater of the sixteenth and seventeenth centuries) male member of the audience who stood at the back of the pit

**mosquitero** /moski'tero/ *m,* mosquito net

**mosquito** /mos'kito/ *m,* mosquito; midge, gnat; *Inf.* tippler, drunkard

**mostacera** /mosta'θera; mosta'sera/ *f,* mustard pot

**mostacho** /mos'tatʃo/ *m,* mustache, whiskers; *Inf.* smudge on the face

**mostaza** /mos'taθa; mos'tasa/ *f,* mustard plant or seed; *Cul.* mustard

**mostela** /mos'tela/ *f,* sheaf (of corn, etc.)

**mosto** /'mosto/ *m,* must, unfermented wine

**mostrador** /mostra'ðor/ **(-ra)** *n* one who shows, exhibitor. *m,* shop counter; face of a watch

**mostrar** /mos'trar/ *vt irr* to show; indicate, point out; demonstrate, prove; manifest, reveal; —*vr* show oneself, be (e.g. *Se mostró bondadoso,* He showed himself to be kind) —*Pres. Indic.* **muestro, muestras, muestra, muestran.** *Pres. Subjunc.* **muestre, muestres, muestre, muestren**

**mostrenco** /mos'trenko/ *a Inf.* stray, vagrant, homeless; *Inf.* dull, ignorant; *Inf.* fat, heavy

**mota** /'mota/ *f,* fault in cloth; mote, defect, fault; mound, hill; thread of cotton, speck of dust, etc.; fleck (of the sun, etc.); spot

**mote** /'mote/ *m,* maxim, saying; motto, device; catchword, slogan; nickname

**motear** /mote'ar/ *vt* to speckle, dot, variegate, spot

**motejar** /mote'har/ *vt* to nickname, call names, dub

**motete** /mo'tete/ *m,* motet

**motín** /mo'tin/ *m,* mutiny; riot

**motivar** /moti'βar/ *vt* to motivate, cause; explain one's reasons

**motivo** /mo'tiβo/ *a* motive. *m,* cause, motive; *Mus.* motif. **con m. de,** on account of, because of. **de m. propio,** of one's own free will

**motocicleta** /motoθi'kleta; motosi'kleta/ *f,* motorcycle

**motociclista** /motoθi'klista; motosi'klista/ *mf* motorcyclist

**motor** /mo'tor/ **(-ra)** *a* motive, driving. *m,* motor, engine —*n* (person) mover, motive force. **m. de combustión interna,** internal combustion engine. **m. de retroacción,** jet engine

**motorista** /moto'rista/ *mf* motorist, driver

**movedizo** /moβe'ðiθo; moβe'ðiso/ *a* movable; insecure, unsteady; shaky; changeable, vacillating

**mover** /mo'βer/ *vt irr* to move; operate, drive; sway; wag; persuade, induce; excite; move (to pity, etc.); (*with prep a*) cause; —*vi* sprout (plants); —*vr* move —*Pres. Indic.* **muevo, mueves, mueve, mueven.** *Pres. Subjunc.* **mueva, muevas, mueva, muevan**

**movible** /mo'βiβle/ *a* movable; insecure, shaky. *m,* motive, cause, incentive

**movilidad** /moβili'ðað/ *f,* mobility; changeableness, inconstancy

**movilización** /moβiliθa'θion; moβilisa'sion/ *f,* mobilization

**movilizar** /moβili'θar; moβili'sar/ *vt* to mobilize

**movimiento** /moβi'miento/ *m,* movement; perturbation, excitement; *Mus.* movement; *Lit.* fire, spirit; *Mech.* motion, movement. *Mil.* **m. envolvente,** encircling movement

**moza** /'moθa; 'mosa/ *f,* maid; girl; waitress. **m. de partido,** party girl, prostitute. **buena m.,** fine, upstanding young woman

**mozalbete** /moθal'βete; mosal'βete/ *m,* lad, stripling, boy

**mozárabe** /mo'θaraβe; mo'saraβe/ *a* Mozarabic. *mf* Mozarab

**mozo** /'moθo; 'moso/ *a* young, unmarried. *m,* boy, youth; bachelor; waiter; porter. **m. de cordel** *or* **m. de esquina,** street porter, message boy. **m. de estación,** railroad porter. **buen m.,** fine, upstanding young man

**muaré** /mua're/ *m,* moiré silk

**muceta** /mu'θeta; mu'seta/ *f, Educ.* hood, short cape (of a graduate's gown)

**muchacha** /mu'tʃatʃa/ *f,* girl, lass; female servant

**muchachada** /mutʃa'tʃaða/ *f,* childish prank

**muchachez** /mutʃa'tʃeθ; mutʃa'tʃes/ *f,* boyhood; girlhood

**muchachil** /mutʃa'tʃil/ *a* boyish; girlish

**muchacho** /mu'tʃatʃo/ *m,* boy, youth; male servant

**muchedumbre** /mutʃe'ðumbre/ *f,* abundance, plenty; crowd, multitude; mass, mob

**muchísimo** /mu'tʃisimo/ *a superl* very much —*adv* very great deal, very much

**mucho** /'mutʃo/ *a* much; plenty of; very; long (time); *pl* many, numerous —*adv* a great deal; much; very much; yes, certainly; frequently, often; very (e.g. *Me alegro m.,* I am very glad); to a great extent; long (time). **con m.,** by far, easily. **ni con m.,** nor anything like it, very far from it. **ni m. menos,** and much less. **por m. que,** however much

**mucílago** /mu'θilago; mu'silago/ *m,* mucilage, gum

**mucosa** /mu'kosa/ *f,* mucous membrane

**mucosidad** /mukosi'ðað/ *f,* mucosity

**mucoso** /mu'koso/ *a* mucous

**muda** /'muða/ *f,* change, transformation; change of clothes; molting season; molt, sloughing of skin (snakes, etc.); change of voice (in boys)

**mudable** /mu'ðaβle/ *a* changeable, inconstant

**mudanza** /mu'ðanθa; muðansa/ *f,* change; furniture removal; step, figure (in dancing); changeability, inconstancy

**mudar** /mu'ðar/ *vt* to change; alter, transform; exchange; remove; dismiss (from employment); molt; slough the skin (snakes, etc.); change the voice (boys); —*vr* alter one's behavior; change one's clothes; change one's residence; change one's expression; *Inf.* go away, depart

**mudéjar** /mu'ðehar/ *m, Archit.* style containing Moorish and Christian elements. *mf* Moor who remained in Spain under Christian rule

**mudez** /mu'ðeθ; mu'ðes/ *f,* dumbness; silence, muteness

**mudo** /'muðo/ *a* dumb; silent, mute, quiet

**mueblaje** /mue'βlahe/ *m,* household goods and furniture

**mueble** /'mueβle/ *m,* piece of furniture; furnishing

**mueblería** /mueβle'ria/ *f,* furniture store or factory

**mueblista** /mue'βlista/ *mf* furniture maker; furniture dealer

**mueca** /'mueka/ *f,* grimace

**muela** /'muela/ *f,* grindstone; molar (tooth); millstone; flat-topped hill. **m. del juicio,** wisdom tooth. **dolor de muelas,** toothache

**muellaje** /mue'ʎahe; mue'yahe/ *m,* wharfage, dock dues

**muelle** /'mueʎe; 'mueye/ *a* soft, smooth; voluptuous, sensuous; luxurious. *m,* spring (of a watch, etc.); wharf, quay; freight platform (railroad). **m. real,** mainspring (of a watch). **m. del volante,** hairspring.

**muérdago** /'mwerðago/ *m*, mistletoe
**muermo** /'mwermo/ *m*, glanders
**muerte** /'mwerte/ *f*, death; destruction, annihilation; end, decline. *Inf.* **una m. chiquita,** a nervous shudder. **a m.,** to the death, with no quarter. **de m.,** implacably, inexorably (of hatred); very seriously (of being ill). **dar m.** ( **a**), to kill. **estar a la m.,** to be on the point of death. **a cada m. de un obispo,** once in a blue moon
**muerto** /'mwerto/ **(-ta)** *a* dead; slaked (lime); *Mech.* neutral; faded, dull (colors); languid, indifferent. **m.** is used in familiar speech as *past part* **matar** (e.g. *Le ha muerto,* He has killed him) —*n* corpse. *Inf.* **desenterrar los muertos,** to speak ill of the dead. *Inf.* **echarle a uno el m.,** to pass the buck. *Inf.* **estar m. por,** to be dying, yearning for. **ser el m.,** to be dummy (at cards)
**muesca** /'mweska/ *f*, notch, mortise, groove
**muestra** /'mwestra/ *f*, shop sign; sample, specimen; pattern, model; demeanor; watch or clock face; sign, indication; poster, placard; *Mil.* muster roll. **hacer m.,** to show
**muestrario** /mues'trario/ *m*, sample book, collection of samples
**mufla** /'mufla/ *f*, muffler (of a furnace)
**mugido** /mu'hiðo/ *m*, mooing or lowing (of cattle)
**mugir** /mu'hir/ *vi* to low or moo (cattle); bellow, shout; rage (elements)
**mugre** /'mugre/ *f*, grease, grime, dirt
**mugriento** /mu'griento/ *a* grimy, greasy
**muguete** /mu'gete/ *m*, lily of the valley
**mujer** /mu'her/ *f*, woman; wife. **m. de la vida airada** or **m. del partido** or **m. pública,** prostitute. **m. de la luna,** man in the moon. **m. de su casa,** good housewife. **tomar m.,** to take a wife
**mujeriego** /muhe'riego/ *a* womanly, feminine; (of men) dissolute, given to philandering. **cabalgar a mujeriegas,** to ride sidesaddle
**mujeril** /muhe'ril/ *a* womanly, feminine
**mula** /'mula/ *f*, female mule; mule (heelless slipper). *Inf.* **Se me fue la m.,** My tongue ran away with me
**muladar** /mula'ðar/ *m*, refuse heap, junkpile, dunghill
**mular** /mu'lar/ *a* mulish
**mulatero** /mula'tero/ *m*, mule hirer; muleteer
**mulato** /mu'lato/ **(-ta)** *a* and *n* mulatto
**muleta** /mu'leta/ *f*, crutch; bullfighter's red flag; support, prop
**mullir** /mu'ʎir/ *vt irr* to make soft, shake out (wool, down, etc.); *Fig.* prepare the way; *Agr.* hoe the roots (of vines, etc.) —*Pres. Part.* **mullendo.** *Preterite* **mulló, mulleron.** *Imperf. Subjunc.* **mullese,** etc.
**mulo** /'mulo/ *m*, mule
**multa** /'multa/ *f*, fine
**multar** /mul'tar/ *vt* to impose a fine on
**multicolor** /multiko'lor/ *a* multicolored
**multiforme** /multi'forme/ *a* multiform
**multilátero** /multi'latero/ *a* multilateral
**multimillonario** /multimiʎo'nario; multimiyo'nario/ **(-ia)** *a* and *n* multimillionaire
**multiplicación** /multiplika'θion; multiplika'sion/ *f*, multiplication
**multiplicador** /multiplika'ðor/ **(-ra)** *a* multiplier. *m*, *Math.* multiplier
**multiplicando** /multipli'kando/ *m*, multiplicand
**multiplicar** /multipli'kar/ **((se)** *vt* and *vr* to multiply; reproduce
**multiplicidad** /multipliθi'ðað; multiplisi'ðað/ *f*, multiplicity
**múltiplo** /'multiplo/ *a* and *m*, multiple
**multisecular** /multiseku'lar/ *a* age-old, many centuries old
**multitud** /multi'tuð/ *f*, multitude, great number; crowd; rabble, masses, mob
**mundanal, mundano** /munda'nal, mun'dano/ *a* worldly, mundane
**mundanalidad** /mundanali'ðað/ *f*, worldliness
**mundial** /mun'dial/ *a* world, worldwide
**mundo** /'mundo/ *m*, world, universe; human race; earth; human society; world (of letters, science, etc.); secular life; *Eccl.* vanities of the flesh; geographical globe. **echar al m.,** to give birth to; produce, bring

forth. **el Nuevo M.,** the New World, America. *Inf.* **medio m.,** half the earth, a great crowd. *Inf.* **ponerse el m. por montera,** to treat the world as one's oyster. **ser hombre del m.,** to be a man of the world. *Inf.* **tener m.** or **mucho m.,** to be very experienced, know the world. **todo el m.,** everyone. **venir al m.,** to be born. **ver m.,** to travel, see the world
**mundología** /mundolo'hia/ *f*, worldliness, experience of the world
**munición** /muni'θion; muni'sion/ *f*, *Mil.* munition; small shot. *Mil.* **m. de boca,** fodder and food supplies
**municionar** /muniθio'nar; munisio'nar/ *vt* to munition, furnish with munitions
**municionero** /muniθio'nero; munisio'nero/ **(-ra)** *n* purveyor, supplier
**municipal** /muniθi'pal; munisi'pal/ *a* municipal. *m*, policeman
**municipalidad** /muniθipali'ðað; munisipali'ðað/ *f*, municipality
**municipio** /muni'θipio; muni'sipio/ *m*, municipality, town council
**munificencia** /munifi'θenθia; munifi'sensia/ *f*, munificence, generosity
**munífico** /mu'nifiko/ *a* munificent, generous
**muñeca** /mu'ɲeka/ *f*, *Anat.* wrist; doll; puppet; dressmaker's dummy; polishing pad; mannequin; boundary marker; *Inf.* flighty young woman
**muñeco** /mu'ɲeko/ *m*, boy doll; puppet; *Inf.* playboy
**muñir** /mu'ɲir/ *vt irr* to summon, convoke; arrange, dispose. See **mullir**
**muñón** /mu'ɲon/ *m*, *Surg.* stump of an amputated limb; *Mech.* gudgeon
**mural** /mu'ral/ *a* mural
**muralla** /mu'raʎa; mu'raya/ *f*, town wall; rampart, fortification
**murar** /mu'rar/ *vt* to surround with a wall, wall in
**murciano** /mur'θiano; mur'siano/ **(-na)** *a* and *n* Murcian
**murciélago** /mur'θielago; mur'sielago/ *m*, *Zool.* bat
**murga** /'murga/ *f*, band of street musicians
**murmullo** /mur'muʎo; mur'muyo/ *m*, whisper; whispering; rustling; purling, lapping, splashing; mumbling, muttering
**murmuración** /murmura'θion; murmura'sion/ *f*, slander, backbiting, gossip
**murmurador** /murmura'ðor/ **(-ra)** *a* gossiping, slanderous —*n* gossip, backbiter
**murmurar** /murmu'rar/ *vi* to rustle (leaves, etc.); purl, lap, splash (water); whisper; mumble, mutter; —*vi* and *vt* *Inf.* slander, backbite
**murmurio** /mur'murio/ *m*, rustling; lapping (of water); whispering; murmur; *Inf.* slander
**muro** /'muro/ *m*, wall; defensive wall, rampart
**musa** /'musa/ *f*, muse
**musaraña** /musa'raɲa/ *f*, *Zool.* shrew; any small animal; *Inf.* ridiculous effigy, guy. *Inf.* **mirar a las musarañas,** to be absent-minded
**muscular** /musku'lar/ *a* muscular
**musculatura** /muskula'tura/ *f*, musculature
**músculo** /'muskulo/ *m*, muscle; strength, brawn
**musculoso** /musku'loso/ *a* strong, brawny
**muselina** /muse'lina/ *f*, muslin
**museo** /mu'seo/ *m*, museum. **m. de pintura,** art gallery, picture gallery
**musgo** /'musgo/ *m*, moss
**musgoso** /mus'goso/ *a* mossy, moss-grown
**música** /'musika/ *f*, music; melody, harmony; musical performance; musical composition; group of musicians; sheet music. *Inf.* **m. celestial,** vain words, moonshine. *Inf.* **m. ratonera,** badly played music. *Inf.* **¡Vaya con su m. a otra parte!** Get out! Go to hell!
**musical** /musi'kal/ *a* musical
**músico** /'musiko/ **(-ca)** *a* music —*n* musician. **m. ambulante,** strolling musician. **m. mayor,** bandleader
**musitar** /musi'tar/ *vi* to mutter, mumble
**muslo** /'muslo/ *m*, thigh
**mustio** /'mustio/ *a* sad, disheartened, depressed; faded, withered
**musulmán** /musul'man/ **(-ana)** *a* and *n* Muslim

**mutabilidad** /mutaβili'ðað/ f, mutability, changeability

**mutación** /muta'θion; muta'sion/ f, change, mutation; sudden change in the weather; *Theat.* change of scene

**mutilación** /mutila'θion; mutila'sion/ f, mutilation; damage; defacement

**mutilar** /muti'lar/ vt to mutilate; spoil, deface, damage; cut short; reduce

**mutis** /'mutis/ m, *Theat.* exit. **hacer m.** *Theat.* to exit; keep quiet, say nothing

**mutismo** /mu'tismo/ m, mutism, dumbness; silence, speechlessness

**mutualidad** /mutuali'ðað/ f, reciprocity, mutuality, interdependence; principle of mutual aid; mutual aid society

**mutualismo** /mutua'lismo/ m, mutualism, organized mutual aid

**mutualista** /mutua'lista/ mf member of a mutual aid society

**mutuante** /mu'tuante/ mf *Com.* lender

**muy** /'mui/ adv very; very much; much. Used to form absolute superlative (e.g. m. *rápidamente,* very quickly). Can modify adjectives, nouns used adjectivally, adverbs, participles (e.g. *María es m. mujer,* Mary is very much a woman (very womanly)). **m. temprano,** very early. **M. señor mío,** Dear Sir (in letters)

# N Ñ

naba /'naβa/ f, swede, turnip
nabar /na'βar/ m, turnip field
nabo /'naβo/ m, turnip; turnip root; any root stem; *Naut.* mast; stock (of a horse's tail)
nácar /'nakar/ m, mother-of-pearl
nacarado, nacáreo /naka'raðo, na'kareo/ a nacreous, mother-of-pearl
nacer /na'θer/ na'ser/ vi irr to be born; rise (rivers, etc.); sprout; grow (plumage, fur, leaves, etc.); descend (lineage); appear (stars, etc.); originate; *Fig.* issue forth; appear suddenly; (*with prep a* or *para*) be destined for, have a natural leaning toward. **n. con pajitas de oro en la cuna,** to be born with a silver spoon in one's mouth —*vr* grow; sprout; *Sew.* split at the seams —*Pres. Indic.* **nazco, naces,** etc —*Pres. Subjunc.* **nazca,** etc.
nacido /na'θiðo; na'siðo/ a and past part born; suitable, fit. m, (gen. pl) the living and the dead. **bien n.,** noble, well-born; well-bred. **mal n.,** base-born; illbred
naciente /na'θiente; na'siente/ a growing; nascent. m, east
nacimiento /naθi'miento; nasi'miento/ m, birth; source (of rivers, etc.); birthplace; origin; lineage; *Astron.* rising; nativity crib, manger. **de n.,** from birth; by birth; born
nación /na'θion; na'sion/ f, nation; country; *Inf.* birth
nacional /naθio'nal; nasio'nal/ a national; native. *mf* citizen, national
nacionalidad /naθionali'ðað; nasionali'ðað/ f, nationality
nacionalismo /naθiona'lismo; nasiona'lismo/ m, nationalism
nacionalista /naθiona'lista; nasiona'lista/ a and *mf* nationalist
nacionalización /naθionaliθa'θion; nasionalisa'sion/ f, naturalization; nationalization; acclimatization
nacionalizar /naθionali'θar; nasionali'sar/ vt to naturalize; nationalize
nacionalsindicalismo /naθio͵nalsindika'lismo; nasio͵nalsindika'lismo/ m, national syndicalism
nacionalsocialismo /naθio͵nalsoθia'lismo; nasio͵nalsosia'lismo/ m, national socialism, nazism
nada /'naða/ f, void, nothingness —*pron indef* nothing —*adv* by no means. **casi n.,** very little, practically nothing. **¡De n.!** Not at all! Don't mention it! You're welcome! **No vale para n.,** He (it, she) is of no use
nadaderas /naða'ðeras/ f pl, water wings (for swimming)
nadador /naða'ðor/ (-ra) n swimmer —a swimming
nadar /na'ðar/ vi to swim; float; have an abundance (of); *Inf.* be too large (of garments, etc.). **n. y guardar la ropa,** *Fig.* to sit on the fence
nadería /naðe'ria/ f, trifle
nadie /'naðie/ pron indef no one. m, *Fig.* a nobody
nadir /na'ðir/ m, nadir
nado /'naðo/ a by swimming; afloat
nafta /'nafta/ f, naphtha
naftalina /nafta'lina/ f, naphthalene
naipe /'naipe/ m, playing card; pack of cards
naire /'naire/ m, elephant keeper or trainer
nalga /'nalga/ f, (gen. pl) buttock(s)
nana /'nana/ f, *Inf.* grandma; lullaby
nao /'nao/ f, ship
napoleónico /napole'oniko/ a Napoleonic
Nápoles /'napoles/ Naples
napolitano /napoli'tano/ (-na) a and n Neapolitan
naranja /na'ranha/ f, orange. **n. dulce,** blood orange. **n. mandarina,** tangerine. *Inf.* **media n.,** better half
naranjada /naran'haða/ f, orangeade
naranjal /naran'hal/ m, orange grove
naranjero /naran'hero/ (-ra) n orange seller
naranjo /na'ranho/ m, orange tree; *Inf.* lout, blockhead

narciso /nar'θiso; nar'siso/ m, narcissus; dandy, fop. **n. trompón,** daffodil
narcótico /nar'kotiko/ a and m, narcotic
narcotizar /narkoti'θar; narkoti'sar/ vt to narcotize
narcotraficante /narkotrafi'kante/ mf drug dealer
nardo /'narðo/ m, tuberose, spikenard, nard
narguile /nar'gile/ m, hookah, hubble-bubble, narghile
narigudo /nari'guðo/ a large-nosed; nose-shaped
nariz /na'riθ; na'ris/ f, nose; nostril; snout; nozzle; sense of smell; bouquet (of wine). **n. perfilada,** well-shaped nose. **n. respingona,** snub nose. *Inf.* **meter las narices,** to meddle, interfere
narración /narra'θion; narra'sion/ f, narration, account
narrador /narra'ðor/ (-ra) a narrative —n narrator
narrar /na'rrar/ vt to narrate, tell, relate
narrativa /narra'tiβa/ f, narrative; account; narrative skill
narrativo, narratorio /narra'tiβo, narra'torio/ a narrative
nata /'nata/ f, cream; *Fig.* the flower, elite; pl whipped cream with sugar
natación /nata'θion; nata'sion/ f, swimming. **n. a la marinera,** trudgen stroke
natal /na'tal/ a natal; native. m, birth; birthday
natalicio /nata'liθio; nata'lisio/ a natal —a and m, birthday
natalidad /natali'ðað/ f, birth rate
natatorio /nata'torio/ a swimming. m, swimming pool
natillas /na'tiʎas; na'tiyas/ f pl, custard
natividad /natiβi'ðað/ f, nativity; birth; Christmas
nativo /na'tiβo/ a indigenous; native; innate
nato /'nato/ a born; inherent; ex officio
natura /na'tura/ f, nature; *Mus.* major scale
natural /natu'ral/ a natural; native; indigenous; spontaneous; sincere, candid; physical; usual, ordinary; *Mus.* natural; unadulterated, pure; *Herald.* proper. mf native, citizen. m, temperament; disposition; instinct (of animals); natural inclination. **al n.,** naturally, without art. **del n.,** *Art.* from life
naturaleza /natura'leθa; natura'lesa/ f, nature; character; disposition; instinct; temperament; nationality, origin; naturalization; kind, class; constitution, physique. **n. humana,** humankind. **n. muerta,** *Art.* still life
naturalidad /naturali'ðað/ f, naturalness; nationality
naturalista /natura'lista/ mf naturalist
naturalización /naturaliθa'θion; naturalisa'sion/ f, naturalization; acclimatization
naturalizar /naturali'θar; naturali'sar/ vt to naturalize; acclimatize; —vr become naturalized; become acclimatized
naturalmente /natural'mente/ adv naturally; of course
naturismo /natu'rismo/ m, nature cure
naufragar /naufra'gar/ vi to be shipwrecked; fail, be unsuccessful
naufragio /nau'frahio/ m, shipwreck; disaster, loss
náufrago /'naufrago/ (-ga) n shipwrecked person. m, shark
náusea /'nausea/ f, nausea (pl more usual); repugnance
nauseabundo, nauseoso /nausea'βundo, nause'oso/ a nauseous; nauseating, repugnant
nauta /'nauta/ mf mariner
náutica /'nautika/ f, navigation; yachting; seamanship
náutico /'nautiko/ a nautical
navaja /na'βaha/ f, razor; clasp knife; boar tusk; sting; *Inf.* slanderous tongue. **n. de afeitar,** (shaving) razor
navajada /naβa'haða/ f, slash with a razor
navajero /naβa'hero/ m, razor case
naval /na'βal/ a naval

**Navarra** /na'βarra/ Navarre

**navarro** /na'βarro/ **(-ra)** *a* and *n* Navarrese

**nave** /'naβe/ *f*, ship; *Archit.* nave. **n. aérea,** airship. *Archit.* **n. lateral,** aisle. **n. principal,** *Archit.* nave

**navegable** /naβe'gaβle/ *a* navigable

**navegación** /naβega'θion; naβega'sion/ *f*, navigation; sea voyage

**navegante** /naβe'gante/ *a* voyaging; navigating. *m*, navigator

**navegar** /naβe'gar/ *vi* to navigate; sail; fly

**navidad** /naβi'ðað/ *f*, nativity; Christmas; *pl* Christmastime

**naviero** /na'βiero/ *a* shipping. *m*, ship owner

**navío** /na'βio/ *m*, warship; ship. **n. de transporte,** transport. **n. de tres puentes,** three-decker

**náyade** /'naiaðe/ *f*, naiad, water nymph

**nazareno** /naθa'reno; nasa'reno/ **(-na)** *a* and *n* Nazarene; Christian

**Nazaret** /naθa'ret; nasa'ret/ Nazareth

**nazismo** /na'θismo; na'sismo/ *m*, nazism

**neblina** /ne'βlina/ *f*, fog; mist

**nebulosidad** /neβulosi'ðað/ *f*, nebulousness; cloudiness

**nebuloso** /neβu'loso/ *a* foggy; misty; cloudy; somber, melancholy; confused, nebulous

**necedad** /neθe'ðað; nese'ðað/ *f*, silliness

**necesario** /neθe'sario; nese'sario/ *a* necessary; unavoidable

**neceser** /neθe'ser; nese'ser/ *m*, dressing case. *Sew.* **n. de costura,** workbox

**necesidad** /neθesi'ðað; nesesi'ðað/ *f*, necessity; poverty, want; shortage, need; emergency. **de n.,** necessarily

**necesitado** /neθesi'taðo; nesesi'taðo/ **(-da)** *a* needy, poor —*n* poor person

**necesitar** /neθesi'tar; nesesi'tar/ *vt* to necessitate; compel, oblige; —*vi* be necessary, need

**necio** /'neθio; 'nesio/ *a* stupid; senseless; unreasonable

**necrología** /nekrolo'hia/ *f*, necrology, obituary

**necromancía** /nekroman'θia; nekroman'sia/ *f*, necromancy

**neerlandés** /neerlan'des/ *a* Dutch

**nefando** /ne'fando/ *a* iniquitous

**nefario** /ne'fario/ *a* nefarious

**nefasto** /ne'fasto/ *a* disastrous, ill-omened

**nefrítico** /ne'fritiko/ *a* nephritic

**nefritis** /ne'fritis/ *f*, nephritis

**negable** /ne'gaβle/ *a* deniable

**negación** /nega'θion; nega'sion/ *f*, negation; privation; negative; nay; *Gram.* negative particle; *Law.* traverse

**negado** /ne'gaðo/ *a* inept, unfitted; stupid

**negar** /ne'gar/ *vt irr* to deny; refuse; prohibit; disclaim; dissemble; disown; *Law.* traverse; —*vr* refuse, avoid; decline (to receive visitors). See **acertar**

**negativa** /nega'tiβa/ *f*, denial; refusal; *Photo.* negative

**negativo** /nega'tiβo/ *a* negative

**negligencia** /negli'henθia; negli'hensia/ *f*, negligence; omission; carelessness; forgetfulness

**negligente** /negli'hente/ *a* negligent; careless; neglectful

**negociable** /nego'θiaβle; nego'siaβle/ *a* negotiable

**negociación** /negoθia'θion; negosia'sion/ *f*, negotiation; business affair, deal

**negociado** /nego'θiaðo; nego'siaðo/ *m*, department, section (of a ministry, etc.); business

**negociante** /nego'θiante; nego'siante/ *m*, businessman —*a* negotiating; trading

**negociar** /nego'θiar; nego'siar/ *vi* to trade, traffic; negotiate

**negocio** /ne'goθio; ne'gosio/ *m*, occupation; trade; business; employment; transaction; *pl* business affairs. **hombre de negocios,** businessman

**negra** /'negra/ *f*, black girl, black woman; *Inf.* honey, *West Hem.* sweetheart

**negrecer** /negre'θer; negre'ser/ *vi irr* to become black. See **conocer**

**negrero** /ne'grero/ **(-ra)** *n* slave trader

**negro** /'negro/ *a* black; dark; melancholy; disas-

trous; *Herald.* sable. *m*, black; black (color). **n. de humo,** lampblack

**negrura** /ne'grura/ *f*, blackness

**negruzco** /ne'gruθko; ne'grusko/ *a* blackish

**nemotécnica** /nemo'teknika/ *f*, mnemonics

**nene** /'nene/ **(-na)** *n Inf.* baby; darling

**nenúfar** /ne'nufar/ *m*, white water lily

**neo** /'neo/ *m*, neon

**neocelandés** /neoθelan'des; neoselan'des/ **(-esa)** *a* New Zealand —*n* New Zealander

**neófito** /ne'ofito/ **(-ta)** *n* neophyte

**neoguineano** /neogine'ano/ *a* New Guinean

**neolítico** /neo'litiko/ *a* neolithic

**neologismo** /neolo'hismo/ *m*, neologism

**neoyorquino** /neoior'kino/ **(-na)** *a* New York —*n* New Yorker

**nepotismo** /nepo'tismo/ *m*, nepotism

**Neptuno** /nep'tuno/ *m*, *Astron.* Neptune; *Poet.* sea

**nereida** /ne'reiða/ *f*, nereid, sea nymph

**nervio** /'nerβio/ *m*, nerve; sinew; *Bot.* vein; vigor; *Mus.* string. **n. ciático,** sciatic nerve

**nervioso** /ner'βioso/ *a* nervous; overwrought, agitated; vigorous; neural; sinewy; jerky (of style, etc.)

**nervosidad** /nerβosi'ðað/ *f*, nervousness; nervosity; flexibility (metals); jerkiness (of style, etc.); force, efficacy

**nervudo** /ner'βuðo/ *a* strong-nerved, vigorous

**nesga** /'nesga/ *f*, *Sew.* gore

**neto** /'neto/ *a* neat; clean; pure; *Com.* net. *m*, *Archit.* dado

**neumático** /neu'matiko/ *a* pneumatic. *m*, rubber tire

**neumococo** /neumo'koko/ *m*, pneumococcus

**neurálgico** /neu'ralhiko/ *a* neuralgic

**neurastenia** /neuras'tenia/ *f*, neurasthenia

**neurasténico** /neuras'teniko/ **(-ca)** *a* and *n* neurasthenic

**neurología** /neurolo'hia/ *f*, neurology

**neurólogo** /neu'rologo/ *m*, neurologist

**neurópata** /neu'ropata/ *mf* neuropath

**neurosis** /neu'rosis/ *f*, neurosis. **n. de guerra,** war neurosis; shell shock

**neurótico** /neu'rotiko/ **(-ca)** *a* and *n* neurotic

**neutral** /neu'tral/ *a* neutral; indifferent

**neutralidad** /neutrali'ðað/ *f*, neutrality; impartiality, indifference

**neutralizar** /neutrali'θar; neutrali'sar/ *vt* to neutralize; counteract, mitigate

**neutro** /'neutro/ *a* neuter; *Chem.* neutral; *Mech.* neuter; sexless

**nevada** /ne'βaða/ *f*, snowfall

**nevar** /ne'βar/ *vi irr impers* to snow —*Pres. Indic.* **nieva.** *Pres. Subjunc.* **nieve**

**nevera** /ne'βera/ *f*, refrigerator; icehouse

**nevero** /ne'βero/ *m*, ice-cream man; iceman

**nevisca** /ne'βiska/ *f*, light snowfall

**nevoso** /ne'βoso/ *a* snowy

**nexo** /'nekso/ *m*, nexus; connection; union

**ni** /ni/ *conjunc* neither, nor. **ni bien ni mal,** neither good nor bad. **ni siquiera,** not even. **¡Ni crea!, ¡Ni creas!** Nonsense!

**niara** /'niara/ *f*, haystack, rick

**nicaragüeño** /nikara'gueɲo/ **(-ña)** *a* and *n* Nicaraguan

**nicho** /'nitʃo/ *m*, niche; recess (in a wall)

**nicotina** /niko'tina/ *f*, nicotine

**nidada** /ni'ðaða/ *f*, nest full of eggs; brood, clutch

**nidal** /ni'ðal/ *m*, nest; nest egg; haunt; cause, foundation

**nido** /'niðo/ *m*, nest; den; hole; dwelling; haunt. **n. de ametralladoras,** *Mil.* pillbox

**niebla** /'nieβla/ *f*, fog; mist; cloud; mildew; haze

**nieto** /'nieto/ **(-ta)** *n* grandchild; descendant

**nieve** /'nieβe/ *f*, snow; whiteness. **deportes de n.,** winter sports

**nigromancia** /nigro'manθia; nigro'mansia/ *f*, necromancy

**nigromante** /nigro'mante/ *m*, necromancer

**nihilismo** /nii'lismo/ *m*, nihilism

**nihilista** /nii'lista/ *mf* nihilist

**Nilo, el** /'nilo, el/ the Nile

**nimbo** /'nimbo/ *m*, halo, nimbus

**nimiedad** /nimie'ðað/ f, prolixity; *Inf.* fussiness; fastidiousness, delicacy
**nimio** /'nimio/ a prolix; *Inf.* fussy; fastidious; *Inf.* parsimonious
**ninfa** /'ninfa/ f, nymph; *Ent.* chrysalis
**ningún** /nin'gun/ a *Abbr.* of **ninguno.** Used before *m, sing* nouns only. **De n. modo,** In no way! Certainly not!
**Nínive** /'niniβe/ Nineveh
**niña** /'nina/ f, girl. **n. del ojo,** pupil (of the eye). **n. de los ojos,** apple of one's eye, darling
**niñada** /ni'naða/ f, childishness, foolish act
**niñera** /ni'nera/ f, nursemaid
**niñería** /nine'ria/ f, childish act; trifle; childishness, folly
**niñez** /ni'neθ; ni'nes/ f, childhood; beginning, early days; *Fig.* cradle
**niño** /'nino/ **(-ña)** a childish; young; inexperienced; imprudent —*n* child; young or inexperienced person. **n. de la doctrina,** charity child. **n. terrible,** enfant terrible. **desde n.,** from childhood
**nipón** /ni'pon/ **(-ona)** a and *n* Japanese
**níquel** /'nikel/ m, *Chem.* nickel
**niquelar** /nike'lar/ *vt* to chrome-plate
**nirvana** /nir'βana/ m, nirvana
**níspero** /'nispero/ m, medlar tree; medlar
**nispola** /'nispola/ f, medlar
**nitidez** /niti'ðeθ; niti'ðes/ f, brightness, neatness, cleanliness
**nítido** /'nitiðo/ a bright, neat, clean (often *Poet.*)
**nitrato** /ni'trato/ m, nitrate
**nítrico** /'nitriko/ a nitric
**nitrógeno** /ni'troheno/ m, nitrogen
**nivel** /ni'βel/ m, level; levelness. **n. de albañil,** plummet. **n. de burbuja,** spirit level. **a n.,** on the level. **estar al n. de las circunstancias,** to rise to the occasion; save the day
**nivelación** /niβela'θion; niβela'sion/ f, leveling
**nivelador** /niβela'ðor/ **(-ra)** a leveling —*n* leveler
**nivelar** /niβe'lar/ *vt* to level; *Fig.* make equal
**níveo** /'niβeo/ a snowy; snow-white
**Niza** /'niθa; 'nisa/ Nice
**no** /no/ *adv* no; not. **no bien,** no sooner. **no sea que,** unless. **no tal,** no such thing
**noble** /'noβle/ a noble, illustrious; generous; outstanding, excellent; aristocratic. *mf* nobleman (-woman)
**nobleza** /no'βleθa; no'βlesa/ f, nobility
**noche** /'notfe/ f, night; darkness; confusion, obscurity. *Inf.* **n. toledana,** restless night. **¡Buenas noches!** Good night! **de n.,** by night. **esta n.,** tonight
**nochebuena** /notfe'βuena/ f, Christmas Eve
**nochebueno** /notfe'βueno/ m, yule log; Christmas cake
**nocherniego** /notfer'niego/ a night, nocturnal
**noción** /no'θion; no'sion/ f, notion, idea; *pl* elementary knowledge
**nocividad** /noθiβi'ðað; nosiβi'ðað/ f, noxiousness
**nocivo** /no'θiβo; no'siβo/ a noxious
**nocturno** /nok'turno/ a nocturnal; melancholy. m, *Mus.* nocturne
**nodriza** /no'ðriθa; no'ðrisa/ f, wet nurse
**nogal** /no'gal/ m, walnut tree; walnut wood
**nómada** /'nomaða/ a nomadic
**nomadismo** /noma'ðismo/ m, nomadism
**nombradia** /nom'βraðia/ f, renown
**nombramiento** /nombra'miento/ m, naming; appointment; nomination
**nombrar** /nom'βrar/ *vt* to name; nominate; appoint; mention (in dispatches, etc.)
**nombre** /'nombre/ m, name; title; reputation; proxy; *Gram.* noun; *Mil.* password. **n. de pila,** Christian name. **por n.,** called; by name. **Su n. anda puesto en el cuerno de la Luna,** He (she) is praised to the skies
**nomenclatura** /nomenkla'tura/ f, nomenclature
**nómina** /'nomina/ f, list, register; payroll; amulet
**nominación** /nomina'θion; nomina'sion/ f, nomination, appointment
**nominador** /nomina'ðor/ **(-ra)** a nominating —*n* nominator

**nominal** /nomi'nal/ a nominal
**nominalismo** /nomina'lismo/ m, nominalism
**nominalista** /nomina'lista/ a nominalistic. *mf* nominalist
**nomo** /'nomo/ m, gnome
**non** /non/ a odd (of numbers)
**nonada** /no'naða/ f, nothing, practically nothing
**nonagenario** /nonahe'nario/ **(-ia)** a and *n* nonagenarian
**nonagésimo** /nona'hesimo/ a ninetieth
**nones** /'nones/ m, *pl* certainly not, definitely not, nope
**nopal** /no'pal/ m, nopal, prickly pear tree
**noque** /'noke/ m, tanner's vat
**noquear** /noke'ar/ *vt* (*Boxing*) to knock out, K.O.
**norabuena** /nora'βuena/ f, congratulation
**nordeste** /nor'ðeste/ m, northeast
**nórdico** /'norðiko/ **(-ca)** a and *n* Nordic
**noria** /'noria/ f, water well; chain pump; *Inf.* hard, monotonous work
**norma** /'norma/ f, square (used by builders, etc.); *Fig.* norm, standard, model
**normal** /nor'mal/ a normal, usual; standard, average. f, normal school, teacher's college (also **escuela n.**)
**normalidad** /normali'ðað/ f, normality
**normalista** /norma'lista/ *mf* student at a teacher's college
**normalización** /normaliθa'θion; normalisa'sion/ f, normalization; standardization
**normalizar** /normali'θar; normali'sar/ *vt* to make normal; standardize
**Normandía** /norman'dia/ Normandy
**normando** /nor'mando/ **(-da)** a Norman —*n* Northman; Norman
**nornordeste** /nornor'ðeste/ m, northnortheast
**nornorueste** /nornor'rueste/ m, northnorthwest
**noroeste** /noro'este/ m, northwest
**norte** /'norte/ m, north pole; north; north wind; polestar; *Fig.* guide
**norteamericano** /norteameri'kano/ **(-na)** a and *n* North American; (*U.S.A.*) American
**norteño** /nor'teno/ a northerly, northern
**Noruega** /no'ruega/ Norway
**noruego** /no'ruego/ **(-ga)** a and *n* Norwegian. m, Norwegian (language)
**nos** /nos/ *pers pron, pl mf acc* and *dat* (direct and indirect object) of **nosotros,** us; to us (e.g. *Nos lo dio,* He gave it to us)
**nosotros, nosotras** /no'sotros, no'sotras/ *pers pron, pl mf* we; us. Also used with preposition (e.g. *Lo hicieron por nosotros,* They did it for us)
**nostalgia** /nos'talhia/ f, nostalgia
**nostálgico** /nos'talhiko/ a nostalgic; melancholy; homesick
**nóstico** /'nostiko/ **(-ca)** a and *n* gnostic
**nota** /'nota/ f, mark, sign; annotation, comment; *Mus.* note; memorandum; *Com.* bill, account; criticism, imputation; mark (in exams); repute, renown; note (diplomatic)
**notabilidad** /notaβili'ðað/ f, notability
**notable** /no'taβle/ a notable, remarkable; outstanding, prominent; with distinction (examination mark). *m pl,* notabilities
**notación** /nota'θion; nota'sion/ f, (*Mus. Math.*) notation; annotation
**notar** /no'tar/ *vt* to mark, indicate; observe, notice; note down; annotate; dictate, read out; criticize, reproach; discredit
**notaría** /nota'ria/ f, profession of a notary; notary's office
**notarial** /nota'rial/ a notarial
**notario** /no'tario/ m, notary public
**noticia** /no'tiθia; no'tisia/ f, rudiment, elementary knowledge; information; news (gen. *pl*); *pl* knowledge. **atrasado de noticias,** *Fig.* behind the times
**noticiar** /noti'θiar; noti'siar/ *vt* to inform, give notice
**noticiario** /noti'θiario; noti'siario/ m, news bulletin; newsreel
**noticiero** /noti'θiero; noti'siero/ m, newspaper
**noticioso** /noti'θioso; noti'sioso/ a informed; learned; newsy

**notificación** /notifika'θion; notifika'sion/ *f, Law.* notification. **n. de reclutamiento,** draft notice

**notificar** /notifi'kar/ *vt* to notify officially; inform; warn

**noto** /'noto/ *a* known. *m,* south wind

**notoriedad** /notorie'ðað/ *f,* notoriety, publicity; flagrancy; fame, renown

**notorio** /no'torio/ *a* well-known; notorious, obvious; flagrant

**novatada** /noβa'taða/ *f, Inf.* ragging (of a freshman); blunder

**novato** /no'βato/ **(-ta)** *a* new, inexperienced —*n* novice, beginner

**novecientos** /noβe'θientos; noβe'sientos/ *a* and *m,* nine hundred

**novedad** /noβe'ðað/ *f,* newness, novelty; change, alteration; latest news; surprise; *pl* novelties. **sin n.,** no change; all well (or as usual); safely, without incident

**novel** /no'βel/ *a* new; inexperienced

**novela** /no'βela/ *f,* novel; tale; falsehood. **n. caballista,** western, cowboy story. **n. por entregas,** serial (story)

**novelero** /noβe'lero/ **(-ra)** *a* fond of novelty and change; fond of novels; fickle —*n* newshound, gossip

**novelesco** /noβe'lesko/ *a* novelistic; imaginary

**novelista** /noβe'lista/ *mf* novelist

**novelística** /noβe'listika/ *f,* art of novel writing

**novena** /no'βena/ *f, Eccl.* novena, religious services spread over nine days

**noveno** /no'βeno/ *a* and *m,* ninth

**noventa** /no'βenta/ *a* and *m,* ninety; ninetieth

**novia** /'noβia/ *f,* bride; fiancée

**noviazgo** /no'βiaθgo; no'βiasgo/ *m,* engagement, betrothal

**noviciado** /noβi'θiaðo; noβi'siaðo/ *m,* novitiate; training, apprenticeship

**novicio** /no'βiθio; no'βisio/ **(-ia)** *n Eccl.* novice; beginner, apprentice; unassuming person

**noviembre** /no'βiembre/ *m,* November

**novillada** /noβi'ʎaða; noβi'yaða/ *f,* herd of young bulls; bullock baiting

**novillo** /no'βiʎo; no'βiyo/ *m,* bullock. **hacer novillos,** to play truant

**novilunio** /noβi'lunio/ *m,* new moon

**novio** /'noβio/ *m,* bridegroom; fiancé; novice, beginner

**novísimo** /no'βisimo/ *a superl* **nuevo** newest; latest, most recent

**nubada** /nu'βaða/ *f,* cloudburst, rainstorm; abundance, plenty

**nubarrón** /nuβa'rron/ *m,* dense, lowering cloud, storm cloud

**nube** /'nuβe/ *f,* cloud; *Fig.* screen, impediment. **n. de verano,** summer cloud; passing annoyance

**nublado** /nu'βlaðo/ *a* cloudy; overcast. *m,* storm cloud; menace, threat; multitude, crowd

**nublarse** /nu'βlarse/ *vr* to cloud over

**nubloso** /nu'βloso/ *a* cloudy; unfortunate, unhappy

**nuca** /'nuka/ *f,* nape

**núcleo** /'nukleo/ *m,* kernel; stone, pip (of fruit); nucleus; *Fig.* core, essence

**nudillo** /nu'ðiʎo; nu'ðiyo/ *m,* knuckle; *Mas.* plug

**nudo** /'nuðo/ *m,* knot; (*Bot. Med.*) node; joint; *Naut.* knot; *Fig.* bond, tie; *Fig.* crux, knotty point. **n. al revés,** granny knot. **n. de comunicaciones,** communication center. **n. de marino,** reef knot. **n. de teje-**

**dor,** sheet bend (knot). **n. en la garganta,** *Fig.* lump in the throat (from emotion)

**nudoso** /nu'ðoso/ *a* knotted, knotty; gnarled

**nuera** /'nuera/ *f,* daughter-in-law

**nuestro, nuestra** /'nuestro, 'nuestra/ *poss pron 1st pers pl mf* our; ours. **los nuestros,** our friends, supporters, party, profession, etc.

**nueva** /'nueβa/ *f,* news

**Nueva Caledonia** /'nueβa kale'ðonia/ New Caledonia

**Nueva Escocia** /'nueβa es'koθia; 'nueβa es'kosia/ Nova Scotia

**Nueva Gales del Sur** /'nueβa 'gales del sur/ New South Wales

**Nueva Guinea** /'nueβa gi'nea/ New Guinea

**nuevamente** /nueβa'mente/ *adv* again

**Nueva Orleans** /'nueβa orle'ans/ New Orleans

**Nueva York** /'nueβa york/ New York

**Nueva Zelanda, Zelandia** /'nueβa θe'landa, θe'landia; 'nueβa se'landa, se'landia/ New Zealand

**nueve** /'nueβe/ *a* nine; ninth. *m,* number nine; ninth (of the month) (e.g. *el nueve de marzo,* March 9th). **a las nueve,** at nine o'clock

**nuevo** /'nueβo/ *a* new; fresh; newly arrived; inexperienced; unused, scarcely worn. **de n.,** again. **¿Qué hay de n.?** What's the news? What's new?

**nuez** /nueθ; nues/ *f,* walnut; *Anat.* Adam's apple. **n. moscada,** nutmeg

**nulidad** /nuli'ðað/ *f,* nullity; incompetence, ineptitude; worthlessness

**nulo** /'nulo/ *a* null, void; incapable; worthless

**numen** /'numen/ *m,* divinity; inspiration

**numeración** /numera'θion; numera'sion/ *f,* calculation; numbering

**numerador** /numera'ðor/ *m,* numerator

**numerar** /nume'rar/ *vt* to number; enumerate; calculate

**numerario** /nume'rario/ *a* numerary. *m,* cash

**numérico** /nu'meriko/ *a* numerical

**número** /'numero/ *m,* number; figure; numeral; size (of gloves, etc.); quantity; issue, copy; rhythm; *Gram.* number; item (of a program); *pl Eccl.* Numbers. **n. del distrito postal,** ZIP code. **n. quebrado,** *Math.* fraction. **sin n.,** numberless

**numeroso** /nume'roso/ *a* numerous; harmonious

**numismática** /numis'matika/ *f,* numismatics

**nunca** /'nunka/ *adv* never. **n. jamás,** nevermore. **N. digas «De esta agua no beberé!»** Never say "Never!"

**nuncio** /'nunθio; 'nunsio/ *m,* messenger; papal nuncio; *Fig.* harbinger

**nupcial** /nup'θial; nup'sial/ *a* nuptial

**nupcialidad** /nupθiali'ðað; nupsiali'ðað/ *f,* marriage rate

**nupcias** /'nupθias; 'nupsias/ *f pl,* nuptials, marriage

**nutria** /'nutria/ *f,* otter, nutria

**nutrición** /nutri'θion; nutri'sion/ *f,* nourishment; nutrition

**nutrido** /nu'triðo/ *a* abundant; numerous

**nutrimento** /nutri'mento/ *m,* nutriment; nourishment; nutrition; *Fig.* food, encouragement

**nutrir** /nu'trir/ *vt* to nourish; encourage; *Fig.* fill

**nutritivo** /nutri'tiβo/ *a* nourishing, nutritive

**ñaques** /'ɲakes/ *m pl,* odds and ends, rubbish

**ñiquiñaque** /ɲiki'ɲake/ *m, Inf.* good-for-nothing, wastrel; *Inf.* trash

**ñoñería** /ɲoɲe'ria/ *f, Inf.* drivel; folly, stupidity. **Déjate de ñoñerías,** *Inf.* Stop being a crybaby

**ñoño** /'ɲoɲo/ **(-ña)** *a Inf.* sentimental; foolish, idiotic. *n* fool.

# O

**o** /o/ *f*, letter O —*conjunc* or, either. **o** becomes **u** before words beginning with **o** or **ho** (e.g. *gloria u honor*)

**oasis** /o'asis/ *m*, oasis; *Fig.* refuge, haven

**obcecación** /oββeka'θion; oββseka'sion/ *f*, blindness; obstinacy; obsession

**obcecar** /oββe'kar; oββse'kar/ *vt* to blind; obsess; *Fig.* dazzle; darken

**obduración** /oββδura'θion; oββδura'sion/ *f*, obstinacy, stubbornness, obduracy

**obedecer** /oββeδe'θer; oββeδe'ser/ *vt irr* to obey; *Fig.* respond; bend, yield (metals, etc.); —*vi* result (from), arise (from). See **conocer**

**obedecimiento** /oββeδeθi'miento; oββeδesi'miento/ *m*, obedience

**obediencia** *f*, obedience

**obediente** /oββe'δiente/ *a* obedient; docile

**obelisco** /oββe'lisko/ *m*, obelisk

**obertura** /oββer'tura/ *f*, *Mus.* overture

**obesidad** /oββesi'δaδ/ *f*, obesity

**obeso** /o'ββeso/ *a* obese

**óbice** /'oββiθe; 'oββise/ *m*, obstacle, impediment

**obispado** /oββis'paδo/ *m*, bishopric

**obispalía** /oββispa'lia/ *f*, bishop's palace; bishopric

**obispo** /o'ββispo/ *m*, bishop. **o. sufragáneo,** suffragan bishop

**óbito** /'oββito/ *m*, death, demise

**obituario** /oββi'tuario/ *m*, obituary; obituary column

**objeción** /oββhe'θion; oββhe'sion/ *f*, objection

**objetar** /oββhe'tar/ *vt* to object to, oppose

**objetivar** /oββheti'ββar/ *vt* to view objectively

**objetividad** /oββhetiββi'δaδ/ *f*, objectivity

**objetivo** /oββhe'tiββo/ *a* objective. *m*, *Opt.* eyepiece; object finder; aim, goal

**objeto** /oββ'heto/ *m*, object; subject, theme; purpose; aim, goal. **sin o.,** without object; aimlessly

**oblea** /o'ββlea/ *f*, seal, wafer

**oblicuidad** /oββlikui'δaδ/ *f*, obliqueness

**oblicuo** /o'ββlikuo/ *a* slanting, oblique

**obligación** /oββliga'θion; oββliga'sion/ *f*, obligation; *Com.* bond; *Com.* debenture; *pl* responsibilities; *Com.* liabilities

**obligacionista** /oββligaθio'nista; oββligasio'nista/ *mf* *Com.* bond holder, debenture holder

**obligado** /oββli'gaδo/ *m*, contractor (to a borough, etc.); *Mus.* obbligato

**obligar** /oββli'gar/ *vt* to compel, oblige, constrain; lay under an obligation; *Law.* mortgage; —*vr* bind oneself, promise

**obligatorio** /oββliga'torio/ *a* obligatory

**oblongo** /o'ββloŋgo/ *a* oblong

**oboe** /o'ββoe/ *m*, oboe; oboe player, oboist

**óbolo** /'oββolo/ *m*, obol, ancient Greek coin

**obra** /'oββra/ *f*, work; anything made; literary, artistic, scientific production; structure, construction; repair, alteration (to buildings, etc.); means, influence, power; labor, or time spent; action, behavior. **o. de caridad,** charitable act. **o. maestra,** masterpiece. **obras públicas,** public works. **poner por o.,** to put into effect; to set to work on. **o. de,** about, approximately

**obrar** /o'ββrar/ *vt* to work; make, do; execute, perform; affect; construct, build; —*vi* be, exist (things); act, behave. **o. mal,** to behave badly, do wrong

**obrero** /o'ββrero/ **(-ra)** *a* working —*n* worker; *pl* workers

**obscenidad** /oββsθeni'δaδ; oββsseni'δaδ/ *f*, obscenity

**obsceno** /oββs'θeno; oββs'seno/ *a* obscene

**obsequiar** /oββse'kiar/ *vt* to entertain, be attentive (to); give presents (to); court, make love to. **Me obsequia con un reloj,** He is presenting me with a watch

**obsequio** /oββ'sekio/ *m*, attention; gift; deference. **en o. de,** as a tribute to

**obsequioso** /oββse'kioso/ *a* obliging, courteous, attentive

**observable** /oββser'ββaββle/ *a* observable

**observación** /oββserββa'θion; oββserββa'sion/ *f*, observation; remark

**observador** /oββserββa'δor/ **(-ra)** *a* observing —*n* observer

**observancia** /oββser'ββanθia; oββser'ββansia/ *f*, observance; respect, reverence

**observar** /oββser'ββar/ *vt* to notice; inspect, examine; fulfill; remark; watch, spy upon; *Astron.* observe

**observatorio** /oββserββa'torio/ *m*, observatory

**obsesión** /oββse'sion/ *f*, obsession

**obsesionar** /oββsesio'nar/ *vt* to obsess

**obseso** /oββ'seso/ *a* obsessed

**obsidiana** /oββsi'δiana/ *f*, obsidian

**obsolecer** /oββsole'θer; oββsole'ser/ *vi* to obsolesce, become obsolete

**obsoleto** /oββso'leto/ *a* obsolete

**obstáculo** /oββs'takulo/ *m*, impediment; obstacle

**obstante, no** /oββs'tante, no/ *adv* in spite of; nevertheless

**obstar** /oββs'tar/ *vi* to impede, hinder

**obstetra** /oββs'tetra/ *mf* obstetrician

**obstetricia** /oββste'triθia; oββste'trisia/ *f*, obstetrics

**obstinación** /oββstina'θion; oββstina'sion/ *f*, obstinacy

**obstinado** /oββsti'naδo/ *a* obstinate, stubborn

**obstinarse** /oββsti'narse/ *vr* (*with en*) to persist in, insist on, be stubborn about

**obstinaz** /oββsti'naθ; oββsti'nas/ *a* obstinate

**obstrucción** /oββstruk'θion; oββstruk'sion/ *f*, obstruction

**obstruccionismo** /oββstrukθio'nismo; oββstruksio'nismo/ *m*, obstructionism

**obstruccionista** /oββstrukθio'nista; oββstruksio'nista/ *mf* obstructionist

**obstruir** /oββs'truir/ *vt irr* to obstruct; block; hinder; —*vr* become choked or stopped up (pipes, etc.). See **huir**

**obtención** /oββten'θion; oββten'sion/ *f*, obtainment; attainment, realization

**obtener** /oββte'ner/ *vt irr* to obtain; attain; maintain, preserve. See **tener**

**obturador** /oββtura'δor/ *m*, stopper; shutter (of a camera)

**obturar** /oββtu'rar/ *vt* to stopper, plug; block, obstruct

**obtuso** /oββ'tuso/ *a* blunt, dull; (*Geom. and Fig.*) obtuse

**obús** /o'ββus/ *m*, howitzer; *Mil.* shell

**obviar** /oββ'ββiar/ *vt* to obviate

**obvio** /'oββββio/ *a* obvious, evident, apparent

**oca** /'oka/ *f*, goose

**ocasión** /oka'sion/ *f*, occasion; opportunity; motive, cause; danger, risk; *Inf.* **asir la o. por la melena,** to take time by the forelock. **de o.,** second-hand

**ocasional** /okasio'nal/ *a* chance, fortuitous; occasional

**ocasionar** /okasio'nar/ *vt* to cause, occasion; excite, provoke; risk, endanger

**ocaso** /o'kaso/ *m*, sunset; west; dusk; decadence, decline

**occidental** /okθiδen'tal; oksiδen'tal/ *a* Western

**occidente** /okθi'δente; oksi'δente/ *m*, West, Occident

**occipital** /okθipi'tal; oksipi'tal/ *a* *Anat.* occipital

**occiso** /ok'θiso; ok'siso/ *a* murdered; killed

**oceánico** /oθe'aniko; ose'aniko/ *a* oceanic

**océano** /o'θeano; o'seano/ *m*, ocean; immensity, abundance

**oceanografía** /oθeanogra'fia; oseanogra'fia/ *f*, oceanography

**ocelote** /oθe'lote; ose'lote/ *m*, ocelot

**ochava** /o'tʃaββa/ *f*, eighth; *Eccl.* octave

**ochavo** /o'tʃaββo/ *m*, *Obs.* small Spanish copper coin

**ochenta** /o'tʃenta/ *a* and *m*, eighty; eightieth

**ochentón** /otʃen'ton/ **(-ona)** *n* octogenarian

**ocho** /'otʃo/ *a* eight; eighth. *m*, figure eight; playing card with eight pips; eight; eighth day (of the month). **las o.,** eight o'clock

**oliente**

**ochocientos** /otʃo'θientos; otʃo'sientos/ *a and m*, eight hundred; eight-hundredth

**ocio** /'oθio; 'osio/ *m*, leisure, idleness; *pl* pastimes; leisure time

**ociosidad** /oθiosi'ðað; osiosi'ðað/ *f*, idleness, laziness; leisure

**ocioso** /o'θioso; o'sioso/ **(-sa)** *a* idle; useless, worthless; unprofitable, fruitless —*n* idle fellow

**ocre** /'okre/ *m*, ocher

**octágono** /ok'tagono/ *m*, octagon

**octava** /ok'taβa/ *f*, octave

**octaviano** /okta'βiano/ *a* Octavian

**octavo** /ok'taβo/ *a* eighth. *m*, eighth. **en o.**, in octavo

**octeto** /ok'teto/ *m*, octet

**octogenario** /oktohe'nario/ **(-ia)** *a and n* octogenarian

**octogésimo** /okto'hesimo/ *a* eightieth

**octubre** /ok'tuβre/ *m*, October

**óctuple** /'oktuple/ *a* octuple, eightfold

**ocular** /oku'lar/ *a* ocular. *m*, eyepiece

**oculista** /oku'lista/ *mf* oculist

**ocultación** /okulta'θion; okulta'sion/ *f*, hiding, concealment

**ocultamente** /okulta'mente/ *adv* secretly

**ocultar** /okul'tar/ *vt* to hide, conceal; disguise; keep secret

**ocultismo** /okul'tismo/ *m*, occultism

**oculto** /o'kulto/ *a* hidden; secret; occult. **en o.**, secretly, quietly

**ocupación** /okupa'θion; okupa'sion/ *f*, occupancy; occupation, pursuit; employment, office, trade

**ocupado** /oku'paðo/ *a* occupied; busy

**ocupante** /oku'pante/ *m*, occupant

**ocupar** /oku'par/ *vt* to take possession of; obtain or hold (job); occupy, fill; inhabit; employ; hinder, embarrass; hold the attention (of); —*vr (with en)* be engaged in, be occupied with; *(with con)* concentrate on (a business affair, etc.)

**ocurrencia** /oku'rrenθia; oku'rrensia/ *f*, occurrence, incident; bright idea; witty remark

**ocurrir** /oku'rrir/ *vi* to anticipate; happen, take place; occur, strike (ideas)

**oda** /'oða/ *f*, ode

**odalisca** /oða'liska/ *f*, odalisk

**odiar** /o'ðiar/ *vt* to hate

**odio** /'oðio/ *m*, hatred; malevolence

**odioso** /o'ðioso/ *a* hateful, odious

**odisea** /oði'sea/ *f*, odyssey

**odontología** /oðontolo'hia/ *f*, odontology

**odontólogo** /oðon'tologo/ *m*, odontologist

**odorífero** /oðo'rifero/ *a* odoriferous, fragrant

**odre** /'oðre/ *m*, goatskin, wineskin; *Inf.* wine bibber

**oesnorueste** /oesno'rueste/ *m*, westnorthwest

**oessudueste** /oessu'ðueste/ *m*, westsouthwest

**oeste** /o'este/ *m*, west

**ofender** /ofen'der/ *vt* to ill-treat, hurt; offend, insult; anger, annoy; —*vr* be offended

**ofendido** /ofen'diðo/ *a* offended; resentful

**ofensa** /o'fensa/ *f*, injury, harm; offense, crime

**ofensiva** /ofen'siβa/ *f*, *Mil.* offensive. **tomar la o.**, to take the offensive

**ofensivo** /ofen'siβo/ *a* offensive

**ofensor** /ofen'sor/ **(-ra)** *n* offender

**oferta** /o'ferta/ *f*, offer; gift; proposal; *Com.* tender. **o. y demanda**, supply and demand

**ofertorio** /ofer'torio/ *m*, *Eccl.* offertory

**oficial** /ofi'θial; ofi'sial/ *a* official. *m*, official; officer; clerk; executioner; worker

**oficiala** /ofi'θiala; ofi'siala/ *f*, trained female worker

**oficialidad** /ofiθiali'ðað; ofisiali'ðað/ *f*, officialdom; officers

**oficiar** /ofi'θiar; ofi'siar/ *vt Eccl.* to celebrate or serve (mass); communicate officially, inform; *Inf. (with de)* act as

**oficina** /ofi'θina; ofi'sina/ *f*, workshop; office; pharmaceutical laboratory; *pl* cellars, basement (of a house)

**oficinesco** /ofiθi'nesko; ofisi'nesko/ *a* bureaucratic, red-tape

**oficinista** /ofiθi'nista; ofisi'nista/ *mf* clerk, office employee, office worker

**oficio** /o'fiθio; o'fisio/ *m*, occupation, employment; office, function, capacity; craft; operation; trade, business; official communication; office, bureau; *Eccl.* office. **Santo O.**, Holy Office. *Fig.* **buenos oficios**, good offices

**oficiosidad** /ofiθiosi'ðað; ofisiosi'ðað/ *f*, diligence, conscientiousness; helpfulness, friendliness; officiousness

**oficioso** /ofi'θioso; ofi'sioso/ *a* conscientious; helpful, useful; officious; meddlesome; unofficial, informal

**ofrecer** /ofre'θer; ofre'ser/ *vt irr* to offer; present; exhibit; consecrate, dedicate; —*vr* occur, suggest itself; volunteer. **¿Qué se le ofrece?** What do you require? What would you like? See **conocer**

**ofrecimiento** /ofreθi'miento; ofresi'miento/ *m*, offer, offering

**ofrenda** /o'frenda/ *f*, *Eccl.* offering; gift, present

**oftalmología** /oftalmolo'hia/ *f*, ophthalmology

**oftalmólogo** /oftal'mologo/ *m*, oculist, ophthalmologist

**ofuscación** /ofuska'θion; ofuska'sion/ *f*. **ofuscamiento** *m*, obfuscation, dazzle, dimness of sight; mental confusion, bewilderment

**ofuscar** /ofus'kar/ *vt* to dazzle, daze; dim, obfuscate; confuse, bewilder

**ogro** /'ogro/ *m*, ogre

**ohmio** /'omio/ *m*, ohm

**oídas, de** /o'iðas, de/ *adv* by hearsay

**oído** /o'iðo/ *m*, sense of hearing; ear. **de o.**, by ear. **decir al o.**, to whisper in a person's ear. *Mus.* **duro de o.**, hard of hearing; having a bad ear (for music). **estar sordo de un o.**, to be deaf in one ear

**oidor** /oi'ðor/ *m*, hearer; judge, *Obs.* magistrate

**oir** /o'ir/ *vt irr* to hear; give ear to, listen; understand —*Pres. Part.* **oyendo**. *Pres. Indic.* **oigo, oyes, oye, oyen**. *Preterite* **oyó, oyeron**. *Pres. Subjunc.* **oiga**, etc. —*Imperf. Subjunc.* **oyese**, etc.

**oíslo** /o'islo/ *mf Inf.* better half

**ojal** /o'hal/ *m*, buttonhole; slit, hole

**¡ojalá!** /oha'la/ *interj* If only that were so! God grant!

**ojeada** /ohe'aða/ *f*, glance

**ojear** /ohe'ar/ *vt* to look at, stare at; bewitch; scare, startle

**ojera** /o'hera/ *f*, dark shadow (under the eye); eye bath

**ojeriza** /ohe'riθa; ohe'risa/ *f*, ill-will, spite

**ojeroso** /ohe'roso/ *a* having dark shadows under the eyes, wan, haggard

**ojete** /o'hete/ *m*, eyelet

**ojinegro** /ohi'negro/ *a* black-eyed

**ojiva** /o'hiβa/ *f*, ogive

**ojo** /'oho/ *m*, eye; hole; slit; socket; keyhole; eye (of a needle); span (of a bridge); core (of a corn); attention, care; mesh; spring, stream; well (of a staircase); *pl* darling. **¡Ojo!** Take care! **o. avizor**, sharp watch; lynx eye. **Ojos que no ven, corazón que no siente**, Out of sight, out of mind. **o. saltón**, prominent, bulging eye. **o. vivo**, bright eye. **a o. de buen cubero**, at a guess. **a ojos vistas**, visibly; patently

**ola** /'ola/ *f*, billow; wave (atmospheric)

**ole** /'ole/ *m*, Andalusian dance

**¡olé!** /o'le/ *interj* Bravo!

**oleada** /ole'aða/ *f*, big wave, breaker; swell (of the sea); *Fig.* surge (of a crowd)

**oleaginoso** /oleahi'noso/ *a* oleaginous

**oleaje** /ole'ahe/ *m*, swell, surge, billowing

**olear** /ole'ar/ *vt* to administer extreme unction

**óleo** /'oleo/ *m*, oil; *Eccl.* holy oil (gen. *pl*). **al ó.**, in oils

**oleoducto** /oleo'ðukto/ *m*, oil pipeline

**oler** /o'ler/ *vt irr* to smell; guess, discover; pry, smell out; —*vi* smell; *(with prep a)* smell of; smack of, be reminiscent of —*Pres. Indic.* **huelo, hueles, huele, huelen**. *Pres. Subjunc.* **huela, huelas, huela, huelan**

**olfatear** /olfate'ar/ *vt* to sniff, snuff, smell; *Inf.* pry into

**olfativo, olfatorio** /olfa'tiβo, olfa'torio/ *a* olfactory

**olfato** /ol'fato/ *m*, sense of smell; shrewdness

**olfatorio** /olfa'torio/ *a* olfactory

**oliente** /o'liente/ **(mal)** *a* evil-smelling

**oligarquía** /oligar'kia/ f, oligarchy

**oligárquico** /oli'garkiko/ a oligarchic

**olímpico** /o'limpiko/ a Olympic; Olympian

**oliva** /o'liβa/ f, olive tree; olive; barn owl; peace

**olivar** /oli'βar/ m, olive grove

**olivo** /o'liβo/ m, olive tree

**olla** /'oʎa; 'oya/ f, stew pot; Spanish stew; whirlpool. **o. podrida**, rich Spanish stew containing bacon, fowl, meat, vegetables, ham, etc. **las ollas de Egipto**, the fleshpots of Egypt

**olmeda** /ol'meða/ f, **olmedo** m, elm grove

**olmo** /'olmo/ m, elm tree

**olor** /o'lor/ m, odor, scent, smell; hope, promise; suspicion, hint; reputation. **o. de santidad**, odor of sanctity

**oloroso** /olo'roso/ a fragrant, perfumed

**olvidadizo** /olβiða'ðiθo; olβiða'ðiso/ a forgetful

**olvidar** /olβi'ðar/ **(se)** vt and vr to forget; neglect, desert. **Se me olvidó el libro**, I forgot the book. **Me olvidé de lo pasado**, I forgot the past

**olvido** /ol'βiðo/ m, forgetfulness; indifference, neglect; oblivion

**ombligo** /om'βligo/ m, navel; Fig. core, center

**ominoso** /omi'noso/ a ominous

**omisión** /omi'sion/ f, omission; carelessness, negligence; neglect

**omiso** /o'miso/ a omitted; remiss; careless. **hacer caso o. de**, to set aside, ignore

**omitir** /omi'tir/ vt to omit

**ómnibus** /'omniβus/ m, bus

**omnímodo** /om'nimoðo/ a all-embracing

**omnipotencia** /omnipo'tenθia; omnipo'tensia/ f, omnipotence

**omnipotente** /omnipo'tente/ a omnipotent, all-powerful

**omnisciencia** /omnis'θienθia; omnis'siensia/ f, omniscience

**omniscio** /om'nisθio; om'nissio/ a omniscient

**omnívoro** /om'niβoro/ a omnivorous

**omoplato** /omo'plato/ m, scapula, shoulder blade

**once** /'onθe; 'onse/ a eleven; eleventh. m, eleven; eleventh (of the month). **las o.**, eleven o'clock

**onceno** /on'θeno; on'seno/ a eleventh

**onda** /'onda/ f, wave; Fig. flicker (of flames); Sew. scallop; Phys. wave; ripple; pl waves (in hair). Radio. **o. corta**, short wave. **o. etérea**, ether wave. **o. sonora**, sound wave

**ondeado** /onde'aðo/ a undulating; wavy; scalloped

**ondeante** /onde'ante/ a waving; flowing

**ondear** /onde'ar/ vi to wave; ripple; undulate; roll (of the sea); float, flutter, stream; Sew. scallop; —vr swing, sway

**ondeo** /on'deo/ m, waving; undulation

**ondina** /on'dina/ f, undine, water sprite

**ondulación** /ondula'θion; ondula'sion/ f, undulation; wave; wriggling; twisting. **o. permanente**, permanent wave, perm

**ondulado** /ondu'laðo/ a wavy; undulating; scalloped

**ondular** /ondu'lar/ vi to writhe, squirm, wriggle; twist; coil; —vt wave (in hair)

**oneroso** /one'roso/ a onerous, heavy; troublesome

**ónice** /'oniθe; 'onise/ m, onyx

**onomástico** /ono'mastiko/ a onomastic. **día o.**, saint's day

**onomatopeya** /onomato'peia/ f, onomatopoeia

**onza** /'onθa; 'onsa/ f, ounce. **por onzas**, by ounces; sparingly

**onzavo** /on'θaβo; on'saβo/ a and m, eleventh

**opacidad** /opaθi'ðað; opasi'ðað/ f, opacity; obscurity; gloom

**opaco** /o'pako/ a opaque; dark; gloomy, sad

**opalescente** /opales'θente; opales'sente/ a opalescent

**opalino** /opa'lino/ a opaline

**ópalo** /'opalo/ m, opal

**opción** /op'θion; op'sion/ f, option; choice, selection; Law. option

**ópera** /'opera/ f, opera

**operación** /opera'θion; opera'sion/ f, Surg. operation; execution, performance; Com. transaction

**operar** /ope'rar/ vt Surg. to operate; —vi act, have an effect; operate, control; Com. transact

**operario** /ope'rario/ **(-ia)** n worker, hand; operator; mechanic

**opereta** /ope'reta/ f, operetta, light opera

**opinar** /opi'nar/ vi to have or form an opinion, think; judge, consider

**opinión** /opi'nion/ f, opinion, view; reputation

**opio** /'opio/ m, opium. **fumadero de o.**, opium den

**opíparo** /o'piparo/ a magnificent, sumptuous (banquets, etc.)

**oponer** /opo'ner/ vt irr to oppose; resist, withstand; protest against; —vr oppose; be contrary or hostile (to); face, be opposite; object (to), set oneself against; compete (in public exams.). See **poner**

**oporto** /o'porto/ m, port (wine)

**oportunidad** /oportuni'ðað/ f, opportunity, occasion

**oportunismo** /oportu'nismo/ m, opportunism

**oportunista** /oportu'nista/ a and mf opportunist

**oportuno** /opor'tuno/ a opportune, timely

**oposición** /oposi'θion; oposi'sion/ f, opposition; resistance; antagonism; public competitive exam for a post; (Astron. Polit.) opposition

**opositor** /oposi'tor/ **(-ra)** n opponent; competitor

**opresión** /opre'sion/ f, oppression; hardship; pressure. **o. de pecho**, difficulty in breathing

**opresor** /opre'sor/ **(-ra)** a oppressive —n oppressor

**oprimir** /opri'mir/ vt to oppress; treat harshly; press, crush; choke

**oprobio** /o'proβio/ m, opprobrium

**optar** /op'tar/ vt to take possession of; (with por) choose

**óptica** /'optika/ f, Phys. optics; peepshow

**óptico** /'optiko/ a optic, optical. m, optician

**optimismo** /opti'mismo/ m, optimism

**optimista** /opti'mista/ mf optimist —a optimistic

**óptimo** /'optimo/ a superl bueno best, optimal, optimum

**opugnar** /opug'nar/ vt to resist violently; Mil. assault, attack; impugn, challenge

**opulencia** /opu'lenθia; opu'lensia/ f, opulence, riches; excess, superabundance

**opulento** /opu'lento/ a opulent, rich

**opúsculo** /o'puskulo/ m, monograph, opuscule

**oquedad** /oke'ðað/ f, hollow, cavity; superficiality, banality

**ora** /'ora/ adv now

**oración** /ora'θion; ora'sion/ f, oration, speech; prayer; Gram. sentence

**oráculo** /o'rakulo/ m, oracle

**orador** /ora'ðor/ **(-ra)** n orator; speech maker. m, preacher

**oral** /o'ral/ a oral; verbal; buccal

**orangután** /orangu'tan/ m, orangutan

**orar** /o'rar/ vi to harangue, make an oration; pray; —vt request, beg

**orate** /o'rate/ mf lunatic

**oratoria** /ora'toria/ f, oratory, eloquence

**oratorio** /ora'torio/ a oratorical. m, oratory, chapel; Mus. oratorio

**orbe** /'orβe/ m, sphere; orb; world

**órbita** /'orβita/ f, Astron. orbit; Fig. sphere; Anat. orbit, eye socket

**Órcades, las** /'orkaðes, las/ the Orkneys

**ordalía** /orða'lia/ f, (medieval hist.) ordeal

**orden** /'orðen/ mf order, mode of arrangement; succession, sequence; group; system; orderliness, neatness; coherence, plan; Eccl. order, brotherhood; (Zool. Bot.) group, class; Archit. order; Math. degree. f, precept, command; Com. order; pl Eccl. ordination. (Mil. Naut.) **o. de batalla**, battle array. **o. de caballería**, order of knighthood. **o. del día**, order of the day. Eccl. **dar órdenes**, to ordain. **en o.**, in order; with regard (to). **por su o.**, in its turn; successively

**ordenación** /orðena'θion; orðena'sion/ f, order, orderly arrangement; disposition; ordinance; precept; Eccl. ordination

**ordenador** /orðena'ðor/ m Spain computer

**ordenamiento** /orðena'miento/ m, ordaining; ordinance; edict

**ordenancista** /orðenan'θista; orðenan'sista/ *mf Mil.* martinet; disciplinarian

**ordenanza** /orðe'nanθa; orðe'nansa/ *f*, order, method; command, instruction; ordinance, regulation (gen. *pl*). *m*, *Mil.* orderly

**ordenar** /orðe'nar/ *vt* to put in order, arrange; command, give instructions to; decree; direct, regulate; *Eccl.* ordain; —*vr* (*with de*) *Eccl.* be ordained as

**ordeñadero** /orðeɲa'ðero/ *m*, milk pail

**ordeñar** /orðe'ɲar/ *vt* to milk

**ordinal** /orði'nal/ *a* ordinal. *m*, ordinal number

**ordinariez** /orðina'rieθ; orðina'ries/ *f*, rudeness, uncouthness; vulgarity

**ordinario** /orði'nario/ *a* ordinary, usual; vulgar, coarse, uncultured; rude; commonplace, average, mediocre. *m*, *Eccl.* ordinary; carrier; courier. **de o.**, usually, ordinarily

**orear** /ore'ar/ *vt* to ventilate; —*vr* dry; air; take the air

**orégano** /o'regano/ *m*, wild marjoram

**oreja** /o'reha/ *f*, external ear; lug; tab, flap; tongue (of a shoe). *Inf.* **con las orejas caídas**, down in the mouth, depressed

**orejera** /ore'hera/ *f*, earflap; mold board (of a plow)

**orejudo** /ore'huðo/ *a* large- or long-eared

**oreo** /o'reo/ *m*, zephyr; ventilation; airing

**orfanato** /orfa'nato/ *m*, orphanage, orphan asylum

**orfandad** /orfan'dað/ *f*, orphanhood; defenselessness, lack of protection

**orfebre** /or'feβre/ *mf* gold- or silversmith

**orfebrería** /orfeβre'ria/ *f*, gold- or silverwork

**orfeón** /orfe'on/ *m*, choral society

**organdí** /organ'di/ *m*, organdy

**orgánico** /or'ganiko/ *a* organic; harmonious; *Fig.* organized

**organillero** /organi'ʎero; organi'yero/ (**-ra**) *n* organ grinder

**organillo** /orga'niʎo; orga'niyo/ *m*, barrel organ

**organismo** /orga'nismo/ *m*, organism; organization, association

**organista** /orga'nista/ *mf* organist

**organización** /organiθa'θion; organisa'sion/ *f*, organization; order, arrangement

**organizador** /organiθa'ðor; organisa'ðor/ (**-ra**) *a* organizing —*n* organizer

**organizar** /organi'θar; organi'sar/ *vt* to organize; regulate; constitute

**órgano** /'organo/ *m*, *Mus.* organ; (*Anat. Bot.*) organ; means, agency. **o. de manubrio,** barrel organ

**orgasmo** /or'gasmo/ *m*, orgasm

**orgía** /or'hia/ *f*, orgy

**orgullo** /or'guʎo; or'guyo/ *m*, pride; arrogance

**orgulloso** /orgu'ʎoso; orgu'yoso/ *a* proud; haughty

**orientación** /orienta'θion; orienta'sion/ *f*, orientation; exposure, prospect; bearings

**oriental** /orien'tal/ *a* Oriental, Eastern. *mf* Oriental

**orientalismo** /orienta'lismo/ *m*, Orientalism

**orientalista** /orienta'lista/ *mf* Orientalist

**orientar** /orien'tar/ *vt* to orientate; —*vr* find one's bearings; familiarize oneself (with)

**oriente** /o'riente/ *m*, Orient, the East; luster (of pearls); youth, childhood; origin, source

**orificio** /ori'fiθio; ori'fisio/ *m*, orifice; hole

**oriflama** /ori'flama/ *f*, oriflamme; standard, flag

**origen** /o'rihen/ *m*, origin, source, root; stock, extraction; reason, genesis. **dar o. a,** to give rise to. **país de o.,** native land

**original** /orihi'nal/ *a* original; earliest, primitive; new, first-hand; novel, fresh; inventive, creative; eccentric; quaint. *m*, original manuscript; original; sitter (for portraits); eccentric

**originalidad** /orihinali'ðað/ *f*, originality

**originar** /orihi'nar/ *vt* to cause, originate; invent; —*vr* spring from, originate (in)

**originario** /orihi'nario/ *a* original, primary; primitive; native (of)

**orilla** /o'riʎa; o'riya/ *f*, limit, edge; hem, border; selvage; shore, margin; bank (of a river, etc.); sidewalk; brink, edge. **a la o.,** on the brink; nearly

**orillar** /ori'ʎar; ori'yar/ *vt* to settle, arrange, conclude;

—*vi* reach the shore or bank; *Sew.* leave a hem; *Sew.* border; leave a selvage on cloth

**orillo** /o'riʎo; o'riyo/ *m*, selvage (of cloth)

**orín** /o'rin/ *m*, rust; *pl* urine

**orinal** /ori'nal/ *m*, chamber pot, urinal

**orinar** /ori'nar/ *vi* to urinate

**oriundo** /o'riundo/ *a* native (of); derived (from)

**orla** /'orla/ *f*, border, fringe; selvage (of cloth, garments); ornamental border (on diplomas, etc.)

**orlar** /or'lar/ *vt* to border; edge, trim

**ornamentación** /ornamenta'θion; ornamenta'sion/ *f*, ornamentation

**ornamental** /ornamen'tal/ *a* ornamental

**ornamentar** /ornamen'tar/ *vt* to ornament; embellish

**ornamento** /orna'mento/ *m*, ornament; decoration; gift, virtue, talent; *pl Eccl.* vestments

**ornar** /or'nar/ *vt* to ornament, adorn, embellish

**ornato** /or'nato/ *m*, decoration, ornament

**ornitología** /ornitolo'hia/ *f*, ornithology

**ornitológico** /ornito'lohiko/ *a* ornithological

**ornitólogo** /orni'tologo/ *m*, ornithologist

**oro** /'oro/ *m*, gold; gold coins or jewelery; *Fig.* riches; *pl* diamonds (cards). **o. batido,** gold leaf. **o. en polvo,** gold dust. *Fig.* **como un o.,** shining with cleanliness. **el as de oros,** the ace of diamonds

**orondo** /o'rondo/ *a* hollow; *Inf.* pompous; *Inf.* swollen, spongy

**oropel** /oro'pel/ *m*, brass foil; showy, cheap thing; trinket; tinsel

**oropéndola** /oro'pendola/ *f*, oriole

**orquesta** /or'kesta/ *f*, orchestra

**orquestación** /orkesta'θion; orkesta'sion/ *f*, orchestration

**orquestal** /orkes'tal/ *a* orchestral

**orquestar** /orkes'tar/ *vt* to orchestrate

**orquídea** /or'kiðea/ *f*, orchid

**ortega** /or'tega/ *f*, *Ornith.* grouse

**ortiga** /or'tiga/ *f*, *Bot.* nettle

**orto** /'orto/ *m*, rising (of sun, stars)

**ortodoxia** /orto'ðoksia/ *f*, orthodoxy

**ortodoxo** /orto'ðokso/ *a* orthodox

**ortografía** /ortogra'fia/ *f*, orthography

**ortográfico** /orto'grafiko/ *a* orthographical

**ortopedia** /orto'peðia/ *f*, orthopedics

**ortopédico** /orto'peðiko/ (**-ca**) *a* orthopedic —*n* orthopedist

**ortopedista** /ortope'ðista/ *mf* orthopedist

**oruga** /o'ruga/ *f*, caterpillar

**orzuelo** /or'θuelo; or'suelo/ *m*, *Med.* sty; trap (for wild animals)

**os** /os/ *pers pron 2nd pl mf dat* and *acc* of **vos** and **vosotros,** you, to you

**osa** /'osa/ *f*, she-bear; *Astron.* **O. mayor,** Big Bear; **O. menor,** Little Bear

**osadía** /osa'ðia/ *f*, boldness, audacity

**osado** /o'saðo/ *a* daring, bold

**osamenta** /osa'menta/ *f*, skeleton; bones (of a skeleton)

**osar** /o'sar/ *vi* to dare; risk, venture

**osario** /o'sario/ *m*, charnel house, ossuary

**oscilación** /osθila'θion; ossila'sion/ *f*, oscillation

**oscilante** /osθi'lante; ossi'lante/ *a* oscillating

**oscilar** /osθi'lar; ossi'lar/ *vi* to oscillate, sway; hesitate, vacillate

**ósculo** /'oskulo/ *m*, kiss, osculation

**oscurantismo** /oskuran'tismo/ *m*, obscurantism

**oscurantista** /oskuran'tista/ *a* and *mf* obscurantist

**oscurecer** /oskure'θer; oskure'ser/ *vt irr* to darken; *Fig.* tarnish, dim, sully; confuse, bewilder; express obscurely; *Art.* shade; —*vr* grow dark; —*vr* cloud over (sky); *Inf.* disappear (things, gen. by theft). See **conocer**

**oscuridad** /oskuri'ðað/ *f*, darkness; gloom, blackness; humbleness; obscurity, abstruseness

**oscuro** /os'kuro/ *a* dark; humble, unknown; abstruse, involved; obscure; uncertain, dangerous. **a oscuras,** in the dark; ignorant

**óseo** /'oseo/ *a* osseous

**osera** /o'sera/ *f*, bear's den

**osezno** /o'seθno; o'sesno/ *m*, bear cub

**osificación** /osifika'θion; osifika'sion/ *f*, ossification

**osificarse** /osifiˈkarse/ *vr* to ossify
**ósmosis** /ˈosmosis/ *f,* osmosis
**oso** /ˈoso/ *m,* bear. **o. blanco,** polar bear
**Ostende** /osˈtende/ Ostend
**ostensible** /ostenˈsiβle/ *a* ostensible; obvious
**ostensión** /ostenˈsion/ *f,* show, display, manifestation
**ostensivo** /ostenˈsiβo/ *a* ostensive
**ostentación** /ostentaˈθion; ostentaˈsion/ *f,* manifestation; ostentation
**ostentar** /ostenˈtar/ *vt* to exhibit, show; boast, show off
**ostentoso** /ostenˈtoso/ *a* magnificent, showy, ostentatious
**osteología** /osteoloˈhia/ *f,* osteology
**osteópata** /osteˈopata/ *mf* osteopath
**osteopatía** /osteopaˈtia/ *f,* osteopathy
**ostra** /ˈostra/ *f,* oyster. **vivero de ostras,** oyster bed
**ostracismo** /ostraˈθismo; ostraˈsismo/ *m,* ostracism
**otear** /oteˈar/ *vt* to observe; look on at
**otero** /oˈtero/ *m,* hill, height, eminence
**otología** /otoloˈhia/ *f,* otology
**otólogo** /oˈtologo/ *m,* otologist
**otomana** /otoˈmana/ *f,* ottoman, couch
**otomano** /otoˈmano/ *a* Ottoman
**otoñal** /otoˈɲal/ *a* autumnal, autumn, fall
**otoño** /oˈtoɲo/ *m,* autumn, fall
**otorgamiento** /otorgaˈmiento/ *m,* granting; consent, approval; license, award

**otorgar** /otorˈgar/ *vt* to grant; concede, approve; *Law.* grant, stipulate, execute
**otro** /ˈotro/ **(-ra)** *a* other, another —*n* another one
**otrosí** /otroˈsi/ *adv* besides, moreover
**ovación** /oβaˈθion; oβaˈsion/ *f,* ovation, triumph; applause
**ovacionar** /oβaθioˈnar; oβasioˈnar/ *vt* to applaud
**oval** /oˈβal/ *a* oval
**óvalo** /ˈoβalo/ *m,* oval
**ovario** /oˈβario/ *m,* ovary
**oveja** /oˈβeha/ *f,* ewe
**ovejuno** /oβeˈhuno/ *a* relating to ewes or sheep, sheep-like
**ovillar** /oβiˈʎar; oβiˈyar/ *vi* to wind thread into a ball; —*vr* curl up; huddle
**ovillo** /oˈβiʎo; oˈβiyo/ *m,* ball, bobbin (of thread); tangled heap (of things)
**ovíparo** /oˈβiparo/ *a* oviparous
**OVNI** /ˈoβni/ *m,* UFO
**ovulación** /oβulaˈθion; oβulaˈsion/ *f,* ovulation
**óvulo** /ˈoβulo/ *m,* ovule
**oxidación** /oksiðaˈθion; oksiðaˈsion/ *f,* oxidation
**oxidar** /oksiˈðar/ *vt* oxidize; —*vr* become oxidized
**óxido** /ˈoksiðo/ *m,* oxide. **ó. de carbono,** carbon monoxide. **ó. de cinc,** zinc oxide
**oxígeno** /okˈsiheno/ *m,* oxygen
**oyente** /oˈiente/ *mf* hearer; *pl* audience
**ozono** /oˈθono; oˈsono/ *m,* ozone

# P

**pabellón** /paβe'ʎon; paβe'yon/ *m*, pavilion; colors, flag; bell tent. **p. británico,** Union Jack. **p. de reposo,** rest home. **en p.,** stacked (of arms)

**pábulo** /'paβulo/ *m*, food; *Fig.* pabulum

**pacedero** /paθe'ðero; pase'ðero/ *a Agr.* grazing, meadow

**pacer** /pa'θer; pa'ser/ *vi irr Agr.* to graze; —*vt* nibble away; eat away. See **nacer**

**paciencia** /pa'θienθia; pa'siensia/ *f*, patience

**paciente** /pa'θiente; pa'siente/ *a* patient; long-suffering; complacent. *mf Med.* patient

**pacienzudo** /paθien'θuðo; pasien'suðo/ *a* extremely patient or long-suffering

**pacificación** /paθifika'θion; pasifika'sion/ *f*, pacification; serenity, peace of mind

**pacificador** /paθifika'ðor; pasifika'ðor/ **(-ra)** *a* peace making; pacifying —*n* peace maker

**pacificar** /paθifi'kar; pasifi'kar/ *vt* to pacify; —*vi* make peace; —*vr* grow quiet, become calm (sea, etc.)

**pacífico** /pa'θifiko; pa'sifiko/ *a* pacific, meek, mild; peace-loving, peaceful. **el Océano P.,** the Pacific Ocean

**pacifismo** /paθi'fismo; pasi'fismo/ *m*, pacifism

**pacifista** /paθi'fista; pasi'fista/ *a* and *mf* pacifist

**pacotilla** /pako'tiʎa; pako'tiya/ *f*, goods. *Inf.* **hacer su p.,** to make one's packet or fortune. **ser de p.,** to be poor stuff; be jerry-built (of houses)

**pactar** /pak'tar/ *vt* to stipulate, arrange; contract

**pacto** /'pakto/ *m*, agreement, contract; pact

**padecer** /paðe'θer; paðe'ser/ *vt irr* to suffer; feel keenly; experience, undergo; tolerate. **p. desnudez,** to go unclothed. **p. hambre,** to go hungry. See **conocer**

**padecimiento** /paðeθi'miento; paðesi'miento/ *m*, suffering

**padrastro** /pa'ðrastro/ *m*, stepfather; cruel father; *Fig.* impediment, obstacle; hangnail

**padrazo** /pa'ðraθo; pa'ðraso/ *m*, *Inf.* indulgent father

**padre** /'paðre/ *m*, father; stallion; head (of the family, etc.); *Eccl.* father; genesis, source; author, creator; *pl* parents; ancestors. **p. adoptivo,** foster father. **p. de familia,** paterfamilias. **P. Eterno,** Eternal Father. **p. nuestro,** Lord's Prayer. **P. Santo,** Holy Father, the Pope

**padrear** /paðre'ar/ *vi* to take after one's father; *Zool.* reproduce, breed

**padrino** /pa'ðrino/ *m*, godfather; sponsor; second (in duels, etc.); patron; best man

**padrón** /pa'ðron/ *m*, census; pattern, model; memorial stone

**paella** /pa'eʎa; pa'eya/ *f*, *Cul.* savory rice dish of shellfish, chicken, and meat

**paga** /'paga/ *f*, payment; amends, restitution; pay; payment of fine; reciprocity (in love, etc.)

**pagadero** /paga'ðero/ *a* payable. *m*, date and place when payment is due

**pagador** /paga'ðor/ **(-ra)** *n* payer. *m*, teller; wages clerk; paymaster

**pagaduría** /pagaðu'ria/ *f*, pay office

**paganismo** /paga'nismo/ *m*, paganism; heathenism

**pagano** /pa'gano/ **(-na)** *a* and *n* pagan; heathen

**pagar** /pa'gar/ *vt* to pay; make restitution, expiate; return, requite (love, etc.); —*vr* (*with de*) become fond of; be proud of. **p. adelantado,** to prepay. *Com.* **p. al contado,** to pay cash. **p. la casa,** to pay the rent (for one's residence)

**pagaré** /paga're/ *m*, *Com.* promissory note, I.O.U.

**página** /'pahina/ *f*, page (of a book); episode, occurrence

**paginación** /pahina'θion; pahina'sion/ *f*, pagination

**paginar** /pahi'nar/ *vt* to paginate

**pago** /'pago/ *m*, payment; recompense, reward; region of vineyards, olive groves, etc.

**pagoda** /pa'goða/ *f*, pagoda, temple; idol

**paguro** /pa'guro/ *m*, hermit crab

**pailebote** /paile'βote/ *m*, schooner

**país** /pa'is/ *m*, country, nation; region; *Art.* landscape. **del p.,** typical of the country of origin (gen. of food)

**paisaje** /pai'sahe/ *m*, countryside; landscape, scenery

**paisajista, paisista** /paisa'hista, pai'sista/ *mf* landscape painter

**paisano** /pai'sano/ **(-na)** *n* compatriot; peasant; civilian

**Países Bajos, los** /pa'ises 'bahos, los/ the Low Countries, the Netherlands

**paja** /'paha/ *f*, straw; chaff; trash; *Fig.* padding. **ver la p. en el ojo del vecino y no la viga en el nuestro,** to see the mote in our neighbor's eye and not the beam in our own

**pajar** /pa'har/ *m*, barn

**pájara** /'pahara/ *f*, hen (bird); kite (toy); *Inf.* jay; prostitute. **p. pinta,** game of forfeits

**pajarear** /pahare'ar/ *vt* to snare birds; loaf, idle about

**pajarera** /paha'rera/ *f*, aviary

**pajarero** /paha'rero/ *m*, bird catcher or seller —*a Inf.* frivolous, giddy; *Inf.* gaudy (colors)

**pajarita** /paha'rita/ *f*, bow tie

**pájaro** /'paharo/ *m*, bird. **p. bobo,** penguin. **p. carpintero,** woodpecker. *Fig. Inf.* **p. gordo,** big gun. **p. mosca,** hummingbird

**pajarota** /paha'rota/ *f*, *Inf.* canard, false report

**paje** /'pahe/ *m*, page; *Naut.* cabin boy

**pajera** /pa'hera/ *f*, hayloft

**pajizo** /pa'hiθo; pa'hiso/ *a* made of straw; covered or thatched with straw; strawcolored

**pala** /'pala/ *f*, paddle; blade (of an oar); shovel; spade; baker's peel (long-handled shovel); cutting edge of a spade, hoe, etc.; *Sports.* racket; vamp, upper (of a shoe); pelota or jai alai racket; tanner's knife; *Inf.* guile, cunning; cleverness, dexterity. **p. de hélice,** propeller blade. **p. para pescado,** fish server. *Inf.* **corta p.,** ignoramus; blockhead

**palabra** /pa'laβra/ *f*, word; power of speech; eloquence; offer, promise; *pl* magic formula, spell. **p. de clave,** code word. **p. de matrimonio,** promise of marriage. **p. de rey,** inviolable promise. **palabras cruzadas,** crossword puzzle. **bajo p. de,** under promise of. **cuatro palabras,** a few words; short conversation. **de p.,** verbally, by word of mouth. **dirigir la p. a,** to address, speak to. **faltar a su p.,** to break one's promise. **llevar la p.,** to be spokesperson. **medias palabras,** half-words; hint, insinuation. **su p. empeñada,** one's solemn word. **tener la p.,** to have the right to speak (in meetings, etc.) (e.g. *El señor Martínez tiene la p.,* Mr. Martinez has the floor)

**palabrería** /palaβre'ria/ *f*, verbosity, wordiness

**palabrota** /pala'βrota/ *f*, *Inf.* coarse language; long word

**palaciego** /pala'θiego; pala'siego/ **(-ga)** *a* pertaining to palaces; *Fig.* courtesan —*n* courtier

**palacio** /pa'laθio; pa'lasio/ *m*, palace; mansion

**palada** /pa'laða/ *f*, shovelful, spadeful; oar stroke

**paladar** /pala'ðar/ *m*, *Anat.* palate; taste; discernment, sensibility

**paladear** /palaðe'ar/ *vt* to taste with pleasure, savor; enjoy, relish

**paladín** /pala'ðin/ *m*, paladin

**paladino** /pala'ðino/ *a* public, clear, open

**palafrén** /pala'fren/ *m*, palfrey

**palafrenero** /palafre'nero/ *m*, groom; stablehand

**palanca** /pa'lanka/ *f*, *Mech.* lever; handle; bar; (high) diving board. **p. de arranque,** starting gear. **p. de cambio de velocidad,** gear-changing lever. **p. de mando,** control stick

**palangana** /palaŋ'gana/ *f*, washbasin

**palanganero** /palaŋga'nero/ *m*, washstand

**palanqueta** /palan'keta/ *f*, *dim* small lever; jimmy

**palastro** /pa'lastro/ *m*, sheet iron or steel

**palatinado** /palati'naðo/ *m*, Palatinate

**palatino** /pala'tino/ *a* palatine

**palatizar** /palati'θar; palati'sar/ *vt* to palatalize

**palazón** /pala'θon; pala'son/ f, woodwork

**palco** /'palko/ m, Theat. box; stand, raised platform, enclosure. **p. de platea**, orchestra

**palenque** /pa'lenke/ m, enclosure; stand; platform; palisade

**paleografía** /paleogra'fia/ f, paleography

**paleógrafo** /pale'ografo/ m, paleographer

**paleolítico** /paleo'litiko/ a paleolithic

**paleología** /paleolo'hia/ f, paleology

**paleontología** /paleontolo'hia/ f, paleontology

**Palestina** /pales'tina/ Palestine

**palestra** /pa'lestra/ f, tilt yard

**paleta** /pa'leta/ f, dim little shovel; trowel; Art. palette; fireplace shovel; mason's trowel; Anat. shoulder blade; blade (of a propeller, ventilator, etc.); Chem. spatula

**paliación** /palia'θion; palia'sion/ f, palliation; excuse

**paliar** /pa'liar/ vt to dissemble, excuse; palliate, mitigate

**paliativo** /palia'tiβo/ a palliative; extenuating

**palidecer** /paliðe'θer; paliðe'ser/ vi irr to turn pale. See **conocer**

**palidez** /pali'ðeθ; pali'ðes/ f, pallor, paleness

**pálido** /'paliðo/ a pale, pallid

**paliducho** /pali'ðutʃo/ a somewhat pale, palish; sallow

**palillo** /pa'liʎo; pa'liyo/ m, dim small stick; toothpick; bobbin (for lacemaking); drumstick; Fig. chatter; pl castanets

**palimpsesto** /palimp'sesto/ m, palimpsest

**palinodia** /pali'noðia/ f, Lit. palinode. **cantar la p.**, to eat one's words, recant

**palio** /'palio/ m, Greek mantle; cape; Eccl. pallium; canopy, awning

**palique** /pa'like/ m, Inf. chat. **estar de p.**, to be having a chat

**paliquear** /palike'ar/ vi to chat

**paliza** /pa'liθa; pa'lisa/ f, caning, beating

**palizada** /pali'θaða; pali'saða/ f, paling, fence; palisade, stockade. **p. de tablas**, hoarding

**palma** /'palma/ f, palm tree; palm leaf; date palm; palm (of the hand); hand; triumph. **llevarse la p.**, to bear away the palm; take the cake

**palmada** /pal'maða/ f, slap; pl hand-clapping

**palmado** /pal'maðo/ a web (of feet); palmy

**palmar** /pal'mar/ a palmaceous; palmar; clear, obvious. m, palm grove

**palmatoria** /palma'toria/ f, ferule, ruler; candlestick

**palmear** /palme'ar/ vi to clap hands

**palmera** /pal'mera/ f, palm tree

**palmeta** /pal'meta/ f, ferrule, ruler

**palmetazo** /palme'taθo; palme'taso/ m, slap on the hand with a ruler; Fig. slap in the face

**Palmira** /pal'mira/ Palmyra

**palmo** /'palmo/ m, span; hand's breadth. **p. a p.**, inch by inch, piecemeal

**palmotear** /palmote'ar/ vt to applaud; clap

**palo** /'palo/ m, stick; rod; pole; timber, wood; wooden log; Naut. mast; blow with a stick; execution by hanging; suit (of playing cards); fruit stalk; Herald. pale. **p. de Campeche**, logwood. **p. de hule**, rubber tree. **p. de rosa**, tulipwood. Naut. **p. mayor**, mainmast. Naut. **a p. seco**, under bare poles. **de tal p., tal astilla**, a chip off the old block; like father like son. **estar del mismo p.**, to be of the same mind, agree

**paloma** /pa'loma/ f, dove; pigeon; gentle person; pl Naut. white horses. **p. buchona**, pouter pigeon. **p. mensajera**, carrier pigeon. **p. torcaz**, wood pigeon

**palomar** /palo'mar/ m, dovecote; pigeon loft

**palomero** /palo'mero/ (-ra) n pigeon fancier; pigeon dealer

**palomino** /palo'mino/ m, young pigeon

**palomo** /pa'lomo/ m, male pigeon; wood pigeon

**palotes** /pa'lotes/ m pl, drumsticks; pothooks (in writing)

**palpabilidad** /palpaβili'ðað/ f, palpability

**palpable** /pal'paβle/ a palpable, tangible

**palpación** /palpa'θion; palpa'sion/ f, Med. palpation

**palpar** /pal'par/ vt to palpate, examine by touch; grope, walk by touch; Fig. see clearly

**palpitación** /palpita'θion; palpita'sion/ f, beating (of a heart); Med. palpitation; convulsive movement

**palpitante** /palpi'tante/ a palpitating; quivering; beating; (of a question) burning

**palpitar** /palpi'tar/ vi to beat (heart); throb, palpitate; shudder, move convulsively; Fig. manifest itself (passions, etc.)

**palpo** /'palpo/ m, palp, feeler

**palúdico** /pa'luðiko/ a marshy, swampy; malarial

**paludismo** /palu'ðismo/ m, malaria; paludism

**palurdo** /pa'lurðo/ (-da) a Inf. gross, rude, boorish —n boor

**palustre** /pa'lustre/ m, mason's trowel —a marshy, swampy

**pamela** /pa'mela/ f, wide-brimmed straw sailor (woman's hat)

**pamema** /pa'mema/ f, Inf. unimportant trifle; Inf. caress

**pampa** /'pampa/ f, pampa, treeless plain

**pámpano** /'pampano/ m, young vine shoot; vine leaf

**pamplina** /pam'plina/ f, Inf. nonsense, rubbish

**pan** /pan/ m, bread; loaf; Cul. piecrust; Fig. food; wheat; gold leaf; pl cereals. **p. ázimo**, unleavened bread. **p. de oro**, gold leaf. **llamar al p. p. y al vino vino**, to call a spade a spade. **venderse como p. bendito**, to sell like hot cakes

**pana** /'pana/ f, velveteen, velours

**panacea** /pana'θea; pana'sea/ f, panacea; cure-all

**panadería** /panaðe'ria/ f, bakery trade or shop; bakery

**panadero** /pana'ðero/ (-ra) n baker. m pl, Spanish dance

**panadizo** /pana'ðiθo; pana'ðiso/ m, Med. whitlow; Inf. ailing person, crock

**panal** /pa'nal/ m, honeycomb; wasp's nest

**Panamá** /pana'ma/ Panama

**panameño** /pana'meɲo/ (-ña) a and n Panamanian

**panamericanismo** /panamerika'nismo/ m, pan-Americanism

**panarra** /pa'narra/ m, Inf. simpleton

**páncreas** /'pankreas/ m, pancreas

**pancreático** /pankre'atiko/ a pancreatic

**panda** /'panda/ f, gallery of a cloister. mf Zool. panda

**pandémico** /pan'demiko/ a pandemic

**pandemónium** /pande'monium/ m, pandemonium

**pandereta** /pande'reta/ f, tambourine

**pandero** /pan'dero/ m, tambourine; Inf. windbag

**pandilla** /pan'diʎa; pan'diya/ f, league, group; gang (of burglars, etc.); party, crowd, band

**pane** /'pane/ f, breakdown

**panecillo** /pane'θiʎo; pane'siyo/ m, dim roll (of bread)

**panegírico** /pane'hiriko/ a and m, panegyric

**panegirista** /panehi'rista/ mf panegyrist; eulogizer

**panel** /pa'nel/ m, panel

**panetela** /pane'tela/ f, panada

**pánfilo** /'panfilo/ (-la) a sluggish, phlegmatic, slow-moving —n sluggard

**panfleto** /pan'fleto/ m, pamphlet

**paniaguado** /pania'guaðo/ m, servant; favorite, protégé

**pánico** /'paniko/ a and m, panic

**panoja** /pa'noha/ f, Bot. panicle; Bot. ear, beard, awn

**panoli** /pa'noli/ a Inf. doltish, stupid

**panoplia** /pa'noplia/ f, panoply; collection of arms

**panorama** /pano'rama/ m, panorama; view

**panorámico** /pano'ramiko/ a panoramic

**pantalla** /pan'taʎa; pan'taya/ f, lampshade; face screen; movie screen; shade, reflector

**pantalón** /panta'lon/ m, pant, trouser (gen. pl); knickers. **p. de corte**, striped trousers. **pantalones bombachos**, plus fours

**pantano** /pan'tano/ m, marsh, swamp; impediment; artificial pool

**pantanoso** /panta'noso/ a marshy, swampy; Fig. awkward, full of pitfalls

**panteísmo** /pante'ismo/ m, pantheism

**panteísta** /pante'ista/ a pantheistic. mf pantheist

**panteón** /pante'on/ m, pantheon

**pantera** /pan'tera/ f, panther

**pantomima** /panto'mima/ f, pantomime; mime

**pantoque** /pan'toke/ *m*, *Naut.* bilge

**pantorrilla** /panto'rriʎa; panto'rriya/ *f*, calf (of the leg)

**pantuflo** /pan'tuflo/ *m*, house slipper

**panza** /'panθa; 'pansa/ *f*, paunch, stomach; belly (of jugs, etc.). *Inf.* **un cielo de p. de burra,** a dark gray sky

**panzudo** /pan'θuðo; pan'suðo/ *a* paunchy

**pañal** /pa'ɲal/ *m*, diaper; shirttail; *pl* long clothes, swaddling clothes; infancy

**pañería** /paɲe'ria/ *f*, drapery stores; drapery

**pañero** /pa'ɲero/ **(-ra)** *n* draper

**paño** /'paɲo/ *m*, woolen material; cloth, fabric; drapery, hanging; tapestry; linen, bandage; tarnish or other mark; *Naut.* canvas; *Sew.* breadth, width (of cloth); panel (in a dress); floor cloth, duster; livid mark on the face; *pl* garments. **p. de lágrimas,** consoler, sympathizer. **p. mortuorio,** pall (on a coffin). **paños menores,** underwear. **p. verde,** gambling table. **al p.,** *Theat.* from the wings, from without. *Inf.* **poner el p. al púlpito,** to hold forth, spread oneself

**pañoleta** /paɲo'leta/ *f*, kerchief, triangular scarf; fichu

**pañuelo** /pa'ɲuelo/ *m*, kerchief; handkerchief

**papa** /'papa/ *m*, pope; *Inf.* papa, daddy. *f*, *Inf.* potato; stupid rumor; nonsense; *pl* pap; *Cul.* sop; food

**papá** /pa'pa/ *m*, *Inf.* papa, daddy

**papada** /pa'paða/ *f*, double chin; dewlap

**papado** /pa'paðo/ *m*, papacy

**papagayo** /papa'gaio/ *m*, parrot

**papamoscas** /papa'moskas/ *m*, *Ornith.* flycatcher; *Inf.* simpleton

**papanatas** /papa'natas/ *m*, *Inf.* simpleton

**papar** /pa'par/ *vt* to sip, take soft food; *Inf.* eat; neglect, be careless about

**paparrucha** /papa'rrutʃa/ *f*, *Inf.* stupid rumor; nonsense

**papel** /pa'pel/ *m*, paper; document; manuscript; *Theat.* role, part; pamphlet; sheet of paper; paper, monograph, essay; guise, role; *Theat.* character. **p. carbón, p. carbónico,** carbon paper. **p. celofán,** cellophane. **p. cuadriculado,** graph paper, cartridge paper. **p. de calcar,** carbon paper; tracing paper. **p. de escribir,** writing paper. **p. de estaño,** tinfoil. **p. de estraza,** brown paper. **p. de fumar,** cigarette paper. **p. de lija,** emery- or sandpaper. **p. de paja de arroz,** rice paper. **p. de seda,** tissue paper. **p. de tornasol,** litmus paper. **p. del estado,** government bonds. **p. higiénico,** toilet paper. **p. moneda,** paper money. **p. pintado,** wallpaper. **p. secante,** blotting paper. **p. sellado,** official stamped paper. **hacer buen ( mal) p.,** to do well (badly). **hacer el p. ( de),** *Theat.* to act the part (of); feign, pretend

**papelear** /papele'ar/ *vi* to turn over papers, search among them; *Inf.* cut a dash

**papeleo** /pape'leo/ *m*, bureaucracy, red tape

**papelera** /pape'lera/ *f*, mass of papers; desk (for keeping papers)

**papelería** /papele'ria/ *f*, heap of papers; stationer's shop; stationery

**papelero** /pape'lero/ **(-ra)** *a* paper, stationery —*n* paper maker; stationer

**papeleta** /pape'leta/ *f*, slip or scrap of paper

**papelista** /pape'lista/ *mf* paper maker; stationer; paperhanger

**papelucho** /pape'lutʃo/ *m*, old or dirty piece of paper; trash, worthless writing; *Inf.* rag (newspaper)

**papera** /pa'pera/ *f*, mumps

**papilla** /pa'piʎa; pa'piya/ *f*, pap; guile, wiliness

**papillote** /papi'ʎote; papi'yote/ *m*, curl-paper

**papiro** /pa'piro/ *m*, papyrus

**papista** /pa'pista/ *a* and *mf* papist

**papo** /'papo/ *m*, dewlap; gizzard (of a bird); goiter. **p. de cardo,** thistledown

**paquebote** /pake'βote/ *m*, *Naut.* packet; mail boat; liner

**paquete** /pa'kete/ *m*, packet; parcel, package

**paquidermo** /paki'ðermo/ *m*, pachyderm

**par** /par/ *a* equal; alike; corresponding. *m*, pair, couple; team (of oxen, mules); peer (title); rafter (of a roof); *Mech.* torque, couple; *Elec.* cell. *f*, par. **a la p.,** jointly; simultaneously; *Com.* at par. **a pares,** two by two. **de p. en p.,** wide-open (doors, etc.). **sin p.,** peerless, excellent

**para** /'para/ *prep* in order to; for; to; for the sake of (e.g. *Lo hice p. ella,* I did it for her sake); enough to (gen. with *bastante,* etc.); in the direction of, toward; about to, on the point of (e.g. *Está p. salir,* He is on the point of going out). Expresses:
1. *Purpose* (e.g. *La educan p. bailarina,* They are bringing her up to be a dancer. *Lo dije p. ver lo que harías,* I said it to (in order to) see what you would do)
2. *Destination* (e.g. *Salió p. Londres,* He left for London)
3. *Use* (e.g. *seda p. medias,* silk for stockings. *un vaso p. flores,* a vase for flowers)
4. *An appointed time* (e.g. *Lo pagaré p. Navidad,* I will pay it at Christmas)
**p. con,** toward (a person) (e.g. *Ha obrado muy bien p. con mi hermano,* He has behaved very well toward my brother)
**p. coneretar,** to be exact, to wit
**p. que,** in order to, so that (e.g. *Lo puse en la mesa p. que lo vieses,* I put it on the table so that you would see it)
**¿P. qué?** Why? For what reason?
**p. siempre,** forever. **decir p. sí,** to say to oneself. **sin qué ni p. qué,** without rhyme or reason

**parábola** /pa'raβola/ *f*, parable; *Geom.* parabola

**parabrisas** /para'βrisas/ *m*, windshield

**paracaídas** /paraka'iðas/ *m*, parachute

**paracaidista** /parakai'ðista/ *mf* parachutist

**parachoques** /para'tʃokes/ *m*, *Auto.* bumper; buffer (railroad)

**paráclito** /pa'raklito/ *m*, Paraclete

**parada** /pa'raða/ *f*, stopping, halting; stop; stoppage, suspension; halt; *Mil.* review; interval, pause; cattle stall; dam; gambling stakes; parry (in fencing); relay (of horses). **p. de coches,** taxi rank. **p. de tranvía,** streetcar stop. **p. discrecional,** request stop (buses, etc.)

**paradero** /para'ðero/ *m*, railroad station; stopping place; end, conclusion; whereabouts

**paradisíaco** /paraði'siako/ *a* paradisaical

**parado** /pa'raðo/ *a* still; indolent, lazy; unoccupied, leisured; silent, reserved; timid; unemployed

**paradoja** /para'ðoha/ *f*, paradox

**paradójico** /para'ðohiko/ *a* paradoxical

**parador** /para'ðor/ *m*, inn, tavern, hostelry

**parafina** /para'fina/ *f*, paraffin

**parafinar** /parafi'nar/ *vt* to paraffin

**parafrasear** /parafrase'ar/ *vt* to paraphrase

**paráfrasis** /pa'rafrasis/ *f*, paraphrase

**paraguas** /pa'raguas/ *m*, umbrella

**paraguayo** /para'guayo/ **(-ya)** *a* and *n* Paraguayan

**paragüería** /parague'ria/ *f*, umbrella shop

**paragüero** /para'guero/ **(-ra)** *n* umbrella maker, umbrella seller. *m*, umbrella stand

**paraíso** /para'iso/ *m*, paradise; garden of Eden; heaven; (*Inf. Theat.*) gallery, gods

**paraje** /pa'rahe/ *m*, place, locality, spot; state, condition

**paralela** /para'lela/ *f*, *Mil.* parallel; *pl* parallel bars (for gymnastic exercises)

**paralelismo** /parale'lismo/ *m*, parallelism

**paralelo** /para'lelo/ *a* parallel; analogous; similar. *m*, parallel, similarity; *Geog.* parallel

**paralelogramo** /paralelo'gramo/ *m*, parallelogram

**parálisis** /pa'ralisis/ *f*, paralysis

**paralítico** /para'litiko/ **(-ca)** *a* and *n* paralytic

**paralización** /paraliθa'θion; paralisa'sion/ *f*, paralysis; cessation; *Com.* dullness, quietness

**paralizar** /parali'θar; parali'sar/ *vt* to paralyze; stop a horse); face (of a wall); facing (of a building)

**paramento** /para'mento/ *m*, ornament; trappings (of a horse); face (of a wall); facing (of a building)

**paramentos sacerdotales,** liturgical vestments or ornaments

**páramo** /'paramo/ *m*, paramo, treeless plain; desert, wilderness

**parangón** /paraŋ'gon/ *m*, comparison; similarity

**parangonar** /paraŋgo'nar/ *vt* to compare

**paraninfo** /para'ninfo/ *m*, *Archit.* paranymph, university hall; best man (weddings); messenger of good

**paranoico** /para'noiko/ *m*, paranoiac

**parapetarse** /parape'tarse/ *vr* to shelter behind a parapet; take refuge behind

**parapeto** /para'peto/ *m*, parapet

**parapoco** /para'poko/ *mf Inf.* ninny, numskull

**parar** /pa'rar/ *vi* to stop, halt; end, finish; lodge; come into the hands of; —*vt* stop; detain; prepare; bet, stake; point (hunting dogs); parry (fencing); —*vr* halt; be interrupted **p. mientes en,** to notice; consider. **sin p.,** immediately, at once; without stopping

**pararrayos** /para'rraios/ *m*, lightning conductor

**parasitario, parasítico** /parasi'tario, para'sitiko/ *a* parasitic

**parásito** /pa'rasito/ *m*, parasite; *Fig.* sponger; *pl Radio.* interference —*a* parasitic

**parasitología** /parasitolo'hia/ *f*, parasitology

**parasol** /para'sol/ *m*, sunshade; *Bot.* umbel

**paratifoidea** /paratifoi'ðea/ *f*, paratyphoid

**parca** /'parka/ *f*, Fate; *Poet.* death. **las Parcas,** the Three Fates

**parcela** /par'θela/ par'sela/ *f*, plot, parcel (of land); atom, particle

**parche** /'partʃe/ *m*, *Med.* plaster; *Auto.* patch; drum; drumhead, parchment of drum; patch, mend

**parcial** /par'θial/ par'sial/ *a* partial, incomplete; biased, prejudiced; factional, party; participatory

**parcialidad** /parθiali'ðað/ parsiali'ðað/ *f*, partiality, bias, prejudice; party, faction, group; intimacy, friendship

**parco** /'parko/ *a* scarce, scanty; temperate, moderate; frugal

**¡pardiez!** /par'ðieθ/ par'ðies/ *interj Inf.* By god!

**pardo** /'parðo/ *a* brown; gray, drab, dun-colored; cloudy, dark; husky (voices). *m*, leopard

**pardusco** /par'ðusko/ *a* grayish; fawn-colored

**parear** /pare'ar/ *vt* to pair, match; put in pairs; compare

**parecer** /pare'θer; pare'ser/ *vi irr* to appear; look, seem; turn up (be found) —*impers* believe, think (e.g. *me parece,* it seems to me, I think, my opinion is); —*vr* look alike, resemble one another. See **conocer**

**parecer** /pare'θer; pare'ser/ *m*, opinion, belief; appearance, looks

**parecido** /pare'θiðo; pare'siðo/ *a* (*with bien or mal*) good- or bad-looking. *m*, resemblance

**pared** /pa'reð/ *f*, wall; partition wall; side, face. **p. maestra,** main wall. **p. medianera,** party wall. **Las paredes oyen,** The walls have ears. *Inf.* **pegado a la p.,** confused, taken aback

**pareja** /pa'reha/ *f*, pair; dance partner; couple. **p. desparejada,** mismatched pair. **parejas mixtas,** mixed doubles (in tennis). **correr parejas** or **correr a las parejas,** to be equal; go together, happen simultaneously; be on a par

**parejo** /pa'reho/ *a* equal; similar; smooth, flat; even, regular

**parentela** /paren'tela/ *f*, relatives, kindred; parentage

**parentesco** /paren'tesko/ *m*, kinship; relationship; affinity; *Inf.* connection, link

**paréntesis** /pa'rentesis/ *m*, parenthesis; digression. **entre p.,** incidentally

**paresa** /pa'resa/ *f*, peeress

**paria** /'paria/ *mf* pariah; outcast

**parida** /pa'riða/ *a f*, newly delivered of a child

**paridad** /pari'ðað/ *f*, parity; analogy, similarity

**pariente** /pa'riente/ **(-ta)** *n* relative, relation; *Inf.* husband (wife)

**parihuela** /pari'uela/ *f*, wheelbarrow; stretcher

**parir** /pa'rir/ *vt* to give birth to; *Fig.* bring forth; reveal, publish; —*vi* lay eggs

**París** /pa'ris/ Paris

**parisiense** /pari'siense/ *a* and *mf* Parisian

**parla** /'parla/ *f*, speech; loquaciousness, eloquence; verbiage

**parlamentar** /parlamen'tar/ *vi* to converse; discuss (contracts, etc.); *Mil.* parley

**parlamentario** /parlamen'tario/ *a* parliamentarian. *m*, member of parliament

**parlamentarismo** /parlamenta'rismo/ *m*, parliamentarianism

**parlamento** /parla'mento/ *m*, legislative assembly; parliament; discourse, speech; *Theat.* long speech; *Mil.* parley

**parlanchín** /parlan'tʃin/ *a Inf.* talkative, chattering, loquacious

**parlar** /par'lar/ *vt* and *vi* to speak freely or easily; chatter; reveal, speak indiscreetly; babble (of streams, etc.)

**parlero** /par'lero/ *a* talkative; gossiping, indiscreet; talking (birds); *Fig.* expressive (eyes, etc.); prattling, babbling (brook, etc.)

**parlotear** /parlote'ar/ *vi Inf.* to chatter, gossip

**parloteo** /parlo'teo/ *m*, chattering, gossip

**parmesano** /parme'sano/ *(-na)* *a* and *n* Parmesan

**parnaso** /par'naso/ *m*, Parnassus; anthology of verse

**paro** /'paro/ *m*, *Inf.* work stoppage; lockout; *Ornith.* tit. **p. forzoso,** unemployment

**parodia** /pa'roðia/ *f*, parody

**parodiar** /paro'ðiar/ *vt* to parody

**parodista** /paro'ðista/ *mf* parodist

**parótida** /pa'rotiða/ *f*, parotid gland; parotitis, mumps

**parotiditis** /paroti'ðitis/ *f*, parotitis, mumps

**paroxismo** /parok'sismo/ *m*, *Med.* paroxysm; frenzy, ecstasy, fit

**parpadear** /parpaðe'ar/ *vi* to blink

**parpadeo** /parpa'ðeo/ *m*, blinking

**párpado** /'parpaðo/ *m*, eyelid

**parque** /'parke/ *m*, park; depot, park; paddock, pen. **p. de atracciones,** pleasure ground. **p. de** ( *or* **para**) **automóviles,** car park, parking lot

**parquedad** /parke'ðað/ *f*, scarcity; moderation, temperance; parsimony, frugality

**parra** /'parra/ *f*, vine. **hoja de p.,** *Fig.* fig leaf

**párrafo** /'parrafo/ *m*, paragraph; *Gram.* paragraph sign. **p. aparte,** new paragraph. **echar un p.,** to chat, gossip

**parranda** /pa'rranda/ *f*, *Inf.* binge; strolling band of musicians. **ir de p.,** to go on a binge

**parricida** /parri'θiða; parri'siða/ *mf* parricide (person)

**parricidio** /parri'θiðio; parri'siðio/ *m*, parricide (act)

**parrilla** /pa'rriʎa; pa'rriya/ *f*, *Cul.* griller, broiler; grill, gridiron; *Engin.* grate. *Cul.* **a la p.,** grilled

**párroco** /'parroko/ *m*, parish priest; parson

**parroquia** /pa'rrokia/ *f*, parish church; parish; clergy of a parish; clientele, customers

**parroquial** /parro'kial/ *a* parochial

**parroquiano** /parro'kiano/ **(-na)** *a* parochial —*n* parishioner; client, customer

**parsi** /'parsi/ *m*, Parsee; Parseeism

**parsimonia** /parsi'monia/ *f*, frugality, thrift; prudence, moderation

**parsimonioso** /parsimo'nioso/ *a* parsimonious

**parte** /'parte/ *f*, part; share; place; portion; side, faction; *Law.* party; *Theat.* part, role. *m*, communication, message; telegraph or telephone message; (*Mil. Nav.*) communiqué. *f pl*, parts, talents. **p. actora,** *Law.* prosecution. **p. de la oración,** part of speech. **partes litigantes,** *Law.* contending parties. **dar p.,** to notify; (*Mil. Naut.*) report; give a share (in a transaction). **de algún tiempo a esta p.,** for some time past. **de p. de,** in the name of, from. **en p.,** partly. **por todas partes,** on all sides, everywhere. **ser p. a** *or* **ser p. para que,** to contribute to. **tener de su p.** ( **a**), to count on the favor of. **la quinta p.,** one-fifth, etc.

**partear** /parte'ar/ *vt* to assist in childbirth

**partera** /par'tera/ *f*, midwife

**partero** /par'tero/ *m*, accoucheur

**partición** /parti'θion; parti'sion/ *f*, partition, distribution; (*Aer. Naut.*) accommodation

**participación** /partiθipa'θion; partisipa'sion/ *f*, participation; notice, warning; announcement (of an engagement, etc.); *Com.* share

**participante** /partiθi'pante; partisi'pante/ *a* and *mf* participant

**participar** /partiθi'par; partisi'par/ *vi* to participate, take part (in), share; —*vt* inform; announce (an engagement, etc.)

**partícipe** /par'tiθipe; par'tisipe/ *a* sharing. *mf* participant

**participio** /parti'θipio; parti'sipio/ *m*, participle

**partícula** /par'tikula/ *f*, particle, grain; *Gram.* particle

**particular** /partiku'lar/ *a* private; peculiar; special, particular; unusual; individual. *mf* private individual. *m*, matter, subject. **en p.,** especially; privately

**particularidad** /partikulari'ðað/ *f*, individuality; specialty; rareness, unusualness; detail, circumstance; intimacy, friendship

**particularizar** /partikulari'θar; partikulari'sar/ *vt* to detail, particularize; single out, choose; —*vr* (with *en*) be characterized by

**partida** /par'tiða/ *f*, departure; entry, record (of birth, etc.); certificate (of marriage, etc.); *Com.* item; *Com.* lot, allowance; *Mil.* guerrilla; armed band; expedition, excursion; game (of cards, etc.); rubber (at bridge, etc.); *Inf.* conduct, behavior; place, locality; death. *Com.* **p. doble,** double entry. **Las siete Partidas,** code of Spanish laws compiled by Alfonso X (1252–84)

**partidario** /parti'ðario/ **(-ia)** *a* partisan —*n* adherent, disciple. *m*, partisan, guerrilla

**partidarismo** /partiða'rismo/ *m*, partisanship

**partido** /par'tiðo/ *m*, party, group, faction; profit; *Sports.* match; team; agreement, pact. **p. conservador,** *Polit.* conservative party. **p. obrero** or **p. laborista,** *Polit.* labor party. **buen p.,** *Fig.* good match, catch. **sacar p. de,** to take advantage of, make the most of. **tomar p.,** to enlist; join, become a supporter (of)

**partidor** /parti'ðor/ *m*, divider, apportioner; cleaver, chopper; hewer

**partir** /par'tir/ *vt* to divide; split; crack, break; separate; *Math.* divide; —*vi* go, depart; start (from). **p. como el rayo,** be off like a flash —*vr* disagree, become divided; leave, depart

**partitura** /parti'tura/ *f*, *Mus.* score

**parto** /'parto/ *m*, parturition, birth; newborn child; *Fig.* creation, offspring; important event

**parturienta** /partu'rienta/ *a f*, parturient

**parva** /'parβa/ *f*, light breakfast; threshed or unthreshed grain; heap, mass

**parvedad** /parβe'ðað/ *f*, smallness; scarcity; light breakfast (taken on fast days)

**parvo** /'parβo/ *a* little, small

**párvulo** /'parβulo/ **(-la)** *n* child —*a* small; innocent, simple; lowly, humble

**pasa** /'pasa/ *f*, raisin; *Naut.* channel; passage, flight (of birds). **p. de Corinto,** currant

**pasacalle** /pasa'kaλe; pasa'kaye/ *m*, *Mus.* lively march

**pasada** /pa'saða/ *f*, passing, passage; money sufficient to live on; passage, corridor. **dar p.,** to let pass, put up with. *Inf.* **mala p.,** bad turn, dirty trick

**pasadera** /pasa'ðera/ *f*, steppingstone

**pasadero** /pasa'ðero/ *a* passable, traversable; fair (health); tolerable, passable. *m*, steppingstone

**pasadizo** /pasa'ðiθo; pasa'ðiso/ *m*, narrow corridor or passage; alley, narrow street; *Naut.* alleyway

**pasado** /pa'saðo/ *m*, past; *pl* ancestors. **Lo p., p.,** What's past is past. **p. de moda,** out of fashion, unfashionable

**pasador** /pasa'ðor/ *m*, bolt, fastener; *Mech.* pin, coupler; pin (of brooches, etc.); colander; *Naut.* marlin spike; shirt stud

**pasajaretas** /pasaha'retas/ *m*, bodkin

**pasaje** /pa'sahe/ *m*, passing; passage; fare; passage money; *Naut.* complement of passengers; channel, strait; (*Mus. Lit.*) passage; *Mus.* modulation, transition (of voice); voyage; passage; covered way; road

**pasajero** /pasa'hero/ **(-ra)** *a* crowded public (thoroughfare); transitory, fugitive; passing; temporary —*n* passenger

**pasamanería** /pasamane'ria/ *f*, passementerie work, industry or shop

**pasamano** /pasa'mano/ *m*, passementerie; banister, handrail; *Naut.* gangway

**pasante** /pa'sante/ *a Herald.* passant. *m*, student teacher; articled clerk; apprentice; student. **p. de pluma,** law clerk

**pasaporte** /pasa'porte/ *m*, passport; license, permission. **dar el p.** ( **a**), *Inf.* to give the sack (to)

**pasar** /pa'sar/ *vt* to pass; carry, transport; cross over; send; go beyond, overstep; run through, pierce; up-

set; overtake; transfer; suffer, undergo; sieve; study; dry (grapes, etc.); smuggle; surpass; omit; swallow (food); approve; dissemble; transform; spend (time); —*vi* pass; be transferred; be infectious; have enough to live on; cease; last; die; pass away; pass (at cards); be transformed; be current (money); be salable (goods); (with prep *a* + *infin*) begin to; (with *por* ) pass as; have a reputation as; visit; (with *sin*) do without —*impers* happen, occur —*vr* end; go over to another party; forget; go stale or bad; *Fig.* go too far, overstep the mark; permeate. **p. contrato,** to draw up a contract; sign a contract. **p. la voz,** to pass the word along. **p. por alto** ( **de**), to omit, overlook. **p. de largo,** to go by without stopping. **pasarse de listo,** to be too clever. **¡No pases cuidado!** Don't worry!

**pasarela** /pasa'rela/ *f*, gangplank

**pasatiempo** /pasa'tiempo/ *m*, pastime, hobby, amusement

**pasavante** /pasa'βante/ *m*, *Naut.* safe conduct; navicert

**pascua** /'paskua/ *f*, Passover; Easter; Christmas; Twelfth Night; Pentecost; *pl* twelve days of Christmas. **P. florida,** Easter Sunday. **dar las pascuas,** to wish a merry Christmas. **¡Felices pascuas!** Merry Christmas!

**pascual** /pas'kual/ *a* paschal

**pase** /'pase/ *m*, pass (with the hands and in football, etc.); safe conduct; free pass; thrust (in fencing)

**paseante** /pase'ante/ *mf* stroller, promenader, passerby

**pasear** /pase'ar/ *vt* to take a walk; parade up and down, display; —*vi* take a walk; go for a drive; go for a ride (on horseback, etc.); stroll up and down; —*vr* touch upon lightly, pass over; loaf, be idle; drift; float

**paseo** /pa'seo/ *m*, walk, stroll; drive; outing, expedition; promenade; boulevard. **p. a caballo,** ride on horseback

**pasiega** /pa'siega/ *f*, wet nurse

**pasillo** /pa'siλo; pa'siyo/ *m*, gallery; corridor; lobby; railway corridor; *Sew.* basting stitch

**pasión** /pa'sion/ *f*, suffering; passivity; passion; desire; *Ecl.* passion. **con p.,** passionately

**pasional** /pasio'nal/ *a* passionate; of passion

**pasionaria** /pasio'naria/ *f*, passionflower

**pasiva** /pa'siβa/ *f*, *Gram.* passive

**pasividad** /pasiβi'ðað/ *f*, passivity

**pasivo** /pa'siβo/ *a* passive; inactive; *Com.* sleeping (partner); *Gram.* passive. *m*, *Com.* liabilities

**pasmar** /pas'mar/ *vt* to freeze to death (plants); dumbfound, amaze, stun; chill; —*vr* be stunned or amazed

**pasmo** /'pasmo/ *m*, amazement, astonishment; wonder, marvel; *Med.* tetanus, lockjaw

**pasmoso** /pas'moso/ *a* astounding, amazing; wonderful

**paso** /'paso/ *a* dried (of fruit)

**paso** /'paso/ *m*, step; pace; passage, passing; way; footstep; progress, advancement; passage (in a book); *Sew.* tacking stitch; occurrence, event; *Theat.* short play; gait, walk; strait, channel; migratory flight (birds); *Mech.* pitch; event or scene from the Passion; armed combat; death; *pl* measures, steps —*adv* softly, in a low voice; gently. **p. a nivel,** level crossing. **p. a p.,** step by step. **p. doble,** quick march; Spanish dance. **p. volante,** (gymnastics) giant stride. **a cada p.,** at every step; often. **al p.,** without stopping; on the way, in passing. **ceder el p.,** to allow to pass. **de p.,** in passing; incidentally. **llevar el p.,** to keep in step. **marcar el p.,** to mark time. **salir al p.** ( **a**), to waylay, confront; oppose. **seguir los pasos** ( **a**), to follow; spy upon

**pasquín** /pas'kin/ *m*, pasquinada *f*, pasquinade, lampoon

**pasta** /'pasta/ *f*, *Cul.* dough; paste; pastry; piecrust; batter; *Cul.* noodle paste; paper pulp; board (bookbinding). **ser de buena p.,** to be good-natured

**pastar** /pas'tar/ *vt* to take to pasture; —*vi* graze, pasture

**pastel** /pas'tel/ *m*, cake; *Art.* pastel; pie; *Inf.* plot, secret understanding; cheating (at cards); *Print.* pie; *Inf.* fat, stocky person

**pastelear** /pastele'ar/ *vi Inf.* to indulge in shady business (especially in politics)

**pastelería** /pastele'ria/ *f,* cake bakery; cake shop; confectioner's art; confectionery

**pastelero** /paste'lero/ **(-ra)** *n* confectioner, pastry cook; *Fig. Inf.* spineless person, jellyfish

**pastelillo** /paste'liʎo; paste'liyo/ *m, Cul.* turnover

**pastelista** /paste'lista/ *mf* pastelist

**pastelón** /paste'lon/ *m,* meat or game pie

**pasteurización** /pasteuriθa'θion; pasteurisa'sion/ *f,* pasteurization

**pasteurizar** /pasteuri'θar; pasteuri'sar/ *vt* to pasteurize

**pastilla** /pas'tiʎa; pas'tiya/ *f,* tablet, cake; lozenge; pastille, drop; tread (of a tire)

**pasto** /'pasto/ *m,* grazing land, pasture; fodder; *Fig.* fuel, food; spiritual food. **a p.,** in plenty, abundantly. **de p.,** of daily use

**pastor** /pas'tor/ **(-ra)** *n* shepherd. *m, Eccl.* pastor

**pastoral** /pasto'ral/ *a* rustic, country; *Eccl.* pastoral, *f,* pastoral poem; *Eccl.* pastoral letter

**pastorear** /pastore'ar/ *vt* to graze, put to grass; *Eccl.* have charge of souls

**pastorela** /pasto'rela/ *f,* pastoral

**pastoreo** /pasto'reo/ *m,* pasturage, grazing

**pastoría** /pasto'ria/ *f,* pastorate

**pastoril** /pasto'ril/ *a* shepherd, pastoral

**pastoso** /pas'toso/ *a* doughy; mealy; pasty; mellow

**pata** /'pata/ *f,* paw and leg (animals); foot (of table, etc.); duck; *Inf.* leg. **p. de gallo,** blunder; crow's-foot, wrinkle. **meter la p.,** to interfere, put one's foot in it. *Inf.* **tener mala p.,** to be unlucky

**patada** /pa'taða/ *f,* kick, stamp; *Inf.* step, pace

**patagón** /pata'gon/ **(-ona)** *a* and *n* Patagonian

**patalear** /patale'ar/ *vi* to stamp (with the feet)

**pataleo** /pata'leo/ *m,* kicking; stamping

**pataleta** /pata'leta/ *f, Inf.* convulsion; feigned hysterics

**patán** /pa'tan/ *m, Inf.* yokel; boor, churl

**patanería** /patane'ria/ *f, Inf.* boorishness, churlishness

**patarata** /pata'rata/ *f,* trash, useless thing; extravagant courtesy

**patata** /pa'tata/ *f,* potato

**patatal, patatar** /pata'tal, pata'tar/ *m,* potato patch

**patatús** /pata'tus/ *m, Inf.* petty worry; mishap; *Med.* stroke, fit

**patear** /pate'ar/ *vt Inf.* to stamp; *Fig.* walk on, treat badly; —*vi Inf.* stamp the feet; be furiously angry; (*Golf*) putt

**patena** /pa'tena/ *f,* engraved medal worn by country women; *Eccl.* paten

**patentar** /paten'tar/ *vt* to issue a patent; take out a patent, patent

**patente** /pa'tente/ *a* obvious, patent; *f,* patent; warrant, commission; letters patent. **p. de invención,** patent. **p. de sanidad,** clean bill of health

**patentizar** /patenti'θar; patenti'sar/ *vt* to make evident

**paternidad** /paterni'ðað/ *f,* paternity

**paterno** /pa'terno/ *a* paternal

**patético** /pa'tetiko/ *a* pitiable; pathetic, moving

**patiabierto** /patia'βierto/ *a Inf.* knock-kneed

**patibulario** /patiβu'lario/ *a* heartrending, harrowing

**patíbulo** /pa'tiβulo/ *m,* scaffold

**paticojo** /pati'koho/ *a Inf.* lame; wobbly; unsteady

**patilla** /pa'tiʎa; pa'tiya/ *f,* side whisker (gen. *pl*); *pl* old Nick, the Devil

**patín** /pa'tin/ *m,* skate; runner (of a sled); (*Aer.* and of vehicles) skid; *Mech.* shoe. **p. del diablo,** scooter. **p. de ruedas,** roller skate

**patinador** /patina'ðor/ **(-ra)** *n* skater

**patinaje** /pati'nahe/ *m,* skating; skidding (of planes and vehicles)

**patinar** /pati'nar/ *vi* to skate; slip, lose one's footing; skid (vehicles and planes)

**patinazo** /pati'naθo; pati'naso/ *m,* skid (of a vehicle)

**patinete** /pati'nete/ *m,* child's scooter

**patio** /'patio/ *m,* courtyard; *Theat.* pit

**patitieso** /pati'tieso/ *a Inf.* paralyzed in the hands or feet; open-mouthed, amazed; stiff, unbending, proud

**patituerto** /pati'tuerto/ *a* crooked-legged; pigeon-toed; *Inf.* lopsided

**patizambo** /pati'θambo; pati'sambo/ *a* knock-kneed

**pato** /'pato/ *m,* duck; *Inf.* **pagar el p.,** to be a scapegoat

**patógeno** /pa'toheno/ *a* pathogenic

**patojo** /pa'toho/ *a* waddling

**patología** /patolo'hia/ *f,* pathology

**patológico** /pato'lohiko/ *a* pathological

**patólogo** /pa'tologo/ *m,* pathologist

**patoso** /pa'toso/ *a Fig.* heavy, pedestrian, tedious

**patraña** /pa'traɲa/ *f,* nonsense, rubbish, fairy tale

**patria** /'patria/ *f,* motherland, native country; native place. **p. chica,** native region

**patriarca** /pa'triarka/ *m,* patriarch

**patriarcado** /patriar'kaðo/ *m,* patriarchy

**patriarcal** /patriar'kal/ *a* patriarchal

**patricio** /pa'triθio; pa'trisio/ **(-ia)** *a* and *n* patrician

**patrimonio** /patri'monio/ *m,* patrimony

**patriota** /pa'triota/ *mf* patriot

**patriótico** /pa'triotiko/ *a* patriotic

**patriotismo** /patrio'tismo/ *m,* patriotism

**patrocinar** /patroθi'nar; patrosi'nar/ *vt* to protect, defend; favor, sponsor; patronize

**patrocinio** /patro'θinio; patro'sinio/ *m,* protection, defense; sponsorship; patronage

**patrón** /pa'tron/ **(-ona)** *n* patron, sponsor; patron saint; landlord; employer. *m,* coxswain; *Naut.* master, skipper; pattern, model; standard. **p. de oro,** gold standard

**patronato** /patro'nato/ *m,* patronage, protection; employers' association; charitable foundation. **p. de turismo,** tourist bureau

**patronímico** /patro'nimiko/ *a* and *m,* patronymic

**patrono** /pa'trono/ **(-na)** *n* protector; sponsor; patron; patron saint; employer

**patrulla** /pa'truʎa; pa'truya/ *f, Mil.* patrol; group, band

**patrullar** /patru'ʎar; patru'yar/ *vi Mil.* patrol; march about

**patudo** /pa'tuðo/ *a Inf.* large-footed

**paulatinamente** /paulatina'mente/ *adv* slowly, by degrees

**pauperismo** /paupe'rismo/ *m,* destitution, pauperism

**paupérrimo** /pau'perrimo/ *a superl* **pobre** exceedingly poor

**pausa** /'pausa/ *f,* pause, interruption; delay; *Mus.* rest; *Mus.* pause. **a pausas,** intermittently

**pausado** /pau'saðo/ *a* deliberate, slow —*adv* slowly, deliberately

**pausar** /pau'sar/ *vi* to pause

**pauta** /'pauta/ *f,* standard, norm, design; *Fig.* guide, model

**pavada** /pa'βaða/ *f,* flock of turkeys

**pavana** /pa'βana/ *f,* pavan, stately dance

**pavero** /pa'βero/ **(-ra)** *a* vain; strutting —*n* turkey keeper or vendor. *m,* broad-brimmed Andalusian hat

**pavimentación** /paβimenta'θion; paβimenta'sion/ *f,* paving, flagging

**pavimento** /paβi'mento/ *m,* pavement

**pavo** /'paβo/ **(-va)** *n Ornith.* turkey. **p. real,** peacock. *Inf.* **pelar la pava,** to serenade, court

**pavón** /pa'βon/ *m, Ornith.* peacock; peacock butterfly; preservative paint (for steel, etc.); gunmetal

**pavonear** /paβone'ar/ *vi* to strut, peacock (also *vr*); *Inf.* hoodwink, dazzle

**pavor** /pa'βor/ *m,* terror, panic

**pavoroso** /paβo'roso/ *a* fearful, awesome, dreadful

**payasada** /paia'saða/ *f,* clowning, practical joke; clown's patter

**payaso** /pa'iaso/ *m,* clown

**paz** /paθ; pas/ *f,* peace; harmony, concord; peaceableness. **¡P. sea en esta casa!** Peace be upon this house! (salutation). **estar en p.,** to be at peace; be quits, be even. **poner** ( *or* **meter) p.,** to make peace (between dissentients). **venir de p.,** to come with peaceful intentions

**pazguato** /paθ'guato; pas'guato/ **(-ta)** *n* simpleton, booby

**pazpuerca** /paθ'puerka; pas'puerka/ *f*, slattern

**pe** /pe/ *f*, name of the letter P. *Inf*. **de pe a pa**, from A to Z, from beginning to end

**peaje** /pe'ahe/ *m*, toll (on bridges, roads, etc.)

**peatón** /pea'ton/ *m*, pedestrian; walker; country postman

**pebete** /pe'βete/ *m*, joss stick; fuse; *Inf*. stench

**peca** /'peka/ *f*, mole, freckle

**pecado** /pe'kaðo/ *m*, sin; fault; excess; defect; *Inf*. the Devil. **p. capital**, mortal sin

**pecador** /peka'ðor/ *a* sinful. *m*, sinner. **¡P. de mí!** Poor me!

**pecadora** /peka'ðora/ *f*, sinner; *Inf*. prostitute

**pecaminoso** /pekami'noso/ *a* sinful

**pecar** /pe'kar/ *vi* to sin; trespass, transgress; (*with de* ) *be too... (e.g. El libro peca de largo*, The book is too long)

**peceño** /pe'θeɲo; pe'seɲo/ *a* pitch-black (horses, etc.); tasting of pitch

**pecera** /pe'θera; pe'sera/ *f*, goldfish bowl; aquarium

**pechera** /pe'tʃera/ *f*, shirt front; chest protector; bib, tucker; shirt frill; *Inf*. bosom

**pecho** /'petʃo/ *m*, *Anat*. chest; breast; bosom; mind, conscience; courage, endurance; *Mus*. quality (of voice); incline, slope. **p. arriba**, uphill. **abrir su p. a** ( *or* **con**), to unbosom oneself to. **dar el p. (a)**, to suckle. **de pechos**, leaning on. **echar el p. al agua**, *Fig*. to embark courageously upon. **tomar a pechos** (**una cosa**), to take (a thing) very seriously; take to heart

**pechuga** /pe'tʃuga/ *f*, breast (of a bird); *Inf*. breast, bosom; slope, incline

**pecio** /'peθio; 'pesio/ *m*, flotsam

**pécora** /'pekora/ *f*, sheep, head of sheep; wily woman, serpent

**pecoso** /pe'koso/ *a* freckled; spotted (with warts)

**pecuario** /pe'kuario/ *a* *Agr*. stock; cattle

**peculiar** /peku'liar/ *a* peculiar, individual

**peculiaridad** /pekuliari'ðað/ *f*, peculiarity

**peculio** /pe'kulio/ *m*, private money or property

**pecunia** /pe'kunia/ *f*, *Inf*. cash

**pecuniario** /peku'niario/ *a* pecuniary

**pedagogía** /peðago'hia/ *f*, education, pedagogy

**pedagógico** /peða'gohiko/ *a* educational, pedagogic

**pedagogo** /peða'gogo/ *m*, schoolmaster; educationalist; *Fig*. mentor

**pedal** /pe'ðal/ *m*, *Mech*. treadle, lever, *Mus*. pedal; *Mus*. sustained harmony. *Auto*. **p. de embrague**, clutch pedal

**pedalear** /peðale'ar/ *vi* to pedal

**pedante** /pe'ðante/ *a* pedantic. *mf* pedant

**pedantería** /peðante'ria/ *f*, pedantry

**pedazo** /pe'ðaθo; pe'ðaso/ *m*, bit, piece; lump; fragment, portion. *Inf*. **p. del alma, p. del corazón, p. de las entrañas**, loved one, dear one. **a pedazos** *or* **en pedazos**, in pieces, in bits. **hacer pedazos**, to break into fragments

**pedernal** /peðer'nal/ *m*, flint; anything very hard

**pedestal** /peðes'tal/ *m*, pedestal; base; stand; *Fig*. foundation

**pedestre** /pe'ðestre/ *a* pedestrian; dull, uninspired

**pediatra** /pe'ðiatra/ *mf* pediatrician

**pedicuro** /peði'kuro/ *m*, chiropodist

**pedido** /pe'ðiðo/ *m*, *Com*. order; request, petition

**pedigüeño** /peði'gueɲo/ *a* importunate, insistent

**pedimento** /peði'mento/ *m*, petition, demand; *Law*. claim; *Law*. motion

**pedir** /pe'ðir/ *vt irr* to ask, request; *Com*. order; demand; necessitate; desire; ask in marriage. **p. en juicio**, *Law*. to bring an action against. *Inf*. **pedírselo** ( a uno) **el cuerpo**, to desire (something) ardently. **a p. de boca**, according to one's wish —*Pres. Part*. **pidiendo**. *Pres. Indic*. **pido, pides, pide, piden**. *Preterite* **pidió, pidieron**. *Pres. Subjunc*. **pida**, etc —*Imperf. Subjunc*. **pidiese**, etc.

**pedo** /'peðo/ *m*, fart

**pedómetro** /pe'ðometro/ *m*, pedometer

**pedrada** /pe'ðraða/ *f*, casting a stone; blow with a stone; innuendo

**pedrea** /pe'ðrea/ *f*, stone throwing; fight with stones; shower of hailstones

**pedregal** /peðre'gal/ *m*, stony ground

**pedregoso** /peðre'goso/ *a* stony

**pedrera** /pe'ðrera/ *f*, stone quarry

**pedrería** /peðre'ria/ *f*, precious stones

**pedrisco** /pe'ðrisko/ *m*, hailstone; shower of stones; pile of stones

**pedrusco** /pe'ðrusko/ *m*, *Inf*. rough, unpolished stone

**pega** /'pega/ *f*, sticking; cementing; joining; pitch; varnish; *Inf*. joke; beating; *Ornith*. magpie

**pegadizo** /pega'ðiθo; pega'ðiso/ *a* sticky, gummy, adhesive; detachable, removable; *Fig*. clinging, importunate (of people)

**pegado** /pe'gaðo/ *m*, sticking plaster; patch

**pegajoso** /pega'hoso/ *a* sticky, gluey; viscid; contagious, catching; *Inf*. oily, unctuous; *Fig*. *Inf*. cadging; sponging

**pegar** /pe'gar/ *vt* to stick; cement; join, fasten; press (against); infect with (diseases); hit, strike; give (a shout, jump, etc.); patch; —*vi* spread, catch (fire, etc.); *Fig*. make an impression, have influence; be opportune; —*vr Cul*. stick, burn; meddle; become enthusiastic about; take root in the mind. **p. un tiro (a)**, to shoot

**Pegaso** /pe'gaso/ *m*, Pegasus

**pegote** /pe'gote/ *m*, sticking plaster; *Fig*. *Inf*. sponger; *Inf*. patch

**peinado** /pei'naðo/ *m*, hairdressing or style; headdress —*a Inf*. effeminate, overelegant (men); overcareful (style). **un p. al agua**, a finger wave

**peinador** /peina'ðor/ **(-ra)** *m*, peignoir, dressing gown —*n* hairdresser

**peinadura** /peina'ðura/ *f*, brushing or combing of hair; *pl* hair combings

**peinar** /pei'nar/ *vt* to comb, dress the hair; card (wool); cut away (rock)

**peine** /'peine/ *m*, comb; *Mech*. hackle, reed; instep; *Inf*. crafty person

**peinería** /peine'ria/ *f*, comb factory or shop

**peinero** /pei'nero/ *m*, comb manufacturer or seller

**peineta** /pei'neta/ *f*, high comb (for mantillas, etc.)

**peladilla** /pela'ðiʎa; pela'ðiya/ *f*, sugared almond; smooth, small pebble

**pelado** /pe'laðo/ *a* plucked; bare, unadorned; needy, poor; hairless; skinned; peeled; without shell; treeless

**peladura** /pela'ðura/ *f*, peeling; shelling; skinning; plucking (feathers)

**pelafustán** /pelafus'tan/ *m*, *Inf*. good-for-nothing, scamp

**pelagatos** /pela'gatos/ *m*, *Inf*. miserable wretch

**pelágico** /pe'lahiko/ *a* pelagian, oceanic

**pelagra** /pe'lagra/ *f*, pellagra

**pelaje** /pe'lahe/ *m*, fur, wool

**pelamesa** /pela'mesa/ *f*, brawl, fight; lock, tuft (of hair)

**pelapatatas** /pelapa'tatas/ *m*, potato peeler

**pelar** /pe'lar/ *vt* to tear out or cut the hair; pluck; skin; peel; shell; rob, fleece; —*vr* lose one's hair

**peldaño** /pel'daɲo/ *m*, step, stair, tread, rung

**pelea** /pe'lea/ *f*, battle; quarrel, dispute; fight (among animals); effort, exertion; *Fig*. struggle

**peleador** /pelea'ðor/ *a* fighting; quarrelsome, aggressive

**pelear** /pele'ar/ *vi* to fight; quarrel; struggle, strive. **p. como perro y gato**, to fight like cat and mouse —*vr* come to blows; fall out, become enemies

**pelechar** /pele'tʃar/ *vi* to get a new coat (of animals); grow new feathers (of birds); *Inf*. prosper, flourish; grow well

**pelele** /pe'lele/ *m*, effigy; *Inf*. nincompoop

**peletería** /pelete'ria/ *f*, furrier; fur shop

**peletero** /pele'tero/ *m*, furrier; skinner

**peliagudo** /pelia'guðo/ *a* long-haired (animals); *Inf*. complicated, difficult; wily, downy

**pelícano** /pe'likano/ *m*, pelican

**pelicorto** /peli'korto/ *a* short-haired

**película** /pe'likula/ *f*, film. **p. fotográfica,** roll of film. **p. sonora,** sound film

**peligrar** /peli'grar/ *vi* to be in danger

**peligro** /pe'ligro/ *m*, danger, peril. **correr p.** *or* **estar en p.,** to be in danger

**peligroso** /peli'groso/ *a* dangerous, perilous, risky
**pelilargo** /peli'largo/ *a* long-haired
**pelirrojo** /peli'rroho/ *a* red-haired
**pelleja** /pe'ʎeha; pe'yeha/ *f*, hide, skin (of animals); sheepskin
**pellejo** /pe'ʎeho; pe'yeho/ *m*, hide; pelt; skin; wine-skin; *Inf.* drunkard; peel, skin (of fruit)
**pelliza** /pe'ʎiθa; pe'yisa/ *f*, fur or fur-trimmed coat
**pellizcar** /peʎiθ'kar; peyis'kar/ *vt* to pinch, tweak, nip; pilfer
**pellizco** /pe'ʎiθko; pe'yisko/ *m*, pinch, nip, tweak; pilfering, pinching; bit, pinch
**pelmazo** /pel'maθo; pel'maso/ *m*, squashed mass; *Inf.* idler, sluggard; *Inf.* bore
**pelo** /'pelo/ *m*, hair; down (on birds and fruit); fiber, filament; hair trigger (firearms); hairspring (watches); kiss (in billiards); nap (of cloth), grain (of wood); flaw (in gems); raw silk. **p. de camello,** camel's hair. **a p.,** in the nude; without a hat; opportunely. **en p.,** bareback (of horses). **hacerse el p.,** to do one's hair; have one's hair cut. *Inf.* **no tener p. de tonto,** to be smart, clever. *Inf.* **no tener pelos en la lengua,** to be outspoken. *Inf.* **tomar el p.** ( **a),** to pull a person's leg. **venir a p.,** to be apposite; come opportunely
**pelón** /pe'lon/ *a* hairless; *Fig. Inf.* broke, fleeced
**pelonería** /pelone'ria/ *f*, *Inf.* poverty, misery
**peloponense** /pelopo'nense/ *a* and *mf* Peloponnesian
**pelota** /pe'lota/ *f*, ball; ball game. **p. base,** baseball. **p. vasca,** pelota. **en p.,** stark naked
**pelotari** /pelo'tari/ *m*, professional pelota player
**pelotazo** /pelo'taθo; pelo'taso/ *m*, knock or blow with a ball
**pelotear** /pelote'ar/ *vt* to audit accounts; —*vi* play ball; throw, cast; quarrel; argue
**pelotera** /pelo'tera/ *f*, *Inf.* brawl
**pelotón** /pelo'ton/ *m*, big ball; lump of hair; crowd, multitude; *Mil.* platoon. **p. de ejecución,** firing squad
**peltre** /'peltre/ *m*, pewter
**peluca** /pe'luka/ *f*, wig; periwig; *Inf.* scolding
**peludo** /pe'luðo/ *a* hairy. *m*, long-haired rug
**peluquería** /peluke'ria/ *f*, hairdressing establishment; hairdressing trade
**peluquero** /pelu'kero/ **(-ra)** *n* hairdresser; barber
**peluquín** /pelu'kin/ *m*, small wig
**pelusa** /pe'lusa/ *f*, down, soft hair; fluff, nap
**pena** /'pena/ *f*, punishment, penalty; grief; pain, suffering; difficulty, trouble; mourning veil; hardship; anxiety; embarrassment; tail feather. **p. capital** *or* **p. de la vida,** capital punishment. **a duras penas,** with great difficulty. **so p. de,** under penalty of. **valer** (*or* **merecer) la p.,** to be worth while
**penable** /pe'naβle/ *a* punishable
**penacho** /pe'natʃo/ *m*, topknot, crest (of birds); plume, panache; *Inf.* pride, arrogance
**penado** /pe'naðo/ **(-da)** *a* difficult, laborious; painful, troubled, afflicted —*n* convict
**penal** /pe'nal/ *a* penal; punitive
**penalidad** /penali'ðað/ *f*, trouble, labor, difficulty; *Law.* penalty
**penar** /pe'nar/ *vt* to penalize; punish; —*vi* suffer; undergo purgatorial pains; —*vr* suffer anguish. **p. por,** to long for
**penca** /'penka/ *f*, *Bot.* fleshy leaf; lash, strap, cat-o'-nine-tails
**penco** /'penko/ *m*, *Inf.* wretched nag
**pendejo** /pen'deho/ *m*, pubic hair; *Inf.* coward; jerk
**pendencia** /pen'denθia; pen'densia/ *f*, fight; quarrel
**pendenciar** /penden'θiar; penden'siar/ *vi* to fight; quarrel
**pendenciero** /penden'θiero; penden'siero/ *a* quarrelsome, aggressive
**pender** /pen'der/ *vi* to hang; depend; be pending
**pendiente** /pen'diente/ *a* pending; hanging; *Com.* outstanding. *m*, earring; pendant. *f*, slope, incline; gradient
**péndola** /'pendola/ *f*, feather, plume; quill pen; pendulum (of a clock)
**pendolista** /pendo'lista/ *mf* calligrapher
**pendón** /pen'don/ *m*, pennon, banner; *Bot.* shoot; *Inf.* lanky, slatternly woman; *pl* reins

**péndulo** /'pendulo/ *a* pendulous, hanging. *m*, pendulum
**pene** /'pene/ *m*, penis
**penetrabilidad** /penetraβili'ðað/ *f*, penetrability
**penetración** /penetra'θion; penetra'sion/ *f*, penetration; understanding, perspicuity; sagacity, shrewdness
**penetrador** /penetra'ðor/ *a* penetrating, perspicacious; sagacious, acute
**penetrante** /pene'trante/ *a* penetrating; deep; piercing (of sounds); acute, shrewd
**penetrar** /pene'trar/ *vt* to penetrate; permeate; master, comprehend; (*with en*) enter
**penetrativo** /penetra'tiβo/ *a* piercing
**penicilina** /peniθi'lina; penisi'lina/ *f*, penicillin
**península** /pe'ninsula/ *f*, peninsula. **la P.** the Iberian Peninsula
**Península Ibérica, la** /pe'ninsula i'βerika, la/ the Iberian Peninsula
**penique** /pe'nike/ *m*, penny
**penitencia** /peni'tenθia; peni'tensia/ *f*, penitence, repentance; penance
**penitencial** /peniten'θial; peniten'sial/ *a* penitential
**penitenciaría** /penitenθia'ria; penitensia'ria/ *f*, penitentiary
**penitenciario** /peniten'θiario; peniten'siario/ *a* penitentiary
**penitente** /peni'tente/ *a* penitent, repentant. *mf* penitent
**penoso** /pe'noso/ *a* laborious, difficult; grievous; painful; troublesome; *Inf.* foppish
**pensado** /pen'saðo/ *a* premeditated, deliberate. **de p.,** intentionally. **mal p.,** malicious, evil-minded
**pensador** /pensa'ðor/ *a* thinking; pensive. *m*, thinker
**pensamiento** /pensa'miento/ *m*, mind; thought; idea; suspicion, doubt; heartsease pansy; maxim; intention, project
**pensar** /pen'sar/ *vt irr* to think; purpose, intend; (*with en, sobre*) reflect upon; think about; —*vt* feed (animals). **p. entre sí, p. para consigo** *or* **p. para sí,** to think to oneself. See **acertar**
**pensativo** /pensa'tiβo/ *a* reflective, pensive
**pensil** /pen'sil/ *a* hanging. *m*, hanging garden; delightful garden
**pensión** /pen'sion/ *f*, pension, allowance; boarding house, private hotel; scholarship grant; cost of board; trouble, drudgery
**pensionado** /pensio'naðo/ **(-da)** *a* pensioned; retired —*n* scholarship holder. *m*, boarding school
**pensionar** /pensio'nar/ *vt* to pension, grant a pension to; charge a pension on
**pensionista** /pensio'nista/ *mf* pensioner; boarder
**pentágono** /pen'tagono/ *m*, pentagon —*a* pentagonal
**pentagrama** /penta'grama/ *or* **pentágrama** *m*, *Mus.* pentagram, stave
**pentámetro** /pen'tametro/ *m*, pentameter
**Pentateuco** /penta'teuko/ *m*, Pentateuch
**Pentecostés** /pentekos'tes/ *m*, Pentecost, Whitsuntide
**penúltimo** /pe'nultimo/ *a* next to the last, penultimate
**penuria** /pe'nuria/ *f*, scarcity; want, penury
**peña** /'peɲa/ *f*, crag, rock; boulder; group of friends; club. **ser una p.,** to be stony-hearted
**peñasco** /pe'ɲasko/ *m*, craggy peak
**peñascoso** /peɲas'koso/ *a* craggy, rocky
**peñón** /pe'ɲon/ *m*, rock; cliff; peak
**peón** /pe'on/ *m*, pedestrian; laborer; *South America* farmhand; top (toy); piece (chess, checkers); *Mech.* axle; infantryman. **p. caminero,** road mender. **p. de ajedrez,** pawn (in chess)
**peonada** /peo'naða/ *f*, day's manual labor; gang of laborers
**peonía** /peo'nia/ *f*, peony
**peonza** /pe'onθa; pe'onsa/ *f*, top; teetotum
**peor** /pe'or/ *a compar* **malo** worse —*adv compar* **mal,** worse —*a superl* **el** ( **la, lo) peor; los** ( **las) peores,** the worst. **p. que p.,** worse and worse. **tanto p.,** so much the worse
**pepino** /pe'pino/ *m*, cucumber plant; cucumber; *Fig.* pin, straw

**pepita** /pe'pita/ f, Mineral. nugget; pip, seed (of fruit)

**peplo** /'peplo/ m, Greek tunic, peplum

**péptico** /'peptiko/ a peptic

**pequeñez** /peke'neθ; peke'nes/ f, littleness, smallness; pettiness; childhood; infancy; trifle, insignificant thing; meanness, baseness

**pequeño** /pe'keno/ a little, small; petty; very young; short, brief; humble, lowly

**pera** /'pera/ f, pear; goatee; Fig. plum, sinecure

**peral** /pe'ral/ m, pear tree; pearwood

**perca** /'perka/ f, Ichth. perch

**percal** /per'kal/ m, percale, calico

**percalina** /perka'lina/ f, percaline, binding cloth

**percance** /per'kanθe; per'kanse/ m, perquisite, attribute (gen. pl); disaster, mischance

**percebe** /per'θeβe; per'seβe/ m, (gen. pl) goose barnacle

**percentaje** /perθen'tahe; persen'tahe/ m, percentage

**percepción** /perθep'θion; persep'sion/ f, perception; idea, conception

**perceptible** /perθep'tiβle; persep'tiβle/ a perceptible

**perceptivo** /perθep'tiβo; persep'tiβo/ a perceptive

**perceptor** /perθep'tor; persep'tor/ (-ra) a perceptive —n observer

**percha** /'pertʃa/ f, stake, pole; coat hanger; perch (for birds); rack (for hay); hall stand, coat and hat stand, coatrack

**perchero** /per'tʃero/ m, hall stand; clothes rack; row of perches (for fowl, etc.)

**percibir** /perθi'βir; persi'βir/ vt to collect, draw, receive; perceive; understand, grasp

**percibo** /per'θiβo; per'siβo/ m, perceiving; collecting, drawing, receiving

**percolador** /perkola'ðor/ m, percolator (coffee)

**percusión** /perku'sion/ f, percussion; shock, vibration

**percusor** /perku'sor/ m, hammer (of a firearm)

**percutir** /perku'tir/ vt to percuss, strike

**perdedor** /perðe'ðor/ (-ra) a losing —n loser

**perder** /per'ðer/ vt to lose; throw away, squander; spoil, destroy; —vi fade (of colors); —vr lose one's way, be lost; be confused or perplexed; be shipwrecked; take to vice, become dissolute; be spoiled or destroyed; disappear; love madly. **p. la chaveta** (**por),** to go out of one's head (for), be wild (about). **p. la ocasión,** to let the chance slip. **p. los estribos,** to lose patience. **p. terreno,** to lose ground. **perderse de vista,** to be lost to sight. **echarse a p.,** to spoil, be damaged. See **entender**

**perdición** /perðí'θion; perði'sion/ f, loss; perdition; ruin; damnation; depravity, viciousness

**pérdida** /'perðiða/ f, loss; waste. **p. cuantiosa,** heavy losses

**perdidamente** /perðiða'mente/ adv ardently, desperately; uselessly

**perdigón** /perði'gon/ m, young partridge; decoy partridge; hailstone, pellet, shot

**perdigonada** /perðigo'naða/ f, volley of hailstone; hailstone wound

**perdiguero** /perði'gero/ (-ra) n game dealer; setter, retriever

**perdiz** /per'ðiθ; per'ðis/ f, partridge. **p. blanca,** ptarmigan

**perdón** /per'ðon/ m, pardon, forgiveness; remission. **con p.,** with your permission; excuse me

**perdonable** /perðo'naβle/ a pardonable, excusable

**perdonar** /perðo'nar/ vt to pardon, forgive; remit, excuse; exempt; waste, lose; give up (a privilege)

**perdonavidas** /perðona'βiðas/ m, Inf. bully, braggart

**perdulario** /perðu'lario/ a careless, negligent; slovenly; vicious, depraved

**perdurable** /perðu'raβle/ a perpetual, everlasting; enduring, lasting

**perdurar** /perðu'rar/ vi to last, endure

**perecedero** /pereθe'ðero; perese'ðero/ a brief, fugitive, transient; perishable. m, Inf. poverty, want

**perecer** /pere'θer; pere'ser/ vi irr to end, finish; perish, die; suffer (damage, grief, etc.); be destitute; —vr (with por) long for, crave; desire ardently. See **conocer**

**peregrinación** /peregrina'θion; peregrina'sion/ f, journey, peregrination; pilgrimage

**peregrinamente** /peregrina'mente/ adv rarely, not often; beautifully, perfectly

**peregrinar** /peregri'nar/ vi to journey, travel; make a pilgrimage

**peregrino** /pere'grino/ (-na) a and n pilgrim —a migratory (birds); rare, unusual; extraordinary, strange; beautiful, perfect

**perejil** /pere'hil/ m, parsley; Inf. ornament or apparel (gen. pl); pl honors, titles

**perengano** /peren'gano/ (-na) n so-and-so, such a one

**perenne** /pe'renne/ a incessant, constant; Bot. perennial

**perennidad** /perenni'ðað/ f, perpetuity

**perentoriedad** /perentorie'ðað/ f, peremptoriness; urgency

**perentorio** /peren'torio/ a peremptory; conclusive, decisive; urgent, pressing

**pereza** /pe'reθa; pe'resa/ f, laziness; languor, inertia; slowness, deliberateness

**perezoso** /pere'θoso; pere'soso/ a lazy; languid; slothful; slow, deliberate. m, Zool. sloth

**perfección** /perfek'θion; perfek'sion/ f, perfection; perfecting, perfect thing, virtue, grace

**perfeccionamiento** /perfekθiona'miento; perfeksiona'miento/ m, perfecting; progress, improvement

**perfeccionar** /perfekθio'nar; perfeksio'nar/ vt to perfect; complete

**perfectamente** /perfekta'mente/ adv perfectly, quite, entirely

**perfecto** /per'fekto/ a perfect; excellent, very good; complete; whole; Gram. perfect

**perfidia** /per'fiðia/ f, perfidy, treachery

**pérfido** /'perfiðo/ a perfidious, treacherous

**perfil** /per'fil/ m, ornament, decoration; outline, contour; profile; section (of metal); fine stroke (of letters); pl finishing touches; politeness, attention, courtesy. **de p.,** in profile; sideways

**perfilado** /perfi'laðo/ a long, elongated (of faces, etc.)

**perfilar** /perfi'lar/ vt to draw in profile; outline; —vr place oneself sideways, show one's profile; Inf. dress up, titivate

**perforación** /perfora'θion; perfora'sion/ f, perforation, boring; hole

**perforador** /perfora'ðor/ a perforating, boring. m, Mech. drill

**perforar** /perfo'rar/ vt to perforate, pierce; bore, drill, make a hole in

**perfumador** /perfuma'ðor/ (-ra) a perfuming —n perfumer. m, perfume burner

**perfumar** /perfu'mar/ vt to perfume; —vi give off perfume

**perfume** /per'fume/ m, perfume; scent, fragrance

**perfumería** /perfume'ria/ f, scent factory; perfumery; perfume shop

**perfumista** /perfu'mista/ mf perfumer

**perfunctorio** /perfunk'torio/ a perfunctory

**pergamino** /perga'mino/ m, parchment, vellum; document; diploma; pl aristocratic descent

**pericardio** /peri'karðio/ m, pericardium

**pericia** /pe'riθia; pe'risia/ f, expertness; skilled workmanship

**pericial** /peri'θial; peri'sial/ a expert, skillful

**perico** /pe'riko/ m, parakeet

**periferia** /peri'feria/ f, periphery

**periférico** /peri'feriko/ a peripheral

**perifollos** /peri'foʎos; peri'foyos/ m pl, Inf. frills, flounces, finery

**perifrástico** /peri'frastiko/ a periphrastic

**perilla** /pe'riʎa; pe'riya/ f, pear-shaped ornament; goatee; imperial. **p. de la oreja,** lobe of the ear. **venir de p.,** to be most opportune

**perillán** /peri'ʎan; peri'yan/ m, Inf. rascal, rogue

**perímetro** /pe'rimetro/ m, perimeter; precincts

**perínclito** /pe'rinklito/ a distinguished, illustrious; heroic

**perineo** /peri'neo/ m, perineum

**perinola** /peri'nola/ f, top, teetotum

**periodicidad** /perioðiθi'ðað; perioðisi'ðað/ f, periodicity

**periódico** /pe'rioðiko/ a periodic. m, newspaper; periodical publication

**periodicucho** /perioði'kutʃo/ m, rag (bad newspaper)

**periodismo** /perio'ðismo/ m, journalism

**periodista** /perio'ðista/ mf journalist

**periodístico** /perio'ðistiko/ a journalistic

**período** /pe'rioðo/ m, period; Phys. cycle; menstruation period; Gram. clause; age, era

**periostio** /pe'riostio/ m, periosteum

**peripatético** /peripa'tetiko/ a peripatetic

**peripecia** /peri'peθia; peri'pesia/ f, sudden change of fortune, vicissitude

**peripuesto** /peri'puesto/ a Inf. overelegant, spruce, too well-dressed; smart

**periquete** /peri'kete/ m, Inf. jiffy, trice

**periquito** /peri'kito/ m, parakeet; budgerigar

**periscopio** /peris'kopio/ m, periscope

**perito** /pe'rito/ **(-ta)** a expert; skillful, experienced —n expert

**peritoneo** /perito'neo/ m, peritoneum

**perjudicador** /perhuðika'ðor/ **(-ra)** a injurious, prejudicial —n injurer

**perjudicar** /perhuði'kar/ vt to harm, damage, injure; prejudice

**perjudicial** /perhuði'θial; perhuði'sial/ a injurious, noxious, harmful; prejudicial

**perjuicio** /per'huiθio; per'huisio/ m, injury, damage; harm; Law. prejudice

**perjurador** /perhura'ðor/ **(-ra)** n perjurer

**perjurar** /perhu'rar/ vi to perjure oneself, commit perjury; swear, curse

**perjurio** /per'hurio/ m, perjury

**perjuro** /per'huro/ **(-ra)** a perjured, forsworn —n perjurer

**perla** /'perla/ f, pearl; Archit. bead; Fig. treasure, jewel, dear. **de perlas,** excellent; exactly right

**perlero** /per'lero/ a pearl

**perlesía** /perle'sia/ f, paralysis; palsy

**perlino** /per'lino/ a pearl, pearl-colored

**permanecer** /permane'θer; permane'ser/ vi irr to stay, remain. **p. en posición de firme,** to stand at attention. See **conocer**

**permanencia** /perma'nenθia; perma'nensia/ f, stay, sojourn; permanence

**permanente** /perma'nente/ a permanent; lasting, enduring

**permanganato** /permaŋga'nato/ m, permanganate

**permeabilidad** /permeaβili'ðað/ f, permeability

**permisible** /permi'siβle/ a permissible, allowable

**permisivo** /permi'siβo/ a permissive

**permiso** /per'miso/ m, permission, leave; permit; (Mil. etc.) pass. **¡Con p.!** Excuse me!; Allow me!

**permitir** /permi'tir/ vt to permit, allow

**permuta** /per'muta/ f, exchange

**permutación** /permuta'θion; permuta'sion/ f, permutation, interchange

**permutar** /permu'tar/ vt to exchange

**pernear** /perne'ar/ vi to kick; Inf. bustle; fret, be impatient

**pernetas, en** /per'netas, en/ adv barelegged

**perniciosidad** /perniθiosi'ðað; pernisiosi'ðað/ f, perniciousness

**pernicioso** /perni'θioso; perni'sioso/ a pernicious

**pernil** /per'nil/ m, Anat. hock; ham; leg of pork; leg (of trousers)

**pernio** /'pernio/ m, hinge (of doors, windows)

**perniquebrar** /pernike'βrar/ vt irr to break the legs of. See **quebrar**

**perno** /'perno/ m, bolt, pin, spike

**pernoctar** /pernok'tar/ vi to spend the night (away from home)

**pero** /'pero/ conjunc but. m, Inf. defect; difficulty, snag

**perogrullada** /perogru'ʎaða; perogru'yaða/ f, Inf. truism

**perol** /pe'rol/ m, Cul. pan

**peroné** /pero'ne/ m, fibula

**peroración** /perora'θion; perora'sion/ f, peroration

**perorar** /pero'rar/ vi to make a speech; Inf. speak pompously; ask insistently

**peróxido** /pe'roksiðo/ m, peroxide

**perpendicular** /perpendiku'lar/ a perpendicular. f, perpendicular

**perpetración** /perpetra'θion; perpetra'sion/ f, perpetration

**perpetrar** /perpe'trar/ vt to perpetrate

**perpetua** /per'petua/ f, Bot. immortelle, everlasting

**perpetuación** /perpetua'θion; perpetua'sion/ f, perpetuation

**perpetuar** /perpe'tuar/ vt to perpetuate; —vr last, endure

**perpetuidad** /perpetui'ðað/ f, perpetuity

**perpetuo** /per'petuo/ a everlasting; lifelong

**perplejidad** /perplehi'ðað/ f, perplexity, bewilderment, doubt

**perplejo** /per'pleho/ a perplexed, bewildered, doubtful

**perquirir** /perki'rir/ vt irr to search carefully. See **adquirir**

**perra** /'perra/ f, bitch; Inf. sot, drunkard; tantrums. **p. chica,** five-cent coin. **p. gorda,** ten-cent coin

**perrada** /pe'rraða/ f, pack of dogs; Inf. dirty trick

**perrengue** /pe'rreŋgue/ m, Inf. short-tempered person

**perrera** /pe'rrera/ f, dog kennel; useless toil; Inf. tantrums

**perrería** /perre'ria/ f, pack of dogs; Inf. dirty trick; fit of anger

**perrero** /pe'rrero/ m, dog fancier; kennel worker

**perro** /'perro/ m. **p. caliente** hot dog. **p. danés,** Great Dane. **p. de aguas,** poodle; spaniel. **p. de casta,** thoroughbred dog. **p. de lanas** poodle. **p. de muestra,** pointer. **p. de presa,** bulldog. **p. de San Bernardo,** St. Bernard (dog). **p. de Terranova,** Newfoundland (dog). **p. del hortelano,** dog in the manger. **p. dogo** bulldog. **p. esquimal** husky. **p. faldero,** lap dog. **p. lobo,** wolfhound. **p. pachón,** dachshund. **p. pastor alemán** or **p. policía,** German shepherd. **p. pequinés,** Pekingese. **p. perdiguero,** retriever. **p. pomerano,** spitz, Pomeranian (dog). **p. sabueso español,** spaniel. **p. zorrero,** foxhound. Inf. **A p. viejo no hay tus tus,** You can't fool an old dog. **vivir como perros y gatos,** Inf. to live like cat and dog

**perruno** /pe'rruno/ a dog, dog-like

**persa** /'persa/ a and mf Persian. m, Persian (language)

**persecución** /perseku'θion; perseku'sion/ f, pursuit; persecution; annoyance, importuning

**perseguidor** /persegi'ðor/ **(-ra)** a pursuing; tormenting —n pursuer; tormentor, persecutor

**perseguimiento** /persegi'miento/ m, pursuit

**perseguir** /perse'gir/ vt irr to pursue; persecute, torment; importune. See **seguir**

**perseverancia** /perseβe'ranθia; perseβe'ransia/ f, perseverance

**perseverante** /perseβe'rante/ a persevering; constant

**perseverar** /perseβe'rar/ vi to persevere; last, endure

**persiana** /per'siana/ f, Venetian blind; flowered silk material

**pérsico** /'persiko/ a Persian. m, peach tree; peach

**persignar** /persig'nar/ vt to sign; make the sign of the cross over; —vr cross oneself

**persistencia** /persis'tenθia; persis'tensia/ f, persistence

**persistente** /persis'tente/ a persistent

**persistir** /persis'tir/ vi to persist

**persona** /per'sona/ f, person; personage; character (in a play, etc.); (Gram. Eccl.) person. **de p. a p.,** in private, face to face

**personaje** /perso'nahe/ m, important person, personage; character (in a play, etc.)

**personal** /perso'nal/ a personal. m, staff, personnel

**personalidad** /personali'ðað/ f, personality

**personalismo** /persona'lismo/ m, personality; personal question

**personalizar** /personali'θar; personali'sar/ vt to become personal, be offensive

**personalmente** /personal'mente/ adv personally

**personarse** /perso'narse/ *vr* to present oneself, call, appear

**personificación** /personifika'θion; personifika'sion/ *f*, personification

**personificar** /personifi'kar/ *vt* to personify

**perspectiva** /perspek'tiβa/ *f*, perspective; view; outlook; aspect, appearance. **p. aérea,** bird's-eye view

**perspicacia** /perspi'kaθia; perspi'kasia/ *f*, perspicacity, shrewdness

**perspicaz** /perspi'kaθ; perspi'kas/ *a* perspicacious, clear-sighted

**perspicuidad** /perspikui'ðað/ *f*, perspicuity

**perspicuo** /pers'pikuo/ *a* lucid, clear

**persuadir** /persua'ðir/ *vt* to persuade

**persuasible** /persua'siβle/ *a* persuadable

**persuasión** /persua'sion/ *f*, persuasion; belief, conviction, opinion

**persuasiva** /persua'siβa/ *f*, persuasiveness

**persuasivo** /persua'siβo/ *a* persuasive

**pertenecer** /pertene'θer; pertene'ser/ *vi irr* to belong; relate, concern. See **conocer**

**perteneciente** /pertene'θiente; pertene'siente/ *a* belonging (to), pertaining (to)

**pertenencia** /perte'nenθia; perte'nensia/ *f*, ownership, proprietorship; property, accessory

**pértiga** /'pertiga/ *f*, long rod; pole. **salto de p.,** pole vaulting

**pertinacia** /perti'naθia; perti'nasia/ *f*, pertinacity, doggedness

**pertinaz** /perti'naθ; perti'nas/ *a* pertinacious, stubborn, dogged

**pertinencia** /perti'nenθia; perti'nensia/ *f*, relevance, appropriateness

**pertinente** /perti'nente/ *a* relevant, apposite; appropriate

**pertrechar** /pertre'tʃar/ *vt* to supply, equip; prepare, make ready

**pertrechos** /per'tretʃos/ *m pl, Mil.* armaments, stores; equipment, appliances

**perturbación** /perturβa'θion; perturβa'sion/ *f*, disturbance; agitation

**perturbador** /perturβa'ðor/ **(-ra)** *a* disturbing —*n* disturber; heckler

**perturbar** /pertur'βar/ *vt* to disturb; agitate

**Perú** /pe'ru/ Peru

**peruano** /pe'ruano/ **(-na)** *a* and *n* Peruvian

**perversidad** /perβersi'ðað/ *f*, wickedness, depravity

**perversión** /perβer'sion/ *f*, perversion; wickedness, evil

**perversivo** /perβer'siβo/ *a* perversive

**perverso** /per'βerso/ *a* wicked, iniquitous, depraved

**pervertir** /perβer'tir/ *vt irr* to pervert, corrupt; distort. See **sentir**

**pesa** /'pesa/ *f*, weight; clock weight; gymnast's weight. **pesas y medidas,** weights and measures

**pesacartas** /pesa'kartas/ *m*, letter scale, letter balance

**pesada** /pe'saða/ *f*, weighing

**pesadez** /pesa'ðeθ; pesa'ðes/ *f*, heaviness; obesity; tediousness, tiresomeness; slowness; fatigue

**pesadilla** /pesa'ðiʎa; pesa'ðiya/ *f*, nightmare

**pesado** /pe'saðo/ *a* heavy; obese; deep (of sleep); oppressive (of weather); slow; unwieldy; tedious; impertinent; dull, boring; offensive

**pesadumbre** /pesa'ðumbre/ *f*, heaviness; grief, sorrow; trouble, anxiety

**pésame** /'pesame/ *m*, expression of condolence. **dar el p.,** to present one's condolences

**pesantez** /pesan'teθ; pesan'tes/ *f*, weight, heaviness; seriousness, gravity

**pesar** /pe'sar/ *m*, grief, sorrow; remorse. **a p. de,** in spite of

**pesar** /pe'sar/ *vi* to weigh; be heavy; be important; grieve, cause regret (e.g. *Me pesa mucho,* I am very sorry); influence, affect; —*vt* weigh; consider. **Mal que me** ( **te,** etc.) **pese...,** Much as I regret...

**pesario** /pe'sario/ *m*, pessary

**pesaroso** /pesa'roso/ *a* regretful, remorseful; sorrowful

**pesca** /'peska/ *f*, fishery; angling, fishing; catch of fish. **p. a la rastra,** trawling. **p. deportiva** sport fishing. **p. mayor,** deep-sea fishing

**pescadería** /peskaðe'ria/ *f*, fishery; fish store; fish market

**pescadilla** /peska'ðiʎa; peska'ðiya/ *f, Ichth.* whiting

**pescado** /pes'kaðo/ *m*, fish (out of the water); salt cod

**pescador** /peska'ðor/ **(-ra)** *n* fisherman; angler

**pescante** /pes'kante/ *m*, driving seat; coach box; jib (of a crane)

**pescar** /pes'kar/ *vt* to fish; *Inf.* catch in the act; acquire. **p. a la rastra,** to trawl

**pescozón** /pesko'θon; pesko'son/ *m*, slap on the neck or head

**pescuezo** /pes'kueθo; pes'kueso/ *m*, neck; throat; haughtiness, arrogance. **torcer el p.,** to wring the neck (of chickens, etc.)

**pesebre** /pe'seβre/ *m*, manger, stable; feeding trough

**pésimamente** /'pesimamente/ *adv* extremely badly

**pesimismo** /pesi'mismo/ *m*, pessimism

**pesimista** /pesi'mista/ *a* pessimistic. *mf* pessimist

**pésimo** /'pesimo/ *a superl* **malo** extremely bad

**peso** /'peso/ *m*, weighing; weight; heaviness; gravity; importance; influence; load; peso (coin); scale, balance. **p. bruto,** gross weight. **p. de joyería,** troy weight. **p. específico,** *Phys.* specific gravity. **p. pluma,** (*Boxing*) featherweight

**pespunte** /pes'punte/ *m*, backstitch

**pesquera** /pes'kera/ *f*, fishing ground, fishery

**pesquería** /peske'ria/ *f*, fishing, angling; fisherman's trade; fishing ground, fishery

**pesquero** /pes'kero/ *a* fishing (of boats, etc.)

**pesquisa** /pes'kisa/ *f*, investigation, examination; search

**pesquisar** /peski'sar/ *vt* to investigate, look into; search

**pestaña** /pes'taɲa/ *f*, eyelash; *Sew.* edging, fringe; ear, lug; *Naut.* fluke

**pestañear** /pestaɲe'ar/ *vi* to wink; blink; flutter the eyelashes

**pestañeo** /pesta'ɲeo/ *m*, winking; blinking

**peste** /'peste/ *f*, plague, pestilence; nauseous smell; epidemic; pest; vice; *pl* oaths, curses. **p. bubónica,** bubonic plague. **p. roja** syphilis. **p. de las abejas,** foul brood. **echar pestes,** to swear; fume

**pestífero** /pes'tifero/ *a* noxious

**pestilencia** /pesti'lenθia; pesti'lensia/ *f*, plague, pestilence

**pestilente** /pesti'lente/ *a* pestilential

**pestillo** /pes'tiʎo; pes'tiyo/ *m*, latch; lock bolt. **p. de golpe,** safety latch

**petaca** /pe'taka/ *f*, cigarette or cigar case; tobacco pouch

**pétalo** /'petalo/ *m*, petal

**petardista** /petar'ðista/ *mf* swindler, impostor

**petardo** /pe'tarðo/ *m*, detonator; torpedo; firecracker; fraud

**petición** /peti'θion; peti'sion/ *f*, petition, request

**peticionario** /petiθio'nario; petisio'nario/ **(-ia)** *n* petitioner —*a* petitionary

**petimetra** /peti'metra/ *f*, stylish and affected young woman

**petimetre** /peti'metre/ *m*, fop

**petirrojo** /peti'rroho/ *m*, robin

**petitorio** /peti'torio/ *a* petitionary. *m, Inf.* importunity

**peto** /'peto/ *m*, breastplate; front (of a shirt); bib

**pétreo** /'petreo/ *a* petrous

**petrificación** /petrifika'θion; petrifika'sion/ *f*, petrifaction

**petrificar** /petrifi'kar/ *vt* to petrify; —*vr* become petrified

**petrografía** /petrogra'fia/ *f*, petrology

**petróleo** /pe'troleo/ *m*, petroleum; oil, mineral oil. **p. bruto,** crude oil. **p. de lámpara,** kerosene

**petrolero** /petro'lero/ **(-ra)** *a* oil, petroleum —*n* petroleum seller; incendiarist. *m*, oil tanker

**petrolífero** /petro'lifero/ *a* oil-bearing

**petroso** /pe'troso/ *a* stony, rocky

**petulancia** /petu'lanθia; petu'lansia/ *f*, insolence; vanity

**petulante** /petu'lante/ *a* insolent; vain

**pez** /peθ/ *pes/ *m*, fish; *pl* Pisces. *f*, *Chem*. pitch. **p. sierra,** swordfish

**pezón** /pe'θon; pe'son/ *m*, *Bot*. stalk; nipple; axle pivot; point (of land, etc.)

**pezonera** /peθo'nera; peso'nera/ *f*, linchpin

**pezuña** /pe'θuɲa; pe'suɲa/ *f*, cloven hoof (of cows, pigs, etc.)

**piada** /'piaða/ *f*, chirping, twittering

**piadoso** /pia'ðoso/ *a* compassionate; kind, pitiful; pious, religious

**piafar** /pia'far/ *vi* to stamp, paw the ground (horses)

**piamontés** /piamon'tes/ **(-esa)** *a* and *n* Piedmontese

**pianista** /pia'nista/ *mf* piano maker; piano dealer; pianist

**piano** /'piano/ *m*, pianoforte. **p. de cola,** grand piano. **p. de media cola,** baby grand. **p. vertical,** upright piano

**piante** /'piante/ *a* chirping, twittering

**piar** /pi'ar/ *vi* to chirp, twitter

**piara** /'piara/ *f*, herd of swine; pack (of horses, etc.)

**pica** /'pika/ *f*, *Mil*. pike; bullfighter's goad; pike soldier; stonecutter's hammer. **a p. seca,** in vain. **pasar por las picas,** to suffer hardship. **poner una p. en Flandes,** to triumph over great difficulties

**picacho** /pi'katʃo/ *m*, peak, summit

**picada** /pi'kaða/ *f*, prick; bite; peck; *Aer*. dive

**picadero** /pika'ðero/ *m*, riding school; paddock (of a racetrack)

**picado** /pi'kaðo/ *a* *Sew*. pinked. *m*, *Cul*. hash

**picador** /pika'ðor/ *m*, horse trainer; meat chopper; horseman armed with a goad (bullfights)

**picadura** /pika'ðura/ *f*, puncture; prick; sting; *Sew*. pinking; peck (of birds); cut tobacco; black tobacco; beginning of caries in teeth

**picajoso** /pika'hoso/ *a* hypersensitive, touchy, peevish

**picamaderos** /pikama'ðeros/ *m*, woodpecker

**picante** /pi'kante/ *a* piquant; mordant; hot, highly seasoned. *m*, mordancy; pungency

**picapleitos** /pika'pleitos/ *m*, *Inf*. shady lawyer, pettifogger

**picaporte** /pika'porte/ *m*, latch, door catch; door knocker

**picar** /pi'kar/ *vt* to prick; sting; peck; bite; chop fine; mince; nibble (of fishing); irritate (the skin); *Sew*. pink; burn (the tongue); eat (grapes); goad; spur; stipple (walls); stimulate, encourage; split, cleave; *Mil*. harass; vex; *Mus*. play staccato; —*vi* burn (of the sun); smart (of cuts, etc.); eat sparingly; *Auto*. knock; (*with en*) knock at (doors, etc.); —*vr* be motheaten; go rotten (fruit, etc.); grow choppy (of the sea); be piqued; boast

**pícaramente** /'pikaramente/ *adv* knavishly, cunningly

**picardear** /pikarðe'ar/ *vi* to play the rogue; behave mischievously

**picardía** /pikar'ðia/ *f*, knavery, roguery; mischievousness; practical joke; wantonness

**picaresco** /pika'resko/ *a* roguish, picaresque, knavish

**pícaro** /'pikaro/ **(-ra)** *a* knavish; base, vile; astute; mischievous —*n* rogue

**picatoste** /pika'toste/ *m*, kind of fritter

**picaza** /pi'kaθa; pi'kasa/ *f*, magpie

**picazo** /pi'kaθo; pi'kaso/ *m*, blow with a pike or anything pointed; peck, tap with a beak (of birds); sting

**picazón** /pika'θon; pika'son/ *f*, itch, irritation; annoyance

**pícea** /'piθea; 'pisea/ *f*, *Bot*. spruce

**píceo** /'piθeo; 'piseo/ *a* piscine, fish-like

**pichel** /pi'tʃel/ *m*, tankard

**pichón** /pi'tʃon/ **(-ona)** *m*, male pigeon —*n* *Inf*. darling

**pico** /'piko/ *m*, beak (of birds); peak; woodpecker; odd amount (e.g. *treinta y p.,* thirty-odd); sharp point; spout (of a jug, etc.); *Inf*. mouth; blarney, gab. **p. de cigüeña,** crane's-bill. **p. de oro,** silver-tongued orator

**picor** /pi'kor/ *m*, burning sensation in the mouth; smarting; itching, irritation

**picoso** /pi'koso/ *a* pitted, marked by smallpox

**picota** /pi'kota/ *f*, pillory; peak; spire

**picotazo** /piko'taθo; piko'taso/ *m*, peck; dab; sting; bite

**picoteado** /pikote'aðo/ *a* peaked, having points

**picotear** /pikote'ar/ *vt* to peck (of a bird); —*vi* toss the head (of horses); *Inf*. chatter senselessly; —*vr Inf*. slang each other

**picotero** /piko'tero/ *a* *Inf*. chattering, talkative; indiscreet

**pictografía** /piktogra'fia/ *f*, picture writing

**pictórico** /pik'toriko/ *a* pictorial

**picudo** /pi'kuðo/ *a* pointed, peaked; having a spout; *Inf*. chattering

**pie** /pie/ *m*, foot; stand, support; stem (of a glass, etc.); standard (of a lamp); *Bot*. trunk, stem; sapling; lees, sediment; *Theat*. cue; foot (measure); custom; (metrics) foot; motive, cause; pretext; (metrics) meter. **p. de cabra,** crowbar. **p. de imprenta,** printer's mark, printer's imprint. **p. de piña,** clubfoot. **p. de rey,** calliper. **p. palmado,** webfoot. **al p. de la letra,** punctiliously. *Inf*. **andar con pies de plomo,** to walk warily. **a p.,** on foot. **a p. firme,** without budging; steadfastly. *Inf*. **buscar tres pies al gato,** to look for something that isn't there; twist a person's words. **de a p.,** on foot. **en p. de guerra,** on a wartime footing. *Inf*. **poner pies en polvorosa,** to quit

**piedad** /pie'ðað/ *f*, piety; pity, compassion; *Art*. pietà

**piedra** /'pieðra/ *f*, stone; tablet; *Med*. gravel. **p. de amolar,** whetstone, grindstone. **p. angular,** cornerstone (also *Fig*.). **p. caliza,** limestone. **p. clave,** keystone. **p. de construcción,** building stone; child's block. **p. de toque,** touchstone, test. **p. filosofal,** philosopher's stone. **p. fundamental,** foundation stone. **p. miliaria,** milestone. **p. mortuoria,** tombstone. *Fig. Inf*. **no dejar p. sin remover,** to leave no stone unturned. **no dejar p. sobre p.,** to demolish, destroy completely

**piel** /piel/ *f*, skin; fur; hide; leather; peel (of some fruits); rind (of bacon). **p. de gallina,** *Fig*. goose flesh. **p. de rata,** horse blanket. **p. de Rusia,** Russian leather.

**piélago** /'pielago/ *m*, high seas; sea, ocean; glut, superabundance

**pienso** /'pienso/ *m*, *Agr*. fodder

**pierna** /'pierna/ *f*, *Anat*. leg; *Mech*. shank; leg of a compass. *Inf*. **a p. suelta,** at one's ease. **en piernas,** barelegged

**pietismo** /pie'tismo/ *m*, pietism

**pietista** /pie'tista/ *a* pietistic. *mf* pietist

**pieza** /'pieθa; 'piesa/ *f*, portion; piece; component part; room; *Theat*. play; roll (of cloth); piece (in chess, etc.); coin; piece (of music). **p. de recambio** *or* **p. de repuesto,** spare part. **p. de recibo,** reception room. *Inf*. **quedarse en una p.,** to be struck dumb

**pífano** /'pifano/ *m*, fife; fife player, fifer

**pigmentación** /pigmenta'θion; pigmenta'sion/ *f*, pigmentation

**pigmentario** /pigmen'tario/ *a* pigmentary

**pigmento** /pig'mento/ *m*, pigment

**pigmeo** /pig'meo/ **(-ea)** *a* and *n* pygmy

**pignoración** /pignora'θion; pignora'sion/ *f*, hypothecation; pawning; mortgage

**pignorar** /pigno'rar/ *vt* to hypothecate; pawn; mortgage

**pigre** /'pigre/ *a* lazy; negligent, careless

**pigricia** /pi'griθia; pi'grisia/ *f*, laziness; negligence

**pijama** /pi'hama/ *m*, pajamas

**pila** /'pila/ *f*, trough, basin; heap, pile; *Elec*. battery; *Eccl*. parish; pier, pile; *Phys*. cell. **p. atómica,** atomic pile. **p. bautismal,** *Eccl*. font

**pilar** /pi'lar/ *m*, fountain basin; milestone; pillar

**pilastra** /pi'lastra/ *f*, pier, pile; pilaster

**píldora** /'pildora/ *f*, *Med*. pill; *Inf*. disagreeable news

**pillador** /piʎa'ðor; piya'ðor/ **(-ra)** *a* pillaging, plundering —*n* plunderer

**pillaje** /pi'ʎahe; pi'yahe/ *m*, pillaging, looting, robbery, theft

**pillar** /pi'ʎar; pi'yar/ *vt* to pillage; steal, rob; seize; snatch; *Inf*. surprise, find out (in a lie, etc.). **pillarse el dedo,** to get one's finger caught (in a door, etc.)

**pillastre** /pi'ʎastre; pi'yastre/ *m*, *Inf*. rogue, ragamuffin

**pillear** /piʎe'ar; piye'ar/ *vi Inf*. to lead a rogue's life

**pillería** /piʎe'ria; piye'ria/ *f, Inf.* gang of rogues; *Inf.* rogue's trick

**pillo** /'piʎo; 'piyo/ *m,* rogue, knave

**pilón** /pi'lon/ *m,* fountain basin; pestle; loaf sugar; pylon

**pilongo** /pi'longo/ *a* thin, lean

**píloro** /'piloro/ *m,* pylorus

**pilotaje** /pilo'tahe/ *m,* pilotage; piling, pilework. **examen de p.,** flying test

**pilotar** /pilo'tar/ *vt* to pilot

**pilote** /pi'lote/ *m, Engin.* pile

**pilotear** /pilote'ar/ *vt* to pilot

**piloto** /pi'loto/ *m,* pilot; mate (in merchant ships). **p. de pruebas,** test pilot

**pimentero** /pimen'tero/ *m,* pepper plant; pepper shaker

**pimentón** /pimen'ton/ *m,* red pepper, cayenne

**pimienta** /pi'mienta/ *f,* pepper. **p. húngara,** paprika. *Inf.* **ser como una p.,** to be sharp as a needle

**pimiento** /pi'miento/ *m,* pimento; capsicum; red pepper; pepper plant. **p. de cornetilla,** chili pepper

**pimpollo** /pim'poʎo; pim'poyo/ *m,* sapling; sprout, shoot; rosebud

**pina** /'pina/ *f,* conical stone; felloe (of a wheel)

**pinacoteca** /pinako'teka/ *f,* art gallery, picture gallery

**pináculo** /pi'nakulo/ *m,* pinnacle; summit; climax, culmination; *Archit.* finial

**pinar** /pi'nar/ *m,* pinewood

**pincarrasco** /pinka'rrasko/ *m,* pin oak

**pincel** /pin'θel; pin'sel/ *m,* paintbrush; artist, painter; painting technique. **p. para las cejas,** eyebrow pencil

**pincelada** /pinθe'laða; pinse'laða/ *f,* brushstroke. **dar la última p.,** to add the finishing touch

**pincelero** /pinθe'lero; pinse'lero/ **(-ra)** *n* seller or maker of paintbrushes; brush box

**pinchadura** /pintʃa'ðura/ *f,* prick, puncture, piercing; sting; nipping, biting

**pinchar** /pin'tʃar/ *vt* to prick; puncture; pierce; sting; nip, bite. **no p. ni cortar,** to be ineffective (of persons)

**pinchazo** /pin'tʃaθo; pin'tʃaso/ *m,* prick; puncture; sting; incitement

**pinche** /'pintʃe/ *m,* scullion

**pineda** /pi'neða/ *f,* pinewood

**pingajo** /piŋ'gaho/ *m, Inf.* tatter, rag

**pingajoso** /piŋga'hoso/ *a Inf.* tattered, ragged

**pingo** /'piŋgo/ *m, Inf.* tatter, rag; *pl Inf.* cheap clothes

**pingüe** /'piŋgue/ *a* fat, greasy; fertile, rich

**pingüino** /piŋ'guino/ *m,* penguin

**pino** /'pino/ *a* steep. *m, Bot.* pine, deal; *Poet.* ship. **p. de tea,** pitch pine. **p. silvestre,** red fir

**pinocha** /pi'notʃa/ *f,* pine needle

**pinta** /'pinta/ *f,* spot; marking; mark; fleck; look, appearance; pint (measure); drop, drip; spot ball (in billiards)

**pintamonas** /pinta'monas/ *mf Inf.* dauber

**pintar** /pin'tar/ *vt* to paint; describe, picture; exaggerate; —*vi* show, manifest itself; —*vr* make up (one's face). *Inf.* **pintarse solo para,** to be very good at, excel at

**pintiparado** /pintipa'raðo/ *a* most similar, very alike; fitting, apposite

**pintiparar** /pintipa'rar/ *vt Inf.* to compare

**pintor** /pin'tor/ **(-ra)** *n* painter, artist. **p. callejero,** sidewalk artist, pavement artist. **p. de brocha gorda,** house painter

**pintoresco** /pinto'resko/ *a* picturesque, quaint, pretty

**pintoresquismo** /pintores'kismo/ *m,* picturesqueness

**pintorrear** /pintorre'ar/ *vt Inf.* to daub, paint badly

**pintura** /pin'tura/ *f,* painting; paint, pigment; picture, painting; description. **p. a la aguada,** watercolor painting. **p. al fresco,** fresco. **p. al látex,** latex paint. **p. al óleo,** oil painting. **p. al pastel,** pastel drawing

**pinturería** /pinture'ria/ *f,* paint store

**pinturero** /pintu'rero/ *a Inf.* affected, conceited; dandified, overdressed

**pinza** /'pinθa; 'pinsa/ *f,* clamp. **p. de la ropa,** clothes peg

**pinzas** /'pinθas; 'pinsas/ *f pl,* pincers; pliers; tweezers; forceps. **p. hemostáticas,** arterial forceps

**pinzón** /pin'θon; pin'son/ *m,* chaffinch

**piña** /'piɲa/ *f,* pineapple; cluster, knot (of people, etc.); pinecone

**piñón** /pi'ɲon/ *m,* pine nut; *Mech.* pinion, chain wheel

**pío** /'pio/ *a* pious; compassionate; good; piebald. *m,* chirping, cheep; *Inf.* longing

**piojo** /'pioho/ *m,* louse

**piojoso** /pio'hoso/ *a* lousy; avaricious, stingy

**pionero** /pio'nero/ *m,* pioneer

**piorrea** /pio'rrea/ *f,* pyorrhea

**pipa** /'pipa/ *f,* barrel, cask; tobacco pipe; pip (of fruits)

**pipar** /pi'par/ *vi* to smoke a pipe

**pipeta** /pi'peta/ *f,* pipette

**pipiar** /pi'piar/ *vi* to chirp, twitter

**pique** /'pike/ *m,* pique, resentment. **a p. de,** on the verge of, about to. **echar a p.,** *Naut.* to sink; destroy. **irse a p.,** to sink, founder

**piquero** /pi'kero/ *m,* pike soldier

**piqueta** /pi'keta/ *f,* pick, mattock; mason's hammer

**piquete** /pi'kete/ *m,* puncture, small wound; *Mil.* picket; pole, stake; small hole (in garments); picket (in strikes)

**pira** /'pira/ *f,* funeral pyre; bonfire

**piragua** /pi'ragua/ *f,* piragua, canoe

**pirámide** /pi'ramiðe/ *f,* pyramid

**pirarse** /pi'rarse/ *vr Inf.* to slip away

**pirata** /pi'rata/ *a* piratical *mf* pirate; savage, cruel person

**piratear** /pirate'ar/ *vi* to play the pirate

**piratería** /pirate'ria/ *f,* piracy; plunder, robbery

**pirático** /pi'ratiko/ *a* piratical

**pirenaico, pirineo** /pire'naiko, piri'neo/ *a* Pyrenean

**pirético** /pi'retiko/ *a* pyretic

**piriforme** /piri'forme/ *a* pear-shaped

**Pirineos, los** /piri'neos, los/ the Pyrenees

**piromancia** /piro'manθia; piro'mansia/ *f,* pyromancy

**piropear** /pirope'ar/ *vt Inf.* to pay compliments to

**piropo** /pi'ropo/ *m,* carbuncle; *Inf.* compliment. **echar piropos,** to pay compliments

**pirotecnia** /piro'teknia/ *f,* pyrotechnics

**pirotécnico** /piro'tekniko/ *a* pyrotechnical. *m,* pyrotechnist

**pirrarse** /pi'rrarse/ *vr Inf.* to desire ardently

**pírrico** /'pirriko/ *a* Pyrrhic

**pirueta** /pi'rueta/ *f,* pirouette, twirl

**pisada** /pi'saða/ *f,* treading, stepping; footprint, footstep; stepping on a person's foot. **seguir las pisadas de alguien,** *Fig.* to follow in someone's footsteps, imitate someone

**pisano** /pi'sano/ **(-na)** *a* and *n* Pisan

**pisapapeles** /pisapa'peles/ *m,* paperweight

**pisar** /pi'sar/ *vt* to tread upon; trample upon; crush; *Mus.* press (strings); trespass upon

**pisaverde** /pisa'βerðe/ *m, Inf.* fop, dandy

**piscicultura** /pisθikul'tura; pissikul'tura/ *f,* pisciculture, fish farming

**piscina** /pis'θina; pis'sina/ *f,* fishpond; swimming pool; *Eccl.* piscina

**piscolabis** /pisko'laβis/ *m, Inf.* snack, light meal

**piso** /'piso/ *m,* treading, trampling; story; flooring; apartment. **p. bajo,** ground floor

**pisón** /pi'son/ *m,* rammer, ram

**pisotear** /pisote'ar/ *vt* to trample; crush under foot; tread on; step on; humiliate, treat inconsiderately

**pisoteo** /piso'teo/ *m,* trampling under foot; treading

**pista** /'pista/ *f,* track, trail (of animals); circus ring; racetrack, racecourse. **p. de patinar,** skating rink. **p. de vuelo,** *Aer.* landing field. *Inf.* **seguir la p. a,** to spy upon

**pistacho** /pis'tatʃo/ *m,* pistachio

**pistar** /pis'tar/ *vt* to pestle, pound

**pistero** /pis'tero/ *m,* feeding cup

**pistilo** /pis'tilo/ *m,* pistil

**pistola** /pis'tola/ *f,* pistol. **p. ametralladora,** machine gun.

**pistolera** /pisto'lera/ *f,* holster; pistol case

**pistolero** /pisto'lero/ *m,* gangster

**pistoletazo** /pistole'taθo; pistole'taso/ *m*, pistol shot; pistol wound

**pistón** /pis'ton/ *m*, *Mus.* piston; *Mil.* percussion cap; *Mech.* piston

**pitada** /pi'taða/ *f*, blast on a whistle, whistling; impertinence

**pitagórico** /pita'goriko/ **(-ca)** *a* and *n* Pythagorean

**pitanza** /pi'tanθa; pi'tansa/ *f*, alms, charity; *Inf.* daily food; pittance, scanty remuneration

**pitar** /pi'tar/ *vi* to play the whistle; —*vt* pay (debts); smoke; give alms to

**pitido** /pi'tiðo/ *m*, blast on a whistle; whistling (of birds)

**pitillera** /piti'ʎera; piti'yera/ *f*, cigarette case; female cigarette maker

**pito** /'pito/ *m*, whistle; *Mus.* fife. *Inf.* **Cuando pitos flautas, cuando flautas pitos,** It's always the unexpected that happens. *Inf.* **no valer un p.,** to be not worth a straw

**pitoflero** /pito'flero/ **(-ra)** *n* mediocre performer (gen. on a wind instrument); *Inf.* talebearer, gossip

**pitón** /pi'ton/ *m*, *Zool.* python; nascent horn (of goats, etc.); spout; protuberance; *Bot.* sprout

**pitonisa** /pito'nisa/ *f*, *Myth.* pythoness; witch, enchantress

**pitorrearse** /pitorre'arse/ *vr* to ridicule, mock

**pituitario** /pitui'tario/ *a* pituitary

**pituso** /pi'tuso/ *a* small and amusing (of children)

**pivote** /pi'βote/ *m*, pivot, swivel, gudgeon

**piyama** /pi'yama/ *m*, pajamas

**pizarra** /pi'θarra; pi'sarra/ *f*, slate; blackboard

**pizarral** /piθa'rral; pisa'rral/ *m*. **pizarrería** *f*, slate quarry

**pizarrero** /piθa'rrero; pisa'rrero/ *m*, slater

**pizarrín** /piθa'rrin; pisa'rrin/ *m*, slate pencil

**pizca** /'piθka; 'piska/ *f*, *Inf.* atom, speck, crumb; jot, whit. **¡Ni p.!** Not a scrap!

**pizpireta** /piθpi'reta; pispi'reta/ *a f*, *Inf.* coquettish; smart; dressed up

**placa** /'plaka/ *f*, plate, disk; *Art.* plaque; *Photo.* plate; star (insignia). **p. recordatorio,** commemorative plaque

**placabilidad** /plakaβili'ðað/ *f*, placability, appeasability

**pláceme** /'plaθeme; 'plaseme/ *m*, congratulation

**placentero** /plaθen'tero; plasen'tero/ *a* agreeable, pleasant

**placer** /pla'θer; pla'ser/ *vt irr* to please, give pleasure to, gratify. *m*, *Naut.* reef, sandbank; pleasure; wish, desire; permission, consent; entertainment, diversion. **a p.,** at one's convenience; at leisure —*Pres. Indic.* **plazco, places,** etc —*Preterite* **plugo, pluguieron.** *Pres. Subjunc.* **plazca,** etc —*Imperf. Subjunc.* **pluguiese,** etc.

**placibilidad** /plaθiβili'ðað; plasiβili'ðað/ *f*, agreeableness, pleasantness

**placible** /pla'θiβle; pla'siβle/ *a* agreeable, pleasant

**placidez** /plaθi'ðeθ; plasi'ðes/ *f*, placidity, calmness, serenity

**plácido** /'plaθiðo; 'plasiðo/ *a* placid, calm, serene

**placiente** /pla'θiente; pla'siente/ *a* pleasing, attractive

**plácito** /'plaθito; 'plasito/ *m*, decision, judgment, opinion

**plafón** /pla'fon/ *m*, ceiling light; *Archit.* panel

**plaga** /'plaga/ *f*, plague; disaster, calamity; epidemic; glut; pest; grief

**plagar** /pla'gar/ *vt (with de)* to infect with; —*vr (with de)* be covered with; be overrun by; be infested with

**plagiar** /pla'hiar/ *vt* to plagiarize, copy; kidnap, hold for ransom

**plagiario** /pla'hiario/ **(-ia)** *n* plagiarist

**plagio** /'plahio/ *m*, plagiary; kidnapping

**plan** /plan/ *m*, plan; scheme; plane. **p. quinquenal,** five-year plan

**plana** /'plana/ *f*, sheet, page; mason's trowel; plain. **p. mayor,** (*Mil. Nav.*) staff

**planadora** /plana'ðora/ *f*, steamroller

**plancha** /'plantʃa/ *f*, sheet, slab, plate; flatiron; horizontal suspension (in gymnastics); *Naut.* gangway, gangplank; *Inf.* howler

**planchado** /plan'tʃaðo/ *m*, ironing; ironing to be done or already finished

**planchador** /plantʃa'ðor/ **(-ra)** *n* ironer

**planchar** /plan'tʃar/ *vt* to iron, press with an iron

**planchear** /plantʃe'ar/ *vt* to plate (with metal)

**planeador** /planea'ðor/ *m*, *Aer.* glider

**planear** /plane'ar/ *vt* to plan out; make plans for; —*vi Aer.* glide

**planeo** /pla'neo/ *m*, *Aer.* glide

**planeta** /pla'neta/ *m*, planet

**planetario** /plane'tario/ *a* planetary. *m*, planetarium

**planicie** /pla'niθie; pla'nisie/ *f*, levelness, evenness; plain

**plano** /'plano/ *a* flat, level; plane. *m*, *Geom.* plane; plan, map; *Aer.* aileron, wing

**planta** /'planta/ *f*, *Bot.* plant; sole (of the foot); plantation; layout, plan; position of the feet (in dancing, fencing); scheme, project. **p. baja,** ground floor. **p. vivaz,** perennial plant. *Inf.* **buena p.,** good appearance

**plantación** /planta'θion; planta'sion/ *f*, planting; plantation, nursery

**plantador** /planta'ðor/ **(-ra)** *n* planter. *m*, *Agr.* dibble. *f.* **plantadora,** mechanical planter

**plantar** /plan'tar/ *vt* to plant; erect; place; found, set up; pose (a problem); raise (a question, etc.); *Inf.* leave in the lurch; —*vr* take up one's position; jib (of horses); oppose

**planteamiento** /plantea'miento/ *m*, execution; putting into practice; planning; statement (of problems)

**plantel** /plan'tel/ *m*, nursery garden; training school, nursery

**plantilla** /plan'tiʎa; plan'tiya/ *f*, young plant; insole (of shoes); *Mech.* template, jig

**plantío** /plan'tio/ *m*, plantation, afforestation; planting —*a* planted or ready for planting (ground)

**plantón** /plan'ton/ *m*, plant or sapling ready for transplanting; *Bot.* cutting; doorkeeper, porter. **dar un p.** ( a), to keep (a person) waiting a long time

**plañidera** /plaɲi'ðera/ *f*, paid mourner

**plañidero** /plaɲi'ðero/ *a* mournful, piteous, anguished

**plañido** /pla'ɲiðo/ *m*, lament, weeping, wailing

**plañir** /pla'ɲir/ *vi* and *vt irr* to lament, wail, weep. See **tañer**

**plasma** /'plasma/ *m*, plasma

**plasmar** /plas'mar/ *vt* to mold, throw (pottery)

**plástica** /'plastika/ *f*, art of clay modeling; plastic

**plasticidad** /plastiθi'ðað; plastisi'ðað/ *f*, plasticity

**plástico** /'plastiko/ *a* plastic; flexible, malleable, soft

**plata** /'plata/ *f*, silver; silver (coins); money; white. **p. labrada,** silverware

**plataforma** /plata'forma/ *f*, platform; running board (of a train); *Rail.* turntable

**plátano** /'platano/ *m*, banana tree, banana; plantain; plane tree

**platea** /pla'tea/ *f*, *Theat.* pit. **butaca de p.,** pit stall

**plateado** /plate'aðo/ *a* silvered; silver-plated; silvery

**plateador** /platea'ðor/ *m*, plater

**platear** /plate'ar/ *vt* to electroplate, silver

**platería** /plate'ria/ *f*, silversmith's art or trade; silversmith's shop or workshop

**platero** /pla'tero/ *m*, silversmith; jeweler

**plática** /'platika/ *f*, conversation; exhortation; sermon; address, discourse

**platicar** /plati'kar/ *vt* and *vi* to converse (about)

**platija** /pla'tiha/ *f*, plaice

**platillo** /pla'tiʎo; pla'tiyo/ *m*, saucer; kitty (in card games); pan (of a scale); *pl* cymbals

**platinado** /plati'naðo/ *m*, plating

**platino** /pla'tino/ *m*, platinum

**platívolo** /pla'tiβolo/ *m*, flying saucer

**plato** /'plato/ *m*, plate; dish; *Cul.* course, dish; pan (of a scale). **p. sopero,** soup plate. **p. trinchero,** meat dish. *Inf.* **comer en un mismo p.,** to be on intimate terms. **nada entre dos platos,** much ado about nothing

**platónico** /pla'toniko/ *a* Platonic

**platonismo** /plato'nismo/ *m*, Platonism

**plausibilidad** /plausiβili'ðað/ *f*, plausibility

**plausible** /plau'siβle/ *a* plausible, reasonable

**playa** /'plaia/ *f,* beach, seashore, strand

**plaza** /'plaθa; 'plasa/ *f,* square (in a town, etc.); marketplace; fortified town; space; duration; employment, post.; *Com.* market. **p. de armas,** garrison town; military camp. **p. de toros,** bullring. **p. fuerte,** strong place, fortress. **sentar p.,** to enlist in the army

**plazo** /'plaθo; 'plaso/ *m,* term, duration; expiration of term, date of payment; installment. **a plazos,** *Com.* by installments, on the installment system

**plazoleta** /plaθo'leta; plaso'leta/ *f,* small square (in gardens, etc.)

**pleamar** /plea'mar/ *f, Naut.* high water

**plebe** /'pleβe/ *f,* common people; rabble, mob

**plebeyo** /ple'βeio/ **(-ya)** *a* plebeian —*n* commoner, plebeian

**plebiscito** /pleβis'θito; pleβis'sito/ *m,* plebiscite

**plectro** /'plektro/ *m,* plectrum

**plegable** /ple'gaβle/ *a* foldable

**plegadera** /plega'ðera/ *f,* folder; folding knife; paper folder

**plegadizo** /plega'ðiθo; plega'ðiso/ *a* folding; collapsible; jointed

**plegado** /ple'gaðo/ *m,* pleating; folding

**plegador** /plega'ðor/ *a* folding. *m,* folding machine

**plegadura** /plega'ðura/ *f,* folding, doubling; fold, pleat

**plegar** /ple'gar/ *vt irr* to fold; pleat; *Sew.* gather; —*vr* submit, give in. See **acertar**

**plegaria** /ple'garia/ *f,* fervent prayer

**pleitear** /pleite'ar/ *vt* to go to court about; indulge in litigation

**pleitista** /plei'tista/ *a* quarrelsome, litigious

**pleito** /'pleito/ *m,* action, lawsuit; dispute, quarrel; litigation. **p. de familia,** family squabble. **ver el p.,** *Law.* to try a case

**plenamente** /plena'mente/ *adv* fully, entirely

**plenario** /ple'nario/ *a* full, complete; *Law.* plenary

**plenilunio** /pleni'lunio/ *m,* full moon

**plenipotencia** /plenipo'tenθia; plenipo'tensia/ *f,* full powers (diplomatic, etc.)

**plenipotenciario** /plenipoten'θiario; plenipoten'siario/ *a* and *m,* plenipotentiary

**plenitud** /pleni'tuð/ *f,* fullness, completeness; plenitude, abundance

**pleno** /'pleno/ *a* full. *m,* general meeting

**pleonasmo** /pleo'nasmo/ *m, Gram.* pleonasm

**pleonástico** /pleo'nastiko/ *a* pleonastic

**pleuresía** /pleure'sia/ *f,* pleurisy

**plexo** /'plekso/ *m,* plexus

**pléyades** /'pleiaðes/ *f pl,* Pleiades

**pliego** /'pliego/ *m,* sheet (of paper); letter, packet of papers

**pliegue** /'pliege/ *m,* fold, pleat; *Sew.* gather

**plinto** /'plinto/ *m, Archit.* plinth (of a column); baseboard

**plisar** /pli'sar/ *vt* to pleat; fold

**plomada** /plo'maða/ *f,* plummet; sounding lead; plumb, lead

**plomería** /plome'ria/ *f,* plumbing; plumbing business; lead roofing

**plomero** /plo'mero/ *m,* plumber

**plomizo** /plo'miθo; plo'miso/ *a* lead-like; lead-colored, gray

**plomo** /'plomo/ *m,* lead (metal); plummet; bullet; *Inf.* bore, tedious person

**pluma** /'pluma/ *f,* feather; pen; plumage; quill; penmanship; writer; writing profession. **p. estilográfica,** fountain pen. **a vuela p.,** as the pen writes, written in a hurry

**plumado** /plu'maðo/ *a* feathered

**plumaje** /plu'mahe/ *m,* plumage, feathers; plume

**plúmbeo** /'plumbeo/ *a* plumbeous, leaden

**plúmeo** /'plumeo/ *a* feathered, plumed

**plumero** /plu'mero/ *m,* feather duster; plume, feather; plumage

**plumón** /plu'mon/ *m,* down; feather bed

**plumoso** /plu'moso/ *a* feathered

**plural** /plu'ral/ *a* and *m,* plural

**pluralidad** /plurali'ðað/ *f,* plurality; multitude, number

**pluralizar** /plurali'θar; plurali'sar/ *vt* to pluralize

**plurilingüe** /pluri'liŋgue/ *a* multilingual

**pluscuamperfecto** /pluskuamper'fekto/ *m,* pluperfect

**plusmarquista** /plusmar'kista/ *mf Sports.* recordholder

**plutocracia** /pluto'kraθia; pluto'krasia/ *f,* plutocracy

**plutócrata** /plu'tokrata/ *mf* plutocrat

**plutocrático** /pluto'kratiko/ *a* plutocratic

**plutónico** /plu'toniko/ *a Geol.* Plutonic

**pluviómetro** /plu'βiometro/ *m,* rain gauge

**poblacho** /po'βlatʃo/ *m,* miserable town or village

**población** /poβla'θion; poβla'sion/ *f,* peopling; population; town

**poblado** /po'βlaðo/ *m,* inhabited place; town; village

**poblador** /poβla'ðor/ **(-ra)** *a* populating —*n* colonist, settler

**poblar** /po'βlar/ *vt irr* to colonize; people, populate; breed fast; stock, supply; —*vr* put forth leaves (of trees). See **contar**

**pobre** /'poβre/ *a* poor; indigent, needy; mediocre; unfortunate; humble, meek. *mf* beggar, pauper, needy person. *Inf.* **ser p. de solemnidad,** to be down and out

**pobrero** /po'βrero/ *m, Eccl.* distributor of alms

**pobretería** /poβrete'ria/ *f,* poverty; needy people

**pobretón** /poβre'ton/ *a* extremely needy

**pobreza** /po'βreθa; po'βresa/ *f,* poverty, need; shortage; timidity; *Mineral.* baseness; poorness (of soil, etc.)

**pocero** /po'θero; po'sero/ *m,* well digger

**pocilga** /po'θilga; po'silga/ *f,* pigsty; *Inf.* filthy place

**poción** /po'θion; po'sion/ *f,* potion, drink; mixture, dose

**poco** /'poko/ *a* little, scanty; *pl* few. *m,* small amount, a little —*adv* little; shortly, in a little while. **p. a p.,** by degrees, little by little; slowly. **p. más o menos,** more or less, approximately. **por p.,** almost, nearly (always used with the present tense, e.g. *Por p. me caigo,* I almost fell). **tener en p.** ( a), to have a poor opinion of; undervalue

**poda** /'poða/ *f, Agr.* pruning; pruning season

**podadera** /poða'ðera/ *f,* pruning knife

**podar** /po'ðar/ *vt Agr.* to prune, trim

**poder** /po'ðer/ *m,* power; authority, jurisdiction; *Law.* power of attorney; strength; ability; proxy; efficacy; possession; *pl* authority; power of attorney. **los poderes constituidos,** the established authorities; the powers that be. **p. de adquisición,** purchasing power. **casarse por poderes,** to be married by proxy

**poder** /po'ðer/ *vt irr* to be able to (e.g. *Podemos comprar estas naranjas,* We can (are able to) buy these oranges). **Dice que la calamidad podía haberse evitado,** He says that the disaster could have been averted). **p.** also expresses possibility (e.g. *Pueden haber ido a la ciudad,* They may have gone to the city. *¡Qué distinta pudo haber sido su vida!* How different his life might have been!) —*impers* be possible. **a más no p.,** of necessity, without being able to help it; to the utmost. **no p. con,** to be unable to control or manage. **no p. hacer más,** to have no alternative, have to; be unable to do more. **no p. menos de,** to be obliged to, have no alternative but. **no p. contener su emoción,** to be overcome with emotion. **no p. ver a,** to hate (persons) —*impers* **Puede que venga esta tarde,** He may come (perhaps he will come) this afternoon —*Pres. Part.* **pudiendo.** *Pres. Indic.* **puedo, puedes, puede, pueden.** *Fut.* **podré,** etc —*Condit.* **podría,** etc —*Preterite* **pude, pudiste,** etc —*Pres. Subjunc.* **pueda, puedas, pueda, puedan.** *Imperf. Subjunc.* **pudiese,** etc

**poderío** /poðe'rio/ *m,* power, authority; sway, rule; dominion; wealth

**poderoso** /poðe'roso/ *a* powerful; opulent; effective, efficacious; mighty, magnificent

**podredumbre** /poðre'ðumbre/ *f,* decay; pus; *Fig.* canker, anguish

**podredura, podrición** /poðre'ðura, poðri'θion; poðre'ðura, poðri'sion/ *f,* putrefaction; decay

**podrido** /po'ðriðo/ *a* rotten; putrid; corrupt; decayed

**podrir** /po'ðrir/ *vt* See **pudrir**

**poema** /po'ema/ *m,* poem. **p. sinfónico,** tone poem

**poesía** /poe'sia/ *f,* poetry, verse; lyric, poem

**poeta** /po'eta/ *m,* poet

**poetastro** /poe'tastro/ *m,* poetaster
**poética** /poe'etika/ *f,* poetics
**poético** /po'etiko/ *a* poetical
**poetisa** /poe'tisa/ *f,* poetess
**poetizar** /poeti'θar; poeti'sar/ *vi* to write verses; —*vt* poeticize
**polaco** /po'lako/ **(-ca)** *a* Polish —*n* Pole. *m,* Polish (language)
**polainas** /po'lainas/ *f pl,* leggings, puttees, gaiters
**polar** /po'lar/ *a* polar
**polaridad** /polari'ðað/ *f,* polarity; polarization
**polarización** /polariθa'θion; polarisa'sion/ *f,* polarization
**polarizar** /polari'θar; polari'sar/ *vt* to polarize
**polca** /'polka/ *f,* polka
**polea** /po'lea/ *f,* pulley; *Naut.* block
**polémica** /po'lemika/ *f,* polemic, controversy, dispute
**polémico** /po'lemiko/ *a* polemical
**polemista** /pole'mista/ *mf* disputant, controversialist
**polen** /'polen/ *m,* pollen
**poliandria** /po'liandria/ *f,* polyandry
**polichinela** /politʃi'nela/ *m,* Punchinello
**policía** /poli'θia; poli'sia/ *f,* police; government, polity, administration; civility, courtesy; cleanliness, tidiness. *m,* policeman. **p.** **urbana,** city police
**policíaco** /poli'θiako; poli'siako/ *a* police; detective
**policromo** /poli'kromo/ *a* polychrome
**poliedro** /po'lieðro/ *m,* polyhedron
**polifacético** /polifa'θetiko; polifa'setiko/ *a* many-sided
**polifonía** /polifo'nia/ *f,* polyphony
**polifónico** /poli'foniko/ *a* polyphonic
**poligamia** /poli'gamia/ *f,* polygamy
**polígamo** /po'ligamo/ **(-ma)** *a* polygamous —*n* polygamist
**poligloto** /poli'gloto/ **(-ta)** *n* polyglot. *f,* polyglot Bible
**polígono** /po'ligono/ *a* polygonal. *m,* polygon
**polilla** /po'liʎa; po'liya/ *f,* moth; moth grub; destroyer, ravager
**polimorfismo** /polimor'fismo/ *m,* Chem. polymorphism
**polimorfo** /poli'morfo/ *a* polymorphous
**Polinesia** /poli'nesia/ Polynesia
**polinesio** /poli'nesio/ **(-ia)** *a* and *n* Polynesian
**polinización** /poliniθa'θion; polinisa'sion/ *f,* pollination
**poliomielitis** /poliomie'litis/ *f,* poliomyelitis, polio
**pólipo** /'polipo/ *m,* Zool. polyp; octopus; Med. polyp
**polisílabo** /poli'silaβo/ *a* polysyllabic. *m,* polysyllable
**polista** /po'lista/ *mf* polo player
**politécnico** /poli'tekniko/ *a* polytechnic
**politeísmo** /polite'ismo/ *m,* polytheism
**politeísta** /polite'ista/ *a* polytheistic. *mf* polytheist
**política** /po'litika/ *f,* politics; civility, courtesy; diplomacy; tact; policy
**politicastro** /politi'kastro/ *m,* corrupt politician
**político** /po'litiko/ *a* political; civil, courteous; in-law, by marriage (relationships). *m,* politician
**politiquear** /politike'ar/ *vi* Inf. to dabble in politics, talk politics
**politizarse** /politi'θarse; politi'sarse/ *vr* to enter the political arena
**póliza** /'poliθa; 'polisa/ *f,* Com. policy; Com. draft; share certificate; revenue stamp; admission ticket; lampoon. **p. a prima fija,** fixed-premium policy. **p. de seguros,** insurance policy. **p. dotal,** endowment policy
**polizón** /poli'θon; poli'son/ *m,* loafer, tramp; stowaway; bustle (of a dress)
**polla** /'poʎa; 'poya/ *f,* pullet; Inf. flapper, young woman
**pollada** /po'ʎaða; po'yaða/ *f,* brood, hatch (especially of chickens)
**pollastro** /po'ʎastro; po'yastro/ **(-ra)** *n* pullet.
**pollera** /po'ʎera; po'yera/ *f,* female poultry breeder or seller; chicken coop; go-cart
**pollería** /poʎe'ria; poye'ria/ *f,* poultry market or shop
**pollero** /po'ʎero; po'yero/ *n* poultry breeder; poulterer. *m,* hen coop
**pollino** /po'ʎino; po'yino/ **(-na)** *n* young ass; donkey

**pollo** /'poʎo; 'poyo/ *m,* chicken; Inf. youth, stripling; Fig. Inf. downy bird. Inf. **p. pera,** young blood, lad.
**sacar pollos,** to hatch chickens
**polo** /'polo/ *m,* pole (all meanings); Fig. support; popular Andalusian song; Sports. polo. **de p. a p.,** from pole to pole
**polonés** /polo'nes/ **(-esa)** *a* Polish —*n* Pole
**polonesa** /polo'nesa/ *f,* polonaise; short coat
**Polonia** /po'lonia/ Poland
**poltrón** /pol'tron/ *a* lazy, idle
**poltronería** /poltrone'ria/ *f,* idleness, laziness
**polución** /polu'θion; polu'sion/ *f,* Med. ejaculation
**poluto** /po'luto/ *a* filthy, unclean
**Pólux** /'poluks/ *m,* Pollux
**polvareda** /polβa'reða/ *f,* dust cloud; storm, agitation
**polvera** /pol'βera/ *f,* powder bowl; powder puff; powder compact
**polvo** /'polβo/ *m,* dust; powder; pinch (of snuff, etc.); *pl* face or dusting powder. **Se hizo como por polvos de la madre celestina,** It was done as if by magic. Inf. **limpio de p. y paja,** gratis, for nothing; net (of profit)
**pólvora** /'polβora/ *f,* gunpowder; bad temper. **p. de algodón,** guncotton.
**polvorear** /polβore'ar/ *vt* to powder, dust with powder
**polvoriento** /polβo'riento/ *a* dusty; powdery, covered with powder
**polvorín** /polβo'rin/ *m,* very fine powder; powder magazine; powder flask
**polvoroso** /polβo'roso/ *a* dusty; covered with powder
**pomada** /po'maða/ *f,* pomade; salve, ointment
**pomar** /po'mar/ *m,* orchard (especially an apple orchard)
**pómez** /'pomeθ; 'pomes/ *f,* pumice stone **(piedra p.)**
**pomo** /'pomo/ *m,* Bot. pome; pomander; nosegay; pommel, hilt (of a sword); handle; rose (of watering can)
**pomología** /pomolo'hia/ *f,* pomology, art of fruit growing
**pompa** /'pompa/ *f,* pomp, splendor; ceremonial procession; air bubble; peacock's outspread tail; Naut. pump; billowing of clothes in the wind
**Pompeya** /pom'peia/ Pompeii
**pompeyano** /pompe'iano/ *a* Pompeian
**pomposidad** /pomposi'ðað/ *f,* pomposity
**pomposo** /pom'poso/ *a* stately, ostentatious, magnificent; inflated, pompous; florid, bombastic
**pómulo** /'pomulo/ *m,* cheekbone
**ponche** /'pontʃe/ *m,* punch, toddy
**ponchera** /pon'tʃera/ *f,* punch bowl
**poncho** /'pontʃo/ *a* lazy, negligent. *m,* military cloak; poncho, cape
**ponderación** /pondera'θion; pondera'sion/ *f,* weighing; reflection, consideration; exaggeration
**ponderador** /pondera'ðor/ *a* reflective, deliberate; exaggerated
**ponderar** /ponde'rar/ *vt* to weigh; consider, ponder; exaggerate; overpraise
**ponderosidad** /ponderosi'ðað/ *f,* heaviness; ponderousness, dullness
**ponderoso** /ponde'roso/ *a* heavy; ponderous; circumspect
**ponedero** /pone'ðero/ *a* egg-laying (of hens). *m,* nest
**ponencia** /po'nenθia; po'nensia/ *f,* clause, section; office of referee or arbitrator; report, referendum
**poner** /po'ner/ *vt irr* to place, put; arrange; set (the table); bet; stake; appoint (to an office); call, name; lay (eggs); set down (in writing); calculate, count; suppose; leave to a person's judgment; risk; contribute; prepare; need, take; cause, inspire (emotions); make, cause; adapt; add; cause to become (angry, etc.); insult; praise; *(with prep a + infin)* begin to. **p. a contribución,** to lay under contribution, turn to account, utilize. **ponerle el cascabel al gato** *or* **el collar al gato,** to bell the cat. **p. los cuernos (a),** to cuckold. **p. al corriente,** to bring up to date, inform. **p. a prueba,** to test. **p. casa,** to set up house. Inf. **p. colorado a,** to make blush. **p. coto a,** to put a stop to, check. **p. en comparación,** to compare. **p. conato en,** to put a great deal of effort into. **p. en cotejo,** to

collate. **p. en limpio,** to make a fair copy (of). **p. en marcha,** to start, set in motion. **p. en práctica,** to put into effect. **p. por caso,** to take as an example (e.g. *Pongamos por caso...* For example,...). **p. por encima (de),** to prefer —*vr* to place oneself; become; put on (garments, etc.); dirty or stain oneself; set (of the sun, stars); oppose; deck oneself, dress oneself up; arrive; (*with prep a* + *infin*) begin to. **ponerse al corriente,** to bring oneself up to date. **ponerse bien,** to improve; get better (in health). **ponerse colorado,** to blush, flush. **p. una base racional a la fe,** to give faith a rational foundation. **p. los cimientos de,** lay the foundation of, lay the foundations for. **p. una conferencia,** to make a long-distance call —*Pres. Indic.* **pongo, pones,** etc —*Fut.* **pondré,** etc —*Condit.* **pondría,** etc —*Imperat.* **pon.** *Past Part.* **puesto.** *Preterite* **puse, pusiste,** etc —*Pres. Subjunc.* **ponga,** etc —*Imperf. Subjunc.* **pusiese,** etc.

**ponientada** /ponien'taða/ *f,* steady west wind
**poniente** /po'niente/ *m,* west; west wind
**pontazgo** /pon'taθgo; pon'tasgo/ *m,* bridge toll
**pontear** /ponte'ar/ *vt* to bridge; make bridges
**pontificado** /pontifi'kaðo/ *m,* pontificate, papacy
**pontifice** /pon'tifiθe; pon'tifise/ *m,* pontifex; pope, pontiff; archbishop; bishop
**pontifical** /pontifi'θial; pontifi'sial/ *a* and *m,* pontifical
**pontificio** /ponti'fiθio; ponti'fisio/ *a* pontifical
**pontón** /pon'ton/ *m, Mil.* pontoon; hulk used as a prison, hospital, store, etc.; wooden bridge
**pontonero** /ponto'nero/ *m,* pontonier, military engineer
**ponzoña** /pon'θoɲa; pon'soɲa/ *f,* poison, venom
**ponzoñoso** /ponθo'ɲoso; ponso'ɲoso/ *a* poisonous, venomous; noxious; harmful
**popa** /'popa/ *f, Naut.* stern, poop. **en p.,** abaft, astern, aft
**popelina** /pope'lina/ *f,* poplin
**populachería** /populatʃe'ria/ *f,* cheap popularity with the rabble
**populachero** /popula'tʃero/ *a* mob, vulgar
**populacho** /popu'latʃo/ *m,* mob, rabble
**popular** /popu'lar/ *a* popular
**popularidad** /populari'ðað/ *f,* popularity
**popularizar** /populari'θar; populari'sar/ *vt* to popularize; —*vr* grow popular
**popularmente** /popular'mente/ *adv* popularly
**populoso** /popu'loso/ *a* populous, crowded
**popurrí** /popu'rri/ *m, Cul.* stew; potpourri; miscellany
**poquedad** /poke'ðað/ *f,* paucity, scarcity; timidity, cowardice; trifle, mere nothing
**poquísimo** /po'kisimo/ *a superl* **poco** very little
**poquito** /po'kito/ *m,* very little
**por** /por/ *prep* for; by; through, along; during; because, as (e.g. *Lo desecharon p. viejo,* They threw it away because it was old); however (e.g. *p. bonito que sea,* however pretty it is); during; in order to (e.g. *Lo hice p. no ofenderla,* I did it in order not to offend her); toward, in favor of, for; for the sake of; on account of, by reason of (e.g. *No pudo venir p. estar enfermo,* He could not come on account of his illness); via, by (e.g. *p. correo aéreo,* by airmail); as for (e.g. *P. mí, lo rechazo,* As for me, I refuse it. *p. mi cuenta,* to my way of thinking; on my own); in exchange for (e.g. *Me vendió dos libros p. seis dólares,* He sold me two books for six dollars); in the name of; as a substitute for, instead of (e.g. *Hace mi trabajo p. mí,* He is doing my work for me); per. **Por** has several uses: 1. Introduces the agent after a passive (e.g. *La novela fue escrita p. él,* The novel was written by him). 2. Expresses movement through, along or about (e.g. *Andaban p. la calle,* They were walking along (or down) the street). 3. Denotes time at or during which an action occurs (e.g. *Ocurrió p. entonces un acontecimiento de importancia,* About that time an important event occurred). 4. Expresses rate or proportion (e.g. *seis por ciento,* six percent). 5. With certain verbs, means "to be" and expresses vague futurity (e.g. *El libro queda p. escribir,* The book remains to be written). **p. cortesía,** by courtesy, out of politeness. **p. cortesía de,** by courtesy of. **p. escrito,** in writing. **p.**

**fas or p. nefas,** by fair means or foul; at any cost. **p. mucho que,** however great, however much; in spite of, notwithstanding. **¿P. qué?** Why? **p. si acaso,** in case, if by chance. **estar p.,** to be about to; be inclined to. **P. un clavo se pierde la herradura,** For want of a nail, the shoe was lost.

**porcelana** /porθe'lana; porse'lana/ *f,* porcelain, china; chinaware
**porcentaje** /porθen'tahe; porsen'tahe/ *m,* percentage
**porche** /'portʃe/ *m,* porch, portico
**porcino** /por'θino; por'sino/ *a* porcine. *m,* young pig; bruise
**porción** /por'θion; por'sion/ *f,* portion; *Com.* share; *Inf.* crowd; allowance, pittance
**porcionista** /porθio'nista; porsio'nista/ *mf* shareholder; sharer; boarding school student
**porcuno** /por'kuno/ *a* porcine, hoggish
**pordiosear** /porðiose'ar/ *vi* to ask alms, beg
**pordioseo** /porðio'seo/ *m,* asking alms, begging
**pordiosero** /porðio'sero/ **(-ra)** *a* begging —*n* beggar
**porfía** /por'fia/ *f,* obstinacy; importunity; tenacity. **a p.,** in competition
**porfiadamente** /porfiaða'mente/ *adv* obstinately
**porfiado** /por'fiaðo/ *a* obstinate, obdurate, persistent
**porfiar** /por'fiar/ *vi* to be obstinate, insist; persist
**pórfido** /'porfiðo/ *m,* porphyry
**pormenor** /porme'nor/ *m,* particular, detail (gen. *pl*); secondary matter
**pormenorizar** /pormenori'θar; pormenori'sar/ *vt* to describe in detail
**pornografía** /pornogra'fia/ *f,* pornography
**pornográfico** /porno'grafiko/ *a* pornographic, obscene
**poro** /'poro/ *m,* pore
**porosidad** /porosi'ðað/ *f,* porosity, permeability
**poroso** /po'roso/ *a* porous, leaky
**porque** /'porke/ *conjunc* because, for; in order that
**porqué** /por'ke/ *m,* reason, wherefore, why; *Inf.* money. **el cómo y el p.,** the why and the wherefore
**porquería** /porke'ria/ *f, Inf.* filth, nastiness; dirty trick; rudeness, gross act; trifle, thing of no account
**porquerizo, porquero** /porke'riθo, por'kero; porke'riso, por'kero/ *m,* swineherd
**porra** /'porra/ *f,* club, bludgeon; last player (in children's games); *Inf.* vanity, boastfulness; bore, tedious person
**porrada** /po'rraða/ *f,* blow with a club; buffet, knock, fall; *Inf.* folly; glut, abundance
**porrazo** /po'rraθo; po'rraso/ *m,* blow with a club; buffet, knock, fall
**porrear** /porre'ar/ *vi Inf.* to insist, harp on
**porrería** /porre'ria/ *f, Inf.* folly; obduracy, persistence
**porreta** /po'rreta/ *f,* green leaves of leeks, onions, and cereals. *Inf.* **en p.,** stark-naked
**porrino** /po'rrino/ *m,* seed of a leek; young leek plant
**porrón** /po'rron/ *m,* winebottle with a spout; earthenware jug
**portaaviones** /portaa'βiones/ *m,* aircraft carrier
**portacartas** /porta'kartas/ *m,* mailbag
**portachuelo** /porta'tʃuelo/ *m,* defile, narrow mountain pass
**portada** /por'taða/ *f,* front, facade; frontispiece, title page; portal, doorway
**portado** /por'taðo/ **(bien** *or* **mal)** *a* well- or ill-dressed or behaved
**portador** /porta'ðor/ **(-ra)** *n* carrier. *m, Com.* bearer; *Mech.* carrier
**portaestandarte** /ˌportaestan'darte/ *m,* standard-bearer
**portafolio** /porta'folio/ *m,* portfolio
**portafusil** /porta'fusil/ *m,* rifle sling
**portal** /por'tal/ *m,* entrance, porch; portico; city gate
**portalámpara** /porta'lampara/ *f,* lamp holder; *Elec.* socket
**portalibros** /porta'liβros/ *m,* bookstrap
**portalón** /porta'lon/ *m,* gangway
**portamanteo** /portaman'teo/ *m,* traveling bag
**portamonedas** /portamo'neðas/ *m,* pocketbook; handbag, purse

**portanuevas** /porta'nueβas/ *mf* bringer of news, newsmonger

**portaobjetos** /portaoβ'hetos/ *m*, stage (of a microscope)

**portaplumas** /porta'plumas/ *m*, pen holder

**portar** /por'tar/ *vt* to retrieve (of dogs); carry (arms); —*vr* behave (well or badly); bear oneself, act; be well, or ill (in health)

**portátil** /por'tatil/ *a* portable

**portatostadas** /portatos'taðas/ *m*, toast rack

**portavoz** /porta'βoθ; porta'βos/ *m*, megaphone; spokesman, mouthpiece

**portazgo** /por'taθgo; por'tasgo/ *m*, toll; tollbooth

**portazguero** /portaθ'gero; portas'gero/ *m*, toll collector

**portazo** /por'taθo; por'taso/ *m*, bang of the door; slamming the door in a person's face

**porte** /'porte/ *m*, transport; *Com.* carriage; postage; freight, transport cost; porterage; behavior, conduct; bearing, looks; capacity, volume; size, dimension; nobility (of descent); *Naut.* tonnage. **p. pagado,** charges prepaid

**porteador** /portea'ðor/ *m*, carrier; porter; carter

**portear** /porte'ar/ *vt* to carry, transport; —*vr* migrate (of birds)

**portento** /por'tento/ *m*, marvel, prodigy, portent

**portentoso** /porten'toso/ *a* marvelous, portentous

**porteo** /por'teo/ *m*, porterage, cartage

**portería** /porte'ria/ *f*, porter's lodge; porter's employment; *Sports.* goal

**portero** /por'tero/ **(-ra)** *n* doorman, doorkeeper; porter; concierge; janitor; *Sports.* goalkeeper. **p. eléctrico,** door buzzer

**portezuela** /porte'θuela; porte'suela/ *f*, *dim* small door; carriage door; pocket flap

**pórtico** /'portiko/ *m*, portico, piazza; porch; vestibule, hall

**portillo** /por'tiʎo; por'tiyo/ *m*, breach, opening; defile, narrow pass; *Fig.* loophole

**portón** /por'ton/ *m*, hall door, inner door

**portorriqueño** /portorri'keno/ **(-ña)** *a* and *n* Puerto Rican

**portuario** /por'tuario/ *a* dock, port

**portugués** /portu'ges/ **(-esa)** *a* and *n* Portuguese. *m*, Portuguese (language)

**portuguesada** /portuge'saða/ *f*, exaggeration

**porvenir** /porβe'nir/ *m*, future time

**¡porvida!** /por'βiða/ *interj* By the saints! By the Almighty!

**pos** /pos/ *prefix* after; behind. Also *adv* **en p.,** with the same meanings

**posa** /'posa/ *f*, tolling bell; *pl* buttocks

**posada** /po'saða/ *f*, dwelling; inn, tavern; lodging; hospitality

**posaderas** /posa'ðeras/ *f pl*, buttocks

**posadero** /posa'ðero/ **(-ra)** *n* innkeeper; boardinghouse keeper

**posar** /po'sar/ *vi* to lodge, live; rest; alight, perch; —*vt* set down (a burden); —*vr* settle (liquids); (*with en or sobre*) perch upon

**posdata** /pos'ðata/ *f*, P.S., postscript

**pose** /'pose/ *f*, *Photo.* time exposure; *Inf.* pose

**poseedor** /posee'ðor/ **(-ra)** *n* possessor, holder

**poseer** /pose'er/ *vt irr* to own, possess; know (a language, etc.); —*vr* restrain oneself. **estar poseído por,** to be possessed by (passion, etc.); be thoroughly convinced of. See **creer**

**posesión** /pose'sion/ *f*, ownership, occupancy; possession; property, territory (often *pl*)

**posesionarse** /posesio'narse/ *vr* to take possession; lay hold (of)

**posesivo** /pose'siβo/ *a* possessive

**poseso** /po'seso/ *a* possessed of an evil spirit

**posesor** /pose'sor/ **(-ra)** *n* owner, possessor

**posfecha** /pos'fetʃa/ *f*, postdate

**posguerra** /pos'gerra/ *f*, postwar period

**posibilidad** /posiβili'ðað/ *f*, possibility; probability; opportunity, means, chance; *pl* property, wealth

**posibilitar** /posiβili'tar/ *vt* to make possible, facilitate

**posible** /po'siβle/ *a* possible. *m pl*, property, personal

wealth. **hacer lo p.** *or* **hacer todo lo p.,** to do everything possible; do one's best

**posición** /posi'θion; posi'sion/ *f*, placing; position; situation; status

**positivamente** /positiβa'mente/ *adv* positively, definitely

**positivismo** /positi'βismo/ *m*, positivism

**positivista** /positi'βista/ *a* positivistic. *mf* positivist

**positivo** /posi'tiβo/ *a* positive; certain, definite; (*Math. Elec.*) plus; true, real

**pósito** /'posito/ *m*, public granary; cooperative association

**posma** /'posma/ *f*, *Inf.* sluggishness, sloth

**posmeridiano** /posmeri'ðiano/ *a* and *m*, postmeridian

**poso** /'poso/ *m*, sediment; lees, dregs; repose, quietness

**posponer** /pospo'ner/ *vt irr* (*with prep a*) to place after; make subordinate to; value less than. See **poner**

**posta** /'posta/ *f*, post horse; stage, post; stake (cards)

**postal** /pos'tal/ *a* postal. *f*, postcard, postal card

**poste** /'poste/ *m*, post, stake

**postema** /pos'tema/ *f*, tumor, abscess; bore, tedious person

**postergación** /posterga'θion; posterga'sion/ *f*, delay; delaying; relegation; disregard of seniority (in promotion)

**postergar** /poster'gar/ *vt* to delay; disregard a senior claim to promotion

**posteridad** /posteri'ðað/ *f*, descendants; posterity

**posterior** /poste'rior/ *a* back, rear; hind; subsequent

**posterioridad** /posteriori'ðað/ *f*, posteriority

**posteriormente** /posterior'mente/ *adv* later, subsequently

**postigo** /pos'tigo/ *m*, secret door; grating, hatch; postern; shutter (of a window)

**postillón** /posti'ʎon; posti'yon/ *m*, postilion

**postizo** /pos'tiθo; pos'tiso/ *a* false, artificial, not natural. *m*, switch of false hair

**postor** /pos'tor/ *m*, bidder (at an auction)

**postración** /postra'θion; postra'sion/ *f*, prostration; exhaustion; depression; distress

**postrar** /pos'trar/ *vt* to cast down, demolish; prostrate, exhaust; —*vr* kneel down; be prostrated or exhausted

**postre** /'postre/ *a* last (in order). *m*, *Cul.* dessert. **a la p.,** at last, finally

**postrero** /pos'trero/ *a* last (in order); rearmost, hindmost

**postrimeramente** /postrimera'mente/ *adv* lastly, finally

**postrimería** /postrime'ria/ *f*, *Eccl.* last period of life

**postulación** /postula'θion; postula'sion/ *f*, entreaty, request

**postulado** /postu'laðo/ *m*, assumption; supposition; working hypothesis; *Geom.* postulate

**postulante** /postu'lante/ **(-ta)** *n* *Eccl.* postulant, applicant, candidate

**postular** /postu'lar/ *vt* to postulate

**póstumo** /'postumo/ *a* posthumous

**postura** /pos'tura/ *f*, posture, bearing; laying (of an egg); bid (at an auction); position; agreement, pact; bet, stake; planting; transplanted tree. **p. de vida,** way of life

**potable** /po'taβle/ *a* drinkable. **agua p.,** drinking water

**potación** /pota'θion; pota'sion/ *f*, potation, drink

**potaje** /po'tahe/ *m*, stew, potage; dried vegetables; mixed drink; hotchpotch

**potasa** /po'tasa/ *f*, potash

**potasio** /po'tasio/ *m*, potassium

**pote** /'pote/ *m*, pot; jar; flowerpot; *Cul.* cauldron; *Cul.* stew

**potencia** /po'tenθia; po'tensia/ *f*, power; potency; *Mech.* performance, capacity; strength, force; *Math.* power; rule, dominion

**potencial** /poten'θial; poten'sial/ *a* potential

**potentado** /poten'taðo/ *m*, potentate

**potente** /po'tente/ *a* potent; powerful; *Inf.* enormous

**potestad** /potes'tað/ *f*, authority, power; podesta,

Italian magistrate; potentate; *Math.* power; *pl* angelic powers

**potestativo** /potesta'tiβo/ *a Law.* facultative

**potingue** /po'tiŋgue/ *m, Inf.* brew; mixture; lotion; medicine; filthy place, pigsty

**potra** /'potra/ *f,* filly

**potrada** /po'traða/ *f,* herd of colts

**potrear** /potre'ar/ *vt Inf.* to tease, annoy

**potro** /'potro/ *m,* colt, foal; rack (for torture); vaulting horse. **p. mesteño,** mustang

**poyo** /'poio/ *m,* stone seat

**pozal** /po'θal; po'sal/ *m,* pail, bucket

**pozo** /'poθo; 'poso/ *m,* well; shaft (in a mine). *Auto.* **p. colector,** crankcase

**práctica** /'praktika/ *f,* practice; custom; habit; method; exercise

**practicabilidad** /praktikaβili'ðað/ *f,* feasibility

**practicable** /prakti'kaβle/ *a* feasible, practicable

**prácticamente** /'praktikamente/ *adv* practically, in practice

**practicante** /prakti'kante/ *m,* medical practitioner; medical student; *Med.* intern; first-aid practitioner

**practicar** /prakti'kar/ *vt* to execute, perform; practice; make

**práctico** /'praktiko/ *a* practical; experienced, expert; workable. *m, Naut.* pilot

**pradeño** /pra'ðeɲo/ *a* meadow, prairie

**pradera** /pra'ðera/ *f,* meadow, field; lawn

**pradería** /praðe'ria/ *f,* meadowland, prairie

**prado** /'praðo/ *m,* meadow; grassland; field; lawn; walk (in cities)

**Praga** /'praga/ Prague

**pragmatismo** /pragma'tismo/ *m,* pragmatism

**pragmatista** /pragma'tista/ *a* pragmatic. *mf* pragmatist

**pravedad** /praβe'ðað/ *f,* wickedness, immorality, depravity

**pravo** /'praβo/ *a* wicked, immoral, depraved

**pre** /pre/ *m, Mil.* daily pay —*prep insep* pre-

**preámbulo** /pre'ambulo/ *m,* preamble, preface; important inopportune digression

**prebenda** /pre'βenda/ *f, Eccl.* prebend, benefice; *Inf.* sinecure

**preboste** /pre'βoste/ *m,* provost

**precario** /pre'kario/ *a* precarious, uncertain, insecure

**precaución** /prekau'θion; prekau'sion/ *f,* precaution, safeguard

**precaucionarse** /prekauθio'narse; prekausio'narse/ *vr* to take precautions, safeguard oneself

**precautelar** /prekaute'lar/ *vt* to forewarn; take precautions

**precaver** /preka'βer/ *vt* to prevent, avoid; —*vr* (*with de or contra*) guard against

**precavido** /preka'βiðo/ *a* cautious, forewarned

**precedencia** /preθe'ðenθia; prese'ðensia/ *f,* priority, precedence; superiority; preference, precedence

**precedente** /preθe'ðente; prese'ðente/ *a* preceding. *m,* antecedent; precedent

**preceder** /preθe'ðer; prese'ðer/ *vt* to precede; have precedence over, be superior to

**preceptivo** /preθep'tiβo; presep'tiβo/ *a* preceptive; didactic

**precepto** /pre'θepto; pre'septo/ *m,* precept; order, injunction; rule, commandment. **de p.,** obligatory

**preceptor** /preθep'tor; presep'tor/ **(-ra)** *n* teacher, instructor, tutor, preceptor

**preces** /'preθes; 'preses/ *f pl, Eccl.* prayers; entreaties

**preciado** /pre'θiaðo; pre'siaðo/ *a* excellent, esteemed, precious; boastful

**preciar** /pre'θiar; pre'siar/ *vt* to esteem, value; valuate, price; —*vr* boast

**precintar** /preθin'tar; presin'tar/ *vt* to seal; rope, string, tie up

**precinto** /pre'θinto; pre'sinto/ *m,* sealing; roping, tying up; strap

**precio** /'preθio; 'presio/ *m,* price, cost; recompense, reward; premium; rate; reputation, importance; esteem. **p. de tasa,** controlled price

**preciosidad** /preθiosi'ðað; presiosi'ðað/ *f,* preciousness; exquisiteness, fineness; richness; wittiness; *Inf.* loveliness, beauty; thing of beauty

**precioso** /pre'θioso; pre'sioso/ *a* precious; exquisite, fine, rare; rich; witty; *Inf.* lovely, delicious, attractive

**precipicio** /preθi'piθio; presi'pisio/ *m,* precipice; heavy fall; ruin, disaster

**precipitación** /preθipita'θion; presipita'sion/ *f,* precipitancy, haste; rashness; *Chem.* precipitation

**precipitadamente** /preθipitaða'mente; presipitaða'mente/ *adv* precipitately, in haste; rashly, foolishly

**precipitado** /preθipi'taðo; presipi'taðo/ *a* precipitate; rash, thoughtless. *m, Chem.* precipitate

**precipitar** /preθipi'tar; presipi'tar/ *vt* to precipitate, hurl headlong; hasten; *Chem.* precipitate; —*vr* hurl oneself headlong; hasten, rush

**precipitoso** /preθipi'toso; presipi'toso/ *a* precipitous; rash, heedless

**precisamente** /preθisa'mente; presisa'mente/ *adv* exactly, precisely, just; necessarily. **Y p. en aquel instante llegó,** And just at that moment he arrived

**precisar** /preθi'sar; presi'sar/ *vt* to fix, arrange; set forth, draw up, state; compel, force, oblige

**precisión** /preθi'sion; presi'sion/ *f,* accuracy, precision; necessity, conciseness, clarity; compulsion, obligation

**preciso** /pre'θiso; pre'siso/ *a* necessary, unavoidable; concise, clear; precise, exact

**precitado** /preθi'taðo; presi'taðo/ *a* aforementioned

**preclaro** /pre'klaro/ *a* illustrious, distinguished, celebrated

**precocidad** /prekoθi'ðað; prekosi'ðað/ *f,* precocity

**precognición** /prekogni'θion; prekogni'sion/ *f,* foreknowledge

**preconcebido** /prekonθe'βiðo; prekonse'βiðo/ *a* preconceived

**preconcepto** /prekon'θepto; prekon'septo/ *m,* preconceived idea, preconceived notion

**preconizar** /prekoni'θar; prekoni'sar/ *vt* to eulogize, praise publicly

**preconocer** /prekono'θer; prekono'ser/ *vt irr* to know beforehand; foresee. See **conocer**

**precoz** /pre'koθ; pre'kos/ *a* precocious

**precursor** /prekur'sor/ **(-ra)** *a* precursory; preceding, previous —*n* precursor

**predecesor** /preðeθe'sor; preðese'sor/ **(-ra)** *n* predecessor

**predecir** /preðe'θir; preðe'sir/ *vt irr* to foretell, prophesy. See **decir**

**predestinación** /preðestina'θion; preðestina'sion/ *f,* predestination

**predestinado** /preðesti'naðo/ **(-da)** *a* predestined; foreordained —*n* one of the predestined

**predestinar** /preðesti'nar/ *vt* to predestine, foreordain

**predeterminación** /preðetermina'θion; preðetermina'sion/ *f,* predetermination

**predeterminar** /preðetermi'nar/ *vt* to predetermine

**prédica** /'preðika/ *f, Inf.* (contemptuous) sermon

**predicación** /preðika'θion; preðika'sion/ *f,* preaching; homily, sermon

**predicadera** /preðika'ðera/ *f,* pulpit; *pl Inf.* talent for preaching

**predicado** /preði'kaðo/ *m,* (*Gram. Philos.*) predicate

**predicador** /preðika'ðor/ **(-ra)** *a* preaching —*n* preacher

**predicamento** /preðika'mento/ *m,* predicament; reputation

**predicar** /preði'kar/ *vt* to publish; manifest; preach; —*vi* overpraise; *Inf.* lecture, scold. **p. en el desierto,** to preach to the wind

**predicción** /preðik'θion; preðik'sion/ *f,* prediction, prophecy

**predilección** /preðilek'θion; preðilek'sion/ *f,* predilection, preference, partiality

**predilecto** /preði'lekto/ *a* favorite, preferred

**predisponer** /preðispo'ner/ *vt irr* to predispose. See **poner**

**predisposición** /preðisposi'θion; preðisposi'sion/ *f,* predisposition; tendency, prejudice

**predominación** /preðomina'θion; preðomina'sion/ *f,* predominance

**predominante** /preðomi'nante/ *a* predominant; prevailing

**predominar** /preðomi'nar/ *vi and vt* to predominate; prevail; tower above; overlook

**predominio** /preðo'minio/ *m,* predominance, ascendancy, preponderance

**preeminencia** /preemi'nenθia; preemi'nensia/ *f,* preeminence

**preeminente** /preemi'nente/ *a* preeminent

**preexistencia** /preeksis'tenθia; preeksis'tensia/ *f,* preexistence

**preexistente** /preeksis'tente/ *a* preexistent

**preexistir** /preeksis'tir/ *vi* to preexist, exist before

**prefacio** /pre'faθio; pre'fasio/ *m,* introduction, preface, prologue; *Eccl.* preface

**prefecto** /pre'fekto/ *m,* prefect

**prefectura** /prefek'tura/ *f,* prefecture

**preferencia** /prefe'renθia; prefe'rensia/ *f,* preference; superiority. **de p.,** preferred, favorite; preferably

**preferente** /prefe'rente/ *a* preferable; preferential; preferred (of stock)

**preferible** /prefe'riβle/ *a* preferable

**preferir** /prefe'rir/ *vt irr* to prefer; excel, exceed —*Pres. Part.* **prefiriendo.** *Pres. Indic.* **prefiero, prefieres, prefiere, prefieren.** *Preterite* **prefirió, prefirieron.** *Pres. Subjunc.* **prefiera, prefieras, prefiera, prefieran.** *Imperf. Subjunc.* **prefiriese,** etc.

**prefijar** /prefi'har/ *vt* to prefix

**prefijo** /pre'fiho/ *m,* prefix

**prefinir** /prefi'nir/ *vt* to fix a time limit for

**prefulgente** /preful'hente/ *a* brilliant, shining, resplendent

**pregón** /pre'gon/ *m,* public proclamation; marriage banns

**pregonar** /prego'nar/ *vt* to proclaim publicly; cry one's wares; publish abroad; eulogize, praise; proscribe, outlaw. **p. a los cuatro vientos,** *Inf.* to shout from the rooftops

**pregonería** /pregone'ria/ *f,* office of the town crier

**pregonero** /prego'nero/ *m,* town crier

**preguerra** /pre'gerra/ *f,* prewar period

**pregunta** /pre'gunta/ *f,* question; *Com.* inquiry; questionnaire, interrogation. *Inf.* **andar** ( *or* **estar**) **a la cuarta p.,** to be very hard up, be on the rocks. **hacer una p.,** to ask a question

**preguntador** /pregunta'ðor/ **(-ra)** *a* questioning; inquisitive —*n* questioner; inquisitive person

**preguntar** /pregun'tar/ *vt* to question, ask; (*with por*) inquire for; —*vr* ask oneself, wonder

**prehistoria** /preis'toria/ *f,* prehistory

**prehistórico** /preis'toriko/ *a* prehistoric

**prejuicio** /pre'huiθio; pre'huisio/ *m,* prejudice

**prejuzgar** /prehuθ'gar; prehus'gar/ *vt* to prejudge, judge hastily

**prelacía** /prela'θia; prela'sia/ *f,* prelacy

**prelación** /prela'θion; prela'sion/ *f,* preference

**prelado** /pre'laðo/ *m,* prelate

**preliminar** /prelimi'nar/ *a* preliminary, prefatory. *m,* preliminary

**preludiar** /prelu'ðiar/ *vi and vt Mus.* to play a prelude (to); —*vt* prepare, initiate

**preludio** /pre'luðio/ *m,* introduction, prologue; *Mus.* prelude; *Mus.* overture

**prematuro** /prema'turo/ *a* premature, untimely; unseasonable; immature, unripe

**premeditación** /premeðita'θion; premeðita'sion/ *f,* premeditation

**premeditar** /premeði'tar/ *vt* to premeditate, plan in advance

**premiador** /premia'ðor/ **(-ra)** *a* rewarding —*n* rewarder

**premiar** /pre'miar/ *vt* to reward, requite

**premio** /'premio/ *m,* prize; reward; premium; *Com.* interest. **p. en metálico,** cash prize. *Inf.* **p. gordo,** first prize (in a lottery)

**premioso** /pre'mioso/ *a* tight; troublesome, annoying; stern, strict; slow-moving; burdensome, hard; labored (of speech or style)

**premisa** /pre'misa/ *f,* premise; sign, indication

**premonitorio** /premoni'torio/ *a* premonitory

**premura** /pre'mura/ *f,* urgency, haste

**prenda** /'prenda/ *f,* pledge; token, sign; jewel; article of clothing; talent, gift; loved one; *pl* game of forfeits

**prendador** /prenda'ðor/ **(-ra)** *n* pledger

**prendamiento** /prenda'miento/ *m,* pawning

**prendar** /pren'dar/ *vt* to pawn; charm, delight; —*vr* (*with de*) take a liking to

**prender** /pren'der/ *vt* to seize; arrest; capture, catch —*vi* take root (plants); catch fire; be infectious

**prendería** /prende'ria/ *f,* second-hand shop

**prendero** /pren'dero/ **(-ra)** *n* second-hand dealer

**prendimiento** /prendi'miento/ *m,* seizure, capture; arrest

**prenombre** /pre'nombre/ *m,* given name, praenomen

**prensa** /'prensa/ *f,* press; printing press; newspapers, the press. **dar a la p.,** to publish

**prensado** /pren'saðo/ *m,* **prensadura** *f,* pressing; flattening; squeezing

**prensar** /pren'sar/ *vt* to press; squeeze

**prensil** /pren'sil/ *a* prehensile

**preñado** /pre'ñaðo/ *a* pregnant; bulging, sagging (walls, etc.); swollen. *m,* pregnancy

**preñez** /pre'ñeθ; pre'ñes/ *f,* pregnancy; suspense

**preocupación** /preokupa'θion; preokupa'sion/ *f,* anxiety, preoccupation; prejudice

**preocupadamente** /preokupaða'mente/ *adv* preoccupiedly, absentmindedly; with prejudice

**preocupar** /preoku'par/ *vt* to preoccupy; make anxious; bias, prejudice; —*vr* be anxious; be prejudiced

**preordinar** /preorði'nar/ *vt Eccl.* to predestine

**preparación** /prepara'θion; prepara'sion/ *f,* preparation; treatment; compound, specific

**preparado** /prepa'raðo/ *a* ready, prepared. *m,* preparation, patent food, etc.

**preparar** /prepa'rar/ *vt* to prepare; —*vr* prepare oneself; qualify

**preparativo** /prepara'tiβo/ *a* preparatory. *m,* preparation

**preparatorio** /prepara'torio/ *a* preparatory

**preponderancia** /preponde'ranθia; preponde'ransia/ *f,* preponderance

**preponderante** /preponde'rante/ *a* preponderant; dominant

**preponderar** /preponde'rar/ *vi* to preponderate; dominate; outweigh

**preponer** /prepo'ner/ *vt irr* to put before. See **poner**

**preposición** /preposi'θion; preposi'sion/ *f,* preposition

**prepósito** /pre'posito/ *m,* chairman, head, president; *Eccl.* provost

**prepucio** /pre'puθio; pre'pusio/ *m,* prepuce

**prerrafaelista** /prerrafae'lista/ *a and mf* Pre-Raphaelite

**prerrogativa** /prerroga'tiβa/ *f,* prerogative

**presa** /'presa/ *f,* hold, grasp; seizure, capture; booty; dam; lock (on rivers, canals); weir; ditch, trench; embankment; slice, bit. **hacer p.,** to seize; take advantage of (circumstances)

**presagiar** /presa'hiar/ *vt* to prophesy, presage, bode

**presagio** /pre'sahio/ *m,* presage, sign; presentiment, foreboding

**présbita** /'presβita/ *a* long-sighted, farsighted

**presbiterado** /presβite'raðo/ *m,* priesthood; holy orders

**presbiteriano** /presβite'riano/ **(-na)** *a and n* Presbyterian

**presbítero** /pres'βitero/ *m,* priest

**presciencia** /pres'θienθia; pres'siensia/ *f,* prescience, foresight

**presciente** /pres'θiente; pres'siente/ *a* prescient, farsighted

**prescindible** /presθin'diβle; pressin'diβle/ *a* nonessential, able to be dispensed with

**prescindir** /presθin'dir; pressin'dir/ *vi* (*with de*) to pass over, omit; do without. **Prescindiendo de esto...,** Leaving this aside....

**prescribir** /preskri'βir/ *vt* to prescribe, order

**prescripción** /preskrip'θion; preskrip'sion/ *f,* prescription

**presea** /pre'sea/ *f,* jewel, object of value

**presencia** /pre'senθia; pre'sensia/ *f,* presence, attendance; appearance, looks; ostentation. **p. de ánimo,** presence of mind

**presenciar** /presen'θiar; presen'siar/ *vt* to be present at; witness, behold

**presentación** /presenta'θion; presenta'sion/ *f*, presentation; introduction

**presentar** /presen'tar/ *vt* to show; present, make a gift of; introduce (persons); —*vr* occur; present oneself; offer one's services

**presente** /pre'sente/ *a* present. *m*, gift; present time. *Law*. **Por estas presentes...,** By these presents.... **tener p.,** to remember

**presentimiento** /presenti'miento/ *m*, presentiment, apprehension

**presentir** /presen'tir/ *vt irr* to have a presentiment of. See **sentir**

**preservación** /preserβa'θion; preserβa'sion/ *f*, preservation, protection, saving

**preservar** /preser'βar/ *vt* to preserve, protect, save

**preservativo** /preserβa'tiβo/ *a* preservative. *m*, preservative, safeguard, protection

**presidencia** /presi'ðenθia; presi'ðensia/ *f*, presidency; chairmanship; presidential seat or residence

**presidencial** /presiðen'θial; presiðen'sial/ *a* presidential

**presidenta** /presi'ðenta/ *f*, female president; president's wife; chairwoman

**presidente** /presi'ðente/ *m*, president; chairman; head, director; presiding judge

**presidiar** /presi'ðiar/ *vt* to garrison

**presidiario** /presi'ðiario/ *m*, convict

**presidio** /pre'siðio/ *m*, garrison; garrison town; fortress; penitentiary; imprisonment; *Law*. hard labor; assistance, protection

**presidir** /presi'ðir/ *vt* to preside over; act as chairperson for; influence, determine

**presilla** /pre'siʎa; pre'siya/ *f*, loop, shank, noose; press stud

**presión** /pre'sion/ *f*, pressure

**preso** /'preso/ **(-sa)** *n* prisoner, captive; convict

**prestación** /presta'θion; presta'sion/ *f*, lending, loan. **p. vecinal,** corvée

**prestador** /presta'ðor/ **(-ra)** *a* lending, loan —*n* lender

**prestamente** /presta'mente/ *adv* expeditiously, promptly

**prestamista** /presta'mista/ *mf* moneylender; pawnbroker

**préstamo** /'prestamo/ *m*, loan; lending. **casa de préstamos,** pawnshop

**prestar** /pres'tar/ *vt* to lend; assist; pay (attention); give; —*vi* be useful; give, expand; —*vr* be suitable; lend itself; offer oneself. **tomar prestado,** to borrow

**prestatario** /presta'tario/ **(-ia)** *n* money borrower, debtor

**preste** /'preste/ *m*, celebrant of high mass. **el p. Juan,** title of Prester John

**presteza** /pres'teθa; pres'tesa/ *f*, speed; promptness, dispatch

**prestidigitación** /prestiðihita'θion; prestiðihita'sion/ *f*, prestidigitation

**prestidigitador** /prestiðihita'ðor/ **(-ra)** *n* juggler, conjurer

**prestigio** /pres'tihio/ *m*, magic spell, sorcery; trick, illusion (of conjurers, etc.); influence, prestige

**prestigioso** /presti'hioso/ *a* illusory; influential

**presto** /'presto/ *a* quick, speedy; prompt, ready. *m*, pressure cooker —*adv* immediately; soon; quickly. **de p.,** speedily

**presumido** /presu'miðo/ *a* conceited, vain; presumptuous

**presumir** /presu'mir/ *vt* to suppose, presume; —*vi* be conceited

**presunción** /presun'θion; presun'sion/ *f*, supposition, presumption; vanity, presumptuousness

**presuntivo** /presun'tiβo/ *a* presumptive

**presuntuosidad** /presuntuosi'ðað/ *f*, presumptuousness

**presuntuoso** /presun'tuoso/ *a* presumptuous, vain

**presuponer** /presupo'ner/ *vt irr* to presuppose, assume; budget, estimate. See **poner**

**presuposición** /presuposi'θion; presuposi'sion/ *f*, presupposition

**presupuesto** /presu'puesto/ *m*, motive, reason; supposition, assumption; estimate; *Com*. tender; national budget

**presuroso** /presu'roso/ *a* swift, speedy

**pretencioso** /preten'θioso; preten'sioso/ *a* pretentious, vain

**pretender** /preten'der/ *vt* to seek, solicit; claim; apply for; attempt, try; woo, court

**pretendiente** /preten'diente/ **(-ta)** *n* pretender; candidate; petitioner; suitor

**pretensión** /preten'sion/ *f*, pretension; claim; *pl* ambitions

**pretérito** /pre'terito/ *a* past. *m*, preterite

**pretextar** /preteks'tar/ *vt* to allege as a pretext or excuse

**pretexto** /pre'teksto/ *m*, pretext, excuse

**prevalecer** /preβale'θer; preβale'ser/ *vi irr* to prevail; be dominant; take root (plants). See **conocer**

**prevaleciente** /preβale'θiente; preβale'siente/ *a* prevailing; prevalent

**prevaricación** /preβarika'θion; preβarika'sion/ *f*, prevarication

**prevaricador** /preβarika'ðor/ **(-ra)** *n* prevaricator

**prevaricar** /preβari'kar/ *vi* to prevaricate

**prevención** /preβen'θion; preβen'sion/ *f*, prevention; precaution; prejudice; police station; *Mil*. guard room; foresight, prevision; preparation. **de p.,** as a precaution

**prevenido** /preβe'niðo/ *a* prepared; cautious, forewarned

**prevenir** /preβe'nir/ *vt irr* to prepare; prevent, avoid; warn; prejudice; occur, happen; *Fig*. overcome (obstacles); —*vr* be ready; be forewarned. See **venir**

**preventivo** /preβen'tiβo/ *a* preventive

**prever** /pre'βer/ *vt irr* to foresee, forecast, anticipate. See **ver**

**previamente** /preβia'mente/ *adv* previously, in advance

**previo** /'preβio/ *a* previous, advance

**previsión** /preβi'sion/ *f*, forecast; foresight, prevision, prescience. **p. social,** social insurance

**previsor** /preβi'sor/ *a* farsighted, provident

**prieto** /'prieto/ *a* almost black, blackish; tight; mean, avaricious

**prima** /'prima/ *f*, *Eccl*. prime; *Com*. premium; female cousin

**primacía** /prima'θia; prima'sia/ *f*, supremacy, preeminence; primacy; primateship

**primada** /pri'maða/ *f*, *Inf*. act of sponging on, taking advantage of

**primado** /pri'maðo/ *m*, primate; primateship

**primario** /pri'mario/ *a* primary. *m*, professor who gives the first lecture of the day

**primavera** /prima'βera/ *f*, springtime; primrose; figured silk material; beautifully colored thing; youth; prime

**primaveral** /primaβe'ral/ *a* spring, spring-like

**primeramente** /primera'mente/ *adv* first; in the first place

**primerizo** /prime'riθo; prime'riso/ **(-za)** *n* novice; beginner; apprentice; firstborn

**primero** /pri'mero/ *a* first; former; excellent, first-rate —*adv* first; in the first place. **primera enseñanza,** primary education. **primera materia,** raw material. **primer plano,** *Art*. foreground. **primera cura,** first aid. **de buenas a primeras,** all at once, suddenly

**primicia** /pri'miθia; pri'misia/ *f*, first fruits; offering of first fruits; *pl* first effects

**primitivo** /primi'tiβo/ *a* original, early; primitive

**primo** /'primo/ **(-ma)** *a* first; excellent, fine —*n* cousin; *Inf*. simpleton; *Inf*. pigeon, dupe. **p. carnal,** first cousin. *Inf*. **hacer el p.,** to be a dupe. *Inf*. **ser prima hermana de,** to be the twin of (of things)

**primogénito** /primo'henito/ **(-ta)** *a* and *n* firstborn

**primogenitura** /primoheni'tura/ *f*, primogeniture

**primor** /pri'mor/ *m*, exquisite care; beauty, loveliness; thing of beauty

**primoroso** /primo'roso/ *a* beautiful; exquisitely done; dexterous, skillful

**princesa** /prin'θesa; prin'sesa/ *f*, princess

**principado** /prinθi'paðo; prinsi'paðo/ *m*, principality; princedom; superiority, preeminence

**principal** /prinθi'pal; prinsi'pal/ *a* chief, principal; illustrious; fundamental, first. *m*, head, principal (of a firm); *Com.* capital, principal; first floor

**principalmente** /prinθipal'mente; prinsipal'mente/ *adv* principally, chiefly

**príncipe** /'prinθipe; 'prinsipe/ *m*, leader; prince. **p. de Asturias,** prince of Asturias. **p. de la sangre,** prince of the blood royal

**principesco** /prinθi'pesko; prinsi'pesko/ *a* princely

**principiante** /prinθi'piante; prinsi'piante/ **(-ta)** *n* beginner, novice; apprentice

**principiar** /prinθi'piar; prinsi'piar/ *vt* to begin, commence

**principio** /prin'θipio; prin'sipio/ *m*, beginning; principle; genesis, origin; rudiment; axiom; constituent. **al p.,** at first. **a principios,** at the beginning (of the month, year, etc.). **en p.,** in principle

**pringar** /prin'gar/ *vt Cul.* to soak in fat; stain with grease; *Inf.* wound; take part in a business deal; slander; —*vr Inf.* appropriate, misuse (funds, etc.)

**pringoso** /prin'goso/ *a* greasy

**pringue** /'pringue/ *mf*, animal fat, lard; grease spot

**prior** /prior/ *m*, prior; parish priest

**priora** /'priora/ *f*, prioress

**prioridad** /priori'ðað/ *f*, priority

**prisa** /'prisa/ *f*, haste, speed; skirmish, foray. **a toda p.,** with all speed. **correr p.,** to be urgent. **dar p.,** to hasten, speed up. **darse** ( *or* **estar de) p.,** to hurry

**prisión** /pri'sion/ *f*, prison, jail; seizure; captivity, imprisonment; *Fig.* bond; obstacle; shackle; *pl* fetters

**prisma** /'prisma/ *m*, prism

**prismáticos** /pris'matikos/ *m pl*, field glasses

**prisonero** /priso'nero/ **(-ra)** *n* prisoner; *Fig.* victim (of passion, etc.)

**pristino** /pris'tino/ *a* pristine

**privación** /priβa'θion; priβa'sion/ *f*, privation; lack, shortage; deprivation; degradation

**privada** /pri'βaða/ *f*, toilet, privy, water closet

**privadamente** /priβaða'mente/ *adv* privately; individually, separately

**privado** /pri'βaðo/ *a* private; individual, personal. *m*, favorite; confidant

**privanza** /pri'βanθa; pri'βansa/ *f*, court favor, intimacy of princes

**privar** /pri'βar/ *vt* to deprive; dismiss (from office); interdict, forbid; —*vi* prevail, be in favor; —*vr* swoon; deprive oneself

**privilegiar** /priβile'hiar/ *vt* to privilege; bestow a favor on

**privilegio** /priβi'lehio/ *m*, privilege; prerogative; concession; copyright; patent

**pro** /pro/ *mf* advantage, benefit. **el p. y el contra,** the pros and cons. **en p.,** in favor

**proa** /'proa/ *f*, prow, bow

**probabilidad** /proβaβili'ðað/ *f*, probability

**probable** /pro'βaβle/ *a* probable; likely; provable

**probación** /proβa'θion; proβa'sion/ *f*, proof, test; novitiate, probation

**probado** /pro'βaðo/ *a* tried, tested, proved

**probar** /pro'βar/ *vt irr* to prove; test; taste; try on (clothes); —*vi* suit; (*with prep a* + *infin*) try to. **p. fortuna,** to try one's luck —*Pres. Indic.* **pruebo, pruebas, prueba, prueban.** *Pres. Subjunc.* **pruebe, pruebes, prueben**

**probatorio** /proβa'torio/ *a* probationary

**probidad** /proβi'ðað/ *f*, probity, trustworthiness, honesty

**problema** /pro'βlema/ *m*, problem

**problemático** /proβle'matiko/ *a* problematical, uncertain

**probo** /'proβo/ *a* honest, trustworthy

**procacidad** /prokaθi'ðað; prokasi'ðað/ *f*, insolence, pertness

**procaz** /pro'kaθ; pro'kas/ *a* insolent, pert, brazen

**procedencia** /proθe'ðenθia; prose'ðensia/ *f*, origin, source; parentage, descent; port of sailing or call

**procedente** /proθe'ðente; prose'ðente/ *a* arriving or coming from

**proceder** /proθe'ðer; prose'ðer/ *vi* to proceed; be-

have; originate, arise; continue, go on; act. *Law.* **p. contra,** to proceed against (a person)

**procedimiento** /proθeði'miento; proseði'miento/ *m*, proceeding, advancement; procedure; legal practice; process

**proceloso** /proθe'loso; prose'loso/ *a* tempestuous

**prócer** /'proθer; 'proser/ *a* exalted, eminent; lofty. *m*, exalted personage

**procesado** /proθe'saðo; prose'saðo/ **(-da)** *n* defendant

**procesamiento** /proθesa'miento; prosesa'miento/ *m*, suing, suit; indictment. **p. de textos,** word processing.

**procesar** /proθe'sar; prose'sar/ *vt Law.* to proceed against, sue

**procesión** /proθe'sion; prose'sion/ *f*, proceeding, emanating; procession; *Inf.* train, string. **andar** ( *or* **ir) por dentro la p.,** to feel keenly without betraying one's emotion

**proceso** /pro'θeso; pro'seso/ *m*, process; progress; advancement; lapse of time; lawsuit

**proclama** /pro'klama/ *f*, proclamation; announcement; publication of marriage banns

**proclamación** /proklama'θion; proklama'sion/ *f*, proclamation; acclaim, applause

**proclamar** /prokla'mar/ *vt* to proclaim; acclaim; publish abroad; reveal, show

**proclividad** /prokliβi'ðað/ *f*, proclivity, tendency

**procomún** /proko'mun/ *m*, social or public welfare

**procreación** /prokrea'θion; prokrea'sion/ *f*, procreation

**procreador** /prokrea'ðor/ **(-ra)** *a* procreative —*n* procreator

**procrear** /prokre'ar/ *vt* to procreate, beget, engender

**procuración** /prokura'θion; prokura'sion/ *f*, procurement; assiduity, care; *Law.* power of attorney; *Law.* attorneyship

**procurador** /prokura'ðor/ **(-ra)** *m*, proxy; *Law.* attorney; proctor —*n* procurer

**procurar** /proku'rar/ *vt* to try, attempt; procure, get; exercise the profession of a lawyer

**prodigalidad** /proðigali'ðað/ *f*, prodigality, lavishness; waste, extravagance

**prodigar** /proði'gar/ *vt* to waste, squander; lavish; bestow freely; —*vr* make oneself cheap

**prodigio** /pro'ðihio/ *m*, marvel, wonder; prodigy; monster; miracle

**prodigiosidad** /proðihiosi'ðað/ *f*, prodigiousness

**prodigioso** /proði'hioso/ *a* wonderful; prodigious; monstrous; miraculous

**pródigo** /'proðigo/ **(-ga)** *a* wasteful, extravagant; lavish, generous —*n* spendthrift, wastrel, prodigal

**producción** /proðuk'θion; proðuk'sion/ *f*, production; output, yield; generation (of heat, etc.); crop

**producir** /proðu'θir; proðu'sir/ *vt irr* to produce; generate; yield, give; cause, occasion; publish; —*vr* explain oneself; arise, appear, be produced. **p. efecto,** to have effect; take effect. See **conducir**

**productividad** /proðuktiβi'ðað/ *f*, productivity

**productivo** /proðuk'tiβo/ *a* productive; fertile; profitable

**producto** /pro'ðukto/ *m*, produce; product; profit; yield, gain; *Math.* product. *Chem.* **p. derivado,** by-product

**productor** /proðuk'tor/ **(-ra)** *a* productive —*n* producer

**proemio** /pro'emio/ *m*, prologue, preface, introduction

**proeza** /pro'eθa; pro'esa/ *f*, prowess, gallantry; skill

**profanación** /profana'θion; profana'sion/ *f*, profanation

**profanador** /profana'ðor/ **(-ra)** *n* profaner, transgressor

**profanar** /profa'nar/ *vt* to profane

**profanidad** /profani'ðað/ *f*, profanity

**profano** /pro'fano/ *a* profane; dissolute; pleasure-loving, worldly; immodest; lay, ignorant

**profecía** /profe'θia; profe'sia/ *f*, prophecy; *Eccl.* Book of the Prophets; opinion, view

**proferir** /profe'rir/ *vt irr* to utter, pronounce. See **herir**

**profesar** /profe'sar/ *vt* to exercise, practice (professions); *Eccl.* profess; believe in; teach

**profesión** /profe'sion/ *f*, profession; trade, occupation; avowal, admission

**profesional** /profesio'nal/ *a* professional

**profesionalismo** /profesiona'lismo/ *m*, professionalism

**profeso** /pro'feso/ **(-sa)** *a* *Eccl.* professed —*n* professed monk

**profesor** /profe'sor/ **(-ra)** *n* teacher; professor

**profesorado** /profeso'raðo/ *m*, teaching staff; teaching profession; professorship; professorate

**profeta** /pro'feta/ *m*, prophet; seer

**profético** /pro'fetiko/ *a* prophetic

**profetisa** /profe'tisa/ *f*, prophetess

**profetizar** /profeti'θar; profeti'sar/ *vt* to prophesy; imagine, suppose

**proficiente** /profi'θiente; profi'siente/ *a* proficient

**profiláctico** /profi'laktiko/ *a* and *m*, prophylactic

**prófugo** /'profugo/ **(-ga)** *a* and *n* fugitive from justice. *m*, *Mil.* one who evades military service

**profundamente** /profunda'mente/ *adv* profoundly; acutely, deeply

**profundidad** /profundi'ðað/ *f*, depth; profundity, obscurity; *Geom.* depth; concavity; intensity (of feeling); vastness (of knowledge, etc.)

**profundizar** /profundi'θar; profundi'sar/ *vt* to deepen; hollow out; *Fig.* go into deeply, fathom

**profundo** /pro'fundo/ *a* deep; low; *Fig.* intense, acute; abstruse, profound; *Fig.* vast, extensive; high. *m*, depth, profundity; *Poet.* ocean, the deep; *Poet.* hell

**profuso** /pro'fuso/ *a* profuse, abundant; extravagant, wasteful

**progenie** /pro'henie/ *f*, descendants

**prognosis** /prog'nosis/ *f*, prognosis; forecast

**programa** /pro'grama/ *m*, program; edict, public notice; plan, scheme; *Educ.* calendar; syllabus; timetable

**progresar** /progre'sar/ *vt* and *vi* to make progress; progress, advance

**progresión** /progre'sion/ *f*, progression; advancement, progress

**progresista** /progre'sista/ *a* *Polit.* progressive. *mf* progressive

**progresivo** /progre'siβo/ *a* progressive; advancing

**progreso** /pro'greso/ *m*, progress, advancement; growth; improvement, development

**prohibente** /proi'βente/ *a* prohibitory, prohibitive

**prohibición** /proiβi'θion; proiβi'sion/ *f*, forbidding, prohibition

**prohibicionista** /proiβiθio'nista; proiβisio'nista/ *mf* prohibitionist —*a* prohibitionist

**prohibir** /proi'βir/ *vt* to forbid, prohibit. «**Prohibido el paso,**» "No thoroughfare"

**prohibitivo, prohibitorio** /proiβi'tiβo, proiβi'torio/ *a* prohibitive

**prohijador** /proiha'ðor/ **(-ra)** *n* adopter (of a child)

**prohijamiento** /proiha'miento/ *m*, child adoption; fathering (of a bill, etc.)

**prohijar** /proi'har/ *vt* to adopt (children, ideas); *Fig.* father

**prohombre** /pro'ombre/ *m*, master of a guild; respected, wellliked man

**prójimo** /'prohimo/ *m*, fellow man, brother, neighbor.

**prole** /'prole/ *f*, progeny, young offspring

**proletariado** /proleta'riaðo/ *m*, proletariat

**proletario** /prole'tario/ *a* poor; common, vulgar. *m*, plebeian; pauper; proletarian

**prolífico** /pro'lifiko/ *a* prolific; abundant, fertile

**prolijidad** /prolihi'ðað/ *f*, verbosity, prolixity; nicety, scruple; importunity, tediousness

**prolijo** /pro'liho/ *a* verbose, prolix; fussy, fastidious; tedious, importunate

**prologar** /prolo'gar/ *vt* to prologue; provide with a preface

**prólogo** /'prologo/ *m*, preface; prologue; introduction

**prolongación** /proloŋga'θion; proloŋga'sion/ *f*, lengthening; prolongation; protraction; extension

**prolongado** /proloŋ'gaðo/ *a* prolonged; oblong, long

**prolongar** /proloŋ'gar/ *vt* to lengthen; *Geom.* produce; prolong, spin out

**promediar** /prome'ðiar/ *vt* to distribute or divide into two equal portions; average; —*vi* arbitrate; place oneself between two people; reach half-time

**promedio** /pro'meðio/ *m*, average; middle, center

**promesa** /pro'mesa/ *f*, promise; augury, favorable sign

**prometedor** /promete'ðor/ **(-ra)** *a* promising —*n* promiser

**prometer** /prome'ter/ *vt* to promise; attest, certify; —*vi* promise well, look hopeful; —*vr* devote oneself to service of God; anticipate confidently, expect; become engaged (marriage). *Inf.* **prometérselas muy felices,** to have high hopes

**prometido** /prome'tiðo/ **(-da)** *n* betrothed. *m*, promise

**prometimiento** /prometi'miento/ *m*, promise; promising

**prominencia** /promi'nenθia; promi'nensia/ *f*, prominence, protuberance; eminence, hill

**prominente** /promi'nente/ *a* prominent, protuberant; eminent, elevated

**promiscuar** /promis'kuar/ *vi* to eat meat and fish on fast days

**promiscuidad** /promiskui'ðað/ *f*, promiscuity; ambiguity

**promiscuo** /pro'miskuo/ *a* indiscriminate, haphazard, promiscuous; ambiguous

**promisión** /promi'sion/ *f*, promise

**promisorio** /promi'sorio/ *a* promissory

**promoción** /promo'θion; promo'sion/ *f*, promotion; batch, class, year (of recruits, students, etc.)

**promontorio** /promon'torio/ *m*, headland; promontory; cumbersome object

**promotor** /promo'tor/ **(-ra)** *a* promotive —*n* promoter; supporter

**promover** /promo'βer/ *vt irr* to promote, further, advance; promote (a person). **p. un proceso ( a),** to bring a suit (against). See **mover**

**promulgación** /promulga'θion; promulga'sion/ *f*, promulgation

**promulgar** /promul'gar/ *vt* to publish officially, proclaim; promulgate. *Law.* **p. sentencia,** to pass judgment

**pronombre** /pro'nombre/ *m*, pronoun

**pronosticación** /pronostika'θion; pronostika'sion/ *f*, prognostication; presage

**pronosticar** /pronosti'kar/ *vt* to prognosticate, forecast; presage

**pronóstico** /pro'nostiko/ *m*, omen, prediction; almanac; prognosis; sign, indication. **p. del tiempo,** weather forecast

**prontitud** /pronti'tuð/ *f*, quickness, promptness; quick-wittedness; *Fig.* sharpness, liveliness; celerity, dispatch

**pronto** /'pronto/ *a* quick, speedy; prompt; ready, prepared. *m*, *Inf.* sudden decision —*adv* immediately; with all speed; soon. **de p.,** suddenly; without thinking. **por lo p.,** temporarily, provisionally

**prontuario** /pron'tuario/ *m*, compendium, handbook; summary

**pronunciación** /pronunθia'θion; pronunsia'sion/ *f*, pronunciation

**pronunciamiento** /pronunθia'miento; pronunsia'miento/ *m*, military uprising; political manifesto; *Law.* pronouncement of sentence

**pronunciar** /pronun'θiar; pronun'siar/ *vt* to pronounce, articulate; decide, determine; *Law.* pronounce judgment; give or make (a speech)

**propagación** /propaga'θion; propaga'sion/ *f*, propagation; dissemination; transmission

**propagador** /propaga'ðor/ *a* propagative. *m*, propagator

**propaganda** /propa'ganda/ *f*, propaganda organization; propaganda

**propagandista** /propagan'dista/ *mf* propagandist

**propagar** /propa'gar/ *vt* to reproduce; propagate, disseminate; —*vr* reproduce, multiply; propagate, spread

**propalar** /propa'lar/ *vt* to disseminate, spread abroad

**propasarse** /propa'sarse/ *vr* to go too far, forget oneself; overstep one's authority

**propender** /propen'der/ *vi* to be inclined, have a leaning toward

**propensión** /propen'sion/ *f*, propensity, inclination; tendency

**propenso** /pro'penso/ *a* inclined, disposed; liable

**propiamente** /propia'mente/ *adv* properly, suitably

**propiciación** /propiθia'θion; propisia'sion/ *f*, propitiation

**propiciador** /propiθia'ðor; propisia'ðor/ **(-ra)** *a* propitiatory —*n* propitiator

**propiciar** /propi'θiar; propi'siar/ *vt* to propitiate, appease

**propiciatorio** /propiθia'torio; propisia'torio/ *a* propitiatory

**propicio** /pro'piθio; pro'pisio/ *a* propitious, auspicious; kind, favorable

**propiedad** /propie'ðað/ *f*, estate, property; ownership; landed property; attribute, quality, property; *Art.* resemblance, naturalness

**propietario** /propie'tario/ **(-ia)** *a* proprietary —*n* proprietor, owner

**propina** /pro'pina/ *f*, gratuity, tip. *Inf.* **de p.,** in addition, extra

**propinar** /propi'nar/ *vt* to treat to a drink; administer (medicine); *Inf.* give (slaps, etc.)

**propincuidad** /propinkui'ðað/ *f*, propinquity, proximity

**propincuo** /pro'pinkuo/ *a* near, contiguous, adjacent

**propio** /'propio/ *a* own, one's own; typical, characteristic; individual, peculiar; suitable, apt; natural, real; same. *m*, messenger; *pl* public lands

**proponente** /propo'nente/ *a* proposing. *m*, proposer; *Com.* tenderer

**proponer** /propo'ner/ *vt irr* to propose, suggest; make a proposition; propose (for a post, office, etc.); *Math.* state; —*vr* intend, purpose. **proponerse para un empleo,** to apply for a post. See **poner**

**proporción** /propor'θion; propor'sion/ *f*, proportion; chance, opportunity; size; *Math.* proportion

**proporcionado** /proporθio'naðo; proporsio'naðo/ *a* fit, suitable; proportionate; symmetrical

**proporcional** /proporθio'nal; proporsio'nal/ *a* proportional

**proporcionar** /proporθio'nar; proporsio'nar/ *vt* to allot, proportion; supply, provide, give; adapt

**proposición** /proposi'θion; proposi'sion/ *f*, proposition; motion (in a debate)

**propósito** /pro'posito/ *m*, purpose; intention, aim; subject, question, matter. **a p.,** suitable, apropos; by the way, incidentally. **de p.,** with the intention, proposing. **fuera de p.,** irrelevant

**propuesta** /pro'puesta/ *f*, proposal, tender

**propugnar** /propug'nar/ *vt* to defend, protect

**propulsar** /propul'sar/ *vt* to repulse, throw back; propel, drive

**propulsión** /propul'sion/ *f*, repulse; propulsion

**propulsor** /propul'sor/ *a* driving, propelling. *m*, propeller

**prorrata** /pro'rrata/ *f*, quota, share, apportionment. **a p.,** in proportion

**prorratear** /prorrate'ar/ *vt* to apportion, distribute proportionately, prorate

**prorrogación** /prorroga'θion; prorroga'sion/ *f*, prorogation, adjournment; extension (of time); renewal (of a lease, etc.)

**prorrogar** /prorro'gar/ *vt* to extend, prolong; defer, suspend, prorogue; renew (leases, etc.)

**prorrumpir** /prorrum'pir/ *vt* (*with en*) to burst out; utter, give vent to, burst into

**prosa** /'prosa/ *f*, prose; prosaism, prosaic style; *Inf.* dull verbosity; monotony, tediousness

**prosaico** /pro'saiko/ *a* prosaic; prosy; monotonous, tedious; matter-of-fact

**prosapia** /pro'sapia/ *f*, family, lineage, descent

**proscenio** /pros'θenio; pros'senio/ *m*, proscenium

**proscribir** /proskri'βir/ *vt* to proscribe, outlaw; forbid, prohibit —*Past Part.* **proscrito**

**proscripción** /proskrip'θion; proskrip'sion/ *f*, proscription

**proscrito** /pros'krito/ **(-ta)** *n* outlaw, exile

**prosecución** /proseku'θion; proseku'sion/ *f*, prosecution, performance; pursuit

**proseguir** /prose'gir/ *vt irr* to continue, proceed with. See **pedir**

**proselitismo** /proseli'tismo/ *m*, proselytism

**prosélito** /pro'selito/ *m*, convert, proselyte

**prosificar** /prosifi'kar/ *vt* to turn verse into prose

**prosista** /pro'sista/ *mf* prose writer

**prosodia** /pro'soðia/ *f*, prosody

**prospecto** /pros'pekto/ *m*, prospectus

**prosperar** /prospe'rar/ *vt* to prosper; protect; —*vi* flourish, prosper

**prosperidad** /prosperi'ðað/ *f*, prosperity; wealth; success

**próspero** /'prospero/ *a* favorable, propitious, fortunate; prosperous

**próstata** /'prostata/ *f*, prostate

**prostitución** /prostitu'θion; prostitu'sion/ *f*, prostitution

**prostituir** /prosti'tuir/ *vt irr* to prostitute; —*vr* become a prostitute; sell oneself, debase oneself. See **huir**

**prostituta** /prosti'tuta/ *f*, prostitute

**protagonista** /protago'nista/ *mf* hero or heroine, principal character; leading figure, protagonist

**protección** /protek'θion; protek'sion/ *f*, protection, defense; favor, aid

**proteccionismo** /protekθio'nismo; proteksio'nismo/ *m*, protectionism

**proteccionista** /protekθio'nista; proteksio'nista/ *mf* protectionist

**protector** /protek'tor/ *a* protective. *m*, protector; guard

**protectorado** /protekto'raðo/ *m*, protectorate

**protectriz** /protek'triθ; protek'tris/ *f*, protectress

**proteger** /prote'her/ *vt* to protect, defend; favor, assist

**protegido** /prote'hiðo/ **(-da)** *n* protégé

**proteico** /pro'teiko/ *a* protean

**proteína** /prote'ina/ *f*, protein

**protervia** /pro'terβia/ *f*, depravity, perversity

**protervo** /pro'terβo/ *a* depraved, perverse

**protesta, protestación** /pro'testa, protesta'θion; pro'testa, protesta'sion/ *f*, protest; protestation, declaration

**protestante** /protes'tante/ *a* and *mf* Protestant

**protestantismo** /protestan'tismo/ *m*, Protestantism

**protestar** /protes'tar/ *vt* to declare, attest; (*with contra*) protest against; (*with de*) affirm vigorously

**protesto** /pro'testo/ *m*, *Com.* protest; objection

**protocolizar** /protokoli'θar; protokoli'sar/ *vt* to protocol, draw up

**protocolo** /proto'kolo/ *m*, protocol

**protoplasma** /proto'plasma/ *m*, protoplasm

**prototipo** /proto'tipo/ *m*, model, prototype

**protuberancia** /protuβe'ranθia; protuβe'ransia/ *f*, protuberance, projection; swelling

**provecho** /pro'βetʃo/ *m*, gain, benefit; profit; advantage; progress, proficiency. **¡Buen p.!** Enjoy your food! Enjoy your meal! **ser de p.,** to be advantageous or useful

**provechoso** /proβe'tʃoso/ *a* beneficial; profitable; advantageous; useful

**provecto** /pro'βekto/ *a* ancient, venerable; mature, experienced

**proveedor** /proβee'ðor/ **(-ra)** *n* provider; purveyor, supplier

**proveer** /proβe'er/ *vt irr* to provide; furnish; supply; confer (an honor or office); transact, arrange. **p. de,** to furnish or supply with; fit with. See **creer**

**provenir** /proβe'nir/ *vi irr* (*with de*) to originate in, proceed from. See **venir**

**Provenza** /pro'βenθa; pro'βensa/ Provence

**provenzal** /proβen'θal; proβen'sal/ *a* and *mf* Provençal. *m*, Provençal (language)

**proverbio** /pro'βerβio/ *m*, proverb; omen; *pl* Book of Proverbs

**providencia** /proβi'ðenθia; proβi'ðensia/ *f*, precaution, foresight; provision, furnishing; measure, preparation. **la Divina P.,** Providence

**providencial** /proβiðen'θial; proβiðen'sial/ *a* providential

**próvido** /'proβiðo/ a provident, thrifty, careful; kind, favorable

**provincia** /pro'βinθia; pro'βinsia/ f, province; *Fig.* sphere

**provincial** /proβin'θial; proβin'sial/ a provincial. m, *Eccl.* provincial

**provincialismo** /proβinθia'lismo; proβinsia'lismo/ m, provincialism

**provinciano** /proβin'θiano; proβin'siano/ (-na) a provincial —n provincial, rustic, countryman; native of Biscay

**provisión** /proβi'sion/ f, stock, store; provision; supply; food supply (gen. *pl*); catering; means, way

**provisional** /proβisio'nal/ a temporary, provisional

**provisor** /proβi'sor/ m, purveyor, supplier; *Eccl.* vicar general

**provocación** /proβoka'θion; proβoka'sion/ f, provocation

**provocador** /proβoka'ðor/ (-ra) a provocative —n provoker; instigator

**provocar** /proβo'kar/ vt to provoke; incite; irritate; help, assist; *Inf.* vomit

**provocativo** /proβoka'tiβo/ a provocative

**próximamente** /'proksimamente/ adv proximately; soon; approximately

**proximidad** /proksimi'ðað/ f, nearness, proximity (in time or space)

**próximo** /'proksimo/ a near, neighboring; next; not distant (of time)

**proyección** /proiek'θion; proiek'sion/ f, projection (all meanings)

**proyectante** /proiek'tante/ a projecting, jutting

**proyectar** /proiek'tar/ vt to throw, cast; plan, contrive; design; project; —vr jut out; be cast (a shadow, etc.)

**proyectil** /proyek'til/ m, projectile

**proyectista** /proiek'tista/ mf planner

**proyecto** /pro'iekto/ a placed in perspective. m, project, plan, scheme; planning; intention, idea

**proyector** /proiek'tor/ (-ra) n designer, planner. m, searchlight; spotlight; projector

**prudencia** /pru'ðenθia; pru'ðensia/ f, prudence, sagacity, caution; moderation

**prudencial** /pruðen'θial; pruðen'sial/ a prudent, discreet; safe

**prudente** /pru'ðente/ a prudent, cautious; provident

**prueba** /'prueβa/ f, proof; test; testing; trial; fitting (of garments); sample; taste; *Law.* evidence; (*Photo. Print.*) proof. *Law.* p. de indicios or p. indiciaria, circumstantial evidence. *Photo.* p. negativa, negative. *Com.* a p., on approval; on trial; up to standard, perfect. a p. de, proof against (water, etc.). poner a p., to put to the test, try out

**prurito** /pru'rito/ m, pruritus; desire, longing

**Prusia** /'prusia/ Prussia

**ps-** /ps-/ For words so beginning (e.g. *psicología, psiquiatría*), see spellings without **p**

**púa** /'pua/ f, prong; tooth (of a comb); quill (of a porcupine); *Agr.* graft; plectrum (for playing the mandolin, etc.); anxiety, grief; pine needle; *Inf.* crafty person

**púber** /'puβer/ a pubescent

**pubertad** /puβer'tað/ f, puberty

**púbico** /'puβiko/ a pubic

**publicación** /puβlika'θion; puβlika'sion/ f, publication; announcement, proclamation; revelation; publishing of marriage banns

**publicador** /puβlika'ðor/ (-ra) a publishing —n publisher; announcer

**publicar** /puβli'kar/ vt to publish; reveal; announce, proclaim; publish (marriage banns)

**publicidad** /puβliθi'ðað; puβlisi'ðað/ f, publicity; advertising, propaganda

**publicista** /puβli'θista; puβli'sista/ mf publicist; publicity agent

**público** /'puβliko/ a well-known, universal; common, general; public. m, public; audience; gathering, attendance. dar al p. or sacar al p., to publish

**pucherazo** /putʃe'raθo; putʃe'raso/ m, *Inf.* electoral fraud, vote-fixing

**puchero** /pu'tʃero/ m, *Cul.* kind of stew; stew pot; *Inf.* daily food; puckering of the face preceding tears

**pudendo** /pu'ðendo/ a shameful, monstrous, obscene

**pudicia** /pu'ðiθia; pu'ðisia/ f, modesty; bashfulness; chastity

**púdico** /'puðiko/ a modest; bashful; chaste

**pudiente** /pu'ðiente/ a rich, wealthy; powerful

**pudín** /pu'ðin/ m, pudding

**pudor** /pu'ðor/ m, modesty; bashfulness, shyness

**pudoroso** /puðo'roso/ a modest; shy

**pudrición** /puðri'θion; puðri'sion/ f, putrefaction

**pudrir** /pu'ðrir/ vt to rot, putrefy; irritate, worry, provoke; —vi rot in the grave; —vr rot; be consumed with anxiety

**puebla** /'pueβla/ f, town; population; gardener's seed setting

**pueblo** /'pueβlo/ m, town; village, hamlet; people, population, inhabitants; common people; working classes; nation

**puente** /'puente/ mf bridge; *Mus.* bridge (of stringed instruments); *Naut.* bridge; crossbeam, transom. p. colgante, suspension bridge. p. levadizo, drawbridge. hacer p. de plata ( a), to remove obstacles for, make plain sailing

**puerca** /'puerka/ f, sow; *Inf.* slattern; harridan, termagant

**puerco** /'puerko/ m, pig; wild boar —a filthy; rough, rude; low, mean. p. espín or p. espino, porcupine. p. marino, dolphin. p. montés or p. salvaje, wild boar

**puericultura** /puerikul'tura/ f, child care

**pueril** /pue'ril/ a childish, puerile; foolish, silly; trivial

**puerilidad** /puerili'ðað/ f, puerility; foolishness; triviality

**puerro** /'puerro/ m, leek

**puerta** /'puerta/ f, door; gate; goal (football, soccer, hockey); means, way. p. batiente, swinging door. p. caediza, trapdoor. p. corrediza, sliding door. p. de servicio, tradesman's entrance. p. falsa or p. secreta, secret door; side door. p. trasera, back door. a p. cerrada, in camera; in secret. *Inf.* dar con la p. en las narices ( de), to slam the door in a person's face; offend, insult. llamar a la p., to knock at the door; be on the verge of happening. tomar la p., to depart, go away

**puerto** /'puerto/ m, harbor; port; defile, narrow pass; refuge, haven. p. fluvial, river port. p. franco, free port. tomar p., to put into port; take refuge

**pues** /pues/ conjunc then; since, as; for, because; well —adv yes, certainly —conjunc p. que, since, as

**puesta** /'puesta/ f, *Astron.* setting, sinking; stake (in gambling). p. al día, aggiornamento, updating; modernization. p. de largo, coming of age; coming-out party. p. del sol, sunset

**puesto** /'puesto/ m, post, job; booth, stall; beat, pitch; place, position; state, condition; *Mil.* encampment, barracks; office, position. p. de los testigos, witness box. p. de mando, command, position of authority.

**puesto** /'puesto/ a (with bien or mal) well-or badly dressed —conjunc p. que, since, as; although

**púgil** /'puhil/ mf pugilist, boxer

**pugilato** /puhi'lato/ m, boxing; boxing match

**pugilista** /puhi'lista/ mf boxer

**pugna** /'pugna/ f, fight, struggle; rivalry, conflict

**pugnante** /pug'nante/ a hostile, conflicting, rival

**pugnar** /pug'nar/ vi to fight; quarrel; (with con, contra) struggle against, oppose; (with por, para) strive to

**pugnaz** /pug'naθ; pug'nas/ a pugnacious

**puja** /'puha/ f, outbidding (at an auction); higher bid; push, thrust

**pujador** /puha'ðor/ (-ra) n bidder or outbidder (at an auction)

**pujante** /pu'hante/ a strong, powerful, vigorous

**pujanza** /pu'hanθa; pu'hansa/ f, strength, vigor

**pujar** /pu'har/ vt to push on; bid or outbid (at an auction); —vi stutter; hesitate, falter; *Inf.* show signs of weeping

**pujo** /'puho/ m, irresistible impulse; desire; will; purpose, intention

**pulchinela** /pultʃi'nela/ m, Punchinello

**pulcritud** /pulkri'tuð/ *f*, beauty, loveliness, delicacy; fastidiousness, subtlety

**pulcro** /'pulkro/ *a* beautiful, lovely; delicate, fine; fastidious, subtle

**pulga** /'pulga/ *f*, flea; small top (toy). **el juego de la p.,** tiddlywinks. *Inf.* **tener malas pulgas,** to be irritable

**pulgada** /pul'gaða/ *f*, inch

**pulgar** /pul'gar/ *m*, thumb

**pulgón** /pul'gon/ *m*, aphid, greenfly

**pulgoso** /pul'goso/ *a* full of fleas

**pulidez** /puli'ðeθ; puli'ðes/ *f*, elegance, fineness; polish, smoothness; neatness

**pulido** /pu'liðo/ *a* elegant, fine; polished, smooth; neat

**pulidor** /puli'ðor/ *m*, polisher (machine)

**pulimentar** /pulimen'tar/ *vt* to polish, burnish

**pulir** /pu'lir/ *vt* to polish, burnish; give the finishing touch to; beautify, decorate; *Fig.* polish up, civilize; —*vr* beautify oneself; become polished and polite

**pulla** /'puʎa; 'puya/ *f*, lewd remark; strong hint; witty comment

**pulmón** /pul'mon/ *m*, lung

**pulmonar** /pulmo'nar/ *a* pulmonary

**pulmonía** /pulmo'nia/ *f*, pneumonia

**pulpa** /'pulpa/ *f*, fleshy part of fruit; *Anat.* pulp; wood pulp

**pulpejo** /pul'peho/ *m*, *Anat.* fleshy part, fat portion (of thumbs, etc.)

**pulpería** /pulpe'ria/ *f*, *West Hem.* grocery, grocery store, general store

**púlpito** /'pulpito/ *m*, pulpit

**pulpo** /'pulpo/ *m*, octopus. *Inf.* **poner como un p.,** to beat to a pulp

**pulposo** /pul'poso/ *a* pulpy, pulpous

**pulquérrimo** /pul'kerrimo/ *a superl* **pulcro** most lovely, most exquisite

**pulsación** /pulsa'θion; pulsa'sion/ *f*, pulsation; throb, beat

**pulsar** /pul'sar/ *vt* to touch, feel; take the pulse of; *Fig.* explore (a possibility); —*vi* beat (the heart, etc.)

**pulsera** /pul'sera/ *f*, bracelet; wrist bandage. **p. de pedida,** betrothal bracelet

**pulso** /'pulso/ *m*, pulse; steadiness of hand; tact, diplomacy, circumspection. **a p.,** freehand (drawing). **tomar a p.** ( **una cosa**), to try a thing's weight. **tomar el p.** ( **a**), to take a person's pulse

**pulular** /pulu'lar/ *vi* to pullulate, sprout; abound, be plentiful; swarm, teem; multiply (of insects)

**pulverización** /pulβeriθa'θion; pulβerisa'sion/ *f*, pulverization; atomization

**pulverizador** /pulβeriθa'ðor; pulβerisa'ðor/ *m*, atomizer, sprayer; scent spray

**pulverizar** /pulβeri'θar; pulβeri'sar/ *vt* to pulverize, grind, make into powder; atomize; spray

**¡pum!** /pum/ *interj* Bang! Thump!

**pundonor** /pundo'nor/ *m*, (**punto de honor**) point of honor, sense of honor

**pundonoroso** /pundono'roso/ *a* careful of one's honor; honorable, punctilious

**pungir** /pun'hir/ *vt* to prick, pierce; revive an old sorrow; *Fig.* wound, sting (passions)

**punible** /pu'niβle/ *a* punishable

**púnico** /'puniko/ *a* Punic

**punitivo** /puni'tiβo/ *a* punitive, punitory

**punta** /'punta/ *f*, sharp end, point; butt (of a cigarette); end, point, tip; cape, headland; trace, touch, suspicion; nib (of a pen); pointing (pointer dogs); *Herald.* point; *pl* point lace. **p. de París,** wire nail. **p. seca,** drypoint, engraving needle. **sacar p.,** to sharpen; *Inf.* twist (a remark)

**puntación** /punta'θion; punta'sion/ *f*, dotting, placing dots over (letters)

**puntada** /pun'taða/ *f*, *Sew.* stitch; innuendo, hint

**puntal** /pun'tal/ *m*, *Naut.* draft, depth; stanchion, prop, brace, pile; *Fig.* basis, foundation

**puntapié** /punta'pie/ *m*, kick

**punteado** /punte'aðo/ *m*, plucking the strings of a guitar, etc.; sewing

**puntear** /punte'ar/ *vt* to make dots; *Mus.* pluck the strings of; play the guitar; sew; *Art.* stipple; —*vi* *Naut.* tack

**puntera** /pun'tera/ *f*, mend in the toe of a stocking; toe cap; new piece on the toe of shoe; *Inf.* kick

**puntería** /punte'ria/ *f*, aiming (of a firearm); aim, sight (of a firearm); marksmanship

**puntero** /pun'tero/ *a* of a good aim, having a straight eye. *m*, pointer, wand; stonecutter's chisel

**puntiagudo** /puntia'guðo/ *a* pointed, sharp-pointed

**puntilla** /pun'tiʎa; pun'tiya/ *f*, narrow lace edging; headless nail, wire nail; brad, tack. **de puntillas,** on tiptoe

**puntillismo** /punti'ʎismo; punti'yismo/ *m*, pointillism

**puntilloso** /punti'ʎoso; punti'yoso/ *a* punctilious; overfastidious, fussy

**punto** /'punto/ *m* dot; point; pen nib; gun sight; *Sew.* stitch; dropped stitch, hole; weaving stitch, mesh; *Gram.* full stop, period; hole (in belts for adjustment); place, spot; point, mark; subject matter; *Mech.* cog; degree, extent; taxi stand; instant; infinitesimal amount; opportunity, chance; vacation, recess; aim, goal; point of honor. **p. de congelación,** freezing point. **p. de ebullición,** boiling point. **p. de fuga,** vanishing point. **p. de fusión,** melting point. **p. de partida,** starting point. **p. de vista,** point of view. **p. final,** *Gram.* period, full stop. **p. interrogante,** question mark. **p. menos,** a little less. **p. y coma,** semicolon. **p. cardinal,** cardinal point. **p. suspensivo,** *Gram.* ellipsis point, suspension point, leader, dot. **a p.,** in readiness; immediately. **en p.,** sharp, prompt (e.g. *a las seis en p.,* at six o'clock sharp)

**puntoso** /pun'toso/ *a* many-pointed

**puntuación** /puntua'θion; puntua'sion/ *f*, punctuation; *Sports.* score

**puntual** /pun'tual/ *a* punctual; punctilious; certain, indubitable; suitable, convenient

**puntualidad** /puntuali'ðað/ *f*, punctuality; punctiliousness; certainty; exactitude, accuracy

**puntualizar** /puntuali'θar; puntuali'sar/ *vt* to describe in detail; give the finishing touch to, perfect; impress on the mind

**puntualmente** /puntual'mente/ *adv* punctually; carefully, diligently; exactly

**puntuar** /pun'tuar/ *vt* to punctuate

**punzada** /pun'θaða; pun'saða/ *f*, prick, sting; puncture, piercing; sudden pain, twinge, stitch; *Fig.* anguish, pain

**punzar** /pun'θar; pun'sar/ *vt* to pierce, puncture; prick; punch, perforate; —*vi* revive, make itself felt (pain or sorrow)

**punzón** /pun'θon; pun'son/ *m*, awl; punch; die; engraver's burin

**puñado** /pu'ɲaðo/ *m*, handful; a few, some, a small quantity. **a puñados,** in handfuls; liberally, lavishly

**puñal** /pu'ɲal/ *m*, dagger

**puñalada** /puɲa'laða/ *f*, dagger thrust; stab, wound; *Fig.* unexpected blow (of fate). **p. por la espalda,** stab in the back

**puñalero** /puɲa'lero/ *m*, dagger maker or seller

**puñetazo** /puɲe'taθo; puɲe'taso/ *m*, blow with the fist

**puño** /'puɲo/ *m*, fist; handful; cuff (of a sleeve); wristband; handle, head, haft; hilt (of a sword); *pl* *Inf.* guts, courage. **p. de amura,** *Naut.* tack. **p. de un manillar,** handlebar grip. *Inf.* **meter en un p.,** to overawe. *Inf.* **ser como un p.,** to be tightfisted; be small (in stature)

**pupila** /pu'pila/ *f*, female child ward; *Anat.* pupil; *Inf.* cleverness, talent

**pupilaje** /pupi'lahe/ *m*, pupilage, minority; boarding house, guesthouse; boarding school; price of board residence; dependence, bondage

**pupilo** /pu'pilo/ **(-la)** *n* ward, minor; boarder; boarding school student

**pupitre** /pu'pitre/ *m*, desk, school desk

**puramente** /pura'mente/ *adv* purely; simply, solely; *Law.* unconditionally, without reservation

**puré** /pu're/ *m*, purée, thick soup

**pureza** /pu'reθa; pu'resa/ *f*, purity; perfection, excellence; chastity; disinterestedness, genuineness; clearness

**purga** /'purga/ *f,* laxative, purge; waste product

**purgación** /purga'θion; purga'sion/ *f,* purging; menstruation; gonorrhea

**purgante** /pur'gante/ *a* purgative. *m,* purge, cathartic

**purgar** /pur'gar/ *vt* to cleanse, purify; expiate, atone for; (*Med. Law.*) purge; suffer purgatorial pains; clarify, refine; —*vr* rid oneself, purge oneself

**purgativo** /purga'tiβo/ *a* purgative

**purgatorio** /purga'torio/ *m,* purgatory —*a* purgatorial

**puridad** /puri'ðað/ *f,* purity; secrecy, privacy. **en p.,** openly, without dissembling; secretly, in private

**purificación** /purifika'θion; purifika'sion/ *f,* purification; cleansing

**purificador** /purifika'ðor/ **(-ra)** *a* purifying; cleansing —*n* purifier; cleanser

**purificar** /purifi'kar/ *vt* to purify; cleanse; —*vr* be purified

**purificatorio** /purifika'torio/ *a* purificatory

**Purísima** /pu'risima/ **(la)** *f,* the Most Blessed Virgin

**purista** /pu'rista/ *mf* purist

**puritanismo** /purita'nismo/ *m,* Puritanism

**puritano** /puri'tano/ **(-na)** *a* puritanical —*n* Puritan

**puro** /'puro/ *a* pure; undiluted; unalloyed; unmixed; disinterested, honest; virgin; absolute, sheer; mere, simple. *m,* cigar. **de p.,** by sheer..., by dint of

**púrpura** /'purpura/ *f,* purple; *Poet.* blood; purpura; *Herald.* purpure; purple (cloth); dignity of an emperor, cardinal, consul

**purpurear** /purpure'ar/ *vi* to look like purple; be tinged with purple

**purpúreo, purpurino** /pur'pureo, purpu'rino/ *a* purple

**purulencia** /puru'lenθia; puru'lensia/ *f,* purulence

**purulento** /puru'lento/ *a* purulent

**pus** /pus/ *m,* pus, matter

**pusilánime** /pusi'lanime/ *a* pusillanimous, timid, cowardly

**pusilanimidad** /pusilanimi'ðað/ *f,* pusillanimity, timidity, cowardice

**pústula** /'pustula/ *f,* pustule

**puta** /'puta/ *f,* whore

**putativo** /puta'tiβo/ *a* putative

**puto** /'puto/ *m,* male prostitute

**putrefacción** /putrefak'θion; putrefak'sion/ *f,* putrefaction; rottenness, putrescence

**putrefacto** /putre'fakto/ *a* rotten, decayed

**pútrido** /'putriðo/ *a* putrid, rotten

**puya** /'puya/ *f,* goad

**puyazo** /pu'yaθo; pu'yaso/ *m,* prick with a goad

# Q

**que** /ke/ *pron rel* all genders sing. and pl. who; which; that; whom; when (e.g. *Un poema con que habla de su juventud,* A poem in which he speaks of his youth. *El libro que tengo aquí,* The book (that) I have here. **No es oro todo lo que reluce,** All that glitters is not gold. **Un día que nos vimos,** One day when we met —*interr* **¿qué?** what? *interj* what a ------! what! how! (e.g. *¿Qué hay?* What's the matter? *¡Qué día más hermoso!* What a lovely day! *¿qué de...?* how many? *¿qué tal?* how? *Inf. ¿Qué tal estás hoy?* How are you today? *¿qué tanto?* how much?) **¿a qué?** why? for what reason? (e.g. *¿A qué negarlo?* Why deny it?) —*conjunc* that (e.g. *Me dijo que vendría,* He said (that) he would come). Means "so that," "that," "for," in commands (e.g. *Mandó que le trajesen el libro,* He ordered that they bring him the book (He ordered them to bring him the book)). Note that the translation of **que** is often omitted in English. In compound tenses where the participle is placed first, **que** means "when" (e.g. *llegado que hube,* when I had arrived). In comparisons, **que** means "than" (e.g. *más joven que yo,* younger than I). With subjunctives and expressing commands or wishes, **que** means "let" (e.g. *¡Que venga!* Let him come!) Preceding a subjunctive, **que** is generally translated to 'to' (e.g. *Quiero, que venga or que llueva,* I want him to come *or* I want it to rain). Also means "may" (e.g. *¡Que lo pase bien!* May you enjoy yourself! (I hope you...)). **es** ( **era**) **que,** the fact is (was) that... **que... que,** whether... or...

**quebrada** /ke'βraða/ *f,* mountain gorge; *Com.* bankruptcy

**quebradizo** /keβra'ðiθo; keβra'ðiso/ *a* brittle, fragile; ailing, infirm; delicate, frail

**quebrado** /ke'βraðo/ **(-da)** *m, Math.* fraction; —*n Com.* bankrupt *a* rough, uneven (ground); *Med.* ruptured; bankrupt; ailing, broken-down

**quebradura** /keβra'ðura/ *f,* snap, breaking; gap, crevice; hernia

**quebraja** /ke'βraha/ *f,* split, crack; flaw (in wood, metal, etc.)

**quebrantahuesos** /keβranta'uesos/ *m,* sea eagle, osprey; *Inf.* bore, tedious person

**quebrantamiento** /keβranta'miento/ *m,* crushing; splitting, cleaving; fracture, rupture; profanation, desecration; burglary; violation, breaking, infringement; fatigue; *Law.* annulment; exhaustion

**quebrantanueces** /keβranta'nueθes; keβranta'nueses/ *m,* nutcrackers

**quebrantaolas** /keβranta'olas/ *m,* breakwater

**quebrantar** /keβran'tar/ *vt* to break, shatter; crush, pound; transgress, infringe; break out, force; tone down, soften; moderate, lessen; bore, exhaust; move to pity; *Inf.* break in (horses); profane; overcome (difficulties); assuage, placate; *Law.* revoke (wills); —*vr* be shaken or bruised, suffer from aftereffects

**quebranto** /ke'βranto/ *m,* breaking, shattering; crushing, pounding; infringement; breaking out (from prison); weakness, exhaustion; compassion, pity; loss, damage; pain, suffering

**quebrar** /ke'βrar/ *vt irr* to break, shatter; crush; impede, hinder; make pale (color, gen. of complexion); mitigate, moderate; bend, twist; overcome (difficulties); —*vi* break off (a friendship); weaken, give way; go bankrupt; —*vr Med.* suffer from hernia; be interrupted (of mountain ranges). **quebrarse los ojos,** to strain one's eyes —*Pres. Indic.* **quiebro, quiebras, quiebra, quiebran.** *Pres. Subjunc.* **quiebre, quiebres, quiebre, quiebren**

**queche** /'ketʃe/ *m,* ketch

**queda** /'keða/ *f,* curfew; curfew bell

**quedada** /ke'ðaða/ *f,* stay, sojourn

**quedar** /ke'ðar/ *vi* to stay, sojourn; remain; be left over; (*with por* + *infin.*) remain to be (e.g. *Queda por escribir,* It remains to be written); (*with por*) be won by or be knocked down to; be, remain in a place; end, cease; (*with en*) reach an agreement (e.g. *Quedamos en no ir,* We have decided not to go). **q. en esta alternativa...,** to face this alternative:... —*vr* remain; abate (wind); grow calm (sea); (*with con*) keep, retain possession of. **q. bien o mal,** to behave well or badly, come off well or badly (in business affairs, etc.). **quedarse muerto,** to be astounded

**quedo** /'keðo/ *a* still, motionless; quiet, tranquil —*adv* in a low voice; quietly, noiselessly. **de q.,** slowly, gradually —*interj* **¡Q.!** Quiet!

**quehacer** /kea'θer; kea'ser/ *m,* odd job; task; business (gen. *pl*)

**queja** /'keha/ *f,* lamentation, grief; complaint, grudge; quarrel

**quejarse** /ke'harse/ *vr* to lament; complain, grumble; *Law.* lodge an accusation (against)

**quejido** /ke'hiðo/ *m,* complaint, moan

**quejoso** /ke'hoso/ *a* querulous, complaining

**quejumbre** /ke'humbre/ *f,* complaint, whine; querulousness

**quejumbroso** /kehum'βroso/ *a* complaining, grumbling

**quema** /'kema/ *f,* burn; burning; fire, conflagration

**quemadero** /kema'ðero/ *a* burnable. *m,* stake (for burning people)

**quemado** /ke'maðo/ *m,* burned patch of forest; *Inf.* anything burned or burning

**quemador** /kema'ðor/ **(-ra)** *m,* jet, burner —*n* incendiary

**quemadura** /kema'ðura/ *f,* burn; scald; burning

**quemajoso** /kema'hoso/ *a* smarting, burning, pricking

**quemar** /ke'mar/ *vt* to burn; dry up, parch; scorch; tan, bronze; scald; throw away, sell at a loss; —*vi* burn, be excessively hot; —*vr* be very hot; be dried up with the heat; burn with (passions); *Inf.* be near the attainment of a desired end. **quemarse las cejas,** to burn the midnight oil, study too hard

**quemazón** /kema'θon; kema'son/ *f,* burning; conflagration; intense heat; *Inf.* smarting; *Inf.* hurtful remark; *Inf.* vexation, soreness

**querella** /ke'reʎa; ke'reya/ *f,* complaint; quarrel, fight

**querellarse** /kere'ʎarse; kere'yarse/ *vr* to complain; lament, bemoan; *Law.* lodge an accusation; *Law.* contest a will

**querelloso** /kere'ʎoso; kere'yoso/ *a* complaining, grumbling, querulous

**querencia** /ke'renθia; ke'rensia/ *f,* love, affection; homing instinct; lair; natural inclination or desire

**querer** /ke'rer/ *vt irr* to desire, wish; want, will; attempt, endeavor; (*with a*) love —*impers* be on the point of. **q. decir,** to mean. **¿Qué quiere decir esto?** What does this mean? **sin q.,** unintentionally. See **entender**

**querer** /ke'rer/ *m,* affection, love

**querido** /ke'riðo/ **(-da)** *n* lover; beloved; darling —*a* dear

**querub, querube** /ke'ruβ, ke'ruβe/ *Poet.* **querubín** *m,* cherub

**querúbico** /ke'ruβiko/ *a* cherubic

**quesera** /ke'sera/ *f,* dairymaid; dairy; cheese vat; cheese board; cheese dish

**quesería** /kese'ria/ *f,* dairy; cheese shop; season for making cheese

**queso** /'keso/ *m,* cheese. **q. de bola,** Dutch cheese. **q. rallado,** grated cheese

**quetzal** /ket'θal; ket'sal/ *m,* quetzal

**quevedos** /ke'βeðos/ *m pl,* glasses, eyeglasses; pince-nez

**¡quia!** /kia/ *interj Inf.* You don't say so!

**quianti** /'kianti/ *m,* chianti

**quicial** /ki'θial; ki'sial/ *m,* doorjamb

**quicio** /'kiθio; 'kisio/ *m,* threshold; hinge; *Mech.* bushing. **fuera de q.,** out of order; unhinged. **sacar de q.,** to displace (things); annoy, irritate; drive crazy

**quiebra** /'kieβra/ *f,* breach, crack; rut, fissure; loss; bankruptcy

**quiebro** /'kieβro/ *m*, twisting of the body, dodging; *Mus*. trill

**quien** /kien/ *rel pron mf pl* **quienes**. *interr* **quién, quiénes** who; whom; he (she, etc.) who, anyone who, whoever; which; whichever (e.g. *mis padres a quienes respeto*, my parents whom I respect. *Quien te quiere te hará llorar*, Whoever (he, those, who) love(s) you will make you weep. **¿Quién está a la puerta?** Who is at the door? **¿De quién es?** Whose is it? To whom does it belong?) —*indef pron* one (*pl* some)

**quienquiera** /kien'kiera/ *indef pron mf pl* **quienesquiera**, whosoever, whichever, whomsoever

**quietación** /kieta'θion; kieta'sion/ *f*, quieting, soothing

**quietador** /kieta'ðor/ **(-ra)** *a* tranquilizing, soothing —*n* soother

**quietismo** /kie'tismo/ *m*, quietism

**quietista** /kie'tista/ *mf* quietist —*a* quietistic

**quieto** /'kieto/ *a* quiet, still; peaceful, tranquil; virtuous, respectable

**quietud** /kie'tuð/ *f*, stillness, repose; peacefulness; rest, quietness

**quif** /kif/ *m*, hashish, marijuana

**quijada** /ki'haða/ *f*, jawbone, jaw; *Mech*. jaw

**quijo** /'kiho/ *m*, ore (gold or silver)

**quijotada** /kiho'taða/ *f*, quixotic action, quixotism

**quijote** /ki'hote/ *m*, cuisse; thigh guard; quixotic person

**quijotería** /kihote'ria/ *f*, **quijotismo** *m*, quixotism

**quijotesco** /kiho'tesko/ *a* quixotic

**quilate** /ki'late/ *m*, carat; degree of excellence (gen. *pl*). *Inf*. **por quilates**, in small bits, parsimoniously

**quilla** /'kiʎa/ 'kiya/ *f*, *Naut*. keel; breastbone (of birds)

**quillotrar** /kiʎo'trar; kiyo'trar/ *vt Inf*. to encourage, incite; woo, make love to; consider; —*vr Inf*. fall in love; dress up; whine, complain

**quillotro** /ki'ʎotro; ki'yotro/ *m*, *Inf*. incentive; indication, sign; love affair; puzzle, knotty point; compliment; dressing up

**quimera** /ki'mera/ *f*, chimera; fancy, vision; quarrel, dispute

**quimérico** /ki'meriko/ *a* chimerical, fanciful

**quimerista** /kime'rista/ *mf* dreamer, visionary; quarreler, disputant

**química** /'kimika/ *f*, chemistry

**químico** /'kimiko/ *a* chemical. *m*, chemist. **productos químicos,** chemicals

**quimono** /ki'mono/ *m*, kimono

**quina** /'kina/ *f*, cinchona; quinine; *pl* Arms of Portugal. *Inf*. **tragar q.,** to suffer in patience, put up with

**quinario** /ki'nario/ *a* quinary

**quincalla** /kin'kaʎa; kin'kaya/ *f*, cheap jewelery; fancy goods

**quincallería** /kinkaʎe'ria; kinkaye'ria/ *f*, cheap jewelry shop; hardware factory or industry; cheap jewelry; fancy goods

**quince** /'kinθe; 'kinse/ *a* and *m*, fifteen; fifteenth

**quinceañero** /kinθea'ɲero; kinsea'ɲero/ *f*, sweet sixteen party, sweet sixteen (in Spanish-speaking areas, held at age fifteen)

**quincena** /kin'θena; kin'sena/ *f*, fortnight, two weeks; bimonthly pay; fifteen

**quincenal** /kinθe'nal; kinse'nal/ *a* fortnightly; lasting a fortnight, lasting two weeks

**quinceno** /kin'θeno; kin'seno/ *a* fifteenth

**quincuagenario** /kinkuahe'nario/ *a* quinquagenarian

**quincuagésimo** /kinkua'hesimo/ *a* fiftieth

**quindécimo** /kin'deθimo; kin'desimo/ *a* fifteenth

**quinientos** /ki'nientos/ *a* five hundred; five-hundredth. *m*, five hundred

**quinina** /ki'nina/ *f*, quinine

**quinqué** /kin'ke/ *m*, oil lamp, student's lamp, table lamp; perspicuity, talent

**quinquenio** /kin'kenio/ *m*, period of five years, lustrum

**quinta** /'kinta/ *f*, country house; *Mus*. fifth; conscripting men into army by drawing lots; *Mil*. draft

**quintaesencia** /kintae'senθia; kintae'sensia/ *f*, quintessence

**quintal** /kin'tal/ *m*, hundredweight

**quintar** /kin'tar/ *vt* to draw one out of every five; draw lots for conscription into the army; —*vi* reach the fifth (day, etc., gen. of the moon)

**quintería** /kinte'ria/ *f*, farm

**quintero** /kin'tero/ *m*, farmer; farmworker

**quinteto** /kin'teto/ *m*, quintet

**quintilla** /kin'tiʎa; kin'tiya/ *f*, five-line stanza of eight syllables

**Quintín, San. armarse** /kin'tin, san ar'marse/ (*or* **haber**) **la de San Q.** to quarrel, make trouble; be a row

**quinto** /'kinto/ *a* fifth. *m*, one-fifth; *Mil*. conscript; duty of twenty percent; *Law*. fifth part of an estate. **quinta columna,** fifth column. **quinta esencia,** quintessence

**quintuplicar** /kintupli'kar/ *vt* to quintuplicate

**quintuplo** /'kintuplo/ *a* fivefold, quintuple

**quinzavo** /kin'θaβo; kin'saβo/ *a* and *m*, fifteenth

**quiñón** /ki'ɲon/ *m*, share of land owned jointly, share of the profits

**quiosco** /'kiosko/ *m*, kiosk, stand; pavilion, pagoda. **q. de música,** bandstand

**quiquiriquí** /kikiri'ki/ *m*, cock-a-doodle-doo; *Fig. Inf*. cock of the walk

**quiromancia** /kiro'manθia; kiro'mansia/ *f*, chiromancy, palmistry

**quiromántico** /kiro'mantiko/ **(-ca)** *n* chiromancer, palmist

**quirúrgico** /ki'rurhiko/ *a* surgical

**quirurgo** /ki'rurgo/ *m*, surgeon

**quisicosa** /kisi'kosa/ *f*, *Inf*. riddle, puzzle, enigma

**quisquilla** /kis'kiʎa; kis'kiya/ *f*, trifle, quibble, scruple; prawn, shrimp

**quisquilloso** /kiski'ʎoso; kiski'yoso/ *a* quibbling, overscrupulous, fastidious; hypersensitive; irascible, touchy

**quistarse** /kis'tarse/ *vr* to make oneself well-liked or loved

**quiste** /'kiste/ *m*, *Med*. cyst

**quita** /'kita/ *f*, *Law*. discharge (of part of a debt)

**quitaesmalte** /kitaes'malte/ *m*, nail polish remover (for fingernails)

**quitamanchas** /kita'mantʃas/ *mf*, dry cleaner, clothes cleaner

**quitamotas** /kita'motas/ *mf Inf*. flatterer, adulator

**quitanieve** /kita'nieβe/ *m*, snowplow

**quitanza** /ki'tanθa; ki'tansa/ *f*, quittance; quietus

**quitapesares** /kitape'sares/ *m*, *Inf*. consolation, solace, comfort

**quitar** /ki'tar/ *vt* to remove; take off or away; clear (the table); rob, steal; prevent, impede; parry (in fencing); separate; redeem (pledges); forbid; annul, repeal (laws, etc.); free from (obligations); —*vr* shed, take off, remove; get rid of; leave, quit. **quitarse de encima** ( **a),** to get rid of someone or something. **q. el polvo,** to dust. **de quita y pon,** detachable, removable; adjustable

**quitasol** /kita'sol/ *m*, parasol, sunshade

**quitasueño** /kita'sueɲo/ *m*, *Inf*. sleep banisher, anxiety

**quite** /'kite/ *m*, hindering, impeding; obstruction; parry (in fencing). **estar al q.,** to be ready to protect someone

**quizá, quizás** /ki'θa, ki'θas; ki'sa, ki'sas/ *adv* perhaps. **q. y sin q.,** without doubt, certainly

# R

**rabadán** /rraβa'ðan/ *m*, head shepherd or herdsman
**rabadilla** /rraβa'ðiʎa; rraβa'ðiya/ *f*, rump, croup
**rábano** /'rraβano/ *m*, radish. **r. picante,** horseradish
**rabel** /rra'βel/ *m*, *Mus.* rebec; *Inf.* backside, seat
**rabera** /rra'βera/ *f*, tail-end; chaff, siftings
**rabí** /rra'βi/ *m*, rabbi
**rabia** /'rraβia/ *f*, rabies, hydrophobia; anger, fury. *Inf.* **tener r. ( a),** to hate
**rabiar** /rra'βiar/ *vi* to suffer from hydrophobia; groan with pain; be furious; (*with por*) yearn for, desire. **a r.,** excessively
**rabicorto** /rraβi'korto/ *a* short-tailed
**rabieta** /rra'βieta/ *f*, *Inf.* tantrum
**rabilargo** /rraβi'largo/ *a* long-tailed
**rabínico** /rra'βiniko/ *a* rabbinical
**rabinismo** /rraβi'nismo/ *m*, rabbinism
**rabino** /rra'βino/ *m*, rabbi. **gran r.,** chief rabbi
**rabioso** /rra'βioso/ *a* rabid; furious, angry; vehement. **perro r.,** mad dog
**rabo** /'rraβo/ *m*, tail; *Bot.* stalk; *Inf.* train (of a dress); shank (of a button). **r. del ojo,** corner of the eye. *Fig. Inf.* **ir r. entre piernas,** to have one's tail between one's legs
**rabón** /rra'βon/ *a* tailless, docked; bobtailed
**rabudo** /rra'βuðo/ *a* big-tailed
**racimo** /rra'θimo; rra'simo/ *m*, bunch (of grapes or other fruits); cluster; raceme
**racimoso** /rraθi'moso; rrasi'moso/ *a* racemose
**raciocinación** /rraθioθina'θion; rrasiosina'sion/ *f*, ratiocination
**raciocinar** /rraθioθi'nar; rrasiosi'nar/ *vi* to reason
**raciocinio** /rraθio'θinio; rrasio'sinio/ *m*, reasoning; ratiocination; discourse, speech
**ración** /rra'θion; rra'sion/ *f*, ration; portion (in a restaurant); meal allowance; *Eccl.* prebendary. *Inf.* **r. de hambre,** starvation diet; pittance, starvation wages
**racional** /rraθio'nal; rrasio'nal/ *a* reasonable, logical; rational
**racionalidad** /rraθionali'ðað; rrasionali'ðað/ *f*, reasonableness; rationality
**racionalismo** /rraθiona'lismo; rrasiona'lismo/ *m*, rationalism
**racionalista** /rraθiona'lista; rrasiona'lista/ *a* and *mf* rationalist —*a* rationalistic
**racionalización** /rraθionaliθa'θion; rrasionalisa'sion/ *f*, rationalization
**racionamiento** /rraθiona'miento; rrasiona'miento/ *m*, rationing. *f.* **cartilla de r.,** ration book
**racionar** /rraθio'nar; rrasio'nar/ *vt* to ration
**rada** /'rraða/ *f*, bay, cove; *Naut.* road, roadstead
**radar** /rra'ðar/ *m*, radar
**radiación** /rraðia'θion; rraðia'sion/ *f*, radiation; *Radio.* broadcasting
**radiactividad** /rraðiaktiβi'ðað/ *f*, radioactivity
**radiactivo** /rraðiak'tiβo/ *a* radioactive
**radiador** /rraðia'ðor/ *m*, radiator (for heating); *Auto.* radiator
**radial** /rra'ðial/ *a* radial
**radiante** /rra'ðiante/ *a Phys.* radiating; brilliant, shining; *Fig.* beaming (with satisfaction)
**radiar** /rra'ðiar/ *vi Phys.* to radiate; —*vt* broadcast (by radio)
**radical** /rraði'kal/ *a* radical; fundamental; *Polit.* radical. *m*, *Gram.* root; (*Math. Chem.*) radical. *mf Polit.* radical
**radicalismo** /rraðika'lismo/ *m*, radicalism
**radicar** /rraði'kar/ **(se)** *vi* and *vr* to take root. **r. una solicitud,** file an application, submit an application —*vi* be (in a place)
**radio** /'rraðio/ *m*, (*Geom. Anat.*) radius; radium. *f*, radio
**radioaficionado** /rraðioafiθio'naðo; rraðioafisio-'naðo/ **(-da)** *n* radio amateur; *Inf.* ham, wireless fan or enthusiast
**radioaudición** /rraðioauði'θion; rraðioauði'sion/ *f*, radio broadcast

**radiocomunicación** /rraðiokomunika'θion; rraðioko-munika'sion/ *f*, radio transmission
**radiodifundir** /rraðioðifun'dir/ *vt Radio.* to broadcast
**radiodifusión, radioemisión** /rraðioðifu'sion, rra-ðioemi'sion/ *f*, *Radio.* broadcast; broadcasting
**radioemisora** /rraðioemi'sora/ *f*, radio station
**radioescucha** /rraðioes'kutʃa/ *mf* radio listener
**radiofotografía** /rraðiofotogra'fia/ *f*, radiophotography; x-ray photograph. **tomar una r. de,** to x-ray
**radiofrecuencia** /rraðiofre'kuenθia; rraðio-fre'kuensia/ *f*, radiofrequency
**radiografía** /rraðiogra'fia/ *f*, radiography
**radiografiar** /rraðiogra'fiar/ *vt* to x-ray, radiograph
**radiografista** /rraðiogra'fista/ *mf* radiographer
**radiograma** /rraðio'grama/ *m*, radiogram, cable
**radiolocación** /rraðioloka'θion; rraðioloka'sion/ *f*, radiolocation
**radiología** /rraðiolo'hia/ *f*, radiology
**radiólogo** /rra'ðiologo/ *mf* radiologist
**radiometría** /rraðiome'tria/ *f*, radiometry
**radiómetro** /rra'ðiometro/ *m*, radiometer
**radiorreceptor** /rraðiorreθep'tor; rraðiorresep'tor/ *m*, receiver, wireless set
**radioscopia** /rraðio'skopia/ *f*, radioscopy
**radiotelefonía** /rraðiotelefo'nia/ *f*, radiotelephony
**radiotelegrafía** /rraðiotelegra'fia/ *f*, radiotelegraphy
**radiotelegrafiar** /rraðiotelegra'fiar/ *vt* to radiotelegraph
**radiotelegráfico** /rraðiotele'grafiko/ *a* radiotelegraphic, wireless
**radiotelegrafista** /rraðiotelegra'fista/ *mf* wireless operator
**radiotelegrama** /rraðiotele'grama/ *m*, radiogram, radiotelegram
**radioterapia** /rraðiote'rapia/ *f*, radiotherapy, radiotherapeutics
**radiotransmisor** /rraðiotransmi'sor/ *m*, (radio) transmitter
**radioyente** /rraðio'yente/ *mf* radio listener
**raedera** /rrae'ðera/ *f*, scraper
**raedor** /rrae'ðor/ *a* scraping; abrasive
**raedura** /rrae'ðura/ *f*, scraping; rubbing; fraying
**raer** /rra'er/ *vt irr* to scrape; abrade; fray; *Fig.* extirpate. See **caer**
**ráfaga** /'rrafaga/ *f*, gust or blast of wind; light cloud; flash (of light)
**rafe** /'rrafe/ *m*, eaves
**rafia** /'rrafia/ *f*, raffia
**raído** /'rraiðo/ *a* frayed, threadbare; brazen, barefaced
**raíz** /rra'iθ; rra'is/ *f*, root. **r. amarga,** horseradish. **r. cuadrada ( cúbica),** square (cubed) root. **r. pivotante,** tap root. **a r.,** close to the root, closely. **a r. de,** as a result of; after. **de r.,** from the root, entirely. **echar raíces,** to take root
**raja** /'rraha/ *f*, split, crack; chip, splinter (of wood); slice (of fruit, etc.)
**rajá** /rra'ha/ *m*, rajah
**rajadura** /rraha'ðura/ *f*, splitting; crack, split, crevice; *Geol.* break
**rajar** /rra'har/ *vt* to crack, split; slice; —*vi Inf.* boast; chatter; —*vr* crack, split; *Inf.* take back one's words
**ralea** /rra'lea/ *f*, kind, quality; (*Inf.* scornful) race, lineage
**ralear** /rrale'ar/ *vi* to grow thin (cloth, etc.); behave true to type (gen. in a bad sense)
**rallador** /rraʎa'ðor; rraya'ðor/ *m*, *Cul.* grater
**rallar** /rra'ʎar; rra'yar/ *vt Cul.* to grate; *Inf.* bother, annoy
**rallo** /'rraʎo; 'rrayo/ *m*, *Cul.* grater; rasp
**ralo** /'rralo/ *a* sparse, thin
**rama** /'rrama/ *f*, bough, branch; *Fig.* branch (of family). *Fig. Inf.* **andarse por las ramas,** to beat around the bush. **en r.,** *Com.* raw; unbound (of books)
**ramaje** /rra'mahe/ *m*, thickness of branches, denseness of foliage

**ramal** /rraˈmal/ *m,* strand (of rope); halter; branch line (of a railroad); fork (of a road, etc.); ramification, division

**ramalazo** /rramaˈlaθo; rramaˈlaso/ *m,* blow with a rope; mark left by this; bruise

**rambla** /ˈrrambla/ *f,* bed, channel, course; avenue; boulevard (in Catalonia)

**ramera** /rraˈmera/ *f,* whore

**ramificación** /rramifikaˈθion; rramifikaˈsion/ *f,* ramification; *Anat.* bifurcation

**ramificarse** /rramifiˈkarse/ *vr* to branch, fork; *Fig.* spread

**ramillete** /rramiˈʎete; rramiˈyete/ *m,* bouquet; table centerpiece; *Bot.* cluster

**ramo** /ˈrramo/ *m, Bot.* branch; twig, spray; bouquet, bunch; wreath; *Fig.* branch (of learning, etc.); *Com.* line (of business); *Fig.* touch, slight attack. **Domingo de Ramos,** Palm Sunday

**ramoso** /rraˈmoso/ *a* branchy, thick with branches

**rampa** /ˈrrampa/ *f,* gradient, incline; *Mil.* ramp; launching site

**ramplón** /rramˈplon/ *a* stout, heavy (of shoes); coarse; vulgar; bombastic

**rana** /ˈrrana/ *f,* frog. **r. de San Antonio,** tree frog

**ranchero** /rranˈtʃero/ *m, Mil.* cook; small farmer; *West Hem.* rancher

**rancho** /ˈrrantʃo/ *m,* mess, rations; settlement, camp; hut, cabin; *Inf.* group, huddle; *West Hem.* ranch; *Naut.* gang. **hacer r.,** *Inf.* to make room

**rancidez** /rranθiˈðeθ; rransiˈðes/ *f,* rancidness; staleness; rankness; antiquity

**ranciedad** /rranθieˈðað; rransieˈðað/ *f,* rancidness; antiquity, oldness; mustiness

**rancio** /ˈrranθio; ˈrransio/ *a* rancid, rank; mellow (of wine); ancient; traditional; musty

**rango** /ˈrranɡo/ *m,* grade, class; range; (*Mil. Nav.* and social) rank; file, line

**ranúnculo** /rraˈnunkulo/ *m,* buttercup

**ranura** /rraˈnura/ *f,* groove, rabbet; slot, notch

**rapacidad** /rrapaθiˈðað; rrapasiˈðað/ *f,* rapacity, avidity, greed

**rapador** /rrapaˈðor/ *a* scraping. *m, Inf.* barber

**rapapolvo** /rrapaˈpolβo/ *m, Inf.* severe scolding, dressing-down

**rapar** /rraˈpar/ **(se)** *vt* and *vr* to shave; —*vt* crop, cut close (hair); *Inf.* steal, pinch

**rapaz** /rraˈpaθ; rraˈpas/ *a* rapacious. *m,* young boy. **ave r.,** bird of prey

**rapaza** /rraˈpaθa; rraˈpasa/ *f,* young girl

**rape** /ˈrrape/ *m, Inf.* hasty shave or haircut. **al r.,** close-cropped

**rapé** /rraˈpe/ *m,* snuff

**rapidez** /rrapiˈðeθ; rrapiˈðes/ *f,* speed, swiftness, rapidity

**rápido** /ˈrrapiðo/ *a* quick, swift; express (trains). *m,* torrent, rapid; express train

**rapiña** /rraˈpiɲa/ *f,* robbery, plundering, sacking

**rapiñar** /rrapiˈɲar/ *vt Inf.* to steal, pinch

**raposa** /rraˈposa/ *f,* vixen, fox; *Inf.* wily person

**raposear** /rraposeˈar/ *vi* to behave like a fox

**raposo** /rraˈposo/ *m,* (male) fox

**rapsodia** /rrapˈsoðia/ *f,* rhapsody

**raptar** /rrapˈtar/ *vt* to abduct; rob

**rapto** /ˈrrapto/ *m,* abduction, rape; snatching, seizing; ecstasy, trance; *Med.* loss of consciousness

**raptor** /rrapˈtor/ *m,* kidnapper, abductor

**raquero** /rraˈkero/ *a* pirate. *m,* wrecker; pickpocket, dock rat

**raqueta** /rraˈketa/ *f,* racket (tennis, badminton, squash rackets); croupier's rake. **r. de nieve,** snowshoe

**raquianestesia** /rrakianesˈtesia/ *f,* spinal anesthesia

**raquídeo** /rraˈkiðeo/ *a* spinal

**raquítico** /rraˈkitiko/ *a Med.* rachitic; small, minute; weak, feeble; rickety

**raquitismo** /rrakiˈtismo/ *m,* rickets

**rarefacción** /rrarefakˈθion; rrarefakˈsion/ *f,* rarefaction

**rarefacer** /rrarefaˈθer; rrarefaˈser/ **(se)** *vt* and *vr irr* to rarefy. See **satisfacer**

**rareza** /rraˈreθa; rraˈresa/ *f,* rareness, unusualness; eccentricity, whim; oddity, curio

**raridad** /rrariˈðað/ *f,* rarity; thinness; scarcity

**raro** /ˈrraro/ *a* rare, unusual, uncommon; notable, outstanding; odd, eccentric, queer; rarefied (gases, etc.). **rara vez,** seldom. **lo r. de,** the strange thing about (e.g. *Lo r. del caso es...,* the strange thing about the case is...)

**ras** /rras/ *m,* level. **a r.,** flush (with), nearly touching

**rasa** /ˈrrasa/ *f,* worn place in cloth; clearing, glade

**rasar** /rraˈsar/ *vt* to level with a strickle; graze, brush, touch lightly; —*vr* grow clear (of the sky, etc.)

**rascacielos** /rraskaˈθielos; rraskaˈsielos/ *m,* skyscraper

**rascador** /rraskaˈðor/ *m,* scraper; ornamental hairpin

**rascadura** /rraskaˈðura/ *f,* scraping; scratching

**rascar** /rrasˈkar/ *vt* to scratch; claw; scrape; twang (a guitar, etc.). *Inf.* **¡Que se rasque!** Let him put up with it! Let him lump it!

**rascatripas** /rraskaˈtripas/ *m, Inf.* caterwauler, squeaker (of violinists, etc.)

**rascón** /rrasˈkon/ *a* sour, tart

**rasgadura** /rrasɡaˈðura/ *f,* tearing; tear, rip, rent

**rasgar** /rrasˈɡar/ **(se)** *vt* and *vr* to tear, rip; —*vt* strum the guitar

**rasgo** /ˈrrasɡo/ *m,* flourish (of the pen); felicitous expression; characteristic, quality; *pl* features (of the face)

**rasgón** /rrasˈɡon/ *m,* rip, tear

**rasguear** /rrasɡeˈar/ *vt* to strum, twang (the guitar); —*vi* write with a flourish

**rasgueo** /rrasˈɡeo/ *m,* flourish (on a guitar); scratch (of a pen)

**rasguñar** /rrasɡuˈɲar/ *vt* to scratch, scrape; claw; *Art.* sketch

**rasguño** /rrasˈɡuɲo/ *m,* scratch; *Art.* sketch, outline

**raso** /ˈrraso/ *a* flat; free of obstacles; glossy; clear (sky, etc.); plain; undistinguished; backless (chairs). *m,* satin. **al r.,** in the open air

**raspa** /ˈrraspa/ *f, Bot.* beard (of cereals); fishbone; bunch of grapes; *Bot.* husk; scraper

**raspador** /rraspaˈðor/ *m,* eraser; scraper, rasp

**raspadura** /rraspaˈðura/ *f,* scraping; erasing; shavings, filings

**raspar** /rrasˈpar/ *vt* to scrape; erase; rob, steal; burn, bite (wine, etc.)

**rastra** /ˈrrastra/ *f,* trace, sign; sled; string of onions, etc.; anything dragging; *Agr.* harrow; *Agr.* rake. **a la r.,** dragging; reluctantly. **pescar a la r.,** to trawl

**rastreador** /rrastreaˈðor/ *m, Naut.* minesweeper —*a* dragging

**rastrear** /rrastreˈar/ *vt* to trace, trail; drag, trawl; surmise, conjecture, investigate; —*vi Agr.* rake; fly low

**rastreo** /rrasˈtreo/ *m,* dragging (of lakes, etc.)

**rastrero** /rrasˈtrero/ *a* dragging, trailing; low-flying; servile, abject; *Bot.* creeping. *m,* slaughterhouse employee

**rastrillador** /rrastriˈʎaðor; rrastriyaˈðor/ **(-ra)** *n* raker; hackler

**rastrilladora** /rrastriˈʎaðora; rrastriyaˈðora/ *f,* mechanical harrow

**rastrillaje** /rrastriˈʎahe; rrastriˈyahe/ *m,* raking

**rastrillar** /rrastriˈʎar; rrastriˈyar/ *vt* to rake; dress, comb (flax)

**rastrillo** /rrasˈtriʎo; rrasˈtriyo/ *m, Agr.* rake; hackle; portcullis; *Agr.* rack

**rastro** /ˈrrastro/ *m, Agr.* rake; track, trail; wholesale meat market; slaughterhouse; trace, vestige; second-hand market (in Madrid)

**rastrojo** /rrasˈtroho/ *m,* stubble; stubble field

**rasura** /rraˈsura/ *f,* shaving

**rasurar** /rrasuˈrar/ **(se)** *vt* and *vr* to shave

**rata** /ˈrrata/ *f,* rat. *m, Inf.* pickpocket. **r. almizclera,** muskrat. *Inf.* **más pobre que las ratas,** poorer than a church mouse

**rataplán** /rrataˈplan/ *m,* rub-a-dub-dub, beating of a drum

**ratear** /rrateˈar/ *vt* to rebate pro rata; apportion; thieve on a small scale, filch; —*vi* crawl, creep

**ratería** /rrateˈria/ *f,* filching, petty theft, picking pockets; meanness, parsimony

**ratero** /rra'tero/ **(-ra)** *n* pilferer, petty thief, pickpocket

**ratificación** /rratifika'θion; rratifika'sion/ *f*, ratification

**ratificador** /rratifika'ðor/ **(-ra)** *n* ratifier

**ratificar** /rratifi'kar/ *vt* to ratify

**ratificatorio** /rratifika'torio/ *a* ratifying, confirmatory

**rato** /'rrato/ *m*, short interval of time, while. **buen (mal) r.**, pleasant (unpleasant) time. **r. perdido**, leisure moment. **a ratos**, sometimes, occasionally. **de r. en r.**, from time to time. **pasar el r.**, *Inf.* to while away the time

**ratón** /rra'ton/ **(-ona)** *n* mouse

**ratonera** /rrato'nera/ *f*, mousetrap; mousehole; mouse nest. *Fig.* **caer en la r.**, to fall into a trap

**ratonero, ratonesco, ratonil** /rrato'nero, rrato'nesko, rrato'nil/ *a* mousy

**rauco** /'rrauko/ *a Poet.* hoarse

**raudal** /rrau'ðal/ *m*, torrent, cascade; *Fig.* flood, abundance

**raudo** /'rrauðo/ *a* swift, rapid

**ravioles** /rra'βioles/ *m pl*, ravioli

**raya** /'rraya/ *f*, stripe, streak; limit, end; part (of the hair); boundary; *Gram.* dash; score (some games). *m, Ichth.* ray. **pasar de r.**, to go too far; misbehave

**rayadillo** /rraya'ðiʎo; rraya'ðiyo/ *m*, striped cotton

**rayano** /rra'yano/ *a* neighboring; border; almost identical, very similar

**rayar** /rra'yar/ *vt* to draw lines; streak; stripe; cross out; underline; rifle (a gun); —*vi* verge (on), border (on); appear (of dawn, daylight); excel; be similar. **Raya en los catorce años**, He is about fourteen

**rayo** /'rrayo/ *m, Phys.* beam, ray; thunderbolt; flash of lightning; spoke; quick-witted person; capable, energetic person; sudden pain; disaster, catastrophe. **r. de sol**, sunbeam. **r. catódico**, cathode ray. **r. x**, x-ray. *Fig.* **echar rayos**, to breathe forth fury

**rayón** /rra'yon/ *m*, rayon

**raza** /'rraθa, 'rrasa/ *f*, race; breed; lineage; family; kind, class; crack, crevice. **de r.**, purebred

**razón** /rra'θon; rra'son/ *f*, reason; reasoning; word, expression; speech, argument; motive, cause; order, method; justice, equity; right, authority; explanation; *Math.* ratio, proportion. **r. de estado**, raison d'état, reasons of state. *Com.* **r. social**, firm, trade name. **a r. de**, at a rate of. **dar la r.** ( a), to agree with. **estar puesto en r.**, to stand to reason. **tener r.**, to be in the right

**razonable** /rraθo'naβle; rraso'naβle/ *a* reasonable; moderate

**razonador** /rraθona'ðor; rrasona'ðor/ **(-ra)** *n* reasoner

**razonamiento** /rraθona'miento; rrasona'miento/ *m*, reasoning

**razonar** /rraθo'nar; rraso'nar/ *vi* to reason; speak; —*vt* attest, confirm

**razzia** /'rraθθia; 'rrassia/ *f*, foray; pillaging, sacking; police raid

**re** /rre/ *m, Mus.* re, D

**reabsorción** /rreaβsor'θion; rreaβsor'sion/ *f*, reabsorption

**reacción** /rreak'θion; rreak'sion/ *f*, reaction. **r. de Bayardo**, quick reaction of someone always ready to help those in distress

**reaccionar** /rreakθio'nar; rreaksio'nar/ *vi* to react

**reaccionario** /rreakθio'nario; rreaksio'nario/ **(-ia)** *a* and *n* reactionary

**reaccionarismo** /rreakθiona'rismo; rreaksiona'rismo/ *m*, reactionism

**reacio** /rre'aθio; rre'asio/ *a* recalcitrant

**reactivo** /rreak'tiβo/ *m*, reagent —*a* reactive; reacting

**readmisión** /rreaðmi'sion/ *f*, readmission

**readmitir** /rreaðmi'tir/ *vt* to readmit

**reajustar** /rreahus'tar/ *vt* to readjust

**real** /rre'al/ *a* actual, real; kingly; royal; royalist; *Fig.* regal; *Inf.* fine, handsome. *m*, silver coin, real; *m pl*, encampment, camp. **alzar el r.**, *Mil.* to strike camp. **asentar el r.**, *Mil.* to encamp. **r. decreto**, royal decree. **sitio r.**, royal residence. **un r., sobre otro**, *Inf.* cash in full

**realce** /rre'alθe; rre'alse/ *m*, raised or embossed work; renown, glory; *Art.* high light

**realeza** /rrea'leθa; rrea'lesa/ *f*, royalty, royal majesty

**realidad** /rreali'ðað/ *f*, reality; sincerity, truth. **en r.**, in fact, actually

**realismo** /rrea'lismo/ *m*, realism; regalism; royalism

**realista** /rrea'lista/ *a* realistic; royalist. *mf* realist; royalist; regalist

**realizable** /rreali'θaβle; rreali'saβle/ *a* realizable; practicable

**realización** /rrealiθa'θion; rrealisa'sion/ *f*, realization; performance, execution

**realizar** /rreali'θar; rreali'sar/ *vt* to perform, execute, carry out; *Com.* realize. **r. beneficio**, to make a profit

**realmente** /rreal'mente/ *adv* really, truly; actually

**realzar** /rreal'θar; rreal'sar/ *vt* to heighten, raise; emboss; exalt; enhance; *Art.* intensify (colors, etc.)

**reanimar** /rreani'mar/ *vt* to reanimate; revive, restore, resuscitate; encourage

**reanudación** /rreanuða'θion; rreanuða'sion/ *f*, resumption, renewal

**reanudar** /rreanu'ðar/ *vt* to resume, continue

**reaparecer** /rreapare'θer; rreapare'ser/ *vi irr* to reappear. See **conocer**

**reaparición** /rreapari'θion; rreapari'sion/ *f*, reappearance

**rearmamento** /rrearma'mento/ *m*, rearmament

**rearmar** /rrear'mar/ *vi* to rearm

**reasegurador** /rreasegura'ðor/ *m*, underwriter

**reasegurar** /rreasegu'rar/ *vt* to reinsure, underwrite

**reaseguro** /rrease'guro/ *m*, reinsurance, underwriting

**reasumir** /rreasu'mir/ *vt* to reassume; resume

**reasunción** /rreasun'θion; rreasun'sion/ *f*, reassumption; resumption

**reata** /rre'ata/ *f*, string of horses or mules. **de r.**, in single file; *Inf.* blindly, unquestioningly; *Inf.* at once

**rebaja** /rre'βaha/ *f*, diminution; *Com.* discount, rebate; remission

**rebajar** /rreβa'har/ *vt* to lower; curtail, lessen; remit; *Com.* reduce in price; *Mech.* file; *Elec.* step down; humble, humiliate; —*vr* cringe, humble oneself

**rebajo** /rre'βaho/ *m*, reduction (in price, etc.); rabbet

**rebanada** /rreβa'naða/ *f*, slice, piece (of bread, etc.)

**rebanar** /rreβa'nar/ *vt* to cut into slices; split

**rebaño** /rre'βaɲo/ *m*, flock, drove, herd; *Eccl.* flock

**rebasar** /rreβa'sar/ *vt* to exceed, go beyond; *Mil.* bypass

**rebate** /rre'βate/ *m*, altercation, dispute, quarrel

**rebatiña** /rreβa'tiɲa/ *f*, grab; scrimmage. **andar a la r.**, to scuffle

**rebatir** /rreβa'tir/ *vt* to repulse, repel; fight again; fight hard; oppose, resist; *Com.* deduct; refuse, reject

**rebato** /rre'βato/ *m*, alarm, tocsin; *Mil.* surprise attack; panic, dismay

**rebeca** /rre'βeka/ *f*, cardigan, jersey

**rebeco** /rre'βeko/ *m, Zool.* chamois

**rebelarse** /rreβe'larse/ *vr* to mutiny, rebel; oppose, resist

**rebelde** /rre'βelde/ *a* mutinous, rebellious; wilful, disobedient; stubborn. *mf* rebel

**rebeldía** /rreβel'dia/ *f*, rebelliousness; willfulness; stubbornness; *Law.* nonappearance

**rebelión** /rreβe'lion/ *f*, insurrection, revolt

**rebién** /rre'βien/ *adv* very well, extremely well

**rebisabuelo** /rreβisa'βuelo/ **(-la)** *n*. See **tatarabuelo**

**reblandecer** /rreβlande'θer; rreβlande'ser/ *vt irr* to soften; —*vr* become soft. See **conocer**

**reblandecimiento** /rreβlandeθi'miento; rreβlandesi'miento/ *m*, softening; *Med.* flabbiness

**reborde** /rre'βorðe/ *m*, rim, edge; *Mech.* flange. **r. de acera**, curb

**rebordear** /rreβorðe'ar/ *vt* to flange

**rebosar** /rreβo'sar/ *vi* to overflow, run over; *Fig.* abound in; express one's feelings

**rebotar** /rreβo'tar/ *vi* to rebound; clinch (nails, etc.); refuse; —*vr* change color; *Inf.* be vexed

**rebote** /rre'βote/ *m*, rebounding; rebound

**rebotica** /rreβo'tika/ *f*, back room of a pharmacy; back of a shop

**rebozar** /rreβo'θar; rreβo'sar/ *vt* to muffle up; coat with batter

**rebozo** /rre'βoθo; rre'βoso/ *m*, muffling up, hiding

the face; head shawl; pretense, excuse. *Fig.* **sin r.,** openly

**rebramo** /rre'βramo/ *m,* barking of deer, stags, etc.

**rebueno** /rre'βueno/ *a Inf.* extremely good, fine

**rebullicio** /rreβu'ʎiθio; rreβu'yisio/ *m,* uproar, clamor

**rebullir** /rreβu'ʎir; rreβu'yir/ *vi* to stir, show signs of movement; *Fig.* swarm, seethe

**rebusca** /rre'βuska/ *f,* close search; gleaning; remains

**rebuscado** /rreβus'kaðo/ *a* affected, unnatural (of style)

**rebuscar** /rreβus'kar/ *vt* to search for; glean

**rebuznar** /rreβuθ'nar; rreβus'nar/ *vi* to bray

**rebuzno** /rre'βuθno; rre'βusno/ *m,* braying

**recadero** /rreka'ðero/ **(-ra)** *n* messenger, errand boy

**recado** /rre'kaðo/ *m,* message; greeting, note; gift, present; daily marketing; outfit, implements; precaution, safeguard

**recaer** /rreka'er/ *vi irr* to fall again; *Med.* relapse; lapse, backslide; devolve, fall upon. See **caer**

**recaída** /rreka'iða/ *f,* falling again; *Med.* relapse; lapse

**recalar** /rreka'lar/ *vt* to impregnate; *Naut.* call at (a port), come within sight of land

**recalcada** /rrekal'kaða/ *f,* pressing down, squeezing; emphasis; *Naut.* list

**recalcar** /rrekal'kar/ *vt* to press down; squeeze; pack tight; stress, emphasize; —*vi Naut.* list; —*vr Inf.* say over and over, savor one's words

**recalcitrante** /rrekalθi'trante; rrekalsi'trante/ *a* obdurate, recalcitrant

**recalentador** /rrekalenta'ðor/ *m, Mech.* superheater

**recalentar** /rrekalen'tar/ *vt irr* to overheat; superheat; reheat. See **sentar**

**recamado** /rreka'maðo/ *m,* raised embroidery

**recámara** /rre'kamara/ *f,* dressing room; explosives chamber; breech of a gun; *Inf.* caution

**recambio** /rre'kambio/ *m,* spare, spare part; *Com.* re-exchange

**recantación** /rrekanta'θion; rrekanta'sion/ *f,* retraction, recantation

**recapacitar** /rrekapaθi'tar; rrekapasi'tar/ *vi* to search one's memory; think over

**recapitulación** /rrekapitula'θion; rrekapitula'sion/ *f,* summary, résumé

**recapitular** /rrekapitu'lar/ *vt* to recapitulate, summarize

**recargar** /rrekar'gar/ *vt* to recharge; load again; reaccuse; overcharge; overdress or overdecorate; —*vr Med.* become more feverish. **r. acumuladores,** to recharge batteries

**recargo** /rre'kargo/ *m,* charge; new load; *Law.* new accusation; overcharge, extra cost; *Med.* temperature increase

**recatado** /rreka'taðo/ *a* prudent, discreet, circumspect; modest, shy

**recatar** /rreka'tar/ *vt* to hide, conceal; —*vr* be prudent or cautious

**recato** /rre'kato/ *m,* caution, prudence; modesty, shyness, reserve

**recauchutar** /rrekautʃu'tar/ *vt* to retread (tires)

**recaudación** /rrekauða'θion; rrekauða'sion/ *f,* collecting; collection (of taxes, etc.); tax collector's office

**recaudador** /rrekauða'ðor/ *m,* tax collector

**recaudar** /rrekau'ðar/ *vt* to collect, recover (taxes, debts, etc.); deposit, place in custody

**recaudo** /rre'kauðo/ *m,* collecting; collection (of taxes, etc.); precaution, safeguard; *Law.* surety

**recelar** /rreθe'lar; rrese'lar/ *vt* to suspect, fear, mistrust; —*vr* (*with de*) be afraid or suspicious of

**recelo** /rre'θelo; rre'selo/ *m,* suspicion, mistrust, doubt, fear

**receloso** /rreθe'loso; rrese'loso/ *a* suspicious, distrustful, doubtful

**recepción** /rreθep'θion; rresep'sion/ *f,* receiving, reception; admission, acceptance; reception, party; *Law.* cross-examination

**receptáculo** /rreθep'takulo; rresep'takulo/ *m,* receptacle, container; *Fig.* refuge; *Bot.* receptacle

**receptador** /rreθepta'ðor; rresepta'ðor/ **(-ra)** *n* receiver (of stolen goods); accomplice

**receptivo** /rreθep'tiβo; rresep'tiβo/ *a* receptive

**receptor** /rreθep'tor; rresep'tor/ **(-ra)** *a* receiving —*n* recipient. *m, Elec.* receiver; wireless set. **r. de galena,** crystal set. **r. telefónico,** telephone receiver

**receta** /rre'θeta; rre'seta/ *f, Med.* prescription; *Cul.* recipe

**recetar** /rreθe'tar; rrese'tar/ *vt Med.* to prescribe; *Inf.* demand

**rechapear** /rretʃape'ar/ *vt* to replate

**rechazar** /rretʃa'θar; rretʃa'sar/ *vt* to repulse; resist; refuse; oppose, deny (the truth of); contradict

**rechazo** /rre'tʃaθo; rre'tʃaso/ *m,* recoil; rebound; refusal

**rechinamiento, rechino** /rretʃina'miento, rre'tʃino/ *m,* squeaking, creaking; gnashing (of teeth)

**rechinar** /rretʃi'nar/ *vi* to squeak, creak; gnash (teeth); chatter (teeth); do with a bad grace

**rechoncho** /rre'tʃontʃo/ *a* squat, stocky

**reciamente** /rreθia'mente; rresia'mente/ *adv* hard; strongly, firmly, vigorously

**recibí** /rreθi'βi; rresi'βi/ *m, Com.* receipt

**recibidor** /rreθiβi'ðor; rresiβi'ðor/ **(-ra)** *a* receiving —*n* recipient. *m,* reception room

**recibimiento** /rreθiβi'miento; rresiβi'miento/ *m,* reception; welcome, greeting; reception room, waiting room; hall, vestibule

**recibir** /rreθi'βir; rresi'βir/ *vt* to obtain, receive; support, bear; suffer, experience (attack, injury); approve; accept, receive; entertain; stand up to (attack); —*vr* (*with de*) graduate as, take office as

**recibo** /rre'θiβo; rre'siβo/ *m,* reception; *Com.* receipt; reception room, waiting room; hall, vestibule. *Com.* **acusar r.,** to acknowledge receipt

**recidiva** /rreθi'ðiβa; rresi'ðiβa/ *f, Med.* relapse

**recién** /rre'θien; rre'sien/ *adv* recently, newly. Shortened form of **reciente** before a past participle (e.g. *r. llegado,* newly arrived)

**reciente** /rre'θiente; rre'siente/ *a* recent; new; fresh

**recinto** /rre'θinto; rre'sinto/ *m,* precincts; neighborhood; premises, place

**recio** /'rreθio; 'rresio/ *a* strong; robust; bulky, thick; rough, uncouth; grievous, hard; severe (weather); impetuous, precipitate

**recipiente** /rreθi'piente; rresi'piente/ *a* receiving. *m,* receptacle, container, vessel

**reciprocar** /rreθipro'kar; rresipro'kar/ *vt* to reciprocate

**reciprocidad** /rreθiproθi'ðað; rresiprosi'ðað/ *f,* reciprocity; reciprocation

**recíproco** /rre'θiproko; rre'siproko/ *a* reciprocal

**recitación** /rreθita'θion; rresita'sion/ *f,* recitation

**recitado** /rreθi'taðo; rresi'taðo/ *m,* recitative

**recitador** /rreθita'ðor; rresita'ðor/ **(-ra)** *n* elocutionist, reciter

**recitar** /rreθi'tar; rresi'tar/ *vt* to recite, declaim

**reclamación** /rreklama'θion; rreklama'sion/ *f,* reclamation; objection, opposition; *Com.* claim

**reclamar** /rrekla'mar/ *vi* to oppose, object to; *Poet.* resound; —*vt* call repeatedly; *Com.* claim; decoy (birds)

**reclamo** /rre'klamo/ *m,* decoy bird; enticement, allurement; *Law.* reclamation; advertisement. **objeto de r.,** advertising sample. **venta de r.,** bargain sale

**reclinación** /rreklina'θion; rreklina'sion/ *f,* reclining; leaning

**reclinatorio** /rreklina'torio/ *m,* couch; prie-dieu

**recluir** /rre'kluir/ *vt irr* to immure, shut up; detain, arrest. See **huir**

**reclusión** /rreklu'sion/ *f,* confinement, seclusion; prison

**recluso** /rre'kluso/ **(-sa)** *n* recluse

**recluta** /rre'kluta/ *f,* recruiting. *mf Mil.* recruit

**reclutador** /rrekluta'ðor/ *m,* recruiting office

**reclutamiento** /rrekluta'miento/ *m,* recruiting

**reclutar** /rreklu'tar/ *vt* to enlist recruits, recruit

**recobrar** /rreko'βrar/ *vt* to recover, regain; —*vr* recuperate; regain consciousness

**recobro** /rre'koβro/ *m,* recovery; *Mech.* pick-up

**recocer** /rreko'θer; rreko'ser/ *vt irr* to reboil; recook; overboil; overcook; anneal (metals); —*vr Fig.* be tormented (by emotion), be all burned up. See **cocer**

**recodo** /rre'koðo/ *m*, bend, turn, loop

**recogedor** /rrekohe'ðor/ *a* sheltering. *m*, *Agr.* gleaner

**recoger** /rreko'her/ *vt* to gather, pick; pick up; retake; collect (letters from a mailbox, etc.); amass; shrink, narrow; keep; hoard; shelter; reap, pick; —*vr* withdraw, retire; go home; go to bed; retrench, economize; give oneself to meditation

**recogida** /rreko'hiða/ *f*, collection (of letters from a mailbox); withdrawal; retirement; harvest

**recogido** /rreko'hiðo/ *a* recluse; cloistered, confined

**recogimiento** /rrekohi'miento/ *m*, gathering, picking; collection, accumulation; seclusion; shelter; women's reformatory

**recolección** /rrekolek'θion; rrekolek'sion/ *f*, summary, résumé; harvest; collection (of taxes, etc.); *Eccl.* convent of a reformed order; mystic ecstasy

**recoleto** /rreko'leto/ *a* *Eccl.* reformed (of religious orders); recluse

**recomendable** /rrekomen'daβle/ *a* commendable, recommendable

**recomendación** /rrekomenda'θion; rrekomenda-'sion/ *f*, recommendation (all meanings)

**recomendar** /rrekomen'dar/ *vt irr* to recommend (all meanings); entrust, commend —*Pres. Indic.* **recomiendo, recomiendas, recomienda, recomiendan.** *Pres. Subjunc.* **recomiende, recomiendes, recomiende, recomienden**

**recompensa** /rrekom'pensa/ *f*, compensation; recompense, reward

**recompensar** /rrekompen'sar/ *vt* to compensate; requite; reward, recompense

**recomposición** /rrekomposi'θion; rrekomposi'sion/ *f*, recomposition

**recomprar** /rrekom'prar/ *vt* to repurchase

**reconcentrar** /rrekonθen'trar; rrekonsen'trar/ *vt* to concentrate; dissemble; —*vr* withdraw into oneself, meditate

**reconciliable** /rrekonθi'liaβle; rrekonsi'liaβle/ *a* reconcilable

**reconciliación** /rrekonθilia'θion; rrekonsilia'sion/ *f*, reconciliation

**reconciliador** /rrekonθilia'ðor; rrekonsilia'ðor/ **(-ra)** *a* reconciliatory —*n* reconciler

**reconciliar** /rrekonθi'liar; rrekonsi'liar/ *vt* to reconcile; *Eccl.* reconsecrate; *Eccl.* hear a short confession; —*vr* become reconciled; *Eccl.* make an additional confession

**recondicionar** /rrekondiθio'nar; rrekondisio'nar/ *vt* to rebuild, overhaul, recondition

**recóndito** /rre'kondito/ *a* recondite

**reconocer** /rrekono'θer; rrekono'ser/ *vt irr* to examine, inspect; recognize; admit, acknowledge; own, confess; search; *Polit.* reconnoiter; (*with por*) adopt as (a son, etc.); recognize as; —*vr* be seen, show; acknowledge, confess; know oneself. **Bien se reconoce que no está aquí,** It's easy to see he's not here. See **conocer**

**reconocido** /rrekono'θiðo; rrekono'siðo/ *a* grateful

**reconocimiento** /rrekonoθi'miento; rrekonosi-'miento/ *m*, examination, inspection; recognition; acknowledgement, admission; search; *Mil.* reconnoitering; adoption; gratitude

**reconquista** /rrekon'kista/ *f*, reconquest

**reconquistar** /rrekonkis'tar/ *vt* to reconquer; *Fig.* recover, win back

**reconstitución** /rrekonstitu'θion; rrekonstitu'sion/ *f*, reconstitution

**reconstituir** /rrekonsti'tuir/ *vt irr* to reconstitute. See **huir**

**reconstituyente** /rrekonstitu'yente/ *m*, *Med.* tonic

**reconstrucción** /rrekonstruk'θion; rrekonstruk'sion/ *f*, reconstruction

**reconstruir** /rrekons'truir/ *vt irr* to reconstruct, rebuild; recreate. See **huir**

**reconvención** /rrekomben'θion; rrekomben'sion/ *f*, rebuke, reproof; recrimination; *Law.* countercharge

**reconversión** /rrekomber'sion/ *f*, reconversion

**recopilación** /rrekopila'θion; rrekopila'sion/ *f*, summary, compendium; collection (of writings); digest (of laws)

**recopilador** /rrekopila'ðor/ *m*, compiler

**recopilar** /rrekopi'lar/ *vt* to compile, collect

**recordar** /rrekor'ðar/ *vt irr* to cause to remember, remind; remember; —*vi* remember; awake. See **acordar**

**recordatorio** /rrekorða'torio/ *m*, reminder —*a* commemorative (e.g. a plaque)

**recorrer** /rreko'rrer/ *vt* to travel over; pass through; wander around; examine, inspect; read hastily; overhaul, renovate

**recorrido** /rreko'rriðo/ *m*, journey, run; *Mech.* stroke; overhaul. **r. de despegue,** *Aer.* take-off run

**recortado** /rrekor'taðo/ *a Bot.* jagged, incised. *m*, paper cutout

**recortar** /rrekor'tar/ *vt* to clip, trim, pare; cut out; *Art.* outline; —*vr* stand out (against), be outlined (against)

**recorte** /rre'korte/ *m*, clipping, paring; cutting; cutout; *Art.* outline; *pl* snippets, clippings. **r. de periódico,** newspaper cutting, newspaper clipping

**recostar** /rrekos'tar/ *vt irr* (*with en or contra*) to lean, rest against; —*vr* (*with en or contra*) lean against, rest on; lean back; recline. See **contar**

**recreación** /rrekrea'θion; rrekrea'sion/ *f*, recreation, hobby

**recrear** /rrekre'ar/ *vt* to entertain, amuse; —*vr* amuse oneself; delight (in), enjoy

**recreo** /rre'kreo/ *m*, recreation, hobby; playtime, recess (in schools); place of amusement. **salón de r.,** recreation room

**recriminación** /rrekrimina'θion; rrekrimina'sion/ *f*, recrimination

**recriminador** /rrekrimina'ðor/ *a* recriminatory

**recriminar** /rrekrimi'nar/ *vt* to recriminate

**recrudecer** /rrekruðe'θer; rrekruðe'ser/ **(se)** *vi* and *vr irr* to recur, return. See **conocer**

**recrudescencia** /rrekruðes'θenθia; rrekruðes'sensia/ *f*, recrudescence, recurrence

**rectángulo** /rrek'tangulo/ *m*, rectangle —*a* rectangular

**rectificable** /rrektifi'kaβle/ *a* rectifiable

**rectificación** /rrektifika'θion; rrektifika'sion/ *f*, rectification; *Mech.* grinding

**rectificador** /rrektifika'ðor/ *m*, rectifier

**rectificar** /rrektifi'kar/ *vt* to rectify; *Mech.* grind; —*vr* mend one's ways; *Mil.* **r. el frente,** to straighten the line

**rectilíneo** /rrekti'lineo/ *a* rectilinear

**rectitud** /rrekti'tuð/ *f*, straightness; rectitude, integrity; exactness; righteousness

**recto** /'rrekto/ *a* straight; upright; erect; literal (meaning); just, fair; single-breasted (of coats); *m*, right angle; rectum

**rector** /rrek'tor/ **(-ra)** *n* director; principal, headmaster. *m*, *Eccl.* rector

**rectorado** /rrekto'raðo/ *m*, principalship, headmaster-(mistress-) ship, directorship; *Eccl.* rectorship

**rectoría** /rrekto'ria/ *f*, rectorate, rectorship

**recua** /'rrekua/ *f*, drove of beasts of burden; *Inf.* string or line (of things)

**recubrir** /rreku'βrir/ *vt* to re-cover; coat; plate —*Past Part.* **recubierto**

**recuento** /rre'kuento/ *m*, calculation; recount; inventory

**recuerdo** /rre'kuerðo/ *m*, memory, remembrance; memento; *pl* greetings, regards

**reculada** /rreku'laða/ *f*, drawing back; recoil

**recular** /rreku'lar/ *vi* to recoil, draw back; *Inf.* go back on, give up

**recuperable** /rrekupe'raβle/ *a* recoverable, recuperable

**recuperación** /rrekupera'θion; rrekupera'sion/ *f*, recovery, recuperation; *Chem.* recovery

**recurrente** /rreku'rrente/ *a* recurrent

**recurrir** /rreku'rrir/ *vi* to recur; (*with prep a*) have recourse to; appeal to

**recurso** /rre'kurso/ *m*, recourse, resort; choice, option; reversion; petition; *Law.* appeal; *pl* means of livelihood; *Fig.* way out, last hope

**recusar** /rreku'sar/ *vt* to refuse; challenge the authority (of)

**red** /rreð/ *f*, net; network; hairnet; railing, grating; *Fig.* snare; system (of communications, etc.); *Fig.* combination (of events, etc.); *Elec.* mains. **r. de**

**arrastre,** trawl net. *Fig. Inf.* **caer en la r.,** to fall into the trap

**redacción** /rreðak'θion; rreðak'sion/ *f,* phrasing; editorial office; editing; editorial board

**redactar** /rreðak'tar/ *vt* to write, phrase; draw up; edit

**redactor** /rreðak'tor/ **(-ra)** *a* editorial —*n* editor

**redada** /rre'ðaða/ *f,* cast (of a fishing net); haul, catch

**redecilla** /rreðe'θiʎa; rreðe'siya/ *f, dim* small net; netting; hairnet

**redención** /rreðen'θion; rreðen'sion/ *f,* redemption; ransom; deliverance, salvation; redeeming, paying off (a mortgage, etc.)

**redentor** /rreðen'tor/ **(-ra)** *a* redeeming, redemptive —*n* redeemer

**redificar** /rreðifi'kar/ *vt* to rebuild

**redifusión** /rreðifu'sion/ *f, Radio.* relay

**redil** /rre'ðil/ *m,* sheepfold

**redimible** /rreði'miβle/ *a* redeemable

**redimir** /rreði'mir/ *vt* to ransom; redeem, buy back; pay off (a mortgage, etc.); deliver, free; *Eccl.* redeem

**reditar** /rreði'tar/ *vt* to reprint, reissue

**rédito** /'rreðito/ *m, Com.* income, revenue, interest, profit

**redoblamiento** /rreðoβla'miento/ *m,* redoubling; bending back (of nails, etc.); rolling (of a drum)

**redoblar** /rreðo'βlar/ *vt* to redouble; repeat; bend back (nails, etc.); —*vi* roll (a drum)

**redoble** /rre'ðoβle/ *m,* doubling; redoubling; repetition; roll (of a drum)

**redoma** /rre'ðoma/ *f,* flask, vial

**redomado** /rreðo'maðo/ *a* astute, crafty, sly; complete, perfect

**redonda** /rre'ðonda/ *f,* district; pasture ground; *Naut.* square sail; *Mus.* semibreve. **a la r.,** around

**redondear** /rreðonde'ar/ *vt* to make round; round; free (from debt, etc.); —*vr* acquire a fortune; clear oneself (of debts, etc.)

**redondel** /rreðon'del/ *m,* traffic circle, rotary, roundabout

**redondez** /rreðon'deθ; rreðon'des/ *f,* roundness

**redondo** /rre'ðondo/ *a* round; circular; unequivocal, plain. *m,* round, circle; *Inf.* cash

**reducción** /rreðuk'θion; rreðuk'sion/ *f,* reduction; *Mil.* defeat, conquest; decrease; *Com.* rebate; *(Math. Chem.)* reduction

**reducible** /rreðu'θiβle; rreðu'siβle/ *a* reducible

**reducir** /rreðu'θir; rreðu'sir/ *vt irr* to reduce; decrease, cut down; break up; *Art.* scale down; *Elec.* step down; subdue; *(Chem. Math. Surg.)* reduce; exchange; divide into small fragments; persuade; —*vr* be obliged to, have to; live moderately. See **conducir**

**reducto** /rre'ðukto/ *m, Mil.* redoubt (of fortifications)

**redundancia** /rreðun'danθia; rreðun'dansia/ *f,* redundance

**redundante** /rreðun'dante/ *a* redundant

**redundar** /rreðun'dar/ *vi* to overflow; be excessive or superfluous; *(with en)* redound to

**reduplicación** /rreðuplika'θion; rreðuplika'sion/ *f,* reduplication

**reduplicar** /rreðupli'kar/ *vt* to reduplicate

**ree** /rree/ For words so beginning (e.g. *reeditar, reexportar*), see spellings with the **e**

**refacción** /rrefak'θion; rrefak'sion/ *f,* refection, light meal; compensation, reparation

**refajo** /rre'faho/ *m,* skirt, underskirt

**refección** /rrefek'θion; rrefek'sion/ *f,* refection, light meal

**refectorio** /rrefek'torio/ *m,* refectory

**referencia** /rrefe'renθia; rrefe'rensia/ *f,* report, account; allusion; regard, relation; *Com.* reference (gen. *pl*); consideration

**referente** /rrefe'rente/ *a* concerning, related (to)

**referir** /rrefe'rir/ *vt irr* to narrate; describe; direct, guide; relate, refer, concern; —*vr* allude (to); refer (to); concern. See **sentir**

**refinación** /rrefina'θion; rrefina'sion/ *f,* refining

**refinado** /rrefi'naðo/ *a* refined; polished, cultured; crafty

**refinador** /rrefina'ðor/ *m,* refiner

**refinamiento** /rrefina'miento/ *m,* refinement, subtlety, care

**refinar** /rrefi'nar/ *vt* to refine, purify; polish, perfect

**refinería** /rrefine'ria/ *f,* refinery

**reflector** /rreflek'tor/ *a* reflecting. *m,* reflector, searchlight; shade (for lamps, etc.)

**reflejar** /rrefle'har/ *vi Phys.* to reflect; —*vt* consider; show, mirror; —*vr Fig.* be reflected, be seen

**reflejo** /rre'fleho/ *m,* reflection; image; glare —*a* reflex; considered, judicious

**reflexión** /rreflek'sion/ *f, Phys.* reflection; consideration, thought

**reflexionar** /rrefleksio'nar/ *vt (with en or sobre)* to consider, reflect upon

**reflexivo** /rreflek'siβo/ *a Phys.* reflective; thoughtful

**reflorecer** /rreflore'θer; rreflore'ser/ *vi irr* to flower again; return to favor (ideas, etc.). See **conocer**

**reflujo** /rre'fluho/ *m,* reflux, refluence; ebb tide

**refocilar** /rrefoθi'lar; rrefosi'lar/ *vt* to warm up, brace up; give pleasure to; —*vr* enjoy oneself

**reforma** /rre'forma/ *f,* reform; improvement; reformation; *Hist.* Reformation

**reformación** /rreforma'θion; rreforma'sion/ *f,* reform, improvement

**reformador** /rreforma'ðor/ **(-ra)** *a* reformatory, reforming —*n* reformer

**reformar** /rrefor'mar/ *vt* to remake; reshape; repair, mend, restore; improve, correct; *Eccl.* reform; reorganize; —*vr* mend one's ways, improve; control oneself

**reformatorio** /rreforma'torio/ *m,* reformatory —*a* reforming, reformatory

**reformista** /rrefor'mista/ *mf* reformist, reformer —*a* reformatory

**reforzador** /rreforθa'ðor; rreforsa'ðor/ *m, Photo.* reinforcing bath; *Elec.* booster

**reforzamiento** /rreforθa'miento; rreforsa'miento/ *m,* stiffening, reinforcing

**reforzar** /rrefor'θar; refor'sar/ *vt irr* to reinforce, strengthen, stiffen; encourage, inspirit. See **forzar**

**refractar** /rrefrak'tar/ *vt* to refract

**refractario** /rrefrak'tario/ *a* stubborn; *(Phys. Chem.)* refractory; unmanageable, unruly; fireproof

**refrán** /rre'fran/ *m,* proverb

**refranero** /rrefra'nero/ *m,* collection of proverbs

**refregamiento** /rrefrega'miento/ *m,* rubbing; scrubbing, scouring

**refregar** /rrefre'gar/ *vt irr* to rub; scrub, scour; *Fig. Inf.* rub in, insist on. See **cegar**

**refrenamiento** /rrefrena'miento/ *m,* curbing; control, restraint

**refrenar** /rrefre'nar/ *vt* to curb, check (horses); control, restrain

**refrendar** /rrefren'dar/ *vt* to countersign, endorse, legalize

**refrescante** /rrefres'kante/ *a* refreshing, cooling

**refrescar** /rrefres'kar/ *vt* to cool, chill; repeat; *Fig.* brush up, revise; —*vi* be rested or refreshed; grow cooler; take the air; freshen (wind); take a cool drink; —*vr* grow cooler; take the air; take a cool drink

**refresco** /rre'fresko/ *m,* refreshment; cool drink

**refriega** /rre'friega/ *f,* affray, scuffle, rough-and-tumble

**refrigeración** /rrefrihera'θion; rrefrihera'sion/ *f,* refrigeration

**refrigerador** /rrefrihera'ðor/ *m,* refrigerator

**refrigerante** /rrefrihe'rante/ *a* refrigerative; chilling; cooling. *m,* cooling chamber, cooler

**refrigerar** /rrefrihe'rar/ *vt* to chill; cool; freeze, refrigerate; refresh

**refrigerio** /rrefri'herio/ *m,* coolness; consolation; refreshment, food

**refringente** /rrefrin'hente/ *a Phys.* refringent

**refuerzo** /rre'fuerθo; rre'fuerso/ *m,* reinforcement; strengthening; aid, help

**refugiado** /rrefu'hiaðo/ **(-da)** *a* and *n* refugee

**refugiar** /rrefu'hiar/ *vt* to protect, shelter; —*vr* take refuge

**refugio** /rre'fuhio/ *m,* refuge, shelter, protection; traffic island. **r. antiaéreo,** air raid shelter. **r. para peatones,** traffic island

**refulgencia** /rreful'henθia; rreful'hensia/ f, resplendence, splendor, brilliance

**refulgente** /rreful'hente/ a resplendent, refulgent, dazzling

**refulgir** /rreful'hir/ vi to shine, be dazzling

**refundición** /rrefundi'θion; rrefundi'sion/ f, recasting (of metals); adaptation; rehash, refurbishing

**refundir** /rrefun'dir/ vt to recast (metals); include, comprise; adapt; rehash, refurbish; —vi Fig. promote, contribute to

**refunfuñador** /rrefunfuɲa'ðor/ a grumbling, fuming

**refunfuñar** /rrefunfu'ɲar/ vi to grumble, growl, fume

**refunfuño** /rrefun'fuɲo/ m, grumble, fuming; snort

**refutable** /rrefu'taβle/ a refutable

**refutación** /rrefuta'θion; rrefuta'sion/ f, refutation

**refutar** /rrefu'tar/ vt to refute

**regadera** /rrega'ðera/ f, watering can; irrigation canal; sprinkler

**regadío** /rrega'ðio/ m, irrigated land; irrigation, watering —a irrigated

**regajal, regajo** /rrega'hal, rre'gaho/ m, pool, puddle; stream, brook

**regalado** /rrega'laðo/ a delicate, highly bred; luxurious, delightful

**regalar** /rrega'lar/ vt to make a gift of, give; caress, fondle; indulge, cherish; entertain, regale; —vr live in luxury

**regalía** /rrega'lia/ f, royal privilege; right, exemption; perquisite, emolument

**regalismo** /rrega'lismo/ m, regalism

**regalista** /rrega'lista/ a and mf regalist

**regaliz** /rrega'liθ; rrega'lis/ m, **regaliza** f, licorice

**regalo** /rre'galo/ m, gift, present; satisfaction, pleasure; entertainment, regalement; luxury, comfort

**regalón** /rrega'lon/ a Inf. pampered

**regañadientes, a** /rregaɲa'ðientes, a/ adv unwillingly, grumblingly

**regañar** /rrega'ɲar/ vi to snarl (dogs); crack (skin of fruits); grumble, mutter; Inf. quarrel; —vt Inf. scold

**regaño** /rre'gaɲo/ m, angry look or gesture; Inf. scolding

**regañón** /rrega'ɲon/ **(-ona)** a Inf. grumbling, complaining; scolding —n Inf. grumbler

**regar** /rre'gar/ vt irr to water, sprinkle with water; flow through, irrigate; spray; Fig. shower (with), strew. See **cegar**

**regata** /rre'gata/ f, regatta; small irrigation channel (for gardens, etc.)

**regate** /rre'gate/ m, twist of the body, sidestep; dribbling; (in soccer); Inf. dodging, evasion

**regatear** /rregate'ar/ vt to haggle over, beat down (prices); resell, retail; dribble (a ball); Fig. Inf. dodge, avoid; —vi bargain, haggle; Naut. take part in a regatta, race

**regateo** /rrega'teo/ m, haggling, bargaining

**regatero** /rrega'tero/ **(-ra)** a retail —n retailer

**regatón** /rrega'ton/ **(-ona)** m, ferrule, tip —a haggling, bargaining —n haggler; retailer

**regatonear** /rregatone'ar/ vt to resell at retail

**regazo** /rre'gaθo; rre'gaso/ m, lap, knees; Fig. heart, bosom

**regencia** /rre'henθia; rre'hensia/ f, regency

**regeneración** /rrehenera'θion; rrehenera'sion/ f, regeneration

**regenerador** /rrehenera'ðor/ **(-ra)** n regenerator —a regenerative, reforming

**regenerar** /rrehene'rar/ vt to regenerate, reform

**regenta** /rre'henta/ f, wife of the president of a court of session

**regentar** /rrehen'tar/ vt to fill temporarily (offices); rule, govern; manage, run (businesses)

**regente** /rre'hente/ a ruling. mf regent. m, president of a court of session; manager

**regicida** /rrehi'θiða; rrehi'siða/ mf regicide (person)

**regicidio** /rrehi'θiðio; rrehi'siðio/ m, regicide (act)

**regidor** /rrehi'ðor/ a ruling, governing. m, magistrate, alderman

**régimen** /'rrehimen/ m, administration, management; regime; (Med. Gram.) regimen; Mech. rating

**regimentación** /rrehimenta'θion; rrehimenta'sion/ f, regimentation

**regimentar** /rrehimen'tar/ vt irr to form into regiments; regiment —Pres. Indic. **regimiento, regimientas, regimienta, regimientan.** Pres. Subjunc. **regimiente, regimientes, regimiente, regimienten**

**regimiento** /rrehi'miento/ m, Mil. regiment; administration, rule

**regio** /'rrehio/ a royal; magnificent, regal

**región** /rre'hion/ f, region, country; area, tract, space. **r. industrial,** industrial area

**regionalismo** /rrehiona'lismo/ m, regionalism

**regionalista** /rrehiona'lista/ mf regionalist —a regional

**regir** /rre'hir/ vt irr to govern, rule; administer, conduct; Gram. govern; —vi be in force (laws, etc.); work, function; Naut. obey the helm. See **pedir**

**registrador** /rrehistra'ðor/ a recording. m, registrar, keeper of records; recorder. **caja ( registradora),** (cash) register

**registrar** /rrehis'trar/ vt to examine, inspect; search; copy, record; mark the place (in a book); observe, note; (of thermometers, etc.) record, show; look on to (houses, etc.); —vr register (hotels, etc.)

**registro** /rre'histro/ m, search; registration, entry; record; recording; reading (of a thermometer, etc.); Mech. damper; registry; register (book); Mus. range, compass (voice); Mus. register (organ); (Mech. Print.) register; bookmark. **r. civil,** register of births, marriages, and deaths

**regla** /'rregla/ f, ruler, measuring stick; rule, principle, guide, precept; system, policy; Med. period; moderation; method, order. **r. de cálculo,** slide rule. **r. T,** T-square. **en r.,** in due form. **por r.,** general, generally, as a rule

**reglamentación** /rreglamenta'θion; rreglamenta'sion/ f, regulation; rules and regulations

**reglamentar** /rreglamen'tar/ vt to regulate

**reglamento** /rregla'mento/ m, bylaw; regulation, ordinance

**reglar** /rre'glar/ vt to rule (lines); regulate; govern; control; —vr restrain oneself, mend one's ways

**regocijado** /rregoθi'haðo; rregosi'haðo/ a merry, joyful, happy

**regocijar** /rregoθi'har; rregosi'har/ vt to cheer, delight; —vr enjoy oneself, rejoice

**regocijo** /rrego'θiho; rrego'siho/ m, happiness, joy; cheer, merriment

**regordete** /rregor'ðete/ a Inf. chubby

**regresar** /rregre'sar/ vi to return

**regresión** /rregre'sion/ f, return; retrogression; regression

**regreso** /rre'greso/ m, return

**reguera** /rre'gera/ f, irrigation channel, ditch

**reguero** /rre'gero/ m, trickle

**regulación** /rregula'θion; rregula'sion/ f, regulation; Mech. control, timing

**regulador** /rregula'ðor/ m, Mech. governor, regulator —a regulating, controlling

**regular** /rregu'lar/ vt to adjust, regulate; Mech. govern —a methodical, ordered; moderate; average, medium; (Eccl. Mil. Geom. Gram.) regular; so-so, not bad; probable. **por lo r.,** generally

**regularidad** /rregulari'ða ð/ f, regularity

**regularización** /rregulariθa'θion; rregularisa'sion/ f, regularization; regulation

**regularizar** /rregulari'θar; rregulari'sar/ vt to regularize; regulate

**regurgitar** /rregurhi'tar/ vi to regurgitate

**rehabilitación** /rreaβilita'θion; rreaβilita'sion/ f, rehabilitation

**rehabilitar** /rreaβili'tar/ vt to rehabilitate; —vr rehabilitate oneself

**rehacer** /rrea'θer; rrea'ser/ vt irr to remake; repair, mend; —vr recover one's strength; control one's emotions; Mil. rally. See **hacer**

**rehén** /rre'en/ m, hostage (gen. pl); Mil. pledge, security

**rehenchir** /rreen'tʃir/ vt irr to restuff; refill, recharge. See **henchir**

**reherir** /rree'rir/ vt irr to repulse. See **herir**

**rehilar** /rrei'lar/ *vt* to spin too much or twist the yarn; —*vi* totter, stagger; whizz (arrows, etc.). See **prohibir**

**rehuir** /rre'uir/ *vt irr* to withdraw; avoid; reject. See **huir**

**rehusar** /rreu'sar/ *vt* to refuse, reject. See **desahuciar**

**reimponer** /rreimpo'ner/ *vt irr* to reimpose. See **poner**

**reimportación** /rreimporta'θion; rreimporta'sion/ *f,* reimportation

**reimpresión** /rreimpre'sion/ *f,* reprint

**reimprimir** /rreimpri'mir/ *vt* to reprint

**reina** /'rreina/ *f,* queen; queen (in chess); queen bee; peerless beauty, belle

**reinado** /rrei'naðo/ *m,* reign; heyday, fashion

**reinante** /rrei'nante/ *a* reigning; prevalent

**reinar** /rrei'nar/ *vi* to reign; influence; endure, prevail

**reincidencia** /rreinθi'ðenθia; rreinsi'ðensia/ *f,* relapse (into crime, etc.), recidivism

**reincidente** /rreinθi'ðente; rreinsi'ðente/ *mf* backslider

**reincidir** /rreinθi'ðir; rreinsi'ðir/ *vi* to relapse (into crime, etc.)

**reincorporar** /rreinkorpo'rar/ *vt* to reincorporate; —*vr* join again, become a member again

**reingresar** /rreiŋgre'sar/ *vi* to reenter

**reingreso** /rreiŋ'greso/ *m,* reentry

**reino** /'rreino/ *m,* kingdom

**reinstalación** /rreinstala'θion; rreinstala'sion/ *f,* reinstatement

**reinstalar** /rreinsta'lar/ *vt* to reinstate; —*vr* be reinstalled

**reintegración** /rreintegra'θion; rreintegra'sion/ *f,* reintegration

**reintegrar** /rreinte'grar/ *vt* to reintegrate; —*vr* be reinstated, recuperate, recover

**reir** /rre'ir/ *vi irr* to laugh; sneer, jeer; *Fig.* smile (nature); —*vt* laugh at; —*vr Inf.* (*with de*) scorn. **reírse a carcajadas,** to shout with laughter —*Pres. Part.* **riendo.** *Pres. Indic.* **río, ríes, ríe, ríen.** *Preterite* **rió, rieron.** *Pres. Subjunc.* **ría,** etc —*Imperf. Subjunc.* **riese,** etc.

**reiteración** /rreitera'θion; rreitera'sion/ *f,* reiteration, repetition

**reiteradamente** /rreiteraða'mente/ *adv* repeatedly, reiteratively

**reiterar** /rreite'rar/ *vt* to reiterate, repeat

**reiterativo** /rreitera'tiβo/ *a* reiterative

**reivindicación** /rreiβindika'θion; rreiβindika'sion/ *f, Law.* recovery

**reivindicar** /rreiβindi'kar/ *vt Law.* to recover

**reja** /'rreha/ *f,* colter, plowshare; plowing, tilling; grating, grille

**rejado** /rre'haðo/ *m,* railing, grating

**rejilla** /rre'hiʎa; rre'hiya/ *f,* grating; grille, lattice; luggage rack (in a train); cane (for chairs, seats, etc.); wire mesh; small brazier; *Elec.* grid; *Mech.* grate

**rejuntar** /rrehun'tar/ *vt* to point (a wall)

**rejuvenecer** /rrehuβene'θer; rrehuβene'ser/ *vt irr* to rejuvenate; *Fig.* revive; bring up to date; —*vi and vr* be rejuvenated, grow young again, rejuvenesce. See **conocer**

**rejuvenecimiento** /rrehuβeneθi'miento; rrehuβenesi'miento/ *m,* rejuvenation

**relación** /rrela'θion; rrela'sion/ *f,* relation; connection (of ideas); report, statement; narrative, account; *Math.* ratio; *Law.* brief; intercourse, association, dealings (gen. *pl*); list; analogy, relation. **tener relaciones con,** to have dealings with; be engaged or betrothed to; woo, court

**relacionar** /rrelaθio'nar; rrelasio'nar/ *vt* to recount, narrate, report; connect, relate; —*vr* be connected

**relajación** /rrelaha'θion; rrelaha'sion/ *f,* relaxation; recreation; laxity, dissoluteness

**relajar** /rrela'har/ *vt* to relax; recreate, amuse; make less rigorous; *Law.* remit; —*vr* become relaxed; be dissolute, lax, or vicious

**relamer** /rrela'mer/ *vt* to lick again; —*vr* lick one's lips; *Fig.* overpaint, make up too much; ooze satisfaction, brag

**relamido** /rrela'miðo/ *a* overdressed; affected

**relámpago** /rre'lampago/ *m,* lightning; flash, gleam;

streak of lightning (of quick persons or things); flash of wit, witticism

**relampaguear** /rrelampage'ar/ *vi* to lighten (of lightning); flash, gleam

**relapso** /rre'lapso/ *a* relapsed, lapsed (into error, vice)

**relatar** /rrela'tar/ *vt* to relate, narrate, report

**relatividad** /rrelatiβi'ðað/ *f,* relativeness; *Phys.* relativity

**relativo** /rrela'tiβo/ *a* relevant, pertinent; relative, comparative; *Gram.* relative

**relato** /rre'lato/ *m,* narration, account, report

**relator** /rrela'tor/ **(-ra)** *a* narrating —*n* narrator. *m, Law.* reporter

**relavar** /rrela'βar/ *vt* to rewash, wash again

**relección** /rrelek'θion; rrelek'sion/ *f,* reelection

**releer** /rrele'er/ *vt irr* to reread; revise. See **creer**

**relegación** /rrelega'θion; rrelega'sion/ *f,* relegation

**relegar** /rrele'gar/ *vt* to banish; relegate, set aside

**relegir** /rrele'hir/ *vt irr* to reelect. See **elegir**

**relente** /rre'lente/ *m,* night dew, dampness; *Inf.* cheek, impudence

**relevación** /rreleβa'θion; rreleβa'sion/ *f, Art.* relief; release; remission, exemption

**relevar** /rrele'βar/ *vt Art.* to work in relief; emboss; relieve, free; dismiss; excuse, pardon; aid, succor; *Fig.* aggrandize; *Mil.* relieve; —*vi* carve in relief

**relevo** /rre'leβo/ *m,* relay; *Mil.* relief

**relicario** /rreli'kario/ *m,* reliquary

**relieve** /rre'lieβe/ *m, Art.* relief; *pl* leftovers, remains (of food). **alto r.,** high relief. **bajo r.,** low relief

**religar** /rreli'gar/ *vt* to retie, fasten again; fasten more securely; solder

**religión** /rreli'hion/ *f,* religion; creed, faith, philosophy; devotion, religious practice. **r. reformada,** Protestantism. **entrar en r.,** *Eccl.* to profess

**religionario** /rrelihio'nario/ *m,* Protestant

**religiosidad** /rrelihiosi'ðað/ *f,* religiosity; religiousness; conscientiousness, punctiliousness

**religioso** /rreli'hioso/ **(-sa)** *a* religious; punctilious, conscientious; moderate —*n* religious

**relinchar** /rrelin'tʃar/ *vi* to whinny, neigh

**relincho** /rre'lintʃo/ *m,* neigh, whinny

**reliquia** /rre'likia/ *f,* residue (gen. *pl*); *Eccl.* relic; vestige, remnant, memento; permanent disability or ailment

**rellanar** /rreʎa'nar; rreya'nar/ *vt* to make level again; —*vr* stretch oneself at full length

**rellano** /rre'ʎano; rre'yano/ *m,* landing (of a staircase); level stretch (of ground)

**rellenar** /rreʎe'nar; rreye'nar/ *vt* to refill, replenish; fill up; *Mas.* plug, point; *Cul.* stuff; *Inf.* cram with food (gen —*vr*)

**relleno** /rre'ʎeno; rre'yeno/ *m, Cul.* stuffing; replenishing; filling; *Fig.* padding (of speeches, etc.)

**reloj** /rre'loh/ *m,* clock; watch. **r. de arena,** hourglass. **r. de bolsillo,** watch. **r. de la muerte,** deathwatch beetle. **r. de péndulo,** grandfather clock. **r. de pulsera,** wristwatch. **r. de repetición,** repeater. **r. de sol** *or* **r. solar,** sundial

**relojera** /rrelo'hera/ *f,* clock stand; watch case

**relojería** /rrelohe'ria/ *f,* watch or clock making; jeweler, watch maker's shop

**relojero** /rrelo'hero/ **(-ra)** *n* watch maker, watch repairer

**reluciente** /rrelu'θiente; rrelu'siente/ *a* shining, sparkling; shiny

**relucir** /rrelu'θir; rrelu'sir/ *vi irr* to glitter, sparkle, gleam; *Fig.* shine, excel. See **lucir**

**reluctante** /rreluk'tante/ *a* unruly, refractory, disobedient

**relumbrante** /rrelum'βrante/ *a* resplendent, dazzling

**relumbrar** /rrelum'βrar/ *vi* to be resplendent, shine, glitter

**remachar** /rrema'tʃar/ *vt* to rivet; *Fig.* clinch

**remache** /rre'matʃe/ *m,* riveting; rivet

**remanente** /rrema'nente/ *m,* remains, residue

**remanso** /rre'manso/ *m,* backwater; stagnant water; sloth, dilatoriness

**remar** /rre'mar/ *vi* to row, paddle, scull; toil, strive

**rematadamente** /rremata'ða'mente/ *adv* completely, entirely, absolutely

**rematado** /rrema'taðo/ *a* beyond hope, extremely ill; utterly lost; *Law.* convicted

**rematar** /rrema'tar/ *vt* to end, finish; finish off, kill; knock down at auction; *Sew.* finish; —*vi* end; —*vr* be ruined or spoiled

**remate** /rre'mate/ *m*, end, conclusion; extremity; *Archit.* coping; *Archit.* terminal; highest bid; auction. **de r.,** utterly hopeless

**rembarcar** /rrembar'kar/ *vt* to reembark, reship

**rembarque** /rrem'βarke/ *m*, reembarkation, reshipment

**rembolsable** /rrembol'saβle/ *a* repayable

**rembolsar** /rrembol'sar/ *vt* to recover (money); refund, return (money)

**rembolso** /rrem'βolso/ *m*, repayment. **contra r.,** cash on delivery, C.O.D.

**remedar** /rreme'ðar/ *vt* to copy, imitate; mimic

**remediador** /rremeðia'ðor/ **(-ra)** *a* remedying —*n* benefactor, helper

**remediar** /rreme'ðiar/ *vt* to remedy; aid, help; save from danger; prevent (trouble)

**remedio** /rre'meðio/ *m*, remedy; emendation, correction; help; refuge, protection; *Med.* remedy. **No hay más r.,** There's nothing else to do, It's the only way open. **no tener más r.,** to be unable to help (doing something), be obliged to

**remedo** /rre'meðo/ *m*, imitation; poor copy

**remembranza** /rremem'βranθa; rremem'βransa/ *f*, remembrance, memory

**rememorar** /rrememo'rar/ *vt* to remember, recall to mind

**remendar** /rremen'dar/ *vt irr* to mend, patch; darn; repair; correct. See **recomendar**

**remendón** /rremen'don/ **(-ona)** *n* cobbler; mender of old clothes

**remero** /rre'mero/ **(-ra)** *n* oarsman, rower; sculler

**remesa** /rre'mesa/ *f*, remittance; consignment, shipment

**remesar** /rreme'sar/ **(se)** *vt* and *vr* to pluck out (hair); —*vt Com.* remit; consign

**remiendo** /rre'miendo/ *m*, *Sew.* patch; mend, darn; emendation; *Inf.* insignia of one of the Spanish military orders. **a remiendos,** *Inf.* piecemeal

**remilgarse** /rremil'garse/ *vr* to preen oneself, be overdressed

**remilgo** /rre'milgo/ *m*, affectation; mannerism; prudery, squeamishness

**reminiscencia** /rreminis'θenθia; rreminis'sensia/ *f*, reminiscence; memory, recollection

**remirado** /rremi'raðo/ *a* wary, cautious, prudent, circumspect

**remirar** /rremi'rar/ *vt* to revise, go over again; —*vr* take great care over; behold with pleasure

**remisión** /rremi'sion/ *f*, sending; remission; pardon, forgiveness; foregoing, relinquishment; abatement, diminution; *Lit.* reference, allusion

**remiso** /rre'miso/ *a* timid, spiritless; languid, slow

**remitente** /rremi'tente/ *mf* sender —*a* sending

**remitir** /rremi'tir/ *vt* to remit, send; pardon, forgive; defer, postpone; abate, diminish; relinquish, forgo; *Lit.* refer; —*vr* remit, submit, consult; refer (to), cite

**remo** /'rremo/ *m*, oar, scull, paddle; arm or leg (of men or animals, gen. *pl*); wing (gen. *pl*); hard, continuous toil; galleys. **al r.,** by dint of rowing; *Inf.* struggling with hardships

**remojar** /rremo'har/ *vt* to soak, steep; celebrate by drinking

**remojo** /rre'moho/ *m*, soaking, steeping

**remolacha** /rremo'latʃa/ *f*, beet

**remolcador** /rremolka'ðor/ *m*, *Naut.* tow, tug —*a Naut.* towing

**remolcar** /rremol'kar/ *vt* (*Naut. Auto.*) to tow; *Fig.* press into service, use

**remolinar** /rremoli'nar/ *vi* to spin, whirl, eddy; —*vr* throng, swarm

**remolino** /rremo'lino/ *m*, whirlwind; eddy, swirl; whirlpool; crowd, throng, swarm; disturbance, riot

**remolonear** /rremolone'ar/ *vi Inf.* to loiter, lag; avoid work; be lax or dilatory

**remolque** /rre'molke/ *m*, towage, towing; towline; barge; *Auto.* trailer. **a r.,** on tow

**remonta** /rre'monta/ *f*, resoling (of shoes); leather gusset (of riding breeches); *Mil.* remount

**remontar** /rremon'tar/ *vt* to scare off (game); *Mil.* supply with fresh horses; resole (shoes); *Fig.* rise to great heights (of oratory, etc.); —*vr* soar (of birds); (*with prep a*) date from, go back to; originate in

**remoquete** /rremo'kete/ *m*, blow with the fist; witticism; *Inf.* flirtation, courtship

**rémora** /'rremora/ *f*, *Ichth.* remora; delay, hindrance

**remorder** /rremor'ðer/ *vt irr* to bite again or repeatedly; *Fig.* gnaw, nag, cause uneasiness or remorse; —*vr* show one's feelings. See **morder**

**remordimiento** /rremorði'miento/ *m*, remorse

**remotamente** /rremota'mente/ *adv* distantly, remotely; unlikely; vaguely, confusedly

**remoto** /rre'moto/ *a* distant, remote; unlikely, improbable

**remover** /rremo'βer/ *vt irr* to remove, move; stir; turn over; dismiss, discharge. See **mover**

**remozar** /rremo'θar; rremo'sar/ *vt* to cause to appear young; freshen up, bring up to date; —*vr* look young

**remplazar** /rrempla'θar; rrempla'sar/ *vt* to replace; exchange, substitute; succeed, take the place of

**remplazo** /rrem'plaθo; rrem'plaso/ *m*, replacement; exchange, substitute; successor; *Mil.* replacement

**remuda** /rre'muða/ *f*, replacement, exchange

**remudar** /rremu'ðar/ *vt* to replace

**remuneración** /rremunera'θion; rremunera'sion/ *f*, remuneration; reward

**remunerador** /rremunera'ðor/ **(-ra)** *a* remunerative, recompensing —*n* remunerator

**remunerar** /rremune'rar/ *vt* to recompense, reward

**remusgar** /rremus'gar/ *vi* to suspect, imagine

**renacentista** /rrenaθen'tista; rrenasen'tista/ *a* renaissance

**renacer** /rrena'θer; rrena'ser/ *vi irr* to be reborn. See **nacer**

**renacimiento** /rrenaθi'miento; rrenasi'miento/ *m*, rebirth; Renaissance

**renacuajo** /rrena'kuaho/ *m*, tadpole; *Mech.* frog; *Inf.* twerp

**renano** /rre'nano/ *a* Rhenish

**rencarcelar** /rrenkarθe'lar; rrenkarse'lar/ *vt* to reimprison

**rencarnación** /rrenkarna'θion; rrenkarna'sion/ *f*, reincarnation

**rencarnar** /rrenkar'nar/ **(se)** *vi* and *vr* to be reincarnated

**rencilla** /rren'θiʎa; rren'siya/ *f*, grudge, grievance, resentment

**rencilloso** /rrenθi'ʎoso; rrensi'yoso/ *a* peevish, easily offended, touchy

**rencor** /rren'kor/ *m*, rancor, spite, old grudge. **guardar r.,** to bear malice

**rencoroso** /rrenko'roso/ *a* rancorous, malicious, spiteful

**rencuadernar** /rrenkuaðer'nar/ *vt* to rebind (books)

**rencuentro** /rren'kuentro/ *m*, collision; *Mil.* encounter, clash

**rendición** /rrendi'θion; rrendi'sion/ *f*, surrender; yield, profit

**rendido** /rren'diðo/ *a* submissive, obsequious

**rendija** /rren'diha/ *f*, crevice, cleft, crack, fissure

**rendimiento** /rrendi'miento/ *m*, weariness, fatigue; submissiveness, obsequiousness; yield, profit; *Mech.* efficiency

**rendir** /rren'dir/ *vt irr Mil.* to cause to surrender; defeat; overcome, conquer; give back, return; yield, provide; tire, exhaust; vomit; pay, render; —*vr* be exhausted, be worn out; surrender. *Mil.* **r. el puesto,** to retire from or give up a post. See **pedir**

**renegado** /rrene'gaðo/ **(-da)** *n* renegade, apostate; turncoat; *Inf.* malignant person —*a* renegade

**renegador** /rrenega'ðor/ **(-ra)** *n* blasphemer; foul-mouthed person

**renegar** /rrene'gar/ *vt irr* to deny, disown; loathe, hate; —*vi* (*with de*) apostatize; blaspheme; *Inf.* curse. See **cegar**

**renganchar** /rrengan'tʃar/ **(se)** *vt* and *vr Mil.* to reenlist

**renganche** /rreŋˈgantʃe/ *m, Mil.* reenlistment

**renglón** /rreŋˈglon/ *m, Print.* line; *pl* writing, composition

**reniego** /rreˈniego/ *m,* blasphemy; *Inf.* foul language, cursing

**renitencia** /rreniˈtenθia; rreniˈtensia/ *f,* repugnance

**reno** /ˈrreno/ *m,* reindeer

**renombrado** /rrenomˈβraðo/ *a* illustrious, famous

**renombre** /rreˈnombre/ *m,* surname; renown, reputation, fame

**renovable** /rrenoˈβaβle/ *a* renewable, replaceable

**renovación** /rrenoβaˈθion; rrenoβaˈsion/ *f,* replacement; renewal; renovation; transformation, reform

**renovador** /rrenoβaˈðor/ **(-ra)** *n* reformer; renovator —*a* renovating; reforming

**renovar** /rrenoˈβar/ *vt irr* to renew; renovate; replace; exchange; reiterate, repeat. See **contar**

**renta** /ˈrrenta/ *f,* yield, profit; income; revenue; government securities; rent; tax

**rentar** /rrenˈtar/ *vt* to yield, produce an income

**rentero** /rrenˈtero/ **(-ra)** *n* tenant farmer. *m,* one who farms out land

**rentista** /rrenˈtista/ *mf* financier; bondholder; person who lives on a private income, rentier

**rentístico** /rrenˈtistiko/ *a* revenue, financial

**renuente** /rreˈnuente/ *a* refractory, willful

**renuevo** /rreˈnueβo/ *m, Bot.* shoot; renewal

**renuncia, renunciación** /rreˈnunθia, rrenunθiaˈθion; rreˈnunsia, rrenunsiaˈsion/ *f,* renunciation; resignation; abandonment, relinquishment

**renunciar** /rrenunˈθiar; rrenunˈsiar/ *vt* to renounce; refuse; scorn; abandon, relinquish; resign; revoke (at cards). **r. a,** to give up

**renuncio** /rreˈnunθio; rreˈnunsio/ *m,* revoke (cards); *Inf.* falsehood

**reñidamente** /rreɲiðaˈmente/ *adv* strongly, stubbornly, fiercely

**reñir** /rreˈɲir/ *vi irr* to quarrel, dispute; fight; be on bad terms, fall out; —*vt* scold; fight (battles, etc.). See **ceñir**

**reo** /ˈrreo/ *mf* criminal; offender, guilty party; *Law.* defendant

**reojo** /rreˈoho/ *m,* (**mirar de**) to look out of the corner of the eye; *Fig.* look askance

**reorganizador** /rreorganiθaˈðor; rreorganisaˈðor/ **(-ra)** *a* reorganizing —*n* reorganizer

**reorganizar** /rreorganiˈθar; rreorganiˈsar/ *vt* to reorganize

**reóstato** /rreˈostato/ *m,* rheostat

**repantigarse** /rrepantiˈgarse/ *vr* to stretch out one's legs, make oneself comfortable

**reparable** /rrepaˈraβle/ *a* remediable, reparable; worthy of note

**reparación** /rreparaˈθion; rreparaˈsion/ *f,* repair, mending; reparation, satisfaction; indemnity, compensation

**reparada** /rrepaˈraða/ *f,* shying (of horses)

**reparador** /rreparaˈðor/ *a* repairing, mending; fault-finding; restoring; satisfying, compensating

**reparar** /rrepaˈrar/ *vt* to repair; restore; consider; correct, remedy; atone for, expiate; indemnify; hold up, detain; protect, guard; (*with en*) notice; —*vi* halt, be detained; —*vr* control oneself

**reparo** /rreˈparo/ *m,* repair; restoration; remedy; note, reflection; warning; doubt, scruple; guard, protection; parry (at fencing)

**repartición** /rrepartiˈθion; rrepartiˈsion/ *f,* distribution

**repartidero** /rrepartiˈðero/ *a,* distributable

**repartidor** /rrepartiˈðor/ **(-ra)** *a* distributing —*n* distributor; tax assessor

**repartimiento** /rrepartiˈmiento/ *m,* distribution, allotment; assessment

**repartir** /rrepartˈir/ *vt* to distribute; share out; allot; deal (cards); assess; *Com.* deliver

**reparto** /rreˈparto/ *m,* distribution; assessment; delivery (of letters, etc.); *Theat.* cast; deal (at cards)

**repasar** /rrepaˈsar/ *vt* to pass by again; peruse, reexamine; brush up, revise; skim, glance over; mend, repair (garments); edit, revise; hone

**repaso** /rreˈpaso/ *m,* second passage through; reexamination, perusal; revision, editing; brushing up, revision; repair, mending; *Inf.* dressing-down, scolding

**repatriación** /rrepatriaˈθion; rrepatriaˈsion/ *f,* repatriation

**repatriado** /rrepaˈtriaðo/ **(-da)** *n* repatriate

**repatriar** /rrepaˈtriar/ *vt* to repatriate; —*vi* and *vr* return to one's own country

**repecho** /rreˈpetʃo/ *m,* steep slope. **a r.,** uphill

**repelar** /rrepeˈlar/ *vt* to pull by the hair; put through its paces (of a horse); clip, cut; remove, diminish

**repeler** /rrepeˈler/ *vt* to repel, throw back; reject, refute

**repelo** /rreˈpelo/ *m,* anything against the grain; *Inf.* skirmish; reluctance, repugnance

**repente** /rreˈpente/ *m, Inf.* sudden or unexpected movement. **de r.,** suddenly

**repentino** /rrepenˈtino/ *a* sudden, unexpected

**repentizar** /rrepentiˈθar; rrepentiˈsar/ *vi Mus.* to sight-read

**repercusión** /rreperkuˈsion/ *f,* repercussion; vibration

**repercutir** /rreperkuˈtir/ *vi* to recoil, rebound; —*vr* reverberate; reecho; *Fig.* have repercussions; —*vt Med.* repel

**repertorio** /rreperˈtorio/ *m,* repertory

**repesar** /rrepeˈsar/ *vt* to reweigh, weigh again

**repetición** /rrepetiˈθion; rrepetiˈsion/ *f,* repetition; *Art.* replica, copy; repeater (in clocks); recital

**repetidamente** /rrepetiðaˈmente/ *adv* repeatedly

**repetidor** /rrepetiˈðor/ *a* repeating

**repetir** /rrepeˈtir/ *vt irr* to repeat, do over again; reiterate; *Art.* copy, make a replica of; recite. See **pedir**

**repicar** /rrepiˈkar/ *vt* to chop, mince; peal (of bells); prick again; —*vr* pride oneself (on), boast

**repique** /rreˈpike/ *m,* chopping, mincing; peal, pealing (of bells); disagreement, grievance

**repisa** /rreˈpisa/ *f, Archit.* bracket; ledge; shelf. **r. de chimenea,** mantelpiece

**replantar** /rreplanˈtar/ *vt* to replant; transplant

**repleción** /rrepleˈθion; rrepleˈsion/ *f,* repletion, satiety

**replegar** /rrepleˈgar/ *vt irr* to refold, fold many times; —*vr Mil.* retreat in good order. See **cegar**

**repleto** /rreˈpleto/ *a* replete

**réplica** /ˈrreplika/ *f,* reply, answer; replica

**replicar** /rrepliˈkar/ *vi* to contradict, dispute; answer, reply. **¡No me repliques!** *Inf.* Don't answer back!

**repliegue** /rreˈpliege/ *m,* double fold, crease; doubling, folding; *Mil.* withdrawal

**repoblación** /rrepoβlaˈθion; rrepoβlaˈsion/ *f,* repeopling, repopulation

**repoblar** /rrepoˈβlar/ *vt* to repeople, repopulate

**repollo** /rreˈpoʎo; rreˈpoyo/ *m,* white cabbage; heart (of lettuce, etc.)

**reponer** /rrepoˈner/ *vt irr* to replace; reinstate; restore; reply; —*vr* recover, regain (possessions); grow well again; grow calm. See **poner**

**reportación** /rreportaˈθion; rreportaˈsion/ *f,* serenity, moderation

**reportaje** /rreporˈtahe/ *m,* journalistic report

**reportar** /rreporˈtar/ *vt* to restrain, moderate; achieve, obtain; carry; bring; —*vr* control oneself

**reporte** /rreˈporte/ *m,* report, news; rumor

**reporterismo** /rreporteˈrismo/ *m,* newspaper reporting

**reportero** /rreporˈtero/ **(-ra)** *a* news, report —*n* reporter

**reposado** /rrepoˈsaðo/ *a* quiet, peaceful, tranquil

**reposar** /rrepoˈsar/ *vi* to rest, repose oneself; sleep, doze; lie in the grave; settle (liquids); rest (on)

**reposición** /rreposiˈθion; rreposiˈsion/ *f,* replacement; restoration; renewal; recovery (of health); *Theat.* revival

**repositorio** /rreposiˈtorio/ *m,* repository

**reposo** /rreˈposo/ *m,* rest, repose; peace, tranquility; sleep

**repostería** /rreposteˈria/ *f,* confectioner's shop; pantry; butler's pantry

**repostero** /rreposˈtero/ *m,* confectioner, pastry cook

**repregunta** /rrepreˈgunta/ *f,* cross-examination

**repreguntar** /rrepregunˈtar/ *vt* to cross-examine

**reprender** /rrepren'der/ vt to scold, reprimand, rebuke

**reprensible** /rrepren'siβle/ a reprehensible, censurable

**reprensión** /rrepren'sion/ f, scolding, reprimand, rebuke

**represa** /rre'presa/ f, damming, holding back (water); dam, lock; restraining, controlling

**represalia** /rrepre'salia/ f, reprisal (gen. pl); retaliation

**represar** /rrepre'sar/ vt to dam, harness (water); Naut. retake, recapture; Fig. restrain, control

**representación** /rrepresenta'θion; rrepresenta'sion/ f, representation; Theat. performance; authority; dignity; Com. agency; portrait, image; depiction, expression; petition

**representador** /rrepresenta'ðor/ a representative

**representante** /rrepresen'tante/ a representative. mf representative; actor; performer

**representar** /rrepresen'tar/ vt to represent; Theat. perform; depict, express; describe, portray; —vr imagine, picture to oneself

**representativo** /rrepresenta'tiβo/ a representative

**represión** /rrepre'sion/ f, repression; recapture

**represivo** /rrepre'siβo/ a repressive

**reprimenda** /rrepri'menda/ f, rebuke, reprimand

**reprimir** /rrepri'mir/ vt to repress, restrain, control; —vr restrain oneself

**reprobación** /rreproβa'θion; rreproβa'sion/ f, censure; reprobation

**reprobar** /rrepro'βar/ vt irr to reprove; censure; fail (in an exam). See **probar**

**réprobo** /'rreproβo/ (-ba) n reprobate

**reprochar** /rrepro'tʃar/ vt to reproach

**reproche** /rre'protʃe/ m, reproaching; rebuke, reproach

**reproducción** /rreproðuk'θion; rreproðuk'sion/ f, reproduction. **r. a gran escala,** large-scale model

**reproducir** /rreproðu'θir; rreproðu'sir/ vt irr to reproduce. See **conducir**

**reproductor** /rreproðuk'tor/ (-ra) a reproductive —n breeding animal

**reps** /rreps/ m, rep (fabric)

**reptil** /rrep'til/ a reptilian; crawling. m, reptile

**república** /rre'puβlika/ f, republic; state, commonwealth. **la r. de las letras,** the republic of letters

**República Dominicana** /rre'puβlika domini'kana/ Dominican Republic

**República Malgache** /rre'puβlika mal'gatʃe/ Republic of Madagascar

**republicanismo** /rrepuβlika'nismo/ m, republicanism

**republicano** /rrepuβli'kano/ (-na) a and n republican

**repudiación** /rrepuðia'θion; rrepuðia'sion/ f, repudiation

**repudiar** /rrepu'ðiar/ vt to cast off (a wife); repudiate, renounce

**repuesto** /rre'puesto/ a retired, hidden. m, stock, provision; serving table; pantry; stake (at cards, etc.). **de r.,** spare, extra

**repugnancia** /rrepug'nanθia; rrepug'nansia/ f, inconsistency, contradiction; aversion, dislike; reluctance; repugnance

**repugnante** /rrepug'nante/ a repugnant, loathsome

**repugnar** /rrepug'nar/ vt to contradict, be inconsistent with; hate, be averse to (e.g. La idea me repugna, I hate the idea)

**repujado** /rrepu'haðo/ m, repoussé work

**repujar** /rrepu'har/ vt to work in repoussé

**repulir** /rrepu'lir/ vt to repolish, reburnish; —vt and vr make up too much, overdress

**repulsa** /rre'pulsa/ f, snub, rebuff; rejection; repulse

**repulsar** /rrepul'sar/ vt to decline, reject; repulse; deny, refuse; rebuff

**repulsión** /rrepul'sion/ f, repulsion; rebuff; aversion, dislike

**repulsivo** /rrepul'siβo/ a repellent

**repunta** /rre'punta/ f, headland, cape; Fig. first sign; Inf. disgust; caprice; fight

**reputación** /rreputa'θion; rreputa'sion/ f, reputation

**reputar** /rrepu'tar/ vt to believe, consider (e.g. Le re-

puto por honrado, I believe him to be an honorable man); appreciate, esteem

**requebrar** /rreke'βrar/ vt irr to break into smaller pieces; make love to, woo; compliment, flatter. See **quebrar**

**requemado** /rreke'maðo/ a sunburned; brown

**requemar** /rreke'mar/ vt to burn again; overcook; dry up, parch (of plants, etc.); burn (the mouth) (of spicy foods, etc.); —vr Fig. suffer inwardly

**requerimiento** /rrekeri'miento/ m, requirement, demand; Law. summons

**requerir** /rreke'rir/ vt irr to inform, notify; examine; need, necessitate; require; summon; woo; persuade. See **sentir**

**requesón** /rreke'son/ m, cream cheese; curd

**requetebién** /rrekete'βien/ adv Inf. exceedingly well

**requiebro** /rre'kieβro/ m, compliment, expression of love; wooing, flirtation

**requisa** /rre'kisa/ f, inspection, visitation; Mil. requisitioning

**requisar** /rreki'sar/ vt Mil. to requisition

**requisito** /rreki'sito/ m, requisite

**res** /rres/ f, animal, beast; head of cattle

**resabiar** /rresa'βiar/ vt to make vicious, cause bad habits; —vr contract bad habits or vices; be discontented; relish

**resabio** /rre'saβio/ m, disagreeable aftertaste; bad habit, vice

**resaca** /rre'saka/ f, surf, undertow, surge; Com. redraft

**resalado** /rresa'laðo/ a Inf. very witty; most attractive

**resaltar** /rresal'tar/ vi to rebound; project, jut out; grow loose, fall out; Fig. stand out, be prominent

**resalto** /rre'salto/ m, rebound; projection

**resarcir** /rresar'θir; rresar'sir/ vt to compensate, indemnify

**resbaladizo** /rresβala'ðiθo; rresβala'ðiso/ a slippery; difficult, delicate (of a situation)

**resbalar** /rresβa'lar/ vi to slip; slide; skid; err, fall into sin

**resbalón** /rresβa'lon/ m, slip; slide; skid; temptation, error

**rescatador** /rreskata'ðor/ (-ra) n ransomer; rescuer

**rescatar** /rreska'tar/ vt to ransom; redeem, buy back; barter; free, rescue; Fig. redeem (time, etc.)

**rescate** /rres'kate/ m, ransom; redemption; barter; amount of ransom

**rescindir** /rresθin'dir; rressin'dir/ vt to annul, repeal, rescind

**rescisión** /rresθi'sion; rressi'sion/ f, annulment, abrogation

**rescoldo** /rres'koldo/ m, ember, cinder; scruple, qualm, doubt

**resentimiento** /rresenti'miento/ m, deterioration, impairment; annoyance, resentment

**resentirse** /rresen'tirse/ vr irr to deteriorate, be impaired; be hurt or offended. See **sentir**

**reseña** /rre'seɲa/ f, Mil. review; short description; review (of a book)

**reseñar** /rrese'ɲar/ vt Mil. to review; describe briefly, outline

**reserva** /rre'serβa/ f, store, stock; exception, qualification; reticence; restraint, moderation; (Eccl. Law.) reservation; (Mil. Naut.) reserve. **sin r.,** frankly, without reserve

**reservación** /rreserβa'θion; rreserβa'sion/ f, reservation; scruple

**reservado** /rreser'βaðo/ a reserved, reticent; prudent, moderate; kept, reserved. m, reserved compartment; private apartment, private garden, etc.

**reservar** /rreser'βar/ vt to keep, hold; postpone; reserve (rooms, etc.); exempt; keep secret; withhold (information); Eccl. reserve; —vr await a better opportunity; be cautious

**reservista** /rreser'βista/ a (Mil. Nav.) reserved. mf reservist

**resfriado** /rres'friaðo/ m, Med. cold, chill

**resfriar** /rres'friar/ vt to chill; Fig. cool, moderate; —vi grow cold; —vr catch a cold; Fig. cool off (of love, etc.)

**resguardar** /rresguar'ðar/ vt to protect; shelter; —vr

take refuge; (*with de*) guard against; (*with con*) shelter by

**resguardo** /rres'ɡuarðo/ *m,* protection, guard; *Com.* guarantee, security; *Com.* voucher; preservation; vigilance (to prevent smuggling, etc.); contraband guards

**residencia** /rresi'ðenθia; rresi'ðensia/ *f,* stay, residence; home, domicile; *Eccl.* residence

**residencial** /rresiðen'θial; rresiðen'sial/ *a* residential; resident, residentiary

**residente** /rresi'ðente/ *a* resident. *mf* inhabitant. *m,* resident, minister resident (diplomatic)

**residir** /rresi'ðir/ *vi* to live, inhabit; reside officially; be found, be, exist

**residuo** /rre'siðuo/ *m,* residuum, remainder; *Math.* remainder; *Chem.* residue

**resignación** /rresiɡna'θion; rresiɡna'sion/ *f,* resignation; fortitude, submission

**resignar** /rresiɡ'nar/ *vt* to resign, relinquish; —*vr* submit, resign oneself

**resina** /rre'sina/ *f,* resin

**resinoso** /rresi'noso/ *a* resinous

**resistencia** /rresis'tenθia; rresis'tensia/ *f,* resistance, opposition; endurance; (*Phys. Mech. Psychol.*) resistance

**resistente** /rresis'tente/ *a* resistant; tough; hardy (of plants)

**resistir** /rresis'tir/ *vi* to resist, oppose; reject; —*vt* endure, bear; resist; —*vr* fight, resist

**resma** /'rresma/ *f,* ream (of paper)

**resollar** /rreso'ʎar/ rreso'yar/ *vi irr* to breathe; pant. See **degollar**

**resolución** /rresolu'θion; rresolu'sion/ *f,* decision; boldness, daring; determination, resolution; decree

**resoluto** /rreso'luto/ *a* resolute, bold; brief, concise; able, expert

**resolver** /rresol'βer/ *vt irr* to determine, decide; summarize; solve; dissolve; analyze; (*Phys. Med.*) resolve; —*vr* decide, determine; be reduced to, become; *Med.* resolve —*Pres. Indic.* **resuelvo, resuelves, resuelve, resuelven.** *Past Part.* **resuelto.** *Pres. Subjunc.* **resuelva, resuelvas, resuelva, resuelvan**

**resonancia** /rreso'nanθia; rreso'nansia/ *f,* resonance, sonority, ring; fame, reputation

**resonante** /rreso'nante/ *a* resonant; resounding

**resonar** /rreso'nar/ *vi irr* to resound, echo. See **tronar**

**resoplido, resoplo** /rreso'pliðo, rre'soplo/ *m,* heavy breathing, pant, snort

**resorber** /rresor'βer/ *vt* to reabsorb

**resorción** /rresor'θion; rresor'sion/ *f,* reabsorption

**resorte** /rre'sorte/ *m, Mech.* spring; elasticity; *Fig.* means, instrument

**respaldo** /rres'paldo/ *m,* back (of chairs, etc.); reverse side (of a piece of paper)

**respectivo** /rrespek'tiβo/ *a* respective

**respecto** /rres'pekto/ *m,* relation, regard, reference. **con r. a,** *or* **r. a,** with regard to, with respect to, concerning

**respetabilidad** /rrespetaβili'ðað/ *f,* respectability; worthiness

**respetable** /rrespe'taβle/ *a* worthy of respect; respectable; *Fig.* considerable, large

**respetar** /rrespe'tar/ *vt* to respect, revere

**respeto** /rres'peto/ *m,* respect, honor; consideration, reason. **de r.,** spare, extra; special, ceremonial

**respetuoso** /rrespe'tuoso/ *a* venerable, worthy of honor; respectful, courteous

**respingar** /rrespiŋ'ɡar/ *vi* to flinch, wince, kick; *Inf.* be uneven, rise (hem of garments); *Inf.* do (a thing) grumblingly

**respingo** /rrespiŋ'ɡo/ *m,* wincing; jerk, shake; *Inf.* gesture of reluctance or dislike

**respirable** /rrespi'raβle/ *a* breathable

**respiración** /rrespira'θion; rrespira'sion/ *f,* breathing, respiration; ventilation

**respiradero** /rrespira'ðero/ *m,* ventilator; air hole, vent; rest, breathing space

**respirador** /rrespira'ðor/ *a* breathing; respiratory. *m,* respirator

**respirar** /rrespi'rar/ *vi* to breathe; exhale, give off; take courage; have a breathing space, rest; *Inf.* speak. **sin r.,** continuously, without stopping for breath

**respiratorio** /rrespira'torio/ *a* respiratory

**respiro** /rres'piro/ *m,* breathing; breathing space, respite

**resplandecer** /rresplande'θer; rresplande'ser/ *vi irr* to glitter, gleam; shine, excel. See **conocer**

**resplandeciente** /rresplande'θiente; rresplande'siente/ *a* glittering, resplendent, shining

**resplandor** /rresplan'dor/ *m,* radiance, brilliance; glitter, gleam; majesty, splendor

**responder** /rrespon'der/ *vt* to reply; satisfy, answer; —*vi* reecho; requite, return; produce, provide; *Fig.* answer, have the desired effect; *Com.* (*with de*) answer for, guarantee; *Com.* correspond

**respondón** /rrespon'don/ *a Inf.* pert, impudent, cheeky, given to answering back

**responsabilidad** /rresponsaβili'ðað/ *f,* responsibility

**responsable** /rrespon'saβle/ *a* responsible

**responso** /rres'ponso/ *m, Eccl.* response, responsory

**respuesta** /rres'puesta/ *f,* answer, reply; response; refutation; repartee

**resquebradura** /rreskeβra'ðura/ *f,* fissure, crevice, crack

**resquebrajarse** /rreskeβra'harse/ *vr* to crack, split

**resquemar** /rreske'mar/ *vt* to bite, sting (of hot dishes)

**resquicio** /rres'kiθio; rres'kisio/ *m,* crack, chink, slit; opportunity

**resta** /'rresta/ *f, Math.* subtraction; *Math.* remainder

**restablecer** /rrestaβle'θer; rrestaβle'ser/ *vt irr* to reestablish; restore; —*vr* recover one's health; reestablish oneself. See **conocer**

**restablecimiento** /rrestaβleθi'miento; rrestaβlesi'miento/ *m,* reestablishment; restoration

**restañar** /rresta'ɲar/ *vt* to re-tin; staunch

**restar** /rres'tar/ *vt Math.* to subtract; deduct; return (a ball); —*vi* remain. **No me resta más que decir adiós,** It only remains for me to say good-by

**restauración** /rrestaura'θion; rrestaura'sion/ *f,* restoration; renovation

**restaurador** /rrestaura'ðor/ **(-ra)** *a* restorative —*n* restorer

**restaurante** /rrestau'rante/ *m,* restaurant

**restaurantero** /rrestauran'tero/ *m,* restaurant operator; restaurant owner; restaurateur

**restaurar** /rrestau'rar/ *vt* to recover, recuperate; renovate, repair; restore

**restaurativo** /rrestaura'tiβo/ *a* and *m,* restorative

**restinga** /rres'tiŋɡa/ *f,* sandbank, bar

**restitución** /rrestitu'θion; rrestitu'sion/ *f,* restitution

**restituible** /rresti'tuiβle/ *a* returnable, replaceable

**restituir** /rresti'tuir/ *vt irr* to return, give back; restore; reestablish; —*vr* return to one's place of departure. See **huir**

**resto** /'rresto/ *m,* rest, balance; *Math.* remainder; *pl* remains

**restorán** /rresto'ran/ *m,* restaurant

**restricción** /rrestrik'θion; rrestrik'sion/ *f,* limitation, restriction

**restrictivo** /rrestrik'tiβo/ *a* restrictive; restraining

**restringir** /rrestriŋ'hir/ *vt* to limit, restrict; contract

**resucitar** /rresuθi'tar; rresusi'tar/ *vt* to raise from the dead; *Fig. Inf.* revive; —*vi* resuscitate

**resuello** /rre'sueʎo; rre'sueyo/ *m,* breathing; panting, hard breathing

**resuelto** /rre'suelto/ *a* audacious, daring; resolute, capable

**resulta** /rre'sulta/ *f,* consequence, result; decision, resolution; vacant post. **de resultas de,** as the result of; in consequence of

**resultado** /rresul'taðo/ *m,* result, consequence, outcome

**resultante** /rresul'tante/ *a* resulting. *f, Mech.* resultant

**resultar** /rresul'tar/ *vi* to result, follow; turn out, happen; result (in); *Inf.* turn out well. **El vestido no me resulta,** The dress isn't a success on me

**resumen** /rre'sumen/ *m,* summary. **en r.,** in short

**resumir** /rresu'mir/ *vt* to summarize, abridge; sum up, recapitulate; —*vr* be contained, be included

**resurgimiento** /rresurhi'miento/ *m,* resurgence, revival

**resurgir** /rresur'hir/ *vi* to reappear, rise again, revive; resuscitate
**resurrección** /rresurrek'θion; rresurrek'sion/ *f,* resurrection
**resurtir** /rresur'tir/ *vi* to rebound
**retablo** /rre'taβlo/ *m, Archit.* altarpiece, retable; frieze; series of pictures
**retaguardia** /rreta'guarðia/ *f,* rear guard. **a r.,** in the rear. **picar la r.,** to harass the rear guard
**retajar** /rreta'har/ *vt* to cut in the round; circumcise
**retal** /rre'tal/ *m,* clipping, filing, shaving; remnant
**retama** /rre'tama/ *f, Bot.* broom. **r. común** *or* **r. de olor,** Spanish broom. **r. de escobas,** common broom
**retar** /rre'tar/ *vt* to challenge; *Inf.* reproach, accuse
**retardación** /rretarða'θion; rretarða'sion/ *f,* retardment
**retardar** /rretar'ðar/ *vt* to retard, delay
**retardo** /rre'tarðo/ *m,* delay, retardment
**retazo** /rre'taθo; rre'taso/ *m,* remnant, cutting; excerpt, fragment
**retemblar** /rretem'βlar/ *vi* to quiver, tremble constantly
**retén** /rre'ten/ *m,* stock, reserve, provision; *Mil.* reserve
**retención** /rreten'θion; rreten'sion/ *f,* retention
**retener** /rrete'ner/ *vt irr* to keep, retain; recollect, remember; keep back; *Law.* detain; deduct. See **tener**
**retenidamente** /rreteniða'mente/ *adv* retentively
**retentiva** /rreten'tiβa/ *f,* retentiveness, memory
**retentivo** /rreten'tiβo/ *a* retentive
**reticencia** /rreti'θenθia; rreti'sensia/ *f,* reticence
**reticente** /rreti'θente; rreti'sente/ *a* reticent
**retículo** /rre'tikulo/ *m,* reticulum, network; *Phys.* reticle
**retina** /rre'tina/ *f,* retina
**retintín** /rretin'tin/ *m,* ringing; tinkling; *Inf.* sarcastic tone
**retiñir** /rreti'ɲir/ *vi* to tinkle, clink; jingle
**retirada** /rreti'raða/ *f,* withdrawal; retirement; seclusion, refuge; *Mil.* retreat
**retirado** /rreti'raðo/ *a* remote, secluded; *Mil.* retired
**retirar** /rreti'rar/ *vt* to withdraw; remove; repel, throw back; hide, put aside; —*vr* withdraw; retire; *Mil.* retreat
**retiro** /rre'tiro/ *m,* withdrawal; removal; seclusion, privacy; *Mil.* retreat; retirement; *Eccl.* retreat. **dar el r. ( a),** to place on the retired list
**reto** /'rreto/ *m,* challenge; threat
**retocar** /rreto'kar/ *vt* to touch again or repeatedly; *Photo.* retouch; restore (pictures); *Fig.* put the finishing touch to
**retoñar** /rreto'ɲar/ *vi* to sprout, shoot; *Fig.* revive, resuscitate
**retoño** /rre'toɲo/ *m,* sprout, shoot
**retoque** /rre'toke/ *m,* frequent touching; finishing touch; touch, slight attack
**retorcer** /rretor'θer; rretor'ser/ *vt irr* to twist; contort; confound with one's argument; misconstrue, distort; —*vr* contort; writhe. See **torcer**
**retórica** /rre'torika/ *f,* rhetoric; *pl Inf.* quibbling
**retórico** /rre'toriko/ **(-ca)** *a* rhetorical —*n* rhetorician
**retornar** /rretor'nar/ *vt* to return, give back; turn, twist; turn back; —*vi* and *vr* return, go back
**retorno** /rre'torno/ *m,* return, going back; recompense, repayment; exchange; return journey
**retorsión** /rretor'sion/ *f,* twisting, writhing; *Fig.* misconstruction
**retorta** /rre'torta/ *f, Chem.* retort
**retortijón** /rretorti'hon/ *m,* twisting, curling. **r. de tripas,** stomachache
**retozar** /rreto'θar; rreto'sar/ *vi* to skip, frisk, frolic, gambol; romp; *Fig.* be aroused (passions)
**retozón** /rreto'θon; rreto'son/ *a* frolicsome
**retracción** /rretrak'θion; rretrak'sion/ *f,* drawing back, retraction
**retractación** /rretrakta'θion; rretrakta'sion/ *f,* retractation, recantation
**retractar** /rretrak'tar/ *vt* to retract, recant, withdraw
**retráctil** /rre'traktil/ *a* retractile
**retraer** /rretra'er/ *vt irr* to bring back again; dissuade;

buy back, redeem; —*vr* take refuge; retire; withdraw; go into seclusion. See **traer**
**retraído** /rre'traiðo/ *a* fugitive, refugee; retired, solitary; timid, nervous, unsociable
**retraimiento** /rretrai'miento/ *m,* withdrawal; seclusion, privacy; refuge, asylum, sanctuary; timidity, unsociability
**retrasar** /rretra'sar/ *vt* to postpone, delay; turn back (the clock); —*vi* be slow (of clocks); —*vr* be behind time, be late; be backward (persons)
**retraso** /rre'traso/ *m,* lateness; delay, dilatoriness; loss of time (clocks); setting back (of the clock) (e.g. *El reloj lleva cinco minutos de r.,* The clock is five minutes slow)
**retratar** /rretra'tar/ *vt* to paint or draw the portrait of; portray, describe; photograph; copy, imitate
**retratista** /rretra'tista/ *mf* portrait painter; photographer; portrayer
**retrato** /rre'trato/ *m,* portrait; portrayal; *Fig.* image, likeness
**retrechería** /rretretʃe'ria/ *f, Inf.* craftiness, evasiveness
**retreta** /rre'treta/ *f, Mil.* retreat; tattoo
**retrete** /rre'trete/ *m,* toilet, water closet
**retribución** /rretriβu'θion; rretriβu'sion/ *f,* recompense, reward
**retribuir** /rretri'βuir/ *vt irr* to recompense, reward. See **huir**
**retroactivo** /rretroak'tiβo/ *a* retroactive
**retroceder** /rretroθe'ðer; rretrose'ðer/ *vi* to withdraw, move back, draw back; recede
**retroceso** /rretro'θeso; rretro'seso/ *m,* retrocedence, withdrawal; *Med.* retrogression
**retrogradación** /rretrograða'θion; rretrograða'sion/ *f,* retrogression
**retrógrado** /rretro'graðo/ *a* retrogressive, retrograde; *Polit.* reactionary
**retronar** /rretro'nar/ *vi irr* to bang, thunder, resound with noise. See **tronar**
**retrospección** /rretrospek'θion; rretrospek'sion/ *f,* retrospection
**retrospectivo** /rretrospek'tiβo/ *a* retrospective
**retrotraer** /rretrotra'er/ *vt irr* to antedate. See **traer**
**retruécano** /rre'truekano/ *m,* antithesis; play on words, pun
**retumbante** /rretum'βante/ *a* resounding; pompous, high-flown
**retumbar** /rretum'βar/ *vi* to resound, echo, reverberate; roll (of thunder); roar (of a cannon)
**retumbo** /rre'tumbo/ *m,* reverberation, echo; rumble; roll (of thunder); roar (of a cannon, etc.)
**reuma** /'rreuma/ *m,* rheumatism
**reumático** /rreu'matiko/ *a* rheumatic
**reumatismo** /rreuma'tismo/ *m,* rheumatism
**reunión** /rreu'nion/ *f,* reunion, union; meeting; assembly, gathering
**reunir** /rreu'nir/ *vt* to reunite; unite; join; gather, assemble; —*vr* meet, assemble; unite
**revacunación** /rreβakuna'θion; rreβakuna'sion/ *f,* revaccination
**revacunar** /rreβaku'nar/ *vt* to revaccinate
**revalidación** /rreβaliða'θion; rreβaliðasion/ *f,* ratification, confirmation
**revalidar** /rreβali'ðar/ *vt* to ratify, confirm; —*vr* pass a final examination
**revejido** /rreβe'hiðo/ *a* prematurely old
**revelación** /rreβela'θion; rreβela'sion/ *f,* revelation; *Photo.* developing
**revelador** /rreβela'ðor/ *a* revealing. *m, Photo.* developer
**revelar** /rreβe'lar/ *vt* to reveal; *Photo.* develop
**revendedor** /rreβende'ðor/ **(-ra)** *a* reselling, retail —*n* retailer
**revender** /rreβen'der/ *vt* to resell; retail (goods)
**reventa** /rre'βenta/ *f,* resale; retail
**reventar** /rreβen'tar/ *vi irr* to burst, explode; break in foam (waves); burst forth; *Fig.* burst (with impatience, etc.); *Inf.* explode (with anger, etc.); —*vt* break, crush; *Fig.* wear out, exhaust; *Inf.* irritate, vex; —*vr* burst; *Fig.* be exhausted. See **sentar**
**reventón** /rreβen'ton/ *a* bursting. *m,* explosion,

bursting; steep hill; hole, fix, difficulty; uphill work, heavy toil

**rever** /rre'βer/ *vt irr* to look at again, revise; *Law.* retry. See **ver**

**reverberación** /rreβerβera'θion; rreβerβera'sion/ *f*, reflection (of light); reverberation, resounding

**reverberar** /rreβerβe'rar/ *vi* to reflect; resound, reverberate

**reverbero** /rreβer'βero/ *m*, reverberation; reflector

**reverdecer** /rreβerðe'θer; rreβerðe'ser/ *vi irr* to grow green again; revive, acquire new vigor. See **conocer**

**reverencia** /rreβeren'θia; rreβeren'sia/ *f*, respect, veneration; bow; curtsy; *Eccl.* reverence (title)

**reverencial** /rreβeren'θial; rreβeren'sial/ *a* reverential, respectful

**reverenciar** /rreβeren'θiar; rreβeren'siar/ *vt* to revere; honor; respect

**reverendo** /rreβe'rendo/ *a* reverend; venerable; *Inf.* overprudent

**reversibilidad** /rreβersiβili'ðað/ *f*, reversibility

**reversión** /rreβer'sion/ *f*, reversion

**reverso** /rre'βerso/ *m*, wrong side, back; reverse side (of coins)

**reverter** /rreβer'ter/ *vi irr* to overflow. See **entender**

**revertir** /rreβer'tir/ *vi Law.* to revert

**revés** /rre'βes/ *m*, wrong side, back, reverse; cuff, slap; backhand (in ballgames); check, setback, reverse; disaster, misfortune. **al r.,** on the contrary; wrong side out. **de r.,** from left to right, counterclockwise

**revesado** /rreβe'saðo/ *a* complicated, difficult; willful

**revestimiento** /rreβesti'miento/ *m*, *Mas.* lining, coating

**revestir** /rreβes'tir/ *vt irr* to dress; *Mas.* coat, line; *Fig.* cover, clothe; —*vr* be dressed or dress oneself; *Fig.* be captivated (by an idea); become haughty or full of oneself; rise to the occasion, develop qualities necessary. See **pedir**

**reviejo** /rre'βieho/ *a* very old. *m,* dead branch (of trees)

**revisar** /rreβi'sar/ *vt* to revise; examine

**revisión** /rreβi'sion/ *f*, revision; reexamination; *Law.* retrial

**revisor** /rreβi'sor/ *a* revising, examining. *m,* reviser; ticket inspector

**revista** /rre'βista/ *f*, reexamination, revision; review, periodical; *Theat.* revue; reinspection; review (of a book, etc.); *Law.* new trial; *Mil.* review. **pasar r.,** to inspect; review

**revistero** /rreβis'tero/ **(-ra)** *n* reviewer, writer of reviews

**revivificación** /rreβiβifika'θion; rreβiβifika'sion/ *f*, revivification

**revivificar** /rreβiβifi'kar/ *vt* to revivify, revive

**revivir** /rreβi'βir/ *vi* to resuscitate; revive

**revocación** /rreβoka'θion; rreβoka'sion/ *f*, revocation, cancellation, annulment

**revocar** /rreβo'kar/ *vt* to revoke, annul; dissuade; repel, throw back; wash (walls); *Law.* discharge

**revolcadero** /rreβolka'ðero/ *m,* bathing place (of animals)

**revolcar** /rreβol'kar/ *vt irr* to knock down, trample underfoot; lay flat (in an argument); —*vr* wallow; dig one's heels in, be obstinate. See **volcar**

**revolotear** /rreβolote'ar/ *vi* to flutter, fly around; twirl; —*vt* hurl, toss

**revoltillo** /rreβol'tiλo; rreβol'tiyo/ *m,* jumble, hodgepodge; confusion, tangle

**revoltoso** /rreβol'toso/ *a* rebellious; mischievous, willful; intricate

**revolución** /rreβolu'θion; rreβolu'sion/ *f*, turn, revolution; rebellion, uprising; revolution

**revolucionar** /rreβoluθio'nar; rreβolusio'nar/ *vt* to revolutionize

**revolucionario** /rreβoluθio'nario; rreβolusio'nario/ **(-ia)** *a* and *n* revolutionary

**revolver** /rreβol'βer/ *vt irr* to turn over; turn upside down; wrap up; revolve; stir; reflect upon, consider; upset, cause disharmony; search through, disorder (papers, etc.); —*vr* move from side to side; change (in the weather). See **resolver**

**revólver** /rre'βolβer/ *m,* revolver

**revoque** /rre'βoke/ *m, Mas.* washing, whitewash; plastering

**revuelco** /rre'βuelko/ *m,* wallowing

**revuelo** /rre'βuelo/ *m,* second flight (of birds); irregular course of flight; disturbance, upset

**revuelta** /rre'βuelta/ *f*, second turn or revolution; revolt, rebellion; quarrel, fight; turning point; change of direction, turn; change (of opinions, posts, etc.)

**revueltamente** /rreβuelta'mente/ *adv* in confusion, higgledy-piggledy

**revulsión** /rreβul'sion/ *f*, revulsion

**rexaminación** /rreksamina'θion; rreksamina'sion/ *f*, reexamination

**rexaminar** /rreksami'nar/ *vt* to reexamine

**rexpedir** /rrekspe'ðir/ *vt* to forward, send on

**rexportación** /rreksporta'θion; rreksporta'sion/ *f*, reexport

**rexportar** /rrekspor'tar/ *vt Com.* to reexport

**rey** /rrei/ *m,* king (in cards, chess); queen bee; *Inf.* swineherd; *Fig.* king, chief. *Herald.* **r. de armas,** king-of-arms. **reyes magos,** magi. **día de Reyes,** Twelfth Night. **servir al r.,** to fight for the king

**reyerta** /rre'yerta/ *f*, quarrel, row, rumpus

**reyezuelo** /rreye'θuelo; rreye'suelo/ *m,* kinglet, petty king; golden-crested wren

**rezagar** /rreθa'gar; rresa'gar/ *vt* to leave behind; postpone, delay; —*vr* lag behind, straggle

**rezar** /rre'θar; rre'sar/ *vt* to pray, say prayers; say mass; *Inf.* state, say; —*vi* pray; *Inf.* fume, grumble. **El edicto reza así,** The edict runs like this, The edict reads like this

**rezo** /'rreθo; 'rreso/ *m,* prayer; devotions

**rezongar** /rreθoŋ'gar; rresoŋ'gar/ *vi* to grouse, grumble

**rezumar** /rreθu'mar; rresu'mar/ **(se)** *vr* and *vi* to percolate, ooze through; *Inf.* leak out, be known

**ría** /'rria/ *f*, estuary, river mouth, firth

**riachuelo** /rria'tʃuelo/ *m,* rivulet, stream

**riada** /'rriaða/ *f*, flood. *Aer.* **r. de acero,** rain of flak

**ribaldería** /rriβalde'ria/ *f*, ribaldry

**ribaldo** /rri'βaldo/ *a* ribald. *m,* knave

**ribazo** /rri'βaθo; rri'βaso/ *m,* slope, incline

**ribera** /rri'βera/ *f*, bank, margin, shore, strand

**ribereño** /rriβe'reno/ **(-ña)** *a* and *n* riparian

**ribero** /rri'βero/ *m,* embankment, wall

**ribete** /rri'βete/ *m,* binding, border, trimming; stripe; increase, addition; dramatic touch, exaggeration; *pl* indications, signs

**ribetear** /rriβete'ar/ *vt Sew.* to bind, trim, edge

**ricacho** /rri'katʃo/ **(-cha)** *n Inf.* newly rich person, nouveau riche

**ricahembra** /rrika'embra/ *f*, lady; daughter or wife of a Spanish noble *Obs.*

**ricamente** /rrika'mente/ *adv* richly, opulently; beautifully, splendidly; luxuriously

**ricino** /rri'θino; rri'sino/ *m,* castor oil plant

**rico** /'rriko/ *a* wealthy, rich; abundant; magnificent, splendid; delicious. **r. como Creso,** rich as Croesus

**ricohombre** /rriko'ombre/ *m,* nobleman *Obs.*

**ricura** /rri'kura/ *f*, *Inf.* richness, wealth

**ridiculez** /rriðiku'leθ; rriðiku'les/ *f*, absurd action or remark; ridiculousness; affectation; folly

**ridiculizar** /rriðikuli'θar; rriðikuli'sar/ *vt* to ridicule, poke fun at

**ridículo** /rri'ðikulo/ *a* ridiculous, absurd; grotesque; preposterous, outrageous. *m,* reticule

**riego** /'rriego/ *m,* watering, spraying; irrigation

**riel** /'rriel/ *m,* ingot; rail (of a train or streetcar)

**rielar** /rrie'lar/ *vi* to glimmer, glisten; glitter; shimmer

**rienda** /'rrienda/ *f*, rein (gen. *pl*); restraint; *pl* administration, government. **a r. suelta,** swiftly; without restraint

**riesgo** /'rriesgo/ *m,* risk, danger

**rifa** /'rrifa/ *f*, raffle; quarrel, disagreement

**rifar** /rri'far/ *vt* to raffle; —*vi* quarrel, fall out

**rifle** /'rrifle/ *m,* rifle

**rigidez** /rrihi'ðeθ; rrihi'ðes/ *f*, stiffness; rigidity; harshness

**rígido** /'rrihiðo/ *a* stiff; rigid; inflexible; severe, harsh

**rigodón** /rrigo'ðon/ *m,* rigadoon

**rigor** /rri'gor/ *m*, severity, sternness; rigor; hardness; inflexibility; *Med.* rigor. **en r.**, strictly speaking. **ser de r.**, to be essential, be indispensable

**rigorista** /rrigo'rista/ *mf* martinet

**riguroso** /rrigu'roso/ *a* rigorous; harsh, cruel; austere, rigid; strict, exact, scrupulous

**rijoso** /rri'hoso/ *a* quarrelsome; lascivious

**riksha** /'rriksa/ *m*, rickshaw

**rima** /'rrima/ *f*, rhyme, rime; heap; *pl* lyrics

**rimador** /rrima'ðor/ **(-ra)** *a* rhyming, rimer —*n* rhymer, rimer

**rimar** /rri'mar/ *vi* to compose verses; —*vi* and *vt* rhyme, rime

**rimbombo** /rrim'βombo/ *m*, reverberation (of a sound)

**rimero** /rri'mero/ *m*, heap, pile

**Rin, el** /rrin, el/ the Rhine

**rincón** /rrin'kon/ *m*, corner, angle; retreat, hiding place; *Inf.* home, nest, nook

**rinconada** /rrinko'naða/ *f*, corner, angle

**rinconera** /rrinko'nera/ *f*, corner cupboard; corner table

**ringlera** /rriŋ'glera/ *f*, file, line, row

**ringlero** /rriŋ'glero/ *m*, guiding line for writing

**ringorrangos** /'rriŋgo'rraŋgos/ *m pl*, *Inf.* exaggerated flourishes in writing; *Inf.* unnecessary frills or ornaments

**rinoceronte** /rrinoθe'ronte; rrinose'ronte/ *m*, rhinoceros

**riñón** /rri'ɲon/ *m*, kidney; *Fig.* center, heart; *pl Anat.* back

**río** /'rrio/ *m*, river; *Fig.* stream, flood

**rioja** /rrioha/ *m*, red wine from Rioja

**ripio** /'rripio/ *m*, remains, rest; debris, rubbish; *Lit.* padding; verbiage, prolixity. **no perder r.**, to lose no occasion or opportunity

**riqueza** /rri'keθa; rri'kesa/ *f*, riches, wealth; abundance; richness, magnificence

**risa** /'rrisa/ *f*, laugh; laughter; cause of amusement, joke

**risco** /'rrisko/ *m*, crag

**riscoso** /rris'koso/ *a* craggy

**risible** /rri'siβle/ *a* laughable

**risoles** /rri'soles/ *m pl*, rissoles

**risotada** /rriso'taða/ *f*, loud laugh

**ristra** /'rristra/ *f*, string (of onions, etc.); file, line, row

**risueño** /rri'sueɲo/ *a* smiling; cheerful; pleasant, agreeable; favorable, hopeful

**rítmico** /'rritmiko/ *a* rhythmic

**ritmo** /'rritmo/ *m*, rhythm

**rito** /'rrito/ *m*, rite

**ritualismo** /rritua'lismo/ *m*, ritualism

**ritualista** /rritua'lista/ *mf* ritualist

**rivalidad** /rriβali'ðað/ *f*, rivalry, competition; hostility

**rivalizar** /rriβali'θar; rriβali'sar/ *vi* to compete, rival

**rizado** /rri'θaðo; rri'saðo/ *m*, curling; pleating, crimping; rippling, ruffling

**rizar** /rri'θar; rri'sar/ *vt* to curl (hair); ripple, ruffle (of water); pleat, crimp; —*vr* be naturally wavy (of hair)

**rizo** /'rriθo; 'rriso/ *m*, curl, ringlet; cut velvet. *Aer.* **hacer el r.**, to loop the loop; *Naut.* to take in reefs

**rizoso** /rri'θoso; rri'soso/ *a* naturally curly or wavy (hair)

**ro, ro** /rro, rro/ *m*, hushaby!

**roano** /rro'ano/ *a* roan (of horses)

**robador** /rroβa'ðor/ **(-ra)** *a* robbing —*n* robber, thief. *m*, abductor

**robar** /rro'βar/ *vt* to rob; abduct; wash away, eat away (rivers, sea); remove honey from the hive; draw (in cards, dominoes); *Fig.* capture (love, etc.)

**roblar** /rro'βlar/ *vt* to reinforce, strengthen; clinch

**roble** /'rroβle/ *m*, oak tree; oak; *Fig.* bulwark, tower of strength

**robledo** /rro'βleðo/ *m*, oak grove

**roblón** /rro'βlon/ *m*, rivet

**robo** /'rroβo/ *m*, theft, robbery; booty

**robustecer** /rroβuste'θer; rroβuste'ser/ *vt irr* to strengthen. See **conocer**

**robustez** /rroβus'teθ; rroβus'tes/ *f*, strength, robustness

**robusto** /rro'βusto/ *a* vigorous, robust, hearty, strong

**roca** /'rroka/ *f*, rock; *Fig.* tower of strength

**roce** /'rroθe; 'rrose/ *m*, rubbing, brushing, touching, friction; social intercourse

**rociada** /rro'θiaða; rro'siaða/ *f*, dewing; sprinkling; dew-wet grass given as medicine to horses and mules; *Fig.* shower; general slander; harsh rebuke

**rociar** /rro'θiar; rro'siar/ *vi* to fall as dew; drizzle; —*vt* sprinkle, spray; *Fig.* shower (with)

**rocín** /rro'θin; rro'sin/ *m*, sorry nag; hack; *Inf.* ignoramus, boor

**rocinante** /rroθi'nante; rrosi'nante/ *m*, poor nag (alluding to Don Quixote's horse)

**rocío** /'rroθio; 'rrosio/ *m*, dew; dewdrop; drizzle, light shower; *Fig.* sprinkling, spray

**rocoso** /rro'koso/ *a* rocky

**rodaballo** /rroða'βaʎo; rroða'βayo/ *m*, turbot; *Inf.* crafty man

**rodada** /rro'ðaða/ *f*, wheel mark or track

**rodado** /rro'ðaðo/ *a* dappled (of horses)

**rodaje** /rro'ðahe/ *m*, wheeling; shooting (of a film)

**rodante** /rro'ðante/ *a* rolling

**rodar** /rro'ðar/ *vi* to roll; revolve, turn; run on wheels; wander, roam; be moved about; be plentiful, abound; happen successively; *(with por)* fall down, roll down

**Rodas** /'rroðas/ Rhodes

**rodear** /rroðe'ar/ *vi* to walk around; go by a roundabout way; *Fig.* beat around the bush; —*vt* encircle, surround; besiege; *West Hem.* round up (cattle)

**rodela** /rro'ðela/ *f*, round shield; buckler

**rodeno** /rro'ðeno/ *a* red (of rocks, earth, etc.)

**rodeo** /rro'ðeo/ *m*, encirclement; indirect and longer way; trick to evade pursuit; *West Hem.* rodeo, roundup; stockyard, cattle enclosure; *Fig.* beating around the bush; evasive reply

**rodera** /rro'ðera/ *f*, rail, track, line; cart rut or track

**Rodesia** /rro'ðesia/ Rhodesia

**rodilla** /rro'ðiʎa; rro'ðiya/ *f*, knee; floor cloth. **de rodillas**, on one's knees. **ponerse de rodillas,** *or* **hincar las rodillas,** to kneel down

**rodillazo** /rroði'ʎaθo; rroði'yaso/ *m*, push with the knee

**rodillera** /rroði'ʎera; rroði'yera/ *f*, kneecap, kneepad; mend at the knee of garments; bagginess of trouser knees

**rodillo** /rro'ðiʎo; rro'ðiyo/ *m*, roller; traction engine; *Print.* inking roller; garden roller. **r. de pastas,** *Cul.* rolling pin

**rododendro** /rroðo'ðendro/ *m*, rhododendron

**rodrigón** /rroðri'gon/ *m*, stake, prop (for plants); *Inf.* old retainer who serves as a ladies' escort

**roedor** /rroe'ðor/ *a* gnawing; *Fig.* nagging; biting —*a* and *m*, rodent

**roedura** /rroe'ðura/ *f*, biting, gnawing; corrosion

**roer** /rro'er/ *vt irr* to gnaw, nibble, eat; corrode, wear away; trouble, afflict —*Pres. Indic.* **roigo, roes,** etc —*Preterite* **royó, royeron.** *Imperf. Subjunc.* **royese,** etc.

**rogación** /rroga'θion; rroga'sion/ *f*, request, supplication, entreaty; *Eccl.* rogation

**rogador** /rroga'ðor/ **(-ra)** *a* requesting; beseeching —*n* suppliant

**rogar** /rro'gar/ *vt irr* to request; beseech, beg. See **contar**

**rogativo** /rroga'tiβo/ *a* supplicatory, petitioning

**roído** /rroi'ðo/ *a* gnawed, eaten; *Inf.* miserable, stingy

**rojal** /rro'hal/ *a* red (of soil, etc.). *m*, red earth

**rojear** /rrohe'ar/ *vi* to appear red; be reddish

**rojete** /rro'hete/ *m*, rouge

**rojez** /rro'heθ; rro'hes/ *f ʹ*, redness

**rojizo** /rro'hiθo; rro'hiso/ *a* reddish

**rojo** /'rroho/ *a* red; fair; red-gold (of hair); *Polit.* radical, red

**rol** /rrol/ *m*, roll, list

**roldana** /rrol'dana/ *f*, pulley wheel

**rollizo** /rro'ʎiθo; rro'yiso/ *a* round; plump, sturdy. *m*, log

**rollo** /'rroʎo; 'rroyo/ *m*, roll; *Cul.* rolling pin; log;

town cross or pillar; anything rolled (paper, etc.); twist (of tobacco)

**Roma** /'rroma/ Rome

**romance** /rro'manθe; rro'manse/ *a* and *m*, romance (language). *m*, Spanish; ballad; romance of chivalry; *pl Fig.* fairy tales, excuses. **en buen r.,** *Fig.* in plain words

**romancear** /rromanθe'ar; rromanse'ar/ *vt* to translate from Latin into the spoken language; translate into Spanish; paraphrase the Spanish to assist translation

**romancero** /rroman'θero; rroman'sero/ **(-ra)** *n* balladeer. *m,* collection of ballads

**romancista** /rroman'θista; rroman'sista/ *mf* romancist

**románico** /rro'maniko/ *a Archit.* Romanesque

**romanista** /rroma'nista/ *mf* expert in Roman law or Romance languages and literature

**romanizar** /rromani'θar; rromani'sar/ *vt* to romanize; —*vr* become romanized

**romano** /rro'mano/ **(-na)** *a* and *n* Roman. **a la romana,** in the Roman way. **cabello a la romana,** *Inf.* bobbed hair

**romanticismo** /rromanti'θismo; rromanti'sismo/ *m,* romanticism

**romántico** /rro'mantiko/ **(-ca)** *a* romantic; emotional; fanciful —*n* romantic; romanticist

**rombo** /'rrombo/ *m,* rhombus

**romería** /rrome'ria/ *f,* pilgrimage; excursion, picnic (made on a saint's day)

**romero** /rro'mero/ **(-ra)** *m,* rosemary —*n* pilgrim

**romo** /'rromo/ *a* blunt, dull, unsharpened; flat (of noses)

**rompecabezas** /rrompeka'βeθas; rrompeka'βesas/ *m,* bludgeon; knuckleduster; *Inf.* teaser, puzzle, riddle; jigsaw puzzle

**rompeimágenes** /rrompei'mahenes/ *mf* iconoclast

**rompeolas** /rrompe'olas/ *m,* jetty, breakwater

**romper** /rrom'per/ *vt* to break; shatter, break into fragments; spoil, ruin; break up, plow; *Fig.* cut, divide (of water, etc.); *Fig.* end, break; interrupt; infringe, break; —*vi* break; break (of waves); sprout, flower; (*with prep a*) begin to. **Rompió a hablar,** He broke into speech —*Past Part.* **roto**

**rompiente** /rrom'piente/ *a* breaking. *m,* reef, shoal

**rompimiento** /rrompi'miento/ *m,* break, rupture; crack, split; breakage; infringement; plowing up; *Fig.* dividing (water, etc.); spoiling, ruining; opening (of buds, etc.)

**ron** /rron/ *m,* rum

**roncar** /rron'kar/ *vi* to snore; *Fig.* roar, howl (of the sea, wind, etc.); *Inf.* brag

**roncear** /rronθe'ar; rronse'ar/ *vi* to be dilatory or unwilling; *Inf.* flatter, cajole; *Naut.* lag behind, sail slowly

**roncero** /rron'θero; rron'sero/ *a* dilatory, slow; grumbling, complaining; cajoling, flattering

**roncha** /'rrontʃa/ *f,* wheal; bruise, bump; *Inf.* money lost through trickery; thin, round slice

**ronco** /'rronko/ *a* hoarse, husky

**ronda** /'rronda/ *f,* round, beat, patrol; serenading party; *Inf.* round (of drinks)

**rondador** /rronda'ðor/ *m,* watchman; roundsman; serenader; night wanderer

**rondalla** /rron'daʎa; rron'daya/ *f,* tale, fairy tale

**rondar** /rron'dar/ *vi* to patrol, police; walk the streets by night; serenade; —*vt* haunt; hover about; *Inf.* overcome (of sleep, etc.)

**rondó** /rron'do/ *m,* rondo

**ronquear** /rronke'ar/ *vi* to be hoarse

**ronquera** /rron'kera/ *f,* hoarseness

**ronquido** /rron'kiðo/ *m,* snore; hoarse sound

**ronronear** /rronrone'ar/ *vi* to purr (of cats)

**ronzal** /rron'θal; rron'sal/ *m,* halter

**ronzar** /rron'θar; rron'sar/ *vt* to munch, crack with the teeth

**roña** /'rroɲa/ *f,* mange (in sheep); grime, filth; mold; moral corruption; *Inf.* stinginess; *Inf.* trick, deception

**roñería** /rroɲe'ria/ *f, Inf.* meanness, stinginess

**roñoso** /rro'ɲoso/ *a* scabby; filthy; rusty; *Inf.* mean, stingy

**ropa** /'rropa/ *f,* fabric, material, stuff; clothes, wearing apparel; garment, outfit; robe (of office). **r. blanca,** underclothes; (domestic) linen. **r. hecha,** ready-made clothing. **r. talar,** long gown; cassock

**ropaje** /rro'pahe/ *m,* clothes, garments; vestments; drapery; *Fig.* form, outline

**ropavejería** /rropaβehe'ria/ *f,* old-clothes shop

**ropavejero** /rropaβe'hero/ **(-ra)** *n* old-clothes dealer

**ropería** /rrope'ria/ *f,* clothier's shop or trade; wardrobe; cloakroom

**ropero** /rro'pero/ **(-ra)** *n* clothier; keeper of the wardrobe. *m,* wardrobe; charitable organization

**ropilla** /rro'piʎa; rro'piya/ *f,* doublet

**ropón** /rro'pon/ *m,* a loose-fitting gown generally worn over clothes

**roque** /'rroke/ *m,* rook (in chess)

**roqueño** /rro'keɲo/ *a* rocky; hard as rock

**roquete** /rro'kete/ *m, Eccl.* rochet; barb of a lance

**rorro** /'rrorro/ *m, Inf.* infant, baby

**rosa** /'rrosa/ *f,* rose; anything rose-shaped; artificial rose; red spot on the body; *Archit.* rose window; *pl* rosettes. *m,* rose color. **r. de los vientos,** mariner's compass. **r. laurel,** oleander

**rosado** /rro'saðo/ *a* rose-colored; rose; rosé (wines)

**rosal** /rro'sal/ *m,* rose tree. **r. de tallo,** standard rose tree

**rosaleda, rosalera** /rrosa'leða, rrosa'lera/ *f,* rose garden

**rosario** /rro'sario/ *m,* rosary; *Fig.* string; chain pump; *Inf.* backbone

**rosbif** /rros'βif/ *m,* roast beef

**rosca** /'rroska/ *f,* screw and nut; *Cul.* twist (of bread or cake); spiral

**roscado** /rros'kaðo/ *a* twisted, spiral

**rosear** /rrose'ar/ *vi* to turn to rose, become rosecolored

**Rosellón** /rrose'ʎon; rrose'yon/ Rousillon

**róseo** /'rroseo/ *a* rose-colored

**roseta** /rro'seta/ *f, dim* small rose; rosette; rose of a watering can; rosette copper; *pl* toasted maize. **r. de fiebre,** rush of fever

**rosetón** /rrose'ton/ *m,* large rosette; *Archit.* rose window

**rosicler** /rrosi'kler/ *m,* rose-pink (first flush of dawn)

**rosillo** /rro'siʎo; rro'siyo/ *a* light red; roan (of horses)

**rosmaro** /rros'maro/ *m,* manatee, sea cow

**roso** /'rroso/ *a* bald, worn; red

**rosquilla** /rros'kiʎa; rros'kiya/ *f,* ring-shaped cake

**rosquillero** /rroski'ʎero; rroski'yero/ **(-ra)** *n* seller of rosquillas

**rostrituerto** /rrostri'tuerto/ *a Inf.* wry-faced (from sadness or anger)

**rostro** /'rrostro/ *m,* bird's beak; face, visage. **conocer de r.,** to know by sight. **dar en r.,** *Fig.* to throw in one's face

**rota** /'rrota/ *f, Mil.* defeat; *Eccl.* Rota; *Bot.* rattan

**rotación** /rrota'θion; rrota'sion/ *f,* rotation. **r. de cultivos,** rotation of crops

**rotativa** /rrota'tiβa/ *f,* rotary printing press

**rotativo** /rrota'tiβo/ *a* rotary

**rotatorio** /rrota'torio/ *a* rotatory

**roto** /'rroto/ *a* shabby, ragged; vicious, debauched

**rotograbado** /rrotogra'βaðo/ *m,* rotogravure

**rotonda** /rro'tonda/ *f,* rotunda

**rótula** /'rrotula/ *f,* rotula, patella

**rotular** /rrotu'lar/ *vt* to label; give a title or heading to

**rótulo** /'rrotulo/ *m,* title; poster, placard; label

**rotundamente** /rrotunda'mente/ *adv* tersely, roundly, plainly

**rotundidad** /rrotundi'ðað/ *f,* rotundity; roundness; finality (of words, etc.)

**rotundo** /rro'tundo/ *a* round; rotund; sonorous; final, plain (of words, etc.)

**rotura** /rro'tura/ *f,* breaking, shattering; plowing up; breakage; rupture

**roturar** /rrotu'rar/ *vt Agr.* to break up, plow up

**roya** /'rroya/ *f,* rust, mildew; tobacco

**roza** /'rroθa; 'rrosa/ *f, Agr.* clearing (of weeds, etc.);

ground ready for sowing. **de r. abierta,** open cast (of mining)

**rozadura** /rroθa'ðura; rrosa'ðura/ *f,* rubbing, friction; abrasion, chafing

**rozagante** /rroθa'gante; rrosa'gante/ *a* long and elaborate (dresses); upstanding; handsome; strapping, fine

**rozamiento** /rroθa'miento; rrosa'miento/ *m,* grazing, brushing, rubbing; discord, disharmony, disagreement; *Mech.* friction

**rozar** /rro'θar; rro'sar/ *vt Agr.* to clear of weeds; crop, nibble; scrape; brush against, touch; —*vi* brush, rub, touch; —*vr* have dealings with, know; stammer; be like, resemble

**rúa** /'rrua/ *f,* village street; highway

**ruar** /rru'ar/ *vi* to walk or ride through the streets; parade through the streets flirting with the ladies

**rubeola** /rruβe'ola/ *f,* rubella

**rubí** /rru'βi/ *m,* ruby; jewel (of a watch)

**rubia** /'rruβia/ *f, Bot.* madder; blonde (girl, woman)

**rubicundez** /rruβikun'deθ; rruβikun'des/ *f,* rubicundity, ruddiness, redness

**rubicundo** /rruβi'kundo/ *a* red-gold; ruddy-complexioned; reddish

**rubio** /'rruβio/ *a* red-gold, gold; fair, blond

**rublo** /'rruβlo/ *m,* ruble

**rubor** /rru'βor/ *m,* blush, flush; bashfulness

**ruborizarse** /rruβori'θarse; rruβori'sarse/ *vr* to blush; be shamefaced

**ruboroso** /rruβo'roso/ *a* shamefaced; blushing

**rúbrica** /'rruβrika/ *f,* rubric; personal mark, flourish added to one's signature

**rubricar** /rruβri'kar/ *vt* to sign and seal; sign with an X or other symbol; sign with a flourish

**rubro** /'rruβro/ *a* red

**rucio** /'rruθio; 'rrusio/ *a* fawn, light-gray (of animals); *Inf.* going gray, gray-haired

**rudamente** /rruða'mente/ *adv* rudely, abruptly, churlishly; roughly

**rudeza** /rru'ðeθa; rru'ðesa/ *f,* roughness; rudeness, uncouthness; stupidity

**rudimentario** /rruðimen'tario/ *a* rudimentary

**rudimento** /rruði'mento/ *m,* embryo; *pl* rudiments

**rudo** /'rruðo/ *a* rough; unfinished; uncouth, boorish, rude; stupid

**rueca** /'rrueka/ *f,* distaff (in spinning); spinning wheel; curve, twist

**rueda** /'rrueða/ *f,* wheel; group, circle; spread of a peacock's tail; roller, castor; round piece or slice; turn, chance; succession (of events); wheel (used for torture). **r. libre,** freewheeling. *Inf.* **hacer la r.** (**a**), to flatter, make a fuss of

**ruedero** /rrue'ðero/ *m,* wheelwright

**ruedo** /'rrueðo/ *m,* turning, rotation; circumference; lined hem of a cassock; circuit

**ruego** /'rruego/ *m,* request, entreaty

**rufián** /rru'fian/ *m,* ruffian; pimp

**rufianesco** /rrufia'nesko/ *a* ruffianly

**rufo** /'rrufo/ *a* fair; red-haired; curly-haired

**rugido** /rru'hiðo/ *m,* roaring, roar; creaking; gnashing; rumbling

**rugir** /rru'hir/ *vi* to roar; squeak, creak; gnash (the teeth)

**ruibarbo** /rrui'βarβo/ *m,* rhubarb

**ruido** /'rruiðo/ *m,* noise, din; disturbance; rumor. **hacer** ( *or* **meter**) **r.,** to cause a sensation. *Inf.* **ser más el r. que las nueces,** to be much ado about nothing

**ruidoso** /rrui'ðoso/ *a* noisy; notable

**ruin** /rru'in/ *a* base, vile; despicable; mean; puny

**ruina** /'rruina/ *f,* ruin, downfall; financial ruin; fall, decline; *pl* ruins

**ruinar** /rrui'nar/ *vt* to ruin

**ruindad** /rruin'dað/ *f,* baseness; meanness; pettiness, unworthiness; mean trick, despicable action

**ruinoso** /rrui'noso/ *a* half-ruined; ruinous; useless, worthless

**ruiseñor** /rruise'ɲor/ *m,* nightingale

**ruleta** /rru'leta/ *f,* roulette

**rumano** /rru'mano/ **(-na)** *a* and *n* Romanian. *m,* Romanian (language)

**rumbo** /'rrumbo/ *m, Naut.* course, way, route; direction; *Inf.* swank. **con r. a,** headed for, in the direction of. **hacer r. a,** to sail for; make for

**rumboso** /rrum'βoso/ *a Inf.* pompous, dignified; open-handed, generous

**rumia** /'rrumia/ *f,* rumination; cud

**rumiante** /rru'miante/ *a* and *mf Zool.* ruminant —*a Inf.* reflective, meditative

**rumiar** /rru'miar/ *vt Zool.* to ruminate; *Inf.* reflect upon, chew on; *Inf.* fume, rage

**rumor** /rru'mor/ *m,* noise; rumor; murmur, babble; dull sound

**runa** /'rruna/ *f,* rune

**rúnico** /'rruniko/ *a* runic

**runrunearse** /rrunrune'arse/ *v impers* to be rumored

**rupia** /'rrupia/ *f,* rupee

**ruptura** /rrup'tura/ *f, Fig.* rupture; *Surg.* hernia

**rural** /rru'ral/ *a* rustic, rural

**ruralmente** /rrural'mente/ *adv* rurally

**Rusia** /'rrusia/ Russia

**rusificar** /rrusifi'kar/ *vt* to russianize

**ruso** /'rruso/ **(-sa)** *a* and *n* Russian. *m,* Russian (language)

**rusticación** /rrustika'θion; rrustika'sion/ *f,* rustication

**rusticar** /rrusti'kar/ *vi* to rusticate

**rusticidad** /rrustiθi'ðað; rrustisi'ðað/ *f,* rusticity; boorishness, coarseness

**rústico** /'rrustiko/ *a* rustic, country; boorish, uncouth. *m,* countryman; yokel; peasant. **en rústica,** in paper covers (of books)

**ruta** /'rruta/ *f,* route; *Fig.* way. **r. de evitación,** by-pass, detour

**ruteno** /rru'teno/ **(-na)** *a* and *n* Ruthenian. *m,* Ruthenian (language)

**rutilante** /rruti'lante/ *a Poet.* sparkling, glowing

**rutilar** /rruti'lar/ *vi Poet.* to gleam, sparkle

**rutina** /rru'tina/ *f,* routine

**rutinario** /rruti'nario/ *a* routine

**rutinero** /rruti'nero/ **(-ra)** *a* routinistic —*n* routinist

# S

**sábado** /'saβaðo/ *m*, Saturday; Jewish sabbath. **s. de gloria,** Easter Saturday

**sábalo** /'saβalo/ *m*, *Ichth.* shad

**sabana** /sa'βana/ *f*, savannah

**sábana** /'saβana/ *f*, bed sheet; altar cloth. *Inf.* **pegársele ( a uno) las sábanas,** to be tied to the bed, get up late

**sabandija** /saβan'diha/ *f*, any unpleasant insect or reptile; *Fig.* vermin

**sabanero** /saβa'nero/ **(-ra)** *n* savannah dweller —*a* savannah

**sabanilla** /saβa'niʎa; saβa'niya/ *f*, small piece of linen (kerchief, towel, etc.); altar cloth

**sabañón** /saβa'ɲon/ *m*, chilblain

**sabatario** /saβa'tario/ *a* sabbatarian

**sabático** /sa'βatiko/ *a* sabbatical

**sabatino** /saβa'tino/ *a* Saturday, Sabbath

**sabedor** /saβe'ðor/ *a* aware; knowledgeable, knowing

**sabelotodo** /saβelo'toðo/ *mf Inf.* know-it-all

**saber** /sa'βer/ *m*, learning; wisdom

**saber** /sa'βer/ *vt irr* to know; be able to, know how; —*vi* know; be shrewd, be well aware of; (*with prep a*) taste of; be like or similar to. **a s.,** viz., namely. *Inf.* **no s. cuántas son cinco,** not to know how many beans make five. **no s. dónde meterse,** to be overcome by shame; have the jitters. **No sé cuántos,** I don't know how many. **no sé quién,** I don't know who (which person). **No sé qué,** I don't know what. **un no sé qué,** a certain something; a touch (of). **¡Quién sabe!** Who knows!; Time will tell —*Pres. Indic.* **sé, sabes,** etc —*Fut.* **sabré,** etc —*Condit.* **sabría,** etc —*Preterite* **supe,** etc —*Pres. Subjunc.* **sepa,** etc —*Imperf. Subjunc.* **supiese,** etc.

**sabiamente** /saβia'mente/ *adv* wisely, prudently

**sabidillo** /saβi'ðiʎo; saβi'ðiyo/ **(-lla)** *a* and *n Inf.* know-it-all

**sabiduría** /saβiðu'ria/ *f*, prudence, wisdom; erudition; learning; knowledge, awareness. **Libro de la S. de Salomón,** Book of Wisdom

**sabiendas, a** /sa'βiendas, a/ *adv* knowingly, consciously

**sabihondo** /sa'βiondo/ **(-da)** *n Inf.* know-it-all

**sabino** /sa'βino/ **(-na)** *a* and *n* Sabine —*a* roan (of horses)

**sabio** /'saβio/ **(-ia)** *a* wise; learned, erudite; prudent, sagacious; knowing (of animals); performing (of animals) —*n* wise person; scholar, erudite person

**sablazo** /sa'βlaθo; sa'βlaso/ *m*, saber thrust or wound; *Inf.* sponging, taking advantage of. **dar un s. ( a),** *Inf.* to sponge on; touch for money

**sable** /'saβle/ *m*, saber; *Herald.* sable; *Inf.* talent for sponging on people —*a Herald.* sable

**sablear** /saβle'ar/ *vi Inf.* to touch for invitations, loans, etc.; cadge

**sablista** /sa'βlista/ *mf Inf.* sponger, cadger

**saboneta** /saβo'neta/ *f*, hunting case watch, hunter

**sabor** /sa'βor/ *m*, taste, flavor; impression, effect. **a s.,** to taste; at pleasure

**saboreamiento** /saβorea'miento/ *m*, savoring; relishing, enjoyment

**saborear** /saβore'ar/ *vt* to flavor, season; relish, savor; appreciate, enjoy; —*vr* relish, savor; enjoy

**saboreo** /saβo'reo/ *m*, tasting; savoring; relishing

**sabotaje** /saβo'tahe/ *m*, sabotage

**saboteador** /saβotea'ðor/ *m*, saboteur

**Saboya** /sa'βoya/ Savoy

**saboyano** /saβo'yano/ **(-na)** *a* and *n* Savoyard

**sabroso** /sa'βroso/ *a* tasty, savory, well-seasoned; delightful, delicious; *Inf.* piquant, racy

**sabueso** /sa'βueso/ *m*, cocker spaniel. **s. de artois,** hound

**sabuloso** /saβu'loso/ *a* sandy

**saburra** /sa'βurra/ *f*, fur (on the tongue)

**saca** /'saka/ *f*, drawing out, removing; export, transport, shipping; removal, extraction; legal copy (of a document). **estar de s.,** to be on sale; *Inf.* be marriageable (of women)

**sacabocados** /sakaβo'kaðos/ *m*, punch (tool); *Inf.* cinch, easy matter

**sacabotas** /saka'βotas/ *m*, bootjack

**sacabrocas** /saka'βrokas/ *m*, tack puller

**sacabuche** /saka'βutʃe/ *m*, *Mus.* sackbut; sackbut player; *Inf.* insignificant little man; *Naut.* hand pump

**sacacorchos** /saka'kortʃos/ *m*, corkscrew

**sacacuartos** /saka'kuartos/ *m*, *Inf.* catchpenny

**sacada** /sa'kaða/ *f*, territory cut off from a province

**sacadineros** /sakaði'neros/ *m*, *Inf.* catchpenny

**sacamanchas** /saka'mantʃas/ *mf.* See **quitamanchas**

**sacamantas** /saka'mantas/ *m*, *Inf.* tax collector

**sacamiento** /saka'miento/ *m*, removing, taking out

**sacamuelas** /saka'muelas/ *mf* dentist; charlatan, quack; *Inf.* windbag

**sacapotras** /saka'potras/ *m*, *Inf.* unskilled surgeon

**sacar** /sa'kar/ *vt* to draw out; extract; pull out; take out; remove; dispossess, turn out; free from, relieve; examine, investigate; extort (the truth); extract (sugar, etc.); win (prizes, games); copy; discover, find out; elect by ballot; obtain, achieve; exclude; show, exhibit; quote, mention; produce, invent; manufacture; note down; put forth; unsheath (swords); bowl (in cricket); serve (in tennis). **s. a bailar,** to invite to dance. **s. a luz,** to publish, print; reveal, bring out. **s. a paseo,** to take for a walk. **s. de pila,** to be a godfather or godmother to. **s. en claro** *or* **s. en limpio,** to copy; conclude, infer, gather. **sacarse en conclusión que...,** the conclusion is that...

**sacarificar** /sakarifi'kar/ *vt* to saccharify

**sacarina** /saka'rina/ *f*, saccharin

**sacasillas** /saka'siʎas; saka'siyas/ *m*, *Inf. Theat.* stagehand

**sacerdocio** /saθer'ðoθio; saser'ðosio/ *m*, priesthood

**sacerdotal** /saθerðo'tal; saserðo'tal/ *a* priestly

**sacerdote** /saθer'ðote; saser'ðote/ *m*, priest

**sacerdotisa** /saθerðo'tisa; saserðo'tisa/ *f*, priestess. **sumo s.,** high priestess

**sachar** /sa'tʃar/ *vt* to weed

**sacho** /'satʃo/ *m*, weeder

**saciable** /sa'θiaβle; sa'siaβle/ *a* satiable

**saciar** /sa'θiar; sa'siar/ *vt* to satisfy; satiate; —*vr* be satiated

**saciedad** /saθie'ðað; sasie'ðað/ *f*, satiety, surfeit

**saco** /'sako/ *m*, handbag; sack, bag; sackful; sack coat; *Biol.* sac; *Mil.* sack, plundering. **s. de noche,** dressing case, weekend case. *Inf.* **no echar en s. roto,** not to forget, to remember

**sacramentalmente** /sakramental'mente/ *adv* sacramentally; in confession

**sacramentar** /sakramen'tar/ *vt* to consecrate; administer the Blessed Sacrament; hide, conceal

**sacramentario** /sakramen'tario/ **(-ia)** *n* sacramentalist; sacramentarian

**sacramento** /sakra'mento/ *m*, sacrament; *Eccl.* Host; *Eccl.* mystery. **s. del altar,** Eucharist. **con todos los sacramentos,** with all the sacraments; done in order, complete with all formalities. **recibir los sacramentos,** to receive the last sacraments

**sacratísimo** /sakra'tisimo/ *a* most sacred

**sacrificadero** /sakrifika'ðero/ *m*, place of sacrifice

**sacrificador** /sakrifika'ðor/ **(-ra)** *a* sacrificing —*n* sacrificer

**sacrificar** /sakrifi'kar/ *vt* to sacrifice; slaughter; —*vr* consecrate oneself to God; sacrifice oneself; devote or dedicate oneself (to)

**sacrificio** /sakri'fiθio; sakri'fisio/ *m*, sacrifice; offering, dedication; surrendering, forgoing; compliance, submission. **s. del altar,** sacrifice of the mass

**sacrilegio** /sakri'lehio/ *m*, sacrilege

**sacrílego** /sa'krilego/ *a* sacrilegious

**sacristán** /sakris'tan/ *m*, sacristan; sexton; hoop (for dresses). *Inf.* **s. de amén,** yes-man. *Inf.* **ser gran s.,** to be very crafty

**sacristana** /sakris'tana/ *f*, wife of a sacristan or sexton; nun in charge of a convent sacristy

**sacristanía** /sakrista'nia/ *f*, office of a sacristan or sexton

**sacristía** /sakris'tia/ *f*, sacristy; vestry; office of a sacristan or sexton

**sacro** /'sakro/ *a* sacred; *Anat.* sacral

**sacrosanto** /sakro'santo/ *a* sacrosanct

**sacudida** /saku'ðiða/ *f*, shake, shaking; jerk, jar, jolt; twitch, pull; *Aer.* bump

**sacudido** /saku'ðiðo/ *a* unsociable; difficult, wayward; determined, bold

**sacudidor** /sakuði'ðor/ **(-ra)** *a* shaking; jerking —*n* shaker. *m*, carpet beater; duster

**sacudidura** /sakuði'ðura/ *f*, shaking (especially to remove dust); jerking

**sacudimiento** /sakuði'miento/ *m*, shake, shaking; jerk; twitch, pull; jolt

**sacudir** /saku'ðir/ *vt* to shake; flap, wave; jerk, twitch; beat, bang; shake off; —*vr* shake off, avoid

**sadismo** /sa'ðismo/ *m*, sadism

**sadista** /sa'ðista/ *mf* sadist

**sadístico** /sa'ðistiko/ *a* sadistic

**saduceo** /saðu'θeo; saðu'seo/ **(-ea)** *a* Sadducean —*n* Sadducee

**saeta** /sa'eta/ *f*, arrow, dart; clock hand, watch hand; magnetic needle; short sung expression of religious ecstasy; *Astron.* Sagitta

**saetada** /sae'taða/ *f*, **saetazo** *m*, arrow wound

**saetera** /sae'tera/ *f*, loophole; small window

**saetero** /sae'tero/ *a* arrow, arrow-like. *m*, archer, bowman

**sáfico** /'safiko/ *a* Sapphic

**saga** /'saɣa/ *f*, saga

**sagacidad** /saɣaθi'ðað; saɣasi'ðað/ *f*, sagacity

**sagaz** /sa'ɣaθ; sa'ɣas/ *a* sagacious, shrewd; farseeing; quick on the scent (dogs)

**sagital** /sahi'tal/ *a* arrow-shaped

**sagitario** /sahi'tario/ *m*, archer; *Astron.* Sagittarius

**sagrado** /sa'ɣraðo/ *a* sacred; holy; sacrosanct, venerable; accursed, detestable. *m*, sanctuary, refuge; haven

**sagrario** /sa'ɣrario/ *m*, sanctuary; sacrarium

**sagú** /sa'ɣu/ *m*, sago

**Sáhara, el** /'saara, el/ the Sahara

**sahornarse** /saor'narse/ *vr* to chafe, grow sore

**sahorno** /sa'orno/ *m*, chafing, abrasion

**sahumado** /sau'maðo/ *a* improved, rendered more excellent; perfumed; fumigated

**sahumador** /sauma'ðor/ *m*, perfumer; fumigating vessel

**sahumar** /sau'mar/ *vt* to perfume; fumigate. See **desahuciar**

**sahumerio** /sau'merio/ *m*, perfuming; fumigation; fume, smoke

**saín** /sa'in/ *m*, fat, grease; sardine oil (for lamps); grease spot (on clothes)

**sainar** /sai'nar/ *vt* to fatten up (animals)

**sainete** /sai'nete/ *m*, *Cul.* sauce; *Theat.* one-act parody or burlesque; farce; delicacy, tidbit; delicate taste (of food)

**sainetero** /saine'tero/ *m*, writer of sainetes

**sainetesco** /saine'tesko/ *a* pertaining to sainetes; burlesque, satirical

**sajar** /sa'har/ *vt* *Surg.* to scarify

**sajón** /sa'hon/ **(-ona)** *a* and *n* Saxon

**Sajonia** /sa'honia/ Saxony

**sal** /sal/ *f*, salt; wit; grace, gracefulness. **s. de cocina,** common kitchen salt. **s. de la Higuera,** Epsom salts. **s. gema,** rock salt. **s. marina,** sea salt. **sales inglesas,** smelling salts. *Inf.* **estar hecho de s.,** to be full of wit. *Inf.* **hacerse s. y agua,** to melt away, disappear (of riches, etc.)

**sala** /'sala/ *f*, drawing room; large room, hall; *Law.* courtroom; *Law.* bench; **s. de apelación,** court of appeal. **s. de hospital,** hospital ward. **s. de justicia,** court of justice. **s. de lectura,** reading room. *Law.* **guardar s.,** to respect the court

**salacidad** /salaθi'ðað; salasi'ðað/ *f*, lewdness, salaciousness

**saladar** /sala'ðar/ *m*, salt marsh

**saladero** /sala'ðero/ *m*, salting or curing place; *West Hem.* meat packing factory

**saladillo** /sala'ðiʎo; sala'ðiyo/ *m*, salt pork

**salado** /sa'laðo/ *a* salty, briny; brackish; witty; attractive, amusing

**salador** /sala'ðor/ **(-ra)** *a* salting, curing —*n* salter, curer. *m*, curing place

**saladura** /sala'ðura/ *f*, salting, curing

**salamandra** /sala'mandra/ *f*, salamander; fire sprite

**salar** /sa'lar/ *vt* to salt; season with salt; oversalt; cure, pickle (meat, etc.)

**salario** /sa'lario/ *m*, salary

**salaz** /sa'laθ; sa'las/ *a* lewd, lecherous

**salazón** /sala'θon; sala'son/ *f*, salting, curing; salt meat or fish trade

**salazonero** /salaθo'nero; salaso'nero/ *a* salting, curing

**salchicha** /sal'tʃitʃa/ *f*, sausage

**salchichería** /saltʃitʃe'ria/ *f*, sausage shop

**salchichero** /saltʃi'tʃero/ **(-ra)** *n* sausage maker, sausage seller

**salchichón** /saltʃi'tʃon/ *m*, *Cul.* salami, kind of sausage

**saldar** /sal'dar/ *vt* *Com.* to settle, pay in full; sell out cheap; balance

**saldista** /sal'dista/ *mf* remnant buyer

**saldo** /'saldo/ *m*, *Com.* balance; closing of an account; bargain sale. **s. acreedor,** credit balance. **s. deudor,** debit balance. **s. líquido,** net balance

**salero** /sa'lero/ *m*, saltshaker, saltcellar; salt storage warehouse; *Inf.* wit

**saleta** /sa'leta/ *f*, *dim* small hall; royal antechamber; court of appeal

**salida** /sa'liða/ *f*, going out; leaving; departure; sailing; exit, way out; projection, protrusion; *Fig.* escape, way out; outcome, result; witty remark; *Mil.* sally; *Com.* outlay, expense. *Com.* opening, sale, salability; environs, outskirts. **s. de dólares,** dollar drain. **s. de tono,** *Inf.* an impertinent remark. **dar s.,** *Com.* to enter on the credit side

**salidero** /sali'ðero/ *a* fond of going out; *m*, exit, way out

**salidizo** /sali'ðiθo; sali'ðiso/ *m*, *Archit.* projection —*a* projecting

**saliente** /sa'liente/ *a* outgoing; salient, projecting. *m*, east; projection; salient. **s. continental,** continental shelf

**salina** /sa'lina/ *f*, salt mine; saltworks

**salinero** /sali'nero/ *m*, salt merchant; salter; salt worker

**salino** /sa'lino/ *a* saline. *m*, *Med.* saline

**salir** /sa'lir/ *vi irr* to go out; depart, leave; succeed in getting out; escape; appear (of the sun, etc.); sprout, show green; fade, come out (of stains); project, stand out; grow, develop; turn out, result; happen, take place; cost; sail; end (of seasons, time); lead off, start (some games); be published (books); do (well or badly), succeed or fail; appear, show oneself; be drawn, win (lottery tickets); balance, come out right (accounts); be elected; become; give up (posts); lead to (of streets, etc.); *Naut.* overtake; (*with prep a*) guarantee, be surety for; resemble, be like; (*with con*) utter, come out with; commit, do inopportunely; succeed in, achieve (e.g. *Salió con la suya,* He got his own way); (*with de*) originate in; break away from (traditions, conventions); get rid of; (*with por*) stand up for, protect; go surety for, guarantee —*vr* leak; boil over; overflow; (*with con*) achieve, get; (*with de*) *Fig.* break away from. *Theat.* **s. a la escena,** to enter, come on to the stage. **s. de,** to recover from (an illness). **no acabar de s. de,** to not be completely recovered from. **s. del apuro,** to get out of trouble. **s. de estampía,** to stampede (of animals). **s. pitando,** *Inf.* to get out in a hurry. **Esta idea no sale de Juan,** This wasn't John's idea. **salga lo que saliere,** *Inf.* come what may... —*Pres. Indic.* **salgo, sales,** etc —*Fut.* **saldré,** etc —*Condit.* **saldría,** etc —*Pres. Subjunc.* **salga,** etc.

**salitral** /sali'tral/ *a* nitrous. *m*, saltpeter bed

**salitre** /sa'litre/ *m*, saltpeter

**salitrería** /salitre'ria/ *f*, saltpeter works

**salitrero** /sali'trero/ *n* saltpeter worker or dealer

**saliva** /sa'liβa/ *f,* saliva. *Inf.* **tragar s.,** to put up with; be unable to speak through emotion

**salivación** /saliβa'θion; saliβa'sion/ *f,* salivation

**salival** /sali'βal/ *a* salivary

**salivar** /sali'βar/ *vi* to salivate; spit

**sallar** /sa'ʎar; sa'yar/ *vt* to weed

**salmantino** /salman'tino/ **(-na)** *a* and *n* Salamanca

**salmear** /salme'ar/ *vi* to intone psalms

**salmista** /sal'mista/ *mf* psalmist; psalmodist, psalm chanter

**salmo** /'salmo/ *m,* psalm

**salmodia** /sal'moðia/ *f,* psalmody; *Inf.* drone; psalter

**salmodiar** /salmo'ðiar/ *vi* to chant psalms; —*vt* drone

**salmón** /sal'mon/ *m,* salmon

**salmonado** /salmo'naðo/ *a* salmon-like

**salmonera** /salmo'nera/ *f,* salmon net

**salmonete** /salmo'nete/ *m,* red mullet

**salmuera** /sal'muera/ *f,* brine

**salobre** /sa'loβre/ *a* salt, salty; brackish

**salobridad** /saloβri'ðað/ *f,* saltiness

**salomar** /salo'mar/ *vi Naut.* to sing chanteys

**salón** /sa'lon/ *m,* drawing room; large room or hall; reception room; salon, reception, social gathering. **s. de muestras,** showroom

**saloncillo** /salon'θiʎo; salon'siyo/ *m, dim* small room; *Theat.* greenroom; rest room

**salpicadura** /salpika'ðura/ *f,* sprinkling, spattering, splashing

**salpicar** /salpi'kar/ *vt* to sprinkle, scatter; bespatter, splash

**salpicón** /salpi'kon/ *m, Cul.* kind of salmagundi; *Inf.* hodgepodge; spattering

**salpimentar** /salpimen'tar/ *vt irr* to season with pepper and salt; sprinkle; *Fig.* leaven, enliven (a speech, etc.). See **regimentar**

**salpresar** /salpre'sar/ *vt* to preserve in salt, salt

**salpullido** /salpu'ʎiðo; salpu'yiðo/ *m,* rash, skin eruption

**salsa** /'salsa/ *f,* sauce; gravy. **s. mahonesa** or **s. mayonesa,** mayonnaise sauce. **s. mayordoma,** sauce maître d'hôtel

**salsera** /sal'sera/ *f,* sauce boat, gravy boat

**saltabanco** /salta'βanko/ *m,* mountebank; street entertainer, juggler

**saltabarrancos** /saltaβa'rrankos/ *mf Inf.* madcap, harum-scarum

**saltable** /sal'taβle/ *a* jumpable

**saltadero** /salta'ðero/ *m,* jumping ground; fountain, jet

**saltador** /salta'ðor/ **(-ra)** *a* jumping —*n* jumper; acrobat. *m,* jump rope, skip rope

**saltamontes** /salta'montes/ *m,* grasshopper

**saltaojos** /salta'ohos/ *m,* peony

**saltaparedes** /saltapa'reðes/ *mf Inf.* madcap, romp

**saltar** /sal'tar/ *vi* to jump, leap, spring; prance; frisk; gambol; rebound; blow up; burst, break asunder; pop (of corks); fly off, come off (buttons, etc.); gush out, shoot up (liquids); break apart, be shattered; be obvious, stand out; come to mind, suggest itself; show anger; *Fig.* let slip, come out with (remarks); —*vt* leap or jump over; poke out (eyes); cover (the female); omit, pass over; blow up, explode. **s. a la cuerda,** to jump rope, play with a skip rope. **s. a la vista,** to be obvious, leap to the eye. **s. diciendo,** *Inf.* to come out with, say

**saltarín** /salta'rin/ **(-ina)** *a* dancing —*n* dancer

**saltatriz** /salta'triθ; salta'tris/ *f,* ballet dancer, female acrobat

**saltatumbas** /salta'tumbas/ *m,* (*Inf.* contemptuous) cleric who makes his living off funerals

**salteador** /saltea'ðor/ *m,* highwayman

**salteamiento** /saltea'miento/ *m,* highway robbery, holdup; assault, attack

**saltear** /salte'ar/ *vt* to hold up and rob; assault, attack; jump from one thing to another, do intermittently; forestall; surprise, amaze

**salterio** /sal'terio/ *m,* psaltery

**saltimbanco, saltimbanqui** /saltim'βanko, saltim'βanki/ *m, Inf..* See **saltabanco**

**salto** /'salto/ *m,* jump, leap, bound; leapfrog (game); precipice, ravine; waterfall; assault; important promotion; omission (of words). **s. de agua,** waterfall. **s. de cama,** peignoir, bathrobe. **s. de campana,** overturning. *Inf.* **s. de mal año,** sudden improvement in circumstances. **s. de mata,** flight, escape. **s. mortal,** leap of death; somersault. **s. de pie,** spillway. **dar un s.,** to leap. **en un s.,** at one jump; swiftly

**saltón** /sal'ton/ *a* jumping, leaping; prominent (teeth, eyes). *m,* grasshopper

**salubérrimo** /salu'βerrimo/ *a superl* **salubre** most healthy

**salubre** /sa'luβre/ *a* salubrious, healthful

**salubridad** /saluβri'ðað/ *f,* healthfulness

**salud** /sa'luð/ *f,* health; salvation; welfare, well-being; *Eccl.* state of grace; *pl* civilities, greetings. **¡S. y pesetas!** Here's to your good health and prosperity! (on drinking). **gastar s.,** to enjoy good health. *Inf.* **vender** ( or **verter**) **s.,** to look full of health

**saludable** /salu'ðaβle/ *a* healthy, wholesome

**saludador** /saluða'ðor/ **(-ra)** *a* greeting, saluting —*n* greeter. *m,* charlatan, quack

**saludar** /salu'ðar/ *vt* to greet, salute; hail (as king, etc.); send greetings to; bow; *Mil.* fire a salute

**saludo** /sa'luðo/ *m,* greeting, salutation; bow; (*Mil. Nav.*) salute

**salutación** /saluta'θion; saluta'sion/ *f,* greeting, salutation; Ave Maria

**salutífero** /salu'tifero/ *a* salubrious

**salva** /'salβa/ *f,* salutation, greeting; (*Mil. Nav.*) salvo, volley; salute (of guns); salver; ordeal (to establish innocence); solemn assurance, oath; sampling, tasting (of food, drink). **s. de veintiún cañonazos,** twenty-one-gun salute

**salvación** /salβa'θion; salβa'sion/ *f,* liberation, deliverance; salvation

**salvado** /sal'βaðo/ *m,* bran

**salvador** /salβa'ðor/ **(-ra)** *a* saving, redeeming —*n* deliverer. *m,* redeemer

**salvadoreño** /salβaðore'ɲo/ **(-ña)** *a* and *n* Salvadorean

**salvaguardia** /salβa'guarðia/ *m,* guard, watch. *f,* safeguard; protection, defense; safe conduct, passport

**salvajada** /salβa'haða/ *f,* savagery, brutal action

**salvaje** /sal'βahe/ *a* wild (plants, animals); rough, uncultivated; uncultured, uncivilized. *mf* savage

**salvajismo** /salβa'hismo/ *m,* savagery

**salvamano, a** /salβa'mano, a/ *adv* safely

**salvamente** /salβa'mente/ *adv* safely, securely

**salvamento** /salβa'mento/ *m,* salvation; deliverance, security, safety; place of safety; salvage

**salvante** /sal'βante/ *adv Inf.* except, save

**salvar** /sal'βar/ *vt* to save; *Eccl.* redeem; avoid (difficulty, danger); exclude, except; leap, jump; pass over, clear; *Law.* prove innocent; *Naut.* salute. **s. la diferencia,** to bridge the gap —*vi* taste, sample (food, drink); —*vr* be saved from danger; *Eccl.* be redeemed

**salvavidas** /salβa'βiðas/ *m,* life belt; safety belt; life preserver; traffic island

**¡salve!** /'salβe/ *interj Poet.* hail!; Hail Mary, Salve Regina

**salvedad** /salβe'ðað/ *f,* qualification, reservation

**salvia** /'salβia/ *f, Bot.* sage

**salvilla** /sal'βiʎa; sal'βiya/ *f,* salver

**salvo** /'salβo/ *a* safe, unharmed; excepting, omitting —*adv* except. **a s.,** safely, without harm. **a su s.,** to his (her, their) satisfaction; at his (her, etc.) pleasure. **dejar a s.,** to exclude, leave aside. **en s.,** in safety

**salvoconducto** /salβokon'dukto/ *m,* safe conduct, pass

**samarita** /sama'rita/ *a* and *mf* **samaritano (-na)** *a* and *n* Samaritan

**sambenito** /sambe'nito/ *m,* penitent's gown (Inquisition); disgrace, dishonor

**Samotracia** /samo'traθia; samo'trasia/ Samothrace

**samotracio** /samo'traθio; samo'trasio/ **(-ia)** *a* and *n* Samothracian

**samoyedo** /samo'yeðo/ **(-da)** *n* Samoyed

**san** /san/ *a Abbr.* of **santo.** Used before masculine singular names of saints except **Santos Tomás** (or **Tomé), Domingo, Toribio**

**sanable** /sa'naβle/ *a* curable

**sanador** /sana'ðor/ **(-ra)** *a* healing, curing —*n* healer

**sanalotodo** /sanalo'toðo/ *m, Inf.* cure-all, universal remedy

**sanar** /sa'nar/ *vt* to cure, heal; —*vi* recover, get well; heal

**sanatorio** /sana'torio/ *m,* sanatorium; convalescent home

**sanchopancesco** /santʃopan'θesko; santʃopan'sesko/ *a* like or pertaining to Sancho Panza

**sanción** /san'θion; san'sion/ *f,* authorization, consent; sanction; penalty

**sancionable** /sanθio'naβle; sansio'naβle/ *a* sanctionable

**sancionar** /sanθio'nar; sansio'nar/ *vt* to authorize, approve; sanction

**sancochar** /sanko'tʃar/ *vt Cul.* to parboil, half-cook

**sandalia** /san'dalia/ *f,* sandal

**sándalo** /'sandalo/ *m,* sandalwood

**sandez** /san'deθ; san'des/ *f,* foolishness, stupidity; folly

**sandía** /san'dia/ *f,* watermelon

**sandio** /'sandio/ *a* foolish, inane

**sandunga** /san'duŋga/ *f, Inf.* attractiveness, winsomeness, grace

**sandunguero** /sanduŋ'guero/ *a Inf.* attractive, appealing, winsome

**saneado** /sane'aðo/ *a* unencumbered, nontaxable, free

**saneamiento** /sanea'miento/ *m,* guarantee, security; indemnity; stabilization (of currency); drainage

**sanear** /sane'ar/ *vt Com.* to guarantee, secure; indemnify; stabilize (currency); drain (land, etc.)

**Sanedrín** /sane'ðrin/ *m,* Sanhedrin

**sangradera** /saŋgra'ðera/ *f,* lancet; channel, sluice, drain

**sangrador** /saŋgra'ðor/ *m,* phlebotomist; outlet, drainage

**sangradura** /saŋgra'ðura/ *f,* inner bend of the arm; *Surg.* bleeding; draining off

**sangrar** /saŋ'grar/ *vt Surg.* to bleed; drain off; *Inf.* extort money, bleed; *Print.* indent; draw off resin (from pines, etc.); —*vi* bleed; —*vr* bleed; have oneself bled; run (of colors)

**sangre** /'saŋgre/ *f,* blood; lineage, family. **s. fría,** sang-froid. **a s. fría,** in cold blood, premeditated. **a s. y fuego,** by fire and sword, without quarter. *Inf.* **bullir la s.,** to have youthful blood in one's veins. **llevar en la s.,** *Fig.* to be in the blood. **subírsele la s. a la cabeza,** to grow excited. *Fig. Inf.* **tener s. de horchata,** to have milk and water in one's veins

**sangría** /saŋ'gria/ *f, Surg.* bloodletting; resin cut (on pines, etc.)

**sangriento** /saŋ'griento/ *a* bloody, bloodstained; bloodthirsty, cruel; mortal (insults, etc.); *Poet.* blood-colored

**sangüesa** /saŋ'guesa/ *f,* raspberry

**sanguijuela** /saŋgi'huela/ *f,* leech; *Fig. Inf.* sponger

**sanguina** /saŋ'gina/ *f,* red crayon drawing, sanguine

**sanguinaria** /saŋgi'naria/ *f,* bloodstone

**sanguinario** /saŋgi'nario/ *a* vengeful, bloody, cruel

**sanguíneo** /saŋ'gineo/ *a* blood; sanguineous; sanguine, fresh-complexioned; blood-colored

**sanguinolento** /saŋgino'lento/ *a.* See **sangriento**

**sanidad** /sani'ðað/ *f,* safety, security; healthiness; health department. **s. interior,** Public Health. **S. militar,** army medical corps

**sanitario** /sani'tario/ *a* sanitary, hygienic. *m, Mil.* medical officer

**sano** /'sano/ *a* healthy; safe, secure; healthful, wholesome; unhurt, unharmed; upright, honest; sincere; *Inf.* entire, undamaged; sane. **s. y salvo,** safe and sound. *Inf.* **cortar por lo s.,** to cut one's losses

**sánscrito** /'sanskrito/ *a* and *m,* Sanscrit

**santa** /'santa/ *f,* female saint

**santabárbara** /santa'βarβara/ *f, Nav.* magazine

**santamente** /santa'mente/ *adv* in a saintly manner; simply

**santero** /san'tero/ **(-ra)** *a* given to image worship —*n* accomplice (of a burglar); caretaker (of a hermitage); beggar

**¡Santiago!** /san'tiago/ *interj* St. James! (Spanish war cry). *m,* attack, assault

**santiamén** /santia'men/ *m, Inf.* trice, twinkling

**santidad** /santi'ðað/ *f,* sanctity; saintliness; godliness. **Su S.,** His Holiness

**santificación** /santifika'θion; santifika'sion/ *f,* sanctification

**santificador** /santifika'ðor/ **(-ra)** *a* sanctifying —*n* sanctifier

**santificar** /santifi'kar/ *vt* to sanctify, make holy; consecrate; dedicate; keep (feast days)

**santiguada** /santi'guaða/ *f,* crossing oneself; rough treatment, harsh reproof

**santiguar** /santi'guar/ *vt* to make the sign of the cross over; *Inf.* beat, rain blows on; —*vr* cross oneself; *Inf.* be dumbfounded

**santísimo** /san'tisimo/ *a superl* most saintly, most holy

**santo** /'santo/ *a* holy; saintly; saint (see **san**); consecrated; inviolate, sacred; *Inf.* simple, sincere, ingenuous. *m,* saint; image of a saint; saint's day, name day (of a person); *Mil.* password. **Santa Hermandad,** Holy Brotherhood (former name of the Spanish rural police force). **S. Oficio,** Holy Office, Inquisition. **S. y bueno,** Well and good, All right! *Inf.* **alzarse con el s. y la limosna,** to take the lot, make off with everything. **llegar y besar el s.,** to do in a trice. *Inf.* **No es s. de mi devoción,** I'm not very keen on him. *Inf.* **todo el s. día,** the whole blessed day

**santón** /san'ton/ *m,* dervish, santon. *Inf.* hypocrite, sham saint

**santoral** /santo'ral/ *m,* book of saints; calendar of saints; choir book

**santuario** /san'tuario/ *m,* sanctuary

**santurrón** /santu'rron/ **(-ona)** *a* sanctimonious; hypocritical; prudish —*n* hypocrite

**santurronería** /santurrone'ria/ *f,* sanctimoniousness

**saña** /'saɲa/ *f,* fury, blind rage; lust for revenge, cruelty

**sañoso, sañudo** /sa'ɲoso, sa'ɲuðo/ *a* furious, blind with rage; cruel

**sapidez** /sapi'ðeθ; sapi'ðes/ *f,* flavor, sapidity

**sápido** /'sapiðo/ *a* tasty, savory

**sapiencia** /sa'pienθia; sa'piensia/ *f,* wisdom; knowledge; erudition

**sapino** /sa'pino/ *m,* fir (tree)

**sapo** /'sapo/ *m,* toad

**saque** /'sake/ *m, Sports.* serve, service; service or bowling line; *Sports.* server; *Sports.* bowler; bowling (in cricket)

**saqueador** /sakea'ðor/ **(-ra)** *a* looting, pillaging —*n* pillager, plunderer

**saquear** /sake'ar/ *vt* to pillage, plunder, sack

**saqueo** /sa'keo/ *m,* plundering, pillage, sacking

**saquilada** /saki'laða/ *f,* small sackful (especially of grain)

**sarampión** /saram'pion/ *m,* measles

**sarao** /sa'rao/ *m,* soirée, evening party

**sarasa** /sa'rasa/ *m, (Inf.* and contemptuous) pansy, faggot

**sarcasmo** /sar'kasmo/ *m,* sarcasm

**sarcástico** /sar'kastiko/ *a* sarcastic

**sarcia** /'sarθia; 'sarsia/ *f,* load, cargo

**sarcófago** /sar'kofago/ *m,* sarcophagus

**sarda** /'sarða/ *f,* mackerel

**sardana** /sar'ðana/ *f,* traditional Catalonian dance

**sardina** /sar'ðina/ *f,* sardine. **s. arenque,** herring. **como sardinas en banasta,** *Fig.* packed like sardines

**sardinal** /sarði'nal/ *m,* sardine net

**sardinero** /sarði'nero/ **(-ra)** *a* sardine —*n* sardine seller or dealer. *m,* famous district of Santander

**sardineta** /sarði'neta/ *f,* sprat; small sardine; *Mil.* chevron

**sardo** /'sarðo/ **(-da)** *a* and *n* Sardinian

**sardónico** /sar'ðoniko/ *a* sardonic

**sarga** /'sarga/ *f,* (silk) serge; willow

**sargenta** /sar'henta/ *f,* sergeant's wife; *Inf.* mannish, overbearing woman

**sargentear** /sarhente'ar/ *vt* to be in charge as a sergeant; command, captain; *Inf.* boss

**sargento** /sar'hento/ *m,* sergeant

**sarmentoso** /sarmen'toso/ *a* vine-like; twining

**sarmiento** /sar'miento/ *m,* vine shoot

**sarna** /'sarna/ *f,* scabies. **s. perruna,** mange. **más viejo que la s.,** *Inf.* older than the plague

**sarnoso** /sar'noso/ *a* itchy; mangy

**sarraceno** /sarra'θeno; sarra'seno/ **(-na)** *a* Saracen —*n* Saracen; Moor

**sarracina** /sarra'θina; sarra'sina/ *f,* scuffle

**sarrillo** /sa'rriʎo; sa'rriyo/ *m,* death rattle, rale; arum lily

**sarro** /'sarro/ *m,* furry encrustation, scale; film; tartar (on teeth)

**sarta** /'sarta/ *f,* string, link (of pearls, etc.); file, line

**sartén** /sar'ten/ *f,* frying pan. **tener la s. por el mango,** *Inf.* to be top dog

**sastra** /'sastra/ *f,* female tailor; tailor's wife

**sastre** /'sastre/ *m,* tailor. **ser buen s.,** *Inf.* to be an expert (in)

**sastrería** /sastre'ria/ *f,* tailoring; tailor's shop

**Satanás** /sata'nas/ *m,* Satan; devil

**satánico** /sa'taniko/ *a* satanic

**satélite** /sa'telite/ *m,* satellite; follower, admirer, sycophant

**satén** /sa'ten/ *m,* sateen

**satinar** /sati'nar/ *vt* to calender; glaze; satin (paper)

**sátira** /'satira/ *f,* satire

**satírico** /sa'tiriko/ *a* satiric

**satirizar** /satiri'θar; satiri'sar/ *vi* to write satires; —*vt* satirize

**sátiro** /'satiro/ *m,* satyr; *Theat.* indecent play

**satisfacción** /satisfak'θion; satisfak'sion/ *f,* settlement, payment; atonement, expiation; satisfaction; gratification; amends; complacency, conceit; contentment; apology. **tomar s.,** to avenge oneself

**satisfacer** /satisfa'θer; satisfa'ser/ *vt irr* to pay, settle; atone for, expiate; gratify; quench; fulfill, observe; compensate, indemnify; discharge, meet; convince, persuade; allay, relieve; reward; explain; answer, satisfy; —*vr* avenge oneself; satisfy oneself —*Pres. Indic.* **satisfago, satisfaces,** etc —*Fut.* **satisfaré,** etc —*Condit.* **satisfaría,** etc —*Preterite* **satisfice,** etc —*Past Part.* **satisfecho.** *Pres. Subjunc.* **satisfaga,** etc —*Imperf. Subjunc.* **satisficiese,** etc.

**satisfactorio** /satisfak'torio/ *a* satisfactory

**satisfecho** /satis'fetʃo/ *a* self-satisfied, complacent; happy, contented

**sátrapa** /'satrapa/ *m,* satrap; *Inf.* cunning fellow

**saturación** /satura'θion; satura'sion/ *f,* saturation

**saturar** /satu'rar/ *vt* to satiate, fill; saturate

**saturnino** /satur'nino/ *a* saturnine, melancholy, morose

**saturnismo** /satur'nismo/ *m,* saturnism, lead poisoning

**Saturno** /sa'turno/ *m,* Saturn

**sauce** /'sauθe; 'sause/ *m,* willow. **s. llorón,** weeping willow

**saúco** /sa'uko/ *m,* elder tree

**saurio** /'saurio/ *a* and *m,* saurian

**savia** /'saβia/ *f,* sap; energy, zest

**sáxeo** /'sakseo/ *a* stone, stony

**saxófono** /sak'sofono/ *or* **saxofón** *m,* saxophone

**saya** /'saya/ *f,* skirt; long tunic

**sayal** /sa'yal/ *m,* thick woolen material

**sayo** /'sayo/ *m,* loose smock; *Inf.* any garment. **cortar un s.** ( **a),** *Inf.* to gossip behind a person's back

**sayón** /sa'yon/ *m,* executioner; *Inf.* hideous-looking man

**sazón** /sa'θon; sa'son/ *f,* ripeness, maturity; season; perfection, excellence; opportunity; taste, flavor; seasoning. **a la s.,** at that time, then. **en s.,** in season; opportunely

**sazonador** /saθona'ðor; sasona'ðor/ **(-ra)** *a* seasoning —*n* seasoner

**sazonar** /saθo'nar; saso'nar/ *vt Cul.* to season; mature; —*vr* mature, ripen

**se** /se/ *object pron reflexive 3rd sing* and *pl mf* 1. Used as accusative (direct object) himself, herself, yourself, themselves, yourselves (e.g. *Juan se ha cortado,* John has cut himself). 2. Used as dative or indirect object to himself, at himself, herself, themselves, etc. (e.g. *María se mira al espejo,* Mary looks at herself in the mirror). Reciprocity is also expressed by reflexive (e.g. *No se hablan,* They do not speak to one another). When a direct object pron. (accusative) and an indirect object pron., both in the 3rd pers. (sing. or pl.), are used together, the indirect object pron. becomes **se** (instead of **le** or **les**) (e.g. *Se lo doy,* I give it to him). Many Spanish reflexive verbs have English equivalents that are not reflexive (e.g. *desayunarse,* to breakfast, *arrepentirse,* to repent, *quejarse,* to complain). Some intransitive (neuter) verbs have a modified meaning when used reflexively (e.g. *marcharse,* to go away, *dormirse,* to fall asleep). The passive may be formed by using **se** + 3rd pers. sing. of verb (e.g. *se dice,* it is said, people say). A number of impersonal phrases are also formed in this way (e.g. «*Se alquila,*» "To Let," «*Se vende,*» "For Sale"). The imperative is used in the same way (e.g. *Véase la página dos,* See page two)

**sebáceo** /se'βaθeo; se'βaseo/ *a* sebaceous

**sebo** /'seβo/ *m,* tallow; candle grease; fat, grease

**seboso** /se'βoso/ *a* tallowy; fat, greasy

**seca** /'seka/ *f,* drought; *Naut.* unsubmerged sandbank

**secadero** /seka'ðero/ *m,* drying place, drying room

**secadora** /seka'ðora/ *f,* dryer, drying machine, clothesdryer. **s. de cabello,** hairdryer

**secafirmas** /seka'firmas/ *m,* blotting pad

**secamente** /seka'mente/ *adv* tersely, brusquely, curtly; dryly

**secamiento** /seka'miento/ *m,* drying

**secano** /se'kano/ *m,* nonirrigated land; *Naut.* unsubmerged sandbank; anything very dry

**secante** /se'kante/ *a* drying —*a* and *f,* *Geom.* secant. **papel s.,** blotting paper

**secar** /se'kar/ *vt* to dry; desiccate; annoy, bore; —*vr* dry; dry up (of streams, etc.); wilt, fade (of plants); become parched; grow thin, become emaciated; be very thirsty; become hard-hearted

**sección** /sek'θion; sek'sion/ *f,* act of cutting; section, part, portion; *Geom. Mil.* section. **s. cónica,** conic section. **s. de amenidades,** entertainment section (of a newspaper). **s. de reserva,** *Mil.* reserve list

**seccionar** /sekθio'nar; seksio'nar/ *vt* to divide into sections, section

**seccionario** /sekθio'nario; seksio'nario/ *a* sectional

**secesión** /seθe'sion; sese'sion/ *f,* secession

**secesionista** /seθesio'nista; sesesio'nista/ *a* and *mf* secessionist

**seco** /'seko/ *a* dry; dried up, parched; faded, wilted; dead (plants); dried (fruits); thin, emaciated; unadorned; barren, arid; brusque, curt; severe, strict; indifferent, unenthusiastic; sharp (sounds); dry (wines). **a secas,** only; solely; simply, just. **en s.,** on dry land; curtly. *Inf.* **dejar s.** ( **a),** to dumbfound, petrify

**secreción** /sekre'θion; sekre'sion/ *f,* segregation, separation; *Med.* secretion

**secreta** /se'kreta/ *f, Law.* secret trial or investigation; *Eccl.* secret(s); toilet, water closet

**secretar** /sekre'tar/ *vt Med.* to secrete

**secretaría** /sekreta'ria/ *f,* secretaryship; secretary's office, secretariat

**secretario** /sekre'tario/ **(-ia)** *n* secretary; amanuensis, clerk. *m,* actuary; registrar. **s. de asuntos exteriores** *or* **s. de asuntos extranjeros,** foreign secretary. **s. particular,** private secretary

**secretear** /sekre'tar/ *vi Inf.* to whisper, have secrets

**secreteo** /sekre'teo/ *m, Inf.* whispering, exchanging of secrets

**secreto** /se'kreto/ *m,* secret; secrecy, silence; confidential information; mystery; secret drawer —*a* secret; private, confidential. **en s.,** secretly, confidentially. **s. a voces,** open secret

**secta** /'sekta/ *f,* sect

**sectario** /sek'tario/ **(-ia)** *a* and *n* sectarian —*n* fanatical believer

**sectarismo** /sekta'rismo/ *m,* sectarianism

**sector** /sek'tor/ *m,* sector

**secuaz** /se'kuaθ; se'kuas/ *mf* follower, disciple

**secuela** /se'kuela/ *f,* sequel, result

**secuencia** /se'kuenθia; se'kuensia/ *f, Eccl.* sequence; (cinema) sequence

**secuestrador** /sekuestra'ðor/ **(-ra)** *a* sequestrating —*n* sequestrator

**secuestrar** /sekues'trar/ *vt* to sequester; kidnap

**secuestro** /se'kuestro/ *m*, sequestration; kidnapping; *Surg.* sequestrum

**secular** /seku'lar/ *a* secular, lay; centennial; age-old, ancient; *Eccl.* secular

**secularización** /sekulariθa'θion; sekularisa'sion/ *f*, secularization

**secularizar** /sekulari'θar; sekulari'sar/ *vt* to secularize; —*vr* become secularized

**secundar** /sekun'dar/ *vt* to second, aid

**secundario** /sekun'dario/ *a* secondary; accessory, subordinate; *Geol.* mesozoic

**sed** /seð/ *f*, thirst; desire, yearning, appetite. **apagar** ( *or* **matar**) **la s.,** to quench one's thirst. **tener s.,** to be thirsty

**seda** /'seða/ *f*, silk; bristle (boar, etc.). **s. cordelada,** twist silk. **s. ocal,** floss silk. **s. vegetal** *or* **s. artificial,** artificial silk. *Inf.* **como una s.,** as smooth as silk; sweet-tempered; achieved without any trouble

**sedación** /seða'θion; seða'sion/ *f*, calming, soothing

**sedal** /se'ðal/ *m*, fish line

**sedar** /se'ðar/ *vt* to soothe, calm

**sedativo** /seða'tiβo/ *a* and *m*, *Med.* sedative

**sede** /'seðe/ *f*, *Eccl.* see; bishop's throne; *Fig.* seat (of government, etc.); Holy See (also **Santa S.**)

**sedentario** /seðen'tario/ *a* sedentary

**sedeño** /se'ðeɲo/ *a* silky; silken, made of silk

**sedería** /seðe'ria/ *f*, silk goods; silks; silk shop

**sedero** /se'ðero/ **(-ra)** *a* . silk —*n* silk weaver or worker; silk merchant

**sedición** /seði'θion; seði'sion/ *f*, sedition

**sedicioso** /seði'θioso; seði'sioso/ *a* seditious

**sediento** /se'ðiento/ *a* thirsty; parched, dry (land); eager (for), desirous (of)

**sedimentación** /seðimenta'θion; seðimenta'sion/ *f*, sedimentation

**sedimentar** /seðimen'tar/ *vt* to leave a sediment; —*vr* settle, form a sediment

**sedimento** /seði'mento/ *m*, sediment; dregs, lees; scale (on boilers)

**sedoso** /se'ðoso/ *a* silky, silk-like

**seducción** /seðuk'θion; seðuk'sion/ *f*, seduction; temptation, blandishment, wile; charm, allurement

**seducir** /seðu'θir; seðu'sir/ *vt irr* to seduce; tempt; lead astray; charm, attract; corrupt, bribe. See **conducir**

**seductivo** /seðuk'tiβo/ *a* tempting; seductive, charming

**seductor** /seðuk'tor/ **(-ra)** *a* tempting; charming —*n* seducer; charming person

**sefardí** /sefar'ði/ *mf* Iberian Jew or Jewess; *pl* Sephardim —*a* Sephardic

**segadera** /sega'ðera/ *f*, sickle

**segadero** /sega'ðero/ *a* reapable, able to be reaped

**segador** /sega'ðor/ *m*, reaper, harvester

**segadora** /sega'ðora/ *f*, mowing machine; harvester; woman harvester

**segar** /se'gar/ *vt irr* to scythe, cut down; reap, harvest; mow. See **cegar**

**seglar** /seg'lar/ *a* secular, lay. *mf* layman

**segmento** /seg'mento/ *m*, segment; *Geom.* segment. **s. de émbolo,** piston ring

**segoviano** /sego'βiano/ **(-na)** *a* and *n* Segovian

**segregación** /segrega'θion; segrega'sion/ *f*, segregation

**segregar** /segre'gar/ *vt* to segregate, separate; *Med.* secrete

**seguida** /se'giða/ *f*, continuation, prolongation. **de s.,** continuously; immediately. **en s.,** at once, immediately

**seguidamente** /segiða'mente/ *adv* continuously; immediately

**seguidilla** /segi'ðiʎa; segi'ðiya/ *f*, popular Spanish tune and dance and verse sung to them; *Inf.* diarrhea

**seguido** /se'giðo/ *a* continuous, successive; direct, straight

**seguidor** /segi'ðor/ **(-ra)** *a* following —*n* follower, disciple

**seguimiento** /segi'miento/ *m*, following, pursuit; continuation, resumption

**seguir** /se'gir/ *vt irr* to follow; go after, pursue; prosecute, execute; continue, go on; accompany, go with;

exercise (a profession); subscribe to, believe in; agree with; persecute; pester, annoy; imitate; *Law.* institute (a suit); handle, manage; —*vr* result, follow as a consequence; follow in order, happen by turn; originate —*Pres. Part.* **siguiendo.** *Pres. Indic.* **sigo, sigues, sigue, siguen.** *Pres. Subjunc.* **siga,** etc —*Imperf. Subjunc.* **siguiese**

**según** /se'gun/ *adv* according to; as. **s. parece,** as it seems. **s. y como,** as, according to

**segunda** /se'gunda/ *f*, *Mus.* second

**segundar** /segun'dar/ *vt* to repeat, do again; —*vi* to second, follow the first

**segundero** /segun'dero/ *a Agr.* of the second flowering or fruiting. *m*, second hand (of a watch)

**segundo** /se'gundo/ *a* second. *m*, second in command, deputy head; *Astron. Geom.* second. **segunda intención,** double meaning. **segunda velocidad,** *Auto.* second gear. **de segunda mano,** second-hand. **sin s.,** without peer or equal

**segundogénito** /segundo'henito/ **(-ta)** *a* and *n* secondborn

**segundón** /segun'don/ *m*, second son; any son but the eldest

**segurador** /segura'ðor/ *m*, surety, security (person)

**seguramente** /segura'mente/ *adv* securely, safely; surely, of course, naturally

**seguridad** /seguri'ðað/ *f*, security; safety; certainty; trustworthiness; *Com.* surety. **con toda s.,** with complete safety, surely, absolutely. **de s.,** *a* safety

**seguro** /se'guro/ *a* secure; safe; certain, sure; firm, fixed; reliable, trustworthy; unfailing. *m*, certainty; haven, place of safety; *Com.* insurance; permit; *Mech.* ratchet. **s. contra incendio, accidentes, robo,** fire, accident, burglary insurance. **s. sobre la vida,** life insurance. **de s.,** surely, certainly. **en s.,** in safety

**seis** /seis/ *a* six; sixth. *m*, six; sixth (of the month); playing card or domino with six spots. **Son las s.,** It is six o'clock

**seiscientos** /seis'θientos; seis'sientos/ *a* six hundred; six-hundredth. *m*, six hundred

**selección** /selek'θion; selek'sion/ *f*, selection, choice. **s. natural,** natural selection

**seleccionar** /selekθio'nar; seleksio'nar/ *vt* to select, choose

**selectivo** /selek'tiβo/ *a* selective

**selecto** /se'lekto/ *a* choice, select, excellent

**sellador** /seʎa'ðor; seya'ðor/ **(-ra)** *a* sealing, stamping —*n* sealer, stamper

**selladura** /seʎa'ðura; seya'ðura/ *f*, sealing, stamping

**sellar** /se'ʎar; se'yar/ *vt* to seal; stamp; end, conclude; close

**sello** /'seʎo; 'seyo/ *m*, seal; stamp. **s. fiscal,** stamp duty. **s. postal,** postage stamp

**selva** /'selβa/ *f*, forest, wood; jungle

**Selva Negra, la** /'selβa 'negra, la/ the Black Forest

**selvático** /sel'βatiko/ *a* sylvan, wood, forest; wild

**selvoso** /sel'βoso/ *a* wooded, sylvan

**semafórico** /sema'foriko/ *a* semaphoric

**semáforo** /se'maforo/ *m*, semaphore, traffic light.

**semana** /se'mana/ *f*, week; week's salary. **S. Mayor** *or* **S. Santa,** Holy Week. **entre s.,** during the week, on weekdays; weekdays

**semanal** /sema'nal/ *a* weekly; of a week's duration

**semanario** /sema'nario/ *a* weekly. *m*, weekly periodical

**semanero** /sema'nero/ *a* employed by the week

**semántica** /se'mantika/ *f*, semantics

**semántico** /se'mantiko/ *a* semantic

**semblante** /sem'βlante/ *m*, facial expression, countenance; face; appearance, look, aspect. **componer el s.,** to pull oneself together, straighten one's face. **mudar de s.,** to change color, change one's expression; alter (of circumstances)

**semblanza** /sem'βlanθa; sem'βlansa/ *f*, biographical sketch. **s. literaria,** short literary biography

**sembradera** /sembra'ðera/ *f*, sowing machine

**sembradío** /sembra'ðio/ *a Agr.* ready for sowing

**sembrado** /sem'βraðo/ *m*, sown land

**sembrador** /sembra'ðor/ **(-ra)** *a* sowing —*n* sower

**sembradura** /sembra'ðura/ *f*, *Agr.* sowing

**sembrar** /sem'βrar/ *vt irr Agr.* to sow; scatter, sprinkle; spread, disseminate. See **sentar**

**semeja** /se'meha/ *f,* resemblance, similarity; indication, sign (gen. *pl*)

**semejante** /seme'hante/ *a* like, similar; such a; *Math.* similar. *m,* similarity, imitation. *mf* fellow man

**semejanza** /seme'hanθa; seme'hansa/ *f,* similarity, likeness. **a s. de,** in the likeness of; like

**semejar** /seme'har/ **(se)** *vi* and *vr* to resemble

**semen** /'semen/ *m,* semen; *Bot.* seed

**semental** /semen'tal/ *a Agr.* seed; breeding (of male animals). *m,* stallion

**sementar** /semen'tar/ *vt Agr.* to sow

**sementera** /semen'tera/ *f, Agr.* sowing; sown land; seedbed; seedtime; *Fig.* hotbed, nursery, genesis

**sementero** /semen'tero/ *m,* seed bag; seed bed

**semestral** /semes'tral/ *a* biannual, half-yearly; lasting six months

**semestre** /se'mestre/ *a* biannual. *m,* half-year, period of six months; six months' salary; semester

**semicircular** /semiθirku'lar; semisirku'lar/ *a* semicircular

**semicírculo** /semi'θirkulo; semi'sirkulo/ *m,* semicircle

**semidifunto** /semiði'funto/ *a* half-dead

**semidiós** /semi'ðios/ *m,* demigod

**semidiosa** /semi'ðiosa/ *f,* demigoddess

**semidormido** /semiðor'miðo/ *a* half-asleep

**semiesférico** /semies'feriko/ *a* hemispherical

**semilla** /se'miʎa; se'miya/ *f, Bot.* seed; *Fig.* germ, genesis

**semillero** /semi'ʎero; semi'yero/ *m,* seedbed; nursery; *Fig.* hotbed, origin

**semilunio** /semi'lunio/ *m, Astron.* half-moon

**seminario** /semi'nario/ *m,* seedbed; nursery; genesis, origin; seminary; tutorial. **s. conciliar,** theological seminary

**seminarista** /semina'rista/ *mf* seminarist

**semiótica** /semi'otika/ *f, Med.* symptomatology; semiotics

**semita** /se'mita/ *mf* Semite —*a* Semitic

**semítico** /se'mitiko/ *a* Semitic

**semitismo** /semi'tismo/ *m,* Semitism

**semitono** /semi'tono/ *m, Mus.* semitone

**semitransparente** /semitranspa'rente/ *a* semitransparent

**semivivo** /semi'βiβo/ *a* half-alive

**sémola** /'semola/ *f,* semolina

**sempiterna** /sempi'terna/ *f,* everlasting flower; thick woolen material

**sempiterno** /sempi'terno/ *a* eternal

**sen** /sen/ *m,* senna

**Sena, el** /'sena, el/ the Seine

**sena** /'sena/ *f, Bot.* senna; six-spotted die

**senado** /se'naðo/ *m,* senate; senate house; any grave assembly

**senador** /sena'ðor/ *m,* senator

**senaduría** /sena'ðuria/ *f,* senatorship

**senario** /se'nario/ *a* senary

**senatorio** /sena'torio/ *a* senatorial

**sencillez** /senθi'ʎeθ; sensi'yes/ *f,* simplicity; naturalness; easiness; ingenuousness, candor

**sencillo** /sen'θiʎo; sen'siyo/ *a* simple; unmixed; natural; thin, light (fabric); easy; ingenuous, candid; unadorned, plain; single; sincere

**senda** /'senda/ *f,* path, footpath; way; means

**senderear** /sendere'ar/ *vt* to conduct along a path; make a pathway; —*vi* attain by tortuous means

**sendero** /sen'dero/ *m,* footpath, path

**sendos, sendas** /'sendos, 'sendas/ *a m,* and *f pl,* one each (e.g. *Les dio sendos lápices,* He gave them each a pencil)

**senectud** /senek'tuð/ *f,* old age

**senegalés** /senega'les/ **(-esa)** *a* and *n* Senegalese

**senescal** /senes'kal/ *m,* seneschal

**senil** /se'nil/ *a* senile

**senilidad** /senili'ðað/ *f,* senility

**seno** /'seno/ *m,* hollow; hole; concavity; bosom, breast; chest; uterus, womb; any internal cavity of the body; bay, cove; lap (of a woman); interior (of anything), heart; gulf; *Math.* sine; *Anat.* sinus

**sensación** /sensa'θion; sensa'sion/ *f,* sensation

**sensacional** /sensaθio'nal; sensasio'nal/ *a* sensational

**sensacionalista** /sensaθiona'lista; sensasiona'lista/ *a* sensationalist

**sensatez** /sensa'teθ; sensa'tes/ *f,* prudence, good sense

**sensato** /sen'sato/ *a* prudent, wise

**sensibilidad** /sensiβili'ðað/ *f,* sensibility

**sensibilizar** /sensiβili'θar; sensiβili'sar/ *vt Photo.* to sensitize

**sensible** /sen'siβle/ *a* sensible, sensitive; tender, feeling; perceptible; noticeable, definite; sensitive; sad, regrettable

**sensiblemente** /sensiβle'mente/ *adv* appreciably; perceptibly; painfully, sadly

**sensiblería** /sensiβle'ria/ *f,* sentimentality, sentimentalism

**sensiblero** /sensi'βlero/ *a* oversentimental

**sensitiva** /sensi'tiβa/ *f,* sensitive plant, mimosa

**sensitivo** /sensi'tiβo/ *a* sensuous; sensitive, sensible

**sensorio** /sen'sorio/ *a* sensory. *m,* sensorium

**sensual** /sen'sual/ *a* sensual; sensitive, sensible; carnal, voluptuous

**sensualidad** /sensuali'ðað/ *f,* sensuality; sensualism

**sensualismo** /sensua'lismo/ *m,* sensualism; *Philos.* sensationalism

**sensualista** /sensua'lista/ *mf Philos.* sensationalist; sensualist

**sentadero** /senta'ðero/ *m,* resting place, improvised seat

**sentado** /sen'taðo/ *a* prudent, circumspect

**sentar** /sen'tar/ *vt irr* to seat; —*vi* Inf. suit, agree with (e.g. *No me sienta este clima (este plato),* This climate (dish) doesn't suit me); fit, become; *Inf.* please, satisfy, be agreeable to; —*vr* sit down; *Inf.* leave a mark on the skin —*Pres. Ind.* **siento, sientas, sienta, sientan.** *Pres. Subjunc.* **siente, sientes, siente, sienten**

**sentencia** /sen'tenθia; sen'tensia/ *f,* opinion, belief; maxim; *Law.* verdict, sentence; decision, judgment. *Law.* **fulminar** ( or **pronunciar**) **la s.,** to pass sentence

**sentenciador** /sentenθia'ðor; sentensia'ðor/ *a Law.* sentencing

**sentenciar** /senten'θiar; senten'siar/ *vt Law.* to sentence; *Inf.* destine, intend

**sentencioso** /senten'θioso; senten'sioso/ *a* sententious

**sentidamente** /sentiða'mente/ *adv* feelingly; sadly, regretfully

**sentido** /sen'tiðo/ *m,* sense (hearing, seeing, touch, smell, taste); understanding, sense; meaning, interpretation, signification; perception, discrimination; judgment; direction, way —*a* and *past part* felt; expressive; hypersensitive, touchy. **s. común,** common sense. **costar un s.,** *Fig. Inf.* to cost a fortune. **perder el s.,** to lose consciousness

**sentimental** /sentimen'tal/ *a* emotional; sentimental; romantic

**sentimentalismo** /sentimenta'lismo/ *m,* emotional quality; sentimentalism

**sentimiento** /senti'miento/ *m,* feeling, sentiment; sensation, impression; grief, sorrow. **Le acompaño a usted en su s.,** I sympathize with you in your sorrow (bereavement)

**sentina** /sen'tina/ *f,* well (of a ship); *Naut.* bilge; cesspool; sink of iniquity

**sentir** /sen'tir/ *vt irr* to feel, experience; hear; appreciate; grieve, regret; believe, consider; envisage, foresee; —*vr* complain; suffer; think or consider oneself; crack; feel, be; go rotten, decay (gen. with *estar +* *Past Part.*). *m,* view, opinion; feeling. **sin s.,** without noticing —*Pres. Part.* **sintiendo.** *Pres. Indic.* **siento, sientes, siente, sienten.** *Preterite* **sintió, sintieron.** *Pres. Subjunc.* **sienta, sientas, sienta, sintamos, sintáis, sientan.** *Imperf. Subjunc.* **sintiese,** etc.

**seña** /'seɲa/ *f,* sign, mark; gesture; *Mil.* password; signal; *pl* address, domicile. **s. mortal,** definite or unmistakable sign. **dar señas,** to show signs, manifest. **hablar por señas,** to converse by signs

**señal** /se'ɲal/ *f,* mark, sign; boundary stone; landmark; scar; signal; trace, vestige; indication, symptom, token; symbol, sign; image, representation; prodigy, marvel; deposit, advance payment. **s. de aterrizaje,** *Aer.* landing signal. **s. de niebla,** fog signal. **señales horarias,** *Radio.* time signal. **en s.,** as a sign, in proof of. **s. luminosa de la circulación,** traffic light, traffic robot

**señaladamente** /seɲalaða'mente/ *adv* especially, particularly, notably

**señalado** /seɲa'laðo/ *a* famous, distinguished; important, notable

**señalador** /seɲala'ðor/ *m, Argentina* bookmark

**señalamiento** /seɲala'miento/ *m,* marking; pointing out; appointment, designation

**señalar** /seɲa'lar/ *vt* to mark; indicate, point out; fix, arrange; wound; signal; stamp; appoint (to office); —*vr* excel

**señero** /se'ɲero/ *a* solitary, isolated

**señor** /se'ɲor/ *a Inf.* gentlemanly. *m,* owner, master; mister, esquire; **(S.)** the Lord; lord, sire. **s. de horca y cuchillo,** feudal lord, lord of life and death

**señora** /se'ɲora/ *f,* lady; owner, mistress; madam; wife. **s. de compañía,** chaperon; lady companion. **Nuestra S.,** Our Lady

**señorear** /seɲore'ar/ *vt* to control, run, manage; master; domineer; appropriate, seize; dominate, overlook; restrain (emotions); —*vr* behave with dignity

**señoría** /seɲo'ria/ *f,* lordship (title and person); lordship, jurisdiction; area, territory; control, restraint

**señoría** /seɲo'ria/ *f,* dignity, sedateness; self-control

**señorial** /seɲo'rial/ *a* manorial; noble, dignified, lordly

**señoril** /seɲo'ril/ *a* lordly, noble, aristocratic

**señorío** /seɲo'rio/ *m,* lordship; jurisdiction, dominion

**señorita** /seɲo'rita/ *f,* young lady; miss; *Inf.* mistress of the house

**señorito** /seɲo'rito/ *m,* young gentleman; *Inf.* master of the house; master (address); *Inf.* young man about town

**señuelo** /se'ɲuelo/ *m,* decoy; bait; allurement, attraction. **caer en el s.,** *Fig. Inf.* to fall into the trap

**sepancuantos** /sepan'kuantos/ *m, Inf.* scolding, rebuke; spanking

**separación** /separa'θion; separa'sion/ *f,* separation

**separado** /sepa'raðo/ *a* separate

**separador** /separa'ðor/ **(-ra)** *a* separating —*n* separator. *m,* filter. **s. de aceite,** oil filter

**separar** /sepa'rar/ *vt* to separate; divide; dismiss (from a post); lay aside; —*vr* retire, resign; separate

**separatismo** /separa'tismo/ *m,* separatism

**separatista** /separa'tista/ *a* and *mf* separatist

**septeno** /sep'teno/ *a.* See **séptimo**

**septentrión** /septen'trion/ *m, Astron.* Great Bear; north

**septentrional** /septentrio'nal/ *a* north; northern

**septeto** /sep'teto/ *m,* septet

**septicemia** /septi'θemia; septi'semia/ *f,* septicemia

**séptico** /'septiko/ *a* septic

**septiembre** /sep'tiembre/ *m,* September

**septillo** /sep'tiʎo; sep'tiyo/ *m, Mus.* septuplet

**séptima** /'septima/ *f, Mus.* seventh

**séptimo** /'septimo/ *a* and *m,* seventh

**septuagenario** /septuahe'nario/ **(-ia)** *a* and *n* septuagenarian

**septuagésimo** /septua'hesimo/ *a* seventieth; septuagesimal. *m,* seventieth

**séptuplo** /'septuplo/ *a* sevenfold

**sepulcral** /sepul'kral/ *a* sepulchral

**sepulcro** /se'pulkro/ *m,* sepulcher

**sepultador** /sepulta'ðor/ **(-ra)** *a* burying —*n* gravedigger; burier

**sepultar** /sepul'tar/ *vt* to inter, bury; hide, cover up

**sepultura** /sepul'tura/ *f,* interment; grave; tomb

**sepulturero** /sepultu'rero/ *m,* gravedigger

**sequedad** /seke'ðað/ *f,* dryness, barrenness; acerbity, sharpness

**sequía** /se'kia/ *f,* drought

**séquito** /'sekito/ *m,* following, suite, retinue; general approval, popularity

**ser** /ser/ *m,* essence, nature; being; existence, life. **El S. Supremo,** The Supreme Being, God

**ser** /ser/ *vi irr* to be (e.g. *El sombrero es azul,* The hat

is blue). **Ser** may agree with either subject or complement, though when latter is *pl* the verb tends to be so too (e.g. *Son las once, (horas),* It is eleven o'clock. **Cien libras son poco dinero,** A hundred pounds is a small amount). If verbal complement is pers. pron., **ser** agrees with it both in number and person (e.g. *Son ellos,* It is they. *Soy yo,* It is I). In impers. phrases the pron. is not expressed (e.g. *Es difícil,* It is difficult. *Es sorprendente,* It is surprising). **ser** means to exist (e.g. *Pienso luego soy,* I think, therefore I am). **ser** (also **ser de** with nouns or obj. prons.) means to belong to, be the property of (e.g. *Este gato es mío,* This cat is mine. *El libro es de Juan,* The book belongs to John). Signifies to happen, occur (e.g. *¿Cómo fue eso?* How did that happen?). Means to be suitable or fitting (e.g. *Este vestido no es para una señora mayor,* This dress is not suitable for an elderly lady). Expresses price, to be worth (e.g. *¿A cuánto es la libra?* How much is it a pound?; How much is the pound (sterling) worth?). Means to be a member of, belong to (e.g. *Es de la Academia Española,* He is a member of the Spanish Academy). Means to be of use, be useful for (e.g. *Esta casa no es para una familia numerosa,* This house is no use for a large family). **Ser** expresses nationality (e.g. *Son francesas,* They are French. *Somos de Londres,* We are from London) —*Auxiliary verb* used to form passive tense (e.g. *Esta historia ha sido leída por muchos,* This story has been read by many. *Fueron mandados al Japón,* They were sent to Japan. *s. de ver,* to be worth seeing. *s. para poco,* to be of little use, amount to little. *s. testigo de,* to witness. *¡Cómo es eso!* How can that be! Surely not! *¡Cómo ha de s.!* How should it be!; One must resign oneself. *Érase una vez or que érase,* Once upon a time. *es a saber,* viz., that is to say. *un sí es no es,* a touch of, a suspicion of) —*Pres. Part.* **siendo.** *Pres. Indic.* **soy, eres, es, somos, sois, son.** *Fut.* **seré,** etc —*Condit.* **sería,** etc —*Preterite* **fui, fuiste, fue, fuimos, fuisteis, fueron.** *Imperf.* **era,** etc —*Past Part.* **sido.** *Pres. Subjunc.* **sea,** etc —*Imperf. Subjunc.* **fuese,** etc —*Imperat.* **sé**

**sera** /'sera/ *f,* large frail

**seráfico** /se'rafiko/ *a* seraphic

**serafín** /sera'fin/ *m,* seraphim

**serbal** /ser'βal/ *m,* service tree

**serena** /se'rena/ *f,* serenade; *Inf.* dew

**serenar** /sere'nar/ *vt* to calm; soothe; clear; —*vr* grow calm; clear up (weather); clear (liquids); be soothed or pacified

**serenata** /sere'nata/ *f,* serenade

**serenidad** /sereni'ðað/ *f,* serenity, composure, tranquility; Serene Highness (title)

**sereno** /se'reno/ *a* cloudless, fair; composed, serene. *m,* dew; night watchman

**sericultor** /serikul'tor/ *m,* silk cultivator, sericulturist

**sericultura** /serikul'tura/ *f,* silk culture

**serie** /'serie/ *f,* series, sequence, succession; *Math.* progression; (*Biol. Elec.*) series; break (in billiards)

**seriedad** /serie'ðað/ *f,* seriousness, earnestness; gravity; austerity; sternness; importance; sincerity; solemnity

**serigrafía** /serigra'fia/ *f,* silkscreen printing

**serio** /'serio/ *a* serious, earnest; grave; austere; stern; important; sincere, genuine; solemn. **en s.,** seriously

**sermón** /ser'mon/ *m,* sermon; scolding. **dar un s.,** to give a sermon; scold

**sermonar** /sermo'nar/ *vi* to preach

**sermonear** /sermone'ar/ *vi* to preach sermons; —*vt* scold

**sermoneo** /sermo'neo/ *m, Inf.* scolding

**seroja** /se'roha/ *f,* withered leaves; brushwood

**serpear** /serpe'ar/ *vi* to wind, twist; wriggle, squirm; coil

**serpenteado** /serpente'aðo/ *a* winding

**serpentear** /serpente'ar/ *vi* to wind, twist, meander; stagger along; wriggle; coil; *Aer.* yaw

**serpenteo** /serpen'teo/ *m,* winding, twisting; wriggling; coiling; *Aer.* yaw

**serpentín** /serpen'tin/ *m, Chem.* worm; coil (in industry); *Mineral.* serpentine

**serpentina** /serpen'tina/ *f, Mineral.* serpentine; paper streamer

**serpentino** /serpen'tino/ *a* serpentine; *Poet.* winding, sinuous

**serpiente** /ser'piente/ *f*, snake, serpent; Satan, the Devil; *Astron.* Serpent. **s. de anteojos,** cobra. **s. de cascabel,** rattlesnake

**serpollo** /ser'poʎo; ser'poyo/ *m*, *Bot.* shoot, new branch; sprout; sucker

**serrado** /se'rraðo/ *a* serrate

**serrallo** /se'rraʎo; se'rrayo/ *m*, harem, seraglio; brothel

**serrana, serranilla** /se'rrana; serra'niʎa, serra'niya/ *f*, pastoral poem

**serranía** /serra'nia/ *f*, mountainous territory

**serrano** /se'rrano/ **(-na)** *a* mountain, highland —*n* highlander, mountain dweller

**serrucho** /se'rrutʃo/ *m*, handsaw. **s. de calar,** fretsaw

**Servia** /'serβia/ Serbia

**servible** /ser'βiβle/ *a* serviceable; useful

**servicial** /serβi'θial; serβi'sial/ *a* useful, serviceable; obliging, obsequious

**servicio** /ser'βiθio; ser'βisio/ *m*, service; domestic service; cult, devotion; care, attendance; military service; set, service; department, section; present of money; cover (cutlery, etc., at table); domestic staff, servants. **s. informativo,** news service. **s. nocturno permanente,** all-night service. **hacer un flaco s.** (a), *Inf.* to do someone an ill turn. **prestar servicios,** to render service, serve

**servidor** /serβi'ðor/ **(-ra)** *n* servant, domestic; name by which one refers to oneself (e.g. *Un s. lo hará con mucho gusto,* I (your servant) will do it with much pleasure). *m*, wooer, lover; bowler (in cricket). **los servidores de una ametralladora,** the crew (of a gun). **Quedo de Vd. atento y seguro s.,** I remain your obedient servant (in letters), Yours faithfully

**servidumbre** /serβi'ðumbre/ *f*, serfdom; servitude; servants, domestic staff; obligation, duty; enslavement (by passions); right of way; use, service

**servil** /ser'βil/ *a* servile; humble

**servilismo** /serβi'lismo/ *m*, servility; abjectness; absolutism (Spanish history)

**servilleta** /serβi'ʎeta; serβi'yeta/ *f*, table napkin. **s. higiénica,** sanitary napkin

**servilletero** /serβiʎe'tero; serβiye'tero/ *m*, napkin ring

**servio** /'serβio/ **(-ia)** *a* and *n* Serbian

**servir** /ser'βir/ *vi irr* to be employed (by), be in the service (of); serve (as), perform the duties (of); be of use; wait (on), be subject to. *Mil.* serve in the armed forces; wait at table; be suitable or favorable; *Sports.* serve; perform a service; follow the lead (cards); (*with de*) act as, be a deputy for; be a substitute for; —*vt* serve; worship; do a favor to; woo, court; serve (food, drink); —*vr* be pleased or willing, deign; help oneself to (food); (*with de*) make use of. **no s. para nada,** to be good for nothing, be useless. **No sirves para tales cosas,** You are no good at this sort of thing. **Para s. a Vd,** At your service. **¡Sírvase de...!** (followed by infin.), Please! **s. de,** to serve as (e.g. *s. de base a,* to serve as a basis for). See **pedir**

**sésamo** /'sesamo/ *m*, sesame

**sesenta** /se'senta/ *a* and *m*, sixty; sixtieth

**sesentavo** /sesen'taβo/ *a* and *m*, sixtieth

**sesentón** /sesen'ton/ **(-ona)** *n Inf.* person of sixty

**sesga** /'sesga/ *f*, *Sew.* gore

**sesgadamente** /sesgaða'mente/ *adv* on the slant; askew; obliquely

**sesgado** /ses'gaðo/ *a* oblique, slanting

**sesgar** /ses'gar/ *vt Sew.* to cut on the bias; slant, slope; place askew, twist to one side

**sesgo** /'sesgo/ *a* slanting, oblique; serious-faced. *m*, slope, slant, obliquity; compromise, middle way. **al s.,** on the slant

**sesión** /se'sion/ *f*, session, meeting; conference, consultation; *Law.* sitting; term. **abrir la s.,** to open the meeting. **levantar la s.,** to adjourn the meeting

**seso** /'seso/ *m*, brain; prudence; *pl* brains. **perder el s.,** to go mad; *Fig.* lose one's head

**sestear** /seste'ar/ *vi* to take an afternoon nap; rest; settle

**sesudez** /sesu'ðeθ; sesu'ðes/ *f*, prudence, shrewdness

**sesudo** /se'suðo/ *a* sensible, prudent

**seta** /'seta/ *f*, mushroom. **s. venenosa,** poisonous toadstool

**setal** /se'tal/ *m*, mushroom bed, patch, or field

**setecientos** /sete'θientos; sete'sientos/ *a* and *m*, seven hundred; seven-hundredth

**setenta** /se'tenta/ *a* and *m*, seventy; seventieth

**setentavo** /seten'taβo/ *a* and *m*, seventieth

**setentón** /seten'ton/ **(-ona)** *n* septuagenarian

**seter** /'seter/ *m*, setter (dog)

**setiembre** /se'tiembre/ *m.* See **septiembre**

**seto** /'seto/ *m*, fence; hedge

**seudo** /'seuðo/ *a* pseudo

**seudónimo** /seu'ðonimo/ *m*, pseudonym

**severamente** /seβera'mente/ *adv* severely, harshly

**severidad** /seβeri'ðað/ *f*, severity; harshness; strictness, rigor; austerity, seriousness

**severo** /se'βero/ *a* severe; harsh; strict, rigid, scrupulous, exact; austere, serious

**sevillanas** /seβi'ʎanas; seβi'yanas/ *f pl*, Sevillian dance and its music

**sevillano** /seβi'ʎano; seβi'yano/ **(-na)** *a* and *n* of or from Seville, Sevillian

**sexagenario** /seksahe'nario/ **(-ia)** *n* sexagenarian

**sexagésimo** /seksa'hesimo/ *a* sixtieth

**sexo** /'sekso/ *m*, sex; (sexual) organ

**sexología** /seksolo'hia/ *f*, sexology

**sexólogo** /sek'sologo/ **(-ga)** *n* sexologist

**sexta** /'seksta/ *f*, *Eccl.* sext; *Mus.* sixth

**sextante** /seks'tante/ *m*, *Math.* sextant

**sexteto** /seks'teto/ *m*, sextet

**sexto** /'seksto/ *a* sixth

**sextuplicación** /sekstuplika'θion; sekstuplika'sion/ *f*, multiplication by six

**sextuplicar** /sekstupli'kar/ *vt* to multiply by six, sextuple

**séxtuplo** /'sekstuplo/ *a* sixfold

**sexualidad** /seksuali'ðað/ *f*, sexuality

**si** /si/ *m*, *Mus.* B, seventh note of the scale —*conjunc* if; whether; even if, although. In conditional clause, **si,** meaning if, is followed by indicative tense unless statement be contrary to fact (e.g. *Si pierdes el tren, volverás a casa,* If you miss your train you will return home, *but Si hubieran venido habríamos ido al campo,* If they had come (but they didn't) we would have gone to the country). **Si** is used at the beginning of a clause to make expressions of doubt, desire, or affirmation more emphatic (e.g. *¡Si lo sabrá él, con toda su experiencia!* Of course he knows it, with all his experience. *¿Si será falsa la noticia?* Can the news be false?) **Si** also means whether (e.g. *Me preguntaron si era médico o militar,* They asked me whether I was a doctor or a soldier). Sometimes means even if, although (e.g. *Si viniesen no lo harían,* Even if they came they would not do it. *como si,* as if. *por si acaso,* in case, in the event of. *si bien,* although.

**sí** /si/ *pers pron reflexive 3rd pers m,* and *f, sing* and *pl* himself, herself, itself, themselves. Always used with prep. (e.g. *para sí,* for himself, herself, etc. *de por sí,* separately, on its own. *decir para sí,* to say to oneself)

**sí** /si/ *adv* yes. **sí** or **sí que** is frequently used to emphasize a verb generally in contrast to a previous negative (e.g. *Ellos no lo harán, pero yo sí,* They won't do it but I will). Often translated by "did" (e.g. *No lo vi todo, pero lo que sí vi,* I didn't see it all, but what I did see...). *m*, assent; yes; consent. **dar el sí,** to say yes; agree; accept an offer of marriage

**siamés** /sia'mes/ **(-esa)** *a* and *n* Siamese. *m*, Thai (language)

**sibarita** /siβa'rita/ *a* sybaritic. *mf* sybarite

**sibarítico** /siβa'ritiko/ *a* sybaritic; sensual

**sibaritismo** /siβari'tismo/ *m*, sybaritism

**siberiano** /siβe'riano/ **(-na)** *a* and *n* Siberian

**sibila** /si'βila/ *f*, sibyl

**sibilante** /siβi'lante/ *a* sibilant

**sibilino** /siβi'lino/ *a* sibylline

**sicario** /si'kario/ *m*, paid assassin

**Sicilia** /si'θilia; si'silia/ Sicily

**siciliano** /siθi'liano; sisi'liano/ **(-na)** *a* and *n* Sicilian

**sicoanálisis** /sikoa'nalisis/ *m*, psychoanalysis

**sicoanalista** /sikoana'lista/ *mf* psychoanalyst

**sicoanalizar** /sikoanali'θar; sikoanali'sar/ vt to psychoanalyze

**sicofanta, sicofante** /siko'fanta, siko'fante/ m, sycophant

**sicología** /sikolo'hia/ f, psychology

**sicológico** /siko'lohiko/ a psychological

**sicólogo** /si'kologo/ (**-ga**) n psychologist

**sicomoro** /siko'moro/ m, sycamore

**sicopático** /siko'patiko/ a psychopathic

**sicosis** /si'kosis/ f, Med. psychosis

**sicoterapia** /sikote'rapia/ f, psychotherapy

**SIDA** /'siða/ m, AIDS

**sideral, sidéreo** /siðe'ral, si'ðereo/ a sidereal

**sidra** /'siðra/ f, cider

**siega** /'siega/ f, reaping, harvesting; harvest time; harvest, crop

**siembra** /'siembra/ f, Agr. sowing; seedtime; sown field

**siempre** /'siempre/ adv always. **s. que,** provided that; whenever. **para s.,** forever. **por s. jamás,** for always, for ever and ever

**siempreviva** /siempre'βiβa/ f, Bot. everlasting flower. **s. mayor,** houseleek

**sien** /sien/ f, Anat. temple

**sierpe** /'sierpe/ f, serpent, snake; anything that wriggles; kite (toy); Bot. sucker; hideous person

**sierra** /'sierra/ f, saw; ridge of mountains; sawfish; slope; hillside. **s. de cerrojero,** hacksaw. **s. de cinta,** handsaw

**siervo** /'sierβo/ (**-va**) n slave; servant; serf

**siesta** /'siesta/ f, noonday heat; afternoon nap

**siete** /'siete/ a seven; seventh. m, seven; seventh (days of the month); playing card with seven spots; number seven. **las s.,** seven o'clock. Inf. **más que s.,** more than somewhat, extremely

**sietemesino** /sieteme'sino/ (**-na**) n seven-month-old child; Fig. Inf. young cock

**sífilis** /'sifilis/ f, syphilis

**sifilítico** /sifi'litiko/ (**-ca**) a and n syphilitic

**sifón** /si'fon/ m, siphon; siphon bottle; soda water; Mech. trap

**sigilar** /sihi'lar/ vt to seal; hide, conceal

**sigilo** /si'hilo/ m, seal; secrecy, concealment; silence, reserve

**sigiloso** /sihi'loso/ a secret, silent

**sigla** /'sigla/ f, acronym

**siglo** /'siglo/ m, century; long time, age; social intercourse, society, world. **s. de oro,** golden age. **en** or **por los siglos de los siglos,** for ever and ever

**signar** /sig'nar/ vt to sign; make the sign of the cross over; —vr cross oneself

**signatario** /signa'tario/ (**-ia**) a and n signatory

**signatura** /signa'tura/ f, Print. signature; mark, sign; Mus. signature

**significación** /signifika'θion; signifika'sion/ f, **significado** m, meaning; importance, significance

**significante** /signifi'kante/ a significant

**significar** /signifi'kar/ vt to signify, indicate; mean; publish, make known; —vi represent, mean; be worth

**significativo** /signifika'tiβo/ a significant

**signo** /'signo/ m, sign, indication, token; sign, character; Math. symbol; sign of the zodiac; Mus. sign; Med. symptom; Eccl. gesture of benediction; destiny, fate

**siguemepollo** /sigeme'poʎo; sigeme'poyo/ m, Inf. streamer

**siguiente** /si'giente/ a following; next, subsequent. **el día s.,** the next day

**sílaba** /'silaβa/ f, syllable

**silabario** /sila'βario/ m, speller, spelling book

**silabear** /silaβe'ar/ vi and vt to pronounce by syllables, syllabize

**silabeo** /sila'βe'o/ m, pronouncing syllable by syllable, syllabication

**silábico** /si'laβiko/ a syllabic

**sílabo** /'silaβo/ m, syllabus, list

**silba** /'silβa/ f, hissing (as a sign of disapproval)

**silbador** /silβa'ðor/ (**-ra**) a whistling; hissing —n whistler; one who hisses

**silbar** /sil'βar/ vi to whistle; whizz, rush through the air; —vi and vt Theat. hiss

**silbato** /sil'βato/ m, whistle; air hole

**silbido, silbo** /sil'βiðo, 'silβo/ m, whistle, whistling; hiss, hissing

**silenciador** /silenθia'ðor; silensia'ðor/ m, (Auto. firearms) silencer

**silenciar** /silen'θiar; silen'siar/ vt to silence; keep secret

**silenciario** /silen'θiario; silen'siario/ a vowed to perpetual silence

**silencio** /si'lenθio; si'lensio/ m, silence; noiselessness, quietness; omission, disregard; Mus. rest. **en s.,** in silence; quietly; uncomplainingly. **pasar en s. (una cosa),** to pass over (something) in silence, omit. **s. de muerte,** deathly silence

**silencioso** /silen'θioso; silen'sioso/ a silent; noiseless; tranquil, quiet. m, (Auto. firearms) silencer

**silesio** /si'lesio/ (**-ia**) a and n Silesian

**sílfide** /'silfiðe/ f, sylph

**silicato** /sili'kato/ m, Chem. silicate

**sílice** /'siliθe; 'silise/ f, Chem. silica

**silla** /'siʎa; 'siya/ f, chair; riding saddle; Mech. rest, saddle; Eccl. see. **s. de manos,** sedan chair. **s. de montar,** riding saddle. **s. de posta,** post chaise. **s. de ruedas,** wheelchair. **s. de tijera,** deck chair; campstool. **s. giratoria,** swivel chair. **s. poltrona,** easy chair. Inf. **pegársele la s.,** to overstay one's welcome

**sillar** /si'ʎar; si'yar/ m, ashlar, quarry stone; horseback

**sillería** /siʎe'ria; siye'ria/ f, set of chairs; pew, choir stalls; chair factory; shop where chairs are sold; chair making; Mas. ashlar masonry

**sillero** /si'ʎero; si'yero/ (**-ra**) n chair maker or seller; saddler

**silleta** /si'ʎeta; si'yeta/ f, bedpan; fireman's lift

**silletero** /siʎe'tero; siye'tero/ m, runner, sedan chair carrier

**sillín** /si'ʎin; si'yin/ m, light riding saddle; seat, saddle (of bicycles, etc.)

**sillón** /si'ʎon; si'yon/ m, armchair; sidesaddle. **s.- cama,** reclining chair. **s. de mimbres,** cane chair

**silo** /'silo/ m, Agr. silo; dark cavern, dark cave

**silogismo** /silo'hismo/ m, syllogism

**silogístico** /silo'histiko/ a syllogistic

**silueta** /si'lueta/ f, silhouette; figure

**silúrico** /si'luriko/ a silurian

**siluro** /si'luro/ m, catfish; Nav. self-propelling torpedo

**silva** /'silβa/ f, literary miscellany; metrical form

**silvestre** /sil'βestre/ a Bot. wild; sylvan; uncultivated; savage

**silvicultor** /silβikul'tor/ m, forester

**silvicultura** /silβikul'tura/ f, forestry

**sima** /'sima/ f, abyss, chasm

**simbiosis** /sim'biosis/ f, symbiosis

**simbólico** /sim'boliko/ a symbolical

**simbolismo** /simbo'lismo/ m, symbolism

**simbolista** /simbo'lista/ mf symbolist

**simbolización** /simboliθa'θion; simbolisa'sion/ f, symbolization

**simbolizar** /simboli'θar; simboli'sar/ vt to symbolize, represent

**símbolo** /'simbolo/ m, symbol. **s. de la fe,** Eccl. Creed

**simetría** /sime'tria/ f, symmetry

**simétrico** /si'metriko/ a symmetric; symmetrical

**simetrizar** /simetri'θar; simetri'sar/ vt to make symmetrical

**símico** /'simiko/ a simian

**simiente** /si'miente/ f, seed; semen; germ, genesis, origin

**simiesco** /si'miesko/ a apish, ape-like

**símil** /'simil/ a similar. m, comparison; simile

**similar** /simi'lar/ a similar

**similitud** /simili'tuð/ f, similarity

**simio** /'simio/ (**-ia**) n ape

**simón** /si'mon/ m, horse cab; cabdriver

**simonía** /simo'nia/ f, simony

**simpatía** /simpa'tia/ f, liking, understanding, affection; fellow feeling; sympathy

**simpático** /sim'patiko/ *a* friendly, nice, decent, congenial; sympathetic. **gran s.,** *Anat.* sympathetic

**simpatizar** /simpati'θar; simpati'sar/ *vi* to get on well, be congenial

**simple** /'simple/ *a* simple; single, not double; insipid; easy; plain, unadorned; stupid, silly; pure, unmixed; easily deceived, simple; naïve, ingenuous; mere; mild, meek. *mf* simpleton; fool

**simpleza** /sim'pleθa; sim'plesa/ *f,* foolishness, stupidity; simplicity

**simplicidad** /simpliθi'ðað; simplisi'ðað/ *f,* simplicity; candor, ingenuousness

**simplicísimo** /simpli'θisimo; simpli'sisimo/ *a superl* most simple, exceedingly simple

**simplificable** /simplifi'kaβle/ *a* simplifiable

**simplificación** /simplifika'θion; simplifika'sion/ *f,* simplification, simplifying

**simplificador** /simplifika'ðor/ *a* simplifying

**simplificar** /simplifi'kar/ *vt* to simplify

**simplista** /sim'plista/ *mf* herbalist

**simulación** /simula'θion; simula'sion/ *f,* pretense, simulation

**simulacro** /simu'lakro/ *m,* image, simulacrum; vision, fancy; *Mil.* mock battle

**simuladamente** /simulaða'mente/ *adv* pretendedly

**simulador** /simula'ðor/ **(-ra)** *a* feigned —*n* dissembler

**simular** /simu'lar/ *vt* to feign, pretend

**simultanear** /simultane'ar/ *vt* to perform simultaneously

**simultaneidad** /simultanei'ðað/ *f,* simultaneousness

**simultáneo** /simul'taneo/ *a* simultaneous

**simún** /si'mun/ *m,* sandstorm

**sin** /sin/ *prep* without (e.g. *Lo hizo s. hablar,* He did it without speaking). **s. embargo,** nevertheless. **s. fin,** endless. **s. hilos,** radio, wireless

**sinagoga** /sina'goga/ *f,* synagogue

**sinapismo** /sina'pismo/ *m, Med.* mustard plaster; *Inf.* pest, bore

**sincerarse** /sinθe'rarse; sinse'rarse/ *vr* to justify oneself; vindicate one's actions

**sinceridad** /sinθeri'ðað; sinseri'ðað/ *f,* sincerity

**sincero** /sin'θero; sin'sero/ *a* sincere

**síncopa** /'sinkopa/ *f, Mus.* syncopation; *Gram.* syncope

**sincopar** /sinko'par/ *vt* to syncopate; abbreviate

**síncope** /'sinkope/ *m,* syncope

**sincrónico** /sin'kroniko/ *a* synchronous

**sincronismo** /sinkro'nismo/ *m,* synchronism

**sincronizar** /sinkroni'θar; sinkroni'sar/ *vt* to synchronize; *Radio.* tune in

**sindéresis** /sin'deresis/ *f,* discretion, good sense

**sindicación** /sindika'θion; sindika'sion/ *f,* syndication

**sindicado** /sindi'kaðo/ *m,* syndicate

**sindical** /sindi'kal/ *a* syndical

**sindicalismo** /sindika'lismo/ *m,* syndicalism, trade unionism

**sindicalista** /sindika'lista/ *mf* syndicalist, trade unionist —*a* syndicalistic, trade unionist

**sindicar** /sindi'kar/ *vt* to accuse, charge; censure; syndicate

**sindicato** /sindi'kato/ *m,* syndicate; trade union. **s. gremial,** trade union. **S. Internacional de Trabajadoras de la Aguja,** International Ladies' Garment Workers' Union

**sindicatura** /sindika'tura/ *f,* (official) receivership

**síndico** /'sindiko/ *m, Com.* receiver, trustee

**síndrome** /'sindrome/ *m,* syndrome

**sinecura** /sine'kura/ *f,* sinecure

**sinergia** /si'nerhia/ *f,* synergy

**sinfín** /sin'fin/ *m,* countless number

**sinfonía** /sinfo'nia/ *f,* symphony

**sinfónico** /sin'foniko/ *a* symphonic

**sinfonista** /sinfo'nista/ *mf* composer of symphonies, player in a symphony orchestra

**sinfonola** /sinfo'nola/ *f,* jukebox

**Singapur** /singa'pur/ Singapore

**singladura** /singla'ðura/ *f, Naut.* day's sailing; nautical twenty-four hours (beginning at midday)

**singlar** /sin'glar/ *vi Naut.* to sail a given course

**singular** /singu'lar/ *a* singular, single; individual; extraordinary, remarkable —*a* and *m, Gram.* singular

**singularidad** /singulari'ðað/ *f,* individuality, peculiarity; strangeness, remarkableness; oddness, eccentricity

**singularizar** /singulari'θar; singulari'sar/ *vt* to particularize, single out; *Gram.* make singular, singularize; —*vr* distinguish oneself, stand out; be distinguished (by)

**sinhueso** /sin'ueso/ *f, Inf.* tongue (organ of speech)

**sínico** /'siniko/ *a* Chinese

**siniestra** /si'niestra/ *f,* left, lefthand

**siniestro** /si'niestro/ *a* left (side); vicious, perverse; sinister; unlucky. *m,* viciousness, depravity (gen. *pl*); shipwreck, sinking; disaster, catastrophe; *Com.* damage, loss

**sinnúmero** /sin'numero/ *m,* countless number

**sino** /'sino/ *m,* fate, destiny —*conjunc* but; except (e.g. *No lo hicieron ellos s. yo,* They didn't do it, I did. *no... s.,* not..., but); only (e.g. *No sólo lo dijo él s. ella,* Not only he said it, but she did too)

**sínodo** /'sinoðo/ *m, (Eccl. Astron.)* synod; council

**sinología** /sinolo'hia/ *f,* sinology

**sinólogo** /si'nologo/ *m,* sinologist

**sinonimia** /sino'nimia/ *f,* synonymy

**sinónimo** /si'nonimo/ *a* synonymous. *m,* synonym

**sinopsis** /si'nopsis/ *f,* synopsis

**sinóptico** /si'noptiko/ *a* synoptic

**sinrazón** /sinra'θon; sinra'son/ *f,* injustice, wrong

**sinsabor** /sinsa'βor/ *m,* unpleasantness, trouble; grief, anxiety

**sintáctico** /sin'taktiko/ *a* syntactic

**sintaxis** /sin'taksis/ *f,* syntax

**síntesis** /'sintesis/ *f,* synthesis

**sintético** /sin'tetiko/ *a* synthetic

**sintetizar** /sinteti'θar; sinteti'sar/ *vt* to synthesize

**sintoísmo** /sinto'ismo/ *m,* Shintoism

**síntoma** /'sintoma/ *m,* symptom

**sintomático** /sinto'matiko/ *a* symptomatic

**sintomatología** /sintomatolo'hia/ *f,* symptomatology

**sintonización** /sintoniθa'θion; sintonisa'sion/ *f, Radio.* tuning in

**sintonizador** /sintoniθa'ðor; sintonisa'ðor/ *m, Radio.* tuner

**sintonizar** /sintoni'θar; sintoni'sar/ *vt Radio.* to tune in

**sinuosidad** /sinuosi'ðað/ *f,* sinuosity

**sinuoso** /sin'uoso/ *a* sinuous, winding

**sinvergüenza** /simber'guenθa; simber'guensa/ *mf* rascal, knave, rogue

**Sión** /'sion/ Zion

**sionismo** /sio'nismo/ *m,* Zionism

**sionista** /sio'nista/ *a* and *mf* Zionist

**siquiatra** /si'kiatra/ *m,* psychiatrist

**siquiatría** /sikia'tria/ *f,* psychiatry

**síquico** /'sikiko/ *a* psychic

**siquiera** /si'kiera/ *conjunc* although, even if. **s.... s.,** whether... or —*adv* at least; even (e.g. *Hay que pedir mucho para tener s. la mitad,* One must ask a great deal to get even half). **ni s.,** not even (e.g. *No había nadie, ni s. un perro,* There was no one, not even a dog)

**Siracusa** /sira'kusa/ Syracuse

**siracusano** /siraku'sano/ **(-na)** *a* and *n* Syracusan

**sirena** /si'rena/ *f,* mermaid, siren; siren; foghorn

**sirga** /'sirga/ *f,* towline

**sirgar** /sir'gar/ *vt Naut.* to track, tow

**Siria** /'siria/ Syria

**siríaco** /si'riako/ **(-ca)** *a* and *n* Syriac

**sirio** /'sirio/ **(-ia)** *a* and *n* Syrian. *m,* Sirius

**siroco** /si'roko/ *m,* sirocco

**sirte** /'sirte/ *f,* sandbank, submerged rock

**sirvienta** /sir'βienta/ *f,* female servant

**sirviente** /sir'βiente/ *a* serving. *m,* servant

**sisa** /'sisa/ *f,* pilfering; *Sew.* dart. **s. dorada,** gold lacquer

**sisador** /sisa'ðor/ **(-ra)** *n* filcher, pilferer

**sisar** /si'sar/ *vt* to pilfer, filch, steal; *Sew.* take in, make darts in

**sisear** /sise'ar/ *vi* and *vt* to hiss (disapproval); sizzle

**sísmico** /'sismiko/ *a* seismic

**sismógrafo** /sis'mografo/ *m*, seismograph

**sismología** /sismolo'hia/ *f*, seismology

**sismológico** /sismo'lohiko/ *a* seismological

**sismómetro** /sis'mometro/ *m*, seismometer

**sistema** /sis'tema/ *m*, system. **s. ferroviario,** railroad system. **s. métrico,** metric system

**sistemático** /siste'matiko/ *a* systematic

**sistematización** /sistematiθa'θion; sistematisa'sion/ *f*, systematization

**sistematizar** /sistemati'θar; sistemati'sar/ *vt* to systematize

**sístole** /'sistole/ *f*, systole

**sitiador** /sitia'ðor/ *a* besieging. *m*, besieger

**sitial** /si'tial/ *m*, ceremonial chair

**sitiar** /si'tiar/ *vt* Mil. to lay siege to; surround, besiege

**sitio** /'sitio/ *m*, place, spot; room, space; site; locality; Mil. siege, blockade. **No hay s.,** There's no room

**sito** /'sito/ *past part* situated, located

**situación** /situa'θion; situa'sion/ *f*, situation; position; circumstances; condition, state; location

**situado** /si'tuaðo/ *past part* situated, placed. *m*, income, interest

**situar** /si'tuar/ *vt* to situate, locate, place; assign funds; —*vr* place oneself

**smoking** /'smokiŋ/ *m*, tuxedo, tux, dinner jacket

**snobismo** /sno'βismo/ *m*, snobbery

**so** /so/ *prep* under (used only with **color, pena, pretexto, capa**) (e.g. *so color de,* under the pretext of) —*interj* **¡So!** Whoa! (to horses)

**soba** /'soβa/ *f*, rubbing; kneading; massaging; drubbing, beating; handling, touching

**sobacal** /soβa'kal/ *a* underarm, axillary

**sobaco** /so'βako/ *m*, armpit; Bot. axil

**sobajar** /soβa'har/ *vt* to squeeze, press

**sobaquera** /soβa'kera/ *f*, Sew. armhole; dress shield

**sobar** /so'βar/ *vt* to rub; knead; massage; beat, thrash; handle, touch, paw (persons); soften

**soberanear** /soβerane'ar/ *vi* to tyrannize, domineer

**soberanía** /soβera'nia/ *f*, sovereignty; dominance, sway, rule; dignity, majesty

**soberano** /soβe'rano/ **(-na)** *a* sovereign; superb; regal, majestic —*n* ruler, lord. *m*, sovereign (coin)

**soberbia** /so'βerβia/ *f*, arrogance, haughtiness; conceit, presumption; ostentation, pomp; rage, anger

**soberbio** /so'βerβio/ *a* haughty, arrogant; conceited; superb, magnificent; lofty, soaring; spirited (of horses)

**sobón** /so'βon/ *a* Inf. overdemonstrative, mushy; Inf. lazy

**sobordo** /so'βorðo/ *m*, Naut. manifest, freight list

**sobornación** /soβorna'θion; soβorna'sion/ *f*, bribing; bribery

**sobornador** /soβorna'ðor/ **(-ra)** *a* bribing —*n* briber

**sobornar** /soβor'nar/ *vt* to bribe

**soborno** /so'βorno/ *m*, bribing; bribe; inducement

**sobra** /'soβra/ *f*, excess, surplus; insult, outrage; *pl* leftovers (from a meal); remains, residue; rubbish, trash. **de s.,** in abundance; in excess, surplus; unnecessary, superfluous; too well

**sobradamente** /soβraða'mente/ *adv* abundantly; in excess

**sobrado** /so'βraðo/ *a* excessive; brazen, bold; wealthy, rich. *m*, garret

**sobrante** /so'βrante/ *a* surplus, leftover, remaining. *m*, remainder, surplus, excess

**sobrar** /so'βrar/ *vt* to exceed; have too much of (e.g. *Me sobran mantas,* I have too many blankets); —*vi* be superfluous; remain, be left. Inf. **Aquí sobro yo,** I am in the way here, My presence is superfluous

**sobrasada** /soβra'saða/ *f*, spicy sausage

**sobre** /'soβre/ *prep* upon, on; above, over; concerning, about; apart from, besides; about (e.g. *s. las nueve,* at about nine o'clock) (indicates approximation); toward; after. *m*, envelope; address, superscription. **s. cero,** above freezing (Fahrenheit); above zero (Centigrade). **s. el nivel del mar,** above sea level. **s. manera,** excessively, extremely. **s. todo,** especially

**sobreabundancia** /soβreaβun'danθia; soβreaβun'dansia/ *f*, superabundance, excess

**sobreabundante** /soβreaβun'dante/ *a* superabundant

**sobreabundar** /soβreaβun'dar/ *vi* to be superabundant

**sobreagudo** /soβrea'guðo/ *a* and *m*, Mus. treble (pitch)

**sobrealiento** /soβrea'liento/ *m*, heavy, painful breathing

**sobrealimentación** /soβrealimenta'θion; soβrealimenta'sion/ *f*, overfeeding; Auto. supercharge

**sobrealimentar** /soβrealimen'tar/ *vt* Auto. to supercharge

**sobreasar** /soβrea'sar/ *vt* to roast or cook again

**sobrecama** /soβre'kama/ *f*, bedspread, quilt

**sobrecarga** /soβre'karga/ *f*, overload; rope, etc., for securing bales and packs; additional trouble or anxiety

**sobrecargar** /soβrekar'gar/ *vt* to overload; weigh down; Sew. oversew, fell

**sobrecargo** /soβre'kargo/ *m*, Naut. purser; flight attendant

**sobrecarta** /soβre'karta/ *f*, envelope (for a letter)

**sobreceja** /soβre'θeha; soβre'seha/ *f*, brow, lower forehead; frown

**sobrecejo** /soβre'θeho; soβre'seho/ *m*, frown

**sobrecielo** /soβre'θielo; soβre'sielo/ *m*, canopy

**sobrecoger** /soβreko'her/ *vt* to take by surprise; —*vr* be frightened or apprehensive

**sobrecogimiento** /soβrekohi'miento/ *m*, fright, apprehension

**sobrecomida** /soβreko'miða/ *f*, dessert

**sobrecoser** /soβreko'ser/ *vt* Sew. to oversew, whip

**sobrecrecer** /soβrekre'θer; soβrekre'ser/ *vi irr* to grow too much. See **conocer**

**sobrecubierta** /soβreku'βierta/ *f*, second lid or cover; dust jacket (of a book); Naut. upper deck

**sobrecuello** /soβre'kueʎo; soβre'kueyo/ *m*, overcollar; loose collar

**sobredicho** /soβre'ðitʃo/ *a* aforementioned, aforesaid

**sobredorar** /soβreðo'rar/ *vt* to gild (metals); make excuses for

**sobreedificar** /soβreeðifi'kar/ *vt* to build upon or above

**sobreexcitar** /soβreeksθi'tar; soβreekssi'tar/ *vt* to overexcite

**sobrefaz** /soβre'faθ; soβre'fas/ *f*, surface, exterior

**sobreganar** /soβrega'nar/ *vt* to make an excess profit

**sobreguarda** /soβre'guarða/ *m*, head guard; extra or second guard

**sobreherido** /soβree'riðo/ *a* lightly wounded

**sobrehilar** /soβrei'lar/ *vt* to oversew or overcast. See **prohibir**

**sobrehumano** /soβreu'mano/ *a* superhuman

**sobrellenar** /soβreʎe'nar; soβreye'nar/ *vt* to fill full

**sobrellevar** /soβreʎe'βar; soβreye'βar/ *vt* to help in the carrying of a burden; endure, bear; make excuses for, overlook; help

**sobremesa** /soβre'mesa/ *f*, tablecloth; after-dinner conversation. **de s.,** Fig. at the dinner table

**sobrenadar** /soβrena'ðar/ *vi* to float

**sobrenatural** /soβrenatu'ral/ *a* supernatural; extraordinary, singular

**sobrenombre** /soβre'nombre/ *m*, additional surname; nickname

**sobrentender** /soβrenten'der/ *vt irr* to take for granted, understand as a matter of course; —*vr* go without saying. See **entender**

**sobrepaga** /soβre'paga/ *f*, overpayment; extra pay

**sobreparto** /soβre'parto/ *m*, time after parturition; afterbirth

**sobrepasar** /soβrepa'sar/ *vt* to exceed; outdo, excel

**sobrepelliz** /soβrepe'ʎiθ; soβrepe'yis/ *f*, surplice

**sobreponer** /soβrepo'ner/ *vt irr* to place over; overlap; —*vr* rise above (circumstances); dominate (persons). See **poner**

**sobreprecio** /soβre'preθio; soβre'presio/ *m*, extra charge; rise in price

**sobreproducción** /soβreproðuk'θion; soβreproðuk'sion/ *f*, overproduction

**sobrepuerta** /soβre'puerta/ *f*, curtain pelmet; door curtain

**sobrepujar** /soβrepu'har/ *vt* to excel, surpass, outdo

**sobrequilla** /soβre'kiʎa; soβre'kiya/ *f*, keelson

**sobrerrealismo** /soβrerrea'lismo/ *m*, surrealism

**sobrerrealista** /soβrerrea'lista/ *a* and *mf* surrealist

**sobresaliente** /soβresa'liente/ *a* overhanging; projecting; distinctive, outstanding; excellent, remarkable. *m*, "excellent" (mark in examinations). *mf Theat.* understudge

**sobresalir** /soβresa'lir/ *vi irr* to overhang, project; stand out; be conspicuous or noticeable; excel; distinguish oneself. See **salir**

**sobresaltar** /soβresal'tar/ *vt* to assail, rush upon; startle, frighten suddenly; —*vi Art.* stand out, be striking; —*vr* be startled or frightened

**sobresalto** /soβre'salto/ *m*, sudden attack; unexpected shock; agitation; sudden fear. **de s.,** unexpectedly

**sobresanar** /soβresa'nar/ *vi* to heal superficially but not deeply; conceal, dissemble

**sobrescribir** /soβreskri'βir/ *vt* to label; address, superscribe —*Past Part.* **sobrescrito**

**sobrescrito** /soβres'krito/ *m*, address, superscription

**sobresello** /soβre'seλo; soβre'seyo/ *m*, second seal

**sobrestante** /soβres'tante/ *m*, overseer; supervisor; foreman; inspector

**sobresueldo** /soβre'sueldo/ *m*, additional salary, bonus

**sobresuelo** /soβre'suelo/ *m*, second flooring

**sobretarde** /soβre'tarðe/ *f*, early evening, late afternoon

**sobretodo** /soβre'toðo/ *m*, overcoat

**sobrevenida** /soβreβe'niða/ *f*, sudden arrival

**sobrevenir** /soβreβe'nir/ *vi irr* occur, take place; supervene. See **venir**

**sobrevidriera** /soβreβi'ðriera/ *f*, storm window; wire-mesh window guard

**sobrevienta** /soβre'βienta/ *f*, gust of wind; fury, violence; shock, surprise. **a s.,** suddenly

**sobreviviente** /soβreβi'βiente/ *a* surviving. *mf* survivor

**sobrevivir** /soβreβi'βir/ *vi* to survive

**sobriedad** /soβrie'ðað/ *f*, sobriety, moderation

**sobrina** /so'βrina/ *f*, niece

**sobrino** /so'βrino/ *m*, nephew

**sobrio** /'soβrio/ *a* sober, moderate, temperate

**socaliña** /soka'liɲa/ *f*, cunning, craft

**socaliñero** /sokali'ɲero/ **(-ra)** *a* cunning —*n* trickster

**socalzar** /sokal'θar; sokal'sar/ *vt Mas.* to underpin

**socapa** /so'kapa/ *f*, blind, pretext. **a s.,** secretly; cautiously

**socarra** /so'karra/ *f*, scorching, singeing; craftiness

**socarrón** /soka'rron/ *a* cunning, deceitful; malicious, sly (of humor, etc.)

**socarronería** /sokarrone'ria/ *f*, cunning, craftiness; slyness (of humor, etc.); knavish action

**socava** /so'kaβa/ *f*, undermining; *Agr.* hoeing round tree roots

**socavar** /soka'βar/ *vt* to undermine

**sociabilidad** /soθiaβili'ðað; sosiaβili'ðað/ *f*, sociability

**sociable** /so'θiaβle; so'siaβle/ *a* sociable; social

**social** /so'θial; so'sial/ *a* social

**socialdemócrata** /soθialde'mokrata; sosialde'mokrata/ *a* and *mf* social democrat

**socialismo** /soθia'lismo; sosia'lismo/ *m*, socialism

**socialista** /soθia'lista; sosia'lista/ *mf* socialist —*a* socialistic

**socialización** /soθialiθa'θion; sosialisa'sion/ *f*, socialization

**socializar** /soθiali'θar; sosiali'sar/ *vt* to socialize

**sociedad** /soθie'ðað; sosie'ðað/ *f*, society; association; *Com.* partnership; *Com.* company. *Com.* **S. anónima,** incorporated company, limited company. **S. de las Naciones,** League of Nations. **s. de socorros mutuos,** mutual aid society. **s. en comandita,** private company

**socio** /'soθio; 'sosio/ **(-ia)** *n* associate, partner; member. **s. comanditario,** *Com.* silent partner

**sociología** /soθiolo'hia; sosiolo'hia/ *f*, sociology

**sociológico** /soθio'lohiko; sosio'lohiko/ *a* sociological

**sociólogo** /so'θiologo; so'siologo/ **(-ga)** *n* sociologist

**socollada** /soko'λaða; soko'yaða/ *f*, *Naut.* flapping (of sails); pitching (of a ship)

**socolor** /soko'lor/ *m*, pretext —*adv* (also **so c.**) under pretext

**socorredor** /sokorre'ðor/ **(-ra)** *a* aiding, succoring —*n* helper

**socorrer** /soko'rrer/ *vt* to aid, succor, assist; pay on account

**socorrido** /soko'rriðo/ *a* helpful, generous, prompt to assist; well-equipped, well-furnished; well-supplied

**socorro** /so'korro/ *m*, aid, help, assistance; payment on account; *Mil.* relief (provisions or arms)

**socrático** /so'kratiko/ *a* socratic

**sodio** /'soðio/ *m*, sodium

**sodomía** /soðo'mia/ *f*, sodomy

**sodomita** /soðo'mita/ *mf* sodomite —*a* sodomitic

**soez** /so'eθ; so'es/ *a* base, vile; vulgar

**sofá** /so'fa/ *m*, sofa, couch

**sofaldar** /sofal'dar/ *vt* to tuck up the skirts; disclose, reveal

**sofisma** /so'fisma/ *m*, sophism, fallacy

**sofista** /so'fista/ *a* sophistic. *mf* sophist, quibbler

**sofistería** /sofiste'ria/ *f*, sophistry

**sofístico** /so'fistiko/ *a* sophistic, fallacious

**soflama** /so'flama/ *f*, thin flame; glow; flush, blush; specious promise, deception

**soflamar** /sofla'mar/ *vt* to shame, make blush; promise with intent to deceive, swindle; —*vr Cul.* burn

**sofocación** /sofoka'θion; sofoka'sion/ *f*, suffocation, smothering; shame; anger

**sofocador, sofocante** /sofoka'ðor, sofo'kante/ *a* suffocating; stifling

**sofocar** /sofo'kar/ *vt* to suffocate, smother; extinguish; dominate, oppress; pester, importune; shame, make blush, make angry; agitate; —*vr* be ashamed; be angry

**sofocleo** /sofo'kleo/ *a* Sophoclean

**sofoco** /so'foko/ *m*, mortification, chagrin; shame; anger; suffocation, smothering; hot flush

**sofreír** /sofre'ir/ *vt irr* to fry lightly. See **reír**

**sofrenada** /sofre'naða/ *f*, sudden check, pulling up short (of horses); harsh scolding; moral restraint

**sofrenar** /sofre'nar/ *vt* to pull up, check suddenly (horses); scold harshly; restrain, repress (emotions)

**soga** /'soga/ *f*, rope; land measure (varies in length). *m*, *Inf.* rogue, knave

**soguería** /soge'ria/ *f*, rope making; rope walk; rope shop; ropes

**soguero** /so'gero/ *m*, rope maker or seller

**soja** /'soha/ *f*, soybean

**sojuzgador** /sohuθga'ðor; sohusga'ðor/ **(-ra)** *a* conquering, oppressive —*n* conqueror, oppressor

**sojuzgar** /sohuθ'gar; sohus'gar/ *vt* to conquer, oppress, subdue

**sol** /sol/ *m*, sun; sunlight; day; Peruvian coin; *Mus.* G, fifth note of the scale, sol. **de s. a s.,** from sunrise to sunset. **hacer s.,** to be sunny. **morir uno sin s. sin luz y sin moscas,** *Inf.* to die abandoned by all. **no dejar a s. ni a sombra,** *Inf.* to follow everywhere; pester constantly. **tomar el s.,** to bask in the sun

**solado** /so'laðo/ *m*, paving; tile floor

**solador** /sola'ðor/ *m*, tiler

**solamente** /sola'mente/ *adv* only; exclusively; merely, solely. **s. que,** only that; nothing but

**solana** /so'lana/ *f*, sunny corner; Solarium

**solanera** /sola'nera/ *f*, sunburn; sunny spot

**solapa** /so'lapa/ *f*, lapel; excuse, pretext. **de s.,** *Inf.* secretly

**solapado** /sola'paðo/ *a* cunning, sly

**solapar** /sola'par/ *vt Sew.* to provide with lapels; *Sew.* cause to overlap; dissemble; —*vi Sew.* overlap

**solapo** /so'lapo/ *m*, lapel; *Inf.* slap, buffet. **a s.,** *Inf.* secretly, slyly

**solar** /so'lar/ *vt irr* to pave; sole (shoes). *m*, family seat, manor house; building site; lineage, family —*a* solar. See **color**

**solariego** /sola'riego/ *a* memorial; of an old and noble family

**solas, a** /'solas, a/ *adv* alone, in private

**solaz** /so'laθ; so'las/ *m*, consolation; pleasure; relief, relaxation. **a s.,** enjoyably, pleasantly

**solazar** /sola'θar; sola'sar/ *vt* to solace, comfort; amuse, entertain; rest; —*vr* be comforted; find pleasure (in)

**soldada** /sol'daða/ *f*, salary, wages, emoluments; (*Nav. Mil.*) pay

**soldadesca** /solda'ðeska/ *f*, soldiering, military profession; troops. **a la s.,** in a soldier-like way

**soldadesco** /solda'ðesko/ *a* military, soldier

**soldado** /sol'daðo/ *m*, soldier; defender, partisan. **s. raso,** *Mil.* private

**soldador** /solda'ðor/ *m*, solderer, welder; soldering iron

**soldadura** /solda'ðura/ *f*, welding, soldering; correction, emendation

**soldar** /sol'dar/ *vt irr* to weld; mend by welding; correct, put right; *Mil.* wipe out, liquidate. See **contar**

**solecismo** /sole'θismo; sole'sismo/ *m*, solecism

**soledad** /sole'ðað/ *f*, solitude; loneliness; homesickness; *pl* melancholy Andalusian song and dance (also *f pl.* **soleares**)

**solemne** /so'lemne/ *a* solemn; magnificent; formal; serious, grave, important; pompous; *Inf.* downright, complete

**solemnidad** /solemni'ðað/ *f*, solemnity; magnificence; formality; gravity, seriousness; solemn ceremony; religious ceremony; legal formality

**solemnización** /solemniθa'θion; solemnisa'sion/ *f*, solemnization

**solemnizar** /solemni'θar; solemni'sar/ *vt* to solemnize, celebrate; extol

**soler** /so'ler/ *vi irr defective* to be in the habit, be used; happen frequently (e.g. *Solía hacerlo los lunes,* I generally did it on Mondays. *Suele llover mucho aquí,* It rains a great deal here). See **moler**

**solercia** /so'lerθia; so'lersia/ *f*, shrewdness, ability, astuteness

**solevantado** /soleβan'taðo/ *a* agitated; restless

**solevantar** /soleβan'tar/ *vt* to raise, push up; incite to rebellion. **s. con gatos,** *Mech.* to jack up

**solfa** /'solfa/ *f*, *Mus.* sol-fa

**solfear** /solfe'ar/ *vt Mus.* to sing in sol-fa; *Inf.* spank, buffet; *Inf.* scold

**solfeo** /sol'feo/ *m*, *Mus.* sol-fa; *Inf.* spanking, drubbing

**solicitación** /soliθita'θion; solisita'sion/ *f*, request; application; solicitation; wooing; search (for a post); attraction, inducement

**solicitador** /soliθita'ðor; solisita'ðor/ **(-ra)** *a* soliciting —*n* solicitor. *m*, agent; applicant

**solicitante** /soliθi'tante; solisi'tante/ *mf* applicant, candidate

**solicitar** /soliθi'tar; solisi'tar/ *vt* to solicit; request; apply for; make love to, court; seek (posts, etc.); try to, attempt to; manage (business affairs); *Phys.* attract; appeal to

**solícito** /so'liθito; so'lisito/ *a* solicitous; conscientious; careful

**solicitud** /soliθi'tuð; solisi'tuð/ *f*, diligence, conscientiousness; solicitude; request; application; appeal, entreaty; petition; *Com.* demand. **a s.,** on request

**solidaridad** /soliðari'ðað/ *f*, solidarity

**solidario** /soli'ðario/ *a Law.* jointly responsible or liable

**solideo** /soli'ðeo/ *m*, *Eccl.* small skullcap

**solidez** /soli'ðeθ; soli'ðes/ *f*, solidity; *Fig.* force, weight (of arguments, etc.)

**solidificación** /soliðifika'θion; soliðifika'sion/ *f*, solidification

**solidificar** /soliðifi'kar/ **(se)** *vt and vr* to solidify

**sólido** /'soliðo/ *a* compact, solid; thick; fast or lasting (of colors); indisputable, convincing. *m*, (*Geom. Phys.*) solid; solidus (ancient coin)

**soliloquiar** /solilo'kiar/ *vi Inf.* to soliloquize, talk to oneself

**soliloquio** /soli'lokio/ *m*, soliloquy

**solio** /'solio/ *m*, throne

**solista** /so'lista/ *mf* soloist

**solitario** /soli'tario/ **(-ia)** *a* abandoned, deserted; solitary; secluded; solitude-loving —*n* recluse. *m*, solitaire diamond; hermit; solitaire (card game). **hacer solitarios,** to play solitaire (card game)

**sólito** /'solito/ *a* accustomed, wonted; customary, habitual

**soliviantar** /soliβian'tar/ *vt* to rouse, incite, excite

**soliviar** /soli'βiar/ *vt* to help to lift up; —*vr* half get up, raise oneself

**sollastre** /so'ʎastre; so'yastre/ *m*, scullion; brazen rogue

**sollozante** /soʎo'θante; soyo'sante/ *a* sobbing

**sollozar** /soʎo'θar; soyo'sar/ *vi* to sob

**sollozo** /so'ʎoθo; so'yoso/ *m*, sob

**solo** /'solo/ *a* sole, only; alone; lonely; deserted, forsaken. *m*, solo performance; (cards) solo; solitaire (card game). **a solas,** alone; without help, unaided

**sólo** /'solo/ *or* **solo** *adv* only; merely, solely; exclusively

**solomillo** /solo'miʎo; solo'miyo/ *m*, sirloin; filet (of meat)

**solsticio** /sols'tiθio; sols'tisio/ *m*, solstice. **s. hiemal,** winter solstice. **s. vernal,** summer solstice

**soltar** /sol'tar/ *vt irr* to loosen; let go; disengage; untie; release; let drop; let out (a laugh, etc.); solve; *Inf.* utter; turn on (taps); set free; —*vr* work loose; grow skillful; (*with prep. a* + *infin.*) begin to do (something). See **contar**

**soltera** /sol'tera/ *f*, spinster

**soltería** /solte'ria/ *f*, bachelorhood; spinsterhood

**soltero** /sol'tero/ *a* unmarried, single. *m*, bachelor

**solterón** /solte'ron/ *m*, confirmed bachelor

**solterona** /solte'rona/ *f*, confirmed old maid

**soltura** /sol'tura/ *f*, loosening, untying; freedom from restraint; ease, independence; impudence; immorality, viciousness; facility of speech; *Law.* release

**solubilidad** /soluβili'ðað/ *f*, solubility

**soluble** /so'luβle/ *a* soluble, dissolvable; solvable

**solución** /solu'θion; solu'sion/ *f*, dissolution, loosening; (*Math. Chem.*) solution; answer, solution; payment, satisfaction; *Lit.* climax; conclusion, end (of negotiations)

**solucionar** /soluθio'nar; solusio'nar/ *vt* to solve, find a solution for

**solvencia** /sol'βenθia; sol'βensia/ *f*, *Com.* solvency

**solventar** /solβen'tar/ *vt* to pay or settle accounts; solve (problems, difficulties)

**solvente** /sol'βente/ *a Com.* solvent

**somático** /so'matiko/ *a* somatic, corporeal

**somatología** /somatolo'hia/ *f*, somatology

**sombra** /'sombra/ *f*, shadow; shade; darkness, dimness; specter, phantom; defense, refuge, protection; resemblance, likeness; defect; *Inf.* luck; gaiety, charm; trace, vestige; *Art.* shading, shadow. **sombras chinescas,** shadow show. **a la s.,** in the shade; *Inf.* in jail. **hacer s.,** to shade; *Fig.* stand in the light, be an obstacle; protect. **ni por s.,** by no means; without warning. **no tener s. de,** to have not a trace of.... **tener buena s.,** *Inf.* to be witty or amusing and agreeable. **tener mala s.,** *Inf.* to bring bad luck, exert an evil influence upon; be dull and disagreeable

**sombrear** /sombre'ar/ *vt* to shadow, shade; *Art.* shade; —*vi* begin to show (of mustaches, beards)

**sombrerera** /sombre'rera/ *f*, milliner; hatbox

**sombrerería** /sombrere'ria/ *f*, hat shop or trade; hat factory

**sombrerero** /sombre'rero/ *m*, hatter; hat manufacturer

**sombrerete** /sombre'rete/ *m*, *Mech.* bonnet, cap; cowl

**sombrero** /som'βrero/ *m*, hat; *Mech.* cap, cowl; sounding board; head (of mushrooms, toadstools). **s. calañés,** Andalusian hat. **s. chambergo,** broad-brimmed plumed hat. **s. de canal** *or* **teja,** shovel hat (worn by clergymen). **s. de copa,** top hat. **s. de jipijapa,** Panama hat. **s. de tres picos,** three-cornered hat, cocked hat. **s. flexible,** soft felt hat. **s. hongo,** bowler (hat)

**sombría** /som'βria/ *f*, shady spot

**sombrilla** /som'βriʎa; som'βriya/ *f*, sunshade

**sombrío** /som'βrio/ *a* dark; shadowy; overcast; *Art.* shaded; gloomy, melancholy

**someramente** /somera'mente/ *adv* superficially; briefly, summarily

**somero** /so'mero/ *a* superficial, shallow; summary, rudimentary, brief

**someter** /some'ter/ *vt* to put down, defeat; submit, place before; subject. **s. a votación,** to put to a vote —*vr* yield, surrender; (*with prep a*) undergo

**sometimiento** /someti'miento/ *m,* defeat; submission (to arbitration, etc.); subjection

**somnambulismo** /somnambu'lismo/ *m,* somnambulism, sleepwalking

**somnámbulo** /som'nambulo/ **(-la)** *a* somnambulistic —*n* somnambulist

**somnífero** /som'nifero/ *a* soporiferous

**somnílocuo** /som'nilokuo/ *a* somniloquous, sleeptalking

**somnolencia** /somno'lenθia; somno'lensia/ *f,* somnolence

**son** /son/ *m,* sound; rumor; reason, motive; means, way; guise, manner. **al s. de,** to the sound of; to the music of. **en s. de,** in the manner of, as, like, under pretext of

**sonadera** /sona'ðera/ *f,* nose blowing

**sonado** /so'naðo/ *a* famous; much admired or talked of. **hacer una que sea sonada,** *Inf.* to cause a great scandal; do something noteworthy

**sonaja** /so'naha/ *f,* metal jingles on a tambourine; baby's rattle

**sonajero** /sona'hero/ *m,* baby's rattle

**sonar** /so'nar/ *vi irr* to sound; be quoted, be mentioned; ring; *Inf.* be familiar, remember (e.g. *No me suena el nombre,* I don't remember the name); (*with prep a*) be reminiscent of; —*vt* sound; ring; play on; clink; —*vr* be rumored, be reported; blow one's nose —*Pres. Indic.* **sueno, suenas, suena, suenan.** *Pres. Subjunc.* **suene, suenes, suene, suenen**

**sonata** /so'nata/ *f,* sonata

**sonda** /'sonda/ *f, Naut.* taking of soundings, heaving the lead; sound, plummet, lead; dragrope; probe, sound

**sondar** /son'dar/ *vt Naut.* to take soundings; probe; *Inf.* sound, try to find out; bore, drill

**sondeable** /sonde'aβle/ *a* fathomable

**sondeo** /son'deo/ *m, Naut.* sounding; *Mineral.* drilling; probing

**sonetear, sonetizar** /sonete'ar, soneti'θar; sonete'ar, soneti'sar/ *vi* to write sonnets

**sonetista** /sone'tista/ *mf* sonneteer

**soneto** /so'neto/ *m,* sonnet

**sonido** /so'niðo/ *m,* sound; literal meaning; rumor, report

**sonochar** /sono'tʃar/ *vi* to keep watch in the early hours of the night

**sonoridad** /sonori'ðað/ *f,* sonorousness

**sonoro** /so'noro/ *a* sounding; resonant, loud; sonorous

**sonreir, sonreírse** /son'reir, son'reirse/ *vi* and *vr irr* to smile; —*vi* look pleasant (landscape, etc.); look favorable (of circumstances). **sonreir tras la barba,** to laugh to oneself. See **reír**

**sonriente** /son'riente/ *a* smiling

**sonrisa** /son'risa/ *f,* smile

**sonrojar** /sonro'har/ *vt* to cause to blush; —*vr* blush

**sonrosado** /sonro'saðo/ *a* rosy, rose-colored, pink

**sonrosar** /sonro'sar/ *vt* to make rose-colored; —*vr* blush, flush

**sonroseo** /sonro'seo/ *m,* blush, flush

**sonsaca** /son'saka/ *f,* removal by stealth; pilfering; enticement; *Fig.* pumping (of a person for information)

**sonsacar** /sonsa'kar/ *vt* to remove by stealth; steal, pilfer; entice away; *Fig.* pump (a person for information), draw out

**sonsonete** /sonso'nete/ *m,* rhythmic tapping or drumming; monotonous sound (gen. unpleasant); sarcastic tone of voice

**soñador** /soɲa'ðor/ **(-ra)** *a* dreamy, sleepy —*n* dreamer

**soñar** /so'ɲar/ *vt* to dream; imagine, conjure up; (*with con*) dream of; (*with prep a*) fear (of persons)

**soñoliento** /soɲo'liento/ *a* sleepy, drowsy; soothing; slow, leisurely

**¡Soo!** /soo/ *interj* Whoa! (command to horses, etc.)

**sopa** /'sopa/ *f,* sop, piece of bread; soup. **s. boba,** beggar's portion; life of ease at others' expense. **an-**

**dar a la s.,** to beg one's way. **hecho una s.,** *Inf.* wet through

**sopapo** /so'papo/ *m,* chuck under the chin; *Inf.* slap; valve

**sopera** /so'pera/ *f,* soup tureen

**sopero** /so'pero/ *m,* soup plate, soup bowl —*a* fond of soup

**sopesar** /sope'sar/ *vt* to try the weight of

**sopetón** /sope'ton/ *m,* blow, cuff. **de s.,** suddenly

**soplada** /so'plaða/ *f,* puff of wind

**soplado** /so'plaðo/ *a Inf.* overelegant; haughty, stiff. *m,* fissure, chasm

**soplador** /sopla'ðor/ **(-ra)** *a* instigatory. *m,* blower, fan —*n* instigator; blower

**soplar** /so'plar/ *vi* to blow; —*vt* blow; blow away; inflate, blow up; filch, steal; instigate, inspire; accuse; fan; prompt, help out; —*vr Inf.* eat and drink too much; *Inf.* be puffed up, grow haughty —*interj* **¡Sopla!** *Inf.* You don't say so!

**soplete** /so'plete/ *m,* blowpipe

**soplo** /'soplo/ *m,* blow; blowing; instant, trice; *Inf.* hint, tip; *Inf.* accusation; *Inf.* tale-bearer; puff, breath (of wind)

**soplón** /so'plon/ **(-ona)** *a Inf.* tale-bearing, backbiting —*n* tale-bearer. *m, Auto.* scavenger

**soponcio** /so'ponθio; so'ponsio/ *m, Inf.* fainting fit

**sopor** /so'por/ *m,* stupor; deep sleep

**soporífero** /sopo'rifero/ *a* soporiferous

**soportable** /sopor'taβle/ *a* bearable

**soportador** /soporta'ðor/ **(-ra)** *a* supporting —*n* supporter

**soportal** /sopor'tal/ *m,* portico

**soportar** /sopor'tar/ *vt* to bear; carry, support; put up with, tolerate

**soporte** /so'porte/ *m,* rest, support; *Mech.* bearing; *Mech.* bracket, support

**sopuntar** /sopun'tar/ *vt* to underline in dots

**sor** /sor/ *f, Eccl.* sister (used of nuns)

**sorbedor** /sorβe'ðor/ **(-ra)** *a* supping, sipping —*n* sipper

**sorber** /sor'βer/ *vt* to suck; imbibe; swallow; *Fig.* absorb eagerly (ideas); sip

**sorbete** /sor'βete/ *m,* sherbet, iced drink; French ice cream

**sorbo** /'sorβo/ *m,* sucking; imbibition; swallow; sip; mouthful, gulp

**sordamente** /sorða'mente/ *adv* secretly, quietly

**sordera** /sor'ðera/ *f,* deafness

**sordidez** /sorði'ðeθ; sorði'ðes/ *f,* sordidness

**sórdido** /'sorðiðo/ *a* dirty, squalid; mean, niggardly; sordid

**sordina** /sor'ðina/ *f, Mus.* sordine, mute; *Mus.* damper. **a la s.,** on the quiet, in secret

**sordo** /'sorðo/ *a* deaf; silent, quiet; dull, muted (of sounds); insensible, inanimate; obdurate, uncompliant. **a la sorda** *or* **a lo s.** *or* **a sordas,** in silence, quietly

**sordomudez** /sorðomu'ðeθ; sorðomu'ðes/ *f,* deafmuteness, deaf-mutism

**sordomudo** /sorðo'muðo/ **(-da)** *a* and *n* deaf-mute

**sorna** /'sorna/ *f,* slowness, sluggishness; craftiness, guile, knavery; malice

**sorprendente** /sorpren'dente/ *a* surprising, amazing

**sorprender** /sorpren'der/ *vt* to surprise, amaze

**sorpresa** /sor'presa/ *f,* surprise; amazement; shock

**sortear** /sorte'ar/ *vt* to raffle; draw lots for; avoid artfully (difficulties, etc.); fight (bulls)

**sorteo** /sor'teo/ *m,* raffle; casting lots

**sortero** /sor'tero/ **(-ra)** *n* sorcerer; holder of a draw ticket

**sortija** /sor'tiha/ *f,* ring (for a finger); ring (for a curtain, etc.); curl

**sortilegio** /sorti'lehio/ *m,* sorcery, magic

**sortílego** /sor'tilego/ **(-ga)** *a* magic —*n* sorcerer, fortuneteller

**sosa** /'sosa/ *f,* sodium carbonate, soda ash. **s. cáustica,** sodiumhydroxide, caustic soda, soda

**sosegado** /sose'gaðo/ *a* tranquil, peaceful, calm

**sosegador** /sosega'ðor/ **(-ra)** *a* soothing, calming —*n* appeaser, soother

**sosegar** /sose'gar/ *vt irr* to soothe, quiet; reassure;

## sosería

appease, moderate; —*vi* grow still; rest, sleep; —*vr* grow quiet; calm down, be appeased; grow still. See **cegar**

**sosería** /sose'ria/ *f*, insipidness; lack of wit, dullness; stupidity

**sosia** /'sosia/ *m*, double, exact likeness (of persons)

**sosiego** /so'siego/ *m*, calm; peace, tranquility

**soslayar** /sosla'yar/ *vt* to slant, place in an oblique position; *Fig.* go around (a difficulty)

**soslayo** /sos'layo/ *a* slanting. **al s.,** obliquely, on the slant; askance

**soso** /'soso/ *a* saltless, insipid; dull, uninteresting; heavy (of people)

**sospecha** /sos'petʃa/ *f*, suspicion

**sospechar** /sospe'tʃar/ *vt* and *vi* to suspect

**sospechoso** /sospe'tʃoso/ *a* suspicious. *m*, suspect

**sostén** /sos'ten/ *m*, support; *Mech.* stand, support; brassiere, bra, bustier; steadiness (of a ship)

**sostenedor** /sostene'ðor/ **(-ra)** *a* supporting —*n* supporter

**sostener** /soste'ner/ *vt irr* to support; defend, uphold; bear, tolerate; help, aid; maintain, support. **s. una conversación,** to carry on a conversation. See **tener**

**sostenido** /soste'niðo/ *a Mus.* sostenuto, sustained —*a* and *m*, *Mus.* sharp

**sostenimiento** /losteni'miento/ *m*, support; defense; toleration, endurance; maintenance, sustenance

**sota** /'sota/ *f*, jack, knave (in cards); *Inf.* baggage, hussy. *m*, foreman, supervisor —*prep* deputy, substitute (e.g. *sotamontero*, deputy huntsman)

**sotabanco** /sota'βanko/ *m*, attic, garret

**sotana** /so'tana/ *f*, gown, cassock, robe

**sótano** /'sotano/ *m*, basement, cellar

**sotavento** /sota'βento/ *m*, leeward. **a s.,** on the lee

**sotechado** /sote'tʃaðo/ *m*, hut, shed

**soterrar** /sote'rrar/ *vt irr* to bury in the ground; hide, conceal. See **acertar**

**sotileza** /soti'leθa; soti'lesa/ *f*, fine cord for fishing (in Santander province)

**soto** /'soto/ *m*, thicket, grove, copse

**soviético** /so'βietiko/ *a* soviet

**sovietismo** /soβie'tismo/ *m*, sovietism

**sovietizar** /soβieti'θar; soβieti'sar/ *vt* to sovietize

**sovoz, a** /so'βoθ, a; so'βos, a/ *adv* in a low voice

**su, sus** /su, sus/ *poss pron 3rd pers mf sing* and *pl* his, her, its, one's, your, their

**suasorio** /sua'sorio/ *a* suasive, persuasive

**suave** /'suaβe/ *a* soft, smooth; sweet; pleasant, harmonious, quiet; slow, gentle; meek; delicate, subtle

**suavidad** /suaβi'ðað/ *f*, softness, smoothness; sweetness; pleasantness; quietness; gentleness; meekness; delicacy

**suavizador** /suaβiθa'ðor; suaβisa'ðor/ *a* softening, smoothing; soothing, quietening. *m*, razor strop

**suavizar** /suaβi'θar; suaβi'sar/ *vt* to soften; smooth; strop (a razor); moderate, temper; *Mech.* steady; quieten; ease

**subalpino** /suβal'pino/ *a* subalpine

**subalternar** /suβalter'nar/ *vt* to put down, subdue

**subalterno** /suβal'terno/ *a* subordinate. *m*, subordinate; *Mil.* subaltern

**subarrendar** /suβarren'dar/ *vt irr* to sublet. See **recomendar**

**subarrendatario** /suβarrenda'tario/ **(-ia)** *n* sublessee

**subarriendo** /suβa'rriendo/ *m*, sublease, sublet

**subasta** /su'βasta/ *f*, auction sale. **sacar a pública s.,** to sell by auction

**subastar** /suβas'tar/ *vt* to auction

**subcentral** /suβθen'tral; suβsen'tral/ *f*, substation

**subclase** /suβ'klase/ *f*, subclass

**subcolector** /suβkolek'tor/ *m*, assistant collector

**subcomisión** /suβkomi'sion/ *f*, subcommittee

**subconsciencia** /suβkons'θienθia; suβkons'siensia/ *f*, subconscious

**subcutáneo** /suβku'taneo/ *a* subcutaneous

**subdelegar** /suβðele'gar/ *vt* to subdelegate

**subdirector** /suβðirek'tor/ **(-ra)** *n* deputy, assistant director

**súbdito** /'suβðito/ **(-ta)** *a* dependent, subject —*n* subject (of a state)

**subdividir** /suβðiβi'ðir/ *vt* to subdivide

**subdominante** /suβðomi'nante/ *f*, *Mus.* subdominant

**subgénero** /suβ'henero/ *m*, subgenus

**subgobernador** /suβgoβerna'ðor/ *m*, deputy governor, lieutenant governor

**subibaja** /suβi'βaha/ *f*, seesaw, teetertotter

**subida** /su'βiða/ *f*, ascension, ascent; upgrade; rise; carrying up; raising (of a theater curtain)

**subidero** /suβi'ðero/ *m*, uphill road; mounting block; way up (to a higher level)

**subido** /su'βiðo/ *a* strong (of scents); deep (of colors); expensive, high-priced; best, finest

**subidor** /suβi'ðor/ *m*, porter, carrier; elevator

**subintendente** /suβinten'dente/ *m*, deputy or assistant intendant

**subir** /su'βir/ *vi* to ascend, climb, go up; mount; rise; *Com.* amount (to), reach; prosper, advance, be promoted; grow more acute (of illnesses); intensify; *Mus.* raise the pitch (of an instrument or voice); —*vt* ascend, climb; pick up, take up; raise up; place higher; build up, make taller; straighten up, place in a vertical position; increase, raise (in price or value); —*vr* ascend, climb. **s. a caballo,** to mount a horse. **subirse a la cabeza,** *Inf.* to go to one's head (of alcohol, etc.)

**subitáneo** /suβi'taneo/ *a* sudden

**súbito** /'suβito/ *a* unexpected, unforeseen; sudden; precipitate, impulsive —*adv* suddenly (also **de s.**)

**subjefe** /suβ'hefe/ *m*, deputy chief, second in command

**subjetividad** /suβhetiβi'ðað/ *f*, subjectivity

**subjetivismo** /suβheti'βismo/ *m*, subjectivism

**subjetivo** /suβhe'tiβo/ *a* subjective

**subjuntivo** /suβhun'tiβo/ *a* and *m*, subjunctive

**sublevación** /suβleβa'θion; suβleβa'sion/ *f*, **sublevamiento** *m*, rebellion, mutiny, uprising

**sublevar** /suβle'βar/ *vt* to rouse to rebellion; excite (indignation, etc.); —*vr* rebel

**sublimación** /suβlima'θion; suβlima'sion/ *f*, sublimation

**sublimado** /suβli'maðo/ *m*, *Chem.* sublimate

**sublimar** /suβli'mar/ *vt* to exalt, raise up; *Chem.* sublimate

**sublime** /su'βlime/ *a* sublime

**sublimidad** /suβlimi'ðað/ *f*, sublimity, majesty, nobility

**submarino** /suβma'rino/ *a* submarine. *m*, submarine. **s. de bolsillo** *or* **s. enano,** midget submarine

**suboficial** /suβofi'θial; suβofi'sial/ *m*, *Mil.* subaltern; *Nav.* petty officer

**subordinación** /suβorðina'θion; suβorðina'sion/ *f*, dependence, subordination

**subordinado** /suβorði'naðo/ **(-da)** *a* and *n* subordinate

**subordinar** /suβorði'nar/ *vt* to subordinate

**subpolar** /suβpo'lar/ *a* subpolar

**subprefecto** /suβpre'fekto/ *m*, subprefect

**subproducto** /suβpro'ðukto/ *m*, by-product

**subrayar** /suβra'yar/ *vt* to underline; emphasize

**subrepción** /suβrep'θion; suβrep'sion/ *f*, underhand dealing; *Law.* subreption

**subrepticio** /suβrep'tiθio; suβrep'tisio/ *a* surreptitious; clandestine

**subrogación** /suβroga'θion; suβroga'sion/ *f*, surrogation

**subrogar** /suβro'gar/ *vt Law.* to surrogate, elect as a substitute

**subs** /suβs/ -- For words so beginning not found here, see **sus-**

**subsanar** /suβsa'nar/ *vt* to make excuses for; remedy, put right; indemnify

**subscriptor** /suβskrip'tor/ **(-ra)** *n* subscriber

**subsección** /suβsek'θion; suβsek'sion/ *f*, subsection

**subsecretaría** /suβsekreta'ria/ *f*, assistant secretaryship; assistant secretary's office

**subsecretario** /suβsekre'tario/ **(-ia)** *n* assistant secretary

**subsecuente** /suβse'kuente/ *a* subsequent

**subsidiario** /suβsi'ðiario/ *a* subsidized; subsidiary

**subsidio** /suβ'siðio/ *m*, subsidy

**subsiguiente** /suβsi'giente/ *a* subsequent; next

**subsistencia** /suβsis'tenθia; suβsis'tensia/ *f*, permanence; stability; subsistence, maintenance; livelihood

**subsistir** /suβsis'tir/ *vi* to last, endure; subsist, live; make a livelihood

**subsuelo** /suβ'suelo/ *m*, subsoil, substratum

**subteniente** /suβte'niente/ *m, Mil.* second lieutenant

**subterfugio** /suβter'fuhio/ *m*, subterfuge, trick

**subterráneo** /suβte'rraneo/ *a* underground, subterranean. *m*, subterranean place

**subtítulo** /suβ'titulo/ *m*, subtitle; caption

**subtropical** /suβtropi'kal/ *a* subtropical

**suburbano** /suβur'βano/ **(-na)** *a* suburban —*n* suburbanite

**suburbio** /su'βurβio/ *m*, suburb

**subvención** /suββen'θion; suββen'sion/ *f*, subsidy, subvention, grant

**subvencionar** /suββenθio'nar; suββensio'nar/ *vt* to subsidize

**subvenir** /suββe'nir/ *vt irr* to help, succor; subsidize. See **venir**

**subversivo** /suββer'siβo/ *a* subversive

**subvertir** /suββer'tir/ *vt irr* to subvert, overturn, ruin. See **sentir**

**subyugación** /suβyuga'θion; suβyuga'sion/ *f*, subjugation

**subyugador** /suβyuga'ðor/ **(-ra)** *a* subjugating —*n* conqueror

**subyugar** /suβyu'gar/ *vt* to subjugate, overcome

**succión** /suk'θion; suk'sion/ *f*, suction

**sucedáneo** /suθe'ðaneo; suse'ðaneo/ *m, Med.* succedaneum

**suceder** /suθe'ðer; suse'ðer/ *vi* to follow, come after; inherit, succeed —*impers* happen, occur

**sucedido** /suθe'ðiðo; suse'ðiðo/ *m, Inf.* event, occurrence

**sucesión** /suθe'sion; suse'sion/ *f*, succession; series; offspring, descendants; *Law.* estate

**sucesivo** /suθe'siβo; suse'siβo/ *a* successive. **en lo s.,** in future

**suceso** /su'θeso; su'seso/ *m*, happening, occurrence; course (of time); outcome, result

**sucesor** /suθe'sor; suse'sor/ **(-ra)** *a* succeeding —*n* successor

**suciedad** /suθie'ðað; susie'ðað/ *f*, dirt; filth, nastiness; obscenity

**sucinto** /su'θinto; su'sinto/ *a* succinct, brief, concise

**sucio** /'suθio; 'susio/ *a* dirty, unclean; stained; easily soiled; *Fig.* sullied, spotted; obscene; dirty (of colors); *Fig.* tainted, infected. **jugar s.,** *Sports.* to play in an unsporting manner

**suco** /'suko/ *m*, juice

**sucoso** /su'koso/ *a* juicy

**suculencia** /suku'lenθia; suku'lensia/ *f*, succulence, juiciness

**suculento** /suku'lento/ *a* succulent; juicy

**sucumbir** /sukum'βir/ *vi* to yield, give in; die, succumb; lose a lawsuit

**sucursal** /sukur'sal/ *a* branch. *f, Com.* branch (of a firm)

**sud** /suð/ *m*, south (gen. **sur**). Used in combinations like **sudamericano**

**sudadero** /suða'ðero/ *m*, horse blanket; sudatorium, sweating bath

**sudafricano** /suðafri'kano/ **(-na)** *a* and *n* South African

**sudamericano** /suðameri'kano/ **(-na)** *a* and *n* South American

**Sudán, el** /su'ðan, el/ the Sudan

**sudante** /su'ðante/ *a* sweating, perspiring

**sudar** /su'ðar/ *vi* and *vt* to perspire, sweat; ooze; —*vi Inf.* toil; —*vt* bathe in sweat; *Inf.* give reluctantly. **s. frío,** to break out in a cold sweat. **s. la gota gorda,** *Fig. Inf.* to be in a stew

**sudario** /su'ðario/ *m*, shroud

**sudeste** /su'ðeste/ *m*, southeast; southeast wind

**sudexpreso** /suðeks'preso/ *m*, southern express

**sudoeste** /suðo'este/ *m*, southwest; southwest wind

**sudor** /su'ðor/ *m*, sweat, perspiration; toil; juice, moisture, sap, gum

**sudoroso** /suðo'roso/ *a* sweaty

**sudsudeste** /suðsu'ðeste/ *m*, southsoutheast

**sudsudoeste** /suðsuðo'este/ *m*, southsouthwest

**Suecia** /'sueθia; 'suesia/ Sweden

**sueco** /'sueko/ **(-ca)** *a* Swedish —*n* Swede. *m*, Swedish (language)

**suegra** /'suegra/ *f*, mother-in-law

**suegro** /'suegro/ *m*, father-in-law

**suela** /'suela/ *f*, sole (of a shoe); *Ichth.* sole; tanned leather; base. **no llegarle a uno a la s. del zapato,** *Inf.* to be not fit to hold a candle to.

**sueldo** /'sueldo/ *m*, salary, wages; *Obs.* Spanish coin. **a s.,** for a salary, salaried

**suelo** /'suelo/ *m*, ground, earth; soil; bottom, base; sediment, dregs; site, plot; floor; flooring; story; land, territory; hoof (of horses); earth, world; *pl* chaff of grain. **s. natal,** native land; **besar el s.,** *Inf.* to fall flat. **dar consigo en el s.,** to fall down. **dar en el s. con,** to throw down; damage, spoil. *Inf.* **estar ( una cosa) por los suelos,** to be dirt cheap

**suelta** /'suelta/ *f*, loosening, unfastening; hobble (for horses); relay of oxen. **dar s. a,** to let loose, allow to go out for a time

**suelto** /'suelto/ *a* swift; competent, efficient; odd, separate; licentious; flowing, easy (style); loose, unbound. *m*, single copy (of a newspaper); loose change; newspaper paragraph

**sueño** /'sueɲo/ *m*, dream; sleep; drowsiness, desire for sleep; vision, fancy. **s. pesado,** deep sleep. **conciliar el s.,** to court sleep. **echar un s.,** *Inf.* to take a nap. **en sueños,** in a dream; while asleep. **entre sueños,** between sleeping and waking. **¡Ni por sueño!** *Inf.* Certainly not! I wouldn't dream of it!

**suero** /'suero/ *m*, serum. **s. de la leche,** whey

**suerte** /'suerte/ *f*, chance, luck; good luck; destiny, fate; condition, state; kind, species, sort; way, manner; bullfighter's maneuver; parcel of land. **de s. que,** so that; as a result. **echar suertes,** to draw lots. **tener buena s.,** to be lucky

**sueste** /'sueste/ *m*, southeast; sou'wester (cap)

**suéter** /'sueter/ *m*, sweater

**suevo** /'sueβo/ **(-va)** *a* and *n* Swabian

**suficiencia** /sufi'θienθia; sufi'siensia/ *f*, sufficiency; talent, aptitude; pedantry. **a s.,** enough

**suficiente** /sufi'θiente; sufi'siente/ *a* sufficient, enough; suitable

**sufijo** /su'fiho/ *m*, suffix

**sufismo** /su'fismo/ *m*, Sufism

**sufragar** /sufra'gar/ *vt* to assist, aid; favor; pay, defray

**sufragio** /su'frahio/ *m*, aid, assistance; *Eccl.* suffragium, pious offering; vote; suffrage

**sufragista** /sufra'hista/ *f*, suffragette

**sufrible** /su'friβle/ *a* bearable, endurable

**sufrido** /su'friðo/ *a* long-suffering, resigned; complaisant (of husbands); dirt-resistant (colors)

**sufrimiento** /sufri'miento/ *m*, suffering, pain; affliction; tolerance

**sufrir** /su'frir/ *vt* to suffer, undergo, experience; bear, endure; tolerate, put up with; allow, permit; resist, oppose; expiate; —*vi* suffer

**sugerir** /suhe'rir/ *vt irr* to suggest. See **sentir**

**sugestión** /suhes'tion/ *f*, suggestion

**sugestionable** /suhestio'naβle/ *a* easily influenced, open to suggestion

**sugestionador** /suhestiona'ðor/ *a* suggestive

**sugestionar** /suhestio'nar/ *vt* to suggest hypnotically; dominate, influence

**sugestivo** /suhes'tiβo/ *a* suggestive, stimulating

**suicida** /sui'θiða; sui'siða/ *a* suicidal, fatal. *mf* suicide (person)

**suicidarse** /suiθi'ðarse; suisi'ðarse/ *vr* to commit suicide

**suicidio** /sui'θiðio; sui'siðio/ *m*, suicide (act)

**Suiza** /'suiθa; 'suisa/ Switzerland

**suiza** /'suiθa; 'suisa/ *f*, row, rumpus, scrap

**suizo** /'suiθo; 'suiso/ **(-za)** *a* and *n* Swiss

**sujeción** /suhe'θion; suhe'sion/ *f*, subjection, domination; fastening, fixture; obedience, conformity

**sujetador** /suheta'ðor/ *m*, clamp; clip

**sujetar** /suhe'tar/ *vt* to fasten, fix; hold down; grasp, clutch; subdue; —*vr* (*with prep a*) conform to, obey. **s. con alfileres,** to pin up. **s. con tornillos,** to screw down

**sujeto** /su'heto/ *a* liable, subject. *m*, topic, subject; person, individual; *Gram. Philos.* subject

**sulfatar** /sulfa'tar/ *vt* to sulphate

**sulfato** /sul'fato/ *m*, sulphate

**sulfurar** /sulfu'rar/ *vt* to sulphurate; —*vr* grow irritated, become angry

**sulfúrico** /sul'furiko/ *a* sulphuric

**sulfuro** /sul'furo/ *m*, sulphide

**sulfuroso** /sulfu'roso/ *a* sulphurous

**sultán** /sul'tan/ *m*, sultan

**sultana** /sul'tana/ *f*, sultana

**sultanía** /sulta'nia/ *f*, sultanate

**suma** /'suma/ *f*, total; amount, sum; *Math.* addition; summary, digest; computation. **en s.**, in brief, in short, finally

**sumador** /suma'ðor/ **(-ra)** *n* summarizer; computator; adder

**sumamente** /suma'mente/ *adv* extremely, most

**sumar** /su'mar/ *vt* to sum up, summarize; *Math.* add up

**sumaria** /su'maria/ *f*, written indictment

**sumariamente** /sumaria'mente/ *adv* concisely, in brief; *Law.* summarily

**sumario** /su'mario/ *a* brief, concise, abridged; *Law.* summary. *m*, summary, résumé, digest

**sumergible** /sumer'hiβle/ *a* sinkable; submergible. *m*, submarine

**sumergir** /sumer'hir/ *vt* to dip, immerse; sink, submerge; *Fig.* overwhelm (with grief, etc.); —*vr* sink; dive; be submerged

**sumersión** /sumer'sion/ *f*, immersion, dive, submersion

**sumidero** /sumi'ðero/ *m*, cesspool; drain; sink; pit, gully

**suministración** /suministra'θion; suministra'sion/ *f*. See **suministro**

**suministrador** /suministra'ðor/ **(-ra)** *n* purveyor

**suministrar** /suminis'trar/ *vt* to purvey, supply, provide

**suministro** /sumi'nistro/ *m*, purveyance; provision; supply

**sumir** /su'mir/ *vt* to sink; submerge; *Eccl.* consummate; *Fig.* overwhelm (with grief, etc.); —*vr* fall in, become sunken (of cheeks, etc.); sink; be submerged

**sumisión** /sumi'sion/ *f*, submission, obedience; *Com.* estimate, tender

**sumiso** /su'miso/ *a* submissive, docile

**sumista** /su'mista/ *mf* quick reckoner, computator. *m*, condenser, summarizer, abridger

**sumo** /'sumo/ *a* supreme; high; tremendous, extraordinary. **a lo s.**, at the most; even if, although. **en s. grado**, in the highest degree

**suntuosidad** /suntuosi'ðað/ *f*, magnificence, luxury

**suntuoso** /sun'tuoso/ *a* magnificent, luxurious, sumptuous

**supeditación** /supeðita'θion; supeðita'sion/ *f*, subjection

**supeditar** /supeði'tar/ *vt* to oppress; overcome, conquer; subordinate

**superabundancia** /superaβun'danθia; superaβun'dansia/ *f*, superabundance, excess; glut

**superabundante** /superaβun'dante/ *a* superabundant, excessive

**superádito** /supe'raðito/ *a* superadded

**superar** /supe'rar/ *vt* to overcome, conquer; surpass; do better than

**superávit** /supe'raβit/ *m*, *Com.* balance, surplus

**superchería** /supertʃe'ria/ *f*, trickery, guile

**superchero** /super'tʃero/ *a* guileful, wily

**superconsciencia** /superkons'θienθia; superkons'siensia/ *f*, higher consciousness

**supereminencia** /superemi'nenθia; superemi'nensia/ *f*, supereminence, greatest eminence

**supereminente** /superemi'nente/ *a* supereminent

**superentender** /superenten'der/ *vt irr* to supervise, superintend. See **entender**

**supererogación** /supereroga'θion; supereroga'sion/ *f*, supererogation

**superestructura** /superestruk'tura/ *f*, superstructure

**superficial** /superfi'θial; superfi'sial/ *a* surface, shallow; superficial, rudimentary; futile

**superficialidad** /superfiθiali'ðað; superfisiali'ðað/ *f*, superficiality; futility; shallowness

**superficie** /super'fiθie; super'fisie/ *f*, area; surface; outside, exterior. **s. de rodadura**, tire tread

**superfino** /super'fino/ *a* superfine

**superfluidad** /superflui'ðað/ *f*, superfluity

**superfluo** /su'perfluo/ *a* superfluous, redundant

**superfortaleza volante** /superforta'leθa bo'lante; superforta'lesa bo'lante/ *f*, *Aer.* superfortress

**superhombre** /super'ombre/ *m*, superman

**superintendencia** /superinten'denθia; superinten'densia/ *f*, supervision; superintendentship; higher administration

**superintendente** /superinten'dente/ *mf* superintendent; supervisor

**superior** /supe'rior/ *a* higher, upper; excellent, fine; superior; higher (education, etc.). *m*, head, director; superior

**superiora** /supe'riora/ *f*, mother superior

**superioridad** /superiori'ðað/ *f*, superiority

**superlativo** /superla'tiβo/ *a* and *m*, superlative

**superno** /su'perno/ *a* supreme

**supernumerario** /supernume'rario/ **(-ia)** *a* and *n* supernumerary

**superposición** /superposi'θion; superposi'sion/ *f*, superposition

**superproducción** /superproðuk'θion; superproðuk'sion/ *f*, overproduction; superproduction

**superrealismo** /superrea'lismo/ *m*, surrealism

**superrealista** /superrea'lista/ *a* surrealist

**superstición** /supersti'θion; supersti'sion/ *f*, superstition

**supersticioso** /supersti'θioso; supersti'sioso/ *a* superstitious

**supervención** /superβen'θion; superβen'sion/ *f*, *Law.* supervention

**supervivencia** /superβi'βenθia; superβi'βensia/ *f*, survival

**superviviente** /superβi'βiente/ *a* surviving. *mf* survivor

**supino** /su'pino/ *a* supine; foolish, stupid. *m*, *Gram.* supine

**suplantación** /suplanta'θion; suplanta'sion/ *f*, supplanting

**suplantador** /suplanta'ðor/ **(-ra)** *a* supplanting —*n* supplanter

**suplantar** /suplan'tar/ *vt* to forge, alter (documents); supplant

**suplefaltas** /suple'faltas/ *mf Inf.* scapegoat

**suplementario** /suplemen'tario/ *a* supplementary, additional

**suplemento** /suple'mento/ *m*, supplement; supply, supplying; newspaper supplement; *Geom.* supplement

**suplente** /su'plente/ *m*, substitute, proxy; *Fig.* makeweight

**súplica** /'suplika/ *f*, supplication, prayer; request

**suplicación** /suplika'θion; suplika'sion/ *f*, entreaty, supplication; *Law.* petition

**suplicante** /supli'kante/ *a* supplicating; *Law.* petitioning. *mf* supplicator; *Law.* petitioner

**suplicar** /supli'kar/ *vt* to beg, supplicate; request; *Law.* appeal

**suplicio** /su'pliθio; su'plisio/ *m*, torment, torture; execution; place of torture or execution; affliction, anguish. **último s.**, capital punishment

**suplir** /su'plir/ *vt* to supply, furnish; substitute, take the place of; overlook, forgive

**suponer** /supo'ner/ *vt irr* to suppose, take for granted; simulate; comprise, include; —*vi* carry weight, wield authority. See **poner**

**suposición** /suposi'θion; suposi'sion/ *f*, supposition, conjecture, assumption; distinction, talent, importance; falsity, falsehood

**supositorio** /suposi'torio/ *m*, suppository

**suprasensible** /suprasen'siβle/ *a* supersensible

**supremacía** /suprema'θia; suprema'sia/ *f*, supremacy

**supremo** /su'premo/ *a* supreme; matchless, incomparable; last

**supresión** /supre'sion/ *f*, suppression; destruction, eradication; omission

**suprimir** /supri'mir/ *vt* to suppress; destroy, eradi-

cate; omit, leave out. **s. una calle al tráfico,** to close a street to traffic, ban traffic from a street
**supuesto** /su'puesto/ *a* supposed; so-called; reputed. *m,* supposition, hypothesis. **por s.,** presumably; doubtless
**supuración** /supura'θion; supura'sion/ *f,* suppuration
**supurar** /supu'rar/ *vi* to suppurate
**suputar** /supu'tar/ *vt* to calculate, compute
**sur** /sur/ *m,* south; south wind
**surcador** /surka'ðor/ *m,* plowman
**surcar** /sur'kar/ *vt* to plow furrows; furrow, line; cut, cleave (water, etc.)
**surco** /'surko/ *m,* furrow; wrinkle, line; groove, channel; rut
**surgidero** /surhi'ðero/ *m, Naut.* road, roadstead
**surgir** /sur'hir/ *vi* to spout, gush, spurt; *Naut.* anchor; appear, show itself; come forth, turn up
**surrealismo** /surrea'lismo/ *m,* surrealism
**surrealista** /surrea'lista/ *a* and *mf* surrealist
**surtida** /sur'tiða/ *f,* hidden exit; false door; *Naut.* slipway
**surtidero** /surti'ðero/ *m,* outlet, drain; jet, fountain
**surtido** /sur'tiðo/ *a* mixed, assorted. *m,* variety, assortment; stock, range. **de s.,** in everyday use
**surtidor** /surti'ðor/ **(-ra)** *n* purveyor, supplier. *m,* fountain, jet. **s. de gasolina,** gasoline pump, gas pump
**surtimiento** /surti'miento/ *m,* assortment; stock
**surtir** /sur'tir/ *vt* to provide, supply, furnish; —*vi* spurt, gush
**surto** /'surto/ *a* calm, reposeful; *Naut.* anchored
**¡sus!** /sus/ *interj* Come on! Hurry up!
**susceptibilidad** /susθeptiβili'ðað; susseptiβili'ðað/ *f,* susceptibility
**susceptible** /susθep'tiβle; sussep'tiβle/ *a* susceptible, open to; touchy, oversensitive
**suscitar** /susθi'tar; sussi'tar/ *vt* to cause, originate; provoke, incite; —*vr* arise, take place
**suscribir** /suskri'βir/ *vt* to sign; agree to; —*vr* subscribe, contribute; take out a subscription (to a periodical, etc.) —*Past Part.* **suscrito**
**suscripción** /suskrip'θion; suskrip'sion/ *f,* subscription; agreement, accession
**susodicho** /suso'ðitʃo/ *a* aforesaid
**suspender** /suspen'der/ *vt* to suspend, hang up; postpone, defer, stop; amaze, dumbfound; suspend (from employment); fail (an exam); adjourn (meetings); —*vr* rear (of horses)
**suspensión** /suspen'sion/ *f,* suspension; postponement, stoppage, deferment; amazement; failure (in an exam); adjournment (of a meeting); springs (of a car). *Com.* **s. de pagos,** suspension of payments. **con mala s.,** badly sprung (of a car)
**suspensivo** /suspen'siβo/ *a* suspensive
**suspensivos** /suspen'siβos/ *m, pl* suspension points, ellipsis points
**suspenso** /sus'penso/ *a* amazed, bewildered. *m,* failure slip (in an exam). **en s.,** in suspense
**suspicacia** /suspi'kaθia; suspi'kasia/ *f,* suspiciousness; mistrust, uneasiness
**suspicaz** /suspi'kaθ; suspi'kas/ *a* suspicious, mistrustful
**suspirado** /suspi'raðo/ *a* eagerly desired, longed for
**suspirar** /suspi'rar/ *vt* and *vi* to sigh. **s. por,** to long for
**suspiro** /sus'piro/ *m,* sigh; breath; glass whistle;

*Mus.* brief pause, pause sign. **último s.,** *Inf.* last kick, end
**suspirón** /suspi'ron/ *a* given to sighing
**sustancia** /sus'tanθia; sus'tansia/ *f,* substance, juice, extract, essence; *Fig.* core, pith; *Fig.* meat; wealth, estate; worth, importance; nutritive part; *Inf.* common sense. *Anat.* **s. gris,** gray matter. **en s.,** in short
**sustanciación** /sustanθia'θion; sustansia'sion/ *f,* substantiation
**sustancial** /sustan'θial; sustan'sial/ *a* substantial, real; important, essential; nutritive; solid
**sustanciar** /sustan'θiar; sustan'siar/ *vt* to substantiate; summarize, extract, abridge
**sustancioso** /sustan'θioso; sustan'sioso/ *a* substantial; nutritive
**sustantivo** /sustan'tiβo/ *a* and *m, Gram.* substantive, noun
**sustentable** /susten'taβle/ *a* arguable, defensible
**sustentación** /sustenta'θion; sustenta'sion/ *f,* maintenance; defense
**sustentar** /susten'tar/ *vt* to sustain, keep; support, bear; nourish, feed; uphold, advocate. **s. un ciclo de conferencias,** to give a series of lectures
**sustento** /sus'tento/ *m,* maintenance, preservation; nourishment, sustenance; support
**sustitución** /sustitu'θion; sustitu'sion/ *f,* substitution
**sustituible** /susti'tuiβle/ *a* substitutive, replaceable
**sustituir** /susti'tuir/ *vt irr* to substitute. See **huir**
**sustitutivo** /sustitu'tiβo/ *a* substitutive
**sustituto** /susti'tuto/ **(-ta)** *n* substitute
**susto** /'susto/ *m,* fright, shock; apprehension. **dar un s. ( a),** to scare
**sustracción** /sustrak'θion; sustrak'sion/ *f,* subtraction
**sustraendo** /sustra'endo/ *m, Math.* subtrahend
**sustraer** /sustra'er/ *vt irr* to remove, separate; rob, steal; *Math.* subtract; —*vr* depart, remove oneself; avoid. See **traer**
**sustrato** /sus'trato/ *m,* substratum
**susurrador** /susurra'ðor/ **(-ra)** *a* whispering; murmuring; rustling —*n* whisperer
**susurrante** /susu'rrante/ *a* whispering; murmuring; rustling
**susurrar** /susu'rrar/ *vi* to whisper; murmur; rustle; babble, purl, prattle (of water); —*vi* and *vr* be whispered abroad
**susurro** /su'surro/ *m,* whispering, whisper; murmur; rustle; lapping
**sutil** /'sutil/ *a* fine, thin; penetrating, subtle, keen
**sutileza, sutilidad** /suti'leθa, sutili'ðað; suti'lesa, sutili'ðað/ *f,* fineness, thinness; subtlety, penetration. **sutileza de manos,** dexterity; light-fingeredness; sleight of hand
**sutilizaciones** /sutiliθa'θiones; sutilisa'siones/ *f, pl* casuistry, hairsplitting, quibbling
**sutilizar** /sutili'θar; sutili'sar/ *vt* to make thin, refine; *Fig.* finish, perfect; *Fig.* split hairs, make subtle distinctions
**sutura** /su'tura/ *f,* suture
**suyo, suya** /'suyo, 'suya/ *m,* and *f, pl* **suyos, suyas,** *poss pron* and *a* 3rd pers his; hers; its; yours; theirs; of his, of hers, etc. (e.g. *Este libro es suyo,* This book is his (hers, yours, theirs). **Este libro es uno de los suyos,** This book is one of his (hers, etc.). (**suyo** is often used with def. art. **el, la,** etc.) **los suyos,** (hers, yours, etc.) family, following, adherents, etc. **de suyo,** of its very nature, of itself; spontaneously. **salirse con la suya,** to get one's own way. *Inf.* **ver la suyo,** to see one's opportunity

# T

**tabacal** /taβa'kal/ *m*, tobacco plantation

**tabacalero** /taβaka'lero/ **(-ra)** *a* tobacco —*n* tobacco merchant; tobacco planter

**tabaco** /ta'βako/ *m*, tobacco plant, tobacco leaf; tobacco; cigar. **t. de pipa,** pipe tobacco. **t. flojo,** mild tobacco. **t. rubio,** Virginia tobacco

**tabalear** /taβale'ar/ **(se)** *vt* and *vr* to rock, sway, swing; —*vi* drum with the fingers

**tabaleo** /taβa'leo/ *m*, swaying, rocking; drumming with the fingers

**tabanco** /ta'βanko/ *m*, market stall

**tábano** /'taβano/ *m*, *Ent.* horsefly

**tabanque** /ta'βanke/ *m*, potter's wheel

**tabaque** /ta'βake/ *m*, small osier basket (for fruit, sewing, etc.); large tack

**tabaquera** /taβa'kera/ *f*, tobacco jar, tobacco tin; bowl of pipe tobacco; tobacco pouch; snuffbox

**tabaquería** /taβake'ria/ *f*, tobacconist's shop

**tabaquero** /taβa'kero/ **(-ra)** *n* worker in a tobacco factory; tobacconist

**tabaquismo** /taβa'kismo/ *m*, nicotinism, nicotine poisoning

**tabaquista** /taβa'kista/ *mf* tobacco expert; heavy smoker

**tabardillo** /taβar'ðiʎo; taβarðiyo/ *m*, fever. **t. de tripas,** typhoid. **t. pintado,** typhus

**tabardo** /ta'βarðo/ *m*, tabard

**taberna** /ta'βerna/ *f*, public house, tavern

**tabernáculo** /taβer'nakulo/ *m*, tabernacle

**tabernario** /taβer'nario/ *a* public house, tavern; low, vulgar

**tabernera** /taβer'nera/ *f*, publican's wife; barmaid

**tabernero** /taβer'nero/ *m*, publican; barman, drawer

**tabicar** /taβi'kar/ *vt* to wall or board up; hide, cover up

**tabique** /ta'βike/ *m*, partition wall, inside wall; thin wall

**tabla** /'taβla/ *f*, plank of wood, board; *Metall.* plate; slab; flat side, face (of wood); *Sew.* box pleat; table (of contents, etc.); *Art.* panel; vegetable garden; butcher's slab; butcher's stall; *pl* tablets (for writing); (*Math.* etc.) tables; stalemate (chess, checkers); draw (in an election); *Theat.* boards, stage. **t. de armonía,** sounding board (of musical instruments). **t. de lavar,** washboard. **t. de materias,** table of contents. **t. de multiplicación,** multiplication table. **t. rasa,** clean sheet (of paper, etc.); complete ignorance. **T. Redonda,** Round Table (of King Arthur). **escapar** or **salvarse en una t.,** to have a narrow escape, escape in the nick of time

**tablacho** /ta'βlatʃo/ *m*, sluice gate. **echar el t.,** *Inf.* to interrupt the flow of someone's remarks

**tablado** /ta'βlaðo/ *m*, flooring; platform; *Theat.* stage; scaffold, gibbet. **sacar al t.,** to produce, put on the stage; to make known, publish

**tablazón** /taβla'θon; taβla'son/ *f*, planks, boards; flooring; *Naut.* deck planks or sheathing

**tablear** /taβle'ar/ *vt* to saw into planks; *Sew.* make box pleats in; hammer iron into sheets

**tablero** /ta'βlero/ *m*, board (of wood); paneling, boarding; slab; shop counter; board (checkers, chess). **t. de instrumentos,** dashboard; instrument panel

**tableta** /ta'βleta/ *f*, tablet; pastille, lozenge

**tablilla** /ta'βliʎa; ta'βliya/ *f*, small board; tablet; bulletin board, notice board

**tablón** /ta'βlon/ *m*, thick plank; wooden beam; *Inf.* drinking bout

**tabú** /ta'βu/ *m*, taboo

**tabuco** /ta'βuko/ *m*, miserable little room; hovel

**taburete** /taβu'rete/ *m*, stool; tabouret

**tacañería** /takaɲe'ria/ *f*, miserliness, niggardliness; craftiness

**tacaño** /ta'kaɲo/ *a* miserly, niggardly; crafty

**tacha** /'tatʃa/ *f*, imperfection, defect; spot, stain; fault; large tack. **poner t.,** to criticize, object to

**tachable** /ta'tʃaβle/ *a* censurable, blameworthy

**tachar** /ta'tʃar/ *vt* to criticize, blame; cross out, erase; charge, accuse

**tacho de basura** /'tatʃo de ba'sura/ *m*, *Argentina* garbage can

**tachón** /ta'tʃon/ *m*, round-headed ornamental nail; *Sew.* gold or silver studs, trimming; crossing out, erasure

**tachonar** /tatʃo'nar/ *vt* to stud with round-headed nails; *Sew.* trim with gold or silver studs or trimming

**tachoso** /ta'tʃoso/ *a* imperfect, defective, faulty; spotted, stained

**tachuela** /ta'tʃuela/ *f*, tack

**tácito** /'taθito; 'tasito/ *a* silent, unexpressed; tacit, implied

**taciturnidad** /taθiturni'ðað; tasiturni'ðað/ *f*, taciturnity; reserve; melancholy

**taciturno** /taθi'turno; tasi'turno/ *a* taciturn; reserved; dismal, gloomy, melancholy

**taco** /'tako/ *m*, stopper, plug; billiard cue; rammer; wad, wadding (in a gun); pop gun; taco (food); tearoff calendar; *Inf.* snack; obscenity, oath. **t. de papel,** writing tablet

**tacón** /ta'kon/ *m*, heel (of a shoe)

**taconear** /takone'ar/ *vi* to stamp with one's heels; walk heavily on one's heels; walk arrogantly

**taconeo** /tako'neo/ *m*, drumming or stamping of one's heels (gen. in dancing)

**táctica** /'taktika/ *f*, method, technique; *Mil.* tactics; policy, way, means

**táctico** /'taktiko/ *a* tactical. *m*, *Mil.* tactician

**táctil** /'taktil/ *a* tactile

**tacto** /'takto/ *m*, sense of touch; touch, feel; touching; skill; tact

**tafetán** /tafe'tan/ *m*, taffeta; *pl* flags, standards. **t. de heridas** or **t. inglés,** court plaster

**tafilete** /tafi'lete/ *m*, morocco leather

**tahalí** /taa'li/ *m*, sword shoulder belt

**tahona** /ta'ona/ *f*, horse mill; bakery; baker's shop

**tahonero** /tao'nero/ **(-ra)** *n* miller; baker

**tahúr** /ta'ur/ *m*, gambler; cardsharper

**tahurería** /taure'ria/ *f*, gambling den; gambling; cheating at cards

**Tailandia** /tai'landia/ Thailand

**taimado** /tai'maðo/ *a* knavish, crafty; obstinate, headstrong

**taimería** /taime'ria/ *f*, cunning, craftiness

**taita** /'taita/ *m*, daddy

**taja** /'taha/ *f*, cut, cutting; slice; washboard

**tajada** /ta'haða/ *f*, slice; strip, portion; steak, filet; *Inf.* cough; drinking bout; hoarseness

**tajadera** /taha'ðera/ *f*, cheese knife; chisel; *pl* sluice gate

**tajado** /ta'haðo/ *a* steep, sheer (of cliffs, etc.)

**tajadura** /taha'ðura/ *f*, cut, cutting, dividing, dissection

**tajamar** /taha'mar/ *m*, cutwater; breakwater; raft

**tajar** /ta'har/ *vt* to cut, chop; sharpen, trim (quill pens)

**tajea** /ta'hea/ *f*, culvert; aqueduct; drain; watercourse

**Tajo, el** /'taho, el/ the Tagus

**tajo** /'taho/ *m*, cut, incision; task; cutting (in a mountain, etc.); cut, thrust (of sword); executioner's block; chopping board; washboard; steep cliff, precipice

**tajón** /ta'hon/ *m*, butcher block; chopping board

**tal** /tal/ *a pl* **tales,** such; said (e.g. *el t. Don Juan,* the said Don Juan). **tal** is always used before nouns and (except when meaning "the said") without def. art. **un t.,** a certain (e.g. *un t. hombre,* a certain man) —*pron* some, some people; someone; such a thing —*adv* so, thus. **t. para cual,** two of a kind, a well-matched pair; tit for tat. **con t. que,** *conjunc* on condition that, provided that. **No hay t.,** There is no such thing. *Inf.* **¿Qué t.?** How are you? What's the news? What's new?

**tala** /'tala/ *f,* felling or cutting down (of trees); cropping of grass (ruminants)

**talabarte** /tala'βarte/ *m,* sword belt

**talabartería** /talaβarte'ria/ *f,* saddlery

**talabartero** /talaβar'tero/ *m,* saddler

**talador** /tala'ðor/ **(-ra)** *a* felling, cutting; destructive —*n* feller, cutter; destroyer

**taladrar** /tala'ðrar/ *vt* to drill, bore, gouge holes; pierce, perforate; punch (a ticket); assail or hurt the ear (sounds); *Fig.* go into deeply (a subject)

**taladro** /ta'laðro/ *m,* drill, gimlet, gouge; drill hole, bore; puncher (for tickets, etc.)

**tálamo** /'talamo/ *m,* marriage bed; (*Bot. Anat.*) thalamus

**talán** /ta'lan/ *m,* peal, tolling (of a bell)

**talanquera** /talan'kera/ *f,* barricade; parapet, fence, wall; refuge, asylum; safety, security

**talante** /ta'lante/ *m,* mode of execution, technique; personal appearance, mien; disposition, temperament; wish, desire; aspect, appearance. **de buen ( mal) t.,** willingly (unwillingly)

**talar** /ta'lar/ *a* full-length, long (of gowns, robes, etc.)

**talar** /ta'lar/ *vt* to fell, chop down (trees); ravage, lay waste; prune (gen. olive trees)

**talco** /'talko/ *m, Mineral.* talc; sequin, tinsel

**talcualillo** /talkua'liλo; talkua'liyo/ *a Inf.* not too bad, fairly good; slightly better (of health)

**taled** /ta'leð/ *m,* prayer shawl, tales, tallit

**talega** /ta'lega/ *f,* sack, bag; sackful; money bag; *pl Inf.* cash wealth

**talego** /talego/ *m,* narrow sack; *Inf.* dumpy person

**talento** /ta'lento/ *m,* talent (Greek coin); talent, gift, quality; intelligence, understanding; cleverness

**talentoso** /talen'toso/ *a* talented

**tálero** /'talero/ *m,* thaler (old German coin)

**talión** /ta'lion/ *m,* **(ley de)** law of retaliation

**talismán** /talis'man/ *m,* talisman

**talla** /'taλa; 'taya/ *f,* carving (especially wood); cutting (of gems); reward for apprehension of a criminal; ransom; stature, height, size; height measuring rod

**tallado** /ta'λaðo; ta'yaðo/ *a* **bien** (or **mal**), well (or badly) carved; well (or badly) proportioned, of a good (or bad) figure

**tallado** /ta'λaðo; ta'yaðo/ *m,* carving

**tallador** /taλa'ðor; taya'ðor/ *m,* metal engraver; die sinker

**tallar** /ta'λar; ta'yar/ *vt Art.* to carve; engrave; cut (gems); value, estimate; measure height (of persons)

**tallarín** /taλa'rin; taya'rin/ *m,* (gen. *pl*) *Cul.* noodle

**talle** /'taλe; 'taye/ *m,* figure, physique; waist; fit (of clothes); appearance, aspect. *Inf.* **largo de t.,** longwaisted; long drawn out, overlong. **tener buen t.,** to have a good figure

**tallecer** /taλe'θer; taye'ser/ *vi irr Bot.* to sprout, shoot. See **conocer**

**taller** /ta'λer; ta'yer/ *m,* workshop; factory; mill; workroom, atelier; industrial school; school of arts and crafts; studio

**tallista** /ta'λista; ta'yista/ *mf* engraver; wood carver; sculptor

**tallo** /'taλo; 'tayo/ *m, Bot.* stalk; shoot; slice of preserved fruit; cabbage. **t. rastrero,** *Bot.* runner

**talludo** /ta'λuðo; ta'yuðo/ *a* long-stalked; lanky, overgrown; no longer young, aging (of women); habit-ridden

**talmúdico** /tal'muðiko/ *a* Talmudic

**talón** /ta'lon/ *m,* heel; heel (of a shoe); *Com.* counterfoil; luggage receipt; *Com.* sight draft; coupon; heel (of a violin bow). *Inf.* **apretar los talones,** to take to one's heels. *Inf.* **pisarle ( a uno) los talones,** to follow on a person's heels; rival successfully

**talonada** /talo'naða/ *f,* dig in with the spurs

**talonario** /talo'nario/ *m,* stub book

**tamaño** /ta'maɲo/ *a compar* so big; so small (e.g. *La conocí tamaña,* I knew her when she was so high) (indicating her size with a gesture)); so great, so large (e.g. *tamaña empresa,* so great an undertaking). *m,* size

**tamarindo** /tama'rindo/ *m,* tamarind

**tambaleante** /tambale'ante/ *a* tottering, rickety; staggering

**tambalear** /tambale'ar/ **(se)** *vi* and *vr* to totter, sway, shake; reel, stagger

**tambaleo** /tamba'leo/ *m,* swaying; tottering; rocking; shaking; staggering, reeling

**tambarillo** /tamba'riλo; tambariyo/ *m,* chest with an arched lid

**también** /tam'bien/ *adv* also, too; in addition, as well

**tambor** /tam'bor/ *m, Mus.* drum; drummer; embroidery frame; *Mech.* drum, cylinder; roaster (for coffee, chestnuts, etc.). **t. mayor,** drum major. **a t.** ( *or* **con t.**) **batiente,** with drums beating; triumphantly, with colors flying

**tamborear** /tambore'ar/ *vi* to totter, sway; stagger, reel

**tamboreo** /tambo'reo/ *m,* tottering, swaying; staggering, reeling

**tamboril** /tambo'ril/ *m,* tabor

**tamborilada** /tambori'laða/ *f, Inf.* slap on the back or face; *Inf.* fall on the bottom

**tamborilear** /tamborile'ar/ *vi* to play the tabor; —*vt* eulogize, extol

**tamborilero** /tambori'lero/ *m,* tabor player

**tamborín** /tambo'rin/ *m,* tabor

**Támesis, el** /'tamesis, el/ the Thames

**tamiz** /ta'miθ; ta'mis/ *m,* sieve

**tamizar** /tami'θar; tami'sar/ *vt* to sieve

**tamo** /'tamo/ *m,* fluff; chaff

**tampoco** /tam'poko/ *adv* neither, not... either, nor... either; no more (e.g. *No lo ha hecho María t.,* Mary hasn't done it either)

**tampón** /tam'pon/ *m,* stamp moistener; *Surg.* tampon

**tan** /tan/ *adv Abbr.* **tanto.** so, as. Used before adjectives and adverbs, excepting **más, mejor, menos, peor,** which need **tanto. t.... como,** as... as. **t. siquiera,** even (see **siquiera**). **t. sólo,** only, solely (e.g. *No vengo t. sólo para saludarte,* I do not come merely to greet you). **qué... t.,** what a... (e.g. *¡Qué día t. hermoso!* What a lovely day!)

**tanda** /'tanda/ *f,* turn; opportunity; task; shift, relay; game (of billiards); bad habit; collection, batch, group; round (of a game); (*Dance.*) set

**tándem** /'tandem/ *m,* tandem

**tandeo** /tan'deo/ *m,* allowance of irrigation water, turn for using water

**Tangañica** /taŋga'ɲika/ Tanganyika

**tangente** /tan'hente/ *a* and *f, Geom.* tangent

**Tánger** /'tanher/ Tangier

**tangerino** /tanhe'rino/ **(-na)** *a* and *n* of or from Tangier, Tangerine

**tanque** /'tanke/ *m, Mil.* tank; cistern, tank, reservoir; ladle, dipper

**tanteador** /tantea'ðor/ *m, Sports.* scorer, marker; scoreboard

**tantear** /tante'ar/ *vt* to measure, compare; consider fully; test, try out; *Fig.* probe, pump (persons); estimate roughly; *Art.* sketch, block in; —*vt* and *vi Sports.* keep the score of

**tanteo** /tan'teo/ *m,* measurement, comparison; test; rough estimate; *Sports.* score

**tanto** /'tanto/ *a* so much; as much; very great; as great; *pl* **tantos,** so many; as many (e.g. *Tienen tantas flores como nosotros,* They have as many flowers as we). In comparisons **tanto** is used before **más, mejor, menos, peor,** but generally **tan** is used before adjectives and adverbs (e.g. *¡Tanto peor!* So much the worse!) —*pron dem* that (e.g. *por lo t.,* therefore, on that account). *m,* so much, a certain amount; copy of a document; man, piece (in games); point (score in games); *Com.* rate (e.g. *el t. por ciento,* the percentage, the rate); *pl* approximation, odd (e.g. *Llegaron cien hombres y tantos,* A hundred-odd men arrived) —*adv* so much; as much; so, in such a way. **t.... como,** the same as, as much as. **t.... cuanto,** as much as. **t. más,** the more. **t. menos,** the less (e.g. *Cuanto más* (*menos*) *dinero tiene* **t. más** (**menos**) **quiere,** The more (less) money he has, the more (less) he wants. **t. más ( menos)... cuanto que,** all the more (less).... because. **algún t.,** a certain amount, somewhat. **al t. de ( una cosa),** aware of, acquainted with (a thing). **en t.** *or* **entre t.,** meanwhile. **las tantas,** *Inf.* late hour, wee hours. **No es para t.,** *Inf.* It's not as bad as that, there's no need to make such a fuss; he (she, it) isn't equal to it. **otro t.,** the same, as much; as much more. **un t.,** a bit, somewhat

**tañedor** /taɲe'ðor/ **(-ra)** *n Mus.* player

**tañer** /ta'ɲer/ *vt irr Mus.* to play; —*vi* sway, swing. **t. la occisa,** to sound the death (in hunting) —*Pres. Part.* **tañendo.** *Preterite* **tañó, tañeron.** *Imperf. Subjunc.* **tañese,** etc.

**tañido** /ta'ɲiðo/ *m,* tune, sound, note; toll, peal; ring

**taoísmo** /tao'ismo/ *m,* Taoism

**taoísta** /tao'ista/ *mf* Taoist

**tapa** /'tapa/ *f,* lid; cover; cover (of books)

**tapaboca** /tapa'βoka/ *m,* blow on the mouth; *f,* scarf, muffler; *Inf.* remark that silences someone

**tapada** /ta'paða/ *f,* veiled woman, one whose face is hidden

**tapadera** /tapa'ðera/ *f,* loose lid, top, cover

**tapadero** /tapa'ðero/ *m,* stopper

**tapador** /tapa'ðor/ **(-ra)** *a* covering —*n* coverer. *m,* stopper; lid; cover

**tapagujeros** /tapagu'heros/ *m, Inf.* unskilled mason or bricklayer; *Fig. Inf.* stopgap (person)

**tapar** /ta'par/ *vt* to cover; cover with a lid; muffle up, veil; hide, keep secret; close up, stop up

**taparrabo** /tapa'rraβo/ *m,* loincloth; swimming trunks

**tapete** /ta'pete/ *m,* rug; tablecover. *Inf.* **t. verde,** gaming table. *Fig.* **estar sobre el t.,** to be on the carpet, be under consideration

**tapia** /'tapia/ *f,* adobe; mud wall; fence. *Inf.* **más sordo que una t.,** as deaf as a post

**tapiar** /ta'piar/ *vt* to wall up; put a fence around, fence in

**tapicería** /tapiθe'ria; tapise'ria/ *f,* set of tapestries; tapestry work; art of tapestry making; upholstery; tapestry storehouse or shop

**tapicero** /tapi'θero; tapi'sero/ *m,* tapestry weaver or maker; upholsterer; carpet layer; furnisher

**tapioca** /ta'pioka/ *f,* tapioca

**tapiz** /ta'piθ; ta'pis/ *m,* tapestry; carpet

**tapizar** /tapi'θar; tapi'sar/ *vt* to cover with tapestry; cover, clothe; upholster; carpet; hang with tapestry; furnish with hangings or drapes

**tapón** /ta'pon/ *m,* stopper; cork (of a bottle); plug; *Surg.* tampon

**taponar** /tapo'nar/ *vt* to stopper, cork; plug; *Surg.* tampon; *Mil.* seal off

**taponazo** /tapo'naθo; tapo'naso/ *m,* pop (of a cork)

**tapujarse** /tapu'harse/ *vr* to wrap oneself up, muffle oneself

**tapujo** /ta'puho/ *m,* scarf, muffler, face covering; disguise; *Inf.* pretense, subterfuge

**taquera** /ta'kera/ *f,* rack (for billiard cues)

**taquería** /take'ria/ *f,* taco stand

**taquigrafía** /takigra'fia/ *f,* shorthand

**taquigrafiar** /takigra'fiar/ *vt* to write in shorthand

**taquigráfico** /taki'grafiko/ *a* shorthand

**taquígrafo** /ta'kigrafo/ **(-fa)** *n* shorthand writer, stenographer

**taquilla** /ta'kiʎa; ta'kiya/ *f,* booking office; box office; grille, window (in banks, etc.); rolltop desk, cupboard for papers; *Theat.* takings, cash

**taquillero** /taki'ʎero; taki'yero/ **(-ra)** *n* booking office clerk

**tara** /'tara/ *f,* tally stick; *Com.* tare

**taracea** /tara'θea; tara'sea/ *f,* inlaid work, marquetry

**taracear** /taraθe'ar; tarase'ar/ *vt* to inlay

**tarambana** /taram'bana/ *mf Inf.* madcap

**tarantela** /taran'tela/ *f,* tarantella

**tarántula** /ta'rantula/ *f,* tarantula

**tararear** /tarare'ar/ *vt* to hum a tune

**tarareo** /tara'reo/ *m,* humming, singing under one's breath

**tarasca** /ta'raska/ *f,* figure of a dragon (carried in Corpus Christi processions); *Inf.* hag, trollop

**tarascada** /taras'kaða/ *f,* bite, nip; *Inf.* insolent reply

**tarascar** /taras'kar/ *vt* to bite; wound with the teeth

**tardanza** /tar'ðanθa; tar'ðansa/ *f,* delay, tardiness; slowness

**tardar** /tar'ðar/ *vi* to delay; be tardy, arrive late; take a long time. **a más t.,** at the latest

**tarde** /'tarðe/ *f,* afternoon —*adv* late. **¡Buenas tardes!** Good afternoon! **de t. en t.,** from time to time, sometimes. **hacerse t.,** to grow late. **Más vale t. que nunca,** Better late than never

**tardecer** /tarðe'θer; tarðe'ser/ *vi impers irr* to grow dusk. See **conocer**

**tardecica, tardecita** /tarðe'θika, tarðe'θita; tarðe'sika, tarðe'sita/ *f,* dusk, late afternoon

**tardíamente** /tar'ðiamente/ *adv* late; too late

**tardío** /tar'ðio/ *a* late; backward; behind; slow, deliberate

**tardo** /'tarðo/ *a* slow, slothful, tardy; late; dilatory; stupid, slow-witted; badly spoken, inarticulate

**tarea** /ta'rea/ *f,* task, work

**tarifa** /ta'rifa/ *f,* price list; tariff

**tarifar** /tari'far/ *vt* to put a tariff on

**tarima** /ta'rima/ *f,* stand, raised platform

**tarín barín** /ta'rin ba'rin/ *adv Inf.* more or less, about

**tarja** /'tarha/ *f,* large shield; ancient coin; tally stick. *Inf.* **beber sobre t.,** to drink on credit

**tarjar** /tar'har/ *vt* to reckon by tally

**tarjeta** /tar'heta/ *f,* buckler, small shield; *Archit.* tablet bearing an inscription; title (of maps and charts); visiting card; invitation (card). **t. de visita,** visiting card. **t. postal,** postcard. **t. telefónica,** calling card (phone)

**tarquín** /tar'kin/ *m,* mud, mire

**tárraga** /'tarraga/ *f,* old Spanish dance

**tarro** /'tarro/ *m,* jar, pot

**tarso** /'tarso/ *m, Anat.* tarsus, ankle; *Zool.* hock; *Ornith.* shank

**tarta** /'tarta/ *f,* cake pan; cake; tart

**tártago** /'tartago/ *m,* spurge; *Inf.* misfortune, disappointment

**tartajear** /tartahe'ar/ *vi* to stammer; stutter

**tartajeo** /tarta'heo/ *m,* stammering; stutter

**tartajoso** /tarta'hoso/ **(-sa)** *a* stammering; stuttering —*n* stutterer

**tartalear** /tartale'ar/ *vi Inf.* to stagger, totter; be speechless, be dumbfounded

**tartamudear** /tartamuðe'ar/ *vi* to stammer, stutter

**tartamudeo** /tartamu'ðeo/ *m,* **tartamudez** *f,* stammering; stuttering

**tartamudo** /tarta'muðo/ **(-da)** *n* stammerer

**tartán** /tar'tan/ *m,* tartan

**tartana** /tar'tana/ *f, Naut.* tartan; covered two-wheeled carriage

**tartáreo** /tar'tareo/ *a Poet.* infernal, hellish

**Tartaria** /tar'taria/ Tartary

**tártaro** /'tartaro/ **(-ra)** *m,* cream of tartar; tartar (on teeth); *Poet.* hell, hades —*a* and *n* Tartar

**tartufo** /tar'tufo/ *m,* hypocrite

**tarugo** /ta'rugo/ *m,* thick wooden peg; stopper; wooden block

**tasa** /'tasa/ *f,* assessment, valuation; valuation certificate; fixed price; standard rate; measure, rule

**tasación** /tasa'θion; tasa'sion/ *f,* valuation; assessment

**tasador** /tasa'ðor/ *m,* public assessor; valuer

**tasajo** /ta'saho/ *m,* salt meat; piece of meat

**tasar** /ta'sar/ *vt* to value; price; fix remuneration; tax; regulate; rate; dole out sparingly

**tasca** /'taska/ *f,* gambling den; tavern

**tascar** /tas'kar/ *vt* to dress (hemp, etc.); graze, crop the grass

**tasquera** /tas'kera/ *f, Inf.* quarrel, row; rumpus

**tasquil** /tas'kil/ *m,* wood splinter, chip

**tata** /'tata/ *m, Inf. West Hem.* daddy

**tatarabuela** /tatara'βuela/ *f,* great-great-grandmother

**tatarabuelo** /tatara'βuelo/ *m,* great-great-grandfather

**tataradeudo** /tatara'ðeuðo/ **(-da)** *n* very old relative; ancestor

**tataranieta** /tatara'nieta/ *f,* great-great-granddaughter

**tataranieto** /tatara'nieto/ *m,* great-great-grandson

**tatas, andar a** /'tatas, an'dar a/ *vt* to walk on all fours

**¡tate!** /'tate/ *interj* Stop!; Be careful!; Go slowly!; Now I understand!, Of course!

**tatuaje** /ta'tuahe/ *m,* tattooing

**tatuar** /tatu'ar/ *vt* to tattoo

**taumaturgia** /tauma'turhia/ *f*, thaumaturgy, wonder-working

**taumaturgo** /tauma'turgo/ *m*, thaumaturge, magician

**taurino** /tau'rino/ *a* taurine; pertaining to bullfights

**Tauro** /'tauro/ *m*, Taurus

**tauromaquia** /tauro'makia/ *f*, bullfighting, tauromachy

**tautología** /tautolo'hia/ *f*, tautology

**taxi** /'taksi/ *m*, taxi

**taxidermia** /taksi'ðermia/ *f*, taxidermy

**taxidermista** /taksiðer'mista/ *mf* taxidermist

**taxista** /tak'sista/ *m*, taxi driver

**taxonomía** /taksono'mia/ *f*, taxonomy

**taza** /'taθa; 'tasa/ *f*, cup; cupful; basin (of a fountain)

**tazar** /ta'θar; ta'sar/ **(se)** *vt* and *vr* to fray (of cloth)

**taz a taz** /taθ a taθ; tas a tas/ *adv* in exchange, without payment; even

**tazmía** /taθ'mia; tas'mia/ *f*, tithe contribution; share of tithes; tithe register

**tazón** /ta'θon; ta'son/ *m*, large cup; bowl

**te** /te/ *f*, name of the letter T. *mf* dat. and acc. of *pers pron 2nd pers sing* thee; you; to thee, to you. Never used with a preposition

**té** /te/ *m*, tea

**tea** /tea/ *f*, torch; firebrand

**teatral** /tea'tral/ *a* theatrical

**teatralidad** /teatrali'ðað/ *f*, theatricality

**teatro** /te'atro/ *m*, theater; stage; dramatic works; dramatic art; drama, plays. **t. de variedades,** music hall. **t. por horas,** theater where short, one-act plays are staged hourly

**tebano** /te'βano/ **(-na), tebeo (-ea)** *a* and *n* Theban

**Tebas** /'teβas/ Thebes

**teca** /'teka/ *f*, teak

**techado** /te'tʃaðo/ *m*, ceiling; roof

**techador** /tetʃa'ðor/ *m*, roofer

**techar** /te'tʃar/ *vt* to roof

**techo** /'tetʃo/ *m*, roof; ceiling; dwelling, habitation

**techumbre** /te'tʃumbre/ *f*, ceiling; roof

**tecla** /'tekla/ *f*, key (of keyed instruments); typewriter, linotype, or calculating machine key; *Fig.* difficult or delicate point. *Inf.* **dar en la t.,** to hit on the right way of doing a thing

**teclado** /te'klaðo/ *m*, keyboard

**tecleado** /tekle'aðo/ *m*, *Mus.* fingering

**teclear** /tekle'ar/ *vi* to finger the keyboard; run one's fingers over the keyboard; *Inf.* drum or tap with the fingers; —*vt* tap (the keys, etc.); *Inf.* try out various schemes

**tecleo** /te'kleo/ *m*, fingering the keys; *Inf.* drumming with the fingers; scheme, means

**técnica** /'teknika/ *f*, technique

**tecnicismo** /tekni'θismo; tekni'sismo/ *m*, technical jargon; technicality, technical term

**técnico** /'tekniko/ *a* technical. *m*, technician

**tecnicolor** /tekniko'lor/ *m*, technicolor

**tecnología** /teknolo'hia/ *f*, technology

**tecnológico** /tekno'lohiko/ *a* technological

**tecnólogo** /tek'nologo/ *m*, technologist

**tedero** /te'ðero/ *m*, torch seller; torch holder

**tedio** /'teðio/ *m*, tedium, boredom, ennui

**tedioso** /te'ðioso/ *a* tedious, boring

**tegumento** /tegu'mento/ *m*, integument, tegument

**teísmo** /te'ismo/ *m*, theism

**teísta** /te'ista/ *a* theistic. *mf* theist

**teja** /'teha/ *f*, tile, slate. *Inf.* **de tejas abajo,** in the normal way; in the world of men. **de tejas arriba,** in a supernatural way; in heaven

**tejadillo** /teha'ðiʎo; teha'ðiyo/ *m*, roof (of a vehicle)

**tejado** /te'haðo/ *m*, roof

**tejar** /te'har/ *m*, tile works —*vt* to roof with tiles

**tejavana** /teha'βana/ *f*, penthouse, open shed

**tejedor** /tehe'ðor/ **(-ra)** *a* weaving; *Inf.* scheming —*n* weaver; *Inf.* schemer

**tejedura** /tehe'ðura/ *f*, weaving; fabric; texture

**tejeduría** /teheðu'ria/ *f*, art of weaving; weaving shed or mill

**tejemaneje** /tehema'nehe/ *m*, *Inf.* cleverness, knack

**tejer** /te'her/ *vt* to weave; plait; spin a cocoon; arrange, regulate; concoct, hatch (schemes); wind in and out (in dancing)

**tejero** /te'hero/ *m*, tile manufacturer

**tejido** /te'hiðo/ *m*, texture, weaving; textile; *Anat.* tissue; fabric, material

**tejo** /'teho/ *m*, quoit, discus; metal disk; yew tree

**tejón** /te'hon/ *m*, *Zool.* badger

**tela** /'tela/ *f*, fabric, material, cloth; membrane; film (on liquids); spiderweb, cobweb; inner skin (of fruit, vegetables); film over the eye; matter, subject; scheme, plot. **t. metálica,** wire gauze. **en t. de juicio,** under consideration, in doubt. **llegarle a uno a las telas del corazón,** to hurt deeply, cut to the quick

**telar** /te'lar/ *m*, loom, weaving machine; *Theat.* gridiron

**telaraña** /tela'raɲa/ *f*, cobweb; mere trifle, bagatelle. *Inf.* **mirar las telarañas,** to be absent-minded

**telarañoso** /telara'ɲoso/ *a* cobwebby

**telecomunicación** /telekomunika'θion; telekomunika'sion/ *f*, telecommunication

**telefonear** /telefone'ar/ *vt* to telephone, call

**telefonía** /telefo'nia/ *f*, telephony. **t. sin hilos,** wireless telephony, broadcasting

**telefónico** /tele'foniko/ *a* telephonic

**telefonista** /telefo'nista/ *mf* telephone operator

**teléfono** /te'lefono/ *m*, telephone. **t. automático,** dial telephone. **llamar por t.** ( **a),** to telephone, call, ring up

**telefundir** /telefun'dir/ *vt* to telecast

**telegrafía** /telegra'fia/ *f*, telegraphy. **t. sin hilos,** wireless telegraphy

**telegrafiar** /telegra'fiar/ *vt* to telegraph

**telegráfico** /tele'grafiko/ *a* telegraphic

**telegrafista** /telegra'fista/ *mf* telegraph operator

**telégrafo** /te'legrafo/ *m*, telegraph. **t. sin hilos,** wireless telegraph. *Inf.* **hacer telégrafos,** to talk by signs

**telegrama** /tele'grama/ *m*, telegram

**telemetría** /teleme'tria/ *f*, telemetry

**telémetro** /te'lemetro/ *m*, telemeter, rangefinder

**teleología** /teleolo'hia/ *f*, teleology

**telepatía** /telepa'tia/ *f*, telepathy

**telepático** /tele'patiko/ *a* telepathic

**telescópico** /teles'kopiko/ *a* telescopic

**telescopio** /teles'kopio/ *m*, telescope

**telespectador** /telespekta'ðor/ *m*, TV viewer, member of the television audience

**teletipo** /tele'tipo/ *m*, teleprinter

**televisión** /teleβi'sion/ *f*, television

**telilla** /te'liʎa; te'liya/ *f*, film (on liquids); thin fabric

**telón** /te'lon/ *m*, *Theat.* curtain; drop scene. **t. contra incendios, t. de seguridad,** *Theat.* safety curtain. **t. de boca,** drop curtain. **t. de foro,** drop scene

**tema** /'tema/ *m*, theme, subject; *Mus.* motif, theme; thesis, argument. *f*, obstinacy; obsession, mania; hostility, grudge, rancor

**temático** /te'matiko/ *a* thematic; pigheaded, obstinate

**temblador** /templa'ðor/ **(-ra)** *a* trembling, shaking —*n* Quaker

**temblante** /tem'blante/ *a* shaking; quivering. *m*, bracelet

**temblar** /tem'blar/ *vi irr* to tremble, shake; wave, quiver; shiver with fear. See **acertar**

**temblequear, tembletear** /templeke'ar, templete'ar/ *vi Inf.* tremble; shake with fear

**temblón** /tem'blon/ *a Inf.* trembling, shaking. *m*, *Inf.* aspen

**temblor** /tem'blor/ *m*, shake, trembling, shiver. **t. de tierra,** earthquake

**tembloroso, tembloso** /temblo'roso, tem'bloso/ *a* trembling, shaking, shivering, quivering

**temedero** /teme'ðero/ *a* fearsome, dread

**temedor** /teme'ðor/ **(-ra)** *a* fearful —*n* fearer, dreader

**temer** /te'mer/ *vt* to fear, dread; suspect, imagine; —*vi* be afraid

**temerario** /teme'rario/ *a* reckless, impetuous; thoughtless, hasty

**temeridad** /temeri'ðað/ *f*, recklessness, impetuosity, temerity; thoughtlessness; act of folly; rash judgment

**temerón** /teme'ron/ *a Inf.* swaggering, bombastic

**temeroso** /teme'roso/ *a* frightening, dread; fearful, timid; afraid, suspicious

**temible** /te'miβle/ *a* dread, awesome

**temor** /te'mor/ *m*, fear

**temoso** /te'moso/ *a* obstinate, headstrong

**témpano** /'tempano/ *m*, tabor; drumhead; block, flat piece; side of bacon. **t. de hielo**, iceberg, ice floe

**temperación** /tempera'θion; tempera'sion/ *f*, tempering

**temperamento** /tempera'mento/ *m*, temperament, nature; compromise, agreement

**temperar** /tempe'rar/ *vt* to temper

**temperatura** /tempera'tura/ *f*, temperature

**temperie** /tem'perie/ *f*, weather conditions

**tempestad** /tempes'tað/ *f*, storm

**tempestividad** /tempestiβi'ðað/ *f*, opportuneness, seasonableness

**tempestivo** /tempes'tiβo/ *a* opportune, seasonable

**tempestuoso** /tempes'tuoso/ *a* stormy

**templa** /'templa/ *f*, tempera; *pl Anat.* temples

**templado** /tem'plaðo/ *a* moderate; temperate (of regions); lukewarm; *Mus.* in tune; restrained (of style); *Inf.* brave, long-suffering. **estar bien** ( *or* **mal)**

**templado,** *Inf.* to be well (or badly) tuned (of musical instruments); be in a good (or bad) temper; be good- (*or* ill-) natured

**templador** /templa'ðor/ **(-ra)** *n* tuner. *m*, tuning key

**templadura** /templa'ðura/ *f*, tuning; tempering

**templanza** /tem'planθa; tem'plansa/ *f*, moderation; sobriety; mildness of climate

**templar** /tem'plar/ *vt* to tune; *Metall.* temper; moderate; warm; allay, appease; anneal; *Art.* harmonize, blend; *Naut.* trim the sails; —*vr* control oneself, be moderate; —*vi* grow warm

**templario** /tem'plario/ *m*, Knight Templar

**temple** /'temple/ *m*, weather conditions; temperature; temper (of metals, etc.); nature, disposition; bravery; mean, average; *Mus.* tuning. **al t.**, in tempera

**templete** /tem'plete/ *m*, *dim* shrine; niche (for statues); kiosk, pavilion

**templo** /'templo/ *m*, temple

**temporada** /tempo'raða/ *f*, space of time, season, while. **de t.**, seasonal; temporary. **estar de t.**, to be out of town, on holiday

**temporal** /tempo'ral/ *a* temporal; temporary; secular, lay; transient, fugitive. *m*, storm, tempest; rainy period; seasonal laborer

**temporalidad** /temporali'ðað/ *f*, secular character; temporality secular possession (gen. *pl*)

**temporáneo, temporario** /tempora'neo, tempo'rario/ *a* temporary, impermanent, fleeting

**témporas** /'temporas/ *f pl*, Ember days

**temporejar** /tempore'har/ *vt Naut.* to lie to in a storm

**temporero** /tempo'rero/ *a* temporary (of work)

**temporizar** /tempori'θar; tempori'sar/ *vi* to while away the time; temporize

**tempranal** /tempra'nal/ *a* early fruiting

**tempranero** /tempra'nero/ *a* early

**temprano** /tem'prano/ *a* early —*adv* in the early hours; prematurely, too soon

**temulento** /temu'lento/ *a* intoxicated, drunken

**tenacear** /tenaθe'ar; tenase'ar/ *vi* to insist, be obstinate

**tenacidad** /tenaθi'ðað; tenasi'ðað/ *f*, adhesiveness; resistance, toughness; obstinacy, tenacity

**tenacillas** /tena'θiʎas; tena'siʎas/ *f pl*, *dim* small tongs; candle snuffers; sugar tongs; curling irons; tweezers

**tenaz** /te'naθ; te'nas/ *a* adhesive; hard, resistant, unyielding; tenacious, obstinate

**tenaza** /te'naθa; te'nasa/ *f*, claw (of a lobster, etc.); *pl* tongs; pincers; pliers; dental forceps

**tenazada** /tena'θaða; tena'saða/ *f*, seizing with tongs; strong bite, snap; rattle of tongs

**tenazón** /tena'θon; tena'son/ **(a** or **de)** *adv* without taking aim, wildly; unexpectedly

**tenca** /'tenka/ *f*, tench

**tención** /ten'θion; ten'sion/ *f*, retention, holding; grip

**ten con ten** /ten kon ten/ *m*, *Inf.* tact, diplomacy

**tendal** /ten'dal/ *m*, awning; sheet for catching olives

**tendedero** /tende'ðero/ *m*, drying ground

**tendedura** /tende'ðura/ *f*, laying out; stretching

**tendencia** /ten'denθia; tendensia/ *f*, tendency

**tendencioso** /tenden'θioso; tenden'sioso/ *a* tendentious, biased

**tender** /ten'der/ *vt irr* to hang out; unfold, spread out; extend, hold out; *Mas.* plaster; —*vi* tend, incline; —*vr* lie down at full length; place one's cards on the table; gallop hard (of horses). See **entender**

**tendero** /ten'dero/ **(-ra)** *n* shopkeeper; retailer. *m*, tent maker

**tendido** /ten'diðo/ *m*, row of seats in a bullfight arena; clothes hung out to dry; clear sky; *Mas.* plaster

**tendón** /ten'don/ *m*, tendon

**tenducha** /ten'dutʃa/ *f*, *Inf.* wretched little shop

**tenebrosidad** /teneβrosi'ðað/ *f*, gloom, darkness, obscurity

**tenebroso** /tene'βroso/ *a* dark, gloomy

**tenedero** /tene'ðero/ *m*, *Naut.* anchoring ground, anchorage

**tenedor** /tene'ðor/ *m*, table fork; possessor, retainer; *Com.* holder; payee. **t. de libros**, bookkeeper

**teneduría** /teneðu'ria/ *f*, employment of a bookkeeper. **t. de libros**, bookkeeping

**tenencia** /te'nenθia; te'nensia/ *f*, possession; tenancy, occupation; lieutenancy

**tener** /te'ner/ *vt irr* to have; hold; grasp; possess; own; uphold, maintain; contain; include; hold fast, grip; stop; keep (promises); lodge, accommodate; (*with en*) value, estimate (e.g. *Le tengo en poco,* I have a poor opinion of him); (*with para*) be of the opinion that (e.g. *tengo para mí,* my opinion is); (*with por*) believe, consider; —*vi* be wealthy; —*vr* steady oneself; hold on to; lean (on); rest (on); defend oneself; uphold; rely on; (*with por*) consider oneself as. **tener** is used to express: 1. *Age* (e.g. *¿Cuántos años tiene Vd?* How old are you?). 2. *Possession* (e.g. *Tenemos muchos sombreros,* We have a great many hats). 3. *Measurements* (e.g. *El cuarto tiene dieciocho metros de largo,* The room is eighteen meters long). Translated by "be" when describing some physical and mental states (e.g. *Tenemos miedo,* We are afraid. *Tengo sueño,* I am sleepy. *Tienen frío* (*calor*), They are cold (hot)). Used as *auxiliary verb* replacing **haber** in compound tenses of transitive verbs (e.g. *Tengo escritas las cartas,* I have written the letters). **t. a bien**, to think fit, please, judge convenient. **t. algo en cuenta a uno**, to hold something against someone. **t. a menos de hacer (una cosa)**, to scorn to do (a thing). **t. cruda**, to have a hangover. **t. curiosidad por**, to be curious about. **t. curiosidad por que** + *subj* to be interested in that. **t. en aprecio**, to appreciate, esteem, value. **t. en cuenta**, to bear in mind. **t. en menos (a)**, to despise (a person). **t. gana**, to want, wish; feel disposed; have an appetite. **t. lugar**, to take place, occur. **t. muchas partes cruzadas**, to be well-traveled. **t. mucho colegio** to be well-educated. **t. muy en cuenta**, to certainly bear in mind. **t. poco colegio**, to have had little education. **t. presente**, to remember. **t. que**, to have to (e.g. *tengo que hacerlo,* I must do it). **t. que ver (con)**, to have something to do (with), be related to. **no tenerlas todas consigo**, *Inf.* to have the jitters —*Pres. Ind.* **tengo, tienes, tiene, tenemos, tenéis, tienen.** *Preterite* **tuve**, etc —*Fut.* **tendré**, etc —*Condit.* **tendría**, etc —*Pres. Subjunc.* **tenga**, etc —*Imperf. Subjunc.* **tuviese**, etc.

**tenguerengue, en** /tengue'rengue, en/ *adv Inf.* rickety, insecure

**tenia** /'tenia/ *f*, tapeworm; *Archit.* fillet, narrow molding

**teniente** /te'niente/ *a* owning, holding; unripe (of fruit); *Inf.* slightly deaf; stingy, mean. *m*, deputy, substitute; *Mil.* first lieutenant, lieutenant. **t. coronel**, lieutenant colonel. **t. de navío**, naval lieutenant. **t. general**, *Mil.* lieutenant general. **t. general de aviación**, air marshal

**tenis** /'tenis/ *m*, tennis

**tenor** /te'nor/ *m*, import, contents (of a letter, etc.); constitution, composition; *Mus.* tenor

**tenorio** /te'norio/ *m*, rake, Don Juan, philanderer

**tensar** /ten'sar/ *vt* to tighten; tense

**tensión** /ten'sion/ *f*, tautness; tension; strain, stress; *Elec.* tension

**tenso** /'tenso/ *a* taut; tight; tense

**tentación** /tenta'θion; tenta'sion/ *f*, temptation; attraction, inducement

**tentáculo** /ten'takulo/ *m*, tentacle; feeler

**tentadero** /tenta'ðero/ *m*, yard for trying out young bulls for bullfighting

**tentador** /tenta'ðor/ **(-ra)** *a* tempting; attractive —*n* tempter. *m*, the Devil

**tentalear** /tentale'ar/ *vt* to examine by touch

**tentar** /ten'tar/ *vt irr* to touch, feel; examine by touch; incite, encourage; try, endeavor; test; tempt; *Surg.* probe. See **sentar**

**tentativa** /tenta'tiβa/ *f*, endeavor, attempt; preliminary exam (at some univs.)

**tentativo** /tenta'tiβo/ *a* tentative, experimental

**tentemozo** /tente'moθo; tente'moso/ *m*, support, prop; tumbler (toy)

**tentempié** /tentem'pie/ *m*, *Inf.* snack, bite

**tenue** /'tenue/ *a* thin; slender, delicate; trivial, worthless, insignificant; pale; faint

**tenuidad** /tenui'ðað/ *f*, slenderness; delicacy; triviality, insignificance; paleness; faintness

**teñidura** /teɲi'ðura/ *f*, dyeing, staining

**teñir** /te'ɲir/ *vt irr* to dye; *Art.* darken; color, tinge; —*vr* be dyed; be tinged or colored. See **ceñir**

**teocracia** /teo'kraθia; teo'krasia/ *f*, theocracy

**teocrático** /teo'kratiko/ *a* theocratic

**teodolito** /teoðo'lito/ *m*, theodolite

**teologal** /teolo'gal/ *a* theological

**teología** /teolo'hia/ *f*, theology, divinity

**teológico** /teo'lohiko/ *a* theological

**teologizar** /teolohi'θar; teolohi'sar/ *vi* to theologize

**teólogo** /te'ologo/ *a* theological. *m*, theologian, divine; student of theology

**teorema** /teo'rema/ *m*, theorem

**teoría** /teo'ria/ *f*, theory

**teórica** /te'orika/ *f*, theory

**teórico** /te'oriko/ *a* theoretical, speculative. *m*, theorist

**teorizar** /teori'θar; teori'sar/ *vt* to consider theoretically, theorize about

**teoso** /te'oso/ *a* resinous, gummy

**teosofía** /teoso'fia/ *f*, theosophy

**teosófico** /teo'sofiko/ *a* theosophical

**teósofo** /te'osofo/ *m*, theosophist

**tepe** /'tepe/ *m*, sod, cut turf

**terapeuta** /tera'peuta/ *mf* therapeutist

**terapéutica** /tera'peutika/ *f*, therapeutics

**terapéutico** /tera'peutiko/ *a* therapeutic

**terapia** /te'rapia/ *f*, therapy

**teratología** /teratolo'hia/ *f*, teratology

**tercena** /ter'θena; ter'sena/ *f*, warehouse for storing government monopoly goods (tobacco, etc.)

**tercenista** /terθe'nista; terse'nista/ *mf* person in charge of a tercena

**tercer** /ter'θer; ter'ser/ *a Abbr.* of **tercero** third. Used before *m*, *sing* nouns

**tercera** /ter'θera; ter'sera/ *f*, procuress; *Mus.* third

**tercería** /terθe'ria; terse'ria/ *f*, arbitration, mediation; temporary occupation of a fortress, etc.

**tercero** /ter'θero; ter'sero/ **(-ra)** *a* third; mediatory —*n* third; mediator. *m*, pimp; *Eccl.* tertiary; tithes collector; third person. **¡A la tercera va la vencida!** Third time lucky!

**terceto** /ter'θeto; ter'seto/ *m*, tercet, triplet

**tercia** /'terθia; 'tersia/ *f*, one-third; *Eccl.* tierce, third hour; storehouse for tithes. **tercias reales,** royal share of ecclesiastical tithes

**terciana** /ter'θiana; ter'siana/ *f*, tertian fever

**terciar** /ter'θiar; ter'siar/ *vt* to slant; sling sideways; divide into three; equalize weight (on beasts of burden); plow or dig for the third time; *Agr.* prune; —*vr* be opportune, come at the right time —*vi* mediate, arbitrate; make up a number (for cards, etc.); reach the third day (of the moon); take part, participate

**terciario** /ter'θiario; ter'siario/ *a* third, tertiary; *Geol.* tertiary. *m*, *Eccl.* tertiary

**tercio** /'terθio; 'tersio/ *a* third. *m*, one-third; *Mil.* infantry regiment; *Obs.*, body of foreign volunteers; fishermen's association; *pl* brawny limbs of a man. **hacer t.,** to take part in; make up the number of. **hacer buen ( or mal) t. a alguien,** to do someone a good (or bad) turn

**terciopelo** /terθio'pelo; tersio'pelo/ *m*, velvet; velveteen

**terco** /'terko/ *a* pigheaded, obstinate; hard, tough

**tergiversación** /terhiβersa'θion; terhiβersa'sion/ *f*, tergiversation, vacillation

**tergiversar** /terhiβer'sar/ *vt* to tergiversate, shuffle, vacillate

**termal** /ter'mal/ *a* thermal

**termas** /'termas/ *f pl*, thermal springs, hot mineral baths; thermal

**térmico** /'termiko/ *a* thermic

**terminable** /termi'naβle/ *a* terminable

**terminación** /termina'θion; termina'sion/ *f*, conclusion, termination; end, finish; ending of a word; *Gram.* termination

**terminador** /termina'ðor/ **(-ra)** *a* concluding —*n* finisher

**terminal** /termi'nal/ *a* terminal; final. *m*, *Elec.* terminal. **t. de carga,** cargo terminal

**terminante** /termi'nante/ *a* conclusive, definite; categorical

**terminar** /termi'nar/ *vt* to end, conclude; complete; —*vr* and *vi* end

**término** /'termino/ *m*, limit, end; term, expression; boundary marker; district, suburb; space, period; state, condition; boundary; object, aim; appearance, demeanor, behavior (gen. *pl*); completion; *Mus.* tone; (*Math. Law. Logic.*) term. **t. medio,** *Math.* average; medium; compromise, middle way. **correr el t.,** to lapse (of time). **en primer t.,** *Art.* in the foreground. **medios términos,** evasions, excuses. **primer t.,** (cinema) closeup

**terminología** /terminolo'hia/ *f*, terminology

**termita** /ter'mita/ *f*, thermite. *m*, termite

**termodinámica** /termoði'namika/ *f*, thermodynamics

**termoeléctrico** /termoe'lektriko/ *a* thermoelectric

**termómetro** /ter'mometro/ *m*, thermometer

**Termópilas** /ter'mopilas/ Thermopylae

**termos** /'termos/ *m*, thermos, vacuum bottle

**termoscopio** /termos'kopio/ *m*, thermoscope

**termostático** /termos'tatiko/ *a* thermostatic

**termóstato** /ter'mostato/ *m*, thermostat

**terna** /'terna/ *f*, triad, trio; set of dice

**ternario** /ter'nario/ *a* ternal, ternary

**terne** /'terne/ *a Inf.* bullying, braggartly; persistent, obstinate; robust. *mf* bully

**ternera** /ter'nera/ *f*, female calf; veal

**ternero** /ter'nero/ *m*, male calf

**terneza** /ter'neθa; ter'nesa/ *f*, tenderness, kindness; softness; softheartedness; endearment, caress, compliment (gen. *pl*)

**ternilla** /ter'niʎa; ter'niya/ *f*, cartilage, gristle

**ternísimo** /ter'nisimo/ *a superl* **tierno** most tender

**terno** /'terno/ *m*, triad; suit of clothes, three-piece suit; oath, curse

**ternura** /ter'nura/ *f*, softness; softheartedness; tenderness, kindness, sweetness

**terquedad, terquería, terqueza** /terke'ðað, terke'ria, ter'keθa; ter'kesa/ *f*, obstinacy, obduracy

**terracota** /terra'kota/ *f*, terra cotta

**terrado** /te'rraðo/ *m*, flat roof

**Terranova** /terra'noβa/ Newfoundland

**terraplén** /terra'plen/ *m*, embankment; *Mil.* terreplein

**terraplenar** /terraple'nar/ *vt* to fill up with earth; fill in (a hollow); make into an embankment; terrace

**terrateniente** /terrate'niente/ *mf* landowner

**terraza** /te'rraθa; te'rrasa/ *f*, terrace; flat roof; flower border (of a garden)

**terrazgo** /te'rraθgo; te'rrasgo/ *m*, tillable land; rent for farming land

**terregoso** /terre'goso/ *a* lumpy, full of clods (of soil)

**terremoto** /terre'moto/ *m*, earthquake

**terrenal** /terre'nal/ a terrestrial

**terreno** /te'rreno/ a terrestrial. m, ground, land; Fig. sphere; region; soil; plot of land. **ganar t.,** Fig. to win ground, make progress. **medir el t.,** Fig. to feel one's way

**térreo** /'terreo/ a earthy

**terrero** /te'rrero/ a earthly; low-flying, almost touching the ground; humble. m, flat roof; pile or mound of earth; deposit of earth, alluvium; target; mineral refuse

**terrestre** /te'rrestre/ a terrestrial, earthly

**terrezuela** /terre'θuela; terre'suela/ f, poor soil

**terribilidad** /terriβili'ðað/ f, terribleness, horribleness; rudeness

**terribilísimo** /terriβi'lisimo/ a superl most terrible

**terrible** /te'rriβle/ a terrible, horrible; rude, unsociable, ill-humored; enormous, huge

**terrífico** /te'rrifiko/ a terrible, frightful

**territorial** /territo'rial/ a territorial

**territorialidad** /territoriali'ðað/ f, territoriality

**territorio** /terri'torio/ m, territory; jurisdiction. **t. bajo mandato,** mandated territory

**terrizo** /te'rriθo; te'rriso/ a earthen

**terrón** /te'rron/ m, clod (of earth); lump; pl lands, landed property. **t. de azúcar,** lump of sugar

**terrorismo** /terro'rismo/ m, terrorism

**terrorista** /terro'rista/ mf terrorist

**terrosidad** /terrosi'ðað/ f, earthiness

**terroso** /te'rroso/ a earthy; earthen

**terruño** /te'rruɲo/ m, plot of ground; native earth; country; soil

**terso** /'terso/ a smooth, shiny, glossy; Lit. elegant, polished (style)

**tersura** /ter'sura/ f, smoothness, glossiness; elegance (of style)

**tertulia** /ter'tulia/ f, regular social meeting (gen. in cafés); conversational group; party; part of Spanish cafés set apart for players of chess, etc. **hacer t.,** to meet for conversation

**tertuliano** /tertu'liano/ **(-na)** n **tertuliante,** mf **tertulio (-ia),** n member of a tertulia

**terzuelo** /ter'θuelo; ter'suelo/ m, third, third part

**Tesalia** /te'salia/ Thessaly

**tesar** /te'sar/ vt Naut. to make taut; —vi step backward, back (oxen)

**tesela** /te'sela/ f, tessera, square used in mosaic work

**teselado** /tese'laðo/ a tessellated

**tesina** /te'sina/ f, master's essay, thesis

**tesis** /'tesis/ f, thesis

**teso** /'teso/ a tight, taut, tense. m, hilltop; bulge, lump

**tesón** /te'son/ m, persistence, obstinacy, tenacity

**tesonería** /tesone'ria/ f, stubbornness, obstinacy

**tesorería** /tesore'ria/ f, treasury; treasuryship

**tesorero** /teso'rero/ **(-ra)** n treasurer

**tesoro** /te'soro/ m, treasure; public treasury; hoard; Fig. gem, excellent person; thesaurus. **t. de duende,** fairy gold

**tespíades** /tes'piaðes/ f pl, the muses

**testa** /'testa/ f, head; face, front; Inf. sense, acumen. **t. coronada,** crowned head

**testación** /testa'θion; testa'sion/ f, erasure, crossing out

**testado** /tes'taðo/ a testate

**testador** /testa'ðor/ **(-ra)** n testator

**testaferro** /testa'ferro/ m, Fig. figurehead, proxy

**testamentar** /testamen'tar/ vt to bequeath

**testamentaria** /testamen'taria/ f, execution of a will; Law. estate; executors' meeting

**testamentario** /testamen'tario/ a testamental, testamentary

**testamento** /testa'mento/ m, Law. will; testament. **Antiguo T.,** Old Testament. **ordenar** ( or **otorgar**) **su t.,** to make one's will

**testar** /tes'tar/ vi to make a will; —vt erase, cross out

**testarada** /testa'raða/ f, a blow with the head; pigheadedness, stubbornness

**testarrón** /testa'rron/ a Inf. pigheaded

**testarudez** /testaru'ðeθ; testaru'ðes/ f, obstinacy, obduracy

**testarudo** /testa'ruðo/ a stubborn, obstinate

**testera** /tes'tera/ f, front, face; front seat (in a vehicle); upper half of an animal's face; tester, canopy

**testículo** /tes'tikulo/ m, testicle

**testificación** /testifika'θion; testifika'sion/ f, testification

**testificar** /testifi'kar/ vt to testify; affirm, assert; attest, prove

**testigo** /tes'tigo/ mf witness. m, proof, evidence. Law. **t. de cargo,** witness for the prosecution. Law. **t. de descargo,** witness for the defense. **t. de vista,** eyewitness. Law. **hacer testigos,** to bring forward witnesses

**testimonial** /testimo'nial/ a confirmatory, proven

**testimoniar** /testimo'niar/ vt to attest, confirm, bear witness to

**testimoniero** /testimo'niero/ **(-ra)** a slanderous; hypocritical —n slanderer, hypocrite

**testimonio** /testi'monio/ m, testimony, proof; slander; affidavit

**testuz** /tes'tuθ; tes'tus/ m, front of the head (of some animals); nape (of animals)

**teta** /'teta/ f, mammary gland, breast; teat, dug, udder. **dar la t.** ( **a**), to suckle

**tétano, tétanos** /'tetano, 'tetanos/ m, tetanus

**tetera** /te'tera/ f, teapot; teakettle

**tetilla** /te'tiʎa; te'tiya/ f, dim rudimentary teat or nipple; nipple (of a nursing bottle)

**tétrico** /'tetriko/ a gloomy; somber

**tetuaní** /tetua'ni/ a and mf of or from Tetuan

**teutón** /teu'ton/ **(-ona)** n Teuton —a Teutonic

**teutónico** /teu'toniko/ a Teutonic

**textil** /teks'til/ a and m, textile

**texto** /'teksto/ m, text; quotation, citation; textbook

**textorio** /teks'torio/ a textile

**textual** /teks'tual/ a textual

**textualista** /tekstua'lista/ mf textualist

**textura** /teks'tura/ f, texture; weaving; structure (of a novel, etc.); animal structure

**tez** /teθ; tes/ f, complexion, skin

**ti** /ti/ pers pron 2nd sing mf dat acc abl thee, you. Always used with prep. (e.g. por ti, by thee (you))

**tía** /'tia/ f, aunt; Inf. wife, mother, dame; Inf. coarse creature. **t. abuela,** grandaunt, great-aunt. Inf. **quedarse para t.,** to be left an old maid

**tiara** /'tiara/ f, ancient Persian headdress; papal tiara; coronet; dignity and power of the papacy

**tiberino** /tiβe'rino/ a Tiberine

**tibetano** /tiβe'tano/ **(-na)** a and n Tibetan. m, Tibetan (language)

**tibia** /'tiβia/ f, flute; tibia

**tibieza** /ti'βieθa; ti'βiesa/ f, tepidity; indifference, lack of enthusiasm

**tibio** /'tiβio/ a tepid, warm; indifferent, unenthusiastic

**tiburón** /tiβu'ron/ m, shark

**ticket** /'tikket/ m, ticket; pass, membership card

**tictac** /tik'tak/ m, ticktock (of a clock)

**tiempo** /'tiempo/ m, time; season; epoch, period; chance, opportunity; leisure, free time; weather; Mus. tempo; Gram. tense; Naut. storm. **t. ha,** many years ago, long ago. **t. medio** or **medio t.,** Sports. halftime. **abrir el t.,** to clear up (of the weather). **ajustar los tiempos,** to fix the date (chronology). **a largo t.,** after a long time. **andando el t.,** in the course of time. **a su t.,** in due course, at the proper time. **a t.,** in time, at the right time. **a un t.,** simultaneously, at the same time. **cargarse el t.,** to cloud over (of the sky). **con t.,** in advance, with time; in time. **correr el t.,** to pass, move on (of time). **de t. en t.,** from time to time. **engañar** (or **entretener**) **el t.,** to kill time, while away the hours. **en t. de Maricastaña** or **del rey Perico,** long, long ago. **fuera de t.,** unseasonably, inopportunely; out of season. **ganar t.,** to gain time; Inf. hurry. **hacer t.,** to wait, cool one's heels; Fig. mark time. **perder el t.,** to waste time; misspend or lose time. **sentarse el t.,** to clear up (of the weather). **tomarse t.** ( **para**), to postpone, take time for (or to)

**tienda** /'tienda/ f, tent; Naut. awning, canopy; shop, store. **t. de antigüedades,** antique shop. **t. de campaña,** bell tent, pavilion. **t. oxígena,** oxygen tent

**tienta** /'tienta/ f, astuteness; cleverness; Surg. probe;

trying out young bulls for the bullring. **a tientas,** by touch, gropingly

**tientaparedes** /tientapa'reðes/ *mf* one who gropes one's way

**tiento** /'tiento/ *m*, touching, feeling; touch, feel; blind person's cane; tightrope walker's pole; manual control, steady hand; caution, care, tact; *Mus.* preliminary flourish; *Inf.* slap buffet; tentacle. **a t.,** by touch; unsurely, gropingly

**tierno** /'tierno/ *a* soft; tender; kind; sweet; delicate; softhearted; fresh, recent; affectionate

**tierra** /'tierra/ *f*, world, planet; earth; soil; ground; cultivated ground, land; homeland, native land; region; district, territory. **t. adentro,** inland. **t. de batán,** fuller's earth. **t. de Promisión,** Promised Land. **t. de Siena,** sienna. **besar la t.,** *Inf.* to fall down. **dar en t. con,** to throw down; demolish. **echar en t.,** *Naut.* to put ashore, land. **echar por t.,** *Fig.* to overthrow, destroy. **echar t. a,** *Fig.* to bury, forget. *Inf.* **la t. de María Santísima,** Andalusia. **por t.,** overland. **saltar en t.,** to land, disembark. **venir** ( *or* **venirse**) **a t.,** to fall down, topple over

**Tierra Santa** /'tierra 'santa/ Holy Land

**tieso** /'tieso/ *a* hard, rigid, stiff; healthy, robust; taut; spirited, courageous; obstinate, stiff-necked; distant, formal —*adv* firmly, strongly

**tiesto** /'tiesto/ *m*, flowerpot; broken piece of earthenware

**tiesura** /tie'sura/ *f*, hardness, rigidity, stiffness; physical fitness; courageousness; obstinacy; formality, stiffness

**tifoidea** /tifoi'ðea/ *f*, typhoid

**tifón** /ti'fon/ *m*, typhoon

**tifus** /'tifus/ *m*, typhus. **t. exantemático,** trench fever

**tigre** /'tigre/ *m*, tiger; ferocious person

**tigresa** /ti'gresa/ *f*, tigress

**tigridia** /ti'griðia/ *f*, tiger lily

**tijera** /ti'hera/ *f*, scissors (gen. *pl*); any scissor-shaped instrument; shears; drainage channel; carpenter's horse; scandalmonger, gossip

**tijereta** /tihe'reta/ *f*, vine tendril; earwig

**tijeretada** /tihere'taða/ *f*, cut or snip with scissors

**tijeretear** /tiherete'ar/ *vt* to cut with scissors; *Inf.* interfere arbitrarily

**tijereteo** /tihere'teo/ *m*, scissor cut; click of the scissors

**tila** /'tila/ *f*, lime tree or flower; linden tree or flower; infusion made of lime flowers

**tildar** /til'dar/ *vt* to cross out, erase; stigmatize; place a tilde over a letter

**tilde** /'tilde/ *mf*, bad reputation; tilde; *f*, jot, iota

**tilín** /ti'lin/ *m*, tinkle, peal (of a bell)

**tillar** /ti'ʎar; ti'yar/ *vt* to lay wood floors

**tilo** /'tilo/ *m*, lime tree

**timador** /tima'ðor/ **(-ra)** *n Inf.* swindler, sharper, cheat

**timar** /ti'mar/ *vt* to swindle, cheat, deceive; —*vr Inf.* exchange looks or winks

**timba** /'timba/ *f*, *Inf.* casino, gambling den; game of chance

**timbal** /tim'bal/ *m*, kettledrum

**timbalero** /timba'lero/.*m*, kettledrum player

**timbrador** /timbra'ðor/ *m*, stamper; stamping machine; rubber stamp

**timbrar** /tim'brar/ *vt* to stamp; place the crest over a coat of arms

**timbre** /'timbre/ *m*, postage stamp; heraldic crest; excise stamp; bell, push-button; *Mus.* timbre; noble deed; personal merit

**timidez** /timi'ðeθ; timi'ðes/ *f*, timidity, nervousness

**tímido** /'timiðo/ *a* timid, nervous

**timo** /'timo/ *m*, *Inf.* swindling, trick; thymus

**timón** /ti'mon/ *m*, *Naut.* helm; rudder; management, direction; stick of a rocket. **t. de dirección,** *Aer.* tailfin

**timonear** /timone'ar/ *vi Naut.* to steer

**timonel** /timo'nel/ **timo'nero**/ *m*, helmsman, coxswain

**timorato** /timo'rato/ *a* godfearing; timid, vacillating

**tímpano** /'timpano/ *m*, *Anat.* eardrum, tympanum; *Mus.* kettledrum; *Archit.* tympanum; *Print.* tympan

**tina** /'tina/ *f*, vat; flour bin; large earthenware jar; wooden tub; bath

**tinada** /ti'naða/ *f*, woodpile; cow shed

**tinaja** /ti'naha/ *f*, large earthenware jar; jarful

**tinajero** /tina'hero/ *m*, seller of earthenware jars

**tinelo** /ti'nelo/ *m*, servants' hall

**tinerfeño** /tiner'feɲo/ **(-ña)** *a* and *n* of or from Tenerife

**tinglado** /tiŋ'glaðo/ *m*, overhanging roof; open shed; penthouse; intrigue

**tiniebla** /ti'nieβla/ *f*, gloom, darkness (gen. *pl*); *pl* profound ignorance; confusion of mind; *Eccl.* tenebrae

**tino** /'tino/ *m*, skilled sense of touch; good eye, accurate aim; judgment, shrewdness; vat. **sacar de t.** ( **a**), to bewilder, confuse; irritate, exasperate. **sin t.,** without limit, excessively

**tinta** /'tinta/ *f*, color, tint; ink; staining, dyeing; dye, stain; *pl* shades, colors; *Art.* mixed colors ready for painting. **t. china,** India ink. **t. simpática,** invisible ink. **recargar las tintas,** *Fig.* to overpaint, lay the colors on too thick. *Inf.* **saber de buena t.** ( **una cosa**), to learn (a thing) from a reliable source

**tintar** /tin'tar/ *vt* to dye; color, tinge, stain

**tinte** /'tinte/ *m*, dyeing, staining; color; dye; stain; dye house; pretext, disguise

**tintero** /tin'tero/ *m*, inkwell. *Inf.* **dejar** ( *or* **quedársele a uno**) **en el t.,** to forget, omit (to say, write)

**tintín** /tin'tin/ *m*, ring, peal; clink; chink

**tintinar** /tinti'nar/ *vi* to ring, tinkle; clink; jingle

**tintineo** /tinti'neo/ *m*, ringing, tinkling; clinking; jingle

**tintirintín** /tintirin'tin/ *m*, bray of a trumpet

**tinto** /'tinto/ *a* red (of wine). *m*, red wine; dark red

**tintorería** /tintore'ria/ *f*, dyeing industry; dyeing and dry-cleaning shop

**tintorero** /tinto'rero/ **(-ra)** *n* dyer; dry cleaner

**tintura** /tin'tura/ *f*, dyeing, staining; color, tint; dye; stain; tincture; smattering, slight knowledge

**tinturar** /tintu'rar/ *vt* to dye; color, tinge, stain; give a superficial notion of

**tiña** /'tiɲa/ *f*, ringworm; *Inf.* meanness, stinginess

**tiñoso** /ti'ɲoso/ *a* mangy; afflicted with ringworm; *Inf.* mean, stingy

**tiñuela** /ti'ɲuela/ *f*, shipworm

**tío** /'tio/ *m*, uncle; gaffer; fellow, chap; fool; stepfather; father-in-law. **t. abuelo,** granduncle, great-uncle

**tiovivo** /tio'βiβo/ *m*, merry-go-round

**tipiadora** /tipia'ðora/ *f*, typewriter

**típico** /'tipiko/ *a* typical

**tiple** /'tiple/ *m*, soprano or treble voice. *mf* soprano

**tipo** /'tipo/ *m*, model, pattern; type; print, type; species, group (of animals, etc.); *Inf.* guy, chap

**tipografía** /tipogra'fia/ *f*, typography

**tipográfico** /tipo'grafiko/ *a* typographical

**tipógrafo** /ti'pografo/ *m*, typographer

**tipula** /'tipula/ *f*, daddy-longlegs

**tiquismiquis** /tikis'mikis/ *m pl*, ridiculous scruples; affected courtesies —*a Inf.* faddy, fussy

**tira** /'tira/ *f*, strip, band, ribbon; stripe, rib. **t. cómica,** comic strip

**tirabotas** /tira'βotas/ *m*, buttonhook

**tirabuzón** /tiraβu'θon; tiraβu'son/ *m*, corkscrew; ringlet, curl; hair curler

**tirada** /ti'raða/ *f*, throwing; drawing, pulling; cast, throw; distance, space; *Print.* edition, issue; circulation (of a newspaper, etc.); stroke (in golf); lapse, interval (of time). **t. aparte,** reprint (of an article, etc.)

**tiradero** /tira'ðero/ *m*, shooting butt

**tirado** /ti'raðo/ *a Inf.* dirt-cheap. *m*, wire drawing

**tirador** /tira'ðor/ **(-ra)** *n* thrower, caster; drawer, puller; marksman. *m*, handle, knob; *Mech.* trigger; bell rope, bell pull; *Print.* pressman. **t. de bota,** boot tag. **t. de gomas,** catapult. **t. de oro,** gold wire drawer

**tiralíneas** /tira'lineas/ *m*, ruling pen

**tiramiento** /tira'miento/ *m*, pulling; stretching

**tiramira** /tira'mira/ *f*, long, narrow mountain range; long line of persons or things; distance

**tiranía** /tira'nia/ *f*, tyranny, despotism

**tiranicida** /tirani'θiða; tirani'siða/ *mf* tyrannicide (person)

**tiranicidio** /tirani'θiðio; tirani'siðio/ *m*, tyrannicide (act)

**tiránico** /ti'raniko/ *a* tyrannical

**tiranización** /tiraniθa'θion; tiranisa'sion/ *f*, tyranny, tyrannization

**tiranizar** /tirani'θar; tirani'sar/ *vt* to tyrannize over

**tirano** /ti'rano/ **(-na)** *a* tyrannous, tyrannical; *Fig.* overwhelming, dominating —*n* tyrant

**tirante** /ti'rante/ *a* taut; tense, strained. *m*, trace (of a harness); shoulderstrap; suspender (gen. *pl*); *Archit.* tie

**tirantez** /tiran'teθ; tiran'tes/ *f*, tautness; tension, strain; straight distance between two points. **estado de t.**, *Polit.* strained relations

**tiranuelo** /tira'nuelo/ *m*, petty tyrant

**tirar** /ti'rar/ *vt* to throw, cast; fling, aim, toss; throw down, overthrow; pull; draw; discharge, shoot; stretch, pull out; rule, draw (lines); squander, waste; *Print.* print; —*vi* attract; pull; (*with prep a*) turn to, turn in the direction of; incline, tend to; incline toward, have a tinge of (colors); try, aspire to; (*with de*) wield, unsheath, draw out (firearms, arms); —*vr* cast oneself, precipitate oneself; throw oneself on. *Inf.* **ir tirando,** to carry on, get along somehow

**tirilla** /ti'riʎa; ti'riya/ *f*, *Sew.* shirt neckband

**tiritaña** /tiri'taɲa/ *f*, thin silk material; *Inf.* mere nothing, trifle

**tiritar** /tiri'tar/ *vi* to shiver with cold

**tiritón** /tiri'ton/ *m*, shiver, shudder

**Tiro** /'tiro/ Tyre

**tiro** /'tiro/ *m*, throwing; throw, cast; toss, fling; try (in football); shooting; piece of artillery; report, shot (of a gun); discharge (firearms); shooting range or gallery; team (of horses); range (of firearms, etc.); hoisting cable; flight (of stairs); *Mineral.* shaft; *Inf.* trick; robbery, theft; innuendo, insinuation; grave harm or injury; *pl* sword belt. **t. de pichón,** pigeon shooting. **t. par,** four-in-hand. **a t.,** within firing range; within reach. **de tiros largos,** *Inf.* in full regalia

**tirocinio** /tiro'θinio; tiro'sinio/ *m*, apprenticeship

**tiroideo** /tiroi'ðeo/ *a* thyroid

**tiroides** /ti'roiðes/ *f*, thyroid gland

**Tirol, el** /ti'rol, el/ the Tyrol

**tirón** /ti'ron/ *m*, novice, beginner; pull, tug, heave. **de un t.,** with one tug; at one stroke, at one blow

**tiroriro** /tiro'riro/ *m*, *Inf.* sound of a wind instrument; *pl Inf.* wind instruments

**tirotearse** /tirote'arse/ *vr Mil.* to exchange fire; indulge in repartee

**tiroteo** /tiro'teo/ *m*, shooting, exchange of shots; crackle (of rifle fire)

**Tirreno, el Mar** /ti'rreno, el mar/ the Tyrrhenian Sea

**tirria** /'tirria/ *f*, *Inf.* hostility, grudge, dislike

**tirulato** /tiru'lato/ *a* dumbfounded, stupefied

**tisana** /ti'sana/ *f*, tisane

**tísico** /'tisiko/ **(-ca)** *a* tuberculous —*n* sufferer from tuberculosis, consumptive

**tisis** /'tisis/ *f*, tuberculosis

**tisú** /ti'su/ *m*, silver or gold tissue

**titánico** /ti'taniko/ *a* titanesque; colossal, huge

**títere** /'titere/ *m*, puppet; *Fig. Inf.* dummy, grotesque; *Inf.* fool; obsession, fixed idea; *pl Inf.* circus; Punch and Judy show. *Inf.* **echar los títeres a rodar,** to upset the whole show; quarrel, fall out with. *Inf.* **no dejar t. con cabeza,** to destroy entirely, smash up completely; leave no one

**titerero** /tite'rero/ **(-ra),** **titiritero** **(-ra),** *n* **titerista** *mf* puppet showman; acrobat; juggler

**tití** /ti'ti/ *m*, marmoset

**titilación** /titila'θion; titila'sion/ *f*, quiver, tremor; twinkling, winking, gleam

**titilador, titilante** /titila'ðor, titi'lante/ *a* quivering, trembling; twinkling

**titilar** /titi'lar/ *vi* to quiver, tremble; twinkle

**titiritaina** /titiri'taina/ *f*, *Inf.* muffled strains of musical instruments; merrymaking; uproar

**titiritar** /titiri'tar/ *vi* to tremble, shiver, shudder

**titiritero** /titiri'tero/ **(-ra)** *n* puppet master; acrobat

**titubear** /tituβe'ar/ *vi* to totter, sway, rock; stutter, stammer; toddle; hesitate, vacillate

**titubeo** /titu'βeo/ *m*, tottering, swaying; stuttering; hesitation

**titulado** /titu'laðo/ *m*, titled person; one who holds an academic title

**titular** /titu'lar/ *a* titular —*vt* to entitle, call; —*vi* obtain a title (of nobility); —*vr* style oneself, call oneself

**título** /'titulo/ *m*, title; heading; inscription; pretext, excuse; diploma, certificate; claim, right; noble title and its owner; section, clause; (univ.) degree; *Com.* stock certificate, bond; *Com.* title; caption; qualification, right, merit; basis of a claim or privilege; *pl Com.* securities, stocks. **t. de la columna,** *Print.* running title. **títulos de propiedad,** title deeds. **t. del reino,** title of nobility. **a t.,** under pretext

**tiza** /'tiθa; 'tisa/ *f*, chalk; whiting; calcined stag's antler

**tiznar** /tiθ'nar; tis'nar/ *vt* to make sooty; dirty, stain, begrime; *Fig.* sully, tarnish

**tizne** /'tiθne; 'tisne/ *m*, (sometimes *f*) soot; charcoal; stain (on one's honor, etc.); *Agr.* blight

**tizón** /ti'θon; ti'son/ *m*, firebrand; *Agr.* blight; *Fig.* stain (on one's honor, etc.)

**tizona** /ti'θona; ti'sona/ *f*, *Inf.* sword (by allusion to name of that of the Cid)

**tizonear** /tiθone'ar; tisone'ar/ *vi* to poke or rake the fire

**toalla** /to'aʎa; to'aya/ *f*, towel. **t. continua,** roller towel. **t. rusa,** Turkish towel

**toallero** /toa'ʎero; toa'yero/ *m*, towel rail

**tobillera** /toβi'ʎera; toβi'yera/ *f*, *Inf.* girl, flapper

**tobillo** /to'βiʎo; to'βiyo/ *m*, ankle

**tobogán** /toβo'gan/ *m*, toboggan; chute (in apartment buildings or amusement parks)

**toca** /'toka/ *f*, headdress; toque; wimple; coif

**tocable** /to'kaβle/ *a* touchable

**tocado** /to'kaðo/ *a Fig.* touched, half-crazy. *m*, headdress; coiffure, hairdressing

**tocador** /toka'ðor/ **(-ra)** *n Mus.* player. *m*, dressing table; kerchief; boudoir; cloakroom; dressing room; dressing case

**tocamiento** /toka'miento/ *m*, touching, feeling; touch; *Fig.* inspiration

**tocante** /to'kante/ *a* touching. **t. a,** concerning, with regard to

**tocar** /to'kar/ *vt* to touch, feel; *Mus.* play; knock, rap; summon; ring, peal; brush against; discover by experience; persuade, inspire; mention, touch upon; *Naut.* touch bottom; *Art.* retouch, touch up —*vi* belong; stop (at), touch at; be one's turn; concern, interest; be one's lot; adjoin, be near to; be opportune; be allied or closely related to; find the scent (of dogs). **t. en un puerto,** *Naut.* to touch at a port. **Ahora me toca a mí,** Now it's my turn. **Es un problema que me toca de cerca,** It is a problem that touches me very nearly. **a toca teja,** *Inf.* in ready cash

**tocayo** /to'kayo/ **(-ya)** *n* namesake

**tochedad** /totʃe'ðað/ *f*, boorishness, loutishness

**tocho** /'totʃo/ *a* boorish, loutish, countrified. *m*, iron bar

**tocinería** /toθine'ria; tosine'ria/ *f*, pork butcher's shop

**tocinero** /toθi'nero; tosi'nero/ *m*, pork butcher

**tocino** /to'θino; to'sino/ *m*, bacon; salt pork

**tocología** /tokolo'hia/ *f*, tokology, obstetrics

**tocón** /to'kon/ *m*, stump (of a tree or an amputated limb)

**todavía** /toða'βia/ *adv* still; even; nevertheless; yet. **No han venido t.,** They have not come yet. **Queda mucho que hacer t.,** There is still much to be done.

**todo** /'toðo/ *a* all; whole, entire; every, each. *m*, whole, entirety; whole word (in charades); all; *pl* all; everyone —*adv* wholly, entirely. **t. lo posible,** everything possible; all one can, one's best. **t. lo que,** all that which. **ante t.,** in the first place; especially, particularly. **así y t.,** nevertheless. **a t. esto,** in the meanwhile. **con t.** *or* **con t. esto** *or* **con t. y esto,** nevertheless, in spite of this. **del t.,** wholly, completely. **jugar el t. por el t.,** to risk everything on the outcome. **sobre t.,** especially. **y t.,** in addition, as well. **Todos somos hijos de Adán y Eva, sino que nos diferencia la lana y la seda,** We are all equal, but some of us are more equal than others

**todopoderoso** /toðopoðe'roso/ *a* all-powerful, almighty. *m,* the Almighty, God

**toga** /'toga/ *f,* toga; robe, gown

**toisón** /toi'son/ *m,* fleece. **t. de oro,** Golden Fleece

**Tokío** /'tokio/ Tokyo

**toldadura** /tolda'ðura/ *f,* awning; canopy; hanging, curtain

**toldillo** /tol'diʎo; tol'diyo/ *m,* covered litter or sedan chair; *West Hem.* mosquito net

**toldo** /'toldo/ *m,* awning; canopy; pomp, show

**tole** /'tole/ *m,* outcry, uproar, tumult

**toledano** /tole'ðano/ **(-na)** *a* and *n* Toledan

**tolerable** /tole'raβle/ *a* bearable, tolerable

**tolerancia** /tole'ranθia; tole'ransia/ *f,* tolerance, forbearance; permission

**tolerante** /tole'rante/ *a* tolerant, broad-minded

**tolerantismo** /toleran'tismo/ *m,* religious toleration

**tolerar** /tole'rar/ *vt* to put up with, bear, tolerate; overlook, allow, forgive

**tolla** /'toʎa; 'toya/ *f,* marsh, bog

**tollina** /to'ʎina; to'yina/ *f, Inf.* spanking, whipping

**tolmo** /'tolmo/ *m,* tor

**tolondro** /to'londro/ *a* stupid, heedless, reckless. *m,* bump, bruise

**tolonés** /tolo'nes/ **(-esa)** *a* and *n* of or from Toulon

**Tolosa** /to'losa/ Toulouse

**tolva** /'tolβa/ *f,* chute (for grain, etc.)

**toma** /'toma/ *f,* taking; receiving; conquest, capture; dose (of medicine)

**tomada** /to'maða/ *f,* taking; take; capture

**tomadero** /toma'ðero/ *m,* handle, haft

**tomadura** /toma'ðura/ *f,* taking; receiving; dose (of medicine). *Inf.* **t. de pelo,** leg-pull, joke

**tomar** /to'mar/ *vt* to take; pick up; conquer; eat; drink; adopt; employ; contract (habits); engage (employees); rent; understand; steal; remove; buy; suffer; *Fig.* overcome (by laughter, sleep, etc.); choose; possess physically; —*vi* (*with por*) go in the direction of; —*vr* grow rusty; go moldy; (*with con*) quarrel with. **t. a chacota,** to take as a joke. **t. a pechos,** to take to heart. **t. el fresco,** to take the air. **tomarla con,** to contradict, oppose; bear a grudge. **t. la delantera,** to take the lead; excel, beat. **t. las de Villadiego,** *Inf.* to quit, show one's heels. **t. por su cuenta,** to undertake, take charge of; take upon oneself. **t. su desquite con,** to get even with. **Más vale un toma que dos te daré,** A little help is worth a lot of promises. **¡Toma!** *Inf.* Fancy! You don't say!; Of course! There's nothing new about that!

**tomatal** /toma'tal/ *m,* tomato bed, tomato patch

**tomate** /to'mate/ *m,* tomato; tomato plant; *Inf.* hole, potato (in stockings, etc.)

**tomatera** /toma'tera/ *f,* tomato plant

**tomatero** /toma'tero/ **(-ra)** *n* tomato seller

**tómbola** /'tombola/ *f,* raffle (gen. for charity); jumble sale

**tomillo** /to'miʎo; to'miyo/ *m,* thyme

**tomo** /'tomo/ *m,* volume, book; importance, worth

**ton** /ton/ *m, Abbr.* **tono. sin t. ni son,** *Inf.* without rhyme or reason

**tonada** /to'naða/ *f,* words of a song and its tune

**tonadilla** /tona'ðiʎa; tona'ðiya/ *f, dim* short song; comic song; *Theat.* musical interlude *Obs.*

**tonadillero** /tonaði'ʎero; tonaði'yero/ **(-ra)** *n* composer or singer of tonadillas

**tonal** /to'nal/ *a* tonal

**tonalidad** /tonali'ðað/ *f,* tonality

**tonar** /to'nar/ *vi Poet.* to thunder or lightning

**tonel** /to'nel/ *m,* barrel; cask; butt

**tonelada** /tone'laða/ *f,* ton

**tonelería** /tonele'ria/ *f,* cooperage; collection or stock of casks and barrels

**tonelero** /tone'lero/ *m,* cooper

**tonga, tongada** /'toŋga, toŋ'gaða/ *f,* layer, stratum; *Inf.* task

**tónica** /'tonika/ *f, Mus.* keynote

**tónico** /'toniko/ *a* tonic. *m, Med.* tonic; pick-me-up

**tonificador, tonificante** /tonifika'ðor, tonifi'kante/ *a* strengthening, invigorating tonic

**tonillo** /to'niʎo; to'niyo/ *m, dim* monotonous singsong voice; regional accent

**tonina** /to'nina/ *f,* tuna; dolphin

**tono** /'tono/ *m,* inflection, modulation; (*Mus. Med. Art.*) tone; pitch, resonance; energy, strength; style; manner, behavior; *Mus.* key; mode of speech. **bajar el t.,** *Fig. Inf.* to change one's tune. *Inf.* **darse t.,** to put on side, give oneself airs. **de buen (mal) t.,** in good (bad) taste

**tonsila** /ton'sila/ *f,* tonsil

**tonsilitis** /tonsi'litis/ *f,* tonsillitis

**tonsura** /ton'sura/ *f,* shearing; hair cutting; *Eccl.* tonsure

**tonsurar** /tonsu'rar/ *vt* to shear, clip; cut the hair off; *Eccl.* tonsure

**tontaina** /ton'taina/ *mf Inf.* ninny, fool

**tontear** /tonte'ar/ *vi* to behave foolishly; play the fool

**tontería** /tonte'ria/ *f,* foolishness, stupidity; piece of folly; trifle, bagatelle

**tontillo** /ton'tiʎo; ton'tiyo/ *m,* dress bustle; hoop (for dresses)

**tontiloco** /tonti'loko/ *a Inf.* crazy, daft

**tontivano** /tonti'βano/ *a* vain, conceited

**tonto** /'tonto/ **(-ta)** *a* silly, stupid, simple; foolish, absurd —*n* fool, idiot. *m,* short coat, stroller. **t. de capirote,** *Inf.* an utter fool. **a tontas y a locas,** without rhyme or reason, topsy-turvy. **volver t.** ( **a**), *Fig. Inf.* to drive crazy

**topacio** /to'paθio; to'pasio/ *m,* topaz

**topar** /to'par/ *vt* (*with con*) to run into, collide with, hit; meet unexpectedly; come across, find; —*vi* butt (of horned animals); take a bet (in cards); consist in (of obstacles); meet with (difficulties); *Inf.* be successful

**tope** /'tope/ *m,* projection, part that juts out; obstacle, impediment; collision, bump; crux, difficult point; quarrel, fight; *Mech.* stop; *Naut.* masthead; *Rail.* buffer. **hasta el t.,** completely full, full to the brim

**topera** /to'pera/ *f,* molehill

**topetada** /tope'taða/ *f,* butt (of horned animals); *Inf.* knock, bang

**topetar** /tope'tar/ *vt* and *vi* to butt (of horned animals); —*vt* meet, run into

**topetón** /tope'ton/ *m,* butt; collision, impact, bump; blow on the head

**tópico** /'topiko/ *a* topical. *m,* topic, theme

**topo** /'topo/ *m, Zool.* mole; *Inf.* clumsy or shortsighted person; dolt, ninny

**topografía** /topogra'fia/ *f,* topography

**topográfico** /topo'grafiko/ *a* topographical

**topógrafo** /to'pografo/ *m,* topographer

**toque** /'toke/ *m,* touch, touching; pealing, ringing (of bells); crux, essence; test, proof; touchstone; *Metall.* assay; warning; *Inf.* tap (on the shoulder, etc.); *Art.* touch. **t. de luz,** *Art.* light (in a picture). **t. de obscuro,** *Art.* shade (in a picture). **t. de queda,** curfew. **t. de tambor,** beating of a drum. **dar un t. a,** *Inf.* to put to the test; pump (for information)

**toquero** /to'kero/ **(-ra)** *n* manufacturer of headdresses

**toquetear** /tokete'ar/ *vt* to keep touching, handle repeatedly

**toquilla** /to'kiʎa; to'kiya/ *f,* hatband, hat trimming; kerchief; small shawl

**torácico** /to'raθiko; to'rasiko/ *a* thoracic

**toral** /to'ral/ *a* principal, chief, main

**tórax** /'toraks/ *m,* thorax

**torbellino** /torβe'ʎino; torβe'yino/ *m,* whirlwind; spate of things; *Inf.* madcap

**torcedero** /torθe'ðero; torse'ðero/ *a* twisted, crooked

**torcedor** /torθe'ðor; torse'ðor/ *a* twisting. *m,* twister; cause of continual anxiety

**torcedura** /torθe'ðura; torse'ðura/ *f,* twisting; sprain, wrench

**torcer** /tor'θer; tor'ser/ *vt irr* to twist; bend; turn, bear (of roads, etc.); slant, slope, incline; misconstrue, pervert; dissuade; wrench, sprain (muscles); corrupt (justice). **t. el gesto,** to make a wry face —*vr* turn sour (of wine, milk); *Fig.* go astray; turn out badly (of negotiations) —*Pres. Indic.* **tuerzo, tuerces,** etc —*Pres. Subjunc.* **tuerza, tuerzas, tuerza, tuerzan**

**torcida** /tor'θiða; tor'siða/ *f,* wick (of lamps, etc.)

**torcido** /tor'θiðo; tor'siðo/ *a* bent, crooked, sloping, inclined; curved; dishonest, tortuous. *m,* silk twist

**torcijón** /torθi'hon; torsi'hon/ *m,* stomachache

**torcimiento** /torθi'miento; torsi'miento/ *m,* twisting; twist, turn; circumlocution; digression

**tordo** /'torðo/ *a* piebald, black-and-white. *m, Ornith.* thrush. **t. de campanario** *or* **t. de Castilla,** starling

**toreador** /torea'ðor/ *m,* bullfighter

**torear** /tore'ar/ *vi* and *vt* to fight bulls; —*vt* ridicule; exasperate, provoke; *Inf.* string along, deceive

**toreo** /to'reo/ *m,* bullfighting

**torera** /to'rera/ *f,* bullfighter's jacket

**torero** /to'rero/ *a Inf.* bullfighting. *m,* bullfighter

**torete** /to'rete/ *m, dim* small bull; *Inf.* problem, difficult question; engrossing topic of conversation

**toril** /to'ril/ *m,* pen for fighting bulls

**torio** /'torio/ *m,* thorium

**tormenta** /tor'menta/ *f,* storm; misfortune, calamity; indignation, agitation

**tormento** /tor'mento/ *m,* torment; torture; pain; anxiety, anguish. **dar t. ( a),** to torture; inflict pain (on)

**tormentoso** /tormen'toso/ *a* stormy, tempestuous; *Naut.* pitching, rolling

**torna** /'torna/ *f,* return; restitution; backwater

**tornaboda** /torna'βoða/ *f,* day after a wedding; rejoicings of this day

**tornada** /tor'naða/ *f,* return home; return visit, revisit; *Poet.* envoy

**tornadizo** /torna'ðiθo; torna'ðiso/ **(-za)** *a Inf.* changeable —*n* turncoat

**tornamiento** /torna'miento/ *m,* return; change, transformation

**tornar** /tor'nar/ *vt* to return, give back; change, transform; —*vi* return, go back; continue

**tornasol** /torna'sol/ *m,* sunflower; sheen, changing light; *Chem.* litmus

**tornasolado** /tornaso'laðo/ *a* shot (of silk, etc.)

**tornasolar** /tornaso'lar/ *vt* to look iridescent; change the color of, cause to appear variegated

**tornátil** /tor'natil/ *a* turned (in a lathe); inconstant, changeable; *Poet.* spinning, revolving

**tornatrás** /torna'tras/ *mf* half-caste

**tornaviaje** /torna'βiahe/ *m,* return journey

**tornavoz** /torna'βoθ; torna'βos/ *m,* soundboard, sounding board

**torneador** /tornea'ðor/ *m,* turner; jouster, fighter in a tournament

**tornear** /torne'ar/ *vt Sports.* to put a spin on (balls); turn in a lathe; —*vi* turn around, spin; fight in a tournament; turn over in the mind

**torneo** /tor'neo/ *m,* tournament

**tornería** /torne'ria/ *f,* turnery

**tornero** /tor'nero/ *m,* turner; lathe maker; convent messenger

**tornillero** /torni'ʎero; torni'yero/ *m,* (*Inf. Mil.*) deserter

**tornillo** /tor'niʎo; tor'niyo/ *m,* screw; (*Inf. Mil.*) desertion

**torniquete** /torni'kete/ *m,* turnstile; tourniquet. **dar t. ( a),** to pervert, misinterpret (meanings)

**torniscón** /tornis'kon/ *m, Inf.* slap, buffet, blow; pinch

**torno** /'torno/ *m,* lathe; turntable (of a convent, etc.); turn, rotation; windlass; dumbwaiter; axletree; spinning wheel; bend, loop (in a river). **en t.,** round about, around; in exchange

**toro** /'toro/ *m,* bull; Taurus; *pl* bullfight. *Inf.* **t. corrido,** tough nut to crack, wise guy. *Inf.* **Ciertos son los toros,** So it's true (gen. of bad news)

**toronja** /to'ronha/ *f,* grapefruit

**toroso** /to'roso/ *a* strong, vigorous, robust

**torpe** /'torpe/ *a* heavy, slow, encumbered; torpid; clumsy, unskilled; stupid, dull-witted; obscene, indecent; base, infamous; ugly

**torpedeamiento** /torpeðea'miento/ *m,* torpedoing, sinking

**torpedear** /torpeðe'ar/ *vt* to torpedo

**torpedeo** /torpe'ðeo/ *m,* torpedoing

**torpedero** /torpe'ðero/ *m,* torpedo boat

**torpedo** /tor'peðo/ *m, Ichth.* torpedo fish, electric ray; torpedo; sports car. **t. automóvil,** self-propelling torpedo

**torpeza** /tor'peθa; tor'pesa/ *f,* slowness, heaviness; torpidity; stupidity; lack of skill, clumsiness; indecency; ugliness; baseness, infamy

**tórpido** /'torpiðo/ *a* torpid

**torrar** /to'rrar/ *vt* to toast, brown

**torre** /'torre/ *f,* tower; belfry, steeple; turret; rook (in chess); *Naut.* gun turret; stack, pile (of chairs, etc.); country house with a garden. **t. del tráfico,** traffic light. **t. de viento,** castle in the air, castle in Spain

**torrefacción** /torrefak'θion; torrefak'sion/ *f,* toasting (of coffee, etc.)

**torrencial** /torren'θial; torren'sial/ *a* torrential

**torrente** /to'rrente/ *m,* torrent; *Fig.* spate, rush; crowd

**torreón** /to'rreon/ *m,* large fortified tower

**torrero** /to'rrero/ *m,* lighthouse keeper; gardener

**torreznero** /torreθ'nero; torres'nero/ **(-ra)** *n Inf.* lazybones, idler

**torrezno** /to'rreθno; to'rresno/ *m,* rasher of bacon

**tórrido** /'torriðo/ *a* torrid

**torsión** /tor'sion/ *f,* twisting, torsion

**torta** /'torta/ *f,* cake; pastry, tart; *Inf.* slap. **t. de reyes,** traditional Twelfth Night cake

**tortada** /tor'taða/ *f,* meat pie, game pie

**tortedad** /torte'ðað/ *f,* twistedness, crookedness

**tortera** /tor'tera/ *f,* cake pan; baking dish; whorl (of a spindle)

**tortícolis** /tor'tikolis/ *m,* crick (in the neck)

**tortilla** /tor'tiʎa; tor'tiya/ *f,* omelet. **t. a la española,** potato omelet. **hacer t.,** to smash to atoms. **Se volvió la t.,** *Inf.* The tables are turned

**tórtola** /'tortola/ *f,* turtledove

**tórtolo** /'tortolo/ *m,* male turtledove; *Inf.* devoted lover

**tortuga** /tor'tuga/ *f,* turtle; tortoise. **a paso de t.,** at a snail's pace

**tortuosidad** /tortuosi'ðað/ *f,* tortuousness; winding; indirectness; deceitfulness

**tortuoso** /tor'tuoso/ *a* tortuous; winding; disingenuous, deceitful

**tortura** /tor'tura/ *f,* twistedness; torture, torment; anguish, grief. **una t. china,** excruciating torture

**torturador** /tortura'ðor/ *a* torturing, tormenting

**torturar** /tortu'rar/ *vt* to torture

**torva** /'torβa/ *f,* squall of rain or snow

**torzal** /tor'θal; tor'sal/ *m,* sewing silk; twist, plait

**tos** /tos/ *f,* cough. **t. ferina,** whooping cough

**Toscana** /tos'kana/ Tuscany

**tosco** /'tosko/ *a* rough, unpolished; coarse; boorish, uncouth

**toser** /to'ser/ *vi* to cough

**tósigo** /'tosigo/ *m,* poison, venom; anguish; affliction

**tosigoso** /tosi'goso/ *a* poisoned, venomous

**tosquedad** /toske'ðað/ *f,* roughness, lack of polish; coarseness; boorishness, uncouthness

**tostada** /tos'taða/ *f, Cul.* toast

**tostadera** /tosta'ðera/ *f,* toasting fork

**tostado** /tos'taðo/ *a* golden brown, tanned. *m,* roasting (of coffee, etc.)

**tostador** /tosta'ðor/ **(-ra)** *n* toaster (of peanuts, etc.). *m,* toaster (utensil); coffee or peanut roaster

**tostadura** /tosta'ðura/ *f,* toasting; roasting (of coffee, etc.)

**tostón** /tos'ton/ *m,* buttered toast; anything over-toasted; roast pig; *Inf.* nuisance, bore

**total** /to'tal/ *a* total, entire, whole; general. *m,* total —*adv* in short; so, therefore

**totalidad** /totali'ðað/ *f,* whole; aggregate, entirety

**totalitario** /totali'tario/ *a* totalitarian

**tótem** /'totem/ *m,* totem

**totemismo** /tote'mismo/ *m,* totemism

**toxicidad** /toksiθi'ðað; toksisi'ðað/ *f,* toxicity

**tóxico** /'toksiko/ *a* toxic. *m,* toxic substance

**toxicología** /toksikolo'hia/ *f,* toxicology

**toxicológico** /toksiko'lohiko/ *a* toxicological

**toxicólogo** /toksi'kologo/ *m,* toxicologist

**toxina** /tok'sina/ *f*, toxin
**tozo** /'toθo; 'toso/ *a* dwarfish, small
**tozudez** /toθu'deθ; tosu'ðes/ *f*, obstinacy
**tozudo** /to'θuðo; to'suðo/ *a* obstinate, obdurate
**tozuelo** /to'θuelo; to'suelo/ *m*, scruff, fat nape (of animals)
**traba** /'traβa/ *f*, setting (of a saw's teeth); tether (for horses); difficulty, obstacle; fastening; bond, tie; shackle; *Law*. distraint
**trabacuenta** /traβa'kuenta/ *f*, mistake in accounts; argument, difference of opinion
**trabajado** /traβa'haðo/ *a* and *past part* wrought; fashioned; labored, exhausted, weary
**trabajador** /traβaha'ðor/ **(-ra)** *a* working; conscientious —*n* worker
**trabajar** /traβa'har/ *vi* to work; function; stand the strain, resist (of machines, etc.); exert oneself, strive; toil, labor; operate, work; produce, yield (the earth fruits, etc.); —*vt* work; till, cultivate; exercise (a horse); worry, annoy, weary; operate, drive; —*vr* make every effort, work hard
**trabajo** /tra'βaho/ *m*, work; toil, labor; operation, working; difficulty, obstacle; literary work; hardship, trouble; process; *pl* poverty; hardship. **t. a destajo,** piecework. **t. al ralenti,** go-slow tactics. **trabajos forzados** ( *or* **forzosos**), *Law*. hard labor. **pasar trabajos,** to undergo hardships
**trabajosamente** /traβahosa'mente/ *adv* painstakingly
**trabajoso** /traβa'hoso/ *a* difficult, hard; ailing, delicate; needy; afflicted
**trabalenguas** /traβa'leŋguas/ *m*, *Inf*. tongue twister, jawbreaker
**trabamiento** /traβa'miento/ *m*, joining, fastening; uniting; initiation, commencement; shackling; hobbling (of horses)
**trabar** /tra'βar/ *vt* to join, unite, fasten; grasp, seize; set the teeth (of a saw); thicken; begin, initiate; hobble (of horses); reconcile, bring together, harmonize; shackle; *Law*. distrain; —*vr* speak with an impediment; stutter, hesitate. **t. amistad,** to make friends. **t. conversación,** to get into conversation. **Se me trabó la lengua,** I began to stutter
**trabazón** /traβa'θon; traβa'son/ *f*, join, union, fastening; connection; thickness, consistency
**trabilla** /tra'βiʎa; tra'βiya/ *f*, vest strap; dropped stitch (in knitting)
**trabuca** /tra'βuka/ *f*, squib, Chinese firecracker, riprap
**trabucar** /traβu'kar/ *vt* to turn upside down, upset; confuse, bewilder; mix up, confuse (news, etc.); pronounce or write incorrectly
**trabucazo** /traβu'kaθo; traβu'kaso/ *m*, shot or report of a blunderbuss; *Inf*. calamity, unexpected misfortune
**trabuco** /tra'βuko/ *m*, *Mil*. catapult; blunderbuss
**trabuquete** /traβu'kete/ *m*, catapult
**tracamundana** /trakamun'dana/ *f*, *Inf*. barter, exchange of trash; hubbub, uproar
**tracción** /trak'θion; trak'sion/ *f*, pulling; traction
**Tracia** /'traθia; 'trasia/ Thrace
**tracoma** /tra'koma/ *f*, trachoma
**tracto** /'trakto/ *m*, tract, area, expanse; lapse of time
**tractor** /trak'tor/ *m*, tractor. **t. de orugas,** caterpillar tractor
**tractorista** /trakto'rista/ *mf* driver of a tractor, tractor driver
**tradición** /traði'θion; traði'sion/ *f*, tradition
**tradicional** /traðiθio'nal; traðisio'nal/ *a* traditional
**tradicionalismo** /traðiθiona'lismo; traðisiona'lismo/ *m*, traditionalism
**tradicionalista** /traðiθiona'lista; traðisiona'lista/ *a* traditionalistic. *mf* traditionalist
**traducción** /traðuk'θion; traðuk'sion/ *f*, translation; interpretation, explanation
**traducible** /traðu'θiβle; traðu'siβle/ *a* translatable
**traducir** /traðu'θir; traðu'sir/ *vt irr* to translate; interpret, explain; express. See **conducir**
**traductor** /traðuk'tor/ **(-ra)** *n* translator; interpreter
**traedizo** /trae'ðiθo; trae'ðiso/ *a* portable, movable
**traer** /tra'er/ *vt irr* to bring; attract; cause, occasion; wear, have on; quote, cite (as proof); compel, force; persuade; conduct, lead (persons); be engaged in; —*vr* dress (well *or* badly). **t. consigo,** to bring with it;

have or carry or bring with one. **t. entre manos,** to have on hand —*Pres. Indic.* **traigo, traes,** etc —*Pres. Part.* **trayendo.** *Preterite* **traje, trajiste,** etc —*Pres. Subjunc.* **traiga,** etc —*Imperf. Subjunc.* **trajese,** etc.
**trafagador** /trafaga'ðor/ *m*, dealer, trafficker, merchant
**tráfago** /'trafago/ *m*, traffic, trade; toil, drudgery
**trafalmejas** /trafal'mehas/ *a Inf*. rowdy, crazy, *mf Inf*. rowdy
**traficante** /trafi'kante/ *mf* dealer, merchant, trader
**traficar** /trafi'kar/ *vi* to trade; travel
**tráfico** /'trafiko/ *m*, traffic; trade, commerce
**tragaderas** /traga'ðeras/ *f pl*, throat, gullet. *Inf*. **tener buenas t.,** to be very credulous; be tolerant (of evil)
**tragadero** /traga'ðero/ *m*, throat, gullet; sink, drain; hole, plug
**tragador** /traga'ðor/ **(-ra)** *n* glutton, guzzler
**tragahombres** /traga'ombres/ *mf Inf*. braggart, bully
**trágala** /'tragala/ *m*, (**trágala tú, servilón**), title of Spanish Liberal song aimed at Absolutists; *Inf*. take that!
**tragaleguas** /traga'leguas/ *mf Inf*. fast walker
**tragaluz** /traga'luθ; traga'lus/ *m*, skylight; fan light
**tragantón** /tragan'ton/ **(-ona)** *a Inf*. guzzling, greedy —*n* glutton
**tragantona** /tragan'tona/ *f*, *Inf*. spread, large meal; swallowing with difficulty; *Fig. Inf*. hard pill to swallow
**tragaperras** /traga'perras/ *m*, *Inf*. vending machine, catchpenny
**tragar** /tra'gar/ *vt* to swallow; eat ravenously, devour; engulf, swallow up; believe, take in; tolerate, put up with; dissemble; consume, absorb
**tragedia** /tra'heðia/ *f*, tragedy
**trágico** /'trahiko/ **(-ca)** *a* tragic —*n* tragedian; writer of tragedies
**tragicomedia** /trahiko'meðia/ *f*, tragicomedy
**tragicómico** /trahi'komiko/ *a* tragicomic
**trago** /'trago/ *m*, swallow, gulp, draft; *Fig. Inf*. bitter pill. **a tragos,** *Inf*. little by little, slowly
**tragón** /tra'gon/ **(-ona)** *a Inf*. greedy, gluttonous —*n* glutton
**tragonear** /tragone'ar/ *vt Inf*. to devour, eat avidly
**traición** /trai'θion; trai'sion/ *f*, treason, treachery. **a t.,** treacherously
**traicionar** /traiθio'nar; traisio'nar/ *vt* to betray
**traicionero** /traiθio'nero; traisio'nero/ **(-ra)** *a* treacherous —*n* traitor
**traída** /tra'iða/ *f*, conduction. **t. de aguas,** water supply
**traidor** /trai'ðor/ **(-ra)** *a* treacherous —*n* traitor
**traílla** /tra'iʎa; tra'iya/ *f*, lead, leash (for animals)
**traje** /'trahe/ *m*, dress, apparel; outfit, costume; suit. **t. de americana,** lounge suit. **t. de ceremonia** *or* **t. de etiqueta,** full-dress uniform; evening dress (men). **t. de luces,** bullfighter's gala outfit. **t. de montar,** riding habit. **t. de noche,** evening dress (women). **t. paisano,** civilian dress; lounge suit
**trajín** /tra'hin/ *m*, carriage; transport; busyness, moving around; bustle; clatter
**trajinar** /trahi'nar/ *vt* to carry, transport; —*vi* be busy, go about one's business
**tralla** /'traʎa; 'traya/ *f*, rope, cord; lash (of a whip); whip
**trama** /'trama/ *f*, woof, texture (of cloth); twisted silk; intrigue, scheme; *Lit*. plot; olive flower
**tramar** /tra'mar/ *vt* to weave, prepare, hatch (plots); *Fig*. prepare the way for; —*vi* flower (of trees, especially olive)
**tramitación** /tramita'θion; tramita'sion/ *f*, transaction, conduct; procedure, method
**tramitar** /trami'tar/ *vt* to transact, conduct, settle
**trámite** /'tramite/ *m*, transit; negotiation, phase of a business deal; requirement, condition
**tramo** /'tramo/ *m*, plot of ground; flight of stairs, staircase; stretch, expanse, reach, tract
**tramontana** /tramon'tana/ *f*, north wind; arrogance, haughtiness
**tramontano** /tramon'tano/ *a* ultramontane, from beyond the mountains
**tramontar** /tramon'tar/ *vi* to cross the mountains;

sink behind the mountains (of the sun); —*vr* run away, escape

**tramoya** /tra'moya/ *f, Theat.* stage machinery; trick, deception, hoax

**tramoyista** /tramo'yista/ *mf* stage carpenter; stagehand; scene-shifter; trickster, impostor, swindler

**trampa** /'trampa/ *f,* trap, snare; trapdoor; flap of a shop counter; trouser fly; trick, swindle; overdue debt. *Fig. Inf.* **caer en la t.,** to fall into the trap. *Inf.* **coger en la t.,** to catch in a trap; catch in the act

**trampal** /tram'pal/ *m,* bog, marsh

**trampantojo** /trampan'toho/ *m, Inf.* optical illusion, swindle

**trampeador** /trampea'ðor/ *a Inf.* swindling —*n* trickster, swindler

**trampear** /trampe'ar/ *vi Inf.* to obtain money on false pretenses; struggle on (against illness, etc.); keep oneself alive, make shift; —*vt* defraud, swindle

**trampolín** /trampo'lin/ *m,* springboard; diving board; *Fig.* jumping-off place

**tramposo** /tram'poso/ **(-sa)** *n* debtor; cardsharper; swindler

**tranca** /'tranka/ *f,* thick stick, cudgel; bar (of a window, etc.)

**trancada** /tran'kaða/ *f,* stride

**trancar** /tran'kar/ *vt* to bar the door; —*vi Inf.* oppose, resist

**trancazo** /tran'kaθo; tran'kaso/ *m,* blow with a stick; influenza, flu

**trance** /'tranθe; 'transe/ *m,* crisis, difficult juncture; danger, peril. **t. de armas,** armed combat. **a todo t.,** at all costs, without hesitation

**tranco** /'tranko/ *m,* stride; threshold. *Inf.* **en dos trancos,** in a trice

**tranquera** /tran'kera/ *f,* stockade, palisade

**tranquilar** /tranki'lar/ *vt Com.* to check off

**tranquilidad** /trankili'ðað/ *f,* tranquility, peace, quietness; composure, serenity

**tranquilizador** /trankiliθa'ðor; trankilisa'ðor/ *a* tranquilizing, soothing

**tranquilizar** /trankili'θar; trankili'sar/ *vt* to calm, quiet; soothe

**tranquilo** /tran'kilo/ *a* tranquil, quiet, peaceful; serene, composed

**transacción** /transak'θion; transak'sion/ *f,* compromise, arrangement; transaction, negotiation, deal

**transalpino** /transal'pino/ *a* transalpine

**transandino** /transan'dino/ *a* transandean

**transatlántico** /transat'lantiko/ *a* transatlantic. *m,* (transatlantic) liner

**transbordar** /transβor'ðar/ *vt* to transship; transfer, remove goods from one vehicle to another

**transbordo** /trans'βorðo/ *m,* transshipment, transshipping; transfer, removal

**transcendencia** /transθen'denθia; transsen'densia/ *f* See **trascendencia**

**transcendental** /transθenden'tal; transsenden'tal/ *a.* See **trascendental**

**transcribir** /transkri'βir/ *vt* to transcribe; copy —*Past Part.* **transcrito**

**transcripción** /transkrip'θion; transkrip'sion/ *f,* transcription; copy, transcript

**transcurrir** /transku'rrir/ *vi* to elapse, pass (time)

**transcurso** /trans'kurso/ *m,* passage, lapse, course (of time)

**transepto** /tran'septo/ *m,* transept

**transeúnte** /tran'seunte/ *a* transient, temporary. *mf* passerby; visitor, sojourner

**transferencia** /transfe'renθia; transfe'rensia/ *f,* transfer (from one place to another); *Law.* conveyance, transference. **t. bancaria,** bank draft

**transferidor** /transferi'ðor/ **(-ra)** *a* transferring —*n* transferrer; *Law.* transferor

**transferir** /transfe'rir/ *vt irr* to transfer, move from one place to another; *Law.* convey (property, etc.); postpone. See **sentir**

**transfiguración** /transfigura'θion; transfigura'sion/ *f,* transfiguration

**transfigurar** /transfigu'rar/ *vt* to transfigure

**transfijo** /trans'fiho/ *a* transfixed

**transfixión** /transfik'sion/ *f,* transfixion

**transformable** /transfor'maβle/ *a* transformable

**transformación** /transforma'θion; transforma'sion/ *f,* transformation

**transformador** /transforma'ðor/ *a* transformative. *m, Elec.* transformer

**transformar** /transfor'mar/ *vt* to transform; reform (persons); —*vr* be transformed; reform, mend one's ways

**transfregar** /transfre'gar/ *vt irr* to rub, scrub. See **cegar**

**transfretar** /transfre'tar/ *vt Naut.* to cross the sea; —*vi* spread

**tránsfuga** /'transfuga/ *mf* **tránsfugo** *m,* fugitive; political turncoat

**transfundir** /transfun'dir/ *vt* to transfuse, pour from one vessel to another; imbue, transmit

**transfusor** /transfu'sor/ *a* transfusive

**transgredir** /transgre'ðir/ *vt* to transgress, infringe

**transgresión** /transgre'sion/ *f,* infringement, violation, transgression

**transgresor** /transgre'sor/ **(-ra)** *a* infringing —*n* transgressor, violator

**transiberiano** /transiβe'riano/ *a* trans-Siberian

**transición** /transi'θion; transi'sion/ *f,* transition, change

**transido** /tran'siðo/ *a* exhausted, worn-out, spent; niggardly, mean

**transigencia** /transi'henθia; transi'hensia/ *f,* tolerance, forbearance, indulgence

**transigente** /transi'hente/ *a* tolerant, forbearing

**transigir** /transi'hir/ *vi* to be tolerant; be broadminded —*vt* put up with, tolerate

**transitable** /transi'taβle/ *a* passable, traversable

**transitar** /transi'tar/ *vi* to cross, pass through; travel

**transitivo** /transi'tiβo/ *a* transitive

**tránsito** /'transito/ *m,* passage, crossing; transit; stopping place; transition, change; gallery of a cloister; *Eccl.* holy death. **de t.,** temporarily; in transit (of goods). **hacer tránsitos,** to break one's journey, stop

**transitorio** /transi'torio/ *a* transitory, fugitive, fleeting

**translimitación** /translimita'θion; translimita'sion/ *f,* trespass; bad behavior; armed intervention in a neighboring state

**translimitar** /translimi'tar/ *vt* to overstep the boundaries (of a state, etc.); overstep the limits (of decency, etc.)

**translucidez** /transluθi'ðeθ; translusi'ðes/ *f,* translucence, semitransparency

**translúcido** /trans'luθiðo; trans'lusiðo/ *a* translucent, semitransparent

**transmarino** /transma'rino/ *a* transmarine

**transmigración** /transmigra'θion; transmigra'sion/ *f,* transmigration

**transmigrar** /transmi'grar/ *vi* to migrate; transmigrate (of the soul)

**transmisión** /transmi'sion/ *f,* transmission. **t. del pensamiento,** thought transference

**transmisor** /transmi'sor/ *a* transmitting. *m, Elec.* transmitter, sender

**transmitir** /transmi'tir/ *vt* to transmit; *Mech.* drive

**transmutable** /transmu'taβle/ *a* transmutable

**transmutación** /transmuta'θion; transmuta'sion/ *f,* transmutation, transformation, change

**transmutar** /transmu'tar/ *vt* to transmute, transform, change

**transmutativo** /transmuta'tiβo/ *a* transmutative

**transoceánico** /transoθe'aniko; transose'aniko/ *a* transoceanic

**transpacífico** /transpa'θifiko; transpa'sifiko/ *a* transpacific

**transparencia** /transpa'renθia; transpa'rensia/ *f,* transparency; obviousness

**transparentarse** /transparen'tarse/ *vr* to be transparent; show through; *Fig.* reveal, give away (secrets)

**transparente** /transpa'rente/ *a* transparent; translucent; evident, obvious. *m,* windowshade, blind

**transpiración** /transpira'θion; transpira'sion/ *f,* transpiration; perspiration

**transpirar** /transpi'rar/ *vi* to perspire; transpire

**transpirenaico** /transpire'naiko/ *a* trans-Pyrenean

**transponer** /transpo'ner/ *vt irr* to move, transfer; transplant; transpose; —*vr* hide behind; sink behind the horizon (of the sun, stars); be half-asleep. See **poner**

**transportable** /transpor'taβle/ *a* transportable

**transportación** /transporta'θion; transporta'sion/ *f.* See **transporte**

**transportador** /transporta'ðor/ **(-ra)** *a* transport —*n* transporter. *m, Geom.* protractor

**transportamiento** /transporta'miento/ *m.* See **transporte**

**transportar** /transpor'tar/ *vt* to transport; *Mus.* transpose; carry; —*vr Fig.* be carried away by (anger, rapture)

**transporte** /trans'porte/ *m,* transport, carriage; cartage; *Naut.* transport; strong emotion, transport, ecstasy

**transposición** /transposi'θion; transposi'sion/ *f,* transposition

**transpositivo** /transposi'tiβo/ *a* transpositive

**transubstanciación** /transuβstanθia'θion; transuβstansia'sion/ *f,* transubstantiation

**transubstanciar** /transuβstan'θiar; transuβstan'siar/ *vt* to transubstantiate, transmute

**transversal, transverso** /transβer'sal, trans'βerso/ *a* transverse

**tranvía** /tram'bia/ *m,* street railway; streetcar. **t. de sangre,** horse-drawn streetcar.

**tranviario** /tram'biario/ *a* streetcar. *m,* streetcar employee

**trapacear** /trapaθe'ar; trapase'ar/ *vi* to cheat, swindle

**trapacete** /trapa'θete; trapa'sete/ *m, Com.* daybook

**trapacista** /trapa'θista; trapa'sista/ *mf* trickster, swindler, knave

**trapajoso** /trapa'hoso/ *a* ragged, shabby, tattered

**trápala** /'trapala/ *f,* noise, confusion, hubbub; noise of horse's hoofs, gallop; *Inf.* trick, swindle; prattling, babbling. *mf Inf.* babbler, prattler; trickster

**trapalear** /trapale'ar/ *vi* to walk noisily, tramp; *Inf.* chatter, babble

**trapatiesta** /trapa'tiesta/ *f, Inf.* brawl, row, quarrel

**trapaza** /tra'paθa; tra'pasa/ *f,* hoax, swindle

**trapecio** /tra'peθio; tra'pesio/ *m,* trapeze; *Geom.* trapezium, trapezoid

**trapería** /trape'ria/ *f,* old-clothes shop; old clothes, rags, trash, frippery

**trapero** /tra'pero/ **(-ra)** *n* old-clothes seller; rag merchant; ragpicker

**trapezoide** /trape'θoiðe; trape'soiðe/ *m,* trapezium, trapezoid

**trapichear** /trapitʃe'ar/ *vi Inf.* to make shift, endeavor

**trapiento** /tra'piento/ *a* ragged, shabby

**trapillo** /tra'piʎo; tra'piyo/ *m, Inf.* poverty-stricken lover; nest egg, savings. *Inf.* **de t.,** in a state of undress, in négligé

**trapío** /tra'pio/ *m, Inf.* spirit of a fighting bull; verve, dash, independent air (of women)

**trapisonda** /trapi'sonda/ *f, Inf.* uproar, brawl; hubbub, bustle; snare, fix

**trapisondear** /trapisonde'ar/ *vi Inf.* to be given to brawling; scheme, intrigue

**trapisondista** /trapison'dista/ *mf* brawler; schemer, trickster

**trapo** /'trapo/ *m,* rag; *Naut.* canvas; bullfighter's cape; *pl* garments, bits and pieces. *Inf.* **poner como un t.** ( **a**), to dress down, scold. *Inf.* **soltar el t.,** to burst out crying or laughing

**trapujo** /tra'puho/ *m, Inf.* trick; subterfuge

**traque** /'trake/ *m,* report, bang (of a rocket, etc.); fuse (of a firework)

**tráquea** /'trakea/ *f,* trachea

**traqueotomía** /trakeoto'mia/ *f,* tracheotomy

**traquetear** /trakete'ar/ *vi* to crack, bang, go off with a report; rattle; jolt (of trains, etc.) —*vt* shake, stir; *Inf.* paw, handle too much

**traqueteo** /trake'teo/ *m,* banging (of fireworks); creaking; rattling; jolting (of trains, etc.)

**traquido** /tra'kiðo/ *m,* report (of a gun); crack (of a whip); creak

**tras** /tras/ *prep* after; behind; following, in pursuit of; trans- (in compounds). *m, Inf.* buttock; sound of a

blow, bang, bump. **t. t.,** knocking (at a door); banging

**trasalcoba** /trasal'koβa/ *f,* dressing room

**trasbarrás** /trasβa'rras/ *m,* bang, bump, noise

**trascendencia** /trasθen'denθia; trassen'densia/ *f,* transcendence, excellence; consequence, result

**trascendental** /trasθenden'tal; trassenden'tal/ *a* transcendental; important, farreaching

**trascender** /trasθen'der; trassen'der/ *vi irr* to spread to, influence; become known, leak out; exhale a scent; —*vt* investigate, discover. See **entender**

**trascocina** /trasko'θina; trasko'sina/ *f,* back kitchen

**trascolar** /trasko'lar/ *vt irr* to filter, strain; cross over, traverse. See **colar**

**trascordarse** /traskor'ðarse/ *vr irr* to mix up, make a muddle of, forget. See **acordar**

**trasechar** /trase'tʃar/ *vt* to ambush, waylay

**trasegar** /trase'gar/ *vt irr* to upset, turn upside down; transfer, move from one place to another; empty, pour out, upset (liquids). See **cegar**

**traseñalar** /traseɲa'lar/ *vt* to re-mark, mark again

**trasera** /tra'sera/ *f,* rear, back, rear portion

**trasero** /tra'sero/ *a* rear, back. *m,* hindquarters, rump; buttocks, seat; *pl Inf.* ancestors

**trasgo** /'trasgo/ *m,* imp, sprite, puck

**trashumante** /trasu'mante/ *a* nomadic (of flocks)

**trashumar** /trasu'mar/ *vi* to go from winter to summer pasture (or vice versa) (of flocks)

**trasiego** /tra'siego/ *m,* emptying, pouring out, upsetting (of liquids); decanting (of wines)

**traslación** /trasla'θion; trasla'sion/ *f,* removal, transfer; alteration (of the date for a meeting); metaphor

**trasladable** /trasla'ðaβle/ *a* removable, movable, transferable

**trasladar** /trasla'ðar/ *vt* to remove, transfer; move from one place to another; alter (the date of a meeting); translate; copy, transcribe; —*vr* remove (from a place)

**traslado** /tras'laðo/ *m,* removal; transfer; transcription

**traslapar** /trasla'par/ *vt* to cover, overlap

**traslapo** /tras'lapo/ *m,* overlap, overlapping

**traslucirse** /traslu'θirse; traslu'sirse/ *vr irr* to be transparent or translucent; shine through; come out (of secrets); infer, gather. See **lucir**

**traslumbramiento** /traslumbra'miento/ *m,* dazzle, glare, brilliance

**traslumbrar** /traslum'βrar/ *vt* to dazzle; —*vr* flicker, glimmer; fade quickly, disappear

**trasluz** /tras'luθ; tras'lus/ *m,* reflected light. **al t.,** against the light

**trasmañana** /trasma'ɲana/ *adv* the day after tomorrow

**trasmañanar** /trasmaɲa'nar/ *vt* to put off from day to day

**trasminar** /trasmi'nar/ *vt* to undermine, excavate; —*vi* percolate, ooze; penetrate, spread

**trasnochada** /trasno'tʃaða/ *f,* previous night, last night; night's vigil; sleepless night; *Mil.* night attack

**trasnochado** /trasno'tʃaðo/ *a* stale, old; weary; hackneyed; drawn, pinched

**trasnochador** /trasnotʃa'ðor/ **(-ra)** *n* one who watches by night or stays up all night; *Inf.* night owl, reveler

**trasnochar** /trasno'tʃar/ *vi* to stay up all night; watch through the night; spend the night; —*vt* sleep on, leave for the following day

**trasnoche, trasnocho** /tras'notʃe, tras'notʃo/ *m, Inf.* night out; night vigil

**trasoir** /traso'ir/ *vt irr* to hear incorrectly, misunderstand. See **oir**

**trasojado** /traso'haðo/ *a* haggard, tired-eyed

**trasoñar** /traso'ɲar/ *vt irr* to imagine, mistake a dream for reality. See **contar**

**traspalar** /traspa'lar/ *vt* to fork (grain); shovel; transfer, move

**trasparencia** /traspa'renθia; traspa'rensia/ *f.* See **transparencia**

**traspasar** /traspa'sar/ *vt* to transfer, move; cross; *Law.* convey, make over to; pierce; transgress, flout; exceed one's authority; *Fig.* go too far; reexamine, go over again; give intolerable pain (of illness, grief). **se traspasa,** to be disposed of (houses, etc.)

**traspaso** /tras'paso/ *m,* transport, transfer; *Law.* conveyance; property transferred; price agreed upon

**traspié** /tras'pie/ *m,* slip, catching of the foot, stumble; heel of the foot. **dar traspiés,** *Inf.* to blunder

**trasplantación** /trasplanta'θion; trasplanta'sion/ *f,* **trasplante** *m,* transplantation; emigration

**trasplantar** /trasplan'tar/ *vt Agr.* to transplant; —*vr* emigrate

**trasplante** /tras'plante/ *m,* planting out

**traspuesta** /tras'puesta/ *f,* transposition; back quarters; rear (of a house); back yard

**traspunte** /tras'punte/ *m, Theat.* prompter

**traspuntín** /traspun'tin/ *m, Auto.* folding seat

**trasquilar** /traski'lar/ *vt* to cut the hair unevenly; shear (sheep); *Inf.* cut down, diminish

**trasquilón** /traski'lon/ *m,* cropping (of hair); shearing; *Inf.* money stolen by pilfering

**trastada** /tras'taða/ *f, Inf.* dirty trick, mean act

**traste** /'traste/ *m,* fret (of stringed instruments); tasting cup. **dar al t. con,** to spoil, upset, damage. *Inf.* **sin trastes,** topsy-turvy, without method

**trastear** /traste'ar/ *vt* to play well (on the mandolin, etc.); *Inf.* manage tactfully; —*vi* move around, change (furniture, etc.); discuss excitedly

**trastejar** /traste'har/ *vt* to repair the roof; renew slates; overhaul

**trastienda** /tras'tienda/ *f,* back of a shop; room behind a shop; *Inf.* wariness, caution

**trasto** /'trasto/ *m,* piece of furniture; (household) utensil; lumber, useless furniture; *Theat.* wing or set piece; *Inf.* useless person, ne'er-do-well; oddment, thing; *pl* implements, equipment

**trastornable** /trastor'naβle/ *a* easily overturned or upset; easily agitated

**trastornar** /trastor'nar/ *vt* to turn upside down; perturb, disturb; *Fig.* overpower (of scents, etc.); disorder, upset; dissuade; make mad; derange the mind

**trastorno** /tras'torno/ *m,* upset; perturbation, anxiety; disorder; mental derangement; confusion (of the senses)

**trastrabillar** /trastraβi'ʎar; trastraβi'yar/ *vi* to stumble, slip; totter, sway; hesitate; stutter, be tongue-tied

**trastrás** /tras'tras/ *m, Inf.* last but one (in games)

**trastrocamiento** /trastroka'miento/ *m,* alteration, change; disarrangement

**trastrocar** /trastro'kar/ *vt irr* to alter, change, disarrange; change the order of. See **contar**

**trasudar** /trasu'ðar/ *vt* to perspire

**trasudor** /trasu'ðor/ *m,* light perspiration

**trasuntar** /trasun'tar/ *vt* to copy, transcribe; summarize

**trasunto** /tra'sunto/ *m,* copy, transcript; imitation

**trasver** /tras'βer/ *vt irr* to see through or between, glimpse; see incorrectly. See **ver**

**trasverter** /trasβer'ter/ *vi irr* to overflow. See **entender**

**trata** /'trata/ *f,* slave trade. **t. de blancas,** white slave traffic

**tratable** /tra'taβle/ *a* easily accessible, sociable, unpretentious

**tratadista** /trata'ðista/ *mf* writer of a treatise; expert, writer on special subjects

**tratado** /tra'taðo/ *m,* pact, agreement; treaty; treatise

**tratador** /trata'ðor/ **(-ra)** *n* arbitrator

**tratamiento** /trata'miento/ *m,* treatment; courtesy title; address, style; *Med.* treatment; process. **t. de textos,** word processing

**tratante** /tra'tante/ *m,* merchant, dealer

**tratar** /tra'tar/ *vt* to handle, use; conduct, manage; have dealings with, meet, know (e.g. *Yo no le trato,* I don't know him); behave well or badly toward; care for, treat; discuss, deal with (e.g. *¿De qué trata el libro?* What is the book about?); propose, suggest; *Chem.* treat; (*with de*) address as, call; —*vi* have amorous relations; (*with de*) try to, endeavor to; (*with en*) trade in; —*vr* look after oneself, treat oneself; conduct oneself

**trato** /'trato/ *m,* use, handling; management; conduct, behavior; manner, demeanor; appellation, title; commerce, traffic; dealings, intercourse; treatment;

agreement, arrangement. **t. colectivo,** collective bargaining

**traumático** /trau'matiko/ *a* traumatic

**traumatismo** /trauma'tismo/ *m,* traumatism

**través** /tra'βes/ *m,* slant, slope; mishap; (*Mil. Archit.*) traverse. **a t.** *or* **al t.,** across; through. **de t.,** athwart; through

**travesaño** /traβe'saɲo/ *m,* crossbar; bolster; rung (of a ladder); traverse

**travesear** /traβese'ar/ *vi* to run about, romp, be mischievous; lead a vicious life; speak wittily; move ceaselessly (of water, etc.)

**travesía** /traβe'sia/ *f,* crossing; traverse; crossroad; side road or street; distance, space; sea crossing; crosswise position; stretch of road within a town

**travestido** /traβes'tiðo/ *a* disguised, dressed up

**travesura** /traβe'sura/ *f,* romping, frolic; mischief; prank; quick-wittedness

**traviesa** /tra'βiesa/ *f,* sleeping car, sleeper (railroad); *Archit.* rafter; distance between two points

**travieso** /tra'βieso/ *a* transverse, crosswise; mischievous, willful; debauched; clever, subtle; ever-moving (of streams, etc.)

**trayecto** /tra'yekto/ *m,* run, distance, journey; stretch, expanse, tract; fare stage

**trayectoria** /trayek'toria/ *f,* trajectory; journey

**traza** /'traθa; 'trasa/ *f,* plan, design, draft; scheme, project; idea, proposal; aspect, appearance; means, manner. **Hombre pobre para todo es trazas,** A poor man is full of schemes (for bettering himself)

**trazado** /tra'θaðo; tra'saðo/ *m,* designing, drawing; design, draft, model, plan; course, direction (of a canal, etc.)

**trazador** /traθa'ðor; trasa'ðor/ **(-ra)** *n* draftsman, designer; planner, schemer

**trazar** /tra'θar; tra'sar/ *vt* to plan, draft, design; make a drawing of; trace; describe; map out, arrange

**trazo** /'traθo; 'traso/ *m,* line, stroke; outline, contour, form, line; *Art.* fold in drapery; stroke of the pen

**trebejar** /treβe'har/ *vi* to frolic, skip, play

**trebejo** /tre'βeho/ *m,* chessman, chess piece; utensil, article (gen. *pl*); plaything

**trébol** /'treβol/ *m,* clover

**trece** /'treθe; 'trese/ *a* and *m,* thirteen, thirteenth. *m,* thirteenth (day of the month)

**trecemesino** /treθeme'sino; treseme'sino/ *a* thirteen months old

**trecho** /'tretʃo/ *m,* distance, space; interval (of time). **a trechos,** at intervals. **de t. en t.,** from time to time

**trefe** /'trefe/ *a* pliable, flexible; light; spurious (of coins)

**tregua** /'tregua/ *f,* truce, respite, rest. **dar treguas,** to afford relief, give a respite; give time

**treinta** /'treinta/ *a* and *m,* thirty; thirtieth. *m,* thirtieth (day of the month)

**treintañal** /treinta'nal/ *a* thirty years old

**treintavo** /trein'taβo/ *a* thirtieth

**treintena** /trein'tena/ *f,* thirtieth (part)

**tremebundo** /treme'βundo/ *a* fearsome, dread

**tremedal** /treme'ðal/ *m,* bog; quagmire

**tremendo** /tre'mendo/ *a* fearful, formidable; awesome; *Inf.* tremendous, enormous

**trementina** /tremen'tina/ *f,* turpentine

**tremesino** /treme'sino/ *a* three months old

**tremolar** /tremo'lar/ *vt* and *vi* to wave, fly (of banners); *Fig.* make a show of

**tremolina** /tremo'lina/ *f,* noise of the wind; *Inf.* hubbub, confusion

**trémulo** /'tremulo/ *a* trembling, tremulous

**tren** /tren/ *m,* supply, provision; outfit; equipment; pomp, show; railroad train; following, train. **t. ascendente,** up train (from coast to interior). *Inf.* **t. botijo,** excursion train. **t. con coches corridos,** corridor train. **t. correo,** mail train. **t. descendente,** down train (from interior to coast). **t. mixto,** train carrying passengers and freight. **t. ómnibus,** accommodation train, slow, stopping train. **t. rápido,** express

**trencilla** /tren'θiʎa; tren'siya/ *f,* braid, trimming

**trencillar** /trenθi'ʎar; trensi'yar/ *vt* to trim with braid, braid

**treno** /'treno/ *m,* threnody

**Trento** /'trento/ Trento

**trenza** /'trenθa; 'trensa/ f, plait, braid; plait of hair; bread twist. **en t.,** in plaits, plaited (of hair)

**trenzadera** /trenθa'ðera; trensa'ðera/ f, linen tape

**trenzar** /tren'θar; tren'sar/ vt to plait, braid; —vi curvet, prance

**trepa** /'trepa/ f, perforation, boring, piercing; climbing; creeping; *Inf.* half-somersault; grain, surface (of wood); craftiness, slyness; deception, fraud; beating, drubbing

**trepador** /trepa'ðor/ a climbing; crawling; *Bot.* creeping, climbing. m, climbing place

**trepanación** /trepana'θion; trepana'sion/ f, trepanning

**trepanar** /trepa'nar/ vt to trepan

**trepante** /tre'pante/ a creeping; *Bot.* twining, climbing

**trepar** /tre'par/ vi to climb, ascend; *Bot.* climb or creep; bore, perforate

**trepatrepa** /trepa'trepa/ m, jungle gym, monkey bars

**trepidación** /trepiða'θion; trepiða'sion/ f, trepidation, dread; vibration; jarring; shaking

**trepidar** /trepi'ðar/ vi to shiver, shudder; vibrate; shake; jar

**trépido** /'trepiðo/ a shuddering, shivering; vibrating

**tres** /tres/ a three; third. m, figure three; third (day of the month); three (of playing cards); trio. *Inf.* **como t. y dos son cinco,** as sure as two and two make four

**trescientos** /tres'θientos; tres'sientos/ a and m, three hundred; three-hundredth

**tresillo** /tre'siʎo; tre'siyo/ m, omber (card game); *Mus.* triplet

**tresnal** /tres'nal/ m, *Agr.* stook, cock, sheaf

**treta** /'treta/ f, scheme; trick, hoax; feint (in fencing)

**trezavo** /tre'θaβo; tre'saβo/ a thirteenth

**tría** /'tria/ f, selection, choice; worn place (in cloth)

**triangulación** /triangula'θion; triangula'sion/ f, triangulation

**triángulo** /tri'angulo/ a triangular. m, (*Geom. Mus.*) triangle. **t. acutángulo,** acute triangle. **t. obtusángulo,** obtuse triangle. **t. rectángulo,** right-angled triangle

**triar** /triar/ vt to select, pick out; —vi fly in and out of the hive (of bees); —vr grow threadbare, become worn

**tribu** /'triβu/ f, tribe; species, family

**tribulación** /triβula'θion; triβula'sion/ f, tribulation, suffering

**tribuna** /tri'βuna/ f, tribune; platform, rostrum, pulpit; spectators' gallery; stand. **t. de la prensa,** press gallery. **t. del jurado,** jury box. **t. del órgano,** organ loft

**tribunado** /triβu'naðo/ m, tribunate

**tribunal** /triβu'nal/ m, law court; *Law.* bench; judgment seat; tribunal; board of examiners. **t. de menores,** children's court, juvenile court. *Naut.* **t. de presas,** prize court. **t. de primera instancia,** *Law.* petty sessions. **t. militar,** court-martial

**tribuno** /tri'βuno/ m, tribune; political speaker

**tributar** /triβu'tar/ vt to pay taxes; offer, render (thanks, homage, etc.)

**tributario** /triβu'tario/ **(-ia)** a tributary; tax-paying, contributive —n taxpayer. m, tributary (of a river)

**tributo** /tri'βuto/ m, contribution; tax; tribute, homage; census

**tricenal** /triθe'nal; trise'nal/ a of thirty years' duration; occurring every thirty years

**tricentésimo** /triθen'tesimo; trisen'tesimo/ a three-hundredth

**triciclo** /tri'θiklo; tri'siklo/ m, tricycle

**tricolor** /triko'lor/ a three-colored

**tricorne** /tri'korne/ a *Poet.* three-cornered, three-horned

**tricornio** /tri'kornio/ a three-cornered. m, three-cornered hat

**tricotomía** /trikoto'mia/ f, trichotomy, division into three

**tricromía** /trikro'mia/ f, three-color process

**tridente** /tri'ðente/ a tridentate, three-pronged. m, trident

**tridentino** /triðen'tino/ a Tridentine

**trienal** /trie'nal/ a triennial

**trienio** /'trienio/ m, space of three years

**trifásico** /tri'fasiko/ a three-phase

**trifolio** /tri'folio/ m, trefoil

**trigal** /tri'gal/ m, wheat field

**trigésimo** /tri'hesimo/ a thirtieth

**trigo** /'trigo/ m, wheat plant; ear of wheat; wheat field (gen. *pl*); wealth, money. **t. sarraceno,** buckwheat. **t. tremés** or **t. trechel** or **t. tremesino** or **t. de marzo,** summer wheat

**trigonometría** /trigonome'tria/ f, trigonometry

**trigueño** /tri'geɲo/ a brunette, dark

**triguero** /tri'gero/ a wheat; wheat-growing. m, grain sieve; grain merchant

**trilátero** /tri'latero/ a three-sided, trilateral

**trilingüe** /tri'lingue/ a trilingual

**trilla** /'triʎa; 'triya/ f, red mullet; *Agr.* harrow; threshing; threshing season

**trillado** /tri'ʎaðo; tri'yaðo/ a frequented, trodden, worn (of paths); hackneyed

**trilladora** /triʎa'ðora; triya'ðora/ f, threshing machine

**trillar** /tri'ʎar; tri'yar/ vt to thresh; *Inf.* frequent; ill-treat

**trillo** /'triʎo; 'triyo/ m, threshing machine; harrow

**trillón** /tri'ʎon; tri'yon/ m, trillion

**trilogía** /trilo'hia/ f, trilogy

**trimestral** /trimes'tral/ a quarterly; terminal (in schools, etc.)

**trimestre** /tri'mestre/ a quarterly; terminal. m, quarter, three months; term (in schools, etc.); quarterly payment; quarterly rent

**trinado** /tri'naðo/ m, *Mus.* trill; twittering, shrilling (of birds)

**trinar** /tri'nar/ vi *Mus.* to trill; twitter, shrill; *Inf.* get in a temper, be furious

**trincapiñones** /trinkapi'ɲones/ m, *Inf.* scatterbrained youth

**trincar** /trin'kar/ vt to fasten securely; tie tightly; pinion; *Naut.* lash, make fast; cut up, chop; *Inf.* tipple; —vi *Naut.* sail close to the wind

**trincha** /'trintʃa/ f, vest strap

**trinchante** /trin'tʃante/ m, table carver; carving fork; stonecutter's hammer

**trinchar** /trin'tʃar/ vt to carve (at table); *Inf.* decide, dispose

**trinchera** /trin'tʃera/ f, *Mil.* trench; cutting (for roads, etc.); trench coat

**trinchero** /trin'tʃero/ m, platter, trencher; serving table, side table

**trineo** /tri'neo/ m, sled, sledge, sleigh

**trinidad** /trini'ðað/ f, trinity

**trinitaria** /trini'taria/ f, *Bot.* heartsease

**trinitario** /trini'tario/ **(-ia)** a and n *Eccl.* Trinitarian

**trino** /'trino/ a triune; ternary. m, *Mus.* trill

**trinomio** /tri'nomio/ m, trinomial

**trinquete** /trin'kete/ m, *Naut.* mainmast; mainsail; *Sports.* rackets; *Mech.* ratchet

**trinquis** /'trinkis/ m, *Inf.* draft, drink

**trío** /'trio/ m, trio

**tripa** /'tripa/ f, entrail, gut; *Inf.* belly; inside (of some fruits). **hacer de tripas corazón,** *Inf.* to take heart, buck up. **revolver las tripas** ( **a**), *Fig. Inf.* to make one sick

**tripartición** /triparti'θion; triparti'sion/ f, tripartition

**tripartir** /tripar'tir/ vt to divide into three

**tripartito** /tripar'tito/ a tripartite

**tripicallos** /tripi'kaʎos; tripi'kayos/ m pl, *Cul.* tripe

**triple** /'triple/ a triple; three-ply (of yarn)

**triplicación** /triplika'θion; triplika'sion/ f, trebling

**triplicar** /tripli'kar/ vt to treble

**trípode** /'tripoðe/ m, (sometimes f) three-legged stool or table; tripod; trivet

**Trípoli** /'tripoli/ Trípoli

**tríptico** /'triptiko/ m, triptych

**triptongo** /'triptongo/ m, triphthong

**tripulación** /tripula'θion; tripula'sion/ f, crew (ships and aircraft)

**tripulante** /tripu'lante/ m, crew member

**tripular** /tripu'lar/ vt to provide with a crew, man; equip, furnish; serve in, work as the crew of

**trique** /'trike/ *m*, crack, creak. *Inf.* **a cada t.**, at every moment

**triquiñuela** /triki'ɲuela/ *f*, *Inf.* evasion, subterfuge

**triquitraque** /triki'trake/ *m*, tap, rap; crack; firework

**tris** /tris/ *m*, crack, noise of glass, etc., cracking; *Inf.* instant, trice. **estar en un t.** ( **de),** to be on the verge (of), within an inch (of)

**trisar** /tri'sar/ *vt* to crack, break, splinter (of glass); —*vi* chirp, twitter (especially of swallows)

**trisca** /'triska/ *f*, cracking, crushing, crackling (of nuts, etc.); noise, tumult

**triscar** /tris'kar/ *vi* to make a noise with the feet; gambol, frolic; creak, crack; —*vt* blend, mingle; set the teeth of a saw

**trisecar** /trise'kar/ *vt* to trisect

**trisección** /trisek'θion; trisek'sion/ *f*, trisection

**trisemanal** /trisema'nal/ *a* three times weekly; every three weeks

**trisílabo** /tri'silaβo/ *a* trisyllabic

**trismo** /'trismo/ *m*, lockjaw, trismus

**triste** /'triste/ *a* unhappy, sorrowful; melancholy, gloomy; sad; piteous, unfortunate; useless, worthless

**tristeza, tristura** /tris'teθa, tris'tura; tris'tesa/ *f*, unhappiness; melancholy, gloom; sadness; piteousness

**tritón** /tri'ton/ *m*, merman

**triturar** /tritu'rar/ *vt* to crumble, crush; chew; masticate; ill-treat, bruise; refute, contradict

**triunfada** /triun'faða/ *f*, trumping (at cards)

**triunfador** /triunfa'ðor/ **(-ra)** *a* triumphant —*n* victor

**triunfal** /triun'fal/ *a* triumphal

**triunfante** /triun'fante/ *a* triumphant

**triunfar** /triun'far/ *vi* to triumph; be victorious, win; trump (at cards); spend ostentatiously

**triunfo** /'triunfo/ *m*, triumph; victory; trump card; success; booty, spoils of war; conquest

**triunvirato** /triumbi'rato/ *m*, triumvirate

**trivial** /tri'βial/ *a* well-known, hackneyed; frequented, trodden; commonplace, mediocre; trivial, unimportant

**trivialidad** /triβiali'ðað/ *f*, banality, triteness; mediocrity; triviality

**trivio** /'triβio/ *m*, road junction

**triza** /'triθa; 'trisa/ *f*, fragment, bit; *Naut.* rope. **hacer trizas,** to smash to bits

**trizar** /tri'θar; tri'sar/ *vt* to smash up, destroy

**trocable** /tro'kaβle/ *a* exchangeable

**trocada, a la** /tro'kaða, a la/ *adv* contrariwise; in exchange

**trocador** /troka'ðor/ **(-ra)** *n* exchanger

**trocar** /tro'kar/ *vt irr* to exchange; vomit; distort, misconstrue, mistake; —*vr* change, alter one's behavior; change places with another; be transferred. See **contar**

**trocear** /troθe'ar; trose'ar/ *vt* to divide into pieces

**trocha** /'trotʃa/ *f*, short cut; trail, path, track

**trochemoche, a** /trotʃe'motʃe, a/ *adv Inf.* without rhyme or reason, pell-mell

**trofeo** /tro'feo/ *m*, trophy; victory; military booty

**troglodita** /troglo'ðita/ *a* and *mf* troglodyte. *m*, *Fig.* savage, barbarian. *mf* glutton

**troglodítico** /troglo'ðitiko/ *a* troglodytic

**troj** /troh/ *f*, granary

**trojero** /tro'hero/ *m*, granary keeper

**trola** /'trola/ *f*, *Inf.* lie, nonsense, hoax

**trole** /'trole/ *m*, trolley

**trolebús** /trole'βus/ *m*, trolley car

**trolero** /tro'lero/ *a Inf.* deceiving, lying

**tromba** /'tromba/ *f*, waterspout

**trombón** /trom'bon/ *m*, trombone; trombone player. **¡Trombones y platillos!** Great Scot!

**trombosis** /trom'bosis/ *f*, thrombosis

**trompa** /'trompa/ *f*, elephant's trunk; *Mus.* horn; proboscis (of insects); waterspout; humming top. **t. de Falopio,** fallopian tube

**trompada** /trom'paða/ *f*, *Inf.* bang, bump; blow, buffet, slap; collision

**trompazo** /trom'paθo; trom'paso/ *m*, heavy blow, knock, bang

**trompear** /trompe'ar/ *vi* to play with a top; —*vt* knock about

**trompero** /trom'pero/ *m*, top maker —*a* deceiving, swindling

**trompeta** /trom'peta/ *f*, trumpet; bugle. *m*, trumpeter; bugler; *Inf.* ninny. **t. de amor,** sunflower

**trompetada** /trompe'taða/ *f*, *Inf.* stupid remark, piece of nonsense

**trompetazo** /trompe'taθo; trompe'taso/ *m*, bray of a trumpet; bugle blast; *Inf.* stupid remark

**trompetear** /trompete'ar/ *vi Inf.* to play the trumpet or bugle

**trompeteo** /trompe'teo/ *m*, trumpeting, trumpet call; sound of the bugle

**trompetería** /trompete'ria/ *f*, collection of trumpets; metal organ pipes

**trompetero** /trompe'tero/ *m*, trumpet or bugle maker or player

**trompetilla** /trompe'tiʎa; trompe'tiya/ *f*, *dim* little trumpet; ear trumpet

**trompicar** /trompi'kar/ *vt* to make stumble, trip —*vi* stumble, trip up

**trompicón** /trompi'kon/ *m*, stumble

**trompo** /'trompo/ *m*, humming or spinning top; *Inf.* dolt, idiot

**tronada** /tro'naða/ *f*, thunderstorm

**tronado** /tro'naðo/ *a* worn-out; threadbare, old; poor, poverty-stricken; down at the heels

**tronar** /tro'nar/ *v impers irr* to thunder; —*vi* growl, roar (of guns); *Inf.* go bankrupt, be ruined; *Inf.* protest against, attack; (*with con*) quarrel with —*Pres. Indic.* **trueno, truenas, truena, truenan.** *Pres. Subjunc.* **truene, truenes, truene, truenen**

**troncal** /tron'kal/ *a* trunk; main, principal

**tronchar** /tron'tʃar/ *vt* to break off, lop off (branches)

**troncho** /'trontʃo/ *m*, *Bot.* stem, stalk, branch

**tronco** /'tronko/ *m*, *Anat. Bot.* trunk; main body or line (of communications); trunk line; common origin, stock; *Inf.* blockhead, dolt; callous person. *Fig.* **estar hecho un t.,** to lie like a log; sleep like a log

**tronera** /tro'nera/ *f*, *Naut.* porthole; embrasure; slit window; pocket of a billiards table. *mf Inf.* madcap, harumscarum

**tronido** /tro'niðo/ *m*, roll of thunder

**trono** /'trono/ *m*, throne; *Eccl.* tabernacle; shrine; kingly might; *pl* thrones, hierarchy of angels

**tronzador** /tronθa'ðor; tronsa'ðor/ *m*, two-handled saw

**tronzar** /tron'θar; tron'sar/ *vt* to smash, break into bits; *Sew.* pleat; exhaust, overtire

**tropa** /'tropa/ *f*, crowd (of people); troops, military; *Mil.* call to arms; *pl* army. **t. de línea,** regiment of the line. **tropas de asalto,** storm troopers. **tropas de refresco,** fresh troops. **en t.,** in a crowd; in groups

**tropel** /tro'pel/ *m*, rush, surge (of crowds, etc.); bustle, confusion; crowd, multitude; heap, jumble (of things). **en t.,** in a rush; in a crowd

**tropelía** /trope'lia/ *f*, rush, dash; violence; outrage

**tropezar** /trope'θar; trope'sar/ *vi irr* to stumble, slip; (*with con*) meet unexpectedly or accidentally come up against, be faced with (difficulties); quarrel with or oppose; fall into (bad habits). See **empezar**

**tropezón** /trope'θon; trope'son/ *m*, stumbling, slipping; stumbling block, obstacle. **a tropezones,** *Inf.* stumblingly; by fits and starts

**tropical** /tropi'kal/ *a* tropical

**trópicos** /'tropikos/ *m pl*, tropics

**tropiezo** /tro'pieθo; tro'pieso/ *m*, stumble; stumbling block, obstacle; hitch; impediment; slip, peccadillo, fault; difficulty, embarrassment; fight, skirmish; quarrel

**tropismo** /tro'pismo/ *m*, tropism

**tropo** /'tropo/ *m*, trope, figure of speech

**troquel** /tro'kel/ *m*, die, mold

**trotaconventos** /trotakon'bentos/ *f*, *Inf.* go-between, procuress

**trotamundos** /trota'mundos/ *m*, *Inf.* globetrotter

**trotar** /tro'tar/ *vi* to trot; *Inf.* hurry, get a move on

**trote** /'trote/ *m*, trot; toil, drudgery. **t. corto,** jog-trot. **al t.,** with all speed

**trotón** /tro'ton/ **(-ona)** *a* trotting. *m*, horse. *f*, chaperone

**trova** /'troβa/ *f*, verse; song, lay, ballad; love song

**trovador** /troβa'ðor/ **(-ra)** *m*, troubadour, minstrel —*n* poet

**trovadoresco** /troβaðo'resko/ *a* pertaining to minstrels, troubadour

**trovar** /tro'βar/ *vi* to compose verses; write ballads; misconstrue, misinterpret

**Troya** /'troia/ Troy

**troyano** /tro'iano/ **(-na)** *a* and *n* Trojan

**trozo** /'troθo; 'troso/ *m*, part, fragment; piece, portion; *Lit.* selection. **t. de abordaje,** *Nav.* landing party

**trucha** /'trutʃa/ *f*, trout. **t. asalmonada,** salmon trout

**truchuela** /tru'tʃuela/ *f*, small trout; salt cod

**truco** /'truko/ *m*, trick, deception

**truculencia** /truku'lenθia; truku'lensia/ *f*, harshness, cruelty, truculence

**truculento** /truku'lento/ *a* fierce, harsh, truculent

**trueco** /'trueko/ *m*, exchange. **a t. de,** in exchange for; on condition that

**trueno** /'trueno/ *m*, thunder; report, noise (of firearms); *Inf.* rake, scapegrace

**trueque** /'trueke/ *m*, exchange. **a.** ( *or* **en) t.,** in exchange

**trufa** /'trufa/ *f*, *Bot.* truffle; nonsense, idle talk

**trufar** /tru'far/ *vt Cul.* to stuff with truffles; —*vi Inf.* lie, tell fibs

**truhán** /tru'an/ **(-ana)** *a* knavish, roguish, comic —*n* knave, rogue; clown, buffoon

**truhanear** /truane'ar/ *vi* to be a trickster, behave like a knave; play the clown

**truhanería** /truane'ria/ *f*, knavery, act of a rogue; clowning, buffoonery; collection of rogues

**truhanesco** /trua'nesko/ *a* knavish, scoundrelly; clownish

**trujal** /tru'hal/ *m*, oil or grape press; oil mill; vat for soap making

**trujar** /tru'har/ *vt* to partition off

**trulla** /'truʎa; 'truya/ *f*, uproar, tumult; crowd, throng

**truncar** /trun'kar/ *vt* to shorten, truncate; decapitate, mutilate; omit, cut out (words, etc.); curtail, abridge; mutilate, deform (texts, etc.)

**truque** /'truke/ *m*, card game; kind of hopscotch

**trust** /trust/ *m*, *Com.* trust

**tú** /tu/ *pers pron 2nd sing mf* thou, you. **tratar de t. (a),** to address familiarly; be on intimate terms with

**tu** /tu/ *poss pron mf* thy, your. Used only before nouns

**tuberculina** /tuβerku'lina/ *f*, tuberculin

**tubérculo** /tu'βerkulo/ *m*, (*Zool. Med.*) tubercle; *Bot.* tubercle, tuber

**tuberculoso** /tuβerku'loso/ *a* tubercular, tuberculous

**tubería** /tuβe'ria/ *f*, piping, tubing; pipe system; pipe factory

**tuberosa** /tuβe'rosa/ *f*, tuberose

**tuberoso** /tuβe'roso/ *a* tuberous

**tubo** /'tuβo/ *m*, pipe, tube; lamp chimney; flue; *Anat.* duct, canal. **t. acústico,** speaking tube. **t. de ensayo,** test tube. **t. de escape,** exhaust pipe. **t. lanzatorpedos,** torpedo tube. **t. termiónico,** *Radio.* thermionic valve

**tubular** /tuβu'lar/ *a* tubular

**tucán** /tu'kan/ *m*, toucan

**tudesco** /tu'ðesko/ *a* German

**tueco** /'tueko/ *m*, stump (of a tree); wormhole (in wood)

**tuerca** /'tuerka/ *f*, nut (of a screw)

**tuerto** /'tuerto/ *a* one-eyed. *m*, *Law.* tort; *pl* afterpains. **a t.,** unjustly

**tueste** /'tueste/ *m*, toasting

**tuétano** /'tuetano/ *m*, marrow. *Inf.* **hasta los tuétanos,** to the depths of one's being

**tufillas** /tu'fiʎas; tu'fiyas/ *mf Inf.* easily irritated person

**tufo** /'tufo/ *m*, strong smell, poisonous vapor; *Inf.* stink; side, airs, conceit (often *pl*); lock of hair over the ears

**tugurio** /tu'gurio/ *m*, shepherd's hut; miserable little room; *Inf.* haunt, low dive

**tul** /tul/ *m*, tulle

**tulipa** /tu'lipa/ *f*, small tulip; lampshade

**tulipán** /tuli'pan/ *m*, tulip

**tullido** /tu'ʎiðo; tu'yiðo/ *a* partially paralyzed; maimed, crippled

**tullir** /tu'ʎir; tu'yir/ *vt irr* to maim, cripple; paralyze; —*vr* become paralyzed; be crippled. See **mullir**

**tumba** /'tumba/ *f*, tomb; tumble, overbalancing; somersault; Catherine wheel

**tumbar** /tum'bar/ *vt* to knock down; kill, drop; *Inf.* overpower, overcome (of odors, wine) —*vi* fall down; *Naut.* run aground; —*vr Inf.* lie down, stretch oneself out

**tumbo** /'tumbo/ *m*, tumble, overbalancing; undulation (of ground); rise and fall of sea waves; imminent danger; book containing deeds and privileges of monasteries and churches

**tumbón** /tum'bon/ *a Inf.* crafty, sly; idle, lazy. *m*, trunk with an arched lid

**tumefacción** /tumefak'θion; tumefak'sion/ *f*, swelling

**tumefacto, túmido** /tume'fakto, 'tumiðo/ *a* swollen

**tumor** /tu'mor/ *m*, tumor

**túmulo** /'tumulo/ *m*, tumulus; catafalque; mound of earth

**tumulto** /tu'multo/ *m*, riot, uprising; tumult, commotion, disturbance

**tumultuario, tumultuoso** /tumul'tuario, tumul'tuoso/ *a* noisy, tumultuous, confused

**tuna** /'tuna/ *f*, prickly pear tree or fruit; vagrant life; strolling student musicians (playing to raise money for charity)

**tunante** /tu'nante/ *a* rascally, roguish. *mf* rascal, scoundrel

**tunantuelo** /tunan'tuelo/ **(-la)** *n Inf.* imp, little rascal

**tunda** /'tunda/ *f*, shearing of cloth; *Inf.* sound beating, hiding

**tundear** /tunde'ar/ *vt* to beat, drub, buffet

**tundidora** /tundi'ðora/ *f*, woman who shears cloth; cloth-shearing machine; lawn mower

**tundir** /tun'dir/ *vt* to shear (cloth); mow (grass); *Inf.* beat, wallop

**tunecino** /tune'θino; tune'sino/ **(-na)** *a* and *n* Tunisian

**túnel** /'tunel/ *m*, tunnel

**Túnez** /'tuneθ; 'tunes/ Tunis, Tunisia

**tungsteno** /tungs'teno/ *m*, tungsten

**túnica** /'tunika/ *f*, tunic, chiton; tunicle; robe

**Tunicia** /tu'niθia; tu'nisia/ Tunisia

**tuno** /'tuno/ **(-na)** *a* knavish, rascally —*n* rascal, scoundrel

**tupé** /tu'pe/ *m*, forelock (of a horse); toupee; *Inf.* cheek, nerve

**tupido** /tu'piðo/ *a* thick, dense; obtuse, dull, stupid

**tupir** /tu'pir/ *vt* to thicken, make dense; press tightly; —*vr* stuff oneself with food or drink

**turba** /'turβa/ *f*, crowd, multitude; peat

**turbación** /turβa'θion; turβa'sion/ *f*, disturbance; upset; perturbation; bewilderment, confusion; embarrassment

**turbador** /turβa'ðor/ **(-ra)** *a* disturbing, upsetting —*n* disturber, upsetter

**turbamulta** /turβa'multa/ *f*, *Inf.* mob, rabble

**turbante** /tur'βante/ *a* upsetting, perturbing. *m*, turban

**turbar** /tur'βar/ *vt* to disturb, upset; make turbid, muddy; bewilder, confuse; embarrass

**turbera** /tur'βera/ *f*, peat bog

**turbiedad** /turβie'ðað/ *f*, muddiness (of liquids); obscurity

**turbina** /tur'βina/ *f*, turbine

**turbio** /'turβio/ *a* turbid, muddy; troublous; turbulent, disturbed; obscure, confused (style); indistinct, blurred, *m pl*, lees, sediment (of oil)

**turbión** /tur'βion/ *m*, brief storm, squall; *Fig.* shower, rush

**turbulencia** /turβu'lenθia; turβu'lensia/ *f*, turbidity, muddiness; turbulence, commotion; disturbance, confusion

**turbulento** /turβu'lento/ *a* muddy, turbid; turbulent; disturbed; confused

**turca** /'turka/ *f*, *Inf.* drinking bout

**turco** /'turko/ **(-ca)** *a* Turkish —*n* Turk. *m*, Turkish (language)

**turgencia** /tur'henθia; tur'hensia/ *f,* swelling, turgidity

**turgente** /tur'hente/ *a Med.* turgescent; *Poet.* turgid, prominent, swollen

**Turingia** /tu'rinhia/ Thuringia

**turismo** /tu'rismo/ *m,* touring, tourist industry. **coche de t.,** touring car

**turista** /tu'rista/ *mf* tourist

**turno** /'turno/ *m,* turn. **por t.,** in turn

**turquesa** /tur'kesa/ *f,* turquoise

**turquesco** /tur'kesko/ *a* Turkish

**Turquía** /tur'kia/ Turkey

**turrón** /tu'rron/ *m,* kind of nougat; almond paste; *Inf.* soft job, sinecure; civil service job

**turulato** /turu'lato/ *a Inf.* dumbfounded, speechless, inarticulate

**¡tus!** /tus/ *interj* word for calling dogs. **sin decir t. ni mus,** *Inf.* without saying anything

**tutear** /tute'ar/ *vt* to address as tú (instead of the formal usted); treat familiarly

**tutela** /tu'tela/ *f,* guardianship; tutelage; protection, defense

**tuteo** /tu'teo/ *m,* the use in speaking to a person of the familiar tú instead of the formal usted

**tutor** /tu'tor/ **(-ra)** *n* guardian. *m,* stake (for plants); protector, defender

**tutoría** /tuto'ria/ *f.* See **tutela**

**tuyo, tuya, tuyos, tuyas** /'tuyo, 'tuya, 'tuyos, 'tuyas/ *poss pron 2nd sing* and *pl mf* thine, yours. Used sometimes with def. art. (e.g. *Este sombrero es el tuyo,* This hat is yours)

# U

**u** /u/ *f*, letter U —*conjunc* Used instead of **o** or before words beginning with **o** or **ho** (e.g. *fragante u oloroso*)

**ubérrimo** /u'βerrimo/ *a superl* most fruitful; very abundant

**ubicación** /uβika'θion; uβika'sion/ *f*, situation, position, location

**ubicar** /uβi'kar/ *vt* to place, situate; —*vi* and *vr* be situated

**ubicuidad** /uβikui'ðað/ *f*, ubiquity

**ubicuo** /u'βikuo/ *a* omnipresent; ubiquitous

**ubre** /'uβre/ *f*, udder

**ucelele** /uθe'lele; use'lele/ *m*, ukulele

**Ucrania** /u'krania/ Ukraine

**ucranio** /u'kranio/ (**-ia**) *a* and *n* Ukrainian

**¡uf!** /uf/ *interj* ugh!

**ufanarse** /ufa'narse/ *vr* to pride oneself, put on airs

**ufanía** /ufa'nia/ *f*, pride, conceit

**ufano** /u'fano/ *a* conceited, vain; satisfied, pleased; expeditious, masterly

**ujier** /u'hier/ *m*, usher

**úlcera** /'ulθera; 'ulsera/ *f*, ulcer

**ulceración** /ulθera'θion; ulsera'sion/ *f*, ulceration

**ulcerar** /ulθe'rar; ulse'rar/ (**se**) *vt* and *vr* to ulcerate

**ulceroso** /ulθe'roso; ulse'roso/ *a* ulcerous

**ulterior** /ulte'rior/ *a* farther, ulterior; subsequent

**ulteriormente** /ulterior'mente/ *adv* subsequently, later

**ultimación** /ultima'θion; ultima'sion/ *f*, ending, finishing

**ultimar** /ulti'mar/ *vt* to end, conclude

**ultimátum** /ulti'matum/ *m*, ultimatum

**último** /'ultimo/ *a* last; farthermost; ultimate; top; final, definitive; most valuable, best; latter; recent. **«Última Hora.»** "Stop Press." **a última hora,** *Fig.* at the eleventh hour. **en estos últimos años,** in recent years. **a últimos de mes,** towards the end of the month. **el ú. piso,** the top floor. **por ú.,** finally. *Inf.* **estar en las últimas,** to be at the end, be finishing

**ultra** /'ultra/, *adv* besides; (with words like *mar*) beyond; (as prefix) excessively

**ultrajar** /ultra'har/ *vt* to insult; scorn, despise

**ultraje** /ul'trahe/ *m*, insult, outrage

**ultrajoso** /ultra'hoso/ *a* offensive, insulting, abusive

**ultramar** /ultra'mar/ *m*, overseas, abroad

**ultramarino** /ultrama'rino/ *a* oversea; ultramarine. *m*, foreign produce (gen. *pl*)

**ultramontano** /ultramon'tano/ *a* ultramontane

**ultrarrojo** /ultra'rroho/ *a* infrared

**ultratumba** /ultra'tumba/ *adv* beyond the grave

**ultravioleta** /ultraβio'leta/ *a* ultraviolet

**úlula** /'ulula/ *f*, screech owl

**ululación** /ulula'θion; ulula'sion/ *f*, screech, howl; hoot of an owl

**ulular** /ulu'lar/ *vi* to howl, shriek, screech; hoot (of an owl)

**ululato** /ulu'lato/ *m*, ululation

**umbilical** /umbili'kal/ *a* umbilical

**umbral** /um'bral/ *m*, threshold; *Fig.* starting point; *Archit.* lintel. **atravesar** ( *or* **pisar**) **los umbrales,** to cross the threshold

**umbría** /um'bria/ *f*, shady place

**umbrío** /um'brio/ *a* shady, dark

**umbroso** /um'broso/ *a* shady

**un** /un/ *Abbr.* of **uno, a,** one. Used before *m*, *sing f*, **una,** *indef art* a, an; a; one

**unánime** /u'nanime/ *a* unanimous

**unanimidad** /unanimi'ðað/ *f*, unanimity. **por u.,** unanimously

**unción** /un'θion; un'sion/ *f*, anointing; *Eccl.* Extreme Unction; unction, fervor

**uncir** /un'θir; un'sir/ *vt* to yoke

**undécimo** /un'deθimo; un'desimo/ *a* eleventh

**undísono** /un'disono/ *a* *Poet.* sounding, sonorous (waves, etc.)

**undoso** /un'doso/ *a* wavy, rippling

**undulación** /undula'θion; undula'sion/ *f*, undulation; *Phys.* wave

**undular** /undu'lar/ *vi* to undulate; wriggle; float, wave (flags, etc.)

**undulatorio** /undula'torio/ *a* undulatory

**ungimiento** /unhi'miento/ *m*, anointment

**ungir** /un'hir/ *vt* to anoint

**ungüento** /un'guento/ *m*, ointment; lotion; *Fig.* balm, unguent

**unicelular** /uniθelu'lar; uniselu'lar/ *a* unicellular

**único** /'uniko/ *a* unique; sole, solitary, only. **Lo ú. que se puede hacer es...,** The only thing one can do is...

**unicolor** /uniko'lor/ *a* of one color

**unicornio** /uni'kornio/ *m*, unicorn

**unidad** /uni'ðað/ *f*, unity; unit; (*Math. Mil.*) unit. **u. de bagaje,** piece of baggage. (of drama) **u. de lugar,** unity of place. **u. de tiempo,** unity of time

**unidamente** /uniða'mente/ *adv* jointly; harmoniously

**unificación** /unifika'θion; unifika'sion/ *f*, unification

**unificar** /unifi'kar/ (**se**) *vt* and *vr* to unify, unite

**uniformación** /uniforma'θion; uniforma'sion/ *f*, standardization

**uniformar** /unifor'mar/ *vt* to make uniform, standardize; put into uniform; —*vr* become uniform

**uniforme** /uni'forme/ *a* uniform; same, similar. *m*, uniform

**uniformidad** /uniformi'ðað/ *f*, uniformity

**unigénito** /uni'henito/ *a* only-begotten. *m*, Christ

**unilateral** /unilate'ral/ *a* one-sided, unilateral

**unión** /u'nion/ *f*, union; correspondence, conformity; agreement; marriage; alliance, federation; composition, mixture; combination; proximity, nearness; (mystic) union

**unionista** /unio'nista/ *mf* *Polit.* unionist

**Unión Soviética** /u'nion so'βietika/ Soviet Union

**unir** /u'nir/ *vt* to unite, join; mix, combine; bind, fasten; connect, couple; bring together; marry; *Fig.* harmonize, conciliate; —*vr* join together, unite; be combined; marry; (*with prep a or con*) be near to; associate with

**unísono** /u'nisono/ *a* unisonant. **al u.,** in unison; unanimously

**unitario** /uni'tario/ (**-ia**) *a* and *n* Unitarian

**universal** /uniβer'sal/ *a* universal; well-informed; widespread

**universalidad** /uniβersali'ðað/ *f*, universality

**universalizar** /uniβersali'θar; uniβersali'sar/ *vt* to make universal, generalize

**universidad** /uniβersi'ðað/ *f*, university; universality; universe

**universitario** /uniβersi'tario/ *a* university

**universo** /uni'βerso/ *a* universal. *m*, universe

**uno** /'uno/ (*f*, **una**) *a* a, one; single, only; same; *pl* some; about, nearly. *m*, one (number). **Tiene unos doce años,** He is about twelve. **unas pocas manzanas,** a few apples —*pron* someone; one thing, same thing; *pl* some people. **No sabe uno qué creer,** One doesn't know what to believe. **Unos dicen que no, otros que sí,** Some (people) say no, others yes. **Juan no tiene libros y le voy a dar uno,** John has no books and I am going to give him one. **Todo es uno,** It's all the same. **u. a u.,** one by one. **u. que otro,** a few. **u. y otro,** both. **unos cuantos,** a few, some. **Es la una,** It is one o'clock

**untar** /un'tar/ *vt* to anoint; grease, oil; *Inf.* bribe; —*vr* smear oneself with grease or similar thing; *Fig. Inf.* line one's pockets. **u. el carro,** *Fig.* to grease the wheels

**unto** /'unto/ *m*, grease; animal fat; *Fig.* balm

**untuoso** /un'tuoso/ *a* fat, greasy

**uña** /'uɲa/ *f*, nail (of fingers or toes); hoof, trotter, claw; stinging tail of scorpion; thorn; stump of tree branch; *Naut.* fluke; *Fig. Inf.* light fingers (gen. *pl*). **afilarse las uñas,** to sharpen one's claws, prepare for trouble. **comerse las uñas,** to bite one's nails. **caer en las uñas de,** to fall into the clutches of. **hincar la u.** ( **en),** to stick the claws into; to defraud, overcharge. **ser u. y carne,** to be devoted friends

**uñarada** /uɲa'raða/ *f,* scratch with nails

**uñero** /u'ɲero/ *m,* ingrowing nail, ingrown nail

**¡upa!** /'upa/ *interj* Up you get! Up you go! Upsy daisy! (gen. to children)

**Urales, los** /u'rales, los/ the Urals

**uranio** /u'ranio/ *m,* uranium

**urbanidad** /urβani'ðað/ *f,* civility, good manners, urbanity

**urbanismo** /urβa'nismo/ *m,* town planning; housing scheme

**urbanización** /urβaniθa'θion; urβanisa'sion/ *f,* urbanization

**urbanizar** /urβani'θar; urβani'sar/ *vt* to civilize, polish; urbanize

**urbano** /ur'βano/ *a* urban, city; urbane

**urbe** /'urβe/ *f,* city, metropolis

**urbícola** /ur'βikola/ *mf* city dweller

**urdemalas** /urðe'malas/ *m,* schemer, intriguer

**urdidera** /urði'ðera/ *f,* warping-frame

**urdimbre** /ur'ðimbre/ *f,* warp; scheming, plotting

**urdir** /ur'ðir/ *vt* to warp; weave; scheme, intrigue

**uréter** /u'reter/ *m,* ureter

**uretra** /u'retra/ *f,* urethra

**urgencia** /ur'henθia; ur'hensia/ *f,* urgency; necessity; compulsion

**urgente** /ur'hente/ *a* urgent

**urgir** /ur'hir/ *vi* to be urgent; be valid, be in force (laws)

**úrico** /'uriko/ *a* uric

**urinario** /uri'nario/ *a* urinary. *m,* urinal

**urna** /'urna/ *f,* urn; ballot box; glass case

**urraca** /u'rraka/ *f,* magpie

**uruguayo** /uru'guayo/ **(-ya)** *a* and *n* Uruguayan

**usado** /u'saðo/ *a* worn out; accustomed, efficient. *Com.* **al u.,** in the usual form. **ropa usada,** secondhand clothing, worn clothing

**usanza** /u'sanθa; usansa/ *f,* custom, usage

**usar** /u'sar/ *vt* to use; wear, make use of; follow (trade, occupation); —*vi* be accustomed

**uso** /'uso/ *m,* use; custom; fashion; habit; wear and tear. **al u.,** according to custom. **al u. de,** in the manner of

**usted** /us'teð/ *mf* you *pl* **ustedes.** Often abbreviated to **Vd, V, Vds, VV** or **Ud, Uds**

**usual** /u'sual/ *a* usual; general, customary; sociable

**usufructo** /usu'frukto/ *m, Law.* usufruct; life-interest; profit

**usura** /u'sura/ *f,* usury; profiteering. **pagar con u.,** to pay back a thousandfold

**usurario** /usu'rario/ *a* usurious

**usurear** /usure'ar/ *vi* to lend or borrow with usury; profiteer, make excess profits

**usurero** /usu'rero/ **(-ra)** *n* usurer; profiteer

**usurpación** /usurpa'θion; usurpa'sion/ *f,* usurpation

**usurpador** /usurpa'ðor/ **(-ra)** *a* usurping —*n* usurper

**usurpar** /usur'par/ *vt* to usurp

**utensilio** /uten'silio/ *m,* utensil; tool, implement (gen. *pl*)

**uterino** /ute'rino/ *a* uterine

**útero** /'utero/ *m,* uterus

**útil** /'util/ *a* useful; profitable; *Law.* lawful (of days, etc.). *m,* usefulness, profit; *pl* **útiles,** utensils, tools

**utilidad** /utili'ðað/ *f,* utility; usefulness; profit

**utilitario** /utili'tario/ *a* utilitarian

**utilitarismo** /utilita'rismo/ *m,* utilitarianism

**utilizable** /utili'θaβle; utilisaβle/ *a* utilizable

**utilización** /utiliθa'θion; utilisa'sion/ *f,* utilization

**utilizar** /utili'θar; utili'sar/ *vt* to utilize

**utillaje** /uti'ʎahe; uti'yahe/ *m,* machinery

**utópico** /u'topiko/ *a* Utopian

**uva** /'uβa/ *f,* grape. **u. espina,** kind of gooseberry. **u. moscatel,** muscatel grape. *Inf.* **hecho una u.,** deaddrunk

**uvero** /u'βero/ **(-ra)** *a* pertaining or relating to grapes, grape —*n* grape seller

**uxoricidio** /uksori'θiðio; uksori'siðio/ *m,* uxoricide (act)

**uxorio** /uk'sorio/ *a* uxorious

# V

**v** /be/ *f*, letter V. **v doble** *or* **doble v,** letter W. **V** *or* **Vd, VV,** *Abbr.* **vuestra (s) merced (es),** *mf sing* and *pl* you

**vaca** /'baka/ *f*, cow. **v. de San Antón,** *Ent.* ladybug

**vacación** /baka'θion; baka'sion/ *f*, vacation, holiday (gen. *pl*); vacancy; act of vacating (employment). **vacaciones retribuídas,** paid vacation

**vacada** /ba'kaða/ *f*, herd of cows

**vacancia** /ba'kanθia; ba'kansia/ *f*, vacancy

**vacante** /ba'kante/ *a* vacant. *f*, vacancy

**vacar** /ba'kar/ *vi* to be vacant; take a holiday; retire temporarily; (*with prep a*) dedicate oneself to, engage in

**vaciadero** /baθia'ðero; basia'ðero/ *m*, rubbish dump; sewer, drain

**vaciado** /ba'θiaðo; ba'siaðo/ *m*, plaster cast; *Archit.* excavation

**vaciamiento** /baθia'miento; basia'miento/ *m*, emptying; molding, casting; depletion

**vaciar** /ba'θiar; ba'siar/ *vt* to empty; drain, drink; mold, cast; *Archit.* excavate; hone; copy; —*vi* flow (into) (rivers); —*vr Inf.* blurt out

**vaciedad** /baθie'ðað; basie'ðað/ *f*, emptiness; foolishness, inanity

**vacilación** /baθila'θion; basila'sion/ *f*, swaying; tottering; staggering; hesitation, perplexity

**vacilante** /baθi'lante; basi'lante/ *a* swaying; tottering; staggering; hesitating, vacillating

**vacilar** /baθi'lar; basi'lar/ *vi* to sway; totter; stagger; flicker; hesitate

**vacío** /ba'θio; ba'sio/ *a* empty, void; fruitless, vain; unoccupied, vacant, deserted; imperfect; hollow, empty; conceited, immature. *m*, hollow; *Anat.* flank; vacancy; shortage; *Phys.* vacuum. **v. de aire,** airpocket. **de v.,** unloaded (carts, etc.). **en v.,** in vacuo. *Inf.* **hacer el v.** ( **a**), to send to Coventry

**vacuidad** /bakui'ðað/ *f*, emptiness; vacuity

**vacuna** /ba'kuna/ *f*, cowpox; vaccine. **v. antivariolosa,** smallpox vaccine

**vacunación** /bakuna'θion; bakuna'sion/ *f*, vaccination

**vacunar** /baku'nar/ *vt* to vaccinate; inoculate

**vacuno** /ba'kuno/ *a* bovine

**vacuo** /'bakuo/ *a* empty; vacant. *m*, void; vacuum

**vadeable** /baðe'aβle/ *a* fordable (rivers, etc.); *Fig.* surmountable

**vadear** /baðe'ar/ *vt* to ford, wade; *Fig.* overcome (obstacles); *Fig.* sound, find out the opinion (of); —*vr* behave

**vademécum** /baðe'mekum/ *m*, vade mecum; school satchel

**vado** /'baðo/ *m*, ford; expedient, help

**vagabundear** /bagaβunde'ar/ *vi* to wander, roam, loiter

**vagabundeo** /bagaβun'deo/ *m*, vagabondage

**vagabundo** /baga'βundo/ **(-da)** *a* roving, wandering; vagrant —*n* tramp, vagabond

**vagamundear** /bagamunde'ar/ *vi.* See **vagabundear**

**vagancia** /ba'ganθia; ba'gansia/ *f*, vagrancy

**vagar** /ba'gar/ *m*, leisure; interval, pause —*vi* be idle or at leisure; wander, roam

**vagido** /ba'hiðo/ *m*, cry, wail (infants)

**vagneriano** /bagne'riano/ *a* Wagnerian

**vago** /'bago/ **(-ga)** *a* vagrant, idle; vague; *Art.* indefinite, blurred —*n* idler. *m*, tramp; loafer. **en v.,** unsuccessfully, vainly

**vagón** /ba'gon/ *m*, wagon; (railway) coach. **v. comedor,** dining car

**vagoneta** /bago'neta/ *f*, open truck (railways, mines, etc.)

**vaguear** /bage'ar/ *vi* to roam, wander; loaf

**vaguedad** /bage'ðað/ *f*, vagueness; vague remark

**vaharada** /baa'raða/ *f*, whiff, exhalation

**vahído** /ba'iðo/ *m*, vertigo

**vaho** /'bao/ *m*, vapor, fume

**vaina** /'baina/ *f*, scabbard; *Bot.* sheath, pod; case (scissors, etc.)

**vainilla** /bai'niʎa; bai'niya/ *f*, *Bot.* vanilla; *Sew.* drawn-thread work

**vaivén** /bai'βen/ *m*, swing, sway, seesaw; instability, fluctuation

**vajilla** /ba'hiʎa; ba'hiya/ *f*, china; dinner service

**val** /bal/ *m*, *Abbr.* **valle**

**Valdepeñas** /balde'peɲas/ *m*, red wine from Valdepeñas

**vale** /'bale/ *m*, *Com.* bond, I.O.U., promissory note; voucher; valediction

**valedero** /bale'ðero/ *a* valid, binding

**valedor** /bale'ðor/ **(-ra)** *n* protector, sponsor

**valencia** /ba'lenθia; ba'lensia/ *f*, valency

**valenciano** /balen'θiano; balen'siano/ **(-na)** *a* and *n* Valencian

**valentía** /balen'tia/ *f*, bravery; heroic deed; boast; (*Art. Lit.*) dash, imagination, fire; superhuman effort

**valentón** /balen'ton/ *a* boastful, blustering

**valer** /ba'ler/ *vt irr* to protect; defend; produce (income, etc.); cost; —*vi* be worth; deserve; have power or authority; be of importance or worth; be a protection; be current (money); be valid; —*vr* (*with de*) make use of. *m*, value, worth. **v. la pena,** to be worthwhile. **v. tanto como cualquiera,** to be as good as the next guy, be as good as the next fellow. **¡Válgame Dios!** Heavens! Bless me! **Más vale así,** It's better thus. **Vale más ser cola de león que cabeza de ratón.** Better a big frog in a small puddle than a small frog in a big puddle —*Pres. Indic.* **valgo, vales,** etc —*Fut.* **valdré,** etc —*Condit.* **valdría,** etc —*Pres. Subjunc.* **valga,** etc.

**valeriana** /bale'riana/ *f*, valerian

**valeroso** /bale'roso/ *a* active, energetic; courageous; powerful

**valetudinario** /baletuði'nario/ *a* valetudinarian

**valía** /ba'lia/ *f*, value, price; influence, worth; faction, party. **a las valías,** at the highest price

**validación** /baliða'θion; baliða'sion/ *f*, validation; force, soundness

**validar** /bali'ðar/ *vt* to make strong; validate

**validez** /bali'ðeθ; bali'ðes/ *f*, validity

**valido** /ba'liðo/ *a* favorite, esteemed. *m*, court favorite; prime minister

**válido** /'baliðo/ *a* firm, sound, valid; strong, robust

**valiente** /ba'liente/ *a* strong, robust; courageous; active; excellent; excessive, enormous (gen. *iron*); boastful

**valija** /ba'liha/ *f*, valise, suitcase, grip; mail bag; mail

**valimiento** /bali'miento/ *m*, value; favor; protection, influence

**valioso** /ba'lioso/ *a* valuable; powerful; wealthy

**valisoletano** /balisole'tano/ **(-na)** *a* and *n* of or from Valladolid

**valla** /'baʎa; 'baya/ *f*, barricade, paling; stockade; *Fig.* obstacle. **v. publicitaria,** billboard

**vallado** /ba'ʎaðo; ba'yaðo/ *m*, stockade; enclosure

**valle** /'baʎe; 'baye/ *m*, valley; vale; river-basin

**valón** /ba'lon/ *a* Walloon

**valona** /ba'lona/ *f*, Vandyke collar

**valor** /ba'lor/ *m*, worth, value; price; courage; validity; power; yield, income; insolence; *pl Com.* securities

**valoración** /balora'θion; balora'sion/ *f*, valuation; appraisement

**valorar** /balo'rar/ *vt* to value; appraise

**valorización** /baloriθa'θion; balorisa'sion/ *f*, valuation

**valquiria** /bal'kiria/ *f*, Valkyrie

**vals** /bals/ *m*, waltz

**valsar** /bal'sar/ *vi* to waltz

**valuación** /balua'θion; balua'sion/ *f*. See **valoración**

**valuar** /balu'ar/ *vt* to value; appraise; assess

**valva** /'balβa/ *f*, *Zool.* valve

**válvula** /'balβula/ *f*, *Mech.* valve. *Auto.* **v. de cámara**

( **del neumático**), tire-valve. **v. de seguridad,** safety-valve

**vampiro** /bam'piro/ *m*, vampire; *Fig.* bloodsucker

**vanagloria** /bana'gloria/ *f*, vaingloriousness, conceit

**vanagloriarse** /banaglo'riarse/ *vr* to be conceited

**vanaglorioso** /banaglo'rioso/ **(-sa)** *a* conceited —*n* boaster

**vanamente** /bana'mente/ *adv* vainly; without foundation; superstitiously; arrogantly

**vandálico** /ban'daliko/ *a* Vandal

**vandalismo** /banda'lismo/ *m*, vandalism; destructiveness

**vándalo** /'bandalo/ **(-la)** *a* and *n* Vandal

**vanguardia** /baŋ'guarðia/ *f*, vanguard; *pl* outerworks. **a v.,** in the forefront

**vanidad** /bani'ðað/ *f*, vanity; ostentation; empty words; illusion. *Inf.* **ajar la v. de,** to take (a person) down a peg

**vanidoso** /bani'ðoso/ **(-sa)** *a* vain; ostentatious —*n* conceited person

**vano** /'bano/ *a* vain; hollow, empty; useless, ineffectual; unsubstantial, illusory. *m*, span (bridge). **v. único,** single span. **en v.,** uselessly, in vain

**vapor** /ba'por/ *m*, steam, vapor; fainting fit; steamboat; *pl* hysterics. **v. de ruedas, v. de paleta,** paddle steamer. **v. volandero,** tramp steamer. **al v.,** full steam ahead; *Inf.* with all speed

**vaporable** /bapo'raβle/ *a* vaporizable

**vaporación** /bapora'θion; bapora'sion/ *f*, evaporation

**vaporización** /baporiθa'θion; baporisa'sion/ *f*, vaporization

**vaporizador** /baporiθa'ðor; baporisa'ðor/ *m*, vaporizer; spray, sprayer

**vaporizar** /bapori'θar; bapori'sar/ *vt* to vaporize; spray

**vaporoso** /bapo'roso/ *a* vaporous; ethereal; gauzy

**vapulación** /bapula'θion; bapula'sion/ *f*, **vapulamiento** *m*, whipping

**vapular** /bapu'lar/ *vt* to whip

**vapuleo** /bapu'leo/ *m*, whipping, spanking

**vaquería** /bake'ria/ *f*, herd of cattle; dairy; dairy farm

**vaquero** /ba'kero/ **(-ra)** *n* cowboy; **vaqueros,** *m*, *pl* jeans

**vaquilla** /ba'kiʎa; ba'kiya/ *f*, heifer

**vara** /'bara/ *f*, staff; rod; wand (of authority); vara (nearly one yard); shaft (of cart). **v. de aforar,** water gauge

**varada** /ba'raða/ *f*, *Naut.* running aground

**varadero** /bara'ðero/ *m*, shipyard

**varar** /ba'rar/ *vi Naut.* to run aground; *Fig.* be held up (negotiations, etc.); —*vt Naut.* put in dry dock

**varear** /bare'ar/ *vt* to knock down (fruit from tree); beat (with a rod); measure with a rod; sell by the rod; —*vr* grow thin

**variabilidad** /bariaβili'ðað/ *f*, variableness

**variable** /ba'riaβle/ *a* variable; changeable, inconsistent

**variación** /baria'θion; baria'sion/ *f*, variation

**variado** /ba'riaðo/ *a* varied; variegated

**variante** /ba'riante/ *a* varying. *f*, variant; discrepancy

**variar** /ba'riar/ *vt* to vary; change; —*vi* change; be different

**varice** /ba'riθe; ba'rise/ *f*, varix

**varicela** /bari'θela; bari'sela/ *f*, chicken pox

**varicoso** /bari'koso/ *a* varicose

**variedad** /barie'ðað/ *f*, variety; change; inconstancy, instability; alteration; variation; *Biol.* variety

**varilla** /ba'riʎa; ba'riya/ *f*, *dim* rod; rib (fan, umbrella). **v. de virtudes,** conjurer's wand. *Mech.* **v. percusora,** tappet rod

**vario** /'bario/ *a* different, diverse; inconstant, changeable; variegated; *pl* some, a few

**variopinto** /bario'pinto/ *a* motley

**varón** /ba'ron/ *m*, male; man

**varonil** /baro'nil/ *a* male; manly

**Varsovia** /bar'soβia/ Warsaw

**varsoviano** /barso'βiano/ **(-na)** *a* and *n* of or from Warsaw

**vasallaje** /basa'ʎahe; basa'yahe/ *m*, vassalage; dependence; tribute money

**vasallo** /ba'saʎo; ba'sayo/ **(-lla)** *n* vassal —*a* vassal; dependent

**vasco** /'basko/ **(-ca), vascongado (-da)** *a* and *n* Basque

**vascuence** /bas'kuenθe; bas'kuense/ *m*, Basque (language); *Inf.* gibberish

**vaselina** /base'lina/ *f*, vaseline

**vasija** /ba'siha/ *f*, vessel, receptacle, jar

**vaso** /'baso/ *m*, receptacle; glass, tankard, mug; glassful; (*Naut. Anat. Bot.*) vessel; garden-urn; vase

**vástago** /'bastago/ *m*, stem, shoot; offspring, descendant; piston rod

**vastedad** /baste'ðað/ *f*, extensiveness, largeness, vastness

**vasto** /'basto/ *a* vast, extensive

**vate** /'bate/ *m*, bard; seer

**vaticano** /bati'kano/ *a* and *m*, Vatican

**vaticinar** /batiθi'nar; batisi'nar/ *vt* to prophesy, foretell

**vaticinio** /bati'θinio; bati'sinio/ *m*, prediction

**vatímetro** /ba'timetro/ *m*, water meter

**vatio** /'batio/ *m*, watt. **v. hora,** watt hour

**ve** /be/ *f*, name of the letter V. **v. doble** *or* **doble v.,** name of the letter W

**vecinal** /beθi'nal; besi'nal/ *a* neighboring

**vecindad** /beθin'dað; besin'dað/ *f*, neighborhood. **buena v.,** good neighborliness. **hacer mala v.,** to be a nuisance to one's neighbors

**vecindario** /beθin'dario; besin'dario/ *m*, neighborhood; population of a district

**vecino** /be'θino; be'sino/ **(-na)** *a* neighboring; near; similar —*n* neighbor; citizen; inhabitant

**vector** /bek'tor/ *m*, carrier (of disease)

**veda** /'beða/ *f*, close season; prohibition

**vedamiento** /beða'miento/ *m*, prohibition

**vedar** /be'ðar/ *vt* to forbid; prevent

**vedija** /be'ðiha/ *f*, tangled lock of hair; piece of matted wool; curl (of smoke)

**veedor** /bee'ðor/ **(-ra)** *a* prying —*n* busy-body. *m*, inspector; overseer

**vega** /'bega/ *f*, fertile lowland plain; meadow

**vegada** /be'gaða/ *f*. See **vez**

**vegetable** /behe'taβle/ *a* and *m*, vegetable

**vegetación** /beheta'θion; beheta'sion/ *f*, vegetation

**vegetal** /behe'tal/ *a* vegetal; plant. *m*, vegetable, plant

**vegetar** /behe'tar/ *vi* to flourish, grow (plants); *Fig.* vegetate

**vegetarianismo** /behetaria'nismo/ *m*, vegetarianism

**vegetariano** /beheta'riano/ **(-na)** *a* and *n* vegetarian

**vegetativo** /beheta'tiβo/ *a* vegetative

**vehemencia** /bee'menθia; bee'mensia/ *f*, vehemence

**vehemente** /bee'mente/ *a* vehement; vivid

**vehículo** /be'ikulo/ *m*, vehicle; means, instrument

**veinte** /'beinte/ *a* and *m*, twenty; twentieth

**veintena** /bein'tena/ *f*, a score

**veinticinco** /beinti'θinko; beinti'sinko/ *a* and *m*, twenty-five; twenty-fifth

**veinticuatro** /beinti'kuatro/ *a* and *m*, twenty-four; twenty-fourth

**veintidós** /beinti'ðos/ *a* and *m*, twenty-two; twenty-second

**veintinueve** /beinti'nueβe/ *a* and *m*, twenty-nine; twenty-ninth

**veintiocho** /bein'tiotʃo/ *a* and *m*, twenty-eight; twenty-eighth

**veintiséis** /beinti'seis/ *a* and *m*, twenty-six; twenty-sixth

**veintisiete** /beinti'siete/ *a* and *m*, twenty-seven; twenty-seventh

**veintitrés** /beinti'tres/ *a* and *m*, twenty-three; twenty-third

**veintiuno** /bein'tiuno/ *a* and *m*, twenty-one; twenty-first. Abbreviates to **veintiún** before a noun (even if one or more adjectives intervene)

**vejación** /beha'θion; beha'sion/ *f*, ill-treatment, persecution

**vejamen** /be'hamen/ *m*, irritation, provocation; taunt; lampoon

**vejar** /be'har/ *vt* to ill-treat, persecute; plague

**vejatorio** /beha'torio/ *a* vexing, annoying

**vejete** /be'hete/ *m, Inf.* silly old man

**vejez** /be'heθ/ *f,* oldness; old age; platitude. *Inf.* **a la v., viruelas,** the older the madder

**vejeces,** *pl* ailments of old age.

**vejiga** /be'hiɣa/ *f,* bladder; blister. **v. natatoria,** float (of a fish)

**vela** /'bela/ *f,* vigil; watch; pilgrimage; sentinel, watchman; candle; *Naut.* sail; awning; night work, overtime. **v. de cangreja,** boom sail. **v. de mesana,** mizzen sail. **v. de trinquete,** foresail. **v. latina,** lateen sail. **a toda v.,** with all speed. **alzar velas,** to hoist sail. **en v.,** wakeful, without sleep. *Inf.* **estar entre dos velas,** to be tipsy

**velación** /bela'θion; bela'sion/ *f,* vigil; watch; marriage ceremony of veiling (gen. *pl*)

**velada** /be'laða/ *f,* vigil; watch; evening party

**velado** /be'laðo/ *a* veiled; dim; (of voice) thick, indistinct

**velador** /bela'ðor/ **(-ra)** *a* watchful; vigilant. *m,* candlestick; small round table —*n* watcher, guard

**velar** /be'lar/ *vi* to watch, be wakeful; work overtime or at night; *Eccl.* watch; *Fig.* (*with por*) watch over, defend; —*vt* veil; conceal; *Photo.* blur; (*with prep a*) wake (corpse); sit with (patient at night)

**veleidad** /belei'ðað/ *f,* velleity; fickleness

**veleidoso** /belei'ðoso/ *a* inconstant, changeable

**velero** /be'lero/ **(-ra)** *m,* sailing ship; sailmaker —*n* candlemaker

**veleta** /be'leta/ *f,* weathercock; float, quill (fishing). *mf* changeable person

**vello** /'beʎo; 'beyo/ *m,* down, soft hair

**vellocino** /beʎo'θino; beyo'sino/ *m,* wool; fleece

**vellón** /be'ʎon; be'yon/ *m,* fleece; copper and silver alloy formerly used in sense of "sterling"; *Obs.* copper coin

**vellosidad** /beʎosi'ðað; beyosi'ðað/ *f,* downiness, hairiness

**velloso** /be'ʎoso; be'yoso/ *a* downy, hairy

**velludo** /be'ʎuðo; be'yuðo/ *a* hairy, downy. *m,* plush, velvet

**velo** /'belo/ *m,* veil; curtain; *Eccl.* humeral veil; excuse, pretext; *Zool.* velum. **v. del paladar,** soft palate. **correr el v.,** to disclose a secret. **tomar el v.,** to take the veil, become a nun

**velocidad** /beloθi'ðað; belosi'ðað/ *f,* speed; *Mech.* velocity. *Aer.* **v. ascensional,** rate of climb. *Mech.* **v. del choque,** speed of impact. **en gran v.,** by passenger train. **en pequeña v.,** by goods train

**velocípedo** /belo'θipeðo; belo'sipeðo/ *m,* velocipede

**velódromo** /be'loðromo/ *m,* velodrome

**velón** /be'lon/ *m,* oil lamp

**veloz** /be'loθ; be'los/ *a* swift; quick-thinking or acting

**vena** /'bena/ *f,* (*Bot. Anat.*) vein; streak, veining (in wood or stone); *Mineral.* seam; underground spring; inspiration. **estar de v.,** to be in the mood; be inspired

**venablo** /be'naβlo/ *m,* javelin

**venado** /be'naðo/ *m,* venison; deer

**venal** /be'nal/ *a* venous; saleable; venal

**venalidad** /benali'ðað/ *f,* saleableness; venality

**vencedor** /benθe'ðor; bense'ðor/ **(-ra)** *a* conquering —*n* conqueror

**vencer** /ben'θer; ben'ser/ *vt* to conquer; defeat; overcome, rise above; outdo, excel; restrain, control (emotions); convince, persuade; —*vi* succeed, triumph; *Com.* fall due, mature; *Com.* expire; —*vr* control oneself; twist, incline

**vencible** /ben'θiβle; ben'siβle/ *a* conquerable; superable

**vencimiento** /benθi'miento; bensi'miento/ *m,* defeat; conquest, victory; bend, twist (of things); *Com.* expiration; *Com.* maturity (of a bill)

**venda** /'benda/ *f,* bandage; fillet. **tener una v. en los ojos,** to be blind (to the truth)

**vendaje** /ben'dahe/ *m,* bandage

**vendar** /ben'dar/ *vt* to bandage; *Fig.* blind (generally passions)

**vendaval** /benda'βal/ *m,* strong wind

**vendedor** /bende'ðor/ **(-ra)** *a* selling —*n* seller

**vender** /ben'der/ *vt* to sell; betray; —*vr* sell oneself; be sold; risk all (for someone); *Fig.* give away (se-

cret); (*with por*) sell under false pretences. **v. al contado,** to sell for cash. **v. al por mayor,** to sell wholesale. **v. al por menor,** to sell retail. **venderse caro,** to be unsociable

**vendí** /ben'di/ *m, Com.* certificate of sale

**vendible** /ben'diβle/ *a* purchasable; saleable

**vendimia** /ben'dimia/ *f,* vintage; profit, fruits

**vendimiador** /bendimia'ðor/ **(-ra)** *n* vintager

**vendimiar** /bendi'miar/ *vt* to harvest the grapes; take advantage of; *Inf.* kill

**Venecia** /be'neθia; be'nesia/ Venice

**veneciano** /bene'θiano; bene'siano/ **(-na)** *a* and *n* Venetian

**veneno** /be'neno/ *m,* poison; venom; danger (to health or soul); evil passion

**venenosidad** /benenosi'ðað/ *f,* poisonousness

**venenoso** /bene'noso/ *a* poisonous, venomous

**venera** /be'nera/ *f,* scallop-shell (pilgrim's badge); badge, decoration

**veneración** /benera'θion; benera'sion/ *f,* respect, veneration

**venerador** /benera'ðor/ **(-ra)** *a* venerating —*n* venerator, respector

**venerar** /bene'rar/ *vt* to venerate; worship

**venéreo** /be'nereo/ *a* venereal

**venero** /be'nero/ *m,* spring of water; horary line on sundial; origin, genesis; *Mineral.* bed

**venezolano** /beneθo'lano; beneso'lano/ **(-na)** *a* and *n* Venezuelan

**vengador** /benga'ðor/ **(-ra)** *a* avenging —*n* avenger

**venganza** /ben'ganθa; ben'gansa/ *f,* revenge

**vengar** /ben'gar/ *vt* to avenge; —*vr* avenge oneself

**vengativo** /benga'tiβo/ *a* vindictive

**venia** /'benia/ *f,* pardon, forgiveness; permission; inclination of head (in greeting); *Law.* license issued to minors to manage their own estate

**venial** /be'nial/ *a* venial

**venialidad** /beniali'ðað/ *f,* veniality

**venida** /be'niða/ *f,* arrival, coming; return; attack (fencing); precipitancy

**venidero** /beni'ðero/ *a* future

**venideros** /beni'ðeros/ *m pl,* successors; posterity

**venir** /be'nir/ *vi irr* to come; arrive; turn up (at cards); fit, suit; consent, agree; *Agr.* grow; follow, come after, succeed; result, originate; occur (to the mind); feel, experience; (*with prep a + infin.*) happen finally, come to pass; (*with en*) decide, resolve; —*vr* ferment. **v. a menos,** to deteriorate, decline; come upon evil days. **v. a pelo,** to come opportunely, be just right. **v. a ser,** to become. **venirse abajo,** to fall, collapse. **¿A qué viene este viaje?** What is the purpose of this journey? **el mes que viene,** next month. **El vestido te viene muy ancho,** The dress is too wide for you. **Me vino la idea de marcharme,** It occurred to me to leave. **en lo por venir,** in the future —*Pres. Indic.* **vengo, vienes, viene, venimos, venís, vienen.** *Pres. Part.* **viniendo.** *Fut.* **vendré,** etc —*Condit.* **vendría,** etc —*Preterite* **vine, viniste, vino, vinimos, vinisteis, vinieron.** *Pres. Subjunc.* **venga,** etc —*Imperf. Subjunc.* **viniese,** etc.

**venoso** /be'noso/ *a* veined; venous

**venta** /'benta/ *f,* selling; sale; inn; *Inf.* wilderness; *pl Com.* turnover. **v. pública,** auction. **a la v.,** on sale. **la V. de la Mesilla,** the Gadsden Purchase

**ventada** /ben'taða/ *f,* gust of wind

**ventaja** /ben'taha/ *f,* advantage; profit

**ventajoso** /benta'hoso/ *a* advantageous

**ventana** /ben'tana/ *f,* window. **v. de guillotina,** sash window. **v. salediza,** bay window. **echar algo por la v.,** to waste a thing

**ventanal** /benta'nal/ *m,* large window

**ventanilla** /benta'niʎa; benta'niya/ *f,* small window (as in railway compartments); grill (ticket office, bank, etc.); nostril

**ventarrón** /benta'rron/ *m,* high wind

**ventear** /bente'ar/ *v impers* to blow (of the wind); —*vt* sniff air (animals); air, dry; investigate; —*vr* be spoiled by air (tobacco, etc.)

**ventero** /ben'tero/ **(-ra)** *n* innkeeper

**ventilación** /bentila'θion; bentila'sion/ *f,* ventilation; ventilator; current of air

**ventilador** /bentila'ðor/ *m,* ventilating fan; ventilator

**ventilar** /benti'lar/ *vt* to ventilate; shake, winnow; air; discuss

**ventisca** /ben'tiska/ *f*, snowstorm

**ventiscar, ventisquear** /bentis'kar, bentiske'ar/ *v impers* to snow with a high wind

**ventisquero** /bentis'kero/ *m*, glacier; snowfield, snowdrift; snowstorm

**ventolera** /bento'lera/ *f*, gust of wind; *Inf.* boastfulness; whim, caprice

**ventor** /ben'tor/ **(-ra)** *n* pointer (dog)

**ventosa** /ben'tosa/ *f*, vent (pipes, etc.); *Zool.* sucker; *Surg.* cupping glass

**ventosidad** /bentosi'ðað/ *f*, flatulence

**ventoso** /ben'toso/ *a* windy; flatulent

**ventrículo** /ben'trikulo/ *m*, ventricle

**ventrílocuo** /ben'trilokuo/ **(-ua)** *a* ventriloquial —*n* ventriloquist

**ventriloquia** /bentri'lokia/ *f*, ventriloquism

**ventrudo** /ben'truðo/ *a* big-bellied

**ventura** /ben'tura/ *f*, happiness; chance, hazard; risk, danger. **a la v.,** at a venture. **buena v.,** good luck. **por v.,** perhaps; by chance; fortunately

**venturoso** /bentu'roso/ *a* fortunate

**Venus** /'benus/ *m*, Venus. *f*, beautiful woman, beauty

**ver** /ber/ *vt irr* to see; witness, behold; visit; inspect, examine; consider; observe; know, understand; (*with de* + *infin.*) try to; —*vr* be seen; show oneself, appear; experience, find oneself; exchange visits; meet. **v. mundo,** to travel. **V. y creer,** Seeing is believing. **A mi v.,** In my opinion. **¡A v.!** Let's see!; Wait and see! **no tener nada que v. con,** to have no connection with, nothing to do with. **Veremos,** Time will tell. **Verse en la casa,** to be a stay-at-home. **Ya se ve,** Of course, Naturally —*Pres. Indic.* **veo, ves,** etc —*Imperf.* **veía,** etc —*Past Part.* **visto.** *Pres. Subjunc.* **vea,** etc —*Imperf. Subjunc.* **viese,** etc.

**vera** /'bera/ *f*, edge; border; shore. **a la v.,** on the edge, on the verge

**veracidad** /beraθi'ðað; berasi'ðað/ *f*, truthfulness, veracity

**veranadero** /berana'ðero/ *m*, summer pasture

**veraneante** /berane'ante/ *mf* summer resident, summer vacationist, holiday-maker

**veranear** /berane'ar/ *vi* to spend the summer

**veraneo** /bera'neo/ *m*, summer vacation, summer holidays, summering

**veraniego** /bera'niego/ *a* summer; light, unimportant

**verano** /be'rano/ *m*, summer; dry season *West Hem.*

**veras** /'beras/ *f pl*, reality, truth; fervor, earnestness. **de v.,** really; in earnest

**veraz** /be'raθ; be'ras/ *a* truthful, veracious

**verbal** /ber'βal/ *a* verbal; oral

**verbena** /ber'βena/ *f*, *Bot.* verbena, vervain; fair held on eve of a saint's day

**verbigracia** /berβi'graθia; berβi'grasia/ *adv* for instance. *m*, example

**verbo** /'berβo/ *m*, word; vow; *Gram.* verb. **v. activo** *or* **v. transitivo,** active or transitive verb. **v. auxiliar,** auxiliary verb. **v. intransitivo** *or* **v. neutro,** intransitive or neuter verb. **v. reflexivo** *or* **v. recíproco,** reflexive verb

**verbosidad** /berβosi'ðað/ *f*, verbosity

**verboso** /ber'βoso/ *a* verbose, prolix

**verdad** /ber'ðað/ *f*, truth, veracity; reality. **a la v.,** indeed; without doubt. **en v.,** in truth; indeed. **cantar cuatro verdades a alguien,** to tell someone a few home truths. **la pura v.,** the plain truth

**verdadero** /berða'ðero/ *a* true; real; sincere; truthful

**verdal** /ber'ðal/ *a* green. **ciruela v.,** greengage

**verde** /'berðe/ *a* green; unripe; fresh (vegetables); youthful; immature, undeveloped; obscene, dissolute. *m*, green (color); verdure, foliage

**verdear** /berðe'ar/ *vi* to look green; be greenish; grow green

**verdecer** /berðe'θer; berðe'ser/ *vi irr* to grow green, be verdant. See **conocer**

**verdegay** /berðe'gai/ *a* and *m*, bright green

**verdemar** /berðe'mar/ *a* and *m*, sea-green

**verdín** /ber'ðin/ *m*, verdure; mold; verdigris

**verdinegro** /berði'negro/ *a* dark green

**verdor** /ber'ðor/ *m*, verdure; greenness; strength; youth (also *pl*)

**verdoso** /ber'ðoso/ *a* greenish

**verdugo** /ber'ðugo/ *m*, hangman, executioner; wale, mark; shoot of tree; switch; whip; *Fig.* scourge; tyrant

**verdulera** /berðu'lera/ *f*, greengrocer; market woman; *Inf.* harridan

**verdulería** /berðule'ria/ *f*, greengrocer's shop

**verdulero** /berðu'lero/ *m*, greengrocer

**verdura** /ber'ðura/ *f*, verdure; green garden produce; vegetables (gen. *pl*); *Art.* foliage; obscenity

**verecundo** /bere'kundo/ *a* bashful

**vereda** /be'reða/ *f*, footpath; sheep track

**veredicto** /bere'ðikto/ *m*, *Law.* verdict; judgment, considered opinion

**verga** /'berga/ *f*, steel bow of crossbow; *Naut.* yard; *Inf.* penis

**vergajo** /ber'gaho/ *m*, rod (for punishment)

**vergel** /ber'hel/ *m*, orchard

**vergonzoso** /bergon'θoso; bergon'soso/ **(-sa)** *a* shameful; bashful, shamefaced —*n* shy person

**vergüenza** /ber'guenθa; ber'guensa/ *f*, shame; self-respect; bashfulness, timidity; shameful act; public punishment

**vericueto** /beri'kueto/ *m*, narrow, stony path

**verídico** /be'riðiko/ *a* veracious; true, exact

**verificación** /berifika'θion; berifika'sion/ *f*, verification, checking; *Law.* **v. de un testamento,** probate

**verificador** /berifika'ðor/ **(-ra)** *a* verifying, checking —*n* inspector, checker

**verificar** /berifi'kar/ *vt* to prove; verify; —*vr* take place, happen; check; come true. *Elec.* **v. las conexiones,** to check the connections

**verisímil** /beri'simil/ *a* credible, probable

**verisimilitud** /berisimili'tuð/ *f*, credibility

**verismo** /be'rismo/ *m*, realism; truthfulness

**verja** /'berha/ *f*, grating, grill; railing

**vermífugo** /ber'mifugo/ *a* and *m*, vermifuge

**verminoso** /bermi'noso/ *a* verminous

**vermut** /ber'mut/ *m*, vermouth

**vernáculo** /ber'nakulo/ *a* native, vernacular

**vernal** /ber'nal/ *a* vernal

**veronés** /bero'nes/ **(-esa)** *a* and *n* Veronese

**verónica** /be'ronika/ *f*, *Bot.* speedwell; veronica (bullfighting)

**verosímil** /bero'simil/ *a* credible, probable

**verosimilitud** /berosimili'tuð/ *f*, verisimilitude, probability

**verraco** /be'rrako/ *m*, boar

**verruga** /be'rruga/ *f*, *Med.* wart; *Inf.* bore; defect

**versar** /ber'sar/ *vi* to revolve; (*with sobre*) concern, deal with (book, etc.); —*vr* become versed (in)

**versátil** /ber'satil/ *a* *Zool.* versatile; changeable; fickle

**versatilidad** /bersatili'ðað/ *f*, *Zool.* versatility; changeableness; fickleness

**versículo** /ber'sikulo/ *m*, versicle; verse (of the Bible)

**versificación** /bersifika'θion; bersifika'sion/ *f*, versification

**versificador** /bersifika'ðor/ **(-ra)** *n* versifier

**versificar** /bersifi'kar/ *vi* to write verses; —*vt* put into verse, versify

**versión** /ber'sion/ *f*, translation; version; account

**verso** /'berso/ *m*, poetry, verse; stanza; line (of a poem). **v. suelto,** blank verse

**vertebrado** /berte'βraðo/ *a* and *m*, *Zool.* vertebrate

**vertedor** /berte'ðor/ *m*, drain, sewer; chute

**verter** /ber'ter/ *vt irr* to pour, spill; empty; translate; —*vi* flow. See **entender**

**vertical** /berti'kal/ *a* and *f*, vertical

**verticalidad** /bertikali'ðað/ *f*, verticality

**vértice** /'bertiθe; 'bertise/ *m*, vertex

**vertiente** /ber'tiente/ *a* emptying. *mf*, slope, incline; watershed

**vertiginoso** /bertihi'noso/ *a* giddy; vertiginous

**vértigo** /'bertigo/ *m*, giddiness, faintness

**vesícula** /be'sikula/ *f*, blister; (*Anat. Bot.*) vesicle

**vespertino** /besper'tino/ *a* evening

**vestíbulo** /bes'tiβulo/ *m*, hall, vestibule foyer

**vestido** /bes'tiðo/ *m*, dress; clothes

**vestidura** /besti'ðura/ *f*, garment; *pl* vestments

**vestigio** /bes'tihio/ *m*, footprint; trace, mark; remains; *Fig.* vestige

**vestir** /bes'tir/ *vt irr* to clothe, dress; adorn; embellish (ideas); *Fig.* disguise (truth); simulate, pretend; —*vi* be dressed; —*vr* dress oneself; *Fig.* be covered. See **pedir**

**vestuario** /bes'tuario/ *m*, clothing, dress; *Theat.* wardrobe or dressing room; *Eccl.* vestry; *Mil.* uniform

**Vesubio** /be'suβio/ Vesuvius

**veta** /'beta/ *f*, vein; stripe, rib (fabric)

**veterano** /bete'rano/ **(-na)** *a* and *n* veteran

**veterinaria** /beteri'naria/ *f*, veterinary science

**veterinario** /beteri'nario/ *a* veterinary. *m*, veterinary surgeon

**veto** /'beto/ *m*, veto; prohibition

**vetustez** /betus'teθ/ betus'tes/ *f*, antiquity, oldness

**vetusto** /be'tusto/ *a* ancient, very old

**vez** /beθ/ bes/ *f*, time, occasion; turn; *pl* proxy, deputy, substitute. **a la v.**, simultaneously. **alguna v.**, sometime. **a su v.**, in its (her, his, their) turn. **a veces**, sometimes. **de una v.**, at the one time. **de v. en cuando**, from time to time. **en v. de**, instead of. **hacer las veces de**, to be a substitute for. **otra v.**, again. **Su cuarto es dos veces más grande que éste**, His room is twice as large as this one

**vía** /'bia/ *f*, way; road; railway track or gauge; *Anat.* tract; (mystic) way; route; conduct; *pl* procedure. **v. ancha**, broad gauge (railway). **v. angosta**, narrow gauge. **v. de agua**, *Naut.* leak. *Law.* **v. ejecutiva**, seizure, attachment. **v. férrea**, railway. **v. láctea**, Milky Way. **v. muerta**, railway siding. **v. principal**, main line. **v. pública**, public thoroughfare. **v. romana**, Roman road. **v. secundaria**, *Rail.* side line. **por v. aérea**, by air, by airplane

**viabilidad** /biaβili'ðað/ *f*, viability

**viable** /'biaβle/ *a* viable; practicable; workable; passable

**viaducto** /bia'ðukto/ *m*, viaduct

**viajante** /bia'hante/ *mf* traveling salesman, commercial traveler

**viajar** /bia'har/ *vi* to travel, journey, voyage

**viaje** /'biahe/ *m*, journey; voyage; water-supply; travel journal; *Naut.* **v. de ensayo**, trial trip. **v. redondo**, circular tour. **¡Buen v.!** Have a good trip! Bon voyage!

**viajero** /bia'hero/ **(-ra)** *a* traveling —*n* traveler; passenger

**vianda** /'bianda/ *f*, viand, victual (gen. *pl*); meal

**viático** /'biatiko/ *m*, *Eccl.* viaticum; provisions for a journey

**víbora** /'biβora/ *f*, viper

**viborezno** /biβo're ñ no; biβo'resno/ *m*, young viper

**vibración** /biβra'θion; biβra'sion/ *f*, vibration; jar, jolt; thrill

**vibrante** /bi'βrante/ *a* shaking; vibrant; thrilling

**vibrar** /bi'βrar/ *vt* to shake, oscillate; —*vi* vibrate; jar, jolt; quiver, thrill

**vibratorio** /biβra'torio/ *a* vibratory, vibrative

**vicaría** /bika'ria/ *f*, vicarage; vestry

**vicario** /bi'kario/ *a* vicarious. *m*, vicar; curate; deputy

**vicealmirante** /biθealmi'rante; bisealmi'rante/ *m*, vice-admiral

**vicecanciller** /biθekanθi'ʎer; bisekansi'yer/ *m*, vice-chancellor

**vicecónsul** /biθe'konsul; bise'konsul/ *m*, vice-consul

**viceconsulado** /biθekonsu'laðo; bisekonsu'laðo/ *m*, vice-consulate

**vicepresidente** /biθepresi'ðente; bisepresi'ðente/ **(-ta)** *n* vice president

**vicesecretario** /biθesekre'tario; bisesekre'tario/ **(-ia)** *n* assistant secretary

**viciar** /bi'θiar; bi'siar/ *vt* to corrupt; adulterate; forge; annul; interpret maliciously, misconstrue; —*vr* become vicious

**vicio** /'biθio; 'bisio/ *m*, vice; defect; error, fraud; bad habit; excess, exaggerated desire; viciousness (animals); overgrowth (plants); peevishness (children). **tener el v. de**, to have the bad habit of. **el v. del juego**, fondness for gambling

**vicioso** /bi'θioso; bi'sioso/ *a* vicious; vigorous, overgrown; abundant; *Inf.* spoiled (children)

**vicisitud** /biθisi'tuð; bisisi'tuð/ *f*, vicissitude

**víctima** /'biktima/ *f*, victim

**¡víctor!** /'biktor/ *interj* Victor!; Long live!; Hurrah!

**victoria** /bik'toria/ *f*, victory, triumph; victoria

**victoriano** /bikto'riano/ **(-na)** *a* and *n* Victorian

**victorioso** /bikto'rioso/ *a* victorious

**vid** /bið/ *f*, vine

**vida** /'biða/ *f*, life; livelihood; human being; biography; vivacity. **v. airada**, dissolute life. **la v. allende la muerte**, life after death. **de por v.**, for life. **darse buena v.**, to live comfortably; enjoy one's life. **dar mala v.**, to ill-treat. **en la v.**, in life; never. **ganarse la v.**, to make one's living

**vidente** /bi'ðente/ *m*, clairvoyant; seer

**videocámara** *f*, video camera, camcorder

**videograbación** /biðeograβa'θion; biðeograβa'sion/ *f*, videotape

**vidriar** /bi'ðriar/ *vt* to glaze (earthenware)

**vidriera** /bi'ðriera/ *f*, glass window (gen. stained or colored)

**vidriero** /bi'ðriero/ *m*, glazier —*a* made of glass

**vidrio** /'biðrio/ *m*, glass; anything made of glass; fragile thing; touchy person. **v. inastillable**, safetyglass. **v. jaspeado**, frosted glass. **v. pintado** or **v. de color**, stainedglass. **v. plano**, plate glass. **v. soplado**, blown glass

**vidrioso** /bi'ðrioso/ *a* brittle; slippery; fragile; hypersensitive; *Fig.* glazed (eyes)

**vieja** /'bieha/ *f*, old woman

**viejo** /'bieho/ *a* old; ancient; former; old-fashioned; worn out. *m*, old man

**Viena** /'biena/ Vienna

**vienés** /bie'nes/ **(-esa)** *a* and *n* Viennese

**viento** /'biento/ *m*, wind; scent (of game, etc.); guy (rope); upheaval; vanity. **v. en popa**, *Naut.* following wind; without a hitch, prosperously. **vientos alisios**, trade-winds. **v. terral**, land wind. **a los cuatro vientos**, in all directions. **contra v. y marea**, *Fig.* against all obstacles. **correr malos vientos**, to be unfavorable (of circumstances). **refrescar el v.**, to stiffen (of the breeze)

**vientre** /'bientre/ *m*, stomach; belly; vitals; *Law.* venter

**viernes** /'biernes/ *m*, Friday. **V. Santo**, Good Friday

**viga** /'biga/ *f*, beam, rafter; girder; joist; mill beam. **v. maestra**, main beam or girder

**vigente** /bi'hente/ *a* valid; in force (laws, customs)

**vigésimo** /bi'hesimo/ *a* twentieth

**vigía** /bi'hia/ *f*, watch tower; (gen. *m*) look-out, watch

**vigilancia** /bihi'lanθia; bihi'lansia/ *f*, watchfulness, vigilance; watch patrol

**vigilante** /bihi'lante/ *a* watchful. *m*, watcher; watchman. **v. escolar**, truant officer

**vigilar** /bihi'lar/ *vt* to watch over; supervise

**vigilia** /bi'hilia/ *f*, vigil; wakefulness; night study; *Eccl.* vigil, eve; wake; *Mil.* watch. **día de v.**, fast-day

**vigor** /bi'gor/ *m*, strength; activity; vigor, efficiency; validity

**vigorizar** /bigori'θar; bigori'sar/ *vt* to invigorate; exhilarate; encourage

**vigorosidad** /bigorosi'ðað/ *f*, vigorousness

**vigoroso** /bigo'roso/ *a* strong, vigorous

**vihuela** /bi'uela/ *f*, lute

**vil** /bil/ *a* vile, infamous; base; despicable; untrustworthy

**vileza** /bi'leθa; bi'lesa/ *f*, baseness; vileness, infamy

**vilipendiar** /bilipen'diar/ *vt* to revile

**vilipendio** /bili'pendio/ *m*, vilification; contempt

**villa** /'biʎa; 'biya/ *f*, villa; country house; town

**villancico** /biʎan'θiko; biyan'siko/ *m*, carol

**villanesco** /biʎa'nesko; biya'nesko/ *a* peasant; rustic, country

**villanía** /biʎa'nia; biya'nia/ *f*, humbleness of birth; vileness; villainy

**villano** /bi'ʎano; bi'yano/ **(-na)** *n* peasant —*a* rustic, country; boorish; base

**vilo, en** /'bilo, en/ *adv* hanging in the air; *Fig.* in suspense

**vilorta** /bi'lorta/ *f*, hoop; *Mech.* washer

**vinagre** /bi'nagre/ *m*, vinegar

**vinagrera** /bina'grera/ f, vinegar bottle; table cruet

**vinagreta** /bina'greta/ f, vinegar sauce

**vinagroso** /bina'groso/ a vinegary; Inf. bad-tempered, acid

**vinatero** /bina'tero/ **(-ra)** n wine merchant —a wine

**vincapervinca** /binkaper'βinka/ f, Bot. periwinkle

**vinculación** /binkula'θion; binkula'sion/ f, Law. entail

**vincular** /binku'lar/ vt Law. to entail; Fig. base; —vr perpetuate —a Law. entail

**vínculo** /'binkulo/ m, tie, bond; Law. entail

**vindicación** /bindika'θion; bindika'sion/ f, vindication; justification; excuse

**vindicador** /bindika'ðor/ **(-ra)** n vindicator —a vindicative

**vindicar** /bindi'kar/ vt to avenge; vindicate; justify; excuse

**vindicativo** /bindika'tiβo/ a avenging; vindicatory

**vinícola** /bi'nikola/ a wine-growing; wine

**vinicultor** /binikul'tor/ **(-ra)** n wine grower, viniculturalist

**vinicultura** /binikul'tura/ f, wine-growing, viniculture

**vinificación** /binifika'θion; binifika'sion/ f, vinification

**vinillo** /bi'niʎo; bi'niyo/ m, thin, weak wine

**vino** /'bino/ m, wine; fermented fruit juice. **v. de Oporto,** port wine. **v. generoso,** well-matured wine. **v. tinto,** red wine

**vinosidad** /binosi'ðað/ f, vinosity

**vinoso** /bi'noso/ a vinous; fond of wine

**viña** /'biɲa/ f, vineyard

**viñador** /biɲa'ðor/ m, vineyard-keeper; vine-cultivator

**viñedo** /bi'ɲeðo/ m, vineyard

**viñeta** /bi'ɲeta/ f, vignette

**viola** /'biola/ f, Mus. viola; Bot. viola, pansy. mf viola player

**violación** /biola'θion; biola'sion/ f, violation; infringement

**violado** /bio'laðo/ a violet

**violador** /biola'ðor/ **(-ra)** n violator. m, seducer

**violar** /bio'lar/ vt to violate; infringe; rape; spoil, harm

**violencia** /bio'lenθia; bio'lensia/ f, violence; outrage; rape

**violentar** /biolen'tar/ vt to force; falsify, misinterpret; force an entrance; —vr force oneself

**violento** /bio'lento/ a violent; repugnant; impetuous, hasty-tempered; unnatural, false; unreasonable

**violeta** /bio'leta/ f, Bot. violet. m, violet color. **v. de febrero,** snowdrop

**violín** /bio'lin/ m, violin

**violinista** /bioli'nista/ mf violinist

**violón** /bio'lon/ m, double-bass, bass viol; double-bass player

**violoncelista** /biolonθe'lista; biolonse'lista/ mf cellist

**violoncelo** /biolon'θelo; biolon'selo/ m, cello

**viperino** /bipe'rino/ a viperine; venomous, evil

**vira** /'bira/ f, welt (of a shoe); dart

**viraje** /bi'rahe/ m, Auto. change of direction; bend, turn

**virar** /bi'rar/ vt Naut. to put about; Photo. tone; —vi Naut. tack; Auto. change direction. **v. de bordo,** Naut. to lay off

**virgen** /bir'hen/ mf virgin. f, Astron. Virgo

**virgiliano** /birhi'liano/ a Virgilian

**virginal** /birhi'nal/ a virginal; pure, unspotted

**virginidad** /birhini'ðað/ f, virginity

**virgulilla** /birgu'liʎa; birgu'liya/ f, comma; cedilla; accent; apostrophe; fine line

**viril** /bi'ril/ a manly, virile. m, clear glass screen

**virilidad** /birili'ðað/ f, virility

**virote** /bi'rote/ m, arrow; shaft; Inf. young blood

**virreina** /bi'rreina/ f, vicereine

**virreinato** /birrei'nato/ m, viceroyship

**virrey** /bi'rrei/ m, viceroy

**virtual** /bir'tual/ a virtual; implicit

**virtualidad** /birtuali'ðað/ f, virtuality

**virtualmente** /birtual'mente/ adv virtually; tacitly

**virtud** /bir'tuð/ f, virtue; power; strength, courage; efficacy. **en v. de,** in virtue of

**virtuosidad** /birtuosi'ðað/ f, virtuosity

**virtuoso** /bir'tuoso/ a virtuous; powerful, efficacious. m, virtuoso, artist

**viruela** /bi'ruela/ f, smallpox (gen. pl)

**virulencia** /biru'lenθia; biru'lensia/ f, virulence

**virulento** /biru'lento/ a virulent

**virus** /'birus/ m, virus

**viruta** /bi'ruta/ f, wood-shaving

**visaje** /bi'sahe/ m, grimace

**visar** /bi'sar/ vt to visa; endorse

**vis cómica** /bis 'komika/ f, the comic spirit

**viscosidad** /biskosi'ðað/ f, viscosity

**viscoso** /bis'koso/ a viscous, sticky

**visera** /bi'sera/ f, visor; eye-shade; peak (of a cap)

**visibilidad** /bisiβili'ðað/ f, visibility

**visigodo** /bisi'goðo/ **(-da)** a Visigothic —n Visigoth

**visigótico** /bisi'gotiko/ a Visigothic

**visillo** /bi'siʎo; bi'siyo/ m, window-blind

**visión** /bi'sion/ f, seeing, sight; queer sight; vision; hallucination; Inf. scarecrow, sight

**visionario** /bisio'nario/ **(-ia)** a and n visionary

**visir** /bi'sir/ m, vizier. **gran v.,** grand vizier

**visita** /bi'sita/ f, visit; visitor; inspection. **v. de cumplido,** formal call. **v. de sanidad,** health inspection. **hacer una v.,** to pay a call

**visitación** /bisita'θion; bisita'sion/ f, visitation; visit

**visitador** /bisita'ðor/ **(-ra)** n regular visitor. m, inspector —a visiting; inspecting

**visitar** /bisi'tar/ vt to visit; inspect; Med. attend; Eccl. examine. **v. los monumentos,** to see the sights, go sightseeing

**visiteo** /bisi'teo/ m, receiving or paying of visits

**vislumbrar** /bislum'βrar/ vt to glimpse; surmise, conjecture

**vislumbre** /bis'lumbre/ f, glimmer, glimpse; surmise, glimmering (gen. pl); semblance, appearance

**viso** /'biso/ m, view point, elevation; glare; shimmer, gleam; colored slip under transparent dress; semblance. **de v.,** prominent (persons)

**visón** /bi'son/ m, mink

**víspera** /'bispera/ f, eve; Eccl. day before festival; prelude, preliminary pl Eccl. vespers. **en vísperas de,** on the eve of

**vista** /'bista/ f, vision, sight; view; eyes; eyesight; meeting, interview; Law. hearing (of a case); apparition; picture of a view; clear idea; connection (of things); proposition, intention; glance; pl window, door, skylight, opening for light. **v. corta,** short sight. **v. de lince,** sharp eyes. **a primera v.,** at first sight. **a v. de,** in sight of; in the presence of. **conocer de v.,** to know by sight. **dar una v.,** to take a look. **doble v.,** second sight; clairvoyance. **en v. de,** in view of, considering. **estar a la v.,** to be evident. Inf. **hacer la v. gorda,** to turn a blind eye. **¡Hasta la v.!** Good-bye! **perder de v. ( a),** to lose sight of

**vistazo** /bis'taθo; bis'taso/ m, glance. **echar un v.,** to cast a glance

**visto** /'bisto/ past part irr **ver.** Law. whereas. **bien v.,** approved. **mal v.,** disapproved. **V. Bueno ( V° B°)** Approved, Passed. **v. que,** since, inasmuch as

**vistoso** /bis'toso/ a showy, gaudy; beautiful

**visual** /bi'sual/ a visual

**vital** /bi'tal/ a vital; essential

**vitalicio** /bita'liθio; bita'lisio/ a lifelong. m, life-insurance

**vitalidad** /bitali'ðað/ f, vitality

**vitalizar** /bitali'θar; bitali'sar/ vt to vitalize

**vitamina** /bita'mina/ f, vitamin

**vitando** /bi'tando/ a odious; bad; vital

**vitela** /bi'tela/ f, vellum

**vitícola** /bi'tikola/ a viticultural. mf viticulturist

**viticultura** /bitikul'tura/ f, viticulture

**¡vítor!** /'bitor/ interj Victor!; Hurrah!; Long live!

**vitorear** /bitore'ar/ vt to cheer; applaud, acclaim

**vítreo** /'bitreo/ a glassy, vitreous

**vitrificar** /bitrifi'kar/ **(se)** vt and vr to vitrify

**vitrina** /bi'trina/ f, show-case; display cabinet

**vitriólico** /bi'trioliko/ a vitriolic

**vitriolo** /bi'triolo/ m, vitriol

**vitualla** /biˈtuaʎa; biˈtuaya/ *f*, (gen. *pl*) victuals, provisions

**vituperable** /bitupeˈraβle/ *a* blameworthy, vituperable

**vituperador** /bitupera'ðor/ **(-ra)** *a* vituperative —*n* vituperator

**vituperar** /bitupe'rar/ *vt* to censure, blame, vituperate

**vituperio** /bitu'perio/ *m*, vituperation

**viuda** /'biuða/ *f*, widow

**viudedad** /biuðe'ðað/ *f*, widow's pension

**viudez** /biu'ðeθ; biu'ðes/ *f*, widowhood

**viudita** /biu'ðita/ *f*, young widow

**viudo** /'biuðo/ *m*, widower

**¡viva!** /'biβa/ *interj* Long live!; Hurrah!

**vivacidad** /biβaθi'ðað; biβasi'ðað/ *f*, vivacity, gaiety; ardor, warmth; brightness

**vivamente** /'biβa'mente/ *adv* quickly, lively

**vivandera** /biβan'dera/ *f*, vivandiere

**vivandero** /biβan'dero/ *m*, sutler

**vivaque** /bi'βake/ *m*, bivouac

**vivaquear** /biβake'ar/ *vi* to bivouac

**vivar** /bi'βar/ *m*, warren; aquarium; breeding ground; well (of a fishing boat)

**vivaracho** /biβa'ratʃo/ *a Inf.* sprightly, cheery, lively

**vivaz** /bi'βaθ; bi'βas/ *a* vigorous; quick-witted; sprightly; *Bot.* perennial; vivid, bright

**víveres** /'biβeres/ *m pl*, provisions; *Mil.* stores

**vivero** /bi'βero/ *m*, *Bot.* nursery; vivarium; small marsh

**viveza** /bi'βeθa; bi'βesa/ *f*, quickness, briskness; vehemence; perspicuity; witticism; resemblance; brightness (eyes, colors); thoughtless word or act

**vividero** /biβi'ðero/ *a* habitable

**vívido** /'biβiðo/ *a Poet.* vivid

**vividor** /biβi'ðor/ **(-ra)** *a* frugal, thrifty; dissolute —*n* liver; long-liver; libertine, rake

**vivienda** /bi'βienda/ *f*, dwelling

**viviente** /bi'βiente/ *a* living

**vivificación** /biβifika'θion; biβifika'sion/ *f*, vivification

**vivificante** /biβifi'kante/ *a* vivifying

**vivificar** /biβifi'kar/ *vt* to vivify; comfort

**vivir** /bi'βir/ *vi* to be alive, live; last, endure; (*with en*) inhabit. *m*, life. **¿Quién vive?** *Mil.* Who goes there? **v. a costillas ajenas,** to live at someone else's expense, live off someone else

**vivisección** /biβisek'θion; biβisek'sion/ *f*, vivisection

**vivo** /'biβo/ *a* alive; intense, strong; bright; *Mil.* active; subtle, ingenious; precipitate; *Fig.* lasting, enduring; diligent; hasty; persuasive, expressive. *m*, edge. **al v., a lo v.,** to the life; vividly

**vizcaíno** /biθ'kaino; bis'kaino/ **(-na)** *a* and *n* Biscayan

**Vizcaya, el Golfo de** /biθ'kaya, el 'golfo de; bis'kaya, el 'golfo de/ the Bay of Biscay

**vizcondado** /biθkon'daðo; biskon'daðo/ *m*, viscounty

**vizconde** /biθ'konde; bis'konde/ *m*, viscount

**vizcondesa** /biθkon'desa; biskon'desa/ *f*, viscountess

**vocablo** /bo'kaβlo/ *m*, word

**vocabulario** /bokaβu'lario/ *m*, vocabulary

**vocación** /boka'θion; boka'sion/ *f*, vocation; trade, profession

**vocal** /bo'kal/ *a* vocal; oral. *f*, *Gram.* vowel. *mf* voting member

**vocalismo** /boka'lismo/ *m*, vocalism, vowel system

**vocalización** /bokaliθa'θion; bokalisa'sion/ *f*, vocalization

**vocalizar** /bokali'θar; bokali'sar/ *vi* to vocalize

**vocear** /boθe'ar; bose'ar/ *vi* to cry out, shout; —*vt* proclaim; call for; acclaim

**vocerío** /boθe'rio; bose'rio/ *m*, shouting; clamor, outcry

**vociferación** /boθifera'θion; bosifera'sion/ *f*, vociferation, outcry

**vociferar** /boθife'rar; bosife'rar/ *vt* to boast (of); —*vi* shout, vociferate

**vocinglería** /boθiŋgle'ria; bosiŋgle'ria/ *f*, clamor; babble, chatter

**vocinglero** /boθiŋ'glero; bosiŋ'glero/ *a* vociferous; prattling, babbling

**vodca** /'boðka/ *m*, vodka

**volada** /bo'laða/ *f*, short flight. *Mech.* **v. de grúa,** jib

**voladura** /bola'ðura/ *f*, explosion; blasting

**volandas (en), volandillas (en)** /bo'landas, bolan'diʎas; bo'landas, bolan'diyas/ *adv* in the air, as though flying; *Inf.* in a trice

**volante** /bo'lante/ *a* flying; wandering, restless. *m*, frill, flounce; screen; fan (of a windmill); *Mech.* flywheel; *Mech.* balance wheel (watches); coiner's stamp mill; shuttle-cock. *Auto.* **v. de dirección,** steering-wheel

**volantón** /bolan'ton/ **(-ona)** *n* fledgling

**volar** /bo'lar/ *vi irr* to fly (birds, insects, aviation); float in the air; hurry; disappear suddenly; burst, explode; jut out (buttresses, etc.); cleave (air) (arrows, etc.); *Fig.* spread (rumors); —*vt* explode; blast; anger. See **contar**

**volatería** /bolate'ria/ *f*, fowling; fowls; poultry; flock of birds; *Fig.* crowd (of ideas)

**volátil** /bo'latil/ *a* volatile; inconstant

**volatilizar** /bolatili'θar; bolatili'sar/ *vt* to volatilize

**volatinero** /bolati'nero/ **(-ra)** *n* tight-rope walker, acrobat

**volcán** /bol'kan/ *m*, volcano; violent passion. **v. extinto,** extinct volcano

**volcánico** /bol'kaniko/ *a* volcanic

**volcar** /bol'kar/ *vt irr* to overturn, capsize; make dizzy; cause a change (of opinion); annoy; —*vi* overturn —*Pres. Indic.* **vuelco, vuelcas, vuelca, vuelcan.** *Preterite* **volqué, volcaste,** etc —*Pres. Subjunc.* **vuelque, vuelques, vuelque, vuelquen**

**volear** /bole'ar/ *vt* to strike in the air, volley; *Agr.* sow broadcast

**voleo** /bo'leo/ *m*, volley (tennis, etc.); high kick; straight punch

**volframio** /bol'framio/ *m*, wolfram, tungsten

**volición** /boli'θion; boli'sion/ *f*, volition

**volquete** /bol'kete/ *m*, tip-cart

**voltaico** /bol'taiko/ *a* voltaic

**voltaje** /bol'tahe/ *m*, voltage

**voltario** /bol'tario/ *a* versatile; capricious, headstrong

**volteador** /boltea'ðor/ **(-ra)** *n* acrobat

**voltear** /bolte'ar/ *vt* to whirl, turn; overturn; change place (of); *Archit.* construct an arch or vault; —*vi* revolve; tumble, twirl (acrobats)

**volteo** /bol'teo/ *m*, turning, revolution; whirl; overturning; twirling; *Elec.* voltage

**voltereta** /bolte'reta/ *f*, somersault

**volteriano** /bolte'riano/ *a* Voltairian

**voltímetro** /bol'timetro/ *m*, voltmeter

**voltio** /'boltio/ *m*, volt

**volubilidad** /boluβili'ðað/ *f*, inconstancy, fickleness

**voluble** /bo'luβle/ *a* easily turned; inconstant, changeable; *Bot.* twining

**volumen** /bo'lumen/ *m*, bulk, size; volume, book

**volumétrico** /bolu'metriko/ *a* volumetric

**voluminoso** /bolumi'noso/ *a* voluminous, bulky

**voluntad** /bolun'tað/ *f*, will, volition; wish; decree; free will; intention; affection; free choice; consent. **a v.,** at will; by choice. **de buena v.,** of good will; willingly, with pleasure. **de su propia v.,** of one's own free will. **mala v.,** hostility, ill-will

**voluntario** /bolun'tario/ **(-ia)** *a* voluntary; strong-willed —*n* volunteer

**voluntarioso** /bolunta'rioso/ *a* self-willed

**voluptuosidad** /boluptuosi'ðað/ *f*, voluptuousness

**voluptuoso** /bolup'tuoso/ *a* voluptuous

**volver** /bol'βer/ *vt irr* to turn; turn over; return; pay back; direct, aim; translate; restore; change, alter; close (doors, etc.); vomit; reflect, reverberate; —*vi* come back; continue (speech, etc.); bend, turn (roads); (*with prep a* + *infin.*) do something again (e.g. *v. a leer,* to read over again); (*with por* + *noun*) protect; —*vr* become; go sour; turn. **v. a las filas,** *Mil.* to reduce to the ranks. **v. en sí,** to regain consciousness. **v. la cabeza,** to turn one's head. **volverse atrás,** *Fig.* to back out. **volverse loco,** to go mad. See **resolver**

**vomitar** /bomi'tar/ *vt* to vomit; *Fig.* vomit forth; *Fig.* spit out (curses, etc.); *Inf.* burst into confidences

**vomitivo** /bomi'tiβo/ *a* and *m*, emetic

**vómito** /'bomito/ *m,* vomit
**voracidad** /boraθi'ðað; borasi'ðað/ *f,* voracity
**vorágine** /bo'rahine/ *f,* vortex, whirlpool
**voraz** /bo'raθ; bo'ras/ *a* voracious
**vórtice** /'bortiθe; 'bortise/ *m,* whirlpool; *Fig.* vortex
**vortiginoso** /bortihi'noso/ *a* vortical
**vos** /bos/ *pers pron 2nd pers sing* and *pl* you.
**vosotros, vosotras** /bo'sotros, bo'sotras/ *pers pron 2nd pers pl mf* you
**votación** /bota'θion; bota'sion/ *f,* voting
**votador** /bota'ðor/ **(-ra)** *n* voter; swearer
**votar** /bo'tar/ *vi* and *vt* to vote; make a vow; curse; swear. **v. una proposición de confianza,** to pass a vote of confidence
**votivo** /bo'tiβo/ *a* votive
**voto** /'boto/ *m,* vote; vow; voter; prayer; curse; desire; opinion. **v. de calidad,** casting vote. **v. de confianza,** vote of confidence
**voz** /boθ; bos/ *f,* voice; sound, noise; cry, shout (gen. *pl*); word; expression; *Mus.* singer or voice; *Gram.* mood; vote; rumor; instruction, order. **v. común,** general opinion. **a voces,** in a shout, loudly. **llevar la v. cantante,** *Inf.* to have the chief say
**vuelco** /'buelko/ *m,* overturning
**vuelo** /'buelo/ *m,* flight; wing; *Sew.* skirt-fullness; ruffle, frill; *Archit.* buttress. **v. de distancia,** long-distance flight. **v. de patrulla,** patrol or reconnaissance flight. **v. de reconocimento,** reconnaissance flight. **v. nocturno,** *Aer.* night flying. **v. sin parar,** non-stop flight. **al v.,** on the wing; in passing; quickly. **alzar** ( *or* **levantar**) **el v.,** to take flight

**vuelta** /'buelta/ *f,* revolution, turn; bend, curve; return; restitution; recompense; repetition; wrong side; beating; *Sew.* facing, cuff; change (money); conning (lessons, etc.); stroll, walk; change; vault, ceiling; *Sports.* round; *Mech.* **vueltas por minuto,** revolutions per minute. **a v. de correo,** by return mail, by return of post. **a la v.,** on returning; overleaf. **dar la v.,** to turn round, make a détour. **dar una v.,** to take a stroll. **dar vueltas,** to revolve; search (for); consider. **media v.,** half turn
**vuestro, vuestra, vuestros, vuestras** /'buestro, 'buestra, 'buestros, 'buestras/ *poss pron 2nd pl mf* your, yours
**vulcanita** /bulka'nita/ *f,* vulcanite
**vulcanización** /bulkaniθa'θion; bulkanisa'sion/ *f,* vulcanization
**vulcanizar** /bulkani'θar; bulkani'sar/ *vt* to vulcanize
**vulgar** /bul'gar/ *a* popular; general, common; vernacular; mediocre
**vulgaridad** /bulgari'ðað/ *f,* vulgarity
**vulgarismo** /bulga'rismo/ *m,* vulgarism
**vulgarización** /bulgariθa'θion; bulgarisa'sion/ *f,* vulgarization; popularization
**vulgarizar** /bulgari'θar; bulgari'sar/ *vt* to vulgarize; popularize; translate into the vernacular; —*vr* grow vulgar
**vulgata** /bul'gata/ *f,* Vulgate
**vulgo** /'bulgo/ *m,* mob
**vulnerabilidad** /bulneraβili'ðað/ *f,* vulnerability
**vulnerable** /bulne'raβle/ *a* vulnerable
**vulpeja** /bul'peha/ *f,* vixen
**vulpino** /bul'pino/ *a* vulpine; crafty

# WXYZ

**wagneriano** /wagne'riano/ *a* Wagnerian

**wáter** /'water/ *m*, toilet, water-closet

**whisky** /'wiski/ *m*, whiskey

**xenofobia** /seno'foβia/ *f*, xenophobia, hatred of foreigners

**xilófago** /si'lofago/ *a* xylophagous, wood-boring. *m*, wood-borer

**xilófono** /si'lofono/ *m*, xylophone

**xilografía** /silogra'fia/ *f*, xylography

**y** /i/ *conjunc* and. See **e**

**ya** /ya/ *adv* already; formerly; soon; now; finally; immediately; well, yes, quite. Used of past, present and future time, and in various idiomatic ways. **Ha venido ya,** He has already come. **¡Ya caerá!** His time will come!, He will get his comeuppance! **Ya vendrá,** He will come soon. **¡Ya voy!** Coming! **¡Ya lo creo!** Of course!; I should think so! **¡Ya!** Quite!; I understand. **ya no,** no longer. **ya que,** since

**yacente** /ya'θente; ya'sente/ *a* recumbent, reclining (statues, etc.)

**yacer** /ya'θer; ya'ser/ *vi irr* to be lying at full length; lie (in the grave); be situated, be; lie (with), sleep (with); graze by night —*Pres. Indic.* **yazgo** or **yazco, yaces,** etc —*Pres. Subjunc.* **yazga** or **yazca,** etc.

**yaciente** /ya'θiente; ya'siente/ *a* recumbent

**yacija** /ya'θiha; ya'siha/ *f*, bed; couch; tomb

**yacimiento** /yaθi'miento; yasi'miento/ *m*, *Geol.* bed, deposit

**yacio** /'yaθio; 'yasio/ *m*, india-rubber tree

**yak** /yak/ *m*, yak

**yámbico** /'yambiko/ *a* and *m*, (metrics) iambic

**yanqui** /'yanki/ *a* and *mf contemptuous and offensive* North American (gen. U.S.A.)

**yarda** /'yarða/ *f*, yard (English measure)

**yate** /'yate/ *m*, *Naut.* yacht

**ye** /ye/ *f*, name of the letter Y

**yegua** /'yegua/ *f*, mare

**yelmo** /'yelmo/ *m*, helmet

**yema** /'yema/ *f*, bud; yolk (of egg); sweetmeat; *Fig.* best of anything. **y. del dedo,** finger-tip

**yermo** /'yermo/ *a* uninhabited, deserted; uncultivated. *m*, wilderness, desert

**yerno** /'yerno/ *m*, son-in-law

**yerro** /'yerro/ *m*, error; mistake; fault

**yerto** /'yerto/ *a* stiff, rigid

**yesca** /'yeska/ *f*, tinder; fuel, stimulus

**yeso** /'yeso/ *m*, gypsum, calcium sulphate; plaster; plaster cast

**yidish** /'yiðis/ *n* and *a* Yiddish

**yo** /yo/ *pers pron 1st sing mf* I. **el yo,** the ego

**yodo** /'yoðo/ *m*, iodine

**yuca** /'yuka/ *f*, yucca

**yucateco** /yuka'teko/ **(-ca)** *a* and *n* from or pertaining to Yucatan

**yugo** /'yugo/ *m*, yoke; nuptial tie; oppression; *Naut.* transom; *Fig.* **sacudir el y.,** to throw off the yoke

**Yugo** /'yugo/ **(e) slavia** Yugoslavia

**yugo** /'yugo/ **(e) slavo (-va)** *a* and *n* Yugoslav

**yugular** /yugu'lar/ *a Anat.* jugular. *m*, jugular vein

**Yukón, el** /yu'kon/ the Yukon

**yunque** /'yunke/ *m*, anvil; patient, undaunted person; hard worker; *Anat.* incus

**yunta** /'yunta/ *f*, yoke (of oxen, etc.)

**yute** /'yute/ *m*, jute fiber or fabric

**yuxtaponer** /yukstapo'ner/ *vt irr* to juxtapose. See **poner**

**yuxtaposición** /yukstaposi'θion; yukstaposi'sion/ *f*, juxtaposition

**zabarcera** /θaβar'θera; saβar'sera/ *f*, vegetable seller

**zaborda** /θa'βorða; sa'βorða/ *f*, **zabordamiento** *m*, *Naut.* grounding, stranding

**zabordar** /θaβor'ðar; saβor'ðar/ *vi Naut.* to run aground, strand

**zacatín** /θaka'tin; saka'tin/ *m*, street or square where clothes are sold

**zafar** /θa'far; sa'far/ *vt* to embellish, garnish, adorn; *Naut.* lighten (a ship); —*vr* escape, hide oneself; (*with de*) excuse oneself, avoid; get rid of

**zafarrancho** /θafa'rrantʃo; safa'rrantʃo/ *m*, *Naut.* clearing the decks; *Inf.* damage; *Inf.* scuffle

**zafiedad** /θafie'ðað; safie'ðað/ *f*, rudeness, ignorance, boorishness

**zafio** /'θafio; 'safio/ *a* rude, unlettered, boorish

**zafiro** /θa'firo; sa'firo/ *m*, sapphire

**zafra** /'θafra; 'safra/ *f*, olive oil container; sugar crop or factory; *Mineral.* waste

**zaga** /'θaga; 'saga/ *f*, rear. *m*, last player. **en z.,** behind. *Inf.* **no quedarse en z.,** not to be left behind; be not inferior

**zagal** /θa'gal; sa'gal/ *m*, youth; strong, handsome lad; young shepherd; full skirt

**zagala** /θa'gala; sa'gala/ *f*, maiden, girl; young shepherdess

**zagual** /θa'gual; sa'gual/ *m*, paddle

**zaguán** /θa'guan; sa'guan/ *m*, entrance hall; vestibule

**zaguero** /θa'gero; sa'gero/ *a* loitering, straggling. *m*, *Sports.* back

**zahareño** /θaa'reɲo; saa'reɲo/ *a* untamable, wild (birds); unsociable, disdainful

**zaherimiento** /θaeri'miento; saeri'miento/ *m*, upbraiding, nagging

**zaherir** /θae'rir; sae'rir/ *vt irr* to upbraid, reprehend; nag. See **herir**

**zahína** /θa'ina; sa'ina/ *f*, *Bot.* sorghum

**zahón** /θa'on; sa'on/ *m*, leather apron (worn by cowboys)

**zahorí** /θao'ri; sao'ri/ *m*, soothsayer; waterfinder; sagacious person

**zahúrda** /θa'urða; sa'urða/ *f*, pigsty

**zaino** /'θaino; 'saino/ *a* treacherous; vicious (horses); chestnut (horses); black (cows)

**zalagarda** /θala'garða; sala'garða/ *f*, ambush; skirmish; snare, trap; *Inf.* trick, ruse; *Inf.* mock battle

**zalamería** /θalame'ria; salame'ria/ *f*, adulation, flattery

**zalamero** /θala'mero; sala'mero/ **(-ra)** *a* wheedling, flattering —*n* flatterer

**zalea** /θa'lea; sa'lea/ *f*, sheepskin

**zalear** /θale'ar; sale'ar/ *vt* to shake; frighten away (dogs)

**zalema** /θa'lema; sa'lema/ *f*, salaam

**zamacuco** /θama'kuko; sama'kuko/ *m*, *Inf.* oaf, dolt; *Inf.* drinking bout

**zamarra** /θa'marra; sa'marra/ *f*, sheepskin jacket

**zamarrear** /θamarre'ar; samarre'ar/ *vt* to worry, shake (prey); *Fig. Inf.* beat up; *Inf.* floor, confound

**zambo** /'θambo; 'sambo/ *a* knock-kneed

**zambomba** /θam'βomba; sam'βomba/ *f*, rustic drum

**zambra** /'θambra; 'sambra/ *f*, Moorish festival; *Inf.* merrymaking; Moorish boat

**zambuco** /θam'βuko; sam'βuko/ *m*, *Inf.* concealment (especially of cards)

**zambullida** /θambu'ʎiða; sambu'yiða/ *f*, plunge, submersion; thrust (in fencing)

**zambullir** /θambu'ʎir; sambu'yir/ *vt* to plunge in water, submerge; —*vr* dive; hide oneself, cover oneself

**zampar** /θam'par; sam'par/ *vt* to conceal (one thing in another); eat greedily; (*with en*) arrive suddenly

**zampatortas** /θampa'tortas; sampa'tortas/ *mf Inf.* glutton

**zampoña** /θam'poɲa; sam'poɲa/ *f*, rustic flute; *Inf.* unimportant work

**zanahoria** /θana'oria; sana'oria/ *f*, carrot

**zanca** /'θanka; 'sanka/ *f*, long leg (birds); *Inf.* long thin leg; *Archit.* stringboard (of stairs)

**zancada** /θan'kaða; san'kaða/ *f*, swift stride

**zancadilla** /θanka'ðiʎa; sanka'ðiya/ *f*, trip (wrestling); *Inf.* trick, deceit. **echar la z.** (**a**), to trip up

**zancajear** /θankahe'ar; sankahe'ar/ *vi* to stride about

**zancajo** /θan'kaho; san'kaho/ *m*, heel-bone; torn

heel (stocking, shoe); *Inf.* ill-shaped person. *Inf.* **no llegarle al z.,** to be immensely inferior to someone

**zancajoso** /θanka'hoso; sanka'hoso/ *a* flatfooted; slovenly

**zanco** /'θanko; 'sanko/ *m,* stilt. *Fig. Inf.* **andar** ( *or* **estar) en zancos,** to have gone up in the world

**zancudo** /θan'kuðo; san'kuðo/ *a* long-legged

**zangandungo** /θaŋgan'duŋgo; saŋgan'duŋgo/ **(-ga)** *n Inf.* loafer

**zanganear** /θaŋgane'ar; saŋgane'ar/ *vi Inf.* to loaf

**zángano** /'θaŋgano; 'saŋgano/ *m, Ent.* drone; *Inf.* idler, parasite

**zangolotear** /θaŋgolote'ar; saŋgolote'ar/ *vt Inf.* to shake violently; —*vi* fuss about, bustle; —*vr* rattle (windows, etc.)

**zangoloteo** /θaŋgolo'teo; saŋgolo'teo/ *m,* shaking; rattling

**zanguango** /θaŋ'guaŋgo; saŋ'guaŋgo/ *m, Inf.* lazybones

**zanja** /'θanha; 'sanha/ *f,* trench, ditch; drain; furrow

**zanjar** /θan'har; san'har/ *vt* to excavate; *Fig.* remove (obstacles)

**Zanzíbar** /θan'θiβar; san'siβar/ Zanzibar

**zapa** /'θapa; 'sapa/ *f,* shovel, spade; *Mil.* sap; sandpaper

**zapador** /θapa'ðor; sapa'ðor/ *m, Mil.* sapper

**zapapico** /θapa'piko; sapa'piko/ *m,* pick-ax; mattock

**zapaquilda** /θapa'kilda; sapa'kilda/ *f, Inf.* she-cat

**zapar** /θa'par; sa'par/ *vi Mil.* to sap

**zaparrastrar** /θaparras'trar; saparras'trar/ *vi Inf.* to trail along the floor (dresses)

**zapata** /θa'pata; sa'pata/ *f,* half-boot; piece of leather used to stop creaking of a hinge; *Archit.* lintel; (*Naut. Mech.*) shoe

**zapatazo** /θapa'taθo; sapa'taso/ *m,* blow with a shoe; fall, thud; stamping (horses); flap (of sail)

**zapateado** /θapate'aðo; sapate'aðo/ *m,* dance in which rhythmic drumming of heels plays important part

**zapatear** /θapate'ar; sapate'ar/ *vt* to hit with a shoe; stamp feet; drum heels (in dancing); *Inf.* ill-treat; thump ground (rabbits); —*vi* stamp (horses); *Naut.* flap (sails); —*vr Fig.* stand one's ground

**zapateo** /θapa'teo; sapa'teo/ *m,* stamping; rhythmic drumming of heels

**zapatera** /θapa'tera; sapa'tera/ *f,* cobbler's wife; woman who makes or sells shoes

**zapatería** /θapate'ria; sapate'ria/ *f,* shoemaking; shoe shop

**zapatero** /θapa'tero; sapa'tero/ *m,* shoemaker; shoe seller. **z. remendón,** cobbler

**zapateta** /θapa'teta; sapa'teta/ *f,* caper, leap

**zapatilla** /θapa'tiʎa; sapa'tiya/ *f,* slipper; trotter, hoof

**zapato** /θa'pato; sa'pato/ *m,* shoe

**¡zape!** /'θape; 'sape/ *interj Inf.* shoo! Used for frightening away cats; exclamation of surprise or warning

**zapear** /θape'ar; sape'ar/ *vt* to scare away cats; *Inf.* frighten off

**zaque** /'θake; 'sake/ *m,* leather bottle, wineskin; *Inf.* drunkard, sot

**zaquizamí** /θaki'θami; sakisa'mi/ *m,* garret; dirty little house or room

**zar** /θar; sar/ *m,* tsar

**zarabanda** /θara'βanda; sara'βanda/ *f,* saraband; *Inf.* racket, row

**zaragata** /θara'gata; sara'gata/ *f, Inf.* fight, brawl

**Zaragoza** /θara'goθa; sara'gosa/ Saragossa

**zaragozano** /θarago'θano; sarago'sano/ **(-na)** *a* and *n* Saragossan

**zaragüelles** /θara'gueʎes; sara'gueyes/ *m, pl* wide pleated breeches

**zaranda** /θa'randa; sa'randa/ *f,* sieve, strainer, colander

**zarandajas** /θaran'dahas; saran'dahas/ *f, pl Inf.* odds and ends

**zarandar** /θaran'dar; saran'dar/ *vt* to sieve (grapes, grain); strain; *Inf.* pick out the best; —*vr Inf.* move quickly

**zarandillo** /θaran'diʎo; saran'diyo/ *m,* small sieve, strainer; *Inf.* a live wire, energetic person; Spanish dance

**zaraza** /θa'raθa; sa'rasa/ *f,* chintz

**zarcillo** /θar'θiʎo; sar'siyo/ *m,* earring; *Bot.* tendril; *Agr.* trowel

**zarco** /'θarko; 'sarko/ *a* light blue (generally eyes or water)

**zarina** /θa'rina; sa'rina/ *f,* tsarina

**zarpa** /'θarpa; 'sarpa/ *f, Naut.* weighing anchor; paw

**zarpada** /θar'paða; sar'paða/ *f,* blow with a paw

**zarpar** /θar'par; sar'par/ *vt* and *vi Naut.* to weigh anchor, sail

**zarza** /'θarθa; 'sarsa/ *f, Bot.* bramble, blackberry bush

**zarzal** /θar'θal; sar'sal/ *m,* bramble patch

**zarzamora** /θarθa'mora; sarsa'mora/ *f,* blackberry

**zarzaparrilla** /θarθapa'rriʎa; sarsapa'rriya/ *f,* sarsaparilla

**zarzo** /'θarθo; 'sarso/ *m,* hurdle; wattle

**zarzoso** /θar'θoso; sar'soso/ *a* brambly

**zarzuela** /θar'θuela; sar'suela/ *f,* comic opera; musical comedy

**zarzuelista** /θarθue'lista; sarsue'lista/ *mf* writer or composer of comic operas

**¡zas!** /θas; sas/ *m,* sound of a bang or blow

**zascandil** /θaskan'dil; saskan'dil/ *m, Inf.* busybody

**zatara** /θa'tara; sa'tara/ *f,* raft

**zeda** /'θeða; 'seða/ *f,* name of the letter Z

**zedilla** /θe'ðiʎa; se'ðiya/ *f,* cedilla

**zenit** /'θenit; 'senit/ *m.* See **cenit**

**zepelín** /θepe'lin; sepe'lin/ *m,* Zeppelin

**zeta** /'θeta; 'seta/ *f.* See **zeda**

**zigzag** /θig'θag; sig'sag/ *m,* zigzag

**zigzaguear** /θigθage'ar; sigsage'ar/ *vi* to zigzag

**zinc** /θink; sink/ *m,* zinc

**zipizape** /θipi'θape; sipi'sape/ *m, Inf.* row, quarrel

**zoca** /'θoka; 'soka/ *f,* square

**zócalo** /'θokalo; 'sokalo/ *m, Archit.* socle

**zoclo** /'θoklo; 'soklo/ *m,* clog, sabot

**zoco** /'θoko; 'soko/ *m,* square; market; clog, sabot

**zodiaco** /θo'ðiako; so'ðiako/ *m,* zodiac

**zona** /'θona; 'sona/ *f,* girdle, band; strip (of land); zone; *Med.* shingles. **z. de depresión,** air pocket. **z. templada,** temperate zone. **z. tórrida,** torrid zone

**zonal** /θo'nal; so'nal/ *a* zonal

**zoología** /θoolo'hia; soolo'hia/ *f,* zoology

**zoológico** /θoo'lohiko; soo'lohiko/ *a* zoological

**zoólogo** /θo'ologo; so'ologo/ *m,* zoologist

**zopenco** /θo'penko; so'penko/ *a* oafish

**zopo** /'θopo; 'sopo/ *a* maimed, deformed (hands, feet)

**zoquete** /θo'kete; so'kete/ *m,* block; dowel; hunk of bread; *Inf.* short, ugly man; *Inf.* dunderhead

**zorcico** /θor'θiko; sor'siko/ *m,* Basque song and dance

**zorra** /'θorra; 'sorra/ *f,* vixen; fox; *Inf.* cunning person; *Inf.* prostitute; *Inf.* drinking bout; truck, dray

**zorrera** /θo'rrera; so'rrera/ *f,* foxhole

**zorrería** /θorre'ria; sorre'ria/ *f,* foxiness; *Inf.* cunning

**zorro** /'θorro; 'sorro/ *m,* fox; fox-skin; *Inf.* knave

**zóster** /'θoster; 'soster/ *f, Med.* shingles

**zote** /'θote; 'sote/ *a* dull, ignorant

**zozobra** /θo'θoβra; so'soβra/ *f, Naut.* foundering, capsizing; anxiety

**zozobrar** /θoθo'βrar; soso'βrar/ *vi Naut.* to founder, sink; *Naut.* plunge, shiver; be anxious, vacillate

**zueco** /'θueko; 'sueko/ *m,* sabot, clog

**zulú** /θu'lu; su'lu/ *a* and *mf* Zulu

**Zululandia** /θulu'landia; sulu'landia/ Zululand

**zumaque** /θu'make; su'make/ *m, Bot.* sumach tree; *Inf.* wine

**zumba** /'θumba; 'sumba/ *f,* cow bell; jest

**zumbar** /θum'βar; sum'βar/ *vi* to buzz, hum; ring (of the ears); whizz; twang (of a guitar, etc.); *Fig. Inf.* be on the brink

**zumbido** /θum'βiðo; sum'βiðo/ *m,* buzzing, humming; ringing (in the ears); whizz; twanging (of a guitar, etc.); *Inf.* slap, blow

**zumbón** /θum'βon; sum'βon/ *a* waggish, jocose

**zumo** /'θumo; 'sumo/ *m,* sap; juice; profit, advantage

**zumoso** /θu'moso; su'moso/ *a* succulent, juicy

**zupia** /'θupia; 'supia/ *f,* wine lees; cloudy wine; *Fig.* dregs

**zurcido** /θur'θiðo; sur'siðo/ *m, Sew.* darn; mend
**zurcidor** /θurθi'ðor; sursi'ðor/ **(-ra)** *n* darner, mender. **z. de voluntades,** *humorous* pimp
**zurcidura** /θurθi'ðura; sursi'ðura/ *f,* darning; mending; darn
**zurcir** /θur'θir; sur'sir/ *vt* to darn; mend, repair; join; *Fig.* concoct, weave
**zurdo** /'θurðo; 'surðo/ *a* left-handed
**zurra** /'θurra; 'surra/ *f, Tan.* currying; *Inf.* spanking; *Inf.* quarrel
**zurrador** /θurra'ðor; surra'ðor/ *m, Tan.* currier, dresser
**zurrapa** /θu'rrapa; su'rrapa/ *f,* (gen. *pl*) sediment, lees, dregs
**zurrar** /θu'rrar; su'rrar/ *vt* to curry (leather); *Inf.* spank; *Inf.* dress down, scold

**zurriagazo** /θurria'gaθo; surria'gaso/ *m,* lash with a whip; *Fig.* blow of fate
**zurriago** /θu'rriago; su'rriago/ *m,* whip
**zurribanda** /θurri'βanda; surri'βanda/ *f, Inf.* whipping; fight, quarrel
**zurriburri** /θurri'βurri; surri'βurri/ *m, Inf.* ragamuffin; mob; uproar
**zurrido** /θu'rriðo; su'rriðo/ *m, Inf.* blow; dull noise
**zurrir** /θu'rrir; su'rrir/ *vi* to have a confused sound, hum, rattle
**zurrón** /θu'rron; su'rron/ *m,* shepherd's pouch; leather bag; *Bot.* husk
**zutano** /θu'tano; su'tano/ **(-na)** *n Inf.* so-and-so, such a one
**Zuyderzee, el** /θuiðer'θee, el; suiðer'see, el/ the Zuider Zee

# English-Spanish
## Dictionary

# A

**a** /ei/ *n* (letter) a, *f; Mus.* la, *m.* **symphony in A major,** sinfonía en la mayor, *f.* **A1,** de primera clase; de primera calidad, excelente

**a, an** /ə, ən; *when stressed* ei;, æn/ *indef art.* (one) un, *m;* una, *f;* (with weights, quantities) el, *m;* la, *f;* (with weeks, months, years, etc.) por, al, *m;* a la, *f.* The indef. art. is omitted in Spanish before nouns expressing nationality, profession, rank, and generally before a noun in apposition. It is omitted also before certain words such as **mil, ciento, otro, semejante, medio,** etc. Not translated in book titles, e.g., *A History of Spain,* Historia de España. *prep* a. In phrases such as *to go hunting,* ir a cazar. As prefix, see *abed, ashore,* etc. *Madrid, a Spanish city,* Madrid, ciudad de España. *three times a month,* tres veces al mes. *ten dollars an hour,* diez dólares por hora. *thirty miles an hour,* treinta millas por hora. *a certain Mrs. Brown,* una tal Sra. Brown. *a thousand soldiers,* mil soldados. *half an hour later,* media hora después

**aback** /ə'bæk/ *adv Naut.* en facha; *Fig.* sorprendido, desconcertado. **to take a.,** desconcertar, coger desprevenido (a)

**abacus** /'æbəkəs, ə'bækəs/ *n* ábaco, *m*

**abaft** /ə'bæft/ *adv Naut.* hacia la popa, en popa; atrás

**abandon** /ə'bændən/ *vt* abandonar; dejar; desertar, desamparar; renunciar; entregar. —*n* entusiasmo, fervor, *m;* naturalidad, *f.* **to a. oneself to,** (despair, vice, etc.) entregarse a

**abandoned** /ə'bændənd/ *a* entregado a los vicios, vicioso

**abandonment** /ə'bændənmənt/ *n* abandono, *m;* renunciación, *f;* deserción, *f*

**abase** /ə'beis/ *vt* humillar; degradar; abatir

**abasement** /ə'beismənt/ *n* humillación, degradación, *f;* abatimiento, *m*

**abash** /ə'bæʃ/ *vt* avergonzar; confundir, desconcertar

**abashed** /ə'bæʃt/ *a* avergonzado, confuso, consternado

**abate** /ə'beit/ *vt* disminuir, reducir; (a price) rebajar; (suppress) suprimir, abolir; (remit) condonar, remitir; (annul) anular; (moderate) moderar; (of pride, etc.) humillar; (of pain) aliviar. —*vi* disminuir; moderarse; (of the wind and *Fig.*) amainar; cesar; apaciguarse, calmarse

**abatement** /ə'beitmənt/ *n* disminución, *f;* reducción, *f;* mitigación, *f;* (of price) rebaja, *f;* supresión, *f;* remisión, *f;* (annulment) anulación, *f;* (of pride) humillación, *f;* (of the wind and of enthusiasm, etc.) amaine, *m;* (of pain, etc.) alivio, *m*

**abattoir** /'æbə,twɑr/ *n* matadero, *m*

**abbey** /'æbi/ *n* abadía, *f*

**abbreviate** /ə'brivi,eit/ *vt* abreviar; condensar, resumir

**abbreviation** /ə,brivi'eiʃən/ *n* abreviación, *f;* resumen, *m,* condensación, *f;* (of a word) abreviatura, *f*

**abdicate** /'æbdɪ,keit/ *vt* renunciar; (a throne) abdicar

**abdication** /,æbdɪ'keiʃən/ *n* renuncia, *f;* abdicación, *f*

**abdomen** /'æbdəmən/ *n* abdomen, *m*

**abdominal** /æb'dɒmənl/ *a* abdominal

**abduct** /æb'dʌkt/ *vt* raptar, secuestrar

**abduction** /æb'dʌkʃən/ *n* rapto, *m;* (Anat., Philos.) abducción, *f*

**abductor** /æb'dʌktər/ *n Anat.* abductor, *m;* ·raptor, *m*

**aberration** /,æbə'reiʃən/ *n* aberración (also *Astron., Phys., Biol.*), *f*

**abet** /ə'bɛt/ *vt* ayudar, apoyar, favorecer; incitar, alentar; (in bad sense) ser cómplice de

**abetment** /ə'bɛtmənt/ *n* ayuda, *f,* apoyo, *m;* instigación, *f*

**abettor** /ə'bɛtər/ *n* instigador (-ra); cómplice, *mf*

**abeyance** /ə'beiəns/ *n* suspensión, *f;* expectativa, esperanza, *f.* **in a.,** en suspenso; vacante; latente

**abhor** /æb'hɔr/ *vt* detestar, odiar, aborrecer; repugnar

**abhorrence** /æb'hɔrəns/ *n* detestación, *f,* odio, aborrecimiento, *m;* repugnancia, *f*

**abhorrent** /æb'hɔrənt/ *a* detestable, odioso, aborrecible; repugnante

**abide** /ə'baid/ *vi* morar, quedar. —*vt* aguardar; *Inf.* aguantar, sufrir. **to a. by,** atenerse a, cumplir; sostener

**abiding** /ə'baidɪŋ/ *a* permanente, constante, perenne

**ability** /ə'bɪlɪti/ *n* habilidad, facultad, *f,* poder, *m;* talento, *m,* capacidad, *f.* **to the best of my a.,** lo mejor que yo pueda

**abject** /'æbdʒɛkt/ *a* abyecto, miserable; despreciable, vil; servil

**abjure** /æb'dʒʊr/ *vt* abjurar; renunciar; retractar

**ablaze** /ə'bleiz/ *adv* en llamas, ardiendo. —*a* brillante; (with, of anger, etc.) dominado por

**able** /'eibəl/ *a* capaz (de); (clever) hábil; competente; en estado (de); *Law.* apto legalmente, capaz; bueno, excelente. **to be a. to,** poder; ser capaz de; (know how) saber. **a.-bodied,** fuerte, fornido. **a.-bodied seaman,** marinero práctico, *m*

**abloom** /ə'blum/ *adv* en flor

**ablution** /ə'bluʃən/ *n* ablución, *f*

**ably** /'eibli/ *adv* hábilmente; competentemente

**abnegation** /,æbnɪ'geiʃən/ *n* abnegación, *f*

**abnormal** /æb'nɔrməl/ *a* anormal; irregular

**abnormality** /,æbnɔr'mælɪti/ *n* anormalidad, *f;* irregularidad, *f*

**abnormally** /æb'nɔrməli/ *adv* anormalmente; demasiado

**aboard** /ə'bɔrd/ *adv* a bordo. —*prep* a bordo de. **to go a.,** embarcarse, ir a bordo. **All a.!** ¡Viajeros a bordo!; (a train) ¡Viajeros al tren!

**abode** /ə'boud/ *n* morada, habitación, *f;* residencia, *f;* (stay) estancia, *f*

**abolish** /ə'bɒlɪʃ/ *vt* abolir, suprimir, anular

**abolition** /,æbə'lɪʃən/ *n* abolición, supresión, *f;* anulación, *f*

**abolitionism** /,æbə'lɪʃə,nɪzəm/ *n* abolicionismo, *m*

**abolitionist** /,æbə'lɪʃənɪst/ *n* abolicionista, *mf*

**abominable** /ə'bɒmənəbəl/ *a* abominable, aborrecible; repugnante, execrable; *Inf.* horrible

**abominably** /ə'bɒmənəbli/ *adv* abominablemente

**abominate** /ə'bɒmə,neit/ *vt* abominar, aborrecer, detestar

**abomination** /ə,bɒmə'neiʃən/ *n* abominación, *f;* aborrecimiento, *m;* horror, *m*

**aboriginal** /,æbə'rɪdʒənl/ *a* aborigen; primitivo

**aborigines** /,æbə'rɪdʒə,niz/ *n pl* aborígenes, *m pl*

**abort** /ə'bɔrt/ *vi* abortar, malparir; *Fig.* malograrse

**abortion** /ə'bɔrʃən/ *n* aborto, *m; Fig.* fracaso, malogro, *m*

**abortive** /ə'bɔrtɪv/ *a* abortivo

**abound** /ə'baund/ *vi* abundar (en)

**about** /ə'baut/ *adv* (around) alrededor; (round about) a la redonda, en torno; (all over) por todas partes; (up and down) acá y acullá; por aquí, por ahí; en alguna parte; por aquí; (in circumference) en circunferencia; (almost) casi, aproximadamente; (by turns) por turnos, en rotación. —*prep* alrededor de; en torno; por; (near to) cerca de; (on one's person) sobre; (on the subject of) sobre; (concerning) acerca de; (over) por, a causa de; en; (of) de; (with time to spare) a eso de, sobre; (towards) hacia; (engaged in) ocupado en; (on the point of) a punto de. **a. here,** por aquí. **a. nothing,** por nada. **a. supper time,** hacia la hora de cenar. **a. three o'clock,** a eso de las tres. **A. turn!** ¡Media vuelta! (a la izquierda or a la derecha). **He wandered a. the streets,** Vagaba por las calles. **somewhere a.,** en alguna parte. **to be a. to,** estar para, estar a punto de. **to bring a.,** ocasionar. **to come a.,** suceder, tener lugar. **to know a.,** saber de. **to set a.,** empezar; (a person) acometer. **What are you thinking a.?** ¿En qué piensas?

**above** /ə'bʌv/ *adv* arriba; en lo alto; encima; (superior) superior; (earlier) antes; (higher up on a page, etc.) más arriba; (in heaven) en el cielo. —*prep* encima de; por encima de; sobre; (beyond) fuera de;

fuera del alcance de; (superior to) superior a; (more than) más de; (too proud to) demasiado orgulloso para; (too good to) demasiado bueno para; (in addition to) además de, en adición a; (with degrees of temperature) sobre. —*a* anterior; (with past participles) antes. **from a.**, desde arriba. **a. all**, sobre todo. **over and a.**, además de. **a. board**, *adv* abiertamente, con las cartas boca arriba. —*a* franco y abierto. **a. mentioned**, supradicho, susodicho, antes citado

**abrasion** /ə'breiʒən/ *n* abrasión, *f;* rozadura, *f; Geol.* denudación, *f*

**abrasive** /ə'breisɪv/ *a* abrasivo. —*n* substancia abrasiva, *f*, abrasivo, *m*

**abreast** /ə'brɛst/ *adv* de frente, al lado uno de otro; *Naut.* por el través. **to keep a. of the times**, mantenerse al dia. **to ride six a.**, cabalgar a seis de frente. **a. with**, al nivel de, a la altura de

**abridge** /ə'brɪdʒ/ *vt* abreviar; resumir, condensar, compendiar; disminuir; reducir

**abridgment** /ə'brɪdʒmənt/ *n* abreviación, *f;* resumen, *m*, sinopsis, *f;* disminución, *f;* reducción, *f*

**abroad** /ə'brɔd/ *adv* (out) fuera, afuera; (gone out) salido; ausente; (everywhere) en todas partes; (in foreign lands) en el extranjero. **to go a.**, salir de casa, echarse a la calle; ir al extranjero; (of rumors, etc.) propagarse, rumorearse

**abrogation** /,æbrə'geiʃən/ *n* abrogación, anulación, *f*

**abrupt** /ə'brʌpt/ *a* (precipitous) escarpado, precipitado, abrupto; (unexpected) repentino, inesperado; (of persons) brusco, descortés; (of style) seco

**abruptly** /ə'brʌptli/ *adv* bruscamente; repentinamente

**abruptness** /ə'brʌptnɪs/ *n* precipitación, *f;* brusquedad, *f*

**abscess** /'æbsɛs/ *n* absceso, *m*

**abscond** /æb'skɒnd/ *vi* evadirse; huir, escaparse; (with money) desfalcar

**absence** /'æbsəns/ *n* ausencia, *f;* alejamiento, *m;* (of mind) abstracción, *f,* ensimismamiento, *m;* (lack) falta, *f.* **leave of a.**, permiso para ausentarse, *m; Mil.* licencia, *f,* permiso, *m*

**absent** /*a* 'æbsənt; *v* æb'sɛnt/ *a* ausente; alejado (de); (in mind) abstraído, ensimismado, distraído. —*vt* ausentarse; alejarse. **the a.**, los ausentes. **a.-mindedness**, ensimismamiento, *m,* abstracción, *f*

**absentee** /,æbsən'ti/ *n* ausente, *mf*

**absenteeism** /,æbsən'tiizəm/ *n* absentismo, *m*

**absently** /'æbsəntli/ *adv* distraídamente

**absinthe** /'æbsɪnθ/ *n* ajenjo, *m*

**absolute** /'æbsə,lut/ *a* absoluto; perfecto; puro; (unconditional) incondicional; (downright) categórico; completo; (true) verdadero; (unlimited) ilimitado. **the a.**, lo absoluto

**absolutely** /,æbsə'lutli/ *adv* absolutamente; enteramente, completamente; realmente, categóricamente

**absolution** /,æbsə'luʃən/ *n* (Eccl. Law.) absolución, *f*

**absolutism** /'æbsəlu,tɪzəm/ *n* absolutismo, despotismo, *m*

**absolutist** /'æbsə,lutɪst/ *n* absolutista, *mf*

**absolve** /æb'zɒlv, -'sɒlv/ *vt* absolver; (free) exentar, eximir; librar; exculpar

**absorb** /æb'sɔrb, -'zɔrb/ *vt* absorber; (drink) beber; (use) gastar; (of shocks) amortiguar; (Fig. digest) asimilar; (engross) ocupar (el pensamiento, etc.). **to be absorbed in**, Fig. enfrascarse en, engolfarse en, estar entregado a

**absorbent** /æb'sɔrbənt, -'zɔr-/ *a and n* absorbente, *m.* **a. cotton**, algodón hidrófilo, *m*

**absorbing** /æb'sɔrbɪŋ, -'zɔr-/ *a* absorbente; Fig. sumamente interesante

**absorption** /æb'sɔrpʃən, -'zɔrp-/ *n* absorción, *f;* (Fig. digestion) asimilación, *f;* (engrossment) enfrascamiento, *m,* preocupación, abstracción, *f*

**abstain** /æb'stein/ *vi* abstenerse (de); evitar

**abstemious** /æb'stimiəs/ *a* abstemio, abstinente; sobrio; moderado

**abstention** /æb'stɛnʃən/ *n* abstención, *f;* abstinencia, *f;* privación, *f*

**abstinence** /'æbstənəns/ *n* abstinencia, *f.* **day of a.**, día de ayuno, *m*

**abstinent** /'æbstənənt/ *a* abstinente; sobrio

**abstract** /*a,* *v* æb'strækt, 'æbstrækt; *n* 'æbstrækt/ *a*

abstracto. —*n* extracto, resumen, *m;* abstracción, *f.* —*vt* abstraer; separar; extraer; (précis) resumir; (steal) substraer. **in the a.**, en abstracto

**abstracted** /æb'stræktɪd/ *a* distraído, desatento, absorto, ensimismado

**abstraction** /æb'strækʃən/ *n* abstracción, *f;* (of mind) preocupación, desatención, *f;* (stealing) substracción, *f*

**abstruse** /æb'strus/ *a* abstruso, ininteligible; obscuro; recóndito

**absurd** /æb'sɜrd/ *a* absurdo, grotesco; ridículo, disparatado; cómico

**absurdity** /æb'sɜrdɪti/ *n* absurdidad, ridiculez, *f;* disparate, *m,* tontería, *f*

**abundance** /ə'bʌndəns/ *n* abundancia, copia, *f;* muchedumbre (de), multitud (de), *f;* riqueza, *f;* prosperidad, *f*

**abundant** /ə'bʌndənt/ *a* abundante, copioso; rico. **to be a. in**, abundar en

**abundantly** /ə'bʌndəntli/ *adv* en abundancia, abundantemente

**abuse** /*n* ə'byus; *v* ə'byuz/ *n* abuso, *m;* (bad language) insulto, *m,* injuria, *f.* —*vt* (ill-use) maltratar; (misuse) abusar (de); (revile) insultar, injuriar; (deceive) engañar

**abuser** /ə'byuzər/ *n* abusador (-ra); injuriador (-ra); (defamer) denigrante, *mf*

**abusive** /ə'byusɪv/ *a* abusivo; (scurrilous) insultante, injurioso, ofensivo

**abusively** /ə'byusɪvli/ *adv* insolentemente, ofensivamente

**abut (on)** /ə'bʌt/ *vi* lindar con; terminar en; estar adosado a

**abysmal** /ə'bɪzməl/ *a* abismal

**abyss** /ə'bɪs/ *n* abismo, *m,* sima, *f;* (hell) infierno, *m*

**acacia** /ə'keiʃə/ *n* acacia, *f*

**academic** /,ækə'dɛmɪk/ *a* académico

**academician** /,ækədə'mɪʃən/ *n* académico, miembro de la Academia, *m*

**academy** /ə'kædəmi/ *n* academia, *f;* conservatorio, *m;* (school) colegio, *m;* (of riding, etc.) escuela, *f.* **A. of Music**, Conservatorio de Música, *m*

**accede** /æk'sid/ *vi* (to a throne) ascender (al trono); tomar posesión (de); (join) hacerse miembro (de); aceptar; (agree) acceder (a), consentir (en), convenir (en)

**accelerate** /æk'sɛlə,reit/ *vt* acelerar; apresurar; (shorten) abreviar

**acceleration** /æk,sɛlə'reiʃən/ *n* aceleración, *f*

**accelerator** /æk'sɛlə,reitər/ *n* (of a vehicle) acelerador, *m*

**accent** /'æksɛnt/ *n* acento (all meanings), *m.* —*vt* acentuar

**accentuate** /æk'sɛntʃu,eit/ *vt* acentuar; dar énfasis a

**accept** /æk'sɛpt/ *vt* aceptar; (believe) creer; recibir; admitir; (welcome) acoger

**acceptability** /æk,sɛptə'bɪlɪti/ *n* aceptabilidad, *f;* mérito, *m*

**acceptable** /æk'sɛptəbəl/ *a* aceptable; admisible; agradable; (welcome) bien acogido

**acceptably** /æk'sɛptəbli/ *adv* aceptablemente, agradablemente

**acceptance** /æk'sɛptəns/ *n* aceptación, *f.* **a. speech** discurso aceptatorio; (approval) aprobación, *f;* (welcome) buena acogida, *f; Com.* aceptación, *f*

**access** /'æksɛs/ *n* acceso, *m;* entrada, *f;* (way) camino, *m; Med.* ataque, *m;* (fit) transporte, *m;* (advance) avance, *m.* **easy of a.**, accesible; fácil de encontrar

**accessibility** /æk,sɛsə'bɪlɪti/ *n* accesibilidad, *f*

**accessible** /æk'sɛsəbəl/ *a* accesible; asequible

**accession** /æk'sɛʃən/ *n* (to the throne, etc.) advenimiento, *m;* aumento, *m;* (acquisition) adición, *f;* adquisición, *f; Law.* accesión, *f*

**accessory** /æk'sɛsəri/ *a* accesorio; secundario; suplementario, adicional. —*n* accesorio, *m; Law.* cómplice, *mf.* **a. before the fact**, instigador (-ra). **a. after the fact**, encubridor (-ra)

**accident** /'æksɪdənt/ *n* accidente, *m;* (chance) casualidad, *f;* (mishap) contratiempo, *m.* **by a.**, por casualidad, accidentalmente. **a. insurance**, seguro contra accidentes, *m*

**accidental** /ˌæksɪ'dɛntḷ/ *a* accidental, casual, fortuito. —*n Mus.* accidente, *m*

**accidentally** /ˌæksɪ'dɛntḷi/ *adv* accidentalmente; por casualidad; sin querer

**acclaim** /ə'kleim/ *vt* aclamar; proclamar; vitorear, aplaudir

**acclamation** /ˌæklə'meifən/ *n* aclamación, *f*; aplauso, vítor, *m*

**acclimatization** /ə'klaimətə,zeishən/ *n* aclimatación, *f*

**acclimatize** /ə'klaimə,taiz/ *vt* aclimatar

**accolade** /'ækə,leid/ *n* acolada, *f*, espaldarazo, *m*

**accommodate** /ə'kɒmə,deit/ *vt* acomodar; ajustar; adaptar; (reconcile) reconciliar; (provide) proveer, proporcionar; (oblige) complacer; (fit) poner, instalar; (lodge) hospedar; (lend) prestar; (hold) tener espacio para, contener; (give a seat to) dar un sitio a. **to a. oneself to,** adaptarse a

**accommodating** /ə'kɒmə,deitɪŋ/ *a* acomodadizo; (obliging) servicial

**accommodation** /ə,kɒmə'deifən/ *n* acomodación, *f*; ajuste, *m*; adaptación, *f*; (arrangement) arreglo, *m*; (reconciliation) reconciliación, *f*; (lodging) alojamiento, *m*; (*Aer. Naut.*) partición, *f*; (space, room or seat) sitio, *m*; (loan) préstamo, *m*. **We found the accommodations good in this hotel,** Estuvimos muy bien en este hotel. **a. ladder,** escalera real, *f*

**accompaniment** /ə'kʌmpənimənt/ *n* acompañamiento, *m*

**accompanist** /ə'kʌmpənɪst/ *n* acompañante (-ta)

**accompany** /ə'kʌmpəni/ *vt* acompañar

**accompanying** /ə'kʌmpəniɪŋ/ *a* anexo *n* acompañamiento, *m*

**accomplice** /ə'kɒmplɪs/ *n* cómplice, comparte, *mf*

**accomplish** /ə'kɒmplɪʃ/ *vt* llevar a cabo, efectuar; terminar; (fulfil) cumplir; perfeccionar; (achieve) conseguir, lograr

**accomplished** /ə'kɒmplɪʃt/ *a* consumado; perfecto; culto; (talented) talentoso

**accomplishment** /ə'kɒmplɪʃmənt/ *n* efectuación, *f*; realización, *f*, logro, *m*; (fulfilment) cumplimiento, *m*; (gift) prenda, *f*, talento, *m*; *pl* **accomplishments,** partes, dotes, *f pl*; conocimientos, *m pl*

**accord** /ə'kɔrd/ *n* acuerdo, *m*; unión, *f*; consentimiento, *m*; concierto, *m*, concordia, *f*; voluntad, *f*. —*vt* otorgar, conceder. —*vi* estar de acuerdo (con); armonizar (con). **of one's own a.,** espontáneamente. **with one a.,** unánimemente

**accordance** /ə'kɔrdns/ *n* acuerdo, *m*, conformidad, *f*; arreglo, *m*. **in a. with,** de acuerdo con, según, con arreglo a

**according** /ə'kɔrdɪŋ/ *adv* según, conforme. **a. as,** conforme a, a medida que. **a. to,** según

**accordingly** /ə'kɔrdɪŋli/ *adv* en consecuencia, por consiguiente; pues

**accordion** /ə'kɔrdiən/ *n* acordeón, *m*. **to a.-pleat,** *vt* plisar

**accost** /ə'kɔst/ *vt* abordar, acercarse a; dirigirse a, hablar

**account** /ə'kaunt/ *vt* (judge) considerar, creer, juzgar, tener por. —*vi* (for) explicar; (understand) comprender; (be responsible) responder de, dar razón de; justificar

**account** /ə'kaunt/ *n* (bill) cuenta, *f*; factura, *f*; (narrative) narración, relación, *f*; (description) descripción, *f*; historia, *f*; versión, *f*; (list) enumeración, *f*; (reason) motivo, *m*, causa, *f*; (importance) importancia, *f*; (weight) peso, *m*; (news) noticias, *f pl*; (advantage) provecho, *m*, ventaja, *f*. **by all accounts,** según lo que se oye, según voz pública. **current a.,** cuenta corriente, *f*. **outstanding a.,** cuenta pendiente, *f*. **on a.,** a cuenta. **on a. of,** a causa de, por motivo de. **on no a.,** de ninguna manera. **on that a.,** por lo tanto. **to be of no a.,** ser insignificante; ser de poca importancia; *Inf.* ser la última mona. **to give an a.,** contar, hacer una relación (de). **to give an a. of oneself,** explicarse. **to keep a.,** llevar la cuenta. **to settle accounts,** ajustar cuentas. **to take into a.,** considerar. **to turn to a.,** sacar provecho de. **a. book,** libro de cuentas, *m*

**accountability** /ə,kauntə'bɪliti/ *n* responsabilidad, *f*

**accountable** /ə'kauntəbəl/ *a* responsable

**accountancy** /ə'kauntnsi/ *n* contabilidad, *f*

**accountant** /ə'kauntnt/ *n* contador, *m*. **chartered a.,** contador autorizado, *m*. **accountant's office,** contaduría, *f*

**accouterment** /ə'kutərmənt/ *n* atavío, *m*; equipo, *m*

**accredit** /ə'krɛdɪt/ *vt* acreditar

**accretion** /ə'krifən/ *n* acrecentamiento, aumento, *m*; *Law.* accesión, *f*

**accrue** /ə'kru/ *vi* resultar (de), proceder (de); originarse (en); aumentar

**accumulate** /ə'kyumyə,leit/ *vt* acumular; amontonar, atesorar. —*vi* acumularse; aumentarse, crecer

**accumulation** /ə,kyumyə'leifən/ *n* acumulación, *f*; amontonamiento, *m*

**accumulative** /ə'kyumyə,leitɪv/ *a* acumulador; adquisitivo, ahorrador

**accumulator** /ə'kyumyə,leitər/ *n Elec.* acumulador, *m*

**accuracy** /'ækyərəsi/ *n* exactitud, corrección

**accurate** /'ækyərɪt/ *a* exacto, correcto, fiel; (of persons) exacto, minucioso; (of apparatus) de precisión

**accurately** /'ækyərɪtli/ *adv* con exactitud, correctamente; con precisión

**accursed** /ə'kɜrsɪd, ə'kɜrst/ *a* maldito.

**accusation** /ˌækyu'zeifən/ *n* acusación, *f*. **to lodge an a.,** querellarse ante el juez

**accusatory** /ə'kyuzə,tɔri/ *a* acusatorio

**accuse** /ə'kyuz/ *vt* acusar

**accused** /ə'kyuzd/ *n Law.* acusado (-da)

**accuser** /ə'kyuzər/ *n* acusador (-ra)

**accustom** /ə'kʌstəm/ *vt* acostumbrar (a), habituar (a)

**accustomed** /ə'kʌstəmd/ *a* acostumbrado, usual; general; característico

**ace** /eis/ *n* as, *m*; *Fig.* pelo, *m*. **to be within an ace of,** estar a dos dedos de

**acerbity** /ə'sɜrbɪti/ *n* acerbidad, *f*; *Fig.* aspereza, *f*; severidad, *f*; sequedad, *f*

**acetate** /'æsɪ,teit/ *n* acetato, *m*

**acetic** /ə'sitɪk/ *a* acético

**acetylene** /ə'sɛtl,in/ *n* acetileno, *m*. **a. lamp,** lámpara de acetileno, *f*

**ache** /eik/ *n* dolor, *m*; pena, *f*. —*vi* doler. **My head aches,** Me duele la cabeza, Tengo dolor de cabeza

**achievable** /ə'tʃivəbəl/ *a* alcanzable, asequible; factible

**achieve** /ə'tʃiv/ *vt* conseguir, lograr; (reach) alcanzar; (obtain) obtener, ganar

**achievement** /ə'tʃivmənt/ *n* logro, *m*, realización, *f*; obtención, *f*; (deed) hazaña, *f*; (work) obra, *f*; (success) éxito, *m*; (discovery) descubrimiento, *m*; (victory) victoria, *f*

**aching** /'eikɪŋ/ *n* dolor, *m*; pena, angustia, *f*. —*a* doliente; afligido

**achromatic** /ˌeikrə'mætɪk/ *a* acromático

**achromic** /ei'kroumɪk/ *a* acrómico

**acid** /'æsɪd/ *a* and *n* ácido, *m*. **fatty a.,** ácido graso, *m*

**acidify** /ə'sɪdə,fai/ *vt* acidificar

**acidity** /ə'sɪdɪti/ *n* acidez, *f*

**acidosis** /ˌæsɪ'dousɪs/ *n Med.* acidismo, *m*

**acidulous** /ə'sɪdʒələs/ *a* acídulo

**acknowledge** /æk'nɒlɪdʒ/ *vt* reconocer; confesar; (reply to) contestar a; (appreciate) agradecer. **to a. receipt,** *Com.* acusar recibo

**acknowledgment** /æk'nɒlɪdʒmənt/ *n* reconocimiento, *m*; confesión, *f*; (appreciation) agradecimiento, *m*; (reward) recompensa, *f*; (of a letter) acuse de recibo, *m*

**acme** /'ækmi/ *n* cumbre, *f*; *Fig.* auge, apogeo, *m*

**acne** /'ækni/ *n* acné, *m*

**acolyte** /'ækə,lait/ *n* acólito, monacillo (male) *m*, acólita, monacilla *f*, (female)

**acorn** /'eikɔrn/ *n* bellota, *f*. **a. cup,** capullo de bellota, *m*. **a.-shaped,** en forma de bellota, abellotado

**acoustic** /ə'kustɪk/ *a* acústico

**acoustics** /ə'kustɪks/ *n pl* acústica, *f*

**acquaint** /ə'kweint/ *vt* dar a conocer, comunicar, informar (de), dar parte (de); familiarizar (con). **to be acquainted with,** conocer; saber. **to make oneself acquainted with,** familiarizarse con; entablar amistad con

**acquaintance** /ə'kweintns/ *n* conocimiento, *m*; (person) conocido (-da); *pl* **acquaintances,** amistades, *f pl.* **to make their a.,** conocer (a), llegar a conocer (a)

**acquiesce** /ˌækwi'es/ *vi* asentir (en), consentir (a)

**acquiescence** /ˌækwi'esəns/ *n* acquiescencia, *f*, consentimiento, *m*

**acquiescent** /ˌækwi'esənt/ *a* conforme; resignado

**acquire** /ə'kwaiər/ *vt* adquirir, obtener; (diseases, habits) contraer; ganar; (learn) aprender

**Acquired Immune Deficiency Syndrome** /ə'kwaiərd/ *n* el síndrome de Inmunodeficiencia Adquirida, *m*

**acquirement** /ə'kwaiərmənt/ *n* adquisición, *f*; (learning) conocimiento, *m*; (talent) talento, *m*

**acquirer** /ə'kwaiərər/ *n* adquisidor (-ra)

**acquisition** /ˌækwə'zıʃən/ *n* adquisición, *f*

**acquisitive** /ə'kwızıtıv/ *a* adquisitivo

**acquit** /ə'kwıt/ *vt* (a debt) pagar; exonerar; *Law.* absolver; (a duty) cumplir. **to a. oneself well ( badly),** portarse bien (mal); salir bien (mal)

**acquittal** /ə'kwıtl/ *n* (of a debt) pago, *m*; *Law.* absolución, *f*; (of a duty) cumplimiento, *m*

**acquittance** /ə'kwıtns/ *n* descargo, *m*; quitanza, *f*

**acre** /'eikər/ *n* (measure) acre, *m*; *pl* **acres,** terrenos, campos, *m pl*

**acreage** /'eikəridʒ/ *n* acres, *m pl*

**acrid** /'ækrid/ *a* acre

**acrimonious** /ˌækrə'mouniəs/ *a* acrimonioso, áspero, mordaz, sarcástico

**acrimony** /'ækrə,mouni/ *n* acrimonia, acritud, *f*; sarcasmo, *m*

**acrobat** /'ækrə,bæt/ *n* acróbata, *mf*

**acrobatic** /ˌækrə'bætık/ *a* acrobático

**acrobatics** /ˌækrə'bætıks/ *n pl* acrobacia, *f*

**acronym** /'ækrənım/ *n* sigla, *f*

**acropolis** /ə'krɒpəlıs/ *n* acrópolis, *f*

**across** /ə'krɒs/ *adv* a través, de través, transversalmente; (on the other side) al otro lado; de una parte a otra; (of the arms, etc.) cruzados, *m pl.* —*prep* a través de; al otro lado de; (upon) sobre; por. **He went a. the road,** Cruzó la calle. **to run a.,** correr por; tropezar con; dar con. **a. country,** a campo travieso. **a. the way,** en frente

**acrostic** /ə'krɒstık/ *n* (poema) acróstico, *m*, *a* acróstico

**act** /ækt/ *n* acción, obra, *f*, hecho, *m*; acto, *m*; *Law.* ley, *f*; *Theat.* acto, *m*. **in the act,** en el acto. **in the act (of doing),** en acto de (hacer algo). **in the very act,** en flagrante. **the Acts of the Apostles,** los Actos de los Apóstoles. **act of God,** fuerza mayor, *f*. **act of indemnity,** bill de indemnidad, *m*

**act** /ækt/ *vt* (a play) representar, hacer; (a part) desempeñar, hacer (un papel); (pretend) simular, fingir. —*vi* obrar, actuar; (behave) portarse, conducirse; (function) funcionar; producir su efecto; (feign) fingir; (as a profession) ser actor. **to act as,** hacer de; cumplir las funciones de. **to act as a second,** (in a duel) apadrinar. **to act for,** representar; ser el representante de. **to act upon,** obrar sobre; afectar; influir en

**acting** /'æktıŋ/ *n* (of a play) representación (de una comedia), *f*; (of an actor) interpretación (de un papel), *f*; (as a hobby) el hacer comedia; (dramatic art) arte dramática, *f*. —*a* interino, suplente; comanditario. **He is a. captain,** Está de capitán. **a. partner,** socio (-ia) comanditario (-ia)

**action** /'ækʃən/ *n* acción, *f*; función, *f*; operación, *f*; (movement) movimiento, *m*; (effect) efecto, *m*; influencia, *f*; *Law.* proceso, *m*; *Mil.* batalla, acción, *f*; *Lit.* acción, *f*. **in a.,** en actividad; en operación; *Mil.* en el campo de batalla. **man of a.,** hombre de acción, *m*. **to be killed in a.,** morir en el campo de batalla. **to bring an a. against,** pedir en juicio, entablar un pleito contra. **to put into a.,** hacer funcionar; introducir. **to take a.,** tomar medidas (para). **to take a. against,** prevenirse contra; *Law.* proceder contra

**actionable** /'ækʃənəbəl/ *a* procesable, punible

**active** /'æktıv/ *a* activo; ágil; diligente; *Mil.* vivo; enérgico. *Gram.* activo. **to make a.,** activar, estimular

**activity** /æk'tıvıti/ *n* actividad, *f*

**actor** /'æktər/ *n* actor, *m*; (in comedy) comediante, *m*

**actress** /'æktrıs/ *n* actriz, *f*; (in comedy) comediante, *f*

**actual** /'æktʃuəl/ *a* actual, existente; real, verdadero

**actuality** /ˌæktʃu'ælıti/ *n* realidad, *f*

**actually** /'æktʃuəli/ *adv* en efecto, realmente, en realidad

**actuary** /'æktʃu,eri/ *n* actuario de seguros, *m*

**actuate** /'æktʃu,eit/ *vt* mover, animar, excitar

**acumen** /ə'kyumən/ *n* cacumen, *m*, agudeza, sagacidad, *f*

**acute** /ə'kyut/ *a* agudo; (shrewd) perspicaz; (of a situation) crítico. **a. accent,** acento agudo, *m*. **a.-angled,** acutángulo

**acutely** /ə'kyutli/ *adv* agudamente; (deeply) profundamente

**acuteness** /ə'kyutnıs/ *n* agudeza, *f*; (shrewdness) perspicacia, penetración, *f*

**ad** /æd/ *n* anuncio, *m*. See **advertisement**

**adage** /'ædıdʒ/ *n* refrán, proverbio, decir, *m*

**adagio** /ə'dadʒou/ *n* adagio, *m*

**Adam** /'ædəm/ *n* Adán, *m*. **Adam's apple,** nuez de la garganta, *f*

**adamant** /'ædəmənt/ *a* firme, duro, inexorable

**adamantine** /ˌædə'mæntin/ *a* adamantino

**adapt** /ə'dæpt/ *vt* adaptar; ajustar, acomodar; aplicar; (a play, etc.) refundir, arreglar; *Mus.* arreglar

**adaptability** /ə,dæptə'bılıti/ *n* adaptabilidad, *f*

**adaptable** /ə'dæptəbəl/ *a* adaptable

**adaptation** /ˌædəp'teiʃən/ *n* adaptación, *f*; (of a play, etc.) refundición, *f*; (Mus. etc.) arreglo, *m*

**adapter** /ə'dæptər/ *n* (of a play, etc.) refundidor (-ra); *Elec.* enchufe de reducción, *m*

**add** /æd/ *vt* añadir; juntar; (up) sumar. **add insult to injury,** al mojado echarle agua, añadir a una ofensa otra mayor. **to add to,** añadir a; (increase) aumentar, acrecentar. **to add up,** sumar. **to add up to,** subir a; (mean) querer decir.

**adder** /'ædər/ *n* víbora, serpiente, *f*

**addict** /'ædıkt/ *n* adicto (-ta).

**addicted** /ə'dıktıd/ *a* aficionado (a), amigo (de), dado (a); adicto (a)

**addiction** /ə'dıkʃən/ *n* afición, propensión, *f*; adicción, *f*

**addition** /ə'dıʃən/ *n* añadidura, *f*; *Math.* adición, suma, *f*. **in a. (to),** además (de), también

**additional** /ə'dıʃənl/ *a* adicional

**addled** /'ædld/ *a* huero, podrido; *Fig.* confuso

**address** /*n* ə'dres, 'ædres; *v* ə'dres/ *n* (on a letter) sobrescrito, *m*; (of a person) dirección, *f*, señas, *f pl*; (speech) discurso, *m*; (petition) memorial, *m*, petición, *f*; (dedication) dedicatoria, *f*; (invocation) invocación, *f*; (deportment) presencia, *f*; (tact) diplomacia, habilidad, *f*; *pl* **addresses,** corte, *f*. —*vt* (a ball) golpear; (a letter) dirigir, poner el sobrescrito a; (words, prayers) dirigir (a); hablar, hacer un discurso. **to a. oneself to a task,** dedicarse a (or entregarse a emprender) una tarea. **to deliver an a.,** pronunciar un discurso. **to pay one's addresses to,** cortejar, hacer la corte a; galantear

**addressee** /ˌædre'si/ *n* destinatario (-ia)

**adduce** /ə'dus/ *vt* aducir, alegar; aportar

**Aden** /'adn/ Adén *m*

**adenoids** /'ædn,ɔidz/ *n pl* amígdalas, *f pl*

**adept** /*a* ə'dept; *n* 'ædept/ *a* adepto, versado, consumado. —*n* adepto, *m*

**adequacy** /'ædıkwəsi/ *n* adecuación, *f*; suficiencia, *f*; competencia, *f*

**adequate** /'ædıkwıt/ *a* adecuado; proporcionado; suficiente; competente; a la altura (de)

**adequately** /'ædıkwıtli/ *adv* adecuadamente

**adhere** /æd'hiər/ *vi* adherirse; pegarse; ser fiel (a); persistir (en)

**adherence** /æd'hiərəns/ *n Fig.* adhesión, *f*

**adherent** /æd'hiərənt/ *n* partidario (-ia)

**adhesion** /æd'hiʒən/ *n* adherencia, *f*; (to a party, etc.) adhesión, *f*

**adhesive** /æd'hisıv/ *a* adhesivo; (sticky) pegajoso. **a. tape,** esparadrapo, *m*; *Elec.* cinta aisladora adherente, *f*

**adipose** /'ædə,pous/ *a* adiposo

**adjacent** /ə'dʒeisənt/ *a* próximo, contiguo, adyacente, vecino

**adjective** /'ædʒıktıv/ *n* adjetivo, *m*

**adjoin** /ə'dʒɔin/ vt estar contiguo a, lindar con; juntar. —vi colindar

**adjoining** /ə'dʒɔiniŋ/ a vecino, de al lado, adyacente; cercano

**adjourn** /ə'dʒɜrn/ vt aplazar, diferir; (a meeting, etc.) suspender, levantar. —vi retirarse. **The debate was adjourned,** Se suspendió el debate. **to a. a meeting,** levantar la sesión

**adjournment** /ə'dʒɜrnmənt/ n aplazamiento, m; (of a meeting) suspensión (de la sesión), f

**adjudicate** /ə'dʒudɪ,keit/ vt adjudicar; Law. declarar; juzgar. —vi ejercer las funciones del juez; fallar, dictar sentencia

**adjudication** /ə,dʒudɪ'keiʃən/ n adjudicación, f; Law. fallo, m, sentencia, f; (of bankruptcy) declaración (de quiebra), f; concesión, f, otorgamiento, m

**adjudicator** /ə'dʒudɪ,keitər/ n adjudicador (-ra)

**adjunct** /'ædʒʌŋkt/ n atributo, m; accesorio, m; adjunto, m; Gram. adjunto, m

**adjure** /ə'dʒʊr/ vt conjurar; rogar encarecidamente

**adjust** /ə'dʒʌst/ vt ajustar; regular; arreglar; (correct) corregir; adaptar

**adjustable** /ə'dʒʌstəbəl/ a ajustable; regulable; desmontable; de quita y pon

**adjustment** /ə'dʒʌstmənt/ n ajuste, m; regulación, f; arreglo, m; (correction) corrección, f; adaptación, f; Com. prorrateo, m

**adjutant** /'ædʒətənt/ n Mil. ayudante, m

**administer** /æd'mɪnəstər/ vt administrar; (laws) aplicar; (blows, etc.) dar; (an office) ejercer; (govern) regir, gobernar; (provide) suministrar; (an oath) tomar; (justice) hacer; (the sacraments) administrar; (with to) contribuir a. **to a. an oath,** tomar juramento (a)

**administration** /æd,mɪnə'streiʃən/ n administración, f; (government) gobierno, m; dirección, f; (of laws) aplicación, f; distribución, f

**administrative** /æd'mɪnə,streitɪv/ a administrativo; gubernativo

**administrator** /æd'mɪnə,streitər/ n administrador, m

**administratrix** /æd,mɪnə'streitrɪks/ n administradora, f

**admirable** /'ædmərəbəl/ a admirable

**admirably** /'ædmərəbli/ adv admirablemente

**admiral** /'ædmərəl/ n almirante, m. **A. of the Fleet,** almirante supremo, m. **admiral's ship,** capitana, f

**admiration** /,ædmə'reiʃən/ n admiración, f

**admire** /æd'maiᵊr/ vt sentir admiración por; (love) amar; (like) gustar; (respect) respetar

**admirer** /æd'maiᵊrər/ n admirador (-ra); (amateur) aficionado (-da), apasionado (-da); (partisan) satélite, m; (lover) enamorado, amante, m

**admiring** /æd'maiəriŋ/ a admirativo, de admiración

**admissible** /æd'mɪsəbəl/ a admisible; aceptable; lícito, permitido

**admission** /æd'mɪʃən/ n admisión, f; recepción, f; entrada, f; confesión, f, reconocimiento, m. **No a.!** Entrada prohibida. **right of a.,** derecho de entrada, m. **A. free,** Entrada libre. **a. ticket,** entrada, f

**admit** /æd'mɪt/ vt admitir; recibir; dejar entrar; hacer entrar, introducir; (hold) contener; (concede) conceder; (acknowledge) reconocer, confesar. **to a. of,** permitir; sufrir

**admittance** /æd'mɪtns/ n admisión, f; entrada, f. **No a.!** Prohibida la entrada. **to gain a.,** lograr entrar

**admittedly** /æd'mɪtɪdli/ adv según opinión general; sin duda

**admonish** /æd'mɒnɪʃ/ vt (advise) aconsejar; amonestar, advertir; (reprimand) reprender

**admonition** /,ædmə'nɪʃən/ n amonestación, f; advertencia, f; admonición, f

**admonitory** /æd'mɒnɪ,tɔri/ a amonestador

**ad nauseam** /'æd nɔziəm/ adv hasta la saciedad

**ado** /ə'du/ n (noise) ruido, m; (trouble) trabajo, m, dificultad, f; (fuss) barahúnda, f. **much ado about nothing,** mucho ruido y pocas nueces, nada entre dos platos. **without more ado,** sin más ni más

**adolescence** /,ædl'ɛsəns/ n adolescencia, f

**adolescent** /,ædl'ɛsənt/ a and n adolescente, mf

**adopt** /ə'dɒpt/ vt adoptar

**adopted** /ə'dɒptɪd/ a adoptivo

**adoption** /ə'dɒpʃən/ n adopción, f; (choice) elección, f

**adoptive** /ə'dɒptɪv/ a adoptivo

**adorable** /ə'dɔrəbəl/ a adorable

**adoration** /,ædə'reiʃən/ n adoración, f. **A. of the Magi,** Adoración de los Reyes, f

**adore** /ə'dɔr/ vt adorar

**adorer** /ə'dɔrər/ n adorador (-ra); amante, m

**adoringly** /ə'dɔriŋli/ adv con adoración

**adorn** /ə'dɔrn/ vt adornar, embellecer; (Fig. of persons) adornar con su presencia

**adornment** /ə'dɔrnmənt/ n adorno, m; ornamento, m; embellecimiento, m

**adrenalin** /ə'drɛnlɪn/ n adrenalina, f

**Adriatic, the** /,eidri'ætɪk/ el (Mar) Adriático, m

**adrift** /ə'drɪft/ a and adv a merced de las olas; a la ventura. **to turn a.,** Inf. poner de patitas en la calle

**adroit** /ə'drɔit/ a hábil

**adulate** /'ædʒə,leit/ vt adular

**adulation** /,ædʒə'leiʃən/ n adulación, f

**adulatory** /'ædʒələ,tɔri/ a adulador

**adult** /ə'dʌlt/ a and n adulto (-ta)

**adult education** n educación de los adultos, f

**adulterate** /v ə'dʌltə,reit; a ə'dʌltə,reit; -tərɪt/ vt adulterar; falsificar; contaminar. —a adulterado; falsificado; impuro

**adulteration** /ə,dʌltə'reiʃən/ n adulteración, f; falsificación, f; impureza, f; contaminación, f

**adulterer** /ə'dʌltərər/ n adúltero, m

**adulteress** /ə'dʌltərɪs/ n adúltera, f

**adulterous** /ə'dʌltərəs/ a adúltero

**adultery** /ə'dʌltəri/ n adulterio, m. **to commit a.,** cometer adulterio, adulterar

**advance** /æd'væns/ n avance, m; (progress) progreso, adelantamiento, m; (improvement) mejora, f; (of shares) alza, f; (of price) subida, f; (loan) préstamo, m; (in rank) ascenso, m; pl **advances,** (overtures) avances, m pl; (proposals) propuestas, f pl; (of love) requerimientos amorosos, m pl. **in a.,** de antemano, con anticipación, con tiempo, previamente; (of money) por adelantado. **a. guard,** Mil. avanzada, f. **a. payment,** anticipo, m, paga por adelantado, f

**advance** /æd'væns/ vt avanzar; (suggest) sugerir, proponer; (encourage) fomentar; (a person) ascender; (improve) mejorar; (of events, dates) adelantar; (of prices, stocks) hacer subir; (money) anticipar; (of steps) tomar. —vi avanzar; (progress) progresar; (in rank, studies, etc.) adelantar; (of prices) subir

**advanced** /æd'vænst/ a avanzado; (developed) desarrollado; (mentally, of children) precoz; (course) superior. **a. research,** investigaciones superiores. **a. standing,** equivalencias, f pl. **a. views,** ideas avanzadas, f pl

**advancement** /æd'vænsmənt/ n adelantamiento, m; progreso, m; (encouragement) fomento, m; (in employment) promoción, f; prosperidad, f

**advancing** /æd'vænsiŋ/ a que avanza; (of years) que pasan

**advantage** /æd'væntɪdʒ/ n ventaja, f; superioridad, f; (benefit) provecho, beneficio, m; interés, m; ocasión favorable, oportunidad, f; (tennis) ventaja, f. **to have the a. of,** tener la ventaja de. **to show to a.,** embellecer, realzar; aumentar la belleza (etc.) de. **to take a. of,** sacar ventaja de, aprovecharse de; (deceive) engañar. **to take a. of the slightest pretext,** asirse de un cabello

**advantageous** /,ædvən'teidʒəs/ a ventajoso, provechoso. **to be a.,** ser de provecho

**advent** /'ædvɛnt/ n advenimiento, m, llegada, f; Eccl. Adviento, m

**adventitious** /,ædvən'tɪʃəs/ a adventicio (all uses)

**adventure** /æd'vɛntʃər/ n aventura, f; riesgo, m; (chance) casualidad, f; Com. especulación, f, vt aventurar, arriesgar. —vi arriesgarse, osar

**adventurer** /æd'vɛntʃərər/ n aventurero, m; (one living by his wits) caballero de industria, m; (in commerce) especulador, m

**adventuresome** /æd'vɛntʃərsəm/ a de aventura

**adventuress** /æd'vɛntʃərɪs/ n aventurera, f

**adventurous** /æd'vɛntʃərəs/ a aventurero; osado, audaz; (dangerous) peligroso, arriesgado

**adverb** /'ædvɜrb/ n adverbio, m

**adversary** /'ædvər,sɛri/ n adversario (-ia)

**adverse** /æd'vɜrs/ *a* adverso; hostil (a); malo; desfavorable; (opposite) opuesto

**adversity** /æd'vɜrsɪti/ *n* adversidad, *f*

**advertise** /'ædvər,taiz/ *vt* anunciar. —*vi* poner un anuncio; (oneself) llamar la atención

**advertisement** /,ædvər'taizmənt, æd'vɜrtismənt/ *n* anuncio, *m;* (poster) cartel, *m;* (to attract attention) reclamo, *m.* **to put an a. in the paper,** poner un anuncio en el periódico. **a. hoarding,** cartelera, *f*

**advertiser** /'ædvər,taizər/ *n* anunciante, *mf*

**advertising** /'ædvər,taizɪŋ/ *n* anuncios, *m pl;* publicidad, propaganda, *f;* medios publicitarios, *m pl*

**advice** /æd'vais/ *n* consejo, *m;* (warning) advertencia, amonestación, *f;* (news) noticia, *f,* aviso, *m; Com.* comunicación, *f;* (belief) parecer, *m,* opinión, *f.* **piece of a.,** consejo, *m.* **to follow the a. of,** seguir los consejos de. **to give a.,** dar consejos

**advisability** /æd,vaizə'bɪlɪti/ *n* conveniencia, *f;* prudencia, *f*

**advisable** /æd'vaizəbəl/ *a* conveniente, aconsejable; prudente

**advise** /æd'vaiz/ *vt* aconsejar; (inform) avisar, informar

**advised** /æd'vaizd/ *a* avisado; premeditado. **ill-a.,** mal aconsejado; imprudente. **well-a.,** bien aconsejado; prudente

**adviser** /æd'vaizər/ *n* consejero (-ra)

**advisory** /æd'vaizəri/ *a* asesor, consultivo, consultativo

**advocacy** /'ædvəkəsi/ *n* defensa, *f;* apología, *f;* abogacía, intercesión, *f*

**advocate** /*n* 'ædvəkɪt; *v* -,keit/ *n Law.* abogado (-da); defensor (-ra); (champion) campeón, *m.* —*vt* abogar, defender; sostener, apoyar; recomendar

**adze** /ædz/ *n* azuela, *f*

**Aegean, the** /ə'dʒiən/ el (Mar) Egeo, *m*

**aegis** /'idʒɪs/ *n* égida, *f;* protección, *f*

**aerated** /'ɛə,reitid/ *a* aereado; (of lemonade, etc.) gaseoso. **a. waters,** aguas gaseosas, *f pl*

**aeration** /,ɛə'reiʃən/ *n* aeración, *f*

**aerial** /'ɛəriəl/ *a* aéreo, de aire; etéreo; fantástico. —*n* (radio) antena, *f.* **indoor a.,** antena interior, *f*

**aerobics** /ɛə'roubɪks/ *n* aerobismo *m*

**aerodynamics** /,ɛəroudai'næmɪks/ *n* aerodinámica, *f*

**aeronaut** /'ɛərə,nɔt/ *n* aeronauta, *mf*

**aeronautical** /,ɛərə'nɔtɪkəl/ *a* aeronáutico

**aeronautics** /,ɛərə'nɔtɪks/ *n* aeronáutica, *f*

**afar** /ə'fɑr/ *adv* a lo lejos, en la distancia. **from a.,** desde lejos

**affability** /,æfə'bɪlɪti/ *n* afabilidad, condescendencia, urbanidad, *f*

**affable** /'æfəbəl/ *a* afable, condescendiente

**affably** /'æfəbli/ *adv* afablemente

**affair** /ə'fɛər/ *n* asunto, *m,* cosa, *f;* cuestión, *f;* (business) negocio, *m; (Fam.* applied to a machine, carriage, etc.) artefacto, *m;* (of the heart) amorío, *m.* **a. of honour,** lance de honor, *m*

**affect** /ə'fɛkt/ *vt* afectar; influir; *Med.* atacar; (move) impresionar, conmover; enternecer; (harm) perjudicar; (frequent) frecuentar; (like) gustar de; (love) amar; (wear) vestir; (use) gastar, usar; (feign) aparentar; (boast) hacer alarde de

**affectation** /,æfɛk'teiʃən/ *n* afectación, *f*

**affected** /ə'fɛktid/ *a* afectado; influido; *Med.* atacado; (moved) conmovido, impresionado; enternecido; (inclined) dispuesto, inclinado; (artificial) artificioso, amanerado, afectado; (of style) rebuscado, artificial

**affecting** /ə'fɛktɪŋ/ *a* conmovedor, emocionante

**affection** /ə'fɛkʃən/ *n* afecto, cariño, *m;* amor, *m;* apego, *m;* simpatía, *f;* (emotion) emoción, *f,* sentimiento, *m; Med.* afección, enfermedad, *f*

**affectionate** /ə'fɛkʃənɪt/ *a* afectuoso, cariñoso; mimoso; (tender) tierno; expresivo

**affectionately** /ə'fɛkʃənɪtli/ *adv* afectuosamente. **Yours a.,** tu cariñoso..., tu..., que te quiere

**affective** /'æfɛktɪv/ *a* afectivo

**affidavit** /,æfi'deivɪt/ *n* declaración jurada, declaración jurídica *f,* atestiguación, *f*

**affiliate** /ə'fɪli,eit/ *vt* afiliar; adoptar; *Law.* imputar; *Law.* legitimar

**affiliation** /ə,fɪli'eiʃən/ *n* afiliación, *f;* adopción, *f;* legitimación de un hijo, *f*

**affinity** /ə'fɪnɪti/ *n* afinidad, *f*

**affirm** /ə'fɜrm/ *vt* afirmar, aseverar, declarar; confirmar. —*vi Law.* declarar ante un juez

**affirmation** /,æfər'meiʃən/ *n* afirmación, aserción, *f;* confirmación, *f; Law.* declaración, deposición, *f*

**affirmative** /ə'fɜrmətɪv/ *a* afirmativo. —*n* afirmativa, *f*

**affix** /*v* ə'fɪks; *n* 'æfɪks/ *vt* fijar; pegar; añadir; (seal, one's signature) poner. —*n Gram.* afijo, *m*

**afflict** /ə'flɪkt/ *vt* afligir, atormentar, aquejar

**affliction** /ə'flɪkʃən/ *n* aflicción, *f;* tribulación, pesadumbre, *f;* calamidad, *f;* miseria, *f;* (ailment) achaque, *m*

**affluence** /'æfluəns/ *n* afluencia, *f;* abundancia, *f;* riqueza, *f;* opulencia, *f*

**affluent** /'æfluənt/ *a* abundante; rico; opulento

**afflux** /'æflʌks/ *n* afluencia, *f; Med.* aflujo, *m*

**afford** /ə'fɔrd/ *vt* dar, proporcionar; producir; ofrecer; (bear) soportar; poder con; (financially) tener medios para; permitirse el lujo de; (be able) poder. **I could not a. to pay so much,** No puedo (podía) pagar tanto

**afforest** /ə'fɔrɪst/ *vt* convertir en bosque

**afforestation** /ə,fɔrə'steiʃən/ *n* conversión en bosque, *f;* plantación de un bosque, *f*

**affray** /ə'frei/ *n* riña, refriega, *f*

**affront** /ə'frʌnt/ *n* afrenta, *f,* insulto, agravio, *m.* —*vt* insultar, ultrajar, afrentar; (offend) ofender

**Afghan** /'æfgæn/ *a* and *n* afgano (-na)

**Afghanistan** /æf'gænə,stæn/ Afganistán, *m*

**afield** /ə'fild/ *adv* en el campo; lejos. **to go far a.,** ir muy lejos

**afire** /ə'faiər/ *adv* en fuego, en llamas; *Fig.* ardiendo

**aflame** /ə'fleim/ *adv* en llamas; *Fig.* encendido

**afloat** /ə'flout/ *adv* a flote; *Naut.* a bordo; (solvent) solvente; en circulación; (floating) flotante; (swamped) inundado; (in full swing) en marcha, en movimiento

**afoot** /ə'fut/ *adv* a pie; en marcha, en movimiento; en preparación. **to set a.,** iniciar, poner en marcha

**aforementioned** /ə'fɔr,menʃənd/ *a* antedicho, ya mencionado

**aforesaid** /ə'fɔr,sɛd/ *a* consabido, dicho, susodicho

**afraid** /ə'freid/ *a* espantado; temeroso, miedoso. **I'm a. that...,** Me temo que.... **to be a.,** tener miedo. **to make a.,** dar miedo (a)

**afresh** /ə'freʃ/ *adv* de nuevo, otra vez

**African** /'æfrɪkən/ *a* and *n* africano (-na)

**aft** /æft/ *adv* en popa; a popa. **fore and aft,** de proa a popa

**after** /'æftər/ *prep* (of place) detrás de; (of time) después de; (behind) en pos de; (following) tras; (in spite of) a pesar de; (in consequence of) después de, a consecuencia de; (in accordance with) según; (in the style of) al estilo de, en imitación de. —*adv* (later) después, más tarde; (subsequently) después (que); (when) cuando. —*a* futuro, venidero. **day a. day,** día tras día. **on the day a.,** al día siguiente. **soon a.,** poco después. **to look a.,** cuidar de. **to go a.,** ir a buscar; seguir. **the day a. tomorrow,** pasado mañana. **What are you a.?** ¿Qué buscas? **a. all,** después de todo. **a. the manner of,** a la moda de, según la moda de; al estilo de. **a.-dinner conversation,** conversación de sobremesa, *f.* **a. glow,** resplandor crepuscular, reflejo del sol poniente en el cielo, *m.* **a. life,** vida futura, *f.* **a. pains,** dolores de sobreparto, *m pl.* **a. taste,** dejo, resabio, *m*

**afterbirth** /'æftər,bɜrθ/ *n* placenta, *f*

**aftermath** /'æftər,mæθ/ *n* consecuencias, *f pl,* resultado, *m*

**afternoon** /,æftər'nun/ *n* tarde, *f.* **Good a.!** ¡Buenas tardes! **a. nap,** siesta, *f.* **a. tea,** el té de las cinco

**afterthought** /'æftər,θɔt/ *n* reflexión tardía, *f;* segunda intención, *f.* **to have an a.,** pensar en segundo lugar

**afterwards** /'æftərwərdz/ *adv* después; más tarde

**again** /ə'gɛn/ *adv* (once more) otra vez, de neuvo; por segunda vez, dos veces; (on the other hand) por otra parte; (moreover) además; (likewise) también; (returned) de vuelta. Sometimes translated by prefix re in verbs. **as much a.,** otro tanto. **never a.,** nunca más. **not a.,** no más. **now and a.,** de vez en cuando.

**to do a.,** volver a hacer, hacer de nuevo. **a. and a.,** repetidas veces

**against** /ə'gɛnst/ *prep* (facing) enfrente de; contra; (in preparation for) para; (contrary to) contrario a; (opposed to) opuesto a; (near) cerca de. **to be a.,** oponer; estar enfrente de. **a. the grain,** a contrapelo

**agate** /'ægɪt/ *n* ágata, *f*; heliotropo, *m*

**age** /eidʒ/ *n* edad, *f*; (generation) generación, *f*; (epoch) siglo, período, *m*; época, *f*; (old age) vejez, *f*; (majority) mayoría de edad, *f*, *vi* envejecer. **at any age,** a cualquier edad. **the golden age,** la edad de oro; (in literature, etc.) el siglo de oro. **from age to age,** por los siglos de los siglos. **to be of age,** ser mayor de edad. **to be under age,** ser menor de edad. **to come of age,** llegar a la mayoría de edad. **She is six years of age,** Ella tiene seis años. **age-old,** secular

**aged** /eidʒd; 'eidʒɪd/ *a* de la edad de; (old) anciano, viejo. **a girl a. four,** una niña de cuatro años

**ageless** /'eidʒlɪs/ *a* siempre joven; eterno

**agency** /'eidʒənsi/ *n* órgano, *m*, fuerza, *f*; acción, *f*; influencia, *f*; intervención, *f*; mediación, *f*; *Com.* agencia, *f*. **through the a. of,** por la mediación (or influencia) de

**agenda** /ə'dʒɛndə/ *n* agenda, *f*

**agent** /'eidʒənt/ *n* agente, *m*; *Com.* representante, *mf*; *Law.* apoderado (-da). **business a.,** agente de negocios, *m*

**agglomerate** /ə'glɒmə,reit/ *vt* and *vi* aglomerar(se)

**agglomeration** /ə,glɒmə'reiʃən/ *n* aglomeración, *f*

**agglutinate** /ə'glutn̩,eit/ *vt* and *vi* aglutinar(se)

**aggrandize** /ə'grændaiz/ *vt* engrandecer

**aggrandizement** /ə'grændɪzmənt/ *n* engrandecimiento, *m*

**aggravate** /'ægrə,veit/ *vt* agravar, hacer peor; intensificar; (annoy) irritar, exasperar

**aggravating** /'ægrə,veitɪŋ/ *a* agravante, agravador; (tiresome) molesto; (annoying) irritante. **a. circumstance,** circunstancia agravante, *f*

**aggravation** /,ægrə'veiʃən/ *n* agravación, *f*, intensificación, *f*; (annoyance)irritación, *f*

**aggregate** /'ægrɪgɪt, -,geit/ *a* total. —*n* agregado, conjunto, *m*. **in the a.,** en conjunto

**aggression** /ə'grɛʃən/ *n* agresión, *f*

**aggressive** /ə'grɛsɪv/ *a* agresivo

**aggressiveness** /ə'grɛsɪvnɪs/ *n* carácter agresivo, *m*, belicosidad, *f*

**aggressor** /ə'grɛsər/ *a* and *n* agresor (-ra)

**aggrieved** /ə'grivd/ *a* afligido; ofendido; lastimero

**aghast** /ə'gæst/ *a* horrorizado, espantado; (amazed) estupefacto

**agile** /'ædʒəl/ *a* ágil; ligero; vivo

**agility** /æ'dʒɪlti/ *n* agilidad, *f*; ligereza, *f*

**agitate** /'ædʒɪ,teit/ *vt* agitar; excitar; inquietar, perturbar; discutir. **a. for,** luchar por; excitar la opinión pública en favor de

**agitating** /'ædʒɪ,teitɪŋ/ *a* agitador

**agitation** /,ædʒɪ'teiʃən/ *n* agitación, *f*; perturbación, *f*; discusión, *f*

**agitator** /'ædʒɪ,teitər/ *n* agitador (-ra); (apparatus) agitador, *m*

**aglow** /ə'glou/ *a* and *adv* brillante, fulgente; encendido

**agnostic** /æg'nɒstɪk/ *a* and *n* agnóstico (-ca)

**agnosticism** /æg'nɒstə,sɪzəm/ *n* agnosticismo, *m*

**ago** /ə'gou/ *adv* hace. **a short while ago,** hace poco. **How long ago?** ¿Cuánto tiempo hace? **long ago,** hace mucho. **many years ago,** hace muchos años. **I last saw him ten years ago,** La última vez que le vi fue hace diez años

**agog** /ə'gɒg/ *a* agitado; ansioso; excitado; impaciente; curioso. —*adv* con agitación; con ansia; con curiosidad

**agonize** /'ægə,naiz/ *vt* atormentar. —*vi* sufrir intensamente; retorcerse de dolor

**agonizing** /'ægə,naizɪŋ/ *a* (of pain) intenso, atormentador

**agonizingly** /'ægə,naizɪŋli/ *adv* dolorosamente

**agony** /'ægəni/ *n* agonía, *f*; angustia, *f*; paroxismo, *m*. **a. column,** columna de los suspiros, *f*

**agrarian** /ə'grɛəriən/ *a* agrario

**agree** /ə'gri/ *vi* estar de acuerdo. **Do you a. or disa-**

**gree?** ¿Coincides o discrepas?; convenir (en); acordar; ponerse de acuerdo, entenderse; (suit) sentar bien, probar; (consent) consentir (en); *Gram.* concordar, (get on well) llevarse bien; (correspond) estar conforme (con). **to a. to,** convenir en, consentir en. **to a. with,** estar de acuerdo con, apoyar; dar la razón a; (suit) sentar bien; *Gram.* concordar

**agreeable** /ə'griəbəl/ *a* agradable; afable, amable; (pleasant) ameno, grato; conforme; dispuesto a (hacer algo); conveniente

**agreeableness** /ə'griəbəlnɪs/ *n* (of persons) afabilidad, amabilidad, *f*; amenidad, *f*; deleite, *m*; conformidad, *f*

**agreeably** /ə'griəbli/ *adv* agradablemente; de acuerdo (con), conforme (a)

**agreed** /ə'grid/ *a* convenido, acordado; (approved) aprobado. —*interj* ¡convenido! ¡de acuerdo!

**agreement** /ə'grimənt/ *n* acuerdo, *m*; pacto, *m*; acomodamiento, concierto, *m*; contrato, *m*; *Com.* convenio, *m*; conformidad, *f*; consentimiento, *f*; *Gram.* concordancia, *f*. **in a.,** conforme. **in a. with,** de acuerdo con; según. **to reach an a.,** ponerse de acuerdo

**agricultural** /,ægrɪ'kʌltʃərəl/ *a* agrícola. **a. engineer,** ingeniero agrónomo, *m*. **a. laborer,** labriego, *m*. **a. show,** exposición agrícola, *f*

**agriculturalist** /,ægrɪ'kʌltʃərəlɪst/ *n* agrícola, *mf*

**agriculture** /'ægrɪ,kʌltʃər/ *n* agricultura, *f*

**agronomist** /ə'grɒnəmɪst/ *n* agrónomo, *m*

**agronomy** /ə'grɒnəmi/ *n* agronomía, *f*

**aground** /ə'graund/ *adv* *Naut.* varado, encallado. **running a.,** varada, *f*. **to run a.,** varar

**ague** /'eigyu/ *n* fiebre intermitente, *f*; *Fig.* escalofrío, *m*

**ah!** /ɑ/ *interj* ¡ah! ¡ay!

**aha!** /ɑ'hɑ/ *interj* ¡ajá!

**ahead** /ə'hɛd/ *adv* delante; enfrente; al frente (de); a la cabeza (de); adelante; hacia delante; *Naut.* por la proa. **Go a.!** ¡Adelante! **It is straight a.,** Está directamente enfrente. **to go straight a.,** ir hacia delante; seguir (haciendo algo)

**ahoy!** /ə'hɔi/ *interj* ¡ah del barco!

**aid** /eid/ *n* ayuda, *f*; socorro, auxilio, *m*; subsidio, *m*, *vt* ayudar; socorrer, auxiliar. **in aid of,** pro, en beneficio de. **first aid,** primera cura, *f*. **first aid post,** puesto de socorro, *m*. **to come or go to the aid of,** acudir en defensa de

**aide-de-camp** /'eid də 'kæmp/ *n* edecán, *m*

**AIDS** /eidz/ *n* el SIDA, *m*

**ail** /eil/ *vt* afligir, doler; pasar. —*vi* estar indispuesto (or enfermo). **What ails you?** *Inf.* ¿Qué te pasa?

**ailing** /'eilɪŋ/ *a* enfermizo, enclenque, achacoso

**ailment** /'eilmənt/ *n* enfermedad, *f*, achaque, *m*

**aim** /eim/ *n* (of firearms) puntería, *f*; (mark) blanco, *m*; *Fig.* objeto, fin, *m*; *Fig.* intención, *f*, propósito, *m*, *vt* (a gun) apuntar; dirigir; (throw) lanzar; (a blow) asestar. —*vi* apuntar (a); (a remark at) decir por; aspirar (a); intentar, proponerse. **Is your remark aimed at me?** ¿Lo dices por mí? **to aim high,** apuntar alto; *Inf.* picar alto. **to miss one's aim,** errar el tiro. **to take aim,** apuntar. **with the aim of,** con objeto de, a fin de

**aimless** /'eimlɪs/ *a* **aimlessly,** *adv* sin objeto, a la ventura

**air** /ɛər/ *n* aire, *m*, (all meanings). **by air,** en avión; (of mail) por avión; (of goods) por vía aérea. **in the air,** al aire; al aire libre; (as though flying) en volandas. **in the open air,** al aire libre, al fresco, a la intemperie. **to be on the air,** *Radio.* hablar por radio. **to give oneself airs,** darse tono, tener humos. **to take the air,** tomar el fresco; despegar. **air balloon,** globo aerostático, *m*; (toy) globo, *m*. **air-base,** base aérea, *f*. **air-bed,** colchón de viento, *m*. **air-borne (to become),** levantar el vuelo, despegar. **air-brake,** *Mech.* freno neumático, *m*. **air-chamber,** cámara de aire, *f*. **air chief marshal,** general del ejército del aire, *m*. **air-cock,** válvula de escape de aire, *f*. **air commodore,** general de brigada de aviación, *m*. **air conditioning,** purificación de aire, *f*. **air-cooled,** enfriado por aire. **air crash,** accidente de avicación, *m*. **air cur-**

rent, corriente de aire, f. **air-cushion,** almohadilla neumática, f. **air-field,** campo de aviación, m. **air fleet,** flotilla aérea, f. **air force,** fuerza aérea, flota aérea, f. **air-gun,** escopeta de viento, f. **air-hole,** respiradero, m. **air-hostess,** azafata, f. **air-lift,** puente aéreo, m. **air-liner,** avión de pasajeros, m. **airline** línea aérea, aerolínea, f. **airmail,** correo aéreo, m. **by airmail,** por avión. **air marshal,** teniente general de aviación, m. **air-pocket,** bolsa (or vacío, m) de aire, f. **air pollution** contaminación atmosférica, f. **air pump,** bomba neumática, f. **air raid,** bombardeo aéreo, m. **air-raid shelter,** refugio antiaéreo, m. **air-raid warning,** alarma aérea, f. **air-route,** vía aérea, f. **air-screw,** hélice de avión, f. **air-shaft,** respiradero de mina, m. **air shuttle,** puente aéreo, m. **air squadron,** escuadrilla aérea, f. **air stream,** chorro de aire, m. **air taxi,** avión taxi, m. **air-tight,** herméticamente cerrado. **air valve,** válvula de aire, f. **air vice-marshal,** general de división de aviación, m

**air** /ɛər/ vt airear, orear; secar al aire; ventilar; *Fig.* sacar a lucir, emitir; *Fig.* ostentar

**aircraft** /'ɛər,kræft/ n aparato, avión, m. **a. barrage,** cortina de fuego de artillería, f. **a.-carrier,** porta-aviones, m. **a. factory,** fábrica de aeroplanos, f

**airily** /'ɛərəli/ adv ligeramente, sin preocuparse; alegremente

**airiness** /'ɛərinɪs/ n airosidad, f; ventilación, f; situación airosa, f; (lightness) ligereza, f; alegría, f; frivolidad, f

**airing** /'ɛərɪŋ/ n aireación, f; ventilación, f; secamiento, m; (walk) vuelta, f, paseo, m. **to take an a.,** dar una vuelta

**airless** /'ɛərlɪs/ a sin aire; falto de ventilación; sofocante

**airman** /'ɛərmən/ n aviador, m

**airplane** /'ɛər,pleɪn/ n aeroplano, avión, m. **jet-propelled a.,** aeroplano de reacción, m. **model a.,** aeroplano en miniatura, m

**airport** /'ɛər,pɔrt/ n aeropuerto, m

**airship** /'ɛər,ʃɪp/ n aeronave, nave aérea, f

**airsick** /'ɛər,sɪk/ a mareado en el aire, mareado

**airway** /'ɛər,weɪ/ n vía aérea, f

**airwoman** /'ɛər,wumən/ n aviadora, f

**airy** /'ɛəri/ a aéreo; (breezy) airoso; ligero; vaporoso; alegre; (vain) vano; (flippant) frívolo

**aisle** /aɪl/ n nave lateral, ala, f

**ajar** /ə'dʒɑr/ a entreabierto, entornado. **to leave a.,** dejar entreabierto, entornar

**akimbo** /ə'kɪmboʊ/ adv en jarras. **with arms a.,** con los brazos en jarras

**akin** /ə'kɪn/ a consanguíneo, emparentado; análogo, relacionado; semejante

**alabaster** /'ælə,bæstər/ n alabastro, m, a alabastrino

**alacrity** /ə'lækrɪti/ n alacridad, f

**alarm** /ə'lɑrm/ n alarma, f, toque de alarma, m; (tocsin) rebato, m; sobresalto, m, alarma, f. —vt alarmar; *Mil.* dar la alarma (a); asustar. **to give the a.,** dar la alarma. **a. bell,** timbre de alarma, m. **a. clock,** despertador, m. **a. signal,** señal de alarma, f

**alarming** /ə'lɑrmɪŋ/ a alarmante

**alarmingly** /ə'lɑrmɪŋli/ adv de un modo alarmante; espantosamente

**alarmist** /ə'lɑrmɪst/ n alarmista, mf

**alas!** /ə'læs/ interj ¡ay!

**alb** /ælb/ n alba, f

**Albanian** /æl'beɪniən/ a and n albanés (-esa); (language) albanés, m

**albatross** /'ælbə,trɔs/ n albatros, m

**albeit** /ɔl'biɪt/ conjunc aunque, si bien; sin embargo

**albinism** /'ælbə,nɪzəm/ n albinismo, m

**albino** /æl'baɪnoʊ/ a albino

**album** /'ælbəm/ n álbum, m

**albumin** /æl'byumən/ n albúmina, f

**alchemist** /'ælkəmɪst/ n alquimista, m

**alchemy** /'ælkəmi/ n alquimia, f

**alcohol** /'ælkə,hɔl/ n alcohol, m. **industrial a.,** alcohol desnaturalizado, m. **wood a.,** alcohol metílico, alcohol de madera, m

**alcoholic** /,ælkə'hɔlɪk/ a alcohólico

**alcoholism** /'ælkəhɔ,lɪzəm/ n alcoholismo, m

**alcove** /'ælkouv/ n alcoba, f; nicho, m

**alder** /'ɔldər/ n (tree and wood) aliso, m

**alderman** /'ɔldərmən/ n concejal, m

**ale** /eɪl/ n cerveza, f. **ale-house,** cervecería, f

**alert** /ə'lɜrt/ a alerto; vigilante; despierto; vivo. —n sirena, f. **to be on the a.,** estar sobre aviso; estar vigilante

**alertly** /ə'lɜrtli/ adv alertamente

**alertness** /ə'lɜrtnɪs/ n vigilancia, f; viveza, f; prontitud, f

**Alexandria** /,ælɪg'zændriə/ Alejandría, f

**alga** /'ælgə/ n alga, f

**algebra** /'ældʒəbrə/ n álgebra, f

**algebraic** /,ældʒə'breɪk/ a algebraico

**Algeria** /æl'dʒɪəriə/ Argelia, f

**Algerian** /æl'dʒɪəriən/ a and n argelino (-na)

**Algiers** /æl'dʒɪərz/ Argel, m

**alias** /'eɪliəs/ adv alias, por otro nombre. —n nombre falso, seudónimo, m

**alibi** /'ælə,baɪ/ n *Law.* coartada, f. **to prove an a.,** probar la coartada

**alien** /'eɪliən/ a ajeno; (foreign) extranjero; extraño; contrario. —n extranjero (-ra). **a. to,** ajeno a; repugnante a. **Aliens Department,** Sección de Extranjeros, f

**alienable** /'eɪliənəbəl/ a enajenable

**alienate** /'eɪliə,neɪt/ vt alejar, hacer indiferente; (property) enajenar, traspasar

**alienation** /,eɪliə'neɪʃən/ n desvío, m; enajenación, f; traspaso, m; enajenación mental, f

**alight** /ə'laɪt/ vi apearse (de), bajar (de); desmontar (de); (of birds, etc.) posarse (sobre)

**alight** /ə'laɪt/ a encendido, iluminado; en llamas

**align** /ə'laɪn/ vt alinear

**alignment** /ə'laɪnmənt/ n alineación, f

**alike** /ə'laɪk/ a semejante; igual. —adv del mismo modo; igualmente

**alimentary** /,ælə'mɛntəri/ a nutritivo; alimenticio. **a. canal,** tubo digestivo, m

**alimentation** /,æləmən'teɪʃən/ n alimentación, f

**alimony** /'ælə,mouni/ n *Law.* alimentos, m pl, pensión alimenticia, f

**alive** /ə'laɪv/ a viviente; vivo; del mundo; (busy) animado, concurrido; (aware) sensible; (alert) lleno de vida, enérgico, despierto. **He is still a.,** Aún vive. **He is the best man a.,** Es el mejor hombre que existe, Es el mejor hombre del mundo. **half-a.,** semivivo. **while a.,** en vida. **a. to,** consciente de, sensible de. **a. with,** plagado de, lleno de

**alkali** /'ælkə,laɪ/ n álcali, m

**alkaline** /'ælkə,laɪn/ a alcalino

**alkaloid** /'ælkə,lɔɪd/ n alcaloide, m

**all** /ɔl/ a todo, m; toda, f; todos, m pl; todas, f pl; (in games) iguales. —adv enteramente, completamente; del todo; absolutamente. **after all,** después de todo; sin embargo. **at all,** nada; de ninguna manera; en absoluto. **fifteen all,** (tennis) quince iguales. **for good and all,** para siempre. **if that's all,** si no es más que eso. **in all,** en conjunto. **It is all one to me,** Me da igual. **not at all,** de ningún modo, nada de eso; nada; (never) jamás; (as a polite formula) No hay de qué. **once for all,** una vez por todas; por última vez. **That is all,** Eso es todo. **all along,** (of time) siempre, todo el tiempo; (of place) a lo largo de, de un extremo a otro de. **all but,** (almost) casi, por poco; (except) todo menos. **all joking aside,** fuera de burla. **all of them,** todos ellos, m pl; todas ellas, f pl. **All right!** ¡Bien! ¡Está bien! ¡Entendido! **all that,** todo eso; (as much as) cuanto. **all that which,** todo lo que. **all those who,** todos los que, m pl; todas las que, f pl. **all the more,** cuanto más. **all the same,** sin embargo, a pesar de todo. **all the worse,** tanto peor

**all** /ɔl/ n todo, m; todos, m pl; todas, f pl; (everyone, all men) todo el mundo. **to lose one's all,** perder todo lo que se tiene. **All is lost,** Todo se ha perdido. **all told,** en conjunto

**all** /ɔl/ (in compounds) **all-absorbing,** que todo lo absorbe; sumamente interesante. **all-bountiful,** de suma bondad. **all-conquering,** invicto. **all-consuming,** que todo lo consume; irresistible; ardiente. **all-enduring,** resignado a todo. **All Fools' Day,** Día de los Inocentes, m, (December 28). **all-fours,** a cuatro patas; a gatas. **to go on all fours,** andar a gatas. **All hail!** ¡Salud! ¡Bienvenido! **all-important,** sumamente importante. **all-in insurance,** seguro contra todo riesgo, *m.* **all-in wrestling,** lucha libre, *f.* **all-loving,** de un amor infinito. **all-merciful,** de una compasión infinita, sumamente misericordioso. **all-powerful,** omnipotente, todo poderoso. **all-round,** completo, cabal; universal. **an all-round athlete,** un atleta completo. **All Souls' Day,** Día de las Ánimas, Día de los difuntos, *m.* **all-wise,** omniscio

**Allah** /'ælə/ *n* Alá, *m*

**allay** /ə'lei/ *vt* calmar; (relieve) aliviar; apaciguar

**allaying** /ə'leiiŋ/ *n* alivio, *m;* apaciguamiento, *m*

**allegation** /,ælɪ'geiʃən/ *n* alegación, *f*

**allege** /ə'ledʒ/ *vt* afirmar, declarar; alegar

**allegiance** /ə'lidʒəns/ *n* lealtad, *f;* fidelidad, *f;* obediencia, *f*

**allegorical** /,ælɪ'gɒrɪkəl/ *a* alegórico

**allegory** /'ælə,gɒri/ *n* alegoría, *f*

**alleluia** /,ælə'luyə/ *n* aleluya, *mf*

**allergic** /ə'lɜrdʒɪk/ *a* alérgico

**allergist** /'ælərdʒɪst/ *n* alergólogo, *m*

**allergy** /'ælərdʒi/ *n* alergia, *f*

**alleviate** /ə'livi,eit/ *vt* aliviar

**alleviation** /ə,livi'eiʃən/ *n* alivio, *m;* mitigación, *f*

**alley** /'æli/ *n* callejuela, *f,* callejón, *m;* avenida, *f;* (skittle a.) pista de bolos, *f.* **a.-way,** *Naut.* pasadizo, *m*

**alliance** /ə'laiəns/ *n* alianza, *f;* parentesco, *m*

**allied** /'ælaid/ *a* aliado; aliado

**alligator** /'ælɪ,geitər/ *n* caimán, *m.* **a. pear,** avocado, *m*

**alliteration** /ə,lɪtə'reiʃən/ *n* aliteración, *f*

**allocate** /'ælə,keit/ *vt* asignar, destinar; distribuir, repartir

**allocation** /,ælə'keiʃən/ *n* asignación, *f;* distribución, *f,* repartimiento, *m*

**allotment** /ə'lɒtmənt/ *n* repartimiento, *m,* distribución, *f;* porción, *f;* lote, *m;* parcela de tierra, huerta, *f*

**allow** /ə'lau/ *vt* permitir; autorizar; dejar; tolerar, sufrir; (provide) dar; conceder, otorgar; (acknowledge) admitir; confesar; (discount) descontar; (a pension) hacer; deducir. **to a. for,** tener en cuenta; ser indulgente con; deducir; dejar (espacio, etc.) para

**allowable** /ə'lauəbəl/ *a* admisible, permisible; lícito, legítimo

**allowance** /ə'lauəns/ *n* ración, *f;* (discount) descuento, *m;* pensión, *f;* concesión, *f;* excusa, *f;* (subsidy) subsidio, *m;* (bonus) abono, *m;* (monthly) mesada, *f.* **to make a. for,** tener presente; hacer excusas para, ser indulgente con

**alloy** /*n* 'ælɔi, *v* ə'lɔi/ *n* aleación, *f;* liga, *f;* mezcla, *f.* —*vt* alear, ligar; mezclar

**allspice** /'ɔl,spais/ *n* guindilla de Indias, *f*

**all-star game** /'ɔl,star/ *n* juego de estrellas, *m*

**allude** /ə'lud/ *vi* aludir (a), referirse (a)

**allure** /ə'lʊr/ *vt* convidar, provocar; atraer; seducir, fascinar

**allurement** /ə'lʊrmənt/ *n* (snare) añagaza, *f;* atracción, *f;* tentación, seducción, *f*

**alluring** /ə'lʊrɪŋ/ *a* atractivo, seductor, tentador; (promising) halagüeño

**allusion** /ə'luʒən/ *n* alusión, referencia, *f;* insinuación, *f*

**allusive** /ə'lusɪv/ *a* alusivo

**ally** /*n* 'ælai, *v* ə'lai/ *n* aliado (-da), allegado (-da); asociado (-da); (state) aliado, *m.* —*vt* unir. **to become allies,** aliarse

**almanac** /'ɔlmə,næk/ *n* almanaque, *m*

**almighty** /ɔl'maiti/ *a* omnipotente

**almond** /'amənd/ *n* almendra, *f;* (tree) almendro, *m.* **bitter a.,** almendra amarga, *f.* **green a.,** almendruco, *m.* **milk of almonds,** horchata de almendras, *f;* (for the hands) loción de almendras, *f.* **sugar a.,** almendra garapiñada, *f.* **a.-eyed,** con, or de, ojos rasgados. **a. paste,** pasta de almendras, *f.* **a.-shaped,** en forma de almendra, almendrado

**almost** /'ɔlmoust/ *adv* casi; por poco

**alms** /amz/ *n* limosna, *f.* **to ask a.,** pedir limosna, mendigar. **to give a.,** dar limosna. **a.-box,** cepillo de limosna, *m*

**almsgiving** /'amz,gɪvɪŋ/ *n* caridad, *f*

**aloe** /'ælou/ *n* áloe, *m; pl* **aloes,** *Med.* acíbar, *m*

**aloft** /ə'lɔft/ *adv* arriba, en alto

**alone** /ə'loun/ *a* solo; solitario. —*adv* a solas, sin compañía; solamente; únicamente. **to leave a.,** dejar solo; dejar en paz

**along** /ə'lɔŋ/ *adv* adelante; a lo largo; todo el tiempo. —*prep* a lo largo de; por; al lado (de); en compañía (de). **Come a.!** ¡Ven! **all a.,** todo el tiempo, desde el principio; a lo largo de. **a. with,** junto con; en compañía de

**alongside** /ə'lɔŋ'said/ *adv* al lado; *Naut.* al costado. —*prep* junto a, al lado de; *Naut.* al costado de. **to bring a.,** *Naut.* abarloar. **to come a.,** *Naut.* acostarse

**aloof** /ə'luf/ *adv* a distancia; lejos. —*a* altanero, esquivo; reservado. **to keep a.,** mantenerse alejado

**aloofness** /ə'lufnɪs/ *n* alejamiento, *m;* esquivez, *f;* reserva, *f*

**aloud** /ə'laud/ *adv* en alta voz, alto

**alpaca** /æl'pækə/ *n* alpaca, *f*

**alphabet** /'ælfə,bet/ *n* alfabeto, *m;* abecedario, *m*

**alphabetical** /,ælfə'betɪkəl/ *a* alfabético

**Alpine** /'ælpain/ *a* alpestre, alpino

**Alps, the** /ælps/ los Alpes, *m*

**already** /ɔl'redi/ *adv* ya; previamente

**Alsace** /æl'sæs, -'seis/ Alsacia, *f*

**Alsatian** /æl'seiʃən/ *a* and *n* alsaciano (-na†). **A. dog,** perro policía, perro pastor alemán, perro lobo, *m*

**also** /'ɔlsou/ *adv* también, igualmente, además

**altar** /'ɔltər/ *n* altar, *m.* **high a.,** altar mayor, *m.* **to lead a woman to the a.,** llevar a una mujer a la iglesia. **a.-cloth,** mantel del altar, *m.* **a.-piece,** retablo, *m.* **a.-rail,** mesa del altar, *f*

**altar boy** *n* acólito, monaguillo, *m*

**altar girl** *n* acólita, monaguilla, *f*

**altar server** *n* acólito, monaguillo, *m* (male), acólita, monaguilla, *f* (female)

**alter** /'ɔltər/ *vt* cambiar; alterar; modificar; corregir; transformar; (clothes) arreglar. —*vi* cambiar

**alterable** /'ɔltərəbəl/ *a* alterable

**alteration** /,ɔltə'reiʃən/ *n* cambio, *m,* alteración, *f;* modificación, *f;* corrección, *f;* innovación, *f;* (to buildings, etc.) reforma, *f;* renovación, *f;* arreglo, *m*

**altercation** /,ɔltər'keiʃən/ *n* altercación, *f*

**alternate** /*a* 'ɔltərnɪt; *v* -,neit/ *a* alternativo; (*Bot.* and of rhymes) alterno. —*vt* and *vi* alternar

**alternately** /'ɔltərnɪtli/ *adv* alternativamente; por turno

**alternating** /'ɔltər,neitɪŋ/ *a* alternador. **a. current,** *Elec.* corriente alterna, *f*

**alternation** /,ɔltər'neiʃən/ *n* alternación, *f;* (of time) transcurso, *m;* turno, *m*

**alternative** /ɔl'tɜrnətɪv/ *n* alternativa, *f,* a alternativo, alterno. **to have no a. but,** no poder menos de

**alternatively** /ɔl'tɜrnətɪvli/ *adv* alternativamente

**alternative medicine** /ɔl'tɜrnətɪv 'mɛdəsɪn/ *n* medicina alternativa, *f*

**alternator** /'ɔltər,neitər/ *n Elec.* alternador, *m*

**although** /ɔl'ðou/ *conjunc* aunque, bien que; si bien; no obstante, a pesar de

**altimeter** /æl'tɪmɪtər/ *n Aer.* altímetro, *m*

**altitude** /'æltɪ,tud/ *n* altitud, elevación, *f;* altura, *f*

**alto** /'æltou/ *n* (voice) contralto, *m;* (singer) contralto, *mf;* viola, *f*

**altogether** /,ɔltə'geðər/ *adv* completamente; del todo; en conjunto

**altruism** /'æltru,izəm/ *n* altruismo, *m*

**altruist** /'æltruist/ *n* altruista, *mf*

**aluminum** /ə'lumənəm/ *n* aluminio, *m*

**aluminum foil** *n* hoja de aluminio, *f*

**always** /'ɔlweiz/ *adv* siempre

**amalgam** /ə'mælgəm/ *n* amalgama, *f;* mezcla, *f*

**amalgamate** /ə'mælgə,meit/ *vt* amalgamar; combinar, unir. —*vi* amalgamarse; combinarse, unirse

**amalgamation** /ə,mælgə'meiʃən/ *n* amalgamación, *f;* combinación, *f;* mezcla, *f*

**amanuensis** /ə,mænyu'ɛnsɪs/ *n* amanuense, *mf;* secretario (-ia)

**amass** /ə'mæs/ *vt* acumular, amontonar

**amateur** /'æmə,tʃʊr/ *a* and *n* aficionado (-da), (sports) no profesional. **a. theatricals,** función de aficionados, *f*

**amateurish** /ˈæmə͵tʃʊrɪʃ/ a no profesional; de aficionado; superficial; (clumsy) torpe

**amatory** /ˈæmə͵tɔri/ a amatorio

**amaze** /əˈmeiz/ vt asombrar, sorprender; pasmar; confundir

**amazed** /əˈmeizd/ a asombrado; sorprendido; admirado; asustado

**amazement** /əˈmeizmənt/ n asombro, pasmo, m; sorpresa, f; (wonderment) admiración, f; estupor, m

**amazing** /əˈmeizɪŋ/ a asombroso, pasmoso; sorprendente

**amazingly** /əˈmeizɪŋli/ adv asombrosamente

**Amazon** /ˈæmə͵zɒn/ n amazona, f

**Amazon River, the** el (Río de las) Amazonas, m

**ambassador** /æmˈbæsədər/ n embajador, m

**ambassadress** /æmˈbæsədrɪs/ n embajadora, f

**amber** /ˈæmbər/ n ámbar, m, a ambarino

**ambergris** /ˈæmbər͵gris/ n ámbar gris, m

**ambidextrous** /͵æmbɪˈdɛkstrəs/ a ambidextro

**ambiguity** /͵æmbɪˈgyuɪti/ n ambigüedad, f

**ambiguous** /æmˈbɪgyuəs/ a ambiguo, equívoco

**ambition** /æmˈbɪʃən/ n ambición, f

**ambitious** /æmˈbɪʃəs/ a ambicioso. **to be a. to,** ambicionar

**amble** /ˈæmbəl/ n (of a horse) paso de andadura, m; paso lento, m. —vi (of a horse) andar a paso de andadura; andar lentamente

**ambulance** /ˈæmbyələns/ n ambulancia, f. **a. corps,** cuerpo de sanidad, m. **a. man,** sanitario, m

**ambulatory** /ˈæmbyələ͵tɔri/ n paseo, m; claustro, m, a ambulante

**ambush** /ˈæmbʊʃ/ n acecho, m, asechanza, f; Mil. emboscada, f. —vt acechar, asechar; Mil. emboscar; sorprender. **to be in a.,** emboscarse, estar en acecho

**ameba** /əˈmibə/ n amiba, f

**amelioration** /ə͵milyəˈreiʃən/ n mejora, f

**amen** /ˈɛiˈmɛn, ˈɑˈmɛn/ n amén, m

**amenable** /əˈminəbəl/ a sujeto (a); responsable; dócil; fácil de convencer, dispuesto a ser razonable; dispuesto a escuchar. **to make a. to reason,** hacer razonable

**amend** /əˈmɛnd/ vt enmendar; modificar. —vi reformarse

**amendment** /əˈmɛndmənt/ n enmienda, f; modificación, f

**amends** /əˈmɛndz/ n pl reparación, f; satisfacción, f; compensación, f. **to make a.,** dar satisfacción

**amenity** /əˈmɛnɪti/ n amenidad, f

**America** /əˈmɛrɪkə/ América, f

**American** /əˈmɛrɪkən/ n americano (-na); (U.S.A.) norteamericano (-na). —a americano, de América; norteamericano, de los Estados Unidos. **Central A.,** a and n centroamericano (-na). **A. bar,** bar americano, m

**Americanism** /əˈmɛrɪkə͵nɪzəm/ n americanismo, m

**Americanize** /əˈmɛrɪkə͵naiz/ vt americanizar

**amethyst** /ˈæməθɪst/ n amatista, f

**amiability** /͵eimiəˈbɪlɪti/ n amabilidad, afabilidad, cordialidad, f

**amiable** /ˈeimiəbəl/ a amable, afable, cordial

**amiably** /ˈeimiəbli/ adv amablemente, con afabilidad

**amicable** /ˈæmɪkəbəl/ a amigable, amistoso

**amicably** /ˈæmɪkəbli/ adv amigablemente

**amice** /ˈæmɪs/ n amito, m

**amid, amidst** /əˈmɪd; əˈmɪdst/ prep en medio de; entre; rodeado por

**amidships** /əˈmɪd͵ʃɪps/ adv en el centro del buque, en medio del navío

**amiss** /əˈmɪs/ adv mal; de más; (ill) indispuesto, enfermo; (inopportunely) inoportunamente. —a malo. **It would not come a.,** No vendría mal. **to take a.,** llevar a mal

**ammeter** /ˈæm͵mitər/ n Elec. amperímetro, m

**ammonia** /əˈmounyə/ n amoníaco, m

**ammunition** /͵æmyəˈnɪʃən/ n munición, f. **a. box,** cajón de municiones, m

**amnesia** /æmˈniʒə/ n amnesia, f

**amnesty** /ˈæmnɛsti/ n amnistía, f. **to concede an a. to,** amnistiar

**amok** /əˈmʌk/ **(to run a.)** atacar a ciegas

**among** /əˈmʌŋ/ prep en medio de; entre; con

**amoral** /eiˈmɔrəl/ a amoral

**amorality** /͵eimɔˈrælɪti/ n amoralidad, f

**amorous** /ˈæmərəs/ a amoroso; (tender) tierno

**amorousness** /ˈæmərəsnɪs/ n erotismo, m; galantería, f

**amorphous** /əˈmɔrfəs/ a amorfo

**amortization** /͵æmərtəˈzeiʃən/ n amorcización, f

**amortize** /ˈæmər͵taiz/ vt amortizar

**amount** /əˈmaunt/ n importe, m, suma, f; cantidad, f, vi (to) subir a, ascender a, llegar a; valer; reducirse a. **gross a.,** importe bruto, m. **net a.,** importe líquido, importe neto, m. **It amounts to the same thing, then,** Es igual entonces, Viene a ser lo mismo pues. **What he says amounts to this,** Lo que dice se reduce a esto

**amperage** /ˈæmpərɪdʒ/ n amperaje, m

**ampere** /ˈæmpɪər/ n amper, amperio, m

**amphibian** /æmˈfɪbiən/ n anfibio, m

**amphibious** /æmˈfɪbiəs/ a anfibio

**amphitheater** /ˈæmfə͵θiətər/ n anfiteatro, m

**amphora** /ˈæmfərə/ n ánfora, f

**ample** /ˈæmpəl/ a amplio; abundante; extenso, vasto; (sufficient) bastante, suficiente

**amplification** /͵æmpləfɪˈkeiʃən/ n amplificación, f

**amplifier** /ˈæmplə͵faiər/ n amplificador, m

**amplify** /ˈæmplə͵fai/ vt amplificar; aumentar, ampliar

**amplitude** /ˈæmplɪ͵tud/ n amplitud, f; abundancia, f; extensión, f

**amply** /ˈæmpli/ adv ampliamente; abundantemente; suficientemente

**amputate** /ˈæmpyʊ͵teit/ vt amputar

**amputation** /͵æmpyʊˈteiʃən/ n amputación, f

**amulet** /ˈæmyəlɪt/ n amuleto, m

**amuse** /əˈmyuz/ vt divertir, entretener, distraer. **to a. oneself,** divertirse; pasarlo bien

**amusement** /əˈmyuzmənt/ n diversión, f, entretenimiento, m; (hobby) pasatiempo, m. **a. park,** parque de atracciones, m

**amusing** /əˈmyuzɪŋ/ a divertido, entretenido; (of people) salado

**amusingly** /əˈmyuzɪŋli/ adv de un modo divertido, entretenidamente

**an** /ən/ See **a**

**Anabaptist** /͵ænəˈbæptɪst/ n anabaptista, mf

**anachronism** /əˈnækrə͵nɪzəm/ n anacronismo, m

**anachronistic** /ə͵nækrəˈnɪstɪk/ a anacrónico

**anagram** /ˈænə͵græm/ n anagrama, m

**analects** /ˈænl͵ɛkts/ n pl analectas, f pl

**analgesia** /͵ænlˈdʒiziə/ n analgesia, f

**analgesic** /͵ænlˈdʒizɪk/ a and n analgésico, m.

**analogous** /əˈnæləgəs/ a análogo

**analogy** /əˈnælədʒi/ n analogía, f

**analysis** /əˈnæləsɪs/ n análisis, m

**analyst** /ˈænlɪst/ n analista, mf

**analytical** /͵ænlˈɪtɪkəl/ a analítico

**analyze** /ˈænl͵aiz/ vt analizar

**anaphora** /əˈnæfərə/ n anáfora, f

**anarchic** /ænˈɑrkɪk/ a anárquico

**anarchism** /ˈænər͵kɪzəm/ n anarquismo, m

**anarchist** /ˈænərkɪst/ n anarquista, mf

**anarchy** /ˈænərki/ n anarquía, f

**anastigmatic** /͵ænəstɪgˈmætɪk/ a anastigmático

**anathema** /əˈnæθəmə/ n anatema, mf

**anathematize** /əˈnæθəmə͵taiz/ vt anatematizar

**anatomic** /͵ænəˈtɒmɪk/ a anatómico

**anatomically** /͵ænəˈtɒmɪkli/ adv anatómicamente; físicamente

**anatomist** /əˈnætəmɪst/ n anatomista, mf

**anatomy** /əˈnætəmi/ n anatomía, f

**ancestor** /ˈænsɛstər/ n antepasado, abuelo, m

**ancestral** /ænˈsɛstrəl/ a de sus antepasados; de familia; hereditario. **a. home,** casa solariega, f

**ancestry** /ˈænsɛstri/ n antepasados, m pl; linaje, abolengo, m; estirpe, f; nacimiento, m; origen, m

**anchor** /ˈæŋkər/ n ancla, f. Fig. áncora, f. —vt sujetar con el ancla. —vi anclar, echar anclas, fondear. **at a.,** al ancla. **drag a.,** ancla flotante, ancla de arrastre, f. **sheet a.,** ancla de la esperanza, f; Fig. ancla de salvación, f. **to drop a.,** anclar. **to ride at a.,** estar al ancla. **to weigh a.,** levar el ancla

**anchorage** /'æŋkərɪdʒ/ *n* anclaje, *m*; anclaje, fondeadero, *m*; derechos de anclaje, *m pl*

**anchorite** /'æŋkə,rait/ *n* anacoreta, *mf*

**anchovy** /'æntʃouvi/ *n* anchoa, *f*, boquerón, *m*

**ancient** /'einʃənt/ *a* anciano; antiguo. —*n pl* **ancients,** los antiguos. **from a. times,** de antiguo. **most a.,** antiquísimo

**and** /ænd, ənd/ *conjunc* y; (before stressed i or hi) e; (after some verbs and before infin.) de, a; que; (with) con; (often not translated before infins.). **Better and better,** Mejor que mejor. **I shall try and do it,** Trataré de hacerlo. **to come and see,** venir a ver. **We shall try and speak to him,** Procuraremos hablar con él

**Andalusia** /,ændl'uʒə/ Andalucía, *f*

**Andalusian** /,ændl'uʒən/ *a* andaluz. —*n* andaluz (-za). **A. hat,** sombrero calañés, *m*

**Andean** /'ændiən/ *a* andino

**Andes, the** /'ændiz/ los Andes, *f*

**andiron** /'ænd,aiⁿrn/ *n* morillo, *m*

**androgynous** /æn'drɒdʒənəs/ *a* andrógino

**anecdotal** /'ænɪk,doutl/ *a* anecdótico

**anecdote** /'ænɪk,dout/ *n* anécdota, *f*

**anemia** /ə'nimiə/ *n* anemia, *f*

**anemic** /ə'nimɪk/ *a* anémico

**anemometer** /,ænə'mɒmɪtər/ *n* anemómetro, *m*

**anemone** /ə'nɛmə,ni/ *n* anémona, anémone, *f*

**aneroid** /'ænə,rɔid/ *a* aneroide. —*n* barómetro aneroide, *m*

**anesthesia** /,ænəs'θiʒə/ *n* anestesia, *f*

**anesthetic** /,ænəs'θɛtɪk/ *a* and *n* acólito, monaguillo, *m*

**anesthetist** /ə'nɛsθɪtɪst/ *n* anestesiador (-ra)

**anesthetize** /ə'nɛsθɪ,taiz/ *vt* anestesiar

**aneurism** /'ænyə,rɪzəm/ *n* aneurisma, *mf*

**angel** /'eindʒəl/ *n* ángel, *m*

**angelic** /æn'dʒɛlɪk/ *a* angélico

**angelica** /æn'dʒɛlɪkə/ *n* angélica, *f*

**angelus** /'ændʒələs/ *n* ángelus, *m*

**anger** /'æŋgər/ *n* cólera, ira, *f*, enojo, *m*, *vt* enojar, encolerizar; hacer rabiar

**angina** /æn'dʒainə/ *n* angina, *f*. **a. pectoris,** angina de pecho, *f*

**angle** /'æŋgəl/ *n* ángulo, *m*; rincón, *m*; esquina, *f*; (of a roof) caballette, *m*; *Fig.* punto de vista, *m*, *vi* pescar con caña. **at an a.,** a un lado. **a.-iron,** hierro angular, *m*. **to a. for,** pescar; *Fig.* procurar obtener

**Angle** /'æŋgəl/ *a* and *n* anglo (-la)

**angler** /'æŋglər/ *n* pescador (-ra) de caña

**Anglican** /'æŋglɪkən/ *a* and *n* anglicano (-na)

**Anglicanism** /'æŋglɪkə,nɪzəm/ *n* anglicanismo, *m*

**Anglicism** /'æŋglə,sɪzəm/ *n* anglicismo, inglesismo, *m*

**Anglicize** /'æŋglə,saiz/ *vt* inglesar

**angling** /'æŋglɪŋ/ *n* pesca con caña, *f*

**Anglo-** (in compounds) anglo-. **A.-American,** *a* and *n* angloamericano (-na). **A.-Indian,** *a* and *n* angloindio (-ia). **A.-Saxon,** *a* and *n* anglosajón (-ona); (language) anglosajón, *m*

**anglomania** /,æŋglə'meiniə/ *n* anglomanía, *f*

**anglophile** /'æŋglə,fail/ *n* anglófilo (-la)

**anglophobia** /,æŋglə'foubiə/ *n* anglofobia, *f*

**angora** /æŋ'gɔrə/ *n* angora, *f*. **a. cat,** gato de angora, *m*. **a. rabbit,** conejo de angora, *m*

**angrily** /'æŋgrəli/ *adv* airadamente

**angry** /'æŋgri/ *a* (of persons) enfadado, enojado, airado; (of waves, etc.) furioso; *Med.* inflamado; (red) rojo; (scowling) cenudo; (dark) obscuro. **to be a.,** estar enojado. **to grow a.,** enojarse, enfadarse; (of waves) encresparse; (of the sky) obscurecerse. **to make a.,** enojar

**anguish** /'æŋgwɪʃ/ *n* agonía, *f*, dolor, *m*; angustia, *f*. —*vt* angustiar

**angular** /'æŋgyələr/ *a* angular; (of features, etc.) anguloso

**angularity** /,æŋgyə'lærɪti/ *n* angulosidad, *f*

**anhydrous** /æn'haidrəs/ *a* anhidro

**aniline** /'ænlɪn/ *n* anilina, *f*

**animal** /'ænəməl/ *a* and *n* animal *m*. **a. fat,** grasa animal, *f*. **a. kingdom,** reino animal, *m*. **a. spirits,** *Philos.* espíritus animales, *m pl*; brío, *m*, energía, *f*

**animalism** /'ænəmə,lɪzəm/ *n* animalidad, *f*; sensualidad, *f*

**animate** /*v* 'ænə,meit; *a* -mɪt/ *vt* animar; inspirar. —*a* animado; viviente

**animated** /'ænə,meitɪd/ *a* animado; vivo, lleno de vida

**animation** /,ænə'meiʃən/ *n* animación, *f*; vivacidad, *f*; calor, fuego, *m*

**animism** /'ænə,mɪzəm/ *n* animismo, *m*

**animosity** /,ænə'mɒsɪti/ *n* animosidad, hostilidad, *f*

**aniseed** /'ænə,sid/ *n* anís, *m*

**anisette** /,ænə'sɛt/ *n* (liqueur) anisete, *m*

**ankle** /'æŋkəl/ *n* tobillo, *m*. **a. bone,** hueso del tobillo, *m*. **a. sock,** calcetín corto, *m*

**anklet** /'æŋklɪt/ *n* brazalete para el tobillo, *m*; (support) tobillera, *f*

**annals** /'ænlz/ *n pl* anales, *m pl*

**anneal** /ə'nil/ *vt* (metals) recocer; (glass) templar; (with oil) atemperar

**annex** /*v* ə'nɛks; 'ænɛks; *n* 'ænɛks/ *vt* unir, juntar; anexar. —*n* anexo, *m*

**annexation** /,ænɪk'seiʃən/ *n* anexión, *f*

**annihilate** /ə'naiə,leit/ *vt* aniquilar

**annihilation** /ə,naiə'leiʃən/ *n* aniquilación,

**anniversary** /,ænə'vɜrsəri/ *a* and *n* aniversario, *m*.

**annotate** /'ænə,teit/ *vt* anotar, acotar, comentar, hacer anotaciones a

**annotation** /,ænə'teiʃən/ *n* anotación, *f*; nota, *f*

**annotator** /'ænə,teitər/ *n* anotador (-ra), comentador (-ra)

**announce** /ə'nauns/ *vt* proclamar; declarar; publicar; anunciar

**announcement** /ə'naunsmənt/ *n* proclama, *f*; declaración, *f*; publicación, *f*; anuncio, *m*; (of a betrothal) participación, *f*

**announcer** /ə'naunsər/ *n* anunciador (-ra); (radio or TV) locutor (-ra)

**annoy** /ə'nɔi/ *vt* exasperar, irritar, disgustar; molestar, incomodar

**annoyance** /ə'nɔiəns/ *n* disgusto, *m*, exasperación, *f*; molestia, *f*, fastidio, *m*

**annoying** /ə'nɔiɪŋ/ *a* enojoso, molesto, fastidioso

**annual** /'ænyuəl/ *a* anual. —*n* anuario, *m*; calendario, *m*; planta anual, *f*

**annually** /'ænyuəli/ *adv* anualmente, cada año

**annuitant** /ə'nuitn̩t/ *n* censualista, *mf*

**annuity** /ə'nuiti/ *n* anualidad, pensión vitalicia, *f*

**annul** /ə'nʌl/ *vt* anular

**annulment** /ə'nʌlmənt/ *n* anulación, *f*

**annunciation** /ə,nʌnsi'eiʃən/ *n* anunciación, *f*. **the A.,** la Anunciación

**anodyne** /'ænə,dain/ *a* and *n* anodino, *m*

**anoint** /ə'nɔint/ *vt* untar; (before death) olear; (a king, etc.) ungir

**anointing** /ə'nɔintɪŋ/ *n* unción, *f*

**anomalous** /ə'nɒmələs/ *a* anómalo

**anomaly** /ə'nɒməli/ *n* anomalía, *f*

**anonymity** /,ænə'nimɪti/ *n* anónimo, *m*

**anonymous** /ə'nɒnəməs/ *a* anónimo. **a. letter,** anónimo, *m*

**anonymously** /ə'nɒnəməsli/ *adv* anónimamente

**another** /ə'nʌðər/ *a* otro; (different) distinto. —*n* otro, *m*; otra, *f*. **For one thing... and for a.,** En primer lugar... y además (y por otra cosa). **one after a.,** uno después de otro. **They love one a.,** Ellos se aman. **They sent it from one to a.,** Lo mandaron de uno a otro

**answer** /'ænsər, 'ɑn-/ *n* contestación, respuesta, *f*; (refutation) refutación, *f*; (pert reply) réplica, *f*; (solution) solución, *f*; *Math.* resultado, *m*; *Law.* contestación a la demanda, *f*

**answer** /'ænsər, 'ɑn-/ *vt* responder, contestar; (a letter, etc.) contestar a; (refute) refutar; (reply pertly) replicar; (write) escribir; (return) devolver; (suit) servir; (a bell, etc.) acudir a; (the door) abrir. —*vi* contestar; (succeed) tener éxito; dar resultado. **to a. by return,** contestar a vuelta de correo, **to a. back,** replicar. **to a. for,** ser responsable por; ser responsable de; (speak for) hablar por; (guarantee) garantizar, responder de

**answerable** /'ænsərəbəl/ *a* responsable; refutable;

(adequate) adecuado. **to make a. for,** hacer responsable de

**answering machine** n contestador telefónico, contestador, m

**ant** /ænt/ n hormiga, f. **ant-eater,** oso hormiguero, m. **ant-hill,** hormiguero, m

**antagonism** /æn'tægə,nɪzəm/ n antagonismo, m, hostilidad, oposición, f

**antagonist** /æn'tægənɪst/ n antagonista, mf

**antagonistic** /æn,tægə'nɪstɪk/ a antagónico, hostil

**antagonize** /æn'tægə,naɪz/ vt contender; hacer hostil (a)

**antarctic** /ænt'ɑrktɪk/ a antártico. —n polo antártico, m

**antecedent** /,æntə'sidn̩t/ a and n antecedente, m.

**antechamber** /'ænti,tʃeimbər/ n antecámara, antesala, f

**antedate** /'ænti,deit/ vt antedatar; anticipar

**antediluvian** /,æntidɪ'luviən/ a antediluviano

**antelope** /'ænt[l,oup/ n antílope, m

**antenna** /æn'tenə/ n antena, f

**anterior** /æn'tɪəriər/ a anterior

**anthem** /'ænθəm/ n antífona, f

**anthologist** /æn'θɒlədʒɪst/ n antólogo, m

**anthology** /æn'θɒlədʒi/ n antología, floresta, f

**anthracite** /'ænθrə,sait/ n antracita, f, carbón mineral, m

**anthrax** /'ænθræks/ n ántrax, m

**anthropological** /,ænθrəpə'lɒdʒɪkəl/ a antropológico

**anthropologist** /,ænθrə'pɒlədʒɪst/ n antropólogo, m

**anthropology** /,ænθrə'pɒlədʒi/ n antropología, f

**anti-aircraft** /,ænti'eər,kræft, ,æntai-/ a antiaéreo. **A.A. gun,** cañón antiaéreo, m

**antibody** /'ænti,bɒdi/ n anticuerpo, m

**antic** /'æntɪk/ n travesura, f

**Antichrist** /'ænti,kraist/ n Anticristo, m

**anticipate** /æn'tɪsə,peit/ vt (foresee) prever; anticipar; adelantarse a; (hope) esperar; (frustrate) frustrar; (enjoy) disfrutar con anticipación de

**anticipation** /æn,tɪsə'peiʃən/ n anticipación, f; adelantamiento, m; esperanza, expectación, f. **in a. of,** en espera de

**anticipatory** /æn'tɪsəpə,tɔri/ a anticipador

**anticlerical** /,ænti'klerɪkəl, ,æntai-/ a anticlerical

**anticlericalism** /,ænti'klerɪkə,lɪzəm, ,æntai-/ n anticlericalismo, m

**anticlimax** /,ænti'klaimæks, ,æntai-/ n anticlímax, m

**antidote** /'ænti,dout/ n antídoto, contraveneno, m

**antifreeze** /'ænti,friz/ n anticongelante, m

**Antilles, the** /æn'tɪliz/ las Antillas, f

**antimony** /'æntə,mouni/ n antimonio, m

**antipathetic** /,æntɪpə'θɛtɪk/ a antipático

**antipathy** /æn'tɪpəθi/ n antipatía, f

**antipode** /'ænti,poud/ n pl antípodas, mf pl

**antiquarian** /,ænti'kwɛəriən/ a anticuario

**antiquary** /'ænti,kwɛri/ n anticuario, m

**antiquated** /'ænti,kweitid/ a anticuado

**antique** /æn'tik/ a antiguo. —n antigüedad, antigualla, f. **a. dealer,** anticuario, m. **a. shop,** tienda de antigüedades, f

**antiquity** /æn'tɪkwɪti/ n antigüedad, f; ancianidad, f

**antireligious** /,æntirɪ'lɪdʒəs, ,æntai-/ a antirreligioso

**antirepublican** /,æntirɪ'pʌblɪkən/ a antirrepublicano

**anti-Semitic** /,æntisə'mitɪk, ,æntai-/ a antisemita

**anti-Semitism** /,ænti'sɛmɪ,tɪzəm, ,æntai-/ n antisemitismo, m

**antiseptic** /,æntə'sɛptɪk/ a and n antiséptico, m

**antisocial** /,ænti'souʃəl, ,æntai-/ a antisocial

**antithesis** /æn'tɪθəsɪs/ n antítesis, f

**antithetic** /,ænti'θɛtɪk/ a antitético

**antitoxin** /,ænti'tɒksɪn/ n antitoxina, f

**antler** /'æntlər/ n asta, f

**antonym** /'æntənɪm/ n contrario, m

**antrum** /'æntrəm/ n antro, m

**Antwerp** /'æntwərp/ Amberes, m

**anus** /'einəs/ n ano, m

**anvil** /'ænvɪl/ n yunque, m, bigornia, f

**anxiety** /æŋ'zaiɪti/ n inquietud, intranquilidad, f; preocupación, f; ansiedad, f; curiosidad, f; impaciencia, f; (wish) deseo, afán, f

**anxious** /'æŋkʃəs, 'æŋʃəs/ a inquieto, intranquilo;

preocupado; ansioso; impaciente; deseoso. **to be a.,** estar inquieto; apurarse. **to be a. to,** ansiar, tener deseos de. **to make a.,** preocupar, inquietar, intranquilizar

**anxiously** /'æŋkʃəsli, 'æŋʃəs-/ adv con inquietud; ansiosamente; impacientemente

**any** /'ɛni/ a cualquiera; (before the noun only) cualquier; (some) algún, m; alguna, f; (every) todo; (expressing condition or with interrogatives or negatives, following the noun) alguno, m; alguna, f, (is often not translated in a partitive sense, e.g. Have you any butter? ¿Tienes mantequilla?) —pron algo; (with the relevant noun) algún, etc.; lo, m, and neut; la, f; los, m pl; las, f pl. **He hasn't any pity,** No tiene piedad alguna. **at any rate,** de todos modos; por lo menos. **If there is any,** Si lo (la, etc.) hay. **in any case,** venga lo que venga. **no more,** ninguno, m; ninguna, f. **Whether any of them...,** Si alguno de ellos... **any further,** más lejos. **any longer,** más largo; (of time) más tiempo. **any more,** nada más; nunca más

**anybody** /'ɛni,bɒdi/ n and pron (someone) alguien; cualquiera, mf; (everyone) todo el mundo; (with a negative) nadie; (of importance) persona de importancia, f. **hardly a.,** casi nadie

**anyhow** /'ɛni,hau/ adv de cualquier modo; (with a negative) de ningún modo; de cualquier manera; (at least) por lo menos, en todo caso; (carelessly) sin cuidado

**anyone** /'ɛni,wʌn/ n. See **anybody**

**anything** /'ɛni,θɪŋ/ n algo, m, alguna cosa, f; (negative) nada; cualquier cosa, f; todo (lo que). **a. but,** todo menos

**anyway** /'ɛni,wei/ adv de todos modos, con todo; venga lo que venga; (anyhow) de cualquier modo

**anywhere** /'ɛni,wɛər/ adv en todas partes, dondequiera; en cualquier parte; (after a negative) en (or a) ninguna parte

**A.O.B.** (any other business) asuntos varios (on an agenda)

**aorta** /ei'ɔrtə/ n aorta, f

**apart** /ə'pɑrt/ adv aparte; a un lado; separadamente; separado (de); apartado (de). **a. from,** aparte de, dejando a un lado. **to keep a.,** mantener aislado; distinguir (entre). **to take a.,** desarmar. **wide a.,** muy distante

**apartment** /ə'pɑrtmənt/ n cuarto, m, habitación, f; (flat) piso, m

**apathetic** /,æpə'θɛtɪk/ a apático; indiferente

**apathy** /'æpəθi/ n apatía, f; indiferencia, f

**ape** /eip/ n simio, m

**Apennines, the** /'æpə,nainz/ los Apeninos, m

**aperitive** /ə'perɪtɪv/ a and n aperitivo, m.

**aperture** /'æpərtʃər/ n abertura, f; agujero, m; orificio, m

**apex** /'eipɛks/ n ápice, m

**aphasia** /ə'feiʒə/ n afasia, f

**aphorism** /'æfə,rɪzəm/ n aforismo, m

**aphrodisiac** /,æfrə'dizi,æk/ a and n afrodisíaco, m

**apiary** /'eipi,ɛri/ n colmenar, m

**apiece** /ə'pis/ adv cada uno; por persona

**apish** /'eipɪʃ/ a simiesco, de simio; (affected) afectado; (foolish) tonto

**aplomb** /ə'plɒm/ n confianza en sí, f, aplomo, m

**apocalypse** /ə'pɒkəlɪps/ n Apocalipsis, m

**apocalyptic** /ə,pɒkə'lɪptɪk/ a apocalíptico

**apocopate** /ə'pɒkə,peit/ vt apocopar

**Apocrypha** /ə'pɒkrəfə/ n libros apócrifos, m pl

**apocryphal** /ə'pɒkrəfəl/ a apócrifo

**apogee** /'æpə,dʒi/ n apogeo, m

**apologetic** /ə,pɒlə'dʒɛtɪk/ a apologético

**apologist** /ə'pɒlədʒɪst/ n apologista, mf

**apologize** /ə'pɒlə,dʒaiz/ vi presentar sus excusas; disculparse, excusarse; (regret) sentir

**apology** /ə'pɒlədʒi/ n excusa, disculpa, f; defensa, apología, f; (makeshift) substituto, m

**apoplectic** /,æpə'plɛktɪk/ a and n apoplético (-ca)

**apoplexy** /'æpə,plɛksi/ n apoplegía, f

**apostasy** /ə'pɒstəsi/ n apostasía, f

**apostate** /ə'pɒsteit/ n apóstata, mf. renegado (-da)

**apostatize** /ə'pɒstə,taiz/ vi apostatar, renegar

**apostle** /ə'pɒsəl/ n apóstol, m. **Apostles' Creed,** el Credo de los Apóstoles

**apostolic** /ˌæpə'stɒlɪk/ a apostólico

**apostrophe** /ə'pɒstrəfi/ n apóstrofe, mf; (punctuation mark) apóstrofo, m

**Apothecaries' weight** peso de boticario, m

**apothecary** /ə'pɒθəˌkɛri/ n apotecario, m

**apothegm** /'æpəˌθɛm/ n apotegma, m

**apotheosis** /əˌpɒθi'ousɪs/ n apoteosis, f

**appall** /ə'pɔl/ vt horrorizar, espantar, aterrar

**appalling** /ə'pɔlɪŋ/ a espantoso, horrible

**apparatus** /ˌæpə'rætəs/ n aparato, m; máquina, f; instrumentos, m pl

**apparel** /ə'pærəl/ n ropa, f; vestiduras, f pl; ornamento, m. —vt vestir

**apparent** /ə'pærənt/ a aparente; visible; evidente, manifiesto; (of heirs) presunto. **to become a.,** manifestarse

**apparently** /ə'pærəntli/ adv al parecer, aparentemente

**apparition** /ˌæpə'rɪʃən/ n aparición, f, fantasma, espectro, m

**appeal** /ə'pil/ n súplica, f; llamamiento, m; (charm) atracción, f, encanto, m; Law. apelación, alzada, f. —vi (to) suplicar (a); hacer llamamiento (a); poner por testigo (a); recurrir a; llamar la atención de; interesar (a); (attract) atraer, encantar; Law. apelar. **It doesn't a. to him,** No le atrae, No le gusta. **To allow an a.,** revocar una sentencia apelada. **without a.,** inapelable

**appealing** /ə'pilɪŋ/ a suplicante; atrayente

**appealingly** /ə'pilɪŋli/ adv de un modo suplicante

**appear** /ə'pɪər/ vi (of persons and things) aparecer; (seem) parecer; (before a judge) comparecer, presentarse (ante el juez); (of books) publicarse; (of lawyers) representar; (of the dawn) rayar; (of the sun, etc.) salir; (show itself) manifestarse. **to cause to a.,** hacer presentarse; (show) hacer ver; (prove) demonstrar, probar

**appearance** /ə'pɪərəns/ n aparición, f; (show, semblance or look, aspect) apariencia, f; presencia, f; aspecto, m; (in court of law) comparecencia, f; (of a book) publicación, f; (arrival) llegada, f; (view) perspectiva, f; (ghost) aparición, f, fantasma, m. **first a.,** (of an actor, etc.) debut, m; (of a play) estreno, m. **to all appearances,** según las apariencias. **to make one's first a.,** aparecer por primera vez; Theat. debutar. **Appearances are deceptive,** Las apariencias engañan

**appease** /ə'piz/ vt apaciguar, aplacar, pacificar; satisfacer

**appeasement** /ə'pizmənt/ n apaciguamiento, aplacamiento, m, pacificación, f; satisfacción, f

**appellant** /ə'pɛlənt/ a and n Law. apelante, mf

**appellation** /ˌæpə'leɪʃən/ n nombre, m; título, m

**append** /ə'pɛnd/ vt añadir; (a seal) poner; (enclose) incluir, anexar

**appendage** /ə'pɛndɪdʒ/ n accesorio, m; (Bot. Zool.) apéndice, m

**appendicitis** /əˌpɛndə'saɪtɪs/ n apendicitis, f

**appendix** /ə'pɛndɪks/ n apéndice, m

**appertain** /ˌæpər'teɪn/ vi pertenecer (a)

**appetite** /'æpɪˌtaɪt/ n apetito, m; Fig. hambre, f; deseo, m. **to have a bad a.,** no tener apetito, estar desganado. **to have a good a.,** tener buen apetito. **to whet the a.,** abrir el apetito

**appetizer** /'æpɪˌtaɪzər/ n aperitivo, m

**appetizing** /'æpɪˌtaɪzɪŋ/ a apetitoso

**applaud** /ə'plɔd/ vt and vi aplaudir; aclamar, ovacionar; celebrar

**applause** /ə'plɔz/ n aplauso, m; ovación, f; aprobación, alabanza, f

**apple** /'æpəl/ n manzana, f. **the a. of one's eye,** la niña de los ojos. **a. orchard,** manzanar, m. **a. sauce,** compota de manzanas, f. **a. tart,** pastel de manzanas, m. **a. tree,** manzano, m

**appliance** /ə'plaɪəns/ n aparato, m; instrumento, m; utensilio, m; máquina, f

**applicability** /ˌæplɪkə'bɪlti/ n aplicabilidad, f

**applicable** /'æplɪkəbəl/ a aplicable

**applicant** /'æplɪkənt/ n candidato, m; aspirante, m; solicitante, mf

**application** /ˌæplɪ'keɪʃən/ n aplicación, f; solicitud, f; petición, f; empleo, m. **on a.,** a solicitar

**appliqué** /ˌæplɪ'keɪ/ a aplicado. —n aplicación, f

**apply** /ə'plaɪ/ vt aplicar; (use) emplear; (place) poner; (give) dar; (the brakes) frenar; vi ser aplicable; ser a propósito; dirigirse (a); acudir (a); (for a post) proponerse para. **a. for,** solicitar, pedir; (a post) proponerse para. **a. for admission (to...),** solicitar el ingreso (en...). **a. oneself to,** ponerse a; dedicarse a, consagrarse a

**appoint** /ə'pɔɪnt/ vt (prescribe) prescribir, ordenar; señalar; asignar; (furnish) amueblar; equipar; (create) crear, establecer; (to a post) nombrar, designar; (manage) gobernar; organizar. **at the appointed hour,** a la hora señalada. **well-appointed,** bien amueblado; bien equipado

**appointive** /ə'pɔɪntɪv/ a por nombramiento

**appointment** /ə'pɔɪntmənt/ n (assignation) cita, f; (to a post) nombramiento, m; (post, office) cargo, m; creación, f. **By Royal A.,** Proveedor de la Real Casa. **to make an a. with,** citar

**apportion** /ə'pɔrʃən/ vt dividir; distribuir; prorratear; (taxes) derramar

**apportionment** /ə'pɔrʃənmənt/ n repartimiento, m, distribución, f; división, f; prorrateo, m

**apposite** /'æpəzɪt/ a a propósito, pertinente, oportuno; justo

**appositeness** /'æpəzɪtnɪs/ n pertinencia, oportunidad, f

**appraisal** /ə'preɪzəl/ n valoración, valuación, f; estimación, f

**appraise** /ə'preɪz/ vt valorar, tasar; estimar

**appreciable** /ə'priʃiəbəl/ a apreciable, perceptible

**appreciably** /ə'priʃiəbli/ adv sensiblemente

**appreciate** /ə'priʃiˌeɪt/ vt (understand) darse cuenta de, comprender; estimar; apreciar; (distinguish) distinguir. —vi encarecer, aumentar en valor; (of shares) subir, estar en alza

**appreciation** /əˌpriʃi'eɪʃən/ n (understanding) comprensión, f; apreciación, f; (recognition, etc.) aprecio, reconocimiento, m; (in value) aumento (en valor), m; subida de precio, f

**appreciative** /ə'priʃətɪv/ a apreciativo

**appreciatively** /ə'priʃətɪvli/ adv con aprecio

**appreciator** /ə'priʃiˌeɪtər/ n apreciador (-ra)

**apprehend** /ˌæprɪ'hɛnd/ vt aprehender, prender; comprender, aprehender; (fear) temer

**apprehension** /ˌæprɪ'hɛnʃən/ n aprehensión, comprensión, f; (fear) aprensión, f; (seizure) aprehensión, presa, f

**apprehensive** /ˌæprɪ'hɛnsɪv/ a aprehensivo; (fearful) aprensivo

**apprehensiveness** /ˌæprɪ'hɛnsɪvnɪs/ n aprehensión, f; (fear) aprensión, f, temor, m

**apprentice** /ə'prɛntɪs/ n aprendiz (-za). **to bind a.,** poner de aprendiz

**apprenticeship** /ə'prɛntɪsˌʃɪp/ n aprendizaje, m. **to serve an a.,** hacer el aprendizaje

**apprise** /ə'praɪz/ vt dar parte (de), informar (de)

**approach** /ə'proutʃ/ vt acercarse a; aproximarse a; (pull, etc. nearer) acercar, aproximar; (resemble) parecerse a, ser semejante a; (speak to) hablar con; entablar negociaciones con. —vi acercarse, aproximarse. —n acercamiento, m; (arrival) llegada, f; aproximación, f; (of night, etc.) avance, m; (entrance) entrada, f; avenida, f; vía, f; (step) paso, m; (to a subject) punto de vista (sobre), concepto (de), m; (introduction) introducción, f; pl approaches, (environs) alrededores, m pl, inmediaciones, f pl; (seas) mares, m pl; (overtures) avances, m pl

**approachable** /ə'proutʃəbəl/ a accesible

**approaching** /ə'proutʃɪŋ/ a venidero, próximo, cercano

**approbation** /ˌæprə'beɪʃən/ n asentimiento, m; aprobación, f

**appropriate** /a ə'prouprit/ v -ˌeɪt/ a apropiado; conveniente; vt adueñarse de, tomar posesión de, apropiar

**appropriately** /ə'proupritli/ adv propiamente; convenientemente; justamente

**appropriateness** /ə'proupriɪtnɪs/ n conveniencia, f; justicia, f

**appropriation** /ə͵prouprɪ'eiʃən/ n apropiación, f; aplicación, f; empleo, m

**approval** /ə'pruvəl/ n aprobación, f; consentimiento, m. **on a.,** a prueba

**approve** /ə'pruv/ vt aprobar; confirmar; (sanction) autorizar, sancionar; ratificar; estar contento (de); (oneself) demostrarse. —vi aprobar

**approved** /ə'pruvd/ a aprobado; bien visto; (on documents) Visto Bueno (V° B°)

**approximate** /a ə'prɒksəmɪt; v -͵meit/ a aproximado. —vt acercar. —vi aproximarse (a)

**approximately** /ə'prɒksəmɪtli/ adv aproximadamente, poco más o menos

**approximation** /ə͵prɒksə'meiʃən/ n aproximación, f

**appurtenance** /ə'pɜrtn̩əns/ n accesorio, m, pertenencia, f

**apricot** /'æprɪ͵kɒt/ n albaricoque, m. **a. tree,** albaricoquero, m

**April** /'eiprəl/ n abril, m, a abrileño. **A. Fool's Day,** el 1° de abril; (in Spain) el Día de los Inocentes (December 28)

**apron** /'eiprən/ n delantal, m; (of artisans and freemasons) mandil, m. **to be tied to a mother's a.-strings,** estar cosido a las faldas de su madre. **a.-stage,** proscenio, m. **a.-string,** cinta del delantal, f

**apse** /æps/ n ábside, mf

**apt** /æpt/ a apto, listo; propenso (a), inclinado (a); expuesto (a); (suitable) apropiado, oportuno

**aptitude** /'æptɪ͵tud/ n aptitud, disposición, facilidad, f

**aptly** /'æptli/ adv apropiadamente; justamente, bien

**aquamarine** /͵ækwəmə'rin/ n aguamarina, f

**aquarelle** /͵ækwə'rel/ n acuarela, f

**aquarellist** /͵ækwə'relɪst/ n acuarelista, mf

**aquarium** /ə'kweəriəm/ n acuario, m

**Aquarius** /ə'kweəriəs/ n Acuario, m

**aquatic** /ə'kwætɪk/ a acuático

**aquatint** /'ækwə͵tɪnt/ n acuatinta, f

**aqueduct** /'ækwɪ͵dʌkt/ n acueducto, m

**aqueous** /'ækwiəs/ a ácueo, acuoso

**aquiline** /'ækwə͵lain/ a aguileño

**Arab** /'ærəb/ a árabe. —n árabe, mf

**arabesque** /͵ærə'besk/ n arabesco, m

**Arabian** /ə'reibiən/ a árabe, arábigo. **The A. Nights,** Las Mil y Una Noches

**Arabic** /'ærəbɪk/ a arábigo. —n (language) arábigo, árabe, m

**Arabist** /'ærəbɪst/ n arabista, mf

**arable** /'ærəbəl/ a cultivable, labrantío

**Aragonese** /͵ærəgə'niz/ a and n aragonés (-esa)

**arbiter** /'arbɪtər/ n árbitro (-ra), arbitrador (-ra)

**arbitrariness** /'arbɪ͵trerinɪs/ n arbitrariedad, f

**arbitrary** /'arbɪ͵treri/ a arbitrario

**arbitrate** /'arbɪ͵treit/ vi arbitrar, juzgar como árbitro; someter al arbitraje

**arbitration** /͵arbɪ'treiʃən/ n arbitraje, m

**arbitrator** /'arbɪ͵treitər/ See **arbiter**

**arbor** /'arbər/ n glorieta, f, emparrado, m

**arc** /ark/ n arco, m. **arc-light,** lámpara de arco, f

**arcade** /ar'keid/ n arcada, f; galería, f; pasaje, m

**arch** /artʃ/ n arco, m; (vault) bóveda, f. —vt abovedar; arquear; encorvar

**arch** /artʃ/ a (roguish) socarrón; (coy) coquetón

**arch-** /artʃ/ prefix archi-

**archaic** /ar'keiɪk/ a arcaico

**archaism** /'arki͵ɪzəm/ n arcaísmo, m

**archangel** /'ark͵eindʒəl/ n arcángel, m

**archbishop** /'artʃ'biʃəp/ n arzobispo, m

**archenemy** /'artʃ'enəmi/ n mayor enemigo (-ga); Demonio, m

**archeological** /͵arkiə'lɒdʒɪkəl/ a arqueológico

**archeologist** /͵arki'ɒlədʒɪst/ n arqueólogo, m

**archeology** /͵arki'ɒlədʒi/ n arqueología, f

**archer** /'artʃər/ n flechero, saltero, m; Mil. arquero, m

**archery** /'artʃəri/ n ballestería, f

**archery range** n campo de tiro con arco, m

**archfiend** /'artʃ'find/ n demonio, m

**arching** /'artʃɪŋ/ n arqueo, m

**archipelago** /͵arkə'pelə͵gou/ n archipiélago, m

**architect** /'arkɪ͵tekt/ n arquitecto, m

**architectural** /͵arkɪ'tektʃərəl/ a arquitectónico

**architecturally** /͵arkɪ'tektʃərəli/ adv arquitectónicamente; desde el punto de vista arquitectónico

**architecture** /'arkɪ͵tektʃər/ n arquitectura, f

**archive** /'arkaiv/ n archivo, m

**archivist** /'arkəvɪst/ n archivero, m

**archness** /'artʃnɪs/ n coquetería, f; malicia, f

**archway** /'artʃ͵wei/ n arcada, f, pasaje abovedado, m; arco, m

**arctic** /'arktɪk, 'artɪk/ a ártico; muy frío. **A. Circle,** Círculo ártico, m

**ardent** /'ardn̩t/ a ardiente; apasionado, vehemente; fogoso

**ardently** /'ardn̩tli/ adv ardientemente; con vehemencia, apasionadamente

**ardor** /'ardər/ n ardor, m

**arduous** /'ardʒuəs/ a arduo, difícil

**arduousness** /'ardʒuəsnɪs/ n dificultad, arduidad, f

**are** /ar/ pl of present indicative of **be**. See **be. There are,** Hay

**area** /'eəriə/ n área, f; superficie, f; (extent) extensión, f; espacio, m; región, f; (of a house) patio, m; (of a concert hall, etc.) sala, f

**area code** n característica, f, (Chile), código territorial (Spain), prefijo (Spain), código interurbano, código (Argentina), m

**arena** /ə'rinə/ n arena, f

**argent** /'ardʒənt/ n Poet. blancura, f; Herald. argén, m

**Argentinian** /͵ardʒən'tiniən/ 'a and n argentino (-na)

**argonaut** /'argə͵nɔt/ n (Zool. and Myth.) argonauta, m

**argot** /'argou, -gət/ n jerga, f; (thieves') germanía, f

**arguable** /'argyuəbəl/ a discutible

**argue** /'argyu/ vt discutir; persuadir; (prove) demostrar. —vi argüir, discutir; sostener. **to a. against,** hablar en contra de, oponer

**arguing** /'argyuɪŋ/ n razonamiento, m; argumentación, f; discusión, f

**argument** /'argyəmənt/ n argumento, m

**argumentative** /͵argyə'mentətɪv/ a argumentador; contencioso

**arid** /'ærɪd/ a árido, seco

**aridity** /ə'rɪdɪti/ n aridez, f

**Aries** /'eəriz/ n Aries, m

**arise** /ə'raiz/ vi levantarse; (appear) surgir, aparecer; ofrecerse, presentarse; (of sound) hacerse oír; provenir (de); proceder (de); (result) hacerse sentir; (rebel) sublevarse

**aristocracy** /͵ærə'stɒkrəsi/ n aristocracia, f

**aristocrat** /ə'rɪstə͵kræt/ n aristócrata, mf

**aristocratic** /ə͵rɪstə'krætɪk/ a aristocrático

**Aristotelian** /͵ærəstə'tiliən/ a aristotélico

**Aristotelianism** /͵ærəstə'tiliyənɪzəm/ n aristotelismo, m

**arithmetic** /ə'rɪθmətɪk/ n aritmética, f

**arithmetical** /͵ærɪθ'metɪkəl/ a aritmético

**ark** /ark/ n arca, f. **Noah's ark,** arca de Noé, f. **Ark of the Covenant,** arca de la alianza, f

**arm** /arm/ n (Anat. Geog. Mech. of a chair, a cross, and Fig.) brazo, m; (lever) palanca, f; (of a tree) rama, f, brazo, m; (sleeve) manga, f; Naut. cabo de una verga, m; (weapon) arma, f; (of army, navy, etc.) ramo, m pl. **arms,** Herald. armas, f pl, escudo, m. **in arms,** en brazos; armado; en oposición. **To arms!** ¡A las armas! **to keep at arm's length,** guardar las distancias; tratar fríamente. **to lay down arms,** rendir las armas. **to present arms,** presentar las armas. **to receive with open arms,** recibir con los brazos abiertos. **to take up arms,** alzarse en armas, empuñar las armas. **under arms,** sobre las armas. **with folded arms,** con los brazos cruzados. **arm in arm,** del bracete, de bracero. **arm of the sea,** brazo de mar, m. **arm-rest,** brazo, m

**arm** /arm/ vt armar; proveer (de); (Fig. fortify) fortificar. —vi armarse

**armada** /ar'madə/ n armada, f

**armament** /'arməmənt/ n armamento, m

**armchair** /'arm͵tʃeər/ n sillón, m, silla poltrona, f

**armed** /armd/ a armado

**Armenian** /ar'miniən/ a and n armenio (-ia); (language) armenio, m

**armful** /'ɑrmˌfʊl/ n brazado, m

**armhole** /'ɑrmˌhoul/ n sobaquera, f

**arming** /'ɑrmɪŋ/ n armamento, m

**armistice** /'ɑrməstɪs/ n armisticio, m

**armless** /'ɑrmlɪs/ a sin brazos

**armor** /'ɑrmər/ n armadura, f; (for ships, etc.) blindaje, m. —vt blindar, acorazar. **(to) a.-plate,** vt blindar. —n coraza, plancha blindada, f

**armored** /'ɑrmərd/ a blindado, acorazado. **a. car,** carro blindado, m. **a. cruiser,** crucero acorazado, m

**armory** /'ɑrməri/ n armería, f

**army** /'ɑrmi/ n ejército, m; multitud, muchedumbre, f. **to be in the a.,** ser del ejército. **to go into the a.,** alistarse. **a. corps,** cuerpo del ejército, m. **a. estimates,** presupuesto del ejército, m. **a. list,** escalafón del ejército, m. **A. Medical Corps,** Sanidad Militar, f. **A. Supply Corps,** Cuerpo de Intendencia, m

**aroma** /ə'roumə/ n aroma, m

**aromatic** /ˌærə'mætɪk/ a aromático

**around** /ə'raund/ prep alrededor de; por todas partes de; cerca de; (with words like corner) a la vuelta de. —adv alrededor; a la redonda, en torno; por todas partes; de un lado para otro

**arouse** /ə'rauz/ vt despertar; excitar. **a. (someone's) suspicions,** despertar las sospechas (de fulano)

**arpeggio** /ɑr'pɛdʒiˌou/ n arpegio, m

**arraign** /ə'rein/ vt acusar; Law. procesar

**arraignment** /ə'reinmənt/ n acusación, f; Law. procesamiento, m

**arrange** /ə'reindʒ/ vt arreglar; acomodar; poner en orden, clasificar; (place) colocar; (order) ordenar, disponer; (contrive) agenciar; organizar; preparar; Mus. adaptar; (of differences) concertar, ajustar. —vi convenir, concertarse; arreglar; hacer preparativos

**arrangement** /ə'reindʒmənt/ n arreglo, m; clasificación, f; disposición, f; (agreement) acuerdo, m; Mus. adaptación, f; pl **arrangements,** preparativos, m pl

**array** /ə'rei/ n (of troops) orden de batalla, mf; formación, f; colección, f; (dress) atavío, m, vt poner en orden de batalla; formar (las tropas, etc.); ataviar, adornar

**arrears** /ə'rɪərz/ n pl atrasos, m pl. **in a.,** atrasado

**arrest** /ə'rɛst/ vt detener, impedir; (the attention) atraer; (capture) arrestar, prender; (judgment) suspender. —n (stop) interrupción, parada, f; (hindrance) estorbo, m; (detention) arresto, m, detención, f; (of a judgment) suspensión, f. **under a.,** bajo arresto

**arresting** /ə'rɛstɪŋ/ a que llama la atención, notable, muy interesante; asombroso, chocador

**arrival** /ə'raivəl/ n llegada, venida, f, advenimiento, m; Naut. arribada, f; entrada, f; el, m, (la, f), que llega. **on a.,** al llegar, a la llegada. **the new arrivals,** los recién llegados

**arrive** /ə'raiv/ vi llegar; aparecer; (happen) suceder; Naut. arribar; entrar. **to a. at,** (a place or conclusion) llegar a

**arrogance** /'ærəgəns/ n arrogancia altivez, soberbia, f

**arrogant** /'ærəgənt/ a altivo, arrogante, soberbio

**arrogate** /'ærəˌgeit/ vt arrogar

**arrow** /'ærou/ n saeta, flecha, f. **a.-head,** punta de flecha, f. **a.-shaped,** en forma de flecha, sagital. **a. wound,** flechazo, saetazo, m

**arsenal** /'ɑrsənl/ n arsenal, m

**arsenic** /'ɑrsənɪk/ n arsénico, m

**arson** /'ɑrsən/ n incendio premeditado, m

**art** /ɑrt/ n arte, mf; (cleverness) habilidad, f; (cunning) artificio, m. **Faculty of Arts,** Facultad de Letras, f. **fine arts,** bellas artes, f pl. **art exhibition,** exposición de pinturas, f. **art gallery,** museo de pinturas, m. **art school,** colegio de arte, m

**arterial** /ɑr'tɪəriəl/ a arterial; (of roads) de primera clase. **a. forceps,** pinzas hemostáticas, f pl

**artery** /'ɑrtəri/ n arteria, f

**artesian** /ɑr'tiʒən/ a artesiano

**artful** /'ɑrtfəl/ a hábil, ingenioso; (crafty) astuto

**artfully** /'ɑrtfəli/ adv ingeniosamente; con astucia

**artfulness** /'ɑrtfəlnɪs/ n habilidad, ingeniosidad, f; astucia, maña, f

**arthritic** /ɑr'θrɪtɪk/ a artrítico

**arthritis** /ɑr'θraitɪs/ n artritis, f

**artichoke** /'ɑrtɪˌtʃouk/ n alcachofa, f. **Jerusalem a.,** aguaturma, f

**article** /'ɑrtɪkəl/ n artículo, m; (object) objeto, m, cosa, f; pl **articles,** escritura, f; contrato, m; estatutos, m pl. —vt escriturar; contratar. **leading a.,** artículo de fondo, m. **articles of apprenticeship,** contrato de aprendizaje, m. **articles of association,** estatutos de asociación, m pl. **articles of war,** código militar, m

**articulate** /v ɑr'tɪkyəˌleit/ a -lɪt/ vt articular; pronunciar, articular. —vi estar unido por articulación; articular. —a articulado; claro; expresivo

**articulation** /ɑrˌtɪkyə'leiʃən/ n articulación, f, (all meanings)

**artifice** /'ɑrtəfɪs/ n artificio, m; arte, m, or f, habilidad, f

**artificer** /ɑr'tɪfəsər/ n artífice, mf

**artificial** /ˌɑrtə'fɪʃəl/ a artificial; falso, fingido; afectado. **a. flowers,** flores de mano, f pl. **a. silk,** seda artificial, seda vegetal, f

**artificial intelligence** /ˌɑrtə'fɪʃəl ɪn'tɛlɪdʒəns/ n inteligencia artificial, f

**artificiality** /ˌɑrtəˌfɪʃiˈælɪti/ n artificialidad, f; falsedad, f; afectación, f

**artificially** /ˌɑrtə'fɪʃəli/ adv artificialmente; con afectación

**artillery** /ɑr'tɪləri/ n artillería, f. **field a.,** artillería volante (or ligera or montada), f. **a. practice,** ejercicio de cañón, m

**artilleryman** /ɑr'tɪlərimən/ n artillero, m

**artisan** /'ɑrtəzən/ n artesano (-na)

**artist** /'ɑrtɪst/ n artista, mf; (painter) pintor (-ra)

**artiste** /ɑr'tist/ n artista, mf

**artistic** /ɑr'tɪstɪk/ a artístico

**artistically** /ɑr'tɪstɪkli/ adv artísticamente

**artistry** /'ɑrtɪstri/ n habilidad artística, f, arte, mf

**artless** /'ɑrtlɪs/ a natural; sencillo, cándido, inocente

**artlessly** /'ɑrtlɪsli/ adv con naturalidad; con inocencia

**artlessness** /'ɑrtlɪsnɪs/ n naturalidad, f; sencillez, candidez, inocencia, f

**art museum** n museo de arte, m

**Aryan** /'ɛəriən/ a ario

**as** /æz/ adv conjunc rel pron como; así como; (followed by infin.) de; (in comparisons) tan... como; (while) mientras; a medida que; (when) cuando, al (followed by infin.); (since) puesto que, visto que; (because) porque; (although) aunque; por; (according to) según; en; (in order that) para (que). **as a rule,** por regla general. **Once as he was walking,** Una vez mientras andaba. **as... as,** tan... como. **as far as,** hasta; en cuanto a. **as from,** desde. **as good as,** tan bueno como. **as if,** como si. **as it were,** por decirlo así, en cierto modo. **as many,** otros tantos (e.g. six embassies in as many countries, seis embajadas en otros tantos países). **as many as,** tanto... como; todos los que. **as soon as,** en cuanto, luego que, así que. **as soon as possible,** cuanto antes. **as sure as can be,** sin duda alguna. **as to,** en cuanto a. **as usual,** como de costumbre. **as well,** también. **as well as,** (besides) además de; tan bien como. **as yet,** todavía.

**asbestos** /æs'bɛstəs/ n asbesto, amianto, m

**ascend** /ə'sɛnd/ vt and vi subir; (on, in) subir a; ascender; (rise) elevarse; (a river) remontar. **to a. the stairs,** subir las escaleras. **to a. the pulpit,** subir al púlpito. **to a. the throne,** subir al trono

**ascendancy** /ə'sɛndənsi/ n ascendiente, influjo, m

**ascendant** /ə'sɛndənt/ n elevación, f. —a ascendente; predominante. **to be in the a.,** Fig. ir en aumento; predominar

**ascending** /ə'sɛndɪŋ/ a ascendente

**ascension** /ə'sɛnʃən/ n subida, ascensión, f; (of the throne) advenimiento (al trono), m. **The A.,** La Ascensión

**ascent** /ə'sɛnt/ n subida, f, ascenso, m; elevación, f; (slope) cuesta, pendiente, f

**ascertain** /ˌæsər'tein/ vt averiguar, descubrir

**ascertainable** /ˌæsər'teinəbəl/ a averiguable, descubrible

**ascertainment** /ˌæsər'teinmənt/ n averiguación, f

**ascetic** /ə'sɛtɪk/ a ascético. —n asceta, mf

**asceticism** /ə'sɛtəˌsɪzəm/ n ascetismo, m

**ascribable** /ə'skraibəbəl/ a imputable, atribuible

**ascribe** 320

**ascribe** /ə'skraib/ *vt* atribuir, adscribir, imputar

**ascription** /ə'skripʃən/ *n* atribución, adscripción, *f*

**asepsis** /ə'sɛpsis/ *n* asepsia, *f*

**aseptic** /ə'sɛptik/ *a* aséptico

**asexual** /ei'sɛkʃuəl/ *a* asexual

**ash** /æʃ/ *n* ceniza, *f*; cenizas, *f pl*; (tree and wood) fresno, *m*; *pl* **ashes**, cenizas, *f pl*; restos mortales, *m pl*. **mountain ash**, serbal, *m*. **ash-bin**, basurero, *m*. **ash-coloured**, ceniciento. **ash grove**, fresneda, *f*. **ashtray**, cenicero, *m*. **Ash Wednesday**, miércoles de ceniza, *m*

**ashamed** /ə'ʃeimd/ *a* avergonzado. **to be a. of**, avergonzarse de. **to be a. of oneself**, avergonzarse, tener vergüenza de sí mismo

**ashen** /'æʃən/ *a* ceniciento; (of ash wood) de fresno; pálido como un muerto

**ashlar** /'æʃlər/ *n* sillar, *m*

**ashore** /ə'ʃɔr/ *adv* a tierra; en tierra. **to go** or **put a.**, desembarcar

**Asia Minor** /'eiʒə/ Asia Menor, *f*

**Asiatic** /ˌeiʒi'ætik/ *a* and *n* asiático (-ca)

**aside** /ə'said/ *adv* a un lado; aparte. —*n Theat.* aparte, *m*. **to set a.**, poner a un lado; (omit) dejar aparte; descontar; abandonar; (a judgment) anular. **to take a.**, llevar aparte

**asinine** /'æsəˌnain/ *a* asnal

**ask** /æsk/ *vt* (a question; enquire) preguntar; (request; demand) pedir; (beg) rogar; (invite) invitar. **to ask a question**, hacer una pregunta. **to ask about**, preguntar acerca de. **to ask after**, preguntar por. **to ask down**, invitar a bajar; invitar a visitar (a alguien). **to ask for**, pedir; preguntar por. **ask for the moon**, pedir cotofas en el golfo. **to ask in**, invitar (a alguien) a entrar

**askance** /ə'skæns/ *adv* al (or de) soslayo, de reojo; con recelo

**askew** /ə'skyu/ *adv* oblicuamente; al lado; a un lado; sesgadamente

**aslant** /ə'slænt/ *prep* a través de

**asleep** /ə'slip/ *a* and *adv* dormido. **to be a.**, estar dormido. **to fall a.**, dormirse

**asparagus** /ə'spærəgəs/ *n* espárrago, *m*. **a. bed**, esparraguera, *f*

**aspect** /'æspɛkt/ *n* aspecto, *m*; vista, *f*; apariencia, *f*, semblante, *m*. **to have a southern a.**, dar (mirar) al sur

**asperity** /ə'spɛriti/ *n* aspereza, *f*

**aspersion** /ə'spɜrʒən/ *n Eccl.* aspersión, *f*; calumnia, *f*; insinuación, *f*

**asphalt** /'æsfɔlt/ *n* asfalto, *m*, *vt* asfaltar

**asphyxia** /æs'fiksiə/ *n* asfixia, *f*

**asphyxiate** /æs'fiksiˌeit/ *vt* asfixiar

**asphyxiating** /æs'fiksiˌeitiŋ/ *a* asfixiante

**aspirant** /'æspərənt/ *n* aspirante, candidato, *m*

**aspirate** /*v* 'æspəˌreit; *n* -pərit/ *vt* aspirar. —*n* letra aspirada, *f*

**aspiration** /ˌæspə'reiʃən/ *n* aspiración, ambición, *f*; deseo, anhelo, *m*; *Gram.* aspiración, *f*

**aspire** /ə'spaiᵊr/ *vi* aspirar (a), pretender, ambicionar; alzarse

**aspirin** /'æspərin/ *n* aspirina, *f*

**ass** /æs/ *n* asno, *m*

**assail** /ə'seil/ *vt* atacar, acometer, arremeter

**assailable** /ə'seiləbəl/ *a* atacable

**assailant** /ə'seilənt/ *n* asaltador (-ra)

**assassin** /ə'sæsin/ *n* asesino, *mf*

**assassinate** /ə'sæsəˌneit/ *vt* asesinar

**assassination** /əˌsæsə'neiʃən/ *n* asesinato, *m*

**assault** /ə'sɔlt/ *n* asalto, *m*; acometida, embestida, *f*; *Fig.* ataque, *m*. —*vt* asaltar; acometer, embestir; atacar. **to take by a.**, tomar por asalto

**assay** /*n* 'æsei; *v* æ'sei/ *n* ensayo, *m*, *vt* ensayar, aquilatar

**assayer** /æ'seiər/ *n* ensayador, *m*

**assaying** /æ'seiiŋ/ *n* ensaye, *m*

**assemblage** /ə'sɛmblidʒ/ *n* reunión, *f*; (of a machine) montaje, *m*; (of people) muchedumbre, *f*, concurso, *m*; (of things) colección, *f*, grupo, *m*

**assemble** /ə'sɛmbəl/ *vt* (persons) reunir, convocar; (things and persons) juntar; (a machine, etc.) armar, ensamblar. —*vi* reunirse, congregarse; acudir

**assembly** /ə'sɛmbli/ *n* asamblea, *f*; reunión, *f*; *Eccl.* concilio, *m*. **a. line**, cadena de montaje, línea de montaje, *f*. **a. room**, sala de reuniones, *f*; sala de baile, *f*

**assent** /ə'sɛnt/ *n* asentimiento, consentimiento, *m*; aprobación, *f*; (parliamentary, *Law.*) sanción, *f*. —*vi* asentir (a), consentir (en); aprobar

**assert** /ə'sɜrt/ *vt* mantener, defender; declarar, afirmar; hacer valer, reclamar. **to a. oneself**, imponerse, hacerse sentir; hacer valer sus derechos

**assertion** /ə'sɜrʃən/ *n* aserción, afirmación, *f*; defensa, *f*; reclamación, *f*

**assertive** /ə'sɜrtiv/ *a* afirmativo; dogmático

**assess** /ə'sɛs/ *vt* tasar, valorar; fijar, señalar; repartir (contribuciones, etc.)

**assessment** /ə'sɛsmənt/ *n* tasación, *f*; fijación, *f*; repartimiento, *m*

**assessor** /ə'sɛsər/ *n Law.* asesor (-ra); (of taxes) repartidor (-ra); (valuer) tasador, *m*. **public a.**, tasador, *m*

**asset** /'æsɛt/ *n* ventaja, *f*; adquisición, *f*; cualidad, *f*; *pl* **assets**, fondos, *m pl*; *Com.* activo, *m*, créditos activos, *m pl*

**assiduity** /ˌæsi'dyuiti/ *n* asiduidad, *f*

**assiduous** /ə'sidʒuəs/ *a* asiduo

**assiduously** /ə'sidʒuəsli/ *adv* asiduamente, con asiduidad

**assign** /ə'sain/ *vt Law.* ceder; señalar, asignar; (appoint) destinar; fijar; atribuir, imputar. —*n* cesionario (-ia)

**assignation** /ˌæsig'neiʃən/ *n* asignación, *f*; cita, *f*; *Law.* cesión, *f*

**assignment** /ə'sainmənt/ *n Law.* cesión, *f*; escritura de cesión, *f*; atribución, *f*; parte, porción, *f*

**assimilable** /ə'siməlabəl/ *a* asimilable

**assimilate** /ə'siməˌleit/ *vt* asimilar; incorporarse. —*vi* mezclarse

**assimilation** /əˌsimə'leiʃən/ *n* asimilación, *f*; incorporación, *f*

**assimilative** /ə'siməlativ/ *a* asimilativo

**assist** /ə'sist/ *vt* ayudar; auxiliar, socorrer; (uphold) apoyar; (further) promover, fomentar. —*vi* (be present) asistir (a)

**assistance** /ə'sistəns/ *n* ayuda, *f*; auxilio, socorro, *m*; apoyo, *m*; (furtherance) fomento, *m*. **public a.**, asistencia pública, *f*

**assistant** /ə'sistənt/ *n* ayudante, *m*; *Eccl.* asistente, *m*; (in a shop) dependiente (-ta); colaborador (-ra); (university) auxiliar, *m*; sub-. **a. secretary**, subsecretario (-ia). **a. secretaryship**, subsecretaría, *f*

**associate** /*n* ə'sousiit; *v* -si,eit/ *n* asociado (-da); miembro, *m*; socio (-ia); compañero (-ra), amigo (-ga); colega, *m*; colaborador (-ra); (confederate) cómplice, *mf a* asociado; auxiliar. —*vt* asociar; unir, juntar. **to a. oneself with**, asociarse con; asociarse a. **to a. with**, frecuentar la compañía de, ir con

**association** /əˌsousi'eiʃən/ *n* asociación, *f*; unión, *f*; sociedad, *f*; compañía, corporación, *f*; (connection) relación, *f*. **a. football**, fútbol, *m*

**assonance** /'æsənəns/ *n* asonancia, *f*

**assort** /ə'sɔrt/ *vt* clasificar; mezclar

**assorted** /ə'sɔrtid/ *a* surtido, mezclado. **They are a well-a. pair**, Son una pareja bien avenida

**assortment** /ə'sɔrtmənt/ *n* clasificación, *f*; arreglo, *m*; surtido, *m*, mezcla, *f*

**assuage** /ə'sweidʒ/ *vt* mitigar; suavizar; calmar; aliviar

**assume** /ə'sum/ *vt* asumir; tomar; apropiarse; (wear) revestir; (suppose) suponer; poner por caso

**assumed** /ə'sumd/ *a* fingido, falso; supuesto

**assumption** /ə'sʌmpʃən/ *n* asunción, *f*; apropiación, arrogación, *f*; suposición, *f*. **Feast of the A.**, Fiesta de la Asunción, *f*

**assurance** /ə'ʃurəns/ *n* garantía, *f*; promesa, *f*; confianza, seguridad, *f*; (in a good sense) aplomo, *m*, naturalidad, *f*; (in a bad sense) presunción frescura, *f*, descaro, *m*; *Com.* seguro, *m*

**assure** /ə'ʃur/ *vt* asegurar

**assured** /ə'ʃurd/ *a* aseguardo; seguro

**assuredly** /ə'ʃurdli/ *adv* seguramente

**asterisk** /'æstərisk/ *n* asterisco, *m*

**astern** /ə'stɜrn/ *adv* a popa; de popa; en popa; atrás

**asthma** /'æzmə/ *n* asma, *f*

**asthmatic** /æz'mætɪk/ *a* asmático

**astigmatic** /ˌæstɪg'mætɪk/ *a* astigmático

**astigmatism** /ə'stɪgmə,tɪzəm/ *n* astigmatismo, *m*

**astir** /ə'stɜr/ *adv* en movimiento; (out of bed) levantado; excitado

**astonish** /ə'stɒnɪʃ/ *vt* sorprender, asombrar

**astonished** /ə'stɒnɪʃt/ *a* atónito, estupefacto

**astonishing** /ə'stɒnɪʃɪŋ/ *a* sorprendente, asombroso

**astonishment** /ə'stɒnɪʃmənt/ *n* asombro, *m*, sorpresa, estupefacción, *f*

**astound** /ə'staund/ *vt* aturdir, pasmar. **to be astounded,** *Inf.* quedarse muerto

**astounding** /ə'staundɪŋ/ *a* asombroso

**astray** /ə'streɪ/ *adv* desviado, extraviado; por el mal camino. **to go a.,** errar el camino, perderse; *Fig.* descarriarse

**astride** /ə'straɪd/ *adv* a horcajadas. —*prep* a horcajadas sobre; a ambos lados de

**astringent** /ə'strɪndʒənt/ *a* astringente

**astrologer** /ə'strɒlədʒər/ *n* astrólogo (-ga)

**astrological** /ˌæstrə'lɒdʒɪkəl/ *a* astrológico

**astrology** /ə'strɒlədʒi/ *n* astrología, *f*

**astronaut** /'æstrə,nɔt/ *n* astronauta, *mf*

**astronomer** /ə'strɒnəmər/ *n* astrónomo, *m*

**astronomical** /ˌæstrə'nɒmɪkəl/ *a* astronómico

**astronomy** /ə'strɒnəmi/ *n* astronomía, *f*

**astrophysics** /ˌæstrou'fɪzɪks/ *n* astrofísica, *f*

**astute** /ə'stut/ *a* astuto, sagaz; (with knave, etc.) redomado, pícaro

**astuteness** /ə'stutnɪs/ *n* astucia, sagacidad, *f*

**asunder** /ə'sʌndər/ *adv* en dos; separadamente; lejos uno de otro

**asylum** /ə'saɪləm/ *n* asilo, *m;* (for the insane) manicomio, *m*

**asymmetrical** /ˌeɪsɪ'mɛtrɪkəl/ *a* asimétrico

**asymmetry** /eɪ'sɪmɪtri/ *n* asimetría, *f*

**at** /æt/ *prep* a; en casa de; en; de; con; por; (before) delante de. Sometimes forms part of verb, e.g. *to aim at,* apuntar. *to look at,* mirar. May be translated by using pres. part., e.g. *They were at play,* Estaban jugando. *at a bound,* de un salto. *at peace,* en paz. *at the doctor's,* en casa del médico. *at the crack of dawn,* al rayar el alba, al romper el alba. *at the head,* a la cabeza. *John is at Brighton,* Juan está en Brighton. *at first,* al principio. *at last,* por fin. *at no time,* jamás. *at once,* en seguida. *at most,* a lo más. *at all events,* en todo caso. *What is he getting at?* ¿Qué quiere saber? *at home,* en casa. *at-home day,* día de recibo, *m*

**atavism** /'ætə,vɪzəm/ *n* atavismo, *m*

**atavistic** /ˌætə'vɪstɪk/ *a* atávico

**atheism** /'eɪθi,ɪzəm/ *n* ateísmo, *m*

**atheist** /'eɪθiɪst/ *n* ateo (-ea)

**atheistic** /ˌeɪθi'ɪstɪk/ *a* ateo

**Atheneum** /ˌæθə'niəm/ *n* ateneo, *m*

**Athenian** /ə'θiniən/ *a* and *n* ateniense *mf*

**Athens** /'æθɪnz/ Atenas, *f*

**athlete** /'æθlit/ *n* atleta, *m*

**athletic** /æθ'lɛtɪk/ *a* atlético

**athletics** /æθ'lɛtɪks/ *n* atletismo, *m*

**athwart** /ə'θwɔrt/ *adv* de través. —*prep* al través de; contra

**Atlantic** /æt'læntɪk/ *a* and *n* atlántico *m*. **A. Charter,** Carta del Atlántico, *f.* **A. liner,** transatlántico, *m*

**Atlantis** /æt'læntɪs/ Atlántida, *f*

**atlas** /'ætləs/ *n* atlas, *m*

**atmosphere** /'ætməs,fɪər/ *n* aire, *m;* atmósfera, *f; Fig.* ambiente, *m*

**atmospheric** /ˌætməs'fɛrɪk/ *a* atmosférico

**atmospherics** /ˌætməs'fɛrɪks/ *n pl* perturbaciones eléctricas atmosféricas, *f pl*

**atoll** /'ætɒl/ *n* atolón, *m*

**atom** /'ætəm/ *n* átomo, *m*. **splitting of the a.,** escisión del átomo, *f*

**atomic** /ə'tɒmɪk/ *a* atómico. **a. bomb,** bomba atómica, *f.* **a. pile,** pila atómica, *f.* **a. theory,** teoría atómica, *f*

**atomize** /'ætə,maɪz/ *vt* pulverizar

**atomizer** /'ætə,maɪzər/ *n* pulverizador, *m*

**atone** /ə'toun/ *vi* (for) expiar

**atonement** /ə'tounmənt/ *n* expiación, *f*

**atonic** /ə'tɒnɪk, eɪ'tɒn-/ *a* átono, atónico

**atrocious** /ə'trouʃəs/ *a* atroz; horrible

**atrocity** /ə'trɒsɪti/ *n* atrocidad, *f*

**atrophy** /'ætrəfi/ *n* atrofia, *f, vi* atrofiarse

**attach** /ə'tætʃ/ *vt* (*Law.* of goods) embargar; (*Law.* of persons) arrestar; (fix) fijar; (tie) atar; (join) juntar; (stick) pegar; (connect) conectar; (hook) enganchar; (with a brooch, etc.) prender; (blame, etc.) imputar; (importance, etc.) dar, conceder; (assign) asignar; (attract) atraer; (enclose) adjuntar, incluir. —*vi* pertenecer (a), ser indivisible (de). **to a. oneself to,** pegarse a; adherirse a, asociarse con; acompañar; hacerse inseparable de

**attaché** /ætæ'ʃeɪ/ *n* agregado, *m.* **a. case,** maletín, *m*

**attachment** /ə'tætʃmənt/ *n* (*Law.* of goods) embargo, *m,* vía ejecutiva, *f;* (*Law.* of persons) arresto, *m;* unión, *f;* conexión, *f;* (hooking) enganche, *m;* (with a brooch, etc.) prendimiento, *m;* (tying) atadura, *f;* (fixing) fijación, *f;* (affection) apego, cariño, *m;* (friendship) amistad, *f*

**attack** /ə'tæk/ *n* ataque, *m; Mil.* ofensiva, *f;* (access) acceso, *m.* —*vt* atacar

**attacker** /ə'tækər/ *n* atacador (-ra), asaltador (-ra)

**attain** /ə'teɪn/ *vt* alcanzar, conseguir, lograr. —*vi* llegar a; alcanzar

**attainable** /ə'teɪnəbəl/ *a* asequible, realizable; accesible

**attainment** /ə'teɪnmənt/ *n* consecución, obtención, *f;* logro, *m; pl* **attainments,** prendas, dotes, *f pl*

**attempt** /ə'tɛmpt/ *vt* (try) procurar, tratar de, intentar; ensayar; querer; *Law.* hacer una tentativa (de), atentar. —*n* tentativa, prueba, *f;* esfuerzo, ensayo, *m;* (criminal) atentado, *m,* tentativa, *f*

**attend** /ə'tɛnd/ *vi* prestar atención (a); escuchar; (look after) cuidar (de); (serve) servir; (accompany) acompañar; (await) esperar. —*vt* (be present) asistir (a); (of a doctor) visitar; (accompany) acompañar; (bring) acarrear, traer; (follow) seguir. **to be attended with,** traer consigo, acarrear

**attendance** /ə'tɛndəns/ *n* asistencia, presencia, *f;* (those present) público, *m,* concurrencia, *f;* servicio, *m;* (train) acompañamiento, *m; Med.* asistencia, *f,* tratamiento médico, *m.* **to be in a.,** acompañar (a)

**attendant** /ə'tɛndənt/ *a* que acompaña; que sigue; concomitante. —*n* criado (-da); (keeper) guardián (-ana); (nurse) enfermero (-ra); (in a cloakroom) guardarropa, *f;* (in a theater) acomodador (-ra); (on a train) mozo, *m;* (waiter) camarero, *m;* (at baths) bañero (-ra)

**attention** /ə'tɛnʃən/ /ə,tɛn'ʃʌn/ *n* atención, *f;* cuidado, *m.* **A.!** ¡Atención!; *Mil.* ¡Firmes! **to pay a.,** prestar atención. **to stand to a.,** cuadrarse, permanecer en posición de firmes

**attentive** /ə'tɛntɪv/ *a* atento; solícito; cortés, obsequioso

**attentively** /ə'tɛntɪvli/ *adv* con atención, atentamente; solícitamente

**attentiveness** /ə'tɛntɪvnɪs/ *n* cuidado, *m;* cortesía, *f*

**attenuate** /ə'tɛnyu,eɪt/ *vt* atenuar

**attenuating** /ə'tɛnyu,eɪtɪŋ/ *a* atenuante. **a. circumstance,** circunstancia atenuante, *f*

**attenuation** /ə,tɛnyu'eɪʃən/ *n* atenuación, *f*

**attest** /ə'tɛst/ *vt* atestar. —*vi* atestiguar, deponer, dar fe

**attestation** /ˌætɛ'steɪʃən/ *n* atestación, deposición, *f;* (certificate) certificado, *m,* fe, *f*

**attic** /'ætɪk/ *n* buhardilla, guardilla, *f,* desván, sotabanco, *m*

**Attic** /'ætɪk/ *a* ático

**attire** /ə'taɪər/ *n* atavío, *m;* (dress) traje, *m;* (finery) galas, *f pl, vt* ataviar, vestir; engalanar

**attitude** /'ætɪ,tud/ *n* actitud, *f;* postura, *f;* posición, *f*

**attorney** /ə'tɜrni/ *n* (solicitor) abogado (-da); (agent) apoderado (-da); (public) procurador, *m.* **power of a.,** poderes, *m pl* procuración, *f.* **A.-general,** fiscal, *m*

**attract** /ə'trækt/ *vt* atraer; (charm) seducir, cautivar, apetecer; (invite) convidar; (goodwill, etc.) captar

**attraction** /ə'trækʃən/ *n* atracción, *f;* atractivo, aliciente, encanto, *m*

**attractive** /ə'træktɪv/ *a* atrayente; atractivo, seductivo; apetecible; encantador

**attractively** /ə'træktɪvli/ *adv* atractivamente

**attributable** /ə'trɪbyutəbəl/ *a* imputable, atribuible

**attribute** /v ə'trıbyut/ n 'ætrə,byut/ vt atribuir (a), achacar (a), imputar (a). —n atributo, m
**attribution** /,ætrə'byuʃən/ n atribución, imputación, f; atributo, m
**attrition** /ə'trıʃən/ n atrición, f
**auburn** /'ɔbərn/ a castaño, rojizo
**auction** /'ɔkʃən/ n subasta, almoneda, f; venta pública, pública subasta, f, vt subastar. **to put up to a.,** sacar a pública subasta
**auctioneer** /,ɔkʃə'nıər/ n subastador (-ra)
**audacious** /ɔ'deıʃəs/ a atrevido, audaz, osado, temerario; (shameless) descarado, impudente
**audaciously** /ə'deıʃəsli/ adv osadamente; descaradamente
**audacity** /ɔ'dæsıti/ n audacia, osadía, temeridad, f, atrevimiento, m; (shamelessness) descaro, m, desvergüenza, f
**audibility** /,ɔdə'bılıti/ n audibilidad, perceptibilidad, f
**audible** /'ɔdəbəl/ a audible, oíble
**audibly** /'ɔdəbli/ adv en forma audible, perceptiblemente, en alta voz
**audience** /'ɔdiəns/ n (interview and Law.) audiencia, f; oyentes, m pl, auditorio, público, m. **to give a.,** dar audiencia. **a. chamber,** sala de recepción, f
**audiofrequency** /'ɔdiou,frikwensi/ n audiofrecuencia, f
**audit** /'ɔdıt/ vt intervenir, examinar (cuentas). —n intervención, f, ajuste (de cuentas), m
**audition** /ɔ'dıʃən/ n audición, f
**auditor** /'ɔdıtər/ n (hearer) oyente, mf; interventor, contador, m
**auditorium** /,ɔdı'tɔriəm/ n sala de espectáculos, f
**auditory** /'ɔdı,tɔri/ a auditivo, auditorio
**Augean** /ɔ'dʒiən/ a de Augeas; muy sucio
**auger** /'ɔgər/ n taladro, m
**aught** /ɔt/ n algo. **For a. I know,** Por lo que yo sepa
**augment** /ɔg'mɛnt/ vt aumentar, acrecentar. —vi aumentarse, acrecentarse
**augmentation** /,ɔgmɛn'teıʃən/ n aumento, acrecentamiento, m; añadidura, f
**augmentative** /ɔg'mɛntətıv/ a aumentativo
**augur** /'ɔgər/ n agorero (-ra). —vt and vi presagiar, anunciar; pronosticar, agorar
**augury** /'ɔgyəri/ n predicción, f; agüero, presagio, pronóstico, m
**August** /'ɔgəst/ n agosto, m
**august** /'ɔgəst/ a augusto
**Augustan** /ɔ'gʌstən/ a (of Roman emperor) augustal. **A. Age,** siglo de Augusto, m
**Augustinian** /,ɔgə'stıniən/ a and n Eccl. agustino (-na)
**aunt** /ænt, ɑnt/ n tía, f. **great-a.,** tía abuela, f. **A. Sally,** el pim, pam, pum
**aura** /'ɔrə/ n exhalación, f; influencia psíquica, f; Med. aura, f
**aural** /'ɔrəl/ a auricular. **a. surgeon,** otólogo, m
**auricle** /'ɔrıkəl/ n (of the heart) aurícula, ala del corazón, f; oreja, f, pabellón de la oreja, m
**aurora** /ə'rɔrə/ n aurora, f. **a. borealis,** aurora boreal, f
**auspice** /'ɔspıs/ n auspicio, m
**auspicious** /ɔ'spıʃəs/ a propicio, favorable, feliz
**auspiciously** /ɔ'spıʃəsli/ adv prósperamente, felizmente
**auspiciousness** /ɔ'spıʃəsnıs/ n buenos auspicios, m pl; felicidad, f
**austere** /ɔ'stıər/ a severo, austero, adusto; ascético; (of style) desnudo
**austerity** /ɔ'stɛrıti/ n austeridad, severidad, f; ascetismo, m; (of style) desnudez, f
**Australian** /ɔ'streılyən/ a and n australiano (-na)
**Austrian** /'ɔstriən/ a and n austríaco (-ca)
**authentic** /ɔ'θɛntık/ a auténtico
**authenticate** /ɔ'θɛntı,keit/ vt autenticar
**authentication** /ɔ,θɛntı'keiʃən/ n autenticación, f
**authenticity** /,ɔθɛn'tısıti/ n autenticidad, f
**author** /'ɔθər/ n autor, m
**authoress** /'ɔθərıs/ n autora, f
**author index** n índice de autores, m
**authoritarian** /ə,θɔrı'tɛəriən/ a autoritario
**authoritative** /ə'θɔrı,teitıv/ a autoritario

**authority** /ə'θɔrıti/ n autoridad, f; poder, m. **to have on the best a.,** tener de muy buena fuente
**authorization** /,ɔθərə'zeiʃən/ n autorización, f
**authorize** /'ɔθə,raiz/ vt autorizar
**authorship** /'ɔθər,ʃıp/ n profesión de autor, f; paternidad (literaria), f; origen, m
**autobiographical** /,ɔtə,baiə'græfıkəl/ a autobiográfico
**autobiography** /,ɔtəbai'ɒgrəfi/ n autobiografía, f
**autocracy** /ɔ'tɒkrəsi/ n autocracia, f
**autocrat** /'ɔtə,kræt/ n autócrata, mf
**autocratic** /,ɔtə'krætık/ a autocrático
**autograph** /'ɔtə,græf/ n autógrafo, m
**autography** /ɔ'tɒgrəfi/ n autografía, f
**automatic** /,ɔtə'mætık/ a automático. **a. gate,** (at level crossings, etc.) barrera de golpe, f. **a. machine,** máquina automática, f; Inf. tragaperras, f. **a. pencil,** lapicero, m
**automatically** /,ɔtə'mætıkəli/ adv automáticamente
**automatism** /ɔ'tɒmə,tızəm/ n automatismo, m
**automaton** /ɔ'tɒmə,tɒn/ n autómata, m
**automobile** /,ɔtəmə'bil/ n automóvil, m
**autonomous** /ɔ'tɒnəməs/ a autónomo
**autonomy** /ɔ'tɒnəmi/ n autonomía, f
**autopsy** /'ɔtɒpsi/ n autopsia, f
**autosuggestion** /,ɔtousəg'dʒɛstʃən/ n autosugestión, f
**autumn** /'ɔtəm/ n otoño, m
**autumnal** /ɔ'tʌmnl/ a otoñal, de otoño
**auxiliary** /ɔg'zılyəri/ a auxiliar. —n auxiliador, m
**avail** /ə'veil/ vi servir; valer; importar. —vt aprovechar. **to a. oneself of,** valerse de, aprovecharse de. **to no a.,** en balde
**availability** /ə,veilə'bılıti/ n utilidad, f; disponibilidad, f; provecho, m; (validity) validez, f
**available** /ə'veiləbəl/ a útil; disponible; aprovechable; válido
**avalanche** /'ævə,læntʃ/ n alud, lurte, m
**avarice** /'ævərıs/ n avaricia, f
**avaricious** /,ævə'rıʃəs/ a avaro, avaricioso
**ave** /'ɑvei/ interj ¡ave! —n avemaría, f; despedida, f
**avenge** /ə'vɛndʒ/ vt vengar; vindicar. **to a. oneself for,** vengarse de
**avenger** /ə'vɛndʒər/ n vengador (-ra)
**avenging** /ə'vɛndʒıŋ/ a vengador
**avenue** /'ævə,nyu/ n avenida, f
**aver** /ə'vɜr/ vt afirmar, asegurar
**average** /'ævərıdʒ/ n promedio, término medio, m; (marine insurance) avería, f, a de promedio; típico; corriente; normal. —vt hallar el término medio (de); prorratear, proporcionar; ser por término medio. **general a.,** (marine insurance) avería gruesa, f. **on the a.,** por término medio
**averse** /ə'vɜrs/ a opuesto (a); desinclinado (a); enemigo (de); repugnante. **to be a. to,** no gustar de; oponerse a; estar desinclinado a; ser enemigo de; repugnar
**aversion** /ə'vɜrʒən/ n aversión, f; repugnancia, f
**avert** /ə'vɜrt/ vt apartar; (avoid) evitar
**aviary** /'eivi,ɛri/ n avería, pajarera, f
**aviation** /,eivi'eiʃən/ n aviación, f
**aviator** /'eivi,eitər/ n aviador (-ra)
**avid** /'ævıd/ a ávido
**avidity** /ə'vıdıti/ n avidez, f
**avidly** /'ævıdli/ adv ávidamente, con avidez
**avocation** /,ævə'keiʃən/ n pasatiempo, m, distracción, f; ocupación, f; profesión, f
**avoid** /ə'vɔid/ vt evitar; (pursuit) evadir, eludir; guardarse (de), rehuir; Law. anular
**avoidable** /ə'vɔidəbəl/ a evitable, eludible
**avoidance** /ə'vɔidns/ n evitación, f
**avow** /ə'vau/ vt confesar; declarar
**avowal** /ə'vauəl/ n confesión, admisión, f
**avowedly** /ə'vauıdli/ adv por confesión propia
**avuncular** /ə'vʌŋkyələr/ a avuncular
**await** /ə'weit/ vt aguardar, esperar
**awake** /ə'weik/ vt despertar. —vi despertarse. —a despierto; vigilante; consciente (de); atento (a)
**awakening** /ə'weikəniŋ/ n despertamiento, m
**award** /ə'wɔrd/ n sentencia, decisión, f; adjudicación, f; (prize) premio, m. —vt adjudicar; otorgar, con-

**ceder.** *She was awarded a professorship in Greek,* Ganó unas oposiciones para una cátedra de griego
**aware** /ə'wɛər/ *a* consciente, sabedor. **to be well a. of,** saber muy bien. **to make a. of,** hacer saber
**awash** /ə'wɒʃ/ *adv* a flor de agua
**away** /ə'wei/ *adv* a distancia, a lo lejos, lejos; (absent) ausente; (out) fuera; (unceasingly) sin parar, continuamente; (wholly) completamente; (visibly) a ojos vistas. In verbs of motion **a.** is rendered by the reflexive, e.g. *to go a.,* marcharse. Sometimes not translated, e.g. *to take a.,* quitar. —*interj* ¡fuera de aquí! ¡márchese Vd.!; ¡vámonos! ¡adelante! *nine miles a.,* a nueve millas de distancia. *a. in the distance,* allá a lo lejos. *She sang a.,* Ella seguía cantando
**awe** /ɔ/ *n* temor reverente, *m;* horror, *m;* respeto, *m;* reverencia, *f, vt* intimidar, aterrar; infundir respeto (a). **to stand in awe of,** tener respeto (a), reverenciar
**awesome** /'ɔsəm/ *a* pavoroso, temible, aterrador; terrible; (august) augusto; (imposing) imponente
**awestruck** /'ɔ,strʌk/ *a* espantado, aterrado
**awful** /'ɔfəl/ *a* terrible, pavoroso; horrible; temible; atroz; *Inf.* enorme. **How a.!** *Inf.* ¡Qué barbaridad!
**awfully** /'ɔfəli, 'ɔfli/ *adv* terriblemente; horriblemente; *Inf.* muy
**awfulness** /'ɔfəlnɪs/ *n* lo terrible; lo horrible; atrocidad, *f;* (of a crime, etc.) enormidad, *f*

**awkward** /'ɔkwərd/ *a* difícil; peligroso; delicado; embarazoso; (of time, etc.) inconveniente, inoportuno; (of things) incómodo; (clumsy) torpe, desmañado; desagradable; (ungraceful) sin gracia. **the a. age,** la edad difícil
**awkwardly** /'ɔkwərdli/ *adv* torpemente; incómodamente; mal; con dificultad; sin gracia. **He is a. placed,** Se encuentra en una situación difícil
**awkwardness** /'ɔkwərdnɪs/ *n* dificultad, *f;* peligro, *m;* delicadeza, *f;* inconveniencia, inoportunidad, *f;* (clumsiness) torpeza, desmaña, *f;* (ungracefulness) falta de gracia, *f*
**awl** /ɔl/ *n* lezna, *f,* punzón, *m*
**awning** /'ɔnɪŋ/ *n* toldo, palio, *m; Naut.* toldilla, *f*
**awry** /ə'rai/ *adv* a un lado; oblicuamente; *Fig.* mal. —*a* torcido; *Fig.* descarriado
**axiom** /'æksiəm/ *n* axioma, *m*
**axiomatic** /,æksiə'mætɪk/ *a* axiomático
**axis** /'æksɪs/ *n* eje, *m; Zool.* axis, *m.* **A. power,** nación del Eje
**axle** /'æksəl/ *n* eje, *m;* peón, árbol (de una rueda), *m.* **back a.,** eje trasero, *m.* **differential a.,** eje diferencial, *m.* **front a.,** eje delantero, *m*
**aye** /ai/ *interj* sí. —*n* voto afirmativo, *m*
**azalea** /ə'zeilyə/ *n* azalea, *f*
**Aztec** /'æztɛk/ *a* and *n* azteca, *mf*
**azure** /'æʒər/ *n* azul celeste, *m*

# B

**b** /bi/ *n* (letter) be, *f; Mus.* si, *m*

**baa** /bæ, ba/ *n* balido, be, *m, vi* balar, dar balidos

**babble** /'bæbəl/ *n* (chatter) charla, *f;* (of a child) gorjeo, *m;* (confused sound) vocinglería, barbulla, *f,* rumor, *m;* (of water) murmullo, susurro, *m.* —*vi* charlar; (of children) gorjearse; (incoherently) balbucir; (water) murmurar, susurrar; (a secret) descubrir

**babbler** /'bæblər/ *n* charlatán (-ana)

**babbling** /'bæblɪŋ/ *n* garrulería, locuacidad, *f;* (incoherent speech) balbuceo, *m.* (of water) murmullo, *m.* —*a* gárrulo, locuaz; balbuciente; murmurante

**babel** /'bæbəl/ *n* babel, *m*

**baboon** /bæ'bun; *esp. Brit.* bə-/ *n* babuino, *m*

**baby** /'beibi/ *n* bebé, crío, *m;* niño (-ña) de pecho; *Fig.* gran bebé, *m;* niño mimado, *m, a* infantil. **b. blue,** azul claro, *m.* **b. doll,** muñeca bebé, *f.* **b. grand piano,** piano de media cola, *m*

**baby carriage** *n* coche de niños, *m*

**baby-faced** /'beibi ,feist/ *a* con mejillas mofletudas

**babyhood** /'beibi,hʊd/ *n* infancia, niñez, *f*

**babyish** /'beibiɪʃ/ *a* infantil, aniñado, pueril

**Babylon** /'bæbələn, -,lɒn/ *n* babilonia, *f*

**babysitter** /'beibi,sɪtər/ *n* cuidaniños, *mf*

**baccalaureate** /,bækə'lɔrɪit, -'lɒr-/ *n* bachillerato, *m*

**baccarat** /,bakə'ra, ,bækə-/ *n* bacará, *m*

**bachelor** /'bætʃələr/ *n* soltero, célibe, *m;* (of a university) licenciado, bachiller, *m;* (as a title) caballero, *m.* **confirmed b.,** solterón, *m.* **degree of b.,** licenciatura, *f.* **to receive the degree of b.,** licenciarse, bachillerarse

**bachelorhood** /'bætʃələr,hʊd/ *n* soltería, *f,* celibato, *m*

**bacillus** /bə'sɪləs/ *n* bacilo, *m*

**back** /bæk/ *n Anat.* espalda, *f;* (of an animal) lomo, espinazo, *m;* (reins, loins) riñones, *m pl;* (of chairs, sofas) respaldo, *m;* (of a book) lomo, *m;* (back, bottom) fondo, *m;* parte posterior, parte de atrás, *f;* (of a hand, brush and other things) dorso, *m;* (of a coin) reverso, *m;* el otro lado de alguna cosa; (in football, hockey) defensa, *m; Theat.* foro, *m;* (of firearms) culata, *f;* (of a knife) canto, *m;* (upper portion) parte superior, *f.* —*a* posterior, trasero; de atrás; (remote) alejado, apartado; inferior; (overdue) past; out of date) atrasado; (earlier) anterior; *Anat.* dorsal. **at the b.,** detrás; en el fondo; en la última fila. **at the b. of one's mind,** por sus adentros, en el fondo del pensamiento. **behind one's b.,** a espaldas de uno, en ausencia de uno. **half-b.,** medio, *m.* **on one's b.,** boca arriba; a cuestas. **to see the b. of,** *Inf.* ver por última vez, desembarazarse de. **to turn one's b. on,** volver la espalda (a). **with one's b. to the engine,** de espaldas a la máquina. **to b. to b.,** espalda con espalda

**back** /bæk/ *vt* empujar hacia atrás; (a vehicle) dar marcha atrás; hacer retroceder; (line) reforzar; (support) apoyar; (sign) endosar; (bind) forrar; (bet on) apostar a; (a sail) fachear. —*vi* retroceder; dar marchar atrás; (of the wind) girar; (with on to) dar sobre, dominar; (with down) abandonar (una pretensión, etc.). **to b. out,** salir, marcharse; volverse atrás; (retract) desdecirse

**back** /bæk/ *adv* detrás; atrás; otra vez, de nuevo; (returned) de vuelta; a alguna distancia; (at home) en casa. —*interj* ¡atrás! **A few weeks b.,** Hace unas semanas, Unas semanas atrás. **It stands b. from the road,** Está a alguna distancia del camino. **to go b. to,** (of families, etc.) remontar a. **to come b.,** regresar. **to come b. again,** regresar de nuevo, regresar por segunda vez

**back axle** *n* eje trasero, *m*

**backbite** /'bæk,bait/ *vt* cortar (a uno) un sayo, desollarle (a uno) vivo, murmurar de

**backbiter** /'bæk,baitər/ *n* mala lengua, *f,* murmurador (-ra)

**backbiting** /'bæk,baitɪŋ/ *n* murmuración, detracción, maledicencia, *f, a* murmurador, detractor

**backbone** /'bæk,boun/ *n* espinazo, *m,* columna vertebral, *f.* **to the b.,** hasta la médula

**backchat** /'bæk,tʃæt/ *n* dimes y diretes, *m pl;* insolencia, *f.* **to indulge in b.-c.,** andar en dimes y diretes

**back door** *n* puerta trasera, puerta de servicio, *f*

**backed** /bækt/ *a* (lined) forrado; (in compounds; of persons) de espalda; (of chairs) de respaldo

**backer** /'bækər/ *n* (better) apostador, *m;* protector (-ra, -triz)

**backfire** /'bæk,fai³r/ *n* contrafuego *m,* falsa explosión, *f*

**backgammon** /'bæk,gæmən/ *n* chaquete, *m*

**back garden** *n* jardín de atrás, *m*

**background** /'bæk,graund/ *n* fondo, *m; Art.* último término, *m.* **in the b.,** en el fondo; *Art.* en último término; *Fig.* en las sombras; alejado, a distancia

**backhand** /'bæk,hænd/ *n Sports.* revés, *m*

**backhanded** /'bæk,hændɪd/ *a* de revés, dado con el revés de la mano; *Fig.* ambiguo, equívoco

**backing** /'bækɪŋ/ *n* forro, *m;* (lining) refuerzo, *m;* (of a vehicle) marcha atrás, *f;* retroceso, *m;* (betting) el apostar (a); (wagers) apuestas, *f pl;* (*Fig.* support) apoyo, *m,* ayuda, *f;* garantía, *f*

**backlog** /'bæk,lɒg/ *n Com.* rezago de pedidos, *m*

**back number** *n* (of a periodical) número atrasado, *m*

**back pedal** *vi* contrapedalear

**back premises** *n* parte trasera (de una casa, etc.), *f*

**backroom** /'bæk'rum/ *n* cuarto interior, *m,* habitación trasera, *f.* **b. boy,** investigador ocupado en trabajos secretos para el gobierno, *m*

**back seat** *n* asiento trasero, *m;* fondo, *m.* **to take a b.-s.,** permanecer en el fondo, ceder el paso

**back shop** *n* trastienda, *f*

**backside** /'bæk,said/ *n* trasero, *m,* posaderas, nalgas, *f pl*

**backslide** /'bæk,slaid/ *vi* recaer, reincidir

**backslider** /'bæk,slaidər/ *n* (in religion or politics) apóstata, *mf;* reincidente, *mf*

**backsliding** /'bæk,slaidɪŋ/ *n* apostasía, *f;* reincidencia, *f*

**backstage** /'bæk'steidʒ/ *n* foro, fondo del escenario, *m, adv* hacia el foro; detrás de bastidores

**backstaircase** /'bæk'stɛər,keis/ *n* escalera de servicio, *f;* escalera secreta, *f*

**backstairs** /'bæk'stɛərz/ *n* escalera de servicio, *f; Fig.* vías secretas, *f pl, a* de cocina; *Fig.* secreto

**backstitch** /'bæk,stɪtʃ/ *n Sew.* pespunte, *m, vt and vi* pespuntar

**back street** *n* calle secundaria, callejuela, *f; pl* **back streets,** barrios bajos, *m pl*

**backstroke** /'bæk,strouk/ *n* reculada, *f; Sports.* revés, *m*

**back tooth** *n* muela, *f*

**back view** *n* vista de detrás, *f*

**backward** /'bækwərd/ *a* hacia atrás; vuelto hacia atrás; (in development) atrasado, poco avanzado; lento; negligente; (shy) modesto; (late) tardío; atrasado; retrógrado; (dull) torpe; retrospectivo. —*adv* hacia atrás; al revés; (of falling) de espaldas; (of time) al pasado. **to go b. and forward,** ir y venir. **b. and forward,** de acá para allá

**backwardness** /'bækwərdnɪs/ *n* atraso, *m;* lentitud, *f;* negligencia, *f;* modestia, *f;* (lateness) tardanza, *f,* atraso, *m;* (dullness) torpeza, *f;* falta de progreso, *f*

**backwards** /'bækwərdz/ *adv* See **backward**

**backwash** /'bæk,wɒʃ/ *n* agua de rechazo, *f*

**backwater** /'bæk,wɔtər/ *n* remanso, *m*

**back wheel** *n* rueda trasera, *f, vi* contrapedalear

**backwoods** /'bæk'wʊdz/ *n* monte, *m,* selva, *f*

**back yard** *n* corral, *m*

**bacon** /'beikən/ *n* tocino, *m*

**bacteria** /bæk'tɪəriə/ *n* bacteria, *f*

**bacterial** /bæk'tɪəriəl/ *a* bacterial, bacteriano

**bactericide** /bæk'tɪərə,said/ *n* bactericida, *m*

**bacteriological** /bæk,tɪəriə'lɒdʒɪkəl/ *a* bacteriológico

**bacteriologist** /,bæktɪəri'ɒlədʒɪst/ *n* bacteriólogo, *m*

**bacteriology** /ˌbæktɪəriˈɒlədʒi/ n bacteriología, f
**bad** /bæd/ a malo; (wicked) perverso; (ill) enfermo, malo (with estar); (naughty; undutiful) malo (with ser); (of coins) falso; (of debts) incobrable; (rotten) podrido; (harmful) nocivo; (dangerous) peligroso; (of pains, a cold) fuerte; intenso; (of a shot) errado; (mistaken) equivocado; (unfortunate) desgraciado. —n el mal, lo malo; (persons) los malos. **extremely bad,** pésimo. **from bad to worse,** de mal en peor. **It's too bad!** ¡Esto es demasiado! **to go bad,** (fruit) macarse; (food) estropearse. **bad habit,** mala costumbre, f, vicio, m. **to have the bad habit of,** tener el vicio de. **bad temper,** malhumor, mal genio, m. **bad tempered,** malhumorado. **bad turn,** flaco servicio, m, mala pasada, f
**badge** /bædʒ/ n insignia, f; (decoration) condecoración, f; símbolo, emblema, m; (mark) marca, f
**badger** /ˈbædʒər/ n tejón, m, vt cansar, molestar
**Bad Lands** (of Nebraska and South Dakota) Tierras malas f pl; (of Argentina) la Travesía, f
**badly** /ˈbædli/ adv mal. **extremely b.,** pésimamente. **to want something b.,** necesitar algo con urgencia. **b. done,** mal hecho. **b. disposed,** malintencionado
**badminton** /ˈbædmɪntn/ n el juego del volante, m
**badness** /ˈbædnɪs/ n maldad, f; mala calidad, f; lo malo
**bad-smelling** /ˈbæd ˌsmɛlɪŋ/ a maloliente
**baffle** /ˈbæfəl/ vt desconcertar; (bewilder) tener perplejo (a); contrariar, frustrar; (obstruct) impedir; (avoid) evitar. **to b. description,** no haber palabras para describir
**baffling** /ˈbæflɪŋ/ a desconcertante; difícil; confuso; perturbador; (of people) enigmático
**bag** /bæg/ n saco, m; talega, f; (hand) bolsa, f, saco (de mano), m; (for tools) capacho, m; (for sewing) costurero, m; (of bagpipes) fuelle, m; (saddle) alforja, f; (briefcase) cartera, f; (suitcase) maleta, f; (under the eye) ojera, f; (game shot) caza, f. —vt entalegar; coger, cazar; matar; tomar. —vi (of garments) arrugarse. **to clear out bag and baggage,** liar el petate. **a bag of bones,** (person) un manojo de huesos. **bag wig,** peluquín, m
**bagatelle** /ˌbægəˈtɛl/ n bagatela, friolera, f; (game) billar romano, m
**bagful** /ˈbægfʊl/ n saco, m; bolsa, f
**baggage** /ˈbægɪdʒ/ n equipaje, m; Mil. bagaje, m; (madcap) pícara, f; (jade) mujerzuela, f. **b. master,** (railway) factor, m. **b. car,** furgón de equipajes, m
**baggage rack** n (of automobile) portaequipajes, m
**baggy** /ˈbægi/ a (creased, of trousers) con rodilleras, arrugado; (wide) bombacho
**bagpipe** /ˈbægˌpaɪp/ n gaita, f
**bagpiper** /ˈbægˌpaɪpər/ n gaitero, m
**bah** /bɑ/ interj ¡bah!
**Bahamas, the** /bəˈhɑməz/ las Islas Bahamas, las Islas Lucayas, f
**bail** /beɪl/ n Law. fianza, caución, f; (person) fiador (-ra); (cricket) travesaño, m, barra, f. —vt Law. poner en libertad bajo fianza; salir fiador (por); (a boat) achicar. **on b.,** en fiado. **to go b.,** dar fianza, fiar.
**bailiff** /ˈbeɪlɪf/ n Law. agente ejecutivo, m; alguacil, m; mayordomo, m; capataz, m
**bait** /beɪt/ n cebo, m; anzuelo, m; (fodder) pienso, m, vt cebar; (feed) dar pienso (a); azuzar; atormentar; (attract) atraer
**baiting** /ˈbeɪtɪŋ/ n cebadura, f; combate, m; tormenta, f
**baize** /beɪz/ n bayeta, f. **green b.,** tapete verde, m
**bake** /beɪk/ vt cocer; hacer (pan, etc.). **I like to bake cakes,** Me gusta hacer pasteles; Fig. endurecer. —vi cocerse
**bakelite** /ˈbeɪklaɪt/ n bakelita, f
**baker** /ˈbeɪkər/ n panadero, hornero, m, **a baker's dozen,** la docena del fraile
**bakery** /ˈbeɪkəri, ˈbeɪkri/ n panadería, f
**baking** /ˈbeɪkɪŋ/ n cocimiento, m, cocción, f; (batch) hornada, f; el hacer (pan, etc.) a Inf. abrasador. **b.-dish,** tortera, f. **b.-powder,** levadura química, f
**balance** /ˈbæləns/ n balanza, f; equilibrio, m; Com. balance, saldo, m; (in a bank) saldo (a favor del cuentacorrentista), m; Math. resto, f; Astron. Libra, f; (pendulum) péndola, f; (counterweight) con-

trapeso, m. **credit b.,** saldo acreedor, m. **debit b.,** saldo deudor, m. **net b.,** saldo líquido, m. **to lose one's b.,** perder el equilibrio. **to strike a b.,** hacer balance. **b. of power,** equilibrio político, m. **b. of trade,** balanza de comercio, f. **b.-sheet,** balance, avanzo, m. **b. wheel,** (of watches) volante, m
**balance** /ˈbæləns/ vt balancear, abalanzar; contrapesar; (accounts) saldar; equilibrar; comparar; considerar, examinar. —vi balancearse; ser de igual peso; equilibrarse; (accounts) saldarse
**balance of trade** n balanza comercial, f
**balancing** /ˈbælənsɪŋ/ n balanceo, m; Com. balance, m. **b.-pole,** balancín, m
**balconied** /ˈbælkənid/ a con balcones, que tiene balcones
**balcony** /ˈbælkəni/ n balcón, m; galería, f; Theat. anfiteatro, m
**bald** /bɔld/ a calvo; (of style) seco, pobre; Fig. desnudo, árido, pelado; sin adorno; (simple) sencillo. **to grow b.,** ponerse calvo, encalvecer
**balderdash** /ˈbɔldərˌdæʃ/ n galimatías, m, jerigonza, f; disparate, m
**baldly** /ˈbɔldli/ adv secamente; sencillamente
**baldness** /ˈbɔldnɪs/ n calvicie, f; (of style) sequedad, pobreza, f; (bareness) desnudez, aridez, f
**bale** /beɪl/ n (bundle) fardo, m; (of cotton, paper, etc.) bala, f
**Balearic** /ˌbæliˈærɪk/ a baleárico
**Balearic Islands, the** las Islas Baleares, f
**baleful** /ˈbeɪlfəl/ a malicioso, siniestro, maligno
**balefully** /ˈbeɪlfəli/ adv malignamente
**balk** /bɔk/ n obstáculo, m; (beam) viga, f; (billiards) cabaña, f. —vt frustrar; impedir. —vi resistirse, rehusar
**Balkan** /ˈbɔlkən/ a balcánico
**Balkans, the** los Balcanes, m
**ball** /bɔl/ n globo, m, esfera, f; (plaything) pelota, f; (as in billiards, cricket, croquet) bola, f; (in football, basket-ball) balón, m; (shot) bala, f; (of wool, etc.) ovillo, m; (of the eye) globo (del ojo), m; (of the thumb) yema (del pulgar), f; (of the foot) planta (del pie), f; (dance) baile, m. —vi apelotonarse. **red b.,** (in billiards) mingo, m. **to play b.,** jugar a la pelota. **to roll oneself into a b.,** aovillarse, hacerse un ovillo. **b.-and-socket joint,** articulación esférica, f. **b.-bearing,** cojinete de bolas, m
**ballad** /ˈbæləd/ n romance, m; (song) balada, f
**balladmonger** /ˈbæləd.mʌŋgər/ n coplero (-ra)
**ballast** /ˈbæləst/ n (Naut. and Fig.) lastre, m; Rail. balasto, m. —vt lastrar; llenar de balasto
**ballerina** /ˌbæləˈrinə/ n bailarina, f
**ballet** /bæˈleɪ/ n baile ruso, ballet, m; baile, m. **b. master,** director de ballet, m
**ballistics** /bəˈlɪstɪks/ n balística, f
**balloon** /bəˈlun/ n globo aerostático, m; Chem. balón, m; (toy) globo, m; Archit. bola, f. **captive b.,** globo cautivo, m. **b. barrage,** cortina de globos de intercepción, f. **b.-tyre,** neumático balón, m
**balloonist** /bəˈlunɪst/ n aeronauta, mf
**ballot** /ˈbælət/ n votación, f; papeleta para votar, cédu&;la de votación, f. —vi votar, balotar. **b. box,** urna electoral, f
**ballpoint pen** /ˈbɔlˌpɔɪnt/ n pluma esférica, f, birome, m (Argentina), punto-bola, m (Bolivia), esfero, m (Colombia)
**ballroom** /ˈbɔlˌrum/ n salón de baile, m; salón de fiestas, m
**ballroom dancing** n baile de salón, m
**balm** /bɑm/ n bálsamo, m; Fig. ungüento, m
**balminess** /ˈbɑmɪnɪs/ n fragancia, f; aroma, m; (gentleness) suavidad, f
**balmy** /ˈbɑmi/ a balsámico; fragante; aromático; (soft) suave; (soothing) calmante
**balsam** /ˈbɔlsəm/ n bálsamo, m
**Baltic** /ˈbɔltɪk/ a báltico
**Baltic, the** el (Mar) Báltico, m
**baluster** /ˈbæləstər/ n balaustre, m
**balustrade** /ˈbæləˌstreɪd/ n balaustrada, barandilla, f, antepecho, m
**bamboo** /bæmˈbu/ n bambú, m
**bamboozle** /bæmˈbuzəl/ vt engatusar, embaucar
**bamboozler** /bæmˈbuzlər/ n embaucador (-ra)

**bamboozling** /bæm'buzlɪŋ/ *n* embaucamiento, engaño, *m*

**ban** /bæn/ *n* interdicción, *f;* prohibición, *f;* bando, *m.* —*vt* prohibir; proscribir

**banal** /bə'næl/ *a* banal, vulgar, trivial

**banality** /bə'nælɪti/ *n* banalidad, vulgaridad, trivialidad, *f*

**banana** /bə'nænə/ *n* (tree and fruit) plátano, *m;* (fruit) banana, *f.* **b. plantation,** platanar, *m*

**band** /bænd/ *n* lista, tira, *f;* zona, *f;* (black mourning) tira de gasa, *f;* (sash) faja, *f;* (ribbon) banda; cinta, *f;* (bandage) venda, *f; Mech.* correa, *f; Archit.* listón, *m; Mus.* banda, *f;* (group) pandilla, *f,* grupo, *m.* —*vi* congregar, reunir. —*vi* reunirse, asociarse. **b.-saw,** sierra de cinta, *f*

**bandage** /'bændɪdʒ/ *n* venda, *f,* vendaje, *m, vt* vendar, poner un vendaje en (limbs, etc. or persons)

**bandaging** /'bændɪdʒɪŋ/ *n* vendaje, *m*

**banderol** /'bændə,roʊl/ *n* banderola, *f*

**bandit** /'bændɪt/ *n* bandido, bandolero, *m*

**bandmaster** /'bænd,mæstər/ *n* músico mayor, *m;* director de orquesta, *m*

**bandsman** /'bændzmən/ *n* músico, *m*

**bandstand** /'bænd,stænd/ *n* quiosco de música, *m*

**bandy** /'bændi/ *vt* cambiar, trocar; pasar de uno a otro

**bandy-legged** /'bændi ˌlɛgɪd/ *a* estevado zanquituerto

**bane** /beɪn/ *n* (poison) veneno, *m;* perdición, ruina, *f;* (nuisance) plaga, *f*

**baneful** /'beɪnfəl/ *a* pernicioso, funesto; dañino; maligno

**banefully** /'beɪnfəli/ *adv* funestamente; malignamente

**bang** /bæŋ/ *n* golpe, golpazo, *m;* (of an explosive, fire-arm) estallido, *m;* detonación, *f;* (of a firework) traque, *m;* (of a door) portazo, *m;* (with the fist) puñetazo, *m;* (noise) ruido, *m;* (fringe) flequillo, *m.* —*vt* golpear; (beat) sacudir; (throw) lanzar, arrojar con violencia; (a door, etc.) cerrar de golpe, cerrar con violencia. —*vi* golpear; estallar; (thunder) retronar; (in the wind) cencerrear. —*interj* ¡pum! ¡zas!

**banging** /'bæŋɪŋ/ *n* golpeadura, *f;* sacudidura, *f;* detonación, *f;* ruido, *m*

**bangle** /'bæŋgəl/ *n* (slave b.) esclava, *f;* pulsera, *f;* brazalete, *m;* (for ankles) ajorca, *f*

**banish** /'bænɪʃ/ *vt* desterrar; apartar; (from the mind) despedir, ahuyentar; (suppress) suprimir

**banishment** /'bænɪʃmənt/ *n* destierro, *m;* expulsión, *f;* relegación, *f;* (suppression) supresión, *f*

**banister** /'bænəstər/ *n* baranda, *f,* pasamano, *m*

**banjo** /'bændʒoʊ/ *n* banjo, *m*

**banjoist** /'bændʒoʊɪst/ *n* tocador (-ra) de banjo

**bank** /bæŋk/ *n* (of rivers, etc.) ribera, orilla, *f,* margen, *m;* (of clouds) banda, capa, *f;* (of sand, fog, snow) banco, *m;* (embankment) terraplén, *m; Com.* banco, *m;* (gaming) banca, *f;* (for foreign exchange) casa de cambio, *f.* **b. account,** cuenta corriente, *f.* **b. book,** libreta de banco, *f.* **b. clerk,** empleado de banco, *m.* **b. holiday,** fiesta oficial, *f,* **b.-note,** billete de banco, *m.* **b. stock,** acciones de un banco, *f pl*

**bank** /bæŋk/ *vt* estancar, represar; amontonar; poner (dinero) en un banco, depositar en un banco. —*vi* tener cuenta corriente en un banco; (gaming) tener la banca; ser banquero; *Aer.* inclinarse al virar

**banker** /'bæŋkər/ *n* banquero, *m,* (also at cards); (money-changer) cambista, *mf*

**banking** /'bæŋkɪŋ/ *n Com.* banca, *f; Aer.* vuelo inclinado, *m, a Com.* bancario. **b. house,** casa de banca, *f*

**bankrupt** /'bæŋkrʌpt/ *a* insolvente, quebrado. —*n* quebrado (-da). **to go b.,** declararse en quiebra, hacer bancarrota

**bankruptcy** /'bæŋkrʌptsi/ *n* bancarrota, quiebra, *f; Fig.* pobreza, decadencia, *f.* **fraudulent b.,** quiebra fraudulenta, *f.* **b. court,** tribunal de quiebras, *m*

**banner** /'bænər/ *n* bandera, *f*

**banns** /bænz/ *n pl* amonestaciones, *f pl.* **to forbid the b.,** impedir las amonestaciones. **to publish the b.,** decir las amonestaciones

**banquet** /'bæŋkwɪt/ *n* banquete, *m, vt and vi* banquetear

**banqueting** /'bæŋkwɪtɪŋ/ *a* de banquetes. **b. hall,** sala de banquetes, *f*

**bantam** /'bæntəm/ *n* gallina enana, *f.* **b. weight,** (*Sports.*) *a* de peso gallo. —*n* peso gallo, *m*

**banter** /'bæntər/ *vt and vi* tomar el pelo (a). —*n* chistes, *m pl,* burlas, *f pl*

**baptism** /'bæptɪzəm/ *n* bautismo, *m; Fig.* bautizo, *m*

**baptist** /'bæptɪst/ *n* bautista, *m.* **St. John the B.,** San Juan Bautista

**baptistry** /'bæptəstri/ *n* baptisterio, bautisterio, *m*

**baptize** /bæp'taɪz, 'bæptaɪz/ *vt* bautizar

**baptizing** /bæp'taɪzɪŋ/ *n* bautizo, *m*

**bar** /bɑr/ *n* barra, *f;* (of chocolate, soap) pastilla, *f; Herald.* banda, *f;* (on a window) reja, *f;* (of a door) tranca, *f,* barrote, *m;* (bar lever) palanca, *f;* (of a balance) astil, *m; Mus.* barra, *f;* (in the sea, etc.) banco, alfaque, *m;* (barrier) barrera, *f;* (barrister's profession) foro, *m,* curia, *f; Fig.* tribunal, *m;* (in a court) barra, *f; Fig.* impedimento, *m;* (of light) rayo, *m;* (stripe) raya, *f;* (for refreshments) bar, *m;* mostrador del bar, *m.* —*vt* atrancar, abarrotar; impedir, obstruir; prohibir; exceptuar, excluir; (streak) rayar. **the b.,** el cuerpo de abogados. **to be called to the b.,** ser recibido como abogado en los tribunales. **b.-tender,** camarero del bar, *m*

**bar association** *n* colegio de abogados, *m*

**barb** /bɑrb/ *n* púa, *f;* (of an arrow, fish-hook, etc.) lengüeta, *f;* (of a lance) roquete, *m;* (of fish) barbilla, *f;* (of a feather) barba, *f;* (horse) caballo berberisco, *m.* —*vt* proveer de púas; armar de lengüetas

**Barbados** /bɑr'beɪdoʊz/ Isla de Barbados, *f*

**barbarian** /bɑr'bɛəriən/ *a* bárbaro, barbárico. —*n* bárbaro (-ra)

**barbaric** /bɑr'bærɪk/ *a* barbárico, salvaje

**barbarism** /'bɑrbə,rɪzəm/ *n* barbarismo, salvajismo, *m;* crueldad, *f;* (of style) barbarismo, *m*

**barbarity** /bɑr'bærɪti/ *n* barbaridad, ferocidad, *f*

**barbarous** /'bɑrbərəs/ *a* feroz, cruel, salvaje; inculto

**barbarously** /'bɑrbərəsli/ *adv* bárbaramente, cruelmente

**barbarousness** /'bɑrbərəsnɪs/ *n* barbaridad, *f;* crueldad, ferocidad, *f*

**Barbary** /'bɑrbəri/ Berbería, *f*

**barbecue** /'bɑrbɪ,kyu/ *n* barbacoa, *f*

**barbed wire** /'bɑrbd/ *n* alambre de púas, alambre espinoso, *m*

**barber** /'bɑrbər/ *n* barbero, *m.* **barber shop,** barbería, *f*

**Barcelona** /,bɑrsə'loʊnə/ (of or from) *a* and *n* barcelonés (-esa)

**bard** /bɑrd/ *n* bardo, vate, *m*

**bare** /bɛər/ *a* desnudo; descubierto; vacío; (mere) mero, solo; (worn) raído, pelado, raso; (unadorned) sencillo; (unsheathed) desnudo; (arid) árido; (curt) seco; (unprotected) desabrigado; pobre. —*vt* desnudar; descubrir; revelar. **He bared his head,** Se descubrió. **to lay b.,** dejar al desnudo; revelar

**bareback** /'bɛər,bæk/ *a* que monta en pelo. —*adv* en pelo

**barefaced** /'bɛər,feɪst/ *a* descarado, desvergonzado, cínico

**barefoot** /'bɛər,fʊt/ *a* descalzo

**bareheaded** /'bɛər,hɛdɪd/ *a* sin sombrero, descubierto

**barelegged** /'bɛər,lɛgɪd/ *a* en pernetas, en piernas

**barely** /'bɛərli/ *adv* apenas; escasamente; meramente, solamente

**bareness** /'bɛərnɪs/ *n* desnudez, *f;* desadorno, *m;* (aridity) aridez, *f;* pobreza, *f*

**bargain** /'bɑrgən/ *n* contrato, *m;* pacto, acuerdo, *m;* (purchase) ganga, *f.* —*vi* negociar; (haggle) regatear; (expect) esperar. **into the b.,** de añadidura, también. **It is a b.,** Es una ganga; Trato hecho. **to get the best of the b.,** salir ganando. **to strike a b.,** cerrar un trato. **b. counter,** sección de saldos, *f.* **b. sale,** venta de saldos, *f*

**bargainer** /'bɑrgənər/ *n* negociador (-ra); regatón (-ona)

**bargaining** /'bɑrgənɪŋ/ *n* negociación, gestión, *f;* (haggling) regateo, *m*

**barge** /bɑrdʒ/ *n* (for freight) barcaza, gabarra, *f;*

falúa, f; lancha, f. —vi (into) tropezar con; dar empujones

**baritone** /'bærɪˌtoun/ n barítono, m

**barium** /'beəriəm/ n Chem. bario, m

**bark** /bɑrk/ n (of a tree) corteza, f; (quinine) quina, f; (boat, Poet.) barca, f; Naut. buque de tres palos, m; (of a dog) ladrido, m; (of a fox) aullido, m; (of a gun) ruido, m. —vi (of a dog) ladrar; (of a fox) aullar; (of a gun) tronar

**barking** /'bɑrkɪŋ/ n ladrido, m; (of stags) rebramo, m; (of foxes) aullidos, m pl; (of guns) trueno, m

**barley** /'bɑrli/ n cebada, f, a de cebada. **pearl b.,** cebada perlada, f. **b.-bin,** cebadera, f. **b. dealer,** cebadero, m. **b. field,** cebadal, m. **b.-water,** hordiate, m

**barm** /bɑrm/ n (froth on beer) giste, m; (leaven) levadura, f

**barmaid** /'bɑrˌmeid/ n moza de bar, camarera, f

**barn** /bɑrn/ n pajar, granero, hórreo, m. **b.-owl,** lechuza, f

**barnacle** /'bɑrnəkəl/ n lapa, f, barnacla, m

**barometer** /bə'rɒmɪtər/ n barómetro, m

**barometric** /ˌbærə'mɛtrɪk/ a barométrico

**baron** /'bærən/ n barón, m

**baroness** /'bærənɪs/ n baronesa, f

**Baron Munchausen** /'bærən 'mʊntʃˌhauzən/ el Baron de la Castaña

**baroque** /bə'rouk/ a barroco. **the b.,** lo barroco

**barrack** /'bærək/ n Mil. cuartel, m, caserna, f, vt acuartelar

**barrage** /bə'rɑʒ/ n presa de contención, f; Mil. cortina de fuego, f; (barrier) barrera, f; (of questions) lluvia, f. **b. balloon,** globo de intercepción, m

**barrel** /'bærəl/ n barril, m; tonel, m, cuba, f; (of a gun) cañón, m; Mech. cilindro, m; (of an animal) cuerpo, m. —vt embarrilar, entonelar. **b.-organ,** organillo, órgano de manubrio, m

**barrelled** /'bærəld/ a embarrilado; (of guns, generally in compounds) de... cañones. **double-b. gun,** escopeta de dos cañones, f

**barren** /'bærən/ a estéril; (of ground) árido; (fruitless) infructuoso

**barrenness** /'bærənˌnɪs/ n esterilidad, f; aridez, sequedad, f; (fruitlessness) inutilidad, f

**barrens** /'bærənz/ n yermo, m sing, yerma, f sing

**barricade** /'bærɪˌkeid/ n barricada, f; barrera, f, vt cerrar con barricadas; obstruir

**barricading** /'bærɪˌkeidɪŋ/ n el cerrar con barricadas; la defensa con barricadas (de)

**barrier** /'bæriər/ n barrera, f; impedimento, m; (for customs duties) portazgo, m

**barring** /'bɑrɪŋ/ prep salvo, excepto, con la excepción de, menos

**barrister** /'bærəstər/ n abogado (-da)

**barrow** /'bærou/ n carretón, m; carretilla, f; (tumulus) túmulo, m

**barter** /'bɑrtər/ n cambio, trueque, m; tráfico, m, vt and vi cambiar, trocar; traficar

**barterer** /'bɑrtərər/ n traficante, mf

**basal** /'beisəl/ a básico, fundamental

**basalt** /bə'sɔlt/ n basalto, m

**base** /beis/ a bajo, vil, ruin; soez; indigno; impuro; (of metals) de mala ley. —n base, f; fundamento, m; pie, m; Archit. pedestal, m; (Mil. Chem. Geom.) base, f; (of a vase) asiento, m, vt basar; fundar. **b. action,** bajeza, f. **b. line,** Sports. línea de base, f. **b. metal,** metal común, m

**baseball** /'beisˌbɔl/ n pelota base, f

**baseless** /'beislɪs/ a sin base; sin fundamento; insostenible

**basely** /'beisli/ adv bajamente, vilmente

**basement** /'beismənt/ n sótano, m

**baseness** /'beisnɪs/ n bajeza, vileza, ruindad, f

**bashful** /'bæʃfəl/ a vergonzoso, ruboroso; tímido, corto; (unsociable) huraño, esquivo

**bashfully** /'bæʃfəli/ adv vergonzosamente; tímidamente

**bashfulness** /'bæʃfəlnɪs/ n vergüenza, f, rubor, m; encogimiento, m, timidez, cortedad, f; (unsociableness) huraña, esquivez, f

**basic** /'beisɪk/ a básico; fundamental

**basic commodity** n artículo básico, producto primario, m

**basilica** /bə'sɪlɪkə/ n basílica, f

**basilisk** /'bæsəlɪsk/ n basilisco, m

**basil (sweet)** /'bæzəl, 'bei-/ n Bot. albahaca, f

**basin** /'beisən/ n vasija, f; (for washing) jofaina, f; (barber's) bacía, f; (of a fountain) taza, f; Anat. bacinete, m; (of a harbor) concha, f; (of a river) cuenca, f (in the earth) hoya, f; (dock) dársena, f

**basis** /'beisɪs/ n base, f; fundamento, m; elemento principal, m

**bask** /bæsk/ vi calentarse; (in the sun) tomar el sol

**basket** /'bæskɪt/ n cesta, f; canasta, f; (frail) espuerta, f. **flat b.,** azafate, m. **large b.,** banasta, f. **b. with a lid,** excusabaraja, f. **b. ball,** baloncesto, m. **b. maker** or **dealer,** banastero, cestero, m. **b. work** or **shop** or **factory,** cestería, f. **b. work chair,** sillón de mimbres, m

**basketful** /'bæskɪtˌfʊl/ n cesta, cestada, f

**Basle** /bɑl/ Basilea, f

**Basque** /bæsk/ a and n vasco (-ca), vascongado (-da). —n (language) vascuence, m

**Basque Provinces, the** las Provincias Vascongadas

**bas-relief** /ˌbɑrɪ'lif, ˌbæs-/ n bajo relieve, m

**bass** /beis/ n Mus. bajo, m; (for tying) esparto, m, a Mus. bajo. **double b.,** contrabajo, m. **figured b.,** bajo cifrado, m. **b. clef,** clave de fa, f. **b. string,** bordón, m. **b. voice,** voz baja, f

**bassinet** /ˌbæsə'nɛt/ n cochecito de niño, m

**bassoon** /bæ'sun/ n Mus. bajón, fagot, m

**bassoonist** /bæ'sunɪst/ n bajonista, fagotista, mf

**bastard** /'bæstərd/ n bastardo (-da), hijo (-ja) natural. —a bastardo, ilegítimo; espurio

**baste** /beist/ vt Sew. bastear, hilvanar, embastar; Cul. enlardar, lardear

**basting** /'beistɪŋ/ n Sew. embaste, m; Cul. lardeamiento, m. **b. spoon,** cacillo, m. **b. stitch,** pasillo, m

**bastion** /'bæstʃən/ n bastión, baluarte, m. **to fortify with bastions,** abastionar

**bastioned** /'bæstʃənd/ a abastionado, con bastiones

**bat** /bæt/ n Zool. murciélago, m; (in cricket) paleta, f; (in table tennis) pala, f. —vi (cricket) golpear con la paleta. **See without**

**batch** /bætʃ/ n (of loaves, etc.) hornada, f; lote, m; (of recruits) promoción, f

**bath** /bæθ/ n baño, m; (room) cuarto de baño, m; (vat) bañador, m; (for swimming) piscina cubierta, f; (in the open air) piscina al aire libre, f; Photo. baño, m, solución, f. —vt bañar, lavar. **hot mineral baths,** termas, f pl. **Order of the B.,** Orden del Baño, f. **public baths,** casa de baños, f. **reinforcing b.,** Photo. reforzador, m. **to take a b.,** bañarse, tomar un baño. **b. -chair,** cochecillo de inválido, m. **b.-robe,** bata de baño, f, albornoz, m. **b. room,** cuarto de baño, m. **b. towel,** toalla del baño, f. **b. tub,** bañera, f, baño, m

**bathe** /beið/ vt bañar, lavar; (of light, etc.) bañar, envolver. —vi bañarse. —n baño, m. **to go for a b.,** ir a bañarse

**bather** /'beiðər/ n bañista, mf; bañador (-ra)

**bathing** /'beiðɪŋ/ a de baño; balneario, m. **b. cap,** gorro de baño, m. **b. dress,** traje de baño, m. **b. gown,** albornoz, m, bata de baño, f. **b. machine,** caseta de baños, f. **b.-pool,** piscina, f. **b.-resort,** estación balnearia, f. **b.-shoes,** calzado de baño, m

**bathos** /'beiθɒs/ n paso de lo sublime a lo ridículo, m; anticlímax, m

**batiste** /bə'tist/ n; batista, f

**baton** /bə'tɒn/ n bastón de mando, m; Mus. batuta, f; (policeman's) porra, f

**battalion** /bə'tælyən/ n batallón, m

**batten** /'bætn̩/ vi engordar (de); medrar, prosperar. **to b. down,** cerrar las escotillas

**batter** /'bætər/ n Cul. batido, m; pasta, f; Sports. lanzador, m. —vt apalear, golpear; (demolish) derribar, demoler; (with artillery) cañonear; batir. **to coat with b.,** rebozar. **to b. down,** derribar

**battering ram** /'bætərɪŋ/ n ariete, m

**battery** /'bætəri/ n (Mil. Nav.) batería, f; Elec. pila, batería, f; Law. agresión, f. **dry b.,** batería de pilas, f. **storage b.,** acumulador, m. **b. cell,** pila de batería eléctrica, f

**battle** /'bætl̩/ n batalla, f; pelea, f, combate, m;

(struggle) lucha, *f.* —*vi* batallar, pelear; luchar. **b.-array,** orden de batalla, *f.* **b.-axe,** hacha de combate, *f.* **b.-cruiser,** acorazado, *m.* **b.-field,** campo de batalla, *m.* **b.-front,** frente de combate, *m.* **b.-piece,** *Art.* batalla, *f.* **b.-ship,** buque de guerra, *m*

**battledore (and shuttlecock)** /'bætļ,dɔr/ *n* raqueta (y volante), *f*

**battlement** /'bætļmənt/ *n* almenaje, *m;* muralla almenada, *f*

**bauble** /'bɔbəl/ *n* (trifle) chuchería, fruslería, *f;* (fool's) cetro de bufón, *m*

**bauxite** /'bɔksait, 'bouzait/ *n* bauxita, *f*

**Bavaria** /bə'vɛəriə/ Baviera, *f*

**Bavarian** /bə'vɛəriən/ *a* and *n* bávaro (-ra)

**bawdy** /'bɔdi/ *a* obsceno, indecente, escabroso

**bawl** /bɔl/ *vi* chillar, vocear

**bawling** /'bɔlɪŋ/ *n* vocerío, *m,* chillidos, *m pl*

**bay** /bei/ *n Geog.* bahía, *f;* (small) abra, *f; Bot.* laurel, *m;* (horse) bayo, *m;* (howl) aullido, *m; Archit.* abertura, *f; Rail.* andén, *m.* —*a* (of horses) bayo, isabelino. —*vi* aullar. **at bay,** en jaque, acorralado. **sick-bay,** enfermería, *f.* **to keep at bay,** tener a distancia; tener alejado; entretener. **bay rum,** ron de malagueta, *m.* **bay window,** ventana salediza, *f*

**baying** /'beiɪŋ/ *n* aullido, *m*

**bayonet** /'beiənɛt/ *n* bayoneta, *f, vt* herir o matar con bayoneta. **fixed b.,** bayoneta calada, *f.* **b. charge,** carga de bayoneta, *f.* **b. thrust,** bayonetazo, *m*

**Bayonne** /ba'yɔn/ Bayona, *f*

**bazaar** /bə'zɑr/ *n* bazar, *m*

**be** /bi/ *vi* ser; (of position, place, state, temporariness) estar; (exist) existir; (in impersonal expressions) haber; (of expressions concerning the weather and time) hacer; (remain) quedar; (leave alone) dejar; (do) hacer; (of one's health) estar; (of feeling cold, hot, afraid, etc. and of years of one's age) tener; (live) vivir; (belong) ser (de), pertenecer (a); (matter, concern) importar (a); (happen) ocurrir, suceder; (find oneself) hallarse, encontrarse, estar; (arrive) llegar (a); (cost) costar; (be worth) valer; (celebrate, hold) celebrarse, tener lugar; (forming continuous tense with present participle active or passive) estar; (with past participle forming passive) ser (this construction is often replaced by reflexive form when no ambiguity is entailed); (with infinitive expressing duty, intention) haber de; (must) tener que. **He is a soldier (doctor, etc.),** Es soldado (médico, etc.). **He is on guard,** Está de guardia. **They were at the door (in the house, etc.),** Estaban a la puerta (en la casa, etc.). **I am writing a letter,** Estoy escribiendo una carta (but this form is often replaced by a simple tense, e.g. escribo...). **It remains to be written,** Queda por escribir. **What is to be done?** ¿Qué hay que hacer? **Woe is me!** ¡Ay de mí! **to be hot (cold),** (of things) estar caliente (frío); (of weather) hacer calor (frío); (of persons) tener calor (frío). **How is John?** He is well, ¿Cómo está Juan? Está bien de salud. **It is daylight,** Es de día. **It is cloudy,** Está nublado. **She is 10,** Tiene diez años. **They are afraid,** Tienen miedo. **I am to go there tomorrow,** He de ir allí mañana. **What is to be will be,** Lo que tiene que ser será. **If John were to come we could go into the country,** Si viniera Juan podríamos ir al campo. **Be that as it may,** Sea como sea. **It is seven years since we saw him,** Hace siete años que no le vemos. **We have been here for three years,** Hace tres años que estamos aquí, Llevamos tres años aquí. **There is** or **there are,** Hay. **There will be many people,** Habrá mucha gente. **There were many people,** Había mucha gente. **There are many people,** Hay mucha gente. **It is three miles to the next village,** Estamos a tres millas del pueblo próximo. **So be it!** Así sea. **Your pen is not to be seen,** Tu pluma no se ve. **It is to be hoped that...,** Se espera que...; ¡Ojalá que...! **The door is open,** La puerta está abierta. **The door was opened by Mary,** La puerta fue abierta por María. **He was accused of being a fascist,** Lo acusaron de fascista. **to be about to,** estar por; (of a more imminent action) estar para, estar a punto de. **to be in,** estar dentro; estar en casa. **to be off,** marcharse, irse. **Be off!** ¡Márchate! ¡Vete!; ¡Fuera! **to be out,** estar fuera; haber salido; no estar en casa; (of a

light, etc.) estar apagado. **to be up,** estar levantado. **to be up to,** proyectar, traer entre manos; urdir, maquinar

**beach** /bitʃ/ *n* playa, *f;* costa, *f.* —*vt* (a boat) encallar en la costa. **b. shoes,** playeras, *f pl.* **b. suit,** vestido de playa, *m*

**beach club** *n* club de playa, *m*

**beacon** /'bikən/ *n* (lighthouse) faro, *m;* (buoy) baliza, *f,* fanal, *m;* (watch-tower) atalaya, *f; Fig.* guía, *f.* —*vt* iluminar. **b. fire,** almenara, *f*

**bead** /bid/ *n* cuenta, *f;* (of glass) abalorio, *m;* (drop) gota, *f; Archit.* perla, *f;* (bubble) burbuja, *f;* (foam) espuma, *f; pl* **beads,** rosario, *m, vt* adornar con abalorios. **to tell one's beads,** rezar el rosario. **b. work,** abalorio, *m*

**beading** /'bidɪŋ/ *n* abalorio, *m; Archit.* friso, listón, *m*

**beadle** /'bidļ/ *n* bedel, *m*

**beadleship** /'bidəl,ʃɪp/ *n* bedelía, *f*

**beagle** /'bigəl/ *n* perro sabueso, *m*

**beak** /bik/ *n* pico, *m;* punta, *f; Naut.* espolón, *m.* **to tap with the b.,** picotear

**beaked** /'bikt/ *a* que tiene pico; (in compounds) de... pico

**beaker** /'bikər/ *n* copa, *f; Chem.* vaso de precipitado, *m*

**beam** /bim/ *n Archit.* madero, *m,* viga, *f;* (width of a ship) manga, *f;* (of a balance) palanca, *f;* (of a plough) cama, *f;* (of light) rayo, destello, *m; Phys.* rayo, *m;* (smile) sonrisa brillante, *f; pl* **beams,** (of a building) envigado, *m;* (of a ship) baos, *m pl.* **main b.,** *Archit.* viga maestra, *f.* **on her b.-ends,** de costado; *Fig.* arruinado; en la miseria. **b. feather,** astil, *m.* **b. of light,** rayo de luz, haz de luz, *m*

**beam** /bim/ *vt* lanzar, emitir; difundir. —*vi* brillar, fulgurar, destellar; estar radiante, estar rebosando de alegría

**beaming** /'bimɪŋ/ *a* brillante; radiante

**bean** /bin/ *n* haba, *f;* judía, alubia, *f;* (of coffee) grano, *m.* **broad b.,** haba, *f.* **French, haricot, kidney b.,** judía, *f.* **string b.,** judía verde, *f.* **b. field,** habar, *m*

**bear** /bɛər/ *n Zool.* oso, *m;* (she-bear) osa, *f;* (Stock Exchange) bajista, *mf.* **Great B.,** *Astron.* Osa Mayor, *f,* Septentrión, *m.* **Little B.,** *Astron.* Osa Menor, *f.* **polar b.,** oso blanco, *m.* **b.-cub,** osezno, *m.* **bear's den,** osera, *f.* **b.-garden,** patio de osos, *m; Inf.* merienda de negros, *f.* **b.-hunting,** caza de osos, *f.* **b.-like,** osuno. **b.-pit,** recinto de los osos, *m*

**bear** /bɛər/ *vt* and *vi* (carry) llevar; (show) ostentar; (company, etc.) hacer; (profess) profesar; (of spite, etc. and of relation) guardar; (have) tener; (fruit) dar; (give birth to) parir; (support) sostener; (endure) aguantar; (suffer) padecer, sufrir; (tolerate) tolerar, sufrir; (a strain, an operation, etc.) resistir; (lean on) apoyarse en; (experience) experimentar; (produce) producir, dar; (enjoy) disfrutar de; (use) usar; (impel) empujar; (occupy, hold) ocupar; (go) dirigirse. **It was suddenly borne in on them that...,** De pronto vieron claro que... **I cannot b. any more,** No puedo más. **We cannot b. him,** No le aguantamos, No le sufrimos. **His language won't b. repeating,** Su lenguaje no puede repetirse. **to bring to b.,** ejercer (presión, etc.). **to b. a grudge,** guardar rencor (a), tener ojeriza (a). **to b. arms,** llevar armas; servir en el ejército o la milicia. **to b. company,** hacer compañía (a), acompañar (a). **to b. in mind,** tener en cuenta, tener presente; acordarse de. **to b. oneself,** conducirse, portarse. **to b. to the right,** ir hacia la derecha. **to b. witness,** atestiguar. **to b. false witness,** levantar falso testimonio. **to b. away,** llevarse; ganar. **to b. down,** hundir; derribar; bajar. **to b. down on,** avanzar rápidamente hacia; correr hacia; *Naut.* arribar sobre; (attack) caer sobre. **to b. in,** llevar adentro. **to b. off,** llevarse; ganar; *Naut.* apartarse de la costa. **to b. on, upon,** apoyarse en; (refer to) referirse a. **to b. out,** llevar fuera; confirmar; apoyar; justificar. **to b. up,** llevar arriba; llevar a la cumbre (de); sostener; (recover) cobrar ánimo; (against) resistir; hacer frente a. **to b. with,** soportar; sufrir; aguantar; llevar con paciencia; ser indulgente con

**bearable** /'bɛərəbəl/ a soportable; aguantable; tolerable

**beard** /bɪərd/ n barba, f; (of cereals) raspa, arista, f, vt desafiar. **thick b.,** barba bien poblada, f

**bearded** /'bɪərdɪd/ a con barba, barbudo

**beardless** /'bɪərdlɪs/ a barbilampiño, desbarbado, imberbe, lampiño

**bearer** /'bɛərər/ n llevador (-ra), portador (-ra); (of a bier) andero, m; Com. dador, portador, m. **good b.,** Agr. árbol fructífero, m. **to b.,** Com. al portador

**bearing** /'bɛərɪŋ/ n porte, m; postura, f; presencia, f; conducta, f; aspecto, m; relación, f; (meaning) significación, f; Naut. demora, orientación, f; Mech. cojinete, soporte, m; (endurance) tolerancia, f; pl **bearings,** (way) camino, m; Herald. escudo de armas, m. **to get one's bearings,** orientarse; encontrar el camino. **to lose one's bearings,** desorientarse; perderse. **to have a b. on,** tener relación con; tener que ver con; influir en

**bearish** /'bɛərɪʃ/ a osuno; rudo, áspero

**bearskin** /'bɛər,skɪn/ n piel de oso, f; birretina, f

**beast** /bist/ n animal, bruto, m; cuadrúpedo, m; (cattle) res, f; bestia, f. **wild b.,** fiera, f. **b. of burden,** acémila, bestia de carga, f. **b. of prey,** animal de rapiña, m

**beastliness** /'bistlɪnɪs/ n bestialidad, brutalidad, f; obscenidad, f

**beastly** /'bistli/ a bestial, brutal; obsceno; Inf. horrible

**beat** /bit/ n latido, m, pulsación, f; golpe, m; (of a drum) toque (de tambor), m; (of a clock) tictac, m; sonido repetido, m; vibración, f

**beat** /bit/ vt and vi batir; golpear; (thrash) pegar, dar una paliza (a); (to remove dust, etc.) sacudir; (shake) agitar; (the wings) aletear; (hunting) batir; (excel) exceder, superar; ganar; (defeat) vencer; (of the rain, etc.) azotar; (a drum) tocar; (of the sun) batir, dar (en); (throb) latir, palpitar, pulsar. **to b. about the bush,** andarse por las ramas. **to stop beating about the bush,** dejarse de historias. **to b. a retreat,** Mil. emprender la retirada; huir. **to b. black and blue,** moler a palos. **to b. hollow,** vencer completamente; ganar fácilmente; aventajar con mucho. **to b. it,** Inf. escaparse corriendo. **to b. time,** Mus. llevar el compás; triunfar sobre la vejez. **to b. to it,** Inf. tomar la delantera. **to b. against,** golpear contra; chocar contra. **to b. back,** rechazar; (sobs, etc.) ahogar; reprimir. **to b. down,** (prices) regatear; (of the sun) caer de plomo, caer de plano; reducir; suprimir; destruir. **to b. off,** rechazar; echar a un lado. **to b. out,** hacer salir; (metals) batir; (a tune) llevar el compás (de). **to b. up,** Cul. batir; (a mattress) mullir; asaltar; maltratar

**beaten** /'bitn/ a (of paths) trillado; (conquered) vencido; (of metals) batido; (dejected) deprimido; (trite) trivial, vulgar

**beater** /'bitər/ n batidor, m; (for carpets) sacudidor (de alfombras), m; Cul. batidor, m

**beatific** /,biə'tɪfɪk/ a beatífico

**beatification** /bi,ætəfɪ'keɪʃən/ n beatificación, f

**beatify** /bi'ætə,faɪ/ vt beatificar

**beating** /'bitɪŋ/ n batimiento, m; vencimiento, m; (thrashing) paliza, f; (of the heart, etc.) palpitación, f; latido, m; (of metals) batida, f; (of a drum) rataplán, toque de tambor, m; (of waves) embate, m; (of wings) aleteo, aletazo, m

**beatitude** /bi'ætɪ,tud/ n beatitud, felicidad, f

**beau** /bou/ n galán, m; (fop) petimetre, m

**beautiful** /'byutəfəl/ a bello, lindo, hermoso; magnífico; excelente; exquisito; elegante; encantador, delicioso

**beautifully** /'byutəfəli/ adv bellamente; (richly) ricamente; admirablemente; magníficamente; elegantemente

**beautify** /'byutə,faɪ/ vt embellecer; hermosear; adornar. **to b. oneself,** arreglarse, ponerse elegante

**beautifying** /'byutəfaɪɪŋ/ n embellecimiento, m; adorno, m

**beauty** /'byuti/ n belleza, hermosura, lindeza, f; magnificencia, f; excelencia, f; elegancia, f; encanto, m; (belle) beldad, Venus, f. **to lose one's b.,** desmejorarse, perder su hermosura. **b. contest,** concurso de belleza, m. **b. parlor,** salón de belleza, instituto de belleza, m. **b. sleep,** el primer sueño de la noche. **b. spot,** lunar, m; lunar postizo, m; (place) sitio hermoso, m. **b. treatment,** masaje facial, m

**beaver** /'bivər/ n castor, m; (hat) sombrero de copa, m; (of helmet) babera, f

**because** /bɪ'kɔz/ conjunc porque. **b. of,** debido a, a causa de

**beckon** /'bɛkən/ vt and vi hacer señas (a); llamar por señas, llamar con la mano

**become** /bɪ'kʌm/ vi volverse; llegar a ser, venir a ser; convertirse en; ponerse; hacerse; (befit) convenir; (suit) ir bien (a), favorecer. **He became red,** Se enrojeció. **The hat becomes you,** El sombrero te va bien. **He became king,** Llegó a ser rey. **What has b. of her?** ¿Qué es de ella?; (Where is she?) ¿Qué se ha hecho de ella? **b. binding,** adquirir carácter de compromiso

**becoming** /bɪ'kʌmɪŋ/ a propio; correcto; decoroso; (suitable) conveniente; (of dress) que favorece, que va bien. **This dress is b. to you,** Este vestido te favorece

**becomingly** /bɪ'kʌmɪŋli/ adv decorosamente

**bed** /bɛd/ n cama, f, lecho, m; (of sea) fondo, m; (of river) cauce, m; Geol. yacimiento, m; (in a garden) cuadro, macizo (de jardín), m; (of a machine) asiento, m; (of a building) cimiento, m; Fig. fundamento, m, base, f, vt (plants) plantar; (fix) fijar, poner. **double bed,** cama de matrimonio, f. **single bed,** cama de monja, f. **in bed,** en cama. **to be gone to bed,** haber ido a la cama. **to be in bed,** estar acostado. **to get into bed,** meterse en cama. **to get out of bed,** levantarse de la cama. **to go to bed,** acostarse, ir a la cama. **to make the beds,** hacer las camas. **to put to bed,** acostar. **to stay in bed,** quedarse en cama, guardar cama. **bed-bug,** chinche, f. **bed-clothes,** ropa de cama, f. **bed-cover,** cubrecama, colcha, f. **bed-head,** cabecera, f. **bed-pan,** silleta, f. **bed-sore,** úlcera de decúbito, f

**bedaub, bedazzle** /bɪ'dɔb; bɪ'dæzəl/. See **daub, dazzle**

**bedchamber** /'bɛd,tʃeɪmbər/ n dormitorio, m, alcoba, f

**bedded** /'bɛdɪd/ a con... cama(s). **a double-b. room,** un cuarto con dos camas; un cuarto con cama de matrimonio

**bedding** /'bɛdɪŋ/ n ropa de cama, f; cama para el ganado, f

**bedeck** /bɪ'dɛk/ vt embellecer, adornar, engalanar

**bedfellow** /'bɛd,felou/ n compañero de almohada, compañero de cama

**bedlam** /'bɛdləm/ n belén, manicomio, m; Fig. babel, m

**Bedouin** /'bɛduɪn/ a and n beduino (-na)

**bedraggled** /bɪ'drægəld/ a mojado y sucio

**bedridden** /'bɛd,rɪdn/ a postrado en cama, inválido

**bedrock** /'bɛd,rɒk/ n lecho de roca, m; Fig. principios fundamentales, fundamentos, m pl

**bedroom** /'bɛd,rum/ n cuarto de dormir, dormitorio, m, habitación, f

**bedside** /'bɛd,saɪd/ n lado de cama, m; cabecera, f. **b. manner,** mano izquierda, diplomacia, f. **b.-table,** mesa de noche, f

**bedspread** /'bɛd,sprɛd/ n colcha, cubrecama, sobrecama, f

**bedstead** /'bɛd,stɛd/ n cama, f

**bedtime** /'bɛd,taɪm/ n hora de acostarse, f

**bee** /bi/ n abeja, f; (meeting) reunión, f, a abejunio. **queen bee,** rey, m, abeja maestra, f. **to have a bee in one's bonnet,** tener una manía (or idea fija). **to make a bee-line for,** ir directamente a. **bee-eater,** Ornith. abejaruco, m. **bee hive,** colmena, f; abejar, m. **bee-keeper,** apicultor (-ra), colmenero (-ra), abejero (-ra). **bee's wax,** cera de abeja, f

**beech** /bitʃ/ n haya, f. **plantation of b. trees,** hayal, m. **b.-nut,** hayuco, m

**beef** /bif/ n carne de vaca, f; (flesh) carne, f; (strength) fuerza, f. **roast b.,** rosbif, m. **b.-tea,** caldo, m

**beefsteak** /'bif,steɪk/ n biftec, bistec, m

**beer** /bɪər/ n cerveza, f. **b. barrel,** barril de cerveza, *m.* **b.-house,** cervecería, *f.* **b. mug,** jarro para la cerveza, *m*

**beery** /'bɪəri/ *a* de cerveza; (tipsy) achispado

**beet** /bit/ *n* remolacha, *f.* **b. sugar,** azúcar de remolacha, *m*

**beetle** /'bitl/ *n* escarabajo, *m.* **b.-browed,** cejijunto

**beetroot** /'bit,rut/ *n* remolacha, *f*

**befall** /bɪ'fɔl/ *vi* acontecer, suceder, ocurrir. —*vt* ocurrir (a), acontecer (a)

**befeathered** /bɪ'fɛðərd/ *a* plumado; adornado con plumas

**befit** /bɪ'fɪt/ *vt* convenir (a), ser digno de

**befitting** /bɪ'fɪtɪŋ/ *a* conveniente, apropiado; digno; oportuno

**before** /bɪ'fɔr/ *adv* delante; al frente; (of time), antes, anteriormente; (of order) antes; (already) ya. —*prep* delante de; en frente de; (of time, order) ante; (in the presence of) ante, en presencia de; (rather than) antes de. **b. going,** antes de marcharse. **B. I did it,** Antes de que lo hiciera; Antes de hacerlo. **as never b.,** como nunca. **b. long,** en breve, dentro de poco. **b.-mentioned,** antes citado. **b. the mast,** al pie del mástil, e.g. *two years b. the mast,* dos años al pie del mástil.

**beforehand** /bɪ'fɔr,hænd/ *adv* previamente, de antemano

**befoul** /bɪ'faul/ *vt* ensuciar; *Fig.* manchar, difamar

**befriend** /bɪ'frɛnd/ *vt* proteger, ayudar, favorecer, amparar

**beg** /bɛg/ *vt* pedir, implorar, suplicar. —*vi* mendigar, pordiosear; vivir de limosna. **I beg to propose,** Me permito proponer; Tengo el gusto de proponer; (the health of) Brindo a la salud de. **I beg your pardon!** ¡Vd. dispense!; (when passing in front of anyone, etc.) Con permiso; (in conversation for repetition of a word) ¿Cómo? **to beg the question,** dar por sentado lo mismo que se trata de probar. **His conduct begs description,** No hay palabras para su comportamiento

**beget** /bɪ'gɛt/ *vt* procrear, engendrar; causar; suscitar

**begetter** /bɪ'gɛtər/ *n* procreador (-ra); creador (-ra)

**begetting** /bɪ'gɛtɪŋ/ *n* procreación, *f;* origen, *m,* causa, *f*

**beggar** /'bɛgər/ *n* mendigo (-ga), pordiosero (-ra). **beggars can't be choosers,** a falta de pan, se conforma con tortillas (Mexico); *vt* empobrecer; arruinar. **to b. description,** no haber palabras para describir

**beggarliness** /'bɛgərlinɪs/ *n* mendicidad, *f;* pobreza, *f*

**beggarly** /'bɛgərli/ *a* miserable, pobre

**beggary** /'bɛgəri/ *n* miseria, pobreza, *f*

**begging** /'bɛgɪŋ/ *n* mendicidad, *f,* pordioseo, *m.* **to go b.,** andar mendigando. **b. letter,** carta pidiendo dinero, *f*

**begin** /bɪ'gɪn/ *vt and vi* empezar; comenzar; iniciar; (a conversation) entablar; (open) abrir; inaugurar; tener su principio; nacer. **to b. to,** empezar a; (start on) ponerse a; (with laughing, etc.) romper a. **to b. with,** empezar por; para empezar, en primer lugar

**beginner** /bɪ'gɪnər/ *n* principiante (-ta); (novice) novato (-ta); iniciador (-ra); autor (-ra)

**beginning** /bɪ'gɪnɪŋ/ *n* principio, comienzo, *m;* origen, *m.* **at the b.,** al principio; (of the month) a principios (de). **from the b. to the end,** desde el principio hasta el fin, *Inf.* de pe a pa. **in the b.,** al principio. **to make a b.,** comenzar, empezar

**begone** /bɪ'gɔn/ *interj* ¡fuera! ¡márchate! ¡vete!

**begonia** /bɪ'gounjə/ *n* begonia, *f*

**begrudge** /bɪ'grʌdʒ/ *vt* envidiar

**beguile** /bɪ'gail/ *vt* engañar; defraudar; (time) entretener; (charm) encantar, embelesar

**beguilement** /bɪ'gailmənt/ *n* engaño, *m;* (of time) entretenimiento, *m;* (charm) encanto, *m*

**beguilingly** /bɪ'gailɪŋli/ *adv* encantadoramente

**behalf** /bɪ'hæf/ *n* (preceded by on or upon) por; (from) de parte (de); a favor (de); en defensa (de)

**behave** /bɪ'heiv/ *vi* (oneself) conducirse, portarse; (act) obrar, proceder. **to b. badly,** portarse mal; obrar mal. **B.!** ¡Pórtate bien!

**behavior** /bɪ'heivjər/ *n* conducta, *f;* comportamiento, *m;* proceder, *m;* (manner) modales, *m pl; Biol.* reacción, *f*

**behaviorism** /bɪ'heivjə,rɪzəm/ *n Psychol.* behaviorismo, *m*

**behead** /bɪ'hɛd/ *vt* decapitar, descabezar

**beheading** /bɪ'hɛdɪŋ/ *n* decapitación, *f*

**behest** /bɪ'hɛst/ *n* precepto, mandato, *m*

**behind** /bɪ'haind/ *adv* detrás; por detrás; atrás; hacia atrás; en pos; (of time and order) después; (late and in arrears) con retraso; (old-fashioned) atrasado. —*prep* detrás de; por detrás de; inferior a; menos avanzado que. —*n Inf.* trasero, *m.* **from b.,** por detrás. **to be b. time,** retrasarse; llegar tarde. **b. the back of,** a espaldas de. **b. the scenes,** entre bastidores. **b. the times,** *Fig.* atrasado de noticias; pasado de moda. **the ideology b. the French Revolution,** la ideología que informó la Revolución Francesa.

**behindhand** /bɪ'haind,hænd/ *a* (out of date) atrasado; (late) tardío; *adv* con retraso

**behold** /bɪ'hould/ *vt* ver, mirar, contemplar; presenciar. —*interj* ¡he aquí! ¡mira!

**beholden** /bɪ'houldən/ *a* obligado, agradecido

**beholder** /bɪ'houldər/ *n* espectador (-ra). **the beholders,** los que lo presenciaban

**beholding** /bɪ'houldɪŋ/ *n* contemplación, vista, *f*

**behoove** /bɪ'houv/ *vt* incumbir, tocar, corresponder

**beige** /beiʒ/ *n* beige, color arena, *m*

**being** /'biɪŋ/ *n* existencia, *f;* operación, *f;* ser, *m;* (spirit) alma, *f,* espíritu, *m;* esencia, *f.* **human b.,** ser humano, *m,* alma viviente, *f.* **for the time b.,** por ahora, por el momento

**bejewel** /bɪ'dʒuəl/ *vt* enjoyar, adornar con joyas

**belabor** /bɪ'leibər/ *vt* apalear, golpear

**belated** /bɪ'leitɪd/ *a* tardío

**belay** /bɪ'lei/ *vt* amarrar

**belch** /bɛltʃ/ *n* eructo, *m;* detonación, *f;* (of a volcano) erupción, *f.* —*vi* eructar. —*vt* vomitar; (curses, etc.) escupir; despedir, arrojar

**belching** /'bɛltʃɪŋ/ *n* eructación, *f;* (of smoke, etc.) vómito, *m,* emisión, *f*

**beleaguer** /bɪ'ligər/ *vt* sitiar

**belfry** /'bɛlfri/ *n* campanario, *m*

**Belgian** /'bɛldʒən/ *a and n* belga, *mf*

**Belgium** /'bɛldʒəm/ Bélgica, *f*

**Belgrade** /'bɛlgreid/ Belgrado, *m*

**belie** /bɪ'lai/ *vt* desmentir, contradecir; defraudar

**belief** /bɪ'lif/ *n* creencia, *f;* fe, *f;* opinión, *f,* parecer, *m;* (trust) confianza, *f.* **in the b. that,** creyendo que, en la creencia de que

**believable** /bɪ'livəbəl/ *a* creíble

**believe** /bɪ'liv/ *vt and vi* creer; opinar, ser de la opinión, parecer (a uno); confiar, tener confianza. **I b. not,** Creo que no, Me parece que no. **I b. so,** Creo que sí, Me parece que sí. **to make (a person) b.,** hacer (a uno) creer. **to b. in,** creer en; confiar en, tener confianza en

**believer** /bɪ'livər/ *n* persona que cree, *f;* creyente, *mf*

**belittle** /bɪ'lɪtl/ *vt* achicar; conceder poca importancia

**bell** /bɛl/ *n* campana, *f;* (hand-bell) campanilla, *f;* (small, round) cascabel, *m;* (on cows, etc.) cencerro, *m,* esquila, *f;* (electric, push, or bicycle) timbre, *m;* (jester's) cascabeles, *m pl;* (cry of stag) bramido, *m.* —*vt* poner un cascabel (a). —*vi* (stags) bramar, roncar. **to bear away the b.,** *Fig.* llevarse la palma. **to ring the b.,** tocar el timbre; agitar la campanilla. **to ring the bells,** tocar las campanas. **to b. the cat,** ponerle el cascabel al gato, ponerle el collar al gato. **b.-boy,** botones, mozo de hotel, *m.* **b.-clapper,** badajo, *m.* **b.-flower,** campanilla, *f.* **b.-founder,** campanero, *m.* **b.-mouthed,** abocinado. **b.-pull,** tirador de campanilla, *m.* **b.-ringer,** campanero, *m.* **b.-shaped,** campanudo. **b.-tent,** pabellón, *m.* **b. tower,** campanario, *m*

**belladonna** /,bɛlə'dɒnə/ *n* belladona, *f*

**belle** /bɛl/ *n* beldad, *f*

**belles-lettres** /bɛl 'lɛtrə/ *n pl* bellas letras, *f pl*

**bellicose** /'bɛlɪ,kous/ *a* belicoso, agresivo

**bellicosity** /,bɛlɪ'kɒsɪti/ *n* belicosidad, *f*

**belligerency** /bə'lɪdʒərənsi/ *n* beligerancia, *f*

**belligerent** /bə'lɪdʒərənt/ *a* beligerante; belicoso, guerrero. —*n* beligerante, *mf*

**bellow** /'bɛlou/ *n* (shout) grito, *m;* rugido, bramido, *m;* (of guns) trueno, *m.* —*vi* gritar, vociferar; rugir, bramar; tronar

**bellowing** /'bɛlouɪŋ/ *n.* See **bellow**

**bellows** /'bɛlouz/ n fuelle, m
**belly** /'bɛli/ n vientre, m, barriga, f; (of a jug, etc.) panza, f; estómago, m; (womb) seno, m. —vt hinchar. —vi hincharse
**belong** /bɪ'lɔŋ/ vi pertenecer (a); tocar (a), incumbir (a); (to a place) ser de; residir en
**belongings** /bɪ'lɔŋɪŋz/ n pl efectos, m pl; posesiones, f pl; (luggage) equipaje, m
**beloved** /bɪ'lʌvɪd/ a muy amado, muy querido. —n querido (-da)
**below** /bɪ'lou/ adv abajo; (under) debajo; (further on) más abajo; (in hell) en el infierno; (in this world) en este mundo, aquí abajo. —prep bajo; (underneath) debajo de; (after) después de; (unworthy of) indigno de; inferior a. **The valley lay b. us,** El valle se extendía a nuestros pies. **b. zero,** bajo cero
**belt** /bɛlt/ n cinturón, m; (of a horse) cincha, f; (corset) faja, f; Geog. zona, f; (of a machine) correa (de transmisión), f
**beltway** /'bɛlt,wei/ n anillo periférico, m
**belvedere** /'bɛlvɪ,dɪər/ n mirador, m
**bemoan** /bɪ'moun/ vt deplorar, lamentar
**bemoaning** /bɪ'mounɪŋ/ n lamentación, f
**bemuse** /bɪ'myuz/ vt confundir, desconcertar
**bench** /bɛntʃ/ n banco, m; (with a back) escaño, m; mesa de trabajo, f; (carpenter's, shoemaker's, in a boat, in parliament) banco, m; (judges) tribunal, m
**bend** /bɛnd/ n corvadura, curva, vuelta, f; (in a river, street) recodo, m; (on a road) codo viraje, m; (of the knee) corva, f; (in a pipe) codo, m; Naut. nudo, m; Herald. banda, f. **sheet b.,** (knot) nudo de tejedor, m
**bend** /bɛnd/ vt encorvar; doblegar; torcer; (the head) bajar; (the body) inclinar; (steps) dirigir, encaminar; (the mind) aplicarse, dedicarse. —vi encorvarse; doblegarse; torcerse; (arch) arquear; inclinarse. **to b. the knee,** arrodillarse. **on bended knee,** de rodillas. **to b. back,** vt redoblar. —vi redoblarse; inclinarse hacia atrás. **to b. down,** agacharse; inclinarse. **b. forward,** inclinarse hacia delante. **to b. over,** inclinarse encima de
**bendable** /'bɛndəbəl/ a que puede doblarse; plegadizo; flexible
**bending** /'bɛndɪŋ/ n doblamiento, m; flexión, f; inclinación, f. —a doblado; inclinado
**beneath** /bɪ'niθ/ adv abajo; debajo; (at one's feet) a los pies de uno. —prep bajo; debajo de; al pie de; (unworthy, inferior) indigno. **He married b. him,** Se casó fuera de su clase
**Benedictine** /,bɛnɪ'dɪktɪn; -tin/ a benedictino. —n benedictino, m; (liqueur) benedictino, m
**benediction** /,bɛnɪ'dɪkʃən/ n bendición, f; gracia divina, merced, f
**benefaction** /'bɛnə,fækʃən/ n beneficiación, f; buena obra, f; beneficio, favor, m
**benefactor** /'bɛnə,fæktər/ n bienhechor, m; protector, m; patrono, m; fundador, m
**benefactress** /'bɛnə,fæktrɪs/ n bienhechora, f; protectora, f; patrona, f; fundadora, f
**benefice** /'bɛnəfɪs/ n beneficio eclesiástico, m, prebenda, f
**beneficence** /bə'nɛfəsəns/ n beneficiencia, caridad, f, buenas obras, f pl
**beneficent** /bə'nɛfəsənt/ a benéfico, caritativo
**beneficial** /,bɛnə'fɪʃəl/ a beneficioso; provechoso, útil
**beneficiary** /,bɛnə'fɪʃi,ɛri/ n beneficiado (-da), beneficiario (-ia)
**benefit** /'bɛnəfɪt/ n beneficio, bien, m; provecho, m, utilidad, f; (favor) favor, m; Theat. beneficio, m; (help) ayuda, f; servicio, m. —vt beneficiar; aprovechar; (improve) mejorar. —vi (with by) sacar provecho de; ganar. **for the b. of,** para; en pro de, a favor de. **b. society,** sociedad benéfica, f
**benevolence** /bə'nɛvələns/ n benevolencia, bondad, f; liberalidad, f; caridad, f; favor, m
**benevolent** /bə'nɛvələnt/ a benévolo; bondadoso; caritativo. **b. society,** sociedad de beneficencia, f
**benevolently** /bə'nɛvələntli/ adv benignamente, con benevolencia
**Bengal** /bɛn'gɔl/ Bengala, f
**benighted** /bɪ'naitɪd/ a sorprendido por la noche; Fig. ignorante
**benign, benignant** /bɪ'nain; bɪ'nɪgnənt/ a benigno

**bent** /bɛnt/ n talento, m; inclinación, afición, f, a torcido, encorvado; resuelto
**benumb** /bɪ'nʌm/ See **numb**
**benzine** /'bɛnzin/ n bencina, f
**bequeath** /bɪ'kwið/ vt legar, dejar (en el testamento); transmitir
**bequest** /bɪ'kwɛst/ n legado, m
**Berber** /'bɜrbər/ a and n bereber, mf
**bereave** /bɪ'riv/ vt privar (de), quitar; arrebatar; afligir. **the bereaved form,** los padres afligidos
**bereavement** /bɪ'rivmənt/ n privación, f; (by death) pérdida, f; aflicción, f
**bereft** /bɪ'rɛft/ a privado (de); desamparado; indefenso. **utterly b.,** completamente solo
**beret** /bə'rei/ n boina, f
**Berlin** /bər'lɪn/ a and n (of or from) berlinés (-esa). —n (carriage) berlina, f
**Bermudas, the** /bər'myudəz/ n pl las Islas Bermudas
**Bernard** /bər'nɑrd/ n Bernardo, m. **St. B. dog,** perro de San Bernardo, m
**Berne** /bɜrn/ Berna, f
**berry** /'bɛri/ n baya, f; (of coffee, etc.) fruto, m, vi dar bayas; coger bayas
**berth** /bɜrθ/ n (bed) litera, f; (cabin) camarote, m; (anchorage) anclaje, fondeadero, m; (job) empleo, m, vt (a ship) fondear. **to give a wide b. to,** Naut. ponerse a resguardo de; apartarse mucho de; evitar
**beseech** /bɪ'sitʃ/ vt suplicar, rogar, implorar; (ask for) pedir con ahinco
**beseeching** /bɪ'sitʃɪŋ/ a suplicante, implorante. —n súplica, f; ruego, m
**beseechingly** /bɪ'sitʃɪŋli/ adv suplicantemente
**beset** /bɪ'sɛt/ vt atacar, acosar; aquejar, acosar, perseguir. **beset by personal misfortune,** acosado por las desgracias personales; (block) obstruir; (surround) rodear, cercar
**besetting** /bɪ'sɛtɪŋ/ a usual, frecuente; obsesionante
**beside, besides** /bɪ'said; bɪ'saidz/ prep al lado de; cerca de; (compared with) en comparación de, comparado con; (in addition) además de; aparte de; excepto. —adv además, también. **to be beside oneself,** estar fuera de sí
**besiege** /bɪ'sidʒ/ vt sitiar; (assail) asaltar, asediar; (surround) rodear; importunar
**besieged** /bɪ'sidʒd/ a sitiado (-da)
**besieger** /bɪ'sidʒər/ n sitiador, m
**besieging** /bɪ'sidʒɪŋ/ a sitiador. —n sitio, asalto, m; asedio, m, importunación, f
**besmear** /bɪ'smɪər/ vt embadurnar, ensuciar
**besotted** /bɪ'sɒtɪd/ a estúpido; embrutecido; atontado
**bespangled** /bɪ'spæŋgəld/ a adornado con lentejuelas; brillante (con); (studded) salpicado (de)
**bespatter** /bɪ'spætər/ vt manchar; derramar; salpicar
**bespeak** /bɪ'spik/ vt reservar; (goods) encargar; (signify) demostrar, indicar expresar; Poet. hablar
**besprinkle** /bɪ'sprɪŋkəl/ vt rociar
**best** /bɛst/ a superl of **good** and **well,** mejor; el (la) mejor, m, f., los (las) mejores, m pl, f pl. —adv mejor; el mejor; (most) más. **as b. I can,** como mejor pueda. **at the b.,** cuando más, en el mejor caso. **He did it for the b.,** Lo hizo con la mejor intención. **the b.,** lo mejor. **to be at one's b.,** brillar; lucirse. **to do one's b.,** hacer todo lo posible. **to get the b. of,** llevar la mejor parte de; triunfar de (or sobre). **to make the b. of,** sacar el mayor provecho de. **The next b. thing to do is...,** Lo mejor que queda ahora por hacer es... **b. man,** padrino de boda, m. **to be b. man to,** apadrinar, ser padrino de boda. **b. seller,** libro que se vende más, libro favorito, m
**bestial** /'bɛstʃəl/ a bestial
**bestiality** /,bɛstʃi'ælɪti/ n bestialidad, f
**bestir (oneself)** /bɪ'stɜr/ vr menearse, moverse; preocuparse; (hurry) darse prisa
**bestow** /bɪ'stou/ vt (place) poner; (with upon) conferir, conceder, otorgar; (a present) regalar
**bestowal** /bɪ'stouəl/ n puesta, f; otorgamiento, m, concesión, f; (of a present) regalo, m, dádiva, f
**bestride** /bɪ'straid/ vt montar a horcajadas en; poner una pierna a cada lado de; cruzar de un tranco
**bestseller** /'bɛst'sɛlər/ n campeón de venta, éxito editorial, triunfo de librería, m

**bet** /bɛt/ n apuesta, postura, f, vi apostar; (gamble) jugar. **What do you bet?** ¿Qué apuesta Vd.?
**betake (oneself)** /bɪ'teik/ vr acudir (a); darse (a); marcharse
**bethink (oneself)** /bɪ'θɪŋk/ vr pensar, reflexionar; (remember) recordar, hacer memoria; ocurrirse
**Bethlehem** /'bɛθlɪ,hɛm/ Belén, m
**betimes** /bɪ'taimz/ adv pronto; de buena hora, temprano; con tiempo
**betoken** /bɪ'toukən/ vt presagiar, prometer; indicar
**betray** /bɪ'trei/ vt traicionar; revelar, descubrir; (a woman) seducir; (show) dejar ver
**betrayal** /bɪ'treiəl/ n traición, f; (of confidence) abuso (de confianza), m; (of a woman) seducción, f
**betrayer** /bɪ'treiər/ n traidor (-ra)
**betroth** /bɪ'trouð/ vt desposar(se) con, prometer(se). **to be betrothed to,** estar desposado con
**betrothal** /bɪ'trouðəl/ n desposorio, m, esponsales, m pl; (duration) noviazgo, m
**betrothed** /bɪ'trouðd/ n desposado (-da), futuro (-ra)
**better** /'bɛtər/ a compar of **good,** mejor; superior. —adv mejor; más. —vt mejorar; exceder. —n apostador (-ra). **He has bettered himself,** Ha mejorado su situación. **It is b. to...,** Es mejor..., Vale más... (followed by infin.). **little b.,** poco mejor; algo mejor; poco más. **much b.,** mucho mejor. **our betters,** nuestros superiores. **so much the b.,** tanto mejor. **the b. to,** para mejor. **to be b.,** ser mejor; (of health) estar mejor. **to get b.,** mejorar. **to get the b. of,** triunfar sobre, vencer. **b. half,** Inf. media naranja, f. **b. off,** mejor situado, más acomodado
**betterment** /'bɛtərmənt/ n mejora, f, mejoramiento, m; adelantamiento, avance, m
**betting** /'bɛtɪŋ/ n apuesta, f
**bettor** /'bɛtər/ n apostador (-ra)
**between** /bɪ'twin/ prep entre; en medio de; de. **the break b. Mr. X and Mrs. Y,** el rompimiento del Sr. X y la Sra. Y. —adv en medio; entre los dos. **far b.,** a grandes intervalos. **b. now and then,** desde ahora hasta entonces. **b. one thing and another,** entre una cosa y otra. **b. ourselves,** entre nosotros
**bevel** /'bɛvəl/ n bisel, m, vt abiselar
**beverage** /'bɛvərɪdʒ/ n brebaje, m, bebida, f
**bevy** /'bɛvi/ n grupo, m; (of birds) bandada, f; (of roes) manada, f
**bewail** /bɪ'weil/ vt lamentar, llorar
**bewailing** /bɪ'weilɪŋ/ n lamentación, f
**beware** /bɪ'wɛər/ vi guardarse (de); cuidar (de); desconfiar (de). —interj ¡cuidado! ¡atención! **B. of imitations!** ¡Desconfiad de las imitaciones!
**bewilder** /bɪ'wɪldər/ vt aturdir, abobar; dejar perplejo (a); confundir
**bewildered** /bɪ'wɪldərd/ a aturdido, abobado; perplejo; confuso
**bewildering** /bɪ'wɪldərɪŋ/ a incomprensible; complicado
**bewilderment** /bɪ'wɪldərmənt/ n aturdimiento, m; perplejidad, f; confusión, f
**bewitch** /bɪ'wɪtʃ/ vt hechizar; fascinar, encantar
**bewitching** /bɪ'wɪtʃɪŋ/ a encantador, hechicero, fascinante. —n embrujamiento, encantamiento, m
**bewitchingly** /bɪ'wɪtʃɪŋli/ adv de un modo encantador
**bewitchment** /bɪ'wɪtʃmənt/ n. See **bewitching**
**beyond** /bɪ'ɒnd/ prep más allá de; más lejos que; (behind) tras, detrás de; (of time) después de; Fig. fuera del alcance de; (without) fuera de; (above) encima de; (not including) aparte. —adv más allá; más lejos; detrás. **b. doubt,** fuera de duda. **b. question,** indiscutible. **b. the sea,** allende el mar. **That is b. me,** Eso es demasiado para mí; Eso no está en mi mano; Eso está fuera de mi alcance. **the back of b.,** donde Cristo dio las tres voces, las quimbambas. **the B.,** la otra vida
**Bhután** /bu'tɑn/ Bután, m
**bias** /'baiəs/ n sesgo, bies, través, m; Fig. prejuicio, m; parcialidad, f, vt influir; predisponer. **to cut on the b.,** cortar al sesgo
**biased** /'baiəst/ a parcial; tendencioso
**bib** /bɪb/ n babero, m; pechera, f, vi beber mucho, empinar el codo
**Bible** /'baibəl/ n Biblia, f

**biblical** /'bɪblɪkəl/ a bíblico. **b. history,** historia sagrada, f
**bibliographer** /,bɪbli'ɒgrəfər/ n bibliógrafo (-fa)
**bibliographical** /,bɪbliə'græfɪkəl/ a bibliográfico
**bibliography** /,bɪbli'ɒgrəfi/ n bibliografía, f
**bibliophile** /'bɪbliə,fail/ n bibliófilo, m
**bibulous** /'bɪbyələs/ a bebedor, borrachín
**bicarbonate** /bai'kɑrbənɪt/ n bicarbonato, m
**bicentenary** /,baisɛn'tɛnəri/ n segundo centenario, m
**biceps** /'baisɛps/ n bíceps, m
**bichloride** /bai'klɔraid/ n bicloruro, m
**bicker** /'bɪkər/ vi disputar, altercar; (of stream, etc.) murmurar, susurrar; (of flame) bailar, centellear
**bickering** /'bɪkərɪŋ/ n altercado, argumento, m
**bicycle** /'baisɪkəl/ n bicicleta, f, vi andar en bicicleta, ir de bicicleta
**bicycling** /'baisɪklɪŋ/ n ciclismo, m
**bicyclist** /'baisɪklɪst/ n biciclista, mf
**bid** /bɪd/ n (at auction) postura, f; (bridge) puja, f; oferta, f, vt mandar, ordenar, invitar a; (at an auction) pujar, licitar. **to make a bid for,** (attempt) hacer un esfuerzo para; procurar. **to bid fair,** prometer; dar indicios de; dar esperanzas de. **to bid goodbye to,** decir adios (a), despedirse de. **to bid welcome,** dar la bienvenida (a)
**biddable** /'bɪdəbəl/ a obediente, dócil; manso
**bidder** /'bɪdər/ n postor, m, pujador (-ra). **the highest b.,** el mejor postor
**bidding** /'bɪdɪŋ/ n (order) orden, f; instrucción, f; invitación, f; (at an auction) postura, licitación, f. **to do a person's b.,** hacer lo que se le manda
**bide** /baid/ vt aguardar, esperar. **to b. by,** (fulfil) cumplir con
**bidet** /bi'dei/ n bidé, m
**biennial** /bai'ɛniəl/ a bianual, bienal
**bier** /bɪər/ n andas, f pl; féretro, ataúd, m
**bifocal** /bai'foukəl/ a bifocal
**bifurcate** /'baifər,keit/ vt and vi bifurcar(se)
**bifurcation** /,baifər'keifən/ n bifurcación, f
**big** /bɪg/ a grande; grueso; (grown up) mayor; (tall) alto; voluminoso; (vast) extenso, vasto; (full) lleno (de); (with young) preñada; importante. **to talk big,** echarla de importante. **big-boned,** huesudo. **big-end,** Auto. biela, f. **big game,** caza mayor, f. **big gun,** Inf. pájaro gordo, m
**bigamist** /'bɪgəmɪst/ n bígamo (-ma)
**bigamous** /'bɪgəməs/ a bígamo
**bigamy** /'bɪgəmi/ n bigamia, f
**bight** /bait/ n (in a rope) vuelta (de un cabo), f; (bay) ensenada, f
**bigness** /'bɪgnɪs/ n grandor, m; gran tamaño, m; altura, f; (tallness of a person) gran talle, m; (vastness) extensión, f; importancia, f
**bigot** /'bɪgət/ n fanático (-ca)
**bigoted** /'bɪgətɪd/ a fanático, intolerante
**bigotry** /'bɪgətri/ n fanatismo, m, intolerancia, f
**bikini** /bɪ'kini/ n bikini, m
**bilateral** /bai'lætərəl/ a bilateral
**bilberry** /'bɪl,bɛri/ n arándano, m
**bile** /bail/ n bilis, hiel, f; mal humor, m, cólera, f
**bilge** /bɪldʒ/ n Naut. pantoque, m, sentina, f. **b. water,** agua de pantoque, f
**bilingual** /bai'lɪŋgwəl/ a bilingüe
**bilious** /'bɪlyəs/ a bilioso
**bill** /bɪl/ n (parliamentary) proyecto de ley, m; Law. escrito, m; Com. cuenta, f; (poster) cartel, m; (program) programa, m; (cast) repertorio, m; (bank note) billete de banco, m; (of a bird) pico, m; (for pruning) podadera, f. **due b.,** Com. abonaré, m. **Post no bills!** Se prohíbe fijar carteles. **b. of exchange,** letra de cambio, f. **b. of fare,** lista de platos, f; Fig. programa, m. **b. of health,** patente de sanidad, f. **b. of lading,** conocimiento de embarque, m. **b. of rights,** declaración de derechos, f. **b. of sale,** contrato de venta, m, carta de venta, f. **b.-broker,** agente de bolsa, agente de cambio, m. **b.-poster,** fijador de carteles, cartelero, m
**bill** /bɪl/ vt anunciar; publicar; poner en el programa; fijar carteles. **to b. and coo,** (doves) arrullar; Inf. besuquearse
**billboard** /'bɪl,bɔrd/ n tablero publicitario, m

**billed** /bɪld/ *a* (in compounds) de pico
**billet** /ˈbɪlɪt/ *n* alojamiento, *m;* (of wood) pedazo (de leña), *m;* (job) empleo, destino, *m, vt* alojar (en or con)
**billeting** /ˈbɪlɪtɪŋ/ *n* alojamiento, *m.* **b. officer,** *Mil.* aposentador, *m;* oficial encargado de encontrar alojamiento, *m*
**billiards** /ˈbɪlyərdz/ *n pl* billar, *m.* **billiard ball,** bola de billar, *f.* **billiard cue,** taco, *m.* **billiard cushion,** baranda de la mesa de billar, *f.* **billiard marker,** marcador, *m.* **billiard match,** partida de billar, *f.* **billiard player,** jugador (-ra) de billar. **billiard room,** sala de billar, *f.* **billiard table,** mesa de billar, *f*
**billing** /ˈbɪlɪŋ/ *n* facturación, *f*
**billion** /ˈbɪlyən/ *n* billón, *m;* (U.S.A. and France) mil millones, *m pl*
**billionth** /ˈbɪlyənθ/ *a* billonésimo; (U.S.A. and France) milmillonésimo
**bill of particulars** *n* relación detallada, *f*
**billow** /ˈbɪlou/ *n* oleada, *f; Poet.* ola, *f; Fig.* onda, *f.*
**—vi** hincharse, encresparse; ondular
**billowy** /ˈbɪloui/ *a* ondulante, ondeante
**bimonthly** /baiˈmʌnθli/ *a* bimestral
**bin** /bɪn/ *n* hucha, *f,* arcón, *m;* recipiente, *m;* depósito, *m;* cajón, *m;* (for wine) estante, *m*
**binary** /ˈbainəri/ *a* binario
**bind** /baind/ *vt* atar; unir, ligar; amarrar; (in sheaves) agavillar; (bandage) vendar; sujetar; fijar; aprisionar; (a book) encuadernar; *Sew.* ribetear; (oblige) obligar; comprometer; (constipate) estreñir; contratar (como aprendiz). **I feel bound to,** Me siento obligado a. **to b. over,** obligar a comparecer ante el juez
**binder** /ˈbaindər/ *n* encuadernador (-ra); *Agr.* agavilladora, *f*
**binding** /ˈbaindɪŋ/ *a* válido, valedero; obligatorio; **become b.,** adquirir carácter de compromiso; *Med.* constrictivo. **—n** atadura, ligación, *f;* (of books) encuadernación, *f; Sew.* ribete, *m*
**binge** /bɪndʒ/ *n* parranda, juerga, *f.* **to go on the b.,** ir de parranda, ir de picos pardos, ir de juerga
**binnacle** /ˈbɪnəkəl/ *n Naut.* bitácora, *f*
**binocular** /bəˈnɒkyələr/ *a* binocular. **—n pl binoculars,** binóculos, gemelos, *m pl*
**binomial** /baiˈnoumiəl/ *a* and *n* binomio *m.*
**biochemist** /ˌbaiouˈkɛmɪst/ *n* bioquímico, *m*
**biochemistry** /ˌbaiouˈkɛməstri/ *n* bioquímica, *f*
**biodiversity** /ˌbaioudɪˈvɜrsɪti/ *n* biodiversidad, *f*
**biographer** /baiˈɒɡrəfər/ *n* biógrafo (-fa)
**biographical** /ˌbaiəˈɡræfɪkəl/ *a* biográfico
**biography** /baiˈɒɡrəfi/ *n* biografía, vida, *f*
**biological** /ˌbaiəˈlɒdʒɪkəl/ *a* biológico
**biologist** /baiˈɒlədʒɪst/ *n* biólogo, *m*
**biology** /baiˈɒlədʒi/ *n* biología, *f*
**bipartite** /baiˈpɑrtait/ *a* bipartido
**biped** /ˈbaipɛd/ *n* bípedo, *m,* a bípedo, bípede
**birch** /bɜrtʃ/ *n Bot.* abedul, *m;* (rod) vara, *f.* **—a** de abedul. **—vt** pegar con una vara, dar una paliza (a)
**bird** /bɜrd/ *n* pájaro, *m;* ave, *f.* **Birds of a feather flock together,** Cada cual se arrima a su cada cual. **hen b.,** pájara, *f.* **b.-call,** voz del pájaro, *f,* canto del ave, *m.* **b. catcher or vendor,** pajarero, *m.* **bird's-eye view,** vista de pájaro, perspectiva aérea, *f.* **b.-fancier,** aficionado (-da) a las aves; criador (-ra) de pájaros. **b. to go b.-nesting,** ir a coger nidos de pájaros. **b. of paradise,** ave del paraíso, *f.* **b. of passage,** ave de paso, *f.* **b. of prey,** ave rapaz, *f.* **b.-seed,** alpiste, *m*
**birth** /bɜrθ/ *n* nacimiento, *m;* (act of) parto, *m;* origen, *m;* (childhood) infancia, *f;* (family) linaje, *m,* familia, *f; Fig.* creación, *f.* **from b.,** de nacimiento. **to give b. to,** dar a luz, echar al mundo, parir. **b. certificate,** partida de nacimiento, certificación de nacimiento, *f.* **b. control,** anticoncepcionismo, *m,* regulación de la fecundidad, *f.* **b.-mark,** antojos, *m pl.* **b.-place,** lugar de nacimiento, *m.* **b.-rate,** natalidad, *f*
**birthday** /ˈbɜrθˌdei/ *n* cumpleaños, *m*
**birthright** /ˈbɜrθˌrait/ *n* derecho de nacimiento, *m;* herencia, *f*
**Biscayan** /ˈbɪsˈkeiən/ *a* and *n* vizcaíno (-na)
**Biscay, the Bay of** /bɪsˈkei/ el Golfo de Vizcaya, *m*

**biscuit** /ˈbɪskɪt/ *n* galleta, *f;* bizcocho, *m.* **b. box or maker,** galletero, *m.* **b.-like,** abizcochado
**bisect** /baiˈsɛkt/ *vt* dividir en dos partes iguales; *Geom.* bisecar
**bisexual** /baiˈsɛkʃuəl/ *a* bisexual
**bishop** /ˈbɪʃəp/ *n* obispo, *m;* (in chess) alfil, *m.* **bishop's crozier,** báculo episcopal, cayado, *m*
**bismuth** /ˈbɪzməθ/ *n* bismuto, *m*
**bison** /ˈbaisən/ *n* bisonte, *m*
**bisque** /bɪsk/ *n* porcelana blanca, *f,* bizcocho, *m*
**bistoury** /ˈbɪstəri/ *n* bisturí, *m*
**bit** /bɪt/ *n* pedazo, *m;* (of grass, etc.) brizna, *f;* (moment) instante, *m;* (quantity) cantidad, *f;* (of a drill) mecha, *f;* (part) parte, *f;* (passage) trozo, *m;* (horse's) bocado, *m; Inf.* miga, *f.* **a bit,** un tanto, algo, un poco. **in bits,** en pedazos. **Not a bit!** ¡Nada!; ¡Ni pizca!; ¡Claro que no! **bit by bit,** poco a poco, gradualmente. **to give someone a bit of one's mind,** contarle cuatro verdades. **to take the bit between one's teeth,** desbocarse; *Fig.* rebelarse. **Wait a bit!** ¡Espera un momento!
**bitch** /bɪtʃ/ *n* (female dog) perra, *f;* (fox) zorra, *f;* (wolf) loba, *f*
**bite** /bait/ *n* mordedura, *f;* mordisco, *m;* (mouthful, snack) bocado, *m;* (of fish and insects) picada, *f;* (hold) asimiento, *m;* (sting, pain) picadura, *f;* (pungency) resquemor, *m;* (offer) oferta, *f; Fig.* mordancy) mordacidad, acritud, *f.* **—vt** and *vi* morder; (gnaw) roer; (of fish, insects) picar; (of hot dishes) resquemar; (of acids) corroer; (deceive) engañar, defraudar; (of wheels, etc.) agarrar; (hurt, wound) herir. **to b. one's tongue,** morderse la lengua. **to b. the dust,** caer al suelo
**biting** /ˈbaitɪŋ/ *a* (stinging) picante; (mordant) mordaz, acre; (of winds, etc.) penetrante; satírico. **—n** mordedura, *f;* roedura, *f*
**bitter** /ˈbɪtər/ *a* amargo; (sour) agrio, ácido; (of winds) penetrante; (of cold) intenso; cruel. **to the b. end,** hasta la muerte; hasta el último extremo. **b.-sweet,** agridulce
**bitterly** /ˈbɪtərli/ *adv* amargamente; intensamente; cruelmente
**bitterness** /ˈbɪtərnɪs/ *n* amargura, *f;* (sourness) acidez, *f;* (of cold) intensidad, *f;* crueldad, *f*
**bitters** /ˈbɪtərz/ *n pl* (of drink) bíter, *m,* angostura, *f*
**bitumen** /baiˈtumən/ *n* betún, *m*
**bituminous** /baiˈtumənəs/ *a* bituminoso, abetunado
**bivalve** /ˈbai,vælv/ *n* bivalvo, *m*
**bivouac** /ˈbɪvuˌæk/ *n Mil.* vivaque, *m, vi* vivaquear
**bizarre** /bɪˈzɑr/ *a* raro, extravagante; grotesco
**black** /blæk/ *a* negro; obscuro; (sad) triste, melancólico; funesto; (wicked) malo, perverso; (sullen) malhumorado. **—n** (color) negro, *m;* (mourning) luto, *m;* (negro) negro, *m;* (negress) negra, *f;* (stain) mancha, *f;* (dirt) tizne, *m.* **—vt** ennegrecer; tiznar. **in b. and white,** por escrito. **to look on the b. side,** verlo todo negro. **b. art,** nigromancia, *f.* **b.-currant,** grosella negra, *f.* **b.-eyed,** ojinegro, con ojos negros. **b.-haired,** pelinegro, de pelo negro. **b.-lead,** plombagina, *f.* **b.-list,** lista negra, *f.* **b.-market,** estraperlo, mercado negro, *m.* **b.-marketeer,** estraperlista, *mf* **b.-out,** oscurecimiento; apagamiento, *m.* **b.-pudding,** morcilla, *f.* **b. sheep,** oveja negra, *f; Fig.* oveja descarriada, *f;* (of a family) garbanzo negro, *m.* **b.-water fever,** melanuria, *f*
**blackberry** /ˈblækˌbɛri/ *n* mora, zarzamora, *f;* (bush) zarza, *f,* moral, *m*
**blackbird** /ˈblækˌbɜrd/ *n* mirlo, *m*
**blackboard** /ˈblækˌbɔrd/ *n* encerado, *m,* pizarra, *f*
**blacken** /ˈblækən/ *vt* ennegrecer; tiznar; *Fig.* denigrar, char, desacreditar. **—vi** ennegrecerse
**black eye** *n* ojo negro con un tomate, ojo morado, *m*
**Black Forest,** la Selva Negra, *f*
**blackguard** /ˈblægɑrd/ *n* tipo de cuidado, perdido, *m*
**blackhead** /ˈblæk,hɛd/ *n* espinilla, *f*
**blacking** /ˈblækɪŋ/ *n* betún, *m*
**blackish** /ˈblækɪʃ/ *a* negruzco
**blackmail** /ˈblæk,meil/ *n* chantaje, *m, vt* hacer víctima de un chantaje; arrancar dinero por chantaje (a)
**blackmailer** /ˈblæk,meilər/ *n* chantajista, *mf*
**blackness** /ˈblæknɪs/ *n* negrura, *f;* obscuridad, *f;* (wickedness) maldad, perversidad, *f*

**Black Sea, the** el Mar Negro, *m*
**blacksmith** /'blæk,smɪθ/ *n* herrero, *m*. **blacksmith's forge,** herrería, *f*
**bladder** /'blædər/ *n* Anat. vejiga, *f*; ampolla, *f*; (of sea-plants) vesícula, *f*; (of fish) vejiga natatoria, *f*
**blade** /bleid/ *n* (leaf) hoja, *f*; (of grass, etc.) brizna, *f*; (of sharp instruments) hoja, *f*; (of oar) pala, *f*; (of propeller) paleta, ala, *f*
**bladed** /'bleidɪd/ *a* de... hojas. **a two-b. knife,** un cuchillo de dos hojas
**blame** /bleim/ *n* culpa, *f*; responsabilidad, *f*; censura, *f*. —*vt* culpar, echar la culpa (a); tachar, censurar, criticar; acusar. **You are to b. for this,** Vd. tiene la culpa de esto
**blameless** /'bleimlɪs/ *a* inculpable; inocente; intachable; elegante
**blamelessness** /'bleimlɪsnɪs/ *n* inculpabilidad, inocencia, *f*; elegancia, *f*
**blameworthy** /'bleim,wɜrði/ *a* culpable, digno de censura, vituperable
**blanch** /blæntʃ/ *vt* Cul. mondar; hacer palidecer. —*vi* palidecer, perder el color
**blanching** /'blæntʃɪŋ/ *n* palidecimiento, *m*; Cul. mondadura, *f*
**blancmange** /blə'mɑndʒ/ *n* manjar blanco, *m*
**bland** /blænd/ *a* afable, cortés; dulce, agradable
**blandish** /'blændɪʃ/ *vt* adular, halagar, acariciar
**blandishment** /'blændɪʃmənt/ *n* adulación, *f*, halago, *m*, caricia, *f*
**blandness** /'blændnɪs/ *n* afabilidad, urbanidad, *f*; dulzura, *f*
**blank** /blæŋk/ *a* en blanco; (empty) vacío; desocupado; pálido; (confused) confuso, desconcertado; (expressionless) sin expresión; (of verse) suelto; sin adorno. —*n* blanco, hueco, *m*; papel en blanco, *m*; laguna, *f*. **b. cartridge,** cartucho para salvas, cartucho de fogueo, *m*. **b. verse,** verso suelto, *m*
**blanket** /'blæŋkɪt/ *n* manta, frazada, *f*; (of a horse) sudadero *m*; Fig. capa, *f*. —*vt* cubrir con una manta. **to toss in a b.,** mantear. **wet b.,** aguafiestas, *mf*. **b. maker or seller,** mantero, *m*. **b. vote,** voto colectivo, *m*
**blanketing** /'blæŋkɪtɪŋ/ *n* manteamiento, *m*
**blankly** /'blæŋkli/ *adv* con indiferencia; sin comprender; (flatly) categóricamente
**blankness** /'blæŋknɪs/ *n* confusión, *f*, desconcierto, *m*; (emptiness) vaciedad, *f*; indiferencia, *f*; incomprensión, *f*
**blare** /blɛər/ *n* sonido de la trompeta o del clarín, Poet. clangor, *m*; (of a car horn) ruido, *m*. —*vi* sonar
**blarney** /'blɑrni/ *n* labia, *f*. —*vt* lisonjear
**blaspheme** /blæs'fim/ *vi* blasfemar. —*vt* renegar de, maldecir
**blasphemer** /blæs'fimər/ *n* blasfemador (-ra), blasfemo (-ma)
**blasphemous** /'blæsfəməs/ *a* blasfemo, blasfematorio
**blasphemy** /'blæsfəmi/ *n* blasfemia, *f*
**blast** /blæst/ *n* (of wind) ráfaga (de viento), *f*; (of a trumpet, etc.) trompetazo, son, *m*; (of a whistle) pitido, *m*; (draft) soplo, *m*; explosión, *f*; Fig. influencia maligna, *f*. —*vt* (rock) barrenar, hacer saltar; (wither) marchitar, secar; Fig. destruir; (curse) maldecir. **in full b.,** en plena marcha. **b.-furnace,** alto horno, horno de cuba, *m*. **b. hole,** barreno, *m*
**blaster** /'blæstər/ *n* barrenero, *m*
**blasting** /'blæstɪŋ/ *n* (of rock) voladura, *f*; (withering) marchitamiento, *m*; Fig. destrucción, ruina, *f*; (cursing) maldiciones, *f pl*. **a. destructor;** Fig. funesto. **b. charge,** carga explosiva, *f*
**blatant** /'bleitnt/ *a* ruidoso; agresivo; llamativo; (boastful) fanfarrón
**blaze** /bleiz/ *n* llama, *f*; fuego, *m*; conflagración, *f*; luz brillante, *f*; (of anger, etc.) acceso, *m*. —*vi* llamear, encenderse en llamas; brillar, resplandecer. **a b. of colour,** una masa de color. **Go to blazes!** ¡Vete al infierno!
**blazon** /'bleizən/ *n* Herald. blasón, *m*; Fig. proclamación, *f*, *vt* blasonar; adornar; proclamar
**bleach** /blitʃ/ *n* lejía, *f*. —*vt* blanquear; descolorar. —*vi* ponerse blanco; descolorarse
**bleaching** /'blitʃɪŋ/ *n* blanqueo, *f*. **b. powder,** hipoclorito de cal, *m*

**bleak** /blik/ *a* yermo, desierto; frío; expuesto; (sad) triste; severo
**bleakness** /'bliknɪs/ *n* situación expuesta, *f*; desnudez, *f*; frío, *m*; (sadness) tristeza, *f*; severidad, *f*
**bleary-eyed** /'blɪəri ,aid/ *a* legañoso, cegajoso
**bleat** /blit/ *n* balido, *m*, *vt* and *vi* balar, dar balidos
**bleating** /'blitɪŋ/ *a* balador, que bala. —*n* balido, *m*
**bleed** /blid/ *vi* sangrar, echar sangre; sufrir. —*vt* sangrar; arrancar dinero a
**bleeding** /'blidɪŋ/ *n* hemorragia, *f*; sangría, *f*
**blemish** /'blɛmɪʃ/ *n* imperfección, *f*, defecto, *m*; (on fruit) maca, *f*; (stain) mancha, *f*; deshonra, *f*
**blend** /blɛnd/ *n* mezcla, mixtura, *f*; combinación, *f*; fusión, *f*. —*vt* mezclar; combinar. —*vi* mezclarse; combinarse
**blende** /blɛnd/ *n* Mineral. blenda, *f*
**blending** /'blɛndɪŋ/ *n* mezcla, *f*; fusión, *f*
**bless** /blɛs/ *vt* bendecir; consagrar; (praise) alabar, glorificar; hacer feliz (a). **B. me!** ¡Válgame Dios!
**blessed** /'blɛsɪd/ *a* bendito; Eccl. beato, bienaventurado; (dear) querido; feliz; Inf. maldito
**blessedness** /'blɛsɪdnɪs/ *n* felicidad, *f*; bienaventuranza, *f*
**blessing** /'blɛsɪŋ/ *n* bendición, *f*; (grace) bendición de la mesa, *f*; (mercy) merced, gracia, *f*; favor, *m*; (good) bien, *m*. **He gave them his b.,** Les echó su bendición
**Bless you!** (to someone who has sneezed) ¡Jesús!
**blight** /blait/ *n* Agr. tizne, tizón, *m*; (of cereals) añublo, *m*; (mould) roña, *f*; (greenfly) pulgón, *m*; Fig. influencia maligna, *f*; (frustration) desengaño, *m*; (spoil-sport) aguafiestas, *mf* *vt* atizonar; anublar; (wither) marchitar, secar; Fig. frustrar, destruir; malograr
**blind** /blaind/ *a* ciego; (secret) secreto; (of a door, etc.) falso; (closed) cerrado, sin salida; (unaware) ignorante; sin apreciación (de). **to be b.,** ser ciego; Fig. tener una venda en los ojos. **to be b. in one eye,** ser tuerto. **to turn a b. eye,** hacer la vista gorda. **b. alley,** callejón sin salida, *m*. **b. as a bat,** más ciego que un topo. **b. flying,** Aer. vuelo a ciegas, *m*. **b. man,** ciego, hombre ciego, *m*. **b. obedience,** obediencia ciega, *f*. **b. side,** (of persons) lado débil, *m*. **b. woman,** ciega, mujer ciega, *f*
**blind** /blaind/ *vt* cegar; poner una venda en los ojos (de); (dazzle) deslumbrar; hacer cerrar los ojos a; hacer ignorar
**blind** /blaind/ *n* persiana, *f*; (Venetian) celosía, *f*; (deception) pretexto, *m*; velo, *m*
**blindfold** /'blaind,fould/ *vt* vendar los ojos (a); Fig. poner una venda en los ojos (de). —*a* and *adv* con los ojos vendados; a ciegas; con los ojos cerrados
**blindly** /'blaindli/ *adv* ciegamente; a ciegas; ignorantemente
**blindman's buff** /'blaind,mænz 'bʌf/ *n* gallina ciega, *f*
**blindness** /'blaindnɪs/ *n* ceguedad, *f*; ofuscación, *f*; ignorancia, *f*
**blink** /blɪŋk/ *n* parpadeo, *m*, guiñada, *f*; (of light) destello, *m*; reflejo, *m*; *vi* parpadear, pestañear; (of lights) destellar
**blinkers** /'blɪŋkərz/ *n pl* anteojeras, *f pl*
**bliss** /blɪs/ *n* felicidad, *f*; deleite, placer, *m*; Eccl. gloria, *f*
**blissful** /'blɪsfəl/ *a* feliz
**blissfully** /'blɪsfəli/ *adv* felizmente
**blissfulness** /'blɪsfəlnɪs/ *n*. See **bliss**
**blister** /'blɪstər/ *n* Med. vesícula, *f*; ampolla, *f*; (bubble) burbuja, *f*. —*vt* ampollar; Fig. herir
**blithe** /blaið/ *a* alegre
**blithely** /'blaiðli/ *adv* alegremente
**blitheness** /'blaiðnɪs/ *n* alegría, *f*
**blitzkrieg** /'blɪts,krig/ *n* blitzkrieg, *m*, guerra relámpago, *f*
**blizzard** /'blɪzərd/ *n* ventisca, nevasca, *f*
**bloated** /'bloutɪd/ *a* abotagado, hinchado; orgulloso; indecente
**bloater** /'bloutər/ *n* arenque ahumado, *m*
**blob** /blɒb/ *n* masa, *f*; mancha, *f*; gota, *f*
**block** /blɒk/ *n* bloque, *m*; (log) leño, *m*; Naut. polea, *f*; (for beheading and of a butcher) tajo, *m*; (for mounting) apeadero, *m*; (of shares, etc.) lote, *m*; (of

houses) manzana, *f;* (jam) atasco, *m;* (obstruction) obstrucción, *f;* (for hats) forma, *f.* **A chip off the old b.,** De tal palo tal astilla. **b. and tackle,** *Naut.* polea con aparejo. **b.-hook,** grapa, *f.* **b.-house,** *Mil.* blocao, *m*

**block** /blɒk/ *vt* bloquear; cerrar (el paso); (stop up) atarugar, atascar; (a wheel) calzar; (a bill, etc.) obstruir; (hats) poner en forma. **to b. the way,** cerrar el paso.

**blockade** /blɒ'keid/ *n* bloqueo, *m, vt* bloquear. **to run the b.,** violar el bloqueo

**blockhead** /'blɒk,hɛd/ *n* leño, zoquete, imbécil, *m*

**blond(e)** /blɒnd/ *a* (of hair) rubio; (of complexion) de tez blanca. —*n* hombre rubio, *m;* (woman) rubia, mujer rubia, *f.* **peroxide b.,** rubia oxigenada, *f.* **b. lace,** blondina, *f*

**blood** /blʌd/ *n* sangre, *f;* (relationship) parentesco, *m;* (family) linaje, *m,* prosapia, *f;* (life) vida, *f;* (sap) savia, *f;* jugo, *m;* (horse) caballo de pura raza, *m;* (dandy) galán, *m.* —*vt* sangrar. **bad b.,** mala sangre, *f;* odio, *m;* mala leche, *f.* **blue b.,** sangre azul, *f.* **in cold b.,** a sangre fría, *f.* **My b. is up,** Se me enciende la sangre. **My b. runs cold,** Se me hiela la sangre. **to be in the b.,** llevar en la sangre. **b.-bank,** banco de sangre, *m.* **b.-bath,** matanza, *f.* **b.-colored,** de color de sangre, sanguíneo. **b.-feud,** venganza de sangre, *f.* **b.-guilt,** culpabilidad de homicidio, *m.* **b.-heat,** calor de sangre, *m.* **b.-letting,** sangría, *f.* **b. orange,** naranja dulce, *f.* **b.-plasma,** plasma sanguíneo, *m.* **b.-poisoning,** septicemia, *f;* infección, *f.* **b.-pressure,** presión sanguínea, *f.* **b. purity,** limpieza de sangre, *f.* **b.-red,** rojo como la sangre. **b.-relation,** pariente (-ta) consanguíneo(a). **b.-relationship,** consanguinidad, *f.* **b.-stain,** mancha de sangre, *f.* **b.-stained,** ensangrentado, manchado de sangre, *f.* **b.-stone,** sanguinaria, *f.* **b.-sucker,** sanguijuela, *f; Fig.* vampiro, *m;* (usurer) avaro (-ra). **b.-vessel,** vaso sanguíneo, *m*

**blooded** /'blʌdɪd/ *a* de sangre...; de casta...

**bloodhound** /'blʌd,haund/ *n* sabueso, *m*

**bloodily** /'blʌdəli/ *adv* sangrientamente; cruentamente; con ferocidad, cruelmente

**bloodiness** /'blʌdinɪs/ *n* estado sangriento, *m;* crueldad, ferocidad, *f*

**bloodless** /'blʌdlɪs/ *a* exangüe; pálido; incruento; anémico; indiferente

**bloodshed** /'blʌd,ʃɛd/ *n* efusión de sangre, *f;* matanza, carnicería, *f*

**bloodshot** /'blʌd,ʃɒt/ *a* (of the eye) inyectado

**bloodthirstiness** /'blʌd,θɜrstinɪs/ *n* sed de sangre, *f*

**bloodthirsty** /'blʌd,θɜrsti/ *a* sanguinario, carnicero

**bloody** /'blʌdi/ *a* sangriento; (of battles) encarnizado; (cruel) sanguinario, cruel

**bloom** /blum/ *n* flor, *f;* florecimiento, *m;* (on fruit) flor, *f;* (prime) lozanía, *f;* (on the cheeks) color sano, *m.* —*vi* florecer. **in b.,** en flor

**blooming** /'blumɪŋ/ *a* florido; en flor; fresco; lozano; brillante

**blossom** /'blɒsəm/ *n* flor, *f.* —*vi* florecer. **to b. out into,** hacerse, llegar a ser; (wear) lucir; (buy) comprarse

**blossomed** /'blɒsəmd/ *a* con flores, de flores

**blossoming** /'blɒsəmɪŋ/ *n* floración, *f*

**blot** /blɒt/ *n* borrón, *m;* mancha, *f.* —*vt* manchar; (erase) tachar; (dry) secar. **to b. out,** borrar; destruir; secar con papel secante

**blotch** /blɒtʃ/ *n* (on the skin, or stain) mancha, *f*

**blotter** /'blɒtər/ *n Com.* libro borrador, *m;* teleta, *f*

**blotting paper** /'blɒtɪŋ/ *n* papel secante, *m*

**blouse** /blaus/ *n* blusa, *f*

**blow** /blou/ *n* golpe, *m;* bofetada, *f;* (with the fist) puñetazo, *m;* (with the elbow) codazo, *m;* (with a club) porrazo, *m;* (with a whip) latigazo, *m;* (blossoming) floración, *f;* (disaster) desastre, *m,* tragedia, *f.* **to come to blows,** venirse a las manos. **at a b.,** con un solo golpe; de una vez. **We are going for a b.,** Vamos a tomar el fresco. **b. below the belt,** golpe bajo, *m.* **b. in the air,** golpe en vago, *m.* **b. of fate,** latigazo de la fortuna, *m*

**blow** /blou/ *vi* (of wind) soplar (el viento), hacer viento, correr aire; (pant) jadear, echar resoplidos; (of fuses) fundirse. —*vt* (wind instruments) tocar; soplar; (inflate) inflar; (swell) hinchar. **to b. a kiss,** ti-

rar un beso. **to b. one's nose,** sonarse las narices. **to b. away,** dispar; ahuyentar; llevar (el viento). **to b. down,** echar por tierra, derribar (el viento). **to b. in,** llevar adentro, hacer entrar (el viento); (windows, etc.) quebrar (el viento). **to b. off,** quitar (el viento). **to b. open,** abrir (el viento). **to b. out,** hacer salir de viento); llevar afuera (el viento); (a light) matar de un soplo, apagar soplando. **to b. over,** pasar por (el viento); soplar por; disiparse; olvidarse. **to b. up,** (inflate) inflar; (the fire) avivar (el fuego); (explode) volar; (swell) hinchar

**blowing** /'blouɪŋ/ *n* soplo, *m;* violencia, *f;* (blossoming) florecimiento, *m.* **b. up,** voleo, *m;* explosión, *f*

**blow-up** /'blou ˌʌp/ *n* (photograph) fotografía ampliada, *f*

**blowzy** /'blauzi/ *a* desaliñado

**blubber** /'blʌbər/ *vi* gimotear; berrear. —*n* (of the whale) grasa de ballena, *f.* **b.-lip,** bezo, *m.* **b.-lipped,** bezudo

**bludgeon** /'blʌdʒən/ *n* cachiporra, porpa, *f;* garrote, *m;* estaca, *f.* —*vt* golpear con una porra, dar garrotazos (a)

**blue** /blu/ *a* azul; (with bruises) amoratado; (sad) deprimido, melancólico; (obscene) verde; (dark) sombrío; (traditionalist) conservador. —*n* azul, *m;* (sky) cielo, *m;* (for clothes) añil de lavandera, *m; pl* **blues,** melancolía, depresión, *f;* (homesickness) morriña, *f.* —*vt* (laundry) añilar. **to look b.,** parecer deprimido; (of prospects, etc.) ser poco halagüeño. **b. black,** azul negro, *m;* (of hair) azabache, *m.* **b.-bottle,** *Ent.* moscón, *m.* **b.-eyed,** con ojos azules. **b. gum,** eucalipto, *m.* **B. Peter,** bandera de salida, *f.* **b. print,** fotocopia, *f;* plan, *m*

**bluebell** /'blu,bɛl/ *n* campanilla, *f*

**blueness** /'blunɪs/ *n* color azul, *m*

**bluestocking** /'blu,stɒkɪŋ/ *n* marisabidilla, doctora, *f*

**bluff** /blʌf/ *a* (of cliffs, etc.) escarpado; (of persons) franco, campechano, brusco

**bluffness** /'blʌfnɪs/ *n* franqueza, brusquedad, *f*

**bluish** /'bluɪʃ/ *a* azulado

**bluishness** /'bluɪʃnɪs/ *n* color azulado, *m*

**blunder** /'blʌndər/ *n* desacierto, desatino, *m;* equivocación, *f;* (in a translation, etc.) falta, *f.* —*vi* tropezar (con); desacertar; equivocarse; *Inf.* meter la pata. —*vt* manejar mal; estropear

**blunderer** /'blʌndərər/ *n* desatinado (-da)

**blundering** /'blʌndərɪŋ/ *a* desacertado; equivocado; imprudente *m.* See **blunder**

**blunt** /blʌnt/ *a* romo, embotado; obtuso; (abrupt) brusco; franco; descortés; (plain) claro. —*vt* enromar, embotar; (the point) despuntar; *Fig.* hacer indiferente; (pain) mitigar

**bluntly** /'blʌntli/ *adv* sin filo; sin punta; bruscamente, francamente; claramente

**bluntness** /'blʌntnɪs/ *n* embotamiento, *m; Fig.* brusquedad, franqueza, *f;* claridad, *f*

**blur** /blɜr/ *n* borrón, *m;* mancha, *f;* imagen indistinta, *f.* —*vt* borrar; manchar; *Photo.* velar

**blurred** /blɜrd/ *a* borroso; indistinto; turbio

**blurt (out)** /blɜrt/ *vt* proferir bruscamente; revelar de querer

**blush** /blʌʃ/ *n* rubor, *m;* rojo, *m.* —*vi* enrojecerse, ruborizarse, ponerse colorado; avergonzarse (por)

**blushing** /'blʌʃɪŋ/ *a* ruboroso; púdico

**bluster** /'blʌstər/ *vi* (of the wind) soplar con furia; (of waves) encresparse, embravecerse; (of persons) bravear, fanfarronear. —*n* furia, violencia, *f;* tumulto, *m;* fanfarronería, *f*

**blustering** /'blʌstərɪŋ/ *a* (of wind) violento, fuerte; (of waves) tumultuoso; (of people) fanfarrón, valentón

**boar** /bɔr/ *n* verraco, *m;* (wild) jabalí, *m*

**board** /bɔrd/ *n* tabla, *f;* (for notices) tablón, *m;* (of residence) pensión, *f;* (table) mesa, *f;* (food) comida, *f;* (for chess, checkers) tablero, *m;* (sign) letrero, *m;* (of instruments) cuadro, *m;* (bookbinding) cartón, *m; Naut.* bordo, *m;* (committee) junta, dirección, *f;* tribunal, *m; pl* **boards** *Theat.* tablas, *f pl.* **above b.,** abiertamente, sin disimulo. **free on b.,** (f.o.b.) franco a bordo. **in boards,** (of books) encartonado. **managerial b.,** junta directiva, *f.* **on b.,** a bordo. **on the boards,** *Theat.* en las tablas. **to go on b.,** a bordo.

**b. and lodging,** pensión completa, casa y comida, f. **b. of directors,** consejo de administración, m. **b. of examiners,** tribunal de exámenes, m. **b. of trade,** junta de comercio, f; ministerio de comercio, m
**board** /bɔrd/ vt entablar, enmaderar; embarcar en; (Nav. a ship) abordar; (lodge) alojar, tomar a pensión
**boarder** /'bɔrdər/ n huésped (-da); (at school) pensionista, mf alumno (-na) interno (-na)
**boarding** /'bɔrdɪŋ/ n entablado, m; (planking) tablazón, f; (of a ship) abordaje, m; (of a train) subida (al tren), f. **b.-house,** casa de huéspedes, pensión, f. **b.-school,** pensionado, m
**boarding gate** n puerta de embarque, f
**boast** /boust/ n jactancia, f; ostentación, f; (honor) gloria, f. —vi jactarse, vanagloriarse; alabarse; ostentar. **to b. about,** jactarse de; hacer gala de; gloriarse en
**boaster** /'boustər/ n vanaglorioso (-sa), jactancioso (-sa)
**boastful** /'boustfəl/ a vanaglorioso, jactancioso; ostentador
**boastfully** /'boustfəli/ adv con jactancia; con ostentación
**boastfulness** /'boustfəlnɪs/ n vanagloria, jactancia, f; fanfarronería, f; ostentación, f
**boasting** /'boustɪŋ/ n alardeo, m; fanfarronería, f
**boat** /bout/ n barco, m; bote, m; (in a fun fair) columpio, m, lancha, f; (for sauce or gravy) salsera, f. —vi ir en barco; (row) remar; navegar. **to b. down,** bajar en barco. **to b. up,** subir en barco. **b. building,** construcción de barcos, f. **b. club,** club náutico, m. **b. crew,** tripulación de un barco, f. **b.-hook,** bichero, garabato, m. **b.-house,** cobertizo de las lanchas, m. **b.-load,** barcada, f. **b.-race,** regata, f. **b.-scoop,** achicador, m. **b.-shaped,** en forma de barco. **b.-train,** tren que enlaza con un vapor, m
**boating** /'boutɪŋ/ n pasear en bote, m; manejo de un bote, m; (rowing) remo, m. **b.-pole,** botador, m
**boatman** /'boutmən/ n barquero, m
**boatswain** /'bousən/ n contramaestre, m. **boat-swain's mate,** segundo contramaestre, m
**bob** /bɒb/ n (curtsey) reverencia, f; (woman's hair) pelo a la romana, m; (of bells) toque (de campana), m. —vi saltar; moverse. —vt cortar corto. **long bob,** (hair) melena, f. **to bob up,** ponerse de pie; surgir. **to bob up and down,** subir y bajar; bailar. **bob-tail,** rabo corto, m. **bob-tailed,** rabón
**Bob** /bɒb/ (pet form of Robert) Beto (Mexico)
**bobbin** /'bɒbɪn/ n carrete, huso, m; (of wool, etc.) ovillo, m; (of looms, sewing machines) bobina, f; (in lace-making) bolillo, palillo, m
**bobsled** /'bɒb,slɛd/ n trineo doble, m
**bode** /boud/ vt presagiar, prometer. **to b. ill,** prometer mal. **to b. well,** prometer bien
**bodice** /'bɒdɪs/ n corpiño, m
**bodied** /'bɒdid/ a (in compounds) de cuerpo-
**bodiless** /'bɒdɪlɪs/ a incorpóreo
**bodily** /'bɒdli/ a del cuerpo; físico; corpóreo; real; material; (of fear) de su persona. —adv corporalmente; en persona, personalmente; en conjunto, enteramente; en una pieza
**boding** /'boudɪŋ/ a ominoso, amenazador. —n presagio, m; agüero, m
**body** /'bɒdi/ n Anat. cuerpo, m; (trunk) tronco, m; (corpse) cadáver, m; (of a vehicle) caja, f; (of a motor-car) carrocería, f; (of a ship) casco, m; (of a church) nave, f; (centre) centro, m; (of a book, persons, consistency and Astron.) cuerpo, m; (person) persona, f; corporación, f; grupo, m; (of an army) grueso (de ejercito), m; organismo, m. **in a b.,** en masa, juntos (juntas); en corporación. **to have enough to keep b. and soul together,** tener de que vivir. **b.-snatcher,** junta cadáveres mf ladrón de cadáveres, m. **b.-snatching,** robo de cadáveres, m
**bodyguard** /'bɒdi,gɑrd/ n guardia de corps, f; guardia, f; (escort) escolta, f
**body language** n el lenguaje del cuerpo, m
**bog** /bɒg/ n pantano, marjal, m, marisma, f
**bogey** /'bougi; 'bugi/ n duende, m; (to frighten children) coco, m; (nightmare) pesadilla, f
**boggy** /'bɒgi/ a pantanoso, fangoso
**bogus** /'bougəs/ a postizo, falso

**Bohemian** /bou'himiən/ a and n bohemio (-ia)
**boil** /bɔil/ vi bullir, hervir; (cook) cocer. —vt hervir; cocer. —n ebullición, f; Med. divieso, m. **to b. away,** consumirse hirviendo; Chem. evaporar a seco. **to b. over,** rebosar
**boiler** /'bɔilər/ n Cul. marmita, olla, f; (of a furnace) caldera, f. **double-b.,** baño de María, m. **steam-b.,** caldera de vapor, f. **b.-maker,** calderero, m. **b. room,** cámara de la caldera, f. **b.-suit,** mono, m
**boiling** /'bɔilɪŋ/ n ebullición, f, hervor, m; (cooking) cocción, f, a hirviente. **b. point,** punto de ebullición, m
**boisterous** /'bɔistərəs/ a (of persons) exuberante, impetuoso; (stormy) tempestuoso, borrascoso; violento
**boisterously** /'bɔistərəsli/ adv impetuosamente, ruidosamente; tempestuosamente; con violencia
**boisterousness** /'bɔistərəsnɪs/ n exuberancia, impetuosidad, f; violencia, f; tempestuosidad, borrascosidad, f
**bold** /bould/ a intrépido, audaz; (determined) resuelto; (forward) atrevido; (showy) llamativo; (clear) claro. **b.-faced,** descarado, desvergonzado. **b.-faced type,** letra negra, f
**boldly** /'bouldli/ adv intrépidamente; descaradamente; resueltamente; claramente
**boldness** /'bouldnɪs/ n intrepidez, valentía, f; resolución, f; (forwardness) osadia, f, descaro, atrevimiento, m; claridad, f
**Bolivian** /bou'lɪviən/ a and n boliviano (-na)
**Bolognese** /,boulə'niz/ a and n boloñés (-esa)
**Bolshevik** /'boulʃəvɪk/ a and n bolchevique, mf
**Bolshevism** /'boulʃə,vɪzəm/ n bolchevismo, m
**Bolshevist** /'boulʃəvɪst/ n bolchevista, mf
**bolster** /'boulstər/ n travesaño, m. —vt apuntalar; Fig. apoyar
**bolt** /boult/ n pasador, cerrojo, m; (pin) perno, m; (knocker) aldaba, f; (roll) rollo, m; (flight) huida, f; (of a crossbow) flecha, f; (from the blue) rayo, m. —adv (upright) recto como una flecha; enhiesto; rígido. **b. and nut,** perno y tuerca, m
**bolt** /boult/ vt echar el cerrojo (a); empernar; (Fam. eat) zampar. —vi huir; (horses) desbocarse, dispararse; (plants) cerner. **to b. down,** cerrar con cerrojo. **to b. in,** entrar corriendo, entrar de repente. **to b. off,** marcharse corriendo. **to b. out,** vi salir de golpe. —vt cerrar fuera
**bolus** /'boulas/ n bolo, m
**bomb** /bɒm/ n bomba, f, vt bombardear. **to be a b.-shell,** Fig. caer como una bomba. **b.-carrier,** portabombas, m. **b. crater,** bombazo, m. **b.-release,** (Aer. Nav.) lanzabombas, m. **b.-sight,** mira de avión de
**bombard** /bɒm'bard/ vt bombardear, bombear; Fig. llover (preguntas, etc.) sobre
**bombardier** /,bɒmbər'dɪər/ n bombardero, m
**bombardment** /bɒm'bardmənt/ n bombardeo, m
**bombast** /'bɒmbæst/ n ampulosidad, pomposidad, f
**bombastic** /bɒm'bæstɪk/ a bombástico, altisonante, pomposo
**bomber** /'bɒmər/ n avión de bombardeo, bombardero, m. **dive b.,** bombardero en picado, m. **heavy b.,** bombardero pesado, m. **light b.,** bombardero ligero, m. **b. command,** servicio de bombardeo, m
**bombproof** /'bɒm,pruf/ a a prueba de bomba
**bonafide** /'bounə,faid/ a fidedigno
**bonbon** /'bɒn,bɒn/ n bombón, confite, dulce, m. **b. box,** bombonera, f
**bond** /bɒnd/ n lazo, vínculo, m; Chem. enlace, m; (financial) obligación, f; (security) fianza, f; (Customs) depósito, m; pl bonds, cadenas, f pl, a esclavo. **in b.,** en depósito. **bonds of interest,** intereses creados, m pl. **b.-holder,** obligacionista, mf
**bondage** /'bɒndɪdʒ/ n esclavitud, f; servidumbre, f; cautiverio, m; prisión, f
**bone** /boun/ n hueso, m; (of fish) espina (de pez), f; (whale b.) ballena, f; pl bones, cuerpo, m, vt deshuesar; poner ballenas (a or en). **to be all skin and bones,** estar en los huesos. **to have a b. to pick with,** tener que arreglar las cuentas con. **b.-ash,** cendra, f

**boned** /bound/ a (in compounds) de huesos; deshuesado, sin hueso
**boner** /'bounər/ n gazapo, m, patochada, plancha, f
**bonfire** /'bɒn,faiᵊr/ n fogata, hoguera, f
**Bonn** /bɒn/ Bona, f
**bonnet** /'bɒnɪt/ n capota, f; (of babies) gorra, f; (of men) boina, f; (of chimney and of machines) sombrerete, m
**bonny** /'bɒni/ a sano; hermoso; (fat) gordo
**bonus** /'bounəs/ n paga extraordinaria, bonificación, f; sobresueldo, m; (of food, etc.) ración extraordinaria, f
**bon vivant** /bɔ̃ viˈvɑ̃/ n alegre, vividor, m
**bon voyage** /bɔ̃ vwaˈyaʒ/ interj ¡buen viaje! ¡feliz viaje!
**bony** /'bouni/ a huesudo; (of fish-bones) lleno de espinas; óseo
**booby** /'bubi/ n pazguato, bobo, m. **b.-prize,** último premio, m. **b.-trap,** trampa, f; Mil. mina, f
**book** /bʊk/ n libro, m; volumen, tomo, m; (of an opera) libreto, m. —vt anotar en un libro; apuntar; (seats) tomar (localidades); (tickets) sacar (billetes); (of the issuing clerk) dar; (reserve) reservar; inscribir; consignar (a suspect); (engage) contratar; (invite) comprometer. **to turn the pages of a b.,** hojear un libro. **b.-ends,** sostén para libros, sujetalibros, m. **b.-keeper,** tenedor de libros, m. **b.-keeping,** teneduría de libros, f. **b.-maker,** apostador de profesión, m. **b. of reference,** libro de consulta, m. **b.-plate,** exlibris, m. **b.-post,** tarifa de impresos, f. **b.-shop,** librería, f. **b.-trade,** venta de libros, f; comercio de libros, m
**bookbinder** /'bʊk,baindər/ n encuadernador (-ra) de libros
**bookbinding** /'bʊk,baindɪŋ/ n encuadernación de libros, f
**bookcase** /'bʊk,keis/ n armario de libros, m
**booking** /'bʊkɪŋ/ n (of rooms, etc.) reservación, f; (of tickets) toma, f; Com. asiento, m; (engagement) contratación, f. **b.-clerk,** vendedor (-ra) de billetes. **b.-office,** despacho de billetes, m; taquilla, f
**bookish** /'bʊkɪʃ/ a aficionado a los libros; docto, erudito
**bookishness** /'bʊkɪʃnɪs/ n afición a los libros, f; erudición, f
**bookmark** /'bʊk,mɑrk/ n marcador, m
**bookseller** /'bʊk,sɛlər/ n librero, m
**bookselling** /'bʊk,sɛlɪŋ/ n venta de libros, f; comercio de libros, m
**bookshelf** /'bʊk,ʃelf/ n estante para libros, m
**bookstall** /'bʊk,stɔl/ n puesto de libros, m
**bookstrap** /'bʊk,stræp/ n portalibros, m
**bookworm** /'bʊk,wɜrm/ n polilla que roe los libros, f; Fig. ratón de biblioteca, m
**boom** /bum/ n Naut. botavara, f; (of a crane) aguilón, m; (noise) ruido, m; (of the sea) bramido, m; (thunder) trueno, m; (in a port) cadena de puerto, f; Com. actividad, f; (Fig. peak) auge, m, vi sonar; bramar; tronar; Com. subir; ser famoso. **b. sail,** vela de cangreja, f
**boomerang** /'bumə,ræŋ/ n bumerang, m
**boon** /bun/ n favor, m, merced, f; bien, m, ventaja, f; don, m; privilegio, m, a (of friends) íntimo
**boor** /bʊr/ n monigote, patán, palurdo, m
**boorish** /'bʊrɪʃ/ a rudo, zafio, rústico, cerril
**boorishness** /'bʊrɪʃnɪs/ n zafiedad, patanería, tosquedad, f
**boost** /bust/ vt Elec. aumentar la fuerza de; Inf. empujar; subir; (advertise) dar bombo (a)
**boot** /but/ n bota, f; (of a car) compartimiento para equipaje, m. **button-boots,** botas de botones, f pl. **riding-boots,** botas de montar, f pl. **to b.,** además, de añadidura. **b.-maker,** zapatero, m. **b.-tag,** tirador de bota, m. **b.-tree,** horma de bota, f
**bootblack** /'but,blæk/ n limpiabotas, m
**booted** /'butɪd/ a con botas, calzado con botas; (in compounds) de botas...
**bootee** /bu'ti/ n botín, m
**booth** /buθ/ n puesto, m, barraca, f
**bootlace** /'but,leis/ n cordón para zapatos, m
**bootlegger** /'but,lɛgər/ n contrabandista de alcohol, m
**boots** /buts/ n mozo de hotel, botones, m

**booty** /'buti/ n botín, m; tesoro, m
**booze** /buz/ vi emborracharse. —n alcohol, m; borrachera, f
**boozer** /'buzər/ n borracho (-cha)
**boracic** /bə'ræsɪk/ a bórico. —n ácido bórico, m
**borax** /'bɒræks/ n bórax, m
**Bordeaux** /bɔr'dou/ a and n (of or from) bordelés (-esa). —n (wine) vino de Burdeos, m
**bordello** /bɔr'delou/ n burdel, m
**border** /'bɔrdər/ n borde, m; (of a lake, etc.) orilla, f; (edge) margen, m; (of a diploma, etc.) orla, f; Sew. ribete, m, orla, f; (fringe) franja, f; (garden) arriate, m; (territory) frontera, f; límite, confín, m. —vt Sew. orlar, ribetear; ornar (de); (of land) lindar con. **to b. on,** (of land) tocar, lindar con; (approach) rayar en. **b. country,** región fronteriza, f
**borderer** /'bɔrdərər/ n habitante de una zona fronteriza, m; escocés (-esa) de la frontera con Inglaterra
**borderland** /'bɔrdər,lænd/ n zona fronteriza, f; lindes, m pl
**borderline** /'bɔrdər,lain/ n frontera, f; límite, m; margen, m, a fronterizo; lindero; (uncertain) dudoso, incierto
**bore** /bɔr/ n taladro, barreno, m; perforación, f; (hole) agujero, m; (of guns) calibre, m; (wave) oleada, f; (nuisance) fastidio, m; (dullness) aburrimiento, tedio, m; (person) pelmazo, m, machaca, mf vt taladrar, barrenar, horadar; perforar; hacer un agujero (en); (exhaust) aburrir; fastidiar. **It's a b.,** Es una lata. **to be bored,** aburrirse, fastidiarse
**boredom** /'bɔrdəm/ n aburrimiento, m; tedio, hastío, m
**boric** /'bɔrɪk/ a bórico
**boring** /'bɔrɪŋ/ a aburrido, pesado, tedioso, molesto; fastidioso. —n taladro, m; horadación, f; sondeo, m; perforación, f
**born** /bɔrn/ a nacido; (by birth) de nacimiento; (b. to be) destinado a; natural (de). **He was b. in 1870.** Nació en 1870. **to be b.,** nacer, venir al mundo. **to be b. again,** renacer, volver a nacer. **well-b.,** bien nacido. **b. with a silver spoon in one's mouth,** Nacido de pie, Nacido un domingo
**-borne** /-bɔrn/ trasmitido por... (e.g. anthropod-b., trasmitido por los antrópodos)
**borough** /'bɜrou/ n burgo, m; villa, f; ciudad, f. **b. surveyor,** arquitecto municipal, m
**borrow** /'bɒrou/ vt pedir prestado; apropiarse, adoptar; copiar; (arithmetic) restar; (a book from a library) tomar prestado. **May I b. your pencil?** ¿Quieres prestarme tu lápiz?
**borrower** /'bɒrouər/ n el (la) que pide o toma prestado
**borrowing** /'bɒrouɪŋ/ n el pedir prestado, acto de pedir prestado, m
**bosh** /bɒʃ/ n patrañas, tonterías, f pl; palabrería, f
**Bosnian** /'bɒzniən/ a bosnio
**bosom** /'bʊzəm/ n pecho, m; (heart) corazón, m; (of the earth, etc.) seno, m. **b. friend,** amigo (-ga) del alma, amigo (-ga) íntimo (-ma)
**Bosphorus, the** /'bɒsfərəs/ el Bósforo, m
**boss** /bɒs/ n (of a shield) corcova saliente, f; tachón, m; Archit. pinjante, m. Inf. amo, m; jefe, m. —vt mandar; dominar. **political b.,** cacique, m
**bossism** /'bɒsɪzəm/ n caudillaje, m
**bossy** /'bɒsi/ a mandón, autoritario
**botanical** /bə'tænɪkəl/ a botánico. **b. garden,** jardín botánico, m
**botanist** /'bɒtnɪst/ n botánico (-ca)
**botany** /'bɒtni/ n botánica, f
**botch** /bɒtʃ/ n (clumsy work) chapucería, f; remiendo, m. —vt chapucear, chafallar; (patch) remendar
**both** /bouθ/ a and pron ambos, m pl; ambas, f pl; los dos, m pl; las dos, f pl, adv tan(to)... como; (and) y; a la vez, al mismo tiempo. **It appealed both to the young and the old,** Gustó tanto a los jóvenes como a los viejos. **b. of you,** ustedes dos, vosotros dos, vosotras dos. **b. pretty and useful,** bonito y útil a la vez
**bother** /'bɒðər/ n molestia, f, fastidio, m; (worry) preocupación, f; dificultad, f; (fuss) alboroto, m. —vt molestar; fastidiar; preocupar. —vi preocuparse

**bottle** /'bɒtḷ/ n botella, f; (smaller) frasco, m; (babies) biberón, m; (for water) cantimplora, f, vt embotellar, envasar, enfrascar. **to b. up,** (liquids, capital, armies, navies) embotellar; (feelings) refrenar. **to bring up on the b.,** criar con biberón. **b.-green,** verde botella, m. **b.-neck,** (in an industry) embotellado, m; (in traffic) atascadero, m. **b.-washer,** fregaplatos, mf; (machine) máquina para limpiar botellas, f
**bottle cap** n corchalata, f
**bottled** /'bɒtḷd/ a en botella; (of fruit, vegetables) conservado
**bottleful** /'bɒtḷˌfʊl/ n botella, f
**bottler** /'bɒtḷər/ n embotellador (-ra)
**bottling** /'bɒtḷɪŋ/ n embotellado, m; envase, m. **b. outfit,** embotelladora, f; (for fruit, etc.) aparato para conservar frutas o legumbres, m
**bottom** /'bɒtəm/ n base, f; (deepest part) fondo, m; (last place) último lugar, m; fundamento, m; (of a chair) asiento, m; (of a page, table, mountain, etc.) pie, m; (posterior) culo, m; (of a river) lecho, m; (of the sea) fondo, m; (of a ship) casco, m; (of a skirt) orilla, f; (truth) realidad, verdad, f; (basis) origen, m, causa, f. **at b.,** en realidad. **at the b.,** en el fondo. **false b.,** fondo doble, fondo secreto, m. **to be at the b. of,** ocupar el último lugar en; ser el causante de. **to get to the b. of,** descubrir la verdad de; profundizar en, analizar. **to sink to the b.,** (of ships) irse a pique
**bottomed** /'bɒtəmd/ a (in compounds) de fondo...
**bottomless** /'bɒtəmlɪs/ a sin fondo; (of chairs, etc.) sin asiento; (unfathomable) insondable
**boudoir** /'budwar/ n tocador, gabinete de señora, m
**bough** /bau/ n rama, f, brazo (de un árbol) m
**boulder** /'bouldər/ n roca, peña, f; canto rodado, m; bloque de roca, m
**boulevard** /'bulə,vard/ n bulevar, m
**Boulogne** /bʊ'loun/ Boloña, f
**bounce** /bauns/ n bote, rebote, m; salto, m; (boasting) fanfaronería, f, vi rebotar; saltar, brincar. —vt hacer botar o saltar
**bouncing** /'baunsɪŋ/ a (healthy) sano, robusto; vigoroso, fuerte
**bound** /baund/ n límite, m; (jump) salto, brinco, m, vt limitar, confinar. —vi saltar, brincar; (bounce) botar. **within bounds,** dentro del límite. **b. for,** con destino a; (of ships) con rumbo a
**boundary** /'baundəri/ n límite, lindero, término, m; frontera, f; raya, f. **b. stone,** mojón, m
**bounden** /'baundən/ a obligatorio, forzoso; indispensable
**boundless** /'baundlɪs/ a sin límites, infinito; inmenso
**bounteous, bountiful** /'bauntiəs; 'bauntɪfəl/ a dadivoso, generoso; bondadoso
**bountifulness** /'bauntɪfəlnɪs/ n munificencia, dadivosidad, generosidad, f
**bounty** /'baunti/ n generosidad, munificencia, f; don, m; (subsidy) subvención, f
**bouquet** /bou'kei, bu-/ n ramo, ramillete (de flores), m; perfume, m; (of wine) nariz, f
**Bourbon** /'bɜrbən; 'burbən/ a borbónico. —n Borbón (-ona)
**bourgeois** /bur'ʒwa/ a and n burgués (-esa)
**bourgeoisie** /ˌburʒwa'zi/ n burguesía, mesocracia, f
**bout** /baut/ n turno, m; (in fencing, boxing, wrestling) asalto, m; (of illness, coughing) ataque, m; (fight) lucha, f, combate, m; (of drinking) borrachera, f
**bovine** /'bouvain/ a bovino, vacuno
**bow** /bou/ n (weapon) arco, m; (of a saddle) arzón (de silla), m; Mus. arco, m; (knot) lazo, m; (greeting) saludo, m; reverencia, inclinación, f; (of a boat) proa, f. **to tie a bow,** hacer un lazo. **bow and arrows,** arco y flechas, m. **bow-legged,** patizambo. **bow window,** ventana saliente, f
**bow** /bau/ vi inclinarse; hacer una reverencia, saludar; (remove the hat) descubrirse; Fig. inclinarse (ante); (submit) someterse (a), reconocer; agobiarse; Mus. manejar el arco. —vt (usher in) introducir en, conducir a; doblar; inclinar. **to bow down (to),** humillarse ante; obedecer; (worship) reverenciar, adorar. **to bow out,** despedir con una inclinación del cuerpo

**bowel** /'bauəl/ n intestino, m; pl **bowels,** Fig. seno, m, entrañas, f pl
**bower** /'bauər/ n (arbor) enramada, f; glorieta, f; (boudoir) tocador de señora, m
**bowing** /'bouɪŋ/ n Mus. arqueada, f; saludo, m, a (of acquaintance) superficial
**bowl** /boul/ n receptáculo, m; (of a fountain) taza, f; (of a pipe) cazoleta, f; (barber's) bacía, f; (for washing) jofaina, f; (for punch) ponchera, f; (goblet) copa, f; (for soup) escudilla, f; (for fruit) frutero, m; (of a spoon) paleta, f; (ball) boliche, m. —vt tirar; (in cricket) sacar; (a hoop) jugar con; (in ninepins) tumbar con una bola. **to b. along,** recorrer; ir en coche o carruaje (por). **to b. over,** Fig. dejar consternado (a), desconcertar
**bowler** /'boulər/ n (in cricket) servidor, m; (hat) sombrero hongo, m; (skittle player) jugador de bolos, m
**bowling** /'boulɪŋ/ n (in cricket) saque, m; (skittles) juego de bolos, m; juego de boliche, m. **b. alley,** bolera, pista de bolos, f, salón de boliche, m. **b.-green,** bolera en cesped, f
**bowls** /boulz/ n juego de boliche, m
**bowsprit** /'bausprɪt/ n bauprés, m
**bowstring** /'bou,strɪŋ/ n cuerda de arco, f
**bow tie** /bou/ n pajarita, f
**bow-wow** /'bau ,wau/ n guau, m
**box** /bɒks/ n caja, f; (case) estuche, m; (luggage) baúl, m, maleta, f; (for a hat) sombrerera, f; Bot. boj, m; Theat. palco, m; (for a sentry, signalman, etc.) garita, casilla, f; (on a carriage) pescante, m; (blow) cachete, m, bofetada, f; (for a horse) vagón, m. **post office box,** apartado de correos, m. **box-kite,** cometa celular, f. **box-maker,** cajero, m. **box office,** taquilla, f. **box-pleat,** Sew. tabla, f
**box** /bɒks/ vt encajonar, meter en una caja. —vi boxear. **to box the ears of,** calentar las orejas de. **to box up,** encerrar
**boxer** /'bɒksər/ n Sports. boxeador, pugilista, m
**boxing** /'bɒksɪŋ/ n encajonamiento, m; envase, m; Sports. boxeo, pugilato, m. **B. Day,** Día de San Esteban, m, (A Spanish child receives its Christmas presents on the Día de Reyes (Twelfth Night).) **b.-gloves,** guantes de boxeo, m pl. **b.-ring,** cuadrilátero de boxeo, m
**box-office success** /'bɒks ˌɔfɪs/ n éxito de taquilla, m
**boy** /bɔi/ n muchacho, niño, rapaz, m; (older) chico, joven, m. **new boy,** nuevo alumno, m. **old boy,** (of a school) antiguo alumno, m; (Fam. address) chico. **small boy,** chiquillo, pequeño, crío, m. **b. doll,** muñeco, m. **boy scout,** muchacho explorador, m
**boycott** /'bɔikɒt/ vt boicotear. —n boicot, m
**boyhood** /'bɔihʊd/ n muchachez, mocedad, f; (childhood) niñez, f
**boyish** /'bɔiɪʃ/ a muchachil; pueril; de niñez
**brace** /breis/ n (prop) puntal, barrote, m; abrazadera, f; berbiquí, m; viento, tirante, m; freno (for the teeth), m, (pair) par, m; pl **braces,** tirantes, m pl. —vt apuntalar; asegurar; ensamblar; Naut. bracear; (trousers) tirar; Fig. fortalecer, refrescar
**bracelet** /'breislɪt/ n pulsera, f, brazalete, m, ajorca, f
**bracing** /'breisɪŋ/ a (of air, etc.) fortificante, tónico; estimulador
**bracken** /'brækən/ n helecho, m
**bracket** /'brækɪt/ n consola, f; Archit. repisa, f; soporte, m; (on furniture, etc.) cantonera, f; Print. paréntesis angular, m; (for a light) brazo (de alumbrado), m. —vt Print. poner entre paréntesis; juntar. **in brackets,** entre paréntesis. **They were bracketed equal,** Fueron juzgados iguales
**brackish** /'brækɪʃ/ a salobre
**brag** /bræg/ vi jactarse, fanfarronear. —n jactancia, f. **to b. about,** hacer alarde de
**braggart** /'brægərt/ a baladrón, jactancioso. —n jactancioso, fanfarrón, m
**bragging** /'brægɪŋ/ n jactancia, f
**Brahmin** /'brɑmɪn/ n brahmán, m
**Brahminism** /'brɑmɪ,nɪzəm/ n brahmanismo, m
**braid** /breid/ n trencilla, f, cordoncillo, m; (for trimming) galón, m; (plait) trenza, f. —vt (hair) trenzar; (trim) galonear; acordonar, trencillar
**brain** /brein/ n cerebro, m; entendimiento, m, inteli-

gencia, *f;* talento, *m;* (common sense) sentido común, *m; pl* **brains,** sesos, *m pl,* (animal and human); cacumen, *m.* —*vt* romper la crisma (a). **to blow one's brains out,** levantarse la tapa de los sesos. **to rack one's brains,** devanarse los sesos. **Brains Trust,** masa cefálica, *f;* consorcio de inteligencias, *m.* **b.-box,** cráneo, *m.* **b.-fever,** fiebre cerebral, *f.* **b.-storm,** crisis nerviosa, *f.* **b.-wave,** idea luminosa, *f.* **b.-work,** trabajo intelectual, *m*

**brainchild** /'breɪn,tʃaɪld/ *n* engendro, *m*

**brain drain** *n* fuga de cerebros, *f*

**brained** /breɪnd/ *a* de cabeza, de cerebro

**brainless** /'breɪnlɪs/ *a* sin seso; tonto

**brainy** /'breɪni/ *a* sesudo, inteligente, talentudo

**braise** /breɪz/ *vt Cul.* asar

**brake** /breɪk/ *n* (of vehicles and *Fig.*) freno, *m;* (flax and hemp) caballete, *m;* (carriage) break, *m;* (thicket) matorral, *m.* —*vt* (vehicles) frenar; (hemp, etc.) rastrillar. **foot-b.,** freno de pedal, *m.* **hand-b.,** freno de mano, *m.* **to b. hard,** frenar de repente. **to release the b.,** quitar el freno

**bramble** /'bræmbəl/ *n* zarza, *f.* **b. patch,** breña, *f,* zarzal, *m*

**brambly** /'bræmbli/ *a* zarzoso

**bran** /bræn/ *n* salvado, *m*

**branch** /bræntʃ, brɑntʃ/ *n* (of a tree, a family) rama, *f;* (of flowers, of learning) ramo, *m;* (of a river) tributario, afluente, *m;* (of roads, railways) ramal, *m;* (of a firm) sucursal, dependencia, *f.* —*a* sucursal, dependiente; (of roads, railways) secundario. —*vi* echar ramas; bifurcarse, dividirse; ramificarse. **to b. off,** bifurcarse, ramificarse. **to b. out,** extenderse; emprender cosas nuevas

**branched** /bræntʃt/ *a* con ramas; *Bot.* ramoso; (of candlesticks) de... brazos

**branchiness** /'bræntʃɪnɪs/ *n* ramaje, *m,* frondosidad, *f*

**branching** /'bræntʃɪŋ/ *n* ramificación, *f;* división, *f.* **b. off,** bifurcación, *f*

**brand** /brænd/ *n* tizón, *m;* (torch) tea, *f;* (on cattle, etc.) hierro, *m;* (trademark) marca de fábrica, *f;* marca, *f;* (stigma) estigma, *m.* —*vt* marcar con el hierro, herrar; marcar; estigmatizar, tildar. **b.-new,** flamante

**branding** /'brændɪŋ/ *n* (of livestock) herradero, *m;* (of slaves, criminals) estigmatización, *f;* difamación, *f.* **b.-iron,** hierro de marcar, *m*

**brandish** /'brændɪʃ/ *vt* blandir

**brandy** /'brændi/ *n* coñac, *m*

**brass** /bræs/ *n* latón, *m; Mus.* metal, *m;* (tablet) placa conmemorativa, *f; Inf.* dinero, *m.* **the b.,** *Mus.* el metal. **b. band,** banda de instrumentos de viento, *f.* **b.-neck,** *Inf.* cara dura, *f.* **b. works** or **shop,** latonería, *f*

**brassiere** /brə'zɪər/ *n* sostén, *m*

**brat** /bræt/ *n* crío, *m*

**bravado** /brə'vɑdou/ *n* bravata, *f*

**brave** /breɪv/ *a* valiente, animoso, intrépido; espléndido, magnífico; bizarro. —*n* valiente, *m.* —*vt* desafiar, provocar; arrostrar

**bravely** /'breɪvli/ *adv* valientemente; espléndidamente; bizarramente

**bravery** /'breɪvəri/ *n* valentía, *f,* valor, *m,* intrepidez, *f,* coraje, *m;* esplendidez, suntuosidad, *f;* bizarría, *f*

**bravo** /'brɑvou/ *n* bandido, *m;* asesino pagado, *m, interj* ¡bravo! ¡olé!

**bravura** /brə'vyʊrə/ *n* bravura, *f*

**brawl** /brɔl/ *n* camorra, reyerta, pelotera, *f.* —*vi* alborotar; (of streams) murmurar. **to start a b.,** armar camorra

**brawler** /'brɔlər/ *n* camorrista, *mf*

**brawling** /'brɔlɪŋ/ *n* alboroto, *m,* vocinglería, *f;* (of streams) murmullo, *m*

**brawn** /brɔn/ *n Cul.* embutido, *m;* músculo, *m;* (strength) fuerza, *f*

**brawny** /'brɔni/ *a* membrudo, musculoso, forzudo

**bray** /breɪ/ *n* rebuzno, *m;* (of trumpets) clangor, *m, vi* rebuznar; sonar

**brazen** /'breɪzən/ *a* de latón; (of voice) bronca; desvergonzado, descarado

**brazier** /'breɪʒər/ *n* (fire) brasero, *m;* latonero, *m*

**Brazil** /brə'zɪl/ el Brasil, *m*

**Brazilian** /brə'zɪlyən/ *a* and *n* brasileño (-ña)

**Brazil nut** *n* nuez del Brasil, *f*

**breach** /britʃ/ *n* violación, contravención, *f;* (gap) abertura, *f; Mil.* brecha, *f.* —*vt Mil.* hacer brecha (en); (in a line of defence) hacer mella (en). **b. of confidence,** abuso de confianza, *m.* **b. of promise,** incumplimiento de la palabra de casamiento, *m.* **b. of the peace,** alteración del orden público, *f,* quebrantamiento de la paz, *m*

**bread** /brɛd/ *n* pan, *m.* **to earn one's b. and butter,** ganarse el pan. **brown b.,** pan moreno, *m.* **unleavened b.,** pan ázimo, *m.* **b. and butter,** pan con mantequilla, *m; Fig.* sustento diario, *m.* **b.-basket,** cesta de pan, *f; Inf.* estómago, *m.* **b.-bin,** caja del pan, *f.* **b.-crumb,** miga, *f;* migaja, *f.* **b.-knife,** cuchillo para cortar el pan, *m.* **b. poultice,** cataplasma de miga de pan, *f.* **b.-winner,** ganador (-ra) de pan, trabajador (-ra)

**breadfruit tree** /'brɛd,frut/ *n* árbol del pan, *m*

**breadth** /brɛdθ/ *n* anchura, *f;* latitud, *f;* liberalidad, *f; Sew.* ancho de una tela, *m*

**breadthways** /'brɛdθ,weiz/ *adv* a lo ancho

**break** /breik/ *n* rotura, *f;* (opening) abertura, *f; Geol.* rajadura, *f;* (fissure) grieta, *f;* solución de continuidad, *f;* interrupción, *f;* (billiards) serie, *f;* (change) cambio, *m;* (in a boy's voice) muda (de la voz), *f;* (blank) vacío, *m;* (in the market) baja, *f;* intervalo, *m;* descanso, *m;* pausa, *f;* (truce) tregua, *f;* (clearing) clara, *f; Mus.* quiebra (de la voz), *f;* (carriage) break, *m; (Fam.* folly) disparate, *m.* **with a b. in one's voice,** con voz entrecortada. **b. of day,** aurora, alba, *f.* **at the b. of day,** al despuntar el alba

**break** /breik/ *vt* romper; quebrar; quebrantar, fracturar; (breach) abrir brecha en; (in two) partir, dividir; (into pieces) hacer pedazos, despedazar; (into small pieces) desmenuzar; (into crumbs) desmigajar; (destroy) destrozar; (a blow) parar; (a law) infringir, violar; (the bank in gambling) quebrar; (a journey, etc.) interrumpir; (a habit) desacostumbrar, hacer perder el vicio de; (a promise) no cumplir, faltar a; (a record) superar; (plow ground) roturar; (spoil) estropear; arruinar; *Com.* ir a la quiebra; (an official) degradar; (an animal) domar, amansar; *(Fig.* crush) subyugar; (betray) traicionar; *(Fig.* of silence, a spell, a lance, peace, the ranks) romper; (cushion) amortiguar; (lessen) mitigar; (disclose) revelar; *Elec.* interrumpir. **to b. one's promise,** faltar a su palabra. **to b. the ice,** *Fig.* romper el hielo. **to b. asunder,** romper en dos (partes); dividir. **to b. down,** derribar; echar abajo; destruir; (suppress) suprimir; subyugar; abolir; disolver. **to b. in,** (animals) domar, amaestrar; (persons) disciplinar; (new shoes) ahormar, romper. **to b. in two,** partir; dividir en dos; (split) hender. **to b. off,** separar, quitar; (a branch) desgajar; *Fig.* romper; interrumpir; cesar. **to b. open,** forzar, abrir a la fuerza. **to b. up,** hacer pedazos; (scatter) poner en fuga, dispersar; hacer levantar la sesión; (the ground) roturar; (parliament) disolver; (a ship) desguazar, deshacer (un buque)

**break** /breik/ *vi* romperse; quebrarse; quebrantarse; (of beads) desgranarse; (burst) reventar, estallar; (of abscesses) abrirse; (of a boy's voice) mudar; *(Fig.* and of clouds, etc.) romperse; desaparecer; (of the dawn) despuntar (el alba), amanecer; (sprout) brotar; (of a ball) torcerse; (of fine weather) terminar; (change) cambiar; (of a storm) estallar. **to b. loose,** desasirse; *Fig.* desencadenarse. **to b. away,** escaparse, fugarse; (from a habit) romper con, independizarse de (another country); disiparse. **to b. down,** (of machinery, cars) averiarse; (fail) frustrarse, malograrse; (weep) deshacerse en lágrimas; (lose one's grip) perder la confianza en sí; (in health) sufrir una crisis de salud. **The car broke down,** El auto tuvo una avería. **to b. in,** (of burglars) forzar la entrada; irrumpir (en); penetrar (en); exclamar. **to b. in on,** sorprender; entrar de sopetón; invadir; interrumpir; caer sobre; molestar. **to b. into,** (force) forzar; (utter) romper a, prorrumpir en; empezar (a); pasar de repente a; (of time, etc.) ocupar; hacer perder. **to b. off,** (of speech) interrumpirse; cesar; (detach) desprenderse, separarse; (of branches) desgajarse. **to b. out,** huir, escaparse; *Fig.* estallar; aparecer; declararse; (of fire) tomar fuego; derramarse; (of an eruption) salir. **to b. over,** derramarse por; bañar. **to b.**

**through,** abrirse paso (por); abrirse salida (por); atravesar; *Fig.* penetrar; (of the sun, etc.) romper (por). **to b. up,** (depart) separarse; (of meetings) levantarse la sesión; dispersarse; (smash) hacerse pedazos; disolverse; (of a school) cerrarse, empezar las vacaciones; (melt) fundir; desbandarse; (of a camp) levantar (el campo); (grow old) hacerse viejo; (be ill) estar agotado. **to b. with,** romper con; cesar; reñir con

**breakable** /'breikəbəl/ *a* quebradizo, frágil
**breakage** /'breikɪdʒ/ *n* rompimiento, quebrantamiento, *m;* cosa rota, *f;* fractura, *f*
**breakdown** /'breik,daun/ *n* accidente, *m;* (of a machine) avería, *f; Auto.* pane, *f;* (failure) fracaso, *m,* falta de éxito, *f;* deterioración, *f;* (in health) crisis de salud, *f.* **b. gang,** pelotón de reparaciones, *m*
**breaker** /'breikər/ *n* oleada, *f*
**breakfast** /'brɛkfəst/ *n* desayuno, *m.* —*vi* desayunar(se), tomar el desayuno. **to have a good b.,** desayunar bien. **b.-cup,** tazón, *m.* **b.-time,** hora del desayuno, *f*
**breaking** /'breikɪŋ/ *n* rompimiento, *m;* quebrantamiento, *m;* fractura, *f;* ruptura, *f;* (in two) división, *f;* (into pieces) despedazamiento, *m;* (into small pieces) desmenuzamiento, *m;* (destruction) destrozo, *m;* (of a blow) parada, *f;* (of a law, etc.) violación, *f;* (of one's word) no cumplimiento, *m;* (of a journey, of sleep, etc.) interrupción, *f;* (escape) escape, *m,* huida, *f;* (of an animal) domadura, *f;* (of a boy's voice) muda (de la voz), *f;* (of news) revelación, *f.* **b. down,** demolición, *f;* (of negotiations) suspensión, *f.* **b. in,** irrupción, *f;* (of an animal) domadura, *f;* (training) entrenamiento, *m.* **b. open,** forzamiento, *m;* quebranto, *m.* **b. out,** huida, *f,* escape, *m; Fig.* estallido, *m;* aparición, *f;* declaración, *f;* (scattering) derramamiento, *m;* (of a rash) erupción, *f.* **b. up,** dispersión, *f;* disolución, *f;* fin, *m;* ruina, *f;* (of a school) cierre, *m;* (change in weather) cambio, *m;* (of a meeting) levantamiento (de una sesión), *m;* (of the earth) roturación, *f*
**breakneck** /'breik,nɛk/ *a* rápido, veloz, precipitado
**breakwater** /'breik,wɔtər/ *n* malecón, rompeolas, *m*
**bream** /brɪm/ *n Ichth.* sargo, *m.* **sea-b.,** besugo, *m*
**breast** /brɛst/ *n* pecho, *m;* (of birds) pechuga, *f;* (of female animals) teta, mama, *f;* (heart) corazón, *m, vt* (the waves) cortar (las olas); luchar con; *Fig.* arrostrar, hacer frente a. **b.-bone,** esternón, *m.* **b. high,** alto hasta el pecho. **b.-pin,** alfiler de pecho, *m.* **b.-pocket,** bolsillo de pecho, *m.* **b.-stroke,** estilo pecho, *m*
**breast cancer** *n* el cáncer del seno, *m*
**breasted** /'brɛstɪd/ *a* de pecho...; de pechuga...; de tetas... **a double-b. jacket,** una chaqueta cruzada. **a single-b. jacket,** una chaqueta
**breastwork** /'brɛst,wɜrk/ *n Mil.* parapeto, *m*
**breath** /brɛθ/ *n* aliento, *m;* suspiro, *m;* (phonetics) aspiración, *f;* (breeze) soplo (de aire), *m;* (of scandal, etc.) murmurio, *m;* (fragrance) perfume, *m,* fragancia, *f;* (life) vida, *f.* **in a b.,** de un aliento. **in the same b.,** sin respirar. **out of b.,** sin aliento. **under one's b.,** por lo bajo, entre dientes. **to draw b.,** tomar aliento. **to get one's b. back,** cobrar aliento. **to hold one's b.,** contener el aliento. **to take one's b. away,** *Fig.* dejar consternado (a)
**breathable** /'briðəbəl/ *a* respirable
**breathe** /brið/ *vi* respirar; vivir; (of air, etc.) soplar; (take the air) tomar el fresco; (rest) tomar aliento. —*vt* (whisper) exhalar; dar aire (a); (whisper) murmurar; (convey) expresar, revelar; (infuse) infundir. **to b. forth fury,** echar rayos. **to b. hard,** jadear. **to b. one's last,** exhalar el último suspiro. **to b. in,** inspirar
**breathing** /'briðɪŋ/ *n* respiración, *f;* (of the air, etc.) soplo, *m;* (phonetics) aspiración, *f.* —*a* que respira; viviente. **hard** or **heavy b.,** jadeo, resuello, resoplido, *m.* **b.-space,** *Fig.* respiro, *m*
**breathless** /'brɛθlɪs/ *a* jadeante, sin aliento; (dead) muerto; (sultry) sin un soplo de aire; intenso, profundo; (of haste) precipitado
**breathlessly** /'brɛθlɪsli/ *adv* anhelosamente; con expectación
**breathlessness** /'brɛθlɪsnɪs/ *n* falta de aliento, *f;* res-

piración difícil, *f;* (death) muerte, *f;* (of weather) falta de aire, *f*
**bred** /brɛd/ *a* criado. **ill (well) b.,** mal (bien) criado. **pure-b.,** de raza
**breech** /britʃ/ *n Anat.* trasero, *m;* (of fire-arms) recámara, *f*
**breeches** /'brɪtʃɪz/ *n* calzones, *m pl;* pantalones, *m pl.* **riding-b.,** pantalones de montar, *m pl.* **to wear the b.,** *Fig.* ponerse los calzones
**breed** /brid/ *n* casta, raza, *f;* tipo, *m;* clase, *f, vt* procrear; engendrar, crear; (bring up) educar; criar. —*vi* reproducirse; sacar cría; multiplicarse. **to b. in-and-in,** procrear sin mezclar razas
**breeder** /'bridər/ *n* criador (-ra); animal reproductor, *m*
**breeding** /'bridɪŋ/ *n* reproducción, *f;* cría, *f;* (up-bringing) crianza, *f;* educación, *f;* instrucción, *f;* producción, *f;* creación, *f, a* de cría; (of male animals) semental; prolífico. **bad b.,** mala crianza, *f.* **good b.,** buena crianza, *f.* **cross b.,** cruzamiento de razas, *m.* **B. will out,** Aunque la mona no se vista de seda, mona se queda. **b. farm,** criadero, *m*
**breeze** /briz/ *n* brisa, *f,* vientecillo, soplo de aire, *m;* (argument) altercación, *f,* argumento, *m;* (of coke) cisco de coque, *m.* **fresh b.,** brisa fresca, *f.* **light b.,** brisa floja, *f.* **strong b.,** viento fuerte, viento muy fresco, *m*
**breezy** /'brizi/ *a* con brisa, fresco; expuesto a la brisa; oreado; (of manner) animado, jovial
**Bremen** /'brɛmən, 'breimən/ Brema, *f*
**brethren** /'brɛðrɪn/ *n pl* hermanos, *m pl*
**Breton** /'brɛtn/ *a* and *n* bretón (-ona). —*n* (language) bretón, *m*
**brevet** /brə'vɛt/ *n Mil.* graduación honoraria, *f;* nombramiento honorario, *m.* —*vt Mil.* graduar
**breviary** /'brivi,ɛri/ *n* breviario, *m*
**brevity** /'brɛvɪti/ *n* brevedad, *f;* concisión, *f*
**brew** /bru/ *n* mezcla, *f;* brebaje, *m.* —*vt* hacer (cerveza, té, etc.); preparar, mezclar; *Fig.* urdir, tramar. —*vi* prepararse; urdirse; (storm) gestarse.
**brewer** /'bruər/ *n* cervecero (-ra)
**brewery** /'bruəri/ *n* cervecería, fábrica de cerveza, *f*
**brewing** /'bruɪŋ/ *n* elaboración de cerveza, *f*
**briar** /'braiər/ *n* (wild rose) rosal silvestre, *m;* (heather) brezo, *m.* **b. pipe,** pipa de brezo, *f*
**bribable** /'braibəbəl/ *a* sobornable
**bribe** /braib/ *n* soborno, cohecho, *m, vt* sobornar, cohechar. **to take bribes,** dejarse sobornar
**briber** /'braibər/ *n* cohechador (-ra)
**bribery** /'braibəri/ *n* soborno, *m*
**brick** /brɪk/ *n* ladrillo, *m;* (for children) piedra de construcción, *f;* bloque, *m; Inf.* buen chico, *m,* joya, *f, a* de ladrillo. —*vt* enladrillar. **b.-floor,** ladrillado, *m;* **b.-kiln,** horno de ladrillo, *m.* **b.-maker,** ladrillero, *m.* **b.-yard,** ladrillar, *m*
**bricklayer** /'brɪk,leiər/ *n* albañil, *m*
**bricklaying** /'brɪk,leiɪŋ/ *n* albañilería, *f*
**brickwork** /'brɪk,wɜrk/ *n* masonería, *f*
**bridal** /'braidl/ *a* nupcial; de la boda; de la novia. **b. bed,** tálamo, *m.* **b. cake,** torta de la boda, *f.* **b. shop,** tienda para novias, *f.* **b. shower,** despedida de soltera, despedida de soltería, *f.* **b. song,** epitalamio, *m.* **b. veil,** velo de la novia, velo nupcial, *m.* **b. wreath,** corona de azahar, *f*
**bride** /braid/ *n* novia, desposada, *f;* (after marriage) recién casada, *f*
**bridegroom** /'braid,grum/ *n* novio, *m;* (after marriage) recién casado, *m*
**bridesmaid** /'braidz,meid/ *n* madrina de boda, *f;* niña encargada de sostener la cola de la novia, *f*
**bridge** /brɪdʒ/ *n* (engineering, *Mus. Naut.*) puente, *m;* lomo (de la nariz), *m;* (game) bridge, *m,* vt construir un puente (sobre); pontear; (obstacles) salvar; evitar; (fill in) ocupar, llenar. **auction b.,** bridge por subasta, *m.* **contract b.,** bridge por contrato, *m.* **suspension-b.,** puente colgante, *m.* **b. toll,** pontazgo, *m*
**bridgehead** /'brɪdʒ,hɛd/ *n* cabeza de puente, *f*
**bridle** /'braidl/ *n* brida, *f;* freno, *m.* —*vt* embridar, enfrenar; *Fig.* reprimir. —*vi* (of horses) levantar la cabeza; (of persons) erguirse; hacer un gesto despreciativo. **snaffle b.,** bridón, *m.* **b. path,** camino de herradura, *m*

**brief** /briːf/ *a* breve, corto; conciso; lacónico, seco; rápido; fugaz, pasajero. —*n* (papal) breve, *m;* *Law.* relación, *f;* escrito, *m.* —*vt* (a barrister) instruir. **to hold a b. for,** defender, abogar por. **b.-case,** portapapeles, *m;* cartera (grande), *f*

**briefly** /ˈbriːfli/ *adv* brevemente; en pocas palabras; sucintamente; (tersely) secamente

**brier** /ˈbraɪər/ *n* rosal silvestre, *m;* zarza, *f*

**brigade** /brɪˈgeɪd/ *n* *Mil.* brigada, *f;* cuerpo, *m;* asociación, *f*

**brigadier** /ˌbrɪgəˈdɪər/ *n* brigadier, *m*

**brigand** /ˈbrɪgənd/ *n* bandolero, bandido, *m*

**brigandage** /ˈbrɪgəndɪdʒ/ *n* bandolerismo, *m*

**bright** /braɪt/ *a* brillante, reluciente; vivo; cristalino; subido; claro; optimista; alegre; inteligente; (quick-witted) agudo; ilustre; (smiling) risueño; (of future, etc.) halagüeño. **to be as b. as a new pin,** estar como una ascua de oro. **b. blue,** azul subido, *m.* **b.-eyed,** con ojos vivos, con ojos chispeantes, ojialegre

**brighten** /ˈbraɪtn̩/ *vt* hacer brillar; (polish) pulir; (make happy) alegrar; (improve) mejorar. —*vi* (of the weather) aclarar, despejarse (el cielo); sentirse más feliz; mejorar

**brightly** /ˈbraɪtli/ *adv* brillantemente; alegremente

**brightness** /ˈbraɪtnɪs/ *n* brillo, *m;* claridad, *f;* esplendor, *m;* (of colors) brillantez, *f;* vivacidad, *f;* inteligencia, *f;* agudeza de ingenio, *f*

**Bright's disease** /braɪts/ *n* enfermedad de Bright, glomerulonefritis, *f*

**brilliance** /ˈbrɪlyəns/ *n* fulgor, brillo, *m,* refulgencia, *f;* esplendor, *m;* lustre, *m;* talento, *m;* brillantez, gloria, *f*

**brilliant** /ˈbrɪlyənt/ *a* brillante. —*n* (gem) brillante, *m.* **to be b.,** (in conversation, etc.) brillar; (be clever) ser brillante

**brilliantine** /ˈbrɪlyənˌtin/ *n* brillantina, *f*

**brim** /brɪm/ *n* (of a glass, etc.) borde, *m;* (of a hat) ala, *f;* margen, *m,* orilla, *f.* **to be full to the b.,** estar lleno hasta los bordes; *Fig.* rebosar. **eyes brimming with tears,** ojos arrasados de lágrimas

**brimful** /ˈbrɪmˈfʊl/ *a* hasta el borde (or los bordes); *Fig.* rebosante

**brimless** /ˈbrɪmlɪs/ *a* (of hats) sin ala

**brimmed** /brɪmd/ *a* (of hats) con ala

**brimstone** /ˈbrɪmˌstoʊn/ *n* azufre, *m*

**brindled** /ˈbrɪndl̩d/ *a* atigrado, abigarrado

**brine** /braɪn/ *n* salmuera, *f;* mar, *m;* *Poet.* lágrimas, *f pl*

**bring** /brɪŋ/ *vt* traer; llevar; transportar; (take a person or drive a vehicle) conducir; *Fig.* acarrear, traer; causar, ocasionar; producir; crear; (induce) persuadir; hacer (ver, etc.); (be worth) valer; (sell for) vender por; *Law.* entablar (un pleito, etc.): (before a judge) hacer comparecer (ante); (present) presentar; (attract) atraer; (place) poner. **to b. home,** llevar a casa; *Fig.* hacer ver, hacer sentir; demostrar; (a crime) probar contra. **to b. near,** acercar. **to b. about,** efectuar, poner por obra; causar, ocasionar; (achieve) lograr, conseguir. **to b. again,** traer otra vez, llevar de nuevo. **to b. away,** llevarse. **to b. back,** devolver; traer; (of memories) recordar. **to b. down,** llevar abajo, bajar; (of persons) hacer bajar; (humble) humillar; hacer caer; (of prices) hacer bajar; arruinar; destruir. **to b. down the house,** *Theat.* hacer venirse el teatro abajo. **to b. forth,** (give birth to) dar a luz; producir; causar; sacar a luz. **to b. forward,** hacer adelantarse; empujar hacia adelante; *Fig.* avanzar; (allege) alegar; *Com.* llevar a nueva cuenta; presentar, producir. **brought forward,** *Com.* suma y sigue. **to b. in,** (things) llevar adentro; (persons) hacer entrar; introducir; aparecer con, presentarse con; (meals) servir; producir; declarar; (a verdict) dictar (sentencia de), fallar. **to b. into being,** poner en práctica; dar origen (a). **to b. off,** (a ship) poner a flote; (rescue) salvar, rescatar; (carry out) efectuar, poner en práctica; (achieve) conseguir, lograr. **B. me the glass off the table,** Tráeme el vaso que hay en la mesa. **to b. on,** causar, inducir; acarrear; iniciar. **He brought a book on to the stage,** Entró en escena llevando un libro (or con un libro). **to b. out,** sacar; poner afuera; (a person) hacer salir; publicar; (a play) poner en escena; sacar a luz; (an idea, jewels,

etc.) sacar a relucir; revelar; demostrar; hacer aparecer; (a girl in society) poner de largo (a). **to b. over,** llevar al otro lado; hacer venir; traer; conducir; hacer cruzar; (convert) convertir. **to b. round,** traer; llevar; (from a swoon) sacar de un desmayo; curar; persuadir; conciliar. **to b. through,** hacer atravesar; llevar a través de; ayudar a salir (de un apuro); (an illness) curar de. **to b. to,** traer a; llevar a; (from a swoon) hacer volver en sí; *Naut.* ponerse a la capa. **He cannot b. himself to,** No puede persuadirse a. **to b. together,** reunir; (things) juntar, amontonar; reconciliar, poner en paz. **to b. under,** someter; sojuzgar; incluir. **to b. up,** llevar arriba, subir; (a person) hacer subir; hacer avanzar; (a price) hacer subir; ir (a); andar; (breed) criar; (educate) educar, criar; (in a discussion) hacer notar; vomitar. **to b. up the rear,** ir al fin (de); *Mil.* ir a la retaguardia. **well** (or **badly**) **brought up,** bien (o mal) educado. **to b. upon oneself,** buscarse, incurrir (en). **to b. up-to-date,** poner al día; refrescar; rejuvenecer

**bringing** /ˈbrɪŋɪŋ/ *n* acción de llevar o traer, *f;* conducción, *f;* transporte, *m.* **b. forth,** producción, *f.* **b. in,** introducción, *f.* **b. out,** producción, *f;* publicación, *f;* (of a girl in society) puesta de largo, *f.* **b. under,** reducción, *f;* subyugación, *f.* **b. up,** educación, crianza, *f*

**brink** /brɪŋk/ *n* borde, margen, *m;* (of water) orilla, *f; Fig.* margen, *m.* **on the b.,** al margen; a la orilla. **to be on the b. of,** (doing something) estar para, estar a punto de

**briny** /ˈbraɪni/ *a* salado

**briquette** /brɪˈkɛt/ *n* briqueta, *f,* aglomerado de carbón, *m*

**brisk** /brɪsk/ *a* activo; vivo; animado; rápido, acelerado; enérgico

**brisket** /ˈbrɪskɪt/ *n* falda, *f*

**briskly** /ˈbrɪskli/ *adv* vivamente; enérgicamente; aprisa

**briskness** /ˈbrɪsknɪs/ *n* actividad, *f;* viveza, *f;* animación, *f;* rapidez, *f;* energía, *f*

**brisling** /ˈbrɪzlɪŋ/ *n* sardina noruega

**bristle** /ˈbrɪsəl/ *n* cerda, seda, *f, vi* erizarse

**bristly** /ˈbrɪsli/ *a* erizado, cerdoso; espinoso; hirsuto

**Bristol board** /ˈbrɪstl̩/ *n* cartulina, *f*

**British** /ˈbrɪtɪʃ/ *a* británico. **the B.,** el pueblo británico; los ingleses

**British Commonwealth, the** la Mancomunidad Británica, *f*

**Briton** /ˈbrɪtn̩/ *n* inglés (-esa). **ancient B.,** britano (-na)

**Brittany** /ˈbrɪtni/ Bretaña, *f*

**brittle** /ˈbrɪtl̩/ *a* frágil, quebradizo, deleznable, friable

**brittleness** /ˈbrɪtlnɪs/ *n* fragilidad, friabilidad, *f*

**broach** /broʊtʃ/ *n Cul.* espetón, asador, *m.* —*vt* espitar (un barril); abrir; *Fig.* introducir

**broad** /brɔd/ *a* ancho; grande; (extensive) vasto, extenso; **a b. confession,** una confesión amplia; (full) pleno; (of accents) marcado; (of words) lato; (clear) claro; (of the mind) liberal, tolerante; (of humor, etc.) grosero; (general) general, comprensivo. **in b. daylight,** en pleno día. **b.-brimmed,** de ala ancha. **b.-faced,** cariancho. **b.-minded,** tolerante, liberal, ancho de conciencia, abierto al mundo. **b.-mindedness,** tolerancia, liberalidad, *f.* **to be b.-minded,** ser tolerante, tener manga ancha. **b.-shouldered,** ancho de espaldas

**broadcast** /ˈbrɔdˌkæst/ *n Agr.* siembra al vuelo, *f; Radio.* radiodifusión, radiotransmisión, emisión, *f, a* radiado. —*adv* por todas partes; extensamente. —*vt Agr.* sembrar a vuelo; *Radio.* radiodifundir, radiar, transmitir por radio; (news, etc.) diseminar

**broadcaster** /ˈbrɔdˌkæstər/ *n* (lecturer) conferenciante, *mf;* radiodifusor (-ra); (announcer) locutor (-ra)

**broadcasting** /ˈbrɔdˌkæstɪŋ/ *n* radiación, radiodifución, *f;* radio, *f.* **b.-station,** estación de radio, emisora, *f.* **b.-studio,** estudio de emisión, *m*

**broaden** /ˈbrɔdn̩/ *vt* ampliar, ensanchar. —*vi* ampliarse, ensancharse

**broad-leaved** /ˈbrɔdˌlivd/ *a* frondoso

**broadly** /ˈbrɔdli/ *adv* anchamente; con marcado acento dialectal; de una manera general

**broadness** /'brɔdnıs/ n anchura, f; extensión, vastedad, f; tolerancia, f; liberalidad, f; grosería, f; (of accent) acento marcado, m
**broadside** /'brɔd,said/ n (of a ship) costado, m; (of guns) andanada, f; Fig. batería, f; Print. cara de un pliego, f. **to be b. on,** dar el costado
**brocade** /brou'keid/ a and n brocado m.. —vt decorar con brocado. **imitation b.,** brocatel, m
**brocaded** /brou'keidıd/ a decorado con brocado; de brocado
**broccoli** /'brɒkəli/ n bróculi, brécol, m
**brochure** /brou'ʃʊr/ n folleto, m
**brogue** /broug/ n acento, m; acento irlandés, m; (shoe) zapato grueso, m
**broil** /brɔil/ vt emparrillar, asar. —vi asarse
**broke** /brouk/ a quebrado
**broken** /'broukən/ a roto; quebrado; (spiritless) abatido, desalentado; (infirm) agotado, debilitado; (ruined) arruinado; (of ground) desigual, escabroso; (of a language) chapucero; (spoilt) estropeado; imperfecto; incompleto; (loose) suelto; (of a horse, etc.) domado; (of the weather) variable; (of sleep) interrumpido; (of the heart, of shoes, etc.) roto; (of the voice, sobs, sighs) entrecortado; (of the voice through old age, etc.) cascada; (incoherent) incoherente. **b.-down,** (tired) rendido, agotado; arruinado; (not working) estropeado. **b.-hearted,** roto el corazón, angustiado. **b.-winged,** aliquebrado. **I speak broken Spanish,** Hablo el español chapuceramente
**brokenly** /'broukənli/ adv (of the voice) con voz entrecortada; a ratos; interrumpidamente
**brokenness** /'broukənnıs/ n interrupción, f; (of the ground) desigualdad, f; (of speech) imperfección, f
**broker** /'broukər/ n corredor, m; (stock) corredor de bolsa, m
**brokerage** /'broukərıdʒ/ n corretaje, m
**bromide** /'broumaid/ n bromuro, m
**bromine** /'broumin/ n bromo, m
**bronchi** /'brɒŋki/ n pl bronquios, m pl
**bronchitis** /brɒŋ'kaitıs/ n bronquitis, f
**broncopneumonia** /'brɒŋkounʊ'mounyə/ n bronconeumonía, f
**Brontosaurus** /ˌbrɒntə'sɔrəs/ n brontosauro, m
**bronze** /brɒnz/ n bronce, m; objeto de bronce, m, a de bronce. —vt broncear. **B. Age,** Edad de Bronce, f
**brooch** /broutʃ/ n broche, m; alfiler de pecho, m
**brood** /brud/ n (of birds) nidada, f; (of chickens) pollada, f; (other animals) cría, f; prole, f, vi empollar. **to b. over,** meditar sobre, rumiar; (of mountains, etc.) dominar
**broody** /'brudi/ a (of hens) clueca, f
**brook** /brʊk/ n arroyo, riachuelo, m, vt tolerar, sufrir, permitir
**broom** /brum/ n escoba, f; Bot. retama, f; hiniesta, f. **common b.,** retama de escobas, f. **Spanish b.,** retama común, retama de olor, hiniesta, f. **b.-handle,** palo de escoba, m
**broomstick** /'brum,stık/ n palo de escoba, m
**broth** /brɔθ/ n caldo, m
**brothel** /'brɒθəl/ n burdel, lupanar, m, casa de trato, f
**brother** /'brʌðər/ n hermano, m; (colleague) colega, m; Inf. compañero, m. **foster-b.,** hermano de leche, m. **half-b.,** medio hermano, m. **step-b.,** hermanastro, m. **b.-in-law,** hermano político, cuñado, m. **b.-officer,** compañero de promoción, m
**brotherhood** /'brʌðər,hʊd/ n fraternidad, f; Eccl. cofradía, f; hermandad, f
**brotherliness** /'brʌðərlinıs/ n fraternidad, f
**brotherly** /'brʌðərli/ a fraterno
**brow** /brau/ n frente, f; ceja, f; (of a hill) cresta, cumbre, f; (edge) borde, m. **to knit one's b.,** fruncir el ceño
**browbeat** /'brau,bit/ vt intimidar, amenazar
**browbeating** /'brau,bitıŋ/ n intimidación, f
**brown** /braun/ a castaño; (gallicism often used of shoes, etc.) marrón; pardo; (of complexion, eyes, hair) moreno; (dark brown) bruno; (blackish) negruzco; (toasted) tostado; (burnt) quemado. —n color moreno, m; color pardo, m; castaño, m; (from the sun) bronce, m. —vt (toast) tostar; (a person) volver moreno, broncear; (meat) asar. —vi tostarse;

volverse moreno, broncearse; asarse. **b. bear,** oso pardo, m. **b. owl,** autillo, m. **b. paper,** papel de estraza, m. **b. study,** ensimismamiento, m. meditación, f. **b. sugar,** azúcar moreno (or quebrado), m
**brownie** /'brauni/ n duende benévolo, m
**brownish** /'braunıʃ/ a morenucho; que tira a castaño o a bruno; parduzco; trigueño
**brownness** /'braunnıs/ n color moreno, m
**browse** /brauz/ vi pacer; (through a publication) hojear (un libro)
**browsing** /'brauzıŋ/ n apacentamiento, m; hojeo (de un libro), m; lectura, f, estudio, m
**Bruges** /'brudʒız/ Brujas, f
**bruise** /bruz/ n cardenal, m; abolladura, f; (in metal) bollo, m; (on fruit) maca, f. —vt acardenalar, magullar; abollar; (fruit) macar
**bruising** /'bruzıŋ/ n magullamiento, m; (of metal) abolladura, f; (crushing) machacadura, f; (boxing) boxeo, pugilato, m
**brunette** /bru'nɛt/ n trigueña, morena, f
**brunt** /brʌnt/ n peso, m; golpe, m; choque, m; esfuerzo, m. **to bear the b.,** soportar el peso; sufrir el choque; Inf. pagar el pato
**brush** /brʌʃ/ n cepillo, m; (broom) escoba, f; (for whitewashing, etc.) brocha, f; (for painting) pincel, m; (of a fox) cola (de zorro), f; (undergrowth) breñal, matorral, m; (fight) escaramuza, f; (argument) altercación, f. **scrubbing-b.,** cepillo para fregar, m. **shoe-b.,** cepillo para limpiar los zapatos, m. **stroke of the b.,** brochada, f; pincelada, f. **whitewash-b.,** brochón, m. **b. maker** or **seller,** escobero (-ra); pincelero (-ra)
**brush** /brʌʃ/ vt cepillar; (sweep) barrer; frotar; (touch) rozar; (touch lightly) acariciar. **to b. against,** rozar, tocar. **to b. aside,** echar a un lado; Fig. no hacer caso de; ignorar. **to b. off,** sacudir(se); quitar(se); (sweep) barrer. **to b. up,** cepillar; (wool) cardar; (tidy) asear; (a subject) refrescar, repasar
**brushing** /'brʌʃıŋ/ n acepilladura, f; (sweeping) barredura, f; (touching) roce, rozamiento, m; (of hair) peinadura, f
**brushwood** /'brʌʃ,wʊd/ n enjutos, m pl, chamarasca, f; matorral, m
**brusque** /brʌsk/ a brusco, seco
**brusquely** /'brʌskli/ adv secamente
**brusqueness** /'brʌsknıs/ n brusquedad, f
**Brussels** /'brʌsəlz/ a bruselense; de Bruselas. **B. lace,** encaje de Bruselas, m
**Brussels sprouts** n pl bretones, m pl
**brutal** /'brutl̩/ a bestial, brutal; salvaje, inhumano
**brutality** /bru'tælıti/ n brutalidad, bestialidad, f; barbaridad, ferocidad, f
**brutalize** /'brutl̩,aiz/ vt embrutecer
**brutally** /'brutl̩i/ adv brutalmente
**brute** /brut/ n bruto, animal, m; salvaje, bárbaro, m. **b. force,** la fuerza bruta
**brutish** /'brutıʃ/ a bruto; sensual, bestial; grosero; salvaje; estúpido; ignorante. **to become b.,** embrutecerse
**bubble** /'bʌbəl/ n burbuja, f; borbollón, m, vi burbujear; borbollar, bullir, hervir
**bubbling** /'bʌbəlıŋ/ n burbujeo, m; hervidero, m; (of brooks) murmullo, m, a burbujeante; hirviente; (of brooks) parlero; (of wine) espumoso, efervescente
**bubonic** /byu'bɒnık/ a bubónico. **b. plague,** peste bubónica, f
**buccaneer** /ˌbʌkə'nıər/ n corsario, m; aventurero, m
**Bucharest** /'bukə,rɛst/ Bucarest, m
**buck** /bʌk/ n Zool. gamo, m; (male) macho, m; (fop) galán, petimetre, m, vi (of a horse) caracolear; fanfarronear. **to pass the b.,** Inf. echarle a uno el muerto. **b.-rabbit,** conejo, m. **to b. up,** hacer de tripas corazón
**bucket** /'bʌkıt/ n cubo, balde, m, cubeta, f
**buckle** /'bʌkəl/ n hebilla, f, vt enhebillar, abrochar con hebilla. —vi doblarse. **to b. to,** ponerse a hacer algo con ahinco
**buckled** /'bʌkəld/ a con hebillas
**buckler** /'bʌklər/ n broquel, m, rodela, tarjeta, f
**buckram** /'bʌkrəm/ n bocací, m
**buckshot** /'bʌk,ʃɒt/ n perdigón, m
**buckskin** /'bʌk,skın/ n ante, m

**buckwheat** /'bʌk,wit/ n alforfón, trigo sarraceno, m
**bucolic** /byu'kɒlɪk/ a bucólico, pastoril
**bud** /bʌd/ n brote, m; botón, capullo, m; (of vines) bollón, m; (of vegetables) gema, f. —vi brotar, germinar. —vt injertar de escudete
**Buddhism** /'budɪzəm/ n budismo, m
**Buddhist** /'budɪst/ n budista, mf
**budding** /'bʌdɪŋ/ n brotadura, f; (of roses, etc) injerto de escudete, m; Fig. germen, m
**budge** /bʌdʒ/ vi moverse, menearse. —vt mover
**budgerigar** /'bʌdʒəri,gɑr/ n periquito, m
**budget** /'bʌdʒɪt/ n presupuesto, m; (of news, etc.) colección, f. —vi presuponer
**Buenos Aires** /'bweɪ'nəs aiᵊrɪz/ (of or from) a and n bonaerense, mf
**buff** /bʌf/ n color de ante, m; piel de ante, f. **b.-colored,** anteado
**buffalo** /'bʌfə,lou/ n búfalo, f
**buffer** /'bʌfər/ n (railway) parachoques, m; (of cars) amortiguador, m. **b. state,** estado tapón, m
**buffet** /bə'feɪ/ n bofetón, m; bofetada, f; bar, m. —vt abofetear; golpear; luchar con las olas
**buffoon** /bə'fun/ n bufón, m
**buffoonery** /bə'funəri/ n bufonería, f
**bug** /bʌg/ n chinche, f
**bugbear** /'bʌg,bɛər/ n pesadilla, f
**bugle** /'byugəl/ n corneta, trompeta, f; (bead) abalorio, m. **b. blast,** trompetazo, m
**bugler** /'byuglər/ n trompetero, m
**build** /bɪld/ vt edificar; (engines, ships, organs, etc.) construir; (a nest and Fig.) hacer; (have built) hacer, edificar; crear; formar; fundar. —n estructura, f; (of the body) hechura, f; talle, m. **to b. castles in Spain,** hacer castillos en el aire. **built-up area,** zona urbana, f. **to b. up,** construir, levantar; (block) tapar; (business, reputation) establecer, crear. **to b. upon,** Fig. contar con, confiar en; esperar de
**builder** /'bɪldər/ n constructor, m; maestro de obras, m; (laborer) albañil, m; creador (-ra), fundador (-ra) arquitecto, m
**building** /'bɪldɪŋ/ n edificación, f; construcción, f; edificio, m; fundación, f; creación, f. **b. contractor,** maestro de obras, m. **b. material,** material de construcción, m. **b. site,** solar, terreno, m. **b. timber,** madera de construcción, f
**built-in** /'bɪlt ,ɪn/ a empotrado. **b. closet,** armario empotrado, m
**bulb** /bʌlb/ n Bot. bulbo, m; (Elec. Phys.) bombilla, f; (of an oil lamp) cebolla, f
**bulbous** /'bʌlbəs/ a bulboso
**Bulgarian** /bʌl'gɛəriən/ a and n búlgaro (-ra)
**bulge** /bʌldʒ/ n bulto, m; hinchazón, f; protuberancia, f; Mil. bolsa (en el frente), f. —vi hincharse; estar lleno (de)
**bulging** /'bʌldʒɪŋ/ a lleno (de); con bultos; hinchado (de)
**bulk** /bʌlk/ n volumen, tamaño, m; bulto, m; (larger part) grueso, m; mayor parte, f; (of people) mayoría, f; (of a ship) capacidad, f. **in b.,** Com. en bruto, en grueso. **to b. large,** tener mucha importancia
**bulkhead** /'bʌlk,hed/ n Naut. mamparo, m
**bulkiness** /'bʌlkɪnɪs/ n abultamiento, m; volumen, tamaño, m
**bulky** /'bʌlki/ a voluminoso, grande, grueso
**bull** /bʊl/ n toro, m; Astron. Tauro, m; (of some animals) macho, m; (Stock Exchange) alcista, mf; (of the Pope) bula (del Papa), f. **a b. in a china shop,** un caballo loco en una cacharrería. **to fight bulls,** torear. **b.-calf,** ternero, m. **bull's eye,** blanco, m; acierto, m. **b. fight,** corrida de toros, f. **b. fighter's gala uniform,** traje de luces, m. **b.-ring,** plaza de toros, f
**bulldog** /'bʊl,dɔg/ n perro dogo, perro de presa, m
**bulldozer** /'bʊl,douzər/ n (excavator) tozadora, f
**bullet** /'bʊlɪt/ n bala, f. **spent b.,** bala fría, f. **stray b.,** bala perdida, f. **b.-proof,** a prueba de bala, blindado
**bulletin** /'bʊlɪtɪn/ n boletín, m
**bulletin board** n tablero de anuncios, tablero de avisos, tablón, m
**bulletproof vest** /'bʊlɪt,pruf/ n chaleco blindado, m
**bullfighter** /'bʊl,faitər/ n torero, m (on foot), toreador, m (on horseback)

**bullfinch** /'bʊl,fɪntʃ/ n pinzón real, m
**bullion** /'bʊlyən/ n Com. metálico, m; oro (or plata) en barras, m, f.
**bullock** /'bʊlək/ n becerro, m; buey, m
**bullpen** /'bʊl,pen/ n toril, m (bullfighting); calentador, m (baseball)
**bully** /'bʊli/ n valentón, perdonavidas, gallito, m; rufián, m. —vt intimidar; tratar mal. **b. beef,** vaca en lata, f
**bulrush** /'bʊl,rʌʃ/ n anea, f
**bulwark** /'bʊlwərk/ n baluarte, m; Naut. antepecho, m
**bumblebee** /'bʌmbəl,bi/ n abejorro, m
**bump** /bʌmp/ n golpe, m; ruido, m; choque, m; (bruise) chichón, m, roncha, f; Aer. sacudida, f; meneo, m. —vi (into, against) tropezar con; (along) saltar en. —vt chocar contra
**bumper** /'bʌmpər/ n copa llena hasta los bordes, f, vaso lleno, m; (of a car) parachoques, m. **a b. harvest,** una cosecha abundante
**bumpkin** /'bʌmpkɪn/ n patán, villano, m
**bumptious** /'bʌmpʃəs/ a fatuo, presuntuoso, presumido
**bumptiousness** /'bʌmpʃəsnɪs/ n fatuidad, presunción, f
**bumpy** /'bʌmpi/ n (of surface) desigual, escabroso; (of a vehicle) incómodo, con mala suspensión
**bun** /bʌn/ n buñuelo, bollo, m; (hair) moño, m
**bunch** /bʌntʃ/ n (of fruit) racimo, m; manojo, m; (of flowers) ramo, m; (tuft) penacho, m; (gang) pandilla, f, vi arracimarse; agruparse
**bundle** /'bʌndl/ n atado, lío, m; (of papers) legajo, m; (of sticks) haz, m; (sheaf) fajo, m; (package) paquete, m; fardo, hatillo, m; (roll) rollo, m, vt atar, liar; envolver; empaquetar; (stuff) meter, introducir. **to b. in,** meter dentro (de). **to b. out,** despachar sin ceremonia, poner de patitas en la calle
**bung** /bʌŋ/ n tapón, tarugo, m, vt atarugar
**bungalow** /'bʌŋgə,lou/ n casa de un solo piso, f
**bungle** /'bʌŋgəl/ vt estropear; hacer mal. —n equivocación, f, yerro, m; cosa (o obra) mal hecha, f
**bungling** /'bʌŋglɪŋ/ a chapucero, torpe
**bunion** /'bʌnyən/ n juanete (del pie), m
**bunk** /bʌŋk/ n litera, f, vi Inf. poner pies en polvorosa, pirarse
**bunker** /'bʌŋkər/ n Naut. pañol, m; (for coal) carbonera, f; (golf) hoya de arena, f
**bunkum** /'bʌŋkəm/ n patrañas, f pl
**bunting** /'bʌntɪŋ/ n gallardete, m
**buoy** /'bui/ n boya, baliza, f, vt boyar; abalizar; Fig. sostener. **light b.,** boya luminosa, f
**buoyancy** /'bɔiənsi/ n flotación, f; Fig. optimismo, m, alegría, f
**buoyant** /'bɔiənt/ a boyante; ligero
**burden** /'bərdṇ/ n carga, f, peso, m; (of a ship) tonelaje, m, capacidad, f; (of a song) estribillo, m; (gist) esencia, f. —vt cargar. **to be a b. on,** pesar sobre
**burdensome** /'bərdṇsəm/ a pesado, oneroso, gravoso; abrumador
**burdensomeness** /'bərdṇsəmnɪs/ n pesadez, f; agobio, m
**bureau** /'byʊrou/ n buró, secreter, m; escritorio, m; (office) dirección, oficina, f; departamento, m
**bureaucracy** /byʊ'rɒkrəsi/ n burocracia, f
**bureaucrat** /'byʊrə,kræt/ n burócrata, mf; Inf. mandarín, m
**bureaucratic** /,byʊrə'krætɪk/ a burocrático
**burgher** /'bərgər/ n ciudadano (-na), vecino (-na)
**burglar** /'bərglər/ n ladrón de casas, escalador, m. **cat b.,** gato, m. **b. alarm,** alarma contra ladrones, f. **b. insurance,** seguro contra robo, m
**burglary** /'bərgləri/ n robo nocturno de una casa, m
**burgle** /'bərgəl/ vi robar una casa de noche. —vt robar
**burgomaster** /'bərgə,mæstər/ n burgomaestre, m
**Burgundian** /bər'gʌndiən/ a and n borgoñón (-ona)
**burgundy** /'bərgəndi/ n vino de Borgoña, borgoña, m
**burial** /'bɛriəl/ n entierro, m. **b.-ground,** campo santo, cementerio, m. **b. service,** misa de difuntos, f. **b. society,** sociedad de entierros, f

**burlap** /'bɜrlæp/ n arpillera, f

**burlesque** /bər'lɛsk/ a burlesco. —n parodia. f. —vt parodiar

**burliness** /'bɜrlınıs/ n corpulencia, f

**burly** /'bɜrli/ a corpulento, fornido

**Burma** /'bɜrmə/ Birmania, f

**Burmese** /bər'miz/ a and n birmano (-na)

**burn** /bɜrn/ vt quemar; calcinar; (bricks) cocer; cauterizar; (the tongue) picar; (dry up) secar; (the skin by sun or wind) tostar. —vi quemar; arder; Fig. abrasarse (en). **b. at the stake,** vt quemar en la hoguera. **to b. to ashes,** reducir a cenizas. **to b. away,** consumir(se). **to b. oneself,** quemarse. **to b. up,** quemar del todo, consumir. **to b. with,** Fig. abrasarse en

**burn** /bɜrn/ n quemadura, f; (stream) arroyo, m

**burnable** /'bɜrnəbəl/ a combustible

**burner** /'bɜrnər/ n quemador (-ra); mechero, m

**burning** /'bɜrnıŋ/ n quema, f; incendio, m; fuego, m; (inflammation) inflamación, f; (pain) quemazón, f; abrasamiento, m. —a en llamas; ardiente; intenso; (notorious) notorio, escandaloso; abrasador; palpitante. **b. question,** cuestión palpitante, f

**burnish** /'bɜrnıʃ/ n bruñido, m; lustre, brillo, m, vt bruñir; pulir, pulimentar, dar brillo a; (weapons) acicalar. —vi tomar lustre

**burnisher** /'bɜrnıʃər/ n bruñidor, acicalador, m

**burnishing** /'bɜrnıʃıŋ/ n bruñido, m; pulimento, m; (of weapons) acicalado, m

**burnoose** /bər'nus/ n albornoz, m

**burr** /bɜr/ n Bot. cáliz de flor con espinas, m; Mech. rebaba, f; sonido fuerte de la erre, m

**burrow** /'bɜrou/ n madriguera, f, vivar, m; (for rabbits) conejera, f. —vt amadrigar; minar

**bursar** /'bɜrsər/ n tesorero, f; becario, m

**bursary** /'bɜrsəri/ n tesorería, f; beca, f

**burst** /bɜrst/ n estallido, m, explosión, f; (in a pipe) avería, f, (fit) acceso, m; transporte, m; (effort) esfuerzo, m; (expanse) extensión, f, panorama, m. **b. of applause,** salva de aplausos, f

**burst** /bɜrst/ vi estallar; reventar; quebrarse; romperse; (overflow) desbordar; (of seams) nacerse; derramarse (por); (into laughter) romper a; (into tears) deshacerse en. —vt quebrar; romper; hacer estallar. **to b. upon the view,** aparecer de pronto. **to b. into,** irrumpir en; (exclamations, etc.) prorrumpir en. **to b. into tears,** romper a llorar, deshacerse en lágrimas. **to b. open,** abrir con violencia; forzar

**bursting** /'bɜrstıŋ/ n estallido, m; quebrantamiento, m; (overflowing) desbordamiento, m

**bury** /'bɛri/ vt enterrar, sepultar; sumergir; (hide) esconder, ocultar; (forget) echar tierra a

**bus** /bʌs/ n autobús, ómnibus, m, Mexico camión, Caribbean guagua, m. **double-decker bus,** ómnibus de dos pisos, m. **to travel by bus,** ir en autobús. **bus station,** estación de autobuses, f

**busby** /'bʌzbi/ n birretina, gorra de húsar, f

**bush** /bʊʃ/ n arbusto, matojo, m; (undergrowth) maleza, f; tierra virgen, f; Mech. manguito, m

**bushel** /'bʊʃəl/ n medida de áridos, f, (In England 8 gallons or 36.37 liters)

**bushiness** /'bʊʃınıs/ n espesura, f; densidad, f

**bushy** /'bʊʃi/ a lleno de arbustos; denso; espeso; grueso; (eyebrows, etc.) poblado

**busily** /'bızəli/ adv diligentemente, solícitamente; afanosamente, laboriosamente. **He was b. occupied in...,** Estaba muy ocupado en...

**business** /'bıznıs/ n ocupación, f; quehaceres, m pl; (matter) asunto, m, cosa, f; empleo, oficio, m; Com. negocio(s), m, pl; casa comercial, f; (trade) comercio, m; (clients, connection) clientela, f; (right) derecho, m; Theat. juego escénico, m, pantomima, f. **He had no b. to do that,** No tenía derecho a hacer eso. **Mind your own b.!** ¡No te metas donde no te llaman! **on b.,** por negocios. **to be in b. for oneself,** tener negocios por su propia cuenta. **to mean b.,** hacer algo en serio; estar resuelto. **to send about his b.,** mandar a paseo (a). **to set up in b.,** establecer un negocio. **b. affairs,** negocios, m pl. **b. agent,** agente de negocios, m. **b. hours,** horas de trabajo, f pl. **b.-like,** formal, práctico, sistemático. **b. man,** hombre de negocios, negociante, m

**business administration** n administración de empresas, f

**bust** /bʌst/ n Art. busto, bulto, m; pecho, m. **b. bodice,** sostén, m

**bustard** /'bʌstərd/ n avutarda, f

**bustle** /'bʌsəl/ n actividad, animación, f; confusión, f; (of a dress) polizón, tontillo, m. —vi menearse, darse prisa. —vt dar prisa (a)

**bustling** /'bʌslıŋ/ a activo; ocupado, atareado; animado; bullicioso, ruidoso

**busy** /'bızi/ a ocupado; atareado; activo, diligente; (of places) animado, bullicioso; (of streets) de gran circulación; (officious) entremetido. **to b. oneself,** ocuparse (en, con); dedicarse (a), entregarse (a); (interfere) entremeterse (con). **to be b.,** estar ocupado; estar atareado, tener mucho que hacer. **b.-body,** bullebulle, mf. entremetido (-da), chismoso (-sa)

**busyness** /'bıznıs/ n ocupación, f; laboriosidad, f; actividad, f

**but** /bʌt/ conjunc prep adv pero; sino; (only) solamente; (except) menos; excepto; (almost) casi; que no; si no; (that) que; (nevertheless) sin embargo, empero, no obstante; (without) sin, sin que; (of time recently passed) no más que, tan recientemente. —n pero, m. **He cannot choose but go,** No puede hacer otra cosa que marcharse. **to do nothing but...,** hacer únicamente..., no hacer más que... **but for,** a no ser por. **but yesterday,** solamente ayer. **but then (or but yet),** pero

**butcher** /'bʊtʃər/ n carnicero, m. —vt matar reses; hacer una carnicería en. **butcher's boy,** mozo del carnicero, m. **butcher's shop,** carnicería, f

**butchery** /'bʊtʃəri/ n carnicería, f; matanza, f

**butler** /'bʌtlər/ n mayordomo, m. **butler's pantry,** despensa, repostería, f

**butt** /bʌt/ n (cask) tonel, m, pipa, f; (for water) barril, m; (of a cigarette, etc.) colilla, f; (of fire-arms) culata, f; (handle) mango, cabo, m; (billiards) mocho, m; (earthwork) terrero, m; (Fig. object) objeto (de), m; (of bulls, etc.) topetada, f; pl **butts,** campo de tiro, m; (target) blanco, m. —vt (toss) topar, acornear; (meet) tropezar (con). **to b. in,** Inf. entrometerse, meter baza; encajarse

**butter** /'bʌtər/ n mantequilla, f, vt untar con mantequilla. **b.-dish,** mantequera, f. **b.-fingers,** torpe, m. **b.-knife,** cuchillo para mantequilla, m. **b.-milk,** suero de mantequilla, m. **b.-print,** molde para mantequilla, m. **b.-sauce,** mantequilla fundida, f

**buttercup** /'bʌtər,kʌp/ n ranúnculo, botón de oro, m

**butterfly** /'bʌtər,flai/ n mariposa, f

**butterscotch** /'bʌtər,skɒtʃ/ n dulce de azúcar y mantequilla, m

**buttery** /'bʌtəri/ n despensa, f

**buttocks** /'bʌtəks/ n pl nalgas, posaderas, f pl

**button** /'bʌtn/ n botón, m; pl **buttons,** botones, paje, m. —vt abotonar, abrochar. —vi abotonarse, abrocharse. **to press the b.,** apretar el botón. **b.-hook,** abotonador, m

**buttonhole** /'bʌtn,houl/ n ojal, m; flor que se lleva en el ojal, f. —vt Sew. hacer ojales; (embroidery) hacer el festón; Inf. importunar

**buttoning** /'bʌtnıŋ/ n abrochamiento, m

**buttress** /'bʌtrıs/ n estribo, macho, contrafuerte, m; Fig. apoyo, sostén, m. —vt afianzar, estribar; Fig. apoyar, sostener. **flying-b.,** arbotante, m

**buxom** /'bʌksəm/ a (of a woman) fresca, guapetona, frescachona

**buxomness** /'bʌksəmnıs/ n frescura, f

**buy** /bai/ vt comprar; obtener; (achieve) lograr; (bribe) sobornar. **to buy on credit,** comprar al fiado. **to buy back,** comprar de nuevo; redimir; (ransom) rescatar. **to buy for,** (a price) comprar por; (purpose or destination) comprar para. **to buy in,** (at an auction) comprar por cuenta del dueño. **to buy off,** librarse de uno con dinero. **to buy out,** (of a business) comprar la parte de un socio. **to buy up,** comprar todo, acaparar

**buyable** /'baiəbəl/ a comprable, que se puede comprar

**buyer** /'baiər/ n comprador (-ra)

**buying** /'baiıŋ/ n compra, f. **b. back,** rescate, m. **b. up,** acaparamiento, m

**buying power** *n* capacidad de compra, *f*, valor adquisitivo, *m*

**buzz** /bʌz/ *n* zumbido, *m;* (whisper) susurro, murmullo, *m;* (of a bell) sonido (del timbre), *m*, *vi* zumbar; susurrar

**buzzer** /'bʌzər/ *n* zumbador, *m;* sirena, *f;* (bell) timbre, *m*

**buzzing** /'bʌzɪŋ/ *a* zumbador, que zumba, *n*. See **buzz**

**by** /bai/ *prep* por; de; en; a; con; (of place) cerca de, al lado de; (according to) según, de acuerdo con; (in front of, past) delante (de); (at the latest) antes de, al más tardar; (expressing agency) por; (by means of) mediante; (through, along) por; (upon) sobre; (for) para; (under) bajo. **He will be here by Wednesday,** Estará aquí para el miércoles; (not later than) Estará aquí antes del miércoles (or el miércoles al más tardar). **How did he come by it?** ¿Cómo llegó a su poder? **He will come by train,** Vendrá en tren. **I know her by sight,** La conozco de vista. **There are three children by the first marriage,** Hay tres niños del primer matrimonio. **He goes by the name of Pérez,** Se le conoce por (or bajo) el nombre de Pérez. **six feet by eight,** seis pies por ocho. **They called her by her name,** La llamaron por su nombre. **two by two,** dos por dos. **The picture was painted by Cézanne,** El cuadro fue pintado por Cézanne. **drop by drop,** gota a gota. **by a great deal,** con mucho. **by all means,** naturalmente; de todos modos; cueste lo que cueste. **by chance,** por ventura. **by day (night),** de día (noche). **by daylight,** a la luz del día. **by doing it,** con hacerlo. **by myself,** solo; sin ayuda. **"By Appointment"** «Cita Previa». **by chance or by mis-**

chance, por ventura o por desdicha. **an hour away by car,** a una hora de automóvil. **music by Brahms,** música de Brahms. **pull by the hair,** tirar por el pelo. **take by the hand,** llevar de la mano.

**by** /bai/ *adv* (near) cerca; (before) delante; al lado; a un lado; aparte; (of time) pasado. **to put by,** (keep) guardar; (throw away) desechar; (accumulate) acumular; (put out of the way) arrinconar. **to pass by,** pasar; pasar delante (de). **by now,** ya, antes de ahora. **by the way,** entre paréntesis, a propósito; de paso; al lado del camino. **by-election,** elección parcial, *f*. **by-law,** reglamento, *m*. **by-pass,** ruta de evitación, *f*, desvío, *m; (Mech. Elec.)* derivación, *f.* —*vi* desviarse de; *Mil.* rebasar. **by-product,** derivado, *m; Chem.* producto derivado, *m; Fig.* consecuencia, *f;* resultado, *m*

**bye** /bai/ *n* (in cricket) meta, *f.* **by the bye,** a propósito, entre paréntesis

**bygone** /'bai,gɔn/ *a* pasado. **Let bygones be bygones,** Lo pasado pasado

**byplay** /'bai,plei/ *n* pantomima, *f*, gestos, *m pl; Theat.* juego escénico, *m*, escena muda, *f*

**bystander** /'bai,stændər/ *n* espectador (-ra); *pl* **bystanders,** los circunstantes

**bystreet** /'bai,strit/ *n* callejuela, *f;* calle pobre, *f*

**byway** /'bai,wei/ *n* camino desviado, *m; Fig.* senda indirecta, *f; pl* **byways,** andurriales, *m pl*

**byword** /'bai,wɜrd/ *n* proverbio, *m;* objeto de burla o escándalo, *m*

**Byzantine** /'bɪzən,tin/ *a* bizantino

**Byzantine Empire, the** el Imperio Bizantino, *m*

**Byzantium** /bɪ'zænʃiəm/ Bizancio, *m*

# C

**c** /si/ *n* (letter) c, *f; Mus.* do, *m*
**cab** /kæb/ *n* (horse-drawn) simón, *m;* (taxi) coche de alquiler, *m;* (of a locomotive) cabina del conductor, *f.*
**cab-rank,** punto de coches, *m*
**cabala** /'kæbələ/ *n* cábala, *f*
**cabaret** /ˌkæbə'rei/ *n* cabaret, *m;* taberna, *f*
**cabbage** /'kæbɪdʒ/ *n* col, berza, *f.* **red c.,** lombarda, *f.* **c. butterfly,** mariposa de col, *f*
**cabin** /'kæbɪn/ *n* cabaña, choza, *f; Naut.* camarote, *m;* (railway) garita, *f; Aer.* cabina, *f.* **c. boy,** grumete, galopín, mozo de cámara, *m.* **c. trunk,** baúl mundo, *m*
**cabinet** /'kæbənɪt/ *n* (piece of furniture) vitrina, *f;* colección, exposición, *f; Polit.* gabinete, *m;* (of a radio) cónsola, *f.* **c.-maker,** ebanista, *m.* **c.-making,** ebanistería, *f.* **c. meeting,** consejo de ministros, *m.* **c. minister,** ministro, *m*
**cable** /'keibəl/ *n* amarra, maroma, *f;* cable, *m;* cable-(grama), *m, vt* cablegrafiar. **electric c.,** cable eléctrico, *m.* **overhead c.,** cable aéreo, *m*
**cabman** /'kæbmən/ *n* cochero de punto, simón, *m*
**caboose** /kə'bus/ *n Naut.* cocina, *f*
**cache** /kæʃ/ *n* escondite, escondrijo, *m*
**cackle** /'kækəl/ *vi* (of a hen) cacarear; (of a goose) graznar; (of humans) chacharear. —*n* cacareo, *m;* graznido, *m;* cháchara, *f*
**cacophony** /kə'kɒfəni/ *n* cacofonía, *f*
**cactus** /'kæktəs/ *n* cacto, *m*
**cad** /kæd/ *n* sinvergüenza, *m;* tipo de cuidado, *m*
**cadaverous** /kə'dævərəs/ *a* cadavérico
**caddish** /'kædɪʃ/ *a* mal educado, grosero
**caddy** /'kædi/ *n* (for tea) cajita para té, *f;* (golf) cadi, *mf*
**cadence** /'keidn̩s/ *n* cadencia, *f*
**cadet** /kə'dɛt/ *n* hermano menor, *m; Mil.* cadete, *m*
**cadge** /kædʒ/ *vi* sablear. —*vt* dar un sablazo (a)
**cadger** /'kædʒər/ *n* sablista, *mf;* mendigo, *m;* (loafer) golfo, *m*
**Cadiz** /'kɑdis/ Cádiz, *m*
**cadmium** /'kædmiəm/ *n* cadmio, *m*
**café** /kæ'fei/ *n* café, *m*
**cafeteria** /ˌkæfɪ'tɪəriə/ *n* bar automático, *m*
**caffeine** /kæ'fin/ *n* cafeína, *f*
**cage** /keidʒ/ *n* (animal's, bird's) jaula, *f;* (of a lift) camarín, *m;* (for transporting miners) jaula, *f.* —*vt* enjaular; encerrar
**Cain** /kein/, **to raise** armar lo de Dios es Cristo
**cairn** /kɛərn/ *n* montón de piedras, *m*
**Cairo** /'kairou/ el Cairo, *m*
**cajole** /kə'dʒoul/ *vt* lisonjear; engatusar; embromar; instar
**cajolery** /kə'dʒouləri/ *n* zalamerías, *f pl;* marrullería, *f,* engatusamiento, *m*
**cake** /keik/ *n Cul.* pastel, *m,* torta, *f;* (of chocolate, etc.) pastilla, *f.* —*vt* and *vi* cuajar; formar costra; (with mud) enlodar. **to sell like hot cakes,** venderse como pan bendito. **to take the c.,** llevarse la palma. **c. of soap,** pastilla de jabón, *f.* **c.-shop,** pastelería, *f*
**calamine** /'kælə,main/ *n* calamina, *f*
**calamitous** /kə'læmɪtəs/ *a* calamitoso, desastroso
**calamity** /kə'læmɪti/ *n* calamidad, *f;* desastre, *m*
**calash** /kə'læʃ/ *n* (carriage) calesa, carretela, *f;* (hood) capota, *f*
**calcium** /'kælsiəm/ *n* calcio, *m*
**calculate** /'kælkyə,leit/ *vt* calcular; adaptar. **to c. on,** contar con
**calculated** /'kælkyə,leitɪd/ *a* premeditado. **to be c. to,** conducir a; ser a propósito para
**calculatedly** /'kælkyə,leitɪdli/ *adv* calculadamente
**calculating** /'kælkyə,leitɪŋ/ *n* cálculo, *m,* a calculador; (of persons) interesado; (shrewd) perspicaz; atento. **c. machine,** máquina de calcular, *f,* calculador, *m*
**calculation** /ˌkælkyə'leifən/ *n* cálculo, *m;* calculación, *f*
**calculus** /'kælkyələs/ *n* cálculo, *m*

**Calcutta** /kæl'kʌtə/ Calcutta, *f*
**calendar** /'kæləndər/ *n* calendario, *m;* almanaque, *m;* (university, etc.) programa, *m*
**calender** /'kæləndər/ *n* calandria, *f, vt* calandrar, cilindrar
**calf** /kæf/ *n* becerro (-rra), ternero (-ra); (young of other animals) hijuelo, *m;* (of the leg) pantorrilla, *f;* (leather) cuero de becerro, *m;* piel, *f.* **calf's-foot,** pie de ternera, *m.* **c. love,** amor de muchachos, *m*
**caliber** /'kælɪbər/ *n* calibre, *m*
**calibrate** /'kælə,breit/ *vt* calibrar
**calico** /'kælɪ,kou/ *n* indiana, *f;* percal, *m.* **c.-printer,** fabricante de estampados, *m*
**Californian** /ˌkælə'fɔrnyən/ *a* californio. —*n* californio (-ia)
**caliph** /'keilɪf/ *n* califa, *m*
**calk** /kɔk/ See **caulk**
**call** /kɔl/ *n* llamada, *f;* (shout) grito, *m;* (of a bird) canto, *m;* (signal) señal, *f;* (visit) visita, *f;* (by a ship) escala, *f; Mil.* toque, *m;* (need) necesidad, *f;* (of religion, etc.) vocación, *f;* invitación, *f;* (demand) demanda, *f;* exigencia, *f.* **They came at my c.,** Acudieron a mi llamada. **c. to arms,** llamada, llamada a filas, *f.* **port of c.,** puerto de escala, *m.* **telephone c.,** llamada telefónica, *f.* **to pay a c.,** hacer una visita. **within c.,** al alcance de la voz. **c.-box,** cabina del teléfono, *f.* **c.-boy,** ayudante del trasponte, *m*
**call** /kɔl/ *vi* llamar; gritar, dar voces; (visit) visitar, hacer una visita (a); venir; (stop) parar; (of a ship) hacer escala. —*vt* llamar; (a meeting, etc.) convocar; (awaken) despertar, llamar; (say) decir; (appoint) nombrar; (at cards) declarar. **She is called Dorothy,** Se llama Dorotea. **Madrid calling!** ¡Aquí Radio Madrid! **Will you c. me at eight o'clock, please?** Haga el favor de despertarme (llamarme) a las ocho. **to c. at a port,** hacer escala en un puerto. **to c. a halt,** hacer alto. **to c. a strike,** declarar una huelga. **to c. names,** vituperar, injuriar. **to c. to account,** pedir cuentas (a). **to c. to arms,** tocar el arma; alarmar. **to c. to mind,** acordarse (de), recordar. **to c. to witness,** hacer testigo (de). **to c. back,** *vt* llamar; hacer volver; (unsay) desdecir. —*vi* (return) volver; venir a buscar; ir a buscar. **I called back for the parcel,** Volví a buscar el paquete. **to c. for,** pedir a gritos; llamar; (demand) pedir; exigir; (collect a person) pasar a buscar; (parcels, etc.) ir (or venir) a recoger. **He called for help,** Pidió socorro a gritos. **to c. forth,** producir; provocar; inspirar; revelar; (bring together) reunir. **to c. in,** hacer entrar; invitar; (a specialist, etc.) llamar; (worn coin) retirar de la circulación. **to c. in question,** poner en duda. **to c. off,** (dogs, etc.) llamar; (a strike) cancelar; parar; terminar; (a person) disuadir (de); (postpone) aplazar; suspender; (refrain) desistir (de). **to c. on,** (visit) hacer una visita (a), ir a ver, visitar; (of a doctor) visitar; (a person to do something) recurrir (a); (for a speech) invitar (a hablar); (invoke) invocar. **I shall now c. on Mr. Martínez,** Doy la palabra al señor Martínez. **to c. out,** *vt* hacer salir; provocar; inspirar; (challenge) desafiar, retar. —*vi* gritar. **c. the roll,** pasar lista. **to c. over,** (names) pasar lista (de). **to c. up,** hacer subir; (to the army) llamar a filas (a); (telephone) llamar por teléfono (a); (memories) evocar. **to c. upon.** See **to c. on**
**caller** /'kɔlər/ *n* visita, *f*
**calligraphist** /kə'lɪgrəfɪst/ *n* calígrafo, *m*
**calligraphy** /kə'lɪgrəfi/ *n* caligrafía, *f*
**calling** /'kɔlɪŋ/ *n* llamamiento, *m;* (occupation) profesión, *f;* empleo, *m;* vocación, *f;* (of a meeting) convocación, *f*
**calling card** /'kɔlɪŋ ˌkɑrd/ *n* (telephone) tarjeta telefónica, *f*
**callipers** /'kælɪpərz/ *n pl* compás de puntas, pie de rey, *m*
**callisthenics** /ˌkæləs'θɛnɪks/ *n pl* calistenia, *f*
**callosity** /kə'lɒsɪti/ *n* callosidad, *f*

**callous** /'kæləs/ *a* (of skin) calloso; *Fig.* insensible, duro, inhumano

**callously** /'kæləsli/ *adv* sin piedad

**callousness** /'kæləsnɪs/ *n* falta de piedad, inhumanidad, dureza, *f*

**callow** /'kælou/ *a* (of birds) implume; (inexperienced) bisoño, inexperto, novato

**callus** /'kæləs/ *n* callo, *m*

**calm** /kɑm/ *n* calma, *f*; paz, tranquilidad, *f*; sosiego, *m*; serenidad, *f*. —*a* (of the sea) en calma; tranquilo; sereno; sosegado. —*vt* calmar; tranquilizar; apaciguar. —*vi* calmarse; tranquilizarse; sosegarse. **dead c.,** calma chicha, *f*

**calming** /'kɑmɪŋ/ *a* calmante

**calmly** /'kɑmli/ *adv* tranquilamente, sosegadamente; con calma

**calmness** /'kɑmnɪs/ *n* calma, tranquilidad, *f*; ecuanimidad, serenidad, *f*

**caloric** /kə'lɔrɪk/ *a* calórico

**calorie** /'kæləri/ *n* caloría, *f*

**calumniation** /kə,lʌmni'eiʃən/ *n* calumnia, *f*

**calumniator** /kə'lʌmni,eitər/ *n* calumniador (-ra)

**calumny** /'kæləmni/ *n* calumnia, *f*

**calvary** /'kælvəri/ *n* calvario, *m*

**calve** /kæv/ *vi* (of a cow, etc.) parir

**Calvinism** /'kælvə,nizəm/ *n* calvinismo, *m*

**Calvinist** /'kælvənɪst/ *n* calvinista, *mf*

**Calvinistic** /,kælvə'nɪstɪk/ *a* calvinista

**calyx** /'keilɪks/ *n* cáliz, *m*

**cam** /kæm/ *n* *Mech.* leva, *f*. **camshaft,** árbol de levas, *m*

**camaraderie** /,kɑmə'rɑdəri/ *n* compañerismo, *m*

**camber** /'kæmbər/ *n* comba(dura), *f*

**cambric** /'keimbrɪk/ *n* batista, *f*

**camcorder** /'kæm,kɔrdər/ *n* videocámara, *f*, camcórder, *m*

**camel** /'kæməl/ *n* camello (-lla). **c.-driver,** camellero, *m*. **camel's hair,** pelo de camello, *m*

**camellia** /kə'milyə/ *n* camelia, *f*

**cameo** /'kæmi,ou/ *n* camafeo, *m*

**camera** /'kæmərə/ *n* *Photo.* máquina fotográfica, *f*. **folding c.,** máquina fotográfica plegable, *f*. **in c.,** a puerta cerrada. **c. obscura,** cámara obscura, *f*

**Cameroons, the** /,kæmə'runz/ el Camerón, los Camerones, *m*

**camouflage** /'kæmə,flɑʒ/ *n* camuflaje, *m*, *vt* camuflar

**camp** /kæmp/ *n* campamento, *m*; campo, *m*; *Fig.* vida de cuartel, *f*; (for school children, etc.) colonia, *f*; (party) partido, *m*. —*vi* acampar; vivir en tiendas de campaña. **to break c.,** levantar el campo. **c.-bed,** cama de campaña, *f*. **c.-stool,** silla de campaña, *f*

**campaign** /kæm'pein/ *n* campaña, *f*. —*vi* hacer una campaña

**campaigner** /kæm'peinər/ *n* veterano, *m*; propagandista, *mf*

**campaigning** /kæm'peinɪŋ/ *n* campañas, *f pl*

**camphor** /'kæmfər/ *n* alcanfor, *m*

**camphorated** /'kæmfə,reitd/ *a* alcanforado

**campus** /'kæmpəs/ *n* recinto, *m* (Puerto Rico), ciudad universitaria, *f*

**can** /kæn/ *v aux* poder; (know how to) saber. **You can go to the village when you like,** Puedes ir al pueblo cuando quieras. **I cannot allow that,** No puedo permitir eso. **What can they mean?** ¿Qué quieren decir? **If only things could have been different!** ¡Si solamente las cosas hubiesen sido distintas! **Can you come to dinner on Saturday?** ¿Puede Vd. venir a cenar el sábado? **I can come later if you like,** Puedo (or Podría) venir más tarde si Vd. quiere. **Mary can** (knows how to) **play the piano,** María sabe tocar el piano **You can't have your cake and eat it too.** No hay rosa sin espinas

**can** /kæn/ *n* lata, *f*; (for carrying sandwiches, etc.) fiambrera, *f*. —*vt* conservar en latas. **canopener,** abrelatas, *m*

**Canada** /'kænədə/ el Canadá, *m*

**Canadian** /kə'neidiən/ *a* canadiense. —*n* canadiense, *mf*

**canaille** /kə'nai/ *n* gentualla, gentuza, *f*

**canal** /kə'næl/ *n* canal, *m*

**canalization** /,kænələ'zeiʃən/ *n* canalización, *f*

**canalize** /'kænl,aiz/ *vt* canalizar

**canary** /kə'neəri/ *n* canario (-ia); color de canario, *m*; vino de Canarias, *m*. **roller c.,** canario de raza flauta, *m*. **c.-seed,** alpiste, *m*

**Canary Islands, the** /kə'neəri/ las Islas Canarias, *m*

**cancel** /'kænsəl/ *vt* cancelar; revocar; borrar; anular. **to c. out,** *Math.* anular

**cancellation** /,kænsə'leiʃən/ *n* cancelación, *f*; revocación, *f*; anulación, *f*

**cancer** /'kænsər/ *n* *Med.* cáncer, *m*; *Astron.* Cáncer, *m*

**cancerous** /'kænsərəs/ *a* canceroso. **to become c.,** cancerarse

**candelabrum** /,kændl'ɑbrəm/ *n* candelabro, *m*

**candescent** /kæn'desənt/ *a* candente

**candid** /'kændɪd/ *a* franco; sincero. **If I am to be c.,** Si he de decir la verdad, Si he de ser franco

**candidate** /'kændɪ,deit/ *n* candidato (-ta); aspirante, *m*

**candidature** /'kændɪdə,tʃʊr/ *n* candidatura, *f*

**candidly** /'kændɪdli/ *adv* francamente; sinceramente

**candidness** /'kændɪdnɪs/ *n* franqueza, *f*; sinceridad, *f*

**candied** /'kændid/ *a* (of peel, etc.) almibarado, garapiñado

**candle** /'kændl/ *n* vela, candela, *f*. **wax c.,** cirio, *m*. **You cannot hold a c. to him,** No llega a la suela de su zapato, Ni llega a sus pies, Ni le llega a los pies. **The game is not worth the c.,** La cosa no vale la pena. **to burn the c. at both ends,** consumir la vida. **c.-grease,** sebo, *m*. **c.-light,** luz de las velas, *f*; luz artificial, *f*. **c.-maker,** candelero, *m*. **c.-power,** *Elec.* potencia luminosa, bujía, *f*. **c.-snuffer,** apagavelas, matacandelas, *m*

**Candlemas** /'kændlməs/ *n* candelaria, *f*

**candlestick** /'kændl,stɪk/ *n* candelero, *m*, palmatoria, *f*; (processional) cirial, *m*

**candor** /'kændər/ *n* franqueza, *f*; sinceridad, *f*; candor, *m*

**candy** /'kændi/ *n* caramelo, bombón, *m*, *vt* garapiñar, almibarar

**candytuft** /'kændi,tʌft/ *n* carraspique, *m*

**cane** /kein/ *n* *Bot.* caña, *f*; (for chair seats, etc.) rejilla, *f*; (walking stick) bastón, *m*; (for punishment) vara, *f*. —*vt* apalear, pegar. **sugar-c.,** caña de azúcar, *f*. **c.-break,** cañaveral, *m*. **c. chair,** sillón de mimbres, *m*. **c.-sugar,** azúcar de caña, *m*. **c.-syrup,** miel de caña, *f*

**canine** /'keinain/ *a* canino. —*n* (tooth) diente canino, *m*

**caning** /'keinɪŋ/ *n* paliza, *f*

**canister** /'kænəstər/ *n* bote, *m*, cajita, *f*

**canker** /'kæŋkər/ *n* úlcera, *f*; (in trees) cancro, *m*; *Fig.* cáncer, *m*, *vt* roer; *Fig.* corromper

**canned** /kænd/ *a* en lata

**cannibal** /'kænəbəl/ *n* caníbal, *mf* antropófago (-ga). —*a* caníbal, antropófago

**cannibalism** /'kænəbə,lizəm/ *n* canibalismo, *m*, antropofagía, *f*

**canning** /'kænɪŋ/ *n* conservación en latas, *f*. **c. factory,** fábrica de conservas alimenticias, *f*

**cannon** /'kænən/ *n* (fire-arm) cañón, *m*; (billiards) carambola, *f*, *vi* carambolear. **to c. into,** chocar con. **c.-ball,** bala de cañón, *f*. **c.-shot,** cañonazo, *m*

**cannonade** /,kænə'neid/ *n* cañoneo, *m*

**canny** /'kæni/ *a* cuerdo, sagaz

**canoe** /kə'nu/ *n* canoa, *f*; piragua, *f*, *vi* ir en canoa

**canoeist** /kə'nuist/ *n* canoero (-ra)

**canon** /'kænən/ *n* (*Eccl. Mus. Print.*) canón, *m*; (dignitary) canónigo, *m*; (criterion) criterio, *m*. **c. law,** derecho canónico, *m*

**canonical** /kə'nɒnikəl/ *a* canónico

**canonization** /,kænənə'zeiʃən/ *n* canonización, *f*

**canonize** /'kænə,naiz/ *vt* canonizar

**canopy** /'kænəpi/ *n* dosel, toldo, *m*; palio, *m*; *Fig.* capa, bóveda, *f*. **the c. of heaven,** la capa (or bóveda) del cielo

**cant** /kænt/ *vt* inclinar; ladear. —*vi* inclinarse; (be a hypocrite) camandulear. —*n* (slope) inclinación, *f*, sesgo, desplomo, *m*; (hypocrisy) gazmoñería, *f*

**Cantabrian** /kæn'teibriən/ *a* cantábrico

**cantankerous** /kæn'tæŋkərəs/ *a* irritable, intratable, malhumorado

**cantankerousness** /kæn'tæŋkərəsnɪs/ *n* mal humor, *m*, irritabilidad, *f*

**cantata** /kən'tɑtə/ *n* cantata, *f*

**canteen** /kæn'tin/ *n* cantina, *f*; (water bottle) cantimplora, *f*. **c. of cutlery,** juego de cubiertos, *m*

**canter** /'kæntər/ *n* medio galope, *m*, *vi* andar a galope corto

**Canterbury** /'kæntər,bɛri/ Cantórbery, Cantuaria, *f*

**canticle** /'kæntɪkəl/ *n* cántico, *m*

**canting** /'kæntɪŋ/ *a* hipócrita

**canto** /'kæntou/ *n* canto, *m*

**canton** /'kæntn/ *n* (province and Herald.) cantón, *m*, *vt* (of soldiers) acantonar

**cantonment** /kæn'tɒnmənt/ *n* acantonamiento, cantón, *m*

**cantor** /'kæntər/ *n* Eccl. chantre, *m*

**canvas** /'kænvəs/ *n* lona, *f*; Art. lienzo, *m*; Naut. vela, *f*, paño, *m*. **under c.,** en tiendas de campaña; (of ships) a toda vela

**canvass** /'kænvəs/ *vt* (votes, etc.) solicitar

**canvasser** /'kænvəsər/ *n* solicitador (-ra) (de votos, etc.)

**canvassing** /'kænvəsɪŋ/ *n* solicitación (de votos, etc.), *f*

**canyon** /'kænyən/ *n* cañón, *m*

**canzonet** /,kænzə'nɛt/ *n* chanzoneta, *f*

**cap** /kæp/ *n* gorra, *f*; (with a peak) montera, *f*; (type of military headgear with brim at front) quépis, *m*; (cardinal's) birrete, *m*; Educ. bonete, *m*; (pointed) caperuza, *f*; (woman's old-fashioned) cofia, *f*; (jester's) gorro de bufón, *m*; (on a bottle) cápsula, tapa, *f*. —*vt* Educ. conferir el grado (a). **cap and bells,** gorro de bufón, *m*. **cap and gown,** birrete y muceta, toga y birrete, toga y bonete. **to throw one's cap over the windmill,** echar la capa al toro. **to cap it all,** ser el colmo

**capability** /,keipə'bɪlɪti/ *n* capacidad, *f*; aptitud, *f*

**capable** /'keipəbəl/ *a* capaz; competente; (of improvement) susceptible; (full of initiative) emprendedor

**capably** /'keipəbli/ *adv* competentemente

**capacious** /kə'peiʃəs/ *a* espacioso; grande; extenso

**capaciousness** /kə'peiʃəsnɪs/ *n* capacidad, *f*; amplitud, *f*

**capacitate** /kə'pæsɪ,teit/ *vt* capacitar

**capacity** /kə'pæsɪti/ *n* capacidad, *f*; calidad, *f*; aptitud, *f*. **in one's c. as,** en calidad de. **seating c.,** número de asientos, *m*; (in aircraft) número de plazas, *m*

**caparison** /kə'pærəsən/ *n* caparazón, *m*

**cape** /keip/ *n* (cloak) capa, *f*; (short) capotillo, *m*, capeta, *f*; (fur) cuello, *m*; Geog. cabo, promontorio, *m*. **c. coat,** capote, *m*

**Cape Horn** /'keip 'hɔrn/ Cabo de Hornos, *m*

**caper** /'keipər/ *vi* (gambol) brincar, saltar; cabriolar, corcovear; (play) juguetear. —*n* travesura, *f*; zapateta, *f*; cabriola, *f*; (whim) capricho, *m*; Bot. alcaparra, *f*. **to c. about,** dar saltos, brincar; juguetear

**capillarity** /,kæpə'lærɪti/ *n* capilaridad, *f*

**capillary** /'kæpə,lɛri/ *a* capilar. —*n* vaso capilar, *m*

**capital** /'kæpɪtl/ *a* capital; mortal; de muerte; de vida; principal; (of letters) mayúscula; (very good) excelente. —*n* (city) capital, *f*; (letter) (letra) mayúscula, *f*; Com. capital, *m*; Archit. capitel, chapitel, *m*. **floating c.,** capital fluctuante, *m*. **idle c.,** fondos inactivos, *m pl*. **c. punishment,** pena de muerte, pena capital, pena de la vida, *f*. **C.!** ¡Estupendo! ¡Excelente! **to make c. out of,** aprovecharse de, sacar ventaja de

**capitalism** /'kæpɪtl,ɪzəm/ *n* capitalismo, *m*

**capitalist** /'kæpɪtlɪst/ *n* capitalista, *mf*

**capitalistic** /,kæpɪtl'ɪstɪk/ *a* capitalista

**capitalization** /,kæpɪtlə'zeiʃən/ *n* capitalización, *f*

**capitalize** /'kæpɪtl,aiz/ *vt* capitalizar

**capitally** /'kæpɪtli/ *adv* estupendamente

**capitation** /,kæpɪ'teiʃən/ *n* capitación, *f*

**Capitol** /'kæpɪtl/ *n* Capitolio, *m*

**capitulate** /kə'pɪtʃə,leit/ *vi* capitular

**capitulation** /kə,pɪtʃə'leiʃən/ *n* capitulación, *f*

**capon** /'keipɒn/ *n* capón, *m*

**caprice** /kə'pris/ *n* capricho, *m*

**capricious** /kə'prɪʃəs/ *a* caprichoso

**capriciousness** /kə'prɪʃəsnɪs/ *n* carácter inconstante, *m*; lo caprichoso

**Capricorn** /'kæprɪ,kɔrn/ *n* Capricornio, *m*

**capsize** /kæp'saiz/ *vt* Naut. hacer zozobrar; volcar. —*vi* Naut. zozobrar; volcarse

**capsizing** /'kæp,saizɪŋ/ *n* Naut. zozobra, *f*; vuelco, *m*

**capsule** /'kæpsəl/ *n* (Bot. Med. Chem. Zool.) cápsula, *f*

**captain** /'kæptən/ *n* (Mil. Nav. Aer. and Sports.) capitán, *m*, *vt* capitanear. **to c. a team,** ser el capitán de un equipo. **group c.,** Aer. capitán de aviación, *m*

**captaincy** /'kæptənsi/ *n* capitanía, *f*

**caption** /'kæpʃən/ *n* (arrest) arresto, *m*; (heading) encabezamiento, título, pie, *m*; (cinema) subtítulo, *m*

**captious** /'kæpʃəs/ *a* capcioso, caviloso

**captivate** /'kæptə,veit/ *vt* cautivar, seducir

**captivating** /'kæptə,veitɪŋ/ *a* encantador, seductor

**captive** /'kæptɪv/ *a* cautivo, *n* cautivo (-va), prisionero (-ra), preso (-sa). **c. balloon,** globo cautivo, globo de observación, *m*

**captivity** /kæp'tɪvɪti/ *n* cautiverio, *m*

**captor** /'kæptər/ *n* el, *m*, (*f*, la) que hace prisionero (-ra)

**capture** /'kæptʃər/ *n* captura, *f*; presa, toma, *f*; Law. captura, *f*. —*vt* prender, capturar; tomar

**Capuchin** /'kæpyətʃɪn/ *a* capuchino. —*n* capuchino, *m*. **C. nun,** capuchina, *f*

**car** /kɑr/ *n* (chariot) carro, *m*; (tram) tranvía, *m*; (motor) automóvil, coche, *m*; (on a train) coche vagón, *m*. **sleeping car,** coche camas, *m*. **car park,** parque de automóviles, *m*

**carabineer** /,kɑrəbə'nɪər/ *n* carabinero, *m*

**carafe** /kə'ræf/ *n* garrafa, *f*

**caramel** /'kærəməl/ *n* caramelo, *m*; azúcar quemado, *m*

**carapace** /'kærə,peis/ *n* carapacho, *m*

**carat** /'kærət/ *n* quilate, *m*

**caravan** /'kærə,væn/ *n* caravana, *f*; coche de gitanos, *m*; coche habitación, *m*

**caraway** /'kærə,wei/ *n* alcaravea, *f*

**carbarn** /'kɑr,bɑrn/ *n* encierro, *m* (Mexico), cochera, cochera de tranvías, *f*, cobertizo, cobertizo para tranvías, *m*

**carbide** /'kɑrbaid/ *n* carburo, *m*

**carbine** /'kɑrbin/ *n* carabina, *f*

**carbohydrate** /,kɑrbou'haidreit/ *n* hidrato de carbono, *m*

**carbolic** /kɑr'bɒlɪk/ *a* carbólico. **c. acid,** ácido fénico, *m*

**carbon** /'kɑrbən/ *n* carbono, *m*. **c. copy,** copia en papel carbón, *f*. **c. dioxide,** anhídrido carbónico, *m*. **c. monoxide,** óxido de carbono, *m*. **c. paper,** papel carbón, papel de calcar, *m*

**carbonate** /'kɑrbə,neit/ *n* carbonato, *m*

**carbonated** /'kɑrbə,neitid/ *a* (beverage) carbónico (formal), con gas (informal)

**carbonic** /kɑr'bɒnɪk/ *a* carbónico

**carbonization** /,kɑrbənə'zeiʃən/ *n* carbonización, *f*

**carbonize** /'kɑrbə,naiz/ *vt* carbonizar

**carboy** /'kɑrbɔi/ *n* damajuana, garrafa, *f*

**carbuncle** /'kɑrbʌŋkəl/ *n* Med. carbunco, *m*; (stone) carbúnculo, *m*

**carburetor** /'kɑrbə,reitər/ *n* carburador, *m*

**carcass** /'kɑrkəs/ *n* (animal) res muerta, *f*; (corpse) cadáver, *m*; (body) cuerpo, *m*; (of a ship) casco, *m*

**carcinoma** /,kɑrsə'noumə/ *n* carcinoma, *m*

**card** /kɑrd/ *n* (playing) naipe, *m*; (pasteboard) cartulina, *f*; (visiting, postal, etc.) tarjeta, *f*; (index) ficha, *f*; (for wool, etc.) carda, *f*. —*vt* (wool, etc.) cardar. **I still have a c. up my sleeve,** Me queda todavía un recurso. **to lay one's cards on the table,** poner las cartas boca arriba. **to play one's cards well,** Fig. jugar el lance. **admission c.,** billete de entrada, *m*. **post c.,** tarjeta postal, *f*. **visiting c.,** tarjeta de visita, *f*. **c.-case,** tarjetero, *m*. **c.-index,** fichero, *m*. —*vt* poner en el fichero. **c.-sharper,** fullero, *m*. **c.-table,** mesa de juego, *f*. **c. trick,** juego de manos con cartas, *m*

**cardboard** /'kɑrd,bɔrd/ *n* cartón, *m*, *a* de cartón

**cardiac** /'kɑrdɪˌæk/ a cardíaco
**cardigan** /'kɑrdɪgən/ n rebeca, chaqueta de punto, f
**cardinal** /'kɑrdn̩l/ a cardinal. —n cardenal, m. **c. number,** número cardinal, m. **c. points,** puntos cardinales, m pl
**cardinalate** /'kɑrdn̩l,eit/ n cardenalato, m
**carding** /'kɑrdɪŋ/ n (of wool, etc.) cardadura, f. **c. machine,** carda mecánica, f
**cardiogram** /'kɑrdɪəˌgræm/ n cardiograma, m
**cardiograph** /'kɑrdɪəˌgræf/ n cardiógrafo, m
**care** /kɛər/ n cuidado, m; atención, f; inquietud, ansia, f; (charge) cargo, m. —vi preocuparse; tener interés; (suffer) sufrir. **I don't c.,** Me es igual; No me importa. **I don't c. a straw,** No se me da un bledo. **They don't c. for eggs,** No les gustan los huevos. **We don't c. what his opinion is,** Su opinión nos tiene sin cuidado (or no nos importa). **to c. for,** cuidar, mirar por; (love) querer (a); (like) gustar. **Take c.!** ¡Cuidado! ¡Ojo! **Take c. not to spoil it!** ¡Ten cuidado que no lo estropees! **Would you c. to...?** ¿Le gustaría...? ¿Tendría inconveniente en...? **c. of,** (on a letter, etc.) en casa de. **c.-free,** a libre de cuidados
**careen** /kə'rin/ vt carenar. —vi dar a la banda
**careening** /kə'rinɪŋ/ n carena, f
**career** /kə'rɪər/ n carrera, f; curso, m. —vi correr a carrera tendida; galopar
**careful** /'kɛərfəl/ a cuidadoso (de); atento (a); prudente. **Be c.!** ¡Cuidado! **to be c.,** tener cuidado
**carefully** /'kɛərfəli/ adv con cuidado. **drive c.,** manejar con cuidado; cuidadosamente; prudentemente; atentamente
**carefulness** /'kɛərfəlnɪs/ n cuidado, m; atención, f; prudencia, f
**careless** /'kɛərlɪs/ a sin cuidado; indiferente (a); insensible (a); negligente; (of mistakes, etc.) de (or por) negligencia
**carelessly** /'kɛərlɪsli/ adv indiferentemente; negligentemente; descuidadamente
**carelessness** /'kɛərlɪsnəs/ n indiferencia, f; negligencia, f; descuido, m; omisión, f
**caress** /kə'rɛs/ n caricia, f, vt acariciar
**caressing** /kə'rɛsɪŋ/ a acariciador
**caretaker** /'kɛərˌteikər/ n (of museums, etc.) guardián (-ana); (of flats, etc.) portero (-ra)
**careworn** /'kɛərˌwɔrn/ a devorado de inquietud, ansioso
**cargo** /'kɑrgou/ n cargamento, m, carga, f. **c.-boat,** barco de carga, m
**Caribbean** /ˌkærə'biən, kə'rɪbi-/ a caribe
**Caribbean Sea, the** el Mar Caribe, m
**caricature** /'kærɪkətʃər/ n caricatura, f, vt caricaturizar
**caricaturist** /'kærɪkəˌtʃʊrɪst/ n caricaturista, mf
**caries** /'kɛəriz/ n caries, f
**carious** /'kɛəriəs/ a cariado. **to become c.,** cariarse
**Carmelite** /'kɑrməˌlait/ a carmelita. —n carmelita, mf
**carmine** /'kɑrmɪn/ n carmín, m, a de carmín
**carnage** /'kɑrnɪdʒ/ n carnicería, f
**carnal** /'kɑrnl̩/ a carnal; sensual
**carnality** /kɑr'nælɪti/ n carnalidad, f
**carnally** /'kɑrnl̩i/ adv carnalmente
**carnation** /kɑr'neiʃən/ n clavel, m
**carnival** /'kɑrnəvəl/ n carnaval, m, a de carnaval, carnavalesco
**carnivore** /'kɑrnəˌvɔr/ n carnívoro, m
**carnivorous** /kɑr'nɪvərəs/ a carnívoro
**carol** /'kærəl/ n villancico, m; canto, m. —vi cantar alegremente; (of birds) trinar, gorjear
**Carolingian** /ˌkærə'lɪndʒiən/ a carolingio
**carotid** /kə'rɒtɪd/ n carótida, f
**carousal** /kə'rauzəl/ n borrachera, f; holgorio, m, jarana, f
**carouse** /kə'rauz/ vi emborracharse. —n borrachera, orgía, f
**carp** /kɑrp/ n carpa, f, vi criticar, censurar
**Carpathian Mountains, the** /kɑr'peiθiən/ los Montes Carpotes, m
**carpel** /'kɑrpəl/ n carpelo, m
**carpenter** /'kɑrpəntər/ n carpintero, m, vi carpintear. **carpenter's bench,** banco de carpintero, m. **carpenter's shop,** carpintería, f
**carpentry** /'kɑrpəntri/ n carpintería, f

**carpet** /'kɑrpɪt/ n alfombra, f; Fig. tapete, m. —vt cubrir de una alfombra, alfombrar; entapizar. **to be on the c.,** estar sobre el tapete. **c.-beater,** sacudidor de alfombras, m. **c. merchant,** alfombrista, m. **c. slippers,** zapatillas de fieltro, f pl. **c.-sweeper,** aspirador de polvo, m
**carpeting** /'kɑrpɪtɪŋ/ n alfombrado, m
**carping** /'kɑrpɪŋ/ a capcioso, criticón
**carriage** /'kærɪ/ n (carrying) transporte, porte, m; (deportment) porte, continente, m, presencia, f; (vehicle) carruaje, m; carroza, f; coche, m; (railway) departamento, m; (chassis) chasis, bastidor, m; (of a typewriter, etc.) carro, m. **c. hackney-c.,** coche de plaza, m. **c. and pair,** carroza de dos caballos, f. **c. door,** portezuela, f. **c.-forward,** porte debido. **c.-free,** franco de porte. **c.-paid,** porte pagado
**carrier** /'kæriər/ n el, m, (f, la) que lleva; portador (-ra); Com. mensajero, m; (on a car, bicycle) portaequipajes, m; (of a disease) vector, m; (aircraft) porta-aviones, m. **c.-pigeon,** paloma mensajera, f
**carrion** /'kæriən/ n carroña, f. **c.-crow,** chova, f
**carrot** /'kærət/ n zanahoria, f
**carry** /'kæri/ vt llevar; transportar; traer; conducir; (Mil. of arms) portar; (have with one) tener consigo; (an enemy position) tomar, ganar; (a motion) aprobar; (oneself) portarse; (one's point, etc.) ganar; (in the mind) retener; (conviction) convencer; (involve) implicar; (influence) influir; (send) despachar, enviar; (contain) incluir, comprender. —vi (of the voice, etc.) alcanzar, llegar. **The noise of the guns carried a long way,** El ruido de los cañones se oía desde muy lejos. **to fetch and c.,** traer y llevar. **to c. all before one,** vencer todos los obstáculos. **to c. into effect,** poner en efecto. **to c. one's audience with one,** captar (or cautivar) su auditorio. **to c. oneself well,** tener buena presencia. **to c. on one's back,** llevar a cuestas. **to c. the day,** quedar victorioso, quedar señor del campo. **to c. weight,** Fig. ser de peso. **to c. along,** llevar; (drag) arrastrar; conducir; acarrear. **to c. away,** llevar; llevarse, llevar consigo; (kidnap) robar, secuestrar; (of emotions) dominar; (by enthusiasm) entusiasmar; (inspire) inspirar. **to c. forward,** llevar a cabo; avanzar; fomentar; (bookkeeping) pasar a cuenta nueva. **to c. off,** (things) llevarse; (persons) llevar consigo (a); (abduct or steal) robar; (kill) matar; (a prize) ganar. **to c. (a thing) off well,** llevar la mejor parte, salir vencedor. **to c. on,** vt (a discussion, etc.) seguir, continuar. **c. on a conversation,** llevar una conversación; mantener; (a business, etc.) tener; dirigir. —vi ir tirando; seguir trabajando. **to c. out,** realizar, llevar a cabo; hacer, ejecutar, efectuar; (a promise) cumplir. **to c. through,** llevar a cabo
**carrying** /'kæriŋ/ n transporte, m; (of a motion) adopción, f
**cart** /kɑrt/ n carro, m. —vt acarrear; llevar. **c.-horse,** caballo de tiro, m. **c.-load,** carretada, f, carro, m. **c.-wheel,** rueda de carro, f; (somersault) voltereta, f
**cartage** /'kɑrtɪdʒ/ n carretaje, transporte, porte, m
**carte blanche** /'kɑrt 'blɑntʃ/ n carta blanca, f
**cartel** /kɑr'tɛl/ n cartel, m
**carter** /'kɑrtər/ n carretero, m
**Cartesian** /kɑr'tiʒən/ a cartesiano. —n cartesiano (-na)
**Carthage** /'kɑrθɪdʒ/ Cartago, m
**Carthaginian** /ˌkɑrθə'dʒɪniən/ a cartaginés. —n cartaginés (-esa)
**Carthusian** /kɑr'θuʒən/ a cartujano. **C. monk,** cartujo, m
**cartilage** /'kɑrtlɪdʒ/ n cartílago, m
**cartilaginous** /ˌkɑrtl̩'ædʒənəs/ a cartilaginoso
**cartographer** /kɑr'tɒgrəfər/ n cartógrafo, m
**cartography** /kɑr'tɒgrəfi/ n cartografía, f
**cartomancy** /'kɑrtəmənsi/ n cartomancia, f
**carton** /'kɑrtn̩/ n caja de cartón, f
**cartoon** /kɑr'tun/ n (design for tapestry, etc.) cartón, m; caricatura, f
**cartoonist** /kɑr'tunɪst/ n caricaturista, mf
**cartridge** /'kɑrtrɪdʒ/ n cartucho, m. **blank c.,** cartucho sin bala, m. **c.-belt,** cartuchera, canana, f. **c.-case,** cápsula de proyectil, f
**carve** /kɑrv/ vt tallar, labrar; grabar; cortar; (meat, etc.) trinchar; (a career, etc.) hacer, forjarse

**carver** /'kɑrvər/ n tallador, m; (at table) trinchador, m; (implement) trinchante, m

**carving** /'kɑrvɪŋ/ n talla, f; (design) tallado, m. **c.-knife,** trinchante, m

**cascade** /kæs'keid/ n cascada, catarata, f, salto de agua, m; *Fig.* chorro, m. —*vi* chorrear

**case** /keis/ n caso, m; *Law.* proceso, m, causa, f; *Gram.* caso, m; *Med.* caso, m; enfermo (-ma); (box) caja, f; (for scissors, etc.) vaina, f; (for a cushion, etc.) funda, f; (for jewels, manicure implements, etc.) estuche, m; (of a piano, watch and *Print.*) caja, f; (for documents) carpeta, f; (glass) vitrina, f; (for a book) sobrecubierta, f; (dressing) neceser, m. —*vt* cubrir; forrar; resguardar. **packing-c.,** caja de embalaje, f. **c. of goods,** caja de mercancías, f; bulto, m. **in any c.,** en todo caso; venga lo que venga. **in c.,** por si acaso. **in c. of emergency,** en caso de urgencia. **in such a c.,** en tal caso. **in the c. of,** en el caso de; respecto a. **lower c.,** *Print.* caja baja, f. **upper c.,** *Print.* caja alta, f. **c.-hardened,** (of iron) templado; *Fig.* endurecido, indiferente

**case closed!** ¡asunto concluido!

**casement window** /'keismənt/ n ventana, f

**cash** /kæʃ/ n efectivo, metálico, m; dinero contante, m; *Inf.* dinero, m; *Com.* caja, f. —*vt* cobrar; pagar, hacer efectivo. **hard or ready c.,** dinero contante, m. **to pay c.,** pagar al contado. **c. on delivery,** (C.O.D.) contra reembolso. **c. on hand,** efectivo en caja, m. **c.-book,** libro de caja, m. **c.-box,** caja, f. **c.-desk,** caja, f. **c. down,** pago al contado, m. **c. prize,** premio en metálico, m. **c.-register,** caja registradora, f

**cashew** /'kæʃu/ n anacardo, m

**cashier** /kæ'ʃiər/ n cajero (-ra). —*vt* degradar. **cashier's desk,** caja, f

**cash machine** n cajero automático, m

**cashmere** /'kæʒmiər/ n cachemira, f

**casino** /kə'sinou/ n casino, m

**cask** /kæsk/ n pipa, barrica, f, tonel, m; cuba, f

**casket** /'kæskɪt/ n cajita, arquilla, f, cofrecito, m

**Caspian** /'kæspiən/ a caspio

**Caspian Sea, the** el (Mar) Caspio, m

**casserole** /'kæsəˌroul/ n cacerola, f

**cassock** /'kæsək/ n sotana, f

**cast** /kæst/ *vt* arrojar, tirar; (in fishing, the anchor, dice, darts, lots, a net, glances, blame, etc.) echar; (skin) mudar; (lose) perder; (a shadow, etc.) proyectar; (a vote) dar; (mold) vaciar; (accounts) echar, calcular; (a horoscope) hacer; (the parts in a play) repartir; (an actor for a part) dar el papel de; (metals) colar, fundir. **the shadow c. by the wall,** la sombra proyectada por el muro. **to c. anchor,** echar anclas, anclar. **to c. in one's lot with,** compartir la suerte de. **to c. something in a person's teeth,** echar en cara (a). **to c. lots,** echar suertes. **to c. about,** meditar, considerar; imaginar; (devise) inventar. **to c. aside,** desechar; poner a un lado; abandonar. **to c. away,** tirar lejos; desechar; (money) derrochar, malgastar. **to be c. away,** *Naut.* naufragar. **to c. down,** (overthrow) derribar, destruir; (eyes) bajar; (depress) desanimar, deprimir; (humiliate) humillar. **to be c. down,** estar deprimido. **c. iron,** n hierro colado, hierro fundido, m. **c.-iron,** a de hierro colado; *Fig.* inflexible. **to c. off,** quitarse; desechar; (a wife) repudiar; (desert) abandonar; (free oneself) librarse (de). **c.-off,** n desecho, m. **c.-off clothing,** ropa de desecho, f. **to c. out,** echar fuera; hacer salir; excluir. **to c. up,** echar; vomitar; (a sum) sumar; (something at a person) reprochar

**cast** /kæst/ n (of dice, fishing-line) echada, f; (of a net) redada, f; (worm) molde, m; (of a play) reparto, m; (of mind) inclinación, f; (in the eye) defecto en la mirada, m; (of colour) matiz, tinte, m. **c. of features,** facciones, f pl, fisonomía, f. **plaster c.,** vaciado, m

**castanets** /ˌkæstə'nɛts/ n pl castañuelas, f pl

**castaway** /'kæstəˌwei/ n náufrago (-ga); *Fig.* perdido (-da)

**caste** /kæst/ n casta, f; clase social, f. **to lose c.,** desprestigiarse

**castigate** /'kæstɪˌgeit/ *vt* castigar

**Castile** /kæ'stil/ Castilla, f

**Castilian** /kæ'stɪlyən/ a castellano. —n castellano (-na); (language) castellano, m

**casting** /'kæstɪŋ/ n lanzamiento, m; (of metals) fundición, colada, f; obra de fundición, f. **c.-net,** esparavel, m. **c.-vote,** voto de calidad, m

**castle** /'kæsəl/ n castillo, m; (in chess) torre, f, roque, m. **to build castles in Spain,** hacer castillos en el aire

**castor** /'kæstər/ n *Zool.* castor, m; (for sugar) azucarero, m; (cruet) convoy, m; (on chairs, etc.) ruedecilla, roldana, f. **c.-oil,** aceite de ricino, m. **c.-sugar,** azúcar en polvo, m

**castrate** /'kæstreit/ *vt* castrar, capar

**castration** /kæs'treiʃən/ n castración, capadura, f

**casual** /'kæʒuəl/ a fortuito, accidental; ligero, superficial; *Inf.* despreocupado. **c. worker,** jornalero, m

**casually** /'kæʒuəli/ adv por casualidad; de paso; negligentemente

**casualness** /'kæʒuəlnɪs/ n *Inf.* negligencia, despreocupación, f

**casualty** /'kæʒuəlti/ n víctima, f; herido, m; *Mil.* baja, f; pl **casualties,** heridos, m pl; muertos, m pl. **c.-list,** lista de víctimas, f; *Mil.* lista de bajas, f

**casuist** /'kæʒuist/ n casuista, mf

**casuistry** /'kæʒuəstri/ n casuística, f

**cat** /kæt/ n gato (-ta). **She is an old cat,** Ella es una vieja chismosa. **to be like a cat on hot bricks,** estar como en brasas, **to let the cat out of the bag,** tirar de la manta. **to lead a cat-and-dog life,** vivir como perros y gatos. **cat's-cradle,** (game) cunas, f pl. **cat's paw,** (person) hombre de paja, m; *Naut.* bocanada de viento, f. **cat o' nine tails,** gato de siete colas, m, penca, f. **catwhisker,** *Radio.* detector, m

**cataclysm** /'kætəˌklizəm/ n cataclismo, m

**catacombs** /'kætəˌkoumz/ n pl catacumbas, f pl

**catafalque** /'kætəˌfɔk/ n catafalco, m

**Catalan** /'kætlˌæn/ a catalán (-ana). —n catalán; (language) catalán, m

**catalepsy** /'kætlˌɛpsi/ n catalepsia, f

**catalogue** /'kætlˌɔg/ n catálogo, m, *vt* catalogar

**Catalonia** /ˌkætl'ouniə/ Cataluña, f

**catalysis** /kə'tæləsis/ n catálisis, f

**cat-and-mouse** /'kæt n 'maus/ n el juego de ratón, m

**catapult** /'kætəˌpʌlt/ n *Mil.* catapulta, f; *Aer.* catapulta (para lanzar aviones), f; (toy) tirador de gomas, m. —*vt* tirar con una catapulta (or con un tirador de gomas); (throw) lanzar

**cataract** /'kætəˌrækt/ n catarata, cascada, f, salto de agua, m; (of the eye) catarata, f

**catarrh** /kə'tɑr/ n catarro, m; constipado, resfriado, m

**catastrophe** /kə'tæstrəfi/ n catástrofe, f, desastre, m; (in drama) desenlace, m

**catastrophic** /ˌkætəs'trɒfɪk/ a catastrófico

**catcall** /'kætˌkɔl/ n silbido, m

**catch** /kætʃ/ *vt* coger; agarrar, asir; (capture) prender, haber; (a disease) contraer; (habit) tomar; (on a hook, etc.) enganchar; (surprise) sorprender; (understand) comprender; (hear) oír; (with blows, etc.) dar. —*vi* (of a lock) encajarse; (become entangled) engancharse; (of a fire) encenderse. **to c. a glimpse of,** ver por un instante (a); alcanzar a ver, entrever. **to c. at,** asir; agarrarse (a); echar mano de; procurar asir; alargar la mano hacia; (an idea, etc.) adoptar con entusiasmo. **to c. on,** (be popular) tener éxito; (understand) comprender. **to c. out,** coger en el acto; coger en un error; *Sports.* coger. **to c. up,** coger; interrumpir. **to c. up with,** (a person) alcanzar; (news) ponerse al corriente de

**catch** /kætʃ/ n presa, f; (of fish) redada, pesca, f; (of a window, etc.) cerradura, f; (latch) pestillo, m; (trick) trampa, f; *Mus.* canon, m. **a good c.,** (matrimonial) un buen partido. **to have a c. in one's voice,** hablar con voz entrecortada. **c.-as-c.-can,** lucha libre, f

**catching** /'kætʃɪŋ/ a contagioso

**catchment** /'kætʃmənt/ n desagüe, m

**catchword** /'kætʃˌwɜrd/ n reclamo, m; (theater cue) pie, apunte, m; (slogan) mote, m

**catchy** /'kætʃi/ a atractivo. **It's a c. tune,** Es una canción que se pega

**catechism** /'kætɪˌkizəm/ n catequismo, m

**categorical** /ˌkætɪ'gɔrɪkəl/ a categórico

**category** /'kætɪˌgɔri/ n categoría, f

**cater** /'keitər/ *vi* proveer, abastecer. **to c. for all tastes,** atender a todos los gustos

**caterer** /'keitərər/ n despensero (-ra)
**catering** /'keitəriŋ/ n provisión, f
**caterpillar** /'kætə,pilər/ n oruga, f. **c. tractor,** tractor de orugas, m
**caterwaul** /'kætər,wɔl/ vi (of a cat) maullar
**caterwauler** /'kætər,wɔlər/ n (violinist, etc.) rascatripas, m
**caterwauling** /'kætər,wɔliŋ/ n maullidos, m pl; música ratonera, f
**catfish** /'kæt,fiʃ/ n siluro, m
**catgut** /'kæt,gʌt/ n Surg. catgut, m; Mus. cuerda, f
**catharsis** /kə'θɑrsɪs/ n Med. purga, f; Fig. catarsis, f
**cathedral** /kə'θidrəl/ n catedral, f
**Catherine wheel** /'kæθrɪn/ n Archit. rosa, f; (firework) rueda de Santa Catalina, f; (somersault) tumba, f
**catheter** /'kæθɪtər/ n catéter, m
**cathode** /'kæθoud/ n cátodo, m. **c. rays,** rayos catódicos, m pl. **c. ray tube,** tubo de rayos catódicos, m
**cathodic** /kæ'θɒdɪk/ a catódico
**catholic** /'kæθəlɪk/ a católico
**Catholicism** /kə'θɒlə,sɪzəm/ n catolicismo, m
**catkin** /'kætkɪn/ n amento, m. **male c.,** amento macho, m
**catlike** /'kæt,laik/ a de gato; gatuno
**cattle** /'kætl/ n ganado vacuno, m; ganado, m; animales, m pl. **c.-dealer,** ganadero, m. **c.-lifter,** hurtador de ganado, m. **c.-pen,** corral, m. **c.-raiser,** criador de ganado, m. **c.-raising,** ganadería, f. **c.-ranch,** hacienda de ganado, estancia, f. **c.-show,** exposición de ganado, f. **c.-truck,** vagón de ferrocarril para ganado, m
**cattle rustler** n abigeo, cuatrero, ladrón de ganado, m
**cattle rustling** n abigeato, m
**catty** /'kæti/ a gatuno; malicioso, chismoso
**Caucasian** /kɔ'keiʒən/ a and n caucáseo (-ea)
**Caucasus, the** /'kɔkəsəs/ el Cáucaso
**cauldron** /'kɔldrən/ n caldera, f
**cauliflower** /'kɔlə,flauər/ n coliflor, f
**caulk** /kɔk/ vt calafatear
**caulker** /'kɔkər/ n calafate, m
**caulking** /'kɔkiŋ/ n calafateado, m. **c. iron,** calador, m
**causality** /kɔ'zælɪti/ n causalidad, f
**causative** /'kɔzətɪv/ a causante
**cause** /kɔz/ n causa, f; (reason) motivo, m, razón, f; (lawsuit) proceso, m. —vt causar; ocasionar; suscitar; (oblige) hacer, obligar (a). **final c.,** Philos. causa final, f. **to have good c. for,** tener buen motivo para
**causeway** /'kɔz,wei/ n dique, m; acera, f
**caustic** /'kɔstɪk/ a cáustico; Fig. mordaz. **c. soda,** sosa cáustica, f
**caustically** /'kɔstɪkli/ adv mordazmente, con sarcasmo
**causticity** /kɔ'stɪsɪti/ n causticidad, f
**cauterization** /,kɔtərə'zeiʃən/ n cauterización, f
**cauterize** /'kɔtə,raiz/ vt cauterizar
**cautery** /'kɔtəri/ n cauterio, m
**caution** /'kɔʃən/ n prudencia, cautela, f; (warning) amonestación, f; aviso, m. —vt amonestar. **to proceed with c.,** ir con prudencia; ir despacio
**"Caution"** /'kɔʃən/ (road sign) «Precaución»
**cautionary** /'kɔʃə,nɛri/ a (of tales) de escarmiento
**cautious** /'kɔʃəs/ a cauteloso, cauto; prudente, circunspecto
**cautiously** /'kɔʃəsli/ adv cautamente; prudentemente. **to go c.,** Inf. ir con pies de plomo
**cavalcade** /,kævəl'keid/ n cabalgata, f
**cavalier** /,kævə'lɪər/ n jinete, m; caballero, m; galán, m, a arrogante, altanero
**cavalry** /'kævəlri/ n caballería, f. **c.-man,** jinete, soldado de a caballo, m
**cave** /keiv/ n cueva, caverna, f. **to c. in,** hundirse; desplomarse; Fig. rendirse. **c.-man,** hombre cavernícola, m
**cavern** /'kævərn/ n caverna, f
**cavernous** /'kævərnəs/ a cavernoso
**caviar** /'kævi,ɑr/ n caviar, m
**cavil** /'kævəl/ vi cavilar
**cavity** /'kævɪti/ n cavidad, f; hoyo, m; hueco, m; (in a lung) caverna, f

**cavy** /'keivi/ n cobayo (-ya), conejillo (-lla) de las Indias
**caw** /kɔ/ n graznido, m, vi graznar, grajear
**cawing** /'kɔiŋ/ n graznidos, m pl
**cayenne** /kai'ɛn/ n pimentón, m
**cease** /sis/ vi cesar (de), dejar de; parar. —vt cesar de; parar de; (payments, etc.) suspender; discontinuar. **C. fire!** ¡Cesar fuego!
**ceaseless** /'sislɪs/ a incesante,continuo, sin cesar
**ceaselessly** /'sislɪsli/ adv sin cesar, incesantemente
**ceasing** /'sisiŋ/ n cesación, f. **without c.,** sin cesar
**cedar** /'sidər/ n (tree and wood) cedro, m. **red c.,** cedro dulce, m
**cede** /sid/ vt ceder, traspasar; (admit) conceder
**cedilla** /sɪ'dɪlə/ n zedilla, f
**ceiling** /'siliŋ/ n techo, m; Aer. altura máxima, f. **c. price,** máximo precio, m
**celebrant** /'sɛləbrənt/ n Eccl. celebrante, m
**celebrate** /'sɛlə,breit/ vt celebrar; solemnizar. **Their marriage was celebrated in the autumn,** Su casamiento se solemnizó en el otoño
**celebrated** /'sɛlə,breitd/ a célebre, famoso
**celebration** /,sɛlə'breiʃən/ n celebración, f; festividad, f
**celebrity** /sə'lɛbrɪti/ n celebridad, f
**celerity** /sə'lɛrɪti/ n celeridad, f
**celery** /'sɛləri/ n apio, m
**celestial** /sə'lɛstʃəl/ a celestial
**celibacy** /'sɛləbəsi/ n celibato, m
**celibate** /'sɛləbɪt/ a célibe. —n célibe, mf
**cell** /sɛl/ n celda, f; (Bot. Biol.) célula, f; (bees, wasps) celdilla, f; Elec. elemento, m
**cellar** /'sɛlər/ n sótano, m; (wine) bodega, f
**cellist** /'tʃɛlɪst/ n violoncelista, mf
**cello** /'tʃɛlou/ n violoncelo, m
**cellophane** /'sɛlə,fein/ n (papel) celofán, m
**cellular** /'sɛlyələr/ a celular, celuloso
**cellular phone** /'sɛlyələr 'foun/ n móvil, m, celular, m (WH)
**cellule** /'sɛlyul/ n célula, f
**celluloid** /'sɛlyə,lɔid/ n celuloide, f
**cellulose** /'sɛlyə,lous/ n celulosa, f
**Celt** /kɛlt, sɛlt/ n celta, mf
**Celtiberian** /,kɛltə'bɪəriən, ,sɛl-/ a celtibérico
**Celtic** /'kɛltɪk, 'sɛl-/ a celta
**cement** /sɪ'mɛnt/ n cemento, m, vt cementar
**cemetery** /'sɛmɪ,tɛri/ n cementerio, m
**cenotaph** /'sɛnə,tæf/ n cenotafio, m
**cense** /sɛns/ vt incensar
**censer** /'sɛnsər/ n incensario, m
**censor** /'sɛnsər/ n censor, m, vt censurar. **banned by the c.,** prohibido por la censura
**censorious** /sɛn'sɔriəs/ a severo; crítico
**censoriousness** /sɛn'sɔriəsnɪs/ n severidad, propensión a censurar, f
**censorship** /'sɛnsər,ʃɪp/ n censura, f
**censure** /'sɛnʃər/ vt censurar, culpar, criticar
**census** /'sɛnsəs/ n censo, m. **to take the c.,** formar el censo, levantar el censo, tomar el censo, empadronar
**census-taking** /'sɛnsəs ,teikiŋ/ n la formación del censo, la formación de los censos, f, el levantamiento del censo, el levantamiento de los censos, m
**cent** /sɛnt/ n (coin) centavo, m. **per c.,** por ciento. **not to have a c., not to have a c. to one's name,** no tener donde caer muerto
**centaur** /'sɛntɔr/ n centauro, m
**centenarian** /,sɛntn'ɛəriən/ a and n centenario (-ia)
**centenary** /sɛn'tɛnɛri/ n centenario, m, a centenario
**center** /'sɛntər/ n centro, m; medio, m. —a central; centro. —vt centrar; concentrar (en). **nervous centers,** centros nerviosos, m pl. **c.-forward,** Sports. delantero centro, m. **c.-half,** Sports. medio centro, m. **c. of gravity,** centro de gravedad, m. **c.-piece,** centro, m
**centerfold** /'sɛntər,fould/ n páginas centrales, f pl
**centigrade** /'sɛnti,greid/ a centígrado
**centigram** /'sɛnti,græm/ n centigramo, m
**centiliter** /'sɛnti,itər/ n centilitro, m
**centime** /'sɑntim/ n céntimo, m
**centimeter** /'sɛntə,mitər/ n centímetro, m. **cubic c.,** centímetro cúbico, m

**centipede** /'sentə,pid/ n ciempiés, m

**central** /'sentrəl/ a central; céntrico. **The house is very c.,** La casa es muy céntrica. **C. American,** a and n centroamericano (-na). **c. depot,** central, f. **c. heating,** calefacción central, f

**centralism** /'sentrə,lizəm/ n centralismo, m

**centralist** /'sentrəlist/ n centralista, mf

**centralization** /,sentrələ'zeiʃən/ n centralización, f

**centralize** /'sentrə,laiz/ vt centralizar

**centrally** /'sentrəli/ adv centralmente; céntricamente

**centric** /'sentrik/ a céntrico; central

**centrifugal** /sen'trifyəgəl/ a centrífugo

**centripetal** /sen'tripitl/ a centrípeto

**centumvir** /'sentəm,viər/ n centunviro, m

**centuple** /'sen'tupəl/ a céntuplo

**centuplicate** /sen'tupli,keit/ vt centuplicar

**centurion** /sen'tyuriən/ n centurión, m

**century** /'sentʃəri/ n siglo, m, centuria, f

**ceramic** /sə'ræmik/ a cerámico

**ceramics** /sə'ræmiks/ n cerámica, f

**Cerberus** /'sɜrbərəs/ n Cancerbero, m

**cereal** /'siəriəl/ a cereal. —n cereal, m

**cerebellum** /,serə'beləm/ n cerebelo, m

**cerebral** /sə'ribrəl/ a cerebral

**cerebrospinal** /sə,ribrou'spainl/ a cerebroespinal

**cerebrum** /sə'ribrəm/ n cerebro, m

**ceremonial** /,serə'mouniəl/ a ceremonial; de ceremonia. —n ceremonial, m

**ceremonially** /,serə'mouniəli/ adv ceremonialmente; con ceremonia

**ceremonious** /,serə'mouniəs/ a ceremonioso

**ceremoniously** /,serə'mouniəsli/ adv ceremoniosamente

**ceremoniousness** /,serə'mouniəsnis/ n ceremonia, formalidad, f

**ceremony** /'serə,mouni/ n ceremonia, f. **to stand on c.,** gastar cumplidos. **without c.,** sin cumplidos

**cerise** /sə'ris/ a de color cereza

**certain** /'sɜrtn/ a (sure) seguro; cierto; (unerring) certero. **a c. man,** cierto hombre. **I am c. that...,** Estoy seguro de que... **to know for c.,** saber con toda seguridad, saber a ciencia cierta. **to make c. of,** asegurarse de

**certainly** /'sɜrtnli/ adv seguramente; ciertamente; (as a reply) sin duda; naturalmente. **c. not,** no, por cierto; claro que no

**certainty** /'sɜrtnti/ n certidumbre, f; seguridad, f; convicción, f. **of a c.,** seguramente

**certificate** /n sər'tifikit/ v -,keit/ n certificado, m; fe, f; partida, f; Com. bono, título, m; diploma, m. —vt certificar. **birth c.,** partida de nacimiento, f. **death c.,** partida de defunción, f. **marriage c.,** partida de casamiento, f

**certificated** /sər'tifi,keitid/ a (of teachers, etc.) con título

**certify** /'sɜrtə,fai/ vt certificar; atestiguar; declarar

**certitude** /'sɜrti,tyud/ n certeza, certidumbre, f

**cerulean** /sə'ruliən/ a cerúleo

**Cervantine** /sər'væntin/ a cervantino

**cervix** /'sɜrviks/ n Anat. cerviz, f

**Cesarean** /sə'zeəriən/ a cesáreo

**cessation** /se'seiʃən/ n cesación, f

**cession** /'seʃən/ n cesión, f

**cessionary** /'seʃənəri/ n cesionario (-ia)

**cesspool** /'ses,pul/ n sumidero, m

**cetacean** /si'teiʃən/ a cetáceo. —n cetáceo, m

**Ceylon** /si'lɒn/ Ceilán, m

**cf.** cfr.

**chafe** /tʃeif/ vt (rub) frotar; (make sore) escocer, rozar. —vi raerse, desgastarse; escocerse; Fig. impacientarse; Fig. irritarse, enojarse

**chaff** /tʃæf/ n (of grain) ahechadura, f; (in a general sense and Fig.) paja, f; tomadura de pelo, burla, f. —vt (a person) tomar el pelo (a), burlarse de

**chaffinch** /'tʃæfintʃ/ n pinzón, m

**chafing** /'tʃeifiŋ/ n frotación, f; (soreness) excoriación, f; Fig. impaciencia, f. **c.-dish,** escalfador, m

**chagrin** /ʃə'grin/ n mortificación, decepción, f, disgusto, m, mortificar

**chain** /tʃein/ n cadena, f, vt encadenar. **c. of mountains,** cadena de montañas, cordillera, f. **c.-gang,** ca-

dena de presidiarios, f. **c.-mail,** cota de malla, f. **c.-stitch,** cadeneta, f. **c.-stores,** empresa con sucursales, f. **in chains,** cargado de cadenas (e.g., prisoners in chains, prisioneros cargados de cadenas)

**chair** /tʃeər/ n silla, f; Educ. cátedra, f; (of a meeting) presidencia, f. —vt llevar en hombros (a). **C.!** ¡Orden! **easy-c.,** (silla) poltrona, f. **to be in the c.,** ocupar la presidencia; presidir. **to take a c.,** sentarse, tomar asiento. **to take the c.,** presidir. **swivel-c.,** silla giratoria, f. **wheel-c.,** silla de ruedas, f. **c.-back,** respaldo de una silla, m

**chairman** /'tʃeərmən/ n presidente (-ta). **to act as c.,** presidir

**chairmanship** /'tʃeərmənʃip/ n presidencia, f

**chaise longue** /'ʃeiz 'lɔŋ/ n meridiana, tumbona, f

**Chaldea** /kæl'diə/ Caldea, f

**Chaldean** /kæl'diən/ a caldeo

**chalet** /ʃæ'lei/ n chalet, m

**chalice** /'tʃælis/ n cáliz, m

**chalk** /tʃɔk/ n creta, f; (for writing, etc.) tiza, f, yeso, m. —vt marcar con tiza; dibujar con tiza. **to c. up,** apuntar. **not by a long c.,** no con mucho

**chalky** /'tʃɔki/ a cretáceo; cubierto de yeso; (of the complexion) pálido

**challenge** /'tʃælindʒ/ n provocación, f; (of a sentry) quién vive, m; (to a duel, etc.) desafío, reto, m; Law. recusación, f; concurso, m. —vt (of a sentry) dar el quién vive (a); desafiar; provocar; Law. recusar

**challenger** /'tʃælindʒər/ n desafiador (-ra)

**challenging** /'tʃælindʒiŋ/ a desafiador, provocador

**chamber** /'tʃeimbər/ n cuarto, m; sala, f; (bed-) dormitorio, m, alcoba, f; cámara, f; Mech. cilindro, m; (in a gun) cámara, f. **c. concert,** concierto de música de cámara, m. **c.-maid,** camarera, f. **c. music,** música de cámara, f. **c. of commerce,** cámara de comercio, f. **c.-pot,** orinal, m

**chamberlain** /'tʃeimbərlin/ n camarero, m. **court c.,** chambelán, m. **Lord C.,** camarero mayor, m

**chameleon** /kə'miliən/ n camaleón, m

**chamfer** /'tʃæmfər/ n chaflán, bisel, m

**chamois** /'ʃæmi/ n gamuza, f, rebeco, m. **c. leather,** piel de gamuza, f

**chamomile** /'kæmə,mail/ n camomila, manzanilla, f

**champ** /tʃæmp/ vt mascar; morder. —vi Fig. impacientarse

**champagne** /ʃæm'pein/ n (vino de) champaña, m

**champion** /'tʃæmpiən/ n campeón, m; defensor (-ra)

**championship** /'tʃæmpiən,ʃip/ n campeonato, m; (of a cause) defensa, f

**chance** /tʃæns/ n casualidad, f; suerte, fortuna, f; posibilidad, f; probabilidad, f; esperanza, f; (opportunity) ocasión, oportunidad, f. —a fortuito; accidental. —vi impers suceder, acontecer. —vt Inf. arriesgar; probar. **by c.,** por casualidad; por ventura. **if by c.,** si acaso. **If it chances that...,** Si sucede que; Si a mano viene que... **The chances are that...,** Las probabilidades son que... **There is no c.,** No hay posibilidad; No hay esperanza. **to let the c. slip,** perder la ocasión. **to take a c.,** aventurarse, arriesgarse. **to c. to do,** hacer algo por casualidad. **to c. upon,** encontrar por casualidad.

**chancel** /'tʃænsəl/ n antealtar, entrecoro, m

**chancellery** /'tʃænsələri/ n cancillería, f

**chancellor** /'tʃænsələr/ n canciller, m; Educ. cancelario, m. **C. of the Exchequer,** Ministro de Hacienda, m

**chancellorship** /'tʃænsələrʃip/ n cancillería, f

**chancery** /'tʃænsəri, 'tʃɑn-/ n chancillería, f; (papal) cancelaría, f

**chandelier** /,ʃændl'iər/ n araña de luces, f

**chandler** /'tʃændlər/ n velero, m

**change** /tʃeindʒ/ vt cambiar; transformar; modificar; (clothes) mudarse (de); (one thing for another) trocar; sustituir (por). —vi cambiar; (clothes) mudarse. **All c.!** ¡Cambio de tren! **to c. a check,** cambiar un cheque. **to c. color,** cambiar de color; (of persons) mudar de color. **to c. countenance,** demudarse. **to c. front,** Fig. cambiar de frente. **to c. hands,** (of shops, etc.) cambiar de dueño. **to c. one's clothes,** cambiar de ropa, mudarse de ropa. **to c. one's mind,** cambiar de opinión. **to c. one's tune,** cambiar de tono. **to c.**

**the subject,** cambiar de conversación. **to c. trains,** cambiar de trenes

**change** /tʃeindʒ/ n cambio, m; transformación, f; modificación, f; variedad, f; (of clothes, feathers) muda, f; (*Theat.* of scene) mutación, f; (money) cambio, m; (small coins) suelto, m; (stock) bolsa, f; lonja, f; vicisitud, f; (of bells) toque (de campanas), m. **for a c.,** para cambiar, como un cambio; para variar. **small c.,** suelto, m, moneda suelta, f. **c. for the better,** cambio para mejor, m. **c. for the worse,** cambio para peor, m. **c. of clothes,** cambio de ropa, m; **c. of front,** *Fig.* cambio de frente, m. **c. of heart,** cambio de sentimientos, m; conversión, f. **c. of life,** menopausia, f. **c.-over,** cambio, m

**changeability** /,tʃeindʒə'bılıti/ n mutabilidad, f; inconstancia, volubilidad, f

**changeable** /'tʃeindʒəbəl/ a voluble; variable; cambiable

**changeless** /'tʃeindʒlıs/ a immutable; constante

**changeling** /'tʃeindʒlıŋ/ n niño (-ña) cambiado (-da) por otro

**changing** /'tʃeindʃıŋ/ a cambiante. **c.-room,** vestuario, m

**channel** /'tʃænl/ n (of a river, etc.) cauce, m; canal, m; (irrigation) acequia, f; (strait) estrecho, m; *Fig.* conducto, m; (furrow) surco, m, estría, f; (of information, etc.) medio, m. —vt acanalar; (furrow) surcar; (conduct) encauzar

**chant** /tʃænt/ n canto llano, m; salmo, m. —vt salmodiar; cantar; recitar

**chantey** /'ʃænti/ n saloma, f

**chaos** /'keiɒs/ n caos, m

**chaotic** /kei'ɒtık/ a caótico, desordenado

**chaotically** /kei'ɒtıkli/ adv en desorden

**chap** /tʃæp/ vt agrietar. —vi agrietarse. —n *Inf.* chico, m

**chapbook** /'tʃæp,bʊk/ n librito de cordel, m

**chapel** /'tʃæpəl/ n capilla, f; templo disidente, m

**chaperon** /'ʃæpə,roun/ n dama de compañía, señora de compañía, dueña, f, vt acompañar

**chaplain** /'tʃæplın/ n capellán, m

**chaplaincy** /'tʃæplınsi/ n capellanía, f

**chaplet** /'tʃæplıt/ n guirnalda, f; rosario, m; (necklace) collar, m

**chapter** /'tʃæptər/ n (in a book) capítulo, m; *Eccl.* cabildo, capítulo, m. **a c. of accidents,** una serie de desgracias. **c. house,** sala capitular, f

**char** /tʃɑr/ vt (a house, etc.) fregar, hacer la limpieza de; (of fire) carbonizar. —n *Inf.* fregona, asistenta, f

**character** /'kærıktər/ n carácter, m; (of a play) personaje, m; (role) papel, m; (eccentric) tipo, m. **Gothic characters,** caracteres góticos, m pl. **in c.,** característico; apropiado. **in the c. of,** en el papel de. **out of c.,** nada característico; no apropiado. **principal c.,** protagonista, mf. **c. actor,** actor de carácter, m. **c. actress,** actriz de carácter

**characteristic** /,kærıktə'rıstık/ a característico, típico. —n característica, peculiaridad, f, rasgo, m

**characterization** /,kærıktərə'zeiʃən/ n caracterización, f

**characterize** /'kærıktə,raiz/ vt caracterizar

**characterless** /'kærıktərlıs/ a sin carácter; insípido, soso

**charade** /ʃə'reid/ n charada, f

**charcoal** /'tʃɑr,koul/ n carbón de leña, m; (for blacking the face, etc.) tizne, m; *Art.* carboncillo, m. **c. burner,** carbonera, f. **c. crayon,** carboncillo, m. **c. drawing,** dibujo al carbón, m

**charge** /tʃɑrdʒ/ vt cargar; (enjoin) encargar; (accuse) acusar (de); (with price) cobrar; (with a mission, etc.) encomendar, confiar; *Mil.* acometer, atacar. —vi *Mil.* atacar; (a price) cobrar, pedir. **How much do you c.?** ¿Cuánto cobra Vd.? **to c. with a crime,** acusar de un crimen

**charge** /tʃɑrdʒ/ n (load) carga, f; (price) precio, m; gasto, m; (on an estate, etc.) derechos, m pl; (task) encargo, m; (office or responsibility) cargo, m; (guardianship) tutela, f; (care) cuidado, m; exhortación, f; *Law.* acusación, f; *Mil.* ataque, m. **He is in c. of...,** Está encargado de...; Es responsable de... **The diamonds are in the c. of...,** Los diamantes están a cargo de. **depth c.,** carga de profundidad, f. **extra c.,**

gasto suplementario, m; (on a train) suplemento, m. **free of c.,** gratis. **c. for admittance,** entrada, f. **to bring a c. against,** acusar de. **to give (someone) in c.,** entregar (una persona) a la policía. **to take c. of,** encargarse de

**chargé d'affaires** /ʃar'ʒei də'fɛər/ n encargado de negocios, m

**charger** /'tʃɑrdʒər/ n caballo de guerra, corcel, m

**chariness** /'tʃɛərınıs/ n cautela, f

**chariot** /'tʃæriət/ n carro, m

**charioteer** /,tʃæriə'tıər/ n auriga, m

**charitable** /'tʃærıtəbəl/ a caritativo; benéfico

**charitableness** /'tʃærıtəbəlnıs/ n caridad, f

**charity** /'tʃærıti/ n caridad, f; beneficencia, f; (alms) limosna, f. **c. child,** niño (-ña) de la doctrina

**charlatan** /'ʃɑrlətṇ/ n charlatán (-ana); (quack) curandero, m

**charlatanism** /'ʃɑrlətṇ,ızəm/ n charlatanismo, m; curanderismo, m

**charm** /tʃɑrm/ n hechizo, m; ensalmo, m; (amulet) amuleto, m; (trinket) dije, m; (general sense) encanto, atractivo, m. —vt encantar, hechizar, fascinar

**charming** /'tʃɑrmıŋ/ a encantador; atractivo, seductor, fascinador

**charm school** n academia de buenos modales, f

**chart** /tʃɑrt/ n *Naut.* carta de marear, f; (graph) gráfica, f. —vt poner en una carta

**charter** /'tʃɑrtər/ n carta, f; (of a city, etc.) fuero, m; cédula, f. —vt (a ship) fletar; (hire) alquilar. **royal c.,** cédula real, f

**Chartism** /'tʃɑrtızəm/ n el cartismo, m

**chartist** /'tʃɑrtıst/ n cartista, mf

**charwoman** /'tʃɑr,wʊmən/ n fregona, asistenta; mujer de hacer faenas, f

**chary** /'tʃɛəri/ a cauteloso; desinclinado; frugal

**chase** /tʃeis/ n caza, f; seguimiento, m. —vt cazar; dar caza (a); perseguir; (drive off) ahuyentar; *Fig.* disipar, hacer desaparecer; (engrave) cincelar. **to give c. to,** dar caza (a). **to go on a wild goose c.,** buscar pan de trastrigo

**chasm** /'kæzəm/ n sima, f, precipicio, m; *Fig.* abismo, m

**chassis** /'tʃæsi/ n chasis, m

**chaste** /tʃeist/ a casto

**chasten** /'tʃeisən/ vt castigar; corregir; humillar, mortificar

**chastened** /'tʃeisənd/ a sumiso, dócil

**chastise** /tʃæs'taiz/ vt castigar

**chastisement** /tʃæs'taizmənt/ n castigo, m

**chastity** /'tʃæstıti/ n castidad, f

**chat** /tʃæt/ vi charlar, conversar. —n conversación, charla, f. **They are having a c.,** Están charlando, Están de palique

**chattels** /'tʃætəlz/ n pl bienes muebles, efectos, m pl

**chatter** /'tʃætər/ vi charlar; hablar por los codos, chacharear; (of water) murmurar; (of birds) piar; (of monkeys, etc.) chillar; (of teeth) rechinar; (of a person's teeth) dar diente con diente. —n charla, f; cháchara, parla, f; (of water) murmurio, m; (of birds) gorjeo, m; (of monkeys, etc.) chillidos, m pl

**chatterbox** /'tʃæt,ər bɒks/ n badajo, m, cotorra, f

**chatterer** /'tʃætərər/ n hablador (-ra)

**chattering** /'tʃætərıŋ/ n charla, cháchara, f; (of teeth) rechinamiento, m, a gárrulo, chacharero, locuaz

**chauffeur** /'ʃoufər/ n chófer, m

**chauvinism** /'ʃouvə,nızəm/ n chauvinismo, m

**cheap** /tʃip/ a barato; (of works of art) cursi. —adv barato. **dirt c.,** baratísimo. **to be dirt c.,** estar por los suelos. **to hold (something) c.,** tener en poco, estimar en poco

**cheapen** /'tʃipən/ vt disminuir el valor de; reducir el precio de

**cheaply** /'tʃipli/ adv barato; a bajo precio

**cheapness** /'tʃipnıs/ n baratura, f; precio módico, m; mal gusto, m, vulgaridad, f

**cheat** /tʃit/ n engaño, fraude, m, estafa, f; (person) fullero (-ra), tramposa, mf embustero (-ra). —vt engañar; defraudar; (at cards) hacer trampas. **He cheated me out of my property,** Me defraudó de mi propiedad

**cheating** /'tʃiːtɪŋ/ n engaño, m; fraude, m; (at cards) fullerías, f pl

**check** /tʃɛk/ n (chess) jaque, m; revés, m; impedimento, m; contratiempo, m; (of a bridle) cama, f; (control) freno, m; control, m; (checking) verificación, f; (ticket) papeleta, f; (counterfoil) talón, m; (square) cuadro, m; (bill) cuenta, f; (bank) cheque, m. —vt (chess) jaquear; (hamper) refrenar; detener; contrarrestar; (test) verificar. —vi detenerse. **to c. off,** marcar. **to c. oneself,** detenerse; contenerse. **to c. up,** comprobar. **crossed c.,** cheque cruzado, m. **c. book,** libro de cheques, m

**checked** /tʃɛkt/ a (cloth) a cuadros

**checker** /'tʃɛkər/ vt escaquear; (variegate) motear, salpicar; diversificar. **a checkered career,** una vida accidentada

**checkers** /'tʃɛkərz/ n. pl. damas, f.

**checking** /'tʃɛkɪŋ/ n represión, f; control, m; verificación, f; comprobación, f

**checkmate** /'tʃɛk,meit/ n mate, jaque, mate, m. —vt dar mate (a); (plans, etc.) frustrar

**checks and balances** n pl frenos y contrapesos, m pl

**cheek** /tʃiːk/ n mejilla, f; Inf. descaro, m; insolencia, f. **They have plenty of c.,** Tienen mucha cara dura. **c. by jowl,** cara a cara; al lado de. **c.-bone,** pómulo, m

**cheekiness** /'tʃiːkɪnɪs/ n cara dura, insolencia, f

**cheeky** /'tʃiːki/ a insolente, descarado; (pert) respondón

**cheep** /tʃiːp/ n pío, m, vi piar

**cheer** /tʃiːər/ n alegría, f, regocijo, m; vítor, m; aplauso, m. —vt animar; alegrar, regocijar; vitorear, aplaudir. **to be of good c.,** estar alegre; ser feliz. **C. up!** ¡Ánimo! **to c. up,** animarse, cobrar ánimo

**cheerful** /'tʃiːərfəl/ a alegre; jovial; de buen humor. **It is a c. room,** Es un cuarto alegre

**cheerfully** /'tʃiːərfəli/ adv alegremente; (willingly) con mucho gusto, de buena gana

**cheerfulness** /'tʃiːərfəlnɪs/ n alegría, f; jovialidad, f; buen humor, m

**cheering** /'tʃiːərɪŋ/ n vítores, m pl, aclamaciones, f pl, a animador

**cheerleader** /'tʃiːər,lidər/ n porro, m

**cheerless** /'tʃiːərlɪs/ a triste; sin alegría; (dank) obscuro, lóbrego

**cheese** /tʃiːz/ n queso, m. **cream c.,** queso de nata, m. **grated c.,** queso rallado, m. **c.-dish,** quesera, f. **c.-mite,** cresa, f. **c.-paring,** n corteza de queso, f. —a Inf. tacaño. **c.-vat,** quesera, f

**cheesy** /'tʃiːzi/ a caseoso

**chemical** /'kɛmɪkəl/ a químico. **c. warfare,** defensa química, f

**chemicals** /'kɛmɪkəlz/ n pl productos químicos, m pl

**chemise** /ʃə'miːz/ n camisa (de mujer), f

**chemist** /'kɛmɪst/ n químico, m. **chemist's shop,** farmacia, f; droguería, f

**chemistry** /'kɛməstri/ n química, f

**chenille** /ʃə'niːl/ n felpilla, f

**cherish** /'tʃɛrɪʃ/ vt amar, querer; (a hope, etc.) abrigar, acariciar

**cherry** /'tʃɛri/ n (fruit) cereza, f; (tree and wood) cerezo, m. **c. brandy,** aguardiente de cerezas, m. **c. orchard,** cerezal, m

**cherub** /'tʃɛrəb/ n querub(e), querubín, m

**cherubic** /tʃə'rubɪk/ a querúbico

**chess** /tʃɛs/ n ajedrez, m. **c.-board,** tablero de ajedrez, m

**chessman** /'tʃɛs,mæn/ n pieza de ajedrez, f

**chest** /tʃɛst/ n arca, f, cofre, m; cajón, m; Anat. pecho, m. **to throw out one's c.,** inflar el pecho. **c.-expander,** extensor, m. **c. of drawers,** cómoda, f

**chested** /'tʃɛstɪd/ a (in compounds) de pecho...

**chestnut** /'tʃɛs,nʌt/ n (tree) castaño, m; (fruit) castaña, f; (color) castaño, color castaño, m; (horse) caballo castaño, m; (joke) chiste del tiempo de Maricastaña, m, a castaño. **horse-c. tree,** castaño de Indias, m

**chevron** /'ʃɛvrən/ n Herald. cabrio, m; (Mil. etc.) sardineta, f

**chew** /tʃu/ vt mascar, mascullar; (ponder) masticar

**chewing** /'tʃuɪŋ/ n masticación, f. **c.-gum,** chicle, m

**chianti** /ki'anti/ n (wine) quianti, m

**chiaroscuro** /ki,ɑrə'skyʊroʊ/ n claroscuro, m

**chic** /ʃik/ n chic, m, elegancia, f

**chicanery** /ʃɪ'keɪnəri/ n sofistería, f

**chicken** /'tʃɪkən/ n pollo, m. **c.-hearted,** medroso, cobarde, timorato. **c.-pox,** varicela, f

**chickenwire** /'tʃɪkən,waɪər/ n alambrillo, m

**chickpea** /'tʃɪk,pi/ n garbanzo, m

**chickweed** /'tʃɪk,wid/ n pamplina, f

**chicory** /'tʃɪkəri/ n achicoria, f

**chide** /tʃaɪd/ vt reprender, reñir

**chidingly** /'tʃaɪdɪŋli/ adv en tono de represión

**chief** /tʃif/ n jefe, m, a principal; primero; en jefe. **mayor. c.-of-staff,** jefe de estado mayor, m

**chiefly** /'tʃifli/ adv principalmente; sobre todo

**chieftain** /'tʃiftən/ n caudillo, m; (of a clan) cabeza, jefe, m

**chiffon** /ʃɪ'fɒn/ n chifón, m, gasa, f

**chiffonier** /ʃɪfə'nɪər/ n cómoda, f

**chignon** /'ʃɪnyɒn/ n moño, m

**chilblain** /'tʃɪlbleɪn/ n sabañón, m

**child** /tʃaɪld/ n niño (-ña); hijo (-ja). **from a c.,** desde niño, desde la niñez. **with c.,** encinta, embarazada. **How many children do you have?** ¿Cuántos hijos tiene Vd.? **child's play,** juegos infantiles, m pl; Fig. niñerías, f pl. **c. welfare,** puericultura, f

**childbirth** /'tʃaɪld,bɜrθ/ n parto, m

**childhood** /'tʃaɪldhʊd/ n niñez, infancia, f. **from his c.,** desde su niñez, desde niño

**childish** /'tʃaɪldɪʃ/ a de niño; aniñado; pueril; fútil. **to grow c.,** chochear

**childishly** /'tʃaɪldɪʃli/ adv como un niño

**childishness** /'tʃaɪldɪʃnɪs/ n puerilidad, f; futilidad, f

**child labor** n trabajo de menores, trabajo infantil, m

**childless** /'tʃaɪldlɪs/ a sin hijos; sin niños

**childlike** /'tʃaɪld,laɪk/ a de niño, aniñado; pueril

**children** /'tʃɪldrən/ See **child**

**Chilean** /'tʃɪliən/ a and n chileno (-na)

**chili** /'tʃɪli/ n chile, pimento de cornetilla, m

**chill** /tʃɪl/ n frío, m; (of fear, etc.) estremecimiento, m; (illness) resfriado, m; (unfriendliness) frialdad, frigidez, f, a frío; (unfriendly) frígido. —vt enfriar; helar; (with fear, etc.) dar escalofríos (de); (discourage) desalentar. —vi tener frío; tener escalofríos. **to take the c. off,** templar, calentar un poco

**chilliness** /'tʃɪlinɪs/ n frío, m; (unfriendliness) frialdad, frigidez, f

**chilly** /'tʃɪli/ a frío; (sensitive to cold) friolero; (of politeness, etc.) glacial, frígido

**chime** /tʃaɪm/ n juego de campanas, m; repique, campaneo, m; armonía, f. —vi (of bells) repicar; Fig. armonizar. **to c. the hour,** dar la hora

**chimera** /kɪ'mɪərə/ n quimera, f

**chimerical** /kɪ'mɛrɪkəl/ a quimérico

**chimney** /'tʃɪmni/ n chimenea, f; (of a lamp) tubo (de lámpara), m. **c.-corner,** rincón de chimenea, m. **c.-pot,** sombrerete de chimenea, m. **c.-stack,** chimenea, f. **c.-sweep,** limpiador de chimeneas, deshollinador, m

**chimpanzee** /,tʃɪmpæn'zi, tʃɪm'pænzi/ n chimpancé, m

**chin** /tʃɪn/ n barbilla, barba, f, mentón, m. **c.-rest,** mentonera, f. **c.-strap,** barboquejo, m; venda para la barbilla, f

**china** /'tʃaɪnə/ n china, porcelana, f; loza, f. —a de porcelana; de loza. **c. cabinet,** chinero, m

**chinchilla** /tʃɪn'tʃɪlə/ n (animal and fur) chinchilla, f

**Chinese** /tʃai'niz/ a and n chino (-na); (language) chino, m. **C. lantern,** farolillo de papel, m. **C. white,** óxido blanco de cinc, m

**chink** /tʃɪŋk/ n resquicio, m, grieta, hendidura, f; (clink) retintín, tintineo, m. —vi tintinar

**chintz** /tʃɪnts/ n zaraza, f

**chip** /tʃɪp/ n astilla, f; (counter) ficha, f. —vt picar; cincelar. **a c. off the old block,** de tal palo tal astilla. **c. potatoes,** patatas fritas, f pl

**chiromancy** /'kaɪrə,mænsi/ n quiromancia, f

**chiropodist** /kɪ'rɒpədɪst/ n pedicuro, m, callista, mf

**chiropody** /kɪ'rɒpədi/ n pedicura, f

**chiropractor** /'kaɪrə,præktər/ n quiropráctico, m

**chirp** /tʃɜrp/ vi piar, gorjear. —n pío, gorjeo, m

**chirping** /'tʃɜrpɪŋ/ n piada, f, a gárrulo, piante

**chisel** /'tʃɪzəl/ n escoplo, cincel, m, vt cincelar. **cold c.,** cortafrío, m

**chitchat** /'tʃɪt,tʃæt/ n charla, f

**chitterlings** /'tʃɪtlɪnz/ n asadura, f

**chivalrous** /'ʃɪvəlrəs/ a caballeroso

**chivalry** /'ʃɪvəlri/ n caballería, f; caballerosidad, f. **novel of c.,** novela de caballería, f

**chive** /tʃaiv/ n Bot. cebollana, f, cebollino, m

**chloral** /'klɔrəl/ n cloral, m

**chlorate** /'klɔreit/ n clorato, m

**chloride** /'klɔraid/ n cloruro, m

**chlorine** /'klɔrin/ n cloro, m

**chloroform** /'klɔrə,fɔrm/ n cloroformo, m, vt cloroformizar

**chlorophyll** /'klɔrəfɪl/ n clorófila, f

**chock-full** /'tʃɒk 'fʊl/ a lleno de bote en bote

**chocolate** /'tʃɒkəlɪt/ n chocolate, m, a de chocolate. **thick drinking-c.,** chocolate a la española, m. **thin drinking-c.,** chocolate a la francesa, m. **c. shop,** chocolatería, f

**choice** /tʃɔis/ n selección, f; preferencia, f; elección, f; opción, f; alternativa, f; lo más escogido. —a escogido, selecto; excelente. **for c.,** con preferencia

**choir** /kwaiⁿr/ n coro, m. **c.-boy,** niño del coro, m. **c.-master,** maestro de capilla, m

**choke** /tʃouk/ vi ahogarse; atragantarse; obstruirse. —vt ahogar; estrangular. **to c. with laughter,** ahogarse de risa. **to c. back,** (words) tragar. **to c. off,** (a person) disuadir (de); quitarse de encima(a). **to c. up,** obstruir, cerrar, obturar; (hide) cubrir, tapar

**choking** /'tʃoukɪn/ a asfixiante, sofocante. —n ahogamiento, m, sofocación, f

**cholera** /'kɒlərə/ n cólera, m

**choleric** /'kɒlərɪk/ a colérico

**cholesterol** /kə'lestə,roul/ n colesterina, f

**choline** /'koulin/ n colina, f

**choose** /tʃuz/ vt escoger; elegir; optar por; (wish) querer, gustar. **They will do it when they c,** Lo harán cuando les parezca bien. **If you c.,** Si Vd. quiere; Si Vd. gusta. **He was chosen as Mayor,** Fue elegido alcalde. **There is nothing to c. between them,** No hay diferencia entre ellos; Tanto vale el uno como el otro. **You cannot c. but love her,** No puedes menos de quererla

**choosing** /'tʃuzɪn/ n selección, f; (for an office, etc.) elección, f

**chop** /tʃɒp/ vt cortar; (mince) picar; (split) hender, partir. —n (meat) chuleta, f; (jaw) quijada, f. **to c. about, round,** (of the wind) girar, virar. **to c. down,** (trees) talar. **to c. off,** separar; cortar; tajar. **to c. up,** cortar en pedazos

**chopper** /'tʃɒpər/ n hacha, f

**choppy** /'tʃɒpi/ a picado, agitado

**chopstick** /'tʃɒp,stɪk/ n palillo chino, m

**choragus** /kə'reigəs/ n corega, corego, m

**choral** /'kɔrəl/ a coral

**chord** /kɔrd/ n cuerda, f; Mus. acorde, m; **the right c.,** Fig. la cuerda sensible

**choreographer** /,kɔri'ɒgrəfər/ n coreógrafo, m

**choreographic** /,kɔriə'græfɪk/ a coreográfico

**choreography** /,kɔri'ɒgrəfi, ,kour-/ n coreografía, f

**chorister** /'kɔrəstər/ n corista, m

**chorus** /'kɔrəs/ n coro, m; (in revues) comparsa, f, acompañamiento, m; (of a song) refrán, m. **to sing in c.,** cantar a coro. **c. girl,** corista, f

**chosen** /'tʃouzən/ a escogido; elegido. **the c.,** los elegidos

**chrestomathy** /kres'tɒməθi/ n crestomatía, f

**Christ** /kraist/ n Cristo, Jesucristo, m

**christen** /'krisən/ vt bautizar

**Christendom** /'krisəndəm/ n cristianismo, m, cristiandad, f

**christening** /'krisənɪn/ n bautizo, m, a bautismal, de bautizo

**Christian** /'kristʃən/ a cristiano. —n cristiano (-na). **C. name,** nombre de pila, m

**Christianity** /,kristʃi'æniti/ n cristianismo, m

**Christmas** /'krisməs/ n Navidad, f. **A Merry C.!** ¡Felices Pascuas (de Navidad)! **Father C.,** Padre Noel, m; (Sp. equivalent) Los Reyes Magos. **C. box,** regalo de Navidad, m. **C. card,** felicitación de Navidad, f. **C.**

**carol,** villancico de Navidad, m. **C. Day,** día de Navidad, m. **C. Eve,** Nochebuena, f. **C.-tide,** Navidades, f pl. **C. tree,** árbol de Navidad, m

**Christopher Columbus** /'krɪstəfər kə'lʌmbəs/ Cristóbal Colón, m

**chromate** /'kroumeit/ n cromato, m

**chromatic** /krou'mætɪk/ a cromático

**chrome** /kroum/ n cromo, m. **c. yellow,** amarillo de cromo, m

**chromic** /'kroumɪk/ a crómico

**chromium** /'kroumiəm/ n cromo, m. **c.-plated,** cromado

**chromosome** /'kroumə,soum/ n cromosoma, m

**chronic** /'krɒnɪk/ a crónico; inveterado

**chronicle** /'krɒnɪkəl/ n crónica, f, vt narrar

**chronicler** /'krɒnɪklər/ n cronista, mf

**chronological** /,krɒnɪ'ɒdʒɪkəl/ a cronológico. **in c. order,** por orden cronológico

**chronology** /krə'nɒlədʒi/ n cronología, f

**chronometer** /krə'nɒmɪtər/ n cronómetro, m

**chrysalis** /'krɪsəlɪs/ n crisálida, f

**chrysanthemum** /krɪ'sænθəməm/ n crisantemo, m

**chubbiness** /'tʃʌbinɪs/ n gordura, f

**chubby** /'tʃʌbi/ a regordete, gordito. **c.-cheeked,** mofletudo

**chuck** /tʃʌk/ vt (throw) lanzar, arrojar; (discontinue) abandonar, dejar. —n (in a lathe) mandril, m. **to c. under the chin,** acariciar la barbilla (a). **to c. away,** derrochar; malgastar, perder. **to c. out,** echar, poner en la calle

**chuckle** /'tʃʌkəl/ vi reír entre dientes. —n risa ahogada, f; risita, f

**chum** /tʃʌm/ n compinche, camarada, mf. **to c. up with,** ser camarada de

**chunk** /tʃʌnk/ n pedazo, trozo, m

**church** /tʃɜrtʃ/ n iglesia, f; (Protestant) templo, m, vt (a woman) purificar. **poor as a c. mouse,** más pobre que las ratas. **the C. of England,** la iglesia anglicana. **to go to c.,** ir a misa; ir al templo. **c. music,** música sagrada, f

**churchyard** /'tʃɜrtʃ,yard/ n cementerio, m

**churl** /tʃɜrl/ n patán, m

**churlish** /'tʃɜrlɪʃ/ a grosero, cazurro; (mean) tacaño, ruin

**churn** /tʃɜrn/ n mantequera, f. —vt (cream) batir; Fig. azotar, agitar

**chute** /ʃut/ n (for grain, etc.) manga de tolva, f; vertedor, m; (in flats and fun fairs) tobogán, deslizadero, m

**ciborium** /sɪ'bɔriəm/ n (chalice) copón, m; (tabernacle) sagrario, m; Archit. ciborio, m

**cicada** /sɪ'keidə/ n cigarra, f

**cicatrice** /'sɪkətrɪs/ n cicatriz, f

**cicatrization** /,sɪkətrə'zeiʃən/ n cicatrización, f

**cicatrize** /'sɪkə,traiz/ vt cicatrizar. —vi cicatrizarse

**cider** /'saidər/ n sidra, f

**cigar** /sɪ'gar/ n cigarro, m. **c.-box,** cigarrera, f. **c.-case,** petaca, cigarrera, f. **c.-cutter,** corta-puros, m

**cigarette** /,sɪgə'ret/ n cigarrillo, pitillo, m. **c.-butt,** colilla, f. **c.-case,** pitillera, f. **c.-holder,** boquilla, f. **c.-lighter,** encendedor de cigarrillos, m. **c.-paper,** papel de fumar, m

**cinch** /sɪntʃ/ n (of a saddle) cincha, f; Inf. ganga, f; Inf. seguridad, f; Inf. suerte, f; látigo, m

**cinchona** /sɪn'kounə/ n quina, cinchona, f

**cinder** /'sɪndər/ n ceniza, f; carbonilla, f. **red-hot c.,** rescoldo, m. **c.-track,** pista de ceniza, f

**cinema** /'sɪnəmə/ n cine, cinematógrafo, m

**cinematographic** /,sɪnə,mætə'græfɪk/ a cinematográfico

**cinematography** /,sɪnəmə'tɒgrəfi/ n cinematografía, f

**cinemogul** /,sɪnə'mougəl/ n magnate del cine, mf

**cinnamon** /'sɪnəmən/ n (spice) canela, f; (tree) canelo, m; color de canela, m

**cipher** /'saifər/ n Math. cero, m; Fig. nulidad, f; (code) cifra, f; monograma, m. **to be a mere c.,** ser un cero

**Circassian** /sər'kæʃən/ a circasiano. —n circasiano (-na)

**circle** /'sɜrkəl/ n círculo, m; (revolution) vuelta, f;

(group) grupo; *m;* (club, etc.) centro, *m;* (cycle) ci-clo, *m.* —*vt* dar vueltas alrededor de; rodear; ceñir; (on an application, examination, etc.) encerrar en un círculo. —*vi* dar vueltas; (aircraft) volar en círculo; (of a hawk, etc.) cernerse. **dress-c.,** *Theat.* anfiteatro, *m.* **the family c.,** el círculo de la familia. **to come full c.,** dar la vuelta. **upper c.,** *Theat.* segundo piso, *m.* **vicious c.,** círculo vicioso, *m*

**circlet** /ˈsɜrklɪt/ *n* (of flowers, etc.) corona, *f;* (ring) anillo, *m*

**circuit** /ˈsɜrkɪt/ *n* circuito, *m;* (tour) gira, *f;* (revolu-tion) vuelta, *f;* (radius) radio, *m.* **short c.,** corto cir-cuito, *m.* **c.-breaker,** corta-circuitos, *m*

**circuit court of appeals** *n* tribunal colegial de cir-cuito, *m*

**circuitous** /sərˈkyuɪtəs/ *a* indirecto; tortuoso

**circuitously** /sərˈkyuɪtəsli/ *adv* indirectamente

**circular** /ˈsɜrkyələr/ *a* circular; redondo. —*n* carta cir-cular, *f;* circular, *f.* **c. tour,** viaje redondo, *m*

**circularize** /ˈsɜrkyələˌraiz/ *vt* enviar circulares (a)

**circulate** /ˈsɜrkyəˌleit/ *vi* circular. —*vt* hacer circular; poner en circulación; (news, etc.) divulgar, diseminar

**circulating library** /ˈsɜrkyəˌleitɪŋ/ *n* biblioteca por subscripción, *f*

**circulation** /ˌsɜrkyəˈleiʃən/ *n* circulación, *f;* (of a newspaper, etc.) tirada, circulación, *f.* **c. of the blood,** circulación de la sangre, *f*

**circulatory** /ˈsɜrkyələˌtɔri/ *a* circulatorio

**circumcise** /ˈsɜrkəmˌsaiz/ *vt* circuncidar

**circumcised** /ˈsɜrkəmˌsaizd/ *a* circunciso

**circumcision** /ˌsɜrkəmˈsɪʒən/ *n* circuncisión, *f*

**circumference** /sərˈkʌmfərəns/ *n* circunferencia, *f*

**circumflex** /ˈsɜrkəmˌfleks/ *a* circunflejo. **c. accent,** acento circunflejo, *m;* (informal) capucha, *f*

**circumlocution** /ˌsɜrkəmlouˈkyuʃən/ *n* circumlocu-ción, *f*

**circumnavigate** /ˌsɜrkəmˈnævɪˌgeit/ *vt* circunnavegar

**circumnavigation** /ˈsɜrkəmˌnævəˈgeiʃən/ *n* circun-navegación, *f*

**circumscribe** /ˈsɜrkəmˌskraib/ *vt* circunscribir; *Fig.* limitar

**circumscribed** /ˈsɜrkəmˌskraibd/ *a* circunscripto; *Fig.* limitado

**circumscription** /ˌsɜrkəmˈskrɪpʃən/ *n* circunscripción, *f; Fig.* limitación, restricción, *f*

**circumspect** /ˈsɜrkəmˌspekt/ *a* circunspecto; discreto, correcto; prudente

**circumspection** /ˌsɜrkəmˈspekʃən/ *n* circunspección, *f;* prudencia, *f*

**circumspectly** /ˈsɜrkəmˌspektli/ *adv* con circunspec-ción; prudentemente

**circumstance** /ˈsɜrkəmˌstæns/ *n* circunstancia, *f;* de-talle, *m.* **aggravating c.,** circunstancia agravante, *f.* **attenuating c.,** circunstancia atenuante, *f.* **in the circumstances,** en las circunstancias. **in easy circumstances,** en buena posición, acomodado. **Do you know what his circumstances are?** ¿Sabes cuál es su situación económica? **under the circumstances,** bajo las circunstancias

**circumstantial** /ˌsɜrkəmˈstænʃəl/ *a* circunstancial; de-tallado. **c. evidence,** prueba de indicios, *f*

**circumvent** /ˌsɜrkəmˈvent/ *vt* frustrar; impedir

**circumvention** /ˌsɜrkəmˈvenʃən/ *n* frustración, *f*

**circumvolution** /ˌsɜrkəmˈvəˈluʃən/ *n* circunvolución, *f*

**circus** /ˈsɜrkəs/ *n* circo, *m;* plaza redonda, *f;* (traffic) redondel, *m*

**cirrhosis** /sɪˈrousɪs/ *n* cirrosis, *f*

**cirrus** /ˈsɪrəs/ *n* (all meanings) cirro, *m*

**cistern** /ˈsɪstərn/ *n* tanque, *m;* cisterna, *f,* aljibe, *m*

**citadel** /ˈsɪtədl̩/ *n* ciudadela, *f*

**citation** /saiˈteiʃən/ *n Law.* citación, *f;* cita, *f*

**citation dictionary** *n* diccionario de autoridades, *m*

**cite** /sait/ *vt* citar

**citizen** /ˈsɪtəzən/ *n* ciudadano (-na); vecino (-na); natural, *mf.* **fellow c.,** conciudadano, *m;* compatriota, *mf*

**citizenship** /ˈsɪtəzənˌʃip/ *n* ciudadanía, *f*

**citrate** /ˈsɪtreit/ *n* citrato, *m*

**citric** /ˈsɪtrɪk/ *a* cítrico

**citrine** /ˈsɪtrin/ *a* cetrino

**citron** /ˈsɪtrən/ *n* (fruit) cidra, *f;* (tree) cidro, *m*

**city** /ˈsɪti/ *n* ciudad, *f,* a municipal

**city-state** /ˈsɪtiˌsteit/ *n* ciudad-estado, *f,* (plural: ciudades-estado)

**civet** /ˈsɪvɪt/ *n* algalia, *f*

**civic** /ˈsɪvɪk/ *a* cívico; municipal

**civics** /ˈsɪvɪks/ *n* civismo, *m*

**civil** /ˈsɪvəl/ *a* civil; doméstico; (polite) cortés, atento; (obliging) servicial. **C. Aeronautics Board,** Dirección general de aeronáutica civil, *f.* **c. defense,** defensa pasiva, *f.* **c. engineer,** ingeniero de caminos, canales y puertos, *m.* **C. Service,** cuerpo de empleados del Es-tado, *m*

**civilian** /sɪˈvɪlyən/ *a* civil. —*n* ciudadano (-na). **c. dress,** traje paisano, *m*

**civility** /sɪˈvɪlɪti/ *n* civilidad, cortesía, *f*

**civilization** /ˌsɪvələˈzeiʃən/ *n* civilización, *f*

**civilize** /ˈsɪvəˌlaiz/ *vt* civilizar

**civilized** /ˈsɪvəˌlaizd/ *a* civilizado

**civilizing** /ˈsɪvəˌlaizɪŋ/ *a* civilizador

**civilly** /ˈsɪvəli/ *adv* civilmente, cortésmente

**clack** /klæk/ *n* golpeo, ruido sordo, *m*

**clad** /klæd/ *a* vestido

**claim** /kleim/ *vt* reclamar; pretender exigir; *Law.* de-mandar; (assert) afirmar. —*vi Law.* pedir en juicio. —*n* reclamación, *f;* pretensión, *f; Law.* demanda, *f;* (in a gold-field, etc.) concesión, *f;* (right) derecho, *m.* **to lay c. to,** pretender a; exigir. **to put in a c. for,** reclamar

**claimant** /ˈkleimənt/ *n Law.* demandante, *mf;* pre-tendiente (-ta); *Com.* acreedor (-ra)

**clairvoyance** /klɛərˈvɔiəns/ *n* doble vista, *f*

**clairvoyant** /klɛərˈvɔiənt/ *n* vidente, *m*

**clam** /klæm/ *n* almeja, chirla, *f*

**clamber** /ˈklæmbər/ *vi* trepar, encaramarse. —*n* subida difícil, *f*

**clamminess** /ˈklæminɪs/ *n* viscosidad, humedad, *f*

**clammy** /ˈklæmi/ *a* viscoso; húmedo, mojado

**clamor** /ˈklæmər/ *n* clamor, estruendo, *m;* gritería, vocería, *f.* —*vi* gritar, vociferar. **to c. against,** protes-tar contra. **to c. for,** pedir a voces

**clamorous** /ˈklæmərəs/ *a* clamoroso, ruidoso, estrepi-toso

**clamp** /klæmp/ *n* grapa, *f;* abrazadera, *f;* tornillo, *m;* (pile) montón, *m.* —*vt* empalmar; sujetar, lañar

**clan** /klæn/ *n* clan, *m;* familia, *f;* partido, grupo, *m*

**clandestine** /klænˈdestɪn/ *a* clandestino, furtivo

**clandestinely** /klænˈdestɪnli/ *adv* en secreto, clandes-tinamente

**clang** /klæŋ/ *vi* sonar; (of a gate, etc.) rechinar. —*vt* hacer sonar. —*n* sonido metálico, *m;* estruendo, *m*

**clank** /klæŋk/ *vi* dar un ruido metálico; crujir. —*vt* hacer sonar; (glasses) hacer chocar. —*n* ruido metá-lico, *m;* el crujir

**clannish** /ˈklænɪʃ/ *a* exclusivista

**clansman** /ˈklænzmən/ *n* miembro de un clan, *m*

**clap** /klæp/ *vt* (hands) batir; (spurs, etc.) poner rápi-damente; (one's hat on) encasquetarse (el sombrero); (shut) cerrar apresuradamente. —*vi* aplaudir. —*n* (of the hands) palmada, *f;* (of thunder) trueno, *m;* (noise) ruido, *m.* **to c. eyes on,** echar la vista encima de. **to c. someone on the back,** dar una palmada en la espalda (a). **to c. the hands,** batir las palmas

**clapper** /ˈklæpər/ *n* (of a bell) badajo, *m*

**clapping** /ˈklæpɪŋ/ *n* aplausos, *m pl*

**claque** /klæk/ *n* claque, *f*

**claret** /ˈklærɪt/ *n* clarete, *m*

**clarification** /ˌklærəfəˈkeiʃən/ *n* clarificación, *f;* eluci-dación, *f*

**clarify** /ˈklærəˌfai/ *vt* clarificar; elucidar, aclarar

**clarinet** /ˌklærəˈnet/ *n* clarinete, *m*

**clarinettist** /ˌklærəˈnetɪst/ *n* clarinete, *m*

**clarion** /ˈklæriən/ *n* clarín, *m*

**clarity** /ˈklærɪti/ *n* claridad, *f;* lucidez, *f*

**clash** /klæʃ/ *vi* chocar; encontrarse; (of events) coin-cidir; (of opinions, etc.) oponerse, estar en desa-cuerdo; (of colors) desentonar, chocar. —*n* estruendo, fragor, *m;* choque, *m; Mil.* encuentro, *m;* (of opinions, etc.) desacuerdo, *m;* disputa, *f*

**clasp** /klæsp/ *vt* (a brooch, etc.) abrochar, enganchar; (embrace) abrazar; (of plants, etc.) ceñir. —*n* (brooch) broche, *m;* (of a belt) hebilla, *f;* (of a necklace, handbag, book) cierre, *m;* (for the hair) pasador, *m.* **to c. someone in one's arms,** tomar en los brazos (a), abrazar. **c.-knife,** navaja, *f*

**class** /klæs/ *n* clase, *f;* (kind) especie, *f;* (of exhibits, etc.) categoría, *f.* —*vt* clasificar. **in a c. by itself,** único en su línea. **the lower classes,** las clases bajas. **the middle classes,** la clase media. **the upper classes,** la clase alta. **c.-mate,** condiscípulo (-la). **c.-room,** sala de clase, *f,* salón de clase, *f.* **c. war,** lucha de clases, *f*

**classic** /'klæsɪk/ *a* clásico. —*n* clásico, *m*

**classical** /'klæsɪkəl/ *a* clásico

**classicism** /'klæsə,sɪzəm/ *n* clasicismo, *m*

**classicist** /'klæsəsɪst/ *a* and *n* clasicista, *mf*

**classifiable** /'klæsə,faiəbəl/ *a* clasificable

**classification** /,klæsəfɪ'keiʃən/ *n* clasificación, *f*

**classified** /'klæsə,faid/ *a* (secreto) reservado, secreto; (advertisement) por palabras

**classified advertisement** *n* anuncio por palabras, *m*

**classify** /'klæsə,fai/ *vt* clasificar

**clatter** /'klætər/ *vi* hacer ruido; (knock) golpear; (of loose horseshoes) chacolotear. —*vt* hacer ruido con; chocar (una cosa contra otra). —*n* ruido, *m;* (hammering) martilleo, *m;* (of horseshoes) chacoloteo, *m;* (of a crowd) estruendo, *m,* bulla, *f.* **John clattered along the street,** Los pasos de Juan resonaban por la calle

**clause** /klɔz/ *n Gram.* cláusula, *f; Law.* condición, estipulación, cláusula, *f*

**claustrophobia** /,klɔstrə'foubiə/ *n* claustrofobia, *f*

**clavichord** /'klævɪ,kɔrd/ *n* clavicordio, *m*

**clavicle** /'klævɪkəl/ *n* clavícula, *f*

**claw** /klɔ/ *n* garra, *f;* (of a lobster, etc.) tenaza, *f;* (hook) garfio, gancho, *m.* —*vt* arañar, clavar las uñas en; (tear) desgarrar. **c.-hammer,** martillo de orejas, *m*

**clay** /klei/ *n* arcilla, *f;* barro, *m;* (pipe) pipa de barro, *f.* **c.-pit,** barrizal, *m*

**clayey** /'kleii/ *a* arcilloso

**clean** /klin/ *a* limpio; puro, casto. —*adv* limpio; completamente; exactamente. **to make a c. sweep (of),** no dejar títere con cabeza. **to make a c. breast of,** confesar sin tormento, no quedarse con nada en el pecho. **to show a c. pair of heels,** tomar las de Villadiego. **c. bill of health,** patente de sanidad, *m.* **c.-cut,** bien definido; claro. **c.-limbed,** bien proporcionado, gallardo. **c.-shaven,** lampiño; sin barba, bien afeitado

**clean** /klin/ *vt* limpiar; (streets) barrer; (a floor) fregar; (dryclean) lavar al seco. **to c. one's hands (teeth),** limpiarse las manos (los dientes). **to c. up,** limpiar; (tidy) asear; poner en orden

**cleaner** /'klinər/ *n* limpiador (-ra); (charwoman) fregona, *f;* (stain remover) sacamanchas, *m;* (drycleaner, person) tintorero (-ra)

**cleaning** /'klinɪŋ/ *n* limpieza, *f,* a de limpiar. **dry-c.,** lavado al seco, *m.* **c. rag,** trapo de limpiar, *m*

**cleanliness** /'klɛnlinɪs/ *n* limpieza, *f;* aseo, *m*

**cleanness** /'klinnɪs/ *n* limpieza, *f;* aseo, *m;* pureza, *f*

**cleanse** /klɛnz/ *vt* limpiar; lavar; purgar; purificar

**cleansing** /'klɛnzɪŋ/ *n* limpieza, *f;* lavamiento, *m;* purgación, *f;* purificación, *f*

**clear** /klɪər/ *a* claro, *m;* (of the sky) sereno, despejado; transparente; (free (from)) libre (de); (open) abierto; (of profit, etc.) neto; (of thoughts, etc.) lúcido; (apparent) evidente; explícito; (of images) distinto; absoluto; (whole) entero, completo. **c. majority,** mayoría absoluta, *f.* **c. profit,** beneficio neto, *m.* **c.-cut,** bien definido. **c.-headed,** perspicaz; inteligente. **c.-sighted,** clarividente

**clear** /klɪər/ *vt* aclarar; despejar; limpiar; librar (de); quitar; (one's throat) carraspear; (*Com.* stock) liquidar; (of a charge) absolver; (one's character) vindicar; (avoid, miss) evitar; (jump) salvar, saltar; (a court, etc.) desocupar; (a debt) satisfacer; (an account) saldar; (a mortgage) cancelar; (win) ganar; hacer un beneficio de; (through customs) despachar en la aduana. —*vi* (of sky, etc.) serenarse; escampar; (of wine, etc.) aclararse; despacharse en la aduana. **to c. the table,** levantar la mesa, levantar los manteles. **to c. the way,** abrir calle; *Fig.* abrir paso. **to c. away,** *vt* quitar; disipar. —*vi* disiparse. **to c. off,** *vt* (finish) terminar; (debts) pagar; (discharge) despedir. —*vi* (of rain) despejarse; escampar; marcharse. **to c.**

**out,** *vt* limpiar; (a drain, etc.) desatascar; vaciar; echar. —*vi* marcharse, escabullirse. **C. out!** ¡Fuera! **c. the decks,** hacer zafarrancho. **c. the decks for action,** hacer zafarrancho. **to c. up,** *vt* poner en orden; (a mystery, etc.) aclarar, resolver, *vi* (of weather) serenarse, escampar, despejarse

**clearance** /'klɪərəns/ *n* (of trees, etc.) desmonte, *m;* eliminación, *f;* expulsión, *f; Mech.* espacio muerto, *m;* despacho de aduana, *m.* **to make a c. of,** deshacerse de. **c. sale,** liquidación, venta de saldos, *f*

**clearing** /'klɪərɪŋ/ *n* (in a wood) claro, *m;* desmonte, *m;* (*Com.* of goods) liquidación, *f;* (of one's character) vindicación, *f.* **c.-house,** casa de compensación, *f*

**clearly** /'klɪərli/ *adv* claramente

**clearness** /'klɪərnɪs/ *n* claridad, *f*

**cleavage** /'klividʒ/ *n* hendimiento, *m;* (in views, etc.) escisión, *f*

**cleave** /kliv/ *vt* partir; abrir; (air, water, etc.) surcar, hender. —*vi* partirse; (stick) pegarse, adherirse

**cleaver** /'klivər/ *n* partidor, *m;* hacha, *f*

**clef** /klɛf/ *n* clave, *f.* **treble c.,** clave de sol, *f*

**cleft** /klɛft/ *n* hendedura, fisura, rendija, abertura, *f.* **c.-palate,** paladar hendido, *m*

**clematis** /'klɛmətɪs/ *n* clemátide, *f*

**clemency** /'klɛmənsi/ *n* (of weather) benignidad, *f;* (of character, etc.) clemencia, *f*

**clement** /'klɛmənt/ *a* (of weather) benigno; (of character, etc.) clemente, benévolo

**clench** /klɛntʃ/ *vt* agarrar; (teeth, etc.) apretar; (a bargain) cerrar, concluir

**clergy** /'klɜrdʒi/ *n* clero, *m,* clérigos, *m pl*

**clergyman** /'klɜrdʒimən/ *n* clérigo, *m*

**cleric** /'klɛrɪk/ *n* eclesiástico, *m*

**clerical** /'klɛrɪkəl/ *a* clerical; de oficina. **c. error,** error de oficina, *m.* **c. work,** trabajo de oficina, *m*

**clericalism** /'klɛrɪkə,lɪzəm/ *n* clericalismo, *m*

**clerk** /klɜrk/ *n* (clergyman) clérigo, *m;* (in an office) oficinista, escribiente, *m;* oficial, *m;* secretario, *m*

**clerkship** /'klɜrkʃɪp/ *n* puesto de oficinista, *m;* escribanía, *f;* secretaría, *f*

**clever** /'klɛvər/ *a* listo, inteligente; ingenioso; hábil; (dexterous) diestro

**cleverly** /'klɛvərli/ *adv* hábilmente; diestramente, con destreza

**cleverness** /'klɛvərnɪs/ *n* talento, *m;* inteligencia, *f;* habilidad, *f;* (dexterity) destreza, *f*

**cliché** /kli'ʃei/ *n* frase hecha, frase de cajón, *f*

**click** /klɪk/ *vi* (of the tongue) dar un chasquido; (of a bolt, etc.) cerrarse a golpe; hacer tictac. —*vt* (one's tongue) chascar; (a bolt, etc.) cerrar a golpe. —*n* golpe seco, *m;* tictac, *m;* (of the tongue) chasquido, *m.* **to c. one's heels together,** hacer chocar los talones

**client** /'klaiənt/ *n* cliente, *mf;* (customer) parroquiano (-na)

**clientele** /,klaiən'tɛl/ *n* clientela, *f*

**cliff** /klɪf/ *n* acantilado, *m,* roca, escarpa, *f*

**cliff dweller** *n* hombre de la roca, hombre de las rocas, *m,* mujer de la roca, mujer de las rocas, *f*

**climate** /'klaimɪt/ *n* clima, *m*

**climatic** /klai'mætɪk/ *a* climático

**climatology** /,klaimə'tɒlədʒi/ *n* climatología, *f*

**climax** /'klaimæks/ *n* culminación, *f;* (rhetoric) clímax, *m;* gradación, *f;* punto más alto, apogeo, cenit, *m;* (of a play, etc.) desenlace, *m*

**climb** /klaim/ *vt* and *vi* trepar; escalar; montar; subir; ascender. **rate of c.,** *Aer.* velocidad ascensional, *f.* **to c. down,** bajar; *Fig.* echar el pie atrás. **to c. over,** (obstacles) salvar. **to c. up,** encaramarse por; subir por; montar

**climber** /'klaimər/ *n* alpinista, *mf;* (plant) trepadera, enredadera, *f;* (social) arribista, *mf*

**clime** /klaim/ *n* clima, *m*

**clinch** /klɪntʃ/ *vt* (nails, etc.) remachar, rebotar; (a bargain, etc.) cerrar; (an argument, etc.) remachar. —*n* (wrestling) cuerpo a cuerpo, *m*

**cling** /klɪŋ/ *vi* pegarse (a); agarrarse (a); (of scents) pegarse; (follow) seguir. **They clung together for an instant,** Quedaron abrazados un instante

**clinging** /'klɪŋɪŋ/ *a* tenaz; (of plants, etc.) trepador; (of persons) manso, dócil. **to be a c. vine,** *Inf.* ser una malva

**clinic** /'klɪnɪk/ n clínica, f

**clinical** /'klɪnɪkəl/ a clínico. **c. thermometer,** termómetro clínico, m

**clink** /klɪŋk/ vi retiñir; (of glasses) chocarse. —vt hacer sonar; (glasses) chocar. —n retintín, m; (of a hammer) martilleo, m; sonido metálico, m; (of glasses) choque, m

**clip** /klɪp/ vt (grasp) agarrar; (sheep, etc.) esquilar; (trim) recortar, cercenar; (prune) podar; (a ticket) taladrar. —n pinza, f; (paper-clip) sujetapapeles, m; Mech. grapa, escarpia, f; (for ornament) sujetador, m. **to c. a person's wings,** Fig. cortar (or quebrar) las alas (a)

**clipper** /'klɪpər/ n (person) esquilador (-ra) (Naut. and Aer.) clíper, m; pl **clippers,** tenazas de cortar, f pl; (for pruning) podaderas, f pl; (punch) taladro, m

**clipping** /'klɪpɪŋ/ n (of sheep, etc.) esquileo, m; (of a newspaper, etc.) recorte, m

**clique** /klik/ n camarilla, f

**cliquish** /'klikɪʃ/ a exclusivista

**cloak** /klouk/ n capa, f; manto, m; Fig. velo, m. —vt encapotar; embozar; (conceal) ocultar, encubrir. **c. and sword play,** comedia de capa y espada, f. **c.-room,** guardarropa, m; (ladies') tocador, m; (on a station) consigna, f

**clock** /klɒk/ n reloj, m; (of a stocking) cuadrado, m. **It is six o'clock,** Son las seis. **c.-face,** esfera de reloj, f. **c.-maker,** relojero, m. **c.-making,** relojería, f. **c.-work,** aparato de relojería, m. **to go like c.-work,** ir como un reloj. **c.-work train,** tren de cuerda, m

**clockwise** /'klɒk,waiz/ a and adv en el sentido de las agujas del reloj; de derecha a izquierda

**clod** /klɒd/ n (of earth) terrón, m; (corpse) tierra, f; (person) zoquete, m. **c.-hopper,** patán, m

**clog** /klɒg/ n (shoe) zueco, zoclo, m; (obstacle) estorbo, obstáculo, m. —vt embarazar; estorbar, impedir; (block) obturar, cerrar; Fig. paralizar

**cloister** /'klɔistər/ n claustro, m; convento, m. —vt enclaustrar

**cloistered** /'klɔistərd/ a enclaustrado; retirado, aislado

**cloistered nun** n monja de claustro, f

**close** /klous/ a estrecho; (of a prisoner) incomunicado; (reticent) reservado; (niggardly) tacaño, avaro; (scarce) escaso; (of friends) íntimo; (equal) igual; (lacking space) apretado; (dense) denso; (thick) tupido; compacto; (of a copy, etc.) fiel, exacto; (thorough) concienzudo; (careful) cuidadoso; (attentive) atento; (to the roots) a raíz; (of shaving) bueno; (of weather) pesado, sofocante; (of rooms) mal ventilado. **at c. quarters,** de cerca. **It is c. to eight o'clock,** Son casi las ocho. **to press c.,** perseguir de cerca; fatigar. **c. at hand, c. by,** cerca; al lado; a mano. **c.-cropped,** (of hair) al rape. **c. fight,** lucha igualada, f. **c.-fisted,** tacaño, apretado. **c.-fitting,** ajustado, ceñido al cuerpo; pequeño. **c. season,** veda, f. **c.-up,** n (cinema) primer plano, m

**close** /klouz/ n (end) fin, m, conclusión, f; (of day) caída, f; Mus. cadencia, f; (enclosure) cercado, m; (square) plazoleta, f; (alley) callejón, m; (of a cathedral) patio, m. **at the c. of day,** a la caída de la tarde. **to bring to a c.,** terminar; llevar a cabo. **to draw to a c.,** tocar a su fin; estar terminando

**close** /klouz/ vt cerrar; (end) concluir, terminar; poner fin a. —vi cerrar(se); (of a wound) cicatrizarse, cerrarse; (end) terminar(se), acabar, concluir. **to c. the ranks,** cerrar filas. **to c. about,** (surround) rodear, cercar; (envelop) envolver. **to c. down,** vt cerrar. —vi cerrar; Radio. cerrarse. **to c. in,** (surround) cercar; (of night) acercar; caer; (envelop) envolver; (of length of days) acortarse. **to c. in on,** cercar. **to c. round,** envolver; (of water) tragar. **to c. up,** vt cerrar; cerrar completamente; obstruir. —vi (of persons) acercarse; (of a wound) cicatrizarse; cerrarse

**closed** /klouzd/ a cerrado. **"Road C.,"** Paso Cerrado. **to have a c. mind,** ser cerrado de mollera; sufrir de estrechez de miras

**closely** /'klousli/ adv estrechamente; de cerca; (carefully) cuidadosamente; (exactly) exactamente; (attentively) con atención, atentamente

**closeness** /'klousnɪs/ n estrechez, f; densidad, f; (nearness) proximidad, f; (of a copy, etc.) fidelidad,

exactitud, f; (stuffiness), falta de aire, f; (of friendship) intimidad, f; (stinginess) tacañería, f; (reserve) reserva.

**closet** /'klɒzɪt/ n camarín, m; (cupboard) alacena, f; (water) excusado, m

**closing** /'klouzɪŋ/ n cerramiento, m; (of an account) saldo, m. **c. time,** cierre, m, hora de cerrar, f

**closure** /'klouʒər/ n conclusión, f; Polit. clausura, f

**clot** /klɒt/ n coágulo, grumo, m. —vt coagular. —vi coagularse, cuajarse

**cloth** /klɔθ/ n tela, f; paño, m; (table) mantel, m; (clergy) clero, m. **She cleaned the books with a c.,** Ella limpió los libros con un paño. **in c.,** (of books) en tela

**clothe** /klouð/ vt vestir; cubrir; (with authority, etc.) revestir. **to c. oneself,** vestirse

**clothes** /klouz/ n pl vestidos, m pl, ropa, f. **a suit of c.,** un traje. **old c. shop,** ropavejería, f. **c.-basket,** cesta de la colada, f. **c.-brush,** cepillo para ropa, m. **c.-hanger,** percha, f. **c.-horse,** enjugador, m. **c.-line,** cuerda de la ropa, f. **c.-peg,** pinza de la ropa, f. **c.-prop,** palo para sostener la cuerda de la colada, m

**clothier** /'klouðiər/ n ropero, m. **clothier's shop,** ropería, f

**clothing** /'klouðɪŋ/ n vestidos, m pl, ropa, f. **article of c.,** prenda de vestir, f

**clotted** /'klɒtɪd/ a grumoso

**cloud** /klaud/ n nube, f. —vt anublar, oscurecer; empañar; (blot out) borrar. —vi anublarse. **to be under a c.,** estar bajo sospecha. **summer c.,** nube de verano, f. **storm-c.,** nubarrón, m. **c.-burst,** nubada, f, chaparrón, m. **c.-capped,** coronado de nubes

**cloudiness** /'klaudinɪs/ n nebulosidad, f; obscuridad, f; (of liquids) turbiedad, f

**cloudless** /'klaudlɪs/ a sin nubes, despejado; sereno; claro

**cloudy** /'klaudi/ a nublado, nubloso; obscuro; (of liquids) turbio

**clove** /klouv/ n clavo de especia, m; (of garlic) diente de ajo, m. **c.-tree,** clavero, m

**cloven** /'klouvən/ a hendido. **to show the c. hoof,** enseñar la oreja. **c. hoof,** pezuña, f

**clover** /'klouvər/ n trébol, m. **to be in c.,** nadar en la abundancia

**clown** /klaun/ n patán, m; bufón, tonto, m; (in a circus) payaso, m. —vi hacer el tonto, hacer el payaso

**clowning** /'klaunɪŋ/ n payasada, f

**clownish** /'klaunɪʃ/ a grosero; palurdo, zafio; bufón

**cloy** /klɔi/ vt empalagar

**cloying** /'klɔiɪŋ/ a empalagoso

**club** /klʌb/ n porra, cachiporra, clava, f; (gymnastic) maza, f; (hockey) bastón de hockey, m; (golf) palo de golf, m; (in cards) basto, m; (social) club, m. —vt golpear. **to c. together,** asociarse, unirse. **We clubbed together to buy him a present,** Entre todos le compramos un regalo. **c.-house,** club, m

**clubfoot** /'klʌb,fot/ n pie calcáneo, pie contrahecho, pie de piña, pie equino, pie talo, pie zambo, m

**clubman** /'klʌb,mæn/ n miembro de un club, m

**cluck** /klʌk/ vi cloquear. —n cloqueo, m

**clucking** /'klʌkɪŋ/ n cloqueo, m

**clue** /klu/ n indicio, m; (to a problem) clave, f; (of a crossword) indicación, f; idea, f

**clump** /klʌmp/ n bloque, pedazo, m; (of trees) grupo, m; (of feet) ruido, m

**clumsily** /'klʌmzəli/ adv torpemente; pesadamente

**clumsiness** /'klʌmzinɪs/ n torpeza, f; falta de maña, f; pesadez, f

**clumsy** /'klʌmzi/ a torpe; desmañado; chapucero, sin arte; (lumbering) pesado; (in shape) disforme

**cluster** /'klʌstər/ n (of currants, etc.) racimo, m; (of flowers) ramillete, m; grupo, m. —vi arracimarse; agruparse. **They clustered round him,** Se agrupaban a su alrededor

**clutch** /klʌtʃ/ vt agarrar; sujetar, apretar. —n Mech. embrague, m; (of eggs) nidada, f; Fig. garras, f pl. **to fall into the clutches of,** caer en las garras de. **to make a c. at,** procurar agarrar. **to throw in the c.,** Mech. embragar. **to throw out the c.,** Mech. desembragar. **c. pedal,** pedal de embrague, m

**clutter** /'klʌtər/ n desorden, m, confusión, f, vt desordenar

**coach** /koutʃ/ n carroza, f; charabán, m; Rail. vagón, coche, m; (hackney) coche de alquiler, m; Sports. entrenador, m; (tutor) profesor particular, m. —vt Sports. entrenar; (teach) preparar, dar lecciones particulares (a). **through c.,** coche directo, m. **c.-box,** pescante, m. **c.-house,** cochera, f

**coaching** /'koutʃɪŋ/ n Sports. entrenamiento, m; le cciones particulares, f pl

**coachman** /'koutʃmən/ n cochero, m

**coagulate** /kou'ægyə,leit/ vi coagularse. —vt coagular, cuajar

**coagulation** /kou,ægyə'leiʃən/ n coagulación, f

**coal** /koul/ n carbón, m; pedazo de carbón, m; (burning) brasa, f. —vi carbonear, hacer carbón. —vt proveer de carbón; carbonear. **to carry coals to Newcastle,** llevar leña al monte, elevar aqua al mar. **to haul a person over the coals,** reprender a alguien. **c.-barge,** (barco) carbonero, m. **c.-black,** negro como el azabache. **c.-cellar, house,** carbonera, f. **c.-dust,** cisco, m. **c.-field,** yacimiento de carbón, m. **c.-gas,** gas de hulla, m. **c.-heaver,** cargador de carbón, m. **c.-merchant,** carbonero, m. **c.-mine,** mina de carbón, f. **c.-miner,** minero de carbón, m. **c.-scuttle,** carbonera, f. **c.-tar,** alquitrán mineral, m

**coalesce** /,kouə'lɛs/ vi fundirse; unirse; incorporarse

**coalescence** /,kouə'lɛsəns/ n fusión, f; unión, f; incorporación, f

**coalition** /,kouə'lɪʃən/ n coalición, f

**coarse** /kɔrs/ a (in texture) basto, burdo; tosco; (gross) grosero; vulgar. **c.-grained,** de fibra gruesa; (of persons) vulgar, poco fino

**coarsen** /'kɔrsən/ vt (of persons) embrutecer. —vi embrutecerse; (of the skin) curtirse

**coarseness** /'kɔrsnɪs/ n basteza, f; tosquedad, f; (of persons) grosería, indelicadeza, f; vulgaridad, f

**coast** /koust/ n costa, f; litoral, m. —vi costear; deslizarse en un tobogán; dejar muerto el motor. **The c. is not clear,** Hay moros en la costa. **c.-guard,** guardacostas, m. **c.-line,** litoral, m

**coastal** /'koustl̩/ a costanero, costero. **c. defences,** defensas costeras, f pl

**coaster** /'koustər/ n Naut. barco costanero, barco de cabotaje, m

**coasting** /'koustɪŋ/ n Naut. cabotaje, m

**coat** /kout/ n abrigo, m; gabán, f; chaqueta, f; (animal's) capa, f; (of paint) mano, f. —vt recubrir; (with paint, etc.) dar una mano de. **fur c.,** abrigo de pieles, m. **sports c.,** Americana sport, f. **c. of arms,** escudo de armas, m. **c. of mail,** cota de malla, f. **c.-hanger,** percha, f

**coating** /'koutɪŋ/ n (of paint, etc.) capa, mano, f

**co-author** /'kou'ɔθər/ n coautor, m

**coax** /kouks/ vt instar; halagar; persuadir (a)

**coaxing** /'kouksɪŋ/ n ruegos, m pl; mimos, m pl, caricias, f pl; persuasión, f. —a mimoso, zalamero; persuasivo

**cob** /kɒb/ n (horse) jaca, f; (lump) pedazo, m; (swan) cisne macho, m

**cobalt** /'koubɔlt/ n cobalto, m. **c. blue,** azul cobalto, m

**cobble** /'kɒbəl/ n (stone) guijarro, m, vt (with stones) empedrar con guijarros; (shoes) remendar

**cobbler** /'kɒblər/ n zapatero remendón, m. **cobbler's last,** horma, f. **cobbler's wax,** cerote, m

**cobblestone** /'kɒbəl,stoun/ n guijarro, m, piedra, f

**cobelligerent** /,koubə'lɪdʒərənt/ n cobeligerante, mf

**cobra** /'koubrə/ n cobra, serpiente de anteojos, f

**cobweb** /'kɒb,wɛb/ n telaraña, f

**cobwebby** /'kɒb,wɛbi/ a cubierto de telarañas; transparente; de gasa

**cocaine** /kou'kein/ n cocaína, f

**coccyx** /'kɒksɪks/ n cóccix, m, Inf. rabadilla, f

**cochlea** /'kɒkliə/ n caracol (del oído), m

**cock** /kɒk/ n gallo, m; (male) macho, m; (tap) grifo, m, espita, f; (of a gun) martillo, m; (weather-vane) veleta, f; (of hay) montón, m. —vt (a gun) amartillar; (a hat) ladear; (raise) erguir, enderezar. **a cocked hat,** un sombrero de tres picos. **at half c.,** (of a gun) desamartillada f.. **He cocked his head,** Erguió la cabeza. **The dog cocked its ears,** El perro aguzó las orejas. **to c. one's eye at,** lanzar una mirada (a). **c.-a-doodle-doo,** quiquiriquí, m. **c.-a-hoop,** triunfante,

jubiloso; arrogante. **c.-crow,** canto del gallo, m. **c.-fight,** riña de gallos, f. **c.-of-the-walk,** gallito, m. **c.-sure,** pagado de sí mismo; completamente convencido

**cockerel** /'kɒkərəl/ n gallo joven, gallito, m

**cocker spaniel** /,kɒkər 'spænyəl/ n cóquer, m

**cockle** /'kɒkəl/ n (bivalve) bucarda, f. —vi arrugarse; (warp) torcerse; doblarse. **c.-shell,** (pilgrims') concha, f; (boat) cascarón de nuez, m

**cockpit** /'kɒk,pɪt/ n gallería, f; Aer. casilla del piloto, f; Fig. arena, f

**cockroach** /'kɒk,routʃ/ n cucaracha, f

**cockscomb** /'kɒks,koum/ n cresta de gallo, f

**cocktail** /'kɒk,teil/ n (drink) cóctel, coctel, m. **to shake a c.,** mezclar un coctel. **c. party,** coctel m. **c. shaker,** cotelera, f

**cocky** /'kɒki/ a fatuo, presuntuoso

**cocoa** /'koukou/ n cacao, m

**coconut** /'kouka,nʌt/ n coco, m; Inf. cabeza, f. **c. milk,** agua de coco, f. **c. shy,** pim, pam, pum, m. **c. tree,** cocotero, m

**cocoon** /kə'kun/ n capullo, m

**cod** /kɒd/ n bacalao, m. **cod-liver oil,** aceite de hígado de bacalao, m

**coddle** /'kɒdl̩/ vt criar con mimo, mimar, consentir

**code** /koud/ n código, m; clave, f; (secret) cifra, f. —vt poner en cifra. **signal c.,** Naut. código de señales, m. **c. word,** palabra de clave, f

**codeine** /'koudin/ n codeína, f

**codex** /'koudɛks/ n códice, m

**codicil** /'kɒdəsəl/ n codicilio, m

**codification** /,kɒdəfɪ'keiʃən/ n codificación, f

**codify** /'kɒdə,fai/ vt codificar

**coeducation** /,kouedʒu'keiʃən/ n coeducación, f

**coefficient** /,kouə'fɪʃənt/ n coeficiente, m

**coequality** /kou'kwɒlɪti/ n coigualdad, f

**coerce** /kou'ɜrs/ vt forzar, obligar; constreñir

**coercion** /kou'ɜrʃən/ n coerción, coacción, f

**coercive** /kou'ɜrsɪv/ a coercitivo, coactivo

**coeval** /kou'ivəl/ a coevo

**coexist** /,kouɪg'zɪst/ vi coexistir

**coexistence** /,kouɪg'zɪstəns/ n coexistencia, f

**coffee** /'kɔfi/ n café, m. **black c.,** café solo, m. **white c.,** café con leche, m. **c.-bean,** grano de café, m. **c.-cup,** taza para café, f. **c.-house,** café, m. **c.-mill,** molinillo de café, m. **c.-plantation,** cafetal, m. **c.-pot,** cafetera, f. **c.-set,** juego de café, m. **c.-tree,** cafeto, m

**coffer** /'kɔfər/ n cofre, m; arca, caja, f

**coffin** /'kɔfɪn/ n ataúd, féretro, m; caja, f

**cog** /kɒg/ n Mech. diente (de rueda), m

**cogency** /'koudʒənsi/ n fuerza, f

**cogent** /'koudʒənt/ a convincente, fuerte; urgente

**cogitate** /'kɒdʒɪ,teit/ vi pensar, considerar, meditar

**cogitation** /,kɒdʒɪ'teiʃən/ n reflexión, meditación, consideración, f

**cognac** /'kounyæk/ n coñac, m

**cognate** /'kɒgneit/ a (of stock) consanguíneo; afín; análogo; semejante

**cognition** /kɒg'nɪʃən/ n cognición, f

**cognitive** /'kɒgnɪtɪv/ a cognoscitivo

**cognizance** /'kɒgnəzəns/ n conocimiento, m; jurisdicción, f

**cogwheel** /'kɒg,wil/ n rueda dentada, f

**cohabit** /kou'hæbɪt/ vi cohabitar

**cohabitation** /kou,hæbɪ'teiʃən/ n cohabitación, f

**coheir** /kou'ɛər/ n coheredero, m

**coheiress** /kou'ɛərɪs/ n coheredera, f

**cohere** /kou'hɪər/ vi pegarse, adherirse; unirse

**coherent** /kou'hɪərənt/ a coherente; consecuente

**cohesion** /kou'hiʒən/ n cohesión, f; coherencia, f

**cohort** /'kouhɔrt/ n cohorte, f

**coif** /kwɔf/ n cofia, f; toca, f

**coiffure** /kwɑ'fyur/ n peinado, m; tocado, f

**coil** /kɔil/ vt arrollar; (Naut. of ropes) adujar. —vi arrollarse; enroscarse; serpentear. —n rollo, m; (of a serpent and ropes) anillo, m; (of hair) trenza, f; Elec. carrete, m. **coil of smoke,** nube de humo, f. **to c. up,** hacerse un ovillo

**coiling** /'kɔilɪŋ/ n arrollamiento, m; serpenteo, m

**coin** /kɔin/ n moneda, f; Inf. dinero, m. —vt acuñar;

(a new word) inventar. **to pay back in the same c.,** pagar en la misma moneda

**coinage** /'kɔɪnɪdʒ/ n acuñación, f; moneda, f; sistema monetario, m; invención, f; (new word) neologismo, m

**coincide** /,kouɪn'saɪd/ vi coincidir (con); estar conforme, estar de acuerdo

**coincidence** /kou'ɪnsɪdəns/ n coincidencia, f; (chance) casualidad, f

**coiner** /'kɔɪnər/ n acuñador de moneda, m; monedero falso, m; (of phrases, etc.) inventor, m

**coitus** /'kouɪtəs/ n coito, m

**coke** /kouk/ n (carbón de) coque, m

**colander** /'kɒləndər/ n colador, m

**cold** /kould/ a frío. —n frío, m; Med. catarro, constipado, m. **I am c.,** Tengo frío. **It is c.,** Está frío; (weather) Hace frío. **to catch a c.,** acatarrarse, resfriarse. **to grow c.,** enfriarse; (of the weather) empezar a hacer frío. **in c. blood,** a sangre fría. **c.-blooded,** (fishes, etc.) de sangre fría; (chilly, of persons) friolero; (pitiless) insensible, sin piedad; (of actions) a sangre fría, premeditado. **c.-chisel,** cortafrío, m. **c. cream,** crema (para el cutis), f. **c.-hearted,** seco, insensible. **c.-shoulder,** n frialdad, f. —vt tratar con frialdad (a). **c.-storage,** conservación refrigerada, f

**coldly** /'kouldli/ adv fríamente

**coldness** /'kouldnɪs/ n frío, m; (of one's reception, etc.) frialdad, f; (of heart) inhumanidad, f

**coleopterous** /,kouli'ɒptərəs/ a coleóptero

**colic** /'kɒlɪk/ n cólico, m

**coliseum** /,kɒlɪ'sɪəm/ n coliseo, m

**colitis** /kə'laɪtɪs/ n colitis, m

**collaborate** /kə'læbə,reɪt/ vi colaborar (con)

**collaboration** /kə,læbə'reɪʃən/ n colaboración, f

**collaborationist** /kə,læbə'reɪʃənɪst/ n colaboracionista, mf

**collaborator** /kə'læbə,reɪtər/ n colaborador (-ra); (quisling) colaboracionista, mf

**collapse** /kə'læps/ n derrumbamiento, m; desplome, m; Med. colapso, m; (of buildings and Fig.) hundimiento, m; (of plans) frustración, f; (failure) fracaso, m. —vi derrumbarse; (of buildings, etc.) hundirse, venirse abajo; (of persons, fall) desplomarse; Med. sufrir colapso; (of plans, etc.) frustrarse, venirse abajo. **George came to us after the c. of France,** Jorge vino a quedarse con nosotros después del hundimiento de Francia

**collapsible** /kə'læpsəbəl/ a plegable

**collar** /'kɒlər/ n (of a garment and of fur) cuello, m; (of a dog, etc., and necklace) collar, m. —vt (seize) agarrar. **detachable c.,** cuello suelto, m. **high c.,** alzacuello, m. **c.-bone,** clavícula, f

**collate** /kou'leɪt/ vt cotejar; (to a benefice) colacionar

**collateral** /kə'lætərəl/ a colateral

**collation** /kə'leɪʃən/ n colación, f

**colleague** /'kɒlig/ n colega, m; compañero (-ra)

**collect** /'kɒlɛkt/ vt (assemble) reunir; (catch) coger; acumular; (call for) pasar a buscar, ir (or venir) a buscar; (pick up) recoger; (taxes, etc.) recaudar; coleccionar; (one's strength, etc. and debts, etc.) cobrar; (letters) recoger. —vi reunirse, congregarse; acumularse. —n Eccl. colecta, f. **to c. oneself,** reponerse

**collected** /kə'lɛktɪd/ a (of persons) seguro de sí.

**collection** /kə'lɛkʃən/ n reunión, f; (of data, etc.) acumulación, f; (of pictures, stamps, etc.) colección, f; (of a debt, etc.) cobranza, f; (of taxes, etc.) recaudación, f; (from a mail box) recogida, f; (of laws, etc.) compilación, f; Eccl. ofertorio, m; (of donations) colecta, f

**collection agency** n agencia de cobros de cuentas, f

**collective** /kə'lɛktɪv/ a colectivo. **c. bargaining,** regateo colectivo, trato colectivo, m

**collectivism** /kə'lɛktə,vɪzəm/ n colectivismo, m

**collector** /kə'lɛktər/ n (of pictures, etc.) coleccionador (-ra), coleccionista, mf; cobrador, m; Elec. colector, m

**college** /'kɒlɪdʒ/ n colegio, m; escuela, f; universidad, f. **C. of Cardinals,** Colegio de Cardenales, m

**collegiate** /kə'lidʒɪt/ a colegial, colegiado. **c. church,** iglesia colegial, f

**collide** /kə'laɪd/ vi chocar (contra), topar (con); estar en conflicto (con). **c. head-on,** chocar frontalmente

**collie** /'kɒli/ n perro de pastor escocés, m

**collier** /'kɒlyər/ n minero de carbón, m; (barco) carbonero, m

**collision** /kə'lɪʒən/ n choque, m, colisión, f; (of interests, etc.) antagonismo, conflicto, m. **to come into c. with,** chocar con

**colloid** /'kɒlɔɪd/ a coloide. —n coloide, m

**colloquial** /kə'loukwiəl/ a familiar

**colloquialism** /kə'loukwiə,lɪzəm/ n expresión familiar, f

**colloquially** /kə'loukwiəli/ adv en lenguaje familiar; familiarmente

**colloquy** /'kɒləkwi/ n coloquio, m

**collusion** /kə'luʒən/ n colusión, f. **to be in c.,** Law. coludir; conspirar, estar de manga

**Cologne** /kə'loun/ Colonia, f

**Colombia** /kə'lʌmbiə/ Colombia, f

**Colombian** /kə'lʌmbiən/ a colombiano. —n colombiano (-na)

**colon** /'koulən/ n Anat. colon, m; (punctuation) dos puntos, m pl

**colonel** /'kɜrnl/ n coronel, m

**colonial** /kə'louniəl/ a colonial. —n habitante de las colonias, m. **C. Office,** Ministerio de Asuntos Coloniales, m

**colonist** /'kɒlənɪst/ n colono, m; colonizador (-ra)

**colonization** /,kɒlənə'zeɪʃən/ n colonización, f

**colonize** /'kɒlə,naɪz/ vt colonizar. —vi establecerse en una colonia

**colonizer** /'kɒlə,naɪzər/ n colonizador (-ra)

**colonizing** /'kɒlə,naɪzɪŋ/ n colonización, f, a colonizador

**colonnade** /,kɒlə'neɪd/ n columnata, f

**colony** /'kɒləni/ n colonia, f

**color** /'kʌlər/ n color, m; colorido, m; tinta, f; materia colorante, f; pl **colors,** insignia, f; bandera, f, estandarte, m; Naut. pabellón, m. —vt colorar; pintar; iluminar; (influence) influir, afectar. —vi colorarse; ruborizarse; encenderse. **fast c.,** color estable, color sólido, m. **regimental colors,** bandera del regimiento, f. **with colors flying,** con tambor batiente, a banderas desplegadas. **to be off c.,** estar malucho, estar indispuesto. **to change c.,** (of persons) mudar de color, mudar de semblante. **to give c. to,** (a story, etc.) hacer verosímil. **to lay the colors on too thick,** recargar las tintas. **to pass with flying colors,** salir triunfante. **under c. of,** so color de, a pretexto de. **c.-blind,** daltoniano. **c.-blindness,** daltonismo, m

**Colorado beetle** /,kɒlə'radou/ n escarabajo de la patata, m

**colored** /'kʌlərd/ a colorado; de color

**colorimeter** /,kʌlə'rɪmɪtər/ n colorímetro, m

**coloring** /'kʌlərɪŋ/ n (substance) colorante, m; (act of) coloración, f; Art. colorido, m; (of complexion) colores, m pl

**colorist** /'kʌlərɪst/ n colorista, mf

**colorless** /'kʌlərlɪs/ a sin color, incoloro; Fig. insípido

**colossal** /kə'lɒsəl/ a colosal, gigantesco; enorme; Inf. estupendo

**colossus** /kə'lɒsəs/ n coloso, m

**colt** /koult/ n potro, m; (boy) muchacho alegre, m

**colter** /'koultər/ n reja, reja del arado, f

**colt's-foot** n Bot. fárfara, f

**columbine** /'kɒləm,baɪn/ n Bot. aguileña, f; (in pantomime) Colombina, f

**column** /'kɒləm/ n columna, f. **Fifth c.,** quinta columna, f

**columned** /'kɒləmd/ a con columnas

**columnist** /'kɒləmnɪst/ n periodista, m

**coma** /'koumə/ n coma, m

**comatose** /'koumə,tous/ a comatoso

**comb** /koum/ n peine, m; (for flax) carda, f; (curry) almohaza, f; (of cock) cresta, carúncula, f; (of a wave) cima, cresta, f; (honey) panal, m, vt (hair) peinar; (flax) rastrillar, cardar. **c. and brush,** cepillo y peine. **high c.,** peineta, f. **to c. one's hair,** peinarse

**combat** /v kəm'bæt; n 'kɒmbæt/ vt luchar contra, combatir, resistir. —vi combatir, pelear. —n combate, m; lucha, batalla, f. **in single c.,** cuerpo a cuerpo

**combatant** /kəm'bætn̩t/ n combatiente, m, a combatiente

**combative** /kəm'bætɪv/ a belicoso, pugnaz

**combination** /ˌkɒmbə'neɪʃən/ n combinación, f; mezcla, f; unión, f; asociación, f; pl **combinations.** camisa pantalón, f. **c. lock,** cerradura de combinación, f

**combine** / v kəm'baɪn; n 'kɒmbaɪn/ vt combinar; reunir, juntar; Chem. combinar. —vi combinarse; asociarse (con); Com. fusionarse. —n asociación, f; Com. monopolio, m

**combings** /'koumɪŋz/ n pl peinaduras, f pl

**combustible** /kəm'bʌstəbəl/ a combustible. —n combustible, m

**combustion** /kəm'bʌstʃən/ n combustión, f. **rapid c.,** combustión rápida, f. **spontaneous c.,** combustión espontánea, f

**come** /kʌm/ vi venir; llegar; avanzar; acercarse: (happen) suceder, acontecer; (result) resultar; (find oneself) encontrarse, hallarse; (become) llegar a ser; (begin to) ponerse (a), empezar (a). **Coming!** ¡Voy! ¡Allá voy! **C., c.!** ¡Vamos! ¡No es para tanto! ¡Ánimo! **I am ready whatever comes,** Estoy preparado venga lo que venga. **He comes of a good family,** Es (Viene) de buena familia. **I came to know him well,** Llegué a conocerle bien. **I don't know what came over me,** No sé lo que me pasó. **When I came to consider it,** Cuando me puse a considerarlo. **The bill comes to six thousand pesetas,** La cuenta sale a seis mil pesetas. **He comes up before the judge tomorrow,** Ha de comparecer ante el juez mañana. **What you say comes to this,** Lo que dice Vd. se reduce a esto. **What is the world coming to?** ¿A dónde va parar el mundo? **It does not c. within my scope,** No está dentro de mi alcance. **to c. apart,** deshacerse; romperse; dividirse. **to c. home to,** Fig. impresionar mucho, tocar en lo más íntimo; hacer comprender (a). **to c. into bloom,** empezar a tener flores, florecer. **to c. into one's head,** venir a las mientes. **to c. into the world,** venir al mundo. **to c. near,** acercarse; aproximarse, estar próximo. **to c. next,** venir después; suceder luego. **to c. to an end,** terminar, acabarse. **to c. to blows,** venir a las manos. **to c. to grief,** salir mal parado; (of schemes, etc.) malograrse. **to c. to hand,** venir a mano; (of letters) llegar a las manos (de). **to c. to life,** despertar; animarse; resucitarse. **to c. to nothing,** frustrarse; no quedar en nada. **to c. to pass,** suceder; realizarse. **to c. to terms,** ponerse de acuerdo. **to c. to true,** cumplirse, verificarse. **to c. about,** suceder, acontecer, tener lugar; (of the wind) girar. **to c. across,** dar con, encontrar por casualidad; tropezar con. **to c. after,** (a situation) solicitar; (follow) seguir (a); venir más tarde (que); (succeed) suceder. **to c. again,** volver. **to c. along,** (come por); andar (por); (arrive) llegar. **C. along!** ¡Ven! ¡Vamos! ¡Andamos! **to c. at,** alcanzar; (attack) embestir, atacar; (gain) obtener, adquirir. **to c. away,** irse, marcharse; (break) deshacerse. **to c. back,** volver. **c.-back,** n Inf. respuesta, f; contraataque, m. **to c. before,** llegar antes; preceder (a). **to c. between,** interponerse (entre), intervenir. **to c. by,** pasar por, pasar junto a; (acquire) obtener, adquirir; (achieve) conseguir. **to c. down,** bajar, descender; (in the world) venir a menos; (be demolished) demolerse; (collapse) derrumbarse, hundirse; (of prices) bajar; (of traditions, etc.) llegar e.g. This work has c. down to us in two fifteenth-century manuscripts Esta obra nos ha llegado en dos manuscritos del siglo quince; (fall) caer. **c.-down,** n caída, f; frustración, f; desengaño, m; despristigio, m; pérdida de posición, f. **to c. down on a person,** cantar la cartilla (a). **to c. forward,** avanzar, adelantarse; (offer) ofrecerse; presentarse. **to c. in,** entrar; (of money) ingresar; (of trains, etc.) llegar; (of the tide) crecer; (of the new year) empezar; (of fashion) ponerse de moda; (be useful) servir (para). **C. in!** ¡Adelante! ¡Pase Vd.! **to c. into,** (a scheme) asociarse con; (property) heredar; (the mind) presentarse a la imaginación, ocurrirse (a). **to c. off,** (happen) tener lugar; realizarse, efectuarse; (be successful) tener éxito; (break off) separarse (de); romperse. **to c. off well,** tener éxito; (of persons) salir bien. **c. off the press,** salir de prensas. **to c. on,** avanzar; (of actors) salir a la escena; (progress) hacer progresos; (develop) desarrollarse; (of pain, etc.) acometer (a); (arrive) llegar; (of a lawsuit) verse. **C. on!** ¡Vamos! ¡En marcha! **to c. out,** salir; (of stars) nacer; (of buds, etc.) brotar; (of the moon, etc.) asomarse; (of stains) borrarse, salir; (of a book) ver la luz, publicarse; (of secrets) divulgarse, saberse; (of a girl, in society) ponerse de largo; (on strike) declararse en huelga; (of fashions, etc.) aparecer. **to c. out with,** (a remark) soltar; (oaths, etc.) prorrumpir (en); (disclose) revelar, hacer público. **to c. round,** (to see someone) venir a ver (a); (coax) engatusar; (after a faint, etc.) volver en sí; (after illness) reponerse; (to another's point of view) aceptar, compartir. **to c. through,** pasar por; (trials, etc.) subir; salir de; (of liquids) salirse. **to c. to,** volver en sí. **to c. together,** reunirse, juntarse; venir juntos; unirse. **to c. under,** venir (or estar) bajo la jurisdicción de; (the influence of) estar dominado por; (figure among) figurar entre, estar comprendido en. **to c. up,** subir; (of sun, moon) salir; (of plants) brotar; (of problems, etc.) surgir; (in conversation) discutirse; (before a court) comparecer. **to c. up to,** (equal) igualar, ser igual (a); rivalizar con; (in height) llegar hasta. **He came up to them in the street,** Les abordó (or se les acercó) en la calle. **We have c. up against many difficulties,** Hemos tropezado con muchas dificultades. **This novel does not c. up to his last,** Esta última novela no es tan buena como la anterior. **The party did not c. up to their expectations,** La reunión no fue tan divertida como esperaban. **to c. up with,** (a person) alcanzar (a). **to c. upon,** encontrar, hallar; tropezar con; encontrar por casualidad. **to c. upon evil days,** venir a menos

**comedian** /kə'midiən/ n actor cómico, comediante, m

**comedy** /'kɒmɪdi/ n comedia, f. **c. of manners,** comedia de costumbres, f

**comeliness** /'kʌmlɪnɪs/ n hermosura, f

**comely** /'kʌmli/ a hermoso

**comer** /'kʌmər/ n el, m, (f, la) que viene. **all comers,** todo el mundo. **first c.,** primer (-ra) venido (-da)

**comet** /'kɒmɪt/ n cometa, m

**comfort** /'kʌmfərt/ vt consolar, confortar; (encourage) animar; (reassure) alegrar. —n consuelo, m; satisfacción, f; comodidad, f; bienestar, m. **He lives in great c.,** Vive con mucha comodidad. **c.-loving,** comodón

**comfortable** /'kʌmftəbəl/ a cómodo; (with income) suficiente; (consoling) consolador. **to make oneself c.,** ponerse cómodo

**comfortably** /'kʌmftəbli/ adv cómodamente; suficientemente; fácilmente; con facilidad; (well) bien. **He is c. off,** Está bien de dinero

**comforter** /'kʌmfərtər/ n consolador (-ra); (baby's) chupador, m; (scarf) bufanda, f

**comforting** /'kʌmfərtɪŋ/ a consolador

**comfortless** /'kʌmfərtlɪs/ a incómodo, sin comodidad; desconsolado; (of persons) inconsolable, desconsolado

**comic** /'kɒmɪk/ a cómico; bufo; satírico. —n cómico, m; pl **comics,** (printed) historietas cómicas, f pl. **c. opera,** ópera cómica, f. **c. paper,** periódico satírico, m

**comical** /'kɒmɪkəl/ a cómico; divertido, gracioso

**coming** /'kʌmɪŋ/ a (with year, etc.) próximo, que viene; (promising) de porvenir; (approaching) que se acerca. —n venida, f; llegada, f; advenimiento, m. **c.-out party,** puesta de largo, f. **comings and goings,** entradas y salidas, f pl

**comma** /'kɒmə/ n coma, f. **inverted commas,** comillas, f pl

**command** /kə'mænd/ vt mandar, ordenar; (silence, respect, etc.) imponer; (an army, fleet, etc.) comandar; capitanear; (one's emotions) dominar; (have at one's disposal) disponer de; (a military position, view) dominar; (sympathy, etc.) despertar, merecer; (of price) venderse por. —vi mandar. —n orden, f; (Mil. Nav.) mando, m; (of an army, etc.) comandancia, f; (of one's emotions, etc.) dominio, m; (of a military position, etc.) dominación, f; disposición, f. **By Royal C.,** Por Real Orden; (of shops, etc.) Proveedor de la Real Casa. **The house commands lovely views of the mountains,** La casa tiene hermosas vistas de las montañas. **word of c.,** orden, f. **Yours to c.,** A la disposición de Vd.

**commandant** /ˌkɒmənˈdænt/ n comandante, m

**commandeer** /ˌkɒmənˈdɪər/ vt (conscript) reclutar; Mil. requisar; expropiar

**commander** /kəˈmændər/ n Mil. comandante, m; Nav. capitán de fragata, m; (of order of Knighthood) comendador, m. **c.-in-chief,** generalísimo, m. **C. of the Faithful,** Comendador de los creyentes, m

**commanding** /kəˈmændɪŋ/ a Mil. comandante; imponente; (of manner) imperioso; dominante. **c. officer,** comandante en jefe, m

**commandment** /kəˈmændmənt/ n precepto, mandamiento, m. **the Ten Commandments,** los diez mandamientos

**commando** /kəˈmændou/ n Mil. comando, m

**commemorate** /kəˈmɛməˌreit/ vt conmemorar

**commemoration** /kəˌmɛməˈreiʃən/ n conmemoración, f

**commemorative** /kəˈmɛməˌreitɪv/ a conmemorativo

**commence** /kəˈmɛns/ vt comenzar, empezar, principiar. —vi comenzar. **He commenced to eat,** Empezó a comer

**commencement** /kəˈmɛnsmənt/ n principio, comienzo, m

**commend** /kəˈmɛnd/ vt (entrust) encomendar; recomendar; alabar

**commendable** /kəˈmɛndəbəl/ a loable; recomendable

**commendation** /ˌkɒmənˈdeiʃən/ n aprobación, alabanza, f, aplauso, m

**commendatory** /kəˈmɛndəˌtɔri/ a (of letters) comendatorio

**commensurable** /kəˈmɛnsərəbəl/ a conmensurable

**commensurate** /kəˈmɛnsərɪt/ a proporcionado (a); conforme (a)

**comment** /ˈkɒmɛnt/ n observación, f; (on a work) comento, m; explicación, nota, f. —vi hacer una observación (sobre); (a work) comentar, anotar. **to c. unfavorably on,** criticar

**commentary** /ˈkɒmənˌtɛri/ n comentario, m; (on a person, etc.) comentos, m pl, observaciones, f pl

**commentator** /ˈkɒmənˌteitər/ n comentador (-ra); (of a work) comentarista, mf

**commerce** /ˈkɒmərs/ n comercio, m; negocios, m pl; (social) trato, m

**commercial** /kəˈmɜrʃəl/ a comercial; mercantil. **c. traveler,** viajante, mf

**commercialism** /kəˈmɜrʃəˌlɪzəm/ n mercantilismo, m

**commercialize** /kəˈmɜrʃəˌlaiz/ vt hacer objeto de comercio

**commercially** /kəˈmɜrʃəli/ adv comercialmente

**commingle** /kəˈmɪŋgəl/ vt mezclar. —vi mezclarse

**commiserate** /kəˈmɪzəˌreit/ vi compadecerse (de), apiadarse (de)

**commiseration** /kəˌmɪzəˈreiʃən/ n conmiseración, compasión, f

**commissariat** /ˌkɒməˈsɛəriət/ n comisaría, f; Inf. despensa, f

**commissary** /ˈkɒməˌsɛri/ n comisario, m

**commission** /kəˈmɪʃən/ n comisión, f; Mil. graduación de oficial, f. —vt comisionar; (a ship) poner en servicio activo, armar; (appoint) nombrar. **in c.,** en servicio, activo. **out of c.,** (of ships) inutilizado; inservible. **c. agent,** comisionista, mf **to gain one's c.,** Mil. graduarse de oficial. **to put out of c.,** retirar del servicio; poner fuera de combate; estropear

**commissionaire** /kəˌmɪʃəˈnɛər/ n portero, m

**commissioned** /kəˈmɪʃənd/ a comisionado. **c. officer,** oficial, m

**commissioner** /kəˈmɪʃənər/ n comisario, m. **High C.,** alto comisario, m. **c. for oaths,** notario, m. **c. of police,** jefe de policía, m

**commit** /kəˈmɪt/ vt entregar (a); (a crime) cometer; (to prison) encarcelar; (for trial) remitir. **to c. oneself,** comprometerse. **to c. to memory,** aprender de memoria. **to c. to writing,** poner por escrito

**commitment** /kəˈmɪtmənt/ n (financial, etc.) obligación, responsabilidad, f; compromiso, m

**committal** /kəˈmɪtl/ n (of an offence) comisión, f;

(placing, entrusting) entrega, f; (to prison) encarcelamiento, m; (legal procedure) auto de prisión, m

**committee** /kəˈmɪti/ n comité, m; comisión, junta, f; consejo, m. **They decided in c.,** Tomaron la resolución en comité. **c. of management,** consejo de administración, m

**commodious** /kəˈmoudiəs/ a espacioso, grande

**commodiousness** /kəˈmoudiəsnɪs/ n espaciosidad, f

**commodity** /kəˈmɒdɪti/ n artículo, m, mercancía, f

**commodore** /ˈkɒməˌdɔr/ n Nav. jefe de escuadra, m; comodoro, m

**common** /ˈkɒmən/ a común; general, corriente; universal; vulgar; (disparaging) cursi; (elementary) elemental. —n pastos comunes, m pl. **He is not a c. man,** No es un hombre cualquiera; No es un hombre vulgar. **in c.,** en común. **the c. man,** el hombre medio. **the c. people,** el pueblo. **c. sense,** sentido común, m. **c. soldier,** soldado raso, m. **c. speech,** lenguaje vulgar, m. **c. usage,** uso corriente, m

**commoner** /ˈkɒmənər/ n plebeyo (-ya)

**commonly** /ˈkɒmənli/ adv comúnmente, por lo general

**commonness** /ˈkɒmənnɪs/ n frecuencia, f; vulgaridad, f

**commonplace** /ˈkɒmənˌpleis/ n lugar común, m; trivialidad, f. —a trivial

**commons** /ˈkɒmənz/ n el pueblo; (House of) Cámara de los Comunes, f; (food) provisiones, f pl. **to be on short c.,** comer mal, estar mal alimentado

**Commonwealth** /ˈkɒmənˌwɛlθ/ n estado, m; república, f; comunidad (de naciones), f; mancomunidad, f. **the Commonwealth of Puerto Rico,** el Estado Libre Asociado de Puerto Rico, m

**commotion** /kəˈmouʃən/ n confusión, f; conmoción, perturbación, f; tumulto, m

**communal** /kəˈmyunl/ a comunal

**commune** /ˈkɒmyun/ n comuna, f; comunión, f, vi conversar (con). **to c. with oneself,** hablar consigo

**communicable** /kəˈmyunɪkəbəl/ a comunicable

**communicant** /kəˈmyunɪkənt/ n Eccl. comulgante, mf; (of information) informante, mf

**communicate** /kəˈmyunɪˌkeit/ vt comunicar; (diseases) transmitir. —vi comunicarse (con); Eccl. comulgar

**communication** /kəˌmyunɪˈkeiʃən/ n comunicación, f. **lines of c.,** comunicaciones, f pl. **to get into c. with,** ponerse en comunicación con. **c.-cord,** (in a railway carriage) timbre de alarma, m

**communicative** /kəˈmyunɪˌkeitɪv/ a comunicativo; expansivo

**communicativeness** /kəˈmyunɪˌkeitɪvnɪs/ n carácter expansivo, m; locuacidad, f

**communion** /kəˈmyunyən/ n comunión, f. **Holy c.,** comunión, f. **to take c.,** comulgar. **c. card,** cédula de comunión, f. **c. cup,** cáliz, f. **c. table,** sagrada mesa, f; altar, m

**communiqué** /kəˌmyunɪˈkei/ n comunicación, parte, f. **to issue a c.,** dar parte

**communism** /ˈkɒmyəˌnɪzəm/ n comunismo, m

**communist** /ˈkɒmyənɪst/ n comunista, mf a comunista

**community** /kəˈmyunɪti/ n comunidad, f. **the c.,** la nación; el público. **c. center,** centro social, m

**commutation** /ˌkɒmyəˈteiʃən/ n conmutación, f; reducción, f

**commute** /kəˈmyut/ vt conmutar; reducir

**compact** / n ˈkɒmpækt/ v kəmˈpækt/ n (pact) acuerdo, pacto, m; (powder) polvorera, f. —a compacto; firme; sólido; apretado, cerrado; (of persons) bien hecho; (of style) conciso, sucinto

**compact disc** /ˈkɒmpækt ˈdɪsk/ n disco compacto, m

**compactness** /kəmˈpæktnɪs/ n compacidad, f; (of style) concisión, f

**companion** /kəmˈpænyən/ n compañero (-ra); camarada, mf; (of an Order) caballero, m, (or dama, f). —vt acompañar. **lady c.,** señora de compañía, f. **c.-hatch,** cubierta de escotilla, f. **c.-ladder,** escala de toldilla, f

**companionable** /kəmˈpænyənəbəl/ a sociable, amistoso

**companionably** /kəmˈpænyənəbli/ adv sociablemente, amistosamente

**companionship** /kəm'pænyən,ʃɪp/ n compañía, f; compañerismo, m

**company** /'kʌmpəni/ n (Com. Mil. etc.) compañía, f; (ship's) tripulación, f. **I will keep you c.,** Te haré compañía. **to part c. with,** separarse de. **Present c. excepted!** ¡Mejorando lo presente! **They are not very good c.,** No son muy divertidos

**company store** n tienda de raya, f (Mexico)

**comparable** /'kɒmpərəbəl/ a comparable

**comparably** /'kɒmpərəbli/ adv comparablemente

**comparative** /kəm'pærətɪv/ a comparativo; relativo

**comparatively** /kəm'pærətɪvli/ adv comparativamente; relativamente

**compare** /kəm'pɛər/ vt comparar. —vi compararse; poder compararse. **beyond c.,** sin comparación; sin igual. **to c. favorably with,** no perder por comparación con. **to c. notes,** cambiar impresiones

**comparison** /kəm'pærəsən/ n comparación, f. **in c. with,** comparado con

**compartment** /kəm'pɑrtmənt/ n compartimiento, m; Rail. departamento, m

**compass** /'kʌmpəs/ n circuito, m; límites, m pl; alcance, m; (of a voice) gama, f; Naut. brújula, f; pl **compasses,** compás, m. —vt (achieve) conseguir; (plan) idear, **mariner's c.,** compás de mar. m, rosa de los vientos, f. **pocket c.,** brújula de bolsillo, f. **to c. about,** cercar, rodear

**compassion** /kəm'pæʃən/ n compasión, f. **to have c. on,** apiadarse de, compadecerse de

**compassionate** /kəm'pæʃənɪt/ a compasivo, piadoso. **c. leave,** permiso, m

**compassionately** /kəm'pæʃənɪtli/ adv compasivamente, con piedad

**compatibility** /kəm,pætə'bɪlɪti/ n compatibilidad, f

**compatible** /kəm'pætəbəl/ a compatible, conciliable

**compatriot** /kəm'peɪtriət/ n compatriota, mf

**compel** /kəm'pɛl/ vt obligar (a), forzar (a); exigir; imponer. **His attitude compels respect,** Su actitud impone el respeto

**compelling** /kəm'pɛlɪŋ/ a compulsivo

**compendious** /kəm'pɛndiəs/ a compendioso, sucinto

**compendium** /kəm'pɛndiəm/ n compendio, m; resumen, m

**compensate** /'kɒmpən,seɪt/ vt compensar; (reward) recompensar; (for loss, etc.) indemnizar. **to c. for,** compensar; indemnizar contra

**compensation** /,kɒmpən'seɪʃən/ n compensación, f; (reward) recompensa, f; (for loss, etc.) indemnización, f

**compensatory** /kəm'pɛnsə,tɔri/ a compensatorio

**compete** /kəm'pit/ vi competir (con); rivalizar; ser rivales; (in a competition) concurrir

**competence** /'kɒmpɪtəns/ n aptitud, f; capacidad, f; competencia, f

**competent** /'kɒmpɪtənt/ a competente; capaz

**competently** /'kɒmpɪtəntli/ adv competentemente

**competition** /,kɒmpɪ'tɪʃən/ n competencia, competición, rivalidad, f; emulación, f; (contest, etc.) concurso, m. **spirit of c.,** espíritu de competencia, m

**competitive** /kəm'pɛtɪtɪv/ a competidor; de competición. **c. examination,** oposición, f

**competitor** /kəm'pɛtɪtər/ n competidor (-ra)

**compilation** /,kɒmpə'leɪʃən/ n compilación, f

**compile** /kəm'paɪl/ vt compilar

**compiler** /kəm'paɪlər/ n compilador (-ra)

**complacence** /kəm'pleɪsəns/ n complacencia, satisfacción, f; contento de sí mismo, m

**complacent** /kəm'pleɪsənt/ a satisfecho; pagado de sí mismo

**complacently** /kəm'pleɪsəntli/ adv con satisfacción

**complain** /kəm'pleɪn/ vi quejarse; lamentarse; Law. querellarse. **He complains about everything,** Se queja de todo

**complainant** /kəm'pleɪnənt/ n Law. demandante, mf

**complaint** /kəm'pleɪnt/ n queja, f; lamento, m; Law. demanda, f; (illness) enfermedad, f. **to lodge a c. (against),** quejarse (de)

**complaisance** /kəm'pleɪsəns/ n afabilidad, cortesía, f

**complaisant** /kəm'pleɪsənt/ a complaciente, cortés, afable; (of husbands) consentido, sufrido

**complement** / n 'kɒmpləmənt; v -,mɛnt/ n complemento, m; total, número completo, m. —vt completar

**complementary** /,kɒmplə'mɛntəri/ a complementario

**complete** /kəm'plit/ a entero; completo; perfecto; acabado. —vt completar; acabar; (happiness, etc.) coronar, poner el último toque (a); (years) cumplir; (forms) llenar

**completely** /kəm'plitli/ adv completamente, enteramente

**completeness** /kəm'plitnɪs/ n entereza, f; totalidad, f; terminación, f, fin, m

**completion** /kəm'pliʃən/ n terminación, f, fin, m

**complex** / a kəm'plɛks; n 'kɒmplɛks/ a complejo. —n complejo, m. **inferiority c.,** complejo de inferioridad, m

**complexion** /kəm'plɛkʃən/ n tez, f, cutis, m; Fig. carácter, m

**complexity** /kəm'plɛksɪti/ n complejidad, f

**compliance** /kəm'plaɪəns/ n condescendencia, f; (subservience) sumisión, f; obediencia, f. **in c. with,** de acuerdo con, en conformidad con

**compliant** /kəm'plaɪənt/ a condescendiente; sumiso, dócil; obediente

**complicate** /'kɒmplɪ,keɪt/ vt complicar

**complicated** /'kɒmplɪ,keɪtɪd/ a complejo; complicado; enredado

**complication** /,kɒmplɪ'keɪʃən/ n complicación, f

**complicity** /kəm'plɪsɪti/ n complicidad, f. **c. in a crime,** complicidad en un crimen

**compliment** / n 'kɒmpləmənt; v -,mɛnt/ n cumplido, m, cortesía, f; requiebro, Inf. piropo, m; favor, m; honor, m; (greeting) saludo, m; (congratulation) felicitación, f. —vt cumplimentar; requebrar; (flatter) adular, lisonjear; (congratulate) felicitar. **They did him the c. of reading his book,** Le hicieron el honor de leer su libro. **to pay compliments,** hacer cumplidos; Inf. echar piropos

**complimentary** /,kɒmplə'mɛntəri/ a lisonjero; galante. **c. ticket,** billete gratuito, m

**comply** /kəm'plaɪ/ vi (with) cumplir, obedecer; conformarse (con); consentir

**component** /kəm'pounənt/ a componente. —n componente, m

**comport** /kəm'pɔrt/ vt (oneself), comportarse

**comportment** /kəm'pɔrtmənt/ n comportamiento, m, conducta, f

**compose** /kəm'pouz/ vt (all meanings) componer. **to c. oneself,** serenarse, calmarse. **to c. one's features,** componer el semblante

**composed** /kəm'pouzd/ a sereno, tranquilo, sosegado

**composer** /kəm'pouzər/ n compositor (-ra)

**composite** /kəm'pɒzɪt/ a compuesto; mixto. —n compuesto, m; Bot. planta compuesta, f

**composition** /,kɒmpə'zɪʃən/ n (all meanings) composición, f

**compositor** /kəm'pɒzɪtər/ n Print. cajista, mf

**composure** /kəm'pouʒər/ n tranquilidad, serenidad, calma, f; sangre fría, f, aplomo, m

**compote** /'kɒmpout/ n compota, f

**compound** /kəm'paʊnd/ vt mezclar, componer; concertar. —a compuesto. —n compuesto, m; mixtura, f. **c. interest,** interés compuesto, m

**comprehend** /,kɒmprɪ'hɛnd/ vt comprender

**comprehensible** /,kɒmprɪ'hɛnsəbəl/ a comprensible

**comprehensibly** /,kɒmprɪ'hɛnsəbli/ adv comprensiblemente

**comprehension** /,kɒmprɪ'hɛnʃən/ n comprensión, f

**comprehensive** /,kɒmprɪ'hɛnsɪv/ a comprensivo

**comprehensiveness** /,kɒmprɪ'hɛnsɪvnɪs/ n alcance, m, extensión, f

**compress** / v kəm'prɛs; n 'kɒmprɛs/ vt comprimir; condensar; reducir, abreviar. —n compresa, f

**compression** /kəm'prɛʃən/ n compresión, f

**compressor** /kəm'prɛsər/ n compresor, m

**comprise** /kəm'praɪz/ vt comprender, abarcar, incluir

**compromise** /'kɒmprə,maɪz/ n compromiso, m, transacción, f; componenda, f. —vt (settle) componer, arreglar; (jeopardize) arriesgar; comprometer. —vi transigir. **to c. oneself,** comprometerse

**compromising** /'kɒmprə,maɪzɪŋ/ a comprometedor

**compulsion** /kəm'pʌlʃən/ n compulsión, fuerza, f. **under c.,** a la fuerza

**compulsory** /kəm'pʌlsəri/ a obligatorio. **c. measures,** medidas obligatorias, f pl. **c. powers,** poderes absolutos, m pl

**compunction** /kəm'pʌŋkʃən/ n compunción, f, remordimiento, m; escrúpulo, m. **without c.,** sin escrúpulo

**computable** /kəm'pyutəbəl/ a calculable

**computation** /ˌkɒmpyu'teiʃən/ n computación, f, cómputo, m

**compute** /kəm'pyut/ vt computar, calcular.

**computer** /kəm'pyutər/ m computador, m (Western Hemisphere), ordenador, m (Spain)

**computer center** n centro calculador, centro de computación, m

**comrade** /'kɒmræd/ n camarada, mf compañero (-ra)

**comradeship** /'kɒmrædˌʃip/ n compañerismo, m

**con** /kɒn/ vt estudiar; leer con atención; Naut. gobernar (el buque)

**concatenation** /kɒnˌkætn'eiʃən/ n concatenación, f

**concave** /kɒn'keiv/ a cóncavo

**conceal** /kən'sil/ vt esconder, ocultar; (the truth, etc.) encubrir, callar; disimular

**concealed** /kən'sild/ a oculto; escondido; disimulado. **c. lighting,** iluminación indirecta, f. **c. turning,** (on a road) viraje oculto, m

**concealment** /kən'silmənt/ n ocultación, f; encubrimiento, m; (place of) escondite, m; secreto, m

**concede** /kən'sid/ vt conceder

**conceit** /kən'sit/ n presunción, vanidad, fatuidad, f, envanecimiento, m. **to have a good c. of oneself,** estar pagado de sí mismo

**conceited** /kən'sitid/ a presumido, fatuo, vanidoso

**conceivable** /kən'sivəbəl/ a concebible, imaginable

**conceivably** /kən'sivəbli/ adv posiblemente

**conceive** /kən'siv/ vt concebir; (affection, etc.) tomar; (an idea, etc.) formar; (plan) formular, idear. —vi concebir; (understand) comprender; (suppose) imaginar, suponer

**concentrate** /'kɒnsən,treit/ vt concentrar. —vi concentrarse; (on, upon) dedicarse (a), entregarse (a); prestar atención (a), concentrar atención (en)

**concentrated** /'kɒnsən,treitid/ a concentrado

**concentration** /ˌkɒnsən'treiʃən/ n concentración, f. **c. camp,** campo de concentración, m

**concentric** /kən'sɛntrɪk/ a concéntrico

**concept** /'kɒnsɛpt/ n concepto, m

**conception** /kən'sɛpʃən/ n concepción, f; conocimiento, m; idea, f, concepto, m. **to have not the remotest c. of,** no tener la menor idea de

**conceptualism** /kən'sɛptʃuə,lizəm/ n conceptualismo, m

**concern** /kən'sɜrn/ vt tocar, tener que vercon, importar, concernir; interesar; referirse (a); tratar (de); (trouble) preocupar, inquietar; (take part in) ocuparse (de or con). —n asunto, m, cosa, f; (share) interés, m; (anxiety) inquietud, f; solicitud, f; (business) casa comercial, firma, f. **as concerns...,** en cuanto a..., respecto a... **It concerns the date of the next meeting,** Es cuestión de la fecha de la próxima reunión. **It is no c. of yours,** No tiene nada que ver contigo. **The book is concerned with the adventures of two boys,** El libro trata de las aventuras de dos muchachos

**concerned** /kən'sɜrnd/ a ocupado (en); afectado; (in a crime) implicado (en); (troubled) preocupado; inquieto, agitado

**concerning** /kən'sɜrnɪŋ/ prep tocante a, con respecto a, referente a, sobre

**concert** /'kɒnsərt/ n acuerdo, concierto, m, armonía, f; Mus. concierto, m, vt concertar, acordar. **in c. with,** de acuerdo con. **c. hall,** sala de conciertos, f

**concerted** /kən'sɜrtɪd/ a concertado

**concertina** /ˌkɒnsər'tinə/ n concertina, f

**concerto** /kən'tʃɛrtou/ n concierto, m

**concession** /kən'sɛʃən/ n concesión, f; privilegio, m

**concessionaire** /kənˌsɛʃə'nɛər/ n concesionario, m

**concierge** /ˌkɒnsi'ɛərʒ/ n conserje, m

**conciliate** /kən'sɪli,eit/ vt conciliar

**conciliation** /kənˌsɪli'eiʃən/ n conciliación, f

**conciliatory** /kən'sɪliə,tɔri/ a conciliador

**concise** /kən'sais/ a conciso, breve, sucinto

**concisely** /kən'saisli/ adv concisamente

**concision** /kən'sɪʒən/ n concisión, f

**conclave** /'kɒnkleiv/ n conciliábulo, m; (of cardinals) conclave, m

**conclude** /kən'klud/ vt concluir. —vi concluirse

**conclusion** /kən'kluʒən/ n conclusión, f. **in c.,** en conclusión, para terminar. **to come to the c. that...,** concluir que...

**conclusive** /kən'klusɪv/ a conclusivo, concluyente, decisivo

**conclusively** /kən'klusɪvli/ adv concluyentemente

**conclusiveness** /kən'klusɪvnɪs/ n carácter decisivo, m, lo concluyente

**concoct** /kɒn'kɒkt/ vt confeccionar; inventar

**concoction** /kɒn'kɒkʃən/ n confección, f; mezcla, f; invención, f; (of a plot) maquinación, f

**concomitant** /kɒn'kɒmɪtənt/ a concomitante. —n concomitante, m

**concord** /'kɒnkɔrd/ n concordia, buena inteligencia, armonía, f; (Mus. Gram.) concordancia, f; (of sounds) armonía, f

**concordance** /kɒn'kɔrdns/ n concordia, armonía, f; (book) concordancias, f pl

**concordat** /kɒn'kɔrdæt/ n concordato, m

**concourse** /'kɒnkɔrs/ n concurrencia, muchedumbre, f

**concrete** /'kɒnkrit/ a concreto; de hormigón. —n hormigón, m. —vt concretar; cubrir de hormigón. **reinforced c.,** hormigón armado, m

**concretion** /kɒn'kriʃən/ n concreción, f

**concubine** /'kɒŋkyə,bain/ n concubina, manceba, f

**concur** /kən'kɜr/ vi coincidir, concurrir; estar de acuerdo, convenir (en)

**concurrence** /kən'kɜrəns/ n (agreement) acuerdo, consentimiento, m, aprobación, f

**concurrent** /kən'kɜrənt/ a concurrente; unánime; coincidente

**concurrently** /kən'kɜrəntli/ adv concurrentemente

**concussion** /kən'kʌʃən/ n concusión, f; Med. concusión cerebral, f

**condemn** /kən'dɛm/ vt condenar; censurar, culpar; (forfeit) confiscar. **condemned cell,** celda de los condenados a muerte, f

**condemnation** /ˌkɒndɛm'neiʃən/ n condenación, f; censura, f

**condensation** /ˌkɒndɛn'seiʃən/ n condensación, f

**condense** /kən'dɛns/ vt condensar. —vi condensarse

**condenser** /kən'dɛnsər/ n (Elec. Mech. Chem.) condensador, m

**condescend** /ˌkɒndə'sɛnd/ vi dignarse; (in a bad sense) consentir (en); (with affability) condescender

**condescending** /ˌkɒndə'sɛndɪŋ/ a condescendiente

**condescendingly** /ˌkɒndə'sɛndɪŋli/ adv con condescendencia

**condescension** /ˌkɒndə'sɛnʃən/ n condescendencia, f; afabilidad, f

**condign** /kən'dain/ a condigno

**condiment** /'kɒndəmənt/ n condimento, m

**condition** /kən'dɪʃən/ n condición, f; estado, m; pl **conditions,** condiciones, f pl; circunstancias, f pl. **on c. that,** con tal que; siempre que, dado que. **to be in no c. to,** no estar en condiciones de. **to change one's c.,** cambiar de estado. **to keep oneself in c.,** mantenerse en buena forma

**conditional** /kən'dɪʃənl/ a condicional. **to be c. on,** depender de

**conditionally** /kən'dɪʃənli/ adv condicionalmente

**conditioned** /kən'dɪʃənd/ a acondicionado. **c. reflex,** reflejo acondicionado, m

**condole** /kən'doul/ vi condolerse (de); (on a bereavement) dar el pésame

**condolence** /kən'douləns/ n condolencia, f. **to present one's condolences,** dar el pésame

**condom** /'kɒndəm/ n condón, m

**condone** /kən'doun/ vt condonar, perdonar

**conduce** /kən'dus/ vi contribuir, conducir

**conducive** /kən'dusɪv/ a que contribuye, conducente; favorable

**conduct** /n 'kɒndʌkt/ v kən'dʌkt/ n conducta, f. —vt conducir; guiar; Mus. dirigir; (oneself) portarse, con-

ducirse; *Phys.* conducir. —*vi Mus.* dirigir (una orquesta, etc.); *Phys.* ser conductor. **conducted tour,** excursión acompañada, *f;* viaje acompañado, *m*
**conduction** /kən'dʌkʃən/ *n* conducción, *f*
**conductive** /kən'dʌktɪv/ *a* conductivo
**conductivity** /ˌkɒndʌk'tɪvɪti/ *n* conductibilidad, *f*
**conductor** /kən'dʌktər/ *n* (guide) guía, *mf;* (of an orchestra) director, *m;* (on a tram, etc.) cobrador, *m; Phys.* conductor, *m*
**conduit** /'kɒnduɪt/ *n* conducto, *m;* cañería, *f;* canal, *m*
**cone** /koun/ *n* (*Bot. Geom.* etc.) cono, *m*
**confabulation** /kən,fæbyə'leiʃən/ *n* confabulación, *f*
**confection** /kən'fɛkʃən/ *n* confección, *f, vt* confeccionar
**confectioner** /kən'fɛkʃənər/ *n* confitero (-ra); pastelero (-ra)
**confectionery** /kən'fɛkʃə,nɛri/ *n* confitería, pastelería, repostería, *f*
**confederate** / *a, n* kən'fɛdərɪt/ *v* -'fɛdə,reit/ *a* confederado; aliado. —*n* confederado, *m;* (in crime) cómplice, *mf.* —*vt* confederar. —*vi* confederarse; aliarse
**confederation** /kən,fɛdə'reiʃən/ *n* confederación, *f*
**confer** /kən'fɜr/ *vt* conceder, conferir; (an honor, etc.) otorgar, investir (con). —*vi* consultar (con); deliberar, considerar
**conference** /'kɒnfərəns/ *n* conferencia, consulta, *f;* conversación, *f*
**conferment** /kən'fɜrmənt/ *n* otorgamiento, *m;* concesión, *f*
**confess** /kən'fɛs/ *vt* confesar, reconocer; *Inf.* admitir; (of a priest) confesar; (of a penitent) confesarse. —*vi* hacer una confesión; (one's sins) confesarse. **I c. that I was surprised,** No puedo negar que me sorprendió
**confessed** /kən'fɛst/ *a* confesado, declarado
**confession** /kən'fɛʃən/ *n* confesión, *f;* reconocimiento, *m;* declaración, *f;* religión, *f;* (creed) credo, *m.* **to go to c.,** confesarse. **to hear a c.,** confesar (a)
**confessional** /kən'fɛʃənl/ *n* confesionario, *m*
**confessor** /kən'fɛsər/ *n* confesor, *m*
**confetti** /kən'fɛti/ *n pl* confeti, papel picado *m,* serpentina, *f*
**confidant** /'kɒnfɪ,dænt/ *n* confidente, *m*
**confidante** /ˌkɒnfɪ'dænt/ *n* confidenta, *f*
**confide** /kən'faid/ *vi* confiar (a o en). —*vt* confiar
**confidence** /'kɒnfɪdəns/ *n* confianza, *f;* seguridad, *f;* (revelation) confidencia, *f.* **in c.,** en confianza. **over-c.,** presunción, *f.* **to have c. in,** tener confianza en. **c. man,** caballero de industria, estafador, *m.* **c. trick,** timo, *m*
**confident** /'kɒnfɪdənt/ *a* confiado; seguro; (conceited) presumido
**confidential** /ˌkɒnfɪ'dɛnʃəl/ *a* confidencial; de confianza. **c. clerk,** empleado (-da) de confianza. **c. letter,** carta confidencial, *f*
**confidentially** /ˌkɒnfɪ'dɛnʃəli/ *adv* en confianza, confidencialmente
**confidently** /'kɒnfɪdəntli/ *adv* confiadamente
**confiding** /kən'faidɪŋ/ *a* confiado
**confidingly** /kən'faidɪŋli/ *adv* con confianza
**configuration** /kən,fɪgyə'reiʃən/ *n* configuración, *f*
**confine** /kən'fain/ *vt* limitar; (imprison) encerrar. **confined space,** espacio limitado, *m.* **to be confined,** (of a woman) estar de parto, parir. **to be confined to one's room,** no poder dejar su cuarto. **to c. oneself to,** limitarse a
**confinement** /kən'fainmənt/ *n* encierro, *m,* prisión, *f;* reclusión, *f;* (of a woman) parto, *m.* **to suffer solitary c.,** estar incomunicado
**confines** /'kɒnfainz/ *n pl* límites, *m pl;* confines, *m pl;* fronteras, *f pl*
**confirm** /kən'fɜrm/ *vt* confirmar; corroborar; *Eccl.* confirmar
**confirmation** /ˌkɒnfər'meiʃən/ *n* confirmación, *f;* (of a treaty) ratificación, *f; Eccl.* confirmación, *f*
**confirmatory** /kən'fɜrmə,tɔri/ *a* confirmatorio
**confirmed** /kən'fɜrmd/ *a* inveterado
**confiscate** /'kɒnfə,skeit/ *vt* confiscar
**confiscation** /ˌkɒnfə'skeiʃən/ *n* confiscación, *f*

**conflagration** /ˌkɒnflə'greiʃən/ *n* conflagración, *f,* incendio, *m*
**conflict** / *n* 'kɒnflɪkt; *v* kən'flɪkt/ *n* conflicto, *m;* lucha, *f.* —*vi* estar opuesto (a), estar en contradicción (con)
**conflicting** /kən'flɪktɪŋ/ *a* opuesto; incompatible; (of evidence) contradictorio
**confluence** /'kɒnfluəns/ *n* confluencia, *f*
**conform** /kən'fɔrm/ *vt* ajustar, conformar. —*vi* ajustarse (a), amoldarse (a); conformarse (a); adaptarse (a)
**conformation** /ˌkɒnfɔr'meiʃən/ *n* conformación, *f*
**conformity** /kən'fɔrmɪti/ *n* conformidad, *f.* **in c. with,** en conformidad con, con arreglo a
**confound** /kɒn'faund/ *vt* confundir. **C. it!** ¡Demonio!
**confounded** /kɒn'faundɪd/ *a* perplejo; *Inf.* maldito
**confraternity** /ˌkɒnfrə'tɜrnɪti/ *n* cofradía, hermandad, *f*
**confront** /kən'frʌnt/ *vt* hacer frente (a), afrontar; salir al paso; confrontar
**Confucianism** /kən'fyuʃə,nɪzəm/ *n* el confucianismo, *m*
**confuse** /kən'fyuz/ *vt* turbar, aturdir; confundir (con); (the issue) obscurecer; (disconcert) desconcertar, dejar confuso (a); dejar perplejo (a). **You have confused one thing with another,** Has confundido una cosa con otra. **My mind was confused,** Mis ideas eran confusas; Tenía la cabeza trastornada
**confused** /kən'fyuzd/ *a* confuso
**confusing** /kən'fyuzɪŋ/ *a* turbador; desconcertante. **It is all very c.,** Todo ello es muy difícil de comprender
**confusion** /kən'fyuʒən/ *n* confusión, *f.* **covered with c.,** confuso, avergonzado. **to be in c.,** estar confuso, estar en desorden
**confute** /kən'fyut/ *vt* (a person) confundir; (by evidence) refutar, confutar
**congeal** /kən'dʒil/ *vt* congelar; (blood) coagular. —*vi* congelarse, helarse; coagularse
**congealment** /kən'dʒilmənt/ *n* congelación, *f;* (of blood) coagulación, *f*
**congenial** /kən'dʒinyəl/ *a* (of persons) simpático; propicio, favorable; agradable
**congenital** /kən'dʒɛnɪtl/ *a* congénito
**congest** /kən'dʒɛst/ *vt* atestar; amontonar; *Med.* congestionar
**congested** /kən'dʒɛstɪd/ *a Med.* congestionado; (of places) atestado de gente; de mayor población, concurrido. **c. area,** área de mayor densidad de población, *f*
**congestion** /kən'dʒɛstʃən/ *n Med.* congestión, *f;* densidad del tráfico, *f;* mayor densidad de población, *f*
**conglomerate** /kən'glɒmərɪt/ *a* conglomerado. —*n* conglomerado, *m*
**conglomeration** /kən,glɒmə'reiʃən/ *n* conglomeración, *f*
**congratulate** /kən'grætʃə,leit/ *vt* felicitar, dar la enhorabuena (a); congratular
**congratulation** /kən,grætʃə'leiʃən/ *n* felicitación, enhorabuena, *f;* congratulación, *f*
**congratulatory** /kən'grætʃələ,tɔri/ *a* de felicitación, congratulatorio
**congregate** /'kɒŋgrɪ,geit/ *vi* congregarse, reunirse, juntarse
**congregation** /ˌkɒŋgrɪ'geiʃən/ *n* congregación, *f;* asamblea, reunión, *f;* (in a church) fieles, *m pl;* (parishioners) feligreses, *m pl*
**congress** /'kɒŋgrɪs/ *n* congreso, *m.* **C.-man,** miembro del Congreso, *m*
**conical** /'kɒnɪkəl/ *a* cónico
**conifer** /'kounəfər/ *n* conífera, *f*
**coniferous** /kou'nɪfərəs/ *a* conífero
**conjectural** /kən'dʒɛktʃərəl/ *a* conjetural
**conjecture** /kən'dʒɛktʃər/ *n* conjetura, *f, vt* conjeturar
**conjoint** /kən'dʒɔint/ *a* asociado, conjunto
**conjointly** /kən'dʒɔintli/ *adv* juntamente, en común
**conjugal** /'kɒndʒəgəl/ *a* conyugal
**conjugate** /'kɒndʒə,geit/ *vt* conjugar. —*vi* conjugarse
**conjugation** /ˌkɒndʒə'geiʃən/ *n* conjugación, *f*
**conjunction** /kən'dʒʌŋkʃən/ *n* conjunción, *f.* **in c. with,** de acuerdo con

**conjunctive** /kən'dʒʌŋktɪv/ *a* conjuntivo. —*n* conjunción, *f*

**conjunctivitis** /kən,dʒʌŋktə'vaɪtɪs/ *n* conjuntivitis, *f*

**conjure** /'kɒndʒər/ *vt* (implore) rogar, suplicar. —*vi* (juggle) hacer juegos de manos. **a name to c. with,** un nombre todopoderoso. **to c. up,** (spirits) conjurar; *Fig.* evocar

**conjurer, conjuror** /'kɒndʒərər/ *n* (magician) nigromante, *m;* prestidigitador, *m.* **conjuror's wand,** varilla de virtudes, *f*

**conjuring** /'kɒndʒərɪŋ/ *n* prestidigitación, *f,* juegos de manos, *m pl.* **c. trick,** juego de manos, *m.* **c. up,** evocación, *f*

**connect** /kə'nɛkt/ *vt* juntar, unir; (relate) relacionar; asociar; (*Elec.* and *Mech.*) conectar. —*vi* juntarse, unirse; relacionarse; asociarse; (of events) encadenarse; (of trains) enlazar. **This train connects with the Madrid express,** Este tren enlaza con el expreso de Madrid. **They are connected with the Borgia family,** Están emparentados con los Borgia, Son parientes de los Borgia

**connected** /kə'nɛktɪd/ *a* conexo; (coherent) coherente; relacionado; asociado; (in a crime) implicado; (by marriage, etc.) emparentado

**connectedly** /kə'nɛktɪdli/ *adv* coherentemente

**connecting** /kə'nɛktɪŋ/ *a* que une; (*Mech.* and *Elec.*) conectivo; (of doors, etc.) comunicante. **c.-link,** *Mech.* varilla de conexión, *f; Fig.* lazo, *m.* **c.-rod,** biela, *f*

**connection** /kə'nɛkʃən/ *n* conexión, *f;* unión, *f;* (of ideas) relación, *f;* (junction) empalme, *m;* (of trains, boats) enlace, *m;* (intimacy) intimidad, *f;* (relative) pariente, *m;* (of a firm, etc.) clientela, *f; Elec.* conexión, *f.* **in c. with,** con referencia a; en asociación con. **in this c.,** respecto a esto

**conning tower** /'kɒnɪŋ/ *n* torre de mando, *f*

**connivance** /kə'naɪvəns/ *n* consentimiento, *m;* complicidad, *f*

**connive (at)** /kə'naɪv/ *vi* hacer la vista gorda, ser cómplice (en)

**connotation** /,kɒnə'teɪʃən/ *n* connotación, *f*

**connote** /kə'nout/ *vt* connotar

**connubial** /kə'nubiəl/ *a* conyugal

**conquer** /'kɒŋkər/ *vt* conquistar; vencer. —*vi* triunfar

**conquering** /'kɒŋkərɪŋ/ *a* conquistador, vencedor; triunfante, victorioso

**conqueror** /'kɒŋkərər/ *n* conquistador, *m;* vencedor, *m*

**conquest** /'kɒŋkwɛst/ *n* conquista, *f.* **to make a c. of,** conquistar

**consanguineous** /,kɒnsæŋ'gwɪniəs/ *a* consanguíneo

**consanguinity** /,kɒnsæŋ'gwɪnɪti/ *n* consanguinidad, *f*

**conscience** /'kɒnʃəns/ *n* conciencia, *f.* **in all c.,** en verdad. **with a clear c.,** con la conciencia limpia. **c.-stricken,** lleno de remordimientos

**conscienceless** /'kɒnʃənslɪs/ *a* desalmado, falto de conciencia

**conscientious** /,kɒnʃi'ɛnʃəs/ *a* concienzudo; diligente. **c. objector,** objetor de conciencia, *m*

**conscientiously** /,kɒnʃi'ɛnʃəsli/ *adv* concienzudamente

**conscientiousness** /,kɒnʃi'ɛnʃəsnɪs/ *n* conciencia, diligencia, *f;* rectitud, *f*

**conscious** /'kɒnʃəs/ *a* consciente. —*n Psychol.* consciente, *m.* **to become c.,** (after unconsciousness) volver en sí. **to become c. of,** darse cuenta de

**consciously** /'kɒnʃəsli/ *adv* conscientemente, a sabiendas

**consciousness** /'kɒnʃəsnɪs/ *n* conciencia, *f;* conocimiento, sentido, *m.* **to lose c.,** perder el conocimiento, perder el sentido. **to recover c.,** recobrar el sentido, volver en sí

**conscript** /*n* 'kɒnskrɪpt; *v* kən'skrɪpt/ *n* conscripto, *m, a* conscripto. —*vt* reclutar

**conscription** /kən'skrɪpʃən/ *n* conscripción, *f*

**consecrate** /'kɒnsɪ,kreɪt/ *vt* consagrar; bendecir

**consecration** /,kɒnsɪ'kreɪʃən/ *n* consagración, *f;* dedicación, *f*

**consecutive** /kən'sɛkyətɪv/ *a* consecutivo

**consecutively** /kən'sɛkyətɪvli/ *adv* consecutivamente

**consensus** /kən'sɛnsəs/ *n* consenso, *m,* unanimidad, *f.* **c. of opinion,** opinión general, *f*

**consent** /kən'sɛnt/ *vi* consentir. —*n* consentimiento,

*m;* permiso, *m,* aquiescencia, *f.* **by common c.,** de común acuerdo

**consequence** /'kɒnsɪ,kwɛns/ *n* consecuencia, *f;* resultado, *m;* importancia, *f,* **in c.,** por consiguiente. **in c. of,** de resultas de. **of no c.,** sin importancia

**consequences** /'kɒnsɪ,kwɛnsɪz/ *n* (game) cartas rusas, *f pl*

**consequent** /'kɒnsɪ,kwɛnt/ *a* consecuente, consiguiente

**consequential** /,kɒnsɪ'kwɛnʃəl/ *a* consecuente; (of persons) fatuo, engreído

**consequently** /'kɒnsɪ,kwɛntli/ *adv* por consiguiente, en consecuencia

**conservation** /,kɒnsər'veɪʃən/ *n* conservación, *f.* **c. of energy,** conservación de energía, *f*

**conservatism** /kən'sɜrvə,tɪzəm/ *n* conservadurismo, *m*

**conservative** /kən'sɜrvətɪv/ *a* preservativo; conservador. —*n* conservador (-ra). **c. party,** partido conservador, *m*

**conservatoire** /kən,sɜrvə'twɑr/ *n* conservatorio de música, *m*

**conservatory** /kən'sɜrvə,tɔri/ *n* invernáculo, invernadero, *m*

**conserve** /kən'sɜrv/ *vt* conservar

**consider** /kən'sɪdər/ *vt* considerar, pensar meditar; tomar en cuenta; examinar; (deem) juzgar; (believe) creer, estar convencido de (que); (of persons) considerar. **all things considered,** considerando todos los puntos, después de considerarlo todo

**considerable** /kən'sɪdərəbəl/ *a* considerable

**considerably** /kən'sɪdərəbli/ *adv* considerablemente

**considerate** /kən'sɪdərɪt/ *a* considerado, solícito

**considerately** /kən'sɪdərɪtli/ *adv* con consideración, solícitamente

**consideration** /kən,sɪdə'reɪʃən/ *n* consideración, *f;* reflexión, deliberación, *f;* remuneración, *f.* **out of c. for,** en consideración de; por consideración a. **to take into c.,** tomar en cuenta, tomar en consideración

**considered** /kən'sɪdərd/ *a* considerado

**considering** /kən'sɪdərɪŋ/ *prep* en consideración de, considerando, en vista de

**consign** /kən'saɪn/ *vt* consignar; *Fig.* enviar. **to c. to oblivion,** sepultar en el olvido

**consignee** /,kɒnsaɪ'ni/ *n* consignatorio, *m*

**consignment** /kən'saɪnmənt/ *n* consignación, *f;* envío, *m*

**consignor** /kən'saɪnər/ *n* consignador, *m*

**consist** /kən'sɪst/ *vi* consistir (en); ser compatible (con). **to c. of,** componerse de, consistir de

**consistence, consistency** /kən'sɪstəns; kən'sɪstənsi/ *n* consistencia, *f;* compatibilidad, *f;* lógica, *f;* (of persons) consecuencia, *f*

**consistent** /kən'sɪstənt/ *a* compatible; lógico; (of persons) consecuente

**consistently** /kən'sɪstəntli/ *adv* conformemente (a); consecuentemente

**consolation** /,kɒnsə'leɪʃən/ *n* consuelo, *m,* consolación, *f*

**console** /'kɒnsoul/ *vt* consolar; confortar. —*n Archit.* cartela, *f.* **c. table,** consola, *f*

**consolidate** /kən'sɒlɪ,deɪt/ *vt* consolidar. —*vi* consolidarse

**consolidation** /kən,sɒlɪ'deɪʃən/ *n* consolidación, *f*

**consoling** /kən'soulɪŋ/ *a* consolador; confortador

**consols** /'kɒnsɒlz, kən'sɒlz/ *n pl* (títulos) consolidados, *m pl*

**consonance** /'kɒnsənəns/ *n* consonancia, *f*

**consonant** /'kɒnsənənt/ *a* consonante

**consort** /*n* 'kɒnsɔrt, *v* kən'sɔrt/ *n* consorte, *mf.* **to c. with,** frecuentar la compañía de; ir con; acompañar (a). **prince c.,** príncipe consorte, *m*

**conspicuous** /kən'spɪkyuəs/ *a* conspicuo; prominente; notable. **to be c.,** destacarse; llamar la atención. **to make oneself c.,** ponerse en evidencia, llamar la atención

**conspicuously** /kən'spɪkyuəsli/ *adv* visiblemente; muy en evidencia

**conspiracy** /kən'spɪrəsi/ *n* conspiración, *f;* complot, *m*

**conspirator** /kən'spɪrətər/ *n* conspirador (-ra)

**conspire** /kən'spaɪər/ *vi* conspirar

**constable** /'kɒnstəbəl/ n agente de policía, m; (historical) condestable, m. **chief c.,** jefe de policía, m

**constabulary** /kən'stæbyə,leri/ n policía, f

**constancy** /'kɒnstənsi/ n constancia, f

**constant** /'kɒnstənt/ a constante; incesante. —n constante, m

**Constantinople** /,kɒnstæntn̩'oupəl/ Constantinopla, f

**constantly** /'kɒnstəntli/ adv constantemente

**constellation** /,kɒnstə'leiʃən/ n constelación, f

**consternation** /,kɒnstər'neiʃən/ n consternación, f; espanto, terror, m

**constipate** /'kɒnstə,peit/ vt estreñir

**constipation** /,kɒnstə'peiʃən/ n estreñimiento, m, constipación de vientre, f

**constituency** /kən'stɪtʃuənsi/ n distrito electoral, m

**constituent** /kən'stɪtʃuənt/ a constituyente. —n constituyente, m; componente, m; elector (-ra)

**constitute** /'kɒnstɪ,tut/ vt constituir; nombrar; autorizar

**constitution** /,kɒnstɪ'tuʃən/ n constitución, f

**constitutional** /,kɒnstɪ'tuʃənl/ a constitucional

**constitutionally** /,kɒnstɪ'tuʃənl̩i/ adv constitucionalmente

**constrain** /kən'strein/ vt obligar, forzar. **I felt constrained to help them,** Me sentí obligado a ayudarles

**constrained** /kən'streind/ a (of smiles, etc.) forzado; (of silences) violento; (of persons) avergonzado

**constraint** /kən'streint/ n fuerza, compulsión, f; (of atmosphere) tensión, f; (reserve) reserva, f; vergüenza, f

**constrict** /kən'strɪkt/ vt apretar, estrechar

**constriction** /kən'strɪkʃən/ n constricción, f

**construct** /kən'strʌkt/ vt edificar; construir

**construction** /kən'strʌkʃən/ n construcción, f; interpretación, f. **to put a wrong c. on,** interpretar mal

**constructional** /kən'strʌkʃənl/ a construccional

**constructive** /kən'strʌktɪv/ a constructor

**constructor** /kən'strʌktər/ n constructor, m

**construe** /kən'stru/ vt construir; (translate) traducir; Fig. interpretar

**consul** /'kɒnsəl/ n cónsul, m

**consular** /'kɒnsələr/ a consular

**consular fees** n pl derechos consulares, m pl

**consulate** /'kɒnsəlɪt/ n consulado, m. **c. general,** consulado general, m

**consult** /kən'sʌlt/ vt consultar. —vi consultar (con), aconsejarse (con)

**consultant** /kən'sʌltənt/ n (Med. and other uses) especialista, m

**consultation** /,kɒnsəl'teiʃən/ n consulta, f

**consultative** /kən'sʌltətɪv/ a consultativo

**consulting** /kən'sʌltɪŋ/ a consultor. **c. hours,** horas de consulta, f pl. **c. rooms,** consultorio, m

**consume** /kən'sum/ vt consumir; (eat) comerse, tragarse. —vi consumirse. **to be consumed by envy,** estar consumido por la envidia. **to be consumed by thirst,** estar muerto de sed

**consumer** /kən'sumər/ n consumidor (-ra)

**consummate** / a 'kɒnsəmɪt; v -,meit/ a consumido, perfecto. —vt consumar

**consummation** /,kɒnsə'meiʃən/ n consumación, f

**consumption** /kən'sʌmpʃən/ n consumo, m; gasto, m; Med. tuberculosis, f. **fuel c.,** consumo de combustible, m

**consumptive** /kən'sʌmptɪv/ a destructivo; Med. tísico, hético. —n tísico (-ca)

**contact** /'kɒntækt/ n contacto, m, vt ponerse en contacto con. **to be in c. with,** estar en contacto con

**contagion** /kən'teidʒən/ n contagio, m

**contagious** /kən'teidʒəs/ a contagioso

**contain** /kən'tein/ vt contener; incluir; Geom. encerrar; (arithmetic) ser divisible por; (oneself) dominarse. **I could not c. myself,** No pude dominarme

**container** /kən'teinər/ n recipiente, m; envase, m; (box) caja, f

**contaminate** /kən'tæmə,neit/ vt contaminar; corromper

**contamination** /kən,tæmə'neiʃən/ n contaminación, f

**contemplate** /'kɒntəm,pleit/ vt contemplar; meditar; considerar; (plan) tener intención de, pensar, proponerse

**contemplation** /,kɒntəm'pleiʃən/ n contemplación, f; meditación, f; expectación, esperanza, f; (plan) proyecto, m. **to have something in c.,** proyectar algo

**contemplative** /kən'templətɪv/ a contemplativo

**contemplatively** adv contemplativamente; atentamente

**contemporaneous** /kən,tempə'reiniəs/ a contemporáneo

**contemporary** /kən'tempə,reri/ a contemporáneo; (of persons) coetáneo; (of events, etc.) actual. —n contemporáneo (-ea)

**contempt** /kən'tempt/ n desprecio, menosprecio, m; desdén, m. **c. of court,** falta de respeto a la sala, f

**contemptible** /kən'temptəbəl/ a menospreciable, despreciable; vil

**contemptibly** /kən'temptəbli/ adv vilmente

**contempt of court** n rebeldía a la corte, f

**contempt of law** n rebeldía a la ley, f

**contemptuous** /kən'temptʃuəs/ a desdeñoso; despectivo; de desprecio. **to be c. of,** desdeñar; menospreciar, tener en poco (a)

**contemptuously** /kən'temptʃuəsli/ adv con desprecio, desdeñosamente

**contend** /kən'tend/ vi contender; (affirm) sostener, mantener. **He contended that...,** Sostuvo que...; **contending party,** Law. parte litigante, f

**content** / n 'kɒntent; a, v kən'tent/ n contenido, m; capacidad, f; (emotion) contento, m; satisfacción, f. —a contento; satisfecho (de). —vt contentar; satisfacer. **to one's heart's c.,** a pedir de boca; a gusto de uno; cuanto quisiera

**contented** /kən'tentid/ a satisfecho, contento

**contentedly** /kən'tentidli/ adv con satisfacción, contentamente

**contention** /kən'tenʃən/ n disputa, controversia, discusión, f; argumento, m, opinión, f

**contentious** /kən'tenʃəs/ a contencioso

**contentment** /kən'tentmənt/ n contentamiento, m; contento, m

**contest** / v kən'test; n 'kɒntest/ vt disputar; (a suit) defender; (a match, an election, etc.) disputar. —n disputa, f; combate, m, lucha, f; (competition) concurso, m

**contestant** /kən'testənt/ n contendiente, mf

**context** /'kɒntekst/ n contexto, m

**contiguity** /,kɒntɪ'gyuɪti/ n contigüidad, f

**contiguous** /kən'tɪgyuəs/ a contiguo, lindero, adyacente

**continence** /'kɒntnəns/ n continencia, f

**continent** /'kɒntnənt/ a continente. —n continente, m

**continental** /,kɒntn̩'entl/ a continental

**continental shelf** n plataforma continental, f

**contingency** /kən'tɪndʒənsi/ n contingencia, f

**contingent** /kən'tɪndʒənt/ a contingente. —n Mil. contingente, m. **to be c. on,** (of events) depender de

**continual** /kən'tɪnyuəl/ a continuo

**continually** /kən'tɪnyuəli/ adv continuamente

**continuance** /kən'tɪnyuəns/ n continuación, f

**continuation** /kən,tɪnyu'eiʃən/ n continuación, f; prolongación, f

**continue** /kən'tɪnyu/ vi continuar; seguir; prolongarse; durar. —vt continuar; seguir; proseguir; perpetuar; (in an office) retener. **to be continued,** se continuará, continuará, seguirá

**continuer** /kən'tɪnyuər/ n continuador (-ra)

**continuity** /,kɒntn̩'uɪti/ n continuidad, f

**continuous** /kən'tɪnyuəs/ a continuo. **c. performance,** sesión continua, f

**continuously** /kən'tɪnyuəsli/ adv de continuo, continuamente

**contort** /kən'tɔrt/ vt retorcer

**contortion** /kən'tɔrʃən/ n contorsión, f

**contortionist** /kən'tɔrʃənɪst/ n contorsionista, m

**contour** /'kɒntʊr/ n contorno, m; curva de nivel, f. **c. map,** mapa con curvas de nivel, m

**contraband** /'kɒntrə,bænd/ n contrabando, m

**contrabandist** /'kɒntrə,bændɪst/ n contrabandista, mf

**contrabass** /'kɒntrə,beis/ n contrabajo, m

**contraception** /,kɒntrə'sepʃən/ n anticoncepción, f

**contraceptive** /,kɒntrə'septɪv/ n anticonceptivo, m

**contract** /n 'kɒntrækt; v kən'trækt/ n pacto, m; (Com. and Law.) contrato, m; (betrothal) esponsales, m pl; (marriage) capitulaciones, f pl; (cards) "Bridge," m. —vt contraer; (acquire) adquirir, contraer; (a marriage, etc.) contraer; (be betrothed to) desposarse con; (by formal contract) contratar; pactar. —vi (shrink) contraerse, encogerse; comprometerse por contrato. **breach of c.,** no cumplimiento de contrato, m. **c. party,** (of matrimony) contrayente, mf

**contractile** /kən'træktl/ a contráctil

**contraction** /kən'trækʃən/ n contracción, f (act or process); forma contracta, f (like isn't or can't)

**contractor** /'kɒntræktər/ n contratista, mf

**contradict** /,kɒntrə'dɪkt/ vt contradecir; desmentir

**contradiction** /,kɒntrə'dɪkʃən/ n contradicción, f; negación, f

**contradictory** /,kɒntrə'dɪktəri/ a contradictorio; opuesto (a), contrario (a)

**contralto** /kən'træltou/ n (voice) contralto, m; (woman) contralto, f

**contraption** /kən'træpʃən/ n Inf. artefacto, m

**contrapuntal** /,kɒntrə'pʌntl/ a Mus. de contrapunto

**contrariness** /'kɒntrerinɪs/ n Inf. testarudez, terquedad, f

**contrariwise** /'kɒntreri,waiz/ adv al contrario; al revés

**contrary** /'kɒntreri/ a contrario; opuesto (a); desfavorable, poco propicio; (of persons) difícil, terco. —n contraria, f; (logic) contrario, m, adv en contra, contrariamente. **on the c.,** al contrario. **to be c.,** (of persons) llevar la contraria

**contrast** /n 'kɒntræst; v kən'træst/ n contraste, m. —vt contrastar (con). —vi contrastar (con), hacer contraste (con)

**contravene** /,kɒntrə'vin/ vt contravenir; atacar, oponerse (a)

**contravention** /,kɒntrə'vɛnʃən/ n contravención, f

**contribute** /kən'trɪbyut/ vt contribuir; (an article) escribir

**contribution** /,kɒntrə'byuʃən/ n contribución, f; (to a review, etc.) artículo, m

**contributor** /kən'trɪbyətər/ n contribuyente, mf; (to a journal) colaborador (-ra)

**contributory** /kən'trɪbyə,tɔri/ a contribuyente

**contrite** /kən'trait/ a penitente, arrepentido, contrito

**contritely** /kən'traitli/ adv contritamente

**contrition** /kən'trɪʃən/ n contrición, penitencia, f, arrepentimiento, m

**contrivance** /kən'traivəns/ n invención, f; (scheme) treta, idea, estratagema, f; (machine) aparato, mecanismo, artefacto, m

**contrive** /kən'traiv/ vt inventar; idear, proyectar. —vi (succeed in) lograr, conseguir; (manage) arreglárselas

**control** /kən'troul/ n autoridad, f; dominio, m; gobierno, m; dirección, f; regulación, f; (restraint) freno, m; (Biol. and Spirit.) control, m; (of a vehicle) conducción, f; manejo, m, manipulación, f; pl **controls,** Mech. mando, m. —vt dirigir, regir; regular; usar, manejar, manipular; controlar; (dominate) dominar; (curb) refrenar, reprimir; (command) mandar. **He lost c. of the car,** Perdió el mando (or control) del automóvil. **out of c.,** fuera de mando, fuera de control. **remote c.,** mando a distancia, m. **to c. oneself,** dominarse, contenerse. **to lose c. of oneself,** no lograr dominarse, perder el control. **c. stick,** Aer. palanca de mando, f. **c. tower,** Aer. torre de mando, f

**controller** /kən'troulər/ n interventor, m; (device) regulador, m

**controlling** /kən'troulɪŋ/ n See **control.** a regulador

**controversial** /,kɒntrə'vɜrʃəl/ a debatible, discutible

**controversy** /'kɒntrə,vɜrsi/ n controversia, f; argumento, m; altercación, disputa, f

**contumacious** /,kɒntu'meiʃəs/ a contumaz

**contumacy** /'kɒntuməsi/ n contumacia, f

**contumely** /'kɒntuməli/ n contumelia, f

**contusion** /kən'tuʒən/ n herida contusa, f

**conundrum** /kə'nʌndrəm/ n acertijo, rompecabezas, m; problema, m

**convalesce** /,kɒnvə'lɛs/ vi convalecer, estar convaleciente

**convalescence** /,kɒnvə'lɛsəns/ n convalecencia, f

**convalescent** /,kɒnvə'lɛsənt/ a convalecente. —n convaleciente, mf. **c. home,** casa de convalecencia, f

**convene** /kən'vin/ vt (a meeting) convocar; (person) citar. —vi reunirse

**convenience** /kən'vinyəns/ n conveniencia, f; (comfort) comodidad, f; utilidad, f; (advantage) ventaja, f; (public) retretes, m pl. **at one's c.,** cuando le sea conveniente a uno. **to make a c. of,** abusar de. **with all modern conveniences,** con todo el confort moderno

**convenient** /kən'vinyənt/ a conveniente; apropiado; cómodo. **I shall make it c. to see him at 6 p.m.,** Arreglaré mis asuntos para verle a las seis

**conveniently** /kən'vinyəntli/ adv cómodamente; oportunamente; sin inconveniente

**convent** /'kɒnvɛnt/ n convento, m

**convention** /kən'vɛnʃən/ n convención, f

**conventional** /kən'vɛnʃənl/ a convencional

**conventual** /kən'vɛntʃuəl/ a conventual. —n conventual, m

**converge** /kən'vɜrdʒ/ vi convergir

**convergence** /kən'vɜrdʒəns/ n convergencia, f

**convergent** /kən'vɜrdʒənt/ a convergente

**conversance** /kən'vɜrsəns/ n familiaridad, f, conocimiento, m

**conversant** /kən'vɜrsənt/ a familiar, versado, conocedor. **c. with,** versado en

**conversation** /,kɒnvər'seiʃən/ n conversación, f. **to engage in c. with,** entablar conversación con

**conversational** /,kɒnvər'seiʃənl/ a de conversación; (talkative) locuaz

**conversationally** /,kɒnvər'seiʃənli/ adv en tono familiar; familiarmente; en conversación

**converse** /kən'vɜrs/ vi conversar. **to c. by signs,** hablar por señas

**conversely** /kən'vɜrsli/ adv recíprocamente

**conversion** /kən'vɜrʒən/ n conversión, f

**convert** /v kən'vɜrt; n 'kɒnvɜrt/ vt convertir; transformar. —n converso (-sa). **to become a c.,** convertirse

**convertible** /kən'vɜrtəbəl/ a convertible; transformable

**convex** /a kɒn'vɛks; n 'kɒnvɛks/ a convexo

**convey** /kən'vei/ vt transportar; conducir, llevar; (a meaning, etc.) comunicar, dar a entender; expresar; Law. traspasar

**conveyance** /kən'veiəns/ n transporte, m; conducción, f; medio de transporte, m; vehículo, m; carruaje, m; (of property) traspaso, m; (document) escritura de traspaso, f. **public c.,** coche de alquiler, m; ómnibus, m

**convict** /n 'kɒnvɪkt; v kən'vɪkt/ n convicto, m; presidiario, m. —vt Law. condenar; culpar. **c. settlement,** colonia penal, f

**conviction** /kən'vɪkʃən/ n (of a prisoner) condenación, f; (belief) convencimiento, m, convicción, f

**convince** /kən'vɪns/ vt convencer

**convincing** /kən'vɪnsɪŋ/ a convincente

**convivial** /kən'vɪviəl/ a convivial

**conviviality** /kən,vɪvi'ælɪti/ n jovialidad, f

**convocation** /,kɒnvə'keiʃən/ n convocación, f

**convoke** /kən'vouk/ vt convocar

**convolution** /,kɒnvə'luʃən/ n circunvolución, f; espira, f

**convoy** /'kɒnvɔi/ vt convoyar, escoltar. —n convoy, m. **to sail in a c.,** navegar en convoy

**convulse** /kən'vʌls/ vt agitar; sacudir; estremecer. **to be convulsed with laughter,** desternillarse de risa, morirse de risa

**convulsion** /kən'vʌlʃən/ n convulsión, f; conmoción, f

**convulsive** /kən'vʌlsɪv/ a convulsivo

**coo** /ku/ vi arrullar; (of infants) gorjearse. —n arrullo, m

**cooing** /'kuɪŋ/ n arrullo, m

**cook** /kʊk/ n cocinero (-ra). —vt guisar, cocer, cocinar; (falsify) falsear

**cooker** /'kʊkər/ n cocina, f. **gas c.,** cocina de gas, f

**cookery** /'kʊkəri/ n cocina, f. **c.-book,** libro de cocina, m

**cooking** /'kʊkɪŋ/ n arte de guisar, m, or f; cocina, f;

(of accounts, etc.) falsificación, *f.* **c. range,** cocina económica, *f.* **c.-stove,** cocina, *f.* **c. utensils,** batería de cocina, *f*

**cool** /kul/ *a* fresco; bastante frío; (not ardent and of receptions, etc.) frío; (calm) sereno, imperturbable. —*n* fresco, *m.* —*vi* enfriarse; (of love, etc.) resfriarse; (of the weather) refrescar; (of persons) refrescarse. —*vt* refrescar; enfriar. **to grow cooler,** (of weather) refrescarse; (of persons) tener menos calor. **It is c.,** Hace fresco. **to be as c. as a cucumber,** tener sangre fría. **c. drink,** bebida fría, *f.* **c.-headed,** sereno, imperturbable

**coolie** /'kuli/ *n* culí, *m*

**cooling** /'kulɪŋ/ *n* enfriamiento, *m,* *a* refrescante

**coolly** /'kuli/ *adv* frescamente; fríamente, con frialdad; imperturbablemente; (impudently) descaradamente

**coolness** /'kulnɪs/ *n* frescura, *f;* (of a welcome, etc.) frialdad, *f;* (sangfroid) sangre fría, serenidad, *f;* aplomo, *m*

**coop** /kup/ *n* gallinero, *m;* caponera, *f,* *vt* enjaular; encerrar. **to keep** (someone) **cooped up,** tener encerrado (a)

**cooper** /'kupər/ *n* tonelero, barrilero, *m,* *vt* hacer barriles

**cooperate** /kou'ɒpə,reit/ *vi* cooperar; colaborar

**cooperation** /kou,ɒpə'reifən/ *n* cooperación, *f*

**cooperative** /kou'ɒpərətɪv/ *a* cooperativo. **c. society,** cooperativa, *f*

**coopt** /kou'ɒpt/ *vt* elegir por votación

**coordinate** /v kou'ɔrdn,eit; *n,* *a* kou'ɔrdnɪt/ *vt* coordinar. —*n Math.* coordenada, *f.* —*a* coordenado

**coordination** /kou,ɔrdn'eifən/ *n* coordinación, *f*

**coot** /kut/ *n* fúlica, *f*

**cop** /kɒp/ *n* (police officer) chapa (Ecuador), polizonte, *mf*

**copartner** /kou'partnər/ *n* copartícipe, *mf;* socio (-ia) *f*

**cope** /koup/ *n Eccl.* capa, *f;* (of heaven) dosel, *m,* bóveda, *f.* **to c. with,** contender con; (a difficulty) hacer cara a, arrostrar

**copeck** /'koupek/ *n* copec, *m*

**Copenhagen** /,koupən'heigən, -'hagən/ Copenhague, *m*

**Copernican** /kou'pɜrnɪkən/ *a* copernicano

**copier** /'kɒpiər/ *n* copiador (-ra)

**coping** /'koupɪŋ/ *n Archit.* albardilla, *f.* **c.-stone,** teja cumbrera, *f; Fig.* coronamiento, *m*

**copious** /'koupiəs/ *a* copioso, abundante

**copiously** /'koupiəsli/ *adv* en abundancia

**copiousness** /'koupiəsnɪs/ *n* abundancia, *f*

**copper** /'kɒpər/ *n* cobre, *m;* (coin) calderilla, *f;* (vessel) caldera, *f.* —*a* de cobre. **c.-colored,** cobrizo. **c.-smith,** calderero, *m.* **c.-sulphate,** sulfato de cobre, *m*

**copperplate** /'kɒpər,pleit/ *n* lámina de cobre, *f;* grabado en cobre, *m*

**coppery** /'kɒpəri/ *a* cobrizo

**coppice** /'kɒpɪs/ *n* soto, bosquecillo, *m.* **c. with standards,** monte medio, *m*

**coproprietor** /,koupro'praitər/ *n* copropietario, *m*

**copse** /kɒps/ *n* arboleda, *f,* bosquecillo, *m*

**Coptic** /'kɒptɪk/ *a* cóptico, copto. —*n* (language) copto, cóptico, *m*

**copulate** /'kɒpyə,leit/ *vi* copularse

**copulation** /,kɒpyə'leifən/ *n* cópula, *f*

**copy** /'kɒpi/ *n* copia, *f;* (of a book) ejemplar, *m;* (of a paper) número, *m;* manuscrito, *m;* (subject-matter) material, *m.* —*vt* copiar; imitar; tomar como modelo (a). **rough c.,** borrador, *m.* **c.-book,** cuaderno de escritura, *m*

**copy editor** *n* redactor de textos, *m*

**copying** /'kɒpiɪŋ/ *n* imitación, *f;* transcripción, *f.* **c. ink,** tinta de copiar, *f*

**copyist** /'kɒpiɪst/ *n* copiador (-ra); (plagiarist) copiante, *mf*

**copyright** /'kɒpi,rait/ *n* derechos de autor, *m pl;* propiedad literaria, *f.* —*a* protegido por los derechos de autor. —*vt* registrar como propiedad literaria. **C. reserved,** Derechos reservados, Queda hecho el depósito que marca la ley

**copywriter** /'kɒpi,raitər/ *n* escritor de anuncios, *m*

**coquet** /kou'ket/ *vi* coquetear; *Fig.* jugar (con)

**coquetry** /'koukɪtri/ *n* coquetería, *f*

**coquette** /kou'ket/ *n* coqueta, *f*

**coquettish** /kou'ketif/ *a* coquetón; atractivo

**coral** /'kɔrəl/ *n* coral, *m;* (polyp) coralina, *f.* —*a* de coral, coralino. **white c.,** madrépora, *f.* **c. beads,** corales, *m pl.* **c.-island,** atolón, *m.* **c.-reef,** escollo de coral, *m.* **c. snake,** coral, *f*

**corbel** /'kɔrbəl/ *n Archit.* ménsula, *f*

**cord** /kɔrd/ *n* cuerda, *f;* cordel, *m;* cordón, *m.* —*vt* encordelar. **spinal c.,** médula espinal, *f.* **umbilical c.,** cordón umbilical, *m*

**cordial** /'kɔrdʒəl/ *a* cordial; sincero, fervoroso. —*n* cordial, *m*

**cordiality** /kɔr'dʒæliti/ *n* cordialidad, *f*

**cordon** /'kɔrdn/ *n* cordón, *m;* cinto, *m.* **to c. off,** acordonar

**Cordova** /'kɔrdəvə/ Córdoba, *f*

**cordovan** /'kɔrdəvən/ *a* cordobés. —*n* (leather) cordobán, *m*

**corduroy** /'kɔrdə,rɔi/ *n* pana de cordoncillo, *f*

**core** /kɔr/ *n* (of a fruit) corazón, *m;* (of a rope) alma, *f,* centro, *m;* (of an abscess) foco, *m;* (of a corn) ojo, *m; Fig.* núcleo, *m;* esencia, *f;* lo esencial

**coreligionist** /,kɔurɪ'lɪdʒənɪst/ *n* correligionario (-ia)

**corespondent** /,kɔurɪ'spɒndənt/ *n* cómplice en un caso de divorcio, *mf*

**Corinth** /'kɔrɪnθ/ Corinto, *m*

**Corinthian** /kə'rɪnθiən/ *a* corintio. —*n* corintio (-ia)

**cork** /kɔrk/ *n* corcho, *m;* (of a bottle) tapón, *m,* *a* de corcho. —*vt* tapar con corcho, taponar; (wine) encorchar; (the face) tiznar con corcho quemado. **pop of a c.,** taponazo, *m.* **to draw a c.,** descorchar. **c.-jacket,** chaleco salvavidas, *m.* **c. tree,** alcornoque, *m*

**corkscrew** /'kɔrk,skru/ *n* sacacorchos, *m*

**cormorant** /'kɔrmərənt/ *n* cormorán, *m*

**corn** /kɔrn/ *n* grano, cereal, *m;* (wheat) trigo, *m;* (maize) maíz, *m;* (single seed) grano, *m;* (on the foot, etc.) callo, *m.* **Indian c.,** maíz, *m.* **c. cure,** callicida, *m.* **c.-exchange,** bolsa de granos, *f.* **c.-field,** campo de trigo, *m.* **c.-flower,** aciano, *m*

**cornea** /'kɔrniə/ *n* córnea, *f*

**corner** /'kɔrnər/ *n* ángulo, *m;* (of a street or building) esquina, *f;* (of a room) rincón, *m;* *Auto.* viraje, *m;* *Com.* monopolio, *m;* (of the eye) rabo, *m;* (Assoc. football) "corner," *m.* —*vt* arrinconar; acorralar; *Com.* acaparar. **the four corners of the earth,** las cinco partes del mundo. **a tight c.,** un lance apretado, un apuro. **to drive into a c.,** *Fig.* poner entre la espada y la pared. **to look out of the c. of the eye,** mirar de reojo. **to turn the c.,** doblar la esquina; *Fig.* pasar la crisis. **c.-cupboard,** rinconera, *f.* **c. seat,** asiento del rincón, *m.* **c.-stone,** piedra angular, *f*

**cornered** /'kɔrnərd/ *a* (of a person) acorralado, en aprieto; (of hats) de... picos. **three-c. hat,** sombrero de tres picos, *m*

**cornet** /kɔr'net/ *n* (musical instrument) corneta, *f; Mil.* corneta, *m;* (paper) cucurucho, *m.* **c. player,** cornetín, *m*

**cornflour** /'kɔrn,flauər/ *n* harina de maíz, *f*

**cornice** /'kɔrnɪs/ *n* cornisa, *f*

**Cornish** /'kɔrnif/ *a* de Cornualles

**cornucopia** /,kɔrnə'koupiə/ *n* cornucopia, *f*

**corollary** /'kɔrə,leri/ *n* corolario, *m*

**corona** /kə'rounə/ *n* (*Astron. Archit.*) corona, *f*

**coronation** /,kɔrə'neifən/ *n* coronación, *f*

**coroner** /'kɔrənər/ *n* juez de guardia, *mf,* médico forense, *m*

**coronet** /,kɔrə'net/ *n* (of a peer, etc.) corona, *f;* tiara, *f;* guirnalda, *f*

**corporal** /'kɔrpərəl/ *a* corporal, *n Mil.* cabo, *m;* (altar-cloth) corporal, *m.* **c. punishment,** castigo corporal, *m*

**corporate** /'kɔrpərɪt/ *a* corporativo

**corporation** /,kɔrpə'reifən/ *n* corporación, *f;* concejo, cabildo municipal, *m;* (*Com.* U.S.A.) sociedad anónima, *f*

**corporeal** /kɔr'pɔriəl/ *a* corpóreo

**corps** /kɔr/ *n* cuerpo, *m*

**corpse** /kɔrps/ *n* cadáver, *m*

**corpulence** /'kɔrpyələns/ *n* gordura, obesidad, *f*

**corpulent** /'kɔrpyələnt/ *a* corpulento, grueso, gordo

**corpus** /'kɔrpəs/ n cuerpo, m. **C. Christi,** Corpus, m. **c. delicti,** cuerpo del delito, m

**corpuscle** /'kɔrpəsəl/ n corpúsculo, m

**correct** /kə'rekt/ a correcto; exacto, justo. —vt corregir; rectificar; amonestar, reprender

**correction** /kə'rekʃən/ n corrección, f; rectificación, f

**corrective** /kə'rektɪv/ a correctivo. —n correctivo, m

**correctness** /kə'rektnɪs/ n corrección, f; exactitud, f; justicia, f

**correlate** /'kɔrə,leit/ vt poner en correlación. —vi tener correlación

**correlation** /,kɔrə'leiʃən/ n correlación, f

**correspond** /,kɔrə'spɒnd/ vi corresponder (a); (by letter) escribirse, corresponderse

**correspondence** /,kɔrə'spɒndəns/ n correspondencia, f; Com. correo, m. **c. course,** curso por correspondencia, m

**correspondent** /,kɔrə'spɒndənt/ n correspondiente, mf; (Com. and journalist) corresponsal, mf. **special c.,** corresponsal extraordinario, m

**corresponding** /,kɔrə'spɒndɪŋ/ a correspondiente. **c. member,** miembro correspondiente, m

**corridor** /'kɔridər/ n corredor, pasillo, m; (railway) pasillo, m; Polit. corredor, m. **c. train,** tren con coches corridos, m

**corroborate** /kə'rɒbə,reit/ vt corroborar, confirmar

**corroboration** /kə,rɒbə'reiʃən/ n corroboración, confirmación, f

**corroborative** /kə'rɒbə,reitɪv/ a corroborativo, confirmatorio

**corrode** /kə'roud/ vt corroer, morder; Fig. roer

**corrosion** /kə'rouʒən/ n corrosión, f

**corrosive** /kə'rousɪv/ a corrosivo; mordaz

**corrugate** /'kɔrə,geit/ vt arrugar. —vi arrugarse

**corrugated** /'kɔrə,geitɪd/ a arrugado; ondulado. **c. iron,** chapa canaleta, f

**corrugation** /,kɔrə'geiʃən/ n corrugación, f, arrugamiento, m

**corrupt** /kə'rʌpt/ a corrompido; vicioso, desmoralizado. —vt corromper. —vi corromperse

**corrupter** /kə'rʌptər/ n corruptor (-ra)

**corruption** /kə'rʌpʃən/ n corrupción, f

**corsage** /kɔr'saʒ/ n corpiño, m

**corset** /'kɔrsɪt/ n corsé, m, vt encorsetar. **c. shop,** corsetería, f

**Corsica** /'kɔrsɪkə/ Córcega, f

**Corsican** /'kɔrsɪkən/ a corso. —n corso (-sa)

**cortege** /kɔr'teʒ/ n séquito, acompañamiento, m; desfile, m

**cortex** /'kɔrteks/ n Bot. Anat. corteza, f

**cortisone** /'kɔrtə,zoun/ n (drug) cortisona, f

**Corunna** /kə'rʌnjə/ La Coruña, f

**coruscation** /,kɔrə'skeiʃən/ n brillo, m

**corvette** /kɔr'vet/ n corbeta, f

**cosignatory** /kou'sɪgnə,tɔri/ n cosignatario (-ia)

**cosine** /'kousain/ n coseno, m

**cosiness** /'kouzɪnɪs/ n comodidad, f

**cosmetic** /kɒz'metɪk/ a cosmético. —n afeite, cosmético, m

**cosmic** /'kɒzmɪk/ a cósmico

**cosmographer** /kɒz'mɒgrəfər/ n cosmógrafo, m

**cosmography** /kɒz'mɒgrəfi/ n cosmografía, f

**cosmopolitan** /,kɒzmə'pɒlɪtn/ a cosmopolita. —n cosmopolita, mf

**cosmopolitanism** /,kɒzmə'pɒlɪtn,izəm/ n cosmopolitismo, m

**cosmos** /'kɒzməs/ n cosmos, universo, m

**Cossack** /'kɒsæk/ a cosaco. —n cosaco (-ca)

**cosset** /'kɒsɪt/ vt mimar, consentir

**cost** /kɔst/ vi costar. —n costa, f, coste, precio, m; Fig. costa, f; pl **costs,** Law. costas, f pl. **at all costs,** cueste lo que cueste, a toda costa. **to my c.,** a mi costa. **c. of living,** coste de la vida, m. **to c. a fortune,** costar un sentido

**Costa Rican** /'kɒstə'rikən/ a costarriqueño. —n costarriqueño (-ña)

**coster** /'kɔstər/ n vendedor (-ra) ambulante

**costliness** /'kɒstlinɪs/ n alto precio, m; suntuosidad, f

**costly** /'kɒstli/ a costoso; suntuoso, magnífico

**costume** /'kɒstum/ n traje, m; (fancy-dress) disfraz,

m; (tailored) traje sastre, m; **"Costume,"** (among credits in films and plays) «Vestuario»

**costumier** /,kɒstu'mɪər/ n modista, mf; sastre, m

**cot** /kɒt/ n (hut) choza, cabaña, f; (child's) camita, f

**coterie** /'koutəri/ n círculo, grupo, m; (clique) camarilla, f

**cotillion** /kə'tɪlyən/ n cotillón, m

**cottage** /'kɒtɪdʒ/ n cabaña, choza, f; casita, f, hotelito, m; torre, villa, f

**cotter** /'kɒtər/ n chaveta, llave, f

**cotton** /'kɒtn/ n algodón, m, a de algodón. **I don't c. to the idea at all,** No me gusta nada la idea; La idea no me seduce. **sewing-c.,** hilo de coser, m. **c. goods,** géneros de algodón, m pl. **c. mill,** hilandería de algodón, algodonería, f. **c. plantation,** algodonal, m. **c.-seed oil,** aceite de semilla de algodón, m. **c.-spinner,** hilandero (-ra) de algodón. **c.-wool,** algodón en rama, m. **c.-yarn,** hilo de algodón, m

**cottony** /'kɒtni/ a algodonoso

**couch** /kautʃ/ n sofá, canapé, m; (bed) lecho, m; (lair) cama, f. —vt (lay down) acostar, echar; (a lance) enristrar; (express) expresar, redactar. —vi acostarse; (crouch) agacharse; estar en acecho

**cough** /kɔf/ vi toser. —n tos, f. **to c. up,** escupir, expectorar. **c.-drop,** pastilla para la tos, f

**coughing** /'kɔfɪŋ/ n tos, f

**could** /kud/. See **can**

**council** /'kaunsəl/ n consejo, m; junta, f; Eccl. concilio, m. **Privy C.,** consejo privado, m. **C. of the Realm,** Concejo del Reino, m. **to hold c.,** celebrar un consejo; aconsejarse (con); consultarse. **town c.,** ayuntamiento, m. **c. chamber,** sala consistorial, f; sala de actos, f. **c. houses,** casas baratas, f pl. **c. of war,** consejo de guerra, m

**councilor** /'kaunsələr/ n concejal, m; miembro de la junta, m

**counsel** /'kaunsəl/ n consultación, f; deliberación, f; consejo, m; Law. abogado, m. —vt aconsejar. **a c. of perfection,** un ideal imposible. **to keep one's own c.,** no decir nada, callarse, guardar silencio. **to take c. with,** consultar (a), aconsejarse con

**counselor** /'kaunsələr/ n consejero, m. **c. of state,** consejero de estado, m

**count** /kaunt/ vt contar; calcular; (consider) creer, considerar. —vi contar. —n cuenta, f; (of votes) escrutinio, m; Law. capítulo, m. **John simply doesn't c.,** Juan no cuenta para nada. **Erudition alone counts for very little,** La mera erudición sirve para muy poco. **to keep c. of,** tener cuenta de. **to lose c. of,** perder cuenta de. **to c. on,** contar con; (doing something) esperar. **to c. up,** contar

**count** /kaunt/ n (title) conde, m

**countenance** /'kauntnəns/ n semblante, m; expresión de la cara, f; aspecto, m; (favor) apoyo, m, ayuda, f. —vt autorizar, aprobar; apoyar, ayudar. **to put (a person) out of c.,** desconcertar

**counter** /'kauntər/ n (in a bank) contador, m; (in a shop) mostrador, m; (in games) ficha, f, adv contra, al contrario; al revés. —a opuesto (a), contrario (a). —vt parar; contestar. **to run c. to my inclinations,** oponerse a mis deseos. **to c. with the left,** (boxing) contestar con la izquierda. **c.-attack,** contraataque, m. **c.-attraction,** atracción contraria, f. **c.-offensive,** contraofensiva, f. **c.-reformation,** contrarreforma, f. **c.-revolution,** contrarrevolución, f

**counteract** /,kauntər'ækt/ vt neutralizar; frustrar

**counterbalance** /'kauntər,bæləns/ n contrapeso, m, vt contrabalancear; compensar, igualar

**counterblast** /'kauntər,blæst/ n denunciación, f; respuesta, f

**countercharge** /'kauntər,tʃardʒ/ n recriminación, f. —vt recriminar; Law. reconvenir

**counterfeit** /'kauntər,fit/ a falso, espurio; fingido. —n falsificación, f; imitación, f; moneda falsa, f; (person) impostor (-ra). —vt imitar; (pretend) fingir; (coins, handwriting, etc.) falsificar

**counterfeiter** /'kauntər,fitər/ n falsario (-ia)

**counterfoil** /'kauntər,fɔil/ n talón, m

**countermand** /v ,kauntər'mænd/ n 'kauntər,mænd/ vt contramandar; (an order) revocar, cancelar. —n contraorden, f; revocación, f

**countermarch** /'kauntər,martʃ/ n contramarcha, f

**countermeasure** /'kauntər,mɛʒər/ *n* contramedida, *f*
**counterpane** /'kauntər,pein/ *n* sobrecama, colcha, *f*
**counterpart** /'kauntər,part/ *n* contraparte, *f*; (of a document) duplicado, *m*
**counterplot** /'kauntər,plɒt/ *n* contratreta, *f*
**counterpoint** /'kauntər,pɔint/ *n Mus.* contrapunto, *m*
**counterpoise** /'kauntər,pɔiz/ *n* contrapeso, *m*; equilibrio, *m*, *vt* contrabalancear, contrapesar
**countersign** /'kauntər,sain/ *n* contraseña, *f*, *vt* refrendar
**countess** /'kauntɪs/ *n* condesa, *f*
**counting** /'kauntɪŋ/ *n* cuenta, *f*; numeración, *f*; (of votes) escrutinio, *m*. **c.-house,** contaduría, *f*
**countless** /'kauntlɪs/ *a* innumerable. **a c. number,** un sinfín, un sinnúmero
**countrified** /'kʌntrə,faid/ *a* rústico, campesino
**country** /'kʌntri/ *n* país, *m*; (fatherland) patria, *f*; región, campiña, tierra, *f*; (as opposed to town) campo, *m*. **—a** del campo; campesino, campestre, rústico. **He lives in the c.,** Vive en el campo. **c. club,** club campestre, *m*. **c. cousin,** provinciano (-na). **c.-dance,** baile campestre, *m*. **c. gentleman,** hacendado, *m*. **c. girl,** campesina, *f*; aldeana, *f*. **c.-house,** finca, *f*; casa de campo, *f*. **c. life,** vida del campo, *f*. **c.-seat,** finca, *f*
**countryman** /'kʌntrimən/ *n* campesino, *m*; hombre del campo, *m*; compatriota, *m*
**countryside** /'kʌntri,said/ *n* campo, *m*; campiña, *f*
**countrywoman** /'kʌntri,wumən/ *n* campesina, *f*; compatriota, *f*
**county** /'kaunti/ *n* condado, *m*; provincia, *f*. **c. council,** diputación provincial, *f*. **c. town,** cabeza de partido, *f*; ciudad provincial, *f*
**county seat** *n* cabecera municipal, cabeza de partido, *f*
**coup** /ku/ *n* golpe, *m*. **c. d'état,** golpe de estado, *m*
**coupe** /kup/ *n* cupé, *m*
**couple** /'kʌpəl/ *n* par, *m*; (in a dance, etc.) pareja, *f*. **—vt** enganchar, acoplar; (in marriage) casar; (animals) aparear; (ideas) asociar; (names) juntar. **the young (married) c.,** el matrimonio joven
**couplet** /'kʌplɪt/ *n* copla, *f*
**coupling** /'kʌplɪŋ/ *n* enganche, acoplamiento, *m*; (of railway carriages) enganche, *m*; (of ideas) asociación, *f*
**coupon** /'kupɒn/ *n* talón, *m*; cupón, *m*
**courage** /'kʌrɪdʒ/ *n* valor, *m*. **C.!** ¡Ánimo! **to muster up c.,** cobrar ánimo
**courageous** /kə'reidʒəs/ *a* valiente
**courageously** /kə'reidʒəsli/ *adv* valientemente
**courier** /'kʌriər/ *n* correo, *m*, estafeta, *f*; (guide) guía, *m*; (newspaper) estafeta, *f*
**course** /kɔrs/ *n* curso, *m*; (of time) transcurso, *m*; (of events) marcha, *f*; (of a river, etc.) cauce, *m*; (of stars) carrera, *f*, curso, *m*; (of a ship) derrota, *f*, rumbo, *m*; (way) camino, *m*, ruta, *f*; (of conduct) línea de conducta, *f*; actitud, *f*; (of study) curso, *m*; (of a meal) plato, *m*; (of an illness) desarrollo, *m*; *Med.* tratamiento, *m*. **He took it as a matter of c.,** Lo tomó sin darle importancia. **in due c.,** a su tiempo debido. **in the c. of time,** andando el tiempo, en el transcurso de los años. **of c.,** claro está; naturalmente. **Are you coming tomorrow? Of c.!** ¿Vienes mañana? ¡Ya lo creo! **the best c. to take,** lo mejor que se puede hacer, el mejor plantamiento, *m*
**course** /kɔrs/ *vt* cazar, perseguir; *Poet.* correr por, cruzar. **—vi** (of blood, etc.) correr; cazar
**court** /kɔrt/ *n* (yard) patio, *m*; (tennis) campo de tenis, *m*; (fives, racquets) cancha, *f*; (royal) corte, *f*; (of justice) tribunal, *m*; (following) séquito, acompañamiento, *m*. **—vt** hacer la corte (a); cortejar, pretender; solicitar; (sleep) conciliar. **to pay c. to,** (a woman) galantear, pretender; (a person) hacer la rueda (a). **to respect the c.,** *Law.* guardar sala. **c. of appeal,** sala de apelación, *f*. **c. of justice,** sala de justicia, *f*; tribunal de justicia, *m*. **supreme c.,** tribunal supremo, *m*. **c.-card,** figura, *f*. **c.-dress,** traje de corte, *m*. **c. house,** palacio de justicia, *m*. **c. jester,** bufón, *m*. **c.-martial,** tribunal militar, *m*. **c.-plaster,** tafetán inglés, tafetán de heridas, *m*. **c.-room,** sala de justicia, *f*
**courteous** /'kɜrtiəs/ *a* cortés

**courteousness** /'kɜrtiəsnɪs/ *n* cortesía, *f*
**courtesan** /'kɔrtəzən/ *n* cortesana, *f*
**courtesy** /'kɜrtəsi/ *n* cortesía, *f*; favor, *m*, merced, *f*; permiso, *m*
**courtier** /'kɔrtiər/ *n* cortesano, palaciego, *m*
**courtliness** /'kɔrtlinɪs/ *n* cortesía, urbanidad, *f*; dignidad, *f*; elegancia, *f*
**courtly** /'kɔrtli/ *a* cortés, galante; digno; elegante
**courtship** /'kɔrtʃip/ *n* noviazgo, *m*; galanteo, *m*
**courtyard** /'kɔrt,yard/ *n* patio, *m*
**cousin** /'kʌzən/ *n* primo (-ma). **first c.,** primo (-ma) carnal. **second c.,** primo (-ma) segundo (-da)
**cove** /kouv/ *n* cala, abra, ensenada, *f*
**covenant** /'kʌvənənt/ *n* contrato, *m*; estipulación, *f*; pacto, *m*; alianza, *f*. **—vt** prometer; estipular
**Coventry, to send to,** /'kʌvəntri/ hacer el vacío (a)
**cover** /'kʌvər/ *vt* cubrir; abrigar; (dissemble) disimular; (a distance) recorrer; (comprise) comprender, abarcar; (with confusion, etc.) llenar (de); (with a revolver, etc.) amenazar (con); (an overdraft, etc.) garantizar; (of stallions) cubrir; (of a hen and eggs) empollar; (a story, journalism) investigar. **—n** cubierta, *f*; (for a chair, umbrella, etc.) funda, *f*; (of a saucepan, jar, etc.) tapa, *f*; (dish-cover) tapadera, *f*; (of a book) cubierta, tapa, *f*; (of a letter) sobre, *m*; (shelter) abrigo, *m*; protección, *f*; (undergrowth) maleza, *f*; *Fig.* velo, manto, *m*; (pretence) pretexto, *m*; *Com.* garantía, *f*. **outer c.,** (of tire) cubierta de neumático, *f*. **to c. oneself with glory,** cubrirse de gloria. **to c. up,** cubrir completamente; (with clothes) arropar; (wrap up) envolver. **to c. with a revolver,** amenazar con un revólver. **to read a book from c. to c.,** leer un libro del principio al fin. **to take c.,** refugiarse, tomar abrigo. **under c.,** bajo tejado; al abrigo
**cover charge** *n* consumo mínimo, precio del cubierto, *m*
**covering** /'kʌvərɪŋ/ *n* cubrimiento, *m*; cubierta, *f*; envoltura, *f*; capa, *f*, abrigo, *m*. **c. letter,** carta adjunta, *f*
**coverlet** /'kʌvərlɪt/ *n* colcha, sobrecama, *f*
**covert** /a 'kouvərt; *n* 'kʌvərt/ *a* oculto; furtivo. **—n** guarida *f*
**covertly** /'kouvərtli/ *adv* secretamente, furtivamente
**covet** /'kʌvɪt/ *vt* codiciar; ambicionar, suspirar por
**covetous** /'kʌvɪtəs/ *a* codicioso; ávido; ambicioso
**covetously** /'kʌvɪtəsli/ *adv* codiciosamente; ávidamente
**covetousness** /'kʌvɪtəsnɪs/ *n* codicia, avaricia, *f*; avidez, *f*; ambición, *f*
**cow** /kau/ *vt* intimidar, acobardar
**cow** /kau/ *n* vaca, *f*; (of other animals) hembra, *f*. **c.-bell,** cencerro, *m*, zumba, *f*. **c.-catcher,** *Auto.* salvavidas, *m*. **c.-hide,** cuero, cuero de vaca, zurriago, *m*; penca, *f*. **c.-house,** establo, *m*, boyera, *f*. **c.-pox,** vacuna, *f*
**coward** /'kauərd/ *n* cobarde, *m*, *a* cobarde
**cowardice** /'kauərdɪs/ *n* cobardía, *f*
**cowardly** /'kauərdli/ *a* cobarde
**cowboy** /'kau,bɔi/ *n* vaquero, *m*; gaucho, "cowboy," *m*
**cower** /'kauər/ *vi* no saber dónde meterse; temblar, acobardarse
**cowherd** /'kau,hɜrd/ *n* vaquero, boyero, *m*
**cowl** /kaul/ *n* capucha, *f*; (of a chimney) sombrerete, *m*
**cowlike** /'kau,laik/ *a* de vaca; bovino
**coworker** /'kou,wɜrkər, kou'wɜr-/ *n* colaborador (-ra)
**cowshed** /'kau,ʃed/ *n* establo, *m*
**cowslip** /'kauslɪp/ *n* prímula, *f*
**cox** /kɒks/ *n* timonel, *m*
**coxcomb** /'kɒks,koum/ *n* (of a jester) gorra de bufón, *f*; mequetrefe, *m*
**coxswain** /'kɒksən/ *n* patrón, *m*; (of a rowboat) timonel, *m*
**coy** /kɔi/ *a* modoso, tímido; coquetón
**coyly** /'kɔili/ *adv* tímidamente; con coquetería
**coyness** /'kɔinɪs/ *n* timidez, modestia, *f*; coquetería, *f*
**cozy** /'kouzi/ *a* cómodo; agradable; caliente. **You are very c. here,** Estás muy bien aquí
**crab** /kræb/ *n* (sea) cangrejo de mar, cámbaro, *m*; (river) cangrejo, *m*; *Astron.* Cáncer, *m*. **—vt** (thwart)

frustrar. **hermit c.,** cangrejo ermitaño, *m.* **c.-apple,** manzana silvestre, *f.* **c.-louse,** ladilla, *f*

**crabbed** /'kræbɪd/ *a* áspero, hosco, desabrido, arisco; (of handwriting) apretado, metido

**crack** /kræk/ *vt* hender; quebrantar, romper; (nuts) cascar; (a whip and fingers) chasquear; (a bottle of wine) abrir. —*vi* (of earth, skin, etc.) agrietarse; romperse, quebrarse; (of the voice) romper; (of the male voice) mudar. —*n* hendedura, rendija, *f;* quebraja, *f;* (of a whip) chasquido, *m;* (of a rifle) estallido, *m;* (blow) golpe, garrotazo, *m, a* excelente, de primera categoría; estupendo. **to c. a joke,** decir un chiste. **to c. up,** *vt* dar bombo (a), alabar. —*vi* (in health) quebrantarse; (airplane) cuartearse, estrellarse. **c.-brained,** chiflado; estúpido, loco

**cracked** /krækt/ *a* grietado; (of a bell, etc.) hendido; (of the voice) cascada; (of a person) chiflado

**cracker** /'krækər/ *n* (firework) petardo, *m;* buscapiés, *m*

**crackle** /'krækəl/ *vi* (of burning wood, etc.) crepitar; (rustle) crujir; (of rifle fire) tirotear. —*n* crepitación, *f;* crujido, *m;* (of rifle fire) tiroteo, *m*

**crackling** /'kræklɪŋ/ *n.* See crackle; *Cul.* chicharrón, *m*

**Cracow** /'krækau/ Cracovia, *f*

**cradle** /'kreidl̩/ *n* cuna, *f; Fig.* niñez, infancia, *f;* (for a limb) arco de protección, *m;* (for winebottle) cesta, *f.* —*vt* mecer. **c.-song,** canción de cuna, *f*

**craft** /kræft/ *n* (guile) astucia, *f;* (skill) habilidad, *f;* arte, *mf;* (occupation) oficio manual, *m;* profesión, *f;* (guild) gremio, *m;* (boat) barco, *m,* embarcación, *f*

**craftily** /'kræftl̩i/ *adv* astutamente

**craftiness** /'kræftɪnɪs/ *n* astucia, *f*

**craftsman** /'kræftsmən/ *n* artífice, *m;* arte sano, *m;* artista, *m*

**craftsmanship** /'kræftsmən,ʃɪp/ *n* arte, *m,* or *f;* habilidad, *f;* artificio, *m*

**crafty** /'kræfti/ *a* astuto, taimado

**crag** /kræg/ *n* peña, *f,* risco, despeñadero, *m*

**cragginess** /'krægɪnɪs/ *n* escabrosidad, aspereza, fragosidad, *f*

**craggy** /'krægi/ *a* escabroso, escarpado, peñascoso, riscoso

**cram** /kræm/ *vt* henchir; atestar; (one's mouth) llenar (de); (poultry) cebar; (a pupil) preparar para un examen; (a subject) empollar. —*vi* (with food) atracarse. **The room was crammed with people,** La sala estaba atestada de gente

**cramp** /kræmp/ *n Med.* calambre, *m;* (numbness) entumecimiento, *m;* (rivet) grapa, *f.* —*vt* dar calambre (a); (numb) entumecer; (fasten) lañar; (*Fig.* hamper) estorbar. **to c. someone's style,** cortar los vuelos (a). **writer's c.,** calambre del escribiente, *m*

**cramped** /kræmpt/ *a* (of space) apretado, estrecho; (of writing) menuda

**cranberry** /'kræn,bɛri/ *n* arándano, *m*

**crane** /krein/ *n Ornith.* grulla, *f;* (machine) grúa, *f.* **jib c.,** grúa de pescante, *f.* **travelling c.,** grúa móvil, *f.* **to c. one's neck,** estirar el cuello. **crane's bill,** pico de cigüeña, *m*

**cranium** /'kreiniəm/ *n* cráneo, *m*

**crank** /kræŋk/ *n* (handle) manivela, *f;* (person) maniático (-ca). —*vt* poner en marcha (un motor) con la manivela

**crankiness** /'kræŋkɪnɪs/ *n* (crossness) irritabilidad, *f,* mal humor, *m;* (eccentricity) excentricidad, *f*

**cranky** /'kræŋki/ *a* (cross) irritable, malhumorado; (eccentric) chiflado, maniático, excéntrico

**cranny** /'kræni/ *n* hendedura, grieta, *f*

**crape** /kreip/ *n* crespón, *m*

**crash** /kræʃ/ *vi* caer estrepitosamente; romperse; estallarse; (of aircraft, cars) estrellarse; *Fig.* hundirse, arruinarse. —*n* estrépito, estruendo, *m;* estallido, *m;* (of aircraft) accidente de aviación, *m;* (car) accidente, *m,* (or choque, *m*) de automóviles; (financial) ruina, *f; Fig.* hundimiento, *m.* **to c. into,** estrellarse contra, chocar con. **c. helmet,** casco, *m.* **c.-landing,** aterrizaje violento, *m*

**crass** /kræs/ *a* craso

**crassness** /'kræsnɪs/ *n* estupidez, *f*

**crate** /kreit/ *n* (box) caja de embalaje, *f;* (basket) canasto, *m,* banasta, *f*

**crater** /'kreitər/ *n* cráter, *m*

**cravat** /krə'væt/ *n* corbata, *f*

**crave** /kreiv/ *vt* suplicar, implorar. **to c. for,** perecer por, suspirar por, anhelar

**craven** /'kreivən/ *a* cobarde, pusilánime. —*n* poltrón, cobarde, *m*

**craving** /'kreivɪŋ/ *n* deseo vehemente, *m,* sed, *f*

**crawfish** /'krɔ,fɪʃ/ *n* cangrejo de río, *m;* cigala, *f*

**crawl** /krɔl/ *vi* arrastrarse; andar a gatas; andar a paso de tortuga; (abase oneself) humillarse; (be full of) abundar (en). —*n* paso de tortuga, *m;* (swimming) arrastne *m*

**crayfish** /'krei,fɪʃ/ *n* cangrejo de río, *m;* cigala, *f*

**crayon** /'kreiən/ *n* carbón, *m;* pastel, *m;* (pencil) lápiz de color, *m.* —*vt* dibujar con pastel, etc. **c. drawing,** dibujo al carbón, *m*

**craze** /kreiz/ *vt* enloquecer, volver loco (a). —*n* manía, *f,* capricho, entusiasmo, *m;* (fashion) moda, *f*

**crazily** /'kreizəli/ *adv* locamente

**craziness** /'kreizɪnɪs/ *n* locura, *f*

**crazy** /'kreizi/ *a* loco; chiflado; (of structure) dilapidado. **He is c. about music,** Está loco por la música. **to be completely c.,** (of persons) ser un loco de atar; ser completamente loco. **to drive c.,** volver loco (a)

**creak** /krik/ *vi* (of shoes, chairs, etc.) crujir; (of gates, etc.) rechinar, chirriar. —*n* crujido, *m;* chirrido, *m*

**creaking** /'krikɪŋ/ *n.* See **creak**

**creaky** /'kriki/ *a* crujiente, que cruje; chirriador

**cream** /krim/ *n* crema, *f;* nata, *f; Fig.* flor, nata, *f.* —*a* de nata. **whipped c.,** nata batida, *f.* **c. cake,** pastel de nata, *m.* **c.-cheese,** queso de nata, *m.* **c.-colored,** de color crema. **c.-jug,** jarro para crema, *m.* **c. of tartar,** cremor, tártaro, *m*

**creamery** /'kriməri/ *n* lechería, *f*

**creamy** /'krimi/ *a* cremoso

**crease** /kris/ *n* (wrinkle) arruga, *f;* (fold) pliegue, *m;* (in trousers) raya, *f;* (in cricket) línea de la meta, *f.* —*vt* (wrinkle) arrugar; (fold) plegar; (trousers) poner la raya en. —*vi* arrugarse

**create** /kri'eit/ *vt* crear; (appoint) nombrar; (produce) suscitar, producir

**creation** /kri'eiʃən/ *n* creación, *f;* establecimiento, *m;* (appointment) nombramiento, *m*

**creative** /kri'eitɪv/ *a* creador; de la creación

**creativeness** /kri'eitɪvnɪs/ *n* facultad creativa, inventiva, *f*

**creator** /kri'eitər/ *n* creador (-ra)

**creature** /'kritʃər/ *n* criatura, *f;* animal, *m.* **c. comforts,** bienestar material, *m*

**crèche** /krɛʃ/ *n* casa cuna, *f*

**credence** /'kridns/ *n* crédito, *m,* fe, creencia, *f; Eccl.* credencia, *f.* **to give c. to,** dar crédito (a), creer

**credentials** /krɪ'dɛnʃəlz/ *n pl* credenciales, *f pl*

**credibility** /,krɛdə'bɪlɪti/ *n* credibilidad, verosimilitud, *f*

**credible** /'krɛdəbəl/ *a* creíble, verosímil; (of persons) digno de confianza

**credibly** /'krɛdəbli/ *adv* creíblemente

**credit** /'krɛdɪt/ *n* crédito, *m;* reputación, *f;* honor, *m;* (Com. and banking) crédito, *m;* (in bookkeeping) data, *f.* —*vt* dar fe (a), dar crédito (a); creer; atribuir; (bookkeeping) acreditar. **It does them c.,** Les hace honor. **on c.,** a crédito, al fiado. **open c.,** *Com.* letra abierta, *f.* **to give on c.,** dar fiado. **c. balance,** haber, *m*

**creditable** /'krɛdɪtəbəl/ *a* loable, honroso, digno de alabanza

**creditably** /'krɛdɪtəbli/ *adv* honrosamente

**creditor** /'krɛdɪtər/ *n* acreedor (-ra); (bookkeeping) haber, *m*

**credulity** /krə'dulɪti/ *n* credulidad, *f*

**credulous** /'krɛdʒələs/ *a* crédulo

**credulously** /'krɛdʒələsli/ *adv* con credulidad, crédulamente

**creed** /krid/ *n* credo, *m*

**creek** /krik/ *n* caleta, abra, *f*

**creel** /kril/ *n* (for fish) cesta de pescador, *f*

**creep** /krip/ *vi* arrastrarse; (of plants and birds) trepar; (of infants) andar a gatas; (totter) hacer pinitos; (slip) deslizarse; (cringe) lisonjear, rebajarse; (of one's flesh) sentir hormigueo. **to c. about on tiptoe,**

andar de puntillas. **to c. into a person's favor,** insinuarse en el favor de. **to c. in,** entrar sin ser notado (en); deslizarse en. **to c. on,** (of time) avanzar lentamente; (of old age, etc.) acercarse insensiblemente. **to c. out,** salir sin hacer ruido; escurrirse. **to c. up,** trepar por; subir a gatas

**creeper** /'kripər/ n Bot. enredadera, f; Ornith. trepador, m; Zool. reptil, m

**creeping** /'kripɪŋ/ a Bot. trepante; Zool. trepador; (servile) rastrero

**cremate** /'krimeit/ vt incinerar

**cremation** /krɪ'meiʃən/ n cremación, f

**crematorium** /ˌkrimə'tɔriəm/ n crematorio, m; horno de incineración, m, inhumadora, f

**creole** /'krioul/ a criollo. —n criollo (-lla)

**creolize** /'kriəˌlaiz/ vt acriollar

**crescent** /'kresənt/ n media luna, f; Herald. creciente, m; calle en forma de semicírculo, f. —a en forma de media luna; Poet. creciente

**cress** /kres/ n Bot. berro, m

**crest** /krest/ n (of a cock, etc.) cresta, f; (plume) penacho, m; (of a helmet) cimera, f; (of a hill) cumbre, cima, f; (of a wave) cresta, f. **family c.,** blasón, escudo, m

**crestfallen** /'krest,fɔlən/ a cabizbajo, cariacontecido

**cretan** /'kritṇ/ a cretense. —n cretense, mf

**Crete** /krit/ Creta, f

**cretin** /'kritṇ/ n cretino (-na)

**cretinism** /'kritṇˌɪzəm/ n cretinismo, m

**crevasse** /krə'væs/ n grieta en un ventisquero, f

**crevice** /'krevɪs/ n intersticio, m, rendija, grieta, f

**crew** /kru/ n (of ships, boats, aircraft) tripulación, f; (of a gun) servidores de una ametralladora, m pl; (gang) pandilla, cuadrilla, f

**crib** /krɪb/ n pesebre, m; (child's) camita de niño, f; (plagiary) plagio, m. —vt (plagiarize) plagiar; (steal) hurtar

**crick** /krɪk/ n (in the neck) tortícolis, m

**cricket** /'krɪkɪt/ n Ent. grillo, m; (game) cricquet, m. **c. ball,** pelota de cricquet, f. **c. bat,** paleta de cricquet, f. **c. ground,** campo de cricquet, m. **c. match,** partido de cricquet, m

**cricketer** /'krɪkɪtər/ n jugador de cricquet, m

**crier** /'kraiər/ n (town) pregonero, m

**crime** /kraim/ n crimen, m; ofensa, f, delito, m

**Crimean War, the** /krai'miən/ la guerra de Crimea, la guerra de Oriente, f

**Crimea, the** /krai'miə/ la Crimea, f

**criminal** /'krɪmənḷ/ a criminal. —n criminal, m; reo, mf **C. Investigation Department,** (nearest equivalent) policía secreta, f. **c. laws,** código penal, m

**criminally** /'krɪmənḷi/ adv criminalmente

**criminologist** /ˌkrɪmə'nɒlədʒɪst/ n criminalista, m

**criminology** /ˌkrɪmə'nɒlədʒi/ n criminología, f

**crimp** /krɪmp/ vt (hair) rizar

**crimson** /'krɪmzən, -sən/ n carmesí, m. —a de carmesí. —vt teñir de carmesí. —vi enrojecerse

**cringe** /krɪndʒ/ vi temblar; asustarse, acobardarse; inclinarse (ante)

**cringing** /'krɪndʒɪŋ/ a servil, humilde; adulador

**crinkle** /'krɪŋkəl/ vi arrugarse; rizarse. —vt arrugar. —n arruga, f

**crinoline** /'krɪnḷɪn/ n crinolina, f, miriñaque, guardainfante, m

**cripple** /'krɪpəl/ n tullido (-da); cojo (-ja). —vt lisiar, tullir, estropear; Fig. paralizar

**crisis** /'kraisɪs/ n crisis, f

**crisp** /krɪsp/ a (of hair and of leaves) crespo; (fresh) fresco; (stiff) tieso; (of style) nervioso, vigoroso; (of manner) decidido; (of repartee) chispeante; (of tone) incisivo

**crisscross** /'krɪsˌkrɔs/ vt (a body of water or land) surcar

**criterion** /krai'tɪəriən/ n criterio, m

**critic** /'krɪtɪk/ n crítico, m; censor, m

**critical** /'krɪtɪkəl/ a crítico

**criticism** /'krɪtəˌsɪzəm/ n crítica, f

**criticize** /'krɪtəˌsaiz/ vt criticar; censurar

**critique** /krɪ'tik/ n crítica, f

**croak** /krouk/ vi (of frogs) croar; (of ravens) graznar; (of persons) lamentarse, gruñir

**croaking** /'kroukɪŋ/ n canto de la rana, m; graznido, m

**Croat** /'krouæt/ a croata. —n croata, mf

**Croatia** /krou'eiʃə/ Crocia, f

**crochet** /krou'ʃei/ n ganchillo, m, vi hacer ganchillo. —vt hacer (algo) de ganchillo. **c. hook,** aguja de gancho, f, ganchillo, m. **c. work,** croché, ganchillo, m

**crockery** /'krɒkəri/ n loza, f, cacharros, m pl. **c. store,** cacharrería, f

**crocodile** /'krɒkəˌdail/ n cocodrilo, m. **c. tears,** lágrimas de cocodrilo, f pl

**crocus** /'kroukəs/ n azafrán, m

**croft** /krɔft/ n campillo, m; (farm) heredad, f

**crofter** /'krɔftər/ n colono, m

**crone** /kroun/ n bruja, f

**crony** /'krouni/ n compinche, mf

**crook** /krʊk/ n curva, f; (staff) cayado, m; (swindler) caballero de industria, estafador, m, vt doblar, encorvar

**crooked** /'krʊkɪd/ a curvo; encorvado; torcido; ladeado; (deformed) contrahecho; (of paths, etc.) tortuoso; (dishonest) torcido, tortuoso

**crookedly** /'krʊkɪdli/ adv torcidamente; de través

**crookedness** /'krʊkɪdnɪs/ n encorvadura, f; tortuosidad, f; sinuosidad, f

**croon** /krun/ vt and vi canturrear; cantar

**crooner** /'krunər/ n cantante, m

**crop** /krɒp/ n (of birds) buche, m; (whip) látigo, m, fusta, f; (handle) mango, m; (harvest) cosecha, f; (of the hair) cortadura, f. —vt cortar; (nibble) rozar; (hair) rapar. **Eton c.,** pelo a la garçonne, m. **to c. up,** aparecer, surgir

**crop rotation** n la rotación de cultivos, f

**croquet** /krou'kei/ n juego de la argolla, juego de croquet, m

**croquette** /krou'ket/ n Cul. croqueta, f

**crosier** /'krouʒər/ n báculo, cayado del obispo, m

**cross** /krɔs/ n cruz, f; Biol. cruzamiento, m; (Sew. bias) bies, m. **in the shape of a c.,** en cruz. **the Red C.,** la Cruz Roja. **c.-bearer,** Eccl. crucero, m

**cross** /krɔs/ vt cruzar; atravesar; pasar por; (a check and animals) cruzar; (thwart) contrariar. **It did not c. my mind,** No se me ocurrió. **Our letters must have crossed,** Nuestras cartas deben haberse cruzado. **to c. oneself,** Eccl. persignarse. **to c. out,** tachar, rayar. **to c. over,** vt atravesar, cruzar. —vi ir al otro lado

**cross** /krɔs/ a transversal; cruzado; oblicuo; (contrary) opuesto (a); (bad-tempered) malhumorado. **c.-breed,** a mestizo, atravesado. **c.-country,** a a campo travieso. **c.-examination,** Law. pregunta, f, contrainterrogatorio, m. **c.-examine,** vt Law. repreguntar; interrogar. **c.-eyed,** bizco. **c.-fire,** Mil. fuego cruzado, m; sing fuegos cruzados, m pl; Fig. tiroteo, m. **c.-grained,** (of wood) vetisegado; (of persons) áspero, intratable, desabrido. **c.-legged,** con las piernas cruzadas. **c.-purpose,** despropósito, m. **at c.-purposes,** a despropósito. **c.-question,** vt Law. repreguntar; interrogar. **c. reference,** contrarreferencia, f. **c. section,** sección transversal, f. **c.-stitch,** punto cruzado, m. **c.-word puzzle,** crucigrama, m

**crossbar** /'krɔs,bɑr/ n travesaño, m

**crossbeam** /'krɔs,bim/ n viga transversal, f

**crossbench** /'krɔs,bentʃ/ a atravesado

**crossbred** /'krɔs,bred/ a cruzado, mestizo; híbrido

**crossbreed** /'krɔs,brid/ n mestizo (-za); híbrido, m

**crossing** /'krɔsɪŋ/ n cruzamiento, m; (of the sea) travesía, f; (intersection) cruce, m; paso, m. **level c.,** paso a nivel, m. **pedestrian c.,** paso para peatones, m. **c.-sweeper,** barrendero, m

**crossly** /'krɔsli/ adv con mal humor, con displicencia, irritablemente

**crossness** /'krɔsnɪs/ n irritabilidad, f, mal humor, m

**crossroad** /'krɔs,roud/ n travesía, f; cruce, m; pl **crossroads,** cruce, cruce de caminos, m sing encrucijada, f sing

**crosswise** /'krɔs,waiz/ adv en cruz; a través

**crotch** /krɒtʃ/ n (of a tree) bifurcación, f; Anat. horcajadura, f; (of breeches) entrepiernas, f pl

**crotchet** /'krɒtʃɪt/ n Mus. semínima, f; (fad) capricho, m; extravagancia, excentricidad, f

**crotchety** /'krɒtʃɪti/ a caprichoso; raro, excéntrico; difícil

**crouch** /krautʃ/ vi acurrucarse, agacharse, acuclillarse
**croup** /krup/ n (disease) crup, garrotillo, m; (of a horse) grupa, anca, f
**croupier** /'krupiər/ n coime, crupié, m
**crow** /krou/ n Ornith. cuervo, m; Ornith. grajo, m; (of a cock) canto del gallo, cacareo, m; (of an infant) gorjeo, m. —vi (of a cock) cantar, cacarear; (of an infant) gorjearse. **as the c. flies**, en línea recta. **to c. over**, gallear, cantar victoria. **crow's-foot**, pata de gallo, f. **crow's-nest**, Naut. gavias, f pl
**crowbar** /'krou,bɑr/ n alzaprima, palanca, f
**crowd** /kraud/ n multitud, muchedumbre, f; concurso, m; vulgo, m; (majority) mayoría, f; Theat. acompañamiento, m. —vi reunirse, congregarse; agolparse, remolinarse, apiñarse. —vt (fill) llenar; atestar. **in a c.**, en tropel. **So many ideas crowded in on me**, Se me ocurrieron tantas ideas a la vez. **to follow the c.**, seguir la multitud; Fig. ir con la mayoría. **to c. in**, entrar en tropel. **to c. round**, cercar, agruparse alrededor de. **to c. together**, apiñarse. **to c. up**, subir en masa, subir en tropel
**crowded** /'kraudɪd/ a lleno; atestado, apiñado; (weighed down) agobiado; (of hours, etc.) lleno
**crowing** /'krouɪŋ/ n cacareo, canto del gallo, m; (of an infant) gorjeos, m pl; (boasting) jactancia, f
**crown** /kraun/ n corona, f; (of the head) coronilla, corona, f; (of a hat) copa, f; Archit. coronamiento, m. —vt coronar. **c. prince**, príncipe heredero, m
**crowning** /'kraunɪŋ/ n coronamiento, m; Archit. remate, m, a final; supremo
**crozier** /'krouʒər/ n. See **crosier**
**crucial** /'kruʃəl/ a decisivo, crítico; difícil
**crucible** /'krusəbəl/ n crisol, m
**crucifix** /'krusəfɪks/ n crucifijo, m
**crucifixion** /,krusə'fɪkʃən/ n crucifixión, f
**cruciform** /'krusə,fɔrm/ a cruciforme
**crucify** /'krusə,fai/ vt crucificar
**crude** /krud/ a crudo; (of colors) chillón, llamativo; (uncivilized) cerril, inculto; (vulgar) cursi; (of truth, etc.) desnudo
**crudity** /'krudɪti/ n crudeza, f
**cruel** /'kruəl/ a cruel
**cruelty** /'kruəlti/ n crueldad, f
**cruet** /'kruɪt/ n ánfora, vinagrera, f; (stand) angarillas, f pl, convoy, m
**cruise** /kruz/ vi cruzar, navegar; (of cars) correr. —n viaje por mar, m
**cruiser** /'kruzər/ n crucero, m
**crumb** /krʌm/ n miga, f; (spongy part of bread) migaja, f. —vt (bread) desmigajar; desmenuzar. **c. brush**, recogemigas, m
**crumble** /'krʌmbəl/ vt desmigajar, desmenuzar. —vi desmoronarse, desmigajarse; Fig. hundirse, derrumbarse; Fig. desaparecer
**crumbling** /'krʌmblɪŋ/ n (of buildings, etc.) desmoronamiento, m; Fig. destrucción, f
**crumple** /'krʌmpəl/ vt arrugar, ajar. —vi arrugarse. **to c. up**, vt (crush) estrujar; (persons) dejar aplastado. —vi (collapse) hundirse, derrumbarse; (of persons) desplomarse; (despair) desalentarse
**crunch** /krʌntʃ/ vt mascar; hacer crujir. —vi crujir
**crupper** /'krʌpər/ n baticola, f
**crusade** /kru'seid/ n cruzada, f
**crusader** /kru'seidər/ n cruzado, m
**crush** /krʌʃ/ vt aplastar; (to powder) moler, triturar; (grapes, etc.) exprimir; (crease) arrugar; (opposition, etc.) vencer; (annihilate) aniquilar, destruir; (abash) humillar, confundir; (hope, etc.) matar; (of sorrow, etc.) agobiar. **We all crushed into his diningroom**, Fuimos en tropel a su comedor. **to c. up**, machacar, moler; (paper, etc.) estrujar
**crushing** /'krʌʃɪŋ/ a (of defeats and replies) aplastante; (of sorrow, etc.) abrumador
**crust** /krʌst/ n (of bread, pie) corteza, f; (scab) costra, f; (of the earth, snow) capa, f. —vt encostrar. —vi encostrarse. **c. of bread**, mendrugo de pan, m
**crustacean** /krʌ'steiʃən/ n crustáceo. —n crustáceo, m
**crustily** /'krʌstli/ adv irritablemente, malhumoradamente
**crustiness** /'krʌstɪnɪs/ n mal humor, m, aspereza, f

**crusty** /'krʌsti/ a costroso; (of persons) malhumorado, irritable; áspero
**crutch** /krʌtʃ/ n muleta, f; (fork) horquilla, f; (crotch) horcajadura, f
**crux** /krʌks/ n problema, m; (knotty point) nudo, m
**cry** /krai/ vi (weep) llorar; (shout) gritar; (exclaim) exclamar. —vt (one's wares) pregonar. —n grito, m. **to cry for help**, pedir socorro a voces. **to cry to high heaven**, poner el grito en el cielo. **to cry one's eyes out**, llorar a mares. **to cry down**, desacreditar. **to cry off**, desdecirse; volverse atrás. **to cry out**, vt gritar. —vi dar gritos; gritar; Fig. clamar. **cry-baby**, niño (-ña) llorón (-ona)
**crying** /'kraiɪŋ/ a urgente; notorio. —n gritos, m pl; (weeping) llanto, m, lamentaciones, f pl; (tears) lágrimas, f pl
**crypt** /krɪpt/ n cripta, f
**cryptic** /'krɪptɪk/ a secreto, oculto
**cryptography** /krɪp'tɒgrəfi/ n criptografía, f
**crystal** /'krɪstl/ n cristal, m. **c. set**, Radio. receptor de galena, m
**crystal ball** n bola de cristal, esfera de cristal, f
**crystalline** /'krɪstlɪn/ a cristalino
**crystallization** /,krɪstlə'zeiʃən/ n cristalización, f
**crystallize** /'krɪstl,aiz/ vt and vi cristalizar
**crystallography** /,krɪstl'ɒgrəfi/ n cristalografía, f
**cub** /kʌb/ n cachorro (-rra)
**Cuban** /'kyubən/ a cubano. —n cubano (-na)
**cubbyhole** /'kʌbi,houl/ n refugio, m; garita, f; cuarto pequeño, m; chiribitil, m
**cube** /kyub/ n cubo, m; (of sugar) terrón, m. —vt cubicar. **c. root**, raíz cúbica, f
**cubic** /'kyubɪk/ a cúbico
**cubicle** /'kyubɪkəl/ n cubículo, m
**cubism** /'kyubɪzəm/ n cubismo, m
**cubist** /'kyubɪst/ n cubista, mf
**cubit** /'kyubɪt/ n codo, m
**cuckold** /'kʌkəld/ n cornudo, m
**cuckoo** /'kuku/ n cuclillo, m; (cry) cucú, m. **c.-clock**, reloj de cuclillo, m
**cucumber** /'kyukʌmbər/ n cohombro m
**cud** /kʌd/ n rumia, f. **to chew the cud**, rumiar
**cuddle** /'kʌdl/ vt abrazar. —n abrazo, m. **to c. up together**, estar abrazados
**cudgel** /'kʌdʒəl/ n porra, estaca, tranca, f, vt aporrear, apalear. **to c. one's brains**, devanarse los sesos. **to take up the cudgels for**, salir en defensa de
**cue** /kyu/ n Theat. pie, m; (lead) táctica, f; (hint) indicación, f; (of hair) coleta, f; (billiard) taco (de billar), m. **to take one's cue from**, tomar como modelo (a); seguir el ejemplo de
**cuff** /kʌf/ n abofetear. —n (blow) bofetón, m; (of sleeve) puño, m, bocamanga, valenciana, f. **c.-links**, gemelos, m pl
**cuisine** /kwɪ'zin/ n cocina, f
**cul-de-sac** /'kʌldə'sæk/ n callejón sin salida, m
**culinary** /'kyulə,neri/ a culinario
**cullender** /'kʌləndər/ n colador, m
**culminate** /'kʌlmə,neit/ vi culminar (en), terminar (en). **culminating point**, punto culminante, m
**culmination** /,kʌlmə'neiʃən/ n culminación, f; Fig. apogeo, punto culminante, m
**culpability** /,kʌlpə'bɪliti/ n culpabilidad, f
**culpable** /'kʌlpəbəl/ a culpable
**culpably** /'kʌlpəbli/ adv culpablemente
**culprit** /'kʌlprɪt/ n culpado (-da)
**cult** /kʌlt/ n culto, m
**cultivable** /'kʌltəvəbəl/ a cultivable, labradero
**cultivate** /'kʌltə,veit/ vt cultivar
**cultivated** /'kʌltə,veitid/ a cultivado; (of persons) culto, fino
**cultivation** /,kʌltə'veiʃən/ n cultivación, f; (of the land) cultivo, m; (of persons, etc.) cultura, f
**cultivator** /'kʌltə,veitər/ n cultivador (-ra); (machine) cultivador, m
**cultural** /'kʌltʃərəl/ a cultural
**culture** /'kʌltʃər/ n cultura, f; (bacteriology) cultivo, m, vt (bacteriology) cultivar
**cultured** /'kʌltʃərd/ a culto, m
**culvert** /'kʌlvərt/ n alcantarilla, f
**cumbersome** /'kʌmbərsəm/ a pesado; incómodo

**cumulative** /'kyumyələtɪv/ *a* cumulativo

**cumulus** /'kyumyələs/ *n* cúmulo, *m*

**cuneiform** /kyu'nɪə,fɔrm/ *a* cuneiforme

**cunning** /'kʌnɪŋ/ *a* astuto, taimado. —*n* (skill) habilidad, *f*; astucia, *f*

**cup** /kʌp/ *n* taza, *f*; (*Eccl.* and *Bot.*) cáliz, *m*; *Sports.* copa, *f*; (hollow) hoyo, *m*, hondonada, *f*. **c.-final,** *Sports.* final de la copa, *m*. **c.-tie,** *Sports.* partido eliminatorio, *m*

**cup-and-ball** /'kʌpən'bɔl/ *n* boliche, *m*

**cupboard** /'kʌbərd/ *n* armario, *m*; (in the wall) alacena, *f*. **c. love,** amor interesado, *m*

**cupful** /'kʌpfʊl/ *n* taza, *f*

**cupidity** /kyu'pɪdɪti/ *n* avaricia, codicia, *f*

**cup of sorrow** *n* ramito de amargura, *m*

**cupola** /'kyupələ/ *n* cúpula, *f*

**cur** /kɜr/ *n* perro mestizo, *m*; canalla, *m*

**curable** /'kyʊrəbəl/ *a* curable

**curableness** /'kyʊrəbəlnɪs/ *n* curabilidad, *f*

**curative** /'kyʊrətɪv/ *a* curativo, terapéutico

**curator** /kyʊ'reɪtər/ *n* (of a museum) director, *m*; (Scots law) curador, *m*

**curb** /kɜrb/ *n* (of a bridle) barbada, *f*; *Fig.* freno, *m*; (stone) bordillo, *m*, guarnición, *f*. —*vt* (a horse) enfrenar; *Fig.* refrenar, reprimir; (limit) limitar

**curd** /kɜrd/ *n* requesón, *m*; cuajada, *f*

**curdle** /'kɜrdl/ *vi* coagularse; (of blood) helarse. —*vt* coagular; (blood) helar

**cure** /kyʊr/ *n* cura, *f*; *Eccl.* curato, *m*. —*vt* curar; (salt) salar; *Fig.* remediar. **to take a c.,** tomar una cura. **c.-all,** panacea, *f*. **c. of souls,** cura de almas, *f*

**curer** /'kyʊrər/ *n* (of fish, etc.) salador, *m*; (of evils, etc.) remediador, *m*

**curfew** /'kɜrfyu/ *n* toque de queda, *m*

**curia** /'kyʊrɪə/ *n* *Eccl.* curia, *f*

**curing** /'kyʊrɪŋ/ *n* curación, *f*; (salting) saladura, *f*

**curio** /'kyʊri,oʊ/ *n* curiosidad, antigüedad, *f*

**curiosity** /,kyʊri'ɒsɪti/ *n* curiosidad, *f*

**curious** /'kyʊriəs/ *a* (all meanings) curioso

**curiously** /'kyʊriəsli/ *adv* curiosamente

**curl** /kɜrl/ *n* (of hair) rizo, bucle, *m*; (of smoke) penacho, *m*. —*vt* rizar. —*vi* rizarse; *Sports.* jugar al curling. **in c.,** rizado. **to c. one's lip,** hacer una mueca de desdén. **to c. up,** *vt* arrollar; *Fig.* dejar fuera de combate (a). —*vi* hacerse un ovillo, enroscarse; (of leaves) abarquillarse; *Fig.* desplomarse; desanimarse. **c.-paper,** papillote, *m*

**curlew** /'kɜrlu/ *n* *Ornith.* zarapito, *m*

**curling** /'kɜrlɪŋ/ *n* (game) curling, *m*, *a* rizado. **c.-tongs,** encrespador, *m*

**curly** /'kɜrli/ *a* rizado, crespo

**curmudgeon** /kər'mʌdʒən/ *n* erizo, misántropo, cara de viernes, *m*

**currant** /'kɜrənt/ *n* (dry) pasa de Corinto, *f*; (fresh) grosella, *f*. **black c.,** grosella negra, *f*; (bush) grosellero negro, *m*. **c.-bush,** grosellero, *m*

**currency** /'kɜrənsi/ *n* uso corriente, *m*; moneda corriente, *f*, dinero, *m*; dinero en circulación, *m*; valor corriente, *m*; estimación, *f*

**current** /'kɜrənt/ *a* corriente; presente, de actualidad; (of money) en circulación. —*n* (of water, etc., *Fig.* *Elec.*) corriente, *f*. **alternating c.,** *Elec.* corriente alterna, *f*. **direct c.,** *Elec.* corriente continua, *f*. **the c. number of a magazine,** el último número de una revista. **c. events,** actualidades, *f pl*

**currently** /'kɜrəntli/ *adv* corrientemente, generalmente

**curricle** /'kɜrɪkəl/ *n* carriola, *f*

**curriculum** /kə'rɪkyələm/ *n* plan de estudios, *m*; curso, *m*

**curriculum vitae** /'vaiti/ *n* hoja de vida, *f*

**curry** /'kɜri/ *vt* (leather) zurrar; (a horse) almohazar; *Cul.* condimentar con cari. **to c. favor with,** insinuarse en el favor de. **c.-comb,** almohaza, *f*

**curse** /kɜrs/ *n* maldición, *f*; blasfemia, *f*; (ruin) azote, castigo, *m*. —*vt* maldecir; (afflict) castigar. —*vi* blasfemar, echar pestes

**cursed** /kɜrst, 'kɜrsɪd/ *a* maldito; abominable, odioso

**cursing** /'kɜrsɪŋ/ *n* maldición, *f*; blasfemias, *f pl*

**cursive** /'kɜrsɪv/ *a* cursivo

**cursorily** /'kɜrsərəli/ *adv* rápidamente; de prisa; superficialmente

**cursory** /'kɜrsəri/ *a* rápido; apresurado; superficial

**curt** /kɜrt/ *a* seco, brusco; corto

**curtail** /kər'teil/ *vt* abreviar; reducir; disminuir

**curtailment** /kər'teilmənt/ *n* abreviación, *f*; reducción, *f*; disminución, *f*

**curtain** /'kɜrtn/ *n* cortina, *f*; *Theat.* telón, *m*. —*vt* poner cortinas (a) **drop c.,** telón de boca, *m*. **iron c.,** *Polit.* telón de acero, *m*. **to c. off,** separar por cortinas. **c.-lecture,** reprimenda conyugal, *f*. **c.-raiser,** entremés, *m*. **c.-ring,** anilla, *f*

**curtly** /'kɜrtli/ *adv* secamente, bruscamente

**curtness** /'kɜrtnɪs/ *n* brusquedad, sequedad, *f*

**curtsey** /'kɜrtsi/ *n* reverencia, cortesía, *f*, *vi* hacer una reverencia

**curvature** /'kɜrvətʃər/ *n* curvatura, *f*

**curve** /kɜrv/ *n* curva, *f*; *Mech.* codo, *m*; (*Auto.* of a road) viraje, *m*. —*vt* encorvar, torcer. —*vi* encorvarse, torcerse; (of a road) hacer un viraje.

**curved** /kɜrvd/ *a* curvo

**curvet** /'kɜrvɪt/ *n* corveta, cabriola, *f*, *vi* corvetear, corcovear, cabriolar

**curvilinear** /,kɜrvə'lɪniər/ *a* curvilíneo

**cushion** /'kʊʃən/ *n* almohada, *f*; cojín, *m*; (billiards) banda, *f*; (of fingers, etc.) pulpejo, *m*. —*vt* proveer de almohadas; (a shock) amortiguar; suavizar

**custard** /'kʌstərd/ *n* flan, *m*, natillas, *f pl*

**custodian** /kʌ'stoudiən/ *n* custodio, *m*; guardián, *m*; (of a museum, etc.) director, *m*

**custody** /'kʌstədi/ *n* custodia, *f*; guarda, *f*; prisión, *f*. **in safe c.,** en lugar seguro. **to take** (a person) **into c.,** arrestar

**custom** /'kʌstəm/ *n* costumbre, *f*; uso, *m*; *Com.* parroquia, clientela, *f*; (sales) ventas, *f pl*; *pl* **Customs,** aduana, *f*. **to go through the Customs,** pasar por la aduana. **Customs duty,** derechos de aduana, *m pl*. **Customs officer,** aduanero, *m*. **c.-house,** aduana, *f*

**customarily** /,kʌstə'merəli/ *adv* habitualmente, por lo general

**customary** /'kʌstə,meri/ *a* acostumbrado, usual, habitual

**customer** /'kʌstəmər/ *n* cliente, *mf* parroquiano (-na). **He is a queer c.,** Es un tipo raro

**customs barrier** *n* barrera aduanera, barrera arancelaria, *f*

**cut** /kʌt/ *vt* cortar; (diamonds) tallar; (hay, etc.) segar; (carve) labrar, tallar; (engrave) grabar; (a lecture, etc.) no asistir a; (cards) destajar, cortar; (*Fig.* wound) herir; (reduce) reducir; abreviar; (teeth) echar; (of lines) cruzar. —*vi* cortar; cortar bien; (*Fam.* go) marcharse a prisa y corriendo. **I must get my hair cut,** He de hacerme cortar el pelo. **That cuts both ways,** Es una arma de dos filos. **His opinion cuts no ice,** Su opinión no cuenta. **Mary cut him dead,** María hizo como si no le reconociera. **to cut a caper,** dar saltos; hacer cabriolas. **to cut a person short,** echar el tablacho (a). **to cut and run,** poner los pies en polvorosa. **to cut for deal,** (cards) cortar para ver quién da las cartas. **to cut short,** (a career) terminar. **to cut to the quick,** herir en lo más vivo. **to cut across,** cortar al través; (a class) atravesar; tomar por un atajo. **to cut away,** *vt* quitar. —*vi* *Inf.* poner pies en polvorosa. **to cut down,** derribar; (by the sword) acuchillar; (by death, etc.) segar, malograr; (expenses, etc.) reducir; (abbreviate) cortar, abreviar. **to cut off,** cortar, separar; amputar; (on a telephone) cortar la comunicación; (gas, water, etc.) cortar; (supply of food, etc.) interrumpir; (of death) llevarse. **to cut off with a shilling,** desheredar (a). **to cut out,** (dresses, etc.) cortar; (oust) suplantar. **He is not cut out for medicine,** No tiene la disposición para la medicina. **to cut up,** trinchar, cortar en pequeños trozos; (afflict) entristecer, afligir. **to cut up rough,** *Inf.* ponerse furioso

**cut** /kʌt/ *a* cortado. **well-cut features,** facciones regulares, *f pl*. **cut and dried opinion,** opinión hecha, idea fija, *f*; ideas cerradas, *f pl*. **cut glass,** cristal tallado, *m*

**cut** /kʌt/ *n* corte, *m*; (with a whip) latigazo, *m*; (with a sword) cuchillada, *f*; (with a sharp instrument) tajo, *m*; cortadura, *f*; (in prices, etc.) reducción, *f*; (en-

graving) grabado, *m;* clisé, *m;* (of cards) corte, *m.*
**short cut,** atajo, *m.* **the cut of a coat,** el corte de un
abrigo. **to give** (someone) **the cut direct,** pasar cerca
de (una persona) sin saludarle. **cut-out,** *n* (paper) recortado, *m; Elec.* cortacircuitos, *m.* **cut-throat,** *n* asesino, *m*

**cutaneous** /kyu'teiniəs/ *a* cutáneo
**cute** /kyut/ *a* cuco, listo; mono
**cuteness** /'kyutnɪs/ *n* cuquería, inteligencia, *f;*
monería, *f*
**cuticle** /'kyutɪkəl/ *n* cutícula, *f*
**cutler** /'kʌtlər/ *n* cuchillero, *m*
**cutlery** /'kʌtləri/ *n* cuchillería, *f*
**cutlet** /'kʌtlɪt/ *n* chuleta, *f*
**cutter** /'kʌtər/ *n* cortador, *m; Naut.* cúter, *m;* escampavía, *f*
**cutting** /'kʌtɪŋ/ *n* corte, *m;* (of diamonds) talla, *f;* (in
a mountain, etc.) tajo, *m; Agr.* plantón, *m;* (of cloth)
retazo, *m;* (newspaper) recorte, *m.* —*a* cortante; (of
remarks) mordaz. **newspaper c.,** recorte de periódico. **c. down,** (of trees) tala, *f;* reducción, *f*
**cuttingly** /'kʌtɪŋli/ *adv* mordazmente, con malicia.
**cuttlefish** /'kʌtl̩fɪʃ/ *n* jibia, *f*
**cyanide** /'saiə,naid/ *n* cianuro, *m*
**cyberspace** /'saibər,speis/ *n* ciberespacio, *m*
**cycle** /'saikəl/ *n* ciclo, *m;* período, *m;* (bicycle) bicicleta, *f.* —*vi* ir en bicicleta
**cyclic** /'saiklɪk/ *a* cíclico

**cycling** /'saiklɪŋ/ *n* ciclismo, *m*
**cyclist** /'saiklɪst/ *n* ciclista, *mf*
**cyclone** /'saikloun/ *n* ciclón, *m*
**Cyclopean** /,saiklə'piən/ *a* ciclópeo
**Cyclopean task** *n* obra ciclopéa, *f*
**cygnet** /'sɪgnɪt/ *n* pollo del cisne, *m*
**cylinder** /'sɪlɪndər/ *n* cilindro, *m; Mech.* tambor, *m.* **c.
head,** culata, *f*
**cylindrical** /sɪ'lɪndrɪkəl/ *a* cilíndrico
**cymbal** /'sɪmbəl/ *n* címbalo, platillo, *m*
**cymbalist** /'sɪmbəlɪst/ *n* cimbalero (-ra)
**cynic** /'sɪnɪk/ *n* cínico, *m*
**cynical** /'sɪnɪkəl/ *a* cínico
**cynicism** /'sɪnə,sɪzəm/ *n* cinismo, *m*
**cynosure** /'sainə,ʃʊr/ *n Astron.* Osa Menor, *f;* blanco,
*m*
**cypress** /'saiprəs/ *n* (tree and wood) ciprés, *m.* **c.
grove,** cipresal, *m*
**Cypriot** /'sɪpriət/ *a* chipriota. —*n* chipriota, *mf*
**Cyprus** /'saiprəs/ Isla de Chipre, *f*
**cyst** /sɪst/ *n* quiste, *m*
**cystic** /'sɪstɪk/ *a* cístico
**Czech** /tʃɛk/ *a* checo. —*n* checo (-ca); (language)
checo, *m*
**Czechoslovak** /'tʃɛkə'slouvæk/ *n* checoslovaco (-ca)
**Czechoslovakia** /,tʃɛkəslə'vakiə/ Checoslovaquia, *f*
**Czechoslovakian** /,tʃɛkəslə'vakiən/ *a* checoslovaco

# D

**d** /di/ *n* (letter) de, *f; Mus.* re, *m*
**dab** /dæb/ *vt* golpear suavemente, tocar; (sponge) esponjar; (moisten) mojar. —*n* golpecito, golpe blando, *m;* (small piece) pedazo pequeño, *m;* (blob) borrón, *m;* (peck) picotazo, *m; Inf.* experto (-ta). **to dab at one's eyes,** secarse los ojos
**dabble** /'dæbəl/ *vt* mojar (en). —*vi* chapotear; (engage in) entretenerse en; (meddle in) meterse en; (speculate in) especular en. **to d. in politics,** meterse en política
**dabbler** /'dæblər/ *n* aficionado (-da)
**dace** /deis/ *n* dardo, albur, *m*
**dachshund** /'dɑks,hʊnt/ *n* perro pachón, *m*
**daddy** /'dædi/ *n* papaíto, *m.* **d.-longlegs,** típula, *f*
**dado** /'deidou/ *n Archit.* dado, neto, *m;* friso, *m*
**daffodil** /'dæfədɪl/ *n* narciso trompón, *m*
**daft** /dæft/ *a* bobo, tonto, chiflado; loco
**dagger** /'dægər/ *n* daga, *f,* puñal, *m; Print.* cruz, *f.* **to be at daggers drawn,** estar a matar. **to look daggers (at),** lanzar miradas de odio (hacia), mirar echando chispas. **d. thrust,** puñalada, *f*
**daguerreotype** /də'gɛərə,taip/ *n* daguerrotipo, *m*
**dahlia** /'dælyə/ *n* dalia, *f*
**daily** /'deili/ *a* diario, de todos los días; cotidiano. —*adv* diariamente, cada día, todos los días; cotidianamente. —*n* (paper) diario, *m.* **d. bread,** pan cotidiano, pan de cada día, *m.* **d. help,** (person) asistenta, *f.* **d. pay,** jornal, *m; Mil.* pre, *m*
**daintily** /'deintli/ *adv* delicadamente; elegantemente; con primor
**daintiness** /'deintinis/ *n* delicadeza, *f;* elegancia, *f;* (beauty) primor, *m*
**dainty** /'deinti/ *a* delicado; elegante; primoroso, exquisito; (fastidious) melindroso, difícil. —*n* bocado exquisito, *m,* golosina, *f*
**dairy** /'dɛəri/ *n* lechería, *f.* **d. cattle,** vacas lecheras, *f pl.* **d.-farm,** granja, *f.* **d.-farmer,** granjero (-ra). **d.-farming,** industria lechera, *f*
**dairymaid** /'dɛəri,meid/ *n* lechera, *f*
**dairyman** /'dɛərimən/ *n* lechero, *m*
**dais** /'deiis/ *n* estrado, *m*
**daisy** /'deizi/ *n* margarita, *f*
**dale** /deil/ *n* valle, *m*
**dalliance** /'dæliəns/ *n* (delay) tardanza, *f;* (play) jugueteo, *m;* diversiones, *f pl;* (caresses) caricias, *f pl,* abrazos, *m pl*
**dally** /'dæli/ *vi* tardar, perder el tiempo; entretenerse, divertirse; (make love) holgar (con); (with an idea) entretenerse con, jugar con
**Dalmatian** /dæl'meifən/ *a* dalmático, dálmata. —*n* dálmata, *mf.* **D. dog,** perro dálmata, *m*
**dalmatic** /dæl'mætɪk/ *n* dalmática, *f*
**daltonism** /'dɔltn,ɪzəm/ *n* daltonismo, *m*
**dam** /dæm/ *n* (of animals) madre, *f;* (of a river, etc.) presa, *f,* embalse, *m;* (mole) dique, *m;* pared de retención, *f.* —*vt* represar, embalsar; cerrar; (restrain) contener, reprimir
**damage** /'dæmɪdʒ/ *n* daño, perjuicio, *m;* mal, *m;* avería, *f;* pérdida, *f;* (*Fam.* price) precio, *m;* *pl* **damages,** *Law.* daños y perjuicios, *m pl.* —*vt* dañar, perjudicar; estropear; deteriorar; (reputation, etc.) comprometer
**damageable** /'dæmɪdʒəbəl/ *a* que puede ser dañado; frágil
**damaging** /'dæmɪdʒɪŋ/ *a* perjudicial; comprometedor
**damascene** /'dæməsin/ *vt* damasquinar
**Damascus** /də'mæskəs/ Damasio, *m*
**damask** /'dæməsk/ *n* (cloth) damasco, *m;* (steel) acero damasquino, *m.* —*a* de damasco; damasquino. —*vt* (metals) damasquinar; (cloth) adamascar. **d.-like,** adamascado. **d. rose,** rosa de Damasco, *f*
**dame** /deim/ *n* dama, señora, *f; Inf.* madre, *f;* (schoolmistress) amiga, *f.* **to attend a d. school,** ir a la amiga
**damming** /'dæmɪŋ/ *n* embalse, *m,* represa, *f;* retención, *f;* represión, *f*

**damn** /dæm/ *vt* condenar al infierno; maldecir; vituperar. **D. it!** ¡Maldito sea!
**damnable** /'dæmnəbəl/ *a* detestable, infame; *Inf.* horrible
**damnably** /'dæmnəbli/ *adv* abominablemente; *Inf.* horriblemente
**damnation** /dæm'neifən/ *n* condenación, perdición, *f;* maldición, *f;* vituperación, *f*
**damned** /dæmd/ *a* condenado; maldito; detestable, odioso
**damning** /'dæmɪŋ/ *a* que condena; irresistible
**damp** /dæmp/ *a* húmedo. —*n* humedad, *f;* (mist) niebla, *f;* exhalación, *f;* (gas) mofeta, *f; Fig.* tristeza, depresión, *f.* —*vt* humedecer; mojar; apagar, amortiguar; (depress) deprimir, entristecer; (stifle) ahogar; (lessen) moderar; (trouble) turbar. **d.-proof,** impermeable
**damper** /'dæmpər/ *n* (of a chimney) registro de humos, *m;* (of a piano) batiente, *m;* (for stamps) mojador, *m;* (gloom) depresión, tristeza, *f;* (restraint) freno, *m*
**dampish** /'dæmpɪʃ/ *a* algo húmedo
**dampness** /'dæmpnɪs/ *n* humedad, *f*
**damsel** /'dæmzəl/ *n* chica, muchacha, *f;* damisela, *f*
**damson** /'dæmzən/ *n* ciruela damascena, *f.* **d. tree,** ciruelo damasceno, *m*
**dance** /dæns/ *n* danza, *f;* baile, *m.* —*vi* bailar, danzar; saltar, brincar. —*vt* bailar; hacer saltar. **to d. attendance on,** servir humildemente; hacer la rueda (a). **to lead someone a d.,** hacer bailar. **d. band,** orquestina, *f;* orquesta de jazz, *f.* **d. floor,** pista de baile, *f.* **d. hall,** salón de baile, *m.* **d. music,** música bailable, *f.* **d.-number,** (in a theater) bailable, *m.* **d. of death,** danza de la muerte, *f*
**dancer** /'dænsər/ *n* bailarín (-ina); danzador (-ra); bailador (-ra); *pl* **dancers,** (partners) parejas de baile, *f pl*
**dancing** /'dænsɪŋ/ *n* baile, *m,* danza, *f.* **d.-girl,** bailarina, *f;* (Indian) bayadera, *f.* **d.-master,** maestro de baile, *m.* **d. school,** academia de baile, *f.* **d. slipper,** zapatilla de baile, *f*
**dandelion** /'dændl,aiən/ *n* diente de león, *m*
**dandle** /'dændl/ *vt* mecer, hacer saltar sobre las rodillas, hacer bailar
**dandruff** /'dændrəf/ *n* caspa, *f*
**dandy** /'dændi/ *n* dandi, petimetre, barbilindo, *m*
**Dane** /dein/ *n* danés (-esa). **Great D.,** perro danés, *m*
**danger** /'deindʒər/ *n* peligro, *m;* riesgo, *m.* **out of d.,** fuera de peligro. **to be in d.,** correr peligro, peligrar, estar en peligro
**dangerous** /'deindʒərəs/ *a* peligroso; arriesgado; nocivo
**dangerously** /'deindʒərəsli/ *adv* peligrosamente
**dangerousness** /'deindʒərəsnɪs/ *n* peligro, *m*
**dangle** /'dæŋgəl/ *vi* colgar, pender. —*vt* dejar colgar; oscilar; (show) mostrar
**Danish** /'deinɪʃ/ *a* danés, de Dinamarca. —*n* (language) danés, *m*
**dank** /dæŋk/ *a* húmedo
**dankness** /'dæŋknɪs/ *n* humedad, *f*
**Danube, the** /'dænyub/ el (Río) Danubio, *m*
**dapper** /'dæpər/ *a* apuesto, aseado; activo, vivaz
**dapple** /'dæpəl/ *vt* motear, salpicar, manchar. **d.-grey,** *a* rucio
**dappled** /'dæpəld/ *a* (of horses) rodado, empedrado
**Dardanelles, the** /,dardn'elz/ los Dardanelos, *m*
**dare** /dɛər/ *vi* atreverse, osar. —*vt* arriesgar; desafiar, provocar; hacer frente a, arrostrar. —*n* reto, *m.* **I d. say!** ¡Ya lo creo! ¡No lo dudo! **I d. say that...,** No me sorprendería que...; Supongo que... **d.-devil,** calavera, *m;* atrevido (-da), valeroso (-sa)
**daring** /'dɛərɪŋ/ *a* intrépido, audaz, atrevido; (dangerous) arriesgado, peligroso. —*n* audacia, osadía, *f,* atrevimiento, *m;* peligro, *m*
**daringly** /'dɛərɪŋli/ *adv* atrevidamente
**dark** /dɑrk/ *a* oscuro; (of complexion, etc.) moreno;

negro; lóbrego; (of colours) oscuro; misterioso; enigmático; secreto, escondido; (sad) funesto, triste; (evil) malo, malévolo; (ignorant) ignorante, supersticioso. —*n* oscuridad, *f;* (shade) sombra, *f;* ignorancia, *f.* **after d.,** *a* nocturno. —*adv* después del anochecer. **in the d.,** a oscuras; de noche; *Fig.* **be in the d.,** quedarse en la luna. **to become d.,** oscurecerse; (cloud over) anublarse; (become night) anochecer. **to keep d.,** *vt* tener secreto. —*vi* esconderse. **d. ages,** los siglos de la ignorancia y de la superstición. **d.-eyed,** de ojos negros, ojinegro. **d. horse,** caballo desconocido, *m; Polit.* batacazo, *m.* **d. lantern,** linterna sorda, *f.* **d. room,** cuarto oscuro, *m; Photo.* laboratorio fotográfico, *m;* (optics) cámara oscura, *f*

**darken** /'dɑrkən/ *vt* obscurecer; sombrear; (of color) hacer más oscuro; (sadden) entristecer. —*vi* obscurecerse; (of the sky) anublarse; (of the face with emotion) inmutarse.

**darkening** /'dɑrkənɪŋ/ *n* oscurecimiento, *m*

**darkly** /'dɑrkli/ *adv* oscuramente; misteriosamente; con malevolencia; secretamente; (archaic) indistintamente

**darkness** /'dɑrknɪs/ *n* oscuridad, *f,* tinieblas, *f pl;* sombra, *f;* (of color) oscuro, *m;* (of the complexion) color moreno, *m;* (of eyes, hair) negrura, *f;* (night) noche, *f;* (ignorance) ignorancia, *f;* (privacy) secreto, *m.* **Prince of d.,** el príncipe de las tinieblas

**darling** /'dɑrlɪŋ/ *a* querido, amado; (greatest) mayor. —*n* querido (-da); (favorite) el predilecto, la predilecta, el favorito, la favorita. **My d.!** ¡Amor mío! ¡Vida mía! ¡Pichoncito mío!

**darn** /dɑrn/ *vt* zurcir, remendar. —*n* zurcido, remiendo, *m*

**darner** /'dɑrnər/ *n* zurcidor (-ra); (implement) huevo de zurcir, *m*

**darning** /'dɑrnɪŋ/ *n* zurcidura, *f;* zurcido, recosido, *m.* **d.-needle,** aguja de zurcir, *f.* **d. wool,** lana de zurcir, *f*

**dart** /dɑrt/ *n* dardo, *m;* movimiento rápido, *m;* avance rápido, *m; Sew.* sisa, *f.* —*vi* lanzarse, abalanzarse (sobre); volar; correr, avanzar rápidamente. —*vt* lanzar, arrojar; dirigir. **to make darts in,** *Sew.* sisar

**Darwinian** /dɑr'wɪniən/ *a* darviniano. —*n* darvinista, *mf*

**Darwinism** /'dɑrwə,nɪzəm/ *n* darvinismo, *m*

**dash** /dæʃ/ *n* (spirit) fogosidad, *f,* brío, *m;* energía, *f;* (impact) choque, golpe, *m;* (mixture) mezcla, *f;* (of a liquid) gota, *f;* (of the pen) rasgo, *m;* (attack) ataque, *m;* avance rápido, *m;* (a little) algo, un poco (de); *Gram.* raya, *f;* (show) ostentación, *f.* **He made a d. for the door,** Se precipitó a la puerta, Corrió hacia la puerta. **to cut a d.,** hacer gran papel. **d.-board,** tablero de instrumentos, *m*

**dash** /dæʃ/ *vt* arrojar con violencia; (break) quebrar, estrellar; (sprinkle) rociar (con), salpicar (con); (mix) mezclar; (knock) golpear; (disappoint) frustrar, destruir; (confound) confundir; (depress) desanimar. —*vi* (rush) precipitarse; quebrarse, estrellarse; chocar (contra); (of waves) romperse. **to d. to pieces,** hacer añicos, estrellar. **to d. along,** avanzar rápidamente; correr. **to d. away,** *vi* marcharse apresuradamente. —*vt* apartar bruscamente. **to d. down,** *vi* bajar aprisa. —*vt* derribar; (overturn) volcar; (throw) tirar. **to d. off,** *vi* marcharse rápidamente. —*vt* hacer apresuradamente; (a letter, etc.) escribir de prisa; (sketch) bosquejar rápidamente. **to d. out,** *vi* salir precipitadamente; lanzarse a la calle. —*vt* (erase) borrar; hacer saltar. **to d. through,** atravesar rápidamente; hacer de prisa. **to d. up,** llegar a prisa; (sprout) saltar

**dashing** /'dæʃɪŋ/ *a* valiente; (spirited) fogoso, gallardo; majo, brillante. —*n* choque, *m;* (breaking) quebrantamiento, *m;* (of the waves) embate, *m*

**dastardly** /'dæstərdli/ *a* cobarde

**data** /'deitə/ *n pl* datos, *m pl*

**database** /'deitə,beis/ *n* base de datos, *f*

**data processing** *n* elaboración electrónica de datos, *f,* recuento de datos, *m*

**date** /deit/ *n* fecha, *f;* (period) época, *f;* (term) plazo, *m;* (duration) duración, *f;* (appointment) cita, *f; Bot.* dátil, *m.* —*vt* fechar, datar; poner fecha a; asignar. —*vi* datar (de), remontar (a). **out of d.,** anticuado;

pasado de moda; (of persons) atrasado de noticias. **to be up to d.,** ser nuevo; ser de última moda; (of persons) estar al día. **to bring up to d.,** renovar; (of persons) poner al corriente. **to fix the d.,** señalar el día; (chronologically) ajustar los tiempos. **to d.,** hasta la fecha. **under d. (of),** con fecha (de). **up to d.,** hasta hoy, hasta ahora. **What is the d.?** ¿Qué fecha es? ¿A cómo estamos hoy? ¿A cuántos estamos hoy? **d. palm,** datilera, *f*

**date of expiry** *n* fecha de caducidad, *f*

**daub** /dɔb/ *vt* barrar, embadurnar; manchar, ensuciar; untar; (paint) pintorrear. —*n* embadurnamiento, *m;* (picture) aleluya, *f*

**dauber** /'dɔbər/ *n* chafalmejas, pintamonas, *mf* pintor (-ra) de brocha gorda

**daughter** /'dɔtər/ *n* hija, *f.* **adopted d.,** hija adoptiva, *f.* **little d.,** hijuela, *f.* **d.-in-law,** nuera, *f*

**daughterly** /'dɔtərli/ *a* de hija

**daunt** /dɔnt, dɑnt/ *vt* intimidar, acobardar; dar miedo (a), espantar; (dishearten) desanimar

**dauntless** /'dɔntlɪs/ *a* impávido, intrépido

**dauphin** /'dɔfɪn/ *n* delfín, *m*

**dawdle** /'dɔdl/ *vi* perder el tiempo; haraganear, gandulear

**dawdler** /'dɔdlər/ *n* gandul (-la)

**dawdling** /'dɔdlɪŋ/ *a* perezoso, lento

**dawn** /dɔn/ *n* alba, madrugada, primera luz, *f; Fig.* aurora, *f.* —*vi* amanecer, alborear, romper el día; (appear) mostrarse, asomar. **at d.,** a primera luz, al amanecer, de madrugada, al alba. **It had not dawned on me,** No me había ocurrido

**day** /dei/ *n* día, *m;* luz del día, *f;* (day's work) jornada, *f;* (battle) batalla, *f;* (victory) victoria, *f; pl* **days,** (time) tiempos, *m pl,* época, *f;* (life) vida, *f;* (years) años, *m pl, a* diario. **all day long,** durante todo el día. **any day,** cualquier día. **by day,** de día. **by the day,** al día. **every day,** todos los días, cada día. **every other day,** un día sí y otro no, cada dos días. **from this day forward,** desde hoy en adelante. **from day to day,** de día en día. **Good day!** ¡Buenos días! **in these days,** en estos días. **in olden days,** en la antigüedad; *Inf.* en tiempos de Maricastaña. **in the days of,** en los tiempos de; durante los años de; durante la vida de. **next day,** el día siguiente. **(on) the next day,** al día siguiente, al otro día. **one of these days,** un día de éstos. **some fine day,** el mejor día, de un día a otro. **the day after tomorrow,** pasado mañana. **the day before yesterday,** anteayer. **the day before,** la víspera. **to win the day,** ganar el día, salir victorioso. **day after day,** cada día, día tras día. **day by day,** día por día. **day in, day out,** un día tras día. **day-book,** *Com.* libro diario, *m.* **day's holiday,** día de asueto, *m;* día libre, *m.* **day laborer,** jornalero, *m.* **day nursery,** guardería de niños, *f.* **day-pupil,** alumno (-na) externo (-na). **day-school,** externado, *m.* **day shift,** turno de día, *m.* **day-star,** lucero del alba, *m.* **day ticket,** billete de excursión, *m*

**daybreak** /'dei,breik/ *n* alba, *f,* amanecer, *m.* **at d.,** al romper el día, al amanecer

**daydream** /'dei,drim/ *n* ensueño, *m;* ilusión, *f;* fantasía, visión, *f.* —*vi Lit.* soñar despierto, dejar volar sus pensamientos, *Fig.* hacerse ilusiones

**daydreamer** /'dei,drimər/ *n* soñador (-ra); visionario (-ia)

**daylight** /'dei,lait/ *n* luz del día, *f,* día, *m;* (contrasted with artificial light) luz natural, *f.* **in broad d.,** a plena calle, a plena luz, en pleno día. **It's d. robbery!** ¡Es un desuello! **d.-saving,** hora de verano, *f*

**daytime** /'dei,taim/ *n* día, *m.* **in the d.,** durante el día

**daze** /deiz/ *vt* aturdir, confundir; (dazzle) deslumbrar. —*n* aturdimiento, *m,* confusión, *f;* perplejidad, *f*

**dazzle** /'dæzəl/ *vt* (camouflage) disfrazar; deslumbrar, ofuscar. —*n* deslumbramiento, *m;* brillo, *m,* refulgencia, *f*

**dazzling** /'dæzlɪŋ/ *a* deslumbrador; brillante

**deacon** /'dikən/ *n* diácono, *m*

**deaconess** /'dikənɪs/ *n* diaconisa, *f*

**dead** /dɛd/ *a* and *past part* muerto; inanimado; (withered) marchito; (deep) profundo; (unconscious) inerte, inmóvil; insensible; (numb) entumecido;

(complete) absoluto, completo; (sure) certero, excelente; (useless) inútil; (of color and human character) apagado; sin espíritu; inactivo; (of eyes) mortecino; (of sound) sordo, opaco; (of villages, etc.) desierto, despoblado; (quiet) silencioso; (empty) vacío; (monotonous) monótono; (of fire) apagado; (with weight, language) muerto; *Elec.* interrumpido; *Law.* muerto civilmente. —*adv* completamente, enteramente; del todo; directamente; exactamente; profundamente. **the d.,** los muertos. **in the d. of night,** en las altas horas de la noche. **to be d.,** estar muerto; haber muerto. **to be d. against,** estar completamente opuesto a. **to drop d.,** caer muerto; morir de repente. **to go d. slow,** ir muy lentamente. **to rise from the d.,** resucitar. **to sham d.,** hacer la mortecina, fingirse muerto. **to speak ill of the d.,** hablar mal de los muertos; *Inf.* desenterrar los muertos. **d. ball,** pelota fuera de juego, *f.* **d.-beat,** muerto de cansancio. **d. body,** cadáver, cuerpo muerto, *m.* **d. calm,** calma profunda, *f; Naut.* calma chicha, *f.* **d. certainty,** seguridad completa, *f.* **d.-drunk,** hecho una uva. **d. end,** callejón sin salida, *m.* **d. heat,** empate, *m.* **d. language,** lengua muerta, *f.* **d.-letter,** letra muerta, *f;* carta devuelta o no reclamada, *f.* **d.-lock,** punto muerto, *m.* **to reach a d.-lock,** llegar a un punto muerto. **d. march,** marcha fúnebre, *f.* **d. season,** temporada de calma, *f.* **d. set,** empeñado (en). **d. shot,** (person) tirador (-ra) certero (-ra) (shot) tiro certero, *m.* **d. silence,** silencio profundo, *m.* **d. stop,** parada en seco, *f.* **d. tired,** rendido. **d. weight,** peso muerto, *m.* **d. wood,** leña seca, *f;* material inútil, *m*

**deaden** /'dɛdn̩/ *vt* amortiguar; (of pain) calmar; (remove) quitar; (of colours) apagar

**deadening** /'dɛdn̩ɪŋ/ *n* amortiguamiento, *m*

**deadliness** /'dɛdlɪnɪs/ *n* carácter mortal, *m;* implacabilidad, *f*

**deadly** /'dɛdli/ *a* mortal; implacable; *Inf.* insoportable. —*adv* mortalmente. **He was d. pale,** Estaba pálido como un muerto. **the seven d. sins,** los siete pecados mortales. **d. nightshade,** belladona, *f*

**deadness** /'dɛdnɪs/ *n* falta de vida, *f;* inercia, *f;* marchitez, *f;* (numbness) entumecimiento, *m;* desanimación, *f;* parálisis, *f*

**Dead Sea Scrolls, the** los rollos del mar Muerto, *m pl*

**Dead Sea, the** el mar Muerto, *m*

**deaf** /dɛf/ *a* sordo. **d. people,** los sordos. **to be d.,** ser sordo; padecer sordera. **to be as d. as a post,** ser más sordo que una tapia. **to become d.,** ensordecer, volverse sordo. **to fall on d. ears,** caer en saco roto. **to turn a d. ear,** hacerse el sordo. **d. aid,** audífono, *m.* **d.-and-dumb,** sordomudo. **d.-and-dumb alphabet,** alfabeto manual, abecedario manual, *m.* **d.-mute,** sordomudo (-da). **d.-mutism,** sordomudez, *f*

**deafen** /'dɛfən/ *vt* asordar, ensordecer

**deafening** /'dɛfənɪŋ/ *a* ensordecedor

**deafly** /'dɛfli/ *adv* sordamente

**deafness** /'dɛfnɪs/ *n* sordera, *f*

**deal** /dil/ *n* (transaction) negocio, trato, *m;* (at cards) reparto, *m;* (wood) pino, *m;* (plank) tablón de pino, *m.* **a d., a great d.,** mucho. **a very great d.,** muchísimo. **to conclude a d.,** cerrar un trato

**deal** /dil/ *vt* repartir; (a blow) asestar, dar; (cards) dar; (justice) dispensar. **to d. a blow at,** asestar un golpe; *Fig.* herir (en); *Fig.* destruir un golpe. **to d. in,** comerciar en, traficar en; ocuparse en; meterse en. **to d. out,** dispensar. **to d. with,** (buy from) comprar de; tener relaciones con, tratar; entenderse con; portarse con; (of affairs) ocuparse en, arreglar, dirigir; (contend) luchar con; (discuss) discutir, tratar de; (of books) versar sobre

**dealer** /'dilər/ *n* traficante, *mf* mercader, *m;* (at cards) el que da las cartas

**dealing** /'dilɪŋ/ *n* conducta, *f;* proceder, *m;* trato, *m;* tráfico, *m; pl* **dealings,** relaciones, *f pl;* transacciones, *f pl*

**dean** /din/ *n Eccl.* deán, *m; Educ.* decano, *m*

**dear** /dɪər/ *a* (beloved) querido, amado; (charming) encantador, simpático; (in letters) estimado, querido; (favorite) predilecto; (expensive) caro. —*n* querido (-da); persona querida, *f,* bien amado (-da). —*adv* caro. **Oh d.!** ¡Dios mío! ¡Ay!

**dearly** /'dɪərli/ *adv* tiernamente, entrañablemente; caro

**dearness** /'dɪərnɪs/ *n* cariño, afecto, *m,* ternura, *f;* (of price) precio alto, *m*

**dearth** /dɜrθ/ *n* carestía, *f;* (of news, etc.) escasez, *f*

**death** /dɛθ/ *n* muerte, *f;* (*Law.* and in announcements) fallecimiento, *m,* defunción, *f.* **to be at death's door,** estar a la muerte. **to put to d.,** ajusticiar. **to the d.,** a muerte. **untimely d.,** muerte repentina, *f;* malogro, *m.* **death's head,** calavera, *f.* **d. certificate,** partida de defunción, *f.* **d.-duties,** derechos de herencia, *m pl.* **d.-like,** cadavérico. **d.-mask,** mascarilla, *f.* **d. penalty,** pena de muerte, *f.* **d.-rate,** mortalidad, *f.* **d.-rattle,** sarrillo, *m.* **d.-trap,** lugar peligroso, *m; Fig.* trampa, *f.* **d.-warrant,** sentencia de muerte, *f.* **d.-watch bettle,** reloj de la muerte, *m*

**deathbed** /'dɛθ,bɛd/ *n* lecho mortuorio, lecho de muerte, *m.* **on one's d.,** en su lecho de muerte

**deathblow** /'dɛθ,blou/ *n* golpe mortal, *m*

**deathless** /'dɛθlɪs/ *a* inmortal, eterno

**deathly** /'dɛθli/ *a* mortal

**death toll** *n* (of a bell) doble, toque de difuntos, *m;* (casualties) número de muertos, saldo de muertos, *m*

**debacle** /də'bɑkəl/ *n Fig.* ruina, *f*

**debar** /dɪ'bɑr/ *vt* excluir, privar

**debase** /dɪ'beis/ *vt* degradar, humillar, envilecer; (the coinage) alterar (la moneda)

**debasement** /dɪ'beismənt/ *n* degradación, humillación, *f,* envilecimiento, *m;* (of the coinage) alteración (de la moneda), *f*

**debasing** /dɪ'beisɪŋ/ *a* degradante, humillante

**debatable** /dɪ'beitəbəl/ *a* discutible

**debate** /dɪ'beit/ *n* debate, *m;* discusión, *f;* disputa, *f.* —*vt* and *vi* debatir; discutir; disputar; considerar

**debater** /dɪ'beitər/ *n* discutidor (-ra); orador (-ra).

**debating** /dɪ'beitɪŋ/ *n* discusión, *f;* argumentación, *f*

**debauch** /dɪ'bɔtʃ/ *vt* corromper, pervertir; (a woman) seducir, violar. —*n* libertinaje, *m;* borrachera, *f*

**debauched** /dɪ'bɔtʃt/ *a* vicioso, licencioso

**debauchee** /,dɛbɔ'tʃi, -'ʃi/ *n* libertino, vicioso, *m*

**debauchery** /dɪ'bɔtʃəri/ *n* libertinaje, mal vivir, *m,* viciosidad, licencia, *f*

**debenture** /dɪ'bɛntʃər/ *n* obligación, *f.* **d. holder,** obligacionista, *mf*

**debilitate** /dɪ'bɪlɪ,teit/ *vt* debilitar

**debilitating** /dɪ'bɪlɪ,teitɪŋ/ *a* debilitante

**debilitation** /dɪ,bɪlɪ'teiʃən/ *n* debilitación, *f*

**debility** /dɪ'bɪliti/ *n* debilidad, *f*

**debit** /'dɛbɪt/ *n* débito, cargo, *m;* saldo deudor, *m;* "debe" de una cuenta, *m.* —*vt* adeudar. **d. and credit,** el cargo y la data. **d. balance,** saldo deudor, *m*

**debonair** /,dɛbə'nɛər/ *a* gallardo, gentil, donairoso; alegre

**debonairly** /,dɛbə'nɛərli/ *adv* gallardamente; alegremente

**débris** /dei'bri/ *n* escombros, desechos, *m pl;* ruinas, *f pl; Geol.* despojos, *m pl*

**debt** /dɛt/ *n* deuda, *f.* **a bad d.,** una deuda incobrable. **to be in the d. of,** ser en cargo a; deber dinero a; *Fig.* sentirse bajo una obligación. **to get into d.,** adeudarse, contraer deudas

**debtor** /'dɛtər/ *n* deudor (-ra); *Com.* debe, *m*

**debunk** /dɪ'bʌŋk/ *vt* demoler

**debut** /dei'byu/ *n* (of a debutante) puesta de largo, *f;* (of a play, etc.) estreno, *m.* **to make one's d.,** ponerse de largo, presentarse en sociedad

**debutante** /'dɛbyu,tant/ *n* debutante, *f*

**decade** /'dɛkeid/ *n* década, *f,* decenio, *m;* (of the rosary) decena, *f*

**decadence** /'dɛkədəns/ *n* decadencia, *f*

**decadent** /'dɛkədənt/ *a* decadente

**decagram** /'dɛkə,græm/ *n* decagramo, *m*

**decaliter** /'dɛkə,litər/ *n* decalitro, *m*

**decalogue** /'dɛkə,lɔg/ *n* decálogo, *m*

**decameter** /'dɛkə,mitər/ *n* decámetro, *m*

**decamp** /dɪ'kæmp/ *vi Mil.* decampar; escaparse, fugarse

**decant** /dɪ'kænt/ *vt* decantar

**decanter** /dɪ'kæntər/ *n* garrafa, *f*

**decapitate** /dɪ'kæpɪ,teit/ *vt* decapitar, descabezar

**decapitation** /dɪˌkæpɪ'teiʃən/ n decapitación, f
**decarbonization** /dɪˌkɑrbənə'zeiʃən/ n descarburación, f
**decarbonize** /di'kɑrbəˌnaiz/ vt descarbonizar
**decay** /dɪ'kei/ vi (rot) pudrirse; degenerar; marchitarse; (of teeth) cariarse; (crumble) desmoronarse, caer en ruinas; decaer, declinar; (come down in the world) venir a menos, arruinarse. —n pudrición, putrefacción, f; (of teeth) caries, f; (withering) marchitez, f; degeneración, f; desmoronamiento, m; ruina, f; (oldness) vejez, f; decadencia, declinación, f; (fall) caída, f
**decease** /dɪ'sis/ n fallecimiento, m, defunción, f, vi fallecer
**deceased** /dɪ'sist/ n finado (-da), difunto (-ta). —a difunto
**deceit** /dɪ'sit/ n engaño, fraude, m; duplicidad, f
**deceitful** /dɪ'sitfəl/ a engañoso, falso; embustero, mentiroso; ilusorio
**deceitfully** /dɪ'sitfəli/ adv engañosamente
**deceitfulness** /dɪ'sitfəlnɪs/ n falsedad, duplicidad, f
**deceivable** /dɪ'sivəbəl/ a fácil a engañar, engañadizo
**deceive** /dɪ'siv/ vt engañar; (disappoint) decepcionar, desilusionar; frustrar. **If my memory does not d. me,** Si la memoria no me engaña, Si mal no me acuerdo
**deceiver** /dɪ'sivər/ n engañador (-ra); seductor, m
**deceiving** /dɪ'sivɪŋ/ a engañador
**December** /dɪ'sɛmbər/ n diciembre, m
**decency** /'disənsi/ n decoro, m, decencia, f; pudor, m, modestia, f; conveniencias, f pl; Inf. bondad, f; (manners) cortesía, f, buenos modales, m pl
**decennial** /dɪ'sɛniəl/ a decenal
**decent** /'disənt/ a decente; decoroso, honesto; púdico; (likable) simpático; (of things) bastante bueno; (honorable) honrado
**decently** /'disəntli/ adv decentemente
**decentralization** /diˌsɛntrələ'zeiʃən/ n descentralización, f
**decentralize** /di'sɛntrəˌlaiz/ vt descentralizar
**deception** /dɪ'sɛpʃən/ n engaño, m; ilusión, f
**deceptive** /dɪ'sɛptɪv/ a engañoso, mentiroso, ilusorio
**deceptively** /dɪ'sɛptɪvli/ adv engañosamente
**decide** /dɪ'said/ vt decidir; Law. determinar. —vi decidir, resolver; acordar, quedar en; juzgar; Law. dictar sentencia, fallar
**decided** /dɪ'saidɪd/ a decidido; (downright) categórico, inequívoco; resuelto; positivo; definitivo
**decidedly** /dɪ'saidɪdli/ adv decididamente; categóricamente; definitivamente
**deciduous** /dɪ'sɪdʒuəs/ a Bot. caedizo
**decigram** /'dɛsɪˌgræm/ n decigramo, m
**decimal** /'dɛsəməl/ a decimal. **d. fraction,** fracción decimal, f. **d. point,** punto decimal, m. **d. system,** sistema métrico, m
**decimate** /'dɛsəˌmeit/ vt diezmar
**decimation** /ˌdɛsə'meiʃən/ n gran mortandad, f; matanza, f
**decimeter** /'dɛsəˌmitər/ n decímetro, m
**decipher** /dɪ'saifər/ vt descifrar; deletrear
**decipherable** /dɪ'saifərəbəl/ a descifrable
**decipherer** /dɪ'saifərər/ n descifrador, m
**decipherment** /dɪ'saifərmənt/ n el descifrar; deletreo, m
**decision** /dɪ'sɪʒən/ n decisión, determinación, f; Law. sentencia, f, fallo, m; (agreement) acuerdo, m; (of character) firmeza, resolución, f
**decisive** /dɪ'saisiv/ a decisivo; terminante, conclusivo; crítico
**decisively** /dɪ'saisivli/ adv decisivamente
**decisiveness** /dɪ'saisivnɪs/ n carácter decisivo, m; firmeza, resolución, f; decisión, f
**deck** /dɛk/ n cubierta, f; (of cards) baraja (de naipes), f. —vt adornar, ataviar; decorar. **between decks,** entrecubiertas, f pl. **lower d.,** cubierta, f. **promenade d.,** cubierta de paseo, f. **upper d.,** cubierta superior, f. **d.-cabin,** camarote de cubierta, m. **d.-chair,** silla de cubierta, silla de tijera, silla extensible, f. **d.-hand,** marinero, estibador, m
**decked** /dɛkt/ a ornado, ataviado; engalanado; Naut. de... puentes

**declaim** /dɪ'kleim/ vt recitar. —vi perorar, declamar
**declamation** /ˌdɛklə'meiʃən/ n declamación, f
**declamatory** /dɪ'klæməˌtɔri/ a declamatorio
**declaration** /ˌdɛklə'reiʃən/ n declaración, f; manifiesto, m; proclamación, f
**declarative** /dɪ'klærətɪv/ a declaratorio, declarativo
**declare** /dɪ'klɛər/ vt declarar; proclamar; afirmar; manifestar; confesar. —vi declarar; Law. deponer, testificar. **to d. war (on)** declarar la guerra (a)
**declaredly** /dɪ'klɛərɪdli/ adv declaradamente, explícitamente, abiertamente
**declension** /dɪ'klɛnʃən/ n declinación, f
**declination** /ˌdɛklə'neiʃən/ n declinación, f
**decline** /dɪ'klain/ n declinación, decadencia, f; disminución, f; debilitación, f; (of the day) caída, f; (of stocks, shares) depresión, f; (illness) consunción, f; (Fig. setting) ocaso, m, vi declinar; inclinarse; decaer; disminuir; debilitarse; (refuse) negarse (a). —vt (refuse) rechazar, rehusar; Gram. declinar; (avoid) evitar
**declining** /dɪ'klainɪŋ/ a declinante. **in one's d. years,** en sus últimos años
**declivity** /dɪ'klɪvɪti/ n cuesta, pendiente, f, declive, m
**declutch** /di'klʌtʃ/ vi desembragar
**decoction** /dɪ'kɒkʃən/ n decocción, f
**decode** /di'koud/ vt descifrar
**decoder** /di'koudər/ n descifrador, m
**décolletee** /ˌdeikɒlə'tei/ a escotado
**decoloration** /diˌkʌlə'reiʃən/ n decoloración, f
**decompose** /ˌdikəm'pouz/ vt descomponer. —vi descomponerse
**decomposition** /ˌdiˌkɒmpə'zɪʃən/ n descomposición, f
**decompressor** /ˌdikəm'prɛsər/ n decompresor, m
**decontaminate** /ˌdikən'tæməˌneit/ vt descontaminar
**decontamination** /ˌdikənˌtæmə'neiʃən/ n descontaminación, f
**decontrol** /ˌdikən'troul/ vt suprimir las restricciones sobre
**decorate** /'dɛkəˌreit/ vt adornar (con), embellecer; (by painting, etc.) decorar, pintar; (honor) investir (con), condecorar
**decoration** /ˌdɛkə'reiʃən/ n decoración, f; Theat. decorado, m; (honor) condecoración, f; ornamento, m
**decorative** /'dɛkərətɪv/ a decorativo
**decorator** /'dɛkəˌreitər/ n decorador, m; (interior) adornista, m
**decorous** /'dɛkərəs/ a decoroso, decente; correcto
**decorum** /dɪ'kɔrəm/ n decoro, m; corrección, f
**decoy** /n 'dikɔi; v dɪ'kɔi/ n señuelo, m; añagaza, f; (trap) lazo, m, trampa, f; Fig. añagaza, f. —vt (birds) reclamar, atraer con señuelo; Fig. tentar (con), seducir (con). **d. bird,** pájaro de reclamo, m
**decrease** /n 'dikris; v dɪ'kris/ n disminución, f; baja, f; reducción, f; (of the moon, waters) mengua, f, vi decrecer, disminuir; bajar; menguar. —vi disminuir; reducir
**decreasingly** /dɪ'krisɪŋli/ adv de menos en menos
**decree** /dɪ'kri/ n decreto, m; edicto, m. —vi and vt decretar, mandar
**decrepit** /dɪ'krɛpɪt/ a decrépito
**decry** /dɪ'krai/ vt desacreditar, rebajar
**dedicate** /v 'dɛdɪˌkeit; a -kɪt/ vt dedicar; consagrar; destinar; aplicar; (a book, etc.) dedicar. **to d. oneself to,** dedicarse a, consagrarse a, entregarse a
**dedication** /ˌdɛdɪ'keiʃən/ n dedicación, f; consagración, f; (of a book, etc.) dedicatoria, f
**dedicatory** /'dɛdɪkəˌtɔri/ a dedicatorio
**deduce** /dɪ'dus/ vt derivar; deducir, inferir
**deduct** /dɪ'dʌkt/ vt deducir; descontar
**deduction** /dɪ'dʌkʃən/ n deducción, f; descuento, m
**deductive** /dɪ'dʌktɪv/ a deductivo
**deed** /did/ n acción, f; hecho, acto, m; hazaña, f; (reality) realidad, f; Law. escritura, f, Law. contrato, m. **d. of gift,** escritura de donación, f
**deem** /dim/ vt juzgar, creer, estimar
**deep** /dip/ a profundo; (wide) ancho; (low) bajo; (thick) espeso; (of colours) subido; (of sounds) grave, profundo; (immersed (in)) absorto (en); (of the mind) penetrante; (secret) secreto; (intense) intenso, hondo; (cunning) astuto, artero; (dark) oscuro; (of mourning) riguroso. —n Poet. piélago, mar, m;

profundidad, *f;* abismo, *m, adv* profundamente; a una gran profundidad. **to be in d. waters,** *Fig.* estar con el agua al cuello. **to be three feet d.,** tener tres pies de profundidad. **to be d. in,** estar absorto en; (of debt) estar cargado de. **three d.,** tres de fondo. **d. into the night,** hasta las altas horas de la noche. **d.-felt,** hondamente sentido. **d. mourning,** luto riguroso, *m.* **d.-rooted,** arraigado. **d.-sea fishing,** pesca mayor, *f.* **d.-sea lead,** escandallo, *m.* **d.-seated,** intimo, profundo; arraigado. **d.-set,** hundido

**deepen** /'dipən/ *vt* profundizar, ahondar; (broaden) ensanchar; (intensify) intensificar; (increase) aumentar; (of colors) aumentar el tono de, intensificar. —*vi* hacerse más profundo, hacerse más hondo; intensificarse; aumentarse; (of sound) hacerse más grave

**deeply** /'dipli/ *adv* profundamente; intensamente; fuertemente

**deepness** /'dipnıs/ *n* (cunning) astucia, *f;* see **depth**

**deer** /dıər/ *n* ciervo (-va), venado, *m, a* cervuno. **d.-hound,** galgo de cazar venados, *m.* **d.-skin,** piel de venado, *f.* **d.-stalking,** caza del ciervo, *f*

**deface** /dı'feis/ *vt* desfigurar, mutilar; estropear; (erase) borrar

**defacement** /dı'feismənt/ *n* desfiguración, mutilación, *f;* afeamiento, *m;* borradura, *f*

**defamation** /ˌdefə'meifən/ *n* difamación, denigración, *f*

**defamatory** /dı'fæmə,tɔri/ *a* difamatorio, denigrante

**defame** /dı'feim/ *vt* difamar, denigrar, calumniar

**default** /dı'fɔlt/ *n* omisión, *f,* descuido, *m;* falta, *f;* ausencia, *f; Law.* rebeldía, *f.* —*vi* dejar de cumplir; faltar; no pagar. —*vt Law.* condenar en rebeldía. **in d. of,** en la ausencia de

**defaulter** /dı'fɔltər/ *n* el, *m,* (*f,* la) que no cumple sus obligaciones; delincuente, *mf;* desfalcador (-ra); *Law.* rebelde, *mf*

**defeat** /dı'fit/ *vt* vencer, derrotar; frustrar; (reject) rechazar; (elude) evitar; *Fig.* vencer, triunfar sobre. —*n* derrota, *f;* vencimiento, *m;* frustración, *f;* rechazamiento, *m.* **to d. one's own ends,** defraudar sus intenciones

**defeatism** /dı'fitizəm/ *n* derrotismo, *m*

**defeatist** /dı'fitıst/ *n* derrotista, *mf*

**defecate** /'defı,keit/ *vt* defecar

**defecation** /ˌdefı'keifən/ *n* defecación, *f*

**defect** /*n* 'difekt, dı'fekt; *v* dı'fekt/ *n* defecto, *m;* imperfección, *f;* falta, *f*

**defection** /dı'fekfən/ *n* defección, *f;* deserción, *f;* (from a religion) apostasía, *f*

**defective** /dı'fektıv/ *a* defectuoso; *Gram.* defectivo; falto; imperfecto; (mentally) anormal. —*n* persona anormal, *f,* anormal, *m*

**defectiveness** /dı'fektıvnıs/ *n* imperfección, *f;* deficiencia, *f;* defecto, *m*

**defend** /dı'fend/ *vt* defender; proteger; preservar; sostener; (a thesis) sustenter

**defendant** /dı'fendənt/ *n Law.* acusado (-da), procesado (-da), demandado (-da)

**defender** /dı'fendər/ *n* defensor (-ra); (of a thesis) sustentante, *mf*

**defense** /dı'fens/ *n* defensa, *f;* justificación, *f; pl* **defenses,** defensas, *f pl;* obras de fortificación, *f pl.* **for the d.,** (of witnesses) de descargo; (of counsel) para la defensa. **in d. of,** en defensa de. **in one's own d.,** en su propia defensa. **d. in depth,** *Mil.* defensa en fondo, *f*

**defenseless** /dı'fenslıs/ *a* indefenso, sin defensa

**defenselessness** /dı'fenslısnıs/ *n* incapacidad de defenderse, *f;* debilidad, *f,* desvalimiento, *m*

**defensible** /dı'fensəbəl/ *a* defendible; justificable

**defensive** /dı'fensıv/ *a* defensivo. —*n* defensiva, *f.* **to be on the d.,** estar a la defensiva

**defensively** /dı'fensıvli/ *adv* defensivamente

**defer** /dı'fər/ *vt* (postpone) diferir, aplazar; suspender. —*vi* (yield) deferir, ceder; (delay) tardar, aguardar. **deferred payment,** pago a plazos, *m*

**deference** /'defərəns/ *n* deferencia, *f,* respeto, *m;* consideración, *f*

**deferential** /ˌdefə'renfəl/ *a* deferente, respetuoso

**deferment** /dı'fərmənt/ *n* aplazamiento, *m;* suspensión, *f*

**defiance** /dı'faiəns/ *n* desafío, *m;* provocación, *f;* oposición, *f;* insolencia, *f.* **in d. of,** en contra de

**defiant** /dı'faiənt/ *a* provocativo; insolente

**defiantly** /dı'faiəntli/ *adv* de un aire provocativo; insolentemente

**deficiency** /dı'fıfənsi/ *n* falta, deficiencia, *f;* imperfección, *f;* defecto, *m;* omisión, *f;* (scarcity) carestía, *f;* (in accounts) déficit, *m*

**deficient** /dı'fıfənt/ *a* deficiente; falto, incompleto; imperfecto; pobre; defectuoso; (not clever at) débil (en); (mentally) anormal. **to be d. in,** carecer de; ser pobre en

**deficit** /'defəsıt/ *n* déficit, *m;* descubierto, *m*

**defile** /dı'fail/ *n* desfiladero, *m.* —*vt* contaminar; profanar; manchar; deshonrar. —*vi Mil.* desfilar

**defilement** /dı'failmənt/ *n* contaminación, *f;* corrupción, *f;* profanación, *f*

**definable** /dı'fainəbəl/ *a* definible

**define** /dı'fain/ *vt* definir; (throw into relief) destacar; fijar; *Law.* determinar

**definite** /'defənıt/ *a* definido; positivo; categórico; exacto; concreto. **d. article,** artículo definido, *m*

**definitely** /'defənıtli/ *adv* positivamente; claramente. **definitely not!** ¡definitivamente no!

**definiteness** /'defənıtnıs/ *n* carácter definido, *m;* exactitud, *f;* lo categórico

**definition** /ˌdefə'nıfən/ *n* definición, *f*

**definitive** /dı'fınıtıv/ *a* definitivo

**deflate** /dı'fleit/ *vi* desinflar. —*vi* desinflarse, deshincharse

**deflation** /dı'fleifən/ *n* desinflación, *f*

**deflect** /dı'flekt/ *vt* desviar; apartar. —*vi* desviarse; apartarse

**deflection** /dı'flekfən/ *n* desviación, *f;* apartamiento, *m*

**defloration** /ˌdeflə'reifən/ *n* desfloración, *f*

**deflower** /dı'flauər/ *vt* desflorar

**deforestation** /dıˌfɔrı'steifən/ *n* desforestación, desmontadura, despoblación forestal, *f*

**deform** /dı'fɔrm/ *vt* deformar, desfigurar; afear

**deformation** /ˌdifɔr'meifən/ *n* deformación, *f*

**deformed** /dı'fɔrmd/ *a* deformado; contrahecho

**deformity** /dı'fɔrmıti/ *n* deformidad, *f*

**defraud** /dı'frɔd/ *vt* defraudar

**defrauder** /dı'frɔdər/ *n* defraudador (-ra)

**defrauding** /dı'frɔdıŋ/ *n* defraudación, *f*

**defray** /dı'frei/ *vt* sufragar, costear, pagar

**defrayal** /dı'freiəl/ *n* pago, *m*

**defrost** /dı'frɔst/ *vt* deshelar

**deft** /deft/ *a* diestro; hábil

**deftly** /'deftli/ *adv* con destreza; hábilmente

**deftness** /'deftnıs/ *n* destreza, *f;* habilidad, *f*

**defunct** /dı'fʌŋkt/ *a* and *n* difunto (-ta)

**defy** /dı'fai/ *vt* desafiar; (face) arrostrar; (violate) contravenir

**degeneracy** /dı'dʒenərəsi/ *n* degeneración, *f;* depravación, degradación, *f*

**degenerate** /*a, n* dı'dʒenərıt; *v* -ˌreit/ *a* and *n* degenerado (-da). —*vi* degenerar

**degeneration** /dıˌdʒenə'reifən/ *n* degeneración, *f*

**degradation** /ˌdegrı'deifən/ *n* degradación, *f;* abyección, *f*

**degrade** /dı'greid/ *vt* degradar; envilecer, deshonrar

**degrading** /dı'greidıŋ/ *a* degradante

**degree** /dı'gri/ *n* grado, *m;* punto, *m;* clase social, *f.* **by degrees,** poco a poco, gradualmente, **five degrees below zero,** cinco grados bajo cero. **in the highest d.,** en sumo grado, en grado superlativo. **to a certain d.,** hasta cierto punto. **to receive a d.,** graduarse

**degree-granting institution** /dı'gri ˌgræntıŋ/ *n* plantel habilitado para expedir títulos, *m*

**dehydrate** /di'haidreit/ *vt* deshidratar

**dehydration** /ˌdihai'dreifən/ *n* deshidratación, *f*

**de-ice** /di'ais/ *vt* deshelar

**deicide** /'diə,said/ *n* (act) deicidio, *m;* (person) deicida, *mf*

**deification** /ˌdiəfı'keifən/ *n* deificación, *f*

**deify** /'diə,fai/ *vt* deificar, endiosar

**deign** /dein/ *vi* dignarse. —*vt* conceder

**deism** /'diizəm/ *n* deísmo, *m*

**deist** /'diist/ *n* deísta, *mf*

**deity** /'diiti/ n deidad, divinidad, f; dios, m
**dejected** /dɪ'dʒɛktɪd/ a abatido, desanimado, deprimido
**dejectedly** /dɪ'dʒɛktɪdli/ adv tristemente, abatidamente
**dejection** /dɪ'dʒɛkʃən/ n abatimiento, desaliento, m, melancolía, f
**delay** /dɪ'lei/ n retraso, m, dilación, tardanza, demora, f. —vt retrasar, demorar; (a person) entretener; (postpone) aplazar; (obstruct) impedir. —vi tardar; entretenerse. **without more d.,** sin más tardar
**delectable** /dɪ'lɛktəbəl/ a deleitoso, delicioso
**delectably** /dɪ'lɛktəbli/ adv deliciosamente
**delectation** /,dilɛk'teiʃən/ n delectación, f, deleite, m
**delegacy** /'dɛlɪɡəsi/ n delegación, f
**delegate** /n 'dɛlɪɡɪt; v -,geit/ n delegado (-da). —vt delegar, diputar
**delegation** /,dɛlɪ'geiʃən/ n delegación, f
**delete** /dɪ'lit/ vt suprimir, borrar
**deleterious** /,dɛlɪ'tɪəriəs/ a deletéreo
**deletion** /dɪ'liʃən/ n supresión, borradura, f
**deliberate** /a dɪ'lɪbərɪt; v -ə,reit/ a premeditado, intencionado; (slow) pausado, lento. —vi and vt deliberar, discurrir, considerar
**deliberately** /dɪ'lɪbərɪtli/ adv (intentionally) con premeditación, a sabiendas; (slowly) pausadamente, lentamente
**deliberation** /dɪ,lɪbə'reiʃən/ n reflexión, deliberación, consideración, f; (slowness) lentitud, pausa, f
**deliberative** /dɪ'lɪbərətɪv/ a deliberativo, de liberante
**delicacy** /'dɛlɪkəsi/ n delicadeza, f; fragilidad, f; suavidad, f; sensibilidad, f; escrupulosidad, f; (of health) debilidad, delicadez, f; (difficulty) dificultad, f; (food) manjar exquisito, m, golosina, f
**delicate** /'dɛlɪkɪt/ a delicado; fino; frágil; suave; exquisito; delicado (de salud); (of situations) difícil
**delicatessen** /,dɛlɪkə'tɛsən/ n (store) fiambrería, f
**delicious** /dɪ'lɪʃəs/ a delicioso
**deliciously** /dɪ'lɪʃəsli/ adv deliciosamente
**deliciousness** /dɪ'lɪʃəsnɪs/ n deleite, m, lo delicioso; excelencia, f; delicias, f pl
**delict** /dɪ'lɪkt/ n delito, m
**delictive** /dɪ'lɪktɪv/ a delictivo
**delight** /dɪ'lait/ n deleite, regocijo, m; encanto, m, delicia, f; placer, gozo, m. —vt deleitar, encantar; halagar. —vi deleitarse, complacerse. **to be delighted with,** estar encantado con. **to d. in,** deleitarse en, complacerse en; tomar placer en
**delightful** /dɪ'laitfəl/ a delicioso, precioso, encantador
**delightfully** /dɪ'laitfəli/ adv deliciosamente
**delimit** /dɪ'lɪmɪt/ vt delimitar
**delimitation** /dɪ,lɪmɪ'teiʃən/ n delimitación, f
**delineate** /dɪ'lɪni,eit/ vt delinear, diseñar; Fig. pintar, describir
**delineation** /dɪ,lɪni'eiʃən/ n delineación, f; retrato, m; Fig. descripción, f
**delineator** /dɪ'lɪnieitər/ n diseñador, m
**delinquency** /dɪ'lɪŋkwənsi/ n delincuencia, f; criminalidad, f; culpa, f; delito, m
**delinquent** /dɪ'lɪŋkwənt/ a delincuente. —n delincuente, mf
**deliquescence** /,dɛlɪ'kwɛsəns/ n delicuescencia, f
**deliquescent** /,dɛlɪ'kwɛsənt/ a delicuescente
**delirious** /dɪ'lɪəriəs/ a delirante; desvariado; Inf. loco. **to be d.,** delirar, desvariar
**delirium** /dɪ'lɪəriəm/ n delirio, desvarío, m. **d. tremens,** delírium tremens, m
**deliver** /dɪ'lɪvər/ vt librar (de); salvar (de); (distribute) repartir; (hand over) entregar; (recite) recitar, decir; (a speech) pronunciar; comunicar; (send) despachar, expedir; (a blow) asestar; (give) dar; (bring) traer; (battle, a lecture) dar; (a woman, of a doctor) asistir en el parto (a); (a child) traer al mundo; (a judgment) pronunciar. **to be delivered (of a child),** dar a luz. **to d. oneself up,** entregarse. **delivered free,** porte pagado.
**deliverance** /dɪ'lɪvərəns/ n libramiento, rescate, m; redención, salvación, f; (of a judgment) pronuncia, f
**deliverer** /dɪ'lɪvərər/ n libertador (-ra); salvador (-ra); (distributor) repartidor (-ra); entregador (-ra)
**delivery** /dɪ'lɪvəri/ n (distribution) reparto, m, distri-

bución, f; entrega, f; Law. cesión, f; (of a judgment) pronuncia, f; (of a speech) pronunciación, f; (manner of speaking) declamación, f; dicción, f; (of a child) parto, m. **on d.,** al entregarse. **The letter came by the first d.,** La carta llegó en el primer reparto. **d. man,** mozo de reparto, m. **d. note,** nota de entrega, f. **d. van,** camión de reparto, m
**delivery truck** n camioneta de reparto, furgoneta, f, sedán de reparto, m
**dell** /dɛl/ n hondonada, f; pequeño valle, m
**delouse** /di'laus/ vt despiojar, espulgar
**Delphi** /'dɛlfai/ Delfos, m
**delta** /'dɛltə/ n (Greek letter) delta, f; (of a river) delta, m
**delude** /dɪ'lud/ vt engañar; ilusionar. **to d. oneself,** engañarse
**deluded** /dɪ'ludɪd/ a iluso, engañado, ciego
**deluge** /'dɛlyudʒ/ n diluvio, m. —vt diluviar; inundar (con)
**delusion** /dɪ'luʒən/ n engaño, m, ceguedad, f; error, m; ilusión, f
**delve** /dɛlv/ vt and vi cavar; Fig. ahondar (en), penetrar (en), investigar
**demagogic** /,dɛmə'gɒdʒɪk/ a demagógico
**demagogue** /'dɛmə,gɒg/ n demagogo (-ga)
**demagogy** /'dɛmə,goudʒi/ n demagogia, f
**demand** /dɪ'mænd/ n exigencia, f; Com. demanda, f; petición, f; Polit. Econ. consumo, m. —vt exigir; requerir; pedir; (claim) reclamar. **in d.,** en demanda. **on d.,** al solicitarse. **to be in d.,** ser popular. **d. note,** apremio, m
**demanding** /dɪ'mændɪŋ/ a exigente
**demarcate** /dɪ'markeit/ vt demarcar
**demarcation** /,dimar'keiʃən/ n demarcación, f
**demean (oneself)** /dɪ'min/ vr degradarse, rebajarse
**demeanor** /dɪ'minər/ n conducta, f; continente, porte, aire, m; (manners) modales, m pl
**demented** /dɪ'mɛntɪd/ a demente, loco
**demerit** /dɪ'mɛrɪt/ n demérito, m
**demi-** prefix semi; casi. **d.-tasse,** taza cafetera, jícara, f
**demigod** /'dɛmi,gɒd/ n semidiós, m
**demigoddess** /'dɛmi,gɒdɪs/ n semidiosa, f
**demijohn** /'dɛmi,dʒɒn/ n damajuana, f
**demilitarize** /di'mɪlɪtə,raiz/ vt desmilitarizar
**demise** /dɪ'maiz/ n Law. traslación de dominio, f; sucesión de la corona, f; (death) óbito, fallecimiento, m
**demisemiquaver** /,dɛmi'sɛmi,kweivər/ n fusa, f
**demobilization** /di,moubələ'zeiʃən/ n desmovilización, f
**demobilize** /di'moubə,laiz/ vt desmovilizar
**democracy** /dɪ'mɒkrəsi/ n democracia, f
**democrat** /'dɛmə,kræt/ n demócrata, mf
**democratic** /,dɛmə'krætɪk/ a democrático. **to make d.,** democratizar
**demolish** /dɪ'mɒlɪʃ/ vt demoler, derribar; Fig. destruir; (eat) engullir, devorar
**demolisher** /dɪ'mɒlɪʃər/ n demoledor, m; Fig. destructor (-ra)
**demolition** /,dɛmə'lɪʃən/ n demolición, f; derribo, m, a demoledor; de demolición. **d. squad,** pelotón de demolición, m
**demon** /'dimən/ n demonio, diablo, m
**demonetization** /di,mɒnɪtə'zeiʃən/ n desmonetización, f
**demonetize** /di'mɒnɪ,taiz/ vt desmonetizar
**demoniacal** /,dimə'naiɪkəl/ a demoníaco
**demonology** /,dimə'nɒlədʒi/ n demonología, f
**demonstrable** /dɪ'mɒnstrəbəl, 'dɛmən-/ a demostrable
**demonstrably** /dɪ'mɒnstrəbli/ adv demostrablemente
**demonstrate** /'dɛmən,streit/ vt demostrar; mostrar; probar. —vi hacer una demostración
**demonstration** /,dɛmən'streiʃən/ n demostración, f; manifestación, f
**demonstrative** /də'mɒnstrətɪv/ a demostrativo; (of persons) expresivo, mimoso. **d. pronoun,** pronombre demostrativo, m
**demonstrator** /'dɛmən,streitər/ n demostrador (-ra)

**demoralization** /dɪ,mɔrələˈzeiʃən/ n desmoralización, f

**demoralize** /dɪˈmɔrə,laiz, -ˈmɒr-/ vt desmoralizar

**demoralizing** /dɪˈmɔrə,laizɪŋ/ a desmoralizador

**demur** /dɪˈmɜr/ vi dudar, vacilar; objetar, protestar; poner dificultades. —n objeción, protesta, f

**demure** /dɪˈmyʊr/ a serio, modoso recatado; púdico; de una coquetería disimulada

**demurely** /dɪˈmyʊrli/ adv modestamente; con recato; con coquetería disimulada

**demureness** /dɪˈmyʊrnɪs/ n seriedad, f, recato, m; modestia fingida, coquetería disimulada, f

**demy** /dəˈmai/ n papel marquilla, m; becario de Magdalen College, Oxford, m

**den** /dɛn/ n madriguera, guardia, f; (of thieves) cueva, f; (in a zoo) cercado, recinto, m; (study) gabinete, m; (squalid room) cuartucho, m

**denaturalization** /di,nætʃərələˈzeiʃən/ n desnaturalización, f

**denaturalize** /diˈnætʃərə,laiz/ vt desnaturalizar

**denial** /dɪˈnaiəl/ n negación, f; rechazo, m; contradicción, f; negativa, f

**denizen** /ˈdɛnəzən/ n habitante, m; ciudadano (-na)

**Denmark** /ˈdɛnmɑrk/ Dinamarca, f

**denominate** /dɪˈnɒmə,neit/ vt denominar, nombrar

**denomination** /dɪ,nɒməˈneiʃən/ n denominación, f; secta, f; clase, f

**denominational** /dɪ,nɒməˈneiʃənl/ a sectario

**denominator** /dɪˈnɒmə,neitər/ n Math. denominador, m

**denote** /dɪˈnout/ vt denotar, indicar; significar

**dénouement** /ˌdeinuˈmɑ̃/ n desenlace, desenredo, m; solución, f

**denounce** /dɪˈnauns/ vt denunciar; delatar, acusar

**denouncer** /dɪˈnaunsər/ n denunciante, mf delator (-ra)

**dense** /dɛns/ a denso; espeso, compacto; tupido; impenetrable; Inf. estúpido

**densely** /ˈdɛnsli/ adv densamente; espesamente. **d. populated,** con gran densidad de población

**density** /ˈdɛnsɪti/ n densidad, f; espesor, m; consistencia, f; Inf. estupidez, f

**dent** /dɛnt/ n mella, f; (in metal) abolladura, f, vt mellar; abollar

**dental** /ˈdɛntl̩/ a dental. —n letra dental, f. **d. forceps,** gatillo, m. **d. mechanic,** mecánico dentista, m. **d. surgeon,** odontólogo, m

**dental floss** n seda dental, f

**dentifrice** /ˈdɛntəfrɪs/ n dentífrico, m

**dentist** /ˈdɛntɪst/ n dentista, mf; odontólogo, m

**dentistry** /ˈdɛntəstri/ n odontología, f

**dentition** /dɛnˈtɪʃən/ n dentición, f

**denture** /ˈdɛntʃər/ n dentadura, f

**denudation** /ˌdinuˈdeiʃən/ n denudación, f

**denude** /dɪˈnud/ vt denudar, despojar, privar (de)

**denunciation** /dɪ,nʌnsiˈeiʃən/ n denuncia, f; acusación, delación, f

**denunciatory** /dɪˈnʌnsiə,tɔri/ a denunciatorio

**Denver boot** /ˈdɛnvər/ n cepo, m

**deny** /dɪˈnai/ vt negar; desmentir; rehusar; rechazar; renegar (de); (give up) renunciar, sacrificar. **to d. oneself,** privarse (de); sacrificar; negarse

**deodorant** /diˈoudərənt/ a and n desodorante m.

**deodorize** /diˈoudə,raiz/ vt desinfectar, destruir el olor de

**depart** /dɪˈpɑrt/ vi marcharse, irse, partir; (of trains, etc., and meaning go out) salir; (deviate) desviarse (de), apartarse (de); (go away) alejarse; (leave) dejar; (disappear) desaparecer; (alter) cambiar; (die) morir

**departed** /dɪˈpɑrtɪd/ a (past) pasado; desaparecido; (dead) difunto, muerto. —n difunto (-ta)

**department** /dɪˈpɑrtmənt/ n departamento, m; sección, f; (of learning) ramo, m; (in France) distrito administrativo, m. **d. store,** grandes tiendas, f pl, (Argentina), grandes almacenes, m pl

**departmental** /dɪ,pɑrtˈmɛntl̩/ a departamental

**departure** /dɪˈpɑrtʃər/ n partida, ida, f; (going out, and of trains, etc.) salida, f; (deviation) desviación, el apartarse. **d. from the rules,** el apartarse de las reglas), f; (disappearance) desaparición, f; (change)

cambio, m; (giving up) renuncia, f; (death) muerte, f. **to take one's d.,** marcharse

**depend** /dɪˈpɛnd/ vi depender. **to d. on,** depender de; (rest on) apoyarse en; (count on) contar con; (trust) fiarse de; tener confianza en, estar seguro de. **That depends!** ¡Eso depende!

**dependable** /dɪˈpɛndəbəl/ a digno de confianza; seguro

**dependence, dependency** /dɪˈpɛndəns; dɪˈpɛndənsi/ n dependencia, f; subordinación, f; (trust) confianza, f

**dependent** /dɪˈpɛndənt/ a dependiente; subordinado; condicional. —n dependiente, m. **to be d. on,** depender de

**depict** /dɪˈpɪkt/ vt representar; pintar; dibujar; Fig. describir, retratar

**depiction** /dɪˈpɪkʃən/ n representación, f; pintura, f; dibujo, m; Fig. descripción, f

**depilate** /ˈdɛpə,leit/ vt depilar

**depilation** /ˌdɛpəˈleiʃən/ n depilación, f

**depilatory** /dɪˈpɪlə,tɔri, -,touri/ a and n depilatorio m.

**deplete** /dɪˈplit/ vt agotar; disipar

**depletion** /dɪˈpliʃən/ n agotamiento, m

**deplorable** /dɪˈplɔrəbəl/ a lamentable, deplorable

**deplorably** /dɪˈplɔrəbli/ adv lamentablemente

**deplore** /dɪˈplɔr/ vt deplorar, lamentar

**deploy** /dɪˈplɔi/ vt desplegar. —vi desplegarse. —n despliegue, m

**deployment** /dɪˈplɔimənt/ n despliegue, m

**deponent** /dɪˈpounənt/ n Law. declarante, deponente, mf a deponente. m

**depopulate** /diˈpɒpyə,leit/ vt despoblar

**depopulation** /di,pɒpyəˈleiʃən/ n despoblación, f

**deport** /dɪˈpɔrt/ vt deportar

**deportation** /ˌdipɔrˈteiʃən/ n deportación, f

**deportment** /dɪˈpɔrtmənt/ n comportamiento, m; porte, aire, m; conducta, f

**depose** /dɪˈpouz/ vt destronar; (give evidence) testificar, declarar

**deposit** /dɪˈpɒzɪt/ n depósito, m; Geol. yacimiento, filón, m; sedimento, m. —vt depositar. **to leave a d.,** dejar un depósito. **d. account,** cuenta corriente, f

**deposition** /ˌdɛpəˈzɪʃən/ n deposición, f; Law. testimonio, m, declaración, f; (from the Cross) descendimiento, m, (de la Cruz)

**depositor** /dɪˈpɒzɪtər/ n depositador (-ra)

**depository** /dɪˈpɒzɪ,tɔri/ n depositaría, f, almacén, m; (of knowledge, etc.) pozo, m

**depot** /ˈdipou/ n almacén, m; (military headquarters) depósito, m; (for army vehicles, etc.) parque, m; (for buses, etc.) estación, f

**depravation** /ˌdɛprəˈveiʃən/ n depravación, f

**depraved** /dɪˈpreivd/ a depravado, perverso, vicioso

**depravity** /dɪˈprævɪti/ n corrupción, maldad, perversión, f

**deprecate** /ˈdɛprɪ,keit/ vt desaprobar, criticar; lamentar, deplorar

**deprecatingly** /ˈdɛprɪ,keitɪŋli/ adv con desaprobación, críticamente

**deprecation** /ˌdɛprɪˈkeiʃən/ n deprecación, f; desaprobación, crítica, f

**deprecatory** /ˈdɛprɪkə,tɔri/ a deprecativo; de desaprobación, de crítica

**depreciate** /dɪˈpriʃi,eit/ vt depreciar, rebajar; Fig. tener en poco, menospreciar. —vi depreciarse, deteriorarse; bajar de precio

**depreciatingly** /dɪˈpriʃi,eitɪŋli/ adv con desprecio

**depreciation** /dɪ,priʃiˈeiʃən/ n (in value) amortización, depreciación, f; Fig. desprecio, m

**depreciatory** /dɪˈpriʃiə,tɔri/ a Fig. despectivo, despreciativo

**depredation** /ˌdɛprəˈdeiʃən/ n depredación, f

**depress** /dɪˈprɛs/ vt deprimir; (weaken) debilitar; (humble) humillar; (dispirit) abatir, entristecer; (trade) desanimar, paralizar

**depressed** /dɪˈprɛst/ a deprimido, desalentado, melancólico, triste; (of an area) necesitado

**depressing** /dɪˈprɛsɪŋ/ a melancólico, triste; pesimista

**depressingly** /dɪˈprɛsɪŋli/ adv con tristeza; con pesimismo

**depression** /dɪ'prɛʃən/ n depresión, f; (hollow) hoyo, m; (sadness) decaimiento, abatimiento, m, melancolía, f; (in prices) baja, f; (in trade) desanimación, parálisis, f; Astron. depresión, f

**deprivation** /ˌdɛprə'veɪʃən/ n privación, f; pérdida, f

**deprive** /dɪ'praɪv/ vt privar (de), despojar (de); defraudar (de); Eccl. destituir (de)

**depth** /dɛpθ/ n profundidad, f; (thickness) espesor, m; fondo, m; (of night, winter, the country) medio, m; (of sound) gravedad, f; (of colour, feeling) intensidad, f; (abstruseness) dificultad, f; (sagacity) sagacidad, f; pl **depths**, profundidades, f pl; abismo, m; lo más hondo; lo más íntimo. **to be 4 feet in d.**, tener cuatro pies de profundidad. **to the depths of one's being**, hasta lo más íntimo de su ser; hasta los tuétanos. **d. charge**, carga de profundidad, f

**deputation** /ˌdɛpyə'teɪʃən/ n deputación, delegación, f

**deputize (for)** /'dɛpyəˌtaɪz/ vi desempeñar las funciones de, substituir

**deputy** /'dɛpyəti/ n (substitute) lugarteniente, m; (agent) representante, m; apoderado, m; (parliamentary) diputado, m; (in compounds) sub, vice. **d.-governor**, subgobernador, m. **d.-head**, subjefe, m; (of a school) subdirector (-ra)

**derail** /di'reil/ vt (hacer) descarrilar

**derailment** /di'reilmənt/ n descarrilamiento, m

**derange** /dɪ'reɪndʒ/ vt desordenar; desorganizar; turbar; (mentally) trastornar, hacer perder el juicio (a)

**derangement** /dɪ'reɪndʒmənt/ n desorden, m; turbación, f; (mental) trastorno, m, locura, f

**derby** /'dɑrbi/ n carrera del Derby, f; (hat) sombrero hongo, m

**deregulate** /di'rɛgyəˌleɪt/ vt desregular

**deregulation** /diˌrɛgyə'leɪʃən/ n desregulación, f

**derelict** /'dɛrəlɪkt/ a abandonado, derrelicto. —n derrelicto, m

**dereliction** /ˌdɛrə'lɪkʃən/ n abandono, m; omisión, negligencia, f; descuido, m

**deride** /di'raid/ vt burlarse de, mofarse de; ridiculizar

**derision** /dɪ'rɪʒən/ n irrisión, f, menosprecio, m

**derisive** /dɪ'raɪsɪv/ a irrisorio; irónico

**derisively** /dɪ'raɪsɪvli/ adv irrisoriamente; con ironía, irónicamente

**derivation** /ˌdɛrə'veɪʃən/ n derivación, f

**derivative** /dɪ'rɪvətɪv/ a derivativo. —n derivado, m

**derive** /dɪ'raɪv/ vt derivar; obtener; extraer; Fig. sacar, hallar. —vi (from) derivar de; proceder de; remontar a

**dermatitis** /ˌdɑrmə'taɪtɪs/ n dermatitis, f

**dermatologist** /ˌdɑrmə'tɒlədʒɪst/ n dermatólogo, m

**dermatology** /ˌdɑrmə'tɒlədʒi/ n dermatología, f

**derogatory** /dɪ'rɒgəˌtɔri/ a despectivo, despreciativo; deshonroso

**derrick** /'dɛrɪk/ n grúa, machina, f; abanico, m

**descant** /n 'dɛskænt; v dɛs'kænt/ n Mus. discante, m. —vi Mus. discantar; discurrir (sobre), disertar (sobre)

**descend** /di'sɛnd/ vi descender, bajar; (be inherited) pasar a; (fall) caer; (of the sun) ponerse. —vt bajar. **to d. from**, descender de. **to d. to**, (lower oneself) rebajarse; (consider) venir a, considerar. **to d. upon**, caer sobre; (arrive unexpectedly) llegar inesperadamente, invadir

**descendant** /dɪ'sɛndənt/ n descendiente, mf; pl **descendants**, descendencia, f

**descent** /dɪ'sɛnt/ n descenso, m; bajada, f; (slope) pendiente, cuesta, f; (attack) invasión, f, ataque, m; (lineage) descendencia, alcurnia, procedencia, f; (inheritance) herencia, f; transmisión, f. **D. from the Cross**, Descendimiento de la Cruz, m

**describable** /dɪ'skraɪbəbəl/ a descriptible

**describe** /dɪ'skraɪb/ vt describir; pintar

**description** /dɪ'skrɪpʃən/ n descripción, f

**descriptive** /dɪ'skrɪptɪv/ a descriptivo

**descry** /dɪ'skraɪ/ vt divisar, descubrir; Poet. ver

**Desdemona** /ˌdɛzdə'moʊnə/ Desdémona, f

**desecrate** /'dɛsɪˌkreɪt/ vt profanar

**desecration** /ˌdɛsɪ'kreɪʃən/ n profanación, f

**desert** /dɪ'zɜrt/ vt abandonar; dejar; (Mil. etc.) desertar. —vi desertar

**desert** /'dɛzərt/ n desierto, m

**desert** /dɪ'zɜrt/ n (merit) mérito, m; **to receive one's deserts**, llevar su merecido

**deserted** /dɪ'zɜrtɪd/ a abandonado; desierto; solitario; inhabitado, despoblado

**deserter** /dɪ'zɜrtər/ n desertor, m

**desertion** /dɪ'zɜrʃən/ n abandono, m, deserción, f; (Mil. etc.) deserción, f

**deserve** /dɪ'zɜrv/ vt and vi merecer

**deservedly** /dɪ'zɜrvɪdli/ adv merecidamente

**deserving** /dɪ'zɜrvɪŋ/ a merecedor; meritorio. **to be d. of**, merecer

**desiccate** /'dɛsɪˌkeɪt/ vt desecar. —vi desecarse

**design** /dɪ'zaɪn/ n proyecto, m; plan, m; intención, f, propósito, m; objeto, m; modelo, m; (pattern) diseño, dibujo, m; arte del dibujo, mf vt idear; proyectar; (destine) destinar, dedicar; diseñar, dibujar, delinear; planear. **by d.**, expresamente, intencionalmente

**designate** /v 'dɛzɪgˌneɪt; a -nɪt/ vt señalar; designar; (appoint) nombrar. —a electo

**designation** /ˌdɛzɪg'neɪʃən/ n designación, f; nombramiento, m

**designedly** /dɪ'zaɪnɪdli/ adv de propósito

**designer** /dɪ'zaɪnər/ n inventor (-ra), autor (-ra); delineador (-ra); dibujante, mf; (of public works, etc.) proyectista, mf

**designing** /dɪ'zaɪnɪŋ/ a intrigante, astuto

**desirability** /dɪˌzaɪərə'bɪlɪti/ n lo deseable; conveniencia, f; ventaja, f

**desirable** /dɪ'zaɪərəbəl/ a deseable; conveniente; ventajoso; agradable; apetecible

**desire** /dɪ'zaɪər/ vt desear; querer; ansiar, ambicionar; (request) rogar, pedir; (order) mandar. —n deseo, m; ansia, aspiración, f; ambición, f; impulso, m; (will) voluntad, f. **to d. ardently**, perecerse por; suspirar por

**desirous** /dɪ'zaɪərəs/ a deseoso (de); ambicioso (de); ansioso (de); impaciente (a); curioso (de)

**desist** /dɪ'sɪst/ vi desistir; dejar (de)

**desk** /dɛsk/ n pupitre, m; escritorio, buró, m; mesa de trabajo, f; (cashier's) caja, f; (teacher's, lecturer's; pulpit) cátedra, f

**desolate** /a 'dɛsəlɪt; v -ˌleɪt/ a solitario; desierto; deshabitado; abandonado; arruinado; árido; (afflicted) desolado, angustiado. —vt desolar; despoblar

**desolation** /ˌdɛsə'leɪʃən/ n desolación, f; aflicción, angustia, f, desconsuelo, m

**despair** /dɪ'spɛər/ n desesperación, f, vi perder toda esperanza. **His life is despaired of**, Se ha perdido la esperanza de salvarle (la vida). **to be in d.**, estar desesperado

**despairing** /dɪ'spɛərɪŋ/ a desesperado

**despairingly** /dɪ'spɛərɪŋli/ adv sin esperanza

**desperate** /'dɛspərɪt/ a desesperado; sin esperanza; irremediable; furioso; violento; (dangerous) arriesgado, peligroso; terrible

**desperately** /'dɛspərɪtli/ adv desesperadamente; furiosamente; terriblemente

**desperation** /ˌdɛspə'reɪʃən/ n desesperación, f; furia, violencia, f

**despicable** /'dɛspɪkəbəl/ a vil, despreciable; insignificante

**despise** /dɪ'spaɪz/ vt despreciar; desdeñar

**despiser** /dɪ'spaɪzər/ n menospreciador (-ra)

**despite** /dɪ'spaɪt/ prep a pesar de

**despoil** /dɪ'spɔɪl/ vt despojar, desnudar

**despoiler** /dɪ'spɔɪlər/ n despojador (-ra)

**despoliation** /dɪˌspoʊli'eɪʃən/ n despojo, m

**despondency** /dɪ'spɒndənsi/ n abatimiento, desaliento, m, desesperación, f

**despondent** /dɪ'spɒndənt/ a abatido, desanimado, deprimido

**despondently** /dɪ'spɒndəntli/ adv con desaliento

**despot** /'dɛspət/ n déspota, m

**despotic** /dɛs'pɒtɪk/ a despótico

**despotism** /'dɛspəˌtɪzəm/ n despotismo, m

**dessert** /dɪ'zɜrt/ n postre, m, a de postre. **d. plate**, plato para postre, m. **d.-spoon**, cuchara de postre, f

**destination** /ˌdɛstə'neɪʃən/ n destinación, f

**destine** /'dɛstɪn/ vt destinar; dedicar; predestinar

**destiny** /'dɛstəni/ n destino, m

**destitute** /'dɛstɪˌtut/ a indigente, menesteroso; desnudo (de); privado (de); desprovisto (de), falto (de); desamparado

**destitution** /ˌdɛstɪˈtuʃən/ *n* destitución, indigencia, miseria, *f;* privación, falta, *f;* desamparo, *m*

**destroy** /dɪˈstrɔi/ *vt* destruir; demoler; deshacer; (kill) matar; exterminar; (finish) acabar con

**destroyer** /dɪˈstrɔiər/ *n* destructor (-ra); *Nav.* destructor, cazatorpedero, *m*

**destructible** /dɪˈstrʌktəbəl/ *a* destructible, destruible

**destruction** /dɪˈstrʌkʃən/ *n* destrucción, *f;* demolición, *f;* ruina, *f;* pérdida, *f;* muerte, *f;* exterminio, *m;* perdición, *f*

**destructive** /dɪˈstrʌktɪv/ *a* destructivo, destructor; (of animals) dañino. **d. animal,** animal dañino, *m,* alimaña, *f*

**destructiveness** /dɪˈstrʌktɪvnɪs/ *n* destructividad, *f;* instinto destructor, *m*

**desultory** /ˈdɛsəlˌtɔri/ *a* inconexo; sin método, descosido; irregular

**detach** /dɪˈtætʃ/ *vt* separar, desprender; (unstick) despegar; *Mil.* destacar

**detachable** /dɪˈtætʃəbəl/ *a* separable, de quita y pon

**detached** /dɪˈtætʃt/ *a* suelto, separado; (*Fig.* with outlook, etc.) imparcial; indiferente, despegado. **d. house,** hotelito, *m*

**detachment** /dɪˈtætʃmənt/ *n* separación, *f; Mil.* destacamento, *m;* (*Fig.* of mind) imparcialidad, *f;* independencia (de espíritu, etc.), *f;* indiferencia, *f*

**detail** /dɪˈteil/ *n* detalle, *m;* pormenor, *m,* particularidad, *f;* circunstancia, *f; Mil.* destacamento, *m.* —*vt* detallar; particularizar, referir con pormenores; *Mil.* destacar. **in d.,** detalladamente; al por menor; *Inf.* ce por be. **to go into details,** entrar en detalles

**detain** /dɪˈtein/ *vt* detener; (arrest) arrestar, prender; (withhold) retener; (prevent) impedir

**detect** /dɪˈtɛkt/ *vt* descubrir; averiguar; (discern) discernir, percibir; *Elec.* detectar

**detectable** /dɪˈtɛktəbəl/ *a* perceptible

**detection** /dɪˈtɛkʃən/ *n* descubrimiento, *m;* averiguación, *f;* percepción, *f*

**detective** /dɪˈtɛktɪv/ *n* detective, *m, a* de detectives, policíaco. **d. novel,** novela policíaca, *f*

**detector** /dɪˈtɛktər/ *n* descubridor, *m; Elec.* detector, *m; Mech.* indicador, *m*

**detention** /dɪˈtɛnʃən/ *n* detención, *f;* (arrest) arresto, *m;* (confinement) encierro, *m*

**deter** /dɪˈtɜr/ *vt* desanimar, desalentar; acobardar; (dissuade) disuadir; (prevent) impedir

**detergent** /dɪˈtɜrdʒənt/ *a* detersorio. —*n* detersorio, *m*

**deteriorate** /dɪˈtɪəriəˌreit/ *vt* deteriorar. —*vi* deteriorarse; empeorar

**deterioration** /dɪˌtɪəriəˈreiʃən/ *n* deterioración, *f;* empeoramiento, *m*

**determinable** /dɪˈtɜrmənəbəl/ *a* determinable

**determination** /dɪˌtɜrməˈneiʃən/ *n* determinación, *f;* definición, *f;* resolución, decisión, *f; Law.* fallo, *m; Med.* congestión, *f*

**determine** /dɪˈtɜrmɪn/ *vt* determinar; definir; decidir, resolver; concluir; (fix) señalar; *Law.* sentenciar. —*vi* resolverse, decidirse; (insist (on)) empeñarse en, insistir en

**determined** /dɪˈtɜrmɪnd/ *a* determinado; resuelto, decidido; (of price) fijo

**determining** /dɪˈtɜrmənɪŋ/ *a* determinante

**determinism** /dɪˈtɜrməˌnizəm/ *n* determinismo, *m*

**deterministic** /dɪˌtɜrməˈnɪstɪk/ *a* determinista

**deterrent** /dɪˈtɜrənt/ *a* disuasivo. —*n* freno, *m.* **to act as a d.,** servir como un freno

**deterrent capability** *n* poder de disuasión, *m*

**detest** /dɪˈtɛst/ *vt* detestar, abominar, aborrecer

**detestable** /dɪˈtɛstəbəl/ *a* detestable, aborrecible, abominable

**detestation** /ˌditeˈsteiʃən/ *n* detestación, abominación, *f,* aborrecimiento, *m*

**dethrone** /diˈθroun/ *vt* destronar

**detonate** /ˈdɛtn̩ˌeit/ *vt* hacer detonar. —*vi* detonar, estallar

**detonation** /ˌdɛtn̩ˈeiʃən/ *n* detonación, *f*

**detonator** /ˈdɛtn̩ˌeitər/ *n* detonador, *m;* señal detonante, *f*

**detour** /ˈditur/ *n* rodeo, *m;* desvío, *m,* desviación, *f*

**detract** /dɪˈtrækt/ *vt* quitar; (diminish) disminuir; (slander) detraer, denigrar

**detraction** /dɪˈtrækʃən/ *n* detracción, denigración, *f*

**detractor** /dɪˈtræktər/ *n* detractor (-ra); infamador (-ra)

**detriment** /ˈdɛtrəmənt/ *n* detrimento, *m;* perjuicio, *m;* daño, *m*

**detrimental** /ˌdɛtrəˈmɛntl/ *a* perjudicial

**deuce** /dus/ *n* (dice, cards) dos, *m;* (tennis) "dos," *m.* **The d.!** ¡Diantre! **to be the d. of a row,** haber moros y cristianos. **D. take it!** ¡Demonios!

**Deuteronomy** /ˌdutəˈrɒnəmi/ *n* Deuteronomio, *m*

**devaluation** /diˌvælyuˈeiʃən/ *n* desvalorización, *f*

**devalue** /diˈvælyu/ *vt* rebajar el valor de

**devastate** /ˈdɛvəˌsteit/ *vt* devastar, asolar

**devastation** /ˌdɛvəˈsteiʃən/ *n* devastación, *f*

**develop** /dɪˈvɛləp/ *vt* desarrollar; (make progress) avanzar, fomentar; perfeccionar; *Photo.* revelar. —*vi* desarrollarse; crecer; avanzar, progresar; evolucionar

**developer** /dɪˈvɛləpər/ *n Photo.* revelador, *m*

**development** /dɪˈvɛləpmənt/ *n* desarrollo, *m;* evolución, *f;* progreso, avance, *m;* (encouragement) fomento, *m;* (event) acontecimiento, suceso, *m;* (product) producto, *m;* (working) explotación, *f; Photo.* revelación, *f*

**deviate** /ˈdiviˌeit/ *vi* desviarse (de); (disagree) disentir (de)

**deviation** /ˌdiviˈeiʃən/ *n* desviación, *f*

**device** /dɪˈvais/ *n* (contrivance) aparato, artefacto, mecanismo, *m;* (invention) invento, *m;* (trick) expediente, artificio, *m;* (scheme) proyecto, *m;* (design) dibujo, emblema, *m;* (motto) divisa, leyenda, *f; pl* **devices,** placeres, caprichos, *m pl*

**devil** /ˈdɛvəl/ *n* diablo, Satanás, *m;* demonio, *m;* (printer's) aprendiz de impresor, *m.* **Go to the d.!** ¡Vete enhoramala! **He is a poor d.,** Es un pobre diablo. **little d.,** diablillo, *m.* **The devil's abroad,** Anda el diablo suelto. **The d. take it!** ¡Llévoselo el diablo! **to play the d. with,** arruinar por completo. **What the d.!** ¡Qué diablos! **d.-possessed,** endemoniado

**devilish** /ˈdɛvəlɪʃ/ *a* diabólico, demoníaco; infernal

**devilry** /ˈdɛvəlri/ *n* diablura, *f;* magia, *f;* demonología, *f;* (wickedness) maldad, *f;* crueldad, *f*

**devious** /ˈdiviəs/ *a* desviado; tortuoso

**deviousness** /ˈdiviəsnɪs/ *n* tortuosidad, *f*

**devise** /dɪˈvaiz/ *vt* idear, inventar; fabricar; *Law.* legar

**deviser** /dɪˈvaizər/ *n* inventor (-ra)

**devitalize** /diˈvaitl̩ˌaiz/ *vt* restar vitalidad, privar de vitalidad

**devoid** /dɪˈvɔid/ *a* desprovisto (de), privado (de); libre (de), exento (de)

**devolve** /dɪˈvɒlv/ *vt* traspasar, transmitir. —*vi* (on, upon) incumbir (a), corresponder (a), tocar (a)

**devote** /dɪˈvout/ *vt* dedicar; consagrar. **to d. oneself to,** darse a, dedicarse a; consagrarse a

**devoted** /dɪˈvoutɪd/ *a* fervoroso, apasionado; (faithful) fiel, leal

**devotedly** /dɪˈvoutɪdli/ *adv* con devoción

**devotee** /ˌdɛvəˈti/ *n* devoto (-ta), admirador (-ra); aficionado (-da)

**devotion** /dɪˈvouʃən/ *n* devoción, *f;* dedicación, *f;* (zeal) celo, *m;* afición, *f;* (loyalty) lealtad, *f; pl* **devotions,** rezos, *m pl,* oraciones, *f pl*

**devotional** /dɪˈvouʃənl/ *a* devoto, religioso, de devoción. **devotional literature,** literatura de devoción, *f*

**devour** /dɪˈvaur/ *vt* devorar; consumir

**devourer** /dɪˈvaurər/ *n* devorador (-ra)

**devouring** /dɪˈvaurɪŋ/ *a* devorador; absorbente

**devout** /dɪˈvaut/ *a* devoto, piadoso, practicante (e.g., *a d. Catholic,* un católico practicante)

**devoutly** /dɪˈvautli/ *adv* piadosamente

**devoutness** /dɪˈvautnɪs/ *n* piedad, devoción, *f*

**dew** /du/ *n* rocío, sereno, relente, *m; Fig.* rocío, *m, vt* rociar; humedecer; (refresh) refrescar. **d.-drop,** aljófar, *m,* gota de rocío, *f*

**dewlap** /ˈduˌlæp/ *n* papada, *f,* papo, *m*

**dewy** /ˈdui/ *a* rociado, lleno de rocío; húmedo; (of eyes) lustroso

**dexterity** /dɛkˈstɛrɪti/ *n* destreza, *f*

**dextrine** /'dɛkstrɪn/ n dextrina, f
**dextrose** /'dɛkstrous/ n dextrosa, glucosa, f
**dextrous** /'dɛkstrəs/ a diestro; hábil, listo
**diabetes** /ˌdaiə'bitɪs/ n diabetes, f
**diabetic** /ˌdaiə'bɛtɪk/ a diabético
**diabolical** /ˌdaiə'bɒlɪkəl/ a diabólico
**diadem** /'daiəˌdɛm/ n diadema, f
**diagnose** /'daiəgˌnous/ vt diagnosticar
**diagnosis** /ˌdaiəg'nousɪs/ n diagnóstico, m, diagnosis, f
**diagnostician** /ˌdaiəgnɒ'stɪʃən/ n diagnóstico, m
**diagonal** /dai'ægənl/ n diagonal, f
**diagram** /'daiəˌgræm/ n diagrama, m; esquema, f; gráfico, m
**diagrammatic** /ˌdaiəgrə'mætɪk/ a esquemático
**dial** /'daiəl/ n (sundial) reloj de sol, m; (of clocks, gas-meter) esfera, f; (of machines) indicador, m; (of a wireless set) cuadrante graduado, m; (of a telephone) marcador, disco, m. —vt (a telephone number) marcar. **d. telephone,** teléfono automático, m
**dialect** /'daiəˌlɛkt/ n dialecto, m, habla, f, a dialectal
**dialectic** /ˌdaiə'lɛktɪk/ a dialéctico
**dialectics** /ˌdaiə'lɛktɪks/ n dialéctica, f
**dialogue** /'daiəˌlɒg/ n diálogo, m. **to hold a d.,** dialogar
**dialysis** /dai'æləsɪs/ n diálisis, f
**diameter** /dai'æmɪtər/ n diámetro, m
**diametrical** /ˌdaiə'mɛtrɪkəl/ a diametral
**diamond** /'daimənd/ n diamante, m; brillante, m; (tool) cortavidrios, m; (cards) oros (de baraja), m pl. **rough d.,** diamante bruto, m. **d.-bearing,** diamantífero. **d. cutter,** diamantista, mf **d. cutting,** talla de diamantes, f. **d. edition,** edición diamante, f. **d.-like,** adiamantado. **d. wedding,** bodas de diamante, f pl
**diapason** /ˌdaiə'peizən/ n diapasón, m
**diaper** /'daipər/ n lienzo adamascado, m; (baby's) pañal, m; (woman's) servilleta higiénica, f
**diaphanous** /dai'æfənəs/ a diáfano, transparente
**diaphragm** /'daiəˌfræm/ n diafragma, m
**diarist** /'daiərɪst/ n diarista, mf
**diarrhea** /ˌdaiə'riə/ n diarrea, f
**diary** /'daiəri/ n diario, m
**diastase** /'daiəˌsteis/ n diastasa, f
**diastole** /dai'æstl/ n diástole, f
**diatribe** /'daiəˌtraib/ n diatriba, denunciación violenta, f
**dibble** /'dɪbəl/ n plantador, m, vt and vi plantar con plantador
**dice** /dais/ n pl dados, m pl. **to load the d.,** cargar los dados
**dicky** /'dɪki/ n (front) pechera postiza, f; (seat) trasera, f; (apron) delantal, m. **d. seat,** Inf. ahí te pudras, m
**dictaphone** /'dɪktəˌfoun/ n dictáfono, m
**dictate** /'dɪkteit/ vt dictar; mandar. —n (order) dictamen, m; Fig. dictado, m
**dictation** /dɪk'teiʃən/ n dictado, m. **to write from d.,** escribir al dictado
**dictator** /'dɪkteitər/ n dictador, m
**dictatorial** /ˌdɪktə'tɔriəl/ a dictatorial, dictatorio, imperioso
**dictatorship** /dɪk'teitərˌʃip/ n dictadura, f
**diction** /'dɪkʃən/ n dicción, f
**dictionary** /'dɪkʃəˌnɛri/ n diccionario, m
**dictum** /'dɪktəm/ n dictamen, m; (saying) sentencia, f; Law. fallo, m
**didactic** /dai'dæktɪk/ a didáctico
**die** /dai/ vi morir; fallecer, finar; (wither) marchitarse; (disappear) desvanecerse, desaparecer; (of light) palidecer; extinguirse; (end) cesar; (desire) ansiar, perecerse (por). **Never say die!** ¡Mientras hay vida, hay esperanza! **to die early,** morir temprano; malograrse. **to die a violent death,** tener una muerte violenta, Inf. morir vestido. **to die from natural causes,** morir por causas naturales; Inf. morir en la cama. **to die hard,** luchar contra la muerte; tardar en morir; tardar en desaparecer. **to die of a broken heart,** morir con el corazón destrozado, morir de pena. **to die away,** desaparecer gradualmente; extinguirse poco a poco; dejar de oírse poco a poco; cesar; pasar. **to die down,** extinguirse gradualmente;

palidecer; dejar de oírse; desaparecer; (of the wind) amainar; perder su fuerza. **to die out,** desaparecer; olvidarse; dejar de existir; pasarse de moda
**die** /dai/ n dado, m; Fig. suerte, f; (stamp) cuño, m; quel, m; Archit. cubo, m. **The die is cast,** La suerte está echada. **die-sinker,** grabador en hueco, m
**diehard** /'dai,hɑrd/ n valiente, m; tradicionalista empedernido, m; partidario (-ia) entusiasta
**Dieppe** /di'ɛp/ Diepa, f
**dieresis** /dai'ɛrəsɪs/ n diéresis, crema, f
**diesel** /'dizəl, -səl/ a Diesel. **d. engine,** motor Diesel, m
**diet** /'daiit/ n dieta, f, régimen dietario, m; (assembly) dieta, f. —vi estar a dieta, hacer régimen
**dietetic** /dai'tɛtɪk/ a dietético
**dietetics** /ˌdaii'tɛtɪks/ n dietética, f
**dietician** /ˌdaii'tiʃən/ n dietista, mf
**differ** /'dɪfər/ vi diferenciarse; (contradict) contradecir; (disagree) no estar de acuerdo; disentir
**difference** /'dɪfərəns/ n diferencia, f; disparidad, f; contraste, m; (of opinion) disensión, f; controversia, disputa, f. **to make no d.,** no hacer diferencia alguna; no afectar; dar lo mismo, no importar
**different** /'dɪfərənt/ a distinto; diferente; vario, diverso
**differential** /ˌdɪfə'rɛnʃəl/ a diferencial. **d. calculus,** cálculo diferencial, m
**differentiate** /ˌdɪfə'rɛnʃiˌeit/ vt diferenciar, distinguir. —vi diferenciarse, distinguirse
**differentiation** /ˌdɪfəˌrɛnʃi'eiʃən/ n diferenciación, f
**differently** /'dɪfərəntli/ adv diferentemente
**difficult** /'dɪfɪˌkʌlt/ a difícil. **to make d.,** dificultar
**difficulty** /'dɪfɪˌkʌlti/ n dificultad, f. **d. in breathing,** opresión de pecho, f
**diffidence** /'dɪfɪdəns/ n modestia, timidez, f; huraña, f; falta de confianza en sí mismo, f
**diffident** /'dɪfɪdənt/ a modesto, tímido; huraño; sin confianza en sí mismo
**diffidently** /'dɪfɪdəntli/ adv tímidamente; vergonzosamente
**diffract** /dɪ'frækt/ vt difractar
**diffraction** /dɪ'frækʃən/ n difracción, f
**diffractive** /dɪ'fræktɪv/ a difrangente
**diffuse** /v dɪ'fyuz; a -'fyus/ vt difundir. —a difuso; (long-winded) difuso
**diffuseness** /dɪ'fyusnɪs/ n difusión, f; prolijidad, f
**diffusion** /dɪ'fyuʒən/ n difusión, f; esparcimiento, m; diseminación, f
**diffusive** /dɪ'fyusɪv/ a difusivo
**dig** /dɪg/ vt and vi cavar; excavar; (of animals) escarbar; (mine) zapar, minar; (into a subject) ahondar (en); (with the spurs) aguijonear, dar con las espuelas; (poke) clavar. **to dig in,** enterrarse; Mil. abrir trincheras; Inf. arreglarse las cosas. **to dig out,** excavar; sacar cavando, sacar con azadón; extraer. **to dig up,** desenterrar; descubrir
**digest** /v dɪ'dʒɛst, dai-; n 'daidʒɛst/ vt clasificar; codificar; (food, also chem. and Fig. tolerate and think over) digerir; (of knowledge and territory) asimilar. —vi digerir. —n compendio, resumen, m; Law. digesto, m; recopilación, f. **This food is easy to d.,** Este alimento es fácil de digerir; Este alimento es muy ligero
**digestibility** /dɪˌdʒɛstə'bɪlɪti, dai-/ n digestibilidad, f
**digestible** /dɪ'dʒɛstəbəl, dai-/ a digerible, digestible
**digestion** /dɪ'dʒɛstʃən, dai-/ n digestión, f; (of ideas) asimilación, f; Chem. digestión, f
**digestive** /dɪ'dʒɛstɪv, dai-/ a digestivo
**digger** /'dɪgər/ n cavador (-ra)
**digging** /'dɪgɪŋ/ n cavadura, f; excavación, f; pl **diggings,** minas, f pl; excavaciones, f pl; Inf. alojamiento, m, posada, f
**digit** /'dɪdʒɪt/ n dígito, m
**digital** /'dɪdʒɪtl/ a digital, dígito
**digitalin** /ˌdɪdʒɪ'tælɪn/ n digitalina, f
**digitalis** /ˌdɪdʒɪ'tælɪs/ n digitalina, f
**dignified** /'dɪgnəˌfaid/ a serio, grave; majestuoso; (worthy) digno; solemne; altivo; noble
**dignify** /'dɪgnəˌfai/ vt dignificar, honrar; exaltar; dar dignidad (a); ennoblecer
**dignitary** /'dɪgnɪˌtɛri/ n dignatario, m; dignidad, f

**dignity** /'dɪgnɪti/ *n* dignidad, *f;* (rank) rango, *m;* (post) cargo, puesto, *m;* (honor) honra, *f;* (stateliness) majestad, *f;* mesura, seriedad, *f;* (haughtiness) altivez, *f;* (nobility) nobleza, *f.* **to stand on one's d.,** darse importancia

**digress** /dɪ'grɛs, dai-/ *vi* divagar

**digression** /dɪ'grɛʃən, dai-/ *n* digresión, divagación, *f*

**dike** /daik/ *n* dique, *m;* (ditch) acequia, *f;* canal, *m;* (embankment) zanja, *f, vt* represar

**dilapidated** /dɪ'læpɪˌdeitɪd/ *a* arruinado, destartalado; (of fortune) dilapidado; (of persons, families) venido a menos; (shabby) raído

**dilapidation** /dɪˌlæpə'deiʃən/ *n* deterioración, *f;* ruina, *f,* estado ruinoso, *m*

**dilatation** /ˌdɪlə'teiʃən/ *n* dilatación, *f;* ensanche, *m*

**dilate** /dai'leit/ *vt* dilatar; ensanchar. —*vi* dilatarse.

to d. upon, extenderse sobre, dilatarse en

**dilator** /dai'leitər/ *n* dilatador, *m*

**dilatoriness** /'dɪlətɔrinɪs/ *n* tardanza, *f;* (slowness) lentitud, *f*

**dilatory** /'dɪləˌtɔri/ *a* dilatorio, tardo; (slow) lento

**dilemma** /dɪ'lɛmə/ *n* dilema, *m*

**dilettante** /'dɪlɪˌtɑnt/ *n* diletante, *m;* aficionado (-da)

**dilettantism** /'dɪlɪtɑnˌtizəm/ *n* diletantismo, *m*

**diligence** /'dɪlɪdʒəns/ *n* diligencia, *f;* asiduidad, *f;* (care) cuidado, *m;* (coach) diligencia, *f*

**diligent** /'dɪlɪdʒənt/ *a* diligente, asiduo, aplicado, industrioso; (painstaking) concienzudo

**dilute** /dɪ'lut, dai-/ *vt* diluir; *Fig.* adulterar. —*a* diluido

**dilution** /dɪ'luʃən, dai-/ *n* dilución, *f; Fig.* adulteración, *f*

**diluvian** /dɪ'luviən/ *a* diluviano

**dim** /dɪm/ *a* (of light) apagado, débil, tenue; (of sight) turbio; (dark) sombrío, oscuro; (blurred, etc.) empañado; indistinto, confuso. —*vt* obscurecer; empañar; (dazzle) ofuscar; (eclipse) eclipsar; reducir la intensidad (de una luz); (of memories) borrar. **dim intelligence,** de brumoso seso

**dimension** /dɪ'mɛnʃən/ *n* dimensión, *f;* (size) tamaño, *m;* (scope) extensión, *f,* alcance, *m*

**dimensional** /dɪ'mɛnʃənl/ *a* dimensional

**diminish** /dɪ'mɪnɪʃ/ *vt* disminuir; reducir; debilitar, atenuar. —*vi* disminuir; reducirse; debilitarse, atenuarse

**diminishing** /dɪ'mɪnɪʃɪŋ/ *a* menguante

**diminution** /ˌdɪmə'nuʃən/ *n* disminución, *f;* reducción, *f;* atenuación, *f*

**diminutive** /dɪ'mɪnyətɪv/ *a* diminutivo. —*n* diminutivo, *m*

**diminutiveness** /dɪ'mɪnyətɪvnɪs/ *n* pequeñez, *f*

**dimly** /'dɪmli/ *adv* obscuramente; vagamente; indistintamente. **dimly lit,** apenas alumbrado

**dimness** /'dɪmnɪs/ *n* oscuridad, *f;* deslustre, *m;* (of light) tenuidad (de la luz), *f;* confusión, *f*

**dimple** /'dɪmpəl/ *n* hoyuelo, *m*

**dimpled** /'dɪmpəld/ *a* con hoyuelos, que tiene hoyuelos

**din** /dɪn/ *n* estrépito, estruendo, ruido, *m;* algarabía, barahúnda, *f, vt* ensordecer

**dine** /dain/ *vi* (in the evening) cenar; (at midday) comer. —*vt* convidar a cenar o a comer. **to d. out,** cenar o comer fuera

**diner** /'dainər/ *n* (on a train) coche comedor, coche restaurante, *m;* cenador, *m;* comedor, *m*

**ding-dong** /'dɪŋˌdɔŋ/ *n* tintín, *m*

**dinghy** /'dɪŋgi/ *n* lancha, *f;* canoa, *f,* bote, *m.* **rubber d.,** canoa de goma, *f*

**dinginess** /'dɪndʒinɪs/ *n* deslustre, *m;* suciedad, *f;* oscuridad, *f;* (of a person) desaseo, *m*

**dingy** /'dɪndʒi/ *a* deslucido, empañado; sucio; oscuro; (of persons) desaseado

**dining car** /'dainɪŋ/ *n* coche comedor, vagón restaurante, *m*

**dining room** *n* comedor, *m;* refectorio, *m*

**dining table** *n* mesa del comedor, *f*

**dinner** /'dɪnər/ *n* (in the evening) cena, *f;* (at midday) comida, *f.* **over the d. table,** de sobremesa. **d.-jacket,** smoking, *m.* **d. party,** cena, *f.* **d. plate,** plato, *m.* **d. roll,** panecillo, *m.* **d. service,** vajilla, *f*

**dinosaur** /'dainəˌsɔr/ *n* dinosauro, *m*

**dint** /dɪnt/ **(by d. of)** a fuerza de, a costa de

**diocesan** /dai'ɒsəsən/ *a* diocesano

**diocese** /'daiəsis/ *n* diócesis, *f*

**Dionysus Thrax** /ˌdaiə'naisəs 'θræks/ Dionisio el Tracio, *m*

**dioxide** /dai'ɒksaid, -sɪd/ *n* dióxido, *m*

**dip** /dɪp/ *n* inmersión, *f;* baño, *m;* (in the ground) declive, *m;* (in the road) columpio, *m,* depresión, *f;* (slope) pendiente, *f;* (candle) vela de sebo, *f;* (of the horizon) depresión (del horizonte), *f;* (of the needle) inclinación (de la aguja), *f.* —*vt* sumergir; bañar; (put) poner. —*vi* inclinarse hacia abajo. **to dip into a book,** hojear un libro. **to dip the colors,** saludar con la bandera. **to dip the headlights,** bajar los faros

**diphtheria** /dɪf'θɪəriə/ *n* difteria, *f*

**diphthong** /'dɪfθɔŋ/ *n* diptongo, *m*

**diploma** /dɪ'ploumə/ *n* diploma, *m*

**diplomacy** /dɪ'plouməsi/ *n* diplomacia, *f;* tacto, *m*

**diploma mill** *n* fábrica de títulos académicos, *f*

**diplomat** /'dɪpləˌmæt/ *n* diplomático, *m*

**diplomatic** /ˌdɪplə'mætɪk/ *a* diplomático. **d. bag,** valija diplomática, *f.* **d. corps,** cuerpo diplomático, *m*

**diplomatically** /ˌdɪplə'mætɪkəli/ *adv* diplomáticamente

**dipper** /'dɪpər/ *n* (ladle) cazo, *m; Astron.* Osa Mayor, *f*

**dipsomania** /ˌdɪpsə'meiniə/ *n* dipsomanía, *f*

**dipsomaniac** /ˌdɪpsə'meiniæk/ *n* dipsómano (-na)

**diptych** /'dɪptɪk/ *n* díptica, *f*

**dire** /dai³r/ *a* espantoso, horrible; cruel; funesto

**direct** /dɪ'rɛkt, dai-/ *a* directo; claro, inequívoco; (of descent) recto; (of electric current) continuo; exacto. —*adv* directamente. —*vt* dirigir; (command) ordenar, encargar; dar instrucciones. **d. action,** acción directa, *f.* **d. current,** corriente continua, *f.* **d. line,** línea directa, *f;* (of descent) línea recta, *f.* **d. object,** acusativo, *m.* **d. speech,** oración directa, *f*

**direct dialing** *n* discado directo, *m*

**direction** /dɪ'rɛkʃən, 'dai-/ *n* dirección, *f;* rumbo, *m;* instrucción, *f;* (on a letter) sobrescrito, *m;* señas, *f pl.* **in the d. of,** en la dirección de; hacia; *Naut.* con rumbo a. **in all directions,** por todas partes; a los cuatro vientos. **to go in the d. of,** ir en la dirección de; tomar por. **Directions for use,** Direcciones para el uso. **d. indicator, d. signal,** (on car) indicador de dirección, *m*

**directive** /dɪ'rɛktɪv, dai-/ *a* directivo, director

**directly** /dɪ'rɛktli, dai-/ *adv* directamente; inmediatamente, en seguida

**directness** /dɪ'rɛktnɪs, dai-/ *n* derechura, *f*

**director** /dɪ'rɛktər, dai-/ *n* director (-triz, -ora), **managing d.,** director gerente, *m*

**directorate** /dɪ'rɛktərɪt, dai-/ *n* directorio, *m,* junta directiva, *f;* cargo de director, *m*

**directory** /dɪ'rɛktəri, dai-/ *n* directorio, *m,* guía, *f.* **telephone d.,** guía de teléfonos, *f*

**dirge** /dɜrdʒ/ *n* endecha, *f,* lamento, *m;* canto fúnebre, *m*

**dirigible** /'dɪrɪdʒəbəl/ *n* dirigible, *m*

**dirt** /dɜrt/ *n* mugre, suciedad, *f;* (mud) lodo, *m;* (earth) tierra, *f;* (dust) polvo, *m; Fig.* inmundicia, *f.* **d.-cheap,** sumamente barato. **to be d. cheap,** (of goods) estar por los suelos. **d.-track,** pista de ceniza, *f.* **d.-track racing,** carreras en pista de ceniza, *f pl*

**dirtiness** /'dɜrtinɪs/ *n* suicedad, *f;* (untidiness) desaseo, *m;* sordidez, *f;* (meanness) bajeza, *f*

**dirty** /'dɜrti/ *a* sucio; (untidy) desaseado; (muddy) enlodado; (dusty) polvoriento; (of weather) borrascoso; (sordid) sórdido; (base, mean) vil; (indecent) indecente, verde, obsceno. —*vt* ensuciar. **d. trick,** mala pasada, *f*

**disability** /ˌdɪsə'bɪlɪti/ *n* incapacidad, *f;* impotencia, *f;* desventaja, *f*

**disable** /dɪs'eibəl/ *vt* (cripple) estropear, tullir; hacer incapaz (de), incapacitar; imposibilitar; (destroy) destruir; *Law.* incapacitar legalmente

**disabled** /dɪs'eibəld/ *a* inválido; impedido, lisiado; (in the hand) manco; incapacitado; (of ships, etc.) fuera de servicio, estropeado. **d. soldier,** inválido, *m*

**disablement** /dɪs'eibəlmənt/ *n* (physical) invalidez, *f;* inhabilitación, *f; Law.* impedimento, *m*

**disabuse** /ˌdɪsəˈbyuz/ *vt* desengañar, sacar de un error

**disadvantage** /ˌdɪsədˈvæntɪdʒ/ *n* desventaja, *f*. **to be under the d. of,** sufrir la desventaja de

**disadvantaged** /ˌdɪsədˈvæntɪdʒd/ *a* (financially) de escasos recursos

**disadvantageous** /dɪsˌædvənˈteɪdʒəs/ *a* desventajoso.

**disaffected** /ˌdɪsəˈfɛktɪd/ *a* desafecto

**disaffection** /ˌdɪsəˈfɛkʃən/ *n* desafecto, descontento, *m*

**disagree** /ˌdɪsəˈgri/ *vi* no estar de acuerdo; diferir; (quarrel) reñir; (not share the opinion of) no estar de la opinión (de); (of food, etc.) sentar mal; no probar. **The meat disagreed with me,** La carne me sentó mal

**disagreeable** /ˌdɪsəˈgriəbəl/ *a* desagradable; repugnante; (of persons) antipático, displicente

**disagreeableness** /ˌdɪsəˈgriəbəlnɪs/ *n* lo desagradable; (of persons) displicencia, *f*

**disagreeably** /ˌdɪsəˈgriəbli/ *adv* desagradablemente; con displicencia

**disagreement** /ˌdɪsəˈgrimənt/ *n* desacuerdo, *m*; diferencia, *f*; desavenencia, *f*; discordia, *f*; (quarrel) riña, disputa, *f*; discrepancia, *f*

**disallow** /ˌdɪsəˈlau/ *vt* negar; rechazar

**disappear** /ˌdɪsəˈpɪər/ *vi* desaparecer. **to cause to d.,** hacer desaparecer

**disappearance** /ˌdɪsəˈpɪərəns/ *n* desaparición, *f*

**disappoint** /ˌdɪsəˈpɔɪnt/ *vt* desilusionar; frustrar; (hopes) defraudar; (deprive) privar de; (annoy) contrariar; (break a promise) faltar (a la palabra)

**disappointedly** /ˌdɪsəˈpɔɪntɪdli/ *adv* con desilusión, con desengaño

**disappointing** /ˌdɪsəˈpɔɪntɪŋ/ *a* desengañador; pobre; triste; poco halagüeño

**disappointment** /ˌdɪsəˈpɔɪntmənt/ *n* desengaño, *m*, decepción, *f*; frustración, *f*; desilusión, *f*; (vexation) contrariedad, *f*; contratiempo, *m*. **to suffer a d.,** sufrir un desengaño; *Inf.* llevarse un chasco

**disapproval** /ˌdɪsəˈpruvəl/ *n* desaprobación, *f*

**disapprove** /ˌdɪsəˈpruv/ *vt* desaprobar

**disapproving** /ˌdɪsəˈpruvɪŋ/ *a* de desaprobación, severo

**disapprovingly** /ˌdɪsəˈpruvɪŋli/ *adv* con desaprobación

**disarm** /dɪsˈɑrm/ *vt* desarmar. —*vi* desarmarse; deponer las armas

**disarmament** /dɪsˈɑrməmənt/ *n* desarme, *m*

**disarrange** /ˌdɪsəˈreɪndʒ/ *vt* desarreglar; descomponer, desajustar; (hair) despeinar

**disarrangement** /ˌdɪsəˈreɪndʒmənt/ *n* desarreglo, *m*; desajuste, *m*; desorden, *m*

**disarray** /ˌdɪsəˈreɪ/ *n* desorden, desarreglo, *m*; confusión, *f*. —*vt* desordenar, desarreglar

**disarticulate** /ˌdɪsɑrˈtɪkyəˌleɪt/ *vt* desarticular

**disarticulation** /ˌdɪsɑrˌtɪkyəˈleɪʃən/ *n* desarticulación, *f*

**disaster** /dɪˈzæstər/ *n* desastre, *m*; catástrofe, *m*; infortunio, *m*

**disastrous** /dɪˈzæstrəs/ *a* desastroso; funesto, trágico

**disastrously** /dɪˈzæstrəsli/ *adv* desastrosamente

**disastrousness** /dɪˈzæstrəsnɪs/ *n* carácter desastroso, *m*

**disavow** /ˌdɪsəˈvau/ *vt* repudiar; retractar

**disavowal** /ˌdɪsəˈvauəl/ *n* repudiación, *f*

**disband** /dɪsˈbænd/ *vt* licenciar. —*vi* desbandarse, dispersarse

**disbelief** /ˌdɪsbɪˈlif/ *n* incredulidad, *f*; desconfianza, *f*

**disbelieve** /ˌdɪsbɪˈliv/ *vt* and *vi* descreer, no creer; desconfiar (de)

**disburse** /dɪsˈbɜrs/ *vt* desembolsar, pagar

**disbursement** /dɪsˈbɜrsmənt/ *n* desembolso, *m*

**disc** /dɪsk/ *n* disco, *m*

**discard** /*v* dɪˈskɑrd; *n* ˈdɪskɑrd/ *vt* desechar, arrinconar; despedir; (at cards) descartar. —*n* (at cards) descarte, *m*

**discern** /dɪˈsɜrn/ *vt* discernir, distinguir, percibir

**discerner** /dɪˈsɜrnər/ *n* discernidor (-ra)

**discernible** /dɪˈsɜrnəbəl/ *a* distinguible, perceptible

**discerning** /dɪˈsɜrnɪŋ/ *a* perspicaz, discernidor

**discernment** /dɪˈsɜrnmənt/ *n* discernimiento, *m*

**discharge** /*v* dɪsˈtʃɑrdʒ/ *vt* descargar; (a gun) disparar, tirar; (an arrow) lanzar; *Elec.* descargar; emitir; (dismiss) destituir, despedir; arrojar; *Mil.* licenciar; (exempt) dispensar (de); (exonerate) absolver, exonerar; (free) dar libertad (a); (from hospital) dar de baja (a); *Law.* revocar; (perform) cumplir, ejecutar; (pay) pagar, saldar; (of an abscess, etc.) supurar.

**discharge** /*n* ˈdɪstʃɑrdʒ/ *n* (of firearms) disparo, tiro, *m*; (of artillery) descarga, *f*; (of goods, cargo) descargue, *m*; *Elec.* descarga, *f*; (from a wound, etc.) pus, *m*, supuración, *f*; (from the intestine) flujo, *m*; (of a debt) pago, m.; *Com.* descargo, *m*; (receipt) carta de pago, quitanza, *f*; *Mil.* licencia absoluta, *f*; (dismissal) despedida, destitución, *f*; (exoneration) exoneración, *f*; (freeing) liberación, *f*; (from hospital) baja, *f*; (performance) cumplimiento, *m*; ejecución, *f*

**disciple** /dɪˈsaipəl/ *n* discípulo (-la)

**disciplinarian** /ˌdɪsəpləˈnɛəriən/ *n* disciplinario (-ia)

**disciplinary** /ˈdɪsəpləˌnɛri/ *a* disciplinario

**discipline** /ˈdɪsəplɪn/ *n* disciplina, *f*, *vt* disciplinar

**disclaim** /dɪsˈkleim/ *vt* renunciar (a); (repudiate) rechazar, repudiar

**disclaimer** /dɪsˈkleimər/ *n* *Law.* renunciación, *f*; repudiación, *f*

**disclose** /dɪˈsklouz/ *vt* descubrir, revelar

**disclosure** /dɪˈsklouʒər/ *n* descubrimiento, *m*, revelación, *f*

**discolor** /dɪsˈkʌlər/ *vt* descolorar. —*vi* descolorarse

**discoloration** /dɪsˌkʌləˈreɪʃən/ *n* descoloramiento, *m*

**discomfit** /dɪsˈkʌmfɪt/ *vt* desconcertar

**discomfiture** /dɪsˈkʌmfɪtʃər/ *n* desconcierto, *m*

**discomfort** /dɪsˈkʌmfərt/ *n* falta de comodidades, *f*; incomodidad, *f*; malestar, *m*; molestia, *f*; inquietud, *f*; dolor, *m*

**discomposure** /ˌdɪskəmˈpouʒər/ *n* confusión, agitación, inquietud, *f*

**disconcert** /ˌdɪskənˈsɜrt/ *vt* desconcertar, turbar; (of plans, etc.) frustrar

**disconnect** /ˌdɪskəˈnɛkt/ *vt* separar; (of railway engines, etc.) desacoplar; desconectar; (of electric plugs) desenchufar

**disconnected** /ˌdɪskəˈnɛktɪd/ *a* inconexo; incoherente, deshilvanado

**disconnectedness** /ˌdɪskəˈnɛktɪdnɪs/ *n* inconexión, *f*; incoherencia, *f*

**disconsolate** /dɪsˈkɒnsəlɪt/ *a* desconsolado, triste

**disconsolately** /dɪsˈkɒnsəlɪtli/ *adv* desconsoladamente, tristemente

**disconsolateness** /dɪsˈkɒnsəlɪtnɪs/ *n* desconsuelo, *m*

**discontent** /ˌdɪskənˈtɛnt/ *n* descontento, disgusto, *m*, *vt* descontentar, desagradar

**discontented** /ˌdɪskənˈtɛntɪd/ *a* descontentadizo, descontento, disgustado

**discontinuance** /ˌdɪskənˈtɪnyuəns/ *n* descontinuación, cesación, *f*; interrupción, *f*

**discontinue** /ˌdɪskənˈtɪnyu/ *vt* descontinuar; cesar; interrumpir; (of payments, etc.) suspender. —*vi* cesar

**discontinuous** /ˌdɪskənˈtɪnyuəs/ *a* descontinuo; interrumpido; intermitente

**discord** /ˈdɪskɔrd/ *n* discordia, *f*; *Mus.* disonancia, *f*, desentono, *m*

**discordant** /dɪsˈkɔrdənt/ *a* discorde, poco armonioso; incongruo; *Mus.* disonante, desentonado. **to be d.,** discordar; ser incongruo; *Mus.* disonar

**discount** /ˈdɪskaunt; *v* also dɪsˈkaunt/ *n* descuento, *m*; rebaja, *f*. —*vt* descontar; rebajar; balancear; (disconsider) desechar. **at a d.,** al descuento; bajo la par; fácil de obtener; superfluo; *Fig.* en disfavor, en descrédito. **rate of d.,** tipo de descuento, *m*. **d. for cash,** descuento por venta al contado, *m*

**discourage** /dɪˈskɜrɪdʒ/ *vt* desalentar, desanimar; oponerse a; disuadir; frustrar

**discouragement** /dɪˈskɜrɪdʒmənt/ *n* desaliento, *m*; desaprobación, oposición, *f*; disuasión, *f*; (obstacle) estorbo, *m*

**discouraging** /dɪˈskɜrɪdʒɪŋ/ *a* poco animador, que ofrece pocas esperanzas; (with prospect, etc.) nada halagüeño

**discourse** /*n* ˈdɪskɔrs; *v* dɪsˈkɔrs/ *n* discurso, *m*; plática, *f*; (treatise) disertación, *f*. —*vi* (converse) platicar, conversar; (with on, upon) disertar sobre, discurrir sobre; tratar de

**dislocation**

**discourteous** /dɪs'kɜrtiəs/ a descortés, desconsiderado
**discourtesy** /dɪs'kɜrtəsi/ n descortesía, f
**discover** /dɪ'skʌvər/ vt descubrir; (see) ver; (realize) darse cuenta de; (show) manifestar; revelar
**discoverable** /dɪ'skʌvərəbəl/ a que se puede descubrir; averiguable; distinguible, perceptible
**discoverer** /dɪ'skʌvərər/ n descubridor (-ra); revelador (-ra)
**discovery** /dɪ'skʌvəri/ n descubrimiento, m; revelación, f
**discredit** /dɪs'krɛdɪt/ n descrédito, m; des honra, f; duda, f. —vt dudar (de), no creer (en); desacreditar; deshonrar
**discreditable** /dɪs'krɛdɪtəbəl/ a deshonroso, ignominioso, vergonzoso
**discreet** /dɪ'skrit/ a discreto; prudente, circunspecto
**discreetly** /dɪ'skritli/ adv discretamente; prudentemente
**discrepancy** /dɪ'skrɛpənsi/ n discrepancia, diferencia, f; contradicción, f
**discrepant** /dɪ'skrɛpənt/ a discrepante; contradictorio, inconsistente
**discretion** /dɪ'skrɛʃən/ n discreción, f; prudencia, circunspección, f; juicio, m; voluntad, f. **at d.,** a discreción. **at one's own d.,** a voluntad (de uno). **years of d.,** edad de discreción, f
**discriminate** /dɪ'skrɪm,əneit/ vi distinguir (entre); hacer una distinción (en favor de or en perjuicio de). —vt distinguir
**discriminating** /dɪ'skrɪmə,neitɪŋ/ a discerniente, que sabe distinguir, juicioso; culto; diferencial
**discrimination** /dɪ,skrɪmə'neiʃən/ n discernimiento, m; gusto, m; distinción, f; discriminación, f
**discursive** /dɪ'skɜrsɪv/ a discursivo; digresivo
**discus** /'dɪskəs/ n disco, m. **d. thrower,** discóbolo, m
**discuss** /dɪ'skʌs/ vt discutir; hablar de; debatir; (deal with) tratar; (Fam. a dish) probar; (a bottle of wine) vaciar
**discussion** /dɪ'skʌʃən/ n discusión, f; debate, m
**disdain** /dɪs'dein/ n dɛsdén, m; altivez, f. —vt desdeñar, desairar, despreciar. **to d. to,** desdeñarse de
**disdainful** /dɪs'deinfəl/ a desdeñoso; altivo
**disdainfully** /dɪs'deinfəli/ adv desdeñosamente
**disease** /dɪ'ziz/ n enfermedad, f; Fig. mal, m. **infectious d.,** enfermedad contagiosa, f
**diseased** /dɪ'zizd/ a enfermo; (of fruit, etc.) malo
**disembark** /,dɪsɛm'bɑrk/ vt and vi desembarcar
**disembarkation** /dɪs,ɛmbɑr'keiʃən/ n desembarque, m; Mil. desembarco (de tropas), m
**disembodied** /,dɪsɛm'bɒdid/ a incorpóreo
**disembowel** /,dɪsɛm'bauəl/ vt desentrañar, destripar
**disenchant** /,dɪsɛn'tʃænt/ vt desencantar; deschechizar; desilusionar
**disenchantment** /,dɪsɛn'tʃæntmənt/ n desencanto, m; desilusión, f
**disengage** /,dɪsɛn'geidʒ/ vt desasir; soltar; (gears) desembragar; (uncouple) desacoplar; (free) librar
**disengaged** /,dɪsɛn'geidʒd/ a (free) libre
**disentangle** /,dɪsɛn'tæŋgəl/ vt (undo) desatar, desanudar; separar; (of threads, etc., and Fig.) desenredar, desenmarañar. —vi desenredarse
**disentanglement** /,dɪsɛn'tæŋgəlmənt/ n desatadura, f; separación, f; desenredo, m
**disestablish** /,dɪsɪ'stæblɪʃ/ vt separar (la Iglesia del Estado)
**disestablishment** /,dɪsɪ'stæblɪʃmənt/ n separación (de la Iglesia del Estado), f
**disfavor** /dɪs'feivər/ n disfavor, m; (disapproval) desaprobación, f. —vt desaprobar
**disfigure** /dɪs'fɪgyər/ vt desfigurar, afear; deformar; (mar) estropear
**disfigurement** /dɪs'fɪgyərmənt/ n desfiguración, f; deformidad, f; defecto, m
**disfranchise** /dɪs'fræntʃaiz/ vt privar de los derechos civiles (a)
**disfranchisement** /dɪs'fræntʃaizmənt/ n privación de los derechos civiles, privación del derecho de votar, f
**disgorge** /dɪs'gɔrdʒ/ vt and vi vomitar; (of a river) desembocar (en); hacer restitución (de lo robado)
**disgrace** /dɪs'greis/ n vergüenza, ignominia, f; des-

honra, f; (insult) afrenta, f; (scandal) escándalo, m; disfavor, m. —vt deshonrar; despedir con ignominia. **in d.,** fuera de favor; desacreditado; (of children and animals) castigado
**disgraceful** /dɪs'greisfəl/ a deshonroso; ignominioso; escandaloso
**disgracefully** /dɪs'greisfəli/ adv escandalosamente
**disgracefulness** /dɪs'greisfəlnɪs/ n ignominia, vergüenza, f; deshonra, f
**disgruntled** /dɪs'grʌntld/ a refunfuñador, enfurruñado, malhumorado
**disguise** /dɪs'gaiz/ n disfraz, m; (mask) máscara, f. —vt disfrazar; cubrir, tapar; (Fig. conceal) ocultar. **in d.,** disfrazado
**disgust** /dɪs'gʌst/ n repugnancia, aversión, f; aborrecimiento, m; asco, m. —vt repugnar, inspirar aversión; disgustar; dar asco (a)
**disgusted** /dɪs'gʌstid/ a asqueado; disgustado; furioso; (bored) aburrido
**disgusting** /dɪs'gʌstɪŋ/ a repugnante; odioso, horrible; asqueroso
**dish** /dɪʃ/ n (for meat, vegetables, fruit, etc.) fuente, f; (food) plato, m; pl **dishes,** platos, m pl, vajilla, f. —vt servir; Inf. frustrar. **cooked d.,** guiso, m. **special d. for today,** plato del día, m. **to wash the dishes,** fregar los platos. **d.-cloth,** (for washing) fregador, m; (for drying) paño de los platos, m. **d.-cover,** cubreplatos, m. **d.-rack,** escurre-platos, m. **d.-washer,** lavaplatos, lavavajillas, m. **d.-water,** agua de lavar los platos, f
**disharmony** /dɪs'hɑrməni/ n falta de armonía, f; (disagreement) discordia, desavenencia, f; incongruencia, f; Mus. disonancia, f
**dishearten** /dɪs'hɑrtn/ vt desalentar, desanimar; desesperar; disuadir (de)
**disheveled** /dɪ'ʃɛvəld/ a despeinado, desgreñado; (untidy) desaseado
**dishonest** /dɪs'ɒnɪst/ a falto de honradez, tramposo; fraudulento; falso, desleal
**dishonestly** /dɪs'ɒnɪstli/ adv de mala fe, sin honradez; fraudulentamente; deslealmente
**dishonesty** /dɪs'ɒnɪsti/ n falta de honradez, falta de integridad, f; fraude, m; falsedad, deslealtad, f
**dishonor** /dɪs'ɒnər/ n deshonra, f, or deshonor, m; Com. no pagar, o no aceptar, un giro
**dishonorable** /dɪs'ɒnərəbəl/ a deshonroso
**dishonorer** /dɪs'ɒnərər/ n deshonrador (-ra); profanador (-ra)
**disillusion** /,dɪsɪ'luʒən/ vt desengañar, desilusionar
**disillusionment** /,dɪsɪ'luʒənmənt/ n desilusión, f, desengaño, desencanto, m
**disinclination** /dɪs,ɪnklə'neiʃən/ n aversión, f
**disincline** /,dɪsɪn'klain/ vt desinclinar
**disinfect** /,dɪsɪn'fɛkt/ vt desinfectar
**disinfectant** /,dɪsɪn'fɛktənt/ a and n desinfectante, m
**disinfection** /,dɪsɪn'fɛkʃən/ n desinfección, f
**disingenuous** /,dɪsɪn'dʒɛnyuəs/ a tortuoso, doble, falso, insincero
**disinherit** /,dɪsɪn'hɛrɪt/ vt desheredar
**disinheritance** /,dɪsɪn'hɛrɪtəns/ n desheredación, f
**disintegrate** /dɪs'ɪntə,greit/ vt despedazar, disgregar. —vi disgregarse; desmoronarse
**disintegration** /dɪs,ɪntə'greiʃən/ n disgregación, f; disolución, f; desmoronamiento, m
**disinter** /,dɪsɪn'tɜr/ vt desenterrar
**disinterested** /dɪs'ɪntə,rɛstid, -trɪstid/ a desinteresado
**disinterestedness** /dɪs'ɪntə,rɛstidnɪs, -trɪstid-/ n desinterés, m
**disinterment** /,dɪsɪn'tɜrmənt/ n desenterramiento, m
**disjointed** /dɪs'dʒɔintid/ a desarticulado; desarticulado; incoherente, inconexo; (of a speech, etc.) descosido
**disjointedness** /dɪs'dʒɔintidnɪs/ n descoyuntura, f; desencajamiento, m; incoherencia, f
**disk** /dɪsk/ n disco, m
**dislike** /dɪs'laik/ n aversión, f; antipatía, f; (hostility) animosidad, f. —vt desagradar, no gustar; repugnar. **I d. the house,** No me gusta la casa. **I d. them,** No me gustan
**dislocate** /'dɪslou,keit/ vt dislocar, descoyuntar; Fig. interrumpir
**dislocation** /,dɪslou'keiʃən/ n dislocación, f, descoyuntamiento, m; Fig. interrupción, f

**dislodge** /dɪs'lɒdʒ/ vt desalojar
**dislodgement** /dɪs'lɒdʒmənt/ n desalojamiento, m
**disloyal** /dɪs'lɔɪəl/ a desleal, infiel, falso
**disloyalty** /dɪs'lɔɪəlti/ n deslealtad, infidelidad, falsedad, f
**dismal** /'dɪzməl/ a lóbrego, sombrío; lúgubre; funesto; triste
**dismantle** /dɪs'mæntl/ vt (a ship or fort) desmantelar; (a machine) desmontar; (a house, etc.) desamueblar
**dismantling** /dɪs'mæntlɪŋ/ n desmantelamiento, m
**dismay** /dɪs'mei/ n desmayo, desaliento, m; consternación, f; espanto, terror, m. —vt desanimar; consternar; espantar, horrorizar
**dismember** /dɪs'mɛmbər/ vt desmembrar
**dismemberment** /dɪs'mɛmbərmənt/ n desmembración, f
**dismiss** /dɪs'mɪs/ vt (from a job) despedir (de); (from an official position) destituir (de); (bid good-bye to) despedirse de; (after military parade) dar la orden de romper filas; (thoughts) apartar de sí; ahuyentar; (discard) desechar, descartar; (omit) pasar por alto de; (disregard) rechazar; (a parliament, etc.) disolver; (a law case) absolver de la instancia. **to d. in a few words,** tratar someramente; hablar brevemente de
**dismissal** /dɪs'mɪsəl/ n despedida, f; (from an official post) destitución, f; apartamiento, m; (discard) descarte, m; (of a parliament, etc.) disolución, f
**dismount** /v dɪs'maunt/ n also 'dɪs,maunt/ vi apearse, desmontar, echar pie a tierra; bajar. —vt desmontar; (dismantle) desarmar
**disobedience** /,dɪsə'bidiəns/ n desobediencia, f
**disobedient** /,dɪsə'bidiənt/ a desobediente
**disobey** /,dɪsə'bei/ vt and vi desobedecer
**disobliging** /,dɪsə'blaidʒɪŋ/ a poco servicial
**disobligingly** /,dɪsə'blaidʒɪŋli/ adv descortésmente
**disorder** /dɪs'ɔrdər/ n desorden, m; confusión, f; (unrest) perturbación del orden público, f; motín, m; (disease) enfermedad, f; (mental) enajenación mental, f; trastorno, m. —vt desordenar, desarreglar; (of health) perjudicar; (the mind) trastornar. **in d.,** en desorden, desarreglado; (helter-skelter) atropelladamente
**disordered** /dɪs'ɔrdərd/ a en desorden; irregular, desordenado; (of the mind and bodily organs) trastornado; (ill) enfermo; (confused) confuso
**disorganization** /dɪs,ɔrgənə'zeifən/ n desorganización, f
**disorganize** /dɪs'ɔrgə,naiz/ vt desorganizar
**disorganizing** /dɪs'ɔrgə,naizɪŋ/ a desorganizador
**disorientate** /dɪs'ɔriən,teit/ vt desorientar
**disorientation** /dɪs,ɔriən'teifən/ n desorientación, f
**disown** /dɪs'oun/ vt repudiar; negar; renegar de
**disparage** /dɪ'spærɪdʒ/ vt menospreciar; desacreditar; denigrar; (spoil) perjudicar; (scorn) despreciar
**disparagement** /dɪ'spærɪdʒmənt/ n menosprecio, m; denigración, f; desprecio, m
**disparagingly** /dɪ'spærɪdʒɪŋli/ adv con desprecio
**disparity** /dɪ'spærɪti/ n disparidad, f
**dispassionate** /dɪs'pæfənɪt/ a desapasionado, sereno; imparcial; moderado
**dispassionately** /dɪs'pæfənɪtli/ adv con imparcialidad; serenamente; con moderación
**dispatch** /dɪ'spætʃ/ n despacho, m; Com. envío, m; (message) mensaje, m; (communiqué) parte, f; (cable) telegrama, m; (promptness) prontitud, presteza, f; (execution) ejecución, muerte, f. —vt despachar; enviar, remitir; (Fam. kill) despachar. **d.-case,** cartera, f. **d.-rider,** mensajero motociclista, m
**dispel** /dɪ'spɛl/ vt disipar
**dispensable** /dɪ'spɛnsəbəl/ a dispensable
**dispensary** /dɪ'spɛnsəri/ n dispensario, m
**dispensation** /,dɪspən'seifən/ n dispensación, f; (of the Pope, etc.) dispensa, f; (decree) ley, f, decreto, m; (of justice) administración, f
**dispense** /dɪ'spɛns/ vt vi dispensar; (of justice) administrar. **to d. with,** pasar sin, prescindir de
**dispenser** /dɪ'spɛnsər/ n dispensador (-ra); administrador (-ra)
**dispersal** /dɪ'spɜrsəl/ n dispersión, f; disipación, f; esparcimiento, m
**disperse** /dɪ'spɜrs/ vt dispersar; disipar; esparcir. —vi dispersarse disiparse

**dispirited** /dɪ'spɪrɪtɪd/ a abatido, desanimado, deprimido; lánguido
**dispiritedly** /dɪ'spɪrɪtɪdli/ adv desanimadamente, con desaliento; lánguidamente
**displace** /dɪs'pleis/ vt desalojar; cambiar de situación; (of liquids) desplazar; (oust) quitar el puesto (a), destituir
**displacement** /dɪs'pleismənt/ n desalojamiento, m; cambio de situación, m; (of liquid) desplazamiento, m; (from a post) destitución, f
**display** /dɪ'splei/ n exhibición, f; ostentación, f; presentación, f; (development) desarrollo, m; manifestación, f; (naval or military) maniobras, f pl; espectáculo, m; (pomp) pompa, f; fausto, m. —vt exhibir; mostrar, manifestar; ostentar; (unfold) desplegar, extender; (develop) desarrollar. **d. cabinet,** vitrina, f
**displease** /dɪs'pliz/ vt desagradar; ofender; enojar
**displeasing** /dɪs'plizɪŋ/ a desagradable
**displeasure** /dɪs'plɛʒər/ n desagrado, m; disgusto, m; disfavor, m; indignación, f; enojo, m; (grief) angustia, f
**disport** /dɪ'spɔrt/ vi (**oneself**), divertirse, entretenerse, recrearse; retozar, jugar
**disposal** /dɪ'spouzəl/ n disposición, f; (transfer) cesión, enajenación, f; (sale) venta, f; (gift) donación, f. **I am at your d.,** Estoy a la disposición de Vd. **the d. of the troops,** la disposición de las tropas
**dispose** /dɪ'spouz/ vt disponer; inclinar. —vi disponer. **to d. of,** disponer de; (finish) terminar, concluir; (get rid of) deshacerse de; (give away) regalar; (sell) vender; (transfer) ceder; (of houses, etc.) traspasar; (kill) matar; (send) enviar; (use) servirse de; (refute) refutar. **"To be disposed of,"** (a business, etc.) «Se traspasa»
**disposed** /dɪ'spouzd/ a (in compounds) intencionado, dispuesto. **well-d.,** bien intencionado
**disposition** /,dɪspə'zɪfən/ n disposición, f; (temperament) naturaleza, índole, f, temperamento, carácter, m; (humor) humor, m
**dispossess** /,dɪspə'zɛs/ vt desposeer (de); privar (de); desahuciar
**dispossession** /,dɪspə'zɛfən/ n desposeimiento, m; desahúcio, m
**disproportion** /,dɪsprə'pɔrfən/ n desproporción, f
**disproportionate** /,dɪsprə'pɔrfənɪt/ a desproporcionado
**disproportionately** /,dɪsprə'pɔrfənɪtli/ adv desproporcionadamente
**disprovable** /dɪs'pruvəbəl/ a refutable
**disprove** /dɪs'pruv/ vt refutar
**disputable** /dɪ'spyutəbəl/ a disputable; discutible
**disputant** /dɪ'spyutənt/ n disputador (-ra)
**dispute** /dɪ'spyut/ n disputa, controversia, f; altercación, f; discusión, f; debate, m. —vt and vi disputar. **beyond d.,** a incontestable —adv incontestablemente; fuera de duda
**disqualification** /dɪs,kwɒləfɪ'keifən/ n incapacidad, f; inhabilitación, f; impedimento, m; Sports. descalificación, f
**disqualify** /dɪs'kwɒlə,fai/ vt incapacitar; inhabilitar; Sports. descalificar
**disquiet** /dɪs'kwaiɪt/ n desasosiego, m; intranquilidad, inquietud, agitación, f. —vt desasosegar, intranquilizar, perturbar, agitar
**disquieting** /dɪs'kwaiɪtɪŋ/ a intranquilizador, perturbador
**disquisition** /,dɪskwə'zɪfən/ n disquisición, f
**disregard** /,dɪsrɪ'gɑrd/ n indiferencia, f; omisión, f; descuido, m; (scorn) desdén, m. —vt no hacer caso de, desatender; omitir; desconocer; descuidar; despreciar
**disregardful** /,dɪsrɪ'gɑrdfəl/ a indiferente; negligente; desatento; desdeñoso
**disrepair** /,dɪsrɪ'pɛər/ n deterioro, mal estado, m
**disreputable** /dɪs'rɛpyətəbəl/ a de mala fama; (shameful) vergonzoso, vil; (compromising) comprometedor; de mal aspecto, horrible; ruin
**disreputably** /dɪs'rɛpyətəbli/ adv ruinmente; vergonzosamente
**disrepute** /,dɪsrɪ'pyut/ n disfavor, m; mala fama, f; deshonra, f; descrédito, m. **to come into d.,** caer en disfavor; perder su reputación

**disrespect** /ˌdɪsrɪ'spɛkt/ n falta de respeto, f; irreverencia, f

**disrespectful** /ˌdɪsrɪ'spɛktfəl/ a irrespetuoso, irreverente

**disrobe** /dɪs'roub/ vt desnudar. —vi desnudarse

**disrupt** /dɪs'rʌpt/ vt quebrar; desorganizar; interrumpir; separar

**disruption** /dɪs'rʌpʃən/ n quebrantamiento, m; desorganización, f; interrupción, f; separación, f

**dissatisfaction** /ˌdɪssætɪs'fækʃən/ n descontento, desagrado, disgusto, m

**dissatisfied** /dɪs'sætɪsˌfaid/ a descontentado, malcontento, no satisfecho

**dissect** /dɪ'sɛkt/ vt disecar; Fig. analizar

**dissecting table** n mesa de disección, f

**dissection** /dɪ'sɛkʃən/ n disección, f; análisis, m

**dissector** /dɪ'sɛktər/ n disector, m; Fig. analizador (-ra)

**dissemble** /dɪ'sɛmbəl/ vt and vi disimular, fingir

**dissembler** /dɪ'sɛmblər/ n hipócrita, mf; disimulador (-ra)

**disseminate** /dɪ'sɛməˌneit/ vt diseminar; propagar, sembrar

**dissemination** /dɪˌsɛmə'neiʃən/ n diseminación, f; propagación, f

**dissension** /dɪ'sɛnʃən/ n disensión, f; disidencia, f

**dissent** /dɪ'sɛnt/ n disentimiento, m, vi disentir, disidir

**dissenter** /dɪ'sɛntər/ n disidente, mf

**dissentient** /dɪ'sɛnʃənt/ a disidente, divergente. **without one d. voice,** unánimemente

**dissertation** /ˌdɪsər'teiʃən/ n disertación, f

**disservice** /dɪs'sɜrvɪs/ n deservicio, m

**dissimilar** /dɪ'sɪmələr/ a disímil, desemejante, diferente

**dissimilarity** /dɪˌsɪmə'lærɪti/ n desemejanza, diferencia, disparidad, f

**dissimulation** /dɪˌsɪmyə'leiʃən/ n disimulación, f, disimulo, m

**dissipate** /'dɪsəˌpeit/ vt disipar; dispersar; (waste) derrochar, desperdiciar. —vi disiparse; dispersarse; (vanish) desvanecerse; (of persons) ser disoluto

**dissipated** /'dɪsəˌpeitɪd/ a (of persons) disipado, disoluto, vicioso

**dissipation** /ˌdɪsə'peiʃən/ n disipación, f; (waste) derroche, m; libertinaje, m

**dissociate** /dɪ'souʃiˌeit/ vt disociar

**dissociation** /dɪˌsousi'eiʃən/ n disociación, f

**dissoluble** /dɪ'sɒlyəbəl/ a disoluble

**dissolute** /'dɪsəˌlut/ a disoluto, vicioso, licencioso

**dissoluteness** /'dɪsəˌlutnɪs/ n disolución, inmoralidad, f

**dissolution** /ˌdɪsə'luʃən/ n disolución, f; separación, f; muerte, f

**dissolvable** /dɪ'zɒlvəbəl/ a soluble

**dissolve** /dɪ'zɒlv/ vt disolver; derretir; (of parliament) prorrogar; (a marriage, etc.) anular; Fig. disipar. —vi disolverse; derretirse; (vanish) desvanecerse, disiparse, evaporarse. **to d. into tears,** deshacerse en lágrimas

**dissolvent** /dɪ'zɒlvənt/ a disolutivo. —n disolvente, m

**dissonance** /'dɪsənəns/ n disonancia, f; Fig. discordia, falta de armonía, f

**dissonant** /'dɪsənənt/ n disonancia, f, a disonante

**dissuade** /dɪ'sweid/ vt disuadir (de), apartar (de)

**dissuasion** /dɪ'sweiʒən/ n disuasión, f

**distaff** /'dɪstæf/ n rueca, f

**distance** /'dɪstəns/ n distancia, f; lontananza, f; lejanía, f; trecho, m; (of time) intervalo, m; (difference) diferencia, f. **at a d.,** a alguna distancia; lejos; (from afar) desde lejos. **from a d.,** desde (or de) lejos. **in the d.,** a lo lejos, en lontananza. **to keep at a d.,** mantener lejos; guardar las distancias (con). **to keep one's d.,** mantenerse a distancia; no intimarse, guardar las distancias. **What is the d. from London to Madrid?** ¿Qué distancia hay desde Londres a Madrid?

**distant** /'dɪstənt/ a distante; lejano; remoto; (of manner) frío, reservado; (slight) ligero; (of references, etc.) indirecto. **He is a d. relation,** Es un pariente le-

jano. **They are always rather d. with her,** La tratan siempre con bastante frialdad

**distantly** /'dɪstəntli/ adv a distancia; a lo lejos; desde lejos; remotamente; (of manner) con frialdad; (slightly) ligeramente

**distaste** /dɪs'teist/ n aversión, repugnancia, f; disgusto, hastío, m

**distasteful** /dɪs'teistfəl/ a desagradable

**distemper** /dɪs'tɛmpər/ n enfermedad, f; (in animals) moquillo, m; Fig. mal, m; (for walls) pintura al temple, f. —vt desordenar, perturbar; (walls) pintar al temple

**distend** /dɪ'stɛnd/ vt ensanchar; dilatar; inflar, henchir; Med. distender. —vi ensancharse, etc.

**distension** /dɪs'tɛnʃən/ n dilatación, f; inflación, f; henchimiento, m; Med. distensión, f

**distill** /dɪ'stɪl/ vt destilar; extraer. —vi destilar; exudar

**distillation** /ˌdɪstl'eiʃən/ n destilación, f; extracción, f; exudación, f

**distiller** /dɪ'stɪlər/ n destilador (-ra)

**distillery** /dɪ'stɪləri/ n destilería, f, destilatorio, m

**distinct** /dɪ'stɪŋkt/ a distinto; diferente; claro; notable, evidente

**distinction** /dɪ'stɪŋkʃən/ n distinción, f

**distinctive** /dɪ'stɪŋktɪv/ a distintivo; característico

**distinctive feature** n Ling. rasgo pertinente, m

**distinctly** /dɪ'stɪŋktli/ adv claramente; distintamente

**distinctness** /dɪ'stɪŋktnɪs/ n claridad, f; distinción, f; carácter distintivo, m

**distinguish** /dɪ'stɪŋgwɪʃ/ vt distinguir; discernir; caracterizar; (honor) honrar. —vi distinguir, diferenciar

**distinguishable** /dɪ'stɪŋgwɪʃəbəl/ a distinguible; perceptible, discernible

**distinguished** /dɪ'stɪŋgwɪʃt/ a distinguido; eminente; famoso, ilustre, egregio

**distinguishing** /dɪ'stɪŋgwɪʃɪŋ/ a distintivo

**distort** /dɪ'stɔrt/ vt (twist) torcer; deformar; falsear; pervertir

**distorting mirror** n (at fairs) espejo de la risa, m; espejo deformador, m

**distortion** /dɪ'stɔrʃən/ n deformación, f; torcimiento, m; contorsión, f; perversión, f; Radio. deformación, f

**distract** /dɪ'strækt/ vt distraer; interrumpir; perturbar; (turn aside) desviar, apartar; (madden) enloquecer, volver loco (a)

**distracted** /dɪ'stræktɪd/ a aturdido; demente, loco

**distractedly** /dɪ'stræktɪdli/ adv locamente; perdidamente

**distraction** /dɪ'strækʃən/ n distracción, f; (amusement) diversion, f, pasatiempo, m; (bewilderment) confusión, f, aturdimiento, m; (madness) locura, f; frenesí, m. **to drive to d.,** trastornar, sacar de quicio.

**distrain** /dɪ'strein/ vi embargar

**distraint** /dɪ'streint/ n embargo, m

**distraught** /dɪ'strɔt/ a aturdido; desesperado; enloquecido

**distress** /dɪ'strɛs/ n dolor, m, aflicción, f; pena, f; miseria, penuria, f; (exhaustion) fatiga, f, cansancio, m; (pain) dolor, m; (misfortune) desdicha, f; apuro, m; (danger) peligro, m; Law. embargo, m. —vt afligir, dar pena (a), llenar de angustia; cansar, fatigar; (pain) doler

**distressed** /dɪ'strɛst/ a afligido; necesitado, pobre

**distressing** /dɪ'strɛsɪŋ/ a congojoso, doloroso, penoso

**distributable** /dɪ'strɪbyutəbəl/ a repartible

**distribute** /dɪ'strɪbyut/ vt (of justice, etc.) administrar; distribuir; repartir

**distribution** /ˌdɪstrə'byuʃən/ n (of justice) administración, f; distribución, f; reparto, m

**distributive** /dɪ'strɪbyətɪv/ a distributivo

**distributor** /dɪ'strɪbyətər/ n distribuidor (-ra); repartidor (-ra). **d. of false money,** expendedor (-ra) de moneda falsa

**district** /'dɪstrɪkt/ n distrito, m; comarca, f; (of a town) barrio, m; (judicial) partido judicial, m; jurisdicción, f; región, zona, f

**distrust** /dɪs'trʌst/ n desconfianza, f; recelo, m, sospecha, f. —vt desconfiar de, sospechar

**distrustful** /dɪs'trʌstfəl/ a desconfiado, receloso, suspicaz

**distrustfully** /dɪs'trʌstfəli/ *adv* desconfiadamente, con recelo

**disturb** /dɪ'stɜrb/ *vt* perturbar; interrumpir; incomodar; (make anxious) inquietar; (alter) cambiar; (disarrange) desordenar, desarreglar. **to d. the peace,** perturbar el orden público

**disturbance** /dɪ'stɜrbəns/ *n* perturbación, *f;* disturbio, *m,* conmoción, *f;* incomodidad, *f;* agitación, *f;* confusión, *f;* tumulto, *m;* desorden, *m; Radio.* parásitos, *m pl*

**disturber** /dɪ'stɜrbər/ *n* perturbador (-ra)

**disturbing** /dɪ'stɜrbɪŋ/ *a* perturbador; inquietador; conmovedor, impresionante, emocionante

**disunion** /dɪs'yunyən/ *n* desunión, *f;* discordia, *f*

**disunite** /ˌdɪsyu'nait/ *vt* desunir; separar, dividir. —*vi* separarse

**disuse** /*n* dɪs'yus; *v* -'yuz/ *n* desuso, *m.* —*vt* desusar; desacostumbrar. **to fall into d.,** caer en desuso

**ditch** /dɪtʃ/ *n* zanja, *f;* (for defense, etc.) foso, *m;* (irrigation) acequia, *f.* —*vt* zanjar; abarrancar. **to die in the last d.,** morir en la brecha

**ditto** /'dɪtou/ *adv* ídem; también

**ditty** /'dɪti/ *n* canción, cantinela, *f*

**diuretic** /ˌdaiə'rɛtɪk/ *a* diurético

**divan** /dɪ'væn/ *n* diván, *m*

**dive** /daiv/ *n* buceo, *m;* (bird) picada, *f, vi* bucear; sumergirse (en); *Aer.* volar en picado; penetrar (en); (into a book) enfrascarse en. **to d. out,** salir precipitadamente. **to d.-bomb,** bombardear en picado. **d.-bomber,** avión en picado, *m.* **d.-bombing,** bombardeo en picado, *m*

**diver** /'daivər/ *n* buceador, *m;* buzo, *m;* (bird) somorgujo, *m*

**diverge** /dɪ'vɜrdʒ/ *vi* divergir

**divergence** /dɪ'vɜrdʒəns/ *n* divergencia, *f*

**divergent** /dɪ'vɜrdʒənt/ *a* divergente

**diverse** /dɪ'vɜrs/ *a* diverso, vario

**diversify** /dɪ'vɜrsəˌfai/ *vt* diversificar

**diversion** /dɪ'vɜrʒən/ *n* diversión, *f;* entretenimiento, *m,* recreación, *f;* pasatiempo, *m;* placer, *m; Mil.* diversión, *f*

**diversity** /dɪ'vɜrsiti/ *n* diversidad, variedad, *f*

**divert** /dɪ'vɜrt/ *vt* desviar; (amuse) divertir, entretener

**diverting** /dɪ'vɜrtɪŋ/ *a* divertido, entretenido

**divide** /dɪ'vaid/ *vt* dividir; partir; separar; (cut) cortar; (share) repartir, distribuir; (hair) hacer la raya (del pelo); (of voting) provocar una votación. —*vi* dividirse; separarse; (of roads, etc.) bifurcarse; (of voting) votar. **divided skirt,** *n* falda pantalón, *f*

**dividend** /'dɪvɪˌdɛnd/ *n* dividendo, *m.* **d. warrant,** cupón de dividendo, *m*

**dividers** /dɪ'vaidərz/ *n pl* compás de puntas, *m*

**dividing** /dɪ'vaidɪŋ/ *a* divisorio, divisor

**divination** /ˌdɪvə'neiʃən/ *n* adivinación, *f*

**divine** /dɪ'vain/ *a* divino; sublime; *Inf.* estupendo. —*n* teólogo, *m.* —*vt* (foretell) vaticinar, pronosticar; presentir; (guess) adivinar

**diving** /'daivɪŋ/ *n* buceo, *m; Aer.* picado, *m.* **d.-bell,** campana de bucear, *f.* **d.-board,** (low) trampolín, *m;* (high) palanca, *f.* **d.-suit,** escafandra, *f*

**divining rod** /dɪ'vainɪŋ/ *n* vara divinatoria, *f*

**divinity** /dɪ'vɪnɪti/ *n* divinidad, *f;* teología, *f*

**divisibility** /dɪˌvɪzə'bɪlɪti/ *n* divisibilidad, *f*

**divisible** /dɪ'vɪzəbəl/ *a* divisible

**division** /dɪ'vɪʒən/ *n* división, *f;* separación, *f;* (distribution) repartimiento, *m;* (*Mil. Math.*) división, *f;* sección, *f;* grupo, *m;* (voting) votación, *f;* (discord) discordia, desunión, *f.* **without a d.,** por unanimidad, sin votar

**divisor** /dɪ'vaizər/ *n Math.* divisor, *m*

**divorce** /dɪ'vɔrs/ *n* divorcio, *m.* —*vt* divorciarse de; *Fig.* divorciar, separar. **to file a petition of d.,** poner una petición de divorcio

**divorcee** /dɪvɔr'sei/ *n* (wife) divorciada, *f;* (husband) divorciado, *m*

**divulge** /dɪ'vʌldʒ/ *vt* divulgar, revelar

**dizzily** /'dɪzəli/ *adv* vertiginosamente

**dizziness** /'dɪzɪnɪs/ *n* vértigo, *m;* mareo, *m;* (bewilderment) aturdimiento, *m,* confusión, *f*

**dizzy** /'dɪzi/ *a* vertiginoso; mareado; confuso, perplejo, aturdido

**do** /du/ *vt* hacer; ejecutar; (one's duty, etc.) cumplir con; concluir; (cause) causar; (homage) rendir; (commit) cometer; (arrange) arreglar; (cook) cocer, guisar; (roast) asar; (*Fam.* cheat) engañar; (suit) convenir; (suffice) bastar; (act) hacer el papel (de); (*Fam.* treat) tratar (bien o mal); (learn) aprender; (exhaust) agotar; (walk) andar; (travel, journey) recorrer; (translate) traducir; (prepare) preparar. —*vi* hacer; (behave) conducirse; (of health) estar (bien o mal); (act) obrar; (get on) ir; (be suitable, suit) convenir; (suffice) bastar; (of plants) florecer; (cook) cocerse; (last) durar. **Don't!** ¡No lo hagas! ¡Quieto! ¡Calla! **How do you do?** ¿Cómo está Vd.? ¡Buenos días! **Have done!** ¡Acaba de una vez! **It will do you good,** Te conviene; Te hará bien; Te sentará bien. **It will do you no harm,** No te perjudicará; No te hará daño. **I could do with one,** Me gustaría (tener) uno; (of drinks) Me bebería uno con mucho gusto. **That will do,** Eso basta; Se puede servirse de eso; Está bien así; (leave it alone) ¡Déjate de eso! (be quiet!) ¡No digas más! ¡Cállate! **That won't do,** Eso no es bastante; Eso no sirve; Eso no se hace así; Eso no se hace. **That will never do,** Eso no servirá; Eso no puede ser. **This will do,** (when buying an article) Me quedaré con éste; Me serviré de esto; Esto basta; Esto será suficiente; (is all right) Está bien así. **Thy will be done!** ¡Hágase tu voluntad! **to be doing,** estar haciendo; estar ocupado en (or con) hacer; (of food) estar cocinando. **to be done for,** estar perdido; estar muerto. **to do better,** hacer mejor (que); (mend one's ways) enmendarse, corregirse; (improve) mejorar, hacer progresos; (in health) encontrarse mejor. **to do nothing,** no hacer nada. **to do reverence,** rendir homenaje; inclinarse. **to do to death,** matar; asesinar; ejecutar. **to do violence to,** *Fig.* hacer fuerza a. **to do well,** hacer bien; obrar bien; (be successful) tener éxito; hacer buena impresión; (prosperous) tener una buena posición. **to do wonders,** hacer maravillas. **to have done with,** renunciar (a); dejar de usar; dejar de hacer, cesar; concluir, terminar; no tener más que ver con; (forsake) abandonar; (a person) romper con. **to have nothing to do,** no tener nada que hacer. **to have nothing to do with,** no tener nada que ver con; (of people) no tratar; (end a friendship) romper su amistad con, dejar de ver. **well done,** bien hecho; (of food) bien guisado; (of meat) bien asado. **What is to be done?** ¿Qué hay que hacer? ¿Qué se puede hacer? **What is to do?** ¿Qué pasa? ¿Qué hay? **When he had done speaking,** Cuando hubo terminado de hablar. **to do again,** hacer de nuevo, volver a hacer, rehacer; repetir. **He will not do it again,** No lo hará más. **to do away with,** quitar; eliminar; suprimir; hacer desaparecer; poner fin a; hacer cesar; destruir; matar. **to do by,** tratar (a), portarse con. **to do for,** arruinar; matar; (suffice) bastar para; ser a propósito para, servir para; (look after) cuidar; (as a housekeeper) dirigir la casa para. **to do out,** (a room) limpiar. **to do out of,** quitar; privar de; (steal) robar. **to do up,** (tie) atar; (fold) enrollar, plegar; envolver; (parcel) empaquetar; (arrange) arreglar; decorar; poner en orden; poner como nuevo; (iron) planchar; (launder) lavar y planchar; (tire) fatigar. **to do with,** (of people) tratar; (of things) tener que ver con; (put up with) poder con; poder sufrir. **to do without,** prescindir de; pasarse sin

**do** /du/ as an auxiliary verb is not translated in Spanish, e.g. *I do believe,* creo. *Do not do that,* no hagas eso. *I did not know,* no sabía. When it is used for emphasis, *do* is translated by *sí, ciertamente, claro* and similar words, e.g.: *She did not know, but he did,* Ella no lo sabía pero él sí. *You do paint well,* Pintas muy bien por cierto. *Do come this time,* No dejes de venir esta vez.

**docile** /'dɒsəl/ *a* dócil

**docility** /dɒ'sɪlɪti/ *n* docilidad, *f*

**dock** /dɒk/ *n* dique, *m,* dársena, *f;* (wharf) muelle, *m;* (in a law court) banquillo de los acusados, *m; Bot.* romaza, *f.* —*vt* (a tail) descolar; cortar, cercenar; reducir; (money) descontar; (a ship) poner en dique. —*vi* entrar en dársena, entrar en dique, entrar en muelle. **dry-d.,** dique seco, *m.* **floating-d.,** dique flotante, *m.* **d.-dues,** muellaje, *m.* **d.** **rat,** (thief) raquero, *m*

**docker** /'dɒkər/ *n* estibador, descargador del muelle, *m*

**docket** /'dɒkɪt/ *n* (bundle) legajo, *m;* extracto, *m;* minuta, *f;* (label) etiqueta, *f,* marbete, *m*

**dockyard** /'dɒk,yɑrd/ *n* arsenal, astillero, *m*

**doctor** /'dɒktər/ *n* doctor (-ra); (medical practitioner) médico (-ca), asistir; (repair) reparar, componer; adulterar; mezclar drogas con; falsificar. —*vi* ejercer la medicina. **family d.,** médico de cabecera, *m.* **to graduate as a d.,** doctorarse. **d. of divinity, laws, medicine,** doctor (-ra) en teología, en derecho, en medicina, *m*

**doctoral** /'dɒktərəl/ *a* doctoral

**doctorate** /'dɒktərɪt/ *n* doctorado, *m*

**doctrinaire** /'dɒktrə'nɛər/ *a* and *n* doctrinario (-ia)

**doctrinal** /'dɒktrənl/ *a* doctrinal

**doctrine** /'dɒktrɪn/ *n* doctrina, *f*

**document** /*n* 'dɒkyəmənt; *v* -,ment/ *n* documento, *m.* —*vt* documentar; probar con documentos. **d.-case,** carpeta, *f*

**documentary** /,dɒkyə'mentəri/ *a* documental; escrito, auténtico. **d. film,** película documental, *f*

**documentation** /,dɒkyəmen'teifən/ *n* documentación, *f*

**Dodecanese, the** /,dɒdɪkə'niz/ el Dodecaneso, *m*

**dodge** /dɒdʒ/ *n* esguince, regate, *m;* evasiva, *f;* (trick) estratagema, *m,* maniobra, *f;* artefacto, *m.* —*vt* esquivar, evadir

**doe** /dou/ *n* gama, *f.* **doe rabbit,** coneja, *f*

**doer** /'duər/ *n* hacedor (-ra); autor (-ra)

**doeskin** /'dou,skɪn/ *n* ante, *m,* piel de gama, *f*

**doff** /dɒf/ *vt* quitar; (of hats, etc.) quitarse; desnudarse de

**dog** /dɔg/ *n* perro, *m;* (male) macho, *m;* (andiron) morillo, *m; Astron.* Can Mayor (or Menor), Sirio, *m.* —*vt* perseguir; seguir los pasos de; espiar. **You can't deceive an old dog,** A perro viejo no hay tus tus. **to go to the dogs,** ir a las carreras de galgos; *Fig.* ir cuesta abajo. **mongrel dog,** perro mestizo, *m.* **thoroughbred dog,** perro de raza pura, *m.* **dog-collar,** collar de perro, *m; Eccl.* alzacuello, *m.* **dog-days,** días caniculares, *m pl,* canícula, *f.* **dog-eared** (of books) con las puntas de las hojas dobladas. **dog-fight,** lucha de perros, *f;* combate aéreo, *m.* **dog-fish,** lija, *f,* cazón, *m.* **dog in the manger,** el perro del hortelano. **dog-kennel,** perrera, *f.* **dog-latin,** bajo latín, *m.* **dog license,** matrícula de perros, *f.* **dog-racing,** carrera de galgos, *f.* **dog-rose,** escaramujo, *m.* **dog show,** exposición canina, *f.* **dog-tooth,** *Archit.* diente de perro, *m.* **dog-vane,** *Naut.* cataviento, *m*

**doge** /doudʒ/ *n* dux, *m*

**dogged** /'dɔgɪd/ *a* persistente, tenaz, pertinaz, obstinado

**doggedly** /'dɔgɪdli/ *adv* tenazmente

**doggedness** /'dɔgɪdnɪs/ *n* pertinacia, tenacidad, terquedad, persistencia, *f*

**doggerel** /'dɔgərəl/ *n* malos versos, *m pl;* aleluyas, coplas de ciego, *f pl, a* malo, irregular

**dogma** /'dɔgmə/ *n* dogma, *m*

**dogmatic** /dɔg'mætɪk/ *a* dogmático

**dogmatize** /'dɔgmə,taiz/ *vt* and *vi* dogmatizar; mostrarse dogmático

**doh** /dou/ *n Mus.* do, *m*

**doily** /'dɔili/ *n* carpeta, *f,* pañito de adorno, *m*

**doings** /'duɪŋz/ *n pl* acciones, *f pl;* (deeds) hechos, *m pl;* (behavior) conducta, *f;* (happenings) acontecimientos, *m pl;* (works) obras, *f pl;* (things) cosas, *f pl*

**doldrums** /'douldrəmz/ *n pl* calmas ecuatoriales, *f pl*

**dole** /doul/ *n* limosna, *f;* porción, *f.* **to d. out,** repartir; distribuir en porciones pequeñas; racionar; dar contra la voluntad de uno.

**doleful** /'doulfəl/ *a* triste, lúgubre, melancólico; doloroso

**dolefulness** /'doulfəlnɪs/ *n* tristeza, melancolía, *f;* dolor, *m*

**doll** /dɒl/ *n* muñeca, *f*

**dollar** /'dɒlər/ *n* dólar, *m*

**dolly** /'dɒli/ *n* muñeca, *f;* (for clothes) moza, *f.* **d.-tub,** cubo para la colada, *m*

**dolman** /'doulmən/ *n* dormán, *m*

**dolphin** /'dɒlfɪn/ *n* delfín, *m*

**dolt** /doult/ *n* cabeza de alcornoque, *mf,* zamacuco, *m*

**domain** /dou'mein/ *n* territorio, *m;* heredad, posesión, propiedad, *f;* (empire) dominio, *m*

**dome** /doum/ *n* cúpula, *f;* bóveda, *f;* (palace) palacio, *m*

**domestic** /də'mestɪk/ *a* doméstico; familiar; (homeloving) casero; (of animals) doméstico; (national) interior, nacional. —*n* doméstico, sirviente, *m;* criada, *f.* **d. economy,** economía doméstica, *f*

**domesticate** /də'mestɪ,keit/ *vt* domesticar

**domesticated** /də'mestɪ,keitɪd/ *a* (of animals) domesticado; (of persons) casero

**domestication** /də,mestɪ'keifən/ *n* domesticación, *f*

**domesticity** /,doume'stɪsɪti/ *n* domesticidad, *f*

**domicile** /'dɒmə,sail/ *n* domicilio, *m,* vt domiciliar

**domiciliary** /,dɒmə'sɪli,ɛri/ *a* domiciliario

**dominant** /'dɒmənənt/ *a* dominante; imperante. —*n Mus.* dominante, *f.* **to be d.,** prevalecer

**dominate** /'dɒmə,neit/ *vt* and *vi* dominar

**domination** /,dɒmə'neifən/ *n* dominación, *f*

**domineer** /,dɒmə'nɪər/ *vi* dominar, tiranizar. **to d. over,** mandar en

**domineering** /,dɒmə'nɪərɪŋ/ *a* dominante, mandón, tiránico

**Dominican** /də'mɪnɪkən/ *a* dominicano. —*n* dominicano, *m*

**Dominican Republic, the** la República Dominicana, *f*

**dominion** /də'mɪnyən/ *n* dominio, *m;* autoridad, soberanía, *f;* imperio, *m; pl* **dominions,** *Eccl.* dominaciones, *f pl*

**Dominions, the** /də'mɪnyənz/ los Dominios, *m*

**domino** /'dɒmə,nou/ *n* dominó, *m.* **to go d.,** nacer domino

**don** /dɒn/ *n* (Spanish and Italian title) don, *m;* señor, *m.* —*vt* ponerse, vestirse

**donation** /dou'neifən/ *n* donación, dádiva, *f;* contribución, *f*

**done** /dʌn/ *a* and *past part* hecho; (of food) cocido; (roasted) asado; (tired) rendido; (*Fam.* deceived) engañado. **Well d.!** ¡Bien hecho! **d. for,** arruinado; muerto; perdido; vencido; (spoilt) estropeado

**donkey** /'dɒŋki/ *n* borrico (-ca), burro (-rra). **d.-engine,** máquina auxiliar, *f*

**donor** /'dounər/ *n* donador (-ra); dador (-ra)

**doodle** /'dudl/ *v* borrajear, garabatear, hacer garabatos

**doom** /dum/ *n* condena, *f;* (fate) suerte, *f;* (judgment) destino, *m;* ruina, *f;* juicio, *m.* —*vt* sentenciar; condenar

**doomsday** /'dumz,dei/ *n* día del juicio final, *m*

**door** /dɔr/ *n* puerta, *f;* entrada, *f.* **front d.,** puerta de entrada, *f.* **next d.,** la casa vecina; la puerta de al lado, la puerta vecina. **next d. neighbor,** vecino (-na) de al lado. **out of doors,** al aire libre; en la calle. **to knock at the d.,** llamar a la puerta. **to slam the d. in a person's face,** dar con la puerta en las narices de alguien. **d.-bell,** timbre (non-electric, campanilla, *f*) de llamada, *m.* **d.-jamb,** quicial, *m.* **d. keeper,** portero, *m.* **d.-knob,** tirador, *m.* **d.-knocker,** manija, *f;* picaporte, *m,* aldaba, *f.* **d.-plate,** placa, *f.* **d.-shutter,** cierre metálico, *m.* **d.-step,** peldaño de la puerta, *m;* umbral, *m.* **d.-way,** portal, *m*

**dope** /doup/ *n* drogas, *f pl,* narcóticos, *m pl;* (news) información, *f.* **d. fiend,** morfinómano (-na)

**dope-pusher** /'doup ,pufər/ *n* narcotraficante, *mf*

**Doric** /'dɔrɪk/ *a* dórico

**dormant** /'dɔrmənt/ *a* durmiente; latente; secreto; inactivo. **to go d.,** dormirse

**dormer window** /'dɔrmər/ *n* lumbrera, *f*

**dormitory** /'dɔrmɪ,tɔri/ *n* dormitorio, *m*

**dormouse** /'dɔr,maus/ *n* lirón, *m*

**dorsal** /'dɔrsəl/ *a* dorsal

**dorsum** /'dɔrsəm/ *n* dorso, *m*

**dory** /'dɔri/ *n* (fish) dorado, *m*

**dose, dosage** /dous; 'dousɪdʒ/ *n;* dosis, *f*

**dossier** /'dɒsi,ei/ *n* documentación, *f*

**dot** /dɒt/ *n* punto, *m; Mus.* puntillo, *m; pl* **dots,** *Gram.* puntos suspensivos, *m pl.* —*vt* poner punto (a

una letra); (scatter) salpicar. **on the dot,** (of time) en punto. **to dot one's i's,** poner los puntos sobre las íes
**dotage** /'doutɪdʒ/ *n* senectud, chochera, *f*
**dotard** /'doutərd/ *n* viejo chocho, *m;* vieja chocha, *f; Inf.* carcamal, *m*
**dote** /dout/ *vi* chochear. **to d. on,** adorar en, idolatrar
**doting** /'doutɪŋ/ *a* chocho
**double** /'dʌbəl/ *a* and *adv* doble; dos veces; (in a pair) en par; en dos; doblemente; (deceitful) doble, de dos caras, falso; ambiguo. —*n* doble, *m;* duplicado, *m; Theat.* contrafigura, *f; pl* **doubles,** (tennis) dobles, *m pl,* juego doble, *m.* —*vt* doblar; duplicar; (fold) doblegar; (the fist) cerrar (el puño); (*Theat.* and *Naut.*) doblar. —*vi* doblarse; (dodge) volverse atrás, hacer un rodeo, dar una vuelta; esquivarse. **to d. up,** *vt* envolver; arrollar; (a person) doblar. —*vi* doblegarse; arrollarse; (collapse) desplomarse. **at the d.,** corriendo. **He was doubled up with pain,** El dolor le hacía retorcerse. **mixed doubles,** parejas mixtas, *f pl;* dobles mixtos, *m pl.* **double two,** (telephone) dos dos. **with a d. meaning,** con segunda intención. **d.-barrelled,** de dos cañones. **d.-bass,** contrabajo, *m.* **d. bed,** cama de matrimonio, *f.* **d.-bedded,** con cama de matrimonio; con dos camas. **d.-breasted,** cruzado. **d.-chin,** papada, *f.* **d.-dealing,** duplicidad, *f.* **d.-edged,** de doble filo. **d.-entry,** *Com.* partida doble, *f.* **d.-faced,** de dos caras. **d.-jointed,** con articulaciones dobles
**double-spaced** /'dʌbəl 'speist/ *a* a doble espacio, a dos espacios
**doublet** /'dʌblɪt/ *n* (garment) jubón, justillo, *m;* pareja, *f,* par, *m*
**doubling** /'dʌblɪŋ/ *n* doblamiento, *m;* doblez, plegadura, *f;* duplicación, *f;* (dodging) evasiva, *f,* esguince, *m*
**doubloon** /dʌ'blun/ *n* doblón, *m*
**doubly** /'dʌbli/ *adv* doblemente; con duplicidad
**doubt** /daut/ *n* duda, *f;* incertidumbre, *f;* sospecha, *f.* —*vt* and *vi* dudar; sospechar; titubear, hesitar; temer. **beyond all d.,** fuera de duda. **no d.,** sin duda. **There is no d. that,** No hay duda de que, No cabe duda de que. **When in d....,** En caso de duda...
**doubter** /'dautər/ *n* incrédulo (-la)
**doubtful** /'dautfəl/ *a* dudoso; incierto; perplejo; ambiguo; (of places) sospechoso
**doubtfully** /'dautfəli/ *adv* dudosamente; inciertamente; irresolutamente; ambiguamente
**doubtfulness** /'dautfəlnɪs/ *n* duda, incertidumbre, *f;* ambigüedad, *f*
**doubtless** /'dautlɪs/ *adv* sin duda, por supuesto; probablemente
**douche** /duʃ/ *n* ducha, *f, vt* duchar
**dough** /dou/ *n* pasta, masa, *f;* (money) lana, *f*
**dour** /dʊr/ *a* huraño, adusto, austero
**dourly** /'dʊrli/ *adv* severamente
**douse** /daus/ *vt* zambullir; (a sail) recoger; *Inf.* apagar
**dove** /duv/ *n* paloma, *f.* **d.-cote,** palomar, *m*
**Dover** /'douvər/ Dóver, *m*
**dovetail** /'dʌv,teil/ *n* cola de milano, *f, vt* machihembrar, empalmar; *Fig.* encajar
**dowager** /'dauədʒər/ *n* viuda, *f;* matrona, *f.* **d. countess,** condesa viuda, *f*
**dowager empress** *n* emperatriz viuda, *f*
**dowdiness** /'daudinɪs/ *n* desaliño, desaseo, *m;* falta de elegancia, *f*
**dowdy** /'daudi/ *a* desaliñado, desaseado; poco elegante. —*n* mujer poco elegante, *f*
**dowel** /'dauəl/ *n* espiga, clavija, *f,* zoquete, *m, vt* enclavijar
**down** /daun/ *n* (of a bird) plumón, *m;* (on a peach, etc.) pelusilla, *f;* (hair) vello, *m;* (before the beard) bozo, *m;* (of a thistle, etc.) vilano, *m.* **ups and downs,** vicisitudes, *f pl*
**down** /daun/ *a* pendiente; (of trains, etc.) descendente. —*adv* abajo; hacia abajo; (lowered) bajado; (of the eyes) bajos; (on the ground) en tierra, por tierra; (stretched out) tendido a lo largo; (depressed) triste, abatido; (ill) enfermo; (fallen) caído; (of the wind) cesado; (closed) cerrado; (exhausted) agotado; *Com.* al contado; (of temperature) más bajo. —*prep*

abajo de; abajo; en la dirección de; (along) a lo largo de; por. **"Down"** (on elevators) «Para bajar». —*interj* ¡Abajo!; ¡A tierra! **He went d. the hill,** Bajaba la colina. **He is d. now,** Ha bajado ahora; Está abajo ahora; Está derribado ahora. **The sun has gone d.,** Se ha puesto el sol. **His stock has gone d.,** *Fig. Inf.* Ha caído en disfavor. **Prices have come d.,** Los precios han bajado. **Their numbers have gone d.,** Sus números han disminuido. **to be d. and out,** estar completamente arruinado, ser pobre de solemnidad. **to boil d.,** reducir hirviendo. **to come d. in the world,** venir a menos. **while I was going d. the river,** mientras iba río abajo, mientras bajaba al río. **d. below,** allá abajo; abajo; en el piso de abajo. **D. on your knees!** ¡De rodillas! **d. to,** hasta. **d. spout,** tubo de bajada, *m.* **D. with!** ¡Abajo! ¡Muera! **d.-stream,** agua abajo. **d. train,** tren descendente, *m*
**down** /daun/ *vt* derribar; vencer. **to d. tools,** declararse en huelga
**downcast** /'daun,kæst/ *a* bajo; cabizbajo, deprimido, abatido
**downfall** /'daun,fɔl/ *n* caída, *f;* derrumbamiento, *m;* (failure) fracaso, *m;* (*Fig.* ruin) decadencia, ruina, *f*
**downhearted** /'daun'hɑrtɪd/ *a* descorazonado, alicaído, desalentado
**downhill** /*n* 'daun'hɪl; *a* 'daun,hɪl/ *adv* cuesta abajo, hacia abajo. —*a* en declive, inclinado. **to go d.,** ir cuesta abajo
**downiness** /'dauninɪs/ *n* vellosidad, *f*
**downpour** /'daun,pɔr/ *n* chubasco (Mexico), aguacero, chaparrón, *m*
**downright** /'daun,rait/ *a* franco, sincero; categórico, terminante; absoluto. —*adv* muy; completamente
**downstairs** /'daun'stɛərz/ *adv* escalera abajo; al piso de abajo; en el piso bajo; abajo. —*a* del piso de abajo. —*n* planta baja, *f;* piso de abajo, *m.* **to go d.,** bajar la escalera; ir al piso de abajo
**downtrodden** /'daun,trodṇ/ *a* oprimido, esclavizado
**downward** /'daunwərd/ *a* descendente; inclinado. —*adv* hacia abajo
**downy** /'dauni/ *a* velloso; (*Fam.* of persons) con más conchas que un galápago
**dowry** /'dauri/ *n* dote, *mf.* **to give as a d.,** dotar
**dowse** /dauz/ *vt.* See **douse**
**doze** /douz/ *vi* dormitar. —*n* sueño ligero, *m*
**dozen** /'dʌzən/ *n* docena, *f*
**drab** /dræb/ *a* pardo, parduzco, grisáceo; *Fig.* gris, monótono. —*n* (slut) pazpuerca, *f;* (prostitute) ramera, *f*
**drachma** /'drækmə/ *n* dracma, *f*
**draft** /dræft/ *n* (act of drawing) tiro, *m;* (of liquid) trago, *m;* (of a ship) calado, *m;* (of air) corriente de aire, *f; Com.* giro, *m,* letra de cambio, *f;* (for the army, navy) conscripción, leva, *f;* (outline) bosquejo, *m;* proyecto, *m;* borrador, *m.* —*vt* (recruit) reclutar; (outline) bosquejar, delinear; (draw up) redactar; proyectar. **on d.,** (of beer, etc.) por vaso. **d. horse,** caballo de tiro, *m.*
**draft card** *n* cartilla (Mexico), libreta de enrolamiento (Argentina), *m*
**draft dodger** *n* emboscado, prófugo, *m*
**drafting** /'dræftɪŋ/ *n* (*Mil. Nav.*) reclutamiento, *m;* (of a bill, etc.) redacción, *f;* (wording) términos, *m pl*
**draftsman** /'dræftsmən/ *n* dibujante, *m;* delineante, *m;* redactor, *m*
**drag** /dræg/ *n* (for dredging) draga, *f;* (harrow) rastrillo, *m;* (break) freno, *m;* (obstacle) estorbo, *m; Aer.* sonda, *f.* —*vt* arrastrar; (fishing nets) rastrear; (harrow) rastrillar. —*vi* (of the anchor) garrar; arrastrarse por el suelo; (of time) pasar lentamente; ir más despacio (que); (of interest) decaer, disminuir. **d.-hook,** garfio, *m.* **d.-net,** brancada, *f*
**dragging** /'drægɪŋ/ *n* arrastre, *m;* (of lakes, etc.) rastreo, *m,* a rastrero; cansado
**draggled** /'drægəld/ *a* mojado y sucio
**dragon** /'drægən/ *n* dragón, *m.* **d.-fly,** libélula, *f,* caballito del diablo, *m*
**dragoon** /drə'gun/ *n Mil.* dragón, *m, vt* someter a una disciplina rigurosa; obligar a la fuerza (a)
**drain** /drein/ *n* desaguadero, *m;* (sewer) cloaca, alcantarilla, *f;* sumidero, *m; Agr.* acequia, *f.* —*vt* desaguar; sanear; (lakes, etc.) desangrar; secar;

(bail) achicar; (empty and drink) vaciar; (swallow) tragar; (*Fig.* of sorrow, etc.) apurar; (despoil) despojar; (deprive) privar (de); (impoverish) empobrecer; (exhaust) agotar. —*vi* desaguarse; vaciarse; (with off) escurrirse. **to be well drained,** tener buen drenaje. **to d. the sump,** vaciar la culata. **to d. away,** vaciar. **d.-pipe,** tubo de desagüe, *m*

**drainage** /'dreinɪdʒ/ *n* (of land) drenaje, *m*; desagüe, *m*; (of wounds) drenaje, *m*; (sewage) aguas del alcantarillado, *f pl*. **main d.,** drenaje municipal, *m*

**draining** /'dreinɪŋ/ *a* de desagüe; de drenaje. **d.-board,** escurridor, *m*

**drake** /dreik/ *n* ánade macho, *m*

**dram** /dræm/ *n* dracma, *f*; (of liquor) trago, *m*

**drama** /'drɑmə, 'dræmə/ *n* drama, *m*

**dramatic** /drə'mætɪk/ *a* dramático

**dramatically** /drə'mætɪkli/ *adv* dramáticamente

**dramatis personae** /'dræmətɪs pər'souni/ *n pl* personajes, *m pl*

**dramatist** /'dræmətɪst, 'drɑmə-/ *n* dramaturgo, *m*

**dramatization** /ˌdræmətə'zeiʃən, ˌdrɑmə-/ *n* versión escénica, *f*; descripción dramática, *f*; (of emotions) dramatización, *f*

**dramatize** /'dræməˌtaiz, 'drɑmə-/ *vt* dramatizar

**drape** /dreip/ *vt* colgar, cubrir; vestir

**draper** /'dreipər/ *n* pañero (-ra)

**drapery** /'dreipəri/ *n* colgaduras, *f pl*; ropaje, *m*, ropas, *f pl*; pañería, *f*

**drastic** /'dræstɪk/ *a* drástico; enérgico, fuerte; **a drastic measure,** una medida avanzada, *f*

**draw** /drɔ/ *vt* tirar; arrastrar; traer; (pluck) arrancar; (attract) atraer; (extract) extraer; sacar; hacer salir; (unsheath) desenvainar; (a bow-string) tender; (cards, dominoes) tomar, robar; (threads) deshilar; (disembowel) destripar; (a check, etc.) girar, librar; (of a ship) calar; (of lines) hacer (rayas); (curtains) correr; (to draw curtains back) descorrer; (salary, money) cobrar, percibir; (obtain) obtener; (persuade) persuadir, inducir; (inhale) respirar; (a sigh) dar; (win) ganar; (a conclusion) deducir, inferir; (a distinction) hacer formular; *Sports.* empatar; (a number, etc.) sortear; (suck) chupar; (tighten) estirar; (lengthen) alargar; (comfort, etc.) tomar; (inspiration) inspirarse en; (obtain money) procurarse (recursos); (withdraw funds) retirar; (write) escribir; (draw) dibujar; (trace) trazar; (provoke) provocar. **to be drawn,** (of tickets in a lottery and cards) salir. **to d. lots,** echar suertes. **to d. water,** sacar agua. **to d. along,** arrastrar; conducir. **to d. aside,** tomar a un lado, tomar aparte; quitar de en medio, poner a un lado; (curtains) descorrer. **to d. away,** (remove) quitar; (a person) llevarse (a); apartar. **to d. back,** hacer recular; hacer retirarse; hacer volverse atrás; (curtains) descorrer. **to d. down,** hacer bajar; tirar a lo largo de (por por); bajar; (attract) atraer. **to d. forth,** hacer salir; hacer avanzar; tirar hacia adelante; conducir; (develop) desarrollar; sacar; hacer aparecer; (comment, etc.) suscitar. **to d. in,** tirar hacia adentro; sacar; acercar; atraer. **to d. off,** sacar; retirar; quitar; (water from pipes, etc.) vaciar; *Print.* tirar; (turn aside) desviar. **to d. on,** (of apparel) ponerse; (boots) calzarse; (occasion) ocasionar. **to d. out,** sacar fuera; hacer salir; tirar (de); (extract) extraer; (trace) trazar; (a person) hacer hablar. **to d. over,** poner encima de; arrastrar por; hacer acercarse (a), tirar hacia; atraer; persuadir. **d. prestige (from),** cobrar prestigio (de). **to d. round,** poner alrededor de. **to d. together,** reunir; acercar. **to d. up,** tirar hacia arriba; subir; sacar; extraer; (raise) levantar; alzar; (bring) traer; (bring near) acercar; (order) ordenar; *Mil.* formar; (a document) redactar; formular. **to d. oneself up,** erguirse

**draw** /drɔ/ *vi* tirar; (shrink) encogerse; (wrinkle) arrugarse; (of chimneys, etc.) tirar; (a picture) dibujar; *Sports.* empatar; (move) moverse; avanzar, adelantarse; (of a ship) calar; (a sword) desnudar (la espada); (lots) echar suertes; (attract people) atraer gente; *Com.* girar. **to d. aside,** ponerse a un lado; retirarse. **to d. back,** retroceder, recular; retirarse; vacilar. **to d. in,** retirarse; (of days) hacerse corto; (of dusk) caer. **to d. off,** alejarse; apartarse, retirarse. **to d. on,** (approach) acercarse; avanzar; *Com.* girar con-

tra; inspirarse en. **to d. out,** hacerse largo; (of a vehicle) ponerse en marcha, empezar a andar. **to d. round,** ponerse alrededor; reunirse alrededor. **to d. together,** reunirse. **to d. up,** parar.

**draw** /drɔ/ *n* tirada, *f*; (of lotteries) sorteo, *m*; *Sports.* empate, *m*; atracción, *f*; (*Fig.* feeler) tanteo, *m*. **to be a big d.,** ser una gran atracción

**drawback** /'drɔˌbæk/ *n* desventaja, *f*, inconveniente, *m*

**drawbridge** /'drɔˌbrɪdʒ/ *n* puente levadizo, *m*

**drawee** /drɔ'i/ *n Com.* girado, *m*

**drawer** /'drɔər for / n tirador (-ra); (of water) aguador (-ra); extractor (-ra); (in a public-house) mozo de taberna, *m*; (designer) diseñador, *m*; (sketcher) dibujante, *mf*; *Com.* girador, *m*; (receptacle) cajón, *m*; *pl* **drawers,** (men's) calzoncillos, *m pl*; (women's) pantalones, *m pl*

**drawing** /'drɔɪŋ/ *n* (pulling) tiro, *m*; atracción, *f*; (extraction) extracción, *f*; saca, *f*; (in raffles, etc. and of lots) sorteo, *m*; (of money) percibo, *m*; *Com.* giro, *m*; (sketch) dibujo, *m*; (plan) esquema, *f*. **free-hand d.,** dibujo a pulso, *m*. **d. from life,** dibujo del natural, *m*. **d.-board,** tablero de dibujo, *m*. **d.-paper,** papel para dibujar, *m*. **d.-pin,** chinche, *f*. **d.-room,** salón, *m*

**drawl** /drɔl/ *vi* hablar arrastrando las palabras

**drawn** /drɔn/ *past part* See **draw**. *a* (tired) ojeroso, con ojeras, con un aspecto de cansancio; (with pain) desencajado. **long d. out,** demasiado largo. **d. sword,** espada desnuda, *f*. **d.-thread work,** deshilados, *m pl*

**dray** /drei/ *n* carro, *m*. **d.-horse,** caballo de tiro, *m*

**dread** /dred/ *n* pavor, temor, terror, espanto, *m*; trepidación, *f*, miedo, *m*. —*a* temible, espantoso, terrible; augusto. —*vt* temer. —*vi* tener miedo, temer. **in d. of,** con miedo de, con terror de

**dreader** /'dredər/ *n* el, *m*, (*f*, la) que teme, temedor (-ra)

**dreadful** /'dredfəl/ *a* terrible, pavoroso, espantoso, horroroso; formidable; augusto

**dreadfully** /'dredfəli/ *adv* terriblemente, horriblemente

**dreadfulness** /'dredfəlnɪs/ *n* horror, *m*

**dreadnought** /'dredˌnɔt/ *n* acorazado de línea, *m*

**dream** /drim/ *n* sueño, *m*; ilusión, *f*; ensueño, *m*; fantasía, *f*. —*vt* and *vi* soñar; imaginar. **He dreamed away the hours,** Pasaba las horas soñando. **I wouldn't d. of it!** ¡Ni por sueño! **in a d.,** en sueños; (waking) como en sueños; mecánicamente. **Sweet dreams!** ¡Duerme bien! **to d. of,** soñar con

**dreamer** /'drimər/ *n* soñador (-ra); visionario (-ia)

**dreamily** /'driməli/ *adv* como en sueños; soñolientamente; vagamente

**dreaming** /'drimɪŋ/ *n* sueños, *m pl*

**dreamland** /'drimˌlænd/ *n* reino de los sueños, *m*

**dreamy** /'drimi/ *a* soñador; soñoliento; fantástico; (empty) vacío

**dreariness** /'drɪərinɪs/ *n* tristeza, *f*; melancolía, *f*; lobreguez, *f*

**dreary** /'drɪəri/ *a* triste; melancólico; lóbrego

**dredge** /dredʒ/ *vt* dragar; (with sugar, etc.) espolvorear

**dredger** /'dredʒər/ *n* draga, *f*; (for sugar) azucarera, *f*; (for flour) harinero, *m*

**dredging** /'dredʒɪŋ/ *n* dragado, *m*; (sprinkling) salpicadura, *f*. **d. bucket,** cangilón, *m*

**dregs** /dregz/ *n pl* heces, *f pl*, posos, *m pl*. **to drain to the d.,** vaciar hasta las heces

**drench** /drentʃ/ *vt* mojar, calar. **He is drenched to the skin,** Está calado hasta los huesos

**Dresden** /'drezdən/ *n* Dresde, *f*. **D. china,** loza de Dresde, *f*

**dress** /dres/ *vt* (with clothes) vestir; (arrange) arreglar; (the hair) peinar(se); (a wound) curar; (hides) adobar; (cloth) aprestar; (flax) rastrillar; (stone) labrar; (wood) desbastar; (prune) podar; (a garden) cultivar; (manure) abonar; *Cul.* aderezar; preparar; (season) condimentar; (a table) poner; (adorn) asaviar, adornar; revestir; (a dead body) amortajar. —*vi* vestirse; ataviarse; (of troops) alinearse. **all dressed up and nowhere to go,** compuesta y sin novio. **dressed up to the nines,** vestido de veinticinco alfileres. **Left (Right) d.!** ¡A la izquierda (A la derecha) alinearse! **to d. down,** (scold) poner como un trapo (a), al mar una calada (a). **to d. up,** *vt* ataviar; (disguise) disfrazar. —*vi* ponerse muy elegante; disfrazarse

**dress** /drɛs/ *n* (in general) el vestir; (clothes) ropa, *f;* (frock) vestido, traje, *m;* (uniform) uniforme, *m;* (*Fig.* covering) hábitos, *m pl;* (appearance) aspecto, *m;* forma, *f.* **full d.,** (uniform) uniforme de gala, *m;* (civilian, man's) traje de etiqueta, *m;* (woman's) traje de gala, *m.* **morning d.,** (man's) traje de paisano, *m;* (woman's) vestido de todos los días, *m;* (man's formal dress) chaqué, *m.* **ready-made d.,** traje hecho, *m.* **d. allowance,** alfileres, *m pl.* **d.-circle,** anfiteatro, *m.* **d.-coat,** frac, *m.* **d. protector,** sobaquera, *f.* **d. rehearsal,** ensayo general, *m.* **d. shirt,** camisa de pechera dura, *f.* **d. suit,** (with white tie) traje de frac, *m;* (with black tie) smoking, *m.* **d. sword,** espada de gala, *f.* **d. tie,** corbata de smoking (or de frac), *f*

**dresser** /'drɛsər/ *n* el que adereza; (of wounds) practicante (de hospital), *m;* (valet) ayuda de cámara, *m;* (maid) doncella, *f;* (of skins) adobador de pieles, *m;* (furniture) aparador, *m;* (in the kitchen) armario de la cocina, *m*

**dressing** /'drɛsɪŋ/ *n* el vestir(se); aderezamiento, *m;* (for cloth) apresto, *m;* (of leather) adobo, *m;* (of wood) desbaste, *m;* (of stone) labrado, *m;* (manuring) estercoladura, *f;* (sauce) salsa, *f;* (seasoning) condimentación, *f;* (of a wound) cura, *f;* (bandage) apósito, *m,* vendaje, *m.* **d.-case,** neceser, saco de noche, *m.* **d.-down,** *Inf.* rapapolvo, *m.* **d.-gown,** (woman's) salto de cama, quimono, *m;* (man's) batín, *m.* **d.-jacket,** chambra, *f,* peinador, *m.* **d.-room,** *Theat.* camarín, *m;* (in a house) trasalcoba, recámara, *f.* **d.-station,** puesto de socorro, *m.* **d.-table,** tocador, *m,* mesa de tocador, *f*

**dressmaker** /'drɛsˌmeikər/ *n* modista, *mf*

**dressmaking** /'drɛsˌmeikɪŋ/ *n* confección de vestidos, *f;* arte de la modista, *mf*

**dribble** /'drɪbəl/ *vi* gotear; (slaver) babear. —*vt* (in football) regatear. —*n* (in football) regate, *m*

**dried** /draid/ *a* seco; (of fruit) paso. **d. up,** (withered) marchito; (of people) enjuto. **d. fish,** cecial, *m.'* **d. meat,** cecina, *f*

**drift** /drɪft/ *n* (in a ship or airplane's course) deriva, *f;* (of a current) velocidad, *f;* (tendency) tendencia, *f;* (meaning) significación, *f;* (heap) montón, *m;* (aim) objeto, propósito, fin, *m; Mineral.* galería, *f;* (of dust, etc.) nube, *f;* (shower) lluvia, *f;* (impulsion) impulso, *m;* violencia, *f.* —*vi* flotar, ir arrastrado por la corriente; amontonarse; *Naut.* derivar; *Aer.* abatir. —*vt* llevar; amontonar. **drifts of sand,** arena movediza, *f.* **to d. into,** (war, etc.) entrar sin querer en; (habits) dar en la flor de; (a room, etc.) deslizarse en. **d.-wood,** madera de deriva, *f*

**drill** /drɪl/ *n* (instrument) taladro, perforador, *m,* barrena, *f;* ejercicio, *m,* educación física, *f; Mil.* instrucción militar, *f;* (cloth) dril, *m; Agr.* sembradora mecánica, *f;* (for seeds) hilera, *f;* (discipline) disciplina, *f;* (teaching) instrucción, *f.* —*vt* taladrar, barrenar; enseñar el ejercicio (a); enseñar la instrucción; disciplinar; (seed) sembrar en hileras. —*vi* hacer el ejercicio; hacer la instrucción militar. **d. ground,** (in a barracks) patio de un cuartel, *m;* (in a school) patio de recreo, *m.* **d.-sergeant,** sargento instructor, *m*

**drilling** /'drɪlɪŋ/ *n* (boring) perforación, *f,* barrenamiento, *m;* (of seeds) sembradura en hileras, *f;* ejercicios, *m pl;* (maneuvers) maniobras, *f pl*

**drink** /drɪŋk/ *n* bebida, *f;* (glass of wine, etc.) copita, *f;* (of water, etc.) vaso, *m.* —*vt* beber; tomar; (empty) vaciar. —*vi* beber. **to d. the health of,** beber a la salud de, brindar por. **to give someone a d.,** dar a beber. **Would you like a d.?** ¿Quieres tomar algo? **to d. in,** absorber. **to d. off, up,** beber de un trago

**drinkable** /'drɪŋkəbəl/ *a* potable, bebedero

**drinker** /'drɪŋkər/ *n* bebedor (-ra)

**drinking** /'drɪŋkɪŋ/ *n* acción de beber, *f;* el beber, *m;* (alcoholism) bebida, *f.* —*a* que bebe; aficionado a la bebida; (of things) para beber. **d.-fountain,** (habit) potable; (tavern) de taberna. **d.-fountain,** fuente pública para beber agua, *f.* **d. place,** bebedero, *m;* bar, *m.* **d.-**

**song,** canción de taberna, *f.* **d.-trough,** abrevadero, *m;* **d.-water,** agua potable, *f*

**drip** /drɪp/ *vi* and *vt* chorrear, gotear; caer gota a gota; escurrir; destilar; chorrear. —*n* goteo, *m;* gota, *f; Archit.* goterón, *m*

**dripping** /'drɪpɪŋ/ *n* goteo, *m;* chorreo, *m;* (fat) grasa, *f,* a que gotea; mojado; que chorrea agua. **d.-pan,** grasera, *f*

**drive** /draiv/ *vt* empujar; arrojar; conducir; (grouse, etc.) batir; (a ball) golpear; (a nail, etc.) clavar; (oblige) compeler, forzar a; (a horse, plough, etc.) manejar; (*Mech.* work) mover; (cause to work, of machines) hacer funcionar; (a tunnel, etc.) abrir, construir; (a bargain, etc.) hacer; (cause) impulsar, hacer; (mad, etc.) volver. —*vi* lanzarse; (of rain) azotar; (a vehicle) conducir; (in a vehicle) ir en (coche, etc.). **to let d. at,** (aim) asestar. **to d. a wedge,** hacer mella. **to d. home an argument,** convencer; hacer convincente. **What is he driving at?** ¿Qué se propone?; ¿Qué quiere?; ¿Qué quiere decir con sus indirectas? ¿A dónde quiere llegar con esto? **to d. along,** ir en coche o carruaje por; pasearse en coche o carruaje; conducir un auto, etc., por. **to d. away,** *vt* echar; (chase) cazar; (flies, etc.) sacudirse, espantar; (care, etc.) ahuyentar; (of persons) apartar, alejar. —*vi* (depart) marcharse (en coche, etc.). **to d. back,** *vt* rechazar; (a ball) devolver. —*vi* volver (en auto, etc.); (arrive) llegar. **to d. down,** hacer bajar; arrojar hacia abajo; (in a vehicle) bajar (por). **to d. in, into,** *vt* hacer entrar; (of teeth, etc.) hincar; (nails) clavar; *Fig.* introducir. —*vt* entrar (en coche, carruaje); llegar (en coche, etc.). **to d. off,** See **away. to d. off the stage,** hacer dejar la escena, silbar. **to d. on,** *vt* empujar; hacer avanzar; (attack) atacar. —*vi* seguir su marcha; seguir avanzando; emprender la marcha. **to d. out,** *vt* expulsar; hacer salir; (chase) cazar. —*vi* salir (en coche, etc.). **to d. up,** *vi* illegar (en coche, etc.); parar. **to d. up to,** avanzar hasta, llegar hasta; conducir (el coche, etc.) hasta

**drive** /draiv/ *n* paseo (en coche, etc.), *m;* (avenue) avenida, *f;* (distance) trayecto, *m;* (journey) viaje, *m; Mech.* acción, *f;* conducción, *f; m; Mil.* ataque, *m;* (of a person) energía, *f;* campaña vigorosa, *f;* impulso, *m.* **left (right) hand d.,** conducción a la izquierda (derecha). **to take a d.,** dar un paseo en (auto, etc.). **to take for a d.,** llevar a paseo en (auto, etc.)

**drive-in** /'draiv,ɪn/ *n* autocine, autocinema, *m*

**drivel** /'drɪvəl/ *n* vaciedades, patrañas, *f pl,* disparates, *m pl,* *vi* decir disparates, chochear

**driver** /'draivər/ *n* conductor (-ra); chófer, *m;* (of an engine) maquinista, *m;* (of a cart) carretero, *m;* (of a coach, carriage) cochero, *m;* (of cattle, etc.) ganadero, *m;* (golf) conductor, *m*

**"Driveway"** «Vado Permanente», «Paso de Carruajes»

**driving** /'draivɪŋ/ *n* conducción, *f;* modo de conducir, *m;* paseo (en coche, etc.), *m;* impulsión, *f.* —*a* de conducir; de chófer; para choferes; motor; propulsor; impulsor; de transmisión; *Fig.* impulsor; (violent) violento, impetuoso. **to go d.,** ir de paseo en un auto o carruaje). **d. license,** carnet de chófer, *m.* **d. mirror,** espejo retrovisor, *m.* **d. seat,** asiento del conductor, *m;* (of an old-fashioned coach, etc.) pescante, *m.* **d.-shaft,** *Mech.* árbol motor, *m.* **d. test,** examen para choferes, *m.* **d.-wheel,** volante, *m;* rueda motriz, *f.* **d.-whip,** látigo, *m*

**drizzle** /'drɪzəl/ *n* llovizna, *f, vi* lloviznar

**droll** /droul/ *a* chusco, gracioso. —*n* bufón, *m*

**dromedary** /'drɒmɪˌdɛri/ *n* dromedario, *m*

**drone** /droun/ *n* abejón, *m; Fig.* zángano, *m;* (hum) zumbido, *m;* (of a song, voice) salmodia, *f, vt* and *vi* (hum) zumbar; (of a song, voice) salmodiar; (idle) zanganear

**droning** /'drounɪŋ/ *a* zumbador; confuso

**droop** /drup/ *vi* inclinarse; colgar; caer; (wither) marchitarse; (fade) consumirse; (pine) desanimarse. —*vt* bajar; dejar caer. —*n* caída, *f,* inclinación, *f*

**drooping** /'drupɪŋ/ *a* caído; debilitado; lánguido; (of ears) gacho; (depressed) alicaído, deprimido

**drop** /drɒp/ *n* gota, *f;* (tear) lágrima, *f;* (for the ear) pendiente, *m;* (sweet) pastilla, *f;* (of a chandelier) almendra, *f;* (fall) caída, *f;* (in price, etc.) baja, *f;*

(slope) pendiente, cuesta, *f.* **by drops,** a gotas. **d. bottle,** frasco cuentagotas, *m.* **d.-curtain,** telón de boca, *m.* **d.-hammer,** martinete, *m.* **d.-head coupé,** cupé descapotable, *m.* **d.-scene,** telón de foro, *m*

**drop** /drɒp/ *vt* verter a gotas; destilar; (sprinkle) salpicar, rociar; dejar caer; soltar; (lower) bajar; (of clothes, etc.) desprenderse de, quitar; (lose) perder; (a letter in a mailbox) echar; (leave) dejar; (give up) renunciar (a); desistir (de); abandonar; (kill) tumbar; (a hint) soltar; (a curtsey) hacer. —*vi* gotear, caer en gotas, destilar; (descend) bajar, descender; caer muerto; caer desmayado; (sleep) dormirse; (fall) caer; (of the wind) amainar; (of prices, temperature) bajar. **to let the matter d.,** poner fin a una cuestión. **to d. a line,** poner unas líneas. **to d. anchor,** anclar. **to d. behind,** quedarse atrás. **to d. down,** caer (a tierra). **to d. in,** entrar al pasar. **d. in on somebody,** pasarse por casa de fulano, pasarse por el despacho de (etc.). **to d. off,** separarse (de); disminuir; (sleep) quedar dormido; (die) morir de repente. **to d. out,** separarse; (from a race, etc.) retirarse (de); quedarse atrás; desaparecer; ausentarse, apartarse; (decrease) disminuir; decaer. **He has dropped out of my life,** Le he perdido de vista. **to d. through,** caer por; frustrarse; no dar resultado

**dropping** /'drɒpɪŋ/ *n* gotera, *f*; gotas, *f pl*; (fall) caída, *f*; **droppings** (of a candle) moco, *m*; (dung) cagadas, *f pl.* **Constant d. wears away the stone,** La gotera cava la piedra

**dropsy** /'drɒpsi/ *n* hidropesía, *f*

**dross** /drɔs/ *n* escoria, *f*; (rubbish) basura, *f*

**drought** /draut/ *n* aridez, *f*; (thirst) sed, *f*; (dry season) sequía, *f*

**drove** /drouv/ *n* manada, *f*, hato, *m*; (of sheep) rebaño, *m*; (crowd) muchedumbre, *f*

**drown** /draun/ *vi* ahogarse. —*vt* ahogar; sumergir; inundar; (*Fig.* of cries, sorrow, etc.) ahogar

**drowning** /'draunɪŋ/ *n* ahogamiento, *m*; sumersión, *f*; inundación, *f*. —*a* que se ahoga

**drowse** /drauz/ *vi* adormecerse

**drowsily** /'drauzəli/ *adv* soñolientamente

**drowsiness** /'drauzɪnɪs/ *n* somnolencia, *f*; sueño, *m*; (laziness) indolencia, pereza, *f*

**drowsy** /'drauzi/ *a* soñoliento; adormecedor, soporífero; (heavy) amodorrado. **to grow d.,** adormecerse. **to make d.,** adormecer

**drubbing** /'drʌbɪŋ/ *n* tunda, zurra, felpa, *f*

**drudgery** /'drʌdʒəri/ *n* trabajo arduo, *m*, faena monótona, *f*

**drug** /drʌg/ *n* droga, *f*; medicamento, *m*; narcótico, *m.* —*vt* mezclar con drogas; administrar drogas (a); narcotizar. —*vi* tomar drogas. **d. trade,** comercio de drogas, *m.* **d. traffic,** contrabando de drogas, narcotráfico *m*

**drug addict** *n* toxicómano, *m*

**drug addiction** *n* toxicomanía, *f*

**druggist** /'drʌgɪst/ *n* droguero (-ra)

**druid** /'druɪd/ *n* druida, *m*

**drum** /drʌm/ *n* tambor, *m*; (of the ear) tímpano (del oído), *m*; (cylinder) cilindro, *m*; (box) caja, *f*; *Archit.* cuerpo de columna, *m.* **bass d.,** bombo, *m.* **with drums beating,** con tambor batiente. **d.-head,** parche (del tambor), *m.* **d.-head service,** misa de campaña, *f.* **d.-major,** tambor mayor, *m*

**drum** /drʌm/ *vt* and *vi* tocar el tambor; (with the fingers) tabalear, teclear; (with the heels) zapatear; (into a person's head) machacar. **to d. out,** *Mil.* expulsar a tambor batiente

**drummer** /'drʌmər/ *n* tambor, *m*

**drumming** /'drʌmɪŋ/ *n* ruido del tambor, *m*; (of the heels) taconeo, *m*; (of the fingers) tabaleo, tecleo, *m*

**drumstick** /'drʌm,stɪk/ *n* palillo (de tambor), *m*

**drunk** /drʌŋk/ *a* borracho, ebrio. —*n* borracho, *m.* **to be d.,** estar borracho. **to get d.,** emborracharse. *Inf.* pillar un lobo. **to make d.,** emborrachar

**drunkard** /'drʌŋkərd/ *n* borracho (-cha)

**drunken** /'drʌŋkən/ *a* borracho, ebrio

**drunkenness** /'drʌŋkənnɪs/ *n* embriaguez, borrachera, ebriedad, *f*

**dry** /drai/ *vi* secarse. —*vt* secar; desaguar; (wipe) enjugar. **to dry one's tears,** enjugarse las lágrimas, *Fig.* secarse las lágrimas. **to dry up,** secarse; (of persons)

acecinarse; (with old age) apergaminarse; (of ideas, etc.) agotarse; (be quiet) callarse

**dry** /drai/ *a* seco; árido; estéril; (thirsty) sediento; (of wine) seco; (U.S.A.) prohibicionista; (squeezed) exprimido; (of toast) sin mantequilla; (*Fig.* chilly) aburrido; (sarcastic) sarcástico; (of humour) agudo. **on dry land,** en seco. **dry battery,** pila seca, *f.* **to dry-clean,** lavar al seco. **dry-cleaner,** tintorero (-ra). **dry-cleaning,** lavado al seco, *m.* **dry-cleaning shop,** tintorería, *f.* **dry goods,** lencería, *f.* **dry land,** tierra firme, *f.* **dry measure,** medida para áridos, *f.* **dry-nurse,** ama seca, *f.* **dry-point,** punta seca, *f.* **dry-rot,** carcoma, *f.* **dry-shod,** con los pies secos

**drying** /'draiɪŋ/ *n* secamiento, *m*; desecación, *f*, *a* secante; seco; para secar. **d. ground,** tendedero, *m.* **d. machine,** secadora, *f*; (for the hair) secadora de cabello, *f.* **d. room,** secadero, *m*

**dryly** /'draili/ *adv* secamente

**dryness** /'drainɪs/ *n* sequedad, *f*; aridez, *f*; (of humour) agudeza, *f*

**dual** /'duəl/ *a* doble; *Gram.* dual. **d. control,** mandos gemelos, *m pl.* **d. personality,** conciencia doble, *f*

**dualism** /'duə,lɪzəm/ *n* dualismo, *m*

**duality** /du'ælɪti/ *n* dualidad, *f*

**dub** /dʌb/ *vt* (a knight) armar caballero; (call) apellidar; (nickname) motejar, apodar

**dubbing** /'dʌbɪŋ/ *n* (of films) doblaje, *m*

**dubious** /'dubiəs/ *a* dudoso, incierto; indeciso; problemático; ambiguo

**dubiously** /'dubiəsli/ *adv* dudosamente

**dubiousness** /'dubiəsnɪs/ *n* carácter dudoso, *m*; incertidumbre, *f*; ambigüedad, *f*

**Dublin** /'dʌblɪn/ Dublín, *f*

**Dubliner** /'dʌblənər/ *n* dublinés (-esa)

**ducat** /'dʌkət/ *n* ducado, *m*

**duchess** /'dʌtʃɪs/ *n* duquesa, *f*

**duchy** /'dʌtʃi/ *n* ducado, *m*

**duck** /dʌk/ *n* pato (-ta), ánade, *mf*; *Sports.* cero, *m*; (darling) vida mía, querida, *f*; (jerk) agachada, *f*; (under the water) chapuz, *m*; (material) dril, *m*; *Mil.* auto anfibio, *m*; *pl* **ducks,** pantalones de dril, *m pl.* —*vi* agacharse; (under water) chapuzarse. —*vt* zabullir, sumergir; bajar, inclinar

**ducking** /'dʌkɪŋ/ *n* chapuz, *m.* **d.-stool,** silla de chapuzar, *f*

**duckling** /'dʌklɪŋ/ *n* anadino (-na)

**duct** /dʌkt/ *n* conducto, canal, *m*; *Bot.* tubo, *m*

**ductile** /'dʌktl/ *a* dúctil

**ductility** /dʌk'tɪlɪti/ *n* ductilidad, *f*

**ductless** /'dʌktlɪs/ *a* sin tubos

**due** /du/ *a* debido; (payable) pagadero; (fallen due) vencido; (fitting) propio; (expected) esperado. —*n* impuesto, *m*; derecho, *m.* **in due form,** en regla. **in its due time,** a su tiempo debido. **to fall due,** vencerse. **due bill,** *Com.* abonaré, *m.* **due west,** poniente derecho, *m*

**duel** /'duəl/ *n* duelo, lance de honor, *m*; *Fig.* lucha, *f.* **to fight a d.,** batirse en duelo

**dueling** /'duəlɪŋ/ *n* el (batirse en) duelo

**duelist** /'duəlɪst/ *n* duelista, *m*

**duenna** /du'ɛnə/ *n* dueña, *f*

**duet** /du'ɛt/ *n* dúo, *m*

**duettist** /du'ɛtɪst/ *n* duetista, *mf*

**duffer** /'dʌfər/ *n* estúpido (-da); ganso, *m*; (at games, etc.) maleta, *m*

**dug** /dʌg/ *n* teta, *f*

**dugout** /'dʌg,aut/ *n* trinchera, *f*

**duke** /duk/ *n* duque, *m*

**dukedom** /'dukdəm/ *n* ducado, *m*

**dulcet** /'dʌlsɪt/ *a* dulce

**dulcimer** /'dʌlsəmər/ *n* dulcémele, *m*

**dull** /dʌl/ *a* (stupid) lerdo, estúpido, obtuso; (boring, tedious) aburrido; (of pain, sounds) sordo; (of colors and eyes) apagado; (of light, beams, etc.) sombrío; (not polished) mate; (pale) pálido; (insipid) insípido, insulso; (of people) soso, poco interesante; (dreary, sad) triste; (gray) gris; (of mirrors, etc.) empañado; (of weather) anublado; (of hearing) duro; (slow) lento; lánguido; insensible; (blunt) romo; *Com.* encalmado, inactivo. **to find life d.,** encontrar la vida aburrida. **d. of hearing,** duro de oído, algo sordo. **d.**

pain, dolor sordo, *m*. **d. season,** temporada de calma, *f*. **d.-eyed,** con ojos apagados. **d.-witted,** lerdo

**dull** /dʌl/ *vt* (make stupid) entontecer; (lessen) mitigar; (weaken) debilitar; (pain) calmar, aliviar; (sadden) entristecer; (blunt) embotar; (spoil) estropear; (a mirror, etc.) empañar; (a polished surface) hacer mate, deslustrar; (of enthusiasm, etc.) enfriar; (tire) fatigar; (obstruct) impedir

**dullness** /'dʌlnɪs/ *n* (stupidity) estupidez, *f*; (boredom) aburrimiento, *m*; (heaviness) pesadez, *f*; (drowsiness) somnolencia, *f*; (insipidity) insipidez, insulsez, *f*; (of literary style) prosaísmo, *m*; (of persons) sosería, *f*; (of a surface) deslustre, *m*; (laziness) pereza, languidez, *f*; (slowness) lentitud, *f*; (tiredness) cansancio, *m*; (sadness) tristeza, *f*; (bluntness) embotamiento, *m*; (of hearing) dureza, *f*; *Com.* desanimación, *f*

**dully** /'dʌli/ *adv* (stupidly) estúpidamente; sin comprender; (insipidly) insípidamente; (not brightly) sin brillo; (slowly) lentamente; (sadly) tristemente; (tiredly) con cansancio; (of sound) sordamente

**duly** /'duli/ *adv* debidamente; puntualmente

**dumb** /dʌm/ *a* mudo; callado; silencioso; *Inf.* tonto, estúpido. **to become d.,** enmudecer. **to strike d.,** dejar sin habla. **d.-bell,** barra con pesas, *f*. **d. show,** pantomima, *f*. **d. waiter,** bufete, *m*

**dumbfound** /dʌm'faund/ *vt* dejar sin habla; confundir; pasmar

**dumbness** /'dʌmnɪs/ *n* mudez, *f*, mutismo, *m*; silencio, *m*

**dummy** /'dʌmi/ *n* (tailor's, etc.) maniquí, *m*; (puppet) títere, *m*; cabeza para pelucas, *f*; (figurehead) hombre de paja, testaferro, *m*; (baby's) chupador, *m*; (at cards) el muerto. —*a* fingido. **to be d.,** (at cards) ser el muerto

**dump** /dʌmp/ *n* depósito, *m*; vaciadero, *m*. —*vt* depositar; (goods on a market) inundar (con)

**dumping** /'dʌmpɪŋ/ *n* depósito, *m*; vaciamiento, *m*; (of goods on a market) inundación, *f*. **"D. prohibited,"** «Se prohibe arrojar la basura»

**dumps** /dʌmps/ *n* murria, *f*

**dun** /dʌn/ *vt* apremiar, importunar

**dunce** /dʌns/ *n* asno, bobo, zoquete, *m*. **dunce's cap,** coroza, *f*

**dun-colored** /'dʌn,kʌlərd/ *a* pardo

**dunderhead** /'dʌndər,hɛd/ *n* cabeza de alcornoque, zoquete, *m*

**dune** /dun/ *n* duna, *f*

**dung** /dʌŋ/ *n* estiércol, *m*; (of rabbits, mice, deer, sheep, goats) cagarruta, *f*; (of cows) boñiga, *f*; (of hens) gallinaza, *f*. **d.-cart,** carro de basura, *m*

**dungarees** /,dʌŋgə'riz/ *n* mono, *m*, pantalones-vaquero, *m pl*

**dungeon** /'dʌndʒən/ *n* mazmorra, *f*, calabozo, *m*

**dunghill** /'dʌŋ,hɪl/ *n* muladar, *m*

**Dunkirk** /'dʌnkɜrk/ Dunquerque, *m*

**duodenum** /,duə'dinəm/ *n* duodeno, *m*

**dupe** /dup/ *n* víctima, *f*; tonto (-ta). —*vt* embelecar, engañar. **to be a d.,** *Inf.* hacer el primo

**duplicate** /a, n 'duplɪkɪt, 'dyu-; v -,keit/ *a* duplicado, doble. —*n* duplicado, *m*; copia, *f*. —*vt* duplicar

**duplication** /,duplɪ'keiʃən/ *n* duplicación, *f*

**duplicator** /'duplɪ,keitər/ *n* copiador, *m*

**duplicity** /du'plɪsɪti/ *n* duplicidad, *f*

**durability** /,dʊrə'bɪliti/ *n* duración, *f*. **This is a cloth of great d.,** Este es un paño que dura mucho, Este es un paño muy duradero

**durable** /'dʊrəbəl/ *a* duradero

**duration** /dʊ'reiʃən/ *n* duración, *f*

**duress** /dʊ'rɛs/ *n* compulsión, *f*; (prison) prisión, *f*

**during** /'dʊrɪŋ/ *prep* durante

**dusk** /dʌsk/ *n* atardecer, anochecer, *m*; (twilight) crepúsculo, *m*; (darkness) oscuridad, *f*. **at d.,** al atardecer, a la caída de la tarde

**dusky** /'dʌski/ *a* (swarthy) moreno; (black) negro; (dim, dark) oscuro; (of colors) sucio

**dust** /dʌst/ *n* polvo, *m*; (cloud of dust) polvareda, *f*; (ashes) cenizas, *f pl*; (of coal) cisco, *m*; (sweepings) barreduras, *f pl*; (of grain) tamo, *m*. —*vt* desempolvar, quitar (or sacudir) el polvo de; (cover with dust) polvorear; (scatter) salpicar; (sweep) barrer; (clean) limpiar. **d.-bin,** basurero, *m*. **d.-cart,** carro de la basura, *m*. **d. cloud,** polvareda, *f*. **d. jacket,** (books) sobrecubierta, *f*. **d.-pan,** recogedor de basura, *m*. **d.-sheet,** guardapolvo, *m*. **d. storm,** vendaval de polvo, *m*

**duster** /'dʌstər/ *n* el, *m*, que quita el polvo; paño (para quitar el polvo), *m*; (of feathers) plumero, *m*

**dustiness** /'dʌstinɪs/ *n* empolvoramiento, *m*; estado polvoriento, *m*

**dusting** /'dʌstɪŋ/ *n* limpieza, *f*; (sweeping) barredura, *f*; (powder) polvos antisépticos, *m pl*

**dusty** /'dʌsti/ *a* polvoriento, polvoroso, empolvado; del color del polvo; (of colours) sucio. **It is very d.,** Hay mucho polvo. **to get d.,** llenarse (or cubrirse) de polvo

**Dutch** /dʌtʃ/ *a* holandés. **the D.,** los holandeses. **double D.,** griego, galimatías, *m*. **D. cheese,** queso de bola, *m*. **D. courage,** coraje falso, *m*. **D. woman,** holandesa, *f*

**Dutchman** /'dʌtʃmən/ *n* holandés, *m*

**dutiable** /'dutiəbəl/ *a* sujeto a derechos de aduana

**dutiful** /'dutəfəl/ *a* que cumple con sus deberes; obediente, sumiso; respetuoso; excelente, muy bueno

**dutifully** /'dutəfəli/ *adv* obedientemente; respetuosamente

**dutifulness** /'dutəfəlnɪs/ *n* obediencia, docilidad, *f*; respeto, *m*

**duty** /'duti/ *n* deber, *m*; obligación, *f*; (greetings) respetos, *m pl*; (charge, burden) carga, *f*; (tax) derecho, impuesto, *m*; *Mil.* servicio, *m*; (guard) guardia, *f*. **off d.,** libre. **on d.,** de servicio. **to be on sentry d.,** estar de guardia. **to do d. as,** servir como. **to do one's d.,** hacer (or cumplir con) su deber. **to pay d. on,** pagar derechos de aduana sobre. **d.-free,** franco de derechos

**dwarf** /dwɔrf/ *a* enano. —*n* enano (-na). —*vt* impedir el crecimiento de; empequeñecer

**dwarfish** /'dwɔrfɪʃ/ *a* enano

**dwell** /dwel/ *vi* vivir, habitar; (with on, upon) (think about) meditar sobre, pensar en; (deal with) tratar de; hablar largamente de; (insist on) insistir en; apoyarse en, hacer hincapié en; (pause over) detenerse en

**dweller** /'dwelər/ *n* habitante, *mf*; (more poetic) morador (-ra)

**dwelling** /'dwelɪŋ/ *n* vivienda, *f*; (abode) morada, habitación, *f*; residencia, *f*; casa, *f*; (domicile) domicilio, *m*. **d.-house,** casa, *f*

**dwindle** /'dwɪndḷ/ *vi* disminuirse; consumirse; (decay) decaer; (degenerate) degenerar. **to d. to,** reducirse a

**dwindling** /'dwɪndlɪŋ/ *n* disminución, *f*

**dye** /dai/ *vt* teñir, colorar. —*vi* teñirse. —*n* tinte, *m*; (colour) color, *m*. **fast dye,** tinte estable, *m*. **dye-house,** tintorería, *f*. **dye-stuff,** materia colorante, *f*. **dye-works,** tintorería, *f*

**dyed-in-the-wool** /'daid ən ðə 'wʊl/ *a* de pies a cabeza

**dyeing** /'daiɪŋ/ *n* teñidura, tintura, *f*; (as a trade) tintorería, *f*. **d. and dry-cleaning shop,** tintorería, *f*

**dyer** /'daiər/ *n* tintorero (-ra)

**dyestuff** /'dai,stʌf/ *n* materia colorante, materia de tinte, materia tintórea, *f*

**dying** /'daiɪŋ/ *a* moribundo, agonizante; de la muerte; (of light) mortecino; (last) último; supremo; (languishing) lánguido; (deathbed) hecho en su lecho mortuorio, *m*; estar agonizando; (of light) fenecer. **to be d. for,** estar muerto por

**dynamic** /dai'næmɪk/ *a* dinámico

**dynamics** /dai'næmɪks/ *n* dinámica, *f*

**dynamite** /'dainə,mait/ *n* dinamita, *f*

**dynamo** /'dainə,mou/ *n* dinamo, *f*

**dynastic** /dai'næstɪk/ *a* dinástico

**dynasty** /'dainəsti/ *n* dinastía, *f*

**dysentery** /'dɪsən,teri/ *n* disentería, *f*

**dyspepsia** /dɪs'pɛpʃə/ *n* dispepsia, *f*

**dyspeptic** /dɪs'pɛptɪk/ *a* dispéptico. —*n* dispéptico (-ca)

# E

e /i/ n (letter) e, f; Mus. mi, m
**each** /itʃ/ a cada (invariable), todo. —pron cada uno, m; cada una, f. **e. of them,** cada uno de ellos. **They help e. other,** Se ayudan mutuamente, Se ayudan entre sí. **to love e. other,** amarse
**eager** /'igər/ a impaciente; ansioso, deseoso; ambicioso
**eagerly** /'igərli/ adv con impaciencia; con ansia; ambiciosamente
**eagerness** /'igərnɪs/ n impaciencia, f; ansia, f, deseo, m; (promptness) alacridad, f; (zeal) fervor, m
**eagle** /'igəl/ n águila, f. **royal e.,** águila caudal, águila real, f. **e.-eyed,** con ojos de lince, de ojo avizor. **have the eyes of an e.,** tener ojos de lince, tener vista de lince
**ear** /ɪr/ n (outer ear) oreja, f; (inner ear and sense of hearing) oído, m; Bot. espiga, panoja, f. **to begin to show the ear,** (grain) espigar. **to be all ears,** ser todo oídos. **to give ear,** dar oído. **to have a good ear,** tener buen oído. **to play by ear,** tocar de oído. **to turn a deaf ear,** hacerse el sordo. **ear-ache,** dolor de oídos, m. **ear-drum,** tímpano (del oído), m. **ear-flap,** orejera, f. **ear-phone, ear-piece,** auricular, m. **ear-piercing,** penetrante, agudo. **ear-shot,** alcance del oído, m. **to be within ear-shot,** estar al alcance del oído. **ear-trumpet,** trompetilla, f. **ear wax,** cerilla, f
**eared** /ɪrd/ a con orejas; de orejas; Bot. con espigas
**earl** /ɜrl/ n conde, m
**earldom** /'ɜrldəm/ n condado, m
**earlier, earliest** /'ɜrliər; 'ɜrliɪst/ a compar and superl más temprano; más primitivo; más antiguo; (first, of time) primero. —adv más temprano; más pronto; antes
**earliness** /'ɜrlinɪs/ n lo temprano; antigüedad, f, lo primitivo; (precocity) precocidad, f. **The e. of his arrival,** La llegada de buena hora
**early** /'ɜrli/ a temprano; primitivo; (of fruit, etc.) temprano, adelantado; (movement) primero (e.g. early Romanticism, el primer romanticismo); (person) de la primera época (e.g. the early Cervantes, Cervantes de la primera época); (work) un primer (e.g. an early work of Unamuno's, una primera obra de Unamuno); (advanced) avanzado; (precocious) precoz; (first, of time) primero; (in the morning) matutino; (near) próximo; cercano; (premature) prematuro; (of child's age) tierno; joven. **in the e. hours,** en las primeras horas; en las altas horas (de la noche). **e. age,** edad temprana, tierna edad, f. **e.-fruiting,** Agr. tempranal. **e. riser,** madrugador (-ra). **e.-rising,** a madrugador. **e. years,** primeros años, años de la niñez, m pl
**early** /'ɜrli/ adv temprano; al principio (de); en los primeros días (de); desde los primeros días (de); (in the month, year) a principios (de); (in time) a tiempo; (in the day) de buena hora; (soon) pronto; (among the first) entre los primeros (de). **as e. as possible,** lo más temprano posible; lo más pronto posible. **to be e.,** llegar antes de tiempo; llegar de buena hora. **to get up e.,** madrugar. **to go to bed e.,** acostarse temprano. **too e.,** demasiado temprano. **e. in the morning,** de madrugada
**earmark** /'ɪr,mɑrk/ vt marcar; Fig. destinar, reservar
**earn** /ɜrn/ vt ganar; obtener, adquirir; (deserve) merecer
**earnable** /'ɜrnəbəl/ a ganable
**earnest** /'ɜrnɪst/ a serio; fervoroso; diligente; sincero. **to be in e. about something,** tomarlo en serio; ser sincero (en). **e. money,** arras, f pl
**earnestly** /'ɜrnɪstli/ adv seriamente; fervorosamente; con diligencia; sinceramente, de buena fe
**earnestness** /'ɜrnɪstnɪs/ n seriedad, f; fervor, celo, m; diligencia, f; sinceridad, buena fe, f
**earnings** /'ɜrnɪŋz/ n pl Com. ingresos, m pl; (salary) salario, m; estipendio, m; (of a workman) jornal, m
**earring** /'ɪr,rɪŋ/ n pendiente, arete, m
**earth** /ɜrθ/ n tierra, f; (of a badger, etc.) madriguera,

f; Radio. tierra, f. —vt cubrir con tierra; Radio. conectar con tierra. **clod of e.,** terrón, m. **half the e.,** Inf. medio mundo, m. **on e.,** en este mundo, sobre la tierra
**earthen** /'ɜrθən/ a terrizo, terroso; (of mud) de barro
**earthenware** /'ɜrθən,weər/ n alfar, m, —a de loza, de barro
**earthiness** /'ɜrθinɪs/ n terrosidad, f
**earthly** /'ɜrθli/ a terrestre, terrenal; de la tierra; (fleshly) carnal; (worldly) mundano; material. **There is not an e. chance,** No hay la más mínima posibilidad
**earthquake** /'ɜrθ,kweik/ n terremoto, temblor de tierra, m
**earth tremor** movimiento sísmico, m
**earthwork** /'ɜrθ,wɜrk/ n terraplén, m
**earthworm** /'ɜrθ,wɜrm/ n gusano de tierra, m
**earthy** /'ɜrθi/ a térreo, terroso
**earwig** /'ɪr,wɪg/ n tijereta, f
**ease** /iz/ n bienestar, m; tranquilidad, f; descanso, m; (leisure) ocio, m; (comfortableness) comodidad, f; (freedom from embarrassment) naturalidad, f, desembarazo, desenfado, m; (from pain) alivio, m; (simplicity) facilidad, f. —vt (widen) ensanchar; aflojar; (pain) aliviar; (lighten) aligerar; (moderate) moderar; (soften) suavizar; (free) librar; (one's mind) tranquilizar. **in my moments of e.,** en mis ocios, en mis momentos de ocio. **Stand at e.!** Mil. ¡En su lugar descansen! **to be at e.,** estar a sus anchas; encontrarse bien; comportarse con toda naturalidad. **with e.,** fácilmente. **to e. off,** vt (Naut. cables, sails) arriar. —vi sentirse menos, cesar
**easel** /'izəl/ n caballete (de pintor) m
**easily** /'izəli/ adv fácilmente. **The engine runs e.,** El motor marcha bien
**easiness** /'izinɪs/ n facilidad, f; sencillez, f; (of manner) desembarazo, m, naturalidad, f
**east** /ist/ n este, m; oriente, m, (of countries) Oriente, m; Levante, m. —a del este; del oriente; (of countries) de Oriente, oriental; levantino. **e. North e.,** estenordeste, m. **e. South e.,** estesudeste, m. **e. wind,** viento del este, m
**Easter** /'istər/ n Pascua de Resurrección, f. **E. egg,** huevo de Pascua, m. **E. Saturday,** sábado de gloria, m. **E. Sunday,** domingo de Pascua, m
**easterly** /'istərli/ a del este; al este. —adv hacia el este
**eastern** /'istərn/ a del este; de Oriente; oriental. —n oriental, mf
**easternmost** /'istərn,moust/ a situado más al este
**East Indies** Indias Orientales, f pl
**eastward** /'istwərd/ adv hacia el este, hacia oriente
**easy** /'izi/ a fácil; sencillo; (comfortable) cómodo; (free from pain) aliviado; Com. flojo; (well-off) acomodado, holgado; (calm) tranquilo; tolerante; natural; afable, condescendiente; (of virtue, women) fácil. —adv con calma; despacio. **I must make myself e. about,** he de tranquilizarme sobre. **Stand e.!** ¡En su lugar descansen! **to take it e.,** tomarlo con calma. **e.-chair,** (silla) poltrona, f. **easy come, easy go,** lo que por agua, agua (Mexico and Colombia), los dineros del sacristán cantando vienen y cantando se van (Spain). **e.-going,** acomodadizo; indolente; (morally) de manga ancha; (casual) descuidado
**eat** /it/ vt comer; (meals, soup, refreshments) tomar; (with a good, bad appetite) hacer; consumir; (corrode) corroer; desgastar. —vi comer; (Fam. of food) ser de buen (or mal) comer. **to eat one's breakfast (lunch),** tomar el desayuno, desayunar (almorzar). **to eat one's words,** retractarse. **to eat away,** comer; consumir; corroer. **to eat into,** (of chemicals) morder; (a fortune) consumir; gastar. **eat out of s. b.'s hand,** comer de la mano de fulano, comer en la mano de fulano. **to eat up,** devorar (also Fig.)
**eatable** /'itəbəl/ a comestible, comedero. —n pl **eatables,** comestibles, m pl

**eater** /'itər/ *n* el, *m*, (*f*, la) que come
**eating** /'itɪŋ/ *n* el comer; comida, *f*. **e. and drinking,** el comer y beber. **e.-house,** casa de comidas, *f*
**eau de cologne** /'ou də kə'loun/ *n* agua de Colonia, *f*
**eaves** /ivz/ *n* rafe, alero, *m*. **under the e.,** debajo del alero
**eavesdrop** /'ivzˌdrɒp/ *vi* escuchar a las puertas; fisgonear, espiar
**eavesdropper** /'ivzˌdrɒpər/ *n* fisgón (-ona)
**eavesdropping** /'ivzˌdrɒpɪŋ/ *n* fisgoneo, *m*
**ebb** /ɛb/ *n* (of the tide) reflujo, *m;* menguante, *f; Fig.* declinación, *f; Fig.* decadencia, *f;* (of life) vejez, *f*. —*vi* (of tide) menguar; declinar; decaer. **to ebb and flow,** fluir y refluir. **to ebb away from,** dejar; dejar aislado. **ebb-tide,** marea menguante, *f*
**ebonite** /'ɛbəˌnait/ *n* ebonita, *f*
**ebony** /'ɛbəni/ *n* ébano, *m*
**ebullience** /ɪ'bʌlyəns/ *n* efervescencia, exuberancia, *f*
**ebullient** /ɪ'bʌlyənt/ *a* efervescente, exuberante
**ebullition** /ˌɛbə'lɪʃən/ *n* (boiling) ebullición, *f*, hervor, *m; Fig.* efervescencia, *f*, estallido, *m*
**eccentric** /ɪk'sɛntrɪk/ *a Geom.* excéntrico; raro, original; extravagante, excéntrico. —*n* persona excéntrica, *f*, original, *m*
**eccentrically** /ɪk'sɛntrɪkəli/ *adv* excéntricamente
**eccentricity** /ˌɛksən'trɪsɪti/ *n Geom.* excentricidad, *f;* rareza, extravagancia, excentricidad, *f*
**Ecclesiastes** /ɪˌkliziˈæstiz/ *n* Eclesiastés, *m*
**ecclesiastic** /ɪˌkliziˈæstɪk/ *a* eclesiástico. —*n* eclesiástico, clérigo, *m*
**ecclesiastically** /ɪˌkliziˈæstɪkəli/ *adv* eclesiásticamente
**echo** /'ɛkou/ *n* eco, *m;* reverberación, resonancia, *f*. —*vt* repercutir; *Fig.* repetir. —*vi* resonar, retumbar, reverberar
**echoing** /'ɛkouɪŋ/ *a* retumbante. —*n* eco, *m*
**eclectic** /ɪ'klɛktɪk/ *a* and *n* ecléctico (-ca)
**eclecticism** /ɪ'klɛktəˌsɪzəm/ *n* eclecticismo, *m*
**eclipse** /ɪ'klɪps/ *n Astron.* eclipse, *m*, *vt* eclipsar, hacer eclipse a. **to be in e.,** estar en eclipse
**ecliptic** /ɪ'klɪptɪk/ *n Astron.* eclíptica, *f*, *a* eclíptico
**eclogue** /'ɛklɔg/ *n* égloga, *f*
**economic** /ˌɛkə'nɒmɪk, ˌikə-/ *a* económico
**economical** /ˌɛkə'nɒmɪkəl, ˌikə-/ *a* económico
**economics** /ˌɛkə'nɒmɪks, ˌikə-/ *n* economía política, *f*
**economist** /ɪ'kɒnəmɪst/ *n* economista, *mf*
**economize** /ɪ'kɒnəˌmaiz/ *vt* economizar, ahorrar. —*vi* hacer economías
**economy** /ɪ'kɒnəmi/ *n* economía, *f*. **domestic e.,** economía doméstica, *f*. **political e.,** economía política, *f*
**ecstasy** /'ɛkstəsi/ *n* éxtasis, arrebato, *m;* transporte, *m*. **to be in e.,** estar en éxtasis
**ecstatic** /ɛk'stætɪk/ *a* extático
**Ecuador** /'ɛkwəˌdɔr/ el Ecuador
**Ecuadorian** /ˌɛkwə'dɔriən/ *a* and *n* ecuatoriano (-na)
**ecumenical** /'ɛkyʊ'mɛnɪkəl/ *a* ecuménico
**eczema** /'ɛksəmə/ *n* eczema, *f*
**eddy** /'ɛdi/ *n* remolino, *m*, *vi* remolinar; *Fig.* remolinear
**edelweiss** /'eidlˌwais/ *n* inmortal de las nieves, *f*
**edema** /ɪ'dimə/ *n Med.* edema, *m*
**Eden** /'idn/ *n* Edén, *m*
**edge** /ɛdʒ/ *n* (of sharp instruments) filo, *m;* (of a skate) cuchilla, *f;* margen, *mf;* (shore) orilla, *f;* (of two surfaces) arista, *f;* (of books) borde, *m;* (of a coin) canto, *m;* (of a chair, a precipice, a forest, a curb, etc.) borde, *m;* (extreme) extremidad, *f*. **on e.,** de canto; *Fig.* ansioso. **to be on e.,** *Fig.* tener los nervios en punta. **to set on e.,** poner de canto; (of teeth) dar dentera
**edge** /ɛdʒ/ *vt* (sharpen) afilar; *Sew.* ribetear; orlar; poner un borde (a); (cut) cortar. **to e. away,** escurrirse. **to e. into,** *vt* insinuarse. —*vi* deslizarse en. **to e. out,** salir poco a poco
**edged** /ɛdʒd/ *a* afilado, cortante; (in compounds) de... filos; (bordered) bordeado; (of books) de bordes...
**edgeways** /'ɛdʒweiz/ *adv* de lado; de canto. **He couldn't get a word in e.,** No pudo meter baza en la conversación

**edging** /'ɛdʒɪŋ/ *n* borde, *m;* ribete, *m*
**edibility** /ˌɛdə'bɪlɪti/ *n* el ser comestible
**edible** /'ɛdəbəl/ *a* comestible
**edict** /'idɪkt/ *n* edicto, *m*
**edification** /ˌɛdəfɪ'keiʃən/ *n* edificación, *f*
**edifice** /'ɛdəfɪs/ *n* edificio, *m*
**edify** /'ɛdəˌfai/ *vt* edificar
**edifying** /'ɛdəˌfaiɪŋ/ *a* edificante, edificador, de edificación
**Edinburgh** /'ɛdnˌbərə/ Edinburgo, *m*
**edit** /'ɛdɪt/ *vt* editar; (a newspaper, journal) ser director de; (prepare for press) redactar; (correct) corregir
**editing** /'ɛdɪtɪŋ/ *n* trabajo editorial, *m;* redacción, *f;* dirección, *f;* corrección, *f*
**edition** /ɪ'dɪʃən/ *n* edición, *f; Print.* tirada, *f*. **first e.,** edición príncipe, *f*. **miniature e.,** edición diamante, *f*
**editor** /'ɛdɪtər/ *n* (of a book) editor (-ra); (of a newspaper, journal) director (-ra)
**editorial** /ˌɛdɪ'tɔriəl/ *a* de redacción; editorial. —*n* editorial, artículo de fondo, *m*. **e. staff,** redacción, *f*
**editorial board** consejo de redacción, *m*
**editorship** /'ɛdɪtərˌʃɪp/ *n* dirección (de un periódico, de una revista), *f*
**educability** /ˌɛdʒəkə'bɪlɪti/ *n* educabilidad, *f*
**educable** /'ɛdʒʊkəbəl/ *a* educable
**educate** /'ɛdʒʊˌkeit/ *vt* educar; formar; (accustom) acostumbrar
**educated** /'ɛdʒʊˌkeitɪd/ *a* culto
**education** /ˌɛdʒʊ'keiʃən/ *n* educación, *f;* enseñanza, *f;* pedagogía, *f*. **chair of e.,** cátedra de pedagogía, *f*. **early e.,** primeras letras, *f pl*. **higher e.,** enseñanza superior, *f*
**educational** /ˌɛdʒʊ'keiʃənl/ *a* educativo; pedagógico; instructivo
**educationalist** /ˌɛdʒə'keiʃənlɪst/ *n* pedagogo, *m*
**educative** /'ɛdʒʊˌkeitɪv/ *a* educativo
**educator** /'ɛdʒʊˌkeitər/ *n* educador (-ra)
**educe** /ɪ'dus/ *vt* educir; deducir; *Chem.* extraer
**eduction** /ɪ'dʌkʃən/ *n* educción, *f*
**Edwardian** /ɛd'wɔrdiən/ *a* and *n* eduardiano (-na)
**eel** /il/ *n* anguila, *f*. **electric eel,** gimnoto, *m*. **eel-basket,** nasa para anguilas, *f*
**eerie** /'ɪəri/ *a* misterioso, fantástico; sobrenatural; lúgubre
**eerily** /'ɪərəli/ *adv* fantásticamente; de modo sobrenatural
**eeriness** /'ɪərinɪs/ *n* ambiente de misterio, *m;* efecto misterioso, *m*
**efface** /ɪ'feis/ *vt* borrar, destruir; quitar. **to e. oneself,** retirarse; permanecer en el fondo
**effacement** /ɪ'feismənt/ *n* borradura, *f*
**effect** /ɪ'fɛkt/ *n* efecto, *m;* impresión, *f;* (result) resultado, *m*, consecuencia, *f,* (meaning) substancia, *f,* significado, *m; pl* **effects,** efectos, bienes, *m pl*. —*vt* efectuar; producir. **in e.,** en efecto, efectivamente. **of no e.,** inútil. **striving after e.,** efectismo, *m*. **to feel the effects of,** sentir los efectos de; padecer las consecuencias de. **to put into e.,** poner en práctica; hacer efectivo. **to take e.,** producir efecto; ponerse en vigor
**effective** /ɪ'fɛktɪv/ *a* eficaz; (striking) de mucho efecto, poderoso, vistoso. **to make e.,** llevar a efecto
**effectively** /ɪ'fɛktɪvli/ *adv* eficazmente; (strikingly) con gran efecto; efectivamente, en efecto
**effectiveness** /ɪ'fɛktɪvnɪs/ *n* eficacia, *f;* efecto, *m*
**effectuate** /ɪ'fɛktʃuˌeit/ *vt* efectuar
**effeminacy** /ɪ'fɛmənəsi/ *n* afeminación, *f*
**effeminate** /ɪ'fɛmənɪt/ *a* afeminado, adamado. **to make e.,** afeminar
**efferent** /'ɛfərənt/ *a* eferente
**effervesce** /ˌɛfər'vɛs/ *vi* estar efervescente, hervir
**effervescence** /ˌɛfər'vɛsəns/ *n* efervescencia, *f*
**effervescent** /ˌɛfər'vɛsənt/ *a* efervescente
**effete** /ɪ'fit/ *a* gastado; estéril; decadente
**effeteness** /ɪ'fitnɪs/ *n* decadencia, *f;* esterilidad, *f*
**efficacious** /ˌɛfɪ'keiʃəs/ *a* eficaz
**efficacy** /'ɛfɪkəsi/ *n* eficacia, *f*
**efficiency** /ɪ'fɪʃənsi/ *n* eficiencia, *f;* buen estado, *m;* habilidad, *f; Mech.* rendimiento, *m*
**efficient** /ɪ'fɪʃənt/ *a* (e.g. medicine) eficaz; eficiente; (person) competente, capaz

**efficiently** /ɪˈfɪʃəntli/ *adv* eficientemente; eficazmente; competentemente

**effigy** /ˈɛfɪdʒi/ *n* efigie, imagen, *f*

**efflorescence** /ˌɛfləˈrɛsəns/ *n Chem.* eflorescencia, *f; Bot.* florescencia, *f*

**effluvium** /ɪˈfluviəm/ *n* efluvio, *m*

**effort** /ˈɛfərt/ *n* esfuerzo, *m.* **to make an e.,** hacer un esfuerzo. **make every effort to,** hacer lo posible por + *Inf.*; empeñar sus máximos esfuerzos en el sentido de + *Inf.*

**effortless** /ˈɛfərtlɪs/ *a* sin esfuerzo

**effrontery** /ɪˈfrʌntəri/ *n* descaro, *m,* insolencia, *f*

**effulgence** /ɪˈfʌldʒəns/ *n* esplendor, fulgor, *m*

**effulgent** /ɪˈfʌldʒənt/ *a* fulgente, resplandeciente

**effusion** /ɪˈfyuʒən/ *n* efusión, *f*

**effusive** /ɪˈfyusɪv/ *a* efusivo, expansivo

**egg** /ɛg/ *n* huevo, *m.* **to egg on,** incitar (a). **boiled egg,** huevo cocido, *m.* **fried egg,** huevo frito, *m.* **hard egg,** huevo duro, *m.* **poached egg,** huevo escalfado, *m.* **scrambled egg,** huevos revueltos, *m pl.* **soft egg,** huevo pasado por agua, *m.* **to lay eggs,** poner huevos. **to put all one's eggs in one basket,** *Fig.* poner toda la carne en el asador. **egg-cup,** huevera, *f.* **egg dealer,** vendedor (-ra) de huevos. **egg flip,** huevo batido con ron, *m.* **eggplant,** berenjena, *f.* **egg-shaped,** aovado. **egg-shell,** cascarón, *m,* cáscara de huevo, *f.* **egg-shell china,** loza muy fina, *f.* **egg-spoon,** cucharita para comer huevos, *f.* **egg-whisk,** batidor de huevos, *m*

**ego** /ˈigou/ *n* yo

**egoism** /ˈigou,ɪzəm/ *n* egoísmo, *m*

**egoist** /ˈigouɪst/ *n* egoísta, *mf*

**egoistic** /ˌigouˈɪstɪk/ *a* egoísta

**egoistically** /ˌigouˈɪstɪkəli/ *adv* egoístamente

**egotism** /ˈigə,tɪzəm/ *n* egotismo, *m,* egolatría, *f*

**egotist** /ˈigətɪst/ *n* egotista, *mf*

**egotistic** /ˌigəˈtɪstɪk/ *a* egotista

**egregious** /ɪˈgridʒəs/ *a* notorio

**egress** /ˈigrɛs/ *n* salida, *f*

**Egypt** /ˈidʒɪpt/ Egipto, *m*

**Egyptian** /ɪˈdʒɪpʃən/ *a* egipcio. —*n* egipcio (-ia); cigarrillo egipcio, *m*

**Egyptologist** /ˌidʒɪpˈtɒlədʒɪst/ *n* egiptólogo (-ga)

**Egyptology** /ˌidʒɪpˈtɒlədʒi/ *n* egiptología, *f*

**eh?** /ei/ *interj* ¿eh? ¿qué?

**eider** /ˈaidər/ *n Ornith.* pato de flojel, *m*

**eiderdown** /ˈaidər,daun/ edredón, *m*

**eight** /eit/ *a* and *n* ocho *m.* **He is e. years old,** Tiene ocho años. **It is e. o'clock,** Son las ocho. **e.-day clock,** reloj con cuerda para ocho días, *m.* **e. hundred,** *a* and *n* ochocientos *m..* **e.-syllabled,** octosilábico

**eighteen** /ˈeiˈtin/ *a* and *n* diez y ocho, *m.*

**eighteenth** /ˈeiˈtinθ/ *a* décimoctavo; (of the month) (el) diez y ocho, diec-iocho; (of monarchs) diez y ocho. —*n* décimoctava parte, *f.* **Louis the E.,** Luis diez y ocho

**eightfold** /ˈeit,fould/ *a* óctuple

**eighth** /eitθ, eiθ/ *a* octavo, *m;* (of the month) (el) ocho; (of monarchs) octavo. —*n* octavo, *m*

**eighthly** /ˈeitθli/ *adv* en octavo lugar

**eightieth** /ˈeitiɪθ/ *a* octogésima

**eighty** /ˈeiti/ *a* and *n* ochenta, *m.*

**either** /ˈiðər/ *a* and *pron* uno u otro, cualquiera de los dos; ambos (-as). —*conjunc* o (becomes **u** before words beginning with **o** or **ho**). —*adv* tampoco. **I do not like e.,** No me gusta ni el uno ni el otro (ni la una ni la otra). **e.... or,** o.... o

**ejaculate** /ɪˈdʒækyə,leit/ *vt* exclamar, lanzar; *Med.* eyacular

**ejaculation** /ɪ,dʒækyəˈleiʃən/ *n* exclamación, *f; Med.* eyaculación, *f*

**ejaculatory** /ɪˈdʒækyələ,tɔri/ *a* jaculatorio

**eject** /ɪˈdʒɛkt/ *vt* echar, expulsar; *Law.* desahuciar; (emit) despedir, emitir

**ejection** /ɪˈdʒɛkʃən/ *n* echamiento, *m,* expulsión, *f; Law.* desahúcio, *m;* (emission) emisión, *f*

**eke** /ik/ (out) *vt* aumentar, añadir a

**elaborate** /*a* ɪˈlæbərɪt/ *v* -ə,reit/ *a* elaborado; primoroso; elegante; complicado; (detailed) detallado;

(of meals) de muchos platos; (of courtesy, etc.) estudiado. —*vt* elaborar; amplificar

**elaborately** /ɪˈlæbərɪtli/ *adv* primorosamente; elegantemente; complicadamente; con muchos detalles

**elaborateness** /ɪˈlæbərɪtnɪs/ *n* primor, *m;* elegancia, *f;* complicación, *f;* (care) cuidado, *m;* minuciosidad, *f*

**elaboration** /ɪ,læbəˈreiʃən/ *n* elaboración, *f*

**elapse** /ɪˈlæps/ *vi* transcurrir, andar, pasar

**elastic** /ɪˈlæstɪk/ *a* elástico. —*n* elástico, *m.* **e. band,** anillo de goma, *m;* cinta de goma, *f.* **e. girdle,** faja elástica, *f*

**elasticity** /ɪlæˈstɪsɪti/ *n* elasticidad, *f*

**elate** /ɪˈleit/ *vt* alegrar; animar

**elatedly** /ɪˈleitɪdli/ *adv* alegremente; triunfalmente

**elation** /ɪˈleiʃən/ *n* alegría, *f,* júbilo, *m;* triunfo, *m*

**elbow** /ˈɛlbou/ *n* codo, *m;* ángulo, *m;* (of a chair) brazo, *m.* —*vt* codear, dar codazos (a). **at one's e.,** a la mano. **nudge with the e.,** codazo, *m.* **to be out at e.,** enseñar los codos, tener los codos raídos; ser harapiento. **to e. one's way,** abrirse paso a codazos. **e.-chair,** silla de brazos, *f.* **e.-grease,** jugo de muñeca, *m.* **e.-piece** or **patch,** codera, *f.* **e. room,** libertad de movimiento, *f*

**elder** /ˈɛldər/ *a compar* mayor. —*n* persona mayor, *f;* señor mayor, *m;* (among Jews and in early Christian Church) anciano, *m; Bot.* saúco, *m*

**elderly** /ˈɛldərli/ *a* mayor

**eldest** /ˈɛldɪst/ *a superl* old (el, la, etc.) mayor. **e. daughter,** hija mayor, *f.* **e. son,** hijo mayor, *m*

**elect** /ɪˈlɛkt/ *vt* elegir. —*a* elegido; predestinado. —*n* electo, *m;* elegido, *m*

**election** /ɪˈlɛkʃən/ *n Theol.* predestinación, *f;* elección, *f.* **by-e.,** elección parcial, *f*

**electioneer** /ɪ,lɛkʃəˈnɪər/ *vi* solicitar votos; distribuir propaganda electoral

**electioneering** /ɪ,lɛkʃəˈnɪərɪŋ/ *n* solicitación de votos, *f;* propaganda electoral, *f*

**elective** /ɪˈlɛktɪv/ *a* electivo. —*n* (subject at school) materia optativa, *f*

**elector** /ɪˈlɛktər/ *n* elector (-ra); (prince) elector, *m*

**electoral** /ɪˈlɛktərəl/ *a* electoral. **e. register,** lista electoral, *f*

**electoral college** colegio de compromisarios, *m*

**electorate** /ɪˈlɛktərɪt/ *n* electorado, *m*

**electric, electrical** /ɪˈlɛktrɪk; ɪˈlɛktrɪkəl/ *a* eléctrico; *Fig.* vivo, instantáneo. **e. arc,** arco voltaico, *m.* **e. engineer,** ingeniero electricista, *m.* **electric fan,** (Spain) ventilador, (Western Hemisphere) ventilador eléctrico, *m.* **e. fire,** estufa eléctrica, *f.* **e. immersion heater,** calentador de agua eléctrico, *m.* **e. light,** luz eléctrica, *f.* **e. pad,** alfombrilla eléctrica, *f.* **e. shock,** conmoción eléctrica, *f.* **e. washing-machine,** lavadora eléctrica, *f.* **e. wire** or **cable,** conductor eléctrico, *m*

**electrically** /ɪˈlɛktrɪkəli/ *adv* por electricidad

**electrician** /ɪlɛkˈtrɪʃən/ *n* electricista, *mf*

**electricity** /ɪlɛkˈtrɪsɪti/ *n* electricidad, *f*

**electrification** /ɪ,lɛktrəfɪˈkeiʃən/ *n* electrificación, *f*

**electrify** /ɪˈlɛktrə,fai/ *vt* electrificar; *Fig.* electrizar

**electro-** *prefix* (in compounds) electro. **e.-chemistry,** electroquímica, *f.* **e.-dynamics,** electrodinámica, *f.* **e.-magnet,** electroimán, *m.* **e.-magnetic,** electromagnético. **e.-plate,** *vt* galvanizar, platear. —*n* artículo galvanizado, *m.* **e.-therapy,** electroterapia, *f*

**electrocute** /ɪˈlɛktrə,kyut/ *vt* electrocutar

**electrocution** /ɪ,lɛktrəˈkyuʃən/ *n* electrocución, *f*

**electrode** /ɪˈlɛktroud/ *n* electrodo, *m*

**electrolysis** /ɪlɛkˈtrɒləsɪs/ *n* electrólisis, *f*

**electrolyte** /ɪˈlɛktrə,lait/ *n* electrólito, *m*

**electrolyze** /ɪˈlɛktrə,laiz/ *vt* electrolizar

**electrometer** /ɪlɛkˈtrɒmɪtər/ *n* electrómetro, *m*

**electromotive** /ɪ,lɛktrəˈmoutɪv/ *a* electromotriz. **e. force,** fuerza electromotriz, *f*

**electron** /ɪˈlɛktrɒn/ *n* electrón, *m*

**electroscope** /ɪˈlɛktrə,skoup/ *n* electroscopio, *m*

**elegance** /ˈɛlɪgəns/ *n* elegancia, *f*

**elegant** /ˈɛlɪgənt/ *a* elegante; bello

**elegantly** /ˈɛlɪgəntli/ *adv* elegantemente, con elegancia

**elegiac** /ˌɛlɪˈdʒaiək/ *a* elegíaco

**elegy** /ˈɛlɪdʒi/ *n* elegía, *f*

**element** /ˈɛləmənt/ *n* elemento, *m;* factor, *m;* in-

grediente, *m;* *Elec.* par, elemento, *m;* *Chem.* *Phys.*
cuerpo simple, *m;* *pl* **elements,** rudimentos, *m pl,*
nociones, *f pl;* (weather) intemperie, *f;* (Eucharist) el
pan y el vino. **to be in one's e.,** estar en su elemento
**elemental** /ˌɛləˈmɛntḷ/ *a* elemental; rudimentario, lo
elemental
**elementariness** /ˌɛləˈmɛntərɪnɪs/ *n* el carácter, elemental
**elementary** /ˌɛləˈmɛntəri/ *a* elemental; rudimentario;
primario. **e. education,** enseñanza primaria, *f*
**elephant** /ˈɛləfənt/ *n* elefante (-ta). **e. keeper** or
**trainer,** naire, *m*
**elephantiasis** /ˌɛləfənˈtaɪəsɪs/ *n* elefantíasis, *f*
**elephantine** /ˌɛləˈfæntin/ *a* elefantino
**elevate** /ˈɛləˌveɪt/ *vt* (the Host) alzar; elevar; (the
eyes, the voice) levantar; (honor) enaltecer
**elevated** /ˈɛləˌveɪtɪd/ *a* noble, elevado, sublime; edificante; (drunk) achispado
**elevation** /ˌɛləˈveɪʃən/ *n* elevación, *f;* enaltecimiento,
*m;* (of style, thought) nobleza, sublimidad, *f;* (hill)
eminencia, altura, *f*
**elevator** /ˈɛləˌveɪtər/ *n* (lift) ascensor, *m;* (for grain,
etc.) montacargas, *m*
**elevator shaft** caja, *f,* hueco pozo, *m*
**eleven** /ɪˈlɛvən/ *a* once. **—n** once, *m.* **It is e. o'clock,**
Son las once
**eleventh** /ɪˈlɛvənθ/ *a* onceno, undécimo; (of month)
(el) once; (of monarchs) once. **—n** onzavo, *m;* undé-
cima parte, *f.* **at the e. hour,** *Fig.* a última hora.
**Louis the E.,** Luis once (XI)
**elf** /ɛlf/ *n* elfo, duende, *m;* (child) trasgo, *m;* (dwarf)
enano, *m*
**elfin** /ˈɛlfɪn/ *a* de duendes; de hada
**elicit** /ɪˈlɪsɪt/ *vt* sacar; hacer contestar; hacer confesar;
descubrir
**elicitation** /ɪˌlɪsɪˈteɪʃən/ *n* descubrimiento, *m*
**elide** /ɪˈlaɪd/ *vt* elidir
**eligibility** /ˌɛlɪdʒəˈbɪlɪti/ *n* elegibilidad, *f*
**eligible** /ˈɛlɪdʒəbəl/ *a* elegible; deseable
**eliminate** /ɪˈlɪməˌneɪt/ *vt* eliminar; quitar
**elimination** /ɪˌlɪməˈneɪʃən/ *n* eliminación, *f*
**eliminatory** /ɪˈlɪmənəˌtɔri/ *a* eliminador
**elision** /ɪˈlɪʒən/ *n* elisión, *f*
**elite** /ɪˈlit/ *n* nata, flor, *f*
**elixir** /ɪˈlɪksər/ *n* elixir, *m*
**Elizabethan** /ɪˌlɪzəˈbiθən/ *a* de la época de la Reina
Isabel I de Inglaterra
**elk** /ɛlk/ *n* ante, *m*
**ell** /ɛl/ *n* (measure) ana, *f*
**ellipse** /ɪˈlɪps/ *n* *Geom.* elipse, *f;* óvalo, *m*
**ellipsis** /ɪˈlɪpsɪs/ *n* *Gram.* elipsis, *f*
**elliptic** /ɪˈlɪptɪk/ *a* *Geom.* *Gram.* elíptico
**elm** /ɛlm/ *n* olmo, *m.* **e. grove,** olmeda, *f*
**elocution** /ˌɛləˈkyuʃən/ *n* elocución, *f;* (art of elocution) declamación, *f*
**elocutionist** /ˌɛləˈkyuʃənɪst/ *n* recitador (-ra), declamador (-ra)
**elongate** /ɪˈlɔŋɡeɪt/ *vt* alargar; extender. **—vi**
alargarse; extenderse. **—a** alargado; (of face) perfilado
**elongation** /ɪlɔŋˈɡeɪʃən/ *n* alargamiento, *m;* prolongación, *f;* extensión, *f*
**elope** /ɪˈloup/ *vi* evadirse, huir; fugarse (con un
amante)
**elopement** /ɪˈloupmənt/ *n* fuga, *f*
**eloquence** /ˈɛləkwəns/ *n* elocuencia, *f*
**eloquent** /ˈɛləkwənt/ *a* elocuente
**eloquently** /ˈɛləkwəntli/ *adv* elocuentemente
**else** /ɛls/ *adv* (besides) más; (instead) otra cosa, más;
(otherwise) si no, de otro modo. **anyone e.,** (cualquier) otra persona; alguien más. **Anything e.?** ¿Algo
más? **everyone e.,** todos los demás. **everything e.,**
todo lo demás. **nobody e.,** ningún otro, nadie más.
**nothing e.,** nada más. **or e.,** o bien, de otro modo; si
no. **someone e.,** otra persona, otro. **somewhere e.,**
en otra parte. **There's nothing e. to do,** No hay nada
más que hacer; No hay más remedio
**elsewhere** /ˈɛlsˌwɛər/ *adv* a, or en, otra parte
**elucidate** /ɪˈlusɪˌdeɪt/ *vt* elucidar, aclarar
**elucidation** /ɪˌlusɪˈdeɪʃən/ *n* elucidación, aclaración, *f*
**elucidatory** /ɪˈlusɪdəˌtɔri/ *a* aclaratorio

**elude** /ɪˈlud/ *vt* eludir, evitar
**elusive** /ɪˈlusɪv/ *a* (of persons) esquivo; fugaz; difícil
de comprender
**elusiveness** /ɪˈlusɪvnɪs/ *n* esquivez, *f;* fugacidad, *f*
**Elysian** /ɪˈlɪʒən/ *a* elíseo. **E. Fields,** campos elíseos, *m*
*pl*
**Elysium** /ɪˈlɪʒiəm/ *n* elíseo, *m*
**emaciate** /ɪˈmeɪʃiˌeɪt/ *vt* extenuar, demacrar, enflaquecer
**emaciated** /ɪˈmeɪʃiˌeɪtɪd/ *a* extenuado, demacrado. **to
become e.,** demacrarse
**emaciation** /ɪˌmeɪʃiˈeɪʃən/ *n* demacración, emaciación, *f;* *Med.* depauperación, *f*
**e-mail** /ˈiˌmeɪl/ *n* correo electrónico, *m*
**emanate** /ˈɛməˌneɪt/ *vi* emanar (de), proceder (de)
**emanation** /ˌɛməˈneɪʃən/ *n* emanación, *f;* exhalación,
*f*
**emancipate** /ɪˈmænsəˌpeɪt/ *vt* emancipar
**emancipated** /ɪˈmænsəˌpeɪtɪd/ *a* emancipado
**emancipation** /ɪˌmænsəˈpeɪʃən/ *n* emancipación, *f*
**emancipator** /ɪˈmænsəˌpeɪtər/ *n* emancipador (-ra),
libertador (-ra)
**emancipatory** /ɪˈmænsəpəˌtɔri/ *a* emancipador
**emasculate** /a ɪˈmæskyəlɪt/ *v* -ˌleɪt/ *a* afeminado.
**—vt** emascular; *Fig.* afeminar; mutilar
**emasculation** /ɪˌmæskyəˈleɪʃən/ *n* emasculación, *f*
**embalm** /ɛmˈbam/ *vt* embalsamar; *Fig.* conservar el
recuerdo de; perfumar
**embalmer** /ɛmˈbamər/ *n* embalsamador, *m*
**embalmment** /ɛmˈbammənt/ *n* embalsamamiento, *m*
**embankment** /ɛmˈbæŋkmənt/ *n* declive, *m;* ribera, *f;*
terraplén, *m;* dique, *m;* (quay) muelle, *m*
**embargo** /ɛmˈbargou/ *n* embargo, *m,* *vt* embargar.
**to put an e. on,** embargar. **to remove an e.,** sacar
de embargo
**embark** /ɛmˈbark/ *vi* embarcarse; lanzarse (a). **—vt**
embarcar
**embarkation** /ˌɛmbarˈkeɪʃən/ *n* (of persons) embarcación, *f;* (of goods) embarque, *m*
**embarrass** /ɛmˈbærəs/ *vt* impedir; (financially) apurar; (perplex) tener perplejo; (worry) preocupar;
(confuse) desconcertar, turbar; (annoy) molestar
**embarrassed** /ɛmˈbærəst/ *a* turbado
**embarrassing** /ɛmˈbærəsɪŋ/ *a* embarazoso; desconcertante; molesto
**embarrassingly** /ɛmˈbærəsɪŋli/ *adv* de un modo desconcertante; demasiado
**embarrassment** /ɛmˈbærəsmənt/ *n* impedimento, *m;*
(financial) apuro, *m;* (obligation) compromiso, *m;*
(perplexity) perplejidad, *f;* (worry) preocupación, *f;*
(confusion) turbación, *f*
**embassy** /ˈɛmbəsi/ *n* embajada, *f*
**embattled** /ɛmˈbætḷd/ *a* en orden de batalla; *Herald.*
almenado
**embed** /ɛmˈbɛd/ *vt* empotrar, enclavar; fijar
**embellish** /ɛmˈbɛlɪʃ/ *vt* embellecer; adornar
**embellishment** /ɛmˈbɛlɪʃmənt/ *n* embellecimiento, *m;*
adorno, *m*
**ember** /ˈɛmbər/ *n* rescoldo, *m.* **E. days,** témporas, *f*
*pl*
**embezzle** /ɛmˈbɛzəl/ *vt* desfalcar
**embezzlement** /ɛmˈbɛzəlmənt/ *n* desfalco, *m*
**embezzler** /ɛmˈbɛzlər/ *n* desfalcador (-ra)
**embitter** /ɛmˈbɪtər/ *vt* *Fig.* amargar; envenenar
**embittering** /ɛmˈbɪtərɪŋ/ *a* amargo
**embitterment** /ɛmˈbɪtərmənt/ *n* amargura, *f*
**emblazon** /ɛmˈbleɪzən/ *vt* blasonar; *Fig.* ensalzar
**emblem** /ˈɛmbləm/ *n* emblema, *m*
**emblematic** /ˌɛmbləˈmætɪk/ *a* emblemático
**embodiment** /ɛmˈbɒdimənt/ *n* incarnación, *f;* expresión, *f;* personificación, *f;* símbolo, *m;* síntesis, *f*
**embody** /ɛmˈbɒdi/ *vt* encarnar; expresar; personificar; incorporar; contener; formular; sintetizar. **to be
embodied in,** quedar plasmado en
**embolden** /ɛmˈbouldən/ *vt* animar, dar valor (a)
**embolism** /ˈɛmbəˌlɪzəm/ *n* *Med.* embolia, *f*
**emboss** /ɛmˈbɔs/ *vt* repujar, abollonar; estampar en
relieve
**embossment** /ɛmˈbɔsmənt/ *n* abolladura, *f;* relieve,
*m*
**embrace** /ɛmˈbreɪs/ *n* abrazo, *m.* **—vt** abrazar, dar un

abrazo (a); (*Fig.*. seize) aprovechar; (accept) aceptar; adoptar; (engage in) dedicarse a; (comprise) incluir, abarcar; (comprehend) comprender. **They embraced,** Se abrazaron

**embroider** /ɛm'brɔɪdər/ *vt* bordar; embellecer; (a tale, etc.) exagerar; *vi* hacer bordado

**embroiderer** /ɛm'brɔɪdərər/ *n* bordador (-ra)

**embroidery** /ɛm'brɔɪdəri, dri/ *n* bordado, *m;* labor, *f.* **e.-frame,** bastidor, *m.* **e. silk,** hilo de bordar, *m*

**embroil** /ɛm'brɔɪl/ *vt* enredar, embrollar; desordenar

**embryo** /'ɛmbri,ou/ *n* embrión, *m; Fig.* germen, *m.* —*a* embrionario

**embryology** /ˌɛmbri'ɒlədʒi/ *n* embriología, *f*

**embryonic** /ˌɛmbri'ɒnɪk/ *a* embrionario

**emend** /ɪ'mɛnd/ *vt* enmendar; corregir

**emendation** /ˌimən'deɪʃən/ *n* enmienda, *f;* corrección, *f*

**emerald** /'ɛmərəld/ *n* esmeralda, *f, a* de color de esmeralda. **e. green,** verde esmeralda, *m*

**emerge** /ɪ'mɜrdʒ/ *vt* emerger; surgir; *Fig.* salir; aparecer

**emergence** /ɪ'mɜrdʒəns/ *n* emergencia, *f;* salida, *f;* aparición, *f*

**emergency** /ɪ'mɜrdʒənsi/ *n* urgencia, *f;* necesidad, *f;* emergencia, *f;* aprieto, *m.* **e. exit,** salida de urgencia, *f.* **e. port,** *Naut.* puerto de arribada, *m*

**emergent** /ɪ'mɜrdʒənt/ *a* emergente; que sale; naciente

**emery** /'ɛməri/ *n* esmeril, *m.* **to polish with e.,** esmerilar. **e.-paper,** papel de lija, *m*

**emetic** /ɪ'mɛtɪk/ *a* and *n* emético, vomitivo, *m*

**emigrant** /'ɛmɪɡrənt/ *a* emigrante. —*n* emigrante, *mf* emigrado, *m*

**emigrate** /'ɛmɪˌɡreɪt/ *vi* emigrar; *Inf.* trasladarse

**emigration** /ˌɛmə'ɡreɪʃən/ *n* emigración, *f.* **e. officer,** oficial de emigración, *m*

**eminence** /'ɛmənəns/ *n* (hill) elevación, prominencia, *f;* eminencia (also as title), *f;* distinción, *f*

**eminent** /'ɛmənənt/ *a* distinguido, eminente; famoso, ilustre; notable; conspicuo

**eminently** /'ɛmənəntli/ *adv* eminentemente

**emir** /ə'mɪər/ *n* amir, *m*

**emissary** /'ɛmə,sɛri/ *n* emisario (-ia); embajador (-ra); agente, *m*

**emission** /ɪ'mɪʃən/ *n* emisión, *f*

**emit** /ɪ'mɪt/ *vt* despedir; exhalar; emitir

**emollient** /ɪ'mɒlyənt/ *a* emoliente, lenitivo. —*n* emoliente, *m*

**emolument** /ɪ'mɒlyəmənt/ *n* emolumento, *m*

**emotion** /ɪ'mouʃən/ *n* emoción, *f.* **to cause e.,** emocionar

**emotional** /ɪ'mouʃənḷ/ *a* emocional, sentimental; emocionante

**emotionalism** /ɪ'mouʃənḷ'ɪzəm/ *n* sentimentalismo, *m*

**emotionalize** /ɪ'mouʃənḷˌaɪz/ *vt* considerar bajo un punto de vista sentimental

**emotionally** /ɪ'mouʃənḷi/ *adv* con emoción, sentimentalmente

**emotionless** /ɪ'mouʃənlɪs/ *a* sin emoción

**emotive** /ɪ'moutɪv/ *a* emotivo

**emperor** /'ɛmpərər/ *n* emperador, *m*

**emphasis (on)** /'ɛmfəsɪs/ *n* énfasis (en), *mf;* insistencia especial (en), especial atención (a), *f;* accentuación, *f*

**emphasize** /'ɛmfə,saɪz/ *vt* subrayar, dar énfasis a, poner de relieve, hacer resaltar, dar importancia a; acentuar; insistir en, hacer hincapié (en)

**emphatic** /ɛm'fætɪk/ *a* enfático

**emphatically** /ɛm'fætɪkəli/ *adv* con énfasis

**empire** /'ɛmpaɪər/ *n* imperio, *m*

**empiric** /ɛm'pɪrɪk/ *a* empírico

**empiricism** /ɛm'pɪrə,sɪzəm/ *n* empirismo, *m*

**employ** /ɛm'plɔɪ/ *n* empleo, *m;* servicio, *m.* —*vt* emplear; ocupar; tomar; servirse de, usar. **How do you e. yourself?** ¿Cómo te ocupas? ¿Cómo pasas el tiempo?

**employable** /ɛm'plɔɪəbəl/ *a* empleable; utilizable

**employee** /ɛm'plɔɪi/ *n* empleado (-da)

**employer** /ɛm'plɔɪər/ *n* el, *m,* (*f,* la) que emplea; dueño (-ña), amo (-a); patrón (-ona)

**employment** /ɛm'plɔɪmənt/ *n* empleo, *m;* uso, *m;* ocupación, *f;* aprovechamiento, *m;* (post) puesto, cargo, *m;* (situation) colocación, *f.* **e. exchange,** bolsa de trabajo, *f*

**emporium** /ɛm'pɔriəm/ *n* emporio, *m;* (store) almacén, *m*

**empower** /ɛm'pauər/ *vt* autorizar; permitir; ayudar (a); dar el poder (para)

**empress** /'ɛmprɪs/ *n* emperatriz, *f*

**emptiness** /'ɛmptɪnɪs/ *n* vaciedad, *f;* futilidad, *f;* vacuidad, *f;* (verbosity) palabrería, *f*

**empty** /'ɛmpti/ *a* vacío; (of a house, etc.) deshabitado, desocupado; (deserted) desierto; (vain) vano, inútil; frívolo; (hungry) hambriento. —*n* envase vacío, *m.* —*vt* vaciar; descargar. —*vi* vaciarse; (river, etc.) desembocar, venir a morir en. **e.-handed,** con las manos vacías. **e.-headed,** casquivano

**emptying** /'ɛmptiɪŋ/ *n* vaciamiento, *m;* abandono, *m; pl* **emptyings,** heces de la cerveza, *f pl*

**emu** /'imyu/ *n* emu, *m*

**emulate** /'ɛmyə,leɪt/ *vt* emular

**emulation** /ˌɛmyə'leɪʃən/ *n* emulación, *f*

**emulative** /'ɛmyə,leɪtɪv/ *a* emulador

**emulsify** /ɪ'mʌlsɪfaɪ/ *vt* emulsionar

**emulsion** /ɪ'mʌlʃən/ *n* emulsión, *f*

**emulsive** /ɪ'mʌlsɪv/ *a* emulsivo

**enable** /ɛn'eibəl/ *vt* (to) hacer capaz (de); ayudar (a); autorizar (para); permitir (de)

**enact** /ɛn'ækt/ *vt Law.* promulgar; decretar; (a part) hacer, desempeñar (un papel); (a play) representar; (happen) ocurrir, tener lugar

**enaction** /ɛn'ækʃən/ *n Law.* promulgación, *f*

**enamel** /ɪ'næməl/ *n* esmalte, *m, vt* esmaltar

**enameler** /ɪ'næmələr/ *n* esmaltador (-ra)

**enameling** /ɪ'næməlɪŋ/ *n* esmaltadura, *f*

**enamor** /ɪ'næmər/ *vt* enamorar. **to be enamored of,** estar enamorado de; estar aficionado a

**encamp** /ɛn'kæmp/ *vt* and *vi* acampar

**encampment** /ɛn'kæmpmənt/ *n* campamento, *m*

**encase** /ɛn'keis/ *vt* encajar; encerrar; (line) forrar

**encasement** /ɛn'keismənt/ *n* encaje, *m;* encierro, *m*

**encephalitis** /ɛn,sɛfə'laitɪs/ *n* encefalitis, *f.* **e. lethargica,** encefalitis letárgica, *f*

**enchant** /ɛn'tʃænt/ *vt* encantar, hechizar; fascinar, embelesar, deleitar

**enchanter** /ɛn'tʃæntər/ *n* encantador, *m*

**enchanting** /ɛn'tʃæntɪŋ/ *a* encantador, fascinador

**enchantment** /ɛn'tʃæntmənt/ *n* encantamiento, *m;* fascinación, *f,* encanto, deleite, *m*

**enchantress** /ɛn'tʃæntrɪs/ *n* bruja, *f; Fig.* mujer seductora, *f*

**encircle** /ɛn'sɜrkəl/ *vt* cercar; rodear; dar la vuelta (a)

**enclose** /ɛn'klouz/ *vt* cercar; meter dentro de; encerrar; (with a letter, etc.) incluir, adjuntar

**enclosed** /ɛn'klouzd/ *a* (of letters) adjunto

**enclosure** /ɛn'klouʒər/ *n* cercamiento, *m;* cercado, *m;* recinto, *m;* (wall) tapia, cerca, *f;* (with a letter) contenido adjunto, *m*

**encomium** /ɛn'koumiəm/ *n* encomio, *m*

**encompass** /ɛn'kʌmpəs/ *vt* cercar, rodear

**encore** /'ɑŋkɔr/ *n* repetición, *f, interj* ¡bis!

**encounter** /ɛn'kauntər/ *n* encuentro, *m;* combate, *m;* conflicto, *m;* lucha, *f.* —*vt* encontrar; atacar; tropezar con

**encourage** /ɛn'kɜrɪdʒ/ *vt* animar; alentar; estimular; incitar; ayudar; (approve) aprobar; (foster) fomentar

**encouragement** /ɛn'kɜrɪdʒmənt/ *n* ánimos, *m pl;* estímulo, incentivo, *m;* ayuda, *f;* (approval) aprobación, *f;* (promotion) fomento, *m*

**encourager** /ɛn'kɜrɪdʒər/ *n* instigador (-ra); ayudador (-ra); aprobador (-ra); fomentador (-ra)

**encouraging** /ɛn'kɜrɪdʒɪŋ/ *a* alentador; estimulante; fomentador; (favorable) halagüeño, favorable

**encouragingly** /ɛn'kɜrɪdʒɪŋli/ *adv* de un modo alentador; con aprobación

**encroach** /ɛn'kroutʃ/ *vi* usurpar; abusar (de); invadir; robar; (of sea, river) hurtar

**encroaching** /ɛn'kroutʃɪŋ/ *a* usurpador; invadiente

**encroachment** /ɛn'kroutʃmənt/ *n* usurpación, *f;* abuso, *m;* invasión, *f*

**encrust** /ɛn'krʌst/ *vt* encostrar; incrustar

**encumber** /ɛn'kʌmbər/ vt impedir, estorbar; llenar; (burden) cargar; (mortgage) hipotecar; (overwhelm) agobiar

**encumbrance** /ɛn'kʌmbrəns/ n impedimento, estorbo, m; gravamen, m; carga, f; (mortgage) hipoteca, f

**encyclical** /ɛn'sɪklɪkəl/ n encíclica, f

**encyclopedia** /ɛn,saɪklə'pidiə/ n enciclopedia, f

**encyclopedic** /ɛn,saɪklə'pidɪk/ a enciclopédico

**encyclopedist** /ɛn,saɪklə'pidɪst/ n enciclopedista, m

**end** /ɛnd/ n fin, m; extremidad, f; extremo, m; conclusión, f; (point) punta, f; cabo, m; (district) barrio, m; cabeza, f; (death) muerte, f; (aim) objeto, intento, m; (purpose) propósito, m; (issue) resultado, m; (bit) fragmento, pedazo, m; (of a word) terminación, f. —vi terminar; acabar; concluir; cesar; (in) terminar en; resultar en; (with) terminar con. —vt terminar; acabar, dar fin a. **at an end,** terminado. **at the end,** al cabo (de); al extremo (de). **end of quotation,** fin de cita, final de la cita, m. **from end to end,** de un extremo a otro; de un cabo a otro. **in the end,** por fin, finalmente. **on end,** de pie, de cabeza, derecho; de punta; (of hair) erizado. **no end of,** un sinnúmero de. **to make both ends meet,** pasar con lo que se tiene. **to make an end of,** acabar con. **to put an end to,** poner fin a. **to the end that,** a fin de que, para que; con objeto de. **toward the end of,** (months, years, etc.) a fines de, a últimos de; hacia el fin de. **two hours on end,** dos horas seguidas. **end-paper,** guarda, f

**endanger** /ɛn'deɪndʒər/ vt arriesgar, poner en peligro

**endear** /ɛn'dɪər/ vt hacer querer

**endearing** /ɛn'dɪərɪŋ/ a que inspira cariño; atrayente; cariñoso

**endearment** /ɛn'dɪərmənt/ n cariño, amor, m; caricia, terneza, f; palabra de cariño, f

**endeavor** /ɛn'dɛvər/ vi procurar, intentar, hacer un esfuerzo. —n esfuerzo, m, tentativa, f

**endemic** /ɛn'dɛmɪk/ a Med. endémico

**ending** /'ɛndɪŋ/ n fin, m; conclusión, f; Gram. terminación, f; cesación, f; (climax) desenlace, m

**endive** /'ɛndaɪv/ n Bot. escarola, f

**endless** /'ɛndlɪs/ a eterno; inacabable; infinito; sin fin; interminable; incesante

**endlessly** /'ɛndlɪsli/ adv sin fin; incesantemente; sin parar

**endlessness** /'ɛndlɪsnɪs/ n eternidad, f; infinidad, f; continuidad, f

**endocrine** /'ɛndəkrɪn/ a endocrino. —n secreción interna, f

**endocrinology** /,ɛndoukrə'nɒlədʒi/ n endocrinología, f

**end-of-season** /'ɛnd əv 'sizən/ a por final de temporada (e.g., end-of-season reductions, rebajos por final de temporada, m pl. end-of-season sale, liquidación por final de temporada, f)

**endogenous** /ɛn'dɒdʒənəs/ a endógeno

**endorse** /ɛn'dɔrs/ vt Com. endosar; garantizar; (uphold) apoyar; confirmar

**endorsee** /ɛndɔr'si/ n endosatario (-ia)

**endorsement** /ɛn'dɔrsmənt/ n Com. endoso, m; aval, m, garantía, f; corroboración, confirmación, f

**endorser** /ɛn'dɔrsər/ n Com. endosante, m

**endow** /ɛn'dau/ vt dotar; fundar; crear

**endowment** /ɛn'daumənt/ n dotación, f; fundación, f; creación, f; (mental) inteligencia, f; cualidad, f, don, m. **e. policy,** póliza dotal, f

**endurable** /ɛn'durəbəl/ a sufrible, soportable; tolerable

**endurance** /ɛn'durəns/ n aguante, m; resistencia, f; sufrimiento, m; tolerancia, f; paciencia, f; (lastingness) duración, continuación, f. **beyond e.,** intolerable, inaguantable. **e. test,** prueba de resistencia, f

**endure** /ɛn'dur/ vt soportar; tolerar, aguantar; sufrir; resistir. —vi sufrir; (last) durar, continuar

**enduring** /ɛn'durɪŋ/ a permanente, perdurable; continuo; constante

**enduringness** /ɛn'durɪŋnɪs/ n (lastingness) permanencia, f; paciencia, f; aguante, m

**enema** /'ɛnəmə/ n lavativa, enema, f

**enemy** /'ɛnəmi/ n enemigo (-ga); adversario (-ia); (in war) enemigo, m. —a del enemigo, enemigo. **to be**

**one's own e.,** ser enemigo de sí mismo. **to become an e. of,** enemistarse con; hacerse enemigo de, volverse hostil a

**energetic** /,ɛnər'dʒɛtɪk/ a enérgico

**energy** /'ɛnərdʒi/ n energía, fuerza, f, vigor, m

**enervate** / v 'ɛnər,veit/ a 'ɪnɜrvɪt/ vt enervar; debilitar. —a enervado

**enervation** /,ɛnər'veiʃən/ n enervación, f; debilitación, f

**enfeeble** /ɛn'fibəl/ vt debilitar

**enfeeblement** /ɛn'fibəlmənt/ n debilitación, f, desfallecimiento, m

**enfold** /ɛn'fould/ vt envolver; abrazar

**enforce** /ɛn'fɔrs/ vt (a law) poner en vigor; (impose) imponer a la fuerza; hacer cumplir; conseguir por fuerza; (demonstrate) demostrar

**enforcement** /ɛn'fɔrsmənt/ n (of a law) ejecución (de una ley), f; imposición a la fuerza, f; observación forzosa, f

**enfranchise** /ɛn'fræntʃaɪz/ vt emancipar; conceder derechos civiles (a)

**enfranchisement** /ɛn'fræntʃaɪzmənt/ n emancipación, f; concesión de derechos civiles, f

**engage** /ɛn'geɪdʒ/ vt empeñar; contratar; tomar en alquiler; tomar a su servicio; (seats, etc.) reservar; (occupy) ocupar; (attention) atraer; (in) aplicarse a, dedicarse a; Mil. combatir con, librar batalla con; atacar; (of wheels) endentar con. —vi obligarse; dedicarse (a); tomar parte (en); (bet) apostar; Mil. librar batalla; (fight) venir a las manos. **to be engaged in,** traer entre manos, ocuparse en. **to become engaged,** prometerse. **Number engaged!** (telephone) ¡Están comunicando!

**engaged** /ɛn'geɪdʒd/ a ocupado; (betrothed) prometido; reservado

**engagement** /ɛn'geɪdʒmənt/ n obligación, f; compromiso, m; (date) cita, f; (betrothal) palabra de casamiento, f; (battle) combate, m, batalla, f. **I have an e. at two o'clock.** Tengo una cita a las dos

**engagement gift** regalo de esponsales, m

**engaging** /ɛn'geɪdʒɪŋ/ a simpático, atractivo

**engagingly** /ɛn'geɪdʒɪŋli/ adv de un modo encantador

**engender** /ɛn'dʒɛndər/ vt Fig. engendrar; excitar

**engine** /'ɛndʒɪn/ n máquina, f; motor, m; (locomotive) locomotora, f; (pump) bomba, f. **to sit with one's back to the e.,** estar sentado de espaldas a la máquina (or locomotora). **e. builder,** constructor de máquinas, m. **e. driver,** maquinista, mf. **e. room,** cuarto de máquinas, m. **e. works,** taller de maquinaria, m

**engineer** /,ɛndʒə'nɪər/ n ingeniero, m; mecánico, m. —vt Fig. gestionar; arreglar. **civil e.,** ingeniero de caminos, canales y puertos, m. **Royal Engineers,** Cuerpo de Ingenieros, m

**engineering** /,ɛndʒə'nɪərɪŋ/ n ingeniería, f; Fig. manejo, m. —a de ingeniería

**England** /'ɪŋglənd/ Inglaterra, f

**English** /'ɪŋglɪʃ/ a inglés. —n (language) inglés, m. **in E. fashion,** a la inglesa. **to speak E.,** hablar inglés. **to speak plain E.,** hablar sin rodeos; hablar en cristiano. **E. Church,** iglesia anglicana, f. **E.-teacher,** maestro (-ra) de inglés. **English-translator,** traductor al inglés, m

**English Channel, the** el Canal de la Mancha

**Englishman** /'ɪŋglɪʃmən/ n inglés, m

**Englishwoman** /'ɪŋglɪʃ,wʊmən/ n inglesa, f

**engrain** /ɛn'greɪn/ vt inculcar

**engrave** /ɛn'greɪv/ vt grabar; esculpir, cincelar; Fig. grabar

**engraver** /ɛn'greɪvər/ n grabador (-ra); (tool) cincel, m

**engraving** /ɛn'greɪvɪŋ/ n grabadura, f; (picture) grabado, m. **e. needle,** punta seca, f

**engross** /ɛn'grous/ vt (a document) poner en limpio; redactar; (absorb) absorber

**engrossing** /ɛn'grousɪŋ/ a absorbente

**engulf** /ɛn'gʌlf/ vt hundir, sumir, sumergir

**enhance** /ɛn'hæns/ vt realzar; intensificar; aumentar; mejorar

**enhancement** /ɛn'hænsmənt/ n realce, m; intensificación, f; aumento, m; mejoría, f

**enigma** /ə'nɪgmə/ *n* enigma, *m*

**enigmatic** /ˌɛnɪg'mætɪk/ *a* enigmático

**enjoin** /ɛn'dʒɔɪn/ *vt* imponer; ordenar, mandar; encargar

**enjoy** /ɛn'dʒɔi/ *vt* disfrutar; gustar de; gozar de; poseer, tener. **to e. oneself,** recrearse, regocijarse; (amuse oneself) divertirse; entretenerse; pasarlo bien. **Did you e. yourself?** ¿Lo pasaste bien?

**enjoyable** /ɛn'dʒɔiəbəl/ *a* agradable; divertido, entretenido

**enjoyableness** /ɛn'dʒɔiəbəlnɪs/ *n* lo agradable; lo divertido

**enjoyably** /ɛn'dʒɔiəbli/ *adv* de un modo muy agradable

**enjoyer** /ɛn'dʒɔiər/ *n* el, *m*, (*f*, la) que disfruta; poseedor (-ra); (amateur) aficionado (-da)

**enjoyment** /ɛn'dʒɔimənt/ *n* posesión, *f*; goce, disfruto, *m*; (pleasure) placer, *m*; aprovechamiento, *m*; utilización, *f*; (satisfaction) satisfacción, *f*

**enlarge** /ɛn'lardʒ/ *vt* agrandar; aumentar; ensanchar; extender; *Photo.* ampliar; dilatar; (the mind, etc.) ensanchar. —*vi* agrandarse; ensancharse; aumentarse; extenderse. **an enlarged heart,** dilatación del corazón, *f*. **to e. upon,** tratar detalladamente, explayarse en

**enlargement** /ɛn'lardʒmənt/ *n* engrandecimiento, *m*; ensanchamiento, *m*; *Photo.* ampliación, *f*; *Med.* dilatación, *f*; aumento, *m*; amplificación, *f*; (of a town, etc.) ensanche, *m*

**enlarger** /ɛn'lardʒər/ *n* *Photo.* ampliadora, *f*

**enlighten** /ɛn'laitn/ *vt* iluminar; aclarar; informar

**enlightened** /ɛn'laitnd/ *a* culto; ilustrado; inteligente

**enlightening** /ɛn'laitnɪŋ/ *a* instructivo

**enlightenment** /ɛn'laitnmənt/ *n* ilustración, *f*; cultura, civilización, *f*

**enlist** /ɛn'lɪst/ *vt* *Mil.* reclutar; alistar; obtener, conseguir. —*vi Mil.* sentar plaza, sentar plaza de soldado; engancharse; alistarse

**enlistment** /ɛn'lɪstmənt/ *n* *Mil.* enganche, *m*; reclutamiento, *m*; alistamiento, *m*

**enliven** /ɛn'laivən/ *vt* animar; avivar; alegrar

**enmity** /'ɛnmɪti/ *n* enemistad, enemiga, hostilidad, *f*

**ennoble** /ɛn'noubəl/ *vt* ennoblecer; ilustrar

**ennui** /ɑn'wi/ *n* tedio, *m*; aburrimiento, *m*

**enormity** /ɪ'nɔrmɪti/ *n* enormidad, *f*; gravedad, *f*; atrocidad, *f*

**enormous** /ɪ'nɔrməs/ *a* enorme, colosal

**enormously** /ɪ'nɔrməsli/ *adv* enormemente

**enormousness** /ɪ'nɔrməsnɪs/ *n* enormidad, *f*

**enough** /ɪ'nʌf/ *a* bastante, suficiente. —*n* lo bastante, lo suficiente. —*adv* bastante; suficientemente. —*interj* ¡bastante! ¡basta! **to be e.,** ser suficiente; bastar. **two are enough,** con dos tenemos bastante, con dos tengo bastante

**enquire** /ɛn'kwaiər/ *vt*. See **inquire**

**enrage** /ɛn'reidʒ/ *vt* enfurecer, hacer furioso; *Inf.* hacer rabiar

**enraged** /ɛn'reidʒd/ *a* furioso

**enrapture** /ɛn'ræptʃər/ *vt* entusiasmar, extasiar; (intoxicate) embriagar; (charm) encantar, deleitar

**enrich** /ɛn'rɪtʃ/ *vt* enriquecer; (adorn) adornar, embellecer; (the land) fertilizar

**enrichment** /ɛn'rɪtʃmənt/ *n* enriquecimiento, *m*; embellecimiento, *m*; (of the land) abono, *m*

**enroll** /ɛn'roul/ *vt* alistar; matricular; inscribir; (perpetuate) inmortalizar

**enrollment** /ɛn'roulmənt/ *n* alistamiento, *m*; inscripción, *f*

**ensconce** /ɛn'skɒns/ *vt* acomodar, colocar; ocultar

**ensemble** /ɑn'sɑmbəl/ *n* conjunto, *m*

**enshrine** /ɛn'ʃrain/ *vt* poner en sagrario; guardar con cuidado; *Fig.* guardar como una reliquia

**enshroud** /ɛn'ʃraud/ *vt* amortajar; envolver; esconder

**ensign** /'ɛnsən/ *n* (badge) insignia, *f*; (flag) enseña, bandera, *f*; pabellón, *m*; bandera de popa, *f*; *Mil.* alférez, *m*; (U.S.A. navy) subteniente, *m*

**enslave** /ɛn'sleiv/ *vt* esclavizar; *Fig.* dominar

**enslavement** /ɛn'sleivmənt/ *n* esclavitud, *f*

**ensue** /ɛn'su/ *vt* conseguir. —*vi* resultar; suceder, sobrevenir

**ensuing** /ɛn'suɪŋ/ *a* (next) próximo; (resulting) resultante

**ensure** /ɛn'ʃʊr/ *vt* asegurar; estar seguro de que; garantizar

**entail** /ɛn'teil/ *vt* traer consigo, acarrear; *Law.* vincular; *n Law.* vinculación, *f*; herencia, *f*

**entangle** /ɛn'tæŋgəl/ *vt* enredar; coger; *Fig.* embrollar

**entanglement** /ɛn'tæŋgəlmənt/ *n* enredo, *m*; complicación, *f*; intriga, *f*; (*Mil.* of wire) alambrada, *f*

**entangling** /ɛn'tæŋglɪŋ/ *a* enmarañador (e.g., *entangling alliances,* alianzas enmarañadoras, *f pl*)

**enter** /'ɛntər/ *vt* entrar en; penetrar; (of thoughts) ocurrirse; (join) ingresar en; entrar en; (become a member of) hacerse miembro de; (enroll) alistarse; (a university) matricularse; (inscribe) inscribir, poner en la lista; (note) anotar, apuntar; (a protest) hacer constar; (make) hacer; formular. —*vi* entrar; *Theat.* salir (a la escena); penetrar; *Com.* anotarse. **to e. for,** *vt* inscribir. —*vi* inscribirse, tomar parte en. **to e. into,** entrar en; formar parte de; (conversation) entablar (conversación); (negotiations) iniciar; considerar; (another's emotion) acompañar en; (an agreement, etc.) hacer; (sign) firmar; (bind oneself) obligarse a, comprometerse a; tomar parte en; (undertake) emprender; empezar; adoptar. **to e. up,** anotar; poner en la lista; registrar. **to e. upon,** comenzar, emprender; tomar posesión de; encargarse de, asumir; inaugurar, dar principio a

**enteric** /ɛn'tɛrɪk/ *a* entérico

**enteritis** /ˌɛntə'raitɪs/ *n* enteritis, *f*

**enterprise** /'ɛntər,praiz/ *n* empresa, *f*; aventura, *f*; (spirit) iniciativa, *f*, empuje, *m*

**enterprising** /'ɛntər,praizɪŋ/ *a* emprendedor, acometedor; de mucha iniciativa

**entertain** /ˌɛntər'tein/ *vt* (an idea, etc.) acariciar, abrigar; considerar; (as a guest) agasajar, obsequiar; recibir en casa; (amuse) divertir, entretener. —*vi* ser hospitalario; tener invitados en casa; dar fiestas

**entertaining** /ˌɛntər'teinɪŋ/ *a* entretenido, divertido

**entertainingly** /ˌɛntər'teinɪŋli/ *adv* entretenidamente; (witty) graciosamente

**entertainment** /ˌɛntər'teinmənt/ *n* convite, *m*; fiesta, *f*; reunión, *f*; banquete, *m*; (hospitality) hospitalidad, *f*; (amusement) diversión, *f*, entretenimiento, *m*; espectáculo, *m*; función, *f*; concierto, *m*

**enthrall** /ɛn'θrɔl/ *vt* seducir, atraer, encantar; absorber, captar la atención

**enthralling** /ɛn'θrɔlɪŋ/ *a* absorbente; atrayente, halagüeño

**enthrallment** /ɛn'θrɔlmənt/ *n* absorción, *f*; atracción, *f*

**enthrone** /ɛn'θroun/ *vt* entronizar

**enthronement** /ɛn'θrounmənt/ *n* entronización, *f*

**enthusiasm** /ɛn'θuzi,æzəm/ *n* entusiasmo, *m*

**enthusiast** /ɛn'θuzi,æst, -ɪst/ *n* entusiasta, *mf*

**enthusiastic** /ɛn,θuzi'æstɪk/ *a* entusiasta. **to make e.,** entusiasmar. **to be e.,** entusiasmarse

**enthusiastically** /ɛn,θuzi'æstɪkəli/ *adv* con entusiasmo

**entice** /ɛn'tais/ *vt* tentar, inducir; atraer, seducir

**enticement** /ɛn'taismənt/ *n* tentación, *f*; atractivo, *m*

**enticing** /ɛn'taisɪŋ/ *a* seduciente, atrayente; halagüeño

**entire** /ɛn'taiər/ *a* entero; completo; intacto; absoluto; perfecto; íntegro; total

**entirely** /ɛn'taiərli/ *adv* enteramente; completamente; integralmente; totalmente

**entirety** /ɛn'taiərti/ *n* totalidad, *f*; integridad, *f*; todo, *m*

**entitle** /ɛn'taitl/ *vt* (designate) intitular; dar derecho (a); autorizar. **to be entitled to,** tener derecho a

**entity** /'ɛntɪti/ *n* entidad, *f*; ente, ser, *m*

**entombment** /ɛn'tummənt/ *n* sepultura, *f*, entierro, *m*

**entomological** /ˌɛntəmə'lɒdʒɪkəl/ *a* entomológico

**entomologist** /ˌɛntə'mɒlədʒɪst/ *n* entomólogo, *m*

**entomology** /ˌɛntə'mɒlədʒi/ *n* entomología, *f*

**entourage** /ˌɑntu'rɑʒ/ *n* séquito, *m*; (environment) medio ambiente, *m*

**entr'acte** /ɑn'trækt/ *n* entreacto, *m*

**entrails** /'ɛntreilz/ n entrañas, tripas, f pl, intestinos, m pl

**entrain** /ɛn'trein/ vi tomar el tren, subir al tren

**entrance** /ɛn'trəns/ n entrada, f; Theat. salida (a la escena), f; (into a profession, etc.) ingreso, m; alistamiento, m; (beginning) principio, m; (door) puerta, f; (porch) portal, m; (of a cave) boca, f. **e. fee,** cuota de entrada, f. **e. hall,** zaguán, m. **e. money,** entrada, f

**entrance** /ɛn'træns/ vt Fig. encantar, fascinar; ecstasiar

**entrancing** /ɛn'trænsɪŋ/ a encantador

**entreat** /ɛn'trit/ vt suplicar, implorar, rogar

**entreating** /ɛn'tritɪŋ/ a suplicante, implorante

**entreatingly** /ɛn'tritɪŋli/ adv de un modo suplicante; insistentemente

**entreaty** /ɛn'triti/ n súplica, instancia, f, ruego, m

**entree** /'ɑntrei/ n entrada, f

**entrench** /ɛn'trɛntʃ/ vt atrincherar

**entrenchment** /ɛn'trɛntʃmənt/ n atrincheramiento, m; Mil. parapeto, m; (encroachment) invasión, f

**entresol** /'ɛntər,sɒl/ n entresuelo, m

**entrust** /ɛn'trʌst/ vt confiar a (or en), encomendar a; encargar

**entry** /'ɛntri/ n entrada, f; (passage) callejuela, f; (note) inscripción, apuntación, f; Com. partida, f; (registration) registro, m. **double e.,** Com. partida doble, f. **single e.,** Com. partida simple, f

**entwine** /ɛn'twain/ vt entrelazar, entretejer

**enumerate** /ɪ'numə,reit/ vt enumerar

**enumeration** /ɪ,numə'reiʃən/ n enumeración, f

**enumerative** /ɪ'numə,reitɪv/ a enumerativo

**enunciate** /ɪ'nʌnsi,eit/ vt enunciar; articular

**enunciation** /ɪ,nʌnsi'eiʃən/ n enunciación, f; articulación, f

**envelop** /ɛn'vɛləp/ vt envolver, cubrir

**envelope** /'ɛnvə,loup/ n sobre, m

**envelopment** /ɛn'vɛləpmənt/ n envolvimiento, m; cubierta, f

**enviable** /'ɛnviəbəl/ a envidiable

**envious** /'ɛnviəs/ a envidioso. **an e. look,** una mirada de envidia

**enviously** /'ɛnviəsli/ adv con envidia

**environment** /ɛn'vairənmənt/ n medio ambiente, m

**environs** /ɛn'vairənz/ n inmediaciones, f pl, alrededores, m pl

**envisage** /ɛn'vɪzɪdʒ/ vt hacer frente a; contemplar; imaginar

**envoy** /'ɛnvɔi/ n enviado, m; mensajero (-ra)

**envy** /'ɛnvi/ n envidia, f, vt envidiar

**enzyme** /'ɛnzaim/ n fermento, m, enzima, f

**eon** /'iən/ n eón, m

**epaulette** /'ɛpə,lɛt/ n hombrera, f

**ephemeral** /ɪ'fɛmərəl/ a efímero; Fig. fugaz, pasajero

**Ephesus** /'ɛfəsəs/ Efiso, m

**Ephraim** /'ifriəm/ Efraín, m

**Ephraimite** /'ifriə,mait/ n and a efraíta, mf

**epic** /'ɛpɪk/ a épico. —n epopeya, f

**epicenter** /'ɛpə,sɛntər/ n epicentro, m

**epicure** /'ɛpɪ,kyʊr/ n epicúreo (-ea)

**epicurean** /,ɛpɪkyʊ'riən/ a epicúreo

**Epicureanism** /,ɛpɪkyʊ'riə,nɪzəm/ n epicureísmo, m

**epidemic** /,ɛpɪ'dɛmɪk/ n epidemia, f; plaga, f, a epidémico

**epidermis** /,ɛpɪ'dɜrmɪs/ n epidermis, f

**epiglottis** /,ɛpɪ'glɒtɪs/ n epiglotis, f

**epigram** /'ɛpɪ,græm/ n epigrama, m

**epigrammatic** /,ɛpɪgrə'mætɪk/ a epigramático

**epigraph** /'ɛpɪ,græf/ n epígrafe, m

**epigraphy** /ɪ'pɪgrəfi/ n epigrafía, f

**epilepsy** /'ɛpə,lɛpsi/ n epilepsia, alferecía, f

**epileptic** /,ɛpə'lɛptɪk/ a and n epiléptico (-ca). **e. fit,** ataque epiléptico, m. **e. aura,** aura epiléptica, f

**epilogue** /'ɛpə,lɔg/ n epílogo, f

**epiphany** /ɪ'pɪfəni/ n epifanía, f

**Epirus** /ɪ'pairəs/ Epiro, m

**episcopacy** /ɪ'pɪskəpəsi/ n episcopado, m

**episcopal** /ɪ'pɪskəpəl/ a episcopal

**episcopalianism** /ɪ,pɪskə'peilyə,nɪzəm/ n episcopalismo, m

**episode** /'ɛpə,soud/ n suceso, incidente, m; Lit. episodio, m

**episodic** /,ɛpə'sɒdɪk/ a episódico

**epistle** /ɪ'pɪsəl/ n epístola, f

**epistolary** /ɪ'pɪstl,ɛri/ a epistolar

**epitaph** /'ɛpɪ,tæf/ n epitafio, m

**epithet** /'ɛpə,θɛt/ n epíteto, m

**epitome** /ɪ'pɪtəmi/ n epítome, m

**epitomize** /ɪ'pɪtə,maiz/ vt resumir, abreviar

**epoch** /'ɛpək/ n época, edad, f

**epode** /'ɛpoud/ n épodo, m

**Epsom salts** /'ɛpsəm/ n sal de la Higuera, f

**equability** /,ɛkwə'bɪlɪti/ n igualdad (de ánimo), ecuanimidad, f; uniformidad, f

**equable** /'ɛkwəbəl/ a igual, ecuánime; uniforme

**equably** /'ɛkwəbli/ adv con ecuanimidad; igualmente; uniformemente

**equal** /'ikwəl/ a igual; uniforme; imparcial; equitativo, justo. —n igual, mf. —vt ser igual a; equivaler a; igualar; Sports. empatar. **to be e. to,** (of persons) ser capaz de; servir para; atreverse a; (circumstances) estar al nivel de; sentirse con fuerzas para. **without e.,** sin igual; (of beauty, etc.) sin par. **e. sign,** Math. igual, m

**equality** /ɪ'kwɒlɪti/ n igualdad, f; uniformidad, f

**equalization** /,ikwələ'zeiʃən/ n igualación, f

**equalize** /'ikwə,laiz/ vt igualar

**equalizing** /'ikwə,laizɪŋ/ a igualador; compensador

**equally** /'ikwəli/ adv igualmente; imparcialmente

**equanimity** /,ikwə'nɪmɪti/ n ecuanimidad, f

**equation** /ɪ'kweiʒən/ n ecuación, f

**equator** /ɪ'kweitər/ n ecuador, m

**equatorial** /,ikwə'tɔriəl/ a ecuatorial

**equerry** /'ɛkwəri/ n caballerizo del rey, m

**equestrian** /ɪ'kwɛstriən/ a ecuestre

**equiangular** /,ikwi'æŋgyələr/ a equiángulo

**equidistance** /,ikwɪ'dɪstəns/ n equidistancia, f

**equidistant** /,ikwɪ'dɪstənt/ a equidistante

**equilateral** /,ikwə'lætərəl/ a equilátero

**equilibrist** /ɪ'kwɪləbrɪst/ n equilibrista, mf

**equilibrium** /,ikwə'lɪbriəm/ n equilibrio, m

**equine** /'ikwain/ a equino; hípico; de caballo

**equinoctial** /,ikwə'nɒkʃəl/ a equinoccial. **e. gale,** tempestad equinoccial, f

**equinox** /'ikwə,nɒks/ n equinoccio, m

**equip** /ɪ'kwɪp/ vt proveer; pertrechar; equipar

**equipage** /'ɛkwəpɪdʒ/ n (train) séquito, tren, m; (carriage) carruaje, m

**equipment** /ɪ'kwɪpmənt/ n habilitación, f; equipo, m; pertrechos, m pl; material, m; aparatos, m pl; armamento, m

**equitable** /'ɛkwɪtəbəl/ a equitativo, justo

**equitableness** /'ɛkwɪtəbəlnɪs/ n equidad, justicia, f

**equitably** /'ɛkwɪtəbli/ adv equitativamente, con justicia

**equity** /'ɛkwɪti/ n equidad, f; imparcialidad, justicia, f

**equivalence** /ɪ'kwɪvələns/ n equivalencia, f

**equivalent** /ɪ'kwɪvələnt/ a and n equivalente, m. **to be e. to,** equivaler a

**equivocal** /ɪ'kwɪvəkəl/ a equívoco, ambiguo

**equivocally** /ɪ'kwɪvəkəli/ adv equivocadamente

**equivocate** /ɪ'kwɪvə,keit/ vi usar frases equívocas, emplear equívocos, tergiversar

**equivocation** /ɪ,kwɪvə'keiʃən/ n equívoco, m

**era** /'iərə, 'ɛrə/ n época, era, f

**eradiation** /ɪ,reidi'eiʃən/ n irradiación, f

**eradicable** /ɪ'rædɪkəbəl/ a erradicable

**eradicate** /ɪ'rædɪ,keit/ vt erradicar; destruir, extirpar; suprimir

**eradication** /ɪ,rædɪ'keiʃən/ n erradicación, f; destrucción, f; supresión, f

**erasable** /ɪ'reisəbəl/ a borrable

**erase** /ɪ'reis/ vt borrar; tachar

**eraser** /ɪ'reisər/ n goma de borrar, f. **ink e.,** goma para tinta, f

**erasure** /ɪ'reiʃər/ n borradura, f; tachón, m

**ere** /ɛər/ conjunc antes de (que), antes de. —prep antes de

**erect** /ɪ'rɛkt/ a (upright) derecho; erguido; vertical; (uplifted) levantado; (standing) de pie; (firm) firme, resuelto; (alert) vigilante. —*vt* (build) edificar, construir; instalar; (raise) alzar; convertir

**erectile** /ɪˈrɛktl/ *a* eréctil

**erection** /ɪˈrɛkʃən/ *n* erección, *f*; construcción, edificación, *f*; (building) edificio, *m*; (structure) estructura, *f*; instalación, *f*; (assembling) montaje, *m*

**erectly** /ɪˈrɛktli/ *adv* derecho

**erectness** /ɪˈrɛktnɪs/ *n* derechura, *f*

**erg** /ɜrg/ *n Phys.* ergio, *m*

**ermine** /ˈɜrmɪn/ *n* armiño, *m, a* de armiño

**erode** /ɪˈroud/ *vt* corroer; comer; *Geol.* denudar

**erosion** /ɪˈrouʒən/ *n* erosión, *f*

**erotic** /ɪˈrɒtɪk/ *a* erótico

**err** /ɜr, ɛr/ *vi* desviarse; errar; desacertar; pecar

**errand** /ˈɛrənd/ *n* mensaje, recado, *m*; encargo, *m*; misión, *f.* **e.-boy,** mandadero, mensajero, motril, mozo, recadero, *m*

**errant** /ˈɛrənt/ *a* errante; (of knights) andante

**erratic** /ɪˈrætɪk/ *a* (of conduct) excéntrico, irresponsable; (of thoughts, etc.) errante; *Med.* errático

**erratum** /ɪˈrɑtəm/ *n* errata, *f*

**erring** /ˈɛrɪŋ/ *a* extraviado; pecaminoso

**erroneous** /əˈrouniəs/ *a* erróneo; falso; injusto

**erroneously** /əˈrouniəsli/ *adv* erróneamente; falsamente; injustamente

**erroneousness** /əˈrouniəsnɪs/ *n* falsedad, *f*

**error** /ˈɛrər/ *n* error, *m*; equivocación, *f*, desacierto, *m*; (sin) pecado, *m.* **in e.,** por equivocación

**erudite** /ˈɛryʊˌdaɪt/ *a* erudito; sabio

**erudition** /ˌɛryʊˈdɪʃən/ *n* erudición, *f*

**erupt** /ɪˈrʌpt/ *vi* entrar en erupción, estar en erupción; *Fig.* salir con fuerza

**eruption** /ɪˈrʌpʃən/ *n* erupción, *f*

**erysipelas** /ˌɛrəˈsɪpələs/ *n* erisipela, *f*

**escalade** /ˌɛskəˈleɪd/ *n* escalada, *f, vt* escalar

**escalator** /ˈɛskəˌleɪtər/ *n* escalera automática, escalera eléctrica, escalera mecánica, escalera móvil, escalera rodante, *f*

**escapable** /ɪˈskeɪpəbəl/ *a* evitable, eludible

**escapade** /ˈɛskəˌpeɪd/ *n* escapada, *f*; aventura, *f*

**escape** /ɪˈskeɪp/ *n* huida, fuga, *f*; evasión, evitación, *f*; (leak) escape, *m*; *Fig.* salida, *f.* —*vt* eludir, evitar; (of cries, groans, etc.) dar, salir de. —*vi* huir, fugarse, escapar; (slip away) escurrirse; librarse; salvarse; (leak) escaparse. **His name escapes me,** Se me escapa (or se me olvida) su nombre. **to e. notice,** pasar inadvertido. **to have a narrow e.,** salvarse en una tabla. **to e. from,** escaparse de; librarse de; huir de

**escape clause** *n* cláusula de salvaguardia, *f*

**escaping** /ɪˈskeɪpɪŋ/ *a* fugitivo

**escarpment** /ɪˈskɑrpmənt/ *n* escarpa, *f*

**eschew** /ɛsˈtʃu/ *vt* evitar

**eschewal** /ɛsˈtʃuəl/ *n* evitación, *f*

**escort** /*n* ˈɛskɔrt; *v* ɪˈskɔrt/ *n Mil.* escolta, *f*; (of ships) convoy, *m*; acompañamiento, *m*; acompañante, *m.* —*vt Mil.* escoltar; (of ships) convoyar; acompañar

**escritoire** /ˌɛskrɪˈtwɑr/ *n* escritorio, *m*

**escudo** /eˈskudou/ *n* escudo, *m*

**escutcheon** /ɪˈskʌtʃən/ *n* escudo, blasón, *m*

**Eskimo** /ˈɛskəˌmou/ *a* and *n* esquimal *mf*

**esoteric** /ˌɛsəˈtɛrɪk/ *a* esotérico

**esparto** /ɪˈspɑrtou/ *n* esparto, *m*

**especial** /ɪˈspɛʃəl/ *a* especial; particular

**especially** /ɪˈspɛʃəli/ *adv* especialmente; ante todo; en particular

**Esperantist** /ˌɛspəˈrɑntɪst/ *n* esperantista, *mf*

**Esperanto** /ˌɛspəˈrɑntou/ *n* esperanto, *m*

**espionage** /ˈɛspiəˌnɑʒ/ *n* espionaje, *m*

**esplanade** /ˈɛspləˌnɑd/ *n Mil.* explanada, *f*; bulevar, paseo, *m*

**espousal** /ɪˈspauzəl/ *n* desposorio, *m*; *Fig.* adhesión (a una causa), *f*

**espouse** /ɪˈspauz/ *vt* desposar; (a cause) abrazar; defender

**espy** /ɪˈspai/ *vt* divisar, ver, observar

**esquire** /ˈɛskwaɪʳr/ *n* escudero, *m*; (landowner) hacendado, *m*; (as a title) don (before given name)

**essay** /ˈɛsei; *v* ɛˈsei/ *n* tentativa, *f*; *Lit.* ensayo, *m*, *vt* probar; procurar; (on an examination) tema, *m.* **essay question,** tema, *m*

**essayist** /ˈɛseiɪst/ *n* ensayista, *mf*

**essence** /ˈɛsəns/ *n* esencia, *f*

**essential** /əˈsɛntʃəl/ *a* esencial; indispensable, imprescindible; intrínseco. —*n* artículo de primera necesidad, *m*; elemento necesario, *m*

**essentially** /əˈsɛntʃəli/ *adv* esencialmente

**establish** /ɪˈstæblɪʃ/ *vt* establecer; fundar; crear; erigir; (constitute) constituir; (order) disponer; (prove) demostrar, probar; (take root, settle) arraigarse

**established** /ɪˈstæblɪʃt/ *a* establecido; arraigado; (proved) demostrado; bien conocido; (author) consagrado; (of churches) oficial

**establishment** /ɪˈstæblɪʃmənt/ *n* establecimiento, *m*; fundación, *f*; creación, *f*; institución, *f*; (building) erección, *f*; arraigo, *m*; (house) casa, *f*; (church) iglesia oficial, *f*; demostración, *f*; reconocimiento, *m*

**estate** /ɪˈsteɪt/ *n* estado, *m*; clase, *f*; condición, *f*; (land) propiedad, finca, *f*; fortuna, *f*; (inheritance) heredad, *f*, patrimonio, *m*; *Law.* bienes, *m pl.* **personal e.,** bienes muebles, *m pl*; fortuna personal, *f.* **third e.,** estado llano, *m.* **e. agent,** agente de fincas, *m*; agente de casas, *m*

**esteem** /ɪˈstim/ *n* estima, *f*, aprecio, *m*; consideración, *f*, *vt* estimar, apreciar; creer, juzgar

**ester** /ˈɛstər/ *n Chem.* éster, *m*

**esthete** /ˈɛsθit/ *n* estético, *m*

**esthetic** /ɛsˈθɛtɪk/ *a* estético

**esthetically** /ɛsˈθɛtɪkli/ *adv* estéticamente

**esthetics** /ɛsˈθɛtɪks/ *n* estética, *f*

**estimable** /ˈɛstəməbəl/ *a* apreciable, estimable

**estimableness** /ˈɛstəməbəlnɪs/ *n* estimabilidad, *f*

**estimate** /*n* ˈɛstəˌmɪt; *v* -ˌmeɪt/ *n* estimación, tasa, *f*; cálculos, *m pl*; apreciación, *f*; opinión, *f*; *pl* **estimates,** presupuesto, *m.* —*vt* (value) avaluar, tasar; calcular, computar; considerar. —*vi* hacer un presupuesto

**estimation** /ˌɛstəˈmeɪʃən/ *n* opinión, *f*; cálculo, cómputo, *m*; (esteem) aprecio, *m*, estima, *f*

**Estonian** /ɛˈstouniən/ *a* and *n* estonio (-ia); (language) estonio, *m*

**estrange** /ɪˈstreɪndʒ/ *vt* enajenar; ofender

**estrangement** /ɪˈstreɪndʒmənt/ *n* enajenación, alienación, *f*

**estuary** /ˈɛstʃuˌɛri/ *n* estuario, *m*, ría, *f*

**etcetera** /ɛtˈsɛtərə/ etcétera. (Used as noun, *f*)

**etch** /ɛtʃ/ *vt* grabar al agua fuerte

**etcher** /ˈɛtʃər/ *n* grabador (-ra) al agua fuerte

**etching** /ˈɛtʃɪŋ/ *n* aguafuerte, *f*; grabado al agua fuerte, *m.* **e. needle,** punta seca, aguja de grabador, *f*

**eternal** /ɪˈtɜrnl/ *a* eterno; incesante. —*n* (E.) el Eterno

**eternally** /ɪˈtɜrnli/ *adv* eternamente

**eternity** /ɪˈtɜrnɪti/ *n* eternidad, *f*

**eternize** /ɪˈtɜrnaiz/ *vt* eternizar

**ether** /ˈiθər/ *n* éter, *m*

**ethereal** /ɪˈθɪəriəl/ *a* etéreo; vaporoso, aéreo

**etheric** /ɪˈθɛrɪk/ *a* etéreo

**etherize** /ˈiθəˌraiz/ *vt* eterizar

**ethical** /ˈɛθɪkəl/ *a* ético, moral; *n* droga de ordenanza, *f*

**ethics** /ˈɛθɪks/ *n* ética, *f*; (filosofía) moral, *f*

**Ethiopia** /ˌiθiˈoupiə/ Etiopía, *f*

**ethnic** /ˈɛθnɪk/ *a* étnico

**ethnographic** /ˌɛθnouˈgræfɪk/ *a* etnográfico

**ethnography** /ɛθˈnɒgrəfi/ *n* etnografía, *f*

**ethnologist** /ɛθˈnɒlədʒɪst/ *n* etnólogo, *m*

**ethnology** /ɛθˈnɒlədʒi/ *n* etnología, *f*

**ethyl** /ˈɛθəl/ *n Chem.* etilo, *m*

**ethylene** /ˈɛθəˌlin/ *n Chem.* etileno, *m*

**etiquette** /ˈɛtɪkɪt/ *n* etiqueta, *f*

**Etna, Mount** /ˈɛtnə/ el Etna

**Eton coat** /ˈitn/ *n* chaquetilla, *f*

**Eton collar** *n* cuello de colegial, *m*

**Eton crop** *n* pelo a la garçonne, *m*

**Etruscan** /ɪˈtrʌskən/ *a* and *n* etrusco (-ca)

**etymological** /ˌɛtəməˈlɒdʒɪkəl/ *a* etimológico

**etymologist** /ˌɛtəˈmɒlədʒɪst/ *n* etimólogo, *m*, etimologista, *m*

**etymology** /ˌɛtəˈmɒlədʒi/ *n* etimología, *f*

**eucalyptus** /ˌyukəˈlɪptəs/ *n* eucalipto, *m*

**Eucharist** /ˈyukərɪst/ *n* Eucaristía, *f*

**eucharistic** /ˌyukə'rɪstɪk/ a eucarístico
**Euclidean** /yu'klɪdiən/ a euclídeo
**eugenic** /yu'dʒɛnɪk/ a eugenésico
**eugenics** /yu'dʒɛnɪks/ n eugenesia, f
**eulogist** /'yulədʒɪst/ n elogiador (-ra), loador (-ra)
**eulogistic** /ˌyulə'dʒɪstɪk/ a elogiador
**eulogize** /'yulə,dʒaiz/ vt elogiar, alabar, encomiar
**eulogy** /'yulədʒi/ n elogio, encomio, m; alabanza, f; panegírico, m
**eunuch** /'yunək/ n eunuco, m
**euphemism** /'yufə,mɪzəm/ n eufemismo, m
**euphonious** /yu'founiəs/ a eufónico
**euphony** /'yufəni/ n eufonía, f
**euphuistic** /ˌyufyu'ɪstɪk/ a alambicado, gongorino
**Eurasian** /yʊ'reiʒən/ a and n eurasio (-ia)
**eurhythmic** /yʊ'rɪðmɪk/ a eurítmico
**eurhythmics** /yʊ'rɪðmɪks/ n euritmia, f
**European** /ˌyʊrə'piən/ a and n europeo (-ea)
**europeanize** /ˌyʊrə'piə,naiz/ vt europeanizar
**euthanasia** /ˌyuθə'neiʒə, -ʒiə, -ziə/ n eutanasia, f
**evacuate** /ɪ'vækyu,eit/ vt evacuar
**evacuation** /ɪ,vækyu'eifən/ n evacuación, f
**evade** /ɪ'veid/ vt evadir, eludir; evitar, esquivar; rehuir
**evaluate** /ɪ'vælyu,eit/ vt evaluar, estimar; calcular
**evaluation** /ɪ,vælyu'eifən/ n evaluación, estimación, f
**evanescent** /ˌevə'nɛsənt/ a transitorio, fugaz, pasajero
**evangelical** /ˌivæn'dʒɛlɪkəl/ a evangélico
**evangelicalism** /ˌivæn'dʒɛlɪkə,lɪzəm/ n evangelismo, m
**evangelist** /ɪ'vændʒəlɪst/ n evangelista, m
**evangelize** /ɪ'vændʒə,laiz/ vt evangelizar
**evaporate** /ɪ'væpə,reit/ vi evaporarse; desvanecerse. —vt evaporar
**evaporation** /ɪ,væpə'reifən/ n evaporación, f; desvanecimiento, m
**evaporative** /ɪ'væpə,reitɪv/ a evaporatorio
**evasion** /ɪ'veiʒən/ n (escape) fuga, f; evasión, f; evasiva, f, efugio, m
**evasive** /ɪ'veisɪv/ a evasivo, ambiguo
**evasively** /ɪ'veisɪvli/ adv evasivamente
**evasiveness** /ɪ'veisɪvnɪs/ n carácter evasivo, m
**eve** /iv/ n víspera, f; Eccl. vigilia, f. **on the eve of,** la víspera de; Fig. en vísperas de
**even** /'ivən/ a (flat) llano; (smooth) liso; igual; (level with) al mismo nivel (de); uniforme; (of numbers) par; (approximate, of sums) redondo; rítmico; invariable, constante; (of temper) apacible; (just) imparcial; (monotonous) monótono, igual; (paid) pagado; (Com. of date) mismo. **to get e. with,** pagar en la misma moneda, vengarse de
**even** /'ivən/ adv siquiera; aun; hasta; (also) también. **not e.,** ni siquiera. **e. as,** así como, del mismo modo que. **e. if,** aun cuando, si bien. **e. now,** aun ahora; ahora mismo. **e. so,** aun así; (nevertheless) sin embargo. **e. though,** aunque; suponiendo que
**even** /'ivən/ vt igualar; (level) allanar, nivelar; (accounts) desquitar; compensar; hacer uniforme
**evening** /'ivnɪŋ/ n tarde, f, atardecer, m; noche, f; Fig. fin, m, a occaso; declive, m. **Good e.!** ¡Buenas tardes! ¡Buenas noches! **in the e.,** al atardecer. **tomorrow e.,** mañana por la tarde. **yesterday e.,** ayer por la tarde. **e. class,** clase nocturna, f. **e. dress,** (women) traje de noche, m; (men) traje de etiqueta, m. **e. meal,** cena, f. **e. paper,** periódico (or diario) de la noche, m. **evening primrose,** hierba del asno, onagra, f. **e. star,** estrella vespertina, estrella de la tarde, f; (Venus) lucero de la tarde, m
**evenly** /'ivənli/ adv igualmente; (on a level) a nivel; uniformemente; imparcialmente; (of speech) con suavidad
**evenness** /'ivənnɪs/ n igualdad, f; (smoothness) lisura, f; uniformidad, f; imparcialidad, f; (of temper) ecuanimidad, serenidad, f
**evensong** /'ivən,sɔŋ/ n vísperas, f pl
**event** /ɪ'vɛnt/ n incidente, suceso, acontecimiento, m; (result) consecuencia, f; resultado, m; caso, m; (athletics) prueba, f; (race) carrera, f. **at all events,** de todas maneras. **in such an e.,** en tal caso. **in the e. of,** en el caso de

**eventful** /ɪ'vɛntfəl/ a lleno de acontecimientos; accidentado; memorable
**eventual** /ɪ'vɛntfuəl/ a eventual; final, último
**eventuality** /ɪ,vɛntfu'ælɪti/ n eventualidad, f
**eventually** /ɪ'vɛntfuəli/ adv a la larga, al fin
**ever** /'ɛvər/ adv siempre; (at any time) jamás; alguna vez; nunca; (even) siquiera; (very) muy; (in any way) en modo alguno. **As fast as e. he can,** Lo más aprisa que pueda. **Be it e. so big,** Por grande que sea. **Did you e.!** ¡Habráse visto! ¡Qué cosa! **for e.,** para siempre. **for e. and e.,** para siempre jamás; (mostly ecclesiastical) por los siglos de los siglos; eternamente. **He is e. so nice,** Es muy simpático. **Hardly e.,** casi nunca. **I don't think I have e. been there,** No creo que haya estado nunca allí. **if e.,** si alguna vez; (rarely) raramente. **nor... e.,** ni nunca. **not... e.,** nunca. **e. after,** desde entonces; (afterward) después. **e. and anon,** de vez en cuando. **e. so little,** siquiera un poco; muy poco
**evergreen** /'ɛvər,grin/ a siempre verde. —n planta vivaz, f. **e. oak,** encina, f
**everlasting** /ˌɛvər'læstɪŋ/ a eterno, perpetuo; (of colors) estable; incesante. **e. flower,** perpetua, f
**evermore** /ˌɛvər'mɔr/ adv eternamente
**every** /'ɛvri/ a todo; cada (invariable); todos los, m pl; todas las, f pl. **e. day,** todos los días, cada día. **e. now and then,** de cuando en cuando. **e. other day,** cada dos días
**everybody** /'ɛvri,bɒdi, -,bʌdi/ n todo el mundo, m; todos, m pl; todas, f pl; cada uno, m; cada una, f
**everyday** /'ɛvri,dei/ a diario, cotidiano; corriente, de cada día, usual
**everything** /'ɛvri,θɪŋ/ n todo, m; (e. that, which) todo lo (que). **e. possible,** todo lo posible
**everywhere** /'ɛvri,wɛər/ adv por todas partes
**evict** /ɪ'vɪkt/ vt desahuciar; expulsar
**eviction** /ɪ'vɪkfən/ n evicción, f, desahúcio, m; expulsión, f
**evidence** /'ɛvidəns/ n Law. testimonio, m, deposición, f; indicios, m pl; evidencia, f; prueba, f; hecho, m, vt patentizar, probar. **to give e.,** dar testimonio, deponer
**evident** /'ɛvidənt/ a evidente, patente, manifiesto; claro. **to be e.,** ser patente, estar a la vista
**evidently** /'ɛvidəntli/ adv evidentemente; claramente
**evil** /'ivəl/ a malo; malvado, perverso; de maldad; (unfortunate) aciago; de infortunio; (of spirits) diabólico, malo. —n mal, m; maldad, perversidad, f; (misfortune) desgracia, f. **the E. one,** el Malo. **e.-doer,** malhechor (-ra). **e. eye,** mal de ojo, aojo, m. **e.-minded,** mal pensado; malintencionado. **e.-speaking,** maledicencia, calumnia, f. **e. spirit,** demonio, espíritu malo, m
**evince** /ɪ'vɪns/ vt evidenciar; mostrar
**eviscerate** /ɪ'vɪsə,reit/ vt destripar, desentrañar
**evocation** /ˌɛvə'keifən/ n evocación, f
**evocative** /ɪ'vɒkətɪv/ a evocador
**evoke** /ɪ'vouk/ vt evocar
**evolution** /ˌɛvə'lufən/ n evolución, f; desarrollo, m; (Nav. Mil.) maniobra, f; Math. extracción de una raíz, f; (revolution) revolución, vuelta, f
**evolutionism** /ˌɛvə'lufə,nɪzəm/ n evolucionismo, m
**evolutive** /ˌɛvə'lutɪv/ a evolutivo
**evolve** /ɪ'vɒlv/ vi evolucionar; desarrollarse. —vt producir por evolución; desarrollar; pensar
**ewe** /yu/ n oveja, f. **ewe lamb,** cordera, f
**ewer** /'yuər/ n aguamanil, m
**exacerbate** /ɪg'zæsər,beit/ vt exacerbar; agravar, empeorar
**exacerbation** /ɪg,zæsər'beifən/ n exacerbación, f; agravación, f
**exact** /ɪg'zækt/ a exacto; fiel; metódico; estricto. —vt exigir
**exacting** /ɪg'zæktɪŋ/ a exigente; severo, estricto; (hard) agotador, arduo
**exaction** /ɪg'zækfən/ n exigencia, f; extorsión, exacción, f
**exactly** /ɪg'zæktli/ adv exactamente; precisamente
**exactness** /ɪg'zæktnɪs/ n exactitud, f
**exaggerate** /ɪg'zædʒə,reit/ vt exagerar; acentuar. —vi exagerar
**exaggerated** /ɪg'zædʒə,reitɪd/ a exagerado

**exaggeration** /ɪgˌzædʒəˈreɪʃən/ n exageración, f

**exaggerator** /ɪgˈzædʒəˌreɪtər/ n exagerador (-ra)

**exalt** /ɪgˈzɔlt/ vt exaltar; enaltecer, elevar; (praise) glorificar, magnificar; (intensify) realzar; intensificar

**exaltation** /ˌɛgzɔlˈteɪʃən/ n exaltación, elevación, f; alegría, f, júbilo, m; (ecstasy) éxtasis, arrobamiento, m; (of the Cross) exaltación, f

**exalted** /ɪgˈzɔltɪd/ a exaltado, eminente

**exaltedness** /ɪgˈzɔltɪdnɪs/ n exaltación, f

**examination** /ɪgˌzæməˈneɪʃən/ n examen, m; inspección, f; investigación, f; Law. interrogatorio, m; prueba, f. **to sit an e.**, examinarse. **written e.**, prueba escrita, f

**examine** /ɪgˈzæmɪn/ vt examinar; inspeccionar; investigar; Law. interrogar; (search) reconocer; (by touch) tentar; observar; analizar. **to e. into**, examinar; considerar detenidamente; ahondar en

**examinee** /ɪgˌzæməˈni/ n examinando (-da)

**examiner** /ɪgˈzæmɪnər/ n examinador (-ra); inspector (-ra)

**examinership** /ɪgˈzæmɪnərˌʃɪp/ n cargo de examinador, m

**examining** /ɪgˈzæmɪnɪŋ/ a que examina; de examen; Law. interrogante

**example** /ɪgˈzæmpəl/ n ejemplo, m; ilustración, f; (parallel) ejemplar, m; (warning) escarmiento, m. **for e.**, por ejemplo. **to set an e.**, dar ejemplo, dar el ejemplo.

**exasperate** /ɪgˈzæspəˌreɪt/ vt exasperar, irritar; (increase) aumentar; (worsen) agravar

**exasperating** /ɪgˈzæspəˌreɪtɪŋ/ a exasperante, irritante, provocador

**exasperation** /ɪgˌzæspəˈreɪʃən/ n exasperación, irritación, f; (worsening) agravación, f; enojo, m

**excavate** /ˈɛkskəˌveɪt/ vt excavar; (hollow) vaciar

**excavation** /ˌɛkskəˈveɪʃən/ n excavación, f; Archit. vaciado, m

**excavator** /ˈɛkskəˌveɪtər/ n excavador (-ra); (machine) excavadora, f

**exceed** /ɪkˈsid/ vt exceder; (excel) superar, aventajar; (one's hopes, etc.) sobrepujar. —vi excederse. **e. all expectations,** exceder a toda ponderación. **to e. one's rights,** abusar de sus derechos, ir demasiado lejos

**exceedingly** /ɪkˈsidɪŋli/ adv sumamente, extremadamente; sobre manera

**excel** /ɪkˈsel/ vt aventajar, superar; vencer. —vi sobresalir; distinguirse, señalarse; ser superior

**excellence** /ˈɛksələns/ n excelencia, f; superioridad, f; perfección, f; mérito, m; buena calidad, f

**excellency** /ˈɛksələnsi/ n (title) Excelencia, f. **Your E.,** Su Excelencia

**excellent** /ˈɛksələnt/ a excelente; superior; perfecto; magnífico; (in examinations) sobresaliente

**excellently** /ˈɛksələntli/ adv excelentemente; perfectamente; magníficamente

**except** /ɪkˈsept/ vt exceptuar; omitir

**except, excepting** /ɪkˈsept; ɪkˈseptɪŋ/ prep excepto, con excepción de; exceptuando; menos; salvo; fuera de. —conjunc a menos que. **except for,** si no fuese por; con excepción de; fuera de

**exception** /ɪkˈsepʃən/ n excepción, f; objeción, protesta, f. **to make an e.,** hacer una excepción. **to take e. to,** protestar contra; tachar, criticar; desaprobar

**exceptional** /ɪkˈsepʃənl/ a excepcional

**excerpt** /n ˈɛksɜrpt; v ɪkˈsɜrpt/ n excerpta, f, extracto, m. —vt extraer

**excess** /ɪkˈses, ˈɛkses/ n exceso, m; superabundancia, f; demasía, f; Com. superávit, m. **in e.,** en exceso, de sobra. **in e. of,** en exceso de; arriba de. **to e.,** excesivamente, demasiado. **e. fare,** suplemento, m. **e. luggage,** exceso de equipaje, m; (overweight) exceso de peso, m

**excessive** /ɪkˈsesɪv/ a excesivo; superabundante; inmoderado, desmesurado; exagerado

**excessively** /ɪkˈsesɪvli/ adv excesivamente; exageradamente

**excessiveness** /ɪkˈsesɪvnɪs/ n exceso, m; superabundancia, f; exageración, f

**exchange** /ɪksˈtʃeɪndʒ/ n cambio, trueque, m; (of prisoners) canje, m; (financial) cambio, m; (building) bolsa, lonja, f; (telephone) oficina central de telé-

fonos, f. —vt cambiar (for, por); trocar; (replace) reemplazar; (prisoners) canjear; (of blows) darse; (pass from, into) pasar de... a. —vi hacer un cambio. **in e. for,** en cambio de, a trueque de; por. **to e. greetings,** saludarse; cambiar saludos. **They exchanged looks,** Se miraron. **What is the rate of e.?** ¿Cuál es el tipo de cambio? **e. of prisoners,** canje de prisioneros, m

**exchangeable** /ɪksˈtʃeɪndʒəbəl/ a cambiable; trocable

**exchequer** /ˈɛkstʃekər/ n (public finance) Hacienda pública, f; tesorería, f; (funds) fondos, m pl. **Chancellor of the E.,** Ministro de Hacienda, m

**excise** /n ˈɛksaiz; v ɪkˈsaiz/ n contribución indirecta, f; (customs and e.) Aduana, f. —vt (cut) cortar, extirpar; imponer una contribución indirecta. **e. duty,** derecho de aduana, m

**excise tax** arbitrios, m pl

**excision** /ɛkˈsɪʒən/ n excisión, f; extirpación, f

**excitability** /ɪkˌsaitəˈbɪlti/ n excitabilidad, f

**excitable** /ɪkˈsaitəbəl/ a excitable

**excitation** /ˌɛksaiˈteɪʃən/ n excitación, f

**excite** /ɪkˈsait/ vt emocionar; conmover; agitar; excitar; suscitar, provocar; incitar, instigar; (attention, interest) despertar; estimular. **to become excited,** emocionarse; exaltarse; (annoyed) acalorarse; (upset) agitarse

**excitedly** /ɪkˈsaitɪdli/ adv con emoción; acaloradamente; agitadamente

**excitement** /ɪkˈsaitmənt/ n conmoción, f; agitación, f; (annoyance) acaloramiento, m; emoción, f; estímulo, m; instigación, f, fomento, m; (amusement) placer, m

**exciting** /ɪkˈsaitɪŋ/ a emocionante; conmovedor; agitador; muy interesante

**exclaim** /ɪkˈskleim/ vt and vi exclamar. **to e. against,** clamar contra

**exclamation** /ˌɛkskləˈmeɪʃən/ n exclamación, f. **e. mark,** punto de exclamación, m

**exclamatory** /ɪkˈsklæməˌtɔri/ a exclamatorio

**exclude** /ɪkˈsklud/ vt excluir; exceptuar; evitar; (refuse) rechazar

**exclusion** /ɪkˈskluʒən/ n exclusión, f; exceptuación, f; eliminación, f

**exclusive** /ɪkˈsklusɪv/ a exclusivo; (snobbish) exclusivista. **e. of,** no incluido; aparte de

**exclusively** /ɪkˈsklusɪvli/ adv exclusivamente; únicamente

**exclusiveness** /ɪkˈsklusɪvnɪs/ n carácter exclusivo, m

**exclusivism** /ɪkˈsklusəˌvɪzəm/ n exclusivismo, m

**exclusivist** /ɪkˈsklusəvɪst/ n exclusivista, mf

**excommunicate** /v ˌɛkskəˈmyunɪˌkeit; -kɪt/ vt excomulgar. —a excomulgado

**excommunication** /ˌɛkskəˌmyunɪˈkeiʃən/ n excomunión, f

**excrement** /ˈɛkskrəmənt/ n excremento, m

**excrescence** /ɪkˈskresəns/ n excrecencia, f

**excrescent** /ɪkˈskresənt/ a que forma excrecencia; superfluo

**excrete** /ɪkˈskrit/ vt excretar

**excretion** /ɪkˈskriʃən/ n excreción, f

**excretory** /ˈɛkskrɪˌtɔri/ a excretorio

**excruciating** /ɪkˈskruʃiˌeitɪŋ/ a atormentador, angustioso; (of pain) agudísimo

**excursion** /ɪkˈskɜrʒən/ n excursión, f; expedición, f; (digression) digresión, f. **e. ticket,** billete de excursión, m. **e. train,** tren de excursionistas, m

**excursionist** /ɪkˈskɜrʒənɪst/ n excursionista, mf; turista, m

**excusable** /ɪkˈskyuzəbəl/ a disculpable, excusable

**excusably** /ɪkˈskyuzəbli/ adv excusablemente

**excuse** /ɪkˈskyus/ n excusa, f; disculpa, f; pretexto, m; justificación, defensa, f. **to give as an e.,** pretextar

**excuse** /ɪkˈskyuz/ vt disculpar, excusar; dispensar (de); librar (de); (forgive) perdonar; (defend) justificar, defender; (minimize) paliar; (oneself) disculparse. **E. me!** ¡Con permiso!; ¡Perdone Vd.!; ¡Dispense Vd.!

**execrable** /ˈɛksɪkrəbəl/ a execrable, abominable

**execrate** /ˈɛksɪˌkreit/ vt execrar, abominar. —vi maldecir

**execration** /ˌɛksɪˈkreiʃən/ n execración, abominación, f; maldición, f

**execute** /ˈɛksɪˌkyut/ vt (perform) ejecutar, poner en

efecto, realizar; (*Art. Mus.*) ejecutar; (part in a play) hacer, desempeñar; (fulfil) cumplir; *Law.* otorgar (un documento); (kill) ajusticiar

**execution** /ˌɛksɪˈkyuʃən/ *n* efectuación, realización, *f;* (*Art., Mus.*) ejecución, *f;* (of part in a play) desempeño (de un papel), *m;* (fulfilment) cumplimiento, *m; Law.* otorgamiento (de un documento), *m;* (killing) suplicio, *m,* ejecución de la pena de muerte, *f;* (*Law.* seizure) ejecución, *f*

**executioner** /ˌɛksɪˈkyuʃənər/ *n* verdugo, *m*

**executive** /ɪgˈzɛkyətɪv/ *a* ejecutivo; administrativo. —*n* poder ejecutivo, *m*

**executor** /ɪgˈzɛkyətər/ *n* administrador testamentario, *m*

**executorship** /ɪgˈzɛkyətərˌʃɪp/ *n* ejecutoría, *f*

**executrix** /ɪgˈzɛkyətrɪks/ *n* administradora testamentaria, *f*

**exegesis** /ˌɛksɪˈdʒisɪs/ *n* exégesis, *f*

**exegetical** /ˌɛksɪˈdʒɛtɪkəl/ *a* exegético

**exemplary** /ɪgˈzɛmpləri/ *a* ejemplar

**exemplification** /ɪgˌzɛmpləfɪˈkeɪʃən/ *n* ejemplificación, ilustración, demostración, *f*

**exemplify** /ɪgˈzɛmpləˌfaɪ/ *vt* ejemplificar; ilustrar, demostrar

**exempt** /ɪgˈzɛmpt/ *vt* exentar, eximir; librar; dispensar, excusar. —*a* exento; libre; excusado; inmune

**exemption** /ɪgˈzɛmpʃən/ *n* exención, *f;* libertad, *f;* inmunidad, *f*

**exercise** /ˈɛksərˌsaɪz/ *n* ejercicio, *m;* uso, *m;* (essay) ensayo, *m; pl* **exercises,** (on land or sea) maniobras, *f pl.* —*vt* ejercer; usar, emplear; (train) ejercitar, entrenar; adiestrar; pasear, dar un paseo; (worry) preocupar. —*vi* hacer ejercicio; ejercitarse; adiestrarse. **spiritual exercises,** ejercicios espirituales, *m pl.* **to take e. in the open air,** tomar ejercicio al aire libre. **to write an e.,** escribir un ejercicio. **e. book,** cuaderno de ejercicios, *m*

**exert** /ɪgˈzɜrt/ *vt* hacer uso de, emplear, ejercer, poner en juego; (deploy) desplegar. **to e. oneself,** hacer un esfuerzo (para); esforzarse (de); trabajar mucho; tratar (de); apurarse, tomarse mucha molestia; preocuparse

**exertion** /ɪgˈzɜrʃən/ *n* esfuerzo, *m;* uso, *m;* (exercise) ejercicio, *m;* (good offices) diligencias, gestiones, *f pl;* buenos oficios, *m pl*

**exhalation** /ˌɛkshəˈleɪʃən/ *n* exhalación, *f;* efluvio, *m;* vapor, *m;* humo, *m*

**exhale** /ɛksˈheɪl/ *vt* exhalar; emitir, despedir. —*vi* evaporarse; disiparse

**exhaust** /ɪgˈzɔst/ *vt* agotar; (empty) vaciar; (end) acabar; apurar; consumir; (tire) rendir, cansar mucho; (weaken) debilitar; (a subject) tratar detalladamente. —*n Mech.* escape, *m;* emisión de vapor, *f;* vapor de escape, *m.* **e. pipe,** tubo de escape, *m*

**exhaustible** /ɪgˈzɔstəbəl/ *a* agotable

**exhausting** /ɪgˈzɔstɪŋ/ *a* cansado, agotador

**exhaustion** /ɪgˈzɔstʃən/ *n* agotamiento, *m;* rendimiento, cansancio, *m;* lasitud, *f;* postración, *f*

**exhaustive** /ɪgˈzɔstɪv/ *a* completo; minucioso

**exhaustively** /ɪgˈzɔstɪvli/ *adv* detenidamente; detalladamente; minuciosamente

**exhaustiveness** /ɪgˈzɔstɪvnɪs/ *n* lo completo; minuciosidad, *f*

**exhibit** /ɪgˈzɪbɪt/ *vt* exhibir; manifestar, ostentar; revelar, descubrir; presentar. —*vi* exhibir, ser expositor. —*n* objeto exhibido, *m; Law.* prueba, *f*

**exhibition** /ˌɛksəˈbɪʃən/ *n* exposición, *f;* (performance) función, *f;* espectáculo, *m;* exhibición, *f;* (showing) manifestación, *f;* (grant) bolsa de estudio, beca, *f*

**exhibitionism** /ˌɛksəˈbɪʃəˌnɪzəm/ *n* exhibicionismo, *m*

**exhibitionist** /ˌɛksəˈbɪʃənɪst/ *n* exhibicionista, *mf*

**exhibitor** /ɪgˈzɪbɪtər/ *n* expositor (-ra)

**exhilarate** /ɪgˈzɪləˌreɪt/ *vt* alegrar, alborozar

**exhilarating** /ɪgˈzɪləˌreɪtɪŋ/ *a* alegre; estimulador; vigorizador, tonificante

**exhilaration** /ɪgˌzɪləˈreɪʃən/ *n* alegría, *f,* alborozo, regocijo, *m*

**exhort** /ɪgˈzɔrt/ *vt* and *vi* exhortar

**exhortation** /ˌɛgzɔrˈteɪʃən/ *n* exhortación, *f*

**exhumation** /ˌɛkshyuˈmeɪʃən/ *n* exhumación, *f*

**exhume** /ɪgˈzum/ *vt* exhumar

**exigence** /ˈɛksɪdʒəns/ *n* exigencia, *f;* urgencia, *f;* (need) necesidad, *f*

**exigent** /ˈɛksɪdʒənt/ *a* exigente; urgente

**exiguous** /ɪgˈzɪgyuəs/ *a* exiguo

**exiguousness** /ɪgˈzɪgyuəsnɪs/ *n* exigüidad, *f*

**exile** /ˈɛgzaɪl/ *n* destierro, *m;* (person) desterrado (-da). —*vt* desterrar

**exist** /ɪgˈzɪst/ *vi* existir

**existence** /ɪgˈzɪstəns/ *n* existencia, *f;* (being) ser, *m;* (life) vida, *f.* **to bring into e.,** causar; producir

**existentialism** /ˌɛgzɪˈstɛnʃəˌlɪzəm/ *n* existencialismo, *m*

**existing** /ɪgˈzɪstɪŋ/ *a* existente

**exit** /ˈɛgzɪt, ˈɛksɪt/ *n* salida, *f;* partida, *f;* (death) muerte, *f; Theat.* mutis, *m.* —*vi Theat.* hacer mutis. **to make one's e.,** salir; marcharse; irse; morir; *Theat.* hacer mutis

**exodus** /ˈɛksədəs/ *n* éxodo, *m;* salida, *f;* emigración, *f;* (Old Testament) Éxodo, *m*

**exonerate** /ɪgˈzɒnəˌreɪt/ *vt* exonerar

**exoneration** /ɪgˌzɒnəˈreɪʃən/ *n* exoneración, *f*

**exorbitance** /ɪgˈzɔrbɪtəns/ *n* exorbitancia, *f*

**exorbitant** /ɪgˈzɔrbɪtənt/ *a* exorbitante

**exorcism** /ˈɛksɔrˌsɪzəm/ *n* exorcismo, *m*

**exorcist** /ˈɛksɔrsɪst/ *n* exorcista, *m*

**exorcize** /ˈɛksɔrˌsaɪz/ *vt* exorcizar, conjurar

**exotic** /ɪgˈzɒtɪk/ *a* exótico. —*n* planta exótica, *f; Fig.* flor de estufa, *f*

**expand** /ɪkˈspænd/ *vt* extender; abrir; (wings, etc.) desplegar; (the chest, etc.) expandir; dilatar; (amplify) ampliar; (an edition) ampliar, aumentar; (develop) desarrollar; *Fig.* ensanchar; (increase) aumentar. —*vi* dilatarse; hincharse; abrirse; extenderse; *Fig.* ensancharse; (increase) aumentarse

**expanse** /ɪkˈspæns/ *n* extensión, *f*

**expansibility** /ɪkˌspænsəˈbɪlɪti/ *n Phys.* expansibilidad, *f;* dilatabilidad, *f*

**expansible** /ɪkˈspænsəbəl/ *a Phys.* expansible; dilatable

**expansion** /ɪkˈspænʃən/ *n* expansión, *f;* extensión, *f;* dilatación, *f;* (amplification) ampliación, *f;* (development) desarrollo, *m; Fig.* ensanchamiento, *m;* (increase) aumento, *m*

**expansionism** /ɪkˈspænʃəˌnɪzəm/ *n* expansionismo, *m*

**expansive** /ɪkˈspænsɪv/ *a* expansivo; (of persons) efusivo, expresivo, comunicativo, afable

**expansiveness** /ɪkˈspænsɪvnɪs/ *n* expansibilidad, *f;* (of persons) afabilidad, *f*

**expatiate** /ɪkˈspeɪʃiˌeɪt/ **(upon)** *vi* extenderse en

**expatiation** /ɪkˌspeɪʃiˈeɪʃən/ *n* discurso, *m;* digresión, *f*

**expatriation** /ɛksˌpeɪtriˈeɪʃən/ *n* expatriación, *f*

**expect** /ɪkˈspɛkt/ *vt* esperar; (await) aguardar; (suppose) suponer; (demand) exigir; (count on) contar con. —*vi* creer

**expectance** /ɪkˈspɛktəns/ *n* expectación, *f;* esperanza, *f*

**expectant** /ɪkˈspɛktənt/ *a* expectante; (hopeful) esperanzado; (pregnant) embarazada

**expectantly** /ɪkˈspɛktəntli/ *adv* con expectación

**expectation** /ˌɛkspɛkˈteɪʃən/ *n* expectación, *f;* (hope) esperanza, expectativa, *f;* probabilidad, *f*

**expectorate** /ɪkˈspɛktəˌreɪt/ *vt* expectorar. —*vi* escupir

**expectoration** /ɪkˌspɛktəˈreɪʃən/ *n* expectoración, *f*

**expedience** /ɪkˈspidiəns/ *n* conveniencia, *f;* oportunidad, *f;* aptitud, *f;* (self-interest) egoísmo, *m*

**expedient** /ɪkˈspidiənt/ *a* conveniente; oportuno; apto; prudente; político. —*n* expediente, recurso, medio, *m*

**expedite** /ˈɛkspɪˌdaɪt/ *vt* acelerar; facilitar; (send off) despachar

**expedition** /ˌɛkspɪˈdɪʃən/ *n* expedición, *f;* (haste) celeridad, diligencia, *f*

**expeditionary** /ˌɛkspɪˈdɪʃəˌnɛri/ *a* expedicionario. **e. force,** fuerza expedicionaria, *f*

**expeditious** /ˌɛkspɪˈdɪʃəs/ *a* expedito, pronto

**expeditiously** /ˌɛkspɪˈdɪʃəsli/ *adv* expeditamente, prontamente

**expeditiousness** /ˌɛkspɪˈdɪʃəsnɪs/ *n* prontitud, *f*

**expel** /ɪk'spɛl/ *vt* expeler, expulsar; echar, arrojar; despedir

**expend** /ɪk'spɛnd/ *vt* gastar, expender; (time) perder

**expenditure** /ɪk'spɛndɪtʃər/ *n* gasto, desembolso, *m;* (of time) pérdida, *f*

**expense** /ɪk'spɛns/ *n* gasto, *m;* pérdida, *f;* costa, *f; pl* **expenses,** expensas, *f pl,* gastos, *m pl.* **at the e. of,** a costa de. **to be put to great e.,** tener que gastar mucho. **to pay one's expenses,** pagar sus gastos

**expensive** /ɪk'spɛnsɪv/ *a* costoso; caro

**expensively** /ɪk'spɛnsɪvli/ *adv* costosamente

**expensiveness** /ɪk'spɛnsɪvnɪs/ *n* lo costoso; costa, *f*

**experience** /ɪk'spɪəriəns/ *n* experiencia, *f.* —*vt* experimentar; sentir; sufrir. **by e.,** por experiencia

**experienced** /ɪk'spɪəriənst/ *a* experimentado; experto; hábil; (lived) vivido

**experiment** /*n* ɪk'spɛrəmənt; *v* -ˌmɛnt/ *n* experimento, *m;* prueba, *f;* ensayo, *m,* tentativa, *f.* —*vi* experimentar; hacer una prueba

**experimental** /ɪk,spɛrə'mɛntl/ *a* experimental; tentativo

**experimentally** /ɪk,spɛrə'mɛntl̩i/ *adv* experimentalmente; por experiencia

**expert** /'ɛkspɜrt/ *a* experto; perito; hábil; (finished) acabado. —*n* experto, *m,* especialista, *mf*

**expertly** /'ɛkspɜrtli/ *adv* expertamente; hábilmente

**expertness** /'ɛkspɜrtnɪs/ *n* pericia, *f;* maestría, *f;* habilidad, *f;* (knowledge) conocimiento, *m*

**expiable** /'ɛkspiəbəl/ *a* que se puede expiar

**expiate** /'ɛkspiˌeit/ *vt* expiar; reparar

**expiation** /ˌɛkspi'eiʃən/ *n* expiación, *f*

**expiatory** /'ɛkspiəˌtɔri/ *a* expiatorio

**expiration** /ˌɛkspə'reiʃən/ *n* (breathing out) espiración, *f;* (ending) expiración, *f;* terminación, *f; Com.* vencimiento, *m;* (death) muerte, *f*

**expiration date** fecha de caducidad, *f*

**expire** /ɪk'spaiᵊr/ *vi* (exhale) espirar; (die) morir, dar el último suspiro; (of fire, light) extinguirse; (end) expirar; terminar; *Com.* vencer

**expiry** /ɪk'spaiᵊri/ *n* terminación, *f;* expiración, *f; Com.* vencimiento, *m*

**explain** /ɪk'splein/ *vt* explicar; aclarar; demostrar; exponer; (justify) justificar, defender. —*vi* explicarse. **to e. away,** explicar; justificar

**explainable** /ɪk'spleinəbəl/ *a* explicable

**explanation** /ˌɛksplə'neiʃən/ *n* explicación, *f;* aclaración, *f*

**explanatory** /ɪk'splænəˌtɔri/ *a* explicativo; aclaratorio

**expletive** /'ɛksplɪtɪv/ *a* expletivo. —*n* interjección, *f*

**explicable** /'ɛksplɪkəbəl/ *a* explicable

**explicit** /ɪk'splɪsɪt/ *a* explícito

**explode** /ɪk'sploud/ *vi* estallar; detonar; reventar. —*vt* hacer estallar; (a mine) hacer saltar; (a belief, etc.) hacer abandonar; desechar

**exploit** /ɪk'splɔit/ *n* hazaña, proeza, *f;* aventura, *f.* —*vt* explotar

**exploitation** /ˌɛksplɔi'teiʃən/ *n* explotación, *f*

**exploiter** /ɪk'splɔitər/ *n* explotador (-ra)

**exploration** /ˌɛksplə'reiʃən/ *n* exploración, *f*

**exploratory** /ɪk'splɔrəˌtɔri/ *a* exploratorio

**explore** /ɪk'splɔr/ *vt* explorar; examinar; averiguar; investigar; (*Med. Surg.*) explorar

**explorer** /ɪk'splɔrər/ *n* explorador (-ra)

**explosion** /ɪk'splouʒən/ *n* explosión, *f;* estallido, *m,* detonación, *f*

**explosive** /ɪk'splousɪv/ *a and n* explosivo, *m.* **high e.,** explosivo violento, *m.* **explosives chamber,** recámara, *f*

**explosiveness** /ɪk'splousɪvnɪs/ *n* propiedad explosiva, *f;* lo explosivo; violencia, *f*

**exponent** /ɪk'spounənt/ *a and n* exponente, *mf*

**export** /*n* 'ɛkspɔrt; *v* ɪk'spɔrt/ *n* exportación, *f.* —*vt* exportar. **e. license,** permiso de exportación, *m.* **e. trade,** comercio de exportación, *m*

**exportation** /ˌɛkspɔr'teiʃən/ *n* exportación, *f*

**exporter** /ɪk'spɔrtər/ *n* exportador (-ra)

**expose** /ɪk'spouz/ *vt* exponer; arriesgar; (exhibit) exhibir, (unmask) desenmascarar; descubrir; revelar; *Photo.* exponer; (ridicule) ridiculizar

**exposed** /ɪk'spouzd/ *a* descubierto; no abrigado; expuesto, peligroso

**exposition** /ˌɛkspə'zɪʃən/ *n* explicación, interpretación, *f;* declaración, *f;* (exhibition) exposición, *f*

**expostulate** /ɪk'spɒstʃəˌleit/ *vi* protestar, **to e. with,** reprochar; reconvenir

**expostulation** /ɪk,spɒstʃə'leiʃən/ *n* protesta, *f;* reconvención, *f*

**exposure** /ɪk'spouʒər/ *n* exposición, *f;* (aspect) orientación, *f;* (scandal) revelación, *f,* escándalo, *m;* peligro, *m;* exposición al frío o al calor, *f*

**expound** /ɪk'spaund/ *vt* exponer, explicar; comentar

**expounder** /ɪk'spaundər/ *n* intérprete, *mf;* comentador (-ra)

**express** /ɪk'sprɛs/ *a* (clear) categórico, explícito, claro; expreso; (exact) exacto; (quick) rápido. —*n* (messenger, post) expreso, *m;* (train) (tren) expreso, (tren) rápido, *m;* (goods) exprés, *m.* —*vt* expresar; (a letter, etc.) mandar por expreso

**expressible** /ɪk'sprɛsəbəl/ *a* decible

**expression** /ɪk'sprɛʃən/ *n* expresión, *f*

**expressionless** /ɪk'sprɛʃənlɪs/ *a* sin expresión

**expressive** /ɪk'sprɛsɪv/ *a* expresivo; que expresa

**expropriate** /ɛks'prouprɪˌeit/ *vt* expropiar

**expropriation** /ɛks,prouprɪ'eiʃən/ *n* expropiación, *f*

**expulsion** /ɪk'spʌlʃən/ *n* expulsión, *f*

**expunge** /ɪk'spʌndʒ/ *vt* borrar; testar; omitir

**expunging** /ɪk'spʌndʒɪŋ/ *n* borradura, *f;* testación, *f;* omisión, *f*

**expurgate** /'ɛkspərˌgeit/ *vt* expurgar

**expurgation** /ˌɛkspər'geiʃən/ *n* expurgación, *f*

**expurgator** /ɪk'spɜrgeitər/ *n* expurgador, *m*

**expurgatory** /ɪk'spɜrgəˌtɔri/ *a* expurgatorio

**exquisite** /ɪk'skwɪzɪt/ *a* exquisito, precioso, primoroso; excelente; (acute) agudo, intenso; (keen) vivo. —*n* elegante, petimetre, *m*

**exquisitely** /ɪk'skwɪzɪtli/ *adv* primorosamente, pulcramente; a la perfección

**exquisiteness** /ɪk'skwɪzɪtnɪs/ *n* primor, *m;* pulcritud, perfección, *f;* excelencia, *f;* (of pain) intensidad, *f;* (keenness) viveza, *f*

**ex-serviceman** /'ɛks'sɜrvɪsmən/ *n* excombatiente, antiguo soldado, *m*

**extant** /'ɛkstənt/ *a* estante; existente; viviente

**extempore** /ɪk'stɛmpəri/ *a* improvisado

**extemporize** /ɪk'stɛmpəˌraiz/ *vt and vi* improvisar

**extend** /ɪk'stɛnd/ *vt* extender; (hold out) tender, alargar; (lengthen) prolongar; (a period of time) prorrogar, diferir; (make larger) ensanchar; (increase) aumentar; dilatar; ampliar; (offer) ofrecer; *vi* extenderse; dilatarse; continuar; (give) dar de sí, estirarse; (last) prolongarse, durar; (become known) propagarse

**extensible** /ɪk'stɛnsəbəl/ *a* extensible

**extension** /ɪk'stɛnʃən/ *n* extensión, *f;* expansión, *f;* (increase) aumento, *m;* prolongación, *f;* ampliación, *f; Com.* prórroga, *f;* (telephone number) extensión, *f,* interno, *m*

**extension cord** *n* cordón de extensión, *m;* ladrón *m,* (Mexico; slang)

**extensive** /ɪk'stɛnsɪv/ *a* extenso, ancho, vasto; grande, considerable; (comprehensive) comprensivo

**extensively** /ɪk'stɛnsɪvli/ *adv* extensamente; generalmente

**extensiveness** /ɪk'stɛnsɪvnɪs/ *n* extensión, *f;* amplitud, *f*

**extensor** /ɪk'stɛnsər, -sɔr/ *n Anat.* extensor, *m*

**extent** /ɪk'stɛnt/ *n* extensión, *f;* (degree) punto, *m;* (limit) límite, *m.* **to a great e.,** en gran parte; considerablemente. **to some e.,** hasta cierto punto. **to the full e.,** en toda su extensión; completamente. **to what e.?** ¿hasta qué punto?

**extenuate** /ɪk'stɛnyuˌeit/ *vt* atenuar, desminuir, mitigar, paliar

**extenuating** /ɪk'stɛnyuˌeitɪŋ/ *a* atenuante

**extenuation** /ɪk,stɛnyu'eiʃən/ *n* atenuación, mitigación, *f*

**exterior** /ɪk'stɪəriər/ *a* exterior, externo; de fuera; (foreign) extranjero. —*n* exterior, *m;* aspecto, *m;* forma, *f*

**exterminate** /ɪk'stɜrməˌneit/ *vt* exterminar

**extermination** /ɪk,stɜrmə'neiʃən/ *n* exterminio, *m*

**exterminator** /ɪk'stɜrməˌneitər/ *n* exterminador (-ra)

**exterminatory** /ɪk'stɜrmənə,tɔri/ a exterminador

**external** /ɪk'stɜrnḷ/ a externo, exterior; (foreign) extranjero. —n pl **externals**, apariencias, f pl; aspecto exterior, m; comportamiento, m

**externally** /ɪk'stɜrnḷi/ adv exteriormente

**exterritorial** /,ɛkstɛrɪ'tɔriəl/ a extraterritorial

**exterritoriality** /,ɛkstɛrɪtɔri'ælɪti/ n extraterritorialidad, f

**extinct** /ɪk'stɪŋkt/ a extinto; (of light, fire) extinguido; suprimido

**extinction** /ɪk'stɪŋkʃən/ n extinción, f

**extinguish** /ɪk'stɪŋgwɪʃ/ vt extinguir; apagar; Fig. eclipsar

**extinguishable** /ɪk'stɪŋgwɪʃəbəl/ a apagable

**extinguisher** /ɪk'stɪŋgwɪʃər/ n apagador (-ra); (for fires) extintor, m; (snuffer) matacandelas, m

**extinguishment** /ɪk'stɪŋgwɪʃmənt/ n apagamiento, m; extinción, f; abolición, f; (destruction) aniquilamiento, m

**extirpate** /'ɛkstər,peit/ vt extirpar

**extirpation** /,ɛkstər'peiʃən/ n extirpación, f

**extol** /ɪk'stoul/ vt elogiar, encomiar, alabar; cantar

**extoller** /ɪk'stoulər/ n alabador (-ra)

**extort** /ɪk'stɔrt/ vt arrancar, sacar por fuerza; exigir por amenazas

**extortion** /ɪk'stɔrʃən/ n extorsión, f; exacción, f

**extortionate** /ɪk'stɔrʃənɪt/ a injusto; opresivo; (of price) exorbitante, excesivo

**extra** /'ɛkstrə/ a and adv adicional; extraordinario; suplementario; (spare) de repuesto. —prefix (in compounds) extra. —n extra, m; suplemento, m; (of a paper) hoja extraordinaria, f; (actor) supernumerario (-ia). **e. charge**, gasto suplementario, m; (on the railway, etc.) suplemento, m. **e.-mural**, a de extramuros.

**extract** /v ɪk'strækt; n 'ɛkstrækt/ vt sacar; (Chem. Math.) extraer; extractar; (obtain) obtener. —n Chem. extracto, m; (excerpt) cita, f

**extraction** /ɪk'strækʃən/ n saca, f; extracción, f; obtención, f

**extradite** /'ɛkstrə,dait/ vt entregar por extradición

**extradition** /,ɛkstrə'dɪʃən/ n extradición, f

**extraneous** /ɪk'streiniəs/ a extraño; (irrelevant) ajeno (a)

**extraordinarily** /ɪk,strɔrdṇ'ɛrəli/ adv extraordinariamente, singularmente

**extraordinariness** /ɪk'strɔrdṇ,ɛrinɪs/ n lo extraordinario; singularidad, f; (queerness) rareza, f

**extraordinary** /ɪk'strɔrdṇ,ɛri/ a extraordinario; singular; (queer) raro, excéntrico; (incredible) increíble

**extravagance** /ɪk'strævəgəns/ n (in spending) prodigalidad, f, derroche, m; (of dress, speech) extravagancia, f; (foolishness) disparate, m; (luxury) lujo, m

**extravagant** /ɪk'strævəgənt/ a extravagante; (queer) extraño, raro; (wasteful) pródigo; (of persons) gastador, manirroto; (of price) exorbitante; excesivo

**extravagantly** /ɪk'strævəgəntli/ adv extravagantemente; de un modo extraño; pródigamente; profusamente; excesivamente

**extreme** /ɪk'strim/ a extremo. —n extremo, m. **in e.**, extremamente, en extremo, en sumo grado. **to carry**

**to extremes,** llevar a extremos; **E. Unction,** Extremaunción, f

**extremely** /ɪk'strimli/ adv sumamente; Inf. muy

**extremism** /ɪk'stri,mɪzəm/ n extremismo, m

**extremist** /ɪk'strimɪst/ a and n extremista, mf

**extremity** /ɪk'strɛmɪti/ n extremidad, f; (point) punta, f; necesidad, f; pl **extremities,** Anat. extremidades, f pl; (measures) medidas extremas, f pl

**extricate** /'ɛkstrɪ,keit/ vt desenredar; librar; sacar

**extrication** /,ɛkstrɪ'keiʃən/ n liberación, f

**extrinsic** /ɪk'strɪnsɪk/ a extrínseco

**extrovert** /'ɛkstrə,vɜrt/ n Psychol. extravertido, ma

**exuberance** /ɪg'zubərəns/ n exuberancia, f

**exuberant** /ɪg'zubərənt/ a exuberante

**exudation** /,ɛksyʊ'deiʃən/ n exudación, f

**exude** /ɪg'zud/ vt exudar; rezumar; sudar. —vi exudar; rezumarse

**exult** /ɪg'zʌlt/ vi exultar; alegrarse

**exultant** /ɪg'zʌltṇt/ a exultante, triunfante

**exultantly** /ɪg'zʌltṇtli/ adv con exultación; triunfalmente

**exultation** /,ɛgzʌl'teiʃən/ n exultación, f; triunfo, m

**eye** /ai/ n ojo, m; (sight) vista, f; (look) mirada, f; atención, f; (opinion) opinión, f, juicio, m; (of a needle, of cheese) ojo, m; (of a hook) corcheta, f; Bot. yema, f; (of a potato) grillo, m. —vt ojear; fijar los ojos en; examinar, mirar detenidamente. **bright eyes,** ojos vivos, m pl. **prominent eyes,** ojos saltones, m pl. **He couldn't keep his eyes off Mary,** Se le fueron los ojos tras María. **as far as the eye can reach,** hasta donde alcanza la vista. **before one's eyes,** a la vista de uno, ante los ojos de uno. **in my (etc.) eyes,** Fig. según creo yo, en mi opinión. **in the twinkling of an eye,** en un abrir y cerrar de ojos. **with an eye to,** pensando en. **with my own eyes,** con mis propios ojos. **with the naked eye,** con la simple vista. **to keep an eye on,** vigilar. **to make eyes at,** guiñar el ojo; mirar con ojos de enamorado. **to have one's eyes opened,** Fig. caérsele la venda. **eye-bath,** ojera, f. **eye-opener,** revelación, sorpresa, f. **eye-pencil,** pincel para las cejas, m. **eye-piece,** objetivo, ocular, m. **eye-shade,** visera, f. **eye-tooth,** colmillo, m. **eye-witness,** testigo ocular, testigo de vista, testigo presencial, mf

**eyeball** /'ai,bɔl/ n globo ocular, m

**eyebrow** /'ai,brau/ n ceja, f

**eye care** atención de la vista, f

**eyed** /aid/ a que tiene ojos; (in compounds) de ojos..., con ojos...; con los ojos; (of a needle) con el ojo... **She is a blue-eyed child,** Es una niña de ojos azules

**eyeglass** /'ai,glæs/ n lente, m

**eyelash** /'ai,læʃ/ n pestaña, f

**eyeless** /'ailɪs/ a sin ojos

**eyelet** /'ailɪt/ n ojete, m

**eyelid** /'ai,lɪd/ n párpado, m

**eyesight** /'ai,sait/ n vista, f

**eyewash** /'ai,wɒʃ/ n colirio, m; Inf. camelo, m. **That's all e.!** ¡Eso es un camelo!

**eyrie** /'ɛəri/ n nido (of any bird of prey), nido de águila (eagle's) m

# F

**f** /ɛf/ n (letter) efe, f; Mus. fa, m. **f sharp,** fa sostenido, m

**fa** /fɑ/ n Mus. fa, m

**fable** /'feibəl/ n fábula, leyenda, historia, f, apólogo, cuento, m; (untruth) invención, mentira, f

**fabled** /'feibəld/ a celebrado, famoso

**fabric** /'fæbrɪk/ n obra, fábrica, f; estructura, construcción, f; (making) manufactura, f; (cloth) tejido, paño, m; textura, f

**fabricate** /'fæbrɪ,keit/ vt fabricar, construir; (invent) fingir, inventar

**fabrication** /,fæbrɪ'keiʃən/ n fabricación, manufactura, f; construcción, f; (lie) invención, ficción, f

**fabulist** /'fæbyəlɪst/ n fabulista, mf

**fabulous** /'fæbyələs/ a fabuloso

**fabulousness** /'fæbyələsnɪs/ n fabulosidad, f

**façade** /fə'sɑd/ n fachada, frente, f

**face** /feis/ n superficie, f; (of persons) cara, f, rostro, m; (look) semblante, aire, m; (of coins) anverso, m; (grimace) mueca, f, gesto, m; (dial) esfera, f; (of gems) faceta, f; (of a wall) paramento, m; (front) fachada, frente, f; (effrontery) cara dura, f, descaro, m. **in the f. of,** ante; en presencia de. Mil. **Left f.!** ¡Izquierda! **on the f. of it,** juzgando por las apariencias. **to bring f. to f.,** confrontar (con). **to laugh in a person's f.,** reírse a la cara (de). **to make a f.,** hacer muecas. **to my f.,** en mi cara, en mis barbas. **to put a good f. on,** Fig. poner (or hacer) buena cara a. **to set one's f. against,** oponerse resueltamente a. **to straighten one's f.,** componer el semblante. **to throw in one's f.,** Fig. dar en rostro, dar en cara. **to wash one's f.,** lavarse la cara. **f. card,** figura (de la baraja), f. **f.-cloth,** paño para lavar la cara, m. **f. downward,** boca abajo. **f. lift,** operación estética facial, f. **f. of the waters,** faz de las aguas, f. **f. powder,** polvos de arroz, m pl. **f. to f.,** cara a cara, de persona a persona; frente a frente. **f. value,** significado literal, m; Com. valor nominal, m

**face** /feis/ vt mirar hacia; confrontar, hacer cara (a); (of buildings, etc.) mirar a, caer a (or hacia); Fig. arrostrar, enfrentarse con; Sew. guarnecer, aforrar. —vi estar orientado. **to f. the facts,** enfrentarse con la realidad. **to f. the music,** Fig. arrostrar las consecuencias. **to f. about,** volver la espalda; Mil. dar una vuelta, cambiar de frente. **to f. up to,** Fig. hacer cara a

**faced** /feist/ a con cara..., de cara...; Sew. forrado (de). **to be two-f.,** Fig. ser de dos haces

**facer** /'feisər/ n puñetazo en la cara, m; Fig. dificultad insuperable, f, problema muy grande, m

**facet** /'fæsɪt/ n faceta, f

**facetious** /fə'siʃəs/ a chancero, chistoso, jocoso

**facetiousness** /fə'siʃəsnɪs/ n jocosidad, festividad, f

**facial** /'feiʃəl/ a facial. **f. expression,** expresión de la cara, f, semblante, m

**facile** /'fæsɪl/ a (frivolous) ligero (e.g., a deduction or inference)

**facilitate** /fə'sɪlɪ,teit/ vt facilitar

**facilitation** /fə,sɪlɪ'teiʃən/ n facilitación, f

**facility** /fə'sɪlɪti/ n facilidad, f; habilidad, destreza, f

**facing** /'feisɪŋ/ n Sew. vuelta, f; (of a building) paramento, m; (of lumber) chapa f; encaramiento, m

**facsimile** /fæk'sɪməli/ n facsímile, m

**fact** /fækt/ n (event) hecho, suceso, m; (datum) dato, m; realidad, verdad, f; **as a matter of f.,** en realidad. **in f.,** en efecto, en realidad. **I know as a f.,** Tengo por cierto. **The f. is...,** La verdad es (que)... **the f. that,** el hecho de que

**fact-finding** /'fækt ,faindɪŋ/ informador (e.g. send s.b. on a fact-finding mission, enviar a fulano en misión informadora)

**faction** /'fækʃən/ n facción, f, partido, bando, m; (tumult) alboroto, m

**factional** /'fækʃənl/ a partidario

**factious** /'fækʃəs/ a faccioso, sedicioso

**factiousness** /'fækʃəsnɪs/ n espíritu de facción, m; rebeldía, f

**factitious** /fæk'tɪʃəs/ a falso; artificial

**factor** /'fæktər/ n (fact) factor, elemento, m; consideración, f; Math. factor, m; Com. agente, factor, m

**factory** /'fæktəri/ n fábrica, manufactura, f; taller, m. **F. Act,** ley de trabajadores industriales, f. **f. hand,** operario (-ia)

**factotum** /fæk'toutəm/ n factótum, m

**factual** /'fæktʃuəl/ a basado en hechos, objetivo

**faculty** /'fækəlti/ n facultad, f; (talent) habilidad, f, talento, m; (university division) facultad, f; (teachers as a group) claustro de profesores, claustro, profesorado, m; (authorization) privilegio, m, autoridad, f

**fad** /fæd/ n capricho, m, chifladura, f, dengue, m

**faddiness** /'fædinɪs/ n manías, f pl, excentricidad, f

**faddist** /'fædɪst/ n chiflado (-da)

**faddy** /'fædi/ a caprichoso, dengoso, difícil, excéntrico

**fade** /feid/ vi (of plants) marchitarse, secarse; (of color) palidecer, descolorarse; (vanish) disiparse, desaparecer; (of persons) desmejorarse; (of stains) salir. —vt descolorar. **to f. away,** desvanecer; (of persons) consumirse. **f.-out,** n (cinema) desaparecimiento gradual, m

**faded** /'feidɪd/ a (of plants) seco, marchito, mustio; (of colors) descolorado, pálido; (of people) desmejorado

**fadeless** /'feidlɪs/ a de colores resistentes; eterno, no olvidado; siempre joven

**fading** /'feidɪŋ/ a que palidece; (of flowers) medio marchito; (of light) mortecino, pálido; decadente. —n desaparecimiento, m, marchitez, f; decadencia, f

**fag** /fæg/ n Inf. pitillo, m. **f.-end,** fin, m; restos, m pl, sobras, f pl; (of a cigarette) colilla, f; (offensive) maricón. —vi trabajar mucho. —vt fatigar mucho; hacer trabajar.

**faggot** /'fægət/ n haz (or gavilla) de leña, f

**faience** /fai'ɑns/ n fayenza, f

**fail** /feil/ vi faltar; fracasar, malograrse; no tener éxito, salir mal; (of strength) decaer, acabarse; (be short of) carecer (de); Com. hacer bancarrota, suspender pagos. —vt abandonar; (disappoint) decepcionar, engañar; (in exams) suspender. **Do not f. to see her,** No dejes de verla. **He failed to do his duty,** Faltó a su deber

**fail** /feil/ n **without f.,** sin falta

**failing** /'feilɪŋ/ n falta, f; (shortcoming) vicio, flaco, m, debilidad, f; malogro, fracaso, m; decadencia, f

**failure** /'feilyər/ n fracaso, m; falta de éxito, f; (in exams) suspensión, f; (of power) no funcionamiento, m; omisión, f, descuido, m; Com. quiebra, bancarrota, f; (decay) decadencia, f. **on f. of,** al fracasar; bajo pena de

**fain** /fein/ a deseoso, muy contento. **He was f. to...,** Se sintió obligado a...; Quería

**faint** /feint/ a débil; (dim) indistinto, vago, borroso; (of colors) pálido, desmayado; (weak) lánguido, desfallecido; (slight) superficial, rudimentario. —vi perder el sentido, desmayarse. —n desmayo, m. **to be f. with hunger,** estar muerto de hambre. **to cause to f.,** hacer desmayar. **f.-hearted,** pusilánime, medroso. **f.-heartedness,** pusilanimidad, f

**faintly** /'feintli/ adv débilmente; en voz débil; indistintamente

**faintness** /'feintnɪs/ n languidez, debilidad, f; (swoon) desmayo, m; lo indistinto; lo borroso.

**fair** /fɛər/ n feria, f; (sale) mercado, m; (exhibition) exposición, f

**fair** /fɛər/ a (beautiful) hermoso, lindo, bello; (of hair) rubio; (of skin) blanco; (clear, fresh) limpio, claro; (good) bueno; (favorable) favorable, propicio, próspero; (of weather) despejado, sereno; (just) imparcial; (straightforward) honrado, recto, justo; (passable) regular, mediano; (of writing) legible; (proper) conveniente. —adv honradamente; (politely) cortésmente; exactamente. **by f. means,** por medios honrados. **It's not f.!** ¡No hay derecho! **to become f.,** (of weather) serenarse. **to give a f. trial,** juzgar imparcialmente; dar una buena oportunidad; *Law.* procesar imparcialmente. **to make a f. copy,** poner en limpio. **f.-haired,** de pelo rubio, rubio. **f. one,** una beldad, *f.* **f. play,** *Sports.* juego limpio, *m;* proceder leal, *m.* **f.-skinned,** de tez blanca, rubio. **f.-weather,** buen tiempo, *m,* bonanza, *f.* **f.-weather friends,** amigos de los días prósperos, *m pl*

**fairing** /'fɛərɪŋ/ *n Brit* regalo de feria, *m.* **to give fairings,** feriar

**fairly** /'fɛərli/ *adv* (justly) con imparcialidad; (moderately) bastante; totalmente, enteramente. **f. good,** bastante bueno; regular

**fairness** /'fɛərnɪs/ *n* belleza, hermosura, *f;* (of skin) blancura, *f;* (justness) imparcialidad, *f;* (reasonableness) justicia, equidad, *f;* (of hair) color rubio, oro, *m*

**fairway** /'fɛər,wei/ *n Naut.* canalizo, paso, *m;* (golf) terreno sin obstáculos, *m*

**fairy** /'fɛəri/ *n* hada, *f,* duende, *m.* —*a* de hada, de duendes. *Fig.* delicado. **f.-gold,** tesoro de duendes, *m;* **f.-light,** lucecillo, *m;* luminaria, *f.* **f.-like,** aduendado, como una hada. **f.-ring,** círculo mágico, *m.* **f.-tale,** cuento de hadas, *m;* patraña, *f,* cuento de viejas, *m*

**fairyland** /'fɛəri,lænd/ *n* país de las hadas, *m*

**faith** /feiθ/ *n* fe, *f;* confianza, *f;* (doctrine) creencia, religión, filosofía, *f;* (honor) palabra, *f.* **in good f.,** de buena fe. **to break f.,** faltar a la palabra dada. **f.-healing,** curanderismo, *m*

**faithful** /'feiθfəl/ *a* fiel, leal; (accurate) exacto; (trustworthy) veraz. **the f.,** los creyentes

**faithfully** /'feiθfəli/ *adv* fielmente, lealmente; (accurately) con exactitud. **Yours f.,** Queda de Vd. su att. s.s.

**faithfulness** /'feiθfəlnɪs/ *n* fidelidad, lealtad, *f;* (accuracy) exactitud, *f*

**faithless** /'feiθlɪs/ *a* infiel, desleal, pérfido.

**faithlessness** /'feiθlɪsnɪs/ *n* infidelidad, deslealtad, traición, *f*

**fake** /feik/ *vt* imitar, falsificar. —*n* imitación, falsificación, *f.* **to f. up,** inventar

**Falangist** /fei'lɑndʒɪst/ *a* and *n* falangista *mf*

**falcon** /'fɔlkən/ *n* halcón, *m.* **f. gentle,** *Ornith.* neblí, *m*

**falconer** /'fɔlkənər/ *n* halconero, *m*

**falconry** /'fɔlkənri/ *n* cetrería, *f*

**fall** /fɔl/ *n* caída, *f;* (of temperature, mercury) baja, *f;* (of water) salto de agua, *m,* catarata, cascada, *f;* (in value) depreciación, *f;* (in price and Stock Exchange) baja, *f;* (descent) bajada, *f;* (autumn) otoño, *m;* (declivity) declinación, *f,* declive, desnivel, *m;* (ruin) ruina, *f,* destrucción, *f;* (of night, etc.) caída (de la noche), *f;* (of snow) nevada, *f;* (of rain) golpe, *m;* (*Theat.* of curtain) caída, bajada, *f;* (surrender) capitulación, rendición, *f;* (of earth) desprendimiento de tierras, *m;* (of the tide) reflujo, *m*

**fall** /fɔl/ *vi* caer; (of mercury, temperature) bajar; (collapse) desplomarse, hundirse, derrumbarse; (die) caer muerto; (descend) descender; (*Theat.* of the curtain) bajar, caer; (of a river into the sea, etc.) desembocar, desaguar; (of hair, draperies) caer; (decrease) disminuir; (of spirits) ponerse triste, sentirse deprimido; (sin) caer; (come upon) sobrevenir; (of dusk, etc.) caer, llegar; (strike, touch) tocar; (as a share) tocar en suerte; (as a duty, responsibility) tocar, corresponder; (of seasons) caer en; (of words from the lips) caer de (los labios); (say) decir, pronunciar palabras; (of exclamations) escaparse; (become) venir a ser; (happen) suceder; (be) ser. **fallen upon evil days,** venido a menos. **His face fell,** Puso una cara de desengaño. **Christmas falls on a Thursday this year,** Navidad cae en jueves este año. **to let f.,** dejar caer. **to f. a-** (followed by verb) empezar a. **He fell a-crying,** Empezó a llorar. **to f. again,** volver a caer, recaer. **to f. among,** caer entre. **to f. astern,** quedarse atrás. **to f. away,** (leave) abandonar, dejar; (grow thin) enflaquecer; marchitarse; (crumble) desmoronarse. **to f. back,** retroceder, volver hacia atrás. **to f. back upon,** recurrir a; *Mil.* replegarse hacia. **to f. backward,** caer de espaldas.

caer hacia atrás. **to f. behind,** quedarse atrás. **to f. down,** venirse a tierra; venirse abajo, dar consigo en el suelo, caer. **to f. due,** vencer. **to f. flat,** caer de bruces; (be unsuccessful) no tener éxito. **to f. in,** caer en; (collapse) desplomarse; *Mil.* alinearse; (expire) vencer. **to f. into,** caer en. **to f. in with,** tropezar con; reunirse con, juntarse con; (agree) convenir en; **to f. off,** caer de; (of leaves, etc.) desprenderse de, separarse de; (abandon) abandonar; (diminish) disminuir. **to f. on,** caer de (e.g. *to f. on one's back,* caer de espaldas); (of seasons) caer en; (attack) echarse encima de, atacar. **to f. out,** (of a window, etc.) caer por; (happen) acontecer, suceder; (quarrel) pelearse, reñir; *Mil.* romper filas. **to f. out with,** reñir con. **to f. over,** volcar, caer; (stumble) tropezar con. **to f. short,** faltar; carecer, ser deficiente; (fail) malograrse, no llegar a sus expectaciones; (of shooting) errar el tiro. **to f. through,** caer por; (fail) malograrse, fracasar. **to f. to,** empezar a, ponerse a; (be incumbent on) tocar a, corresponder a; (attack) atacar. **to f. under,** caer debajo; caer bajo; sucumbir, perecer; (incur) incurrir en, merecer. **to f. upon,** (attack) caer sobre, acometer; acaecer, tener lugar; (be incumbent) tocar a

**fallacious** /fə'leiʃəs/ *a* falaz, engañoso, ilusorio

**fallaciousness** /fə'leiʃəsnɪs/ *n* falacia, *f,* engaño, *m*

**fallacy** /'fæləsi/ *n* error, *m,* ilusión, *f*

**fallen** /'fɔlən/ *a* caído; arruinado; degradado. **f. angel,** ángel caído, *m.* **f. woman,** perdida, mujer caída, *f*

**fallibility** /ˌfælə'bɪlɪti/ *n* falibilidad, *f*

**fallible** /'fæləbəl/ *a* falible

**falling** /'fɔlɪŋ/ *a* que cae, cayente. —*n* caída, *f;* (of mercury, temperature) baja, *f;* (crumbling) desmoronamiento, *m;* (collapse) hundimiento, derrumbamiento, *m;* (of tide) reflujo, *m;* (of waterlevel) bajada, *f;* (in value) depreciación, *f;* (of prices and Stock Exchange) baja, *f;* (diminishment) disminución, *f;* (in level of earth) declinación, *f;* (*Com.* expiry) vencimiento, *m;* (*Theat.* of curtain) bajada, caída, *f.* **f. away,** (crumbling) desmoronamiento, *m;* desprendimiento de tierras, *m;* (desertion) deserción, *f;* abandono, *m.* **f. back,** retirada, *f,* retroceso, *m.* **f. down,** caída, *f;* derrumbamiento, *m.* **f. due,** vencimiento, *m.* **f. in,** hundimiento, *m;* (crumbling) desmoronamiento, *m.* **f. off,** caída de, *f;* (disappearance) desaparición, *f;* (diminution) disminución, *f;* (deterioration) deterioración, *f.* **f. out,** caída por, *f,* disensión, *f.* **f. short,** falta, *f;* carácter inferior, *m;* frustración, *f.* **f. star,** estrella fugaz, *f*

**fallout** /'fɔl,aut/ *n* caída radiactiva, llovizna radiactiva, precipitación radiactiva, *f*

**fallow** /'fæloʊ/ *a* (of color) leonado; *Agr.* barbechado; descuidado. —*n* barbecho, *m.* —*vt* barbechar. **to leave f.,** dejar en barbecho. **f. deer,** corzo (-za)

**false** /fɔls/ *a* incorrecto, erróneo, equivocado; falso; (unfounded) infundado; (disloyal) infiel, traidor, desleal; (not real) postizo; artificial; de imitación; *Mus.* desafinado; (pretended) fingido; engañoso, mentiroso. **to play a person f.,** traicionar (a). **f. bottom,** fondo doble, *m;* **f. claim,** pretensión infundada, *f.* **f. door,** surtida, *f.* **f.-hearted,** pérfido, desleal. **f. teeth,** dientes postizos, *m pl,* dentadura postiza, *f*

**falsehood** /'fɔlshʊd/ *n* mentira, *f*

**falseness** /'fɔlsnɪs/ *n* falsedad, *f;* (disloyalty) duplicidad, perfidia, traición, *f*

**falsetto** /fɔl'sɛtoʊ/ *n* falsete, *m,* voz de cabeza, *f*

**falsification** /ˌfɔlsəfɪ'keiʃən/ *n* falsificación, *f;* (of texts) corrupción, *f*

**falsifier** /'fɔlsəfaiər/ *n* falsificador (-ra)

**falsify** /'fɔlsəfai/ *vt* falsear, falsificar; (disappoint) defraudar, frustrar, contrariar

**falter** /'fɔltər/ *vi* (physically) titubear; (of speech) balbucir, tartamudear; (of action) vacilar. **to f. out,** balbucir; hablar con voz entrecortada; decir con vacilación

**faltering** /'fɔltərɪŋ/ *a* titubeante; (of speech) entrecortado; vacilante. —*n* temblor, *m;* vacilación, *f*

**falteringly** /'fɔltərɪŋli/ *adv* (of speech) balbuciente, en una voz temblorosa; con dificultad, vacilantemente

**fame** /feim/ *n* fama, *f;* reputación, *f;* (renown) celebridad, *f,* renombre, *m.* **of ill f.,** de mala fama

**famed** /feimd/ *a* reputado; renombrado, célebre, famoso

**familiar** /fəˈmɪlyər/ *a* íntimo, familiar; afable, amistoso; (ill-bred) insolente, demasiado familiar; (usual) corriente, usual, común; conocido. —*n* amigo (-ga) íntimo (-ma); *Eccl.* familiar, *m;* demonio familiar, *m.* **to be f. with,** (a subject) estar versado en, conocer muy bien; (a person) tratar con familiaridad. **to become f. with,** acostumbrarse a; familiarizarse con; (a person) hacerse íntimo de

**familiarity** /fə,mɪliˈærɪti/ *n* intimidad, familiaridad, confianza, *f;* (friendliness) afabilidad, *f;* (over-familiarity) insolencia, demasiada familiaridad, *f;* (with a subject) conocimiento (de), *m,* experiencia (de), *f*

**familiarize** /fəˈmɪlyə,raiz/ *vt* familiarizar, acostumbrar, habituar. —*vr* familiarizarse

**familiarly** /fəˈmɪlyərli/ *adv* familiarmente; amistosamente

**family** /ˈfæməli/ *n* familia, *f;* (lineage) linaje, abolengo, *m;* (Bot. Zool.) familia, *f;* (of languages) grupo, *m.* —*a* de familia; familiar; casero. **f. doctor,** médico de cabecera, *m.* **f. life,** vida de familia, *f;* hogar, *m.* **f. man,** padre de familia, *m.* **f. name,** apellido, *m.* **f. seat,** casa solar, *f.* **f. tree,** árbol genealógico, *m*

**family quarrel** disputa de familia, *f*

**famine** /ˈfæmɪn/ *n* hambre, *f;* carestía, escasez, *f*

**famish** /ˈfæmɪʃ/ *vt* matar de hambre. —*vi* morirse de hambre

**famished** /ˈfæmɪʃt/ *a* hambriento

**famous** /ˈfeiməs/ *a* famoso, célebre, renombrado; insigne, distinguido; *Inf.* excelente

**famously** /ˈfeiməsli/ *adv Inf.* muy bien, excelentemente

**fan** /fæn/ *n* abanico, *m; Agr.* aventador, *m; Mech.* ventilador, *m;* (on a windmill) volante, *m;* (amateur) aficionado (-da); (admirer) admirador (-ra); *Archit.* abanico, *m.* —*vt* abanicar; *Agr.* aventar; ventilar. **fan oneself,** abanicarse; *Agr.* aventar viento. **tap with a f.,** abanicazo, golpecito con el abanico, *m.* **f.-belt,** *Mech.* correa de transmisión del ventilador, *f.* **f.-light,** tragaluz, *m.* **f. maker** or **seller,** abaniquero (-ra). **f.-shaped,** en abanico, abanicado, en forma de abanico

**fanatic** /fəˈnætɪk/ *a* and *n* fanático (-ca)

**fanaticism** /fəˈnætə,sɪzəm/ *n* fanatismo, *m*

**fanaticize** /fəˈnætə,saiz/ *vt* fanatizar

**fancied** /ˈfænsid/ *a* imaginario

**fancier** /ˈfænsiər/ *n* aficionado (-da); (of animals) criador (-ra)

**fanciful** /ˈfænsɪfəl/ *a* romántico, caprichoso; fantástico

**fancifulness** /ˈfænsɪfəlnɪs/ *n* extravagancia, *f;* romanticismo, *m*

**fancy** /ˈfænsi/ *n* fantasía, imaginación, *f;* (idea) idea, *f,* ensueño, *m;* (caprice) capricho, antojo, *m;* (liking) afecto, cariño, *m;* gusto, *m,* afición, *f;* (wish) deseo, *m;* (fantasy) quimera, *f, a* imaginario; elegante, ornado; *Com.* de capricho, de fantasía; fantástico, extravagante. —*vt* imaginar, figurarse; (like) gustar de; aficionarse a; antojarse. **I have a f. for...,** Se me antoja.... **Just f.!** ¡Toma! ¡Quia! ¡Parece mentira! **to take a f. to,** (things) tomar afición a; (people) tomar cariño (a). **f.-dress,** disfraz, *m.* **f.-dress ball,** baile de trajes, *m*

**fancy goods** *n pl* artículos suntuarios *m pl*

**fane** /fein/ *n* templo, *m*

**fanfare** /ˈfænfeər/ *n* tocata de trompetas, *f*

**fang** /fæŋ/ *n* colmillo, *m;* raíz de un diente, *f*

**fanged** /fæŋd/ *a* que tiene colmillos; (of teeth) acolmillado

**fangless** /ˈfæŋlɪs/ *a* sin colmillos

**fanner** /ˈfænər/ *n* abanicador (-ra); *Agr.* aventador, *m*

**fanning** /ˈfænɪŋ/ *n* abaniqueo, *m; Agr.* avienta, *f*

**fantastic** /fænˈtæstɪk/ *a* fantástico; extravagante

**fantastically** /fænˈtæstɪkəli/ *adv* fantásticamente; extravagantemente

**fantasy** /ˈfæntəsi/ *n* imaginación, *f;* fantasía, quimera, visión, *f;* creación imaginativa, *f*

**far** /fɑr/ *adv* lejos; a lo lejos; (much, greatly) mucho,

en alto grado; (very) muy; (mostly) en gran parte. —*a* lejano, distante; (farther) ulterior. **as far as,** tan lejos como; (up to, until) hasta; en cuanto, por lo que, según que. (e.g. *As far as we know,* Por lo que nosotros sepamos. *As far as we are concerned,* En cuanto a nosotros toca). **by far,** con mucho. **from far and near,** de todas partes. **from far off,** desde lejos. **He read far into the night,** Leyó hasta las altas horas de la noche. **how far?** ¿a qué distancia?; (to what extent) ¿hasta qué punto? ¿hasta dónde? **How far is it to...?** ¿Qué distancia hay a...? **in so far as,** en tanto que. **on the far side,** al lado opuesto; al otro extremo. **so far,** tan lejos; (till now) hasta ahora. **to go far,** ir lejos. **far away,** a distante, remoto, lejano; *Fig.* abstraído. —*adv* muy lejos. **far beyond,** mucho más allá. **far-fetched,** increíble, improbable. **far-off,** distante. —*adv* a lo lejos, en lontananza. **far-reaching,** de gran alcance. **far-sighted,** sagaz, presciente, previsor. **far-sightedness,** sagacidad, previsión, *f*

**farce** /fɑrs/ *n* farsa, *f.* —*vt Cul.* embutir, rellenar

**farcical** /ˈfɑrsɪkəl/ *a* burlesco, cómico, sainetesco; absurdo, grotesco, ridículo

**fare** /feər/ *n* (price) pasaje, precio del billete, *m;* (traveler) viajero (-ra), pasajero (-ra); (food) comida, *f.* —*vi* pasarlo (e.g. *to f. well,* pasarlo bien). **bill of f.,** menú, *m.* **full f.,** billete entero, *m.* **f. stage,** trayecto, *m*

**farewell** /ˌfeərˈwɛl/ *n* despedida, *f,* adiós, *m.* —*a* de despedida. —*interj* ¡adiós! ¡quede Vd. con Dios! **to bid f. to,** despedirse de

**farewell address** *n* discurso de despedida *m*

**farflung** /ˈfɑrˈflʌŋ/ de gran alcance, extenso, vasto; (empire) dilatado

**farina** /fəˈrinə/ *n* harina (de cereales), *f; Chem.* fécula, *f,* almidón, *m; Bot.* polen, *m*

**farm** /fɑrm/ *n* granja, hacienda, quintería, finca, chacra, *f,* cortijo, *m.* —*vi* cultivar, labrar (la tierra); (taxes) arrendar. —*vi* ser granjero. **to f. out,** (taxes) dar en arriendo. **f. girl,** labradora, *f.* **f. house,** alquería, casa de labranza, granja, *f.* **f. laborer,** labriego, peón, *m.* **f. yard,** corral de una granja, *m*

**farmer** /ˈfɑrmər/ *n* granjero, hacendado, quintero, *m,* agrícola, *mf;* (small) colono, labrador, *m;* (of taxes) arrendatario, *m*

**farmhand** /ˈfɑrmˌhænd/ *n* gañán, mozo, mozo de granja, peón *m*

**farming** /ˈfɑrmɪŋ/ *n* labranza, *f,* cultivo, *m;* agricultura, labor agrícola, *f;* (of taxes) arriendo, *m.* —*a* de labranza, labradoríl; agrícola

**faro** /ˈfeərou/ *n* (card game) faraón, *m*

**farouche** /fəˈruʃ/ *a* huraño, esquivo

**farrago** /fəˈrɑgou/ *n* fárrago, *m,* mezcla, *f*

**farrier** /ˈfæriər/ *n* herrador, *m*

**farther** /ˈfɑrðər/ *adv* más lejos; (beyond) más adelante; (besides) además. —*a* ulterior; más distante. **at the f. end,** al otro extremo; en el fondo. **f. on,** más adelante; más allá

**farthest** /ˈfɑrðɪst/ *adv* más lejos. —*a* más lejano, más distante; extremo

**farthing** /ˈfɑrðɪŋ/ *n* cuarto, *m; Fig.* ardite, maravedí, *m.* **He hasn't a brass f.,** No tiene dos maravedís

**fasces** /ˈfæsiz/ *n pl* fasces, *f pl*

**fascicle** /ˈfæsɪkəl/ *n Bot.* hacecillo, *m*

**fascinate** /ˈfæsə,neit/ *vt* fascinar; encantar, hechizar, seducir

**fascinating** /ˈfæsə,neitɪŋ/ *a* fascinador; encantador, seduciente

**fascination** /ˌfæsəˈneiʃən/ *n* fascinación, *f;* encanto, hechizo, *m*

**Fascism** /ˈfæʃ,ɪzəm/ *n* fascismo, *m*

**Fascist** /ˈfæʃɪst/ *a* and *n* fascista *mf*

**fashion** /ˈfæʃən/ *n* (form) forma, hechura, *f;* (way) modo, *m;* (custom) costumbre, *f,* uso, *m;* (vogue) moda, *f;* (high life) alta sociedad, *f;* (tone) buen tono, *m.* —*vt* hacer, labrar; inventar. **in Spanish f.,** a la española, al uso de España. **the latest f.,** la última moda. **to be in f.,** estar de moda. **to go out of f.,** dejar de ser de moda, perder la popularidad. **f. book,** revista de modas, *f.* **f. plate,** figurín, *m*

**fashionable** /ˈfæʃənəbəl/ *a* de moda; elegante; de

buen tono. **to be f.,** estar en boga, ser de moda. **f. world,** mundo elegante, mundo de sociedad, *m*

**fashionableness** /'fæʃənəbəlnıs/ *n* buen tono, *m;* elegancia, *f*

**fashionably** /'fæʃənəbli/ *adv* a la moda, elegantemente

**fashion show** desfile de modas, *m,* exhibición de modas, *f*

**fast** /fæst/ *a* (firm) firme; (secure) seguro; (strong) fuerte; (fixed) fijo; (closed) cerrado; (of boats) amarrado; (tight) apretado; (of colors) estable; (of trains) rápido; (of sleep) profundo; (of friends) leal, seguro; (quick) rápido, veloz; (of a watch) adelantado; (dissipated) disoluto. —*adv* firmemente, seguramente; (quickly) rápidamente; (of sleep) profundamente; (tightly) estrechamente, apretadamente; (of rain) (llover) a cántaros; (ceaselessly) continuamente; (often) frecuentemente; (entirely) completamente. **to be f.,** (clocks) adelantar. **to make f.,** *Naut.* amarrar, trincar. **f. asleep,** profundamente dormido. **f. color,** color estable, color sólido, *m*

**fast** /fæst/ *n* ayuno, *m, vi* ayunar. **to break one's f.,** romper el ayuno. **f.-day,** día de ayuno, día de vigilia, *m*

**fasten** /'fæsən/ *vt* (tie) atar; (fix) fijar; sujetar; (stick) pegar; (a door) cerrar; (bolt) echar el cerrojo; *Naut.* trincar; (together) juntar, unir; (with buttons, hooks, etc.) abrochar; (on, upon) fijar en; *Fig.* imputar (a). —*vi* fijarse; pegarse; (upon) agarrarse a, asir. **to f. one's eyes on,** fijar los ojos en. **to f. up,** cerrar; atar; (nail) clavar

**fastener** /'fæsənər/ *n* (bolt) pasador, *m;* (for bags, jewelery, etc.) cierre, *m;* (buckle) hebilla, *f;* (of a coat, etc.) tiador, *m;* (of a book, file) sujetador, *m;* (lock) cerrojo, *m.* **paper-f.,** sujetador de papeles, *m.* **patent-f.,** botón automático, *m*

**fastening** /'fæsənıŋ/ *n* atadura, *f;* sujeción, *f,* afianzamiento, *m;* (together) union, *f;* (of a garment) brochadura, *f;* (of a handbag) cierre, *m*

**fastidious** /fæ'stıdiəs/ *a* dengoso, melindroso, desdeñoso; (sensitive) sensitivo, delicado; (critical) discerniente, crítico

**fastidiously** /fæs'tıdiəsli/ *adv* melindrosamente

**fastidiousness** /fæs'tıdiəsnıs/ *n* dengues, melindres, *m pl,* nimiedad, *f,* desdén, *m;* sensibilidad, delicadeza, *f;* sentido crítico, *m*

**fasting** /'fæstıŋ/ *n* ayuno, *m.* —*a* and *part* de ayuno; en ayunas

**fastness** /'fæstnıs/ *n* firmeza, solidez, *f;* (stronghold) fortaleza, *f;* (retreat) refugio, *m;* (speed) velocidad, rapidez, *f;* (dissipation) disipación, *f,* libertinaje, *m*

**fat** /fæt/ *a* (stout) gordo, grueso; mantecoso, graso, seboso; (greasy) grasiento; (rich) fértil, pingüe; (productive) lucrativo. —*n* (stoutness) gordura, *f;* (for cooking) manteca, *f;* (lard) lardo, *m;* (of animal or meat) grasa, *f;* sebo, saín, *m;* *Fig.* riqueza, *f;* *Fig.* fertilidad, *f.* **to grow fat,** engordarse, ponerse grueso

**fatal** /'feitl/ *a* fatal, mortal; funesto

**fatalism** /'feitl,ızəm/ *n* fatalismo, *m*

**fatalist** /'feitlıst/ *n* fatalista, *mf*

**fatalistic** /,feitl'ıstık/ *a* fatalista

**fatality** /fei'tælıti/ *n* fatalidad, *f;* infortunio, *m,* calamidad, *f;* muerte, *f*

**fatally** /'feitli/ *adv* mortalmente, fatalmente; inevitablemente

**fate** /feit/ *n* destino, sino, hado, *m,* providencia, *f;* fortuna, suerte, *f;* destrucción, ruina, *f;* muerte, *f.* **the Three Fates,** las Parcas

**fated** /'feitıd/ *a* fatal, destinado; predestinado

**fateful** /'feitfəl/ *a* decisivo, fatal; aciago, ominoso

**father** /'faðər/ *n* padre, *m.* —*vt* prohijar, adoptar; (on or upon) atribuir (a), imputar (a). **Eternal F.,** Padre Eterno, *m.* **Holy F.,** Padre Santo, *m.* **indulgent f.,** padre indulgente, padrazo, *m.* **Like f. like son,** De tal palo tal astilla. **f. confessor,** *Eccl.* director espiritual, *m.* **f.-in-law,** suegro, *m*

**fatherhood** /'faðər,hʊd/ *n* paternidad, *f*

**fatherland** /'faðər,lænd/ *n* patria, madre patria, *f*

**fatherless** /'faðərlıs/ *a* sin padre, huérfano de padre

**fatherliness** /'faðərlınıs/ *n* amor paternal, *m;* sentimiento paternal, *m*

**fatherly** /'faðərli/ *a* paternal, de padre

**fathom** /'fæðəm/ *n* *Naut.* braza, *f.* —*vt* sondear; *Fig.* profundizar, tantear; (a mystery) desentrañar

**fathomless** /'fæðəmlıs/ *a* insondable; *Fig.* incomprensible, impenetrable

**fatigue** /fə'tig/ *n* fatiga, *f,* cansancio, *m;* *Mil.* faena, *f;* *Mech.* pérdida de resistencia, *f.* —*vt* fatigar, cansar. **to be fatigued,** estar cansado, cansarse, fatigarse. **f. party,** *Mil.* pelotón de castigo, *m*

**fatiguing** /fə'tigıŋ/ *a* fatigoso

**fatness** /'fætnıs/ *n* (stoutness) gordura, carnosidad, *f;* grasa, *f,* gordo, *m;* (richness) fertilidad, *f;* lo lucrativo

**fatten** /'fætn/ *vt* engordar; (animals) cebar, sainar; (land) abonar, fertilizar. —*vi* ponerse grueso, echar carnes

**fatty** /'fæti/ *a* untoso, grasiento; *Chem.* graso. **f. acid,** ácido graso, *m.* **f. degeneration,** degeneración grasienta, *f*

**fatuity** /fə'tuıti/ *n* fatuidad, necedad, *f*

**fatuous** /'fætʃuəs/ *a* fatuo, necio, lelo

**faucet** /'fɔsıt/ *n* canilla, llave, *f,* grifo, *m*

**fault** /fɔlt/ *n* defecto, *m,* imperfección, *f;* (blame) culpa, *f;* (mistake) falta, *f,* error, *m;* (in cloth) canilla, barra, *f;* *Geol.* falla, quiebra, *f;* *Elec.* avería, *f;* *Sports.* falta, *f, vi Sports.* cometer una falta. **to a f.,** excesivamente. **to be at f.,** (to blame) tener la culpa; (mistaken) estar equivocado; (puzzled) estar perplejo; (of dogs) perder el rastro. **to find f.,** tachar, culpar, criticar. **Whose f. is it?** ¿Quién tiene la culpa?

**faultfinder** /'fɔlt,faindər/ *n* criticón (-ona)

**faultiness** /'fɔltınıs/ *n* defectuosidad, imperfección, *f*

**faultless** /'fɔltlıs/ *a* sin faltas; perfecto, sin tacha; impecable

**faulty** /'fɔlti/ *a* defectuoso, imperfecto

**faun** /fɔn/ *n* fauno, *m*

**fauna** /'fɔnə/ *n* fauna, *f*

**favor** /'feivər/ *n* favor, *m;* (protection) amistad, protección, *f,* amparo, *m;* (permission) permiso, *m,* licencia, *f;* (kindness) merced, gracia, *f;* (gift) obsequio, *m;* (favoritism) favoritismo, *m,* preferencia, *f;* (benefit) beneficio, *m;* (badge) colores, *m pl; Com.* grata, atenta, *f.* —*vt* favorecer, apoyar; mirar con favor, mostrar parcialidad (hacia); (suit) favorecer; (be advantageous) ser propicio (a); (contribute to) contribuir a, ayudar; (resemble) parecerse (a). **Circumstances f. the idea,** Las circunstancias son propicias a la idea, Las circunstancias militan en pro de la idea. **I f. the teaching of modern languages,** Soy partidario de la enseñanza de lenguas vivas. **in f. of,** a favor de, en pro de. **in the f. of,** en el favor de. **out of f.,** fuera de favor; (not fashionable) fuera de moda. **to count on the f. of,** tener de su parte (a), contar con el apoyo de. **to do a f.,** hacer un favor. **to enjoy the f. of,** gozar del favor de. **to fall out of f.,** caer en desgracia; (go out of fashion) pasar de moda. **to grow in f.,** aumentar en favor

**favorable** /'feivərəbəl/ *a* favorable; propicio, próspero

**favorableness** /'feivərəbəlnıs/ *n* lo favorable; lo propicio; benignidad, benevolencia, *f*

**favorably** /'feivərəbli/ *adv* favorablemente

**favored** /'feivərd/ *a* favorecido; predilecto; (in compounds) parecido, encarado

**favoring** /'feivərıŋ/ *a* favorecedor, propicio

**favorite** /'feivərıt/ *a* favorito; predilecto, preferido. —*n* favorito (-ta). **court f.,** valido, privado, *m;* (mistress) querida (de un rey), *f;* (lover) amante (de una reina), *m.* **to be a f.,** ser favorito

**favoritism** /'feivərı,tızəm/ *n* favoritismo, *m*

**fawn** /fɔn/ *n* *Zool.* cervato, *m;* (color) color de cervato, color de ante, *m.* —*a* de color de cervato, anteado, pardo; (of animals) rucio, pardo. —*vt* and *vi* parir la cierva. —*vi* acariciar; (on, upon) adular, lisonjear

**fawning** /'fɔnıŋ/ *n* adulación, *f, a* adulador, lisonjero

**fear** /fıər/ *n* miedo, temor, *m;* (apprehension) ansiedad, aprensión, *f,* recelo, *m;* (respect) veneración, *f.* —*vt* temer; recelar; (respect) reverenciar. —*vi* tener miedo; estar receloso, estar con cuidado. **for f. of,** por miedo de. **for f. that,** por temor de que, por miedo de que. **from f.,** por miedo. **There is no f. of...,** No hay miedo de (que)...

**fearer** /'fıərər/ *n* temedor (-ra), el (la) que teme

**fearful** /'fɪərfəl/ a miedoso, aprensivo, receloso; (cowardly) tímido, pusilánime; (terrible) horrible, espantoso, pavoroso; *Inf.* tremendo, enorme

**fearfully** /'fɪərfəli/ adv con miedo; tímidamente; (terribly) horriblemente; *Inf.* enormemente

**fearfulness** /'fɪərfəlnɪs/ n temor, miedo, m; (horribleness) lo horrible

**fearless** /'fɪərlɪs/ a sin miedo, intrépido, audaz

**fearlessness** /'fɪərlɪsnɪs/ n intrepidez, valentía, f

**fearsome** /'fɪərsəm/ a temible, horrible, espantoso

**feasibility** /ˌfizə'bɪlɪti/ n practicabilidad, posibilidad, f

**feasible** /'fizəbəl/ a factible, hacedero, practicable, ejecutable

**feast** /fist/ n *Eccl.* fiesta, f; banquete, m; *Fig.* abundancia, f, vi regalarse. —vt festejar, agasajar; (delight) recrear, deleitar. **immovable f.,** *Eccl.* fiesta fija, f. **movable f.,** fiesta movible, f. **f. day,** día de fiesta, m, festividad f

**feasting** /'fistɪŋ/ n banquetes, m pl; fiestas, f pl

**feat** /fit/ n hazaña, proeza, f, hecho, m

**feather** /'fɛðər/ n pluma, f; (of the tail) pena, f; pl **feathers,** plumaje, m; plumas, f pl. —vt emplumar; adornar con plumas; (rowing) poner casi horizontal la pala del remo. **to f. one's nest,** *Inf.* hacer su agosto. **f.-bed,** plumón, colchón de plumas, m. **f.-brained,** casquivano, alocado, aturdido; **f.-duster,** plumero, m. **f.-stitch,** *Sew.* diente de perro, m. **f. weight,** (boxing) peso pluma, m

**feathered** /'fɛðərd/ a plumado, plumoso; adornado con plumas; (winged) alado

**feathery** /'fɛðəri/ a plumoso; como plumas

**feature** /'fitʃər/ n rasgo, m, característica, f; (cinema) número de programa, m; pl **features** (of the face) facciones, f pl. —vt dar importancia (a); (cinema) presentar. **f. film,** documentaria, f

**febrile** /'fibrəl/ a febril

**February** /'fɛbru,ɛri, 'fɛbyu-/ n febrero, m

**fecal** /'fikəl/ a fecal

**feces** /'fisiz/ n heces, f pl; excremento, m

**fecund** /'fikʌnd/ a fecundo, fértil

**fecundate** /'fikən,deit/ vt fecundar

**fecundity** /fɪ'kʌndɪti/ n fecundidad, fertilidad, f

**federal** /'fɛdərəl/ a federal, federalista

**federalism** /'fɛdərə,lɪzəm/ n federalismo, m

**federalist** /'fɛdərəlɪst/ n federalista, federal, mf

**federate** /v 'fɛdə,reit; -ərɪt/ vt confederar. —vi confederarse. —a confederado

**federation** /ˌfɛdə'reiʃən/ n confederación, federación, f; liga, unión, asociación, f

**federative** /'fɛdə,reitɪv/ a federativo

**fee** /fi/ n (feudal law) feudo, m; (homage) homenaje, m; (duty) derecho, m; (professional) honorario, estipendio, m; (to a servant) gratificación, f; (entrance, university, etc.) cuota, f; (payment) paga, f

**feeble** /'fibəl/ a débil; lánguido; enfermizo; (of light, etc.) tenue; *Fig.* flojo. **to grow f.,** debilitarse; disminuir. **f.-minded,** anormal

**feebleness** /'fibəlnɪs/ n debilidad, f; *Fig.* flojedad, f

**feebly** /'fibli/ adv débilmente; lánguidamente

**feed** /fid/ n alimento, m; (meal) comida, f; (of animals) pienso, forraje, m; *Mech.* alimentación, f. —vt alimentar; dar de comer (a); (animals) cebar; *Mech.* alimentar; mantener; *Fig.* nutrir. —vi comer, alimentarse; (graze) pastar. **to be fed up,** *Inf.* estar hasta la coronilla, estar harto. **to f. on,** alimentarse de; *Fig.* nutrirse de. **f. pipe,** tubo de alimentación, m

**feedback** /'fid,bæk/ n retrocomunicación, f

**feeder** /'fidər/ n el, m, (f, la) que da de comer a; (eater) comedor (-ra); (of a river) tributario, afluente, m; (bib) babero, m; *Mech.* alimentador, m; (cup for invalids) pistero, m

**feeding** /'fidɪŋ/ n alimentación, f, a alimenticio, de alimentación. **f.-bottle,** biberón, m. **f.-cup,** pistero, m. **f.-trough,** pesebre, m

**feel** /fil/ n (touch) tacto, m; (feeling) sensación, f; (instinct) instinto, m, percepción innata, f

**feel** /fil/ vt (touch) tocar, tentar, palpar; (experience) sentir, experimentar; (understand) comprender; (believe) creer; (be conscious of) estar consciente de; (the pulse) tomar; examinar. —vi sentir, ser sensible; sentirse, encontrarse; (to the touch) ser... al tacto, estar. **How do you f.?** ¿Cómo se siente Vd.? **I f. cold,**

Tengo frío. **I f. for you,** Lo siento en el alma; Estoy muy consciente de ello. **I f. strongly that...,** Estoy convencido de que... **I f. that it is a difficult question,** Me parece una cuestión difícil. **It feels like rain,** Creo que va a llover. **to f. at home,** sentirse a sus anchas, sentirse como en su casa. **to f. hungry (thirsty),** tener hambre (sed). **to f. one's way,** andar a tientas; *Fig.* medir el terreno. **to f. soft,** ser blando al tacto. **to make itself felt,** hacerse sentir. **Your hands f. cold,** Tus manos están frías

**feeler** /'filər/ n (of insects) palpo, m, antena, f; tentáculo, m; *Fig.* tentativa, f, balón de ensayo, m

**feeling** /'filɪŋ/ n (touch) tacto, m; (sensation) sensación, f; (sentiment) sentimiento, m; emoción, f; (premonition) corazonada, intuición, premonición, f; (tenderness) ternura, f; (perception) sensibilidad, percepción, f; (passion) pasión, f; (belief) opinión, f, sentir, m. —a sensible; tierno; (compassionate) compasivo; apasionado; (moving) conmovedor

**feelingly** /'filɪŋli/ adv con emoción; (strongly) enérgicamente, vivamente; (understandingly) comprensivamente

**feign** /fein/ vt fingir; (invent) inventar, imaginar; simular; (allege) pretextar; (dissemble) disimular. —vi disimular

**feint** /feint/ n artificio, engaño, m; (in fencing) treta, finta, f. —vi hacer finta

**feldspar** /'fɛld,spɑr/ n *Mineral.* feldespato, m

**felicitate** /fɪ'lɪsɪ,teit/ vt felicitar, congratular, dar el parabién (a)

**felicitation** /fɪ,lɪsɪ'teiʃən/ n felicitación, f, parabién, m

**felicitous** /fɪ'lɪsɪtəs/ a feliz, dichoso, afortunado; (of phrases, etc.) feliz, acertado; oportuno

**felicity** /fɪ'lɪsɪti/ n felicidad, dicha, f

**feline** /'filain/ a felino, gatuno, de gato. —n felino, m

**fell** /fɛl/ n (skin) piel, f; (upland) altura, cuesta de montaña, f. —a cruel, feroz; (unhappy) aciago, funesto. —vt talar, cortar; (knock down) derribar; *Sew.* sobrecoser

**feller** /'fɛlər/ n talador, leñador, m

**felling** /'fɛlɪŋ/ n corta, tala, f

**fellow** /'felou/ n compañero (-ra); (equal) igual, mf; (in crime) cómplice, mf; (man) hombre, m; (boy, youth) chico, m; (colleague) colega, m; (of a society) miembro, m; (of a pair of objects) pareja, f; *Inf.* tipo, chico, m. **He's a good f.,** Es un buen chico. **How are you, old f.?** ¡Hombre! ¡Cómo estás? **f.-citizen,** conciudadano (-na). **f.-countryman,** compatriota, m; paisano (-na). **f.-creature,** semejante, mf. **f.-feeling,** simpatía, comprensión mutua, f. **f.-member,** compañero (-ra); colega, m. **f.-passenger,** compañero (-ra) de viaje. **f.-prisoner,** compañero (-ra) de prisión. **f.-student,** condiscípulo (-la). **f.-worker,** compañero (-ra) de trabajo; (collaborator) colaborador (-ra); (colleague) colega, m

**fellowship** /'felou,ʃɪp/ n coparticipación, f; (companionship) compañerismo, m; (brotherhood) comunidad, confraternidad, f; (society) asociación, f; (grant) beca, f; (of a university) colegiatura, f

**felon** /'fɛlən/ n reo, criminal, mf; felón (-ona); malvado (-da); (swelling) panadizo, m

**felonious** /fə'louniəs/ a criminal; pérfido, traidor

**felony** /'fɛləni/ n felonía, f

**felt** /fɛlt/ n fieltro, m. **a f. hat,** un sombrero de fieltro

**female** /'fimeil/ n hembra, f, a femenino. (**f.** is often rendered in Sp. by the feminine ending of the noun, e.g. *a f. cat,* una gata; *a f. friend,* una amiga.) **This is a f. animal,** Este animal es una hembra. **f. screw,** hembra de tornillo, tuerca, f

**feminine** /'fɛmənɪn/ a femenino; mujeril, afeminado. **in the f. gender,** en el género femenino

**feminism** /'fɛmə,nɪzəm/ n feminismo, m

**feminist** /'fɛmənɪst/ n feminista, mf

**feministic** /ˌfɛmə'nɪstɪk/ a feminista

**femur** /'fimər/ n *Anat.* fémur, m

**fen** /fɛn/ n marjal, pantano, m

**fence** /fɛns/ n cerca, f; (of stakes) estacada, palizada, f; (hedge) seto, m; (fencing) esgrima, f; *Mech.* guía, f; *Inf.* comprador (-ra) de efectos robados. —vi esgrimir; *Fig.* defenderse; *Inf.* recibir efectos robados. —vt cercar; estacar; *Fig.* defender; proteger. **to sit on the f.,** *Fig.* estar a ver venir

**fencer** /'fɛnsər/ n esgrimidor, m

**fencesitter** /'fɛns,sɪtər/ bailarín de la cuerda flaja, m

**fencing** /'fɛnsɪŋ/ n esgrima, f; palizada, empalizada, f. **f. mask,** careta, f. **f. master,** maestro de esgrima, maestro de armas, m. **f. match,** asalto de esgrima, m

**fend** /fɛnd/ (off) vt parar; defenderse de, guardarse de. —vi (for) mantener, cuidar de. **to f. for oneself,** ganarse la vida; defenderse

**fender** /'fɛndər/ n (round hearth) guardafuegos, m; Naut. espolón, m, defensas, f pl; Auto. parachoques, m

**fennel** /'fɛnl̩/ n Bot. hinojo, m

**ferment** /n 'fɜrmɛnt; v fər'mɛnt/ n fermento, m; fermentación, f; Fig. agitación, conmoción, efervescencia f. —vt hacer fermentar; Fig. agitar, excitar. —vi fermentar, estar en fermentación; Fig. hervirse, agitarse, excitarse

**fermentation** /,fɜrmɛn'teiʃən/ n fermentación, f

**fern** /fɜrn/ n helecho, m

**ferny** /'fɜrni/ a cubierto de helechos

**ferocious** /fə'rouʃəs/ a feroz, bravo, salvaje

**ferocity** /fə'rɒsɪti/ n ferocidad, braveza, fiereza, f

**ferreous** /'fɛriəs/ a férreo

**ferret** /'fɛrɪt/ n Zool. hurón (-ona); **to f. out,** cazar con hurones; (discover) husmear, descubrir

**Ferris wheel** /'fɛris/ n estrella giratoria, gran rueda, novia, rueda de feria, f

**ferroconcrete** /,fɛrou'kɒnkrit/ n hormigón armado, m

**ferrous** /'fɛrəs/ a ferroso

**ferruginous** /fə'rudʒənəs/ a ferruginoso; aherrumbrado, rojizo

**ferrule** /'fɛrəl/ n herrete, regatón, m, contera, f; garrucha de tornillos, f

**ferry** /'fɛri/ n barca de transporte, f; barca de pasaje, f, transbordador, m. —vt transportar de una a otra orilla, llevar en barca. —vi cruzar un río en barca. **ferry across** vt transbordar. **F.-Command,** servicio de entrega y transporte de aeroplanos, m

**ferryman** /'fɛrimən/ n barquero, m

**fertile** /'fɜrtl̩/ a fértil, fecundo; (rich) pingüe; Fig. prolífico, abundante

**Fertile Crescent, the** el Creciente Fértil m

**fertility** /fər'tɪlɪti/ n fertilidad, fecundidad, f

**fertilization** /,fɜrtlə'zeiʃən/ n Biol. fecundación, f; Agr. fertilización, f, abono, m

**fertilize** /'fɜrtl̩,aiz/ vt Biol. fecundar; Agr. fertilizar, abonar

**fertilizer** /'fɜrtl̩,aizər/ n abono, m

**ferule** /'fɛrəl/ n palmatoria, palmeta, férula, f

**fervent** /'fɜrvənt/ a ardiente; fervoroso, intenso; (enthusiastic) entusiasta, apasionado

**fervently** /'fɜrvəntli/ adv con fervor, con vehemencia

**fervor** /'fɜrvər/ n ardor, fervor, m, pasión, f; (enthusiasm) entusiasmo, celo, m; vehemencia, f

**festal** /'fɛstl̩/ a de fiesta; alegre, festivo, regocijado

**fester** /'fɛstər/ vi ulcerarse, enconarse; Fig. inflamarse, amargarse. —vt ulcerar

**festival** /'fɛstəvəl/ a de fiesta. —n festividad, f; Eccl. fiesta, f; (musical, etc.) festival, m

**festive** /'fɛstɪv/ a de fiesta; festivo, alegre

**festivity** /fɛ'stɪvɪti/ n festividad, fiesta, f; (merriment) alegría, f, júbilo, m

**festoon** /fɛ'stun/ n festón, m, guirnalda, f. —vt festonear

**festschrift** /'fɛst,ʃrɪft/ n libro de homenaje, libro jubilar, m

**fetal** /'fitl̩/ a fetal

**fetch** /fɛtʃ/ vt traer; ir a buscar; ir por; llevar; (conduct) conducir; (of tears) hacer derramar lágrimas, hacer saltársele las lágrimas; (blood) hacer correr la sangre; (produce, draw) sacar; (a blow, a sigh) dar; (acquire) conseguir; (charm) fascinar; (of price) venderse por. **to go and f.,** ir a buscar. **to f. and carry,** vt (news) divulgar, publicar. —vi estar ocupado en oficios humildes, trajinar. **to f. away,** llevarse; ir a buscar; venir a buscar. **to f. back,** devolver; (of persons) traer a casa, etc.); traer otra vez. **to f. down,** bajar, llevar abajo; hacer bajar. **to f. in,** hacer entrar; (place inside) poner adentro; (persons and things) llevar adentro. **to f. out,** hacer salir; (bring out things) sacar; (put out) poner afuera; (an idea,

etc.) sacar a relucir. **to f. up,** (a parcel, etc.) subir; (a person) hacer subir; llevar arriba

**fete** /feit/ n fiesta, f

**fetid** /'fɛtid/ a fétido, hediondo

**fetidness** /'fɛtidnɪs/ n fetidez, f, hedor, m

**fetish** /'fɛtɪʃ/ n fetiche, m

**fetishism** /'fɛti,ʃizəm/ n fetichismo, m

**fetter** /'fɛtər/ n grillete, m; pl **fetters,** grillos, m pl, cadenas, f pl; prisión, cárcel, f. —vt encadenar, atar

**fettle** /'fɛtl̩/ n condición, f, estado, m

**fetus** /'fitəs/ n feto, m

**feud** /fyud/ n enemistad, riña, f; (feudal law) feudo, m

**feudal** /'fyudl̩/ a feudal. **f. lord,** señor feudal, señor de horca y cuchillo, m

**feudalism** /'fyudl̩,izəm/ n feudalismo, m

**feudatory** /'fyudə,tɔri/ a and n feudatario (-ia)

**fever** /'fivər/ n fiebre, f; calentura, f; (enthusiasm) pasión, afición, f. **to be in a f.,** tener fiebre; (agitated) estar muy agitado. **to be in a f. to,** estar muy impaciente de. **puerperal f.,** fiebre puerperal, f. **tertian f.,** fiebre terciana, f. **yellow f.,** fiebre amarilla, f

**feverish** /'fivərɪʃ/ a febril; Fig. ardiente, febril, vehemente. **to grow f.,** empezar a tener fiebre, acalenturarse

**feverishness** /'fivərɪʃnɪs/ n calentura, f; (impatience) impaciencia, f

**few** /fyu/ a and n pocos, m pl; pocas, f pl; algunos, m pl; algunas, f pl; (few in number) número pequeño (de), m. **a good f.,** bastantes, mf pl. **not a f.,** no pocos, m pl, (pocas, f pl). **the f.,** la minoría, f. **f. and far between,** raramente, en raras ocasiones; pocos y contados

**fewer** /'fyuər/ a compar menos. **The f. the better,** Cuantos menos mejor

**fewest** /'fyuist/ a superl (el) menos, m; el menor número (de), m; (el) menos posible de, m

**fewness** /'fyunɪs/ n corto número, m

**fez** /fɛz/ n fez, m

**fiancé(e)** /,fiɑn'sei/ n novio (-ia); desposado (-da), prometido (-da)

**fiasco** /fi'æskou/ n fiasco, mal éxito, fracaso, malogro, m

**fiat** /'fiɑt/ n fiat, mandato, m, orden, f

**fib** /fɪb/ n mentirilla, f, vt decir mentirillas, mentir

**fibber** /'fɪbər/ n embustero (-ra), mentiroso (-sa)

**fiber** /'faibər/ n fibra, f; filamento, m, hebra, f; (of grass, etc.) brizna, f; Fig. naturaleza, f

**fibroid** /'faibrɔid/ a fibroso. —n fibroma, m

**fibrous** /'faibrəs/ a fibroso

**fibula** /'fɪbyələ/ n Anat. peroné, m

**fichu** /'fiʃu/ n pañoleta, f, fichú, m

**fickle** /'fɪkəl/ a inconstante; mudable; (of persons) liviano, ligero, voluble

**fickleness** /'fɪkəlnɪs/ n inconstancia, f; mudanza, f; liviandad, ligereza, veleidad, volubilidad, f

**fiction** /'fɪkʃən/ n ficción, f; invención, f; literatura narrativa, f; novelas, f pl. **legal f.,** ficción legal, ficción de derecho, f

**fictitious** /fɪk'tɪʃəs/ a ficticio; imaginario; fingido

**fictitiousness** /fɪk'tɪʃəsnɪs/ n carácter ficticio, m; falsedad, f

**fiddle** /'fɪdl̩/ n violín, m. —vt tocar... en el violín. —vi tocar el violín; (fidget) jugar; perder el tiempo. **to play second f.,** tocar el segundo violín; Fig. ser plato de segunda mesa

**fiddler** /'fɪdlər/ n violinista, mf

**fiddling** /'fɪdlɪŋ/ a insignificante, trivial, frívolo

**fidelity** /fɪ'dɛlɪti/ n fidelidad, f

**fidget** /'fɪdʒɪt/ vi estar nervioso, estar inquieto; impacientarse; trajinar; (with) jugar con. —vt molestar; impacientar

**fidgetiness** /'fɪdʒɪtinɪs/ n inquietud, nerviosidad, f

**fidgety** /'fɪdʒɪti/ a inquieto, nervioso. **to be f.,** tener hormiguillo

**fiduciary** /fɪ'duʃɪ,ɛri/ a fiduciario. —n fideicomisario (-ia)

**fief** /fif/ n feudo, m

**field** /fild/ n campo, m; (meadow) prado, m, pradera, f; (sown field) sembrado, m; (Phys. Herald.) campo, m; (of ice) banco, m; Mineral. yacimiento, m;

(background) fondo, *m;* (campaign) campaña, *f;* (battle) batalla, lucha, *f;* (space) espacio, *m;* (of knowledge, etc.) especialidad, esfera, *f;* (hunting) caza, *f; Sports.* campo, *m;* (competitors) todos los competidores en una carrera, etc.; (horses in a race) el campo. —*a* campal, pradeño; de campo; de los campos. —*vt Sports.* parar y devolver la pelota. **in the f.,** *Mil.* en el campo de batalla, en campaña. **magnetic f.,** campo magnético, *m.* **to take the f.,** entrar en campaña. **f.-artillery,** artillería ligera, artillería montada, *f.* **f.-day,** (holiday) día de asueto, *m;* (day out) día en el campo, *m; Mil.* día de maniobras, *m.* **f.-glasses,** anteojos, gemelos, *m pl.* **f.-hospital,** hospital de sangre, *m;* ambulancia fija, *f.* **f.-kitchen,** cocina de campaña, *f.* **f.-marshal,** capitán general de ejército, *m.* **f.-mouse,** ratón silvestre, *m.* **f. of battle,** campo de batalla, *m.* **f. of vision,** campo visual, *m.* **f.-telegraph,** telégrafo de campaña, *m*

**fielder** /'fildər/ *n* (baseball) jardinero (-ra)

**field work** prácticas de campo, *f pl*

**fiend** /find/ *n* diablo, demonio, *m;* malvado (-da); (addict) adicto (-ta). **morphia f.,** morfinómano (-ma)

**fiendish** /'findɪʃ/ *a* diabólico, infernal; malvado, cruel, malévolo

**fiendishness** /'findɪʃnɪs/ *n* perversidad, crueldad, *f*

**fierce** /fɪərs/ *a* salvaje, feroz, cruel; (of the elements) violento, furioso; (intense) intenso, vehemente

**fiercely** /'fɪərsli/ *adv* ferozmente; violentamente, con furia; intensamente, con vehemencia

**fierceness** /'fɪərsnɪs/ *n* ferocidad, fiereza, *f;* violencia, furia, *f;* intensidad, vehemencia, *f*

**fieriness** /'faiərinɪs/ *n* ardor, *m;* (flames) las llamas, *f pl;* (redness) rojez, *f;* (irritability) ferocidad, irritabilidad, *f;* (vehemence) pasión, vehemencia, *f;* (of horses) fogosidad, *f*

**fiery** /'faiəri/ *a* ardiente; (red) rojo; (irritable) feroz, colérico, irritable; (vehement) apasionado, vehemente; (of horses) fogoso

**fife** /faif/ *n Mus.* pífano, pito, *m*

**fifteen** /'fif'tin/ *a* and *n* quince *m.;* (of age) quince años, *m pl*

**fifteenth** /'fif'tinθ/ *a* and *n* décimoquinto *m.;* (part) quinzavo, *m,* décimoquinta parte, *f;* (of the month) (el) quince, *m;* (of monarchs) quince; *Mus.* quincena, *f*

**fifth** /fifθ/ *a* quinto; (of monarchs) quinto; (of the month) (el) cinco. —*n* quinto, *m;* (part) quinto, *m,* quinta parte, *f; Mus.* quinta, *f,* **Charles V,** Carlos quinto. **f. column,** quinta columna, *f*

**fifthly** /'fifθli/ *adv* en quinto lugar

**fiftieth** /'fiftiiθ/ *a* quincuagésimo; (part) quincuagésima parte, *f,* cincuentavo, *m*

**fifty** /'fifti/ *a* and *n* cincuenta *m.;* (of age) cincuenta años, *m pl*

**fiftyfold** /'fifti,fould/ *a* and *adv* cincuenta veces

**fig** /fig/ *n* higo, *m;* (tree) higuera, *f; Fig.* bledo, ardite, *m.* **green fig,** higo, *m,* breva, *f.* **I don't care a fig,** No se me da un higo. **to be not worth a fig,** no valer un ardite. **fig-leaf,** hoja de higuera, *f; Fig.* hoja de parra, *f*

**fight** /fait/ *n* lucha, pelea, *f,* combate, *m;* batalla, *f;* (struggle) lucha, *f;* (quarrel) riña, pelea, *f;* (conflict) conflicto, *m;* (valor) coraje, brío, *m.* **hand-to-hand f.,** cachetina, *f.* **in fair f.,** en buena lid. **to have a f.,** tener una pelea. **to show f.,** mostrarse agresivo

**fight** /fait/ *vt* luchar contra, batirse con; (a battle) dar (batalla); (oppose) oponer; (defend) defender, pelear por; hacer batirse. —*vi* luchar, batirse, pelear; (with words) disputar; (struggle) luchar; (make war) hacer la guerra; (in a tournament) tornear. **to f. one's way,** abrirse paso con las armas. **to f. against,** luchar contra. **to f. off,** librarse de; sacudirse. **to f. with,** luchar con; pelear con; reñir con

**fighter** /'faitər/ *n* luchador (-ra); combatiente, *m;* guerrero, *m;* duelista, *m;* (boxer) boxeador, *m; Aer.* (avión de) caza, *m.* **night f.,** *Aer.* (avión de) caza nocturno, *m.* **f.-bomber,** *Aer.* caza bombardero, *m.* **Command,** *Aer.* servicio de aviones de caza, *m*

**fighting** /'faitin/ *n* lucha, *f,* combate, *m;* el pelear; (boxing) boxeo, *m,* a combatiente; (bellicose) agresivo, belicoso. **f.-man,** combatiente, guerrero, *m*

**figment** /'figmənt/ *n* ficción, invención, *f*

**figurative** /'figyərətɪv/ *a* figurado, metafórico; figurativo; simbólico

**figuratively** /'figyərətɪvli/ *adv* en sentido figurativo; metafóricamente

**figure** /'figyər/ *n* figura, *f;* forma, *f;* (statue) estatua, figura, *f;* (of a person) silueta, *f;* talle, *m;* (number) cifra, *f,* número, *m;* (quantity) cantidad, *f;* (price) precio, *m; Geom. Gram. Dance.* (skating) figura, *f;* (appearance) presencia, *f,* aire, *m;* (picture) imagen, *m;* (on fabric) diseño, *m; Mus.* cifra, *f; pl* **figures,** aritmética, *f,* matemáticas, *f pl.* —*vt* figurar; (imagine) figurarse, imaginar; *Mus.* cifrar. —*vi* figurar, hacer un papel; (calculate) calcular, hacer cuentas. **to f. out,** calcular; (a problem, etc.) resolver. **a fine f. of a woman,** *Inf.* una real hembra. **lay f.,** maniquí, *m.* **to be good at figures,** estar fuerte en matemáticas. **to cut a f.,** *Fig.* hacer figura. **to have a good f.,** tener buen talle. **f. of speech,** figura retórica, figura de dicción *f;* (manner of speaking) metáfora *f.* **f. dance,** baile de figuras, *m,* contradanza, *f.* **f.-head,** *Naut.* mascarón, *m,* (or figura, *f*) de proa; *Fig.* figura decorativa, *f*

**figured** /'figyərd/ *a* estampado, con diseños, labrado

**figurine** /,figyə'rin/ *n* figurilla, *f*

**filament** /'filəmənt/ *n* filamento, *m;* hebra, *f*

**filamentous** /,filə'mentəs/ *a* filamentoso, fibroso

**filbert** /'filbərt/ *n* avellana, *f;* (tree) avellano, *m*

**filch** /filtʃ/ *vt* sisar, ratear

**filching** /'filtʃin/ *n* sisa, *f*

**file** /fail/ *n* (line) fila, hilera, sarta, línea, *f; Mil.* fila, *f;* (tool) lima, *f;* (rasp) escofina, *f;* (list) lista, *f,* catálogo, *m;* (for documents) carpeta, *f,* cartapacio, *m;* (bundle of papers) legajo, *m;* (for bills, letters, etc.) clasificador, *m;* archivo, *m;* (in an archives) expediente *m.* **in a f.,** en fila; en cola

**file** /fail/ *vt* hacer marchar en fila; (smooth) limar; (literary work) pulir; (classify) clasificar; (note particulars) fichar; (keep) guardar; (a petition, etc.) presentar, registrar. —*vi* marchar en fila. **to f. in,** entrar en fila. **to f. off,** desfilar. **to file a brief,** presentar un escrito. **to f. letters,** clasificar correspondencia. **to f. past,** *Mil.* desfilar

**filial** /'filiəl/ *a* filial

**filiation** /,fili'eifən/ *n* filiación, *f*

**filibuster** /'filə,bʌstər/ *n* filibustero, pirata, *m*

**filigree** /'filə,gri/ *n* filigrana, *f, a* afiligranado

**filing** /'failin/ *n* (with a tool) limadura, *f;* clasificación, *f;* (of a petition, etc.) presentación, *f,* registro, *m; pl* **filings,** limaduras, *f pl,* retales, *m pl.* **f.-cabinet,** fichero, *m.* **f.-card,** ficha, *f*

**fill** /fil/ *vt* llenar; (stuff) rellenar; (appoint to a post) proveer; (occupy a post) desempeñar; (imbue) henchir; (saturate) saturar; (occupy) ocupar; (a tooth) empastar; (fulfil) cumplir; (charge, fuel) cargar; (with food) hartar. —*vi* llenarse. **fill an order,** servir un pedido. **fill a prescription,** surtir una receta. **to f. the chair,** ocupar la presidencia; (university) ocupar la cátedra. **to f. the place of,** ocupar el lugar de; substituir; suplir. **It will be difficult to find someone to f. his place,** Será difícil de encontrar uno que haga lo que hizo él. **to f. to the brim,** llenar hasta los bordes. **to f. in, f. out,** (a form) llenar (or completar) (una hoja); (insert) insertar, añadir; (a hollow) terraplenar. **to f. out,** *vt* hinchar. —*vi* hincharse; echar carnes; (of the face) redondearse. **to f. up,** colmar, llenar hasta los bordes; (an office) proveer; (block) macizar; (a form) completar, llenar

**fillet** /'filit/ *n* venda, cinta, *f;* (of meat or fish) filete, *m;* (of meat) solomillo, *m; Archit.* filete, *m.* —*vt* atar con una venda o cinta; *Cul.* cortar en filetes

**filling** /'filin/ *n* envase, *m;* (swelling) henchimiento, *m;* (of a tooth) empastadura, *f;* (in or up, of forms, etc.) llenar, *m.* **f. station,** depósito de gasolina, *m*

**fillip** /'filəp/ *n* capirotazo, *m;* (stimulus) estímulo, *m;* (trifle) bagatela, *f.* —*vt* and *vi* dar un capirotazo (a); *vt* estimular, incitar

**filly** /'fili/ *n* jaca, potra, *f*

**film** /film/ *n* (on liquids) tela, *f;* membrana, *f;* (coating) capa ligera, *f;* (on eyes) tela, *f;* (cinema) película, cinta, *f; Photo.* película, *f; Fig.* velo, *m;* nube, *f, vi* cubrirse de un velo, etc. —*vt* cubrir de un velo, etc.; filmar, fotografiar para el cine. **roll f.,**

película fotográfica, *f.* **silent f.**, película muda, *f.* **talking f.**, película sonora, *f.* **to shoot a f.**, hacer una película. **to take part in a f.**, actuar, or tomar parte, en una película. **f. pack**, película en paquetes *f.* **f. star**, estrella de la pantalla (or del cine), *f*

**film industry** industria fílmica, *f*

**filminess** /'filminis/ *n* transparencia, diafanidad, *f*

**filmy** /'filmi/ *a* transparente, diáfano

**filter** /'filtər/ *n* filtro, *m.* —*vt* filtrar. —*vi* infiltrarse; (*Fig.* of news) trascender, divulgarse. **f.-bed**, filtro, *m.* **f.-paper**, papel filtro, *m*

**filth** /filθ/ *n* inmundicia, suciedad, *f; Fig.* corrupción, *f; Fig.* obscenidad, *f*

**filthiness** /'filθinis/ *n* suciedad, *f;* escualidez, *f; Fig.* asquerosidad, *f; Fig.* obscenidad, *f*

**filthy** /'filθi/ *a* inmundo, sucio; escuálido; *Fig.* asqueroso; *Fig.* obsceno

**filtrate** /'filtreit/ *n* filtrado, *m, vt* filtrar

**filtration** /fil'treiʃən/ *n* filtración, *f*

**fin** /fin/ *n* (of fish) aleta, ala, *f;* (of whale) barba, *f; Aer.* aleta, *f*

**final** /'fainl/ *a* último, final; (conclusive) conclusivo, decisivo, terminante. —*n Sports.* finales, *m pl; Educ.* último examen, *m.* **f. blow**, *Fig.* golpe decisivo, *m.* **f. cause**, *Philos.* causa final, *f*

**finale** /fi'næli/ *n* final, *m*

**finalist** /'fainlist/ *n Sports.* finalista, *mf*

**finality** /fai'næliti/ *n* finalidad, *f;* (decision) determinación, resolución, decisión, *f*

**finally** /'fainli/ *adv* por fin, finalmente, por último, a la postre; (irrevocably) irrevocablemente

**finance** /'fainæns/ *n* hacienda pública, *f,* asuntos económicos, *m pl;* finanzas, *f pl.* —*vt* financiar

**financial** /fi'nænʃəl/ *a* financiero, monetario. **f. year**, año económico, *m*

**financially** /fi'nænʃəli/ *adv* del punto de vista financiero

**financier** /ˌfinən'siər, ˌfainən-/ *n* financiero, *m*

**find** /faind/ *vt* encontrar, hallar; (discover) descubrir, dar con; (invent) inventar, crear; (supply) facilitar, proporcionar; (provide) proveer; (instruct) instruir; *Law.* declarar. —*vi Law.* fallar, dar sentencia. —*n* hallazgo, *m;* descubrimiento, *m.* **I found him out a long time ago,** *Fig.* Hace tiempo que me di cuenta de cómo era él. **I found it possible to go out,** Me fue posible salir. **The judge found them guilty,** El juez les declaró culpables. **to f. a verdict,** *Law.* dar sentencia, fallar. **to f. one's way,** encontrar el camino. **to f. oneself,** hallarse, verse, encontrarse. **to f. out,** averiguar, descubrir. **to f. out about,** informarse sobre (or de)

**finder** /'faindər/ *n* hallador (-ra); (inventor) inventor (-ra), descubridor (-ra); (telescope, camera) buscador, *m*

**finding** /'faindiŋ/ *n* hallazgo, *m;* (discovery) descubrimiento, *m; Law.* fallo, *m,* sentencia, *f*

**fine** /fain/ *n* multa, *f;* (end) fin, *m.* **in f.**, en fin, en resumen

**fine** /fain/ *vt* multar, cargar una multa de

**fine** /fain/ *a* (thin) delgado; (sharp) agudo; (delicate) fino, delicado; (minute) menudo; (refined) refinado, puro; (healthy) saludable; (of weather) bueno; magnífico; (beautiful) hermoso, lindo; excelente; (perfect) perfecto; (good) bueno; elegante; (showy) ostentoso, vistoso; (handsome) guapo; (subtle) sutil; (acute) agudo; (noble) noble; (eminent, accomplished) distinguido, eminente; (polished) pulido; (affected) afectado; (clear) claro; (transparent) transparente, diáfano. —*adv* muy bien. **a f. upstanding young man,** un buen mozo. **a f. upstanding young woman,** una real moza. **He's a f. fellow,** (ironically) Es una buena pieza. **That is all very f. but...,** Todo eso está muy bien pero.... **to become f.,** (weather) mejorar

**finely** /'fainli/ *adv* finamente; menudamente; elegantemente; (ironically) lindamente

**fineness** /'fainnis/ *n* (thinness) delgadez, *f;* (excellence) excelencia, *f;* delicadeza, *f;* (softness) suavidad, *f;* elegancia, *f;* (subtlety) sutileza, *f;* (acuteness) agudeza, *f;* (perfection) perfección, *f;* (nobility) nobleza, *f;* (beauty) hermosura, *f*

**finery** /'fainəri/ *n* galas, *f pl,* atavíos magníficos, *m pl;* adornos, *m pl;* primor, *m,* belleza, *f*

**finesse** /fi'nɛs/ *n* sutileza, diplomacia, *f;* estratagema, artificio, *m;* (cunning) astucia, *f, vi* valerse de estratagemas y artificios

**finger** /'fiŋgər/ *n* dedo, *m;* (of a clock, etc.) manecilla, *f;* (measurement) dedada, *f; Fig.* mano, *f.* —*vt* manosear, tocar; (soil) ensuciar con los dedos; (steal) sisar; (*Mus.* a keyed instrument) teclear, (a stringed instrument) tocar. **first f.**, dedo índice, *m.* **fourth f.**, dedo anular, *m.* **little f.**, dedo meñique, *m.* **second f.**, dedo de en medio, dedo del corazón, *m.* **to burn one's fingers**, quemarse los dedos; *Fig.* cogerse los dedos. **to have at one's f.-tips**, *Fig.* saber al dedillo. **f.-board**, (of piano) teclado, *m;* (of stringed instruments) diapasón, *m.* **f.-bowl**, lavadedos, lavafrutas, *m.* **finger's breadth**, dedo, *m.* **f.-mark**, huella digital, *f.* **f.-nail**, uña del dedo, *f.* **f.-print**, impresión digital, *f.* **f.-stall**, dedil, *m.* **f.-tip**, punta del dedo, yema del dedo, *f.* **f.-wave**, peinado al agua, *m*

**fingered** /'fiŋgərd/ *a* (in compounds) con dedos, que tiene los dedos...

**fingering** /'fiŋgəriŋ/ *n* (touching) manoseo, *m; Mus.* digitación, *f;* (*Mus.* the keys) tecleo, *m;* (wool) estambre, *m*

**finial** /'finiəl/ *n* pináculo, *m*

**finicky** /'finiki/ *a* (of persons) dengoso, remilgado; (of things) nimio

**finish** /'finiʃ/ *n* fin, *m,* conclusión, terminación, *f;* (final touch) última mano, *f;* perfección, *f;* (of an article) acabado, *m; Sports.* llegada, (*horse race*) meta, *f.* —*vt* terminar, acabar, concluir; llevar a cabo, poner fin a; (perfect) perfeccionar; (put finishing touch to) dar la última mano a; (kill) matar; (exhaust) agotar, rendir; (overcome) vencer. —*vi* acabar; concluirse. **to f. off,** acabar, terminar; (kill) matar, acabar con; (destroy) destruir. **to f. up,** acabar; (eat) comer; (drink) beber

**finishable** /'finiʃəbəl/ *a* acabable

**finished** /'finiʃt/ *a* acabado, terminado, completo; perfecto; (careful) cuidadoso

**finished goods** *n pl* bienes terminados, *m pl*

**finisher** /'finiʃər/ *n* terminador (-ra), acabador (-ra); pulidor (-ra); (final blow) golpe de gracia, *m*

**finishing** /'finiʃiŋ/ *a* concluyente. —*n* terminación, *f,* fin, *m;* perfección, *f;* (last touch) última mano, *f.* **to put the f. touch,** dar la última pincelada

**finite** /'fainait/ *a* finito

**Finland** /'finlənd/ Finlandia, *f*

**Finn** /fin/ *n* finlandés (-esa)

**Finnish** /'finiʃ/ *a* finlandés. —*n* (language) finlandés, *m*

**fir** /fɜr/ *n* abeto, sapino, pino, *m.* **red fir,** pino silvestre, *m.* **fir-cone,** piña de abeto, *f.* **fir grove,** abetal, *m*

**fire** /faiər/ *n* fuego, *m;* (conflagration) incendio, *m;* (on the hearth) lumbre, *f,* fuego, *m; Fig.* ardor, *m,* pasión, *f;* (shooting) fuego, tiro, *m.* **by f. and sword,** a sangre y fuego. **by the f.,** cerca del fuego; (in a house) al lado de la chimenea. **long-range f.,** *Mil.* fuego de largo alcance, *m.* **short-range f.,** *Mil.* fuego de corto alcance, *m.* **on f.,** en fuego, ardiendo, en llamas; *Fig.* impaciente; *Fig.* lleno de pasión. **to be between two fires,** *Fig.* estar entre dos aguas. **to make a f.,** encender un fuego. **to miss f.,** no dar en el blanco, errar el tiro. **to open f.,** *Mil.* hacer una descarga. **to set on f.,** prender fuego a, incendiar. **to take f.,** encenderse. **under f.,** bajo fuego. **f.-alarm,** alarma de incendios, *f.* **f.-arm,** arma de fuego, *f.* **f.-box,** hogar, *m.* **f.-brand,** tea, *f.* **f.-brigade,** cuerpo de bomberos, *m.* **f.-damp,** aire detonante, grisú, *m,* mofeta, *f.* **f.-dog,** morillo, *m.* **f.-drill,** (firefighters') instrucción de bomberos, *f,* (others') simulacro de incendio, *m.* **f.-engine,** autobomba, bomba, de incendios, *f.* **f.-escape,** escalera de incendios, *f.* **f.-extinguisher,** apagador de incendio, extintor, matafuego, *m.* **f.-guard,** vigilante de incendios, *m;* alambrera, *f.* **f.-hose,** manguera de incendios, *f.* **f.-insurance,** seguro contra incendios, *m.* **f.-irons,** badil *m.* y tenazas *f pl.* **f.-lighter,** encendedor, *m.* **f.-screen,** pantalla, *f.* **f.-ship,** brulote, *m.* **f.-shovel,** badil, *m,* paleta, *f.* **f.-spotter,** vigilante de incendios, *m.* **f.-sprite,** salamandra, *f.* **f.-watching,** servicio de vigilancia de incendios, *m*

**fire** /faiᵊr/ *vt* incendiar, prender (or pegar) fuego a; quemar; (bricks) cocer; (fire-arms) disparar; (cauterize) cauterizar; (*Fig.* stimulate) estimular, excitar; (inspire) inspirar; (*Inf.* of questions) disparar; (*Inf.* sack) despedir. —*vi* encenderse; (shoot) hacer fuego, disparar (un tiro); (*Inf.* away) disparar; (up) enojarse. **to f. a salute,** disparar un saludo. *Mil.* **F.!** ¡Fuego!

**fire department** *n* parque de bomberos, servicis de bomberos, servicio de incendios, parque de bombas (Puerto Rico), *m*

**firefly** /'faiᵊr,flai/ *n* cocuyo, *m*

**fireman** /'faiᵊrmən/ *n* bombero, *m;* (of an engine, etc.) fogonero, *m.* **fireman's lift,** silleta, *f*

**fireplace** /'faiᵊr,pleis/ *n* chimenea francesa, chimenea, *f;* (hearth) hogar, *m*

**fireproof** /'faiᵊr,pruf/ *a* a prueba de incendios; incombustible

**firer** /'faiᵊrər/ *n* disparador, *m*

**firewood** /'faiᵊr,wʊd/ *n* leña, *f.* **f. dealer,** leñador (-ra), vendedor (-ra) de leña

**firework** /'faiᵊr,wɜrk/ *n* fuego artificial, *m*

**firing** /'faiᵊrɪŋ/ *n* (of fire-arms) disparo, *m;* (burning) incendio, *m,* quema, *f;* (of bricks, etc.) cocimiento, *m;* (of pottery) cocción, *f;* (cauterization) cauterización, *f;* (fuel) combustible, *m;* (*Inf.* sacking) despedida, *f.* **within f. range,** a tiro. **f.-line,** línea de fuego, *f.* **f.-oven,** (pottery) horno alfarero, *m.* **f.-squad,** pelotón de ejecución, *m*

**firm** /fɜrm/ *a* firme; (strong) fuerte; (secure) seguro; sólido; (resolute) inflexible, resoluto; severo; (steady) constante; (persistent) tenaz. —*n Com.* casa (de comercio), empresa, *f;* razón social, *f*

**firmament** /'fɜrməmənt/ *n* firmamento, *m*

**firmly** /'fɜrmli/ *adv* firmemente; inflexiblemente; constantemente

**firmness** /'fɜrmnɪs/ *n* firmeza, *f;* solidez, *f;* inflexibilidad, resolución, *f;* severidad, *f;* constancia, *f;* tenacidad, *f*

**first** /fɜrst/ *a* primero (primer before *m sing* nouns); (of monarchs) primero; (of dates) (el) primero. —*n* primero, *m;* (beginning) principio, *m.* —*adv* primero, en primer lugar; (before, of time) antes; (for the first time) por primera vez; (at the beginning) al principio; (ahead) adelante. **at f.,** al principio. **from the very f.,** desde el primer momento. **to appear for the f. time,** aparecer (or presentarse) por primera vez; *Theat.* debutar. **to go f.,** ir delante de todos, ir a la cabeza; ir adelante. **f. and foremost,** en primer lugar; ante todo. **f.-aid,** primera cura, *f.* **f.-aid post,** casa de socorro, *f.* **f.-aider,** practicante, *m.* **f.-born,** *a* and *n* primogénito (-ta). **f.-class,** de primera clase; *Fig.* excelente. **f.-cousin,** primo (-ma) carnal, primo (-ma) hermano (-na). **f. edition,** edición príncipe, *f.* **f. floor,** primer piso, *m.* **f. fruits,** frutos primerizos, *m pl; Fig.* primicias, *f pl.* **f.-hand,** *a* original, de primera mano. **f. letters,** primeras letras, *f pl.* **f. night,** *Theat.* estreno, *m.* **f. of all,** primero, ante todo. **f.-rate,** *a* de primera clase

**firstly** /'fɜrstli/ *adv* en primer lugar, primero

**firth** /fɜrθ/ *n* ría, *f*

**fiscal** /'fɪskəl/ *a* and *n* fiscal *m.*. **f. year,** año económico, *m*

**fish** /fɪʃ/ *n* pez, *m;* (out of the water) pescado, *m; Inf.* tipo, indivíduo, *m.* —*vt* pescar; (out) sacar. —*vi* pescar; *Fig.* buscar. **fried f.,** pescado frito, *m.* **He is a queer f.,** Es un tipo muy raro. **to be neither f. nor fowl,** no ser ni carne ni pescado. **to feel like a f. out of water,** sentirse fuera de su ambiente. **to f. in troubled waters,** *Fig.* a río revuelto ganancia de pescadores. **f.-eating,** *a* ictiófago. **f.-fork,** tenedor de pescado, *m.* **f.-glue,** cola de pescado, *f.* **f.-hook,** anzuelo, *m.* **f.-knife,** cuchillo de pescado, *m.* **f.-like,** de pez; como un pez, parecido a un pez. **f. roe,** hueva, *f.* **f.-server,** pala para pescado, *f*

**fishbone** /'fɪʃ,boʊn/ *n* espina de pescado, raspa de pescado, *f*

**fisherman** /'fɪʃərmən/ *n* pescador, *m*

**fishery** /'fɪʃəri/ *n* pesquería, *f*

**fishing** /'fɪʃɪŋ/ *n* pesca, *f, a* de pescar. **to go f.,** ir de pesca. **f.-boat,** bote de pesca, *m.* **f.-floats,** levas, *f pl.* **f.-line,** sedal, *m.* **f.-net,** red de pesca, *f.* **f.-reel,** carretel, carrete, *m.* **f.-rod,** caña de pescar, *f.* **f.-tackle,**

aparejo de pesca, *m.* **f. village,** pueblo de pescadores, *m*

**fishmeal** /'fɪʃ,mil/ *n* harina de pescado, *f*

**fishmonger** /'fɪʃ,mʌŋgər/ *n* pescadero (-ra).

**fishmonger's shop** *n* pescadería, *f*

**fishpond** /'fɪʃ,pɒnd/ *n* vivero, *m,* piscina, *f*

**fishwife** /'fɪʃ,waif/ *n* pescadora, *f*

**fishy** /'fɪʃi/ *a* de pescado; (of eyes, etc.) de pez, como un pez; (in smell) que huele a pescado; *Inf.* sospechoso; (of stories) inverosímil

**fissure** /'fɪʃər/ *n* grieta, hendidura, rendija, *f;* (*Anat. Geol.*) fisura, *f*

**fissured** /'fɪʃərd/ *a* hendido

**fist** /fɪst/ *n* puño, *m; Print.* manecilla, *f;* (handwriting) letra, *f.* **with clenched fists,** a puño cerrado

**fisticuff** /'fɪstɪ,kʌf/ *n* puñetazo, *m; pl* **fisticuffs,** agarrada, riña, *f*

**fit** /fɪt/ *n* espasmo, paroxismo, *m;* ataque, *m;* (impulse) acceso, arranque, *m;* (whim) capricho, *m;* (of a garment) corte, *m;* (adjustment) ajuste, encaje, *m.* **by fits and starts,** a tropezones, espasmódicamente

**fit** /fɪt/ *a* a propósito (para), bueno (para); (opportune) oportuno; (proper) conveniente; apto; (decent) decente; (worthy) digno; (ready) preparado, listo; (adequate) adecuado; (capable) capaz, en estado (de); (appropriate) apropiado; (just) justo. **It is not in a fit state to be used,** No está en condiciones para usarse. **to be not fit for,** no servir para; (through ill-health) no tener bastante salud para. **to think fit,** creer (or juzgar) conveniente. **fit for use,** usable. **fit to eat,** comestible

**fit** /fɪt/ *vt* ajustar, acomodar, encajar; adaptar (a); (furnish) proveer de; surtir (con); (of tailor, dressmaker) entallar, probar; (of shoemaker) calzar; (of garments, shoes) ir (bien o mal); (prepare) preparar; (go with) ser apropiado (a); (adapt itself to) adaptarse a. —*vi* ajustarse, acomodarse, encajarse; adaptarse; (clothes) ir (bien o mal). **to fit in,** *vt* encajar; incluir. —*vi* encajarse; caber; adaptarse. **to fit out,** equipar; proveer (de); preparar. **to fit up,** montar, instalar; proveer (de). **to fit with,** proveer de

**fitful** /'fɪtfəl/ *a* intermitente; espasmódico; caprichoso

**fitfully** /'fɪtfəli/ *adv* por intervalos, a ratos; caprichosamente

**fitly** /'fɪtli/ *adv* adecuadamente; justamente; apropiadamente

**fitment** /'fɪtmənt/ *n* equipo, *m;* instalación, *f;* (of bookcase, etc.) sección, *f;* (furniture) pieza, *f,* mueble, *m*

**fitness** /'fɪtnɪs/ *n* conveniencia, *f;* aptitud, capacidad, *f;* oportunidad, *f;* salud, *f;* (good health) vigor, *m*

**fitted** /'fɪtɪd/ *a* (of clothes) ajustado

**fitter** /'fɪtər/ *n* ajustador, *m;* (mechanic) armador, mecánico, *m;* (tailoring) cortador, *m;* (dressmaking) probador (-ra)

**fitting** /'fɪtɪŋ/ *n* encaje, ajuste, *m;* adaptación, *f;* (of a garment) prueba, *f;* (size) medida, *f;* (installation) instalación, *f;* **pl. fittings,** guarniciones, *f pl;* instalaciones, *f pl;* accesorios, *m pl.* —*a* conveniente, justo; apropiado; adecuado; (worthy) digno; (of coats, etc.) ajustado. **f. room,** cuarto de pruebas, *m.* **f. in,** encaje, *m.* **f. out,** equipo, *m.* **f. up,** arreglo, *m;* (of machines) montaje, *m;* (of a house) mueblaje, *m*

**five** /faiv/ *a* and *n* cinco *m.;* (of the clock) las cinco, *f pl;* (of age) cinco años, *m pl.* **to be f.,** tener cinco años. **f. feet deep,** de cinco pies de profundidad. **f. feet high,** cinco pies de altura. **f.-finger exercises,** ejercicios de piano, *m pl.* **F.-Year Plan,** Plan Quinquenal, *m*

**fivefold** /'faiv,foʊld/ *a* quíntuplo

**fix** /fɪks/ *n* aprieto, apuro, *m;* callejón sin salida, *m.* —*vt* fijar; sujetar, afianzar; (bayonets) calar; (with nails) clavar; (*Photo., Chem., Med.*) fijar; (decide) establecer; (a date) señalar; (eyes, attention) clavar; (on the mind) grabar, estampar; (one's hopes) poner; (base) basar, fundar; (*Inf.* put right) arreglar, componer. —*vi* fijarse; establecerse; determinarse. **to get in a fix,** hacerse un lío. **to fix a price,** fijar un precio. **to fix on, upon,** elegir, escoger; decidir, determinar. **to fix up,** arreglar; decidir; organizar; (differences) olvidar (sus disensiones)

**fixation** /fɪk'seɪʃən/ n obsesión, idea fija, f; (scientific) fijación, f

**fixative** /'fɪksətɪv/ n (Med., Photo.) fijador, m; (dyeing) mordiente, m. **—a** que fija

**fixed** /fɪkst/ a fijo; inmóvil; permanente; (of ideas) inflexible. **f. bayonet,** bayoneta calada, f. **f. price,** precio fijo, m. **f. star,** estrella fija, f

**fixedly** /'fɪksɪdli/ adv fijamente; resueltamente; firmemente

**fixing** /'fɪksɪŋ/ n fijación, f; afianzamiento, m; arreglo, m; (of a date) señalamiento, m. **f. bath,** Photo. baño fijador, m

**fixity** /'fɪksɪti/ n permanencia, f; inmovilidad, f; invariabilidad, f; firmeza, f

**fixture** /'fɪkstʃər/ n instalación, f; accesorio fijo, m; Sports. partido, m; Inf. permanencia, f. **f. card,** Sports. calendario deportivo, m

**fizz** /fɪz/ n espuma, f; chisporroteo, m. Inf. champaña, m. **—vi** (liquids) espumear; (sputter) chisporrotear

**fizzle** /'fɪzəl/ n (failure) fiasco, fracaso, m. **—vi** chisporrotear; (out) apagarse; (fail) fracasar, no tener éxito

**fjord** /fyɔrd/ n fiordo, m

**flabbergast** /'flæbər,gæst/ vt dejar con la boca abierta, dejar de una pieza

**flabbiness, flaccidity** /'flæbɪnɪs; flæk'sɪdɪti/ n flaccidez, flojedad, f; Med. reblandecimiento, m; (of character) debilidad, flaqueza del ánimo, f

**flabby, flaccid** /'flæbi; 'flæksɪd/ a fláccido, flojo; Fig. débil

**flag** /flæg/ n bandera, f; pabellón, estandarte, m; (small) banderola, f; (iris) (yellow) cala, f; (purple) lirio cárdeno, m; (stone) losa, f. **to dip the f.,** saludar con la bandera. **to hoist the f.,** izar la bandera. **to strike the f.,** bajar la bandera; (in defeat) rendir la bandera. **f. bearer,** portaestandarte, abanderado, m. **f.-day,** día de la bandera, m; (in U.S.A.) día de la bandera, m. **f.-officer,** almirante, m; vicealmirante, m; jefe de escuadra, m. **f. of truce,** bandera blanca, bandera de paz, f

**flag** /flæg/ vi flaquear, debilitarse; languidecer; (wither) marchitarse; decaer, disminuir. **—vt** adornar con banderas; (signal) hacer señales con una bandera; (for a race, etc.) marcar con banderas; (with stones) enlosar, embaldosar.

**flagellant** /'flædʒələnt/ n flagelante, m

**flagellate** /'flædʒə,leit/ vt flagelar

**flagellation** /,flædʒə'leiʃən/ n flagelación, f

**flageolet** /,flædʒə'lɛt/ n Mus. caramillo, m, chirimía, f. **f. player,** chirimía, m

**flagging** /'flægɪŋ/ n pavimentación, f; (floor) enlosado, m. **—a** lánguido, flojo

**flagon** /'flægən/ n frasco, m; botella, f

**flagrancy** /'fleigrənsi/ n escándalo, m, notoriedad, f

**flagrant** /'fleigrənt/ a escandaloso, notorio

**flagship** /'flægʃɪp/ n capitana, f

**flagstaff** /'flæg,stæf/ n asta de bandera, f

**flagstone** /'flæg,stoun/ n losa, lancha, f

**flail** /fleil/ n mayal, m

**flair** /flɛər/ n instinto natural, m, comprensión innata, f; habilidad natural, f

**flak** /flæk/ n cortina (or barrera) antiaérea, f

**flake** /fleik/ n escama, f; laminilla, hojuela, f; (of snow) copo, m; (of fire) chispa, f. **—vt** cubrir con escamas, etc.; exfoliar; (crumble) hacer migas de, desmigajar. **—vi** escamarse; (off) exfoliarse; caer en copos

**flaky** /'fleiki/ a escamoso; en laminillas; (of pastry) hojaldrado. **f. pastry,** hojaldre, f

**flamboyance** /flæm'bɔiəns/ n extravagancia, f, Lit. ampulosidad, f

**flamboyant** /flæm'bɔiənt/ a Archit. flamígero; extravagante, llamativo, rimbombante; (of style) ampuloso. **f. gothic,** gótico florido, m

**flame** /fleim/ n llama, f; Fig. fuego, m. Inf. amorío, m, vi flamear, llamear; arder, abrasarse; (shine) brillar; (up, Fig.) inflamarse; acalorarse. **f.-colored,** de color de llama, anaranjado. **f.-thrower,** lanzallamas, m

**flaming** /'fleimɪŋ/ a llameante; abrasador; (of colors)

llamativo, chillón; (of feelings) ardiente, fervoroso, apasionado.

**flamingo** /flə'mɪŋgou/ n Ornith. flamenco, m

**Flanders** /'flændərz/ flandes, m

**flange** /flændʒ/ n Mech. reborde, m, vt rebordear

**flank** /flæŋk/ n (of animal) ijada, f; (human) costado, m; (of hill, etc.) lado, m, falda, f; Mil. flanco, m. **—a** (Mil. Nav.) por el flanco. **—vt** lindar con, estar contiguo a; (Mil., Nav.) flanquear. **—vi** estar al lado de; tocar a, lindar con.

**flannel** /'flænl/ n franela, f, a de franela

**flannelette** /,flænl'ɛt/ n moletón, m

**flap** /flæp/ n golpe, m; (of a sail) zapatazo, m, sacudida, f; (of a pocket) cartera, tapa, f; (of skin) colgajo, m; (of a shoe, etc.) oreja, f; (of a shirt, etc.) falda, f; (of a hat) ala, f; (of trousers) bragueta, f; (rever) solapa, f; (of a counter) trampa, f; (of a table) hoja plegadiza, f; (of the wings) aletazo, m; (of w.c.) tapa, f. **—vt** sacudir, golpear, batir; agitar; (the tail) menear. **—vi** agitarse; (of wings) aletear; (of sails) zapatear, sacudirse; colgar. **f.-eared,** de orejas grandes y gachas

**flapjack** /'flæp,dʒæk/ n Cul. torta de sartén, f; (for powder) polvorera, f

**flapper** /'flæpər/ n Inf. polla, tobillera, chica "topolino," f

**flapping** /'flæpɪŋ/ n batimiento, m; (waving) ondulación, f; (of sails) zapatazo, m; (of wings) aleteo, m

**flare** /flɛər/ n fulgor, m, llama, f; hacha, f; Aer. cohete de señales, m; Sew. vuelo, m. **—vi** relampaguear, fulgurar; brillar; (of a lamp) llamear; (up) encolerizarse, salirse de tino; (of epidemic) declararse; (war, etc.) desencadenarse

**flash** /flæʃ/ n relámpago, centelleo, m, ráfaga de luz, f; brillo, m; (from a gun) fuego, fogonazo, m; (of wit, genius) rasgo, m; (of joy, etc.) acceso, m. **—vi** relampaguear, fulgurar, centellear; brillar; cruzar rápidamente, pasar como un relámpago. **—vt** hacer relampaguear; hacer brillar; (a look, etc.) dar; lanzar; (light) encender; (powder) quemar; transmitir señales por heliógrafo; Inf. sacar a relucir, enseñar. **shoulder-f.,** Mil. emblema, m. **to be gone like a f.,** desaparecer como un relámpago. **to f. out,** brillar, centellear. **f. of lightning,** relámpago, rayo, m. **f. of wit,** agudeza, f, rasgo de ingenio, m

**flashback** /'flæʃ,bæk/ n episodio intercalado, m, retrospección, f

**flashily** /'flæʃəli/ adv llamativamente, con mal gusto

**flashing** /'flæʃɪŋ/ n centelleo, m, llamarada, f. **—a** centellador, relampagueante; brillante; chispeante

**flashlight** /'flæʃ,lait/ n luz de magnesio, f; (torch) lamparilla eléctrica, f, rayo, m (Mexico); **f. photograph,** magnesio, m

**flashy** /'flæʃi/ a llamativo, de mal gusto, charro; frívolo, superficial

**flask** /flæsk/ n frasco, m, redoma, botella, f; (for powder) frasco, m; (vacuum) termos, m

**flat** /flæt/ a llano; (smooth) liso; (lying) tendido, m; (flattened) aplastado; (destroyed) arrasado; (stretched out) extendido; (of nose, face) chato, romo; (of tire) desinflado; (uniform) uniforme; (depressed) desanimado; (uninteresting) monótono; (boring) aburrido; Com. paralizado; (downright) categórico; absoluto; (net) neto; Mus. bemol; (of boats) de fondo plano. **—adv** See **flatly.** n planicie, f; (of a sword) hoja, f; (of the hand) palma, f; (land) llanura, f; (apartment) piso, m; Mus. bemol, m. **to fall f.,** caer de bruces; Fig. no tener éxito. **to make f.,** allanar. **to sing f.,** desafinar. **f. boat,** barco de fondo plano, m. **f.-footed,** de pies achatados; Fig. pedestre. **f.-iron,** plancha, f. **f. roof,** azotea, f

**flatly** /'flætli/ adv de plano; a nivel; (plainly) llanamente, netamente; (dully) indiferentemente; (categorically) categóricamente

**flatness** /'flætnɪs/ n planicie, f; llanura, f; (smoothness) lisura, f; (evenness) igualdad, f; (uninterestingness) insulsez, insipidez, f; aburrimiento, m; (depression) desaliento, abatimiento, m

**flatten** /'flætn/ vt aplanar, allanar; aplastar; (smooth) alisar; (even) igualar; (destroy) derribar, arrasar, destruir; (dismay) desconcertar; (out) extender. **—vi** aplanarse, allanarse; aplastarse

**flattening** /'flætnɪŋ/ *n* achatamiento, *m*, allanamiento, *m*; aplastamiento, *m*; igualación, *f*

**flatter** /'flætər/ *vt* adular, lisonjear, halagar; (of a dress, photograph, etc.) favorecer, (please the senses) regalar, deleitar; (oneself) felicitarse

**flatterer** /'flætərər/ *n* adulador (-ra), lisonjero (-ra)

**flattering** /'flætərɪŋ/ *a* adulador, lisonjero; (promising) halagüeño; favoreciente; deleitoso

**flattery** /'flætəri/ *n* adulación, *f*

**flat tire** llanta desinflada, *f*

**flatulence** /'flætʃələns/ *n* flatulencia, *f*

**flatulent** /'flætʃələnt/ *a* flatulento

**flaunt** /flɔnt/ *vi* (flutter) ondear; pavonearse. —*vt* desplegar; ostentar, sacar a relucir; enseñar

**flaunting** /'flɔntɪŋ/ *n* ostentación, *f*, alarde, *m*. —*a* ostentoso; magnífico; (fluttering) ondeante

**flautist** /'flɔtɪst/ *n* flautista, *mf*

**flavor** /'fleivər/ *n* sabor, gusto, *m*; *Cul.* condimento, *m*; *Fig.* dejo, *m*. —*vt Cul.* sazonar, condimentar; dar un gusto (de), hacer saborear (a); *Fig.* dar un dejo (de)

**flavored** /'fleivərd/ *a* (in compounds) de sabor...; sazonado; que tiene sabor de...

**flavoring** /'fleivərɪŋ/ *n Cul.* condimento, *m*; *Fig.* sabor, dejo, *m*

**flavorless** /'fleivərlɪs/ *a* insípido, soso, sin sabor

**flaw** /flɔ/ *n* desperfecto, *m*, imperfección, *f*; (crack) grieta, hendedura, *f*; (in wood, metals) quebraja, *f*; (in gems) pelo, *m*; (in fruit) maca, *f*; (in cloth) gabarro, *m*; *Fig.* defecto, error, *m*; (wind) ráfaga de viento, *f*

**flawless** /'flɔlɪs/ *a* sin defecto; perfecto; impecable

**flawlessness** /'flɔlɪsnɪs/ *n* perfección, *f*; impecabilidad, *f*

**flax** /flæks/ *n* lino, *m*. **to dress f.,** rastrillar lino. **f.-comb,** rastrillo, *m*. **f. field,** linar, *m*

**flaxen** /'flæksən/ *a* de lino; (fair) rubio, blondo. **f.-haired,** de pelo rubio

**flay** /flei/ *vt* desollar; (criticize) despellejar

**flaying** /'fleiɪŋ/ *n* desuello, *m*, desolladura, *f*

**flea** /fli/ *n* pulga, *f*. **f. bite,** picada de pulga, *f*

**fleck** /flɛk/ *n* pinta, mancha, *f*, lunar, *m*; (of sun) mota, *f*; (speck) partícula, *f*; (freckle) peca, *f*. —*vt* abigarrar; manchar; (dapple) salpicar, motear

**fledged** /flɛdʒd/ *a* emplumecido, plumado; alado; *Fig.* maduro

**fledgling** /'flɛdʒlɪŋ/ *n* volantón, *m*; *Fig.* niño (-ña); *Fig.* novato (-ta)

**flee** /fli/ *vi* huir, fugarse, escapar; (vanish) desaparecer; (avoid) evitar, huir de. —*vt* abandonar

**fleece** /flis/ *n* vellón, *m*; lana, *f*; toisón, *m*. —*vt* esquilar; *Fig. Inf.* pelar. **Order of the Golden F.,** Orden del Toisón de Oro, *f*

**fleecy** /'flisi/ *a* lanoso, lanar; (white) blanquecino; (of clouds) borreguero. **f. clouds,** borregos, *m pl*

**fleet** /flit/ *n* (navy) armada, *f*; escuadra, flota, *f*; *Fig.* serie, *f*. *a* alado, rápido, veloz. **F. Air Arm,** Aviación Naval, *f*. **f.-footed,** ligero de pies

**fleeting** /'flitɪŋ/ *a* fugaz, momentáneo, efímero, pasajero

**Flemish** /'flɛmɪʃ/ *a* flamenco. —*n* (language) flamenco, *m*

**flesh** /flɛʃ/ *n* carne, *f*; (mankind) género humano, *m*, humanidad, *f*; (of fruit) pulpa, *f*. **a man of f. and blood,** un hombre de carne y hueso. **of one's own f. and blood,** de la misma sangre de uno. **to make one's f. creep,** dar carne de gallina (a). **f.-coloured,** encarnado, de color de carne. **f.-eating,** carnívoro. **f. wound,** herida superficial, *f*

**fleshiness** /'flɛʃinɪs/ *n* carnosidad, gordura, *f*

**fleshpot** /'flɛʃ,pɒt/ *n* marmita, *f*; *Fig.* olla, *f*. **the fleshpots of Egypt,** las ollas de Egipto

**fleshy** /'flɛʃi/ *a* carnoso, grueso; (of fruit) pulposo; suculento

**fleur-de-lis** /,flɜrdl'i/ *n* flor de lis, *f*

**flex** /flɛks/ *n Elec.* flexible, *m*, *vt* doblar. —*vi* doblarse

**flexibility** /,flɛksə'bɪlɪti/ *n* flexibilidad, *f*; (of style) plasticidad, *f*; docilidad, *f*

**flexible** /'flɛksəbəl/ *a* flexible; dúctil, maleable; (of style) plástico; of) voice) quebradizo; adaptable; dócil

**flexion** /'flɛkʃən/ *n* flexión, *f*; *Gram.* inflexión, *f*; *Gram.* flexión, *f*

**flexor** /'flɛksər/ *n Anat.* músculo flexor, *m*

**flick** /flɪk/ *n* golpecito, toque, *m*; (of the finger) capirotazo, *m*; *Inf.* cine, *m*, *vt* dar un golpecito a; dar ligeramente con un látigo; sacudir. **flick one's wrist** hacer girar la muñeca **to f. over the pages of,** hojear

**flicker** /'flɪkər/ *n* estremecimiento, temblor, *m*; fluctuación, *f*; (of bird) aleteo, *m*; (of flame) onda (de una llama), *f*; (of eyelashes) pestañeo, *m*; (of a smile) indicio, *f*, *vi* agitarse; (of flags) ondear; vacilar

**flickering** /'flɪkərɪŋ/ *a* tenue; vacilante

**flier** /'flaiər/ *n* volador (-ra); aviador (-ra); piloto, *m*; fugitivo (-va)

**flight** /flait/ *n* vuelo, *m*; (of bird of prey) colada, *f*; (flock of birds) bandada, *f*; (migration) migración, *f*; (of time) transcurso, *m*; (of imagination, etc.) arranque, *m*; (volley) lluvia, *f*; (of aeroplanes) escuadrilla (de aviones), *f*; (of stairs) tramo, tiro, *m*; (staircase) escalera, *f*; (of locks on canal, etc.) ramal, *m*; (escape) huida, fuga, *f*. **long-distance f.,** *Aer.* vuelo de distancia, *m*. **non-stop f.,** *Aer.* vuelo sin parar, *m*. **reconnaissance f.,** *Aer.* vuelo de reconocimiento, vuelo de patrulla, *m*. **test f.,** *Aer.* vuelo de pruebas, *m*. **to put to f.,** ahuyentar, poner en fuga. **to take f.,** alzar el vuelo. **f.-lieutenant,** teniente aviador, *m*. **f.-sergeant,** sargento aviador, *m*

**flight attendant** sobrecarbo *mf*

**flightiness** /'flaitinɪs/ *n* frivolidad, veleidad, ligereza, *f*

**flighty** /'flaiti/ *a* frívolo, inconstante, veleidoso

**flimsiness** /'flɪmzinɪs/ *n* falta de solidez, endeblez, *f*; fragilidad, *f*; (of arguments) futilidad, *f*

**flimsy** /'flɪmzi/ *a* endeble; frágil; fútil, insubstancial

**flinch** /flɪntʃ/ *vi* echarse atrás, retirarse (ante); vacilar, titubear. **without flinching,** sin vacilar; sin quejarse

**fling** /flɪŋ/ *vt* arrojar, echar, tirar; lanzar; (scatter) derramar; (oneself) echarse; (oneself upon) echarse encima; *Fig.* confiar en. —*vi* lanzarse; marcharse precipitadamente; saltar. —*n* tiro, *m*; (of dice, etc.) echada, *f*; (gibe) sarcasmo, *m*, burla, chufleta, *f*; (of horse) respingo, brinco, *m*; baile escocés, *m*. **in full f.,** en plena operación; en progreso. **to have one's f.,** darse un verde, correrla. **to f. away,** *vt* desechar; (waste) desperdiciar, malgastar, perder. —*vi* marcharse enfadado; marcharse rápidamente. **to f. back,** (a ball) devolver; (the head) echar atrás. **to f. down,** tirar al suelo; arrojar; derribar. **to f. off,** *vt* rechazar; apartar; (a garment, etc.) quitar. —*vi* marcharse sin más ni más. **to f. oneself down,** tumbarse, echarse; despeñarse (por). **to f. oneself headlong,** despeñarse. **to f. open,** abrir violentamente, abrir de repente. **to f. out,** *vt* echar a la fuerza; (a hand) alargar, extender. —*vi* salir apresuradamente. **to f. over,** (upset) volcar; arrojar por; abandonar. **to f. up,** lanzar al aire; levantar, erguir; renunciar (a), abandonar; dejar

**flint** /flɪnt/ *n* pedernal, *m*; (for producing fire) piedra de encendedor, *f*

**flinty** /'flɪnti/ *a* pedernalino; *Fig.* endurecido

**flippancy** /'flɪpənsi/ *n* levedad, ligereza, *f*; frivolidad, *f*; impertinencia, *f*

**flippant** /'flɪpənt/ *a* poco serio, ligero, frívolo; impertinente

**flipper** /'flɪpər/ *n* aleta, *f*

**flirt** /flɜrt/ *n* (man) coquetón, castigador, *m*; (woman) coqueta, castigadora, *f*. —*vt* (shake) sacudir; (move) agitar; (wave) menear. —*vi* flirtear, coquetear; (toy with) jugar con; divertirse con

**flirtation** /flɜr'teiʃən/ *n* flirteo, amorío, *m*

**flirtatious** /flɜr'teiʃəs/ *a* (of men) galanteador, castigador; (of women) coqueta

**flit** /flɪt/ *vi* revolotear, mariposear; (move silently) deslizarse, pasar silenciosamente; (depart) irse, marcharse; mudarse por los aires. **to f. about,** ir y venir silenciosamente. **to f. past,** pasar como una sombra

**flitch** /flɪtʃ/ *n* (of bacon) hoja de tocino, *f*

**float** /flout/ *n* masa flotante, *f*; (raft) balsa, *f*; *Mech.* flotador, *m*; (of fishing rod or net) corcho, *m*; (of fish) vejiga natatoria, *f*; (for swimming) nadadera, calabaza, *f*; (for tableaux) carroza, *f*; *pl* **floats,** *Theat.*

candilejas, *f pl.* —*vi* flotar; (flags, hair, etc.) ondear; (wander) vagar; *Naut.* boyar. —*vt* poner a flote; hacer flotar; (a grounded ship) desencallar; (*Com.* a company) fundar; (a loan, etc.) emitir, poner en circulación; (launch a ship) botar; (flood) inundar

**floating** /'floutɪŋ/ *n* flotación, *f*, flote, *m;* Com. fundación (de una compañía), *f;* (of a loan) emisión, *f* (of a ship) botadura, *f.* —*a* flotante; boyante; *Com.* en circulación, flotante; fluctuante, variable. **f. capital,** capital fluctuante, *m.* **f. debt,** deuda flotante, *f.* **f. dock,** dique flotante, *m.* **f. light,** buque faro, *m.* **f. population,** población flotante, *f.* **f. rib,** costilla flotante, *f*

**flock** /flɒk/ *n* rebaño, *m*, manada, *f;* (of birds) bandada, *f; Fig.* grey, *f;* (crowd) multitud, muchedumbre, *f;* (parishioners) congregación, *f;* (of wool or cotton) vedija (de lana o de algodón), *f; pl* **flocks,** (for stuffing) borra, *f.* —*vi* concurrirse, reunirse, congregarse; ir en tropel, acudir; (birds) volar en bandada. **f.-bed,** colchón de borra, *m*

**floe** /flou/ *n* banco de hielo, *m*

**flog** /flɒg/ *vt* azotar; castigar

**flogging** /'flɒgɪŋ/ *n* azotamiento, vapuleo, *m*

**flood** /flʌd/ *n* inundación, *f;* (Bible) diluvio, *m;* (of the tide) flujo, *m; Fig.* torrente, *m;* (abundance) copia, abundancia, *f;* (fit) paroxismo, *m.* —*vt* inundar; sumergir; (of tears) mojar. —*vi* desbordar. **f. lighting,** iluminación intensiva, *f*

**floodgate** /'flʌd,geit/ *n* compuerta (de esclusa), *f*

**flooding** /'flʌdɪŋ/ *n* inundación, *f;* desbordamiento, *m; Med.* hemorragia uterina, *f*

**floodtide** /'flʌd,taid/ *n* marea creciente, *f*

**floor** /flɔr/ *n* suelo, piso, *m;* (wooden) entarimado, *m;* (story) piso, *m;* (of a cart) cama, *f; Agr.* era, *f.* —*vt* entablar; echar al suelo, derribar; *Fig.* desconcertar, confundir. **on the f.,** en el suelo. **on the ground f.,** en el piso bajo. **to take the f.,** *Fig.* tener la palabra. **f.-polisher,** lustrador de piso, *m*

**flooring** /'flɔrɪŋ/ *n* tablado, *m*, tablazón, *f;* piso, *m*

**flop** /flɒp/ *n* golpe, *m;* ruido sordo, *m;* (splash) chapoteo, *m; Inf.* fiasco, *m.* —*vi* dejarse caer

**flora** /'flɔrə/ *n* flora, *f*

**floral** /'flɔrəl/ *a* floral. **f. games,** juegos florales, *m pl*

**Florence** /'flɔrəns/ Florencia, *f*

**Florentine** /'flɔrən,tin/ *a* and *n* florentino (-na)

**florescence** /flɔ'resəns/ *n* florescencia, *f*

**florid** /'flɔrɪd/ *a* florido; demasiado ornado, cursi, llamativo; (of complexion) rubicundo

**floridness** /'flɔrɪdnɪs/ *n* floridez, *f*, estilo florido, *m;* demasiada ornamentación, vulgaridad, *f*, mal gusto, *m;* (of complexion) rubicundez, *f*

**florin** /'flɔrɪn/ *n* florín, *f*

**florist** /'flɔrɪst/ *n* florista, *mf*

**floss** /flɔs/ *n* seda floja, filoseda, *f;* (of maize) penacho, *m;* (of a cocoon) cadarzo, *m.* **f. silk,** seda floja, *f*

**flotilla** /flou'tɪlə/ *n* flotilla, *f*

**flotsam** /'flɒtsəm/ *n* pecio, *m*

**flounce** /flauns/ *n* volante, *m, vi* saltar de impaciencia. **to f. out,** salir airadamente

**flounder** /'flaundər/ *n* (nearest equivalent) *Ichth.* platija, *f;* tumbo, *m.* —*vi* tropezar; revolcarse; andar dificultosamente

**flour** /flauər/ *n* harina, *f, vt* enharinar. **f.-bin,** tina, *f,* harinero, *m.* **f. merchant,** harinero, *m*

**flourish** /'flɔrɪʃ/ *n* movimiento, *m;* gesto, saludo, *m;* (of a pen) plumada, *f;* (on the guitar, in fencing) floreo, *m;* preludio, *m;* (fanfare) tocata (de trompetas), *f;* (of a signature) rúbrica, *f;* (in rhetoric) floreo, *m.* —*vi* (of plants) vegetar; (prosper) prosperar, medrar; florecer; (of the guitar, in fencing) florear; *Mus.* preludiar; (with a pen) hacer plumadas (or rasgos de pluma); (of a signature) firmar con rúbrica; (sound a fanfare) hacer una tocata (de trompetas). —*vt* agitar en el aire, blandir

**flourishing** /'flɔrɪʃɪŋ/ *a* (of plants) lozano; floreciente; (prosperous) próspero; (happy) feliz

**flourmill** /'flauər,mɪl/ *n* molino de harina, *m*, fábrica de harina, *f*, molina harinero, *m*

**floury** /'flauəri, 'flauəri/ *a* harinoso

**flout** /flaut/ *vt* burlarse de; despreciar, no hacer caso de

**flow** /flou/ *n* flujo, *m;* corriente, *f;* chorro, *m;* (of water) caudal, *m;* (output) producción total, cantidad, *f;* (of the tide) flujo (de la marea), *m;* (of words) facilidad, *f.* —*vi* fluir, manar; correr; (of the tide) crecer (la marea); (pass) pasar, correr; (result) resultar (de), provenir (de); (of hair, drapery) caer, ondular; (abound) abundar (en). **to f. away,** escaparse, salir. **to f. back,** refluir. **to f. down,** descender, fluir hacia abajo; (of tears) correr por. **to f. from,** dimanar de; manar de; *Fig.* provenir de. **to f. in,** llegar en abundancia. **to f. into,** (rivers) desaguar en, desembocar en. **to f. over,** derramarse por. **to f. through,** fluir por; atravesar; (water) regar. **to f. together,** (rivers) confluir

**flower** /'flauər/ *n* flor, *f;* (best) flor y nata, crema, *f.* —*vi* florecer. **in f.,** en flor. **No flowers by request,** (for a funeral) No flores por deseo del finado. **f.-bud,** capullo, *m.* **f.-garden,** jardín, *m.* **f. girl,** florista, vendedora de flores, *f.* **f. market,** mercado de flores, *m.* **f.-piece,** florero, *m.* **f. pot,** tiesto, *m*, maceta, *f.* **f. show,** exposición de flores, *f.* **f. vase,** florero, *m*

**flowerbed** /'flauər,bed/ *n* cuadro, macizo, *m*

**flower car** coche portacoronas, *m*

**flowered** /'flauərd/ *a* (in compounds) con flores; con dibujos de flores

**floweriness** /'flauərinɪs/ *n* abundancia de flores, *f;* (of style) floridez, *f*, estilo florido, *m*

**flowering** /'flauərɪŋ/ *n* florecimiento, *m.* —*a* floreciente; con flores; (of shrubs) de adorno. **f. season,** época de la floración, *f*

**flowery** /'flauəri/ *a* florido

**flowing** /'flouɪŋ/ *n* flujo, *m;* derrame, *m.* —*a* fluente, corriente, *f;* (of tide) creciente; (waving) ondeante; suelto; (of style) flúido

**flow of capital** corriente de capital, *f*

**fluctuate** /'flʌktʃu,eit/ *vi* fluctuar, vacilar; variar

**fluctuating** /'flʌktʃu,eitɪŋ/ *a* fluctuante, vacilante; variable; (hesitating) irresoluto, dudoso

**fluctuation** /,flʌktʃu'eiʃən/ *n* fluctuación, *f;* cambio, *m*, variación, *f;* (hesitancy) indecisión, vacilación, *f*

**flue** /flu/ *n* (of a chimney) cañón, *m;* (of a boiler) tubo, *m*

**fluency** /'fluənsi/ *n* fluidez, *f*

**fluent** /'fluənt/ *a* flúido; fácil

**fluently** /'fluəntli/ *adv* corrientemente, con facilidad, de corrido

**fluff** /flʌf/ *n* borra, pelusa, *f*, tamo, *m*

**fluffy** /'flʌfi/ *a* velloso; (feathered) plumoso; (woolly) lanudo; (of hair) encrespado

**fluid** /'fluɪd/ *n* flúido, líquido, *m*, *a* flúido

**fluidity** /flu'ɪdɪti/ *n* fluidez, *f*

**fluke** /fluk/ *n* (in billiards) chiripa, *f; Naut.* uña, *f; Inf.* carambola, chiripa, chambonada, *f.* **by a f.,** de carambola, por suerte. **f.-worm,** duela del hígado, *f*

**flunkey** /'flʌŋki/ *n* lacayo, *m; Fig.* adulador, *m*

**fluorescence** /flo'resəns/ *n* fluorescencia, *f*

**fluorescent** /flo'resənt/ *a* fluorescente

**fluorine** /'florin/ *n* Chem. flúor, *m*

**fluorite** /'florait/ *n* fluorita, *f*

**flurry** /'flɜri/ *n* (of wind) ráfaga, *f;* (squall) chubasco, *m;* agitación, *f.* —*vt* agitar

**flush** /flʌʃ/ *n* rubor, *m;* (in the sky) arrebol, rojo, color de rosa, *m;* emoción, *f*, acceso, *m;* sensación, *f;* (at cards) flux, *m;* vigor, *m;* (flowering) floración, *f;* abundancia, *f;* (of youth, etc.) frescura, *f.* —*a* (level) igual, parejo; abundante; (generous) pródigo, liberal; (rich) adinerado. —*vi* ruborizarse, enrojecerse, ponerse colorado; (flood) inundarse, llenarse (de agua, etc.); (of sky) arrebolarse. —*vt* inundar, limpiar con un chorro de agua, etc., lavar; (of blood) circular por; (redden) enrojecer; (make blush) hacer ruborizarse; (exhilarate) excitar, animar; (inflame) inflamar, encender; (make level) igualar, nivelar. **f. with,** a ras de

**flushing** /'flʌʃɪŋ/ *n* rojez, *f;* (cleansing) limpieza, lavadura, *f;* (flooding) inundación, *f*

**fluster** /'flʌstər/ *n* agitación, confusión, *f*, aturdimiento, *m.* —*vt* agitar, poner nervioso (a), aturdir; (oneself) preocuparse. —*vi* agitarse; estar nervioso, estar perplejo; (with drink) estar entre dos velas

**flute** /flut/ *n* flauta, *f; Archit.* estría, *f;* (organ-stop) flautado, *m.* —*vi* tocar la flauta, flautear; tener la voz

**flauteada.** —*vt* tocar (una pieza) en la flauta; (groove) encanutar, acanalar, estriar. **f. player,** flautista, *mf*

**fluted** /ˈflutɪd/ *a* (grooved) acanalado

**fluting** /ˈflutɪŋ/ *n Mus.* son de la flauta, *m;* (of birds) trinado, *m; Archit.* estría, *f; Sew.* rizado, *m*

**flutter** /ˈflʌtər/ *n* (of wings) aleteo, *m;* (of leaves, etc.) murmurio, *m;* (of eyelashes) pestañeo, *m;* (of flags, etc.) ondeo, *m,* ondulación, *f;* (excitement) agitación, *f;* (stir) sensación, *f;* (gamble) jugada, *f.* —*vi* (of birds) aletear; revolotear; (of butterflies) mariposear; (of flags) ondear; palpitar; (of persons) estar agitado. —*vt* agitar; (the eyelashes) pestañear; (agitate) agitar, alarmar

**fluttering** /ˈflʌtərɪŋ/ *n* mariposeo, *m;* revoloteo, *m;* (of birds) aleteo, *m;* (of leaves, etc.) murmurio, *m;* (of flags, etc.) ondeo, *m,* ondulación, *f;* (of eyelashes) pestañeo, *m*

**fluvial** /ˈfluvɪəl/ *a* fluvial

**flux** /flʌks/ *n* flujo, *m*

**fly** /flai/ *n* (insect) mosca, *f;* (on a fishhook) mosca artificial, *f;* (carriage) calesín, *m;* (of breeches) bragueta, *f; Theat.* bambalina, *f;* (of a tent) toldo, *m;* (flight) vuelo, *m;* (of a flag) vuelo, *m.* **fly-blown,** manchado por las moscas. **fly-by-night,** trasnochador (-ra). **fly-catcher,** *Ornith.* papamoscas, *m;* matamoscas, *m.* **fly-fishing,** pesca con moscas artificiales, *f.* **fly-leaf,** guarda (de un libro), *f.* **fly-paper,** papel matamoscas, *m.* **fly-swatter,** matamoscas, *m.* **fly-wheel,** *Mech.* volante, *m*

**fly** /flai/ *vi* volar; (flutter) ondear; (jump) saltar; (rush) lanzarse, precipitarse; (pass away) pasar volando, volar; (run off) marcharse a todo correr; (escape) huir, escapar; (seek refuge) refugiarse; (of the head, of intoxicants) subirse; (vanish) desaparecer. —*vt* hacer volar; hacer ondear, enarbolar; (an airplane) pilotar, dirigir; (flee from) huir de; evitar. **to let fly (at),** descargar, tirar; *Fig.* saltar la sinhueso. **to fly about,** volar en torno de; revolotear. **to fly at,** lanzarse sobre; acometer, asaltar. **to fly away,** emprender el vuelo. **to fly back,** volar hacia el punto de partida; (of doors, etc.) abrir, o cerrar, de repente. **to fly down,** volar abajo. **to fly in,** volar dentro de; volar adentro; (of airplanes) llegar (el avión). **to fly in pieces,** hacerse pedazos. **to fly into a rage,** montarse en cólera. **to fly low,** rastrear; *Aer.* volar a poca altura. **to fly off,** emprender el vuelo; (hasten) marcharse volando; (of buttons, etc.) saltar (de), separarse (de). **to fly open,** abrirse de repente. **to fly over,** volar por, volar por encima de. **to fly upwards,** volar hacia arriba; subir

**flying** /ˈflaiɪŋ/ *n* vuelo, *m.* —*a* volante, volador; que vuela; de volar; volátil; (hasty) rápido; (flowing) ondeante, ondulante. **to shoot f.,** tirar al vuelo. **with f. colors,** con banderas desplegadas, triunfante. **f.-boat,** hidroavión, *m.* **f.-buttress,** botarel, arbotante, *m.* **f.-column,** *Mil.* cuerpo volante, *m.* **f.-fish,** (pez) volador, *m.* **f.-fortress,** *Aer.* fortaleza volante, *f.* **f.-officer,** oficial de aviación, *m.* **f.-sickness,** mal de altura, *m.* **f.-squad,** escuadra ligera, *f.* **f.-test,** *Aer.* examen de pilotaje, *m*

**foal** /foul/ *n* potro (-ra). —*vi and vt* parir una yegua

**foam** /foum/ *n* espuma, *f.* —*vi* espumar; (of horses, etc.) echar espumarajos. **to f. and froth,** (of the sea) hervir. **f. at the mouth,** echar espuma por la boca.

**foam rubber** *n* caucho esponjoso, *m,* espuma de caucho, *f,* espuma sintética, *f*

**foamy** /ˈfoumi/ *a* espumoso

**fob** /fɒb/ *n* bolsillo del reloj, *m;* faltriquera pequeña, *f.* —*vt* (off) engañar con

**focal** /ˈfoukəl/ *a* focal

**focus** /ˈfoukəs/ *n* foco, *m;* centro, *m.* —*vt* enfocar; concentrar. —*vi* convergir. **in f.,** en foco

**fodder** /ˈfɒdər/ *n Agr.* pienso, forraje, *m.* —*vt* dar forraje (a)

**foe** /fou/ *n* enemigo, *m*

**fog** /fɒg/ *n* neblina, niebla, *f; Fig.* confusión, *f; Fig.* perplejidad, *f, vt* obscurecer; *Photo.* velar; *Fig.* ofuscar. —*vi* hacerse nebuloso; *Photo.* velarse. **fog-signal,** señal de niebla, *f*

**fogbound** /ˈfɒgˌbaund/ *a* rodeado de niebla; detenido por la niebla

**fogey** /ˈfougi/ *n* obscurantista, *m.* **He is an old f.,** Es un señor chapado a la antigua

**fogginess** /ˈfɒgɪnɪs/ *n* oscuridad, neblina, *f*

**foggy** /ˈfɒgi/ *a* nebuloso; *Photo.* velado. **It is f.,** Hay niebla

**foghorn** /ˈfɒgˌhɔrn/ *n* sirena, *f;* bocina, *f*

**foible** /ˈfɔibəl/ *n* flaco, *m,* debilidad, *f*

**foil** /fɔil/ *n* (sword) florete, *m;* (coat) hoja, *f;* (of a mirror) azogado, *m.* —*vt* frustrar. **f. a plot,** desbaratar un complot. **She makes a good f. for her sister's beauty,** Hace resaltar la belleza de su hermana

**foiling** /ˈfɔilɪŋ/ *n* frustración, *f*

**foist** /fɔist/ *vt* imponer, insertar, incluir; engañar (con)

**fold** /fould/ *n* doblez, *f,* pliegue, *m;* arruga, *f; Sew.* cogido, *m;* (for sheep) redil, aprisco, *m; Fig.* iglesia, congregación de los fieles, *f;* (in compounds) vez, *f.* —*vt* doblar, plegar, doblegar; (the arms) cruzar (los brazos); (embrace) abrazar; (wrap) envolver; (clasp) entrelazar; (sheep) meter en redil, encerrar. —*vi* doblarse, plegarse; cerrarse

**folder** /ˈfouldər/ *n* doblador (-ra); plegadera, *f*

**folding** /ˈfouldɪŋ/ *n* plegadura, *f,* doblamiento, *m;* (of sheep) encerramiento, *m,* a plegadizo. **f.-door,** puerta plegadiza, *f.* **f.-machine,** plegador, *m.* **f.-seat,** *Auto.* traspuntín, *m.* **f.-table,** mesa de tijeras, *f;* mesa plegadiza, *f*

**foliage** /ˈfouliɪdʒ/ *n* follaje, *m,* frondas, *f pl.* **thick f.,** frondosidad, *f*

**folio** /ˈfouliˌou/ *n* folio, *m;* (a volume) infolio, *m.* —*a* de infolio. —*vt* foliar

**folk** /fouk/ *n* (nation) pueblo, *m,* nación, *f;* gente, *f; pl* **folks,** *Inf.* familia, *f;* parientes, *m pl.* **f.-dance,** danza popular, *f*

**folklore** /ˈfoukˌlɔr/ *n* folclore, *m,* tradiciones folclóricas, *f pl*

**folklorist** /ˈfoukˌlɔrɪst/ *n* folclorista, *mf*

**folksong** /ˈfoukˌsɔŋ/ *n* canción popular, *f;* romance, *m;* copla, *f*

**folktale** /ˈfoukˌteil/ *n* conseja, *f,* cuento popular, *m*

**follicle** /ˈfɒlɪkəl/ *n* (*Anat., Bot.*) folículo, *m*

**follow** /ˈfɒlou/ *vt* seguir; (pursue) perseguir; (hunt) cazar; (adopt) adoptar; (understand) comprender; (notice) observar. —*vi* ir, o venir, detrás; (of time) venir después; (gen. impers.) seguir, resultar; seguirse. **as follows,** como sigue. **I shall f. your advice,** Seguiré tus consejos. **to f. on the heels of,** *Fig.* pisar los talones (a). **to f. suit,** (at cards) asistir, jugar el mismo palo; *Fig.* imitar. **to f. up,** proseguir, continuar; (pursue) perseguir; (enhance) reforzar. **f.-me-lads,** *Inf.* siguemepollo, *m*

**follower** /ˈfɒlouər/ *n* seguidor (-ra); adherente, secuaz, *m;* (imitator) imitador (-ra); (lover) novio, *m; pl* **followers,** acompañamiento, sequito, *m*

**following** /ˈfɒlouɪŋ/ *n* séquito, acompañamiento, *m,* comitiva, *f;* partidarios, *m pl,* adherentes, *mf pl.* —*a* siguiente; próximo. **f. wind,** viento en popa, *m*

**folly** /ˈfɒli/ *n* locura, extravagancia, absurdidad, tontería, *f,* disparate, *m*

**foment** /fouˈment/ *vt* (poultice) fomentar; provocar, incitar, instigar; (assist) fomentar, proteger, promover

**fomentation** /ˌfoumenˈteifən/ *n Med.* fomentación, *f;* provocación, instigación, *f;* fomento, *m,* protección, *f*

**fomenter** /ˈfoumentər/ *n* fomentador (-ra), instigador (-ra)

**fond** /fɒnd/ *a* (credulous) vano, crédulo, vacío; (doting) demasiado indulgente; (loving) cariñoso, tierno, afectuoso; (addicted to) aficionado a, adicto a, amigo de. **to be f. of,** (things) tener afición a, estar aficionado de; (people) tener cariño (a). **to grow f. of,** (things) aficionarse a; (people) tomar cariño (a)

**fondle** /ˈfɒndl/ *vt* mimar, acariciar; jugar (con.)

**fondly** /ˈfɒndli/ *adv* (vainly) vanamente, sin razón; cariñosamente, tiernamente

**fondness** /ˈfɒndnɪs/ *n* cariño, afecto, *m;* (for things) afición, inclinación, *f;* gusto, *m*

**font** /fɒnt/ *n* pila bautismal, *f; Poet.* fuente, *f; Print.* fundición, *f*

**food** /fud/ *n* alimento, *m;* comida, *f,* el comer; (of animals) pasto, *m; Fig.* pábulo, *m;* materia, *f.* **She gave him f.** Le dio de comer. **You have given me f. for thought,** Me has dado en qué pensar. **f.-card,**

cartilla de racionamiento, **food, clothing, and shelter** comida, abrigo y vivienda, *f*. **F. Ministry,** Ministerio de Alimentación, *m*. **f. value,** valor nutritivo, *m*.

**food poisoning,** intoxicación alimenticia, *f*

**foodstuffs** /'fud,stʌfs/ *n pl* comestibles, víveres, *m pl*

**fool** /ful/ *n* tonto (-ta), mentecato (-ta), majadero (ra) necio (-ia); (jester) bufón, *m*; (butt of jest) hazmerreír, *m*; víctima, *f*; *Cul.* compota de frutas con crema, *f*, *vi* tontear, hacer tonterías. —*vt* poner en ridículo (a); (deceive) engañar, embaucar; (with) jugar con. **to make a f. of oneself,** ponerse en ridículo. **to f. about,** *vi* perder el tiempo, vagabundear. **to f. away,** malgastar, malbaratar. **fool's bauble,** cetro de bufón, *m*. **fool's cap,** gorro de bufón, *m*

**foolhardiness** /'ful,hɑrdinəs/ *n* temeridad, *f*

**foolhardy** /'ful,hɑrdi/ *a* temerario, atrevido

**fooling** /'fuliŋ/ *n* payasada, bufonada, *f*; (deceiving) engaño, *m*, burla, *f*

**foolish** /'fuliʃ/ *a* imprudente, estúpido, tonto; ridículo, absurdo; imbécil

**foolishly** /'fuliʃli/ *adv* imprudentemente; tontamente; imbécilmente

**foolishness** *n* /'fuliʃnis/ imprudencia, *f*; estupidez, tontería, *f*, disparate, *m*; ridiculez, *f*; imbecilidad, *f*

**foolproof** /'ful,pruf/ *a* (of utensils, etc.) con garantía absoluta

**foolscap** /'fulz,kæp/ *n* (nearest equivalent) papel de barba, *m*

**fool's gold** *n* pirita amarilla, *f*, sulfuro de hierro *m*

**foot** /fut/ *n* pie, *m*; (of animals, furniture) pata, *f*; (of bed, sofa, grave, ladder, page, etc.) pie, *m*; (hoof) pezuña, *f*; (metric unit and measure) pie, *m*; *Mil.* infantería, *f*; (base) base, *f*; (step) paso, *m*. —*a Mil.* de a pie; a pie. —*vi* ir a pie; venir a pie; bailar. —*vt* hollar; (account) pagar (una cuenta); (stockings) poner pie (a). **on f.,** a pie; (of soldiers) de a pie; (in progress) en marcha. **to go on f.,** ir a pie, andar. **to put one's best f. forward,** apretar el paso; *Fig.* hacer de su mejor. **to put one's f. down,** poner pies en pared, pararle fulano el alto. **to put one's f. in it,** meter la pata. **to rise to one's feet,** ponerse de pie. **to set f. on,** pisar, hollar. **to set on f.,** poner en pie; *Fig.* poner en marcha. **to trample under f.,** pisotear. **f.-and-mouth disease,** glosopeda, *f*. **f.-brake,** freno de pedal, *m*. **f.-pump,** fuelle de pie, *m*. **f.-rule,** (nearest equivalent) doble decímetro, *m*. **f.-soldier,** soldado de a pie, infante, *m*

**football** /'fut,bɔl/ *n* (game) fútbol, *m*; (ball) pelota de fútbol, *f*. **f. field,** campo de fútbol, *m*. **f. match,** partida de fútbol, *f*. **f. pools,** apuestas de fútbol, *f pl*; (in Spain) apuestas benéficas de fútbol, *f pl*

**footballer** /'fut,bɔlər/ *n* futbolista, *m*

**footbath** /'fut,bæθ/ *n* baño de pies, *m*

**footbridge** /'fut,brɪdʒ/ *n* puente para peatones, *m*

**footed** /'futɪd/ *a* con pies; de pies...; de patas...

**footfall** /'fut,fɔl/ *n* pisada, *f*, paso, *m*

**foothills** /'fut,hɪlz/ *n pl* faldas de la montaña, *f pl*

**foothold** /'fut,hould/ *n* hincapié, *m*; posición establecida, *f*

**footing** /'futɪŋ/ *n* hincapié, *m*; posición firme, *f*; condiciones, *f pl*; relaciones, *f pl*. **on a peacetime f.,** en pie de paz. **to be on an equal f.,** estar en pie de igualdad, estar en iguales condiciones. **to miss one's f.,** resbalar

**footlights** /'fut,laɪts/ *n pl* canilejas, candilejas, *f pl*. **to get across the f.,** hacer contacto con el público

**footman** /'futmən/ *n* lacayo, *m*

**footnote** /'fut,nout/ *n* llamada a pie de página, nota a pie de página, *f*

**footpath** /'fut,pæθ/ *n* senda, vereda, *f*, sendero, *m*

**footprint** /'fut,prɪnt/ *n* huella, pisada, *f*, vestigio, *m*

**footsore** /'fut,sɔr/ *a* con los pies lastimados

**footstep** /'fut,stɛp/ *n* paso, *m*; (trace) pisada, huella, *f*. **to follow in the footsteps of,** *Fig.* seguir las pisadas de

**footstool** /'fut,stul/ *n* escabel, banquito, *m*

**footwarmer** /'fut,wɔrmər/ *n* calientapiés, *m*

**footwear** /'fut,wɛər/ *n* calzado, *m*

**fop** /fɒp/ *n* petimetre, *m*

**foppery** /'fɒpəri/ *n* afectación en el vestir, *f*; vanidad, *f*

**foppish** /'fɒpɪʃ/ *a* presumido, afectado; elegante

**for** /fɔr; *unstressed* fər/ *prep* (expressing exchange, price or penalty of, instead of, in support or favor of, on account of) por; (expressing destination, purpose, result) para; (during) durante, por; (for the sake of) para; (because of) a causa de; (in spite of) a pesar de; (as) como; (with) de; (in favor of) en favor de; (in election campaign) con (e.g., "Ecuadorians for Martínez!" ¡Ecuatorianos con Martínez!) (toward) hacia; (that) que, para que (with *subjunc*); a, (before) antes de; (searching for) en busca de; (bound for) con rumbo a; (regarding) en cuanto a; (until) hasta. What's for dinner? ¿Qué hay de comida? **center for...** centro de... (e.g., *Center for Applied Linguistics*, Centro de Lingüística Aplicada). **He is in business for himself,** Tiene negocios por su propia cuenta. **It is raining too hard for you to go there,** Llueve demasiado para que vayas allí. **It is not for him to decide,** No le toca a él decidirlo. **Were it not for...,** Si no fuese por... **She has not been to see me for a week,** Hace una semana que no viene a verme. **It is impossible for them to go out,** Les es imposible salir. **but for all that,** pero con todo. **for ever,** por (or para) siempre. **for fear that,** por miedo de que. **for myself,** en cuanto a mí, personalmente. **for the present,** por ahora. **for what reason?** ¿para qué? ¿por cuál motivo? **for brevity's sake, for the sake of brevity,** por causa de la brevedad

**for** /fɔr; *unstressed* fər/ *conjunc* porque; visto que, pues, puesto que, en efecto, ya que

**forage** /'fɔrɪdʒ/ *n* forraje, *m*. —*vt* and *vi* forrajear. **to f. for,** buscar. **f. cap,** gorra de cuartel, *f*

**forager** /'fɔrɪdʒər/ *n* forrajeador, *m*

**foraging** /'fɔrɪdʒɪŋ/ *n* forraje, *m*

**forasmuch as** /,fɔrəz'mʌtʃ ,æz/ *conjunc* puesto que, como que, ya que

**foray** /'fɔreɪ/ *n* correría, cabalgada, *f*; saqueo, *m*

**forbear** /'fɔr,bɛər/ *vt* and *vi* dejar (de), guardarse (de); abstenerse de; evitar; reprimirse (de); rehusarse (de); (cease) cesar (de); (be patient) ser paciente; ser tolerante

**forbearance** /fɔr'bɛərəns/ *n* abstención, *f*; tolerancia, transigencia, *f*; indulgencia, *f*; paciencia, *f*

**forbearing** /fɔr'bɛərɪŋ/ *a* tolerance, transigente; generoso, magnánimo; paciente

**forbid** /fər'bɪd/ *vt* prohibir, defender (de); impedir. **I f. you to do it,** Te prohibo hacerlo. **The game is forbidden,** El juego está prohibido. **They have forbidden me to...,** Me han defendido de... **Heaven f.!** ¡Dios no lo quiera!

**forbidden** /fər'bɪdn/ *a* prohibido; ilícito. **f. fruit,** fruto prohibido, *m*

**forbidding** /fər'bɪdɪŋ/ *a* repugnante, horrible; antipático, desagradable; (dismal) lúgubre; (threatening) amenazador. —*n* prohibición, *f*

**force** /fɔrs/ *n* fuerza, *f*; violencia, *f*; vigor, *m*; (efficacy) eficacia, *f*; (validity) validez, *f*; (power) poder, *m*; (motive) motivo, *m*, razón, *f*; (weight) peso, *m*, importancia, *f*; (police) policía, *f*; *pl* **forces,** *Mil.* fuerzas, tropas, *f pl*. **by main f.,** por fuerza mayor. **in f.,** vigente, en vigor. **to be in f.,** estar vigente

**force** /fɔrs/ *vt* forzar; (compel) obligar, constreñir, precisar; (ravish) violar; *Cul.* rellenar; (impose) imponer; (plants) forzar; (the pace) apresurar; (cause) hacer; (a lock, etc.) forzar. **to f. oneself into,** entrar a la fuerza en; (a garment) ponerse con dificultad; imponerse a la fuerza. **to f. oneself to,** esforzarse a. **to f. the pace,** forzar el paso. **to f. away,** ahuyentar. **to f. back,** hacer retroceder; rechazar; (a sigh, etc.) ahogar. **to f. down,** hacer bajar, obligar a bajar; (make swallow) hacer tragar; (of airplanes) hacer tomar tierra. **to f. in,** introducir a la fuerza; obligar a entrar. **to f. into,** meter a la fuerza; obligar a entrar (en). **to f. on, upon,** imponer. **to f. open,** abrir a la fuerza; (a lock) romper, forzar. **to f. out,** hacer salir; empujar hacia fuera; (words) pronunciar con dificultad. **to f. up,** obligar a subir; hacer subir; hacer vomitar

**forced** /fɔrst/ *a* forzado; forzoso; afectado. **f. landing,** *Aer.* aterrizaje forzoso, *m*. **f. march,** *Mil.* marcha forzada, *f*

**forceful** /'fɔrsfəl/ *a* See **forcible**

**forcemeat** /'fɔrs‚mit/ n picadillo, m; relleno, m. **f. ball**, albóndiga, f

**forceps** /'fɔrsəps/ n pl fórceps, m pl; pinzas, f pl. **arterial f.**, pinzas hemostáticas, f pl

**forcible** /'fɔrsəbəl/ a fuerte; a la fuerza; violento; enérgico, vigoroso; poderoso; Lit. vívido, gráfico, vehemente. **f. feeding**, alimentación forzosa, f

**forcibleness** /'fɔrsəbəlnɪs/ n fuerza, f; vigor, m, energía, f; vehemencia, f

**forcibly** /'fɔrsəbli/ adv a la fuerza

**forcing** /'fɔrsɪŋ/ n forzamiento, m; compulsión, f. **f. frame**, semillero, m, especie de invernadero, f

**ford** /fɔrd/ n esguazo, vado, m. —vt esguazar, vadear

**fordable** /'fɔrdəbəl/ a esguazable, vadeable

**fore** /fɔr/ a delantero; Naut. de proa. —adv delante; Naut. de proa. **f.-and-aft**, Naut. de popa a proa.

**forearm** /fɔr'ɑrm/ n antebrazo, m. —vt armar de antemano; preparar

**forebear** /'fɔr‚bɛər/ n antecesor, m, ascendiente, mf

**forebode** /fɔr'boud/ vt presagiar, augurar, anunciar; presentir

**foreboding** /fɔr'boudɪŋ/ n presagio, augurio, m; presentimiento, m, corazonada, f

**forecast** /'fɔr‚kæst/ n pronóstico, m; proyecto, plan, m, vt pronosticar; proyectar. **weather f.**, pronóstico del tiempo, m

**forecastle** /'fouksəl/ n Naut. castillo de proa, m

**foreclose** /fɔr'klouz/ vt excluir; impedir; vender por orden judicial; anticipar el resultado de; decidir de antemano

**foreclosure** /fɔr'klouʒər/ n venta por orden judicial, f; juicio hipotecario, m

**foredoom** /fɔr'dum/ vt predestinar

**forefather** /'fɔr‚fɑðər/ n antepasado, antecesor, m

**forefinger** /'fɔr‚fɪŋgər/ n índice, dedo índice, m

**forefoot** /'fɔr‚fʊt/ n pata delantera, f

**forefront** /'fɔr‚frʌnt/ n delantera, primera línea, f; frente, m; vanguardia, f. **in the f.**, en la vanguardia; en el frente

**foregoing** /fɔr'gouɪŋ/ a precedente, anterior

**foregone** /fɔr'gɔn/ a decidido de antemano; previsto

**foreground** /'fɔr‚graund/ n primer plano, primer término, frente, m. **in the f.**, Art. en primer término

**forehand** /'fɔr‚hænd/ a derecho. **f. stroke**, golpe derecho, m

**forehead** /'fɔrɪd/ n frente, f

**foreign** /'fɔrɪn/ a extranjero; extraño; exótico; exterior; (alien) ajeno. **f. affairs**, asuntos extranjeros, m pl. **f. body**, cuerpo extraño, m. **f. debt**, deuda exterior, f. **F. Legion**, tercio extranjero, m. **F. Office**, Ministerio de Relaciones Extranjeras, m. **f. parts**, extranjero, m. **f. policy**, política internacional, f. **F. Secretary**, Secretario de Asuntos Extranjeros, Secretario de Asuntos Exteriores, Ministro de Relaciones Extranjeras, m. **f. trade**, comercio con el extranjero, m

**foreigner** /'fɔrənər/ n extranjero (-ra)

**foreignness** /'fɔrənnɪs/ n extranjerismo, m; (strangeness) extrañeza, f; lo exótico

**foreknowledge** /'fɔr‚nɒlɪdʒ/ n presciencia, precognición, f

**foreland** /'fɔr‚lænd/ n promontorio, cabo, m

**foreleg** /'fɔr‚lɛg/ n pata delantera, f

**forelock** /'fɔr‚lɒk/ n guedeja, vedeja, f; (of a horse) copete, tupé, m. **to take time by the f.**, asir la ocasión por la melena

**foreman** /'fɔrmən/ n (of jury) presidente (del jurado), m; (of a farm) mayoral, m; (in a works) capataz, m

**foremost** /'fɔr‚moust/ a delantero; de primera fila; más importante. —adv en primer lugar; en primera fila

**forensic** /fə'rɛnsɪk/ a forense, legal. **f. medicine**, medicina legal, f

**foreordained** /‚fɔrɔr'deind/ a predestinado

**forerunner** /'fɔr‚rʌnər/ n precursor (-ra), predecessor (-ra); (presage) anuncio, presagio, m

**foresee** /fɔr'si/ vt prever, anticipar

**foreseeing** /fɔr'siɪŋ/ a presciente, sagaz

**foreseer** /fɔr'siər/ n previsor (-ra)

**foreshadow** /fɔr'ʃædou/ vt anunciar, prefigurar; simbolizar; hacer sentir.

**foreshorten** /fɔr'ʃɔrtn/ vt Art. escorzar

**foreshortening** /fɔr'ʃɔrtnɪŋ/ n Art. escorzo, m

**foresight** /'fɔr‚sait/ n presciencia, f; previsión, prudencia, f; (of gun) punto de mira, m; (optical) croquis de nivel, m

**forest** /'fɔrɪst/ n bosque, m, selva, f. —vt arbolar

**forestall** /fɔr'stɔl/ vt anticipar, saltear; prevenir; Com. acaparar

**forestalling** /fɔr'stɔlɪŋ/ n anticipación, f

**forestation** /‚fɔrə'steiʃən/ n repoblación forestal, f

**forester** /'fɔrəstər/ n silvicultor, guardamonte, ingeniero forestal, m; habitante de los bosques, m

**forest fire** incendio forestal, m

**forestry** /'fɔrəstri/ n silvicultura, f

**foresworn** /fɔr'swɔrn/ a perjuro

**foretaste** /n 'fɔr‚teist/ v fɔr'teist/ n muestra, f; presagio, m. —vt gustar con anticipación

**foretell** /fɔr'tɛl/ vt predecir, profetizar; anunciar, presagiar

**foreteller** /fɔr'tɛlər/ n profeta, m; presagio, m

**foretelling** /fɔr'tɛlɪŋ/ n profecía, predicción, f

**forethought** /'fɔr‚θɔt/ n presciencia, previsión, f; prevención, f

**forewarn** /fɔr'wɔrn/ vt prevenir

**forewarning** /fɔr'wɔrnɪŋ/ n presagio, m

**forewoman** /'fɔr‚wʊmən/ n encargada, f; primera oficiala, f

**foreword** /'fɔr‚wɜrd/ n prefacio, m, introducción, f

**forfeit** /'fɔrfɪt/ n pérdida, f; (fine) multa, f; (in games) prenda, f; (of rights, goods, etc.) confiscación, f. —a confiscado. —vt perder; perder el derecho o el título de

**forfeiture** /'fɔrfɪtʃər/ n pérdida, f; confiscación, f; secuestro, m

**forge** /fɔrdʒ/ n fragua, f; (smithy) herrería, f. —vt and vi fraguar, forjar; (fabricate) inventar, fabricar; falsificar; (advance) avanzar lentamente. **to f. ahead**, abrirse camino; avanzar

**forged** /fɔrdʒd/ a (of iron) forjado; (of checks, etc.) falso, falsificado

**forger** /'fɔrdʒər/ n falsificador (-ra), falsario (-ia); (creator) artífice, mf

**forgery** /'fɔrdʒəri/ n falsificación, f

**forget** /fər'gɛt/ vt olvidar; descuidar. —vi olvidarse. **to f. about**, olvidarse de, desacordarse de. **to f. oneself**, olvidarse de sí mismo; propasarse; (in anger) perder los estribos

**forgetful** /fər'gɛtfəl/ a olvidadizo; descuidado, negligente

**forgetfulness** /fər'gɛtfəlnɪs/ n olvido, m; descuido, m; falta de memoria, f

**forget-me-not** /fər'gɛtmi‚nɒt/ n Bot. miosota nomeolvides, f

**forging** /'fɔrdʒɪŋ/ n fraguado, m; falsificación, f

**forgivable** /fər'gɪvəbəl/ a perdonable, excusable

**forgive** /fər'gɪv/ vt perdonar, disculpar, condonar; (debts) remitir

**forgiveness** /fər'gɪvnɪs/ n perdón, m; condonación, f; (remission) remisión, f

**forgiving** /fər'gɪvɪŋ/ a misericordioso, clemente, dispuesto a perdonar

**forgo** /fɔr'gou/ vt renunciar, sacrificar, privarse de; abandonar, ceder

**forgoing** /fɔr'gouɪŋ/ n renunciación, f, sacrificio, m; cesión, f

**"For Immediate Occupancy"** «De Ocupación Inmediata»

**fork** /fɔrk/ n Agr. horca, horquilla, f; (table fork) tenedor, m; bifurcación, f; (of rivers) confluencia, f; (of branches) horcadura, f; (of legs) horcajadura, f; (for supporting trees, etc.) horca, f; Mus. diapasón normal, m. —vt hacinar con horca. —vi bifurcarse; ramificarse

**forked** /fɔrkt/ a bifurcado, hendido, ahorquillado. **f. lightning**, relámpago, m. **f. tail**, cola hendida, f

**forlorn** /fɔr'lɔrn/ a abandonado, desamparado, desesperado. **f. hope**, aventura desesperada, f

**forlornness** /fɔr'lɔrnnɪs/ n desamparo, m, miseria, f; desolación, f, desconsuelo, m

**form** /fɔrm/ n forma, f; figura, f; (shadowy) bulto, m; (formality) formalidad, f; ceremonia, f; Eccl. rito, *m;* método, *m;* regla, *f;* (in a school) clase, *f;* (lair) cama, *f;* (seat) banco, *m;* (system) sistema, *m;* (ghost) espectro, *m;* aparición, *f;* (to fill up) documento, *m;* hoja, *f;* (state) condición, *f; Lit.* construcción, forma, *f.* **It is a matter of f.,** Es una pura formalidad. **in due f.,** en debida forma, en regla. **in the usual f.,** *Com.* al usado. **It is not good f.,** No es de buena educación

**form** /fɔrm/ *vt* formar; (a habit) contraer; (an idea) hacerse (una idea). —*vi* formarse. **to f. fours,** *Mil.* formar a cuatro

**formal** /'fɔrməl/ *a* esencial; formal; ceremonioso, solemne; (of person) etiquetero, formalista. **f. call,** visita de cumplido, *f*

**formaldehyde** /fɔr'mældə,haid/ *n* formaldehído. *m*

**formalism** /'fɔrmə,lɪzəm/ *n* formalismo, *m*

**formality** /fɔr'mælɪti/ *n* formalidad, *f;* ceremonia, solemnidad, *f*

**formally** /'fɔrməli/ *adv* formalmente

**format** /'fɔrmæt/ *n* formato, *m*

**formation** /fɔr'meiʃən/ *n* formación, *f;* disposición, *f,* arreglo, *m;* organización, *f;* (*Mil., Geol.*) formación, *f*

**formative** /'fɔrmətɪv/ *a* formativo

**former** /'fɔrmər/ *a* primero; antiguo; anterior; pasado. **in f. times,** antes, antiguamente. **the f.,** ése, aquél, *m;* ésa, aquélla, *f;* aquéllos, *m pl;* aquéllas, *f pl*

**former** /'fɔrmər/ *n* formador (-ra); creador (-ra), autor (-ra)

**formerly** /'fɔrmərli/ *adv* antiguamente, antes

**formidable** /'fɔrmɪdəbəl/ *a* formidable; terrible, espantoso

**formless** /'fɔrmlɪs/ *a* informe

**formlessness** /'fɔrmlɪsnɪs/ *n* falta de forma, *f*

**formula** /'fɔrmyələ/ *n* fórmula, *f.* **standard f.,** (*Math. ,Chem.*) fórmula clásica, *f*

**formulate** /'fɔrmyə,leit/ *vt* formular

**fornicate** /'fɔrnɪ,keit/ *vi* fornicar

**fornication** /,fɔrnɪ'keiʃən/ *n* fornicación, *f*

**fornicator** /'fɔrnɪ,keitər/ *n* fornicador (-ra)

**forsake** /fɔr'seik/ *vt* dejar, desertar; abandonar, desamparar; separarse de; (of birds, the nest) aborrecer;∙ (one's faith) renegar de

**forsaker** /fɔr'seikər/ *n* el, *m,* (la, *f*) que abandona; desertor, *m;* renegado (-da)

**"For Sale"** «Se Vende»

**forsooth** /fɔr'suθ/ *adv* ciertamente, claro está

**forswear** /fɔr'swɛər/ *vt* abjurar; renunciar a. **to f. oneself,** perjurarse

**forswearing** /fɔr'swɛərɪŋ/ *n* abjuración, *f;* renuncia, *f;* perjurio, *m*

**fort** /fɔrt/ *n* fortaleza, *f,* fuerte, *m*

**forte** /'fɔrtei/ *n* fuerte, *m.* —*a Mus.* fuerte

**forth** /fɔrθ/ *adv* (on) adelante, hacia adelante; (out) fuera; (in time) en adelante, en lo consecutivo; (show) a la vista. **and so f.,** y así en lo sucesivo; etcétera

**forthcoming** /fɔrθ'kʌmɪŋ/ *a* próximo; futuro; en preparación

**forthwith** /,fɔrθ'wɪθ/ *adv* en seguida, sin tardanza

**fortieth** /'fɔrtiɪθ/ *a* cuadragésimo; cuarenta. —*n* cuarentavo, *m*

**fortifiable** /'fɔrtə,faiəbəl/ *a* fortificable

**fortification** /,fɔrtəfɪ'keiʃən/ *n* fortificación, *f*

**fortify** /'fɔrtə,fai/ *vt* fortificar; fortalecer; confirmar; *Fig.* proveer (de)

**fortitude** /'fɔrtɪ,tud/ *n* aguante, *m,* fortaleza, *f,* estoicismo, *m*

**fortnight** /'fɔrt,nait/ *n* quince días, *m pl,* dos semanas, *f pl;* quincena, *f.* **a f. ago,** hace quince días. **a f. tomorrow,** mañana en quince. **in a f.,** dentro de quince días; al cabo de quince días. **once a f.,** cada quince días

**fortnightly** /'fɔrt,naitli/ *a* quincenal. —*adv* cada dos semanas, dos veces al mes. —*n* revista quincenal, *f*

**fortress** /'fɔrtrɪs/ *n* fortaleza, plaza fuerte, *f*

**fortuitous** /fɔr'tuitəs/ *a* fortuito, accidental

**fortuitously** /fɔr'tuitəsli/ *adv* accidentalmente

**fortuity** /fɔr'tuiti/ *n* casualidad, *f;* accidente, *m*

**fortunate** /'fɔrtʃənɪt/ *a* dichoso, feliz; afortunado; próspero. **to be f.,** (of persons) tener suerte

**fortunately** /'fɔrtʃənɪtli/ *adv* afortunadamente, por dicha, felizmente

**fortune** /'fɔrtʃən/ *n* suerte, fortuna, *f,* destino, *m;* (money) caudal, *m,* fortuna, *f;* bienes, *m pl;* buena ventura, *f.* **good f.,** buena fortuna, dicha, *f.* **ill f.,** mala suerte, *f.* **to cost a f.,** costar un sentido. **to make one's f.,** enriquecerse; *Inf.* hacer su pacotilla. **to tell fortunes,** echar las cartas. **f. hunter,** buscador de dotes, cazador de dotes, cazador de fortunas, aventurero, *m.* **f.-teller,** adivinadora, *f;* echadora de cartas, *f.* **f.-telling,** buenaventura, *f*

**forty** /'fɔrti/ *a and n* cuarenta, *m.* **He is turned f.,** Ha cumplido los cuarenta. **person of f.,** cuarentón (-ona). **She is f.,** Tiene cuarenta años

**forum** /'fɔrəm/ *n* foro, tribuna *f.* (e.g., *to serve as a forum for discussion*, servir de tribuna de discusión)

**forward** /'fɔrwərd/ *a* avanzado; adelantado; (of position) delantero; (ready) pronto; (eager) pronto, listo, impaciente; activo, emprendedor; (of persons, fruit, etc.) precoz; (pert) insolente, desenvuelto, atrevido. —*adv* adelante; hacia adelante; (of time) en adelante; (farther on) más allá; hacia el frente; en primera linea. —*vt* ayudar, promover; adelantar; (letters) hacer seguir; *Com.* expedir, remitir; (a parcel) despachar; (hasten) apresurar; (plants) hacer crecer. —*n Sports.* delantero, *m. center-f., Sports.* delantero centro, *m.* **from this time f.,** de hoy en adelante. **Please f.,** ¡Haga seguir! **putting f. of the clock,** el adelanto de la hora. **to carry f.,** *Com.* pasar a cuenta nueva. **to go f.,** adelantarse; estar en marcha, estar en preparación. **f. line,** *Sports.* delantera, *f.* **F.!** ¡Adelante!

**forwarder** /'fɔrwərdər/ *n* promotor (-ra); *Com.* remitente, *m*

**forwarding** /'fɔrwərdɪŋ/ *n* fomento, *m,* promoción, *f; Com.* expedición, *f,* envío, *m*

**forwardness** /'fɔrwərdnɪs/ *n* progreso, adelantamiento, *m;* (haste) apresuramiento, *m;* (of persons, fruit, etc.) precocidad, *f;* (pertness) desenvoltura, insolencia, frescura, *f,* descaro, *m;* (eagerness) impaciencia, *f*

**fosse** /fɒs/∙*n* foso, *m*

**fossil** /'fɒsəl/ *a and n* fósil, *m.*

**fossilization** /,fɒsələ'zeiʃən/ *n* fosilización, *f*

**fossilize** /'fɒsə,laiz/ *vt* fosilizar; petrificar. —*vi* fosilizarse

**foster** /'fɒstər/ *vt* provocar, promover, suscitar; (favor) favorecer, ser propicio a. **f.-brother,** hermano de leche, *m.* **f.-child,** hijo (-ja) de leche. **f.-father,** padre adoptivo, *m.* **f.-mother,** ama de leche, *f.* **f.-sister,** hermana de leche, *f*

**foul** /faul/ *a* sucio, asqueroso, puerco; (evil-smelling) hediondo, fétido; (of air) viciado; impuro; (language) ofensivo; (coarse) indecente, obsceno; (harmful) nocivo, dañino; (wicked) malvado; infame; vil; (unfair) injusto; *Sports.* sucio; (ugly) feo; (entangled) enredado; (with corrections) lleno de erratas; (choked) atascado; (of weather) borrascoso, tempestuoso, malo, desagradable; (repulsive) repugnante. —*n Sports.* juego sucio, *m.* —*vt* ensuciar; *Naut.* chocar, abordar; (block) atascar; (the anchor) enredar; (dishonor) deshonrar. —*vi* atascarse; (anchor) enredarse; *Naut.* chocar. **to fall f. of,** *Naut.* abordar (un buque); *Fig.* habérselas con. **by fair means or f.,** a las buenas o a las malas. **f. breath,** aliento fétido, aliento corrompido, *m.* **f. brood,** peste de las abejas, *f.* **f. language,** palabras ofensivas, *f pl;* lenguaje obsceno, *m.* **f. play,** juego sucio, *m.* **f. weather,** mal tiempo, tiempo borrascoso, *m*

**found** /faund/ *vt* fundar; (metal, glass) fundir; (create, etc.) establecer

**foundation** /faun'deiʃən/ *n* fundación, *f;* establecimiento, *m;* creación, *f; Archit.* cimiento, embasamiento, *m;* (basis) base, *f;* (cause) causa, *f,* origen, principio, *m;* (endowment) dotación, *f; Sew.* refuerzo, *m.* **to lay the f.,** poner las fundaciones. **f. stone,** piedra angular, *f; Fig.* primera piedra, *f.* **to lay the f. stone,** poner la piedra angular

**founder** /'faundər/ *n* fundador (-ra); (of metals) fundidor, *m.* —*vt* (a ship) hacer zozobrar. —*vi* zozobrar, irse a pique; *Fig.* fracasar

**foundering** /'faundərɪŋ/ *n Naut.* zozobra, *f*

**founding** /'faundɪŋ/ n fundación, f; establecimiento, m; (of metals) fundición, f

**foundling** /'faundlɪŋ/ n hijo (-ja) de la cuna, expósito (-ta). **f. hospital** or **home,** casa de cuna, casa de expósitos, inclusa, f

**foundry** /'faundri/ n fundición, f

**fountain** /'fauntn/ n fuente, f; (spring) manantial, m; (jet) chorro, m; (artificial) fuente, f, surtidero, m; (source) origen, principio, m. **f.-head,** fuente, f. **Fountain of Youth,** Fuente de la juventud, Fuente de Juvencio, f. **f. pen,** pluma estilográfica, f

**four** /fɔr/ a and n cuatro, m. **It is f. o'clock,** Son las cuatro. **She is f.,** Tiene cuatro años. **on all fours,** a gatas. **f.-course,** (of meals) de cuatro platos. **f.-engined,** cuadrimotor. **f.-engined plane,** cuadrimotor, m. **f.-footed,** cuadrúpedo. **f.-horse,** de cuatro caballos. **f. hundred,** cuatrocientos. **f.-inhand,** tiro par, m. **f.-part,** (of a song) a cuatro voces. **f.-wheel brakes,** freno en las cuatro ruedas, m

**fourfold** /'fɔr,fould/ a cuádruple

**fourposter** /'fɔr'poustər/ n cama de matrimonio, f

**fourscore** /'fɔr'skɔr/ a and n ochenta, m.

**foursome** /'fɔrsəm/ n partido de cuatro personas, m

**fourteen** /'fɔr'tin/ a and n catorce, m. **He is f.,** Tiene catorce años

**fourteenth** /'fɔr'tinθ/ a and n décimocuarto m.; (of the month) (el) catorce, m; (of monarchs) catorce. **April f.,** El 14 (catorce) de abril

**fourth** /fɔrθ/ a cuarto; (of the month) el cuatro; (of monarchs) cuarto. —n (fourth part) cuarta parte, f; Mus. cuarta, f. **f. dimension,** cuarta dimensión, f. **f. term,** (U.S.A. Polit.) cuarto mandato, m

**fourthly** /'fɔrθli/ adv en cuarto lugar

**fowl** /faul/ n gallo. m; gallina, f; (chicken) pollo, m; (bird) ave, f; (barndoor f.) ave de corral, f. —vi cazar aves. **f.-house or run,** gallinero, m

**fox** /fɒks/ n zorro, m; (vixen) zorra, raposa, f; Fig. zorro, taimado, m. —vi disimular. —vt (books) descolorar. **f.-brush,** cola de raposa, f. **f.-earth,** zorrera, f. **f.-hunting,** caza de zorras, f. **f. terrier,** fox-térrier, m

**foxglove** /'fɒks,glʌv/ n digital, dedalera, f

**foxhound** /'fɒks,haund/ n perro zorrero, m

**foxiness** /'fɒksinɪs/ n zorrería, astucia, f

**foxtrot** /'fɒks,trɒt/ n foxtrot, m

**foxy** /'fɒksi/ a de zorro; zorrero, astuto

**foyer** /'fɔiər/ n foyer, salón de descanso, m

**fraction** /'frækʃən/ n Math. fracción, f, número quebrado, m; pequeña parte, f; fragmento, m. **improper f.,** Math. fracción impropia, f. **proper f.,** Math. fracción propia, f

**fractional** /'frækʃən/ a fraccionario

**fractious** /'frækʃəs/ a malhumorado, enojadizo

**fractiousness** /'frækʃəsnɪs/ n mal humor, m

**fracture** /'fræktʃər/ n Surg. fractura, f. —vt fracturar. **compound f.,** fractura conminuta, f

**fragile** /'frædʒəl/ a frágil, quebradizo; (of persons) delicado

**fragility** /frə'dʒɪliti/ n fragilidad, f

**fragment** /'frægmənt/ n fragmento, m; trozo, pedazo, m. **to break into fragments,** hacer pedazos, hacer añicos

**fragmentary** /'frægmən,teri/ a fragmentario

**fragrance** /'freigrəns/ n fragancia, f, buen olor, perfume, aroma, m

**fragrant** /'freigrənt/ a fragante, oloroso. **to make f.,** perfumar

**frail** /freil/ a frágil, quebradizo; débil, endeble. —n capacho, m, espuerta, f

**frailty** /'freilti/ n fragilidad, f; debilidad, f

**frame** /freim/ n constitución, f; sistema, m; organización, f; (of the body) figura, f, talle, m; (of window, picture) marco, m; (of machine, building) armadura, f; (of a bicycle) cuadro (de bicicleta), m; Agr. cajonera, f; (embroidery) bastidor (para bordar), m; (skeleton) esqueleto, m; Lit. composición, construcción, f; (of spectacles) armadura, f; (of mind) disposición (de ánimo), f; humor, m. —vt formar; construir; arreglar; ajustar; (a picture) enmarcar; componer, hacer; (draw up) redactar; (think up) idear, inventar; (words) articular, pronunciar. **f. a constitution,** elaborar una constitución

**framer** /'freimər/ n fabricante de marcos, m; autor (-ra), creador (-ra), inventor (-ra)

**framework** /'freim,wɜrk/ n armadura, armazón, f, esqueleto, m; organización, f; (basis) base, f

**franc** /fræŋk/ n (coin) franco, m

**France** /fræns/ Francia, f

**Franche-Comté** /frãʃ kɔ̃'tei/ Franco-Condado, m

**franchise** /'fræntʃaiz/ n (exemption) franquicia, f; privilegio, m; (vote) derecho de sufragio, m; (citizenship) derecho político, m

**Franciscan** /fræn'siskən/ a and n franciscano (-na)

**Franco-** (in compounds) franco-... —a (referring to General Franco) franquista

**Francophile** /'fræŋkə,fail/ a and n afrancesado (-da)

**Frank** /fræŋk/ n franco (-ca), galo (-la)

**frank** /fræŋk/ a franco, franco, cándido, sincero; abierto. —vt franquear

**frankincense** /'fræŋkin,sens/ n incienso, m

**frankly** /'fræŋkli/ adv francamente; sinceramente; cara a cara; sin rodeos, claramente; abiertamente. **to speak f.,** hablar claro, hablar sin rodeos

**frankness** /'fræŋknɪs/ n franqueza, f; sinceridad, f, candor, m

**frantic** /'fræntik/ a frenético, furioso, loco. **He drives me f.,** Me vuelve loco

**fraternal** /frə'tɜrnl/ a fraterno, fraternal

**fraternity** /frə'tɜrniti/ n fraternidad, hermandad, f

**fraternization** /,frætərnə'zeiʃən/ n fraternización, f

**fraternize** /'frætər,naiz/ vi fraternizar

**fratricidal** /,frætri'saidl/ a fratricida

**fratricide** /'frætri,said/ n (person) fratricida, mf; (action) fratricidio, m

**fraud** /frɔd/ n fraude, m; engaño, embuste, m; (person) farsante, m, embustero (-ra)

**fraudulence** /'frɔdʒələns/ n fraudulencia, fraude, f

**fraudulent** /'frɔdʒələnt/ a fraudulento

**fraught** /frɔt/ a (with) cargado de; lleno de, preñado de

**fray** /frei/ n refriega, riña, f; combate, m, batalla, f; (rubbing) raedura, f. —vt raer, tazar. —vi tazarse, deshilarse

**frayed** /freid/ a raído

**fraying** /'freiɪŋ/ n raedura, deshiladura, f

**freak** /frik/ n monstruo, m; fenómeno, m; (whim) capricho, m

**freakish** /'frikiʃ/ a monstruoso; caprichoso; extravagante; raro, singular

**freakishness** /'frikiʃnɪs/ n carácter caprichoso, m; extravagancia, f; rareza, extrañeza, f

**freckle** /'frekəl/ n peca, f. —vi tener pecas; salir pecas (a la cara, etc.)

**freckled** /'frekəld/ a pecoso, con pecas

**free** /fri/ a (in most senses) libre; independiente; emancipado; desembarazado; abierto; limpio (de); franco; (voluntary) voluntario; (self-governing) autónomo, independiente; accesible; (disengaged) desocupado; (vacant) vacío; (exempt) exento (de); (immune) immune (de); ajeno; gratuito; (loose) suelto; (generous) generoso, liberal; (vicious) disoluto, licencioso; (bold) atrevido; (impudent) insolente, demasiado familiar. —adv gratis, gratuitamente. **There are two f. seats in the train,** Hay dos asientos libres en el tren. **to get f.,** libertarse. **to make f. with,** tomarse libertades con; usar como si fuera suyo. **to set f.,** poner en libertad. **f. agent,** libre albedrío, m. **f. and easy,** familiar, sin ceremonia. **f. gift,** Com. objeto de reclamo, m. **f.-hand drawing,** dibujo a pulso, m. **f. kick,** Sports. golpe franco, m. **f. love,** amor libre, m. **f. play,** rienda suelta, f; Mech. holgura, f. **f. port,** puerto franco, m. **f. speech,** libertad de palabra, f. **f. thought,** libre pensamiento, m. **f. ticket,** Theat. billete de favor, m. **f. trade,** a librecambista. —n librecambio, m. **f. trader,** librecambista, mf. **f. verse,** verso libre, verso suelto, m. **f.-wheeling,** desenfrenado, libre. **f. will,** propia voluntad, f; (theology) libre albedrío, m

**free** /fri/ vt libertar, poner en libertad (a); librar (de); (slave) salvar; emancipar; exentar; (of obstacles, difficulties) desembarazar; **to f. from,** libertar de; librar de; (clean) limpiar de

**freebooter** /'fri,butər/ n pirata, filibustero, m

**freeborn** /'fri,bɔrn/ a nacido libre, libre por herencia

**freedman** /'fridmən/ n liberto, m

**freedom** /'fridəm/ n libertad, f; independencia, f; exención, f; inmunidad, f; soltura, facilidad, f, franqueza, f; (over-familiarity) insolencia, f; (boldness) audacia, intrepidez, f; (of customs) licencia, f. **to receive the f. of a city,** ser recibido como ciudadano de honor. **f. of speech,** libertad de palabra, f. **f. of the press,** libertad de la prensa, f. **f. of worship,** libertad de cultos, f

**freehold** /'fri,hould/ n feudo franco, m

**freeing** /'friɪŋ/ n liberación, f; emancipación, f; salvación, f; (from obstruction) desembarazo, m; limpieza, f

**freelance** /'fri,læns/ n Mil. soldado libre, m; Polit. independiente, m; aventurero (-ra). **f. journalist,** periodista libre, m

**freely** /'frili/ adv libremente; francamente; generosamente; sin reserva

**freeman** /'frimən/ n hombre libre, m; (of a city) ciudadano de honor, m

**freemason** /'fri,meisən/ n francmasón, m. **freemason's lodge,** logia masónica, f

**freemasonry** /'fri,meisənri/ n francmasonería, masonería, f

**freethinker** /'fri'θɪŋkər/ n librepensador (-ra)

**freeze** /friz/ vt helar; (meat, etc.) congelar; Fig. helar. —vi helarse; congelarse; (impers, of the weather) helar. **to f. to death,** morir de frío

**freezing** /'frizɪŋ/ n hielo, m; congelación, f. —a glacial; congelante, frigorífico. **f. mixture,** mezcla frigorífica, f. **f. of assets,** bloqueo de los depósitos bancarios, m. **f.-point,** punto de congelación, m. **above f.-point,** sobre cero. **below f.-point,** bajo cero

**freight** /freit/ n flete, m; porte, m. —vt fletar

**freighter** /'freitər/ n fletador, m; (ship) buque de carga, m

**French** /frentʃ/ a francés. —n (language) francés, m; (people) los franceses, m pl. **in F. fashion,** a la francesa. **to take F. leave,** despedirse a la inglesa. **What is the F. for "hat"?** ¿Cómo se dice «sombrero» en francés? **F. spoken,** Se habla francés. **F. bean,** judía, f. **F. chalk,** jabón de sastre, m. **F. horn,** trompa, f. **F. lesson,** lección de francés, f. **F. marigold,** flor del estudiante, f. **F. polish,** barniz de muebles, m. **F. poodle,** perro (-rra) de aguas. **F. roll,** panecillo, m. **F. window,** puerta ventana, f

**Frenchify** /'frentʃə,fai/ vt afrancesar

**Frenchman** /'frentʃmən/ n francés, m. **a young F.,** un joven francés

**Frenchwoman** /'frentʃ,wumən/ n francesa, mujer francesa, f. **a young F.,** una joven francesa, una muchacha francesa, f

**frenzied** /'frenzid/ a frenético

**frenzy** /'frenzi/ n frenesí, delirio, paroxismo, m

**frequency** /'frikwənsi/ n frecuencia, f. **high f.,** alta frecuencia, f. **low f.,** baja frecuencia, f

**frequent** /'frikwənt/ v fri'kwent/ a frecuente; (usual) común, corriente. —vt frecuentar

**frequentation** /,frikwən'teiʃən/ n frecuentación, f

**frequenter** /'frikwəntər/ n frecuentador (-ra)

**frequently** /'frikwəntli/ adv frecuentemente, con frecuencia, muchas veces; comúnmente

**fresco** /'freskou/ n Art. fresco, m, pintura al fresco, f. —vt pintar al fresco

**fresh** /freʃ/ a fresco; nuevo; reciente; (newly arrived) recién llegado; (inexperienced) inexperto, bisoño; (of water, not salt) dulce; puro; (healthy) sano; (brisk) vigoroso, enérgico; (vivid) vivo, vívido; (bright) brillante; (cheeky) fresco. —adv neuvamente, recién (with past participle). **He came to us f. from school,** Vino a nosotros recién salido de su colegio. **We are going to take the f. air,** Vamos a tomar el fresco. **The milk is not f.,** La leche no está fresca. **f.-complexioned,** de buenos colores. **f. news,** noticias nuevas, f pl. **f. troops,** tropas nuevas, f pl, (reinforcements) tropas de refuerzo, f pl. **f. water,** agua fresca, f; (not salt) agua dulce, f. **f. wind,** viento fresco, m

**freshen** /'freʃən/ vt refrescar; (remove salt) desalar. —vi (wind) refrescar. **to f. up,** renovar; refrescar; (of dress, etc.) arreglar

**freshly** /'freʃli/ adv nuevamente; recientemente

**freshness** /'freʃnɪs/ n frescura, f; (newness) novedad, f; (vividness, brightness) intensidad, f; pureza, f; (beauty) lozanía, hermosura, f; (cheek) frescura, f, descaro, m

**freshwater** /'freʃ,wɔtər/ n agua dulce, f. **f. sailor,** marinero de agua dulce, m

**fret** /fret/ n agitación, f; ansiedad, preocupación, f; Archit. greca, f; (of stringed instrument) traste, m. —vt roer; (of a horse) bocezar; (corrode) desgastar, corroer; (of the wind, etc.) rizar; (worry) tener preocupado (a); irritar, enojar; (lose) perder; (oneself) apurarse, consumirse; Archit. calar. —vi torturarse, preocuparse, inquietarse; (complain) quejarse; (mourn) lamentarse, estar triste

**fretful** /'fretfəl/ a mal humorado, mohíno, quejoso, irritable

**fretfully** /'fretfəli/ adv irritablemente, con mal humor

**fretwork** /'fret,wɜrk/ n calado, m

**Freudian** /'frɔidiən/ a freudiano

**friar** /'fraiər/ n fraile, m. **Black f.,** dominicano, m. **Gray f.,** franciscano, m. **White f.,** carmelita, m. **f.-like,** frailesco

**friction** /'frikʃən/ n frote, frotamiento, roce, m; Phys. rozamiento, m; fricción, f. **to give a f.,** friccionar, dar fricciones (a). **f. gearing,** engranaje de fricción, m. **f. glove,** guante de fricciones, m

**Friday** /'fraidei/ n viernes, m. **Good F.,** Viernes Santo, m

**fried** /fraid/ a frito. **f. egg,** huevo frito, m

**friend** /frend/ n amigo (-ga); (acquaintance) conocido (-da); (Quaker) cuáquero (-ra); (follower) adherente, m; partidario (-ia); (ally) aliado (-da); pl **friends,** amistades, f pl; amigos, m pl. **a f. of yours,** un amigo tuyo, uno de tus amigos. **to make friends,** hacer amigos; (become friends) hacerse amigos; (after a quarrel) hacer las paces. **Friends!** (to sentinel) ¡Gente de paz!

**friendless** /'frendlɪs/ a sin amigos; desamparado

**friendliness** /'frendlinɪs/ n amabilidad, afabilidad, cordialidad, amigabilidad, f

**friendly** /'frendli/ a amistoso, amigable, amigo; afable, acogedor, simpático; propicio, favorable. **to be f. with,** ser amigo de. **f. society,** sociedad de socorros, f

**friendship** /'frendʃip/ n amistad, intimidad, f

**Friesland** /'frizlənd/ Frisia, f

**frieze** /friz/ n friso, m; (cloth) frisa, jerga, f

**frigate** /'frɪgɪt/ n Nav. fragata, f

**fright** /frait/ n terror, susto, m; (guy) espantajo, m. —vt asustar. **to have a f.,** tener un susto. **to take f.,** asustarse

**frighten** /'fraitn/ vt espantar, dar un susto (a), alarmar, asustar; horrorizar; (overawe) acobardar. **to be frightened out of one's wits,** estar muerto de miedo. **to f. away,** ahuyentar, espantar

**frightened** /'fraitnd/ a miedoso, tímido, medroso, nervioso

**frightening** /'fraitnɪŋ/ a que da miedo; alarmante, amedrentador; horrible

**frightful** /'fraitfəl/ a horrible, espantoso, horroroso; Inf. tremendo, enorme

**frightfully** /'fraitfəli/ adv horrorosamente; Inf. enormemente

**frigid** /'frɪdʒɪd/ a frío; helado; Med. impotente

**frigidity** /frɪ'dʒɪdɪti/ n frialdad, frigidez, f; Med. impotencia, f

**frigidly** /'frɪdʒɪdli/ adv fríamente

**frill** /frɪl/ n Sew. volante, m; (jabot) chorrera, f; (round a bird's neck) collarín de plumas, m; (of paper) frunce, m. —vt alechugar; fruncir

**fringe** /frɪndʒ/ n fleco, m, franja, f; (of hair) flequillo, m; (edge) borde, m, margen, mf. —vt guarnecer con fleco, franjar; adornar; (grow by) crecer al margen (de)

**Frisian** /'frɪʒən/ a and n frisón (-ona); (language) frisón, m

**frisk** /frɪsk/ vi retozar, brincar

**friskiness** /'frɪskinɪs/ n viveza, agilidad, f

**frisky** /'frɪski/ a retozón, juguetón

**fritter** /'frɪtər/ n Cul. fruta de sartén, f. —vt (away) malgastar, desperdiciar; perder

**frivolity** /frɪ'vɒlɪti/ n frivolidad, ligereza, f; futilidad, f

**frivolous** /'frɪvələs/ a frívolo, ligero, liviano; (futile) trivial, fútil

**frizz** /frɪz/ vt (cloth) frisar; (hair) rizar

**frizzy** /'frɪzɪ/ a (of hair) crespo, rizado

**fro** /frou/ adv hacia atrás. **movement to and fro,** vaivén, m. **to and fro,** de un lado a otro. **to go to and fro,** ir y venir

**frock** /frɒk/ n vestido, m; (of a monk) hábito, m; (of priest) sotana, f. **f.-coat,** levita, f

**frog** /frɒg/ n rana, f. **to have a f. in the throat,** padecer carraspera

**frolic** /'frɒlɪk/ n (play) juego, m; (mischief) travesura, f; (folly) locura, extravagancia, f; (joke) chanza, f; (amusement) diversión, f; (wild party) holgorio, m, parranda, f. —vi retozar, juguetear; divertirse

**frolicsome** /'frɒlɪksəm/ a retozón, juguetón

**from** /frʌm, frɒm; unstressed frəm/ prep de; desde; (according to) según; (in the name of, on behalf of) de parte de; (through, by) por; (beginning on) a contar de; (with) con; **F.** (on envelope) Remite, Remitente. **He is coming here f. the dentist's,** Vendrá aquí desde de casa del dentista. **Give him this message f. me,** Dale este recado de mi parte. **Judging f. his appearance,** Juzgando por su apariencia. **prices f. five hundred pesetas upward,** precios desde quinientos pesetas en adelante. **f. what I hear,** según mi información, según lo que oigo. **f. above,** desde arriba. **f. among,** de entre. **f. afar,** de lejos, desde lejos. **f. time to time,** de cuando en cuando, de vez en cuando

**frond** /frɒnd/ n Bot. fronda, f

**front** /frʌnt/ n frente, f; cara, f; Mil. frente, m; (battle line) línea de combate, f; (of a building) fachada, f; (of shirt) pechera, f; (at the seaside) playa, f; (promenade) paseo de la playa, m; (forefront) primera línea, f; (forepart) parte delantera, f; Theat. auditorio, m; (organization) organización de fachada, f; (impudence) descaro, m, a delantero; anterior; de frente; primero. —adv hacia delante. —vi mirar a, dar a; hacer frente a. **in f.,** en frente. **in f. of,** en frente de; (in the presence of) delante de, en la presencia de. **to face f.,** hacer frente. **to put on a bold f.,** hacer de tripas corazón. **f. door,** puerta de entrada, puerta principal, f. **f. line,** Mil. línea del frente, f; primera línea, f. **f. seat,** (at an entertainment, etc.) delantera, f. **f. organization** organización de fachada, f. **f. tooth,** diente incisivo, m. **f. view,** vista de frente, f; vista de cerca, f

**frontage** /'frʌntɪdʒ/ n (of a building) fachada, f; (site) terreno de... metros de fachada, m

**frontal** /'frʌntl/ a Mil. de frente; Anat. frontal

**frontier** /frʌn'tɪər/ n frontera, f; Fig. límite, m. —a fronterizo

**frontispiece** /'frʌntɪsˌpis/ n (of a building) frontispicio, m, fachada, f; (of a book) portada, f

**frontless** /'frʌntlɪs/ a sin frente

**frost** /frɒst/ n escarcha, f; helada, f. —vt helar; Cul. escarchar; (glass) deslustrar; Fig. escarchar. —vi helar. **f.-bitten,** helado

**frostbite** /'frɒstˌbaɪt/ n efectos del frío, m pl

**frosted** /'frɒstɪd/ a escarchado; helado; (of glass) deslustrado, opaco; Cul. escarchado

**frostily** /'frɒstəli/ adv Fig. glacialmente, con frialdad.

**frostiness** /'frɒstɪnɪs/ n; frío glacial, m

**frosting** /'frɒstɪŋ/ n escarcha, f; (of glass) deslustre, m; Cul. cobertura, escarcha, f

**frosty** /'frɒsti/ a helado; de hielo; (of hair) canoso; Fig. glacial, frío. **It was f. last night,** Anoche heló

**froth** /frɒθ/ n espuma, f; Fig. frivolidad, vanidad, f, vi espumar, hacer espuma; echar espuma. —vt hacer espumar; hacer echar espuma

**frothiness** /'frɒθɪnɪs/ n espumosidad, f; Fig. frivolidad, superficialidad, vaciedad, f

**frothy** /'frɒθi/ a espumoso, espumajoso; Fig. frívolo, superficial

**frown** /fraun/ n ceño, m; cara de juez, expresión severa, f; desaprobación, f; (of fortune) revés, golpe, m. —vi fruncir el ceño. **to f. at, on, upon,** mirar con desaprobación, ver con malos ojos; ser enemigo de; desaprobar

**frowning** /'fraunɪŋ/ a ceñudo; severo; amenazador

**frowningly** /'fraunɪŋli/ adv severamente

**frowsiness** /'frauzɪnɪs/ n mal olor, m; (dirtiness) suciedad, f; (untidiness) desaliño, desaseo, m

**frowsy** /'frauzi/ a fétido, mal oliente; mal ventilado; (dirty) sucio; (untidy) desaliñado, desaseado

**frozen** /'frouzən/ a helado; cubierto de hielo; congelado; (Geog. and Fig.) glacial. **to be f. up,** estar helado. **f. meat,** carne congelada, f

**frugal** /'frugəl/ a económico; frugal; sobrio

**frugality** /fru'gælɪti/ n economía, f; frugalidad, sobriedad, f

**fruit** /frut/ n (in general sense) fruto, m; (off a tree or bush) fruta, f; Fig. fruto, m; resultado, m, consecuencia, f. —vi frutar, dar fruto. **bottled f.,** fruta en almíbar, f. **candied f.,** fruta azucarada, f. **dried f.,** fruta seca, f. **first fruits,** primicias, f pl. **soft f.,** frutas blandas, f pl. **stone f.,** fruta de hueso, f. **f.-bearing,** frutal. **f.-cake,** pastel de fruta, m. **f.-dish,** frutero, m. **f. farming,** fruticultura, f. **f.-knife,** cuchillo de postres, m. **f. shop,** frutería, f. **f. tree,** frutal, m

**fruiterer** /'frutərər/ n frutero (-ra)

**fruitful** /'frutfəl/ a fructuoso, fértil; prolífico, fecundo; provechoso

**fruitfulness** /'frutfəlnɪs/ n fertilidad, f; fecundidad, f; provecho, m

**fruition** /fru'ɪʃən/ n fruición, f

**fruitless** /'frutlɪs/ a infructuoso, estéril; inútil

**fruitlessness** /'frutlɪsnɪs/ n infructuosidad, esterilidad, f; inutilidad, f

**fruity** /'fruti/ a de fruta; (wines) vinoso; (of voice) melodioso

**frump** /frʌmp/ n estantigua, f

**frumpish** /'frʌmpɪʃ/ a estrafalario; fuera de moda

**frustrate** /'frʌstreit/ vt frustrar; defraudar; malograr; destruir; anular

**frustration** /frʌ'streiʃən/ n frustración, f; defraudación, f; malogro, m; destrucción, f; desengaño, m

**fry** /frai/ n Cul. fritada, f, vt freír. —vi freírse. **small fry,** Inf. gente menuda, f

**frying** /'fraiɪŋ/ n fritura, f, el freír. **to fall out of the f.-pan into the fire,** ir de mal en peor, andar de zocos en colodros, ir de Guatemala en Guatepeor. **f.-pan,** sartén, f

**fuchsia** /'fyuʃə/ n Bot. fuscia, f

**fuddle** /'fʌdl/ vt atontar, aturdir; embriagar, emborrachar

**fudge** /fʌdʒ/ n patraña, tontería, f, disparate, m. —interj ¡qué disparate! ¡qué va!

**fuel** /'fyuəl/ n combustible, m; Fig. cebo, pábulo, m. —vt cebar, echar combustible en. —vi tomar combustible. **to add f. to the flame,** echar leña al fuego. **f. consumption,** consumo de combustible, m. **f.-oil,** aceite combustible, aceite de quemar, m. **f.-tank,** depósito de combustible, m

**fueling** /'fyuəlɪŋ/ n aprovisionamiento de combustible, m

**fugitive** /'fyudʒɪtɪv/ a fugitivo; pasajero, perecedero; transitorio, efímero, fugaz. —n fugitivo (-va); (from justice) prófugo (-ga); Mil. desertor, m; (refugee) refugiado (-da)

**fugue** /fyug/ n Mus. fuga, f

**fulcrum** /'fʌlkrəm/ n Mech. fulcro, m

**fulfill** /fʊl'fɪl/ vt cumplir; (satisfy) satisfacer; (observe) observar; guardar. **to be fulfilled,** cumplirse, realizarse

**fulfillment** /fʊl'fɪlmənt/ n cumplimiento, m; desempeño, ejercicio, m; (satisfaction) satisfacción, realización, f; (observance) observancia, f

**full** /fʊl/ a lleno; colmado; todo; pleno; (crowded) atestado; (replete) harto; abundante; (intent on) preocupado con, pensando en; (loose) amplio; (plentiful) copioso; (occupied) ocupado; completo; (resonant) sonoro; (mature) maduro; puro; perfecto; (satiated) saciado (de); (of the moon, sails) lleno; (weighed down) agobiado, abrumado; (detailed) detallado; (with uniform, etc.) de gala; (with years, etc.) cumplido. —n colmo, m; totalidad, f. —adv muy; completamente, totalmente. **f. many a flower,** muchas flores. **at f. gallop,** a galope tendido. **at f. speed,** a todo correr; a toda velocidad. **His hands are f.,** Sus manos están llenas. **The moon was at the f.,** La luna estaba llena. **in f.,** por completo; sin abreviaciones; integralmente. **in f. swing,** en plena actividad. **in f.**

**vigor,** en pleno vigor. **to the f.,** completamente; hasta la última gota; a la perfección. **to be f. to the brim,** estar lleno hasta el tope. **f.-blooded,** sanguíneo; de pura raza; *Fig.* viril, vigoroso; *Fig.* apasionado. **f.-blown,** en plena flor, abierto. **f. dress,** a de gala. —*n* traje de etiqueta, traje de ceremonia, *m.* **f.-face,** de cara. **f.-flavored,** (wine) abocado. **f.-grown,** adulto; completamente desarrollado. **f.-length,** de cuerpo entero. **f. moon,** luna llena, *f;* plenilunio, *m.* **f. name,** nombre y apellidos, *m.* **f. powers,** plenos poderes, *m pl.* **f. scale,** tamaño natural, *m.* **f. scope,** carta blanca, *f;* toda clase de facilidades. **f. steam ahead,** a todo vapor. **f. stop,** *Gram.* punto final, *m*

**full** /fʊl/ *vt* (cloth) abatanar

**full-color** /'fʊl 'kʌlər/ *a* a todo color. **full-color plates,** láminas a todo color

**fuller** /'fʊlər/ *n* batanero, *m.* **fuller's earth,** tierra de batán, galactita, *f*

**fulling** /'fʊlɪŋ/ *n* abatanadura, *f.* **f.-mill,** batán, *m*

**fullness** /'fʊlnɪs/ *n* abundancia, *f;* plenitud, *f;* (repletion) hartura, *f;* (of clothes) amplitud, *f;* (stoutness) gordura, *f;* (swelling) hinchazón, *f.* **She wrote with great f. of all that she had seen,** Describía muy detalladamente todo lo que había visto. **in the f. of time,** andando el tiempo

**full-page** /fʊl 'peɪdʒ/ *a* a toda plana. **full-page advertisement,** anuncio a toda plana.

**full-time** /fʊl 'taɪm/ *a* de tiempo completo

**fully** /'fʊli/ *adv* plenamente; enteramente. **It is f. six years since...,** Hace seis años bien cumplidos que... **It is f. 9 o'clock,** Son las nueve bien sonadas. **f. dressed,** completamente vestido

**fulminant** /'fʌlmənənt/ *a Med.* fulminante

**fulminate** /'fʌlmə,neɪt/ *n Chem.* fulminato, *m.* —*vi* estallar; fulminar. —*vt* volar; fulminar

**fulminous** /'fʌlmənəs/ *a* fulmíneo, fulminoso

**fulsome** /'fʊlsəm/ *a* servil; insincero, hipócrita; asqueroso, repugnante

**fumble** /'fʌmbəl/ *vi* (grope) ir a tientas; procurar hacer algo; chapucear (con); (for a word) titubear

**fumbling** /'fʌmblɪŋ/ *n* hesitación, *f;* tacto incierto, *m.* —*a* incierto; vacilante

**fumblingly** /'fʌmblɪŋli/ *adv* de manera incierta; a tientas

**fume** /fyum/ *n* vaho, humo, gas, *m;* emanación, *f;* mal olor, *m,* fetidez, *f; Fig.* vapor, *m;* (state of mind) agitación, *f;* frenesí, *m.* —*vi* humear; refunfuñar, echar pestes

**fumigate** /'fyumɪ,geɪt/ *vt* fumigar; sahumar, perfumar; desinfectar

**fumigation** /,fyumə'geɪʃən/ *n* fumigación, *f;* sahumerio, *m*

**fumigator** /'fyumɪ,geɪtər/ *n* fumigador (-ra); (apparatus) fumigador, *m*

**fumigatory** /'fyuməgə,tɔri/ *a* fumigatorio

**fuming** /'fyumɪŋ/ *n* refunfuño, *m.* —*a* refunfuñador

**fumy** /'fyumi/ *a* humoso

**fun** /fʌn/ *n* diversión, *f,* entretenimiento, *m;* (joke) chanza, broma, *f.* **for fun,** para divertirse; en chanza. **in fun,** de burlas. **to have fun,** divertirse. **to poke fun at,** burlarse de, mofarse de, ridiculizar

**funambulist** /fyu'næmbyəlɪst/ *n* funámbulo (-la)

**function** /'fʌŋkʃən/ *n* función, *f.* —*vi* funcionar

**functional** /'fʌŋkʃənl/ *a* funcional

**functionary** /'fʌŋkʃə,nɛri/ *n* funcionario, *m.* —*a* funcional

**functioning** /'fʌŋkʃənɪŋ/ *n* funcionamiento, *m*

**fund** /fʌnd/ *n* fondo, *m; pl* **funds,** fondos, *m pl; Inf.* dinero, *m.* **public funds,** fondos públicos, *m pl.* **sinking f.,** fondo de amortización, *m*

**fundamental** /,fʌndə'mɛntl/ *a* fundamental, básico; esencial. —*n* fundamento, *m*

**fundamentally** /,fʌndə'mɛntli/ *adv* fundamentalmente, básicamente; esencialmente

**funeral** /'fyunərəl/ *a* funeral, fúnebre, funerario. —*n* funerales, *m pl;* entierro, *m.* **to attend the f. ( of),** asistir a los funerales (de). **f. feast,** banquetes fúnebres, *m pl.* **f. director, f. furnisher,** director de pompas fúnebres, *m.* **f. procession,** cortejo fúnebre, *m.* **f. pyre,** pira funeraria, *f.* **f. service,** misa de difuntos, *f*

**funereal** /fyu'nɪəriəl/ *a* fúnebre, lúgubre

**fungicide** /'fʌndʒə,saɪd/ *n* anticriptógamo, *m*

**fungous** /'fʌŋgəs/ *a* fungoso

**fungus** /'fʌŋgəs/ *n* hongo, *m*

**funicular** /fyu'nɪkyələr/ *a* funicular. **f. railway,** ferrocarril funicular, *m*

**funnel** /'fʌnl/ *n Chem.* embudo, *m; Naut.* chimenea, *f;* (of a chimney) cañón (de chimenea), *m.* **f.-shaped,** en forma de embudo

**funnily** /'fʌnli/ *adv* de un modo raro

**funniness** /'fʌnɪnɪs/ *n* lo divertido; rareza, extrañeza, *f*

**funny** /'fʌni/ *a* cómico, gracioso; divertido; (strange) extraño, raro; (mysterious) misterioso. **It struck me as f.,** (amused me) Me hizo gracia; (seemed strange) Me pareció raro. **f.-bone,** hueso de la alegría, *m*

**fur** /fɜr/ *n* piel, *f;* depósito, sarro, *m;* (on tongue) saburra, *f.* —*a* hecho de pieles. —*vt* forrar, o adornar, or cubrir, con pieles; depositar sarro sobre; (the tongue) ensuciarse la lengua. —*vi* estar forrado, or adornado, or cubierto, con pieles; formarse incrustaciones; (of the tongue) tener la lengua sucia. **fur cap,** gorra de pieles, *f.* **fur cape,** cuello de piel, *m;* capa de pieles, *f.* **fur trade,** peletería, *f*

**furbish** /'fɜrbɪʃ/ *vt* pulir; renovar; limpiar

**furious** /'fyʊriəs/ *a* furioso. **to become f.,** ponerse furioso, enfurecerse

**furiously** /'fyʊriəsli/ *adv* furiosamente, con furia

**furiousness** /'fyʊriəsnɪs/ *n* furia, *f*

**furl** /fɜrl/ *vt* plegar; enrollar; *Naut.* aferrar

**furlong** /'fɜrlɔŋ/ *n* estadio, *m*

**furlough** /'fɜrloʊ/ *n Mil.* permiso, *m.* —*vt* conceder un permiso (a). **on f.,** de permiso

**furnace** /'fɜrnɪs/ *n* horno, *m;* (of steam boiler) fogón, *m;* (for central heating) caldera de calefacción central, *f;* (for smelting) cubilote, *m*

**furnish** /'fɜrnɪʃ/ *vt* proveer (de), equipar (de), suplir (de); amueblar; (an opportunity) proporcionar; producir

**furnished** /'fɜrnɪʃt/ *a* amueblado, con muebles. **f. house,** casa amueblada, *f*

**furnisher** /'fɜrnɪʃər/ *n* decorador, *m;* proveedor (-ra)

**furnishing** /'fɜrnɪʃɪŋ/ *n* provisión, *f,* equipo, *m; pl* **furnishings,** accesorios, *m pl;* mobiliario, mueblaje, *m*

**furniture** /'fɜrnɪtʃər/ *n* mobiliario, mueblaje, *m;* ajuar, equipo, *m;* avíos, *m pl; Naut.* aparejo, *m.* **a piece of f.,** un mueble. **to empty of f.,** desamueblar, quitar los muebles (de). **f. dealer** or **maker,** mueblista, *mf.* **f. factory,** mueblería, *f.* **f. polish,** crema para muebles, *f.* **f. mover,** transportador de muebles, *m;* (packer) embalador, *m.* **f. repository,** guardamuebles, *m.* **f. van,** carro de mudanzas, *m*

**furor** /'fyʊrɔr/ *n* furor, *m*

**furred** /fɜrd/ *a* forrado or cubierto or adornado de piel; (of the tongue) sucia

**furrier** /'fɜriər/ *n* peletero, *m.* **furrier's shop,** peletería, *f*

**furrow** /'fɜroʊ/ *n* surco, *m;* muesca, *f; Archit.* estría, *f;* (wrinkle) arruga, *f.* —*vt* surcar

**furry** /'fɜri/ *a* cubierto de piel; parecido a una piel; hecho de pieles

**further** /'fɜrðər/ *a* ulterior, más distante; (other) otro; opuesto; adicional, más. —*adv* más lejos; más allá; además; también; por añadidura. —*vt* promover, fomentar; ayudar. **on the f. side,** al otro lado. **till f. orders,** hasta nueva orden. **f. on,** más adelante; más allá

**furtherance** /'fɜrðərəns/ *n* fomento, *m,* promoción, *f;* progreso, avance, *m*

**furthermore** /'fɜrðər,mɔr/ *adv* además, por añadidura

**furthest** /'fɜrðɪst/ *a* (el, la, lo) más lejano or más distante; extremo. —*adv* más lejos

**furtive** /'fɜrtɪv/ *a* furtivo

**furtively** /'fɜrtɪvli/ *adv* furtivamente, a hurtadillas. **to look at f.,** mirar de reojo

**fury** /'fyʊri/ *n* furor, enfurecimiento, *m,* rabia, *f;* violencia, *f;* frenesí, arrebato, *m;* furia, *f.* **like a f.,** hecho una furia. **to breathe forth f.,** echar rayos

**fuse** /fyuz/ *n* (of explosives) espoleta, mecha, *f; Elec.* fusible, *m.* —*vt* (metals) fundir; fusionar, mezclar. —*vi* (metals) fundirse; mezclarse. **safety-f.,** espoleta de seguridad, *f.* **time-f.,** espoleta de tiempo, *f.* **to**

**fuzzy**

**blow a f.,** fundir un fusible. **f. box,** caja de fusibles, *f.* **f. wire,** fusible, *m*

**fuselage** /'fyusə,lɑʒ/ *n Aer.* fuselaje, *m*

**fusible** /'fyuzəbəl/ *a* fusible

**fusillade** /'fyusə,lɑd/ *n* descarga cerrada, *f*

**fusion** /'fyuʒən/ *n* fusión, *f;* unión, *f;* (melting) fundición, *f*

**fuss** /fʌs/ *n* agitación, *f;* (bustle) conmoción, bulla, *f;* bullicio, *m.* —*vi* agitarse, preocuparse. —*vt* poner nervioso. **There's no need to make such a f.,** No es para tanto. **to make a f. of,** (a person) hacer la rueda (a), ser muy atento (a); (spoil) mimar mucho (a). **to f. about,** andar de acá para allá

**fussily** /'fʌsəli/ *adv* nerviosamente; de un aire importante

**fussy** /'fʌsi/ *a* meticuloso, nimio; nervioso; (of style) florido, hinchado; (of dress) demasiado adornado

**fustigate** /'fʌstɪ,geit/ *vt* fustigar

**fusty** /'fʌsti/ *a* (moldy) mohoso; mal ventilado; mal oliente; (of views, etc.) pasado de moda

**futile** /'fyutḷ/ *a* fútil, superficial, frívolo; inútil

**futility** /fyu'tɪlɪti/ *n* futilidad, superficialidad, frivolidad, *f;* (action) tontería, estupidez, *f*

**future** /'fyutʃər/ *a* futuro, venidero. —*n* futuro, porvenir, *m.* **in the f.,** en adelante, en lo venidero, en lo sucesivo. **for f. reference,** para información futura. **f. perfect tense,** *Gram.* futuro perfecto, *m.* **f. tense,** *Gram.* futuro, *m*

**futurism** /'fyutʃə,rɪzəm/ *n* futurismo, *m*

**futurist** /'fyutʃərɪst/ *n* futurista, *mf*

**futuristic** /ˌfyutʃə'rɪstɪk/ *a* futurístico

**fuzz** /fʌz/ *n* tamo, *m*, pelusa, *f.* **f.-ball,** *Bot.* bejín, *m*

**fuzzy** /'fʌzi/ *a* crespo rizado; velloso

# G

**g** /dʒi/ n (letter) ge, f; Mus. sol, m. **G clef,** clave de sol, f

**gab** /gæb/ n Inf. labia, f. **to have the gift of the gab,** tener mucha labia

**gabardine** /ˈgæbərˌdin/ n gabardina, f

**gabble** /ˈgæbəl/ vi chacharear, garlar; hablar indistintamente; (of goose and some birds) graznar. —vt decir indistintamente; decir rápidamente; (a language) chapurrear; mascullar. —n cháchara, f; vocerío, m; (of goose and some birds) graznido, m

**gabbler** /ˈgæblər/ n charlatán (-ana), chacharero (-ra)

**gabbling** /ˈgæblɪŋ/ n See **gabble**

**gable** /ˈgeibəl/ n Archit. gablete, hastial, m. **g.-end,** alero, m

**gad** /gæd/ vi corretear, callejear. **to gad about,** correr por todos lados; divertirse.

**gadabout** /ˈgædəˌbaut/ n azotacalles, mf; gandul (-la), vagabundo (-da)

**gadding** /ˈgædɪŋ/ a callejero; vagabundo. —n vagancia, f; vida errante, f; gandulería, f

**gadfly** /ˈgædˌflai/ n Ent. tábano, m; Inf. moscardón, m

**gadget** /ˈgædʒɪt/ n accesorio, m; aparato, m; chuchería, f

**Gadsden Purchase** /ˈgædzdən/ la Venta de la Meseta, f

**Gael** /geil/ n escocés (-esa) del norte; celta, mf

**Gaelic** /ˈgeilɪk/ a gaélico. —n gaélico, m

**gaff** /gæf/ n (hook) garfio, m; Naut. pico de cangrejo, m; Theat. teatrucho, m

**gaffer** /ˈgæfər/ n viejo, tío, abuelo, m

**gag** /gæg/ n mordaza, f; Theat. morcilla, f. —vt amordazar; Fig. hacer callar. —vi Theat. meter morcillas

**gage** /geidʒ/ n prenda, fianza, f; (symbol of challenge) guante, m; (challenge) desafío, m. See **gauge**

**gagging** /ˈgægɪŋ/ n amordazamiento, m

**gaggle** /ˈgægəl/ n (cry) graznido, m; (of geese) manada (de ocas), f. —vi graznar; cacarear

**gaiety** /ˈgeiti/ n alegría, f; animación, vivacidad, f; (entertainment) diversión, festividad, f

**gaily** /ˈgeili/ adv alegremente

**gain** /gein/ n ganancia, f; provecho, beneficio, m; (increase) aumento, m; (riches) riqueza, f. —vt ganar; (acquire) conseguir; adquirir; obtener; conquistar; (friends) hacerse; (reach) llegar a, alcanzar. —vi ganar; (improve) mejorar; (of a watch) adelantarse. **What have they gained by going to Canada?** ¿Qué han logrado con marcharse al Canadá? **to g. ground,** Fig. ganar terreno. **to g. momentum** adquirir velocidad **to g. time,** ganar tiempo. **to g. on, upon,** acercarse a; (overtake) alcanzar; (outstrip) dejar atrás, pasar; (of sea) invadir; (of habits) imponerse

**gainful** /ˈgeinfəl/ a gananciso, lucrativo; ventajoso

**gainfully** /ˈgeinfəli/ adv ventajosamente; lucrativamente

**gainsay** /ˈgeinˌsei/ vt contradecir; oponer; negar

**gainsaying** /ˈgeinˌseiɪŋ/ n contradicción, f; oposición, f; negación, f

**gait** /geit/ n porte, andar, m; paso, m, andadura, f

**gaiter** /ˈgeitər/ n polaina, f; (spat) botín, m

**gala** /ˈgeilə/ n gala, fiesta, f. **g.-day.** día de fiesta, m. **g.-dress,** traje de gala, m

**galaxy** /ˈgæləksi/ n Astron. vía láctea, f; Fig. constelación, f; grupo brillante, m

**gale** /geil/ n vendaval, ventarrón, m; (storm) temporal, m; tempestad, f

**Galician** /gəˈlɪʃən/ a and n gallego (-ga).

**Galilean** /ˌgæləˈleiən/ a and n galileo (-ea)

**Galilee** /ˈgæləˌli/ Galilea, f

**gall** /gɔl/ n (on horses) matadura, f; (abrasion) rozadura, f; hiel, bilis, f; Fig. hiel, amargura, f; rencor, m; (American slang) descaro, m, impertinencia, f; Bot. agalla, f. —vt rozar; Fig. mortificar, herir. **g.-apple,**

---

agalla, f. **g.-bladder,** vejiga de la hiel, f. **g.-stone,** cálculo hepático, m

**gallant** /ˈgælənt, gəˈlænt, -ˈlɑnt/ a hermoso; (imposing) imponente, majestuoso; (brave) valiente, gallardo, valeroso, intrépido; (chivalrous) caballeroso; noble; (attentive to ladies, or amorous) galante. —n galán, m. —vt galantear, cortejar

**gallantly** /ˈgæləntli/ adv (bravely) valientemente; caballerosamente; cortésmente; galantemente

**gallantry** /ˈgæləntri/ n (bravery) valentía, f, valor, m; heroísmo, m, proeza, f; (chivalry) caballerosidad, f; (toward women, or amorousness) galantería, f

**galleon** /ˈgæliən/ n galeón, m

**gallery** /ˈgæləri/ n galería, f; pasillo, m; (of a cloister) tránsito, m; (cloister) claustro, m; (for spectators) tribuna, f; Theat. paraíso, gallinero, m; (theater audience) galería, f; (of portraits, etc.) galería, colección, f; (Mineral., Mil.) galería, f; (building) museo, m. **art g.,** museo de pinturas, m

**galley** /ˈgæli/ n (Naut., Print.) galera, f; (kitchen) cocina, f; (rowboat) falúa de capitán, f. **to condemn to the galleys,** echar a galeras. **wooden g.,** Print. galerín, m. **g.-proof,** galerada, f. **g.-slave,** galeote, m

**Gallic** /ˈgælik/ a gálico, galicano; francés

**gallicism** /ˈgælɪsɪzəm/ n galicismo, m

**galling** /ˈgɔliŋ/ a Fig. irritante; mortificante

**gallivant** /ˈgæləˌvænt/ vi callejear, corretear; divertirse; ir de parranda

**gallon** /ˈgælən/ n galón, m

**galloon** /gəˈlun/ n galón, m, trencilla, f

**gallop** /ˈgæləp/ n galope, m. —vi galopar; ir aprisa. —vt hacer galopar, **at full g.,** a rienda suelta, a galope tendido. **to g. back,** volver al galope. **to g. down,** bajar a galope. **to g. off,** marcharse galopando; alejarse corriendo. **to g. past,** desfilar a galope ante. **to g. through,** cruzar a galope. **to g. up,** vt subir a galope. —vi llegar a galope

**gallopade** /ˌgæləˈpeid/ n (dance) galop, m

**galloping** /ˈgæləpɪŋ/ n galope, m; galopada, f. —a que va a galope; Med. galopante. **g. consumption,** tisis galopante, f

**gallows** /ˈgælouz/ n patíbulo, m, horca, f; (framework) montante, m. **g.-bird,** criminal digno de la horca, m

**galop** /ˈgæləp/ n galop, m

**galore** /gəˈlɔr/ adv a granel, en abundancia (e.g. sunshine galore, sol a granel)

**galosh** /gəˈlɒʃ/ n chanclo, m

**galvanic** /gælˈvænɪk/ a Elec. galvánico; espasmódico

**galvanism** /ˈgælvəˌnɪzəm/ n Elec. galvanismo, m

**galvanize** /ˈgælvəˌnaiz/ vt galvanizar

**gambit** /ˈgæmbɪt/ n (chess) gambito, m; Fig. táctica, f

**gamble** /ˈgæmbəl/ n juego de azar, m; jugada, f; aventura, f; Com. especulación, f. —vi jugar por dinero; especular; (with) Fig. aventurar, arriesgar. **to g. on the Stock Exchange,** jugar en la bolsa. **to g. away,** perder al juego

**gambler** /ˈgæmblər/ n jugador (-ra)

**gambling** /ˈgæmblɪŋ/ n juego, m. —a jugador; de juego. **g.-den,** casa de juego, f, garito, m

**gambol** /ˈgæmbəl/ n salto, brinco, retozo, m; cabriola, f; juego, m. —vi saltar, brincar, retozar; juguetear

**game** /geim/ n juego, m; (match) partido, m; (jest) chanza, f; (trick) trampa, f; (birds, hares, etc.) caza menor, f; (tigers, lions, etc.) caza mayor, f; (flesh of game) caza, f; pl **games,** deportes, m pl. —a de caza; (courageous) valiente, animoso, brioso; resuelto. —vi jugar por dinero. **He is g. for anything,** Se atreve a todo. **big g. hunting,** caza mayor, f. **head of g.,** pieza de caza, f. **It is a g. at which two can play,** Donde las dan las toman. **The g. is not worth the candle,** La cosa no vale la pena. **The g. is up,** Fig. El proyecto se ha frustrado. **to make g. of,** (things) burlarse de; (persons) tomar el pelo a; mofarse de. **to**

**play the g.,** *Fig.* jugar limpio. **to g. away,** perder al juego. **g. of cards,** juego de naipes, *m.* **g. of chance,** juego de azar, *m.* **g.-bag,** morral, *m.* **g. drive,** batida de caza, *f.* **g.-laws,** leyes de caza, *f pl.* **g.-licence,** licencia de caza, *f.* **g.-pie,** tortada, *f.* **g. preserve,** coto de caza, *m*

**gamekeeper** /'geim,kipər/ *n* guardabosque, *m*

**gamely** /'geimli/ *adv* valientemente

**gameness** /'geimnis/ *n* valentía, resolución, fortaleza, *f*

**gamete** /'gæmit/ *n* gameto, *m*

**gaming** /'geimiŋ/ *n* juego, *m, a* de juego. **g.-house,** garito, *m.* **g.-table,** mesa de juego, *f; Fig.* juego, *m*

**gammon** /'gæmən/ *n* (of bacon) jamón, *m.* —*vt* curar (jamón)

**gamut** /'gæmət/ *n* gama, *f*

**gander** /'gændər/ *n* ganso, *m*

**gang** /gæŋ/ *n* cuadrilla, pandilla, *f;* (squad) pelotón, *m;* (of workers) brigada, cuadrilla, *f;* group, *m.* **g.-plank,** plancha, *f*

**ganglion** /'gæŋgliən/ *n* ganglio, *m; Fig.* centro, *m*

**gangrene** /'gæŋgrin/ *n* gangrena, *f.* —*vt* gangrenar. —*vi* gangrenarse

**gangrenous** /'gæŋgrinəs/ *a* gangrenoso

**gangster** /'gæŋstər/ *n* pistolero, gángster, *m*

**gangway** /'gæŋ,wei/ *n* pasillo, *m; Naut.* plancha, *f,* pasamano, *m;* (opening in ship's side) portalón, *m.* **midship g.,** crujía, *f*

**gap** /gæp/ *n* brecha, *f;* abertura, *f;* (hole) boquete, *m;* (pass) desfiladero, paso, *m;* (ravine) hondonada, barranca, *f;* (blank) laguna, *f,* vacío, *m;* (crack) intersticio, *m,* hendedura, *f,* resquicio, *m.* **to fill a gap,** llenar un boquete; llenar un vacío

**gape** /geip/ *vi* estar con la boca abierta, papar moscas. **to g. at,** mirar con la boca abierta

**gaping** /'geipiŋ/ *n* huelgo, *m;* abertura, *f, a* que bosteza; boquiabierto; abierto

**garage** /gə'rɑʒ/ *n* garaje, *m.* —*vt* poner (un coche, etc.) en un garaje. **g. owner,** garajista, *mf*

**garb** /gɑrb/ *n* traje, vestido, *m;* uniforme, *m; Herald.* espiga, *f.* —*vt* vestir, ataviar

**garbage** /'gɑrbidʒ/ *n* basura, inmundicia, *f*

**garbage can** basurero, tarro de la basura, *m*

**garble** /'gɑrbəl/ *vt* falsear, mutilar, pervertir

**garden** /'gɑrdn/ *n* jardín, *m;* huerto, *m;* (fertile region) huerta, *f.* —*a* de jardín. —*vi* trabajar en el jardín, cultivar un huerto. **g. city,** ciudad jardín, *f.* **g.-frame,** semillero, *m.* **g. mold,** tierra vegetal, *f.* **g.-party,** fiesta de jardín, *f.* **g.-plot,** parterre, *m.* **g. produce,** hortalizas, legumbres, *f pl.* **g. roller,** rodillo, *m.* **g.-seat,** banco de jardín, *m.* **g. urn,** jarrón, *m*

**gardener** /'gɑrdnər/ *n* jardinero, *m*

**gardenia** /gɑr'dinyə/ *n* gardenia, *f,* jazmín de la India, *m*

**gardening** /'gɑrdniŋ/ *n* jardinería, *f;* horticultura, *f.* —*a* de jardinería

**gargantuan** /gɑr'gæntʃuən/ *a* gargantuesco; tremendo, enorme

**gargle** /'gɑrgəl/ *n* (liquid) gargarismo, *f;* gárgaras, *f pl.* —*vi* hacer gárgaras, gargarizar

**gargling** /'gɑrgliŋ/ *n* gargarismo, *m*

**gargoyle** /'gɑrgɔil/ *n* gárgola, *f*

**garish** /'gɛərɪʃ/ *a* cursi, llamativo, charro, chillón

**garishness** /'gɛərɪʃnɪs/ *n* cursería, ostentación, *f,* lo llamativo

**garland** /'gɑrlənd/ *n* guirnalda, *f;* corona, *f;* (anthology) florilegio, *m; Archit.* festón, *m.* —*vt* enguirnaldar

**garlic** /'gɑrlɪk/ *n* ajo, *m*

**garment** /'gɑrmənt/ *n* prenda de vestir, *f;* traje, vestido, *m; Fig.* vestidura, *f;* (Fig. cloak) capa, *f*

**garner** /'gɑrnər/ *n* granero, *m;* tesoro, *m;* colección, *f.* —*vt* atesorar, guardar

**garnet** /'gɑrnɪt/ *n* granate, *m*

**garnish** /'gɑrnɪʃ/ *n Cul.* aderezo, *m;* adorno, *m.* —*vt Cul.* aderezar; embellecer, adornar

**garnishing** /'gɑrnɪʃɪŋ/ *n.* See **garnish**

**garret** /'gærɪt/ *n* guardilla, buhardilla, *f,* desván, *m*

**garrison** /'gærəsən/ *n* guarnición, *f,* presidio, *m.* —*vt* guarnecer, presidiar. **g. town,** plaza de armas, *f*

**garrote** /gə'rɒt/ *n* garrote, *m.* —*vt* agarrotar, dar garrote (a)

**garrulity** /gə'rulɪti/ *n* garrulidad, locuacidad, charlatanería, *f*

**garrulous** /'gærələs/ *a* gárrulo, locuaz, charlatán

**garter** /'gɑrtər/ *n* liga, *f;* (G.) Jarretera, *f, vt* atar con liga; investir con la Jarretera. **Order of the G.,** Orden de la Jarretera, *f*

**gas** /gæs/ *n* gas, *m; Fig. Inf.* palabrería, *f;* (petrol) bencina, *f, a* de gas; con gas; para gases. —*vt* asfixiar con gas; *Mil.* atacar con gas; saturar de gas. **gas attack,** ataque con gases asfixiantes, *m.* **gas-bag,** bolsa de gas, *f; Inf.* charlatán (-ana). **gas-burner,** mechero de gas, *m.* **gas-chamber,** cámara de gas, *f.* **gas detector,** detector de gases, *m.* **gas-fire,** estufa de gas, *f.* **gas-fitter,** gasista, *m.* **gas-fittings,** lámparas de gas, *f pl.* **gas-light,** luz de gas, *f;* mechero de gas, *m.* **gas-main,** cañería maestra de gas, *f.* **gas-man,** gasista, *m.* **gas-mantle,** camiseta incandescente, *f.* **gas-mask,** máscara para gases, *f.* **gas-meter,** contador de gas, *m.* **gas-pipes,** cañerías (or tuberías) de gas, *f pl.* **gas-ring,** fogón de gas, *m.* **gas-shell,** obús de gases asfixiantes, *m.* **gas-stove,** cocina de gas, *f.* **gas warfare,** guerra química, *f.* **gas-works,** fábrica de gas, *f*

**Gascon** /'gæskən/ *a* and *n* gascón (-ona)

**Gascony** /'gæskəni/ Gascuña, *f*

**gaseous** /'gæsiəs/ *a* gaseoso

**gash** /gæʃ/ *n* cuchillada, *f;* herida extensa, *f.* —*vt* acuchillar; herir extensamente

**gasket** /'gæskɪt/ *n* aro de empaquetadura, *m*

**gasoline** /,gæsə'lin/ *n* gasolina, *f*

**gasp** /gæsp/ *n* boqueada, *f.* —*vi* boquear. **to be at the last g.,** estar agonizando. **to g. for breath,** luchar por respirar. **to g. out,** decir anhelante, decir con voz entrecortada

**gastric** /'gæstrɪk/ *a* gástrico

**gastritis** /gæ'straitis/ *n* gastritis, *f*

**gastronome** /'gæstrə,noum/ *n* gastrónomo (-ma)

**gastronomic** /,gæstrə'nɑmɪk/ *a* gastronómico

**gastronomy** /gæ'strɒnəmi/ *n* gastronomía, *f*

**gate** /geit/ *n* puerta, *f;* cancela, verja, *f;* entrada, *f;* (of a lock, etc.) compuerta, *f;* (across a road, etc.) barrera, *f;* (money) entrada, *f; Fig.* puerta, *f.* **automatic g.,** (at level crossings, etc.) barrera de golpe, *f.* **to g.-crash,** asistir sin invitación. **g.-keeper,** portero, *m;* guardabarrera, *mf* **g.-money,** entrada, *f.* **g.-post,** soporte de la puerta, *m*

**gateway** /'geit,wei/ *n* entrada, *f;* puerta, *f;* paso, *m;* vestíbulo, *m; Fig.* puerta, *f*

**gather** /'gæðər/ *vt* (assemble) reunir; (amass) acumular, amontonar; (acquire) obtener, adquirir; hacer una colección (de); cobrar; (harvest) cosechar, recolectar; (pick up) recoger; (pluck) coger; (infer) sacar en limpio, aprender; *Sew.* fruncir; (the brows) fruncir (el ceño). —*vi* reunirse, congregarse; amontonarse; (threaten) amenazar; (sadden) amargar; (Fig. hover over) cernerse (sobre); (increase) aumentar, crecer; (be covered) cubrirse; (fester) supurar. —*n Sew.* frunce, pliegue, *m.* **to g. breath,** tomar aliento. **to g. speed,** ganar velocidad. **to g. strength,** cobrar fuerzas. **I g. from Mary that they are going abroad,** Según lo que me ha dicho María, van al extranjero. **to g. in,** juntar; reunir; (harvest) cosechar; coger. **to g. together,** *vt* reunir. —*vi* reunirse. **to g. up,** recoger; coger; tomar; (one's limbs) encoger. **to g. up the threads,** *Fig.* recoger los hilos.

**gatherer** /'gæðərər/ *n* cogedor, colector, *m;* (harvester) segador, *m;* (of grapes) vendimiador (-ra); (of taxes) recaudador, *m*

**gathering** /'gæðəriŋ/ *n* cogedura, *f;* (fruit, etc.) recolección, *f;* (of taxes) recaudación, *f;* amontonamiento, *m;* colección, *f; Med.* absceso, *m; Sew.* fruncimiento, *m;* (assembly) reunión, asamblea, *f;* (crowd) concurrencia, muchedumbre, *f*

**gathers** /'gæðərz/ *n Sew.* fruncidos, pliegues, *m pl*

**gauche** /gouʃ/ *a* torpe, huraño

**gaudily** /'gɔdəli/ *adv* ostentosamente; brillantemente

**gaudiness** /'gɔdinis/ *n* ostentación, *f;* brillantez, *f*

**gaudy** /'gɔdi/ *a* llamativo, vistoso, brillante, ostentoso

**gauge** /geidʒ/ *n* (of gun) calibre, *m;* (railway) entrevía, *f;* (for measuring) indicator, *m;* regla de medir, *f; Naut.* calado, *m; Fig.* medida, *f;* (test) indicación, *f;* (model) norma, *f.* —*vt* calibrar; medir; estimar; (ship's capacity) arquear; (judge) juzgar; (size up) tomar la medida (de); *Fig.* interpretar; *Sew.* fruncir; (liquor) aforar. **broad (narrow) g. railway,** ferrocarril de vía ancha (estrecha), *m.* **pressure g.,** manómetro, *m.* **water g.,** indicador del nivel de agua, *m*

**gauging** /'geɪdʒɪŋ/ *n* medida, *f;* (of ship's capacity) arqueo, *m;* (of liquor) aforamiento, *m; Fig.* apreciación, *f;* interpretación, *f*

**Gaul** /gɔl/ Galia, *f*

**gaunt** /gɔnt/ *a* anguloso, huesudo, desvaído; (of houses, etc.) lúgubre

**gauntlet** /'gɔntlɪt/ *n* guante de manopla, *m;* (part of armor) manopla, *f,* guantelete, *m.* **to throw down the g.,** echar el guante, desafiar

**gauntness** /'gɔntnɪs/ *n* angulosidad, flaqueza, *f*

**gauze** /gɔz/ *n* gasa, *f;* (mist) bruma, *f.* **wire-g.,** tela metálica, *f*

**gauziness** /'gɔzɪnɪs/ *n* diafanidad, *f*

**gauzy** /'gɔzi/ *a* diáfano; de gasa

**gavotte** /gə'vɒt/ *n* gavota, *f*

**gawkiness** /'gɔkinɪs/ *n* torpeza, desmaña, *f*

**gawky** /'gɔki/ *a* anguloso, desgarbado, torpe

**gay** /gei/ *a* alegre; festivo, animado; ligero de cascos, disipado; homosexual; (of colors) brillante, llamativo

**Gaza Strip** /'gɑzə/ la franja de Gaza, *f*

**gaze** /geiz/ *n* mirada, *f;* mirada fija, *f.* —*vi* mirar; mirar fijamente, contemplar

**gazelle** /gə'zɛl/ *n* gacel (-la)

**gazer** /'geizər/ *n* espectador (-ra)

**gazette** /gə'zɛt/ *n* gaceta, *f.* —*vt* publicar en la gaceta.

**gazing** /'geizɪŋ/ *n* contemplación, *f,* a contemplador; que presencia, que asiste a

**gear** /gɪər/ *n* (apparel) atavíos, *m pl;* (harness) guarniciones, *f pl,* arneses, *m pl;* (tackle) utensilios, *m pl,* herramientas, *f pl; Naut.* aparejo, *m; Mech.* engranaje, *m;* juego, *m,* marcha, *f.* —*vt* aparejar, enjaezar; *Mech.* poner en marcha, hacer funcionar. —*vi Mech.* engranar, endentar. **low g.,** pimera velocidad, *f.* **neutral g.,** punto muerto, *m.* **reverse g.,** marcha atrás, *f.* **second g.,** segunda velocidad, *f.* **three-speed g.,** cambio de marchas de tres velocidades, *m.* **top g.,** tercera (or cuarta--according to gear-box) velocidad, *f.* **to change g.,** cambiar de marcha, cambiar de velocidad. **to throw out of g.,** *Fig.* desquiciar. **g.-box,** caja de velocidades, *f.* **g.-changing,** cambio de velocidad, *m.* **g.-changing lever,** palanca de cambio de velocidad, palanca de cambio de marchas, *f*

**gearing** /'gɪərɪŋ/ *n* engranaje, *m*

**gee up** /dʒi/ *interj* ¡arre!

**gehenna** /gɪ'hɛnə/ *n* gehena, *m*

**geisha** /'geiʃə/ *n* geisha, *f*

**gelatin** /'dʒɛlətn/ *n* gelatina, *f.* **cooking g.,** gelatina seca, *f*

**gelatinous** /dʒə'lætnəs/ *a* gelatinoso

**geld** /gɛld/ *vt* capar, castrar

**gelder** /'gɛldər/ *n* castrador, *m*

**gelding** /'gɛldɪŋ/ *n* castración, capadura, *f;* caballo castrado, *m;* animal castrado, *m*

**gelid** /'dʒɛlɪd/ *a* gélido, helado; *Fig.* frío, frígido

**gem** /dʒɛm/ *n* piedra preciosa, *f;* joya, alhaja, *f; Fig.* joya, *f.* —*vt* adornar con piedras preciosas; enjoyar

**Gemini** /'dʒɛmə,nai/ *n* (los) Gemelos

**gender** /'dʒɛndər/ *n Gram.* género, *m;* sexo, *m*

**gene** /dʒin/ *n Biol.* gene, *m*

**genealogical** /,dʒiniə'lɒdʒɪkəl/ *a* genealógico. **g. tree,** árbol genealógico, *m*

**genealogist** /,dʒini'ɒlədʒɪst/ *n* genealogista, *mf*

**genealogy** /,dʒini'ɒlədʒi/ *n* genealogía, *f*

**general** /'dʒɛnərəl/ *a* general; universal; común; corriente; (usual) acostumbrado, usual; del público, público. —*n* lo general; (*Mil., Eccl.*) general, *m; Inf.* criada para todo, *f.* **in g.,** por lo general, en general, generalmente. **to become g.,** generalizarse. **to make g.,** generalizar, hacer general. **g. average,** (marine insurance) avería gruesa, *f.* **g. election,** elección general, *f.* **g. meeting,** pleno, mitin general, *m.* **g. opinion,** voz común, opinión general, *f.* **G. Post Office,** Oficina Central de Correos, *f.* **g. practitioner,** médico (-ca) general. **g. public,** público, *m.* **the general reader** el lector de tipo general *m*

**generalissimo** /,dʒɛnərə'lɪsə,mou/ *n* generalísimo, *m*

**generality** /,dʒɛnə'rælɪti/ *n* generalidad, *f*

**generalization** /,dʒɛnərələ'zeiʃən/ *n* generalización, *f*

**generalize** /'dʒɛnərə,laiz/ *vt* and *vi* generalizar

**generally** /'dʒɛnərəli/ *adv* en general, por regla general, por lo general, generalmente; comúnmente, por lo común

**generalship** /'dʒɛnərəl,ʃɪp/ *n Mil.* generalato, *m;* (strategy) táctica, estrategia, *f;* dirección, jefatura, *f*

**generate** /'dʒɛnə,reit/ *vt* (beget) engendrar, procrear; (*Phys., Chem.*) generar; *Fig.* producir, crear

**generation** /,dʒɛnə'reiʃən/ *n* procreación, *f;* generación, *f; Fig.* producción, creación, *f.* **the younger g.,** los jóvenes

**generative** /'dʒɛnərətɪv/ *a* generador

**generator** /'dʒɛnə,reitər/ *n Mech.* generador, *m;* dínamo, *f*

**generic** /dʒə'nɛrɪk/ *a* genérico

**generosity** /,dʒɛnə'rɒsɪti/ *n* generosidad, *f;* liberalidad, *f*

**generous** /'dʒɛnərəs/ *a* generoso; liberal, dadivoso; magnánimo; (plentiful) abundante; (of wines) generoso

**generously** /'dʒɛnərəsli/ *adv* generosamente; abundantemente

**genesis** /'dʒɛnəsɪs/ *n* principio, origen, *m;* (G.) Génesis, *m*

**genetic** /dʒə'nɛtɪk/ *a* genético

**genetics** /dʒə'nɛtɪks/ *n* genética, *f*

**Geneva** /dʒə'nivə/ Ginebra *f*

**Genevan** /dʒə'nivən/ *a* and *n* ginebrés (-esa), ginebrino (-na)

**genial** /'dʒinyəl/ *a* (of climate) agradable, bueno; (of persons) afable, bondadoso; de buen humor, bonachón

**geniality** /,dʒini'ælɪti/ *n* afabilidad, bondad, *f;* buen humor, *m*

**genially** /'dʒinyəli/ *adv* afablemente

**genie** /'dʒini/ *n* genio, *m*

**genital** /'dʒɛnɪtl/ *a* genital, sexual. —*n pl* **genitals,** genitales, *m pl*

**genitive** /'dʒɛnɪtɪv/ *a* and *n Gram.* genitivo *m.*

**genius** /'dʒinyəs/ *n* genio, *m;* carácter, *m,* índole, *f;* ingenio, *m; Inf.* talento, *m*

**Genoa** /'dʒɛnouə/ Genova, *f*

**Genoese** /,dʒɛnou'iz/ *a* and *n* genovés (-esa)

**genre** /'ʒɑnrə/ *n* género, *m.* **g. painting,** cuadro de género, *m*

**genteel** /dʒɛn'til/ *a* fino; (affected) remilgado, melindroso; de buen tono; de buena educación

**gentile** /'dʒɛntail/ *a* and *n* gentil *mf*

**gentility** /dʒɛn'tɪlɪti/ *n* aristocracia, *f;* respetabilidad, *f*

**gentle** /'dʒɛntl/ *a* noble, bien nacido, de buena familia; amable; suave; ligero; dulce; (docile) manso, dócil; (affectionate) cariñoso; bondadoso; sufrido, paciente; cortés; pacífico, tolerante. **He was a man of g. birth,** Era un hombre bien nacido. **"G. reader,"** «Querido lector»

**gentlefolk** /'dʒɛntl,fouk/ *n pl* gente de bien, gente fina, *f;* gente de buena familia, *f*

**gentleman** /'dʒɛntlmən/ *n* caballero, señor, *m;* gentilhombre, *m.* **Ladies and gentlemen,** Señoras y caballeros, Señores. **young g.,** señorito, *m.* **to be a perfect g.,** ser un caballero perfecto. **g.-inwaiting,** gentilhombre de la cámara, *m*

**gentlemanliness** /'dʒɛntlmənlinɪs/ *n* caballerosidad, *f*

**gentlemanly** /'dʒɛntlmənli/ *a* caballeroso

**gentleness** /'dʒɛntlnɪs/ *n* amabilidad, *f;* suavidad, *f;* dulzura, *f;* mansedumbre, docilidad, *f;* bondad, *f;* paciencia, *f;* cortesía, *f;* tolerancia, *f*

**gentlewoman** /'dʒɛntl,wumən/ *n* dama, *f;* dama de servicio, *f*

**gently** /'dʒɛntli/ *adv* suavemente; dulcemente; silenciosamente, sin ruido; (slowly) despacio, poco a poco. **g. born,** bien nacido

**gentry** /'dʒɛntri/ *n* pequeña aristocracia, alta clase media, *f;* (disparaging) gentle, *f*

**genuflect** /'dʒɛnyu,flɛkt/ *vi* doblar la rodilla

**genuflection** /,dʒɛnyə'flɛkʃən/ *n* genuflexión, *f*

**genuine** /'dʒɛnyuɪn/ *a* puro; genuino; verdadero; real; sincero; auténtico

**genuinely** /ˈdʒɛnyuɪnli/ *adv* genuinamente; verdaderamente; realmente; sinceramente

**genuineness** /ˈdʒɛnyuɪnɪs/ *n* pureza, *f*; autenticidad, *f*; verdad, *f*; sinceridad, *f*

**genus** /ˈdʒinəs/ *n* género, *m*

**geodesic** /ˌdʒiəˈdɛsɪk/ *a* geodésico

**geodesy** /dʒiˈɒdəsi/ *n* geodesia, *f*

**geographer** /dʒiˈɒgrəfər/ *n* geógrafo, *m*

**geographical** /ˌdʒiəˈgræfɪkəl/ *a* geográfico

**geographically** /ˌdʒiəˈgræfɪkəli/ *adv* geográficamente; desde el punto de vista geográfico

**geography** /dʒiˈɒgrəfi/ *n* geografía, *f*

**geological** /ˌdʒiəˈlɒdʒɪkəl/ *a* geológico

**geologically** /ˌdʒiəˈlɒdʒɪkəli/ *adv* geológicamente; desde el punto de vista geológico

**geologist** /dʒiˈɒlədʒɪst/ *n* geólogo, *m*

**geologize** /dʒiˈɒlə,dʒaiz/ *vi* estudiar la geología. —*vt* estudiar desde un punto de vista geológico

**geology** /dʒiˈɒlədʒi/ *n* geología, *f*

**geometric** /ˌdʒiəˈmɛtrɪk/ *a* geométrico

**geometry** /dʒiˈɒmɪtri/ *n* geometría, *f*

**geophysics** /ˌdʒiouˈfɪzɪks/ *n* geofísica, *f*

**Georgian** /ˈdʒɔrdʒən/ *a Geog.* georgiano; del principio del siglo diez y nueve

**georgic** /ˈdʒɔrdʒɪk/ *n* geórgica, *f*

**geotropism** /dʒiˈɒtrə,pɪzəm/ *n* geotropismo, *m*

**geranium** /dʒəˈreiniəm/ *n* geranio, *m*

**germ** /dʒɜrm/ *n* embrión, germen, *m*; microbio, bacilo, *m*; *Fig.* germen, *m*. **g.-cell,** célula germinal, *f*

**German** /ˈdʒɜrmən/ *a* alemán; germánico. —*n* alemán (-ana); (language) alemán, *m*; germano (-na), germánico (-ca). **Sudeten G.,** alemán (-ana) sudete. **G. measles,** rubeola, *f*. **G. silver** alpaca, *f*, melchor *m*, plata alemana *f*

**germander** /dʒɜrˈmændər/ *n Bot.* camedrio, *m*

**germane** /dʒɜrˈmein/ *a* pertinente (a), a propósito (a)

**Germanic** /dʒɜrˈmænɪk/ *a* germánico. —*n* (language) germánico, *m*

**Germanization** /ˌdʒɜrmənɪˈzeiʃən/ *n* germanización, *f*

**Germanize** /ˈdʒɜrmə,naiz/ *vt* germanizar. —*vi* germanizarse

**Germanophile** /dʒɜrˈmænə,fail/ *n* germanófilo (-la)

**Germany** /ˈdʒɜrməni/ Alemania, *f*

**germicidal** /ˌdʒɜrməˈsaidl/ *a* bactericida

**germicide** /ˈdʒɜrmə,said/ *n* desinfectante, *m*

**germinal** /ˈdʒɜrmənl/ *a* germinal. —*n* (G.) germinal, *m*

**germinate** /ˈdʒɜrmə,neit/ *vi* germinar, brotar. —*vt* hacer germinar

**germination** /ˌdʒɜrməˈneiʃən/ *n* germinación, *f*

**germinative** /ˈdʒɜrmə,neitɪv/ *a* germinativo

**gerund** /ˈdʒɛrənd/ *n* gerundio, *m*

**gerundive** /dʒəˈrʌndɪv/ *n* gerundio adjetivado, *m*

**Gestapo** /gəˈstɑpou/ *n* Gestapo, *f*

**gestation** /dʒɛˈsteiʃən/ *n* gestación, *f*

**gesticulate** /dʒɛˈstɪkyə,leit/ *vi* gesticular, hacer gestos; accionar. —*vt* expresar por gestos

**gesticulation** /dʒɛˌstɪkyəˈleiʃən/ *n* gesticulación, *f*

**gesticulatory** /dʒɛˈstɪkyələ,tɔri/ *a* gesticulatorio

**gesture** /ˈdʒɛstʃər/ *n* movimiento, *m*; gesticulación, *f*; (of the face) gesto, *m*, mueca, *f*; ademán, *m*, acción, *f*. —*vi* gesticular. —*vt* decir por gestos; acompañar con gestos

**get** /gɛt/ *vt* (obtain) obtener; (acquire) adquirir; (buy) comprar; (take) tomar; (receive) recibir; (gain, win) ganar; (hit) acertar, dar; (place) poner; (achieve) alcanzar, lograr; (make) hacer; (call) llamar; (understand) comprender; (catch) coger; (procreate) procrear, engendrar; (induce) persuadir; (invite) convidar, invitar; (cause) hacer; (with have and past part.) tener; (with have and past part. followed by infin.) tener que; (followed by noun and past part.) hacer; (fetch) buscar, ir a buscar; (order) mandar, disponer; (procure) procurar; (bring) traer; (money) hacer; (a reputation, etc.) hacerse; (a prize, an advantage) llevar; (learn) aprender; (be) ser. —*vi* (become) hacerse; ponerse; venir a ser; (old) envejecerse; (angry) montar (en cólera), enojarse; (arrive) llegar a; (attain) alcanzar; (accomplish) conseguir, lograr; (drunk) emborracharse; (hurt) hacerse daño;

(wet) mojarse; (cool) enfriarse; (money) hacer (dinero); (of health) ponerse; (find oneself) hallarse, encontrarse; (late) hacerse (tarde); (dark) empezar a caer (la noche), empezar a caer (la noche), empezar a oscurecer; (put oneself) meterse; (grow, be) estar; (on to or on top of) montar sobre, subir a. **He has got run over,** Ha sido atropellado. **It gets on my nerves,** Se me pone los nervios en punta. **Let's get it over!** ¡Vamos a concluir de una vez! **How do you get on with her?** ¿Cómo te va con ella? **She must be getting on for twenty,** Tendrá alrededor de veinte años. **to get a suit made,** mandar hacerse un traje. **to get better,** (in health) mejorar de salud; hacer progresos adelantar. **to get dark,** obscurecer. **to get into conversation with,** trabar conversación con. **to get into bad company,** frecuentar malas compañías. **to get into the habit of,** acostumbrarse a. **to get married,** casarse. **to get near,** acercarse. **to get one's own way,** salir con la suya. **to get oneself up as,** disfrazarse de. **to get out in a hurry,** salir apresuradamente; marcharse rápidamente, *Inf.* salir pitando. **to get out of the way,** quitarse de en medio, apartarse. **to get rid of,** desembarazarse de, librarse de; salir de; perder. **to have got,** poseer; tener; padecer. **Get on!** ¡Adelante!; (to a horse) ¡Arre!; (continue) ¡Sigue! **Get out!** ¡Fuera! ¡Largo de aquí! ¡Sal! **Get up!** ¡Levántate!; (to a horse) ¡Arre! **to get about,** moverse mucho; andar mucho; (attend to business affairs) ir a sus negocios; (travel) viajar; (get up from sick bed) levantarse; (go out) salir; (be known) saberse, divulgarse, hacerse público. **to get above,** subir a un nivel más alto (de). **to get across,** *vi* cruzar, atravesar. —*vt* hacer cruzar. **to get along,** *vi* (depart) marcharse; (continue) seguir, vivir; (manage) ir, ir tirando. —*vt* llevar; traer; hacer andar por. **How are you getting along?** ¿Cómo le va? **I am getting along all right, thank you,** Voy tirando, gracias. **to get along without,** pasarse sin. **to get at,** (remove) sacar; (find) encontrar; (reach) llegar a; alcanzar; (discover) descubrir; (allude to) aludir a; (understand) comprender. **to get away,** *vi* dejar (un lugar); marcharse, irse; (escape) escaparse. —*vt* ayudar a marcharse; ayudar a escaparse. **to get away with,** llevarse, marcharse con; *Inf.* salir con la suya. **to get back,** *vi* regresar, volver; (get home) volver a casa; (be back) estar de vuelta. —*vt* (recover) recobrar; (receive) recibir; (find again) hallar de nuevo. **to get down,** *vi* bajar, descender. —*vt* bajar; (take off a hook) descolgar; (swallow) tragar; (note) anotar; escribir. **to get down on all fours,** ponerse en cuatro patas. **to get down to,** ponerse a (estudiar, trabajar, etc.). **to get in,** *vi* entrar en; lograr entrar en; (slip in) colarse en; (of political party) entrar en el poder; (of a club) hacerse socio de; (return) regresar; (home) volver a casa; (find oneself) hallarse, estar; (a habit) adquirir. —*vt* hacer entrar en; (a club, etc.) hacer socio de; (a word) decir. **to get into.** See **to get in. to get off,** *vt* apearse de; bajar de; (send) enviar; (from punishment) librar; (bid goodbye) despedirse de; (remove) quitar, sacar. —*vi* apearse; bajar; (from punishment) librarse; (leave) ponerse en camino, marcharse. **to get on,** *vi* (wear) tener puesto; (progress) hacer progresos, adelantar; (prosper) medrar, prosperar; (succeed) tener éxito; avanzar; seguir el camino; (agree) avenirse. —*vt* (push) empujar; (place) poner; (cause) hacer; (clothes) ponerse; (mount) subir a. **to get open,** abrir. **to get out,** *vt* hacer salir; sacar; (publish) publicar; divulgar. —*vi* salir; escapar; **to get out of a jam,** salir de un paso; (descend) bajar (de). **to get over,** (cross) atravesar, cruzar; (an illness, grief, etc.) reponerse, reponerse de; (excuse) perdonar; (surmount) superar; (ground) recorrer. **to get round,** (a person) persuadir; (surround) rodear; (avoid) evitar; (difficulties) superar, vencer. **to get through,** pasar por; (time) pasar, entretener; (money) gastar; (finish) terminar, acabar; (pierce or enter) penetrar; (communicate) comunicar (con); (difficulties) vencer; (an exam) aprobar. **to get to,** llegar a; encontrar; (begin) empezar a. **to get together,** reunir, juntar. —*vi* reunirse, juntarse. **to get under,** ponerse debajo de; (control) dominar. **to get up,** *vt* (raise) alzar, levantar; (carry up things) subir; hacer subir; organizar;

preparar; (learn) aprender; (linen) blanquear, colar; (ascend) subir; hacer; (dress) ataviar; (steam) generar; (a play) ensayar, poner en escena. —*vi* levantarse; (on a horse) montar a caballo; (of the wind) refrescarse; (of the fire) avivarse; (of the sea) embravecerse. **to get up to,** llegar a; alcanzar

**get-at-able** /'get ,æt əbəl/ *a* accesible

**getting** /'getɪŋ/ *n* adquisición, *f;* (of money) ganancia, *f.* **g. up,** preparación, *f;* organización, *f;* (of a play) representación (de una comedia), puesta en escena, *f*

**get-up** /'get ,ʌp/ *n* atavío, *m;* (of a book, etc.) aspecto, *m*

**gewgaw** /'gyugɔ/ *n* chuchería, *f*

**geyser** /'gaizər/ *n* géiser, *m;* (for heating water) calentador (de agua), *m*

**ghastliness** /'gæstlinɪs/ *n* horror, *m;* palidez mortal, *f;* aspecto miserable, *m;* (boringness) tedio, aburrimiento, *m;* lo desagradable

**ghastly** /'gæstli/ *a* horrible; de una palidez mortal; cadavérico; (boring) aburrido; muy desagradable

**gherkin** /'gɑrkɪn/ *n* cohombrillo, *f*

**ghetto** /'getou/ *n* gueto *m*

**ghost** /goust/ *n* fantasma, espectro, aparecido, *m;* (spirit) alma, *f,* espíritu, *m;* (shadow) sombra, *f;* (writer) mercenario, *m.* **Holy G.,** Espíritu Santo, *m.* **to give up the g.,** entregar el alma; perder la esperanza, desesperarse. **to look like a g.,** parecer un fantasma

**ghostliness** /'goustlinɪs/ *n* espiritualidad, *f;* lo misterioso; palidez, *f;* tenuidad, *f*

**ghostly** /'goustli/ *a* espiritual; espectral; misterioso; pálido; vaporoso, tenue; indistinto

**ghost town** *n* pueblo-fantasma, *m*

**ghost word** *n* palabra-fantasma, *m*

**ghoul** /gul/ *n* vampiro, *m*

**ghoulish** /'gulɪʃ/ *a* insano; cruel; sádico

**giant** /'dʒaiənt/ *n* gigante, *m;* Fig. coloso, *m, a* gigantesco; de gigantes; de los gigantes. **g.-killer,** matador de gigantes, *m.* **g.-stride,** (gymnastics) paso volante, *m*

**giantess** /'dʒaiəntɪs/ *n* giganta, *f*

**gibber** /'dʒɪbər/ *vi* hablar incoherentemente, hablar entre dientes; farfullar, hablar atropelladamente; decir disparates

**gibberish** /'dʒɪbərɪʃ/ *n* galimatías, *m;* jerigonza, *f,* griego, *m*

**gibbet** /'dʒɪbɪt/ *n* horca, *f,* patíbulo, *m.* **to die on the g.,** morir ahorcado

**gibbon** /'gɪbən/ *n* Zool. gibón, *m*

**gibe** /dʒaib/ *n* improperio, escarnio, *m,* burla, mofa, *f.* —*vi* criticar. **to g. at,** burlarse de, ridiculizar, mofarse de

**gibing** /'dʒaibɪŋ/ *a* burlón, mofador. —*n* mofas, burlas, *f pl*

**gibingly** /'dʒaibɪŋli/ *adv* burlonamente, con sorna

**giblets** /'dʒɪblɪts/ *n* menudillos, *m pl*

**giddily** /'gɪdli/ *adv* vertiginosamente; frívolamente, atolondradamente

**giddiness** /'gɪdinɪs/ *n* vértigo, *m;* atolondramiento, *m;* inconstancia, *f;* frivolidad, ligereza de cascos, *f*

**giddy** /'gɪdi/ *a* vertiginoso; mareado; atolondrado, casquivano, frívolo; inconstante. **She felt very g.,** Se sintió muy mareada. **to make g.,** dar vértigo (a), marear

**gift** /gɪft/ *n* regalo, *m,* dádiva, *f;* (quality) don, talento, *m;* prenda, *f;* poder, *m;* Law. donación, *f;* (offering) ofrenda, oblación, *f.* —*vt* dotar. **deed of g.,** Law. escritura de donación, *f.* **in the g. of,** en el poder de, en las manos de. **I wouldn't have it as a g.,** No lo tomaría ni regalado. **Never look a g. horse in the mouth,** A caballo regalado no se le mira el diente. **g. of tongues,** don de las lenguas, genio de las lenguas, *m*

**gifted** /'gɪftɪd/ *a* talentoso

**gig** /gɪg/ *n* (carriage) carrocín, *m;* (boat) falúa, lancha, *f;* (for wool) máquina de cardar paño, *f;* (harpoon) arpón, *m*

**gigantic** /dʒai'gæntɪk/ *a* gigantesco; colosal, enorme

**giggle** /'gɪgəl/ *vi* reírse sin motivo; reírse disimuladamente. —*n* risa disimulada, *f*

**giggling** /'gɪglɪŋ/ *n* risa estúpida, *f;* risa nerviosa, *f*

**gigolo** /'dʒɪgə,lou/ *n* gigolo, mantenido, jinetero (Cuba), *m*

**gild** /gɪld/ *vt* dorar; (metals) sobredorar; embellecer. **to g. the pill,** dorar la píldora

**gilder** /'gɪldər/ *n* dorador, *m*

**gilding** /'gɪldɪŋ/ *n* dorado, *m,* doradura, *f;* embellecimiento, *m*

**Gileadite** /'gɪliə,dait/ *n* and *a* galaadita, *mf*

**gill** /gɪl/ *n* (of fish) agalla, branquia, *f;* (ravine) barranco, *m;*

**gill** /dʒɪl/ *n* (measure) cierta medida de líquidos, *f,* (⅛ litro)

**gilt** /gɪlt/ *n* dorado, *m;* pan de oro, *m;* relumbrón, *m;* Fig. encanto, *m, a* dorado, áureo. **g.-edged,** (of books) con los bordes dorados. **g.-edged security,** papel del Estado, *m;* valores de toda confianza, *m pl*

**gimcrack** /'dʒɪm,kræk/ *n* chuchería, *f.* —*a* de baratillo, cursi; mal hecho

**gimlet** /'gɪmlɪt/ *n* barrena, *f,* taladro, *m*

**gin** /dʒɪn/ *n* (drink) ginebra, *f;* (snare) trampa, *f.* —*vt* (snare) coger con trampa. **g. block,** Mech. garrucha, *f*

**ginger** /'dʒɪndʒər/ *n* jengibre, *m;* Inf. energía, *f,* brío, *m, a* rojo. —*vt* sazonar con jengibre; Inf. animar, estimular. **g.-beer,** gaseosa, *f*

**gingerly** /'dʒɪndʒərli/ *adv* con gran cuidado; delicadamente

**gingham** /'gɪŋəm/ *n* guinga, *f*

**gingivitis** /,dʒɪndʒə'vaitɪs/ *n* gingivitis, *f*

**gipsy** /'dʒɪpsi/ *n.* See **gypsy**

**giraffe** /dʒə'ræf/ *n* jirafa, *f*

**gird** /gɑrd/ *vt* ceñir; (invest) investir; (surround) cercar, rodear; (put on) revestir. **to g. oneself for the fray,** prepararse para la lucha

**girder** /'gɑrdər/ *n* viga, jácena, *f.* **main g.,** viga maestra, *f*

**girdle** /'gɑrdl/ *n* (belt) cinturón, *m;* (corset) faja, *f;* circunferencia, *f;* zona, *f.* —*vt* ceñir; Fig. cercar, rodear

**girl** /gɑrl/ *n* niña, *f;* chica, muchacha, *f;* (maidservant) criada, muchacha, *f;* (young lady) señorita, *f.* **a young g.,** una jovencita, (a little older) una joven. **old g.,** (of a school) antigua alumna, *f;* Inf. vieja, *f;* (Inf. affectionate) chica, *f.* **g. friend,** amiguita, *f.* **g. guide, girl scout,** exploradora, *f.* **girls' school,** colegio de niñas, colegio de señoritas, *m*

**girlhood** /'gɑrlhʊd/ *n* niñez, *f;* juventud, *f*

**girlish** /'gɑrlɪʃ/ *a* de niña, de muchacha; (of boys) afeminado; joven

**girth** /gɑrθ/ *n* (of horse, etc.) cincha, *f;* circunferencia, *f;* (of person) talle, *m;* (obesity) corpulencia, obesidad, *f*

**gist** /dʒɪst/ *n* esencia, substancia, *f,* importe, *m*

**give** /gɪv/ *vt* dar; (a present) regalar; (infect) contagiar; (impart) comunicar; (grant) otorgar; (allow, concede) conceder; (assign) asignar, señalar; (appoint) nombrar; (a toast) brindar (a la salud de); (a party, ball, etc.) dar; (a bill) presentar; (wish) desear; (punish) castigar; (pay) pagar; (hand over) entregar; (names at baptism) imponer; (produce) producir; dar; (cause) causar; (of judicial sentences) condenar a; (evoke) proporcionar; (provoke) provocar; (devote) dedicar, consagrar; (sacrifice) sacrificar; (evidence, an account, orders, a lesson, a performance, a concert) dar; (a cry, shout) lanzar, proferir; (a laugh) soltar; (describe) describir; (paint) pintar; (write) escribir; (offer) ofrecer; (show) mostrar; (transmit) transmitir; (heed, pain) hacer; (a speech) pronunciar, hacer; (award, adjudge) adjudicar; (ear) prestar (oído (a)). —*vi* dar; ser dadivoso, mostrarse generoso; (give in) ceder; (be elastic) dar de sí; ablandarse; (collapse) hundirse. **G. them my best wishes!** ¡Dales mis mejores recuerdos! **G. us a song!** ¡Cántanos algo! **I can g. him a lift in my car,** Puedo ofrecerle un asiento en mi auto. **I g. you my word,** Os doy mi palabra. **to g. a good account of oneself,** defenderse bien; hacer bien; salir bien. **to g. a person a piece of one's mind,** contarle cuatro verdades. **to g. chase,** dar caza (a). **to g. it to a person,** poner a uno como nuevo; reprender; (beat) pegar, dar de palos. **to g. of itself,** dar de sí. **to g. rise to,** dar lugar a, ocasionar, causar. **to g. way,** no poder resistir; (break) romperse;

(yield) ceder; (collapse) hundirse; (retreat) retroceder. **to g. way to,** (retreat before) retirarse ante; (abandon oneself to) entregarse a, abandonarse a. **to g. away,** enajenar; dar; regalar; (sell cheaply) vender a un precio muy bajo; (get rid of) deshacerse de; (sacrifice) sacrificar; (a secret) revelar; (betray) traicionar; (expose) descubrir; (tell) contar; (a bride) conducir al altar. **He gave himself away,** Reveló su pensamiento sin querer. **to g. back,** *vt* devolver; restituir. —*vi* retirarse, cejar. **to g. forth,** divulgar, publicar; (scatter) derramar; (emit) emitir, despedir; (smoke, rays) echar. **to g. in,** *vt* entregar; presentar. —*vi* darse por vencido. **to g. in to,** (agree with) asentir en, consentir en; rendirse ante. **Mary always gives in to George,** María hace siempre lo que Jorge quiere. **to g. off,** (of odors, etc.) emitir, exhalar, despedir. **to g. out,** *vt* (distribute) distribuir, repartir; (allocate) asignar; (publish) publicar; (announce) anunciar; (reveal) divulgar; (allege) afirmar, hacer saber; (emit) emitir. —*vi* (be exhausted) agotarse; (end) acabarse; (be lacking) faltar. **to g. over,** *vt* entregar; (transfer) traspasar; cesar de. —*vi* cesar. **to g. up,** entregar; ceder; (renounce) renunciar (a); (sacrifice) sacrificar; (abandon) abandonar; (cease) dejar de; (as lost) dar por perdido; (of a patient) desahuciar; (a post) dimitir de; (return) devolver, restituir; (a problem) renunciar (a resolver un problema); (lose hope) perder la esperanza; (give in) darse por vencido. **I had given you up,** (didn't expect you), Creí que no ibas a venir. **to g. oneself up to,** entregarse a; dedicarse a; *Mil.* rendirse a. **to g. up one's seat,** ceder su sitio (or asiento). **to g. upon,** (overlook) dar sobre
**give** /gɪv/ *n* elasticidad, *f*; el dar de sí; (concession) concesión, *f.* **g. and take,** concesiones mutuas, *f pl.* **g. away,** *Inf.* revelación indiscreta, *f*
**given** /'gɪvən/ *a* dado; especificado; convenido; (with to) dado a, adicto a. **in a g. time,** en un tiempo dado. **g. that,** dado que
**giver** /'gɪvər/ *n* dador (-ra); donador (-ra)
**gizzard** /'gɪzərd/ *n* molleja, *f.* **It sticks in my g.,** *Inf.* No lo puedo tragar
**glacial** /'gleɪʃəl/ *a* glacial
**glacier** /'gleɪʃər/ *n* glaciar, *m*
**glad** /glæd/ *a* feliz, alegre; contento, satisfecho; *Inf.* elegante. **to be g.,** alegrarse, estar contento; estar satisfecho. **to give the g. eye,** hacer ojos
**gladden** /'glædn̩/ *vt* alegrar, regocijar
**glade** /gleɪd/ *n* claro, *m*; rasa, *f*
**gladiator** /'glædi,eitər/ *n* gladiador, *m*
**gladiatorial** /,glædiə'tɔriəl/ *a* gladiatorio
**gladiolus** /,glædi'ouləs/ *n Bot.* gladíolo, gladio, *m*; espadaña, *f*
**gladly** /'glædli/ *adv* alegremente; con mucho gusto, gustoso, de buena gana
**gladness** /'glædnɪs/ *n* alegría, felicidad, *f*, contento, *m*; placer, *m*
**glamorous** /'glæmərəs/ *a* exótico; garboso
**glamour** /'glæmər/ *n* encanto, *m*, fascinación, *f*; garbo, *m.* **g. girl,** belleza exótica, *f*
**glance** /glæns/ *n* (of a projectile) desviación, *f*; (of light) vislumbre, *m*; relumbrón, centelleo, *m*; (look) vistazo, *m*, ojeada, *f*; mirada, *f*, *vi* desviarse; relumbrar, centellear; (with at) ojear, echar un vistazo a, lanzar miradas a; (a book) hojear; mirar; mirar de reojo; *Fig.* indicar brevemente. **at a g.,** con un vistazo; en seguida. **at the first g.,** a primera vista. **to g. off,** desviarse (al chocar). **to g. over,** repasar, echar un vistazo a; (a book) hojear
**glancing** /'glænsɪŋ/ *a* (of a blow) que roza
**gland** /glænd/ *n* (*Anat.*, *Bot.*) glándula, *f*; (in the neck) ganglio, *m.* **to have swollen glands,** tener inflamación de los ganglios
**glandular** /'glændʒələr/ *a* glandular
**glare** /glɛr/ *n* brillo, fulgor, *m*; luminosidad, *f*; reflejo, *m*; (look) mirada feroz, *f.* —*vi* relumbrar, centellear; (stare) mirar con ferocidad, mirar fijamente
**glaring** /'glɛrɪŋ/ *a* deslumbrante, brillante; (of colors) chillón, llamativo; (of looks) de mirada feroz; (flagrant) notorio, evidente
**glaringly** /'glɛrɪŋli/ *adv* brillantemente; con mirada feroz; notoriamente

**glass** /glæs/ *n* vidrio, *m*; cristal, *m*; (glassware) artículos de vidrio, *m pl*; cristalería, *f*; (for drinking) vaso, *m*, copa, *f*; (pane) cristal, *m*; (mirror) espejo, *m*; (telescope) telescopio, *m*; catalejo, *m*; (barometer) barómetro, *m*; (hour-glass) reloj de arena, *m*; (of a watch) vidrio (de reloj), *m*; *pl* **glasses,** (binoculars) anteojos, *m pl*; (spectacles) gafas, lentes, *m pl*; (opera glasses) gemelos de teatro, *m pl*, *a* de vidrio; de cristal. —*vt* vidriar. **John wears glasses,** Juan lleva gafas. **The g. is falling (rising),** El barómetro baja (sube). **to clink glasses,** trincar las copas. **to look in the g.,** mirarse en el espejo. **clear g.,** vidrio transparente, *m.* **cut g.,** cristal tallado, *m.* **frosted g.,** vidrio jaspeado, *m.* **plate-g.,** vidrio plano, *m*; **safety g.,** vidrio inastillable, *m.* **stained g.,** vidrio de color, vidrio pintado, *m.* **under g.,** bajo vidrio; en invernáculo. **g. bead,** abalorio, *m*; cuenta de vidrio, *f.* **g.-blower,** soplador de vidrio, *m.* **g.-blowing,** el soplar de vidrio. **g. case,** escaparate, *m.* **g.-cloth,** paño para vasos, *m.* **g. eye,** ojo de cristal, *m.* **g. paper,** papel de vidrio, *m.* **g. roof,** techo de cristal, *m.* **g. window,** vidriera, *f*
**glasscutter** /'glæs,kʌtər/ *n* cortador de vidrio, *m*
**glassful** /'glæsfʊl/ *n* contenido de un vaso, *m*; vaso, vaso lleno, *m*, copa, *f*
**glasshouse** /'glæs,haʊs/ *n* fábrica de vidrio, *f*; vidriería, *f*; invernáculo, invernadero, *m*, estufa, *f*
**glassware** /'glæsi/ *n* cristalería, *f*
**glassy** /'glæsi/ *a* vitreo; (of eyes) vidrioso; *Fig.* cristalino; (smooth) liso, raso
**glaucous** /'glɔkəs/ *a* de color verdemar; *Bot.* glauco
**glaze** /gleɪz/ *n* barniz, *m*; lustre, brillo, *m.* —*vt* poner vidrios (a); vidriar; barnizar; (paper, leather, etc.) satinar. —*vi* (of eyes) vidriarse, ponerse vidrioso
**glazier** /'gleɪʒər/ *n* vidriero, *m*
**glazing** /'gleɪzɪŋ/ *n* vidriado, *m*; barnizado, *m*; satinado, *m*; (material) barniz, *m*
**gleam** /glim/ *n* rayo, destello, *m*; (of color) viso, *m*, mancha, *f*; *Fig.* rayo, *m*; (in the eye) chispa, *f.* —*vi* relucir, centellear, resplandecer; brillar; reflejar la luz; *Fig.* brillar. **g. of hope,** rayo de esperanza, *m*
**gleaming** /'glimɪŋ/ *a* reluciente, centelleante; brillante. —*n* see **gleam**
**glean** /glin/ *vt* espigar, rebuscar; recoger. —*vi* espigar
**gleaner** /'glinər/ *n* espigador, *m*; recogedor (-ra)
**gleaning** /'glinɪŋ/ *n* espigueo, *m*; rebusca, recolección, *f*; *pl* **gleanings,** fragmentos, *m pl*
**glee** /gli/ *n* alegría, *f*, júbilo, alborozo, *m*; *Mus.* canción para voces solas, *f*
**gleeful** /'glifəl/ *a* alegre, jubiloso, gozoso
**gleefully** /'glifəli/ *adv* alegremente, con júbilo
**glen** /glɛn/ *n* cañada, *f*, cañón, *m*, hondonada, *f*
**glib** /glɪb/ *a* locuaz, voluble; (easy) fácil
**glibness** /'glɪbnɪs/ *n* locuacidad, volubilidad, *f*; (easiness) facilidad, *f*
**glide** /glaɪd/ *n* deslizamiento, *m*; *Aer.* planeo, *m.* —*vi* deslizarse; resbalar; *Aer.* planear. **to g. away,** escurrirse; desaparecer silenciosamente
**glider** /'glaɪdər/ *n Aer.* deslizador, planeador, *m*
**gliding** /'glaɪdɪŋ/ *n Aer.* vuelo sin motor, *m*
**glimmer** /'glɪmər/ *n* luz trémula, luz débil, *f*, tenue resplandor, *m*; vislumbre, *m.* —*vi* brillar con luz trémula, rielar *Fig.*; tener vislumbres (de)
**glimpse** /glɪmps/ *n* vistazo, *m*; vislumbre, *m*; indicio, *m*; impresión, *f*; vista, *f.* —*vt* entrever, divisar; tener una vista (de); ver por un instante; vislumbrar
**glint** /glɪnt/ *n* tenue resplandor, *m*; lustre, *m*; centelleo, *m*; reflejo, *m*; (in the eye) chispa, *f.* —*vi* relucir, destellar, rutilar; reflejar
**glisten** /'glɪsən/ *vi* brillar, relucir
**glistening** /'glɪsənɪŋ/ *a* coruscante; brillante, reluciente
**glitter** /'glɪtər/ *n* brillo, resplandor, *m*, rutilación, *f.* —*vi* brillar, resplandecer, relucir; rutilar. **All that glitters is not gold,** Todo lo que reluce no es oro
**glittering** /'glɪtərɪŋ/ *a* reluciente, resplandeciente; *Fig.* brillante
**gloat (over)** /glout/ *vi* recrearse en, gozarse en, deleitarse en
**globe** /gloub/ *n* globo, *m*; esfera, *f*; (for fish) pecera, *f*; (for gas, electric light) globo, *m.* **geographical g.,** globo terrestre, *m.* **g.-trotter,** trotamundos, *m*

**globular** /'glɒbyələr/ a globular, esférico

**globule** /'glɒbyul/ n glóbulo, m

**globulous** /'glɒbyələs/ a globuloso

**gloom** /glum/ n obscuridad, f; lobreguez, f, tinieblas, f pl; Fig. melancolía, tristeza, f; taciturnidad, f. —vi Fig. ponerse melancólico; ser taciturno

**gloomily** /'gluməli/ adv obscuramente; Fig. tristemente; taciturnamente

**gloomy** /'glumi/ a obscuro; sombrío, lóbrego; melancólico, triste; taciturno; (of prospects, etc.) poco halagüeño, nada atrayente

**glorification** /ˌglɔrəfɪ'keɪʃən/ n glorificación, f

**glorify** /'glɔrə,faɪ/ vt glorificar; exaltar; alabar

**glorious** /'glɔriəs/ a glorioso; espléndido, magnífico; insigne; Inf. estupendo

**glory** /'glɔri/ n gloria, f; esplendor, m, magnificencia, f; Art. gloria, f. —vi recrearse, gozarse; glorificarse, jactarse. **to be in one's g.,** estar en la gloria. **to g. in,** hacer gala de, glorificarse en

**gloss** /glɒs/ n (sheen) lustre, brillo, m; Fig. apariencia, f; (note) glose, m; (excuse) disculpa, f. —vt pulir; glosar. **to g. over,** (faults) disculpar, excusar

**glossary** /'glɒsəri/ n glosario, m

**glossiness** /'glɒsɪnɪs/ n lustre, m, tersura, f; brillo, m

**glossy** /'glɒsi/ a lustroso, terso; brillante; (of hair) liso

**glottal stop** /'glɒtl/ n choque glótica, golpe de glotis, m

**glottis** /'glɒtɪs/ n Anat. glotis, f

**glove** /glʌv/ n guante, f. **evening gloves,** guantes largos, m pl. **to be hand in g. with,** juntar diestra con diestra. **to fit like a g.,** sentar como un guante. **to put on one's gloves,** ponerse los guantes. **g. shop,** guantería, f. **g.-stretcher,** ensanchador (or abridor) de guantes, m

**glove compartment** gaveta, guantera, f, guantero, m portaguantes m

**glove-compartment light** luz de portaguantes, f

**glover** /'glʌvər/ n guantero (-ra)

**glow** /glou/ n incandescencia, f; claridad, f; luz difusa, f; (heat) calor, m; (of color) intensidad, f; color vivo, m; (enthusiasm) ardor, entusiasmo, m; (redness) rojez, f; (in the sky) arrebol, m; (of pleasure, etc.) sentimiento de placer, m; sensación de bienestar, f. —vi estar incandescente; arder; abrasarse; sentir entusiasmo; mostrarse rojo; experimentar un sentimiento de placer o una sensación de bienestar. **to g. with health,** estar rebosando de salud. **g.-worm,** luciérnaga, f

**glower** /'glauər/ n ceño, m; mirada amenazadora, f. —vi poner cara de pocos amigos, mirar airadamente; tener los ojos puestos (en)

**glowing** /'glouɪŋ/ a candente, incandescente; ardiente; entusiasta; satisfecho; intenso; (bright) vivo; (red) encendido; (with health) rebosante de salud. —n see **glow**

**glowingly** /'glouɪŋli/ adv encendidamente; Fig. con entusiasmo

**glucose** /'glukous/ n glucosa, f

**glue** /glu/ n engrudo, m, cola, f. —vt encolar, engrudar; pegar; Fig. fijar, poner. **He kept his eyes glued on them,** Tenía los ojos fijados (or pegados) en ellos. **g.-pot,** pote de cola, m

**gluey** /'glui/ a gomoso; pegajoso, viscoso

**glueyness** /'gluinɪs/ n viscosidad, f

**gluing** /'gluɪŋ/ n encoladura, f

**glum** /glʌm/ a deprimido, taciturno, sombrío

**glumly** /'glʌmli/ adv taciturnamente

**glut** /glʌt/ n superabundancia, f, exceso, m. —vt (satiate) hartar; Fig. saciar; (the market) inundar

**gluteal** /'glutiəl/ a glúteo

**glutinous** /'glutnəs/ a glutinoso, pegajoso, viscoso

**glutton** /'glʌtn/ n glotón (-ona); Fig. ávido (-da)

**gluttonous** /'glʌtnəs/ a glotón, comilón

**gluttony** /'glʌtni/ n glotonería, gula, f

**glycerin** /'glɪsərɪn/ n glicerina, f

**gnarled** /narld/ a nudoso; (of human beings) curtido

**gnash** /næʃ/ vt rechinar, crujir (los dientes)

**gnashing** /'næʃɪŋ/ n rechinamiento (de dientes), m

**gnat** /næt/ n mosquito, m

**gnaw** /nɔ/ vt roer; morder; (of wood by worms) carcomer; Fig. roer

**gnawing** /'nɔɪŋ/ n roedura, f; mordedura, f, a roedor; mordedor

**gnome** /noum/ n nomo, m

**gnostic** /'nɒstɪk/ a and n nóstico (-ca)

**gnosticism** /'nɒstɪsɪzəm/ n nosticismo, m

**go** /gou/ vi ir; (depart) irse, marcharse; (go toward) dirigirse a, encaminarse a; (lead to, of roads, etc.) conducir a, ir a; (vanish) desaparecer; (leave) dejar, salir de; (lose) perder; (pass) pasar; (of time) transcurrir, pasar; (be removed) quitarse; (be prohibited) prohibirse; (fall) caer; (collapse) hundirse; (be torn off) desprenderse; desgajarse; Mech. funcionar, trabajar, andar; (sound) sonar; (of the heart) palpitar, latir; (follow) seguir; (gesture) hacer un gesto; (be stated) decirse, afirmarse; (live) vivir; (wear) llevar; (turn out) salir, resultar; (improve) mejorar; (prosper) prosperar; (turn, become) ponerse; volverse; (to sleep) dormirse; (into a faint) desmayarse; (decay) echarse a perder, estropearse; (turn sour) agriarse; (become, adopt views, etc.) hacerse; (be sold) venderse; (be decided); decidirse, ser decidido; (have) tener; (by will) pasar; (belong) pertenecer; (receive) recibir; (have its place) estar; (put) ponerse; (going plus infin.) ir a; (die) morir, irse; (do a journey, a given distance) hacer; (a pace, step) dar; (take) tomar; (escape) escaparse, (contribute) contribuir (a); (harmonize) armonizar (con); (be current) ser válido; (be) ser; (of a document, etc., run) rezar, decir; (attend) asistir a; (be broken) estar roto; (be worn) estar raído; (be granted) darse, otorgarse. **It's gone five,** Ya dieron las cinco. **It's time to be going,** Es hora de marcharse. **Let's go!** ¡Bueno, ¡qué tal? ¿Cómo te va? **Who goes there?** Mil. ¿Quién va? **to go and fetch,** ir a buscar. **to let go,** soltar; dejar ir. **to go one's way,** seguir su camino. **to go wrong,** salir mal, fracasar; (sin) descarriarse. **"Go!"** (traffic sign) «¡Siga!» **Go on!** ¡Adelante!; (continue) ¡Siga!; Inf. ¡Qué va! **to go about,** dar la vuelta a; rodear; recorrer; (undertake) emprender, hacer; intentar; (of news, etc.) circular; Naut. virar de bordo. **Go about your business!** ¡Métete en lo que te importa! **to go abroad,** ir al extranjero; salir a la calle; publicarse, divulgarse. **to go across,** cruzar, atravesar; pasar. **to go after,** andar tras; seguir; (seek) ir a buscar; (persecute) perseguir. **to go again,** ir de nuevo; (be present) asistir otra vez; volver. **to go against,** ir contra; militar contra; oponerse a; ser desfavorable a. **to go ahead,** adelantar, avanzar; progresar; prosperar; (lead) ir a la cabeza (de), conducir; Naut. marchar hacia adelante. **to go along,** andar por; recorrer; (depart) irse, marcharse. **go apartment-hunting,** ir en busca de piso. **to go along with,** acompañar (a). **to go aside,** quitarse de en medio; apartarse, retirarse. **to go astray,** perderse; extraviarse, descarriarse. **to go at,** atacar, acometer; (undertake) emprender; empezar a. **to go at it again,** Inf. volver a la carga. **to go away,** irse, marcharse; ausentarse; alejarse; desaparecer. **to go away with,** marcharse con; (an object) llevarse; volver; (retreat) retroceder, volverse atrás; (in history) remontarse a. **to go back on,** (a promise, etc.) faltar a; (retract) retractarse; (betray) traicionar. **to go backwards,** retroceder, cejar; desandar lo andado; Fig. deteriorar, empeorar. **to go backwards and forwards,** ir y venir; oscilar. **to go before,** (lead) ir a la cabeza de, conducir; anteceder; proceder; (a judge, etc.) comparecer ante. **to go behind,** ir detrás de; esconderse detrás de; seguir; (evidence, etc.) mirar más allá de. **to go between,** ponerse entre; interponerse; (as a mediator) mediar; (insert) intercalarse; (travel) ir entre; llevar cartas entre, ser mensajero de. **to go beyond,** ir más allá; exceder. **to go by,** pasar por; pasar cerca de, pasar junto a; ir por; (of time) transcurrir, pasar; (follow) seguir; guiarse por, atenerse a; (judge by) juzgar por; (a name) pasar por; tomar el nombre de. **to go down,** bajar, descender; (of the sun) ponerse; (sink) hundirse; sumergirse; (fall) caer; (be remembered) ser recordado; (believe) tragar; ser creído. **to go down again,** bajar de nuevo; volver a caer. **go Dutch,** ir a escote, ir a la gringa, ir a la par, ir a limón. **to go far,** ir lejos; influir mucho (en); impresionar mucho; (contribute) contribuir (a). **to go for,** (seek) ir en busca de; procurar tener; (attack) echarse encima de, atacar. **to go for a ride (by car, bicycle, on horseback),** dar un paseo (en coche, en bicicleta, a caballo). **to go forth,** salir; publicarse. **to go forward,** adelantar, avanzar; progresar; continuar; (happen) tener lugar. **to go from,** dejar, abandonar; separarse de, apartarse de; marcharse de. **to go in,** entrar en; (a railway carriage, etc.) subir a; (compete) concurrir. **to go in again,** volver a entrar en, entrar de nuevo en. **to go in and out,** entrar y salir; ir y venir. **to go in for,** entrar a buscar; dedicarse a, entregarse a; (buy) comprarse; tomar parte en; (an examination) tomar (un examen); (for a competition) entrar en (un concurso); (try) ensayar; arriesgar. **to go into,** entrar en; examinar; investigar; ocuparse con. **to go near,** acercarse a. **to go off,** marcharse; (explode) estallar; (of fire-arms) dispararse; (of the voice, etc.) perder (la voz, etc.); (run away) huir, fugarse. **to go off badly,** salir mal, fracasar, no tener éxito. **to go off well,** salir bien, tener éxito. **to go on,** subirse a; continuar; durar; avanzar; proseguir su marcha; progresar; prosperar; *Theat.* entrar en escena; (of clothes) ponerse; (rely on) apoyarse en. **Don't go on like that,** No seas así, No te pongas así. **This glove will not go on me,** No puedo ponerme este guante. **to be gone on a person,** *Inf.* estar loco por. **I went on to say...,** Después dije; Continuando mi discurso dije... **It was going on for six o'clock when...** Serían alrededor de las seis cuando... **He is going on for fifty,** Raya en los cincuenta años. **to go on foot,** ir a pie. **to go on with,** continuar con; empezar. **to go out,** salir; (descend) bajar; (of fires, lights) extinguirse, apagarse; (of fashion, etc.) pasar (de); (the tide) menguar; (retire) retirarse; (in society) frecuentar la alta sociedad; (die) morir; (arouse) excitar. **to go out of fashion,** pasar de moda. **to go out of one's way (to),** dejar su camino (para); (lose oneself) perder el camino, extraviarse; (take trouble) desvivirse (por), tomarse molestia (para). **to go over,** cruzar; pasar por encima; (to another party or to the other side) pasarse a; (read) repasar; examinar. **to go past,** pasar; pasar en frente de. **to go round,** dar la vuelta a; (revolve) girar; (surround) rodear; (of news, etc.) divulgarse; (be enough) ser suficiente para todos. **to go through,** ir por, pasar por; recorrer; (pierce) penetrar, atravesar; (examine) examinar; (suffer) padecer, sufrir; (experience) experimentar; (live) vivir; (of time) pasar; (of money) malgastar, derrochar. **to go through with,** llevar a cabo; terminar. **to go to,** ir a, encaminarse a; (a person) acercarse a, dirigirse a; (help, be useful) servir para; (be meant for) destinarse a; (rise of price) subir a; (find) encontrar; (of a bid) subir una apuesta hasta. **to go to war,** declarar la guerra. **to go together,** ir juntos (juntas). **to go toward,** encaminarse hacia; ir hacia; (help) ayudar a. **to go under,** pasar por debajo de; (sink) hundirse; (fail) fracasar; (be bankrupt) arruinarse, declararse en quiebra; (the name of) hacerse pasar por. **to go up,** subir; ir arriba; (a tree) trepar; (a ladder, etc.) subir; (a river) ir río arriba; (to town) ir a; (explode) estallar. **to go up and down,** subir y bajar; oscilar; ir de una parte a otra. **to go upon,** subirse a; (rely on) apoyarse en; obrar según; emprender. **to go upstairs,** ir arriba; (to another story, as in a flat) subir al otro piso; subir la escalera. **to go up to,** acercarse a; (of a bid) subir una apuesta hasta. **to go with,** acompañar; (agree with) estar de acuerdo con; (of principles) seguir, ser fiel a; (harmonize) armonizar con; (be suitable to) ir bien con; convenir a; (*Inf.* get along) ir. **to go without,** marcharse sin; (lack) pasarse sin. **It goes without saying that...,** Huelga decir que **Where are you going with this?** (What do you mean?) ¿A dónde quieres llegar con esto?

**go** /gou/ *n* (fashion) moda, boga, *f;* (happening) suceso, *m;* (fix) apuro, *m;* (energy) energía, *f,* empuje, brío, *m;* (turn) turno, *m;* (attempt) tentativa, *f,* (action) movimiento, *m,* acción, *f;* (bargain) acuerdo, *m.* **It's a go!** (agreed) ¡Trato hecho! ¡Acordado! ¡Entendidos! ¡Entendidas! **It is all the go,** Hace furor, Es

la gran moda. **It is no go,** No puede ser, Es imposible. **Now it's my go,** Ahora me toca a mí, Ahora es mi turno. **on the go,** en movimiento; entre manos; ocupado. **to have a go,** probar suerte; procurar, tratar de; tener un turno

**goad** /goud/ *n* garrocha, aguijada, *f,* aguijón, *m; Fig.* acicate, estímulo, *m.* —*vt* aguijar, picar; *Fig.* incitar, estimular, empujar. **prick with a g.,** aguijonazo, *m*

**go-ahead** /'gou ə,hɛd/ *a* emprendedor; progresivo

**goal** /goul/ *n* (posts in football, etc.) meta, portería, *f;* (score) gol, *m;* (in racing) meta, *f;* (destination) destinación, *f; Fig.* ambición, *f;* (purpose, objective) fin, objeto, *m.* **to score a g.,** marcar un gol. **g.-keeper,** guardameta, *m,* portero (-ra). **g.-post,** palo de la portería, *m*

**goat** /gout/ *n* cabra, *f; Astron.* capricornio, *m.* **he-g.,** cabrón, *m.* **young g.,** cabrito, *m,* chivo (-va). **g.-herd,** cabrero, *m.* **g. skin,** piel de cabra, *f;* (wineskin) odre, *m*

**goatee** /gou'ti/ *n* pera, perilla, *f*

**goatish** /'goutiʃ/ *a* cabruno; de cabra; lascivo

**gobble** /'gɒbəl/ *vt and vi* engullir, tragar. —*vi* (of turkey) gluglutear. —*n* gluguteo, *m,* voz del pavo, *f*

**gobbler** /'gɒblər/ *n* engullidor (-ra), tragón (-ona); *Inf.* pavo, *m*

**go-between** /'gou bɪ,twin/ *n* trotaconventos, *f;* alcahuete, *m;* (mediator) medianero (-ra)

**goblet** /'gɒblɪt/ *n* copa, *f*

**goblin** /'gɒblɪn/ *n* trasgo, duende, *m*

**go-by, to give the** /'gou ,bai/ evitar; pasar por alto de; omitir

**go-cart** /'gou ,kɑrt/ *n* andaderas, *f pl;* pollera, *f;* cochecito de niño, *m*

**god** /gɒd/ *n* dios, *m; pl* **gods,** dioses, *m pl;* (in a theater) público del paraíso, *m;* paraíso, *m.* **By God!** ¡Vive Dios! **For God's sake,** ¡Por el amor de Dios!; ¡Por Dios! **Please God,** ¡Plegue a Dios! **Thank God!** ¡Gracias a Dios! **God Bless You!** (to someone who has sneezed) ¡Jesús! **God forbid!** ¡No lo quiera Dios! **God grant it!** ¡Dios lo quiera! **God keep you!** ¡Dios le guarde! ¡Vaya Vd. con Dios! **God willing,** Dios mediante. **My father, God rest his soul, was...,** Mi padre, que Dios perdone, era...

**godchild** /'gɒd,tʃaild/ *n* ahijado (-da)

**goddaughter** /'gɒd,dɔtər/ *n* ahijada, *f*

**goddess** /'gɒdɪs/ *n* diosa, *f; Poet.* dea, *f*

**godfather** /'gɒd,faðər/ *n* padrino, *m.* **to be a g. to,** ser padrino de, sacar de pila (a)

**godfearing** /'gɒd,fiərɪŋ/ *a* timorato, temeroso de Dios; religioso

**godforsaken** /'gɒdfər,seikən/ *a* dejado de la mano de Dios; (of places) remoto, solitario

**Godhead** /'gɒd,hɛd/ *n* divinidad, *f*

**godless** /'gɒdlɪs/ *a* impío, irreligioso; sin Dios

**godlessness** /'gɒdlɪsnɪs/ *n* impiedad, irreligiosidad, *f*

**godlike** /'gɒd,laik/ *a* divino

**godliness** /'gɒdlinɪs/ *n* piedad, *f;* santidad, *f*

**godling** /'gɒdlɪŋ/ *n* diosecillo, *m*

**godly** /'gɒdli/ *a* devoto, piadoso, religioso

**godmother** /'gɒd,mʌðər/ *n* madrina, *f.* **fairy g.,** hada madrina, *f.* **to be a g. to,** ser madrina de

**godparent** /'gɒd,pɛərənt/ *n* padrino, *m;* madrina, *f, pl* **godparents,** padrinos, *m pl*

**godsend** /'gɒd,sɛnd/ *n* bien, *m;* buena suerte, *f;* fortuna, *f*

**go-getter** /'gou ,gɛtər/ *n* buscavidas, *mf*

**goggle** /'gɒgəl/ *n* mirada fija, *f; pl* **goggles,** anteojos, *m pl,* gafas, *f pl;* (of a horse) anteojeras, *f pl.* —*vi* mirar fijamente; salirse a uno los ojos de la cabeza. **g.-eyed,** de ojos saltones. **g.-eyes,** ojos saltones, *m pl*

**going** /'gouɪŋ/ *n* ida, *f;* (departure) partida, marcha, *f;* salida, *f;* (pace) paso, *m;* (speed) velocidad, *f.* **It was heavy g.,** El avance era lento; El progreso era lento; (of parties, etc.) Era aburrido. **The g. was difficult on those mountainous roads,** El conducir (or el ir or el andar) era difícil en aquellos caminos de montaña. **g. back,** vuelta, *f,* regreso, *m.* **g. down,** bajada, *f,* descenso, *m;* (of the sun, etc.) puesta, *f.* **g. forward,** avance, *m;* progreso, *m.* **g. in,** entrada, *f.* **g. in and out,** idas y venidas, *f pl.* **g. out,** salida, *f;* (of a fire, light) apagamiento, *m*

**going** /'gouɪŋ/ *a and pres part* que va, yendo; que

funciona. **G., g., gone** (at an auction) A la una, a las dos, a las tres. **goings-on,** (tricks) trapujos, *m pl*; (conduct) conducta, *f.* **g. concern,** empresa próspera, *f.* **g. to,** con destino a
**going-away present** /'gouɪŋ ə,wei/ *n* regalo de despedida, *m*
**goiter** /'gɔɪtər/ *n* bocio, *m*
**gold** /gould/ *n* oro, *m*; color de oro, *m.* —*a* de oro; áureo. **All that glitters is not g.,** No es oro todo lo que reluce. **cloth of g.,** tela de oro, *f.* **dull g.,** oro mate, *m.* **light g.,** oro pálido, *m.* **old g.,** oro viejo, *m.* **g.-beater,** batidor de oro, *m.* **g.-digger,** minero de oro, *m*; (woman) aventurera, *f.* **g. dust,** oro en polvo, *m.* **g.-fever,** fiebre de oro, *f.* **g. lace,** galón de oro, *m.* **g. lacquer,** sisa dorada, *f.* **g. leaf,** pan de oro, oro batido, *m.* **g.-mine,** mina de oro, *f.* **g. piece,** moneda de oro, *f.* **g. plate,** vajilla de oro, *f.* **g. standard,** patrón oro, *m.* **g.-thread,** hilo de oro, *m.* **g.-yielding,** *a* aurífero
**golden** /'gouldən/ *a* de oro; dorado; áureo; amarillo; *Fig.* feliz; excelente. **to become g.,** dorarse. **g. age,** edad de oro, *f.* **g.-crested wren,** abadejo, *m.* **g. hair,** cabellos dorados (or de oro), *m pl.* **G. Legend,** leyenda áurea, *f.* **g. mean,** justo medio, *m.* **g. rose,** rosa de oro, *f.* **g. rule,** regla áurea, *f.* **g. syrup,** jarabe de arce, *m.* **g. voice,** voz de oro, *f.* **g. wedding,** bodas de oro, *f pl*
**goldfinch** /'gould,fɪntʃ/ *n* jilguero, *m*
**goldfish** /'gould,fɪʃ/ *n* carpa dorada, *f.* **g. bowl,** pecera, *f*
**goldrush** /'gould,rʌʃ/ carrera de oro, *f*
**goldsmith** /'gould,smɪθ/ *n* orfebre, oribe, orífice, *m*
**golf** /gɒlf/ *n* golf, *m.* **g.-club,** (stick) palo de golf, *m*; (organization) club de golf, *m.* **g.-course,** campo de golf, *m*
**golfer** /'gɒlfər/ *n* jugador (-ra) de golf
**gonad** /'gounæd/ *n* gonada, *f*
**gondola** /'gɒndlə/ *n* góndola, *f*
**gondolier** /ˌgɒndl'ɪər/ *n* gondolero, *m*
**gone** /gɔn/ *a* and *past part* ido; (lost) perdido; (ruined) arruinado; (dead) muerto; (past) pasado; (disappeared) desaparecido; (fainted) desmayado; (suppressed) suprimido; (pregnant) encinta; (drunk) borracho; (ended) terminado; (exhausted) agotado; (ill) enfermo. **far g.,** avanzado; (in years) de edad avanzada; (of illness) cerca de la muerte, muy enfermo; (in love) loco de amor; (drunk) muy borracho. **It is all g.,** No hay más. **It is g. seven o'clock,** Son las siete y pico, Son las siete ya
**gong** /gɔŋ/ *n* gong, *m*; (Chinese) batintín, *m*
**gonorrhea** /ˌgɒnə'riə/ *n* gonorrea, *f*
**good** /gʊd/ *a* bueno (before *m sing* nouns) buen; agradable; afortunado; (appropriate) apropiado, oportuno; (beneficial) provechoso, ventajoso; (wholesome) sano, saludable; (suitable) apto; (useful) útil; (kind) bondadoso; (much) mucho; (obliging) amable; (virtuous) virtuoso; (skilled) experto; (fresh) fresco; (genuine) genuino, legítimo; verdadero. —*adv* bien. —*interj* ¡bueno! ¡bien! **a g. deal,** mucho. **a g. many,** bastantes. **a g. turn,** un favor. **a g. way,** (distance) un buen trecho; mucho. **a g. while,** un buen rato. **as g. as,** tan bueno como. **Be so g. as to...!** Haga el favor de, Tenga Vd. la bondad de (followed by infin.). **fairly g.,** *a* bastante bueno. —*adv* bastante bien. **I'm g. for another five miles,** Tengo fuerzas para cinco millas más. **It was g. of you to do it,** Vd. fue muy amable de hacerlo, Vd. tuvo mucha bondad de hacerlo. **to be no g. at this sort of thing,** no servir para tales cosas. **to have a g. time,** pasarlo bien. **to make g.,** reparar; indemnizar; (accomplish) llevar a cabo, poner en práctica; justificar; (a promise) cumplir. **very g.,** *a* muy bueno. —*adv* muy bien. **g.-feeling,** buena voluntad, *f.* **g.-fellowship,** compañerismo, *m*; buena compañía, *f.* **g.-for-nothing,** *a* papanatas, badulaque, *m.* **to be g.-for-nothing,** no servir para nada. **g. luck,** buena suerte, *f.* **g. manners,** buenos modales, *m pl.* **g. nature,** buena crianza, educación, *f.* **g. nature,** buen natural, *m*; buen humor, *m.* **g.-natured,** de buen natural; de buen humor, bonachón. **g. offices,** buenos oficios, *m pl.* **g.-tempered,** de buen humor
**good** /gʊd/ *n* bien, *m*; provecho, *m*; utilidad, *f*; pl

**goods.** See separate entry. **I am saying this for your g.,** Lo digo para tu bien. **Much g. may it do you!** ¡Buen provecho te haga! **for g. and all,** para siempre jamás. **It is no g.,** Es inútil; No vale la pena. **the g.,** el bien; (people) los buenos. **They have gone for g.,** Se han marchado para no volver. **to do one g.,** hacer bien a uno; mejorar; ser provechoso (a uno); (suit) sentar bien (a uno). **What is the g. of...?** ¿Para qué sirve...?; ¿Qué vale...? **g. and evil,** el bien y el mal
**good-bye** /ˌgʊd 'bai/ *interj* ¡adiós! —*n* adiós, *m*, despedida, *f.* **to bid g.-b.,** decir adiós. **G.-b. for the present!** ¡Hasta la vista! ¡Hasta luego! **G.-b. until tomorrow, then,** Hasta mañana pues, adiós, Hasta mañana entonces
**goodness** /'gʊdnɪs/ *n* bondad, *f*; (of quality) buena calidad, *f*; (of persons) amabilidad, benevolencia, *f*; (essence) esencia, substancia, *f*; bien, *m*; excelencia, *f*; *interj* ¡Jesús! ¡Dios mío! **For g. sake!** ¡Por Dios! **I wish to g. that,** ¡Ojalá que...!
**goods** /gʊdz/ *n pl* bienes, efectos, *m pl*; artículos, *m pl*; *Com.* mercancías, *f pl*, géneros, *m pl.* **by g.-train,** en pequeña velocidad. **stolen g.,** objetos robados, *m pl.* **g. lift,** montacargas, *m.* **g. office,** depósito de mercancías, *m.* **g. station,** estación de carga, *f.* **g.-train,** tren de mercancías, *m.* **g. van,** furgón, *m.* **g. wagon,** vagon de mercancías, *m*
**good-smelling** /'gʊd ˌsmɛlɪŋ/ *a* oloroso
**goodwill** /'gʊd'wɪl/ *n* benevolencia, *f*; buena voluntad, *f*; (of a business) clientela, *f*
**goose** /gus/ *n* oca, *f*, ganso (-sa); plancha de sastre, *f.* —*a* de oca. **g.-flesh,** *Fig.* carne de gallina, *f.* **g. girl,** ansarera, *f.* **g.-step,** paso de oca, *m*
**gooseberry** /'gus,bɛri/ *n* uva espina, *f*
**Gordian** /'gɔrdiən/ *a* gordiano. **G. knot,** nudo gordiano, *m*
**gore** /gɔr/ *n* sangre, *f*; *Sew.* sesga, nesga, *f.* —*vt* acornear; desgarrar; herir (con arma blanca)
**gorge** /gɔrdʒ/ *n* (valley) cañón, barranco, *m*; (heavy meal) comilona, *f*, atracón, *m.* —*vt* engullir, tragar. —*vi* hartarse, atracarse
**gorgeous** /'gɔrdʒəs/ *a* magnífico; espléndido, suntuoso; *Inf.* maravilloso, estupendo
**gorgeously** /'gɔrdʒəsli/ *adv* magníficamente
**gorgeousness** /'gɔrdʒəsnɪs/ *n* magnificencia, *f*; suntuosidad, *f*, esplendor, *m*
**gorilla** /gə'rɪlə/ *n* gorila, *m*
**gormandize** /'gɔrmən,daiz/ *vi* glotonear
**gormandizer** /'gɔrmən,daizər/ *n* glotón (-ona)
**gorse** /gɔrs/ *n* tojo, *m*, aulaga, *f*
**gory** /'gɔri/ *a* ensangrentado; sangriento
**gosh** /gɒʃ/ *interj* ¡caray! ¡caramba!
**goshawk** /'gɒs,hɔk/ *n* *Ornith.* azor, *m*
**gosling** /'gɒzlɪŋ/ *n* ansarino, *m*
**gospel** /'gɒspəl/ *n* evangelio, *m*; doctrina, *f.* **The G. according to St. Mark,** El Evangelio según San Marcos. **to believe as g. truth,** creer como si fuese el evangelio. **to preach the G.,** predicar el evangelio
**gossamer** /'gɒsəmər/ *n* hilo de araña, *m*, red de araña, telaraña, *f*; (filmy material) gasa, *f*; hilo finísimo, *m*, *a* de gasa; sutil, delgado, fino
**gossip** /'gɒsəp/ *n* murmurador (-ra), chismoso (-sa), hablador (-ra); (scandal) chisme, *m*; habladuría, murmuración, *f*; (obsolete, of a woman) comadre, *f*; (talk) charla, *f.* —*vi* charlar, conversar; (in bad sense) murmurar, chismear; criticar. **to g. about,** charlar de; poner lenguas en, cortar un sayo (a); hablar mal de. **g. column,** gacetilla, *f*
**gossiping** /'gɒsəpɪŋ/ *a* charlatán, hablador; chismoso, murmurador. —*n* See **gossip**
**Goth** /gɒθ/ *n* godo (-da); bárbaro (-ra)
**Gothic** /'gɒθɪk/ *a* *Art.* gótico; (of race) godo; bárbaro. —*n* (language) gótico, *m*; arquitectura gótica, *f.* **G. characters,** letra gótica, *f*
**gouge** /gaudʒ/ *n* gubia, *f.* —*vt* escoplear. **to g. out,** vaciar; sacar
**gourd** /gɔrd/ *n* calabaza, *f*
**gourmand** /gʊr'mɑnd/ *n* glotón, *m*
**gourmet** /gʊr'mei/ *n* gastrónomo, *m*
**gout** /gaut/ *n* *Med.* gota, *f*
**gouty** /'gauti/ *a* gotoso
**govern** /'gʌvərn/ *vt* gobernar; regir; (guide) guiar;

dominar; domar, refrenar; *Gram.* regir; (regulate) regular

**governable** /'gʌvərnəbəl/ *a* gobernable; manejable; dócil

**governess** /'gʌvərnɪs/ *n* institutriz, *f;* (in a school) maestra, *f*

**governing** /'gʌvərnɪŋ/ *a* gubernante; director; (with principle, etc.) directivo. —*n* See **government**

**government** /'gʌvərnmənt, -ərmənt/ *n* gobierno, *m;* dirección, *f;* autoridad, *f.* **g. bond,** bono del gobierno, *m.* **g. house,** palacio del gobernador, *m.* **g. office,** oficina del gobierno, *f.* **g. stock,** papel del Estado, *m*

**governmental** /ˌgʌvərn'mɛntl, ˌgʌvər-/ *a* gubernamental, gubernativo

**Government Printing Office** Talleres Gráficos de la Nación, *m pl*

**governor** /'gʌvərnər/ *n* gobernador (-ra); vocal de la junta de gobierno, *mf;* (of a prison) director (-ra) (de una prisión); *Mech.* regulador, *m.* **g.-general,** gobernador general, *m*

**governorship** /'gʌvərnərˌʃɪp/ *n* gobierno, *m; ;* dirección, *f*

**gown** /gaun/ *n* toga, *f;* (cassock) sotana, *f;* (dressing-g.) bata, *f;* (for sleeping) camisa de noche, *f;* (bathing-wrap) albornoz, *m;* (dress) vestido, traje, *m*

**Goyesque** /gɔi'ɛsk/ *a* goyesco

**grab** /græb/ *n* asimiento, *m,* presa, *f; Mech.* gancho, *m.* —*vt* arrebatar, asir, agarrar; *Fig.* alzarse con, tomar

**grabber** /'græbər/ *n* cogedor (-ra); codicioso (-sa)

**grace** /greis/ *n* elegancia, *f;* simetría, armonía, *f;* gracia, gentileza, *f,* donaire, *m;* encanto, *m;* (goodness) bondad, *f;* gracia, *f;* merced, *f,* favor, *m;* (period of time) plazo, *m;* (privilege) privilegio, *m; Theol.* gracia divina, *f;* (at table) bendición de la mesa, *f;* (as a title) excelentísimo, (to an archbishop) ilustrísimo. —*vt* adornar; favorecer; honrar. **airs and graces,** humos, *m pl.* **the Three Graces,** las Gracias. **three days' g.,** plazo de tres días, *m.* **to get into a person's good graces,** congraciarse con; caer en gracia con. **to say g.,** bendecir la mesa. **with a bad g.,** a regañadientes. **with a good g.,** de buena gana. **g.-note,** *Mus.* nota de adorno, *f*

**graceful** /'greisfəl/ *a* airoso, gentil, gracioso; elegante; bonito

**gracefully** /'greisfəli/ *adv* airosamente, gentilmente; con gracia; elegantemente

**gracefulness** /'greisfəlnɪs/. See **grace**

**graceless** /'greislɪs/ *a* réprobo; dejado de la mano de Dios; sin gracia

**gracious** /'greiʃəs/ *a* (merciful) piadoso, clemente; (urbane) afable, condescendiente, agradable. **Good g.!** ¡Vamos!, ¡Dios mío!

**graciously** /'greiʃəsli/ *adv* afablemente; con benevolencia. **to be g. pleased,** tener a bien

**graciousness** /'greiʃəsnɪs/ *n* amabilidad, afabilidad, condescendencia, *f*

**gradate** /'greideit/ *vt* graduar; *Art.* degradar

**gradation** /grei'deiʃən/ *n* graduación, *f; Mus.* gradación, *f;* paso gradual, *m;* serie, *f*

**grade** /greid/ *n* grado, *m;* (quality) calidad, clase, *f;* (in a school) clase, *f;* (gradient) pendiente, *f,* declive, *m.* —*vt* graduar, clasificar; (cattle breeding) cruzar. **down g.,** cuesta abajo. **up g.,** cuesta arriba. **highest g.,** *n* primera clase, *f.* —*a* de primera clase; de calidad excelente

**gradient** /'greidiənt/ *n* declive, *m.* cuesta, pendiente, *f*

**gradual** /'grædʒuəl/ *a* gradual. —*n Eccl.* gradual, *m*

**gradually** /'grædʒuəli/ *adv* gradualmente; poco a poco

**graduate** /*n, a* 'grædʒuit; *v* -ˌeit/ *n* licenciado (-da). —*a* graduado. —*vt* graduar. —*vi* graduarse; (as a doctor) doctorarse. **to g. as,** recibirse de

**graduation** /ˌgrædʒu'eiʃən/ *n* graduación, *f*

**graft** /græft/ *n Bot.* injerto, *m; Surg.* injerto de piel, *m;* (swindle) estafa, *f;* (bribery) soborno, *m.* —*vt Bot.* injertar; *Surg.* injertar un trozo de piel; *Fig.* injerir

**grafting** /'græftɪŋ/ *n Bot.* injerto, *m; Surg.* injerto de piel, *m; Fig.* inserción, *f*

**grain** /grein/ *n* (corn) grano, *m;* (cereal) cereal, *m,* or *f;* (seed, weight) grano, *m;* (trace) pizca, *f;* (of wood,

etc.) hila, *m,* fibra, hebra, veta, *f;* (of leather) flor, *f;* (texture) textura, *f.* —*vt* granear; granular; (wood, marble, etc.) vetear. **against the g.,** a contrapelo. **g. lands,** mieses, *f pl*

**gram** /græm/ *n* gramo, *m*

**grammar** /'græmər/ *n* gramática, *f.* **g. school,** instituto de segunda enseñanza, *m*

**grammarian** /grə'mɛəriən/ *n* gramático, *m*

**grammatical** /grə'mætɪkəl/ *a* gramatical

**grammatically** /grə'mætɪkəli/ *adv* gramaticalmente, como la gramática lo quiere. (e.g., *She now speaks Catalan g.,* Ahora habla el catalán como la gramática lo quiere)

**grammaticalness** /grə'mætɪkəlnɪs/ *n* corrección gramatical, *f*

**gramophone** /'græməˌfoun/ *n* gramófono, *m.*

**granary** /'greinəri/ *n* granero, hórreo, *m,* troj, *f.* **g. keeper,** trojero, *m*

**grand** /grænd/ *a* magnífico, soberbio; imponente; (of dress) espléndido, vistoso; (of people) distinguido, importante; aristocrático; (proud) orgulloso; (of style) elevado, sublime; (morally) noble; augusto; (main) principal; (full) completo; *Inf.* estupendo, magnífico; (with duke, etc.) gran. —*n* piano de cola, *m.* **g.-aunt,** tía abuela, *f.* **g. cross,** gran cruz, *f.* **g. duchess,** gran duquesa, *f.* **g. duke,** gran duque, *m.* **g. lodge,** (of freemasons) Gran Oriente, *m.* **g. master,** gran maestre, *m.* **g.-nephew,** resobrino, *m.* **g.-niece,** resobrina, *f.* **g. opera,** ópera, *f.* **g. piano,** piano de cola, *m.* **g.-stand,** tribuna, *f.* **g.-uncle,** tío abuelo, *m.* **g. vizier,** gran visir, *m*

**grandchild** /'græn,tʃaild/ *n* nieto (-ta). **great-g.,** bisnieto (-ta). **great-great-g.,** tataranieto (-ta)

**granddaughter** /'græn,dɔtər/ *n* nieta, *f.* **great-g.,** bisnieta, *f.* **great-great-g.,** tataranieta, *f*

**grandee** /græn'di/ *n* grande (de España, grande de Portugal), *m*

**grandeur** /'grændʒər/ *n* magnificencia, *f;* grandiosidad, *f;* magnitud, grandeza, *f;* (pomp) pompa, *f,* fausto, *m*

**grandfather** /'græn,faðər/ *n* abuelo, *m.* **great-g.,** bisabuelo, *m.* **great-great-g.,** tatarabuelo, *m*

**grandfatherly** /'græn,faðərli/ *a* de abuelo

**grandfather's clock** reloj de péndulo, *m*

**grandiloquence** /græn'dɪləkwəns/ *n* grandilocuencia, *f*

**grandiloquent** /græn'dɪləkwənt/ *a* grandílocuo

**grandiose** /'grændiˌous/ *a* grandioso, sublime; impresionante; imponente; (in a bad sense) extravagante: (of style) bombástico, hinchado

**grand jury** *n* jurado de acusación, jurado de jucio, *m*

**grandmother** /'græn,mʌðər/ *n* abuela, *f.* **great-g.,** bisabuela, *f.* **great-great-g.,** tatarabuela, *f*

**grandness** /'grændnɪs/ *n* magnificencia, *f;* aristocracia, *f;* (pride) orgullo, *m;* grandiosidad, *f;* (of style) sublimidad, *f;* (of character) nobleza, *f*

**grandparent** /'græn,pɛərənt/ *n* abuelo, *m;* abuela, *f; pl* **grandparents,** abuelos, *m pl.* **great-grand-parents,** bisabuelos, *m pl.* **great-great-grandparents,** tatarabuelos, *m pl*

**grandson** /'græn,sʌn/ *n* nieto, *m.* **great-g.,** bisnieto, *m.* **great-great-g.,** tataranieto, *m*

**grange** /greindʒ/ *n* granja, *f;* casa de campo, *f*

**granite** /'grænɪt/ *n* granito, *m.*

**granny** /'græni/ *n* abuelita, nana, *f;* abuela, *f.* **g. knot,** nudo al revés, *m*

**grant** /grænt/ *n* concesión, *f;* otorgamiento, *m;* donación, *f;* privilegio, *m;* (for study) beca, bolsa de estudio, *f;* (transfer) traspaso, *m,* cesión, *f.* —*vt* conceder; (bestow) otorgar, dar; donar; (agree to) acceder a, asentir en; permitir; (transfer) traspasar; (assume) suponer. **to g. a degree,** expedir un título. **to g. a motion,** dar por entrada a una moción. **to take for granted,** descontar; dar por hecho, dar por sentado. **God g. it!** ¡Dios lo quiera! **granted that,** dado que

**grantee** /græn'ti/ *n* cesionario (-ia), adjudicatorio (-ia)

**grantor** /'græntər/ *n* cesionista, *mf;* otorgador (-ra)

**granulated** /'grænyəˌleitɪd/ *a* granulado

**granule** /'grænyul/ *n* gránulo, *m.*

**granulous** /'grænyələs/ *a* granuloso

**grape** /greip/ *n* uva, *f.* **bunch of grapes,** racimo de

**graph** 444

uvas, *m.* **muscatel g.,** uva moscatel, *f.* **sour grapes,** uvas agrias, *f pl;* (phrase) ¡están verdes! **g.-fruit,** toronja, *f.* **g. gatherer,** vendimiador (-ra). **g. harvest,** vendimia, *f.* **g. juice,** mosto, *m.* **g.-shot,** metralla, *f.* **g. stone,** granuja, *f.* **g.-sugar,** glucosa, *f.* **g.-vine,** vid, parra, *f*

**graph** /græf/ *n* gráfica, *f;* diagrama, *m*

**graphic** /'græfɪk/ *a* gráfico

**graphite** /'græfaɪt/ *n* grafito, *m*

**graphology** /græ'fɒlədʒi/ *n* grafología, *f*

**grapple** /'græpəl/ *n Naut.* rezón, arpeo, *m;* lucha a brazo partido, *f.* —*vt Naut.* aferrar; asir, agarrar. —*vi Naut.* aferrarse. **to g. with,** luchar a brazo partido (con); *Fig.* luchar con

**grappling** /'græplɪŋ/ *n Naut.* aferramiento, *m;* lucha cuerpo a cuerpo, *f;* (with a problem) lucha con, *f*

**grasp** /græsp/ *n* agarro, *m;* (reach) alcance, *m;* (of a hand) apretón, *m;* (power) garras, *f pl,* poder, *m;* (understanding) comprensión, *f;* inteligencia, capacidad intelectual, *f.* —*vt* agarrar, asir; empuñar; abrazar; *Fig.* comprender, alcanzar; (a hand) estrechar. —*vi* agarrarse. **within one's g.,** al alcance de uno. **to g. at,** asirse de

**grasping** /'græspɪŋ/ *n* asimiento, *m;* (understanding) comprensión, *f, a* codicioso, tacaño, mezquino

**graspingness** /'græspɪŋnɪs/ *n* codicia, *f*

**grass** /græs/ *n* hierba, *f;* (pasture) pasto, herbaje, *m;* (sward) césped, *m.* —*vt* cubrir de hierba; sembrar de hierba; apacentar. **to hear the g. grow,** sentir crecer la hierba. **to let the g. grow,** *Fig.* dejar crecer la hierba. **to turn out to g.,** echar al pasto. **g.-blade,** brizna de hierba, *f.* **g.-green,** *a* and *n* verde como la hierba *m..* **g.-grown,** cubierto de hierba. **g.-land,** pradera, *f.* **g.-snake,** culebra *f.* **g. widow,** mujer cuyo marido está ausente

**grasshopper** /'græs,hɒpər/ *n* saltamontes, *m.* **grasshopper's chirp,** chirrido (del saltamontes), *m*

**grassy** /'græsi/ *a* parecido a la hierba, como la hierba; cubierto de hierba; de hierba

**grate** /greit/ *n* parrilla, *f;* (grating) reja, *f.* —*vt* raspar, raer; *Cul.* rallar; (make a noise) hacer rechinar. —*vi* rozar; rechinar, chirriar. **to g. on, upon,** (of sounds) irritar, molestar; chocar con. **to g. on the ear,** herir el oído

**grateful** /'greitfəl/ *a* agradecido, reconocido; (pleasant) agradable, grato

**gratefully** /'greitfəli/ *adv* agradecidamente; gratamente

**gratefulness** /'greitfəlnɪs/ *n* agradecimiento, *m,* gratitud, *f;* (pleasantness) agrado, *m*

**grater** /'greitər/ *n Cul.* rallador, *m*

**gratification** /,grætəfɪ'keiʃən/ *n* satisfacción, *f;* (pleasure) placer, gusto, *m*

**gratified** /'grætə,faid/ *a* satisfecho, contento

**gratify** /'grætə,fai/ *vt* satisfacer; (please) gratificar, agradar

**gratifying** /'grætə,faiɪŋ/ *a* satisfactorio, agradable

**grating** /'greitɪŋ/ *n* reja, *f;* rejilla, *f;* *Naut.* jareta, *f;* (optics) retículo, *m;* (sound) rechinamiento, chirrido, *m.* —*a* rechinante, chirriador; áspero

**gratis** /'grætɪs/ *a* and *adv* gratis

**gratitude** /'grætɪ,tud/ *n* agradecimiento, *m,* gratitud, *f*

**gratuitous** /grə'tuɪtəs/ *a* gratuito

**gratuitousness** /grə'tuɪtəsnɪs/ *n* gratuidad, *f*

**gratuity** /grə'tuiti/ *n* gratificación, propina, *f*

**grave** /greiv/ *n* (hole) sepultura, fosa, *f;* (monument) tumba, *f,* sepulcro, *m;* *Fig.* muerte, *f.* **g.-digger,** enterrador, sepulturero, *m*

**grave** /a greiv; *n* grɒv/ *a* grave; importante; serio; sobrio; (anxious) preocupado; (of accent) grave. —*n* (grave accent) acento grave, *m*

**gravel** /'grævəl/ *n* grava, *f;* cascajo, casquijo, *m;* *Med.* arenillas, *f pl,* cálculo, *m*

**gravely** /'greivli/ *adv* gravemente; seriamente

**Graves' disease** /greivz/ *n* bocio exoftálmico, *m*

**gravestone** /'greiv,stoun/ *n* lápida mortuoria, *f*

**graveyard** /'greiv,yɑrd/ *n* camposanto, cementerio, *m*

**gravitate** /'grævɪ,teit/ *vi* gravitar; tender

**gravitation** /,grævɪ'teiʃən/ *n* gravitación, *f;* tendencia, *f*

**gravitational** /,grævɪ'teiʃənl/ *a* de gravitación, gravitacional, gravitatorio

**gravitational pull** *n* atracción gravitatoria, *f*

**gravity** /'grævɪti/ *n Phys.* gravedad, *f;* seriedad, *f;* solemnidad, *f;* gravedad, *f;* (weight) peso, *m;* importancia, *f;* (enormity) enormidad, *f;* (danger) peligro, *m.* **center of g.,** centro de gravedad, *m.* **law of g.,** ley de la gravedad, *f.* **specific g.,** peso específico, *m*

**gravy** /'greivi/ *n* salsa, *f;* jugo (de la carne), *m.* **g.-boat,** salsera, *f*

**gray** /grei/ *a* gris; (of animals) rucio. —*n* color gris, gris, *m;* caballo gris, *m.* **His hair is turning g.,** El pelo se le vuelve gris. **g.-haired,** de pelo gris. **g. matter,** materia gris, *f;* cacumen, *m.* **g. mullet,** *Ichth.* mújol, *m.* **g. squirrel,** gris, *m.* **g. wolf,** lobo gris, *m*

**grayish** /'greiɪʃ/ *a* grisáceo, agrisado; (of hair) entrecano

**grayness** /'greinɪs/ *n* color gris, gris, *m;* *Fig.* monotonía, *f*

**graze** /greiz/ *n* abrasión, *f;* (brush) roce, *m, vi* pacer, apacentarse. —*vt* pastorear, apacentar; (brush) rozar

**grazing** /'greizɪŋ/ *n Agr.* apacentamiento, pastoreo, *m;* (brushing) rozadura, *f.* —*a* que pace, herbívoro; (of land) pacedero. **g. land,** pasto, *m*

**grease** /gris/ *n* grasa, *f;* (dirt) mugre, *f;* (of a candle) sebo, *m,* cera, *f.* —*vt* engrasar; manchar con grasa; *Fig. Inf.* untar. **to g. the wheels,** *Fig.* untar el carro. **g.-box,** *Mech.* caja de sebo, *f.* **g.-gun,** engrasador de compresión, *m.* **g.-paint,** afeites de actor (or de actriz), *m pl.* **g.-proof paper,** papel impermeable, *m.* **g. spot,** lámpara, mancha de grasa, *f,* saín, *m*

**greaser** /'grisər/ *n* engrasador, *m*

**greasiness** /'grisinɪs/ *n* graseza, *f;* lo aceitoso; untuosidad, *f*

**greasing** /'grisɪŋ/ *n* engrasado, *m*

**greasy** /'grisi/ *a* grasiento; (oily) aceitoso; (grubby) mugriento, bisunto; *Fig.* lisonjero. **g. pole,** cucaña, *f*

**great** /greit/ *a* gran; grande; enorme; vasto; (much) mucho; (famous) famoso, ilustre; noble, sublime; (intimate) íntimo; important; principal; poderoso; magnífico, impresionante; *Inf.* famoso, estupendo; (of time) largo; (clever) fuerte. **Alexander the G.,** Alejandro Magno. **the G. Mogul,** el Gran Mogul. **a g. deal,** mucho. **a g. man,** un grande hombre, un hombre famoso. **a g. many,** muchos (muchas). **He lived to a g. age,** Vivió hasta una edad avanzada. **so g.,** tan grande, tamaño. **the g.,** los grandes hombres. **g. on,** aficionado a. **g.-aunt,** tía abuela, *f.* **g.-grandchild,** etc. See **grandchild,** etc. **g.-hearted,** valeroso; magnánimo, generoso. **g. power,** gran poder, *m.* **G. War,** Gran Guerra, *f.* **the Great Schism,** el Gran Cisma, *m*

**greater** /'greitər/ *a* comp. of **great,** mayor; más grande. **to make g.,** agrandar. **G. London,** el Gran Londres, *m*

**greatest** /'greitɪst/ *a* sup. of **great,** más grande; mayor; máximo; más famoso; sumo

**greatly** /'greitli/ *adv* mucho; con mucho; (very) muy; noblemente

**greatness** /'greitnɪs/ *n* grandeza, *f;* grandiosidad, *f;* extensión, vastedad, *f;* importancia, *f;* poder, *m;* majestad, *f;* esplendor, *m;* (intensity) intensidad, *f;* (enormity) enormidad, *f*

**Grecian** /'griʃən/ *a* griego

**Greco-** *prefix* (in compounds) greco-, greco

**Greece** /gris/ *n* Grecia, *f*

**greed** /grid/ *n* (cupidity) codicia, rapacidad, avaricia, *f;* avidez, ansia, *f;* (of food) gula, glotonería, *f*

**greedily** /'gridəli/ *adv* codiciosamente; con avidez; (of eating) vorazmente

**greedy** /'gridi/ *a* (for food) glotón; codicioso; ambicioso; ávido; deseoso

**Greek** /grik/ *a* and *n* griego (-ga); (language) griego, *m.* **It's all G. to me,** Para mí es como si fuese en latín, Me es chino. **G. tunic,** peplo, *m*

**green** /grin/ *a* verde; (inexpert) inexperto, bisoño; (recent) nuevo, reciente; (fresh) fresco; (of complexion) pálido, descolorido; (flowery) floreciente; (vigorous) lozano; (young) joven; (unripe) verde; (credulous) crédulo; (raw) crudo; (of wood, vegetables) verde. —*n* verde, color verde, *m;* (vegetables) verdura, *f;* (meadow) prado, *m;* (turf) césped, *m;* (grass) hierba, *f;* (bowling) campo de juego, *m.* —*vt* teñir (or pintar) de verde. **bright g.,** *n* verdegay, verde claro, *m*. **dark g.,** *n* verdinegro, *m*. **light g.,** *n* verde pálido, *m*. **to grow** or **look g.,** verdear. **g.-eyed,** de ojos verdes. **g. peas,** guisantes, *m pl*. **g. table,** tapete verde, *m*

**greenery** /'grinəri/ *n* follaje, *m;* verdura, *f*

**greengrocer** /'grin,grousər/ *n* verdulero (-ra)

**greengrocery** /'grin,grousəri/ *n* verduleria, *f*

**greenhorn** /'grin,hɔrn/ *n* bisoño (-ña); papanatas, *m*

**greenhouse** /'grin,haus/ *n* invernáculo, invernadero, *m*

**greenish** /'griniʃ/ *a* verdoso. **g.-yellow,** cetrino

**Greenland** /'grinlənd/ Groenlandia, *f*

**Greenlander** /'grinləndər/ *n* groenlandés (-esa)

**greenness** /'grinnis/ *a* lo verde; verdor, *m*, verdura, *f;* (inexperience) falta de experiencia, *f;* (vigor) vigor, *m*, lozanía, *f;* (newness) novedad, *f;* (of wood, fruit) falta de madurez, *f*

**greenroom** /'grin,rum/ *n* Theat. saloncillo, *m*

**greenstuff** /'grin,stʌf/ *n* hortalizas, legumbres, *f pl*

**greet** /grit/ *vt* saludar; recibir; (express pleasure) dar la bienvenida (a)

**greeting** /'gritɪŋ/ *n* salutación, *f*, saludo, *m;* recepción, *f;* (welcome) bienvenida, *f; pl* **greetings,** recuerdos, *m pl*

**gregarious** /grɪ'gɛəriəs/ *a* gregario

**gregariousness** /grɪ'gɛəriəsnis/ *n* gregarismo, *m*

**Gregorian** /grɪ'gɔriən/ *a* gregoriano

**grenade** /grɪ'neid/ *n* granada, bomba, *f*. **hand-g.,** bomba de mano, *f*

**grey** /grei/ See **gray**

**greyhound** /'grei,haund/ *n* galgo, lebrel, *m*. **g. bitch,** galga, *f;* **g. racing,** carreras de galgos, *f pl*

**grid** /grid/ *n* (of electric power) red, *f;* rejilla, *f;* (for water, etc.) alcantarilla, *f*

**gridiron** /'grid,aiərn/ *n* Cul. parrilla, *f;* (of electric power) red, *f; Theat.* telar, *m*

**grief** /grif/ *n* angustia, pena, aflicción, *f;* dolor, suplicio, *m*. **to come to g.,** pasarlo mal, tener un desastre

**grievance** /'grivəns/ *n* injusticia, *f;* motivo de queja, *m*

**grieve** /griv/ *vt* entristecer, afligir, angustiar; atormentar. —*vi* entristecerse, afligirse, acongojarse. **to g. for,** lamentar: echar de menos

**grievous** /'grivəs/ *a* (heavy) oneroso, gravoso; opresivo; doloroso, penoso; lamentable; cruel. **g. error,** error lamentable

**grievousness** /'grivəsnis/ *n* (weight) peso, *m;* carácter opresivo, *m;* dolor, *m*, aflicción, *f;* enormidad, *f;* crueldad, *f*

**griffin** /'grifin/ *n* grifo, *m;* (Fig. chaperon) carabina, *f;* (dog) grifón, *m*

**grill** /gril/ *n* Cul. parrilla, *f;* (grating) rejilla, *f;* (before a window) reja, *f;* (food) asado a la parrilla, *m*. —*vt* Cul. asar a la parrilla; (burn) quemar; (question) interrogar; (torture) torturar. —*vi* Cul. asarse a la parrilla; (be burnt) quemarse. **g.-room,** parrilla, *f*

**grille** /gril/ *n* reja, *f;* rejilla, *f;* (screen) verja, *f*

**grilled** /grild/ *a* Cul. a la parrilla; con rejilla

**griller** /'grilər/ *n* Cul. parrilla, *f*

**grim** /grim/ *a* (fierce) feroz, salvaje; (severe) severo, ceñudo, adusto; inflexible; (frightful) horrible

**grimace** /'griməs/ *n* mueca, *f*, gesto, mohín, visaje, *m*, *vi* hacer muecas

**grime** /graim/ *n* mugre, *f;* suciedad, *f*. **to cover with g.,** enmugrecer

**grimly** /'grimli/ *adv* severamente; sin sonreír; inflexiblemente; (without retreating) sin cejar; (frightfully) horriblemente; de un modo espantoso

**grimness** /'grimnis/ *n* (ferocity) ferocidad, *f;* (severity) severidad, *f;* inflexibilidad, *f;* (frightfulness) horror, *m*, lo espantoso

**grimy** /'graimi/ *a* mugriento, sucio

**grin** /grin/ *n* sonrisa grande, *f;* sonrisa burlona, *f;* (grimace) mueca, *f*. —*vi* sonreír mostrando los dientes; sonreír bonachonamente; sonreír de un modo burlón

**grind** /graind/ *vt* (to powder) pulverizar; moler; (break up) quebrantar; (oppress) agobiar, oprimir; (sharpen) afilar, amolar; (a barrel-organ) tocar (un manubrio); (the teeth) crujir, rechinar (los dientes); (into) reducir a; (Inf. teach) empollar. —*vi* moler;

*Fig. Inf.* trabajar laboriosamente. —*n Fig. Inf.* trabajo pesado, *m; n Fig. Inf.* estudiantón, *m*

**grinder** /'graindər/ *n* (of scissors, etc.) afilador, *m;* (of an organ) organillero; (mill-stone) piedra de moler, *f;* (molar) muela, *f*

**grinding** /'graindɪŋ/ *a* (tedious) cansado, aburrido; opresivo; (of pain) incesante. —*n* pulverización, *f;* amoladura, *f;* (of grain) molienda, *f;* (polishing) pulimento, bruñido, *m;* (oppression) opresión, *f;* (of teeth) rechinamiento, *m*

**grindstone** /'graind,stoun/ *n* amoladera, afiladera, piedra de amolar, *f*. **to have one's nose to the g.,** batir el yunque

**grinning** /'grinɪŋ/ *a* sonriente; riente; (mocking) burlón

**grip** /grip/ *n* asimiento, agarro, *m;* (claws, clutches) garras, *f pl;* (hand) mano, *f;* (of shaking hands) apretón de manos, *m;* (of a weapon, etc.) empuñadura, *f;* (reach) alcance, *m;* (understanding) comprensión, *f;* (control) dominio, *m;* (bag) portamanteo, *m;* maleta, *f*. —*vt* asir, agarrar; (of wheels) agarrarse, *f; Mech.* morder; (a sword, etc.) empuñar; (pinch) pellizcar; (surround) cercar; (understand) comprender; (press; to grip the hand and *Fig.* the heart) apretar; (fill) llenar; (the attention) atraer, llamar; (sway, hold) dominar

**gripe** /graip/ *n* (Inf. pain) retortijón (de tripas), *m*

**grisly** /'grizli/ *a* espantoso; repugnante

**grist** /grist/ *n* molienda, *f*. **Everything is g. to their mill,** Sacan partido de todo

**gristle** /'grisəl/ *n* cartílago, *m*, ternilla, *f*

**gristly** /'grisli/ *a* cartilaginoso

**grit** /grit/ *n* cascajo, *m;* polvo, *m; Fig.* firmeza (de carácter), *f;* (courage) valor, *m;* (endurance) aguante, *m*

**gritty** /'griti/ *a* arenoso, arenisco

**grizzled** /'grizəld/ *a* (of hair, etc.) gris; canoso; grisáceo

**grizzly bear** /'grizli/ *n* oso (-sa) pardo (-da)

**groan** /groun/ *n* gemido, *m*. —*vi* gemir; (creak) crujir. **to g. out,** decir (o contar) entre gemidos. **to g. under,** sufrir bajo, gemir bajo; (of weight) crujir bajo

**groaning** /'grounɪŋ/ *n* gemidos, *m pl*. —*a* que gime, gemidor; (under a weight) crujiente

**grocer** /'grousər/ *n* abacero (-ra) vendedor (-ra) de comestibles. **grocer's shop,** tienda de comestibles, bodega, *f*

**grocery** /'grousəri/ *n* tienda de comestibles, tienda de ultramarinos, abarrotería, lonja, bodega, *f*, negocio de comestibles, *m; pl* **groceries,** provisiones, *f pl*, comestibles, *m pl*

**grog** /grɒg/ *n* grog, *m*

**groin** /grɔin/ *n Anat.* ingle, *f*

**groom** /grum/ *n* (in a royal household) gentilhombre, *m;* lacayo, *m;* mozo de caballos, *m;* (of a bride) novio, *m*. —*vt* (a horse) cuidar; (oneself) arreglarse. **She is always well groomed,** Está siempre muy bien arreglada

**groomsman** /'grumzmən/ *n* padrino de boda, *m*

**groove** /gruv/ *n* ranura, muesca, *f;* estría, *f;* surco, *m; Fig.* rutina, *f*. —*vt* entallar; estriar

**grooved** /gruvd/ *a* con ranura; estriado

**grope** /group/ *vi* andar a tientas; (with for) buscar a tientas; procurar, encontrar, buscar. **to g. one's way toward,** avanzar a tientas hacia; *Fig.* avanzar poco a poco hacia

**gropingly** /'groupɪŋli/ *adv* a tientas; irresolutamente

**gross** /grous/ *n Com.* gruesa, *f;* totalidad, *f, a* grueso; denso, espeso; (unrefined) grosero; (great) grande; (crass) craso; total; *Com.* bruto; (tremendous) enorme. **in g.,** en grueso. **g. amount,** total, *m; Com.* importe bruto, *m*. **g. weight,** peso bruto, *m*

**grossly** /'grousli/ *adv* groseramente; (much) enormemente

**grossness** /'grousnis/ *n* gordura, *f;* (vulgarity) grosería, *f;* obscenidad, *f;* (enormity) enormidad, *f*

**grotesque** /grou'tɛsk/ *a* grotesco; extravagante, estrambótico; ridículo. —*n* grotesco, *m*

**grotesqueness** /grou'tɛsknis/ *n* lo grotesco; ridiculez, *f*

**grotto** /'grɒtou/ *n* gruta, *f*

**ground** /graund/ *n* suelo, *m;* (of water and Naut.)

fondo, *m;* (earth) tierra, *f; Fig.* terreno, *m;* (strata) capa, *f; Sports.* campo, *m;* (parade) plaza (de armas), *f;* (background) fondo, *m;* (basis) base, *f,* fundamento, *m;* (reason) causa, *f;* motivo, *m;* (excuse) pretexto, *m; pl* **grounds,** jardines, *m pl,* parque, *m;* (sediment) sedimento, *m,* heces, *f pl;* (reason) causa, *f.* —*vi Naut.* varar, encallar. —*vt* poner en tierra; *Naut.* hacer varar; *Elec.* conectar con tierra; (base) fundar (en), basar (en); (teach) enseñar los rudimentos (de). —*a* molido; en polvo; (of floors, stories) bajo; (of glass) deslustrado; *Bot.* terrestre. **common g.,** tierra comunal, *f; Fig.* tierra común, *f.* **He is on his own g.,** Está en terreno propio. **It fell to the g.,** Cayó al suelo; *Fig.* Fracasó. **It is on the g.,** Está en el suelo. **It suits me to the g.,** Me viene de perilla. **to break fresh g.,** *Fig.* tratar problemas nuevos. **to be well grounded in,** conocer bien los elementos (or rudimentos) de. **to cover g.,** cubrir terreno; recorrer; (in discussion) tocar muchos puntos. **to cut the g. from beneath one's feet,** hacer perder la iniciativa (a). **to give g.,** retroceder; perder terreno. **to raze to the g.,** echar por tierra, arrasar. **to stand one's g.,** resistir el ataque; no darse por vencido; *Fig.* mantenerse firme, mantenerse en sus trece. **to win g.,** ganar terreno. **g. coffee,** café molido, *m.* **g.-color,** (of paint) primera capa, *f;* (color de) fondo, *m;* **g.-floor,** piso bajo, *m.* **g. glass,** vidrio deslustrado, *m.* **g.-ivy,** hiedra terrestre, *f.* **g. nut,** cacahuete, *m.* **g.-plan,** *Archit.* planta, *f.* **g.-rent,** censo, *m.* **g.-sheet,** tela impermeable, *f;* **g. staff,** *Aer.* personal del aeropuerto, *m.* **g.-swell,** mar de fondo, *m.*

**grounded** /'graundɪd/ *a* fundado. **The airplanes are g.,** Los aviones están sin volar. **His suspicions are well g.,** Tiene motivos para sus sospechas

**grounding** /'graundɪŋ/ *n Naut.* encalladura, *f;* (teaching) instrucción en los rudimentos, *f*

**groundless** /'graundlɪs/ *a* sin fundamento, inmotivado, sin causa, sin motivo

**groundwork** /'graund,wɜrk/ *n* fundamento, *m;* base, *f;* principio, *m*

**group** /grup/ *n* grupo, *m.* —*vt* agrupar. —*vi* agruparse. **g. captain,** coronel de aviación, *m*

**grouping** /'grupɪŋ/ *n* agrupación, *f*

**grouse** /graus/ *n Ornith.* ortega, *f.* —*vi* rezongar, refunfuñar

**grove** /grouv/ *n* soto, boscaje, *m;* arboleda, *f*

**grovel** /'grɒvəl/ *vi* arrastrarse; *Fig.* humillarse

**groveling** /'grɒvəlɪŋ/ *a Fig.* servil; ruin

**grow** /grou/ *vi* crecer; (increase) aumentar; (become) hacerse; empezar a; llegar a; (turn) volverse; ponerse; (flourish) progresar, adelantar; (develop) desarrollarse; (extend) extenderse. —*vt* cultivar; dejar crecer. **I grew to fear it,** Llegué a temerlo. **to g. cold,** ponerse frío; enfriarse; (of weather) empezar a hacer frío; *Fig.* endurecerse. **to g. fat,** engordar. **to g. hard,** ponerse duro; *Fig.* endurecerse. **to g. hot,** ponerse caliente; calentarse; (of weather) empezar a hacer calor. **to g. like Topsy,** crecer a la buena de Dios. **to g. old,** envejecer. **to g. tall,** crecer mucho; ser alto. **to g. again,** crecer de nuevo. **to g. into,** hacerse, llegar a ser; venir a ser. **to g. out of,** brotar de; originarse en; (a habit) desacostumbrarse poco a poco. **He is growing out of his clothes,** La ropa se le hace pequeña. **to g. up,** (of persons) hacerse hombre (mujer); desarrollarse; (of a custom, etc.) imponerse. **to g. on, upon,** crecer sobre; llegar a dominar; (make think) hacer creer, empezar a pensar; (of a habit) arraigar en

**grower** /'grouər/ *n* cultivador (-ra)

**growing** /'grouɪŋ/ *n* crecimiento, *m;* desarrollo, *m;* (increase) aumento, *m;* (of flowers, etc.) cultivación, *f,* a creciente

**growing pains** *n pl* crisis de desarrollo, *f*

**growl** /graul/ *n* gruñido, *m;* reverberación, *f;* trueno, *m.* —*vi* gruñir; (of guns) tronar; (of thunder) reverberar. **to g. out,** decir gruñendo

**grown** /groun/ *a* crecido; maduro; adulto. **a g. up,** una persona mayor. **to be full-g.,** estar completamente desarrollado; haber llegado a la madurez. **g. over with,** cubierto de

**growth** /grouθ/ *n* crecimiento, *m;* (development) desarrollo, *m;* (progress) progreso, adelanto, *m;* (in-

crease) aumento, *m;* (cultivation) cultivo, *m;* (vegetation) vegetación, *f; Med.* tumor, *m.* **He has a week's g. on his chin,** Tiene una barba de una semana

**grub** /grʌb/ *n* larva, *f,* gusano, *m.* —*vt* (with up, out) desarraigar; cavar; desmalezar; *Fig. Inf.* buscar

**grubbiness** /'grʌbinɪs/ *n* suciedad, *f;* (untidiness) desaliño, *m*

**grubby** /'grʌbi/ *a* lleno de gusanos; sucio; bisunto; desaliñado

**grudge** /grʌdʒ/ *n* motivo de rencor, *m;* rencor, resentimiento, *m,* ojeriza, *f;* mala voluntad, *f;* aversión, *f.* —*vt* envidiar. **to bear a g.,** tener ojeriza

**grudging** /'grʌdʒɪŋ/ *a* (niggardly) mezquino; envidioso; poco generoso; de mala gana; nada afable

**grudgingly** /'grʌdʒɪŋli/ *adv* de mala gana, contra su voluntad; con rencor; a regañadientes

**gruel** /'gruəl/ *n* gachas, *f pl*

**gruesome** /'grusəm/ *a* pavoroso, horrible; macabro

**gruff** /grʌf/ *a* (of the voice) bronco, grave, áspero; (of manner) brusco, malhumorado

**gruffly** /'grʌfli/ *adv* en una voz bronca (or áspera); bruscamente, con impaciencia, malhumoradamente

**gruffness** /'grʌfnɪs/ *n* aspereza, bronquedad, *f;* brusquedad, sequedad, impaciencia, *f,* mal humor, *m*

**grumble** /'grʌmbəl/ *n* ruido sordo, trueno, *m;* estruendo, *m;* (complaint) refunfuño, rezongo, *m.* —*vi* tronar; refunfuñar, rezongar; hablar entre dientes; quejarse; protestar (contra). —*vt* decir refunfuñando

**grumbler** /'grʌmblər/ *n* murmurador (-ra), refunfuñador (-ra)

**grumbling** /'grʌmblɪŋ/ *a* gruñón, refunfuñador; regañón; descontento. —*n See* **grumble**

**grumblingly** /'grʌmblɪŋli/ *adv* a regañadientes, refunfuñando

**grumpiness** /'grʌmpinɪs/ *n* mal humor, *m,* irritabilidad, *f*

**grumpy** /'grʌmpi/ *a* malhumorado, irritable

**grunt** /grʌnt/ *n* gruñido, *m.* —*vi* gruñir

**grunting** /'grʌntɪŋ/ *a* gruñidor

**guarantee** /ˌgærən'ti/ *n Law.* persona de quien otra sale fiadora, *f;* garantía, *f;* abono, *m.* —*vt* garantizar; responder de; abonar; (assure) asegurar, acreditar

**guarantor** /'gærən,tɔr/ *n* garante, *mf*

**guard** /gɑrd/ *n* (watchfulness) vigilancia, *f;* (in fencing) guardia, *f;* (of a sword) guarnición, *f;* (sentry) centinela, *m;* (soldier) guardia, *m;* (body of soldiers) guardia, *f;* (escort) escolta, *f;* (keeper) guardián, *m;* (protection) protección, defensa, *f;* (of a train) jefe de tren, *m.* —*vt* guardar; proteger, defender; vigilar; (escort) escoltar. **to g. against,** guardarse de. **the changing of the g.,** el relevo de la guardia. **to be on g.,** *Mil.* estar de guardia; (in fencing) estar en guardia. **to be on one's g.,** estar prevenido, estar alerta. **to be off one's g.,** estar desprevenido. **to mount g.,** *Mil.* montar la guardia; vigilar. **guard's van,** furgón de equipajes, *m.* **g.-house,** cuerpo de guardia, *m;* prisión militar, *f*

**guarded** /'gɑrdɪd/ *a* (reticent) reservado, circunspecto, prudente, discreto

**guardedly** /'gɑrdɪdli/ *adv* prudentemente, con circunspección, discretamente

**guardian** /'gɑrdiən/ *n* protector (-ra); guardián (-ana); *Law.* tutor, *m.* —*a* que guarda; tutelar. **g. angel,** ángel de la guarda, ángel custodio, *m;* deidad tutelar, *f*

**guardianship** /'gɑrdiən,ʃɪp/ *n* protección, *f;* patronato, *m; Law.* curaduría, tutela, *f*

**guardsman** /'gɑrdzmən/ *n* guardia, *m*

**Guatemalan** /ˌgwɑtə'mɑlən/ *a and n* guatemalteco (-ca)

**guava** /'gwɑvə/ *n Bot.* guayaba, *f*

**Guernsey** /'gɜrnzi/ Guenesy, *m*

**guerrilla** /gə'rɪlə/ *n* guerrilla, *f;* (soldier) guerrillero, *m.* —*a* de guerrilla. **g. warfare,** guerra de guerrillas, *f*

**guess** /gɛs/ *n* adivinación, *f;* estimación, *f;* conjetura, *f;* sospecha, *f.* —*vt* and *vi* adivinar; conjeturar; sospechar; imaginar; (suppose) suponer, creer; calcular. **to g. at,** formar una opinión sobre; imaginar. **a rough g.,** estimación aproximada, *f.* **at a g.,** a poco más o menos, a ojo de buen cubero. **g.-work,** conjeturas, suposiciones, *f pl*

**guest** /gɛst/ *n* (at a meal) convidado (-da), invitado

(-da); (at a hotel, etc.) cliente (-da); *Biol.* parásito, *m*.

**g.-room,** alcoba de respeto, alcoba de honor, alcoba de huéspedes, *f*, cuarto de amigos, cuarto para invitados, *m*

**guffaw** /gʌ'fɔ/ *n* carcajada, *f*. —*vi* reírse a carcajadas, soltar el trapo

**Guiana** /gi'ænə/ Guayana, *f*

**guidance** /'gaidn̩s/ *n* dirección, *f*; gobierno, *m*; (advice) consejos, *m pl*; inspiración, *f*

**guide** /gaid/ *n* (person) guía, *mf*; (girl g.) exploradora, *f*; (book and *Fig.*) guía, *f*; mentor, *m*; modelo, *m*; (inspiration) norte, *m*; *Mech.* guía, *f*. —*vt* guiar; conducir; encaminar; dirigir; (govern) gobernar. **g.-book,** guía (de turistas), *f*. **g.-post,** poste indicador, *m*

**guided tour** /'gaidɪd/ *n* visita explicada, visita programada, *f*

**guideline** /'gaid,lain/ *Lit.* falsarregla, falsilla, *f*; *Fig.* pauta, *f*

**guiding** /'gaidɪŋ/ *a* que guía; directivo; decisivo. —*n* See **guidance**

**guild** /gɪld/ *n* gremio, *m*. —*a* gremial. **g. member,** gremial, *m*

**guilder** /'gɪldər/ *n* (coin) florín holandés, *m*

**guile** /gail/ *n* astucia, superchería, maña, *f*

**guileful** /'gailfəl/ *a* astuto

**guileless** /'gaillɪs/ *a* cándido, sin malicia, inocente

**guilelessly** /'gaillɪsli/ *adv* inocentemente

**guilelessness** /'gaillɪsnɪs/ *n* inocencia, candidez, *f*

**guillotine** /'gɪlə,tin/ *n* guillotina, *f*. —*vt* guillotinar

**guilt** /gɪlt/ *n* culpabilidad, *f*; crimen, *m*; (sin) pecado, *m*

**guilt complex** complejo de culpa, *m*

**guiltily** /'gɪltəli/ *adv* culpablemente; como si fuese culpable

**guiltless** /'gɪltlɪs/ *a* libre de culpa, inocente; puro; ignorante

**guilty** /'gɪlti/ *a* culpable; delincuente; criminal. **to find g.,** encontrar culpable. **to plead g.,** confesarse culpable. **g. party,** culpable, *m*

**Guinea** /'gɪni/ Guinea, *f*

**guinea** /'gɪni/ *n* guinea, *f*. **g.-fowl,** gallina de Guinea, *f*. **g.-pig,** conejillo de Indias, cobayo, *m*

**guise** /gaiz/ *n* manera, guisa, *f*; (garb) traje, *m*; máscara, *f*; *Fig.* pretexto, *m*. **under the g. of,** bajo el pretexto de; bajo la apariencia de

**guitar** /gɪ'tar/ *n* guitarra, *f*

**guitarist** /gɪ'tarɪst/ *n* guitarrista, *mf*

**gulf** /gʌlf/ *n* golfo, *m*; abismo, *m*

**Gulf Stream, the** la Corriente del Golfo

**gull** /gʌl/ *n* *Ornith.* gaviota, *f*; (dupe) primo, *m*. —*vt* engañar, timar, defraudar

**gullet** /'gʌlɪt/ *n* esófago, *m*; garganta, *f*

**gullibility** /ˌgʌlə'bɪlɪti/ *n* credulidad, *f*

**gullible** /'gʌləbəl/ *a* crédulo

**gully** /'gʌli/ *n* hondonada, barranca, *f*; (gutter) arroyo, *f*

**gulp** /gʌlp/ *n* trago, sorbo, *m*. —*vt* engullir, tragar; (repress) ahogar; (believe) tragar. **to g. up,** vomitar

**gum** /gʌm/ *n* (of the mouth) encía, *f*; goma, *f*. —*vt* engomar; pegar con goma. **gum arabic,** goma arábiga, *f*. **gum boots,** botas de goma, *f*. **gum-resin,** gomorresina, *f*. **gum starch,** aderezo, *m*. **gum tree,** eucalipto, *m*

**gumminess** /'gʌminɪs/ *n* gomosidad, *f*

**gummy** /'gʌmi/ *a* gomoso

**gumption** /'gʌmpʃən/ *n* sentido común, seso, *m*

**gun** /gʌn/ *n* arma de fuego, *f*; (handgun) fusil, *m*; (sporting g.) escopeta, *f*; (pistol) pistola, *f*, revólver, *m*; (cannon) cañón, *m*; (firing) cañonazo, *m*. **big gun,** *Inf.* pájaro gordo, *m*. **heavy gun,** cañón de grueso calibre, *m*. **gun-barrel,** cañón de escopeta, *m*. **gun-carriage,** cureña, *f*. **gun-cotton,** pólvora de algo-

dón, *f*. **gun-fire,** cañonazos, *m pl*, fuego, *m*. **gun-metal,** bronce de cañón, *m*; pavón, *m*. **gun-room,** armería, *f*; (on a ship) polvorín, *m*. **gun-running,** contrabanda de armas, *f*. **gun-turret,** torre, *f*. **gun wound,** balazo, *m*

**gunboat** /'gʌn,bout/ *n* cañonero, *m*, lancha bombardera, *f*

**gunflint** /'gʌn,flɪnt/ *n* piedra de escopeta, *f*

**gunman** /'gʌnmən/ *n* escopetero, armero, *m*; bandido armado, *m*; gángster, apache, *m*

**gunner** /'gʌnər/ *n* artillero, *m*; escopetero, *m*

**gun permit** *n* licencia de armas, *f*, permiso de armas, *m*

**gunpowder** /'gʌn,paudər/ *n* pólvora, *f*

**gunshot** /'gʌn,ʃɒt/ *n* escopetazo, *m*; tiro de fusil, *m*

**gunsmith** /'gʌn,smɪθ/ *n* escopetero, armero, *m*

**gunwale** /'gʌnl̩/ *n* *Naut.* regala, borda, *f*

**gurgle** /'gɜrgəl/ *n* murmullo, murmurio, gorgoteo, *m*; gluglú, *m*; (of a baby) gorjeo, *m*. —*vi* murmurar; hacer gluglú; (of babies) gorjear

**gurgling** /'gɜrglɪŋ/ *a* murmurante; (of babies) gorjeador. —*n* See **gurgle**

**gush** /gʌʃ/ *n* chorro, *m*; (of words) torrente, *m*; (of emotion) efusión, *f*. —*vi* chorrear, borbotar; surtir, surgir. **to g. out,** saltar, brotar a borbotones, salir a borbollones, salira borbotones. **to g. over,** *Fig.* hablar con efusión de

**gushing** /'gʌʃɪŋ/ *a* hirviente; (of people) efusivo, extremoso, empalagoso

**gusset** /'gʌsɪt/ *n* *Sew.* escudete, *m*

**gust** /gʌst/ *n* (of wind) ráfaga, bocanada (de aire), *f*; *Fig.* arrebato, acceso, *m*

**gusto** /'gʌstou/ *n* brío, *m*; entusiasmo, *m*

**gusty** /'gʌsti/ *a* borrascoso

**gut** /gʌt/ *n* intestino, *m*, tripa, *f*; (catgut) cuerda de tripa, *f*; *Naut.* estrecho, *m*; *pl* **guts,** tripas, *f pl*; (content) meollo, *m*, substancia, *f*; (stamina) aguante, espíritu, *m*. —*vt* (of fish, etc.) destripar; (plunder) saquear; destruir por completo; quemar completamente

**gutta-percha** /'gʌtə 'pɜrtʃə/ *n* gutapercha, *f*

**gutter** /'gʌtər/ *n* canal, *m*; (of a street) arroyo (de la calle), *m*; (ditch) zanja, *f*; *Fig.* hampa, *f*. —*vt* surcar. —*vi* gotear; (of a candle) cerotear, gotear la cera. **g. spout,** canalón, *m*

**guttersnipe** /'gʌtər,snaip/ *n* golfillo, *m*, niño (-ña) del hampa

**guttural** /'gʌtərəl/ *a* gutural. —*n* letra gutural, *f*

**guy** /gai/ *n* (rope) viento, *m*; *Naut.* guía, *f*; (effigy) mamarracho, *m*; (scarecrow) espantajo, *m*, *vt* sujetar con vientos o guías; burlarse de

**guzzle** /'gʌzəl/ *vt* tragar, engullir. —*vi* atracarse, engullir; emborracharse. —*n* comilón, *m*; borrachera, *f*

**guzzler** /'gʌzlər/ *n* tragador (-ra); borracho (-cha)

**gymnasium** /dʒɪm'naziəm/ *n* gimnasio, *m*

**gymnast** /'dʒɪmnæst/ *n* gimnasta, *mf*

**gymnastic** /dʒɪm'næstɪk/ *a* gimnástico. **g. rings,** anillas, *f pl*

**gymnastics** /dʒɪm'næstɪks/ *n* gimnasia, *f*

**gynecological** /ˌgainɪkə'lɒdʒɪkəl/ *a* ginecológico

**gynecologist** /ˌgainɪ'kɒlədʒɪst/ *n* ginecólogo (-ga)

**gynecology** /ˌgainɪ'kɒlədʒi/ *n* ginecología, *f*

**gypsum** /'dʒɪpsəm/ *n* yeso, *m*

**gypsy** /'dʒɪpsi/ *n* gitano (-na). —*a* gitano, gitanesco; (music) flamenco

**gyrate** /'dʒaireit/ *vi* girar, rodar

**gyration** /dʒai'reiʃən/ *n* giro, *m*, vuelta, *f*

**gyratory** /'dʒairə,tɔri/ *a* giratorio

**gyro-compass** /'dʒairou ,kʌmpəs/ *n* brújula giroscópica, *f*

**gyroscope** /'dʒairə,skoup/ *n* *Phys.* giroscopio, *m*

# H

**h** /eitʃ/ n (letter) hache, f
**ha** /hɑ/ interj ¡ah!
**haberdasher** /'hæbər,dæʃər/ n mercero, m
**haberdashery** /'hæbər,dæʃəri/ n mercería, f
**habiliment** /hə'bɪləmənt/ n vestidura, f; pl **habiliments**, indumentaria, f
**habilitate** /hə'bɪlɪ,teit/ vt habilitar
**habilitation** /hə,bɪlɪ'teiʃən/ n habilitación, f
**habit** /'hæbɪt/ n costumbre, f, hábito, m; (temperament) temperamento, carácter, m; (use) uso, m; (of body) complexión, constitución, f; Eccl. hábito, m. **to be in the h. of,** soler, acostumbrar, estar acostumbrado a. **to have bad habits,** estar malacostumbrado. **to have the bad h. of,** tener el vicio (or la mala costumbre) de. **to contract the h. of,** contraer la costumbre de. **h. maker,** sastre de trajes de montar, m
**habitable** /'hæbɪtəbəl/ a habitable, vividero
**habitat** /'hæbɪ,tæt/ n (Bot., Zool.) medio, m, habitación, f
**habitation** /,hæbɪ'teiʃən/ n habitación, f
**habit-forming** /'hæbɪt,fɔrmɪŋ/ a enviciador, que crea vicio
**habitual** /hə'bɪtʃuəl/ a habitual, acostumbrado, usual; constante; común
**habitually** /hə'bɪtʃuəli/ adv habitualmente; constantemente; comúnmente
**habituate** /hə'bɪtʃu,eit/ vt habituar, acostumbrar
**habituation** /hə,bɪtʃu'eiʃən/ n habituación, f
**habitué** /hə'bɪtʃu,ei/ n parroquiano (-na); veterano (-na)
**hack** /hæk/ n caballo de alquiler, m; rocín, jaco, m; (writer) escritor mercenario, m. —vt acuchillar; tajar, cortar. —vi cortar. **to h. to pieces,** cortar en pedazos; pasar a cuchillo
**hacking** /'hækɪŋ/ a (of coughs) seco
**hackle** /'hækəl/ n (for flax, hemp) rastrillo, m
**hackney carriage** /'hækni/ n coche de plaza, coche de alquiler, m
**hackneyed** /'hæknid/ a gastado, trillado, muy usado, repetido, resobado
**hacksaw** /'hæk,sɔ/ n sierra de cerrajero, sierra para metal, f
**hackwork** /'hæk,wɜrk/ n trabajo de rutina, m
**haddock** /'hædək/ n merlango, m, pescadilla, f
**Hades** /'heidiz/ n Hades, m; Inf. el infierno, m
**haft** /hæft/ n mango, tomadero, m, manija, f; puño, m
**hag** /hæg, hɑg/ n bruja, f
**haggard** /'hægərd/ a ojeroso, trasnochado, trasojado
**haggardly** /'hægərdli/ adv ansiosamente
**haggardness** /'hægərdnɪs/ n aspecto ojeroso, m
**haggle** /'hægəl/ vi regatear; vacilar
**haggling** /'hæglɪŋ/ n regateo, m, a regatón
**hagiographer** /,hægi'ɒgrəfər/ n hagiógrafo, m
**hagiography** /,hægi'ɒgrəfi/ n hagiografía, f
**Hague, The** /heig/ La Haya
**ha, ha!** /'hɑ 'hɑ/ interj ¡ja, ja!
**hail** /heil/ n (salutation) saludo, m; (shout) grito, m; aclamación, f; (frozen rain) granizo, m; (of blows) lluvia, f. —interj ¡salve! —vt saludar; llamar; aclamar; Fig. lanzar, echar. —vi (hailstones) granizar; (blows, etc.) llover. **to h. from,** proceder de, ser natural de. **within h.,** al habla. **H. Mary,** Salve Regina, Avemaría, f
**hailstone** /'heil,stoun/ n granizo, pedrisco, m
**hailstorm** /'heil,stɔrm/ n granizada, f
**hair** /hɛər/ n (single h.) cabello, m; (Zool. Bot.) pelo, m; (of horse's mane) crin, f; (head of h.) cabellera, mata de pelo, f, pelo, m; (superfluous) vello, m; (fiber) fibra, f, filamento, m; (on the pen) raspa, f, pelo, m; Fig. pelo, m. **lock of h.,** bucle, rizo, m; mecha, f. **to dress one's h.,** peinarse. **to have one's h. cut,** hacerse cortar el pelo. **to part the h.,** hacer(se) la raya del pelo. **to put up one's h.,** hacerse el moño; (to "come out") ponerse de largo. **to tear one's h.,** mesarse los cabellos. **h. combings,** peinaduras, f pl.

**h.-curler,** tirabuzón, m. **h. dryer,** secadora de cabello, f. **h. dye,** tinte para el pelo, m. **h.-net,** redecilla, f. **h.-oil,** brillantina, f. **h.-raising,** horripilante, espeluznante. **h.-ribbon,** cinta para el pelo, f. **h.-shirt,** cilicio, m. **h. slide,** pasador, m. **h.-splitting,** sofistería, argucia, f; mez quinas argucias, quis quillas, f pl. **h.-spring,** muelle del volante, m. **h.-switch,** añadido, m. **h.-trigger,** pelo de una pistola, m
**hairbrush** /'hɛər,brʌʃ/ n cepillo para el cabello, m
**hairdresser** /'hɛər,drɛsər/ n peluquero (-ra), peinadora, f
**hairdressing** /'hɛər,drɛsɪŋ/ n peinado, m. **h. establishment or trade,** peluquería, f
**haired** /hɛərd/ a peludo, con pelo; (in compounds) de pelo...
**hairiness** /'hɛərinɪs/ n vellosidad, f
**hairless** /'hɛərlɪs/ a sin pelo; calvo
**hairlike** /'hɛər,laik/ a filiforme
**hairpin** /'hɛər,pɪn/ n horquilla, f. **h. bend,** viraje en horquilla, m
**hairsbreadth** /'hɛərz,brɛdθ/ n pelo, m. **to have a h. escape,** escapar por un pelo.
**hairy** /'hɛəri/ a peludo; velloso; Bot. hirsuto
**Haiti** /'heiti/ Haití, m
**Haitian** /'heiʃən/ a and n haitiano (-na)
**hake** /heik/ n merluza, f
**halcyon** /'hælsiən/ n alción, martín pescador, m. —a Fig. feliz, sereno, tranquilo
**hale** /heil/ a fuerte, sano, robusto. —vt hacer comparecer
**half** /hæf/ n mitad, f; (school term) trimestre, m. —a medio; semi. —adv a medias; mitad; (almost) casi; insuficientemente; imperfectamente. **I don't h. like it,** No me gusta nada. **It is h.-past two,** Son las dos y media. **an hour and a h.,** una hora y media. **better h.,** Inf. media naranja, cara mitad, f. **by halves,** a medias. **in h.,** en dos mitades. **one h.,** la mitad. **to go halves,** ir a medias. **to h. close,** entornar. **to h. open,** entreabrir. **h. a bottle,** media botella, f. **h. a crown,** media corona, f. **h.-alive,** semivivo. **h. an hour,** media hora, f. **h.-and-h.,** mitad y mitad; en partes iguales. **h.-asleep,** semidormido, medio dormido. **h.-awake,** medio despierto, entre duerme y vela. **h.-back,** Sports. medio, m. **h.-baked,** medio cocido, crudo; Fig. poco maduro. **h.-binding,** encuadernación en media pasta, f. **h.-breed,** a mestizo. —n cruce, m. **h.-brother,** hermanastro, hermano de padre, hermano de madre, m. **h.-caste,** mestizo. **h. circle,** semicírculo, m. **h.-closed,** entreabierto; medio cerrado. **h.-dead,** medio muerto; más muerto que vivo. **h.-done,** hecho a medias, sin acabar. **h.-dozen,** media docena, f. **h.-dressed,** medio desnudo. **h. fare,** medio billete, m. **h.-full,** medio lleno. **h.-hearted,** débil, poco eficaz, lánguido; indiferente, sin entusiasmo. **h.-heartedness,** debilidad, f; indiferencia, f. **h.-holiday,** media fiesta, f. **h.-hourly,** cada media hora. **h.-length,** (portrait) de medio cuerpo. **h.-length coat,** abrigo de tres cuartos, m. **h.-light,** media luz, f. **h.-mast,** a media asta. **h.-measure,** medida poco eficaz, f. **h.-moon,** n media luna, f; Astron. semilunio, m; (of a nail) blanco (de la uña), m. **h.-mourning,** medio luto, m. **h.-pay,** media paga, f. **h.-price,** a mitad de precio. **h.-seas-over,** Inf. entre dos velas. **h.-sister,** hermanastra, hermana de padre, hermana de madre, f. **h.-time,** Sports. media parte, f, medio tiempo, m. **h.-tone,** de medio tono. **h.-tone illustration,** fotograbado a media tinta, m. **h.-truth,** verdad a medias, f. **h.-turn,** media vuelta, f. **h.-way,** a medio camino; medio. **h.-witted,** medio loco, tonto, imbécil. **h.-year,** medio año, m. **h.-yearly,** semestral
**halfpenny** /'heipəni/ n medio penique, m; Inf. perra gorda, f
**half title** anteportada, falsa portada, portadilla, preportada, f
**halibut** /'hæləbət/ n halibut, m; (genus) hipogloso, m
**halitosis** /,hælɪ'tousɪs/ n halitosis, f
**hall** /hɔl/ n (mansion) mansión, casa de campo, f,

caserón, *m;* (public building) edificio, *m,* casa (de); (town h.) casa del ayuntamiento, *f;* (room) sala, *f;* (entrance) vestíbulo, *m;* (dining room) comedor, *m;* (of residence for students) residencia, *f.* **h. door,** portón, *m,* puerta del vestíbulo, *f.* **h. porter,** conserje, *m.* **h.-stand,** perchero, *m*

**hallelujah** /ˌhælə'luyə/ *n* aleluya, *f*

**hallmark** /'hɔl,mɑrk/ *n* marca de ley, *f; Fig.* señal, *f;* indicio, *m.* —*vt* poner la marca de ley sobre; *Fig.* sellar

**halloo** /hə'lu/ *vt* (hounds) azuzar; perseguir dando voces; (call) llamar

**hallow** /'hælou/ *vt* santificar; reverenciar; (consecrate) consagrar

**Halloween** /ˌhælə'win/ *n* la víspera de Todos los Santos, *f*

**hallucination** /hə,lusə'neiʃən/ *n* alucinación, ilusión, *f;* visión, *f;* fantasma, *m*

**hallucinatory** /hə'lusənə,tɔri/ *a* alucinador

**halo** /'heilou/ *n* halo, nimbo, *m*

**halogen** /'hælədʒən/ *n Chem.* halógeno, *m*

**halt** /hɔlt/ *n Mil.* alto, *m;* cesación, *f;* interrupción, *f;* (on a railway) apeadero, *m;* (for trams, buses) parada, *f.* —*vt* parar, detener. —*vi* pararse, detenerse; *Mil.* hacer alto; cesar; interrumpirse; (in speech) titubear; (of verse) estar cojo; (doubt) dudar; (limp) cojear. **H.!** *Mil.* ¡Alto!

**halter** /'hɔltər/ *n* ronzal, cabestro, *m;* (for hanging) dogal, *m.* —*vt* encabestrar, cabestrar

**halting** /'hɔltɪŋ/ *n* parada, *f;* interrupción, *f.* —*a* (of gait) cojo; incierto; vacilante; (of speech) titubeante

**halve** /hæv/ *vt* partir (or dividir) en dos mitades

**ham** /hæm/ *n* jamón, *m; Anat.* pernil, *m;* (radiooperator) radioaficionado, *m*

**Hamburg** /'hæmbɜrg/ Hamburgo, *m*

**hamlet** /'hæmlɪt/ *n* aldea, *f,* pueblecito, *m*

**hammer** /'hæmər/ *n* martillo, *m;* (stone cutter's) maceta, *f;* (mason's) piqueta, *f;* (of fire-arms) percusor, *m;* (of piano) macillo, *m.* —*vt* amartillar, martillar, batir. **to throw the h.,** lanzar el martillo. **under the h.,** en subasta, al remate. **h. blow,** martillazo, *m*

**hammering** /'hæmərɪŋ/ *n* martilleo, martillazos, *m.* **by h.,** a martillo

**hammock** /'hæmək/ *n* hamaca, *f; Naut.* coy, *m*

**hamper** /'hæmpər/ *n* banasta, canasta, *f,* cesto grande, *m.* —*vt* estorbar, dificultar, impedir; *Fig.* embarazar

**hamster** /'hæmstər/ *n Zool.* hámster, *m,* marmota de Alemania, rata del trigo, *f*

**hand** /hænd/ *n* mano, *f;* (of animal) pata, mano, *f;* (worker) operario (-ia); obrero (-ra); (skill) habilidad, *f;* (side) mano, *f,* lado, *m;* (measure) palmo, *m;* (of a clock) manecilla, *f;* (of instruments) aguja, *f;* (applause) aplauso, *m;* (power) poder, *m;* las manos; (at cards) mano, *f;* (card player) jugador, *m;* (signature) firma, *f;* (handwriting) letra, escritura, *f;* (influence) influencia, parte, mano, *f.* **old h.,** veterano; perro viejo. **at h.,** a mano, al lado, cerca. **have at hand,** tener a la mano. **at the hands of,** de manos de. **by h.,** a mano; (on the bottle) con biberón. **from h. to h.,** de mano a mano. **in h.,** entre manos; (of money) de contado. **in the hands of,** *Fig.* en el poder de. **"Hands wanted,"** «Se desean trabajadores.» **h. over h.,** mano sobre mano. **hand's breadth,** palmo, *m.* **Hands off!** ¡Fuera las manos! **Hands up!** ¡Manos arriba! **lost with all hands,** (of a ship) perdido con toda su tripulación. **off one's hands,** despachado; (of a daughter) casada. **on all hands,** por todas partes. **on h.,** entre manos; (of goods) existente; (present) presente. **on one's hands,** a cargo de uno. **on the one h.,** por un lado; a un lado. **on the other h.,** por otra parte; en cambio. **out of h.,** luego, inmediatamente; revoltoso. **to come to h.,** venir a mano; (of letters) llegar a las manos (de). **to get onto one's h. in,** ejercitarse. **to have a h. in,** tener parte en; intervenir en. **to have no h. in,** no tener arte ni parte en. **to have on h.,** traer entre manos. **to have the upper h.,** tener la sartén por el mango, llevar la ventaja. **to hold one's h.,** abstenerse; detenerse. **to hold hands,** cogerse de las manos. **to lay hands on,** tocar; poner mano en; echar manos a. **to set one's h. to,** emprender; (sign) firmar. **to shake hands,** estrechar la

mano. **to stretch out one's hands,** tender las manos. **to take one's hands off,** no tocar. **with folded hands,** mano sobre mano. **with his hands behind his back,** con las manos en la espalda. **h.-in-h.,** cogidos (cogidas) de las manos. **h.-lever,** manija, *f.* **h.-loom,** telar de mano, *m.* **h. luggage,** equipaje de mano, *m.* **h.-made,** hecho a mano. **h.-mill,** molinillo, *m.* **h.-pump,** *n Naut.* sacabuche, *m.* **h. rail,** pasamano, *m,* baranda, balustrada, *f.* **h.-sewn,** cosido a mano. **h.-to-h.,** de mano en mano; (of a fight) a brazo partido, cuerpo a cuerpo. **h.-to-h. fight,** cachetina, *f.* **h.-to-mouth,** precario. **to live from h.-to-mouth,** vivir de día en día

**hand** /hænd/ *vt* dar; entregar; alargar. **to h. down,** bajar; (a person) ayudar a bajar; transmitir. **to h. in,** entregar; (a person) ayudar a entrar; (one's resignation) dimitir; (send) mandar, enviar. **to h. on,** transmitir. **to h. out,** *vt* distribuir; (a person) ayudar a salir; (from a vehicle) ayudar a bajar. —*vi Inf.* pagar. **to h. over,** *vt* entregar. —*vi Mil.* traspasar los poderes (a). **to h. round,** pasar de mano en mano; pasar; ofrecer. **to h. up,** subir; (a person) ayudar a subir

**handbag** /'hænd,bæg/ *n* bolso, saco, monedero, *m*

**handbill** /'hænd,bɪl/ *n* anuncio, *m*

**handbook** /'hænd,bʊk/ *n* manual, compendio, tratado, *m;* anuario, *m;* (guide) guía, *f*

**handcart** /'hænd,kɑrt/ *n* carretilla de mano, *f,* carretón, *m*

**handcuff** /'hænd,kʌf/ *n* esposa, *f,* grillo, *m,* (gen. —*pl*). —*vt* poner las esposas (a), maniatar

**handed** /'hændɪd/ *a* (in compounds) que tiene manos; de manos...; con las manos... **four-h.,** *Sports.* de cuatro personas. **one-h.,** manco

**handful** /'hændfʊl/ *n* puño, puñado, manojo, *m.* **to be a h.,** *Inf.* tener el diablo en el cuerpo. **in handfuls,** a manojos

**handgrip** /'hænd,grɪp/ *n* apretón de manos, *m*

**handicap** /'hændi,kæp/ *n* desventaja, *f;* obstáculo, *m; Sports.* handicap, *m;* ventaja, *f.* —*vt Fig.* perjudicar, impedir, dificultar. **the handicapped,** los lisiados, *m pl*

**handicraft** /'hændi,kræft/ *n* mano de obra, *f;* (skill) destreza manual, *f,*

**handiwork** /'hændi,wɜrk/ *n* mano de obra, *f;* trabajo manual, *m;* obra, *f;* (deed) acción, *f,* hecho, *m*

**handkerchief** /'hæŋkərtʃɪf/ *n* pañuelo, *m*

**handle** /'hændl/ *n* mango, puño, *m;* (lever) palanca, *f;* (of baskets, dishes, jugs) asa, *f;* (of doors, windows, drawers) pomo, *m,* (of a car door) picaporte *m;* (to one's name) designación, *f;* título, *m;* (excuse) pretexto, *m.* —*vt* (touch) tocar; manejar, manipular; (treat) tratar; **h. with kid gloves,** tratar con guantes de seda; (deal in) comerciar en; tomar; (paw) manosear; (direct) dirigir; (control) gobernar; (pilot) pilotar; (a theme) explicar, tratar de. **h.-bar,** manillar, *m.* **h.-bar grip,** puño de un manillar, *m*

**handless** /'hændlɪs/ *a* sin manos; manco; *Fig.* torpe

**handling** /'hændlɪŋ/ *n* manejo, *m;* manipulación, *f;* (treatment) trato, *m,* relaciones (con), *f pl;* (thumbing) manoseo, *m;* interpretación, *f; Art.* tratamiento, *m,* técnica, *f*

**handmaid** /'hænd,meid/ *n* sirvienta, criada, *f; Fig.* mayordomo, *m*

**handsaw** /'hænd,sɔ/ *n* sierra de mano, *f,* serrucho, *m*

**handsbreadth** /'hændz,bredθ/ *n* palmo, *m*

**handshake** /'hænd,ʃeik/ *n* apretón de manos, *m*

**handsome** /'hænsəm/ *a* (generous) generoso; magnánimo; considerable; hermoso, bello; elegante; (of people) guapo, distinguido; excelente; (flattering) halagüeño. **He was a very h. man,** Era un hombre muy guapo

**handsomely** /'hænsəmli/ *adv* generosamente; con magnanimidad; elegantemente; bien

**handsomeness** /'hænsəmnɪs/ *n* generosidad, *f;* magnanimidad, *f;* hermosura, *f;* elegancia, *f;* distinción, *f*

**handspring** /'hænd,sprɪŋ/ *n* voltereta sobre las manos, *f*

**handwork** /'hænd,wɜrk/ *n* obra hecha a mano, *f,* trabajo a mano, *m;* (needlework) labor de aguja, *f*

**handworked** /'hænd,wɜrkt/ *a* hecho a mano; (embroidered) bordado

**handwriting** /'hænd,raitɪŋ/ *n* caligrafía, letra, escritura, *f.* **the h. on the wall,** la mano que escribía en la pared, *f*

**handy** /'hændi/ *a* (of persons) diestro, mañoso, hábil; (of things) conveniente; útil; (near) cercano, a mano. —*adv* cerca. **h.-man,** hombre de muchos oficios, *m;* factótum, *m*

**hang** /hæŋ/ *vt* colgar; suspender; (execute) ahorcar; (the head) bajar; dejar caer; (upholster) entapizar; (with wallpaper) empapelar; (drape) poner colgaduras en; (place) poner; (cover) cubrir. —*vi* colgar, pender; estar suspendido; (be executed) ser ahorcado; (of garments) caer. —*n* (of garments) caída, *f;* (of a machine) mecanismo, *m;* (meaning) sentido, *m,* significación, *f.* **to h. by a thread,** pender de un hilo. **to h. in the balance,** estar en la balanza. **to h. fire,** estar (una cosa) en suspenso. **to h. loose,** caer suelto; (clothes) venir ancho. **to h. about,** (surround) rodear, pegarse a; (frequent) frecuentar; (haunt) rondar; (be imminent) ser inminente, amenazar; (embrace) abrazar. **to h. back,** retroceder; quedarse atrás; *Fig.* vacilar, titubear. **to h. down,** colgar, pender; estar caído; caerse. **to h. on,** seguir agarrado (a); apoyarse en; *Fig.* persistir; (a person's words) estar pendiente de, beber; (remain) quedarse. **to h. out,** *vt* tender. —*vi* (lean out) asomarse (por); (*Inf.* live) habitar. **to h. over,** colgar por encima; (brood) cernerse sobre; (lean over) inclinarse sobre; quedarse cerca de; (overhang) sobresalir; (overarch) abovedar; (threaten) amenazar. **to h. together,** (of persons) permanecer unidos; (of things) tener cohesión; (be consistent) ser lógico, ser consistente. **to h. up,** colgar; suspender; *Fig.* dejar pendiente, interrumpir. **to h. upon,** apoyarse en; (a person's words) beber las palabras de uno

**hangar** /'hæŋər/ *n* cobertizo; *Aer.* hangar, *m*

**hanger** /'hæŋər/ *n* colgadero, *m;* percha *f.* **h.-on,** parásito, *m;* dependiente, *m*

**hanging** /'hæŋɪŋ/ *n* colgamiento, *m;* (killing) ahorcamiento, *m; pl* **hangings,** colgaduras, *f pl,* cortinajes, *m pl.* —*a* pendiente colgante; péndulo; (of gardens) pensil. **It's not a h. matter,** No es una cuestión de vida y muerte. **h. bridge,** puente colgante, *m.* **h. committee,** junta (de una exposición,) *f.* **h. lamp,** lámpara de techo, *f*

**hangman** /'hæŋmən/ *n* verdugo, *m*

**hangnail** /'hæŋ,neɪl/ *n* padrastro, *m*

**hangover** /'hæŋ,ouvər/ *n* (after drinking) resaca, cruda (Mexico), *f*

**hank** /hæŋk/ *n* madeja, *f*

**hanker** /'hæŋkər/ *vi* (with after) ansiar, ambicionar; (with for) anhelar, suspirar por, desear con vehemencia

**hankering** /'hæŋkərɪŋ/ *n* ambición, *f;* deseo vehemente, *m*

**hanky-panky** /'hæŋki 'pæŋki/ *n* superchería, *f;* engaño, *m*

**hap** /hæp/ *n* casualidad, suerte, *f;* suceso fortuito, *m*

**haphazard** /*n* 'hæp,hæzərd/ *a* hæp'hæzərd/ *n* casualidad, *f.* —*a* fortuito, casual

**hapless** /'hæplɪs/ *a* desgraciado, desdichado

**haplessness** /'hæplɪsnɪs/ *n* desgracia, desdicha, *f*

**happen** /'hæpən/ *vi* suceder, acontecer, ocurrir, pasar; (to be found, be) hallarse por casualidad; (take place) tener lugar, verificarse; (arise) sobrevenir. **Do you know what has happened to...?** ¿Sabes qué se ha hecho de...? **as if nothing had happened,** como si no hubiese pasado nada. **He turned up as if nothing had happened,** Se presentó como si tal cosa. **How did it h.?** ¿Cómo fue esto? **If they h. to see you,** Si acaso te vean. **I happened to be in London,** Me hallaba por casualidad en Londres. **It won't h. again,** No volverá a suceder. **whatever happens,** venga lo que venga

**happening** /'hæpənɪŋ/ *n* suceso, acontecimiento, hecho, *m,* ocurrencia, *f*

**happily** /'hæpəli/ *adv* felizmente; por suerte

**happiness** /'hæpɪnɪs/ *n* felicidad, dicha, *f;* alegría, *f,* regocijo, *m*

**happy** /'hæpi/ *a* (lucky) afortunado; (felicitous) feliz, oportuno; feliz, dichoso; alegre, regocijado. **to be h.,** estar contento, ser feliz. **to be h. about,** alegrarse de.

**to make h.,** hacer feliz, alegrar. **h.-go-lucky,** irresponsable, descuidado

**harangue** /hə'ræŋ/ *n* arenga, *f.* —*vt* arengar. —*vi* pronunciar una arenga

**harass** /hə'ræs/ *vt* hostigar, acosar; atormentar; preocupar; *Mil.* picar. **to h. the rear-guard,** picar la retaguardia

**harbinger** /'hɑrbɪndʒər/ *n Fig.* precursor, heraldo, *m;* presagio, anuncio, *m.* —*vt* anunciar, presagiar

**harbor** /'hɑrbər/ *n* puerto, *m;* (bay) bahía, *f;* (haven) asilo, refugio, *m.* —*vt* dar refugio (a), albergar, acoger; (cherish) abrigar, acariciar; (conceal) esconder. **inner h.,** puerto, *m.* **outer h.,** rada del puerto, *f.* **to put into h.,** entrar en el puerto. **h. bar,** barra del puerto, *f.* **h.-dues,** derechos de puerto, *m pl.* **h.-master,** capitán de puerto, contramaestre de puerto, *m*

**harborer** /'hɑrbərər/ *n* amparador (-ra), protector (-ra); (criminal) encubridor (-ra)

**hard** /hɑrd/ *a* duro; (firm) firme; difícil; laborioso, agotador; violento; poderoso; arduo; fuerte, recio; vigoroso, robusto; insensible, inflexible; cruel; (of weather) inclemente, severo; (unjust) injusto, opresivo; (stiff) tieso; (of water) cruda; (of wood) brava. —*adv* duro; duramente; con ahínco; con fuerza; de firme; difícilmente; (of gazing) fijamente; severamente; (firmly) firmemente; vigorosamente; (of raining) a cántaros, mucho; (quickly) rápidamente; (of bearing misfortune) a pechos; (attentively) atentamente; (heavily) pesadamente; (much) mucho; (of bearing misfortune) a pechos; (attentively) atentamente; (heavily) pesadamente; (badly) mal; (closely) de cerca, inmediatamente. **It was a h. blow,** Fue un golpe recio. **to be h. put to,** encontrar difícil. **to go h.,** endurecerse. **to go h. with,** irle mal a uno. **to have a h. time,** pasar apuros, pasarlo mal. **to look h. at,** mirar atentamente, examinar detenidamente; mirar fijamente. **to be a h. drinker,** ser un bebedor empedernido. **h. and fast rule,** regla inalterable, *f.* **h.-bitten,** de carácter duro. **h.-boiled egg,** un huevo duro. **h. breathing,** resuello, *m.* **h. by,** muy cerca. **h. cash,** efectivo, *m.* **h.-earned,** difícilmente conseguido; ganado con el sudor de la frente. **h.-featured,** de facciones duras. **h.-fisted,** tacaño. **h.-fought,** arduo, reñido. **h.-headed,** práctico, perspicaz. **h.-hearted,** duro de corazón, insensible. **h.-heartedness,** insensibilidad, *f.* **h. labor,** *Law.* trabajos forzados, *m pl,* presidio, *m.* **h.-mouthed,** (of horses) boquiduro. **h. of hearing,** duro de oído. **h.-up,** apurado. **to be very h.-up,** ser muy pobre; *Inf.* estar a la cuarta pregunta. **h.-wearing,** duradero; sufrido. **h.-won,** See **h.-earned. h.-working,** trabajador, hacendoso, diligente

**harden** /'hɑrdn/ *vt* endurecer; (metal) templar; robustecer; (to war) aguerrir; (make callous) hacer insensible. —*vi* endurecerse; hacerse duro; templarse; robustecerse; (of shares) entonarse

**hardening** /'hɑrdnɪŋ/ *n* endurecimiento, *m;* (of metal) temple, *m.* **h. of the arteries,** arteriosclerosis, *f*

**hardiness** /'hɑrdɪnɪs/ *n* vigor, *m,* fuerza, robustez, *f;* audacia, *f*

**hardly** /'hɑrdli/ *adv* duramente; difícilmente; (badly) mal; severamente; (scarcely) apenas, casi. **h. ever,** casi nunca

**hardness** /'hɑrdnɪs/ *n* dureza, *f;* severidad, *f;* inhumanidad, insensibilidad, *f;* (stiffness) tiesura, *f;* (difficulty) dificultad, *f;* (of water) crudeza, *f;* (of hearing) dureza de oído, *f*

**hardship** /'hɑrdʃɪp/ *n* penas, *f pl,* trabajos, *m pl;* infortunio, *m,* desdicha, *f;* (suffering) sufrimiento, *m;* (affliction) aflicción, *f;* (privation) privación, *f.* **to undergo h.,** pasar trabajos

**hardware** /'hɑrd,wɛər/ *n* ferretería, *f*

**hardwood** /'hɑrd,wʊd/ *n* madera brava, *f*

**hardy** /'hɑrdi/ *a* audaz, intrépido; (strong) fuerte, robusto; *Bot.* resistente

**hare** /hɛər/ *n* liebre, *f.* **young h.,** lebrato, *m.* **h. and hounds,** rally paper, *m,* caza de papelitos, *f.* **h.-brained,** casquivano, atronado, con cabeza de chorlito. **hare's foot,** mano de gato, *f.* **h.-lip,** labio leporino, *m.* **h.-lipped,** labihendido

**harebell** /'hɛər,bɛl/ *n* campanilla, campánula, *f*

**harem** /'hɛərəm/ *n* harén, serrallo, *m*

**haricot** /'hærə,kou/ *n* (green bean) judia, *f;* (dried bean) alubia, *f*

**hark** /hɑrk/ *vt* escuchar; oír. **to h. back,** volver al punto de partida; volver a la misma canción

**harlequin** /'hɑrləkwɪn/ *n* arlequín, *m*

**harlequinade** /,hɑrləkwɪ'neid/ *n* arlequinada, *f*

**harlot** /'hɑrlət/ *n* ramera, prostituta, meretriz, *f*

**harlotry** /'hɑrlətri/ *n* prostitución, *f*

**harm** /hɑrm/ *n* mal, *m;* daño, *m;* perjuicio, *m;* (danger) peligro, *m;* (detriment) menoscabo, *m;* (misfortune) desgracia, *f, vt* hacer mal (a); dañar, hacer daño (a); perjudicar. **And there's no h. in that,** Y en eso no hay mal. **to keep out of harm's way,** evitar el peligro; guardarse del mal

**harmful** /'hɑrmfəl/ *a* malo; dañino, perjudicial, nocivo; (dangerous) peligroso. **to be h.,** (of food, etc.) hacer mal (a); (of pests) ser dañino; (of behavior, etc.) perjudicar

**harmfulness** /'hɑrmfəlnɪs/ *n* lo malo; perniciosidad, *f;* daño, *m;* peligro, *m*

**harmless** /'hɑrmlɪs/ *a* innocuo; inofensivo; inocente

**harmlessness** /'hɑrmlɪsnɪs/ *n* innocuidad, *f;* inocencia, *f*

**harmonic** /hɑr'mɒnɪk/ *n* (*Phys. Math.*) harmónica, *f; Mus.* armónico, *m, a Mus.* armónico

**harmonica** /hɑr'mɒnɪkə/ *n* armónica, *f*

**harmonics** /hɑr'mɒnɪks/ *n* armonía, *f;* (tones) armónicos, *m pl*

**harmonious** /hɑr'mouniəs/ *a* armonioso

**harmoniously** /hɑr'mouniəsli/ *adv* armoniosamente; *Fig.* en armonía

**harmoniousness** /hɑr'mouniəsnɪs/ *n* armonía, *f*

**harmonium** /hɑr'mouniəm/ *n* armonio, *m*

**harmonization** /,hɑrmənɪ'zeiʃən/ *n* armonización, *f*

**harmonize** /'hɑrmə,naiz/ *vt* armonizar. —*vi* armonizarse, estar en armonía

**harmony** /'hɑrməni/ *n* armonía, *f; Fig.* paz, *f,* buenas relaciones, *f pl;* música, *f.* **to live in h.,** vivir en paz

**harness** /'hɑrnɪs/ *n* guarniciones, *f pl,* jaeces, *m pl;* (armor) arnés, *m.* —*vt* enjaezar; (yoke) enganchar; (water) represar. **to die in h.,** *Fig.* morir en la brecha. **h. maker,** guarnicionero, *m.* **h. room,** guadarnés, *m*

**harp** /hɑrp/ *n* arpa, *f.* **to h. on,** volver a la misma canción, volver a repetir

**harpist** /'hɑrpɪst/ *n* arpista, *mf*

**harpoon** /hɑr'pun/ *n* arpón, *m.* —*vt* arponear

**harpooner** /hɑr'punər/ *n* arponero, *m*

**harpsichord** /'hɑrpsɪ,kɔrd/ *n* arpicordio, *m*

**harpy** /'hɑrpi/ *n* arpía, *f*

**harridan** /'hærədn̩/ *n* bruja, *f*

**harrow** /'hærou/ *n Agr.* rastra, *f,* escarificador, *m.* —*vt Agr.* escarificar; *Fig.* lastimar, atormentar

**harrowing** /'hærouɪŋ/ *a* patibulario, conmovedor, atormentador, angustioso

**harry** /'hæri/ *vt* devastar, asolar; (persons) robar; perseguir; (worry) atormentar; (annoy) molestar

**harsh** /hɑrʃ/ *a* áspero; (of voice) ronco; (of sound) discordante; (of colors) áspero; duro; chillón; severo; duro; (of features) duro; (of taste) ácido, acerbo

**harshly** /'hɑrʃli/ *adv* severamente

**harshness** /'hɑrʃnɪs/ *n* (roughness) aspereza, *f;* (of voice) ronquedad, aspereza, *f;* (of sound) disonancia, *f;* (of colors) aspereza, *f;* severidad, *f;* dureza, *f;* (of taste) acidez, *f*

**hart** /hɑrt/ *n* ciervo, *m*

**harum-scarum** /'hɛərəm 'skɛərəm/ *n* tronera, saltabarrancos, *mf* molino, *m, a* irresponsable

**harvest** /'hɑrvɪst/ *n* cosecha, siega, *f;* recolección, *f; Fig.* producto, fruto, *m.* —*vt* cosechar; recoger. **h. festival,** fiesta de la cosecha, *f*

**harvester** /'hɑrvəstər/ *n* segador, *m,* cosechero (-ra); (machine) segadora, *f*

**hash** /hæʃ/ *n Cul.* picado, *m.* —*vt Cul.* picar

**hashish** /'hæʃiʃ/ *n* hachich, hachís, quif, *m*

**hasp** /hæsp/ *n* pasador, *f;* sujetador, *m*

**hassock** /'hæsək/ *n* cojín, *m*

**haste** /heist/ *n* prisa, rapidez, *f;* precipitación, *f;* urgencia, *f.* —*vt* dar prisa (a); acelerar; precipitar. —*vi* darse prisa; acelerarse; precipitarse. **in h.,** de prisa, aprisa. **to be in h.,** estar de prisa, llevar prisa. **in**

**great h.,** muy aprisa, aprisa y corriendo, precipitadamente; con mucha prisa. **More h. less speed,** (Spanish equivalent. Words said by Charles III of Spain to his valet) ¡Vísteme despacio que voy de prisa!

**hasten** /'heisən/ *vt* acelerar, apresurar; precipitar. —*vi* darse prisa, apresurarse; moverse con rapidez; correr. **to h. one's steps,** apretar el paso. **to h. away,** marcharse rápidamente. **to h. back,** regresar apresuradamente. **to h. down,** bajar rápidamente. **to h. on,** seguir el camino sin descansar; seguir rápidamente. **to h. out,** salir rápidamente. **to h. towards,** ir rápidamente hacia; correr hacia. **to h. up,** subir aprisa, correr hacia arriba; darse prisa

**hastily** /'heistli/ *adv* de prisa, rápidamente; con precipitación, precipitadamente; (angrily) impacientemente, airadamente; (thoughtlessly) sin reflexión

**hastiness** /'heistinɪs/ *n* rapidez, *f;* precipitación, *f;* (anger) impaciencia, irritación, *f*

**hasty** /'heisti/ *a* rápido, apresurado; precipitado; (superficial) superficial, ligero; (ill-considered) desconsiderado, imprudente; (angry) impaciente, irritable; violento, apasionado

**hat** /hæt/ *n* sombrero, *m.* **to pass round the h.,** pasar el platillo. **Andalusian h.,** sombrero calañés, *m.* **bowler h.,** sombrero hongo, *m.* **broad-brimmed h.,** sombrero chambergo, *m.* **Panama h.,** sombrero de jipijapa, *m.* **picture h.,** pamela, *f.* **shovel h.,** sombrero de teja, *m.* **soft felt h.,** sombrero flexible, *m.* **straw h.,** sombrero de paja, *m.* **three-cornered h.,** sombrero de tres picos, *m.* **top-h.,** sombrero de copa, *m.* **h. shop** or **trade,** sombrerería, *f*

**hatband** /'hæt,bænd/ *n* cinta de sombrero, *f,* cintillo, *m*

**hatblock** /'hæt,blɒk/ *n* formillón, *f*

**hatbox** /'hæt,bɒks/ *n* sombrerera, *f*

**hatbrush** /'hæt,brʌʃ/ *n* cepillo para sombreros, *m*

**hatch** /hætʃ/ *n* (wicket) compuerta, *f;* (trap-door) puerta caediza, *f; Naut.* escotilla, *f;* compuerta de esclusa, *f;* (of chickens) pollada, *f;* (of birds) nidada, *f.* —*vt* (birds) empollar; incubar, encobar; *Fig.* tramar, urdir. —*vi* empollarse, salir del cascarón; incubarse; *Fig.* madurarse. **to h. a plot,** urdir un complot, conspirar. **to h. chickens,** sacar pollos

**hatchet** /'hætʃɪt/ *n* hacha pequeña, *f,* machado, *m.* **to bury the h.,** hacer la paz. **h.-faced,** de cara de cuchillo

**hatching** /'hætʃɪŋ/ *n* incubación, *f;* (of a plot) maquinación, *f*

**hatchway** /'hætʃ,wei/ *n Naut.* escotilla, *f*

**hate** /heit/ *n* odio, aborrecimiento, *m,* aversión, *f;* abominación, *f.* —*vt* odiar, aborrecer, detestar; repugnar; saber mal, sentir. **I h. to trouble you,** Me sabe mal molestarle, Siento mucho molestarle. **to h. the sight of,** *Inf.* no poder ver (a)

**hateful** /'heitfəl/ *a* odioso, aborrecible; repugnante

**hatefulness** /'heitfəlnɪs/ *n* odiosidad, *f,* lo odioso; maldad, *f*

**hater** /'heitər/ *n* aborrecedor (-ra). **to be a good h.,** saber odiar

**hatful** /'hætfəl/ *n* un sombrero lleno (de)

**hatless** /'hætlɪs/ *a* sin sombrero, descubierto

**hatpin** /'hæt,pɪn/ *n* horquilla de sombrero, *f*

**hatred** /'heitrɪd/ *n* odio, aborrecimiento, *m,* detestación, *f;* aversión, enemistad, *f*

**hatstand** /'hæt,stænd/ *n* perchera, *f*

**hatter** /'hætər/ *n* sombrerero, *m.* **as mad as a h.,** loco como una cabra

**haughtiness** /'hɔtinɪs/ *n* altanería, arrogancia, altivez, soberbia, *f,* orgullo, *m*

**haughty** /'hɔti/ *a* altanero, arrogante, altivo, orgulloso

**haul** /hɔl/ *n* (pull) tirón, *m;* (of fish) redada, *f;* (booty) botín, *m.* —*vt* arrastrar, tirar de; *Naut.* halar. **to h. at, upon,** (ropes, etc.) aflojar, soltar, arriar. **to h. down,** (flags, sails) arriar

**haulage** /'hɔlɪdʒ/ *n* transporte, acarreo, *m;* coste de transporte, *m.* **h. contractor,** contratista de transporte, *m*

**haunch** /hɔntʃ/ *n* anca, culata, *f;* (of meat) pierna, *f.* **h.-bone,** hueso ilíaco, *m*

**haunt** /hɔnt/ *n* punto de reunión, lugar frecuentado (por), *m;* (lair) cubil, nido, *m,* guarida, *f.* —*vt* frecuentar; rondar; (of ideas) perseguir; (of ghosts) aparecer, visitar. **It is a h. of thieves,** Es una cueva de ladrones

**haunted** /'hɔntɪd/ *a* (by spirits) encantado

**haunter** /'hɔntər/ *n* frecuentador (-ra); (ghost) fantasma, espectro, *m*

**haunting** /'hɔntɪŋ/ *n* frecuentación, *f;* aparición de un espectro, *f.* —*a* persistente

**hautboy** /'houbɔi, 'oubɔi/ *n* oboe, *m*

**hauteur** /hou'tɜr/ *n* altivez, *f*

**Havana** /hə'vænə/ la Habana, *f.* —*n* (cigar) habano, *m.* (native) habanero (-ra), habano (-na)

**have** /hæv; *unstressed* həv, əv/ *vt* tener; poseer; (suffer) padecer; (spend) pasar; (eat or drink) tomar; (eat) comer; (a cigarette) fumar; (a bath, etc.) tomar; (a walk, a ride) dar; (cause to be done) mandar (hacer), hacer (hacer); (deceive) engañar; (defeat) vencer; (catch) coger; (say) decir; (allow) permitir; (tolerate) tolerar, sufrir; (obtain) lograr, conseguir; (wish) querer; (know) saber; (realize) realizar; (buy) comprar; (acquire) adquirir. As an auxiliary verb, haber (e.g. *I h. done it,* Lo he hecho, etc.). **As fate would h. it,** Según quiso la suerte. **Do you h. to go?** ¿Tiene Vd. que marcharse? **H. him come here,** Hazle venir aquí. **I h. been had,** Me han engañado. **I h. a good mind to...,** Tengo ganas de... **I had all my books stolen,** Me robaron todos los libros. **You had better go,** Es mejor que te vayas. **I had rather,** Preferiría, Me gustaría más bien. **I h. had a suit made,** Mandé hacerme un traje, Hice hacerme un traje. **I would not h. had it otherwise,** No lo hubiese querido de otra manera. **I will not h. it,** No lo quiero; No quiero tomarlo; (object) No lo permitiré. **If we had known,** Si lo hubiésemos sabido. **It has to do with the sun,** Está relacionado con el sol, Tiene que ver con el sol. **Have a good trip!** ¡Buen viaje!, ¡Feliz viaje! **What are you going to h.?** ¿Qué quiere Vd. tomar? **Will you h. some jam?** ¿Quiere Vd. mermelada? **to h. breakfast,** desayunar. **to h. dinner, supper,** cenar. **to h. lunch,** almorzar. **to h. for tea,** invitar a tomar el té; (of food) merendar. **to h. tea,** tomar el té. **to h. it out with,** habérselas con. **to h. just,** acabar de. **I h. just done it,** Acabo de hacerlo. **to h. on hand,** traer entre manos. **to h. one's eye on,** no perder de vista (a), vigilar. **to h. one's tail between one's legs,** ir rabo entre piernas. **to h. to,** tener que; deber. **It has to be so,** Tiene que ser así. **to h. too much of,** sobrar, tener demasiado de. **He has too much time,** Le sobra tiempo. **to h. about one,** tener (or llevar) consigo. **to h. back,** aceptar; recibir. **to h. down,** hacer bajar. **She had her hair down,** El pelo le caía por las espaldas. **to h. in,** hacer entrar. **to h. on,** vestir, llevar puesto; (engagements) tener (compromisos). **to h. out,** hacer salir; llevar a paseo; llevar fuera; (have removed) hacerse sacar; quitar. **to h. up,** (persons) hacer subir; (things) subir; *Law.* llevar a (ante) los tribunales. **I h. her with me,** La tengo conmigo, Ella me acompaña

**haven** /'heivən/ *n* puerto, *m,* abra, *f; Fig.* oasis, abrigo, refugio, *m*

**haversack** /'hævər,sæk/ *n* mochila, *f,* morral, *m*

**havoc** /'hævək/ *n* destrucción, ruina, *f; Fig.* estrago, *m.* **to wreak h. among,** destruir; *Fig.* hacer estragos entre (or en)

**Hawaii** /hə'waii/ Hawai, *m*

**Hawaiian** /hə'waiən/ *a* and *n* hawaiano; *n* (language) hawaiano, *m*

**hawk** /hɔk/ *n* halcón, *m;* gavilán, milano, *m.* —*vi* cazar con halcón. —*vt* vender mercancías por las calles; *Fig.* difundir. **h.-eyed,** de ojos de lince. **h.-nosed,** de nariz aguileña

**hawker** /'hɔkər/ *n* halconero, *m;* (vendor) buhonero, *m,* vendedor (-ra) ambulante

**hawking** /'hɔkɪŋ/ *n* caza con halcones, cetrería, *f;* (expectorating) gargajeo, *m;* (selling) buhonería, *f*

**hawser** /'hɔzər/ *n* maroma, *f,* calabrote, *m*

**hawthorn** /'hɔ,θɔrn/ *n* espino, *m.* **white h.,** espino blanco, *m*

**hay** /hei/ *n* heno, *m.* **to make hay while the sun shines,** hacer su agosto. **hay fever,** fiebre del heno, *f.* **hay-fork,** horca, *f*

**hayloft** /'hei,lɔft/ *n* henil, *m*

**haymaker** /'hei,meikər/ *n* segador (-ra); (machine) segadora, *f*

**haymaking** /'hei,meikɪŋ/ *n* recolección del heno, *f*

**haystack** /'hei,stæk/ *n* almiar, *m,* niara, *f*

**hazard** /'hæzərd/ *n* azar, *m,* suerte, *f;* riesgo, peligro, *m;* (game) juego de azar, *m.* —*vt* arriesgar, aventurar. **at all hazards,** a todo riesgo

**hazardous** /'hæzərdəs/ *a* azaroso, arriesgado, peligroso

**haze** /heiz/ *n* bruma, *f;* confusión, *f*

**hazel** /'heizəl/ *n* avellano, *m.* **h.-nut,** avellana, *f*

**hazy** /'heizi/ *a* brumoso, calinoso; confuso

**he** /hi/ *pers pron* él. —*n* (of humans) varón, *m;* (of animals) macho, *m.* **he who,** el que, quien. **he-goat,** macho cabrío, *m.* **he-man,** todo un hombre, hombre cabal, *m*

**head** /hɛd/ *vt* golpear con la cabeza; encabezar; (lead) capitanear; (direct) dirigir, guiar; (wine) cabecear. —*vi* estar a la cabeza de; dirigirse a. **headed for,** con rumbo a, en dirección a. **to h. off,** interceptar; desviar; *Fig.* distraer

**head** /hɛd/ *n Anat.* cabeza, *f;* (upper portion) parte superior, *f;* (of a coin) cara, *f;* (hair) cabellera, *f;* (individual) persona, *f;* (of cattle) res, *f;* (of a mountain) cumbre, *f;* (of a ladder) último peldaño, *m;* (of toadstools) sombrero, *m;* (of trees) copa, *f;* (of a stick) puño, *m;* (of a cylinder) culata, *f;* (of a river, etc.) manantial, origen, *m;* (of a bed) cabecera, *f;* (of nails, pins) cabeza, *f;* (froth) espuma, *f;* (flower) flor, *f;* (leaves) hojas, *f pl;* (first place) primer puesto, *m;* (of game, fish) pieza, *f;* (of a page, column) cabeza, *f;* (cape) cabo, *m;* (of an arrow, dart, lance) punta, *f;* (front) frente, *m;* (leader) jefe, cabeza, *m;* (chief) director (-ra), superior (-ra); presidente (-ta); (of a school) director (-ra); (of a cask) fondo, *m; Mech.* cabezal, *m;* (of an ax) filo, *m;* (of a bridge) cabeza, *f;* (of a jetty, pier) punta, *f;* (of a ship) proa, *f;* (of a flower) cabezuela, *f;* (of asparagus) punta, *f;* (of a table) cabeza, *f;* (of the family) jefe, cabeza, *m;* (seat of honor) cabecera, *f;* (title) título, *m;* (aspect) punto de vista, *m;* (division) capítulo, *m;* (management, direction) dirección, *f;* (talent) talento, *m,* cabeza, *f;* (intelligence) inteligencia, *f.* —*a* principal; primero; en jefe. **at the h. of,** a la cabeza de. **crowned h.,** testa coronada, *f.* **from h. to foot,** de pies a cabeza; de hito en hito; de arriba abajo. **He took it into his h. to...,** Se le ocurrió de... **This story has neither h. nor tail,** Este cuento no tiene pies ni cabeza. **with h. held high,** con la frente levantada. **to come to a h.,** llegar a la crisis; llegar al punto decisivo. **to get an idea out of a person's h.,** quitar una idea a uno de la cabeza. **to keep one's h.,** *Fig.* conservar la sangre fría, no perder la cabeza. **to lose one's h.,** *Fig.* perder la cabeza. **to put into a person's h.,** *Fig.* meter (a uno) en la cabeza. **to run one's h. against,** golpear la cabeza contra. **h. first,** de cabeza. **h. of cattle,** res, *f.* **h. office,** central, *f.* **h. of hair,** cabellera, *f;* mata de pelo, *f.* **h.-on,** de cabeza. **h.-on collision,** choque de frente, *m.* **h. opening,** (of a garment) cabezón, *m.* **heads or tails,** cara o cruz, águila o sol (Mexico). **h. over heels,** de patas arriba. **h. over heels in love,** calado hasta los huesos. **h.-dress,** tocado, *m;* peinado, *m;* sombrero, *m.* **h. voice,** voz de cabeza, *f.* **h. waiter,** encargado de comedor, jefe de camareros, *m*

**headache** /'hɛd,eik/ *n* dolor de cabeza, *m; Fig.* quebradero de cabeza, *m*

**headboard** /'hɛd,bɔrd/ *n* cabecera de una cama, *f*

**headed** /'hɛdɪd/ *a* con cabeza...; que tiene la cabeza...; de cabeza...; (of an article) intitulado. **large h.,** cabezudo

**header** /'hɛdər/ *n* caída de cabeza, *f;* salto de cabeza, *m*

**headgear** /'hɛd,gɪər/ *n* tocado, *m;* sombrero, gorro, *m*

**head-hunting** /'hɛd,hʌntɪŋ/ *n* la caza de cabezas, *f*

**heading** /'hɛdɪŋ/ *n Naut.* el poner la proa en dirección (a); el guiar en dirección (a); (of a book, etc.) título, encabezamiento, *m;* (soccer) golpe de cabeza, *m.* **to come under the h. of,** estar incluido entre; clasificarse bajo

**headland** /'hɛdlənd/ n cabo, promontorio, m

**headless** /'hɛdlɪs/ a sin cabeza

**headlight** /'hɛd,laɪt/ n Auto. faro, m; (Rail. Naut.) farol, m. **to dip the headlights,** bajar los faros. **to switch on the headlights,** encender los faros (or los faroles)

**headline** /'hɛd,laɪn/ n (of a newspaper) titular, m; (to a chapter) título de la columna, m

**headlong** /'hɛd,lɔŋ/ a precipitado; despeñado. —adv de cabeza; precipitadamente. **to fall h.,** caer de cabeza

**headman** /'hɛd'mæn/ n cacique, cabecilla, m; (foreman) capataz, contramaestre, m

**headmaster** /'hɛd'mæstər/ n director de colegio, rector, m

**headmistress** /'hɛd'mɪstrɪs/ n directora de colegio, rectora, f

**head nurse** enfermero-jefe, m

**head-on collision** /'hɛd ˌɒn/ n choque frontal, m

**headphones** /'hɛd,founz/ n pl auriculares, m pl

**headquarters** /'hɛd,kwɔrtərz/ n Mil. cuartel general, m; oficina central, f; jefatura, f; centro, m

**headrest** /'hɛd,rɛst/ n respaldo, m; apoyo para la cabeza, m

**headstone** /'hɛd,stoun/ n piedra mortuoria, f

**headstrong** /'hɛd,strɔŋ/ a impetuoso, terco, testarudo

**headway** /'hɛd,weɪ/ n marcha, f; Fig. progreso, avance, m. **to make h.,** avanzar; Fig. hacer progresos; Fig. prosperar

**headwind** /'hɛd,wɪnd/ n viento en contra, m

**heady** /'hɛdi/ a apasionado, violento; impetuoso, precipitado; (obstinate) terco; (of alcohol) encabezado; Fig. embriagador

**heal** /hil/ vt curar, sanar; (flesh) cicatrizar. —vi curar, sanar; cicatrizarse; (superficially) sobresanar

**healable** /'hiləbəl/ a curable

**healer** /'hilər/ n sanador (-ra), curador (-ra); curandero, m

**healing** /'hilɪŋ/ a curador, sanador; médico. —n curación, f; cura, f; remedio, m

**health** /hɛlθ/ n salud, f; higiene, sanidad, f. **Here's to your very good h.!** ¡Salud y pesetas! **He is in good h.,** Disfruta de buena salud. **to drink a person's h.,** beber a la salud de. **to enjoy good h.,** gozar de buena salud. **to look full of h.,** vender salud. **h.-giving,** saludable. **h. inspection,** visita de sanidad, f. **h. officer,** inspector de sanidad, m. **h. resort,** balneario, m

**healthiness** /'hɛlθɪnɪs/ n buena salud, f; sanidad, salubridad, f

**healthy** /'hɛlθi/ a sano; con buena salud; (healthful) saludable. **to be h.,** tener buena salud

**heap** /hip/ n montón, m; rima, pila, f, acervo, m; (of people) muchedumbre, f, tropel, m. —vt amontonar; apilar; colmar. **in heaps,** a montones. **We have heaps of time,** Nos sobra tiempo, Tenemos tiempo de sobra. **to h. together,** juntar, mezclar. **to h. up, upon,** colmar; amontonar; Agr. hacinar; Fig. acumular

**hear** /hɪər/ vt oír; (listen) escuchar; (attend) asistir a; (give audience) dar audiencia (a); (a lawsuit) ver (un pleito); (speak) hablar; (be aware of, feel) sentir. —vi oír; tener noticias; (learn) enterarse de; (allow) permitir. **H.! H.!** ¡Muy bien! ¡Bravo! **I have heard it said that...** He oído decir que... **Let me h. from you!** ¡Mándame noticias tuyas! **They were never heard of again,** No se volvió a saber de ellos, No se supo más de ellos. **to h. about,** oír de; (know) saber de, tener noticias de; recibir información sobre. **to h. from,** ser informado por; tener noticias de: recibir carta de. **to h. of,** enterarse de, saber; recibir información sobre; (allow) permitir

**hearer** /'hɪərər/ n oyente, mf

**hearing** /'hɪərɪŋ/ n (sense of) oído, m; alcance del oído, m; (audience) audición, f; Law. vista (de una causa) f. **It was said in my h.,** Fue dicho en mi presencia. **out of h.,** fuera del alcance del oído. **within h.,** al alcance del oído. **have a h. problem,** ser parcialmente sordo

**hearing aid** acústica, aparato auditivo, aparato acústico, audífono, m

**hearsay** /'hɪər,seɪ/ n fama, f, rumor, m. **by h.,** de oídas

**hearse** /hɜrs/ n coche fúnebre, m

**heart** /hɑrt/ n corazón, m; (feelings) entrañas, f pl; (of the earth, etc.) seno, corazón, m; (of lettuce, etc.) cogollo, repollo, m; (suit in cards) copas, f pl; Bot. médula, f; (soul) alma, f; (courage) valor, m; ánimo, m. **at h.,** en el fondo, esencialmente. **by h.,** de memoria. **from the h.,** con toda sinceridad, de todo corazón. **He is a man after my own h.,** Es un hombre de los que me gustan. **I have no h. to do it,** No tengo valor de hacerlo. **in the h. of the country,** en medio del campo. **to break one's h.,** partirse el corazón. **to have one's h. in one's mouth,** tener el alma en un hilo, estar muerto de miedo. **to have no h.,** Fig. no tener entrañas. **to lose h.,** desanimarse, descorazonarse. **to set one's h. on,** poner el corazón en. **to take h.,** cobrar ánimo; Inf. hacer de tripas corazón. **to take to h.,** tomar a pechos. **to wear one's h. on one's sleeve,** tener el corazón en la mano. **with all my h.,** con todo el alma. **h.-ache,** angustia, pena, f; **h.-beat,** latido del corazón, m. **h.-breaker,** (woman) coqueta, f; (man) ladrón de corazones, m. **h. disease,** enfermedad del corazón, enfermedad cardíaca, f. **h. failure,** colapso cardíaco, m. **h.-rending,** desgarrador, angustioso. **h.-searching,** examen de conciencia, m. **h.-shaped,** acorazonado, en forma de corazón. **h.-strings,** fibras del corazón, f pl. **h.-to-h. talk,** conversación íntima, f. **h.-whole,** libre de afectos

**heartbreaking** /'hɑrt,breɪkɪŋ/ a desgarrador, angustioso, doloroso, lastimoso

**heartbroken** /'hɑrt,broukən/ a acongojado, afligido, transido de dolor

**heartburn** /'hɑrt,bɜrn/ n acidez del estómago, acedia, pirosis, rescoldera, f

**heartburning** /'hɑrt,bɜrnɪŋ/ n rencor, m, animosidad, envidia, f

**hearted** /'hɑrtɪd/ a de corazón... que tiene el corazón... **kind-h.,** de buen corazón, bondadoso

**hearten** /'hɑrtn/ vt alentar, animar

**heartfelt** /'hɑrt,fɛlt/ a hondo; de todo corazón, sincero; más expresivo

**hearth** /hɑrθ/ n hogar, m; chimenea, f; Fig. hogar, m

**heartily** /'hɑrtli/ adv cordialmente; sinceramente; enérgicamente; con entusiasmo; (of eating) con buen apetito; (very) muy, completamente. **I am h. sick of it all,** Inf. Estoy harto hasta los dientes

**heartiness** /'hɑrtɪnɪs/ n cordialidad, f; sinceridad, f; energía, f, vigor, m; vehemencia, f; entusiasmo, m; (of appetite) buen diente, buen apetito, m

**heartless** /'hɑrtlɪs/ a sin corazón, sin piedad, despiadado, inhumano, cruel

**heartlessness** /'hɑrtlɪsnɪs/ n falta de corazón, inhumanidad, crueldad, f

**hearty** /'hɑrti/ a cordial; sincero; enérgico; vigoroso; robusto; (frank) campechano; (of appetite) voraz; bueno; (big) grande

**heat** /hit/ n calor, m; (in animals) celo, m; (of an action) calor, m; Fig. vehemencia, fogosidad, f; Fig. fuego, m; (passion) ardor, m, pasión, f; (of a race) carrera eliminatoria, f. —vt calentar; (excite) conmover, acalorar, excitar; (annoy) irritar. —vi calentarse. **dead h.,** empate, m. **in h.,** en celo. **in the h. of the moment,** en el calor del momento. **to become heated,** Fig. acalorarse, exaltarse. **white h.,** candencia, incandescencia, f. **h. lightning,** fucilazo, m. **h. spot,** pápula, f; terminación sensible, f. **h. stroke,** insolación, f. **h. wave,** onda de calor, f

**heated** /'hitɪd/ a calentado; caliente; excitado; apasionado

**heatedly** /'hitdli/ adv con vehemencia, con pasión

**heater** /'hitər/ n calentador, m; calorífero, m; (stove) estufa, f; (for plates) calientaplatos, m. **water-h.,** calentador de agua, m

**heath** /hiθ/ n brezal, m; yermo, páramo, m; Bot. brezo, m

**heathen** /'hiðən/ n pagano (-na); idólatra, mf; ateo (-ea), descreído (-da). —a pagano; ateo; bárbaro

**heathenism** /'hiðə,nɪzəm/ n paganismo, m; idolatría, f; ateísmo, m

**heather** /'hɛðər/ n brezo, m

**heating** /'hitɪŋ/ n calefacción, f, a calentador; (of drinks) fortificante. **central h.,** calefacción central, f
**heave** /hiv/ vt alzar, levantar; Naut. izar; (the anchor, etc.) virar; (throw) arrojar, lanzar; elevar; (extract) extraer; (emit) dar, exhalar. —vi subir y bajar; palpitar; agitarse. —n tirón, m; (of the sea) vaivén, m. **to h. in sight,** aparecer, surgir. **to h. out sail,** Naut. desenvergar. **to h. the lead,** Naut. escandallar. **to h. to,** Naut. estarse a la capa
**heaven** /'hɛvən/ n cielo, m; firmamento, m; paraíso, m. **Heavens!** ¡Cielos! ¡Por Dios! **Thank H.!** ¡Gracias a Dios! **h.-born,** celeste. **h.-sent,** Fig. providencial
**heavenliness** /'hɛvənlinɪs/ n carácter celestial, m; delicia, f
**heavenly** /'hɛvənli/ a celeste, celestial; divino; Fig. delicioso. **h. body,** astro, m
**heavily** /'hɛvəli/ adv pesadamente; torpemente; penosamente; (slowly) lentamente; severamente; excesivamente; (of sighing) hondamente; (sadly) tristemente; (of rain, etc.) reciamente, fuertemente; (of wind) con violencia. **He fell h.,** Cayó de plomo. **to lie h. upon,** pesar mucho sobre. **to rain h.,** llover mucho, diluviar
**heaviness** /'hɛvinɪs/ n peso, m; (lethargy) torpor, letargo, m; sueño, m, languidez, f; (clumsiness) torpeza, f; (severity) severidad, f; importancia, responsabilidad, f; dificultad, f; (gravity) gravedad, f; tristeza, melancolía, f; (boredom) sosería, insulsez, f; (of style) monotonía, ponderosidad, f
**heaving** /'hivɪŋ/ n levantamiento, m; (of the anchor, etc.) virada, f; (of the sea) vaivén, m; (of the breast) palpitación, f
**heavy** /'hɛvi/ a pesado; torpe; sin gracia; (slow) lento; (thick) grueso; (strong) fuerte; (hard) duro; grave; difícil; oneroso; responsable, importante; (oppresive) opresivo; penoso; grande; (sad) triste, melancólico; (of the sky) anublado; (of food) indigesto; (tedious) aburrido, soso; (pompous) pomposo; (of roads) malo; (of scents) fuerte, penetrante; (of sleep, weather) pesado; (weary) rendido; (charged with) cargado de; (of a meal) grande, abundante; (violent) violento; (of a cold, etc.) malo; (drowsy) soñoliento; (torpid) tórpido; (of rain, snow, hail) fuerte, recio; (of firing) intenso; (of sighs) profundo; (of soil) recio, de mucha miga; (Phys. Chem.) pesado. **How h. are you?** ¿Cuánto pesa Vd.? **h.-armed,** pesado; armado hasta los dientes. **h.-eyed,** con ojeras. **h. guns,** artillería pesada, f. **h.-handed,** de manos torpes; Fig. tiránico, opresivo. **h.-hearted,** triste, apesadumbrado. **h. industry,** la gran industria, la industria pesada, f. **h.-laden,** muy cargado. **h. losses,** Mil. pérdidas cuantiosas, f pl. **h.weight,** Sports. peso pesado, m
**Hebraic** /hɪ'breiɪk/ a hebraico, hebreo, judaico
**Hebraism** /'hibrei,ɪzəm/ n judaísmo, hebraísmo, m
**Hebraist** /'hibreiɪst/ n hebraísta, m
**Hebrew** /'hibru/ n hebreo (-ea), judío (-ía): (language) hebreo, m
**Hebrides, the** /'hɛbrɪdiz/ las Hébridas
**hecatomb** /'hɛkə,toum/ n hecatombe, f
**heckle** /'hɛkəl/ vt Fig. interrumpir, importunar con preguntas
**heckler** /'hɛklər/ n perturbador (-ra)
**heckling** /'hɛklɪŋ/ n interrupción, f
**hectare** /'hɛktɛər/ n hectárea, f
**hectic** /'hɛktɪk/ a (consumptive) hético; (feverish) febril; Fig. Inf. agitado
**hectogram** /'hɛktə,græm/ n hectogramo, m
**hectoliter** /'hɛktə,litər/ n hectolitro, m
**hector** /'hɛktər/ vt intimidar, amenazar
**hectoring** /'hɛktərɪŋ/ a imperioso; amenazador
**hectowatt** /'hɛktə,wɑt/ n Elec. hectovatio, m
**hedge** /hɛdʒ/ n seto, m; barrera, f. —vt cercar con un seto; rodear. —vi Fig. titubear, vacilar. **h.-hopping,** Aer. vuelo a ras de tierra, m. **h.-sparrow,** acentor de bosque, m
**hedgehog** /'hɛdʒ,hɒg/ n erizo, m. **h. position,** Mil. puesto fuerte, m
**hedonism** /'hidn,ɪzəm/ n hedonismo, m
**hedonist** /'hidnɪst/ n hedonista, mf
**heed** /hid/ n atención, f, cuidado, m. —vt atender; observar, considerar; escuchar. —vi hacer caso

**heedful** /'hidfəl/ a atento; cuidadoso
**heedless** /'hidlɪs/ a desatento; descuidado, negligente; distraído
**heedlessly** /'hidlɪsli/ adv sin hacer caso; negligentemente; distraídamente
**heedlessness** /'hidlɪsnɪs/ n desatención, distracción, f; descuido, m; negligencia, f; inconsideración, f
**heel** /hil/ n Anat. talón, calcañar, m; (of shoe) tacón, m; (of a violin, etc., bow) talón, m; (remains) restos, m pl. —vt poner tacón a; poner talón a; Naut. hacer zozobrar. —vi Naut. zozobrar. **rubber h.,** tacón de goma, m. **She let him cool his heels for half an hour,** le dio un plantón de media hora. **to follow on a person's heels,** pisarle (a uno) los talones. **to be down at h.,** (of shoes) estar gastados los tacones; estar desaseado. **to take to one's heels,** apretar a correr, poner pies en polvorosa. **to turn on one's h.,** dar media vuelta. **h.-bone,** zancajo, m. **h.-piece,** talón, m
**heeltap** /'hil,tæp/ n tapa de tacón, f; escurridura, f
**heft** /hɛft/ vt sopesar, tomar al peso
**hegemony** /hɪ'dʒɛməni/ n hegemonía, f
**heifer** /'hɛfər/ n ternera, vaquilla, f
**heigh** /hei/ interj (calling attention) ¡oye! ¡ioiga! **h.-ho!** ¡ay!
**height** /hait/ n altura, f; elevación, f; altitud, f; (stature) estatura, f; (high ground) cerro, m, colina, f; (sublimity) sublimidad, excelencia, f; colmo, m; (zenith) auge, m, cumbre, f
**heighten** /'haitn/ vt hacer más alto; (enhance) realzar; (exaggerate) exagerar; (perfect) perfeccionar; (intensify) intensificar
**heightening** /'haitnɪŋ/ n elevación, f; (enhancement) realce, m; (exaggeration) exageración, f; (perfection) perfección, f; (intensification) intensificación, f
**heinous** /'heinəs/ a atroz, nefando, horrible.
**heinousness** /'heinəsnɪs/ n atrocidad, enormidad, f
**heir** /ɛər/ n heredero, m. **h. apparent,** heredero aparente, m. **h.-at-law,** heredero forzoso, m. **h. presumptive,** presunto heredero, m
**heiress** /'ɛərɪs/ n heredera, f
**heirloom** /'ɛər,lum/ n reliquia de familia, f; Fig. herencia, f
**helicopter** /'hɛli,kɒptər/ n helicóptero, m
**helium** /'hiliəm/ n Chem. helio, m
**helix** /'hilɪks/ n Geom. hélice, f; (Archit. Geom.) espira, f
**hell** /hɛl/ n infierno, m. **h.-fire,** fuego del infierno, m, llamas del infierno, f pl
**Hellenic** /hɛ'lɛnɪk/ a helénico
**Hellenism** /'hɛlə,nɪzəm/ n helenismo, m
**Hellenist** /'hɛlənɪst/ n helenista, mf
**Hellenistic** /,hɛlə'nɪstɪk/ a helenístico
**Hellenize** /'hɛlə,naiz/ vt helenizar
**hellish** /'hɛlɪʃ/ a infernal; Inf. horrible, detestable
**hello** /'hɛlou/ interj ¡hola!; (on telephoning someone) ¡oiga! ¡alo!; (answering telephone) ¡diga! ¡alo!
**helm** /hɛlm/ n caña del timón, f; timón, gobernalle, m. **to obey the h.,** obedecer el timón. **to take the h.,** gobernar el timón; ponerse a pilotar
**helmet** /'hɛlmɪt/ n casco, m; (in olden days) yelmo, capacete, m; (sun) casco colonial, m
**helminthic** /hɛl'mɪnθɪk/ a helmíntico, vermífugo
**helmsman** /'hɛlmzmən/ n timonero, m
**help** /hɛlp/ n ayuda, f; auxilio, socorro, m; (protection) favor, m, protección, f; (remedy) remedio, m; (cooperation) cooperación, f, concurso, m; (domestic) criada, f. **A little h. is worth a lot of sympathy,** Más vale un toma que dos te daré. **There's no h. for it,** No hay más remedio. **to call for h.,** pedir socorro a gritos. **without h.,** a solas, sin la ayuda de nadie
**help** /hɛlp/ vt ayudar; socorrer, auxiliar; (favor) favorecer; (mitigate) aliviar; (contribute to) contribuir a, facilitar; (avoid) evitar. —vi ayudar. **He cannot h. worrying,** No puede menos de preocuparse. **God h. you!** ¡Dios te ampare! **So h. me God!** ¡Así Dios me salve! **to h. one another,** ayudarse mutuamente, ayudarse los unos a los otros. **to h. oneself,** (to food) servirse. **to h. down, off,** ayudar a bajar; ayudar a apearse. **to h. in,** ayudar a entrar. **to h. along, forward, on,** avanzar, fomentar, promover; contribuir a. **Shall I h. you on with the dress?** ¿Quieres que te

ayude a ponerte el vestido? **to h. out,** ayudar a salir; (from a vehicle) ayudar a bajar; (of a difficulty, etc.) sacar; suplir la falta de; ayudar. **to h. over,** ayudar a cruzar; (a difficulty) ayudar a salir (de un apuro); ayudar a vencer (un obstáculo, etc.); (a period) ayudar a pasar. **to h. to,** contribuir a, ayudar en; (food) servir. **to h. up,** ayudar a subir; ayudar a levantarse, levantar

**helper** /'hɛlpər/ n auxiliador (-ra); asistente (-ta); (protector) favorecedor (-ra); bienhechor (-ra); (colleague) colega, m; (co-worker) colaborador (-ra). **He thanked all his helpers,** Dio las gracias a todos los que le habían ayudado

**helpful** /'hɛlpfəl/ a útil, provechoso; (obliging) servicial, atento; (favorable) favorable; (healthy) saludable

**helpfulness** /'hɛlpfəlnɪs/ n utilidad, f; bondad, f

**helping** /'hɛlpɪŋ/ n ayuda, f; (of food) porción, ración, f, plato, m. **Won't you have a second h.?** ¿No quiere usted servirse más (or otra vez)? ¿No quiere usted repetir? **to lend a h. hand (to),** prestar ayuda (a)

**helpless** /'hɛlplɪs/ a desamparado, abandonado; (through infirmity) imposibilitado; impotente, sin fuerzas (para); (shiftless) incompetente, inútil

**helplessness** /'hɛlplɪsnɪs/ n desamparo, m; invalidez, debilidad, f; impotencia, f; incompetencia, f

**helpmeet** /'hɛlp,mit/ n compañero (-ra) perfecto (-ta); esposa, f

**helter-skelter** /'hɛltər 'skɛltər/ adv atropelladamente; en desorden. —n barahunda, f

**hem** /hɛm/ n Sew. dobladillo, filete, m, bastilla, f; (edge) orilla, f. —interj ¡ejem! —vt hacer dobladillo en, dobladillar. —vi (cough) fingir toser. **false hem,** Sew. dobladillo falso, m. **running hem,** Sew. jareta, f. **to hem and haw,** tartamudear; vacilar. **to hem in,** cercar, sitiar

**hemisphere** /'hɛmɪ,sfɪər/ n hemisferio, m

**hemispherical** /,hɛmɪ'sfɛrɪkəl/ a hemisférico, semiesférico

**hemlock** /'hɛm,lɒk/ n Bot. cicuta, f

**hemoglobin** /'himə,gloubɪn/ n Chem. hemoglobina, f

**hemophilia** /,himə'filiə/ n Med. hemofilia, f

**hemorrhage** /'hɛmərɪdʒ/ n hemorragia, f, flujo de sangre, m

**hemorrhoids** /'hɛmə,rɔidz/ n pl Med. hemorroides, f

**hemp** /hɛmp/ n cáñamo, m. **h. cloth,** lienzo, m. **h.-seed,** cañamón, m

**hemstitch** /'hɛm,stɪtʃ/ n vainica, f. —vt hacer vainica en

**hen** /hɛn/ n gallina, f; (female bird) hembra, f. **the hen pheasant,** la hembra del faisán. **hen bird,** pájara, f. **hen-coop** or **house,** gallinero, m. **hen party,** Inf. reunión de mujeres, f. **hen-roost,** nidal, ponedero, m

**hence** /hɛns/ adv (of place) de aquí; (of time) de ahora, de aquí a, dentro de; (therefore) por eso, por lo tanto, por consiguiente. —interj ¡fuera! ¡fuera de aquí! **I shall come to see you a month h.,** Vendré a verte en un mes (or al cabo de un mes). **ten years h.,** de aquí a diez años. **h. the fact that...,** de aquí que.... **H. it happens that...,** Por eso sucede que....

**henceforth** /,hɛns'fɔrθ/ adv desde aquí en adelante, de hoy en adelante

**henchman** /'hɛntʃmən/ n escudero, m; satélite, secuaz, m

**henna** /'hɛnə/ n alheña, f

**henpecked** /'hɛn,pɛkt/ a gobernado por su mujer, que se deja mandar por su mujer

**her** /hɜr; unstressed hər, ər/ pers pron direct object la; (with prepositions) ella. —pers pron indirect object le, a ella. —poss a su, mf; sus, mf pl, de ella. **I saw her on Wednesday,** La vi el miércoles. **The message is for her,** El recado es para ella. **It is her book,** Es su libro, Es el libro de ella

**herald** /'hɛrəld/ n heraldo, m; presagio, anuncio, m. —vt proclamar; anunciar, presagiar

**heraldic** /hɛ'rældɪk/ a heráldico

**heraldry** /'hɛrəldri/ n heráldica, f

**herb** /ɜrb; esp. Brit. hɜrb/ n hierba, f

**herbaceous** /hɜr'beiʃəs, ɜr-/ a herbáceo

**herbage** /'ɜrbɪdʒ, 'hɜr-/ n herbaje, m; pasto, m

**herbal** /'ɜrbəl, 'hɜr-/ a herbario. —n herbolaria, f

**herbalist** /'ɜrbəlɪst, 'hɜr-/ n herbario, m, simplista, mf

**herbarium** /hɜr'bɛəriəm, ɜr-/ n herbario, m

**herbivorous** /hɜr'bɪvərəs, ɜr-/ a herbívoro

**herby** /'ɜrbi, 'hɜr-/ a herbáceo

**Herculean** /,hɜrkyə'liən/ a hercúleo

**herd** /hɜrd/ n manada, f; (of cattle) hato, m; (race) raza, f; (Fig. contemptuous) populacho, m, masa, f. —vt reunir en manadas; reunir en hatos; (sheep) reunir en rebaños; guiar las manadas, etc. —vi ir en manadas, hatos o rebaños; asociarse, reunirse. **h.-instinct,** instinto gregario, m; instinto de las masas, m

**herdsman** /'hɜrdzmən/ n ganadero, pastor, manadero, m; (head herdsman) rabadán, m

**here** /hɪər/ adv aquí; (at roll-call) ¡presente!; acá; an este punto; ahora. —n presente, m. **And h. he looked at me,** Y a este punto me miró. **Come h.!** ¡Ven acá! **in h.,** aquí dentro. **h. below,** aquí abajo, en la tierra. **h. and there,** aquí y allá. **h., there and everywhere,** en todas partes. **H. I am,** Heme aquí. **h. is...,** he aquí.... **H. they are,** Aquí los tienes, Aquí están. **Here's to you!** (on drinking) ¡Salud y pesetas! ¡A tu salud!

**hereabouts** /'hɪərə,bauts/ adv por aquí cerca

**hereafter** /hɪər'æftər/ adv en lo futuro; desde ahora, en adelante. —n futuro, m. **the H.,** la otra vida

**hereat** /hɪər'æt/ adv en esto

**hereby** /hɪər'bai/ adv por esto, por las presentes

**hereditarily** /hə,rɛdɪ'tɛrəli/ adv hereditariamente, por herencia

**hereditary** /hə'rɛdɪ,tɛri/ a hereditario

**heredity** /hə'rɛdɪti/ n herencia, f

**herein** /hɪər'ɪn/ adv en esto; aquí dentro; incluso

**hereinafter** /,hɪərɪn'æftər/ adv después, más abajo, más adelante, en adelante, en lo sucesivo

**hereinbefore** /,hɪərɪnbɪ'fɔr/ adv en la anterior, en lo arriba citado, en lo antes mencionado, en lo precedente

**hereof** /hɪər'ʌv/ adv de esto

**heresy** /'hɛrəsi/ n herejía, f

**heretic** /'hɛrɪtɪk/ n hereje, mf

**heretical** /hə'rɛtɪkəl/ a herético

**hereunder** /hɪər'ʌndər/ adv abajo

**hereupon** /,hɪərə'pɒn/ adv en esto, en seguida

**herewith** /hɪər'wɪθ/ adv junto con esto, con esto; ahora, en esta ocasión

**heritage** /'hɛrɪtɪdʒ/ n herencia, f

**hermaphrodite** /hɜr'mæfrə,dait/ a and n hermafrodita, mf

**hermetic** /hɜr'mɛtɪk/ a hermético

**hermit** /'hɜrmɪt/ n ermitaño, m. **h. crab,** paguro, cangrejo ermitaño, m

**hernia** /'hɜrniə/ n hernia, f

**hero** /'hɪərou/ n héroe, m. **h.-worship,** culto a los héroes, m

**heroic** /hɪ'rouɪk/ a heroico, épico

**heroin** /'hɛrouɪn/ n Chem. heroína, f

**heroine** /'hɛrouɪn/ n heroína, f

**heroism** /'hɛrou,ɪzəm/ n heroísmo, m

**heron** /'hɛrən/ n garza, f

**herpes** /'hɜrpiz/ n pl herpes, mf pl

**herring** /'hɛrɪŋ/ n arenque, m

**hers** /hɜrz/ poss pron 3rd sing (el) suyo, m; (la) suya, f; (los) suyos, m pl; (las) suyas, f pl; de ella. **This book is h.,** Este libro es suyo. **This book is h., not mine,** Este libro es el suyo no el mío. **a sister of h.,** una de sus hermanas, una hermana suya

**herself** /hər'sɛlf/ pron sí misma, sí; ella misma; (with reflexive verb) se. **She has done it by h.,** Lo ha hecho por sí misma. **She told me so,** Ella misma me lo dijo. **She is by h.,** Está a solas, Está sola

**hesitancy** /'hɛzɪtənsi/ n. See **hesitation**

**hesitant** /'hɛzɪtənt/ a indeciso, vacilante, irresoluto. **to be h.,** mostrarse irresoluto

**hesitate** /'hɛzɪteit/ vi vacilar, dudar; titubear. **I do not h. to say...,** No vacilo en decir... **He hesitated over his reply,** Tardaba en dar su respuesta

**hesitatingly** /'hɛzɪ,teitɪŋli/ adv irresolutamente; titubeando

**hesitation** /,hɛzɪ'teiʃən/ n vacilación, hesitación, f;

irresolución, indecisión, f; (reluctance) aversión, repugnancia, f; titubeo, m

**heterodox** /'hetərə,dɒks/ a heterodoxo

**heterodoxy** /'hetərə,dɒksi/ n heterodoxia, f

**heterogeneity** /,hetəroudʒə'niiti/ n heterogeneidad, f

**heterogeneous** /,hetərə'dʒiniəs/ a heterogéneo

**hew** /hyu/ vt cortar, tajar; (trees) talar; (a career, etc.) hacerse

**hewer** /'hyuər/ n partidor, talador, m

**hexagon** /'heksə,gɒn/ n hexágono, m

**hey** /hei/ interj ¡eh!

**heyday** /'hei,dei/ n apogeo, colmo, m; buenos tiempos, m pl; reinado, m; pleno vigor, m

**hi** /hai/ interj ¡oye! ¡hola!

**hiatus** /hai'eitəs/ n hiato, m; laguna, f, vacío, m

**hibernate** /'haibər,neit/ vi invernar

**hibernation** /,haibər'neiʃən/ n invernada, f

**hibiscus** /hai'bɪskəs/ n Bot. hibisco, m

**hiccup** /'hɪkʌp/ n hipo, m. —vi hipar. —vt decir con hipo

**hidden** /'hɪdn/ a escondido, secreto, oculto

**hide** /haid/ n piel, f; pellejo, cuero, m

**hide** /haid/ vt esconder, ocultar; (cover) cubrir, tapar; (dissemble) disimular; (meaning) obscurecer. —vi esconderse; ocultarse; refugiarse. **to h. from each other,** esconderse el uno del otro. **h.-and-seek,** escondite, dormirlas, m

**hidebound** /'haid,baund/ a Fig. muy conservador, reaccionario, de ideas muy tradicionales

**hideous** /'hɪdiəs/ a horrible, repulsivo, horroroso; repugnante, odioso

**hideously** /'hɪdiəsli/ adv horriblemente. **to be h. ugly,** (of people) ser más feo que Picio

**hideousness** /'hɪdiəsnɪs/ n fealdad, horribilidad, f; repugnancia, f

**hiding** /'haidɪŋ/ n ocultación, f; encubrimiento, m; refugio, m; Inf. paliza, tunda, f. **h.-place,** escondite, escondrijo, m

**hie** /hai/ vi apresurarse, ir a prisa

**hierarch** /'haiə,rɑrk/ n jerarca, m

**hierarchical** /,haiə'rɑrkikəl/ a jerárquico

**hierarchy** /'haiə,rɑrki/ n jerarquía, f

**hieroglyph** /'haiərə,glɪf/ n jeroglífico, m

**higgledy-piggledy** /'hɪgəldi 'pɪgəldi/ adv revueltamente, en confusión; en montón, en desorden

**high** /hai/ a alto; elevado; (with altar, Mass, street, festival) mayor; grande; eminente; aristocrático; (of shooting) fijante; (of quality) superior; excelente; (haughty) orgulloso; (solemn) solemne; (good) bueno; noble; supremo; sumo; (of price) subido; Mus. agudo; (of the sea) tempestuoso, borrascoso; (of wind and explosives) violento, fuerte; (of polish) brillante; (with speed) grande; (with tension, frequency) alto; (with number, etc.) importante, grande; (with colors) subido; (of food) pasado; (angry) enojado, airado; (of cheek bones) saliente, prominente; (well-seasoned) picante; (flattering) lisonjero. —adv alto; hacia arriba; arriba; (deeply) profundamente; fuertemente; con violencia; (of price) a un precio elevado; (luxuriously) lujosamente; Mus. agudo. **a room 12 ft. h.,** un cuarto de doce pies de altura. **I knew her when she was so h.,** La conocí tamaña. **It is h. time he came,** Ya es hora de que viniese. **on h.,** en alto, arriba; en los cielos. **h. altar,** altar mayor, m. **h. and dry,** en la playa, varado; Fig. en seco. **h. and low,** de arriba abajo; por todas partes. **h.-born,** aristocrático, de alta alcurnia. **h.-bred,** (of people) de buena familia; (of animals) de buena raza. **h.-class,** de buena clase; de alta calidad. **h. collar,** alzacuello, m. **h. colored,** de colores vivos; Fig. exagerado. **h. command,** (Mil. Nav.) alto mando, m. **h. court,** tribunal supremo, m. **h. day,** día festivo, m. **h. explosive,** explosivo violento, m. **h.-flown,** hinchado, retumbante, altisonante. **h. frequency,** alta frecuencia, f. **h.-handed,** arbitrario, dominador, despótico. **h.-heeled,** a de tacón alto. **h. jump,** salto de altura, m. **h. land,** tierras altas, f pl; eminencia, f. **h. light,** Art. realce, m; acontecimiento de más interés, m; momento culminante, m. **h. mass,** misa mayor, f. **h.-minded,** de nobles pensamientos; arrogante. **h.-necked,** con cuello alto. **h.-pitched,** de tono alto, agudo. **h.-powered,** de alta potencia. **h.-powered car,** coche de

muchos caballos, m. **h. precision,** suma precisión, f. **h. pressure,** m alta presión, f; Fig. urgencia, f; n de alta presión; Fig. urgente. **h.-priced,** caro. **h. priest,** sumo pontífice, sumo sacerdote, alto sacerdote, m. **h. relief,** alto relieve, m. **h. road,** carretera mayor, f. **h. school,** instituto de segunda enseñanza, instituto, colegio, liceo, m; colegio, liceo, instituto, m, escuela secundaria, secundaria, f. **h. sea,** marejada, f. **h. seas,** alta mar, f. **h.-seasoned,** picante. **h. society,** alta sociedad, f. **h.-sounding,** altisonante, bombástico. **h.-speed,** de alta velocidad. **h.-spirited,** brioso; alegre. **h.-strung,** nervioso, excitable, sensitivo. **h. tension,** alta tensión, f. **h. tide,** marea alta, f. **h.-toned,** Mus. agudo; Inf. de alto copete; aristocrático. **h. treason,** alta traición, f. **h. water,** marea alta, pleamar, f. **h.-water mark,** límite de la marea, m; Fig. colmo, m; apogeo, m

**highbrow** /'hai,brau/ a and n intelectual, mf

**high-ceilinged** /'hai 'silɪŋd/ a alto de techo

**higher** /'haiər/ a compar of **high,** más alto; más elevado; superior. **on a h. plane,** en un nivel más alto. **h. education,** enseñanza superior, f. **h. mathematics,** la alta matemática, f. **h. criticism,** la alta crítica, f. **h. up,** más arriba. **h. up the river,** río arriba

**highest** /'haiist/ a superl of **high,** el más alto; la más alta; los más altos; las más altas; sumo, supremo; excelente. **h. common factor,** Math. máximo común divisor, m. **h. references,** (of cook, gardener, etc.) informes inmejorables, m pl; Com. referencias excelentes, f pl

**highland** /'hailənd/ n altiplanicie, f; montañas, f pl, distrito montañoso, m. —a montañoso

**highlander** /'hailəndər/ n montañés (-esa); esocés (-esa) del norte

**highlight** /'hai,lait/ vt dar relieve a, destacar

**highly** /'haili/ adv altamente; mucho; muy; extremadamente; grandemente; bien; favorablemente; con lisonja, lisonjeramente. **h. seasoned,** picante. **h. strung,** nervioso, excitable

**highness** /'hainis/ n altura, f; elevación, f; excelencia, f; nobleza, f; (title) Alteza, f. **His Royal H., Her Royal Highness,** Su Alteza Real

**high-ranking** /'hai 'ræŋkɪŋ/ a de alta jerarquía, de alto rango

**highway** /'hai,wei/ n camino real, m, carretera, f. **h. code,** código de la vía pública (or de la circulación), m. **h. robbery,** salteamiento de caminos, atraco, m

**highwayman** /'hai,weimən/ n salteador de caminos, m

**highways and byways** /'hai,weiz ən 'bai,weiz/ caminos y veredas

**hike** /haik/ vi ir de excursión. —n marcha con equipo, f

**hiker** /'haikər/ n excursionista, mf

**hiking** /'haikɪŋ/ n excursionismo, m; marcha con equipo, f

**hilarious** /hɪ'lɛəriəs/ a alegre

**hilarity** /hɪ'lɛrɪti/ n hilaridad, f

**hill** /hɪl/ n colina, f, cerro, otero, m; monte, m, montaña, f; (pile) montón, m. **h.-side,** falda de montaña, ladera de una colina, f. **h.-top,** cumbre de una colina, f

**hilliness** /'hɪlinɪs/ n montuosidad, f, lo montañoso

**hillman** /'hɪl,mæn/ n montañés, m

**hillock** /'hɪlək/ n altozano, montículo, collado, m

**hilly** /'hɪli/ a montañoso

**hilt** /hɪlt/ n puño, m, empuñadura, f

**him** /hɪm/ pron 3rd sing direct object le, lo; (with prep.) él; indirect object le, a él; (with a direct obj. in 3rd person) se. **I gave him the magazine,** Le di la revista. **I gave it to him,** Se lo di a él. **This is for him,** Esto es para él

**Himalayan** /,hɪmə'leiən/ a himalayo

**Himalayas, the** /,hɪmə'leiəz/ los Himalayas, m pl

**himself** /hɪm'sɛlf/ pron sí, sí mismo; él mismo; (reflexive) se. **He did it by h.,** Lo hizo por sí mismo. For more examples see **herself**

**hind** /haind/ n corza, cierva, f. —a trasero, posterior. **h.-quarters,** cuarto trasero, m; (of a horse) ancas, f pl

**hinder** /'hindər/ a trasero, posterior

**hinder** /'hindər/ vt impedir, estorbar; embarazar, di-

**hold**

ficultar; interrumpir. —*vi* ser un obstáculo; formar un obstáculo

**hinderer** /'hɪndərər/ *n* estorbador (-ra); interruptor (-ra)

**hindmost** /'haind,moust/ *a* posterior, postrero, último

**hindrance** /'hɪndrəns/ *n* obstáculo, estorbo, impedimento, *m;* perjuicio, *m;* interrupción, *f*

**Hindu** /'hɪndu/ *a* hindú, *mf*

**Hinduism** /'hɪndu,ɪzəm/ *n* indoísmo, *m*

**Hindustani** /,hɪndʊ'stɑni/ *a* indostanés. —*n* (language) indostani, *m*

**hinge** /hɪndʒ/ *n* gozne, pernio, *m,* bisagra, *f;* articulación, *f; Fig.* eje, *m.* —*vi* moverse (or abrirse) sobre goznes; *Fig.* depender (de). —*vt* engoznar

**hinged** /hɪndʒd/ *a* con goznes

**hint** /hɪnt/ *n* indirecta, insinuación, sugestión, *f;* (advice) consejo, *m.* —*vt* dar a entender, decir con medias palabras, insinuar, sugerir. —*vi* insinuar. **to take the h.,** darse por aludido

**hinterland** /'hɪntər,lænd/ *n* interior (de un país), *m*

**hip** /hɪp/ *n Anat.* cadera, *f; Bot.* fruto del rosal silvestre, *m.* **h.-bath,** baño de asiento, *m.* **h.-bone,** hueso ilíaco, *m.* **h.-joint,** articulación de la cadera, *f.* **h.-pocket,** faltriquera, *f*

**hipped** /hɪpt/ *a* de caderas

**hippodrome** /'hɪpə,droum/ *n* hipódromo, *m*

**hippopotamus** /,hɪpə'pɒtəməs/ *n* hipopótamo, *m*

**hire** /haiər/ *n* alquiler, arriendo, *m;* salario, *m.* —*vt* alquilar, arrendar; tomar en arriendo; (person) contratar; tomar a su servicio. **to h. out,** alquilar. **for** or **on h.,** de alquiler. **h.-purchase,** compra a plazos, *f*

**hireling** /'haiərlɪŋ/ *n* mercenario, *m*

**hirer** /'haiərər/ *n* alquilador (-ra), arrendador (-ra)

**hirsute** /'hɜrsut/ *a* hirsuto. **non-h.** *Bot.* lampiño

**his** /hɪz; *unstressed* ɪz/ *poss pron 3rd sing* (el) suyo, *m;* (la) suya, *f;* (los) suyos, *m pl;* (las) suyas, *f pl;* de él. —*poss a* su, *mf;* sus, *mf pl;* de él. **his handkerchiefs,** sus pañuelos. **his mother,** su madre, la madre de él. **a sister of his,** una de sus hermanas, una hermana suya. See **hers** for more examples.

**Hispanism** /'hɪspə,nɪzəm/ *n* hispanismo, *m*

**Hispanist** /'hɪspənɪst/ *n* hispanista, *mf*

**hispanize** /'hɪspə,naiz/ *vt* españolizar

**Hispano-American** /hɪs'pænou ə'mɛrɪkən/ *a* hispano-americano

**hiss** /hɪs/ *n* silbido, *m;* (sputter) chisporroteo, *m.* —*vi* silbar

**hissing** /'hɪsɪŋ/ *n* silbido, *m;* chisporroteo, *m.* —*a* silbante

**hist** /hɪst/ *interj* ¡chist!

**histologist** /hɪs'tɒlədʒɪst/ *n* histólogo, *m*

**histology** /hɪ'stɒlədʒi/ *n* histología, *f*

**historian** /hɪ'stɔriən/ *n* historiador (-ra)

**historic** /hɪ'stɔrɪk/ *a* histórico

**historical** /hɪ'stɔrɪkəl/ *a* histórico. **h. truth,** verdad histórica, *f*

**historically** /hɪs'tɔrɪkəli/ *adv* históricamente

**historiographer** /hɪ,stɔri'ɒgrəfər/ *n* historiógrafo, *m*

**historiography** /hɪ,stɔri'ɒgrəfi/ *n* historiografía, *f*

**history** /'hɪstəri/ *n* historia, *f.* **Biblical h.,** historia sagrada, *f.* **natural h.,** historia natural, *f*

**histrionic** /,hɪstri'ɒnɪk/ *a* histriónico

**hit** /hɪt/ *n* golpe, *m; Aer.* impacto, *m;* (success) éxito, *m;* (piece of luck) buena suerte, *f;* (satire) sátira, *f.* —*vt* golpear; (buffet) abofetear, pegar; (find) dar con, tropezar con; (attain) acertar; (guess) adivinar; (attract) atraer; (deal) lanzar, dar; (wound) herir, hacer daño (a). **The sun hits me right in the eyes,** El sol me da en la cabeza. **direct hit,** *Aer.* impacto de lleno, *m.* **lucky hit,** acierto, *m.* **to hit a straight left,** (boxing) lanzar un directo con la izquierda. **to hit the mark,** dar en el blanco; *Fig.* dar en el clavo. **hit or miss,** acierto o error. **to hit against,** dar contra, estrellar contra. **to hit back,** defenderse; devolver golpe por golpe. **to hit off,** imitar; (a likeness) coger. **to hit out,** abofetear; *Fig.* atacar; golpear (la pelota) fuera. **to hit upon,** dar con; tropezar con; encontrar por casualidad; (remember) acordarse de

**hitch** /hɪtʃ/ *n* (jerk) sacudida, *f;* nudo fácil de soltar, *m; Fig.* obstáculo, *m; Fig.* dificultad, *f.* **give s.b. a hitch,** levantar a fulano. —*vt* sacudir; (a chair, etc.)

arrastrar, empujar; amarrar, enganchar; atar. —*vi* (along a seat, etc.) correrse (en); (get entangled) enredarse, cogerse; (rub) rascarse. **without a h.,** sin dificultad alguna, viento en popa; (smoothly) a pedir de boca. **to h. up,** sacudir, dar una sacudida (a)

**hitchhike** /'hɪtʃ,haik/ *vi* ir a dedo (Argentina), pedir aventón (Mexico), pedir botella (Cuba), hacer autostop, ir por autostop (Spain)

**hither** /'hɪðər/ *adv* acá, hacia acá; *a* citerior, más cercano. **h. and thither,** acá y aculla allá

**hitherto** /'hɪðər,tu/ *adv* hasta ahora, hasta el presente

**Hitlerian** /hɪt'lɛəriən/ *a* hitleriano, nacista

**Hitlerism** /'hɪtlə,rɪzəm/ *n* hitlerismo, nacismo, *m*

**Hittite** /'hɪtait/ *a* and *n* heteo (-ea)

**hive** /haiv/ *n* (for bees) colmena, *f;* (swarm) enjambre, *m; Fig.* centro, *m.* —*vt* (bees) enjambrar. **h. of industry,** centro de industria

**hoard** /hɔrd/ *n* acumulación, *f;* provisión, *f;* tesoro, *m.* —*vt* acumular, amasar, amontonar; guardar

**hoarder** /'hɔrdər/ *n* acaparador (-ra)

**hoarding** /'hɔrdɪŋ/ *n* amontonamiento, *m;* acaparamiento, *m;* (fence) empalizada, cerca, *f;* palizada de tablas, *f*

**hoarfrost** /'hɔr,frɔst/ *n* escarcha, helada blanca, *f*

**hoariness** /'hɔrinɪs/ *n* (of the hair) canicie, *f;* blancura, *f;* (antiquity) vejez, vetustez, *f*

**hoarse** /hɔrs/ *a* ronco; discordante. **to be h.,** tener la voz ronca. **to grow h.,** enronquecerse

**hoarsely** /'hɔrsli/ *adv* roncamente

**hoarseness** /'hɔrsnɪs/ *n* ronquera, *f; Inf.* carraspera, *m*

**hoary** /'hɔri/ *a* (of the hair) canoso; blanco; (old) vetusto, antiguo, viejo

**hoax** /houks/ *n* estafa, *f,* engaño, *m;* broma pesada, *f;* burla, *f.* —*vt* estafar, engañar; burlar

**hoaxer** /'houksər/ *n* burlador (-ra); estafador (-ra)

**hob** /hɒb/ *n* repisa interior del hogar, *f*

**hobble** /'hɒbəl/ *n* (gait) cojera, *f;* traba, maniota, *f.* —*vi* cojear. —*vt* manear. **h. skirt,** falda muy estrecha, *f*

**hobby** /'hɒbi/ *n* pasatiempo, *m,* recreación, *f;* manía, afición, *f.* **h.-horse,** caballo de cartón, *m; Fig.* caballo de batalla, *m*

**hobgoblin** /'hɒb,gɒblɪn/ *n* trasgo, duende, *m*

**hobnail** /'hɒb,neil/ *n* clavo de herradura, clavo de botas, *m*

**hobnailed** /'hɒb,neild/ *a* (of boots) con clavos

**hobnob** /'hɒb,nɒb/ *vi* codearse, tratar con familiaridad

**hock** /hɒk/ *n Anat.* pernil, *m;* (wine) vino del Rin, *m*

**hockey** /'hɒki/ *n* chueca, *m.* **h. ball,** bola, pelota de chueca, *f.* **h. stick,** bastón de chueca, *m*

**hocus-pocus** /'houkəs 'poukəs/ *n* juego de pasa pasa, *m;* engaño, *m,* treta, *f*

**hod** /hɒd/ *n* cuezo, *m*

**hodgepodge** /'hɒdʒ,pɒdʒ/ See **hotchpotch**

**hoe** /hou/ *n* azadón, *m.* —*vt* azadonar; sachar

**hoeing** /'houɪŋ/ *n* cavadura con azadón, *f;* sachadura, *f*

**hoer** /'houər/ *n* azadonero, *m*

**hog** /hɔg/ *n* cerdo, puerco, *m.* **to go the whole hog,** ir al extremo. **hogskin,** piel de cerdo, *f*

**hoggish** /'hɔgɪʃ/ *a* porcuno; (greedy) comilón, tragón; (selfish) egoísta

**hoist** /hɔist/ *n* levantamiento, *m;* (lift) montacargas, *m;* (winch) cabria, *f;* (crane) grúa, *f.* —*vt* levantar, alzar; (flags) enarbolar; suspender; *Naut.* izar

**hoity-toity** /'hɔiti 'tɔiti/ *a* picajoso, quisquilloso; presuntuoso

**hold** /hould/ *n* asimiento, agarro, *m,* presa, *f;* asidero, *m; Fig.* autoridad, *f,* poder, *m; Fig.* comprensión, *f;* (of a ship) cala, bodega, *f.* **to loose one's h.,** aflojar su presa. **to lose one's h.,** perder su presa. **to seize h. of,** asirse de, echar mano de. **h.-all,** funda, *f.* **h.-up,** (robbery) atraco, robo a mano armada, *m;* (in traffic) atasco (or obstáculo) en el tráfico, *m;* (in work) parada, cesación (de trabajo), *f*

**hold** /hould/ *vt* tener; asir, agarrar; coger; retener; (embrace) abrazar; (a post) ocupar; (a meeting, etc.) celebrar; (bear weight of) aguantar, soportar; (own) poseer; *Mil.* ocupar, defender; (contain) contener; (have in store) reservar; tener capacidad para; (retain) retener; (believe) creer, sostener; (consider) opinar, tener para (mí, etc.); juzgar; (restrain) detener; contener; (of attention, etc.) mantener; (maneuvers) hacer; (observe) guardar. —*vi* resistir, aguantar; (be valid) ser válido; regir; (apply) aplicarse; (last) continuar, seguir. —*interj* ¡tente! ¡para! **The room won't h. more,** En este cuarto no caben más. **They h. him in great respect,** Le tienen mucho respeto. **The theory does not h. water,** La teoría es falsa, La teoría no es lógica. **to h. one's own,** defenderse, mantenerse en sus trece. **to h. one's breath,** contener la respiración. **to h. one's tongue,** callarse. **to h. sway,** mandar; reinar. **to h. tightly,** agarrar fuertemente; (clasp) estrechar. **H. the line!** (telephone) ¡Aguarde un momento! **to h. back,** *vt* detener; contener; retener; esconder; abstenerse de entregar. —*vi* quedarse atrás; vacilar, dudar; tardar en. **to h. by,** seguir; basarse en, apoyarse en. **to h. down,** sujetar; (oppress) oprimir. **to h. fast,** *vt* sujetar fuertemente. —*vi* mantenerse firme; *Fig.* estar agarrado (a). **to h. forth,** *vt* ofrecer; expresar. —*vi* hacer un discurso, perorar. **to h. in,** *vt* contener; retener. —*vi* contenerse. **to h. off,** *vt* apartar, alejar. —*vi* apartarse, alejarse, mantenerse alejado. **to h. on,** seguir, persistir en; aguantar. **to h. out,** *vt* alargar, extender; ofrecer. —*vi* aguantar; durar, resistir. **to h. over,** *vt* tener suspendido sobre; (postpone) aplazar; *Fig.* amenazar con. **to h. to,** agarrarse a; atenerse a. **to h. together,** *vt* unir; juntar. —*vi* mantenerse juntos. **to h. up,** *vt* (display) mostrar, enseñar; levantar; sostener, soportar; (rob) atracar, saltear; (delay) atrasar; (stop) interrumpir, parar. —*vi* mantenerse en pie; (of weather) seguir bueno. **The train has been held up by fog,** El tren viene con retraso a causa de la niebla

**holder** /'houldər/ *n* el *m*, (*f*, la) que tiene; poseedor (-ra); *Com.* tenedor (-ra); inquilino (-na); propietario (-ia); (support) soporte, *m*; mango, *m*; asa, *f*; (in compounds) porta...

**holding** /'houldɪŋ/ *n* tención, *f*; posesión, *f*; propiedad, *f*; (leasing) arrendamiento, *m*; (celebration) solemnización, *f*; (of a meeting) el celebrar, el tener; *pl* **holdings,** *Com.* valores habidos, *m pl*

**holding company** *n* compañía de cartera, *f*

**hole** /houl/ *n* hoyo, *m*; boquete, *m*; agujero, *m*; cavidad, *f*; (hollow) depresión, *f*, hueco, *m*; orificio, *m*; (tear) roto, desgarro, *m*; (eyelet) punto, *m*; (in cheese) ojo, *m*; (in stocking) rotura, *f*, punto, *m*; (lair) madriguera, *f*; (nest) nido, *m*; (golf) hoyo, *m*; (fix) aprieto, *m*. —*vt* agujerear; excavar; (bore) taladrar; *Sports.* meter la pelota (en). **to h. out,** (golf) meter la pelota en el hoyo. **h.-and-corner,** *a Inf.* bajo mano, secreto

**hole-puncher** /'houl ˌpʌntʃər/ *n* agujereadora, *f*

**holiday** /'hɒlɪˌdei/ *n* día feriado, *m*; día de fiesta, día festivo, *m*; vacación, *f*. —*a* festivo, alegre; de vacación; de vacaciones; de excursión; (summer) veraniego. **day's h.,** día de asueto, *m*. **to take a h.,** tomar una vacación; hacer fiesta. **h. camp,** colonia veraniega, *f*. **h.-maker,** excursionista, turista, *mf*; (in the summer) veraneante, *mf* **holidays with pay,** vacaciones retribuidas, *f pl*

**holiness** /'houlɪnɪs/ *n* santidad, *f*

**Holland** /'hɒlənd/ Holanda, *f*

**holland** /'hɒlənd/ *n* lienzo crudo. —*a* holandés. **H. gin,** ginebra holandesa, *f*

**hollow** /'hɒlou/ *a* hueco; cóncavo; (empty) vacío; (of eyes, etc.) hundido; (of sound) sordo; (of a cough) cavernoso; (echoing) retumbante; (*Fig.* unreal) vacío, falso; insincero. —*adv* vacío; *Inf.* completamente. —*n* hueco, *m*; concavidad, *f*; (hole) hoyo, *m*; cavidad, *f*; (valley) hondanada, *f*, barranco, *m*; (groove) ranura, *f*; (depression) depresión, *f*; (in the back) curvadura, *f*. —*vt* excavar, ahuecar; vaciar. **h.-cheeked,** con las mejillas hundidas. **h.-eyed,** con los ojos hundidos, de ojos hundidos

**hollowness** /'hɒlounɪs/ *n* concavidad, *f*; (falseness) falsedad, *f*; insinceridad, *f*

**holly** /'hɒli/ *n* acebo, agrifolio, *m*

**holocaust** /'hɒləˌkɔst/ *n* holocausto, *m*

**holograph** /'hɒləˌgræf/ *n* hológrafo, *m*

**holster** /'houlstər/ *n* pistolera, *f*

**holy** /'houli/ *a* santo; sagrado; (blessed) bendito.

**most h.,** *a* santísimo. **to make h.,** santificar. **H. Father,** Padre Santo, el Papa, *m*. **H. Ghost,** Espíritu Santo, *m*. **H. Office,** Santo Oficio, *m*, Inquisición, *f*. **H. Orders,** órdenes sagradas, *f pl.* **h. places,** santos lugares, *m pl.* **H. Scripture,** Sagrada Escritura, *f*. **H. See,** Cátedra de San Pedro, *f*. **h. water,** agua bendita, *f*. **H. Souls,** las Ánimas Benditas. **h. water stoup,** acetre, *m*. **H. Week,** Semana Santa, *f*

**Holy Land,** the la Tierra Santa, *f*

**homage** /'hɒmɪdʒ/ *n* homenaje, *m*; culto, *m*; reverencia, *f*. **to pay h.,** rendir homenaje

**home** /houm/ *n* casa, *f*; hogar, *m*; domicilio, *m*, residencia, *f*; (institution) asilo, *m*; (haven) refugio, *m*; (habitation) morada, *f*; (country of origin) país de origen, *m*; (native land) patria, *f*; (environment) ambiente natural, *m*; *Sports.* meta, *f*. —*a* casero, doméstico; nativo; nacional, del país; indígena. —*adv* a casa, hacia casa; (in one's country) en su patria; (returned) de vuelta; (of the feelings) al corazón, al alma; (to the limit) al límite. **at h.,** en casa; *Fig.* en su elemento; (of games) en campo propio; de recibo. **at-h. day,** día de recibo, *m*. **He shot the bolt h.,** Echó el cerrojo. **one's long h.,** su última morada. **to be at h.,** estar en casa; estar de recibo. **to be away from h.,** estar fuera de casa; estar ausente. **to bring h.,** traer (o llevar) a casa; hacer ver; convencer; llegar al alma; (a crime) probar (contra). **to go h.,** volver a casa; volver a la patria; (be effective) hacer su efecto; (move) herir en lo más vivo. **to make oneself at h.,** ponerse a sus anchas, sentirse como en casa de uno. **Please make yourself at home!** ¡Ha tomado posesión de su casa! **to strike h.,** dar en el blanco; herir; (hit) golpear; herir en lo más vivo; hacerse sentir. **h. affairs,** asuntos domésticos, *m pl*, (Ministry of) Gobernación, *f*. **h.-bred,** criado en el país. **h.-brewed,** fermentado en el país; fermentado en casa. **h.-coming,** regreso al hogar, *m*. **h. counties,** condados alrededor de Londres, *m pl.* **H. Defense,** defensa nacional, *f*. **h. farm,** residencia del propietario de una finca, *f*. **h. for the aged,** asilo de ancianos, *m*. **h. front,** frente doméstico, *m*. **H. Guard,** milicia nacional, *f*. **h. life,** vida de familia, *f*. **h.-made** casero, de fabricación casera, hecho en casa. **H. Office,** Ministerio de Gobernación, *m*. **H. Rule,** autonomía, *f*. **H. Secretary,** Ministro de Gobernación, *m*. **h. stretch,** último trecho (de una carrera), *m*. **h. truth,** verdad, *Inf.* fresca, *f*. **to tell someone a few h. truths,** contarle cuatro verdades

**homeless** /'houmlɪs/ *a* sin casa; sin hogar. **the h.,** los sin techo

**homeliness** /'houmlɪnɪs/ *n* comodidad, *f*; sencillez, *f*; (ugliness) fealdad, *f*

**homely** /'houmli/ *a* doméstico; familiar; (unpretentious) sencillo; llano; (ugly) feo; desabrido

**homemaker** /'houmˌmeikər/ *n* ama de casa, *f*

**homeopath** /'houmiəˌpæθ/ *n* homeópata, *mf*

**homeopathic** /ˌhoumiə'pæθɪk/ *a* homeópata

**homeopathy** /ˌhoumi'ɒpəθi/ *n* homeopatía, *f*

**Homeric** /hou'mɛrɪk/ *a* homérico

**homesick** /'houmˌsɪk/ *a* nostálgico. **to be h.,** tener morriña

**homesickness** /'houmˌsɪknɪs/ *n* nostalgia, añoranza, morriña, *f*

**homespun** /'houmˌspʌn/ *a* tejido en casa; hecho en casa; basto, grueso

**homestead** /'houmstɛd/ *n* hacienda, *f*; casa solariega, *f*; casa, *f*

**homeward** /'houmwərd/ *adv* hacia casa, en dirección al hogar; de vuelta; hacia la patria. **h.-bound,** en dirección a casa; (of ships) con rumbo al puerto de origen; (of other traffic) de vuelta

**homicidal** /ˌhɒmə'saidl/ *a* homicida

**homicide** /'hɒməˌsaid/ *n* (act) homicidio, *m*; (person) homicida, *mf*

**homily** /'hɒməli/ *n Eccl.* homilía, *f*; sermón, *m*

**homing pigeon** /'houmɪŋ/ *n* palomo (-ma) mensajero (-ra)

**homogeneity** /ˌhoumədʒə'niiti/ *n* homogeneidad, *f*

**homogeneous** /ˌhoumə'dʒiniəs/ *a* homogéneo

**homologous** /hə'mɒləgəs/ *a* homólogo

**homonym** /'hɒmənɪm/ *n* homónimo, *m*

**homonymous** /hə'mɒnəməs/ *a* homónimo

**homosexual** /ˌhoumə'sɛkʃuəl/ a and n homosexual, mf

**Honduran** /hɒn'durən/ a and n hondureño (-ña)

**hone** /houn/ n piedra de afilar, f. —vt afilar, vaciar

**honest** /'ɒnɪst/ a honrado; decente, honesto; (chaste) casto; (loyal) sincero, leal; (frank) franco; imparcial. **an h. man,** un hombre de buena fe, un hombre honrado, un hombre decente

**honesty** /'ɒnəsti/ n honradez, f; honestidad, f; (chastity) castidad, f; sinceridad, f; rectitud, imparcialidad, f

**honey** /'hʌni/ n miel, f. **h.-bee,** abeja obrera, f. **h.-colored,** melado. **h.-pot,** jarro de miel, m. **h.-tongued,** melifluo; de pico de oro

**honeycomb** /'hʌni,koum/ n panal, m

**honeycombed** /'hʌni,koumd/ a apanalado

**honeydew** /'hʌni,du/ n mielada, f; Fig. ambrosia, f

**honeyed** /'hʌnid/ a de miel; Fig. meloso, adulador

**honeymoon** /'hʌni,mun/ n luna de miel, f; viaje de novios, viaje nupcial, m. —vi hacer un viaje nupcial

**honeysuckle** /'hʌni,sʌkəl/ n madreselva, f

**honor** /'ɒnər/ n honor, m; honra, f; honradez, rectitud, integridad, f; pl **honors,** honores, m pl; condecoraciones, f pl; (last h.) honras, pompas fúnebres, f pl. —vt honrar; (God) glorificar; (decorate) condecorar, laurear; (respect) respetar; reverenciar; Com. aceptar; (a toast) beber. **On my h.,** A fe mía. **point of h.,** punto de honor, pundonor, m. **word of h.,** palabra de honor, f. **Your H.,** (to a judge) Excelentísimo Señor Juez

**honorable** /'ɒnərəbəl/ a honorable; glorioso; digno; ilustre; (sensitive of honor) pundonoroso

**honorable mention** n accésit, m

**honorableness** /'ɒnərəbəlnɪs/ n honradez, f

**honorably** /'ɒnərəbli/ adv honorablemente; dignamente

**honorarium** /ˌɒnə'rɛəriəm/ n honorario, m

**honorary** /'ɒnə,rɛri/ a honorario, honorífico. **h. member,** socio (-ia) honorario (-ia). **h. mention,** mención honorífica, f

**hood** /hʊd/ n capucha, caperuza, f; (folding of vehicles) capota, cubierta, cubierta del motor f; (of a carriage) caparazón, fuelle, m; (of a car) capó, m, (university) muceta, f; (of a fireplace) campana (de hogar), f; (cowl of chimney) sombrerete (de chimenea), m. —vt cubrir con capucha; cubrir; (the eyes) ocultar, cubrir, velar

**hooded** /'hʊdɪd/ a con capucha

**hoodwink** /'hʊd,wɪŋk/ vt vendar (los ojos); Fig. engañar, embaucar, burlar

**hoof** /hʊf/ n casco, m; (cloven) pezuña, f

**hoofed** /hʊft/ a ungulado

**hoof it** ir a golpe de calcetín

**hook** /hʊk/ n gancho, garfio, m; (boat-) bichero, m; (fish-) anzuelo, m; (on a dress) corchete, m; (hanger) colgadero, m; (claw) garra, f. —vt enganchar; (a dress) abrochar; (fish) pescar, coger; (nab) atrapar, pescar. **by h. or by crook,** a tuertas o a derechas. **left h.,** (boxing) izquierdo, m. **right h.,** (boxing) derecho, m. **to catch oneself on a h.,** engancharse. **h. and eye,** los corchetes. **h.-nosed,** con nariz de gancho, con nariz aguileña. **h.-up,** Radio. circuito, m; transmisión en circuito, f

**hooked** /hʊkt/ a con ganchos; corvo, ganchoso

**hooking** /'hʊkɪŋ/ n enganche, m; (of a dress) abrochamiento, m; (of fish and Inf.) pesca, f

**hookworm** /'hʊk,wɜrm/ n anquilostoma, m

**hooligan** /'huligən/ n rufián, m

**hooliganism** /'huligə,nɪzəm/ n rufianería, f

**hoop** /hup/ n aro, arco, m; (of a skirt) miriñaque, m; (croquet) argolla, f; (toy) aro, m; círculo, m. —vt poner aros a; Fig. rodear

**hoot** /hut/ n (of owls) ululación, f, grito, m; (whistle) silbido, m; ruido, clamor, m. —vi (of owls) ulular, gritar; silbar; Auto. avisar con la bocina. **to h. off the stage,** hacer abandonar la escena. **to h. down,** silbar

**hooter** /'hutər/ n sirena, f; Auto. bocina, f; (whistle) pito, m

**hooting** /'hutɪŋ/ n See **hoot**

**hop** /hɒp/ n salto, brinco, m; Bot. lúpulo, m; Bot. flores de oblón, f pl; (dance) baile, m. —vi saltar con un

pie; andar dando brincos; saltar; (limp) cojear; recoger lúpulo; (of plant) dar lúpulo. —vt saltar. **hop-garden,** huerto de lúpulo, m. **hop-kiln,** horno para secar lúpulo, m. **hop-picker,** recolector (-ra) de lúpulo. **hop-picking,** recolección de lúpulos, f

**hope** /houp/ n esperanza, f; (faith) confianza, f; (expectation) anticipación, expectación, f; (probability) probabilidad, f; (illusion) ilusión, f; sueño, m. —vi esperar. **to live in h. that,** vivir con la esperanza de que. **to lose h.,** desesperarse. **to h. against h.,** esperar sin motivo, esperar lo imposible. **to h. for,** desear. **to h. in,** confiar en

**hopeful** /'houpfəl/ a lleno de esperanzas, confiado; optimista; (Fig.) risueño. —n Inf. la esperanza de la casa. **to look h.,** Fig. prometer bien

**hopefully** /'houpfəli/ adv con esperanza

**hopefulness** /'houpfəlnɪs/ n optimismo, m; Fig. aspecto prometedor, m

**hopeless** /'houplɪs/ a desesperado, sin esperanza; irremediable; (of situations) imposible; (of disease) incurable. **to be h.,** (lose hope) desesperarse; (have no remedy) ser irremediable; (of disease) no tener cura. **to make h.,** hacer perder la esperanza, desesperar; dejar sin remedio; (a situation) hacer imposible; (an illness) hacer imposible de curar

**hopelessly** /'houplɪsli/ adv sin esperanza; sin remedio; imposiblemente; incurablemente

**hopelessness** /'houplɪsnɪs/ n desesperación, f; (of an illness) imposibilidad de curar, f; lo irremediable; imposibilidad, f

**hopscotch** /'hɒp,skɒtʃ/ n infernáculo, m, rayuela, f

**horal, horary** /'hɔrəl; 'hɔrəri/ a horario

**horde** /hɔrd/ n horda, f

**horizon** /hə'raizən/ n horizonte, m

**horizontal** /ˌhɔrə'zɒntl/ a horizontal. **h. suspension,** (gymnastics) plancha, f

**horizontality** /ˌhɔrəzɒn'tælɪti/ n horizontalidad, f

**horizontally** /ˌhɔrə'zɒntli/ adv horizontalmente

**hormone** /'hɔrmoun/ n hormona, f

**horn** /hɔrn/ n (of bull, etc.) cuerno, m; (antler) asta, f; (of an insect) antena, f; (of a snail) tentáculo, m; Mus. cuerno, m; trompa, f; (of motor and phonograph) bocina, f; (of moon) cuerno (de la luna), m. **article made of h.,** objeto de cuerno, m. **on the horns of a dilemma,** entre la espada y la pared. **h. of plenty,** cuerno de abundancia, m; cornucopia, f. **h.-rimmed spectacles,** anteojos de concha, m pl. **h. thrust,** cornada, f

**horned** /hɔrnd/ a cornudo; (antlered) enastado

**hornet** /'hɔrnɪt/ n avispón, abejón, m

**horny** /'hɔrni/ a córneo; calloso; duro. **h.-handed,** con manos callosas

**horoscope** /'hɔrə,skoup/ n horóscopo, m

**horrible** /'hɔrəbəl/ a horrible, repugnante, espantoso; (of price) enorme; Inf. horrible

**horribleness** /'hɔrəbəlnɪs/ n horribilidad, f, horror, m, lo espantoso

**horribly** /'hɔrəbli/ adv horriblemente

**horrid** /'hɔrɪd/ a horroroso; desagradable

**horridness** /'hɔrɪdnɪs/ n horror, m; lo desagradable

**horrific** /hɔ'rɪfɪk/ a horrífico, horrendo

**horrify** /'hɔrə,fai/ vt horrorizar; escandalizar

**horrifying** /'hɔrə,faiɪŋ/ a horroroso, horripilante

**horror** /'hɔrər/ n horror, m. **h.-stricken,** horrorizado

**hors d'œuvres** /ɔr'dɜrvz/ n pl entremeses, m pl

**horse** /hɔrs/ n caballo, m; (cavalry) caballería, f; (frame) caballete, m; (gymnastics and as punishment) potro, m. —a caballar, caballuno. —vt montar a caballo. **pack of horses,** caballada, f. **to ride a h.,** cabalgar, montar a caballo. **H. Artillery,** artillería montada, f. **h. blanket,** manta para caballos, f; sudadero, m. **h.-block,** montador, m. **h.-box,** vagón para caballos, m. **h.-breaker,** domador de caballos, m. **h.-cab,** simón, m. **h.-chestnut,** castaña pilonga, f. **h.-chestnut flower,** candela, f. **h.-collar,** collera, f. **h.-dealer,** chalán, m. **h.-doctor,** veterinario, m. **h.-flesh,** carne de caballo, f. **h.-fly,** tábano, m. **H. Guards,** guardias montadas, f pl. **h.-latitudes,** calmas de Cáncer, f pl. **h.-laugh,** carcajada, f. **h.-master,** maestro de equitación, m. **h. meat,** carne de caballo, f. **h. pistol,** pistola de arzón, f. **h.-play,** payasada, f. **h.-power,** caballo de vapor, m; potencia, f. **a twelve-**

**h.p. car,** un coche de doce caballos. **h.-race,** carrera de caballos, f. **h.-radish,** rábano picante, raíz amarga, m. **h.-sense,** sentido común, m, gramática parda, f. **h. show,** exposición de caballos, feria equina f; concurso de caballos, m. **h.-trainer,** entrenador de caballos, m. **h. tram,** tranvía de sangre, m. **h. trappings,** monturas, f pl

**horseback** /'hɔrs,bæk/ n lomo de caballo, m. **on h.,** a caballo. **to ride on h.,** ir a caballo

**horseman** /'hɔrsmən/ n jinete, cabalgador, m

**horsemanship** /'hɔrsmən,ʃip/ n equitación, f, manejo del caballo, m

**horseshoe** /'hɔrs,ʃu/ n herradura, f. **h. arch,** arco de herradura, arco morisco, m

**horsewhip** /'hɔrs,wip/ n látigo, m. —vt zurriagar, pegar con látigo

**horsewoman** /'hɔrs,wumən/ n amazona, f

**horsey** /'hɔrsi/ a de caballo; aficionado a caballos; grosero

**horticultural** /,hɔrtɪ'kʌltʃərəl/ a horticultural. **h. show,** exposición de flores, f

**horticulturalist** /,hɔrtɪ'kʌltʃərɪst/ n horticultor (-ra)

**horticulture** /'hɔrtɪ,kʌltʃər/ n horticultura, f

**hosanna** /hou'zænə/ n hosanna, m

**hose** /houz/ n (tube) manga, f; (breeches) calzón, m; (stockings) medias, f pl; (socks) calcetines, m pl. **h. man,** manguero, m. **h.-pipe,** manga de riego, manguera, f

**hosier** /'houʒər/ n calcetero (-ra)

**hosiery** /'houʒəri/ n calcetería, f. **h. trade,** calcetería, f

**hospice** /'hɒspɪs/ n hospicio, m; asilo, refugio, m

**hospitable** /'hɒspɪtəbəl/ a hospitalario

**hospitableness** /'hɒspɪtəbəlnɪs/ n hospitalidad, f

**hospitably** /'hɒspɪtəbəli/ adv hospitalariamente

**hospital** /'hɒspɪtḷ/ n hospital, m; (school) colegio, m. **h. nurse,** enfermera, f. **h. ship,** buque hospital, m

**hospital bed** cama hospitalaria, f

**hospitality** /,hɒspɪ'tæliti/ n hospitalidad, f

**host** /houst/ n huésped, convidador, (of radio or tv program) presentador, m; (at an inn) patrón, mesonero, m; (army) ejército, m; (crowd) multitud, muchedumbre, f; Eccl. hostia, f; pl **hosts,** huestes, f pl. **h.-plant,** planta huésped, f

**hostage** /'hɒstɪdʒ/ n rehén, m; Fig. prenda, f

**host country** n (of an organization) país-sede, m

**hostel** /'hɒstḷ/ n hostería, f; club, m; residencia de estudiantes, f

**hostelry** /'hɒstḷri/ n hospedería, f; parador, mesón, m

**hostess** /'houstɪs/ n ama de la casa, f; la que recibe a los invitados; la que convída; (of an inn) patrona, mesonera, f

**hostile** /'hɒstḷ/ a enemigo; hostil, contrario (a); (of circumstances, etc.) desfavorable

**hostility** /hɒ'stɪlɪti/ n enemistad, f, antagonismo, m, mala voluntad, f; hostilidad, guerra, f. **suspension of hostilities,** suspensión de hostilidades, f

**hot** /hɒt/ a caliente; (of a day, etc.) caluroso; (piquant) picante; ardiente; vehemente, impetuoso; violento; impaciente; colérico; entusiasta; lleno de deseo; Art. intenso; (great) grande, mucho; (vigorous) enérgico. **You are getting very hot now,** Inf. (in a game, etc.) Te estás quemando. **It is hot,** Está caliente; (of weather) Hace calor. **to grow hot,** calentarse; Fig. acalorarse; (of weather) empezar a hacer calor. **to make hot,** calentar; dar calor (a); Inf. dar vergüenza. **hot-blooded,** de sangre caliente; apasionado; colérico. **hot-foot,** aprisa, apresuradamente. **hot-headed,** impetuoso. **hot-plate,** Elec. calientaplatos, m. **hot springs,** termas, f pl. **hot-tempered,** colérico, irascible. **hot water,** agua caliente, f. **hot-water bottle,** bolsa de goma, f. **hot-water pipes,** las cañerías del agua caliente

**hotbed** /'hɒt,bɛd/ n semillero, vivero, m; Fig. semillero, foco, m

**hotchpotch** /'hɒtʃ,pɒtʃ/ n potaje, m; Fig. mezcolanza, f, fárrago, m

**hotel** /hou'tɛl/ n hotel, m. **h.-keeper,** hotelero (-ra)

**hothead** /'hɒt,hɛd/ n exaltado (-da), fanático (-ca)

**hothouse** /'hɒt,haus/ n invernáculo, m, estufa, f. **h. plant,** Fig. planta de estufa, f

**hotly** /'hɒtli/ adv calurosamente; con vehemencia; coléricamente

**hough** /hɒk/ n Zool. pernil, m; (in man) corva, f

**hound** /haund/ n perro de caza, sabueso de artois, m; perro, m; Inf. canalla, m. —vt cazar con perros; Fig. perseguir; Fig. incitar. **master of hounds,** montero, m. **pack of hounds,** jauría, f

**hour** /auᵊr/ n hora, f; momento, m; ocasión, oportunidad, f pl. **hours,** horas, f pl. **after hours,** fuera de horas. **at the eleventh h.,** en el último minuto. **by the h.,** por horas; horas enteras. **small hours,** altas horas de la noche, Inf. las tantas, f pl. **to keep late hours,** acostarse tarde. **to strike the h.,** dar la hora. **h.-glass,** reloj de arena, m. **h.-hand,** horario, m. **h. of death,** hora suprema, hora de la muerte, f

**hourly** /'auᵊrli/ a cada hora; por hora; continuo. —adv a cada hora; de un momento a otro

**house** /n haus; v hauz/ n casa, f; (home) hogar, m; (lineage) familia, f, abolengo, m; (Theat.) sala, f, teatro, m; Com. casa comercial, f; (takings) entrada, f; (audience) público, m; (of Lords, Commons) cámara, f; (college) colegio, m; (parliament) parlamento, m; (building) edificio, m. —a de casa; de la casa; doméstico. —vt dar vivienda (a); alojar, recibir (or tener) en casa de uno; (store) poner, guardar. **The cottage will not h. them all,** No habrá bastante lugar para todos ellos en la cabaña, No cabrán todos en la cabaña. **country-h.,** finca, f; casa de campo, f. **full h.,** casa llena, f; Theat. lleno, m. **to bring down the h.,** Theat. hacer venirse el teatro abajo. **to keep h.,** llevar la casa; ser ama de casa. **to keep open h.,** tener mesa puesta, ser hospitalario. **to set up h.,** poner casa. **h. of cards,** castillo de naipes, m. **H. of Commons,** Cámara de los Comunes, f. **H. of Lords,** Cámara de los Lores, f. **h.-agent,** agente de casas, m. **h.-boat,** barco-habitación, m, casa flotante, f. **h.-dog,** perro de guardia, m; perro de casa, m. **h.-fly,** mosca doméstica, f. **h. furnisher,** mueblista, mf. **h. painter,** pintor de brocha gorda, m. **h. party,** reunión en una casa de campo, f. **h.-physician,** médico (-ca) interno (-na). **h. porter,** portero, m. **h. property,** propiedad inmueble, f. **h.-room,** capacidad de una casa, f. **h. slipper,** zapatilla, f, pantuflo, m. **h.-surgeon,** cirujano interno, m. **h.-to-h.,** de casa en casa. **h.-warming,** reunión para colgar la cremallera, f

**housebreaker** /'haus,breikər/ n ladrón de casas, m

**housebreaking** /'haus,breikɪŋ/ n robo de una casa, m

**houseful** /'hausful/ n casa, f

**house furnishings** n pl artefactos para el hogar, accesorios caseros, aparatos electrodomésticos, m pl

**household** /'haus,hould/ n casa, f; familia, f; hogar, m. —a de la casa; doméstico; del hogar. **to be a h. word,** andar en lenguas. **h. accounts,** cuentas de la casa, f pl. **h. duties,** labores de la casa, f pl. **h. gods,** penates, m pl. **h. goods,** ajuar, mobiliario, m. **h. management,** gobierno de la casa, m

**householder** /'haus,houldər/ n padre de familia, m; dueño (-ña) (or inquilino (-na)) de una casa

**housekeeper** /'haus,kipər/ n ama de llaves, f; mujer de su casa, f

**housekeeping** /'haus,kipɪŋ/ n gobierno de la casa, m; economía doméstica, f. —a doméstico. **to set up h.,** poner casa

**housemaid** /'haus,meid/ n camarera, sirvienta, f. **housemaid's knee,** rodilla de fregona, f

**house of ill repute** n burdel, m, casa de citas, casa de zorras, casa pública, f; lupanar, m

**housetops** /'haus,tɒps/ n tejado, m; (flat roof) azotea, f. **to shout from the h.,** pregonar a los cuatro vientos

**housewife** /'haus,waif/ n madre de familia, mujer de su casa, f; (sewing-bag) neceser de costura, m

**housewifely** /'haus,waifli/ a propio de una mujer de su casa; doméstico; (of a woman) hacendosa

**housewifery** /'haus,waifəri/ n economía doméstica, f

**housing** /'hauzɪŋ/ n provisión de vivienda, f; (storage) almacenaje, m; alojamiento, m; Inf. casa, vivienda, f. **h. scheme,** urbanización, f. **h. shortage,** crisis de vivienda, f, déficit habitacional, m

**hovel** /'hʌvəl/ n casucha, f

**hover** /'hʌvər/ vi revolotear; (of hawks, etc.)

cernerse; estar suspendido; rondar; seguir de cerca, estar al lado (de); *Fig.* vacilar, dudar

**hovering** /'hʌvərɪŋ/ *n* revoloteo, *m;* (of birds of prey) calada, *f; Fig.* vacilación, *f.* —*a* revolante, que revolotea; que se cierne (sobre); (menacing) que amenaza, inminente

**how** /hau/ *adv* cómo; (by what means, in what manner) de qué modo; (at what price) a qué precio; qué; cuánto. —*n* el cómo. **to know how,** saber. **For how long?** ¿Por cuánto tiempo? **How are you?** ¿Cómo está Vd.? *Inf.* ¡Qué tal? **How do you do!** ¡Mucho gusto (en conocerlo/conocerla/conocerlos/conocerlas)! **How old are you?** ¿Qué edad tiene Vd.? **How beautiful!** ¡Qué hermoso! **How big!** ¡Cuán grande! **How early?** ¿Cuán temprano?; ¿Cuándo a más tardar? **How far?** ¿A qué distancia? ¡Hasta qué punto? ¡Hasta dónde? **How fast?** ¿A qué velocidad? **How few!** ¡Qué pocos! **How little!** ¡Qué pequeño!; ¡Qué poco! **How long?** ¿Cuánto tiempo? **How many?** ¿Cuántos? *m pl;* ¿Cuántas? *f pl.* **How much is it?** ¿Cuánto vale? **How much cloth do you want?** ¿Cuánta tela quieres? **How often?** ¿Cuán a menudo? ¿Cuántas veces? **How would you like to go for a walk?** ¿Te gustaría pasearte? **How are you going to Lisbon?** ¿En qué vas a Lisboa?

**however** /hau'ɛvər/ *adv* como quiera (que) (followed by subjunctive); por más que (followed by subjunctive); por... que (followed by subjunctive). —*conjunc* (nevertheless) sin embargo, no obstante. **h. good it is,** por bueno que sea. **h. he does it,** como quiera que lo haga. **h. it may be,** sea como sea. **h. much,** por mucho que

**howl** /haul/ *n* aullido, *m;* (groan) gemido, *m;* (cry) grito, *m;* (roar) rugido, bramido, *m;* lamento, *m.* —*vi* aullar; gemir; gritar; rugir, bramar. —*vt* chillar. **Each time he opened his mouth he was howled down,** Cada vez que abrió la boca se armó una bronca

**howler** /'haulər/ *n* aullador (-ra); *Zool.* mono (-na) chillón (-ona); (blunder) coladura, plancha, *f*

**howling** /'haulɪŋ/ *a* aullante; gemidor; (crying) que llora; bramante, rugiente. —*n* los aullidos; (groaning) el gemir, los gemidos; (crying) los gritos; (weeping) el lloro; (roaring) los bramidos, el rugir; los lamentos

**hub** /hʌb/ *n* (of a wheel) cubo (de rueda) *m; Fig.* centro, *m.* **hub cap,** tapa de cubo, *f*

**hubbub** /'hʌbʌb/ *n* algarada, barahúnda, *f*

**huckster** /'hʌkstər/ *n* revendedor (-ra). —*vi* revender; (haggle) regatear

**huddle** /'hʌdl/ *n* (heap) montón, *m;* colección, *f;* (group) corrillo, grupo, *m;* (mixture) mezcla, *f.* —*vt* arrebujar, amontonar; acurrucar, arrebujar; (throw on) echarse. —*vi* amontonarse; apiñarse; acurrucarse, arrebujarse

**hue** /hyu/ *n* color, *m;* matiz, tono, *m;* (of opinion) matiz, *m;* (clamor) clamor, *m,* gritería, *f.* **hue and cry,** alarma, *f*

**huff** /hʌf/ *n* acceso de cólera, *m*

**huffily** /'hʌfəli/ *adv* malhumoradamente; petulantemente

**huffiness** /'hʌfɪnɪs/ *n* mal humor, *m;* petulancia, *f;* arrogancia, *f*

**hug** /hʌg/ *n* abrazo, *m.* —*vt* abrazar, apretujar; *Fig.* acariciar; *Naut.* navegar muy cerca de. **to hug oneself,** *Fig.* congratularse

**huge** /hyudʒ/ *a* enorme, inmenso; gigante; vasto

**hugely** /'hyudʒli/ *adv* inmensamente, enormemente

**hugeness** /'hyudʒnɪs/ *n* inmensidad, enormidad, *f;* vastedad, *f*

**Huguenot** /'hyugə,nɒt/ *a and n* hugonote (-ta)

**hulk** /hʌlk/ *n* barco viejo, *m;* pontón, *m*

**hulking** /'hʌlkɪŋ/ *a* pesado, desgarbado

**hull** /hʌl/ *n Naut.* casco (de un buque), *m;* (shell) cáscara, *f;* (pod) vaina, *f, vt* mondar

**hullabaloo** /'hʌləbə,lu/ *n* alboroto, tumulto, *m;* vocerío, *m*

**hullo** /hə'lou/ *interj* See **hallo**

**hum** /hʌm/ *n* zumbido, *m;* ruido confuso, *m.* —*vi* (sing) canturrear; zumbar; (confused sound) zurrir; (hesitate) vacilar. —*vt* (a tune) tararear

**human** /'hyumən/ *a* humano. **the h. touch,** el don de gentes. **h. being,** ser humano, hombre, *m*

**humane** /hyu'mein/ *a* humanitario, humano

**humanely** /hyu'meinli/ *adv* humanitariamente

**humaneness** /hyu'meinnɪs/ *n* humanidad, *f*

**humanism** /'hyumə,nɪzəm/ *n* humanismo, *m*

**humanist** /'hyumənɪst/ *n* humanista, *mf*

**humanistic** /,hyumə'nɪstɪk/ *a* humanista

**humanitarian** /hyu,mænɪ'tɛəriən/ *a* humanitario

**humanitarianism** /hyu,mænɪ'tɛəriə,nɪzəm/ *n* humanitarismo, *m*

**humanity** /hyu'mænɪti/ *n* humanidad, *f;* raza humana, *f.* **the humanities,** las humanidades

**humanize** /'hyumə,naiz/ *vt* humanizar; (milk) maternizar. —*vi* humanizarse

**humanly** /'hyumənli/ *adv* humanamente

**humble** /'hʌmbəl/ *a* humilde; modesto; (cringing) servil; sumiso; pobre. —*vt* humillar; mortificar. **to h. oneself,** humillarse

**humbleness** /'hʌmbəlnɪs/ *n* humildad, *f;* modestia, *f;* (abjectness) servilismo, *m;* sumisión, *f;* pobreza, *f;* (of birth, etc.) obscuridad, *f*

**humbling** /'hʌmblɪŋ/ *n* humillación, *f;* mortificación, *f*

**humbly** /'hʌmbli/ *adv* humildemente; modestamente; servilmente

**humbug** /'hʌm,bʌg/ *n* (fraud) embuste, engaño, *m;* (nonsense) disparate, *m,* tontería, *f;* mentira, *f;* (person) farsante, charlatán, *m;* (sweetmeat) caramelo de menta, *m.* —*vt* engañar, embaucar; burlarse de

**humdrum** /'hʌm,drʌm/ *a* monótono; aburrido

**humeral** /'hyumərəl/ *a* humeral. —*n Eccl.* velo humeral, *m*

**humerus** /'hyumərəs/ *n Anat.* húmero, *m*

**humid** /'hyumɪd/ *a* húmedo

**humidity** /hyu'mɪdɪti/ *n* humedad, *f*

**humiliate** /hyu'mɪli,eit/ *vt* humillar, mortificar. **to h. oneself,** humillarse

**humiliating** /hyu'mɪli,eitɪŋ/ *a* humillante; degradante

**humiliation** /hyu,mɪli'eifən/ *n* humillación, mortificación, *f;* degradación, *f*

**humility** /hyu'mɪlɪti/ *n* humildad, *f;* modestia, *f*

**humming** /'hʌmɪŋ/ *n* zumbido, *m;* (of a tune) tarareo, *m.* —*a* zumbador. **h.-bird,** pájaro mosca, colibrí, *m.* **h.-top,** trompa, *f*

**humor** /'hyumər/ *n* humor, *m;* humorismo, *m;* (temperament) disposición, *f,* carácter, *m;* (whim) capricho, *m.* —*vt* seguir el humor (a), complacer; satisfacer, consentir en; (a lock, etc.) manejar. **in a good (bad) h.,** de buen (mal) humor. **I am not in the h. to...** No estoy de humor para... **sense of h.,** sentido de humor, *m*

**humored** /'hyumərd/ *a* (in compounds) de humor... **good-h.,** de buen humor. **ill-h.,** malhumorado, de mal humor

**humoresque** /,hyumə'rɛsk/ *n Mus.* capricho musical, *m*

**humorist** /'hyumərɪst/ *n* humorista, *mf*

**humorless** /'hyumərlɪs/ *a* sin sentido humorístico, sin sentido de humor

**humorous** /'hyumərəs/ *a* humorístico; cómico, risible

**humorously** /'hyumərəsli/ *adv* humorísticamente; cómicamente

**humorousness** /'hyumərəsnɪs/ *n* humorismo, *m;* lo cómico

**hump** /hʌmp/ *n* joroba, giba, *f;* (hillock) montecillo, *m; Fig.* depresión, *f*

**humpback** /'hʌmp,bæk/ *n* giba, joroba, *f;* (person) jorobado (-da), giboso (-sa)

**humpbacked** /'hʌmp,bækt/ *a* jorobado, giboso, corcovado

**humph** /an inarticulate expression resembling a snort or grunt; spelling pron. hʌmf/ *interj* ¡qué va!; ¡patrañas!

**humus** /'hyuməs/ *n* humus, mantillo, *m*

**hunchback** /'hʌntʃ,bæk/ *n* joroba, giba, *f;* (person) jorobado (-da), corcovado (-da), giboso (-sa)

**hunchbacked** /'hʌntʃ,bækt/ *a* jorobado, giboso, corcovado

**hundred** /'hʌndrɪd/ *n* ciento, *m;* centenar, *m,* centena, *f.* —*a* ciento; (before nouns and adjectives, excluding numerals, with the exception of mil and millón) cien. **a h. thousand,** cien mil. **one h. and one,** ciento uno, ciento uno. **by the h.,** a centenares. **hundreds of people,** centenares de personas, *m pl.* **h.-millionth,** *a* and *n* cienmillonésimo *m*. **h.-thousandth,** *a* and *n* cienmilésimo *m*.

**hundredfold** /'hʌndrɪd,fould/ *adv* cien veces. —*n* céntuplo, *m*

**hundredth** /'hʌndrɪdθ/ *a* centésimo, céntimo. —*n* centésimo, *m*, centésima parte, *f*

**hundredweight** /'hʌndrɪd,weit/ *n* quintal, *m*

**Hungarian** /hʌŋ'gɛəriən/ *a* and *n* húngaro (-ra); (language) húngaro, *m*

**Hungary** /'hʌŋgəri/ Hungría, *f*

**hunger** /'hʌŋgər/ *n* hambre, *f*; apetito, *m*; (craving) deseo, *m*, ansia, *f*. —*vi* estar hambriento, tener hambre. **to h. for,** desear, ansiar. **h.-strike,** huelga de hambre, *f*

**hungrily** /'hʌŋgrəli/ *adv* hambrientamente, con hambre; ansiosamente

**hungry** /'hʌŋgri/ *a* hambriento; (of land) pobre; (anxious) deseoso. **to be h.,** tener hambre. **to make h.,** dar hambre

**hunk** /hʌŋk/ *n* rebanada, *f*, pedazo, *m*

**hunt** /hʌnt/ *n* caza, cacería, montería, *f*; grupo de cazadores, *m*; (search) busca, *f*; (pursuit) persecución, *f*. —*vt* cazar; cazar a caballo; (search) buscar; rebuscar, explorar; (pursue) perseguir. **to h. down,** perseguir. **to h. for,** buscar. **to h. out,** buscar; descubrir, desenterrar

**hunter** /'hʌntər/ *n* cazador, *m*; caballo de caza, *m*; (watch) saboneta, *f*

**hunting** /'hʌntɪŋ/ *n* caza, *f*; caza a caballo, *f*; persecución, *f*. —*a* cazador, de caza. **to go h.,** ir a cazar. **h.-box,** pabellón de caza, *m*. **h.-cap,** gorra de montar, *f*. **h.-crop,** látigo para cazar, *m*. **h.-ground,** coto de caza, terreno de caza, *m*. **h.-horn,** cuerno de caza, *m*, corneta de monte, *f*. **h. party,** partido de caza, *m*, cacería, *f*

**hunting lodge** *n* pabellón *m*

**huntress** /'hʌntrɪs/ *n* cazadora, *f*

**huntsman** /'hʌntsmən/ *n* cazador, montero, *m*

**huntsmanship** /'hʌntsmən,ʃɪp/ *n* montería, arte de cazar, *f*

**hurdle** /'hɜrdl/ *n* valla, *f*; zarzo, *m*. **h.-race,** carrera de obstáculos, *f*; carrera de vallas, *f*

**hurdy-gurdy** /'hɜrdi'gɜrdi/ *n* organillo, *m*

**hurl** /hɜrl/ *vt* lanzar, tirar, arrojar, echar. **to h. one-self,** lanzarse. **to h. oneself against,** arrojarse a (or contra). **to h. oneself upon,** abalanzarse sobre

**hurly-burly** /'hɜrli'bɜrli/ *n* alboroto, tumulto, *m*

**hurrah** /hə'rɑ/ *interj* ¡hurra! ¡viva! —*n* vítor, *m*. **H. for...!** ¡Viva...!, ¡Vivan...! **to shout h.,** vitorear

**hurricane** /'hɜrɪ,kein/ *n* huracán, *m*. **h.-lamp,** lámpara sorda, *f*

**hurried** /'hɜrid/ *a* apresurado, precipitado; hecho a prisa; superficial

**hurriedly** /'hɜrɪdli/ *adv* apresuradamente, precipitadamente, con prisa; superficialmente; (of writing) a vuela pluma

**hurry** /'hɜri/ *n* prisa, *f*; precipitación, *f*; urgencia, *f*; confusión, *f*; alboroto, *m*. **in a h.,** aprisa. **in a great h.,** aprisa y corriendo. **to be in a h.,** llevar prisa, estar de prisa. **There is no h.,** No corre prisa, No hay prisa

**hurry** /'hɜri/ *vt* apresurar, dar prisa (a); llevar aprisa; hacer andar aprisa; enviar apresuradamente; precipitar; acelerar. —*vi* darse prisa; apresurarse. **to h. after,** correr detrás de, seguir apresuradamente. **to h. away,** *vi* marcharse aprisa, marcharse corriendo; huir; salir precipitadamente. —*vt* hacer marcharse aprisa; llevar con prisa. **to h. back,** *vi* volver aprisa, apresurarse a volver. —*vt* hacer volver aprisa. **to h. in,** *vi* entrar aprisa, entrar corriendo. —*vt* hacer entrar aprisa. **to h. off.** See **to h. away. to h. on,** *vi* apresurarse. —*vt* apresurar, precipitar. **to h. out,** salir rápidamente. **to h. over,** hacer rápidamente; concluir aprisa; despachar rápidamente; (travel over) atravesar aprisa; pasar rápidamente por. **to h. toward,** llevar rápidamente hacia; arrastrar hacia; impeler hacia. **to h. up,** *vi* darse prisa. —*vt* apresurar, precipitar; estimular

**hurt** /hɜrt/ *n* herida, *f*; (harm) daño, mal, *m*; perjuicio, *m*. —*vt* (wound) herir; (cause pain) doler; hacer daño (a); hacer mal (a); (damage) perjudicar, estropear; (offend) ofender; (the feelings) mortificar, lasti-

mar, herir. —*vi* doler; hacer mal; perjudicarse, estropearse. **I haven't h. myself,** No me he hecho daño. **Does it still h. you?** ¿Te duele todavía? **to h. deeply,** *Fig.* herir en el alma. **to h. a person's feelings,** herirle (a uno) el amor propio, lastimar, ofender

**hurtful** /'hɜrtfəl/ *a* nocivo, dañino; injurioso, pernicioso

**hurtfulness** /'hɜrtfəlnɪs/ *n* nocividad, *f*; perniciosidad, *f*

**hurtle** /'hɜrtl/ *vt* lanzar. —*vi* lanzarse; volar; caer

**husband** /'hʌzbənd/ *n* esposo, marido, *m*. —*vt* economizar, ahorrar. **h. and wife,** los esposos, los cónyuges

**husbandry** /'hʌzbəndri/ *n* labor de los campos, agricultura, *f*; (thrift) frugalidad, parsimonia, *f*

**hush** /hʌʃ/ *n* silencio, *m*, tranquilidad, *f*. —*interj* ¡chitón! ¡calla! ¡silencio! —*vt* silenciar, hacer callar, imponer silencio (a); (a baby) adormecer; *Fig.* sosegar, calmar. —*vi* callarse, enmudecer. **to h. up,** mantener secreto, ocultar. **h.-h.,** secreto. **h. money,** soborno, chantaje, *m*

**hushaby** /'hʌʃə,bai/ *interj* ¡duerme!

**husk** /hʌsk/ *n* (of grain) cascabillo, *m*; zurrón, *m*; cáscara, *f*; (of chestnut) erizo, *m*

**huskily** /'hʌskəli/ *adv* roncamente

**huskiness** /'hʌskɪnɪs/ *n* ronquera, *f*; *Inf.* robustez, *f*

**husky** /'hʌski/ *a* (of voice) ronco; *Bot.* cascarudo; (Eskimo) esquimal; *Inf.* robusto, fuerte. —*n* perro esquimal, *m*

**hussy** /'hʌsi/ *n* pícara, bribona, *f*

**hustle** /'hʌsəl/ *vt* empujar, codear; *Fig.* precipitar; *Inf.* acelerar. —*vi* codearse; andarse de prisa

**hut** /hʌt/ *n* choza, cabaña, barraca, *f*

**hutch** /hʌtʃ/ *n* (chest) arca, *f*, cofre, *m*; (cage) jaula, *f*; (for rabbits) conejera, *f*; (for rats) ratonera, *f*; *Inf.* choza, *f*

**hutment** /'hʌtmənt/ *n* campamento de chozas, *m*

**hyacinth** /'haiəsɪnθ/ *n* jacinto, *m*

**hybrid** /'haibrɪd/ *a* híbrido; mestizo, mixto. —*n* híbrido, *m*

**hybridism** /'haibrɪ,dɪzəm/ *n* hibridismo, *m*

**hybridization** /,haibrɪdə'zeifən/ *n* hibridación, *f*

**hybridize** /'haibrɪ,daiz/ *vt* cruzar. —*vi* producir (o generar) híbridos

**hydrangea** /hai'dreindʒə/ *n* *Bot.* hortensia, *f*

**hydrant** /'haidrənt/ *n* boca de riego, *f*

**hydrate** /'haidreit/ *n* *Chem.* hidrato, *m*. —*vt* hidratar

**hydration** /hai'dreifən/ *n* hidratación, *f*

**hydraulic** /hai'drɔlɪk/ *a* hidráulico. **h. engineering,** hidrotecnia, *f*

**hydraulics** /hai'drɔlɪks/ *n* hidráulica, *f*

**hydrocarbon** /,haidrə'kɑrbən/ *n* *Chem.* hidrocarburo, *m*

**hydrochloric** /,haidrə'klɔrɪk/ *a* clorhídrico. **h. acid,** ácido clorhídrico, *m*

**hydrogen** /'haidrədʒən/ *n* hidrógeno, *m*. **h. peroxide,** agua oxigenada, *f*

**hydrogenation** /,haidrədʒə'neifən/ *n* hidrogenación, *f*

**hydrogenize** /'haidrədʒə,naiz/ *vt* hidrogenizar

**hydrolysis** /hai'drɒləsɪs/ *n* hidrólisis, *f*

**hydromel** /'haidrə,mɛl/ *n* aguamiel, *f*, hidromel, *m*

**hydropathic** /,haidrə'pæθɪk/ *a* hidropático. **h. establishment,** balneario, *m*

**hydrophobia** /,haidrə'foubiə/ *n* hidrofobia, rabia, *f*

**hydrophobic** /,haidrə'foubɪk/ *a* hidrofóbico, rabioso

**hydroplane** /'haidrə,plein/ *n* hidroplano, *m*

**hydrotherapic** /,haidrouθə'ræpɪk/ *a* hidroterápico

**hydrotherapy** /,haidrə'θɛrəpi/ *n* hidroterapia, *f*

**hyena** /hai'inə/ *n* hiena, *f*

**hygiene** /'haidʒin/ *n* higiene, *f*. **personal h.,** higiene privada, *f*

**hygienic** /,haidʒi'ɛnɪk/ *a* higiénico

**hymen** /'haimən/ *n* *Anat.* himen, *m*; himeneo, *m*

**hymeneal** /,haimə'niəl/ *a* nupcial

**hymn** /hɪm/ *n* himno, *m*. **h.-book,** himnario, *m*

**hyperbole** /hai'pɜrbəli/ *n* hipérbole, *f*

**hyperbolical** /,haipər'bɒlɪkəl/ *a* hiperbólico

**hypercorrection** /,haipərkə'rɛkʃən/ *n* seudocultismo, supercultismo, *m*, ultracorrección, *f*

**hypercritic** /ˌhaipər'krɪtɪk/ *n* hipercrítico, *m*
**hypercritical** /ˌhaipər'krɪtɪkəl/ *a* hipercrítico, criticón
**hypersensitive** /ˌhaipər'sɛnsɪtɪv/ *a* vidrioso, quisquilloso
**hypertrophy** /hai'pərtrəfi/ *n* hipertrofia, *f.* —*vi* hipertrofiarse
**hyphen** /'haifən/ *n* guión, *m*
**hypnosis** /hɪp'nousɪs/ *n* hipnosis, *f*
**hypnotic** /hɪp'nɒtɪk/ *a* hipnótico. —*n* (person) hipnótico (-ca); (drug) hipnótico, narcótico, *m*
**hypnotism** /'hɪpnə,tɪzəm/ *n* hipnotismo, *m*
**hypnotist** /'hɪpnətɪst/ *n* hipnotizador (-ra)
**hypnotization** /ˌhɪpnətə'zeiʃən/ *n* hipnotización, *f*
**hypnotize** /'hɪpnə,taiz/ *vt* hipnotizar
**hypo** /'haipou/ *n* (sodium hyposulphite) hiposulfito sólido, *m*
**hypochondria** /ˌhaipə'kɒndriə/ *n* hipocondria, *f*
**hypochondriac** /ˌhaipə'kɒndri,æk/ *n* hipocondríaco (-ca)

**hypochondriacal** /ˌhaipoukən'draiəkəl/ *a* hipocondríaco
**hypocrisy** /hɪ'pɒkrəsi/ *n* hipocresía, *f;* mojigatería, gazmoñería, *f*
**hypocrite** /'hɪpəkrɪt/ *n* hipócrita, *mf;* mojigato (-ta). **to be a h.,** ser hipócrita
**hypocritical** /ˌhɪpə'krɪtɪkəl/ *a* hipócrita; mojigato, gazmoño
**hypocritically** /ˌhɪpə'krɪtɪkəli/ *adv* hipócritamente, con hipocresía
**hypodermic** /ˌhaipə'dɜrmɪk/ *a* hipodérmico. **h. syringe,** jeringa de inyecciones, *f*
**hypotenuse** /hai'pɒtn̩,us/ *n Geom.* hipotenusa, *f*
**hypothesis** /hai'pɒθəsɪs/ *n* hipótesis, *f*
**hypothetical** /ˌhaipə'θɛtɪkəl/ *a* hipotético
**hysterectomy** /ˌhɪstə'rɛktəmi/ *n Surg.* histerectomía, *f*
**hysteria** /hɪ'stɛriə/ *n Med.* histerismo, *m;* histeria, *f,* ataque de nervios, *m*
**hysterical** /hɪ'stɛrɪkəl/ *a* histérico. **to become h.,** tener un ataque de nervios. **hysterics,** *n pl* ataque de nervios, *m*

# I

**i** /ai/ *n* (letter) i. —*1st pers pron* yo. **It is I,** Soy yo. Normally omitted, the verb alone being used except when **yo** is needed for emphasis, e.g. *Hablo a María, I speak to Mary, but Yo toco el violín, pero Juan toca el piano, I play the violin, but John plays the piano*
**Iago** /i'ɑgou/ Yago, *m*
**Iberian** /ai'bɪərɪən/ *a* ibero, ibérico. —*n* ibero (-ra)
**Iberian Peninsula, the** la Peninsula Ibérica
**ibex** /'aibɛks/ *n* Zool. íbice, *m*
**ice** /ais/ *n* hielo, *m;* (ice cream) helado, *m.* —*vt* helar; cubrir de hielo; congelar, cuajar; (a cake, etc.) azucarñar, escarchar, alcorzar. **to ice up,** (Aer., Auto.) helarse. **to be as cold as ice,** *Inf.* estar hecho un hielo. **His words cut no ice,** Sus palabras ni pinchan ni cortan. **ice-age,** edad del hielo, *f.* **ice-ax,** piolet, *m.* **icebox,** nevera, *f.* **ice-cream,** helado, mantecado, *m.* **ice-cream cone,** cucurucho de helado, *m.* **ice-cream freezer,** heladora, *f.* **ice-cream vendor,** mantequero (-ra). **ice-field,** campo de hielo, *m.* **ice-floe,** témpano de hielo flotante, *m.* **ice hockey,** hockey sobre patines, *m.* **ice-pack,** bolsa para hielo, *f.* **ice-skates,** patines de cuchilla, *m pl.* **ice water,** agua helada, *f*
**iceberg** /'aisbɜrg/ *n* iceberg, témpano de hielo, banco de hielo, *m*
**icebound** /'ais,baund/ *a* aprisionado por el hielo; atascado en el hielo; (of roads, etc.) helado
**iced** /aist/ *a* helado; congelado, cuajado; (cakes) garapiñado, escarchado; (of drinks) con hielo. **i. drink,** sorbete, *m*
**Iceland** /'aislənd/ Islandia, *f*
**Icelander** /'ais,lændər/ *n* islandés (-esa)
**icelandic** /ais'lændɪk/ *a* islandes, islándico. —*n* (language) islandés, *m*
**icicle** /'aisɪkəl/ *n* carámbano, canelón, cerrión, *m*
**icily** /'aisəli/ *adv* fríamente; *Fig.* frígidamente, con indiferencia, con frialdad
**iciness** /'aisinɪs/ *n* frialdad, frigidez, *f; Fig.* indiferencia, frigidez, *f*
**icing** /'aisɪŋ/ *n* helada, *f,* hielo, *m;* (on a cake, etc.) alcorza, capa de azúcar, *f*
**icon** /'aikɒn/ *n* icono, *m*
**iconoclast** /ai'kɒnə,klæst/ *n* iconoclasta, *mf*
**iconoclastic** /ai,kɒnə'klæstɪk/ *a* iconoclasta
**iconography** /,aikə'nɒgrəfi/ *n* iconografía, *f*
**iconology** /,aikə'nɒlədʒi/ *n* iconología, *f*
**icy** /'aisi/ *a* helado; glacial, frío; Med. álgido; *Fig.* indiferente, desabrido; *Poet.* frígido, gélido
**idea** /ai'diə/ *n* idea, *f,* concepto, *m;* (opinion) juicio, *m,* opinión, *f;* (notion) impresión, noción, *f;* (plan) proyecto, plan, designio, *m.* **to form an i. of,** hacerse una idea de, formar un concepto de. **to have an i. of,** tener una idea de; tener nociones de. **An i. struck me,** Se me ocurrió una idea. **full of ideas,** preñado (or lleno) de ideas. **I had no i. that...** No tenía la menor idea de que... No sabía que... **What an i.!** ¡Qué idea!
**ideal** /ai'diəl/ *a* ideal; excelente, perfecto; (utopian) utópico; (imaginary) imaginario, irreal, ficticio. —*n* ideal, *m;* modelo, prototipo, *m*
**idealism** /ai'diə,lizəm/ *n* idealismo, *m*
**idealist** /ai'diəlɪst/ *n* idealista, *mf*
**idealistic** /ai,diə'lɪstɪk/ *a* idealista
**idealization** /ai,diəlɪ'zeiʃən/ *n* idealización, *f*
**idealize** /ai'diə,laiz/ *vt* idealizar
**ideally** /ai'diəli/ *adv* idealmente
**ideation** /,aidi'eiʃən/ *n* Philos. ideación, *f*
**idem** /'aidɛm/ *adv* ídem
**identical** /ai'dɛntɪkəl/ *a* idéntico, mismo, igual; muy parecido, semejante
**identically** /ai'dɛntɪkəli/ *adv* idénticamente
**identifiable** /ai,dɛntɪ'faiəbəl/ *a* identificable
**identification** /ai,dɛntəfɪ'keiʃən/ *n* identificación, *f.* **i. number,** placa de identidad, *f*
**identify** /ai'dɛntə,fai/ *vt* identificar. **to i. oneself with,** identificarse con
**identity** /ai'dɛntɪti/ *n* identidad, *f.* **i. card,** cédula personal, *f;* carnet de identidad, *m.* **i. disc,** disco de identidad, *m*
**ideogram** /'ɪdiə,græm/ *n* ideograma, *m*
**ideography** /,ɪdi'ɒgrəfi/ *n* ideografía, *f*
**ideological** /,aidiə'lɒdʒɪkəl/ *a* ideológico
**ideologist** /,aidi'ɒlədʒɪst/ *n* ideólogo (-ga)
**ideology** /,aidi'ɒlədʒi/ *n* ideología, *f*
**Ides** /aidz/ *n pl* idus, *m pl*
**idiocy** /'ɪdiəsi/ *n* idiotez, imbecilidad, *f;* (foolishness) necedad, tontería, sandez, *f*
**idiom** /'ɪdiəm/ *n* idiotismo, *m;* modismo, *m,* locución, *f;* (language) habla, *f,* lenguaje, *m*
**idiomatic** /,ɪdiə'mætɪk/ *a* idiomático
**idiopathy** /,ɪdi'ɒpəθi/ *n* Med. idiopatía, *f*
**idiosyncrasy** /,ɪdiə'sɪŋkrəsi/ *n* idiosincrasia, *f*
**idiosyncratic** /,ɪdiousɪn'krætɪk/ *a* idiosincrásico
**idiot** /'ɪdiət/ *n* idiota, imbécil, *mf;* (fool) necio (-ia), tonto (-ta), mentecato (-ta)
**idiotic** /,ɪdi'ɒtɪk/ *a* idiota, imbécil; (foolish) necio, tonto, sandío
**idle** /'aidl/ *a* desocupado; indolente, ocioso; (unemployed) cesante, sin empleo; (lazy) perezoso, holgazán; (of machines) parado, inactivo; (useless) vano, inútil, sin efecto; (false) falso, mentiroso, infundado; (stupid) fútil, frívolo. —*vi* holgar, estar ocioso; holgazanear, haraganear, gandulear. **to i. away,** malgastar, perder. **to i. away the time,** pasar el rato, matar el tiempo. **i. efforts,** vanos esfuerzos, *m pl.* **i. fancies,** ilusiones, fantasías, *f pl,* sueños, *m pl.* **i. hours,** horas desocupadas, *f pl,* ratos perdidos, *m pl.* **i. question,** pregunta ociosa, *f.* **i. tale,** cuento de viejas, *m.* **i. threat,** reto vacuo, *m*
**idleness** /'aidlnɪs/ *n* ociosidad, indolencia, inacción, *f;* pereza, holgazanería, gandulería, *f;* (uselessness) inutilidad, futilidad, *f*
**idler** /'aidlər/ *n* ocioso (-sa); haragán (-ana); perezoso (-sa), holgazán (-ana), gandul (-la)
**idly** /'aidli/ *adv* ociosamente, perezosamente; (uselessly) vanamente
**idol** /'aidl/ *n* ídolo, *m.* **a popular i.,** el ídolo de las masas, *m*
**idolater** /ai'dɒlətər/ *n* idólatra, *mf;* (admirer) amante, *mf* esclavo (-va), admirador (-ra)
**idolatrous** /ai'dɒlətrəs/ *a* idólatra, idolátrico
**idolatrously** /ai'dɒlətrəsli/ *adv* idolatradamente, con idolatría
**idolatry** /ai'dɒlətri/ *n* idolatría, *f;* (devotion) adoración, pasión, *f*
**idolization** /,aidlə'zeiʃən/ *n* idolatría, *f*
**idolize** /'aidl,aiz/ *vt* idolatrar, adorar
**idyll** /'aidl/ *n* idilio, *m*
**idyllic** /ai'dɪlɪk/ *a* idílico
**if** /ɪf/ *conjunc* si, ; (even if) aunque, aun cuando; (whenever) cuando, en caso de que; (whether) si. **as if,** como si. (foll. by subjunc.) **If he comes, we shall tell him,** Si viene se lo diremos. **If he had not killed the tiger, she would be dead,** Si él no hubiera matado al tigre, ella estaría muerta. **If ever there was one,** Si alguna vez lo hubiera. **if necessary,** si fuese necesario. **if not,** si no, si no es que (e.g., *Poet and philosopher are twins, if not one and the same,* Poeta y filósofo son hermanos gemelos, si no es que la misma cosa). **If only!** ¡Ojalá que! (foll. by subjunc.)
**igloo** /'ɪglu/ *n* iglú, *m*
**igneous** /'ɪgniəs/ *a* ígneo
**ignite** /ɪg'nait/ *vt* encender, pegar fuego (a), incendiar. —*vi* prender fuego, incen&diarse; arder
**ignition** /ɪg'nɪʃən/ *n* ignición, *f; Auto.* encendido, *m.* **i. coil,** *Auto.* carrete de inducción del encendido, *m.* **i. key,** *Auto.* llave del contacto, *f*
**ignoble** /ɪg'noubəl/ *a* innoble, vil, indigno
**ignobly** /ɪg'noubli/ *adv* bajamente, vilmente
**ignominious** /,ɪgnə'mɪniəs/ *a* ignominioso
**ignominiously** /,ɪgnə'mɪniəsli/ *adv* ignominiosamente
**ignominy** /'ɪgnə,mɪni/ *n* ignominia, deshonra, afrenta, *f*

**ignoramus** /ˌɪgnəˈreiməs/ *n* ignorante, *mf*
**ignorance** /ˈɪgnərəns/ *n* ignorancia, *f;* (unawareness) desconocimiento, *m.* **to plead i.,** pretender ignorancia
**ignorant** /ˈɪgnərənt/ *a* ignorante; inculto. **He is an i. fellow,** Es un ignorante. **to be i. of,** no saber, ignorar. **to be very i.,** ser muy ignorante, *Inf.* ser muy burro
**ignorantly** /ˈɪgnərəntli/ *adv* ignorantemente, por ignorancia; neciamente
**ignore** /ɪgˈnɔr/ *vt* no hacer caso de, desatender; (omit) pasar por alto de; *Law.* rechazar; (pretend not to recognize) hacer semblante de no reconocer; (not recognize) no reconocer
**iguana** /ɪˈgwɑnə/ *n Zool.* iguana, *f*
**ileac** /ˈɪliæk/ *a Anat.* ilíaco
**ileum** /ˈɪliəm/ *n Anat.* íleon, *m*
**Iliad** /ˈɪliəd/ *n* Ilíada, *f*
**ilium** /ˈɪliəm/ *n Anat.* ilion, *m*
**ill** /ɪl/ *n* mal, *m.* —*a* (sick) enfermo, malo; (bad) malo; (unfortunate) desdichado, funesto. —*adv* mal. **to be ill,** estar malo. **to be taken ill,** caer enfermo. **ill-advised,** mal aconsejado; desacertado, imprudente. **ill-advisedly,** imprudentemente. **ill at ease,** incómodo. **ill-bred,** mal criado, mal educado, mal nacido. **ill-breeding,** mala crianza, mala educación, *f.* **ill-disposed,** malintencionado. **ill fame,** mala fama, *f.* **ill-fated,** malhadado, malaventurado, aciago, fatal. **ill-favored,** mal parecido, feúcho. **ill-feeling,** hostilidad, *f,* rencor, *m.* **ill-gotten,** maladquirido. **ill-humor,** mal humor, *m.* **ill-humored,** de mal humor, malhumorado. **ill-luck,** desdicha, mala suerte, malaventura, *f;* infortunio, *m.* **ill-mannered,** mal educado. **ill-natured,** malévolo, perverso. **ill-naturedly,** malignamente. **ill-omened,** nefasto. **ill-spent,** malgastado, perdido. **ill-spoken,** mal hablado. **ill-suited,** malavenido. **ill-timed,** inoportuno, intempestivo. **ill-treat,** maltratar, malparar, tratar mal. **ill-treated,** que ha sido tratado mal; maltrecho. **ill-treatment,** maltratamiento, *m,* crueldad, *f.* **ill-turn,** mala jugada, *f.* **to do an ill-turn,** hacer un flaco servicio. **ill will,** mala voluntad, *f;* rencor, *m,* ojeriza, *f.* **to bear a person ill will,** guardarle rencor
**illegal** /ɪˈligəl/ *a* ilegal; indebido, ilícito
**illegality** /ˌɪliˈgæliti/ *n* ilegalidad, *f*
**illegally** /ɪˈligəli/ *adv* ilegalmente
**illegibility** /ɪˌledʒəˈbɪliti/ *n* ilegibilidad, *f*
**illegible** /ɪˈledʒəbəl/ *a* ilegible, indescifrable
**illegibly** /ɪˈledʒəbli/ *adv* de un modo ilegible
**illegitimacy** /ˌɪliˈdʒɪtəməsi/ *n* ilegitimidad, *f;* falsedad, *f*
**illegitimate** /ˌɪliˈdʒɪtəmɪt/ *a* ilegítimo, bastardo; falso; ilícito, desautorizado
**illegitimately** /ˌɪliˈdʒɪtəmɪtli/ *adv* ilegítimamente
**illiberal** /ɪˈlɪbərəl/ *a* iliberal; intolerante, estrecho de miras; (mean) avaro, tacaño, ruin
**illiberality** /ɪˌlɪbəˈræliti/ *n* iliberalidad, *f;* intolerancia, *f;* (avarice) tacañería, avaricia, ruindad, *f*
**illiberally** /ɪˈlɪbərəli/ *adv* avariciosamente, ruinmente
**illicit** /ɪˈlɪsɪt/ *a* ilícito, indebido, ilegal
**illicitly** /ɪˈlɪsɪtli/ *adv* ilícitamente, ilegalmente
**illicitness** /ɪˈlɪsɪtnɪs/ *n* ilicitud, ilegalidad, *f*
**illimitable** /ɪˈlɪmɪtəbəl/ *a* ilimitado, sin límites, infinito
**illiteracy** /ɪˈlɪtərəsi/ *n* analfabetismo, *m*
**illiterate** /ɪˈlɪtərɪt/ *a and n* analfabeto (-ta), iliterato (-ta)
**illness** /ˈɪlnɪs/ *n* enfermedad, dolencia, *f,* mal, *m*
**illogical** /ɪˈlɒdʒɪkəl/ *a* ilógico; absurdo, irracional
**illogicality** /ɪˌlɒdʒɪˈkæliti/ *n* falta de lógica, *f;* absurdo, *m,* irracionalidad, *f*
**illuminant** /ɪˈlumənənt/ *a* iluminador, alumbrador
**illuminate** /ɪˈluməˌneit/ *vt* iluminar, alumbrar; *Art.* iluminar; (explain) aclarar, ilustrar
**illuminated** /ɪˈluməˌneitɪd/ *a* iluminado, encendido; *Art.* iluminado. **i. sign,** letrero luminoso, *m*
**illuminati** /ɪˌluməˈnɑti/ *n pl* secta de los alumbrados, *f*
**illuminating** /ɪˈluməˌneitɪŋ/ *a* iluminador; (explanatory) aclaratorio. —*n Art.* iluminación, *f*
**illumination** /ɪˌluməˈneiʃən/ *n* iluminación, *f,* alumbrado, *m;* (for decoration) luminaria, *f; Art.* iluminación, *f; Fig.* inspiración, *f*

**illuminator** /ɪˈluməˌneitər/ *n Art.* iluminador (-ra)
**illumine** /ɪˈlumɪn/ *vt* encender, alumbrar; *Fig.* inspirar
**illusion** /ɪˈluʒən/ *n* ilusión, *f,* engaño, *m;* (dream) esperanza, ilusión, *f,* ensueño, *m.* **to harbor illusions,** tener ilusiones
**illusive** /ɪˈlusɪv/ *a* ilusivo, engañoso, falso
**illusively** /ɪˈlusɪvli/ *adv* falsamente, aparentemente
**illusoriness** /ɪˈlusərɪnɪs/ *n* ilusión, falsedad, *f,* engaño, *m*
**illusory** /ɪˈlusəri/ *a* ilusorio, deceptivo, falso, irreal
**illustrate** /ˈɪləˌstreit/ *vt* ilustrar, aclarar, explicar, elucidar; *Art.* ilustrar; (prove) probar, demostrar
**illustration** /ˌɪləˈstreiʃən/ *n* ejemplo, *m;* ilustración, *f; Art.* grabado, *m;* estampa, *f;* (explanation) elucidación, aclaración, *f*
**illustrative** /ɪˈlʌstrətɪv/ *a* ilustrativo, ilustrador, explicativo, aclaratorio
**illustrator** /ˈɪləˌstreitər/ *n* ilustrador (-ra), grabador (-ra)
**illustrious** /ɪˈlʌstriəs/ *a* ilustre, famoso, renombrado, distinguido
**illustriously** /ɪˈlʌstriəsli/ *adv* ilustremente, noblemente
**illustriousness** /ɪˈlʌstriəsnɪs/ *n* eminencia, *f,* renombre, *m,* grandeza, *f*
**image** /ˈɪmɪdʒ/ *n* (optics) imagen, *f;* efigie, imagen, *f;* (religious) imagen, estatua, *f; Art.* figura, *f;* (metaphor) metáfora, expresión, *f;* (of a person) retrato, *m.* **to be the i. of,** ser el retrato de. **sharp i.,** imagen nítida, *f.* **i. breaker,** iconoclasta, *mf.* **i. vendor,** vendedor (-ra) de imágenes
**imagery** /ˈɪmɪdʒri/ *n Art.* imaginería, *f;* (style) metáforas, *f pl*
**imaginable** /ɪˈmædʒənəbəl/ *a* imaginable
**imaginary** /ɪˈmædʒəˌnɛri/ *a* imaginario; fantástico, de ensueño
**imagination** /ɪˌmædʒəˈneiʃən/ *n* imaginación, *f;* imaginativa, fantasía, inventiva, *f,* ingenio, *m*
**imaginative** /ɪˈmædʒənətɪv/ *a* imaginativo; fantástico
**imagine** /ɪˈmædʒɪn/ *vt* imaginar, concebir; idear, proyectar, inventar; figurarse, suponer. **Just i.!** ¡Imagínese usted!
**imam** /ɪˈmɑm/ *n,* imán, *m*
**imbecile** /ˈɪmbəsɪl/ *a* imbécil; (foolish) necio, estúpido, tonto. —*n* imbécil, *mf;* (fool) necio (-ia), tonto (-ta), estúpido (-da)
**imbecility** /ɪmbəˈsɪlɪti/ *n* imbecilidad, *f;* (folly) necedad, sandez, *f*
**imbibe** /ɪmˈbaib/ *vt* embeber, absorber; (drink) sorber, chupar; empaparse de
**imbibing** /ɪmˈbaibɪŋ/ *n* imbibición, absorción, *f*
**imbricate** /ˈɪmbrɪkɪt/ *a* (Zool. Bot.) imbricado
**imbroglio** /ɪmˈbroulyou/ *n* embrollo, lío, *m*
**imbue** /ɪmˈbyu/ *vt* imbuir, calar, empapar; teñir. **to i. with,** infundir de
**imitable** /ˈɪmɪtəbəl/ *a* imitable
**imitate** /ˈɪmɪˌteit/ *vt* imitar; copiar, reproducir; (counterfeit) contrahacer
**imitation** /ˌɪmɪˈteiʃən/ *n* imitación, *f;* copia, *f;* remedo, traslado, *m.* —*a* imitado; falso, artificial
**imitative** /ˈɪmɪˌteitɪv/ *a* imitativo; imitador
**imitativeness** /ˈɪmɪˌteitɪvnɪs/ *n* facultad imitativa (or de imitacion), *f*
**imitator** /ˈɪmɪˌteitər/ *n* imitador (-ra); contrahacedor (-ra), falsificador (-ra)
**immaculate** /ɪˈmækyəlɪt/ *a* inmaculado, puro; (of dress) elegante. **I. Conception,** la Purísima Concepción
**immaculately** /ɪˈmækyəlɪtli/ *adv* inmaculadamente, elegantemente
**immaculateness** /ɪˈmækyəlɪtnɪs/ *n* pureza, *f;* (of dress) elegancia, *f*
**immanence** /ˈɪmənəns/ *n* inmanencia, inherencia, *f*
**immanent** /ˈɪmənənt/ *a* inmanente; inherente
**immaterial** /ˌɪməˈtɪəriəl/ *a* inmaterial, incorpóreo; sin importancia. **It is i. to me,** Me es indiferente, No me importa, Me da lo mismo, Me da igual
**immateriality** /ˌɪməˌtɪəriˈæliti/ *n* inmaterialidad, *f*
**immature** /ˈɪməˈtʃʊr/ *a* inmaturo; precoz; (of fruit) verde

**immaturity** /ˌɪmə'tʃʊrɪti/ n falta de madurez, f; precocidad, f

**immeasurability** /ɪˌmɛʒərə'bɪlɪti/ n inmensurabilidad, inmensidad, f

**immeasurable** /ɪ'mɛʒərəbəl/ a inmensurable, inmenso, imponderable

**immeasurably** /ɪ'mɛʒərəbli/ adv inmensamente, enormemente

**immediate** /ɪ'midɪit/ a (of place) inmediato, cercano, contiguo; (of time) próximo, inmediato, directo; (of action) inmediato, perentorio; (on letters) urgente. **to take i. action,** tomar acción inmediata

**immediately** /ɪ'midɪitli/ adv (of place) próximamente, contiguamente; (of time) luego, seguidamente, en el acto, ahora mismo, enseguida; directamente; (as soon as) así que

**immemorial** /ˌɪmə'mɔriəl/ a inmemorial, inmemorable

**immemorially** /ˌɪmə'mɔriəli/ adv desde tiempo inmemorial

**immense** /ɪ'mɛns/ a inmenso, enorme; vasto, extenso; infinito

**immensely** /ɪ'mɛnsli/ adv inmensamente, enormemente

**immensity** /ɪ'mɛnsɪti/ n inmensidad, f; extensión, vastedad, f

**immerse** /ɪ'mɜrs/ vt sumergir, hundir en, zambullir; bautizar por sumersión. *Fig.* **to be immersed in,** estar absorto en

**immersion** /ɪ'mɜrʒən/ n sumersion, f, hundimiento, m; *Astron.* inmersión, f

**immigrant** /'ɪmɪgrənt/ a and n inmigrante, mf

**immigrate** /'ɪmɪˌgreit/ vi inmigrar

**immigration** /ˌɪmɪ'greiʃən/ n inmigración, f

**imminence** /'ɪmənəns/ n inminencia, f

**imminent** /'ɪmənənt/ a inminente

**immobile** /ɪ'moubəl/ a inmóvil, inmoble; impasible, imperturbable

**immobility** /ˌɪmou'bɪlɪti/ n inmovilidad, f; impasibilidad, imperturbabilidad, f

**immobilization** /ɪˌmoubələ'zeiʃən/ n inmovilización, f

**immobilize** /ɪ'moubəˌlaiz/ vt inmovilizar

**immoderate** /ɪ'mɒdərɪt/ a inmoderado, excesivo, indebido

**immoderately** /ɪ'mɒdərɪtli/ adv inmoderadamente, excesivamente

**immoderateness** /ɪ'mɒdərɪtnɪs/ n inmoderación, f, exceso, m

**immodest** /ɪ'mɒdɪst/ a inmodesto; indecente, deshonesto; (pert) atrevido, descarado

**immodestly** /ɪ'mɒdɪstli/ adv impúdicamente, inmodestamente

**immodesty** /ɪ'mɒdɪsti/ n inmodestia, impudicia, f; deshonestidad, licencia, f; (forwardness) descaro, atrevimiento, m

**immolate** /'ɪməˌleit/ vt inmolar, sacrificar

**immolation** /ˌɪmə'leiʃən/ n inmolación, f, sacrificio, m

**immolator** /'ɪməˌleitər/ n inmolador (-ra)

**immoral** /ɪ'mɔrəl/ a inmoral; licencioso, vicioso; incontinente

**immorality** /ˌɪmə'rælɪti/ n inmoralidad, f

**immortal** /ɪ'mɔrtl/ a inmortal; perenne, eterno, imperecedero. —n inmortal, mf

**immortality** /ˌɪmɔr'tælɪti/ n inmortalidad, f; fama inmortal, f

**immortalize** /ɪ'mɔrtlˌaiz/ vt inmortalizar, perpetuar

**immortally** /ɪ'mɔrtli/ adv inmortalmente, eternamente, para siempre

**immovability** /ɪˌmuvə'bɪlɪti/ n inamovibilidad, inmovilidad, f; (of purpose) inflexibilidad, tenacidad, constancia, f

**immovable** /ɪ'muvəbəl/ a inmoble, fijo, inmóvil; (of purpose) inconmovible, inalterable, constante. —n pl. **immovables** *Law.* bienes inmuebles, m pl. *Eccl.* **i. feast,** fiesta fija, f

**immovably** /ɪ'muvəbli/ adv inmóvilmente, fijamente

**immune** /ɪ'myun/ a inmune, libre; *Med.* inmune. **i. from,** exento de; libre de

**immunity** /ɪ'myunɪti/ n inmunidad, libertad, f; exención, f; *Med.* inmunidad, f

**immunization** /ɪˌmyunə'zeiʃən/ n *Med.* inmunización, f

**immunize** /'ɪmyəˌnaiz/ vt inmunizar

**immure** /ɪ'myʊr/ vt emparedar, recluir, encerrar

**immutability** /ɪˌmyutə'bɪlɪti/ n inmutabilidad, inalterabilidad, f

**immutable** /ɪ'myutəbəl/ a inmutable, inalterable, constante

**immutably** /ɪ'myutəbli/ adv inmutablemente

**imp** /ɪmp/ n trasgo, diablillo, duende, m; (child) picaruelo (-la)

**impact** /'ɪmpækt/ n impacto, m, impacción, f; choque, m, colisión, f

**impair** /ɪm'pɛər/ vt perjudicar, echar a perder, deteriorar, empeorar, desmejorar. **to be impaired,** deteriorarse, perjudicarse

**impairment** /ɪm'pɛərmənt/ n deterioración, perjuicio, empeoramiento, m

**impale** /ɪm'peil/ vt (punishment) empalar; (with a sword) atravesar, espetar

**impalement** /ɪm'peilmənt/ n (punishment) empalamiento, m; atravesamiento, m, transfixión, f

**impalpability** /ɪmˌpælpə'bɪlɪti/ n impalpabilidad, intangibilidad, f

**impalpable** /ɪm'pælpəbəl/ a impalpable, intangible; incorpóreo

**impart** /ɪm'part/ vt comunicar, dar parte (de); conferir

**impartial** /ɪm'parʃəl/ a imparcial, ecuánime

**impartiality** /ɪmˌparʃi'ælɪti/ n imparcialidad, ecuanimidad, entereza, f, desinterés, m

**impartially** /ɪm'parʃəli/ adv imparcialmente, con desinterés

**impassability** /ɪmˌpæsə'bɪlɪti/ n impracticabilidad, f

**impassable** /ɪm'pæsəbəl/ a intransitable, impracticable; (of water) invadeable

**impasse** /'ɪmpæs/ n callejón sin salida, m

**impassibility** /ɪmˌpæsə'bɪlɪti/ n impasibilidad, imperturbabilidad, indiferencia, f

**impassible** /ɪm'pæsəbəl/ a impasible, insensible; indiferente, imperturbable

**impassion** /ɪm'pæʃən/ vt apasionar, conmover

**impassioned** /ɪm'pæʃənd/ a apasionado, vehemente, ardiente

**impassive** /ɪm'pæsɪv/ a impasible, insensible; indiferente, imperturbable; apático

**impassively** /ɪm'pæsɪvli/ adv indiferentemente

**impassivity** /ˌɪmpæ'sɪvɪti/ n impasibilidad, f; indiferencia, f; apatía, f

**impatience** /ɪm'peiʃəns/ n impaciencia, f

**impatient** /ɪm'peiʃənt/ a impaciente; intolerante. **to make i.,** impacientar. **to grow i.,** impacientarse, perder la paciencia. **to grow i. at,** impacientarse ante. **to grow i. to,** impacientarse a or por. **to grow i. under,** impacientarse bajo

**impatiently** /ɪm'peiʃəntli/ adv con impaciencia, impacientemente

**impeach** /ɪm'pitʃ/ vt *Law.* denunciar, delatar, acusar, hacer juicio político (Argentina); censurar, criticar, tachar

**impeachable** /ɪm'pitʃəbəl/ a *Law.* delatable, denunciable, acusable; censurable

**impeacher** /ɪm'pitʃər/ n acusador (-ra), denunciador (-ra), delator (-ra)

**impeachment** /ɪm'pitʃmənt/ n *Law.* acusación, denuncia, f; reproche, m, queja, f

**impeccability** /ɪmˌpɛkə'bɪlɪti/ n (perfection) impecabilidad, perfección, f; elegancia, f

**impeccable** /ɪm'pɛkəbəl/ a impecable, intachable, perfecto; elegante

**impeccably** /ɪm'pɛkəbli/ adv perfectamente; elegantemente

**impecuniosity** /ˌɪmpəˌkyuni'ɒsɪti/ n indigencia, pobreza, f

**impecunious** /ˌɪmpə'kyuniəs/ a indigente, pobre

**impede** /ɪm'pid/ vt impedir, obstruir, estorbar; *Fig.* dificultar, embarazar

**impediment** /ɪm'pɛdəmənt/ n obstáculo, estorbo, m; *Fig.* dificultad, f; *Law.* impedimento, m. **to have an i. in one's speech,** tener una dificultad en el hablar

**impel** /ɪm'pɛl/ vt impulsar, impeler; *Fig.* estimular,

obligar, mover, constreñir. **I felt impelled (to),** Me sentí obligado (a)

**impend** /ɪmˈpɛnd/ vi ser inminente, amenazar

**impending** /ɪmˈpɛndɪŋ/ a inminente, pendiente

**impenetrability** /ɪmˌpɛnɪtrəˈbɪlɪti/ n impenetrabilidad, f; Fig. enigma, secreto, misterio, m

**impenetrable** /ɪmˈpɛnɪtrəbəl/ a impenetrable; intransitable; denso, espeso; Fig. enigmático, insondable, secreto

**impenetrably** /ɪmˌpɛnɪtrəˈbɪlɪti/ adv impenetrablemente, densamente

**impenitence** /ɪmˈpɛnɪtəns/ n impenitencia, f

**impenitent** /ɪmˈpɛnɪtənt/ a impenitente, incorregible

**impenitently** /ɪmˈpɛnɪtəntli/ adv sin penitencia

**imperative** /ɪmˈpɛrətɪv/ a imperioso, perentorio; Gram. imperativo; (necessary) esencial, urgente. —n mandato, m, orden, f; Gram. imperativo, m. **in the i.,** en el imperativo

**imperatively** /ɪmˈpɛrətɪvli/ adv imperativamente

**imperativeness** /ɪmˈpɛrətɪvnɪs/ n perentoriedad, f; urgencia, importancia, f

**imperceptible** /ˌɪmpərˈsɛptəbəl/ a imperceptible, insensible

**imperceptibly** /ˌɪmpərˈsɛptəbli/ adv imperceptiblemente

**imperceptive** /ˌɪmpərˈsɛptɪv/ a insensible

**imperfect** /ɪmˈpɜrfɪkt/ a imperfecto; incompleto, defectuoso. —a and n Gram. imperfecto m

**imperfection** /ˌɪmpərˈfɛkʃən/ n imperfección, f; defecto, desperfecto, m; falta, tacha, f

**imperfectly** /ɪmˈpɜrfɪktli/ adv imperfectamente

**imperial** /ɪmˈpɪəriəl/ a imperial, imperatorio. —n (beard) pera, f. **i. preference,** preferencia dentro del Imperio, f

**imperial** /ɪmˈpɪəriəl/ vt arriesgar, poner en peligro, aventurar

**imperialism** /ɪmˈpɪəriəˌlɪzəm/ n imperialismo, m

**imperialist** /ɪmˈpɪəriəlɪst/ n imperialista, mf

**imperialistic** /ɪmˌpɪəriəˈlɪstɪk/ a imperialista

**imperious** /ɪmˈpɪəriəs/ a imperioso, altivo, arrogante; (pressing) urgente, apremiante

**imperiously** /ɪmˈpɪəriəsli/ adv imperiosamente, con arrogancia

**imperiousness** /ɪmˈpɪəriəsnɪs/ n autoridad, arrogancia, altivez, f; necesidad, urgencia, f, apremio, m

**imperishability** /ɪmˌpɛrɪʃəˈbɪlɪti/ n (immortality) inmortalidad, perennidad, f

**imperishable** /ɪmˈpɛrɪʃəbəl/ a imperecedero, inmarchitable, perenne, eterno

**impermanence** /ɪmˈpɜrmənəns/ n inestabilidad, interinidad, f; brevedad, fugacidad, f

**impermanent** /ɪmˈpɜrmənənt/ a interino, no permanente

**impermeability** /ɪmˌpɜrmiəˈbɪlɪti/ n impermeabilidad, f

**impermeable** /ɪmˈpɜrmiəbəl/ a impermeable

**impersonal** /ɪmˈpɜrsənḷ/ a impersonal, objetivo; Gram. impersonal

**impersonality** /ɪmˌpɜrsəˈnælɪti/ n objetividad, f

**impersonally** /ɪmˈpɜrsənḷi/ adv impersonalmente

**impersonate** /ɪmˈpɜrsəˌneɪt/ vt personificar, simbolizar; Theat. representar

**impersonation** /ɪmˌpɜrsəˈneɪʃən/ n personificación, simbolización, f; Theat. representación, f

**impertinence** /ɪmˈpɜrtṇəns/ n impertinencia, majadería, insolencia, f; inoportunidad, f; despropósito, m

**impertinent** /ɪmˈpɜrtṇənt/ a impertinente, insolente; (unseasonable) intempestivo, inoportuno; (irrelevant) fuera de propósito

**impertinently** /ɪmˈpɜrtṇəntli/ adv con insolencia, impertinentemente

**imperturbability** /ˌɪmpərtɜrbəˈbɪlɪti/ n imperturbabilidad, serenidad, impasibilidad, f; impavidez, f

**imperturbable** /ˌɪmpərˈtɜrbəbəl/ a imperturbable, impasible, sereno; impávido

**imperturbably** /ˌɪmpərˈtɜrbəbli/ adv con serenidad, imperturbablemente

**impervious** /ɪmˈpɜrviəs/ a impermeable, impenetrable; Fig. insensible. **He is i. to arguments,** No hace caso de argumentos

**imperviousness** /ɪmˈpɜrviəsnɪs/ n impermeabilidad, impenetrabilidad, f; Fig. insensibilidad, f

**impetigo** /ˌɪmpɪˈtaɪɡou/ n Med. impétigo, m

**impetuosity** /ɪmˌpɛtʃuˈɒsɪti/ n impetuosidad, temeridad, irreflexión, f

**impetuous** /ɪmˈpɛtʃuəs/ a impetuoso, temerario, irreflexivo; violento, vehemente

**impetuously** /ɪmˈpɛtʃuəsli/ adv impetuosamente; con vehemencia

**impetus** /ˈɪmpɪtəs/ n Mech. ímpetu, m, impulsión, f; Fig. incentivo, estímulo, impulso, m

**impiety** /ɪmˈpaɪɪti/ n impiedad, irreligión, irreligiosidad, f

**impinge (upon)** /ɪmˈpɪndʒ/ vi chocar con, tropezar con

**impious** /ˈɪmpiəs/ a impío, irreligioso, sacrílego; (wicked) malvado, perverso, malo

**impish** /ˈɪmpɪʃ/ a travieso, revoltoso, enredador

**implacability** /ɪmˌplækəˈbɪlɪti/ n implacabilidad, f

**implacable** /ɪmˈplækəbəl/ a implacable, inexorable, inflexible, riguroso

**implacably** /ɪmˈplækəbli/ adv implacablemente

**implant** /ɪmˈplænt/ vt Fig. implantar, inculcar, instilar

**implantation** /ˌɪmplænˈteɪʃən/ n Fig. implantación, instilación, inculcación, f

**implement** /n ˈɪmpləmənt; v also -ˌmɛnt/ n instrumento, utensilio, m, herramienta, f; (of war) elemento, m. —vt cumplir, hacer efectivo; llevar a cabo

**implicate** /ˈɪmplɪˌkeɪt/ vt enredar, envolver; (imply) implicar, contener, llevar en sí; (in a crime) comprometer. **to be implicated in a crime,** estar implicado en un crimen.

**implication** /ˌɪmplɪˈkeɪʃən/ n implicación, inferencia, repercusión, sugestión, f; (in a crime) complicidad, f

**implicit** /ɪmˈplɪsɪt/ a implícito, virtual, tácito; (absolute) ciego, absoluto, implícito. **with i. faith,** con fe ciega

**implicitness** /ɪmˈplɪsɪtnɪs/ n carácter implícito, m, lo implícito

**implied** /ɪmˈplaɪd/ a tácito, implícito

**implore** /ɪmˈplɔr/ vt implorar, suplicar

**imploring** /ɪmˈplɔrɪŋ/ a suplicante, implorante

**imploringly** /ɪmˈplɔrɪŋli/ adv con encarecimiento, a súplica, de un modo suplicante

**imply** /ɪmˈplaɪ/ vt implicar, indicar, presuponer; (mean) querer decir, significar; (hint) insinuar, sugerir

**impolicy** /ɪmˈpɒləsi/ n indiscreción, imprudencia, impolítica, f

**impolite** /ˌɪmpəˈlaɪt/ a descortés, mal educado

**impolitely** /ˌɪmpəˈlaɪtli/ adv con descortesía

**impoliteness** /ˌɪmpəˈlaɪtnɪs/ n descortesía, falta de urbanidad, f

**impolitic** /ɪmˈpɒlɪtɪk/ a impolítico

**imponderability** /ɪmˌpɒndərəˈbɪlɪti/ n imponderabilidad, f

**imponderable** /ɪmˈpɒndərəbəl/ a imponderable

**import** /v ɪmˈpɔrt; a, n ˈɪmpɔrt/ vt Com. importar; (mean) significar, querer decir. —a Com. importado, de importación. —n Com. importación, f; (meaning) significado, sentido, m; (value) importe, valor, m; (contents) contenido, tenor, m; importancia, f. **i. duty,** derechos de importación derechos de entrada, m pl, gravamen a la importación, m. **i. licence,** permiso de importación, m. **i. trade,** negocios de importación, m pl

**importable** /ɪmˈpɔrtəbəl/ a importable, que se puede importar

**importance** /ɪmˈpɔrtṇs/ n importancia, f; valor, alcance, m, magnitud, f; consideración, eminencia, f. **to be fully conscious of one's i.,** tener plena conciencia de su importancia

**important** /ɪmˈpɔrtṇt/ a importante; distinguido; presuntuoso, vanidoso. **to be i.,** importar, ser importante. **i. person,** personaje, m, persona importante, f

**importantly** /ɪmˈpɔrtṇtli/ adv importantemente, con importancia

**importation** /ˌɪmpɔrˈteɪʃən/ n importación, f; Com. introducción (or importación) de géneros extranjeros, f

**importer** /ɪmˈpɔrtər/ n importador (-ra)

**importunate** /ɪmˈpɔrtʃənɪt/ a (of a demand) insistente, importuno; (of persons) impertinente, pesado

**importunately** /ɪmˈpɔrtʃənɪtli/ adv importunadamente

**importune** /ˌɪmpɔrˈtun/ vt importunar, asediar, perseguir

**importuning** /ˌɪmpɔrˈtunɪŋ/ n persecución, importunación, f

**importunity** /ˌɪmpɔrˈtunɪti/ n importunidad, insistencia, impertinencia, f

**impose** /ɪmˈpouz/ vt (on, upon) imponer, infligir, cargar; Print. imponer. —vi (on, upon) (deceive) engañar, embaucar

**imposing** /ɪmˈpouzɪŋ/ a imponente, impresionante; (of persons) majestuoso, importante

**imposition** /ˌɪmpəˈzɪʃən/ n imposición, f; (burden) impuesto, tributo, m, carga, f; (Print., etc.) imposición, f; (trick) fraude, engaño, m, decepción, f

**impossibility** /ɪmˌpɒsəˈbɪlɪti/ n imposibilidad, f

**impossible** /ɪmˈpɒsəbəl/ a imposible. **Nothing is i.,** No hay nada imposible, Inf. De menos nos hizo Dios. **to do the i.,** hacer lo imposible

**impost** /ˈɪmpoust/ n impuesto, m, contribución, gabela, f

**impostor** /ɪmˈpɒstər/ n impostor (-ra), bribón (-ona), embustero (-ra)

**imposture** /ɪmˈpɒstʃər/ n impostura, f, engaño, fraude, m

**impotence** /ˈɪmpətəns/ n impotencia, f

**impotent** /ˈɪmpətənt/ a impotente

**impound** /ɪmˈpaund/ vt acorralar; (water) embalsar; (goods) confiscar

**impoverish** /ɪmˈpɒvərɪʃ/ vt empobrecer, depauperar, arruinar; (health) debilitar; (land) agotar

**impoverished** /ɪmˈpɒvərɪʃt/ a indigente, necesitado; (of land) agotado

**impoverishment** /ɪmˈpɒvərɪʃmənt/ n empobrecimiento, m, ruina, f; (of land) agotamiento, m

**impracticability** /ɪmˌpræktɪkəˈbɪlɪti/ n impracticabilidad, imposibilidad, f

**impracticable** /ɪmˈpræktɪkəbəl/ a impracticable, no factible, imposible

**imprecation** /ˌɪmprɪˈkeɪʃən/ n imprecación, maldición, f

**imprecatory** /ˈɪmprɪkəˌtɔri/ a imprecatorio, maldiciente

**impregnable** /ɪmˈpregnəbəl/ a inexpugnable, inconquistable

**impregnate** /ɪmˈpregneit/ vt impregnar, empapar; Biol. fecundar. **to become impregnated,** impregnarse

**impregnation** /ˌɪmpregˈneiʃən/ n impregnación, f; Biol. fecundación, fertilización, f; Fig. inculcación, f

**impresario** /ˌɪmprəˈsɑri,ou/ n empresario, m

**imprescriptible** /ˌɪmprəˈskrɪptəbəl/ a imprescriptible, inalienable

**impress** /v ɪmˈpres; n ˈɪmpres/ vt imprimir; (on the mind) impresionar; inculcar, imbuir; (with respect) imponer; Mil. reclutar; (of goods) confiscar. —n impresión, marca, señal, huella, f

**impression** /ɪmˈpreʃən/ n impresión, f; marca, señal, huella, f; Print. impresión, f; tirada, f. **He has the i. that they do not like him,** Sospecha que no les es simpático. **to be under the i.,** tener la impresión

**impressionability** /ɪmˌpreʃənəˈbɪlɪti/ n susceptibilidad, sensibilidad, f

**impressionable** /ɪmˈpreʃənəbəl/ a susceptible, impresionable, sensitivo

**impressionism** /ɪmˈpreʃəˌnɪzəm/ n impresionismo, m

**impressionist** /ɪmˈpreʃənɪst/ n impresionista, mf

**impressionistic** /ɪmˌpreʃəˈnɪstɪk/ a impresionista

**impressive** /ɪmˈpresɪv/ a impresionante; emocionante; imponente, majestuoso, enfático

**impressively** /ɪmˈpresɪvli/ adv solemnemente, de modo impresionante; enfáticamente

**impressiveness** /ɪmˈpresɪvnɪs/ n efecto impresionante, m; grandiosidad, pompa, f; majestuosidad, f; fuerza, f

**imprint** /n ˈɪmprɪnt; v ɪmˈprɪnt/ n impresión, señal, marca, huella, f; Print. pie de imprenta, m. —vt imprimir; (on the mind) grabar, fijar

**imprison** /ɪmˈprɪzən/ vt encerrar, encarcelar, aprisionar

**imprisonment** /ɪmˈprɪzənmənt/ n encarcelación, prisión, f, encierro, m

**improbability** /ɪmˌprɒbəˈbɪlɪti/ n improbabilidad, f; inverosimilitud, f

**improbable** /ɪmˈprɒbəbəl/ a improbable; inverosímil

**improbity** /ɪmˈproubɪti/ n improbidad, f

**impromptu** /ɪmˈprɒmptu/ a indeliberado, impremeditado, espontáneo. —adv de improviso, in promptu. —n improvisación, f

**improper** /ɪmˈprɒpər/ a impropio, inadecuado; incorrecto; indebido; indecente, indecoroso. **i. fraction,** Math. quebrado impropio, m

**improperly** /ɪmˈprɒpərli/ adv impropiamente, incorrectamente; indecorosamente

**impropriety** /ˌɪmprəˈpraiiti/ n inconveniencia, f; incorrección, f; (style) impropiedad, f; falta de decoro, f

**improvable** /ɪmˈpruvəbəl/ a mejorable, perfectible

**improve** /ɪmˈpruv/ vt mejorar; perfeccionar; (beautify) embellecer, hermosear; (land) bonificar; Lit. corregir, enmendar; (cultivate) cultivar; (increase) aumentar; (an opportunity) aprovechar; (strengthen) fortificar; (business) sacar provecho de, explotar. —vi mejorar; perfeccionarse; (progress) hacer progresos, progresar, adelantarse; Com. subir; (become beautiful) hacerse hermoso, embellecerse; (increase) aumentarse. **to i. upon,** mejorar, perfeccionar; pulir

**improvement** /ɪmˈpruvmənt/ n mejora, f; perfeccionamiento, m; aumento, m; adelantamiento, progreso, m; (in health) mejoría, f; embellecimiento, m; cultivación, f; (of land) abono, m

**improver** /ɪmˈpruvər/ n aprendiz (-za)

**improvidence** /ɪmˈprɒvɪdəns/ n imprevisión, f; improvidencia, f

**improvident** /ɪmˈprɒvɪdənt/ a impróvido, desprevenido

**improvidently** /ɪmˈprɒvɪdəntli/ adv impróvidamente

**improvisation** /ɪmˌprɒvəˈzeiʃən/ n improvisación, f

**improvise** /ˈɪmprə,vaiz/ vt improvisar

**improviser** /ˈɪmprə,vaizər/ n improvisador (-ra)

**imprudence** /ɪmˈprudns/ n imprudencia, f; desacierto, m, indiscreción, f

**imprudent** /ɪmˈprudnt/ a imprudente; desacertado, indiscreto, mal avisado, irreflexivo

**imprudently** /ɪmˈprudntli/ adv imprudentemente; sin pensar

**impudence** /ˈɪmpyədəns/ n impudencia, f, descaro, m, insolencia, desvergüenza, f, atrevimiento, m

**impudent** /ˈɪmpyədənt/ a impudente, descarado, insolente, desvergonzado, atrevido

**impudently** /ˈɪmpyədəntli/ adv descaradamente, con insolencia

**impugn** /ɪmˈpyun/ vt impugnar, contradecir, atacar

**impugnable** /ɪmˈpyunəbəl/ a impugnable, atacable

**impugnment** /ɪmˈpyunmənt/ n impugnación, f

**impulse** /ˈɪmpʌls/ n ímpetu, m, impulsión, f; impulso, estímulo, m; incitación, instigación, f; motivo, m; (fit) arranque, arrebato, acceso, m

**impulsion** /ɪmˈpʌlʃən/ n ímpetu, m, impulsión, f; empuje, m, arranque, m

**impulsive** /ɪmˈpʌlsɪv/ a impelente; irreflexivo, impulsivo

**impulsively** /ɪmˈpʌlsɪvli/ adv por impulso

**impulsiveness** /ɪmˈpʌlsɪvnɪs/ n irreflexión, f; carácter impulsivo, m

**impunity** /ɪmˈpyunɪti/ n impunidad, f. **with i.,** impunemente

**impure** /ɪmˈpyʊr/ a impuro; adulterado, mezclado; (indecent) deshonesto, indecente; (dirty) turbio, sucio

**impurity** /ɪmˈpyʊrɪti/ n impureza, f; adulteración, mezcla, f; deshonestidad, liviandad, f; suciedad, turbiedad, f

**imputable** /ɪmˈpyutəbəl/ a imputable, atribuible

**imputation** /ˌɪmpyuˈteiʃən/ n imputación, atribución, f; (in a bad sense) acusación, f, reproche, m

**impute** /ɪmˈpyut/ vt imputar, achacar, atribuir; acusar, reprochar

**imputer** /ɪmˈpyutər/ n imputador (-ra); recriminador (-ra), acusador (-ra)

**in** /ɪn/ prep en; a; (of duration) durante, mientras; (with) con; (through) por; dentro de; (under) bajo;

(following a superlative) de; (of specified time) dentro de, de aquí a; (with afternoon, etc.) por; (out of) sobre. **course in medieval Catalan literature,** curso de literatura catalana medioeval. **dressed in black,** vestido de negro. **in London,** en Londres. **in the morning,** por la mañana; (in the course of) durante la mañana. **in time,** a tiempo; dentro de algún tiempo. **in a week,** dentro de una semana. **in the best way,** del mejor modo. **in writing,** por escrito. **in anger,** con enojo. **in one's hand,** en la mano. **in addition to,** además de, a más de. **in case,** por si acaso; en caso de que. **in order to,** a fin de, para (foll. by infin.). **in order that,** para que (foll. by subjunc.). **in so far as,** en cuanto. **in spite of,** a pesar de. **in the distance,** a lo lejos, en lontananza. **in the meantime,** entre tanto. **in the middle of,** en el medio de; a la mitad de. **in the style of,** al modo de; a la manera de, a la (francesa, etc.)

**in** /ɪn/ *adv* adentro, dentro; (at home) en casa; (of sun) escondido; (of fire) alumbrado; (in power) en el poder; (of harvest) cosechado; (of boats) entrado (with haber); (of trains) llegado (with haber). **to be in,** estar dentro; haber llegado; estar en casa. **to be in for,** estar expuesto a, correr el riesgo de. **to be in with a person,** ser muy amigo de, estar muy metido con. **Come in!** ¡Adelante!; ¡Pase usted! **ins and outs,** sinuosidades, *f pl;* (of river) meandros, *m pl;* (of an affair) pormenores, detalles, *m pl.* **in less time than you can say Jack Robinson,** en menos de Jesús, en un credo, en menos que canta un gallo, en menos que se persigna un cura loco. **in the middle of nowhere,** donde Cristo dio las tres voces, (Western Hemisphere) donde el diablo perdió el poncho.

**in** /ɪn/ *a* interno. **in-law** (of relations) político. **inpatient,** enfermo (-ma) de hospital

**inability** /ˌɪnəˈbɪlɪti/ *n* incapacidad, inhabilidad, ineptitud, incompetencia, *f;* impotencia, *f*

**inaccessibility** /ˌɪnækˌsesəˈbɪlɪti/ *n* inaccesibilidad, *f*

**inaccessible** /ˌɪnəkˈsesəbəl/ *a* inaccesible

**inaccuracy** /ɪnˈækyərəsi/ *n* inexactitud, incorrección, *f*

**inaccurate** /ɪnˈækyərɪt/ *a* inexacto, incorrecto

**inaccurately** /ɪnˈækyərɪtli/ *adv* inexactamente, erróneamente

**inaction** /ɪnˈækʃən/ *n* inacción, *f*

**inactive** /ɪnˈæktɪv/ *a* inactivo, pasivo; (of things) inerte; (lazy) perezoso, indolente; (machinery) parado; (motionless) inmóvil; (at leisure) desocupado, sin empleo

**inactivity** /ˌɪnækˈtɪvɪti/ *n* inactividad, pasividad, *f;* (of things) inercia, *f;* pereza, indolencia, *f;* (of machinery) paro, *m;* inmovilidad, *f;* (leisure) desocupación, *f*

**inadaptable** /ˌɪnəˈdæptəbəl/ *a* inadaptable, no adaptable

**inadequacy** /ɪnˈædɪkwəsi/ *n* insuficiencia, escasez, *f;* imperfección, *f,* defecto, *m*

**inadequate** /ɪnˈædɪkwɪt/ *a* inadecuado, insuficiente, escaso; imperfecto, defectuoso

**inadequately** /ɪnˈædɪkwɪtli/ *adv* inadecuadamente

**inadmissible** /ˌɪnədˈmɪsəbəl/ *a* inadmisible, no admisible

**inadvertence** /ˌɪnədˈvɜrtns/ *n* inadvertencia, *f;* equivocación, *f,* descuido, *m*

**inadvertent** /ˌɪnədˈvɜrtn̩t/ *a* inadvertido, accidental, casual; negligente

**inadvertently** /ˌɪnədˈvɜrtn̩tli/ *adv* inadvertidamente, sin querer

**inalienability** /ˌɪnˌeilyənəˈbɪlɪti/ *n* inalienabilidad, *f*

**inalienable** /ɪnˈeilyənəbəl/ *a* inajenable, inalienable

**inalterability** /ɪnˌɔltərəˈbɪlɪti/ *n* inalterabilidad, *f*

**inalterable** /ɪnˈɔltərəbəl/ *a* inalterable

**inalterably** /ɪnˈɔltərəbli/ *adv* inalterablemente, sin alteración

**inane** /ɪˈnein/ *a* lelo, fatuo, vacío, necio

**inanimate** /ɪnˈænəmɪt/ *a* (of matter) inanimado; sin vida, exánime, muerto

**inanition** /ˌɪnəˈnɪʃən/ *n* inanición, *f*

**inanity** /ɪˈnænɪti/ *n* vacuidad, fatuidad, necedad, *f*

**inappeasable** /ˌɪnəˈpizəbəl/ *a* implacable, riguroso

**inapplicability** /ˌɪnˌæplɪkəˈbɪlɪti/ *n* no aplicabilidad, *f*

**inapplicable** /ɪnˈæplɪkəbəl/ *a* inaplicable

**inapposite** /ɪnˈæpəzɪt/ *a* fuera de propósito, no pertinente, inoportuno

**inappreciable** /ˌɪnəˈpriʃiəbəl/ *a* inapreciable, imperceptible

**inappreciation** /ˌɪnəpriʃiˈeiʃən/ *n* falta de apreciación, *f*

**inappreciative** /ˌɪnəˈpriʃiətɪv/ *a* desagradecido, ingrato. **i. of,** insensible a, indiferente a

**inapproachable** /ˌɪnəˈproutʃəbəl/ *a* inaccesible, huraño, adusto

**inappropriate** /ˌɪnəˈproupriɪt/ *a* impropio, inconveniente, inadecuado, incongruente; inoportuno

**inappropriately** /ˌɪnəˈproupriɪtli/ *adv* impropiamente; inoportunamente

**inappropriateness** /ˌɪnəˈproupriɪtnɪs/ *n* impropiedad, inconveniencia, incongruencia, *f;* inoportunidad, *f*

**inapt** /ɪnˈæpt/ *a* inepto, inhábil; impropio

**inaptitude** /ɪnˈæptɪˌtud/ *n* ineptitud, inhabilidad, *f;* impropiedad, *f*

**inarticulate** /ˌɪnɑrˈtɪkyəlɪt/ *a* (of speech) inarticulado; (reticent) inexpresivo, reservado; indistinto; *Anat.* inarticulado

**inarticulately** /ˌɪnɑrˈtɪkyəlɪtli/ *adv* indistintamente, de un modo inarticulado

**inarticulateness** /ˌɪnɑrˈtɪkyəlɪtnɪs/ *n* tartamudez, *f;* inexpresión, reserva, *f;* silencio, *m*

**inartistic** /ˌɪnɑrˈtɪstɪk/ *a* antiartístico, antiestético

**inartistically** /ˌɪnɑrˈtɪstɪkli/ *adv* sin gusto (estético)

**inasmuch (as)** /ˌɪnəzˈmʌtʃ/ *adv* puesto que, visto que, dado que

**inattention** /ˌɪnəˈtenʃən/ *n* desatención, inaplicación, abstracción, *f;* falta de solicitud, *f*

**inattentive** /ˌɪnəˈtentɪv/ *a* desatento, distraído; poco solícito, no atento

**inattentively** /ˌɪnəˈtentɪvli/ *adv* sin atención, distraídamente

**inaudibility** /ɪnˌɔdəˈbɪlɪti/ *n* imposibilidad de oír, *f*

**inaudible** /ɪnˈɔdəbəl/ *a* inaudible, no audible, ininteligible

**inaudibly** /ɪnˈɔdəbli/ *adv* indistintamente, de modo inaudible

**inaugurate** /ɪnˈɔgyəˌreit/ *vt* inaugurar; (open) estrenar, abrir, dedicar; (install) investir, instalar; (initiate) originar, iniciar, dar lugar (a)

**inauguration** /ɪnˌɔgyəˈreiʃən/ *n* inauguración, *f;* (opening) estreno, *m,* apertura, *f;* (investiture) instalación, investidura, *f*

**inauspicious** /ˌɪnɔˈspɪʃəs/ *a* poco propicio, desfavorable; ominoso, triste, infeliz

**inauspiciously** /ˌɪnɔˈspɪʃəsli/ *adv* en condiciones desfavorables, desfavorablemente; infelizmente, bajo malos auspicios

**inauspiciousness** /ˌɪnɔˈspɪʃəsnɪs/ *n* condiciones desfavorables, *f pl;* infelicidad, *f;* malos auspicios, *m pl*

**inborn** /ɪnˈbɔrn/ *a* innato, instintivo, inherente

**inbred** /ˈɪnˈbred/ *a* innato, inherente, instintivo

**Inca** /ˈɪŋkə/ *a* incaico, de los incas. —*n* inca, *m*

**incalculability** /ɪnˌkælkyələˈbɪlɪti/ *n* imposibilidad de calcular, *f;* (of persons) volubilidad, veleidad, *f;* infinidad, immensidad, *f*

**incalculable** /ɪnˈkælkyələbəl/ *a* incalculable, innumerable; (of persons) voluble, veleidoso, caprichoso; infinito, inmenso

**incalculably** /ɪnˈkælkyələbli/ *adv* enormemente, infinitamente; caprichosamente

**incandescence** /ˌɪnkənˈdesəns/ *n* incandescencia, candencia, *f*

**incandescent** /ˌɪnkənˈdesənt/ *a* incandescente, candente. **i. light,** luz incandescente, *f.* **to make i.,** encandecer

**incantation** /ˌɪnkænˈteiʃən/ *n* hechizo, *m,* encantación, *f,* ensalmo, *m*

**incapability** /ɪnˌkeipəˈbɪlɪti/ *n* incapacidad, *f;* inhabilidad, ineptitud, incompetencia, *f*

**incapable** /ɪnˈkeipəbəl/ *a* incapaz; inhábil, incompetente; (physically) imposibilitado

**incapacitate** /ˌɪnkəˈpæsɪˌteit/ *vt* imposibilitar, incapacitar, inutilizar; (disqualify) inhabilitar, incapacitar

**incapacitation** /ˌɪnkəˌpæsɪˈteiʃən/ *n* inhabilitación, *f*

**incapacity** /ˌɪnkəˈpæsɪti/ *n* incapacidad, inhabilidad, *f*

**incarcerate** /ɪnˈkɑrsəˌreit/ *vt* encarcelar

**incarceration** /ɪnˌkɑrsəˈreiʃən/ *n* encarcelación, prisión, *f*

**incarnate** /a ɪn'kɑrnɪt/ v -neit/ a encarnado. —vt encarnar

**incarnation** /ˌɪnkɑr'neɪʃən/ n encarnación, f

**incautious** /ɪn'kɔʃəs/ a incauto, imprudente

**incautiously** /ɪn'kɔʃəsli/ adv incautamente

**incautiousness** /ɪn'kɔʃəsnɪs/ n imprudencia, negligencia, falta de cautela, f

**incendiary** /ɪn'sendiˌɛri/ a incendiario. **i. bomb,** incendiaria, f

**incense** /ɪn'sɛns/ n incienso, m; Fig. adulación, f. —vt Eccl. incensar; (annoy) irritar, exasperar, enojar. **i. burner,** incensario, m

**incentive** /ɪn'sɛntɪv/ n incentivo, estímulo, motivo, m. —a estimular, incitativo

**inception** /ɪn'sɛpʃən/ n comienzo, principio, m; inauguración, f

**incertitude** /ɪn'sɜrtɪˌtud/ n incertidumbre, f

**incessant** /ɪn'sesənt/ a incesante, continuo, constante

**incessantly** /ɪn'sesəntli/ adv incesantemente, sin cesar

**incest** /'ɪnsest/ n incesto, m

**incestuous** /ɪn'sestʃuəs/ a incestuoso

**inch** /ɪntʃ/ n pulgada, f. **every i. a man,** hombre hecho y derecho. **Not an i.!** ¡Ni pizca! **within an i. of,** a dos dedos de. **i. by i.,** palmo a palmo, paso a paso. **i. tape,** cinta métrica, f

**inchoate** /ɪn'kouɪt/ a rudimentario; imperfecto, incompleto

**incidence** /'ɪnsɪdəns/ n incidencia, f

**incident** /'ɪnsɪdənt/ a propio, característico, incidental. —n incidente, acontecimiento, m, ocurrencia, f

**incidental** /ˌɪnsɪ'dɛntl/ a incidente, incidental; accidental, accesorio, no esencial. **i. expense,** gasto imprevisto, m

**incidentally** /ˌɪnsɪ'dɛntli/ adv (secondarily) incidentalmente; (by the way) de propósito

**incident of navigation** n accidente de navegación, m

**incinerate** /ɪn'sɪnəˌreit/ vt incinerar

**incineration** /ɪnˌsɪnə'reiʃən/ n incineración, cremación, f

**incinerator** /ɪn'sɪnəˌreitər/ n incinerador, m

**incipient** /ɪn'sɪpiənt/ a incipiente, naciente, rudimentario

**incise** /ɪn'saiz/ vt cortar; Art. grabar, tajar

**incision** /ɪn'sɪʒən/ n incisión, f; corte, tajo, m; Med. abscisión, f

**incisive** /ɪn'saisɪv/ a (of mind) agudo, penetrante; (of words) mordaz, incisivo, punzante

**incisively** /ɪn'saisɪvli/ adv en pocas palabras; mordazmente, incisivamente

**incisiveness** /ɪn'saisɪvnɪs/ n (of mind) agudeza, penetración, f; (of words) mordacidad, f, sarcasmo, m

**incisor** /ɪn'saizər/ n diente incisivo, m

**incite** /ɪn'sait/ vt incitar, estimular, animar; provocar, tentar. **to i. to,** mover a, incitar a

**incitement** /ɪn'saitmənt/ n incitación, instigación, f; estímulo, m; tentación, f; aliciente, m

**incivility** /ˌɪnsə'vɪlɪti/ n incivilidad, descortesía, f

**inclemency** /ɪn'klɛmənsi/ n inclemencia, f, rigor, m

**inclement** /ɪn'klɛmənt/ a inclemente, riguroso, borrascoso

**inclination** /ˌɪnklə'neiʃən/ n inclinación, f; (slope) declive, m, pendiente, cuesta, f; (tendency) propensión, tendencia, f; (liking) afición, f; amor, m; (bow) reverencia, f; Geom. inclinación, f

**incline** /v ɪn'klain; n 'ɪnklain/ vt inclinar, torcer; doblar; (cause) inclinar (a), hacer. —vi inclinarse, torcerse; (tend) tender, propender, inclinarse; (colors) tirar (a). —n declive, m, pendiente, cuesta, inclinación, f. **I am inclined to believe it,** Me inclino a creerlo. **I am inclined to do it,** Estoy por hacerlo, Creo que lo haré

**inclined** /ɪn'klaind/ a torcido, inclinado, doblado; Fig. propenso, adicto. **i. plane,** plano inclinado, m

**include** /ɪn'klud/ vt incluir, contener, encerrar; comprender, abrazar

**including** /ɪn'kludɪŋ/ present part incluso, inclusive. **not i.,** no comprendido

**inclusion** /ɪn'kluʒən/ n inclusión, f

**inclusive** /ɪn'klusɪv/ a inclusivo. **January 2 to January 12 i.,** del 2 al 12 de enero, ambos inclusivos. **not**

**i. of,** sin contar, exclusivo de. **i. of,** que incluye. **i. terms,** todo incluido, todos los gastos incluidos

**incognito** /ˌɪnkɒg'nitou/ a and adv and n incógnito, m.

**incoherence** /ˌɪnkou'hɪərəns/ n incoherencia, inconsecuencia, f

**incoherent** /ˌɪnkou'hɪərənt/ a incoherente, inconexo, inconsecuente. **an i. piece of writing,** un escrito sin pies ni cabeza

**incoherently** /ˌɪnkou'hɪərəntli/ adv con incoherencia

**incombustibility** /ˌɪnkəmˌbʌstə'bɪlɪti/ n incombustibilidad, f

**incombustible** /ˌɪnkəm'bʌstəbəl/ a incombustible

**income** /'ɪnkʌm/ n renta, f, ingreso, m; Com. rédito, m. **i.-tax,** impuesto de utilidades, m. **i.-tax commissioners,** inspectores de impuestos de utilidades, m pl. **i.-tax return,** declaración de utilidades, f

**incoming** /'ɪnˌkʌmɪŋ/ a entrante; nuevo. —n entrada, llegada, f. —n pl **incomings,** ingresos, m pl

**incommensurability** /ˌɪnkəˌmɛnsərə'bɪlɪti/ n inconmensurabilidad, f

**incommensurable** /ˌɪnkə'mɛnsərəbəl/ a inconmensurable, no conmensurable

**incommensurate** /ˌɪnkə'mɛnsərɪt/ a desproporcionado, desmedido

**incommode** /ˌɪnkə'moud/ vt incomodar, molestar, fastidiar

**incommodious** /ˌɪnkə'moudiəs/ a estrecho; incómodo, inconveniente

**incommodiousness** /ˌɪnkə'moudiəsnɪs/ n estrechez, f; incomodidad, f

**incommunicable** /ˌɪnkə'myunɪkəbəl/ a incommunicable, indecible, inexplicable

**incommunicative** /ˌɪnkə'myunɪkətɪv/ a insociable, intratable, adusto, huraño

**incomparable** /ɪn'kɒmpərəbəl/ a incomparable; sin par, sin igual, excelente

**incomparableness** /ɪn'kɒmpərəbəlnɪs/ n excelencia, perfección, f

**incomparably** /ɪn'kɒmpərəbli/ adv incomparablemente, con mucho

**incompatibility** /ˌɪnkəmˌpætə'bɪlɪti/ n incompatibilidad, f

**incompatible** /ˌɪnkəm'pætəbəl/ a incompatible

**incompetence** /ɪn'kɒmpɪtəns/ n incompetencia, ineptitud, inhabilidad, f; Law. incapacidad, f

**incompetent** /ɪn'kɒmpɪtənt/ a incompetente, incapaz, inepto, inhábil; Law. incapaz

**incompetently** /ɪn'kɒmpɪtəntli/ adv inhábilmente

**incomplete** /ˌɪnkəm'plit/ a incompleto; imperfecto, defectuoso; (unfinished) sin terminar, inacabado, inconcluso. **incomplete sentence,** frase que queda colgando, f

**incompletely** /ˌɪnkəm'plitli/ adv incompletamente; imperfectamente

**incompleteness** /ˌɪnkəm'plitnɪs/ n estado incompleto, m; imperfección, f; inconclusión, f

**incomprehensibility** /ˌɪnkɒmprɪˌhɛnsə'bɪlɪti/ n incomprensibilidad, f

**incomprehensible** /ˌɪnkɒmprɪ'hɛnsəbəl/ a incomprensible

**incomprehension** /ˌɪnkɒmprɪ'hɛnʃən/ n incomprensión, falta de comprensión, f

**inconceivable** /ˌɪnkən'sivəbəl/ a inconcebible, inimaginable

**inconclusive** /ˌɪnkən'klusɪv/ a inconcluyente, cuestionable, dudoso, no convincente

**inconclusiveness** /ˌɪnkən'klusɪvnɪs/ n carácter inconcluso, m, falta de conclusiones, f

**incongruity** /ˌɪnkən'gruɪti/ n incongruencia, desproporción, disonancia, f

**incongruous** /ɪn'kɒŋgruəs/ a incongruente, incongruo; chocante, desproporcionado, disonante

**incongruously** /ɪn'kɒŋgruəsli/ adv incongruentemente, incongruamente

**inconsequence** /ɪn'kɒnsɪˌkwɛns/ n inconsecuencia, f

**inconsequent, inconsequential** /ɪn'kɒnsɪˌkwɛnt; ɪnˌkɒnsɪ'kwɛnʃəl/ a inconsecuente, ilógico; inconsistente

**inconsiderable** /ˌɪnkən'sɪdərəbəl/ a insignificante

**inconsiderate** /ˌɪnkən'sɪdərɪt/ a desconsiderado, irreflexivo, irrespetuoso

**inconsiderately** /ˌɪnkən'sɪdərɪtli/ adv sin consideración, desconsideradamente
**inconsiderateness** /ˌɪnkən'sɪdərɪtnɪs/ n desconsideración, falta de respeto, f
**inconsistency** /ˌɪnkən'sɪstənsi/ n inconsistencia, inconsecuencia, incompatibilidad, contradicción, anomalía, f
**inconsistent** /ˌɪnkən'sɪstənt/ a inconsistente, inconsiguiente, incompatible, contradictorio, anómalo
**inconsistently** /ˌɪnkən'sɪstəntli/ adv contradictoriamente
**inconsolable** /ˌɪnkən'souləbəl/ a inconsolable, desconsolado. **to be i.**, estar inconsolable, (Inf. of a woman) estar hecha una Magdalena
**inconsolably** /ˌɪnkən'souləbli/ adv desconsoladamente
**inconspicuous** /ˌɪnkən'spɪkyuəs/ a que no llama la atención; insignificante, humilde, modesto
**inconspicuously** /ˌɪnkən'spɪkyuəsli/ adv humildemente, modestamente
**inconspicuousness** /ˌɪnkən'spɪkyuəsnɪs/ n modestia, humildad, f
**inconstancy** /ɪn'kɒnstənsi/ n inconstancia, movilidad, f; mudanza, veleidad, f
**inconstant** /ɪn'kɒnstənt/ a inconstante, mudable, variable; veleidoso, volátil, voluble
**incontestable** /ˌɪnkən'tɛstəbəl/ a incontestable, evidente, indisputable
**incontinence** /ɪn'kɒntɪnəns/ n incontinencia, f
**incontinent** /ɪn'kɒntɪnənt/ a incontinente
**incontrollable** /ˌɪnkən'trouləbəl/ a ingobernable, indomable
**incontrovertible** /ˌɪnkɒntrə'vɜrtəbəl/ a incontrovertible, incontrastable
**inconvenience** /ˌɪnkən'vinyəns/ n incomodidad, inconveniencia, f; (of time) inoportunidad, f. —vt incomodar, causar inconvenientes (a)
**inconvenient** /ˌɪnkən'vinyənt/ a incómodo, inconveniente, molesto, embarazoso; (of time) inoportuno. **at an i. time**, a deshora
**inconveniently** /ˌɪnkən'vinyəntli/ adv incómodamente; (of time) inoportunamente
**incorporate** /v ɪn'kɔrpə,reit; a -pərɪt/ vt incorporar, agregar; comprender, incluir, encerrar. —vi asociarse, incorporarse. —a incorpóreo, inmaterial; incorporado, asociado
**incorporation** /ɪn,kɔrpə'reiʃən/ n incorporación, agregación, f; asociación, f
**incorporeal** /ˌɪnkɔr'pɔriəl/ a incorpóreo, inmaterial
**incorporeity** /ɪn,kɔrpə'riɪti/ n incorporeidad, inmaterialidad, f
**incorrect** /ˌɪnkə'rɛkt/ a incorrecto; inexacto, erróneo, falso
**incorrectness** /ˌɪnkə'rɛktnɪs/ n incorrección, f
**incorrigibility** /ɪn,kɔrɪdʒə'bɪlɪti/ n incorregibilidad, f
**incorrigible** /ɪn'kɔrɪdʒəbəl/ a incorregible, empecatado
**incorrigibly** /ɪn'kɔrɪdʒəbli/ adv incorregiblemente, obstinadamente
**incorrupt** /ˌɪnkə'rʌpt/ a incorrupto; recto, honrado
**incorruptibility** /ˌɪnkə,rʌptə'bɪlɪti/ n incorruptibilidad, f; honradez, probidad, f
**incorruptible** /ˌɪnkə'rʌptəbəl/ a incorrupto; honrado, incorruptible
**incorruption** /ˌɪnkə'rʌpʃən/ n incorrupción, f
**increase** /v ɪn'kris; n 'ɪnkris/ vt aumentar, acrecentar; (in numbers) multiplicar; (extend) ampliar, extender; (of price) encarecer, aumentar. —vi aumentar, crecer; multiplicarse; extenderse; encarecerse, aumentar. —n aumento, crecimiento, m; multiplicación, f; (in price) encarecimiento, m, alza, f; (of water) crecida, f; (of moon) creciente, f. **It is on the i.**, Va en aumento. **to i. and multiply**, crecer y multiplicar
**increasingly** /ɪn'krisɪŋli/ adv más y más; en creciente, en aumento
**incredibility** /ɪn,krɛdə'bɪlɪti/ n incredibilidad, f
**incredible** /ɪn'krɛdəbəl/ a increíble; fabuloso, extraordinario. **It seems i.**, Es increíble, Inf. Parece mentira
**incredibly** /ɪn'krɛdəbli/ adv increíblemente
**incredulity** /ˌɪnkrɪ'dulɪti/ n incredulidad, f, escepticismo, m

**incredulous** /ɪn'krɛdʒələs/ a incrédulo, escéptico
**incredulously** /ɪn'krɛdʒələsli/ adv con incredulidad, escépticamente
**increment** /'ɪnkrəmənt/ n aumento, incremento, m; adición, añadidura, f; Math. incremento, m. **unearned i.**, plusvalía, mayor valía, f
**incriminate** /ɪn'krɪmə,neit/ vt incriminar
**incriminating** /ɪn'krɪmə,neitɪŋ/ a incriminante, acriminador
**incrust** /ɪn'krʌst/ vt incrustar, encostrar
**incrustation** /ˌɪnkrʌ'steiʃən/ n incrustación, f; (scab) costra, f
**incubate** /'ɪnkyə,beit/ vt empollar; Med. incubar
**incubation** /ˌɪnkyə'beiʃən/ n empolladura, incubación, f; Med. incubación, f
**incubator** /'ɪnkyə,beitər/ n incubadora, f
**incubus** /'ɪnkyəbəs/ n íncubo, m; (burden) carga, f
**inculcate** /ɪn'kʌlkeit/ vt inculcar, implantar, instilar
**inculcation** /ˌɪnkʌl'keiʃən/ n inculcación, implantación, instilación, f
**incumbency** /ɪn'kʌmbənsi/ n posesión, duración de, posesión, duración (de cualquier puesto), f
**incumbent** /ɪn'kʌmbənt/ a obligatorio. —n Eccl. beneficiado, m. **to be i. on**, incumbir a, ser de su obligación
**incur** /ɪn'kɜr/ vi incurrir (en), incidir (en). **to i. an obligation**, contraer una obligación
**incurability** /ɪn,kyʊrə'bɪlɪti/ n incurabilidad, f
**incurable** /ɪn'kyʊrəbəl/ a incurable, insanable; Fig. sin solución, irremediable. —n incurable, mf
**incurably** /ɪn'kyʊrəbli/ adv incurablemente, irremediablemente
**incurious** /ɪn'kyʊriəs/ a indiferente, sin interés; incurioso, negligente, descuidado
**incursion** /ɪn'kɜrʒən/ n incursión, invasión, irrupción, f, acometimiento, m
**indebted** /ɪn'dɛtɪd/ a empeñado, adeudado; (obliged) reconocido
**indebtedness** /ɪn'dɛtɪdnɪs/ n deuda, f; (gratitude) obligación, f; agradecimiento, m
**indecency** /ɪn'disənsi/ n indecencia, f
**indecent** /ɪn'disənt/ a indecente; obsceno, deshonesto
**indecently** /ɪn'disəntli/ adv torpemente, indecentemente
**indecision** /ˌɪndɪ'sɪʒən/ n indecisión, vacilación, irresolución, f
**indecisive** /ˌɪndɪ'saisɪv/ a indeciso, irresoluto, vacilante
**indeclinable** /ˌɪndɪ'klainəbəl/ a indeclinable
**indecorous** /ɪn'dɛkərəs/ a indecoroso, indecente, indigno
**indecorum** /ˌɪndɪ'kɔrəm/ n indecoro, m, indecencia, f; incorrección, f
**indeed** /ɪn'did/ adv en efecto, de veras, a la verdad, realmente, por cierto, claro está. —interr ¿de veras? ¿es posible? **I shall be very glad i.**, Estaré contento de veras. **It is i. an excellent book**, Es en efecto un libro excelente. **There are differences i. between this house and the other**, Hay diferencias, claro está, entre esta casa y la otra
**indefatigability** /ˌɪndɪ,fætɪgə'bɪlɪti/ n resistencia, f, aguante, m, tenacidad, f
**indefatigable** /ˌɪndɪ'fætɪgəbəl/ a incansable, infatigable, resistente
**indefatigably** /ˌɪndɪ'fætɪgəbli/ adv infatigablemente
**indefensible** /ˌɪndɪ'fɛnsəbəl/ a indefendible, insostenible
**indefinable** /ˌɪndɪ'fainəbəl/ a indefinible
**indefinite** /ɪn'dɛfənɪt/ a indefinido, incierto; (delicate) sutil, delicado; Gram. indefinido; (vague) vago. Gram. **i. article**, artículo indefinido, m
**indefinitely** /ɪn'dɛfənɪtli/ adv indefinidamente
**indefiniteness** /ɪn'dɛfənɪtnɪs/ n lo indefinido, el carácter indefinido, m; vaguedad, f
**indelibility** /ɪn,dɛlə'bɪlɪti/ n resistencia, f, lo indeleble; Fig. duración, tenacidad, f
**indelible** /ɪn'dɛləbəl/ a indeleble, imborrable; Fig. inolvidable
**indelibly** /ɪn'dɛləbli/ adv indeleblemente

**indelicacy** /ɪn'dɛlɪkəsɪ/ n falta de buen gusto, grosería, f; (tactlessness) indiscreción, falta de tacto, f
**indelicate** /ɪn'dɛlɪkɪt/ a grosero, descortés; indecoroso, inmodesto; (tactless) inoportuno, indiscreto
**indemnification** /ɪn,dɛmnəfɪ'keɪʃən/ n indemnización, compensación, f
**indemnify** /ɪn'dɛmnəˌfaɪ/ vt indemnizar, compensar
**indemnity** /ɪn'dɛmnɪtɪ/ n indemnización, reparación, f
**indent** /ɪn'dɛnt/ vt endentar, mellar; Print. sangrar
**indentation** /,ɪndɛn'teɪʃən/ n impresión, depresión, f; corte, m, mella, f; línea quebrada, f, zigzag, m
**indenture** /ɪn'dɛntʃər/ n escritura, f, instrumento, m. —vt escriturar
**independence** /,ɪndɪ'pɛndəns/ n independencia, libertad, f; (autonomy) autonomía, f. I. Day, Fiesta de la Independencia, f. i. movement, movimiento en favor de la independencia, m
**independent** /,ɪndɪ'pɛndənt/ a independiente; libre; (autonomous) autónomo; i. of, libre de; aparte de. a person of i. means, una persona acomodada
**independently** /,ɪndɪ'pɛndəntlɪ/ adv independientemente
**indescribability** /,ɪndɪˌskraɪbə'bɪlɪtɪ/ n imposibilidad de describir, f, lo indescriptible
**indescribable** /,ɪndɪ'skraɪbəbəl/ a indescriptible; indefinible, indecible, inexplicable; incalificable
**indestructibility** /,ɪndɪˌstrʌktə'bɪlɪtɪ/ n indestructibilidad, f
**indestructible** /,ɪndɪ'strʌktəbəl/ a indestructible
**indeterminable** /,ɪndɪ'tɜrmənəbəl/ a indeterminable
**indeterminate** /,ɪndɪ'tɜrmənɪt/ a indeterminado, indefinido, vago; Math. indeterminado
**indetermination** /,ɪndɪˌtɜrmə'neɪʃən/ n irresolución, indecisión, duda, vacilación, f
**index** /'ɪndɛks/ n (forefinger) dedo índice, m; (of book) tabla de materias, f, índice, m; (on instruments) manecilla, aguja, f; Math. índice, m; (sign) señal, indicación, f. —vt poner índice (a); poner en el índice. i. card, ficha, f. I. expurgatorius, Índice expurgatorio, m
**India** /'ɪndɪə/ n la India, f. I. paper, papel de China, m. i.-rubber, Bot. caucho, m; (eraser) goma de borrar, f. i.-rubber tree, yacio, m
**Indian** /'ɪndɪən/ a and n indio (-ia). I. chief, cacique, m. I. club, maza, f. I. corn, maíz, m. I. ink, tinta china, f. I. summer, veranillo, veranillo de San Martín, m
**Indian Ocean, the** el Océano Indico, m
**indicate** /'ɪndɪˌkeɪt/ vt indicar, señalar; (show) denotar, mostrar, anunciar
**indication** /,ɪndɪ'keɪʃən/ n indicación, f; señal, f, indicio, síntoma, m; prueba, f
**indicative** /ɪn'dɪkətɪv/ a indicador, indicativo, demostrativo; Gram. indicativo. —n Gram. indicativo, m. to be i. of, indicar, señalar
**indicator** /'ɪndɪˌkeɪtər/ n indicador, señalador, m
**indict** /ɪn'daɪt/ vt acusar; Law. demandar, enjuiciar
**indictable** /ɪn'daɪtəbəl/ a procesable, denunciable, enjuiciable
**indictment** /ɪn'daɪtmənt/ n acusación, f; Law. procesamiento, m
**indifference** /ɪn'dɪfərəns/ n indiferencia, apatía, f; desinterés, desapego, m; imparcialidad, neutralidad, f; (coldness) frialdad, tibieza, f
**indifferent** /ɪn'dɪfərənt/ a indiferente, apático; imparcial, neutral; frío; (ordinary) regular, ordinario, ni bien ni mal
**indifferently** /ɪn'dɪfərəntlɪ/ adv con indiferencia; imparcialmente; friamente
**indigence** /'ɪndɪdʒəns/ n indigencia, necesidad, penuria, f
**indigenous** /ɪn'dɪdʒənəs/ a indígena, nativo, natural
**indigent** /'ɪndɪdʒənt/ a indigente, necesitado, menesteroso
**indigestible** /,ɪndɪ'dʒɛstəbəl/ a indigesto
**indigestion** /,ɪndɪ'dʒɛstʃən/ n indigestión, f; Fig. empacho, ahíto, m
**indignant** /ɪn'dɪgnənt/ a indignado. to make i., indignar
**indignantly** /ɪn'dɪgnəntlɪ/ adv con indignación
**indignation** /,ɪndɪg'neɪʃən/ n indignación, cólera, f

**indignity** /ɪn'dɪgnɪtɪ/ n indignidad, f; ultraje, m
**indigo** /'ɪndɪˌgoʊ/ n añil, índigo, m
**indirect** /,ɪndə'rɛkt/ a indirecto; oblicuo; tortuoso; Gram. i. case, caso oblicuo, m
**indirectness** /,ɪndə'rɛktnɪs/ n (of route) rodeo, m, desviación, f; oblicuidad, f; (falsity) tortuosidad, f
**indiscernible** /,ɪndɪ'sɜrnəbəl/ a imperceptible
**indiscipline** /ɪn'dɪsəplɪn/ n indisciplina, falta de disciplina, f
**indiscreet** /,ɪndɪ'skrit/ a indiscreto, imprudente, impolítico
**indiscreetly** /,ɪndɪ'skritlɪ/ adv indiscretamente
**indiscretion** /,ɪndɪ'skrɛʃən/ n indiscreción, imprudencia, f; (slip) desliz, m
**indiscriminate** /,ɪndɪ'skrɪmənɪt/ a general, universal; indistinto, promiscuo
**indiscriminately** /,ɪndɪ'skrɪmənɪtlɪ/ adv promiscuamente
**indiscrimination** /,ɪndɪˌskrɪmə'neɪʃən/ n universalidad, indistinción, f
**indispensability** /,ɪndɪˌspɛnsə'bɪlɪtɪ/ n indispensabilidad, precisión, necesidad, f
**indispensable** /,ɪndɪ'spɛnsəbəl/ a imprescindible, indispensable, insustituible
**indispensably** /,ɪndɪ'spɛnsəblɪ/ adv forzosamente, indispensablemente
**indispose** /,ɪndɪ'spoʊz/ vt indisponer. to be indisposed, estar indispuesto, indisponerse
**indisposed** /,ɪndɪ'spoʊzd/ a indispuesto, enfermo, destemplado; (reluctant) maldispuesto
**indisposition** /,ɪndɪspə'zɪʃən/ n indisposición, enfermedad, f
**indisputability** /,ɪndɪˌspyutə'bɪlɪtɪ/ n verdad manifiesta, certeza, evidencia, f
**indisputable** /,ɪndɪ'spyutəbəl/ a innegable, incontestable; irrefutable, evidente
**indisputably** /,ɪndɪ'spyutəblɪ/ adv indisputablemente
**indissolubility** /,ɪndɪˌsɒlyə'bɪlɪtɪ/ n indisolubilidad, f
**indissoluble** /,ɪndɪ'sɒlyəbəl/ a indisoluble
**indistinct** /,ɪndɪ'stɪŋkt/ a indistinto; indeterminado, confuso, vago
**indistinctly** /,ɪndɪ'stɪŋktlɪ/ adv indistintamente; confusamente, vagamente
**indistinctness** /,ɪndɪ'stɪŋktnɪs/ n incertidumbre, vaguedad, indistinción, indeterminación, f
**indistinguishable** /,ɪndɪ'stɪŋgwɪʃəbəl/ a indistinguible
**individual** /,ɪndə'vɪdʒuəl/ a (single) solo, único; individual, individuo, particular, propio; personal. —n individuo, m, particular, mf
**individualism** /,ɪndə'vɪdʒuəˌlɪzəm/ n individualismo, m
**individualist** /,ɪndə'vɪdʒuəlɪst/ n individualist, mf
**individualistic** /,ɪndəˌvɪdʒuə'lɪstɪk/ a individualista
**individuality** /,ɪndəˌvɪdʒu'ælɪtɪ/ n individualidad, personalidad, f; carácter, m, naturaleza, f
**individualize** /,ɪndə'vɪdʒuəˌlaɪz/ vt particularizar, individuar
**individually** /,ɪndə'vɪdʒuəlɪ/ adv individualmente, particularmente
**indivisibility** /,ɪndəˌvɪzə'bɪlɪtɪ/ n indivisibilidad, f
**indivisible** /,ɪndə'vɪzəbəl/ a incompartible, impartible, indivisible
**indivisibly** /,ɪndə'vɪzəblɪ/ adv indivisiblemente
**Indo** /'ɪndoʊ/ (in compounds) indo-. I.-Chinese, a and n indochino (-na). I.-European, indoeuropeo. I.-Germanic, indogermánico
**indocile** /ɪn'dɒsɪl/ a indócil, desobediente, rebelde
**indocility** /ɪn'dɒsɪlɪtɪ/ n indocilidad, desobediencia, falta de docilidad, f
**indolence** /'ɪndələns/ n indolencia, pereza, desidia, f
**indolent** /'ɪndələnt/ a indolente, perezoso, holgazán; Med. indoloro
**indolently** /'ɪndələntlɪ/ adv perezosamente
**indomitable** /ɪn'dɒmɪtəbəl/ a indomable, indómito
**indoor** /'ɪnˌdɔr/ a de casa; de puertas adentro, interno. i. swimming pool, piscina bajo techo, f. i. tennis, tenis en pistas cubiertas, tenis bajo techo, m
**indoors** /ɪn'dɔrz/ adv en casa; adentro, bajo techo
**indorsee** /ɪndɔr'si/ n endosatario (-ia)
**indubitable** /ɪn'dubɪtəbəl/ a indudable

**indubitably** /ɪnˈdubɪtəbli/ *adv* indudablemente, sin duda

**induce** /ɪnˈdus/ *vt* inducir, mover; instigar, incitar; producir, ocasionar; *Elec.* inducir. **Nothing would i. me to do it,** Nada me induciría a hacerlo

**inducement** /ɪnˈdusmənt/ *n* incitamiento, *m;* estímulo, *m;* aliciente, atractivo, *m;* tentación, *f*

**induct** /ɪnˈdʌkt/ *vt* instalar; introducir, iniciar

**induction** /ɪnˈdʌkʃən/ *n* instalación, *f;* iniciación, introducción, *f; Phys.* inducción, *f.* **i. coil,** carrete de inducción, *m*

**inductive** /ɪnˈdʌktɪv/ *a* (of reasoning) inductivo; *Phys.* inductor

**indulge** /ɪnˈdʌldʒ/ *vt* (children) consentir, mimar; (a desire) satisfacer, dar rienda suelta a; (with a gift) agasajar (con), dar gusto (con). **to i. in,** *vt* consentir en. —*vi* entregarse a, permitirse, gustar de

**indulgence** /ɪnˈdʌldʒəns/ *n* (of children) mimo, cariño excesivo, *m;* (of a desire) propensión (a), afición (a), *f;* (toward others) tolerancia, transigencia, *f; Eccl.* indulgencia, *f*

**indulgent** /ɪnˈdʌldʒənt/ *a* indulgente; tolerante, transigente

**indult** /ɪnˈdʌlt/ *n Eccl.* indulto, *m*

**industrial** /ɪnˈdʌstrɪəl/ *a* industrial. **i. alcohol,** alcohol desnaturalizado, *m.* **i. school,** escuela de artes y oficios, *f, Com.* **i. shares,** valores industriales, *m pl*

**industrialism** /ɪnˈdʌstrɪə‚lɪzəm/ *n* industrialismo, *m*

**industrialist** /ɪnˈdʌstrɪəlɪst/ *n* industrial, *m*

**industrialization** /ɪnˌdʌstrɪəlɪˈzeɪʃən/ *n* industrialización, *f*

**industrialize** /ɪnˈdʌstrɪə‚laiz/ *vt* industrializar

**industrious** /ɪnˈdʌstrɪəs/ *a* industrioso, aplicado, diligente

**industriously** /ɪnˈdʌstrɪəsli/ *adv* industriosamente, diligentemente

**industriousness** /ɪnˈdʌstrɪəsnɪs/ *n* industria, laboriosidad, *f*

**industry** /ˈɪndəstri/ *n* diligencia, aplicación, *f;* (work) trabajo, *m,* labor, *f; Com.* industria, *f*

**inebriate** /*a, n* ɪˈnibriɪt; *v* -bri‚eit/ *a* borracho, ebrio. —*n* borracho (-cha). —*vt* embriagar, emborrachar

**inebriation** /ɪˌnibriˈeiʃən/ *n* embriaguez, borrachera, *f*

**inedible** /ɪnˈɛdəbəl/ *a* incomible, no comestible

**inedited** /ɪnˈɛdɪtɪd/ *a* inédito

**ineffable** /ɪnˈɛfəbəl/ *a* indecible, inefable

**ineffaceable** /ˌɪnɪˈfeisəbəl/ *a* imborrable, indeleble

**ineffective** /ˌɪnɪˈfɛktɪv/ *a* ineficaz; vano, fútil. **to be i.,** (of persons) no pinchar ni cortar. **to prove i.,** quedar sin efecto; no tener influencia

**ineffectiveness** /ˌɪnɪˈfɛktɪvnɪs/ *n* ineficacia, *f;* futilidad, *f*

**inefficiency** /ˌɪnɪˈfɪʃənsi/ *n* ineficacia, incompetencia, ineptitud, *f*

**inefficient** /ˌɪnɪˈfɪʃənt/ *a* ineficaz, incapaz

**inefficiently** /ˌɪnɪˈfɪʃəntli/ *adv* ineficazmente

**inelastic** /ˌɪnɪˈlæstɪk/ *a* inelástico

**inelegance** /ɪnˈɛlɪgəns/ *n* inelegancia, fealdad, vulgaridad, *f*

**inelegant** /ɪnˈɛlɪgənt/ *a* inelegante, ordinario, de mal gusto

**inelegantly** /ɪnˈɛlɪgəntli/ *adv* sin elegancia

**ineligibility** /ɪnˌɛlɪdʒəˈbɪlɪti/ *n* ineligibilidad, *f*

**ineligible** /ɪnˈɛlɪdʒəbəl/ *a* inelegible

**inept** /ɪnˈɛpt/ *a* inepto, inoportuno; absurdo, ridiculo; (of persons) incompetente, ineficaz

**ineptitude** /ɪnˈɛpti‚tud/ *n* ineptitud, *f;* necedad, *f;* (of persons) incapacidad, incompetencia, *f*

**ineptly** /ɪnˈɛptli/ *adv* ineptamente, neciamente

**inequality** /ˌɪnɪˈkwɒlɪti/ *n* desigualdad, desemejanza, disparidad, *f;* (of surface) escabrosidad, aspereza, *f; Fig.* injusticia, *f;* (of opportunity) diferencia, *f*

**inequitable** /ɪnˈɛkwɪtəbəl/ *a* desigual, injusto

**inequity** /ɪnˈɛkwɪti/ *n* injusticia, desigualdad, *f*

**ineradicable** /ˌɪnɪˈrædɪkəbəl/ *a* indeleble, imborrable

**ineradicably** /ˌɪnɪˈrædɪkəbli/ *adv* indeleblemente

**inert** /ɪnˈɜrt/ *a* inerte, inactivo, pasivo; ocioso, flojo, perezoso

**inertia** /ɪnˈɜrʃə/ *n* inercia, inacción, *f;* abulia, pereza, *f; Phys.* inercia, *f*

**inertly** /ɪnˈɜrtli/ *adv* indolentemente, sin mover, pasivamente

**inescapable** /ˌɪnəˈskeipəbəl/ *a* ineludible, inevitable

**inessential** /ˌɪnɪˈsɛnʃəl/ *a* no esencial

**inestimable** /ɪnˈɛstəməbəl/ *a* inestimable

**inevitability** /ɪnˌɛvɪtəˈbɪlɪti/ *n* fatalidad, necesidad, *f;* lo inevitable

**inevitable** /ɪnˈɛvɪtəbəl/ *a* inevitable, necesario, fatal, forzoso, ineludible

**inevitably** /ɪnˈɛvɪtəbli/ *adv* inevitablemente, necesariamente, forzosamente

**inexact** /ˌɪnɪgˈzækt/ *a* inexacto, incorrecto

**inexactitude** /ˌɪnɪgˈzæktɪ‚tud/ *n* inexactitud, *f*

**inexcusable** /ˌɪnɪkˈskyuzəbəl/ *a* imperdonable, inexcusable, irremisible

**inexcusableness** /ˌɪnɪkˈskyuzəbəlnɪs/ *n* enormidad, *f;* lo inexcusable

**inexcusably** /ˌɪnɪkˈskyuzəbli/ *adv* inexcusablemente

**inexhaustible** /ˌɪnɪgˈzɔstəbəl/ *a* inagotable, inexhausto

**inexorability** /ɪnˌɛksərəˈbɪlɪti/ *n* inflexibilidad, inexorabilidad, *f*

**inexorable** /ɪnˈɛksərəbəl/ *a* inexorable, inflexible, duro

**inexorably** /ɪnˈɛksərəbli/ *adv* inexorablemente, implacablemente

**inexpediency** /ˌɪnɪkˈspidiənsi/ *n* inoportunidad, inconveniencia, imprudencia, *f*

**inexpedient** /ˌɪnɪkˈspidiənt/ *a* inoportuno; inconveniente; impolítico, imprudente. **to deem i.,** creer inoportuno

**inexpensive** /ˌɪnɪkˈspɛnsɪv/ *a* poco costoso, barato

**inexpensiveness** /ˌɪnɪkˈspɛnsɪvnɪs/ *n* baratura, *f,* bajo precio, *m*

**inexperience** /ˌɪnɪkˈspɪəriəns/ *n* inexperiencia, falta de experiencia, *f*

**inexperienced** /ˌɪnɪkˈspɪəriənst/ *a* inexperto, novato

**inexpert** /ɪnˈɛkspɜrt/ *a* inexperto, imperito

**inexpertly** /ɪnˈɛkspɜrtli/ *adv* sin habilidad

**inexpertness** /ɪnˈɛkspɜrtnɪs/ *n* impericia, torpeza, *f*

**inexpiable** /ɪnˈɛkspiəbəl/ *a* inexpiable

**inexplicable** /ɪnˈɛksplɪkəbəl/ *a* inexplicable

**inexplicit** /ˌɪnɪkˈsplɪsɪt/ *a* no explícito

**inexplosive** /ˌɪnɪkˈsplousɪv/ *a* inexplosible

**inexpressible** /ˌɪnɪkˈsprɛsəbəl/ *a* inexplicable, indecible, inefable

**inexpressive** /ˌɪnɪkˈsprɛsɪv/ *a* inexpresivo; (of persons) reservado, callado, poco expresivo, retraído

**inexpressiveness** /ˌɪnɪkˈsprɛsɪvnɪs/ *n* falta de expresión, *f;* (of persons) reserva, *f,* silencio, retraimiento, *m*

**inexpugnable** /ˌɪnɪkˈspʌgnəbəl/ *a* inexpugnable

**inextinguishable** /ˌɪnɪkˈstɪŋgwɪʃəbəl/ *a* inapagable, inextinguible

**inextricable** /ɪnˈɛkstrɪkəbəl/ *a* inextricable, intrincado, enmarañado

**inextricably** /ɪnˈɛkstrɪkəbli/ *adv* intrincadamente

**infallibility** /ɪnˌfæləˈbɪlɪti/ *n* infalibilidad, *f*

**infallible** /ɪnˈfæləbəl/ *a* infalible

**infamous** /ˈɪnfəməs/ *a* infame, torpe, vil, ignominioso; odioso, repugnante

**infamously** /ˈɪnfəməsli/ *adv* infamemente

**infamy** /ˈɪnfəmi/ *n* infamia, torpeza, vileza, ignominia, *f;* deshonra, *f*

**infancy** /ˈɪnfənsi/ *n* infancia, niñez, *f; Law.* minoridad, *f*

**infant** /ˈɪnfənt/ *n* criatura, *f;* crío (-ía), niño (-ña); *Law.* menor, *mf* **i. school,** escuela de párvulos, *f*

**infanticidal** /ɪnˈfæntəˈsaidl/ *a* infanticida

**infanticide** /ɪnˈfæntə‚said/ *n* (act) infanticidio, *m;* (person) infanticida, *mf*

**infantile** /ˈɪnfən‚tail/ *a* infantil. **i. paralysis,** parálisis infantil, *f*

**infantry** /ˈɪnfəntri/ *n Mil.* infantería, *f*

**infantryman** /ˈɪnfəntrimən/ *n Mil.* infante, peón, *m*

**infatuate** /ɪnˈfætʃu‚eit/ *vt* infatuar, embobar

**infatuation** /ɪnˌfætʃuˈeiʃən/ *n* infatuación, *f,* encaprichamiento, *m*

**infect** /ɪnˈfɛkt/ *vt* infectar, contagiar; *Fig.* pegar, influir; (*Fig.* in a bad sense) corromper, pervertir, inficionar. **to become infected,** infectarse

**infected** /ɪnˈfɛktɪd/ a infecto

**infection** /ɪnˈfɛkʃən/ n infección, f, contagio, m; Fig. influencia, f; (Fig. in a bad sense) corrupción, perversión, f

**infectious** /ɪnˈfɛkʃəs/ a infeccioso, contagioso; (Fig. in a bad sense) corruptor; Fig. contagioso

**infectiousness** /ɪnˈfɛkʃəsnɪs/ n contagiosidad, f

**infelicitous** /ˌɪnfəˈlɪsɪtəs/ a poco apropiado, desacertado

**infelicity** /ˌɪnfəˈlɪsɪti/ n infelicidad, desdicha, f, infortunio, m; desacierto, m, inoportunidad, f

**infer** /ɪnˈfɜr/ vt inferir, concluir, educir, deducir, implicar

**inferable** /ɪnˈfɜrəbəl/ a deducible, demostrable

**inference** /ˈɪnfərəns/ n inferencia, deducción, conclusión, f

**inferential** /ˌɪnfəˈrɛnʃəl/ a ilativo, deductivo

**inferior** /ɪnˈfɪəriər/ a inferior; (in rank) subordinado, subalterno; (of position) secundario. —n inferior, mf subordinado (-da). **to be not i.,** no ser inferior, Inf. no quedarse en zaga

**inferiority** /ɪnˌfɪəriˈɔrɪti/ n inferioridad, f. **i. complex,** complejo de inferioridad, m

**infernal** /ɪnˈfɜrnl/ a infernal; Poet. inferno, tartáreo

**infernally** /ɪnˈfɜrnli/ adv infernalmente

**inferno** /ɪnˈfɜrnou/ n infierno, m

**infertile** /ɪnˈfɜrtl/ a infértil, infecundo, estéril

**infertility** /ˌɪnfərˈtɪlɪti/ n infertilidad, infecundidad, esterilidad, f

**infest** /ɪnˈfɛst/ vt infestar. **to be infested with,** plagarse de

**infestation** /ˌɪnfɛsˈteɪʃən/ n infestación, f

**infidel** /ˈɪnfɪdl/ n infiel, gentil, mf pagano (-na); (atheist) descreído (-da), ateo (-ea). —a pagano; infiel, descreído, ateo

**infidelity** /ˌɪnfɪˈdɛlɪti/ n infidelidad, alevosía, perfidia, f

**infiltrate** /ɪnˈfɪltreit/ vt infiltrar. —vi infiltrarse

**infiltration** /ˌɪnfɪlˈtreiʃən/ n infiltración, f

**infinite** /ˈɪnfənɪt/ a infinito, ilimitado; inmenso, enorme; (of number) innumerable, infinito. —n infinito, m

**infinitely** /ˈɪnfənɪtli/ adv infinitamente

**infinitesimal** /ˌɪnfɪnɪˈtɛsəməl/ a infinitesimal. **i. calculus,** cálculo infinitesimal, m

**infinitive** /ɪnˈfɪnɪtɪv/ a and n Gram. infinitivo, m.

**infinitude, infinity** /ɪnˈfɪnɪtud; ɪnˈfɪnɪti/ n infinidad, infinitud, f; (extent) inmensidad, f; (of number) sinfín, m; Math. infinito, m

**infirm** /ɪnˈfɜrm/ a achacoso, enfermizo, enclenque; (shaky) inestable, inseguro; (of purpose) irresoluto, vacilante

**infirmary** /ɪnˈfɜrməri/ n enfermería, f, hospital, m

**infirmity** /ɪnˈfɜrmɪti/ n achaque, m, enfermedad, dolencia, f; (fault) flaqueza, falta, f

**inflame** /ɪnˈfleim/ vt encender; (excite) acalorar, irritar, provocar; Med. inflamar. —vi encenderse, arder; acalorarse, irritarse; Med. inflamarse

**inflammability** /ɪnˌflæməˈbɪlɪti/ n inflamabilidad, f

**inflammable** /ɪnˈflæməbəl/ a inflamable

**inflammation** /ˌɪnfləˈmeiʃən/ n inflamación, f

**inflammatory** /ɪnˈflæməˌtɔri/ a inflamador; Med. inflamatorio

**inflate** /ɪnˈfleit/ vt inflar, hinchar; (with pride) engreír, ensoberbecer

**inflation** /ɪnˈfleiʃən/ n inflación, hinchazón, f; Com. inflación, f

**inflationism** /ɪnˈfleiʃəˌnɪzəm/ n inflacionismo, m

**inflator** /ɪnˈfleitər/ n Mech. bomba para inflar, f

**inflect** /ɪnˈflɛkt/ vt torcer; (voice) modular; Gram. conjugar, declinar

**inflection** /ɪnˈflɛkʃən/ n dobladura, f; (of voice) tono, acento, m, modulación, f; Gram. conjugación, declinación, f

**inflexibility** /ɪnˌflɛksəˈbɪlɪti/ n inflexibilidad, dureza, rigidez, f

**inflexible** /ɪnˈflɛksəbəl/ a inflexible, rígido; Fig. inexorable, inalterable

**inflexibly** /ɪnˈflɛksəbli/ adv inflexiblemente

**inflict** /ɪnˈflɪkt/ vt infligir, imponer

**infliction** /ɪnˈflɪkʃən/ n imposición, f; castigo, m

**inflorescence** /ˌɪnflɔˈrɛsəns/ n Bot. inflorescencia, f

**inflow** /ˈɪnˌflou/ n afluencia, f, flujo, m

**influence** /ˈɪnfluəns/ n influencia, f, influjo, m; ascendiente, m; (importance) influencia, importancia, f. —vt influir, afectar; persuadir, inducir. **to have i. over,** (a person) tener ascendiente sobre. Law. **undue i.,** influencia indebida, f

**influential** /ˌɪnfluˈɛnʃəl/ a influyente; (of person) prestigioso, importante

**influenza** /ˌɪnfluˈɛnzə/ n Med. gripe, f, trancazo, m

**influx** /ˈɪnˌflʌks/ n influjo, m; (of rivers) desembocadura, afluencia, f

**inform** /ɪnˈfɔrm/ vt (fill) infundir, llenar; (tell) informar, enterar, advertir; instruir; (with about) poner al corriente de, participar. —vi (with against) delatar (a), denunciar. **to i. oneself,** informarse, enterarse. **to be informed about,** estar al corriente de

**informal** /ɪnˈfɔrməl/ a irregular; sin ceremonia, de confianza; (meeting) no oficial, extraoficial

**informality** /ˌɪnfɔrˈmælɪti/ n irregularidad, f; falta de ceremonia, sencillez, f; intimidad, f

**informally** /ɪnˈfɔrməli/ adv sin ceremonia

**informant** /ɪnˈfɔrmənt/ n informante, mf; informador (-ra)

**information** /ˌɪnfərˈmeiʃən/ n información, instrucción, f; noticia, f, aviso, m; Law. denuncia, delación, f. **piece of i.,** información, f. **i. bureau,** oficina de información, f

**informative** /ɪnˈfɔrmətɪv/ a informativo

**informer** /ɪnˈfɔrmər/ n delator (-ra), denunciador (-ra)

**infraction** /ɪnˈfrækʃən/ n contravención, infracción, transgresión, f

**infrared** /ˌɪnfrəˈrɛd/ a Phys. infrarrojo, ultrarrojo

**infrequency** /ɪnˈfrikwənsi/ n infrecuencia, rareza, irregularidad, f

**infrequent** /ɪnˈfrikwənt/ a infrecuente, raro, irregular

**infrequently** /ɪnˈfrikwəntli/ adv rara vez, infrecuentemente

**infringe** /ɪnˈfrɪndʒ/ vt infringir, violar, contravenir, quebrantar

**infringement** /ɪnˈfrɪndʒmənt/ n contravención, violación, infracción, f

**infringer** /ɪnˈfrɪndʒər/ n infractor (-ra), contraventor (-ra), violador (-ra), transgresor (-ra)

**infuriate** /ɪnˈfyʊriˌeit/ vt enfurecer, enloquecer, enojar. **to be infuriated,** estar furioso

**infuse** /ɪnˈfyuz/ vt vaciar, infiltrar; Fig. infundir, inculcar, instilar

**infusible** /ɪnˈfyuzəbəl/ a infundible

**infusion** /ɪnˈfyuʒən/ n infusión, f; Fig. instilación, inculcación, f

**ingathering** /ɪnˈgæðərɪŋ/ n cosecha, recolección, f

**ingenious** /ɪnˈdʒinyəs/ a ingenioso; mañoso, hábil

**ingeniously** /ɪnˈdʒinyəsli/ adv ingeniosamente, hábilmente

**ingenuity** /ˌɪndʒəˈnuɪti/ n ingeniosidad, inventiva, listeza, habilidad, f

**ingenuous** /ɪnˈdʒɛnyuəs/ a ingenuo, franco, sincero, cándido, sencillo, inocente

**ingenuousness** /ɪnˈdʒɛnyuəsnɪs/ n ingenuidad, franqueza, sinceridad, f; candor, m

**ingest** /ɪnˈdʒɛst/ vt ingerir

**ingestion** /ɪnˈdʒɛstʃən/ n ingestión, f

**inglorious** /ɪnˈglɔriəs/ a vergonzoso, ignominioso, deshonroso; desconocido, obscuro

**ingloriously** /ɪnˈglɔriəsli/ adv vergonzosamente, ignominiosamente; obscuramente

**ingloriousness** /ɪnˈglɔriəsnɪs/ n deshonra, ignominia, f; obscuridad, f

**ingoing** /ˈɪnˌgouɪŋ/ a entrante, que entra. —n ingreso, m, entrada, f; Com. **i. and outgoing,** entradas y salidas, f pl

**ingot** /ˈɪŋgət/ n pepita, f, lingote, m; (of any metal) barra, f

**ingrained** /ɪnˈgreind, ˈɪnˌgreind/ a innato, natural

**ingratiate** /ɪnˈgreiʃiˌeit/ vt (oneself with) congraciarse con, captarse la buena voluntad de, insinuarse en el favor de

**ingratiating** /ɪnˈgreiʃiˌeitɪŋ/ a obsequioso

**ingratitude** /ɪnˈɡrætɪˌtud/ *n* ingratitud, *f*, desagradecimiento, *m*

**ingredient** /ɪnˈɡridiənt/ *n* ingrediente, *m*

**ingress** /ˈɪnɡrɛs/ *n* ingreso, *m;* derecho de entrada, *m*

**ingrowing** /ˈɪnˌɡrouɪŋ/ *a* que crece hacia adentro. **i. nail,** uñero, *m*

**inhabit** /ɪnˈhæbɪt/ *vt* habitar, ocupar, vivir en, residir en

**inhabitable** /ɪnˈhæbɪtəbəl/ *a* habitable, vividero

**inhabitant** /ɪnˈhæbɪtənt/ *n* habitante, residente, *m;* vecino (-na)

**inhabited** /ɪnˈhæbɪtɪd/ *a* habitado, poblado

**inhalation** /ˌɪnhəˈleiʃən/ *n* inspiración, *f; Med.* inhalación, *f*

**inhale** /ɪnˈheil/ *vt* aspirar; *Med.* inhalar

**inharmonious** /ˌɪnhɑrˈmouniəs/ *a Mus.* disonante, inarmónico; desavenido, discorde, desconforme. **to be i.,** disonar; (of people) llevarse mal

**inhere** /ɪnˈhɪər/ *vi* ser inherente; pertenecer (a), residir (en)

**inherence** /ɪnˈhɪərəns/ *n* inherencia, *f*

**inherent** /ɪnˈhɪərənt/ *a* inherente; innato, intrínseco, natural

**inherently** /ɪnˈhɪərəntli/ *adv* intrínsecamente

**inherit** /ɪnˈhɛrɪt/ *vt* heredar

**inheritance** /ɪnˈhɛrɪtəns/ *n* herencia, *f;* patrimonio, abolengo, *m*

**inheritor** /ɪnˈhɛrɪtər/ *n* heredero (-ra)

**inhibit** /ɪnˈhɪbɪt/ *vt* inhibir, impedir; *Eccl.* prohibir. **be inhibited, became inhibited,** cohibirse

**inhibition** /ˌɪnɪˈbɪʃən/ *n* inhibición, *f*

**inhibitory** /ɪnˈhɪbɪˌtɔri/ *a* inhibitorio

**inhospitable** /ɪnˈhɒspɪtəbəl/ *a* inhospitalario

**inhospitably** /ɪnˈhɒspɪtəbli/ *adv* desabridamente

**inhospitality** /ˌɪnhɒspɪˈtælɪti/ *n* inhospitalidad, *f*

**inhuman** /ɪnˈhyumən/ *a* inhumano; cruel, bárbaro

**inhumanity** /ˌɪnhyuˈmænɪti/ *n* inhumanidad, crueldad, *f*

**inhumanly** /ɪnˈhyumənli/ *adv* inhumanamente, cruelmente

**inhume** /ɪnˈhyum/ *vt* inhumar, sepultar

**inimical** /ɪˈnɪmɪkəl/ *a* enemigo, hostil, opuesto, contrario

**inimically** /ɪˈnɪmɪkəli/ *adv* hostilmente

**inimitable** /ɪˈnɪmɪtəbəl/ *a* inimitable

**inimitably** /ɪˈnɪmɪtəbli/ *adv* inimitablemente

**iniquitous** /ɪˈnɪkwɪtəs/ *a* inicuo, malvado, perverso, nefando; *Inf.* diabólico

**iniquity** /ɪˈnɪkwɪti/ *n* iniquidad, maldad, injusticia, *f*

**initial** /ɪˈnɪʃəl/ *a* inicial. —*n* inicial, letra inicial, *f.* —*vt* firmar con las iniciales

**initially** /ɪˈnɪʃəli/ *adv* al principio, en primer lugar

**initiate** /a ɪˈnɪʃiɪt; v ɪˈnɪʃiˌeit/ *a* iniciado. —*vt* iniciar, poner en pie, empezar, entablar; (a person) admitir

**initiation** /ɪˌnɪʃiˈeiʃən/ *n* principio, *m;* (of a person) iniciación, admisión, *f*

**initiative** /ɪˈnɪʃiətɪv/ *n* iniciativa, *f.* **to take the i.,** tomar la iniciative

**initiator** /ɪˈnɪʃiˌeitər/ *n* iniciador (-ra)

**inject** /ɪnˈdʒɛkt/ *vt* inyectar

**injection** /ɪnˈdʒɛkʃən/ *n* inyección, *f.* **i. syringe,** jeringa de inyecciones, *f*

**injudicious** /ˌɪndʒuˈdɪʃəs/ *a* imprudente, indiscreto

**injudiciously** /ˌɪndʒuˈdɪʃəsli/ *adv* imprudentemente

**injudiciousness** /ˌɪndʒuˈdɪʃəsnɪs/ *n* imprudencia, indiscreción, *f*

**injunction** /ɪnˈdʒʌŋkʃən/ *n* precepto, mandato, *m; Law.* embargo, *m*

**injure** /ˈɪndʒər/ *vt* perjudicar, dañar; menoscabar, deteriorar; (hurt) lastimar, lisiar. **to i. oneself,** hacerse daño

**injured** /ˈɪndʒərd/ *a* (physically) lisiado; (morally) ofendido

**injurer** /ˈɪndʒərər/ *n* perjudicador (-ra)

**injurious** /ɪnˈdʒʊriəs/ *a* dañoso, perjudicial, malo; ofensivo, injurioso

**injuriously** /ɪnˈdʒʊriəsli/ *adv* perjudicialmente

**injury** /ˈɪndʒəri/ *n* perjuicio, daño, *m;* (physical) lesión, *f;* (insult) agravio, insulto, *m*

**injustice** /ɪnˈdʒʌstɪs/ *n* injusticia, desigualdad, *f.* **You do him an i.,** Le juzgas mal

**ink** /ɪŋk/ *n* tinta, *f.* —*vt* entintar. **copying-ink,** tinta de copiar, *f.* **marking-ink,** tinta indeleble, *f.* **printer's ink,** tinta de imprenta, *f.* **ink-stand** or **ink-well,** tintero, *m*

**inker** /ˈɪŋkər/ *n Print.* rodillo, *m*

**inkling** /ˈɪŋklɪŋ/ *n* sospecha, noción, *f*

**inky** /ˈɪŋki/ *a* manchado de tinta. **i. black,** negro como el betún

**inland** /ˈɪnlænd/ *n* el interior de un país, *a* interior, mediterráneo; del país, regional. —*adv* tierra adentro. **to go i.,** internarse en un país. **I. Revenue,** delegación de contribuciones, *f.* **i. town,** ciudad del interior, *f*

**inlay** /ɪnˈlei/ *vt* taracear, ataracear, embutir; incrustar. —*n* taracea, *f,* embutido, *m*

**inlet** /ˈɪnlɛt/ *n* entrada, admisión, *f; Geog.* ensenada, *f.* **i. valve,** válvula de admisión, *f*

**inmate** /ˈɪnˌmeit/ *n* residente, habitante, *m;* (of hospital) paciente, *mf;* enfermo (-ma); (of prison) prisionero

**inmost** /ˈɪnmoust/. See **innermost**

**inn** /ɪn/ *n* posada, fonda, venta, *f,* mesón, *m.* **Inns of Court,** Colegio de Abogados, *m*

**innate** /ɪˈneit/ *a* innato, inherente, instintivo, nativo

**innately** /ɪˈneitli/ *adv* naturalmente, instintivamente

**innavigable** /ɪˈnævɪɡəbəl/ *a* innavegable

**inner** /ˈɪnər/ *a* interior, interno. **i. tube** *Auto.* cámara de neumatico, cámara de aire, *f*

**innermost** /ˈɪnərˌmoust/ *a* más adentro; *Fig.* más íntimo, más hondo

**innings** /ˈɪnɪŋz/ *n* (sport) turno, *m*

**innkeeper** /ˈɪnˌkipər/ *n* fondista, *mf;* tabernero (-ra), mesonero (-ra), posadero (-ra)

**innocence** /ˈɪnəsəns/ *n* inocencia, *f;* pureza, *f;* (guilelessness) simplicidad, *f,* candor, *m*

**innocent** /ˈɪnəsənt/ *a* inocente, puro; (guiltless) inocente, inculpable; (foolish) simple, tonto, candoroso, inocentón; (harmless) innocuo. —*n* inocente, *mf* **Holy Innocents,** Santos Inocentes, *m pl*

**innocuous** /ɪˈnɒkyuəs/ *a* innocuo, inofensivo

**innocuousness** /ɪˈnɒkyuəsnɪs/ *n* inocuidad, *f*

**innovate** /ˈɪnəˌveit/ *vt* innovar

**innovation** /ˌɪnəˈveifən/ *n* innovación, *f*

**innovator** /ˈɪnəˌveitər/ *n* innovador (-ra)

**innuendo** /ˌɪnyuˈɛndou/ *n* indirecta, insinuación, *f*

**innumerable** /ɪˈnumərəbəl/ *a* innumerable, incalculable. **i. things,** un sinfín de cosas

**inobservance** /ˌɪnəbˈzɜrvəns/ *n* inobservancia, *f,* incumplimiento, *m*

**inoculate** /ɪˈnɒkyəˌleit/ *vt* inocular

**inoculation** /ɪˌnɒkyəˈleiʃən/ *n* inoculación, *f*

**inoculator** /ɪˈnɒkyəˌleitər/ *n* inoculador, *m*

**inodorous** /ɪnˈoudərəs/ *a* inodoro

**inoffensive** /ˌɪnəˈfɛnsɪv/ *a* inofensivo, innocuo; (of people) pacífico, apacible, manso

**inoffensively** /ˌɪnəˈfɛnsɪvli/ *adv* inofensivamente

**inoffensiveness** /ˌɪnəˈfɛnsɪvnɪs/ *n* inocuidad, *f;* (of people) mansedumbre, *f*

**inoperable** /ɪnˈɒpərəbəl/ *a* inoperable

**inoperative** /ɪnˈɒpərətɪv/ *a* ineficaz, impracticable, inútil

**inopportune** /ɪnˌɒpərˈtun/ *a* inoportuno, intempestivo, inconveniente

**inopportunely** /ɪnˌɒpərˈtunli/ *adv* inoportunamente, a destiempo

**inopportuneness** /ɪnˌɒpərˈtunnɪs/ *n* inoportunidad, inconveniencia, *f*

**inordinate** /ɪnˈɔrdnɪt/ *a* desordenado, excesivo

**inordinately** /ɪnˈɔrdnɪtli/ *adv* desmedidamente

**inorganic** /ˌɪnɔrˈɡænɪk/ *a* inorgánico

**inoxidizable** /ɪnˈɒksɪˌdaizəbəl/ *a* inoxidable

**input** /ˈɪnˌpʊt/ *n* capacidad instalada, *f,* insumo, *m*

**inquest** /ˈɪnkwɛst/ *n Law.* indagación, investigación, *f*

**inquietude** /ɪnˈkwaiɪˌtud/ *n* inquietud, *f,* desasosiego, *m,* agitación, preocupación, *f*

**inquire** /ɪnˈkwaiər/ *vt* and *vi* preguntar, averiguar, indagar. **to i. about,** (persons) preguntar por; (things) hacer preguntas sobre. **to i. into,** investigar, examinar, averiguar. **to i. of,** preguntar a. **"I. within,"** «dan informaciones»

**inquirer** /ɪn'kwaɪᵊrər/ n indagador (-ra), inquiridor (-ra)

**inquiring** /ɪn'kwaɪᵊrɪŋ/ a indagador, inquiridor

**inquiringly** /ɪn'kwaɪᵊrɪŋli/ adv interrogativamente

**inquiry** /ɪn'kwaɪᵊri/ n interrogación, pregunta, f; indagación, pesquisa, investigación, f; examen, m. **i. office,** oficina de informaciones, f. **on i.,** al preguntar

**inquisition** /ˌɪnkwə'zɪʃən/ n investigación, indagación, f; inquisición, f. **Holy I.,** Santo Oficio, m, Inquisición, f

**inquisitive** /ɪn'kwɪzɪtɪv/ a curioso, inquiridor; preguntador, impertinente, mirón

**inquisitively** /ɪn'kwɪzɪtɪvli/ adv con curiosidad, impertinentemente

**inquisitiveness** /ɪn'kwɪzɪtɪvnɪs/ n curiosidad, f; impertinencia, f

**Inquisitor** /ɪn'kwɪzɪtər/ n Eccl. inquisidor, m

**inquisitorial** /ɪn,kwɪzɪ'tɔriəl/ a inquisitorial, inquisidor

**inroad** /'ɪn,roud/ n incursión, f

**insalubrious** /ˌɪnsə'lubriəs/ a malsano, insalubre

**insane** /ɪn'sein/ a loco, demente, insano; (senseless) insensato, ridículo. **to become i.,** enloquecer, volverse loco, perder la razón. **to drive i.,** volver a uno el juicio, enloquecer, trastornar. **i. person,** demente, mf. loco (-ca)

**insanely** /ɪn'seinli/ adv locamente

**insanitary** /ɪn'sænɪ,teri/ a antihigiénico, malsano

**insanity** /ɪn'sænɪti/ n demencia, locura, f; enloquecimiento, m; (folly) insensatez, ridiculez, f

**insatiability** /ɪn,seiʃə'bɪlɪti/ n insaciabilidad, f

**insatiable** /ɪn'seiʃəbəl/ a insaciable

**insatiably** /ɪn'seiʃəbli/ adv insaciablemente

**inscribe** /ɪn'skraib/ vt inscribir

**inscription** /ɪn'skrɪpʃən/ n inscripción, f; letrero, m; (of a book) dedicatoria, f; Com. inscripción, anotación, f, asiento, m

**inscrutability** /ɪn,skrutə'bɪlɪti/ n enigma, misterio, m; incomprensibilidad, f

**inscrutable** /ɪn'skrutəbəl/ a enigmático, insondable, incomprensible, inescrutable

**inscrutably** /ɪn'skrutəbli/ adv incomprensiblemente, enigmáticamente

**insect** /'ɪnsɛkt/ n insecto, m. **i. powder,** polvos insecticidas, m pl

**insecticide** /ɪn'sɛktə,said/ a and n insecticida m.

**insecure** /ˌɪnsɪ'kyʊr/ a inseguro, precario

**insecurely** /ˌɪnsɪ'kyʊrli/ adv inseguramente

**insecurity** /ˌɪnsɪ'kyʊrɪti/ n inseguridad, f; incertidumbre, inestabilidad, f

**inseminate** /ɪn'sɛmə,neit/ vt Fig. implantar; Med. fecundar

**insemination** /ɪn,sɛmə'neiʃən/ n Fig. implantación, f; Med. fecundación, f

**insensate** /ɪn'sɛnseit/ a (unfeeling) insensible, insensitivo; (stupid) insensato, sin sentido, necio

**insensibility** /ɪn,sɛnsə'bɪlɪti/ n insensibilidad, inconsciencia, f; (stupor) sopor, letargo, m; impasibilidad, indiferencia, f

**insensible** /ɪn'sɛnsəbəl/ a insensible, inconsciente; indiferente, impasible, duro de corazón; (scarcely noticeable) imperceptible. **to make i.,** (to sensations) hacer indiferente (a); insensibilizar

**insensibly** /ɪn'sɛnsəbli/ adv insensiblemente, imperceptiblemente

**insensitive** /ɪn'sɛnsɪtɪv/ a insensible, insensitivo; (person) hecho un tronco, hecho un leño

**insensitiveness** /ɪn'sɛnsɪtɪvnɪs/ n insensibilidad, f

**insentient** /ɪn'sɛnʃiənt/ a insensible

**inseparability** /ɪn,sɛpərə'bɪlɪti/ n inseparabilidad, f

**inseparable** /ɪn'sɛpərəbəl/ a inseparable

**inseparably** /ɪn'sɛpərəbli/ adv inseparablemente

**insert** /ɪn'sɜrt/ vt insertar, intercalar; (introduce) meter dentro, introducir, encajar; (in a newspaper) publicar

**insertion** /ɪn'sɜrʃən/ n inserción, intercalación, f; (introduction) introducción, f; metimiento, encaje, m; Sew. entredós, m; (in a newspaper) publicación, f

**inshore** /'ɪn'ʃɔr/ a cercano a la orilla. —adv cerca de la orilla. **i. fishing,** pesca de arrastre, f

**inside** /ˌɪn'said/ a interior, interno. —adv adentro,

dentro. —n interior, m; (contents) contenido, m; (lining) forro, m; (Inf. stomach) entrañas, f pl. **to turn i. out,** volver al revés. **to walk on the i. of the pavement,** andar a la derecha de la acera. **from the i.,** desde el interior; por dentro. **on the i.,** por dentro, en el interior. **i. information,** información confidencial, f. **i. out,** al revés, de dentro afuera

**insidious** /ɪn'sɪdiəs/ a insidioso, enganoso, traidor

**insidiously** /ɪn'sɪdiəsli/ adv insidiosamente

**insidiousness** /ɪn'sɪdiəsnɪs/ n insidia, f; engaño, m, traición, f

**insight** /'ɪn,sait/ n percepción, perspicacia, intuición, f. atisbo, m

**insignia** /ɪn'sɪgniə/ n pl insignias, f pl

**insignificance** /ˌɪnsɪg'nɪfɪkəns/ n insignificancia, futilidad, pequeñez, f

**insignificant** /ˌɪnsɪg'nɪfɪkənt/ a insignificante; fútil, trivial

**insincere** /ˌɪnsɪn'sɪr/ a insincero, hipócrita, falso

**insincerely** /ˌɪnsɪn'sɪrli/ adv falsamente, hipócritamente

**insincerity** /ˌɪnsɪn'sɛrɪti/ n insinceridad, hipocresía, falsedad, falta de sinceridad, doblez, f

**insinuate** /ɪn'sɪnyu,eit/ vt insinuar, introducir; (hint) soltar una indirecta, sugerir; (oneself) insinuarse, introducirse con habilidad

**insinuation** /ɪn,sɪnyu'eiʃən/ n insinuación, introducción, f; (hint) indirecta, f

**insipid** /ɪn'sɪpɪd/ a insípido, insulso; (dull) soso

**insipidity** /ˌɪnsə'pɪdɪti/ n insipidez, insulsez, f, desabor, m; (dullness) sosería, f

**insist** /ɪn'sɪst/ vi insistir; persistir, obstinarse. **to i. on,** insistir en; obstinarse en, hacer hincapié en, aferrarse en (or a)

**insistence** /ɪn'sɪstəns/ n insistencia, f; obstinación, pertinacia, f

**insistent** /ɪn'sɪstənt/ a insistente; porfiado, obstinaz

**insistently** /ɪn'sɪstəntli/ adv con insistencia; porfiadamente

**insobriety** /ˌɪnsə'braiɪti/ n falta de sobriedad, f; embriaguez, ebriedad, f

**insole** /'ɪn,soul/ n (of shoes) plantilla, f

**insolence** /'ɪnsələns/ n insolencia, altanería, majadería, frescura, f, atrevimiento, descaro, m

**insolent** /'ɪnsələnt/ a insolente, arrogante, atrevido, descarado, desmesurado, fresco

**insolently** /'ɪnsələntli/ adv insolentemente, con descaro

**insolubility** /ɪn,sɒlyə'bɪlɪti/ n insolubilidad, f

**insoluble** /ɪn'sɒlyəbəl/ a insoluble

**insolvency** /ɪn'sɒlvənsi/ n in olvencia, f

**insolvent** /ɪn'sɒlvənt/ a insolvente

**insomnia** /ɪn'sɒmniə/ n insomnio, m

**insomuch** /ˌɪnsə'mʌtʃ/ adv (gen. with as or that) de modo (que), así (que), de suerte (que)

**inspect** /ɪn'spɛkt/ vt examinar, investigar, inspeccionar; (officially) registrar, reconocer

**inspection** /ɪn'spɛkʃən/ n inspección, investigación, f; examen, m; (official) reconocimiento, registro, m

**inspector** /ɪn'spɛktər/ n inspector, m, veedor, interventor, m

**inspectorate** /ɪn'spɛktərɪt/ n inspectorado, m; cargo de inspector, m

**inspiration** /ˌɪnspə'reiʃən/ n (of breath) inspiración, aspiración, f; numen, m, inspiración, vena, f. **to find i. in,** inspirarse en.

**inspire** /ɪn'spaiᵊr/ vt (inhale) aspirar, inspirar; (stimulate) animar, alentar, iluminar; (suggest) sugerir, inspirar; infundir. **to i. enthusiasm,** entusiasmar. **to i. hope,** dar esperanza, esperanzar

**inspired** /ɪn'spaiᵊrd/ a inspirado, intuitivo, iluminado; (of genius) genial

**inspirer** /ɪn'spaiᵊrər/ n inspirador (-ra)

**inspiring** /ɪn'spaiᵊrɪŋ/ a alentador, animador; inspirador

**inspirit** /ɪn'spɪrɪt/ vt alentar, inspirar, estimular, animar

**inspiriting** /ɪn'spɪrɪtɪŋ/ a alentador, estimulador

**instability** /ˌɪnstə'bɪlɪti/ n inestabilidad, mutabilidad, inconstancia, f

**install** /ɪn'stɔl/ *vt* (all meanings) instalar. **to i. one-self,** instalarse, establecerse

**installation** /ˌɪnstə'leiʃən/ *n* (all meanings) instalación, *f*

**installment** /ɪn'stɔlmənt/ *n* (of a story) entrega, *f; Com.* plazo, *m,* cuota, *f.* **by installments,** *Com.* a plazos. **i. plan,** pago a plazos, pago por cuotas, *m*

**instance** /'ɪnstəns/ *n* ejemplo, caso, *m;* (request) solicitación, *f,* ruego, *m; Law.* instancia, *f.* —*vt* citar como ejemplo, mencionar; demostrar, probar. **for i.,** por ejemplo, verbigracia. **in that i....,** en el caso... **in the first i.,** en primer lugar, primero

**instant** /'ɪnstənt/ *a* immediato, urgente; *Com.* corriente, actual. —*n* instante, momento, *m; Inf.* tris, santiamén, *m. Com.* **the 2nd i.,** el 2º (segundo) del corriente. **this i.,** (immediately) en seguida

**instantaneous** /ˌɪnstən'teiniəs/ *a* instantáneo. *Photo.* **i. exposure,** instantánea, *f*

**instantaneously** /ˌɪnstən'teiniəsli/ *adv* instantáneamente

**instantaneousness** /ˌɪnstən'teiniəsnɪs/ *n* instantaneidad, *f*

**instantly** /'ɪnstəntli/ *adv* en seguida, al instante, inmediatamente

**instead** /ɪn'stɛd/ *adv* en cambio; (with of) en vez de, en lugar de

**instep** /'ɪnˌstɛp/ *n* empeine, *m*

**instigate** /'ɪnstɪˌgeit/ *vt* instigar, incitar, aguijar, animar, provocar; fomentar

**instigating** /'ɪnstɪˌgeitɪŋ/ *a* instigador, provocador, fomentador

**instigation** /ˌɪnstɪ'geiʃən/ *n* instigación, incitación, *f;* estímulo, *m*

**instigator** /'ɪnstɪˌgeitər/ *n* instigador (-ra), provocador (-ra), fomentador (-ra)

**instill** /ɪn'stɪl/ *vt* instilar; (ideas) inculcar, infundir

**instillment** /ɪn'stɪlmənt/ *n* inculcación, implantación, insinuación, *f*

**instinct** /'ɪnstɪŋkt/ *n* instinto, *m.* **i. with,** imbuido de, lleno de. **by i.,** por instinto, movido por instinto

**instinctive** /ɪn'stɪŋktɪv/ *a* instintivo, espontáneo

**instinctively** /ɪn'stɪŋktɪvli/ *adv* por instinto

**institute** /'ɪnstɪˌtut/ *vt* instituir, fundar, establecer; (an inquiry) iniciar, empezar. —*n* instituto, *m; pl* **institutes,** *Law.* instituta, *f*

**institution** /ˌɪnstɪ'tuʃən/ *n* (creation) fundación, creación, *f;* institución, *f,* instituto, *m;* (beginning) comienzo, *m,* iniciación, *f;* (charitable) asilo, *m;* (custom) uso, *m,* costumbre, tradición, *f*

**institutional** /ˌɪnstɪ'tuʃənl/ *a* institucional

**instruct** /ɪn'strʌkt/ *vt* (teach) instruir, enseñar; (order) mandar, dar orden (a)

**instruction** /ɪn'strʌkʃən/ *n* (teaching) instrucción, enseñanza, *f; pl* **instructions,** (orders) instrucciones, *f pl* orden, *f,* mandato, *m*

**instructive** /ɪn'strʌktɪv/ *a* instructivo, instructor, informativo

**instructively** /ɪn'strʌktɪvli/ *adv* instructivamente

**instructiveness** /ɪn'strʌktɪvnɪs/ *n* el carácter informativo, lo instructivo

**instructor** /ɪn'strʌktər/ *n* instructor, preceptor, *m*

**instrument** /'ɪnstrəmənt/ *n* instrumento, *m;* (tool) herramienta, *f,* utensilio, aparato, *m;* (agent) órgano, agente, medio, *m; Law.* instrumento, *m,* escritura, *f.* —*vt Mus.* instrumentar. **percussion i.,** instrumento de percusión, *m.* **scientific i.,** instrumento científico, *m.* **stringed i.,** instrumento de cuerda, *m.* **wind i.,** instrumento de viento, *m*

**instrumental** /ˌɪnstrə'mɛntl/ *a* instrumental; influyente. **to be i. in,** contribuir a

**instrumentalist** /ˌɪnstrə'mɛntlɪst/ *n Mus.* instrumentista, *m*

**instrumentality** /ˌɪnstrəmən'tælɪti/ *n* mediación, intervención, agencia, *f,* buenos oficios, *m pl*

**instrumentation** /ˌɪnstrəmən'teiʃən/ *n Mus.* instrumentación, *f;* mediación, *f*

**insubordinate** /ˌɪnsə'bɔrdnɪt/ *a* insubordinado, rebelde, desobediente, refractario

**insubordination** /ˌɪnsəˌbɔrdn̩'eiʃən/ *n* insubordinación, rebeldía, desobediencia, *f*

**insubstantial** /ˌɪnsəb'stænʃəl/ *a* irreal; insubstancial

**insubstantiality** /ˌɪnsəbˌstænʃi'ælɪti/ *n* irrealidad, *f;* insubstancialidad, *f*

**insufferable** /ɪn'sʌfərəbəl/. See **intolerable**

**insufficiency** /ˌɪnsə'fɪʃənsi/ *n* insuficiencia, falta, carestía, *f*

**insufficient** /ˌɪnsə'fɪʃənt/ *a* insuficiente, falto. **"I. Postage,"** «Falta de franqueo»

**insufficiently** /ˌɪnsə'fɪʃəntli/ *adv* insuficientemente

**insular** /'ɪnsələr/ *a* isleño, insular; (narrow-minded) intolerante, iliberal

**insularity** /ˌɪnsə'lɛarɪti/ *n* carácter isleño, *m;* (narrow-mindedness) iliberalidad, intolerancia, *f*

**insulate** /'ɪnsəˌleit/ *vt* aislar

**insulating** /'ɪnsəˌleitɪŋ/ *a* aislador. **i. tape,** *Elec.* cinta aisladora, *f*

**insulation** /ˌɪnsə'leiʃən/ *n* aislamiento, *m*

**insulator** /'ɪnsəˌleitər/ *n Elec.* aislador, *m*

**insulin** /'ɪnsəlɪn/ *n Med.* insulina, *f*

**insult** /*n.* 'ɪnsʌlt; *v.* ɪn'sʌlt/ *n* insulto, agravio, ultraje, *m,* afrenta, ofensa, *f.* —*vt* insultar, ofender, afrentar. **He was insulted,** Fue insultado; Se mostró ofendido

**insulter** /ɪn'sʌltər/ *n* insultador (-ra)

**insulting** /ɪn'sʌltɪŋ/ *a* insultante, injurioso, ofensivo. **He was very i. to them,** Les insultó, Les trató con menosprecio

**insultingly** /ɪn'sʌltɪŋli/ *adv* con insolencia, ofensivamente

**insuperability** /ɪnˌsupərə'bɪlɪti/ *n* dificultades insuperables, *f pl,* imposibilidad, *f,* lo insuperable

**insuperable** /ɪn'supərəbəl/ *a* insuperable, invencible

**insuperably** /ɪn'supərəbli/ *adv* invenciblemente

**insupportable** /ˌɪnsə'pɔrtəbəl/ *a* insoportable, inaguantable, intolerable, insufrible

**insupportably** /ˌɪnsə'pɔrtəbli/ *adv* insufriblemente, insoportablemente

**insurable** /ɪn'ʃʊrəbəl/ *a* asegurable

**insurance** /ɪn'ʃʊrəns/ *n* aseguramiento, *m; Com.* seguro, *m;* aseguración, *f.* **accident i.,** seguro contra accidentes, *m.* **fire-i.,** seguro contra incendio, *m.* **life i.,** seguro sobre la vida, *m.* **maritime i.,** seguro marítimo, *m.* **National I. Act,** Ley del Seguro Nacional Obligatorio, *f.* **i. broker,** corredor de seguros, *m.* **i. company,** compañía de seguros, *f.* **i. policy,** póliza de seguros, *f.* **i. premium,** prima de seguros, *f*

**insure** /ɪn'ʃʊr, -'ʃɜr/ *vt Com.* asegurar. **to i. oneself,** asegurarse. **the insured,** (person) el asegurado

**insurer** /ɪn'ʃʊrər/ *n* asegurador (-ra)

**insurgent** /ɪn'sɜrdʒənt/ *a* insurgente, rebelde; (of sea) invasor. —*n* rebelde, *mf* insurrecto (-ta)

**insurmountable** /ˌɪnsər'mauntəbəl/ *a* insalvable, insuperable, invencible, intransitable

**insurrection** /ˌɪnsə'rɛkʃən/ *n* insurrección, sublevación, *f,* levantamiento, *m*

**insurrectionary** /ˌɪnsə'rɛkʃəˌnɛri/ *a* rebelde, amotinado, insurgente

**insusceptible** /ˌɪnsə'sɛptəbəl/ *a* no susceptible, indiferente, insensible

**intact** /ɪn'tækt/ *a* intacto, íntegro, indemne

**intake** /'ɪnˌteik/ *n* (of a stocking) menguado, *m; Mech.* aspiración, *f;* válvula de admisión, *f; Aer.* admisión, toma, *f;* orificio de entrada, *m*

**intangibility** /ɪnˌtændʒə'bɪlɪti/ *n* intangibilidad, *f*

**intangible** /ɪn'tændʒəbəl/ *a* intangible; incomprensible

**integer** /'ɪntɪdʒər/ *n Math.* número entero, *m*

**integral** /'ɪntɪgrəl/ *a* íntegro, intrínseco, inherente; *Math.* entero. —*n Math.* integral, *f.* **i. calculus,** cálculo integral, *m*

**integrate** /'ɪntɪˌgreit/ *vt* integrar, completar; formar en un todo; *Math.* integrar

**integrity** /ɪn'tɛgrɪti/ *n* integridad, honradez, rectitud, entereza, *f*

**intellect** /'ɪntlˌɛkt/ *n* intelecto, entendimiento, *m*

**intellectual** /ˌɪntl'ɛktʃuəl/ *a* intelectual, mental. —*n* intelectual

**intellectualism** /ˌɪntl'ɛktʃuəˌlɪzəm/ *n* intelectualismo, *m,* intelectualidad, *f*

**intellectually** /ˌɪntl'ɛktʃuəli/ *adv* intelectualmente, mentalmente

**intelligence** /ɪn'tɛlɪdʒəns/ *n* inteligencia, comprensión, mente, *f;* (quickness of mind) agudeza, perspi-

cacia, *f;* (news) noticia, *f,* conocimiento, informe, *m.*
**the latest i.,** las últimas noticias. **i. quotient,** cociente de inteligencia, *m.* **I. Service,** Inteligencia, *f;*
policía secreta, *f.* **i. test,** prueba de inteligencia, *f*
**intelligent** /ɪn'telɪdʒənt/ *a* inteligente
**intelligentsia** /ɪnˌtelɪ'dʒentsiə/ *n* clase intelectual, intelectualidad, *f, Inf.* masa cefálica, *f*
**intelligibility** /ɪnˌtelɪdʒə'bɪlɪti/ *n* comprensibilidad, inteligibilidad, *f*
**intelligible** /ɪn'telɪdʒəbəl/ *a* inteligible, comprensible
**intelligibly** /ɪn'telɪdʒəbəl/ *adv* inteligiblemente
**intemperance** /ɪn'tempərəns/ *n* intemperancia, inmoderación, *f;* exceso en la bebida, *m*
**intemperate** /ɪn'tempərɪt/ *a* intemperante, destemplado, descomedido; inmoderado; bebedor en exceso
**intemperately** /ɪn'tempərɪtli/ *adv* inmoderadamente
**intend** /ɪn'tend/ *vt* intentar, proponerse, pensar; destinar, dedicar; (mean) querer decir. **to be intended,**
estar destinado; tener por fin; querer decir
**intendant** /ɪn'tendənt/ *n* intendente, *m*
**intended** /ɪn'tendɪd/ *a* pensado, deseado. —*n Inf.*
novio (-ia), futuro (-ra), prometido (-da)
**intense** /ɪn'tens/ *a* intenso, vivo, fuerte; (of emotions) profundo, hondo, vehemente; (of colors) subido, intenso; (great) extremado, sumo, muy grande
**intensification** /ɪnˌtensəfɪ'keɪʃən/ *n* intensificación, *f;*
aumento, *m*
**intensify** /ɪn'tensə,faɪ/ *vt* intensar, intensificar; aumentar
**intensity** /ɪn'tensɪti/ *n* intensidad, fuerza, *f;* (of emotions) profundidad, vehemencia, violencia, *f;* (of
colors) intensidad, *f*
**intensive** /ɪn'tensɪv/ *a* intensivo
**intensive-care unit** /ɪn'tensɪv'keər/ *n* sala de terapia
intensiva, unidad de cuidados intensivos, unidad de
vigilancia intensiva, *f*
**intent** /ɪn'tent/ *n* intento, propósito, deseo, *m.* —*a*
atento; (absorbed) absorto, interesado; (on doing) resuelto a, decidido a. **to all intents and purposes,** en
efecto, en realidad. **to be i. on,** (reading, etc.) estar
absorto en, entregarse a. **with i. to defraud,** con el
propósito deliberado de defraudar
**intention** /ɪn'tenʃən/ *n* intención, voluntad, *f,* propósito, pensamiento, proyecto, *m*
**intentional** /ɪn'tenʃənl/ *a* intencional, deliberado,
premeditado
**intentionally** /ɪn'tenʃənli/ *adv* a propósito, intencionalmente, de pensado
**intentioned** /ɪn'tenʃənd/ *a* intencionado
**intently** /ɪn'tentli/ *adv* atentamente
**inter** /ɪn'tɜr/ *vt* enterrar, sepultar
**inter-** *prefix* inter, entre. **i.-allied,** interaliado, de los
aliados. **i.-denominational,** intersectario. **i.-
university,** interuniversitario. **i.-urban,** interurbano
**interaction** /ˌɪntər'ækʃən/ *n* interacción, acción recí-
proca, acción mutua, *f*
**intercalate** /ɪn'tɜrkə,leɪt/ *vt* intercalar, interpolar
**intercede** /ˌɪntər'sid/ *vi* interceder, mediar. **to i. for,**
hablar por
**intercept** /ˌɪntər'sept/ *vt* interceptar, detener; entrecoger, atajar
**interception** /ˌɪntər'sepʃən/ *n* interceptación, detención, *f*
**intercession** /ˌɪntər'seʃən/ *n* mediación, intercesión, *f*
**intercessor** /ˌɪntər'sesər/ *n* intercesor (-ra), mediador
(-ra)
**interchange** /*n.* 'ɪntərˌtʃeɪndʒ; *v.* ˌɪntər'tʃendʒ/ *n* intercambio, *f;* (of goods) comercio, tráfico, *m.* —*vt*
cambiar, trocar; alternar
**interchangeable** /ˌɪntər'tʃeɪndʒəbəl/ *a* intercambiable
**intercom** /'ɪntərˌkɒm/ *n* teléfono interior, *m*
**intercommunicate** /ˌɪntərkə'myunɪˌkeɪt/ *vi* comunicarse
**intercommunication** /ˌɪntərkəˌmyunɪ'keɪʃən/ *n*
comunicación mutua, *f;* comercio, *m*
**intercostal** /ˌɪntər'kɒstl/ *a Anat.* intercostal
**intercourse** /'ɪntərˌkɔrs/ *n* (social) trato, *m,* relaciones, *f pl; Com.* comercio, tráfico, *m;* (of ideas) intercambio, *m;* (sexual) coito, trato sexual, *m*
**interdependence** /ˌɪntərdɪ'pendənt/ *n* dependencia
mutua, mutualidad, *f*
**interdependent** /ˌɪntərdɪ'pendənt/ *a* mutuo

**interdict** /*n* 'ɪntərˌdɪkt; *v* ˌɪntər'dɪkt/ *n* interdicto,
veto, *m,* prohibición, *f; Eccl.* entredicho, *m.* —*vt*
interdecir, prohibir, privar; *Eccl.* poner entredicho
**interdiction** /ˌɪntər'dɪkʃən/ *n* interdicción, prohibición, *f*
**interest** /'ɪntərɪst/ *n* interés, *m;* provecho, *m; Com.*
premio, rédito, interés, *m;* (in a firm) participación, *f;*
(curiosity) interés, *m;* curiosidad, *f;* simpatía, *f;* (influence) influencia, *f.* —*n pl* **interests,** (commercial
undertakings) empresas, *f pl,* intereses, negocios, *m
pl.* —*vt* interesar. **to be interested in,** interesarse en,
(on behalf of) por. **to be in one's own i.,** ser en provecho de uno, ser en su propio interés. **to bear eight
per cent. i.,** dar interés del ocho por ciento. **to pay
with i.,** pagar con creces. **to put out at i.,** dar a interés. **in the interests of,** en interés de. **compound
i.,** interés compuesto, *m.* **simple i.,** interés sencillo,
*m.* **vested interests,** intereses creados, *m pl*
**interesting** /'ɪntərəstɪŋ/ *a* interesante, curioso, atractivo
**interestingly** /'ɪntərəstɪŋli/ *adv* amenamente, de
modo interesante
**interfere** /ˌɪntər'fɪər/ *vi* intervenir, meterse, entremeterse, mezclarse; *Inf.* mangonear, meter las narices; (with) meterse con; (impede) estorbar, impedir
**interference** /ˌɪntər'fɪərəns/ *n* intervención, *f,* entrometimiento, *m;* (obstacle) estorbo, obstáculo, *m;*
*Phys.* interferencia, *f; Radio.* parásitos, *m pl*
**interfering** /ˌɪntər'fɪərɪŋ/ *a* entremetido, oficioso; *Inf.*
mangoneador
**interim** /'ɪntərəm/ *n* ínterin, intermedio, *m.* —*a*
interino, provisional. **in the i.,** entre tanto, en el ínterin. *Com.* **i. dividend,** dividendo interino, *m*
**interior** /ɪn'tɪəriər/ *a* interior, interno; doméstico. —*n*
interior, *m*
**interject** /ˌɪntər'dʒekt/ *vt* interponer
**interjection** /ˌɪntər'dʒekʃən/ *n* exclamación, interjección, *f;* interposición, *f*
**interlace** /ˌɪntər'leɪs/ *vt* entrelazar, entretejer
**interleave** /ˌɪntər'liv/ *vt* interfoliar, interpaginar
**interline** /'ɪntərˌlaɪn/ *vt* entrerrenglonar, interlinear
**interlinear** /ˌɪntər'lɪniər/ *a* interlineal
**interlineation** /ˌɪntərˌlɪni'eɪʃən/ *n* interlineación, *f*
**interlining** /'ɪntərˌlaɪnɪŋ/ *n* entretela, *f*
**interlock** /ˌɪntər'lɒk/ *vt* (of wheels, etc.). endentar;
trabar; cerrar. —*vi* endentarse; entrelazarse, unirse;
cerrar
**interlocutor** /ˌɪntər'lɒkyətər/ *n* interlocutor (-ra)
**interloper** /'ɪntərˌloupər/ *n* intruso (-sa); *Com.* intérlope, *m*
**interloping** /ˌɪntər'loupɪŋ/ *a* intérlope
**interlude** /'ɪntərˌlud/ *n* intervalo, intermedio, *m;*
*Mus.* interludio, *m; Theat.* entremés, *m*
**intermarriage** /ˌɪntər'mærɪdʒ/ *n* casamiento entre
parientes próximos, entre razas distintas, o entre
grupos étnicos distintos, *m*
**intermarry** /ˌɪntər'mæri/ *vi* contraer matrimonio entre
parientes próximos, entre personas de razas distintas,
o entre grupos étnicos distintos
**intermediary** /ˌɪntər'midiˌeri/ *a and n* intermediario
(-ia)
**intermediate** /ˌɪntər'midiˌeit/ *a* intermedio, medio,
medianero. —*n* sustancia intermedia, *f.* —*vi*
intervenir, mediar
**interment** /ɪn'tɜrmənt/ *n* entierro, *m*
**intermezzo** /ˌɪntər'metsou/ *n Theat.* intermedio, *m;*
*Mus.* intermezzo, *m*
**interminable** /ɪn'tɜrmənəbəl/ *a* interminable, inacabable
**interminably** /ɪn'tɜrmənəbli/ *adv* interminablemente,
sin fin, sin cesar
**intermingle** /ˌɪntər'mɪŋgəl/ *vt* entremezclar, entreverar. —*vi* mezclarse
**intermission** /ˌɪntər'mɪʃən/ *n* intermisión, interrupción, pausa, *f; Theat.* entreacto, *m.* **without i.,** sin
pausa, sin tregua
**intermittence** /ˌɪntər'mɪtns/ *n* intermitencia, alternación, *f*
**intermittent** /ˌɪntər'mɪtnt/ *a* intermitente, discontinuo; (of fever) intermitente
**intermittently** /ˌɪntər'mɪtntli/ *adv* a intervalos, a ratos, a pausas

**intern** /ɪn'tɜrn/ *n Med.* practicante de hospital *m*, interno (-na), interno de hospital, alumno interno, *m*.
—*vt* confinar, encerrar
**internal** /ɪn'tɜrnḷ/ *a* interno, interior; (of affairs) doméstico, civil; intrínseco; íntimo. **i.-combustion engine,** motor de combustión interna, *m*
**internally** /ɪn'tɜrnḷi/ *adv* interiormente
**international** /ˌɪntər'næʃənḷ/ *a* internacional. —*n Sports.* un partido internacional. **i. law,** derecho internacional, *m*
**internationalism** /ˌɪntər'næʃənḷ,ɪzəm/ *n* internacionalismo, *m*
**internationalist** /ˌɪntər'næʃənḷɪst/ *n* internacionalista, *mf*
**internationalization** /ˌɪntər,næʃənḷə'zeɪʃən/ *n* internacionalización, *f*
**internationalize** /ˌɪntər'næʃənḷ,aɪz/ *vt* hacer internacional, poner bajo un control internacional
**internecine** /ˌɪntər'nisin/ *a* sanguinario, feroz
**internee** /ˌɪntər'ni/ *n* internado (-da)
**Internet, the** /'ɪntər,nɛt/ *n* el Internet, *m*
**internment** /ɪn'tɜrnmənt/ *n* internamiento, *m*. **i. camp,** campo de internamiento, *m*
**interoceanic** /ˌɪntər,ouʃi'ænɪk/ *a* interoceánico
**interpolate** /ɪn'tɜrpə,leɪt/ *vt* interpolar, intercalar, interponer
**interpolation** /ɪn,tɜrpə'leɪʃən/ *n* interpolación, inserción, añadidura, *f*
**interpolator** /ɪn'tɜrpə,leɪtər/ *n* interpolador (-ra)
**interpose** /ˌɪntər'pouz/ *vt* interponer; (a remark) interpolar. —*vi* interponerse, intervenir; (interfere) entrometerse; interrumpir
**interposition** /ˌɪntərpə'zɪʃən/ *n* interposición, *f*; entrometimiento, *m*
**interpret** /ɪn'tɜrprɪt/ *vt* interpretar; (translate) traducir; (explain) explicar, descifrar. —*vi* interpretar.
**interpretation** /ɪn,tɜrprɪ'teɪʃən/ *n* interpretación, *f*; (translation) traducción, *f*; (explanation) explicación, *f*
**interpretative** /ɪn'tɜrprɪ,tʃitɪv/ *a* interpretativo, interpretador
**interpreter** /ɪn'tɜrprɪtər/ *n* intérprete, *mf*
**interregnum** /ˌɪntər'rɛgnəm/ *n* interregno, *m*
**interrelation** /ˌɪntərrɪ'leɪʃən/ *n* relación mutua, *f*
**interrogate** /ɪn'tɛrə,geɪt/ *vt* interrogar, examinar, preguntar
**interrogating** /ɪn'tɛrə,geɪtɪŋ/ *a* interrogante
**interrogation** /ɪn,tɛrə'geɪʃən/ *n* interrogación, *f*, examen, *m*; pregunta, *f*. **mark of i.,** punto de interrogación, *m*
**interrogative** /ˌɪntə'rɒgətɪv/ *a* interrogativo. —*n* palabra interrogativa, *f*
**interrogatively** /ˌɪntə'rɒgətɪvli/ *adv* interrogativamente
**interrogator** /ɪn'tɛrə'getər/ *n* examinador (-ra), interrogador (-ra)
**interrogatory** /ˌɪntə'rɒgə,tɔri/ *a* interrogativo. —*n* interrogatorio, *m*
**interrupt** /ˌɪntə'rʌpt/ *vt* interrumpir
**interruptedly** /ˌɪntə'rʌptɪdli/ *adv* interrumpidamente
**interrupter** /ˌɪntə'rʌptər/ *n* interruptor (-ra); *Elec.* interruptor, *m*
**interruption** /ˌɪntə'rʌpʃən/ *n* interrupción, *f*
**intersect** /ˌɪntər'sɛkt/ *vt* cruzar. —*vi* cruzarse, intersecarse
**intersection** /ˌɪntər'sɛkʃən/ *n* intersección, *f*; cruce, *m*, (of streets) bocacalle, *f*
**intersperse** /ˌɪntər'spɜrs/ *vt* diseminar, esparcir; interpolar, entremezclar
**interstice** /ɪn'tɜrstɪs/ *n* intervalo, intermedio, *m*; (chink) intersticio, *m*, hendedura, *f*
**intertwine** /ˌɪntər'twaɪn/ *vt* entretejer, entrelazar. —*vi* entrelazarse
**interval** /'ɪntərvəl/ *n* intervalo, intermedio, *m*, pausa, *f*; *Theat.* entreacto, *m*, intermisión, *f*; (in schools) recreo, *m*. **at intervals,** a trechos, de vez en cuando. **lucid i.,** intervalo claro, intervalo lúcido, *m*
**intervene** /ˌɪntər'vin/ *vi* intervenir, tomar parte (en); mediar; (occur) sobrevenir, acaecer; *Law.* interponerse
**intervening** /ˌɪntər'vinɪŋ/ *a* intermedio; interventor

**intervention** /ˌɪntər'vɛnʃən/ *n* intervención, mediación, *f*
**interventionist** /ˌɪntər'vɛnʃənɪst/ *n Polit.* partidario (-ia) de la intervención
**interview** /'ɪntər,vyu/ *n* entrevista, *f*, interviev, *m*. —*vt* entrevistarse con
**interviewer** /'ɪntər,vyuər/ *n* interrogador (-ra); (reporter) reportero, periodista, *m*
**interweave** /ˌɪntər'wiv/ *vt* entretejer, entrelazar
**interweaving** /ˌɪntər'wivɪŋ/ *n* entretejimiento, *m*
**intestacy** /ɪn'tɛstəsi/ *n* ausencia de un testamento, *f*
**intestate** /ɪn'tɛsteɪt/ *a* and *n* intestado (-da)
**intestinal** /ɪn'tɛstənḷ/ *a* intestinal, intestino. **i. worm,** lombriz intestinal, *f*
**intestine** /ɪn'tɛstɪn/ *n* intestino, *m*. **large i.,** intestino grueso, *m*. **small i.,** intestino delgado, *m*
**intimacy** /'ɪntəməsi/ *n* intimidad, *f*, familiaridad, *f*; (of nobility and others) privanza, *f*
**intimate** /'ɪntəmɪt/ *a* íntimo; (of relations) entrañable, estrecho; intrínseco, esencial; (of knowledge) profundo, completo, detallado. —*n* amigo (-ga) de confianza. —*vt* intimar, dar a entender, indicar. **to become i.,** intimarse. **to be on i. terms with,** tratar de tú (a), ser amigo íntimo de
**intimately** /'ɪntəmɪtli/ *adv* íntimamente, al fondo
**intimation** /ˌɪntə'meɪʃən/ *n* intimación, indicación, *f*; (hint) insinuación, indirecta, *f*
**intimidate** /ɪn'tɪmɪ,deɪt/ *vt* intimidar, aterrar, infundir miedo (a), espantar, acobardar, amedrentar
**intimidation** /ɪn,tɪmɪ'deɪʃən/ *n* intimidación, *f*
**intimidatory** /ɪn'tɪmɪdə,tɔri/ *a* aterrador, amenazador
**into** /'ɪntu; *unstressed* -tʊ, -tə/ *prep* en; a, al, a la; dentro, adentro; (of transforming, forming, etc.) en. **Throw it i. the fire,** Échalo al (or en el) fuego. **She went i. the house,** Entró en la casa. **to look i.,** mirar dentro de; mirar hacia el interior (de); investigar
**intolerable** /ɪn'tɒlərəbəl/ *a* intolerable, insufrible, inaguantable, insoportable, inllevable
**intolerableness** /ɪn'tɒlərəbəlnɪs/ *n* intolerabilidad, *f*
**intolerably** /ɪn'tɒlərəbli/ *adv* intolerablemente, insufriblemente
**intolerance** /ɪn'tɒlərəns/ *n* intolerancia, intransigencia, *f*
**intolerant** /ɪn'tɒlərənt/ *a* intolerante, intransigente; *Med.* intolerante
**intonation** /ˌɪntou'neɪʃən/ *n* entonación, *f*
**intone** /ɪn'toun/ *vt* entonar; *Eccl.* salmodiar
**intoxicant** /ɪn'tɒksɪkənt/ *a* embriagador. —*n* bebida alcohólica, *f*
**intoxicate** /ɪn'tɒksɪ,keɪt/ *vt* emborrachar, embriagar; *Med.* intoxicar, envenenar; (excite) embriagar, embelesar
**intoxicated** /ɪn'tɒksɪ,keɪtɪd/ *a* borracho; (excited) ebrio, embriagado; *Med.* intoxicado
**intoxicating** /ɪn'tɒksɪ,keɪtɪŋ/ *a* embriagador
**intoxication** /ɪn,tɒksɪ'keɪʃən/ *n* borrachera, embriaguez, *f*; *Med.* intoxicación, *f*, envenenamiento, *m*; (excitement) entusiasmo, *m*, ebriedad, *f*
**intractability** /ɪn,træktə'bɪlɪti/ *n* insociabilidad, hurañería, *f*
**intractable** /ɪn'træktəbəl/ *a* intratable, insociable, huraño
**intramural** /ˌɪntrə'myʊrəl/ *adv* intramuros
**intransigence** /ɪn'trænsɪdʒəns/ *n* intransigencia, intolerancia, *f*
**intransigent** /ɪn'trænsɪdʒənt/ *a* intransigente, intolerante
**intransitive** /ɪn'trænsɪtɪv/ *a* intransitivo, neutro
**intrauterine** /ˌɪntrə'yutərɪn/ *a Med.* intrauterino
**intravenous** /ˌɪntrə'vinəs/ *a Med.* intravenoso
**intrepid** /ɪn'trɛpɪd/ *a* intrépido, osado, audaz
**intrepidity** /ˌɪntrə'pɪdɪti/ *n* intrepidez, osadía, audacia, *f*
**intrepidly** /ɪn'trɛpɪdli/ *adv* intrépidamente, audazmente
**intricacy** /'ɪntrɪkəsi/ *n* intrincación, complejidad, *f*
**intricate** /'ɪntrɪkɪt/ *a* intrincado, complejo
**intricately** /'ɪntrɪkɪtli/ *adv* intrincadamente
**intrigue** /ɪn'trig/ *n. also* 'ɪntrɪg/ *n* intriga, maquinación, *f*, enredo, *m*; (amorous) lío, *m*. —*vi* intrigar, en-

redar; (amorous) tener un lío. —*vt* (interest) atraer, interesar; (with) intrigar con

**intriguer** /ɪn'trigər/ *n* intrigante, *mf.* urdemalas, *m,* enredador (-ra)

**intriguing** /ɪn'trigɪŋ/ *a* enredador; (attractive) atrayente, interesante, seductor

**intrinsic** /ɪn'trɪnsɪk/ *a* intrínseco, innato, inherente, esencial

**intrinsically** /ɪn'trɪnsɪkli/ *adv* intrínsecamente, esencialmente

**introduce** /ˌɪntrə'dus/ *vt* introducir; hacer entrar; insertar, injerir; (a person) presentar; poner de moda, introducir; (a bill) presentar; (a person to a thing) llamar la atención sobre. **Permit me to i. my friend,** Permítame que le presente mi amigo

**introduction** /ˌɪntrə'dʌkʃən/ *n* introducción, *f;* (of a book) prefacio, prólogo, *m,* advertencia, *f;* (of a person) presentación, *f;* inserción, *f*

**introductory** /ˌɪntrə'dʌktəri/ *a* introductor, preliminar, preparatorio

**intromission** /ˌɪntrə'mɪʃən/ *n* intromisión, *f*

**introspection** /ˌɪntrə'spɛkʃən/ *n* introspección, *f*

**introspective** /ˌɪntrə'spɛktɪv/ *a* introspectivo

**introversion** /ˌɪntrə'vɜrʒən/ *n Psychol.* introversión *f*

**introvert** /'ɪntrə,vɜrt/ *a* and *n Psychol.* introverso (-sa)

**intrude** /ɪn'trud/ *vt* introducir, imponer. —*vi* entremeterse, inmiscuirse. **Do I i.?** ¿Estorbo?

**intruder** /ɪn'trudər/ *n* intruso (-sa)

**intrusion** /ɪn'truʒən/ *n* intrusión, *f; Geol.* intromisión, *f*

**intrusive** /ɪn'trusɪv/ *a* intruso

**intuition** /ˌɪntu'ɪʃən/ *n* intuición, *f.* **to know by i.,** intuir, saber por intuición

**intuitive** /ɪn'tuɪtɪv/ *a* intuitivo

**inundate** /'ɪnən,deɪt/ *vt* inundar, anegar; *Fig.* abrumar

**inundation** /ˌɪnən'deɪʃən/ *n* inundación, anegación, *f; Fig.* diluvio, *m,* abundancia, *f*

**inure** /ɪn'yʊr/ *vt* endurecer, habituar

**inurement** /ɪn'yʊrmənt/ *n* habituación, *f*

**invade** /ɪn'veɪd/ *vt* invadir, irrumpir, asaltar; *Med.* invadir

**invader** /ɪn'veɪdər/ *n* invasor (-ra), acometedor (-ra), agresor (-ra)

**invading** /ɪn'veɪdɪŋ/ *a* invasor, irruptor

**invalid** /ɪn'vælɪd/ *a* inválido, nulo. **to become i.,** caducar

**invalid** /'ɪnvəlɪd/ *n* inválido (-da), enfermo (-ma). **to become an i.,** quedarse inválido. **to i. out of the army,** licenciar por invalidez. **i. carriage,** cochecillo de inválido, *m*

**invalidate** /ɪn'vælɪ,deɪt/ *vt* invalidar, anular

**invalidation** /ɪn,vælɪ'deɪʃən/ *n* invalidación, *f*

**invalidity** /ˌɪnvə'lɪdɪti/ *n* invalidez, nulidad, *f*

**invaluable** /ɪn'vælyuəbl/ *n* inestimable

**invariability** /ɪn,vɛəriə'bɪlɪti/ *n* invariabilidad, invariación, inalterabilidad, inmutabilidad, *f*

**invariable** /ɪn'vɛəriəbl/ *a* invariable, inmutable, inalterable

**invariably** /ɪn'vɛəriəbli/ *adv* invariablemente, inmutablemente

**invariant** /ɪn'vɛəriənt/ *n Math.* invariante, *m*

**invasion** /ɪn'veɪʒən/ *n* invasión, irrupción, *f; Med.* invasión, *f*

**invective** /ɪn'vɛktɪv/ *n* invectiva, diatriba, *f*

**inveigh (against)** /ɪn'veɪ/ *vi* desencadenarse (contra), prorrumpir en invectivas (contra)

**inveigle** /ɪn'veɪgl/ *vt* seducir, engatusar, persuadir

**inveiglement** /ɪn'veɪglmənt/ *n* seducción, persuasión, *f*

**invent** /ɪn'vɛnt/ *vt* inventar, descubrir, originar; (a falsehood) fingir; (create) idear, componer

**invention** /ɪn'vɛnʃən/ *n* invención, *f,* invento, descubrimiento, *m;* (imagination) ingeniosidad, inventiva, *f;* (falsehood) ficción, mentira, *f;* (finding) invención, *f,* hallazgo, *m*

**inventive** /ɪn'vɛntɪv/ *a* inventor, inventivo; ingenioso, despejado

**inventiveness** /ɪn'vɛntɪvnɪs/ *n* inventiva, *f*

**inventor** /ɪn'vɛntər/ *n* inventor (-ra), autor (-ra)

**inventory** /'ɪnvən,tɔri/ *n* inventario, *m;* descripción, *f.* —*vt* inventariar

**inverse** /ɪn'vɜrs/ *a* inverso. **i. proportion,** razón inversa, *f*

**inversely** /ɪn'vɜrsli/ *adv* inversamente, a la inversa

**inversion** /ɪn'vɜrʒən/ *n* inversión, *f,* trastrocamiento, *m; Gram.* hipérbaton, *m*

**invert** /ɪn'vɜrt/ *vt* invertir, trastornar, trastrocar. **inverted commas,** comilla, *f*

**invertebrate** /ɪn'vɜrtəbrɪt/ *a* and *n* invertebrado *m.*

**invest** /ɪn'vɛst/ *vt Com.* invertir; *Mil.* sitiar, cercar; (foll. by with) poner, cubrir con; (of qualities) conferir, otorgar, dar. —*vi* (with in) poner dinero en, echar caudal en; *Inf.* comprar

**investigable** /ɪn'vɛstɪgəbl/ *a* averiguable

**investigate** /ɪn'vɛstɪ,geɪt/ *vt* investigar, estudiar; examinar, averiguar; explorar

**investigation** /ɪn,vɛstɪ'geɪʃən/ *n* investigación, *f,* estudio, *m;* examen, *m,* averiguación, *f;* encuesta, pesquisa, *f*

**investigator** /ɪn'vɛstɪ,geɪtər/ *n* investigador (-ra); averiguador (-ra)

**investigatory** /ɪn'vɛtɪgə,tɔri/ *a* investigador

**investiture** /ɪn'vɛstɪtʃər/ *n* investidura, instalación, *f*

**investment** /ɪn'vɛstmənt/ *n* (Com. of money) inversión, *f,* empleo, *m; Mil.* cerco, *m;* (investiture) instalación, *f; pl* **investments,** *Com.* acciones, *f pl,* fondos, *m pl*

**investor** /ɪn'vɛstər/ *n* inversionista, *m;* accionista, *mf*

**inveteracy** /ɪn'vɛtərəsi/ *n* antigüedad, *f,* lo arraigado

**inveterate** /ɪn'vɛtərɪt/ *a* inveterado, antiguo, arraigado, incurable

**invidious** /ɪn'vɪdiəs/ *a* odioso, repugnante, injusto

**invidiousness** /ɪn'vɪdiəsnɪs/ *n* injusticia, *f,* lo odioso

**invigorate** /ɪn'vɪgə,reɪt/ *vt* vigorizar, dar fuerza (a), avivar

**invigorating** /ɪn'vɪgə,reɪtɪŋ/ *a* fortaleciente, fortificador, vigorizador

**invincibility** /ɪn,vɪnsə'bɪlɪti/ *n* invencibilidad, *f*

**invincible** /ɪn'vɪnsəbl/ *a* invencible, indomable; *Fig.* insuperable

**inviolability** /ɪn,vaɪələ'bɪlɪti/ *n* inviolabilidad, *f*

**inviolable** /ɪn'vaɪələbl/ *a* inviolable

**inviolate** /ɪn'vaɪəlɪt/ *a* inviolado

**invisibility** /ɪn,vɪzə'bɪlɪti/ *n* invisibilidad, *f*

**invisible** /ɪn'vɪzəbl/ *a* invisible. **i. ink,** tinta simpática, *f.* **i. mending,** zurcido invisible, *m*

**invitation** /ˌɪnvɪ'teɪʃən/ *n* invitación, *f;* convite, *m;* (card) tarjeta de invitación, *f*

**invite** /ɪn'vaɪt/ *vt* invitar, convidar; (request) pedir, rogar; (of things) incitar, tentar

**inviting** /ɪn'vaɪtɪŋ/ *a* atrayente, incitante; (of food) apetitoso; (of looks) provocativo

**invocation** /ˌɪnvə'keɪʃən/ *n* invocación, *f*

**invocatory** /ɪn'vɒkətɔri/ *a* invocatorio, invocador

**invoice** /'ɪnvɔɪs/ *n Com.* factura, *f.* —*vt* facturar. **proforma i.,** factura simulada, *f.* **shipping i.,** factura de expedición, *f.* **i. book,** libro de facturas, *m*

**invoke** /ɪn'vouk/ *vt* invocar; suplicar, implorar; (laws) acogerse (a)

**involuntarily** /ɪn,vɒlən'tɛərəli/ *adv* sin querer, involuntariamente

**involuntariness** /ɪn'vɒlən,tɛrɪnɪs/ *n* involuntariedad, *f*

**involuntary** /ɪn'vɒlən,tɛri/ *a* involuntario; instintivo, inconsciente

**involve** /ɪn'vɒlv/ *vt* (entangle) enredar, embrollar, enmarañar; (implicate) comprometer; (imply) implicar, ocasionar, suponer, traer consigo

**involved** /ɪn'vɒlvd/ *a* complejo, intrincado; (of style) confuso, obscuro

**invulnerability** /ɪn,vʌlnərə'bɪlɪti/ *n* invulnerabilidad, *f*

**invulnerable** /ɪn'vʌlnərəbl/ *a* invulnerable

**inward** /'ɪnwərd/ *a* interior, interno; íntimo, espiritual. —*adv* adentro

**inwardly** /'ɪnwərdli/ *adv* interiormente; para sí, entre sí

**inwards** /'ɪnwərdz/ *adv* hacia dentro; adentro

**iodine** /'aɪə,daɪn/ *n* yodo, *m.* **i. poisoning,** yodismo, *m*

**ion** /'aiən/ n Chem. ion, m
**Ionian** /ai'ouniən/ a and n jónico (-ca)
**Ionic** /ai'ɒnɪk/ a jónico. **i. foot** Poet. jónico, m
**iota** /ai'outə/ n (letter) iota, f; jota, pizca, f, ápice, m. **not an i.,** ni pizca
**I.O.U.** n Com. abonaré, m
**ipecacuanha** /,ɪpɪ,kækyə'wany'ə/ n ipecacuana, f
**Iranian** /ɪ'reiniən/ a and n iranio (-ia)
**Iraq** /ɪ'ræk/ Irak, m
**irascibility** /ɪ,ræsə'bɪlɪti/ n irascibilidad, iracundia, irritabilidad, f
**irascible** /ɪ'ræsəbəl/ a irascible, iracundo, irritable
**irate** /ai'reit/ a airado, colérico, enojado
**ire** /aiᵊr/ n ira, cólera, furia, f
**Ireland** /'aiᵊrlənd/ Irlanda, f
**iridescence** /,ɪrɪ'dɛsəns/ n iridiscencia, f
**iridescent** /,ɪrɪ'dɛsənt/ a iridiscente. **to look i.,** irisar, tornasolarse
**iridium** /ɪ'rɪdiəm/ n Chem. iridio, m
**iris** /'airɪs/ n Anat. iris, m; Bot. irídea, f
**Irish** /'airɪʃ/ a and n irlandés (-esa). **the I.,** los irlandeses
**Irish Sea** Mar de Irlanda, f
**irksome** /'ᵊrksəm/ a fastidioso, tedioso, aburrido
**irksomeness** /'ᵊrksəmnis/ n tedio, fastidio, aburrimiento, m
**iron** /'aiərn/ n hierro, m; (for clothes) plancha, f; (tool) utensilio, m, herramienta, f; (golf) hierro, m; pl **irons,** grillos, m pl, cadenas, f pl. —a de hierro, férreo; Fig. duro, severo. —vt (linen) planchar; (with out) allanar. **to have too many irons in the fire,** tener demasiados asuntos entre manos. **to put in irons,** echar grillos (a). **to strike while the i. is hot,** A hierro caliente batir de repente. **cast-i.,** hierro colado, m. **scrap i.,** hierro viejo, m. **sheet i.,** hierro en planchas, m. **wrought i.,** hierro dulce, m. **i. age,** edad de hierro, f. **i.-foundry,** fundición de hierro, f. **i. lung,** Med. pulmón de hierro, pulmón de acero, m. **i.-mold,** mancha de orín, f. **i. smelting furnace,** alto horno, m. **i. tonic,** Med. reconstituyente ferruginoso, m. **i. will,** voluntad de hierro, f
**ironclad** /'aiərn 'klæd/ n -,klæd/ a blindado, acorazado. —n buque de guerra blindado, acorazado, m
**ironer** /'aiərnər/ n planchador (-ra)
**ironical** /ai'rɒnɪkəl/ a irónico
**ironically** /ai'rɒnɪkli/ adv con ironía, irónicamente
**ironing** /'aiərnɪŋ/ n planchado, m; ropa por planchar, f. —a de planchar. **i. board,** tabla de planchar, f
**ironist** /'aiərnɪst/ n ironista, mf
**ironmonger** /'aiərn,mʌŋgər/ n ferretero (-ra). **ironmonger's shop,** ferretería, f
**ironmongery** /'aiərn,mʌŋgəri/ n ferretería, quincallería, f
**iron sulphide** sulfuro de hierro, m
**ironwork** /'aiərn,wɜrk/ n herraje, m; obra de hierro, f
**ironworks** /'aiərn,wɜrks/ n herrería, f
**irony** /'airəni/ n ironía, f. —a (like iron) ferrugiento
**Iroquois** /'ɪrə,kwɔi/ a and n iroqués (-esa)
**irradiate** /ɪ'reidi,eit/ vt irradiar; Fig. iluminar, aclarar
**irradiation** /ɪ,reidi'eiʃən/ n irradiación, f; Fig. iluminación, f
**irrational** /ɪ'ræʃənl/ a ilógico, ridículo, irracional
**irrationality** /ɪ,ræʃə'nælɪti/ n irracionalidad, f
**irreclaimable** /,ɪrɪ'kleiməbəl/ a irrecuperable, irredimible; (of land) inservible, improductivo; irreformable
**irreconcilable** /ɪ'rɛkən,sailəbəl/ a irreconciliable
**irreconcilably** /ɪ'rɛkən,sailəbli/ adv irremediablemente
**irrecoverable** /,ɪrɪ'kʌvərəbəl/ a irrecuperable, incobrable
**irredeemable** /,ɪrɪ'diməbəl/ a irredimible, perdido. **i. government loan,** deuda perpetua, f
**irredeemably** /,ɪrɪ'diməbli/ adv perdidamente
**irreducible** /,ɪrɪ'dusəbəl/ a irreducible
**irrefutability** /ɪ,rɛfyətə'bɪlɪti/ n verdad, f
**irrefutable** /ɪ'rɛfyətəbəl/ a irrefutable, indisputable, innegable, irrebatible
**irregular** /ɪ'rɛgyələr/ a irregular; anormal; (of shape) disforme; desordenado; Gram. irregular; (of surface) desigual, escabroso

**irregularity** /ɪ,rɛgyə'lærɪti/ n irregularidad, f; anormalidad, f; (of shape) desproporción, irregularidad, f; (of surface) escabrosidad, desigualdad, f; exceso, m, demasía, f
**irrelevance** /ɪ'rɛləvəns/ n inconexión, f; inoportunidad, f; futilidad, poca importancia, f; (stupidity) desatino, m, impertinencia, f
**irrelevant** /ɪ'rɛləvənt/ a inaplicable, fuera de propósito; inoportuno; sin importancia, fútil; (stupid) impertinente
**irreligion** /,ɪrɪ'lɪdʒən/ n irreligión, impiedad, f
**irreligious** /,ɪrɪ'lɪdʒəs/ a irreligioso, impío
**irremediable** /,ɪrɪ'midiəbəl/ a irremediable, irreparable
**irremediably** /,ɪrɪ'midiəbli/ adv sin remedio, irremediablemente
**irreparable** /ɪ'rɛpərəbəl/ a irreparable
**irreplaceable** /,ɪrɪ'pleisəbəl/ a irreemplazable
**irrepressible** /,ɪrɪ'prɛsəbəl/ a incontrolable, indomable
**irreproachable** /,ɪrɪ'proutʃəbəl/ a irreprochable, intachable
**irresistible** /,ɪrɪ'zɪstəbəl/ a irresistible
**irresistibleness** /,ɪrɪ'zɪstəbəlnɪs/ n superioridad, f
**irresolute** /ɪ'rɛzə,lut/ a irresoluto, indeciso, vacilante
**irresoluteness** /ɪ'rɛzə,lutnɪs/ n irresolución, indecisión, f
**irrespective** /,ɪrɪ'spɛktɪv/ a (with of) independiente de, aparte de, sin distinción de
**irresponsibility** /,ɪrɪ,spɒnsə'bɪlɪti;/ n irresponsabilidad, f
**irresponsible** /,ɪrɪ'spɒnsəbəl/ a irresponsable
**irretrievable** /,ɪrɪ'trivəbəl/ a irrecuperable
**irretrievably** /,ɪrɪ'trivəbli/ adv irreparablemente, sin remedio
**irreverence** /ɪ'rɛvərəns/ n irreverencia, f
**irreverent** /ɪ'rɛvərənt/ a irreverente, irrespetuoso
**irrevocability** /ɪ,rɛvəkə'bɪlɪti/ n irrevocabilidad, f
**irrevocable** /ɪ'rɛvəkəbəl/ a irrevocable; inquebrantable
**irrigable** /'ɪrɪgəbəl/ a regadío
**irrigate** /'ɪrɪ,geit/ vt Agr. poner en regadío; regar; Med. irrigar
**irrigation** /,ɪrɪ'geiʃən/ n Agr. riego, m; Med. irrigación, f. **i. channel,** cacera, acequia, f, canal de riego, m
**irritability** /,ɪrɪtə'bɪlɪti/ n irritabilidad, iracundia, f
**irritable** /'ɪrɪtəbəl/ a irritable, irascible, iracundo
**irritably** /'ɪrɪtəbli/ adv con irritación, airadamente
**irritant** /'ɪrɪtn̩t/ a irritante, irritador. —n irritador, m; Med. medicamento irritante, m
**irritate** /'ɪrɪ,teit/ vt provocar, estimular; irritar, molestar, exasperar; Med. irritar
**irritating** /'ɪrɪ,teitɪŋ/ a irritador, irritante
**irritatingly** /'ɪrɪ,teitɪŋli/ adv de un modo irritante
**irritation** /,ɪrɪ'teiʃən/ n irritación, f, enojo, m; Physiol. picazón, f, picor, m
**irruption** /ɪ'rʌpʃən/ n irrupción, invasión, f
**isinglass** /'aizən,glæs/ n cola de pescado, f
**Islamic** /ɪs'læmɪk/ a islámico
**Islamism** /ɪs'lɑmɪzəm/ n islamismo, m
**Islamite** /ɪs'læmait/ a and n islamita mf
**island** /'ailənd/ n isla, f, a isleño
**islander** /'ailəndər/ n isleño (-ña)
**islet** /'ailɪt/ n isleta, f; isolote, m
**isobaric** /,aisə'bærɪk/ a isobárico
**isolate** /v. 'aisə,leit/ vt aislar, apartar
**isolated** /'aisə,leitɪd/ a aislado, apartado, solitario; único, solo
**isolation** /,aisə'leiʃən/ n aislamiento, apartamiento, m, soledad, f
**isolationism** /,aisə'leiʃə,nɪzəm/ n Polit. aislacionismo, aislamientismo, m
**isolationist** /,aisə'leiʃənɪst/ a and n Polit. aislacionista, aislamientista, mf
**isomerism** /ai'sɒmə,rɪzəm/ n Chem. isomería, f
**isometric** /,aisə'mɛtrɪk/ a isométrico
**isosceles** /ai'sɒsə,liz/ a isósceles
**isotope** /'aisə,toup/ n isotope, isotopo, m
**Israelite** /'ɪzriə,lait/ a and n israelita mf
**issue** /'ɪʃu/ n salida, f; (result) resultado, m, consecuencia, f; (of a periodical) número, m; Print. edi-

ción, tirada, *f;* (offspring) prole, sucesión, *f;* (of notes, bonds) emisión, *f; Med.* flujo, *m;* cuestión, *f,* problema, *m.* —*vi* salir, fluir, manar; nacer, originarse; resultar, terminarse. —*vt* (an order) expedir, emitir, dictar; publicar, dar a luz; (of notes, bonds) poner en circulación, librar. **at i.,** en disputa, en cuestión. **to join i.,** llevar la contraria, oponer

**isthmian** /ˈɪsmiən/ *a* ístmico

**isthmus** /ˈɪsməs/ *n* istmo, *m*

**it** /ɪt/ *pron* (as subject) él, *m;* ella, *f;* (gen. omitted with all verbs in Sp.); (as object) lo, *m;* la, *f;* (as indirect object) le (se with an object in 3rd pers.); (meaning that thing, that affair) eso, ello. Sometimes omitted in other cases, e.g. *He has thought it necessary to stay at home,* Ha creído necesario de quedarse en casa. *We heard it said that...,* Oímos decir que... *to make it perfectly clear that...,* dejar bien claro que... —*n* (slang) garbo, aquél, *m;* atractivos, *m pl.* **Is it not so?** ¿No es así? **That is it,** Eso es. **It's me,** Soy yo

**Italian** /ɪˈtælyən/ *a* and *n* italiano (-na) (language) italiano, *m. Art.* **I. School,** escuela italiana, *f*

**italic** /ɪˈtælɪk/ *a* (of Italy) itálico; *Print.* itálico, bastardillo. —*n* letra bastardilla, bastardilla, letra itálica, *f.* **italics mine,** el subrayado es mío, los subrayados son míos

**italicize** /ɪˈtælə‚saɪz/ *vt* imprimir en bastardilla; dar énfasis (a)

**Italy** /ˈɪtli/ Italia, *f*

**itch** /ɪtʃ/ *n* sarna, *f; Fig.* picazón, *f;* prurito, capricho, *m.* —*vi* picar; *Fig.* sentir picazón; (with to) rabiar por, suspirar por.

**itching** /ˈɪtʃɪŋ/ *n* picazón, *f,* picor, *m.* —*a* sarnoso, picante; *Med.* pruriginoso. **to have an i. palm,** *Fig.* ser de la virgen del puño

**item** /*n* ˈaɪtəm; *adv* ˈaɪtɛm/ *n* ítem, artículo, *m; Com.* partida, *f;* punto, detalle, *m;* (of a program) número, *m;* asunto, *m.* —*adv* ítem

**iterative** /ˈɪtə‚reɪtɪv/ *a* iterativo

**Ithaca** /ˈɪθəkə/ Ítaca, *f*

**itinerant** /aɪˈtɪnərənt/ *a* nómada, errante

**itinerary** /aɪˈtɪnəˈrɛri/ *n* itinerario, *m,* ruta, *f*

**its** /ɪts/ *poss a* su (with pl. obj.) sus. **a book and its pages,** un libro y sus páginas.

**itself** /ɪtˈsɛlf/ *pron* él mismo, *m;* ella misma, *f;* (with prep.) sí; (with reflex. verb) se; (with noun) el mismo, la misma; (meaning alone) solo. **in i.,** en sí

**ivied** /ˈaɪvid/ *a* cubierto de hiedra

**ivory** /ˈaɪvəri/ *n* marfil, *m.* —*a* ebúrneo, de marfil, marfileño. **vegetable i.,** marfil vegetal, *m.* **i. carving,** talla de marfil, *f*

**ivory tower** *n* torre de marfil, *f*

**ivory-tower** /ˈaɪvəri ˈtauər/ *a* de torre de marfil

**ivy** /ˈaɪvi/ *n* hiedra, *f*

# J

**j** /dʒeɪ/ n (letter) jota, f

**jab** /dʒæb/ vt (with a hypodermic needle, etc.) pinchar; introducir (en); clavar (con); (scrape) hurgar; (place) poner. —n pinchazo, m; golpe, m. **He jabbed his pistol in my ribs,** Me puso la pistola en las costillas

**jabber** /'dʒæbər/ vt and vi chapurrear; (of monkeys) chillar

**jabbering** /'dʒæbərɪŋ/ n chapurreo, m; (of monkeys) chillidos, m pl

**Jack** /dʒæk/ n Juan, m; (man) hombre, m; (sailor) marinero, m; (in cards) sota, f; (for raising weights) gato, m; (of a spit) torno, m; (of some animals) macho, m; (bowls) boliche, m. —vt (with up) solevantar con gatos. **Union J.,** pabellón británico, m. **j.-boot,** bota de montar, f. **J.-in-office,** mandarín, funcionario impertinente, m. **J.-in-the-box,** faca, f. **j.-knife,** navaja, f. **J. of all trades,** hombre de muchos oficios, m. **jack of all trades, master of none,** aprendiz de todo, oficial de nada. **j.-rabbit,** liebre americana, f. **J.-tar,** marinero, m

**jackal** /'dʒækəl/ n chacal, adive, m

**jackanapes** /'dʒækə,neɪps/ n impertinente, m; mequetrefe, m

**jackass** /'dʒæk,æs/ n asno, m; (fool) tonto, asno, m. **laughing j.,** martín pescador, m

**jacket** /'dʒækɪt/ n chaqueta, f; americana, f; (for boilers, etc.) camisa, f; (of a book) forro, m, sobrecubierta, f. **strait j.,** camisa de fuerza, f

**jacks** /dʒæks/ n (game) matatenas, f pl, cantillos, m pl

**jade** /dʒeɪd/ n Mineral. jade, m; (horse) rocín, m; (woman) mala pécora, f; (saucy wench) mozuela, picaruela, f

**jaded** /'dʒeɪdɪd/ a fatigado, agotado, rendido; (of the palate) saciado

**jagged** /'dʒægɪd/ a dentado

**jaguar** /'dʒægwɑr/ n jaguar, m

**jail** /dʒeɪl/ cárcel, prisión, f; encierro, m. —vt encarcelar. —a carcelario, carcelero.

**jailbird** /'dʒeɪl,bɜrd/ n malhechor; presidiario, m

**jailer** /'dʒeɪlər/ n carcelero (-ra)

**jalopy** /dʒə'lɒpi/ carcacho, m, (Mexico), cafetera rusa, f, (Spain)

**jalousie** /'dʒælə,si/ n celosía, f

**jam** /dʒæm/ vt (ram) apretar; apiñar; estrujar; (a machine) atascar; (radio) causar interferencia (a); (preserve) hacer confitura de. —vi atascarse. —n (of people) agolpamiento, m; (traffic) atasco, m; (preserve) confitura, mermelada, compota, f. **He jammed his hat on,** Se encasquetó el sombrero. **She suddenly jammed down on the brakes,** Frenó de repente. **jam-dish,** compotera, f. **jam-jar,** pote para confitura, m

**Jamaican** /dʒə'meɪkən/ a jamaicano, n jamaicano (-na)

**jamboree** /,dʒæmbə'ri/ n campamento, m

**jamming** /'dʒæmɪŋ/ n Radio. interferencias, f pl

**jangle** /'dʒæŋgəl/ vi cencerrear; chocar; rechinar. —n cencerreo, m; choque, m; rechinamiento, m

**janissary** /'dʒænə,sɛri/ n jenízaro, m

**janitor** /'dʒænɪtər/ n portero, m; (in a university, etc.) bedel, m

**Jansenist** /'dʒænsənɪst/ a and n jansenista, mf

**January** /'dʒænyu,ɛri/ n enero, m

**Japan** /dʒə'pæn/ el Japón, m

**japan** /dʒə'pæn/ n charol, m. —vt charolar

**Japanese** /,dʒæpə'niz/ a japonés. —n japonés (-esa); (language) japonés, m

**jar** /dʒɑr/ n chirrido, m; choque, m; sacudida, f; vibración, trepidación, f; (quarrel) riña, f; (receptacle) jarra, f; (for tobacco, honey, cosmetics, etc.) pote, m; (Leyden) botella (de Leyden), f. —vi chirriar; vibrar; trepidar; chocar; (of sounds) ser discorde; (of colors) chillar. —vt sacudir; hacer vibrar. **It jarred on my nerves,** Me atacaba los nervios. **It gave me a nasty**

---

**jar,** Fig. Me hizo una impresión desagradable. **on the jar,** entreabierto

**jardiniere** /,dʒɑrdn̩'ɪər/ n jardinera, f

**jargon** /'dʒɑrgən/ n jerga, jerigonza, f; monserga, f; (technical) lenguaje especial, m

**jarring** /'dʒɑrɪŋ/ a discorde, disonante; en conflicto, opuesto; (to the nerves) que ataca a los nervios

**jasmine** /'dʒæzmɪn/ n jazmín, m. **yellow j.,** jazmín amarillo, m

**jasper** /'dʒæspər/ n Mineral. jaspe, m

**jaundice** /'dʒɔndɪs/ n ictericia, f

**jaundiced** /'dʒɔndɪst/ a envidioso; desengañado, desilusionado

**jaunt** /dʒɔnt/ n excursión, f, vi ir de excursión

**jauntily** /'dʒɔntli/ adv airosamente, con garbo

**jauntiness** /'ʒɔntɪnɪs/ n garbo, m, gentileza, ligereza, f

**jaunty** /'dʒɔnti/ a garboso, airoso

**Javanese** /,dʒævə'niz/ a javanés. —n javanés (-esa)

**javelin** /'dʒævlɪn/ n jabalina, f. **j. throwing,** lanzamiento de la jabalina, m

**jaw** /dʒɔ/ n quijada, f; maxilar, m; pl **jaws,** boca, f; (of death, etc.) garras, f pl; Mech. quijada, f; (narrow entrance) boca, abertura, f. **jaw-bone,** mandíbula, f; Anat. hueso maxilar, m

**jay** /dʒeɪ/ n arrendajo, m

**jazz** /dʒæz/ n jazz, m. —vi bailar el jazz. **j. band,** orquesta de jazz, f

**jealous** /'dʒɛləs/ a celoso; envidioso. **to be j. of,** tener celos de. **to make j.,** dar celos (a)

**jealously** /'dʒɛləsli/ adv celosamente

**jealousy** /'dʒɛləsi/ n celos, m pl

**jeans** /dʒinz/ n vaqueros, m pl

**jeep** /dʒip/ n Mil. yip, m

**jeer** /dʒɪər/ n burla, mofa, f; insulto, m, vi burlarse; (with at) mofarse de

**jeerer** /'dʒɪərər/ n mofador (-ra)

**jeering** /'dʒɪərɪŋ/ a mofador. —n burlas, f pl; insultos, m pl

**jeeringly** /'dʒɪərɪŋli/ adv burlonamente

**jellied** /'dʒɛlid/ a en gelatina

**jelly** /'dʒɛli/ n jalea, f; gelatina, f, vi solidificarse. **j.-bag,** manga, f. **j.-fish,** aguamala, aguaviva, malagna, medusa, f

**jeopardize** /'dʒɛpər,daɪz/ vt arriesgar, poner en juego; comprometer

**jeopardy** /'dʒɛpərdi/ n peligro, m

**jeremiad** /,dʒɛrə'maɪəd/ n jeremiada, f

**jerk** /dʒɜrk/ n sacudida, f. —vt sacudir, dar una sacudida (a); lanzar bruscamente; (pull) tirar de; (push) empujar. —vi moverse a sacudidas. **I jerked myself free,** Me libré de una sacudida

**jerkily** /'dʒɜrkəli/ adv con sacudidas; espasmódicamente; nerviosamente

**jerkin** /'dʒɜrkɪn/ n justillo, m

**jerky** /'dʒɜrki/ a espasmódico; nervioso (also of style)

**jerry-built** /'dʒɛri,bɪlt/ a mal construido, de pacotilla

**jersey** /'dʒɜrzi/ n jersey, m. —a de jersey; de Jersey. **football j.,** camiseta de fútbol, f, jersey de fútbol, m. **J. cow,** vaca jerseysa, f

**Jerusalem** /dʒɪ'rusələm/ Jerusalén, m

**jest** /dʒɛst/ n broma, chanza, f; (joke) chiste, m; (laughingstock) hazmerreír, m. —vi bromear; burlarse (de). **in j.,** en broma, de guasa

**jester** /'dʒɛstər/ n burlón (-ona); (practical joker, etc.) bromista, mf; (at a royal court) bufón, m

**jesting** /'dʒɛstɪŋ/ n bromas, f pl; chistes, m pl; burlas, f pl. —a de broma; burlón

**jestingly** /'dʒɛstɪŋli/ adv en broma

**Jesuit** /'dʒɛʒuɪt/ n Jesuita, m

**Jesuitical** /,dʒɛʒu'ɪtɪkəl/ a jesuítico

**jet** /dʒɛt/ n Mineral. azabache, m; (stream) chorro, m; (pipe) mechero, m; (burner) mechero, m, vi chorrear. **jet-black,** negro como el azabache, de azabache. **jet-propelled engine,** motor de retroacción, m. **jet-propelled plane,** aeroplano de reacción, m

**jetsam** /'dʒɛtsəm/ n echazón, f; Fig. víctima, f
**jettison** /'dʒɛtəsən/ n echazón, f. —vt echar (mercancías) al mar; Fig. librarse de, abandonar
**jetty** /'dʒɛti/ n dique, malecón, m; (landing pier) embarcadero, muelle, m
**Jew** /dʒu/ n judío, m. **Jew's harp,** birimbao, m
**jewel** /'dʒuəl/ n joya, alhaja, f; (of a watch) rubí, m; Fig. alhaja, f. —vt enjoyar, adornar con piedras preciosas. **j.-box, -case,** joyero, m
**jeweled** /'dʒuəld/ a adornado con piedras preciosas, enjoyado; (of a watch) con rubíes
**jeweler** /'dʒuələr/ n joyero (-ra). **jeweler's shop,** joyería, f
**jewelry** /'dʒuəlri/ n joyas, f pl; artículos de joyería, m pl
**Jewess** /'dʒuɪs/ n judía, f
**Jewish** /'dʒuɪʃ/ a judío
**Jewry** /'dʒuri/ n judería, f
**jib** /dʒɪb/ n Naut. foque, m. —vi (of a horse) plantarse; (refuse) rehusar. **to jib at,** vacilar en; mostrarse desinclinado. **jib-boom,** Naut. botalón de foque, m
**jiffy** /'dʒɪfi/ n instante, credo, m. **in a j.,** en un decir Jesús, en un credo, en un santiamén
**jig** /dʒɪg/ n (dance) jiga, f. —vi bailar una jiga; bailar, agitarse, sacudirse. —vt agitar, sacudir; (sieve) cribar
**jigger** /'dʒɪgər/ n Naut. cangreja de mesana, f; aparejo de mano, m; jigger, m
**jigsaw puzzle** /'dʒɪg,sɔ/ n rompecabezas, m
**jilt** /dʒɪlt/ vt dar calabazas (a)
**jingle** /'dʒɪŋgəl/ n tintineo, m; ruido, m; verso, m; estribillo, m. —vi tintinar; sonar; rimar
**jingoism** /'dʒɪŋgou,ɪzəm/ n jingoísmo, m
**jitters, to have the** /'dʒɪtərz/ no tenerlas todas consigo, no saber dónde meterse
**job** /dʒɒb/ n tarea, f; trabajo, m; empleo, m; (affair) asunto, m; (thing) cosa, f; (unscrupulous transaction) intriga, f. **It is a good (bad) job that...,** Es una buena (mala) cosa que... **He has done a good job,** Ha hecho un buen trabajo. **He has lost his job,** Ha perdido su empleo, Le han declarado cesante. **odd-job man,** factótum, m. **job-lot,** colección miscelánea, f; Com. saldo de mercancías, f
**jobber** /'dʒɒbər/ n (workman) destajista, m; (in stocks) agiotista, m; Com. corredor, m
**jobless** /'dʒɒblɪs/ a sin trabajo
**jockey** /'dʒɒki/ n jockey, m. —vt engañar; (with into) persuadir, hacer; (with out of) quitar, robar. **j. cap,** gorra de jockey, f. **J. Club,** jockey-club, m
**jocose** /dʒou'kous/ a jocoso, gracioso, guasón
**jocosity** /dʒou'kɒsɪti/ n jocosidad, f
**jocular** /'dʒɒkyələr/ a gracioso, alegre; chistoso, zumbón
**jocularity** /,dʒɒkyə'lærɪti/ n alegría, jocosidad, f
**jocularly** /'dʒɒkyələrli/ adv en broma; alegremente
**jocund** /'dʒɒkənd/ a alegre, jovial; jocundo
**jocundity** /dʒou'kʌndɪti/ n alegría, f; jocundidad, f
**jog** /dʒɒg/ vt empujar; (the memory) refrescar. —vi ir despacio; andar a trote corto. —n empujón, m. **He jogged me with his elbow,** Me dio con el codo. **jog-trot,** trote corto, m
**joie de vivre** /ʒwɑdə'vivrə/ n goce de vivir, arregosto de vivir, m
**join** /dʒɔin/ vt juntar; unir; añadir; (railway lines) empalmar; juntarse con; (meet) encontrarse (con); reunirse (con); (a club, etc.) hacerse miembro (de); (share) acompañar; (regiments, ships) volver (a). —vi juntarse; unirse; asociarse. —n unión, f; (railway) empalme, m; (roads) bifurcación, f. **At what time will you j. me?** ¿A qué hora me vendrás a buscar? **He has joined his ship,** Ha vuelto a su buque. **Will you j. me in a drink?** ¿Me quieres acompañar en una bebida? **to j. battle,** librar batalla. **to j. forces,** combinar; Inf. juntar meriendas. **to j. in,** tomar parte en, participar en. **to j. together,** vt unir, juntar. —vi juntarse; asociarse. **to j. up,** alistarse
**joiner** /'dʒɔinər/ n carpintero, ensamblador, m
**joinery** /'dʒɔinəri/ n ensambladuría, f; carpintería, f
**joining** /'dʒɔinɪŋ/ n juntura, conjunción, f; (etc.) ensambladura, f; Fig. unión, f
**joint** /dʒɔint/ n juntura, junta, f; Anat. coyuntura, articulación, f; (knuckle) nudillo, m; (of meat) cuarto,

m; (hinge) bisagra, f; Bot. nudo, m, a unido; combinado; colectivo; mixto; mutuo; (in compounds) co. —vt juntar; (meat) descuartizar. **out of j.,** dislocado; (of the times) fuera de compás. **j. account,** cuenta corriente mutua, f. **j.-heir,** coheredero, m. **j. stock company,** compañía por acciones, sociedad anónima, f
**jointed** /'dʒɔintɪd/ a articulado; (foldable) plegadizo
**jointly** /'dʒɔintli/ adv juntamente, en común, colectivamente
**joist** /dʒɔist/ n sopanda, viga, f
**joke** /dʒouk/ n chiste, m; burla, broma, f. —vi bromear, chancearse. —vt burlarse (de). **Can he take a j.?** ¿Sabe aguantar una broma? **practical j.,** broma pesada, f. **to play a j.,** gastar una broma, hacer una burla
**joker** /'dʒoukər/ n bromista, mf; (in cards) comodín, m
**joking** /'dʒoukɪŋ/ n chistes, m pl, bromas, f pl. —a chistoso; cómico
**jokingly** /'dʒoukɪŋli/ adv en broma, de guasa
**jollification** /,dʒɒləfɪ'keiʃən/ n regocijo, m; festividades, fiestas, f pl
**jollity** /'dʒɒlɪti/ n alegría, f, regocijo, m
**jolly** /'dʒɒli/ a alegre, jovial; (tipsy) achispado; (amusing) divertido; (nice) agradable. —adv muy. **He is a j. good fellow,** Es un hombre estupendo. **I am j. glad,** Estoy contentísimo, Me alegro mucho
**jolt** /dʒoult/ n sacudida, f. —vt sacudir. —vi (of a vehicle) traquetear
**jolting** /'dʒoultɪŋ/ n sacudidas, f pl, sacudimiento, m; (of a vehicle) traqueteo, m
**jongleur** /'dʒɒŋglər/ n juglar, m
**jonquil** /'dʒɒŋkwɪl/ n Bot. junquillo, m
**Jordan** /'dʒɔrdn/ Jordania, f
**joss** /dʒɒs/ n ídolo chino, m. **j.-stick,** pebete, m
**jostle** /'dʒɒsəl/ vt empujar, empellar. —vi dar empujones, codear
**jot** /dʒɒt/ n jota, pizca, f. —vt (down) apuntar. **not a jot,** ni jota, ni pizca. **to be not worth a jot,** no valer un comino
**jotter** /'dʒɒtər/ n taco para notas, m; (exercise book) cuaderno, m
**jotting** /'dʒɒtɪŋ/ n apunte, m; observación, f
**journal** /'dʒɜrnl/ n (diary) diario, m; (ship's) diario de navegación, m; (newspaper) periódico, m; (review) revista, f
**journalese** /,dʒɜrnl'iz/ n lenguaje periodístico, m
**journalism** /'dʒɜrnl,ɪzəm/ n periodismo, m
**journalist** /'dʒɜrnlɪst/ n periodista, mf
**journalistic** /,dʒɜrnl'ɪstɪk/ a periodístico
**journey** /'dʒɜrni/ n viaje, m; expedición, f; trayecto, m; camino, m. —vi viajar. **j. by sea,** viaje por mar. **Pleasant j.!** ¡Buen viaje! ¡Feliz viaje! **outward j.,** viaje de ida, m. **return j.,** viaje de regreso, m
**Jove** /dʒouv/ n Júpiter, m. **By J.!** ¡Pardiez! ¡Caramba!
**jovial** /'dʒouviəl/ a jovial
**joviality** /,dʒouvi'ælɪti/ n jovialidad, f
**jowl** /dʒaul/ n (cheek) carrillo, m; (of cattle, etc.) papada, f; (jaw) quijada, f
**joy** /dʒɔi/ n alegría, f; felicidad, f; deleite, placer, m; vi alegrarse. **I wish you joy,** Te deseo la felicidad. **joy-ride,** excursión en coche, f; vuelo en avión, m. **joy-stick,** (of an airplane) palanca de gobierno, f
**joyful** /'dʒɔifəl/ a alegre
**joyfulness** /'dʒɔifəlnɪs/ n alegría, f
**joyless** /'dʒɔilɪs/ a sin alegría, triste
**joylessness** /'dʒɔilɪsnɪs/ n falta de alegría, tristeza, f
**joyous** /'dʒɔiəs/. See **joyful**
**jubilant** /'dʒubələnt/ a jubiloso; triunfante
**jubilantly** /'dʒubələntli/ adv con júbilo, alegremente; triunfalmente
**jubilation** /,dʒubə'leiʃən/ n júbilo, m, alegría, f; ruido triunfal, m
**jubilee** /'dʒubə,li/ n jubileo, m
**jubilee volume** n libro de homenaje, libro jubilar, m
**Judaic** /dʒu'deiɪk/ a judaico
**Judaism** /'dʒudi,ɪzəm/ n judaísmo, m
**Judas** /'dʒudəs/ n (traitor and hole) judas, m
**Judezmo** /dʒu'dɛzmou/ el judesmo, m
**judge** /dʒʌdʒ/ n juez, m; (connoisseur) conocedor

(-ra) (de); (umpire) arbitrio, *m.* —*vt* juzgar; considerar, tener por. —*vi* servir como juez; juzgar. **judging by,** a juzgar por. **to be a good j. of,** ser buen juez de. **to j. for oneself,** formar su propia opinión

**judgment** /'dʒʌdʒmənt/ *n Law.* fallo, *m;* sentencia, *f;* juicio, *m;* (understanding) entendimiento, discernimiento, *m;* (opinion) opinión, *f,* parecer, *m.* **In my j....,** Según mi parecer,... Según creo yo... **Last J.,** Juicio Final, *m.* **to pass j. on,** *Law.* pronunciar sentencia (en or sobre); dictaminar sobre; juzgar. **to sit in j. on,** ser juez de; juzgar. **j.-day,** Día del Juicio, *m.* **j.-seat,** tribunal, *m*

**judicature** /'dʒudɪˌkeitʃər/ *n* judicatura, *f;* (court) juzgado, *m*

**judicial** /dʒu'dɪʃəl/ *a* judicial; legal; (of the mind) juicioso. **j. inquiry,** investigación judicial, *f.* **j. separation,** separación legal, *f*

**judiciary** /dʒu'dɪʃiˌɛri/ *a* judicial. —*n* judicatura, *f*

**judicious** /dʒu'dɪʃəs/ *a* juicioso, prudente.

**judiciously** /dʒu'dɪʃəsli/ *adv* prudentemente, juiciosamente

**judiciousness** /dʒu'dɪʃəsnɪs/ *n* juicio, *m,* prudencia, sensatez, *f*

**judo** /'dʒudou/ *n* yudo, *m*

**judoka** /'dʒudou‚ka/ *n* yudoca, *mf*

**jug** /dʒʌg/ *n* jarro, *m;* cántaro, *m;* pote, *m.* —*vt Cul.* estofar. —*vi* (of nightingale) trinar, cantar. **jugged hare,** *n* liebre en estofado, *f*

**juggle** /'dʒʌgəl/ *vi* hacer juegos malabares. **to j. out of,** (money, etc.) quitar con engaño, estafar. **to j. with,** *Fig.* (facts, etc.) tergiversar, falsificar; (person) engañar

**juggler** /'dʒʌglər/ *n* malabarista, *mf;* (deceiver) estafador (-ra)

**jugglery** /'dʒʌgləri/ *n* prestidigitación, *f;* juegos malabares, *m pl;* (imposture) engaño, *m,* estafa, *f;* trampas, *f pl*

**jugular** /'dʒʌgyələr/ *a Anat.* yugular. **j. vein,** yugular, *m*

**juice** /dʒus/ *n* jugo, *m;* *Fig.* zumo, *m.* **digestive j.,** jugo digestivo, *m*

**juiciness** /'dʒusinɪs/ *n* jugosidad, *f;* suculencia, *f*

**juicy** /'dʒusi/ *a* jugoso; suculento

**jujube** /'dʒudʒub/ *n* pastilla, *f*

**jukebox** /'dʒuk‚bɒks/ *n* tocadiscos, vitrola, sinfonola, *f*

**July** /dʒu'lai/ *n* julio, *m*

**jumble** /'dʒʌmbəl/ *vt* mezclar, confundir. —*n* mezcla confusa, colección miscelánea, confusión, *f.* **j. sale,** tómbola, *f*

**jump** /dʒʌmp/ *n* salto, *m;* (in prices, etc.) aumento, *m.* **at one j.,** de un salto. **high j.,** salto de altura, *m.* **long j.,** salto de longitud, *m.* **to be on the j.,** *Inf.* estar nervioso, tener los nervios en punta

**jump** /dʒʌmp/ *vi* saltar; dar un salto; brincar; (of tea-cups, etc.) bailar; (throb) pulsar. —*vt* saltar; hacer saltar; (a child) brincar; (omit) pasar por alto de, omitir. **The train jumped the rails,** El tren se descarriló. **to j. out of bed,** saltar de la cama. **to j. to the conclusion that...,** darse prisa a concluir que... **to j. about,** dar saltos, brincar; revolverse, moverse de un lado para otro. **to j. at,** saltar sobre; precipitarse sobre, abalanzarse hacia; (an offer) apresurarse a aceptar; (seize) coger con entusiasmo. **to j. down,** bajar de un salto. **to j. over,** saltar; saltar por encima de. **to j. up,** saltar; (on to a horse, etc.) montar rápidamente; levantarse apresuradamente. **to j. with,** (agree) convenir en, estar conforme con

**jumper** /'dʒʌmpər/ *n* saltador (-ra); (sailor's) blusa, *f* jersey, sweater, *m*

**jumpiness** /'dʒʌmpinɪs/ *n* nerviosidad, *f*

**jumping** /'dʒʌmpɪŋ/ *n* saltos, *m pl.* —*a* saltador. **j.-off place,** base avanzada, *f;* *Fig.* trampolín, *m.* **j.-pole,** pértiga, *f*

**jumpy** /'dʒʌmpi/ *a* nervioso, agitado

**junction** /'dʒʌŋkʃən/ *n* unión, *f;* (of roads) bifurcación, *f;* (railway) empalme, *m;* (connection) conexión, *f*

**juncture** /'dʒʌŋktʃər/ *n* coyuntura, *f;* momento, *m;* crisis, *f,* momento crítico, *m;* (joint) junta, *f*

**June** /dʒun/ *n* junio, *m*

**jungle** /'dʒʌŋgəl/ *n* selva, *f.* **j.-fever,** fiebre de los grandes bosques, *f*

**junior** /'dʒunyər/ *a* joven; hijo; más joven; menos antiguo; subordinado, segundo. —*n* joven, *mf* **Carmen is my j. by three years,** Carmen es tres años más joven que yo. **James Thomson, Jr.,** James Thomson, hijo. **the j. school,** los pequeños. **j. partner,** socio menor, *m*

**juniper** /'dʒunəpər/ *n Bot.* enebro, *m*

**junk** /dʒʌŋk/ *n* trastos viejos, *m pl;* (nonsense) patrañas, *f pl;* *Naut.* junco, *m;* (salt meat) tasajo, *m.* **j.-shop,** tienda de trastos viejos, *f*

**junk bond** bono-basura, *m*

**junketing** /'dʒʌŋkɪtɪŋ/ *n* festividades, *f pl*

**juridical** /dʒʊ'rɪdɪkəl/ *a* jurídico

**jurisconsult** /‚dʒʊrɪskən'sʌlt/ *n* jurisconsulto, *m*

**jurisdiction** /‚dʒʊrɪs'dɪkʃən/ *n* jurisdicción, *f;* competencia, *f*

**jurisprudence** /‚dʒʊrɪs'prudns/ *n* jurisprudencia, *f*

**jurist** /'dʒʊrɪst/ *n* jurista, legista, *mf*

**juror** /'dʒʊrər/ *n* (miembro del) jurado, *m*

**jury** /'dʒʊri/ *n* jurado, *m.* **to be on the j.,** formar parte del jurado. **j.-box,** tribuna del jurado, *f*

**juryman** /'dʒʊrimən/ *n* miembro del jurado, *m*

**just** /dʒʌst/ *a* justo; justiciero; exacto; fiel. **Peter the J.,** Pedro el justiciero

**just** /dʒʌst/ *adv* justamente, exactamente; precisamente; (scarcely) apenas; (almost) casi; (entirely) completamente; (simply) meramente, solamente, tan sólo; (newly) recién (followed by past part.), recientemente. **He only j. missed being run over,** Por poco le atropellan. **It is j. near,** Está muy cerca. **It is j. the same to me,** Me es completamente igual. **J. as he was leaving,** Cuando estaba a punto de marcharse, En el momento de marcharse. **Just as you arrive in Spain, you must...,** Nada más llegar a España, tienes que... **That's j. it!** ¡Eso es! ¡Exactamente! **to have j.,** acabar de. **They have j. dined,** Acaban de cenar. **J. as you wish,** Como Vd. quiera. **j. at that moment,** precisamente en aquel momento. **j. by,** muy cerca; al lado. **j. now,** ahora mismo; hace poco; pronto, dentro de poco. **j. yet,** todavía. **They will not come j. yet,** No vendrán todavía. **Just looking** (browser to shopkeeper) Estoy viendo, Estamos viendo

**justice** /'dʒʌstɪs/ *n* justicia, *f;* (judge) juez, *m;* (magistrate) juez municipal, *m.* **to bring to j.,** llevar ante el juez (a). **to do j. to,** (a person) hacer justicia (a); (a meal) hacer honor (a). **to do oneself j.,** quedar bien

**justifiable** /'dʒʌstəˌfaiəbəl/ *a* justificable

**justifiably** /'dʒʌstəˌfaiəbli/ *adv* con justicia, justificadamente

**justification** /‚dʒʌstəfɪ'keiʃən/ *n* justificación, *f*

**justify** /'dʒʌstəˌfai/ *vt* justificar, vindicar; (excuse) disculpar; *Print.* justificar. **to be justified (in),** tener derecho (a), tener motivo (para), tener razón (en)

**justly** /'dʒʌstli/ *adv* justamente; con justicia; con derecho; con razón; exactamente; debidamente

**justness** /'dʒʌstnɪs/ *n* justicia, *f;* exactitud, *f*

**jute** /dʒut/ *n* yute, *m*

**jut (out)** /dʒʌt/ *vi* salir, proyectar; sobresalir

**juvenile** /'dʒuvənl/ *a* juvenil; de la juventud; para la juventud; joven; de niños; para niños. —*n* joven, *mf.* **j. court,** tribunal de menores, *m.* **j. lead,** *Theat.* galancete, galán joven, *m.* **j. offender,** delincuente infantil, *m*

**juxtapose** /'dʒʌkstəˌpouz/ *vt* yuxtaponer

**juxtaposition** /‚dʒʌkstəpə'zɪʃən/ *n* yuxtaposición, *f*

# K

**k** /kei/ n (letter) ka, f
**kaiser** /'kaizər/ n káiser, emperador, m. **the K.**
el emperador alemán, m
**kaleidoscope** /kə'laidə,skoup/ n calidoscopio, m
**kaleidoscopic** /kə,laidə'skɒpɪk/ a calidoscópico
**kangaroo** /,kæŋgə'ru/ n canguro, m
**kaolin** /'keiəlɪn/ n caolín, m
**kapok** /'keipɒk/ n miraguano, m
**keel** /kil/ n quilla, f. —vt carenar. **to k. over,** volcar; caer; Naut. zozobrar
**keelson** /'kelsən/ n sobrequilla, f
**keen** /kin/ a (of edges) afilado; agudo; penetrante; vivo; sutil; ardiente; celoso, entusiasta; mordaz; (desirous) ansioso; (of appetite) grande, bueno. **He is a k. tennis player,** Es tenista entusiasta. **Joan has a very k. ear,** Juana tiene un oído muy agudo. **I'm not very k. on apples,** No me gustan mucho las manzanas
**keenly** /'kinli/ adv agudamente; vivamente; (of feeling) hondamente; (of looking) atentamente
**keenness** /'kinnɪs/ n (of a blade) afiladura, f; agudeza, f; viveza, f; sutileza, f; perspicacia, f; (enthusiasm) entusiasmo, m, afición, f; (desire) ansia, f
**keep** /kip/ vt guardar; tener; que darse con; retener; conservar; mantener; (a shop, hotel, etc.) dirigir, tener; (a school) ser director de; (a promise, etc.) cumplir; (the law, etc.) observar, guardar; (celebrate) solemnizar; (a secret) guardar; (books, accounts, a house, in step) llevar; (sheep, etc., one's bed) guardar; (a city, etc.) defender; (domestic animals, cars, etc.) tener; (lodge) alojar; (detain) detener; (reserve) reservar; (cause) hacer. **They had kept this room for me,** Me habían reservado este cuarto. **Dorothy has kept the blue dress,** Dorotea se ha quedado con el vestido azul. **The government could not k. order,** El gobierno no sabía mantener el orden. **I did not know how to k. their attention,** No sabía retener su atención. **Carmen kept quiet,** Carmen guardó silencio, Carmen se calló. **Can you k. a secret?** ¿Sabes guardar un secreto? **to k. an appointment,** acudir a una cita. **to k. in repair,** conservar en buen estado. **to k. someone from doing something,** evitar que uno haga algo. **to k. someone waiting,** hacer que espere uno. **to k. something from someone,** ocultar algo de uno. **We were kept at it night and day,** Nos hacían trabajar día y noche. **I always k. it by me,** Lo tengo siempre a mi lado (or conmigo). **to k. away,** alejar; mantener a distancia; no dejar venir. **to k. back,** (a crowd, etc.) detener; cortar el paso (a); no dejar avanzar; (retain) guardar, retener; reservar; (tears, words) reprimir, contener; (evidence, etc.) callar, suprimir. **to k. down,** no dejar subir (a); sujetar; (a nation, etc.) oprimir, subyugar; (emotions) dominar; (prices, expenses) mantener bajo; (check) moderar, reprimir. **to k. in,** (feelings) contener; reprimir; (the house) hacer quedarse en casa, no dejar salir; (imprison) encerrar; (school) hacer quedar en la escuela (a). **to k. off,** alejar; tener a distancia (a); cerrar el paso (a), no dejar avanzar; no andar sobre; no tocar; (a subject) no tratar de, no discutir, no tocar. **K. your hands off!** ¡No toques! **to k. on,** guardar; retener; (eyes) fijar en, poner en. **to k. out,** no dejar entrar; excluir. **It is difficult to k. him out of trouble,** Es difícil de evitar que se meta en líos. **to k. to,** seguir; limitarse a; adherirse a; **K. to the Left,** «Tome su izquierda», **K. to the right,** «Tome su derecha»; (a path, etc.) seguir por; (one's bed) guardar; (fulfil) cumplir; (oblige) hacer, obligar. **to k. under,** subyugar, oprimir; dominar; controlar. **to k. up,** mantener; (appearances) guardar; conservar; persistir en; (prices) sostener; (in good repair) conservar en buen estado; (go on doing) continuar. **He kept me up late last night,** Anoche me entretuvo hasta muy tarde; Ayer me hizo trasnochar; Anoche me hizo velar. **to k. one's end up,** volver por sí, hacerse fuerte. **to k. up one's spirits,** no desanimarse
**keep** /kip/ vi quedar; (be) estar; (continue) seguir,

continuar; mantenerse; (at home, etc.) quedarse, permanecer; (be accustomed) acostumbrar, soler; (persist) perseverar; (of food) conservarse fresco. **How is he keeping?** ¿Cómo está? **to k. in with someone,** cultivar a alguien. **to k. up with the times,** mantenerse al corriente. **to k. at,** seguir; persistir; perseverar; (pester) importunar. **John keeps at it,** Juan trabaja sin descansar. **to k. away,** mantenerse apartado; mantenerse a distancia; no acudir. **to k. back,** hacerse a un lado, apartarse, alejarse. **to k. down,** quedarse tumbado; seguir acurrucado; no levantarse; esconderse. **to k. from,** (doing something) guardarse de. **to k. off,** mantenerse a distancia. **If the storm keeps off,** Si no estalla una tempestad. **If the rain keeps off,** Si no empieza a llover, Si no hay lluvia. **to k. on,** continuar; seguir. **to k. straight on,** seguir derecho. **I'm tired, but I still k. on,** Estoy cansado, pero sigo trabajando. **to k. out,** quedarse fuera. **to k. out of,** (quarrels, trouble, etc.) no meterse en, evitar. **to k. out of sight,** no dejarse ver, no mostrarse, mantenerse oculto. **to k. together,** quedarse juntos; reunirse
**keep** /kip/ n (of a castle) mazmorra, f; (maintenance) subsistencia, f; comida, f. **for keeps,** para siempre jamás
**keeper** /'kipər/ n guarda, mf; (in a park, zoo, of a lunatic) guardián, m; (of a museum, etc.) director, m; (of animals) criador (-ra); (gamekeeper) guardabosque, m; (of a boardinghouse, shop, etc.) dueño (-ña); (of accounts, books) tenedor, m. **Am I my brother's k.?** ¿Soy yo responsable por mi hermano?
**keeping** /'kipɪŋ/ n guarda, f; conservación, f; protección, f; (of a rule) observación, f; (of an anniversary, etc.) celebración, f; (of a person) mantenimiento, m. **in k. with,** en armonía con; de acuerdo con. **out of k. with,** en desacuerdo con. **to be in safe k.,** estar en buenas manos; estar en un lugar seguro. **k. back,** retención, f
**keepsake** /'kip,seik/ n recuerdo, m
**keg** /kɛg/ n barrilete, m
**ken** /kɛn/ n alcance de la vista, m; vista, f; comprensión, f
**Kennedy Round** /'kɛnidi/, **the** la serie Kénnedy, f
**kennel** /'kɛnḷ/ n (of a dog) perrera, f; (of hounds) jauría, f; (dwelling) cuchitril, m; (gutter) arroyo, m. **k. man,** perrero, m
**kepi** /'keipi/ n quepis, m
**Kepler** /'kɛplər/ Keplero
**kerchief** /'kɜrtʃɪf/ n pañuelo, m; pañoleta, f. **brightly-colored k.,** pañuelo de hierbas, m
**kernel** /'kɜrnḷ/ n almendra, semilla, f; Fig. meollo, m, esencia, f
**kerosene** /'kɛrə,sin/ n petróleo de lámpara, m; kerosén, m
**ketchup** /'kɛtʃəp/ n salsa de tomate y setas, f
**kettle** /'kɛtḷ/ n caldero, m. **pretty k. of fish,** olla de grillos, f. **k.-drum,** timbal, m. **k.-drum player,** timbalero, m
**key** /ki/ n llave, f; (Fig. Archit. Mus.) clave, f; (tone) tono, m; (of a piano, typewriter, etc.) tecla, f; Mech. chaveta, f; (of a wind instrument) pistón, m; (winged fruit) sámara, f; Elec. conmutador, m. **major (minor) key,** tono mayor (menor), m. **latch-key,** llave de la puerta, f; (Yale) llavín, m. **master key,** llave maestra, f. **skeleton key,** ganzúa, f. **He is all keyed up,** Tiene los nervios en punta. **key industry,** industria clave, f. **key man,** hombre indispensable, m. **key point,** punto estratégico, m. **key-ring,** llavero, m. **key signature,** Mus. clave, f. **key word,** palabra clave, f
**keyboard** /'ki,bɔrd/ n teclado, m
**keyhole** /'ki,houl/ n ojo de la cerradura, m. **through the k.,** por el ojo de la cerradura
**keynote** /'ki,nout/ n Mus. tónica, f. Fig. piedra clave, idea fundamental, f
**keystone** /'ki,stoun/ n piedra clave, f
**khaki** /'kæki/ n caqui, m

**kick** /kɪk/ *vt* dar un puntapié (a); golpear; (a goal) chutar. —*vi* (of horses, etc.) dar coces, cocear; (of guns) recular. **to k. one's heels,** hacer tiempo. **to kick the bucket,** palmarla. **to k. up a row,** hacer un ruido de mil diablos; (quarrel) armar camorra. **to k. about,** dar patadas (a). **to k. away,** quitar con el pie; lanzar con el pie. **to k. off,** quitar con el pie; lanzar; sacudirse. **k.-off,** *n* golpe de salida, puntapié inicial, saque, *m.* **to k. out,** echar a puntapiés

**kick** /kɪk/ *n* puntapié, *m;* golpe, *m;* coz, *f;* (of guns) culatazo, *m.* **free k.,** golpe franco, *m*

**kicking** /'kɪkɪŋ/ *n* coces, *f pl;* acoceamiento, *m;* pataleo, *m;* golpeamiento, *m*

**kid** /kɪd/ *n* cabrito, *m,* chivo (-va); carne de cabrito, *f;* (leather) cabritilla, *f; Inf.* crío, *m.* **kid gloves,** guantes de cabritilla, *m pl*

**kidnap** /'kɪdnæp/ *vt* secuestrar

**kidnapper** /'kɪdnæpər/ *n* secuestrador (-ra); ladrón (-ona) de niños

**kidnapping** /'kɪdnæpɪŋ/ *n* secuestro, *m*

**kidney** /'kɪdni/ *n* riñón, *m; Fig.* especie, índole, *f.* **k.-bean,** (plant) judía, *f;* (fruit) habichuela, judía, *f,* fréjol, *m*

**Kidron** /'kɪdrən/ Cedrón, *m*

**kill** /kɪl/ *vt* matar; destruir; suprimir. **to k. off,** exterminar. **to k. time,** entretener el tiempo, pasarse las horas muertas. **to k. two birds with one stone,** matar dos pájaros de un tiro. **k.-joy,** aguafiestas, *mf*

**killer** /'kɪlər/ *n* matador (-ra); (murderer) asesino, *mf*

**killing** /'kɪlɪŋ/ *n* matanza, *f;* (murder) asesinato, *m.* —*a* matador; destructivo; (comic) cómico; ridículo, absurdo; (ravishing) irresistible

**kiln** /kɪl/ *n* horno de cerámica, horno, *m*

**kilo** /'kilou/ *n* kilo, *m*

**kilocycle** /'kɪlə,saikəl/ *n Elec.* kilociclo, *m*

**kilogram** /'kɪlə,græm/ *n* kilogramo, *m*

**kiloliter** /'kɪlə,litər/ *n* kilolitro, *m*

**kilometer** /kɪ'lɒmɪtər/ *n* kilómetro, *m*

**kilometric** /,kɪlə'mɛtrɪk/ *a* kilométrico

**kilowatt** /'kɪlə,wɒt/ *n Elec.* kilovatio, *m*

**kilt** /kɪlt/ *n* enagüillas, *f pl*

**kimono** /kə'mounə/ *n* quimono, *m*

**kin** /kɪn/ *n* parientes, *m pl;* familia, *f;* clase, especie, *f.* **the next of kin,** los parientes próximos, la familia

**kind** /kaind/ *n* género, *m,* clase, *f;* especie, *f; Inf.* tipo, *m.* **He is a queer k. of person,** Es un tipo muy raro. **What k. of cloth is it?** ¿Qué clase de tela es? **Nothing of the k!** ¡Nada de eso! **payment in k.,** pago en especie, *m*

**kind** /kaind/ *a* bondadoso, bueno; cariñoso, tierno; amable; favorable, propicio. **Will you be so k. as to...** Tenga Vd. la bondad de... **With k. regards,** Con un saludo afectuoso. **You have been very k. to her,** Vd. ha sido muy bueno para ella. **k.-hearted,** bondadoso. **k.-heartedness,** bondad, benevolencia, *f*

**kindergarten** /'kɪndər,gɑrtn̩/ *n* jardín de la infancia, kindergarten, *m*

**kindle** /'kɪndl̩/ *vt* encender; hacer arder; *Fig.* avivar. —*vi* prender, empezar a arder; encenderse; *Fig.* inflamarse

**kindliness** /'kaindlinɪs/ *n* bondad, *f*

**kindling** /'kɪndlɪŋ/ *n* encendimiento (del fuego), *m;* (wood) leña menuda, *f*

**kindly** /'kaindli/ *a* bondadoso; bueno; benévolo; propicio, favorable; (of climate) benigno. —*adv* con bondad, bondadosamente; fácilmente. **K. sit down,** Haga el favor de sentarse

**kindness** /'kaindnɪs/ *n* bondad, *f;* benevolencia, *f;* amabilidad, *f;* cariño, *m;* favor, *m,* atención, *f*

**kindred** /'kɪndrɪd/ *n* parentesco, *m;* parientes, *m pl;* familia, *f;* afinidad, *f, a* emparentado; hermano

**king** /kɪŋ/ *n* (ruler, important person, chess, cards) rey, *m;* (in draughts) dama, *f.* **king's evil,** escrófula, *f.* **k.-bolt,** perno real, *m.* **k.-craft,** arte de reinar, *m,* or *f.* **k.-cup,** *Bot.* botón de oro, *m.* **K.-of-Arms,** rey de armas, *m.* **k.-post,** pendolón, *m*

**kingdom** /'kɪŋdəm/ *n* reino, *m.* **animal k.,** reino animal, *m*

**kingfisher** /'kɪŋ,fɪʃər/ *n* martín pescador, alción, *m*

**kink** /kɪŋk/ *n* nudo, *m;* pliegue, *m;* (curl) rizo, *m; Fig.* peculiaridad, *f*

**kinsfolk** /'kɪnz,fouk/ *n* parientes, *m pl,* familia, *f*

**kinship** /'kɪnʃɪp/ *n* parentesco, *m;* afinidad, *f*

**kinsman** /'kɪnzmən/ *n* pariente, deudo, *m*

**kinswoman** /'kɪnz,wumən/ *n* parienta, *f*

**kiosk** /'kiɒsk/ *n* quiosco, *m*

**kipper** /'kɪpər/ *n* arenque ahumado, *m.* —*vt* ahumar

**kiss** /kɪs/ *n* beso, *m;* (in billiards) pelo, *m.* —*vt* besar; dar un beso (a); (of billiard balls) tocar. **to k. each other,** besarse. **k.-curl,** rizo de la sien, *m,* sortijilla, *f*

**kit** /kɪt/ *n* (tub) cubo, *m;* (for tools, etc.) cajita, caja, *f;* (soldier's) equipo, *m.* **kit-bag,** mochila, *f*

**kitchen** /'kɪtʃən/ *n* cocina, *f.* **k.-boy,** pinche (de cocina), *m.* **k.-garden,** huerta, *f.* **k.-maid,** fregona, *f.* **k.-range,** cocina económica, *f.* **k.-sink,** fregadero, *m.* **k.-stove,** horno de cocina, *m.* **k. utensils,** batería de cocina, *f*

**kitchenette** /,kɪtʃə'nɛt/ *n* cocinilla, *f*

**kite** /kait/ *n Ornith.* milano, *m;* cometa, pájara, *f.* **to fly a k.,** hacer volar una cometa. **box-k.,** cometa celular, *f*

**kith and kin** /kɪθ/ *n pl* parientes y amigos, *m pl*

**kitten** /'kɪtn̩/ *n* gatito (-ta). —*vi* (of a cat) parir

**kittenish** /'kɪtnɪʃ/ *a* de gatito; juguetón

**kitty** /'kɪti/ *n* michito, *m;* (in card games) platillo, *m*

**kleptomania** /,klɛptə'meiniə/ *n* cleptomanía, *f*

**kleptomaniac** /,klɛptə'meiniæk/ *a* cleptómano. —*n* cleptómano (-na)

**knack** /næk/ *n* destreza, *f;* talento, *m;* (trick) truco, *m*

**knapsack** /'næp,sæk/ *n* mochila, *f; Mil.* alforja, *f*

**knave** /neiv/ *n* bellaco, truhán, tunante, *m;* (at cards) sota, *f*

**knavery** /'neivəri/ *n* bellaquería, truhanería, *f*

**knavish** /'neivɪʃ/ *a* de bribón; taimado, truhanesco

**knead** /nid/ *vt* amasar; (massage) sobar; *Fig.* formar

**kneading** /'nidɪŋ/ *n* amasijo, *m;* (massaging) soba, *f.* **k.-trough,** amasadera artesa *f*

**knee** /ni/ *n* rodilla, *f; Fig.* ángulo, codillo, *m.* **on bended k.,** de hinojos. **on one's knees,** de rodillas, arrodillado. **to go down on one's knees,** arrodillarse, ponerse de rodillas. **k.-breeches,** calzón corto, *m;* calzón ceñido, *m;* (Elizabethan) gregüescos, *m pl.* **k.-cap,** rótula, *f.* **k.-deep,** hasta las rodillas. **k.-joint,** articulación de la rodilla, *f; Mech.* junta de codillo, *f.* **k.-pad,** rodillera, *f*

**kneel (down)** /nil/ *vi* arrodillarse, hincarse de rodillas, ponerse de rodillas

**kneeling** /'nilɪŋ/ *a* arrodillado, de rodillas

**knell** /nɛl/ *n* toque de difuntos, tañido fúnebre, *m;* toque de campanas, *m; Fig.* muerte, *f.* —*vi* tocar a muerto. —*vt Fig.* anunciar, presagiar

**knickerbockers** /'nɪkər,bɒkərz/ *n pl* bragas, *f pl;* calzón corto, *m;* (women's) pantalones, *m pl*

**knickknack** /'nɪk,næk/ *n* chuchería, *f*

**knife** /naif/ *n* cuchillo, *m.* **to have one's k. in someone,** tener enemiga (a), querer mal (a). **war to the k.,** guerra a muerte, *f.* **k.-edge,** filo de cuchillo, *m;* fiel de soporte, *m.* **k. grinder,** amolador, *m.* **k.-handle,** mango de cuchillo, *m.* **k. thrust,** cuchillada, *f*

**knife, fork, and spoon** cuchara, tenedor, y cuchillo

**knight** /nait/ *n* caballero, *m;* (chess) caballo, *m.* —*vt* armar caballero, calzar la espuela; (in modern usage) dar el título de caballero. **untried k.,** caballero novel, *m.* **k. commander,** comendador, *m.* **k.-errant,** caballero andante, *m.* **k.-errantry,** caballería andante, *f.* **Knight of Labor,** Caballero del Trabajo *m.* **k. of the rueful countenance,** el caballero de la triste figura

**knighthood** /'naithʊd/ *n* caballería, *f;* (in modern usage) título de caballero, *m*

**knightly** /'naitli/ *a* caballeresco; de caballero; de caballería

**knit** /nɪt/ *vt and vi* hacer calceta, hacer media; juntar; ligar; unir. **Isabel is knitting me a jumper,** Isabel me hace un jersey de punto de media. **to k. one's brows,** fruncir el ceño

**knitted** /'nɪtɪd/ *a* de punto. **k. goods,** géneros de punto, *m pl*

**knitter** /'nɪtər/ *n* calcetero (-ra); (machine) máquina de hacer calceta, *f*

**knitting** /'nɪtɪŋ/ *n* acción de hacer calceta, *f;* trabajo de punto, *m,* labor de calceta, *f;* unión, *f.* **k.-machine,** máquina de hacer calceta, *f.* **k.-needle,** aguja de media, aguja de hacer calceta, *f*

**knob** /nɒb/ n protuberancia, f; (of a door, etc.) perilla, borlita, f; (ornamental) bellota, f; (of sugar) terrón, m; (of a stick) puño, m

**knock** /nɒk/ n golpe, m; choque, m; (with a knocker) aldabada, f

**knock** /nɒk/ vt golpear; chocar (contra). —vi llamar a la puerta; (of an engine) picar. **to k. one's head against,** chocar con la cabeza contra, dar con la cabeza contra. **to k. about,** vt pegar; aporrear. —vi viajar; vagar, rodar; callejear. **to k. against,** golpear contra; chocar contra. **to k. down,** derribar; (of vehicles) atropellar; (houses, etc.) demoler; (an argument, etc.) destruir; (a tender, etc.) rebajar; (of an auctioneer) rematar al mejor postor. **to k. in,** (nails, etc.) clavar. **to k. into one another,** toparse. **to k. off,** hacer caer; sacudir; quitar; (from price) descontar; (from speed, etc.) reducir; (finish) terminar pronto; (runs in cricket) hacer. **to k. out,** (remove) quitar; (boxing) dejar fuera de combate, noquear; (Fig. stun) atontar; (an idea, etc.) bosquejar. **to k. over,** volcar. **to k. up,** hacer saltar; (call) llamar; (runs in cricket) hacer; (tire) agotar, rendir; (building) construir toscamente. **to k. up against,** chocar contra; tropezar con. **k.-kneed,** a patiabierto. **k.-out,** "knock-out," m

**knocker** /'nɒkər/ n (on a door) aldaba, f. **k.-up,** despertador, m

**knocking** /'nɒkɪŋ/ n golpes, m pl, golpeo, m; (with a knocker) aldabeo, m. **k. over,** vuelco, m; (by a vehicle) atropello, m

**knoll** /noul/ n altillo, otero, m

**knot** /nɒt/ n nudo, m; (bow) lazo, m; (of hair) moño, m; Naut. nudo, m, milla náutica, f; (of people) corrillo, grupo, m; (on timber) nudo, m. —vt anudar. —vi hacer nudos; enmarañarse. **to tie a k.,** hacer un nudo

**knotted** /'nɒtɪd/ a nudoso

**knotty** /'nɒti/ a nudoso; Fig. intrincado, difícil, complicado. **a k. problem,** problema espinoso

**know** /nou/ vt conocer; saber; (understand) comprender; (recognize) reconocer. **I k. her very well by sight,** La conozco muy bien de vista. **John knows Latin,** Juan sabe latín. **How can I k.?** ¿Cómo lo voy a saber yo? **I knew you at once,** Te reconocí en seguida. **They always k. best,** Siempre tienen razón. **Did you k. about Philip?** ¿Has oído lo de Felipe? **to be in the k.,** estar bien informado, saber de buena tinta. **to get to k.,** (a person) llegar a conocer, trabar amistad con. **to make known,** dar a conocer; manifestar. **Who knows?** ¿Quién sabe? **to k. by heart,** saber de coro. **to k. how,** (to do something) saber. **to k. oneself,** conocerse a sí mismo. **k.-it-all,** sabelotodo, mf, marisabidilla, f

**knowing** /'nouɪŋ/ a inteligente; malicioso; (of animals) sabio. **There is no k.,** No hay modo de saberlo. **worth k.,** digno de saberse

**knowingly** /'nouɪŋli/ adv a sabiendas, de intento; conscientemente; (cleverly) hábilmente; (with look, etc.) de un aire malicioso

**knowledge** /'nɒlɪdʒ/ n conocimiento, m. **To the best of my k. the book does not exist,** El libro no existe que yo sepa. **He has a thorough k. of...,** Conoce a fondo... **lack of k.,** ignorancia, f. **He did it without my k.,** Lo hizo sin que lo supiera yo. **It is a matter of common k. that...** Es notorio que...

**knowledgeable** /'nɒlɪdʒəbəl/ a sabedor

**known** /noun/ a conocido

**knuckle** /'nʌkəl/ n (of a finger) nudillo, m, articulación del dedo, f; (of meat) jarrete, m. **He knuckled down to his work,** Se puso a trabajar con ahínco. **to k. under,** someterse. **k.-duster,** rompecabezas, m

**kopeck** /'koupɛk/ n copec, f

**Koran** /ka'ran/ n Corán, Alcorán, m

**Korea** /kə'riə/ Corea, f

**kosher** /'koufər/ a cosher; (slang) genuino

**kowtow** /'kau'tau/ vi saludar humildemente; Fig. bajar la cerviz

**Kremlin** /'krɛmlɪn/ n Kremlín, m

**kudos** /'kudouz/ n prestigio, m, gloria, f

**Kurdish** /'kɜrdɪʃ/ a curdo

**kyrie eleison** /'kɪəri,ei ɛ'leiə,sɒn/ n kirieleisón, m

# L

**l** /ɛl/ n (letter) ele, f
**la** /lɑ/ n Mus. la, m
**label** /'leibəl/ n etiqueta, (on a garment), rótula, m, (on a can), f; (on a museum specimen, etc.) letrero, m; Fig. calificación, f. —vt poner etiqueta en; marcar, rotular; Fig. calificar, designar, clasificar
**labial** /'leibiəl/ a labial. —n letra labial, f
**labor** /'leibər/ n trabajo, m; labor, f; fatiga, pena, f; clase obrera, f; (manual workers) mano de obra, f; (effort) esfuerzo, m; (of childbirth) dolores de parto, m pl. —vi trabajar; (strive) esforzarse, afanarse; (struggle) forcejar, luchar; (try) procurar, tratar de; avanzar con dificultad; (in childbirth) estar de parto. —vt elaborar; pulir, perfeccionar. **to l. under,** sufrir; tener que luchar contra. **hard l.,** trabajo arduo, m; Law. trabajos forzosos, m pl, presidio, m. **Ministry of L.,** Ministerio de Trabajo, m. **to be in l.,** estar de parto. **to l. in vain,** trabajar en balde, arar en el mar. **to l. under a delusion,** estar en el error, estar equivocado. **L. Exchange,** Bolsa de Trabajo, f. **l. leader,** dirigente sindical, m. **L. party,** partido laborista, partido obrero, m. **l. question,** cuestión obrera, f; (domestic) problema del servicio, m. **l.-saving,** a que ahorra trabajo. **l. union,** sindicato, m
**laboratory** /'læbrə,tɔri/ n laboratorio, m
**labored** /'leibərd/ a (of style) premioso, artificial; forzado; (of breathing) fatigoso; (slow) torpe, lento
**laborer** /'leibərər/ n obrero, m; (on the land) labrador, labriego, m; (on the roads, etc.) peón, m; (by the day) jornalero, m
**laborious** /lə'bɔriəs/ a laborioso; arduo, difícil, penoso
**laboriously** /lə'bɔriəsli/ adv laboriosamente; con dificultad, penosamente
**laboriousness** /lə'bɔriəsnɪs/ n laboriosidad, f; dificultad, f
**Labrador dog** /'læbrə,dɔr/ n perro de Labrador, m
**labyrinth** /'læbərɪnθ/ n laberinto, m
**labyrinthine** /,læbə'rɪnθɪn/ a laberíntico; intrincado
**lace** /leis/ n (of shoes, corsets, etc.) cordón, m; (tape) cinta, f; encaje, m; (narrow, for trimming) puntilla, f; (of gold or silver) galón, m. —vt and vi (shoes, etc.) atarse los cordones; (trim) guarnecer con encajes, etc.; Fig. ornar; (a drink) echar (coñac, etc.) en. **blond l.,** blonda, f. **gold l.,** galón de oro, m. **point l.,** encaje de aguja, m. **l. curtain,** cortina de encaje, f; (of net) visillo, m. **l. maker** or **seller,** encajera, f. **l. making,** obra de encaje, f. **l.-pillow,** almohadilla para encajes, f. **l. shoes,** zapatos con cordones, m pl
**lacerate** /'læsə,reit/ vt lacerar
**laceration** /,læsə'reiʃən/ n laceración, f
**lachrymal** /'lækrəməl/ a lagrimal, lacrimal
**lachrymose** /'lækrə,mous/ a lacrimoso
**lack** /læk/ n falta, f. **l. of evidence,** falta de pruebas, f; carestía, escasez, f; (absence) ausencia, f; (need) necesidad, f. —vt carecer de; no tener; necesitar. —vi hacer falta; necesitarse. **to l. confidence in oneself,** no tener confianza en sí mismo, carecer de confianza en sí mismo. **l.-luster,** (of eyes) apagado, mortecino. **l. of evidence,** falta de pruebas, f
**lackadaisical** /,lækə'deizɪkəl/ a lánguido; indiferente; (dreamy) ensimismado, distraído
**lackey** /'læki/ n lacayo, m
**laconic** /lə'kɒnɪk/ a lacónico
**lacquer** /'lækər/ n laca, f, vt dar laca (a), barnizar con laca. **gold l.,** sisa dorada, f. **l. work,** laca, f
**lacquering** /'lækərɪŋ/ n barnizado de laca, m; laca, capa de barniz de laca, f
**lactate** /'lækteit/ n lactato, m, vi lactar
**lactation** /læk'teiʃən/ n lactancia, f
**lacteal** /'læktiəl/ a lácteo
**lactic** /'læktɪk/ a láctico
**lactose** /'læktous/ n lactosa, f
**lacuna** /lə'kyunə/ n laguna, f
**lacy** /'leisi/ a de encaje; parecido a encaje; Fig. transparente, etéreo

**lad** /læd/ n muchacho, joven, mozalbete, m; zagal, m; (stable, etc.) mozo, m. **He's some l.!** ¡Qué tío que es! **l. of the village,** chulo, m
**ladder** /'lædər/ n escalera de mano, f; Naut. escala, f; (in a stocking, etc.) carrera, f. **companion l.,** escala de toldilla, f. **to l. one's stocking,** escurrirse un punto de las medias
**Ladies and gentlemen** /'leidiz/ n pl Señoras y señores, Señoras y caballeros. **ladies' man,** hombre de salón, Perico entre ellas, mujeriego, m
**lading** /'leidɪŋ/ n flete, m, carga, f
**ladle** /'leidl/ n cucharón, cazo, m. —vt servir con cucharón; (a boat) achicar; Inf. distribuir, repartir
**lady** /'leidi/ n dama, f; señora, f; (English title) milady, f; (woman) mujer, f. **to be a l.,** ser una señora. **leading l.,** Theat. dama primera, f. **Our L.,** Nuestra Señora. **young l.,** señorita, f; Inf. novia, f. **L. Day,** día de la Anunciación (de Nuestra Señora), m. **l.-help,** asistenta, f. **l.-in-waiting,** dama de servicio, f. **l.-killer,** ladrón de corazones, castigador, tenorio, m. **l.-love,** querida, amada, f. **l. mayoress,** alcaldesa, f. **l. of the house,** señora de la casa, f. **l. bug,** Ent. catalina mariquita, vaca de San Antonio, f. **l. of the house,** señora de la casa, f. **l.'s maid,** doncella, f. **l. of the house,** señora de la casa, f
**ladylike** /'leidi,laik/ a de dama; elegante; distinguido; bien educado; delicado; (of men) afeminado
**ladyship** /'leidi,ʃɪp/ n señoría, f. **Your L.,** Su Señoría
**lag** /læg/ vt recubrir; aislar. —vi retrasarse; quedarse atrás; ir (or andar) despacio; rezagarse; Naut. roncear. —n retraso, m; Mech. retardación de movimiento, f
**laggard** /'lægərd/ n holgazán (-ana), haragán (-ana)
**lagoon** /lə'gun/ n laguna, f
**laid** /leid/ past part of verb **to lay. l. up,** (ill) enfermo; Naut. inactivo; (of cars, etc.) fuera de circulación
**lair** /lɛar/ n cubil, m; guarida, madriguera, f
**laity** /'leiti/ n legos, m pl
**lake** /leik/ n lago, m; (pigment) laca, f. **small l.,** laguna, f. **l. dwelling,** vivienda palustre, f
**lama** /'lɑmə/ n lama, m
**lamb** /læm/ n cordero (-ra). —vi parir corderos. **lamb's wool,** lana de cordero. f
**lambent** /'læmbənt/ a ondulante, vacilante; centelleante
**lamblike** /'læm,laik/ a manso como un cordero; inocente
**lambskin** /'læm,skɪn/ n corderina, piel de cordero, f
**lame** /leim/ a estropeado, lisiado; (in the feet) cojo; (of meter) que cojea, malo; (of arguments) poco convincente; frívolo, flojo. —vt lisiar; hacer cojo. **l. excuse,** pretexto frívolo. **to be l.,** (in the feet) (permanently) ser cojo; (temporarily) estar cojo
**lamely** /'leimli/ adv cojeando, con cojera; Fig. sin convicción; mal
**lameness** /'leimnɪs/ n cojera, f; falta de convicción, f
**lament** /lə'mɛnt/ n lamento, m; queja, lamentación, f. —vi lamentarse; quejarse. —vt lamentar, deplorar, llorar
**lamentable** /lə'mɛntəbəl/ a lamentable, deplorable; lastimero
**lamentation** /,læmən'teiʃən/ n lamentación, f, lamento, m. **Book of Lamentations,** Libro de los lamentos, m
**lamenting** /lə'mɛntɪŋ/ n lamentación, f
**lamina** /'læmənə/ n lámina, f
**laminate** /'læmə,neit/ a laminado, laminar. —vt laminar
**lamp** /læmp/ n lámpara, f; (on vehicles, trains, ships and in the street) farol, m; luz, f; (oil) candil, m, lámpara de aceite, f. **safety-l.,** lámpara de seguridad, lámpara de los mineros, f. **street l.,** farol (de las calles), m. **l.-black,** negro de humo, m. **l.-chimney,** tubo de una lámpara, m. **l. factory** or **shop,** lamparería, f. **l.-holder,** portalámpara, f. **l.-lighter,**

farolero, lamparero, *m.* **l.-post,** farola, *f.* **l.-shade,** pantalla (de lámpara,) *f.* **l. stand,** pie de lámpara, *m*

**lamplight** /'læmp,lait/ *n* luz de la lámpara, *f;* luz artificial, *f.* **in the l.,** a la luz de la lámpara; en luz artificial

**lampoon** /læm'pun/ *n* pasquinada, *f,* pasquín, *m, vt* pasquinar, satirizar

**lampooner** /læm'punər/ *n* escritor (-a) de pasquinadas, libelista, *m*

**lamprey** /'læmpri/ *n* lamprea, *f*

**lance** /læns/ *n* lanza, *f;* (soldier) lancero, *m.* —*vt* alancear; *Med.* lancinar. **l. in rest,** lanza en ristre, *f.* **l. thrust,** lanzada, *f.* **l.-corporal,** soldado de primera clase, *m*

**lancer** /'lænsər/ *n Mil.* lancero, *m; pl* lancers, (dance and music) lanceros, *m pl*

**lancet** /'lænsɪt/ *n* apostemero, *m,* lanceta, *f.* **l. arch,** arco puntiagudo, *m*

**land** /lænd/ *n* tierra, *f;* terreno, *m;* (country) país, *m;* (region) región, *f;* territorio, *m;* (estate) bienes raíces, *m pl,* tierras, fincas, *f pl.* —*vt* desembarcar; echar en tierra; (Fig. place) poner; Inf. dejar plantado (con); (obtain) obtener; (a fish) sacar del agua; (a blow) dar (un golpe); (leave) dejar. —*vi* desembarcar; saltar en tierra; (of a plane) aterrizar; (arrive) llegar; (fall) caer. **cultivated l.,** tierras cultivadas, *f pl.* **dry l.,** (not sea) tierra firme, *f.* **native l.,** patria, *f;* suelo natal, *m.* **on l.,** en tierra. **to see how the l. lies,** *Fig.* tantear el terreno. **l. of milk and honey,** jauja, *f,* paraíso, *m.* **l. of promise,** tierra de promisión, *f.* **l. agent,** procurador de fincas, *m.* **l. breeze,** brisa de tierra, *f.* **l. forces,** fuerzas terrestres, *f pl.* **l. law,** leyes agrarias, *f pl.* **l.-locked,** cercado de tierra, mediterráneo *l.-lubber,** marinero de agua dulce, *m.* **l. mine,** mina terrestre, *f.* **l. surveying,** agrimensura, *f.* **l. surveyor,** agrimensor, *m.* **l. tax,** contribución territorial, *f*

**landau** /'lændɔ/ *n* landó, *m*

**landed** /'lændɪd/ *a* hacendado. **l. gentry,** hacendados, terratenientes, *m pl.* **l. property,** bienes raíces, *m pl*

**landfall** /'lænd,fɔl/ *n* derrumbamiento de tierras, *m*

**landing** /'lændɪŋ/ *n* desembarque, desembarco, *m;* (landing place) desembarcadero, *m;* Aer. aterrizaje, *m;* (of steps) descanso, rellano, *m,* mesa, mesilla, *f.* **forced l.,** aterrizaje forzoso, *m.* **l. certificate,** *Com.* tornaguía, *f.* **l. craft,** barcaza de desembarco, *f.* **l. field,** campo de aterrizaje, *m,* pista de vuelo, *f.* **l.-net,** salabardo, *m.* **l. party,** trozo de abordaje, *m.* **l. signal,** Aer. señal de aterrizaje, *f.* **l.-stage,** desembarcadero, *m;* (jetty) atracadero, *m*

**landlady** /'lænd,leidi/ *n* patrona, huéspeda, *f*

**landlord** /'lænd,lɔrd/ *n* (of houses, land) propietario, *m;* hotelero, patrón, *m*

**landmark** /'lænd,mɑrk/ *n* (of a hill or mountain) punto destacado, *m;* lugar conocido, *m;* característica, *f;* Fig. monumento, *m*

**landmass** /'lænd,mæs/ *n* unidad territorial, *f*

**landowner** /'lænd,ounər/ *n* hacendado, terrateniente, *m*

**landscape** /'lænd,skeip/ *n* paisaje, *m;* perspectiva, *f.* **l. gardener,** arquitecto de jardines, *m.* **l. painter,** paisajista, *mf*

**landslide** /'lænd,slaid/ *n* desprendimiento de tierras, *m;* Fig. cambio brusco de la opinión pública, *m*

**landward** /'lændwərd/ *adv* hacia tierra

**lane** /lein/ *n* vereda, senda, *f;* (of traffic) carril, *m,* (Argentina, Spain), línea, *f*

**language** /'læŋgwɪdʒ/ *n* lenguaje, *m;* lengua, *f,* idioma, *m.* **modern l.,** lengua viva, *f.* **strong l.,** palabras mayores, *f pl*

**languid** /'læŋgwid/ *a* lánguido

**languidness** /'læŋgwɪdnɪs/ *n* languidez, *f*

**languish** /'læŋgwɪʃ/ *vi* languidecer

**languishing** /'læŋgwɪʃɪŋ/ *a* lánguido; amoroso, sentimental

**languishingly** /'læŋgwɪʃɪŋli/ *adv* lánguidamente; amorosamente

**languor** /'læŋgər/ *n* languidez, *f*

**languorous** /'læŋgərəs/ *a* lánguido

**languorously** /'læŋgərəsli/ *adv* con langor

**lank** /læŋk/ *a* flaco, descarnado, alto y delgado; (of hair) lacio

**lankiness** /'læŋkinis/ *n* flacura, *f*

**lanky** /'læŋki/ *a* larguirucho, descarnado

**lanolin** /'lænlɪn/ *n* lanolina, *f*

**lantern** /'læntərn/ *n* linterna, *f;* (Naut. and of a lighthouse) farol, *m;* Archit. linterna, *f;* (small) farolillo, *m.* **dark l.,** linterna sorda, *f.* **magic l.,** linterna mágica, *f.* **l.-jawed,** carilargo. **l. maker,** farolero, *m.* **l. slide,** diapositiva, *f*

**lap** /læp/ *n* regazo, *m;* falda, *f;* (knees) rodillas, *f pl;* (lick) lamedura, *f;* (of water) murmurio, susurro, *m;* (in a race) vuelta, *f;* (stage) etapa, *f.* —*vt* (wrap) envolver; (cover) cubrir; (fold) plegar; (lick) lamer; (swallow) tragar. —*vi* (overlap) traslaparse; estar replegado; (lick) lamer; (of water) murmurar, susurrar, besar. **l.-dog,** perro de faldas, perro faldero, *m*

**lapel** /lə'pɛl/ *n* solapa, *f*

**lapidary** /'læpɪ,dɛri/ *a* lapidario

**lapidate** /'læpɪ,deit/ *vt* lapidar

**lapis lazuli** /'læp'ɪs læzʊli/ *n* lapislázuli, *m*

**Lapland** /'læp,lænd/ Laponia, *f*

**Laplander** /'læp,lændər/ *n* lapón (-ona)

**lapping** /'læpɪŋ/ *n* (licking) lamedura, *f;* (of water) murmurio, susurro, chapaleteo, *m*

**lapse** /læps/ *n* lapso, *m;* (fault) desliz, *m,* falta, *f;* (of time) transcurso, intervalo, *m;* (fall) caída, *f;* (Law. termination) caducidad, *f.* **lapse (into),** *vi* caer (en), recaer (en), reincidir (en); volver a, caer de nuevo (en); (Law. cease) caducar; (Law. pass to) pasar (a); dejar de existir, desaparecer. **after the l. of three days,** después de tres días, al cabo de tres días. **with the l. of years,** en el transcurso de los años

**larboard** /'lɑr,bɔrd/ *n* babor, *m,* a de babor

**larceny** /'lɑrsəni/ *n* latrocinio, *m*

**lard** /lɑrd/ *n* manteca, *f;* lardo, *m.* —*vt Cul.* lardear, mechar; *Fig.* sembrar (con), adornar (con)

**larder** /'lɑrdər/ *n* despensa, *f*

**large** /lɑrdʒ/ *a* grande; grueso; amplio; vasto, extenso; (wide) ancho; considerable; (in number) numeroso; (main, chief) principal; liberal; magnánimo. **at l.,** en libertad, suelto. **on the l. side,** algo grande. **l.-headed,** cabezudo. **l.-hearted,** que tiene un gran corazón, magnánimo. **l. mouth,** boca grande, boca rasgada, *f.* **l.-nosed,** narigudo. **l. scale,** en gran escala. **l.-sized,** de gran tamaño. **l.-toothed,** dentudo, que tiene dientes grandes. **l. type,** letras grandes, *f pl*

**largely** /'lɑrdʒli/ *adv* grandemente; en gran manera; en su mayor parte, considerablemente; muy; ampliamente; liberalmente; extensamente

**largeness** /'lɑrdʒnɪs/ *n* gran tamaño, *m;* (of persons) gran talle, *m;* amplitud, *f;* vastedad, extensión, *f;* (width) anchura, *f;* liberalidad, *f;* (generosity) magnanimidad, *f;* grandeza de ánimo, *f*

**larger** /'lɑrdʒər/ *a compar* más grande, etc. See **large.** **to grow l.,** crecer, aumentarse. **to make l.,** hacer más grande; aumentar

**largesse** /lɑr'dʒɛs/ *n* liberalidad, *f*

**largo** /'lɑrgou/ *n and adv Mus.* largo, *m*

**lariat** /'læriət/ *n* lazo, *m*

**lark** /lɑrk/ *n* alondra, *f;* (spree) juerga, *f;* (joke) risa, *f.* **to rise with the l.,** levantarse con las gallinas

**larva** /'lɑrvə/ *n* larva, *f*

**laryngeal** /lə'rɪndʒiəl/ *a* laríngeo

**laryngitis** /,lærən'dʒaitɪs/ *n* laringitis, *f*

**larynx** /'lærɪŋks/ *n* laringe, *f*

**lascivious** /lə'sɪviəs/ *a* lascivo, lujurioso

**lasciviousness** /lə'sɪviəsnɪs/ *n* lujuria, lascivia, *f*

**lash** /læʃ/ *n* (thong) tralla, *f;* (whip) látigo, *m;* (blow) latigazo, *m;* azote, *m;* (of the eye) pestaña, *f.* —*vt* dar latigazos (a); azotar; (of waves) romper contra; (of hail, rain) azotar; (excite) provocar; (the tail) agitar (la cola); (scold) fustigar; (fasten) sujetar, atar; *Naut.* trincar. **to l. out,** (of horses, etc.) dar coces; (in words) prorrumpir (en)

**lashing** /'læʃɪŋ/ *n* (whipping) azotamiento, *m;* (tying) ligadura, atadura, *f;* amarradura, *f*

**lass** /læs/ *n* muchacha, chica, *f;* mozuela, *f;* zagala, *f;* niña, *f*

**lassitude** /'læsɪ,tud/ *n* lasitud, *f*

**lasso** /'læsou/ *n* lazo, *m,* mangana, *f, vt* lazar, manganear

**last** /læst/ *vi* durar; subsistir, conservarse; continuar

**last** /læst/ *a* último; (with month, week, etc.) pasado;

(supreme) extremo, (el) mayor. —*adv* al fin; finalmente; por último; después de todos; por última vez; la última vez. —*n* el, *m*, (*f*, la) último (-ma); los últimos, *m pl*, (*f pl*, las últimas); (end) fin, *m*; (for shoes) horma, *f*. **at l.**, en fin; por fin, a la postre. **at the l. moment,** a última hora. **I have not been there these l. five years,** Hace cinco años que no voy allá. **John spoke l.,** Juan habló el último. **She came at l.,** Por fin llegó. **to the l.,** hasta el fin. **l. but one,** penúltimo (-ma). **l. hope,** última esperanza, *f*; último recurso, *m*. **l. kick,** *Inf.* último suspiro, *m*. **l. night,** anoche. **l. week,** la semana pasada

**lasting** /'læstɪŋ/ *a* permanente, perdurable; duradero; constante; (of colours) sólido

**lastingness** /'læstɪŋnɪs/ *n* permanencia, *f*; duración, *f*

**lastly** /'læstli/ *adv* en conclusión, por fin, finalmente, por último

**latch** /lætʃ/ *n* pestillo, *m*, *vt* cerrar con pestillo. **l.-key,** llave de la puerta, *f*; (Yale) llavín, *m*

**late** /leit/ *a* tarde; tardío; (advanced) avanzado; (last) último; reciente; (dead) difunto; (former) antiguo, ex...; (new) nuevo. —*adv* tarde. **Better l. than never,** Más vale tarde que nunca. **Helen arrived l.,** Elena llegó tarde. **The train arrived five minutes l.,** El tren llegó con cinco minutos de retraso. **He keeps l. hours,** Se acuesta muy tarde, Se acuesta a las altas horas de la noche (*Inf.* a las tantas). **of l.,** últimamente. **to grow l.,** hacerse tarde. **l.-eighteenth-century poetry,** la poesía de fines del siglo diez y ocho; llorado, malogrado (e.g. *the l. Mrs. Smith,* la llorada Sra. Smith, la malograda Sra. Smith);

**lateen** /læ'tin/ *a* latino. **l. sail,** vela latina, *f*

**lately** /'leitli/ *adv* recientemente; últimamente, hace poco

**latency** /'leitnsi/ *n* estado latente, *m*

**lateness** /'leitnɪs/ *n* lo tarde; lo avanzado; retraso, *m*. **the l. of the hour,** la hora avanzada

**latent** /'leitnt/ *a* latente

**later** /'leitər/ *a* más tarde; posterior; más reciente. —*adv* más tarde; (afterwards) luego, después; posteriormente. **sooner or l.,** tarde o temprano. **l. on,** más tarde

**lateral** /'lætərəl/ *a* lateral, ladero

**late registration** *n* matrícula tardía, *f*

**latest** /'leitɪst/ *a* and *adv superl* último; más reciente, etc. See **late. at the l.,** a lo más tarde, a más tardar. **l. fashion,** última moda, *f*. **l. news,** últimas noticias, *f pl*; novedad, *f*

**latex** /'leiteks/ *n* (*Bot. Chem.*) látex, *m*

**lath** /læθ/ *n* listón, *m*. **to be as thin as a l.,** no tener más que el pellejo, estar en los huesos

**lathe** /leið/ *n* torno, *m*

**lather** /'læðər/ *n* espuma de jabón, *f*, jabonaduras, *f pl*; (of sweat) espuma, *f*. —*vt* enjabonar; *Inf.* zurrar. —*vi* hacer espuma

**lathering** /'læðərɪŋ/ *n* jabonadura, *f*; *Inf.* tunda, zurra, *f*

**Latin** /'lætn/ *n* latín, *m*, *a* latino. **Low L.,** bajo latín, *m*. **L.-American,** *a* latinoamericano. —*n* latinoamericano (-na)

**Latinism** /'lætn,ɪzəm/ *n* latinismo, *m*

**Latinist** /'lætnɪst/ *n* latinista, *mf*

**latitude** /'læti,tud/ *n* latitud, *f*; libertad, *f*

**latitudinal** /,læti'tudnl/ *a* latitudinal

**latrine** /lə'trin/ *n* letrina, *f*

**latter** /'lætər/ *a* más reciente; último, posterior; moderno. **the l.,** éste, *m*; ésta, *f*; esto, *neut*; éstos, *m pl*; éstas, *f pl*. **the l. half,** la segunda mitad. **toward the l. end of the year,** hacia fines del año. **L.-Day Saint,** santo de los últimos días *m*, santa de los últimos días, *f*

**latterly** /'lætərli/ *adv* recientemente, últimamente; en los últimos tiempos; hacia el fin

**lattice** /'lætɪs/ *n* rejilla, *f*; celosía, reja, *f*. —*vt* poner celosía (a); entrelazar. **l.-work,** enrejado, *m*

**latticed** /'lætɪst/ *a* (of windows, etc.) con reja

**Latvia** /'lætviə/ Latvia, Letonia, *f*

**Latvian** /'lætviən/ *a* latvio. —*n* latvio (-ia)

**laud** /lɔd/ *n* alabanza, *f*; *pl.* **lauds,** *Eccl.* laudes, *f pl.* —*vt* alabar, elogiar

**laudability** /,lɔdə'bɪliti/ *n* mérito, *m*, lo meritorio

**laudable** /'lɔdəbəl/ *a* loable, meritorio

**laudably** /'lɔdəbli/ *adv* laudablemente

**laudatory** /'lɔdə,tɔri/ *a* laudatorio

**laugh** /læf/ *n* risa, *f*; carcajada, *f*. —*vi* reír; (smile) sonreír; reírse. **loud l.,** risa estrepitosa, *f*. **to l. in a person's face,** reírsele a uno en las barbas. **to l. loudly,** reírse a carcajadas. **to l. to oneself,** reírse interiormente. **to l. to scorn,** poner en ridículo. **to l. at,** reírse de; burlarse de, ridiculizar

**laughable** /'læfəbəl/ *a* risible, irrisible, ridículo, absurdo

**laughing** /'læfɪŋ/ *a* risueño, alegre; (absurd) risible, *n* risa, *f*. **to burst out l.,** reírse a carcajadas. **l.-gas,** gas hilarante, *m*. **l.-stock,** hazmerreír, *m*

**laughingly** /'læfɪŋli/ *adv* riendo

**laughter** /'læftər/ *n* risa, *f*; (in a report) risas, *f pl.* **burst of l.,** carcajada, *f*. **to burst into l.,** soltar el trapo, reírse a carcajadas, desternillarse de risa

**launch** /lɔntʃ/ *n* botadura (de un buque), *f*; lancha, *f*; bote, *m*; canoa, *f*. —*vt* (throw) lanzar; (a blow) asestar; (a vessel) botar, echar al agua; (begin) iniciar, dar principio a; (make) hacer. **to l. an offensive,** *Mil.* emprender una ofensiva. **to l. into,** arrojarse en; entregarse a. **motor l.,** canoa automóvil, *f*. **steam l.,** bote de vapor, *m*

**launching** /'lɔntʃɪŋ/ *n* botadura (de un buque), *f*; (throwing) lanzamiento, *m*; (beginning) iniciación, *f*; inauguración, *f*; (of a loan, etc.) emisión, *f*. **l. site,** rampa, *f*

**launder** /'lɔndər/ *vt* lavar y planchar (ropa)

**laundress** /'lɔndrɪs/ *n* lavandera, *f*

**laundromat** /'lɔndrə,mæt/ *n* lavandería automática, *f*

**laundry** /'lɔndri/ *n* lavadero, *m*, lavandería, *f*; (washing) colada, *f*; *Inf.* ropa lavada o ropa para lavar, *f*. **l.-man,** lavandero, *m*

**laureate** /'lɔriit/ *a* laureado. —*n* poeta laureado, *m*

**laurel** /'lɔrəl/ *n* laurel, cerezo, *m*, *a* láureo. **to crown with l.,** laurear. **l. wreath,** lauréola, *f*

**Lausanne** /lou'zæn/ Lausana, Losana, *f*

**lava** /'lɑvə/ *n* lava, *f*

**lavabo** /lə'veibou/ *n* lavabo, *m*; *Eccl.* lavatorio, *m*

**lavatory** /'lævə,tɔri/ *n* lavabo, *m*; retrete, excusado, *m*

**lave** /leiv/ *vt* bañar

**lavender** /'lævəndər/ *n* espliego, *m*, lavanda, *f*. **l.-water,** agua de lavanda, *f*

**lavish** /'lævɪʃ/ *a* pródigo; profuso, abundante. —*vt* prodigar

**lavishly** /'lævɪʃli/ *adv* pródigamente; en profusión

**lavishness** /'lævɪʃnɪs/ *n* prodigalidad, *f*; profusión, abundancia, *f*

**law** /lɔ/ *n* ley, *f*; derecho, *m*; jurisprudencia, *f*; código de leyes, *m*. **according to law,** según derecho. **canon law,** derecho civil, *m*. **constitutional law,** derecho político, *m*. **criminal law,** derecho penal, *m*. **in law,** por derecho, de acuerdo con la ley; desde el punto de vista legal. **international law,** derecho internacional, *m*. **maritime law,** código marítimo, *m*. **sumptuary law,** ley suntuaria, *f*. **to be the law,** ser la ley. **to go to law,** pleitear (sobre). **to sue at law,** pedir en juicio, poner pleito. **to take the law into one's own hands,** tomar la ley por su propia mano. **law-abiding,** observante de la ley; amigo del orden. **law-breaker,** transgresor (-ra). **law court,** tribunal de justicia, *m*; palacio de justicia, *m*. **law of nature,** ley natural, *f*. **law report,** revista de tribunales, *f*. **law school,** escuela de derecho, *f*. **law student,** estudiante de derecho, *mf*

**lawful** /'lɔfəl/ *a* legítimo; legal; lícito; válido

**lawfully** /'lɔfəli/ *adv* legalmente; legítimamente, lícitamente

**lawfulness** /'lɔfəlnɪs/ *n* legalidad, *f*; legitimidad, *f*

**lawgiver** /'lɔ,gɪvər/ *n* legislador (-ra)

**lawless** /'lɔlɪs/ *a* ilegal; desordenado; ingobernable, rebelde

**lawlessness** /'lɔlɪsnɪs/ *n* ilegalidad, *f*; desorden, *m*; rebeldía, *f*

**lawn** /lɔn/ *n* césped, prado, *m*; (cloth) estopilla, *f*. **l.-mower,** cortacésped *m*, tundidora de césped, *f*, máquina segadora del césped, *f*. **l.-tennis,** tenis (en pista de hierba), *m*

**lawsuit** /'lɔ,sut/ *n* pleito, litigio, *m*, causa, acción, *f*

**lawyer** /'lɔyər/ *n* abogado (-da). **lawyer's office** or **practice,** bufete, *m*

**lax** /læks/ *a* laxo; indisciplinado; vago; descuidado

**laxative** /'læksətɪv/ *n* laxante, *m*, purga, *f*, *a* laxativo

**laxity** /'læksɪti/ *n* laxitud, *f*; descuido, *m*; indiferencia, *f*

**lay** /lei/ *a* laico, seglar, lego; profano. —*n* poema, *m*, trova, *f*; romance, *m*; (song) canción, *f*. **the lay of the land,** la configuración del terreno. **lay brother,** confeso, monigote, *m*. **lay figure,** maniquí, *m*. **lay sister,** (hermana) lega, *f*

**lay** /lei/ *vt* and *vi* poner; colocar; dejar; (strike) tumbar; (demolish) derribar; (the dust) matar; (pipes, etc.) instalar; (hands on) asentar (la mano en); (deposit) depositar; (beat down corn, etc.) encamar, abatir; (eggs, keel) poner; (the table) cubrir, poner; (stretch) extender(se); (bury) depositar en el sepulcro; (a bet) hacer; (wager) apostar; (an accusation) acusar; (the wind, etc.) sosegar, amainar; (a ghost) exorcizar; (impute) atribuir, imputar; (impose) imponer; (prepare) prepara; (make) hacer; (open) abrir; (blame, etc.) echar; (claim) reclamar; (reveal) revelar. **Don't lay the blame on me!** ¡No me eches la culpa! **We laid our plans,** Hicimos nuestros planes; Hicimos nuestros preparativos. **to lay siege to,** asediar. **to lay the colors on too thick,** *Fig.* recargar las tintas. **to lay the foundations,** abrir los cimientos; *Fig.* crear, establecer; fundar. **to lay about one,** dar garrotazos de ciego. **to lay aside,** poner a un lado; arrinconar; (save) ahorrar; (cast away) desechar; abandonar; (reserve) reservar; (a person) apartar de sí; (incapacitate) incapacitar. **lay something at somebody's feet,** embutir algo en el guante de fulano. **to lay before,** mostrar; presentar; poner a la vista; revelar. **to lay by,** See **to lay aside. to lay down,** acostar; depositar; (a burden) posar; (arms) rendir; (one's life); entregar; (give up) renunciar (a); (sketchout) trazar, dibujar; (plan) proyectar; (keep) guardar; (as a principle) establecer, sentar; (the law) dictar. **to lay oneself down,** echarse, tumbarse. **to lay in,** (a stock) proveerse de, hacer provisión de; (hoard) ahorrar; (buy) comprara. **to lay off,** *Naut.* virar de bordo; *Inf.* quitarse de encima. **to lay on,** *vt* colocar sobre; (thrash) pegar; (blows) descargar; (paint, etc.) dar; (water, etc.) instalar; (impose) imponer; (exaggerate) exagerar. —*vi* atacar. **to lay open,** abrir; descubrir, revelar; manifestar; exponer. **to lay oneself open to attack,** exponerse a ser atacado. **to lay out,** poner; arreglar; (the dead) amortajar; (one's money) invertir, emplear; (at interest) poner a rédito; (plan) planear; (knock down) derribar. **to lay oneself out to,** esforzarse a; tomarse la molestia de. **to lay over,** cubrir; sobreponer; extender sobre. **to lay to,** *vi Naut.* estar a la capa. **to lay up,** guardar, acumular, atesorar; poner a un lado; (a ship) desarmar; (a car) poner fuera de circulación; (a person) obligar a guardar cama, incapacitar

**layer** /'leiər/ *n* capa, *f*; *Geol.* estrato, *m*; *Mineral.* manto, *m*; (bird) gallina (pata, etc.) ponedera, *f*; (one who bets) apostador (-ra); *Agr.* acodo, *m*. —*vt* (of plants) acodar

**layette** /lei'et/ *n* canastilla, *f*

**laying** /'leiɪŋ/ *n* colocación, *f*; puesta, *f*; (of an egg) postura, *f*. **l. down,** depósito, *m*; conservación, *f*; (explanation) exposición, *f*. **l. on of hands,** imposición de manos, *f*. **l. out,** tendedura, *f*; (of money) empleo, *m*; inversión, *f*; (arrangement) arreglo, *m*

**layman** /'leimən/ *n* seglar, *mf*; profano (-na)

**layout** /'lei,aut/ *n* plan, *m*; diagramación, disposición, *f*; distribución, *f*; esquema, *m*

**laze** /leiz/ *vi* holgazanear, gandulear, no hacer nada; encontrarse a sus anchas

**lazily** /'leizəli/ *adv* perezosamente; indolentemente; lentamente

**laziness** /'leizɪnɪs/ *n* pereza, holgazanería, *f*; indolencia, *f*; lentitud, *f*

**lazy** /'leizi/ *a* perezoso, holgazán; indolente. **l.-bones,** gandul (-la)

**lead** /lɛd/ *n* (metal) plomo, *m*; (in a pencil) mina, *f*; (plummet) sonda, *f*; *Print.* interlínea, *f*; *pl* **leads,** (roofs) tejados, *m pl.* —*vt* emplomar; guarnecer con plomo; *Print.* interlinear. **black-l.,** grafito, *m*. **deep-**

**sea l.,** *Naut.* escandallo, *m*. **white l.,** albayalde, *m*. **to heave the l.,** echar el escandallo, sondar. **l.-colored,** de color de plomo, plomizo. **l. mine,** mina de plomo, *f*. **l. poisoning,** saturnismo, *m*

**lead** /lid/ *n* delantera, *f*; primer lugar, *m*; dirección, *f*, mando, *m*; (suggestion) indicación, *f*; (influence) influencia, *f*; (dog's) traílla, *f*; *Theat.* protagonista, *mf*; *Theat.* papel principal, *m*; (at cards) mano, *f*

**lead** /lid/ *vt* and *vi* (conduct) conducir, llevar; guiar; (induce) mover, persuadir, inducir; inclinar; (cause) hacer, causar; (captain) capitanear, encabezar; dirigir; (channel) encauzar; (with life) llevar; (give) dar; (head) ir a la cabeza de; *Mil.* mandar; (at cards) salir; (at games) jugar en primer lugar; tomar la delantera; *Fig.* superar a los demás; (of roads) conducir. **to take the l.,** ir delante; ir a la cabeza, tomar la delantera; tomar la iniciativa. **to l. one to think,** hacer pensar. **to l. the way,** mostrar el camino; ir adelante. **to l. along,** llevar (por la mano, etc.), conducir; conducir por; guiar. **to l. astray,** descarriar; desviar (de), seducir (de). **to l. away,** conducir (a otra parte); llevarse (a). **to l. back,** conducir de nuevo; hacer volver. **This path leads back to the village,** Por esta senda se vuelve al pueblo. **to l. in, into,** conducir a (or ante); introducir en; hacer entrar en; invitar a entrar en; (of rooms) comunicarse con; (sin, etc.) inducir a. **to l. off,** *vi* ir adelante; (begin) empezar; (of rooms) comunicarse con. —*vt* hacer marcharse, llevarse (a). **to l. on,** *vt* conducir; guiar; hacer pensar en; (make talk) dar cuerda (a). —*vi* ir a la cabeza; tomar la delantera. **to l. out,** conducir afuera; (to dance) sacar. **to l. to,** conducir a; desembocar en, salir a; (cause) dar lugar a, causar; (make) hacer; (incline) inclinar. **This street leads to the square,** Por esta calle se va a la plaza, Esta calle conduce a la plaza. **to l. up to,** conducir a; (in conversation, etc.) preparar el terreno para; preparar; tener lugar antes de, ocurrir antes de

**leaden** /'lɛdn/ *a* hecho de plomo, plúmbeo; (of skies, etc.) plomizo, de color de plomo, aplomado. **l.-footed,** pesado; lento

**leader** /'lidər/ *n* conductor (-ra); guía, *mf*; jefe (-fa); general, *m*; director (-ra); (in a journal) artículo de fondo, *m*; (of an orchestra) primer violín, *m*. **follow-the-l.,** (game) juego de seguir la fila, *m*

**leadership** /'lidər,ʃɪp/ *n* dirección, *f*; jefatura, *f*; *Mil.* mando, *m*

**lead-in** /'lid ,ɪn/ *a Radio.* de entrada. —*n Radio.* conductor de entrada, *m*

**leading** /'lɛdɪŋ/ *n* (leadwork) emplomadura, *f*

**leading** /'lidɪŋ/ *n* (guidance) dirección, *f*. —*a* principal; primero; importante; eminente. **l. article,** artículo de fondo, *m*; editorial, *m*. **l. card,** primer naipe, *m*. **l. counsel,** abogado (-da) principal. **l. lady,** *Theat.* dama primera, primera actriz, *f*; (cinema) estrella (de la pantalla), *f*. **l. man,** *Theat.* primer galán, *m*. **l. question,** pregunta que sugiere la respuesta, *f*; cuestión importante, *f*. **l. strings,** andadores, *m pl*; *Fig.* tutelaje, *m*

**leaf** /lif/ *n* (*Bot.* and of a page, door, table, screen, etc.) hoja, *f*; (petal) pétalo, *m*, *vi* echar hojas. **gold l.,** pan de oro, *m*. **to turn over a new l.,** volver la hoja, hacer libro nuevo, hacer vida nueva. **to turn over the leaves of a book,** hojear (un libro). **l.-bud,** yema, *f*. **l.-mold,** abono verde, *m*. **l. tobacco,** tabaco en hoja, *m*

**leafiness** /'lifinɪs/ *n* frondosidad, *f*

**leafless** /'liflɪs/ *a* sin hojas

**leaflet** /'liflɪt/ *n* hojuela, *f*; (pamphlet) folleto, *m*

**leafy** /'lifi/ *a* frondoso

**league** /lig/ *n* (measure) legua, *f*; liga, federación, sociedad, *f*; (football) liga, *f*. —*vt* aliar; asociar. —*vi* aliarse; asociarse, confederarse. **to be in l.,** *Inf.* estar de manga. **L. of Nations,** Sociedad de las Naciones, *f*

**leak** /lik/ *n* (hole) agujero, *m*, grieta, *f*; *Naut.* vía de agua, *f*; (of gas, liquids, etc.) escape, *m*; (in a roof, etc.) gotera, *f*; *Elec.* resistencia de escape, *f*. —*vi Naut.* hacer agua; (gas, liquids, etc.) escaparse, salirse; (drip) gotear. **to l. out,** (of news, etc.) trascender, saberse. **to spring a l.,** aparecer una vía de agua, hacer agua

**leakage** /'likɪdʒ/ n (of gas, liquids) escape, m, fuga, f; derrame, m; pérdida, f; (of information) revelación, f
**leaky** /'liki/ a Naut. que hace agua; agujereado; poroso; que tiene goteras
**lean** /lin/ a magro, seco, enjuto, delgado; (of meat) magro; Fig. pobre, estéril. —n carne magra, f, magro, m. **to grow l.,** enflaquecer
**lean** /lin/ vi inclinarse; apoyarse (en). —vt apoyar (en); dejar arrimado (en). **to l. out of the window,** asomarse a la ventana. **to l. against,** apoyarse en, recostarse en (or contra). **to l. back,** echarse hacia atrás; recostarse. **to l. over,** inclinarse. **to l. upon,** apoyarse en; descansar sobre
**leaning** /'linɪŋ/ n inclinación, tendencia, f; predilección, afición, f
**leanness** /'linnɪs/ n magrura, flaqueza, f; (of meat) magrez, f; Fig. pobreza, f
**leap** /lip/ n salto, m; brinco, m; (caper) zapateta, f; Fig. salto, m. —vi saltar, dar un salto; brincar. —vt saltar; hacer saltar. **at one l.,** en un salto. **by leaps and bounds,** en saltos. **My heart leaped,** Mi corazón dio un salto. **to l. to the conclusion that...,** saltar a la conclusión de que... **to l. to the eye,** saltar a la vista. **l. frog,** salto, salto de la muerte, m, pídola f. **l. year,** año bisiesto, m, salta cabrillas, f pl
**leaping** /'lipɪŋ/ a saltador. —n saltos, m pl
**learn** /lɜrn/ vt and vi aprender; instruirse; enterarse de. **to l. by heart,** aprender de memoria. **to l. from a reliable source,** saber de buena tinta. **to l. from experience,** aprender por experiencia
**learned** /'lɜrnɪd/ a sabio, docto; erudito; (of professions) liberal; versado (en), entendido (en). **a l. society,** una sociedad erudita
**learner** /'lɜrnər/ n aprendedor (-ra)
**learning** /'lɜrnɪŋ/ n saber, m; conocimientos, m pl; erudición, f; estudio, m; (literature) literatura, f
**lease** /lis/ n arrendamiento, arriendo, m; contrato de arrendamiento, m. —vt dar en arriendo, arrendar. **on l.,** en arriendo. **to take a new l. on life,** recobrar su vigor. **Lend L. Act,** ley de préstamo y arriendo, f
**leasehold** /'lis,hould/ n censo, m, a censatario
**leaseholder** /'lis,houldər/ n concesionario, m; arrendatario (-ia)
**leash** /liʃ/ n (of a dog) traílla, f
**least** /list/ a superl little, mínimo; el (la, etc.) menor; más pequeño. —adv menos. —n lo menos. **at l.,** siquiera; por lo menos, al menos. **at the very l.,** a lo menos. **not in the l.,** de ninguna manera, nada. **to say the l. of,** sin exagerar, para no decir más
**leather** /'leðər/ n cuero, m; piel, f, a de cuero; de piel. **patent l.,** charol, m. **Spanish l.,** cordobán, m. **tanned l.,** curtido, m. **l. apron,** mandil, m. **l. bag,** saco de cuero, m. **l. bottle,** bota, f. **l. breeches,** pantalón de montar, m. **l. jerkin,** coleto, m. **l. shield,** adarga, f. **l. strap,** correa, f. **l. trade,** comercio en cueros, m
**leatherette** /ˌlɛðəˈrɛt/ n cartón cuero, m
**leathery** /'leðəri/ a de cuero, f; (of the skin) curtido por la intemperie; (tough) correoso
**leave** /liv/ n (permission) permiso, m; (Mil. etc.) licencia, f; (farewell) despedida, f. —vt and vi dejar; abandonar; salir de, quitar, marcharse (de); (as surety) empeñar; (by will) legar, mandar; (an employment) darse de baja (de), dejar; (give into the keeping of) entregar; (bid farewell) despedirse (de). **By your l.,** Con permiso de Vd. (Vds.). Con la venia de Vd. (Vds.) **on l.,** de permiso. **l.-taking,** despedidas, f pl. **to be left,** quedar. **to be left over,** quedar; sobrar. **Two from four leaves two,** De cuatro a dos van dos. **to take French l.,** despedirse a la inglesa. **to take l. of,** despedirse de. **to take one's l.,** marcharse; despedirse. **to l. a deep impression,** Fig. impresionar mucho; quedar grabado (en). **to l. undone,** dejar de hacer, no hacer; dejar sin terminar. **to l. about,** vt dejar por todas partes. —vi (of time) marcharse a eso de... **to l. ajar,** entreabrir, entornar. **to l. alone,** dejar a solas; dejar en paz; no molestar, no meterse con. **to l. aside,** omitir; prescindir de; olvidar. **to l. behind,** dejar atrás; olvidar. **l. much to be desired,** tener mucho que desear. **to l. off,** vt dejar de; abandonar; (garments) no ponerse, quitarse. —vi terminar. **to l. out,** dejar fuera; dejar a un lado, des-

contar; omitir; pasar por; (be silent about) callar; suprimir. **to l. to,** dejar para; dejar hacer
**leaven** /'levən/ n levadura, f, fermento, m, vt fermentar; (Fig. permeate) penetrar (en), infiltrar en, imbuir; (a speech) salpimentar (con)
**leaving** /'livɪŋ/ n salida, partida, marcha, f; pl **leavings,** sobras, f pl; desechos, m pl
**Lebanon** /'lebənən/ el Líbano, m
**lecherous** /'letʃərəs/ a lascivo, lujurioso
**lechery** /'letʃəri/ n lascivia, lujuria, f
**lectern** /'lektərn/ n atril, m; (in a church) facistol, m
**lecture** /'lektʃər/ n conferencia, f; (in a university) lección, clase, f; discurso, m; (Inf. scolding) sermoneo, m. —vi dar una conferencia; (in a university) dar clase. —vt (Inf. scold) predicar, sermonear. **l. room,** sala de conferencias, f; (in a university) sala de clase, aula, f
**lecturer** /'lektʃərər/ n conferenciante, mf; (in a university) auxiliar, m; (professor) catedrático (-ca), profesor (-ra)
**lectureship** /'lektʃər,ʃip/ n auxiliaría, f
**ledge** /ledʒ/ n borde, m; capa, f; (of a window) alféizar, m; (shelf) anaquel, m
**ledger** /'ledʒər/ n libro mayor, m
**lee** /li/ n Naut. sotavento, m, a sotavento
**leech** /litʃ/ n sanguijuela, f
**leek** /lik/ n puerro, m
**leer** /lɪər/ vi mirar de soslayo; guiñar el ojo; mirar con los ojos llenos de deseo. —n mirada de soslayo, f; mirada de lascivia, f
**lees** /liz/ n pl heces, f pl; sedimento, m
**leeward** /'liwərd/ n sotavento, m. **on the l. side,** a sotavento
**leeway** /'li,wei/ n Naut. deriva, f; Fig. amplitud, margen de holgura, márgenes de maniobra, f pl
**left** /left/ past part dejado, etc. See **leave.** a izquierdo. —adv a la izquierda; hacia la izquierda. —n izquierda, f. **on the l.,** a la izquierda. **the L.,** Polit. las izquierdas. **the Left Bank** ( of Paris) la Ribera izquierda, la Orilla izquierda **L. face!** ¡Izquierda! **l.-hand,** mano izquierda, f; izquierda, f. **l.-hand drive,** conducción a la izquierda, f. **l.-handed,** zurdo. **l. luggage office,** consigna, f. **l.-overs,** sobras, f pl, desperdicios, m pl
**leg** /leg/ n pierna, f; (of animals, birds, furniture) pata, f; (of a triangle) cateto, m; (of a pair of compasses, trousers, lamb, veal) pierna, f; (of boots, stockings) caña, f; (of pork) pernil, m; (support) pie, m; (stage) etapa, f. **to be on one's last legs,** estar en las últimas; estar acabándose; estar sin recursos. **to pull a person's leg,** tomar el pelo (a). **leg-pull,** tomadura de pelo, f. **leg-of-mutton sleeve,** manga de pernil, f
**legacy** /'legəsi/ n legado, m, manda, f; herencia, f
**legal** /'ligəl/ a legal; de derecho; jurídico; (lawful, permissible) legítimo, lícito; (of a lawyer) de abogado. **l. expenses,** litisexpensas, f pl. **l. inquiry,** investigación jurídica, f
**legality** /li'gæliti/ n legalidad, f
**legalization** /ˌligələ'zeiʃən/ n legalización, f
**legalize** /'ligə,laiz/ vt legalizar; autorizar, legitimar
**legally** /'ligəli/ adv según la ley; según derecho; legalmente
**legal tender** n moneda de curso liberatorio, f
**legate** /'legɪt/ n legado, m. **papal l.,** legado papal, m
**legatee** /ˌlegə'ti/ n legatario (-ia)
**legation** /lɪ'geiʃən/ n legación, f
**legend** /'ledʒənd/ n leyenda, f
**legendary** /'ledʒən,deri/ a legendario
**legerdemain** /ˌledʒərdə'mein/ n juegos de manos, m pl
**legged** /'legɪd/ a con piernas; de piernas...; de patas... **a three-l. stool,** un taburete de tres patas. **long l.,** zancudo
**leggings** /'legɪnz/ n pl polainas, f pl
**legibility** /ˌledʒə'biliti/ n legibilidad, f
**legible** /'ledʒəbəl/ a legible
**legion** /'lidʒən/ n legión, f. **L. of Honor,** Legión de Honor, f
**legionary** /'lidʒə,neri/ a legionario. —n legionario, m
**legislate** /'ledʒɪs,leit/ vt legislar
**legislation** /ˌledʒɪs'leiʃən/ n legislación, f

**legislative** /'lɛdʒɪs,leɪtɪv/ *a* legislativo, legislador

**legislator** /'lɛdʒɪs,leɪtər/ *n* legislador (-ra)

**legislature** /'lɛdʒɪs,leɪtʃər/ *n* legislatura, *f*

**legitimacy** /lɪ'dʒɪtəməsɪ/ *n* legitimidad, *f;* justicia, *f*

**legitimate** /lɪ'dʒɪtəmɪt/ *a* legítimo; justo

**legitimation** /lɪ,dʒɪtə'meɪʃən/ *n* legitimación, *f*

**leguminous** /lɪ'gyumənəs/ *a* leguminoso

**leisure** /'liʒər/ *n* ocio, *m*, desocupación, *f;* tiempo libre, *m*. **at one's l.,** con sosiego, despacio. **You can do it at your l.,** Puedes hacerlo cuando tengas tiempo. **to be at l.,** estar desocupado, no tener nada que hacer. **l. moments,** ratos perdidos, momentos de ocio, *m pl*

**leisured** /'liʒərd/ *a* desocupado, libre; sin ocupación; (wealthy) acomodado

**leisurely** /'liʒərli/ *a* pausado, lento, deliberado; tardo

**lemon** /'lɛmən/ *n* limón, *m;* (tree) limonero, *m, a* limonado, de color de limón; hecho o sazonado con limón. **l. drop,** pastilla de limón, *f.* **l.-grove,** limonar, *m.* **l.-squash,** limonada natural, *f.* **l.-squeezer,** exprime limones, *m,* exprimidera, *f*

**lemonade** /,lɛmə'neɪd/ *n* limonada, *f.* **l. powder,** limonada seca, *f*

**lemur** /'limər/ *n* lemur, *m*

**lend** /lɛnd/ *vt* prestar. **to l. an ear to,** prestar atención a. **It does not l. itself to...,** No se presta a... **to l. a hand,** echar una mano, dar una mano

**lender** /'lɛndər/ *n* el, *m,* (*f,* la) que presta; prestador (-ra); (of money) prestamista, *mf;* *Com.* mutuante, *mf*

**lending** /'lɛndɪŋ/ *n* prestación, *f;* préstamo, *m.* **l.-library,** biblioteca circulante, *f*

**length** /lɛŋkθ/ *n* largo, *m;* longitud, *f;* (of fabric) corte, *m;* (of a ship) eslora, *f;* (in racing) largo, *m;* distancia, *f;* (in time) duración, *f;* alcance, *m.* **at l.,** por fin, finalmente; (in full) extensamente, largamente. **by a l.,** por un largo. **full-l.,** de cuerpo entero. **three feet in l.,** tres pies de largo. **to go the l. of...,** llegar al extremo de...

**lengthen** /'lɛŋkθən/ *vt* alargar; prolongar; extender. —*vi* alargarse; prolongarse; extenderse; (of days) crecer

**lengthening** /'lɛŋkθənɪŋ/ *n* alargamiento, *m;* prolongación, *f;* crecimiento, *m*

**lengthily** /'lɛŋkθəli/ *adv* largamente

**lengthiness** /'lɛŋkθɪnɪs/ *n* largueza, *f;* prolijidad, *f*

**lengthy** /'lɛŋkθi/ *a* largo; demasiado largo, larguísimo; (of speech) prolijo; verboso

**leniency** /'liniənsi/ *n* lenidad, *f;* indulgencia, *f*

**lenient** /'liniənt/ *a* indulgente; poco severo

**leniently** /'liniəntli/ *adv* con indulgencia

**Leningrad** /'lɛnɪn,græd/ *n* Leningrado, *m*

**lenitive** /'lɛnɪtɪv/ *a* lenitivo. —*n* lenitivo, *m*

**lens** /lɛnz/ *n* lente, *m;* (of the eye) cristalino, *m*

**Lent** /lɛnt/ *n* Cuaresma, *f*

**Lenten** /'lɛntn/ *a* de Cuaresma, cuaresmal

**lentil** /'lɛntɪl/ *n* lenteja, *f*

**lentitude** /'lɛntɪ,tud/ *n* lentitud, *f*

**Leo** /'liou/ *n* León, *m*

**leonine** /'liə,naɪn/ *a* leonino

**leopard** /'lɛpərd/ *n* leopardo, *m*

**leper** /'lɛpər/ *n* leproso (-sa). **l. colony,** colonia de leprosos, *f*

**leprosy** /'lɛprəsi/ *n* lepra, *f*

**leprous** /'lɛprəs/ *a* leproso

**lesbian** /'lɛzbiən/ *a* and *n* lesbiana

**lesion** /'liʒən/ *n* lesión, *f*

**less** /lɛs/ *a* menor; más pequeño; menos; inferior. —*adv* menos; sin. **l. than,** menos de (que). **more or l.,** poco más o menos. **no l.,** nada menos. **none the l.,** sin embargo. **to grow l.,** disminuir. **l. and l.,** cada vez menos

**lessee** /lɛ'si/ *n* arrendatario (-ia); inquilino (-na)

**lessen** /'lɛsən/ *vi* disminuir; reducirse. —*vt* disminuir; reducir; (lower) rebajar; (disparage) menospreciar

**lessening** /'lɛsənɪŋ/ *n* disminución, *f;* reducción, *f*

**lesser** /'lɛsər/ *a compar* menor; más pequeño. See **little**

**lesson** /'lɛsən/ *n* lección, *f.* **to give a l.,** dar lección, dar clase; *Fig.* dar una lección (a). **to hear a l.,** tomar la lección

**lessor** /'lɛsɔr/ *n* arrendador (-ra)

**lest** /lɛst/ *conjunc* para que no; por miedo de (que), no sea que. **I did not do it l. they should not like it,** No lo hice por miedo de que no les gustase

**let** /lɛt/ *vt* dejar, permitir; (lease) arrendar. —*vi* alquilarse, ser alquilado. **Let** as an expression of the imperative is rendered in Spanish by the subjunctive or the imperative, e.g. *Let them go!* ¡Que se vayan! ¡Déjalos marchar! *He let them go,* Les dejó marchar. *to let fall,* dejar caer. *to let go,* dejar marchar; soltar; poner en libertad (a). **to let loose,** dar suelta a; *Fig.* desencadenar. **to let one know,** hacer saber, comunicar. **to let the cat out of the bag,** tirar de la manta. **to let th chance slip,** perder la ocasión. **to let alone,** (a thing) no tocar; (a person) dejar en paz, dejar tranquilo; (an affair) no meterse (en or con); (omit) no mencionar, omitir toda mención de. **to let down,** bajar; (by a rope) descolgar; (hair, etc.) dejar caer; (a dress, etc.) alargar; *Naut.* calar; (disappoint) dejar plantado. **to let in,** dejar entrar; hacer entrar; invitar a entrar; recibir; (insert) insertar. **to let into,** (initiate) iniciar en, admitir en; (a secret) revelar. Other meanings, see **to let in. to let off,** dejar salir; dejar en libertad; exonerar; perdonar; (a gun) disparar; (fireworks, etc.) hacer estallar. **to let out,** dejar salir; poner en libertad; (from a house) acompañar a la puerta; abrir la puerta; *Sew.* ensanchar; (hire) alquilar; (the fire, etc.) dejar extinguirse. **to let up,** dejar subir; (decrease) disminuir; (end) terminar

**let** /lɛt/ *n* estorbo, impedimento, obstáculo, *m.* **without let or hindrance,** sin estorbo ni obstáculo

**lethal** /'liθəl/ *a* letal. **l. weapon,** instrumento de muerte, *m*

**lethargic** /lə'θɑrdʒɪk/ *a* aletargado; letárgico

**lethargy** /'lɛθərdʒɪ/ *n* letargo, *m;* *Med.* letargía, *f*

**letter** /'lɛtər/ *n* (of the alphabet) letra, *f;* (epistle) carta, *f;* *Print.* carácter, *m;* (lessor) arrendador (-ra); *pl* **letters,** letras, *f pl;* (correspondence) correo, *m;* correspondencia, *f.* —*vt* inscribir; imprimir. **capital l.,** letra mayúscula, *f.* **first letters,** *Fig.* primeras letras, *f pl.* **registered l.,** carta certificada, *f,* certificado, *m.* **small l.,** letra minúscula, *f.* **the l. of the law,** la ley escrita. **to be l.-perfect,** saber de memoria. **to the l.,** *Fig.* a la letra. **letters patent,** patente, *f;* título de privilegio, *m.* **l.-balance,** pesacartas, *m.* **l.-book,** *Com.* libro copiador, *m.* **l.-box,** buzón de correos, *m.* **l.-card,** tarjeta postal del gobierno, *f.* **l. of credit,** carta de crédito, *f.* **l. of introduction,** carta de presentación, *f.* **l.-writer,** escritor (-ra) de cartas

**lettered** /'lɛtərd/ *a* culto, instruido; (printed) impreso

**lettering** /'lɛtərɪŋ/ *n* inscripción, *f;* letrero, rótulo, *m*

**letterpress** /'lɛtər,prɛs/ *n* imprenta, *f;* (not illustrations) texto, *m*

**letting** /'lɛtɪŋ/ *n* (hiring) arrendamiento, *m*

**lettuce** /'lɛtɪs/ *n* lechuga, *f.* **l. plant,** lechuguino, *m.* **l. seller,** lechuguero (-ra)

**Leuven** /'luvən/ Lovaina, *f*

**Levantine** /'lɛvən,taɪn/ *a* and *n* levantino (-na)

**Levant, the** /lɪ'vænt/ el Levante, *m*

**levee** /'lɛvi/ *n* besamanos, *m,* recepción, *f*

**level** /'lɛvəl/ *n* nivel, *m;* ras, *m,* flor, *f;* llano, *m;* (plain) llanura, *f;* (instrument) nivel, *a,* llano; igual; al nivel (de); uniforme; imparcial. —*adv* a nivel; igualmente. —*vt* nivelar; igualar; allanar; (a blow) asestar; (a gun) apuntar; (raze) arrasar, derribar; adaptar; hacer uniforme. **on the l.,** a nivel; *Fig.* de buena fe. **spirit l.,** nivel de burbuja, *m.* **to make l. again,** rellanar. **l. country,** campaña, llanura, *f.* **l. with the ground,** a ras de la tierra. **l. with the water,** a flor de agua. **l. crossing,** paso a nivel, *m.* **l.-headed,** sensato, cuerdo. **l. stretch,** rellano, *m;* llanura, *f*

**leveler** /'lɛvələr/ *n* nivelador (-ra)

**leveling** /'lɛvəlɪŋ/ *a* nivelador; de nivelación; igualador. —*n* nivelación, *f;* allanamiento, *m;* (to the ground) arrasamiento, *m;* igualación, *f*

**levelness** /'lɛvəlnɪs/ *n* nivel, *m;* planicie, *f;* igualdad, *f*

**lever** /'lɛvər/ *n* palanca, *f;* (handle) manivela, *f;* escape de reloj, *m;* (excuse) pretexto, *m;* (means) modo, *m.* —*vt* sopalancar. **control l.,** *Aer.* palanca de mando, *f.* **hand-l.,** palanca de mano, *f*

**leverage** /'lɛvərɪdʒ/ n sistema de palancas, m; acción de palanca, f; Fig. influencia, fuerza, f, poder, m

**Leviathan** /lɪ'vaɪəθən/ n leviatán, m

**levitation** /ˌlɛvɪ'teɪʃən/ n levitación, f

**Levite** /'livaɪt/ n levita, m

**Levitical** /lɪ'vɪtɪkəl/ a levítico

**Leviticus** /lɪ'vɪtɪkəs/ n Levítico, m

**levity** /'lɛvɪti/ n levedad, frivolidad, ligereza, f

**levy** /'levi/ n exacción (de tributos), f; impuesto, m; (of a fine) imposición, f; Mil. leva, f. —vt (taxes) exigir; (a fine) imponer; (troops) reclutar, enganchar

**levying** /'leviɪŋ/ n (of a tax) exacción (de tributos), f; (of a fine) imposición, f; (of troops) leva, f

**lewd** /lud/ a lascivo, lujurioso, impúdico

**lewdness** /'ludnɪs/ n lascivia, lujuria, impudicia, f

**lexicographer** /ˌleksɪ'kɒgrəfər/ n lexicógrafo, m

**lexicography** /ˌleksɪ'kɒgrəfi/ n lexicografía, f

**lexicon** /'leksɪˌkɒn/ n léxico, m

**liability** /ˌlaɪə'bɪlɪti/ n responsabilidad, obligación, f; tendencia, f; riesgo, m; pl **liabilities**, obligaciones, f pl; Com. pasivo, m

**liable** /'laɪəbəl/ a responsable; propenso (a); ex-puesto (a); sujeto (a)

**liaison** /li'eɪzɒn/ n lío, m; coordinación, f. **l. officer,** oficial de coordinación, m

**liar** /'laɪər/ n mentiroso (-sa)

**libation** /laɪ'beɪʃən/ n libación, f

**libel** /'laɪbəl/ n libelo, m; difamación, f, vt difamar, calumniar

**libeler** /'laɪbələr/ n libelista, mf difamador (-ra)

**libelous** /'laɪbələs/ a difamatorio

**liberal** /'lɪbərəl/ a liberal; generoso; abundante. —n liberal, mf **l. profession,** carrera liberal, f. **l.-minded,** tolerante. **l.-mindedness,** tolerancia, f

**liberalism** /'lɪbərəˌlɪzəm/ n liberalismo, m

**liberality** /ˌlɪbə'rælɪti/ n liberalidad, f; generosidad, f

**liberalize** /'lɪbərəˌlaɪz/ vt liberalizar

**liberate** /'lɪbəˌreɪt/ vt (a prisoner) poner en libertad; librar (de); (a gas, etc.) dejar escapar

**liberation** /ˌlɪbə'reɪʃən/ n liberación, f; (of a captive) redención, f; (of a slave) manumisión, f

**liberator** /'lɪbəˌreɪtər/ n libertador (-ra)

**libertinage** /'lɪbərˌtɪnɪdʒ/ n libertinaje, m

**libertine** /'lɪbərˌtin/ n libertino, m

**libertinism** /'lɪbərtɪˌnɪzəm/ n libertinaje, m

**liberty** /'lɪbərti/ n libertad, f; (familiarity) familiari-dad, f; (right) privilegio, m, prerrogativa, f; (leave) permiso, m. **at l.,** en libertad; desocupado, libre. **I have taken the l. of giving them your name,** Me he tomado la libertad de darles su nombre. **to set at l.,** poner en libertad (a). **to take liberties with,** tratar con familiaridad; (a text) tergiversar. **l. of speech,** li-bertad de palabra, libertad de expresión, f. **l. of thought,** libertad de pensamiento, f

**libidinous** /lɪ'bɪdnəs/ a libidinoso

**Libra** /'lɪbrə/ n Libra, f

**librarian** /laɪ'brɛəriən/ n bibliotecario (-ia)

**librarianship** /laɪ'brɛəriənˌʃɪp/ n carrera f, or empleo m, de bibliotecario

**library** /'laɪˌbrɛri/ n biblioteca, f; (book shop) librería, f. **l. catalog,** catálogo de la biblioteca, m

**librettist** /lɪ'brɛtɪst/ n libretista, mf

**libretto** /lɪ'brɛtou/ n libreto, m

**Libya** /'lɪbiə/ Libia, f

**Libyan** /'lɪbiən/ a and n libio (-ia)

**license** /'laɪsəns/ n licencia, f, permiso, m; autoriza-ción, f; (driving) carnet de chófer, permiso de con-ducción, m; (of a car) permiso de circulación, m; (for a wireless, etc.) licencia, f; (marriage) licencia de ca-samiento, f; (excess) libertinaje, desenfreno, m. **im-port l.,** permiso de importación, m. **poetic l.,** licencia poética, f. **l. number,** (of a car) número de matrícula-ción, m. —vt licenciar; autorizar; (a car) sacar la li-cencia del automóvil

**licensee** /ˌlaɪsən'si/ n concesionario (-ia)

**licentiate** /laɪ'sɛnʃɪt/ n licenciado (-da)

**licentious** /laɪ'sɛnʃəs/ a licencioso, disoluto

**licentiousness** /laɪ'sɛnʃəsnɪs/ n libertinaje, m, disipa-ción, f

**lichen** /'laɪkən/ n liquen, m

**licit** /'lɪsɪt/ a lícito

**lick** /lɪk/ vt lamer; (of waves) besar; (of flames) bai-lar; (thrash) azotar; (defeat) vencer. **to l. one's lips,** relamerse los labios, chuparse los dedos. **to l. the dust,** morder el polvo

**licking** /'lɪkɪŋ/ n lamedura, f; (beating) paliza, tunda, f; (defeat) derrota, f

**licorice** /'lɪkərɪʃ, 'lɪkrɪʃ, 'lɪkərɪs/ n regaliz, m

**lid** /lɪd/ n cobertera, f; tapa, f; (of the eye) párpado, m

**lie** /laɪ/ n mentira, f; invención, falsedad, f; mentís, m, vi mentir. **to give the lie to,** desmentir, dar el mentís. **to lie barefacedly,** mentir por la mitad de la barba. **white lie,** mentira oficiosa, f

**lie** /laɪ/ vi estar tumbado, estar echado; estar re-costado; descansar, reposar; (in the grave) yacer; (be) estar; (be situated) hallarse, estar situado; (stretch) extenderse; (sleep) dormir; (depend) de-pender; (consist) consistir, estribar; (as an obligation) incumbir. **Here lies...,** Aquí descansa..., Aquí yace... **It does not lie in my power,** No depende de mí. **to let lie,** dejar; dejar en paz. **to lie at anchor,** estar an-clado. **to lie fallow,** estar en barbecho; Fig. descan-sar. **to lie about,** estar esparcido por todas partes; estar en desorden. **to lie along,** estar tendido a lo largo de; Naut. dar a la banda. **to lie back,** re-costarse; apoyarse (en). **to lie by,** estar acostado al lado de; (of things, places) estar cerca (de); descan-sar. **to lie down,** tenderse, tumbarse, echarse, acos-tarse; reposar. **Lie down!** (to a dog) ¡Echate! **to lie down under,** tenderse bajo; (an insult) tragar, sufrir. **to lie in,** consistir en; depender de; (of childbirth) es-tar de parto. **to lie open,** estar abierto; estar ex-puesto (a); estar al descubierto, estar a la vista. **to lie over,** (be postponed) quedar aplazado. **to lie to,** Naut. estarse a la capa, ponerse en facha. **to lie un-der,** estar bajo, hallarse bajo; estar bajo el peso de; (be exposed to) estar expuesto a. **to lie with,** dormir con; (concern) tocar (a); corresponder (a)

**lie** /laɪ/ n configuración, f; disposición, f; posición, f. **the lie of the land,** la configuración del terreno

**lieu** /lu/ n lugar, m. **in l. of,** en lugar de, en vez de

**lieutenant** /lu'tɛnənt/ n teniente, lugarteniente, m; (naval) alférez, m. **first l.,** (in the army) primer te-niente, teniente, m; (in the navy) alférez de navío, m. **naval l.,** teniente de navío, m. **second l.,** (in the army) segundo teniente, m; (in the navy) alférez de fragata, m. **l.-colonel,** teniente coronel, m. **l.-commander,** capitán de fragata, m. **l.-general,** te-niente general, m. **l.-governor,** subgobernador, m

**life** /laɪf/ n vida, f; (being) ser, m; (society) mundo, m, sociedad, f; (vitality) vitalidad, f; vigor, m, a de vida; (of annuities, etc.) vitalicio; (life-saving) de salvamento. **for l.,** de por vida. **from l.,** del natural. **high l.,** gran mundo, m, alta sociedad, f. **low l.,** vida del hampa, vida de los barrios bajos, f. **to the l.,** al vivo. **to lay down one's l.,** entregar la vida. **to take one's l. in one's hands,** jugarse la vida. **l. annuity,** fondo vitalicio, m. **l.-belt,** (cinturón) salvavidas, m. **l.-blood,** sangre vital, f; Fig. nervio, m; vigor, m. **l.-boat,** (on a ship) bote salvavidas, m; (on the coast) lancha de salvamento, f. **l.-boat station,** estación de salvamento, f. **l.-giving,** vivificante, que da vida; tonificante. **l.-guard,** (soldier) guardia militar, f; Guardia de Corps, f; (at beach or swimming pool) guardavivas, mf. **l.-insurance,** seguro sobre la vida, m. **l.-interest,** usufructo, m. **l.-jacket,** chaleco salvavidas, m. **l.-like,** natural. **l.-line,** cable de salva-mento, m. **l.-saving,** a de salvamento; curativo. **l.-saving apparatus,** aparato salvavidas, m. **l.-sized,** de tamaño natural

**life cycle** n ciclo vital, m

**life imprisonment** n reclusión perpetua, f

**life jacket** n chaleco salvavidas, f

**lifeless** /'laɪflɪs/ a sin vida, muerto; inanimado; Fig. desanimado

**lifelong** /'laɪfˌlɔŋ/ a de toda la vida

**lifetime** /'laɪfˌtaɪm/ n vida, f

**lift** /lɪft/ n esfuerzo para levantar, m; acción de levan-tar, f; alza, f; (blow) golpe, m; (help) ayuda, f; (ele-vator) ascensor, m; (for goods) montacargas, m; pl **lifts,** Naut. balancines, m pl. **to give a l. to,** (help) ayudar; (hitchhiker etc.) dar un aventón. **l. attend-ant,** ascensorista, *mf*

**lift** /lɪft/ *vt* levantar; alzar, elevar; (pick up) coger; (one's hat) quitarse; (steal) hurtar; exaltar. —*vi* (of mist) disiparse; desaparecer. **to l. the elbow,** empinar el codo. **to l. down,** quitar (de); (a person) bajar en brazos. **to l. up,** alzar; erguir, levantar; levantar en brazos

**lifting** /'lɪftɪŋ/ *n* acción de levantar, *f;* levantamiento, alzamiento, *m*

**ligament** /'lɪgəmənt/ *n* ligamento, *m*

**ligature** /'lɪgətʃər/ *n* (*Surg. Mus.*) ligadura, *f*

**light** /laɪt/ *a* (not dark) claro, con mucha luz, bañado de luz; (of colors) claro; (not heavy, and of sleep, food, troops, movements) ligero; (of reading) de entretenimiento; (irresponsible) frívolo; (easy) fácil; (slight) leve; (of hair) rubio; (happy) alegre; (fickle) inconstante, liviano; (of complexion) blanco. —*adv* ligero. **to be l.,** no pesar mucho; estar de día. **to grow l.,** (dawn) clarear; iluminarse. **to make l. of,** no tomar en serio; no preocuparse de; (suffering) sufrir sin quejarse. **l.-colored,** (de color) claro. **l.-fingeredness,** sutileza de manos, *f.* **l.-footed,** ligero de pies. **l.-haired,** de pelo rubio. **l.-headed,** casquivano, ligero de cascos; delirante. **l.-headedness,** ligereza de cascos, frivolidad, *f;* delirio, *m.* **l.-hearted,** alegre (de corazón). **l.-heartedness,** alegría, *f.* **l. horse,** *Mil.* caballería ligera, *f.* **l. troops,** tropas ligeras, *f pl.* **l.-weight,** *n* (boxing) peso ligero, *m, a* de peso ligero

**light** /laɪt/ *n* luz., *f;* (day) día, *m;* (match) cerilla, *f;* (of a cigarette, etc.) fuego, *m;* (of a window) cristal, vidrio, *m;* (point of view) punto de vista, *m;* (in a picture) toque de luz, *m; pl* **lights,** (offal) bofes, *m pl.* **against the l.,** al trasluz. **by the l. of,** a la luz de; según. **half-l.,** media luz, *f.* **high light ( s),** *Art.* claros, *m pl; Fig.* momento culminante, *m;* acontecimiento de más interés, *m.* **to come to l.,** descubrirse. **to put a l. to the fire,** encender el fuego. **l.-year,** año de luz, *m*

**light** /laɪt/ *vt* (a lamp, fire, etc.) encender; iluminar. —*vi* encenderse; iluminarse; *Fig.* animarse; brillar. **to l. upon,** encontrar por casualidad; tropezar con

**lighten** /'laɪtn̩/ *vt* (illuminate) iluminar; (of weight) aligerar; (cheer) alegrar; (mitigate) aliviar. —*vi* (grow light) clarear; (of lightning) relampaguear; (become less heavy) disminuir de peso, aligerarse; volverse más alegre

**lightening** /'laɪtn̩ɪŋ/ *n* aligeramiento, *m;* (easing) alivio, *m;* luz, *f*

**lighter** /'laɪtər/ *n* (boat) lancha, barcaza, gabarra, *f;* (device) encendedor, *m.* **pocket l.,** encendedor de bolsillo, *m.* **l. man,** gabarrero, *m*

**light-fingered** *a* ligero de manos

**lighthouse** /'laɪtˌhaʊs/ *n* faro, *m.* **l.-keeper,** guardafaro, *m*

**lighting** /'laɪtɪŋ/ *n* iluminación, *f;* alumbrado, *m.* **flood l.,** iluminación intensiva, *f.* **l.-up time,** hora de encender los faros, *f*

**lightly** /'laɪtli/ *adv* ligeramente; fácilmente; (slightly) levemente; ágilmente; sin seriedad. **l. wounded,** levemente herido

**lightness** /'laɪtnɪs/ *n* ligereza, *f;* poco peso, *m;* agilidad, *f;* (brightness) claridad, *f;* (inconstancy) liviandad, inconstancia, *f;* frivolidad, *f*

**lightning** /'laɪtnɪŋ/ *n* relámpago, rayo, *m.* **as quick as l.,** como un relámpago. **to be struck by l.,** ser herido por un relámpago. **l.-rod,** pararrayos, *m*

**lightship** /'laɪtˌʃɪp/ *n* buque faro, *m*

**ligneous** /'lɪgnɪəs/ *a* leñoso

**lignite** /'lɪgnaɪt/ *n* lignito, *m*

**likable** /'laɪkəbəl/ *a* simpático

**like** /laɪk/ *a* semejante; parecido; igual, mismo; (characteristic) típico, característico; (likely) probable; (equivalent) equivalente. —*adv* como; igual (que); del mismo modo (que). —*n* semejante, igual, *mf;* tal cosa, *f;* cosas semejantes, *f pl.* **Don't speak to me l. that,** No me hables así. **He was l. a fury,** Estaba hecho una furia. **They are very l. each other,** Se parecen mucho. **to be l.,** parecerse a; semejar. **to look l.,** parecer ser (que); tener el aspecto de; (of

persons) parecerse (a). **to return l. for l.,** pagar en la misma moneda

**like** /laɪk/ *vt* gustar, agradar; estar aficionado (a), gustar de; (wish) querer. **As you l.,** Como te parezca bien, Como quieras. **If you l.,** Si quieres. **James likes painting,** Jaime está aficionado a la pintura. **Judith does not l. the north of England,** A Judit no le gusta el norte de Inglaterra. **I don't l. to do it,** No me gusta hacerlo. **I should l. him to go to Madrid,** Me gustaría que fuese a Madrid

**likelihood** /'laɪkliˌhʊd/ *n* posibilidad, *f;* probabilidad, *f*

**likely** /'laɪkli/ *a* probable; verosímil, creíble, plausible; posible; (suitable) satisfactorio, apropiado; (handsome) bien parecido. —*adv* probablemente. **They are not l. to come,** No es probable que vengan

**liken** /'laɪkən/ *vt* comparar

**likeness** /'laɪknɪs/ *n* parecido, *m,* semejanza, *f;* (portrait) retrato, *m*

**likewise** /'laɪkˌwaɪz/ *adv* igualmente, asimismo, también. —*conjunc* además

**liking** /'laɪkɪŋ/ *n* (for persons) simpatía, *f,* cariño, *m;* (for things) gusto, *m,* afición, *f;* (appreciation) aprecio, *m.* **I have a l. for old cities,** Me gustan (or me atraen) las viejas ciudades. **to take a l. to,** (things) aficionarse a; (persons) prendarse de, tomar cariño (a)

**lilac** /'laɪlək/ *n* lila, *f.* **l. color,** color de lila, *m*

**Lilliputian** /ˌlɪlɪ'pyuʃən/ *a* liliputiense. —*n* liliputiense, *mf*

**lilt** /lɪlt/ *n* canción, *f;* ritmo, *m;* armonía, *f*

**lily** /'lɪli/ *n* lirio, *m,* azucena, *f;* (of France) flor de lis, *f.* **l. of the valley,** lirio de los valles, muguete, *m.* **l.-white,** blanco como la azucena

**limb** /lɪm/ *n* *Anat.* miembro, *m;* (of a tree) rama, *f*

**limbless** /'lɪmlɪs/ *a* mutilado

**limbo** /'lɪmboʊ/ *n* limbo, *m*

**lime** /laɪm/ *n* *Chem.* cal, *f;* (for catching birds) liga, hisca, *f;* (linden tree) tilo, *m;* (tree like a lemon) limero, *m;* (fruit) lima, *f.* —*vt* (whiten) encalar; *Agr.* abonar con cal. **slaked l.,** cal muerta, *f.* **l.-flower,** flor del tilo, tila, *f;* flor del limero, *f.* **l.-juice,** jugo de lima, *m.* **l.-kiln,** calera, *f.* **l.-pit,** pozo de cal, *m*

**limelight** /'laɪmˌlaɪt/ *n* luz de calcio, *f;* *Fig.* centro de atención, *m;* publicidad, *f.* **to be in the l.,** ser el centro de atención, estar a la vista (de público)

**limestone** /'laɪmˌstoʊn/ *n* piedra caliza, *f.* **l. deposit,** calar, *m*

**limit** /'lɪmɪt/ *n* límite, *m;* confín, *m;* linde, *m,* or *f;* limitación, *f, vt* limitar; fijar; (restrict) restringir. **This is the l.!** ¡Este es el colmo! ¡No faltaba más!

**limitation** /ˌlɪmɪ'teɪʃən/ *n* limitación, *f;* restricción, *f*

**limitative** /'lɪmɪˌteɪtɪv/ *a* restrictivo, limitativo

**limited** /'lɪmɪtɪd/ *a* limitado; restringido; escaso; (of persons) de cortos alcances; *Com.* anónimo. **l. company,** sociedad anónima, *f*

**limited monarchy** *n* monarquía moderada, *f*

**limiting adjective** /'lɪmɪtɪŋ/ *n* adjetivo determinativo, *m*

**limitless** /'lɪmɪtlɪs/ *a* sin límites; ilimitado, inmenso

**limousine** /'lɪməˌzin/ *n* limusina, *f,* coche cerrado, *m*

**limp** /lɪmp/ *a* flojo; débil; fláccido; lánguido. —*n* cojera, *f.* —*vi* cojear. **to l. off,** marcharse cojeando. **to l. up,** acercarse cojeando; subir cojeando

**limpid** /'lɪmpɪd/ *a* límpido, cristalino, puro

**limpidity** /lɪm'pɪdɪti/ *n* limpidez, *f*

**limping** /'lɪmpɪŋ/ *a* cojo

**limply** /'lɪmpli/ *adv* flojamente; débilmente; lánguidamente

**limpness** /'lɪmpnɪs/ *n* flojedad, *f;* debilidad, *f;* languidez, *f*

**linchpin** /'lɪntʃˌpɪn/ *n* pezonera, *f*

**linden** /'lɪndən/ *n* tilo, *m*

**line** /laɪn/ *vt* (furrow) surcar; (troops, etc.) poner en fila; alinear; (clothes, nests, etc.) forrar; (building) revestir; (one's pocket) llenar. —*vi* estar en línea, alinearse

**line** /laɪn/ *n* (most meanings) línea, *f;* (cord) cuerda, *f; Naut.* cordel, *m;* (fishing) sedal, *m;* (railway) vía, *f;* (wrinkle) surco, *m;* arruga, *f;* (row) hilera, ringlera, fila, *f;* (of verse) verso, *m; Print.* renglón, *m;* (of business) ramo, *m;* profesión, *f;* (interest) especialidad, *f.* **bowling** or **serving l.,** línea de saque, *f;* **hard lines,** mala suerte, *f;* apuro, *m,* situación difícil, *f.* **in a l.,** en fila; en cola. **in direct l.,** (of descent) en línea recta. **It is not in my l.,** No es una especialidad mía; No es uno de mis intereses. **on the lines of,** conforme a; parecido a. **to cross the l.,** (equator) pasar la línea; (railway) cruzar la vía. **to drop a l.,** escribir unas líneas, poner unas líneas. **to read between the lines,** leer entre líneas. **l.-drawing,** dibujo de líneas, *m.* **l. of battle,** línea de batalla, *f*

**lineage** /'lɪnɪdʒ/ *n* linaje, *m,* familia, raza, *f*

**lineal** /'lɪnɪəl/ *a* lineal

**lineament** /'lɪnɪəmənt/ *n* lineamento, *m;* (of the face) facciones, *f pl*

**linear** /'lɪnɪər/ *a* lineal. **l. equation,** ecuación de primer grado, *f*

**lined** /laɪnd/ *a* rayado, con líneas; (of the face) surcado, arrugado; (of gloves, etc.) forrado. **lined paper,** papel rayado, *m*

**linen** /'lɪnən/ *n* lino, *m; Inf.* ropa blanca, *f; a* de lino. **clean l.,** ropa limpia, *f.* **dirty l.,** ropa sucia, *f;* ropa para lavar, *f.* **table-l.,** mantelería, *f.* **l. cupboard,** armario para ropa blanca, *m.* **l. draper,** lencero (-ra). **l.-draper's shop,** lencería, *f.* **l. room,** lencería, *f.* **l. tape,** trenzadera, *f.* **l. thread,** hilo de lino, *m*

**liner** /'laɪnər/ *n* (ship) transatlántico, *m;* buque de vapor, *m; Aer.* avión de pasaje, *m*

**linesman** /'laɪnzmən/ *n* soldado de línea, *m; Sports.* juez de línea, *m*

**ling** /lɪŋ/ *n Bot.* brezo, *m; Ichth.* especie de abadejo, *f*

**linger** /'lɪŋgər/ *vi* (remain) quedarse; tardar en marcharse; ir lentamente; hacer algo despacio

**lingerie** /ˌlɑnʒə'reɪ/ *n* ropa blanca, *f*

**lingering** /'lɪŋgərɪŋ/ *a* lento; largo; prolongado; melancólico, triste

**lingeringly** /'lɪŋgərɪŋli/ *adv* lentamente; largamente; melancólicamente

**linguist** /'lɪŋgwɪst/ *n* lingüista, *mf*

**linguistic** /lɪŋ'gwɪstɪk/ *a* lingüístico

**linguistics** /lɪŋ'gwɪstɪks/ *n* lingüística, *f*

**liniment** /'lɪnəmənt/ *n* linimento, *m*

**lining** /'laɪnɪŋ/ *n* (of a garment, etc.) forro, *m;* (building) revestimiento, *m*

**link** /lɪŋk/ *n* (in a chain) eslabón, *m;* (of beads) sarta, *f; Fig.* enlace, *m,* cadena, *f;* conexión, *f; Mech.* corredera, *f;* (torch) hacha de viento, *f.* —*vt* enlazar, unir; *Fig.* encadenar. **missing l.,** *Fig.* eslabón perdido, *m.* **to l. arms,** cogerse del brazo

**linking** /'lɪŋkɪŋ/ *n* encadenamiento, *m; Fig.* conexión, *f*

**links** /lɪŋks/ *n pl* campo de golf, *m*

**linoleum** /lɪ'nouliəm/ *n* linóleo, *m*

**linotype** /'laɪnəˌtaɪp/ *n* linotipia, *f*

**linseed** /'lɪnˌsɪd/ *n* linaza, *f.* **l. cake,** bagazo, *m.* **l.-oil,** aceite de linaza, *m*

**lint** /lɪnt/ *n Med.* hilas, *f pl;* (fluff) borra, *f*

**lintel** /'lɪntl/ *n* dintel, *m;* (threshold) umbral, *m*

**lion** /'laɪən/ *n* león, *m; Fig.* celebridad, *f.* **l. cage** or **den,** leonera, *f.* **l.-hearted,** valeroso. **l.-hunter,** cazador (-ra) de leones. **l.-keeper,** leonero (-ra). **lion's mane,** melena, *f.* **l.-tamer,** domador (-ra) de leones

**lioness** /'laɪənɪs/ *n* leona, *f*

**lionize** /'laɪəˌnaɪz/ *vt* dar bombo (a), hacer la rueda (a), tratar como una celebridad (a)

**lion's share** *n* parte del león, tajada del león, *f*

**lip** /lɪp/ *n* labio, *m;* (of a vessel) pico, *m;* (of a crater) borde, *m; Fig.* boca, *f;* **to open one's lips,** abrir la boca. **to smack one's lips,** chuparse los dedos. **lip reading,** lectura labial, *f.* **lip-service,** amor fingido, *m;* promesas hipócritas, *f pl.* **lip stick,** lápiz para los labios, *m*

**lipped** /lɪpt/ *a* (in compounds) con labios..., que tiene labios; (of vessels in compounds) con... picos

**liquefaction** /ˌlɪkwə'fækʃən/ *n* licuefacción, *f*

**liquefiable** /'lɪkwəˌfaɪəbəl/ *a* liquidable

**liquefy** /'lɪkwəˌfaɪ/ *vt* liquidar. —*vi* liquidarse

**liqueur** /lɪ'kɜr/ *n* licor, *m.* **l.-glass,** copita de licor, *f.* **l.-set,** licorera, *f*

**liquid** /'lɪkwɪd/ *n* líquido, *m, a* líquido; límpido. **l.**

air, aire líquido, *m.* **l. measure,** medida para líquidos, *f*

**liquidate** /'lɪkwɪˌdeɪt/ *vt* liquidar; saldar (cuentas); *Mil.* soldar

**liquidation** /ˌlɪkwɪ'deɪʃən/ *n* liquidación, *f*

**liquidness** /'lɪkwɪdnɪs/ *n* liquidez, *f;* fluidez, *f*

**liquor** /'lɪkər/ *n* licor, *m.* **l. shop,** aguardentería, *f.* **l. traffic,** negocio de vinos y licores, *m;* contrabando, *m*

**lira** /'lɪərə/ *n* lira, *f*

**Lisbon** /'lɪzbən/ Lisboa, *f*

**lisp** /lɪsp/ *n* ceceo, *m;* balbuceo, *m, vi* cecear; balbucir

**lisping** /'lɪspɪŋ/ *a* ceceoso; balbuciente. —*n* ceceo, *m;* (of a child, etc.) balbuceo, *m*

**lissome** /'lɪsəm/ *a* flexible; ágil

**list** /lɪst/ *n* lista, *f;* catálogo, *m;* matrícula, *f; Naut.* recalcada, *f;* inclinación, *f;* (tournament) liza, *f.* —*vt* hacer una lista de; catalogar; matricular, inscribir. —*vi Naut.* recalcar; inclinarse a un lado. **to enter the lists,** entrar en liza. **l. of wines,** lista de vinos, *f*

**listen** /'lɪsən/ *vi* escuchar; (attend) atender. **Don't you want to l. to the music?** ¿No quieres escuchar la música? **to l. in,** (to the radio) escuchar la radio; (eavesdrop) escuchar a hurtadillas

**listener** /'lɪsənər/ *n* oyente, *mf;* (to radio) radiooyente, *mf*

**listless** /'lɪstlɪs/ *a* lánguido, apático, indiferente

**listlessly** /'lɪstlɪsli/ *adv* lánguidamente, indiferentemente

**listlessness** /'lɪstlɪsnɪs/ *n* apatía, languidez, indiferencia, inercia, *f*

**litany** /'lɪtn̩i/ *n* letanía, *f*

**liter** /'lɪtər/ *n* litro, *m*

**literal** /'lɪtərəl/ *a* literal. **l.-minded,** sin imaginación

**literalness** /'lɪtərəlnɪs/ *n* literalidad, *f*

**literary** /'lɪtəˌreri/ *a* literario

**literary executor** *n* depositario de la obra literaria, *m*

**literate** /'lɪtərɪt/ *a and n* literato (-ta)

**literature** /'lɪtərətʃər/ *n* literatura, *f*

**lithe** /laɪð/ *a* flexible; sinuoso y delgado; ágil

**litheness** /'laɪðnɪs/ *n* flexibilidad, *f;* sinuosidad, *f;* delgadez, *f;* agilidad, *f*

**lithograph** /'lɪθəˌgræf/ *n* litografía, *f, vt* litografiar

**lithographer** /lɪ'θɒgrəfər/ *n* litógrafo, *m*

**lithographic** /ˌlɪθə'græfɪk/ *a* litográfico

**lithography** /lɪ'θɒgrəfi/ *n* litografía, *f*

**Lithuania** /ˌlɪθu'einiə/ Lituania, *f*

**Lithuanian** /ˌlɪθu'einiən/ *a* lituano, *n* lituano (-na); (language) lituano, *m*

**litigant** /'lɪtɪgənt/ *n* litigante, *mf*

**litigate** /'lɪtɪˌgeit/ *vi and vt* litigar, pleitear

**litigation** /ˌlɪtɪ'geiʃən/ *n* litigación, *f*

**litigious** /lɪ'tɪdʒəs/ *a* litigioso

**litmus** /'lɪtməs/ *n* tornasol, *m.* **l. paper,** papel de tornasol, *m*

**litter** /'lɪtər/ *n* litera, *f;* (stretcher) camilla, *f;* (bed) lecho, *m;* cama de paja, *f;* (brood) camada, cría, *f;* (rubbish) cosas en desorden, *f pl;* (papers) papeletas, *f pl;* (untidiness) desarreglo, desorden, *m,* confusión, *f, vt* poner en desorden

**little** /'lɪtl/ *a* pequeño; poco; (scanty) escaso; insignificante; bajo, mezquino. —*adv* poco. **a l.,** un poco (de); un tanto. **in l.,** en pequeño. **not a l.,** no poco; bastante. **l. by l.,** poco a poco. **l. or no,** poco o nada. **however l.,** por pequeño que. **as l. as possible,** lo menos posible. **to make l. of,** no dar importancia a; sacar poco en claro de, no comprender bien; no hacer caso de; (persons) acoger mal. **l. by l.,** poco a poco. **l. finger,** dedo meñique, *m.* **l. one,** pequeñuela, *f,* pequeñito, *m*

**littleness** /'lɪtlnɪs/ *n* pequeñez, *f;* poquedad, *f;* mezquindad, *f;* trivialidad, *f*

**littoral** /'lɪtərəl/ *a and n* litoral, *m*

**liturgical** /lɪ'tɜrdʒɪkəl/ *a* litúrgico. **l. calendar,** calendario litúrgico, *m*

**liturgical vestment** *n* paramento litúrgico, *m*

**liturgy** /'lɪtərdʒi/ *n* liturgia, *f*

**live** /laiv/ *a* vivo, viviente; (alight) encendido; (of a wire, etc.) cargado de electricidad. **l. cartridge,** cartucho con bala, *m.* **l. coal,** ascua, *f.* **l.-stock,**

ganadería, f. **l. wire,** conductor eléctrico, m; Fig. fuerza viva, f

**live** /laiv/ vi vivir; residir, habitar; (of ships) mantenerse a flote; salvarse; subsistir. —vt (one's life) llevar, pasar. **Long l.! ¡Viva! to have enough to l. on,** tener de que vivir. **to l. together,** convivir. **to l. again,** volver a vivir. **to l. at,** vivir en, habitar. **to l. down,** sobrevivir a; (a fault) lograr borrar. **to l. on,** vivir de. **to l. up to,** vivir con arreglo a, vivir en conformidad con; estar al nivel de, merecer. **to l. up for one's income,** vivir al día, gastarse toda la renta

**live broadcast** n emisión en directo, f

**livelihood** /'laivli,hʊd/ n vida, subsistencia, f. **to make a l.,** ganarse la vida

**liveliness** /'laivlɪnɪs/ n vivacidad, vida, f; animación, f; alegría, f

**livelong** /'lɪv,lɔŋ/ a entero, todo; eterno. **all the l. day,** todo el santo día

**lively** /'laivli/ a vivo; vivaracho; brioso, enérgico; alegre; bullicioso; animado; (fresh) fresco; (of colors) brillante; intenso

**liver** /'lɪvər/ n vividor (-ra), el, m, (f, la) que vive; habitante, m; Anat. hígado, m. **l. cancer,** cáncer del hígado, m. **l. complaint,** mal de hígado, m. **l. extract,** extracto de hígado, m

**livery** /'lɪvəri/ n librea, f; uniforme, m; Poet. vestiduras, f pl. **l. stables,** pensión de caballos, f; cochería de alquiler, f

**livid** /'lɪvɪd/ a lívido; cárdeno, amoratado

**lividness** /'lɪvɪdnɪs/ n lividez, f

**living** /'lɪvɪŋ/ a viviente; vivo, vital. —n vida, f; modo de vivir, m; beneficio eclesiástico, m. **the l.,** los vivos. **to make one's l.,** ganarse la vida. **l. memory,** memoria de personas vivientes, memoria de los que aún viven, f. **l.-room,** sala de estar, f. **l. soul,** ser viviente, m. Inf. bicho viviente, m. **l. wage,** jornal básico, m

**lizard** /'lɪzərd/ n lagarto (-ta). **giant l.,** dragón, m. **wall l.,** lagartija, f. **l. hole,** lagartera, f

**llama** /'lɑmə/ n llama, f

**load** /loud/ n carga, f; peso, m; (cart) carretada, f; Elec. carga, f; (quantity) cantidad, f. —vt cargar (con); (with honors) llenar (de); (Fig. weigh down) agobiar (con); (a stick with lead) emplomar; (Elec. and of dice) cargar; (wine) mezclar vino con un narcótico. **to be loaded with fruit,** estar cargado de fruta. **to l. oneself with,** cargarse de. **to l. the dice,** cargar los dados. **to l. again,** recargar

**loader** /'loudər/ n cargador, m

**loading** /'loudɪŋ/ n carga, f. **l. depot,** cargadero, m

**loaf** /louf/ n pan, m; (French) barra de pan, f. —vi golfear, vagabundear, gandulear. **l. sugar,** azúcar de pilón, f

**loafer** /'loufər/ n vago (-ga); azotacalles, mf; gandul (-la); golfo (-fa)

**loafing** /'loufɪŋ/ n gandulería, f, vagabundeo, m

**loam** /loum/ n marga, f

**loamy** /'loumi/ a margoso

**loan** /loun/ n empréstito, m; (lending) prestación, f; préstamo, m. —vt prestar. **l. fund,** caja de empréstitos, f. **l. company office,** casa de préstamos, f

**loath** /louθ/ a desinclinado, poco dispuesto

**loathe** /louð/ vt abominar, detestar, odiar, aborrecer; repugnar

**loather** /'louðər/ n el, m, (f, la) que odia; aborrecedor (-ra)

**loathing** /'louðɪŋ/ n aborrecimiento, odio, m; repugnancia, aversión, f

**loathsome** /'louðsəm/ a odioso, aborrecible; asqueroso; repugnante

**loathsomeness** /'louðsəmnɪs/ n carácter repugnante, m; asquerosidad, f

**lobby** /'lɒbi/ n pasillo, m; antecámara, f; (in a hotel, house) vestíbulo, recibidor, m; (waiting-room) sala de espera, f; (in Parliament) sala de los pasos perdidos, f. —vt and vi cabildear

**lobe** /loub/ n Bot. lobo, m; (Anat. Archit.) lóbulo, m

**lobster** /'lɒbstər/ n langosta, f; bogavante, m. **l.-pot,** cambín, m, nasa, f

**local** /'loukəl/ a local; de la localidad. **l. anesthetic,** anestésico local, m. **l. color,** color local, m

**locale** /lou'kæl/ n local, m

**locality** /lou'kælɪti/ n localidad, f; situación, f

**localization** /,loukələ'zeiʃən/ n localización, f

**localize** /'loukə,laiz/ vt localizar

**locate** /'loukeit/ vt situar; colocar; localizar. **to be located,** situarse; hallarse

**location** /lou'keiʃən/ n colocación, f; emplazamiento, m; localidad, f; situación, posición, f

**loch** /lɒk/ n lago, m

**lock** /lɒk/ n cerradura (of a door, including a vehicle) f; (of a gun) cerrojo, m; (in wrestling) llave, f; (on rivers, canals) presa, f; (at a dock) esclusa, f; (of hair) mechón, m, guedeja, f; (ringlet) bucle, m; pl **locks,** (hair) cabellos, m pl, pelo, m. **spring l.,** cerradura de golpe, f. **to put a l. on,** poner cerradura a. **under l. and key,** bajo cuatro llaves. **l.-jaw,** trismo, m. **l. keeper,** esclusero, m. **l.-out strike,** huelga patronal, f

**lock** /lɒk/ vt cerrar con llave; Fig. encerrar; (embrace) abrazar estrechamente; (of wheels, etc.) trabar; (twine) entrelazar. —vi cerrarse con llave. **to l. in,** cerrar con llave; encerrar. **to l. out,** cerrar la puerta (a); dejar en la calle (a). **to l. up,** encerrar; (imprison) encarcelar

**locker** /'lɒkər/ n (drawer) cajón, m; (cupboard) armario, m; Naut. cajonada, f

**locket** /'lɒkɪt/ n guardapelo, m; medallón, m

**locksmith** /'lɒk,smiθ/ n cerrajero, m. **locksmith's trade,** cerrajería, f

**locomotion** /,loukə'mouʃən/ n locomoción, f

**locomotive** /,loukə'moutɪv/ a locomotor. —n locomotora, f

**locum tenens** /'loukəm 'tinɛnz/ n interino (-na)

**locust** /'loukəst/ n langosta migratoria, f

**locution** /lou'kyuʃən/ n locución, f

**lode** /loud/ n filón, m

**lodestar** /'loud,stɑr/ n estrella polar, f; Fig. norte, m

**lodge** /lɒdʒ/ n casita, garita, f; casa de guarda, f; (freemason's) logia, f; (porter's) portería, f, vi hospedarse, alojarse vivir, parar; penetrar; entrar (en); fijarse (en). —vt hospedar, alojar; albergar; (a blow) asestar; (a complaint) hacer, dar; (money, etc.) depositar. **to l. an accusation against,** querellarse contra, quejarse de. **l.-keeper,** conserje, m

**lodger** /'lɒdʒər/ n huésped (-eda)

**lodging** /'lɒdʒɪŋ/ n hospedaje, alojamiento, m; (inn) posada, f; residencia, f; casa, f. **l.-house,** casa de huéspedes, f

**loft** /lɒft/ n desván, sotabanco, m; pajar, m

**loftily** /'lɔftli/ adv en alto; (proudly) con arrogancia, con altanería

**loftiness** /'lɔftinɪs/ n altura, f; sublimidad, f; nobleza, f; dignidad, f; (haughtiness) altanería, soberbia, f

**lofty** /'lɔfti/ a alto; sublime; noble; eminente; (haughty) altanero, soberbio

**log** /lɒg/ n madero, tronco, m; palo, m; leño, m; Naut., diario de a bordo m, barquilla, f. **to lie like a log,** estar hecho un tronco. **log-book,** Naut. cuaderno de bitácora, m. **log-cabin,** cabañas de troncos, m. **log-wood,** palo campeche, m

**logarithm** /'lɔgə,rɪðəm/ n logaritmo, m

**logarithmic** /,lɔgə'rɪðmɪk/ a logarítmico

**logic** /'lɒdʒɪk/ n lógica, f

**logical** /'lɒdʒɪkəl/ a lógico, m

**logician** /lou'dʒɪʃən/ n lógico (-ca)

**loin** /lɔin/ n ijar, m; (of meat) falda, f; pl **loins,** lomos, riñones m pl. **to gird up one's loins,** Fig. arremangarse las faldones. **l.-cloth,** taparrabo, m

**loiter** /'lɔitər/ vi vagabundear, vagar, errar; haraganear; rezagarse

**loiterer** /'lɔitərər/ n haragán (-ana); vago (-ga); rezagado (-da)

**loll** /lɒl/ vi recostarse (en), apoyarse (en). —vt (the tongue) sacar

**Lombardy-Venetia** /'lɒmbərdi və'niʃə/ Lombardo-Véneto, m

**London** /'lʌndən/ Londres, m

**Londoner** /'lʌndənər/ n londinense, mf

**lone** /loun/ a. See **lonely**

**loneliness** /'lounlinɪs/ n soledad, f; aislamiento, m

**lonely** /'lounli/ a solitario; solo; aislado, remoto; desierto

**lonesome** /'lounsəm/ a solo, solitario

**long** /lɔŋ/ a largo; prolongado; de largo; (extensive) extenso; (big) grande; (much) mucho. **a l. time,** mucho tiempo. **It is five feet l.,** Tiene cinco pies de largo. **l.-armed,** que tiene los brazos largos. **l.-boat,** falúa, f. **l. clothes,** (infant's) mantillas, f pl. **l.-distance call,** conferencia telefónica, f. **l.-distance race,** carrera de fondo, f. **l.-eared,** de orejas largas. **l.-faced,** de cara larga, carilargo. **l.-forgotten,** olvidado hace mucho tiempo. **l.-haired,** que tiene el pelo largo. **l.-headed,** dolicocéfalo; *Fig.* astuto, sagaz. **l.-legged,** zanquilargo, zancudo. **l.-lived,** que vive hasta una edad avanzada; longevo; duradero. **l.-lost,** perdido hace mucho tiempo. **l.-sighted,** présbita; previsor; sagaz. **l.-standing,** viejo, de muchos años. **l.-suffering,** sufrido, paciente. **l.-tailed,** de cola larga. **l.-waisted,** de talle largo. **l.-winded,** prolijo

**long** /lɔŋ/ adv mucho tiempo; mucho; durante mucho tiempo. **as l. as,** mientras (que). **before l.,** dentro de poco. **the l. and the short of it,** en resumidas cuentas. **How l. has she been here?** ¿Cuánto tiempo hace que está aquí? **not l. before,** poco tiempo antes. **l. ago,** tiempo ha, muchos años ha

**long** /lɔŋ/ vi anhelar, suspirar (por), desear con vehemencia

**longanimity** /ˌlɔŋgəˈnɪmɪti/ n longanimidad, f

**longer** /ˈlɔŋgər/ a compar más largo. —adv compar más tiempo. **How much l. must we wait?** ¿Cuánto tiempo más hemos de esperar? **He can no l. walk as he used,** Ya no puede andar como antes

**longevity** /lɒnˈdʒɛvɪti/ n longevidad, f

**longing** /ˈlɔŋɪŋ/ a anheloso, ansioso; de envidia. —n anhelo, m, ansia, f; deseo vehemente, m; envidia, f

**longingly** /ˈlɔŋɪŋli/ adv con ansia; impacientemente; con envidia

**longish** /ˈlɔŋɪʃ/ a algo largo

**longitude** /ˈlɒndʒɪˌtud/ n longitud, f

**longitudinal** /ˌlɒndʒɪˈtudn̩l/ a longitudinal

**long take** n *Cinema.* toma larga, f

**loofah** /ˈlufə/ n esponja vegetal, f

**look** /lʊk/ n mirada, f; (glance) vistazo, m, ojeada, f; (air) semblante, aire, porte, m; (appearance) aspecto, m; apariencia, f. **good looks,** buen parecer, m; guapeza, f. **the new l.,** la nueva línea, la nueva silueta, la nueva moda. **to be on the l.-out,** andar a la mira

**look** /lʊk/ vi and vt mirar; considerar, contemplar; (appear, seem) parecer; tener aire (de); tener aspecto (de); hacer el efecto (de); (show oneself) mostrarse; (of buildings, etc.) caer (a); dar (a); mirar (a).; (seem to be) revelar (e.g., *You don't l. thirty,* No revelas treinta años) la l. alike, parecerse. **to l. hopeful,** *Fig.* prometer bien. **to l. out of the corner of the eye,** mirar de reojo. **to l. ( a person) up and down,** mirar de hito en hito. **to l. about one,** mirar a su alrededor; observar. **to l. after,** tener la mirada puesta en, mirar; (care for) cuidar; (watch) vigilar; mirar por. **to l. at,** mirar; considerar; examinar. **He looked at his watch,** Miró su reloj. **He looked at her,** La miró. **to l. away,** desviar los ojos, apartar la mirada. **to l. back,** mirar hacia atrás; volver la cabeza; (in thought) pensar en el pasado. **to l. down,** bajar los ojos; mirar el suelo; mirar hacia abajo. **to l. down upon,** dominar, mirar a; (scorn) despreciar; mirar de arriba para abajo. **to l. for,** buscar; buscar con los ojos; (await) aguardar; (expect) esperar. **to l. forward,** mirar hacia el porvenir; pensar en el futuro; esperar con ilusión. **to l. in,** entrar por un instante, hacer una visita corta. **to l. into,** mirar dentro de; mirar hacia el interior de; estudiar, investigar. **to l. on,** vt mirar; considerar; (of buildings, etc.) dar a. —vi ser espectador. **to l. on to,** dar a, mirar a. **to l. out,** vi (be careful) tener cuidado; (look through) mirar por; asomarse a. —vt (search) buscar; (find) hallar; (choose) escoger, elegir. **L. out!** ¡Atención! ¡Ojo! **to l. out for,** buscar; (await) aguardar, esperar; (be careful) tener cuidado con. **to l. out of,** mirar por; asomarse a. **to l. over,** mirar bien; (persons) mirar de hito en hito; examinar; visitar; (a house) inspeccionar; (a book) hojear; mirar superficialmente. **to l. round,** vt (a place) visitar. —vi volver la cabeza, volverse; mirar hacia atrás. **to l. round for,** buscar con los ojos; buscar por todas partes. **to l. through,** mirar por; mirar a través de; examinar;

(search) registrar; (understand) registrar. **to l. to,** (be careful of) tener cuidado de; (attend to) atender a; (care for) cuidar de; (count on) contar con; (resort to) acudir a; (await) esperar. **to l. toward,** mirar hacia, mirar en la dirección de; caer a. **to l. up,** vi mirar hacia arriba; (aspire) aspirar; (improve) mejorar. —vt visitar, ir (o venir) a ver; (turn up) buscar; averiguar. **to l. upon,** mirar. Other meanings see to l. on. **They l. upon her as their daughter,** La miran como una hija suya. **to l. up to,** *Fig.* respetar

**looked-for** /ˈlʊkt ˌfɔr/ a esperado; deseado

**looking** /ˈlʊkɪŋ/ a (in compounds) de... aspecto, de... apariencia. **dirty-l.,** de aspecto sucio. **l.-glass,** espejo, m

**lookout** /ˈlʊkˌaʊt/ vigilancia, observación, f; (view) vista, f, panorama, m; (viewpoint) miradero, m; *Mil.* atalaya, m; *Naut.* gaviero, m; (*Fig.* prospect) perspectiva, f

**loom** /lum/ n telar, m, vi asomar, aparecer

**loop** /lup/ n (turn) vuelta, f; (in rivers, etc.) recodo, m, curva, f; (fold) pliegue, m; bucle, m; (fastening) fiador, m, presilla, f; *Aer.* rizo, m; (knot) nudo corredizo, m. **to l. the l.,** *Aer.* hacer el rizo, hacer rizos. **l.-line,** empalme de ferrocarril, m

**loophole** /ˈlupˌhoʊl/ n saetera, aspillera, f; *Fig.* escapatoria, f; pretexto, m, excusa, f

**loose** /lus/ a suelto; (free) libre; (slack) flojo; (of garments) holgado; (untied) desatado; (unfastened) desprendido; movible; (unchained) desencadenado; en libertad; (of the bowels) suelto (de vientre); (pendulous) colgante; (of a nail, tooth, etc.) inseguro; poco firme; que se mueve; (of knots, etc.) flojo; (of the mind, etc.) incoherente, ilógico; poco exacto; (of style, etc.) vago, impreciso; (of conduct) disoluto, vicioso; (careless) negligente, descuidado. —vt (untie) desatar; desprender; soltar; aflojar; (of a priest) absolver; *Fig.* desencadenar. **to break l.,** desprenderse; soltarse; libertarse; escapar; *Fig.* desencadenarse. **to let l.,** desatar; aflojar; poner en libertad; soltar; *Fig.* desencadenar; (interject) lanzar. **to turn l.,** poner en libertad; dar salida (a); echar de casa, poner en la calle. **to work l.,** desprenderse; aflojarse; desvencijarse. **l.-box,** caballeriza, f. **l. change,** suelto, m. **l.-leaf notebook,** libreta de hojas sueltas, f

**loosely** /ˈlusli/ adv flojamente; sueltamente; (vaguely) vagamente; incorrectamente; incoherentemente; (carelessly) negligentemente; (viciously) disolutamente

**loosen** /ˈlusən/ vt (untie) desatar; aflojar; soltar; desasir; (the tongue) desatar; *Fig.* hacer menos riguroso, ablandar

**looseness** /ˈlusnɪs/ n flojedad, f; (of clothing) holgura, f; soltura, f; relajación, f; (of the bowels) diarrea, f; (viciousness) licencia, f, libertinaje, m; (vagueness) vaguedad, f; incoherencia, f

**loosening** /ˈlusənɪŋ/ n desprendimiento, m; desasimiento, m; aflojamiento, m

**loot** /lut/ n botín, m, vt saquear

**looter** /ˈlutər/ n saqueador (-ra)

**looting** /ˈlutɪŋ/ n saqueo, pillaje, m, a saqueador

**lop** /lɒp/ vt mochar; podar; destroncar; cortar de un golpe. —a (of ears) gacho. **to lop off the ends,** cercenar. **to lop off the top,** desmochar. **lop-sided,** desproporcionado; desequilibrado

**lopping** /ˈlɒpɪŋ/ n desmoche, m; poda, f

**loquacious** /loʊˈkweɪʃəs/ a locuaz, gárrulo

**loquacity** /loʊˈkwæsɪti/ n locuacidad, garrulidad, f

**lord** /lɔrd/ n señor, m; (husband) esposo, m; (English title) lord, m, (pl lores) (Christ) Señor, m. **feudal l.,** señor de horca y cuchillo, m. **my l.,** milord. **my lords,** milores. **Our L.,** Nuestro Señor. **the Lord's Prayer,** el Padrenuestro. **to l. it over,** mandar como señor, mandar a la baqueta. **L. Chamberlain,** camarero mayor, m. **L. Chancellor,** gran canciller, m. **L. Chief Justice,** presidente del tribunal supremo, m. **L.-Lieutenant,** virrey, m. **L. Mayor,** alcalde, m. **L. Privy Seal,** guardasellos del rey, m

**lordliness** /ˈlɔrdlɪnɪs/ n suntuosidad, f; liberalidad, munificencia, f; dignidad, f; (haughtiness) altivez, arrogancia, f

**lordly** /ˈlɔrdli/ a señorial, señoril; altivo, arrogante

**lordship** /'lɔrdʃɪp/ n señoría, f; señorío, poder, m. **his l.,** su señoría

**lore** /lɔr/ n saber, m; erudición, f; tradiciones, f pl

**lorgnette** /lɔrn'yɛt/ n impertinentes, m pl

**lorry** /'lɔri/ n camión, m; carro, m

**lose** /luz/ vt perder; hacer perder, quitar; (forget) olvidar. —vi perder; (of clocks) atrasar. **to be lost in thought,** estar ensimismado, estar absorto. **to l. one-self (in)** perderse (en); abstraerse (en); entregarse (a). **to l. one's footing,** resbalar. **to l. one's way,** extraviarse, perder el camino. **to l. one's self-control,** perder el tino. **to l. one's head,** perder la cabeza. **to l. ground,** perder terreno. **to l. one's voice,** perder la voz. **to l. patience,** perder la paciencia, perder los estribos

**loser** /'luzər/ n perdedor (-ra)

**losing** /'luzɪŋ/ a perdedor. —n pérdida, f

**loss** /lɔs/ n pérdida, f. **at a l.,** Com. con pérdida; perplejo, dudoso. **heavy losses,** Mil. pérdidas cuantiosas, f pl. **We are at a l. for words...,** No tenemos palabras para...

**lot** /lɒt/ n suerte, f; fortuna, f; lote, m; parte, porción, cuota, f; (for building) solar, m. **a lot of people,** muchas personas. **Our lot would have been very different,** Nuestra suerte hubiera sido muy distinta, Otro gallo nos cantara. **to draw lots,** echar suertes, sortear. **to take the lot,** Inf. alzarse con el santo y la limosna

**lotion** /'louʃən/ n loción, f

**lottery** /'lɒtəri/ n lotería, f. **l. ticket,** billete de la lotería, m

**lotus** /'loutəs/ n loto, m. **l.-eating,** lotofagía, f; Fig. indolencia, pereza, f

**loud** /laud/ a fuerte; (noisy) ruidoso, estrepitoso; alto; (gaudy) chillón, llamativo, cursi. —adv ruidosamente. **l.-speaker,** Radio. altavoz, altoparlante, m

**loudly** /'laudli/ adv en alta voz; fuertemente; ruidosamente, con estrépito

**loudness** /'laudnɪs/ n (noise) ruido, m; sonoridad, f; (force) fuerza, f; (of colors, etc.) mal gusto, m, vulgaridad, f

**lounge** /laundʒ/ n sala de estar, f; salón, m, vi reclinarse, ponerse a sus anchas; apoyarse (en); gandulear; vagar. **l. chair,** poltrona, f. **l.-lizard,** Inf. pollo pera, m. **l.-suit,** traje americano, m

**lounger** /'laundʒər/ n holgazán (-ana); golfo (-fa), azotacalles, mf

**louse** /laus/ n piojo, m

**lousy** /'lauzi/ a piojoso

**lout** /laut/ n patán, zamacuco, m

**loutish** /'lautɪʃ/ a rústico

**lovable** /'lʌvəbəl/ a amable; simpático

**lovableness** /'lʌvəbəlnɪs/ n amabilidad, f

**love** /lʌv/ n amor, m; (friendship) amistad, f; (enthusiasm, liking) afición, f; (in tennis) cero, m, vt querer, amar; gustar mucho; tener afición (a). —vi estar enamorado. **I should l. to dine with you,** Me gustaría mucho cenar con Vds. **to be in l. with,** estar enamorado de. **to fall in l. with,** enamorarse de. **They l. each other,** Se quieren. **to make l. to,** hacer el amor (a), galantear. **l. affair,** amorío, lance de amor, m. **l.-bird,** periquito, m. **l.-letter,** carta amatoria, carta de amor, f. **l.-making,** galanteo, m. **l.-philtre,** filtro, m. **l.-song,** canción de amor, f. **l.-story,** historia de amor, f. **l.-token,** prenda de amor, f

**loveless** /'lʌvlɪs/ a sin amor

**loveliness** /'lʌvlinɪs/ n hermosura, belleza, f; encanto, m; amabilidad, f

**lovely** /'lʌvli/ a hermoso, bello; delicioso; amable; Inf. estupendo

**lover** /'lʌvər/ n amante, mf; aficionado (-da)

**lovesick** /'lʌv,sɪk/ a enfermo de amor, enamorado

**loving** /'lʌvɪŋ/ a amoroso; cariñoso; (friendly) amistoso; de amor

**low** /lou/ a bajo; de poca altura; (of dresses, etc.) escotado; (of musical notes) grave; (soft) suave; (feeble) débil; (depressed) deprimido, triste, abatido; (plain) sencillo; (of a fever) lento; (of a bow) profundo; pequeño; inferior; humilde; (ill) enfermo; (vile) vil, ruin; obsceno, escabroso. —adv bajo; cerca de la tierra; en voz baja; (cheaply) barato, a bajo pre-

cio. **in a low voice,** en voz baja, paso. **to lay low,** (kill) tumbar; (knock down) derribar; incapacitar. **to lie low,** descansar; estar muerto; esconderse, agacharse; callar. **to run low,** escasear. **low-born,** de humilde cuna. **low-brow,** nada intelectual. **low comedy,** farsa, f. **low flying,** n bajo vuelo, m, a que vuela bajo; terrero, rastrero; que vuela a ras de tierra. **low frequency,** baja frecuencia, f. **low Latin,** bajo latín, m. **Low Mass,** misa rezada, f. **low neck,** escote, m. **Low-necked,** escotado. **low-pitched,** grave. **low-spirited,** deprimido. **Low Sunday,** domingo de Cuasimodo, m. **low tension,** baja tensión, f. **low trick,** mala pasada, f. **low water,** marea baja, bajamar, f; (of rivers) estiaje, m

**low** /lou/ vi berrear, mugir. —n berrido, mugido, m

**low-ceiling** /'lou 'silɪŋ/ a bajo de techo.

**Low Countries,** the Los Países Bajos, m

**lower** /'louər/ vt bajar; descolgar; disminuir; (price) rebajar; (a boat, sails) arriar. —vi (of persons) fruncir el ceño, mostrarse malhumorado; (of the sky) encapotarse, cargarse; (menace) amenazar. **to l. a boat,** arriar un bote. **to l. oneself,** (by a rope, etc.) descolgarse. **to l. the flag,** abatir la bandera

**lower** /'louər/ a compar más bajo; menos alto; bajo; inferior. **l. classes,** clase obrera, f; clases bajas, f pl. **l. down,** más abajo. **L. House,** Cámara de los Comunes, f; cámara baja, f. **l. jaw,** mandíbula inferior, f. **l. storey,** piso bajo, m; piso de abajo, m

**lowering** /'louərɪŋ/ n abajamiento, m; descenso, m; (of prices) baja, f; (of a boat) arriada, f; (of the flag) abatimiento, m, a (of persons) ceñudo; (of the sky) anublado, encapotado; (threatening) amenazador

**lowest** /'louɪst/ a superl el (la, etc.) más bajo; el (la, etc.) más profundo; ínfimo

**lowing** /'louɪŋ/ n berrido, mugido, m

**lowland** /'loulənd/ n tierra baja, f. **the Lowlands,** las tierras bajas de Escocia

**lowliness** /'loulinɪs/ n humildad, f; modestia, f

**lowly** /'louli/ a humilde

**lowness** /'lounɪs/ n poca altura, f; situación poco elevada, f; pequeñez, f; (of musical notes) gravedad, f; (softness) suavidad, f; (feebleness) debilidad, f; (sadness) tristeza, f, abatimiento, m; (of price) baratura, f; inferioridad, f; humildad, f; (vileness) bajeza, f; obscenidad, f

**loyal** /'lɔiəl/ a leal, fiel

**loyalist** /'lɔiəlɪst/ n realista, mf; defensor (-ra) del gobierno legítimo

**loyalty** /'lɔiəlti/ n lealtad, fidelidad, f

**loyalty oath** n (approximate equivalent) certificado de adhesión, m

**lozenge** /'lɒzɪndʒ/ n pastilla, f

**lubricant** /'lubrɪkənt/ a and n lubricante m

**lubricate** /'lubrɪ,keit/ vt lubricar, engrasar

**lubricating oil** n aceite lubricante, m

**lubrication** /,lubrɪ'keiʃən/ n lubricación, f, engrasado, m

**lubricator** /'lubrɪ,keitər/ n lubricador, m; engrasador, m

**Lucerne** /lu'sɜrn/ Lucerna, f

**lucid** /'lusɪd/ a lúcido; claro

**lucidity** /lu'sɪdɪti/ n lucidez, f; claridad, f

**lucidly** /'lusɪdli/ adv claramente

**luck** /lʌk/ n destino, azar, m; (good) buenaventura, suerte, f. **to bring bad l.,** traer mala suerte. **to try one's l.,** probar fortuna

**luckily** /'lʌkəli/ adv por fortuna, afortunadamente, felizmente

**luckless** /'lʌklɪs/ a desdichado

**lucky** /'lʌki/ a afortunado; dichoso, venturoso; feliz. **to be l.,** tener buena suerte

**lucrative** /'lukrətɪv/ a lucrativo

**lucre** /'lukər/ n lucro, m

**lucubration** /,lukyu'breiʃən/ n lucubración, f

**ludicrous** /'ludɪkrəs/ a absurdo, risible, ridículo

**ludicrousness** /'ludɪkrəsnɪs/ n ridiculez, f

**lug** /lʌg/ n tirón, m; (ear and projection) oreja, f, vt tirar (de); arrastrar. **to lug about,** arrastrar (por); llevar con dificultad. **to lug in,** arrastrar adentro; introducir; hacer entrar. **to lug out,** arrastrar afuera; hacer salir

**luggage** /'lʌgɪdʒ/ n equipaje, m. **excess l.,** exceso de equipaje, *m.* **piece of l.,** bulto, *m.* **to register one's l.,** facturar el equipaje. **l. carrier,** (on buses, etc.) baca, *f;* (on a car) portaequipajes, *m.* **l. porter,** mozo de equipajes, *m.* **l. rack,** (on a car) portaequipajes, *m;* (in a train) rejilla para el equipaje, *f.* **l. receipt,** talón de equipaje, *m.* **l. room,** consigna, *f.* **l. van,** furgón de equipajes, *m*

**lugubrious** /luˈgubriəs/ *a* lúgubre

**lukewarm** /ˈlukˈwɔrm/ *a* tibio, templado; *Fig.* indiferente, frío

**lukewarmness** /ˈlukˈwɔrmnɪs/ *n* tibieza, *f; Fig.* indiferencia, frialdad, *f*

**lull** /lʌl/ *n* momento de calma, *m;* tregua, *f;* silencio, *m, vt* (a child) arrullar, adormecer; (soothe) sosegar, calmar; disminuir, mitigar

**lullaby** /ˈlʌləˌbai/ *n* canción de cuna, *f*

**lumbago** /lʌmˈbeigou/ *n* lumbago, *m*

**lumbar** /ˈlʌmbər/ *a* lumbar

**lumber** /ˈlʌmbər/ *n* (wood) maderas de sierra, *f pl;* (rubbish) trastos viejos, *m pl.* —*vt* amontonar trastos viejos; obstruir. —*vi* andar pesadamente; avanzar ruidosamente, avanzar con ruido sordo. **l.-jack,** maderero, ganchero, *m.* **l.-room,** leonera, *f.* **l.-yard,** maderería, *f,* depósito de maderas, *m*

**lumbering** /ˈlʌmbərɪŋ/ *a* pesado

**luminary** /ˈluməˌneri/ *n* lumbrera, *f*

**luminosity** /ˌluməˈnɒsɪti/ *n* luminosidad, *f*

**luminous** /ˈlumənəs/ *a* luminoso

**lump** /lʌmp/ *n* masa, *f;* bulto, *m;* pedazo, *m;* (of sugar) terrón *m;* (swelling) hinchazón, *f;* protuberancia, *f.* —*vt* amontonar. **to l. together,** mezclar; incluir. **in the l.,** en la masa; en grueso. **Let him l. it!** ¡Que se rasque! **l. in one's throat,** nudo en la garganta, *m.* **l. of sugar,** terrón de azúcar, *m.* **l. sum,** cantidad gruesa, *f*

**lumpishness** /ˈlʌmpɪʃnɪs/ *n* hobachonería, *f*

**lunacy** /ˈlunəsi/ *n* locura, *f*

**lunar** /ˈlunər/ *a* lunar

**lunatic** /ˈlunətɪk/ *n* loco (-ca); demente, *mf a* de locos; loco. **l. asylum,** manicomio, *m*

**lunch, luncheon** /lʌntʃ; ˈlʌntʃən;/ *n* almuerzo, *m;* (snack) merienda, *f.* —*vi* almorzar. **l. basket** or **pail,** fiambrera, *f*

**lunette** /luˈnet/ *n* (*Archit. Mil.*) luneta, *f*

**lung** /lʌŋ/ *n* pulmón, *m*

**lunge** /lʌndʒ/ *n* (fencing) estocada, *f;* embestida, *f, vi* dar una estocada; abalanzarse sobre

**lurch** /lɜrtʃ/ *n* sacudida, *f; Naut.* guiñada, *f;* tambaleo, *m;* movimiento brusco, *m.* —*vi* dar guiñadas; guiñar; tambalearse; andar haciendo eses. **to leave in the l.,** dejar plantado

**lure** /lʊr/ *n* añagaza, *f;* reclamo, *m;* aliciente, atractivo, *m;* seducción, *f.* —*vt* atraer, tentar

**lurid** /ˈlʊrɪd/ *a* misterioso, fantástico; cárdeno; ominoso; funesto, triste; (orange) anaranjado; (vicissitudinous) accidentado

**lurk** /lɜrk/ *vi* acechar, espiar; esconderse

**lurking** /ˈlɜrkɪŋ/ *a* (in ambush) en acecho; (of fear, etc.) vago

**luscious** /ˈlʌʃəs/ *a* delicioso; suculento; meloso; atractivo, *m;* seducción, *f*

**lusciousness** /ˈlʌʃəsnɪs/ *n* suculencia, *f;* melosidad, *f;* atractivo, *m;* sensualidad, *f*

**lush** /lʌʃ/ *a* jugoso; fresco y lozano; maduro

**lust** /lʌst/ *n* lujuria, lascivia, *f;* codicia, *f;* deseo, *m.* **l. for revenge,** deseo de venganza, *m*

**luster** /ˈlʌstər/ *n* lustre, brillo, *m;* brillantez, *f*

**lusterless** /ˈlʌstərlɪs/ *a* sin brillo; mate, deslustrado; (of eyes) apagado

**lustful** /ˈlʌstfəl/ *a* lujurioso, lúbrico, lascivo

**lustrous** /ˈlʌstrəs/ *a* lustroso

**lusty** /ˈlʌsti/ *a* vigoroso, fuerte, lozano

**lute** /lut/ *n* laúd, *m,* vihuela, *f.* **l.-player,** vihuelista, *mf*

**Lutheran** /ˈluθərən/ *a* luterano. —*n* luterano (-na)

**Lutheranism** /ˈluθərəˌnɪzəm/ *n* luteranismo, *m*

**luxation** /lʌkˈseiʃən/ *n* luxación, *f*

**Luxembourg** /ˈlʌksəmˌbɜrg/ Luxemburgo, *m*

**luxuriance** /lʌgˈʒʊriəns/ *n* lozanía, *f;* exuberancia, superabundancia, *f*

**luxuriant** /lʌgˈʒʊriənt/ *a* lozano; fértil; exuberante

**luxuriate** /lʌgˈʒʊriˌeit/ *vi* crecer con exuberancia; complacerse (en); disfrutar (de), gozar (de)

**luxurious** /lʌgˈʒʊriəs/ *a* lujoso

**luxuriously** /lʌgˈʒʊriəsli/ *adv* lujosamente, con lujo

**luxury** /ˈlʌkʃəri/ *n* lujo, *m.* **l. goods,** artículos de lujo, *m pl*

**lyceum** /laiˈsiəm/ *n* liceo, *m*

**lye** /lai/ *n* lejía, *f*

**lying** /ˈlaiɪŋ/ *a* (recumbent) recostado; (untrue) mentiroso, falso. —*n* mentiras, *f pl.* **l.-in,** parto, *m*

**lymph** /lɪmf/ *n* linfa, *f;* vacuna, *f*

**lymphatic** /lɪmˈfætɪk/ *a* linfático; flemático

**lynch** /lɪntʃ/ *vt* linchar

**lynching** /ˈlɪntʃɪŋ/ *n* linchamiento, *m*

**lynx** /lɪŋks/ *n* lince, *m.* **l.-eyed,** de ojos de lince

**lyre** /laiᵊr/ *n* lira, *f.* **l.-bird,** pájaro lira, *m*

**lyric** /ˈlɪrɪk/ *n* poesía lírica, *f;* poema lírico, *m;* letra (de una canción,) *f*

**lyrical** /ˈlɪrɪkəl/ *a* lírico

**lyricism** /ˈlɪrəˌsɪzəm/ *n* lirismo, *m*

# M

**m** /ɛm/ n (letter) eme, f
**ma'am** /mæm/ n señora, f
**macabre** /məˈkɑbrə/ a macabro
**macadam** /məˈkædəm/ n macadán, m, a de macadán
**macadamize** /məˈkædəˌmaiz/ vt macadanizar
**macaroni** /ˌmækəˈrouni/ n macarrones, m pl
**macaronic** /ˌmækəˈrɒnɪk/ a macarrónico
**macaroon** /ˌmækəˈrun/ n macarrón de almendras, m
**Macassar oil** /məˈkæsər/ n aceite de Macasar, m
**macaw** /məˈkɔ/ n macagua, f, guacamayo, m
**mace** /meis/ n maza, f; Cul. macis, f. **m.-bearer,** macero, m
**Macedonian** /ˌmæsɪˈdouniən/ a macedón, macedonio. —n macedonio (-ia)
**macerate** /ˈmæsəˌreit/ vt macerar. —vi macerarse
**Machiavellian** /ˌmækiəˈvɛliən/ a maquiavélico
**Machiavellism** /ˌmækiəˈvɛlɪzəm/ n maquiavelismo, m
**machination** /ˌmækəˈneiʃən/ n maquinación, f
**machine** /məˈʃin/ n máquina, f; mecanismo, m; aparato, m; instrumento, m; organización, f, vt trabajar a máquina; Sew. coser a máquina. **m.-gun,** n ametralladora, f. —vt ametrallar. **m.-gun carrier,** portametralladoras, m. **m.-gunner,** ametrallador, m. **m.-made,** hecho a máquina. **m.-oil,** aceite de motores, m. **m.-shop,** taller de maquinaria, m. **m.-tool,** máquina herramienta, f
**machinery** /məˈʃinəri/ n maquinaria, f; mecanismo, m; organización, f; sistema, m
**machinist** /məˈʃinɪst/ n maquinista, mf; Sew. costurera a máquina, f
**mackerel** /ˈmækərəl/ n caballa, f. **m. sky,** cielo aborregado, m
**mackintosh** /ˈmækɪnˌtɒʃ/ n impermeable, m
**macrocosm** /ˈmækrəˌkɒzəm/ n macrocosmo, m
**mad** /mæd/ a loco; fuera de sí; (of a dog, etc.) rabioso; furioso. **as mad as a hatter,** loco como una cabra. **to drive mad,** volver loco (a). **to go mad,** volverse loco, enloquecer, perder el seso. **mad with joy** ( **pain**), loco de alegría (dolor). **mad dog,** perro rabioso, m
**madam** /ˈmædəm/ n señora, f; (French form) madama, f. **Yes, m.,** Sí señora
**madcap** /ˈmædˌkæp/ n locuelo (-la), f, botarate, m; tarambana, mf
**madden** /ˈmædn/ vt enloquecer; enfurecer, exasperar
**maddening** /ˈmædnɪŋ/ a exasperante, irritador
**madder** /ˈmædər/ n Bot. rubia, f
**made** /meid/ past part and a hecho; formado. **self-m. man,** un hombre hecho y derecho. **m.-to-measure,** hecho a la medida. **m.-up,** compuesto; (of clothes) confeccionado, ya hecho; (of the face) pintado; (fictitious) inventado, ficticio; artificial
**Madeira** /məˈdɪərə/ n vino de Madera, m, a de Madera
**madhouse** /ˈmædˌhaus/ n casa de locos, f, manicomio, m
**madly** /ˈmædli/ adv locamente; furiosamente
**madman** /ˈmædˌmæn/ n loco, m
**madness** /ˈmædnɪs/ n locura, f; (of a dog, etc.) rabia, f; furia, f
**Madonna** /məˈdɒnə/ n Madona, f
**madrigal** /ˈmædrɪgəl/ n madrigal, m
**Madrilenian** /ˌmædrəˈliniən/ a madrileño, matritense. —n madrileño (-ña)
**madwoman** /ˈmædˌwumən/ n loca, f
**Maecenas** /miˈsinəs/ n mecenas, m
**maelstrom** /ˈmeilstrəm/ n remolino, vórtice, m
**magazine** /ˌmægəˈzin/ n (store) almacén, m; (for explosives) polvorín, m, santabárbara, f; (periodical) revista, f. **m. rifle,** rifle de repetición, m
**Magdalene** /ˈmægdəˌlin/ n magdalena, f
**magenta** /məˈdʒɛntə/ n color magenta, m
**maggot** /ˈmægət/ n gusano, m, cresa, f; Fig. manía, f, capricho, m
**maggoty** /ˈmægəti/ a gusanoso
**magic** /ˈmædʒɪk/ n magia, f; mágica, f; Fig. encanto,

m, a mágico. **as if by m.,** por ensalmo. **m. lantern,** linterna mágica, f
**magically** /ˈmædʒɪkli/ adv por encanto
**magician** /məˈdʒɪʃən/ n mago, mágico, brujo, m; (conjurer) jugador de manos, m
**magisterial** /ˌmædʒəˈstɪəriəl/ a magistral
**magistracy** /ˈmædʒəstrəsi/ n magistratura, f
**magistrate** /ˈmædʒəˌstreit/ n magistrado, m; juez municipal, m
**Magi, the** /ˈmeidʒai/ n pl los reyes magos
**Magna Carta** /ˈmægnə ˈkartə/ n Carta Magna, f
**magnanimity** /ˌmægnəˈnɪmɪti/ n magnanimidad, generosidad, f
**magnanimous** /mægˈnænəməs/ a magnánimo, generoso
**magnanimously** /mægˈnænəməsli/ adv magnánimamente
**magnate** /ˈmægneit/ n magnate, m
**magnesia** /mægˈniʒə/ n magnesia, f
**magnesium** /mægˈniziəm/ n magnesio, m. **m. light,** luz de magnesio, f
**magnet** /ˈmægnɪt/ n imán, m
**magnetic** /mægˈnɛtɪk/ a magnético; Fig. atractivo. **m. field,** campo magnético, m. **m. needle,** brújula, f
**magnetics** /mægˈnɛtɪks/ n la ciencia del magnetismo, f
**magnetism** /ˈmægnɪˌtɪzəm/ n magnetismo, m
**magnetization** /ˌmægɪtɪˈzeiʃən/ n imanación, magnetización, f
**magnetize** /ˈmægnɪˌtaiz/ vt magnetizar, imanar; (hypnotize) magnetizar; Fig. atraer
**magnification** /ˌmægnəfɪˈkeiʃən/ n (by a lens, etc.) aumento, m; exageración, f
**magnificence** /mægˈnɪfəsəns/ n magnificencia, f
**magnificent** /mægˈnɪfəsənt/ a magnífico
**magnify** /ˈmægnəˌfai/ vt (by lens) aumentar; exagerar; (praise) magnificar
**magnifying** /ˈmægnəˌfaiɪŋ/ a de aumento, vidrio de aumento. **m. glass,** lente de aumento, m
**magniloquence** /mægˈnɪləkwəns/ n grandilocuencia, f
**magniloquent** /mægˈnɪləkwənt/ a grandílocuo
**magnitude** /ˈmægnɪˌtud/ n magnitud, f
**magnolia** /mægˈnoulyə/ n magnolia, f
**magnum** /ˈmægnəm/ n botella de dos litros, m
**magpie** /ˈmægˌpai/ n marica, picaza, f
**maharajah** /ˌmahəˈradʒə/ n maharajá, m
**mahogany** /məˈhɒgəni/ n caoba, f, a de caoba
**maid** /meid/ n doncella, muchacha, f; virgen, f; soltera, f; (servant) criada, f; (daily) asistenta, f. **old m.,** solterona, f. **m.-of-all-work,** criada para todo, f. **m.-of-honor,** dama de honor, f
**maiden** /ˈmeidn/ n doncella, joven, soltera, f; virgen, f; zagala, f. —a de soltera; soltera f; virginal; (of speeches, voyages, etc.) primero. **m. lady,** dama soltera, f. **m.-name,** apellido de soltera, m. **m. speech,** primer discurso, m
**maidenhood** /ˈmeidnˌhud/ n doncellez, virginidad, f
**maidenly** /ˈmeidnli/ a virginal; modesto, modoso; tímido
**maidservant** /ˈmeidˌsɜrvənt/ n criada, sirvienta, f
**mail** /meil/ n mala, f; (bag) valija, f; correo, m; correspondencia, f; (armour) cota de malla, f. —vt mandar por correo; armar con cota de malla. **coat of m.,** cota de malla, f. **royal m.,** malla real, f. **m.-bag,** valija de correo, f; portacartas, m. **m.-boat,** buque correo, m. **m.-cart,** ambulancia de correos, f. **m.-clad,** vestido de cota de malla; armado, m. **m.-coach,** coche correo, m, diligencia, f. **m.-order,** pedido postal, m. **m.-order business,** negocio de ventas por correo, m. **m.-plane,** avión postal, m. **m. service,** servicio de correos, m. **m. steamer,** vapor correo, m. **m. train,** tren correo, m. **m. van,** (on a train) furgón postal, m
**mailed** /meild/ a de malla; armado. **m. fist,** Fig. puño de hierro, m
**maim** /meim/ vt mancar; mutilar, tullir; estropear

**maimed** /meimd/ *a* manco; tullido, mutilado

**main** /mein/ *a* mayor; principal; más importante, esencial; maestro. —*n* (mainland) continente, *m;* (sea) océano, *m;* (pipe) cañería maestra, *f.* **by m. force,** por fuerza mayor. **in the m.,** en general, generalmente; en su mayoría. **m. beam,** viga maestra, *f.* **m. body,** (of a building) ala principal, *f;* (of a church) cuerpo (de iglesia), *m;* (of an army) cuerpo (del ejército), *m;* mayor parte, mayoría, *f.* **m. line,** línea principal, *f.* **m. mast,** palo mayor, *m.* **m. thing,** cosa principal, *f,* lo más importante. **m. wall,** pared maestra, *f*

**mainland** /'mein,lænd/ *n* continente, *m;* tierra firme, *f*

**mainly** /'meinli/ *adv* principalmente; en su mayoría; generalmente

**mainsail** /'mein,seil/ *n* vela mayor, *f*

**mainspring** /'mein,sprɪŋ/ *n* (of a watch) muelle real, *m;* motivo principal, *m;* origen, *m*

**mainstay** /'mein,stei/ *n* estay mayor, *m; Fig.* sostén principal, *m*

**maintain** /mein'tein/ *vt* mantener; sostener; tener; guardar; afirmar

**maintainable** /mein'teinəbəl/ *a* sostenible; defendible

**maintenance** /'meintənəns/ *n* mantenimiento, *m;* manutención, *f,* sustento, *m;* conservación, *f,* subsistencia, *f*

**maize** /meiz/ *n* maíz, *m.* **m. field,** maizal, *m*

**majestic** /mə'dʒɛstɪk/ *a* majestuoso

**majesty** /'mædʒəsti/ *n* majestad, *f;* majestuosidad, *f.* **His** or **Her M.,** Su Majestad

**majolica** /mə'dʒɒlɪkə/ *n* mayólica, *f*

**major** /'meidʒər/ *a* mayor; principal. —*n* mayor de edad, *m; Mil.* comandante. **anthropology major,** alumno con la especialidad en antropología *m.* **m.-domo,** mayordomo, *m.* **m.-general,** general de división, *m.* **m. road,** carretera, *f;* ruta de prioridad, *f.* **m. scale,** escala mayor, *f*

**Majorca** /mə'dʒɔrkə/ Mallorca, *f*

**majority** /mə'dʒɔrɪti/ *n* mayoría, *f;* mayor número, *m;* generalidad, *f.* **to have attained one's m.,** ser mayor de edad

**make** /meik/ *vt* hacer; crear, formar; (manufacture) fabricar, confeccionar; construir; (produce) producir; causar; (prepare) preparar; (a bed, a fire, a remark, poetry, friends, enemies, war, a curtsey) hacer; (earn, win) ganar; (a speech) pronunciar; (compel) obligar (a), forzar (a); inclinar (a); (arrive at) alcanzar, llegar (a); (calculate) calcular; (arrange) arreglar; deducir (be) ser; (equal) ser igual a; (think) creer; (appoint as) hacer; (behave) portarse (como). —*vi* (begin) ir (a), empezar (a); (make as though) hacer (como si); (of the tide) crecer; contribuir (a); tender (a). **He made as if to go,** Hizo como si de marchara. **to m. as though...,** aparentar, fingir. **It made me ill,** Me hizo sentir mal. **They have made it up,** Han hecho las paces. **They m. a great deal of money,** Hacen (or ganan) mucho dinero. **You cannot m. me believe it,** No puedes hacerme creerlo. **He is making himself ridiculous,** Se está poniendo en ridículo. **to m. ready,** preparar. **to m. the tea,** hacer el té; preparar el té. **Two and two m. four,** Dos y dos son cuatro. **to m. oneself known,** darse a conocer. **to m. one of...,** ser uno de... **to m. after,** seguir; correr detrás de. **to m. again,** hacer de nuevo, rehacer. **to m. away with,** quitar; suprimir; destruir; (kill) matar; (squander) derrochar; (steal) llevarse; hurtar. **to m. away with oneself,** quitarse la vida, suicidarse. **to m. for,** encaminarse a, dirigirse a; (attack) abalanzarse sobre, atacar; (tend to) contribuir a, tender a. **to m. off,** marcharse corriendo, largarse; huir, escaparse. **to m. out,** (discern) distinguir; descifrar; (understand) comprender; (prove) probar, justificar; (draw up) redactar; (fill in a form) complete, llenar; (a check, etc.) extender; (an account) hacer; (get on, succeed or otherwise) ir (with bien or mal); (convey) dar la impresión de que; sugerir. **I cannot m. it out,** No lo puedo comprender. **How did you m. out** (get on)? ¿Cómo te fue? **to m. over,** hacer de nuevo, rehacer; (transfer) ceder, traspasar. **to m. up,** hacer; acabar; (of clothes) confec-

cionar; fabricar; (the face) pintarse, maquillarse; (the fire) echar carbón, etc. a; *Print.* compaginar; (invent) inventar; (lies) fabricar; (compose) formar; (package) empaquetar; reparar; indemnizar; compensar; (an account) ajustar; preparar; arreglar; (conciliate) conciliar; enumerar; *Theat.* caracterizarse. **to m. up for,** reemplazar; compensar; (lost time, etc.) recobrar. **to m. up to,** compensar; indemnizar; (flatter) adular, halagar; procurar congraciarse con, procurar obtener el favor de; (court) galantear (con). **m. an impression (on),** dejar(le a fulano) una impresión

**make** /meik/ *n* forma, *f;* hechura, *f;* estructura, *f;* confección, *f;* manufactura, *f;* producto, *m;* (trade name) marca, *f;* (character) carácter, temperamento, *m.* **m.-believe,** *n* artificio, pretexto, *m,* a fingido, *vi* fingir. **land of m.-believe,** reino de los sueños, *m.* **m.-up,** (for the face, etc.) maquillaje, *m; Theat.* caracterización, *f; Print.* imposición, *f;* (whole) conjunto, *m;* (character) carácter, modo de ser, *m*

**maker** /'meikər/ *n* creador, *m;* autor (-ra); artífice, *mf;* (manufacturer) fabricante, *m;* constructor, *m;* (of clothes, etc.) confeccionador (-ra); (worker) obrero (-ra)

**makeshift** /'meik,ʃɪft/ *n* expediente, *m,* a provisional

**makeweight** /'meik,weit/ *n* añadidura (de peso), *f,* contrapeso, *m; Fig.* suplente, *m*

**making** /'meikɪŋ/ *n* creación, *f;* hechura, *f;* (manufacture) fabricación, *f;* construcción, *f;* (of clothes, etc.) confección, *f;* formación, *f;* preparación, *f;* estructura, *f;* composición, *f; pl* **makings,** (profits) ganancias, *f pl;* (elements) elementos, *m pl;* germen, *m;* rasgos esenciales, *m pl,* características, *f pl.* —*pl* **m.-up,** (of clothes) confección, *f; Print.* ajuste, *m;* (of the face) maquillaje, *m;* (invention) invención, *f;* fabricación, *f*

**Malachite** /'mælə,kait/ *n* malaquita, *f*

**maladjustment** /,mælə'dʒʌstmənt/ *n* mal ajuste, *m;* inadaptación, *f*

**maladministration** /,mæləd,mɪnə'strei'ʃən/ *n* desgobierno, *m,* mala administración, *f;* (of funds) malversación, *f*

**maladroit** /,mælə'drɔit/ *a* torpe

**maladroitness** /,mælə'drɔitnɪs/ *n* torpeza, *f*

**malady** /'mælədi/ *n* enfermedad, *f;* mal, *m*

**Malaga** /'mæləgə/ *n* vino de Málaga, *m*

**malaria** /mə'lɛəriə/ *n* paludismo, *m*

**malarial** /mə'lɛəriəl/ *a* palúdico. **m. fever,** fiebre palúdica, *f*

**Malaya** /mə'leiə/ Malasia, *f,* Archipiélago Malayo, *m*

**Malayan** /mə'leiən/ *a* malayo. —*n* malayo (-ya)

**malcontent** /,mælkən'tɛnt/ *n* malcontento (-ta). —*a* descontento

**Maldives** /'mɔldivz/ Maldivas, *f pl*

**male** /meil/ *a* macho; masculino. —*n* macho, *m;* varón, *m.* **m. child,** niño, *m;* niño varón, *m;* (son) hijo varón, *m.* **m. flower,** flor masculina, *f.* **m. issue,** sucesión masculina, *f.* **m. nurse,** enfermero, *m.* **m. sex,** sexo masculino, *m*

**malediction** /,mælɪ'dɪkʃən/ *n* maldición, *f*

**malefactor** /'mælə,fæktər/ *n* malhechor (-ra)

**malefic** /mə'lefɪk/ *a* maléfico

**malevolence** /mə'lɛvələns/ *n* malevolencia, *f*

**malevolent** /mə'lɛvələnt/ *a* malévolo, maligno

**malformation** /,mælfɔr'meiʃən/ *n* formación anormal, deformidad, deformación congénita, *f*

**malice** /'mælɪs/ *n* malicia, *f; Law.* alevosía, *f.* **to bear m.,** guardar rencor

**malicious** /mə'lɪʃəs/ *a* malicioso; maligno, rencoroso

**maliciousness** /mə'lɪʃəsnɪs/ *n* malicia, mala intención, *f*

**malign** /mə'lain/ *vt* calumniar, difamar. —*a* maligno; malévolo

**malignancy** /mə'lɪgnənsi/ *n* malignidad, *f;* malevolencia, *f*

**malignant** /mə'lɪgnənt/ *a* maligno; malévolo; *Med.* maligno

**malinger** /mə'lɪŋgər/ *vi* fingirse enfermo

**malingerer** /mə'lɪŋgərər/ *n* enfermo (-ma) fingido (-da)

**malingering** /mə'lɪŋgərɪŋ/ *n* enfermedad fingida, *f*

**mallard** /'mælərd/ *n* pato (-ta), silvestre

**malleability** /,mæliə'bɪliti/ *n* maleabilidad, *f*

**malleable** /'mæliəbəl/ *a* maleable
**mallet** /'mælɪt/ *n* mazo, *m;* (in croquet) pala, *f,* mazo, *m;* (in polo) maza (de polo), *f*
**mallow** /'mælou/ *n* malva, *f*
**malmsey** /'mɑmzi/ *n* (wine) malvasía, *f*
**malnutrition** /,mælnu'trɪʃən/ *n* desnutrición, alimentación deficiente, *f*
**malodorous** /mæl'oudərəs/ *a* de mal olor, hediondo, fétido
**malpractice** /mæl'præktɪs/ *n* (wrongdoing) maleficencia, *f;* (by a doctor) tratamiento equivocado, perjudicial o ilegal, *m;* (malversation) malversación, *f;* inmoralidad, *f*
**malt** /mɔlt/ *n* malta, *m.* —*vt* preparar el malta. **m.-house,** fábrica de malta, *f.* **m. vinegar,** vinagre de malta, *m*
**malted milk** /'mɔltɪd/ *n* leche malteada, *f*
**Maltese** /mɔl'tiz/ *a* maltés. —*n* maltés (-esa). **M. cat,** gato maltés, *m.* **M. cross,** cruz de Malta, *f.* **M. dog,** perro maltés, *m*
**Malthusian** /mæl'θuʒən/ *a* maltusiano
**Malthusianism** /mæl'θuʒə,nɪzəm/ *n* maltusianismo, *m*
**maltose** /'mɔltous/ *n* maltosa, *f*
**maltreat** /mæl'trit/ *vt* maltratar
**maltreatment** /mæl'tritmənt/ *n* maltrato, *m,*
**malt shop** *n* café-nevería, *m*
**mamma** /'mæmə for 1; 'mamə for 2/ *n Anat.* mama, *f;* (mother) mamá, *f*
**mammal** /'mæməl/ *n* mamífero, *m*
**mammalian** /mə'meiliən/ *a* mamífero
**mammary** /'mæməri/ *a* mamario. **m. gland,** mama, teta, *f*
**mammon** /'mæmən/ *n* becerro de oro, *m*
**mammoth** /'mæməθ/ *n* mamut, *m, a* gigantesco, enorme
**man** /mæn/ *n* hombre, *m;* varón, *m;* persona, *f;* (servant) criado, *m;* (workman) obrero, *m;* (soldier) soldado, *m;* (sailor) marinero, *m;* (humanity) raza humana, *f;* (husband) marido, *m;* (chess) peón, *m;* (checkers) dama, *f;* (a ship) buque, *m.* **no man,** nadie; ningún hombre. **young man,** joven, *m.* **to a man,** como un solo hombre. **to come to man's estate,** llegar a la edad viril. **Man overboard!** ¡Hombre al agua! **man and wife,** marido y mujer, *m,* cónyuges, esposos, *m pl.* **man about town,** hombre de mundo, señorito, *m.* **man-at-arms,** hombre de armas, *m.* **man-eater,** caníbal, *mf;* tigre, *m.* **man-eating,** *a* antropófago. **man hater,** misántropo, *m;* mujer que odia a los hombres, *f.* **man-hole,** pozo, *m.* **man-hunter,** caníbal, *mf;* (woman) castigadora, *f.* **man in charge,** encargado, *m.* **man in the moon,** mujer de la luna, *f.* **man in the street,** hombre de la calle, hombre medio, *m.* **man of letters,** hombre de letras, literato, *m;* **man of straw,** bausán, *m;* (figure-head) testaferro, *m.* **man of the world,** hombre del mundo, *m.* **man of war,** buque de guerra, *m.* **man-power,** mano de obra, *f,* brazos, *m pl,* (e.g. *lack of man-power,* falta de brazos, *f).* **man servant,** criado, *m*
**man** /mæn/ *vt* armar; *Mil.* poner guarnición (a); ocupar; *Naut.* tripular; dirigir; *Fig.* fortificar
**manacle** /'mænəkəl/ *n* manilla, *f; pl* **manacles,** esposas, *f pl;* grillos, *m pl.* —*vt* poner esposas (a)
**manage** /'mænɪdʒ/ *vt* manejar; (animals) domar; dirigir; gobernar; administrar; (arrange) agenciar, arreglar; (work) explotar; (do) hacer; (eat) comer. —*vi* arreglárselas (para); (get along) ir tirando; (know how) saber hacer; (succeed in) lograr; (do) hacer
**manageability** /,mænɪdʒə'bɪlɪti/ *n* lo manejable; flexibilidad, *f;* (of animals, persons) docilidad, mansedumbre, *f*
**manageable** /'mænɪdʒəbəl/ *a* manejable; flexible; (of persons, animals) dócil
**management** /'mænɪdʒmənt/ *n* manejo, *m;* dirección, *f;* gobierno, *m;* administración, *f;* arreglo, *m;* (working) explotación, *f; Com.* gerencia, *f; Theat.* empresa, *f;* conducta, *f;* (economy) economía, *f;* (skill) habilidad, *f;* prudencia, *f.* **the m.,** la dirección, el cuerpo de directores. **domestic m.,** economía doméstica, *f*
**manager** /'mænɪdʒər/ *n* director, *m;* administrador, *m;* jefe, *m; Theat.* empresario, *m; Com.* gerente, *m;*

regente, *m.* **She is not much of a m.,** No es muy mujer de su casa. **manager's office,** dirección, *f*
**managerial** /,mænɪ'dʒɪəriəl/ *a* directivo; administrativo. **m. board,** junta directiva, *f*
**managership** /'mænɪdʒər,ʃɪp/ *n* puesto de director, *m;* jefatura, *f*
**managing** /'mænɪdʒɪŋ/ *a* directivo; (officious) mandón, dominante; (niggardly) tacaño
**manatee** /'mænə,ti/ *n* manatí, *m*
**Manchurian** /mæn'tʃuriən/ *a* manchuriano. —*n* manchuriano (-na)
**mandarin** /'mændərɪn/ *n* mandarín, *m;* (language) mandarina, *f.* **m. orange,** mandarina, *f*
**mandate** /'mændeit/ *n* mandato, *m.* **mandated territory,** territorios bajo mandato, *m pl*
**mandatory** /'mændə,tɔri/ *a* obligatorio
**mandible** /'mændəbəl/ *n* mandíbula, *f*
**mandolin** /'mændlɪn/ *n* bandolín, *m,* bandurria, *f*
**mandrake** /'mændreik, -drɪk/ *n* mandrágora, *f*
**mandrill** /'mændrɪl/ *n* mandril, *m*
**mane** /mein/ *n* melena, *f;* (of a horse) crines, *f pl*
**maned** /meind/ *a* (in compounds) con melena...; con crines...
**maneuver** /mə'nuvər/ *n* maniobra, *f.* —*vi* maniobrar, hacer maniobras. —*vt* hacer maniobras; manipular
**maneuvering** /mə'nuvərɪŋ/ *n* maniobras, *f pl;* maquinaciones, intrigas, *f pl*
**manfully** /'mænfəli/ *adv* valientemente; vigorosamente
**manganate** /'mæŋgəneit/ *n* manganato, *m*
**manganese** /'mæŋgə,nis, -,niz/ *n* manganeso, *m*
**mange** /meindʒ/ *n* sarna, *f;* (in sheep) roña, *f*
**manger** /'meindʒər/ *n* pesebre, *m*
**manginess** /'meindʒɪnɪs/ *n* estado sarnoso, *m*
**mangle** /'mæŋgəl/ *n* (for clothes) exprimidor de la ropa, *m.* —*vt* pasar por el exprimidor; (mutilate) mutilar, lacerar, magullar; (a text) mutilar
**mangling** /'mæŋglɪŋ/ *n* (mutilation) mutilación, laceración, *f*
**mango** /'mæŋgou/ *n* mango, *m*
**mangy** /'meindʒi/ *a* sarnoso
**manhandle** /'mæn,hændl/ *vt* maltratar
**manhood** /'mænhʊd/ *n* virilidad, *f;* edad viril, *f;* masculinidad, *f;* los hombres; (manliness) hombradía, *f,* valor, *m*
**mania** /'meiniə/ *n* manía, *f;* obsesión, *f;* capricho, *m,* chifladura, *f*
**maniac** /'meini,æk/ *n* maníaco (-ca). —*a* maníaco, maniático
**manicure** /'mænɪ,kyʊr/ *n* manicura, *f.* —*vt* arreglar las uñas. **m.-set,** estuche de manicura, *m*
**manicurist** /'mænɪ,kyʊrɪst/ *n* manicuro (-ra)
**manifest** /'mænə,fest/ *n Naut.* manifiesto, *m.* —*vt* mostrar; hacer patente, probar; manifestarse. —*vi* publicar un manifiesto; (of spirits) manifestarse. —*a* manifiesto, evidente, claro, patente. **to make m.,** poner de manifiesto
**manifestation** /,mænəfə'steiʃən/ *n* manifestación, *f*
**manifestly** /'mænə,festli/ *adv* evidentemente, manifiestamente
**manifesto** /,mænə'festou/ *n* manifiesto, *m*
**manifold** /'mænə,fould/ *a* múltiple; numeroso; diverso, vario
**manikin** /'mænɪkɪn/ *n* enano, *m;* muñeco, *m; Art.* maniquí, *m*
**Manilla** /mə'nɪlə/ *n* Manila, *f;* cigarro filipino, *m.* **M. hemp,** cáñamo de Manila, *m*
**maniple** /'mænəpəl/ *n* manípulo, *m*
**manipulate** /mə'nɪpyə,leit/ *vt* manipular
**manipulation** /mə,nɪpyə'leiʃən/ *n* manipulación, *f*
**manipulative** /mə'nɪpyə,leitɪv/ *a* manipulador
**mankind** /'mæn'kaind/ *n* humanidad, raza humana, *f,* género humano, *m*
**manlike** /'mæn,laik/ *a* de hombre, masculino; varonil; (of a woman) hombruno
**manliness** /'mænlinɪs/ *n* masculinidad, hombradía, *f;* virilidad, *f;* valor, *m;* (of a woman) aire hombruno, *m*
**manly** /'mænli/ *a* masculino, de hombre; varonil, viril; valiente; fuerte. **to be very m.,** ser muy hombre, ser todo un hombre

**manna** /'mænə/ n maná, m

**mannequin** /'mænɪkɪn/ n manequín, modelo, f. **m. parade,** exposición de modelos, f

**manner** /'mænər/ n manera, f, modo, m; aire, porte, m; conducta, f; (style) estilo, m; (sort) clase, f; Gram. modo, m; pl **manners,** modales, m pl, crianza, educación, f; (customs) costumbres, f pl. **after the m. of,** en (or según) el estilo de. **in a m. of speaking,** en cierto modo, para decirlo así. **in this m.,** de este modo. **to have bad ( good) manners,** tener malos (buenos) modales, ser mal (bien) criado. **the novel of manners,** la novela de costumbres

**mannered** /'mænərd/ a amanerado; (in compounds)... educado, de... modales; de costumbres... **well-m.,** bien educado, de buenos modales

**mannerism** /'mænə,rɪzəm/ n amaneramiento, m; afectación, f; Theat. latiguillo, m. **to acquire mannerisms,** amanerarse

**manneriness** /'mænərlɪnɪs/ n cortesía, buena educación, urbanidad, f

**mannerly** /'mænərli/ a cortés, bien educado, atento

**mannish** /'mænɪʃ/ a (of a woman) hombruno; de hombre, masculino

**manor** /'mænər/ n feudo, m; finca, hacienda, f; casa solariega, f; señorío, m

**manorial** /mə'nɔriəl/ a señorial

**mansion** /'mænʃən/ n mansión, f; casa solariega, f; hotel, m. **m.-house,** casa solariega, f; residencia del alcalde de Londres, f

**manslaughter** /'mæn,slɔtər/ n homicidio, m; Law. homicidio sin premeditación, m

**mantelpiece** /'mæntl,pis/ n repisa de chimenea, f

**mantilla** /mæn'tɪlə/ n mantilla, f

**mantle** /'mæntl/ n capa, f, manto, m; Fig. cobertura, f; (gas) camiseta, f, manguito, mf; Zool. manto, m. —vt cubrir; envolver; ocultar. —vi extenderse; (of blushes) inundar, subirse (a las mejillas)

**Mantuan** /'mæntʃuan/ a mantuano

**manual** /'mænyual/ a manual. —n manual, m; Mus. teclado de órgano, m. **m. work,** trabajo manual, m

**manufactory** /,mænyə'fæktəri/ n fábrica, f, taller, m

**manufacture** /,mænyə'fæktʃər/ n fabricación, f; manufactura, f. —vt manufacturar, fabricar

**manufacturer** /,mænyə'fæktʃərər/ n fabricante, industrial, m. **manufacturer's price,** precio de fábrica, m

**manufacturing** /,mænyə'fæktʃərɪŋ/ a manufacturero, fabril. —n fabricación, f

**manure** /mə'nʊr/ n estiércol, abono, m. —vt estercolar, abonar. **m. heap,** estercolero, m

**manuring** /mə'nʊrɪŋ/ n estercoladura, f

**manuscript** /'mænyə,skrɪpt/ n manuscrito, m, a manuscrito

**Manx** /mæŋks/ a manés

**many** /'mɛni/ a muchos (-as); numeroso; diversos (-as); varios (-as). —n muchos (-as); la mayoría; las masas; muchedumbre, multitud, f. **a great m.,** muchísimos, m pl. muchísimas, f pl; un gran número. **as m. as...,** tantos como... **How m. are there?** ¿Cuántos hay? ¿Cuántas hay? **m. a time,** muchas veces. **three too m.,** tres de más. **for m. long years,** por largos años. **m.-colored,** multicolor. **m.-headed,** con muchas cabezas. **m.-sided,** multilátero; polifacético; complicado

**Maori** /'mauri/ n maorí, m, (pl maoríes)

**map** /mæp/ n mapa, m; plano, m; (chart) carta, f. —vt hacer un mapa (or plano) de. **to map out,** Surv. apear; trazar; (plan) proyectar. **ordnance map,** mapa del estado mayor, m. **map of the world,** mapamundi, mapa del mundo, m. **map-making,** cartografía, f

**maple** /'meipəl/ n (tree) arce, m; (wood) madera de arce, f. **m.-syrup,** jarabe de arce, m

**mapping** /'mæpɪŋ/ n cartografía, f

**mar** /mɑr/ vt estropear; desfigurar; (happiness) destruir, aguar; frustrar

**marabou** /'mærə,bu/ n marabú, m

**maraschino** /,mærə'skinou/ n marrasquino, m. **m. cherry,** cerezas en marrasquino, f pl

**maraud** /mə'rɔd/ vi merodear

**marauder** /mə'rɔdər/ n merodeador, m

**marauding** /mə'rɔdɪŋ/ a merodeador, m, merodeo, m

**marble** /'mɑrbəl/ n mármol, m; (for playing with) canica, f, a de marmol, marmóreo; Fig. insensible; (of paper, etc.) jaspeado. —vt jaspear. **m. cutter,** marmolista, m. **m. works,** marmolería, f

**marbled** /'mɑrbəld/ a jaspeado

**March** /mɑrtʃ/ n marzo, m. **as mad as a M. hare,** loco como una cabra, loco de atar

**march** /mɑrtʃ/ n marcha, f; (step) paso, m; Fig. marcha, f, progreso, m. **forced m.,** marcha forzada, f. **quick m.,** paso doble, m. **to steal a m. on,** tomar la delantera (a), ganar por la mano (a). **to strike up a m.,** batir la marcha. **m.-past,** desfile, m

**march** /mɑrtʃ/ vi marchar; (of properties) lindar (con). —vt hacer marchar, poner en marcha (a). **to m. back,** vi regresar (or volver) a pie. —vt hacer volver a pie. **to m. in,** entrar (a pie) en. **to m. off,** marcharse. **to m. on,** seguir marchando; seguir adelante; avanzar. **to m. past,** desfilar ante

**marching** /'mɑrtʃɪŋ/ n marcha, f. —a en marcha; de marcha. **to receive one's m. orders,** recibir la orden de marchar; Inf. ser despedido. **m. order,** orden de marcha, m. **m. song,** canción de marcha, f

**marchioness** /'mɑrʃənɪs/ n marquesa, f

**mardi gras** /'mardi ,gra/ n martes de carnaval, m

**mare** /mɛər/ n yegua, f

**margarine** /'mardʒərɪn/ n margarina, f

**margin** /'mardʒɪn/ n borde, lado, m, orilla, f; (of a page) margen, mf; reserva, f; sobrante, m. **in the m.,** al margen

**marginal** /'mardʒənl/ a marginal. **m. note,** acotación, nota marginal, f

**marigold** /'mæri,gould/ n caléndula, maravilla, f

**marine** /mə'rin/ a marino, de mar; marítimo; naval. —n (fleet) marina, f; (soldier) soldado de marina, m. **Tell that to the marines!** ¡Cuéntaselo a tu tía! **mercantile m.,** marina mercante, f. **m. forces,** infantería de marina, f. **m. insurance,** seguro marítimo, m

**mariner** /'mærənər/ n marinero, marino, m. **mariner's compass,** aguja de marear, brújula, f

**marionette** /,mæriə'nɛt/ n marioneta, f, títere, m

**marital** /'mærɪtl/ a marital

**maritime** /'mæri,taim/ a marítimo

**mark** /mɑrk/ n marca, f; señal, f; mancha, f; impresión, f; (target) blanco, m; (standard) norma, f; (level) nivel, m; (distinction) importancia, distinción, f; (in examinations) nota, f; calificación, f; (signature) cruz, f; (coin) marco, m. —vt marcar; señalar; (price) poner precio (a); (notice) observar, darse cuenta (de); (characterize) caracterizar. **trade-m.,** marca de fábrica, f. **to be beside the m.,** no dar en el blanco; errar el tiro; Fig. no tener nada que ver con; equivocarse. **to hit the m.,** dar en el blanco; Fig. dar en el clavo. **to make one's m.,** firmar con una cruz; distinguirse. **to m. time,** marcar el paso; Fig. hacer tiempo. **to m. down,** (a person) señalar; escoger; (in price) rebajar. **to m. out,** marcar; trazar; definir; (erase) borrar; (a person) escoger; destinar. **m. somebody absent,** ponerle a fulano su ausencia. **m. somebody present,** ponerle a fulano su asistencia

**Mark** /mɑrk/ n Marcos. **the Gospel according to St. M.,** el Evangelio de San Marcos

**marked** /mɑrkt/ a marcado; señalado; notable; acentuado; particular, especial. **He speaks with a m. Galician accent,** Habla con marcado acento gallego

**markedly** /'mɑrkɪdli/ adv marcadamente; notablemente; especialmente, particularmente

**marker** /'mɑrkər/ n (billiards) marcador, m; (football, etc.) tanteador, m

**market** /'mɑrkɪt/ n mercado, m; tráfico, m; venta, f; (price) precio, m; (shop) bazar, emporio, m. —vt and vi comprar en un mercado; vender en un mercado. **black m.,** mercado negro, estraperlo, m. **open m.,** mercado al aire libre, m; Fig. mercado libre, m. **m. day,** día de mercado, m. **m. garden,** huerto, m, huerta, f. **m. gardener,** hortelano, m. **m.-place,** plaza de mercado, f; Fig. mercado de mercado, m. **m. price,** precio corriente, m. **m. stall,** tabanco, puesto de mercado, m. **m.-woman,** verdulera, f

**marketable** /'mɑrkɪtəbəl/ a comerciable, vendible; corriente

**marketing** /'mɑrkɪtɪŋ/ n venta, f; compra en un mercado, f; mercado, m. **to go m.,** ir al mercado

**marking** /'mɑrkɪŋ/ n marca, f; (spot on animals, etc.) pinta, f. **m.-ink,** tinta de marcar, f. **m.-iron,** ferrete, hierro de marcar, m

**marksman** /'mɑrksmən/ n tirador (-ra)

**marksmanship** /'mɑrksmən,ʃɪp/ n puntería, f

**marl** /mɑrl/ n marga, f

**marlinespike** /'mɑrlɪn,spaik/ n pasador, m

**marmalade** /'mɑrmə,leid/ n mermelada de naranjas amargas, f

**marmoset** /'mɑrmə,zɛt/ n tití, m

**marmot** /'mɑrmət/ n Zool. marmota, f

**maroon** /mə'run/ n (color) marrón, m; (slave) cimarrón (-ona); (fireware) petardo, m. **—a** de marrón. **—vt** abandonar, dejar

**marquee** /mɑr'ki/ n marquesina, f

**marquetrie** /'mɑrkɪtri/ n marquetería, f

**marquis** /'mɑrkwɪs/ n marqués, m

**marriage** /'mærɪdʒ/ n matrimonio, m; unión, f; (wedding) boda, f, casamiento, m. **by m.,** (of relationship) político. **She is an aunt by m.,** tía política. **m. articles,** capitulaciones (matrimoniales), f pl. **m. contract,** contrato matrimonial, m. **m. license,** licencia de casamiento, f. **m. portion,** dote, mf. **m. rate,** nupcialidad, f. **m. register,** acta matrimonial, f. **m. song,** epitalamio, m

**marriageable** /'mærɪdʒəbəl/ a casadero

**married** /'mærid/ past part and a casado; matrimonial, conyugal. **newly-m. couple,** los recién casados. **to get m. to,** casarse con. **m. couple,** matrimonio, m, cónyuges, m pl. **m. life,** vida conyugal, f

**married name** n nombre de casada, f

**marrow** /'mærou/ n tuétano, m, médula, f; Fig. meollo, m. **to the m. of one's bones,** hasta los tuétanos.

**marrowbone** /'mærou,boun/ n hueso medular, m. **on one's marrowbones,** de rodillas

**marry** /'mæri/ vt casarse con, contraer matrimonio con; casar; (of a priest) unir en matrimonio; Fig. juntar, unir. **—vi** casarse. **to m. again,** volver a casarse

**Marseillaise** /,mɑrsei'ez/ n marsellesa, f

**Marseilles** /mɑr'sei/ Marsella, f

**marsh** /mɑrʃ/ n marjal, pantano, m. **m.-mallow,** Bot. malvavisco, m. **m. marigold,** calta, f

**marshal** /'mɑrʃəl/ n mariscal, m, vt poner en orden, arreglar; dirigir. **field-m.,** capitán general de ejército, m

**marshaling** /'mɑrʃəlɪŋ/ n ordenación, f; dirección, f. **m.-yard,** (railway) apartadero ferroviario, m

**marshy** /'mɑrʃi/ a pantanoso

**mart** /mɑrt/ n Poet. plaza de mercado, f; mercado, m; emporio, m; (auction rooms) martillo, m

**marten** /'mɑrtn/ n marta, f

**martial** /'mɑrʃəl/ a militar; marcial, belicoso. **m. array,** orden de batalla, m. **m. law,** derecho militar, m; estado de guerra, m. **m. spirit,** marcialidad, f, espíritu belicoso, m

**martially** /'mɑrʃəli/ adv militarmente; marcialmente

**Martian** /'mɑrʃən/ a marciano

**martinet** /,mɑrtn̩'et/ n Mil. ordenancista, m; rigorista, mf

**Martinique** /,mɑrtn̩'ik/ Martinica, f

**Martinmas** /'mɑrtn̩məs/ n día de San Martín, m

**martyr** /'mɑrtər/ n mártir, mf vt martirizar

**martyrdom** /'mɑrtərdəm/ n martirio, m

**martyrize** /'mɑrtə,raiz/ vt martirizar

**marvel** /'mɑrvəl/ n maravilla, f. **to m. at,** maravillarse de, admirarse de

**marvelous** /'mɑrvələs/ a maravilloso

**marvelousness** /'mɑrvələsnɪs/ n maravilla, f, carácter maravilloso, m, lo maravilloso

**Marxism** /'mɑrksɪzəm/ n marxismo, m

.**Marxist** /'mɑrksɪst/ a and n marxista, mf

**marzipan** /'mɑrzə,pæn/ n mazapán, m

**mascot** /'mæskɒt/ n mascota, f

**masculine** /'mæskyəlɪn/ a masculino; viril, macho; de hombre; (of a woman) hombruno. **—n** masculino, m

**masculinity** /,mæskyə'lɪnɪti/ n masculinidad, f

**mash** /mæʃ/ n mezcla, f; amasijo, m; pasta, f, puré, m. **—vt** mezclar; amasar. **mashed potatoes,** puré de patatas (de papas), m

**mask** /mæsk/ n máscara, f; antifaz, m; (death) mascarilla, f; (person) máscara, mf. **—vt** enmascarar; Fig. encubrir, disimular. **—vi** ponerse una máscara; disfrazarse. **masked ball,** n baile de máscaras, m

**masker** /'mæskər/ n máscara, mf

**masochism** /'mæsə,kɪzəm/ n masoquismo, m

**mason** /'meisən/ n albañil, m; (freemason) francmasón, masón, m

**masonic** /mə'sɒnɪk/ a masónico. **m. lodge,** logia de francmasones, f

**masonry** /'meisənri/ n (trade) albañilería, f; (mambostería, f

**masque** /mæsk/ n mascarada, f

**masquerade** /,mæskə'reid/ n mascarada, f

**masquerader** /,mæskə'reidər/ n máscara, mf

**mass** /mæs/ n misa, f. **to hear m.,** oír misa. **to say m.,** celebrar misa. **high m.,** misa mayor, f. **low m.,** misa rezada, f. **m. book,** libro de misa, m

**mass** /mæs/ n masa, f; (shape) bulto, m; (heap) montón, m; (great number) muchedumbre, f; (cloud of steam, etc.) nube, f. **—vt** amasar; Mil. concentrar. **—vi** congregarse en masa. **in a m.,** en masa; en conjunto. **the m. ( of)...,** la mayoría (de)... **the masses,** las masas, el vulgo, el pueblo. **m. formation,** columna cerrada, f. **m.-meeting,** mitin, mitin popular, m. **m.-production,** fabricación en serie, f

**massacre** /'mæsəkər/ n matanza, carnicería, f, vt hacer una carnicería (de)

**massage** /mə'sɑʒ/ n masaje, m; (friction) fricción, f. **—vt** dar un masaje (a)

**masseur, masseuse** /mə'sɜr; mə'sus/ n masajista, mf

**massive** /'mæsɪv/ a macizo; sólido

**massively** /'mæsɪvli/ adv macizamente; sólidamente

**massiveness** /'mæsɪvnɪs/ n macicez, f; solidez, f

**mast** /mæst/ n Naut. palo, árbol, m; (for wireless) mástil, m; poste, m; (beech) hayuco, m; (oak) bellota, f. **—vt** Naut. arbolar. **at half-m.,** a media asta. **m.-head,** calcés, tope, m

**masted** /'mæstɪd/ a arbolado; (in compounds) de... palos

**master** /'mæstər/ n (of the house, etc.) señor, amo, m; maestro, m; Naut. patrón, m; (owner) dueño, m; (teacher) profesor, maestro, m; (young master and an address) señorito, m; director, m; jefe, m; (expert) perito, m; (of a military order) maestre, m, a maestro; superior. **—vt** dominar; ser maestro en; dominar, conocer a fondo. **This picture is by an old m.,** Este cuadro es de un gran maestro antiguo. **to be m. of oneself,** ser dueño de sí. **to be one's own m.,** ser dueño de sí mismo; trabajar por su propia cuenta; ser independiente; estar libre. **m. builder,** maestro de obras, m. **m. hand,** mano maestra, f. **M. of Arts,** maestro (-tra) en artes, m. **M. of Ceremonies,** maestro de ceremonias, m. **M. of Foxhounds,** cazador mayor, m. **M. of the Horse,** caballerizo mayor del rey, m. **M. of the Rolls,** archivero mayor, m. **m.-key,** llave maestra, f. **m. mind,** águila, f, ingenio, m. **m. stroke,** golpe maestro, m

**masterful** /'mæstərfəl/ a imperioso, dominante; autoritario, arbitrario

**masterfulness** /'mæstərfəlnɪs/ n imperiosidad, f; arbitrariedad, f

**masterless** /'mæstərlɪs/ a sin amo

**masterliness** /'mæstərlɪnɪs/ n maestría, f; excelencia, f; perfección, f

**masterly** /'mæstərli/ a maestro; excelente; perfecto. **m. performance,** obra maestra, f; Theat. representación perfecta, f; ejecución excelente, f

**masterpiece** /'mæstər,pis/ n obra maestra, f

**master plan** n plan regulador, m

**masterstroke** /'mæstər,strouk/ n golpe magistral, golpe de maestro, m

**mastery** /'mæstəri/ n dominio, m; autoridad, f; poder, m; ventaja, f; superioridad, maestría, f; conocimiento profundo, m. **to gain the m. of,** hacerse el señor de; llegar a dominar

**mastic** /'mæstɪk/ n masilla, almáciga, f

**masticate** /'mæstɪ,keit/ vt masticar, mascar

**mastication** /,mæstɪ'keiʃən/ n masticación, f

**mastiff** /'mæstɪf/ n mastín, alano, m

**mastodon** /'mæstə,dɒn/ n mastodonte, m

**mastoid** /'mæstɔid/ a mastoides. —n apófisis mastoides, f

**masturbate** /'mæstər,beit/ vi masturbarse

**masturbation** /,mæstər'beiʃən/ n masturbación, f

**mat** /mæt/ n esterilla, f; alfombrilla, f; (on the table) tapete individual, m. —vt (tangle) enmarañar, desgreñar. —vi enmarañarse

**match** /mætʃ/ n Sports. partido, m; (wrestling, boxing) lucha, f; (fencing) asalto, m; (race) carrera, f; (contest) concurso, m; (equal) igual, mf; (pair) pareja, f; compañero (-ra); (marriage) boda, f, casamiento, m; (for lighting) cerilla, f, fósforo, m; (for guns) mecha, f. —vt competir con; (equal) igualar; ser igual (a); hacer juego con; emparejar, aparear; armonizar. —vi ser igual; hacer juego; armonizarse. **good m.,** Inf. buen partido, m. **as thin as a m.,** más delgado que una cerilla. **to meet one's m.,** dar con la horma de su zapato. **to play a m.,** jugar un partido. **m.-box,** cajita de cerillas, fosforera, f. **m.-seller,** fosforero (-ra)

**matchless** /'mætʃlɪs/ a incomparable, sin igual, sin par

**matchwood** /'mætʃ,wʊd/ n madera para cerillas, f

**mate** /meit/ n compañero, camarada, m; (spouse) compañero (-ra); pareja, f; (on merchant ships) piloto, m; (assistant) ayudante, m; (at chess) mate, m. —vt (marry) casar, desposar; (animals, birds) aparear, acoplar; (chess) dar jaque mate (a). —vi casarse; aparearse, acoplarse

**maté** /'mɑtei/ maté, té del Paraguay, m

**materfamilias** /,meitərfə'miliəs/ n madre de familia, f

**material** /mə'tiəriəl/ a material; importante, esencial; considerable; sensible, notable; grave. —n material, m; materia, f; (fabric) tela, f; tejido, m. **raw materials,** materias primas, f pl. **writing materials,** utensilios de escritorio, m pl; papel de escribir, m

**materialism** /mə'tiəriə,lizəm/ n materialismo, m

**materialist** /mə'tiəriəlist/ n materialista, mf

**materialistic** /mə,tiəriə'listik/ a materialista

**materiality** /mə,tiəri'æliti/ n materialidad, f; importancia, f

**materialization** /mə,tiəriəli'zeiʃən/ n materialización, f

**materialize** /mə'tiəriə,laiz/ vt materializar

**maternal** /mə'tɜrnl/ a materno, maternal. **m. grandparents,** abuelos maternos, m pl

**maternity** /mə'tɜrniti/ n maternidad, f. **m. center,** centro de maternidad, m. **m. hospital,** casa de maternidad, f

**mathematical** /,mæθə'mætikəl/ a matemático

**mathematician** /,mæθəmə'tiʃən/ n matemático, m

**mathematics** /,mæθə'mætiks/ n pl; matemáticas, f pl. **applied m.,** matemáticas prácticas, f pl. **higher m.,** matemáticas superiores, f pl. **pure m.,** matemáticas teóricas, f pl

**matinee** /,mætn̩'ei/ n función de tarde, f

**mating** /'meitɪŋ/ n (of animals) apareamiento, acoplamiento, m; unión, f; casamiento, m

**matins** /'mætɪnz/ n pl Eccl. maitines, m pl

**matriarch** /'meitri,ɑrk/ n matriarca, f

**matriarchal** /,meitri'ɑrkəl/ a matriarcal

**matriarchy** /'meitri,ɑrki/ n matriarcado, m

**matricide** /'mætri,said/ n (crime) matricidio, m; (person) matricida, mf

**matriculate** /mə'trikyə,leit/ vt matricular. —vi matricularse

**matriculation** /mə,trikyə'leiʃən/ n matriculación, f

**matrimonial** /,mætrə'mouniəl/ a matrimonial, de matrimonio; marital. **m. agency,** agencia de matrimonios, f

**matrimony** /'mætrə,mouni/ n matrimonio, m

**matrix** /'meitriks/ n matriz, f

**matron** /'meitrən/ n matrona, mujer casada, madre de familia, f; (of a hospital) matrona, f; (of a school) ama de llaves, f; directora, f. **m. of honor,** (at a wedding) madrina, f

**matronly** /'meitrənli/ a de matrona, matronal; respetable; serio

**matte** /mæt/ a mate

**matted** /'mætid/ a enmarañado, enredado

**matter** /'mætər/ n materia, f; substancia, f; caso, m; cuestión, f; asunto, m; causa, f; (distance) distancia, f; (amount) cantidad, f; (duration) espacio de tiempo, m; (importance) importancia, f; Med. pus, m; pl **matters,** asuntos, m pl, etc.; situación, f. **as if nothing were the m.,** como si no hubiese pasado nada. **for that m.,** en cuanto a eso. **grey m.,** substancia gris, f. **in the m. of,** en el caso de. **It is a m. of taste,** Es cuestión de gusto. **printed m.,** impresos, m pl. **What is the m.?** ¿Qué pasa? ¿Qué hay? **What is the m. with him?** ¿Qué tiene? ¿Qué le pasa? **m.-of-course,** cosa natural, f. **m.-of-fact,** práctico; sin imaginación; positivista. **m. of fact,** n hecho positivo, m, realidad, f. **As a m. of fact...,** En realidad..., El caso es que... **m. of form,** cuestión de fórmula, f; pura formalidad, f

**matter** /'mætər/ vi importar; (discharge) supurar. **What does it m.?** ¿Qué importa? **It doesn't m.,** Es igual, No importa, Da lo mismo

**Matterhorn** /'mætər,hɔrn/, **the** el Matterhorn, m

**matting** /'mætɪŋ/ n estera, f

**mattress** /'mætris/ n colchón, m. **spring-m.,** colchón de muelles, m. **m.-maker,** colchonero, m

**mature** /mə'tʃʊr/ a maduro; Com. vencido. —vt madurar. —vi madurarse; Com. vencer

**maturity** /mə'tʃʊriti/ n madurez, f; edad madura, f; (Com. of a bill) vencimiento, m

**matutinal** /mə'tutnl/ a matutino

**maudlin** /'mɔdlin/ a sensiblero; lacrimoso; (tipsy) calamocano

**maul** /mɔl/ vt maltratar; herir

**maundy** /'mɔndi/ n lavatorio, m. **M. Thursday,** Jueves Santo, m

**Mauritius** /mɔ'riʃəs/ Mauricio, m, Isla de Francia, f

**mausoleum** /,mɔsə'liəm/ n mausoleo, m

**mauve** /mouv/ n color purpúreo delicado, color de malva, m, a de color de malva

**maw** /mɔ/ n (of a ruminant) cuajar, m; (of a bird) buche, m; Fig. abismo, m

**mawkish** /'mɔkiʃ/ a insípido, insulso; sensiblero; asqueroso

**mawkishness** /'mɔkiʃnis/ n insipidez, insulsez, f; sensiblería, f; asquerosidad, f

**maxilla** /mæk'silə/ n hueso maxilar, maxilar, m

**maxillary** /'mæksə,leri/ a maxilar

**maxim** /'mæksim/ n máxima, f

**maximum** /'mæksəməm/ a máximo. —n máximo, m

**may** /mei/ v aux poder; ser posible; (expressing wish, hope) ojalá que..., Dios quiera que..., or the present subjunctive may be used, e.g. May you live many years! ¡(qué) Viva Vd. muchos años! (to denote uncertainty, the future tense of the verb is often used, e.g. You may perhaps remember the date, Vd. quizás se acordará de la fecha. Who may he be? ¿Quién será?) **May God grant it!** ¡(que) Dios lo quiera! **It may be that...,** Puede ser que..., Es posible que..., Quizás... **He may come on Saturday,** Es posible que venga el sábado; Puede venir el sábado. **May I come in?** ¿Puedo entrar? ¿Se puede entrar? **May I come and see you?** ¿Me das permiso para hacerme una visita? ¿Me dejas venir a verte? **May I go then?** ¿Puedo irme pues? ¿Tengo permiso para marcharme entonces?

**May** /mei/ n mayo, m; Fig. abril, m; Bot. espina blanca, f. **May Day,** primero de mayo, m. **mayflower,** flor del cuclillo, f. **mayfly,** cachipolla, f. **May queen,** maya, f

**maybe** /'meibi/ adv quizás, tal vez

**mayonnaise** /,meiə'neiz/ n mayonesa, f. **m. sauce,** salsa mayonesa, f

**mayor** /'meiər/ n alcalde, m

**mayoral** /'meiərəl/ a de alcalde

**mayoress** /'meiəris/ n alcaldesa, f

**maypole** /'mei,poul/ n mayo, m. **m. dance,** danza de cintas, f

**maze** /meiz/ n laberinto, m; Fig. perplejidad, f. —vt dejar perplejo, aturdir

**mazurka** /mə'zɜrkə/ n mazurca, f

**me** /mi/ pron me; (after a preposition only) mí. **They sent it for me,** Lo mandaron para mí. **Dear me!** ¡Ay de mí!

**meadow** /'mɛdou/ n prado, m, pradera, f. **m.-sweet,** reina de los prados, f

**meager** /'migər/ *a* magro, enjuto, flaco; (scanty) exiguo, escaso, insuficiente; pobre; *Fig.* árido

**meagerly** /'migərli/ *adv* pobremente

**meagerness** /'migərnıs/ *n* exigüidad, escasez, *f;* pobreza, *f; Fig.* aridez, *f*

**meal** /mil/ *n* comida, *f;* (flour) harina, *f.* **to have a good m.,** comer bien. **test m.,** *Med.* comida de prueba, *f.* **m.-time,** hora de comida, *f*

**mealy** /'mili/ *a* harinoso; (of the complexion) pastoso no; (humble) humilde; pobre; inferior; bajo, vil, **m.-spirited,** vil, de alma ruin

**mean** /min/ *a* (middle) medianero; (average) mediano; (humble) humilde; pobre; inferior; bajo, vil, ruin; (avaricious) tacaño, mezquino. **m.-spirited,** vil, de alma ruin

**mean** /min/ *n* medio, *m;* medianía, *f; pl* **means,** medio, *m;* expediente, *m;* medios, *m pl;* (financial) recursos, *m pl;* modo, *m,* manera, *f.* **by all means,** por todos los medios; (certainly) ¡ya lo creo! ¡no faltaba más! ¡naturalmente! **by means of,** mediante, por medio de; con la ayuda de. **by no means,** de ningún modo; nada. **by some means,** de algún modo, de alguna manera

**mean** /min/ *vt* destinar (para); pretender, proponerse; intentar, pensar; querer decir, significar; importar; (wish) querer; (concern, speak about) tratarse (de). —*vi* tener el propósito, tener la intención. **I did not m. to do it,** Lo hice sin querer. **What does this word m.?** ¿Qué significa esta palabra? **What do you m. by that?** ¿Qué quieres decir con eso? **This portrait is meant to be Joan,** Este retrato quiere ser Juana. **What do they m. to do?** ¿Qué piensan (or se proponen) hacer? **Do you really m. it?** ¿Lo dices en serio? **Charles always means well,** Carlos siempre tiene buenas intenciones

**meander** /mi'ændər/ *n* meandro, serpenteo, *m;* camino tortuoso, *m, vi* serpentear; errar, vagar; (in talk) divagar

**meandering** /mi'ændərıŋ/ *n* meandros, *m pl,* serpenteo, *m;* (in talk) divagaciones, *f pl, a* serpentino, tortuoso

**meaning** /'minıŋ/ *n* intención, voluntad, *f;* significación, *f,* significado, *m;* (of words) acepción, *f;* (sense) sentido, *m;* (thought) pensamiento, *m.* —*a* significante. **double m.,** doble intención, *f.* **He gave me a m. look,** Me miró con intención. **What is the m. of it?** ¿Qué significa? ¿Qué quiere decir?

**meaningful** /'minıŋfəl/ *a* significante

**meaningless** /'minıŋlıs/ *a* sin sentido, insensato; insignificante

**meaningly** /'minıŋli/ *adv* significativamente; con intención

**meanness** /'minnıs/ *n* pobreza, *f;* inferioridad, *f;* mediocridad, *f;* bajeza, ruindad, *f;* (stinginess) mezquindad, tacañería, *f*

**meantime, meanwhile** /'min,taim; 'min,wail/ *n* ínterin, *m, adv* entre tanto, mientras tanto, a todo esto. **in the m.,** mientras tanto, en el ínterin

**measles** /'mizəlz/ *n* sarampión, *m.* **German m.,** rubéola, *f*

**measurable** /'mɛʒərəbəl/ *a* mensurable

**measure** /'mɛʒər/ *n* medida, *f;* capacidad, *f;* (for measuring) regla, *f;* número, *m;* proporción, *f;* (limit) límite, *m;* (*Fig.* step) medida, *f;* (metre) metro, *m; Mus.* compás, *m;* (degree) grado, *m;* manera, *f;* (parliamentary) proyecto (de ley), *m.* —*vt* medir; proporcionar, distribuir; (water) aforar; (land) apear; (height of persons) tallar; (for clothes) tomar las medidas (a); (judge) juzgar; (test) probar; (*Poet.* traverse) recorrer. **A suit made to m.,** un traje hecho a medida. **in great m.,** en gran manera, en alto grado. **in some m.,** hasta cierto punto. **to m. one's length,** caer tendido. **to take a person's m.,** *Fig.* tomar las medidas (a). **to m. up to,** *Fig.* estar al nivel de, ser igual a

**measured** /'mɛʒərd/ *a* mesurado, moderado; uniforme; limitado. **to walk with m. tread,** andar a pasos contados

**measurement** /'mɛʒərmənt/ *n* medición, *f;* medida, *f;* dimensión, *f*

**meat** /mit/ *n* carne, *f;* (food) alimento, *m;* (meal) comida, *f; Fig.* substancia, *f.* **to sit at m.,** estar a la mesa. **cold meats,** fiambres, *m pl.* **m.-ball,** albóndiga, *f.* **m.-chopper,** picador, *m.* **m.-dish,** fuente, *f.* **m.-eater,** comedor (-ra) de carne. **m. extract,** carne concentrada, *f.* **m.-market,** carnicería, *f.* **m.-pie,** pastel de carne, *m.* **m.-safe,** fresquera, *f*

**meaty** /'miti/ *a* carnoso; *Fig.* substancial

**Mecca** /'mɛkə/ la Meca, *f*

**mechanic** /mə'kænık/ *n* mecánico, *m*

**mechanical** /mə'kænıkəl/ *a* mecánico; maquinal

**mechanically** /mə'kænıkli/ *adv* mecánicamente; maquinalmente

**mechanical pencil** *n* lapicero, *m*

**mechanics** /mə'kænıks/ *n* mecánica, *f*

**mechanism** /'mɛkə,nızəm/ *n* mecanismo, *m;* (philosophy) mecanicismo, *m*

**mechanize** /'mɛkə,naiz/ *vt* convertir en máquina; (gen. *Mil.*) mecanizar; motorizar

**medal** /'mɛdl/ *n* medalla, *f*

**medallion** /mə'dælyən/ *n* medallón, *m*

**medallist** /'mɛdlıst/ *n* grabador de medallas, *m;* el, *m,* (*f,* la) que recibe una medalla

**meddle** /'mɛdl/ *vi* tocar; meterse (con or en); entremeterse, inmiscuirse; intrigar

**meddler** /'mɛdlər/ *n* entremetido (-da); intrigante, *mf*

**meddlesome** /'mɛdlsəm/ *a* entremetido; oficioso; impertinente; enredador, intrigante. **to be very m.,** meterse en todo

**meddlesomeness** /'mɛdlsəmnıs/ *n* entremetimiento, *m;* oficiosidad, *f;* impertinencia, *f;* intrigas, *f pl*

**median** /'midiən/ *a* del medio

**mediate** /*v* 'midi,eit/ *a* -ıt/ *vi* intervenir, mediar, arbitrar; abogar (por). —*a* medio; interpuesto

**media** /'midiə/, **the** los medios informativos, *m pl*

**mediation** /,midi'eiʃən/ *n* mediación, intervención, *f;* intercesión, *f;* interposición, *f*

**mediator** /'midi,eitər/ *n* mediador (-ra); arbitrador, *m;* intercesor (-ra)

**mediatory** /'midiə,tɔri/ *a* de mediador; intercesor

**medical** /'mɛdıkəl/ *a* médico; de medicina; de médico. —*n Inf.* estudiante de medicina, *m.* **m. Army M. Service,** Servicio de Sanidad Militar, *m.* **m. books,** libros de medicina, *m pl.* **m. examination,** examen médico, *m,* exploración médica, *f.* **m. jurisprudence,** medicina legal, *f.* **m. knowledge,** conocimientos médicos, *m pl.* **m. practitioner,** médico (-ca). **m. school,** escuela de medicina, *f*

**medicament** /mə'dıkəmənt/ *n* medicamento, *m*

**medicate** /'mɛdı,keit/ *vt* medicar; medicinar

**medicated** /'mɛdı,keitıd/ *a* medicado

**medication** /,mɛdı'keiʃən/ *n* medicación, *f*

**medicinal** /mə'dısənl/ *a* medicinal

**medicine** /'mɛdəsın/ *n* medicina, *f;* medicamento, *m;* (charm) ensalmo, hechizo, *m.* **patent m.,** específico farmacéutico, *m.* **m. ball,** balón medical, *m.* **m. chest,** botiquín, *m.* **m. man,** hechizador, *m*

**medico-** *prefix* médico-. **m.-legal,** médicolegal

**medieval** /,midi'ivəl/ *a* medieval

**medievalism** /,midi'ivə,lızəm/ *n* afición a la edad media, *f;* espíritu medieval, *m*

**mediocre** /,midi'oukər/ *a* mediocre

**mediocrity** /,midi'ɒkrıti/ *n* mediocridad, *f;* medianía, *f*

**meditate** /'mɛdı,teit/ *vt* idear, proyectar, meditar. —*vi* meditar, reflexionar; pensar, intentar

**meditation** /,mɛdı'teiʃən/ *n* meditación, *f*

**meditative** /'mɛdı,teitıv/ *a* meditabundo, contemplativo; de meditación

**meditatively** /'mɛdı,teitıvli/ *adv* reflexivamente

**Mediterranean** /,mɛdıtə'reiniən/ *a* mediterráneo. —*n* Mar Mediterráneo, *m*

**medium** /'midiəm/ *n* medio, *m;* (cooking) término medio, a medio cocer, a medio asar, *m;* (environment) medio ambiente, *m;* (agency) intermediario, *m;* (spiritualism) médium, *m; Art.* medio, *m,* a mediano; regular; mediocre. **through the m. of,** por medio de. **m.-sized,** de tamaño regular

**medlar** /'mɛdlər/ *n* (fruit) níspola, *f;* (tree) níspero, *m*

**medley** /'mɛdli/ *n* mezcla, *f;* miscelánea, *f, a* mezclado, mixto

**medulla** /mə'dʌlə/ *n* medula, *f*

**meek** /mik/ *a* dulce, manso; humilde; modesto; pacífico

**meekly** /'mikli/ *adv* mansamente; humildemente; modestamente

**meekness** /'miknis/ *n* mansedumbre, *f;* humildad, *f;* modestia, *f*

**meet** /mit/ *vt* encontrar; encontrarse con; tropezar con; (by arrangement) reunirse con; (make the acquaintance of) conocer (a); (satisfy) satisfacer; cumplir (con); (a bill) pagar, saldar; (refute) refutar; (fight) batirse (con); (confront) hacer frente (a). —*vi* juntarse; encontrarse; reunirse; verse; (of rivers) confluir. —*n* montería, *f, a* conveniente. **I shall m. you at the station,** Te esperaré en la estación. **Until we m. again!** ¡Hasta la vista! **to go to m.,** ir al encuentro de. **to m. half-way,** encontrar a la mitad del camino; partir la diferencia con; hacer concesiones (a). **to m. the eye,** saltar a la vista. **to m. with,** encontrar; experimentar; sufrir

**meeting** /'mitiŋ/ *n* encuentro, *m;* reunión, *f;* (interview) entrevista, *f;* (of rivers, etc.) confluencia, *f;* (public, etc.) mitin, *m;* (council) concilio, *m;* concurso, *m;* (race) concurso de carreras de caballos, *m.* **creditors' m.,** concurso de acreedores, *m.* **m.-house,** templo de los Cuáqueros, *m.* **m.-place,** lugar de reunión, *m;* lugar de cita, *m;* centro, *m.* **to adjourn the m.,** levantar la sesión. **to call a m.,** convocar una sesión. **to open the m.,** abrir la sesión

**megalomania** /ˌmɛgəlou'meiniə/ *n* megalomanía, monomanía de grandezas, *f*

**megalomaniac** /ˌmɛgəlou'meiniæk/ *n* megalómano (-na)

**megaphone** /'mɛgəˌfoun/ *n* megáfono, portavoz, *m*

**Meknès** /mɛk'nɛs/ Mequínez, *f*

**melancholia** /ˌmɛlən'koulia/ *n* melancolía, *f*

**melancholy** /'mɛlənˌkɒli/ *a* melancólico. —*n* melancolía, *f*

**mellifluence** /mə'lifluəns/ *n* melifluidad, *f*

**mellifluous** /mə'lifluəs/ *a* melifluo; dulce

**mellow** /'mɛlou/ *a* maduro; dulce; (of wine) rancio; blando; suave; (of sound) melodioso; (slang) alegre; (tipsy) entre dos luces. —*vt* madurar; ablandar; suavizar. —*vi* madurarse

**mellowing** /'mɛlouiŋ/ *n* maduración, *f*

**mellowness** /'mɛlounis/ *n* madurez, *f;* dulzura, *f;* (of wine) ranciedad, *f;* blandura, *f;* suavidad, *f;* melodia, *f*

**melodic** /mə'lɒdik/ *a* melódico

**melodious** /mə'loudiəs/ *a* melodioso

**melodiously** /mə'loudiəsli/ *adv* melodiosamente

**melodiousness** /mə'loudiəsnis/ *n* melodía, *f*

**melodrama** /'mɛləˌdrɑmə/ *n* melodrama, *m*

**melodramatic** /ˌmɛlədrə'mætik/ *a* melodramático

**melody** /'mɛlədi/ *n* melodía, *f*

**melon** /'mɛlən/ *n* melón, *m;* sandía, *f.* **slice of m.,** raja de melón, *f.* **m. bed,** sandiar, *m.* **m.-shaped,** amelonado

**melt** /mɛlt/ *vi* derretirse; deshacerse; disolverse; evaporarse; desaparecer; (of money, etc.) hacerse sal y agua; (relent) enternecerse, ablandarse. —*vt* fundir; (snow, etc.) derretir; (*Fig.* soften) ablandar. **He melted away,** *Inf.* Se escurrió. **to m. into tears,** deshacerse en lágrimas. **to m. down,** fundir

**melting** /'mɛltiŋ/ *a* fundente; (forgiving) indulgente; (tender) de ternura; lánguido; dulce. —*n* fusión, *f;* derretimiento, *m.* **m. point,** punto de fusión, *m.* **m. pot,** *Metall.* crisol, *m; Fig.* caldera de razas, *f, m*

**member** /'mɛmbər/ *n* miembro, *m;* (of a club, etc.) socio (-ia). **M. of Parliament,** diputado a Cortes, *m*

**membership** /'mɛmbərˌʃip/ *n* calidad de miembro, socio(-ia); número de miembros (or socios), *m,* composición, integración, *f*

**membrane** /'mɛmbrein/ *n* membrana, *f*

**membranous** /'mɛmbrənəs/ *a* membranoso

**memento** /mə'mɛntou/ *n* recuerdo, *m*

**memoir** /'mɛmwar/ *n* memoria, *f*

**memorable** /'mɛmərəbəl/ *a* memorable

**memorably** /'mɛmərəbli/ *adv* memorablemente

**memorandum** /ˌmɛmə'rændəm/ *n* memorándum, *m*

**memorial** /mə'mɔriəl/ *a* conmemorativo. —*n* monumento conmemorativo, *m;* memorial, *m*

**memorize** /'mɛməˌraiz/ *vt* aprender de memoria

**memory** /'mɛməri/ *n* memoria, *f;* recuerdo, *m.* **from m.,** de memoria. **If my m. does not deceive me,** Si

mal no me acuerdo. **in m. of,** en conmemoración de; en recuerdo de

**memory span** *n* retentiva memorística, *f*

**menace** /'mɛnis/ *n* amenaza, *f, m* amenazar

**menacing** /'mɛnəsiŋ/ *a* amenazador

**menacingly** /'mɛnəsiŋli/ *adv* con amenazas

**menagerie** /mə'nædʒəri/ *n* colección de fieras, *f;* casa de fieras, *f*

**mend** /mɛnd/ *vt* remendar; componer; reparar; (darn) zurcir; (rectify) remediar; reformar; enmendar; (a fire) echar carbón (or leña, etc.) a; (one's pace) avivar. —*vi* (in health and of the weather) mejorar. —*n* remiendo, *m;* (darn) zurcido, *m.* **to be on the m.,** ir mejorando. **to m. one's ways,** reformarse, enmendarse

**mendacious** /mɛn'deiʃəs/ *a* mendaz

**mendacity** /mɛn'dæsiti/ *n* mendacidad, *f*

**Mendelism** /'mɛndlˌizəm/ *n* mendelismo, *m*

**mender** /'mɛndər/ *n* componedor (-ra); (darner) zurcidor (-ra); reparador (-ra); (cobbler and tailor) remendón, *m*

**mendicancy** /'mɛndikənsi/ *n* mendicidad, *f*

**mendicant** /'mɛndikənt/ *a* mendicante. —*n* mendicante, *mf.* **m. friar,** fraile mendicante, *m*

**mending** /'mɛndiŋ/ *n* compostura, *f;* reparación, *f;* (darning) zurcidura, *f;* ropa por zurcir, *f*

**menial** /'miniəl/ *a* doméstico; servil; bajo, ruin. —*n* criado (-da); lacayo, *m*

**meningeal** /ˌmɛnin'dʒiəl/ *a* meningeo

**meningitis** /ˌmɛnin'dʒaitis/ *n* meningitis, *f*

**menopause** /'mɛnəˌpɔz/ *n* menopausia, *f*

**menses** /'mɛnsiz/ *n* menstruación, *f*

**menstrual** /'mɛnstruəl/ *a* menstrual

**menstruate** /'mɛnstruˌeit/ *vi* menstruar

**menstruation** /ˌmɛnstru'eiʃən/ *n* menstruación, *f,*

**mental** /'mɛntl/ *a* mental; intelectual. **m. derangement,** enajenación mental, *f.* **m. hospital,** manicomio, *m*

**mentality** /mɛn'tæliti/ *n* mentalidad, *f*

**mentally** /'mɛntli/ *adv* mentalmente. **m. deficient,** anormal

**menthol** /'mɛnθɒl/ *n* mentol, *m*

**mention** /'mɛnʃən/ *n* mención, *f;* alusión, *f.* —*vt* hacer mención (de), mencionar, mentar, hablar (de); aludir (a); (quote) citar; (in dispatches) nombrar. **Don't m. it!** (keep silent) ¡No digas nada!; (you're welcome) ¡No hay de que!

**mentor** /'mɛntɔr/ *n* mentor, *m*

**menu** /'mɛnyu/ *n* menú, *m;* lista de platos, *f*

**meow** /mi'au/ *vi* maullar. —*n* maullido, *m*

**Mephistophelean** /ˌmɛfəstə'filiən/ *a* mefistofélico

**mephitic** /mə'fitik/ *a* mefítico

**mercantile** /'mɑrkənˌtil/ *a* mercantil; mercante. **m. law,** derecho mercantil, *m.* **m. marine,** marina mercante, *f*

**mercantilism** /'mɑrkəntiˌlizəm/ *n* mercantilismo, *m*

**mercenariness** /'mɑrsəˌnerinis/ *n* lo mercenario

**mercenary** /'mɑrsəˌneri/ *a* mercenario. —*n* (soldier) mercenario, *m*

**mercer** /'mɑrsər/ *n* mercero, *m*

**mercerize** /'mɑrsəˌraiz/ *vt* mercerizar

**mercery** /'mɑrsəri/ *n* mercería, *f*

**merchandise** /'mɑrtʃənˌdaiz/ *n* mercancía, *f*

**merchant** /'mɑrtʃənt/ *n* traficante (en), *mf,* negociante (en), *m;* comerciante, *mf* mercader, *m.* —*a* mercante. **The M. of Venice,** El Mercader de Venecia. **m. navy, service,** marina mercante, *f.* **m. ship,** buque mercante, *m*

**merchantman** /'mɑrtʃəntmən/ *n* buque mercante, *m*

**merciful** /'mɑrsifəl/ *a* misericordioso, piadoso; compasivo; clemente; indulgente

**mercifully** /'mɑrsifəli/ *adv* misericordiosamente; compasivamente; con indulgencia

**mercifulness** /'mɑrsifəlnis/ *n* misericordia, *f;* compasión, *f;* indulgencia, *f*

**merciless** /'mɑrsilis/ *a* despiadado, inhumano

**mercilessly** /'mɑrsilisli/ *adv* sin piedad

**mercilessness** /'mɑrsilisnis/ *n* inhumanidad, *f;* falta de compasión, *f*

**mercurial** /mər'kyuriəl/ *a* mercurial; (changeable) volátil; (lively) vivo

**mercury** /'mɜrkyəri/ n mercurio, m; (Astron. and Myth.) Mercurio, m. **Mercury's wand**, caduceo, m
**mercy** /'mɜrsi/ n misericordia, f; compasión, f; clemencia, f; indulgencia, f; merced, f. **at the m. of the elements**, a la intemperie. **to be at the m. of**, estar a la merced de
**mere** /miər/ a mero; simple; no más que, solo. —n lago, m
**merely** /'miərli/ adv meramente, solamente; simplemente, sencillamente
**meretricious** /,mɛri'trɪʃəs/ a (archaic) meretricio; (flashy) de oropel; llamativo, charro
**meretriciousness** /,mɛri'trɪʃəsnɪs/ n mal gusto, m
**merge** /mɜrdʒ/ vt fundir; Com. fusionar; mezclar. —vi fundirse; Com. fusionarse; mezclarse
**merger** /'mɜrdʒər/ n combinación, f; Com. fusión, f
**meridian** /mə'rɪdiən/ n (Geog. Astron.) meridiano, m; (noon) mediodía, m; (peak) apogeo, m
**meringue** /mə'ræŋ/ n merengue, m
**merino** /mə'rinou/ a de merino; merino. —n (fabric and sheep) merino, m
**merit** /'mɛrɪt/ n mérito, m, vt merecer, ser digno de
**meritorious** /,mɛri'tɔriəs/ a meritorio
**meritoriously** /,mɛri'tɔriəsli/ adv merecidamente
**meritoriousness** /,mɛri'tɔriəsnɪs/ n mérito, m
**merlon** /'mɜrlən/ n merlón, m, almena, f
**mermaid** /'mɜr,meid/ n sirena, f
**merrily** /'mɛrɪli/ adv alegremente
**merriment** /'mɛrɪmənt/ n alegría, f; júbilo, m; regocijo, m; diversión, f; juego, m
**merriness** /'mɛrɪnɪs/ n alegría, f; regocijo, m; Inf. ebriedad, f
**merry** /'mɛri/ a alegre; jovial; feliz; regocijado, divertido; (tipsy) calamocano. **to make m.**, divertirse. **to make m. over**, reírse de. **M. Christmas!** ¡Felices Navidades! **m.-andrew**, bufón, m. **m.-go-round**, caballitos, m pl, tiovivo, m. **m.-making**, festividades, fiestas, f pl
**meseta** n meseta, f
**mesh** /mɛʃ/ n malla, f; Mech. engranaje, m; (network) red, f; (snare) lazo, m. —vt coger con red; Mech. endentar
**mesmerism** /'mɛzmə,rɪzəm/ n mesmerismo, m
**mesmerize** /'mɛzmə,raiz/ vt hipnotizar
**mess** /mɛs/ n (of food) plato de comida, m; porción, ración, f; rancho, m; (mixture) mezcla, f; (disorder) desorden, m; suciedad, f; (failure) fracaso, m. —vt (dirty) ensuciar; desordenar; (mismanage) echar a perder. **to be in a m.**, Inf. estar aviado. **to get in a m.**, Inf. hacerse un lío. **to make a m. of**, ensuciar; desordenar; (spoil) echarlo todo a rodar
**message** /'mɛsɪdʒ/ n mensaje, m; recado, m; (telegraphic) parte, m. **I have to take a m.**, Tengo que hacer un recado
**messenger** /'mɛsəndʒər/ n mensajero (-ra); (of telegrams) repartidor, m; heraldo, m; anuncio, m
**Messiah** /mɪ'saiə/ n Mesías, m
**Messianic** /,mɛsi'ænɪk/ a mesiánico
**messrs.** /'mɛsərz/ n pl (abbreviation) sres. (from señores), m pl
**metabolism** /mə'tæbə,lɪzəm/ n metabolismo, m
**metabolize** /mə'tæbə,laiz/ vt metabolizar
**metal** /'mɛtl/ n metal, m; vidrio en fusión, m; (road) grava, f; Herald. metal, m; (mettle) temple, temperamento, m; brío, fuego, m; (of metals, (of a railway) rieles, m pl. **m. engraver**, grabador en metal, m. **m. polish**, limpiametales, m. **m. shavings**, cizallas, f pl. **m. work**, metalistería, f. **m. worker**, metalario, m
**metallic** /mə'tælɪk/ a metálico
**metalliferous** /,mɛtl'ɪfərəs/ a metalífero
**metalloid** /'mɛtl,ɔid/ n metaloide, m
**metallurgic** /,mɛtl'ɜrdʒɪk/ a metalúrgico
**metallurgist** /'mɛtl,ɜrdʒɪst/ n metalúrgico, m
**metallurgy** /'mɛtl,ɜrdʒi/ n metalurgia, f
**metamorphosis** /,mɛtə'mɔrfəsɪs/ n metamorfosis, f
**metaphor** /'mɛtə,fɔr/ n metáfora, f
**metaphorical** /,mɛtə'fɔrɪkəl/ a metafórico
**metaphysical** /,mɛtə'fɪzɪkəl/ a metafísico
**metaphysician** /,mɛtəfə'zɪʃən/ n metafísico, m
**metaphysics** /,mɛtə'fɪzɪks/ n metafísica, f
**metathesis** /mə'tæθəsɪs/ n metátesis, f

**mete** /mit/ vt repartir, distribuir
**metempsychosis** /mə,tɛmsə'kousɪs/ n metempsicosis, f
**meteor** /'mitiər/ n meteoro, m
**meteoric** /,miti'ɔrɪk/ a meteórico
**meteorite** /'mitiə,rait/ n meteorito, m
**meteorological** /,mitiərə'lɒdʒɪkəl/ a meteorológico
**meteorologist** /,mitiə'rɒlədʒɪst/ n meteorologista, mf
**meteorology** /,mitiə'rɒlədʒi/ n meteorología, f
**meter** /'mitər/ n (for gas, etc.) contador, m; (verse and measure) metro, m
**methane** /'mɛθein/ n metano, m
**method** /'mɛθəd/ n método, m; técnica, f; táctica, f
**methodical** /mə'θɒdɪkəl/ a metódico; ordenado, sistemático
**Methodism** /'mɛθə,dɪzəm/ n metodismo, m
**Methodist** /'mɛθədɪst/ n metodista, mf
**methyl** /'mɛθəl/ n metilo, m. **m. alcohol**, alcohol metílico, m
**methylated spirit** /'mɛθə,leitɪd/ n alcohol desnaturalizado, m
**meticulous** /mə'tɪkyələs/ a meticuloso; minucioso
**meticulously** /mə'tɪkyələsli/ adv con meticulosidad
**meticulousness** /mə'tɪkyələsnɪs/ n meticulosidad, f; minuciosidad, f
**metric** /'mɛtrɪk/ a métrico. **m. system**, sistema métrico, m
**metrics** /'mɛtrɪks/ n métrica, f
**metronome** /'mɛtrə,noum/ n metrónomo, m
**metropolis** /mɪ'trɒpəlɪs/ n metrópoli, f; capital, f
**metropolitan** /,mɛtrə'pɒlɪtn/ a metropolitano; de la capital. —n Eccl. metropolitano, m
**mettle** /'mɛtl/ n temple, temperamento, m; fuego, brío, m; valor, m. **You have put him on his m.**, Le has picado en el amor propio
**mew** /myu/ n (gull) gaviota, f; (of a cat) maullido, m; (of sea-birds) alarido, m. —vi (of a cat) maullar; (of sea-birds) dar alaridos. **to mew up**, encerrar
**mews** /myuz/ n establos, m pl, caballeriza, f
**Mexican** /'mɛksɪkən/ a mejicano. —n mejicano (-na)
**Mexico** /'mɛksɪ,kou/ Méjico, m
**mezzanine** /'mɛzə,nin/ n entresuelo, m
**mezzo soprano** /'mɛtsou sə'prænou/ n mezzo-soprano
**mi** /mi/ n Mus. mi, m
**miaow** /mi'au/ n miau, m, vi maullar
**miasma** /mai'æzmə/ n miasma, m
**miasmatic** /,maiəz'mætɪk/ a miasmático
**mica** /'maikə/ n mica, f
**microbe** /'maikroub/ n microbio, m
**microbial** /mai'kroubiəl/ a microbiano
**microbiologist** /,maikroubai'plədʒɪst/ n microbiólogo, m
**microbiology** /,maikroubai'plədʒi/ n microbiología, f
**microcosm** /'maikrə,kɒzəm/ n microcosmo, m
**microphone** /'maikrə,foun/ n micrófono, m
**microscope** /'maikrə,skoup/ n microscopio, m
**microscopic** /,maikrə'skɒpɪk/ a microscópico
**microwave** /'maikrou,weiv/ n microonda, f
**mid** /mɪd/ a medio. —prep entre; en medio de, a mediados de. **from mid May to August**, desde mediados de mayo hasta agosto. **a mid-fourteenth century castle**, un castillo de mediados del siglo catorce. **in mid air**, en medio del aire. **in mid channel**, en medio del canal. **in mid winter**, en medio del invierno
**midday** /'mɪd'dei/ n mediodía, m, a del mediodía, meridional. **at m.**, a mediodía
**midden** /'mɪdn/ n muladar, m
**middle** /'mɪdl/ a medio; en medio de; del centro; intermedio; (average) mediano. —n medio, m; mitad, f; centro, m; (waist) cintura, f. **in the m. of**, en medio de. **in the m. of nowhere**, donde Cristo dio las tres voces. **toward the m. of the month**, a mediados del mes. **m. age**, edad madura, f. **m.-aged**, de edad madura, de cierta edad. **M. Ages**, edad media, f. **m. class**, clase media, burguesía, f, a de la clase media, burgués. **m. distance**, término medio, m. **m. ear**, oído medio, m. **m. finger**, dedo de en medio (or del corazón), m. **m. way**, Fig. término medio, m. **m. weight**, peso medio, m

**Middle East, the** el Oriente Medio, el Levante, *m*

**middleman** /'mɪdl̩,mæn/ *n* agente de negocios, *m;* (retailer) revendedor, *m;* intermediario, *m*

**middling** /'mɪdlɪŋ/ *a* mediano; mediocre; regular, así, así

**midge** /mɪdʒ/ *n* mosquito, *m,* mosca de agua, *f*

**midget** /'mɪdʒɪt/ *n* enano (-na). **m. submarine,** submarino de bolsillo, *m*

**midnight** /'mɪd,nait/ *n* medianoche, *f.* —*a* de medianoche; nocturno. **at m.,** a medianoche. **to burn the m. oil,** quemarse las cejas. **m. mass,** misa del gallo, *f*

**midriff** /'mɪdrɪf/ *n* diafragma, *m*

**midship** /'mɪd,ʃɪp/ *a* maestro. —*n* medio del buque, *m.* **m. beam,** bao maestro, *m.* **m. gangway,** crujía, *f*

**midshipman** /'mɪd,ʃɪpmən/ *n* guardiamarina, *m*

**midst** /mɪdst/ *n* medio, *m;* seno, *m, prep* entre. **in the m. of,** en medio de. **There is a traitor in our m.,** Hay un traidor entre nosotros (or en nuestra compañía)

**midstream,** /'mɪd'strim/ *n* **in m.** *m.* en medio de la corriente

**midsummer** /'mɪd'sʌmər/ *n* pleno verano, *m;* solsticio estival, *m;* fiesta de San Juan, *f.* **A M. Night's Dream,** El Sueño de la Noche de San Juan

**midway** /*adv,* *a* 'mɪd'wei; *n* -,wei/ *a* and *adv* situado a medio camino; a medio camino, a la mitad del camino; entre. —*n* mitad del camino, *f;* medio, *m.* **m. between…,** equidistante de…, entre

**midwife** /'mɪd,waif/ *n* comadrona, partera, *f*

**midwifery** /mɪd'wɪfəri/ *n* obstetricia, *f*

**midwinter** /*n.* 'mɪd'wɪntər, -,wɪn-; *a* -,wɪn-/ *n* medio del invierno, *m*

**mien** /min/ *n* aire, *m;* porte, semblante, *m*

**might** /mait/ *vi* poder. **It m. or m. not be true,** Podría o no podría ser verdad. **How happy Mary m. have been!** ¡Qué feliz pudo haber sido María! **I thought that you m. have seen him in the theater,** Creí que pudieras haberle visto en el teatro. **That I m….!** ¡Que yo pudiese…! **This m. have been avoided if…** Esto podía haberse evitado si…

**might** /mait/ *n* fuerza, *f;* poder, *m.* **with m. and main,** con todas sus fuerzas

**mightily** /'maitl̩i/ *adv* fuertemente; poderosamente; *Inf.* muchísimo, sumamente

**mightiness** /'maitinɪs/ *n* fuerza, *f;* poder, *m;* grandeza, *f*

**mighty** /'maiti/ *a* fuerte, vigoroso; poderoso; grande; *Inf.* enorme; (proud) arrogante. —*adv Inf.* enormemente, muy

**migraine** /'maigrein/ *n* migraña, jaqueca, *f*

**migrant** /'maigrənt/ *a* migratorio, de paso. —*n* ave migratoria, ave de paso, *f*

**migrate** /'maigreit/ *vi* emigrar

**migration** /mai'greiʃən/ *n* migración, *f*

**migratory** /'maigrə,tɔri/ *a* migratorio, de paso; (of people) nómada, pasajero

**migratory worker** *n* trabajador golondrino, *m*

**Milanese** /,mɪlə'niz/ *a* milanés. —*n* milanés (-esa)

**milch** /mɪltʃ/ *a f,* (of cows) lechera

**mild** /maild/ *a* apacible, pacífico; manso; dulce; suave; (of the weather) blando; *Med.* benigno; (light) leve; (of drinks) ligero; (weak) débil

**mildew** /'mɪl,du/ *n* mildiu, añublo, *m;* moho, *m.* —*vt* anublar; enmohecer. —*vi* anublarse; enmohecerse

**mildly** /'maildli/ *adv* suavemente; dulcemente; con indulgencia

**mildness** /'maildnɪs/ *n* apacibilidad, *f;* mansedumbre, *f;* suavidad, *f;* (of weather) blandura, *f;* dulzura, *f;* indulgencia, *f;* (weakness) debilidad, *f*

**mile** /mail/ *n* milla, *f*

**mileage** /'mailɪdʒ/ *n* distancia en millas, *f;* kilometraje, *m*

**milestone** /'mail,stoun/ *n* hito, *m,* piedra miliaria, *f;* mojón kilométrico, *m*

**milfoil** /'mɪl,fɔil/ *n* milenrama, *f*

**militancy** /'mɪlɪtənsi/ *n* carácter militante, *m;* belicosidad, *f*

**militant** /'mɪlɪtənt/ *a* militante, combatiente; belicoso; agresivo. —*n* combatiente, *mf*

**militarily** /,mɪlɪ'terəli/ *adv* militarmente

**militariness** /'mɪlɪ,terinɪs/ *n* lo militar, el carácter militar

**militarism** /'mɪlɪtə,rɪzəm/ *n* militarismo, *m*

**militarist** /'mɪlɪtərɪst/ *n* militarista, *mf*

**militaristic** /,mɪlɪtə'rɪstɪk/ *a* militarista

**militarization** /,mɪlɪtərɪ'zeiʃən/ *n* militarización, *f*

**militarize** /'mɪlɪtə,raiz/ *vt* militarizar

**military** /'mɪlɪ,teri/ *a* militar; de guerra. **the m.,** los militares. **m. academy,** colegio militar, *m.* **m. camp,** campo militar, *m.* **m. law,** código militar, *m.* **m. man,** militar, *m.* **m. police,** policía militar, *f.* **m. service,** servicio militar, *m*

**militate** /'mɪlɪ,teit/ (**against**) *vi* militar contra

**militia** /mɪ'lɪʃə/ *n* milicia, *f*

**militiaman** /mɪ'lɪʃəmən/ *n* miliciano, *m*

**milk** /mɪlk/ *n* leche, *f.* —*a* de leche; lácteo. —*vt* ordeñar. —*vi* dar leche. **to have m. and water in one's veins,** tener sangre de horchata. **condensed m.,** leche condensada, leche en lata, *f.* **m.-can,** lechera, *f.* **m.-cart,** carro de la leche, *m.* **m. chocolate,** chocolate con leche, *m.* **m. of magnesia,** leche de magnesia, *f.* **m.-pail,** ordeñadero, *m.* **m.-tooth,** diente de leche, *m.* **m.-white,** blanco como la leche

**milkiness** /'mɪlkinɪs/ *n* lactescencia, *f;* carácter lechoso, *m;* (whiteness) blancura, *f*

**milking** /'mɪlkɪŋ/ *n* ordeño, *m.* **m.-machine,** máquina ordeñadora, *f.* **m.-stool,** taburete, banquillo, *m*

**milkmaid** /'mɪlk,meid/ *n* lechera, *f*

**milkman** /'mɪlk,mæn/ *n* lechero, *m*

**milksop** /'mɪlk,sɒp/ *n* marica, *m*

**milky** /'mɪlki/ *a* lechero; de leche; lechoso, como leche; *Astron.* lácteo. **the Milky Way** la Vía láctea *f*

**mill** /mɪl/ *n* molino, *m;* (for coffee, etc.) molinillo, *m;* (factory) fábrica, *f;* taller, *m;* (textile) hilandería, *f;* fábrica de tejidos, *f;* (fight) riña a puñetazos, *f;* pugilato, *m.* —*vt* (grind) moler; (coins) acordonar; (cloth) abatanar; (chocolate) batir. **cotton m.,** hilandería de algodón, *f.* **hand-m.,** molinillo, *m.* **paper-m.,** fábrica de papel, *f.* **saw-m.,** serrería, *f.* **spinning m.,** hilandería, *f.* **water m.,** molino de agua, *m.* **m.-course,** saetín, canal de molino, *m.* **m-dam,** esclusa de molino, *f.* **m.-hand,** obrero (-ra). **m.-pond,** cubo, *m.* **m.-race,** caz, *m.* **m.-wheel,** rueda de molino, *f*

**millennial** /mɪ'lɛniəl/ *a* milenario

**millennium** /mɪ'lɛniəm/ *n* milenario, *m*

**miller** /'mɪlər/ *n* molinero, *m.* **miller's wife,** molinera

**millet** /'mɪlɪt/ *n* mijo, *m*

**milligram** /'mɪlɪ,græm/ *n* miligramo, *m*

**milliliter** /'mɪlə,litər/ *n* mililitro, *m*

**millimeter** /'mɪlə,mitər/ *n* milímetro, *m*

**milliner** /'mɪlənər/ *n* sombrerero (-ra), modista, *mf* **milliner's shop,** sombrerería, tienda de modista, *f*

**millinery** /'mɪlə,nɛri/ *n* sombreros, *m pl;* modas, *f pl;* tienda de modista, *f*

**milling** /'mɪlɪŋ/ *n* molienda, *f;* acuñación, *f;* (edge of coin) cordoncillo, *m.* **m. machine,** fresadora, *f*

**million** /'mɪlyən/ *n* millón, *m.* **the m.,** las masas

**millionaire** /,mɪlyə'nɛər/ *a* millonario. —*n* millonario, *m*

**millionairess** /,mɪlyə'nɛərɪs/ *n* millonaria, *f*

**millionth** /'mɪlyənθ/ *a* millonésimo

**millstone** /'mɪl,stoun/ *n* piedra de moler, muela, *f*

**mime** /maim/ *n* (Greek farce and actor) mimo, *m;* (mimicry) mímica, *f;* pantomima, *f.* —*vi* hacer en pantomima

**mimetic** /mɪ'mɛtɪk/ *a* mímico, imitativo

**mimic** /'mɪmɪk/ *a* mímico; (pretended) fingido. —*n* imitador (-ra). —*vt* imitar, contrahacer; *Biol.* imitar, adaptarse a

**mimicry** /'mɪmɪkri/ *n* mímica, imitación, *f; Biol.* mimetismo, *m*

**minaret** /,mɪnə'rɛt/ *n* minarete, *m;* (of a mosque) alminar, *m*

**minatory** /'mɪnə,tɔri, -,touri/ *a* amenazador

**mince** /mɪns/ *vt* desmenuzar; (meat) picar; (words) medir (las palabras). —*vi* andar con pasos menuditos; andar o moverse con afectación; hacer remilgos. **m.-meat,** carne picada, *f;* (sweet) conserva de fruta y especias, *f*

**mincing** /'mɪnsɪŋ/ *a* afectado. —*n* acción de picar carne, *f.* **m. machine,** máquina de picar carne, *f*

**mincingly** /'mɪnsɪŋli/ *adv* con afectación; con pasos menuditos

**mind** /maind/ *n* inteligencia, *f;* espíritu ánimo, *m;* imaginación, *f;* alma, *f;* (memory) memoria, *f,* recuerdo, *m;* (understanding) entendimiento, *m;* (genius) ingenio, *m;* (cast of mind) mentalidad, *f;* (opinion) opinión, *f;* (liking) gusto, *m;* (thoughts) pensamiento, *m;* (intention) propósito, *m,* intención, *f;* (tendency) propensión, inclinación, *f.* **I have a good m. to go away,** Por poco me marcho; Tengo ganas de marcharme. **I have changed my m.,** He cambiado de opinión. **out of m.,** olvidado. **I shall give him a piece of my m.,** Le diré cuatro verdades. **It had quite gone out of my m.,** Lo había olvidado completamente. **I can see it in my mind's eye,** Está presente a mi imaginación. **I shall bear it in m.,** Lo tendré en cuenta. **I thought in my own m. that...,** Pensé por mis adentros que... **We are both of the same m.,** Ambos somos de la misma opinión. **to be out of one's m.,** estar fuera de juicio. **to call to m.,** acordarse de. **to have something on one's m.,** estar preocupado. **to make up one's m. ( to),** resolverse (a), decidirse (a), determinar; animarse (a). **m.-reader,** adivinador (-ra) del pensamiento

**mind** /maind/ *vt* (remember) recordar, no olvidar; (heed) atender a; hacer caso de; tener cuidado de; (fear) tener miedo de; (obey) obedecer; preocuparse de; (object to) molestar; importar; (care for) cuidar. —*vi* tener cuidado; molestar; (feel) sentir; (fear) tener miedo; (be the same thing) ser igual. **Do you m. being quiet a moment?** ¿Quieres hacer el favor de callarte un momento? **Do you m. if I smoke?** ¿Le molesta si fumo? **They don't m.,** No les importa, Les da igual. **Never m.!** ¡No se moleste!; ¡No se preocupe!; ¡No importa! ¡Vaya! **M. what you are doing!** ¡Cuidado con lo que haces! **M. your own business!** ¡No te metas donde no te llaman!

**minded** /'maindɪd/ *a* dispuesto, inclinado; de... pensamientos; de... disposición

**mindful** /'maindfəl/ *a* atento (a), cuidadoso (de); que se acuerda (de)

**mine** /main/ *a poss* mío, *m,* (mía, *f;* míos, *m pl;* mías, *f pl*); el mío, *m,* (la mía, *f;* lo mío, *neut;* los míos, *m pl;* las mías, *f pl*); mi (*pl* mis). **a friend of m.,** un amigo mío; uno de mis amigos

**mine** /main/ *n* mina, *f.* —*vt* minar; extraer; sembrar minas en, colocar minas en. —*vi* minar; hacer una mina; dedicarse a la minería. **drifting m.,** mina a la deriva, *f.* **land m.,** mina terrestre, *f.* **magnetic m.,** mina magnética, *f.* **to lay mines,** colocar (o sembrar) minas. **m.-sweeper,** dragaminas, buque barreminas, *m*

**minefield** /'main,fild/ *n* campo de minas, *m;* barrera de minas, *f*

**minelayer** /'main,leiər/ *n* barca plantaminas, *f,* barco siembraminas, lanzaminas, *m*

**miner** /'mainər/ *n* minero, *m; Mil.* zapador minador, *m*

**mineral** /'mɪnərəl/ *n* mineral, *m, a* mineral. **m. baths,** baños, *m pl.* **m. water,** agua mineral, *f;* gaseosa, *f*

**mineralogical** /,mɪnərə'lɒdʒɪkəl/ *a* mineralógico

**mineralogist** /,mɪnə'blədʒɪst/ *n* mineralogista, *m*

**mineralogy** /,mɪnə'rɒlədʒi/ *n* mineralogía, *f*

**mingle** /'mɪŋgəl/ *vt* mezclar; confundir. —*vi* mezclarse; confundirse

**mingling** /'mɪŋglɪŋ/ *n* mezcla, *f*

**miniature** /'mɪniətʃər/ *n* miniatura, *f.* —*a* en miniatura. **m. edition,** edición diamante, *f*

**miniature golf** *n* minigolf, *m*

**miniaturist** /'mɪniətʃərɪst/ *n* miniaturista, *mf*

**minimize** /'mɪnə,maiz/ *vt* aminorar, reducir al mínimo; mitigar; (underrate) tener en menos, despreciar

**minimum** /'mɪnəməm/ *n* mínimo, *m, a* mínimo

**mining** /'mainɪŋ/ *n* minería, *f, a* minero; de mina; de minas; de minero. **m. engineer,** ingeniero de minas, *m*

**minion** /'mɪnyən/ *n* favorito (-ta); satélite, *m; Print.* miñona, *f*

**minister** /'mɪnəstər/ *n* ministro, *m.* —*vi* servir; suministrar, proveer de; (contribute) contribuir (a).

**m. of health,** ministro de sanidad, *m.* **m. of war,** ministro de la guerra, *m*

**ministerial** /,mɪnə'stɪəriəl/ *a* ministerial

**ministration** /,mɪnə'streiʃən/ *n Eccl.* ministerio, *m;* servicio, *m;* agencia, *f*

**ministry** /'mɪnəstri/ *n* ministerio, *m.* **m. of food,** Ministerio de Abastecimientos, *m*

**mink** /mɪŋk/ *n* visón, *m*

**minnow** /'mɪnou/ *n* pez pequeño de agua dulce, *m*

**minor** /'mainər/ *a* menor. —*n* menor de edad, *m;* (logic) menor, *f; Mus.* tono menor, *m; Eccl.* menor, *m.* **to be a m.,** ser menor de edad. **m. key,** tono menor, *m.* **m. orders,** *Eccl.* órdenes menores, *f pl.* **m. scale,** escala menor, *f*

**Minorca** /mɪ'nɔrkə/ Menorca, *f*

**minority** /mɪ'nɔriti/ *n* minoría, *f;* (of age) minoridad, *f.* **in the m.,** en la minoría

**minster** /'mɪnstər/ *n* catedral, *f;* monasterio, *m*

**minstrel** /'mɪnstrəl/ *n* trovador, juglar, *m;* músico, *m;* cantante, *m*

**minstrelsy** /'mɪnstrəlsi/ *n* música, *f;* canto, *m;* arte del trovador, *m,* or *f;* gaya ciencia, *f*

**mint** /mɪnt/ *n Bot.* menta, hierbabuena, *f;* casa de moneda, casa de la moneda, ceca, *f; Fig.* mina, *f;* (source) origen, *m.* —*vt* (money) acuñar; *Fig.* inventar, *a* (postage stamp) en estado nuevo

**minter** /'mɪntər/ *n* acuñador, *m; Fig.* inventor (-ra)

**minting** /'mɪntɪŋ/ *n* (of coins) acuñación, *f; Fig.* invención, *f*

**minuet** /,mɪnyu'ɛt/ *n* minué, *m*

**minus** /'mainəs/ *a* menos; negativo; desprovisto de; sin. —*n* signo menos, *m;* cantidad negativa, *f*

**minute** /mai'nut/ *a* menudo, diminuto; insignificante; minucioso

**minute** /'mɪnɪt/ *n* minuto, *m;* momento, *m;* instante, *m;* (note) minuta, *f, pl* **minutes,** actas, *f pl.* **in a m.,** en un instante. **m.-book,** libro de actas, minutario, *m.* **m.-hand,** minutero, *m*

**minutely** /mai'nutli/ *adv* minuciosamente; en detalle; exactamente

**minuteness** /mai'nutnɪs/ *n* suma pequeñez, *f;* minuciosidad, *f*

**minx** /mɪŋks/ *n* picaruela, *f;* coqueta, *f*

**miracle** /'mɪrəkəl/ *n* milagro, *m.* **m.-monger,** milagrero (-ra). **m. play,** milagro, *m*

**miraculous** /mɪ'rækyələs/ *a* milagroso

**miraculously** /mɪ'rækyələsli/ *adv* milagrosamente, por milagro

**miraculousness** /mɪ'rækyələsnɪs/ *n* carácter milagroso, *m,* lo milagroso

**mirage** /mɪ'rɑʒ/ *n* espejismo, *m*

**mire** /maiər/ *n* fango, lodo, *m;* (miry place) lodazal, *m*

**mirror** /'mɪrər/ *n* espejo, *m.* —*vt* reflejar. **to look in the m.,** mirarse al espejo. **full-length m.,** espejo de cuerpo entero, *m.* **small m.,** espejuelo, *m*

**mirth** /mɜrθ/ *n* alegría, *f,* júbilo, *m;* risa, *f;* hilaridad, *f*

**mirthful** /'mɜrθfəl/ *a* alegre

**mirthless** /'mɜrθlɪs/ *a* sin alegría, triste

**miry** /'maiəri/ *a* lodoso, fangoso, cenagoso

**misadventure** /,mɪsəd'vɛntʃər/ *n* desgracia, *f;* accidente, *m*

**misanthrope** /'mɪsən,θroup/ *n* misántropo, *m*

**misanthropic** /,mɪsən'θrɒpɪk/ *a* misantrópico

**misanthropy** /mɪs'ænθrəpi/ *n* misantropía, *f*

**misapplication** /,mɪsæplɪ'keiʃən/ *n* mala aplicación, *f;* mal uso, *m;* abuso, *m*

**misapply** /,mɪsə'plai/ *vt* aplicar mal; hacer mal uso de; abusar de

**misapprehend** /,mɪsæpri'hɛnd/ *vt* comprender mal; equivocarse sobre

**misapprehension** /,mɪsæprə'hɛnʃən/ *n* concepto erróneo, *m;* equivocación, *f,* error, *m*

**misappropriate** /,mɪsə'proupri,eit/ *vt* malversar

**misappropriation** /,mɪsəproupri'eiʃən/ *n* malversación, *f*

**misbehave** /,mɪsbɪ'heiv/ *vi* portarse mal; (of a child) ser malo

**misbehavior** /,mɪsbɪ'heivyər/ *n* mala conducta, *f*

**miscalculate** /mɪs'kælkyəleit/ vt calcular mal; engañarse (sobre)

**miscalculation** /ˌmɪskælkyə'leiʃən/ n mal cálculo, error, m; desacierto, m

**miscall** /mɪs'kɔl/ vt mal nombrar; llamar equivocadamente; (abuse) insultar

**miscarriage** /mɪs'kærɪdʒ/ n Med. aborto, m; (failure) malogro, fracaso, m; (of goods) extravío, m

**miscarriage of justice** n yerro en la administración de la justicia, m

**miscarry** /mɪs'kæri/ vi Med. abortar, malparir; (fail) malograrse, frustrarse; (of goods) extraviarse

**miscellaneous** /ˌmɪsə'leiniəs/ a misceláneo; vario, diverso

**miscellany** /'mɪsəˌleini/ n miscelánea, f

**mischance** /mɪs'tʃæns/ n mala suerte, f; infortunio, m, desgracia, f; accidente, m

**mischief** /'mɪstʃɪf/ n daño, m; mal, m; (wilfulness) travesura, f; (person) diablillo, m. **m.-maker,** enredador (-ra), chismoso (-sa); alborotador, m; malicioso (-sa). **m.-making,** a enredador; chismoso; malicioso; alborotador

**mischievous** /'mɪstʃəvəs/ a dañino, perjudicial, malo; malicioso; chismoso; (wilful) travieso; juguetón; (of glances, etc.) malicioso

**mischievously** /'mɪstʃəvəsli/ adv maliciosamente; con (or por) travesura

**mischievousness** /'mɪstʃəvəsnɪs/ n mal, m; malicia, f; maleficencia, f; travesura, f

**misconceive** /ˌmɪskən'siv/ vt formar un concepto erróneo de; concebir mal, juzgar mal

**misconception** /ˌmɪskən'sɛpʃən/ n concepto erróneo, m, idea falsa, f; error, m, equivocación, f; engaño, m

**misconduct** / n /mɪs'kɒndʌkt; v /ˌmɪskən'dʌkt/ n mala conducta, f. **to m. oneself,** portarse mal

**misconstruction** /ˌmɪskən'strʌkʃən/ n mala interpretación, f; falsa interpretación, f; tergiversación, f; mala traducción, f

**misconstrue** /ˌmɪskən'stru/ vt interpretar mal; entender mal; tergiversar; traducir mal

**miscount** / v /mɪs'kaunt; n /'mɪsˌkaunt/ vt contar mal, equivocarse en la cuenta de; calcular mal. —n error, m; yerro de cuenta, m

**miscreant** /'mɪskriənt/ n malandrín, m; bribón, m, a vil, malandrín

**misdeed** /mɪs'did/ n delito, malhecho, crimen, m

**misdemeanor** /ˌmɪsdɪ'minər/ n mala conducta, f; Law. delito, m; ofensa, f, malhecho, m

**misdirect** /ˌmɪsdɪ'rɛkt/ vt informar mal (acerca del camino); (a letter) dirigir mal, poner unas señas incorrectas en

**miser** /'maizər/ n avaro (-ra)

**miserable** /'mɪzərəbəl/ a infeliz, desgraciado; miserable; despreciable; sin valor

**miserably** /'mɪzərəbli/ adv miserablemente

**miserliness** /'maizərlɪnɪs/ n avaricia, tacañería, f

**miserly** /'maizərli/ a avaro, tacaño

**misery** /'mɪzəri/ n miseria, f; sufrimiento, m; dolor, tormento, m

**misfire** /mɪs'fɪər/ vi no dar fuego; (of a motor-car, etc.) hacer falsas explosiones, errar el encendido

**misfit** /mɪs'fɪt; 'mɪsˌfɪt for person/ n traje que no cae bien, m; zapato que no va bien, m; (person) inadaptado, m

**misfortune** /mɪs'fɔrtʃən/ n infortunio, m, mala suerte, adversidad, f; desdicha, desgracia, f; mal, m

**misgive** /mɪs'gɪv/ vt hacer temer; llenar de duda; hacer recelar; hacer presentir

**misgiving** /mɪs'gɪvɪŋ/ n temor, m; duda, f; recelo, m; presentimiento, m

**misgovern** /mɪs'gʌvərn/ vt gobernar mal; administrar mal; dirigir mal

**misgovernment** /mɪs'gʌvərnmənt/ n desgobierno, m; mala administración, f

**misguided** /mɪs'gaidɪd/ a mal dirigido; extraviado; engañado; (blind) ciego

**misguidedly** /mɪs'gaidɪdli/ adv equivocadamente

**mishap** /'mɪshæp/ n desgracia, f; contratiempo, accidente, m. **to have a m.,** sufrir una desgracia; tener un accidente

**misinform** /ˌmɪsɪn'fɔrm/ vt informar mal; dar informes erróneos (a)

**misinformation** /ˌmɪsɪnfər'meiʃən/ n noticia falsa, f; información errónea, f

**misinterpret** /ˌmɪsɪn'tɜrprɪt/ vt interpretar mal; entender mal; torcer; tergiversar; traducir mal

**misinterpretation** /ˌmɪsɪnˌtɜrprɪ'teiʃən/ n mala interpretación, f; interpretación falsa, f; tergiversación, f; mala traducción, f

**misjudge** /mɪs'dʒʌdʒ/ vt juzgar mal; equivocarse (en or sobre); tener una idea falsa de

**misjudgment** /mɪs'dʒʌdʒmənt/ n juicio errado, m; idea falsa, f; juicio injusto, m

**mislay** /mɪs'lei/ vt extraviar, perder

**mislead** /mɪs'lid/ vt extraviar; llevar a conclusiones erróneas, despistar; engañar

**misleading** /mɪs'lidɪŋ/ a de falsas apariencias; erróneo, falso; engañoso

**mismanage** /mɪs'mænɪdʒ/ vt administrar mal; dirigir mal; echar a perder

**mismanagement** /mɪs'mænɪdʒmənt/ n mala administración, f; desgobierno, m

**misname** /mɪs'neim/ vt mal nombrar; llamar equivocadamente

**misnomer** /mɪs'noumər/ n nombre equivocado, m; nombre inapropiado, m

**misogynist** /mɪ'sɒdʒənɪst/ n misógino, m

**misogyny** /mɪ'sɒdʒəni/ n misoginia, f

**misplace** /mɪs'pleis/ vt colocar mal; poner fuera de lugar

**misplaced** /mɪs'pleist/ a mal puesto; inoportuno, equivocado

**misprint** /n. 'mɪsˌprɪnt; v. mɪs'prɪnt/ n error de imprenta, m, errata, f, vt imprimir con erratas

**mispronounce** /ˌmɪsprə'nouns/ vt pronunciar mal

**mispronunciation** /ˌmɪsprənʌnsi'eiʃən/ n mala pronunciación, f

**misquotation** n cita errónea, f

**misquote** /mɪs'kwout/ vt citar mal, citar erróneamente

**misrepresent** /ˌmɪsrɛprɪ'zɛnt/ vt desfigurar; tergiversar; falsificar

**misrepresentation** /mɪsˌrɛprɪzɛn'teiʃən/ n desfiguración, f; tergiversación, f; falsificación, f

**misrule** /mɪs'rul/ vt gobernar mal. —n mal gobierno, m, desgobierno, m; confusión, f

**miss** /mɪs/ n señorita, f

**miss** /mɪs/ vt (one's aim) errar (el tiro, etc.); no acertar (a); (let fall) dejar caer; (lose a train, the post, etc., one's footing, an opportunity, etc.) perder; (fall short of) dejar de; no ver; no notar; pasar por alto de; omitir; echar de menos; notar la falta de; no encontrar. —vi errar; (fail) salir mal, fracasar. **I m. you,** Te echo de menos. **to be missing,** faltar; estar ausente; haberse marchado; haber desaparecido. **to m. one's mark,** errar el blanco. **to m. out,** omitir, pasar por alto de. **She doesn't miss a beat,** (fig.) No se le escapa nada

**missal** /'mɪsəl/ n misal, m

**misshapen** /mɪs'ʃeipən/ a deforme

**missile** /'mɪsəl/ n arma arrojadiza, f; proyectil, m

**missing** /'mɪsɪŋ/ a que falta; perdido; ausente; Mil. desaparecido

**mission** /'mɪʃən/ n misión, f

**missionary** /'mɪʃəˌneri/ n misionero, m

**missionize** /'mɪʃəˌnaiz/ vi misionar

**missis** /'mɪsəz/ n señora, f; Inf. mujer, f

**Mississippi** /ˌmɪsə'sɪpi/ el Misisipí, m

**missive** /'mɪsɪv/ n misiva, f

**Missouri** /mɪ'zuri/ el Misuri, m

**misspend** /mɪs'spɛnd/ vt malgastar; desperdiciar; perder

**mist** /mɪst/ n bruma, neblina, f; vapor, m; (drizzle) llovizna, f; Fig. nube, f. —vt anublar, empañar. —vi lloviznar

**mistakable** /mɪ'steikəbəl/ a confundible

**mistake** /mɪ'steik/ vt comprender mal; equivocarse sobre; errar; (with for) confundir con, equivocarse con. —n equivocación, f; error, m; inadvertencia, f; (in an exercise, etc.) falta, f. **And no m.!** Inf. Sin duda alguna. **by m.,** por equivocación; (involuntarily) sin querer. **If I am not mistaken,** Si no me engaño, Si no estoy equivocado. **to make a m.,** equivocarse

**mistaken** /mɪ'steikən/ a (of persons and things) equivocado; (of things) erróneo; incorrecto

**mistakenly** adv equivocadamente; injustamente, falsamente

**mister** /'mɪstər/ n señor, m

**mistily** /'mɪstəli/ adv a través de la neblina; obscuramente; indistintamente, vagamente

**mistimed** /mɪs'taimd/ a intempestivo; inoportuno

**mistiness** /'mɪstɪnɪs/ n neblina, bruma, f; vaporosidad, f; obscuridad, f

**mistletoe** /'mɪsəl,tou/ n muérdago, m

**mistranslate** /,mɪstrænz'leit/ vt traducir mal; interpretar mal

**mistranslation** /,mɪstrænz'leiʃən/ n mala traducción, f; traducción inexacta, f

**mistress** /'mɪstrɪs/ n señora, f; maestra, f; (fiancée) prometida, f; (beloved) amada, dulce dueña, f; (concubine) amiga, querida, f. **M. (Mrs.) Gómez,** Sra Gómez. **m. of the robes,** camarera mayor, f

**mistrust** /mɪs'trʌst/ vt desconfiar de, no tener confianza en; dudar de. —n desconfianza, f; recelo, m, suspicacia, f; aprensión, f

**mistrustful** /mɪs'trʌstfəl/ a desconfiado; receloso, suspicaz. **to be m. of,** recelarse de

**misty** /'mɪsti/ a brumoso, nebuloso; vaporoso; (of the eyes) anublado; (of windows, etc.) empañado

**misunderstand** /,mɪsʌndər'stænd/ vt comprender mal; tomar en sentido erróneo; interpretar mal

**misunderstanding** /,mɪsʌndər'stændɪŋ/ n concepto erróneo, error, m; equivocación, f; (disagreement) desavenencia, f

**misuse** /n mɪs'yus; v -'yuz/ vt emplear mal; abusar de; (funds) malversar; (ill-treat) tratar mal. —n abuso, m; (of funds) malversación, f

**mite** /mait/ n (coin) ardite, m; (trifle) pizca, f; óbolo, m; Ent. ácaro, m

**miter** /'maitər/ n mitra, f; inglete, m, vt cortar ingletes en

**mitigate** /'mɪtɪ,geit/ vt (pain) aliviar; mitigar; suavizar

**mitigation** /,mɪtɪ'geiʃən/ n (of pain) alivio, m; mitigación, f

**mitten** /'mɪtn/ n mitón, m

**mix** /mɪks/ vt mezclar; (salad) aderezar; (concrete, etc.) amasar; combinar, unir; (sociably) alternar (con); (confuse) confundir. —vi mezclarse; frecuentar la compañía (de); frecuentar; (get on well) llevarse bien

**mixed** /mɪkst/ a mezclado; vario, surtido; mixto; (confused) confuso. **m. doubles,** parejas mixtas, f pl. **m. up,** (in disorder) revuelto; confuso. **m. up with,** implicado en; asociado con

**mixer** /'mɪksər/ n mezclador, m; (person) mezclador (-ra); Inf. persona sociable, f. **electric m.,** mezclador eléctrico, m

**mixture** /'mɪkstʃər/ n mezcla, f; (medicine) poción, medicina, f

**mizzen** /'mɪzən/ n mesana, f. **m.-mast,** palo de mesana, m. **m.-sail,** vela de mesana, f. **m.-topsail,** sobremesana, f

**mnemonics** /nɪ'mɒnɪks/ n mnemotecnia, f

**Moabite** /'mouə,bait/ n moabita, mf

**moan** /moun/ vt lamentar; llorar. —vi gemir; quejarse, lamentarse. —n gemido, m; lamento, m; quejido, m

**moaning** /'mounɪŋ/ n gemidos, m pl

**moat** /mout/ n foso, m

**mob** /mɒb/ n (crowd) muchedumbre, multitud, f; (rabble) populacho, m, gentuza, f. —vt atropellar; atacar. **mob-cap,** cofia, f

**mobile** /'moubil/ a móvil; ambulante; (fickle) voluble. **m. canteen,** cantina ambulante, f

**mobility** /mou'bɪlɪti/ n movilidad, f

**mobilization** /,moubələ'zeiʃən/ n movilización, f

**mobilize** /'moubə,laiz/ vt movilizar. —vi movilizarse

**moccasin** /'mɒkəsɪn, -zən/ n mocasín, m

**mocha** /'moukə/ n café de Moca, m

**mock** /mɒk/ vt ridiculizar; burlarse (de), mofarse (de); (cause to fail) frustrar; (mimic) imitar; (delude) engañar. —vi mofarse, burlarse, reírse. —a cómico, burlesco; falso; fingido; imitado. **to make a m. of,** poner en ridículo; hacer absurdo; burlarse de. **m.-**

**heroic,** heroico-cómico. **m.-orange,** Bot. jeringuilla, f. **m.-turtle soup,** sopa hecha con cabeza de ternera a imitación de tortuga, f

**mocker** n mofador (-ra); el, m, (f, la) que se burla de

**mockery** /'mɒkəri/ n mofa, burla, f; ridículo, m; ilusión, apariencia, f. **to make a m. of,** mofarse de; hacer ridículo

**mocking** /'mɒkɪŋ/ a burlón. **m. bird,** pájaro burlón, m

**mockingly** /'mɒkɪŋli/ adv burlonamente

**modality** /mou'dælɪti/ n modalidad, f

**mode** /moud/ n modo, m; manera, f; (fashion) moda, f; uso, m, costumbre, f

**model** /'mɒdl/ n modelo, m; (artist's) modelo vivo, m, a modelo; en miniatura. —vt modelar; moldear; formar; hacer; planear. **m. display,** (hats, etc.) exposición de modelos, f. **m. railway,** ferrocarril en miniatura, m

**modeler** /'mɒdlər/ n modelador (-ra); disenador, m

**modeling** /'mɒdlɪŋ/ n modelado, m; modelo, m. **m. wax,** cera para moldear, f

**modem** /'moudəm, -dɛm/ n módem, m

**moderate** /a, n. 'mɒdərɪt v. -ə,reit/ a moderado; (of prices, etc.) módico; (fair, medium) regular, mediano; razonable; mediocre. —n moderado, m. —vt moderar; modificar; calmar. —vi moderarse; calmarse

**moderately** /'mɒdərɪtli/ adv moderadamente; módicamente; medianamente; bastante; razonablemente; mediocremente

**moderation** /,mɒdə'reiʃən/ n moderación, f. **in m.,** en moderación

**moderator** /'mɒdə,reitər/ n moderador, m; (Church of Scotland) presidente, m; Educ. examinador, m; Educ. inspector de exámenes, m. **m. lamp,** lámpara de regulador, f

**modern** /'mɒdərn/ a moderno. —n modernista, mf. **in the m. way,** a la moderna. **m. language,** lengua viva, f

**modernism** /'mɒdər,nɪzəm/ n modernismo, m

**modernist** /'mɒdərnɪst/ n modernista, mf

**modernistic** /,mɒdər'nɪstɪk/ a modernista

**modernity** /mɒ'dɜrnɪti/ n modernidad, f

**modernization** /,mɒdərnə'zeiʃən/ n modernización, f

**modernize** /'mɒdər,naiz/ vt modernizar

**modernness** /'mɒdərnnɪs/ n modernidad, f

**modest** /'mɒdɪst/ a modesto; (of a woman) púdico

**modesty** /'mɒdəsti/ n modestia, f; (of a woman) pudor, m

**modicum** /'mɒdɪkəm/ n porción pequeña, f; poco, m

**modifiable** a modificable

**modification** /,mɒdəfɪ'keiʃən/ n modificación, f

**modify** /'mɒdə,fai/ vt modificar. **It has been much modified,** Se ha modificado mucho; Se han hecho muchas modificaciones

**modifying** a modificante, modificador

**modish** /'moudɪʃ/ a de moda en boga; elegante

**modishness** /'moudɪʃnɪs/ n elegancia, f

**modiste** /mou'dist/ n modista, modista, mf

**modulate** /'mɒdʒə,leit/ vt and vi modular

**modulation** /,mɒdʒə'leiʃən/ n modulación, f

**modus vivendi** /'moudəs vɪ'vɛndi, -dai/ n modo de conveniencia, m

**Mogul** /'mougəl/ a mogol. —n mogol (-la). **the Great M.,** el Gran Mogol

**Mohammedan** /mʊ'hæmɪdn, mou-/ a mahometano, agareno

**Mohammedanism** /mʊ'hæmɪdn,ɪzəm, mou-/ n mahometismo, m

**Mohican** /mou'hikən/ n mohican, m

**moiety** /'mɔiti/ n mitad, f

**moiré** /mwɑ'rei, mɔ-/ n muaré, m

**moist** /mɔist/ a húmedo

**moisten** /'mɔisən/ vt humedecer, mojar

**moisture** /'mɔistʃər/ n humedad, f

**molar** /'moulər/ n muela, f, a molar

**molasses** /mə'læsɪz/ n pl melaza, f

**mold** /mould/ n (fungus) moho, m; (humus) mantillo, m; (iron-mould) mancha de orín, f; (matrix) molde, m, matriz, f; Cul. cubilete, m; Naut. gálibo, m; (for jelly, etc.) molde, m; Archit. moldura, f;

(temperament) temple, *m*, disposición, *f.* —*vt* moldear; (cast) vaciar; moldurar; *Naut.* galibar; *Fig.* amoldar, formar; *Agr.* cubrir con mantillo. **to m. one-self on,** modelarse sobre. **m.-board,** (of a plough) orejera, *f*

**Moldavian** /moul'deiviǝn/ *a* moldavo. —*n* moldavo (-va)

**molder** /'mouldǝr/ *n* moldeador, *m; Fig.* amoldador (-ra); creador (-ra). —*vi* desmoronarse, convertirse en polvo; *Fig.* decaer, desmoronarse; vegetar

**moldiness** /'mouldınıs/ *n* moho, *m*

**molding** /'mouldıŋ/ *n* amoldamiento, *m;* vaciado, *m; Archit.* moldura, *f; Fig.* formación,

**moldy** /'mouldi/ *a* mohoso, enmohecido; *Fig.* anticuado

**mole** /'moulei/ *n* (animal) topo, *m;* (spot) lunar, *m;* (breakwater) dique, malecón, *m;* muelle, *m*

**molecular** /mǝ'lekyǝlǝr/ *a* molecular

**molecule** /'mɒlı,kyul/ *n* molécula, *f*

**molehill** /'moul,hıl/ *n* topera, *f*

**moleskin** /'moul,skın/ *n* piel de topo, *f*

**molest** /mǝ'lɛst/ *vt* molestar; perseguir, importunar; faltar al respeto (a)

**molestation** /,moulǝ'steifǝn/ *n* importunidad, persecución, *f;* molestia, incomodidad, *f*

**mollification** /,mɒlǝfı'keifǝn/ *n* apaciguamiento, *m;* mitigación, *f*

**mollify** /'mɒlǝ,fai/ *vt* apaciguar, calmar; mitigar

**mollusk** /'mɒlǝsk/ *n* molusco, *m*

**mollycoddle** /'mɒli,kɒdl/ *n* alfeñique, mírame y no me toques, *m;* niño (-ña), mimado (-da)

**Moloch** /'moulɒk/ *n* Moloc, *m*

**molt** /moult/ *vi* mudar, *n* muda, *f*

**molten** /'moultn/ *a* fundido; derretido

**Moluccas, the** /mǝ'lukǝz/ las Malucas, *f pl*

**moment** /'moumǝnt/ *n* momento, *m;* instante *m;* (importance) importancia, *f.* **at this m.,** en este momento. **Do it this m.!** ¡Hazlo al instante (or en seguida)!

**momentarily** /,moumǝn'tɛǝrǝli, 'moumǝn,tɛr-/ *adv* momentáneamente; cada momento

**momentariness** /'moumǝn,tɛrınıs/ *n* momentaneidad, *f*

**momentary** /'moumǝn,tɛri/ *a* momentáneo

**momentous** /mou'mɛntǝs/ *a* de suma importancia; crítico; grave

**momentousness** /mou'mɛntǝsnıs/ *n* importancia, *f;* gravedad, *f*

**momentum** /mou'mɛntǝm/ *n* momento, *m*, velocidad adquirida *f; Fig.* ímpetu, *m.* **to gather m.,** cobrar velocidad, acelerar

**monarch** /'mɒnǝrk/ *n* monarca, *m*

**monarchic** /mǝ'narkık/ *a* monárquico

**monarchism** /'mɒnǝr,kızǝm/ *n* monarquismo, *m*

**monarchist** *n* monárquico (-ca)

**monarchy** /'mɒnǝrki/ *n* monarquía, *f*

**monastery** /'mɒnǝ,stɛri/ *n* monasterio, *m*

**monastic** /mǝ'næstık/ *a* monástico. **m. life,** vida de clausura, *f*

**monasticism** *n* vida monástica, *f*

**Monday** /'mʌndei, -di/ *n* lunes, *m*

**monetary** /'mɒnı,tɛri/ *a* monetario

**monetization** *n* monetización, *f*

**money** /'mʌni/ *n* dinero, *m;* (coin) moneda, *f;* sistema monetario, *m.* **paper m.,** papel moneda, *m.* **ready m.,** dinero contante, *m.* **to make m.,** ganar (or hacer) dinero; enriquecerse. **M. talks,** Poderoso caballero es Don Dinero. **m.-bag,** talega, *f;* (person) ricacho (-cha). **m.-bags,** riqueza, *f.* **m.-box,** alcancía, hucha, *f.* **m.-changer,** cambista, *mf* **m.-lender,** prestamista, *mf* **m.-making,** *n* el hacer dinero; prosperidad, ganancia, *f.* —*a* lucrativo. **m.-order,** giro postal, *m*

**moneyed** /'mʌnid/ *a* adinerado; acomodado

**Mongolian** /mɒŋ'gouliǝn/ *a* mogol. —*n* mogol (-la); (language) mogol, *m*

**mongoose** /'mɒŋ,gus/ *n* mangosta, *f*

**mongrel** /'mʌŋgrǝl/ *a* mestizo, atravesado. —*n* perro mestizo, *m;* (in contempt) mestizo. *m*

**monitor** /'mɒnıtǝr/ *n* monitor, *m*

**monitory** /'mɒnı,tɔri/ *a* monitorio. —*n Eccl.* monitorio, *m*

**monk** /mʌŋk/ *n* monje, *m.* **to become a m.,** hacerse monje, tomar el hábito. **monk's-hood,** acónito, *m*

**monkey** /'mʌŋki/ *n* mono (-na); (imp) diablillo, *m;* (of a pile-driver) pilón de martinete, *m;* (in glass-making) crisol, *m.* **to m. with,** meterse con; entremeterse. **m. nut,** cacahuete, *m.* **m.-puzzle,** (tree) - araucaria, *f.* **m. tricks,** monadas, travesuras, diabluras, *f pl.* **m.-wrench,** llave inglesa, *f*

**monkish** /'mʌŋkıf/ *a* monacal, de monje; monástico

**monochromatic** /,mɒnǝkrou'mætık/ *a* monocromo

**monochrome** /'mɒnǝ,kroum/ *n* monocromo, *m*

**monocle** /'mɒnǝkǝl/ *n* monóculo, *m*

**monogamist** /mǝ'nɒgǝmıst/ *n* monógamo (-ma)

**monogamous** /mǝ'nɒgǝmǝs/ *a* monógamo

**monogamy** /mǝ'nɒgǝmi/ *n* monogamia, *f*

**monogram** /'mɒnǝ,græm/ *n* monograma, *m*

**monograph** /'mɒnǝ,græf/ *n* monografía, *f*, opúsculo, *m*

**monolith** /'mɒnǝlıθ/ *n* monolito, *m*

**monolithic** /,mɒnǝ'lıθık/ *a* monolítico

**monologue** /'mɒnǝ,lɔg/ *n* monólogo, *m*

**monomania** /,mɒnǝ'meiniǝ/ *n* monomanía, *f*

**monomaniac** /,mɒnǝ'meini,æk/ *n* monomaníaco (-ca)

**monomial** /mou'noumiǝl/ *n* monomio, *m*, *a* de un solo término

**monoplane** /'mɒnǝ,plein/ *n* monoplano, *m*

**monopolist** /mǝ'nɒpǝlıst/ *n* monopolista, *mf;* acaparador (-ra)

**monopolization** /mǝ,nɒpǝlǝ'zeifǝn/ *n* monopolio, *m*

**monopolize** /mǝ'nɒpǝ,laiz/ *vt* monopolizar

**monopoly** /mǝ'nɒpǝli/ *n* monopolio, *m*

**monotheism** /'mɒnǝθi,ızǝm/ *n* monoteísmo, *m*

**monotheist** /'mɒnǝ,θiıst/ *n* monoteísta, *mf*

**monotone** /'mɒnǝ,toun/ *n* monotonía, *f*

**monotonous** /mǝ'nɒtnǝs/ *a* monótono

**monotony** /mǝ'nɒtni/ *n* monotonía, *f*

**monoxide** /mɒn'ɒksaid/ *n* monóxido, *m*

**Monroe doctrine** /mǝn'rou/ *n* monroísmo, *m*

**monsignor** /mɒn'sinyǝr/ *n* monseñor, *m*

**monsoon** /mɒn'sun/ *n* monzón, *mf*

**monster** /'mɒnstǝr/ *n* monstruo, *m*

**monstrance** /'mɒnstrǝns/ *n* custodia, *f*

**monstrosity** /mɒn'strɒsıti/ *n* monstruosidad, *f*

**monstrous** /'mɒnstrǝs/ *a* monstruoso; horrible, atroz; enorme

**montage** /mɒn'tɑʒ/ *n* montaje, *m*

**month** /mʌnθ/ *n* mes, *m.* **He arrived a m. ago,** Llegó hace un mes

**monthly** /'mʌnθli/ *a* mensual. —*adv* mensualmente, cada mes. —*n* revista (or publicación) mensual, *f; pl* **monthlies,** menstruación, regla, *f.* **m. salary** or **payment,** mensualidad, *f*

**monument** /'mɒnyǝmǝnt/ *n* monumento, *m*

**monumental** /,mɒnyǝ'mɛntl/ *a* monumental

**moo** /mu/ *vi* (of cattle) mugir. —*n* mugido, *m*

**mood** /mud/ *n* humor, *m;* espíritu, *m; Gram.* modo, *m*

**moodily** /'mudļi/ *adv* taciturnamente; tristemente, pensativamente

**moodiness** /'mudınıs/ *n* mal humor, *m*, taciturnidad, *f;* melancolía, tristeza, *f*

**moody** /'mudi/ *a* taciturno, de mal humor; triste, melancólico, pensativo

**mooing** /'muıŋ/ *n* (of cattle) mugido, *m*

**moon** /mun/ *n* luna, *f;* satélite, *m;* mes lunar, *m;* luz de la luna, *f.* **full m.,** plenilunio, *m;* luna llena, *f.* **new m.,** novilunio, *m,* luna nueva, *f*

**moonbeam** /'mun,bim/ *n* rayo de luna, *m*

**moonless** /'munlıs/ *a* sin luna

**moonlight** /'mun,lait/ *n* luz de la luna, *f.* **in the m.,** a la luz de la luna. **to do a m. flit,** *Inf.* mudarse por el aire

**moonlighting** /'mun,laitıŋ/ *n* el pluriempleo, *m*

**moonlit** /'mun,lıt/ *a* iluminado por la luna. **moonlit night,** noche de luna, *f*

**moonshine** /'mun,fain/ *n* claridad de la luna, *f; Fig.* música celestial, ilusión, *f*

**moonstone** /'mun,stoun/ *n* adularia, *f*

**moonstruck** /'mun‚strʌk/ a lunático
**Moor** /mʊr/ n moro (-ra)
**moor** /mʊr/ n páramo, brezal, m; (marsh) pantano, m; (for game) coto, m. —vt amarrar, aferrar; afirmar con anclas o cables. **m.-hen,** polla de agua, f
**mooring** /'mʊrɪŋ/ n amarre, m. **m.-mast,** Aer. poste de amarre, m
**moorings** /'mʊrɪŋz/ n pl amarradero, m
**Moorish** /'mʊrɪʃ/ a moro; árabe. **M. architecture,** arquitectura árabe, f. **M. girl,** mora, f
**moorland** /'mʊrlənd/ n páramo, brezal, m
**moose** /mus/ n anta, f
**moot** /mut/ n junta, f; ayuntamiento, m. —a discutible. —vt (bring up) suscitar; (discuss) discutir, debatir
**mop** /mɒp/ n (implement) trapeador, m (Ecuador), escoba con fleco, f; (of hair) mata (de pelo), f. —vt trapear (Ecuador); (dry) enjugar, secar. **to mop up,** Inf. limpiar; Mil. acabar con (el enemigo)
**mope** /moup/ vi replace by tristear. **to m. about,** vagar tristemente
**moquette** /mou'kɛt/ n moqueta, f
**moraine** /mə'rein/ n morena, f
**moral** /'mɔrəl/ a moral; (chaste) casto, virtuoso; honrado. —n (maxim) moraleja, f; pl **morals,** moralidad, f; ética, f; moral, f; (conduct) costumbres, f pl. **m. philosophy,** filosofía moral, f. **m. support,** apoyo moral, m. **m. tale,** apólogo, m
**morale** /mə'ræl/ n moral, f
**moralist** /'mɔrəlɪst/ n moralista, m
**morality** /mə'rælɪti/ n moralidad, f; virtud, f; castidad, f. **m. play,** moralidad, f; drama alegórico, m
**moralization** /‚mɔrələ'zeiʃən/ n moralización, f
**moralize** /'mɔrə‚laiz/ vt and vi moralizar
**moralizer** /'mɔrə‚laizər/ n moralizador (-ra)
**moralizing** /'mɔrə‚laizɪŋ/ a moralizador
**morally** /'mɔrəli/ adv moralmente
**morals** /'mɔrəlz/. See **moral**
**morass** /mə'ræs/ n marisma, ciénaga, f
**moratorium** /‚mɔrə'tɔriəm/ n moratoria, f
**Moravian** /mɔ'reiviən/ a moravo. —n moravo (-va)
**morbid** /'mɔrbɪd/ a mórbido, mórboso; (of the mind, etc.) insano
**morbidezza** /‚mɔrbɪ'dɛtsə/ n (Art. and Lit.) morbidez, f
**morbidity** /mɔr'bɪdɪti/ n morbidez, f
**mordacity** /mɔr'dæsɪti/ n mordacidad, f
**mordant** /'mɔrdn̩t/ a mordaz; (of acid) mordiente. —n mordiente, m
**more** /mɔr/ a and adv más. **The m. he earns, the less he saves,** Cuanto más gana, menos ahorra. **The m. the better,** cuanto más, tanto mejor. **without m. ado,** sin más ni más; sin decir nada. **Would you like some m.?** ¿Quiere Vd. más? (of food) ¿Quiere Vd. repetir? **no m.,** no más; (never) nunca más; (finished) se acabó. **once m.,** otra vez, una vez más. **m. and m.,** cada vez más, más y más. **m. or less,** más o menos; (about) poco más o menos
**moreover** /mɔr'ouvər/ adv además, también; por otra parte
**morganatic** /‚mɔrgə'nætɪk/ a morganático
**morgue** /mɔrg/ n depósito de cadáveres, m
**moribund** /'mɔrə‚bʌnd/ a moribundo
**Mormon** /'mɔrmən/ a mormónico. —n mormón (-ona)
**Mormonism** /'mɔrmə‚nɪzəm/ n mormonismo, m
**morning** /'mɔrnɪŋ/ n mañana, f, a matutino, de la mañana. **Good m.!** ¡Buenos días! **the next m.,** la mañana siguiente. **very early in the m.,** muy de mañana. **m. coat,** chaqué, m. **m. dew,** rocío de la mañana, m. **m. paper,** periódico de la mañana, m. **m. star,** lucero del alba, m. **m. suit,** chaqué, m
**Moroccan** /mə'rɒkən/ a marroquí, marrueco. —n marrueco (-ca), marroquí, mf
**Morocco** /mə'rɒkou/ Marruecos, m
**morocco** /mə'rɒkou/ n (leather) marroquí, tafilete, m
**morose** /mə'rous/ a sombrío, taciturno, malhumorado
**morosely** /mə'rousli/ adv taciturnamente
**moroseness** /mə'rousnɪs/ n taciturnidad, f; mal humor, m

**morphine** /'mɔrfin/ n morfina, f. **m. addict,** morfinómano (-na)
**morrow** /'mɒrou/ n mañana, f; día siguiente, m
**Morse code** /mɔrs/ n la clave telegráfica de Morse, f, el alfabeto de Morse, m
**morsel** /'mɔrsəl/ n pedazo, m; (mouthful) bocado, m
**mortal** /'mɔrtl̩/ a mortal. —n mortal, mf. **m. sin,** pecado mortal, pecado capital, m
**mortality** /mɔr'tælɪti/ n mortalidad, f
**mortally wounded** /'mɔrtl̩i/ adv herido de muerte
**mortar** /'mɔrtər/ n (for building) argamasa, f; (for mixing and Mil.) mortero, m. **m. and pestle,** mortero y majador, m. **m.-board,** (in building) cuezo, m; (academic cap) birrete, m
**mortgage** /'mɔrgɪdʒ/ n hipoteca, f. —vt hipotecar. —a hipotecario. **to pay off a m.,** redimir una hipoteca
**mortgageable** /'mɔrgɪdʒəbəl/ a hipotecable
**mortgaged debt** /'mɔrgɪdʒd/ n deuda garantizada con una hipoteca, f
**mortgagee** /‚mɔrgə'dʒi/ n acreedor (-ra) hipotecario (-ia)
**mortgagor** /'mɔrgədʒər/ n deudor (-ra) hipotecario (-ia)
**mortification** /‚mɔrtəfɪ'keiʃən/ n mortificación, f; humillación, f; Med. gangrena, f
**mortify** /'mɔrtə‚fai/ vt mortificar; humillar. —vi Med. gangrenarse
**mortifying** /'mɔrtə‚faiŋ/ a humillante
**mortise** /'mɔrtɪs/ n muesca, f. —vt hacer muescas (en); ensamblar
**mortuary** /'mɔrtʃu‚ɛri/ a mortuorio. —n depósito de cadáveres, m
**Mosaic** /mou'zeiɪk/ a mosaico
**mosaic** /mou'zeiɪk/ n mosaico, m
**Moscow** /'mɒskou,-kau/ Moscú, m
**mosque** /mɒsk/ n mezquita, f
**mosquito** /mə'skitou/ n mosquito, m. **m. net,** mosquitero, m
**moss** /mɔs/ n musgo, m; moho, m; (swamp) marjal, m
**mossgrown** /'mɔs‚groun/ a musgoso, cubierto de musgo; Fig. anticuado
**mossiness** /'mɔsinɪs/ n estado musgoso, m
**mossy** /'mɔsi/ a musgoso
**most** /moust/ a ei (la, los, etc.) más; la mayor parte de; la mayoría de; (el, etc.) mayor. —adv más; el (la, etc.) más; (extremely) sumamente; (very) muy; (before adjectives sometimes expressed by superlative, e.g. m. reverend, reverendisimo, m. holy, santísimo, etc.). —n (highest price) el mayor precio; la mayor parte; el mayor número; lo más. **m. of all,** sobre todo. **m. people,** la mayoría de la gente. **at the m.,** a lo más, a lo sumo. **for the m. part,** en su mayor parte; casi todos; generalmente, casi siempre. **to make the m. of,** sacar el mayor partido posible de; aprovechar bien; exagerar
**mostly** /'moustli/ adv principalmente; en su mayoría; en su mayor parte; casi siempre; en general, generalmente
**mote** /mout/ n átomo, m; mota, f. **to see the m. in our neighbor's eye and not the beam in our own,** ver la paja en el ojo del vecino y no la viga en el nuestro
**motet** /mou'tɛt/ n motete, m
**moth** /mɔθ/ n mariposa nocturna, f; polilla, f. **m.ball,** bola de naftalina, f. **m.-eaten,** apolillado
**mother** /'mʌðər/ n madre, f; madre de familia, f; (of alcoholic beverages) madre, f. —vt cuidar como una madre (a); servir de madre (a); (animals) ahijar. **M. Church,** madre iglesia, f; iglesia metropolitana, f. **m.-in-law,** suegra, f. **m. land,** (madre) patria, f. **m.-of-pearl,** m madreperla, f, nácar, m. —a nacarado, nacáreo. **M. Superior,** (madre) superiora, f. **m. tongue,** lengua materna, f
**motherhood** /'mʌðər‚hʊd/ n maternidad, f
**motherless** /'mʌðərlɪs/ a huérfano de madre, sin madre
**motherlike** a de madre, como una madre
**motherliness** /'mʌðərlinɪs/ n cariño maternal, m
**motherly** /'mʌðərli/ a maternal

**motif** /mou'tif/ n motivo, m; tema, m; Sew. adorno, m

**motion** /'mouʃən/ n movimiento, m; Mech. marcha, operación, f; mecanismo, m; (sign) seña, señal, f; (gesture) ademán, gesto, m; (carriage) aire, porte, m; (of the bowels) movimiento del vientre, m, deyección, f; (will) voluntad, f, deseo, m; (proposal in an assembly or debate) proposición, moción, f; Law. pedimento, m. —vt hacer una señal (a). —vi hacer señas. **to set in m.**, poner en marcha. **m. picture**, fotografía cinematográfica, película, f. **m.-picture theater**, cine, m

**motionless** /'mouʃənlıs/ a inmóvil

**motivate** /'moutə,veit/ vt motivar

**motive** /'moutıv/ n motivo, m. —a **motor** motivo. **with no m.**, sin motivo. **m. power**, fuerza motriz, f

**motley** /'mɒtli/ a abigarrado, multicolor; (mixed) diverso, vario. —n traje de colores, m, botarga, f

**motor** /'moutər/ n motor, m; automóvil, m, a motor; movido por motor; con motor; (traveling) de viaje. —vi ir en automóvil. —vt llevar en automóvil (a). **m. boat**, lancha automóvil, f. **m.bus**, autobús, ómnibus, m. **m.car**, automóvil, m. **m.-coach**, autobús, m. **m. cycle**, motocicleta, f. **m.cyclist**, motociclista, mf **m.-launch**, canoa automóvil, f. **m.oil**, aceite para motores, m. **m.-road**, autopista, f. **m.-rug**, manta de viaje, f. **m.-scooter**, bicicleta con motor, f. **m.-spirit**, bencina, f

**motoring** /'moutərıŋ/ n automovilismo, m

**motorist** /'moutərıst/ n automovilista, motorista, mf

**mottled** /'mɒtļd/ a abigarrado; (of marble, etc.) jaspeado, esquizado; manchado (con), con manchas (de); pintado (con)

**motto** /'mɒtou/ n Herald. divisa, f; mote, m; (in a book, etc.) lema, m

**mound** /maund/ n montón, m; (knoll) altozano, m; (for defence) baluarte, m; (for burial) túmulo, m

**mount** /maunt/ n (hill, and in palmistry) monte, m; (for riding) caballería, f; montadura, f; (for a picture) borde, m. —vt subir; (machines, etc.) montar; (jewels) engastar; (a picture) poner un borde a; (a play) poner en escena; poner a caballo; proveer de caballo. —vi montar; subir; (increase) aumentar. **to m. a horse**, subir a caballo, montar. **to m. guard**, Mil. montar la guardia. **to m. the throne**, subir al trono

**mountain** /'mauntņ/ n montaña, f; (mound) montón, m. —a de montaña(s); montañés; alpino, alpestre. **to make a m. out of a molehill**, convertir un grano de arena en una montaña. hacer de una pulga un camello, hacer de una pulga un elefante. **m.-chain**, cadena de montañas, f. **m. dweller**, montañés (-esa). **m. railway**, ferrocárril de cremallera, m. **m.-side**, falda de una montaña, f

**mountaineer** /,mauntņ'ıər/ n (inhabitant) montañés (-esa); (climber) alpinista, mf. —vi hacer alpinismo

**mountaineering** /,mauntņ'ıərıŋ/ n alpinismo, m

**mountainous** /'mauntņəs/ a montañoso; (huge) enorme

**mountebank** /'mauntə,bæŋk/ n saltabanco, m; charlatán, m

**mounting** /'mauntıŋ/ n (ascent) subida, f; ascensión, f; (of machinery, etc.) armadura, f; montadura, f; (of a precious stone) engaste, m. **m.-block**, subidero, m

**mourn** /mɔrn/ vi afligirse, lamentarse; (wear mourning) estar de luto. —vt llorar; lamentar; llevar luto por

**mourner** /'mɔrnər/ n lamentador (-ra); (paid) plañidera, f; el, m, (f, la) que acompaña al féretro

**mournful** /'mɔrnfəl/ a triste, acongojado; funesto, lúgubre; fúnebre; lamentable

**mournfully** /'mɔrnfəli/ adv tristemente

**mournfulness** /'mɔrnfəlnıs/ n tristeza, f; melancolía, aflicción, f, pesar, m

**mourning** /'mɔrnıŋ/ n aflicción, f; lamentación, f; luto, m. **deep m.**, luto riguroso, m. **half m.**, medio luto, m. **to be in m.**, estar de luto. **to be in m. for**, llevar luto por. **to come out of m.**, dejar el luto. **m.-band**, (on the hat) tira de gasa, f; (on the arm) brazal de luto, m. **m.-coach**, coche fúnebre, m

**mouse** /n. maus/ v. mauz/ n ratón (-na); Naut. barrilete, m. —vi cazar ratones. **m.-coloured**, de color de rata. **m.-hole, m.-trap**, ratonera, f

**mouser** /'mauzər/ n gato ratonero, m

**mousing** /'mausıŋ/ n caza de ratones, f

**moustache** /'mʌstæʃ, mə'stæʃ/ n bigote, mostacho, m

**mousy** /'mausi/ a ratonesco, ratonil

**mouth** /n. mauθ/ v. mauð/ n (Anat. human being, of a bottle, cave) boca, f; (of a river) desembocadura, f; (of a channel) embocadero, m; (of a wind-instrument) boquilla, f. —vt pronunciar con afectación; (chew) mascar. —vi clamar a gritos, vociferar. **down in the m.**, Inf. con las orejas caídas. **It makes my m. water**, Se me hace la boca agua. **large m.**, boca rasgada, f. **m.-gag**, abrebocas, m. **m.-organ**, armónica, f. **m.-wash**, antiséptico bucal, m (Argentina), enjuague, m

**mouthed** /mauðd, mauθd/ a que tiene boca...; de boca... **open-m.**, boquiabierto

**mouthful** /'mauθ,fʊl/ n bocado, m; (of smoke, air) bocanada, f

**mouthpiece** /'mauθ,pis/ n (of wind-instruments, tobacco-pipe, waterpipe) boquilla, f; (of a wineskin) brocal, m; (spokesman) portavoz, m; intérprete, mf

**movable** /'muvəbəl/ a movible; (of goods) mobiliario. **m. feast**, fiesta movible, f

**movables** /'muvəbəlz/ n pl bienes muebles, efectos, m pl

**movable type** n tipos sueltos, m pl

**move** /muv/ n movimiento, m; (of household effects) mudanza, f; (motion) marcha, f; (in a game) jugada, f; (Fig. step) paso, m; (device) maniobra, f. **Whose m. is it?** ¿A quién le toca jugar? **to be on the m.**, estar en movimiento; estar de viaje. **to be always on the m.**, Inf. parecer una lanzadera

**move** /muv/ vt mover; poner en marcha; (furniture) trasladar; cambiar de lugar; (stir) remover; (shake) agitar, hacer temblar; (transport) transportar; (a piece in chess, etc.) jugar; (pull) arrancar; (impel) impulsar; (incline) inclinar, disponer; (affect emotionally) conmover, emocionar, enternecer; impresionar. —vi moverse; ponerse en marcha; (walk) andar; ir; avanzar; (a step forward, etc.) dar; (move house) trasladarse; (act) entrar en acción; (in games) hacer una jugada; (progress) progresar; (shake) agitarse, temblar; removerse; (propose in an assembly) hacer una proposición; (in a court of law) hacer un pedimento; (grow) crecer. **to m. about**, pasearse; ir y venir; (of traffic) circular; (remove) trasladarse; (stir, tremble) agitarse. **to m. along**, caminar por; avanzar por. **to m. aside**, vt apartar; poner a un lado; (curtains) descorrer. —vi ponerse a un lado; quitarse de en medio. **to m. away**, vt alejar. —vi alejarse; marcharse; trasladarse; mudar de casa. **to m. back**, retroceder; volver hacia atrás. **to m. down**, bajar, descender. **to m. forward**, adelantarse; avanzar; progresar. **to m. in**, entrar (en); tomar posesión de una casa. **to m. off**, vt quitar. —vi marcharse; ponerse en marcha; alejarse, apartarse. **to m. on**, avanzar; ponerse en marcha; circular; (of time) pasar, correr. **to m. out**, vt sacar, quitar. —vi salir; (from a house) mudarse, abandonar (una casa, etc.). **to m. round**, dar vueltas, girar; (turn round) volverse. **to m. to**, (make) hacer, animar (a); causar. **to m. up**, vt montar, subir. —vi montar; avanzar

**movement** /'muvmənt/ n movimiento, m; Mech. mecanismo, m; (Stock Exchange) actividad, f. **encircling m.**, Mil. movimiento envolvente, m

**mover** /'muvər/ n motor, m; móvil, m; promotor (-ra); (of a motion, proposer) autor (-ra) de una moción

**movie** /'muvi/ n Inf. cine, m. **m. camera**, máquina de impresionar, f. **m. star**, estrella de la pantalla, f

**moving** /'muvıŋ/ a móvil; motor; (affecting) emocionante, conmovedor; impresionante; patético. —n movimiento, m; traslado, m; cambio de domicilio, m. **m. picture**, fotografía cinematográfica, f. **m. staircase**, escalera móvil, f

**movingly** /'muvıŋli/ adv con emoción; patéticamente

**mow** /mou/ vt segar

**mowing** /'mouıŋ/ n siega, f. **m.-machine**, segadora, f

**Mr.** /'mıstər/ See **mister**

**Mrs.** /'mısəz/ See **mistress**

**much** /mʌtʃ/ a mucho. —adv mucho; (by far) con mucho; (with past part.) muy; (pretty nearly) casi, más o menos. **m. of a size,** más o menos del mismo tamaño. **I was m. angered,** Estuve muy enfadado. **as m. as,** tanto como. **as m. more,** otro tanto. **How m. is it?** ¿Cuánto es? ¿Cuánto cuesta? **however m….,** por mucho que… **not m.,** no mucho. **not to think m. of,** tener en poco (a). **so m. so that,** tanto que. **too m.,** demasiado. **to make m. of,** dar grande importancia a; (a person) apreciar, querer; agasajar; (a child) mimar, acariciar

**mucilage** /'myusəlɪdʒ/ n mucílago, m

**muck** /mʌk/ n (dung) estiércol, m; (filth) porquería, inmundicia, f; suciedad, f; (rubbish, of a literary work, etc.) porquería, n. **to m. up,** ensuciar; (spoil) estropear por completo

**mucky** /'mʌki/ a muy sucio; puerco; asqueroso, repugnante

**mucosity** /mu'kɒsɪti/ n mucosidad, f

**mucous** /'myukəs/ a mucoso. **m. membrane,** mucosa, f

**mucus** /'myukəs/ n mucosidad, f; (from the nose) moco, m

**mud** /mʌd/ n lodo, barro, fango, m. **to stick in the mud,** (of a ship, etc.) embarrancarse. **mudbath,** baño de barro, m. **mud wall,** tapia, f

**muddiness** /'mʌdɪnɪs/ n estado fangoso, m; (of liquids) turbiedad, f; suciedad, f

**muddle** /'mʌdl/ vt (bewilder) dejar perplejo, aturdir; (intoxicate) emborrachar; (stupefy) entontecer; (spoil) estropear; embarullar, dejar en desorden; hacer un lío de. —n desorden, m; confusión, f; lío, embrollo, m. **in a m.,** en desorden; en confusión. **to make a m.,** armar un lío. **to m. away,** derrochar sin ton ni son

**muddled** /'mʌdld/ a desordenado; confuso; estúpido; torpe; (drunk) borracho

**muddy** /'mʌdi/ a fangoso, lodoso, barroso; cubierto de lodo; (of liquids, etc.) turbio; (of the complexion) cetrino. —vt enlodar, cubrir de lodo; ensuciar; (liquids) enturbiar

**mudguard** /'mʌd,gard/ n guardabarro, m

**muezzin** /myu'ɛzɪn, mu-/ n almuecín, almuédano, m

**muff** /mʌf/ n manguito, m; (for a car radiator) cubierta para radiador, f; (Inf. at games, etc.) maleta, m. —vt dejar escapar (una pelota); (an opportunity) perder

**muffin** /'mʌfɪn/ n mollete, m

**muffle** /'mʌfəl/ vt embozar, arrebozar; envolver; encubrir, ocultar, tapar; (stifle sound of) apagar; (oars, bells) envolver con tela para no hacer ruido; Fig. ahogar. **to m. oneself up,** embozarse

**muffled** /'mʌfəld/ a (of sound) sordo; confuso; apagado. **m. drum,** tambor enlutado, m

**muffler** /'mʌflər/ n bufanda, tapaboca, f; (furnace) mufla, f; (of a car radiator) cubierta para radiador, f; (silencer) silencioso, m

**mufti** /'mʌfti/ n mufti, m

**mug** /mʌg/ n vaso, m; (tankard) pichel, tarro, m; (face) jeta, f; (dupe) primo, m; (at games, etc.) maleta, m

**mulatto** /mə'lætou/ a mulato. —n mulato (-ta). **m.-like,** amulatado

**mulberry** /'mʌl,bɛri/ n (fruit) mora, f; (bush) morera, f. **m. plantation,** moreral, m

**mule** /myul/ n mulo (-la); (slipper) mula, chinela, f; (spinning-jenny) huso mecánico, m

**mulish** /'myulɪʃ/ a mular; terco como una mula

**mulishness** /'myulɪʃnɪs/ n terquedad de mula, f

**mullet** /'mʌlɪt/ n (red) salmonete, m, trilla, f; (grey) mújol, m

**multicolored** /'mʌlti,kʌlərd/ a multicolor

**multifarious** /,mʌltə'fɛəriəs/ a numeroso, mucho; diverso, vario

**multiform** /'mʌltə,fɔrm/ a multiforme

**multilateral** /,mʌltɪ'lætərəl/ a multilátero

**multimillionaire** /,mʌltɪ'mɪlyə,nɛər/ a archimillonario, multimillonario, n multimillonario, m

**multiple** /'mʌltəpəl/ a múltiple, múltiplo. —n múltiplo, m

**multiple-choice question** n pregunta optativa, f

**multiplicand** /,mʌltəplɪ'kænd/ n multiplicando, m

**multiplication** /,mʌltəplɪ'keɪʃən/ n multiplicación, f. **m. table,** tabla de multiplicación, f

**multiplicity** /,mʌltə'plɪsɪti/ n multiplicidad, f

**multiplier** /'mʌltə,plaɪər/ n Math. multiplicador, m; máquina de multiplicar, f

**multiply** /'mʌltəpli/ vt multiplicar. —vi multiplicarse

**multitude** /'mʌltɪ,tud/ n multitud, f. **the m.,** las masas

**multitudinous** /,mʌltɪ'tudnəs/ a muy numeroso

**mumble** /'mʌmbəl/ vi and vt musitar, hablar entre dientes; refunfuñar; (chew) mascullar

**mummer** /'mʌmər/ n momero (-ra); máscara, mf

**mummery** /'mʌməri/ n momería, f; mascarada, f

**mummification** /,mʌməfɪ'keɪʃən/ n momificación, f

**mummify** /'mʌmə,fai/ vt momificar. —vi momificarse

**mummy** /'mʌmi/ n momia, f; carne de momia, f; (Inf. mother) mama, f. **m. case,** sarcófago, m

**mumps** /mʌmps/ n pl parotiditis, papera, f

**munch** /mʌntʃ/ vt masticar, mascullar, mascar

**mundane** /mʌn'dein/ a mundano

**municipal** /myu'nɪsəpəl/ a municipal. **m. charter,** fuero municipal, m. **m. government,** gobierno municipal, m

**municipality** /myu,nɪsə'pælɪti/ n municipio, m

**munificence** /myu'nɪfəsəns/ n munificencia, f

**munificent** /myu'nɪfəsənt/ a munífico, generoso

**munition** /myu'nɪʃən/ n munición, f. —vt municionar. **m. dump,** depósito de municiones, m. **m. factory,** fábrica de municiones, f. **m. worker,** obrero (-ra) de una fábrica de municiones

**mural** /'myʊrəl/ a mural. —n pintura mural, f

**murder** /'mɜrdər/ n asesinato, m. —vt asesinar; dar muerte (a), matar; (a work, etc.) degollar. **He was murdered,** Fue asesinado. **willful m.,** homicidio premeditado, m

**murderer** /'mɜrdərər/ n asesino, m

**murderess** /'mɜrdərɪs/ n asesina, f

**murderous** /'mɜrdərəs/ a homicida; cruel, sanguinario; fatal; imposible, intolerable

**murderously** /'mɜrdərəsli/ adv con intento de asesinar; (with look) con ojos asesinos; cruelmente

**murkiness** /'mɜrkɪnɪs/ n obscuridad, lobreguez, f, tinieblas, f pl

**murky** /'mɜrki/ a lóbrego, negro, obscuro; (of one's past, etc.) negro, accidentado

**murmur** /'mɜrmər/ n murmullo, m; rumor, m; susurro, m; (grumble) murmurio, m. —vi murmurar, susurrar; (complain) murmurar, quejarse. —vt murmurar, decir en voz baja

**murmuring** /'mɜrmərɪŋ/ n murmurio, m, a que murmura, susurrante

**muscatel** /,mʌskə'tɛl/ a moscatel. —n moscatel, m. **m. grape,** uva moscatel, f

**muscle** /'mʌsəl/ n músculo, m

**Muscovite** /'mʌskə,vait/ a moscovita. —n moscovita, mf

**muscular** /'mʌskyələr/ a muscular, musculoso; (brawny) membrudo, fornido. **m. pains,** (in the legs, etc.) agujetas, f pl

**muscularity** /,mʌskyə'lærɪti/ n fuerza muscular, f

**musculature** /'mʌskyələtʃər/ n musculatura, f

**Muse** /myuz/ n musa, f

**muse** /myuz/ n meditación, f. —vi meditar, reflexionar, rumiar; mirar las musarañas, estar distraído. **to m. on,** meditar en (or sobre)

**museum** /myu'ziəm/ n museo, m

**museum of arms** n museo de armas, m, aploteca, f

**mushroom** /'mʌʃrum/ n seta, f. —a de setas; de forma de seta; (upstart) advenedizo; (ephemeral) efímero, de un día. **m.-bed,** setal, m. **m.-spawn,** esporas de setas, f pl

**music** /'myuzɪk/ n música, f; armonía, f; melodía, f. —a de música. **to set to m.,** poner en música. **m.-hall,** teatro de variedades, m; salón de conciertos, m. **m. master,** profesor de música, m. **m. publisher,** editor de obras musicales, m. **m. stand,** atril, m; tablado para una orquesta, m. **m. stool,** taburete de piano, m

**musical** /'myuzɪkəl/ a musical; armonioso, melodioso. **She is very m.,** Es muy aficionada a la música; Tiene mucho talento para la música. **m.-box,** caja de música, *f*. **m. comedy,** zarzuela, *f*. **m. instrument,** instrumento de música, *m*

**musical chairs** *n* escobas, *f pl*, el juego de sillas, *m sing*

**musically** /'myuzıklı/ *adv* musicalmente; melodiosamente

**musician** /myu'zıʃən/ *n* músico (-ca)

**musing** /'myuzıŋ/ *n* meditación, *f*; ensueños, *m pl*, a pensativo, meditabundo

**musingly** /'myuzıŋli/ *adv* reflexivamente

**musk** /mʌsk/ *n* (substance) almizcle, *m*; perfume de almizcle, *m*. —*a* de almizcle; almizclero; (of scents) almizcleño. **m.-deer,** almizclero, *m*. **m.-rat,** rata almizclera, *f*

**musket** /'mʌskıt/ *n* mosquete, *m*

**musketeer** /,mʌskı'tıər/ *n* mosquetero, *m*

**Muslim** /'mʌzlım/ *a* musulmán, mahometano. —*n* musulmán (-ana)

**muslin** /'mʌzlın/ *n* muselina, *f*, *a* de muselina

**mussel** /'mʌsəl/ *n* mejillón, *m*. **m.-bed,** criadero de mejillones, *m*

**must** /mʌst/ *vi* haber de; tener que; deber; (expressing probability) deber de, ser. **This question m. be settled without delay,** Esta cuestión debe ser resuelta sin demora. **You m. do it at once,** Tienes que hacerlo en seguida. **I m. have seen him in the street sometime,** Debo haberle visto en la calle alguna vez. **One m. eat to live,** Se ha de comer para vivir. **Well, go if you m.,** Bueno, vete si no hay más remedio. **It m. be a difficult decision for him,** Debe ser una decisión difícil para él. **It m. have been about twelve o'clock when...,** Serían las doce cuando...

**must** /mʌst/ *n* mosto, zumo de la uva, *m*; (mould) moho, *m*

**mustang** /'mʌstæŋ/ *n* potro mesteño, *m*

**mustard** /'mʌstərd/ *n* mostaza, *f*. **m. gas,** iperita, *f*. **m. plaster,** sinapismo, *m*. **m. pot,** mostacera, *f*. **m. spoon,** cucharita para la mostaza, *f*

**muster** /'mʌstər/ *n* lista, *f*, rol, *m*; revista, *f*; reunión, *f*, *vt* pasar lista (de); pasar revista (a); reunir. —*vi* juntarse, reunirse. **to m. out,** (from the army) dar de baja (a). **to m. up sufficient courage,** cobrar ánimos suficientes. **to pass m.,** pasar revista; ser aceptado. **m.-roll,** *Mil*. muestra, *f*; *Naut*. rol de la tripulación, *m*

**mustiness** /'mʌstınıs/ *n* moho, *m*; ranciedad, *f*; (of a room, etc.) olor de humedad, *m*

**musty** /'mʌsti/ *a* mohoso; rancio; que huele a humedad. **to go m.,** enmohecerse

**mutability** /,myutə'bılıti/ *n* mutabilidad, *f*; inconstancia, inestabilidad, *f*

**mutable** /'myutəbəl/ *a* mudable; inconstante, inestable

**mutation** /myu'teıʃən/ *n* mutación, *f*

**mute** /myut/ *a* mudo; silencioso. —*n* mudo (-da); *Mus*. sordina, *f*; (phonetics) letra muda, *f*. **deaf m.,** sordomudo (-da)

**muted** /'myutıd/ *a* (of sounds) sordo, apagado

**mutely** /'myutli/ *adv* mudamente; en silencio

**muteness** /'myutnıs/ *n* mudez, *f*; silencio, *m*

**mutilate** /'myutḷ,eit/ *vt* mutilar; estropear

**mutilation** /,myutḷ'eıʃən/ *n* mutilación, *f*

**mutineer** /,myutṇ'ıər/ *n* amotinador, rebelde, *m*

**mutinous** /'myutṇəs/ *a* amotinado; rebelde, sedicioso; turbulento

**mutiny** /'myutṇi/ *n* motín, *m*; sublevación, insurrección, *f*, *vi* amotinarse, sublevarse

**mutt** /mʌt/ *n* chucho, *m*

**mutter** /'mʌtər/ *vt and vi* murmurar, musitar; mascullar, decir (or hablar) entre dientes; gruñir, refunfuñar; (of thunder, etc.) tronar, retumbar. —*n* murmurio, *m*; rumor, *m*; retumbo, *m*

**mutton** /'mʌtṇ/ *n* carnero, *m*, *a* de carnero. **m.-chop,** chuleta, *f*

**mutual** /'myutʃuəl/ *a* mutuo, recíproco; común. **by m. consent,** de común acuerdo. **m. aid society,** sociedad de socorros mutuos, *f*. **m. insurance company,** sociedad de seguros mutuos, *f*

**mutual fund** *n* fondo de inversiones rentables, *m*

**mutualism** /'myutʃuə,lızəm/ *n* mutualismo, *m*

**mutuality** /,myutʃu'ælıti/ *n* mutualidad, *f*

**mutually** /'myutʃuəli/ *adv* mutuamente, recíprocamente

**muzzle** /'mʌzəl/ *n* (snout) hocico, *m*; (for a dog) bozal, *m*; (of a gun) boca, *f*. —*vt* abozalar, poner un bozal (a); (*Fig*. gag) amordazar, imponer silencio (a)

**muzzling** /'mʌzlıŋ/ *n* acción de abozalar, *f*; (*Fig*. gagging) amordazamiento, *m*

**my** /mai/ *a poss* mi, *mf*; mis, *mf pl* **my relatives,** mis parientes. **My goodness!** ¡Dios mío!

**myelitis** /,maiə'laitıs/ *n* mielitis, *f*

**myopia** /mai'oupiə/ *n* miopía, *f*

**myopic** /mai'ɒpık/ *a* miope

**myriad** /'mıriəd/ *n* miríada, *f*

**myrmidon** /'mɜrmı,dɒn/ *n* rufián, *m*; asesino, *m*; secuaz, *m*

**myrrh** /mɜr/ *n* mirra, *f*

**myrtle** /'mɜrtḷ/ *n* mirto, arrayán, *m*

**myself** /mai'self/ *pron* yo mismo; (as a reflexive with a preposition) mí; (with a reflexive verb) me. **I m. sent it,** yo mismo (-ma) lo mandé

**mysterious** /mı'stıariəs/ *a* misterioso

**mysteriousness** /mı'stıariəsnıs/ *n* misterio, *m*, lo misterioso

**mystery** /'mıstəri/ *n* misterio, *m*. **m. play,** (religious) misterio, drama litúrgico, *m*; (thriller) comedia de detectives, *f*. **m. story,** novela policíaca, *f*; novela de aventuras, *f*

**mystic** /'mıstık/ *a* místico

**mysticism** /'mıstə,sızəm/ *n* misticismo, *m*

**mystification** /,mıstəfı'keıʃən/ *n* mistificación, *f*

**mystify** /'mıstə,fai/ *vt* mistificar

**myth** /mıθ/ *n* mito, *m*

**mythical** /'mıθıkəl/ *a* mítico

**mythologist** /mı'θɒlədʒıst/ *n* mitólogo, *m*

**mythology** /mı'θɒlədʒi/ *n* mitología, *f*

# N

**n** /ɛn/ *n* (letter) ene, *f*

**nab** /næb/ *vt Inf.* atrapar, apresar, agazapar

**nabob** /'neibɒb/ *n* nabab, *m;* ricacho, *m*

**nacre** /'neikər/ *n* nácar, *m*, madreperla, *f*

**nadir** /'neidər/ *n* nadir, *m*

**nag** /næg/ *n* jaca, *f;* (wretched hack) rocín, jamelgo, penco, *m.* —*vt* zaherir, echar en cara, regañar; (of one's conscience) remorder. —*vi* criticar, regañar

**nagging** /'nægɪŋ/ *n* zaherimiento, *m.* —*a* zaheridor, criticón; (pain) continuo, incesante, constante

**naiad** /'neiæd/ *n Myth.* náyade, *f*

**nail** /neil/ *vt* clavar, enclavar; (for ornament) clavetear, tachonar, adornar con clavos. —*n* uña, *f; Mech.* clavo, *m;* (animal's) garra, *f.* **to n. down,** sujetar (or cerrar) con clavos. **to n. to (on to),** clavar en. **to n. together,** fijar con clavos. *Inf.* **on the n.,** en el acto, en seguida. *Inf.* **to hit the n. on the head,** dar en el clavo. **brass-headed n.,** tachón, *m.* **French n.,** punta de París, *f.* **headless n.,** puntilla, *f.* **hob-n.,** clavo de herradura, *m.* **hook n.,** gancho, *m.* **round-headed n.,** bellota, *f.* **n.-brush,** cepillo para las (or de) uñas, *m.* **n.-file,** lima para las uñas, *f.* **n. head,** cabeza de un clavo, *f.* **n.-puller,** sacaclavos, arrancaclavos, botador, *m.* **n.-scissors,** tijeras para las uñas, *f pl.* **n. trade,** ferretería, *f.* **n. varnish,** barniz para las uñas, *m*

**nailed** /neild/ *a* adornado con clavos, claveteado

**nailer** /'neilər/ *n* fabricante de clavos, chapucero, *m*

**nailing** /'neilɪŋ/ *n* enclavación, *f*

**naive** /nɑ'iv/ *a* ingenuo, candoroso, espontáneo

**naively** /nɑ'ivli/ *adv* ingenuamente, espontáneamente

**naiveté** /nɑiv'tei, -,nɑiv'tei, -'ivtei, -'ivə-/ *n* ingenuidad, naturalidad, franqueza, *f;* candor, *m*

**naked** /'neikɪd/ *a* desnudo, nudo; desabrigado, indefenso, desamparado; (birds) implume; calvo; (truth) simple, sencillo, puro; evidente, patente. **stark n.,** en cueros vivos, tal como le parió su madre. **with the n. sword,** con la espada desnuda. **n. eye,** simple vista, *f.* **n. light,** llama descubierta, *f*

**nakedly** /'neikɪdli/ *adv* nudamente; desabrigadamente; abiertamente, claramente

**nakedness** /'neikɪdnɪs/ *n* desnudez, *f; Fig.* desabrigo, *m,* aridez, *f; Fig.* claridad, *f.* **the truth in all its n.,** la verdad desnuda

**namby-pamby** /'næmbi'pæmbi/ *a* soso, insípido, ñoño

**name** /neim/ *n* nombre, *m;* título, *m;* fama, opinión, *f;* renombre, crédito, *m;* autoridad, *f;* apodo, mal nombre, *m.* —*vt* nombrar, llamar, imponer el nombre de, apellidar; mencionar, señalar; (appoint) designar, elegir; (ships) bautizar. **by n.,** por nombre. **Christian n.,** nombre de pila, *m.* **in his n.,** en nombre de él, en nombre suyo; de parte de él. **in n. only,** nada más que en nombre. **to be named,** llamarse. **to call** (a person) **names,** poner como un trapo (a). **to go under the n. of,** vivir bajo el nombre de. **to have a good n.,** tener buena fama. **What is her n.?** ¿Cómo se llama? **n. day,** santo, *m.* **n. plate,** (machinery) placa de fábrica, *f;* (streets) rótulo, *m;* (professional) placa profesional, *f*

**nameless** /'neimlɪs/ *a* anónimo; desconocido; (inexpressible) vago, indecible

**namely** /'neimli/ *adv* a saber, es decir

**namesake** /'neim,seik/ *n* tocayo (-ya)

**naming** /'neimɪŋ/ *n* bautizo, *m;* nombramiento, *m;* designación, *f*

**nannygoat** /'næni,gout/ *n* cabra, *f*

**nap** /næp/ *n* (cloth) pelusa, *f,* pelo, tamo, *m;* (plants) vello, *m,* pelusilla, *f;* (sleep) siesta, *f,* sueño, *m;* (cards) napolitana, *f.* **to take a nap,** *vi* dormitar, echar un sueño, echar una siesta. **to take an afternoon nap,** dormir la siesta. **to be caught napping,** estar desprevenido

**nape** /neip/ *n* nuca, *f,* cogote, *m;* (animal's) testuz, *m,*

**naphtha** /'næfθə, 'næp-/ *n Chem.* nafta, *f.* **wood n.,** alcohol metílico, *m*

**naphthalene** /'næfθə,lin, 'næp-/ *n Chem.* naftalina, *f*

**napkin** /'næpkɪn/ *n* (table) servilleta, *f;* (babies') pañal, *m.* **n.-ring,** servilletero, *m*

**Naples** /'neipəlz/ Nápoles, *m*

**Napoleonic** /nə,pouli'ɒnɪk/ *a* napoleónico

**narcissism** /'nɑrsə,sɪzəm/ *n* narcisismo, *m*

**narcissus** /nɑr'sɪsəs/ *n* narciso, *m*

**narcosis** /nɑr'kousɪs/ *n Med.* narcosis, *f*

**narcotic** /nɑr'kɒtɪk/ *a* Med. narcótico, calmante, soporífero. —*n Med.* narcótico, *m,* opiata, *f*

**nard** /nɑrd/ *n Bot.* nardo, *m,* tuberosa, *f*

**narrate** /'næreit/ *vt* narrar, contar; referir, relatar

**narration** /næ'reiʃən/ *n* narración, narrativa; relación, descripción, *f,* relato, *m*

**narrative** /'nærətɪv/ *a* narrador, narrativo, narratorio. —*n* narrativa, *f;* descripción, *f*

**narrator** /'næreitər/ *n* narrador (-ra), relator (-ra), descriptor (-ra)

**narrow** /'nærou/ *vt* estrechar, angostar; reducir, limitar. —*vi* reducirse, hacerse más estrecho; (eyes) entornarse; (knitting) menguar. —*a* estrecho, angosto; limitado, restringido, reducido, corto; (avaricious) ruin, avaro, mezquino; (ideas) intolerante, intransigente. **"Narrow Road,"** «Camino Estrecho». —*n pl* **narrows,** *Naut.* estrecho, *m;* desfiladero, paso estrecho, *m.* **to have a n. escape,** escapar en una tabla. **n.-brimmed** (hats), de ala estrecha. **n. circumstances,** estrechez, escasez de medios, *f.* **n.-gauge railway,** ferrocarril de vía estrecha (or de vía angosta), *m.* **n. life,** vida de horizontes estrechos, *f.* **n. majority,** escasa mayoría, *f.* **n.-minded,** cerrado al mundo, intolerante, intransigente. **n.-mindedness,** intolerancia, intransigencia, estrechez de miras, *f*

**narrowing** /'nærouɪŋ/ *n* estrechez, *f,* estrechamiento, *m;* reducción, limitación, *f;* (in knitting) menguado, *m*

**narrowly** /'nærouli/ *adv* estrechamente; por poco, con dificultad; atentamente, cuidadosamente. **I n. escaped being run over,** Por poco me atropellan

**narrowness** /'nærounɪs/ *n* estrechez, angostura, *f;* (of means) pobreza, miseria, *f;* (of ideas) intolerancia, intransigencia, *f*

**nasal** /'neizəl/ *a* nasal, gangoso. —*n* letra nasal, *f*

**nasalize** /'neizə,laiz/ *vt* nasalizar

**nasally** /'neizəli/ *adv* nasalmente. **to speak n.,** hablar por las narices, ganguear

**nascent** /'næsənt, 'neisənt/ *a* naciente

**nastily** /'næstəli/ *adv* suciamente; ofensivamente, de un modo insultante; maliciosamente, con malignidad

**nastiness** /'næstinɪs/ *n* suciedad, inmundicia, porquería, *f;* (indecency) obscenidad, indecencia, *f;* (rudeness) insolencia, impertinencia, grosería, *f;* (difficulty) dificultad, *f,* lo malo

**nasturtium** /nə'stɜrʃəm/ *n* mastuerzo, *m,* capuchina, *f*

**nasty** /'næsti/ *a* nauseabundo, repugnante; asqueroso, inmundo, sucio; (obscene) indecente, obsceno; desagradable, malo; (malicious) rencoroso, malicioso; violento; malévolo, amenazador; peligroso; difícil. *Fig.* **to be in a n. mess,** tener el agua al cuello. **to turn n.,** *Inf.* ponerse desagradable

**natal** /'neitl/ *a* natal, natalicio, de nacimiento, nativo

**nation** /'neiʃən/ *n* nación, *f,* estado, país, *m;* (people) pueblo, *m*

**national** /'næʃənl/ *a* nacional; público; patriótico. —*n* nacional, *mf.* **n. anthem,** himno nacional, *m.* **n. debt,** deuda pública, *f.* **n. schools,** escuelas públicas, *f pl.* **n. socialism,** nacionalsocialismo, *m.* **n. socialist,** *a* and *n* nacionalsocialista *mf.* **n. syndicalism,** *Polit.* nacionalsindicalismo, *m.* **n. syndicalist,** *a* and *n Polit.* nacionalsindicalista, *mf*

**nationalism** /'næʃənl,ɪzəm/ *n* nacionalismo, patriotismo, *m*

**nationalist** /'næʃənlɪst/ *a* and *n* nacionalista, *mf*

**nationality** /,næʃ ə'nælɪti/ *n* nacionalidad, *f;* nación, *f*

**nationalization** /ˌnæʃənlə'zeiʃən/ n nacionalización, f
**nationalize** /'næʃənḷ,aiz, 'næʃnə,laiz/ vt nacionalizar
**National Labor Relations Board** n Junta Nacional de Relaciones Laborales
**nationally** /'næʃənḷi/ adv nacionalmente, como nación; del punto de vista nacional
**native** /'neitɪv/ a (of a place) nativo, natal, oriundo; indígena; nacional, típico, del país; (vocabulary) patrimonial (as opposed to borrowed vocabulary); (of genius) natural, innato, instintivo; *Mineral.* nativo; (language) vernáculo. —n nacional, mf; natural, mf; ciudadano (-na) indígena, aborigen (gen. pl.), mf; producto nacional, m. **He is a n. of Madrid,** Nació en Madrid, Es natural de Madrid, Es madrileño. **native informant,** sujeto, m. **n. land,** patria, tierra, f. **n. place,** lugar natal, m. **n. region,** patria chica, f. **n. soil,** terruño, m. **n. tongue,** lengua materna, f
**nativity** /nə'tɪvɪti/ n navidad, natividad, f; (manger) nacimiento, m
**natty** /'næti/ a *Inf.* chulo, majo; coquetón
**natural** /'nætʃərəl/ a natural; (wild) virgen, salvaje; nativo; (of products) crudo; normal; (usual) acostumbrado, corriente, natural; (of likeness) fiel, verdadero; (illegitimate) ilegítimo, bastardo; (of qualities) innato, instintivo; físico; característico, propio; (of people) inafectado, sencillo, genuino; *Mus.* natural. —n *Mus.* becuadro, m; *Mus.* nota natural, f; imbécil, mf **n. features,** geografía física, f. **n. history,** historia natural, f. **n. philosophy,** filosofía natural, f. **n. science,** ciencias naturales, f pl. **n. selection,** selección natural, f. **n. state,** estado virgen, m
**natural child** n hijo ilegítimo, m
**natural daughter** n hija ilegítima, f
**naturalism** /'nætʃərə,lɪzəm/ n naturalismo, m
**naturalist** /'nætʃərəlɪst/ n (*Lit.* and *Science.*) naturalista, mf
**naturalistic** /ˌnætʃərə'lɪstɪk/ a naturalista
**naturalization** /ˌnætʃərələ'zeiʃən/ n naturalización, f; aclimatación, f. **n. papers,** carta de naturaleza, f
**naturalize** /'nætʃərə,laiz/ vt naturalizar; aclimatar. **to become naturalized,** naturalizarse
**naturally** /'nætʃərəli/ adv naturalmente, por naturaleza; normalmente; sin afectación; instintivamente, por instinto; (without art) al natural
**naturalness** /ˌnætʃərəlnɪs/ n naturalidad, f; sencillez, desenvoltura, f; desembarazo, m
**nature** /'neitʃər/ n naturaleza, f; (of people) carácter, fondo, temperamento, genio, natural, modo de ser, m; (kind) género, m, especie, f; (essence) condición, esencia, cualidad, f, *Art.* **from n.,** del natural. **good n.,** bondad natural, afabilidad, f. **ill n.,** mala índole, f. **nature cure,** naturismo, m. **n. curist,** naturista, mf. **n. study,** historia natural, f. **n. worship,** panteísmo, culto de la naturaleza, m
**natured** /'neitʃərd/ a de carácter, de índole, con un modo de ser, de condición
**naught** /nɔt/ n nada, f; cero, m. —a inútil, sin valor. **all for n.,** todo en balde. **to come to n.,** malograrse. **to set at n.,** tener en menos; despreciar
**naughtily** /'nɔtḷi/ adv traviesamente; con picardía, con malicia
**naughtiness** /'nɔtɪnɪs/ n travesura, picardía, mala conducta, f; malicia, f
**naughty** /'nɔti/ a travieso, pícaro, revoltoso, malo; salado, escabroso, verde (stories, etc.). **to be n.,** (children) ser malo
**nausea** /'nɔziə, -ʒə/ n náusea, f, bascas, f pl, mareo, m; *Fig.* asco, m; repugnancia, f
**nauseate** /'nɔzi,eit, -ʒi-/ vt dar náuseas; *Fig.* repugnar, dar asco
**nauseating** /'nɔzi,eitɪŋ, -ʒi-/ a repugnante, horrible; asqueroso
**nauseous** /'nɔʃəs/ a nauseabundo, asqueroso; *Fig.* repugnante
**nauseousness** /'nɔʃəsnɪs/ n náusea, asquerosidad, f; *Fig.* repugnancia, f, asco, m
**nautical** /'nɔtɪkəl/ a náutico, marítimo. **n. day, twenty-four hours,** singladura, f
**nautilus** /'nɔtḷəs/ n *Zool.* argonauta, nautilo, m
**naval** /'neivəl/ a naval; de marina, marítimo. **n. base,** base naval, f. **n. engagement,** batalla naval, f. **n. hospital,** hospital de marina, m. **n. law,** código na-

val, m. **n. officer,** oficial de marina, m. **n. power,** poder marítimo, m. **n. reservist,** marinero de reserva, m. **n. yard,** arsenal, m
**Navarre** /nə'vɑr/ Navarra, f
**Navarrese** /ˌnævə'riz/ a and n navarro (-rra)
**nave** /neiv/ n *Archit.* nave, f; (of wheels) cubo, m
**navel** /'neivəl/ n ombligo, m. **n. string,** cordón umbilical, m
**navigability** /ˌnævɪgə'bɪlɪti/ n navegación, practicabilidad de navegar, f
**navigable** /'nævɪgəbəl/ a navegable, practicable
**navigate** /'nævɪ,geit/ vt navegar, marear, dirigir (unbuque); *Fig.* conducir, guiar. —vi navegar
**navigation** /ˌnævɪ'geiʃən/ n navegación, f; (science of) náutica, marina, f. **n. company,** empresa naviera, f. **n. laws,** derecho marítimo, m. **n. lights,** luces de navegación, f pl
**navigator** /'nævɪ,geitər/ n navegador, navegante, m; piloto, m
**navvy** /'nævi/ n peón, bracero, jornalero, m; *Mech.* máquina, excavadora, f. **road n.,** peón caminero, m. **to work like a n.,** estar hecho un azacán, sudar la gota gorda
**navy** /'neivi/ n marina, f; armada, f; (color) azul marino, m. **n. board,** consejo de la armada, m. **n. department** ministerio de marina, m. **n. estimates,** presupuesto de marina, m. **n. list,** escalafón de marina, m
**nay** /nei/ adv no; al contrario, más bien, mejor dicho. —n negativa, f, voto contrario, m
**Nazarene** /ˌnæzə'rin/ a and n nazareno (-na)
**Nazareth** /'næzərəθ/ Nazaret, m
**Nazi** /'nɑtsi/ a and n nacionalsocialista, naci, mf
**Nazism** /'nɑtsɪzəm/ n nacismo, m
**n.d.** (no date) *s.f.* (sin fecha)
**Neapolitan** /ˌniə'pɒlɪtn/ a and n neapolitano (-na)
**near** /nɪər/ vi acercarse, aproximarse. —a cercano, immediato, contiguo; (of time) inminente, próximo; (relationship) cercano, consanguíneo; (of friends) íntimo, entrañable; (mean) tacaño, avariento
**near** /nɪər/ prep cerca de, junto a; hacia, en la dirección de; (of time) cerca de, casi. —adv cerca; (time) cerca, próximamente. **to be n. to,** estar cerca de. **to bring n.,** acercar, aproximar. **It was a n. thing,** Escapamos por un pelo. **n. at hand,** a la mano; (time) cerca, inminente. **n.-by,** a cercano, inmediato. —adv cerca. **n. side,** (of vehicles) lado de la acera, m. **n.-sighted,** corto de vista, miope. **n.-sightedness,** miopía, cortedad de vista, f
**nearest** /'nɪərɪst/ a compar and superl más cercano, más cerca; más corto. **the n. way,** el camino más corto, el camino directo
**nearly** /'nɪərli/ adv casi; cerca de, aproximadamente; estrechamente; íntimamente. **It touches me n.,** Me toca de cerca, Es de sumo interés para mí. **They n. killed me,** Por poco me matan. **to be n.,** (of age) frisar en, rayar en
**nearness** /'nɪərnɪs/ n (of place) cercanía, proximidad, contigüidad, f; (of time) inminencia, proximidad, f; (relationship) consanguinidad, f; (avarice) avaricia, tacañería, f; (dearness) intimidad, amistad estrecha, f
**neat** /nit/ a *Zool.* vacuno; elegante, sencillo, de buen gusto; (of the body) bien hecho, airoso, esbelto; (clean) limpio, aseado; (of handwriting) legible, bien proporcionado; pulido, esmerado, acabado; hábil, astuto, diestro; (of liquor, spirits) puro, solo. **to make a n. job of,** hacer (algo) bien
**neatly** /'nitli/ adv sencillamente, con elegancia, con primor; con aseo, limpiamente; bien (proporcionado); diestramente, hábilmente
**neatness** /'nitnɪs/ n aseo, m, limpieza, f; elegancia, sencillez, f; buen gusto, m; destreza, habilidad, f; (aptness) pertinencia, f
**nebula** /'nɛbyələ/ n *Astron.* nebulosa, f
**nebulosity** /ˌnɛbyə'lɒsɪti/ n nebulosidad, f; *Astron.* nebulosa, f; vaguedad, imprecisión, f
**nebulous** /'nɛbyələs/ a nebuloso; vago, impreciso, confuso
**necessarily** /ˌnɛsə'sɛərəli/ adv necesariamente; inevitablemente, sin duda
**necessary** /'nɛsə,sɛri/ a necesario, inevitable; imprescindible, preciso, indispensable, esencial; obligatorio,

debido, forzoso. —*n* requisito esencial, *m.* **if n.,** en caso de necesidad; si fuera necesario. **to be n.,** hacer falta; necesitarse

**necessitate** /nə'sɛsɪˌteɪt/ *vt* necesitar, exigir, requerir, obligar

**necessitous** /nə'sɛsɪtəs/ *a* pobre, indigente, miserable, necesitado

**necessity** /nə'sɛsɪti/ *n* necesidad, *f;* menester, *m,* (e.g., *an indispensable n.*), un menester imprescindible); consecuencia, *f,* resultado, efecto, *m;* inevitabilidad, fatalidad, *f;* (poverty) indigencia, pobreza, *f.* **Fire and clothing are necessities,** El fuego y el vestir son cosas necesarias. **from n.,** por necesidad. **in case of n.,** si fuese necesario, en caso de necesidad. **of n.,** de necesidad, sin remedio. **physical necessities,** menesteres físicos, *m pl.* **prime n.,** artículo de primera necesidad, *m.* **to be under the n. of,** tener que, tener la necesidad de

**Necessity is the mother of invention** La necesidad es una gran inventora, La necesidad aguza el ingenio

**neck** /nɛk/ *n* cuello, *m,* garganta, *f;* (of bottles) gollete, cuello, *m;* (of animals) pescuezo, *m; Geog.* istmo, *m,* lengua de tierra, *f;* (of musical instruments) clavijero, mástil, *m; Sew.* escote, *m.* **low-necked,** (of dresses) escotado. **She fell on his n.,** Se colgó de su cuello. **He won by a n.,** Ganó por un cuello; *Fig.* Ganó por un tris. **to break anyone's n.,** romperle el pescuezo. **to wring the n. of,** torcer el pescuezo (a). **n. and n.,** parejos. **n. or nothing,** todo o nada, perdiz o no comerla. **n. stock,** alzacuello, *m*

**neckband** /'nɛkˌbænd/ *n* tirilla de camisa, *f*

**necklace** /'nɛklɪs/ *n* collar, *f*

**necklet** /'nɛklɪt/ *n* collar, *m;* (of fur) cuello, *m*

**necktie** /'nɛkˌtaɪ/ *n* corbata, *f*

**necrological** /ˌnɛkrə'lɒdʒɪkəl/ *a* necrológico

**necrology** /nə'krɒlədʒi/ *n* necrología, *f*

**necropolis** /nə'krɒpəlɪs/ *n* necrópolis, *f*

**nectar** /'nɛktər/ *n* néctar, *f*

**nectarine** /ˌnɛktə'rin/ *n Bot.* variedad de melocotón, *f*

**need** /nid/ *vt* necesitar, haber menester, requerir, exigir. —*vi* ser necesario, hacer falta, carecer; haber (de). **N. I obey?** ¿He de obedecer? **You need to write carefully,** Hay que escribir con cuidado. **The work n. not be done for tomorrow,** No es preciso hacer el trabajo para mañana

**need** /nid/ *n* necesidad, *f;* cosa necesaria, *f;* falta; (poverty) indigencia, pobreza, *f;* urgencia, *f;* (shortage) escasez, carestía, *f.* **in case of n.,** en caso de necesidad, en caso de urgencia. **I have n. of two more books,** Me hacen falta dos libros más

**needful** /'nidfəl/ *a* necesario, preciso; indispensable, esencial. **the n.,** lo necesario

**needfulness** /'nidfəlnɪs/ *n* necesidad, falta, *f*

**neediness** /'nidinɪs/ *n* pobreza, penuria, miseria, estrechez, *f*

**needle** /'nidl/ *n Sew.* aguja, *f;* (of compass) brújula, aguja imanada, *f;* (monument) obelisco, *m;* (of scales) fiel, *m,* lengüeta, *f;* (of phonograph) púa, *f,* (of measuring instruments) índice, *m; Med.* aguja de inyecciones, *f. Inf.* **to be as sharp as a n.,** no tener pelo de tonto. **pack n.,** aguja espartera, *f.* **n.-case,** alfiletero, agujero, *m.* **n. maker,** fabricante de agujas, *m.* **n.-shaped,** en forma de aguja, acicular

**needle and thread** hilo y aguja

**needless** /'nidlɪs/ *a* innecesario, superfluo. **n. to say,** claro está que..., huelga decir que...

**needlessly** /'nidlɪsli/ *adv* innecesariamente, inútilmente; en vano, de balde

**needlessness** /'nidlɪsnɪs/ *n* superfluidad, *f,* lo innecesario

**needlewoman** /'nidlˌwʊmən/ *n* (professional) cosedora, *f;* costurera, *f.* **She is a good n.,** Cose bien (or es una buena cosedora)

**needlework** /'nidlˌwɜrk/ *n* labor de aguja, labor blanca, costura, *f;* bordado, *m.* **to do n.,** hacer costura

**needs** /nidz/ *adv* necesariamente, sin remedio *n pl* necesidades, *f pl.* **if n. must,** si hace falta. **N. must when the devil drives,** A la fuerza ahorcan

**needy** /'nidi/ *a* necesitado, menesteroso, corto de medios, pobre, apurado

**ne'er-do-well** /'nɛərduˌwɛl/ *n* calavera, perdido, *m.* **to be a n.,** ser de mala madera

**nefarious** /nɪ'fɛəriəs/ *a* nefario, vil, nefando

**nefariously** /nɪ'fɛəriəsli/ *adv* vilmente, nefariamente

**negation** /nɪ'geɪʃən/ *n* negación, *f*

**negative** /'nɛgətɪv/ *vt* negar, denegar; votar en contra (de), oponerse (a); (prevent) impedir, imposibilitar. —*a* negativo. —*n* negativa, negación, *f;* repulsa, denegación, *f; Photo.* negativo, *m,* prueba negativa, *f; Elec.* electricidad negativa, *f.* **to reply in the n.,** dar una respuesta negativa

**negativeness** /'nɛgətɪvnɪs/ *n* el carácter negativo, *m*

**neglect** /nɪ'glɛkt/ *vt* descuidar, desatender; abandonar, dejar; (ignore) despreciar, no hacer caso (de); omitir, olvidar. —*n* descuido, *m,* desatención, *f;* inobservancia, *f;* abandono, olvido, *m;* desdén, *m,* frialdad, *f.* **to fall into n.,** caer en desuso. **to n. one's obligations,** descuidar sus obligaciones

**neglectful** /nɪ'glɛktfəl/ *a* negligente, descuidado, omiso

**negligee** /ˌnɛglɪ'ʒeɪ/ *n* salto de cama, quimono, *m,* bata, *f*

**negligence** /'nɛglɪdʒəns/ *n* negligencia, *f,* descuido, *m;* flojedad, pereza, *f;* (of dress) desaliño, *m*

**negligent** /'nɛglɪdʒənt/ *a* negligente, descuidado; remiso, flojo, perezoso

**negligently** /'nɛglɪdʒəntli/ *adv* negligentemente; con indiferencia

**negligible** /'nɛglɪdʒəbəl/ *a* insignificante, escaso, insuficiente; sin importancia, desdeñable

**negotiable** /nɪ'goʊʃiəbəl, -ʃəbəl/ *a* negociable; (of a road) practicable, transitable

**negotiate** /nɪ'goʊʃiˌeɪt/ *vt* gestionar, agenciar, tratar; (a bend) tomar; (an obstacle) salvar, franquear; *vi* negociar. **to n. a bill of exchange,** descontar una letra de cambio. **to n. for a contract,** tratar un contrato

**negotiation** /nɪˌgoʊʃi'eɪʃən/ *n* negociación, *f; Com.* gestión, transacción, *f;* (of a bend) toma, *f;* (of an obstacle) salto, *m*

**negotiator** /nɪ'goʊʃiˌeɪtər/ *n* negociador (-ra)

**neigh** /neɪ/ *vi* relinchar. —*n* relincho, relinchido, *m*

**neighbor** /'neɪbər/ *n* vecino (-na); (biblical) prójimo (-ma)

**neighborhood** /'neɪbərˌhʊd/ *n* vecindad, *f,* vecindario, *m;* cercanía, *f,* afueras, *f pl,* alrededores, *m pl;* *a* de barrio (e.g. *neighborhood moviehouse,* cine del barrio)

**neighboring** /'neɪbərɪŋ/ *a* vecino; cercano, inmediato, adyacente

**neighborliness** /'neɪbərlinɪs/ *n* buena vecindad, *f*

**neighborly** /'neɪbərli/ *a* amistoso, sociable, bondadoso. **to be n.,** ser de buena vecindad.

**neither** /'niðər, 'naɪ-/ *a* ningún; ninguno de los dos, e.g. **N.** *explanation is right,* Ninguna de las dos explicaciones es correcta. —*conjunc* ni, tampoco, e.g. **N.** *Mary nor John,* Ni María ni Juan. *N. will he give it to her,* Tampoco se lo dará. —*pron* ni uno ni otro, ninguno, e.g. **N.** *of them heard it,* Ni uno ni otro lo oyó.

**nemesis** /'nɛməsɪs/ *n* némesis, *f;* justicia, *f*

**neo-** *prefix* neo. **neo-Catholic,** *a* and *n* neo-católico (-ca). **neo-Platonic,** neoplatónico. **neo-Platonism,** neoplatonismo, *m*

**neolithic** /ˌniə'lɪθɪk/ *a* neolítico

**neologism** /ni'ɒləˌdʒɪzəm/ *n* neologismo, *m*

**neon** /'niɒn/ *n Chem.* neón, *m*

**neon sign** anuncio luminoso, *m*

**neophyte** /'niəˌfaɪt/ *n* neófito (-ta); aspirante, *mf*

**nephew** /'nɛfyu/ *n* sobrino, *m*

**nephritis** /nə'fraɪtɪs/ *n Med.* nefritis, *f*

**nepotism** /'nɛpəˌtɪzəm/ *n* nepotismo, *m*

**nerve** /nɜrv/ *n* (*Anat. Bot.*) nervio, *m;* valor, ánimo, *m;* vitalidad, *f; Inf.* descaro, *m,* desvergüenza, frescura, *f.* —*vt* animar, alentar, envalentonar; esforzar; dar fuerza (a). —*vi* animarse, esforzarse (a). **My nerves are all on edge,** Se me crispan los nervios. **n. -cell,** neurona, *f.* **to lose one's n.,** perder la cabeza; perder los nervios. **to strain every n.,** hacer un esfuerzo supremo. **n. center,** centro nervioso, *m.* **n.-racking,** espantoso, horripilante. **n. strain,** tensión nerviosa, *f*

**nerveless** /'nɜrvlɪs/ *a* sin nervio; enervado

**nerviness** /'nɜrvɪnɪs/ *n* nervosidad, *f*

**nervous** /'nɜrvəs/ *a* nervioso, asustadizo, tímido; agitado, excitado; (of style) vigoroso. **n. breakdown,** crisis nerviosa, *f*. **n. system,** sistema nervioso, *m*

**nervously** /'nɜrvəsli/ *adv* nerviosamente; tímidamente

**nervousness** /'nɜrvəsnɪs/ *n* nervosidad, timidez, *f*; agitación, *f*; (of style) vigor, *m*; energía, *f*

**nervy** /'nɜrvi/ *a* nervioso

**nest** /nɛst/ *vi* anidar, hacerse un nido. —*n* (bird's) nido, *m*; (animal's) madriguera, *f*; (of drawers) juego, *m*, serie, *f*; (of thieves) cueva, guarida, *f*; *Inf.* casita, *f*, hogar, *m*. **to feather one's n.,** hacer su agosto. **n.-egg,** *Fig.* nidal, *m*. **n. of eggs,** nidada de huevos, *f*

**nestle** /'nɛsəl/ *vt* apoyar. —*vi* apiñarse, hacerse un ovillo. **to n. up to a person,** apretarse contra

**nestling** /'nɛstlɪŋ/ *n* pichón, pollo, *m*; pajarito, *m*

**net** /nɛt/ *vt* coger con redes; obtener, coger; cubrir con redes. —*vi* hacer redes. —*n* red, *f*; (mesh) malla, *f*; (fabric) tul, *m*. **net making,** manufactura de redes, *f*

**net** /nɛt/ *a Com.* líquido, neto, limpio; (of fabric) de tul. **net amount,** importe líquido, importe neto, *m*. **net balance,** saldo líquido, *m*. **net cost,** precio neto, *m*. **net profit,** beneficio neto (or líquido), *m*

**nether** /'nɛðər/ *a* inferior, bajero, más bajo. **n. regions,** infierno, *m*

**Netherland** /'nɛðərlənd/ *a* neerlandés, holandés

**Netherlander** /'nɛðər,lændər/ *n* neerlandés (-esa), holandés (-esa)

**Netherlands, the** /'nɛðərləndz/ los Países Bajos *m pl*

**nethermost** /'nɛðər,moust/ *a* lo más bajo, ínfimo, más hondo

**netting** /'nɛtɪŋ/ *n* red, (obra de) malla, *f*; *Naut.* jareta, *f*; manufactura de redes, *f*; pesca con redes, *f*. **wire-n.,** tela metálica, malla de alambre, *f*

**nettle** /'nɛtl/ *vt* picar; *Fig.* irritar, picar, fastidiar, disgustar. —*n* ortiga, *f*. **n.-rash,** urticaria, *f*

**network** /'nɛt,wɜrk/ *n* red, malla, randa, *f*; (of communications) sistema, *m*, red, *f*

**neuralgia** /nʊ'rældʒə/ *n* neuralgia, *f*

**neuralgic** /nʊ'rældʒɪk/ *a* neurálgico

**neurasthenia** /,nʊrəs'θiniə/ *n* neurastenia, *f*

**neurasthenic** /,nʊrəs'θɛnɪk/ *a* and *n* neurasténico (-ca)

**neuritis** /nʊ'raitɪs/ *n* neuritis, *f*

**neurologist** /nʊ'rɒlədʒɪst/ *n* neurólogo, *m*

**neurology** /nʊ'rɒlədʒi/ *n* neurología, *f*

**neuropath** /'nʊrə,pæθ/ *n* neurópata, *m*

**neuropathic** /,nʊrə'pæθɪk/ *a* neuropático

**neurosis** /nʊ'rousɪs/ *n* neurosis, *f*

**neurosurgeon** /'nʊrou,sɜrdʒən/ *n* neurocirujano, *m*

**neurotic** /nʊ'rɒtɪk/ *a* and *n* neurótico (-ca)

**neuter** /'nʊtər/ *a* neutro; (of verbs) intransitivo; (*Zool. Bot.*) sin sexo

**neutral** /'nʊtrəl/ *a* neutral; (*Chem. Mech.*) neutro; (of colors) indeciso, indeterminado; (of persons) imparcial, indiferente. —*n* neutral, *mf Mech.* **to go into n.,** pasar a marcha neutra

**neutrality** /nʊ'trælɪti/ *n* neutralidad, *f*; indiferencia, *f*; imparcialidad, *f*

**neutralization** /'nʊtrələ'zeiʃən/ *n* neutralización, *f*

**neutralize** /'nʊtrə,laiz/ *vt* neutralizar

**never** /'nɛvər/ *adv* nunca, jamás; de ningún modo, no; ni aun, ni siquiera. **Better late than n.,** Más vale tarde que nunca. **Never look a gift horse in the mouth,** A caballo regalado no se le mira el diente. **Were the hour n. so late,** Por más tarde que fuese la hora. **n. again,** nunca jamás. **n. a one,** ni siquiera uno. **n. a whit,** ni pizca. **N. mind!** ¡No importa! ¡No te preocupes! ¡No hagas caso! **n.-ceasing,** continuo, incesante. **n.-ending,** inacabable, eterno, sin fin. **n.-failing,** infalible. **n.-to-be-forgotten,** inolvidable

**nevermore** /,nɛvər'mɔr/ *adv* nunca jamás

**nevertheless** /,nɛvərðə'lɛs/ *adv* sin embargo, no obstante, con todo

**new** /nu/ *a* nuevo; novel, fresco; distinto, diferente; moderno; (inexperienced) novato, no habituado; reciente. —*adv* (in compounds) recién. **as good as new,** como nuevo. **brand-new,** flamante, nuevecito. **new-born,** recién nacido. **new-comer,** recién llegado

(-da). **new-fashioned,** de última moda. **new-found,** recién hallado. **new-laid egg,** huevo fresco, *m*. **new moon,** luna nueva, *f*, novilunio, *m*. **new rich,** ricacho (-cha); indio, *m*. **new student,** alumno de nuevo ingreso. **New Testament,** Nuevo Testamento, *m*. **New World,** Nuevo Mundo, *m*. **New York** ( **er** ), *a* and *n* neoyorquino (-na). **New Zealand** ( **er** ), *a* and *n* neozelandés (-esa)

**newel** /'nuəl/ *n* (of stair) alma, *f*, árbol, nabo, *m*. **n.-post,** pilarote (de escalera), *m*

**newest** /'nuɪst/ *a superl* novísimo; más reciente

**Newfoundland** /'nufənlənd/ Terranova, *f*. **N. dog,** perro de Terranova, *m*

**New Guinea** /'gɪni/ Nueva Guinea, *f*

**newish** /'nuɪʃ/ *a* bastante nuevo

**newly** /'nuli/ *adv* nuevamente; hace poco, recientemente. The abb. form **recién** is used only with past part, e.g. *the n. painted door,* la puerta recién pintada. *the n.-weds,* los desposados, los recién casados

**newness** /'nunɪs/ *n* novedad, *f*; inexperiencia, falta de práctica, *f*; innovación, *f*

**New Orleans** /'ɔrliənz, ɔr'linz/ Nueva Orleans, *f*

**news** /nuz/ *n pl* noticias, *f pl*; nueva, *f*; reporte, aviso, *m*; novedad, *f*. **No n. is good n.,** Falta de noticias, buena señal. **piece of n.,** noticia, *f*. **What's the n.?** ¿Qué hay de nuevo? **n. agency,** agencia de noticias, agencia periodística, *f*. **n.-agent,** agente de la prensa, *m*; vendedor (-ra) de periódicos. **n. bulletin,** *Radio.* boletín de noticias, *m*. *Inf.* **n.-hound,** gacetillero (-ra). **n. item,** noticia de actualidad, *f*. **n.-print,** papel para periódicos, *m*. **n.-room,** gabinete de lectura, *m*. **n. reel,** película noticiera, revista cinematográfica, *f*, noticiario cinematográfico, noticiero *m*, actualidades, *f pl*. **n.-stand,** puesto de periódicos, quiosco de periódicos, *m*. **n. theater,** cine de actualidades, *m*

**newscast** /'nuz,kæst/ *n* noticiario, *m*

**newsletter circular** /'nuz,lɛtər/ noticiera, relación de sucesos, *f*

**New South Wales** La Nueva Gales del Sur, *f*

**newspaper** /'nuz,peipər/ *n* periódico, diario, noticiero, *m*. **n. clipping, n. cutting,** recorte de periódico, *m*. **n. paragraph,** suelto, *m*. **n. reporter,** reportero (-ra); periodista, *mf* **n. reporting,** reporterismo, *m*. **n. serial,** folletín, *m*, novela por entregas, *f*. **n. vendor,** vendedor (-ra) de periódicos, *m*

**news report** *n* reportaje, *m*

**newsy** /'nuzi/ *a Inf.* lleno de noticias, noticioso

**newt** /nut/ *n* tritón, *m*

**Newtonian** /nu'touniən/ *a* neutoniano

**New York** /jɔrk/ Nueva York, *f*

**New Zealand** /'zilənd/ Nueva Zelandia, *f*

**next** /nɛkst/ *a* (of place) siguiente, vecino, contiguo; (of time) próximo, siguiente. **on the n. page,** en la página siguiente. **the n. day,** el día siguiente. **the n.-door house,** la casa vecina. **the n. life,** la otra vida. **n. month** ( **yesar**), el mes (año) próximo (or que viene). **n. time,** otra vez, la próxima vez

**next** /nɛkst/ *adv* (of time) luego, en seguida; (of place) inmediatamente después. **I come n.,** Ahora me toca a mí. **It is n. to a certainty that...,** Es casi seguro que... **the n. best,** el segundo. **the n. of kin,** los pariente más cercarro, *m*, parientes más cercanos, *m pl*. **to wear n. to the skin,** llevar sobre la piel. **n. to,** al lado de, junto a; primero después de; casi. **n. to nothing,** casi nada, muy poco. **What n.?** ¿Qué más?; ¿Y ahora qué?

**nib** /nɪb/ *n* punto, tajo (de una pluma), *m*

**nibble** /'nɪbəl/ *vt* mordiscar, mordisquear, roer; (horses) rozar; (fish) picar; *Fig.* considerar, tantear; *vi* picar. —*n* mordisco, *m*; roedura, *f*

**Nicaraguan** /,nɪkə'ragwən/ *a* and *n* nicaragüeño (-ña)

**Nice** /nis/ Niza, *f*

**nice** /nais/ *a* escrupuloso, minucioso, exacto; (of persons) simpático, afable, amable; fino; (of things) agradable, bonito; bueno; sutil, delicado; (*Inf. Ironic.*) bonito. **a n. point,** un punto delicado. **a n. view,** una vista agradable (or bonita). **n.-looking,** guapo. **n. people,** gente fina, *f*; gente simpática, *f*

**nicely** /'naisli/ *adv* muy bien; con elegancia; primorosamente; con amabilidad, gentilmente; agradablemente

**Nicene** /nai'sin/ *a* niceno

**niceness** /'naisnis/ n exactitud, minuciosidad, f; (of persons) bondad, amabilidad, f; amenidad, hermosura, f; lo bonito; sutileza, f; refinamiento, m

**nicety** /'naisiti/ n exactitud, f; sutileza, f, refinamiento, m. **niceties,** n pl detalles, m pl. **to a n.,** con la mayor precisión; a la perfección

**niche** /nɪtʃ/ n nicho, templete, m; (vaulted) hornacina, f, Fig. **to find a n. for oneself,** encontrarse una buena posición; situarse

**nick** /nɪk/ vt cortar en muescas, mellar, tarjar. —n mella, muesca, f. **in the n. of time,** en el momento oportuno, a tiempo

**nickel** /'nɪkəl/ n níquel, m; Com. moneda de níquel, f. **n.-plated,** niquelado

**nickname** /'nɪk,neim/ vt apodar, motejar, apellidar. —n apodo, sobrenombre, mote, mal nombre, m

**nicotine** /'nɪkə,tin/ n nicotina, f

**nicotinism** /'nɪkəti,nɪzəm/ n nicotismo, m

**nictitating membrane** /'nɪktɪ,teitɪŋ/ n Anat. membrana nictitante, f

**niece** /nis/ n sobrina, f

**niggardliness** /'nɪɡərdlinɪs/ n tacañería, avaricia, parsimonia, mezquindad, f

**niggardly** /'nɪɡərdli/ a tacaño, avaricioso, mezquino, ruin, miserable

**niggling** /'nɪɡlɪŋ/ a nimio, meticuloso; escrupuloso, minucioso

**nigh.** /nai/ See **near**

**night** /nait/ n noche, f; Fig. oscuridad, f, tinieblas, f pl. **all n.,** toda la noche, la noche entera. **all n. service,** servicio nocturno permanente, m. **at** or **by n.,** de noche. **every n.,** todas las noches, cada noche. **Good n.!** ¡Buenas noches! **last n.,** ayer por la noche, anoche, la noche pasada. **restless n.,** noche mala, noche toledana, f. **the n. before last,** anteayer por la noche, m. **to-n.,** esta noche. **tomorrow n.,** mañana por la noche. **to be n.,** ser de noche. **to spend the n.,** pernoctar, pasar la noche. **n.-bird,** pájaro nocturno, m; Inf. trasnochador (-ra). **n.-blindness,** nictalopía, f. **n.-cap,** gorro de dormir, m. **n. clothes,** traje de dormir, m. **n. club,** cabaré m. **n. dew,** relente, sereno, m. **n. flying,** vuelo nocturno, m. **n.-jar,** Ornith. chotacabras, m. **n.-light,** mariposa, lamparilla, f. **n. mail,** último correo, m; tren correo de la noche, m. **n. school,** escuela nocturna, f. **n. shift,** turno de noche, m. **n. watch,** ronda de noche, f; Naut. sonochada, f. **n. watchman,** (in the street) sereno, m; (of a building) vigilante nocturno, m

**nightfall** /'nait,fɔl/ n anochecer, crepúsculo, atardecer, m

**nightgown** /'nait,gaun/ n camisa de noche, f

**nightingale** /'naitn̩,geil, 'naitɪŋ-/ n ruiseñor, m

**nightly** /'naitli/ a de noche; nocturno, nocturnal. —adv todas las noches, cada noche

**nightmare** /'nait,mɛər/ n pesadilla, f

**nightmarish** /'nait,mɛərɪʃ/ a de pesadilla, horrible

**nightshade** /'nait,ʃeid/ n Bot. hierba mora, f, solano, m

**nihilism** /'naiə,lɪzəm, 'ni-/ n nihilismo, m

**nihilist** /'naiəlɪst, 'ni-/ n nihilista, mf

**Nile, the** /nail/ el Nilo, m

**nimble** /'nɪmbəl/ a ágil, activo; vivo, listo. **n.-fingered,** ligero de dedos. **n.-witted,** despierto, vivo

**nimbleness** /'nɪmbəlnɪs/ n agilidad, actividad, f; viveza, habilidad, f

**nimbly** /'nɪmbli/ adv ágilmente, ligeramente

**nimbus** /'nɪmbəs/ n nimbo, m, aureola, f

**nincompoop** /'nɪnkəm,pup, 'nɪŋ-/ n papirote, m, papanatas, mf tonto (-ta)

**nine** /nain/ a and n nueve, m. **He is n.,** Tiene nueve años. **the N.,** las nueve Musas. **n. o'clock,** las nueve. **to be dressed up to the nines,** estar hecho un brazo de mar

**ninefold** /a 'nain,fould; adv. 'nain'fould/ a and adv nueve veces

**ninepins** /'nain,pɪnz/ n juego de bolos, m

**nineteen** /'nain'tin/ a and n diez y nueve, diecinueve m

**nineteenth** /'nain'tinθ/ a décimonono. —n (of month) el diez y nueve; (of monarchs) diez y nueve. **the n. century,** el siglo diez y nueve

**ninetieth** /'naintiəθ/ a nonagésimo, noventa

**ninety** /'nainti/ a and n noventa m. **n.-one,** noventa y uno. **n.-two,** noventa y dos. **the n.-first chapter,** el capítulo noventa y uno

**ninny** /'nɪni/ n parapoco, chancleta, mf; mentecato (-ta)

**ninth** /nainθ/ a noveno, nono. —n nueve, m; (of the month) el nueve (of sovereigns) nono. **one n.,** un noveno

**ninthly** /'nainθli/ adv en noveno (or nono) lugar

**nip** /nɪp/ vt pellizcar, pinchar; mordiscar, morder; (wither) marchitar; (freeze) helar; (run) correr. —vi pinchar; picar (el viento). —n pellizco, pinchazo, m; mordisco, m; (of spirits) trago, m; copita, f; (in the air) viento frío, hielo, m. **to nip in,** colarse dentro, deslizarse en. **to nip off,** pirarse, mudarse. Fig. **to nip in the bud,** cortar en flor

**nippers** /'nɪpərz/ pl alicates, m pl; tenacillas, pinzas, f pl

**nipping** /'nɪpɪŋ/ n pinchadura, f; mordedura, f. —a punzante; helado, glacial, mordiente. **n. off,** (of a point) despuntadura, f

**nipple** /'nɪpəl/ n pezón, m; pezón artificial, m

**nit** /nɪt/ n Ent. liendre, f

**niter** /'naitər/ n salitre, m

**nitrate** /'naitreit/ n Chem. nitrato, m

**nitric** /'naitrɪk/ a nítrico

**nitrite** /'naitrait/ n Chem. nitrito, m

**nitro-** prefix Chem. nitro. **n.-cellulose,** algodón pólvora, m. **n.-glycerine,** nitroglicerina, f

**nitrogen** /'naitrədʒən/ n Chem. nitrógeno, m

**nitrous** /'naitrəs/ a nitroso, salitral

**no** /nou/ a ningún, ninguno, ninguna, e.g. by no means, de ningún modo. No is often not translated in Sp., e.g. I have no time, No tengo tiempo. —adv no. —n voto negativo, no, m. to be of no account, no tener importancia; no significar nada. to be no good for, no servir para. to be of no use, ser inútil. to have no connection with, no tener nada que ver con. for no reason, sin motivo alguno. "No Admittance," «Entrada Prohibida.» no, indeed, Cierto que no. no-man's land, tierra de nadie, f. no more, no más. No more of this! ¡No hablemos más de eso! no one, nadie, ninguno. no sooner, no bien, tan pronto (como). no such thing, no tal. "No Thoroughfare," «Prohibido el Paso.» whether or not, sea o no sea

**Noah's Ark** /'nouəz/ n arca de Noé, f

**nobility** /nou'bɪlɪti/ n nobleza, f; (of rank) aristocracia, nobleza, f; (of conduct) caballerosidad, hidalguía, generosidad, bondad, f; (grandeur) grandeza, sublimidad, f. the higher n., los nobles de primera clase

**noble** /'noubəl/ a noble; (in rank) aristocrático, noble, linajudo; (of conduct) caballeroso, generoso; (of buildings) sublime, magnífico. —n noble, m, aristócrata, mf to make n., ennoblecer. n.-mindedness, generosidad, grandeza de alma, f. n. title, título de nobleza, título del reino, m

**noblewoman** /'noubəl,wumən/ n dama noble, mujer noble, aristócrata, f

**nobly** /'noubli/ adv noblemente, generosamente. n. born, nacido de nacimiento

**nobody** /'nou,bɒdi/ n nadie, ninguno. There was n. there, No había nadie allí. Inf. a n., un (una) cualquiera, una persona insignificante. n. else, nadie más, ningún otro

**nocturnal** /nɒk'tɜrnl̩/ a nocturno, nocherniego, nocturnal

**nocturne** /'nɒktɜrn/ n Mus. nocturno, m

**nod** /nɒd/ vt inclinar la cabeza; hacer una señal (or señas) con la cabeza; vi dar cabezadas; cabecear; (of trees) mecerse, inclinarse; inclinar la cabeza. —n señal (or seña) con la cabeza, f; inclinación de la cabeza, f; cabeceo, m, cabezada, f. A nod is as good as a wink, A buen entendedor pocas palabras. He nodded to me as he passed, Me saludó con la cabeza al pasar. He signed to me with a nod, Me hizo una señal con la cabeza

**nodding** /'nɒdɪŋ/ a que cabecea; Bot. colgante, inclinado; temblante. —n cabeceo, m; saludo con la cabeza, m

**noddle** /'nɒdl̩/ n mollera, f

**node** /noud/ n (Bot. Med.) nudo, m

**nodule** /'nɒdʒul/ n nódulo, m; nudillo, m

**noise** /nɔiz/ n ruido, son, m; tumulto, clamor, estruendo, alboroto, m. **to make a n.,** hacer ruido. **to n. abroad,** divulgar, publicar

**noiseless** /'nɔizlɪs/ a silencioso, callado, sin ruido

**noiselessness** /'nɔizlɪsnɪs/ n silencio, m, falta de ruido, f

**noisily** /'nɔizəli/ adv ruidosamente

**noisiness** /'nɔizɪnɪs/ n ruido, estrépito, tumulto, clamor, m; (of voices) gritería, f

**noisome** /'nɔisəm/ a ofensivo; fétido, apestoso

**noisy** /'nɔizi/ a ruidoso; estruendoso; estrepitoso, clamoroso

**nomad** /'noumæd/ a nómada, errante; (of flocks) trashumante. —n nómada, mf

**nomadism** /'noumædɪzəm/ n nomadismo, m

**nomenclature** /'noumən,kleitʃər/ n nomenclatura, f

**nominal** /'nɒmənl/ a nominal; titular; insignificante, de poca importancia. **the n. head,** el director en nombre

**nominalism** /'nɒmənl,ɪzəm/ n nominalismo, m

**nominalist** /'nɒmənlɪst/ a and n nominalista mf

**nominally** /'nɒmənli/ adv nominalmente, en nombre

**nominate** /'nɒmə,neit/ vt nombrar, designar, elegir; fijar, señalar

**nominating** /'nɒmə,neitɪŋ/ a nominador

**nomination** /,nɒmə'neiʃən/ n nombramiento, m, nominación, f; señalamiento, m

**nominator** /'nɒmə,neitər/ n nominador (-ra)

**nominee** /,nɒmə'ni/ n nómino propuesto, m

**non** /nɒn/ adv non; des-; in-; falta de. **non-acceptance,** rechazo, m. **non-acquaintance,** ignorancia, f. **non-admission,** no admisión, f; denegación, f, rechazo, m. **non-aggression,** no agresión, f. **non-alcoholic,** no alcohólico. **non-appearance,** ausencia, f; Law. no comparecencia, contumacia, f. **non-arrival,** ausencia, f; falta de recibo, f. **non-attendance,** falta de asistencia, ausencia, f. **non-carbonated,** sin gas. **non-combatant,** no combatiente. **non-commissioned officer,** oficial subalterno, m. **non-committal,** evasivo, equívoco, ambiguo. **non-compliance,** falta de obediencia, f. **non-concurrence,** falta de acuerdo, f. **non-conducting,** no conductivo. **non-conductor,** mal conductor, m; Elec. aislador, m. **non-contagious,** no contagioso. **non-cooperation,** Polit. resistencia pasiva, f; no cooperación, f. **non-delivery,** falta de entrega, f. **non-essential,** no esencial, prescindible. **non-execution,** no cumplimiento, m. **non-existence,** no existencia, f. **non-existent,** inexistente, no existente. **non-intervention,** no intervención, f. **non-manufacturing,** no industrial. **non-member,** visitante, mf **non-observance,** incumplimiento, m; violación, f. **non-payment,** falta de pago, f. **non-performance,** falta de ejecución, f. **non-poisonous,** no venenoso, innocuo. **non-resistance,** falta de resistencia, f; obediencia pasiva, f. **non-skid,** antideslizante, antirresbaladizo. **non-smoking,** que no fuma; (of a railway compartment, etc.) para no fumadores. **non-stop,** continuo, incesante; directo, sin parar; Aer. sin escalas

**nonagenarian** /,nɒnədʒə'nɛəriən/ a and n nonagenario (-ia)

**non-aligned** /,nɒn ə'laind/ a no abanderado

**non-alignment** /,nɒn ə'lainmənt/ n no abanderamiento m

**nonce word** /nɒns/ n palabra ocasional, f

**nonchalance** /,nɒnʃə'lɑns/ n aplomo, m, indiferencia, frialdad, calma, f

**nonchalant** /,nɒnʃə'lɑnt/ a indiferente, frío, impasible

**nonchalantly** /,nɒnʃə'lɑntli/ adv con indiferencia

**nonconformist** /,nɒnkən'fɔrmɪst/ a and n disidente mf; a inconforme, n, inconformista, mf

**nonconformity** /,nɒnkən'fɔrmɪti/ n disidencia, f

**nondescript** /,nɒndɪ'skrɪpt/ a indeterminado, indefinido, indeciso, mediocre

**none** /nʌn/ pron nadie, ninguno; nada. —a and n ninguno (-na). —adv no; de ningún modo, de ninguna manera. **I have n. of your things,** No tenemos ninguna de tus cosas. **I was n. the worse,** No me hallaba peor. **N. can read his account with pleasure,** Nadie puede leer su narración con gusto. **n. the less,** no menos; sin embargo

**nonentity** /nɒn'ɛntɪti/ n persona sin importancia, medianía, f, cero, m

**nones** /nounz/ n pl Eccl. nona, f; (Roman Calendar) nonas, f pl,

**nonplussed** /nɒn'plʌst/ a cortado, perplejo, confuso

**non-profit** /nɒn 'prɒfɪt/ a sin fines de lucro, sin fines lucrativos

**non-self-governing** /'nɒn sɛlf'gʌvərnɪŋ/ a no autónomo

**nonsense** /'nɒnsɛns/ n disparate, despropósito, desatino, m, absurdidad, f; Inf. galimatías, m; pamplina, patraña, f. **to talk n.,** hablar sin ton ni son. **N.!** ¡otro perro con este hueso! ¡Patrañas!

**nonsensical** /nɒn'sɛnsɪkəl/ a absurdo, ridículo, disparatado

**noodle** /'nudl/ n Cul. tallarín, m; Inf. mentecato (-ta), bobo (-ba)

**nook** /nʊk/ n escondrijo, lugar retirado, rincón, m

**noon** /nun/ n mediodía, m; Fig. punto culminante, apogeo, m, a de mediodía, meridional. **at n.,** a mediodía

**noose** /nus/ vt coger con lazos. —n lazo corredizo, dogal, m

**nopal** /'noupəl/ n Bot. nopal, m

**No Parking** «Se Prohibe Estacionar,» «Se Prohibe Estacionarse»

**nor** /nɔr; unstressed nər/ conjunc ni, no, tampoco. **He removed neither his coat nor his hat,** No se quitó ni el gabán ni el sombrero. **Nor was this the first time,** Y no fue ésta la primera vez. **Nor I,** Ni yo tampoco

**Nordic** /'nɔrdɪk/ a and n nórdico (-ca)

**norm** /nɔrm/ n modelo, m, norma, regla, pauta, f; (of size) marca, f; (Bot. Zool.) tipo, m

**normal** /'nɔrməl/ a normal; común, natural, corriente, regular; Math. perpendicular, normal. —n condición normal, f, estado normal, m; Math. normal, f. **to become n.,** normalizarse, hacerse normal. **to make n.,** normalizar. **n. school,** escuela normal, f

**normality** /nɔr'mælɪti/ n normalidad, f

**normalization** /,nɔrmələ'zeiʃən/ n normalización, f

**normalize** /'nɔrmə,laiz/ vt normalizar

**normally** /'nɔrməli/ adv normalmente

**Norman** /'nɔrmən/ a and n normando (-da)

**Normandy** /'nɔrməndi/ Normandía, f

**Norse** /nɔrs/ n noruego (language), m, a escandinavo

**Norseman** /'nɔrsmən/ n normando, viking (pl -os), hombre del norte, m

**north** /nɔrθ/ n norte, m. —a del norte, septentrional. **n. by west,** norte, cuarta noroeste. **n. of the city,** al norte de la ciudad. **N.-American,** a and n norteamericano (-na). **n.-east,** a and n del nordeste, m. **n.-easter,** viento del nordeste, m. **n.-easterly,** del nordeste (winds). **n.-eastern,** del nordeste (places). **n.-eastward,** hacia al nordeste. **n.-n.-east,** nornordeste, m. **n.-n.-west,** nornorueste, m. **n.-polar,** ártico. **N. Star,** estrella del norte, estrella polar, f. **n.-west,** noroeste, m. **n.-wester,** viento del noroeste, m. **n.-westerly,** del noroeste (winds). **n.-westerly gale,** temporal del noroeste, m. **n.-western,** del noroeste; situado al noroeste, m. **n.-westwards,** hacia el noroeste. **n. wind,** el viento del norte, el cierzo

**North America,** Norteamérica, América del Norte, f

**northern** /'nɔrðərn/ a del norte, septentrional, norteño; (of races) nórdico. **N. Cross,** crucero, m. **n. lights,** aurora boreal, f

**northerner** /'nɔrðərnər/ n hombre del norte, m, habitante del norte, m

**northernmost** /'nɔrðərn,moust/ a superl al extremo norte, más septentrional

**northwards** /'nɔrθwərdz/ adv hacia el norte

**Norway** /'nɔrwei/ Noruega, f

**Norwegian** /nɔr'widʒən/ a and n noruego (-ga); (language) noruego, m

**nose** /nouz/ n nariz, f; (of animals) hocico, m; (sense of smell) olfato, m; (of ships) proa, f; (of jug) pico, m, boca, f; (projecting piece) cuerno, m, nariz, f; (of airplane) cabeza, f, vt acariciar con la nariz; avanzar lentamente. —vi husmear, olfatear. **to n. into,** Inf. meter las narices, poner baza. **to n. out,** descubrir, averiguar. **to bleed at the n.,** echar sangre por las narices. **to blow one's n.,** sonar (or limpiarse) las narices. **to keep one's n. to the grindstone,** estar sobre el yunque, batir el cobre. *Fig.* **to lead by the n.,** tener a uno agarrado por las narices. **to pay through the n.,** costar un ojo de la cara. **to speak through the n.,** ganguear. **to turn up one's n.,** *Fig.* hacer gestos (a), volver la cara. **flat n.,** nariz chata, *f.* **snub n.,** nariz respingona, *f.* **well-shaped n.,** nariz perfilada, *f.* **under one's n.,** bajo las narices de uno. **n.-bag,** cebadera, mochila, *f;* morral, *m.* **n.-bleeding,** *Med.* epistaxis, *f;* hemorragia de las narices, *f.* **n.-dive,** *Aer.* descenso de cabeza, picado, *m.* —*vi* picar. **n.-piece,** (of microscope) ocular, *m.* **n.-ring,** (of a bull, etc.) narigón, *m*

**-nosed** *a* de nariz..., con la nariz...

**nosegay** /'nouz,geɪ/ *n* ramillete, *m*

**nosey Parker** /'nouzi 'pɑrkər/ *n Inf.* mequetrefe, *m;* cócora, *mf*

**No Smoking** «Prohibido Fumar», Se Prohíbe Fumar

**nostalgia** /nɒ'stældʒə/ *n* nostalgia, añoranza, *f*

**nostalgic** /nɒ'stældʒɪk/ *a* nostálgico

**nostril** /'nɒstrəl/ *n* ventana de la nariz, *f, n pl* **nostrils,** narices, *f pl*

**nostrum** /'nɒstrəm/ *n* panacea, *f,* curalotodo, *m;* medicina patentada, *f*

**not** /nɒt/ *adv* no; sin; ni, ni siquiera. **Is it not true? We think not,** ¿No es verdad? No lo creemos. **You have seen Mary, have you not?** Vd. ha visto a María, ¿verdad? **not caring whether he came or not,** sin preocuparse de que viniese o no. **not that he will come,** no es decir que venga. **not at all,** de ningún modo; (courtesy) ¡de nada! **not even,** ni siquiera. **not guilty,** no culpable. **not one,** ni uno. **not so much as,** no tanto como; ni siquiera. **It is not so much that, as it is...** No es tanto eso, cuanto que... **not to say,** por no decir

**notability** /,noutə'bɪlɪti/ *n* notabilidad, *f;* (person) notable, *mf* persona de importancia, *f*

**notable** /'noutəbəl/ *a* notable, señalado, memorable; digno de atención. **n.** persona eminente, *f,* notable, *mf*

**notably** /'noutəbli/ *adv* notablemente, señaladamente

**notary** /'noutəri/ *n* notario, escribano, *m*

**notation** /nou'teɪʃən/ *n* notación, *f*

**notch** /nɒtʃ/ *vt* cortar muescas (en); mellar, ranurar, entallar. —*n* muesca, mella, ranura, entalladura, *f*

**note** /nout/ *vt* notar, observar; anotar, apuntar; advertir, hacerse cuenta de. —*n Mus.* nota, *f;* son, acento, *m;* (letter) recado, billete, *m;* anotación, glosa, *f;* apuntación, *f,* apunte, *m,* nota, *f;* (importance) importancia, distinción, *f; Com.* vale, abonaré, *m;* (sign) marca, señal, *f.* **to n. down,** anotar. **worthy of note,** digno de atención. **n.-book,** libro de apuntes, cuaderno, *m,* libreta, *f.* **n.-case,** cartera, *f, Com.* de mano, pagaré, *m.* **n.-paper,** papel de escribir, *m.* **n.-taker,** apuntador (-ra)

**noted** /'noutɪd/ *a* célebre, famoso, ilustre, eminente, insigne

**noteworthy** /'nout,wɜrði/ *a* digno de nota, notable, digno de atención

**nothing** /'nʌθɪŋ/ *n* nada, *f;* la nada; cero, *m.* —*adv* en nada. **to come to n.,** anonadarse, fracasar. **to do n.,** no hacer nada. **to do n. but,** no hacer más que. **to have n. to do with,** no tener nada que ver con; *Inf.* no tener arte ni parte en. **There is n. else to do,** No hay nada más que hacer; No hay más remedio. **There is n. to fear,** No hay de que tener miedo. **We could make n. of the book,** No llegamos a comprender el libro. **for n.,** de balde, en vano; gratis. **next to n.,** casi nada. **n. else or more,** nada más. **n. like,** ni con mucho. **n. much,** poca cosa. **n. new,** nada nuevo. **n. similar,** nada semejante. **n. to speak of,** poca cosa

**nothingness** /'nʌθɪŋnɪs/ *n* nada, *f*

**notice** /'noutɪs/ *vt* observar, reparar en, darse cuenta (de), marcar, caer en la cuenta (de), fijarse (en). —*n* observación, atención, *f;* aviso, *m,* notificación, *f;* anuncio, *m;* (term) plazo, *m;* (review) crítica, *f.* **at short n.,** a corto aviso. **until further n.,** hasta nuevo aviso (or orden). **to attract n.,** atraer la atención. **I hadn't noticed,** No me había fijado. **to be beneath one's n.,** no merecer su atención. **to be under n.,** es-

tar dimitido. **to bring to the n. of,** dar noticia de. **to escape n.,** pasar desapercibido. **to give n.,** hacer saber, informar; (of employer) despedir (a); (of employee) dimitir, dar la dimisión. **to take n. of,** notar, darse cuenta de; hacer caso, atender (a). **n. board,** letrero, tablero de anuncios, *m.* **n. to quit,** desahúcio, *m*

**noticeable** /'noutɪsəbəl/ *a* perceptible, evidente; digno de observación, notable

**noticeably** /'noutɪsəbli/ *adv* perceptiblemente; notablemente

**notifiable** /,noutə'faɪəbəl/ *a* declarable, notificable

**notification** /,noutəfɪ'keɪʃən/ *n* notificación, intimación, advertencia, *f,* aviso, *m*

**notify** /'noutə,faɪ/ *vt* notificar, comunicar, avisar, intimar, hacer saber

**notion** /'nouʃən/ *n* noción, idea, *f,* concepto, *m;* (view) opinión, *f,* parecer, *m;* (novelty) novedad, *f;* artículo de fantasía, *m.* **I have a n. that...,** Tengo la idea de que..., Sospecho que... **I haven't a n.,** No tengo idea

**No Tipping** «No Se Admiten Propinas»

**notoriety** /,noutə'raɪɪti/ *n* notoriedad, publicidad, *f;* escándalo, *m;* persona notoria, *f*

**notorious** /nou'tɔriəs/ *a* notorio, famoso, conocido; escandaloso, sensacional

**notoriously** /nou'tɔriəsli/ *adv* notoriamente

**notwithstanding** /,nɒtwɪð'stændɪŋ/ *prep* a pesar de. —*adv* sin embargo, no obstante. —*conjunc* aunque, bien que, por más que

**nougat** /'nugət/ *n* turrón, *m*

**nought** /nɔt/ *n Math.* cero, *m;* nada, *f*

**noun** /naun/ *n* substantivo, nombre, *m*

**nourish** /'nɜrɪʃ/ *vt* sustentar, alimentar, nutrir; *Fig.* fomentar, favorecer

**nourishing** /'nɜrɪʃɪŋ/ *a* nutritivo, alimenticio, nutricio

**nourishment** /'nɜrɪʃmənt/ *n* nutrición, *f;* sustento, *m;* alimento, *m; Fig.* fomento, pasto, *m*

**Nova Scotia** /'nouvə 'skouʃə/ Nueva Escocia, *f*

**novel** /'nɒvəl/ *a* nuevo, original, inacostumbrado. —*n* novela, *f.* **n. of roguery,** novela picaresca, *f*

**novelette** /,nɒvə'lɛt/ *n* novela corta, *f*

**novelist** /'nɒvəlɪst/ *n* novelista, *mf*

**novelty** /'nɒvəlti/ *n* novedad, *f;* innovación, *f;* cambio, *m*

**November** /nou'vɛmbər/ *n* noviembre, *m*

**novice** /'nɒvɪs/ *n Eccl.* novicio (-ia); comenzante, principiante, *mf,* aspirante, *m*

**novocain** /'nouvə,keɪn/ *n Med.* novocaína, *f*

**now** /nau/ *adv* ahora, actualmente, al presente, a la fecha; en seguida, ahora, inmediatamente; poco ha, hace poco; pues bien. —*interj* ¡A ver! ¡Vamos! —*conjunc* pero, mas. —*n* presente, *m,* actualidad, *f.* **before now,** antes, en otras ocasiones, ya, previamente. **just now,** ahora mismo, hace poco. **now... now,** ya... ya; sucesivamente, en turno. **now and then,** de vez en cuando, de tarde en tarde. **now that,** ya que, ahora que, dado que. **until now,** hasta el presente, hasta aquí, hasta ahora

**nowadays** /'nauə,deɪz/ *adv* hoy en día, actualmente, en nuestros días

**nowhere** /'nou,wɛr/ *adv* en ninguna parte. **in the middle of n.,** donde Cristo dio las tres voces. **n. else,** en ninguna otra parte. *Inf.* **n. near,** ni con mucho; muy lejos (de)

**nowise** /'nou,waɪz/ *adv* de ningún modo, en modo alguno, de ninguna manera

**noxious** /'nɒkʃəs/ *a* dañoso, nocivo; pestífero

**noxiousness** /'nɒkʃəsnɪs/ *n* nocividad, *f*

**nozzle** /'nɒzəl/ *n* (of a hose-pipe) boquilla, *f; Mech.* gollete, *m;* tubo de salida, *m,* tobera, *f;* inyector, *m*

**n.p.** (no place) s.l. (sin lugar)

**nuance** /'nuans/ *n* matiz, *m,* gradación, sombra, *f*

**nubile** /'nubɪl, -baɪl/ *a* núbil

**nuclear** /'nukliər/ *a* nuclear

**nucleus** /'nukliəs/ *n* núcleo, *m;* centro, foco, *m*

**nude** /nud/ *a* desnudo, nudo

**nudge** /nʌdʒ/ *vt* dar un codazo (a). —*n* codazo, *m*

**nudism** /'nudɪzəm/ *n* nudismo, *m*

**nudist** /'nudɪst/ *n* nudista, *mf*

**nudity** /'nuditi/ *n* desnudez, *f*

**nugget** /'nʌgɪt/ *n Mineral.* pepita, *f*

**nuisance** /'nusəns/ *n* molestia, incomodidad, *f*, fastidio, *m*; *Inf.* tostón, *m*, lata, *f.* **to make a n. of oneself,** meterse donde no le llaman, ser un pelmazo. **What a n.!** ¡Qué lata! ¡Qué fastidio!

**null** /nʌl/ *a* nulo, inválido, sin fuerza legal. **n. and void,** nulo, írrito

**nullification** /ˌnʌləfɪ'keiʃən/ *n* anulación, invalidación, *f*

**nullity** /'nʌlɪti/ *n* nulidad, *f*

**numb** /nʌm/ *vt* entumecer, entorpecer. —*a* entumecido; torpe, dormido; paralizado; *Fig.* insensible, pasmado. **n. with cold,** entumecido de frío

**number** /'nʌmbər/ *vt* numerar, contar; poner número (a); (pages of a book) foliar; ascender a. —*n* número, *m*; (figure) cifra, *f*; (crowd) multitud, muchedumbre, *f*; cantidad, *f*; (of a periodical) ejemplar, *m*; *Gram.* número, *m*; *pl* versos, *m pl.* **Numbers,** (Bible) Números, *m pl*; **to be numbered among,** figurar entre. **among the n. of,** entre la muchedumbre de. **a n. of,** varios, muchos, una cantidad de. **in great n.,** en gran número; en su mayoría. **6 Peace Street,** Calle de la Paz N° (número) 6. **one of their n.,** uno entre ellos. **n. board,** (racing) indicador, *m.* **n. plate,** *Auto.* chapa de identidad, placa de número, *f*

**numbering** /'nʌmbərɪŋ/ *n* numeración, *f*

**numberless** /'nʌmbərlɪs/ *a* innumerable, sin número, sin fin, infinito

**numbness** /'nʌmnɪs/ *n* entumecimiento, entorpecimiento, *m*; *Fig.* insensibilidad, *f*

**numeral** /'numərəl/ *a* numeral. —*n* número, *m*, cifra, *f*; *Gram.* nombre o adjetivo numeral, *m*

**numerator** /'numəˌreitər/ *n* numerador

**numerical** /nu'mɛrɪkəl/ *a* numérico

**numerous** /'numərəs/ *a* numeroso; nutrido, grande; muchos (-as)

**numerousness** /'numərəsnɪs/ *n* numerosidad, multitud, muchedumbre, *f*

**numismatic** /ˌnumɪz'mætɪk/ *a* numismático. —*n pl* **numismatics,** numismática, *f*

**numismatist** /nu'mɪzmətɪst/ *n* numismático, *m*

**numskull** /'nʌm,skʌl/ *n* zote, topo, *m*

**nun** /nun/ *n* monja, religiosa, *f.* **to become a nun,** profesar, tomar el hábito, meterse monja

**nuncio** /'nʌnʃiˌou/ *n* nuncio, *m.* **acting n.,** pronuncio, *m*

**nunnery** /'nʌnəri/ *n* convento de monjas, *m*

**nuptial** /'nʌpʃəl/ *a* nupcial. —*n pl* **nuptials,** nupcias, *f pl*, enlace, *m.* **n. mass,** *Eccl.* misa de velaciones, *f.* **n. song,** epitalamio, *m*

**nurse** /nɜrs/ *vt* criar; dar de mamar (a), amamantar; (the sick) cuidar, asistir; (fondle) acariciar, mecer; *Fig.* fomentar, promover. —*vi* trabajar como enfermera. —*n* (of the sick) enfermera, *f*; (wet) nodriza, ama de leche, *f*; (children's) niñera, *f*; *Fig.* fomentador, *m.* **male n.,** enfermero, *m*

**nursery** /'nɜrsəri/ *n Agr.* plantel, vivero semillero, criadero, *m*; (children's room) cuarto de los niños, *m*; *Fig.* sementera, *f*; semillero, *m.* **n. governess,** aya, *f.* **n. rhyme,** canción infantil, *f*

**nurseryman** /'nɜrsərimən/ *n* horticultor, *m*; jardinero, *m*

**nursing** /'nɜrsɪŋ/ *n* lactancia, crianza, *f*; (of the sick) asistencia, *f*, cuido, *m.* **n. home,** clínica, *f.* **n. mother,** madre lactante, *f*

**nurture** /'nɜrtʃər/ *vt* alimentar; criar, educar. —*n* nutrición, alimentación, *f*; crianza, educación, *f*

**nut** /nʌt/ *vi* coger nueces. —*n Bot.* nuez, *f*; *Mech.* tuerca, hembra de tornillo, *f*, *Inf.* **to be a tough nut to crack,** ser un tío de cuidado. **to crack nuts,** cascar nueces. **to go nutting,** coger nueces. **cashew nut,** anacardo, *m.* **loose nut,** *Mech.* tuerca aflojada, *f.* **nut-brown,** castaño, *m.* **nut tree,** nogal, *m*

**nutcrackers** /'nʌtˌkrækərz/ *n pl* cascanueces, quebrantanueces, *m*

**nutmeg** /'nʌtmɛg/ *n* nuez moscada, nuez de especia, *f*

**nutria** /'nutriə/ *n Zool.* nutria, *f*

**nutriment** /'nutrəmənt/ *n* nutrimento, alimento, *m*

**nutrition** /nu'trɪʃən/ *n* nutrición, alimentación, *f*

**nutritious, nutritive** /nu'trɪʃəs; 'nutrɪtɪv/ *a* nutritivo, alimenticio, atible

**nutshell** /'nʌtˌʃɛl/ *n* cáscara de nuez, *f.* **to put in a n.,** decir en resumidas cuentas, decir en forma apastillada

**nutty** /'nʌti/ *a* de nuez

**nuzzle** /'nʌzəl/ *vt* acariciar con la nariz

**nylon** /'nailɒn/ *n* nilón, nylon, *m.* **n. stockings,** medias de cristal (or de nilón), *f pl*

**nymph** /nɪmf/ *n* ninfa, *f*; *Ent.* crisálida, *f.* **n.-like,** como una ninfa; de ninfa

**nymphomania** /ˌnɪmfə'meiniə/ *n* ninfomanía, *f*, furor uterino, *m*

# O

**o** /ou/ *n* (letter) o, *f, interj* ¡o! **O that...!** ¡Ojalá que!
**oaf** /ouf/ *n* zoquete, zamacuco, *m*
**oafish** /'oufɪʃ/ *a* lerdo, torpe
**oafishness** /'oufɪʃnɪs/ *n* torpeza, estupidez, *f*
**oak** /ouk/ *n* (tree and wood) roble, *m, a* de roble.
  **carved oak,** roble tallado, *m.* **holm-oak,** encina, *f.*
  **oak-apple,** agalla, *f.* **oak grove,** robledo, *m*
**oakum** /'oukəm/ *n* estopa, *f*
**oar** /ɔr/ *n* remo, *m.* **to lie on the oars,** cesar de remar. **to pull at the oars,** bogar, remar. **to put in
  one's oar,** *Inf.* meter baza. **to ship the oars,** armar
  los remos. **to unship the oars,** desarmar los remos.
  **oar-stroke,** palada, *f*
**oarsman** /'ɔrzmən/ *n* remero, bogador, *m*
**oarsmanship** /'ɔrzmən,ʃɪp/ *n* arte de remar, *m, or f*
**oasis** /ou'eisɪs/ *n* oasis, *m*
**OAS (Organization of American States)** OEA (Organización de los Estados Americanos)
**oast** /oust/ *n* horno para secar el lúpulo, *m*
**oat** /out/ *n Bot.* avena, *f.* **wild oat,** avena silvestre, *f.*
  **to sow one's wild oats,** correrla, andarse a la flor del
  berro. **oat field,** avenal, *m*
**oath** /ouθ/ *n* juramento, *m;* (curse) blasfemia, *f,* reniego, *m.* **on o.,** bajo juramento. **to break an o.,** violar el juramento. **to put on o.,** tomar juramento,
  hacer prestar juramento. **to take an o.,** prestar (or
  hacer) juramento. **to take the o. of allegiance,** jurar
  la bandera
**oatmeal** /'out,mil/ *n* harina de avena, *f*
**obduracy** /'ɒbdʊrəsi/ *n* obduración, obstinación, terquedad, *f*
**obdurate** /'ɒbdʊrɪt/ *a* obstinado, terco, porfiado. **He
  is o. to our requests,** Es sordo a nuestros ruegos
**obedience** /ou'bidiəns/ *n* obediencia, sumisión, docilidad, *f.* **blind o.,** obediencia ciega, *f.* **in o. to,** conforme a, de acuerdo con
**obedient** /ou'bidiənt/ *a* obediente, sumiso, dócil. **to
  be o. to,** ser obediente (a), obedecer (a)
**obediently** /ou'bidiəntli/ *adv* obedientemente, dócilmente. **Yours o.,** Su atento servidor (su att. s.)
**obeisance** /ou'beisəns, ou'bi-/ *n* reverencia, cortesía,
  *f,* saludo, *m;* (homage) homenaje, *m*
**obelisk** /'ɒbəlɪsk/ *n* obelisco, *m*
**obese** /ou'bis/ *a* obeso, corpulento, grueso, gordo
**obesity** /ou'bisɪti/ *n* obesidad, gordura, corpulencia, *f*
**obey** /ou'bei/ *vt and vi* obedecer. —*vt* (carry out)
  cumplir, observar. **to be obeyed,** ser obedecido
**obfuscate** /'ɒbfə,skeit/ *vt* ofuscar, cegar
**obfuscation** /,ɒbfə'skeiʃən/ *n* ofuscamiento, *m,* confusión, *f*
**obituary** /ou'bɪtʃu,ɛri/ *a* mortuorio, necrológico. —*n*
  obituario, *m,* necrología, *f.* **o. column,** (in newspaper) sección necrológica, *f.* **o. notice,** esquela de defunción, *f*
**object** /*n.* 'ɒbdʒɪkt; *v.* əb'dʒɛkt/ *n* objeto, artículo, *m,*
  cosa, *f;* (purpose) propósito, intento, *m;* (aim) fin,
  término, *m; Gram.* complemento, *m; Inf.* individuo,
  *m.* —*vt* objetar, poner reparos (a). —*vi* oponerse,
  poner objeciones. **I o. to that remark,** Protesto contra
  esa observación. **If you don't o.,** Si Vd. no tiene inconveniente. **o. finder,** objetivo, *m.* **o. lesson,** lección de cosas, *f;* lección práctica, *f*
**objection** /əb'dʒɛkʃən/ *n* objeción, protesta, *f,* reparo,
  *m;* (obstacle) dificultad, *f,* inconveniente, *m.* **to have
  no o.,** no tener inconveniente. **to raise an o.,** hacer
  constar una protesta, poner una objeción
**objectionable** /əb'dʒɛkʃənəbəl/ *a* censurable, reprensible; desagradable, molesto
**objective** /əb'dʒɛktɪv/ *a* objetivo; *Gram.* acusativo.
  —*n* objetivo, propósito, *m;* destinación, *f; Mil.* objetivo,
  *m, Gram.* **o. case,** caso acusativo, *m,*
**objectivism** /əb'dʒɛktə,vɪzəm/ *n Philos.* objetivismo,
  *m*
**objectivity** /,ɒbdʒɪk'tɪvɪti/ *n* objetividad, *f*
**objector** /əb'dʒɛktər/ *n* objetante, *mf,* impugnador

(-ra). **conscientious o.,** (dissident) el, *m, (f,* la) que
  protesta contra; (pacifist) pacifista, *mf*
**oblation** /ɒ'bleiʃən/ *n* oblación, ofrenda, *f*
**obligation** /,ɒblɪ'geiʃən/ *n* obligación, *f;* deber, *m,*
  precisión, *f;* compromiso, *m.* **of o.,** de deber; de precepto. **to be under an o.,** estar bajo una obligación;
  deber un favor. **to place under an o.,** poner bajo una
  obligación
**obligatory** /ə'blɪgə,tɔri/ *a* obligatorio, forzoso
**oblige** /ə'blaidʒ/ *vt* (insist on) obligar, hacer, forzar;
  (gratify) hacer un favor (a), complacer. **He obliged
  me with a match,** Me hizo el favor de una cerilla.
  **They are much obliged to you,** Le están muy reconocidos. **Much obliged!** ¡Se agradece!
**obliging** /ə'blaidʒɪŋ/ *a* atento, condescendiente, complaciente, servicial
**obligingly** /ə'blaidʒɪŋli/ *adv* cortésmente
**obligingness** /ə'blaidʒɪŋnɪs/ *n* cortesía, amabilidad,
  bondad, *f*
**oblique** /ə'blik/ *a* oblicuo, sesgado; (indirect) indirecto, evasivo; *Gram.* oblicuo
**obliquely** /ə'blikli/ *adv* oblicuamente, al sesgo, sesgadamente; indirectamente. **to place o.,** poner al sesgo
**obliquity** /ə'blɪkwɪti/ *n* oblicuidad, *f,* sesgo, *m;* (of
  conduct, etc.) tortuosidad, *f*
**obliterate** /ə'blɪtə,reit/ *vt* borrar; destruir, aniquilar.
  **to be obliterated,** borrarse; quedar destruido
**obliteration** /ə,blɪtə'reiʃən/ *n* testación, *f;* destrucción, *f.* **o. raid,** bombardeo de saturación, *m*
**oblivion** /ə'blɪviən/ *n* olvido, *m.* **to cast into o.,**
  echar al olvido
**oblivious** /ə'blɪviəs/ *a* olvidadizo, descuidago
**oblong** /'ɒb,lɔŋ/ *a* oblongo, cuadrilongo, rectangular.
  —*n* rectángulo, cuadrilongo, *m*
**obloquy** /'ɒbləkwi/ *n* infamia, maledicencia, deshonra, *f*
**obnoxious** /əb'nɒkʃəs/ *a* odioso, ofensivo, aborrecible
**obnoxiously** /əb'nɒkʃəsli/ *adv* odiosamente
**obnoxiousness** /əb'nɒkʃəsnɪs/ *n* odiosidad, *f*
**oboe** /'oubou/ *n Mus.* oboe, *m.* **o. player,** oboe, *m*
**obol** /'ɒbəl/ *n* óbolo, *m*
**obscene** /əb'sin/ *a* indecente, obsceno, escabroso
**obscenely** /əb'sinli/ *adv* obscenamente, escabrosamente
**obscenity** /əb'sɛnɪti/ *n* indecencia, obscenidad, *f*
**obscurantism** /əb'skyʊrən,tɪzəm/ *n* obscurantismo,
  *m*
**obscurantist** /əb'skyʊrəntɪst/ *a and n* obscurantista
  *mf*
**obscure** /əb'skyʊr/ *a* (indistinct) obscuro, indistinto;
  (dark) lóbrego, tenebroso; (remote) retirado,
  apartado; (puzzling) confuso; (unknown) desconocido; humilde; (difficult to understand) abstruso, obscuro; (vague) vago. —*vt* obscurecer; (hide) esconder;
  (eclipse) eclipsar. **to o. the issue,** hacer perder de
  vista el problema
**obscurely** /əb'skyʊrli/ *adv* obscuramente; humildemente, retiradamente; confusamente; vagamente
**obscurity** /əb'skyʊrɪti/ *n* (darkness) obscuridad, lobreguez, *f;* (difficulty of meaning) ambigüedad, confusión, vaguedad, *f;* humildad, *f*
**obsequies** /'ɒbsɪkwiz/ *n pl* exequias, *f pl,* ritos fúnebres, *m pl*
**obsequious** /əb'sikwiəs/ *a* servil, empalagoso,
  zalamero
**obsequiously** /əb'sikwiəsli/ *adv* servilmente
**obsequiousness** /əb'sikwiəsnɪs/ *n* servilismo, *m,*
  sumisión, *f*
**observable** /əb'zɜrvəbəl/ *a* observable, perceptible,
  visible; notable
**observably** /əb'zɜrvəbli/ *adv* notablemente
**observance** /əb'zɜrvəns/ *n* observancia, *f,* cumplimiento, *m;* práctica, costumbre, *f;* (religious) rito, *m*
**observant** /əb'zɜrvənt/ *a* observador; obediente,
  atento. **o. of,** observador de; atento a
**observation** /,ɒbzɜr'veiʃən/ *n* observación, *f,* exa-

men, escrutinio, *m;* (experience) experiencia, *f;* (remark) advertencia, *f,* comento, *m.* **to escape o.,** no ser advertido. **o. car.,** vagón-mirador, *m,* **o. post,** puesto de observación, *m*

**observatory** /əbˈzɜːrvəˌtɔːri/ *n* observatorio, *m*

**observe** /əbˈzɜːrv/ *vt* (laws) cumplir; (holy days, etc.) guardar; (notice) observar, mirar, notar, ver, reparar en; (remark) decir, advertir; (examine) vigilar, atisbar, examinar; *Astron.* observar. —*vi* ser observador. **to o. silence,** guardar silencio

**observer** /əbˈzɜːrvər/ *n* observador (-ra)

**obsess** /əbˈsɛs/ *vt* obsesionar, obcecar

**obsessed** /əbˈsɛst/ *a* obseso

**obsession** /əbˈsɛʃən/ *n* obsesión, obcecación, idea fija, manía, *f*

**obsidian** /əbˈsɪdiən/ *n Mineral.* obsidiana, *f*

**obsolescent** /ˌɒbsəˈlɛsənt/ *a* que se hace antiguo, que cae en desuso

**obsolete** /ˌɒbsəˈliːt/ *a* obsoleto, anticuado; *Biol.* rudimentario, atrofiado

**obstacle** /ˈɒbstəkəl/ *n* obstáculo, impedimento, *m;* dificultad, *f,* inconveniente, *m.* **to put obstacles in the way of,** *Fig.* dificultar, hacer difícil. **o. race,** carrera de obstáculos, *f*

**obstetric** /əbˈstɛtrɪk/ *a* obstétrico

**obstetrician** /ˌɒbstɪˈtrɪʃən/ *n* obstétrico (-ea), médico (-ca) partero (-ra)

**obstetrics** /əbˈstɛtrɪks/ *n* obstetricia, tocología, *f*

**obstinacy** /ˈɒbstənəsi/ *n* obstinación, terquedad, tenacidad, porfía, *f,* tesón, *m;* persistencia, *f*

**obstinate** /ˈɒbstənɪt/ *a* terco, porfiado, obstinado, tenaz; refractario; persistente, pertinaz. **to be o.,** ser terco; porfiar. **to be o. about,** obstinarse en.

**obstinately** /ˈɒbstənɪtli/ *adv* tercamente

**obstreperous** /əbˈstrɛpərəs/ *a* turbulento, ruidoso

**obstruct** /əbˈstrʌkt/ *vt* obstruir: impedir; cerrar; (thwart) estorbar; (hinder) dificultar, embarazar; (the traffic) obstruir, atascar. —*vi* estorbar. **to become obstructed,** obstruirse, cerrarse

**obstruction** /əbˈstrʌkʃən/ *n* obstrucción, *f;* estorbo, obstáculo, *m.* **to cause a street o.,** obstruir el tráfico

**obstructionism** /əbˈstrʌkʃəˌnɪzəm/ *n* obstruccionismo, *m*

**obstructionist** /əbˈstrʌkʃənɪst/ *n* obstruccionista, *mf*

**obstructive** /əbˈstrʌktɪv/ *a* estorbador, obstructor

**obtain** /əbˈteɪn/ *vt* obtener, conseguir, lograr; recibir; (by threats) arrancar. —*vi* estar en boga, estar en vigor, predominar. **to o. on false pretences,** conseguir por engaño

**obtainable** /əbˈteɪnəbəl/ *a* asequible, alcanzable. **easily o.,** fácil a obtener

**obtainer** /əbˈteɪnər/ *n* conseguidor (-ra), adquisidor (-ra)

**obtainment** /əbˈteɪnmənt/ *n* obtención, *f,* logro, *m*

**obtrude** /əbˈtruːd/ *vt* imponer

**obtrusion** /əbˈtruːʒən/ *n* imposición, *f;* importunidad, *f*

**obtrusive** /əbˈtruːsɪv/ *a* importuno; entremetido; pretencioso

**obtrusiveness** /əbˈtruːsɪvnɪs/ *n* importunidad, *f;* entremetimiento, *m*

**obtuse** /əbˈtuːs/ *a* (blunt) obtuso, romo; (stupid) estúpido, torpe, lerdo. **o. angle,** obtusángulo, *m*

**obtuseness** /əbˈtuːsnɪs/ *n* (bluntness) embotamiento, *m;* (stupidity) estupidez, torpeza, *f*

**obverse** / *a.* ɒbˈvɜːrs; *n.* ˈɒbvɜːrs/ *a* del anverso. —*n* anverso, *m*

**obviate** /ˈɒbviˌeɪt/ *vt* obviar, evitar

**obvious** /ˈɒbviəs/ *a* evidente, manifiesto, patente, obvio, aparente, transparente; poco sutil

**obviously** /ˈɒbviəsli/ *adv* evidentemente, patentemente

**obviousness** /ˈɒbviəsnɪs/ *n* evidencia, transparencia, *f*

**occasion** /əˈkeɪʒən/ *n* ocasión, *f;* oportunidad, *f,* momento oportuno, tiempo propicio, *m;* (reason) motivo, origen, *m,* causa, razón, *f;* (need) necesidad, *f.* —*vt* ocasionar, causar, producir. **as o. demands,** cuando las circunstancias lo exigen, en caso necesario. **for the o.,** para la ocasión. **on one o.,** una vez. **on the o. of,** en la ocasión de. **on that o.,** en tal ocasión, en aquella ocasión. **He has given me no o. to say so,** No me ha dado motivos de decirlo.

**There is no o. for it,** No hay necesidad para ello. **to have o. to,** haber de, tener que, necesitar. **to lose no o.,** no perder ripio (or oportunidad). **to rise to the o.,** estar al nivel de las circunstancias. **to take this o.,** aprovechar esta oportunidad

**occasional** /əˈkeɪʒənl/ *a* (occurring at times) de vez en cuando, intermitente; poco frecuente, infrecuente; (of verse) de ocasión. **o. table,** mesilla, *f*

**occasionally** /əˈkeɪʒənli/ *adv* de vez en cuando

**occiput** /ˈɒksəˌpʌt/ *n Anat.* occipucio, *m*

**occlude** /əˈkluːd/ *vt* obstruir, cerrar; *Med.* ocluír; *Chem.* absorber

**occlusion** /əˈkluːʒən/ *n* cerramiento, *m; Med.* oclusión, *f; Chem.* absorción de gases, *f*

**occlusive** /əˈkluːsɪv/ *a* oclusivo

**occult** /əˈkʌlt/ *a* oculto, escondido; misterioso; mágico. **o. sciences,** creencias ocultas, *f pl*

**occultation** /ˌɒkʌlˈteɪʃən/ *n Astron.* ocultación, *f;* eclipse, *m*

**occultism** /əˈkʌltɪzəm/ *n* ocultismo, *m*

**occultist** /əˈkʌltɪst/ *n* ocultista, *mf*

**occupancy** /ˈɒkyəpənsi/ *n* ocupación, posesión, *f;* (tenancy) tenencia, *f*

**occupant** /ˈɒkyəpənt/ *n* habitante, *mf;* ocupante, *mf;* (tenant) inquilino (-na)

**occupation** /ˌɒkyəˈpeɪʃən/ *n* ocupación *f;* (tenure) inquilinato, *m,* tenencia, *f;* (work) trabajo, quehacer, *m,* labor, *f;* (employment) empleo, oficio, *m;* profesión, *f*

**occupational** /ˌɒkyəˈpeɪʃənl/ *a* de oficio. **o. disease,** enfermedad profesional, *f*

**occupier** /ˈɒkyəˌpaɪər/ *n* ocupante, *mf,* inquilino (-na)

**occupy** /ˈɒkyəˌpaɪ/ *vt* ocupar; (live in) vivir en, habitar; (time) emplear, pasar; (take over) apoderarse de, ocupar. **to o. oneself in** or **with,** ocuparse en, ocuparse con. **to be occupied in** or **with,** estar ocupado con, ocuparse en

**occur** /əˈkɜːr/ *vi* (happen) suceder, tener lugar, acaecer; (exist) encontrarse, existir; (of ideas) ocurrirse, venirse. **to o. to one's mind,** venírsele a las mientes. **to o. again,** volver a suceder, ocurrir de nuevo. **An idea occurred to her,** Se le ocurrió una idea

**occurrence** /əˈkɜːrəns/ *n* ocurrencia, *f;* incidente, suceso, acontecimiento, *m.* **to be of frequent o.,** ocurrir con frecuencia, acontecer a menudo

**ocean** /ˈoʊʃən/ *n* océano, *m; Fig.* mar, abundancia, *f.* **o.-going vessel,** buque de alta mar, *m*

**Oceania** /ˌoʊʃiˈæniə/ el Mundo Novísmo, *m*

**oceanic** /ˌoʊʃiˈænɪk/ *a* oceánico

**oceanography** /ˌoʊʃəˈnɒɡrəfi/ *n* oceanografía, *f*

**ocelot** /ˈoʊsəˌlɒt/ *n Zool.* ocelote, *m*

**ocher** /ˈoʊkər/ *n* ocre, *m*

**octagon** /ˈɒktəˌɡɒn/ *n* octágono, *m*

**octagonal** /ɒkˈtæɡənl/ *a* octagonal

**octave** /ˈɒktɪv/ *n* (Eccl. metrics, Mus.) octava, *f*

**octavo** /ɒkˈteɪvoʊ, -ˈtɑ-/ *n Print.* libro, etc. en octavo (8°), *m.* **in o.,** en octavo. **large o.,** octavo mayor, *m.* **small o.,** octavo menor, *m*

**octet** /ɒkˈtɛt/ *n Mus.* octeto, *m*

**October** /ɒkˈtoʊbər/ *n* octubre, *m,* 2 October 1996, el segundo (2°) de octubre de mil novecientos noventa y seis

**octogenarian** /ˌɒktədʒəˈnɛəriən/ *a* and *n* octogenario (-ia)

**octopus** /ˈɒktəpəs/ *n* pulpo, *m*

**ocular** /ˈɒkyələr/ *a* ocular, visual. —*n* ocular, *m*

**oculist** /ˈɒkyəlɪst/ *n* oculista, *mf*

**odd** /ɒd/ *a* (of numbers) impar; (of volumes, etc.) suelto; (strange) raro, curioso, extraño, extravagante; (casual) casual, accidental; (extra) y pico, y tantos, sobrante; (of gloves, etc.) sin pareja. **at odd moments,** en momentos de ocio. **at odd times,** de vez en cuando. **thirty odd,** treinta y pico. **odd number,** número impare, *m.* **odd or even,** pares o impares. **odd trick,** (at cards) una baza más

**oddity** /ˈɒdɪti/ *n* excentricidad, rareza, extravagancia, *f;* (person) ente singular, *m;* (curio) objeto curioso, *m,* antigüedad, *f*

**oddly** /ˈɒdli/ *adv* singularmente

**oddment** /ˈɒdmənt/ *n* bagatela, baratija, *f*

**oddness** /ˈɒdnɪs/ *n* singularidad, rareza, extravagancia, *f*

**odds** /ɒdz/ *n pl* diferencia, desigualdad, *f;* (superiority) ventaja, superioridad, *f;* (quarrel) disputa, riña, *f.* **The o. are that...,** Lo más probable es que... **to fight against dreadful o.,** luchar contra fuerzas muy superiores. **o. and ends,** (remains) sobras y picos, *f pl;* (trifles) ñaques, *m pl,* chucherías, *f pl*

**Odessa** /ou'desə/ Odesa, *f*

**odious** /'oudiəs/ *a* odioso, detestable, aborrecible, repugnante

**odiousness** /'oudiəsnɪs/ *n* odiosidad, *f*

**odium** /'oudiəm/ *n* odio, *m*

**odor** /'oudər/ *n* olor, *m,* (fragrance) perfume, aroma, *m,* fragancia, *f; Fig.* sospecha, *f.* **in bad o.,** *Fig.* en disfavor. **o. of sanctity,** olor de santidad, *m*

**odoriferous** /ˌoudə'rɪfərəs/ *a* odorífero; (perfumed) oloroso, perfumado

**odorless** /'oudərlɪs/ *a* inodoro

**odorous** /'oudərəs/ *a* fragante, oloroso

**odyssey** /'ɒdəsi/ *n* odisea, *f*

**Oedipus complex** /'ɛdəpəs/ *n* complejo de Edipo, *m*

**of** /əv/ *prep* **de. of** has many idiomatic translations which are given as far as possible under the heading of the word concerned. It is also not translated. **I robbed him of his reward,** Le robé su recompensa. **I was thinking of you,** Pensaba en tí. **It was very good of you to...,** Vd. ha tenido mucha bondad de... **Your naming of the child Mary,** El que Vd. haya dado el nombre de María al niño. **29th of Sept., 1936,** el 29 de septiembre de 1936. **Of course!** ¡Claro está! ¡Ya lo creo! ¡Naturalmente! **of late,** últimamente. **of the** (before *m, sing*) del; (before *f, sing*) de la; (before *m pl*) de los; (before *f pl*) de las. **to dream of,** soñar con. **to smell of,** oler a tener olor de. **to taste of, etc.,** saber a, tener gusto de.

**off** /ɔf/ *prep* de; fuera de; cerca de; desde; *Naut.* a la altura de. **from off,** de. **Take your gloves off the table!** ¡Quítate los guantes de la mesa! **The wheel was off the car,** La rueda se había desprendido del coche. **to be off duty,** no estar de servicio; *Mil.* no estar de guardia. **to lunch off cold meat,** almorzar de carne fría. **off one's head,** chiflado

**off** /ɔf/ *a* (contrasted with near) de la derecha, derecho; (unlikely) improbable, remoto. —*adv* (with intransitive verbs of motion) se (e.g. *He has gone off,* Se ha marchado); (contrasted with on) de (e.g. *He has fallen off the horse,* Ha caído del caballo); (of place at a distance) lejos, a distancia de; (of time) generally a verb is used (e.g. *The wedding is three months off,* Faltan tres meses para la boda); (completely) enteramente. **Off** is often not translated in Sp. (e.g. *to put off,* aplazar, *to cut off,* cortar). **day off,** día libre, día de asueto, *m.* **How far off is the house from here? The house is five miles off.** ¿Cuántas millas está la casa de aquí? La casa está a cinco millas de aquí. **His hat is off,** Está sin sombrero, Se ha quitado el sombrero. **The cover is off,** La cubierta está quitada. **The party is off,** Se ha anulado la reunión. **6% off,** un descuento de seis por ciento. —*interj* **Off with you!** ¡Márchate! ¡Fuera! **off and on,** de vez en cuando, espasmódicamente. **off color,** (ill) malucho; (of jokes) verde. **off season,** estación muerta, *f.* **off-shore,** a vista de tierra. **off-stage,** entre bastidores

**offal** /'ɔfəl/ *n* (butchers') menudencias, *f pl,* asadura, *f,* menudos, despojos, *m pl;* desperdicio, *m*

**offend** /ə'fɛnd/ *vt* ofender, agraviar, insultar; herir; desagradar, disgustar; *vi* ofender, pecar. **to be offended,** resentirse, insultarse. **This offends my sense of justice,** Esto ofende mi sentimiento de justicia. **to o. against,** pecar contra; violar

**offender** /ə'fɛndər/ *n* delincuente, *mf;* agraviador (-ra), pecador (-ra), transgresor (-ra). **old o.,** *Law.* criminal inveterado, *m*

**offense** /ə'fɛns/ *n* ofensa, transgresión, violación, *f;* pecado, *m; Law.* delito, crimen, *m;* (insult) agravio, *m,* afrenta, *f.* **the first o.,** el primer delito, *m.* **fresh o.,** nuevo delito, *m.* **political o.,** crimen político, *m.* **technical o.,** *Law.* cuasidelito, *m.* **to commit an o. against,** ofender contra. **to take o.,** resentirse, darse por ofendido

**offensive** /ə'fɛnsɪv/ *a* ofensivo, desagradable, repugnante; (insulting) injurioso, agraviador, agresivo. —*n Mil.* ofensiva, *f.* **to take the o.,** tomar la ofensiva

**offensiveness** /ə'fɛnsɪvnɪs/ *n* lo desagradable; (insult) ofensa, *f;* lo injurioso

**offer** /'ɔfər/ *n* oferta, *f;* ofrecimiento, *m;* (of help) promesa, *f;* proposición, *f; Com.* oferta, *f.* —*vt* ofrecer; prometer; (opportunities, etc.) deparar, brindar; tributar. —*vi* ofrecerse, ocurrir, surgir. **to o. up,** ofrecer; inmolar, sacrificar. **He did not offer to go,** No hizo ademán de marcharse. **to o. resistance,** oponer resistencia. **o. of marriage,** oferta de matrimonio, *f*

**offerer** /'ɔfərər/ *n* ofrecedor (-ra)

**offering** /'ɔfərɪŋ/ *n* ofrecimiento, *m; Eccl.* ofrenda, oblación, *f,* sacrificio, *m;* regalo, don, *m,* dádiva, *f*

**offhand** /'ɔf'hænd/ *a* sin preparación, de repente; (casual) casual, despreocupado; (discourteous) brusco, descortés

**offhandedly** /'ɔf'hændɪdli/ *adv* sin preparación, espontáneamente; negligentemente; bruscamente

**office** /'ɔfɪs/ *n* oficina, *m;* (post) cargo, puesto, destino, *m;* (state department) ministerio, *m;* (of a Cabinet minister) cartera, *f;* (room) oficina, *f;* despacho, escritorio, *m;* (of a newspaper) redacción, *f;* (lawyer's) bufete, *m;* departamento, *m; Eccl.* oficio, *m pl.* **offices,** negocio, *m;* oficinas, *f pl;* (prayers) rezos, *m pl; Eccl.* oficios, *m pl.* **domestic offices,** dependencias, *f pl. Fig.* buenos oficios, *m pl.* **head o.,** casa central, oficina principal, *f.* **private o.,** despacho particular, *m.* **to be in o.,** estar en el poder. **o.-bearer,** miembro de la junta, *m;* funcionario, *m.* **o.-boy,** mozo de oficina, *m.* **o. employee,** oficinista, *mf.* **o. hours,** horas de oficina, *f pl;* (professions) horas de consulta, *f pl.* **o.-seeker,** aspirante, *m;* pretendiente, *m.* **o. work,** trabajo de oficina, *m*

**officer** /'ɔfəsər/ *n* oficial, funcionario, *m;* (police) agente de policía, *m;* (of the Church) dignatario, *m;* (*Mil. Nav. Aer.*) oficial, *m.* —*vt* mandar. **commissioned o.,** oficial, *m.* **non-commissioned o.,** oficial subalterno, *m.* **to be well officered,** tener buena oficialidad, *f.* **Officers' Training Corps,** Escuela de Oficiales, *f*

**office worker** *n* oficinista, *mf*

**official** /ə'fɪʃəl/ *a* oficial; autorizado; ceremonioso, grave. —*n* funcionario, *m;* oficial público, *m.* **high o.,** funcionario importante. *m.* **o. mourning,** duelo oficial, *m.* **o. receiver,** fiscal de quiebras, *m*

**officialdom** /ə'fɪʃəldəm/ *n* funcionarismo, *m;* círculos oficiales, *m pl*

**officiant** /ə'fɪʃiənt/ *n* oficiante, *m*

**officiate** /ə'fɪʃi,eit/ *vi* celebrar; oficiar, funcionar

**officiating** /ə'fɪʃi,eitɪŋ/ *a* oficiante; celebrante. **o. priest,** sacerdote oficiante, celebrante, *m*

**officious** /ə'fɪʃəs/ *a* oficioso, entremetido

**officiousness** /ə'fɪʃəsnɪs/ *n* oficiosidad, *f*

**offing** /'ɔfɪŋ/ *n Naut.* mar afuera, *m.* **in the o.,** cerca

**off season** fuera de temporada

**offset** /*n.* 'ɔf,sɛt; *v.* ˌɔf'sɛt/ *n* compensación, *f, vt* compensar, neutralizar

**offshoot** /'ɔf,ʃut/ *n* renuevo, vástago, *m*

**offside** /'ɔf'said/ *a* (of a car) del lado derecho (or izquierda); *Sports.* fuera de juego

**offspring** /'ɔf,sprɪŋ/ *n* vástago, *m;* descendiente, *mf;* prole, *f;* hijos, *m pl*

**often** /'ɔfən/ *adv* a menudo, mucho, con frecuencia, frecuentemente, muchas veces. **as o. as,** tan a menudo como, siempre que. **as o. as not,** no pocas veces. **How o.?** ¿Cuántas veces? **It is not o. that...,** No ocurre con frecuencia que... **so o.,** tantas veces, con frecuencia. **Do you go there o.?** ¿Va Vd. allí con frecuencia (or frecuentemente)? **Not o.,** Voy rara vez allá

**ogival** /'oudʒaivəl/ *a Archit.* ojival

**ogive** /'oudʒaiv/ *n Archit.* ojiva, *f*

**ogle** /'ougəl/ *vt* and *vi* comer(se) con los ojos (a), ojear, guiñar el ojo (a). —*n* ojeada, *f,* guiño, *m*

**ogling** /'ouglɪŋ/ *n* guiño, *m,* ojeada, *f*

**ogre** /'ougər/ *n* ogro, *m*

**oh!** /ou/ *interj* ¡o! **O no!** ¡Ca! ¡Claro que no!

**ohm** /oum/ *n Elec.* ohmio, *m*

**oil** /ɔil/ *n* aceite, *m;* petróleo, *m;* óleo, *m.* —*vt* aceitar, engrasar; olear, ungir, untar; (bribe) sobornar, untar la mano; *Fig.* suavizar. —*a* aceitero; petrolero. **to pour oil on troubled waters,** echar aceite sobre aguas turbulentas. **to strike oil,** encontrar un pozo de petróleo; *Fig.* encontrar un filón. **crude oil,** petróleo bruto, *m.* **heavy oil,** aceite pesado, *m.* **thin oil,** aceite ligero, *m. Art.* **in oils,** al óleo. **oil-bearing,** petrolífero. **oil-box,** engrasador, *m.* **oil-burner,** quemador de petróleo, *m.* **oil-can,** aceitera, *f.* **oil-colors,** pinturas al óleo, *f pl.* **oil field,** yacimiento petrolífero, campo de petróleo, *m.* **oil-filter,** separador de aceite, *m.* **oil-gauge,** nivel de aceite, *m.* **oil lamp,** velón, candil, quinqué, *m.* **oil of turpentine,** aceite de trementina, aguarrás, *m.* esencia de trementina, *f.* **oil-painting,** pintura al óleo, *f.* **oil pipeline,** oleoducto, *m.* **oil shop,** aceitería, *f.* **oil-silk,** encerado, *m.* **oil stove,** estufa de petróleo, *f.* **oil tanker,** *Naut.* petrolero, *m.* **oil-well,** pozo de petróleo, *m*

**oilcake** /'ɔɪlˌkeɪk/ *n* bagazo, *m*

**oilcloth** /'ɔɪlˌklɔθ/ *n* hule, *m;* linóleo, *m*

**oiler** /'ɔɪlər/ *n* (can) aceitera, *f; Naut.* petrolero, *m;* lubricador, *m*

**oiliness** /'ɔɪlɪnɪs/ *n* oleaginosidad, untuosidad, *f*

**oiling** /'ɔɪlɪŋ/ *n* engrasado, *m*

**oil seed** *n* semilla oleaginosa, *f*

**oilskin** /'ɔɪlˌskɪn/ *n* encerado, *m*

**oily** /'ɔɪli/ *a* aceitoso, grasiento

**ointment** /'ɔɪntmənt/ *n* ungüento, *m,* pomada, *f*

**old** /ould/ *a* viejo; antiguo, anciano; (of wines, etc.) añejo; (worn out) usado, gastado; (inveterate) arraigado, inveterado. **How old are you?** ¿Cuántos años tiene usted? **to be sixteen years old,** tener dieciséis años. **He is old enough to know his own mind,** Tiene bastante edad para saber lo que quiere. **to grow old,** envejecer. **to remain an old maid,** quedar soltera; *Inf.* quedarse para vestir imágenes. **of old,** antiguamente. **prematurely old,** revejido averiado. **old age,** vejez, senectud, *f.* **old bachelor,** solterón, *m.* **old clothes,** ropa vieja (or usada), ropa de segunda mano, *f.* **old-clothes dealer,** ropavejero (-ra). **old-clothes shop,** ropavejería, *f.* **old-established,** viejo. **old-fashioned,** pasado de moda, viejo; (of people) chapado a la antigua. **old lady,** anciana, dama vieja, *f.* **old-looking,** de aspecto viejo, avejentado. **old maid,** solterona, *f.* **old-maidish,** remilgado. **old man,** viejo, *m; Theat.* barba, *m.* **old salt,** lobo de mar, *m.* **Old Testament,** Antiguo Testamento, *m.* **old wives' tale,** cuento de viejas, *m.* **old woman,** vieja, *f.* **Old World,** Viejo Mundo, mundo antiguo, *m*

**old-age home** /'ould 'eɪdʒ/ *n* asilo de ancianos, *m*

**olden** /'ouldən/ *a* antiguo. **o. days,** días pasados, *m pl*

**older** /'ouldər/ *a compar* más viejo, mayor. **The older the madder,** A la vejez viruelas

**old hat** *n* viejo conocido

**oldish** /'ouldɪʃ/ *a* bastante viejo, de cierta edad

**oldness** /'ouldnɪs/ *n* antigüedad, ancianidad, edad, *f*

**oleaginous** /ˌouli'ædʒənəs/ *a* oleaginoso

**oleander** /'ouliˌændər/ *n Bot.* adelfa, *f,* baladre, *m*

**olfactory** /ɒl'fæktəri/ *a* olfatorio, olfativo

**oligarchic** /ˌɒlɪ'gɑrkɪk/ *a* oligárquico

**oligarchy** /'ɒlɪˌgɑrki/ *n* oligarquía, *f*

**olive** /'ɒlɪv/ *n* (tree) olivo, *m;* (fruit) aceituna, oliva, *f, a* aceitunado. **wild o. tree,** acebuche, *m.* **o.-complexioned,** con tez aceitunada. **o. green,** verde oliva, *m.* **o. grove,** olivar, *m.* **o. oil,** aceite de oliva, *m*

**olympiad** /ə'lɪmpiˌæd/ *n* olimpíada, *f*

**olympian** /ə'lɪmpiən/ *a* olímpico

**olympic** /ə'lɪmpɪk/ *a* olímpico. **o. games,** juegos olímpicos, *m pl*

**olympus** /ə'lɪmpəs/ *n* olimpo, *m*

**omasum** /ou'meɪsəm/ *n Zool.* librillo, libro, *m*

**omber** /'ɒmbər/ *n* tresillo, hombre, *m*

**omega** /ou'migə, ou'mei-/ *n* omega, *f*

**omelet** /'ɒmlɪt/ *n* tortilla, *f,* tortilla dulce, *f.* **sweet o.,** tortilla dulce, *f*

**omen** /'oumən/ *n* pronóstico, presagio, agüero, *m, vt* agorar, anunciar

**ominous** /'ɒmənəs/ *a* ominoso, azaroso, siniestro, amenazante

**ominously** /'ɒmənəsli/ *adv* ominosamente, con amenazas

**omission** /ou'mɪʃən/ *n* omisión, *f;* olvido, descuido, *m;* supresión, *f*

**omit** /ou'mɪt/ *vt* omitir; olvidar, descuidar; (suppress) suprimir, excluir, callar, dejar a un lado

**omitting** /ou'mɪtɪŋ/ *pres part* salvo, excepto

**omnibus** /'ɒmnəˌbʌs/ *n* ómnibus, autobús, *m.* **o. conductor,** cobrador de autobús, *m.* **o. driver,** conductor de autobús, *m.* **o. route,** trayecto de autobús, *m.* **o. service,** servicio de autobuses, *m.* **o. volume,** volumen de obras coleccionadas, *m*

**omnipotence** /ɒm'nɪpətəns/ *n* omnipotencia, *f*

**omnipotent** /ɒm'nɪpətənt/ *a* omnipotente, todopoderoso

**omnipresence** /ˌɒmnə'prɛzəns/ *n* omnipresencia, ubicuidad, *f*

**omnipresent** /ˌɒmnə'prɛzənt/ *a* ubicuo

**omniscience** /ɒm'nɪʃəns/ *n* omnisciencia, *f*

**omniscient** /ɒm'nɪʃənt/ *a* omniscio, omnisciente

**omnivorous** /ɒm'nɪvərəs/ *a* omnívoro

**on** /ɒn/ *prep* (upon) sobre, en, encima de; (concerning) de, acerca de, sobre; (against) contra; (after) después; (according to) según; (with gerund) en; (with infin.) al; (at) a; (connected with, employed in) de; (by means of) por, mediante; (near to) cerca de, sobre; (into) en. Untranslated before days of week, dates of month or time of day (e.g. *on Monday,* el lunes. *on Friday afternoons,* los viernes por la tarde). **She has a bracelet on her wrist,** Tiene una pulsera en la muñeca. **He will retire on a good income,** Se jubilará con una buena renta. **on my uncle's death,** después de la muerte (or a la muerte) de mi tío, al morir. **On seeing them, he stopped,** Al verles se paró. **on leave,** con licencia, en uso de licencia. **on the next page,** en la página siguiente. **on this occasion,** en esta ocasión. **on the other hand,** en cambio. **on second thoughts,** luego de pensarlo bien. **on the way,** en camino. **on one side,** a un lado. **on the left,** a la izquierda. **on time,** a tiempo. **on my honor,** bajo palabra de honor. **on pain of death,** so pena de muerte, bajo pena de muerte. **on an average,** por término medio. **on his part,** por su parte. **on and after,** desde, a partir de. **on credit,** de fiado. **on fire,** ardiendo, en llamas. **on foot,** a pie. **on purpose,** a propósito; con intención. **on,** *adv* puesto (e.g. *She has her gloves on,* Tiene los guantes puestos); (forward) adelante, hacia adelante; (continue, with a verb) seguir, continuar (e.g. *He went on talking,* Siguió hablando). Often **on** is included in Sp. verb (e.g. *The new play is on,* Se ha estrenado la nueva comedia. *The fight is on,* Ya ha empezado la lucha). **On!** *interj* ¡Adelante! **and so on,** y así sucesivamente. **to have on,** llevar puesto. **on and off,** de vez en cuando. **on and on,** sin cesar

**onanism** /'ounəˌnɪzəm/ *n* onanismo, *m*

**once** /wʌns/ *adv* una vez; (formerly) en otro tiempo, antiguamente; *conjunc* si (e.g. *O. you give him the opportunity,* Si le das la oportunidad). **all at o.,** todo junto, a un mismo tiempo; simultáneamente; (suddenly) súbitamente, de repente. **at o.,** en seguida, inmediatamente. **for o.,** por una vez. **more than o.,** más de una vez. **not o.,** ni siquiera una vez. **o. before,** una vez antes. **o. and for all,** una vez para siempre; por última vez. **o. in a while,** una vez en cuando. **o. more,** otra vez. **o. or twice,** una vez o dos, algunas veces. **o. too often,** una vez demasiado. **O. upon a time,** En tiempos pasados, En tiempos de Maricastaña; (as beginning of a story) Érase una vez, Había una vez, Hubo una vez

**once in a blue moon** a cada muerte de un obispo

**one** /wʌn/ *a* un, uno, una; (first) primero; (single) único, solo; (indifferent) igual, indiferente; (some, certain) algún, cierto, un (e.g. *one day,* cierto día). —*n* uno; (hour) la una; (of age) un año. Often not translated in Sp. (e.g. *I shall take the blue one,* Tomaré el azul). —*pron* se; uno. **one's,** su, de uno (e.g. *one's work,* el trabajo de uno). **I for one do not think so,** Yo por uno no lo creo. **It is all one,** Es igual, No hace diferencia alguna. **only one,** un solo. **that one,** ése, *m,* ésa, *f,* eso, *neut.* **this one,** éste, *m,* ésta, *f,* esto, *neut.* **these ones,** éstos, etc. **those ones,** ésos, etc. **the one,** el (que), *m,* la (que), *f.* **with one accord,** unánimemente. **one and all,** todos. **one an-**

other, se, uno a otro, mutuamente. **one by one,** uno a uno. **one day,** un día; un día de éstos, algún día. **one-eyed,** tuerto. **one-handed,** manco. **one-sided,** parcial. **one-way street,** calle de dirección única, *f.* **one-way traffic,** tráfico en una sola dirección, *m*

**oneiric** /ou'nairık/ *a* onírico

**oneness** /'wʌnnıs/ *n* unidad, *f*

**onerous** /'ɒnərəs/ *a* oneroso, pesado, molesto, gravoso

**onerousness** /'ɒnərəsnıs/ *n* pesadez, molestia, dificultad, inconveniencia, *f*

**one-seater** /'wʌn 'sitər/ *n* avión de una plaza, *m*

**oneself** /wʌn'self/ *pron* se, uno mismo (una misma); (after prep.) sí mismo, sí. **It must be done by o.,** Uno mismo ha de hacerlo

**onion** /'ʌnyən/ *n* cebolla, *f.* **string of onions,** ristra de cebollas, *f.* **young o.,** babosa, *f.* **o. bed,** cebollar, *m.* **o. seed,** cebollino, *m.* **o. seller,** cebollero (-ra)

**on-line** /'ɒn'lain, 'ɔn-/ *a* conectado, en línea

**onlooker** /'ɒn,lʊkər/ *n* espectado (-ra), observador (-ra); testigo, *mf*

**only** /'ounli/ *a* único, solo. —*adv* únicamente, sólo; no... más (que), tan sólo; con la excepción de, salvo. —*conjunc* pero, salvo (que), si no fuera (que). **I shall o. give you three,** No te daré más de tres. **The o. thing one can do,** Lo único que se puede hacer. **I o. wished to see her,** Quería verla nada más. **if o.,** ¡ojalá (que)! **not o....,** no sólo... **o.-begotten,** *a* unigénito. **o. child,** hijo (-ja) único (-ca)

**onomatopoeia** /,ɒnə,mætə'piə/ *n* onomatopeya, *f*

**onomatopoeic** /,ɒnə,mætə'piık/ *a* onomatopéyico

**onrush** /'ɒn,rʌʃ/ *n* asalto, ataque, acometimiento, *m*; acometida, embestida, *f*; (of water, etc.) acceso, *m*; torrente, *m*, corriente, *f*

**onset** /'ɒn,set/ *n* ataque, *m*, acometida, *f*; (beginning) principio, *m.* **at the first o.,** al primer ímpetu

**onslaught** /'ɒn,slɔt/ *n* asalto, ataque, *m*

**ontology** /ɒn'tɒlədʒi/ *n* Philos. ontología, *f*

**onus** /'ounəs/ *n* responsabilidad, *f.* **o. of proof,** obligación de probar, *f*

**onward** /'ɒnwərd/ *a* progresivo. —*adv* adelante, hacia adelante; (as a command) ¡Adelante!

**onyx** /'ɒnıks/ *n Mineral.* ónice, *f*

**ooze** /uz/ *n* légamo, limo, fango, *m*, lama, *f.* —*vi* exudar, rezumarse; manar; *vt* sudar. **to o. satisfaction,** caérsele (a uno) la baba. **to o. away,** (of money, etc.) desaparecer, volar. **to o. out,** (news) divulgarse

**oozing** /'uzıŋ/ *a* fangoso, legamoso, lamoso

**opacity** /ou'pæsıti/ *n* opacidad, *f*

**opal** /'oupəl/ *n* ópalo, *m*

**opalescence** /,oupə'lesəns/ *n* opalescencia, *f*

**opalescent** /,oupə'lesənt/ *a* opalescente, iridiscente

**opaline** /'oupəlın/ *a* opalino

**opaque** /ou'peik/ *a* opaco

**opaqueness** /ou'peiknıs/ *n* opacidad, *f*

**op. cit.** /'ɒp' sıt/ (opere citato) obra cit. (obra citada)

**open** /'oupən/ *vt* abrir; (a package) desempaquetar, desenvolver; (remove lid) destapar; (unfold) desplegar; (inaugurate) inaugurar; iniciar, empezar; establecer; (an abscess) cortar; (with arms, heart, eyes) abrir; (with mind, thought) descubrir, revelar; (make accessible) franquear, hacer accesible; (tear) romper; *vi* abrirse; empezar, comenzar; (of a view, etc.) aparecer, extenderse; inaugurarse; (of a career, etc.) prepararse. **to o. fire against,** abrir el fuego contra. **to o. into,** comunicar con, salir a. **to o. into each other,** (of rooms) comunicarse. **to o. on,** mirar a, dar a, caer a. **to o. out,** *vt* abrir; desplegar; revelar. —*vi* extenderse; revelarse. **to o. the eyes of,** *Fig.* desengañar, desilusionar. **to o. up,** abrir; explorar, hacer accesible; revelar; *Fig. Inf.* desabrocharse. **to o. with** or **by,** empezar con

**open** /'oupən/ *a* abierto; descubierto; expuesto; (unfenced) descercado; (not private) público; libre; (unfolded) desplegado, extendido; (persuasible) receptivo; no resuelto, pendiente; (frank) franco, candoroso; (with sea) alto; (liberal) generoso, hospitalario; sin prejuicios; *Com.* abierto, pendiente; sin defensa; (of weather) despejado; (of a letter) sin sellar; (without a lid) destapado; (well-known) manifiesto, bien conocido. —*n* aire libre, *m.* **in the o.,** al

descubierto. **in the o. air,** al aire libre, al raso, a cielo abierto. **to break o.,** forzar. **to cut o.,** abrir de un tajo, cortar. **to leave o.,** dejar abierto. **wide o.,** muy abierto; (of doors) de par en par. **o. boat,** barco descubierto, *m.* **o. car,** coche abierto, *m.* **o. carriage,** carruaje descubierto, *m.* **o. cast,** *Mineral.* roza abierta, *f.* **o.-eyed,** con los ojos abiertos. **o.-handed,** generoso, dadivoso. **o. letter,** carta abierta, *f.* **o.-minded,** imparcial. **o.-mouthed,** con la boca abierta, boquiabierto. **o. question,** cuestión por decidir, cuestión discutible, *f.* **o. secret,** secreto a voces, *m.* **o. sea,** alta mar, *f.* **o. town,** ciudad abierta, *f.* **o. tram-car,** jardinera, *f.* **o. truck,** vagoneta, *f.* **o.-work,** *Sew.* calado, enrejado, *m*

**opener** /'oupənər/ *n* abridor, *m*

**opening** /'oupənıŋ/ *n* abertura, brecha, *f*; orificio, *m*; inauguración, apertura, *f*; principio, *m*; (chance) oportunidad, *f*; (employment) puesto, *m.* **o. price,** *Com.* (on Exchange) precio de apertura, *m*, primer curso *m*

**openly** /'oupənli/ *adv* abiertamente, francamente; públicamente

**openness** /'oupənnıs/ *n* situación expuesta, *f*; espaciosidad, *f*; franqueza, *f*, candor, *m*; imparcialidad, *f*

**opera** /'ɒpərə/ *n* ópera, *f.* **comic o.,** zarzuela, *f.* **o.-cloak,** abrigo de noche, *m.* **o.-glasses,** gemelos de teatro, *m pl.* **o.-hat,** clac, *m.* **o.-house,** teatro de la ópera, *m.* **o. singer,** cantante de ópera, operista, *mf*

**operate** /'ɒpə,reit/ *vi* funcionar, trabajar; obrar; (with on, upon) producir efecto sobre; influir; *Surg.* operar; (on Exchange) especular, jugar a la bolsa; *vt* hacer funcionar, manejar; mover, impulsar; dirigir

**operatic** /,ɒpə'rætık/ *a* de ópera, operístico

**operating** /'ɒpə,reitıŋ/ *a* (of surgeons) operante; de operación. **o. table,** mesa de operaciones, *f.* **o. theater,** anfiteatro, *m*; sala de operaciones, *f*

**operation** /,ɒpə'reiʃən/ *n* funcionamiento, *m*, acción, *f*; *Surg.* intervención quirúrgica, operación, *f*; (*Mil. Naut.*) maniobra, *f*; manipulación, *f.* **to come into o.,** ponerse en práctica; hacerse efectivo. **to continue in o.,** ( laws) seguir en vigor. **to perform an o.,** *Surg.* operar, practicar una intervención quirúrgica; hacer una maniobra. **to put into o.,** poner en práctica

**operative** /'ɒpərətıv/ *a* operativo, activo. —*n* operario (-ia), obrero (-ra). **to become o.,** tener efecto

**operator** /'ɒpə,reitər/ *n* operario (-ia); (telephone) telefonista, *mf*; (machines, engines) maquinista, *mf*; *Surg.* operador, *m*

**operetta** /,ɒpə'retə/ *n* opereta, *f*

**ophthalmologist** /,ɒfθəl'mɒlədʒıst/ *n* oftalmólogo, *m*

**ophthalmology** /,ɒfθəl'mɒlədʒi/ *n* oftalmología, *f*

**opiate** /'oupiıt/ *n* opiata, *f*, narcótico, *m*, a opiado

**opine** /ou'pain/ *vi and vt* opinar, creer

**opinion** /ə'pınyən/ *n* opinión, *f*, parecer, juicio, *m*; concepto, *m*, idea, *f.* **in my o.,** según mi parecer. **to be of the o. that,** ser de la opinión que, opinar que. **to be of the same o.,** estar de acuerdo, concurrir. **public o.,** opinión (or voz) pública, *f*

**opinionated** /ə'pınyə,neitıd/ *a* terco, obstinado

**opium** /'oupiəm/ *n* opio, *m.* **o. addict,** opiónamo (-ma). **o. den,** fumadero de opio, *m.* **o. eater,** mascador de opio, opiófago, *m.* **o. smoker,** fumador (-ra) de opio

**Oporto** /ou'pɔrtou/ Oporto, Porto, *m*

**opponent** /ə'pounənt/ *n* antagonista, *mf*, enemigo (-ga); contrario (-ia), adversario (-ia), competidor (-ra)

**opportune** /,ɒpər'tun/ *a* oportuno, tempestivo, conveniente, a propósito. **to be o.,** venir al caso. **o. moment,** momento oportuno, *m*; hora propicia, *f*

**opportunely** /,ɒpər'tunli/ *adv* oportunamente. **to come o.,** venir a pelo

**opportuneness** /,ɒpər'tunnıs/ *n* oportunidad, tempestividad, conveniencia, *f*

**opportunism** /,ɒpər'tunızəm/ *n* oportunismo, *m*

**opportunist** /,ɒpər'tunıst/ *n* oportunista, *mf*

**opportunity** /,ɒpər'tunıti/ *n* oportunidad, ocasión, posibilidad, *f.* **to give an o. for,** dar margen para. **to open new opportunities,** abrir nuevos horizontes. **to take the o.,** tomar la oportunidad

**opposable** /ə'pouzəbəl/ *a* oponible

**oppose** /ə'pouz/ vt (counterbalance) oponer, contrarrestar; combatir; hacer frente (a), contrariar, pugnar contra, oponerse (a)

**opposed (to)** /ə'pouzd/ a opuesto a, enemigo de, contra

**opposing** /ə'pouziŋ/ a opuesto; enemigo, contrario

**opposite** /'ɒpəzɪt/ a (facing) de cara a, frente a, del otro lado de; opuesto; (antagonistic) contrario, antagónico; otro, diferente. —n contraria, f, lo opuesto; antagonista, mf; adversario (-ia). **the o. sex,** el otro sexo. **o. leaves,** Bot. hojas opuestas, f pl. **o. to,** frente a; distinto de

**opposition** /ˌɒpə'zɪʃən/ n oposición, f; (obstacle) estorbo, impedimento, m, dificultad, f; resistencia, hostilidad, f; (Astron. Polit.) oposición, f; (difference) contraste, m, diferencia, f. —a de la oposición. **in o.,** en oposición; Polit. en la oposición. **to be in o.,** estar en oposición; Polit. ser de la oposición, estar en la oposición

**oppress** /ə'pres/ vt oprimir, tiranizar, sojuzgar, apremiar; (of moral causes) abrumar, agobiar, desanimar; (of heat, etc.) ahogar

**oppression** /ə'preʃən/ n opresión, tiranía, crueldad, f; (moral) agobio, sufrimiento, m, ansia, f; (difficulty in breathing) sofocación, f, ahogo, m

**oppressive** /ə'presɪv/ a opresivo, tiránico, cruel; (taxes, etc.) gravoso; (of heat) sofocante, asfixiante; agobiador, abrumador

**oppressor** /ə'presər/ n opresor (-ra), sojuzgador (-ra), tirano (-na)

**opprobrious** /ə'proubriəs/ a oprobioso, vituperioso; infame

**opprobrium** /ə'proubriəm/ n oprobio, m, ignominia, f

**opt** /ɒpt/ vi optar, escoger, elegir

**optic, optical** a óptico. **o. illusion,** ilusión óptica, f; engaño a la vista, trampantojo, m. **o. nerve,** nervio óptico, m

**optician** /ɒp'tɪʃən/ n óptico, m

**optics** /'ɒptɪks/ n óptica, f

**optimism** /'ɒptəˌmɪzəm/ n optimismo, m

**optimist** /'ɒptəmɪst/ n optimista, mf

**optimistic** /ˌɒptə'mɪstɪk/ a optimista

**optimum** /'ɒptəməm/ n lo óptimo; (used as adjective) óptimo

**option** /'ɒpʃən/ n opción, f, (all meanings)

**optional** /'ɒpʃənl/ a discrecional, facultativo

**opulence** /'ɒpyələns/ n opulencia, riqueza, magnificencia, f; (abundance) abundancia, copia, f

**opulent** /'ɒpyələnt/ a opulento, rico, acaudalado; abundante

**opus** /'oupəs/ n obra, composición, f

**opuscule** /ou'pʌskyul/ n opúsculo, m

**or** /ɔr/ conjunc o; (before a word beginning with o or ho) u; (negative) ni. —n Herald. oro, m. **an hour or so,** una hora más o menos, alrededor de una hora. **either... or,** o.... o. **or else,** o bien. **whether... or,** que... que, siquiera... siquiera, ya... ya. **without... or,** sin... ni

**oracle** /'ɒrəkəl/ n oráculo, m

**oracular** /ɔ'rækyələr/ a profético, vatídico; ambiguo, misterioso, sibilino; dogmático, magistral

**oral** /'ɔrəl/ a verbal, hablado; Anat. oral, bucal

**oral cavity** n cavidad bucal, f

**orange** /'ɒrɪndʒ/ n (tree) naranjo, m; (fruit) naranja, f; **bitter o.,** naranja amarga, f. **blood o.,** naranja dulce, f. **tangerine o.,** naranja mandarina, f. **o. blossom,** azahar, m. **o. color,** color de naranja, m. **o.-colored,** de color de naranja, anaranjado. **o.-flower water,** agua de azahar, f. **o. grove,** naranjal, m. **o. grower** (or **seller**), naranjero (-ra). **o. peel,** piel de naranja, f. **o.-stick,** (for nails) limpiauñas, m

**orangeade** /ˌɒrɪndʒ'eid/ n naranjada, f; (mineral water) gaseosa, f

**orangery** /'ɒrɪndʒri/ n naranjal, m

**orangutan** /ɔ'ræŋʊˌtæn/ n Zool. orangután, m

**oration** /ɔ'reiʃən/ n oración, declamación, f, discurso, m

**orator** /'ɒrətər/ n orador (-ra), declamador (-ra)

**oratorical** /ˌɒrə'tɔrɪkəl/ a oratorio, declamatorio, retórico

**oratorio** /ˌɒrə'tɔriˌou/ n Mus. oratorio, m

**oratory** /'ɒrəˌtɔri/ n oratoria, elocuencia, f; Eccl. oratorio, m, capilla, f

**orb** /ɔrb/ n orbe, m; esfera, f, globo, m; astro, m; Poet. ojo, m

**orbit** /'ɔrbɪt/ n Astron. órbita, f; Anat. órbita, cuenca del ojo, f

**orbital** /'ɔrbɪtl/ a Anat. orbital

**orchard** /'ɔrtʃərd/ n huerto, vergel, m; (especially of apples) pomar, m

**orchestra** /'ɔrkəstrə/ n orquesta, f. **with full o.,** con gran orquesta. Theat. **o. seat, o. stall,** butaca de piatea, f

**orchestral** /ɔr'kestrəl/ a orquestal, instrumental

**orchestrate** /'ɔrkəˌstreit/ vt orquestar, instrumentar

**orchestration** /ˌɔrkə'streiʃən/ n orquestración, instrumentación, f

**orchid** /'ɔrkɪd/ n orquídea, f

**orchitis** /ɔr'kaitɪs/ n Med. orquitis, f

**ordain** /ɔr'dein/ vt mandar, disponer, decretar; Eccl. ordenar. **to be ordained as,** Eccl. ordenarse de

**ordeal** /ɔr'dil/ n Hist. ordalías, f pl; prueba severa, f

**order** /'ɔrdər/ n (most meanings) orden, m; (command) precepto, mandamiento, decreto, m; orden, f; (rule) regla, f; (for money) libranza postal, f; (for goods) pedido, encargo, m; (arrangement) método, arreglo, m, clasificación, f; (condition) estado, m; Archit. estilo, m; (Zool. Bot.) orden, m; (sort) clase, especie, f; (rank) clase social, f; Eccl. orden, f; (badge) condecoración, insignia, f; (association) sociedad, asociación, compañía, f; (to view a house, etc.) permiso, m; (series) serie, f. **in good o.,** en buen estado; arreglado. **in o.,** (alphabetical, etc.) en orden; arreglado; (parliamentary) en regla. **in o. that,** para que, a fin de que. **in o. to,** a fin de para. **out of o.,** estropeado, descompuesto; (on a notice) No funciona; (parliamentary) fuera del orden del día. **till further o.,** hasta nueva orden. **to o.,** Com. por encargo especial. **to give an o.,** dar una orden; Com. poner un pedido. **to go out of o.,** descomponerse. **to keep in o.,** mantener en orden. **to put in o.,** poner en orden, ordenar. **O.!** ¡Orden! orden real, f. **o. of knighthood,** orden de caballería, f. **o. of the day,** orden del día, f. reglamento, m

**order** /'ɔrdər/ vt disponer; arreglar; (command) mandar, ordenar; (request) rogar, pedir; (direct) dirigir, gobernar; Com. encargar, cometer; (a meal, a taxi) encargar. **I ordered them to do it,** Les mandé hacerlo. **to o. about,** mandar. **to o. back,** hacer volver, mandar que vuelva. **to o. down,** hacer bajar, pedir (a uno) que baje. **to o. in,** mandar entrar. **to o. off,** despedir, decir (a uno) que se vaya. **to o. out,** mandar salir; (the troops) hacer salir la tropa; echar. **to o. up,** mandar subir, hacer subir

**orderliness** /'ɔrdərlinɪs/ n orden, aseo, método, m; limpieza, f; buena conducta, formalidad, f; buena administración, f

**orderly** /'ɔrdərli/ a bien arreglado, metódico; aseado, en orden; (of behaviour) formal, bien disciplinado. —n Mil. ordenanza, m; ayudante de hospital m

**ordinal** /'ɔrdnəl/ a and n ordinal m

**ordinance** /'ɔrdnəns/ n ordenanza, f, reglamento, m; Archit. ordenación, f; Eccl. rito, m

**ordinarily** /ˌɔrdn'eərəli/ adv de ordinario, ordinariamente, comúnmente

**ordinary** /'ɔrdnˌeri/ a (usual) corriente, común, usual, ordinario, normal; (average) mediano, mediocre; (somewhat vulgar) ordinario, vulgar. —n Eccl. ordinario, m. **out of the o.,** excepcional; poco común. **o. seaman,** marinero, m. **o. share,** Com. acción ordinaria, f

**ordination** /ˌɔrdn'eiʃən/ n Eccl. ordenación, f

**ordnance** /'ɔrdnəns/ n artillería, f, cañones, m pl; pertrechos de guerra, m pl. **o. survey map,** mapa del estado mayor, m. **o. survey number,** acotación, f

**ore** /ɔr/ n Mineral. mena, f, quijo, m

**organ** /'ɔrgən/ n (all meanings) órgano, m. **barrel-o.,** organillo, órgano de manubrio, m. **o.-blower,** entonador (-ra). **o.-grinder,** organillero (-ra). **o.-loft,** tribuna del órgano, f. **o.-pipe,** cañón de órgano, m. **o.-stop,** registro de órgano, m

**organdy** n organdí, m

**organic** /ɔr'gænɪk/ *a* orgánico. **o. chemistry,** química orgánica, *f*

**organism** /'ɔrgə,nɪzəm/ *n* organismo, *m*

**organist** /'ɔrgənɪst/ *n* organista, *mf*

**organization** /,ɔrgənə'zeifən/ *n* organización, *f*; grupo, *m*, asociación, sociedad, *f*; organismo, *m*

**organize** /'ɔrgə,naiz/ *vt* organizar; arreglar. —*vi* organizarse; asociarse, constituirse

**organizer** /'ɔrgə,naizər/ *n* organizador (-ra)

**organizing** /'ɔrgə,naizɪŋ/ *a* organizador

**orgasm** /'ɔrgæzəm/ *n Med.* orgasmo, *m*

**orgiastic** /,ɔrdʒi'æstɪk/ *a* orgiástico

**orgy** /'ɔrdʒi/ *n* orgía, *f*

**oriel** /'ɔriəl/ *n Archit.* mirador, *m*

**orient** /'ɔriənt/ *a Poet.* naciente, oriental. —*n* Oriente, Este, *m.* **pearl of fine o.,** perla de hermoso oriente, *f*

**oriental** /,ɔri'ɛntl/ *a* and *a* oriental, *mf*

**orientalism** /,ɔri'ɛntlɪzəm/ *n* orientalismo, *m*

**orientalist** /,ɔri'ɛntlɪst/ *n* orientalista, *mf*

**orientate** /'ɔriən,teit/ *vt* orientar; dirigir, guiar. —*vi* mirar (or caer) hacia el este; orientarse

**orientation** /,ɔriən'teifən/ *n* orientación, *f*

**orifice** /'ɔrəfɪs/ *n* orificio, *m*; abertura, boca, *f*

**origin** /'ɔrɪdʒɪn/ *n* origen, génesis, *m*; raíz, causa, *f*; principio, comienzo, *m*; (extraction) descendencia, procedencia, familia, *f*, nacimiento, *m*

**original** /ə'rɪdʒənl/ *a* original; primitivo, primero; ingenioso. —*n* original, *m*; prototipo, modelo, *m.* **o. sin,** pecado original, *m*

**originality** /ə,rɪdʒə'nælɪti/ *n* originalidad, *f*

**originally** /ə'rɪdʒənli/ *adv* originalmente; al principio; antiguamente

**originate** /ə'rɪdʒə,neit/ *vt* (produce) ocasionar, producir, suscitar, iniciar, engendrar; (create) inventar, crear. —*vi* originarse, surgir, nacer. **to o. in,** tener su origen en, surgir de, emanar de, venir de

**origination** /ə,rɪdʒə'neifən/ *n* origen, principio, génesis, *m*

**originator** /ə'rɪdʒə,neitər/ *n* iniciador (-ra), fundador (-ra); autor (-ra), creador (-ra)

**oriole** /'ɔri,oul/ *n Ornith.* oropéndola, *f*

**Orion** /ə'raiən/ *n Astron.* Orión, *m*

**Orkneys, the** /'ɔrkniz/ las Orcades, *f pl*

**ornament** /*n.* 'ɔrnəmənt; *v.* -,mɛnt/ *n* adorno, *m*; decoración, *f*; *Fig.* ornamento, *m*; (trinket) chuchería, *f*, *n pl.* **ornaments,** *Eccl.* ornamentos, *m pl.* —*vt* ornar, adornar, decorar, embellecer

**ornamental** /,ɔrnə'mɛntl/ *a* ornamental, decorativo

**ornamentation** /,ɔrnəmɛn'teifən/ *n* ornamentación, decoración, *f*

**ornate** /ɔr'neit/ *a* vistoso, ornado en demasía, barroco

**ornateness** /ɔr'neitnɪs/ *n* elegancia, vistosidad, magnificencia, *f*

**ornithological** /,ɔrnəθə'lɒdʒɪkəl/ *a* ornitológico

**ornithologist** /,ɔrnə'θɒlədʒɪst/ *n* ornitólogo, *m*

**ornithology** /,ɔrnə'θɒlədʒi/ *n* ornitología, *f*

**orphan** /'ɔrfən/ *a* and *n* huérfano (-na)

**orphanage** /'ɔrfənɪdʒ/ *n* orfanato, hospicio, *m*

**orphanhood** /'ɔrfən,hʊd/ *n* orfandad, *f*

**Orphean** /ɔr'fiən/ *a* órfico

**orthodox** /'ɔrθə,dɒks/ *a* ortodoxo

**orthodoxy** /'ɔrθə,dɒksi/ *n* ortodoxia, *f*

**orthographic** /,ɔrθə'græfɪk/ *a* ortográfico

**orthography** /ɔr'θɒgrəfi/ *n* ortografía, *f*

**orthopedic** /,ɔrθə'pidɪk/ *a* ortopédico

**orthopedics** /,ɔrθə'pidɪks/ *n* ortopedia, *f*

**orthopedist** /,ɔrθə'pidɪst/ *n* ortopedista, *mf* ortopédico (-ca)

**oscillate** /'ɒsə,leit/ *vi* oscilar, fluctuar; (hesitate) dudar, vacilar. —*vt* hacer oscilar

**oscillation** /,ɒsə'leifən/ *n* oscilación, fluctuación, vibración, *f*; *Elec.* oscilación, *f*

**oscillator** /'ɒsə,leitər/ *n* oscilador, *m*

**oscillatory** /'ɒsələ,tɔri/ *a* oscilante

**osculation** /,ɒskyə'leifən/ *n* ósculo, *m*

**osier** /'ouʒər/ *n Bot.* mimbre, *m*, or *f.* **o. bed,** mimbrera, *f*

**osmic** /'ɒzmɪk/ *a Chem.* ósmico

**osmosis** /ɒz'mousɪs/ *n* (*Phys. Chem.*) ósmosis, *f*

**osprey** /'ɒspri, -prei/ *n Ornith.* quebrantahuesos, *m*

**osseous** /'ɒsiəs/ *a* óseo

**ossification** /,ɒsəfɪ'keifən/ *n* osificación, *f*

**ossify** /'ɒsə,fai/ *vt* osificar; *vi* osificarse

**ossuary** /'ɒfu,ɛri/ *n* osario, *m*

**osteitis** /,ɒsti'aitɪs/ *n Med.* osteítis, *f*

**Ostend** /ɒs'tɛnd/ Ostende, *m*

**ostensible** /ɒ'stɛnsəbəl/ *a* ostensible; aparente, engañoso, ilusorio

**ostensibly** /ɒ'stɛnsəbli/ *adv* en apariencia, ostensiblemente

**ostentation** /,ɒstɛn'teifən/ *n* ostentación, *f*; aparato, fausto, boato, alarde, *m*, soberbia, *f*

**ostentatious** /,ɒstɛn'teifəs/ *a* ostentoso; aparatoso, fastuoso, rumboso

**ostentatiously** /,ɒstɛn'teifəsli/ *adv* con ostentación

**osteology** /,ɒsti'ɒlədʒi/ *n* osteología, *f*

**osteomyelitis** /,ɒstiou,maiə'laitɪs/ *n Med.* osteomielitis, *f*

**osteopath** /'ɒstiə,pæθ/ *n* osteópata, *m*

**osteopathy** /,ɒsti'ɒpəθi/ *n* osteopatía, *f*

**osteoplasty** /'ɒstiə,plæsti/ *n Surg.* osteoplastia, *f*

**ostler** /'ɒslər/ *n* mozo de cuadras, establero, *m*

**ostracism** /'ɒstrə,sɪzəm/ *n* ostracismo, *m*

**ostracize** /'ɒstrə,saiz/ *vt* desterrar; excluir del trato, echar de la sociedad

**ostrich** /'ɒstrɪtʃ/ *n* avestruz, *m*.

**otalgia** /ou'tældʒiə/ *n Med.* otalgia, *f*, dolor de oídos, *m*

**other** /'ʌðər/ *a* otro. —*pron* el otro, *m*; la otra, *f*; lo otro, *neut adv* (with than) de otra manera que, de otro modo que; otra cosa que. **this hand, not the o.,** esta mano, no la otra. **every o. day,** un día sí y otro no, cada dos días. **no o.,** ningún otro, *m*; otra ninguna, *f.* **someone or o.,** alguien. **the others,** los (las) demás, *m*, *f pl*; los otros, *m pl*; las otras, *f pl.* **o. people,** otros, *m pl*, los demás

**otherwise** /'ʌðər,waiz/ *adv* de otra manera, de otro modo, otramente; (in other respects) por lo demás, por otra parte; (if not) si no

**otitis** /ou'taitɪs/ *n Med.* otitis, *f*

**otologist** /ou'tɒlədʒɪst/ *n* otólogo, *m*

**otology** /ou'tɒlədʒi/ *n* otología, *f*

**otter** /'ɒtər/ *n Zool.* nutria, *f.* **o. hound,** perro para cazar la nutria

**ottoman** /'ɒtəmən/ *a* otomano, turco. —*n* otomana, *f*

**ouch!** /autʃ/ *interj* ¡ax!, ¡huy!

**ought** /ɔt/ *v aux* deber, tener la obligación (de); ser conveniente, convenir; ser necesario (que), tener que. **I o. to have done it yesterday,** Debía haberlo hecho ayer. **She o. not to come,** No debe (debiera, debería) venir. **He o. to see them tomorrow,** (should) Conviene que les vea mañana; Tiene la obligación de verles mañana; (must) Es necesario que les vea mañana, Tiene que verles mañana.

**ounce** /auns/ *n* (animal and weight) onza, *f.* **He hasn't an o. of common sense,** No tiene pizca de sentido común

**our** /auᵊr *unstressed* ɑr/ *a* nuestro

**ours** /auᵊrz/ *pron* nuestro, *m*; nuestra, *f*; nuestros, *m pl*; nuestras, *f pl*; de nosotros, *m pl*; de nosotras, *f pl*; el nuestro, *m*; la nuestra, *f*; lo nuestro, *neut*; los nuestros, *m pl*; las nuestras, *f pl.* **This book is ours,** Este libro es nuestro (or el nuestro)

**ourselves** /ɑr'sɛlvz/ *pron pl* nosotros mismos, *m pl*; nosotras mismas, *f pl*

**oust** /aust/ *vt* despedir, desahuciar, expulsar, echar

**out** /aut/ *adv* afuera; hacia fuera; (gone out) fuera, salido, ausente; (invested) puesto; (published) publicado, salido; (discovered) conocido, descubierto; (on strike) en huelga; (mistaken) en error, equivocado, (of journeys) de ida, (on ships) de navegación (e.g. *on the second day out,* al segundo día de navegación); (of fire, etc.) extinguido; (at sea) en el mar; (of girls in society) puesta de largo, que ha entrado en sociedad; (of fashion) fuera de moda; (of office) fuera del poder; (in holes) roto, agujereado, andrajoso; (exhausted) agotado; (expired) vencido; (of a watch) llevar... minutos (horas) de atraso or de adelanto; (unfriendly) reñido; (way out) salida, *f*; (sport) fuera de juego; (of flowers) abierto; (of chickens) empollado. **a scene out of one of Shakespeare's plays,** una escena de una de las comedias de Shakespeare. **I am**

**out** $6, He perdido seis dólares. **I am out of tea,** Se me ha acabado el té. **to drink out of a glass,** beber de un vaso. **to read out of a book,** leer en un libro. **to speak out,** hablar claro. **Murder will out,** El asesinato se descubrirá. **out-and-out,** completo; (with rogue, etc.) redomado. **out of,** fuera de; (beyond) más allá de; (through, by) por; (with) con; (without) sin; (from among) entre; (in) en; (with a negative sense) no. **out of breath,** jadeante, sin aliento. **out of character,** impropio. **out of commission,** fuera de servicio. **out of danger,** fuera de peligro. **out of date,** anticuado. **out of hand,** en seguida; indisciplinado. **out of money,** sin dinero. **out of necessity,** por necesidad. **out of one's mind,** loco, demente. **out of order.** See **order. out of print,** agotado. **out of reach,** fuera de alcance, inasequible. **out of season,** fuera de temporada. **out of sight,** fuera del alcance de la vista; invisible. **Out of sight, out of mind,** Ojos que no ven, corazón que no siente. **out of sorts,** indispuesto. **out of temper,** de mal genio. **out of the question,** imposible. **out of the way,** adv (of work) terminado, hecho; (remote) fuera del camino; (put aside) arrinconado; donde no estorbe. **out-of-the-way,** a remoto, aislado; (unusual) extraordinario, singular. **out of this world,** lo máximo, lo último. **out of touch with,** alejado de; sin relaciones con; sin simpatía con. **out of work,** sin empleo, sin trabajo, en paro forzoso. **out-patient,** enfermo (-ma) de un dispensario. **Out!** interj ¡Fuera! ¡Fuera de aquí! ¡Márchate! **Out with it!** ¡Hable Vd.! sin rodeos! ¡Hablen claro!

**outbalance** /ˌautˈbæləns/ vt exceder, sobrepujar
**outbid** /ˌautˈbɪd/ vt pujar, mejorar
**outbidding** /ˌautˈbɪdɪŋ/ n puja, mejora, f
**outbreak** /ˈautˌbreik/ n (of war) declaración, f; comienzo, m; (of disease) epidemia, f; (of crimes, etc.) serie, f
**outbuilding** /ˈautˌbɪldɪŋ/ n dependencia, f, edificio accesorio, anexo, m
**outburst** /ˈautˌbɜrst/ n acceso, arranque, m, explosión, f
**outcast** /ˈautˌkæst/ n paria, mf; desterrado (-da), proscripto (-ta)
**outclass** /ˌautˈklæs/ vt aventajar, ser superior (a), exceder
**outcome** /ˈautˌkʌm/ n consecuencia, f, resultado, m
**outcry** /ˈautˌkrai/ n clamor, grito, m; protesta, f
**outdistance** /ˌautˈdɪstəns/ vt dejar atrás
**outdo** /ˌautˈdu/ vt eclipsar, aventajar, sobrepujar
**outdoor** /ˈautˌdɔr/ a externo; (of activities) al aire libre; fuera de casa
**outdoors** /ˌautˈdɔrz/ adv fuera de casa; al aire libre
**outer** /ˈautər/ a externo, exterior
**outermost** /ˈautərˌmoust/ a superl (el, etc.) más externo, más exterior; extremo, de más allá
**outer space** espacio extraatmosférico, espacio extraterrestre, espacio exterior, espacio sideral, espacio sidéreo, espacio ultraterrestre, m
**outfit** /ˈautˌfɪt/ n equipo, m; (of clothes) traje, m; (of furniture or trousseau) ajuar, m; (gear) pertrechos, avíos, m pl. —vt aviar equipar
**outfitter** /ˈautˌfɪtər/ n proveedor (-ra), abastecedor (-ra)
**outflank** /ˌautˈflæŋk/ vt Mil. flanquear; ser más listo (que)
**outgoing** /ˈautˌgouɪŋ/ a saliente, que sale; cesante. **outgoings,** n pl gastos, m pl
**outgrow** /ˌautˈgrou/ vt hacerse demasiado grande para; crecer más que; (ideas) perder; (illness) curarse de, curarse con la edad; pasar de la edad de, ser ya viejo para. **to o. one's clothes,** quedársele a uno chica la ropa.
**outgrowth** /ˈautˌgrouθ/ n excrecencia, f; resultado, fruto, m, consecuencia, f
**outhouse** /ˈautˌhaus/ n edificio accesorio, m
**outing** /ˈautɪŋ/ n excursión, vuelta, f, paseo, m
**outlandish** /autˈlændɪʃ/ a extraño, singular, raro; absurdo, ridículo
**outlast** /ˌautˈlæst/ vt durar más que; (outlive) sobrevivir a
**outlaw** /ˈautˌlɔ/ n bandido, proscrito, m, vt proscribir
**outlay** /ˈautˌlei/ n gasto, desembolso, m

**outlet** /ˈautlɛt/ n salida, f; orificio de salida, m; (of drains, etc.) desagüe, m; (of streets, rivers) desembocadura, f; Fig. escape, m, válvula de seguridad, f
**outline** /ˈautˌlain/ n perfil, contorno, m; (drawing) esbozo, bosquejo, m; idea general, f; plan general, m, vt esbozar, bosquejar. **in o.,** en esbozo; en perfil. **to be outlined** (against), dibujarse (contra), destacarse (contra)
**outlive** /ˌautˈlɪv/ vt sobrevivir (a); (live down) hacer olvidar
**outlook** /ˈautˌlʊk/ n (view) perspectiva, vista, f; (opinion) actitud, f, punto de vista, m; aspecto, m, apariencia, f; (for trade, etc.) perspectiva, f, posibilidades, f pl. **o. tower,** atalaya, f
**outlying** /ˈautˌlaiŋ/ a remoto, lejano, distante
**outmaneuver** /ˌautməˈnuvər/ vt superar en estrategia
**outmatch** /ˌautˈmætʃ/ vt aventajar, superar
**outmoded** /ˈautˈmoudɪd/ a anticuado, pasado de moda
**outnumber** /ˌautˈnʌmbər/ vt ser más numerosos que, exceder en número
**out-of-court settlement** /ˈaut əv ˌkɔrt/ n arreglo pacífico, m
**out-of-town** a de las provincias
**outpost** /ˈautˌpoust/ n Mil. avanzada, f, puesto avanzado, m
**outpouring** /ˈautˌpɔrɪŋ/ n derramamiento, m; efusión, f
**output** /ˈautˌpʊt/ n producción, f. **o. capacity,** capacidad de producción, f
**outrage** /ˈautreidʒ/ n barbaridad infamia, atrocidad, f; rapto, m, violación, f. —vt ultrajar; violar;
**outrageous** /autˈreidʒəs/ a atroz, terrible; desaforado, monstruoso; injurioso; ridículo
**outrageousness** /autˈreidʒəsnɪs/ n lo atroz; violencia, furia, f; escándalo, m; enormidad, f; lo excesivo; lo horrible
**outré** /uˈtrei/ a cursi, extravagante
**outride** /ˌautˈraid/ vt cabalgar más a prisa que
**outright** /adv. ˈautˈrait; a. ˈautˌrait/ adv (frankly) de plano (e.g. to reject outright, rechazar de plano), francamente, sin reserva; (immediately) en seguida, immediatamente. —a categórico; completo; franco
**outrival** /ˈautˌraivəl/ vt vencer, superar
**outrun** /ˌautˈrʌn/ vt correr más que
**outset** /ˈautˌsɛt/ n principio, comienzo, m
**outshine** /ˌautˈʃain/ vt brillar más que, eclipsar en brillantez; superar, eclipsar
**outside** /adv., prep., a. ˈautˈsaid; n. ˈautˈsaid/ adv afuera, fuera. —prep fuera de, al otro lado de, al exterior de; (besides) aparte de, fuera de. —a externo, exterior; (of labor, etc.) desde fuera; máximo; ajeno. —n exterior, m; superficie, f; aspecto, m, apariencia, f. **at the o.,** a lo sumo, cuando más. **from the o.,** de (o desde) fuera. **on the o.,** (externally) por fuera. **o. the door,** a la puerta
**outsider** /ˌautˈsaidər/ n forastero (-ra); desconocido (-da); caballo desconocido, m; persona poco deseable, f
**outsize** /ˈautˌsaiz/ n artículo de talla mayor que las corrientes, m
**outskirts** /ˈautˌskɜrts/ n pl alrededores, m pl, afueras, inmediaciones, cercanías, f pl
**outspoken** /ˈautˈspoukən/ a franco. **to be o.,** decir lo que se piensa, no tener pelos en la lengua
**outspokenness** /ˈautˈspoukənnɪs/ n franqueza, f,
**outspread** /ˈautˌsprɛd/ a extendido; (of wings) desplegadas
**outstanding** /ˌautˈstændɪŋ/ a excelente; sobresaliente, conspicuo; Com. pendiente, sin pagar. **to be o.,** Com. estar pendiente; Fig. sobresalir. **o. account,** Com. cuenta pendiente, f
**outstay** /ˌautˈstei/ vt quedarse más tiempo que. **to o. one's welcome,** pegársele la silla
**outstretched** /ˌautˈstrɛtʃt/ a extendido
**outstrip** /ˌautˈstrip/ vt dejar atrás, pasar; aventajar, superar
**outvote** /ˌautˈvout/ vt emitir más votos que; rechazar por votación
**outward** /ˈautwərd/ a exterior, externo; aparente, visible. —adv exteriormente; hacia fuera; superficial-

mente. **o. bound,** con rumbo a... **o. voyage,** el viaje de ida

**outwardly** /'autwərdli/ *adv* exteriormente; hacia fuera; en apariencia

**outwear** /,aut'weər/ *vt* durar más que; gastar

**outweigh** /,aut'wei/ *vt* exceder, valer más que

**outwit** /,aut'wit/ *vt* ser más listo que; vencer

**outworn** /'aut'wɔrn/ *a* anticuado, ya viejo

**oval** /'ouval/ *n* óvalo, *m, a* oval, ovalado, aovado

**ovarian** /ou'veəriən/ *a* (*Bot. Zool.*) ovárico

**ovary** /'ouvəri/ *n* ovario, *m*

**ovation** /ou'veifən/ *n* ovación, recepción entusiasta, *f*

**oven** /'ʌvən/ *n* horno, *m*. **o. peel,** pala de horno, *f.* **o. rake,** hurgón, *m*

**over** /'ouvər/ *prep* (above, upon, over) sobre, encima de; (on the other side) al otro lado de; (across) allende, a través de; (more than) más de; (beyond) más allá de; (of rank) superior a; (during) durante; (in addition) además de; (through) por. —*n* en; por encima; al otro lado; de un lado a otro; enfrente; al lado contrario; de un extremo a otro; (finished) terminado; (ruined) arruinado, perdido; (more) más; (excessively) demasiado, excesivamente; (covered) cubierto (de); (extra) en exceso; (completely) enteramente; (from head to foot) de pies a cabeza, de hito en hito; (of time) pasado. **over** is also used as a prefix. Indicating excess, it is generally translated by demasiado or excesivamente. In other meanings, it is either not translated or its meaning forms part of the verb, being translated as re-, super-, trans-, ultra. Very often a less literal translation is more successful than the employment of the above prefixes. **all o.,** (everywhere) en todas partes; (finished) todo acabado; (covered) cubierto (de); (up and down) de pies a cabeza. **all the world o.,** en todo el mundo. **He is o. in Germany,** Está en Alemania. **that which is o., Estaba todo tembloroso. that which is o.,** el exceso, lo que queda. **to read o.,** leer, repasar. **o. again,** de nuevo. **o. and above,** por encima de, fuera de, en exceso de. **o. and o.,** repetidamente, muchas veces. **o. my signature,** bajo mi firma. **o. six months since...,** más de seis meses desde que...

**overabundance** /,ouvərə'bʌndəns/ *n* sobreabundancia, *f*

**overabundant** /,ouvərə'bʌndənt/ *a* sobreabundante

**overact** /,ouvər'ækt/ *vt* exagerar (un papel)

**overall** /'ouvər,ɔl/ *n* bata, *f;* guardapolvo, *m; a* de conjunto (e.g., *overall assessment,* evaluación de conjunto) *pl* **overalls,** mono, *m*

**overanxious** /,ouvər'æŋkfəs/ *a* demasiado ansioso; demasiado inquieto. **to be o.-a.,** preocuparse demasiado

**overarch** /,ouvər'artf/ *vt* abovedar

**overawe** /,ouvər'ɔ/ *vt* intimidar, acobardar

**overbalance** /,ouvər'bæləns/ *vt* hacer perder el equilibrio. hacer caer; preponderar. —*vi* perder el equilibrio, caer

**overbalancing** /'ouvər,bæələnsɪŋ/ *n* pérdida del equilibrio, caída, *f;* preponderancia, *f*

**overbearing** /,ouvər'bɛərɪŋ/ *a* dominante, autoritario, imperioso

**overboard** /'ouvər,bɔrd/ *adv* al agua, al mar.

**overburden** /,ouvər'bɜrdn̩/ *vt* sobrecargar, agobiar

**overcast** /*a.* 'ouvər'kæst; *v.* ,ouvər'kæst/ *a* anublado, cerrado, encapotado. —*vt Sew.* sobrehilar. **to become o.,** anublarse

**overcharge** /*n.* 'ouvər,tfardʒ; *v.* ,ouvər'tfardʒ/ *n* recargo, *m;* (price) recargo de precio, precio excesivo, *m.* —*vt* recargar, cobrar un precio excesivo; *Elec.* sobrecargar. —*vi* cobrar demasiado

**overcloud** /,ouvər'klaud/ *vt* anublar; *Fig.* entristecer

**overcoat** /'ouvər,kout/ *n* abrigo, sobretodo, gabán, *m*

**overcome** /,ouvər'kʌm/ *vt* vencer, rendir, subyugar; (difficulties) triunfar de, allanar, dominar. —*vi* saber vencer. —*a* (by sleep, etc.) rendido; (at a loss) turbado, confundido; (by kindness) agradecidísimo

**overconfidence** /,ouvər'kɒnfɪdəns/ *n* confianza excesiva, *f*

**overcooked** /'ouvər,kukt/ *a* recocido, demasiado cocido

**overcrowd** /,ouvər'kraud/ *vt* atestar, llenar de bote en bote; (over-populate) sobrepoblar

**overcrowding** /'ouvər,kraudɪŋ/ *n* sobrepoblación, *f*

**overdo** /,ouvər'du/ *vt* exagerar; ir demasiado lejos, hacer demasiado; *Cul.* recocer; (overtire) fatigarse demasiado

**overdose** /'ouvər,dous/ *n* dosis excesiva, *f*

**overdraft** /'ouvər,dræft/ *n Com.* giro en descubierto, *m*

**overdraw** /,ouvər'drɔ/ *vt* and *vi Com.* girar en descubierto

**over-dressed** /'ouvər 'drɛst/ *a* que viste demasiado; cursi

**overdue** /,ouvər'du/ *a* atrasado; *Com.* vencido y no pagado

**overeat** /,ouvər'it/ *vi* comer demasiado, atracarse

**overestimate** /,ouvər'estə,meit/ *vt* estimar en valor excesivo; exagerar, sobreestimar, *n* presupuesto excesivo, *m;* estimación excesiva, *f*

**overexcite** /,ouvərɪk'sait/ *vt* sobreexcitar

**overexposure** /,ouvərɪk'spouʒər/ *n Photo.* exceso de exposición, *m*

**overfatigue** /,ouvərfə'tig/ *vt* fatigar demasiado. —*n* cansancio excesivo, *m*

**overfeeding** /'ouvər,fidɪŋ/ *n* sobrealimentación, *f*

**overflow** /*v.* ,ouvər'flou; *n.* 'ouvər,flou/ *vt* inundar, derramarse por; *Fig.* cubrir, llenar; desbordarse. —*vi* (with) rebosar de. —*n* inundación, *f*, desbordamiento, derrame, *m; Fig.* residuo, resto, exceso, *m;* (plumbing) sumidero, vertedero, *m*, descarga, *f.* **The river overflowed its banks,** El río se desbordó, El río salió de cauce

**overflowing** /,ouvər'flouɪŋ/ *a* rebosante; superabundante. **filled to o.,** lleno hasta los bordes.

**overgrown** /,ouvər'groun/ *a* (gawky) talludo; (plants) exuberante, vicioso; frondoso, cubierto de verdura

**overhang** /,ouvər'hæŋ/ *vt* caer a, mirar a; colgar; *Fig.* amenazar. —*vi* colgar, sobresalir; *Fig.* amenazar

**overhanging** /'ouvər,hæŋɪŋ/ *a* saledizo, sobresaliente; colgante, pendiente

**overhaul** /*v.* ,ouvər'hɔl; *n.* 'ouvər,hɔl/ *vt* examinar, investigar; componer, hacer una inspección general de; (of boats overtaking) alcanzar. —*n* examen, *m*, investigación, *f; Med.* exploración general, *f*

**overhead** /'ouvər'hɛd/ *adv* arriba, en lo alto, encima de la cabeza. —*a* aéreo, elevado; general, fijo. **o. cable,** cable eléctrico, *m.* **o. expenses,** gastos generales, *m pl.* **o. railway,** ferrocarril aéreo (or elevado), *m*

**overhear** /,ouvər'hiər/ *vt* (accidentally) oír por casualidad, oír sin querer; (on purpose) alcanzar a oír, lograr oír

**overheat** /,ouvər'hit/ *vt* acalorar, hacer demasiado caliente, recalentar. —*vi* (in argument) acalorarse; hacerse demasiado caliente

**overheating** /,ouvər'hitɪŋ/ *n* recalentamiento, *m*

**overindulge** /,ouvərɪn'dʌldʒ/ *vt* mimar demasiado; dedicarse a algo con exceso; tomar algo con exceso. —*vi* darse demasiada buena vida

**overjoyed** /'ouvər,dʒɔid/ *a* contentísimo, lleno de alegría, encantado

**overland** /'ouvər,lænd/ *adv* por tierra. —*a* terrestre, trascontinental

**overlap** /*v.* ,ouvər'læp; *n.* 'ouvər,læp/ *vi* traslaparse; coincidir. —*n* traslapo, *m*

**overlay** /,ouvər'lei/ *vt* cubrir, dar una capa; (with silver) platear; (with gold) dorar. —*n* capa, *f;* cubierta, *f*

**overleaf** /'ouvər,lif/ *adv* a la vuelta

**overload** /*v.* ,ouvər'loud; *n.* 'ouvər,loud/ *vt* sobrecargar, recargar. —*n* sobrecarga, *f*

**overlook** /,ouvər'luk/ *vt* (face) dar a, mirar a, dominar; (supervise) vigilar, examinar, inspeccionar; (not notice) no notar, pasar por alto, no hacer, caso de, no fijarse en; (neglect) desdeñar; (ignore) no darse cuenta de, ignorar; (excuse) perdonar, tolerar, hacer la vista gorda

**overlord** /'ouvər,lɔrd/ *n* señor de horca y cuchillo, señor, jefe, *m*

**overmuch** /'ouvər'mʌtf/ *adv* demasiado, en exceso

**overnight** /*adv.* 'ouvər'nait; *a.* 'ouvər,nait/ *adv* la noche pasada, durante la noche; toda la noche. —*a* de la víspera, nocturno. **to stay o. with,** pasar la noche con

**overpass** /'ouvər‚pæs/ *n* pasaje elevado, viaducto, *m*

**overpay** /‚ouvər'pei/ *vt* pagar demasiado

**overpayment** /'ouvər‚peimənt/ *n* pago excesivo, *m*

**overpopulate** /‚ouvər'pɒpyə‚leit/ *vt* sobrepoblar, become overpopulated recargarse de habitantes (with people), recargarse de animales (with animals)

**overpower** /‚ouvər'pauər/ *vt* vencer, subyugar; (of scents, etc.) trastornar; rendir, dominar

**overpowering** /‚ouvər'pauəriŋ/ *a* irresistible

**overpraise** /‚ouvər'preiz/ *vt* encarecer, alabar mucho

**overproduce** /‚ouvərprə'dus/ *vt* and *vi* sobreproducir

**overproduction** /‚ouvərprə'dʌkʃən/ *n* sobreproducción, *f*

**overrate** /‚ouvər'reit/ *vt* exagerar el valor de; (of property) sobrevalorar

**overreach** /‚ouvər'ritʃ/ *vt* sobrealcanzar. **to o. oneself,** sobrepasarse, ir demasiado lejos

**override** /‚ouvər'raid/ *vt* (trample) pasar por encima (de); *Fig.* rechazar, poner a un lado; (bully) dominar; (a horse) fatigar, reventar

**overripe** /'ouvər'raip/ *a* demasiado maduro

**overrule** /‚ouvər'rul/ *vt Law.* denegar, no admitir; vencer

**overrun** /‚ouvər'rʌn/ *vt* (flood) inundar; (ravage) invadir; (infest) plagar, infestar; desbordarse, derramarse

**overseas** /*a.* 'ouvər'siz; *adv.* ‚ouvər'siz/ *a* ultramarino, de ultramar. —*adv* en ultramar, allende los mares

**oversee** /‚ouvər'si/ *vt* vigilar, inspeccionar

**overseer** /'ouvər‚siər/ *n* capataz, mayoral, sobrestante, contramaestre, *m;* inspector (-ra), veedor (-ra)

**oversell** /‚ouvər'sɛl/ *vt* and *vi* vender en exceso

**oversensitive** /‚ouvər'sɛnsɪtɪv/ *a* demasiado sensitivo; vidrioso; susceptible

**oversew** /'ouvər‚sou/ *vt* sobrecoser

**overshadow** /‚ouvər'ʃædou/ *vt* sombrear; *Fig.* eclipsar, obscurecer; (sadden) entristecer

**overshoe** /'ouvər‚ʃu/ *n* chanclo, *m;* (for snow) galocha, *f*

**overshoot** /‚ouvər'ʃut/ *vt* tirar más allá del blanco; *Fig.* exceder, rebasar el límite conveniente, **overshoot the target** (fig.) ir más allá del blanco, ir más allá de lo razonable. **to o. oneself,** exagerar; propasarse, descomedirse

**oversight** /'ouvər‚sait/ *n* inadvertencia, omisión, equivocación, *f;* descuido, *m*

**oversimplify** /‚ouvər'sɪmplə‚fai/ *vt* simplificar en exceso

**oversleep** /‚ouvər'slip/ *vi* dormir demasiado; *Inf.* pegársele a uno las sábanas, levantarse demasiado tarde

**overspend** /‚ouvər'spɛnd/ *vt* and *vi* gastar demasiado

**overspread** /‚ouvər'sprɛd/ *vt* desparramar, salpicar, esparcir, sembrar; cubrir

**overstate** /‚ouvər'steit/ *vt* exagerar, encarecer, ponderar

**overstatement** /‚ouvər'steitmənt/ *n* exageración, ponderación, *f*

**overstep** /‚ouvər'stɛp/ *vt* exceder, pasar, violar; rebasar, pasar más allá (de)

**overstrain** /‚ouvər'strein/ *vt* fatigar demasiado, agotar. —*n* fatiga, *f.* **to o. oneself,** esforzarse demasiado, cansarse demasiado

**overstrung** /‚ouvər'strʌŋ/ *a* nervioso, excitable; (piano) de cuerdas cruzadas

**oversubscribe** /‚ouvərsəb'skraib/ *vt* subscribir en exceso

**overt** /ou'vɜrt/ *a* abierto, público; manifiesto, evidente

**overtake** /‚ouvər'teik/ *vt* alcanzar, pasar, dejar atrás; adelantarse (a); (surprise) coger, sorprender; (overwhelm) vencer, dominar

**overtax** /‚ouvər'tæks/ *vt* oprimir de tributos; agobiar, cansar demasiado

**overthrow** /*v.* ‚ouvər'θrou; *n.* 'ouvər‚θrou/ *vt* volcar, echar por tierra, derribar; *Fig.* vencer, destruir, destronar. —*n* vuelco, derribo, *m; Fig.* destrucción, ruina, *f*

**overtime** /'ouvər‚taim/ *adv* fuera de las horas estipuladas. —*n* horas extraordinarias de trabajo, *f pl.* **to work o.,** trabajar horas extraordinarias

**overtone** /'ouvər‚toun/ *n Mus.* armónico, *m*

**overtop** /‚ouvər'tɒp/ *vt* dominar, sobresalir, elevarse encima de

**overture** /'ouvərtʃər/ *n Mus.* obertura, *f*

**overturn** /‚ouvər'tɜrn/ *vt* volcar, derribar, echar a rodar, echar abajo; (upset) revolver, desordenar. —*vi* volcar, venirse abajo, allanarse; estar revuelto

**overturning** /‚ouvər'tɜrniŋ/ *n* vuelco, salto de campana, *m*

**overweening** /'ouvər'winiŋ/ *a* arrogante, insolente, altivo

**overweight** /'ouvər‚weit/ *n* sobrepeso, exceso en el peso, *m.* **to be o.,** pesar más de lo debido

**overwhelm** /‚ouvər'wɛlm/ *vt* (conquer) vencer, aplastar, derrotar; (of waves, etc.) sumergir, hundir, inundar, engolfar; (in argument) confundir, dejar confuso, avergonzar; (of grief, etc.) vencer, postrar, dominar; (of work) inundar

**overwhelming** /‚ouvər'wɛlmiŋ/ *a* irresistible, invencible, abrumador, apabullante

**overwind** /‚ouvər'waind/ *vt* (a watch) dar demasiada cuerda a; romper la cuerda de

**overwork** /*v.* ‚ouvər'wɜrk; *n.* 'ouvər‚wɜrk/ *vt* hacer trabajar demasiado (or con exceso); esclavizar. —*vi* trabajar demasiado. —*n* exceso de trabajo, demasiado trabajo, *m*

**overwrought** /'ouvər'rɔt/ *a* (overworked) agotado por el trabajo, rendido, muy cansado; nerviosísimo, sobreexcitado, exaltado, muy agitado

**ovine** /'ouvain/ *a* ovejuno

**ovoid** /'ouvɔid/ *a* ovoide

**ovulation** /‚ɒvyə'leiʃən/ *n Med.* ovulación, *f*

**owe** /ou/ *vt* deber, tener deudas (de); deber, estar agradecido (por), estar obligado (a). —*vi* estar en deuda, estar endeudado, tener deudas. **He owes his tailor $30,** Le debe treinta dólares a su sastre. **I owe him thanks for his help,** Le estoy agradecido por su ayuda (*or* Le debo las gracias por...). **He owes his success to good fortune,** Su éxito se debe a la suerte

**owing** /'ouiŋ/ *a* sin pagar. **o. to,** debido a, a causa de, por. **We had to stay in o. to the rain,** Tuvimos que quedarnos en casa a causa de la lluvia. **What is o. to you now?** ¿Cuánto se le debe ahora?

**owl** /aul/ *n* búho, mochuelo, *m.* **barn** or **screech owl,** lechuza, *f.* **brown owl,** autillo, *m*

**owlish** /'auliʃ/ *a* parecido a un búho, de búho

**own** /oun/ *a* propio. —*n* (dearest) bien, *m.* —*vt* poseer, tener, ser dueño de; (recognize) reconocer; (admit) confesar. —*vi* confesar. **my (thy, his, our, your) own,** mi (tu, su, nuestro, vuestro) propio, *m,* (*f,* propia); mis (tus, sus, nuestros, vuestros) propios, *m pl,* (*f pl,* propias); (when not placed before a noun) el mío (tuyo, suyo, nuestro, vuestro), la mía (tuya, etc.), los míos (tuyos, etc.), las mías (tuyas, etc.); (relations) los suyos. **in his own house,** en su propia casa. **my (thy, his, etc.) own self,** yo (tú, él) mismo, *m,* (*f,* misma, *m pl,* mismos, *f pl,* mismas). **a room of one's own,** un cuarto para sí (or para uno mismo). **to be on one's own,** ser independiente; estar a solas. **to hold one's own,** mantenerse en sus trece. **to own up,** confesar

**owner** /'ounər/ *n* dueño (-ña), propietario (-ia), posesor (-ra)

**ownerless** /'ounərlis/ *a* sin dueño, sin amo

**ownership** /'ounər‚ʃip/ *n* posesión, *f,* dominio, *m;* propiedad, *f*

**ox** /ɒks/ *n* buey (*pl* bueyes), *m.* **oxeye daisy,** margarita, *f.* **oxstall,** boyera, *f*

**oxidation** /‚ɒksɪ'deiʃən/ *n Chem.* oxidación, *f*

**oxide** /'ɒksaid/ *n Chem.* óxido, *m*

**oxidization** /‚ɒksədɪ'zeiʃən, -‚dai-/ *n* oxidación, *f*

**oxidize** /'ɒksɪ‚daiz/ *vt Chem.* oxidar; *vi* oxidarse

**oxygen** /'ɒksɪdʒən/ *n* oxígeno, *m.* **o. mask,** máscara de oxígeno, *f.* **o. tent,** tienda de oxígeno, *f*

**oxygenate** /'ɒksɪdʒə‚neit/ *vt Chem.* oxigenar

**oxygenation** /‚ɒksɪdʒə'neiʃən/ *n Chem.* oxigenación, *f*

**oyez, oyez!** /'ouyei, 'ouyɛs, 'ouɛz/ *interj* ¡oíd!

**oyster** /'ɔistər/ *n* ostra, *f.* **o. bed,** pescadero (or criadero) de ostras, *m.* **o. culture,** ostricultura, *f*

**ozone** /'ouzoun/ *n* ozono, *m*

# P

**p** /pi/ n (letter) pe, f. **to mind one's p's and q's,** poner los puntos sobre las íes; ir con pies de plomo

**pabulum** /'pæbyələm/ n pábulo, m; sustento, m

**pace** /peis/ n paso, m; (gait) andar, m, marcha, f; (of a horse) andadura, f; (speed) velocidad, f. —vi pasear(se), andar; (of a horse) amblar. —vt recorrer, andar por; marcar el paso para; (with out) medir a pasos. **at a good p.,** a un buen paso. **to keep p. with,** ajustarse al paso de, ir al mismo paso que; andar al paso de; (events) mantenerse al corriente de. **to p. up and down,** pasearse, dar vueltas. **p.-maker,** el que marca el paso

**paced** /peist/ a de andar...; (of a horse) de andadura...; de paso...

**pachyderm** /'pækɪˌdɜrm/ n paquidermo, m

**pacific** /pə'sɪfɪk/ a Geog. pacífico; sosegado, tranquilo, pacífico. **He is of a p. disposition,** Es amigo de la paz

**pacification** /ˌpæsəfɪ'keiʃən/ n pacificación, f

**pacificatory** /pə'sɪfɪkəˌtɔri/ a pacificador

**Pacific, the** el (Océano) Pacífico, m

**pacifier** /'pæsəˌfaiər/ n pacificador (-ra)

**pacifism** /'pæsəˌfɪzəm/ n pacifismo, m

**pacifist** /'pæsəfɪst/ a pacifista. —n pacifista, mf

**pacify** /'pæsəˌfai/ vt pacificar; calmar, tranquilizar; aplacar, conciliar

**pack** /pæk/ n (bundle) fardo, lío, m; paquete, m; (load) carga, f; (of hounds) jauría, f; (herd) hato, m; (of seals) manada, f; (of cards) baraja (de naipes), f; (of rogues) cuadrilla, f; (of lies, etc.) colección, f; masa, f; (of ice) témpanos flotantes, m pl; (Rugby football) delanteros, m pl; (for the face) compresa, f. **p.-horse,** caballo de carga, m. **p.-needle,** aguja espartera, f. **p.-saddle,** albarda, f. **p.-thread,** bramante, m

**pack** /pæk/ vt embalar; empaquetar; envasar; encajonar; (a suit-case, etc.) hacer; (cram) apretar; (crowd) atestar, llenar; (a pipe joint, etc.) empaquetar; (an animal) cargar. —vi llenar; (one's luggage) hacer el equipaje, hacer el baúl, arreglar el equipaje. **packed like sardines,** como sardinas en banasta. **The train was packed,** El tren estababa lleno de bote en bote. **to p. off,** (a person) despachar; poner de partitas en la calle. **to p. up,** hacer el equipaje; empaquetar; embalar; Inf. liar el hato

**package** /'pækɪdʒ/ n paquete, m; bulto, m; (bundle) fardo, m

**packer** /'pækər/ n embalador, m; envasador (-ra)

**packet** /'pækɪt/ n paquete, m; (of cigarettes, etc.) cajetilla, f; (boat) paquebote, m. **to make one's p.,** Inf. hacer su pacotilla

**packing** /'pækɪŋ/ n embalaje, m; envoltura, f; envase, m; (on a pipe, etc.) guarnición, f. **I must do my p.,** Tengo que hacer las maletas. **p.-case,** caja de embalaje, f. **p.-needle,** aguja espartera, f

**pact** /pækt/ n pacto, convenio, m. **to make a p.,** pactar

**pad** /pæd/ n almohadilla, f, cojinete, m; (on a bed, chair) colchoneta, f; (on a wound) cabezal, m; (for polishing) muñeca, f; (hockey) defensa, f; (cricket) espinillera, f; (writing) bloque, m; (of a calendar) taco, m; (blotting) secafirmas, m; (of a quadruped's foot) pulpejo, m; (of fox, hare) pata, f; (leaf) hoja grande, f, vt almohadillar; acolchar; rellenar, forrar; (out, a book, etc.) meter paja en. **inking-pad,** almohadilla de entintar, f. **padded cell,** celda acolchonada, f. **shoulder-pad,** (in a garment) hombrera, f

**padding** /'pædɪŋ/ n relleno, m, almohadilla, f; (material) borra, f, algodón, m; Fig. paja, f, ripio, m,

**paddle** /'pædl/ n (oar) canalete, zagual, m; paleta, f; (flipper) aleta, f, vt and vi remar con canalete; (dabble) chapotear. **double p.,** remo doble, m. **p.-steamer,** vapor de ruedas, vapor de paleta, m. **p.-wheel,** rueda de paletas, f

**paddler** /'pædlər/ n remero (-ra); el, m, (f, la) que chapotea

**paddling** n chapoteo, chapaleo, m

**paddock** /'pædək/ n prado, m, dehesa, f; parque, m; (near a racecourse) en silla dero, picadero, m; (toad) sapo, m

**padlock** /'pædˌlɒk/ n candado, m, vt cerrar con candado, acerrojar

**Paduan** /'pædʒuən/ a and n paduano (-na)

**paean** /'piən/ n himno de alegría, m

**pagan** /'peigən/ a and n pagano (-na)

**paganism** /'peigənɪzəm/ n paganismo, m

**page** /peidʒ/ n (boy) paje, m; (squire) escudero, m; (of a book, etc.) página, f; Fig. hoja, f. —vt compaginar; (a person) vocear. **on p. nine,** en la página nueve. **to turn the p.,** Fig. volver la hoja

**pageant** /'pædʒənt/ n espectáculo, m; (procession) desfile, m; representación teatral, f; fiesta, f; Fig. pompa, f, aparato, m

**pageantry** /'pædʒəntri/ n pompa, f, aparato, m, magnificencia, f

**pager** /'peidʒər/ n buscapersonas, m, bip, m (Mexico)

**paginate** /'pædʒəˌneit/ vt paginar

**pagination** /ˌpædʒə'neiʃən/ n paginación, f

**pagoda** /pə'goudə/ n pagoda, f

**paid** /peid/ a pagado; (on a parcel) porte pagado. **p. mourner,** plañidera, f. **p.-up share,** acción liberada, f

**pail** /peil/ n cubo, pozal, m, cubeta, f

**pailful** /'peilˌfʊl/ n cubo lleno (de agua, etc.), m

**pain** /pein/ n dolor, m; sufrimiento, m; (mental) tormento, m, angustia, f; Law. pena, f; pl **pains,** (effort) trabajo, esfuerzo, m. —vt doler; atormentar, afligir. **dull p.,** dolor sordo, m. **I have a p. in my head,** Me duele la cabeza. **on p. of death,** so pena de muerte. **to be in great p.,** sufrir mucho. **to take pains,** tomarse trabajo, esforzarse, esmerarse

**pained** /peind/ a dolorido; afligido; de angustia

**painful** /'peinfəl/ a doloroso; angustioso; fatigoso; (troublesome) molesto; (embarrassing) embarazoso; difícil; (laborious) arduo

**painfully** /'peinfəli/ adv dolorosamente; penosamente; fatigosamente; con angustia; laboriosamente

**painfulness** /'peinfəlnɪs/ n dolor, m; angustia, aflicción, f; tormento, m; dificultad, f

**painless** /'peinlɪs/ a sin dolor, indoloro

**painlessly** /'peinlɪsli/ adv sin dolor; sin sufrir

**painlessness** /'peinlɪsnɪs/ n falta de dolor, f

**painstaking** /'peinzˌteikɪŋ, 'peinˌstei-/ a concienzudo; diligente, industrioso; cuidadoso. —n trabajo, m; diligencia, industria, f; cuidado, m

**paint** /peint/ n pintura, f; (for preserving metal) pavón, m; (rouge) colorete, m. —vt pintar. —vi pintar; pintarse. **The door is painted blue,** La puerta está pintada de azul. **p.-box,** caja de pinturas, f. **p.-brush,** pincel, m; (for house painting) brocha, f

**painter** /'peintər/ n pintor (-ra); (house) pintor de brocha gorda, pintor de casas, m; (of a boat) boza, f. **sign-p.,** pintor de muestras, m

**painting** /'peintɪŋ/ n pintura, f; (picture) cuadro, m, pintura, f

**pair** /pɛər/ n par, m; (of people) pareja, f; (of oxen) yunta, f. —vt parear, emparejar; (persons) unir, casar; (animals) aparear. —vi parearse; casarse; aparearse. **a carriage and p.,** un landó con dos caballos. **a p. of steps,** una escalera de mano. **a p. of pants a p. of trousers,** unos pantalones. **in pairs,** de dos en dos; por parejas. **to p. off,** vi formar pareja; Inf. casarse

**pal** /pæl/ n camarada, compinche, mf; amigote, m

**palace** /'pælɪs/ n palacio, m

**paladin** /'pælədɪn/ n paladín, m

**palatable** /'pælətəbəl/ a sabroso, apetitoso; Fig. agradable, aceptable

**palatableness** /'pælɪtəbəlnɪs/ n buen sabor, gusto agradable, m; Fig. lo agradable

**palatably** /'pælɪtəbli/ adv agradablemente

**palatal** /'pælətl/ a paladial. —n letra paladial, f

**palatalize** /'pælətlˌaiz/ vt palatizar

**pantry**

**palate** /'pælɪt/ *n* paladar, *m*. **hard p.**, paladar, *m*. **soft p.**, velo del paladar, *m*

**palatial** /pə'leɪʃəl/ *a* (of a palace) palaciego; (sumptuous) magnífico, suntuoso

**pale** /peɪl/ *n* (stake) estaca, *f*; límite, *m*; *Herald.* palo, *m*, *a* pálido; (wan) descolorido; (of colours) claro, desmayado; (of light) tenue, mortecino; (lustreless) sin brillo, muerto. —*vi* palidecer, perder el color; *Fig.* eclipsarse

**palely** /'peɪli/ *adv* pálidamente; vagamente, indistintamente

**paleness** /'peɪlnɪs/ *n* palidez, *f*; (wanness) descoloramiento, *m*, amarillez, *f*; (of light) tenuidad, *f*

**paleographer** /,peɪli'ɒɡrəfər/ *n* paleógrafo, *m*

**paleography** /,peɪli'ɒɡrəfi/ *esp. Brit.* ,pæli-/ *n* paleografía, *f*

**paleolithic** /,peɪliə'lɪθɪk/ *a* paleolítico

**paleology** /,peɪli'ɒlədʒi/ *n* paleología, *f*

**paleontology** /,peɪliən'tɒlədʒi/ *esp. Brit.* ,pæli-/ *n* paleontología, *f*

**Palestine** /'pælə,staɪn/ Palestina, *f*

**palette** /'pælɪt/ *n* paleta, *f*. **p.-knife**, espátula, *f*

**palimpsest** /'pælɪmp,sɛst/ *n* palimpsesto, *m*

**palindrome** /'pælɪn,droʊm/ *n* capicúa *f*, (of numbers), palíndromo *m*

**paling** /'peɪlɪŋ/ *n* palizada, estacada, valla, *f*

**palisade** /,pælə'seɪd/ *n* palenque, *m*, tranquera, palizada, *f*; *Mil.* estacada, *f*

**palish** /'peɪlɪʃ/ *a* algo pálido; paliducho

**pall** /pɔl/ *n* (on a coffin) paño mortuorio, *m*; (*Fig.* covering) manto, *m*, capa, *f*; *Eccl.* palio, *m*; (over a chalice) palia, *f.* —*vi* perder el sabor, hacerse insípido; saciarse (de); aburrirse (de), cansarse (de). **The music of Bach never palls on me,** No me canso nunca de la música de Bach

**palladium** /pə'leɪdiəm/ *n* *Mineral.* paladio, *m;* (safeguard) paladión, *m*

**pallet** /'pælɪt/ *n* jergón, *m;* camilla, *f; Mech.* fiador de rueda, *m;* torno de alfarero, *m*

**palliate** /'pæli,eɪt/ *vt* (pain) paliar, aliviar; mitigar; (excuse) disculpar, excusar

**palliation** /,pæli'eɪʃən/ *n* paliación, *f;* mitigación, *f;* disculpa, *f*

**palliative** /'pæli,eɪtɪv, -iətɪv/ *a* paliativo; (extenuating) atenuante. —*n* paliativo, *m*

**pallid** /'pælɪd/ *a* pálido

**pallidness** /'pælɪdnɪs/ *n* palidez, *f*

**pallor** /'pælər/ *n* palidez, *f*

**palm** /pɑm/ *n* (of the hand, and *Fig.*, victory) palma, *f;* (measurement) ancho de la mano, *m;* (tree) palmera, *f.* —*vt* (a card, etc.) empalmar; (with off) defraudar (con); dar gato por liebre (a). **to bear away the p.**, llevar la palma. **p. branch**, palma, *f.* **p. grove**, palmar, *m.* **p.-oil**, aceite de palma, *m;* (bribe) soborno, *m.* **P. Sunday**, Domingo de Ramos, *m.* **p. tree**, palmera, *f*

**palmate** /'pælmeɪt, -mɪt, 'pɑl-, 'pɑmeɪt/ *a* palmeado

**palmer** /'pɑmər, 'pɑl-/ *n* peregrino, *m;* (caterpillar) oruga velluda, *f*

**palming** /'pɑmɪŋ/ *n* (in conjuring, etc.) empalme, *m*

**palmist** /'pɑmɪst/ *n* quiromántico (-ca)

**palmistry** /'pɑməstri/ *n* quiromancía, *f*

**palmy** /'pɑmi/ *a* palmar; (flourishing) floreciente; (happy) dichoso, feliz; (prosperous) próspero, triunfante

**Palmyra** /pæl'maɪrə/ Palmira, *f*

**palp** /pælp/ *n* palpo, *m*

**palpability** /,pælpə'bɪlɪti/ *n* palpabilidad, *f*

**palpable** /'pælpəbəl/ *a* palpable

**palpate** /'pælpeɪt/ *vt* palpar

**palpation** /pæl'peɪʃən/ *n* palpación, *f*

**palpitate** /'pælpɪ,teɪt/ *vi* palpitar

**palpitating** /'pælpɪ,teɪtɪŋ/ *a* palpitante

**palpitation** /,pælpɪ'teɪʃən/ *n* palpitación, *f*

**palsied** /'pɔlzid/ *a* paralítico

**palsy** /'pɔlzi/ *n* parálisis, *f*, *vt* paralizar

**paltriness** /'pɔltrɪnɪs/ *n* mezquindad, pequeñez, *f*

**paltry** /'pɔltri/ *a* mezquino, insignificante, pobre

**paludism** /'pælyə,dɪzəm/ *n* *Med.* paludismo, *m*

**pampas** /'pæmpəz/ *attributively* 'pæmpəs/ *n* pampa, *f*

**pamper** /'pæmpər/ *vt* mimar, consentir demasiado; criar con mimos, regalar; alimentar demasiado bien

**pampered** /'pæmpərd/ *a* mimado, consentido; demasiado bien alimentado

**pamphlet** /'pæmflɪt/ *n* folleto, *m*

**pamphleteer** /,pæmflɪ'tɪər/ *n* folletinista, *mf*

**pan** /pæn/ *n* (vessel) cazuela, *f;* cacerola, *f;* (brain) cráneo, *m;* (of a balance) platillo, *m;* (of a firelock) cazoleta, *f*, *Cinema.* toma panorámica *f*, *prefix* pan-. **to pan off,** separar el oro en una gamella. **to pan out,** dar oro; *Fig.* suceder. **Pan-Americanism,** panamericanismo, *m*

**Pan** /pæn/ *n* Pan, *m.* **pipes of Pan,** flauta de Pan, *f*

**panacea** /,pænə'siə/ *n* panacea, *f*

**panache** /pə'næʃ/ *n* penacho, *m*

**panada** /pənə'da/ *n* *Cul.* panetela, *f*

**Panama** /'pænə,mɑ/ el Panamá, *m*

**Panama** /'pænə,mɑ/ *a* panameño. (-ña). **P. hat,** sombrero de jipijapa, panamá *m*

**pancake** /'pæn,keɪk/ *n* fruta de sartén, hojuela, *f.* **p. landing,** *Aer.* aterrizaje brusco, *m.* **P. Tuesday,** martes de Carnaval, *m*

**panchromatic** /,pænkroʊ'mætɪk, -krə-/ *a* pancromático

**pancreas** /'pænkriəs, 'pæŋ-/ *n* páncreas, *m*

**pancreatic** /,pænkri'ætɪk/ *a* pancreático

**panda** /'pændə/ *n* *Zool.* panda, *mf*

**pandemic** /pæn'dɛmɪk/ *a* pandémico

**pandemonium** /,pændə'moʊniəm/ *n* pandemonio

**pander** /'pændər/ *n* alcahuete, *m*, *vi* alcahuetear. **to p. to,** prestarse a; favorecer, ayudar

**pandore** /pæn'dɔr/ *n* *Mus.* bandola, *f*

**pane** /peɪn/ *n* hoja de vidrio, hoja de cristal, *f;* cuadro, *m*

**panegyric** /,pænɪ'dʒɪrɪk/ *a* panegírico. —*n* panegírico, *m*

**panegyrist** /,pænɪ'dʒɪrɪst/ *n* panegirista, *mf*

**panel** /'pænl/ *n* panel, entrepaño, *m; Art.* tabla, *f;* (in a dress) paño, *m;* (list) lista, *f*, registro, *m;* (jury) jurado, *m;* lista de jurados, *f*, *vt* labrar a entrepaños; artesonar. **p. doctor,** médico (-ca) de seguros

**paneled** /'pænld/ *a* entrepañado; (of ceilings) artesonado. **p. ceiling,** artesonado, *m*

**paneling** /'pænlɪŋ/ *n* entrepaños, *m pl;* artesonado, *m*

**panful** /'pæn,fʊl/ *n* cazolada, *f*

**pang** /pæŋ/ *n* punzada (de dolor), *f*, dolor agudo, *m;* dolor, *m;* (anguish of mind) angustia, *f*, tormento, *m;* (of conscience) remordimiento, *m*

**panic** /'pænɪk/ *n* pánico, *m;* pavor, espanto, *m;* terror súbito, *m*, *a* pánico. —*vi* espantarse. **p.-monger,** alarmista, *mf* **p.-stricken,** aterrorizado, despavorido

**panicky** /'pænɪki/ *a* *Inf.* lleno de pánico; nervioso

**panicle** /'pænɪkəl/ *n* *Bot.* panoja, *f*

**pannier** /'pænyər/ *n* (basket) alforja, *f;* cesto, *m;* (bustle) caderillas, *f pl*

**panoply** /'pænəpli/ *n* panoplia, *f*

**panorama** /,pænə'ræmə, -'rɑmə/ *n* panorama, *f*

**panoramic** /,pænə'ræmɪk/ *a* panorámico

**pansy** /'pænzi/ *n* pensamiento, *m*, trinitaria, *f*

**pant** /pænt/ *vi* jadear; (of dogs) hipar; resollar; (of the heart) palpitar. —*n* jadeo, *m;* palpitación, *f.* **to p. after,** suspirar por

**pantaloon** /,pæntl'un/ *n* (trouser) pantalón, *m;* (Pantaloon) Pantalón, *m*

**pantechnicon** /pæn'tɛknɪ,kɒn/ *n* almacén de muebles, *m;* (van) carro de mudanzas, *m*

**pantheism** /'pænθi,ɪzəm/ *n* panteísmo, *m*

**pantheist** /'pænθiɪst/ *n* panteísta, *mf*

**pantheistic** /,pænθi'ɪstɪk/ *a* panteísta

**pantheon** /'pænθi,ɒn, -ən *or, esp. Brit.,* pæn'θiən/ *n* panteón, *m*

**panther** /'pænθər/ *n* pantera, *f*

**panties** /'pæntiz/ *n pl* pantalones, *m pl*

**panting** /'pæntɪŋ/ *a* jadeante, sin aliento. —*n* jadeo, *m;* resuello, *m;* respiración difícil, *f;* palpitación, *f*

**pantograph** /'pæntə,græf/ *n* pantógrafo, *m*

**pantomime** /'pæntə,maɪm/ *n* pantomima, *f;* revista, *f.* **in p.,** en pantomima; por gestos

**pantry** /'pæntri/ *n* despensa, *f*

**pants** /pænts/ n pl calzoncillos, m pl; (trousers) pantalones, m pl

**panzer division** /'pænzər/ n división motorizada, f

**pap** /pæp/ n (nipple) pezón, m; (soft food) papilla, f

**papa** /'pɑpə, pə'pɑ/ n papá, m

**papacy** /'peipəsi/ n papado, pontificado, m

**papal** /'peipəl/ a papal, pontificio. **p. bull,** bula pontificia, f. **p. nuncio,** nuncio del Papa, nuncio apostólico, m. **p. see,** sede apostólica, f

**paper** /'peipər/ n papel, m; hoja de papel, f; documento, m; (lecture) comunicación, f; (newspaper) periódico, m; (journal) revista, f; (exam.) examen escrito, trabajo, m; ejercicio, m; pl **papers,** (credentials) documentación, f, credenciales, f pl; Com. valores negociables, m pl; (packet) paquete, m, a de papel; para papeles; parecido al papel. —vt (a room) empapelar; (a parcel) envolver. **daily p.,** diario, m. **in p. covers,** (of books) en rústica. **slip of p.,** papeleta. f. **to send in one's papers,** entregar su dimisión. **p. bag,** saco de papel, m. **p.-chase,** rally-paper," m. **p. clip,** prendedero de oficina, "sujeta papels," m. **p.-cutting machine,** guillotina, f. **p. folder,** plegadera, f. **p.-hanger,** empapelador, m. **p.-hanging,** empapelado, m. **p.-knife,** cortapapel, m. **p.-maker,** fabricante de papel, m. **p.-making,** manufactura de papel, f. **p.-mill,** fábrica de papel, f. **p.-money,** papel moneda, m. **p.-pulp,** pasta, f. **p.-streamer,** serpentina, f. **p.-weight,** pisapapeles, m

**papering** /'peipəriŋ/ n (of a room) empapelado, m

**papery** /'peipəri/ a semejante al papel

**papier-mâché** /,peipərmə'ʃei, pɑ,pyei-/ n cartón piedra, m

**papillary** /'pæpə,leri/ a papilar

**papist** /'peipist/ n papista, mf; católico (-ca)

**papoose** /pæ'pus;/ n niño indio, m

**paprika** /pæ'prikə, pə-, pɑ-, 'pæprikə/ n pimienta húngara, f

**papyrus** /pə'pairəs/ n papiro, m

**par** /pɑr/ n par, f. **at par,** Com. a la par. **above (below) par,** Com. por encima (or debajo) de la par. **He is a little below par,** No está muy bien de salud. **to be on par with,** ser el equivalente de; ser igual a. **par excellence,** por excelencia

**parable** /'pærəbəl/ n parábola, f

**parabola** /pə'ræbələ/ n Geom. parábola, f

**parachute** /'pærəʃut/ n paracaídas, m; Bot. vilano, m **to p. down,** lanzarse en paracaídas. **p. troops,** cuerpo de paracaidistas, m

**parachutist** /'pærəʃutist/ n paracaidista, mf

**parade** /pə'reid/ n alarde, m; Mil. parada, revista, f; (procession) desfile, m, procesión, f; (promenade) paseo, m. —vt (display) hacer alarde de, hacer gala de, ostentar; (troops) formar en parada; pasar revista (a); (patrol) recorrer. —vi Mil. tomar parte en una parada; desfilar. **to p. up and down,** pasearse. **p.-ground,** campo de instrucción, m; plaza de armas, f

**paradigm** /'pærə,daim/ n paradigma, m

**paradise** /'pærə,dais/ n paraíso, edén, m; Fig. jauja, f. **bird of p.,** ave del paraíso, f

**paradisiac** /,pærə'dizi,æk/ a paradisíaco

**paradox** /'pærə,dɒks/ n paradoja, f

**paradoxical** /,pærə'dɒksikəl/ a paradójico

**paradoxicality** /,pærə,dɒksi'kæliti/ n lo paradójico

**paraffin** /'pærəfin/ n parafina, f. —vt parafinar. **p. oil,** parafina líquida, f

**paragon** /'pærə,gɒn/ n modelo perfecto, dechado, m

**paragraph** /'pærə,græf/ n párrafo, m; (in a newspaper) suelto, m, vt dividir en párrafos; escribir un suelto sobre. **new p.,** párrafo aparte, m

**Paraguay** /'pærə,gwai, -,gwei/ el Paraguay, m

**Paraguayan** /,pærə'gwaiən/ a and n paraguayo (-ya)

**parakeet** /'pærə,kit/ n Ornith. perico, m

**parallel** /'pærə,lɛl/ a paralelo; igual; semejante, análogo. —n línea paralela, f; paralelo, m; Mil. paralela, f; Geog. paralelo, m; Print. pleca, f. —vt poner en paralelo; cotejar, comparar; igualar. **to run p. to,** ser paralelo a; ser conforme a. **p. bars,** paralelas, f pl

**parallelism** /'pærələ,lizəm/ n paralelismo, m

**parallelogram** /,pærə'lɛlə,græm/ n paralelogramo, m

**paralysis** /pə'ræləsis/ n parálisis, f

**paralytic** /,pærə'litik/ a and n paralítico (-ca)

**paralyzation** n paralización, f

**paralyze** vt paralizar

**paramount** /'pærə,maunt/ a supremo, sumo

**paramour** /'pærə,mʊr/ n amante, querido, m; querida, amiga, f

**paranoia** /,pærə'nɔiə/ n paranoia, f

**paranoiac** /,pærə'nɔiæk/ n paranoico, m

**parapet** /'pærəpit, -,pɛt/ n (Archit. and Mil.) parapeto, m

**paraphernalia** /,pærəfər'neilyə, -fə'neil-/ n Law. bienes parafernales, m, pl; (finery) atavíos, adornos, m pl; equipo, m; arreos, m pl; insignias, f pl

**paraphrase** /'pærə,freiz/ n paráfrasis, f, vt parafrasear

**parasite** /'pærə,sait/ n parásito, m; Inf. zángano, m, gorrista, mf

**parasitic** /,pærə'sitik/ a parásito, parasitario; Med. parasítico

**parasitology** /,pærəsai'tɒlədʒi, -si-/ n parasitología, f

**parasol** /'pærə,sɔl, -,sɒl/ n parasol, quitasol, m

**parathyroid** /,pærə'θairɔid/ a paratiroides. —n paratiroides, f pl

**paratroops** /'pærə,trups/ n pl paracaidistas, m pl

**paratyphoid** /,pærə'taifɔid/ n paratifoidea, f

**parboil** /'pɑr,bɔil/ vt sancochar

**parcel** /'pɑrsəl/ n paquete, m; fardo, m; (of land) parcela, f. **to p. out,** repartir, distribuir; dividir. **to p. up,** envolver, empaquetar. **p. post,** servicio de paquetes, m

**parceling** /'pɑrsəliŋ/ n empaque, m; (out) reparto, m, distribución, f; división, f

**parch** /pɑrtʃ/ vt secar; abrasar, quemar; (roast) tostar. —vi secarse; quemarse, abrasarse

**parched** /pɑrtʃt/ a seco, sediento. **p. with thirst,** muerto de sed

**parchedness** /'pɑrtʃidnis/ n sequedad, aridez, f

**parchment** /'pɑrtʃmənt/ n pergamino, m; (of a drum) parche, m. **p.-like,** apergaminado

**pardon** /'pɑrdn/ n perdón, m; Eccl. indulgencia, f. —vt perdonar; indultar, amnistiar. **a general p.,** una amnistía. **I beg your p.!** ¡Vd. dispense!; ¡Perdone Vd.! **to beg p.,** pedir perdón; disculparse. **P.?** ¿Cómo?

**pardonable** /'pɑrdn̩əbəl/ a perdonable, disculpable, excusable

**pardonableness** /'pɑrdn̩əbəlnis/ n disculpabilidad, f

**pardonably** /'pɑrdn̩əbli/ adv disculpablemente, excusablemente

**pardoner** /'pɑrdn̩ər/ n vendedor de indulgencias, m; perdonador (-ra)

**pardoning** /'pɑrdn̩iŋ/ n perdón, m; remisión, f

**pare** /pɛər/ vt (one's nails) cortar; (fruit) mondar; (potatoes, etc.) pelar; (remove) quitar; (reduce) reducir

**parent** /'pɛərənt, 'pær-/ n padre, m; madre, f; (ancestor) antepasado, m; (origin) origen, m, fuente, f; (cause) causa, f; (author) autor, m; autora, f; pl **parents,** padres, m pl. —a madre, materno; principal

**parentage** /'pɛərəntidʒ, 'pær-/ n parentela, f; linaje, m, familia, alcurnia, f; procedencia, f, nacimiento, origen, m

**parental** /pə'rɛntl/ a paternal; maternal, de madre

**parentally** /pə'rɛntl̩i/ adv como un padre; como una madre

**parenthesis** /pə'rɛnθəsis/ n paréntesis, m

**parenthetical** /,pɛərən'θɛtikəl/ a entre paréntesis; de paréntesis

**parenthood** /'pɛərənt,hʊd, 'pær-/ n paternidad, f; maternidad, f

**pariah** /pə'raiə/ n paria, mf

**parietal** /pə'raiitl/ a parietal

**paring** /'pɛəriŋ/ n (act) raedura, f; peladura, mondadura, f; (shred) brizna, f; (refuse) desecho, desperdicio, m. **p.-knife,** trinchete, m

**Paris** /'pæris/ París, m

**parish** /'pæriʃ/ n parroquia, f; feligresía, f, a parroquial. **p. church,** parroquia, f. **p. clerk,** sacristán de parroquia, m. **p. priest,** párroco, m. **p. register,** registro de la parroquia, m

**parishioner** /pə'riʃənər/ n parroquiano (-na); feligrés (-esa)

**Parisian** /pə'riʒən, -'riʒən, -'riziən/ a parisiense. —n parisiense, mf

**parity** /'pæriti/ n paridad, f

**park** /park/ *n* parque, *m;* jardín, *m.* —*vt* (vehicles) estacionar; (dump) depositar. **car p.,** parque de automóviles, *m.* **p.-keeper,** guardián del parque, *m*

**parking** /'parkıŋ/ *n* (of vehicles) estacionamiento, *m;* (dumping) depósito, *m.* **p. lights,** *Auto.* luces de estacionamiento, *f pl.* **p. place,** parque de estacionamiento, *m*

**parking meter** *n* parquímetro, *m* (Argentina)

**parlance** /'parlans/ *n* lenguaje, *m.* **in common p.,** en lenguaje vulgar

**parley** /'parli/ *n* plática, conversación, *f;* discusión, *f; Mil.* parlamento, *m.* —*vi Mil.* parlamentar; discutir; conversar. —*vt* hablar

**parliament** /'parlamant/ *n* parlamento, *m;* cortes, *f pl;* cuerpo legislativo, *m*

**parliamentarian** /,parlaman'tɛarian/ *a and n* parlamentario; (of an academy) censor, *m*

**parliamentarianism** /,parlaman'tɛarianızam/ *n* parlamentarismo, *m,*

**parliamentary** /,parla'mɛntari, ,parlya-/ *a* parlamentario. **p. immunity,** inviolabilidad parlamentaria, *f*

**parlor** /'parlar/ *n* salón, gabinete, *m;* sala de recibo, *f;* (in a convent) locutorio, *m.* **p. games,** diversión de salón, *f,* juego de sociedad, *m.* **p.-maid,** camarera, *f*

**parlous** /'parlas/ *a* crítico, malo. —*adv* sumamente, muy

**Parmesan** /'parma,zan, ,parma'zan/ *a* parmesano, de Parma. —*n* parmesano (-na). **P. cheese,** queso de Parma, *m*

**Parnassian** /par'næsian/ *a* del parnaso; parnasiano. —*n* parnasiano, *m*

**Parnassus** /par'næsas/ *n* Parnaso, *m*

**parochial** /pa'roukial/ *a* parroquial, parroquiano; *Fig.* provincial

**parochialism** /pa'roukia,lızam/ *n* provincialismo, *m*

**parochially** /pa'roukiali/ *adv* por parroquias

**parodist** /'pæradıst/ *n* parodista, *mf*

**parody** /'pæradi/ *n* parodia, *f, vt* parodiar

**parole** /pa'roul/ *n* (of convict) libertad vigilada, *f*

**paroxysm** /'pærak,sızam/ *n* paroxismo, *m;* ataque, acceso, *m*

**parquet** /par'kei/ (floor) entarimado *m;* (of theater) platea, *f*

**parricide** /'pæra,said/ *n* (act) parricidio, *m;* (person) parricida, *mf*

**parrot** /'pærat/ *n* papagayo, loro, *m*

**parry** /'pæri/ *vt* (a blow, and in fencing) parar; rechazar; evitar. —*n* parada, *f;* (in fencing) quite, *m,* parada, *f*

**parse** /pars, parz/ *vt* analizar

**Parsee** /'parsi, par'si/ *n* parsi, *m*

**parsimonious** /,parsa'mounias/ *a* parsimonioso

**parsimoniously** /,parsa'mouniasli/ *adv* con parsimonia

**parsimony** /'parsa,mouni/ *n* parsimonia, *f*

**parsley** /'parsli/ *n* perejil, *m*

**parsnip** /'parsnıp/ *n* chirivía, *f*

**parson** /'parsan/ *n* párroco, cura, *m;* (clergyman) clérigo, *m*

**parsonage** /'parsanıdʒ/ *n* rectoría, *f*

**part** /part/ *n* parte, *f;* porción, *f;* trozo, *m; Mech.* pieza, *f;* (Gram. and of a literary work) parte, *f;* (of a living organism) miembro, *m;* (duty) deber, *m,* obligación, *f; Theat.* papel, *m; Mus.* voz, *f; pl* **parts,** (region) partes, *f pl,* lugar, *m;* (talents) partes, dotes, *f pl.* **foreign parts,** países extranjeros, *m pl,* el extranjero. **For my p....,** Por lo que a mí toca, Por mi parte. **for the most p.,** en su mayoría. **from all parts,** de todas partes. **in p.,** en parte; parcialmente. **spare p.,** pieza de recambio, *f.* **The funny p. of it is...,** Lo cómico del asunto es... **the latter p. of the month,** los últimos días del mes, la segunda quincena del mes. **to form p. of,** formar parte de. **to play a p.,** hacer un papel. **to take a person's p.,** apoyar a alguien, ser partidario de alguien. **to take in good p.,** tomar bien. **to take p. in,** tomar parte en, participar en. **p. of speech,** parte de la oración, *f.* **p.-owner,** copropietario (-ia). **p.-time job,** trabajo de unas cuantas horas, *m*

**part** /part/ *vt* distribuir, repartir; dividir; separar (de); (open) abrir. —*vi* partir, marcharse; despedirse; (of roads, etc.) bifurcarse; dividirse; (open) abrirse. **to p. one's hair,** hacerse la raya. **to p. from,** (things) separarse de; (people) despedirse de. **to p. with,** separarse de; deshacerse de; perder; (dismiss) despedir (a)

**partake** /par'teik/ *vt* participar de, compartir; tomar parte en. —*vi* tomar algo (de comer, de beber). **to p. of,** comer (beber) de; tener rasgos de

**partaker** /par'teikar/ *n* partícipe, *mf*

**Parthian** /'parθian/ *a* parto. —*n* parto (-ta). **P. shot,** la flecha del parto

**partial** /'parʃal/ *a* parcial; (fond of) aficionado (a). **p. eclipse,** eclipse parcial, *m*

**partiality** /,parʃi'æliti, par'ʃæl-/ *n* parcialidad, *f;* preferencia, predilección, *f*

**partially** /'parʃali/ *adv* en parte, parcialmente; (with bias) con parcialidad

**participant** /par'tısapant/ *a* participante. —*n* partícipe, *mf*

**participate** /par'tısa,peit/ *vi* participar (de), compartir; tomar parte (en)

**participation** /par,tısa'peiʃan/ *n* participación, *f*

**participial** /,partı'sıpial/ *a Gram.* participial

**participle** /'partə,sıpal, -səpal/ *n Gram.* participio, *m.* **past p.,** participio pasado (or pretérito or pasivo), *m.* **present p.,** participio activo (or presente), *m*

**particle** /'partıkal/ *n* partícula, *f; Fig.* átomo, grano, *m,* pizca, *f; Gram.* partícula, *f*

**parti-colored** /'parti,kʌlard/ *a* bicolor

**particular** /par'tıkyalar/ *a* particular; especial; individual; singular; cierto; exacto; escrupuloso; difícil, exigente. —*n* detalle, pormenor, *m;* circunstancia, *f;* caso particular, *m; pl* **particulars,** informes, detalles, *m pl.* **further particulars,** más detalles. **in p.,** en particular; sobre todo. **He is very p. about...,** Es muy exigente en cuanto a...; Le es muy importante..., Le importa mucho...

**particularize** /par'tıkyala,raiz/ *vt* particularizar, detallar; especificar

**particularly** /par'tıkyalarli/ *adv* en particular; particularmente; sobre todo

**parting** /'partıŋ/ *n* despedida, *f;* partida, *f;* separación, *f;* (of the hair) raya, crencha, *f;* (cross roads) bifurcación, *f.* —*a* de despedida. **at p.,** al despedirse. **to reach the p. of the ways,** *Fig.* llegar al punto decisivo

**partisan** /'partazan, -san/ *n* partidario (-ia); (fighter) guerrillero, *m, a* partidario; de guerrilleros

**partisanship** /'parta,zanʃıp/ *n* partidarismo, *m*

**partition** /par'tıʃan, par-/ *n* partición, *f;* división, *f;* (wall) pared, *f,* tabique, *m.* **the p. of Ireland,** la división de Irlanda

**partly** /'partli/ *adv* en parte

**partner** /'partnar/ *n* asociado (-da); *Com.* socio (-ia); (dancing) pareja, *f;* (in games, and companion) compañero (-ra); (spouse) consorte, *mf;* (in crime) codelincuente, *mf* **sleeping p.,** socio comanditario, *m.* **working p.,** socio industrial, *m*

**partnership** /'partnar,ʃıp/ *n* asociación, *f; Com.* sociedad, compañía, *f.* **deed of p.,** artículos de sociedad, *m pl.* **to take into p.,** tomar como socio (a). **to form a p.,** asociarse

**partridge** /'partrıdʒ/ *n Ornith.* perdiz, *f.* **young p.,** perdigón, *m*

**parturient** /par'turiant/ *a f,* parturienta. —*n* parturienta, *f*

**parturition** /,partu'rıʃan, -tʃu-/ *n* parto, *m*

**party** /'parti/ *n* partido, *m;* grupo, *m;* (of pleasure, etc.) partida, *f;* reunión, fiesta, *f; Mil.* pelotón, destacamento, *m; Law.* parte, *f;* (person) interesado (-da); (accessory) cómplice, *mf.* **rescue p.,** pelotón de salvamento, *m.* **to be a p. to,** prestarse a; ser cómplice en. **to give a p.,** dar una fiesta, dar una reunión. **p.-spirit,** espíritu del partido, *m.* **p.-wall,** pared medianera, *f*

**parvenu** /'parva,nu/ *n* advenedizo (-za)

**parvis** /'parvıs/ *n Archit.* atrio, *m*

**Paschal** /'pæ'skæl/ *a* pascual

**pass** /pæs/ *n* (in an exam.) aprobación, *f;* (crisis) crisis, situación crítica, *f;* estado, *m;* (with the hands) pase, *m;* (permit) permiso, *m; Mil.* licencia, *f;* (safeconduct) salvoconducto, *m;* (in football, etc.) pase, *m;* (membership card) carnet, *m;* (defile) desfiladero, paso, puerto, *m; Naut.* rebasadero, *m;* (fencing) estocada, *f.* **free p.,** billete de favor, *m.* **p.-book,** libreta de banco, *f.* **p. certificate,** (in exams.) aprobado, *m.* **p.-key,** llave maestra, *f*

**pass** /pæs/ *vi* pasar; (of time) correr, pasar, transcurrir; (happen) occurrir, tomar lugar; (end) cesar, desaparecer; (die) morir. —*vt* pasar; hacer pasar; (the butter, etc.) dar, alargar; (in football, hockey) pasar; (excel) aventajar, exceder; (a bill, an examination) aprobar; (sentence) fallar, pronunciar; (a remark) hacer; (transfer) traspasar; (tolerate) sufrir, tolerar; evacuar. **He passed in psychology,** Aprobó sicología. **to allow to p.,** ceder el paso (a). **to bring to p.,** ocasionar. **to come to p.,** suceder. **to let p.,** (put up with) dejar pasar; no hacer caso de; (forgive) perdonar. **to p. a vote of confidence,** votar una proposición de confianza. **to p. the buck,** *Inf.* echarle a uno el muerto. **pass the hat, pass the plate,** pasar la gorra. **to p. along,** pasar por; pasar. **to p. away,** pasar; desaparecer; (die) morir, fallecer; (of time) transcurrir. **to p. by,** pasar por, pasar delante de, pasar al lado de; (omit) pasar por alto de, omitir; (ignore) pasar sin hacer caso de. **to p. for,** pasar por. **to p. in,** entrar. **to p. in and out,** entrar y salir. **to p. off,** *vi* pasar; cesar, acabarse; desaparecer; evaporarse, disiparse; (of events) tener lugar. —*vt* (oneself) darse por; dar por, hacer pasar por. **to p. a cat off as hare,** dar gato por liebre. **to p. on,** *vi* pasar; seguir su camino, continuar su marcha. —*vt* pasar algo de uno a otro. **to p. out,** salir. **to p. over,** pasar por encima de; pasar; cruzar, atravesar; (transfer) traspasar; (disregard) pasar por alto de, dejar a un lado; omitir. **to p. over in silence,** pasar en silencio (por). **to p. round,** circular. **to p. through,** cruzar, atravesar, pasar por; (pierce) traspasar; *Fig.* experimentar

**passable** /'pæsəbəl/ *a* transitable, pasadero; (fairly good) regular, mediano; tolerable

**passably** /'pæsəbli/ *adv* medianamente, pasaderamente, tolerablemente

**passage** /'pæsɪdʒ/ *n* pasaje, *m;* paso, tránsito, *m;* (voyage) viaje, *m,* travesía, *f;* (corridor) pasillo, *m;* (entrance) entrada, *f;* (way) camino, *m;* (alley) callejón, *m;* (in a mine) galería, *f;* (of time) transcurso, *m;* (of birds) pasa, *f;* (in a book, and *Mus.*) pasaje, *m;* (occurrence) episodio, incidente, *m;* (of a bill) aprobación, *f.* **p. money,** pasaje, *m.* **p. of arms,** lucha, *f,* combate, *m;* disputa, *f*

**passementerie** /pæs'mɛntri/ *n* pasamanería, *f*

**passenger** /'pæsəndʒər/ *n* viajero (-ra); (on foot) peatón, *m.* **by p. train,** en gran velocidad

**passerby** /'pæsər'bai/ *n* transeúnte, paseante, *mf*

**passing** /'pæsɪŋ/ *a* pasajero; fugitivo; momentáneo. —*adv* sumamente, extremadamente. —*n* pasada, *f;* paso, *m;* (death) muerte, *f;* (disappearance) desaparición, *f;* (of a law) aprobación, *f.* **in p.,** de paso. **p.-bell,** toque de difuntos, *m*

**passing grade** *n* mínima calificación aprobatoria, *f*

**passion** /'pæʃən/ *n* pasión, *f;* (Christ's) Pasión, *f;* (anger) cólera, *f.* **to fly into a p.,** montar en cólera. **p.-flower,** pasionaria, granadilla, *f.* **P. play,** drama de la Pasión, *m.* **P. Sunday,** Domingo de Pasión, *m.* **P. Week,** Semana Santa, *f*

**passionate** /'pæʃənɪt/ *a* apasionado; (quick-tempered) irascible, colérico; (fervid) vehemente, intenso, ardiente

**passionately** /'pæʃənɪtli/ *adv* con pasión, apasionadamente; (irascibly) coléricamente; (fervidly) con vehemencia, ardientemente

**passionless** /'pæʃənlɪs/ *a* sin pasión, frío; impasible; imparcial

**passive** /'pæsɪv/ *a* pasivo. —*n Gram.* pasiva, *f.* **p. resistance,** resistencia pasiva, *f*

**passivity** /pæ'sɪvɪti/ *n* pasividad, *f*

**Passover** /'pæs,ouvər/ *n* Pascua de los judíos, *f*

**passport** /'pæspɔrt/ *n* pasaporte, *m*

**password** /'pæs,wɜrd/ *n* contraseña, *f*

**past** /pæst/ *a* pasado; último; (expert) consumado; (former) antiguo, ex-. —*n* pasado, *m;* historia, *f,* antecedentes, *m pl, prep* después de; (in front of) delante de; (next to) al lado de; (beyond) más allá de; (without) sin; fuera de; (of age) más de; (no longer

able to) incapaz de. —*adv* más allá. (The translation of **past** as an adverb is often either omitted, or included in the verb, e.g. *The years flew p.,* Los años transcurrieron. *for centuries p.,* durante siglos.) **I am p. caring,** Nada me importa ya. **It is a quarter p. ten,** Son las diez y cuarto. **It is p. four o'clock,** Son las siete pasadas, Son después de las cuatro. **what's p. is p.,** lo pasado, pasado. **p. doubt,** fuera de duda. **p. endurance,** insoportable. **p. help,** sin remedio, irremediable. **p. hope,** sin esperanza. **p.-master,** maestro, consumado, experto, *m.* **p. participle,** participio pasado, *m.* **p. president,** ex-presidente, *m.* **p. tense,** (tiempo) pasado, *m*

**paste** /peist/ *n* pasta, *f;* (gloy) engrudo, *m.* —*vt* (affix) pegar; (glue) engomar, engrudar

**pasteboard** /'peist,bɔrd/ *n* cartón, *m,* cartulina, *f, a* de cartón, de cartulina

**pastel** /pæ'stɛl/ *n Art.* pastel, *m.* **p. drawing,** pintura al pastel, *f*

**pastelist** /'pæstɛlɪst/ *n* pastelista, *mf*

**pasteurization** /,pæstʃərə'zeiʃən/ *n* pasteurización, *f*

**pasteurize** /'pæstʃə,raiz/ *vt* pasteurizar

**pastille** /pæ'stil/ *n* pastilla, *f*

**pastime** /'pæs,taim/ *n* pasatiempo, entretenimiento, *m,* diversión, recreación, *f*

**pastor** /'pæstər/ *n* pastor, *m*

**pastoral** /'pæstərəl/ *a* pastoril; *Eccl.* pastoral. —*n Eccl.* pastoral, *f;* (Poet. Mus.) pastorela, *f*

**pastorate** /'pæstərɪt/ *n* pastoría, *f*

**pastry** /'peistri/ *n* (dough) pasta, *f;* pastel, *m,* torta, *f;* pastelería, *f.* **p.-cook,** repostero, *m,* pastelero (-ra)

**pasturage** /'pæstʃərɪdʒ/ *n* (grass, etc.) pasto, *m;* pastoreo, *m*

**pasture** /'pæstʃər/ *n* (grass, etc.) pasto, herbaje, *m;* pasturaje, *m;* (field) prado, *m,* pradera, dehesa, *f.* —*vi* pacer; pastar. —*vt* apacentar, pastar

**pasty** /'pæsti/ *a* pastoso; (pale) pálido. —*n* empanada, *f*

**pat** /pæt/ *n* toque, *m;* caricia, *f;* (for butter) molde (de mantequilla), *m.* —*vt* tocar; acariciar, pasar la mano (sobre). —*adv* a propósito; oportunamente; fácilmente. **pat of butter,** pedacito de mantequilla, *m.* **pat on the back,** golpe en la espalda, *m; Fig.* elogio, *m*

**Patagonian** /,pætə'gouniən/ *a* and *n* patagón (-ona)

**patch** /pætʃ/ *n* (mend) remiendo, *m;* (piece) pedazo, *m;* (plaster and *Auto.,* etc.) parche, *m;* (beauty spot) lunar postizo, *m;* (of ground) parcela, *f;* (of flowers, etc.) masa, *f;* (stain, and *Fig.*) mancha, *f.* —*vt* (mend) remendar; poner remiendo (a); pegar; (roughly) chafallar; (the face) ponerse lunares postizos. **p. of blue sky,** pedazo de cielo azul. **patch of green grass,** mancha de hierba verde. **to be not a p. on,** no ser de la misma clase que; (of persons) no llegarle a los zancajos de. **to p. up a quarrel,** hacer las paces

**patchwork** /'pætʃ,wɜrk/ *n* labor de retazos, obra de retacitos, *f; Fig.* mezcla, mezcolanza, *f.* **p. quilt,** centón, *m*

**patchy** /'pætʃi/ *a* desigual; manchado

**patella** /pə'tɛlə/ *n Anat.* rótula, *f*

**patency** /'peitnsi/ *n* evidencia, claridad, *f*

**patent** /'pætnt/ *a* evidente, patente; patentado. —*n* patente, *f.* —*vt* patentar. **p. of nobility,** carta de hidalguía, *f.* **"P. Applied For,"** «Patente Solicitada.» **Patent Pending** marca en trámite. **p. leather,** *n* charol, *m.* —*a* de charol. **p. medicine,** específico farmacéutico, *m*

**patentee** /,pætn'ti/ *n* el, *m,* (f, la) que obtiene una patente; inventor (-ra)

**patently** /'pætntli/ *adv* evidentemente, claramente

**paterfamilias** /,peitərfə'miliəs, ,pɑ-, ,pætər-/ *n* padre de familia, *m*

**paternal** /pə'tɜrnl/ *a* paterno, paternal

**paternally** /pə'tɜrnli/ *adv* paternalmente

**paternity** /pə'tɜrnɪti/ *n* paternidad, *f*

**path** /pæθ/ *n* senda, vereda, *f,* sendero, *m;* camino, *m;* (track) pista, *f;* (traject) trayectoria, *f.* **the beaten p.,** el camino trillado

**pathetic** /pə'θɛtɪk/ *a* patético

**pathless** /'pæθlɪs/ *a* sin senda

**pathogenic** /,pæθə'dʒɛnɪk/ *a Med.* patógeno

**pathological** /,pæθə'lɒdʒɪkəl/ *a* patológico

**pathologist** /pə'θɒlədʒɪst/ n patólogo, m

**pathology** /pə'θɒlədʒi/ n patología, f

**pathos** /'peiθɒs/ n lo patético

**patience** /'peiʃəns/ n paciencia, f. **He tries my p. very much,** Me cuesta mucho no impacientarme con él. **to lose p.,** perder la paciencia; (grow angry) perder los estribos. **to play p.,** hacer solitarios

**patient** /'peiʃənt/ a paciente. —n paciente, mf; (ill person) enfermo (-ma); (of a physician) cliente, mf

**patiently** /'peiʃəntli/ adv con paciencia, pacientemente

**patina** /'pætnə, pə'tinə/ n pátina, f

**patriarch** /'peitri,ark/ n patriarca, m

**patriarchal** /,peitri'arkəl/ a patriarcal

**patriarchy** /'peitri,arki/ n patriarcado, m

**patrician** /pə'trɪʃən/ a and n patricio (-ia)

**patrimonial** /,pætrə'mouniəl/ a patrimonial

**patrimony** /'pætrə,mouni/ n patrimonio, m

**patriot** /'peitriət/ n patriota, mf

**patriotic** /,peitri'ɒtɪk/ a patriótico

**patriotism** /'peitriə,tɪzəm/ n patriotismo, m

**patrol** /pə'troul/ n patrulla, f; ronda, f, vi and vt patrullar; rondar; recorrer. **p. boat,** lancha escampavía, f. **p. flight,** vuelo de patrulla, m

**patron** /'peitrən/ n (of a freed slave) patrono, m; (of the arts, etc.) mecenas, protector, m; (customer) parroquiano (-na), cliente, mf. **p. saint,** santo (-ta) patrón (-ona)

**patronage** /'peitrənidʒ/ n (protection) patrocinio, m; protección, f; Eccl. patronato, m; (regular custom) clientela, f; (of manner) superioridad, f

**patroness** /'peitrənɪs/ n patrona, f; protectora, f; (of a charity, etc.) patrocinadora, f; (of a regiment, etc.) madrina, f

**patronize** /'peitrə,naiz/ vt patrocinar; proteger, favorecer; (a shop) ser parroquiano de; (treat arrogantly) tratar con superioridad

**patronizing** /'peitrə,naizɪŋ/ a (with air, behavior, etc.) de superioridad, de altivez

**patten** /'pætn/ n zueco, chanclo, m

**patter** /'pætər/ n (jargon) jerga, f; charla, f; (of rain) azotes, m pl; (of feet) son, m; golpecitos, m pl. —vt (repeat) decir mecánicamente. —vi (chatter) charlar; (of rain) azotar, bailar; correr ligeramente

**pattern** /'pætərn/ n modelo, m; (Sew. and dressmaking) patrón, m; (in founding) molde, m; (template) escantillón, m; (of cloth, etc.) muestra, f; (design) dibujo, diseño, m; (example) ejemplar, m. —vt diseñar, estampar. **p. book,** libro de muestras, m

**patty** /'pæti/ n empanada, f, pastelillo, m

**paucity** /'pɔsɪti/ n poquedad, f; corto número, m; insuficiencia, escasez, f

**paunch** /pɔntʃ/ n panza, barriga, f

**pauper** /'pɔpər/ n pobre, mf

**pauperism** /'pɔpə,rɪzəm/ n pauperismo, m

**pauperization** /,pɔpərə'zeiʃən/ n empobrecimiento, m

**pauperize** /'pɔpə,raiz/ vt empobrecer, reducir a la miseria

**pause** /pɔz/ n pausa, f; intervalo, m; silencio, m; interrupción, f; Mus. pausa, f. —vi pausar, hacer una pausa; detenerse, interrumpirse; vacilar. **to give p. to,** hacer vacilar (a)

**pavan** /'pævən/ n (dance) pavana, f

**pave** /peiv/ vt empedrar, enlosar. **to p. the way for,** facilitar el paso de, preparar el terreno para, abrir el camino de

**pavement** /'peivmənt/ n pavimento, m; (sidewalk) acera, f. **p.-artist,** pintor callejero, m

**pavilion** /pə'vɪlyən/ n pabellón, m; (for a band, etc.) quiosco, m; (tent) tienda de campaña, f

**paving** /'peivɪŋ/ n pavimentación, f; empedrado, m; see **pavement. p.-stone,** losa, f

**paw** /pɔ/ n pata, f; (with claws) garra, f; Inf. manaza, f. —vt tocar con la pata; (scratch) arañar; (handle) manosear. —vi (of a horse) piafar

**pawing** /'pɔiŋ/ n (of a horse) el piafar; (handling) manoseo, m

**pawn** /pɔn/ n (chess) peón (de ajedrez), m; empeño, m; Fig. prenda, f. —vt empeñar, pignorar; dar en prenda. **p.-ticket,** papeleta de empeño, f

**pawnbroker** /'pɔn,broukər/ n prestamista, mf

**pawning** /'pɔnɪŋ/ n empeño, m, pignoración, f

**pawnshop** /'pɔn,ʃɒp/ n casa de préstamos, casa de empeño, f, monte de piedad, m

**pay** /pei/ n paga, f; (Mil. Nav.) soldada, f; salario, m; (of a workman) jornal, m; (reward) recompensa, compensación, f; (profit) beneficio, provecho, m. **pay-day,** día de paga, m. **pay-office,** pagaduría, f. **pay-sheet,** nómina, f

**pay** /pei/ vt pagar; (a debt) satisfacer; (spend) gastar; (recompense) remunerar, recompensar; (hand over) entregar; (yield) producir; (a visit) hacer; (attention) prestar; (homage) rendir; (one's respects) presentar. —vi pagar; producir ganancia; sacar provecho; ser una ventaja, ser provechoso. **It would not pay him to do it,** No le saldría a cuenta hacerlo. **This job doesn't pay,** Este trabajo no da dinero. **to pay a compliment (to),** cumplimentar, decir alabanzas (a), echar una flor (a). **to pay attention,** prestar atención; hacer caso. **to pay cash,** pagar al contado. **to pay in advance,** pagar adelantado. **to pay in full,** saldar. **to pay off old scores,** ajustar cuentas viejas. **to pay one's addresses to,** hacer la corte (a), pretender en matrimonio (a). **to pay the penalty,** sufrir el castigo, hacer penitencia. **to pay with interest,** Fig. pagar con creces. **to pay again,** volver a pagar, pagar de nuevo. **to pay back,** devolver, restituir; (money only) reembolsar; Fig. pagar en la misma moneda, vengarse (de). **to pay down,** pagar al contado. **to pay for,** pagar, costear; satisfacer. **to pay in,** ingresar. **to pay off,** (persons) despedir; (a debt) saldar; (a mortgage) cancelar, redimir. **to pay out,** (persons) vengarse de; (money) pagar; (ropes, etc.) arriar. **to pay up,** pagar; pagar por completo; (shares, etc.) redimir

**payable** /'peiəbəl/ a pagadero; a pagar; que puede ser pagado

**payee** /pei'i/ n tenedor, m

**payer** /'peiər/ n pagador (-ra)

**paying** /'peiɪŋ/ n. See **payment**

**paymaster** /'pei,mæstər/ n pagador, m; tesorero, m. **P.-General,** ordenador general de pagos, m

**payment** /'peimənt/ n pago, m, paga, f; remuneración, f; Fig. recompensa, satisfacción, f; Fig. premio, m. **in p. of,** en pago de. **on p. of,** mediante el pago de. **p. in advance,** pago adelantado, anticipo, m

**pea** /pi/ n guisante, m. **dry or split pea,** guisante seco, m. **sweet pea,** guisante de olor, m. **pea-flour,** harina de guisantes, f. **pea-green,** verde claro, m. **pea-jacket,** chaquetón de piloto, m. **pea-shooter,** cerbatana, f

**peace** /pis/ n paz, f; tranquilidad, quietud, f, sosiego, m; Law. orden público, m. **P.!** ¡Silencio! **to hold one's p.,** callarse, guardar silencio. **to make p.,** hacer las paces. **P. be upon this house!** ¡Paz sea en esta casa! **p.-footing,** pie de paz, m. **p.-loving,** pacífico. **p.-offering,** sacrificio propiciatorio, m; satisfacción, oferta de paz, f

**peaceable** /'pisəbəl/ a pacífico; apacible; tranquilo, sosegado

**peaceableness** /'pisəbəlnɪs/ n paz, f; apacibilidad, f; tranquilidad, quietud, f, sosiego, m

**peaceably** /'pisəbli/ adv pacíficamente; tranquilamente

**peaceful** /'pisfəl/ a pacífico; tranquilo; silencioso. **to come with p. intentions,** venir de paz

**peacefully** /'pisfəli/ adv en paz; pacíficamente; tranquilamente

**peacefulness** /'pisfəlnɪs/ n paz, f; tranquilidad, calma, quietud, f; silencio, m; carácter pacífico, m

**peacemaker** /'pis,meikər/ n pacificador (-ra); conciliador (-ra)

**peach** /pitʃ/ n (fruit) melocotón, m; (tree) melocotonero, melocotón, m; (girl) breva, f. **p.-colour,** color de melocotón, m

**peacock** /'pi,kɒk/ n pavo real, pavón, m. —vi pavonearse; darse humos. **The p. spread its tail,** El pavo real hizo la rueda

**peahen** /'pi,hɛn/ n pava real, f

**peak** /pik/ n punta, f; (of a cap) visera, f; (of a mountain) peñasco, m, cumbre, cima, f; (mountain itself) pico, m; (Naut. of a hull) pico, m; Fig. auge, apogeo, *m;* punto más alto, *m.* —*vi* consumirse, enflaquecer. **p. hours,** horas de mayor tráfico, *f pl*

**peaked** /'pikɪd/ *a* en punta; puntiagudo; picudo; (of a cap) con visera; (wan) ojeroso; (thin) delgaducho, macilento, consumido

**peal** /pil/ *n* toque (or repique) de campanas, *m;* campanillazo, *m;* carillón, *m;* (noise) estruendo, ruido, *m;* (of thunder) trueno, *m;* (of an organ) sonido, *m.* —*vi* repicar; sonar. —*vt* tañer, echar a vuelo (las campanas); (of a bell that one presses) hacer sonar, tocar. **a p. of laughter,** una carcajada

**peanut** /'pi,nʌt/ *n* cacahuete, *m.* **p. butter,** mantequilla de cacahuete, *f*

**pear** /pɛər/ *n* pera, *f.* **p.-shaped,** piriforme, de figura de pera. **p. tree,** peral, *m*

**pearl** /pɜrl/ *n* perla, *f;* (mother-of-pearl) nácar, *m, a* de perla; perlero. —*vt* (dew) rociar, aljofarar. —*vi* pescar perlas; formar perlas. **seed p.,** aljófar, *m.* **p.-ash,** carbonato potásico, *m.* **p.-barley,** cebada perlada, *f.* **p.-button,** botón de nácar, *m.* **p.-fisher,** pescador de perlas, *m.* **p.-fishery,** pescaduría de perlas, *f.* **p.-grey,** gris de perla, *m*

**pearly** /'pɜrli/ *a* perlino; de perla; nacarado; (dewy) aljofarado

**peasant** /'pɛzənt/ *n* campesino (-na), labrador (-ra). —*a* campesino

**peasantry** /'pɛzəntri/ *n* campesinos, *m pl,* gente del campo, *f*

**peat** /pit/ *n* turba, *f.* **p.-bog,** turbera, *f*

**pebble** /'pɛbəl/ *n* guijarro, *m,* pedrezuela, guija, *f;* (gravel) guijo, *m;* cristal de roca, *m;* lente de cristal de roca, *m*

**pebbled, pebbly** /'pɛbəld; 'pɛbli/ *a* guijarroso, enguijarrado

**peccadillo** /,pɛkə'dɪlou/ *n* pecadillo, *m*

**peck** /pɛk/ *n* (of a bird) picotazo, *m,* picada, *f;* (kiss) besito, *m;* (large amount) montón, *m;* multitud, *f.* —*vt* (of a bird) picotear; sacar (or coger) con el pico; (kiss) besar rápidamente. —*vi* (with at) picotear; picar

**pectoral** /'pɛktərəl/ *a* pectoral

**peculiar** /pɪ'kyulyər/ *a* particular, peculiar, individual; propio, característico; (marked) especial; (unusual) extraño, raro, extraordinario

**peculiarity** /pɪ,kyuli'ærɪti/ *n* peculiaridad, particularidad, *f;* singularidad, *f;* (eccentricity) excentricidad, rareza, *f*

**peculiarly** /pɪ'kyulyərli/ *adv* particularmente, peculiarmente; especialmente; extrañamente

**pecuniarily** /pɪ,kyuni'ɛərəli/ *adv* pecuniariamente

**pecuniary** /pɪ'kyuni,ɛri/ *a* pecuniario

**pedagogic** /,pɛdə'gɒdʒɪk/ *a* pedagógico

**pedagogue** /'pɛdə,gɒg/ *n* pedagogo, *m*

**pedagogy** /'pɛdə,goudʒi, -,gɒdʒi/ *n* pedagogía, *f*

**pedal** /'pɛdl/ *n* pedal, *m.* —*vi* pedalear

**pedant** /'pɛdnt/ *n* pedante, *mf*

**pedantic** /pə'dæntɪk/ *a* pedante

**pedantically** /pə'dæntɪkli/ *adv* con pedantería, pedantescamente

**pedantry** /'pɛdntri/ *n* pedantería, *f*

**peddle** /'pɛdl/ *vi* ser buhonero. —*vt* revender

**peddling** /'pɛdlɪŋ/ *n* buhonería, *f.* —*a* trivial, insignificante; mezquino

**pedestal** /'pɛdəstl/ *n* pedestal, *m;* Fig. fundamento, *m,* base, *f.* **to put on a p.,** Fig. poner sobre un pedestal

**pedestrian** /pə'dɛstriən/ *n* peatón, peón, *m, a* pedestre; Fig. patoso. **p. traffic,** circulación de los peatones, *f*

**pedestrian crosswalk,** cruce peatonal (Argentina), cruce de peatones, *m*

**pediatrician** /,pidiə'trɪʃən/ *n* pediatra, *mf*

**pedigree** /'pɛdɪ,gri/ *n* genealogía, *f;* raza, *f;* (of words) etimología, *f.* —*a* (of animals) de raza, de casta. **p. dog,** perro de casta, *m*

**pediment** /'pɛdəmənt/ *n* Archit. frontón, *m*

**pedlar** /'pɛdlər/ *n* buhonero, *m*

**pedometer** /pə'dɒmɪtər/ *n* pedómetro, cuentapasos, *m*

**peel** /pil/ *n* (baker's) pala, *f;* (of fruit, etc.) piel, *f,* hollejo, *m.* —*vt* pelar, mondar; (bark) descortezar.

—*vi* descascararse, desconcharse; (of the bark of a tree) descortezarse

**peeling** /'pilɪŋ/ *n* (of fruit, etc.) peladura, monda, *f;* (of bark) descortezadura, *f;* (of paint, etc.) desconchadura, *f*

**peep** /pip/ *vi* (of birds) piar; (of mice) chillar; (peer) atisbar, mirar a hurtadillas; (appear) asomar; mostrarse; (of the dawn) despuntar. —*n* (of birds) pío, *m;* (of mice) chillido, *m;* (glimpse) vista, *f;* (glance) ojeada, mirada furtiva, *f;* **at the p. of day,** al despuntar el día. **p.-hole,** mirilla, *f,* atisbadero, *m;* escucha, *f.* **p.-show,** óptica, *f*

**peeper** /'pipər/ (eye) avizón *m*

**peer** /pɪər/ *n* par, *m;* igual, *mf.* —*vi* atisbar; escudriñar; Fig. asomar, aparecer

**peerage** /'pɪərɪdʒ/ *n* nobleza, aristocracia, *f;* dignidad de par, *f*

**peeress** /'pɪərɪs/ *n* paresa, *f*

**peerless** /'pɪərlɪs/ *a* sin par, incomparable, sin igual

**peevish** /'pivɪʃ/ *a* displicente, malhumorado; picajoso, vidrioso, enojadizo

**peevishness** /'pivɪʃnɪs/ *n* displicencia, *f,* mal humor, *m;* impaciencia, *f*

**peg** /pɛg/ *n* clavija, *f;* (of a tent) estaca, *f;* (of a barrel) estaquilla, *f;* (of a violin, etc.) clavija, *f;* (for coats, etc.) colgadero, *m;* (of whisky, etc.) trago, *m;* Fig. pretexto, *m.* —*vt* clavar, enclavijar, empernar. **to take down a peg,** bajar los humos (a). **to peg away,** batirse el cobre. **to peg down,** fijar con clavijas; (a tent) sujetar con estacas; (prices) fijar

**Pegasus** /'pɛgəsəs/ *n* Pegaso, *m*

**peignoir** /pein'wɑr/ *n* peinador, salto de cama, *m,* bata, *f*

**pekinese** /,pikə'niz/ *n* perro (-rra) pequinés (-esa)

**pelican** /'pɛlɪkən/ *n* pelícano, *m*

**pellagra** /pə'lægrə/ *n* Med. pelagra, *f*

**pellet** /'pɛlɪt/ *n* bolita, *f;* (pill) píldora, *f;* (shot) perdigón, *m*

**pellmell** /'pɛl'mɛl/ *adv* a trochemoche; atropelladamente

**pellucid** /pə'lusɪd/ *a* diáfano

**Peloponnesian** /,pɛləpə'niʒən/ *a and n* peloponense, *mf*

**pelota** /pə'loutə/ *n* pelota vasca, *f.* **p. player,** pelotari, *m*

**pelt** /pɛlt/ *n* pellejo, *m;* cuero, *m;* (fur) piel, *f;* (blow) golpe, *m.* —*vt* llover (piedras, etc.) sobre, arrojar... sobre; (questions) disparar; (throw) tirar. —*vi* (of rrain) azotar, diluviar

**pelvic** /'pɛlvɪk/ *a* pélvico, pelviano

**pelvis** /'pɛlvɪs/ *n* pelvis, *f*

**pen** /pɛn/ *n* (for sheep, etc.) aprisco, *m;* corral, *m;* (paddock) parque, *m;* (for hens) pollera, *f;* (for writing and Fig., author, etc.) pluma, *f.* —*vt* (shut up) acorralar; encerrar; (write) escribir (con pluma). **pen-and-ink drawing,** dibujo a la pluma, *m.* **pen-holder,** portaplumas, *m.* **pen-name,** seudónimo, *m.* **pen-wiper,** limpiaplumas, *m*

**penal** /'pinl/ *a* penal. **p. code,** código penal, *m.* **p. colony,** colonia penal, *f.* **p. servitude,** trabajos forzados (or forzosos), *m pl.* **p. servitude for life,** cadena perpetua, *f*

**penalization** /,pinlə'zeiʃən/ *n* castigo, *m*

**penalize** /'pinl,aiz/ *vt* penar, imponer pena (a); castigar

**penalty** /'pɛnlti/ *n* Law. penalidad, *f;* castigo, *m;* (fine) multa, *f;* (risk) riesgo, *m;* Sports. sanción, *m.* **the p. of,** la desventaja de. **under p. of,** so pena de. **p. kick,** (football) penalty, *m*

**penance** /'pɛnəns/ *n* penitencia, *f.* **to do p.,** hacer penitencia

**penchant** /'pɛntʃənt/ *n* tendencia, *f;* inclinación, *f*

**pencil** /'pɛnsəl/ *n* lápiz, *m;* (automatic) lapicero, *m.* —*vt* escribir (or dibujar or marcar) con lápiz. **p.-case,** estuche para lápices, *m.* **p.-holder,** lapicero, *m.* **p.-sharpener,** cortalápices, afilalápices, *m*

**pendant** /'pɛndənt/ *n* (jewel) pendiente, *m;* Archit. culo de lámpara, *m;* (Naut. rope) amantillo, *m;* (flag) gallardete, *m*

**pending** /'pɛndɪŋ/ *a* pendiente. —*prep* durante. **to be p.,** pender; amenazar

**pendulous** /'pɛndʒələs/ *a* péndulo; colgante; oscilante

**pendulum** /'pɛndʒələm/ *n* péndola, *f*, péndulo, *m*

**penetrability** /,pɛnɪtrə'bɪlɪti/ *n* penetrabilidad, *f*

**penetrable** /'pɛnɪtrəbəl/ *a* penetrable

**penetrate** /'pɛnɪ,treɪt/ *vt* and *vi* penetrar

**penetrating** /'pɛnɪ,treɪtɪŋ/ *a* penetrante

**penetration** /,pɛnɪ'treɪʃən/ *n* penetración, *f*

**penguin** /'pɛŋgwɪn/ *n* pingüino, pájaro bobo, *m*

**penicillin** /,pɛnə'sɪlɪn/ *n* penicilina, *f*

**peninsula** /pə'nɪnsələ, -'nɪnsyələ/ *n* península, *f*

**peninsular** /pə'nɪnsələr, -'nɪnsyələr/ *a* peninsular. **P. War,** Guerra de la Independencia, *f*

**penis** /'pinɪs/ *n* pene, *m*

**penitence** /'pɛnɪtəns/ *n* penitencia, *f*

**penitent** /'pɛnɪtənt/ *a* penitente. —*n* penitente, *mf*

**penitential** /,pɛnɪ'tɛnʃəl/ *a* penitencial

**penitentiary** /,pɛnɪ'tɛnʃəri/ *n Eccl.* penitenciaria, *f*; casa de corrección, *f*; penitenciaria, *f*, presidio, *m*; cárcel modelo, *f*, *a* penitenciario

**penknife** /'pɛn,naɪf/ *n* cortaplumas, *m*

**penmanship** /'pɛnmən,ʃɪp/ *n* caligrafía, *f*

**pennant** /'pɛnənt/ *n Naut.* gallardete, *m*; banderola, *f*; (ensign) insignia, bandera, *f*

**penniless** /'pɛnɪlɪs/ *a* sin un penique, sin blanca; indigente, pobre de solemnidad. **to leave p.,** dejar en la miseria; *Inf.* dejar sin camisa

**pennilessness** /'pɛnɪlɪsnɪs/ *n* falta de dinero, extrema pobreza, *f*

**penning** /'pɛnɪŋ/ *n* escritura, *f*; (drawing up) redacción, *f*; (of bulls, etc.) acorralamiento, *m*

**pennon** /'pɛnən/ *n* pendón, *m*, banderola, *f*; (ensign) bandera, insignia, *f*

**Pennsylvanian** /,pɛnsəl'veɪnyən/ *a* and *n* pensilvano (-na)

**penny** /'pɛni/ *n* de un centavo, penique, *m*; perra gorda, *f*. —*a* de un penique. **p.-a-liner,** gacetillero, *m*. **p. dreadful,** folletín, *m*, novela por entregas, *f*. **p.-in-the-slot machine,** tragaperras, *m*

**pennyworth** /'pɛni,wɜrθ/ *n* penique, valor de un penique, *m*

**pension** /'pɛnʃən/ *n* pensión, *f*; *Mil.* retiro, *m*; (grant) beca, *f*; (boardinghouse) pensión de familia, *f*. —*vt* pensionar, dar una pensión (a); (with off) jubilar. **old age p.,** pensión para la vejez, *f*. **retirement p.,** pensión vitalicia, *f*

**pensioner** /'pɛnʃənər/ *n* pensionista, *mf*; (*Mil.* and *Nav.*) inválido, *m*

**pensive** /'pɛnsɪv/ *a* pensativo, meditabundo; cabizbajo, triste

**pensively** /'pɛnsɪvli/ *adv* pensativamente; tristemente

**pensiveness** /'pɛnsɪvnɪs/ *n* reflexión, meditación profunda, *f*; tristeza, melancolía, *f*

**pentagon** /'pɛntə,gɒn/ *n* pentágono, *m*

**Pentateuch** /'pɛntə,tuk/ *n* pentateuco, *m*

**Pentecost** /'pɛntɪ,kɔst/ *n* Pentecostés, *m*, Pascua, *f*

**pentecostal** /,pɛntɪ'kɔstl/ *a* de Pentecostés, pascual

**penthouse** /'pɛnt,haʊs/ *n* cobertizo, tinglado, *m*, tejavana, *f*

**pent-up** /pɛnt 'ʌp/ *a* encerrado; enjaulado; (of emotion) reprimido

**penultimate** /pɪ'nʌltəmɪt/ *a* penúltimo. —*n* penúltimo, *m*

**penurious** /pə'nʊriəs/ *a* pobre; escaso; (stingy) tacaño, avaro

**penury** /'pɛnyəri/ *n* penuria, *f*

**peony** /'piəni/ *n* peonía, *f*, saltaojos, *m*, rosa albardera, rosa montés, *f*

**people** /'pipəl/ *n* pueblo, *m*; nación, *f*; gente, *f*; personas, *f pl*; (used disparagingly, mob) populacho, vulgo, *m*; (inhabitants) habitantes, *m pl*; (subjects) súbditos, *m pl*; (relations) parientes, *m pl*; familia, *f*. —*vt* poblar. **little p.,** (children) gente menuda, *f*. **respectable p.,** gente de bien, *f*. **the p. of Burgos,** los habitantes de Burgos. **P. say,** Se dice, La gente dice. **Very few p. think as you do,** Hay muy pocas personas que opinan como Vd. **How are your p.** (family)? ¿Cómo están los de tu casa? ¿Cómo está tu familia? **"People Working"** «Trabajadores»

**peopling** /'piplɪŋ/ *n* población, *f*; colonización, *f*

**pep** /pɛp/ *n Inf.* energía, *f*, ánimo, *m*. **p. talk,** discurso estimulante, *m*. **p. up,** animar

**Pepin the Short** /'pɛpɪn/ Pipino el Breve

**peplum** /'pɛpləm/ *n* peplo, *m*

**pepper** /'pɛpər/ *n* pimienta, *f*; (plant) pimentero, pimiento, *m*, *vt* sazonar con pimienta; (pelt) acribillar; (with questions) disparar; (a literary work with quotations, etc.) salpimentar. **black p.,** pimienta negra, *f*. **red p.,** pimiento, *m*; (cayenne) pimentón, *m*. **p.-castor,** pimentero, *m*

**peppercorn** /'pɛpər,kɔrn/ *n* grano de pimienta, *m*

**peppermint** /'pɛpər,mɪnt/ *n* menta, *f*. **p. drop,** pastilla de menta, *f*

**peppery** /'pɛpəri/ *a* picante; (irascible) colérico, irascible

**pepsin** /'pɛpsɪn/ *n Chem.* pepsina, *f*

**peptic** /'pɛptɪk/ *a* péptico

**per** /pər/ *unstressed* pər/ *prep* por. **ninety miles per hour,** noventa millas por hora. **ten pesetas per dozen,** diez pesetas la docena. **$60 per annum,** sesenta dólares al año. **per cent.,** por ciento

**perambulate** /pər'æmbyə,leɪt/ *vt* recorrer

**perambulator** /pər'æmbyə,leɪtər/ *n* cochecito para niños, *m*

**percale** /pər'keɪl/ *n* percal, *m*

**percaline** /,pɜrkə'lin/ *n* percalina, *f*

**perceive** /pər'siv/ *vt* percibir, comprender, darse cuenta de; percibir, discernir

**percentage** /pər'sɛntɪdʒ/ *n* tanto por ciento, *m*; porcentaje, *m*

**perceptible** /pər'sɛptəbəl/ *a* perceptible, visible; sensible

**perceptibly** /pər'sɛptəbli/ *adv* visiblemente; sensiblemente

**perception** /pər'sɛpʃən/ *n* percepción, *f*; sensibilidad, *f*

**perceptive** /pər'sɛptɪv/ *a* perceptivo

**perch** /pɜrtʃ/ *n Ichth.* perca, *f*; (for birds) percha, *f*; (measure) pértiga, *f*. —*vi* posarse (en o sobre). —*vt* posar (en o sobre)

**percolate** /'pɜrkə,leɪt/ *vi* filtrar; *Fig.* penetrar. —*vt* filtrar, colar

**percolation** /,pɜrkə'leɪʃən/ *n* filtración, *f*

**percolator** /'pɜrkə,leɪtər/ *n* filtro, *m*. **coffee p.,** colador de café, *m*

**percussion** /pər'kʌʃən/ *n* percusión, *f*; choque, *m*. **p. cap,** fulminante, *m*. **p. instrument,** instrumento de percusión, *m*

**perdition** /pər'dɪʃən/ *n* perdición, *f*; ruina, *f*

**peregrination** /,pɛrɪgrə'neɪʃən/ *n* peregrinación, *f*

**peremptorily** /pə'rɛmptərəli/ *adv* perentoriamente

**peremptoriness** /pə'rɛmptərɪnɪs/ *n* perentoriedad, *f*

**peremptory** /pə'rɛmptəri/ *a* perentorio; (of manner, etc.) imperioso, autoritario

**perennial** /pə'rɛniəl/ *a Bot.* vivaz; perenne; eterno, perpetuo. —*n* planta vivaz, *f*

**perennially** /pə'rɛniəli/ *adv* perennemente

**perfect** /*a.*, *n.* 'pɜrfɪkt; *v.* pər'fɛkt/ *a* perfecto; (of a work) acabado; completo. —*n Gram.* (tiempo) perfecto, *m*. —*vt* perfeccionar; (oneself) perfeccionarse. **to have a p. knowledge of...,** conocer a fondo... **They are p. strangers to me,** Me son completamente desconocidos

**perfectible** /pər'fɛktəbəl/ *a* perfectible

**perfecting** /pər'fɛktɪŋ/ *n* perfeccionamiento, *m*; terminación, *f*

**perfection** /pər'fɛkʃən/ *n* perfección, *f*; excelencia, *f*. **to p.,** a la perfección, a las mil maravillas

**perfectionist** /pər'fɛkʃənɪst/ *n* perfeccionista, *mf*

**perfidious** /pər'fɪdiəs/ *a* pérfido

**perfidy** /'pɜrfɪdi/ *n* perfidia, *f*

**perforate** /'pɜrfə,reɪt/ *vt* perforar, agujerear

**perforating** /'pɜrfə,reɪtɪŋ/ *a* perforador

**perforation** /,pɜrfə'reɪʃən/ *n* perforación, *f*; agujero, *m*

**perforce** /pər'fɔrs/ *adv* a la fuerza, forzosamente

**perform** /pər'fɔrm/ *vt* hacer; poner por obra, llevar a cabo; desempeñar, cumplir; ejercer; (a piece of music, etc.) ejecutar; realizar; (a play) representar, dar; (a part in a play) desempeñar (el papel de...); (Divine Service) oficiar. —*vi Theat.* trabajar, representar un papel; (a musical instrument) tocar; (sing) cantar; (of animals) hacer trucos

**performable** /pər'fɔrməbəl/ *a* hacedero, practicable, ejecutable; *Theat.* que puede representarse; *Mus.* tocable

**performance** /pər'fɔrməns/ *n* ejecución, realización, *f*; desempeño, ejercicio, *m*; cumplimiento, *m*; acción, *f*; hazaña, *f*; (work) obra, *f*; *Theat.* función, representación, *f*; (*Theat.* acting of a part) interpretación, *f*; *Mus.* ejecución, *f*; *Mech.* potencia, *f*. **first p.,** *Theat.* estreno, *m*

**performer** /pər'fɔrmər/ *n Mus.* ejecutante, *mf*, músico, *m*; *Theat.* actor (-triz), representante, *mf*; artista, *mf*

**performing** /pər'fɔrmɪŋ/ *a* (of animals) sabio. **p. dog,** perro sabio, *m*

**perfume** /*n.* 'pɜrfyum; *v.* pər'fyum/ *n* perfume, *m*; fragancia, *f*; aroma, *m.* —*vt* perfumar; embalsamar, aromatizar, llenar con fragancia. **p. burner,** perfumador, *m*

**perfumer** /pər'fyumər/ *n* perfumista, *mf*

**perfumery** /pər'fyuməri/ *n* perfumería, *f*

**perfuming** /'pɜrfyumɪŋ/ *n* acción de perfumar, *f*, *a* que perfuma

**perfunctorily** /pər'fʌŋktərəli/ *adv* perfunctoriamente, sin cuidado; superficialmente

**perfunctoriness** /pər'fʌŋktərɪnɪs/ *n* descuido, *m*, negligencia, *f*; superficialidad, *f*

**perfunctory** /pər'fʌŋktəri/ *a* perfunctorio, negligente; superficial; ligero, de cumplido

**pergola** /'pɜrgələ/ *n* emparrado, cenador, *m*

**perhaps** /pər'hæps/ *adv* quizá, quizás(s), tal vez

**peril** /'pɛrəl/ *n* peligro, *m*; riesgo, *m.* —*vt* poner en peligro; arriesgar. **at one's p.,** a su riesgo. **in p.,** en peligro

**perilous** /'pɛrələs/ *a* peligroso, arriesgado

**perimeter** /pə'rɪmɪtər/ *n* perímetro, *m*

**perineum** /ˌpɛrə'niəm/ *n Anat.* perineo, *m*

**period** /'pɪəriəd/ *n* período, *m*; época, *f*; edad, *f*, tiempo, *m*; duración, *f*; término, plazo, *m*; *Gram.* período, *m*; (full stop) punto final, *m*; *Med.* menstruación, regla, *f*. **p. furniture,** muebles de época, *m pl*

**periodic** /ˌpɪəri'ɒdɪk/ *a* periódico

**periodical** /ˌpɪəri'ɒdɪkəl/ *a* periódico. —*n* publicación periódica, revista, *f*

**periodicity** /ˌpɪəriə'dɪsɪti/ *n* periodicidad, *f*

**peripatetic** /ˌpɛrəpə'tɛtɪk/ *a* peripatético

**peripheral** /pə'rɪfərəl/ *a* periférico

**periphery** /pə'rɪfəri/ *n* periferia, *f*

**periphrastic** /ˌpɛrə'fræstɪk/ *a* perifrástico

**periscope** /'pɛrəˌskoup/ *n* periscopio, *m*

**perish** /'pɛrɪʃ/ *vi* perecer; marchitarse; desaparecer, acabar. **to be perished with cold,** estar muerto de frío

**perishable** /'pɛrɪʃəbəl/ *a* perecedero, frágil

**peritoneum** /ˌpɛrɪtṇ'iəm/ *n* peritoneo, *m*

**peritonitis** /ˌpɛrɪtṇ'aitɪs/ *n* peritonitis, *f*

**periwig** /'pɛrɪˌwɪg/ *n* peluca, *f*

**periwinkle** /'pɛrɪˌwɪŋkəl/ *n Zool.* caracol marino, *m*; *Bot.* vincapervinca, *f*

**perjure** /'pɜrdʒər/ *vt* perjurar. **to p. oneself,** perjurarse

**perjurer** /'pɜrdʒərər/ *n* perjuro (-ra); perjurador (-ra)

**perjury** /'pɜrdʒəri/ *n* perjurio, *m.* **to commit p.,** jurar en falso, perjurar

**perkiness** /'pɜrkɪnɪs/ *n* desenvoltura, gallardía, *f*, despejo, *m*

**perk (up)** /pɜrk/ *vi* levantar la cabeza; recobrar sus bríos, alzar la cabeza; sacar la cabeza

**perky** /'pɜrki/ *a* desenvuelto, gallardo; coquetón; atrevido; (gay) alegre

**permanence** /'pɜrmənəns/ *n* permanencia, *f*; estabilidad, *f*

**permanent** /'pɜrmənənt/ *a* permanente; estable; (of posts, etc.) fijo. **p. wave,** ondulación permanente, *f*. **p. way,** *Rail.* vía, *f*

**permanganate** /pər'mæŋgəˌneit/ *n* permanganato, *m*

**permeability** /ˌpɜrmiə'bɪlɪti/ *n* permeabilidad, *f*

**permeable** /'pɜrmiəbəl/ *a* permeable

**permeate** /'pɜrmiˌeit/ *vt* penetrar; impregnar; *Fig.* infiltrar (en)

**permeation** /ˌpɜrmi'eiʃən/ *n* penetración, *f*; impregnación, *f*; *Fig.* infiltración, *f*

**permissible** /pər'mɪsəbəl/ *a* permisible, admisible; lícito

**permission** /pər'mɪʃən/ *n* permiso, *m*, licencia, *f* ⸱

**permissive** /pər'mɪsɪv/ *a* permisivo, tolerado; (optional) facultativo

**permit** /*v* pər'mɪt; *n* 'pɜrmɪt/ *vt* permitir; dar permiso (a), dejar; tolerar, sufrir; admitir. —*n* permiso, *m*; licencia, *f*; pase, *m.* **Will you p. me to smoke?** ¿Me permites fumar?

**permutation** /ˌpɜrmyu'teiʃən/ *n* permutación, *f*

**permute** /pər'myut/ *vt* permutar

**pernicious** /pər'nɪʃəs/ *a* pernicioso. **p. anemia,** anemia perniciosa, *f*

**perniciousness** /pər'nɪʃəsnɪs/ *n* perniciosidad, *f*

**pernickety** /pər'nɪkɪti/ *a* tiquismiquis

**peroration** /ˌpɛrə'reiʃən/ *n* peroración, *f*

**peroxide** /pə'rɒksaid/ *n* peróxido, *m*

**perpendicular** /ˌpɜrpən'dɪkyələr/ *a* perpendicular. —*n* perpendicular, *f*

**perpendicularity** /ˌpɜrpən,dɪkyə'lærɪti/ *n* perpendicularidad, *f*

**perpendicularly** /ˌpɜrpən'dɪkyələrli/ *adv* perpendicularmente

**perpetrate** /'pɜrpɪˌtreit/ *vt Law.* perpetrar; cometer

**perpetration** /ˌpɜrpɪ'treiʃən/ *n Law.* perpetración, *f*; comisión, *f*

**perpetrator** /'pɜrpɪˌtreitər/ *n* el, *m*, (*f*, la) que comete; *Law.* autor (-ra); perpetrador (-ra)

**perpetual** /pər'pɛtʃuəl/ *a* perpetuo, perdurable, eterno; incesante, constante; (life-long) perpetuo

**perpetually** /pər'pɛtʃuəli/ *adv* perpetuamente; sin cesar; continuamente; constantemente

**perpetuate** /pər'pɛtʃuˌeit/ *vt* perpetuar, eternizar; inmortalizar

**perpetuation** /pər,pɛtʃu'eiʃən/ *n* perpetuación, *f*

**perpetuity** /ˌpɜrpɪ'tuiti/ *n* perpetuidad, *f*. **in p.,** para siempre

**perplex** /pər'plɛks/ *vt* dejar perplejo, aturdir, confundir; embrollar

**perplexed** /pər'plɛkst/ *a* perplejo, irresoluto; confuso; (of questions, etc.) complicado, intrincado

**perplexedly** /pər'plɛksɪdli/ *adv* perplejamente

**perplexing** /pər'plɛksɪŋ/ *a* difícil; complicado; confuso

**perplexity** /pər'plɛksɪti/ *n* perplejidad, *f*; confusión, *f*

**perquisites** /'pɜrkwəzɪts/ *n pl* emolumentos, *m pl*; gajes, percances, *m pl*; (tips) propinas, *f pl*

**persecute** /'pɜrsɪˌkyut/ *vt* perseguir; importunar, molestar

**persecution** /ˌpɜrsɪ'kyuʃən/ *n* persecución, *f*

**persecutor** /'pɜrsɪˌkyutər/ *n* perseguidor (-ra)

**perseverance** /ˌpɜrsə'vɪərəns/ *n* perseverancia, *f*

**persevere** /ˌpɜrsə'vɪər/ *vi* perseverar

**persevering** /ˌpɜrsə'vɪərɪŋ/ *a* perseverante

**perseveringly** /ˌpɜrsə'vɪərɪŋli/ *adv* con perseverancia, perseverantemente

**Persia** /'pɜrʒə/ (la) Persia, *f*

**Persian** /'pɜrʒən/ *a* persa; de Persia; pérsico. —*n* persa, *mf*; (language) persa, *m.* **P. blinds,** persianas, *f pl.* **P. cat,** gato (-ta) de Angora

**persiennes** /ˌpɜrzi'ɛnz/ *n pl* persianas, *f pl*

**persist** /pər'sɪst/ *vi* persistir; persistir (en), empeñarse (en), obstinarse (en)

**persistence** /pər'sɪstəns/ *n* persistencia, *f*

**persistent** /pər'sɪstənt/ *a* persistente

**persistently** /pər'sɪstəntli/ *adv* con persistencia, persistentemente

**person** /'pɜrsən/ *n* persona, *f*. **first p.,** *Gram.* primera persona, *f*. **in p.,** en persona. **no p.,** nadie

**personable** /'pɜrsənəbəl/ *a* bien parecido

**personage** /'pɜrsənɪdʒ/ *n* personaje, *m*

**personal** /'pɜrsənl/ *a* personal; íntimo; particular; en persona; (movable) mueble. **He is to make a p. appearance,** Va a estar presente en persona. **p. column,** (in a newspaper) columna de los suspiros, *f*. **p. equation,** ecuación personal, *f*. **p. estate,** (goods) bienes muebles, *m pl*

**personality** /ˌpɜrsə'næliti/ n personalidad, f; (insult) personalismo, m. **dual p.,** conciencia doble, f

**personate** /'pɜrsə,neit/ vt (in a play) hacer el papel de; (impersonate) hacerse pasar por

**personification** /pər,sɒnəfi'keiʃən/ n personificación, f

**personify** /pər'sɒnə,fai/ vt personificar

**personnel** /ˌpɜrsə'nɛl/ n personal, m

**perspective** /pər'spɛktɪv/ n perspectiva, f, a en perspectiva

**perspicacious** /ˌpɜrspɪ'keiʃəs/ a perspicaz, clarividente, sagaz

**perspicacity** /ˌpɜrspɪ'kæsiti/ n perspicacia, clarividencia, sagacidad, f

**perspicuity** /ˌpɜrspɪ'kyuiti/ n perspicuidad, claridad, lucidez, f

**perspicuous** /pər'spɪkyuəs/ a perspicuo, claro

**perspiration** /'pɜrspə'reiʃən/ n sudor, m

**perspire** /pər'spaiᵊr/ vi sudar, transpirar

**persuadable** /pər'sweidəbəl/ a persuasible

**persuade** /pər'sweid/ vt persuadir; inducir (a), instar (a), mover (a), inclinar (a)

**persuasion** /pər'sweiʒən/ n persuasión, f; persuasiva, f; opinión, f; creencia, f; religión, f; secta, f

**persuasive** /pər'sweisɪv/ a persuasivo. —n persuasión, f; aliciente, atractivo, m

**persuasively** /pər'sweisɪvli/ adv de un modo persuasivo, persuasivamente

**persuasiveness** /pər'sweisɪvnɪs/ n persuasiva, f

**pert** /pɜrt/ a petulante; respondón, desparpajado

**pertain** /pər'tein/ vi pertenecer (a); tocar (a), incumbir (a), convenir (a); estar relacionado (con)

**pertinacious** /ˌpɜrtn̩'eiʃəs/ a pertinaz

**pertinaciously** /ˌpɜrtn̩'eiʃəsli/ adv con pertinacia

**pertinacity** /ˌpɜrtn̩'æsiti/ n pertinacia, f

**pertinence** /'pɜrtn̩əns/ n pertinencia, f

**pertinent** /'pɜrtn̩ənt/ a pertinente, atinado

**pertinently** /'pɜrtn̩əntli/ adv atinadamente

**pertly** /'pɜrtli/ adv con petulancia; con descaro

**pertness** /'pɜrtnɪs/ n petulancia, f; desparpajo, descaro, m

**perturb** /pər'tɜrb/ vt perturbar, agitar, turbar, inquietar

**perturbation** /ˌpɜrtər'beiʃən/ n perturbación, agitación, inquietud, f; confusión, f; desorden, m

**perturbed** /pər'tɜrbd/ a perturbado, agitado, ansioso, intranquilo

**perturbing** /pər'tɜrbɪŋ/ a perturbador, inquietador

**Peru** /pə'ru/ el Perú

**peruke** /pə'ruk/ n peluca, f

**perusal** /pə'ruzəl/ n lectura, f; examen, m

**peruse** /pə'ruz/ vt leer con cuidado, estudiar, examinar

**Peruvian** /pə'ruvi ən/ a and n peruano (-na)

**pervade** /pər'veid/ vt penetrar; llenar, saturar; difundirse por; reinar en

**pervasion** /pər'veiʒən/ n penetración, f

**pervasive** /pər'veisɪv/ a penetrante

**perverse** /pər'vɜrs/ a (wicked) perverso, depravado; obstinado; travieso; intratable

**perversion** /pər'vɜrʒən/ n perversión, f

**perversity** /pər'vɜrsiti/ n (wickedness) perversidad, f; obstinacia, f; travesura, f

**perversive** /pər'vɜrsɪv/ a perversivo

**pervert** /pər'vɜrt/ vt pervertir; (words, etc.) torcer, tergiversar

**pervious** /'pɜrviəs/ a penetrable; permeable

**pessary** /'pesəri/ n Surg. pesario, m

**pessimism** /'pesə,mɪzəm/ n pesimismo, m

**pessimist** /'pesəmɪst/ n pesimista, mf

**pessimistic** /ˌpesə'mɪstɪk/ a pesimista

**pessimistically** /ˌpesə'mɪstɪkli/ adv con pesimismo

**pest** /pest/ n insecto nocivo, m; animal dañino, m; parásito, m; (pestilence) peste, f; Fig. plaga, f; (person) mosca, f

**pester** /'pestər/ vt importunar, molestar, incomodar. **to p. constantly,** Inf. no dejar a sol ni a sombra

**pestering** /'pestərɪŋ/ n importunaciones, f pl

**pestilence** /'pestl̩əns/ n pestilencia, peste, f; plaga, f

**pestilential** /ˌpestl̩'ɛnʃəl/ a pestilente, pestífero; pernicioso

**pestle** /'pesəl/ n mano de mortero, f, vt pistar, machacar, majar

**pet** /pet/ n animal doméstico, m; niño (-ña) mimado (-da); favorito (-ta); (dear) querido (-da); (peevishness) despecho, malhumor, m. —vt acariciar; (spoil) mimar. **to be a great pet,** ser un gran favorito

**petal** /'petl/ n pétalo, m, hoja, f

**Peter** /'pitər/ n Pedro, m. **blue P.,** bandera de salida, f. **Peter's pence,** los diezmos de San Pedro

**peter (out)** vi desaparecer; agotarse

**petition** /pə'tɪʃən/ n petición, f; súplica, f; instancia, solicitud, f; memorial, m. —vt suplicar; pedir, demandar; dirigir un memorial (a). **to file a p.,** elevar una instancia

**petitioner** /pə'tɪʃənər/ n peticionario (-ia)

**Petrarchan** /pɪ'trɑrkən/ a petrarquista

**petrel** /'petrəl/ n petrel, m

**petrifaction** /ˌpetrə'fækʃən/ n petrificación, f

**petrify** /'petrə,fai/ vt petrificar; Inf. dejar seco. **to become petrified,** petrificarse

**petrol** /'petrəl/ n bencina, gasolina, f. —a de gasolina, de bencina. **to run out of p.,** tener una pana de bencina. **p. gauge,** indicador del nivel de gasolina, m. **p. pump,** surtidor de gasolina, m. **p. station,** puesto de bencina, m, estación de servicio, f. **p. tank,** depósito de bencina, m

**petroleum** /pə'trouliəm/ n petróleo, m. —a petrolero; de petróleo. **p. works,** refinería de petróleo, f

**petrology** /pɪ'trɒlədʒi/ n petrografía, f

**petrous** /'petrəs/ a pétreo

**petticoat** /'peti,kout/ n enagua, f; pl **petticoats,** (slang) faldas, f pl. —a de faldas, de mujeres; de mujer

**pettifogger** /'peti,fɒgər/ n (lawyer) picapleitos, m, rábula, mf; (quibbler) sofista, mf

**pettifogging** /'peti,fɒgɪŋ/ a charlatán, mezquino, trivial

**pettiness** /'petinɪs/ n trivialidad, insignificancia, f; pequeñez, f; mezquindad, f; ruindad, bajeza, f

**petty** /'peti/ a trivial, sin importancia, insignificante; inferior; pequeño; mezquino; ruin; bajo. **p. cash,** gastos menores de caja, m pl. **p. expense,** gasto menudo, m. **p. officer,** suboficial, m. **p. thief,** ratero (-ra)

**petulance** /'petʃələns/ n mal humor, m, displicencia, irritabilidad, f

**petulant** /'petʃələnt/ a malhumorado, displicente, enojadizo, irritable

**petulantly** /'petʃələntli/ adv displicentemente, con mal humor

**petunia** /pɪ'tunyə/ n petunia, f

**pew** /pyu/ n banco (de iglesia), m. **p.-opener,** sacristán, m

**pewter** /'pyutər/ n peltre, m, a de peltre

**phalange** /'fæləndʒ/ n falange, f

**phalanx** /'feilæŋks/ n falange, f

**phallic** /'fælɪk/ a fálico

**phallus** /'fæləs/ n falo, m

**phantasmagoria** /fæn,tæzmə'gɔriə/ n fantasmagoría, f

**phantasmagoric** /fæn,tæzmə'gɔrɪk/ a fantasmagórico

**phantom** /'fæntəm/ n fantasma, espectro, m; sombra, ficción, f; visión, f

**Pharisaical** /ˌfærə'seiɪkəl/ a farisaico

**Pharisee** /'færə,si/ n fariseo, m

**pharmaceutical** /ˌfɑrmə'sutɪkəl/ a farmacéutico; producto farmacéutico, m

**pharmacist** /'fɑrməsɪst/ n farmacéutico, m

**pharmacological** /ˌfɑrməkə'lɒdʒɪkəl/ a farmacológico

**pharmacologist** /ˌfɑrmə'kɒlədʒɪst/ n farmacólogo, m

**pharmacology** /ˌfɑrmə'kɒlədʒi/ n farmacología, f

**pharmacopeia** /ˌfɑrmə'koupiə/ n farmacopea, f

**pharmacy** /'fɑrməsi/ n farmacia, f

**pharyngeal** /fə'rɪndʒiəl/ a faríngeo

**pharyngitis** /ˌfærɪn'dʒaitɪs/ n faringitis, f

**pharynx** /'færɪŋks/ n faringe, f

**phase** /feiz/ n fase, f; aspecto, m; Astron. fase, f

**pheasant** /'fezənt/ n faisán, m. **hen p.,** faisana, f. **p. shooting,** caza de faisanes, f

**phenic** /'finɪk/ a fénico

**phenol** /'finɔl/ n fenol, m
**phenomenal** /fɪ'nɒmənl/ a fenomenal
**phenomenon** /fɪ'nɒmə,nɒn/ n fenómeno, m
**phial** /'faiəl/ n redoma, f
**philander** /fɪ'lændər/ vi galantear
**philanderer** /fɪ'lændərər/ n Tenorio, galanteador, m
**philandering** /fɪ'lændərɪŋ/ n galanteo, m
**philanthropic** /,fɪlən'θrɒpɪk/ a filantrópico
**philanthropist** /fɪ'lænθrəpɪst/ n filántropo, m
**philanthropy** /fɪ'lænθrəpi/ n filantropía, f
**philatelic** /,fɪlə'telɪk/ a filatélico
**philatelist** /fɪ'lætlɪst/ n filatelista, mf
**philately** /fɪ'lætli/ n filatelia, f
**philharmonic** /,fɪlhɑr'mɒnɪk/ a filarmónico
**philippic** /fɪ'lɪpɪk/ n filípica, f
**Philippine** /'fɪlə,pin/ a and n filipino (-na)
**Philippines, the** /'fɪlə,pinz/ las (Islas) Filipinas, f pl
**Philistine** /'fɪlə,stin/ a and n filisteo (-ea)
**philological** /,fɪlə'lɒdʒɪkəl/ a filológico
**philologist** /fɪ'lɒlədʒɪst/ n filólogo, m
**philology** /fɪ'lɒlədʒi/ n filología, f
**philosopher** /fɪ'lɒsəfər/ n filósofo, m. **philosopher's stone,** piedra filosofal, f
**philosophical** /,fɪlə'sɒfɪkəl/ a filosófico
**philosophize** /fɪ'lɒsə,faiz/ vi filosofar
**philosophy** /fɪ'lɒsəfi/ n filosofía, f. **moral p.,** filosofía moral, f. **natural p.,** filosofía natural, f
**philter** /'fɪltər/ n filtro, m
**phlebitis** /flə'baitɪs/ n flebitis, f
**phlebotomist** /flə'bɒtəmɪst/ n sangrador, flebotomiano, m
**phlebotomy** /flə'bɒtəmi/ n flebotomía, f
**phlegm** /flɛm/ n flema, f
**phlegmatic** /fleg'mætɪk/ a flemático
**phlox** /flɒks/ n flox, m
**Phoenician** /fɪ'nɪʃən/ a and n fenicio (-ia)
**phoenix** /'finɪks/ n fénix, f
**phonetic** /fə'netɪk/ a fonético
**phoneticist** /fe'netəsɪst/ n fonetista, mf
**phonetics** /fə'netɪks, fou–/ n fonética, f
**phonograph** /'founə,græf/ n fonógrafo, m
**phonological** /,fɒn|ɒdʒɪkəl/ a fonológico
**phonology** /fə'nɒlədʒi/ n fonología, f
**phony** /'founi/ a falso; espurio. **p. war,** guerra tonta, guerra falsa, f
**phosphate** /'fɒsfeit/ n fosfato, m
**phosphoresce** /,fɒsfə'rɛs/ vi fosforecer, ser fosforescente
**phosphorescence** /,fɒsfə'rɛsəns/ n fosforescencia, f
**phosphorescent** /,fɒsfə'rɛsənt/ a fosforescente
**phosphoric** /fɒs'fɔrɪk/ a fosfórico
**phosphorus** /'fɒsfərəs/ n fósforo, m
**photo** /'foutou/ n foto, f
**photochemistry** /,foutou'kɛməstri/ n fotoquímica, f
**photogenic** /,foutə'dʒɛnɪk/ a fotogénico
**photograph** /'foutə,græf/ n fotografía, f. —vt fotografiar, retratar. **to have one's p. taken,** hacerse retratar
**photographer** /fə'tɒgrəfər/ n fotógrafo, m
**photographic** /,foutə'græfɪk/ a fotográfico
**photography** /fə'tɒgrəfi/ n fotografía, f
**photogravure** /,foutəgrə'vyur/ n fotograbado, m
**photostat** /'foutə,stæt/ n fotostato, m
**photosynthesis** /,foutə'sɪnθəsɪs/ n fotosíntesis, f
**phrase** /freiz/ n frase, f; Mus. frase musical, f. —vt expresar, frasear; redactar. **p.-book,** libro de frases, m
**phraseology** /,freizi'ɒlədʒi/ n fraseología, f
**phrasing** /'freizɪŋ/ n (drawing up) redacción, f; (style) estilo, m; Mus. frases, f pl
**phrenetic** /frɪ'netɪk/ a frenético
**Phrygian** /'frɪdʒiən/ a and n frigio (-ia)
**Phrygian cap** n gorro frigio, m
**phthisis** /'θaisɪs/ n tisis, f
**phylactery** /fɪ'læktəri/ n filactria, f
**phylloxera** /fɪ'lɒksərə/ n filoxera, f
**physical** /'fɪzɪkəl/ a físico. **p. fitness,** buen estado físico, m. **p. geography,** geografía física, f. **p. jerks,** ejercicios físicos, m pl. **p. sciences,** ciencias físicas, f pl. **p. training,** educación física, f
**physician** /fɪ'zɪʃən/ n médico (-ca)

**physicist** /'fɪzəsɪst/ n físico, m
**physics** /'fɪzɪks/ n física, f
**physiognomist** /,fɪzi'ɒgnəmɪst/ n fisonomista, mf
**physiognomy** /,fɪzi'ɒgnəmi/ n fisonomía, f
**physiological** /,fɪziə'lɒdʒɪkəl/ a fisiológico
**physiologist** /,fɪzi'ɒlədʒɪst/ n fisiólogo, m
**physiology** /,fɪzi'ɒlədʒi/ n fisiología, f
**physiotherapy** /,fɪziou'θerəpi/ n fisioterapia, f
**physique** /fɪ'zik/ n físico, m
**pianist** /pi'ænɪst, 'piənɪst/ n pianista, mf
**pianola** /,piə'noulə/ n piano mecánico, m
**piano, pianoforte** /pi'ænou; pi'ænə,fɔrt/ n piano, m. **baby grand p.,** piano de media cola, m. **grand p.,** piano de cola, m. **upright p.,** piano vertical, m. **p. maker,** fabricante de pianos, m. **p. stool,** taburete de piano, m. **p. tuner,** afinador de pianos, m
**picaresque** /,pɪkə'rɛsk/ a picaresco
**piccolo** /'pɪkə,lou/ n flautín, m
**pick** /pɪk/ n (tool) pico, zapapico, m; (mattock) piqueta, f; (choice) selección, f; derecho de elección, m; (best) lo mejor, lo más escogido; (Fig. cream) flor, nata, f. **tooth-p.,** mondadientes, m. **p.-a-back,** sobre los hombros, a cuestas. **p.-ax,** zapapico, m, alcotana, f. **p.-me-up,** tónico, m; trago, m
**pick** /pɪk/ vt (with a pick-ax, make a hole) picar; (pluck, pick up) coger; (remove) sacar; (clean) limpiar; (one's teeth) mondarse (los dientes); (one's nose) hurgarse (las narices); (a bone) roer; (a lock) abrir con ganzúa; (a pocket) bolsear, robar del bolsillo; (peck) picotear; (choose) escoger; (a quarrel) buscar. —vi (steal) hurtar, robar; (nibble) picar. **I have a bone to p. with you,** Tengo que ajustar unas cuentas contigo. **Take your p.!** ¡Escoja! **to p. and choose,** mostrarse difícil. **to p. to pieces,** Fig. criticar severamente. **to p. one's way through,** abrirse camino entre; andar con precaución por; andar a tientas por. **to p. off,** coger; arrancar; quitar; (shoot) disparar; fusilar. **to p. out,** entresacar; escoger; (recognize) reconocer; (understand) llegar a comprender; (a tune) tocar de oídas; (a song) cantar de oídas; (of colours) contrastar, resaltar. **to p. up,** vt (ground, etc.) romper con pico; coger; tomar; recoger; (raise) levantar, alzar; (information, etc.) cobrar, adquirir; (a living) ganar; (make friends with) trabar amistad con; (recover) recobrar; (find) encontrar, hallar; (buy) comprar; (learn) aprender; (a wireless message) interceptar; (a radio station) oír, tener. —vi recobrar la salud; reponerse; mejorar. —n Mech. recobro, m
**picket** /'pɪkɪt/ n estaca, f; (Mil. and during strikes) piquete, m. —vt cercar con estacas; poner piquetes ante (or alrededor de); poner de guardia; estacionar
**picking** /'pɪkɪŋ/ n (gathering) recolección, f; (choosing) selección, f; (pilfering) robo, m; pl **pickings,** desperdicios, m pl; (perquisites) gajes, m pl; ganancias, f pl
**pickle** /'pɪkəl/ n (solution) escabeche, m; (vegetable, etc.) encurtido, m; (plight) apuro, m; (child) diablillo, m. —vt encurtir, escabechar
**picklock** /'pɪk,lɒk/ n (thief and instrument) ganzúa, f
**pickpocket** /'pɪk,pɒkɪt/ n carterista, mf ratero (-ra)
**picnic** /'pɪknɪk/ n partida de campo, jira, f, picnic, m. —vi llevar la merienda al campo, hacer un picnic
**picnicker** /'pɪknɪkər/ n excursionista, mf
**pictorial** /pɪk'tɔriəl/ a pictórico; ilustrado. —n revista ilustrada, f
**pictorially** /pɪk'tɔriəli/ adv pictóricamente; en grabados; por imágenes
**picture** /'pɪktʃər/ n cuadro, m; (of a person) retrato, m; imagen, f; (illustration) grabado, m, lámina, f; fotografía, f; (outlook) perspectiva, f; idea, f. —vt pintar; describir; imaginar. **to go to the pictures,** ir al cine. **motion p.,** película, f. **talking p.,** película sonora, f. **p. book,** libro con láminas, m. **p. frame,** marco, m. **p. gallery,** museo de pinturas, m; galería de pinturas, f. **p. hat,** pamela, f. **p. palace,** cine, m. **p. postcard,** tarjeta postal, f. **p. restorer,** restaurador de cuadros, m. **p. writing,** pictografía, f
**picturesque** /,pɪktʃə'rɛsk/ a pintoresco
**picturesqueness** /,pɪktʃə'rɛsknɪs/ n carácter pintoresco, m, lo pintoresco; pintoresquismo, m
**pie** /pai/ n (savoury) empanada, f; (sweet) pastel, m, torta, f; (of meat) pastelón, m; Print. pastel, m. **apple**

**pie**, torta de manzanas, *f.* **to eat humble pie,** bajar las orejas. **to have a finger in the pie,** meter baza

**piebald** /'pai,bɔld/ *a* pío; tordo

**piece** /pis/ *n* pedazo, *m;* trozo, *m;* parte, porción, *f;* (literary, artistic work, coin, of fabric, at chess, etc. and slang) pieza, *f;* (of luggage) bulto, *m;* (of paper) hoja, *f;* (of ground) parcela, *f;* (of money) moneda, *f,* *vt* remendar; unir, juntar. **a p. of advice,** un consejo. **a p. of bread,** un pedazo de pan; una rebanada de pan. **a p. of folly,** un acto de locura. **a p. of furniture,** un mueble. **a p. of insolence,** una insolencia. **a p. of news,** una noticia. **a p. of paper,** un papel, una hoja de papel, una cuartilla. **a p. of poetry,** una poesía. **Peter has a five-shilling p.,** Pedro tiene una moneda de cinco chelines. **to break in pieces,** *vt* hacer pedazos, romper. —*vi* hacerse pedazos, romperse. **to come or fall to pieces,** deshacerse; (of machines) desarmarse. **to cut in pieces,** cortar en pedazos; (an army) destrozar. **to give a p. of one's mind (to),** decir cuatro verdades (a), decir cuántas son cinco (a). **to go to pieces,** (of persons) hacerse pedazos. **to take to pieces,** (a machine) desmontar; deshacer. **to tear or pull to pieces,** hacer pedazos, despedazar; desgarrar. **p. goods,** géneros en piezas, *m pl.* **p.-work,** trabajo a destajo, *m.* **to do p.-work,** trabajar a destajo. **p.-worker,** destajista, *mf*

**piecemeal** /'pis,mil/ *adv* en pedazos; a remiendos; en detalle; poco a poco

**piecrust** /'pai,krʌst/ *n* pasta, *f*

**pied** /paid/ *a* bicolor; abigarrado, de varios colores

**pier** /pɪər/ *n* (jetty) dique, *m;* embarcadero, *m;* malecón, *m;* (of a bridge) pila, *f;* (pillar) columna, *f;* (between windows, etc.) entrepaño, *m.* **p.-glass,** espejo de cuerpo entero, *m.* **p. head,** punta del dique, *f.* **p. table,** consola, *f*

**pierce** /pɪərs/ *vt* penetrar; (of sorrow, etc.) traspasar, herir; (bore) agujerear, taladrar. —*vi* penetrar

**pierced ear** /pɪərst/ *n* oreja perforada, *f*

**piercing** /'pɪərsɪŋ/ *a* penetrante; (of the wind, etc.) cortante; (of the voice, etc.) agudo. —*n* penetración, *f*

**piercingly** /'pɪərsɪŋli/ *adv* de un modo penetrante, agudamente

**pietism** /'paiɪ,tɪzəm/ *n* pietismo, *m*

**pietist** /'paiɪtɪst/ *n* pietista, *mf*

**pietistic** /,paiɪ'tɪstɪk/ *a* pietista

**piety** /'paiɪti/ *n* piedad, devoción, *f*

**piezometer** /,paiə'zɒmɪtər/ *n Phys.* piezómetro, *m*

**piffle** /'pɪfəl/ *n* patrañas, tonterías, *f pl*

**pig** /pɪg/ *n* puerco, cerdo, *m; Inf.* cochino, *m;* (metal) lingote, *m.* **to buy a p. in a poke,** cerrar un trato a ciegas. **p.-eyed,** de ojos de cerdo. **p.-iron,** arrabio; hierro colado en barras, lingote de fundición, *m*

**pigeon** /'pɪdʒən/ *n* paloma, *f,* palomo, *m; Inf.* primo, *m.* —*vt* embaucar, engañar. **carrier p.,** paloma mensajera, *f.* **clay p.,** pichón de barro, platillo de arcilla, *m.* **male p.,** pichón, *m.* **pouter p.,** paloma buchona, *f.* **young p.,** palomino, *m.* **p. fancier,** palomero, *m.* **p.-hole,** casilla, *f.* —*vt* encasillar. **set of p.-holes,** encasillado, *m.* **p.-shooting,** tiro de pichón, *m.* **p.-toed,** patituerto

**piggy bank** /'pɪgi/ *n* alcancía, *f*

**pigheaded** /'pɪg,hɛdɪd/ *a* terco, testarudo

**pigheadedness** /'pɪg,hɛdɪdnɪs/ *n* terquedad, testarudez, *f*

**piglet** /'pɪglɪt/ *n* cerdito, *m*

**pigment** /'pɪgmənt/ *n* pigmento, *m*

**pigmentary** /'pɪgmən,tɛri/ *a* pigmentario

**pigmentation** /,pɪgmən'teiʃən/ *n* pigmentación, *f*

**pigskin** /'pɪg,skɪn/ *n* piel de cerdo, *f*

**pigsty** /'pɪg,stai/ *n* pocilga, *f*

**pigtail** /'pɪg,teil/ *n* coleta, *f*

**pike** /paik/ *n Mil.* pica, *f,* chuzo, *m;* (peak) pico, *m*

**pilaster** /pɪ'læstər/ *n* pilastra, *f*

**pile** /pail/ *n* estaca, *f;* poste, *m;* (engineering) pilote, *m;* (heap) pila, *f,* montón, *m;* (pyre) pira, *f;* (building) edificio grande, *m; Elec.* pila, *f;* (hair) pelo, *m;* (nap) pelusa, *f; pl* **piles,** *Med.* almorranas, *f pl.* —*vt* clavar pilotes en; apoyar con pilotes; (heap) amontonar; (load) cargar. **to make one's p.,** *Inf.* hacer su pacotilla. **to p. arms,** poner los fusiles en pabellón. **to p. on,** (coal, etc.) echar; (increase) aumentar. **to p. it on,** exagerar, intensificar; (a table) cargar. **to p.**

**up,** amontonarse; acumularse; (of a ship) encallar. **p. -driver,** machina, *f;* martinete, *m.* **p. dwelling,** vivienda palustre, sostenida por pilares, *f*

**pilfer** /'pɪlfər/ *vt* sisar, sonsacar, hurtar, ratear

**pilferer** /'pɪlfərər/ *n* sisador (-ra), ratero (-ra)

**pilfering** /'pɪlfərɪŋ/ *n* sisa, ratería, *f*

**pilgrim** /'pɪlgrɪm/ *n* peregrino (-na). **pilgrim's staff,** bordón, *m*

**pilgrimage** /'pɪlgrəmɪdʒ/ *n* peregrinación, *f;* romería, *f.* **to make a p.,** hacer una peregrinación, peregrinar; ir en romería

**piling** /'pailɪŋ/ *n* amontonamiento, *m;* (of buildings) pilotaje, *m*

**pill** /pɪl/ *n* píldora, *f.* **to gild the p.,** *Fig.* dorar la píldora. **p.-box,** caja de píldoras, *f;* casamata, *f, Mil.* nido de ametralladoras, *m*

**pillage** /'pɪlɪdʒ/ *vt* pillar, saquear. —*n* saqueo, *m*

**pillager** /'pɪlɪdʒər/ *n* saqueador (-ra)

**pillaging** /'pɪlɪdʒɪŋ/ *n* pillaje, *m,* a pillador, saqueador

**pillar** /'pɪlər/ *n* pilar, *m,* columna, *f;* (person) sostén, soporte, *m.* **from p. to post,** de Ceca en Meca. **p. of salt,** estatua de sal, *f.* **the Pillars of Hercules,** las Columnas de Hércules. **to be a p. of strength,** *Inf.* ser una roca. **p.-box,** buzón, *m*

**pillared** /'pɪlərd/ *a* con columnas, sostenido por columnas; en columnas

**pillion** /'pɪlyən/ *n* (on a horse, etc.) grupera, *f;* (on a motor-cycle) grupa, *f.* **to ride p.,** ir a la grupa

**pillory** /'pɪləri/ *n* picota, argolla, *f.* —*vt* empicotar; *Fig.* poner en ridículo; censurar duramente

**pillow** /'pɪlou/ *n* almohada, *f;* (for lace-making) cojín, *m;* (of a machine) cojinete, *m.* —*vt* apoyar; reposar; servir como almohada. **to take counsel of one's p.,** consultar con la almohada. **p.-case,** funda de almohada, *f*

**pilot** /'pailət/ *n* piloto, *m; Naut.* práctico, piloto (de puerto), *m.* —*vt* guiar, conducir; (*Naut. Aer.*) pilotar, pilotear. **p. boat,** vaporcito del práctico, *m.* **p. jacket,** chaquetón de piloto, *m.* **p. officer,** oficial de aviación, *m*

**pilotage** /'pailətɪdʒ/ *n* pilotaje, *m; Naut.* practicaje, *m*

**pilotless** /'pailətlɪs/ *a* sin piloto

**pimento** /pɪ'mɛntou/ *n* pimiento, *m*

**pimp** /pɪmp/ *n* rufián, alcahuete, *m, vi* alcahuetear

**pimple** /'pɪmpəl/ *n* grano, *m*

**pimply** /'pɪmpli/ *a* con granos

**pin** /pɪn/ *n* alfiler, *m;* prendedor, *m;* clavija, *f;* clavo, *m,* chaveta, *f;* (bolt) perno, *m.* —*vt* prender con alfileres; (with a peg) enclavijar; fijar; sujetar. **to pin up,** sujetar con alfileres; (the hair) sujetar con horquillas. **I don't care a pin,** No me importa un bledo. **to be on pins,** estar en ascuas. **to suffer from pins and needles,** tener agujones. **pin-head,** cabeza de alfiler, *f.* **pin-money,** alfileres, *m pl.* **pin-oak,** *Bot.* pincarrasco, *m,* carrasca, *f.* **pin point,** punta de alfiler, *f.* **pin-prick,** alfilerazo, *m*

**pinafore** /'pɪnə,fɔr/ *n* delantal de niño, *m*

**pince-nez** /'pæns,nei/ *n* quevedos, *m pl*

**pincers** /'pɪnsərz/ *n pl* pinzas, tenazas, *f pl,* alicates, *m pl;* (of crustaceans) pinzas, *f pl.* **p. movement,** movimiento de pinzas, *m*

**pinch** /pɪntʃ/ *vt* pellizcar; (crush) estrujar; aplastar; apretar; (of the cold) helar; (steal) hurtar, birlar; (arrest) coger, prender. —*n* pellizco, torniscón, *m;* pulgarada, *f;* (of snuff) polvo, *m;* (distress) miseria, *f;* (pain) dolor, *m,* angustia. *f.* **at a p.,** en caso de apuro. **to know where the shoe pinches,** saber dónde le aprieta el zapato

**pinched** /pɪntʃt/ *a* (by the cold) helado; (wan) marchito, descolorido

**pincushion** /'pɪn,kuʃən/ *n* acerico, *m*

**Pindaric** /pɪn'dærɪk/ *a* pindárico

**pine** /pain/ *n Bot.* pino, *m.* —*vi* languidecer, marchitarse, consumirse. **to p. for,** anhelar, suspirar por, perecer por. **pitch-p.,** pino de tea, *m.* **p.-apple,** piña de las Indias, *f,* ananás, *m.* **p. cone,** piña, *f.* **p. kernel,** piñón, *m.* **p. needle,** pinocha, *f.* **p. wood,** pinar, *m,* pineda, *f*

**pineal** /'pɪniəl/ *a* en figura de piña; *Anat.* pineal

**ping** /pɪŋ/ *n* silbido de una bala, *m;* zumbido, *m.* **p. pong,** tenis de mesa, pingpong, *m*

**pinion** /'pɪnyən/ *n* (wing) ala, *f;* (small feather) piñón, *m;* (in carving) alón, *m;* (wheel) piñón, *m.* —*vt* atar las alas de; cortar un piñón de; (a person) atar; (the arms of) trincar, asegurar

**pink** /pɪŋk/ *n Bot.* clavel, *m;* color de rosa, *m;* (perfection) modelo, *m;* colmo, *m;* (hunting) color rojo, *m;* levitín rojo de caza, *m.* —*a* de color de rosa, rosado. —*vt Sew.* picar; (pierce) penecrar, atravesar. —*vi* (of an engine) picar

**pinking** /'pɪŋkɪŋ/ *n Sew.* picadura, *f*

**pinkish** /'pɪŋkɪʃ/ *a* rosáceo

**pinnacle** /'pɪnəkəl/ *n Naut.* pinaza, *f*

**pinnacle** /'pɪnəkəl/ *n* pináculo, *m*

**pinpoint** /'pɪn,pɔɪnt/ *vt* precisar

**pint** /paint/ *n* (measure) pinta, *f*

**pintle** /'pɪntl/ *n* (pin) perno, *m*

**piolet** /,piə'lei/ *n* piolet, *m*

**pioneer** /,paiə'nɪər/ *n* pionero, explorador, *m;* introductor, *m.* **to be a p. in...,** ser el primero en (or a)... **pioneering role,** papel de iniciador (e.g. *She played a pioneering role,* jugó un papel de iniciadora)

**pious** /'paiəs/ *a* pío, devoto, piadoso

**piously** /'paiəsli/ *adv* piadosamente, devotamente

**pip** /pɪp/ *n* (of fruit) pepita, *f;* (on cards, dice) punto, *m;* (disease) moquillo, *m;* (of an army, etc., officer) insignia, *f*

**pipe** /paip/ *n* (for tobacco) pipa de fumar, *f; Mus.* caramillo, *m;* (boatswain's) pito, *m;* (of a bird) trino, *m;* (voice) voz aguda, *f;* tubo, *m;* (for water, etc.) cañería, *f;* (of a hose) manga, *f;* (of an organ) cañón, *m;* (of wine) pipa, *f; pl* **pipes,** *Mus.* gaita, *f.* —*vi* tocar el caramillo (or la gaita); empezar a cantar; silbar; (of birds) trinar. —*vt* (a tune) tocar; (sing) cantar; (whistle) llamar con pito; conducir con cañerías; instalar cañerías en. **He smokes a p.,** Fuma una pipa. **I smoked a p.** (of tobacco) **before I went to bed,** Fumé una pipa antes de acostarme. **Put that in your p. and smoke it!** ¡Chúpate eso! **p. clay,** blanquizal, *m.* **p. cleaner,** limpiapipas, *m.* **p. layer,** cañero, fontanero, *m.* **p. laying,** instalación de cañerías, *f.* **p.-line,** cañería, *f;* (oil) oleoducto, *m.* **p. tobacco,** tabaco de pipa, *m*

**pipeful** /'paipful/ *n* pipa, *f*

**piper** /'paipər/ *n* (bagpiper) gaitero, *m;* flautista, *mf*

**pipette** /pai'pet/ *n Chem.* pipeta, *f*

**piping** /'paipɪŋ/ *n* sonido del caramillo, *m;* música de la flauta, etc., *f;* (of birds) trinos, *m pl;* voz aguda, *f;* (for water, etc.) cañería, tubería, *f; Sew.* cordoncillo, *m.* **p.-hot,** hirviente

**pipkin** /'pɪpkɪn/ *n* ollita de barro, *f*

**pippin** /'pɪpɪn/ *n* (apple) camuesa, *f*

**piquancy** /'pikənsi/ *n* picante, *m*

**piquant** /'pikənt/ *a* picante

**pique** /pik/ *n* (resentment, and score in game) pique, *m.* **to p. oneself upon,** preciarse de, jactarse de. **to be piqued,** estar enojado; *Inf.* amoscarse

**piquet** /pɪ'kei/ *n* juego de los cientos, *m*

**piracy** /'pairəsi/ *n* piratería, *f*

**pirate** /'pairət/ *n* pirata, *mf.* —*vi* piratear. —*vt* publicar una edición furtiva de. **p. edition,** edición furtiva, *f*

**piratical** /pɪ'rætɪkəl/ *a* pirata, pirático; de pirata, de piratas

**pirouette** /,pɪru'ɛt/ *n* pirueta, *f*

**Pisces** /'paisiz/ *n pl* peces, *m pl*

**pisciculture** /'pɪsɪ,kʌltʃər/ *n* piscicultura, *f*

**Pisgah** /'pɪzgə/ Fasga, *f*

**pistachio** /pɪ'stæʃɪ,ou/ *n* pistacho, *m*

**pistil** /'pɪstl/ *n Bot.* pistilo, *m*

**pistol** /'pɪstl/ *n* pistola, *f.* **p. belt,** charpa, *f,* cinto de pistolas, *m.* **p. case,** pistolera, *f.* **p. shot,** pistoletazo, *m*

**piston** /'pɪstən/ *n Mech.* émbolo, pistón, *m; Mus.* pistón, *m,* llave, *f.* **p. ring,** anillo de émbolo, segmento de émbolo, *m.* **p. rod,** biela, *f.* **p. stroke,** carrera del émbolo, *f*

**pit** /pɪt/ *n* hoyo, *m;* foso, *m;* (in a garage) foso de reparación, *m; Theat.* platea, *f;* (trap) trampa, *f;* (scar) hoyo, *m;* precipicio, *m;* (hell) infierno, *m.* —*vt* (with smallpox) marcar con viruelas; (against) competir

con. **pithead,** boca de mina, *f.* **pit of the stomach,** boca del estómago, *f.* **pit stall,** butaca de platea, *f*

**pitch** /pɪtʃ/ *n Chem.* pez, brea, *f,* alquitrán, *m;* (place) puesto, *m;* (throwing) lanzamiento, *m;* (distance thrown) alcance, *m;* (for cricket) cancha, *f;* (bowling) saque, *m;* (slope) pendiente, inclinación, *f;* (height) elevación, *f; Mus.* tono, *m;* (Fig. degree) grado, extremo, *m;* (*Naut. Aer.*) cabeceo, *m;* (of threads of a screw, etc.) paso, *m.* —*vt* (camp) asentar; (a tent, etc.) colocar, poner; (throw) lanzar, arrojar, tirar; (cricket, etc.) lanzar; (fix in) clavar; *Mus.* graduar el tono de; (tell) narrar. —*vi* (fall) caer; *Naut.* cabecear, zozobrar; *Aer.* cabecear. **to paint with p.,** embrear. **to p. into,** (attack) acometer, atacar; (scold) desatarse contra; (food) engullir. **p.-black,** negro como la pez; oscuro como boca de lobo. **p.-pine,** pino de tea, *m.* **p.-pipe,** diapasón vocal, *m*

**pitched battle** /pɪtʃt/ *n* batalla campal, *f*

**pitcher** /'pɪtʃər/ *n* jarro, cántaro, *m;* (in baseball) lanzador de pelota, *m*

**pitcherful** /'pɪtʃər,fʌl/ *n* jarro (de), *m*

**pitchfork** /'pɪtʃ,fɔrk/ *n* horquilla, *f,* aventador, *m.* —*vt* levantar con horquilla; *Fig.* lanzar

**pitching** /'pɪtʃɪŋ/ *n* (pavement) adoquinado, *m;* (of a ship) socollada, *f;* cabeceo, *m*

**piteous** /'pɪtiəs/ *a* lastimero; triste; plañidero; compasivo, tierno

**piteousness** /'pɪtiəsnɪs/ *n* estado lastimero, *m;* tristeza, *f;* compasión, ternura, *f*

**pitfall** /'pɪt,fɔl/ *n* trampa, *f; Fig.* añagaza, *f,* lazo, peligro, *m*

**pith** /pɪθ/ *n Bot.* médula, *f;* médula espinal, *f; Fig.* meollo, *m;* fuerza, *f,* vigor, *m;* substancia, *f;* quinta esencia, *f;* importancia, *f*

**pithiness** /'pɪθinɪs/ *n* jugosidad, *f;* fuerza, *f,* vigor, *m*

**pithy** /'pɪθi/ *a* meduloso; *Fig.* jugoso; enérgico, vigoroso

**pitiable** /'pɪtiəbəl/ *a* lastimoso, digno de compasión; (paltry) despreciable

**pitiful** /'pɪtɪfəl/ *a* piadoso, compasivo; conmovedor, doloroso, lastimero; (contemptible) miserable

**pitifully** /'pɪtɪfəli/ *adv* lastimosamente

**pitiless** /'pɪtɪlɪs/ *a* sin piedad, despiadado

**pitilessness** /'pɪtɪlɪsnɪs/ *n* crueldad, inhumanidad, *f*

**pitman** /'pɪtmən/ *n* minero, *m;* aserrador de foso, *m*

**pittance** /'pɪtns/ *n* pitanza, *f;* pequeña porción, *f;* ración de hambre, *f*

**pitted** /'pɪtɪd/ *a* picoso

**pituitary** /pɪ'tuɪ,tɛri/ *a* pituitario

**pity** /'pɪti/ *n* piedad, compasión, *f;* lástima, *f.* —*vt* compadecerse de, tener lástima (a); compadecer. **It is a p. that...,** Es lástima que... **Have p.!** ¡Ten piedad! **to take p. on,** tener lástima (de). **to move to p.,** dar lástima (a), enternecer

**pityingly** /'pɪtiɪŋli/ *adv* con lástima

**pivot** /'pɪvət/ *n* pivote, *m;* eje, *m; Fig.* punto de partida, *m, vi* girar sobre un pivote o eje

**pivotal** /'pɪvətl/ *a Fig.* cardinal, principal, fundamental

**pixy** /'pɪksi/ *n* duende, *m.* **p. hood,** caperuza, *f*

**pizzicato** /,pɪtsɪ'katou/ *a* pichigato

**placability** /,plækə'bɪlɪti/ *n* placabilidad, *f*

**placable** /'plækəbəl/ *a* aplacable, placable

**placard** /'plækard/ *n* cartel, *m.* —*vt* fijar carteles (en); publicar por carteles

**placate** /'pleikeit/ *vt* aplacar, ablandar, apaciguar

**placatory** /'pleikə,tɔri/ *a* placativo

**place** /pleis/ *n* lugar, *m;* sitio, *m;* (position) puesto, *m;* (seat) asiento, *m;* (laid at table) cubierto, *m;* (square) plaza, *f;* (house) residencia, *f;* (in the country) casa de campo, finca, *f;* (in a book) pasaje, *m;* (in an examination) calificación, *f;* (rank) posición, *f,* rango, *m;* situación, *f;* (employment) empleo, *m,* colocación, *f.* —*vt* poner; colocar; (in employment) dar empleo (a); (appoint) nombrar; (an order) dar; (money) invertir; (remember) recordar, traer a la memoria; (size up) fijar; (confidence) poner. **in p.,** en su lugar; apropiado. **in p. of,** en vez de, en lugar de. **in the first p.,** en primer lugar, primero. **in the next p.,** luego, después. **out of p.,** fuera de lugar; inoportuno. **It is not my p. to...,** No me toca a mí de... **to give p. to,** ceder el paso (a); ceder (a). **to**

**take p.,** verificarse, tener lugar, ocurrir. **p. of business,** establecimiento, local de negocios, *m*. **p. of worship,** edificio de culto, *m*

**placenta** /pləˈsɛntə/ *n* placenta, *f*

**placid** /ˈplæsɪd/ *a* plácido, apacible; calmoso; sereno, sosegado; dulce

**placidity** /pləˈsɪdɪti/ *n* placidez, *f*; serenidad, tranquilidad, *f*, sosiego, *m*

**placidly** /ˈplæsɪdli/ *adv* plácidamente

**placing** /ˈpleisɪŋ/ *n* colocación, *f*; posición, *f*; localización, *f*

**placket** /ˈplækɪt/ *n* abertura (en una falda), *f*

**plagiarism** /ˈpleidʒəˌrɪzəm/ *n* plagio, *m*

**plagiarist** /ˈpleidʒərɪst/ *n* plagiario (-ia)

**plagiarize** /ˈpleidʒəˌraiz/ *vt* plagiar, hurtar

**plague** /pleig/ *n* plaga, *f*; peste, pestilencia, *f*. —*vt* importunar, atormentar; plagar

**plaice** /pleis/ *n* (nearest equivalent) platija, *f*

**plaid** /plæd/ *n* manta escocesa, *f*; género de cuadros, *m*, *a* a cuadros

**plain** /plein/ *a* claro; evidente; (simple) sencillo; llano; sin adorno; (flat) liso, igual; (candid) franco; (with truth, etc.) desnudo; mero; puro, sin mezcla; (of words) redondo; (ugly) feo. —*adv* claramente, llanamente; sencillamente; francamente. —*n* llanura, *f*, llano, *m*. **the p. truth,** la pura verdad. **p. clothes,** traje de paisano, *m*. **p. clothes man,** detective, *m*. **p. cooking,** cocina sencilla, cocina casera, *f*. **p. dealing,** buena fe, sinceridad, *f*. **p. dweller,** llanero (-ra). **p. living,** vida sencilla, *f*. **p. people,** gente sencilla, *f*. **p. sailing,** *Fig.* camino fácil, *m*. **p. sewing,** costura, *f*. **p.-song,** canto llano, *m*. **p. speaking,** franqueza, *f*. **p.-spoken,** franco. **in p. English,** sin rodeos, en cristiano (e.g. *Speak in p. English!* Habla sin rodeos! Habla en cristiano!)

**plainly** /ˈpleinli/ *adv* claramente; sencillamente; llanamente; francamente; rotundamente

**plainness** /ˈpleinnɪs/ *n* claridad, *f*; sencillez, *f*; llaneza, *f*; franqueza, *f*; (ugliness) fealdad, *f*

**plainsman** /ˈpleinzmən/ *n* hombre de las llanuras, *m*

**plaint** /pleint/ *n* queja, *f*, lamento, *m*; *Law.* demanda, querella, *f*

**plaintiff** /ˈpleintɪf/ *n* demandante, *mf*, actor, *m*, parte actora, actora, *f*

**plaintive** /ˈpleintɪv/ *a* quejumbroso, dolorido; patético

**plaintively** /ˈpleintɪvli/ *adv* quejumbrosamente

**plaintiveness** /ˈpleintɪvnɪs/ *n* melancolía, tristeza, *f*; voz quejumbrosa, *f*

**plait** /pleit/ *n* trenza, *f*. —*vt* trenzar; tejer. **in plaits,** (of hair) en trenzas

**plan** /plæn/ *n* plan, *m*; (map) plano, *m*; proyecto, *m*. —*vt* planear; proyectar; proponerse. **the Marshall P.,** el Plan Marshall. **to make a p. of,** trazar un plano de. **to make plans,** hacer planes

**planchette** /plænˈʃɛt/ *n* mesa giratoria, *f*

**plane** /plein/ *n* (tree) plátano, *m*; (tool) cepillo, *m*; *Geom.* plano, *m*; (level) nivel, *m*; *Aer.* avión, *m*; plano. —*vt* acepillar, alisar. —*vi Aer.* planear

**planet** /ˈplænɪt/ *n* planeta, *m*

**planetarium** /ˌplænɪˈtɛəriəm/ *n* planetario, *m*

**planetary** /ˈplænɪˌtɛri/ *a* planetario

**planing** /ˈpleinɪŋ/ *n* acepilladura, alisadura, *f*,

**plank** /plæŋk/ *n* tabla, *f*; *Fig.* fundamento, principio, *m*; *pl* **planks,** tablazón, *f*. —*vt* entablar, enmaderar

**planking** /ˈplæŋkɪŋ/ *n* entablado, *m*, tablazón, *f*

**plankton** /ˈplæŋktən/ *n* plancton, *m*

**planned** /plænd/ *a* proyectado, planeado; dirigido. **p. economy,** economía dirigida, *f*

**planner** /ˈplænər/ *n* proyectista, *mf*; autor (-ra) de un plan

**planning** /ˈplænɪŋ/ *n* proyecto, *m*; concepción, *f*

**plant** /plænt/ *n Bot.* planta, *f*; instalación, *f*, material, *m*. —*vt* plantar; (place) colocar; fijar; (a blow) asestar; (people) establecer; (instil) inculcar, imbuir (con); (conceal) esconder. **p. pot,** florero, *m*. **p. stand,** jardinera, *f*

**plantain** /ˈplæntɪn/ *n Bot.* llantén, *m*

**plantation** /plænˈteiʃən/ *n* plantación, *f*; plantío, *f*; *Fig.* colonia, *f*; introducción, *f*; establecimiento, *m*

**planter** /ˈplæntər/ *n* plantador, cultivador, *m*

**planting** /ˈplæntɪŋ/ *n* plantación, *f*; *Fig.* colonia, *f*; introducción, *f*. **p. out,** trasplante, *m*

**plantlike** /ˈplæntˌlaik/ *a* como una planta; de planta

**plaque** /plæk/ *n* placa, *f*; medalla, *f*

**plash** /plæʃ/ *n* (puddle) charco, *m*; (sound) chapaleteo, *m*. —*vt* and *vi* chapotear, chapalear

**plasma** /ˈplæzmə/ *n* plasma, *m*

**plaster** /ˈplæstər/ *n* (for walls, etc.) argamasa, *f*; yeso, *m*; *Med.* parche, emplasto, *m*. —*vt* (walls, etc.) enlucir, enyesar; poner emplastos (a or en); (daub) embadurnar manchar; (cover) cubrir. **p. cast,** vaciado, yeso, *m*. **p. of Paris,** escayola, *f*

**plasterer** /ˈplæstərər/ *n* yesero, *m*

**plastering** /ˈplæstərɪŋ/ *n* revoque, enyesado, guarnecido, *m*. **p. trowel,** fratás, *m*

**plastic** /ˈplæstɪk/ *a* plástico. —*n* plástica, *f*; *pl* **plastics,** materias plásticas, *f pl*. **p. surgery,** cirugía plástica, cirugía estética, *f*

**plasticine** /ˈplæstəˌsin/ *n* plasticina, *f*

**plasticity** /plæˈstɪsɪti/ *n* plasticidad, *f*

**plate** /pleit/ *n* plancha, chapa, *f*; (engraving and *Photo.*, of a doctor, etc.) placa, *f*; (illustration) lámina, *f*; (cutlery, etc.) vajilla, *f*; (for eating) plato, *m*; (for money) platillo, *m*; electrotipo, *m*; (dental) dentadura postiza, *f*. —*vt* (with armor) blindar; (with metal) planchear; (silver) platear; (electro-plate) niquelar. **silver p.,** vajilla de plata, plata, *f*. **p.-armor,** armadura, *f*; (of a ship) blindaje, *m*. **p.-draining rack,** escurreplatos, *m*. **p.-glass,** vidrio plano, *m*. **p.-rack,** escurridero para platos, *m*. **p. warmer,** calientaplatos, *m*

**plateau** /plæˈtou/ *n* meseta, altiplanicie, *f*

**plateful** /ˈpleit,fʌl/ *n* plato (de), *m*

**plater** /ˈpleitər/ *n* plateador, *m*; platero, *m*

**plateresque** /ˌplætəˈrɛsk/ *a Archit.* plateresco

**platform** /ˈplætfɔrm/ *n* plataforma, *f*; (railway) andén, *m*. **p. ticket,** billete de andén, *m*

**plating** /ˈpleitɪŋ/ *n* niquelado, *m*; electrogalvanización, *f*; (with armor) blindaje, *m*

**platinum** /ˈplætnəm/ *n* platino, *m*. **p. blonde,** rubia platino, *f*

**platitude** /ˈplætɪˌtud/ *n* perogrullada, *f*, lugar común, *m*; trivialidad, vulgaridad, *f*

**platitudinous** /ˌplætɪˈtudnəs/ *a* lleno de perogrulladas; trivial

**platonic** /pləˈtɒnɪk/ *a* platónico

**Platonism** /ˈpleitn̩ˌizəm/ *n* platonismo, *m*

**Platonist** /ˈpleitn̩ɪst/ *n* platonista, *mf*

**platoon** /pləˈtun/ *n Mil.* pelotón, *m*

**platter** /ˈplætər/ *n* fuente, *f*, trinchero, *m*; plato, *m*

**plaudit** /ˈplɔdɪt/ *n* aplauso, *m*, aclamación, *f*; (praise) elogio, *m*, alabanza, *f*

**plausibility** /ˌplɔzəˈbɪlɪti/ *n* plausibilidad, *f*

**plausible** /ˈplɔzəbəl/ *a* plausible

**plausibly** /ˈplɔzəbli/ *adv* plausiblemente

**play** /plei/ *vi* jugar; (frolic) juguetear, retozar; recrearse, divertirse; *Mech.* moverse; (on a musical instrument) tocar; (wave) ondear, flotar; *Theat.* representar; (behave) conducirse. —*vt* jugar; (of a searchlight, etc.) enfocar; (direct) dirigir; (a fish) agotar; (a joke, etc.) hacer; (a piece in a game) mover; (a musical instrument or music) tocar; (a string instrument) tañer; (a character in a play) hacer el papel de; (a drama, etc.) representar, poner en escena. **to p. a joke,** gastar una broma, hacer una burla. **to p. fair,** jugar limpio. **to p. false,** jugar sucio, engañar. **to p. the fool,** hacerse el tonto, hacerse el payaso. **to p. at,** jugar a; (pretend) fingir; hacer sin entusiasmo. **to p. off,** confrontar, contraponer. **to p. on.** See to p. **upon. to p. on the...,** (of musical instruments) tocar. **to p. to,** (a person) tocar para. **to p. upon,** (a person's fears, etc.) explotar. **to p. up to,** (a person) adular, hacer la rueda (a). **to p. with,** jugar con; burlarse de; (an idea) acariciar play, *n* juego, *m*; diversión, *f*, recreo, *m*; (reflection) reflejo, *m*; movimiento libre, *m*; (to the imagination, etc.) rienda suelta, *f*; *Mech.* holgura, *f*; *Lit.* pieza dramática, comedia, *f*; (performance) función, representación, *f*; (*Theater.*) teatro, *m*. **fair p.,** juego limpio, *m*. **foul p.,** juego sucio, *m*; traición, perfidia, *f*. **to bring into p.,** poner en juego. **to come into p.,** entrar en juego. **to give**

**p. to,** dar rienda a. **p. on words,** juego de palabras, *m.* **p.-pen,** cuadro enrejado, *m*

**playact** /'plei,ækt/ *vi* hacer la comedia

**playbill** /'plei,bil/ *n* cartel, *m;* programa, *m*

**played-out** /ˌpleid 'aut/ *a* agotado; viejo

**player** /'pleiər/ *n* jugador (-ra); *Theat.* actor (-triz), representante, *mf; Mus.* músico (-ca), tocador (-ra)

**playfellow** /'plei,fɛlou/ *n* camarada, *mf;* compañero (-ra) de juego, compañero de juegos

**playful** /'pleifəl/ *a* juguetón; travieso; alegre

**playfully** /'pleifəli/ *adv* en juego, de broma; alegremente

**playfulness** /'pleifəlnis/ *n* carácter juguetón, *m;* travesuras, *f pl;* alegría, *f*

**playgoer** /'plei,gouər/ *n* persona que frecuenta los teatros, *f;* espectador de comedias, *m*

**playground** /'plei,graund/ *n* patio de recreo, *m*

**playing** /'pleiiŋ/ *n* juego, *m.* **p.-cards,** naipes, *m pl,* cartas, *f pl.* **p.-field,** campo de deportes, *m*

**playlet** /'pleilit/ *n* comedia corta, *f*

**playmate** /'plei,meit/ *n.* See **playfellow**

**plaything** /'plei,θiŋ/ *n* juguete, *m*

**playtime** /'plei,taim/ *n* recreación, *f;* (in schools) hora de recreo, *f,* recreo, *m*

**playwright** /'plei,rait/ *n* dramaturgo, *m,* autor (-ra) de comedias

**plea** /pli/ *n Law.* informe, *m;* declaración, *f; Law.* acción, *f,* proceso, *m;* (excuse) pretexto, *m,* excusa, *f;* (entreaty) súplica, *f.* **under p. of,** bajo pretexto de, con excusa de

**plead** /plid/ *vi Law.* pleitear; *Law.* declarar; suplicar; (of counsel, etc.) abogar (por); interceder (por). —*vt* defender en juicio; aducir, alegar; pretender. **to p. guilty,** confesarse culpable. **to p. not guilty,** negar la acusación. **to p. ignorance,** pretender ignorancia

**pleading** /'plidiŋ/ *n* súplicas, *f pl; Law.* defensa, *f; pl* **pleadings,** alegatos, *m pl,* a implorante

**pleasant** /'plɛzənt/ *a* agradable; placentero; ameno; encantador; dulce; alegre; (of persons) simpático, amable; bueno; divertido

**pleasantly** /'plɛzəntli/ *adv* agradablemente; de un modo muy amable; alegremente

**pleasantness** /'plɛzəntnis/ *n* agrado, *m;* placer, *f;* amabilidad, *f;* alegría, *f*

**pleasantry** /'plɛzəntri/ *n* jocosidad, *f;* broma, chanza, *f*

**please** /pliz/ *vi* dar placer, gustar, dar gusto, agradar; parecer bien, querer, servirse; tener a bien, placer. —*vt* deleitar, agradar, gustar; halagar; contentar, satisfacer. **I will do what I p.,** Haré lo que me parezca bien. **If you p.,** Si te parece bien; Con tu permiso. **She is very easy to p.,** Es muy fácil de darle placer. **When you p.,** Cuando Vd. quiera, Cuando a Vd. le venga bien Cuando Vd. guste. **"Please Do Not Disturb,"** «No Molesten.» **P. sit down!** ¡Haga el favor de sentarse! ¡Sírvase de sentarse! **P. God!** ¡Plegue a Dios!

**pleased** /plizd/ *a* contento (de or con); encantado (de); alegre (de); satisfecho (de or con). **I am p. with my new house,** Estoy contento con mi nueva casa. **I'm p. to meet you,** Mucho gusto (en conocerle), Mucho gusto (en conocerla). **to be p.,** estar contento; complacerse en

**pleasing** /'pliziŋ/ *a* agradable, grato; placentero; halagüeño

**pleasurable** /'plɛʒərəbəl/ *a* agradable; divertido, entretenido

**pleasure** /'plɛʒər/ *n* placer, *m;* gusto, *m;* satisfacción, *f;* (will) voluntad, *f;* recreo, *m;* diversión, distracción, *f.* **to give p. (to),** dar placer (a); deleitar, agradar; complacer. **to take p. in,** gustar de, disfrutar de; complacerse en. **I shall do it with great p.,** Lo haré con mucho gusto, Lo haré con mucho placer. **p.-boat,** barco de recreo, *m.* **p.-ground,** parque de atracciones, *m.* **p.-seeking,** amigo de placeres, frívolo. **p. trip,** viaje de recreo, *m;* excursión, *f*

**pleasure craft** *n* barco de recreo, *m,* (one vessel); barcas de recreo (collectively), *m pl*

**pleat** /plit/ *n* pliegue, *m, vt* plegar, hacer pliegues en

**pleating** /'plitiŋ/ *n* plegado, *m*

**plebeian** /plɪ'biən/ *a* plebeyo. —*n* plebeyo (-ya)

**plebiscite** /'plɛbə,sait/ *n* plebiscito, *m.* **to take a p.,** hacer un plebiscito

**plectrum** /'plɛktrəm/ *n* plectro, *m*

**pledge** /plɛdʒ/ *n* prenda, *f;* empeño, *m;* garantía, *f;* (hostage) rehén, *m;* (toast) brindis, *m.* —*vt* empeñar, dar en prenda; garantizar; brindar por; prometer. **to p. oneself,** comprometerse. **to p. support for,** prometer apoyo para

**Pleiades** /'pliə,diz/ *n pl* pléyades, *f pl*

**plenary** /'plinəri/ *a* pleno; plenario. **p. indulgence,** indulgencia plenaria, *f.* **p. session,** sesión plenaria, *f*

**plenipotentiary** /ˌplɛnəpə'tɛnʃi,ɛri/ *a* plenipotenciario. —*n* plenipotenciario, *m*

**plenitude** /'plɛni,tud/ *n* plenitud, *f*

**plentiful** /'plɛntəfəl/ *a* copioso, abundante. **to be p.,** abundar

**plentifully** /'plɛntəfəli/ *adv* en abundancia

**plenty** /'plɛnti/ *n* abundancia, *f;* en abundancia; de sobra; mucho. —*adv Inf.* bastante. **There is p. of food,** Hay comida en abundancia. **We have p. of time,** Tenemos tiempo de sobra

**pleonasm** /'pliə,næzəm/ *n* pleonasmo, *m*

**plethora** /'plɛθərə/ *n* plétora, *f*

**pleurisy** /'plʊrəsi/ *n* pleuresía, *f*

**plexus** /'plɛksəs/ *n* plexo, *m*

**pliability** /ˌplaiə'biliti/ *n* flexibilidad, *f;* docilidad, *f*

**pliable, pliant** /'plaiəbəl; 'plaiənt/ *a* flexible; dócil

**pliers** /'plaiərz/ *n pl* pinzas, *f pl,* alicates, *m pl,* tenazas, *f pl*

**plight** /plait/ *vt* (one's word) empeñar, dar; prometer en matrimonio. —*n* (fix) aprieto, apuro, *m.* **to p. one's troth,** dar palabra de matrimonio

**plinth** /plinθ/ *n Archit.* plinto, *m*

**Pliny the Elder** /'plini/ Plinio el Antiguo, Plinio el Mayor

**Pliny the Younger** Plinio el Menor

**plod** /plɒd/ *vi* andar despacio, caminar con trabajo; *Fig.* trabajar con ahínco

**plodder** /'plɒdər/ *n* trabajador lento y concienzudo, *m;* (student) empollón (-ona)

**plot** /plɒt/ *n* (of land) parcela, *f;* terreno, solar, *m;* (plan) proyecto, *m;* estratagema, *m;* (literary) intriga, trama, *f;* (story) argumento, *m;* (conspiracy) conjuración, *f,* complot, *m.* —*vt* trazar (un plano, etc.); urdir, tramar. —*vi* conspirar, intrigar

**plotter** /'plɒtər/ *n* conspirador (-ra conjurado (-da)

**plotting** /'plɒtiŋ/ *n* trazado (de un plano, una gráfica), *m;* (conspiracy) conspiración, *f;* maquinaciones, *f pl;* (hatching) trama, *f*

**plover** /'plʌvər, 'plouvər/ *n* ave fría, *f,* chorlito, *m*

**plow** /plau/ *n* arado, *m; Astron.* el Carro, la Osa Mayor; (in an examination) escabechina, *f.* —*vt* and *vi* arar; *Fig.* surcar; (in examinations) escabechar, dar calabazas (a), suspender. **plow the sands,** arar en el mar. **p. handle,** esteva, *f.* **to p. up,** roturar

**plowman** /'plaumən/ *n* arador, surcador, *m;* (peasant) labrador, *m*

**plowshare** /'plau,ʃɛər/ *n* reja de arado, *f*

**pluck** /plʌk/ *vt* (pick) coger; (a bird) desplumar; *Mus.* puntear; (in an examination) calabacear escabechar. —*vi* tirar (de). —*n* (tug) tirón, *m;* (of an animal) asadura, *f;* (courage) coraje, *m.* **to p. up courage,** tomar coraje, sacar ánimos. **to p. off,** quitar. **to p. out,** arrancar; quitar

**pluckily** /'plʌkili/ *adv* valientemente

**pluckiness** /'plʌkinis/ *n* coraje, valor, *m*

**plucky** /'plʌki/ *a* valiente, esforzado, resuelto, animoso

**plug** /plʌg/ *n* tapón, tarugo, *m;* (in building) nudillo, *m;* (of a switchboard) clave, *f; Elec.* enchufe, *m;* (of a w.c.) tirador, *m;* (of a bath, etc.) tapón, *m;* (of tobacco) rollo, *m.* —*vt* atarugar, taponar, obturar; (in building) rellenar. —*vt* (with away) batirse el cobre, sudar la gota gorda. **to p. in,** enchufar

**plum** /plʌm/ *n* (tree) ciruelo, *m;* (fruit) ciruela, *f;* (raisin) pasa, *f; (Inf.* prize) breva, golosina, *f.* **p. cake,** pastel de fruta, *m*

**plumage** /'plumidʒ/ *n* plumaje, *m*

**plumb** /plʌm/ *n* plomada, *f;* (sounding-lead) escandallo, *m.* —*a* perpendículo; recto; completo. —*adv* a plomo, verticalmente; exactamente. —*vt* aplomar; *Naut.* sondar; *(Fig.* pierce) penetrar; (understand) comprender. —*vi* trabajar como plomero. **p.-line,** plomada, *f*

**plumbago** /plʌm'beigou/ *n* plombagina, *f*

**plumber** /'plʌmər/ *n* plomero, fontanero, *m;* instalador de cañerías, *m*

**plumbic** /'plʌmbɪk/ *a Chem.* plúmbico

**plumbing** /'plʌmɪŋ/ *n* plomería, fontanería, *f;* instalación de cañerías, *f*

**plumbless** /'plʌmlɪs/ *a Poet.* insondable

**plume** /plum/ *n* pluma, *f;* penacho, *m.* —*vt* adornar con plumas; desplumar; **to p.** itself, (of a bird) limpiarse las plumas. **to p. oneself on,** echárselas de, hacer alarde de; jactarse de

**plumed** /plumd/ *a* plumado; con plumas; empenachado

**plumelet** /'plumlɪt/ *n* agujas, *f pl*

**plummet** /'plʌmɪt/ *n* plomada, *f;* (weight) plomo, *m;* (sounding-lead) sonda, *f*

**plump** /plʌmp/ *a* gordito, llenito; rollizo; hinchado. —*adv* de golpe; claramente. —*vt* (swell) hinchar, rellenar; (make fall) hacer (or dejar) caer. —*vi* (swell) hincharse; engordar; (fall) caer a plomo; dejarse caer. **to p. for,** escoger, dar apoyo (a); votar por. **p.-cheeked,** mofletudo

**plumpness** /'plʌmpnɪs/ *n* gordura, *f;* lo rollizo

**plumy** /'plumi/ *a* como una pluma; plumado

**plunder** /'plʌndər/ *vt* saquear; pillar; despojar. —*n* saqueo, pillaje, *m;* (booty) botín, despojo, *m*

**plunderer** /'plʌndərər/ *n* saqueador (-ra); ladrón (-ona)

**plundering** /'plʌndərɪŋ/ *n* saqueo, *m;* despojo, *m.* —*a* saqueador

**plunge** /plʌndʒ/ *vt* chapuzar; sumergir; hundir; meter. —*vi* sumergirse; (into water) zambullirse; (rush) precipitarse, lanzarse; *Naut.* zozobrar; (of a horse) encabritarse; (gamble) jugarse el todo. —*n* sumersión, *f;* zambullida, *f;* chapuz, *m;* (rush) salto, *m;* (Fig. step) paso, *m*

**plunger** /'plʌndʒər/ *n Mech.* émbolo, *m*

**plunging** /'plʌndʒɪŋ/ *n* (of a ship) zozobra, *f;* (of a horse) cabriolas, *f pl;* saltos, *m pl,* For other meanings, see **plunge**

**plural** /'plʊrəl/ *a* plural. —*n* plural, *m.* **in the p.,** en el plural. **to make p.,** poner en plural

**plurality** /plʊ'rælɪti/ *n* pluralidad, *f*

**pluralize** /'plʊrə,laiz/ *vt* pluralizar

**plus** /plʌs/ *prep* and *a* más; *(Math. Elec.)* positivo. —*n* signo más, *m; Math.* cantidad positiva, *f.* **p. fours,** pantalones de golf, *m pl*

**plush** /plʌʃ/ *n* felpa, *f;* velludo, *m*

**plushy** /'plʌʃi/ *a* felpudo; de felpa

**Pluto** /'plutou/ *n* Plutón, *m;* (pipe-line) oleoducto, *m*

**plutocracy** /plu'tɒkrəsi/ *n* plutocracia, *f*

**plutocrat** /'plutə,kræt/ *n* plutócrata, *mf*

**plutocratic** /ˌplutə'krætɪk/ *a* plutocrático

**pluviometer** /ˌpluvi'ɒmɪtər/ *n* pluviómetro, *m*

**ply** /plai/ *n* cabo, *m.* —*vt* emplear, usar; manejar; ejercer; ofrecer; servir (con); importunar (con). —*vi* hacer el trayecto; hacer el servicio; ir y venir; hacer viajes. **to ply for hire,** tomar viajeros; ofrecerse para ser alquilado

**plywood** /'plai,wʊd/ *n* madera contrachapada, *f*

**pneumatic** /nʊ'mætɪk/ *a* neumático. —*n* (tire) neumático, *m.* **p. drill,** barreno neumático, *m*

**pneumococcus** /ˌnumə'kɒkəs/ *n* neumococo, *m*

**pneumonia** /nʊ'mounyə/ *n* pulmonía, *f.* **double p.,** pulmonía doble, *f*

**poach** /poutʃ/ *vi* cazar (or pescar) en vedado. —*vt* robar caza de un vedado; *Fig.* invadir; (Fig. steal) hurtar; (eggs) escalfar. **to p. upon another's preserves,** meterse en los asuntos de otro

**poacher** /'poutʃər/ *n* cazador furtivo, *m*

**poaching** /'poutʃɪŋ/ *n* caza (or pesca) furtiva, *f*

**pock** /pɒk/ *n* pústula, *f.* **p.-mark,** hoyo, *m.* **p.-marked,** picado de viruelas

**pocket** /'pɒkɪt/ *n* bolsillo, *m;* bolsillo del reloj, *m;* faltriquera, *f; Mineral.* bolsa, *f,* depósito, *m; Fig.* bolsa, *f;* (in billiards) tronera, *f.* —*vt* meter (or poner) en el bolsillo; (an insult) tragarse; (in billiards) entronerar; (a profit) ganar; apropiarse. **air-p.,** bolsa de aire, *f.* **to be out of p.,** haber perdido, tener una pérdida. **to have a person in one's p.,** calzarse a una

persona. **to p.** one's **pride,** olvidarse de su orgullo. **p. battleship,** acorazado de bolsillo, *m.* **p.-book,** cartera, *f.* **p. dictionary,** diccionario de bolsillo, *m.* **p.-flap,** portezuela, *f.* **p.-handkerchief,** pañuelo (de bolsillo), *m.* **p.-knife,** cortaplumas, *m.* **p.-lighter,** encendedor de bolsillo, *m.* **p.-money,** alfileres, *m pl,* dinero del bosillo, *m.* **p. picking,** ratería de carterista, *f*

**pocketful** /'pɒkɪt,fʊl/ *n* bolsillo lleno (de), *m;* lo que cabe en un bolsillo

**pocket of resistance** *n* foco de resistencia, *m*

**pod** /pɒd/ *n Bot.* vaina, *f;* (of a silkworm) capullo, *m.* —*vt* desvainar; mondar. —*vi* hincharse, llenarse

**podgy** /'pɒdʒi/ *a* gordo, grueso

**poem** /'pouəm/ *n* poema, *m; pl* **poems,** poesías, *f pl,* versos, *m pl*

**poet** /'pouɪt/ *n* poeta, *m.* **p. laureate,** poeta laureado, *m*

**poetaster** /'pouɪt,æstər/ *n* poetastro, *m*

**poetess** /'pouɪtɪs/ *n* poetisa, *f*

**poetic** /pou'ɛtɪk/ *a* poético. **p. licence,** licencia poética, *f*

**poeticize** /pou'ɛtə,saiz/ *vt* poetizar; hacer un poema (de)

**poetics** /pou'ɛtɪks/ *n* poética, *f*

**poetry** /'pouɪtri/ *n* poesía, *f;* versos, poemas, *m pl*

**pogrom** /pə'grʌm/ *n* pogrom, *m*

**poignancy** /'pɔinyənsi/ *n* (of emotions) profundidad, violencia, *f,* lo patético; (of a retort, etc.) mordacidad, acerbidad, *f*

**poignant** /'pɔinyənt/ *a* (moving) conmovedor, hondo, agudo; patético; (mordant) mordaz, agudo

**poignantly** /'pɔinyəntli/ *adv* de un modo conmovedor, patéticamente; mordazmente

**poinsettia** /pɔin'sɛtiə/ *n* flor de nochebuena, *f*

**point** /pɔint/ *n* (usual meanings and *Astrol., Math.,* in cards, in a speech, etc.) punto, *m;* característica, *f;* cualidad, *f;* (purpose) motivo, fin, *m;* (question) cuestión, *f;* asunto, *m;* (wit) agudeza, *f;* (significance) significación, *f;* (detail) detalle, *m;* (in rationing) cupón, *m;* (sharp end) punta, *f;* (of a shawl, etc.) pico, *m;* (of land) promontorio, cabo, *m;* (engraving) buril, *m;* (railway) aguja, *f;* (of horses) cabo, *m.* **Mary has many good points,** María tiene muchas cualidades buenas. **There is no p. in being angry,** No hay para que enfadarse. **in p.,** en cuestión; a propósito. **in p. of fact,** en efecto, en verdad. **on the p. of,** a punto de. **to be to the p.,** venir al caso; ser apropiado. **to carry one's p.,** salir con la suya. **to come to the p.,** ir al grano, ir al caso, ir al mollo del asunto. **to make a p. of,** insistir en; tener por principio. **to win on points,** (boxing) ganar por puntos. **p. at issue,** cuestión bajo consideración, *f,* punto en cuestión, *m.* **p.-blank,** a boca de jarro. **p.-duty,** regulación de tráfico, *f.* **p. lace,** encaje de aguja, *m.* **p. of honor,** punto de honor, *m;* cuestión de honor, *f.* **p. or order,** cuestión de orden, *f.* **p. of view,** punto de vista, *m.* **What's your p.?** ¿A dónde quieres llegar con esto?

**point** /pɔint/ *vt* sacar punta (a), afilar; (a moral, etc.) inculcar; (in building) rejuntar; *Gram.* puntuar; (of dogs) mostrar la caza. **He pointed his gun at them,** Les apuntó con su fusil. **The hands of the clock pointed to seven o'clock,** Las agujas del reloj marcaban las siete. **to p. with the finger,** señalar con el dedo. **to p. at,** señalar, indicar; (with a gun) apuntar; dirigir. **to p. out,** señalar, indicar; enseñar, mostrar; advertir

**pointed** /'pɔintɪd/ *a* (sharpened) afilado; (in shape) puntiagudo, picudo; *Archit.* ojival; *Fig.* mordaz; satírico; (of a remark, etc.) directo; personal, aparente, evidente

**pointedly** /'pɔintɪdli/ *adv* explícitamente, categóricamente; mordazmente; directamente; satíricamente

**pointedness** /'pɔintɪdnɪs/ *n* forma puntiaguda, *f;* (incisiveness) mordacidad, aspereza, *f;* claridad, *f*

**pointer** /'pɔintər/ *n* (of a clock, weighing-machine, etc.) aguja, *f;* (of a balance) fiel, *m;* (wand) puntero, *m; Fig.* índice, *m;* (dog) perro de muestra, *m*

**pointillism** *n Art.* puntillismo, *m*

**pointillisme** /'pwantḷ,izem/ *n Art.* puntillismo, *m*

**pointing** /'pɔɪntɪŋ/ n (in building) rejuntado, m; (of a gun) puntería, f
**pointless** /'pɔɪntlɪs/ a sin motivo, innecesario; fútil; sin importancia
**pointlessly** /'pɔɪntlɪsli/ adv sin motivo, sin necesidad; fútilmente
**pointsman** /'pɔɪntsmən/ n (railway) guardagujas, m; (policeman) guardia del tráfico, m
**poise** /pɔɪz/ vt balancear; pesar. —vi balancearse; posar, estar suspendido. —n equilibrio, m; (of mind) serenidad de ánimo, sangre fría, f; aplomo, m; (bearing) porte, aire, m
**poison** /'pɔɪzən/ n veneno, m; Fig. ponzoña, f, veneno, m. —vt envenenar; intoxicar; Fig. emponzoñar. **p. gas,** gas asfixiante, m
**poisoner** /'pɔɪzənər/ n envenenador (-ra); Fig. corruptor (-ra)
**poisoning** /'pɔɪzənɪŋ/ n envenenamiento, m; intoxicación, f
**poisonous** /'pɔɪzənəs/ a venenoso; tóxico; Fig. ponzoñoso, pernicioso. **p. snake,** serpiente venenosa
**poisonousness** /'pɔɪzənəsnɪs/ n venenosidad, f; toxicidad, f; Fig. veneno, m, ponzoña, f
**poke** /pouk/ vt (thrust) clavar; (make) hacer; (the fire) atizar; hurgar; (push) empujar; (put away) arrinconar. —vi andar a tientas; meterse. **Don't p. your nose into other people's business!** ¡No te metas donde no te llaman! **They poked his eyes out,** Le saltaron los ojos. **to p. fun at,** burlarse de, mofarse de. **to p. the fire,** atizar la lumbre (or el fuego). **to p. about for,** buscar a tientas. **p.-bonnet,** capelina, f
**poker** /'poukər/ n (game) póker, m; (for the fire) hurgón, atizador, m. **p. work,** pirograbado, m
**poky** /'pouki/ a estrecho, ahogado, pequeño; miserable
**Poland** /'poulənd/ Polonia, f
**polar** /'poulər/ a polar. **p. bear,** oso (-sa) blanco (-ca). **p. lights,** aurora boreal, f
**polarimeter** /,poulə'rɪmɪtər/ n polarímetro, m
**polarity** /pou'lærɪti/ n polaridad, f
**polarization** /,poulərə'zeɪʃən/ n polarización, f
**polarize** /'poulə,raɪz/ vt polarizar
**pole** /poul/ n palo largo, m; poste, m; (of a tent) mástil, m; (of a cart) pértiga, f; Sports. pértiga, garrocha, f; (measurement) percha, f; (Astron. Geog. Biol. Math. Elec.) polo, m. —vt (a punt) impeler con pértiga. **from p. to p.,** de polo a polo. **greasy p.,** cucaña, f. **under bare poles,** Naut. a palo seco. **p.-ax,** hachuela de mano, f; hacha de marinero, f; (butcher's) mazo, m. **p. jumping,** salto de pértiga, salto a la garrocha, m. **p.-star,** estrella polar, f
**Pole** /poul/ n polaco (-ca)
**polemic** /pə'lɛmɪk/ n polémica, f
**polemical** /pə'lɛmɪkəl/ a polémico
**police** /pə'lis/ n policía, f. —vt mantener servicio de policía en; mantener el orden público en; administrar, regular. **mounted p.,** policía montada, f. **p. constable,** (agente de) policía, guardia urbano, m. **p. court,** tribunal de la policía, m. **p. dog,** perro de policía, m. **p. force,** cuerpo de policía, m, policía, f. **p. magistrate,** juez municipal, m. **p. station,** comisaría de policía, f. **p. trap,** puesto oculto de la policía del tráfico, m. **p. woman,** policía, f
**policeman** /pə'lismən/ n policía, guardia, m
**policy** /'poləsi/ n política, f; táctica, f; sistema, m; norma de conducta, f; ideas, f pl, principios, m pl; prudencia, f; (insurance) póliza, f. **fixed premium p.,** póliza a prima fija, f. **p.-holder,** asegurado (-da), tenedor (de una póliza), m
**poliomyelitis** /,pouliou,maɪə'laɪtɪs/ n poliomielitis, f
**polish** /'polɪʃ/ vt (metals and wood) pulir; (furniture and shoes) dar brillo (a); (Lit. works) pulir, limar; (persons) descortezar, civilizar. —n (shine) brillo, m; (furniture) cera para los muebles, f; (metal, silver) líquido para limpiar metales, m; (for shoes) betún para zapatos, m; (varnish) barniz, m; (of Lit. works) pulidez, elegancia, f; (of persons) urbanidad, cultura, f. **to p. off,** terminar a prisa; (a person) acabar con; (food) engullir
**Polish** /'poulɪʃ/ a polaco, polonés. —n (language) polaco, m
**polished** /'polɪʃt/ a (of verses, etc.) pulido, elegante;

(of person) culto, distinguido; (of manners) fino, cortés
**polisher** /'polɪʃər/ n (machine) pulidor, m; lustrador, m. **floor-p.,** lustrador de piso, m. **French p.,** barnizador, m
**polite** /pə'laɪt/ a cortés, bien educado; atento; elegante
**politely** /pə'laɪtli/ adv cortésmente; atentamente
**politeness** /pə'laɪtnɪs/ n cortesía, f. **for p. sake,** por cortesía
**politic** /'polɪtɪk/ a político
**political** /pə'lɪtɪkəl/ a político. **p. agent,** agente político, m. **p. economist,** hacendista, mf **p. economy,** economía política, f
**politically** /pə'lɪtɪkli/ adv políticamente
**politician** /,polɪ'tɪʃən/ n político (-ca)
**politics** /'polɪtɪks/ n política, f. **to dabble in p.,** meterse en política
**polity** /'polɪti/ n forma de gobierno, constitución política, f
**polka** /'poulkə/ n polca, f
**polka-dot** /'poukə,dot/ a con puntos
**poll** /poul/ n (head of person) cabeza, f; (voters' register) lista electoral, f; (voting) votación, f; (polling booth) colegio electoral, m; (counting of votes) escrutinio, m. —vt (trees) desmochar; (vote) votar, dar su voto (a); (obtain votes) obtener, recibir; (count votes) escrutar. **p.-tax,** capitación, f
**pollard** /'polərd/ vt desmochar. —n (tree) árbol desmochado, m
**pollen** /'polən/ n polen, m
**pollinate** /'polə,neit/ vt fecundar con polen
**pollination** /,polə'neiʃən/ n polinización, f
**polling** /'poulɪŋ/ n votación, f. **p. booth,** colegio electoral, m
**pollute** /pə'lut/ vt contaminar; ensuciar; profanar; (corrupt morally) corromper
**polluter** /pə'lutər/ n profanador (-ra), corruptor (-ra)
**pollution** /pə'luʃən/ n contaminación, f; profanación, f; corrupción, f
**polo** /'poulou/ n polo, m. **p. mallet,** maza de polo, f. **p. player,** jugador de polo, m, polista, mf
**polonaise** /,polə'neiz/ n polonesa, f
**poltroon** /pol'trun/ n cobarde, m
**polychrome** /'poli,kroum/ a policromo
**polygamist** /pə'lɪgəmɪst/ n polígamo (-ma)
**polygamous** /pə'lɪgəməs/ a polígamo
**polygamy** /pə'lɪgəmi/ n poligamia, f
**polygenesis** /,poli'dʒɛnəsɪs/ n poligenismo, m
**polyglot** /'poli,glot/ a poligloto (-ta). **p. Bible,** poliglota, f
**polygon** /'poli,gon/ n polígono, m
**Polynesia** /,polə'niʒə/ Polinesia, f
**Polynesian** /,polə'niʒən/ a polinesio (-ia)
**polyp** /'polɪp/ n pólipo, m
**polyphonic** /,poli'fonɪk/ a polifónico
**polyphony** /pə'lɪfəni/ n polifonía, f
**polytechnic** /,poli'tɛknɪk/ a politécnico
**polytheism** /'poliθi,ɪzəm/ n politeísmo, m
**polytheistic** /,poliθi'ɪstɪk/ a politeísta
**pomade** /po'meid/ n pomada, f
**pomegranate** /'pom,grænɪt/ n granada, f
**Pomeranian** /,pomə'reiniən/ a pomerano. **P. dog,** perro pomerano, m
**pommel** /'pʌməl/ n pomo, m, vt aporrear
**pomp** /pomp/ n pompa, magnificencia, f, fausto, m; aparato, m; ostentación, f
**Pompeian** /pom'peiən/ a pompeyano
**Pompeii** /pom'pei/ Pompeya, f
**pompom** /'pom,pom/ n pompón, m, pompón, m
**pomposity** /pom'posɪti/ n pomposidad, presunción, f; (of language) ampulosidad, f
**pompous** /'pompəs/ a pomposo, ostentoso; (of style) ampuloso, hinchado; importante. **to be p.,** (of persons) darse tono
**pompously** /'pompəsli/ adv pomposamente
**pond** /pond/ n charca, f, estanque, m
**ponder** /'pondər/ vt ponderar, estudiar, considerar. —vi meditar (sobre), reflexionar (sobre)
**ponderable** /'pondərəbəl/ a ponderable

**ponderous** /'pɒndərəs/ a pesado; macizo, abultado; grave; (dull) pesado, aburrido

**ponderously** /'pɒndərəsli/ adv pesadamente; gravemente

**ponderousness** /'pɒndərəsnɪs/ n pesadez, f; gravedad, importancia, f

**poniard** /'pɒnyərd/ n puñal, m, vt apuñalar

**pontiff** /'pɒntɪf/ n pontífice, m

**pontifical** /pɒn'tɪfɪkəl/ a pontificio

**pontificate** /pɒn'tɪfɪˌkɪt/ n pontificado, m

**pontonier** /ˌpɒntnɪər/ n pontonero, m

**pontoon** /pɒn'tun/ n pontón, m. **p. bridge,** puente de pontones, m

**pony** /'pouni/ n jaca, f

**poodle** /'pudl/ n perro (-rra) de aguas, perro de lanas, perro lanudo

**pooh-pooh** /'pu'pu/ vt despreciar, desdeñar. **Pooh!** ¡Bah!

**pool** /pul/ n (in a river) rebalsa, f; charca, f, estanque, m; (of blood, etc.) charco, m; (in cards) baceta, f; Com. asociación, f; Fig. fuente, f; pl **pools,** (football) apuestas benéficas de fútbol, f pl. —vt (resources, etc.) combinar; juntar

**poop** /pup/ n popa, f. **p. lantern,** fanal, m

**poor** /pʊr/ a pobre; malo; (insignificant or unfortunate) infeliz, desgraciado. **the p.,** los pobres. **to be in p. health,** estar mal de salud. **to be p. stuff,** ser de pacotilla. **to be poorer than a church mouse,** ser más pobre que las ratas. **to have a p. opinion of,** tener en poco (a). **P. me!** ¡Ay de mí! ¡Pecador de mí! **p.-box,** cepillo, m. **p.-law,** ley de asistencia pública, f. **p.-spirited,** apocado

**poorhouse** /'pʊr,haus/ n asilo, m

**poorly** /'pʊrli/ adv pobremente; mal. —a indispuesto, malo

**poorness** /'pʊrnɪs/ n pobreza, f; mala calidad, f; (lack) carestía, f; (of soil) infertilidad, f; (of character) mezquindad, f

**pop** /pɒp/ n (of a cork) taponazo, m; (of a gun) detonación, f; (drink) gaseosa, f, adv ¡pum! —vi (a cork) saltar; (of guns) detonar. —vt (corks) hacer saltar; (a gun, a question, etc.) disparar. **popgun,** escopeta de aire comprimido, f. **to pop down,** bajar a presuradamente. **to pop in,** (visit) dejarse caer; entrar rápidamente. **to pop off,** marcharse a prisa; (die) estirar la pata. **to pop up,** subir corriendo; aparecer de pronto

**pope** /poup/ n Papa, m

**popinjay** /'pɒpɪn,dʒei/ n (fop) pisaverde, m

**popish** /'poupɪʃ/ a papista

**poplar** /'pɒplər/ n (black) chopo, álamo, m; (white) álamo blanco, m. **p. grove,** alameda, f

**poplin** /'pɒplɪn/ n popelina, f

**poppy** /'pɒpi/ n amapola, adormidera, f

**populace** /'pɒpyələs/ n pueblo, m; (scornful) populacho, m

**popular** /'pɒpyələr/ a popular; en boga, de moda; común. **He is a p. hero,** Es un héroe popular

**popularity** /ˌpɒpyə'lærɪti/ n popularidad, f

**popularization** /ˌpɒpyələrə'zeiʃən/ n vulgarización, f

**popularize** /'pɒpyələ,raiz/ vt popularizar, vulgarizar

**popularly** /'pɒpyələrli/ adv popularmente

**populate** /'pɒpyə,leit/ vt poblar

**population** /ˌpɒpyə'leiʃən/ n población, f

**populous** /'pɒpyələs/ a populoso; muy poblado

**porcelain** /'pɔrsəlɪn/ n porcelana, f

**porch** /pɔrtʃ/ n pórtico, m; (of a house) portal, m

**porcine** /'pɔrsain/ a porcino, porcuno

**porcupine** /'pɔrkyə,pain/ n puerco espín, m

**pore** /pɔr/ n poro, m. **to p. over,** estar absorto en; examinar cuidadosamente

**pork** /pɔrk/ n carne de cerdo, f. **salt p.,** tocino, m. **p. butcher,** tocinero, m. **p. pie,** pastel de carne de cerdo, m

**pornographic** /ˌpɔrnə'græfɪk/ a pornográfico

**pornography** /pɔr'nɒgrəfi/ n pornografía, f

**porosity** /pɔ'rɒsɪti/ n porosidad, f

**porous** /'pɔrəs/ a poroso

**porphyry** /'pɔrfəri/ n pórfido, m

**porpoise** /'pɔrpəs/ n marsopa, f, puerco marino, m

**porridge** /'pɔridʒ/ n gachas, f pl, m

**port** /pɔrt/ n puerto, m; (in a ship) porta, f; (larboard) babor, m; (wine) vino de Oporto, m; (mien) porte, m, presencia, f. —vt (the helm) poner a babor; Mil. llevar un fusil terciado. **to put into p.,** tomar puerto. **to stop at a p.,** hacer escala en un puerto. **dues,** derechos de puerto, m pl

**portable** /'pɔrtəbəl/ a portátil; móvil. **p. typewriter,** máquina de escribir portátil (or de viaje), f. **p. wireless,** radio portátil, f

**portal** /'pɔrtl/ n portal, m

**portcullis** /pɔrt'kʌlɪs/ n rastrillo, m

**portend** /pɔr'tend/ vt presagiar, anunciar

**portent** /'pɔrtent/ n augurio, presagio, m; portento, m

**portentous** /pɔr'tentəs/ a ominoso; portentoso; importante

**porter** /'pɔrtər/ n (messenger) mozo de cordel, m; (of a university, hotel) portero, m; (of a block of flats) conserje, m; (railway) mozo de estación, m; (drink) cerveza negra, f. **porter's lodge,** portería, f; conserjería, f

**porterage** /'pɔrtərɪdʒ/ n porte, m

**portfolio** /pɔrt'fouli,ou/ n carpeta, f; (Polit. of a minister) cartera, f; (Polit. ministry) ministerio, m

**porthole** /'pɔrt,houl/ n tronera, f

**portico** /'pɔrtɪ,kou/ n pórtico, m

**portiere** /pɔr'tyeər/ n antepuerta, f

**portion** /'pɔrʃən/ n porción, f; parte, f; (marriage) dote, mf; (piece) pedazo, m; (in a restaurant) ración, f; (in life) fortuna, f. —vt dividir; repartir; (dower) dotar

**portliness** /'pɔrtlinɪs/ n corpulencia, f

**portly** /'pɔrtli/ a corpulento, grueso

**portmanteau** /pɔrt'mæntou/ n maleta, f

**portmanteau word** n palabra de acarreo, f

**portrait** /'pɔrtrɪt/ n retrato, m. **p. painter,** pintor (-ra) de retratos

**portraiture** /'pɔrtrɪtʃər/ n retratos, m pl; descripción, pintura, f

**portray** /pɔr'trei/ vt retratar; pintar, representar; (in words) describir, pintar

**portrayal** /pɔr'treiəl/ n pintura, f; retrato, m; (in words) descripción, f

**portrayer** /pɔr'treiər/ n retratista, mf, pintor (-ra)

**portress** /'pɔrtrɪs/ n portera, f; (in a convent) tornera, f

**Portuguese** /ˌpɔrtʃə'giz/ a portugués. —n portugués (-esa); (language) portugués, m

**pose** /pouz/ vt colocar; (a problem, etc.) plantear; (a question) hacer; vi colocarse; (with as) echárselas de, dárselas de, fingir ser; hacerse pasar por. —n actitud, postura, f; (affected) pose, f; (deception) engaño, m

**poser** /'pouzər/ n problema difícil, m; (in an examination) pega, f; pregunta embarazosa, f

**position** /pə'zɪʃən/ n posición, f; situación, f; actitud, postura, f; condición, f, estado, m; (post) puesto, empleo, m. **He is not in a p. to...,** No está en condiciones de..., No está para... **to place in p.,** poner en posición, colocar

**positive** /'pɒzɪtɪv/ a positivo; absoluto; (convinced) convencido, seguro; (downright) categórico; Inf. completo. —n realidad, f; Photo. (prueba) positiva, f

**positively** /'pɒzɪtɪvli/ adv positivamente; categóricamente

**positiveness** /'pɒzɪtɪvnɪs/ n certitud, seguridad, f; terquedad, obstinacia, f

**positivism** /'pɒzɪtəˌvɪzəm/ n positivismo, m

**positivist** /'pɒzɪtɪvɪst/ n positivista, mf

**positivistic** /ˌpɒzɪtɪ'vɪstɪk/ a positivista

**posse** /'pɒsi/ n pelotón, m; multitud, muchedumbre, f

**possess** /pə'zɛs/ vt poseer; gozar (de); (of ideas, etc.) dominar. **to p. oneself of,** apoderarse de, apropiarse. **What possessed you to do it?** ¿Qué te hizo hacerlo?

**possession** /pə'zɛʃən/ n posesión, f. **to take p. of,** tomar posesión de; hacerse dueño de, apoderarse de; (a house, etc.) entrar en, ocupar

**possessive** /pə'zɛsɪv/ a posesivo. —n posesivo, m

**possessor** /pə'zɛsər/ n poseedor (-ra); dueño (-ña); propietario (-ia)

**possibility** /ˌpɒsə'bɪlɪti/ n posibilidad, f

**possible** /'pɒsəbəl/ a posible. **as soon as p.,** cuanto antes, lo más pronto posible. **to make p.,** hacer posible, posibilitar

**possibly** /'pɒsəbli/ *adv* posiblemente; (perhaps) quizás. **I shall come as soon as I p. can,** Vendré lo más pronto posible

**post** /poust/ *n* (pole) poste, *m;* (of a sentry, etc.) puesto, *m;* (employment) empleo, *m;* (mail) correo, *m; Mil.* toque, *m.* —*vt* (a notice) fijar; anunciar; (to an appointment) destinar; (letters, etc.) echar al correo; *Com.* pasar al libro mayor; (inform) tener al corriente. —*vi* viajar en posta. **"P. no bills!"** «Se prohibe fijar carteles.» **registered p.,** correo certificado, *m.* **p. card,** postal, *f.* **p.-chaise,** silla de posta, *f.* **p.-date,** posfecha, *f.* **p.-free,** franco de porte. **p.-haste,** con gran celeridad. **p.-horse,** caballo de posta, *m.* **p.-impressionism,** post-impresionismo, *m.* **p.-mortem,** *n* autopsia, *f.* **p.-natal,** post-natal. **p.-nuptial,** postnupcial. **p. office,** correo, *m,* correos, *m pl;* (on a train) ambulancia de correos, *f.* **p. office box,** apartado de correos, *m.* **p. office savings bank,** caja postal de ahorros, *f.* **p.-paid,** porte pagado; franco. **p.-war,** *n* postguerra, *f.* —*a* de la postguerra

**postage** /'poustɪdʒ/ *n* porte de correos, franqueo, *m.* **p. stamp,** sello postal, *m*

**postage meter** *n* franqueadora, *f*

**postal** /'poustl/ *a* postal. **p. order,** orden postal de pago, *f.* **p. packet,** paquete postal, *m*

**poster** /'poustər/ *n* cartel, *m.* —*vt* fijar carteles (a or en); anunciar por carteles. **bill-p.,** fijador de carteles, *m*

**poste restante** /ˌpoust re'stɑnt/ *n* lista de correos, *f*

**posterior** /pɒ'stɪəriər/ *a* posterior. —*n* trasero, *m,* asentaderas, *f pl*

**posteriority** /pɒˌstɪəri'ɒriti/ *n* posterioridad, *f*

**posterity** /pɒ'steriti/ *n* posteridad, *f*

**postern** /'poustərn/ *n* postigo, *m; Mil.* poterna, *f*

**postgraduate** /poust'grædʒuit/ *n* estudiante graduado que hace estudios avanzados, *m.* —*a* avanzado; para estudiantes graduados

**posthumous** /'pɒstʃəməs/ *a* póstumo

**posthumously** /'pɒstʃəməsli/ *adv* después de la muerte

**postman** /'poustmən/ *n* cartero, *m*

**postmark** /'poust,mɑrk/ *n* matasellos, *m,* *vt* poner matasellos (a)

**postmaster** /'poust,mæstər/ *n* administrador de correos, *m*

**postmeridian** /ˌpoustmə'ridiən/ *a* postmeridiano

**postmistress** /'poust,mistris/ *n* administradora de correos, *f*

**postpone** /poust'poun/ *vt* aplazar, diferir; retrasar; (subordinate) postergar

**postponement** /poust'pounmənt/ *n* aplazamiento, *m;* tardanza, *f*

**postscript** /'poust,skript/ *n* posdata, *f*

**postulate** /*n.* 'pɒstʃəlit; *v.* -,leit/ *n* postulado, *m, vt* postular

**posture** /'pɒstʃər/ *n* postura, actitud, *f;* (of affairs) estado, *m,* situación, *f.* —*vi* tomar una postura

**posy** /'pouzi/ *n* (nosegay) ramillete de flores, *m;* flor, *f;* (motto) mote, *m*

**pot** /pɒt/ *n* pote, *m;* tarro, *m;* (flower-) tiesto, *m;* (for cooking) olla marmita, *f;* jarro, *m.* —*vt* plantar en tiestos; conservar en potes. **pot-bellied,** panzudo. **pot-boiler,** obra literaria escrita con el sólo propósito de ganar dinero, *f.* **pot-herb,** hierba que se emplea para sazonar, hortaliza, *f.* **pot-hole,** bache, **pot-luck,** comida ordinaria, *f.* **pot-shot,** tiro fácil, *m;* tiro al azar, *m*

**potable** /'poutəbəl/ *a* potable

**potage** /pou'tɑʒ/ *n* potaje, *m*

**potash** /'pɒt,æʃ/ *n* potasa, *f.* **caustic p.,** potasa cáustica, *f*

**potassium** /pə'tæsiəm/ *n* potasio, *m*

**potato** /pə'teitou/ *n* patata, *f.* **sweet p.,** batata, *f.* **p. beetle,** coleóptero de la patata, *m.* **p. omelet,** tortilla a la española, *f.* **p. patch,** patatal, *m.* **p. peeler,** pela-patatas, *m*

**potency** /'poutnsi/ *n* potencia, *f;* fuerza, eficacia, *f*

**potent** /'poutnt/ *a* potente, fuerte; eficaz

**potentate** /'poutn,teit/ *n* potentado, *m*

**potential** /pə'tenʃəl/ *a* potencial; virtual; (*Phys.*

*Gram.*) potencial, *n* poder, *m; Gram.* modo potencial, *m; Phys.* energía potencial, *f; Elec.* tensión potencial, *f*

**potentiality** /pəˌtenʃi'æliti/ *n* potencialidad, *f*

**pothook** /'pɒt,huk/ *n* garabato de cocina, *m;* palote, *m;* (scrawl) garabato, *m*

**potion** /'pouʃən/ *n* poción, *f,*

**potpourri** /ˌpoupʊ'ri/ *n* popurrí, *m*

**potter** /'pɒtər/ *n* alfarero, *m.* —*vi* gandulear. —*vt* perder. **potter's clay,** barro de alfarero, *m.* **potter's wheel,** tabanque, *m.* **potter's workshop,** alfar, *m*

**pottery** /'pɒtəri/ *n* alfarería, *f;* (china) loza, porcelana, *f*

**pouch** /pautʃ/ *n* bolsa, *f; Zool.* bolsa marsupial, *f;* (for tobacco) tabaquera, *f;* (for cartridges) cartuchera, *f.* —*vt* embolsar. —*vi* bolsear

**poulterer** /'poultərər/ *n* pollero (-ra)

**poultice** /'poultis/ *n* apósito, emplasto, *m,* *vt* poner emplastos (a or en)

**poultry** /'poultri/ *n* volatería, *f.* **p. dealer,** gallinero (-ra) vendedor (-ra) de volatería. **p. yard,** gallinero, *m*

**poultry farming** *n* avicultura, *f*

**pounce** /pauns/ *n* (swoop) calada, *f.* —*vi* (swoop) calarse; saltar (sobre); agarrar, hacer presa (en); *Fig.* atacar; descubrir, hacer patente

**pound** /paund/ *n* (weight and currency) libra, *f;* (for cattle) corral de concejo, *m;* (thump) golpe, *m.* —*vt* (break up) machacar, pistar; (beat) batir; (thump) golpear, aporrear. **p. sterling,** libra esterlina, *f.* **p. troy,** libra medicinal, *f*

**pounding** /'paundɪŋ/ *n* machucamiento, *m;* batimiento, *m*

**pour** /pɔr/ *vt* vaciar, verter; derramar. —*vi* correr; (of rain) diluviar, llover a cántaros; (fill) llenar; (of crowds, words, etc.) derramarse. **to p. out the tea,** servir el té. **The crowd poured in,** La multitud entró en tropel

**pouring** /'pɔrɪŋ/ *a* (of rain) torrencial

**pout** /paut/ *vi* torcer el gesto; hacer pucheritos

**poverty** /'pɒvərti/ *n* pobreza, *f.* **p.-stricken,** menesteroso, indigente, necesitado

**powder** /'paudər/ *n* polvo, *m;* (face) polvos de arroz, *m pl;* (gun) pólvora, *f.* —*vt* polvorear; (crush) reducir a polvo, pulverizar. —*vi* ponerse polvos. **p.-flash,** fogonazo, *m.* **p.-flask,** polvorín, *m.* **p.-magazine,** santabárbara, *f.* **p.-mill,** fábrica de pólvora, *f.* **p.-puff,** polvera, borla de empolvarse, *f*

**powdered** /'paudərd/ *a* en polvo

**powdery** /'paudəri/ *a* polvoriento; friable

**power** /'pauər/ *n* poder, *m;* facultad, capacidad, *f;* vigor, *m,* fuerza, *f;* (*Polit.* and *Math.*) potencia, *f; Mech.* fuerza, *f;* influencia, *f.* **as far as lies within my p.,** en cuanto me sea posible. **It does not lie within my p.,** No está dentro de mis posibilidades, No está en mi poder. **the Great Powers,** las grandes potencias. **the powers that be,** los que mandan. **to be in p.,** estar en el poder. **p.-house, p.-station,** central eléctrica, *f.* **p. of attorney,** poderes, *m pl,* procuración, *f.* **to grant p. of attorney (to),** dar poderes (a)

**powerful** /'pauərfəl/ *a* poderoso; fuerte; eficaz; potente; (of arguments, etc.) convincente

**powerfully** /'pauərfəli/ *adv* poderosamente; fuertemente

**powerless** /'pauərlis/ *a* impotente

**power steering** *n* dirección asistida *f* (Spain), servo dirección *f*

**powwow** /'pau,wau/ *n* conferencia, *f;* conversación, *f*

**pox** /pɒks/ *n* sífilis, *f;* (smallpox) viruelas, *f pl;* (chicken-pox) viruelas falsas, *f pl*

**practicability** /ˌpræktikə'biliti/ *n* factibilidad, *f*

**practicable** /'præktikəbəl/ *a* practicable, factible, posible; viable, transitable

**practical** /'præktikəl/ *a* (doable) factible; práctico; virtual. **p. joke,** burla de consecuencias

**practically** /'præktikli/ *adv* prácticamente; en práctica; virtualmente; (in fact) en efecto. **p. nothing,** casi nada

**practicalness** /'præktikəlnis/ *n* carácter práctico, *m*

**practice** /'præktis/ *n* (custom) costumbre, *f,* práctica, *f;* ejercicio, *m;* (of a doctor, etc.) clientela, *f;* profesión, *f;* (religious) rito, *m,* ceremonias, *f pl;* (experience) experiencia, *f.* **It is not his p. to...,** No es su costumbre de... **to be out of p.,** estar desentrenado. **to put into p.,** poner en práctica. **P. makes perfect,** El ejercicio hace maestro. —*vt* tener la costumbre de; practicar; (a profession) ejercer; (a game) entrenarse en; (work at) estudiar; (a musical instrument) tocar; (accustom) acostumbrar. **to p. what one preaches,** predicar con el ejemplo

**practiced** /ˈpræktɪst/ *a* experimentado; experto

**practitioner** /prækˈtɪʃənər/ *n* médico (-ca). **general p.,** médico (-ca) general

**pragmatic** /prægˈmætɪk/ *a* pragmatista; (historical) pragmático; práctico

**pragmatism** /ˈprægməˌtɪzəm/ *n* pragmatismo, *m*

**pragmatist** /ˈprægmətɪst/ *n* pragmatista, *mf*

**Prague** /prɑg/ Praga, *f*

**prairie** /ˈprɛəri/ *n* pradera, sabana, pampa, *f,* a de la pradera, etc.

**praise** /preiz/ *vt* alabar; ensalzar, glorificar; elogiar. —*n* alabanza, *f;* elogio, *m;* glorificación, *f,* ensalzamiento, *m.* **to p. to the skies,** poner en los cuernos de la luna poner por las nubes, poner sobre las estrellas hacerse lenguas de

**praiseworthiness** /ˈpreizˌwɜrðinɪs/ *n* mérito, *m*

**praiseworthy** /ˈpreizˌwɜrði/ *a* digno de alabanza, laudable

**prance** /præns/ *vi* (of a horse) caracolear, encabritarse, cabriolar; saltar; andar airosamente. —*n* corveta, cabriola, *f;* salto, *m*

**prank** /præŋk/ *n* travesura, diablura, *f.* **to play pranks,** hacer diabluras

**prate, prattle** /preit; ˈprætl/ *vi* charlar, chacharear; (lisp) balbucir; (of brooks, etc.) murmurar, susurrar. —*vt* divulgar. —*n* charla, cháchara, *f;* balbuceo, *m*

**prattler** /ˈprætlər/ *n* parlanchín (-ina); (gossip) chismoso (-sa); (child) niño (-ña)

**prattling** /ˈprætlɪŋ/ *n* charla, *f;* (lisping) balbuceo, *m;* (of brooks, etc.) murmullo, susurro, ruido armonioso, *m.* —*a* charlatán, gárrulo; balbuciente; (of brooks, etc.) parlero

**prawn** /prɔn/ *n* camarón, *m*

**pray** /prei/ *vt* and *vi* suplicar; implorar; rezar, orar. **P. be seated,** Haga el favor de sentarse

**prayer** /ˈpreiər/ *n* rezo, *m,* plegaria, oración, *f;* súplica, *f; Law.* petición, *f.* **p. book,** libro de devociones, devocionario, *m.* **p.-meeting,** reunión para rezar, *f.* **p.-rug,** alfombra de rezo, *f*

**praying** /ˈpreiɪŋ/ *n* rezo, *m;* suplicación, *f*

**pre-** *prefix* de antes de (e.g. *pre-World-War-1 publications,* publicaciones de antes de la Primera Guerra Mundial)

**preach** /pritʃ/ *vt* and *vi* predicar

**preacher** /ˈpritʃər/ *n* predicador (-ra). **to turn p.,** meterse a predicador

**preaching** /ˈpritʃɪŋ/ *n* predicación, *f,* a predicador

**preamble** /ˈpriˌæmbəl/ *n* preámbulo, *m*

**prearrange** /ˌpriəˈreindʒ/ *vt* preparar de antemano, predisponer

**precarious** /prɪˈkɛəriəs/ *a* precario; inseguro; incierto, arriesgado

**precariousness** /prɪˈkɛəriəsnɪs/ *n* condición precaria, *f;* inseguridad, *f;* incertidumbre, *f*

**precaution** /prɪˈkɔʃən/ *n* precaución, *f.* **to take precautions,** tomar precauciones

**precautionary** /prɪˈkɔʃəˌnɛri/ *a* de precaución; preventivo

**precede** /prɪˈsid/ *vt* preceder (a), anteceder (a); tomar precedencia (a), exceder en importancia (a). —*vi* ir delante; tener la precedencia

**precedence** /ˈpresɪdəns/ *n* precedencia, *f;* prioridad, *f;* superioridad, *f.* **to take p. over,** tomar precedencia (a), preceder (a)

**precedent** /*n.* ˈpresɪdənt; *a.* prɪˈsidnt/ *n* precedente, *m,* a precedente. **without p.,** sin precedente

**preceding** /prɪˈsidɪŋ/ *a* anterior, precedente

**precept** /ˈprisɛpt/ *n* precepto, *m*

**preceptor** /prɪˈsɛptər/ *n* preceptor, *m*

**precinct** /ˈprisɪŋkt/ *n* (police station) comisaría de sección (Argentina), delegación (Mexico), *f*

**precincts** /ˈprisɪŋkts/ *n pl* recinto, *m;* ámbito, *m;* distrito, barrio, *m*

**preciosity** /ˌprɛʃiˈɒsɪti/ *n* afectación, *f*

**precious** /ˈprɛʃəs/ *a* precioso; de gran valor; hermoso; amado; muy querido; (with rogue, etc.) redomado; completo. **p. little,** muy poco. **p. nearly,** casi, por poco... **p. stone,** piedra preciosa, *f*

**preciousness** /ˈprɛʃəsnɪs/ *n* preciosidad, *f;* gran valor, *m*

**precipice** /ˈpresəpɪs/ *n* precipicio, *m*

**precipitancy** /prɪˈsɪpɪtənsi/ *n* precipitación, *f*

**precipitant** /prɪˈsɪpɪtənt/ *a* precipitado

**precipitate** /*v.* prɪˈsɪpɪˌteit; *n., a.* -tɪt/ *vt* precipitar, despeñar, arrojar; acelerar; *Chem.* precipitar. —*vi* precipitarse. —*n* precipitado, *m.* —*a* precipitado, súbito. **to p. oneself,** tirarse, lanzarse

**precipitately** /prɪˈsɪpɪtɪtli/ *adv* precipitadamente

**precipitation** /prɪˌsɪpɪˈteiʃən/ *n Chem.* precipitación, *f; Chem.* precipitado, *m;* (rain, etc.) precipitación pluvial, *f*

**precipitous** /prɪˈsɪpɪtəs/ *a* precipitoso, escarpado, acantilado

**precipitously** /prɪˈsɪpɪtəsli/ *adv* en precipicio

**precise** /prɪˈsais/ *a* preciso; exacto; justo; puntual; escrupuloso; formal; claro; pedante, afectado; ceremonioso

**precisely** /prɪˈsaisli/ *adv* precisamente; exactamente; puntualmente; escrupulosamente; claramente; con afectación; ceremoniosamente. **at six o'clock p.,** a las seis en punto

**precision** /prɪˈsɪʒən/ *n* precisión, *f;* exactitud, *f;* puntualidad, *f;* escrupulosidad, *f;* claridad, *f;* afectación, *f;* ceremonia, *f*

**preclude** /prɪˈklud/ *vt* excluir; impedir, hacer imposible

**preclusion** /prɪˈkluʒən/ *n* exclusión, *f;* imposibilidad, *f*

**precocious** /prɪˈkouʃəs/ *a* precoz

**precocity** /prɪˈkɒsɪti/ *n* precocidad, *f*

**preconceived** /ˌprikənˈsivd/ *a* preconcebido

**preconception** /ˌprikənˈsɛpʃən/ *n* idea preconcebida, *f;* (prejudice) prejuicio, *m*

**preconcerted** /ˌprikənˈsɜrtɪd/ *a* concertado de antemano

**precursor** /prɪˈkɜrsər/ *n* precursor (-ra)

**precursory** /prɪˈkɜrsəri/ *a* precursor

**predatory** /ˈprɛdəˌtɔri/ *a* rapaz; de rapiña; voraz

**predecease** /ˌpridiˈsis/ *vt* morir antes (de or que); *Law.* premorir. —*n Law.* premuerto, *m*

**predecessor** /ˈprɛdəˌsɛsər/ *n* predecesor (-ra); (ancestor) antepasado, *m*

**predestination** /prɪˌdɛstəˈneiʃən/ *n* predestinación, *f*

**predestine** /prɪˈdɛstɪn/ *vt* predestinar

**predetermination** /ˌpridɪˌtɜrmɪˈneiʃən/ *n* predeterminación, *f*

**predetermine** /ˌpridɪˈtɜrmɪn/ *vt* predeterminar

**predicament** /prɪˈdɪkəmənt/ *n* /ˈprɛdɪkəmənt/ (logic) predicamento, *m;* situación, *f;* (fix) apuro, *m;* pl **predicaments,** categorías, *f pl*

**predicate** /*v.* ˈprɛdɪˌkeit; *n.* -kɪt/ *vt* afirmar. —*n* (logic, *Gram.*) predicado, *m*

**predict** /prɪˈdɪkt/ *vt* predecir, pronosticar, profetizar

**prediction** /prɪˈdɪkʃən/ *n* predicción, *f;* pronóstico, vaticinio, *m,* profecía, *f*

**predilection** /ˌprɛdlˈɛkʃən/ *n* predilección, *f*

**predispose** /ˌpridɪˈspouz/ *vt* predisponer

**predisposition** /ˌpridɪspəˈzɪʃən/ *n* predisposición, *f*

**predominance** /prɪˈdɒmənəns/ *n* predominio, *m*

**predominant** /prɪˈdɒmənənt/ *a* predominante

**predominate** /prɪˈdɒməˌneit/ *vi* predominar

**preeminence** /priˈɛmənəns/ *n* preeminencia, *f;* primacía, superioridad, *f*

**preeminent** /priˈɛmənənt/ *a* preeminente; superior; extraordinario

**preeminently** /priˈɛmənəntli/ *adv* preeminentemente; extraordinariamente; por excelencia; entre todos

**preen** /prin/ *vt* (of birds) limpiarse; (of people) darse humos, jactarse

**preexist** /ˌpriɪgˈzɪst/ *vi* preexistir

**preexistence** /ˌpriɪgˈzɪstəns/ *n* preexistencia, *f*

**prefabricated** /priˈfæbrɪˌkeitɪd/ *a* prefabricado

**preface** /ˈprɛfɪs/ *n* prólogo, *m; Eccl.* prefacio, *m;* introducción, *f.* —*vt* dar principio (a), empezar. **He**

**prefaced his remarks by...,** Dijo a modo de introducción
**prefatory** /ˈprɛfəˌtɔri/ a preliminar, introductorio; a manera de prólogo
**prefect** /ˈprifɛkt/ n prefecto, m
**prefecture** /ˈprifɛktʃər/ n prefectura, f
**prefer** /prɪˈfɜr/ vt preferir, gustar más (a); (promote) ascender, elevar; (a charge, etc.) presentar. **to p. a charge against,** pedir en juicio (a). **I p. oranges to apples,** Me gustan más las naranjas que las manzanas, Prefiero las naranjas a las manzanas
**preferability** /ˌprɛfərəˈbɪliti/ n preferencia, ventaja, f
**preferable** /ˈprɛfərəbəl/ a preferible
**preferably** /ˈprɛfərəbli/ adv preferiblemente, con preferencia
**preference** /ˈprɛfərəns/ n preferencia, f; privilegio, m. **p. share,** acción privilegiada, acción preferente, f
**preferential** /ˌprɛfəˈrɛnʃəl/ a preferente
**preferment** /prɪˈfɜrmənt/ n promoción, f, ascenso, m; puesto eminente, m
**preferred** /prɪˈfɜrd/ a preferente; favorito, predilecto. **p. share,** acción preferente, f
**prefix** /ˈprifɪks/ vt anteponer, prefijar; (to a word) poner prefijo (a). —n prefijo, m
**pregnancy** /ˈprɛɡnənsi/ n embarazo, m, preñez, f
**pregnant** /ˈprɛɡnənt/ a embarazada, encinta, preñada, f; Fig. fértil; Fig. preñado
**prehensile** /prɪˈhɛnsɪl/ a prensil
**prehistoric** /ˌprihɪˈstɔrɪk/ a prehistórico
**prehistory** /priˈhɪstəri/ n prehistoria, f
**prejudge** /priˈdʒʌdʒ/ vt prejuzgar
**prejudice** /ˈprɛdʒədɪs/ n prejuicio, m; Law. perjuicio, m. —vt influir, predisponer; (damage) perjudicar. **without p.,** sin perjuicio
**prejudiced** /ˈprɛdʒədɪst/ a parcial; con prejuicios
**prejudicial** /ˌprɛdʒəˈdɪʃəl/ a perjudicial
**prelacy** /ˈprɛləsi/ n prelacía, f; episcopado, m
**prelate** /ˈprɛlɪt/ n prelado, m
**preliminarily** /prɪˌlɪməˈnɛərəli/ adv preliminarmente
**preliminary** /prɪˈlɪməˌnɛri/ a preliminar. —n preliminar, m
**prelude (to)** /ˈprɛlyud/ n preludio (de) m; presagio (de) m, vt and vi preludiar
**premature** /ˌprɪməˈtʃʊr/ a prematuro
**prematurely** /ˌprɪməˈtʃʊrli/ adv prematuramente
**prematureness** /ˌprɪməˈtʃʊrnɪs/ n lo prematuro
**premeditate** /prɪˈmɛdɪˌteɪt/ vt premeditar
**premeditatedly** /prɪˈmɛdɪˌteɪtɪdli/ adv premeditadamente, con premeditación
**premeditation** /prɪˌmɛdɪˈteɪʃən/ n premeditación, f
**premier** /prɪˈmɪər/ a primero, principal. —n primer minístro, m; (in Spain) presidente del Consejo de Ministros, m
**premiere** /prɪˈmɪər/ n estreno, m
**premiership** /prɪˈmɪərʃɪp/ n puesto de primer ministro, m; (in Spain) presidencia del Consejo de Ministros, f
**premise** /ˈprɛmɪs/ n (logic) premisa, f; pl **premises,** local, m; recinto, m; establecimiento, m; propiedad, f; tierras, f pl. **on the premises,** en el local; en el establecimiento
**premium** /ˈprimiəm/ n (prize) premio, m, recompensa, f; Com. prima, f; precio, m. **at a p.,** a premio; a una prima; (of shares) sobre la par; Fig. en boga, muy solicitado, en gran demanda
**premonition** /ˌpriməˈnɪʃən/ n presentimiento, presagio, m
**premonitory** /prɪˈmɒnɪˌtɔri/ a premonitorio
**prenatal** /priˈneɪtl/ a prenatal, antenatal
**preoccupation** /priˌɒkyəˈpeɪʃən/ n preocupación, f
**preoccupied** /priˈɒkyəˌpaɪd/ a preocupado; abstraído, absorto
**preoccupy** /priˈɒkyəˌpaɪ/ vt preocupar
**prepaid** /priˈpeɪd/ a porte pagado, franco de porte
**preparation** /ˌprɛpəˈreɪʃən/ n preparación, f; preparativo, m, disposición, f; (patent food) preparado, m. **I have made all my preparations,** He hecho todos mis preparativos. **The book is in p.,** El libro está en preparación
**preparative** /prɪˈpærətɪv/ a preparativo. —n preparativo, m

**preparatory** /prɪˈpærəˌtɔri/ a preparatorio, preparativo; preliminar. **p. school,** escuela preparatoria, f, m. **p. to,** como preparación para; antes de
**prepare** /prɪˈpɛər/ vt preparar; aparejar, aviar; equipar; (cloth) aprestar. —vi prepararse; hacer preparativos
**preparedness** /prɪˈpɛərɪdnɪs/ n estado de preparación, m; preparación, f, apercibimiento, m
**prepay** /priˈpeɪ/ vt pagar adelantado; (a letter, etc.) franquear
**prepayment** /priˈpeɪmənt/ n pago adelantado, m; (of a letter, etc.) franqueo, m
**preponderance** /prɪˈpɒndərəns/ n preponderancia, f
**preponderant** /prɪˈpɒndərənt/ a preponderante, predominante
**preponderantly** /prɪˈpɒndərəntli/ adv predominantemente; en su mayoría
**preponderate** /prɪˈpɒndəˌreɪt/ vi preponderar; prevalecer (sobre), predominar (sobre)
**preposition** /ˌprɪpəˈzɪʃən/ n preposición, f
**prepossess** /ˌprɪpəˈzɛs/ vt predisponer; causar buena impresión (a)
**prepossessing** /ˌprɪpəˈzɛsɪŋ/ a atractivo
**preposterous** /prɪˈpɒstərəs/ a ridículo, absurdo
**preposterously** /prɪˈpɒstərəsli/ adv absurdamente
**preposterousness** /prɪˈpɒstərəsnɪs/ n ridiculez, f
**Prep School** /prɛp/ n preparatoria, f
**prepuce** /ˈpripyus/ n prepucio, m
**Pre-Raphaelite** /priˈræfiəˌlaɪt/ a and n prerrafaelista, mf
**prerequisite** /priˈrɛkwəzɪt/ n requisito necesario, esencial, m, a previamente necesario, esencial
**prerogative** /prɪˈrɒɡətɪv/ n prerrogativa, f
**presage** /ˈprɛsɪdʒ/ n presagio, m; anuncio, m. —vt presagiar; anunciar
**Presbyterian** /ˌprɛzbɪˈtɪəriən/ a and n presbiteriano (-na)
**prescience** /ˈprɛʃəns/ n presciencia, previsión, f
**prescient** /ˈprɛʃənt/ a presciente
**prescind** /prɪˈsɪnd/ vt prescindir (de); separar (de). —vi separarse
**prescribe** /prɪˈskraɪb/ vt and vi prescribir; Med. recetar; dar leyes; Law. prescribir
**prescription** /prɪˈskrɪpʃən/ n prescripción, f; Med. receta, f
**presence** /ˈprɛzəns/ n presencia, f; (ghost) aparición, f. **in the p. of,** en presencia de, delante; a vista de. **p. of mind,** presencia de ánimo, serenidad de ánimo, f
**present** /ˈprɛzənt/ a presente; actual; (with month) corriente; Gram. presente. **at p.,** al presente, actualmente. **at the p. day,** a la fecha, en la actualidad, hoy día. **P. company excepted!** ¡Mejorando lo presente! **the present writer,** el que suscribe, el que esto escribe, el que estas líneas traza. **to be p. at,** presenciar, ser testigo de; asistir a, acudir a; hallarse en. **p.-day,** de hoy, actual. **p. tense,** Gram. tiempo presente, m
**present** /ˈprɛzənt/ n (time) presente, m; actualidad, f; Gram. tiempo presente, m; (gift) regalo, m, dádiva, f. **By these presents...,** Law. Por estas presentes... **to make a p. of,** regalar. **Jane made me a p. of a watch,** Juana me regaló un reloj
**present** /prɪˈzɛnt/ vt presentar; ofrecer; manifestar; (a gift) regalar, dar; (Eccl. Mil.) presentar. **New problems presented themselves,** Nuevos problemas surgieron. **to p. arms,** presentar las armas. **He presented himself in the office,** Se presentó en la oficina. **He presented his friend Mr. Moreno to me,** Me presentó a su amigo el Sr. Moreno
**presentable** /prɪˈzɛntəbəl/ a presentable
**presentation** /ˌprɛzənˈteɪʃən/ n presentación, f; homenaje, m; (exhibition) exposición, f. **on p.,** Com. a presentación
**presentiment** /prɪˈzɛntəmənt/ n presentimiento, corazonada, f. **I had a p. that...,** Tuve el presentimiento de que..., Tuve una corazonada que... **to have a p. about,** presentir
**presently** /ˈprɛzəntli/ adv pronto; en seguida; dentro de poco
**preservation** /ˌprɛzərˈveɪʃən/ n conservación, f; (from harm) preservación, f

**preservative** /prɪ'zɜrvətɪv/ *a* preservativo. —*n* preservativo, *m*

**preserve** /prɪ'zɜrv/ *vt* preservar (de); guardar; proteger; conservar; *Cul.* hacer conservas de; (in syrup) almibarar. —*n Cul.* conserva, *f;* (of fruit) compota, confitura, *f;* (covert) coto, *m.* **preserved fruit,** dulce de almíbar, *m.* **p. dish,** compotera, *f*

**preserver** /prɪ'zɜrvər/ *n* conservador (-ra); (saviour) salvador (-ra); (benefactor) bienhechor (-ra)

**preserving** /prɪ'zɜrvɪŋ/ *n* (from harm) preservación, *f;* conservación, *f.* **p. pan,** cazuela para conservas, *f*

**preside** /prɪ'zaɪd/ *vi* (over) presidir; dirigir, gobernar. **He presided at the meeting,** Presidió la reunión

**presidency** /'prezɪdənsi/ *n* presidencia, *f*

**president** /'prezɪdənt/ *n* presidente, *m;* (of a college) rector, *m.* **lady p.,** presidenta, *f*

**presidential** /,prezɪ'denʃəl/ *a* presidencial

**presidentship** /'prezɪdənt,ʃɪp/ *n* presidencia, *f*

**press** /pres/ *vt* prensar; (juice out of) exprimir; (clothes) planchar; (a bell, a hand, and of a shoe, etc.) apretar; (embrace) dar un abrazo (a); (a stamp, a kiss, etc.) imprimir; (an enemy) hostigar, acosar; (in a game) apretar; (crowd upon) oprimir; (emphasize) insistir en; (urge) instar, instigar; (compel) obligar; apremiar; (oppress) abrumar, agobiar; (paper) satinar; (an advantage) aprovecharse de. **Lola pressed his hand,** Lola le apretó la mano. **Time presses,** El tiempo es breve. **I did not p. the point,** No insistí. **to p. against,** pegar(se) contra. **to p. down,** comprimir; *Fig.* agobiar. **to p. for,** exigir, reclamar. **to p. forward, on,** avanzar; seguir el camino, continuar la marcha; (hurry) apretar el paso

**press** /pres/ *n* (pressure) apretón, *m;* (push) golpe, *m;* (throng) muchedumbre, *f;* (of business, etc.) urgencia, *f;* (apparatus) prensa, *f;* (printing press and publishing firm) imprenta, *f;* (cupboard) armario, *m.* **Associated P.,** Prensa Asociada, *f.* **freedom of the p.,** libertad de la prensa, *f.* **in p., in the p.,** en prensa. **in the p. of battle,** en lo más reñido de la batalla. **to go to p.,** entrar en prensa. **p.-agent,** agente de publicidad, *m.* **p.-box,** tribuna de la prensa, *f.* **p. clipping, p.-cutting,** recorte de prensa, *m.* **p.-gallery,** tribuna de la prensa, *f.* **p.-gang,** ronda de enganche, *f.* **p.-mark,** número de catálogo, *m.* **p. proof,** prueba de imprenta, *f.* **p.-room,** taller de imprenta, *m.* **p.-stud,** botón automático, *m.* **p. conference,** rueda de prensa, entrevista de prensa, conferencia de pensa, *f*

**pressing** /'presɪŋ/ *a* urgente, apremiante; importuno. —*n* prensado, *m*, prensadura, *f;* expresión, *f;* (of a garment) planchado, *m*

**pressingly** /'presɪŋli/ *adv* urgentemente, con urgencia; importunamente

**pressman** /'presmən/ *n* tirador, *m;* (journalist) periodista, *m*

**pressure** /'preʃər/ *n* presión, *f;* (of the hand) apretón, *m;* apremio, *m;* opresión, *f;* (weight) peso, *m;* (force) fuerza, *f;* urgencia, *f.* **p.-cooker,** cazuela de presión, olla de presión, *f,* presto, *m.* **p.-gauge,** manómetro, *m*

**prestidigitation** /,prestɪ,dɪdʒɪ'teɪʃən/ *n* prestidigitación, *f,* juegos de manos, *m pl*

**prestige** /pre'stiʒ/ *n* prestigio, *m*

**prestigious** /pre'stɪdʒəs/ *a* prestigiado

**presumable** /prɪ'zuməbəl/ *a* presumible

**presume** /prɪ'zum/ *vt* presumir; suponer, sospechar; (attempt) pretender. —*vi* presumir; tomarse libertades; abusar (de)

**presumption** /prɪ'zʌmpʃən/ *n* presunción, *f;* suposición, *f;* (effrontery) atrevimiento, *m;* insolencia, *f*

**presumptive** /prɪ'zʌmptɪv/ *a* presuntivo; (with heir, etc.) presunto

**presumptuous** /prɪ'zʌmptʃuəs/ *a* presumido, insolente, presuntuoso; atrevido

**presumptuously** /prɪ'zʌmptʃuəsli/ *adv* presuntuosamente

**presumptuousness** /prɪ'zʌmptʃuəsnɪs/ *n* presunción, presuntuosidad, *f;* atrevimiento, *m*

**presuppose** /,prisə'pouz/ *vt* presuponer

**presupposition** /,prisʌpə'zɪʃən/ *n* presuposición, *f*

**pretence** /prɪ'tens/ *n* (claim) pretensión, *f;* afectación, *f;* (simulation) fingimiento, *m;* pretexto, *m.* **false pretences,** apariencias fingidas, *f pl;* engaño, *m,*

estafa, *f.* **to make a p. of,** fingir. **under p. of,** bajo pretexto de

**pretend** /prɪ'tend/ *vt* dar como pretexto de; aparentar, fingir, simular, hacer el papel (de). —*vi* pretender (a); tener pretensiones (de); ser pretendiente (a); fingir

**pretended** /prɪ'tendɪd/ *a* supuesto, fingido; falso

**pretender** /prɪ'tendər/ *n* pretendiente, *m;* hipócrita, *mf*

**pretension** /prɪ'tenʃən/ *n* pretensión, *f;* afectación, simulación, *f*

**pretentious** /prɪ'tenʃəs/ *a* pretencioso; (of persons) presumido

**pretentiousness** /prɪ'tenʃəsnɪs/ *n* pretensiones, *f pl,* lo pretencioso

**preterite** /'pretərɪt/ *n* (tiempo) pretérito, *m,* *a* pretérito, pasado

**pretext** /'pritekst/ *n* pretexto, *m.* —*vt* pretextar. **under p. of,** bajo pretexto de, so color de

**prettily** /'prɪtli/ *adv* lindamente; con gracia; agradablemente

**prettiness** /'prɪtinɪs/ *n* lo bonito; elegancia, *f;* gracia, *f*

**pretty** /'prɪti/ *a* bonito; (of women, children) guapo, mono; (of men) lindo; elegante; excelente; *Ironic.* bueno. —*adv* bastante; medianamente; (very) muy; (almost) casi. **p. good,** bastante bueno. **p.-p.,** de muñeca; mono. —*n* chuchería, *f,* guapos, *m pl.* **p. ways,** monerías, *f pl*

**prevail** /prɪ'veɪl/ *vi* prevalecer, predominar; ser la costumbre. **to p. against or over,** triunfar de, vencer (a). **to p. on, upon,** inducir, convencer, persuadir. **to be prevailed upon to,** dejarse persuadir a

**prevailing** /prɪ'veɪlɪŋ/ *a* prevaleciente; dominante; predominante, reinante; general; común; (fashionable) en boga

**prevalence** /'prevələns/ *n* predominio, *m;* existencia, *f;* (habit) costumbre, *f;* (fashion) boga, *f*

**prevalent** /'prevələnt/ *a* prevaleciente; predominante; general; común; corriente; (fashionable) en boga

**prevaricate** /prɪ'værɪ,keɪt/ *vi* tergiversar; *Law.* prevaricar

**prevarication** /prɪ,værɪ'keɪʃən/ *n* tergiversación, *f,* equívoco, *m*

**prevaricator** /prɪ'værɪ,keɪtər/ *n* tergiversador (-ra)

**prevent** /prɪ'vent/ *vt* evitar; (hinder) impedir (a)

**preventable** /prɪ'ventəbəl/ *a* evitable

**prevention** /prɪ'venʃən/ *n* prevención, *f;* (preventive) estorbo, obstáculo, *m*

**preventive** /prɪ'ventɪv/ *a* preventivo. —*n* preservativo, *m*

**preview** /'priˌvyu/ *n* vista de antemano, *f;* (of a film) avances, *m pl* (Cuba, Mexico), colas, *f pl* (Argentina), cortos *m pl* (Venezuela), sinopsis, *f* (Uruguay), tráiler, *m* (Spain)

**previous** /'priviəs/ *a* previo, anterior. **p. to,** antes de

**previously** /'priviəsli/ *adv* anteriormente, antes, previamente

**previousness** /'priviəsnɪs/ *n* anterioridad, *f;* inoportunidad, *f*

**prevision** /prɪ'vɪʒən/ *n* previsión, *f*

**prewar** /'pri'wɔr/ *a* de antes de la guerra

**prey** /preɪ/ *n* presa, *f; Fig.* víctima, *f;* (booty) botín, *m.* —*vi* (of animals) devorar; (plunder) robar, pillar; (of sorrow, etc.) hacer presa (de); agobiar, consumir; (sponge on) vivir a costa de. **to fall a p. to,** ser víctima de

**price** /praɪs/ *n* precio, *m;* valor, *m;* costa, *f.* —*vt* evaluar, tasar; poner precio a; preguntar el precio de; fijar el precio de. **at any p.,** a cualquier precio; (whatever the cost) cueste lo que cueste. **at a reduced p.,** a precio reducido. **fixed p.,** precio fijo, *m.* **p. ceiling,** precio máximo, precio tope, *m.* **p. control,** control de precios, *m.* **price list,** lista de precios, *f;* tarifa, *f;* (of shares, etc.) boletín de cotización, *m.* **Prices are subject to change without notice,** Los precios están sujetos a variación sin previo aviso.

**priceless** /'praɪslɪs/ *a* sin precio; (amusing) divertidísimo. **These jewels are p.,** Estas joyas no tienen precio

**prick** /prɪk/ *n* pinchazo, *m;* picadura, *f;* punzada, *f;* (prickle) espina, *f;* (with a goad) aguijonazo, *m;*

(with a pin) alfilerazo, *m;* (with a spur) espolada, *f;* (of conscience) remordimiento, escrúpulo, *m.* —*vt* pinchar, punzar; picar; (with remorse) atormentar, causar remordimiento (a); (urge on) incitar. **to p. the ears,** aguzar las orejas

**pricking** /'prɪkɪŋ/ *n* picadura, *f;* punzada, *f.* **prickings of conscience,** remordimientos, *m pl*

**prickle** /'prɪkəl/ *n* espina, *f;* (irritation) escozor, *m*

**prickly** /'prɪkli/ *a* espinoso; erizado. **p. heat,** salpullido causado por exceso de calor, *m.* **p. pear,** higo chumbo, *m,* chumbera, *f*

**pride** /praid/ *n* orgullo, *m;* arrogancia, *f;* (splendour) pompa, *f,* fausto, aparato, *m;* belleza, *f;* vigor, *m;* (of lions) manada, *f.* **to take p. in,** estar orgulloso de. **to p. oneself,** sentirse orgulloso, ufanarse. **to p. oneself upon,** jactarse de, preciarse de

**prie-dieu** /'pri'dyʊ/ *n* reclinatorio, *m*

**prier** /'praiər/ *n* espía, *mf;* curioso (-sa)

**priest** /prist/ *n* sacerdote, *m;* cura, *m.* **high-p.,** sumo sacerdote, *m.* **p.-ridden,** dominado por el clero

**priestess** /'pristɪs/ *n* sacerdotisa, *f*

**priesthood** /'pristhʊd/ *n* sacerdocio, *m*

**priestly** /'pristli/ *a* sacerdotal

**prig** /prɪg/ *n* fatuo (-ua), mojigato (-ta)

**priggish** /'prɪgɪʃ/ *a* fatuo, gazmoño

**priggishness** /'prɪgɪʃnɪs/ *n* gazmoñería, fatuidad, *f*

**prim** /prɪm/ *a* almidonado, etiquetero; peripuesto; afectado

**primacy** /'praiməsi/ *n* primacía, *f*

**prima donna** /,primə 'dɒnə/ *n* cantatriz, *f*

**primarily** /prai'mɛərəli/ *adv* en primer lugar principalmente

**primary** /'praimɛri/ *a* primario; primitivo; principal. **p. education,** enseñanza primaria, *f.* **p. color,** color primario, *m.* **p. school,** escuela primaria, *f.* **p. election,** elección interna (dentro de un partido), *f*

**primate** /'praimeit/ *n* primado, *m*

**prime** /praim/ *a* primero; principal; excelente; de primera calidad; de primera clase. —*n* (spring) primavera, *f;* (of life, etc.) flor, *f,* vigor, *m;* (best) nata, crema, *f; Eccl.* prima, *f;* (number) número primo, *m.* —*vt* preparar, aprestar; (fire-arms) cebar. **p. the pump,** cebar la bomba; (with paint, etc.) imprimar; (instruct) dar instrucciones (a), informar. **in his p.,** en la flor de su edad. **of p. quality,** de primera calidad. **P. Minister,** Primer Ministro, *m.* **p. necessity,** artículo de primera necesidad, *m*

**primer** /'praimər/ *n* cartilla, *f,* abecedario, *m;* libro de lectura, *m;* (prayer book) devocionario, *m*

**primeval** /prai'mivəl/ *a* primevo, primitivo

**priming** /'praimɪŋ/ *n* preparación, *f;* (of fire-arms) cebo, *m;* (of paint, etc.) imprimación, *f;* instrución, *f*

**primitive** /'prɪmɪtɪv/ *a* primitivo; anticuado. —*n* primitivo, *m*

**primitiveness** /'prɪmɪtɪvnɪs/ *n* lo primitivo; carácter primitivo, *m*

**primly** /'prɪmli/ *adv* afectadamente, con afectación; gravemente

**primness** /'prɪmnɪs/ *n* afectación, *f;* gravedad, *f*

**primogeniture** /,praimə'dʒɛnɪtʃər/ *n* primogenitura, *f*

**primordial** /prai'mɔrdiəl/ *a* primordial

**primrose** /'prɪm,rouz/ *n* primavera, *f;* color amarillo pálido, *m*

**prince** /prɪns/ *n* príncipe, *m.* **P. Consort,** príncipe consorte, *m.* **P. of Wales,** (Britain) príncipe heredero, *m;* (Spanish equivalent) Príncipe de Asturias, *m.* **p. regent,** príncipe regente, *m.* **P. Charming,** el Príncipe Azul, *m*

**princeliness** /'prɪnslɪnɪs/ *n* magnificencia, *f;* nobleza, *f*

**princely** /'prɪnsli/ *a* principesco; magnífico; noble

**princess** /'prɪnsɪs/ *n* princesa, *f*

**principal** /'prɪnsəpəl/ *a* principal; fundamental; mayor. —*n* principal, jefe, *m;* (of a university) rector, *m;* (of a school) director (-ra); *Law.* causante, *m; Com.* capital, *m*

**principality** /,prɪnsə'pælɪti/ *n* principado, *m*

**principally** /'prɪnsəpli/ *adv* principalmente

**principle** /'prɪnsəpəl/ *n* principio, *m.* **in p.,** en principio

**principled** /'prɪnsəpəld/ *a* de principios...

**print** /prɪnt/ *n* (mark) impresión, marca, *f;* (type) letra de molde, *f,* tipo, *m;* (of books) imprenta, *f;* (fabric) estampado, *m;* (picture) grabado, *m;* (photograph) positiva impresa, *f;* (mold) molde, *m.* —*vt* marcar; imprimir; (on the mind) grabar; *Print.* tirar, hacer una tirada (de); (in photography) tirar una prueba (de); (publish) sacar a luz, publicar; (fabrics) estampar. **in p.,** impreso; publicado; **He likes to see his name in print,** Le gusta ver su nombre en letras de molde; (available) existente. **to be out of p.,** estar agotado. **p. dress,** vestido estampado, *m*

**printed** /'prɪntɪd/ *a* impreso. **p. fabric,** estampado, *m.* **p. matter,** impresos, *m pl*

**printer** /'prɪntər/ *n* impresor, *m;* tipógrafo, *m.* **printer's devil,** aprendiz de impresor, *m.* **printer's ink,** tinta de imprenta, tinta tipográfica, *f.* **printer's mark,** pie de imprenta, *m*

**printing** /'prɪntɪŋ/ *n* imprenta, *f;* impresión, *f;* (of fabrics) estampación, *f;* (art of) tipografía, *f.* **p. house,** imprenta, *f.* **p. machine,** máquina de imprimir, *f.* **p. press,** prensa tipográfica, *f.* **p. types,** caracteres de imprenta, *m pl*

**prior** /'praiər/ *n* prior, *m, a* anterior, previo. **p. to,** anterior a, antes de

**prioress** /'praiərɪs/ *n* priora, *f*

**priority** /prai'ɔrɪti/ *n* prioridad, *f*

**prism** /'prɪzəm/ *n* prisma, *m;* espectro solar, *m*

**prismatic** /prɪz'mætɪk/ *a* prismático

**prison** /'prɪzən/ *n* prisión, cárcel, *f.* **p.-breaking,** huida de la prisión, *f.* **p. camp,** campo de prisioneros, *m.* **p. van,** coche celular, *m.* **p. yard,** patio de la prisión, *m*

**prisoner** /'prɪzənər/ *n* prisionero (-ra), preso (-sa). **to take p.,** prender, hacer prisionero (a)

**pristine** /'prɪstin/ *a* pristino, original

**privacy** /'praivəsi/ *n* soledad, *f,* aislamiento, retiro, *m;* intimidad, *f;* secreto, *m*

**private** /'praivɪt/ *a* particular; privado; secreto; confidencial; reservado; íntimo; personal; doméstico; (of hearings, etc.) a puertas cerradas, secreto; (own) propio. —*n* (soldier) soldado raso, *m.* **in p.,** en secreto; confidencialmente, de persona a persona. **They wish to be p.,** Quieren estar a solas. **p. company,** sociedad en comandita, *f.* **p. hotel,** pensión, *f.* **p. house,** casa particular, *f.* **p. individual,** particular, *mf.* **p. interview,** entrevista privada, *f.* **p. life,** vida privada, *f.* **p. office,** despacho particular, *m.* **p. secretary,** secretario (-ia) particular. **p. viewing, (of a film)** función privada, *f;* **(of an exhibition)** día de inauguración, *m*

**privateer** /,praivə'tɪər/ *n* corsario, *m*

**privately** /'praivɪtli/ *adv* privadamente; en secreto; personalmente; confidencialmente; (of hearings) a puertas cerradas

**privation** /prai'veiʃən/ *n* privación, *f;* carencia, escasez, *f*

**privet** /'prɪvɪt/ *n* alheña, *f*

**privilege** /'prɪvəlɪdʒ/ *n* privilegio, *m;* derecho, *m;* inmunidad, *f.* —*vt* privilegiar

**privileged** /'prɪvəlɪdʒd/ *a* privilegiado; confidencial

**privy** /'prɪvi/ *a* privado; cómplice; enterado; personal, particular. —*n* (latrine) retrete, *m.* **p. council,** consejo privado, *m*

**prize** /praiz/ *n* premio, *m;* recompensa, *f,* galardón, *m;* (capture) presa, *f.* —*a* que ha ganado un premio; premiado; (huge) enorme; (complete) de primer orden. —*vt* estimar, apreciar. **to p. open,** abrir con una palanca. **to carry off the p.,** ganar el premio. **cash p.,** premio en metálico, *m.* **first p.,** primer premio, *m;* (in a lottery) premio gordo, *m.* **p. court,** tribunal de presas, *m.* **p. fight,** partido de boxeo, *m.* **p. fighter,** boxeador, *m.* **p. giving,** distribución de premios, *f.* **p. money,** premio en metálico, *m;* (boxing) bolsa, *f*

**pro** /prou/ *prep* pro. **pro forma invoice,** factura simulada, *f*

**probability** /,prɒbə'bɪlɪti/ *n* probabilidad, *f*

**probable** /'prɒbəbəl/ *a* probable

**probably** /'prɒbəbli/ *adv* probablemente

**probate** /'proubeit/ *n* verificación de un testamento, *f*

**probation** /prou'beiʃən/ *n* probación, *f; Law.* libertad vigilada, *f*

**probationary** /prou'beiʃə,nɛri/ *a* de probación; de prueba

**probationer** /prou'beɪʃənər/ *n* novicio, *m;* estudiante de enfermera, *f;* candidato, *m;* aspirante, *m*
**probe** /proub/ *n Surg.* sonda, cala, tienta, *f.* —*vt Surg.* tentar; escudriñar
**probing** /'proubɪŋ/ *n* sondeo, *m*
**probity** /'proubɪti/ *n* probidad, integridad, *f*
**problem** /'prɒbləm/ *n* problema, *m;* cuestión, *f.* **p. play,** drama de tesis, *m*
**problematic** /,prɒblə'mætɪk/ *a* problemático
**problem child** *n* niño problemático, *m* (male), niña problemática, *f* (female)
**proboscis** /prou'bɒsɪs/ *n* (of an elephant) trompa, *f;* (of an insect) trompetilla, *f*
**Probus** /'proubəs/ Probo, *m*
**procedure** /prə'sidʒər/ *n* procedimiento, *m*
**proceed** /prə'sid/ *vi* seguir el camino, continuar la marcha; avanzar, seguir adelante; ir; proceder; ponerse (a); empezar (a); (say) proseguir; (come to) llegar a, ir a; (of a play, etc.) desarrollarse. **Before we p. any further...** Antes de ir más lejos... **to p. to blows,** llegar a las manos. **to p. against,** proceder contra, procesar. **to p. from,** venir de. **to p. with,** proseguir; poner por obra; usar
**proceeding** /prə'sidɪŋ/ *n* modo de obrar, *m;* conducta, *f;* procedimiento, *m;* transacción, *f;* *pl* **proceedings,** (measures) medidas, *f pl,* actos, *m pl;* (of a learned society or a conference) actas, *f pl.* **to take proceedings against,** *Law.* procesar
**proceeds** /'prousidz/ *n pl* producto, *m;* ganancias, *f pl;* beneficios, *m pl.* **net p.,** producto neto, *m*
**process** /'prɒsɛs/ *n* proceso, *m;* (method) procedimiento, *m;* (course) curso, *m;* marcha, *f;* (*Law. Zool.*) proceso, *m.* —*vt* beneficiar (ore), trasformar, elaborar. **in p. of,** en curso de. **in the p. of time,** con el tiempo marchando el tiempo
**processing industry** /'prɒsɛsɪŋ/ *n* industria de trasformación, industria de elaboración, *f*
**procession** /prə'sɛʃən/ *n* desfile, *m;* cortejo, *m;* (religious) procesión, *f.* **funeral p.,** cortejo fúnebre, *m.* **to walk in p.,** desfilar
**processional** /prə'sɛʃənl/ *a* procesional
**proclaim** /prou'kleɪm/ *vt* proclamar; publicar, pregonar; anunciar; (reveal) revelar; (outlaw) denunciar
**proclamation** /,prɒklə'meɪʃən/ *n* proclamación, *f;* proclama, *f,* anuncio, *m;* declaración, *f*
**proclivity** /prou'klɪvɪti/ *n* proclividad, propensión, *f*
**procrastinate** /prou'kræstə,neit/ *vi* tardar (en decidirse), aplazar su decisión; vacilar; perder el tiempo
**procrastination** /prou,kræstə'neɪʃən/ *n* dilación, tardanza, *f;* vacilación, *f,* pereza, *f*
**procrastinator** /prou'kræstə,neitər/ *n* perezoso (-sa)
**procreate** /'proukri,eit/ *vt* procrear
**procreation** /,proukri'eiʃən/ *n* procreación, *f*
**procreator** /'proukri,eitər/ *n* procreador (-ra)
**proctor** /'prɒktər/ *n* procurador, *m; Educ.* censor, *m*
**procurable** /prou'kyʊrəbəl/ *a* procurable; asequible
**procure** /prou'kyʊr/ *vt* obtener, conseguir, lograr
**procurement** /prou'kyʊrmənt/ *n* obtención, *f,* logro, *m*
**procurer** /prou'kyʊrər/ *n* alcahuete, *m*
**procuress** /prou'kyʊrɪs/ *n* alcahueta, celestina, trotaconventos, *f*
**prod** /prɒd/ *n* (with a bayonet, etc.) punzada, *f; Fig.* pinchazo, *m.* —*vt* punzar; (in the ribs, etc.) clavar; *Fig.* pinchar
**prodigal** /'prɒdɪgəl/ *a* and *n* pródigo (-ga)
**prodigality** /,prɒdɪ'gælɪti/ *n* prodigalidad, *f*
**prodigally** /'prɒdɪgəli/ *adv* pródigamente
**prodigious** /prə'dɪdʒəs/ *a* prodigioso
**prodigiousness** /prə'dɪdʒəsnɪs/ *n* prodigiosidad, *f;* enormidad, *f*
**prodigy** /'prɒdɪdʒi/ *n* prodigio, *m;* portento, *m.* **child p.,** niño prodigio
**produce** /*v.* prə'dus; *n.* 'prɒdus, 'proudus/ *vt* producir; dar frutos; (show) mostrar, presentar; (take out) sacar; (occasion) causar, traer consigo, ocasionar; (goods) fabricar, manufacturar; (of shares, etc.) rendir; *Geom.* prolongar; (a play) poner en escena. —*n* producto, *m;* víveres, comestibles, *m pl*
**producer** /prə'dusər/ *n* productor (-ra); *Theat.* director de escena, *m*

**product** /'prɒdəkt/ *n* producto, *m;* (result) fruto, resultado, *m,* consecuencia, *f; Math.* producto, *m*
**production** /prə'dʌkʃən/ *n* producción, *f;* producto, *m; Geom.* prolongación, *f;* (of a play) dirección escénica, *f;* (performance) producción, *f.* **p. cost,** coste de producción, *m*
**productive** /prə'dʌktɪv/ *a* productivo
**productivity** /,proudʌk'tɪvɪti/ *n* productividad, *f*
**profanation** /,prɒfə'neɪʃən/ *n* profanación, *f*
**profane** /prə'fein/ *a* profano; sacrílego, blasfemo. —*vt* profanar
**profaner** /prə'feinər/ *n* profanador (-ra)
**profanity** /prə'fænɪti/ *n* profanidad, *f;* blasfemia, *f*
**profess** /prə'fɛs/ *vt* (assert) afirmar, manifestar; declarar; (a faith, a profession, teach) profesar; (feign) fingir; (pretend) tener pretensiones de. —*vi* (as a monk or nun) tomar estado, entrar en religión. **He professed himself surprised,** Se declaró sorprendido
**professed** /prə'fɛst/ *a* declarado; *Eccl.* profeso; ostensible, fingido
**profession** /prə'fɛʃən/ *n* profesión, *f;* carrera, *f;* declaración, *f.* **p. of faith,** profesión de fe, *f.* **the learned professions,** las carreras liberales
**professional** /prə'fɛʃənl/ *a* profesional; de la profesión; de profesión; de carrera. **p. diplomat,** diplomático (-ca) de carrera. **p. etiquette,** etiqueta profesional, *f.* **p. man,** hombre profesional, *m;* hombre de carrera liberal, *m*
**professor** /prə'fɛsər/ *n* catedrático (-ca), profesor (-ra)
**professorate** /prə'fɛsərɪt/ *n* profesorado, *m*
**professorial** /,proufə'sɔriəl/ *a* de catedrático; de profesor
**professorship** /prə'fɛsər,ʃɪp/ *n* cátedra, *f*
**proffer** /'prɒfər/ *vt* proponer; ofrecer. —*n* oferta, *f*
**proficiency** /prə'fɪʃənsi/ *n* pericia, habilidad, *f*
**proficient** /prə'fɪʃənt/ *a* proficiente, experto, adepto, perito
**profile** /'proufail/ *n* perfil, *m.* —*vt* perfilar. **in p.,** de perfil
**profit** /'prɒfɪt/ *n* provecho, *m;* utilidad, *f;* ventaja, *f; Com.* ganancia, *f, vt* aprovechar. —*vi* ganar; *Com.* sacar ganancia. **to p. by,** aprovechar. **gross p.,** ganancia total, *f.* **p. and loss,** ganancias y pérdidas, *f pl.* **p. sharing,** participación en las ganancias, participación de utilidades, *f*
**profitable** /'prɒfɪtəbəl/ *a* provechoso, útil, ventajoso; lucrativo. **p. use,** aprovechamiento, *m*
**profitably** /'prɒfɪtəbli/ *adv* con provecho, provechosamente; lucrativamente
**profiteer** /,prɒfɪ'tɪər/ *n* estraperlista, *mf*
**profit incentive** *n* acicate del lucro, *m*
**profitless** /'prɒfɪtlɪs/ *a* sin provecho, infructuoso, inútil
**profligacy** /'prɒflɪgəsi/ *n* libertinaje, *m*
**profligate** /'prɒflɪgɪt/ *a* licencioso, disoluto. —*n* libertino, *m*
**profound** /prə'faund/ *a* profundo
**profundity** /prə'fʌndɪti/ *n* profundidad, *f*
**profuse** /prə'fyus/ *a* profuso; pródigo; lujoso
**profusely** /prə'fyusli/ *adv* profusamente; pródigamente; lujosamente
**profusion** /prə'fyuʒən/ *n* profusión, abundancia, *f;* prodigalidad, *f;* exceso, *m*
**progenitor** /prou'dʒɛnɪtər/ *n* progenitor, *m;* (ancestor) antepasado, *m*
**progeny** /'prɒdʒəni/ *n* prole, *f*
**prognosis** /prɒg'nousɪs/ *n* prognosis, *f;* presagio, *m; Med.* pronóstico, *m*
**prognosticate** /prɒg'nɒstɪ,keit/ *vt* pronosticar, presagiar
**prognostication** /prɒg,nɒstɪ'keiʃən/ *n* pronosticación, *f;* pronóstico, presagio, augurio, *m*
**program** /'prougræm/ *n* programa, *m*
**progress** /*n.* 'prɒgrɛs; *v.* prə'grɛs/ *n* progreso, *m;* avance, *m;* (betterment) mejora, *f;* (of events) marcha, *f.* —*vi* avanzar, marchar; (improve) progresar, adelantar; mejorar. **to make p.,** adelantarse; hacer progresos
**progression** /prə'grɛʃən/ *n* progresión, *f*
**progressive** /prə'grɛsɪv/ *a* progresivo; avanzado; *Polit.* progresista. —*n Polit.* progresista, *mf*

**progressiveness** /prəˈgresɪvnɪs/ n carácter progresivo, m

**prohibit** /prouˈhɪbɪt/ vt prohibir; defender; (prevent) impedir, privar. **His health prohibited him from doing it,** Su salud le impidió hacerlo

**prohibition** /ˌprouəˈbɪʃən/ n prohibición, f; interdicción, f; (of alcohol) prohibicionismo, m

**prohibitionist** /ˌprouəˈbɪʃənɪst/ n prohibicionista, mf

**prohibitive** /prouˈhɪbɪtɪv/ a prohibitivo, prohibitorio

**project** /v. prəˈdʒɛkt; n. ˈprɒdʒɛkt/ vt (all meanings) proyectar. —vi sobresalir; destacarse. —n proyectil, plan, m

**projectile** /prəˈdʒɛktɪl/ n proyectil, m, a arrojadizo

**projecting** /prəˈdʒɛktɪŋ/ a saliente; (of teeth) saltón

**projection** /prəˈdʒɛkʃən/ n (hurling) lanzamiento, m; prominencia, protuberancia, f; (other meanings) proyección, f

**projector** /prəˈdʒɛktər/ n proyectista, mf; proyector, m

**proletarian** /ˌprouliˈtɛəriən/ a proletario

**proletariate** /ˌprouliˈtɛərɪt/ n proletariado, m

**prolific** /prəˈlɪfɪk/ a prolífico; fecundo, fértil

**prolix** /prouˈlɪks/ a prolijo

**prolixity** /prouˈlɪksɪti/ n prolijidad, f

**prolog** /ˈproulɔg/ n prólogo, m, vt prologar

**prolong** /prəˈlɔŋ/ vt prolongar

**prolongation** /ˌproulɔŋˈgeɪʃən/ n prolongación, f

**promenade** /ˌprɒməˈneɪd, -ˈnɑd/ n paseo, m; bulevar, m; avenida, f. —vi pasearse. —vt recorrer, andar por, pasearse por. **p. deck,** cubierta de paseo, f

**Promethean** /prəˈmiθiən/ a de Prometeo

**prominence** /ˈprɒmənəns/ n prominencia, f; protuberancia, f; eminencia, f; importancia, f

**prominent** /ˈprɒmənənt/ a prominente, saliente; (of eyes, teeth) saltón; (distinguished) eminente, distinguido. **They placed the vase in a p. position,** Pusieron el florero muy a la vista. **to play a p. part,** desempeñar un papel importante. **p. eyes, ojos** saltones, m pl

**promiscuous** /prəˈmɪskyuəs/ a promiscuo

**promiscuousness** /prəˈmɪskyuəsnɪs/ n promiscuidad, f

**promise** /ˈprɒmɪs/ n promesa, f; (hope) esperanza, f; (word) palabra, f; (future) porvenir, m. —vt and vi prometer. **a young man of p.,** un joven de porvenir. **to break one's p.,** faltar a su palabra; no cumplir una promesa. **to keep one's p.,** guardar su palabra; cumplir su promesa. **to p. and do nothing,** apuntar y no dar. **under p. of,** bajo palabra de. **p. of marriage,** palabra de matrimonio, f

**promised** /ˈprɒmɪst/ a prometido. **P. Land,** Tierra de promisión, f

**promising** /ˈprɒməsɪŋ/ a que promete bien, que promete mucho; prometedor; (of the future, etc.) halagüeño; (of persons) que llegará

**promissory** /ˈprɒməˌsɔri/ a promisorio. **p. note,** pagaré, abonaré, m

**promontory** /ˈprɒmənˌtɔri/ n promontorio, m

**promote** /prəˈmout/ vt fomentar, promover; provocar; (aid) favorecer, proteger; avanzar; estimular; (to a post) ascender; (an act bill) promover; Com. negociar

**promoter** /prəˈmoutər/ n promotor (-ra); instigador (-ra); (Theat. etc.) empresario, m

**promotion** /prəˈmouʃən/ n (encouragement) fomento, m; (furtherance) adelanto, m; protección, f, favorecimiento, m; (in employment, etc.) promoción, f, ascenso, m; (of a company, etc.) creación, f

**prompt** /prɒmpt/ a pronto; diligente; presuroso; puntual; rápido; Com. inmediato. —vt impulsar, incitar, mover; dictar; insinuar; Theat. apuntar; (remind) recordar. **He came at five o'clock p.,** Vino a las cinco en punto. **p. book,** libro del traspunte, m. **p. box,** concha (del apuntador), f

**prompter** /ˈprɒmptər/ n Theat. apuntador, (in the wings) traspunte, m

**prompting** /ˈprɒmptɪŋ/ n sugestión, f; instigación, f; pl **promptings,** impulso, m; (of the heart, etc.) dictados, m pl

**promptitude** /ˈprɒmptɪˌtud/ n prontitud, presteza, f; prisa, expedición, f; puntualidad, f

**promptly** /ˈprɒmptli/ adv inmediatamente, en seguida; con prontitud, con celeridad; puntualmente

**promptness** /ˈprɒmptnɪs/ n See **promptitude**

**promulgate** /ˈprɒməlˌgeɪt/ vt promulgar; divulgar, diseminar

**promulgation** /ˌprɒməlˈgeɪʃən/ n promulgación, f; divulgación, diseminación, f

**prone** /proun/ a postrado; inclinado, propenso

**proneness** /ˈprounɪs/ n postración, f; inclinación, tendencia, propensión, f

**prong** /prɔŋ/ n (pitchfork) horquilla, f; (of a fork) diente, m, púa, f

**pronged** /prɔŋd/ a dentado, con púas

**pronoun** /ˈprouˌnaun/ n pronombre, m

**pronounce** /prəˈnauns/ vt pronunciar; declarar; articular

**pronounced** /prəˈnaunst/ a marcado; perceptible; bien definido

**pronouncement** /prəˈnaunsmənt/ n pronunciamiento, m

**pronunciation** /prəˌnʌnsiˈeɪʃən/ n pronunciación, f; articulación, f

**proof** /pruf/ n prueba, f; demostración, f; ensayo, m; Law. testimonio, m; (Photo. Print.) prueba, f; Math. comprobación, f, a hecho a prueba (de); impenetrable (a); Fig. insensible (a). —vt (raincoats, etc.) impermeabilizar. **in p. whereof,** en fe de lo cual. **p. against bombs,** a prueba de bombas. **p. reading,** corrección de pruebas, f

**prop** /prɒp/ n apoyo, puntal, estribadero, m; (for a tree) horca, f, rodrigón, m; Naut. escora, f; Fig. báculo, m, columna, f, apoyo, m. —vt apoyar; apuntalar; (a tree) ahorquillar; (a building) acodalar; Naut. escorar; Fig. sostener. **He propped himself against the wall,** Se apoyó en el muro, Se arrimó al muro

**propaganda** /ˌprɒpəˈgændə/ n propaganda, f

**propagandist** /ˌprɒpəˈgændɪst/ n propagandista, mf

**propagate** /ˈprɒpəˌgeɪt/ vt propagar. —vi propagarse

**propagation** /ˌprɒpəˈgeɪʃən/ n propagación, f

**propagator** /ˈprɒpəˌgeɪtər/ n propagador (-ra)

**propel** /prəˈpɛl/ vt propulsar, empujar, mover

**propeller** /prəˈpɛlər/ n propulsor, m; Mech. hélice, f

**propelling** /prəˈpɛlɪŋ/ n propulsión, f. **p. pencil,** lapicero, m

**propensity** /prəˈpɛnsɪti/ n propensión, tendencia, inclinación, f

**proper** /ˈprɒpər/ a propio; apropiado; correcto; decente; (prim) afectado; serio, formal; (exact) justo, exacto; (suitable (for)) bueno (para), apto (para); (true) verdadero; (characteristic) peculiar; Herald. natural; (with rascal, etc.) redomado; (handsome) guapo. **If you think it p.,** Si te parece bien. **p. noun,** nombre propio, m

**properly** /ˈprɒpərli/ adv decentemente; correctamente; propiamente; bien. **to do (a thing) p.,** hacer algo bien. **p. speaking,** propiamente dicho, hablando con propiedad

**propertied** /ˈprɒpərtid/ a propietario, hacendado; (rich) pudiente, adinerado

**property** /ˈprɒpərti/ n propiedad, f; (belongings) bienes, m pl; posesiones, f pl; (estate) hacienda, f; (quality) cualidad, f; pl **properties,** Theat. accesorios, m pl. **personal p.,** bienes muebles, m pl; cosas personales, f pl. **real p.,** bienes raíces, m pl. **p. man,** Theat. encargado de los accesorios, m. **p. owner,** propietario (-ia). **p. tax,** contribución sobre la propiedad, f

**prophecy** /ˈprɒfəsi/ n profecía, f; predicción, f

**prophesier** /ˈprɒfəˌsiər/ n See **prophet**

**prophesy** /ˈprɒfəˌsai/ vt profetizar; presagiar, predecir. —vi hacer profecías

**prophet** /ˈprɒfɪt/ n profeta, m

**prophetess** /ˈprɒfɪtɪs/ n profetisa, f

**prophetic** /prəˈfɛtɪk/ a profético

**prophylactic** /ˌproufəˈlæktɪk/ a and n profiláctico, m

**propinquity** /prouˈpɪŋkwɪti/ n propincuidad, proximidad, f; (relationship) parentesco, m

**propitiate** /prəˈpɪʃiˌeɪt/ vt propiciar; apaciguar, conciliar

**propitiation** /prəˌpɪʃiˈeɪʃən/ n propiciación, f

**propitiator** /prəˈpɪʃiˌeɪtər/ n propiciador (-ra)

**propitiatory** /prə'pɪʃɪə,tɔri/ *a* propiciador
**propitious** /prə'pɪʃəs/ *a* propicio, favorable
**propitiousness** /prə'pɪʃəsnɪs/ *n* lo propicio
**proportion** /prə'pɔrʃən/ *n* proporción, *f*; parte, *f*; porción, *f*; *pl* **proportions**, proporciones, *f pl*; dimensiones, *f pl.* —*vt* proporcionar; repartir, distribuir. **in p.**, en proporción; conforme (a), según; *Com.* a prorrata. **in p. as**, a medida que. **out of p.**, desproporcionado. **He has lost all sense of p.**, Ha perdido su equilibrio (mental)
**proportional** /prə'pɔrʃənl/ *a* proporcional; en proporción (a); proporcionado (a). **p. representation**, representación proporcional, *f*
**proportionally** /prə'pɔrʃənļi/ *adv* proporcionalmente, en proporción
**proportionate** /*a.* prə'pɔrʃənɪt; *v.* -,neit/ *a* proporcionado; proporcional. —*vt* proporcionar
**proportionately** /prə'pɔrʃənɪtli/ *adv* See **proportionally**
**proposal** /prə'pouzəl/ *n* proposición, *f*; oferta, *f*; (plan) propósito, proyecto, *m.* **p. of marriage**, oferta de matrimonio, *f*
**propose** /prə'pouz/ *vt* proponer; ofrecer; (a toast) dar, brindar. —*vi* pretender, intentar, tener la intención de; pensar; (marriage) declararse
**proposer** /prə'pouzər/ *n* proponente, *m*; (of a motion) autor (-ra) de una proposición
**proposition** /,prɒpə'zɪʃən/ *n* proposición, *f*; (plan) proyecto, propósito, *m*
**propound** /prə'paund/ *vt* proponer; plantear, presentar
**proprietary** /prə'praiɪ,tɛri/ *a* propietario; de propiedad
**proprietor** /prə'praiɪtər/ *n* propietario, *m*; dueño, *m*
**proprietorship** /prə'praiɪtərˌʃɪp/ *n* propiedad, pertenencia, *f*
**proprietress** /prə'praiɪtrɪs/ *n* propietaria, *f*; dueña, *f*
**propriety** /prə'praiɪti/ *n* decoro, *m*; conveniencia, *f*; corrección, *f*
**propulsion** /prə'pʌlʃən/ *n* propulsión, *f*
**propulsive** /prə'pʌlsɪv/ *a* propulsor
**prorogation** /,prourou'geiʃən/ *n* prorrogación, *f*
**prorogue** /prou'roug/ *vt* prorrogar, suspender (la sesión de una asamblea legislativa)
**prosaic** /prou'zeiɪk/ *a* prosaico
**pros and cons** /'prouz ən 'kɒnz/ el pro y el contra
**proscenium** /prou'siniəm/ *n* proscenio, *m*
**proscribe** /prou'skraib/ *vt* proscribir
**proscription** /prou'skrɪpʃən/ *n* proscripción, *f*
**prose** /prouz/ *n* prosa, *f.* **p. writer**, prosista, *mf*
**prosecute** /'prɒsɪ,kyut/ *vt* proseguir, llevar adelante; (*Law.* a person) procesar; (*Law.* a claim) pedir en juicio
**prosecution** /,prɒsɪ'kyuʃən/ *n* prosecución, *f*; cumplimiento, *m*; *Law.* acusación, *f*; (*Law.* party) parte actora, *f.* **in the p. of his duty**, en el cumplimiento de su deber
**prosecutor** /'prɒsɪ,kyutər/ *n* demandante, actor, *m.* **public p.**, fiscal, *m*
**proselyte** /'prɒsə,lait/ *n* prosélito, *m*
**proselytism** /'prɒsəlɪ,tɪzəm/ *n* proselitismo, *m*
**prose writer** *n* prosador, *m*
**prosody** /'prɒsədi/ *n* prosodia, *f*
**prospect** /'prɒspɛkt/ *n* perspectiva, *f*; esperanza, *f*; probabilidad, *f*; (in mining) indicio de filón, *m*; criadero (de oro, etc.), *m.* —*vi* explorar; (of a mine) prometer (bien), dar buenas esperanzas. —*vt* explorar, inspeccionar; examinar. **He is a man with good prospects**, Es un hombre de porvenir
**prospecting** /'prɒspɛktɪŋ/ *n* la prospección, *f*
**prospective** /prə'spɛktɪv/ *a* en expectativa, futuro; previsor
**prospector** /'prɒspɛktər/ *n* explorador, operador, *m*
**prospectus** /prə'spɛktəs/ *n* prospecto, programa, *m*
**prosper** /'prɒspər/ *vi* prosperar. —*vt* favorecer, prosperar
**prosperity** /prɒ'spɛrɪti/ *n* prosperidad, *f*
**prosperous** /'prɒspərəs/ *a* próspero; favorable
**prostate** /'prɒsteit/ *n* próstata, *f*
**prostitute** /'prɒstɪ,tut/ *n* prostituta, *f*, *vt* prostituir
**prostitution** /,prɒstɪ'tuʃən/ *n* prostitución, *f*

**prostrate** /'prɒstreit/ *a* tendido; postrado; abatido. —*vt* derribar; arruinar; (by grief, etc.) postrar; (oneself) postrarse
**prostration** /prɒ'streiʃən/ *n* postración, *f*; abatimiento, *m.* **nervous p.**, neurastenia, *f*
**prosy** /'prouzi/ *a* aburrido, árido; pedestre, prosaico; verboso, prolijo
**protagonist** /prou'tægənɪst/ *n* protagonista, *mf*
**protean** /'proutiən/ *a* proteico
**protect** /prə'tɛkt/ *vt* proteger
**protection** /prə'tɛkʃən/ *n* protección, *f*; defensa, *f*; garantía, *f*; abrigo, *m*; refugio, *m*; (passport) salvoconducto, *m*; *Polit.* proteccionismo, *m*
**protectionism** /prə'tɛkʃə,nɪzəm/ *n* proteccionismo, *m*
**protectionist** /prə'tɛkʃənɪst/ *n* proteccionista, *mf*
**protective** /prə'tɛktɪv/ *a* protector; *Polit.* proteccionista
**protector** /prə'tɛktər/ *n* protector, *m*
**protectorate** /prə'tɛktərɪt/ *n* protectorado, *m*
**protectress** /prou'tɛktrɪs/ *n* protectriz, *f*
**protein** /'proutin, -tiɪn/ *n* proteína, *f*
**protest** /*v.* prə'tɛst, 'proutɛst; *n.* 'proutɛst/ *vt* protestar; *Law.* hacer el protesto de una letra de cambio. —*vi* declarar; insistir (en); hacer una protesta. —*n* protesta, *f*; *Law.* protesto, *m.* **under p.**, bajo protesta. **to p. against**, protestar contra
**Protestant** /'prɒtəstənt/ *a* and *n* protestante, *mf*
**Protestantism** /'prɒtəstən,tɪzəm/ *n* protestantismo, *m*
**protestation** /,prɒtə'steiʃən/ *n* protestación, *f*
**protester** /'proutɛstər/ *n* el, *m*, (*f*, la) que protesta
**protest literature** *n* literatura de denuncia, *f*
**protocol** /'proutə,kɔl/ *n* protocolo, *m*, *vt* protocolizar
**protoplasm** /'proutə,plæzəm/ *n* protoplasma, *m*
**prototype** /'proutə,taip/ *n* prototipo, *m*
**protract** /prou'trækt/ *vt* prolongar; dilatar
**protracted** /prou'træktɪd/ *a* prolongado; largo
**protraction** /prou'trækʃən/ *n* prolongación, *f*
**protractor** /prou'træktər/ *n* (*Geom.* and *Surv.*) transportador, *m.* **p. muscle**, músculo extensor, *m*
**protrude** /prou'trud/ *vt* sacar fuera. —*vi* salir fuera; sobresalir
**protuberance** /prou'tubərəns/ *n* protuberancia, *f*
**protuberant** /prou'tubərənt/ *a* protuberante, prominente
**proud** /praud/ *a* orgulloso; arrogante; noble; glorioso; magnífico; soberbio. **to be p.**, enorgullecerse. **to make p.**, enorgullecer; hacer orgulloso. **to be p. of**, ser orgulloso de, pagarse de, gloriarse en. **p. flesh**, carnosidad, *f*, bezo, *m*
**proudly** /'praudli/ *adv* con orgullo, orgullosamente
**provable** /'pruvəbəl/ *a* demostrable
**prove** /pruv/ *vt* probar; demostrar; (experience) experimentar, sufrir; poner a prueba; (a will) verificar; (show) mostrar; confirmar. —*vi* resultar, salir (bien or mal)
**provenance** /'prɒvənəns/ *n* origen, *m*
**Provençal** /,prouvən'sal, ,prɒvã-/ *a* provenzal. —*n* provenzal, *mf*; (language) provenzal, *m*
**Provence** /prə'vɒns/ Provenza, *f*
**provender** /'prɒvəndər/ *n* forraje, *m*; *Inf.* provisiones, *f pl*
**proverb** /'prɒvərb/ *n* refrán, *m*; proverbio, *m.* **collection of proverbs**, refranero, *m.* **Book of Proverbs**, Proverbios, *m pl*
**proverbial** /prə'vɜrbiəl/ *a* proverbial
**proverbially** /prə'vɜrbiəli/ *adv* proverbialmente
**provide** /prə'vaid/ *vt* proporcionar, dar; proveer, surtir, suplir; (stipulate) estipular; preparar (por); tomar precauciones (contra); sufragar los gastos (de); proporcionar medios de vida (a); señalar una pensión (a). **to p. oneself with**, proveerse de
**provided (that)** /prə'vaidɪd/ *conjunc* si; a condición de que, siempre que, con tal que
**providence** /'prɒvɪdəns/ *n* providencia, *f*
**provident** /'prɒvɪdənt/ *a* próvido, previsor, prudente; económico
**providential** /,prɒvɪ'dɛnʃəl/ *a* providencial
**providentially** /,prɒvɪ'dɛnʃəli/ *adv* providencialmente
**providently** /'prɒvɪdəntli/ *adv* próvidamente, prudentemente
**provider** /prə'vaidər/ *n* proveedor (-ra)

**province** /'prɒvɪns/ n provincia, f; esfera, f; función, incumbencia, f

**provincial** /prə'vɪnʃəl/ a provincial, de provincia; provinciano. —n provinciano (-na); *Eccl.* provincial, m

**provincialism** /prə'vɪnʃə,lɪzəm/ n provincialismo, m

**provision** /prə'vɪʒən/ n provisión, f; (stipulation) estipulación, f; pl **provisions**, provisiones, f pl; víveres, comestibles, m pl. —vt abastecer, aprovisionar. **to make p. for,** hacer provisión para, proveer de. **to make p. for one's family,** asegurar el porvenir de su familia. **p. merchant,** vendedor (-ra) de comestibles

**provisional** /prə'vɪʒənl/ a provisional, interino

**provisioning** /prə'vɪʒənɪŋ/ n aprovisionamiento, abastecimiento, m

**proviso** /prə'vaizou/ n condición, estipulación, disposición, f

**provisory** /prə'vaizəri/ a provisional; condicional

**provocation** /,prɒvə'keiʃən/ n provocación, f

**provocative** /prə'vɒkətɪv/ a provocativo, provocador

**provocatively** /prə'vɒkətɪvli/ adv de un modo provocativo

**provoke** /prə'vouk/ vt provocar; suscitar; incitar, excitar; (irritate) sacar de madre (a), indignar

**provoker** /prə'voukər/ n provocador (-ra); instigador (-ra)

**provoking** /prə'voukɪŋ/ a provocativo; (irritating) enojoso, irritante

**provost** /'prouvoust *or, esp. in military usage,* 'prouvou/ n preboste, m; (of a college) director, m; (in Scotland) alcalde, m. **p.-marshal,** capitán preboste, m

**prow** /prau/ n proa, f

**prowess** /'prauɪs/ n valor, m, destreza, f; proeza, f

**prowl** /praul/ vi and vt rondar; cazar al acecho

**prowler** /'praulər/ n rondador (-ra); ladrón (-ona)

**proximity** /prɒk'sɪmɪti/ n proximidad, f

**proximo** /'prɒksə,mou/ adv en (or del) mes próximo

**proxy** /'prɒksi/ n poder, m; delegación, f; apoderado, m; delegado (-da); substituto (-ta). **to be married by p.,** casarse por poderes

**prude** /prud/ n mojigata, beata, f

**prudence** /'prudns/ n prudencia, f

**prudent** /'prudnt/ a prudente

**prudently** /'prudntli/ adv con prudencia

**prudery** /'prudəri/ n mojigatería, beatería, damería, gazmoñería, f

**prudish** /'prudɪʃ/ a mojigato, gazmoño, remilgado

**prune** /prun/ n ciruela pasa, f; color de ciruela, m, vt podar; (cut) cortar; reducir

**pruning** /'prunɪŋ/ n poda, f; reducción, f. **p. knife,** podadera, f

**prurient** /'pruriənt/ a lascivo, lujurioso, salaz

**Prussia** /'prʌʃə/ Prusia, f

**Prussian** /'prʌʃən/ a and n prusiano (-na). **P. blue,** azul de Prusia, f

**prussic acid** /'prʌsɪk/ n acido prúsico, m

**pry** /prai/ vi escudriñar; acechar, espiar, fisgonear; (meddle) entremeterse, meterse donde no le llaman. —vt See **prize**

**prying** /'praiɪŋ/ n fisgoneo, m; curiosidad, f, a fisgón, curioso

**psalm** /sɑm/ n salmo, m. **to sing psalms,** salmodiar

**psalmist** /'sɑmɪst/ n salmista, m

**psaltery** /'sɔltəri/ n salterio, m

**pseudo-** a seudo. **p.-learned,** erudito a la violeta

**pseudonym** /'sudnɪm/ n seudónimo, m

**psychiatrist** /sɪ'kaiətrɪst, sai-/ n siquiatra, m

**psychiatry** /sɪ'kaiətri, sai-/ n siquiatría, f

**psychic** /'saikɪk/ a síquico

**psychoanalysis** /,saikouə'næləsɪs/ n sicoanálisis, mf

**psychoanalyst** /,saikou'ænlɪst/ n sicoanalista, mf

**psychoanalyze** /,saikou'ænl,aiz/ vt sicoanalizar

**psychological** /,saikə'lɒdʒɪkəl/ a sicológico

**psychologist** /sai'kɒlədʒɪst/ n sicólogo (-ga)

**psychology** /sai'kɒlədʒi/ n sicología, f

**psychopathic** /,saikə'pæθɪk/ a sicopático

**psychosis** /sai'kousɪs/ n sicosis, f

**psychotherapy** /,saikou'θerəpi/ n sicoterapia, f

**ptomaine poisoning** /'toumein/ n intoxicación por tomaínas, f

**puberty** /'pyubərti/ n pubertad, f

**pubescent** /pyu'besənt/ a púber

**pubic** /'pyubɪk/ a púbico

**pubis** /'pyubɪs/ n pubis, m

**public** /'pʌblɪk/ a and n público m. **in p.,** en público. **p. assistance,** asistencia pública, f. **p. funds,** hacienda pública, f. **p. health,** higiene pública, f. **p.-house,** taberna, f. **p. opinion,** opinión pública, f. *Inf.* el qué dirán. **p.-spirited,** patriótico. **p. thoroughfare,** vía pública, f. **p. works,** obras públicas, f pl

**publican** /'pʌblɪkən/ n tabernero, m

**publication** /,pʌblɪ'keiʃən/ n publicación, f

**publicist** /'pʌbləsɪst/ n publicista, mf

**publicity** /pʌ'blɪsɪti/ n publicidad, f

**publicity agent** n publicista, mf

**publish** /'pʌblɪʃ/ vt publicar, divulgar, difundir; (a book, etc.) dar a luz, dar a la prensa, publicar; (of a publisher) editar. **to p. abroad,** pregonar a los cuatro vientos. **to p. banns of marriage,** correr las amonestaciones

**publisher** /'pʌblɪʃər/ n publicador (-ra); (of books) editor (-ra)

**publishing** /'pʌblɪʃɪŋ/ n publicación, f. **p. house,** casa editorial, f. **the p. world,** el mundo de la edición, m

**puck** /pʌk/ n trasgo, m; diablillo, picaruelo, m

**pucker** /'pʌkər/ vt (one's brow, etc.) fruncir; (crease) arrugar. —vi arrugarse. —n frunce, m; arruga, f; (fold) bolsa, f

**puckering** /'pʌkərɪŋ/ n fruncido, m; arrugas, f pl

**puckish** /'pʌkɪʃ/ a travieso

**pudding** /'pudɪŋ/ n pudín, budín, m. **black p.,** morcilla, f

**puddle** /'pʌdl/ n charco, m

**puerile** /'pyuəril/ a pueril

**puerility** /pyuə'rɪlɪti/ n puerilidad, f

**puerperal** /pyu'ɜrpərəl/ a puerperal. **p. fever,** fiebre puerperal, f

**Puerto Rican** /'pwɛrtə 'rikən, 'pɔr-/ a and n puertorriqueño (-ña)

**puff** /pʌf/ vt and vi (blow) soplar; (at a pipe, etc.) chupar; (smoke) lanzar bocanadas de humo; (make pant) hacer jadear; (advertise) dar bombo (a); (distend) hinchar; (make conceited) envanecerse; (of a train, etc.) bufar; resoplar. —n soplo, m; (of smoke, etc.) bocanada, f; (of an engine, etc.) resoplido, bufido, m; (for powder) borla (para polvos), f; (pastry) bollo, m; (advertisement) bombo, m. **to be puffed up,** *Fig.* hincharse, inflarse. **p. of wind,** ráfaga de aire, f. **p.-ball,** bejín, m. **p.-pastry,** hojaldre, m, or f. **p.-sleeve,** manga de bullón, f

**puffiness** /'pʌfinɪs/ n hinchazón, f

**puffy** /'pʌfi/ a (of the wind) a ráfagas; (panting) jadeante; (swollen) hinchado

**pug** /pʌg/ n (dog) doguino, m. **p.-nosed,** de nariz respingona

**pugilism** /'pyudʒə,lɪzəm/ n boxeo, pugilato, m

**pugilist** /'pyudʒəlɪst/ n pugilista, mf; boxeador, m

**pugnacious** /pʌg'neiʃəs/ a pugnaz, belicoso

**pugnacity** /pʌg'næsɪti/ n pugnacidad, belicosidad, f

**pull** /pul/ n tirón, m; sacudida, f; golpe, m; (row) paseo en barco, m; (with the oars) golpe (de remos), m; (at a bell) tirón, m; (bell-rope) tirador, m; (at a bottle) trago, m; (strain) fuerza, f; atracción, f; (struggle) lucha, f; (advantage) ventaja, f; (influence) influencia, f. **to give a p.,** tirar (de), dar un tirón (a). **to have plenty of p.,** *Inf.* tener buenas aldabas

**pull** /pul/ vt tirar (de); (drag) arrastrar; (extract) sacar; (a boat) remar; (gather) coger; *Print.* imprimir. **He pulled the trigger (of his gun),** Apretó el gatillo. **He was sitting by the fire pulling at his pipe,** Estaba sentado cerca del fuego fumando su pipa. **to p. a hat well down on the head,** calarse el sombrero. **to p. a person's leg,** tomar el pelo (a). **to p. oneself together,** componer el semblante, serenarse; recobrar el aplomo; (tidy oneself) arreglarse. **to p. apart,** vt separar; romper en dos. —vi separarse; romper en dos. **to p. away,** vt arrancar; quitar. —vi tirar con esfuerzo. **to p. back,** tirar hacia atrás; hacer retroceder (a); retener. **to p. down,** hacer bajar, obligar a bajar; (objects) bajar; (buildings) derribar, demoler; (humble) humillar; degradar; (weaken) debilitar. **to p. in,** tirar hacia dentro; hacer entrar; (a horse) enfrenar;

(expenditure) reducir. **to p. off,** arrancar; (clothes) quitarse; (a deal) cerrar (un trato), concluir con éxito; (win) ganar. **to p. on,** *vt* (gloves, etc.) meterse; ponerse. —*vi* seguir remando. **to p. open,** abrir; abrir rápidamente. **to p. out,** hacer salir; obligar a salir; (teeth, daggers, etc.) sacar; (hair) arrancar. **to p. round, through,** *vt* ayudar a reponerse (a); sacar de un aprieto. —*vi* restablecerse; reponerse, cobrar la salud, sanar. **to p. together,** obrar de acuerdo; (get on) llevarse (bien or mal). **He pulled himself together very quickly,** Se repuso muy pronto. **to p. up,** *vt* montar, subir; (a horse) sofrenar; (stop) parar; (by the root) desarraigar, extirpar; (interrupt) interrumpir; (scold) reñir. —*vi* parar(se); (restrain oneself) reprimirse, contenerse

**pullet** /'pʊlɪt/ *n* polla, *f*

**pulley** /'pʊli/ *n* polea, *f*; *Naut.* garrucha, *f.* **p. wheel,** roldana, *f*

**pulling** /'pʊlɪŋ/ *n* tracción, *f*; tirada, *f*; arranque, *m*

**pullover** /'pʊl,oʊvər/ *n* jersey, *m*

**pullulate** /'pʌlyə,leit/ *vi* pulular

**pulmonary** /'pʌlmə,nɛri/ *a* pulmonar

**pulp** /pʌlp/ *n* pulpa, *f*; (of fruit) carne, *f*; (paper) pasta, *f*; (of teeth) bulbo dentario, *m.* —*vt* reducir a pulpa; deshacer (el papel). **to beat to a p.,** *Inf.* poner como un pulpo

**pulpit** /'pʊlpɪt, 'pʌl-/ *n* púlpito, *m*

**pulpy** /'pʌlpi/ *a* pulposo; *Bot.* carnoso

**pulsate** /'pʌlseit/ *vi* pulsar, latir

**pulsation** /pʌl'seiʃən/ *n* pulsación, *f*, latido, *m*

**pulsatory** /'pʌlsə,tɔri/ *a* pulsante, pulsativo, latiente

**pulse** /pʌls/ *n* pulso, *m*; pulsación, *f*, latido, *m*; vibración, *f*; (vegetable) legumbre, *f*, *vi* pulsar, latir; vibrar. **to take a person's p.,** tomar el pulso (a)

**pulverization** /,pʌlvərə'zeiʃən/ *n* pulverización, *f*

**pulverize** /'pʌlvə,raiz/ *vt* pulverizar

**puma** /'pyumə, 'pu-/ *n* puma, *f*

**pumice** /'pʌmɪs/ *n* piedra pómez, *f*

**pummel** /'pʌməl/ *vt* aporrear

**pump** /pʌmp/ *n* *Mech.* bomba, *f*; (for water, etc.) aguatocha, *f*; *Naut.* pompa, *f*; (slipper) escarpín, *m*, *vt* bombear, extraer por medio de una bomba; (inflate) inflar; (for information) sondear, sonsacar. **hand-p.,** bomba de mano, *f.* **to work a p.,** darle a la bomba

**pumpkin** /'pʌmpkɪn/ *n* calabaza, *f*, (Chile) zapallo *m*; (plant) calabacera, *f*

**pun** /pʌn/ *n* retruécano, *m*

**punch** /pʌntʃ/ *n* (drink) ponche, *m*; (blow) puñetazo, golpe, *m*; *Mech.* punzón, *m*; (for tickets, etc.) taladro, *m*; *Inf.* fuerza, *f.* —*vt* (perforate) taladrar, punzar; estampar; (hit) dar un puñetazo (a). **p.-ball,** pelota de boxeo, *f.* **p.-bowl,** ponchera, *f*

**Punchinello** /,pʌntʃə'nɛloʊ/ *n* Polichinela, *m.* **Punch and Judy show,** títeres, *m pl*

**punctilious** /pʌŋk'tiliəs/ *a* formal, puntual, puntilloso

**punctiliousness** /pʌŋk'tiliəsnɪs/ *n* formalidad, puntualidad, *f*

**punctual** /'pʌŋktʃuəl/ *a* puntual

**punctually** /'pʌŋktʃuəli/ *adv* puntualmente

**punctuate** /'pʌŋktʃu,eit/ *vt* puntuar

**punctuation** /,pʌŋktʃu'eiʃən/ *n* puntuación, *f*

**puncture** /'pʌŋktʃər/ *n* pinchazo, *m*; perforación, *f*; *Surg.* punción, *f.* —*vt* pinchar; perforar; punzar. **We have a p. in the right tire,** Tenemos un pinchazo en el neumático derecho

**pungency** /'pʌndʒənsi/ *n* picante, *m*; acerbidad, mordacidad, *f*

**pungent** /'pʌndʒənt/ *a* picante; acerbo, mordaz

**Punic** /'pyunɪk/ *a* púnico, cartaginés

**punish** /'pʌnɪʃ/ *vt* castigar; maltratar

**punishable** /'pʌnɪʃəbəl/ *a* punible

**punishment** /'pʌnɪʃmənt/ *n* castigo, *m*; pena, *f*; maltrato, *m*

**punitive** /'pyunɪtɪv/ *a* punitivo

**punt** /pʌnt/ *n* batea, *f.* —*vt* impeler una batea con una pértiga; ir en batea; (a ball) golpear, dar un puntapié (a)

**puny** /'pyuni/ *a* débil, encanijado; insignificante; pequeño

**pup** /pʌp/ *n* cachorro (-rra). —*vi* parir la perra

**pupa** /'pyupə/ *n* crisálida, *f*

**pupil** /'pyupəl/ *n* alumno (-na), discípulo (-la); (of the eye) pupila, niña (del ojo), *f*; *Law.* pupilo (-la). —*a* escolar. **day p.,** alumno (-na) externo (-na). **p. teacher,** maestro (-tra) alumno (-na)

**puppet** /'pʌpɪt/ *n* títere, marioneta, *f*; muñeca, *f*; (person) maniquí, *m.* **p. show,** función de títeres, *f.* **p. showman,** titiritero, titerero, *m*

**puppy** /'pʌpi/ *n* perrito (-ta), cachorro (-rra)

**purblind** /'pɜr,blaind/ *a* ciego; (short-sighted and *Fig.*) miope

**purchasable** /'pɜrtʃəsəbəl/ *a* comprable, que puede comprarse; *Fig.* sobornable

**purchase** /'pɜrtʃəs/ *vt* comprar; adquirir; *Fig.* lograr, conseguir. —*n* compra, *f*; adquisición, *f*; *Mech.* apalancamiento, *m*; fuerza, *f*; (lever) palanca, *f*, aparejo, *m*; *Fig.* influencia, *f.* **p. tax,** impuesto de lujo, *m*

**purchaser** /'pɜrtʃəsər/ *n* comprador (-ra)

**purchasing** /'pɜrtʃəsɪŋ/ *n* See **purchase. p. power,** poder de adquisición, *m*

**pure** /pyʊr/ *a* puro. **p.-bred,** de raza

**pureness** /'pyʊrnɪs/ *n* pureza, *f*

**purgation** /pɜr'geiʃən/ *n* purgación, *f*

**purgative** /'pɜrgətɪv/ *a* purgativo. —*n* purga, *f*

**purgatorial** /,pɜrgə'tɔriəl/ *a* del purgatorio; (expiatory) purgatorio

**purgatory** /'pɜrgə,tɔri/ *n* purgatorio, *m*

**purge** /pɜrdʒ/ *n* purgación, *f*; (laxative) purga, *f*; *Polit.* depuración, *f*; purificación, *f.* —*vt* purgar; *Polit.* depurar; purificar; expurgar

**purging** /'pɜrdʒɪŋ/ *n* purgación, *f*; *Polit.* depuración, *f*; *Fig.* purificación, *f*

**purification** /,pyʊrəfɪ'keiʃən/ *n* purificación, *f*

**purificatory** /pyʊ'rɪfɪkə,tɔri/ *a* purificador, purificatorio, que purifica

**purifier** /'pyʊrə,faiər/ *n* purificador (-ra)

**purify** /'pyʊrə,fai/ *vt* purificar; (metals) acrisolar; refinar; depurar; (purge) purgar

**purist** /'pyʊrɪst/ *n* purista, *mf*

**puritan** /'pyʊrɪtn/ *a and n* puritano (-na)

**Puritanism** /'pyʊrɪtn,ɪzəm/ *n* puritanismo, *m*

**purity** /'pyʊrɪti/ *n* pureza, *f*

**purl** /pɜrl/ *vi* (of a stream, etc.) murmurar, susurrar. —*n* (of a stream, etc.) susurro, murmullo, *m*

**purlieu** /'pɜrlu/ *n* límite, *m*; *pl* **purlieus,** alrededores, *m pl*, inmediaciones, *f pl*; (slums) barrios bajos, *m pl*

**purling** /'pɜrlɪŋ/ *a* murmurante, que susurra, parlero. —*n* murmullo, susurro, *m*

**purloin** /pər'lɔin/ *vt* hurtar, robar

**purple** /'pɜrpəl/ *n* púrpura, *f*, *a* purpúreo. —*vt* purpurar, teñir de púrpura. —*vi* purpurear

**purplish** /'pɜrplɪʃ/ *a* purpurino, algo purpúreo

**purport** /v. pər'pɔrt; n. 'pɜrpɔrt/ *vt* dar a entender, querer decir; significar; indicar; parecer; tener el objeto de; pretender. —*n* importe, *m*; sentido, significado, *m*; objeto, *m*

**purpose** /'pɜrpəs/ *n* objeto, *m*; propósito, fin, *m*; intención, *f*; proyecto, *m*; designio, *m*; determinación, *f*; efecto, *m*; ventaja, utilidad, *f*, *vi* and *vt* proponerse; pensar, tener el propósito (de), intentar. **It will serve my p.,** Servirá para lo que yo quiero. **for the p. of...,** con el propósito de..., con el fin de... **for purposes of...,** para efectos de... **on p.,** de propósito, expresamente. **to no p.,** inútilmente; en vano

**purposeful** /'pɜrpəsfəl/ *a* resuelto; de substancia

**purposeless** /'pɜrpəslɪs/ *a* irresoluto, vacilante, vago; sin objeto; inútil

**purposely** /'pɜrpəsli/ *adv* expresamente, de intento

**purr** /pɜr/ *vi* ronronear. —*n* ronroneo, *m*

**purse** /pɜrs/ *n* bolsa, *f*; monedero, portamonedas, *m.* **to p. one's lips,** apretar los labios

**purser** /'pɜrsər/ *n* *Naut.* contador, sobrecargo, *m.* **purser's office,** contaduría, *f*

**pursuance** /pər'suəns/ *n* cumplimiento, desempeño, *m*, prosecución, *f.* **in p. of,** en cumplimiento de; en consecuencia de

**pursuant** /pər'suənt/ *a and adv* según; conforme (a), de acuerdo (con); en consecuencia (de)

**pursue** /pər'su/ *vt* perseguir; seguir; (search) buscar; (hunt) cazar; (a submarine, etc.) dar caza (a); (continue) proseguir, continuar; (an occupation) dedicarse (a), ejercer

**pursuer** /pər'suər/ *n* perseguidor (-ra)

**pursuit** /pər'sut/ *n* perseguimiento, *m;* (search) busca, *f;* (hunt) caza, *f;* (performance) prosecución, *f,* desempeño, *m;* (employment) ocupación, *f.* **in p. of,** en busca de. **p. plane,** avión de caza, *m*

**purulence** /'pyʊrələns/ *n* purulencia, *f*

**purulent** /'pyʊrələnt/ *a* purulento

**purvey** /pər'vei/ *vt* proveer, surtir, suministrar; abastecer; procurar

**purveyance** /pər'veiəns/ *n* suministro, abastecimiento, *m;* provisión, *f*

**purveyor** /pər'veiər/ *n* suministrador (-ra), proveedor (-ra), bastecedor (-ra)

**pus** /pʌs/ *n* pus, *m*

**push** /pʊʃ/ *n* empujón, *m;* empellón, *m;* impulso, *m;* (of a person) empuje, *m,* energía, *f;* (attack) ataque, *m;* ofensiva, *f;* (effort) esfuerzo, *m;* crisis, *f,* momento crítico, *m.* **at a push,** *Inf.* en caso de necesidad; en un aprieto, si llegara el caso. **to give the p. to,** *Inf.* despedir. **p.-bicycle,** bicicleta, *f.* **p.-button,** botón, *m;* botón de llamada, *m.* **p.-cart,** carretilla de mano, *f;* (child's) cochecito de niño, *m*

**push** /pʊʃ/ *vt* empujar; (jostle) empellar, dar empellones (a); (a finger in one's eye, etc.) clavar; (a button) apretar; (*Fig.* a person) proteger, ayudar; dar publicidad (a); (a claim, etc.) insistir en; (compel) obligar. —*vi* empujar; dar empujones, empellar. **I am pushed for time,** Me falta tiempo. **He is pushed for money,** Está apurado por dinero. **I have pushed my finger in my eye,** Me he clavado el dedo en el ojo. **to p. against,** empujar contra; lanzarse contra; empellar, dar empellones (a). **to p. aside, away,** apartar con la mano; rechazar, alejar. **to p. back,** (hair, etc.) echar hacia atrás; (people) hacer retroceder; rechazar. **to p. by,** pasar. **to p. down,** hacer bajar; hacer caer; (demolish) derribar. **to p. forward,** *vt* empujar hacia delante, hacer avanzar; (a plan, etc.) llevar adelante. —*vi* adelantarse a empujones; avanzar; seguir el camino. **to p. oneself forward,** *Fig.* abrirse camino; entremeterse; darse importancia. **to p. in,** *vt* empujar; hacer entrar; clavar, hincar. —*vi* entrar a la fuerza; entremeterse. **to p. off,** *vt* apartar con la mano (a); *Inf.* quitar de encima (a). —*vi Naut.* desatracar; *Inf.* ponerse en camino. **to p. open,** empujar, abrir. **to p. out,** *vt* empujar hacia fuera; hacer salir; echar. —*vi Naut.* zarpar. **to p. through,** *vt* (business, etc.) despachar rápidamente; (a crowd) abrirse camino por. —*vi* aparecer, mostrarse. **to p. to,** cerrar. **to p. up,** empujar; hacer subir; (windows, etc.) levantar. **be pushing up the daises,** mirar los árboles de raíz

**pushing** /'pʊʃɪŋ/ *a* enérgico, emprendedor; ambicioso; agresivo. **by p. and shoving,** a empellones, a empujones

**pusillanimity** /ˌpyusələ'nɪmɪti/ *n* pusilanimidad, *f*

**pusillanimous** /ˌpyusə'lænəməs/ *a* pusilánime

**puss** /pʊs/ *n* micho (-cha). **P.! P.!** ¡Miz, Miz!

**pustule** /'pʌstʃʊl/ *n* pústula, *f*

**put** /pʊt/ *vt* poner; colocar; (pour out) echar; aplicar; emplear; (estimate) calcular; presentar; (ask) preguntar; (say) decir; (express) expresar; (a question) hacer; (a problem) plantear; (the weight) lanzar; (rank) estimar. **As the Spanish put it,** Como dicen los españoles. **If I may put it so,** Si puedo expresarlo así, Por así decirlo. **hard put to it,** en dificultades, apurado. **How will you put it to her?** ¿Cómo se lo vas a explicar a ella? **to put ashore,** echar en tierra (a). **to put a child to bed,** acostar a un niño. **to put in order,** arreglar; ordenar. **to put out of joint,** dislocar. **to put out of order,** estropear. **to put to death,** matar; (judicially) ajusticiar. **to put about,** *vt* (a rumor) diseminar, divulgar; (worry) preocupar. —*vi Naut.* virar, cambiar de rumbo. **to put aside,** poner a un lado; descartar; (omit) omitir, pasar por alto de; (fears, etc.) desechar. **to put away,** quitar; guardar; poner en salvo; arrinconar; (thoughts) desechar, ahuyentar; (save) ahorrar; (banish) despedir, alejar; (a wife) repudiar, divorciar; (food) tragar. **to put back,** *vt* echar hacia atrás; hacer retroceder; (replace) devolver, restituir; (the clock) retrasar; (retard) retardar, atrasar. —*vi* volver; *Naut.* volver a puerto. **to put down,** depositar; poner en el suelo; (the blinds) bajar; (an umbrella) cerrar; (a rebellion) sofocar; (gambling, etc.) suprimir; (humble) abatir,

humillar; degradar; (silence) hacer callar; (reduce) reducir, disminuir; (write) apuntar, anotar; (a name) inscribir; (to an account) poner a la cuenta de; (estimate) juzgar, creer; (impute) atribuir. **The book is so interesting that it's hard to put down,** El libro es tan interesante que es difícil dejarlo. **to put forth,** (leaves, flowers, sun's rays) echar; (a book) publicar, dar a luz; (a hand) alargar; (an arm) extender; (show) manifestar, mostrar; (strength, etc.) desplegar; (use) emplear. **to put forward,** avanzar; (a clock) adelantar; (a suggestion, etc.) hacer; (propose) proponer; (a case) presentar. **to put oneself forward,** ponerse en evidencia. **to put in,** poner dentro; (a hand, etc.) introducir; (liquids) echar en; (a government) poner en el poder; (an employment) nombrar, colocar; (insert) insertar; (a claim) presentar; (say) decir. **I shall put in two hours' work before bedtime,** Trabajaré por dos horas antes de acostarme. **He put in a good word for you,** Habló en tu favor. **to put in writing,** poner por escrito. **to put in for,** (an employment) solicitar (un empleo); (as a candidate) presentarse como candidato para. **to put into,** meter dentro (de); (words) expresar; (port) arribar, hacer escala en (un puerto). **to put off,** desechar; (garments) quitarse, despojarse (de); (postpone) diferir, aplazar; (evade) evadir, entretener; quitarse de encima (a), desembarazarse (de); (confuse) desconcertar; (discourage) desanimar; quitar el apetito (a). **to put on,** poner sobre; (clothes) ponerse; (pretend) fingir, afectar; poner; (a play) poner en escena; (the hands of a clock) adelantar; (weight) engordar, poner carnes; (add) añadir; (*Sports.* score) hacer; (bet) apostar; (the light) encender; (assume) tomar; (the brake) frenar; (abuse) abusar (de). engañar. **He put the kettle on the fire,** Puso la tetera en el fuego. **to put on airs and graces,** darse humos. **to put on probation,** dar el azul a, poner a prueba a. **to put on more trains,** poner más trenes. **put one's foot down,** ponerle a fulano el alto. **to put out,** *vt* (eject) echar, expulsar; hacer salir; poner en la calle; (a tenant) deshauciar; (one's hand) alargar; (one's arm) extender; (one's tongue) sacar; (eyes) saltar; (fire, light) apagar, extinguir; (leaves, etc.) echar; (horns) sacar; (head) asomar, sacar; (use) emplear; (give) entregar, dar; (at interest) dar a interés; (finish) terminar; (dislocate) dislocar; (worry) desconcertar; turbar; poner los nervios en punta (a); (anger) enojar; (inconvenience) incomodar; (a book) publicar; (a boat) echar al mar. —*vi* (of a ship) hacerse a la vela, zarpar. **to put out to grass,** mandar a pacer. **We put out to sea,** Nos hicimos a la mar. **to put the cart before the horse,** poner la carreta por delante de los bueyes. **to put through,** (perform) desempeñar; concluir, terminar; (thrust) meter; (subject to) someter a; (exercise) ejercitar; (on the telephone) poner en comunicación (con). **to put together,** juntar; (a machine, etc.) montar, armar. **to put two and two together,** atar cabos. **to put up,** *vt* (sails, a flag) izar; (raise a window) levantar, cerrar; (open a window, or an umbrella) abrir; (one's hands, etc.) poner en alto; (one's fists) alzar; (a prayer) ofrecer, hacer; (as a candidate) nombrar; (for sale) poner (a la venta); (the price) aumentar; (a prescription) preparar; (food) conservar; (pack) empaquetar; (a sword) envainar; (lodge) alojar; (a petition) presentar; (build) construir; *Mech.* montar; (*Inf.* plan) arreglar. —*vi* alojarse. **to put upon,** abusar (de); arruinar; (accuse) imputar, acusar (de). **to put up to,** incitar (a), instigar (a); dar informaciones sobre; poner al corriente (de). **to put up with,** tolerar, soportar, aguantar; resignarse a; contentarse con, conformarse con

**putative** /'pyutətɪv/ *a* supuesto; (of relationship) putativo

**putrefaction** /ˌpyutrə'fækʃən/ *n* putrefacción, *f*

**putrefy** /'pyutrəˌfai/ *vt* pudrir. —*vt* pudrirse, descomponerse

**putrid** /'pyutrɪd/ *a* pútrido, *f; Inf.* apestoso

**putt** /pʌt/ *vt* and *vi* patear.

**putting** /'pʊtɪŋ/ *n* acción de poner, *f;* colocación, *f.* **p. forward of the clock,** adelanto de la hora, *m.* **p. off,** tardanza, dilación, *f.* **p. the weight,** lanzamiento del peso, *m.* **p. up,** (for office) candidatura, *f.* /'pʌtɪŋ/ **p. green,** pista de golf en miniatura, *f*

**putty** /'pʌti/ n masilla, f, vt enmasillar, rellenar con masilla
**puzzle** /'pʌzəl/ vt dejar perplejo; desconcertar; confundir; embrollar. —n problema, m; dificultad, f; enigma, m; (perplexity) perplejidad, f; (game) rompecabezas, m. **to p. out,** procurar resolver; encontrar la solución de. **to p. over,** pensar en, meditar sobre. **I am puzzled by...,** Me trae (or tiene) perplejo...
**pygmy** /'pɪgmi/ a and n pigmeo (-ea)
**pyjamas** /pə'dʒɑməz, -'dʒæməz/ n pijama, m
**pylon** /'pailɒn/ n pilón, m; poste, m; (at an airport) poste de señales, m
**pylorus** /pai'lɔrəs/ n píloro, m
**pyorrhea** /,paiə'riə/ n piorrea, f
**pyramid** /'pɪrəmɪd/ n pirámide, f

**pyramidal** /pɪ'ræmɪdl̩/ a piramidal
**pyre** /pai³r/ n pira, f
**Pyrenean** /,pɪərə'niən/ a pirineo, pirenaico
**Pyrenees, the** /'pɪərə,niz/ los Pirineos, m pl
**pyrites** /pai'raitiz/ n pirita, f
**pyromancy** /'pairə,mænsi/ n piromancia, f
**pyrotechnic** /,pairə'tɛknɪk/ a pirotécnico
**pyrotechnics** /,pairə'tɛknɪks/ n pirotecnia, f
**pyrotechnist** /,pairə'tɛknɪst/ n pirotécnico, m
**Pyrrhic** /'pɪrɪk/ a pírrico
**Pythagorean** /pɪ,θægə'riən/ a and n pitagórico (-ca)
**Pythian** /'pɪθiən/ a pitio
**python** /'paiθɒn/ n pitón, m
**pythoness** /'paiθənɪs/ n pitonisa, f

# Q

**q** /kyu/ *n* (letter) cu, *f*
**quack** /kwæk/ *vi* (of a duck) graznar. —*n* (of a duck) graznido, *m;* (charlatan) charlatán, farsante, *m;* curandero, *m.* **q. doctor,** matasanos, medicastro, curandero, *m.* **q. medicine,** curanderismo, *m*
**quackery** /'kwækəri/ *n* charlatanería, *f,* charlatanismo, *m*
**quadrangle** /'kwɒd,ræŋgəl/ *n* cuadrángulo, *m;* (courtyard) patio, *m*
**quadrangular** /kwɒd'ræŋgyələr/ *a* cuadrangular
**quadrant** /'kwɒdrənt/ *n* (Geom. Astron. etc.) cuadrante, *m*
**quadratic** /kwɒ'drætɪk/ *a* cuadrático. **q. equation,** cuadrática, ecuación de segundo grado, *f*
**quadrature** /'kwɒdrətʃər/ *n* (Math. Astron.) cuadratura, *f*
**quadrennial** /kwɒ'drɛniəl/ *a* cuadrienal
**quadrilateral** /,kwɒdrə'lætərəl/ *a* and *n* cuadrilátero *m*
**quadrille** /kwɒ'drɪl/ *n* cuadrilla, *f;* (card game) cuatrillo, *m*
**quadruped** /'kwɒdrʊ,pɛd/ *a* and *n* cuadrúpedo *m*
**quadruple** /kwɒ'drupəl/ *a* cuádruple. —*vt* cuadruplicar. —*n* cuádruplo, *m*
**quadruplet** /kwɒ'drʌplɪt/ *n* serie de cuatro cosas, *f;* bicicleta de cuatro asientos, *f;* uno (una) de cuatro niños (-as) gemelos (-as)
**quadruplication** /kwɒ,druplɪ'keɪʃən/ *n* cuadruplicación, *f*
**quaff** /kwɒf/ *vt* beber a grandes tragos, vaciar de un trago
**quagmire** /'kwæg,maiᵊr/ *n* tremedal, pantano, *m; Fig.* cenagal, *m*
**quail** /kweil/ *n* codorniz, *f;* (U.S.A.) parpayuela, *f.* —*vi* cejar, retroceder; temblar, acobardarse
**quaint** /kweint/ *a* pintoresco; curioso, raro; (eccentric) excéntrico, extravagante
**quaintly** /'kweintli/ *adv* de un modo pintoresco; curiosamente; con extravagancia
**quaintness** /'kweintnɪs/ *n* lo pintoresco; rareza, singularidad, *f;* (eccentricity) extravagancia, *f*
**quake** /kweik/ *vi* estremecerse, vibrar; temblar. —*n* estremecimiento, *m;* (of the earth) terremoto, *m.* **to q. with fear,** temblar de miedo
**Quaker** /'kweikər/ *n* cuáquero (-ra)
**Quakerism** /'kweikə,rɪzəm/ *n* cuaquerismo, *m*
**quaking** /'kweikɪŋ/ *a* temblón; tembloroso. —*n* temblor, *m;* estremecimiento, *m.* **q. ash,** álamo temblón, *m*
**quakingly** /'kweikɪŋli/ *adv* trémulamente
**qualifiable** /'kwɒlə,faiəbəl/ *a* calificable
**qualification** /,kwɒləfɪ'keɪʃən/ *n* calificación, *f,* requisito, *m;* capacidad, aptitud, *f;* (reservation) reservación, salvedad, *f*
**qualified** /'kwɒlə,faid/ *a* apto, competente; (of professions) con título universitario; habilitado; limitado
**qualify** /'kwɒlə,fai/ *vt* habilitar; calificar; modificar; suavizar; *vi* habilitarse; prepararse; llenar los requisitos
**qualifying** /'kwɒlə,faiɪŋ/ *a Gram.* calificativo
**qualitative** /'kwɒlɪ,teitɪv/ *a* cualitativo
**quality** /'kwɒlɪti/ *n* cualidad, *f;* calidad, *f;* propiedad, *f.* **This cloth is of good q.,** Esta tela es de buena calidad. **the q.,** la alta sociedad, la aristocracia
**qualm** /kwɑm/ *n* náusea, *f;* mareo, desmayo, *m;* (of conscience) escrúpulo, remordimiento, *m*
**quandary** /'kwɒndəri/ *n* incertidumbre, perplejidad, *f;* dilema, apuro, *m.* **to be in a q.,** estar perplejo
**quantitative** /'kwɒntɪ,teitɪv/ *a* cuantitativo
**quantity** /'kwɒntɪti/ *n* cantidad, *f;* gran cantidad, *f.* **unknown q.,** incógnita, *f*
**quantum** /'kwɒntəm/ *n* cantidad, *f;* tanto, *m.* **q. theory,** teoría de la quanta, *f*
**quarantine** /'kwɔrən,tin/ *n* cuarentena, *f, vt* someter a cuarentena
**quarrel** /'kwɔrəl/ *vi* pelear, disputar; (scold) reñir;

(find fault) criticar. —*n* pelea, disputa, *f;* (glazier's) diamante de vidriero, *m.* **to pick a q. with,** armar pleito con, reñir con. **to q. with,** reñir con, romper con; quejarse de
**quarreller** /'kwɔrələr/ *n* reñidor (-ra)
**quarrelling** /'kwɔrəlɪŋ/ *n* disputas, altercaciones, *f pl*
**quarrelsome** /'kwɔrəlsəm/ *a* pendenciero, peleador, belicoso
**quarrelsomeness** /'kwɔrəlsəmnɪs/ *n* belicosidad, pugnacidad, *f*
**quarry** /'kwɔri/ *n* cantera, *f; Fig.* mina, *f;* (prey) presa, *f;* víctima, *f.* —*vt* explotar una cantera; examinar
**quarrying** /'kwɔriɪŋ/ *n* explotación de canteras, *f;* cantería, *f*
**quarryman** /'kwɔrimən/ *n* cantero, *m*
**quart** /kwɔrt/ *n* cuarto de galón, *m*
**quartan** /'kwɔrtn̩/ *a* cuartanal. —*n* (fever) cuartana, *f*
**quarter** /'kwɔrtər/ *n* (fourth part) cuarta parte, *f,* cuarto, *m;* (of a year) trimestre, *m;* (of an hour, the moon, a ton, an animal, etc.) cuarto, *m;* (of the compass) cuarta, *f; Naut.* cuartelada, *f;* (of a town) barrio, *m;* (mercy) cuartel, *m; Herald.* cuartel, *m;* dirección, *f;* origen, *m,* fuente, *f; pl* **quarters,** vivienda, *f;* alojamiento, *m;* (barracks) cuartel, *m.* —*vt* cuartear; (a body) descuartizar, hacer cuartos (a); (troops) alojar; (in barracks) acuartelar; *Herald.* cuartelar. **a q. of an hour,** un cuarto de hora. **at close quarters,** de cerca. **hind quarters,** cuartos traseros, *m pl.* **It is a q. to four,** Son las cuatro menos cuarto. **It is a q. past four,** Son las cuatro y cuarto. **q.-day,** primer día de un trimestre, *m.* **q.-deck,** alcázar, *m;* cuerpo de oficiales de un buque, *m.* **q.-mile,** cuarto de milla, *m.* **q.-plate,** cuarto de placa, *m.* **q.-sessions,** sesión trimestral de los juzgados municipales, *f.* **q.-staff,** barra, *f.* **q.-tone,** cuarto de tono, *m*
**quartering** /'kwɔrtərɪŋ/ *n* (punishment) descuartizamiento, *m; Herald.* cantón, *m*
**quarterly** /'kwɔrtərli/ *a* trimestral, trimestre. —*n* publicación trimestral, *f, adv* trimestralmente
**quartermaster** /'kwɔrtər,mæstər/ *n Mil.* cabo furriel, *m; Nav.* maestre de víveres, cabo de mar, *m.* **q.-general,** intendente de ejército, *m*
**quartet** /kwɔr'tɛt/ *n* cuarteto, *m*
**quarto** /'kwɔrtou/ *n* papel en cuarto, *m;* libro en cuarto, *m.* **in q.,** en cuarto
**quartz** /kwɔrts/ *n* cuarzo, *m*
**quash** /kwɒʃ/ *vt Law.* anular, derogar; *Inf.* sofocar, reprimir
**quasi** /'kweizai, 'kwɑsi/ *a* and *adv* cuasi
**quasimodo** /,kwɑsə'moudou/ *n* cuasimodo, *m*
**quatrain** /'kwɒtrein/ *n* cuarteta, *f*
**quaver** /'kweivər/ *vi* vibrar; temblar; (trill) trinar, hacer quiebros. —*vt* decir con voz temblorosa. —*n* vibración, *f;* trémolo, *m;* (trill) trino, *m;* (musical note) corchea, *f*
**quaveringly** /'kweivərɪŋli/ *adv* con voz temblorosa
**quavery** /'kweivəri/ *a* trémulo, tembloroso
**quay** /ki, kei/ *n* muelle, *m*
**queasiness** /'kwizinɪs/ *n* náusea, *f;* escrupulosidad, *f*
**queasy** /'kwizi/ *a* propenso a la náusea; nauseabundo; delicado, escrupuloso
**queen** /kwin/ *n* reina, *f;* (in a Spanish pack of cards) caballo, *m;* (in a French or English pack and in chess) reina, *f.* **to q. it,** conducirse como una reina; mandar. **q. bee,** maestra, abeja reina, *f.* **q. cell,** maestril, *m.* **q. mother,** reina madre, *f.* **q. regent,** reina regente, *f*
**queenliness** /'kwinlinɪs/ *n* majestad de reina, *f*
**queenly** /'kwinli/ *a* de reina; regio
**queer** /kwiər/ *a* raro; extraño, singular; ridículo; (shady) sospechoso; (ill) malucho, algo enfermo; (mad) chiflado
**queerly** /'kwiərli/ *adv* extrañamente; ridículamente
**queerness** /'kwiərnɪs/ *n* rareza, extrañeza, singularidad, *f;* ridiculez, *f*

**quell** /kwel/ *vt* subyugar; reprimir; apaciguar, calmar

**quench** /kwentʃ/ *vt* apagar; calmar; satisfacer. **to q. one's thirst,** apagar la sed

**quenching** /'kwentʃɪŋ/ *n* apagamiento, *m;* satisfacción, *f*

**querulous** /'kwerələs/ *a* quejumbroso

**querulousness** /'kwerələsnɪs/ *n* hábito de quejarse, *m;* quejumbre, *f*

**query** /'kwɪəri/ *n* pregunta, *f;* duda, *f;* punto de interrogación, *m.* —*vt* preguntar; dudar (de); poner en duda. —*vi* hacer una pregunta; expresar una duda

**quest** /kwest/ *n* busca, *f;* (adventure) demanda, *f.* **in q. of,** en busca de

**question** /'kwestʃən/ *n* pregunta, *f;* problema, *m;* asunto, *m;* cuestión, *f;* (discussion) debate, *m,* discusión, *f.* —*vt* and *vi* interrogar; examinar; poner en duda, dudar de; preguntarse; hacer preguntas. **beyond q.,** fuera de duda. **to ask a q.,** hacer una pregunta. **without q.,** sin duda. **It is a q. of whether...,** Se completamente imposible. **It is a q. of whether...,** Se trata de si... **q.-mark,** punto interrogante, *m*

**questionable** /'kwestʃənəbəl/ *a* cuestionable, discutible, dudoso; equívoco, sospechoso

**questionableness** /'kwestʃənəbəlnɪs/ *n* lo discutible; carácter dudoso, *m;* carácter sospechoso, *m*

**questioner** /'kwestʃənər/ *n* preguntador (-ra); interrogador (-ra)

**questioning** /kwəstʃənɪŋ/ *n* preguntas, *f pl;* interrogatorio, *m*

**questioningly** /kwestʃənɪŋli/ *adv* interrogativamente

**questionnaire** /ˌkwestʃə'neər/ *n* cuestionario, *m*

**quetzal** /ket'sal/ *n* (money and *Ornith.*) quetzal, *m*

**queue** /kyu/ *n* coleta, *f;* cola, *f, vi* formar cola; hacer cola

**quibble** /'kwɪbəl/ *n* equívoco, subterfugio, *m;* sutileza, *f;* (pun) retruécano, *m.* —*vi* hacer uso de subterfugios; sutilizar

**quibbler** /'kwɪblər/ *n* sofista, *mf*

**quibbling** /'kwɪblɪŋ/ *n* sofistería, *f,* sofismas, *m pl,* sutilezas, *f pl*

**quick** /kwɪk/ *a* vivo; agudo; penetrante; sagaz; rápido, veloz; (ready) pronto; ágil, activo; (light) ligero. —*adv* rápidamente; (soon) pronto. —*n* carne viva, *f; Fig.* lo vivo. **Be q.!** ¡Date prisa! **He was very q.,** Lo hizo muy aprisa; Volvió (or Fue, according to sense) rápidamente. **the q. and the dead,** los vivos y los muertos. **to cut to the q.,** herir en lo más vivo. **q. march,** paso doble, *m.* **q.-sighted,** de vista aguda; perspicaz. **q. step,** paso rápido, *m.* **q.-tempered,** de genio vivo, colérico. **q. time,** compás rápido, *m; Mil.* paso doble, *m.* **q.-witted,** de ingenio agudo

**quicken** /'kwɪkən/ *vt* vivificar; animar; acelerar; excitar, avivar. —*vi* vivificarse; despertarse; renovarse; acelerarse; (stir) moverse. **to q. one's step,** acelerar el paso

**quicklime** /'kwɪkˌlaɪm/ *n* cal viva, *f*

**quickly** /'kwɪkli/ *adv* rápidamente; (soon) pronto; (immediately) en seguida; (promptly) con presteza; vivamente

**quickness** /'kwɪknɪs/ *n* viveza, *f;* (of wit, etc.) agudeza, *f;* rapidez, velocidad, *f;* (promptness) prontitud, *f;* agilidad, *f;* (lightness) ligereza, *f;* (understanding) penetración, sagacidad, *f*

**quicksand** /'kwɪkˌsænd/ *n* arena movediza, *f; Fig.* cenagal, *m*

**quicksilver** /'kwɪkˌsɪlvər/ *n* azogue, mercurio, *m, vt* azogar

**quiescence** /kwi'esəns/ *n* reposo, *m;* quietud, tranquilidad, *f;* inactividad, *f;* pasividad, *f*

**quiescent** /kwi'esənt/ *a* quieto; inactivo; pasivo

**quiet** /'kwaɪɪt/ *a* tranquilo; quieto; silencioso; quedo; monótono; inactivo; (informal) sin ceremonia; (simple) sencillo; (of the mind) sereno; (of colours, etc.) suave. —*n* tranquilidad, quietud, *f;* silencio, *m;* paz, *f;* (of mind) serenidad, *f.* —*vt* tranquilizar, sosegar; calmar. **to be q.,** callarse; no hacer ruido. **Be q.!** ¡Estate quieto! ¡A callar!

**quietism** /'kwaɪɪˌtɪzəm/ *n* quietismo, *m*

**quietist** /'kwaɪɪtɪst/ *n* quietista, *mf*

**quietistic** /ˌkwaɪɪ'tɪstɪk/ *a* quietista

**quietly** /'kwaɪɪtli/ *adv* tranquilamente; en silencio; sin ruido; en calma; (simply) sencillamente; dulcemente

**quietness** /'kwaɪɪtnɪs/ *n* tranquilidad, quietud, *f;* calma, *f;* paz, *f;* silencio, *m*

**quietus** /kwai'itəs/ *n* (quittance) quitanza, *f,* finiquito, *m;* golpe de gracia, *m;* muerte, *f*

**quill** /kwɪl/ *n* pluma de ave, *f;* (of a feather) cañón, *m;* (pen) pluma, *f;* (of a porcupine) púa, *f.* **q.-driver,** cagatintas, *mf*

**quilt** /kwɪlt/ *n* colcha, *f,* edredón, *m.* —*vt* acolchar. **q. maker,** colchero, *m*

**quilting** /'kwɪltɪŋ/ *n* acolchamiento, *m;* colchadura, *f*

**quince** /kwɪns/ *n* (tree and fruit) membrillo, *m.* **q. cheese,** carne de membrillo, *f.* **q. jelly,** jalea de membrillo, *f*

**quincentenary** /ˌkwɪnsen'tenəri/ *n* quinto centenario, *m*

**quinine** /'kwaɪnaɪn/ *n* quinina, *f*

**quinsy** /'kwɪnzi/ *n* angina, *f*

**quintessence** /kwɪn'tesəns/ *n* quinta esencia, *f*

**quintessential** /ˌkwɪntə'senʃəl/ *a* quintaesenciado

**quintet** /kwɪn'tet/ *n* quinteto, *m*

**quintuple** /kwɪn'tupəl/ *a* quíntuplo

**quintuplet** /kwɪn'tʌplɪt/ *n* quintupleto, *m;* uno (una) de cinco niños (-as) gemelos (-as)

**quip** /kwɪp/ *n* agudeza, salida, *f;* (hint) indirecta, *f;* donaire, *m,* chanza, burla, *f*

**quire** /kwaɪər/ *n* (of paper) mano (de papel), *f*

**quirk** /kwɜrk/ *n* (quip) agudeza, salida, *f;* (quibble) sutileza, evasiva, *f,* (gesture) gesto, *m*

**quit** /kwɪt/ *vt* abandonar; dejar; renunciar (a). —*vi* marcharse, *Inf.* tomar las de Villadiego, poner pies en polvorosa; (slang) dejar de, cesar de. **notice to q.,** aviso de desahúcio, *m*

**quite** /kwaɪt/ *adv* completamente, enteramente; totalmente; del todo; (very) muy; (fairly) bastante. **It is not q. the thing to do,** Esto es algo que no se hace. **Q. so!** ¡Claro!; ¡Eso es! Se comprende. **It is not q. so good as we hoped,** No es tan bueno como esperábamos. **Peter is q. grown-up,** Pedro está hecho un hombre (or es todo un hombre)

**quits** /kwɪts/ *adv* quito, descargado. **be q.,** estar en paz

**quittance** /'kwɪtns/ *n* quitanza, *f;* recibo, *m;* recompensa, *f*

**quitter** /'kwɪtər/ *n* desertor (-ra); cobarde, *mf*

**quiver** /'kwɪvər/ *vi* temblar; vibrar; estremecerse; palpitar; (of light) titilar. —*n* (for arrows) aljaba, *f,* carcaj, *m.* See also **quivering**

**quivering** /'kwɪvərɪŋ/ *a* tremulante; vibrante; palpitante. —*n* temblor, *m;* estremecimiento, *m*

**quixotic** /kwɪk'sɒtɪk/ *a* quijotesco

**quixotism** /'kwɪksəˌtɪzəm/ *n* quijotismo, *m*

**quiz** /kwɪz/ *n* examen parcial, *m.* —*vt* tomar el pelo (a); burlarse (de); (stare) mirar de hito en hito (a)

**quizzical** /'kwɪzɪkəl/ *a* burlón; cómico; estrafalario

**quizzically** /'kwɪzɪkli/ *adv* burlonamente; cómicamente

**quoin** /kɔin, kwɔin/ *n* piedra angular, *f;* ángulo, *m;* (wedge) cuña, *f.* —*vt* meter cuñas (a)

**quoit** /kwɔit/ *n* tejo, *m;* pl **quoits,** juego de tejos, *m*

**quondam** /'kwɒndəm/ *a* antiguo

**quorum** /'kwɔrəm/ *n* quórum, *m.* **to form a q.,** hacer un quórum

**quota** /'kwoutə/ *n* cuota, *f*

**quotable** /'kwoutəbəl/ *a* citable; (Stock Exchange) cotizable

**quota system** *n* tablas diferenciales, *f pl*

**quotation** /kwou'teiʃən/ *n* citación, *f;* cita, *f; Com.* cotización, *f.* **q. mark,** comilla, *f*

**quote** /kwout/ *vt* citar; *Com.* cotizar. —*n Inf.* comilla, *f*

**quoth** /kwouθ/ *vt* **q. I,** dije yo. **q. he,** dijo él

**quotient** /'kwouʃənt/ *n* cociente, *m.* **intelligence q.,** cociente intelectual, *m*

# R

**r** /ar/ n (letter) erre, f
**rabbet** /'ræbɪt/ n ranura, f, rebajo, m. —vt ensamblar a rebajo. **r.-joint,** junta a rebajo, f
**rabbi** /'ræbai/ n rabí, rabino, m. **grand r.,** gran rabino, m
**rabbinical** /rə'bɪnɪkəl/ a rabínico
**rabbinism** /'ræbə,nɪzəm/ n rabinismo, m
**rabbit** /'ræbɪt/ n conejo (-ja). —a conejuno, de conejo. —vi cazar conejos. **young r.,** gazapo, m. **r.-hutch,** jaula para conejos, f. **r.-warren,** conejera, f
**rabble** /'ræbəl/ n populacho, vulgo, m, plebe, f
**Rabelaisian** /,ræbə'leizɪən/ a rabelasiano
**rabid** /'ræbɪd/ a rabioso; fanático; furioso, violento
**rabies** /'reibiz/ n rabia, hidrofobia, f
**raccoon** /ræ'kun/ n mapache, m
**race** /reis/ n carrera, f; (current) corriente, f; (prize) premio, m; (breed) raza, f; casta, estirpe, f; (family) linaje, m, familia, f; (scornful) ralea, f; (struggle) lucha, f. —vi tomar parte en una carrera; correr de prisa; asistir a concursos de carreras de caballos; (of a machine) dispararse. —vt (hacer) correr; competir en una carrera (con); desafiar a una carrera. **flat r.,** carrera llana, f. **mill-r.,** caz, m. **to run a r.,** tomar parte en una carrera; Fig. hacer una carrera. **r.-card,** programa de carreras de caballos, m. **r. hatred,** odio de razas, m. **r.-meeting,** concurso de carreras de caballos, m. **r. suicide,** suicidio de la raza, m. **r.-track,** pista, f
**racecourse** /'reis,kɔrs/ n hipódromo, m; estadio, m
**racehorse** /'reis,hɔrs/ n caballo de carrera, m
**racer** /'reisər/ n (horse) caballo de carreras, m; (person) carrerista, mf; (car) coche de carreras, m; (boat) yate de carreras, m; (bicycle) bicicleta de carreras, f
**rachitic** /rə'kɪtɪk/ a raquítico
**racial** /'reiʃəl/ a racial, de raza
**racialism** /'reiʃə,lɪzəm/ n rivalidad de razas, f
**raciness** /'reisinɪs/ n sabor, m; savia, f, picante, m
**racing** /'reisiŋ/ n carreras, f pl; Mech. disparo, m, a de carreras; hípico. **r. calendar,** calendario de concursos de carreras de caballos, m. **r. car,** coche de carreras, m. **r. cycle,** bicicleta de carreras, f
**rack** /ræk/ n (for hay) percha (del pesebre), f; (in a railway compartment) rejilla, f; (for billiard cues) taquera, f; (for clothes) percha, f; (for torture) potro, m; Mech. cremallera, f. —vt poner en el potro, torturar; atormentar. **to be on the r.,** estar en el potro. **to r. one's brains,** devanarse los sesos, quebrarse la cabeza. **r. and ruin,** ruina total, f. **r. railway,** ferrocarril de cremallera, m,
**racket** /'rækɪt/ n Sports. raqueta, f; (din) barahúnda, f; ruido, estrépito, m; confusión, f; (bustle) bullicio, m, agitación, f; (swindle) estafa, f; (binge) parranda, f. **to play rackets,** jugar a la raqueta
**racking** /'rækɪŋ/ n tortura, f; (of wine) trasiego, m, a torturante; (of a pain or cough) persistente
**racoon** /ræ'kun/ n mapache, m
**racquet** /'rækɪt/ n See **racket**
**racy** /'reisi/ a picante; sabroso
**radar** /'reidɑr/ n radar, m
**raddled** /'rædld/ a pintado de almagre; mal pintado
**radial** /'reidiəl/ a radial
**radiance** /'reidiəns/ n resplandor, brillo, m, luminosidad, f
**radiant** /'reidiənt/ a radiante; brillante, luminoso. —n Geom. línea radial, f. **r. heat,** calor radiante, m
**radiantly** /'reidiəntli/ adv con resplandor; brillantemente; con alegría
**radiate** /'reidi,eit/ vi radiar. —vt irradiar
**radiation** /,reidi'eiʃən/ n irradiación, f; Geom. radiación, f
**radiator** /'reidi,eitər/ n (for central heating and of a car) radiador, m; (stove) calorífero, m
**radical** /'rædɪkəl/ a radical. —n (Math. Chem.) radical, m; Polit. radical, mf
**radicalism** /'rædɪkə,lɪzəm/ n radicalismo, m
**radio** /'reidi,ou/ n radio, f; radiocomunicación, f. **r.**

**amateur, r. enthusiast,** radioaficionado (-da). **r. announcer,** locutor (-ra). **r. broadcast,** radioemisión, radiodifusión, f. **r. listener,** radioyente, mf **r. receiver,** (technical) radiorreceptor, m; (usual word) aparato de radio, m. **r. transmitter,** radiotransmisor, m
**radioactive** /,reidiou'æktɪv/ a radiactivo
**radioactive fallout** n caída radiactiva, llovizna radiactiva, precipitación radiactiva, f
**radioactivity** /,reidiouæk'tɪvɪti/ n radiactividad, f
**radiofrequency** /,reidiou'frikwənsi/ n radiofrecuencia, f
**radiolocation** /,reidioulou'keiʃən/ radiolocación, f
**radiologist** /,reidi'ɒlədʒɪst/ n radiólogo, m
**radiology** /reidi'ɒlədʒi/ n radiología, f
**radiometer** /,reidi'ɒmɪtər/ n radiómetro, m
**radiometry** /,reidi'ɒmɪtri/ n radiometría, f
**radioscopy** /,reidi'ɒskəpi/ n radioscopia, f
**radiotherapeutics, radiotherapy** /,reidiou,θɛrə'pyutiks; ,reidiou'θɛrəpi/ n radioterapia, f
**radish** /'rædɪʃ/ n rábano, m. **horse-r.,** rábano picante, m
**radium** /'reidiəm/ n radio, m
**radius** /'reidiəs/ n (Geom. Anat.) radio, m; (of a wheel) rayo, m; (scope) alcance, m
**raffia** /'ræfiə/ n rafia, f
**raffish** /'ræfɪʃ/ a disoluto, libertino
**raffle** /'ræfəl/ n rifa, f, sorteo, m; lotería, f. —vt rifar, sortear
**raffling** /'ræflɪŋ/ n sorteo, m, rifa, f
**raft** /ræft/ n balsa, f; (timber) armadía, f. —vt transportar en balsa; cruzar en balsa
**rafter** /'ræftər/ n (of a roof) viga, traviesa, f; (raftsman) balsero, m
**raftered** /'ræftərd/ a con vigas
**rag** /ræg/ n jirón, guiñapo, m; (for cleaning) paño, trapo, m; (for papermaking) estraza, f; (of smoke, etc.) penacho, m; (newspaper) papelucho, m; pl **rags,** harapos, m pl; Inf. viejos hábitos, m pl. —vt (tease) tomar el pelo (a); burlarse de; hacer una broma pesada (a). **r.-and-bone-man, ragpicker,** andrajero, trapero (Mexico), pepinador, m. **r. doll,** muñeca de trapo, f
**ragamuffin** /'rægə,mʌfɪn/ n galopín, m
**rage** /reidʒ/ n (anger) cólera, rabia, ira, f; (of the elements) furia, violencia, f; (ardour) entusiasmo, ardor, m; (fashion) boga, moda, f; (craze) manía, f; (of the poet) furor, m. —vi (be angry) rabiar, estar furioso; (of the sea) encresparse, alborotarse, enfurecerse; (of wind, fire, animals) bramar, rugir; (of pain) rabiar; (be prevalent) prevalecer, desencadenarse. **to r. against,** protestar furiosamente contra; culpar amargamente (de). **to be all the r.,** Inf. ser la ultima moda. **to fly into a r.,** montar en cólera. **to put into a r.,** hacer rabiar
**ragged** /'rægɪd/ a harapiento, andrajoso; roto; (uneven) desigual; (rugged) peñascoso, áspero, escabroso; (serrated) serrado; dentellado; (of a coastline) accidentado; (unfinished) inacabado, sin terminar; (of style) descuidado, sin pulir
**raggedness** /'rægɪdnɪs/ n harapos, m pl; estado andrajoso, m; aspereza, escabrosidad, f; lo serrado; lo accidentado; (of style) falta de elegancia, tosquedad, f
**raging** /'reidʒɪŋ/ a furioso, rabioso; violento; (roaring) bramante; (of the sea) bravío; intenso. —n furia, f; violencia, f; intensidad, f
**raglan** /'ræglən/ n raglán, m. **r. sleeve,** manga raglán, f
**ragout** /ræ'gu/ n estofado, m
**ragpicker** /'ræg,pɪkər/ n trapero (-ra)
**ragtime** /'ræg,taim/ n música sincopada, f
**raid** /reid/ n incursión, correría, f; asalto, ataque, m; (by the police) razzia, f; (by aircraft) bombardeo, m, vt invadir; atacar, asaltar; apoderarse de; hacer una razzia en; (by aircraft) bombear, bombardear; (pil-

lage) pillar, saquear. **obliteration r.**, hombardeo de saturación, *m*

**raider** /'reidər/ *n* corsario, *m;* atacador, asaltador, *m;* (aircraft) avión enemigo, *m*

**rail** /reil/ *n* barra, *f;* antepecho, *m;* (of a staircase) barandilla, *f,* pasamano, *m;* (track) riel, *m;* (railway) ferrocarril, *m;* (of a ship) barandilla, *f;* (of a chair) travesaño, *m pl.* **rails,** (fence) cerca, barrera, palizada, *f.* —*vt* cercar con una palizada, poner cerca a; mandar por ferrocarril. **by r.,** por ferrocarril. **to run off the rails,** descarrilar. **to r. at,** protestar contra; prorrumpir en invectivas contra, injuriar de palabra (a)

**railing** /'reiliŋ/ *n* barandilla, *f;* antepecho, *m,* enrejado, *m;* (grille) reja, *f;* (jeers) burlas, *f pl;* insultos, *m pl,* injurias, *f pl;* quejas, *f pl*

**raillery** /'reiləri/ *n* jocosidad, tomadura de pelo, *f;* sátiras, *f pl*

**railway** /'reil,wei/ *n* ferrocarril, *m;* vía férrea, *f,* camino de hierro, *m, a* de ferrocarril, ferroviario. **elevated r.,** ferrocarril aéreo, *m.* **narrow gauge r.,** ferrocarril de vía estrecha, *m.* **r. buffet,** fonda, *f,* (or restaurante, *m*) de estación. **r. carriage,** departamento de tren, *m.* **r. company,** compañía de ferrocarriles, *f.* **r. crossing,** paso a nivel, *m.* **r. engine,** locomotora, *f.* **r. guard,** jefe del tren, *m.* **r. guide,** guía de ferrocarriles, *f.* **r. line,** vía férrea, *f.* **r. marshalling yard,** apartadero ferroviario, *m.* **r. passenger,** viajero (-ra) en un tren. **r. platform,** andén, *m.* **r. porter,** mozo de estación, *m.* **r. siding,** vía muerta, *f.* **r. signal,** disco de señales, *m.* **r. station,** estación (de ferrocarril), *f.* **r. system,** sistema ferroviario, *m.* **r. ticket,** billete de tren, *m*

**railwayman** /'reil,weimən/ *n* ferroviario, empleado de los ferrocarriles, *m*

**raiment** /'reimənt/ *n* ropa, *f; Poet.* hábitos, *m pl*

**rain** /rein/ *n* lluvia, *f.* —*vi* and *vt* llover. **a r. of arrows,** una lluvia de flechas. **fine r.,** llovizna, *f.* **to r. cats and dogs,** llover a cántaros. **to r. hard,** diluviar. **r. cloud,** nubarrón, *m.* **r.-gauge,** pluviómetro, *m*

**rainbow** /'rein,bou/ *n* arco iris, arco de San Martín, *m*

**raincoat** /'rein,kout/ *n* abrigo impermeable, *m*

**raindrop** /'rein,drɒp/ *n* gota de lluvia, *f*

**rainfall** /'rein,fɔl/ *n* cantidad llovida, *f;* (shower) aguacero, *m*

**rainless** /'reinlis/ *a* sin lluvia, seco

**rainstorm** /'rein,stɔrm/ *n* chaparrón, *m,* tempestad de lluvia, *f*

**rainwater** /'rein,wɔtər/ *n* lluvia, *f;* agua lluvia, *f*

**rainy** /'reini/ *a* lluvioso. **r. day,** día de lluvia, *m; Fig.* tiempo de escasez, *m*

**raise** /reiz/ *vt* levantar; alzar; (the hat) quitar; solevantar; (dough) fermentar; (erect) erigir, edificar; (dust) levantar; elevar; (promote) ascender; (increase) aumentar; hacer subir; (spirits, memories) evocar; (the dead) resucitar; (cause) causar; dar lugar (a); hacer concebir; (a question, a point) hacer; plantear; (breed or educate) criar; (a crop) cultivar; (an army) alistar; (gather together) juntar; (a subscription) hacer; (money, etc.) obtener, hallar; (a siege, etc.) levantar, alzar; (a laugh, a protest, etc.) suscitar, provocar; (utter) poner, dar; (a fund) abrir. **to r. oneself,** incorporarse. **He succeeded in raising himself,** Logró alzarse; Logró mejorar su posición. **He raised their hopes unduly,** Les hizo concebir esperanzas desmesuradas. **to r. an objection (to),** poner objeción (a). **to r. an outcry,** armar un alboroto. **to r. a point,** hacer una observación; plantear una cuestión. **to r. a siege,** levantar un sitio. **to r. Cain,** armar la de Dios es Cristo. **to r. one's voice,** alzar la voz

**raised** /reizd/ *a* (in relief) en relieve; (embossed) de realce

**raiser** /'reizər/ *n* (breeder) criador (-ra); (cultivator) cultivador (-ra); (educator) educador (-ra); autor (-ra); fundador (-ra); (of objections, etc.) suscitador (-ra)

**raisin** /'reizin/ *n* pasa, *f*

**raising** /'reiziŋ/ *n* levantamiento, *m;* alzamiento, *m;* (of a building, monument) erección, *f;* elevación, *f;* (increase) aumento, *m;* provocación, *f;* fundación, *f;*

(breeding or education) crianza, *f;* (of spirits) evocación, *f;* (of the dead) resucitación, *f;* producción, *f;* (of crops) cultivo, *m*

**rake** /reik/ *n Agr.* rastrillo, *m,* rastra, *f;* (for the fire) hurgón, *m;* (croupier's) raqueta, *f;* (of a mast, funnel) inclinación, *f;* (person) tenorio, calavera, *m.* —*vt Agr.* rastrillar; (a fire, etc.) hurgar; (sweep) barrer; recoger; (ransack) buscar (en); (with fire) enfilar, tirar a lo largo de; (scan) escudriñar. —*vi* trabajar con el rastrillo; (slope) inclinarse. **r. off,** tajada, *f.* **to r. together,** juntar con el rastrillo; amontonar; ahorrar. **to r. up,** (revive) resucitar, desenterrar

**raking** /'reikiŋ/ *n* rastrillaje, *m;* (the fire, etc.) hurgonada, *f*

**rakish** /'reikiʃ/ *a* (of a ship) de palos muy inclinados, (dissolute) disoluto, libertino; (dashing) elegante

**rakishly** /'reikiʃli/ *adv* disolutamente; elegantemente

**rakishness** /'reikiʃnis/ *n* (licentiousness) libertinaje, *m,* disipación, disolución, *f;* (elegance) elegancia, *f*

**rally** /'ræli/ *vt* reunir; *Mil.* rehacer; (faculties) concentrar; (tease) tomar el pelo (a). —*vi* reunirse; *Mil.* rehacerse; (revive) mejorar, recobrar las fuerzas; (of markets, etc.) mejorar *n* reunión, *f*

**rallying** /'ræliiŋ/ *n* reunión, *f;* (of faculties, etc.) concentración, *f;* (recovery) mejora, *f.* **r. point,** punto de reunión, *m*

**ram** /ræm/ *n Zool.* carnero, morueco, *m; Astron.* Aries, Carnero, *m;* (Mil. etc.) ariete, *m;* (tool) pisón, *m; Nav.* espolón, *m, vt* golpear con ariete o espolón; (of a gun) atacar; apisonar; meter a la fuerza; hacer tragar a la fuerza; (squeeze) apretar; (crowd) atestar

**Ramadan** /,ræmə'dɑn/ *n* ramadán, *m*

**ramble** /'ræmbəl/ *vi* vagar, vagabundear; hacer una excursión. —*vt* errar por

**rambler** /'ræmblər/ *n* excursionista, *mf;* paseante, *mf; Bot.* rosa trepante, *f*

**rambling** /'ræmbliŋ/ *a* (of houses) encantado; laberíntico; (straggly) disperso; (of thought, etc.) incoherente, inconexo. —*n* vagabundeo, *m;* excursiones, *f pl;* paseo, *m;* (digression) digresiones, *f pl;* (delirium) desvaríos, *m pl*

**ramification** /,ræməfɪ'keiʃən/ *n* ramificación, *f*

**ramify** /'ræmə,fai/ *vi* ramificarse, tener ramificaciones. —*vt* ramificar; dividir en ramales

**rammer** /'ræmər/ *n* pisón de empedrador, *m;* baqueta (de fusil), *f;* (of a ship) espolón, *m*

**ramp** /ræmp/ *n* rampa, *f;* (swindle) estafa, *f;* (storm, commotion) tormenta, *f*

**rampage** /'ræmpeidʒ/ *vi* alborotarse; bramar

**rampant** /'ræmpənt/ *a* salvaje; *Herald.* rampante; (of persons) impaciente, furioso; (of plants, growth) lozano, exuberante; desenfrenado; (rife) prevaleciente, predominante

**rampart** /'ræmpɑrt/ *n* muralla, *f;* terraplén, *m; Fig.* baluarte, *m.* —*vt* abaluartar, abastionar

**ramrod** /'ræm,rɒd/ *n* baqueta, *f*

**ramshackle** /'ræm,ʃækəl/ *a* destartalado, ruinoso; desvencijado; (badly made) mal hecho

**ranch** /ræntʃ/ *n* rancho, *m,* hacienda (de ganado), *f*

**rancher** /'ræntʃər/ *n* ranchero, *m*

**rancid** /'rænsid/ *a* rancio

**rancidness** /'rænsidnis/ *n* rancidez, *f*

**rancor** /'ræŋkər/ *n* rencor, encono, *m*

**rancorous** /'ræŋkərəs/ *a* rencoroso

**random** /'rændəm/ *n* azar, *m, a* fortuito, al azar; sin orden ni concierto. **at r.,** a la ventura, al azar; sin pensar; (of shooting) sin apuntar. **to talk at r.,** hablar a trochemoche

**range** /reindʒ/ *n* línea, hilera, *f;* (of mountains) cadena, *f;* serie, *f;* clase, *f;* variedad, *f;* (of goods) surtido, *m;* (of a gun, voice, vision, etc.) alcance, *m;* (area) extensión, área, *f;* esfera de actividad, *f;* (scope) alcance, *m;* (of voice, musical instrument) compás, *m;* (of colors) gama, *f;* (for shooting) campo de tiro, *m;* (for cooking) cocina económica, *f.* **at close r.,** de cerca. **out of r.,** fuera de alcance. **within r.,** al alcance. **r.-finder,** (of guns, cameras) telémetro, *m.* **r. of mountains,** cadena de montañas, *f;* sierra, *f*

**range** /reindʒ/ *vt Poet.* arreglar; alinear; ordenar; clasificar; (a gun, etc.) apuntar; (place oneself) ponerse; sumarse (a); (roam) recorrer; (scan) escudriñar. —*vi* extenderse; (roam) vagar; (of plants) crecer (en);

variar, fluctuar; oscilar, vacilar; (of guns, etc.) alcanzar; (of the mind) pasar (por); (include) incluir

**ranger** /'reɪndʒər/ n (wanderer) vagabundo, m; (keeper) guardabosque, m; Mil. batidor, m

**ranging** /'reɪndʒɪŋ/ n arreglo, m; alineación, f; ordenación, f; clasificación, f; (roving) vida errante, f

**rank** /ræŋk/ n línea, f; fila, f; grado, m; clase, f; rango, m; categoría, f; posición, f; calidad, f; distinción, f. —vt ordenar; clasificar; (estimate) estimar; poner (entre). —vi ocupar un puesto; tener un grado, rango, etc.; estar al nivel (de); ser igual (a); contarse (entre). —a (luxuriant) lozano, exuberante; fértil; (thick) espeso; (rancid) rancio; (complete) consumado; completo; (foul-smelling) fétido; Fig. repugnante, aborrecible; (very) muy. **of the first r.**, de primera calidad; de primera clase; de distinción. **the r. and file,** los soldados, la tropa; las masas, hombres de filas, m pl, mujeres de fila, f pl, la mayoría; los socios ordinarios (de un club, etc.). **to break ranks,** Mil. romper filas. **to rise from the ranks,** ascender de las filas. **to r. high,** ocupar alta posición; ser de los mejores (de). **to r. with,** estar al nivel de; (be numbered among) contarse entre, figurar entre

**rankle** /'ræŋkəl/ vi Fig. irritar, molestar; envenenarse la vida, hacerse odioso

**rankly** /'ræŋkli/ adv ranciamente; lozanamente; con exuberancia; abundantemente; groseramente

**rankness** /'ræŋknɪs/ n rancidez, f; olor rancio, m; fertilidad, lozanía, f; exuberancia, f, vigor, m; enormidad, f

**ransack** /'rænsæk/ vt (search) registrar; (pillage) saquear; Fig. buscar en

**ransacking** /'rænsækɪŋ/ n (searching) registro, m; (sacking) saqueo, m

**ransom** /'rænsəm/ n rescate, m, redención, f; liberación, f. —vt rescatar, redimir

**ransomer** /'rænsəmər/ n rescatador (-ra)

**ransoming** /'rænsəmɪŋ/ n redención, f; liberación, f

**rant** /rænt/ vi declamar a gritos, vociferar; despotricar (contra); desvariar; hablar por hablar, hablar sin ton ni son. —n declamación, vociferación, f; desvarío, m

**ranter** /'ræntər/ n declamador (-ra); agitador populachero, m; predicador chillón, m

**rap** /ræp/ n golpecito, m; toque, m; (with the knocker) aldabada, f; (worthless trifle) ardite, maravedí, m. —vt and vi golpear; tocar. **He doesn't care a rap,** No le importa un ardite. **to rap at the door,** tocar a la puerta. **to rap with the knuckles,** golpear con los nudillos. **to rap out an oath,** proferir una blasfemia

**rapacious** /rə'peɪʃəs/ a rapaz

**rapaciously** /rə'peɪʃəsli/ adv con rapacidad

**rapacity** /rə'pæsɪti/ n rapacidad, f

**rape** /reɪp/ n (carrying off) rapto, m. **the Rape of the Sabine Women,** el Rapto de las Sabinas, m; Law. estupro, m; violación, f; Bot. nabo silvestre, m. —vt (carry off) raptar, robar; violar, forzar

**rapid** /'ræpɪd/ a rápido. —n rápido, m. **r. combustion,** combustión activa, f

**rapidity** /rə'pɪdɪti/ n rapidez, f

**rapidly** /'ræpɪdli/ adv rápidamente, con rapidez

**rapier** /'reɪpiər/ n estoque, m; espadín, m

**rapine** /'ræpɪn/ n rapiña, f

**rapping** /'ræpɪŋ/ n golpecitos, m pl; golpeo, m; toques, m pl; (of the knocker) aldabeo, m

**rapscallion** /ræp'skælyən/ n bribón, m

**rapt** /ræpt/ past part and a arrebatado; absorto; extático, extasiado

**rapture** /'ræptʃər/ n arrebato, m; éxtasis, m; transporte, m; embriaguez, f; entusiasmo, m

**rapturous** /'ræptʃərəs/ a embelesado; extático; entusiasta

**rapturously** /'ræptʃərəsli/ adv extáticamente; con entusiasmo

**rare** /rɛər/ a raro; extraordinario; exótico; infrecuente

**raree show** /'rɛəri/ n barracón de los fenómenos, barracón de las atracciones, m

**rarefaction** /,rɛərə'fækʃən/ n rarefacción, f

**rarefy** /'rɛərə,faɪ/ vt rarefacer. —vi rarefacerse

**rareness** /'rɛərnɪs/ n rareza, f; singularidad, f; infrecuencia, f

**rarity** /'rɛərɪti/ n raridad, f; (uncommonness and rare object) rareza, f

**rascal** /'ræskəl/ n sinvergüenza, m; truhán, bribón, pícaro, m; (affectionately) picaruelo, m

**rascality** /ræ'skælɪti/ n bellaquería, truhanería, f

**rascally** /'ræskəli/ a redomado; vil, ruin, canallesco

**rash** /ræʃ/ a temerario, precipitado; imprudente. —n erupción, f, salpullido, m

**rasher** /'ræʃər/ n magra, f; (of bacon) torrezno, m

**rashly** /'ræʃli/ adv temerariamente, precipitadamente; imprudentemente, con imprudencia

**rashness** /'ræʃnɪs/ n temeridad, precipitación, f; imprudencia, f

**rasp** /ræsp/ n escofina, f, rallo, m; sonido áspero, m. —vt raspar, escofinar; (get on one's nerves) poner los nervios en punta (a)

**raspberry** /'ræz,bɛri/ n frambuesa, f. **r.-cane,** frambueso, m. **r. jam,** mermelada de frambuesa, f

**rasping** /'ræspɪŋ/ a (of the voice) áspero, estridente

**rat** /ræt/ n rata, f; desertor, m; (black leg) esquirol, m. —vi cazar ratas; ser desertor; ser esquirol. **rat-catcher,** cazador de ratas, m. **rat poison,** matarratas, m, raticida, f. **rat-trap,** ratonera, f

**ratable** /'reɪtəbəl/ a sujeto a contribución; imponible; valuable

**ratafia** /,rætə'fiə/ n ratafía, f

**rataplan** /,rætə'plæn/ n rataplán, m

**ratchet** /'rætʃɪt/ n Mech. trinquete, m; (of a watch) disparador, m. **r.-drill,** carraca, f. **r.-wheel,** rueda dentada con trinquete, f

**rate** /reɪt/ n velocidad, f; razón, proporción, f; (of exchange) tipo, m; tanto, m; precio, m; clase, f; modo, m, manera, f; Naut. clasificación, f; (tax) contribución, f, impuesto, m; pl **rates,** (of a house) inquilinato, m. —vt tasar; estimar; fijar el precio (a); Naut. clasificar; imponer una contribución (de); (scold) reñir. **at a great r.,** rápidamente, velozmente. **at a r. of,** a razón de; a una velocidad de. **at any r.,** de todos modos; por lo menos; sea como fuere. **at this r.,** de este modo; a este paso; a esa cuenta; en esta proporción; (with seguir) así. **first-r.,** de primera clase. **rates and taxes,** contribuciones e impuestos, f pl. **r. of climb,** Aer. velocidad ascensional, f. **r. of exchange,** tipo de cambio, m. **r.-payer,** contribuyente, mf

**rather** /'ræðər/ adv más bien; antes; (more willingly) de mejor gana; (somewhat) algo, un poco; (perhaps) quizás; mejor dicho; (fairly) bastante; (very) muy; mucho; al contrario. **R.!** ¡Ya lo creo! **or r.,** o más bien. **anything r. than...,** todo menos... **He had r.,** Preferiría. **r. than,** antes que, en vez de

**ratification** /,rætəfɪ'keɪʃən/ n ratificación, f; (of a bill) aprobación, f

**ratifier** /'rætə,faɪər/ n ratificador (-ra)

**ratify** /'rætə,faɪ/ vt ratificar

**ratifying** /'rætə,faɪɪŋ/ n ratificación, f, a ratificatorio

**rating** /'reɪtɪŋ/ n tasación, f; valuación, f; clasificación, f; impuesto, m, contribución, f; repartición de impuestos, f; (of a ship's company) graduación, f; (scolding) represión, f

**ratio** /'reɪʃou/ n razón, f; proporción, f. **in direct r.,** en razón directa

**ratiocinate** /,ræʃi'ɒsə,neɪt/ vi raciocinar

**ratiocination** /,ræʃi,ɒsə'neɪʃən/ n raciocinación, f

**ration** /'ræʃən, 'reɪʃən/ n ración, f. —vt racionar. **r.-book,** cartilla de racionamiento, f

**rational** /'ræʃənl/ a racional; razonable, juicioso. —n ser racional, m

**rationalism** /'ræʃənl,ɪzəm/ n racionalismo, m

**rationalist** /'ræʃənlɪst/ n racionalista, mf

**rationalistic** /,ræʃənl'ɪstɪk/ a racionalista

**rationality** /,ræʃə'nælɪti/ n racionalidad, f; justicia, f

**rationalization** /,ræʃənlə'zeɪʃən/ n racionalización, f; justificación, f

**rationalize** /'ræʃənl,aɪz/ vt hacer racional; concebir racionalmente; Math. quitar los radicales (a); justificar

**rationing** /'ræʃənɪŋ, 'reɪ-/ n racionamiento, m

**rattan** /ræ'tæn/ n rota, f; bejuco, m; junquillo, m

**ratteen** /ræ'tin/ n ratina, f

**ratter** /'rætər/ n perro ratonero, m; gato que caza ratas, m

**ratting** /'rætɪŋ/ n caza de ratas, f; deserción, f
**rattle** /'rætl/ vi hacer ruido; rechinar, crujir; (of loose windows, etc.) zangolotearse; (knock) golpear; tocar; (patter) bailar; sonar; (of the dying) dar un estertor. —vt (shake) sacudir; hacer vibrar; (jolt) traquetear; (do rapidly) acabar rápidamente; (confuse) aturdir, hacer perder la cabeza (a); desconcertar. **to r. along,** deslizarse (or correr) rápidamente. **to r. off,** (repeat) decir rápidamente; terminar apresuradamente. **to r. on about,** charlar mucho de, hablar sin cesar sobre
**rattle** /'rætl/ n rechinamiento, crujido, m; zangoloteo, m; ruido, m; son (de la lluvia, etc.), m; (in the throat) estertor, m; (of a rattlesnake) cascabel, m; (child's) sonajero, m; matraca, f; carraca, f; (chatter) charla, f. **r.-headed,** de cabeza de chorlito, casquivano
**rattlesnake** /'rætl,sneik/ n serpiente de cascabel, f, crótalo, m
**rattling** /'rætlɪŋ/ n See **rattle**
**raucous** /'rɔkəs/ a ronco, estridente
**raucousness** /'rɔkəsnɪs/ n ronquedad, f, estridor, m
**ravage** /'rævidʒ/ vt devastar; (pillage) saquear; destruir; (spoil) estropear. —n devastación, f; destrucción, f; estrago, m
**ravager** /'rævidʒər/ n devastador (-ra); saqueador (-ra)
**rave** /reiv/ vi desvariar, delirar; (of the elements) bramar, rugir. **to r. about,** hablar con entusiasmo de; delirar por. **to r. against,** vociferar contra, despotricarse contra
**ravel** /'rævəl/ vt deshilar, destejer; Fig. enredar. **to r. out,** deshilarse; Fig. desenredarse, desenmarañarse
**raven** /'reivən/ n cuervo, m, a negro como el azabache
**ravening** /'rævənɪŋ/ a rapaz, salvaje
**Ravenna** /rə'vɛnə/ Rávena, f
**ravenous** /'rævənəs/ a voraz
**ravenously** /'rævənəsli/ adv vorazmente
**ravenousness** /'rævənəsnɪs/ n voracidad, f
**ravine** /rə'vin/ n cañada, f, barranco, cañón, m
**raving** /'reivɪŋ/ n delirio, m, desvaríos, m pl. —a delirante; violento; bravío
**ravioli** /,rævi'ouli/ n pl ravioles, m pl
**ravish** /'rævɪʃ/ vt (carry off) arrebatar, raptar; extasiar, encantar; (rape) violar, forzar
**ravisher** /'rævɪʃər/ n raptador, m; violador, m
**ravishing** /'rævɪʃɪŋ/ n violación, f, a encantador
**ravishment** /'rævɪʃmənt/ n violación, f; arrobamiento, m; transporte, éxstasis, m
**raw** /rɔ/ a (of meat, etc., silk, leather, weather) crudo; bruto; (inexpert) bisoño; (of flesh) vivo; Com. en bruto. **raw-boned,** huesudo. **raw hand,** novato (-ta).
**raw material,** primera materia, f. **raw materials,** materias primas, f pl. **raw score,** puntuación bruta, f.
**raw silk,** seda cruda, seda en rama, f. **raw sugar,** azúcar bruto, m
**rawhide** /'rɔ,haid/ a de cuero crudo
**rawness** /'rɔnɪs/ n crudeza, f; inexperiencia, f; (of weather) humedad, f
**ray** /rei/ n rayo, m; (line) raya, f; (radius) radio, m; (fish) raya, f. **cathode rays,** rayos catódicos, m pl
**rayon** /'reiɒn/ n rayón, m
**raze** /reiz/ vt arrasar, asolar; demoler; (erase) borrar, tachar
**razor** /'reizər/ n navaja, f. **electric r.,** máquina de afeitar eléctrica, f. **safety r.,** máquina de afeitar, f. **slash with a r.,** navajada, f. **r. blade,** hoja de afeitar, f. **r. case,** navajero, m. **r. strop,** suavizador, m
**re** /ri, rei/ n Mus. re, m; prep Law. causa, f; Com. concerniente a
**re** /ri/ prefix (attached to verb) re-; (after the verb) de nuevo; (followed by infin.) volver a... **to re-count,** volver a contar, contar de nuevo, recontar
**reabsorb** /,riəb'sɔrb, -'zɔrb/ vt resorber
**reabsorption** /,riəb'sɔrpʃən, -'zɔrp-/ n reabsorción, resorción, f
**reach** /ritʃ/ vt (stretch out) alargar; extender; alcanzar; llegar hasta; (arrive at) llegar a; (achieve) lograr, obtener. —vi extenderse; alcanzar; penetrar. —n alcance, m; extensión, f; poder, m; capacidad, f; (of a river) tabla, f. **as far as the eye could r.,** hasta donde alcanzaba la vista. **He reached home very**

**soon,** Llegó muy pronto a casa. **out of r.,** fuera de alcance. **to r. a deadlock,** llegar a un punto muerto. **within r.,** al alcance. **within easy r.,** de fácil acceso; a corta distancia. **to r. after,** procurar alcanzar; hacer esfuerzos para obtener. **to r. back,** (of time) remontarse. **to r. down,** bajar. **r.-me-downs,** ropa hecha, f
**react** /ri'ækt/ vi reaccionar. —vt hacer de nuevo; Theat. volver a representar
**reaction** /ri'ækʃən/ n reacción, f
**reactionary** /ri'ækʃə,nɛri/ a and n reaccionario (-ia)
**reactive** /ri'æktɪv/ a reactivo
**read** /rid/ vt leer; (a riddle, etc.) adivinar; descifrar; interpretar; (study) estudiar; (the Burial Service, etc.) decir; (correct) corregir; (of thermometers, etc.) marcar. —vi leer; estudiar; (be written) estar escrito, decir. **The play acts better than it reads,** La comedia es mejor representada que leída. **to r. aloud,** leer en voz alta. **to r. between the lines,** leer entre líneas. **to r. proofs,** corregir pruebas. **to r. to oneself,** leer para sí. **to r. about,** leer; (learn) enterarse de. **to r. again,** volver a leer, leer otra vez. **to r. on,** continuar leyendo. **to r. out,** leer en alta voz. **to r. over,** leer; leerlo todo. **to r. over and over again,** leer muchas veces, leer y releer.
**read** /rɛd/ past part leído, etc. **well-r.,** releído; instruido, culto
**readability** /,ridə'bɪlɪti/ n legibilidad, f; interés, m, amenidad, f
**readable** /'ridəbəl/ a legible; interesante
**readdress** /,riə'drɛs/ vt dirigir de nuevo (una carta, etc.); poner la nueva dirección en (una carta, etc.)
**reader** /'ridər/ n lector (-ra); Eccl. lector, m; (proof) corrector de pruebas, m; (citation collector for a dictionary) cedulista, mf; (university) profesor (-ra) auxiliar a cátedra; (book) libro de lectura, m. **to be a great r.,** leer mucho. **the Spanish r.** (reader of Spanish books) el lector de español
**readily** /'rɛdli/ adv fácilmente; en seguida, inmediatamente; de buena gana, con placer
**readiness** /'rɛdɪnɪs/ n prontitud, expedición, f; buena voluntad, f; (of speech, etc.) facilidad, f. **in r.,** preparado. **r. of wit,** viveza de ingenio, f
**reading** /'ridɪŋ/ n lectura, f; (erudition) conocimientos, m pl; (recital) declamación, f; (lecture) conferencia, f; (study) estudio, m; interpretación, f; (of a thermometer, etc.) registro, m; (of a will) apertura, f. **r.-book,** libro de lectura, m. **r.-desk,** atril, m. **r.-glass,** lente para leer, m, carlita, f. **r.-lamp,** lámpara de sobremesa, f. **r.-matter,** material de lectura, m. **r.-room,** gabinete de lectura, m, sala de lectura, f
**readjourn** /,riə'dʒɜrn/ vt (a meeting) suspender (la sesión) de nuevo
**readjust** /,riə'dʒʌst/ vt reajustar, reacomdar; vi reacomodarse
**readjustment** /,riə'dʒʌstmənt/ n reajuste, m, reacomodación, f
**readmission** /,riəd'mɪʃən/ n readmisión, f
**readmit** /,riəd'mɪt/ vt readmitir
**ready** /'rɛdi/ a listo, preparado; dispuesto; pronto; (on the point of) a punto de; (easy) fácil; (near at hand) a la mano; (with money) contante; (with wit, etc.) vivo; (available) disponible; (nimble) ágil, ligero. **I am r. to do it,** Estoy dispuesto a hacerlo. **in r. cash,** en dinero contante. **to get r.,** prepararse; (dress) vestirse. **to make r.,** vt preparar; aprestar; Print. imponer. —vi prepararse, disponerse. **r.-made,** hecho; confeccionado. **r.-made clothing,** ropa hecha, f. **r. money,** dinero contante, m. **r.-witted,** de ingenio vivo
**reaffirm** /,riə'fɜrm/ vt afirmar de nuevo; reiterar, volver a repetir
**reaffirmation** /,riæfər'meiʃən/ n reiteración, f
**reagent** /ri'eidʒənt/ n reactivo, m
**real** /ri'al/ a real; verdadero; efectivo; (with silk, etc.) puro; sincero. **r. estate, r. property,** bienes raíces, m pl
**realism** /'riə,lɪzəm/ n realismo, m
**realist** /'riəlɪst/ n realista, mf
**realistic** /,riə'lɪstɪk/ a realista
**reality** /ri'ælɪti/ n realidad, f; verdad, f
**realizable** /,riə'laizəbəl/ a realizable; factible

**realization** /ˌrɪələˈzeɪʃən/ n realización, f; comprensión, f

**realize** /ˈrɪəˌlaɪz/ vt (understand) darse cuenta de, hacerse cargo de; realizar; (make real) dar vida (a); (accomplish) llevar a cabo; Com. realizar; (gain) adquirir

**really** /ˈrɪəli/ adv realmente; en verdad; en realidad; en efecto; (frankly) francamente. **R.?** ¿De veras?

**realm** /rɛlm/ n reino, m, dominios, m pl; Fig. esfera, f

**realty** /ˈrɪəlti/ n bienes raíces, m pl

**ream** /rim/ n resma, f

**reanimate** /riˈænəˌmeit/ vt reanimar

**reap** /rip/ vt segar; Fig. cosechar, recoger

**reaper** /ˈripər/ n segador (-ra); (machine) segadora mecánica, f

**reaping** /ˈripɪŋ/ n siega, f; Fig. cosecha, f. **r.-machine,** segadora mecánica, f

**reappear** /ˌriəˈpiər/ vi reaparecer

**reappearance** /ˌriəˈpiərəns/ n reaparición, f

**reapplication** /ˌriæpliˈkeiʃən/ n nueva aplicación, f; (of paint, etc.) otra capa, f; (for a post, etc.) neuva solicitud, f

**reapply** /ˌriəˈplai/ vt aplicar de nuevo; (paint, etc.) dar otra capa (de); (for a post, etc.) mandar una nueva solicitud

**reappoint** /ˌriəˈpoint/ vt designar de nuevo

**rear** /riər/ vt (lift) alzar, levantar; (breed, educate) criar; (build) erigir, construir. —vi (of horses) encabritarse, corcovear

**rear** /riər/ n cola, f; parte de atrás, f; parte posterior, f; última fila, f; (background) fondo, m; Inf. trasera, f; Mil. retaguardia, f. —a de atrás; trasero; último; posterior; de última fila; Mil. de retaguardia. **in the r.,** por detrás; a la cola; a retaguardia. **to bring up the r.,** cerrar la marcha. **r.-admiral,** contra almirante, m. **r.-axle,** eje trasero, m. **r.-guard,** retaguardia, f. **r. lamp,** faro trasero, m. **r. rank,** última fila, f. **r. view,** vista por detrás, f; vista posterior, f

**rearing** /ˈriəriŋ/ n (breeding) cría, f; (education) crianza, f

**rearm** /riˈɑrm/ vt rearmar. —vi rearmarse

**rearmament** /riˈɑrməmənt/ n rearmamento, m

**rearrange** /ˌriəˈreindʒ/ vt volver a arreglar; arreglar de otra manera; (a literary work) refundir, adaptar

**rearrangement** /ˌriəˈreindʒmənt/ n nuevo arroglo, m; (of a literary work) refundición, adaptación, f

**reascend** /ˌriəˈsɛnd/ vi and vt subir de nuevo, subir otra vez; montar de nuevo (sobre)

**reason** /ˈrizən/ n razón, f. **I have plenty of r. to...** No me faltarían motivos para... —vi and vt razonar. **to r. out of,** disuadir de. **by r. of,** a causa de, con motivo de; en virtud de. **for this r.,** por esto, por esta razón. **out of all r.,** fuera de razón. **to stand to r.,** ser lógico, estar puesto en razón. **with r.,** con razón. **r. of state,** razón de estado, f

**reasonable** /ˈrizənəbəl/ a razonable; racional

**reasonableness** /ˈrizənəbəlnɪs/ n lo razonable; moderación, f; justicia, f; racionalidad, f

**reasonably** /ˈrizənəbli/ adv razonablemente; con razón; bastante

**reasoning** /ˈrizəniŋ/ n razonamiento, m

**reassemble** /ˌriəˈsɛmbəl/ vt reunir otra vez. —vi juntarse de nuevo

**reassert** /ˌriəˈsɜrt/ vt afirmar de nuevo, reiterar

**reassertion** /ˌriəˈsɜrʃən/ n reiteración, f

**reassess** /ˌriəˈsɛs/ vt tasar de nuevo; repartir de nuevo; (a work of art) hacer una nueva apreciación (de)

**reassessment** /ˌriəˈsɛsmənt/ n nueva tasación, f; nuevo repartimiento, m; (of a work of art) nueva estimación, f

**reassume** /ˌriəˈsum/ vt reasumir

**reassumption** /ˌriəˈsʌmpʃən/ n reasunción, f

**reassurance** /ˌriəˈsʊrəns/ n afirmación repetida, f; confianza restablecida, f

**reassure** /ˌriəˈʃʊr/ vt asegurar de nuevo; tranquilizar, confortar

**reassuring** /ˌriəˈʃʊriŋ/ a tranquilizador, consolador

**rebate** /ˈribeit/ n rebaja, f, descuento, m; reducción, f. —vt rebajar, descontar; reducir. **to r. pro rata,** ratear

**rebec** /ˈribɛk/ n Mus. rabel, m

**rebel** / n. ˈrɛbəl; v. riˈbɛl/ n rebelde, mf, insurrecto (-ta). —vi rebelarse, sublevarse. **r. leader,** cabecilla, m

**rebellion** /rɪˈbɛlyən/ n rebelión, f

**rebellious** /rɪˈbɛlyəs/ a rebelde; revoltoso; refractario

**rebelliousness** /rɪˈbɛlyəsnɪs/ n rebeldía, f

**rebind** /riˈbaind/ vt atar de nuevo; (a book) reencuadernar

**rebirth** /riˈbɜrθ/ n renacimiento, m

**rebore** /riˈbɔr/ vt (an engine) descarbonizar

**reboring** /riˈbɔriŋ/ n (of an engine) descarburación, f

**reborn, to be** /riˈbɔrn/ vi renacer; ser reincarnado

**rebound** /v. riˈbaund; n. ˈri,baund/ a (of books) reencuadernado. —vi rebotar; repercutir; (revive) reavivarse. —n rebote, resalto, m; reacción, f, rechazo, m

**rebuff** /rɪˈbʌf/ n repulsa, f, desaire, m; contrariedad, f. —vt rechazar; contrariar

**rebuild** /riˈbɪld/ vt reedificar

**rebuilding** /riˈbɪldiŋ/ n reedificación, f

**rebuke** /rɪˈbyuk/ n reconvención, reprensión, censura, f, reproche, m, vt reprender, censurar, reprochar

**rebukingly** /rɪˈbyukiŋli/ adv en tono de censura; con reprensión, con reprobación

**rebut** /rɪˈbʌt/ vt refutar

**rebuttal** /rɪˈbʌtl/ n refutación, f

**recalcitrance** /rɪˈkælsɪtrəns/ n terquedad, obstinacia, f; rebeldía, f

**recalcitrant** /rɪˈkælsɪtrənt/ a reacio, recalcitrante

**recall** / v. rɪˈkɔl; n. also ˈrikɔl/ vt llamar; hacer volver; (dismiss) destituir; (ambassador, etc.) retirar; (remind or remember) recordar; (revoke) revocar. —n llamada, f; Mil. toque de llamada, m; (of ambassadors, etc.) retirada, f; (dismissal) destitución, f. **beyond r.,** irrevocable; (forgotten) olvidado

**recant** /rɪˈkænt/ vt retractar, retirar. —vi desdecirse (de), retractarse

**recantation** /ˌrikænˈteiʃən/ n recantación, f

**recapitulate** /ˌrikəˈpitʃəˌleit/ vt recapitular, resumir

**recapitulation** /ˌrikə,pitʃəˈleiʃən/ n recapitulación, f

**recapture** /riˈkæptʃər/ vt volver a prender, hacer prisionero nuevamente; (a place) volver a tomar; (a ship) represar

**recast** /riˈkæst/ vt (metals, a literary work) refundir; (alter) cambiar; (reckon) volver a calcular

**recasting** /riˈkæstiŋ/ n (metals, a literary work) refundición, f

**recede** /riˈsid/ vi retroceder; alejarse (de), separarse (de); desviarse (de); retirarse; desaparecer; (diminish) disminuir; (of prices) bajar

**receding** /riˈsidiŋ/ a que retrocede, etc.

**receipt** /rɪˈsit/ n recibo, m; (for money) recibí, m; (recipe) receta, f; pl **receipts,** ingresos, m pl. —vt firmar (or extender) recibo. **on r. of,** al recibir. **to acknowledge the r. of,** acusar recibo de. **r. book,** libro talonario, m

**receive** /rɪˈsiv/ vt and vi recibir; admitir, aceptar; acoger; (money) percibir, cobrar; (lodge) hospedar, alojar; (contain) contener. **to be well received,** tener buena acogida

**receiver** /rɪˈsivər/ n recibidor (-ra); (of stolen goods) receptador (-ra); (in bankruptcies) síndico, m; (for other legal business) receptor, m; (of a telephone) auricular, m; Elec. receptor, m; Radio. radiorreceptor, m. **to hang up (the r.),** colgar (el auricular)

**receivership** /rɪˈsivərˌʃip/ n sindicatura, f; receptoría, f

**receiving** /rɪˈsiviŋ/ n recibimiento, m; (of money, etc.) cobranza, f, percibo, m; (of stolen goods) encubrimiento, m. —a que recibe; recipiente; de recepción. **r. set,** aparato de radio, m

**recency** /ˈrisənsi/ n lo reciente; novedad, f

**recent** /ˈrisənt/ a reciente; nuevo. **in r. years,** en estos últimos años

**recently** /ˈrisəntli/ adv recientemente; (before past participles) recién. **until r.,** hasta hace poco. **r. painted,** recién pintado

**receptacle** /rɪˈsɛptəkəl/ n receptáculo, recipiente, m; Bot. receptáculo, m

**reception** /rɪˈsɛpʃən/ n recepción, f; recibo, m; (welcome) acogida, f; (of evidence) recepción, f. **r. room,** pieza de recibo, f, gabinete, m

**receptive** /rɪˈsɛptɪv/ a receptivo; susceptible

**receptiveness** /rɪˈsɛptɪvnɛs/ *n* sensibilidad, susceptibilidad, *f*

**recess** /rɪˈsɛs, ˈrisɛs/ *n* (holiday) vacacioneś, *f pl*;
(during school hours) hora de recreo, *f*; (*Fig.* heart)
seno, *m*, entrañas, *f pl*; (of the soul, heart) hondón,
*m*; (in a coastline, etc.) depresión, *f*; (in a wall)
nicho, *m*; (alcove) alcoba, *f*. **parliamentary r.**, interregno parlamentario, *m*

**recessional** /rɪˈsɛʃənl/ *n* himno que se canta mientras
se retiran los eclesiásticos y el coro, *m*

**recharge** /riˈtʃɑrdʒ/ *vt* (a gun, etc.) recargar; acusar
de nuevo

**recipe** /ˈrɛsəpi/ *n* receta, *f*

**recipient** /rɪˈsɪpiənt/ *n* recibidor (-ra); el, *m*, (*f*, la)
que recibe. —*a* recipiente; receptivo

**reciprocal** /rɪˈsɪprəkəl/ *a* recíproco

**reciprocate** /rɪˈsɪprəˌkeɪt/ *vt* reciprocar; *Mech.* producir movimiento de vaivén. —*vi Mech.* oscilar, tener
movimiento alternativo; corresponder; ser recíproco

**reciprocation** /rɪˌsɪprəˈkeɪʃən/ *n* reciprocación, *f*; reciprocidad, correspondencia, *f*

**reciprocity** /ˌrɛsəˈprɒsɪti/ *n* reciprocidad, *f*

**recital** /rɪˈsaɪtl/ *n* narración, relación, *f*; enumeración,
*f*; recitación, *f*; *Mus.* recital, *m*

**recitation** /ˌrɛsɪˈteɪʃən/ *n* recitación, *f*

**recitative** /ˌrɛsɪtəˈtiv/ *n* recitado, *m*

**recite** /rɪˈsaɪt/ *vt* recitar, repetir; narrar; declamar.
—*vi* decir una recitación

**reciter** /rɪˌsaɪtər/ *n* recitador (-ra); declamador (-ra)

**reckless** /ˈrɛklɪs/ *a* temerario, audaz; precipitado; descuidado (de); indiferente (a); excesivo; imprudente

**recklessly** /ˈrɛklɪsli/ *adv* temerariamente; descuidadamente; imprudentemente

**recklessness** /ˈrɛklɪsnɪs/ *n* temeridad, audacia, *f*; descuido, *m*; imprudencia, *f*; indiferencia, *f*

**reckon** /ˈrɛkən/ *vt* calcular, computar; contar; enumerar; (believe) considerar, juzgar; (attribute) atribuir;
(think) creer (que). **to r. up,** echar cuentas, calcular.
**to r. with,** contar con; tomar en serio

**reckoner** /ˈrɛkənər/ *n* calculador (-ra). **ready r.,** tablas matemáticas, *f pl*

**reckoning** /ˈrɛkənɪŋ/ *n* cálculo, *m*, calculación, *f*;
cuenta, *f*; *Fig.* retribución, *f*, castigo, *m*; *Naut.* estima,
*f.* **the day of r.,** el día de ajuste de cuentas; el día
del juicio final. **to be out in one's r.,** equivocarse en
el cálculo; engañarse en el juicio

**reclaim** /rɪˈkleɪm/ *vt* (land) entarquinar; (reform) reformar; (tame) domesticar; (claim) reclamar; (restore) restaurar

**reclamation** /ˌrɛkləˈmeɪʃən/ *n* (of land) entarquina-
miento, *m*; cultivo, *m*; (reform) reformación, *f*; (restoration) restauración, *f*; (claiming) reclamación, *f*

**recline** /rɪˈklaɪn/ *vt* apoyar; recostar; reclinar; descansar, reposar. —*vi* recostarse, reclinarse; estar tumbado; apoyarse; descansar

**reclining** /rɪˈklaɪnɪŋ/ *n* reclinación, *f.* —*a* inclinado;
acostado; (of statues) yacente

**recluse** /ˈrɛklus, rɪˈklus/ *a* solitario, *n* recluso (-sa);
solitario (-ia); ermitaño, *m*, anacoreta, *mf*

**recognition** /ˌrɛkəgˈnɪʃən/ *n* reconocimiento, *m*

**recognizable** /ˌrɛkəgˈnaɪzəbəl/ *a* que puede reconocerse; identificable

**recognizance** /rɪˈkɒgnəzəns, -ˈkɒnə-/ *n* reconocimiento, *m*; *Law.* obligación, *f*

**recognize** /ˈrɛkəgˌnaɪz/ *vt* reconocer; confesar

**recoil** /*n.* ˈriˌkɔɪl; *v.* rɪˈkɔɪl/ *n* reculada, *f*; (of a gun)
culatazo, *m*; (refusal) rechazo, *m*; (result) repercusión, *f*; (repugnance) aversión, repugnancia, *f.* —*vi*
recular; retroceder; repercutir; sentir repugnancia

**recoin** /riˈkɔɪn/ *vt* acuñar de nuevo

**recollect** /ˌrɛkəˈlɛkt/ *vt* acordarse de, recordar. **to r.
oneself,** reponerse, reponerse

**recollection** /ˌrɛkəˈlɛkʃən/ *n* recuerdo, *m*, memoria, *f*

**recommence** /ˌrikəˈmɛns/ *vt* and *vi* empezar de
nuevo

**recommend** /ˌrɛkəˈmɛnd/ *vt* recomendar; aconsejar;
encargar

**recommendable** /ˌrɛkəˈmɛndəbəl/ *a* recomendable

**recommendation** /ˌrɛkəmɛnˈdeɪʃən/ *n* recomendación, *f*

**recommendatory** /ˌrɛkəˈmɛndəˌtɔri/ *a* recomenda-
tario

**recommender** /ˌrɛkəˈmɛndər/ *n* el, *m*, (*f*, la) que recomienda

**recompense** /ˈrɛkəmˌpɛns/ *n* recompensa, *f*, *vt* recompensar

**recomposition** /ˌrikɒmpəˈzɪʃən/ *n* recomposición, *f*

**reconcilability** /ˌrɛkənˌsaɪləˈbɪlɪti/ *n* posibilidad de reconciliación, *f*; compatibilidad, *f*

**reconcilable** /ˌrɛkənˈsaɪləbəl/ *a* reconciliable; compatible; conciliable

**reconcile** /ˈrɛkənˌsaɪl/ *vt* reconciliar; (quarrels) componer, ajustar; (opposing theories, etc.) conciliar. **to
r. oneself ( to),** aceptar; acostumbrarse (a); resignarse (a)

**reconciler** /ˈrɛkənˌsaɪlər/ *n* reconciliador (-ra)

**reconciliation** /ˌrɛkənˌsɪliˈeɪʃən/ *n* reconciliación, *f*;
(of theories, etc.) conciliación, *f*

**reconciliatory** /ˌrɛkənˈsɪliəˌtɔri/ *a* reconciliador

**recondite** /ˈrɛkənˌdaɪt/ *a* recóndito

**recondition** /ˌrikənˈdɪʃən/ *vt* reacondicionar

**reconnaissance** /rɪˈkɒnəsəns, -zəns/ *n* reconocimiento, *m*; exploración, *f.* **r. flight,** vuelo de reconocimiento, *m*. **r. plane,** avión de reconocimiento, *m*

**reconnoiter** /ˌrikəˈnɔɪtər/ *vt Mil.* reconocer; explorar.
—*vi Mil.* practicar un reconocimiento; correr la campaña

**reconnoitering** /ˌrikəˈnɔɪtərɪŋ/ *n* reconocimiento, *m*,
*a* de reconocimiento

**reconquer** /riˈkɒŋkər/ *vt* reconquistar

**reconquest** /riˈkɒŋkwɛst/ *n* reconquista, *f*

**reconsecrate** /riˈkɒnsɪˌkreɪt/ *vt* consagrar de nuevo

**reconsider** /ˌrikənˈsɪdər/ *vt* considerar de nuevo,
volver a considerar; volver a discutir

**reconsideration** /ˌrikənˌsɪdəˈreɪʃən/ *n* nueva consideración, *f*; nueva discusión, *f*

**reconstitute** /riˈkɒnstɪˌtut/ *vt* reconstituir

**reconstitution** /ˌriˌkɒnstɪˈtuʃən/ *n* reconstitución, *f*

**reconstruct** /ˌrikənˈstrʌkt/ *vt* reconstruir

**reconstruction** /ˌrikənˈstrʌkʃən/ *n* reconstrucción, *f*

**reconversion** /ˌrikənˈvɜrʒən/ *n* reconversión, *f*

**recopy** /riˈkɒpi/ *vt* copiar de nuevo

**record** /*v.* rɪˈkɔrd; *n.* ˈrɛkərd/ *vt* apuntar; inscribir;
(recount) contar, escribir; recordar; registrar; (of
thermometers, etc.) marcar, registrar; hacer un disco
de gramófono de; (radio, cinema) impresionar. —*n*
relación, *f*; crónica, *f*; historia, *f*; (soldier's) hoja de
servicios, *f*; (past) antecedentes, *m pl*; documento, *m*;
inscripción, *f*; (entry) partida, *f*; testimonio, *m*;
(memory) recuerdo, *m*; registro, *m*; (gramophone)
disco de gramófono, *m*; *Sports.* record, *m*, plusmarca,
*f*; *pl* **records,** *m pl*; (notes) notas, *f pl*; (facts) datos,
*m pl*; anales, *m pl*. **keeper of the records,** archivero,
*m*. **off the r.,** confidencialmente. **on r.,** escrito; regis-
trado; inscrito en los anales de la historia. **to break a
r.,** supremar precedentes. **r.-holder,** plusmarquista,
*mf*

**recorder** /rɪˈkɔrdər/ *n* registrador, *m*; archivero, *m*;
*Law.* juez, *m*; (historian) historiador, *m*; *Mus.* caramillo, *m*; *Mech.* contador, indicador, *m*; (scientific)
aparato registrador, *m*

**recording** /rɪˈkɔrdɪŋ/ *a* registrador. **r. apparatus,**
(cinema, radio, gramophone) máquina de impresionar, *f*; (scientific) aparato registrador, *m*. **r. van,**
carro de sonido, *m*

**recount** /rɪˈkaʊnt/ *vt* contar de nuevo; (tell) referir,
narrar, contar

**recoup** /rɪˈkup/ *vt* compensar, indemnizar; recobrar,
desquitarse de

**recourse** /ˈrikɔrs/ *n* recurso, *m*. **to have r. to,** recurrir, *a*

**recover** /rɪˈkʌvər/ *vt* (regain) recobrar; *Fig.* reconquistar; (retrieve) rescatar; *Law.* reivindicar. —*vi*
reponerse; (in health) recobrar la salud, sanar, curarse; *Law.* ganar un pleito. **to r. consciousness,**
volver en sí

**recoverable** /rɪˈkʌvərəbəl/ *a* recuperable

**recovery** /rɪˈkʌvəri/ *n* (regaining) recobro, *m*, recuperación, *f*; (of money) cobranza, *f*; (retrieval) rescate,
*m*; *Fig.* reconquista, *f*; (from illness) mejoría, convalecencia, *f*; restablecimiento, *m*; *Law.* reivindicación, *f*

**recreant** /ˈrɛkriənt/ *a* traidor, falso, desleal. —*n*
apóstata, *mf* traidor (-ra)

**recreate** /ˈrɛkriˌeɪt/ *vt* recrear

**recreation** /ˌrɛkri'eɪʃən/ n recreación, f; (break in schools) recreo, m. **r. hall,** sala de recreo, f
**recreative** /'rɛkri,eitɪv/ a recreativo
**recriminate** /rɪ'krɪməˌneɪt/ vi recriminar
**recrimination** /rɪˌkrɪmə'neɪʃən/ n recriminación, reconvención, f
**recriminator** /rɪ'krɪməˌneɪtər/ n recriminador (-ra)
**recriminatory** /rɪ'krɪmənəˌtɔri/ a recriminador
**recross** /ri'krɔs/ vt volver a cruzar, cruzar de nuevo
**recrudesce** /ˌrikru'dɛs/ vi recrudecer
**recrudescence** /ˌrikru'dɛsəns/ n recrudescencia, f
**recrudescent** /ˌrikru'dɛsənt/ a recrudescente
**recruit** /rɪ'krut/ n recluta, m. —vt reclutar; (restore) reponer
**recruiting** /rɪ'krutɪŋ/ n reclutamiento, m. **r. office,** caja de reclutamiento, f
**recruiting flag** n bandera de enganche, f
**rectal** /'rɛktl/ a rectal
**rectangle** /'rɛk,tæŋgəl/ n rectángulo, m
**rectangular** /rɛk'tæŋgyələr/ a rectangular
**rectifiable** /'rɛktə,faɪəbəl/ a rectificable
**rectification** /ˌrɛktəfɪ'keɪʃən/ n rectificación, f
**rectifier** /'rɛktə,faɪər/ n rectificador, m
**rectify** /'rɛktə,faɪ/ vt rectificar
**rectilinear** /ˌrɛktl'ɪniər/ a rectilíneo
**rectitude** /'rɛktɪ,tud/ n rectitud, f
**rector** /'rɛktər/ n (of a university or school) rector, m; (priest) párroco, m
**rectorship** /'rɛktərˌʃɪp/ n rectorado, m
**rectory** /'rɛktəri/ n rectoral, rectoría, f
**rectum** /'rɛktəm/ n recto, m
**recumbent** /rɪ'kʌmbənt/ a recostado, reclinado; (of a statue) yacente
**recuperable** /rɪ'kupərəbəl/ a recuperable
**recuperate** /rɪ'kupə,reit/ vt recuperar, recobrar. —vi restablecerse, reponerse; recuperarse
**recuperation** /rɪkupə'reiʃən/ n recuperación, f
**recuperative** /rɪ'kupərətɪv/ a recuperativo
**recur** /rɪ'kɜr/ vi presentarse a la imaginación; volver (sobre); presentarse de nuevo, aparecer otra vez; repetirse; reproducirse
**recurrence** /rɪ'kɜrəns/ n reaparición, f; repetición, f
**recurrent** /rɪ'kɜrənt/ a periódico; Med. recurrente
**red** /rɛd/ a rojo; (of wine) tinto. —n color rojo, m; (in billiards) mingo, m, bola roja, f; Polit. rojo, m. **to catch red-handed,** coger con el hurto en las manos; coger con las manos en la masa, coger en el acto. **to grow red,** enrojecerse, ponerse rojo; volverse rojo. **red-berried,** con bayas rojas. **red cabbage,** lombarda, f. **red cedar,** cedro dulce, m. **red corpuscle,** glóbulo rojo, m. **Red Cross,** Cruz Roja, f. **red currant,** grosella, f. **red currant bush,** grosellero, m. **red-eyed,** con los ojos inyectados. **red fir,** pino silvestre, m. **red flush,** (in the sky) arrebol, m. **red-gold,** bermejo; (of hair, etc.) rojo. **red-haired,** pelirrojo, de pelo rojo. **red-handed,** con las manos ensangrentadas; Fig. en el acto. **red-head** (person) pelirrojo (-ja). **red-heat,** incandescencia, f. **red-hot,** candente. m. **red-lead,** minio, m. **red-letter,** de fiesta; extraordinario. **red-letter day,** día de fiesta, m; día extraordinario, m. **red mullet,** salmonete, m, trilla, f. **red ocher,** almagre, m. **red pepper,** pimiento, m; (cayenne) pimentón, m, **Red Sea,** mar Rojo, mar Bermejo, m. **red tape,** balduque, m; formulismo, m; burocracia, f. **red wine,** vino tinto, m
**redbreast** /'rɛd,brɛst/ n petirrojo, m
**redden** /'rɛdn/ vt rojear, enrojecer; pintar de rojo. —vi enrojecerse, ponerse rojo; volverse rojo
**reddish** /'rɛdɪʃ/ a rojizo
**redeem** /rɪ'dim/ vt (a mortgage, bonds, etc.) amortizar; (from pawn) desempeñar; (a promise, etc.) cumplir; libertar; redimir; compensar; (a fault) expiar; (reform) reformar; (rescue) rescatar
**redeemable** /rɪ'diməbəl/ a redimible; amortizable
**redeemer** /rɪ'dimər/ n rescatador (-ra); salvador (-ra); Theol. Redentor, m
**redeeming** /rɪ'dimɪŋ/ a redentor; compensatorio. **r. feature,** compensación, f; rasgo bueno, m. **There is no r. feature in his work,** No hay nada bueno en su obra
**redemption** /rɪ'dɛmpʃən/ n (of a mortgage, etc.)

amortización, f; (from pawn) desempeño, m; (of a promise, etc.) cumplimiento, m; (ransom, etc.) rescate, m; Theol. redención, f; compensación, f; (of a fault) expiación, f; reformación, f
**redemptive** /rɪ'dɛmptɪv/ a redentor
**redescend** /ˌridɪ'sɛnd/ vi bajar de nuevo
**rediscovery** /ˌridə'skʌvəri/ n nuevo descubrimiento, m
**redistribute** /ˌridɪ'strɪbyut/ vt distribuir de nuevo, volver a distribuir
**redistribution** /ˌridɪstrə'byuʃən/ n nueva distribución, f
**redness** /'rɛdnɪs/ n rojez, f, color rojo, m
**redolent** /'rɛdlənt/ a fragante, oloroso; Fig. evocador (de)
**redouble** /ri'dʌbəl/ vt redoblar. —vi redoblarse
**redoubling** /ri'dʌblɪŋ/ n redoblamiento, m
**redoubt** /rɪ'daut/ n reducto, m
**redoubtable** /rɪ'dautəbəl/ a formidable, terrible; valiente
**redound** /rɪ'daund/ vi redundar (en)
**redress** /rɪ'drɛs/ vt rectificar; reparar; remediar; hacer justicia (a); corregir
**reduce** /rɪ'dus/ vt reducir; disminuir; (in price) rebajar; abreviar; (exhaust, weaken) agotar; (impoverish) empobrecer; (degrade) degradar. **to r. to the ranks,** Mil. volver a las filas; degradar. **to be in reduced circumstances,** estar en la indigencia
**reducible** /rɪ'dusəbəl/ a reducible
**reduction** /rɪ'dʌkʃən/ n reducción, f; (in price) rebaja, f
**redundance** /rɪ'dʌndəns/ n redundancia, f
**redundant** /rɪ'dʌndənt/ a redundante; superfluo, excesivo
**reduplicate** /rɪ'duplɪ,keit/ vt reduplicar
**reduplication** /rɪˌduplɪ'keiʃən/ n reduplicación, f
**reecho** /ri'ɛkou/ vt repetir; devolver el son de, hacer reverberar. —vi repercutirse, reverberar
**reed** /rid/ n Bot. caña, f; (arrow) saeta, f; (pipe) caramillo, m; (in wind-instruments) lengüeta, f; Archit. junquillo, m; (in a loom) peine, m; (pastoral poetry) poesía bucólica, f. —vt (thatch) bardar con cañas
**reedit** /ri'ɛdɪt/ vt reeditar, volver a editar
**reedy** /'ridi/ a juncoso, lleno de cañas; (of the voice) silbante
**reef** /rif/ n arrecife, escollo, encalladero, m; Mineral. filón, m; Naut. rizo, m. —vt Naut. arrizar. **to take in reefs,** Naut. hacer el rizo. **r.-knot,** nudo de marino, m
**reek** /rik/ n humo, m; olor, m. —vi humear; oler (de); Fig. recordar, hacer pensar (en)
**reeky** /'riki/ a humoso
**reel** /ril/ n carrete, m; carrete, m; devanadera, f; (of a fishing rod) carrete, carretel, m; (cinema) cinta, f; (dance) baile escocés, m. —vt devanar. —vi tambalear, titubear; (of ships, etc.) cabecear; temblar; oscilar. **to r. about drunkenly,** (of persons) andar haciendo eses, arrimarse a las paredes. **to r. off,** recitar; enumerar; decir rápidamente
**reelect** /ˌrii'lɛkt/ vt reelegir
**reelection** /ˌrii'lɛkʃən/ n reelección, f
**reeligible** /ri'ɛlɪdʒəbəl/ a reelegible
**reeling** /'rilɪŋ/ n tambaleo, m; andar vacilante, m; (of a ship, etc.) cabeceo, m; oscilación, f
**reembarcation** /ˌriɛmbɑr'keiʃən/ n reembarque, m
**reembark** /ˌriɛm'bɑrk/ vt reembarcar. —vi reembarcarse
**reemerge** /ˌrii'mɜrdʒ/ vi reaparecer
**reemergence** /ˌrii'mɜrdʒəns/ n reaparición, f
**reenact** /ˌrii'nækt/ vt revalidar (una ley); decretar de nuevo
**reenactment** /ˌrii'næktmənt/ n revalidación (de una ley), f; nuevo decreto, m
**reengage** /ˌriɪn'geidʒ/ vt contratar de nuevo
**reengagement** /ˌriɪn'geidʒmənt/ n nuevo contrato, m
**reenlist** /ˌriɪn'lɪst/ vt and vi alistar(se) de nuevo
**reenlistment** /ˌriɪn'lɪstmənt/ n reenganche, m
**reenter** /ri'ɛntər/ vt volver a entrar (en); reingresar (en)
**reentry** /ri'ɛntri/ n segunda entrada, f, reingreso, m

**reequip** /ˌriː'kwɪp/ vt equipar de nuevo

**reestablish** /ˌriːs'tæblɪʃ/ vt restablecer; restaurar

**reestablishment** /ˌriːs'tæblɪʃmənt/ n restablecimiento, m; restauración, f

**reeve** /riːv/ vt Naut. laborear, guarnir

**reexamination** /ˌriːɡˌzæmɪ'neɪʃən/ n reexaminación, f; nuevo examen, m; Law. nuevo interrogatorio, m

**reexamine** /ˌriːɡ'zæmɪn/ vt reexaminar; Law. interrogar de nuevo

**reexport** /ˌriːk'spɔːt/ vt reexportar

**reexportation** /ˌriːkspɔːr'teɪʃən/ n reexportación, f

**refashion** /riː'fæʃən/ vt volver a hacer; formar de nuevo

**refection** /rɪ'fɛkʃən/ n refección, f

**refectory** /rɪ'fɛktəri/ n refectorio, m

**refer** /rɪ'fɜr/ vt atribuir (a); (send) enviar, remitir; (assign) referir (a), relacionar (con). —vi referirse (a); aludir (a); hablar (de)

**referee** /ˌrɛfə'riː/ n árbitro, m; Law. juez arbitrador, m; (reference) garante, mf fiador (-ra). —vi servir de árbitro

**reference** /'rɛfərəns/ n referencia, f; consulta, f; mención, f; alusión, f; (relation) relación, f; pl **references,** Com. referencias, f pl. **for r.,** para consulta. **in r. to,** con referencia a, respecto a, en cuanto a. **terms of r.,** puntos de consulta, m pl. **work of r.,** libro de consulta, m

**reference book** n libro de consulta, m

**referendum** /ˌrɛfə'rɛndəm/ n referéndum, m

**refill** /v. riː'fɪl; n. 'riːfɪl/ vt rellenar; rehenchir; (pen) llenar de nuevo con tinta. —n (for a pencil) mina de recambio, f

**refine** /rɪ'faɪn/ vt refinar; (metals) acrisolar; (fats) clarificar; Fig. perfeccionar, pulir, refinar

**refined** /rɪ'faɪnd/ a refinado; fino; culto; cortés; elegante; delicado; (subtle) sutil; (affected) afectado

**refinement** /rɪ'faɪnmənt/ n refinamiento, m; finura, f; cultura, f; cortesía, f; elegancia, f; delicadeza, f; (subtlety) sutileza, f; (affectation) afectación, f

**refiner** /rɪ'faɪnər/ n refinador, m

**refinery** /rɪ'faɪnəri/ n refinería, f

**refining** /rɪ'faɪnɪŋ/ n refinación, f; Fig. refinamiento, m

**refit** /riː'fɪt/ vt reparar; Naut. embonar

**refitting** /riː'fɪtɪŋ/ n reparación, f; Naut. embonada, f

**reflect** /rɪ'flɛkt/ vt reflejar; reflexionar. —vi reflejar; reflexionar (sobre), pensar (en), meditar (sobre). **This offer reflects credit on him,** Esta oferta le hace honor. **to r. on, upon,** reflexionar sobre; (disparage) desacreditar; (affect unfavorably) perjudicar

**reflecting** /rɪ'flɛktɪŋ/ a reflector

**reflection** /rɪ'flɛkʃən/ n Phys. reflexión, f; reflejo, m; consideración, f; pensamiento, m; (aspersion) censura, f, reproche, m. **upon mature r.,** después de pensarlo bien

**reflective** /rɪ'flɛktɪv/ a Phys. reflector; reflexivo, pensativo, meditabundo

**reflectively** /rɪ'flɛktɪvli/ adv reflexivamente

**reflector** /rɪ'flɛktər/ n reflector, m; (shade) pantalla, f

**reflex** /'riːflɛks/ a reflejo. —n reflejo, m; acción refleja, f. **r. action,** acción refleja, f

**refloat** /riː'floʊt/ vt (a ship) poner una vex a flote, desvarar

**reflux** /'riːˌflʌks/ n reflujo, m

**reforestation** n nuevas plantaciones, f pl

**reform** /rɪ'fɔrm/ n reforma, f. —a de reforma; reformista. —vt reformar; formar de nuevo. —vi reformarse

**reformation** /ˌrɛfər'meɪʃən/ n reformación, f; **Reformation,** Reforma, f

**reformatory** /rɪ'fɔrmə,tɔri/ a reformatorio, reformador. —n reformatorio, m, casa de corrección, f

**reformer** /rɪ'fɔrmər/ n reformador (-ra), reformista, mf

**refract** /rɪ'frækt/ vt refractar

**refraction** /rɪ'frækʃən/ n refracción, f

**refractive** /rɪ'fræktɪv/ a refringente

**refractoriness** /rɪ'fræktərɪnɪs/ n terquedad, obstinacia, f; rebeldia, indocilidad, f

**refractory** /rɪ'fræktəri/ a (of substances) refractario; recalcitrante, intratable, rebelde

**refrain** /rɪ'freɪn/ n estribillo, estrambote, m

**refrain** /rɪ'freɪn/ vi abstenerse (de), evitar

**refresh** /rɪ'frɛʃ/ vt refrescar

**refreshing** /rɪ'frɛʃɪŋ/ a refrescante; atractivo; estimulante; interesante

**refreshment** /rɪ'frɛʃmənt/ n (solace) solaz, reposo, m; recreación, f, deleite, m; (food and (or) drink) refresco, m. **r.-room,** (at a station) fonda, f

**refrigerate** /rɪ'frɪdʒə,reɪt/ vt refrigerar; enfriar; refrescar

**refrigeration** /rɪˌfrɪdʒə'reɪʃən/ n refrigeración, f; enfriamiento, m. **r. chamber,** cámara frigorífica, f

**refrigerative** /rɪ'frɪdʒərətɪv/ a refrigerante, frigorífico

**refrigerator** /rɪ'frɪdʒə,reɪtər/ n refrigerador, m, nevera, f

**refringent** /rɪ'frɪndʒənt/ a refringente

**refuel** /riː'fjuəl/ vt (a furnace) cargar con carbón, etc.; (of a ship) tomar carbón; (of an airplane, motor vehicle) tomar bencina

**refuge** /'rɛfjudʒ/ n refugio, m; asilo, m; (resort) recurso, m; subterfugio, m; (traffic island) refugio para peatones, m. **to take r.,** refugiarse; resguardarse (de)

**refugee** /ˌrɛfjʊ'dʒi/ n refugiado. —n refugiado (-da)

**refulgence** /rɪ'fʌldʒəns/ n refulgencia, f

**refulgent** /rɪ'fʌldʒənt/ a refulgente

**refund** /rɪ'fʌnd/ vt reembolsar; devolver

**refunding** /rɪ'fʌndɪŋ/ n reembolso, m; devolución, f

**refurbish** /ri'fɜrbɪʃ/ vt restaurar; renovar; (a literary work) refundir

**refurnish** /ri'fɜrnɪʃ/ vt amueblar de nuevo

**refusal** /rɪ'fyuzəl/ n negativa, f; (rejection) rechazo, m; (option) opción, f; preferencia, f

**refuse** /rɪ'fyuz/ vt negar; (reject) rechazar. —vi negarse (a), rehusar; (of a horse) resistirse a saltar

**refuse** /'rɛfyus/ n desecho, m; desperdicios, m pl; residuo, m; basura, f. —a de desecho. **r. dump,** muladar, m

**refutable** /rɪ'fyutəbəl/ a refutable

**refutation** /ˌrɛfyu'teɪʃən/ n refutación, f

**refute** /rɪ'fyut/ vt refutar

**regain** /ri'geɪn/ vt recobrar, recuperar; cobrar; ganar de nuevo; Fig. reconquistar. **to r. one's breath,** cobrar aliento. **to r. consciousness,** volver en sí

**regal** /'riɡəl/ a regio, real

**regale** /rɪ'geɪl/ vt regalar, agasajar; recrear, deleitar

**regalia** /rɪ'geiliə/ n regalía, f; insignias reales, f pl; distintivos, m pl, insignias, f pl

**regally** /'riɡəli/ adv regiamente

**regard** /rɪ'gɑrd/ vt mirar; observar; considerar; (respect) respetar; (concern) importar, concernir; relacionarse con. —n mirada, f; atención, f; (esteem) aprecio, f, estimación, f; respeto, m; veneración, f; (relation) referencia, f; pl **regards,** recuerdos, saludos, m pl. **He has little r. for their feelings,** Le importan poco sus susceptibilidades. **With kindest regards,** Con mis saludos más afectuosos. **as regards, with r. to,** con referencia a, respecto a, en cuanto a

**regardful** /rɪ'gɑrdfəl/ a atento (a), cuidadoso (de); que se preocupa (de)

**regarding** /rɪ'gɑrdɪŋ/ prep tocante a, en cuanto a, respecto de

**regardless** /rɪ'gɑrdlɪs/ a negligente (de); indiferente (a), insensible (a); que no se interesa (en); que no se inqueta (por); sin preocuparse (de)

**regatta** /rɪ'gætə, -'gɑtə/ n regata, f

**regency** /'ridʒənsi/ n regencia, f

**regeneracy** /rɪ'dʒɛnərəsi/ n regeneración, f

**regenerate** /rɪ'dʒɛnə,reɪt/ vt regenerar. —a regenerado

**regeneration** /rɪˌdʒɛnə'reɪʃən/ n regeneración, f

**regenerative** /rɪ'dʒɛnərətɪv/ a regenerador

**regenerator** /rɪ'dʒɛnə,reɪtər/ n regenerador (-ra)

**regent** /'ridʒənt/ n regente, mf

**régime** /rei'ʒim/ n régimen, m

**regimen** /'rɛdʒəmən/ n (Gram. Med.) régimen, m,

**regiment** /n. 'rɛdʒəmənt; v. -,ment/ n regimiento, m. —vt regimentar. **r. of the line,** tropa de línea, f

**regimental** /ˌrɛdʒə'mɛntl/ a de (un) regimiento, perteneciente a un regimiento

**regimentation** /ˌrɛdʒəmən'teɪʃən/ n regimentación, f

**region** /'riːdʒən/ n región, f
**regional** /'riːdʒənl/ a regional
**regionalism** /'riːdʒənl,ɪzəm/ n regionalismo, m
**regionalist** /'riːdʒənlɪst/ n regionalista, mf
**regionalistic** /'riːdʒənl,ɪstɪk/ a regionalista
**register** /'rɛdʒəstər/ n (record and Mech. Mus. Print.) registro, m; (of ships, etc.) matrícula, f; lista, f. —vt registrar; matricular; (a ship) abanderar; inscribir; (one's child in a school) anotar (Argentina), inscribir; (of thermometers, etc.) marcar; (letters) certificar; (luggage) facturar; (in one's mind) grabar; (emotion) mostrar, manifestar. —vi (at a hotel, etc.) registrarse; Print. estar en registro. **cash r.,** caja registradora, f. **r. of births, marriages and deaths,** registro civil, m
**registered letter** /'rɛdʒəstərd/ n carta certificada, f
**registrar** /'rɛdʒə,strɑr/ n registrador, m; archivero, m; secretario, m; (of a school) jefe de inscripciones, secretario general (the latter has many more duties). **r. of births, marriages and deaths,** secretario del registro civil, m. **registrar's office,** oficina del registro civil, f
**registration** /,rɛdʒə'streɪʃən/ n registro, m; inscripción, f; (of a vehicle, etc.) matrícula, f; Naut. abanderamiento, m; (of a letter, etc.) certificación, f. **r. number,** número de matrícula, m
**registry** /'rɛdʒəstri/ n registro, m; inscripción, f; matrícula, f. **r. office,** oficina del registro civil, f; (for servants) agencia doméstica, f
**regression** /rɪ'grɛʃən/ n regresión, f, retroceso, m
**regret** /rɪ'grɛt/ vt sentir; lamentar, pesar; arrepentirse (de); (miss) echar de menos (a). —n sentimiento, pesar, m; (remorse) remordimiento, m. **I r. very much that...,** Me pesa mucho que..., Siento mucho que... **to send one's regrets,** mandar sus excusas
**regretful** /rɪ'grɛtfəl/ a lleno de pesar; arrepentido; lamentable, deplorable. **He was most r. that...,** Lamentaba mucho que...
**regretfully** /rɪ'grɛtfəli/ adv con pesar
**regrettable** /rɪ'grɛtəbəl/ a lamentable, deplorable; doloroso; (with loss, etc.) sensible
**regrettably** /rɪ'grɛtəbli/ adv lamentablemente; sensiblemente
**regroup** /ri'grup/ vt arreglar de nuevo; formar de nuevo; reorganizar
**regular** /'rɛgyələr/ a regular; normal; (ordinary) corriente, común; (in order) en regla; (Gram. Bot. Eccl. Mil. Geom.) regular. —n Eccl. regular, m; (soldier) soldado de línea, m; (officer) militar de carrera, m; (client) parroquiano habitual, m
**regularity** /,rɛgyə'lærɪti/ n regularidad,
**regularization** /,rɛgyələrə'zeɪʃən/ n regularización, f
**regularize** /'rɛgyələ,raiz/ vt regularizar
**regularly** /'rɛgyələrli/ adv regularmente
**regulate** /'rɛgyə,leit/ vt regular; ajustar, arreglar; (direct) dirigir; reglamentar
**regulation** /,rɛgyə'leɪʃən/ n regulación, f; arreglo, m; (rule) reglamento, m, a de reglamento; normal
**regulative** /'rɛgyə,leitiv/ a regulador
**regulator** /'rɛgyə,leitər/ n Mech. regulador, m
**regurgitate** /rɪ'gɜrdʒɪ,teit/ vt and vi regurgitar
**regurgitation** /rɪ,gɜrdʒɪ'teiʃən/ n regurgitación, f
**rehabilitate** /,rihə'bɪlɪ,teit/ vt rehabilitar
**rehabilitation** /,rihə,bɪlɪ'teiʃən/ n rehabilitación, f
**rehash** /ri'hæʃ/ vt (a literary work, etc.) refundir
**rehearing** /ri'hiərɪŋ/ n nueva audición, f, (of a case) revisión, f
**rehearsal** /rɪ'hɜrsəl/ n Theat. ensayo, m; recitación, f; relación, narración, f. **dress r.,** ensayo general, m
**rehearse** /rɪ'hɜrs/ vt Theat. ensayar; recitar; (narrate) narrar; enumerar
**reheat** /ri'hit/ vt recalentar
**reign** /rein/ n reinado, m. —vi reinar; predominar
**reigning** /'reinɪŋ/ a reinante; predominante
**reimburse** /,riɪm'bɜrs/ vt reembolsar
**reimbursement** /,riɪm'bɔrsmənt/ n reembolso, m
**reimport** /ri'impɔrt/ vt importar de nuevo, reimportar, n reimporte, m
**reimportation** /,riɪmpɔr'teiʃən/ n reimportación, f
**reimpose** /,riɪm'pouz/ vt reimponer
**reimposition** /,riɪmpə'zɪʃən/ n reimposición, f

**reimprison** /,riɪm'prɪzən/ vt encarcelar de nuevo, reencarcelar
**reimprisonment** /,riɪm'prɪzənmənt/ n reencarcelamiento, m
**rein** /rein/ n rienda, f. —vt llevar las riendas (de); (hold back) refrenar. **to give r. to,** Fig. dar rienda suelta (a)
**reincarnation** /,riɪnkɑr'neiʃən/ n reencarnación, f
**reincorporate** /,riɪn'kɔrpə,reit/ vt reincorporar
**reincorporation** /,riɪn,kɔrpə'reiSən/ n reincorporación, f
**reindeer** /'rein,diər/ n reno, m
**reinforce** /,riɪn'fɔrs/ vt reforzar; (concrete) armar; fortalecer. **reinforced concrete,** n hormigón armado, m
**reinforcement** /,riɪn'fɔrsmənt/ n reforzamiento, m; (Mil. Nav. Fig.) refuerzo, m
**reins.** n See rein
**reinsert** /,riɪn'sɜrt/ vt volver a insertar
**reinstall** /,riɪn'stɔl/ vt reinstalar; rehabilitar
**reinstallment** /,riɪn'stɔlmənt/ n reinstalación, f; rehabilitación, f; restablecimiento, m
**reinstate** /,riɪn'steit/ vt reponer, restablecer; reinstalar; rehabilitar
**reinstatement** /,riɪn'steitmənt/ n restablecimiento, m; rehabilitación, f
**reinsurance** /,riɪnʃurəns/ n reaseguro, m
**reinsure** /,riɪn'ʃur, -'ʃɜr/ vt reasegurar
**reintegrate** /ri'intə,greit/ vt reintegrar
**reintegration** /,riɪntə'greiʃən/ n reintegración, f
**reinter** /,riɪn'tɜr/ vt enterrar de nuevo
**reinvest** /,riɪn'vɛst/ vt reinvertir
**reinvestment** /,riɪn'vɛstmənt/ n reinversión, f
**reinvigorate** /,riɪn'vɪgə,reit/ vt reanimar, dar nuevo vigor, f
**reinvite** /,riɪn'vait/ vt invitar de nuevo (a)
**reissue** /ri'ɪʃu/ n nueva emisión, f; (of a book, etc.) nueva edición, reimpresión, f. —vt hacer una nueva emisión (de); reeditar, publicar de nuevo
**reiterate** /ri'itə,reit/ vt reiterar, repetir
**reiteration** /ri,itə'reiʃən/ n reiteración, f
**reiterative** /ri'itə,reitiv/ a reiterativo
**reject** /v. rɪ'dʒɛkt/ vt rechazar, rehusar; repudiar; repulsar; desechar
**rejection** /rɪ'dʒɛkʃən/ n rechazamiento, m; repudiación, refutación, f; repulsa, f
**rejoice** /rɪ'dʒɔis/ vt alegrar, regocijar. —vi alegrarse (de), regocijarse (de), gloriarse (en)
**rejoicing** /rɪ'dʒɔisɪŋ/ n regocijo, júbilo, m, alegría, f; algazara, f, fiestas, f pl
**rejoin** /rɪ'dʒɔin/ vt and vi juntar de nuevo; volver a; reunirse con; (reply) contestar, replicar
**rejoinder** /rɪ'dʒɔindər/ n contestación, respuesta, f
**rejuvenate** /rɪ'dʒuvə,neit/ vt rejuvenecer
**rejuvenation** /rɪ,dʒuvə'neiʃən/ n rejuvenecimiento, m
**rekindle** /ri'kɪndl/ vt encender de nuevo; despertar, reavivar. —vi encenderse de nuevo; reavivarse
**relapse** /rɪ'l{ps; n. also 'riːlæps/ n reincidencia, recaída, f; Med. recidiva, f. —vi reincidir (en); Med. recaer
**relapsed** /rɪ'læpst/ a relapso
**relate** /rɪ'leit/ vt (recount) relatar, narrar; relacionar; unir; (of kinship) emparentar. —vi ajustarse (a); referirse (a). **The first fact is not related to the second,** El primer hecho no tiene nada que ver con el segundo
**related** /rɪ'leitid/ a relacionado; (by kinship) emparentado. **John is well-r.,** Juan es de buena familia; Juan es de familia influyente; Juan tiene buenas relaciones
**relater** /rɪ,leitər/ n narrador (-ra)
**relation** /rɪ'leiʃən/ n (narrative) relación, narración, f; conexión, f; relación, f; (kinship) parentesco, m; (person) pariente (-ta). **in r. to,** con relación a, en cuanto a
**relationship** /rɪ'leiʃən,ʃip/ n parentesco, m; conexión, relación, f
**relative** /'rɛlətiv/ a relativo. —n pariente (-ta); pl **relatives,** parientes, m pl, parentela, f
**relativism** /'rɛlətə,vɪzəm/ n relativismo, m
**relativity** /,rɛlə'tɪvɪti/ n relatividad, f

**relator** /rɪ'leitər/ n Law. relator, m

**relax** /rɪ'læks/ vt relajar; aflojar; (make less severe) ablandar; (decrease) mitigar. —vi relajarse; aflojar; (rest) descansar

**relaxation** /,rilæk'seiʃən/ n relajación, f; aflojamiento, m; ablandamiento, m; mitigación, f; (rest) descanso, reposo, m; (pastime) pasatiempo, m; (amusement) diversión, f

**relaxing** /rɪ'læksɪŋ/ a relajante; (of climate) enervante

**relay** /'rilei/ v. rɪ'lei/ n (of horses) parada, f; (shift) tanda, f; relevo, m; Elec. relais, m; Radio. redifusión, f. —vt enviar por posta; Elec. reemitir; Radio. retransmitir; (lay again) colocar de nuevo. **r. race,** carrera de equipo, carrera de relevos, f

**release** /rɪ'lis/ vt soltar; (hurl) lanzar; (set free) poner en libertad (a); librar (de); absolver; (surrender) renunciar (a); dar al público, poner en circulación; (lease again) realquilar. —n soltura, f; lanzamiento, m; liberación, f; (from pain) alivio, m; remisión, f; exoneración, f; publicación, f; (of films) representación, f; Law. soltura, f

**relegate** /'relɪ,geit/ vt relegar

**relegation** /,relɪ'geiʃən/ n relegación, f

**relent** /rɪ'lent/ vi ablandarse, enternecerse; ceder

**relenting** /rɪ'lentɪŋ/ n enternecimiento, desenojo, m

**relentless** /rɪ'lentlis/ a implacable, inexorable; despiadado

**relentlessly** /rɪ'lentlisli/ adv inexorablemente; sin piedad

**relentlessness** /rɪ'lentlisnis/ n inexorabilidad, f; falta de piedad, f

**relet** /ri'let/ vt realquilar

**relevance** /'reləvəns/ n conexión, f; pertinencia, f; aplicabilidad, f

**relevant** /'reləvənt/ a relativo; pertinente, a propósito, oportuno; aplicable

**reliability** /rɪ,laiə'bɪliti/ n seguridad, f; formalidad, f; confianza, f; exactitud, f; veracidad, f

**reliable** /rɪ'laiəbəl/ a seguro; formal; digno de crédito, de confianza, sclvente digno de confianza; exacto; veraz

**reliably** /rɪ'laiəbli/ adv seguramente; de una manera digna de confianza; exactamente

**reliance** /rɪ'laiəns/ n confianza, f. **to place r. on,** tener confianza en

**reliant** /rɪ'laiənt/ a confiado

**relic** /'relɪk/ n vestigio, rastro, m; Eccl. reliquia, f

**relict** /'relɪkt/ n viuda, f

**relief** /rɪ'lif/ n (alleviation) alivio, m; desahogo, m; (help) socorro, m, ayuda, f; beneficencia, f; Mil. relevo, m; (pleasure) placer, m, satisfacción, f; (consolation) consuelo, m; Law. remisión, f; Art. relieve, m. **high r.,** alto relieve, m. **low r.,** bajo relieve, m. **r. map,** mapa en relieve, m. **r. train,** tren de socorro, m

**relieve** /rɪ'liv/ vt aliviar; aligerar, suavizar; mitigar; (one's feelings, etc.) desahogar; (Mil. and to take the place of) relevar; (free) librar; (dismiss) destituir; (remove) quitar; (rob) robar; (help) socorrer, remediar; (redeem) redimir; (ornament) adornar; (from a wrong) hacer justicia (a)

**relieving** /rɪ'livɪŋ/ n alivio, m; aligeramiento, m; mitigación, f; (of the feelings) desahogo, m; Mil. relevo, m; (help) socorro, m. **r. arch,** sobrearco, m

**relight** /ri'lait/ vt volver a encender. —vi encenderse de nuevo

**religion** /rɪ'lɪdʒən/ n religión, f

**religiosity** /rɪ,lɪdʒi'ɒsiti/ n religiosidad, f

**religious** /rɪ'lɪdʒəs/ a religioso; en religión; piadoso, crevente; devoto. —n religioso (-sa). **r. orders,** órdenes religiosas, f pl. **r. toleration,** libertad de cultos, f

**religiousness** /rɪ'lɪdʒəsnis/ n religiosidad, f

**relinquish** /rɪ'lɪŋkwɪʃ/ vt abandonar; (one's grip) soltar; renunciar; desistir (de), dejar (de); (a post) dimitir (de)

**relinquishment** /rɪ'lɪŋkwɪʃmənt/ n abandono, m; renuncia, f; dejamiento, m; (of a post) dimisión, f

**reliquary** /'relɪ,kweri/ n relicario, m

**relish** /'relɪʃ/ n gusto, m; sabor, m; (touch, smack) dejo, m; condimento, m; apetito, m, gana, f. —vt gustar de; comer con apetito; saborear, paladear; Fig.

seducir, atraer, gustar. —vi tener gusto (de). **I do not much r. the idea,** No me seduce la idea

**relishing** /'relɪʃɪŋ/ n saboreo, m; (enjoyment) goce, m, fruición, f; consideración, f

**relive** /ri'lɪv/ vt vivir de nuevo, volver a vivir

**reload** / ri'loud/ vt recargar

**reluctance** /rɪ'lʌktəns/ n repugnancia, desgana, f. **with r.,** a regañadientes, de mala gana

**reluctant** /rɪ'lʌktənt/ a poco dispuesto (a), que tiene repugnancia (a hacer algo), sin gana; (forced) forzado; artificial; (hesitating) vacilante

**reluctantly** /rɪ'lʌktəntli/ adv de mala gana, con repugnancia, a disgusto

**rely on** /rɪ'lai/ vi contar con, confiar en, depender de

**remain** /rɪ'mein/ vi quedar; permanecer; (be left over) sobrar; continuar. **I r. yours faithfully...,** (in a letter) Queda de Vd. su att. s.s.... **It remains to be written,** Queda por escribir

**remainder** /rɪ'meindər/ n resto, m; restos, m pl, sobras, f pl; residuo, m. **The r. of the people went away,** Los demás se marcharon

**remaining** /rɪ'meinɪŋ/ pres part and a que queda; sobrante

**remains** /rɪ'meinz/ n pl restos, m pl; sobras, f pl, desperdicios, m pl; ruinas, f pl

**remake** /v. ri'meik/ vt rehacer; reformar

**remand** /rɪ'mænd/ vt Law. reencarcelar. —n Law. reencarcelamiento, m

**remark** /rɪ'mɑrk/ n observación, f; nota, f; comentario, m. —vt and vi observar; notar. **to r. on,** comentar, hacer una observación sobre

**remarkable** /rɪ'mɑrkəbəl/ a notable, singular, extraordinario

**remarkableness** /rɪ'mɑrkəbəlnis/ n singularidad, f, lo extraordinario

**remarkably** /rɪ'mɑrkəbli/ adv singularmente

**remarriage** /ri'mærɪdʒ/ n segundas nupcias, f pl, segundo casamiento, m

**remarry** /ri'mæri/ vt volver a casar (a). —vi casarse en segundas nupcias; volver a casarse

**remediable** /rɪ'midiəbəl/ a remediable

**remedial** /rɪ'midiəl/ a remediador; curativo, terapéutico

**remedy** /'remɪdi/ n remedio, m; recurso, m, vt remediar; curar

**remember** /rɪ'membər/ vt recordar; tener presente; acordarse de. —vi acordarse; no olvidarse. **R. me to your mother,** Dale recuerdos míos a tu madre. **If I r. rightly...,** Si bien me acuerdo... **And r. that I shall do no more!** ¡Y no olvides que no haré más!

**remembrance** /rɪ'membrəns/ n recuerdo, m; memoria, f; pl **remembrances,** recuerdos, m pl

**remind** /rɪ'maind/ vt recordar

**reminder** /rɪ'maindər/ n recuerdo, m; (warning) advertencia, f. **a gentle r.,** una indirecta, una insinuación

**reminisce** /,remə'nis/ vi Inf. recordar viejas historias

**reminiscence** /,remə'nisəns/ n reminiscencia, f, recuerdo, m

**reminiscent** /,remə'nisənt/ a evocador, que recuerda; de reminiscencia; que piensa en el pasado. **to be r. of,** recordar; Inf. oler a

**reminiscently** /,remə'nisəntli/ adv evocadoramente, como si recordara

**remiss** /rɪ'mis/ a negligente, descuidado

**remission** /rɪ'miʃən/ n remisión, f

**remissly** /rɪ'misli/ adv negligentemente

**remissness** /rɪ'misnis/ n negligencia, f, descuido, m

**remit** /rɪ'mit/ vt remitir; Com. remesar, enviar. —vi (pay) pagar

**remittance** /rɪ'mitns/ n remesa, f, envío, m

**remitter** /rɪ'mitər/ n remitente, mf

**remnant** /'remnənt/ n resto, m; (of fabric) retal, retazo, m; (relic) vestigio, m, reliquia, f. **r. sale,** saldo, m

**remodel** /ri'mɒdl/ vt rehacer; reformar; modelar de nuevo; (a play, etc.) refundir

**remodeling** /ri'mɒdlɪŋ/ n reformación, f; (of a play, etc.) refundición, f

**remonstrance** /rɪ'mɒnstrəns/ n protesta, f; reconvención, f

**remonstrate** /rɪ'mɒnstreɪt/ vi protestar, objetar. **to r. with,** reprochar, reconvenir

**remorse** /rɪ'mɔrs/ n remordimiento, m

**remorseful** /rɪ'mɔrsfəl/ a lleno de remordimientos; penitente, arrepentido

**remorsefully** /rɪ'mɔrsfəli/ adv con remordimiento

**remorseless** /rɪ'mɔrslɪs/ a sin conciencia, sin remordimientos; despiadado, inflexible

**remorselessness** /rɪ'mɔrslɪsnɪs/ n inexorabilidad, crueldad, dureza, f

**remote** /rɪ'mout/ a distante, lejano; remoto; aislado; ajeno; (slight) leve, vago. **r. control,** mando a distancia, m

**remotely** /rɪ'moutli/ adv remotamente

**remoteness** /rɪ'moutnɪs/ n distancia, f; aislamiento, m; alejamiento, m; (vagueness) vaguedad, f

**remount** /v. ri'maunt; n. 'ri,maunt/ vt subir de nuevo, montar de nuevo; Mil. remontar. —vi (go back to) remontar (a), derivarse (de). —n Mil. remonta, f

**removable** /rɪ'muvəbəl/ a que puede quitarse; (of collars, etc.) de quita y pon; transportable; (of officials, etc.) amovible

**removal** /rɪ'muvəl/ n acción de quitar o levantar, f; sacamiento, m; separación, f; eliminación, f; alejamiento, m; traslado, m; (from office, etc.) deposición, f; supresión, f; asesinato, m. **r. van,** carro de mudanzas, m

**remove** /rɪ'muv/ vt quitar; retirar; levantar; sacar; apartar; separar; eliminar; trasladar; (from office) destituir; suprimir; asesinar. —vi trasladarse. —n grado, m; distancia, f; (departure) partida, f. **to r. oneself,** quitarse de en medio. **to r. one's hat,** descubrirse. **first cousin once removed,** hijo de primo carnal, primo hermano del padre, primo hermano de la madre, m

**remunerate** /rɪ'myunə,reɪt/ vt remunerar

**remuneration** /rɪ,myunə'reɪʃən/ n remuneración, f

**remunerative** /rɪ'myunərətɪv/ a remunerador

**renaissance** /'rɛnə,sɑns/ n renacimiento, m, a renacentista

**Renaissance man** /'rɛnə,sɑns/ n hombre del Renacimiento, m

**Renaissance woman** n mujer del Renacimiento, f

**renal** /'rinl/ a renal

**rename** /ri'neɪm/ vt poner otro nombre (a)

**renascent** /rɪ'næsənt, -'neɪsənt/ a renaciente, que renace

**rend** /rɛnd/ vt desgarrar, rasgar; Fig. lacerar; (split) hender; Fig. dividir. **to r. from,** arrancar (a). **to r. the air,** (with cries, etc.) llenar el aire

**render** /'rɛndər/ vt (return) devolver; dar; rendir; (make) hacer; (help, service) prestar; interpretar; (translate) traducir; (fat) derretir y clarificar

**rendering** /'rɛndərɪŋ/ n versión, f; interpretación, f

**rendezvous** /'rɑndə,vu, -deɪ-/ n cita, f; lugar de cita, m; reunión, f. —vi reunirse

**rending** /'rɛndɪŋ/ n desgarro, m; hendimiento, m

**renegade** /'rɛnɪ,geɪd/ a renegado. —n renegado (-da)

**renew** /rɪ'nu/ vt renovar; (resume) reanudar; (a lease, etc.) prorrogar

**renewable** /rɪ'nuəbəl/ a renovable

**renewal** /rɪ'nuəl/ n renovación, f; (resumption) reanudación, f; (of a lease, etc.) prorrogación, f

**renewed** /rɪ'nud/ a renovado; nuevo

**rennet** /'rɛnɪt/ n cuajo, m

**renounce** /rɪ'nauns/ vt renunciar; (a throne) abdicar; renegar (de), repudiar; abandonar. —vi Law. desistir; (cards) renunciar

**renouncement** /rɪ'naunsmənt/ n renuncia, f; (of a throne) abdicación, f; repudiación, f

**renovate** /'rɛnə,veɪt/ vt renovar; limpiar; restaurar

**renovation** /,rɛnə'veɪʃən/ n renovación, f; limpiadura, f; restauración, f

**renovator** /'rɛnə,veɪtər/ n renovador (-ra)

**renown** /rɪ'naun/ n renombre, m, fama, f

**renowned** /rɪ'naund/ a renombrado, famoso

**rent** /rɛnt/ n (tear) rasgadura, f; desgarro, m; abertura, f; raja hendedura, f; (discord) división, f; (hire) alquiler, m; arrendamiento, m. —vt arrendar, alquilar. **r.-free,** sin pagar alquiler

**rentable** /'rɛntəbəl/ a alquilable, arrendable

**rental** /'rɛntl/ See rent

**renter** /'rɛntər/ n arrendador (-ra)

**rentier** n rentista, mf

**renting** /'rɛntɪŋ/ n alquiler, arrendamiento, m

**renumber** /ri'nʌmbər/ vt numerar de nuevo

**renunciation** /rɪ,nʌnsi'eɪʃən/ n renunciación, renuncia, f

**reoccupy** /ri'ɒkyu,paɪ/ vt volver a ocupar, ocupar otra vez

**reopen** /ri'oupən/ vt abrir de nuevo, volver a abrir. —vi abrirse nuevamente, abrirse otra vez

**reopening** /ri'oupənɪŋ/ n reapertura, f

**reorder** /ri'ɔrdər/ vt ordenar de nuevo, Com. volver a pedir. —n Com. nuevo pedido, m

**reorganization** /,riɔrgənə'zeɪʃən/ n reorganización, f

**reorganize** /ri'ɔrgə,naɪz/ vt reorganizar

**reorganizing** /ri'ɔrgə,naɪzɪŋ/ a reorganizador

**repack** /ri'pæk/ vt reembalar; reenvasar; volver a hacer (una maleta)

**repaint** /ri'peɪnt/ vt pintar de nuevo

**repainting** /ri'peɪntɪŋ/ n nueva pintura, f

**repair** /rɪ'pɛər/ vt arreglar (e.g. a machine) componer, remendar; reparar; restaurar; rehacer. —vi (with to) dirigirse a, ir a; acudir a. —n arreglo m, reparación, f; compostura, f; restauración, f. **to keep in r.,** conservar en buen estado

**repairable** /rɪ'pɛərəbəl/ a que se puede componer

**repairer** /rɪ'pɛərər/ n componedor (-ra); restaurador (-ra)

**repairing** /rɪ'pɛərɪŋ/ a reparador

**reparable** /'rɛpərəbəl/ a reparable; remediable

**reparation** /,rɛpə'reɪʃən/ n reparación, f

**repartee** /,rɛpɑr'ti, -'teɪ, -ɑr-/ n respuestas, agudezas, f pl; Inf. dimes y diretes, m pl

**repast** /rɪ'pæst/ n comida, f; (light) colación, f

**repatriate** /v. ri'peɪtri,eɪt/ vt repatriar

**repatriation** /ri,peɪtri'eɪʃən/ n repatriación, f

**repay** /rɪ'peɪ/ vt reembolsar; recompensar, pagar; pagar en la misma moneda. —vi pagar. **It well repays a visit,** Vale la pena de visitarse

**repayable** /rɪ'peɪəbəl/ a reembolsable

**repayment** /rɪ'peɪmənt/ n reembolso, m; pago, retorno, m

**repeal** /rɪ'pil/ n abrogación, revocación, f, vt abrogar, rescindir, revocar

**repeat** /rɪ'pit/ vt repetir; reiterar; (renew) renovar; duplicar. —n repetición, f

**repeated** /rɪ'pitɪd/ a reiterado; redoblado

**repeatedly** /rɪ'pitɪdli/ adv reiteradamente, repetidamente

**repeater** /rɪ'pitər/ n repetidor (-ra); reloj de repetición, m; arma de repetición, f

**repel** /rɪ'pɛl/ vt repeler; ahuyentar; (spurn) rechazar; Phys. resistir; repugnar

**repellent** /rɪ'pɛlənt/ a repulsivo

**repent** /rɪ'pɛnt/ vt arrepentirse de. —vi arrepentirse

**repentance** /rɪ'pɛntns/ n arrepentimiento, m, penitencia, f

**repentant** /rɪ'pɛntnt/ a arrepentido, penitente, contrito

**repentantly** /rɪ'pɛntntli/ adv arrepentido, con contrición

**repeople** /ri'pipəl/ vt repoblar

**repeopling** /ri'pipəlɪŋ/ n repoblación, f

**repercuss** /,ripər'kʌs/ vt repercutir (en)

**repercussion** /,ripər'kʌʃən/ n repercusión, f

**repercussive** /,ripər'kʌsɪv/ a repercusivo

**repertory** /'rɛpər,tɔri/ n repertorio, m

**repetition** /,rɛpɪ'tɪʃən/ n repetición, f; recitación, f

**repetitive** /rɪ'pɛtɪtɪv/ a iterativo

**repine** /rɪ'paɪn/ vi afligirse (de); quejarse (de); padecer nostalgia

**repining** /rɪ'paɪnɪŋ/ n pesares, m pl; quejas, f pl; descontento, m; nostalgia, f

**replace** /rɪ'pleɪs/ vt (put back) reponer, colocar de nuevo; restituir, devolver; (renew) renovar; (in a post, etc.) reemplazar, substituir

**replaceable** /rɪ'pleɪsəbəl/ a restituible; renovable; reemplazable

**replacement** /rɪ'pleɪsmənt/ n reposición, f; restitución, devolución, f; renovación, f; reemplazo, m

**replant** /ri'plænt/ *vt* replantar

**replanting** /ri'plæntɪŋ/ *n* replantación, *f*

**replenish** /rɪ'plɛnɪʃ/ *vt* rellenar

**replenishment** /rɪ'plɛnɪʃmənt/ *n* relleno, *m*

**replete** /rɪ'plit/ *a* repleto

**repletion** /rɪ'pliʃən/ *n* repleción, *f*

**replica** /'rɛplɪkə/ *n* réplica, *f*

**reply** /rɪ'plai/ *n* respuesta, contestación, *f*, *vi* responder, contestar. **Awaiting your r.,** En espera de sus noticias. **in his r.,** en su respuesta

**repolish** /ri'pɒlɪʃ/ *vt* repulir

**repopulate** /ri'pɒpjə,leit/ *vt* repoblar

**repopulation** /ri,pɒpjə'leiʃən/ *n* repoblación, *f*

**report** /rɪ'pɔrt/ *n* (rumor) voz, *f*, rumor, *m*; (reputation) fama, *f*; (news) noticia, *f*; (journalistic) reportaje, *m*; (*Mil. Nav.* and from school) parte, *f*; (weather) boletín, *m*; (proceedings) actas, *f pl*; (statement) informe, *m*; relación, *f*; (of a gun, etc.) detonación, *f*; explosión, *f*. —*vt* dar cuenta de, relatar; informar; (measure) registrar; (*Mil. Nav.*) dar parte de; comunicar; (journalistic) hacer un reportaje de; (transcribe) transcribir; (accuse) denunciar; quejarse de. —*vi* presentar informe; ser reportero; (present oneself) presentarse, comparecer. **It is reported that...,** Se informa que...

**report card** *n* boletín de calificaciones, *m*

**reporter** /rɪ'pɔrtər/ *n* reportero (-ra); *Law.* relator, *m*

**reporting** /rɪ'pɔrtɪŋ/ *n* reporterismo, *m*

**repose** /rɪ'pouz/ *n* reposo, *m*; quietud, *f*; tranquilidad, serenidad, *f*. —*vt* reposar, descansar; reclinar; (place) poner. —*vi* reposar; tener confianza (en); basarse (en)

**repository** /rɪ'pɒzɪ,tɔri/ *n* repositorio, depósito, *m*; almacén, *m*; (furniture) guardamuebles, *m*; (person) depositario (-ia)

**repoussé** /,rəpu'sei/ *n* repujado, *m*. **to work in r.,** repujar

**reprehend** /,rɛprɪ'hɛnd/ *vt* reprender, reprobar

**reprehensible** /,rɛprɪ'hɛnsəbəl/ *a* reprensible

**reprehension** /,rɛprɪ'hɛnʃən/ *n* reprensión, *f*

**represent** /,rɛprɪ'zɛnt/ *vt* representar; significar

**representation** /,rɛprɪzɛn'teiʃən/ *n* representación, *f*

**representational** /,rɛprɪzɛn'teiʃənl/ *a* Art. realista

**representative** /,rɛprɪ'zɛntətɪv/ *a* que representa; representativo. —*n* representante, *mf*

**repress** /rɪ'prɛs/ *vt* reprimir

**repression** /rɪ'prɛʃən/ *n* represión, *f*

**repressive** /rɪ'prɛsɪv/ *a* represivo

**reprieve** /rɪ'priv/ *vt* Law. aplazar la ejecución (de); *Fig.* dar una tregua (a)

**reprimand** /'rɛprə,mænd/ *n* reprimenda, *f*, *vt* reprender

**reprint** /*n.* 'ri,prɪnt; *v.* ri'prɪnt; / *n* reimpresión, tirada aparte, separata, *f*, *vt* reimprimir

**reprinting** /'ri,prɪntɪŋ/ *n* reimpresión, *f*

**reprisal** /rɪ'praizəl/ *n* represalia, *f*. **to take reprisals,** tomar represalias

**reproach** /rɪ'proutʃ/ *n* reproche, *m*; censura, *f*; (shame) vergüenza, *f*. —*vt* reprochar; censurar, echar en cara, afear

**reproachful** /rɪ'proutʃfəl/ *a* severo; lleno de reproches; de censura; (shameful) vergonzoso

**reproachfully** /rɪ'proutʃfəli/ *adv* con reprobación, con reprensión, severamente

**reproachfulness** /rɪ'proutʃfəlnɪs/ *n* severidad, *f*. **the r. of my gaze,** mi mirada llena de reproches

**reprobate** /'rɛprə,beit/ *n* réprobo (-ba)

**reproduce** /,riprə'dus/ *vt* reproducir. —*vi* reproducirse

**reproducible** /,riprə'dusəbəl/ *a* reproductible

**reproduction** /,riprə'dʌkʃən/ *n* reproducción, *f*

**reproductive** /,riprə'dʌktɪv/ *a* reproductor; de reproducción

**reproof** /rɪ'pruf/ *n* reconvención, *f*

**reprove** /rɪ'pruv/ *vt* censurar, culpar; reprender

**reprovingly** /rɪ'pruvɪŋli/ See **rebukingly**

**reptile** /'rɛptɪl, -tail/ *a* and *n* reptil, *m*

**republic** /rɪ'pʌblɪk/ *n* república, *f*. **the r. of letters,** la república de las letras

**republican** /rɪ'pʌblɪkən/ *a* and *n* republicano (-na)

**republicanism** /rɪ'pʌblɪkə,nɪzəm/ *n* republicanismo, *m*

**republish** /ri'pʌblɪʃ/ *vt* publicar de nuevo; volver a editar

**repudiate** /rɪ'pyudi,eit/ *vt* repudiar; negar, rechazar

**repudiation** /rɪ,pyudi'eiʃən/ *n* repudiación, *f*

**repugnance** /rɪ'pʌgnəns/ *n* repugnacia, *f*

**repugnant** /rɪ'pʌgnənt/ *a* repugnante; contrario; opuesto. **to be r. to,** repugnar (a)

**repulse** /rɪ'pʌls/ *vt* repulsar, repeler; rebatir, refutar; (refuse) rechazar, *n* repulsa, *f*; refutación, *f*; rechazo, *m*

**repulsion** /rɪ'pʌlʃən/ *n* Phys. repulsión, *f*; repugnancia, aversión, *f*

**repulsive** /rɪ'pʌlsɪv/ *a* repulsivo, repugnante, repelente

**repulsiveness** /rɪ'pʌlsɪvnɪs/ *n* carácter repulsivo, *m*; aspecto repugnante, *m*

**reputable** /'rɛpyətəbəl/ *a* honrado, respetable, formal

**reputation** /,rɛpyə'teiʃən/ *n* reputación, *f*; fama, *f*, renombre, *m*. **to have the r. of,** ser reputado como, pasar por

**reputed** /rɪ'pyutɪd/ *a* supuesto; putativo

**reputedly** /rɪ'pyutɪdli/ *adv* según la opinión común, según dice la gente

**request** /rɪ'kwɛst/ *n* ruego, *m*, petición, *f*; instancia, *f*; solicitud, *f*; Com. demanda, *f*. —*vt* pedir, rogar; suplicar; solicitar. **in r.,** en boga; solicitado; en demanda, *f*. **on r.,** a solicitud. **r. stop,** (for buses) parada discrecional, *f*

**requiem** /'rɛkwiəm/ *n* réquiem, *m*. **r. mass,** misa de difuntos, *f*

**require** /rɪ'kwaiʳr/ *vt* exigir, requerir; necesitar; (wish) desear; invitar. —*vi* ser necesario

**required** /rɪ'kwaiərd/ *a* necesario; obligatorio

**requirement** /rɪ'kwaiʳrmənt/ *n* deseo, *m*; requisito, *m*; formalidad, *f*; estipulación, *f*; necesidad, *f*

**requisite** /'rɛkwəzɪt/ *n* requisito, *m*. —*a* necesario, requisito, preciso. **to be r.,** ser necesario, ser menester hacer falta

**requisition** /,rɛkwə'zɪʃən/ *vt* Mil. requisar

**requisitioning** /,rɛkwə'zɪʃənɪŋ/ *n* requisa, *f*

**requital** /rɪ'kwaitl/ *n* recompensa, *f*; compensación, *f*; satisfacción, *f*

**requite** /rɪ'kwait/ *vt* pagar, recompensar; (affection) corresponder a

**reread** /ri'rid/ *vt* releer

**reredos** /'rɪərdɒs/ *n* retablo, *m*

**resale** /'ri,seil/ *n* reventa, *f*

**rescind** /rɪ'sɪnd/ *vt* rescindir

**rescission** /rɪ'sɪʒən/ *n* rescisión, *f*

**rescue** /'rɛskyu/ *vt* salvar; librar; Mil. rescatar. —*n* socorro, *m*; salvamento, *m*; Mil. rescate, *m*. **to go to the r. of,** ir al socorro de. **r. party,** expedición de salvamento, *f*; Mil. expedición de rescate, *f*

**rescuer** /'rɛskyuər/ *n* salvador (-ra)

**reseal** /ri'sil/ *vt* resellar

**research** /rɪ'sɜrtʃ, 'risɜrtʃ/ *n* investigación, *f*, *vt* investigar

**researcher** /rɪsɜrtʃər, 'risɜrtʃər/ *n* investigador (-ra)

**reseda** /rɪ'sidə/ *n* Bot. reseda, *f*

**resell** /ri'sɛl/ *vt* revender

**resemblance** /rɪ'zɛmbləns/ *n* parecido, *m*, semejanza, *f*. **The two sisters bear a strong r. to each other,** Las dos hermanas se parecen mucho

**resemble** /rɪ'zɛmbəl/ *vt* parecerse (a). **Mary doesn't r. her mother,** María no se parece a su madre

**resent** /rɪ'zɛnt/ *vt* resentirse de; ofenderse por, indignarse por; tomar a mal

**resentful** /rɪ'zɛntfəl/ *a* resentido; ofendido, indignado, agraviado; vengativo

**resentfully** /rɪ'zɛntfəli/ *adv* con resentimiento; con indignación

**resentment** /rɪ'zɛntmənt/ *n* resentimiento, *m*

**reservation** /,rɛzər'veiʃən/ *n* reservación, *f*, reserva, *f*; territorio reservado, *m*; santuario, *m*. **mental r.,** reserva mental, *f*

**reserve** /rɪ'zɜrv/ *n* reserva, *f*. —*vt* reservar. —*a* de reserva. **without r.,** sin reserva

**reserved** /rɪ'zɜrvd/ *a* reservado; callado, taciturno. **r.**

**compartment,** reservado, *m.* **r. list,** (*Mil. Nav.*) sección de reserva, *f*
**reservedly** /rɪ'zɜrvɪdli/ *adv* con reserva
**reservist** /rɪ'zɜrvɪst/ *n* reservista, *mf*
**reservoir** /'rezər,vwɑr/ *n* depósito, *m;* cisterna, *f,* aljibe, tanque, *m*
**reset** /*v.* rɪ'set/ *vt* montar de nuevo
**resettle** /ri'setl/ *vt* repoblar; rehabilitar; (a dispute) llegar a un nuevo acuerdo sobre
**resettlement** /ri'setlmənt/ *n* repoblación, *f;* rehabilitación, *f;* (of a dispute) nuevo acuerdo, *m*
**reshape** /ri'ʃeip/ *vt* reformar
**reship** /ri'ʃɪp/ *vt* reembarcar
**reshipment** /ri'ʃɪpmənt/ *n* reembarque, *m*
**reshuffle** /ri'ʃʌfəl/ *vt* volver a barajar; *Fig.* cambiar
**reside** /rɪ'zaid/ *vi* residir, habitar; vivir
**residence** /'rezɪdəns/ *n* residencia, *f;* permanencia, estada, *f;* domicilio, *m*
**resident** /'rezɪdənt/ *a* residente; (of a servant) que duerme en casa; interno. —*n* residente, *mf;* (diplomacy) residente, *m*
**residential** /,rezɪ'denʃəl/ *a* residencial
**residue** /'rezɪ,du/ *n* resto, *m;* (*Law., Chem.*) residuo, *m*
**residuum** /rɪ'zɪdʒuəm/ *n* residuo, *m*
**resign** /rɪ'zain/ *vt* renunciar (a); ceder; resignar. —*vi* dimitir. **to r. oneself,** resignarse
**resignation** /,rezɪg'neiʃən/ *n* resignación, *f;* (from a post) dimisión, *f.* **to send in one's r.,** dimitir
**resigned** /rɪ'zaind/ *a* resignado
**resignedly** /rɪ'zainɪdli/ *adv* con resignación
**resilience** /rɪ'zɪlyəns/ *n* elasticidad, *f*
**resilient** /rɪ'zɪlyənt/ *a* elástico
**resin** /'rezɪn/ *n* resina, *f;* (solid, for violin bows, etc.) colofonia, *f*
**resinous** /'rezənəs/ *a* resinoso
**resist** /rɪ'zɪst/ *vt* and *vi* (bear) aguantar; (impede) impedir; (repel, ward off) resistir; rechazar; hacer frente (a); oponerse (a); negarse (a)
**resistance** /rɪ'zɪstəns/ *n* resistencia, *f;* aguante, *m,* tenacidad, *f;* oposición, *f;* repugnancia, *f.* **passive r.,** resistencia pasiva, *f.* **r. coil,** *Elec.* resistencia, *f.* **r. movement,** movimiento de resistencia, *m*
**resistant** /rɪ'zɪstənt/ *a* resistente
**resister** /rɪ'zɪstər/ *n* el, *m,* (*f,* la) que resiste
**resole** /ri'soul/ *vt* remontar
**resoling** /ri'souliŋ/ *n* remonta, *f*
**resolute** /'rezə,lut/ *a* resuelto, decidido
**resolutely** /,rezə'lutli/ *adv* resueltamente
**resolution** /,rezə'luʃən/ *n* resolución, *f;* (proposal placed before a legislative body, etc.) proposición, *f;* propósito, *m*
**resolve** /rɪ'zɒlv/ *vt* resolver; desarrollar, deshacer (an abbreviation, acronym, or initialism). —*vi* resolverse. —*n* propósito, *m;* (of character) resolución, firmeza, *f*
**resonance** /'rezənəns/ *n* resonancia, *f;* sonoridad, *f*
**resonant** /'rezənənt/ *a* resonante; reverberante, sonoro
**resort** /rɪ'zɔrt/ *n* recurso, *m;* punto de reunión. *m;* (frequentation) frecuentación, *f;* (gathering) concurrencia, *f;* reunión, *f.* —*vi* acudir (a), acogerse (a); hacer uso (de); pasar (a); (frequent) frecuentar, concurrir. **health r.,** balneario, *m.* **holiday r.,** playa de verano, *f;* pueblo de veraneo, *m.* **in the last r.,** en último recurso
**resound** /rɪ'zaund/ *vi* resonar, retumbar, retronar; *Fig.* tener fama, ser celebrado. —*vt* hacer reverberar; *Fig.* celebrar
**resounding** /rɪ'zaundɪŋ/ *a* retumbante, resonante
**resource** /'risɔrs/ *n* recurso, *m;* (of character) inventiva, *f; pl* **resources;** recursos, fondos, *m pl*
**resourceful** /rɪ'sɔrsfəl/ *a* ingenioso
**resourcefully** /rɪ'sɔrsfəli/ *adv* ingeniosamente
**resourcefulness** /rɪ'sɔrsfəlnɪs/ *n* ingeniosidad, *f*
**respect** /rɪ'spekt/ *n* respeto, *m;* consideración, *f;* (reference, regard) respecto, *m; pl* **respects,** (greetings) saludos, *m pl;* homenaje, *m.* —*vt* respetar; honrar; (concern, regard) concernir, tocar (a). **in other respects,** por lo demás. **in r. of,** tocante a, respecto a. **in some respects,** desde algunos puntos de vista. **out of r. for,** por consideración a

**respectability** /rɪ,spektə'bɪlɪti/ *n* respetabilidad, *f*
**respectable** /rɪ'spektəbəl/ *a* respetable; pasable; considerable
**respectably** /rɪ'spektəbli/ *adv* respetablemente
**respected** /rɪ'spektɪd/ *a* and *part* respetado; apreciado, estimado; digno de respeto, honrado
**respectful** /rɪ'spektfəl/ *a* respetuoso
**respectfully** /rɪ'spektfəli/ *adv* respetuosamente
**respectfulness** /rɪ'spektfəlnɪs/ *n* aire respetuoso, *m;* conducta respetuosa, *f*
**respecting** /rɪ'spektɪŋ/ *prep* con respecto a, en cuanto a, tocante a; a propósito de
**respective** /rɪ'spektɪv/ *a* respectivo; relativo
**respectively** /rɪ'spektɪvli/ *adv* respectivamente
**respiration** /,respə'reiʃən/ *n* respiración, *f*
**respirator** /'respə,reitər/ *n* respirador, *f*
**respiratory** /'respərə,tɔri/ *a* respiratorio
**respire** /rɪ'spaiᵊr/ *vt* and *vi* respirar; exhalar; descansar
**respite** /'respɪt/ *n* tregua, pausa, *f;* respiro, *m; Law.* espera, *f.* —*vt* dar tregua (a); (postpone) aplazar; (relieve) aliviar
**resplendence** /rɪ'splendəns/ *n* resplandor, *m,* refulgencia, *f,* esplendor, fulgor, *m*
**resplendent** /rɪ'splendənt/ *a* resplandeciente, refulgente, relumbrante. **He was r. in a new uniform,** Lucía (or Ostentaba) un nuevo uniforme. **to be r.,** ser resplandeciente; relumbrar, refulgir
**resplendently** /rɪ'splendəntli/ *adv* esplendorosamente
**respond** /rɪ'spɒnd/ *vi* responder; contestar; (obey) obedecer; reaccionar
**respondent** /rɪ'spɒndənt/ *n* (in a suit) demandado (-da)
**response** /rɪ'spɒns/ *n* respuesta, *f; Eccl.* responso, *m*
**responsibility** /rɪ,spɒnsə'bɪlɪti/ *n* responsabilidad, *f*
**responsible** /rɪ'spɒnsəbəl/ *a* responsable
**responsive** /rɪ'spɒnsɪv/ *a* simpático; sensible, sensitivo
**responsiveness** /rɪ'spɒnsɪvnɪs/ *n* simpatía, *f;* sensibilidad, *f*
**rest** /rest/ *n* descanso, *m;* reposo, *m;* (the grave) última morada, *f;* tranquilidad, paz, *f;* inacción, *f;* (prop) soporte, apoyo, *m;* base, *f;* (for a lance) ristre, *m;* (for a rifle) apoyo, *m; Mus.* silencio, *m,* pausa, *f;* (in verse) cesura, *f.* **in r.,** en ristre. **the r.,** el resto; los demás, los otros. **to set at r.,** calmar, tranquilizar; (remove) quitar. **r.-cure,** cura de reposo, *f.* **r.-house,** hospedería, *f;* refugio, *m.* **r.-room, lounge,** sala de descanso, *f;* (toilet) excusado, retrete, *m;* (in theaters) saloncillo, *m*
**rest** /rest/ *vi* reposar, descansar; (lie down) acostarse, echarse; (stop) cesar, parar; estar en paz; apoyarse (en); descansar (sobre); posar; depender (de); (remain) quedar. —*vt* descansar; dar un descanso (a); (lean) apoyar; basar (en). **It rests with them,** Depende de ellos. **These valuable documents now rest in the Library of Congress,** Estos valiosos documentos han parado en la Biblioteca del Congreso. **May he r. in peace!** ¡Que en paz descanse! **to r. assured,** estar seguro. **to r. on one's oars,** cesar de remar; descansar
**restate** /ri'steit/ *vt* repetir, afirmar de nuevo
**restatement** /ri'steitmənt/ *n* repetición, *f*
**restaurant** /'restərənt/ *n* restaurante, restorán, *m.* **r.-car,** coche-comedor, *m*
**restful** /'restfəl/ *a* descansado; tranquilo, sosegado
**resting** /'restɪŋ/ *n* reposo, *m.* **last r.-place,** última morada, *f.* **r.-place,** descansadero, *m;* refugio, *m*
**restitution** /,restɪ'tuʃən/ *n* restitución, *f*
**restive** /'restɪv/ *a* (of a horse) repropio, ingobernable; inquieto, agitado; impaciente
**restiveness** /'restɪvnɪs/ *n* inquietud, agitación, *f;* impaciencia, *f*
**restless** /'restlɪs/ *a* agitado; inquieto, intranquilo; turbulento; sin reposo; (wakeful) desvelado; (ceaseless) incesante. **r. night,** noche desvelada, noche intranquila, *Inf.* noche toledana, *f*
**restlessly** /'restlɪsli/ *adv* agitadamente; con inquietud; turbulentamente; incesantemente
**restlessness** /'restlɪsnɪs/ *n* agitación, *f;* inquietud, intranquilidad, *f;* turbulencia, *f;* falta de reposo, *f;* (wakefulness) desvelo, *m;* movimiento incesante, *m*

**restock** /rɪ'stɒk/ vt (with goods) surtir de nuevo; proveer de nuevo; restablecer; repoblar

**restoration** /ˌrestə'reɪʃən/ n restauración, f; renovación, f; restablecimiento, m; (returning) restitución, f

**restorative** /rɪ'stɒrətɪv/ a and n restaurativo m

**restore** /rɪ'stɔr/ vt restaurar; restituir; devolver; restablecer; reponer; (repair) reformar, reparar; reconstruir; (to former rank, etc.) rehabilitar. **He restored the book to its place,** Devolvió el libro a su sitio

**restorer** /rɪ'stɔrər/ n restaurador (-ra)

**restrain** /rɪ'streɪn/ vt refrenar; reprimir; (restrict) limitar, restringir; (prevent) impedir; desviar; (detain) recluir. **to r. oneself,** contenerse

**restrained** /rɪ'streɪnd/ a moderado, mesurado; sobrio; (of emotion) contenido

**restraining** /rɪ'streɪnɪŋ/ a restrictivo; moderador, calmante

**restraint** /rɪ'streɪnt/ n freno, m; restricción, f; limitación, f; prohibición, f; compulsión, f; (reserve) reserva, f; moderación, f

**restrict** /rɪ'strɪkt/ vt restringir; limitar

**restriction** /rɪ'strɪkʃən/ n restricción, f; limitación, f

**restrictive** /rɪ'strɪktɪv/ a restrictivo

**result** /rɪ'zʌlt/ n resultado, m; consecuencia, resulta, f; solución, f. —vi resultar. **as the r. of,** de resultas de

**resultant** /rɪ'zʌltnt/ a resultante; consecuente. —n resultado, m; Mech. resultante, f

**resume** /rɪ'zum/ vt reasumir; (continue) reanudar, continuar; (summarize) resumir

**résumé** n resumen, m

**resummon** /rɪ'sʌmən/ vt convocar de nuevo (a); citar de nuevo (a)

**resumption** /rɪ'zʌmpʃən/ n (renewal) reanudación, f; reasunción, f

**resurgence** /rɪ'sɜrdʒəns/ n resurgimiento, m

**resurrect** /ˌrezə'rekt/ vt Inf. desenterrar; resucitar

**resurrection** /ˌrezə'rekʃən/ n resurrección, f

**resuscitate** /rɪ'sʌsɪˌteɪt/ vt and vi resucitar

**resuscitation** /rɪˌsʌsɪ'teɪʃən/ n resurrección, f; renovación, f; renacimiento, m

**retail** /'riteɪl/ n venta al por menor, reventa, f. —adv al por menor. —vt (goods) vender al por menor; revender; (tell) contar; repetir. **r. trade,** comercio al por menor, m

**retailer** /'riteɪlər/ n vendedor (-ra) al por menor; (of a story) narrador (-ra); el, m, (f, la) que cuenta algo

**retain** /rɪ'teɪn/ vt retener; guardar; conservar; (a barrister) ajustar; (hire) contratar

**retainer** /rɪ'teɪnər/ n (dependent) criado, dependiente, m; partidario, adherente, m; (fee) honorario, m; pl **retainers,** séquito, m, adherentes, m pl, gente, f

**retaining wall** /rɪ'teɪnɪŋ/ n muro de contención, m

**retake** /ri'teɪk/ vt volver a tomar; reconquistar

**retaking** /'ri,teɪkɪŋ/ n reconquista, f

**retaliate** /rɪ'tæliˌeɪt/ vt vengarse de, desquitarse de. —vi vengarse, tomar represalias

**retaliation** /rɪˌtæli'eɪʃən/ n represalias, f pl; desquite, m, satisfacción, f. **law of r.,** talión, m,

**retaliatory** /rɪ'tæliə, tɔri/ a de represalias; de desquite

**retard** /rɪ'tɑrd/ vt retardar

**retch** /retʃ/ vi tener náuseas, procurar vomitar

**retching** n náusea, basca, f

**retell** /ri'tel/ vt repetir, volver a contar

**retention** /rɪ'tenʃən/ n retención, f; conservación, f

**retentive** /rɪ'tentɪv/ a retentivo

**retentiveness** /rɪ'tDntlvnls/ n poder de retención, m; (memory) retentiva, f

**reticence** /'retəsəns/ n reticencia, reserva, f

**reticent** /'retəsənt/ a reservado, inexpresivo, taciturno

**retina** /'retnə, 'retnə/ n retina, f

**retinue** /'retn,u, -,yu/ n séquito, acompañamiento, m, comitiva, f

**retire** /rɪ'taɪər/ vi retirarse; (to bed) recogerse, acostarse; (from a post) jubilarse. —vt retirar; jubilar. **to r. from a post,** Mil. rendir el puesto

**retired** /rɪ'taɪərd/ a retirado; (remote) apartado, aislado; (hidden) escondido; (former) antiguo; (from employment, etc.) jubilado; (of an officer) retirado. **to place on the r. list,** jubilar; (Mil. Nav.) dar el retiro (a)

**retirement** /rɪ'taɪərmənt/ n retirada, f; (solitude) apartamiento, aislamiento, m; retiro, m; (superannuation) jubilación, f

**retiring** /rɪ'taɪərɪŋ/ a que se retira; (from a post) dimitente; (with pension, etc.) de jubilación; (reserved) reservado; modesto

**retort** /rɪ'tɔrt/ vi replicar. —vt retorcer; devolver (una acusación, etc.). —n réplica, f; contestación, f; Chem. retorta, f

**retouch** /v. ri'tʌtʃ/ vt retocar

**retrace** /rɪ'treɪs/ vt volver a trazar; volver a andar (un camino); (one's steps) volver sobre sus pasos, volver atrás; (in memory) rememorar, recordar; buscar el origen (de); (recount) narrar, contar

**retract** /rɪ'trækt/ vt retractar, retirar; (draw back) retraer. —vi retractarse

**retraction** /rɪ'trækʃən/ n retracción, f

**retranslate** /ri'trænsleɪt/ vt hacer una nueva traducción (de)

**retransmission** /ˌritrænsm'mɪʃən/ n retransmisión, f

**retread** /v. ri'tred/ vt pisar de nuevo; (tires) recauchetear

**retreat** /rɪ'trit/ n retirada, f; (Mil. signal) retreta, f; (refuge and Eccl.) retiro, m. —vi retirarse; retroceder; refugiarse

**retreat house** n casa de ejercicios, f

**retreating** /rɪ'tritɪŋ/ a que se retira; que retrocede; Mil. que se bate en retirada

**retrench** /rɪ'trentʃ/ vt reducir; disminuir; vi economizar, hacer economías

**retrenchment** /rɪ'trentʃmənt/ n disminución, reducción, f; economías, f pl

**retrial** /'ritraɪl/ n (of a person) nuevo proceso, m; (of a case) revisión, f

**retribution** /ˌretrə'byuʃən/ n retribución, f; justo castigo, m, pena merecida, f

**retrievable** /rɪ'trivəbəl/ a recuperable, que puede recobrarse; reparable

**retrieval** /rɪ'trivəl/ n recuperación, f; reparación, f; (of game) cobra, f; (of one's character) rehabilitación, f

**retrieve** /rɪ'triv/ vt (game, of dogs) cobrar; (regain) recobrar, recuperar; restaurar; reparar; restablecer; (one's character) rehabilitar. —vi cobrar la caza

**retriever** /rɪ'trivər/ n (dog) perdiguero (-ra)

**retroactive** /ˌretrou'æktɪv/ a retroactivo

**retrocede** /ˌretrə'sid/ vi retroceder

**retrograde** /'retrə,greɪd/ a retrógrado

**retrogression** /ˌretrə'greʃən/ n retrogradación, regresión, f; Med. retroceso, m

**retrogressive** /ˌretrə'gresɪv/ a retrógrado

**retrospect** /'retrə,spekt/ n mirada retrospectiva, f, examen del pasado, m. **in r.,** retrospectivamente

**retrospection** /ˌretrə'spekʃən/ n retrospección, f

**retrospective** /ˌretrə'spektɪv/ a retrospectivo

**retrospectively** /ˌretrə'spektɪvli/ adv retrospectivamente

**retry** /ri'traɪ/ vt (a case) rever; (a person) procesar de nuevo

**return** /rɪ'tɜrn/ vi regresar; volver; reaparecer; presentarse de nuevo; Law. revertir; (answer) contestar, responder. —vt (give back or put back) devolver; (a ball) restar; (a kindness, visit) pagar; restituir; (reciprocate) corresponder (a); recompensar; contestar (a); dar; rendir; (yield) producir; (a verdict) fallar, pronunciar; (report) dar parte de; anunciar; (exchange) cambiar; (elect) elegir. —n regreso, m; vuelta, f; (giving or putting back) devolución, f; pago, m; restitución, f; correspondencia, f; recompensa, f; (reply) respuesta, f; (reappearance) reaparición, f; reinstalación, f; repetición, f; (gain) ganancia, f; provecho, m; rendimiento, m; (exchange) cambio, m; (report) parte oficial, f; informe, m; lista, f; (election) elección, f; pl **returns,** tablas estadísticas, f pl; (of election) votación, f, m pl. **Many happy returns!** ¡Feliz cumpleaños! **by return mail,** a vuelta de correo. **on my (his, etc.) r.,** a la vuelta, cuando vuelva. **to r. like for like,** pagar en la misma moneda. **r. journey, r. trip,** viaje de vuelta, m. **r. match,** partido de vuelta, m. **r. ticket,** billete de ida y vuelta, m; billete de vuelta, m

**returnable** /rɪ'tɜrnəbəl/ a restituible; susceptible a

ser devuelto; (on approval) a prueba; *Law.* devolutivo

**returning** /rɪ'tɜrnɪŋ/ *a* que vuelve. —*n* See **return** "Return to Sender" «Al remitente»

**reunion** /ri'yunyən/ *n* reunión, *f*

**reunite** /,riyu'nait/ *vt* reunir. —*vi* reunirse

**revaccinate** /ri'væksə,neit/ *vt* revacunar

**revaccination** /ri,væksə'neifən/ *n* revacunación, *f*

**reveal** /rɪ'vil/ *vt* revelar; descubrir

**revealer** /rɪ'vilər/ *n* revelador (-ra)

**revealing** /rɪ'vilɪŋ/ *a* revelador. —*n* revelación, *f;* descubrimiento, *m*

**reveille** /'revəli; *Brit.* rɪ'væli/ *n Mil.* diana, *f*

**revel** /'revəl/ *vi* divertirse; regocijarse (en), gozarse (en); entregarse (a); (carouse) ir de parranda; emborracharse. —*n* algazara, jarana, *f; pl* **revels,** fiestas, festividades, *f pl*

**revelation** /,revə'leifən/ *n* revelación, *f;* descubrimiento, *m;* (in the Bible) Apocalipsis, *m*

**reveler** /'revələr/ *n* convidado alegre, *m;* (at night) trasnochador (-ra); (drunk) borracho (-cha); (masked) máscara, *mf*

**revelry** /'revəlri/ *n* festividades, *f pl,* regocijo, *m;* orgías, *f pl*

**revenge** /rɪ'vendʒ/ *n* venganza, *f.* —*vt* vengarse de; desquitarse de

**revengeful** /rɪ'vendʒfəl/ *a* vengativo

**revengefully** /rɪ'vendʒfəli/ *adv* vengativamente

**revengefulness** /rɪ'vendʒfəlnɪs/ *n* deseo de venganza, *m;* carácter vengativo, *m*

**revenger** /rɪ'vendʒər/ *n* vengador (-ra)

**revenue** /'revən,yu, -ə,nu/ *n* rentas públicas, *f pl;* (treasury) fisco, *m; Com.* rédito, *m,* ingresos, *m pl;* beneficio, *m.* **Inland R.,** delegación de contribuciones, *f.* **r. officer,** agente fiscal, *m*

**reverberate** /rɪ'vɜrbə,reit/ *vt* and *vi* (of sound) retumbar, resonar; (of light, etc.) reverberar

**reverberation** /rɪ,vɜrbə'reifən/ *n* (reflection) reverberación, *f;* (of sound) retumbo, eco, *m*

**revere** /rɪ'vɪər/ *vt* reverenciar, venerar, honrar

**reverence** /'revərəns/ *n* reverencia, *f, vt* reverenciar

**reverend** /'revərənd/ *a* reverendo

**reverent** /'revərənt/ *a* reverente

**reverently** /'revərəntli/ *adv* reverentemente, con reverencia

**reverie** /'revəri/ *n* ensueño, *m*

**reversal** /rɪ'vɜrsəl/ *n* inversión, *f;* (of a verdict) revocación, *f*

**reverse** /rɪ'vɜrs/ *vt* invertir; (a steam engine) dar contra vapor (a); (a vehicle) poner en marcha atrás; (arms) llevar a la funerala; (a judgment, etc.) revocar, derogar. —*vi* (dancing) dar vueltas al revés. —*n* lo contrario, lo opuesto; (back) dorso, revés, *m;* (change) cambio, *m;* (check) revés, *m,* vicisitud, *f;* (loss) pérdida, *f;* (defeat) derrota, *f; Mech.* marcha atrás, *f,* a inverso; contrario, opuesto. **quite the r.,** todo el contrario. **r. turn,** (of an engine) cambio de dirección, *m;* (in dancing) vuelta al revés, *f*

**reversible** /rɪ'vɜrsəbəl/ *a* reversible

**reversion** /rɪ'vɜrʒən, -ʃən/ *n* reversión, *f; Biol.* atavismo, *m;* (of offices) futura, *f;* (of property) reversión, *f*

**revert** /rɪ'vɜrt/ *vi Law.* revertir; volver (a)

**review** /rɪ'vyu/ *n* examen, análisis, *m;* juicio crítico, *m;* (journal and *Mil.*) revista, *f;* (criticism) revista, reseña, *f; Law.* revisión, *f.* —*vt* examinar, analizar; (*Mil.* etc.) pasar revista (a); revisar; repasar; (a book, etc.) reseñar; *Law.* revisar. —*vi* escribir revistas

**review article** *n* artículo de reseña, *m*

**reviewer** /rɪ'vyuər/ *n* revistero (-ra), crítico, *m*

**revile** /rɪ'vail/ *vt* injuriar, maldecir, difamar

**reviler** /rɪ'vailər/ *n* maldiciente, *m,* insultador (-ra)

**reviling** /rɪ'vailɪŋ/ *n* insultos, *m pl,* injurias, *f pl*

**revisal** /rɪ'vaizəl/ *n* revisión, *f*

**revise** /rɪ'vaiz/ *vt* revisar; repasar; corregir; (change) cambiar

**reviser** /rɪ'vaizər/ *n* revisor, *m;* corrector de pruebas, *m*

**revision** /rɪ'vɪʒən/ *n* revisión, *f;* repaso, *m;* corrección de pruebas, *f*

**revisit** /rɪ'vɪzɪt/ *vt* volver a visitar, visitar de nuevo

**revival** /rɪ'vaivəl/ *n* resurgimiento, *m;* renovación, *f;* (awakening) despertamiento, *m;* restablecimiento, *m;* resurrección, *f;* (of learning) renacimiento, *m; Theat.* reposición, *f;* (religious) despertar religioso, *m*

**revive** /rɪ'vaiv/ *vi* reponerse; restablecerse; resucitar; renovarse; renacer; cobrar fuerzas; (recover consciousness) volver en sí. —*vt* hacer revivir; resucitar; restablecer; renovar; restaurar; despertar; (fire, colors) avivar

**reviver** /rɪ'vaivər/ *n* resucitador (-ra)

**revivification** /rɪ,vɪvəfɪ'keiʃən/ *n* revivificación, *f*

**revivify** /rɪ'vɪvə,fai/ *vt* revivificar

**revocable** /'revəkəbəl, rɪ'vou-/ *a* revocable

**revocation** /,revə'keifən/ *n* revocación, *f*

**revoke** /rɪ'vouk/ *vt* revocar, anular, derogar; (wills) quebrantar. —*vi* revocar, anular; (at cards) renunciar. —*n* (cards) renuncio, *m*

**revolt** /rɪ'voult/ *n* rebelión, *f, vi* rebelarse, sublevarse. —*vt* repugnar, indignar, dar asco (a)

**revolting** /rɪ'voultɪŋ/ *a* repugnante, asqueroso; (rebellious) rebelde

**revolution** /,revə'luʃən/ *n* revolución, *f;* (turn) vuelta, *f,* giro, *m*

**revolutionary** /,revə'luʃə,neri/ *a* and *n* revolucionario (-ia)

**revolutionize** /,revə'luʃə,naiz/ *vt* revolucionar

**revolve** /rɪ'vɒlv/ *vi* dar vueltas, girar; suceder periódicamente. —*vt* hacer girar; (ponder) revolver, discurrir

**revolver** /rɪ'vɒlvər/ *n* revólver, *m*

**revolving** /rɪ'vɒlvɪŋ/ *a* giratorio; que vuelve; periódico. **r. chair,** silla giratoria, *f.* **r. door,** puerta giratoria, *f.* **r. stage,** escenario giratorio, *m*

**revue** /rɪ'vyu/ *n Theat.* revista, *f*

**revulsion** /rɪ'vʌlʃən/ *n* revulsión, *f*

**revulsive** /rɪ'vʌlsɪv/ *a Med.* revulsivo

**rev up** /rev/ *vt* (an engine) calentar

**reward** /rɪ'wɔrd/ *n* recompensa, *f;* retribución, *f.* —*vt* recompensar; satisfacer, premiar

**rewarding** /rɪ'wɔrdɪŋ/ *a* premiador; que recompensa. —*n* recompensación, *f.* **a rewarding experience,** una experiencia compensadora, *f*

**rewrite** /v. ri'rait/ *vt* escribir de nuevo; volver a escribir; redactar otra vez

**rhapsody** /'ræpsədi/ *n* rapsodia, *f*

**rheostat** /'riə,stæt/ *n* reóstato, *m*

**rhetoric** /'retərɪk/ *n* retórica, *f*

**rhetorical** /rɪ'tɔrɪkəl/ *a* retórico; declamatorio

**rhetorician** /,retə'rɪʃən/ *n* retórico (-ca)

**rheumatic** /rʊ'mætɪk/ *a* reumático. **r. fever,** reumatismo poliarticular agudo, *m*

**rheumatism** /'rumə,tɪzəm/ *n* reumatismo, reuma, *m*

**rheumy** /'rumi/ *a* catarroso; (of the eyes) legañoso

**rhinestone** /'rain,stoun/ *n* circón, *m*

**Rhine, the** /rain/ el Rin, *m*

**rhinoceros** /rai'nɒsərəs/ *n* rinoceronte, *m*

**Rhodes** /roudz/ Rodas, *f*

**rhododendron** /,roudə'dendrən/ *n* rododendro, *m*

**rhubarb** /'rubɑrb/ *n* ruibarbo, *m*

**rhyme** /raim/ *n* rima, *f;* verso, *m.* —*vi* and *vt* rimar. **without r. or reason,** sin ton ni son; a tontas y a locas

**rhymer** /'raimər/ *n* rimador (-ra)

**rhyming** /'raimɪŋ/ *a* rimador

**rhythm** /'rɪðəm/ *n* ritmo, *m*

**rhythmic** /'rɪðmɪk/ *a* rítmico

**rib** /rɪb/ *n* (*Anat. Bot. Aer. Naut. Archit.*) costilla, *f;* (of an umbrella or fan) varilla, *f;* (in cloth) cordoncillo, *m,* lista, *f*

**ribald** /'rɪbəld/ *a* escabroso, ribaldo, indecente

**ribaldry** /'rɪbəldri/ *n* ribaldería, escabrosidad, indecencia, *f*

**ribbed** /rɪbd/ *a* con costillas; (of cloth) listado, con listas

**ribbon** /'rɪbən/ *n* cinta, *f;* tira, *f;* (tatter) jirón, *m.* **to tear to ribbons,** hacer jirones

**rice** /rais/ *n* arroz, *m.* —*a* de arroz; con arroz. **r. field,** arrozal, *m.* **r.-paper,** papel de paja de arroz, *m.* **r.-pudding,** arroz con leche, *m*

**rich** /rɪtʃ/ *a* rico; opulento; (happy) dichoso; (of land, etc.) fértil; abundante; (of objects) magnífico, suntuoso, hermoso; precioso; (of food) exquisito;

suculento; (highly seasoned) muy sazonado; (creamy) con mucha nata; (of colours) brillante, vivo. **new r.,** ricacho (-cha). **newly-r.,** advenedizo. **to grow r.,** enriquecerse
**riches** /'rɪtʃɪz/ n riqueza, f
**richly** /'rɪtʃli/ adv ricamente; abundantemente; magníficamente; bien
**richness** /'rɪtʃnɪs/ n riqueza, f; opulencia, f; (of land, etc.) fertilidad, f; abundancia, f; (of objects) magnificencia, suntuosidad, hermosura, f; preciosidad, f; (of food) gusto exquisito, m; suculencia, f; (piquancy) gusto picante, m; (of colours) viveza, f
**rickets** /'rɪkɪts/ n raquitismo, m
**rickety** /'rɪkɪti/ a Med. raquítico; destartalado, desvencijado; (unsteady) tambaleante; cojo
**rickshaw** /'rɪkʃ ɔ/ n riksha, m
**ricochet** /,rɪkə'ʃei/ n rebote, m, vi rebotar
**rid** /rɪd/ vt librar (de). **to get rid of,** librarse de; quitarse de encima (a); perder, quitarse; (dismiss) despedir. **to rid oneself of,** librarse de, deshacerse de
**riddance** /'rɪdns/ n libramiento, m
**riddle** /'rɪdl/ n acertijo, m; enigma, problema, m; misterio, m; (sieve) tamiz de alambre, m; vt (guess) adivinar; (sift) cribar; (with holes) acribillar
**ride** /raid/ vi (a horse) montar a caballo, cabalgar; pasear a caballo; (a mule, a bicycle) montar en, pasear en; (a vehicle, train) ir en; (a carriage, car) andar en, pasear en; (float) flotar; (on the wind) dejarse llevar por el viento; ser llevado por el viento; (go) ir; (come) venir; (a distance) hacer... a caballo, en coche, etc.; Naut. estar al ancla; Mech. tener juego. —vt (a horse, mule, bicycle) montar; ir montado sobre; manejar; (a race) hacer; (float) flotar en; (cleave, the sea, etc.) surcar. —n paseo (a caballo, en bicicleta, en coche, etc.), m; viaje (en un autobús, de tren, etc.), m; (bridle path) camino de herradura, m; cabalgata, f, desfile a caballo, m. **a r. on horseback,** un paseo a caballo. **They gave me a r. in their car,** (e.g. to see the sights) Me llevaron a paseo en su auto, (a lift to a certain place) Me dieron un aventón. **ride at anchor,** estar fondeado. **to r. a bicycle,** montar en bicicleta. **to r. rough-shod over,** mandar a la baqueta (a), mandar a puntapiés (a). **to r. sidesaddle,** cabalgar a mujeriegas. **to r. at,** embestir con. **to r. away,** marcharse, alejarse; marcharse a caballo, etc. **to r. back,** volver; volver a caballo, en bicicleta, etc. **to r. behind,** seguir a caballo; ir inmediatamente detrás (de); (on the back seat) ocupar el asiento de atrás; (on the same animal) cabalgar en la grupa. **to r. down,** atropellar; (trample) pisotear, pasar por encima de. **to r. on,** seguir su camino. **to r. out,** salir a paseo en caballo, etc.; irse a paseo en coche, etc.; (a storm) hacer frente a, luchar con. **to r. over,** pasar por encima de; recorrer. **to r. up,** vi llegar, acercarse; (of a tie, etc.) subir. —vt montar
**rider** /'raidər/ n cabalgador (-ra); jinete, m; persona que va en coche, etc., f; (on a bicycle) ciclista, mf; (on a motorcycle) motociclista, mf; (horsebreaker) domador de caballos, m; (clause) añadidura, f; corolario, m
**ridge** /rɪdʒ/ n cumbre, cima, f; (of mountains) cordillera, sierra, f; (of a roof, of a nose) caballete, m; Agr. lomo, caballón, m; (wrinkle) arruga, f; (on coins) cordoncillo, m. —vt surcar; formar lomos (en); (wrinkle) arrugar
**ridicule** /'rɪdɪ,kyul/ n ridículo, m, vt poner en ridículo, ridiculizar, burlarse (de), mofarse (de)
**ridiculous** /rɪ'dɪkyələs/ a ridículo, absurdo
**ridiculously** /rɪ'dɪkyələsli/ adv absurdamente
**ridiculousness** /rɪ'dɪkyələsnɪs/ n ridiculez, f
**riding** /'raidɪŋ/ a cabalgante; que va a caballo; montado (a, en, sobre); Naut. al ancla; (in compounds) de equitación; de montar. —n equitación, f; paseo a caballo; en bicicleta, etc., m; acción de ir a caballo, etc., f; (district) comarca, f. **r.-boots,** botas de montar, f pl. **r.-habit,** traje de montar, m; (woman's) amazona, f. **r.-master,** profesor de equitación, m. **r.-saddle,** silla de montar, f. **r.-school,** escuela de equitación, f
**rife** /raif/ a común; corriente; frecuente; prevalente; abundante; general. **r. with,** abundante en; lleno de

**riffraff** /'rɪf,ræf/ n desperdicios, m pl; (rabble) gentuza, canalla, f
**rifle** /'raifəl/ n rifle, fusil rayado, m. —vt robar; (a suitcase, etc.) desvalijar; (a gun) rayar. **r.-range,** campo de tiro, m. **r.-sling,** portafusil, m. **r.-shot,** fusilazo, m
**rifleman** /'raifəlmən/ n fusilero, m
**rifler** /'raiflər/ n saqueador (-ra)
**rifling** /'raiflɪŋ/ n (robbing) saqueo, robo, m; (of a suitcase, etc.) desvalijamiento, m
**rift** /rɪft/ n hendedura, abertura, f; grieta, f
**rig** /rɪg/ n Naut. aparejo, m; Inf. atavío, m. —vt (a ship) aparejar; equipar; (elections) falsificar. **to rig out,** proveer de; equipar con; ataviar. **to rig up,** arreglar; armar, construir
**rigging** /'rɪgɪŋ/ n (of a ship) aparejo, m
**right** /rait/ a recto; correcto; conveniente, debido; apropiado; exacto; (opposite of left hand) derecho; (straight) directo; en línea recta; razonable; (true) verdadero, genuino, legítimo; (just) justo; (prudent) prudente; (in health) sano. **All r.!** ¡Está bien! **I feel all r.,** Me siento perfectamente bien, Estoy bien. **He is the r. man for the job,** Él es el hombre que hace falta para el puesto. **It is the r. word,** Es la palabra apropiada. **on the r.,** a la derecha. **to be r.,** (of persons) tener razón. **to make r.,** poner en orden; arreglar. **r.-angle,** ángulo recto, m. **r.-angled,** rectangular. **r.-angled triangle,** triángulo rectángulo, m. **the R. Bank (of Paris),** la Orilla derecha, la Ribera derecha, f. **r. hand,** n (mano) derecha, diestra, f; derecha, f; (person) brazo derecho, m. —a—de la mano derecha; de la derecha; a la derecha. **r.-handed,** derecho; diestro, hábil. **r. mind,** entero juicio, m. **r.-minded,** juicioso, prudente; honrado. **r.-of-way,** derecho a la vía, m
**right** /rait/ adv directamente; inmediatamente; derechamente; correctamente; debidamente; exactamente; bien; (quite, thoroughly) completamente; honradamente; (very) muy. **r. on,** adelante; en frente. **R. about face!** ¡Media vuelta a la derecha! **r. at the bottom,** al fondo; al final; el último (de la clase, etc.). **r. at the end of his speech,** al fin de su discurso. **r. away,** en seguida, inmediatamente
**right** /rait/ n razón, f; verdad, f; justicia, f; (good) bien, m; derecho, m; (not left side) derecha, f; (of political parties) derechas, f pl. **r. and wrong,** el bien y el mal. **"All rights reserved,"** «Derechos reservados.» **by rights,** por derecho. **It is on the r.,** Está a la derecha. **to exercise one's r.,** usar de su derecho. **r. of association,** derecho de asociación, m. **r. of way,** derecho de paso, m. **to be in the r.,** tener razón; estar en su derecho
**right** /rait/ vt enderezar; rectificar; corregir; poner en orden; Naut. enderezar; hacer justicia (a). **to r. wrongs,** deshacer agravios
**righteous** /'raitʃəs/ a recto, virtuoso, justo; justificado
**righteously** /'raitʃəsli/ adv virtuosamente; justamente
**righteousness** /'raitʃəsnɪs/ n rectitud, integridad, virtud, f; justicia, f
**rightful** /'raitfəl/ a justo; legítimo; verdadero
**rightfully** /'raitfəli/ adv justamente; legítimamente; verdaderamente
**rightfulness** /'raitfəlnɪs/ n justicia, f; legitimidad, f; verdad, f
**rightly** /'raitli/ adv justamente; debidamente; correctamente; bien. **r. or wrongly,** mal que bien
**rightness** /'raitnɪs/ n rectitud, f; derechura, f; justicia, f; exactitud, f
**rigid** /'rɪdʒɪd/ a rígido; inflexible; severo, riguroso
**rigidity** /rɪ'dʒɪdɪti/ n rigidez, f; inflexibilidad, f; severidad, f
**rigmarole** /'rɪgmə,roul/ n monserga, f, galimatías, m, jerigonza, f
**rigor** /'rɪgər/ n rigor, m
**rigorous** /'rɪgərəs/ a riguroso
**rigorously** /'rɪgərəsli/ adv rigurosamente
**rile** /rail/ vt Inf. irritar, sacar de tino (a)
**rim** /rɪm/ n borde, m; orilla, f; (of a wheel) llanta, f, aro, m
**rime** /raim/ n escarcha, f, vt cubrir con escarcha. See also **rhyme**

**rind** /raind/ n (of fruit) cáscara, corteza, f; (of cheese) costra, f; (of bacon) piel, f

**ring** /rɪŋ/ n círculo, m; (round the eyes) ojera, f; (for curtains, etc.) anilla, f; (for the finger) anillo, m, sortija, f; (for children's games, etc.) corro, m; (for the ears) arete, m; (of smoke and for the nose) anillo, m; (for hitching, etc.) argolla, f; (for boxing) cuadrilátero, m; (on a racecourse) picadero, m; (at a circus, bull-fight) ruedo, redondel, m; Fig. arena, f; (group) camarilla, f, grupo, m; (metallic sound) sonido metálico, m; resonancia, f; (tinkle) tintín, m; (of a bell) repique, tañido, son (de la campana), m; (of bells) juego de campanas, m; (of laughter, etc.) ruido, m; (of truth, etc.) apariencia, f. **r.-bolt,** Naut. cáncamo, m. **r. finger,** dedo anular, m. **r.-master,** director de circo, m

**ring** /rɪŋ/ vt (surround) cercar, rodear; (a bull, etc.) poner un anillo (a); (sound) hacer sonar; sonar; (a door bell, etc.) tocar, apretar; (bells) echar a vuelo; (announce by pealing the bells) anunciar, proclamar; sonar, tañer. —vi (of bells) sonar; (re-echo) resonar; (of the ears) zumbar; (tinkle) tintinar. **to r. the bell,** tocar la campana; tocar el timbre. **to r. off,** colgar el teléfono. **to r. up,** llamar por teléfono, telefonear

**ringing** /'rɪŋɪŋ/ n acción de tocar las campanas o el timbre, f; toque, m; repique, m; campanilleo, m; (in the ears) zumbido, m. —a resonante, sonoro. **r. signal,** señal de llamada, f. **the r. of the bells,** el son de las campanas

**ringleader** /'rɪŋ,lidər/ n cabecilla, m

**ringlet** /'rɪŋlɪt/ n rizo, bucle, m

**ringworm** /'rɪŋ,wɜrm/ n tiña, f

**rink** /rɪŋk/ n pista, f. **skating-r.,** sala de patinar, f; pista de patinar, f

**rinse** /rɪns/ n enjuague, m; enjuagadura, f; (of clothes) aclarado, m. —vt enjuagar; (clothes) aclarar; lavar

**rinsing** /'rɪnsɪŋ/ n See **rinse;** —pl **rinsings,** lavazas, f pl, a de aclarar

**riot** /'raɪət/ n motín, m; tumulto, m; desorden, m; exceso, m; orgía, f; disipación, f. —vi amotinarse; alborotarse; entregarse a la disipación (or al placer); (enjoy) gozar, disfrutar. **to run r.,** hacer excesos; perder el freno; desmandarse; Fig. extenderse por todas partes; crecer en abundancia, cubrir todo

**rioter** /'raɪətər/ n amotinador (-ra); alborotador (-ra)

**riotous** /'raɪətəs/ a sedicioso; bullicioso; disoluto; desordenado; desenfrenado

**riotously** /'raɪətəs/ adv sediciosamente; bulliciosamente; disolutamente; con exceso

**riotousness** /'raɪətəsnɪs/ n sedición, f; disolución, f; excesos, m pl, desenfreno, m; desorden, m

**rip** /rɪp/ vt rasgar; (unsew) descoser; (wood, etc.) partir; (make) hacer. —vi rasgarse. —n rasgón, m; rasgadura, f; desgarro, m; (libertine) calavera, m. **to rip off,** arrancar; quitar. **to rip open,** abrir; (an animal) abrir en canal

**riparian** /rɪ'pɛəriən/ a and n ribereño (-ña)

**ripe** /raɪp/ a maduro; preparado; perfecto, acabado

**ripen** /'raɪpən/ vt and vi madurar

**ripeness** /'raɪpənɪs/ n madurez, f

**ripening** /'raɪpənɪŋ/ n maduración, f

**ripping** /'rɪpɪŋ/ n rasgadura, f; (unstitching) deshiladura, f. —a Inf. estupendo

**ripple** /'rɪpəl/ n rizo, m; onda, f; (of sound) murmullo, m. —vt rizar. —vi rizarse; murmurar

**rippling** /'rɪplɪŋ/ n rizado, m; murmullo, m

**rise** /raɪz/ vi ascender; subir; levantarse; ponerse de pie; (of a meeting) suspenderse; (from the dead) resucitar; (grow) crecer; (swell) hincharse; (of sun, moon) salir; (of sound, gradient, price, stock exchange quotations) subir; (of river source) nacer; (in revolt) sublevarse, rebelarse; (to the mind) presentarse, surgir; (appear) aparecer; (of buildings, etc.) elevarse, alzarse; (in the world) mejorar de posición; (originate) originarse (en), proceder (de); (of mercury) alzarse; (of fish) picar. **He has risen in my estimation,** Ha ganado en mi estimación. **She rose early,** Se levantó temprano. **The color rose in her cheeks,** Se le subieron los colores a la cara. **to r. to the occasion,** estar al nivel de las circunstancias. **to r. to one's feet,** ponerse de pie. **to r. to the bait,**

morder el anzuelo. **to r. again,** levantarse de nuevo; resucitar; renovarse; suscitarse otra vez. **to r. above,** alzarse por encima de; mostrarse superior a

**rise** /raɪz/ n ascensión, f; subida, f; levantamiento, m; (in price, temperature) alza, f; (increase) aumento, m; (of the sun, moon) salida, f; (of a river) nacimiento, m; (origin) origen, m; (growth, development) desarrollo, crecimiento, m; (promotion) ascenso, m; (slope) cuesta, f; pendiente, f; (high ground) eminencia, altura, f. **to give r. to,** dar lugar a, causar. **r. and fall,** subida y baja, f; (of the voice) ritmo, m; (of music) cadencia, f; (of institutions) grandeza y decadencia, f. **r. to power,** subida al poder, f

**riser** /'raɪzər/ n el, m, (f, la) que se levanta; (of a step) contrahuella, f. **early r.,** madrugador (-ra). **late r.,** el, m, (f, la) que se levanta tarde

**risibility** /,rɪzə'bɪlɪti/ n risibilidad, f

**risible** /'rɪzəbəl/ a risible

**rising** /'raɪzɪŋ/ n subida, f; (of the source of rivers) nacimiento, m; (overflowing of rivers) crecimiento, m; (of sun, moon) salida, f; (from the dead) resurrección, f; (rebellion) sublevación, insurrección, f; (of the tide) crecida, f; (of bread) levadura, f; (of an assembly) suspensión, f; (of a theater curtain) subida, f; (literary) renacimiento, m, a creciente; naciente; saliente; (promising of porvenir; (young) joven. **the r. generation,** los jóvenes, la generación joven. **He is r. forty,** Raya en los cuarenta. **He likes early r.,** Le gusta madrugar. **On the r. of the curtain...,** Al levantarse el telón... **the r. of the moon,** la salida de la luna, f. **the r. tide,** la marea creciente

**risk** /rɪsk/ n riesgo, m; peligro, m. —vt arriesgar; atreverse (a), osar. **at the r. of,** al riesgo de. **to take a r.,** tomar un riesgo; correr peligro. **to r. everything on the outcome,** jugar el todo por el todo

**risk capital** n capital-riesgo, m

**riskiness** /'rɪskɪnɪs/ n peligro, m

**risky** /'rɪski/ a arriesgado, peligroso

**rissole** /'rɪsoul/ n risol, m, (pl risoles)

**rite** /raɪt/ n rito, m

**rite of passage** n rito de tránsito, m

**ritual** /'rɪtʃuəl/ a ritual. —n rito, m, ceremonia, f

**ritualist** /'rɪtʃuəlɪst/ n ritualista, mf

**ritualistic** /,rɪtʃuə'lɪstɪk/ a ritualista

**rival** /'raɪvəl/ n rival, mf a competidor; rival. —vt rivalizar con, competir con

**rivalry** /'raɪvəlri/ n rivalidad, f

**river** /'rɪvər/ n río, m. —a del río; fluvial. **r.-basin,** cuenca de un río, f. **r.-bed,** lecho, cauce (de un río), m. **r. civilization,** civilización fluvial, f. **r.-god,** dios de los ríos, m. **r.-mouth,** ría, f. **r. port,** puerto fluvial, m

**riverside** /'rɪvər,saɪd/ n ribera, orilla de un río, f. —a de la(s) orilla(s) de un río; situado a la orilla de un río; ribereño

**rivet** /'rɪvɪt/ n remache, roblón, m. —vt remachar; clavar; Fig. fijar, concentrar; Fig. cautivar, absorber

**riveter** /'rɪvɪtər/ n remachador, m

**riveting** /'rɪvɪtɪŋ/ n remachado, remache, m; Fig. fijación, concentración, f; Fig. absorción, f. **r. machine,** remachadora, f

**Riviera, the** /,rɪvi'ɛrə/ la Riviera, f

**rivulet** /'rɪvyəlɪt/ n riachuelo, arroyo, m

**road** /roud/ n camino, m; carretera, f; ruta, f; pl **roads,** Naut. rada, f. **high r.,** camino real, m. **main r.,** carretera, f. **secondary r.,** carretera de segunda clase, f. **on the r. to...,** en el camino de... **to get out of the r.,** Inf. quitarse de en medio. **to go by r.,** ir por carretera. **"R. up!"** «Carretera en reparaciones.» **r.-book,** guía de carreteras, f. **r. house,** albergue de carretera, m. **r. maker,** constructor de caminos, m; (navvy) peón caminero, m. **r. making,** construcción de caminos, f. **r. map,** mapa de carreteras, m. **r. sign,** señal de carretera, señal de tránsito, señal vial, f; poste indicador, m. **The r. to hell is paved with good intentions,** El camino del infierno está empedrado de buenas intenciones. **"R. Repairs,"** «Camino en Reparación»

**roadmender** /'roud,mɛndər/ n peón caminero, m

**roadside** /'roud,saɪd/ n borde del camino, m, a al lado del camino

**roadstead** /'roud,stɛd/ n rada, f

**roadster** /'roudstər/ n automóvil de turismo, m; bicicleta de carreras, f; caballo de aguante, m; buque fondeado en rada, m

**roadway** /'roud,wei/ n calzada, carretera, f

**roam** /roum/ vi vagar, vagabundear, andar errante. —vt errar por

**roamer** /'roumər/ n vagabundo (-da), hombre errante, m

**roaming** /'roumɪŋ/ n vagabundeo, m; excursiones, f pl, paseos, m pl; a errante, vagabundo; nómada

**roan** /roun/ a roano, sabino. —n caballo roano, m

**roar** /rɔr/ vi rugir; (of a bull, of the wind, of a person in anger) bramar; dar voces; (of the fire) crepitar; (of cannon) retumbar; (of thunder) estallar. —vt gritar. —n rugido, bramido, m; (shout) grito, m; (of the fire) crepitación, f; (of cannon, thunder) estallido, m; (noise) ruido, m. **to r. with laughter,** reírse a carcajadas

**roaring** /'rɔrɪŋ/ n (of horses) asma de los caballos, f, For other meanings, see under **roar.** a rugiente, bramante; Inf. magnífico. **to do a r. trade,** hacer un buen negocio

**roast** /roust/ n asado, m, carne asada, f. —a asado; tostado. —vt asar; (coffee and to warm one's feet, etc.) tostar; (metals) calcinar; (scold) desollar vivo (a). —vi asarse; tostarse. **r. beef,** rosbif, m

**roaster** /'roustər/ n asador, m; (for coffee or peanuts) tostador, m; (for chestnuts, etc.) tambor, m

**roasting** /'roustɪŋ/ n asación, f; (of coffee) tostado, m; (of metals) calcinación, f. **r. spit,** asador, m

**rob** /rɒb/ vt robar; quitar, privar (de). **They have robbed her of her pocketbook,** Le han robado la cartera

**robber** /'rɒbər/ n ladrón (-ona); (footpad) salteador de caminos, m; (brigand) bandido, m

**robbery** /'rɒbəri/ n robo, m. **It's daylight r.!** ¡Es un desuello! **to commit a r.,** cometer un robo. **r. with violence,** robo armado, m

**robe** /roub/ n traje talar, m, toga, f; (of a monk, nun) hábito, m; (of a priest, etc.) sotana, f; Poet. manto, m; (infant's) mantillas, f pl; pl **robes,** traje de ceremonia, m. —vt vestir; cubrir, revestir (de). —vi vestirse. **bath r.,** albornoz, m

**robin** /'rɒbɪn/ n petirrojo, m

**robot** /'roubət, -bɒt/ n hombre mecánico, m; Aer. piloto mecánico, m. **traffic r.,** torre del tráfico, f, aparato automático, m. **r. plane,** avión sin piloto, m

**robust** /rou'bʌst/ a robusto; fuerte, vigoroso. **to make r.,** robustecer

**robustness** /rou'bʌstnɪs/ n robustez, f; vigor, m, fuerza, f

**rock** /rɒk/ n roca, f; (in the sea) abrojo, escollo, m; peña, f, peñasco, m. **como una roca.** **to be on the rocks,** Inf. estar a la cuarta pregunta. **r. bottom,** n fondo, m. —a mínimo, más bajo. **r. crystal,** cuarzo, m. **r.-garden,** jardincito rocoso, jardín alpestre, m. **r.-plant,** planta alpestre, f. **r.-rose,** heliantemo, m. **r.-salt,** sal gema, f

**rock** /rɒk/ vt mecer; (shake) hacer temblar, sacudir; (to sleep) arrullar. —vi mecerse, balancearse; tambalearse; agitarse; temblar

**rocker** /'rɒkər/ n (of a chair, cradle) balancín, m; (chair) mecedora, f

**rockery** /'rɒkəri/ n jardincito rocoso, m

**rocket** /'rɒkɪt/ n cohete, volador, m. —vi lanzarse. **r.-launching aircraft,** caza lanzacohetes, f

**rockiness** /'rɒkɪnɪs/ n abundancia de rocas, f; fragosidad, escabrosidad, f

**rocking** /'rɒkɪŋ/ n balanceo, m; (staggering) tambaleo, m; oscilación, f; (of an infant) arrullo, m. **r.-chair,** mecedora, f. **r.-horse,** caballo balancín, caballo mecedor, m

**rocky** /'rɒki/ a rocoso; de roca; roqueño; (rough) fragoso, escabroso; (rugged) peñascoso, escarpado. **the R. Mountains,** las Montañas Rocosas, f pl

**rococo** /rə'koukou/ n rococó, m

**rod** /rɒd/ n vara, f; bastón de mando, m; (for fishing) caña, f; (measure) pértiga, f; (surveying) jalón, f; palo, m; (for punishment) vergajo, m; Mech. vástago, m. **connecting rod,** biela, f. **to fish with rod and line,** pescar con caña

**rodent** /'roudn̩t/ a and n roedor, m

---

**roe** /rou/ n (deer) corzo (-za); (of fish) hueva, f. **soft roes,** lechas, f pl

**rogue** /roug/ n bribón, pícaro, pillo, m; Law. vago, m; (affectionate) picaruelo (-la)

**roguery** /'rougəri/ n truhanería, picardía, f; (knaves) pícaros, m pl; (mischief) travesuras, f pl. **novel of r.,** novela picaresca, f

**roguish** /'rougɪʃ/ a picaresco, bellaco; (mischievous) travieso, juguetón; malicioso

**roguishly** /'rougɪʃli/ adv como un pícaro; con malicia

**roguishness** /'rougɪʃnɪs/ n picardía, bribonería, bellaquería, f; (mischievousness) travesuras, f pl; malicia, f

**role** /roul/ n papel, m

**roll** /roul/ n rollo, m; (list) rol, m, lista, f; (of bread) panecillo, m; (of a drum) redoble, m; (of thunder) tronido, m; (of cloth) pieza, f; (of tobacco) rollo, m; (of meat, etc.) pastel, m; (of a ship) balanceo, m; pl **rolls,** (records) archivos, m pl. **He has a nautical r.,** Tiene un aire de marinero. **to call the r.,** pasar lista. **r. film,** película fotográfica, f. **r. of honour,** lista de honor, f. **r.-on corset,** faja elástica, f, corsé de goma, m. **r.-top desk,** buró de cierre enrollable, m

**roll** /roul/ vi rodar; dar vueltas; (wallow) revolcarse; (of a ship) balancearse, bambolearse; (in money, etc.) nadar; (flow) correr, fluir; (Fig. of time) pasar tranquilamente; (of vehicle) rodar; pasar rodando; (of country) ondular; (of the sea) ondear; (of drums) redoblar; (of thunder) retumbar. —vt hacer rodar; arrollar; (a cigarette) liar; (metals) laminar; (move) mover; (the eyes) guiñar (los ojos); (the ground) apisonar; (pastry) aplanar; (of an organ) sonar; (a drum) redoblar. **Mary rolled her eyes heavenwards,** María puso los ojos en blanco. **to r. away,** alejarse; desaparecer; (of time) pasar. **to r. back,** volver, retirarse; desaparecer. **to r. by,** pasar rodando; desaparecer. **to r. down,** bajar rodando, rodar por. **to r. in,** llegar en gran cantidad (or en gran número). **to r. off,** caer de. **to r. on,** seguir su marcha; fluir sin cesar; seguir su curso; (of time) avanzar. **to r. out,** (metal) laminar; (pastry) aplanar; (bring out) sacar; desenrollar. **to r. over,** vt volcar; tumbar; dar la vuelta (a). —vi dar la vuelta; volverse al otro lado. **to r. up,** arrollar; envolver; (of hedgehogs, etc.) enroscarse, hacerse un ovillo

**roll-call vote** /'roul,kɔl/ n votación nominal, f

**roller** /'roulər/ n rodillo, m; cilindro, m; (wheel, castor) rueda, f; (for flattening the ground) apisonadora, f; Print. rodillo, m; (wave) ola grande, f. **r.-bandage,** venda, f. **r. canary,** canario de raza flauta, m. **r.-skate,** patín de ruedas, m. **r.-skating,** patinaje de ruedas, m. **r.-towel,** toalla continua, f

**rollicking** /'rɒlɪkɪŋ/ a alegre, jovial; juguetón

**rolling** /'roulɪŋ/ a rodante; (of landscape) ondulante, quebrado. —n rodadura, f; (wallowing) revuelco, m; (of metals) laminación, f; (of a ship) balanceo, m; (rolling up) enrollamiento, m. **r.-pin,** rodillo, rodillo de pastelero, m. **r.-stock,** material móvil ferroviario, m

**Roman** /'roumən/ a romano, de los romanos; (of noses and Print.) romano. —n romano (-na). **in R. fashion,** a la romana. **R. Catholic,** a católico; católico apostólico romano. —n el católico (-ca). **R. Catholicism,** catolicismo, m. **R. figures,** números romanos, m pl. **R. nose,** nariz romana, f. **R. road,** vía romana, f. **R. type,** Print. tipo romano, m

**Romance** /'roumæns/ a (of languages) romance. —n (language) romance, m

**romance** /rou'mæns/ n novela de caballería, f; romance, m; aventura, f; cuento, m, novela, f; romanticismo, m; Mus. romanza, f. —vi inventar ficciones; exagerar

**romancer** /rou'mænsər/ n romancerista, mf; mentiroso (-sa), embustero (-ra)

**Romanesque** /,roumə'nɛsk/ a románico; romanesco

**Romanian** /ru'meiniən, -'meinyən/ a rumano. —n rumano (-na); (language) rumano, m

**romantic** /rou'mæntɪk/ a and n romántico (-ca)

**romantically** /rou'mæntɪkli/ adv románticamente; de un modo romántico

**romanticism** /rou'mæntə,sɪzəm/ n romanticismo, m

**romanticist** /rou'mæntəsɪst/ n romántico (-ca)

**Rome** /roum/ n Roma, f

**romp** /rɒmp/ vi juguetear, brincar, retozar, loquear; correr rápidamente. —n locuelo (-la), saltaparedes, mf; (game) retozo, m. **The horse romped home easily,** El caballo ganó la carrera fácilmente

**rompers** /'rɒmpərz/ n mono, m

**romping** /'rɒmpɪŋ/ n juegos, m pl, travesuras, f pl

**rondo** /'rɒndou/ n rondó, m

**rood** /rud/ n cruz, f; crucifijo, m; cuarto de acre, m. **By the r.!** ¡Por mi santiguada!

**roof** /ruf/ n tejado, techado, m; (of a motor-car, bus) tejadillo, m; (of coaches, etc.) imperial, f; cubierta, f; (of the mouth) paladar, m; (bower) enramada, f; (of heaven) bóveda (del cielo), f. —vt techar, tejar; (shelter) abrigar. **r.-garden,** azotea, f. **r.-gutter,** canalera, f

**roofer** /'rufər/ n techador, m; constructor de tejados, m

**rook** /rʊk/ n chova, f, grajo, m; (chess) torre, f. —vt engañar, estafar; (overcharge) desollar vivo (a)

**rookery** /'rʊkəri/ n manada de grajos, f; colonia de grajos, aves marinas or focas, f

**room** /rum/ n (in a house) habitación, f, cuarto, m; sala, f; cámara, f; (behind a shop) trastienda, f; (space) sitio, espacio, m; lugar, m; (opportunity) oportunidad, f; (cause) motivo, m, causa, f. —vi alojarse. **bath-r.,** cuarto de baño, m. **dining-r.,** comedor, m. **drawing-r.,** salón, m. **There is no r. for us in this car,** No cabemos en este coche. **There is still r. for improvement,** Se puede mejorar todavía. **There isn't r. for anything else,** No cabe más. **to be r.,** caber, haber sitio. **to make r.,** hacer sitio

**roomed** /rumd/ a (in compounds) de... habitaciones; de... salas

**roominess** /'ruminɪs/ n espaciosidad, amplitud, amplitud de habitación, f; (of garments) holgura, f

**rooming house** /'rutɪd/ n casa de huéspedes, f

**roommate** /'rum,meit, 'rʊm-/ n compañero de cuarto, compañero de pieza, m

**roomy** /'rumi, 'rʊmi/ a espacioso, amplio; (of garments) holgado

**roost** /rust/ n percha de gallinero, f. —vi dormir en una percha; recogerse. **to rule the r.,** ser el amo del cotarro

**rooster** /'rustər/ n gallo, m,

**root** /rut or, sometimes, rʊt/ n raíz, f; Gram. radical, m; Mus. base, f; origen, m; explicación, f. —vt arraigar; Fig. fijar, clavar. —vi echar raíces; Fig. arraigarse; (of pigs, etc.) hozar, escarbar; revolver. **to r. out,** arrancar de raíz; Fig. desarraigar; (destroy) extirpar. **cubed r.,** raíz cúbica, f. **from the r.,** (entirely) de raíz. **square r.,** raíz cuadrada, f. **to cut close to the r.,** cortar a raíz

**rooted** a (in compounds) de raíces...; arraigado

**rope** /roup/ n soga, cuerda, f; (hawser) maroma, f; Naut. cabo, m; (tight-rope) cable, m, cuerda de volatinero, f; (string) ristra, sarta, f; hilo, m; pl **ropes,** (boxing) cuerdas del cuadrilátero, f pl. —vt encordelar, atar con cuerdas. **to r. in,** encerrar; (a person) enganchar, coger. **a r. of pearls,** una sarta de perlas. **to give a person plenty of r.,** dar mucha latitud (a). **to know the ropes,** conocer todos los trucos. **r.-ladder,** escala de cuerda, f. **r.-maker,** cordelero (-ra), soguero, m. **r.-making,** cordelería, soguería, f. **r.-trick,** truco de la cuerda, m. **r.-walk,** cordelería, f. **r.-yarn,** Naut. filástica, f

**rosary** /'rouzəri/ n rosario, m. **to say the r.,** rezar el rosario

**rose** /rouz/ n rosa, f; color de rosa, m; (rosette) roseta, f; Archit. rosetón, m; (of watering-can) pomo, m, roseta, f. —a de rosa, rosado. **to see the world through r.-colored spectacles,** ver las cosas en color de rosa. **to turn to r.,** volverse color de rosa, rosear. **r.-bay,** Bot. rododafne, adelfa, f. **r.-bush,** rosal, m. **r.-color,** color de rosa, rosa, m. **r.-colored,** de color de rosa, rosado. **r.-garden,** rosalera, rosaleda, f. **r. grower,** cultivador (-ra) de rosas. **r. hip,** escaramujo, m. **r. leaf,** hoja de rosa, f; pétalo de rosa, m. **r.-like,** como una rosa, de rosa. **r.-red,** de color de rosa; como una rosa. **climbing r.-tree,** rosal trepador, m. **dwarf r.-tree,** rosal bajo, m. **standard r.-tree,** rosal de tallo, m. **r.-water,** agua de rosas, f. **r.-window,** rosetón, m, rosa, f. **r.-wood,** palo de rosa, m

**rosé** a (of wines) rosado

**rosebud** /'rouz,bʌd/ n capullo de rosa, m

**rosemary** /'rouz,meəri/ n romero, m

**rosin** /'rɒzɪn/ n (solid, for violin-bows, etc.) colofonia, f; resina, f. —vt dar con colofonia; dar con resina

**rosiness** /'rouzinɪs/ n color de rosa, m

**roster** /'rɒstər/ n lista, f; registro, m; matrícula, f

**rostrum** /'rɒstrəm/ n tribuna, f; Zool. pico, m; (of a ship) espolón, m

**rosy** /'rouzi/ a róseo, rosado; sonrosado; Fig. de color de rosa, halagüeño; optimista. **r.-cheeked,** con (de) mejillas sonrosadas

**rot** /rɒt/ n putrefacción, podredumbre, f; (in trees) caries, f; (in sheep) comalía, f; (slang) patrañas, f pl, disparates, m pl, vi pudrirse; descomponerse; Fig. echarse a perder; (slang) decir disparates. —vt pudrir; Fig. corromper; (slang) tomar el pelo (a)

**rota** /'routə/ n lista, f; orden del día, m

**rotary** /'routəri/ a rotativo. **r. printing press,** rotativa, f

**rotary telephone** n teléfono de discado, m

**rotate** /'routeit/ vi girar, dar vueltas; alternarse. —vt hacer girar

**rotating** /'routeitɪŋ/ a rotativo; giratorio

**rotation** /rou'teiʃən/ n rotación, f; turno, m. **in r.,** por turnos. **r. of crops,** rotación de cultivos, f

**rotatory** /'routə,tɔri/ a rotatorio

**rote, to learn by** /rout/ vt aprender de memoria, aprender por repetición, aprender de cotorra

**rotogravure** /,routəgrə'vyʊr/ n rotograbado, m

**rotten** /'rɒtn/ a putrefacto; podrido; (of bones, teeth) cariado; dañado, echado a perder; Fig. corrompido; (slang) pésimo. **to smell r.,** oler a podredumbre; apestar

**rottenness** /'rɒtn̩nɪs/ n putrefacción, podredumbre, f; Fig. corrupción, f

**rotter** /'rɒtər/ n (slang) perdido, m

**rotting** /'rɒtɪŋ/ n pudrición, f, a que se pudre

**rotund** /rou'tʌnd/ a rotundo

**rotunda** /rou'tʌndə/ n rotonda, f

**rotundity** /rou'tʌndɪti/ n redondez, f; rotundidad, f

**roué** /ru'ei, 'ruei/ n calavera, libertino, m

**rouge** /ruʒ/ n colorete, m, vt and vi pintar de rojo, poner(se) colorete

**rough** /rʌf/ a áspero; duro; (of country) fragoso, escabroso; (uneven) desigual; (stormy) borrascoso, tempestuoso; (of the sea) encrespado, bravo; (of movement) violento; (bristling) erizado; (of the hair) despeinado; (unpolished) tosco; basto; (unskilled, clumsy) torpe; (of sounds, tastes) áspero; (of persons) rudo, inculto; (severe) severo; (of behavior) brutal; (of manners) brusco; (rude) grosero; (approximate) aproximado. —adv duramente, mal. —n estado tosco, m; (person) matón, m. **in the r.,** en bruto; (roughed out) bosquejado. **to grow r.,** (of the sea) encresparse, embravecerse. **to take the r. with the smooth,** Fig. aceptar la realidad; tomar lo bueno con lo malo. **to r. it,** luchar contra las dificultades, pasar apuros; llevar una vida sencilla; vivir mal. **to r. out,** bosquejar. **r. and ready,** improvisado; provisional. **r. and tumble,** n camorra, pendencia, f. **r.-cast,** vt dar una primera capa de mezcla gruesa (a); bosquejar. **r. diamond,** diamante bruto (or en bruto), m. **r.-draft,** borrador, m; bosquejo, m. **r.-haired,** (of a dog) de pelo crespo. **r.-hewn,** modelado toscamente; desbastado; Fig. cerril, tosco. **r.-house,** jarana, f. **r.-rider,** domador (de caballos), m. **r. sketch,** bosquejo, esbozo, m. **r.-spoken,** malhablado

**roughen** /'rʌfən/ vt poner áspero. —vi ponerse áspero

**roughly** /'rʌfli/ adv rudamente, toscamente; duramente; brutalmente; bruscamente; (of tastes, sounds) ásperamente; (approximately) aproximadamente, más o menos

**roughness** /'rʌfnɪs/ n aspereza, f; dureza, f; tosquedad, f; rudeza, f; (of the sea, wind) braveza, f; violencia, f; (of manner) brusquedad, f; brutalidad, f; (vulgarity) grosería, f. **the r. of the way,** la aspereza del camino

**roulette** /ru'lɛt/ n ruleta, f

**round** /raund/ a redondo; (plump) rollizo; rotundo, categórico; sonoro. **a r. sum,** una cantidad redonda;

un número redondo. **to walk at a r. pace,** andar a un buen paso. **r. dance,** baile en ruedo, *m.* **r.-faced,** carilleno, de cara redonda. **r.-house,** cuerpo de guardia, *m; Naut.* tumbadillo, *m.* **r.-shouldered,** cargado de espaldas. **r. table,** mesa redonda, *f;* (of King Arthur) Tabla Redonda, *f.* **r. trip,** viaje redondo, viaje de ida y vuelta, *m.* **r.-up,** rodeo de ganado, *m;* arresto, *m*

**round** /raund/ *n* círculo, *m;* esfera, *f;* redondez, *f;* (slice) rodaja, *f;* (of a ladder) peldaño, *m;* (patrol and *Mil.*) ronda, *f;* circuito, *m;* vuelta, *f,* giro, *m;* serie, *f;* rutina, *f;* (of ammunition) andanada, descarga, *f;* (of cartridge) cartucho con bala, *m;* (of applause, etc.) salva, *f;* (of golf) partido, *m;* (in a fight) asalto, *m; Sports.* vuelta, *f;* (of drinks) ronda, *f;* (doctor's) visitas, *f pl*

**round** /raund/ *vt* redondear; (*Fig.* complete) acabar, perfeccionar; (go round, e.g. a corner) dar vuleta (a), doblar, trasponer; rodear, cercar; (of a ship) doblar. —*vi* redondearse. **to r. off,** redondear; terminar; coronar. **to r. up,** (cattle) rodear. **to r. upon,** volverse contra

**round** /raund/ *adv* alrededor, en derredor; por todos lados; a la redonda, en torno; en circunferencia; en conjunto (**r.** is not translated in Spanish, e.g. *I shall come r. to your house,* Vendré a tu casa). —*prep* alrededor de. **all the year r.,** todo el año, el año entero. **r. about,** a la redonda de, al derredor de; (nearly) cerca de; (of time by the clock) a eso de. **The road is closed and we shall have to go r.,** El camino está cerrado y tendremos que dar una vuelta. **to come r.,** volver; dejarse persuadir; recobrar su buen humor. **to go r.,** (spin) dar vueltas; (of the wind) cambiar. **There is enough to go r.,** Hay bastante para todos

**roundabout** /*a.* ˌraundəˈbaut, *n.* ˈraundəˌbaut/ *a* indirecto; desviado; vago. —*n* tiovivo, *m;* (traffic) redondel, *m.* **He spoke in a r. way,** Hablaba con circunloquios. **We went there by a r. way,** Fuimos dando un rodeo

**roundly** /ˈraundli/ *adv* en redondo; rotundamente, claramente

**roundness** /ˈraundnɪs/ *n* redondez, *f;* rotundidad, *f*

**rouse** /rauz/ *vt* despertar; animar; excitar; suscitar; provocar. **to r. oneself,** despertarse; animarse (a hacer algo)

**rousing** /ˈrauzɪŋ/ *a* que despierta; (moving) emocionante; (enthusiastic) entusiasta; grande, bueno

**rout** /raut/ *n* (rabble) chusma, *f;* (party) sarao, *m;* (defeat) derrota, *f;* (meeting) reunión, *f.* —*vt* derrotar, poner en fuga; vencer

**route** /rut, raut/ *n* ruta, *f;* camino, *m;* itinerario, *m.* **r. march,** marcha de maniobras, *f*

**routine** /ruˈtin/ *n* rutina, *f,* a rutinario, de rutina

**rove** /rouv/ *vi* vagar, errar

**rover** /ˈrouvər/ *n* vagabundo (-da); pirata, *m*

**roving** /ˈrouvɪŋ/ *a* vagabundo, errante; ambulante

**row** /rou/ *n* (line) hilera, fila, hila, *f;* (in a theater, etc.) fila, *f;* (string) ristra, *f;* (in a boat) paseo en bote, *m;* (commotion) alboroto, *m;* (noise) ruido, *m,* (shindy) gresca, camorra, *f;* (scolding) regaño, *m, vi* (a boat) remar, bogar. —*vt* conducir remando; (scold) regañar. **to be a row,** (shindy) haber la de San Quintín. **to start a row,** (shindy) armar camorra.

**rowboat** /ˈrouˌbout/ *n* bote de remos, *m*

**rowdiness** /ˈraudɪnɪs/ *n* alboroto, *m*

**rowdy** /ˈraudi/ *a* alborotador. —*n* trafalmejas, *mf* rufián, *m*

**rower** /ˈrouər/ *n* remero (-ra), bogador (-ra)

**rowing** /ˈrouɪŋ/ *a* que rema; de remos. —*n* deporte del remo, *m;* paseo en bote, *m.* **r.-boat,** bote de remos, *m.* **r.-club,** club náutico, *m.* **r.-seat,** bancada, *f.* **r.-stroke,** bogada, *f*

**royal** /ˈrɔiəl/ *a* real; regio. —*n Naut.* sobrejuanete, *m.* **r. academy,** real academia, *f.* **r. eagle,** águila real, *f.* **R. Highness,** Alteza Real, *f.* **R. letters patent,** cédula real, *f.* **R. Mail,** mala real, *f.* **R. Standard,** estandarte real, *m*

**royalism** /ˈrɔiəˌlɪzəm/ *n* realismo, *m*

**royalist** /ˈrɔiəlɪst/ *a* and *a* realista, *mf*

**royally** /ˈrɔiəli/ *adv* realmente; regiamente

**royalty** /ˈrɔiəlti/ *n* realeza, *f;* miembro de la familia

real, *m;* tanto por ciento de los ingresos, *m;* derechos de autor, *m pl*

**R.R.** (abbrev. of *Railroad*) F.R. (abbrev. of *ferrocarril*)

**rub** /rʌb/ *vt* frotar, estregar; fregar; rozar; friccionar; (make sore) raspar. **to rub one's hands together,** frotarse las manos. **to rub the wrong way,** frotar a contrapelo. **to rub against,** rozar. **to rub along,** *Inf.* ir tirando. **to rub down,** (a horse) bruzar; limpiar; (dry) secar; (wear down) desgastar. **to rub in,** dar fricciones con; frotar con; (an idea, etc.) machacar. **to rub off,** *vt* quitar (frotando); borrar. —*vi* borrarse; separarse (de). **to rub out,** *vt* borrar. —*vi* borrarse. **to rub up,** (polish) limpiar; *Fig.* refrescar

**rub** /rʌb/ *n* frotación, *f;* roce, *m;* fricción, *f; Fig.* obstáculo, *m;* dificultad, *f.* **to give a rub,** frotar, etc. **rub-a-dub,** rataplán, *m*

**rubber** /ˈrʌbər/ *n* de caucho, de goma. —*n* caucho, *m,* goma, *f;* (for erasing) goma de borrar, *f;* (masseur) masajista, *mf;* (at whist, etc.) partida, *f;* *Sports.* vuelta, *f.* **r. band,** goma, banda de goma, *f.* **r. belt,** *Mech.* correa de transmisión de caucho, *f.* **r. bers,** zapatos de goma, chanclos, *m pl.* **synthetic r.,** caucho artificial, *m.* **r. band,** goma, banda de goma, *f.* **r. belt,** *Mech.* correa de transmisión de caucho, *f.* **r.-plant, tree,** cauchera, *f.* **r. plantation,** cauchal, *m.* **r. planter,** cauchero, *m.* **r. stamp,** estampilla, *f*

**rubbing** /ˈrʌbɪŋ/ *n* frotación, *f;* fricción, *f;* roce, *m;* (of floors, dishes, etc.) fregado, *m*

**rubbish** /ˈrʌbɪʃ/ *n* basura, *f;* desperdicios, *m pl,* desecho, *m;* (of goods) pacotilla, *f;* (nonsense) pamplinas, patrañas, *f pl,* disparates, *m pl.* **r. cart,** carro del basurero, *m*

**rubbishy** /ˈrʌbɪʃi/ *a* sin valor, malo; (of goods) de pacotilla, de calidad inferior

**rubble** /ˈrʌbəl/ *n* escombros, *m pl;* cascote, *m;* piedra bruta, *f*

**rubicund** /ˈrubɪˌkʌnd/ *a* rubicundo

**ruble** /ˈrubəl/ *n* rublo, *m*

**rubric** /ˈrubrɪk/ *n* rúbrica, *f*

**ruby** /ˈrubi/ *n* rubí, *m.* —*a* de rubíes; de rubí. **r. lips,** labios de rubí, *m pl*

**rucksack** /ˈrʌkˌsæk, ˈruk-/ *n* mochila, *f*

**rudder** /ˈrʌdər/ *n* timón, gobernalle, *m*

**ruddiness** /ˈrʌdinɪs/ *n* rubicundez, *f;* rojez, *f;* frescura, *f*

**ruddy** /ˈrʌdi/ *a* rubicundo; rojo; frescote; (of animals) barcino

**rude** /rud/ *a* rudo; tosco; vigoroso; grosero, descortés

**rudely** /ˈrudli/ *adv* toscamente; groseramente

**rudeness** /ˈrudnɪs/ *n* rudeza, *f;* tosquedad, *f;* grosería, incivilidad, descortesía, *f*

**rudiment** /ˈrudəmənt/ *n* rudimento, *m*

**rudimentary** /ˌrudəˈmɛntəri/ *a* rudimentario

**rue** /ru/ *vt* lamentar, llorar. —*n Bot.* ruda, *f*

**rueful** /ˈrufəl/ *a* triste, melancólico; lamentable

**ruefully** /ˈrufəli/ *adv* tristemente

**ruefulness** /ˈrufəlnɪs/ *n* tristeza, *f*

**ruff** /rʌf/ *n* golilla, lechuguilla, *f;* (of a bird) collarín de plumas, *m;* (of an animal) collarín de pelo, *m*

**ruffian** /ˈrʌfiən/ *n* rufián, *m*

**ruffle** /ˈrʌfəl/ *n Sew.* volante fruncido, *m;* (of a bird) collarín de plumas, *m;* (of an animal) collarín de pelo, *m;* (ripple) rizo, *m;* (annoyance) irritación, *f.* —*vt* (ripple) rizar; (pleat) fruncir; (feathers) erizar; (hair) despeinar; agitar; (annoy) irritar, incomodar

**ruffling** /ˈrʌflɪŋ/ *n* (rippling) rizado, *m;* (pleating) fruncido, *m;* (of the temper) irritación, *f*

**rug** /rʌg/ *n* (floor) alfombra, *f;* manta de viaje, *f.* **rug strap,** portamantas, *m*

**rugged** /ˈrʌgɪd/ *a* áspero, escabroso; escarpado; abrupto; (wrinkled) arrugado; tosco; (harsh) duro, severo; inculto; rudo; mal acabado; vigoroso

**ruggedness** /ˈrʌgɪdnɪs/ *n* aspereza, escabrosidad, *f;* lo escarpado; dureza, severidad, *f;* rudeza, *f;* vigor, *m*

**ruin** /ˈruɪn/ *n* ruina, *f.* —*vt* arruinar; echar a perder, estropear por completo; (a woman) perder

**ruination** /ˌruəˈneɪʃən/ *n* ruina, perdición, *f*

**ruined** /ˈruɪnd/ *a* arruinado; en ruinas

**ruinous** /ˈruənəs/ *a* ruinoso; en ruinas

**ruinously** /ˈruənəsli/ *adv* ruinosamente

**rule** /rul/ *n* regla, *f;* gobierno, *m;* autoridad, *f,* mando, *m;* administración, *f;* (reign) reinado, *m;* (of a court, etc.) orden, *f;* (for measuring) regla, *f; Print.*

regleta, *f; pl* **rules,** reglas, *f pl;* reglamento, *m.* —*vt* gobernar; regentar, regir; (control) dominar; (of a chairman, etc.) disponer, decidir; (guide) guiar; (lines) reglar. —*vi* gobernar; (of a monarch) reinar; (of prices) mantenerse; estar en boga, prevalecer. **as a r.,** por regla general, en general. **slide-r.,** regla de cálculo, *f.* **to make it a r.,** tener por regla; tener por costumbre; tener por máxima. **to r. out,** excluir; *Law.* no admitir. **to r. over,** (of a king, etc.) reinar sobre. **r. of the road,** reglamento del tráfico, *m.* **r. of thumb,** regla empírica, *f;* rutina, *f*

**ruler** /'rulər/ *n* gobernador (-ra); soberano (-na); (master) amo (ama); (for ruling lines) regla, *f*

**ruling** /'rulɪŋ/ *a* regente; dominante; (current) vigente. —*n* gobierno, *m; Law.* decisión, *f,* fallo, *m;* (with lines) rayado, *m.* **r. pen,** tiralíneas, *m*

**rum** /rʌm/ *n* ron, *m*

**rumble** /'rʌmbəl/ *vi* retumbar, tronar; (of vehicles) rugir; crujir. —*n* retumbo, trueno, *m;* rugido, *m;* ruido sordo, *m;* rumor, *m;* crujido, *m*

**rumbling** /'rʌmblɪŋ/ *a* que retumba, etc. —*n* ruido sordo, *m;* retumbo, *m;* crujido, *m;* (in the bowels) rugido, *m*

**ruminant** /'rumənənt/ *a* and *n* rumiante, *mf*

**ruminate** /'rumə,neit/ *vi* and *vt* rumiar

**rumination** /,rumə'neiʃən/ *n* rumia, *f;* meditación, reflexión, *f*

**rummage** /'rʌmɪdʒ/ *vt* revolver, desordenar, trastornar; explorar. **to r. out,** desenterrar

**rumor** /'rumər/ *n* rumor, *m,* fama, *f.* **It is rumored that...,** Hay rumores de que..., La voz corre que..., Se dice que...

**rump** /rʌmp/ *n* (of an animal) nalgas, ancas, *f pl;* cuarto trasero, *m;* (of a bird) rabadilla, *f;* (scornful) culo, *m,* posaderas, *f pl.* **r.-steak,** solomillo, *m*

**rumple** /'rʌmpəl/ *vt* arrugar; desordenar

**run** /rʌn/ *vi* correr; acudir; (flee) huir; (rush) precipitarse, lanzarse; (in a race) tomar parte en una carrera; competir; (pass over) deslizarse (por); (of machines) andar, marchar; (of traffic) circular; (leave, of trains, ships, etc.) salir; (ply between) hacer el trayecto entre... y...; (flow) fluir, correr; (into the sea, of rivers) desembocar (en); (spurt) chorrear, manar; (drip) gotear; (leak) dejar fugar (el agua, etc.); (of colors) correrse; caer; (of tears) correr; derramarse; (of eyes) llorar; (melt) derretirse; (of a sore) supurar; (travel or go) ir; moverse; (work) trabajar; funcionar; (of editions of a book) agotarse; (of a play) representarse; (cross) cruzar; (elapse) correr, transcurrir, pasar; (become) hacerse; (of wording) decir; (be current) correr; (for parliament, etc.) hacerse candidato; (navigate) navegar; (spread) extenderse; (be) estar; ser; (of thoughts) pasar; (last) durar; (tend) tender (a). —*vt* (a race, a horse) correr; (drive) conducir; (a business, etc.) administrar; dirigir; (govern) gobernar, regir; (hunt) cazar; perseguir; (water, etc.) hacer correr; (pierce) clavar; introducir; (push) empujar; (one's hand, eye, etc.) pasar; (risks, etc.) correr; (possess) tener; establecer un servicio de (autobuses, etc.); (smuggle) hacer contrabando de. **The ship ran aground,** El barco encalló. **to run dry,** secarse; agotarse. **to run in the family,** estar en la familia. **to run into debt,** endeudarse, contraer deudas. **to run to seed,** granar; agotarse. **Steamers run daily between Barcelona and Mallorca,** Hay servicio diario de vapores entre Barcelona y Mallorca. **A stab of pain ran up his leg,** Sintió un dolor agudo en la pierna. **Feeling was running high,** Los ánimos estaban excitados. **My arrangements ran smoothly,** Mis planes marchaban bien. **Funds are running low,** El dinero escasea. **The tune runs in my head,** Tengo la canción metida en la cabeza. **The message runs like this,** El mensaje reza así, El mensaje dice así. **He ran his fingers through his hair,** Se mesaba los cabellos. **to run about,** andar de un lado a otro, correr por todas partes; (gad) corretear. **to run across,** cruzar corriendo; (meet) topar con, tropezar con. **to run after,** correr detrás (de); perseguir; buscar. **to run against,** (collide with) dar contra; (meet) tropezar con. **to run at,** abalanzarse hacia, precipitarse sobre; atacar. **to run away,** huir, escaparse; (slip away) escurrirse; (of a horse) dispararse, desbocarse. **to run away with,**

huir con, fugarse con; (carry off) arrebatar; (steal) llevarse; (imagine) imaginarse, figurarse; (of temper, etc.) dominar, poseer. **to run back,** volver corriendo; llegar corriendo; retroceder rápidamente, correr hacia atrás. **to run backwards,** correr hacia atrás; **to run backwards and forwards,** ir y venir. **to run behind,** correr detrás (de); quedarse atrás; (be late) estar atrasado. **to run down,** *vi* bajar corriendo; descender, bajar; (of a clock) parar; (of a battery) gastarse; (of liquids) correr; fluir; (drop by drop) destilar. —*vt* (capture) coger; alcanzar; (a person by a vehicle) atropellar; (a ship) echar a pique; (disparage) hablar mal de. **run-down,** (in health) agotado; (of a clock) parado. **to run for,** buscar corriendo; correr para coger (el autobús, etc.); (president, etc.) ser candidato para. **to run in,** *vi* entrar corriendo. —*vt* arrestar; hacer prisionero; *Print.* encerrar. **to run into,** tropezar con; chocar con; (plunge into) meterse de cabeza en; (of sums of money, etc.) ascender a; (of streets, rivers, etc.) desembocar en. **to run off,** *vi* escaparse corriendo; marcharse corriendo. —*vt* deslizarse por; (drain) vaciar; *Print.* imprimir; (compose) componer. **to run off with,** huir con. **to run on,** correr delante; continuar; (of the mind) pensar en, entregarse a; hablar sin cesar; *Print.* recorrer. **to run out,** *vi* salir corriendo; (of liquids) derramarse; salir; (end) acabarse; agotarse; (project) sobresalir. —*vt* (cricket) coger al lanzador fuera de la línea de saque. **to run out of,** no tener más de, haber terminado. **to run over,** *vi* rebosar; derramarse. —*vt* (of a vehicle) atropellar, pasar por encima de; (peruse) repasar; revisar. **run pell-mell,** salir pitando, salir volando, salvarse por pies. **to run through,** correr por; pasar por; recorrer; (go directly) ir directamente (a); (pierce) traspasar, pasar de parte a parte; (squander) derrochar, malbaratar; (read) hojear, leer por encima. **to run up,** *vt* (hoist) izar; hacer de prisa; construir rápidamente; (incur) incurrir. —*vi* subir corriendo; (of plants) trepar (por); (shrink) encogerse; (of expenses) aumentar. **to run up to time,** llegar a su hora. **to run up against,** tropezar con; (opposition, etc.) encontrar.

**run** /rʌn/ *n* carrera, corrida, *f;* (excursion) visita, excursión, *f;* (cricket) carrera, *f;* (walk) paseo, *m;* (by train or sea) viaje, *m;* (by bus, tram) trayecto, *m;* (sea crossing) travesía, *f;* (distance run) recorrido, *m;* (of events, etc.) curso, *m;* marcha, *f;* (of markets, etc.) tendencia, *f;* (rhythm) ritmo, *m;* dirección, *f;* distancia, *f; Mus.* serie de notas, *f;* serie, *f;* duración, *f; Theat.* serie de representaciones, *f;* (freedom to use) libre uso, *m;* (majority) mayoría, *f;* (on a bank) asedio, *m;* (on a book, etc.) d > f; (for sheep, etc.) terreno de pasto, *m;* (for fowls) gallinero, *m.* **a run of bad luck,** una temporada de mala suerte. **at a run,** corriendo. **in the long run,** a la larga, al fin y al cabo. **on the run,** en fuga; ocupado. **Prices came down with a run,** Los precios bajaron de golpe. **take-off run,** *Aer.* recorrido de despegue, *m*

**runaway** /'rʌnə,wei/ *a* fugitivo; (of a horse) desbocado

**rune** /run/ *n* runa, *f*

**rung** /rʌŋ/ *n* (of a ladder) peldaño, *m;* (of a chair) travesaño, *m;* (lath) listón, *m*

**runic** /'runɪk/ *a* rúnico

**runner** /'rʌnər/ *n* corredor (-ra); (carrier of sedan chair, etc.) silletero, *mf;* (smuggler) contrabandista, *m;* (courier) estafeta, *f;* (messenger) mensajero, *m;* (ring) anillo movible, pasador corredizo, *m;* rueda móvil, *f;* (of a sledge) patín, *m; Bot.* tallo rastrero, *m.* **r.-up,** el segundo

**running** /'rʌnɪŋ/ *a* corredor; (of water, bank accounts) corriente; (of a knot) corredizo; (of a sore) supurante; (continuous) continuo; (consecutive) consecutivo. —*n* carrera, *f;* marcha, *f;* funcionamiento, *m;* administración, *f;* gobierno, *m;* dirección, *f;* (flowing) derrame, *m;* (of trains, buses, etc.) servicio, *m;* (smuggling) contrabando, *m;* (of a sore) supuración, *f.* **six times r.,** seis veces consecutivas. **The car is in r. order,** El auto está en buen estado. **r. away,** fuga, *f.* **r.-board,** (of a car, etc.) estribo, *m;* (of a locomotive) plataforma, *f.* **r. costs,** gastos de mantenimiento, *m pl;* (railway) gastos de tracción, *m pl.* **r.**

**fight,** acción de retirada, *f.* **r.-knot,** lazo corredizo, *m.* **r. title,** *Print.* título de la columna, *m*

**run-off match** /'rʌnɔf/ *n* desempate, *m*

**runway** /'rʌn,wei/ *n* (for launching a ship) grada, *f;* (of an airfield) pista de aterrizaje, *f*

**rupee** /ruˈpi, ˈrupi/ *n* rupia, *f*

**rupestrian** /ruˈpestriən/ *a* rupestre

**rupture** /'rʌptʃər/ *n* rompimiento, *m,* rotura, *f;* ruptura, *f; med* hernia, *f*

**ruptured** /'rʌptʃərd/ *a med* herniado, quebrado

**rupturing** /'rʌptʃərɪŋ/ *n* ruptura, *f*

**rural** /'rʊrəl/ *a* rural, campestre, del campo; agrario

**ruse** /ruz/ *n* artimaña, treta, ardid, *f*

**rush** /rʌʃ/ *n Bot.* junco, *m;* acometida, *f;* ataque, *m;* (of water) torrente, *m;* (bustle) bullicio, *m;* (speed) prisa, *f;* precipitación, *f;* acceso, *m;* (crowd) tropel, *m,* masa, *f;* (struggle) lucha, *f;* furia, *f.* —*vi* precipitarse, lanzarse; agolparse. —*vt* llevar rápidamente (a); despachar rápidamente; precipitar; (attack) asaltar, atacar; (capture) tomar, capturar; hacer de prisa; (a bill) hacer aprobar de prisa. **to r. upon,** abalanzarse hacia; embestir. **in a r.,** en tropel, en masa; de prisa. **to r. to a conclusion,** precipitarse a una conclusión. **r.-bottomed,** con asiento de enea. **r. hour,** hora de mayor circulación, *f,* hora de aglomeración, hora-pico (Argentina), hora brava (Argentina, informal). **r. order,** pedido urgente, *m*

**rushy** /'rʌʃi/ *a* juncoso

**russet** /'rʌsɪt/ *a* rojizo; rojo. **r. apple,** manzana asperiega, *f*

**Russia** /'rʌʃə/ Rusia, *f*

**Russian** /'rʌʃən/ *a* ruso. —*n* ruso (-sa); (language) ruso, *m.* **R. leather,** piel de Rusia, *f*

**rust** /rʌst/ *n* herrumbre, *f,* orín, *m;* moho, *m;* (disease) añublo, tizón, *m.* —*vt* aherrumbrar; enmohecer. —*vi* aherrumbrarse; enmohecerse

**rustic** /'rʌstɪk/ *a* rústico; campesino, aldeano; (scornful) palurdo, grosero. —*n* aldeano, *m;* (scornful) patán, *m*

**rusticate** /'rʌstɪ,keit/ *vi* rusticar, vivir en el campo. —*vt* enviar al campo

**rustication** /,rʌstɪ'keiʃən/ *n* rusticación, *f*

**rusticity** /rʌ'stɪsɪti/ *n* rusticidad, *f*

**rustiness** /'rʌstɪnɪs/ *n* herrumbre, *f;* enmohecimiento, *m;* color rojizo, *m; Fig.* falta de práctica, *f*

**rustle** /'rʌsəl/ *n* susurro, *m;* murmurio, *m;* (of silk, a dress, etc.) frufrú, *m;* (of paper, etc.) crujido, *m.* —*vi* susurrar; murmurar; crujir. —*vt* (a paper) hacer crujir

**rustless** /'rʌstlɪs/ *a* inoxidable

**rustling** /'rʌslɪŋ/ *n* see **rustle**

**rusty** /'rʌsti/ *a* herrumbroso; enmohecido, mohoso; (red) rojizo, (worn out) usado, viejo; (out of practice) desacostumbrado; (forgotten) empolvorado, oxidado (e.g. *My Portuguese is rusty,* Mi portugués está empolvorado)

**rut** /rʌt/ *n* rodera, *f,* bache, surco, *m; fig* sendero trillado, *m; fig* rutina, *f;* (sexual appetite) celo, *m, vi* estar en celo

**ruthless** /'ruθlɪs/ *a* inhumano, insensible, despiadado; inexorable, inflexible

**ruthlessly** /'ruθlɪsnɪs/ *adv* inhumanamente; inflexiblemente, inexorablemente

**ruthlessness** *n* inhumanidad, *f;* inflexibilidad, inexorabilidad, *f*

**Rwanda** /ruˈɑndə/ Ruanda, *f*

**rye** /rai/ *n* centeno, *m.* **rye field,** centenar, *m*

# S

**s** /ɛs/ *n* (letter) ese, *f*
**sabbatarian** /ˌsæbə'tɛəriən/ *a* sabatario
**Sabbath** /'sæbəθ/ *n* (Jewish) sábado, *m;* (Christian) domingo, *m*
**sabbatical** /sə'bætɪkəl/ *a* sabático
**saber** /'seibər/ *n* sable, *m;* (soldier) jinete, *m.* —*vt* dar sablazos (a), acuchillar. **s. cut, thrust,** sablazo, *m*
**sable** /'seibəl/ *n* (animal and fur) marta, *f; herald* sable, *m.* —*a herald* sable; *poet* negro
**sabotage** /'sæbə,taʒ/ *n* sabotaje, *m, vt* cometer un acto de sabotaje en
**saboteur** /ˌsæbə'tɜr/ *n* saboteador, *m*
**sac** /sæk/ *n biol* saco, *m*
**saccharin** /'sækərɪn/ *n* sacarina, *f*
**sachet** /sæ'ʃei/ *n* sachet, *m;* bolsa, *f.* **handkerchief s.,** bolsa para pañuelos, *f*
**sack** /sæk/ *n* (bag) saco, *m; mil* saqueo, saqueamiento, saco, *m.* —*vt* meter en sacos; (dismiss) dar pasaporte (a), despedir; *mil* saquear. **to get the s.,** recibir el pasaporte. **to give the s.,** dar el pasaporte (a), poner de patitas en la calle (a). **s. coat,** saco, *m*
**sackcloth** /'sæk,klɔθ/ *n* harpillera, *f.* **to repent in s. and ashes,** ponerse cenizas en la cabeza
**sacking** /'sækɪŋ/ *n* harpillera, *f; mil* saqueo, *m*
**sacrament** /'sækrəmənt/ *n* sacramento, *m;* Eucaristía, *f.* **the Blessed S.,** el Santísimo Sacramento. **to receive the Holy S.,** comulgar. **to receive the last sacraments,** recibir los sacramentos, recibir la Extremaunción
**sacramental** /ˌsækrə'mɛntl/ *a* sacramental
**sacramentalist** /ˌsækrə'mɛntlɪst/ *n* sacramentario (-ia)
**sacred** /'seikrid/ *a* sagrado; sacro, santo; consagrado. **Nothing is s. to them,** No hay nada sagrado para ellos, No respetan nada. **the S. Heart of Jesus,** el Sagrado Corazón (de Jesús). **S. to the memory of...** Consagrado a la memoria de... **s. music,** música sagrada, *f*
**sacredness** /'seikridnɪs/ *n* carácter sagrado, *m;* santidad, *f;* inviolabilidad, *f*
**sacrifice** /'sækrə,fais/ *n* sacrificio, *m.* —*vt and vi* sacrificar. **s. of the mass,** sacrificio del altar, *m*
**sacrificial** /ˌsækrə'fɪʃəl/ *a* sacrificador; del sacrificio
**sacrilege** /'sækrəlɪdʒ/ *n* sacrilegio, *m*
**sacrilegious** /ˌsækrə'lɪdʒəs/ *a* sacrílego
**sacristan** /'sækrɪstən/ *n* sacristán, *m*
**sacristy** /'sækrɪsti/ *n* sacristía, *f*
**sacrosanct** /'sækrou,sæŋkt/ *a* sacrosanto
**sacrum** /'sækrəm, 'seikrəm/ *n anat* sacro, *m*
**sad** /sæd/ *a* triste; melancólico; (of a mistake) deplorable, funesto; *Inf.* redomado; (pensive) pensativo. **How s.!** ¡Qué lástima! ¡Qué triste! **It made me s.,** Me entristeció
**sadden** /'sædn/ *vt* entristecer, acongojar, afligir
**saddle** /'sædl/ *n* (riding) silla de montar, *f;* (of a bicycle, etc.) sillín, *m; mech* silla, *f; Anat.* espalda, *f.* —*vt* ensillar. **to s. with the responsibility of,** echar la responsabilidad de (a). **s. of mutton,** lomo de carnero, *m.* **s.-bag,** alforja, *f.* **s.-cloth,** mantilla de silla, *f.* **s.-tree,** arzón, *m*
**saddler** /'sædlər/ *n* sillero, guarnicionero, *m*
**Sadducee** /'sædʒə,si/ *n* saduceo (-ea)
**sadism** /'seidɪzəm/ *n* sadismo, *m*
**sadist** /'seidɪst/ *n* sadista, *mf*
**sadistic** /sə'dɪstɪk/ *a* sadístico
**sadly** /'sædli/ *adv* tristemente; (very) muy
**sadness** /'sædnɪs/ *n* tristeza, melancolía, *f*
**safe** /seif/ *a* al abrigo (de); seguro; salvo; (certain) cierto; prudente; digno de confianza. —*n* caja de caudales, *f;* (for food) alacena, *f.* **I stood beneath a tree s. from the rain,** Estaba de pie bajo un árbol, al abrigo de la lluvia. **to put something in a s. place,** poner algo en salvo; poner algo en un lugar seguro. **s. and sound,** sano y salvo. **s.-conduct,** salvoconducto, *m.* **s.-keeping,** lugar seguro, *m;* (of a person) buenas manos, *f pl*

**safeguard** /'seif,gɑrd/ *n* protección, garantía, *f;* precaución, *f.* —*vt* proteger, guardar; tomar precauciones (contra)
**safely** /'seifli/ *adv* seguramente; sin accidente, sin novedad, sano y salvo; sin peligro. **You may s. tell him,** Puedes decírselo con toda seguridad. **to put (something) away s.,** poner (algo) en un lugar seguro
**safety** /'seifti/ *n* seguridad, *f.* —*a* de seguridad; (of locks) de golpe. **a place of s.,** un lugar seguro. **in s.,** en salvo, en seguro; con seguridad. **to believe in s. first,** poner la seguridad en primer lugar. **to play for s.,** jugar seguro. **with complete s.,** con toda seguridad. **s.-belt,** (cinto) salvavidas, *m.* **s.-catch,** fiador, *m.* **s.-curtain,** telón de seguridad, telón contra incendios, *m.* **s.-fuse,** espoleta de seguridad, *f.* **s.-glass,** vidrio inastillable, *m.* **s.-island,** refugio para peatones, *m.* **s.-lamp,** lámpara de seguridad, *f.* **s.-latch,** pestillo de golpe, *m.* **s.-lock,** (of fire-arms) seguro, *m;* (of doors, etc.) cerradura de seguridad, *f.* **s.-pin,** imperdible, *m.* **s.-razor,** máquina de afeitar, *f.* **s.-valve,** válvula de seguridad, *f*
**saffron** /'sæfrən/ *n* azafrán, *m, a* azafranado, de color de azafrán.
**sag** /sæg/ *vi* doblegarse, ceder; inclinarse; *naut* caer a sotavento; (of prices) bajar; (of spirits, etc.) flaquear
**saga** /'sɑgə/ *n* saga, *f;* epopeya, *f*
**sagacious** /sə'geiʃəs/ *a* sagaz, perspicaz; (of animals) sabio
**sagacity** /sə'gæsɪti/ *n* sagacidad, perspicacia, *f;* (of animals) sagacidad, *f*
**sage** /seidʒ/ *n* sabio, *m; bot* salvia, *f.* —*a* sabio; sagaz; cuerdo
**Sagittarius** /ˌsædʒɪ'tɛəriəs/ *n* Sagitario, *m*
**Sahara, the** /sə'hærə/ el Sáhara, *m*
**said** /sɛd/ *a* antedicho; dicho. **No sooner s. than done,** Dicho y hecho. **the s. Mr. Martínez,** el tal Sr. Martínez
**sail** /seil/ *n* (of a ship) vela, *f;* (sailing-ship) velero, *m;* (of a windmill) aspa, *f; mech* ala, *f;* (trip) paseo en barco, *m.* —*vi* navegar; ir en barco; dar un paseo en barco; (leave) salir en barco; zarpar; (of swans, etc.) deslizarse; (of clouds, etc.) flotar. —*vt* (a ship) gobernar; (the sea) navegar por. **She sailed into the room,** Entró majestuosamente en la sala. **The ship sailed at eight knots,** El buque navegaba a ocho nudos. **to go for a s.,** dar un paseo en barco. **to s. round the world,** dar la vuelta al mundo. **to s. the seas,** navegar por mares. **to set s.,** darse a la vela, zarpar. **to take in the sails,** amainar. **s.-maker,** velero, *m.* **to s. into,** entrar en. **to s. round,** (the Cape, etc.) doblar. **to s. up,** subir en barco; (of a boat) ir río arriba
**sailcloth** /'seil,klɔθ/ *n* lona, *f*
**sailing** /'seilɪŋ/ *n* navegación, *f;* (departure) salida, *f.* **It's all plain s.,** Todo va viento en popa. **s.-boat,** bote de vela, *m.* **s.-ship,** buque de vela, velero, *m*
**sailor** /'seilər/ *n* marinero, *m.* **John is a bad s.,** Juan se marea fácilmente. **to be a good s.,** no marearse. **s.-blouse,** marinera, *f.* **s.-suit,** traje de marinero, *m*
**saint** /seint/ *n* santo (-ta); (before masculine names of Sts., excluding Sts. Dominic and Thomas) San; *Inf.* ángel, *m.* **All Saints' Day,** el día de Todos los Santos. **saint's day,** fiesta de un santo (or de una santa), *f;* (of a person) santo, *m.* **St. Bernard dog,** perro de San Bernardo, *m.* **St. John the Baptist,** San Juan Bautista. **St. Martin's summer,** el veranillo de San Martín. **St. Vitus's dance,** el baile de San Vito
**sainthood** /'seinthʊd/ *n* santidad, *f*
**saintliness** /'seintlɪnɪs/ *n* santidad, *f*
**saintly** /'seintli/ *a* de santo; de santa; santo; inf angelical
**Saint Petersburg** /seint 'pitərz,bɜrg/ San Petersburgo, *m*
**sake** /seik/ *n* amor, *m;* causa, *f.* **for God's s.,** por el amor de Dios. **for the s. of,** para; por amor de. **to talk for talking's s.,** hablar por hablar

**salable** /'seiləbəl/ *a* vendible

**salaciousness** /sə'leiʃəsnıs/ *n* salacidad, *f*

**salad** /'sæləd/ *n* ensalada, *f*; (lettuce) lechuga, *f*. **fruit s.,** macedonia de frutas, *f*. **s.-bowl,** ensaladera, *f*. **s.-dressing,** aderezo, aliño, *m*, salsa para ensalada, *f*. **s.-oil,** aceite para ensaladas, *m*

**salamander** /'sælə,mændər/ *n* salamandra, *f*

**salaried** /'sælərid/ *a* a sueldo; (of posts) retribuido

**salary** /'sæləri/ *n* sueldo, salario, *m*

**sale** /seil/ *n* venta, *f*; (auction) almoneda, subasta pública, *f*. **clearance s.,** liquidación, *f*, saldo, *m*. **to be on s.,** estar de venta. **"Piano for s.,"** «Se vende un piano.» **s. price,** precio de venta, *m*; precio de saldo, *m*

**sales contract** *n* contrato de compraventa, *m*

**salesman** /'seilzmən/ *n* dependiente de tienda, *m*; (traveller) viajante, *m*

**salesmanship** /'seilzmən,ʃıp/ *n* arte de vender, *mf*

**salesroom** /'seilz,rum/ *n* salón de ventas, *m*

**saleswoman** /'seilz,wumən/ *n* dependiente de tienda, vendedera, *f*

**salient** /'seiliənt/ *a* saliente; *Fig.* prominente, conspicuo, notable, *n* saliente, *m*. **s. angle,** ángulo saliente, *m*

**saline** /'seilin/ *a* salino. —*n* (marsh) saladar, *m*; *med* salino, *m*

**saliva** /sə'laivə/ *n* saliva, *f*

**salivary** /'sælə,veri/ *a* salival

**salivate** /'sælə,veit/ *vi* salivar

**salivation** /,sælə'veiʃən/ *n* salivación, *f*

**sallow** /'sælou/ *a* cetrino, oliváceo, lívido

**sallowness** /'sælounıs/ *n* amarillez, lividez, *f*; palidez, *f*

**sally** /'sæli/ *n* (mil. etc) salida, *f*; (quip) ocurrencia, salida, *f*. —*vi* hacer una salida, salir. **to s. forth,** ponerse en camino

**salmon** /'sæmən/ *n* salmón, *m*; color de salmón, *m*. **s.-net,** salmonera, *f*. **s. trout,** trucha asalmonada, *f*

**salon** /sə'lɒn/ *n* salón, *m*

**Salonika** /sə'lɒnıkə/ Salónica, *f*

**saloon** /sə'lun/ *n* sala, *f*; (of a steamer) cámara, *f*, salón, *m*; (on train, for sleeping) departamento de coche cama, *m*; (on train, for dining) coche comedor, *m*; *auto* coche cerrado, *m*. **billiard s.,** salón de billares, *m*. **dancing s.,** salón de baile, *m*. **hair-dresser's s.,** salón de peluquero, *m*. **s. bar,** bar, *m*

**salsify** /'sælsəfi/ *n bot* salsifí, *m*

**salt** /sɔlt/ *n* sal, *f*; (spice) sabor, *m*; (wit) sal, agudeza, *f*. —*a* salobre, salino; salado; (of land) salitroso. —*vt* (season) poner sal en; (cure) salar. **kitchen s.,** sal de cocina, *f*. **old s.,** *inf* lobo de mar, *m*. **rock s.,** sal gema, *f*. **sea s.,** sal marina, *f*. **to be not worth one's s.,** no merecer el pan que se come. **to take with a pinch of s.,** tomar con su grano de sal. **s.-cellar,** salero, *m*. **s. lagoon,** albufera, *f*. **s. lake,** lago salado, *m*. **s. marsh,** saladar, *m*. **s. meat,** carne salada, cecina, *f*. **s. merchant,** salinero, *m*. **s.-mine,** mina de sal, *f*. **s.-spoon,** cucharita de sal, *f*. **s. water,** agua salada, *f*; agua de mar, *f*. **s.-water fish,** pez de mar, *m*. **s.-works,** salinas, *f pl*

**saltiness** /'sɔltınıs/ *n* sabor de sal, *m*; salobridad, *f*

**salting** /'sɔltıŋ/ *n* saladura, *f*; (salt marsh) saladar, *m*

**saltless** /'sɔltlıs/ *a* sin sal, soso, insípido; *Fig.* soso

**saltpeter** /,sɔlt'pitər/ *n* salitre, *f*. **s. bed,** salitral, *m*. **s. works,** salitrería, *f*

**salty** /'sɔlti/ *a* salado; salobre

**salubrious** /sə'lubriəs/ *a* salubre, saludable, sano

**salubriousness** /sə'lubriəsnıs/ *n* salubridad, *f*

**salutary** /'sælyə,teri/ *a* saludable, beneficioso

**salutation** /,sælyə'teiʃən/ *n* salutación, *f*, saludo, *m*

**salute** /sə'lut/ *vt and vi* saludar. —*n* saludo, *m*; (of guns) salva, *f*. **to fire a s.,** hacer salvas, saludar con... salvas. **The soldier saluted them,** El soldado les saludó. **to take the s.,** tomar el saludo. **saluting base,** puesto de mando, *m*

**Salvadoran** /'sælvə'dɔrən/ a; **Salvadorian** /,sælvə'dɔrən/ -'dɔriən/ *a and n* salvadoreño (-ña)

**salvage** /'sælvıdʒ/ *n* salvamento, *m*, *vt* salvar

**salvation** /sæl'veiʃən/ *n* salvación, *f*. **to work out one's own s.,** salvar el alma. **the S. Army,** el Ejército de la Salvación, *m*

**salve** /sælv/ *n* pomada, *f*; *fig* bálsamo, *m*. —*vt* curar;

(overcome) vencer; (soothe) tranquilizar; *naut* salvar. **to s. one's conscience,** tranquilizar la conciencia

**salver** /'sælvər/ *n* salva, bandeja, *f*

**salvo** /'sælvou/ *n* (of guns or applause) salva, *f*; (reservation) salvedad, reservación, *f*. **s. of applause,** salva de aplausos, *f*

**Samaritan** /sə'mærıtn/ *a and n* samaritano (-na)

**same** /seim/ *a* mismo; igual; parecido; idéntico. —*adv* lo mismo; del mismo modo. **all the s.,** sin embargo; con todo, a pesar de eso. **at the s. time,** al mismo tiempo; a la vez. **just the s.,** igual; (nevertheless) sin embargo. **He bowed deeply and I did the s.,** Él hizo una profunda reverencia y yo hice lo mismo. **They do not look at things the s. as we do,** No ven las cosas del mismo modo que nosotros. **If it is the s. to her,** Si le da igual. **It's all the s.,** Es igual, Lo mismo da, Es todo uno. **Ávila, capital of the province of the s. name,** Ávila, capital de la provincia de su nombre

**"Same-Day Service"** /'seimdei/ «En el día» (Argentina)

**sameness** /'seimnıs/ *n* identidad, *f*; semejanza, *f*, parecido, *m*; monotonía, *f*

**samovar** /'sæmə,vɑr/ *n* samovar, *m*

**sampan** /'sæmpæn/ *n* (boat) champán, *m*

**sample** /'sæmpəl/ *n* muestra, *f*; prueba, *f*; ejemplo, *m*. —*vt* sacar una muestra de; (try) probar. **s. book,** muestrario, *m*

**sampler** /'sæmplər/ *n* probador, *m*; (of wines) catador, *m*; *sew* dechado, *m*

**sanatorium** /,sænə'tɔriəm/ *n* sanatorio, *m*

**sanctification** /,sæŋktəfı'keiʃən/ *n* santificación, *f*; consagración, *f*

**sanctify** /'sæŋktə,fai/ *vt* santificar; consagrar

**sanctimonious** /,sæŋktə'mouniəs/ *a* santurrón, mojigato, beato

**sanctimoniousness** /,sæŋktə'mouniəsnıs/ *n* beatería, mojigatería, santurronería, *f*

**sanction** /'sæŋkʃən/ *n* sanción, *f*. —*vt* sancionar; autorizar. **to apply sanctions,** *polit* aplicar sanciones

**sanctity** /'sæŋktıti/ *n* santidad, *f*; lo sagrado; inviolabilidad, *f*. **odor of s.,** olor de santidad, *f*

**sanctuary** /'sæŋktʃu,eri/ *n* santuario, *m*; (historical) sagrado, sagrado asilo, *m*; refugio, asilo, *m*. **to take s.,** acogerse a sagrado; refugiarse

**sand** /sænd/ *n* arena, *f*; (for drying writing) arenilla, *f*; granos de arena, *m pl*; *pl* **sands,** playa, *f*; (of life) horas de la vida, *f pl*. —*vt* arenar. **to plough the s.,** arar en el mar. **s.-bag,** *n* saco de arena, *m*, —*vt* (a building) proteger con sacos de arena; (a person) golpear con un saco de arena. **s.-bank,** banco de arena, *m*, barra, *f*. **to run on a s.-bank,** encallar. **s.-colored,** de color de arena. **s.-dune,** médano, *m*. **s.-paper,** *n* papel de lija, *m*. —*vt* pulir con papel de lija, lijar. **s.-pit,** arenal, *m*. **s. shoes,** alpargatas, *f pl*

**sandal** /'sændl/ *n* sandalia, *f*; (rope-soled) alpargata, *f*. **s.-wood,** sándalo, *m*

**sandiness** /'sændınıs/ *n* naturaleza arenosa, *f*; (of hair) color bermejo, *m*

**sandstone** /'sænd,stoun/ *n* arenisca, *f*

**sandstorm** /'sænd,stɔrm/ *n* tempestad de arena, *f*; simún, *m*

**sandwich** /'sændwıtʃ, 'sæn-/ *n* emparedado, bocadillo, *m*. —*vt* insertar. **I found myself sandwiched between two fat men,** Me encontré aplastado entre dos hombres gordos. **s.-man,** hombre sándwich, *m*

**sandy** /'sændi/ *a* arenoso; sabuloso; (of hair) rojo, rufo, bermejo. **a s. beach,** una playa arenosa

**sane** /sein/ *a* de juicio sano; razonable, prudente; sesudo. **He is a very s. person,** Es un hombre con mucho sentido común. **to be s.,** estar en su juicio; (of a policy, etc.) ser prudente, ser razonable

**sangfroid** /san'frwa/ *n* sangre fría, *f*; aplomo, *m*

**sanguinary** /'sæŋgwə,neri/ *a* sanguinario

**sanguine** /'sæŋgwın/ *a* (of complexion) rubicundo; sanguíneo; optimista, confiado. —*n* (drawing) sanguina, *f*. **to be s. about the future,** ser optimista acerca del porvenir, tener confianza en el porvenir

**sanhedrin** /sæn'hedrın/ *n* sanedrín, *m*

**sanitary** /'sænı,teri/ *a* sanitario; higiénico, **s. inspector,** inspector de sanidad, *m*. **s. napkin, s. towel,** servilleta higiénica, toalla sanitaria, *mf*, paño higiénico, *m*

**sanitation** /ˌsænɪ'teiʃən/ *n* higiene, *f*; sanidad pública, *f*; (apparatus) instalación sanitaria, *f*

**sanity** /'sænɪti/ *n* juicio sano, *m*; prudencia, *f*; (common sense) sentido común, *m*, sensatez, *f*

**Sanskrit** /'sænskrɪt/ *a* and *n* sánscrito, *m*

**Santa Claus** /'sæntə klɔz/ *n* (Spanish equivalent) los Reyes Magos, *m pl*

**São Paulo** /'sau 'paulou, -lʊ/ San Pablo, *m*

**sap** /sæp/ *n* (*bot* and *fig*) savia, *f*; *mil* zapa, *f*. —*vt* (undermine) debilitar, agotar; *mil* zapar

**sapidity** /sæ'pɪdɪti/ *n* sapidez, *f*

**sapling** /'sæplɪŋ/ *n* arbolillo, *m*

**sapper** /'sæpər/ *n mil* zapador, *m*

**Sapphic** /'sæfɪk/ *a* sáfico. **S. verse,** verso sáfico, *m*

**sapphire** /'sæfaiªr/ *n* zafiro, *m*. —*a* de zafiros; cerúleo, de zafiro

**Saracen** /'særəsən/ *a* and *n* sarraceno (-na)

**Saragossa** /ˌsærə'gɒsə/ Zaragoza, *f*

**sarcasm** /'sɑrkæzəm/ *n* sarcasmo, *m*

**sarcastic** /sɑr'kæstɪk/ *a* sarcástico

**sarcastically** /sɑr'kæstɪkli/ *adv* con sarcasmo, sarcásticamente

**sarcophagus** /sɑr'kɒfəgəs/ *n* sarcófago, *m*

**sardine** /sɑr'din/ *n* sardina, *f*. **packed like sardines,** como sardinas en banasta. **s.-net,** sardinal, *m*

**Sardinia** /sɑr'dɪniə/ Cerdeña, *f*

**Sardinian** /sɑr'dɪniən/ *a* and *n* sardo (-da)

**sardonic** /sɑr'dɒnɪk/ *a* sardónico

**sarsaparilla** /ˌsæspə'rɪ, ˌsɑrspə-/ *n* zarzaparrilla, *f*

**sash** /sæʃ/ *n* (with uniform) faja, *f*; (belt) cinto, cinturón, *m*; (of a window) cerco, *m*. **s. window,** ventana de guillotina, *f*

**Satan** /'seitn/ *n* Satanás, *m*

**satanic** /sə'tænɪk, sei-/ *a* satánico

**satchel** /'sætʃəl/ *n* saquito de mano, *m*, bolsa, *f*; (school) vademécum, *m*; cartapacio, *m*, cartera, *f*

**sate** /seit/ *vt* saciar, hartar; satisfacer

**sateen** /sæ'tin/ *n* satén, *m*

**satellite** /'sætlˌait/ *n* satélite, *m*

**satiable** /'seiʃəbəl/ *a* saciable

**satiate** /*v.* 'seiʃiˌeit, -ɪt, -ˌeit/ *vt* saciar, hartar; satisfacer. —*a* harto; repleto

**satiety** /sə'taiɪti/ *n* saciedad, *f*

**satin** /'sætn/ *n* raso, *m*. —*a* de raso; (glossy) lustroso, terso. —*vt* (paper) satinar

**satiny** /'sætni/ *a* arrasado; lustroso, brillante

**satire** /'sætaiªr/ *n* sátira, *f*

**satiric** /sə'tɪrɪk/ *a* satírico

**satirist** /'sætərɪst/ *n* escritor (-ra) satírico (-ca)

**satirize** /'sætəˌraiz/ *vt* satirizar

**satisfaction** /ˌsætɪs'fækʃən/ *n* satisfacción, *f*; (contentment) contento, *m*, satisfacción, *f*; (for sin) expiación, *f*; (of a debt) pago, *m*; desquite, *m*; recompensa, *f*. **to demand s.,** pedir satisfacción. **to give** (someone) **s.,** dar contento (a), alegrar

**satisfactorily** /ˌsætɪs'fæktərəli/ *adv* satisfactoriamente

**satisfactoriness** /ˌsætɪs'fæktərɪnɪs/ *n* carácter satisfactorio, *m*, lo satisfactorio

**satisfactory** /ˌsætɪs'fæktəri/ *a* satisfactorio; (for sin) expiatorio

**satisfy** /'sætɪsˌfai/ *vt* satisfacer; (convince) convencer; (allay) tranquilizar, apaciguar. **I am satisfied with him,** Estoy satisfecho (Estoy contento) con él. **The explanation did not s. me,** La explicación no me convenció. **to s. oneself that...,** asegurarse de que... **to s. one's thirst,** apagar la sed

**satisfying** /'sætɪsˌfaiŋ/ *a* que satisface; satisfactorio; (of food) nutritivo

**satrap** /'seitræp, 'sæ-/ *n* sátrapa, *m*

**saturate** /'sætʃəˌreit/ *vt* saturar (de), empapar (de); *chem* saturar; *fig* imbuir; *fig* empapar. **to s. oneself in,** (a subject) empaparse en

**saturation** /ˌsætʃə'reiʃən/ *n* saturación, *f*. **s. point,** (*chem* etc.) punto de saturación, *m*

**Saturday** /'sætərˌdei/ *n* sábado, *m*

**Saturn** /'sætərn/ *n* Saturno, *m*

**saturnine** /'sætərˌnain/ *a* saturnino, taciturno

**satyr** /'seitər, 'sætər/ *n* sátiro, *m*

**sauce** /sɔs/ *n* salsa, *f*; (thick fruit) compota, *f*; *inf* insolencia, *f*. **s.-boat,** salsera, *f*

**saucepan** /'sɔsˌpæn/ *n* cazuela, cacerola, *f*. **double s.,** baño de María, *m*

**saucer** /'sɔsər/ *n* platillo, *m*. **flying s.,** platillo volante, *m*. **s.-eyed,** con ojos redondos

**sauciness** /'sɔsinɪs/ *n* impertinencia, insolencia, *f*

**saucy** /'sɔsi/ *a* respondón, descarado; (cheerful) alegre; (of hats, etc.) coquetón, majo

**sauerkraut** /'sauªr,kraut/ *n* chucruta, *f*

**saunter** /'sɔntər/ *vi* pasearse, vagar, *n* paseo, *m*, vuelta, *f*

**sausage** /'sɔsɪdʒ/ *n* chorizo, *m*; salchicha, *f*. **s.-balloon,** globo cautivo, *m*. **s.-curl,** bucle, *m*. **s.-machine,** choricera, *f*. **s.-maker,** choricero (-ra)

**savage** /'sævɪdʒ/ *a* salvaje; feroz; (cruel) inhumano, cruel; (furious) furioso. —*n* salvaje, *mf*

**savagely** /'sævɪdʒli/ *adv* bárbaramente; ferozmente; furiosamente

**savagery** /'sævɪdʒri/ *n* salvajismo, *m*; ferocidad, *f*; brutalidad, crueldad, *f*

**savannah** /sə'vænə/ *n* sabana, *f*. **s. dweller,** sabanero (-ra)

**save** /seiv/ *vt* salvar; (keep) guardar; conservar; reservar; (money, one's clothes, etc.) ahorrar; (time) ganar; (avoid) evitar. —*vi* salvar; hacer economías; ahorrar. **He saved my life,** Me salvó la vida. **They have saved a room for me,** Me han reservado una habitación. **to s. appearances,** guardar las apariencias. **to s. oneself trouble,** ahorrarse molestias. **to s. the situation,** estar al nivel de las circunstancias

**save** /seiv/ *prep* salvo, excepto, menos. —*conjunc* sino, a menos que; con la excepción de. **all s. one,** todos menos uno. **all the conspirators s. he,** todos los conspiradores con la excepción de él

**saving** /'seiviŋ/ *a* frugal, económico; (stingy) tacaño, avaricioso; (clause) condicional. —*n* salvación, *f*; (of money, time, etc.) ahorro, *m*, economía, *f*; *pl* **savings,** ahorros, *m pl*. —*prep* salvo, excepto, fuera de. —*conjunc* con excepción de que, fuera de que. **s. grace,** único mérito, *m*. **savings bank,** caja de ahorros, *f*. **savings fund,** montepío, *m*

**savior** /'seivjər/ *n* salvador (-ra). **the S.,** el Salvador, el Redentor

**savor** /'seivər/ *n* sabor, gusto, *m*; (aftertaste) dejo, *m*; (zest) salsa, *f*. —*vi* saber (a), tener sabor (de); *fig* oler (a). —*vt* saborear, paladear; (flavor) sazonar

**savoriness** /'seivərinɪs/ *n* buen sabor, *m*; (of a district) respetabilidad, *f*

**savory** /'seivəri/ *a* sabroso, apetitoso; (not sweet) no dulce; (of places) respetable; (of reputation, etc.) bueno. —*n* entremés salado, *m*. **s. omelette,** tortilla, *f*

**Savoy** /sə'vɔi/ Saboya, *f*

**saw** /sɔ/ *n* (maxim) sentencia, *f*; (proverb) refrán, decir, *m*; (tool) sierra, *f*. —*vt* aserrar; (the air) cortar. —*vi* usar una sierra. **two-handled saw,** tronzador, *m*. **saw-fish,** pez sierra, *m*. **saw-mill,** molino de aserrar, *m*. **saw-pit,** aserradero, *m*

**sawdust** /'sɔˌdʌst/ *n* aserrín, *m*

**sawhorse** /'sɔˌhɔrs/ *n* caballete de aserrar, *m*

**sawyer** /'sɔjər/ *n* aserrador, *m*

**Saxon** /'sæksən/ *a* and *n* sajón (-ona)

**Saxony** /'sæksəni/ Sajonia, *f*

**saxophone** /'sæksəˌfoun/ *n* saxófono, saxofón *m*

**say** /sei/ *vt* decir; recitar. —*vi* decir. **Let us say that the house is worth $100,000,** Pongamos por ejemplo que la casa vale cien mil dólares. **He has no say in the matter,** No entra ni sale en el asunto. **I have said my say,** He dicho lo que quería. **They say,** Se dice, Dicen, La gente dice. **You don't say!** ¡Calle! ¡De veras? ¡Imposible! **that is to say...,** es decir...; esto es..., a saber... **to say one's prayers,** rezar, decir sus oraciones. **to say again,** volver a decir; decir otra vez, repetir. **to say over and over again,** repetir muchas veces, decir repetidamente. **What do you say to that?** ¿Qué dices a esto?

**saying** /'seiiŋ/ *n* decir, *m*; (proverb) refrán, *m*; (maxim) sentencia, *f*. **As the s. is,** Como suele decirse; Según el refrán. **It goes without s.,** Huelga decir. **It's only a s.,** Es un decir, nada más

**scab** /skæb/ n (of a wound) costra, f; (disease) escabro, m; (blackleg) esquirol, m

**scabbard** /'skæbərd/ n vaina (de espada), f

**scabby** /'skæbi/ a costroso; (diseased) roñoso, sarnoso

**scabies** /'skeibiz/ n sarna, f. **s. mite,** arador de la sarna, m

**scaffold** /'skæfəld/ n (in building) andamio, m; (for execution) cadalso, patíbulo, m. **to go to the s.,** ir al patíbulo; acabar en el patíbulo

**scaffolding** /'skæfəldɪŋ/ n andamiada, f; (building, scaffold) andamio, m

**scald** /skɔld/ vt escaldar; quemar; (instruments) esterilizar. —n quemadura, escaldadura, f. **to s. oneself,** escaldarse. **scalding hot,** hirviendo

**scale** /skeil/ n (of a balance) platillo, m; zool escama, f; bot bráctea, f; bot hojuela, f; (flake) laminita, f; (mus, math) escala, f; (of charges, etc.) tarifa, f; (of salaries) escalafón, m; (of a thermometer) escala, f. —vt escalar; (fish) escamar. **major s.,** escala mayor, f. **minor s.,** escala menor, f. **on a grand s.,** en gran escala. **on a small s.,** en pequeña escala. **pair of scales,** balanza, f; (for heavy weights) báscula, f. **social s.,** escala social, f. **The Scales,** Astron. Libra, f. **to draw to s.,** dibujar a escala. **to turn the scales,** pesar; Fig. inclinar la balanza. **to s. down,** (Art. and of charges) reducir

**scaling** /skeiliŋ/ n (of fish) escamadura, f; (of buildings) desconchadura, f; (ascent) escalamiento, m

**scallop** /'skɒləp, 'skæl-/ n (ichth and badge) venera, f; concha, f; sew onda, f, festón, m. —vt Cul. guisar en conchas; sew ondear, festonear

**scalp** /skælp/ n anat pericráneo, m; cuero cabelludo, m; fig trofeo, m. —vt escalpar. **s.-hunter,** cazador de cabelleras, m

**scalpel** /'skælpəl/ n escalpelo, m

**scaly** /'skeili/ a escamoso, conchado; (of boilers) incrustado

**scamp** /skæmp/ n bribón, granuja, m, vt (work) frangollar

**scamper** /'skæmpər/ vi retozar, brincar; correr. —n carrerita, f. **to s. off,** salvarse por los pies, huir; marcharse corriendo

**scan** /skæn/ vt (verse) medir, escandir; (examine) escudriñar, examinar; (glance at) dar un vistazo (a)

**scandal** /'skændl/ n escándalo, m; maledicencia, f; (slander) calumnia, f. **to talk s.,** murmurar

**scandalize** /'skændl̩aiz/ vt escandalizar

**scandalous** /'skændləs/ a escandaloso; infame; calumnioso

**scandalously** /'skænd̩ləsli/ adv escandalosamente

**scandalousness** /'skændl̩əsnɪs/ n carácter escandaloso, m

**Scandinavia** /ˌskændə'neiviə/ Escandinavia, f

**Scandinavian** /ˌskændə'neiviən/ a escandinavo. —n escandinavo (-va)

**scant** /skænt/ a escaso; insuficiente

**scantily** /'skæntl̩i/ adv insuficientemente

**scantiness** /'skæntinɪs/ n escasez, f; insuficiencia, f

**scanty** /'skænti/ a insuficiente; escaso; (of hair) ralo; (of crops, etc.) pobre

**scapegoat** /'skeipˌgout/ n víctima propiciatoria, f; cabeza de turco, f. **to be a s. for,** pagar el pato por

**scapegrace** /'skeipˌgreis/ n bribón, m

**scapula** /'skæpyələ/ n anat escápula, f

**scapulary** /'skæpyəˌleri// n eccl escapulario, m

**scar** /skɑr/ n cicatriz, f; fig señal, f. —vt marcar con una cicatriz. **to s. over,** cicatrizarse

**scarab** /'skærəb/ n escarabajo, m; escarabajo sagrado, m

**scarce** /skɛərs/ a escaso; insuficiente; raro. —adv poet apenas. **to make oneself s.,** largarse, pirarse, escabullirse; ausentarse, esconderse

**scarcely** /'skɛərsli/ adv apenas; no bien; casi; (with difficulty) a duras penas, con dificultad. **It is s. likely he said that,** No es muy probable que lo hubiese dicho. **There were s. twenty people in the building,** Había apenas veinte personas en el edificio. **S. anyone likes his pictures,** Sus cuadros no le gustan a casi nadie

**scarcity** /'skɛərsɪti/ n escasez, insuficiencia, f; (famine) carestía, f; (rarity) rareza, f

**scare** /skɛər/ vt asustar, espantar, llenar de miedo (a); intimidar. —n susto, pánico, m; alarma, f. **What a s. I got!** ¡Qué susto me he llevado! **to s. away,** ahuyentar

**scarecrow** /'skɛərˌkrou/ n espantapájaros, m; Inf. estantigua, f, mamarracho, espantajo, m

**scaremonger** /'skɛərˌmʌŋgər/ n alarmista, mf

**scarf** /skɑrf/ n bufanda, f; (tie) corbata, f; mil faja, f

**scarlatina** /ˌskɑrlə'tinə/ n med escarlatina, f

**scarlet** /'skɑrlɪt/ n escarlata, f. —a de color escarlata. **to turn s.,** (of persons) enrojecerse. **s. fever,** escarlatina, f. **s. hat,** eccl capelo (cardenalicio), m. **s. runner,** bot judía verde, f

**scatheless** /'skeiðlɪs/ a ileso, sano y salvo

**scathing** /'skeiðɪŋ/ a mordaz, cáustico

**scathingly** /'skeiðɪŋli/ adv mordazmente, cáusticamente

**scatter** /'skætər/ vt esparcir, sembrar con; (benefits, etc.) derramar; (put to flight) derrotar; dispersar; disipar; fig frustrar; (squander) derrochar, desparramar. —vi dispersarse. **The crowd scattered,** La muchedumbre se dispersó. **s.-brained,** de cabeza de chorlito, atolondrado

**scattered** /'skætərd/ a disperso; esparcido

**scattered showers** n lluvias aisladas, f pl

**scattering** /'skætərɪŋ/ n dispersión, f; (defeat) derrota, f; esparcimiento, m; (small number) número pequeño, m

**scavenge** /'skævɪndʒ/ vt (streets) recoger la basura de, barrer

**scavenger** /'skævɪndʒər/ n (of the streets) barrendero, m; (dustman) basurero, m; zool animal que se alimenta de carne muerta, m; insecto que se alimenta de estiércol, m. —vt See **scavenge**

**scenario** /sɪ'nɛəri,ou, -'nɑr-/ n escenario, m

**scene** /sin/ n escena, f; teatro, lugar, m; espectáculo, m; (theat décor) decoración, f; (of a play) escena, f; (view) vista, perspectiva, f. **behind the scenes,** entre bastidores. **The s. is laid...,** La acción pasa... **to come on the s.,** entrar en escena. **to make a s.,** hacer una escena. **s.-painter,** n escenógrafo (-fa). **s.-shifter,** tramoyista, mf

**scenery** /'sinəri/ n theat decorado, m; (landscape) paisaje, m

**scenic** /'sinik/ a dramático; escénico; pintoresco. **s. railway,** montaña rusa, f

**scenography** /si'nɒgrəfi/ n escenografía, f

**scent** /sɛnt/ vt perfumar; (smell) oler; (out) husmear, olfatear; (suspect) sospechar. —n perfume, m; fragancia, f, aroma, m; (smell) olor, m; (of hounds) viento, m; (of game, etc.) rastro, viento, m; (fig of person) nariz, f; (trail) pista, f. **to lose the s.,** perder la pista. **to s. danger,** oler el peligro. **to throw off the s.,** despistar. **s.-bottle,** frasco de perfume, m. **s.-spray,** pulverizador, m

**scented** /'sɛntɪd/ a perfumado; (of roses, etc.) de olor, oloroso; (in compounds) de... olfato. **s. sweet pea,** guisante de olor, m

**scentless** /'sɛntlɪs/ a sin olor; inodoro

**scepter** /'sɛptər/ n cetro, m

**sceptical** /'skɛptɪk/ a escéptico (-ca)

**sceptical** /'skɛptɪkəl/ a escéptico

**scepticism** /'skɛptə,sɪzəm/ n escepticismo, m

**schedule** /'skɛdʒul/ n lista, m; programa, m; (of taxes) clase, f; (of trains, etc.) horario, m. —vt poner en una lista; inventariar

**scheme** /skim/ n plan, m; proyecto, m; diagrama, esquema, m; (summary) resumen, m; (of colors, etc.) combinación, f; (plot) intriga, maquinación, f. —vt proyectar. —vi planear, formar planes; (intrigue) intrigar, conspirar. **color s.,** combinación de colores, f

**schemer** /'skimər/ n (plotter) intrigante, mf

**scheming** /'skimɪŋ/ a intrigante; astuto. —n planes, proyectos, m pl; intrigas, maquinaciones, f pl

**schism** /'sɪzəm, 'skɪz-/ n cisma, m/f

**schismatic** /sɪz'mætɪk, skɪz-/ a cismático. —n cismático (-ca)

**scholar** /'skɒlər/ n (at school) colegial (-la); (disciple) alumno (-na); (student) estudiante, mf; (learned person) erudito (-ta), hombre de letras, m; (scholarship holder) becario, m

**scholarly** /'skɒlərli/ *a* de sabio, de hombre de letras; erudito
**scholarship** /'skɒlər,ʃɪp/ *n* erudición, *f*; saber, *m*; (exhibition) beca, *f*. **s. holder**, becario, *m*
**scholastic** /skə'læstɪk/ *a* escolar, escolástico; pedante; (medieval) escolástico. —*n* escolástico, *m*. **the s. profession**, el magisterio
**school** /skul/ *n* escuela, *f*; colegio, *m*; academia, *f*; *educ* departamento, *m*; (faculty) facultad, *f*; (of fish) banco, *m*. —*vt* enseñar, instruir; formar; disciplinar. **in s.**, en clase. **day s.**, escuela, *f*, colegio, *m*. **the Florentine s.**, (of painting) la escuela florentina. **the lower s.**, los alumnos del preparatorio. **private s.**, colegio particular, *m*. **s.-bag**, vademécum, *m*. **s.-book**, libro escolar, *m*. **s.-days**, los días de escuela; los años de colegio. **in his s.-days**, cuando él iba a la escuela. **s.-fees**, gastos de la enseñanza, *m pl*, cuota escolar, *f*,
**schoolboy** /'skul,bɔɪ/ *n* muchacho de escuela, colegial, *m*
**school district** *n* sector escolar, *m*
**schoolfellow** /'skul,fɛlou/ *n* compañero de colegio, condiscípulo, *m*
**schoolgirl** /'skul,gɜrl/ *n* colegiala, *f*
**schooling** /'skulɪŋ/ *n* educación, enseñanza, *f*
**schoolmaster** /'skul,mæstər/ *n* maestro de escuela, professor, *m*
**schoolmistress** /'skul,mɪstrɪs/ *n* maestra de escuela, profesora, *f*
**school of hard knocks** *n* universidad sin tejados, *f*
**schoolroom** /'skul,rum/ *n* aula, sala de clase, salón de clase, *m*
**schooner** /'skunər/ *n naut* escuna, goleta, *f*
**sciatic** /saɪ'ætɪk/ *a* ciático
**sciatica** /saɪ'ætɪkə/ *n* ciática, *f*
**science** /'saɪəns/ *n* ciencia, *f*
**scientific** /,saɪən'tɪfɪk/ *a* científico; exacto, sistemático
**scientifically** /,saɪən'tɪfɪkli/ *adv* científicamente
**scientist** /'saɪəntɪst/ *n* hombre de ciencia, *m*, científico (-ca)
**scimitar** /'sɪmɪtər, -,tɑr/ *n* cimitarra, *f*
**scintilla** /sɪn'tɪlə/ *n fig* átomo, vestigio, *m*
**scintillate** /'sɪntḷ,eit/ *vi* centellear, lucir, chispear; (of persons) brillar
**scion** /'saɪən/ *n* (sucker) acodo, *m*; (shoot) vástago, renuevo, *m*; (human) descendiente, *mf*. **s. of a noble race**, vástago de una raza noble, *m*
**scissors** /'sɪzərz/ *n pl* tijeras, *f pl*. **s.-sharpener**, amolador, *m*
**sclerosis** /sklɪ'rousɪs/ *n med* esclerosis, *f*
**sclerotic** /sklɪ'rɒtɪk/ *n anat* esclerótica, *f*
**scoff** /skɒf, skɔf/ *n* burla, mofa, *f*. —*vi* burlarse. **to s. at**, burlarse de, mofarse de
**scoffer** /'skɒfər, 'skɔf-/ *n* mofador (-ra); (at religion, etc.) incrédulo (-la)
**scoffing** /'skɒfɪŋ, 'skɔf-/ *a* burlón. —*n* mofas, burlas, *f pl*
**scold** /skould/ *n* virago, *f*, *vt* reñir, reprender
**scolding** /'skouldɪŋ/ *n* reprensión, increpación, *f*
**sconce** /skɒns/ *n* cubo de candelero, *m*; candelabro de pared, *m*; cornucopia, *f*
**scone** /skoun, skɒn/ *n* bollo, *m*
**scoop** /skup/ *n* pala de mano, *f*; cuchara de draga, *f*; (boat) achicador, *m*; (financial) golpe, *m*; (journalistic) éxito periodístico, *m*. —*vt* sacar con pala (de); sacar con cuchara (de); (shares, etc.) comprar, obtener. **to s. out**, vaciar; excavar; (bail) achicar
**scooter** /'skutər/ *n* (child's) patinete, patín del diablo, *m*; monopatín, *m*
**scope** /skoup/ *n* alcance, *m*; esfera de acción, *f*; lugar, *m*. **to give full s. to**, dar rienda suelta a. **to have full s.**, tener plena oportunidad; tener todas las facilidades. **within the s. of**, dentro del alcance de
**scorbutic** /skɔr'byutɪk/ *a med* escorbútico
**scorch** /skɔrtʃ/ *vt* chamuscar; (the skin) tostar; (of the sun) abrasar, quemar; (wither) agostar. **to s. along**, ir como un relámpago. **scorching**, *a* abrasador, ardiente; *fig* mordaz
**score** /skɔr/ *n* (scratch) rasguño, *m*; señal, *f*; (crossing out) raya, *f*; (reckoning) cuenta, *f*, escote, *m*; (notch) muesca, *f*; *sports* tanteo, *m*, puntuación, *f*; (point) punto, tanto, *m*; (twenty) veintena, *f*; (rea-

son) motivo, *m*, causa, *f*; respecto, *m*; *mus* partitura, *f*. —*vt* marcar; rayar; (erase) tachar, borrar; (cricket runs, etc.) hacer; (goals) marcar; (points) ganar; (reckon) apuntar. **s. a triumph**, apuntarse un triunfo; *mus* instrumentar; (for orchestra) orquestar. —*vi* (be fortunate) llevar la ventaja. **to pay off old scores**, ajustar cuentas viejas. **to s. off someone**, ganar un punto (a), triunfar de. **upon that s.**, a ese respecto; por esa causa. **Upon what s.?** ¿Con qué motivo? **s.-board**, marcador, *m*
**scorer** /'skɔrər/ *n* (of a goal, etc.) tanteador, *m*; (keeper of score) marcador, *m*
**scoria** /'skɔriə/ *n* escoria, *f*
**scorn** /skɔrn/ *n* desprecio, desdén, *m*. —*vt* despreciar, desdeñar; reírse de. **to s. to do**, no dignarse hacer
**scornful** /'skɔrnfəl/ *a* desdeñoso, despreciativo
**scornfully** /'skɔrnfəli/ *adv* desdeñosamente, con desprecio
**Scorpion** /'skɔrpiən/ *n* Escorpión, *m*
**scorpion** /'skɔrpiən/ *n* escorpión, alacrán, *m*; *astron* Escorpión, *m*
**Scot** /skɒt/ *n* escocés, *m*
**scotch** /skɒtʃ/ *vt* (kill) matar; (thwart) frustrar; (a wheel) calzar
**Scotland** /'skɒtlənd/ Escocia, *f*
**Scotswoman** /'skɒts,wʊmən/ *n* escocesa, *f*
**Scottish** /'skɒtɪʃ/ *a* escocés
**scoundrel** /'skaundrəl/ *n* canalla, sinvergüenza, *mf*
**scour** /skauˀr/ *vt* (traverse) recorrer, batir; (pans, etc.) fregar, estregar; (free from) limpiar (de); (of water) arrastrar
**scourge** /skɜrdʒ/ *vt* azotar, flagelar; castigar, mortificar. —*n* disciplinas, *f pl*; *fig* verdugo, *m*, plaga, *f*
**scout** /skaut/ *n mil* batidor, explorador, *m*. —*vi mil* explorar, reconocer. —*vt* (flout) rechazar a mano airada, rechazar con desdén. **boy s.**, muchacho explorador, *m*
**scowl** /skaul/ *vi* fruncir el ceño. —*n* ceño, *m*. **to s. at**, mirar con ceño
**scowling** /'skaulɪŋ/ *a* amenazador
**scragginess** /'skræginɪs/ *n* magrez, flaqueza, *f*
**scraggy** /'skrægi/ *a* flaco, magro, descarnado
**scramble** /'skræmbəl/ *vi* trepar. —*vt* (throw) arrojar; (eggs) revolver. **scrambled eggs**, huevos revueltos, *m pl*. **to s. for**, andar a la rebatiña por; (for coins, etc.) luchar para. **to s. up**, escalar; subir a gatas
**scrap** /skræp/ *n* pedazo, *m*; fragmento, *m*; pizca, brizna, *f*; (shindy) suiza, camorra, *f*; (boxing) combate de boxeo, *m*; *pl* **scraps**, desperdicios, *m pl*; (food) restos de la comida, *m pl*. —*vt* desechar; (expunge) borrar; *vi* (fight) armar camorra. **a few scraps of news**, algunas noticias. **Do you mind not coming? Not a s.**, ¿Te importa no venir? Ni pizca. **s.-book**, álbum de recortes, *m*; **s.-heap**, depósito de basura, *m*; *fig* olvido, *m*. **s. iron**, chatarra, *f*, hierro viejo, *m*
**scrape** /skreip/ *vt* raspar, rascar, raer; (one's shoes) restregar; (a musical instrument) rascar. —*n* rasguño, *m*; ruido de raspar, *m*; (predicament) lío, apuro, *m*; dificultad, *f*. **to s. acquaintance with**, trabar amistad con. **to s. along**, *inf* ir tirando. **to s. away**, rascar; quitar. **to s. through**, (an examination) aprobar justo. **to s. together**, amontonar poco a poco
**scrappy** /'skræpi/ *a* escaso; fragmentario; (incoherent) descosido. **a s. meal**, una comida escasa
**scratch** /skrætʃ/ *vt* arañar; (the earth) escarbar; (rub) rascar; (a hole) hacer; (sketch) dibujar, trazar; (a horse) retirar de una carrera. —*vi* arañar; rascar; escarbar; (of a pen) rasguear; (back out) retirarse. —*n* arañazo, *m*; (of a pen) rasgueo, *m*; (in a race) línea de salida, *f*; (in games) cero, *m*. —*a* improvisado. **The dog scratched at the door**, El perro arañó la puerta. **to come up to s.**, estar al nivel de las circunstancias. **to s. one's head**, rascarse la cabeza. **to s. a person's eyes out**, sacar los ojos con las uñas (a). **to s. the surface of**, (a subject) tratar superficialmente. **to s. out**, tachar
**scrawl** /skrɔl/ *vi* hacer garabatos. —*vt* garabatear, garrapatear. —*n* garabato, *m*
**scream** /skrim/ *vt and vi* chillar. —*n* chillido, *m*. **It was a perfect s.** Era para morirse de risa. **to s. with laughter**, reírse a carcajadas, morirse de risa

**screaming** /'skrimɪŋ/ n chillidos, m pl. —a chillador; (piercing) penetrante, agudo; (funny) divertidisimo

**screech** /skritʃ/ vi chillar; (of owls, etc.) ulular; graznar. —n chillido, m, ululación, f; graznido, m. **s.-owl**, úlula, f

**screed** /skrid/ n arenga, f; cita larga, f

**screen** /skrin/ n biombo, m; (wire) tela metálica, f; (nonfolding) mampara, f; (ecol) cancel, m; (cinema, television) pantalla, f; (of trees, etc., and mil) cortina, f; (fig protection) abrigo, m. —vt proteger; (shelter) abrigar; (hide) esconder, ocultar; (a light) proteger con pantalla; (a film) proyectar; (sieve) cribar, cerner; (examine) investigar. **to s. from view**, ocultar la vista (de), esconder. **s. star**, estrella de la pantalla, f

**screw** /skru/ n tornillo, m; (propeller) hélice, f; vuelta de tornillo, f; presión, f; (miser) tacaño, m; (salary) salario, m. —vt atornillar; torcer; apretar, oprimir. **He has a s. loose**, Le falta un tornillo. **to s. down**, sujetar con tornillos. **to s. up**, cerrar con tornillos. **to s. up one's courage**, tomar coraje. **to s. up one's eyes**, desojarse, entornar los ojos. **s.-driver**, destornillador, m

**scribble** /'skrɪbəl/ vt escribir de prisa, vi garabatear, garrapatear; escribir, ser autor. —n garabato, garrapato, m; mala letra, letra ilegible, f; (note) billete, m

**scribbler** /'skrɪblər/ n el, m, (f, la) que tiene mala letra; (author) autor (-ra) malo (-la)

**scribbling** /'skrɪblɪŋ/ n garabateo, m. **s.-block**, bloque de papel, m

**scribe** /skraib/ n escribiente, copista, mf; (Jewish history) escriba, m

**scrimmage** /'skrɪmɪdʒ/ n reyerta, pelea, camorra, f; (Rugby) mêlée, f

**script** /skrɪpt/ n letra cursiva, f; print plumilla, f; manuscrito, m; law escritura, f; examen escrito, m; (film) escenario, m

**scriptural** /'skrɪptʃərəl/ a bíblico

**Scripture** /'skrɪptʃər/ n Sagrada Escritura, f. **Scriptures**, Escrituras, f pl; (of non-Christian religions) los libros sagrados

**scrivener** /'skrɪvnər/ n chupatintas, mf

**scrofula** /'skrɒfjələ/ n escrófula, f

**scrofulous** /'skrɒfjələs/ a escrofuloso

**scroll** /skroul/ n (of paper, etc.) rollo, m; pergamino, m; (flourish) rúbrica, f; (of an Ionic capital) voluta, f. **s. of fame**, lista de la fama, f

**scrotum** /'skroutəm/ n anat escroto, m

**scrounge** /skraundʒ/ vi sablear. —vt dar un sablazo (a); hurtar

**scrounger** /'skraundʒər/ n sablista, mf

**scrub** /skrʌb/ vt fregar; limpiar; restregar. —n fregado, m; limpieza, f; fricción, f; (brushwood) matorral, breñal, m, maleza, f

**scrubbing** /'skrʌbɪŋ/ n fregado, m. **s.-brush**, cepillo para el suelo, m

**scrubby** /'skrʌbi/ a (of plants) anémico; (of persons) insignificante, pobre; (of land) cubierto de maleza

**scruff** /skrʌf/ n nuca, f; pescuezo, m

**scruple** /'skrupəl/ n escrúpulo, m. —vi tener escrúpulos. **to have no scruples**, no tener escrúpulos

**scrupulous** /'skrupyələs/ a escrupuloso; exacto, meticuloso

**scrupulously** /'skrupyələsli/ adv escrupulosamente; meticulosamente

**scrupulousness** /'skrupyələsnɪs/ n escrupulosidad, f; meticulosidad, f

**scrutinize** /'skrutn̩,aiz/ vt escudriñar, examinar; (votes) escrutar

**scrutinizer** /'skrutn̩,aizər/ n escudriñador (-ra); (of votes) escrutador (-ra)

**scrutinizing** /'skrutn̩,aizɪŋ/ escrutador

**scrutiny** /'skrutn̩i/ n escrutinio, m

**scud** /skʌd/ vi correr; deslizarse; flotar. **to s. before the wind**, ir viento en popa

**scuffle** /'skʌfəl/ vi pelear, forcejear, andar a la rebatiña. —n refriega, pelea, sarracina, arrebatiña, f

**scull** /skʌl/ n remo, m, vi remar

**scullery** /'skʌləri/ n fregadero, m. **s. maid**, fregona, f

**sculptor** /'skʌlptər/ n escultor, m, escultora, f

**sculptural** /'skʌlptʃərəl/ a escultural, escultórico

**sculpture** /'skʌlptʃər/ n escultura, f, vt esculpir

**scum** /skʌm/ n espuma, f; (dregs) heces, f pl. —vt espumar. **s. of the earth**, las heces de la sociedad

**scupper** /'skʌpər/ n Naut. clava, f. —vt abrir las clavas (de); (frustrate) frustrar, destruir

**scurrility** /skə'rɪlɪti/ n grosería, indecencia, f

**scurrilous** /'skɜrələs/ a grosero, indecente

**scurry** /'skɜri/ vi echar a correr. —n fuga precipitada, f; (of rain) chaparrón, m; (of snow) remolino, m. **to s. off**, escabullirse. **to s. through**, hacer de prisa, terminar rápidamente

**S-curve** /'ɛs,kɜrv/ n curva doble, f

**scurvy** /'skɜrvi/ a tiñoso, vil, ruin. —n escorbuto, m. **a s. trick**, una mala pasada

**scuttle** /'skʌtl/ n (trap-door) escotillón, m; naut escotilla, f; (for coal) carbonera, f; (flight) huida precipitada, f. —vt (a boat) echar a pique, vi (run away) escabullirse, apretar a correr

**scythe** /saið/ n dalle, m, guadaña, f, vt dallar, segar

**sea** /si/ n mar, m, or f; ola, f; multitud, f. **Black Sea**, Mar Negro. **Mediteranean Sea**, (Mar) Mediterráneo, m. **at sea**, en el mar; perplejo. **beyond the seas**, allende los mares. **by sea**, por mar. **by the sea**, a la orilla del mar. **high seas**, alta mar, f. **the seven seas**, todos los mares del mundo. **to go to sea**, hacerse marinero. **to put to sea**, hacerse a la mar, hacerse a la vela. **sea-anemone**, anémone de mar. f. **sea-bathing**, baños de mar, m pl. **sea-breeze**, brisa de mar, f. **sea captain**, capitán de mar, m. **sea chart**, carta de marear, f. **sea-coast**, litoral, m, costa marítima, f. **sea-cow**, manatí, m. **sea dog**, lobo de mar, m. **sea-fight**, combate naval, m. **sea-foam**, espuma de mar, f. **sea-girt**, rodeado por el mar. **sea-going**, de altura; navegante. **sea-going craft**, embarcación de alta mar, f. **sea-green**, verdemar, m. **sea-gull**, gaviota, f. **sea-horse**, caballo marino, m. **sea-legs**, piernas de marino, f pl. **sea-level**, nivel del mar, m. **sea-lion**, león marino, m. **sea-mist**, bruma, f. **sea-nymph**, nereida, f. **sea-power**, potencia naval, f. **sea-serpent**, serpiente de mar, f. **sea-sick**, mareado. **to be sea-sick**, marearse. **sea-sickness**, mal de mar, m. **sea-trip**, viaje por mar, m. **sea-urchin**, erizo de mar, m. **sea-wall**, dique de mar, m

**seafarer** /'si,fɛərər/ n (traveller) viajero (-ra) por mar; (sailor) marinero, m

**seafaring** /'si,fɛərɪŋ/ a marinero, marino. —n viajes por mar, m pl; vida del marinero, f

**seal** /sil/ n zool foca, f, lobo marino, m; piel de foca, f; sello, m; (stamp) estampillo, timbre, m; vt sellar; (stamp) estampar; (letters, etc.) cerrar; vi cazar focas. **His fate is sealed**, Su suerte está determinada. **His lips were sealed**, Sus labios estaban cerrados. **under my hand and s.**, firmado y sellado por mí. **s.-ring**, sortija de sello, f

**sealing wax** /'silɪŋ/ n lacre, m

**sealskin** /'sil,skɪn/ n piel de foca, f

**seam** /sim/ n sew costura, f; naut costura de los tablones, f; anat sutura, f; surg cicatriz, f; (wrinkle) arruga, f, surco, m; geol capa, f, yacimiento, m; mineral vena, f, filón, m. —vt coser; juntar; (a face) surcar, arrugar

**seaman** /'simən/ n marinero, m; hombre de mar, m; navegante, m. **able-bodied s.**, marinero práctico, m

**seamanlike** /'simən,laik/ a de marinero, marino; de buen marinero

**seamanship** /'simən,ʃɪp/ n marinería, f; náutica, f

**seamstress** /'simstrɪs/ n costurera, f

**seamy** /'simi/ a con costuras. **the s. side of life**, el lado peor de la vida

**seance** /'seians/ n sesión, junta, f; sesión de espiritistas, f

**seaplane** /'si,plein/ n hidroavión, hidroplano, m

**seaport** /'si,pɔrt/ n puerto de mar, m

**sear** /sɪər/ a marchito. —vt agostar, secar; (a wound) cauterizar; marchitar, ajar; (a conscience) endurecer

**search** /sɜrtʃ/ vt registrar; (a wound) explorar; examinar; escudriñar; investigar. —vi buscar. —n busca, f; (of luggage, etc.) reconocimiento, m. **in s. of**, en busca de. **to s. after, for**, buscar; ir al encuentro de. **to s. out**, ir en busca de; preguntar por. **right of s.**, (international law) derecho de visita, m. **s.-party**, pelotón de salvamento, m. **s.-warrant**, auto de reconocimiento, auto de registro domiciliario, orden de allanamiento, orden de cateo, *m*

**searching** /'sɜrtʃɪŋ/ *a* escrutador; penetrante; minucioso. **a s. look,** una mirada penetrante. **a s. wind,** un viento penetrante. **a s. question,** una pregunta perspicaz

**searchlight** /'sɜrtʃ,lait/ *n* reflector, proyector, *m*

**seashore** /'si,ʃɔr/ *n* playa, *f;* orilla del mar, *f*

**seaside** /'si,said/ *n* orilla del mar, *f;* playa, *f.* **to go to the s.,** ir al mar, ir a la playa

**season** /'sizən/ *n* estación, *f;* sazón, *f;* temporada, *f;* tiempo, *m.* —*vt* (food) sazonar; (wood, wine) madurar; (accustom) acostumbrar, aclimatar; (with wit, etc.) salpimentar; (temper) templar, moderar. —*vi* madurarse. **at that s.,** a la sazón. **close s.,** veda, *f.* **in s.,** en sazón; a su tiempo. **out of s.,** fuera de sazón; fuera de tiempo, inoportuno. **the dead s.,** la estación muerta. **the autumn s.,** el otoño; (for social functions, etc.) la temporada de otoño. **s.-ticket,** billete de abono, *m*

**seasonable** /'sizənəbəl/ *a* de estación; tempestivo, oportuno

**seasonably** /'sizənəbli/ *adv* en sazón; oportunamente

**seasonal** /'sizənl/ *a* estacional; de temporada

**seasonal worker** *n* trabajador por temporada, *m*

**seasoned** /'sizənd/ *a* (of food) sazonado; (of wood, etc.) maduro. **highly-s.,** (of a dish) picante, con muchas especies

**seasoning** /'sizənɪŋ/ *n cul* condimento, *m;* madurez, *f;* aclimatación, *f; fig* salsa, sal, *f*

**seat** /sit/ *n* asiento, *m;* (bench) banco, *m;* (chair) silla, *f;* (in a cinema, etc.) localidad, *f;* (*theat* etc., ticket) entrada, *f;* (of a person) trasero, *m,* asentaderas, *f pl;* (of trousers) fondillos, *m pl;* (of government, etc.) sede, capital, *f;* (of war, etc.) teatro, *m;* (place) sitio, lugar, *m;* (house) casa solar, *f.* —*vt* sentar; poner en una silla (a); encontrar sitio; (of buildings) tener... asientos; (a chair) poner asiento (a). **The hall seats a thousand,** La sala tiene mil asientos, Hay mil asientos en la sala. **Please be seated!** ¡Haga el favor de sentarse! **to be seated,** estar sentado; sentarse. **to have a good s.,** (on a horse) caer bien a caballo. **to hold a s. in parliament,** ser diputado a Cortes. **to keep one's s.,** permanecer sentado. **to take a s.,** tomar asiento, sentarse. **s.-back,** respaldo, *m.* **s. belt,** cinturón de seguridad, *m*

**seater** /'sitər/ *n* de... asientos. **four-s.,** automóvil de cuatro asientos, *m*

**seaweed** /'si,wid/ *n* alga marina, *f*

**seaworthy** /'si,wɜrði/ *a* (of a ship) en buen estado; marinero

**sebaceous** /sɪ'beiʃəs/ *a* sebáceo

**secede** /sɪ'sid/ *vi* retirarse (de); separarse (de)

**secession** /sɪ'sɛʃən/ *n* secesión, *f*

**secessionist** /sɪ'sɛʃənɪst/ *n* secesionista, *mf; polit* separatista, *mf.* —*a* secesionista; *polit* separatista

**secluded** /sɪ'kludɪd/ *a* apartado, retirado; solitario

**seclusion** /sɪ'kluʒən/ *n* reclusión, *f;* apartamiento, retiro, *m;* soledad, *f*

**second** /sɪ'kɒnd/ *a* segundo; otro; igual. —*adv* en segundo lugar; después. —*n* segundo, *m;* (in a duel) padrino, *m;* (helper) ayudante, *m;* (boxing) segundo, *m;* (railway compartment) departamento de segunda (clase), *m; mus* segunda, *f;* (of time) segundo, *m;* (moment) instante, momento, *m.* —*vt* secundar; (a motion) apoyar; *mil* ayudar. **the s. of May,** el dos de mayo. **James the S.,** Jaime el segundo. **on s. thoughts,** después de pensarlo bien. **every s. day,** cada dos días. **They live on the s. floor,** Viven en el primer piso (since the ground floor is not counted separately in Spanish speaking areas, the American second floor = the Spanish **primer piso**). **the s. largest,** el más grande menos uno. **to be s. to none,** no ser inferior a ninguno; (of persons) no ser inferior a nadie; no ceder a nadie. **to come off s.,** llegar el segundo; ser vencido. **seconds hand,** (of watch) segundero, *m.* **s.-in-command,** segundo, *m;* subjefe, *m.* **s.-best,** segundo. **My s.-best hat,** Mi sombrero número dos. **to come off s.-best,** salir mal parado, ser vencido. **s. class,** segunda clase, *f.* **s.-class,** de segunda clase; de calidad inferior; mediocre. **s.**

**cousin,** primo (-ma) segundo (-a). **s. gear,** segunda velocidad, *f.* **s.-hand,** *a* usado; de ocasión; no nuevo. —*adv* de segunda mano. **s.-hand car,** un coche de segunda mano. **s.-hand clothing,** ropa usada, *f.* **s. lieutenant,** *mil* subteniente, segundo teniente, *m; nav* alférez de fragata, *m.* **s.-rate,** *a* inferior, mediocre. **s. sight,** doble vista, *f*

**secondary** /'sɛkən,dɛri/ *a* secundario; subordinado; accesorio; poco importante. **s. education,** enseñanza secundaria, *f*

**seconder** /'sɛkəndər/ *n* ayudante, *m;* el, *m,* (*f,* la) que apoya una proposición

**secondly** /'sɛkəndli/ *adv* en segundo lugar

**secrecy** /'sikrəsi/ *n* secreto, *m;* reserva, *f,* silencio, *m.* **in the s. of one's own heart,** en lo más íntimo de su corazón

**secret** /'sikrɪt/ *a* secreto; clandestino; (of persons) reservado, taciturno; (secluded) remoto, apartado; oculto; misterioso. —*n* secreto, *m;* (key) clave, *f.* **a s. code,** un código secreto. **in s.,** en secreto, secretamente. **open s.,** secreto a voces. **to keep a s.,** guardar un secreto. **to keep s.,** tener secreto, ocultar. **s. drawer,** secreto, *m.*

**secretaire** /,sɛkrɪ'tɛər/ *n* secreter, escritorio, *m*

**secretarial** /,sɛkrɪ'tɛəriəl/ *a* de secretario. **s. college,** academia comercial, *f*

**secretariat** /,sɛkrɪ'tɛəriət/ *n* secretaría, *f*

**secretary** /'sɛkrɪ,tɛri/ *n* secretario (-ia). **private s.,** secretario (-ia) particular. **S. of State,** ministro, *m;* Ministro de Estado, *m*

**secrete** /sɪ'krit/ *vt* esconder, ocultar; *med* secretar

**secretion** /sɪ'kriʃən/ *n* escondimiento, *m; med* secreción, *f*

**secretive** /'sikrɪtɪv/ *a* reservado, callado

**secretly** /'sikrɪtli/ *adv* en secreto, secretamente; ocultamente, a escondidas

**sect** /sɛkt/ *n* secta, *f*

**sectarian** /sɛk'tɛəriən/ *a* and *n* sectario (-ia)

**sectarianism** /sɛk'tɛəriə,nɪzəm/ *n* sectarismo, *m*

**section** /'sɛkʃən/ *n* sección, *f;* porción, *f;* subdivisión, *f;* (of a law) artículo, *m.* —*vt* seccionar. **conic s.,** sección cónica, *f*

**sectional** /'sɛkʃənl/ *a* en secciones. **s. bookcase,** biblioteca desmontable, *f*

**sector** /'sɛktər/ *n* sector, *m*

**secular** /'sɛkyələr/ *a* (very old) secular; (lay) seglar; laico; profano. **s. music,** música profana, *f.* **s. school,** escuela laica, *f*

**secularization** /,sɛkyələrə'zeiʃən/ *n* secularización, *f*

**secularize** /'sɛkyələ,raiz/ *vt* secularizar

**secure** /sɪ'kyʊr/ *a* seguro; (certain) asegurado; (safe) en seguridad; sano y salvo; (firm) firme; fijo; (confident (in)) confiado (en). —*vt* asegurar; (insure) garantizar; (lock) cerrar; (confine) prender; (acquire) adquirir, obtener; lograr, conseguir

**securely** /sɪ'kyʊrli/ *adv* seguramente; en seguridad, sin peligro; con confianza; (firmly) firmemente

**security** /sɪ'kyʊrti/ *n* seguridad, *f;* protección, defensa, *f;* garantía, *f;* (faith) confianza, *f; com* fianza, *f;* (person) fiador, *m; pl* **securities,** valores, títulos, *m pl.* **government securities,** papel del Estado, *m.* **to give s.,** *com* dar fianza. **to stand s. for,** *com* salir fiador de

**sedan-chair** /sɪ'dæn,tʃɛər/ *n* silla de manos, *f*

**sedate** /sɪ'deit/ *a* tranquilo, sosegado; formal, serio, grave

**sedately** /sɪ'deitli/ *adv* sosegadamente; seriamente

**sedateness** /sɪ'deitnɪs/ *n* sosiego, *m,* tranquilidad, *f;* formalidad, compostura, *f*

**sedative** /'sɛdətɪv/ *a* and *n* sedativo, calmante *m*

**sedentary** /'sɛdn,tɛri/ *a* sedentario

**sediment** /'sɛdəmənt/ *n* sedimento, *m*

**sedimentation** /,sɛdəmən'teiʃən/ *n* sedimentación, *f*

**sedition** /sɪ'dɪʃən/ *n* sedición, *f*

**seditious** /sɪ'dɪʃəs/ *a* sedicioso

**seduce** /sɪ'dus/ *vt* seducir

**seducer** /sɪ'dusər/ *n* seductor, *m*

**seduction** /sɪ'dʌkʃən/ *n* seducción, *f*

**seductive** /sɪ'dʌktɪv/ *a* seductivo, atractivo; persuasivo

**sedulous** /'sɛdʒələs/ *a* asiduo, diligente

**see** /si/ *n* sede, *f.* **The Holy S.,** la Santa Sede, *f*

**see** /si/ *vt* and *vi* ver; mirar; (understand) comprender; (visit) visitar; (attend to) atender a; ocuparse de. **He sees the matter quite differently,** Él mira el asunto de un modo completamente distinto, Su punto de vista sobre el asunto es completamente distinto. **You are not fit to be seen,** No eres nada presentable. **See you next Tuesday!** ¡Hasta el miércoles que viene! **I see!** ¡Ya! ¡Ahora comprendo! **Let's see!** ¡Vamos a ver! **Shall I see you home?** ¿Quieres que te acompañe a casa? **to go and see,** ir a ver. **to see red,** echar chispas. **to see the sights,** visitar los monumentos. **to see life,** ver mundo. **to see service,** servir (en el ejército, etc.). **to see about,** atender a; pensar en; ocuparse de. **to see after,** cuidar de; atender (a); ocuparse de. **to see again,** volver a ver. **to see into,** investigar, examinar. **to see off,** (at the station, etc.) ir a despedir; acompañar. **to see out,** (a person) acompañar a la puerta; (a play, etc.) quedarse hasta el fin (de); no dejar el puesto. **to see over,** inspeccionar. **to see through,** (a house, etc.) inspeccionar; (a person) calarle las intenciones; (a mystery) penetrar; (a person through trouble) ayudar. **to see it through,** llevarlo al cabo; quedarse hasta el fin. **to see to,** atender a; ocuparse de; encargarse de. **to see to everything,** encargarse de todo

**seed** /sid/ *n* semilla, *f;* simiente, *f;* (of fruit) pepita, *f,* grano, *m; fig* germen, *m;* (offspring) prole, descendencia, *f.* —*vi* granar. —*vt* sembrar. **s.-bed,** almáciga, *f,* semillero, *m.* **s.-pearl,** aljófar, *m.* **s.-plot,** sementera, *f; fig* semillero, *m.* **s.-time,** tiempo de sembrar, *m*

**seedling** /'sidlɪŋ/ *n* planta de semilla, *f*

**seedsman** /'sidzmən/ *n* tratante en semillas, *m*

**seedy** /'sidi/ *a* granado; (of clothes) raído, roto; (of persons) andrajoso, desharrapado; infeliz, desgraciado; (ill) indispuesto, malucho

**seeing** /'siɪŋ/ *n* vista, *f;* visión, *f.* **It is worth s.,** Vale la pena de verse. **s. that...,** visto que, dado que, como que. **S. is believing,** Ver es creer

**seek** /sik/ *vt* buscar; solicitar, pretender; (demand) pedir; (investigate) investigar; (to do something) procurar, tratar de. **They are much sought after,** Son muy populares, Están en demanda. **to s. after,** buscar; perseguir. **to s. for,** buscar

**seeker** /'siker/ *n* el, *m,* (*f,* la) que busca; investigador (-ra)

**seem** /sim/ *vi* parecer. **He seemed honest,** Parecía honrado. **It seemed to me,** Me pareció a mí. **It seems that they were both at home last night,** Parece ser que ambos estaban en casa anoche

**seeming** /'simɪŋ/ *a* aparente; supuesto

**seemingly** /'simɪŋli/ *adv* aparentemente; en apariencia

**seemliness** /'simlinɪs/ *n* decoro, *m*

**seemly** /'simli/ *a* decoroso, decente

**seep** /sip/ *vi* filtrar; rezumarse

**seer** /sɪər/ *n* profeta, *m*

**seesaw** /'si,sɔ/ *n* columpio, *m.* vaivén, *m.* —*vi* columpiarse; balancearse, oscilar. —*a* de vaivén, oscilante

**seethe** /sið/ *vi* hervir; *fig* bullir

**segment** /'sɛgmənt/ *n* segmento, *m*

**segregate** /*v.* 'sɛgrɪˌgeit/ *a.* -gɪt/ *vt* segregar. —*vi* segregarse. —*a* segregado

**segregation** /ˌsɛgrɪ'geiʃən/ *n* segregación, *f*

**Seine, the** /sɛn/ *n* el Sena, *m*

**seismic** /'saizmɪk/ *a* sísmico

**seismograph** /'saizməˌgræf/ *n* sismógrafo, *m*

**seismological** /ˌsaizmə'lɒdʒɪkəl/ *a* sismológico

**seismology** /saiz'mɒlədʒi/ *n* sismología, *f*

**seize** /siz/ *vt law* embargar; apoderarse de; asir; (a person) prender; coger; (a meaning) comprender; (an occasion, etc.) aprovecharse de; (of emotions) dominar; (of illnesses) atacar. —*vi mech* atascarse. **He was seized by fear,** Le dominó el miedo. **to s. the opportunity,** aprovecharse de la oportunidad. **to s. upon a pretext,** valerse de un pretexto

**seizure** /'siʒər/ *n* asimiento, *m;* (of property) embargo, secuestro, *m;* (of a person) captura, *f;* arresto, *m; med* ataque, *m*

**seldom** /'sɛldəm/ *adv* rara vez, raramente; pocas veces

**select** /sɪ'lɛkt/ *a* escogido, selecto; exclusivista. —*vt* escoger

**selection** /sɪ'lɛkʃən/ *n* selección, *f.* **selections from Cervantes,** trozos escogidos de Cervantes, *m pl.* **to make a s. from,** escoger entre. **s. committee,** comité de selección, *m*

**selective** /sɪ'lɛktɪv/ *a* selectivo

**self** /sɛlf/ *n* mismo (-a), propio (-a); sí mismo (-a), se; personalidad, *f;* ser, *m.* **all by one's s.,** sin ayuda de nadie; solo; *inf* solito. **my other s.,** mi otro yo. **my better s.,** mi mejor parte. **the s.,** el yo. **s.-abasement,** humillación de sí mismo, *f.* **s.-acting,** automático. **s.-apparent,** evidente, patente. **s.-appointed,** nombrado por uno mismo. **s.-assertion,** presunción, (a). **s.-assertive,** presumido. **s.-assurance,** confianza en sí mismo, *f;* aplomo, *m;* (impertinence) cara dura, frescura, *f.* **s.-centered,** egocéntrico. **s.-colored,** del mismo color; de su color natural. **s.-command,** dominio de sí mismo, *m;* sangre fría, ecuanimidad, *f.* **s.-complacent,** satisfecho de sí mismo. **s.-conceit,** vanidad, arrogancia, petulancia, *f.* **s.-confidence,** confianza en sí mismo, *f;* aplomo, *m.* **s.-confident,** seguro de sí mismo, lleno de confianza en sí mismo. **s.-conscious,** turbado, confuso, apocado. **s.-consciousness,** turbación, confusión, *f,* apocamiento, azoramiento, *m.* **s.-contained,** (of a person) reservado, poco comunicativo; dueño de sí mismo; (of things) completo; (of flats, etc.) independiente; con entrada independiente. **s.-contradictory,** contradictorio. **s.-control,** dominio de sí mismo, *m;* ecuanimidad, serenidad, sangre fría, *f.* **s.-controlled,** dueño de sí mismo; ecuánime, sereno. **s.-deception,** engaño de sí mismo, *m;* ilusiones, *f pl.* **s.-defense,** defensa propia, *f.* **s.-denial,** abnegación, *f;* renunciación, *f;* frugalidad, *f.* **s.-destruction,** suicidio, *m.* **s.-determination,** libre albedrío, *m;* (of peoples) autonomía, *f;* independencia, *f.* **s.-educating,** autodidacto. **s.-esteem,** respeto para uno mismo, *m;* amor propio, *m.* **s.-evident,** aparente, que salta a la vista. **s.-explanatory,** que se explica a sí mismo; evidente. **s.-generating,** autógeno. **s.-government,** (of a person) dominio de sí mismo, *m;* (of a state) autonomía, *f.* **s.-importance,** presunción, petulancia, *f.* **s.-important,** pagado de sí mismo. **to be s.-important,** darse importancia, darse tono. **s.-indulgence,** indulgencia con sí mismo, *f;* (of food, drink, etc.) excesos, *m pl,* falta de moderación, *f.* **s.-indulgent,** indulgente con sí mismo; dado a los placeres, sibarita. **s.-interest,** propio interés, *m.* **s.-knowledge,** conocimiento de sí mismo, *m.* **s.-love,** egolatría, *f.* **s.-made man,** hombre que ha llegado a su posición actual por sus propios esfuerzos, *m.* **self-medication,** automedicación, *f.* **s.-opinionated,** terco, obstinaz. **s.-portrait,** autorretrato, *m.* **s.-possessed,** dueño de sí mismo; reservado; de sangre fría. **s.-possession,** aplomo, *m,* sangre fría, serenidad, *f.* **s.-preservation,** protección de sí mismo, *f.* **s.-reliance,** independencia, *f;* confianza en sí mismo, *f.* **s.-reliant,** independiente; confiado en sí mismo. **s.-reproach,** remordimiento, *m.* **s.-respect,** respeto de sí mismo, *m;* amor propio, *m,* dignidad, *f.* **s.-respecting,** que se respeta; que tiene amor propio. **s.-restraint,** dominio de sí mismo, *m;* moderación, *f.* **s.-righteous,** farisaico. **s.-sacrifice,** abnegación, *f.* **s.-sacrificing,** abnegado. **s.-same,** mismo, idéntico. **s.-satisfaction,** satisfacción de sí mismo, *f;* vanidad, *f;* (of desires, etc.) satisfacción, indulgencia, *f.* **s.-satisfied,** satisfecho de sí mismo, pagado de sí mismo. **s.-seeking,** *a* egoísta, interesado. —*n* egoísmo, *m.* **s.-starter,** *Mech.* arranque automático, *m.* **s.-styled,** autodenominado, autotitulado, llamado por sí mismo. **s.-sufficiency,** suficiencia, *f;* presunción, *f.* **s.-sufficient,** que basta a sí mismo; contento de sí mismo. **s.-supporting,** que vive de su propio trabajo; (of an institution, business) independiente. **s.-taught,** autodidacto. **s.-willed,** voluntarioso

**selfish** /'sɛlfɪʃ/ *a* egoísta, interesado

**selfishly** /'sɛlfɪʃli/ *adv* interesadamente; por egoísmo

**selfishness** /'sɛlfɪʃnɪs/ *n* egoísmo, *m*

**sell** /sɛl/ *vt* vender. —*vi* vender; venderse. **They sold him to his enemies,** Le vendieron a sus enemigos. **House to s.,** «Se vende una casa.» **to s. at a loss,** malvender, vender con pérdida. **to s. for cash,** vender al contado. **to s. retail,** vender al por menor.

**to s. wholesale,** vender al por mayor. **to s. one's life dearly,** vender cara la vida. **They sold the chair for $10,** Vendieron la silla por diez dólares. **to s. off,** (goods) liquidar, saldar. **to s. out,** vender; agotar. **The best edition is sold out,** La mejor edición está agotada. **All the nylons have been sold out,** Se han vendido todas las medias de nilón (de cristal). **to s. up,** vender

**seller** /'sɛlər/ n vendedor (-ra); comerciante (en), m

**selling** /'sɛlɪŋ/ n venta, f. **s. off,** liquidación, f. **s. price,** precio de venta, m

**selvage** /'sɛlvɪdʒ/ n (in cloth) orillo, m

**semantics** /sɪ'mæntɪks/ n semántica, f

**semaphore** /'sɛmə,fɔr/ n semáforo, m, vt and vi hacer señales semafóricas (a)

**semaphoric** /,sɛmə'fɔrɪk/ a semafórico

**semblance** /'sɛmbləns/ n apariencia, f. **to put on a s. of woe,** aparentar ser triste

**semen** /'simən/ n semen, m, esperma, f

**semester** /sɪ'mɛstər/ n semestre, m

**semi-** prefix semi; medio. **s.-conscious,** medio consciente. **s.-detached house,** casa doble, f

**semicircle** /'sɛmɪ,sɜrkəl/ n semicírculo, m

**semicircular** /,sɛmɪ'sɜrkyələr/ a semicircular

**semicolon** /'sɛmɪ,koulən/ n punto y coma, m

**semidetached** /,sɛmɪdɪ'tætʃt, ,semai-/ a (house) apartado

**semiformal** /,semi'fɔrməl, ,semai-/ a de media ceremonia

**seminarist** /'sɛmɪnərɪst/ n seminarista, mf

**seminary** /'sɛmə,nɛri/ n seminario, m; (for girls) colegio interno, m

**Semite** /'sɛmait/ n semita, mf

**Semitic** /sə'mɪtɪk/ a semítico, semita

**Semitism** /'sɛmɪ,tɪzəm/ n semitismo, m

**semolina** /,sɛmə'linə/ n sémola, f

**senate** /'sɛnɪt/ n senado, m

**senator** /'sɛnətər/ n senador, m

**senatorial** /,sɛnə'tɔriəl/ a senatorio

**send** /sɛnd/ vt enviar, mandar; com remitir; (a ball) lanzar; (grant) conceder; permitir; (inflict) afligir (con). **I sent Jane for it,** Envié a Juana a buscarlo. **He sent me word that he could not come,** Nos mandó un recado diciéndonos que no podía venir. **to s. mad,** hacer enloquecer. **to s. packing,** mandar a paseo. **to s. again,** volver a mandar. **to s. away,** vt enviar; (dismiss) destituir; despedir; (scare off) ahuyentar, vi enviar a otra parte. **to s. back,** (goods) devolver; (persons) volver. **to s. down,** hacer bajar; (rain, etc.) mandar, derramar; (a student) suspender, expulsar. **to s. in,** mandar; (persons) hacer entrar, introducir; (food) servir; (a bill) presentar; (one's name) dar. **Please s. him in!** ¡Sírvase de invitarle a entrar! **to s. in one's resignation,** mandar su dimisión. **to s. off,** enviar, mandar; (goods) despachar; (persons) destituir; (scare) ahuyentar. **s.-off,** n despedida, f. **a good s.-off,** una despedida afectuosa. **to s. on,** (a letter) hacer seguir; (instructions) trasmitir. **to s. out,** hacer salir; mandar; (emit) despedir, dar; (new shoots, etc.) echar. **to s. round,** (the hat, etc.) hacer circular. **to s. up,** enviar arriba; mandar subir, hacer subir; mandar, enviar; (a ball) lanzar

**sender** /'sɛndər/ n remitente, mf; elec transmisor, m

**sending** /'sɛndɪŋ/ n envío, m

**Senegal** /,sɛnɪ'gɔl, -'gɑl/ Senegal, m

**Senegalese** /,sɛnəgə'liz/ a and n senegalés (-esa)

**senile** /'sinail/ a senil

**senility** /sɪ'nɪlɪti/ n senilidad, f

**senior** /'sinyər/ a mayor, de mayor edad; más antiguo. **Martinez s.,** Martínez padre. **Charles is Mary's s. by five years,** Carlos es cinco años mayor que María. **s. member,** decano, m

**seniority** /sin'yɔrɪti/ n ancianidad, f; antigüedad, f

**senna** /'sɛnə/ n bot sena, f

**sensation** /sɛn'seiʃən/ n sensación, f; sentimiento, m; impresión, f. **to create a s.,** causar una sensación

**sensational** /sɛn'seiʃənl/ a sensacional

**sensationalism** /sɛn'seiʃənl,ɪzəm/ n philos sensualismo, m; efectismo, m

**sensationalist** /sɛn'seiʃənlɪst/ n philos sensualista, mf; efectista, mf

**sense** /sɛns/ n sentido, m. —vt sentir. **in a s.,** hasta

cierto punto; desde un punto de vista. **in the full s. of the word,** en toda la extensión de la palabra. **common s.,** sentido común, m. **He has no s. of smell,** No tiene olfato. **the five senses,** los cinco sentidos. **to be out of one's senses,** estar fuera de sí, estar trastornado. **You must be out of your senses!** ¡Debes de haber perdido el juicio! ¡Estás loco! **to come to one's senses,** (after unconsciousness) volver en sí; (after folly) recobrar el sentido común. **to talk s.,** hablar con sentido común, hablar razonablemente. **s. organ,** órgano de los sentidos, m. **have a good s. of direction,** saber orientarse, tener buena orientación. **have no s. of smell,** ser incapaz de percibir olores. **have no s. of taste,** ser incapaz de distinguir gustos

**senseless** /'sɛnslɪs/ a (unconscious) sin sentido, insensible; desmayado; (silly) necio, estúpido. **to knock s.,** derribar, tumbar

**senselessness** /'sɛnslɪsnɪs/ n falta de sentido común, f; locura, absurdidad, f

**sensibility** /,sɛnsə'bɪlɪti/ n sensibilidad, f

**sensible** /'sɛnsəbəl/ a sensible; (conscious) consciente (de); sesudo. **to be s. of,** estar consciente de; estar persuadido de

**sensibly** /'sɛnsəbli/ adv sensiblemente; sesudamente, cuerdamente

**sensitive** /'sɛnsɪtɪv/ a sensitivo; susceptible (a); impresionable. **s. plant,** sensitiva, f

**sensitivity** /,sɛnsɪ'tɪvɪti/ n sensibilidad, f; susceptibilidad, f; delicadeza, f

**sensitize** /'sɛnsɪ,taiz/ vt photo sensibilizar

**sensory** /'sɛnsəri/ a sensorio

**sensual** /'sɛnʃuəl/ a sensual; voluptuoso

**sensualism** /'sɛnʃuə,lɪzəm/ n sensualismo, m

**sensualist** /'sɛnʃuəlɪst/ n sensualista, mf

**sensuality** /,sɛnʃu'ælɪti/ n sensualidad, f

**sensually** /'sɛnʃuəli/ adv sensualmente

**sensuous** /'sɛnʃuəs/ a sensorio

**sensuousness** /'sɛnʃuəsnɪs/ n sensualidad, f

**sentence** /'sɛntns/ n law sentencia, f; (penalty) pena, f; gram frase, f; (maxim) máxima, sentencia, f. —vt sentenciar, condenar. **to pass s.,** pronunciar sentencia, fallar. **under s. of,** bajo pena de

**sententious** /sɛn'tɛnʃəs/ a sentencioso

**sentient** /'sɛnʃənt/ a sensible

**sentiment** /'sɛntəmənt/ n sentimiento, m; (sentimentality) sentimentalismo, m; opinión, f

**sentimental** /,sɛntə'mɛntl/ a sentimental; (mawkish) sensiblero

**sentimentalist** /,sɛntə'mɛntlɪst/ n romántico (-ca), persona sentimental, f

**sentimentality** /,sɛntəmɛn'tælɪti/ n sentimentalismo, m, sensiblería, f

**sentimentalize** /,sɛntə'mɛntl,aiz/ vt idealizar

**sentimentally** /,sɛntə'mɛntli/ adv sentimentalmente

**sentinel** /'sɛntnl/ n centinela, mf

**sentry** /'sɛntri/ n centinela, m. **to be on s. duty,** estar de guardia. **s.-box,** garita de centinela, f

**separable** /'sɛpərəbəl/ a separable

**separate** /a. 'sɛpərɪt; v. ɹreit/ a separado; distinto; independiente. —vt separar; dividir. —vi separarse; (of husband and wife) separarse de bienes y de cuerpos

**separately** /'sɛpərɪtli/ adv separadamente; aparte

**separation** /,sɛpə'reiʃən/ n separación, f; law separación de bienes y de cuerpos, f

**separatism** /'sɛpərə,tɪzəm/ n separatismo, m

**separatist** /'sɛpərətɪst/ a and n separatista mf

**Sephardic** /sə'fardɪk/ a Sefaradí

**sepia** /'sipiə/ n (color and fish) sepia, f

**September** /sɛp'tɛmbər/ n setiembre, septiembre, m

**septic** /'sɛptɪk/ a séptico

**septicemia** /,sɛptɪ'simiə/ n septicemia, f

**septuagenarian** /,sɛptʃuədʒə'nɛəriən/ n setentón (-ona); septuagenario (-ia)

**septum** /'sɛptəm/ septo, tabique, m

**sepulcher** /'sɛpəlkər/ n sepulcro, m

**sepulchral** /sə'pʌlkrəl/ a sepulcral

**sequel** /'sikwəl/ n (of a story, etc.) continuación, f; consecuencia, f; resultado, m

**sequence** /'sikwəns/ n sucesión, f; serie, f; orden,

*mf;* (at cards) serie, *f; gram* correspondencia, *f;* (*eccl and cinema*) secuencia, *f.* **s. of tenses,** correspondencia de los tiempos, *f*

**sequestered** /sɪ'kwestərd/ *a* aislado, remoto

**sequestrate** /sɪ'kwestreit/ *vt* secuestrar

**sequestration** /,sikwes'treiʃən/ *n* secuestro, *m,*

**sequin** /'sikwɪn/ *n* lentejuela, *f*

**seraglio** /sɪ'rælyou/ *n* serrallo, *m*

**seraph** /'seraf/ *n* serafín, *m*

**seraphic** /sɪ'ræfɪk/ *a* seráfico

**seraphim** /'serafɪm/ *n* serafín, *m*

**Serbia** /'sɜrbiə/ Servia, *f*

**Serbian** /'sɜrbiən/ *a* servio. *—n* servio (-ia); (language) servio, *m*

**serenade** /,serə'neid/ *n* serenata, *f, vt* dar una serenata (a)

**serene** /sə'rin/ *a* sereno. **His S. Highness,** Su Alteza Serenísima

**serenity** /sə'renɪti/ *n* serenidad, *f;* tranquilidad, *f*

**serf** /sɜrf/ *n* siervo (-va)

**serfdom** /'sɜrfdəm/ *n* servidumbre, *f*

**serge** /sɜrdʒ/ *n* estameña, *f;* (silk) sarga, *f*

**sergeant** /'sɑrdʒənt/ *n mil* sargento, *m;* (police) sargento de policía, *m.* **s.-at-arms,** macero, *m.* **s.-major,** sargento instructor, *m*

**serial** /'sɪəriəl/ *a* en serie; (of a story) por entregas. *—n* novela por entregas, *f.* **s. number,** número de serie, *m*

**sericulture** /'sɪrɪ,kʌltʃər/ *n* sericultura, *f*

**series** /'sɪəriz/ *n* serie, *f;* cadena, *f; math* serie, progresión, *f.* **in s.,** en serie

**serious** /'sɪəriəs/ *a* serio; sincero; verdadero; (of illness, etc.) grave; importante. **He was s.** (not laughing) when he said it, Lo dijo en serio. **He is very s. about it,** Lo toma muy en serio. **to grow s.,** (of persons) ponerse serio; (of events) hacerse grave

**seriously** /'sɪəriəsli/ *adv* seriamente; en serio; gravemente. **to take** (something) **s.,** tomar (algo) en serio. **to take oneself s.,** tomarse muy en serio

**seriousness** /'sɪəriəsnɪs/ *n* seriedad, *f;* gravedad, *f.* **in all s.,** en serio, seriamente

**sermon** /'sɜrmən/ *n* sermón, *m*

**sermonize** /'sɜrmə,naiz/ *vt and vi* sermonear

**serpent** /'sɜrpənt/ *n* serpiente, *f; mus* serpentón, *m*

**serpentine** /'sɜrpən,tin, -,tain/ *a* serpentino; (of character) tortuoso. *—n mineral* serpentina, *f*

**serrated** /'sereitɪd/ *a* serrado; dentellado

**serried** /'serid/ *a* apretado, apiñado

**serum** /'sɪərəm/ *n* suero, *m*

**servant** /'sɜrvənt/ *n* servidor (-ra); (domestic) criado (-da); (employee) empleado (-da); (slave and *fig*) siervo (-va); *pl* **servants,** (domestic) servidumbre, *f,* servicio, *m.* **I remain your obedient s.,** Quedo de Vd. atento y seguro servidor (att. y s.s.). **civil s.,** empleado del estado, *m.* **general s.,** criada para todo, *f.* **man s.,** criado, *m.* **the s. problem,** el problema del servicio. **Your s., sir,** Servidor de Vd., señor. **s.-girl,** criada, *f*

**serve** /sɜrv/ *vt* servir (a); ser útil (a); satisfacer; (in a shop) despachar; (an apprenticeship, etc.) hacer; (a prison sentence) cumplir; (treat) tratar; (of stallion) cubrir; (a warrant, etc.) ejecutar; (a notice) entregar; (a ball) servir; (on a jury, etc.) formar parte de; *naut* aforrar. *—vi* servir; (*mil, nav*) hacer el servicio. *—n sports* saque, *m.* **It serves you right!** ¡Lo tienes merecido! **to s. at table,** servir a la mesa. **to s. as,** servir de. **to s. out,** distribuir; servir. **Serves 8,** (recipe) Da 8 porciones

**server** /'sɜrvər/ *n eccl* acólito, *m; sports* saque, *m;* (tray) bandeja, *f;* (for fish, etc.) pala, *f*

**service** /'sɜrvɪs/ *n* servicio, *m; eccl* oficio, *m;* servicio de mesa, *m;* (of a writ) entrega, *f; sports* saque, *m.* **coffee s.,** juego de café, *m.* **diplomatic s.,** cuerpo diplomático, *m.* **At your s.,** Para servir a Vd., A su disposición. **on active s.,** en acto de servicio; en el campo de batalla. **to go into s.,** (of servants) ir a servir. **to render s.,** prestar servicios. **S. tree,** serbal, *m*

**serviceable** /'sɜrvəsəbəl/ *a* (of persons) servicial; (of things) servible, utilizable; útil; práctico; (lasting) duradero

**service road** *n* vía de servicio, *f*

**serviette** /,sɜrvi'ɛt/ *n* servilleta, *f.* **s. ring,** servilletero, *m*

**servile** /'sɜrvɪl/ *a* servil

**servility** /sər'vɪlɪti/ *n* servilismo, *m*

**serving** /'sɜrvɪŋ/ *a* sirviente; al servicio (de). **s. maid,** criada, *f.* **s. table,** trinchero, *m*

**servitude** /'sɜrvɪ,tud/ *n* servidumbre, esclavitud, *f.* **penal s.,** cadena perpetua, *f*

**session** /'seʃən/ *n* sesión, *f;* junta, *f.* **petty sessions,** tribunal de primera instancia, *m*

**set** /set/ *vt* poner; colocar; fijar; (seeds, etc.) plantar; (bones) reducir, componer; (gems) engastar, montar; (a clock) regular; (sails) desplegar; (the teeth of a saw) trabar, triscar; (congeal) hacer coagular; (a trap) armar; (a snare) tender; (a razor) afilar; (make ready) preparar; (type) componer; (cause) hacer; *mus* poner en música; *mus* adaptar; (order) mandar; (prescribe) dar, asignar; (estimate) estimar, evaluar; (an example, etc.) dar; (establish) establecer, crear. *—vi* (of the sun, etc.) ponerse; (solidify) coagularse; solidificarse; (of tides) fluir; (of the wind) soplar; (of dogs) hacer punta. **The joke set him laughing,** El chiste le hizo reír. **set an example,** dar ejemplo, dar el ejemplo. **set a precedent,** sentar precedente. **to set a person's mind at rest,** tranquilizar, sosegar. **to set a trap,** armar lazo. **to set at ease,** poner a sus anchas (a), hacer cómodo (a). **to set at naught,** despreciar. **to set eyes on,** poner los ojos en. **to set fire to,** pegar fuego a, incendiar. **to set free,** poner en libertad, librar (de). **to set in motion,** poner en marcha. **to set one's teeth,** apretar los dientes. **to set people talking,** dar que hablar a la gente. **to set the fashion,** fijar la moda; poner de moda. **to set the alarm at seven o'clock,** poner el despertador a las siete. **to set the table,** poner la mesa. **to set to work,** ponerse a trabajar. **to set about,** *vi* (begin) ponerse (a); empezar; (undertake) emprender. *—vt* (a rumor, etc.) divulgar. **They set about each other,** Empezaron a golpearse, Vinieron a las manos. **to set against,** indisponer (con), enemistar (con); hacer enemigo (de), ser hostil (a); (balance) oponer, balancear. **to set oneself against,** oponerse a; atacar; luchar contra. **to set aside,** poner a un lado; apartar; (discard) desechar; (omit) omitir, pasar por alto de; dejar aparte, excluir; (keep) reservar; (money, etc.) ahorrar; (reject) rechazar; (quash) anular. **to set back,** retrasar; hacer retroceder. **set-back,** *n* revés, *m;* contrariedad, *f.* **to set before,** poner ante; (facts) exponer; (introduce) presentar. **to set down,** poner en tierra; depositar; (of a bus, etc.) dejar; (in writing) poner por escrito; anotar, apuntar; narrar, contar; (attribute) atribuir; (fix) fijar, formular; (believe to be) creer. **Passengers are set down at...,** Los viajeros pueden apearse en... **to set forth,** *vt* (one's opinions, etc.) exponer; publicar; (display) exhibir, mostrar; (make) hacer. *—vi* ponerse en camino. **to set going,** poner en marcha; echar a andar. **to set in,** empezar; (of the tide) fluir. **A reaction has set in,** Se ha hecho sentir una reacción. **to set off,** *vt* (explode) hacer estallar; (cause) hacer; (heighten) realzar; hacer resaltar; (counterbalance) contraponer. *—vi* partir; ponerse en camino. **set-off,** *n* contraste, *m,* contraposición, *f.* **to set off against,** contraponer. **to set on,** *vt* (a dog) azuzar; (incite) instigar, incitar. *—vi* atacar. **to set out,** *vi* (state) exponer, manifestar; (embellish) realzar; (display) arreglar, disponer. *—vi* ponerse en camino, partir. **to set over,** (rule) tener autoridad sobre; gobernar. **to set to,** (begin to) ponerse a, empezar a; (work) ponerse a trabajar. **set-to,** *n* lucha, *f;* (boxing) asalto, *m;* (quarrel) pelea, riña, *f.* **to set up,** *vt* (a monument, etc.) erigir, levantar; (fix) fijar; (apparatus, machinery) montar; (exalt) exaltar; (found) establecer; crear; (propound) exponer; (a howl, etc.) dar; (equip with) proveer de; instalar; (make strong) robustecer; fortificar; (type) componer; (raise) alzar. *—vi* establecerse; dárselas de. **He sets himself up as a painter,** Se las da de pintor. **to set** (a person) **up as a model,** poner como modelo (a). **to set up house,** poner casa. **to set up a business,** establecer un comercio. **set-up,** *n* establecimiento, *m;* arreglo, *m.* **to set upon,** atacar

**set** /set/ *n* (of sun, etc.) puesta, *f,* ocaso, *m;* (of the head, etc.) porte, *m;* (of a garment) corte, *m;* (of the tide, etc.) dirección, f; (slant) inclinación, f; (fig drift) tendencia, f, movimiento, m; (of the teeth of a saw) triscamiento, m; (of men, houses, etc.) grupo, m; (of tools, golf clubs, china, etc.) juego, m; (gang) pandilla, camarilla, f; clase, f; (dance) tanda, f; (tennis) partido, f; theat decoración, f; radio aparato de radio, m, radio, f. **coffee set,** juego de café, m. **allmains set,** radio de corriente eléctrica, f. **battery set,** radio de batería, f. **portable set,** radio portátil, f. **the smart set,** el mundo elegante. **to have a shampoo and set,** hacerse lavar y marcar (el pelo). **to make a set,** hacer juego. **to make a dead set at,** hacer un ataque vigoroso (a), atacar resueltamente; procurar insinuarse en el favor de. **set of teeth,** dentadura, f

**set** /set/ a fijo; inmóvil; (of a smile) forzado; (of a task) asignado; (of times) señalado, fijo; (prescribed) prescrito, establecido; (firm) firme; (resolved) resuelto; (well-known) consabido; (obstinate) terco, nada adaptable. **well set-up,** apuesto, bien plantado. **He is set on doing it,** Se empeña en **to be dead set against,** estar completamente opuesto a. **set phrase,** frase hecha, f. **set-square,** cartabón, m

**settee** /se'ti/ n canapé, m. **s.-bed,** cama turca, f
**setter** /'setər/ n (perro) séter, perdiguero, m. **s.-on,** instigador (-ra)
**setting** /'setɪŋ/ n (of the sun, etc.) puesta, f; (of mortar, etc.) fraguado, m; (of a jelly) solidificación, f; (of jewels) engaste, m, montadura, f; (of bones) aliño, m; (of teeth of saw) traba, f; (of razor) afiladura, f; (of a trap) armadura, f; (of a machine, etc.) ajuste, m; (frame) marco, m; mus arreglo, m; theat decorado, m; (emplacement) lecho, m. **the s. sun,** el sol poniente. **s. free,** liberación, f. **s. off,** partida, salida, f. **s. out,** ida, marcha, f; principio, m. **s.-up,** creación, institución, f; establecimiento, m; (of a machine) montaje, m; print composición, f
**settle** /'setl/ vt colocar; asegurar; afirmar; (a country) colonizar; (live in) establecer (en); (populate) poblar; (in a profession, etc.) dar; (install) instalar; (the imagination, etc.) sosegar, calmar; (resolve) resolver; (arrange) disponer, arreglar; (differences) componer, concertar; (an opponent, etc.) confundir; (a bill) saldar, pagar; (a claim) satisfacer; (clarify) depositar, clarificar; (end) poner fin (a). —vi establecerse; (of weather) serenarse; (to work, etc.) empezar a, ponerse a; aplicarse a; (decide) decidirse; (alight) posarse; (of foundations, etc.) asentarse (of a ship) zozobrar; (of sediment) depositarse; (of liquid) clarificarse. **to s. accounts with,** fig ajustar cuentas con. **to s. down,** establecerse, arraigarse; adaptarse (a); (become calm) sosegarse, calmarse; sentar el juicio; (of foundations) asentarse (of a ship) zozobrar; (of sediment) depositarse. **to s. in,** vt instalar. —vi instalarse. **to s. on,** (choose) escoger; (decide on) decidirse (a). **to s. a pension on,** señalar pensión (a). **to s. up,** vt (one's affairs) poner en orden; (bill) pagar, saldar. —vi llegar a un acuerdo; pagar cuentas
**settled** /'setld/ a fijo; permanente; invariable; (of countries) colonizado; (of weather) sereno
**settlement** /'setlmənt/ n (of a country) colonización, f; (of a dispute) arreglo, ajuste, m; (of a question) solución, f; decisión, f; (of a bill) saldo, pago, m, liquidación, f; (of an obligation) satisfacción, f; (colony) colonia, f; (creation) creación, institución, f; establecimiento, arraigo, m. **deed of s.,** escritura de donación, f. **marriage s.,** contrato matrimonial, m; **s. out of court,** arreglo pacífico, m
**settler** /'setlər/ n colono, m; colonizador (-ra)
**seven** /'sevən/ a and n siete m. **It is s. o'clock,** Son las siete. **the s. deadly sins,** los siete pecados capitales
**seventeen** /'sevən'tin/ a diecisiete, diez y siete. —n diecisiete, m. **She is just s.,** Acaba de cumplir los diez y siete años
**seventeenth** /'sevən'tinθ/ a décimoséptimo; (of monarchs and of the month) diez y siete. —n décimoséptimo, m. **Louis the S.,** Luis diez y siete. **the s. of June,** el diez y siete de junio
**seventh** /'sevənθ/ a séptimo; (of the month) siete. —n séptimo, m; séptima parte, f; mus séptima, f. **Edward the S.,** Eduardo séptimo. **the s. of August,** el siete de agosto

**seventieth** /'sevəntiəθ/ a septuagésimo, setentavo. —n setentavo, m
**seventy** /'sevənti/ a and n setenta, m
**sever** /'sevər/ vt separar; romper; dividir
**several** /'sevərəl/ a distinto, diferente; respectivo; varios, m pl, (f pl, varias); algunos, m pl, (f pl, algunas)
**severally** /'sevərəli/ adv separadamente; individualmente; independientemente
**severance** /'sevərəns/ n separación, f; (of friendship, etc.) ruptura, f ̂
**severe** /sə'vɪər/ a severo; riguroso; fuerte; duro; (of style) austero; (of pain) agudo; (of illness) grave
**severely** /sə'vɪərli/ adv severamente; intensamente; gravemente
**severity** /sə'vɛriti/ n severidad, f; intensidad, f; (of weather) inclemencia, f; (of illness) gravedad, f
**sew** /sou/ vt and vi coser. **to sew on,** coser, pegar
**sewage** /'suɪdʒ/ n aguas residuales, f pl. **s. system,** alcantarillado, m
**sewer** /'suər/ n alcantarilla, cloaca, f, albañal, m
**sewing** /'souɪŋ/ n costura, f. **s. bag,** costurero, m. **s. cotton,** hilo de coser, m. **s.-machine,** máquina de coser, f. **s. silk,** torzal, m
**sex** /seks/ n sexo, m. **the fair sex,** el bello sexo. **the weaker sex,** el sexo débil. **sex appeal,** atractivo, m
**sexagenarian** /,seksədʒə'nɛəriən/ n sexagenario (-ia)
**sexless** /'sekslɪs/ a neutro; frígido
**sexologist** /sek'splədʒɪst/ n sexólogo (-ga)
**sexology** /sek'splədʒi/ n sexología, f
**sextant** /'sekstənt/ n sextante, m
**sexton** /'sekstən/ n sacristán, m; sepulturero, m; (bell-ringer) campanero, m
**sexual** /'sekʃuəl/ a sexual
**sexuality** /,sekʃu'æliti/ n sexualidad, f
**Sforza** /'sfɔrtsa/ Esforcia, f
**sh!** /ʃ/ interj ¡Chitón! ¡Chis!
**shabbily** /'ʃæbəli/ adv (of dressing) pobremente; (of treatment) mezquinamente
**shabbiness** /'ʃæbɪnɪs/ n pobreza, f; estado andrajoso, m; (of behavior) mezquindad, ruindad, f
**shabby** /'ʃæbi/ a (of persons) desharrapado, andrajoso; (of garments) raído, roto; (of a neighborhood, etc.) pobre; (mean) ruin, mezquino
**shack** /ʃæk/ n choza, f
**shackle** /'ʃækəl/ n traba, f; pl **shackles,** grillos, m pl, esposas, f pl; fig cadenas, f pl. —vt poner esposas (a), encadenar; (a horse) apear; fig atar; (impede) estorbar
**shad** /ʃæd/ n sábalo, m
**shade** /ʃeid/ n sombra, f; (in a picture) toque de obscuro, m; (for the eyes) visera, f; (of a lamp) pantalla, f; (ghost) espectro, fantasma, m; (of color) matiz, m; (tinge) dejo, m. —vt sombrear, dar sombra (a); (the face, etc.) proteger, resguardar; (a drawing) esfumar. **in the s.,** a la sombra. **80° in the s.,** ochenta grados a la sombra. **to put** (a person) **in the s.,** eclipsar
**shadiness** /'ʃeidɪnɪs/ n sombra, f
**shading** /'ʃeidɪŋ/ n sombra, f; art degradación, f
**shadow** /'ʃædou/ n sombra, f; obscuridad, f; (in a picture) toque de obscuro, m. —vt sombrear; obscurecer; (a person) seguir **to cast a s.,** proyectar una sombra. **to s. forth,** indicar; simbolizar. **s. show,** sombras chinescas, f pl
**shadowy** /'ʃædoui/ a umbroso; vago, indistinto, indefinido
**shady** /'ʃeidi/ a sombreado, umbrío; sombrío; (of persons, etc.) sospechoso. **It was s. in the wood,** Hacía sombra en el bosque
**shaft** /ʃæft/ n fuste, m; (arrow) flecha, saeta, f, dardo, m; (of a golf club, etc.) mango, m; (of a cart) vara, f; mech árbol, eje, m; (of a column and a feather) cañón, m; (of light) rayo, m; (of a mine) pozo, tiro, m; (air-shaft) conducto de aire, ventilador, m. **cam-s.,** árbol de levas, m. **driving s.,** árbol motor, m
**shaggy** /'ʃægi/ a peludo; lanudo
**shagreen** /ʃə'grin/ n chagrén, m
**shah** /ʃɑ, ʃɔ/ n cha, m
**shake** /ʃeik/ vt sacudir; agitar; hacer temblar; (weaken) debilitar, hacer flaquear. —vi estremecerse; temblar; (trill) trinar. **He managed to s. himself**

**free,** Consiguió librarse por una sacudida. **to s. hands,** darse la mano, estrecharse la mano. **to s. one's finger at,** señalar con el dedo (a). **to s. one's fist at,** amenazar con el puño (a). **to s. one's head,** mover la cabeza; negar con la cabeza. **to s. one's sides,** (with laughter) reírse a carcajadas. **to s. with fear,** temblar de miedo. **to s. down,** sacudir, hacer caer. **s.-down,** n cama improvisada, f. **to s. off,** sacudirse; librarse (de), perder; quitar de encima (a). **to s. out,** (unfurl) desplegar; sacudir. **to s. up,** agitar; sacudir, remover

**shake** /ʃeik/ n sacudida, f; (of the head) movimiento (de la cabeza), m; (of the hand) apretón (de manos), m; temblor, m; trino, gorjeo, m. **in two shakes,** Inf. en un periquete. **to give a person a good s.,** sacudir violentamente (a)

**Shakespearean** /ʃeik'spiəriən/ a shakespeariano

**shakiness** /'ʃeikinis/ n inestabilidad, f; poca firmeza, f; temblor, m; lo dudoso. **the s. of his voice,** su voz trémula

**shaking** /'ʃeikiŋ/ n sacudimiento, m; temblor, m; (of windows, etc.) zangoloteo, m

**shaky** /'ʃeiki/ a inestable; poco firme; (of hands, etc.) tembloroso; (of the voice) trémulo; (of gait) vacilante; dudoso

**shale** /ʃeil/ n esquisto, m

**shall** /ʃæl/ unstressed ʃəl/ v aux (expressing simple future) **I s. arrive tomorrow,** Llegaré mañana. **S. we go to the sea next week?** ¿Iremos al mar la semana próxima?; (expressing obligation, compulsion) **You s. not go out,** No has de salir, No quiero que salgas. **He s. see her immediately,** Tiene que verla en seguida; (as a polite formula) **S. I go?** ¿Quiere Vd. que vaya? **S. we buy the soap?** ¿Quiere Vd. que compremos el jabón? ¿Compraremos el jabón?

**shallot** /ʃæˈlɒt, ʃəˈlɒt/ n bot chalote, m, ascalonia, f

**shallow** /'ʃælou/ a poco profundo; (of a receptacle) llano; (of persons) superficial, frívolo; (of knowledge, etc.) superficial, ligero, somero. —n bajío, m

**shallowness** /'ʃælounis/ n poca profundidad, f; superficialidad, f

**sham** /ʃæm/ vt fingir, simular. —n farsa, f; imitación, f; engaño, m; (person) farsante, m. —a fingido; falso; espurio. **to s. illness,** fingirse enfermo. **to s. dead,** hacer la mortecina. **You're just a s.,** Eres un farsante

**sham battle** n mil simulacro de combate, simulacro guerrero, m

**shamble** /'ʃæmbəl/ vi andar arrastrándose. —n andar pesado, m; pl **shambles,** matadero, m; fig carnicería, f

**shambling** /'ʃæmbliŋ/ a pesado, lento

**shame** /ʃeim/ n vergüenza, f; ignominia, f; deshonra, f. —vt avergonzar; deshonrar. **For s.!** ¡Qué vergüenza! **What a s.!** ¡Qué lástima! **to put to s.,** avergonzar

**shamefaced** /'ʃeim,feist/ a (bashful) vergonzoso, tímido; (ashamed) avergonzado

**shamefacedly** /,ʃeim'feisidli/ adv vergonzosamente, tímidamente; con vergüenza

**shameful** /'ʃeimfəl/ a vergonzoso, escandaloso; indecente

**shamefully** /'ʃeimfəli/ adv escandalosamente

**shamefulness** /'ʃeimfəlnis/ n vergüenza, infamia, f; indecencia, f

**shameless** /'ʃeimlis/ a desvergonzado; impúdico, indecente

**shamelessly** /'ʃeimlisli/ adv desvergonzadamente

**shamelessness** /'ʃeimlisnis/ n desvergüenza, poca vergüenza, f; impudicia, deshonestidad, f

**shampoo** /ʃæm'pu/ vt dar un champú, m. —vt dar un champú (a); dar un masaje (a). **dry s.,** champú seco, m

**shamrock** /'ʃæmrɒk/ n trébol blanco, m

**shank** /ʃæŋk/ n zanca, f; mech pierna, f; (handle) mango, m; (of a button) rabo, m, cola, f. **go on Shank's mare, ride on Shank's mare,** caminar en coche de San Francisco, ir en la boridad de Villadiego

**shanty** /'ʃænti/ n choza, f

**shanty town** n barriada (Peru), callampa, población, población callampa (Chile), f. Rancho (Venezuela), m, villa-miseria (Argentina), f

**shape** /ʃeip/ n forma, f; bulto, m; fantasma, m; (of a garment) corte, m; (of a person) talle, m; cul molde, m; (of a hat) forma, f. —vt formar; (a garment) cortar; (ideas) dar forma (a); adaptar; (stone, etc.) labrar; (one's life) dominar. —vi (of events) desarrollarse. **to go out of s.,** perder la forma. **to take s.,** tomar forma. **to s. one's course,** dirigirse (hacia, a); naut dar el rumbo. **to s. well,** prometer bien

**shaped** /ʃeipt/ a de forma de..., que tiene figura de... **pear-s.,** piriforme

**shapeless** /'ʃeiplis/ a informe; disforme

**shapelessness** /'ʃeiplisnis/ n informidad, f; deformidad, f

**shapeliness** /'ʃeiplinis/ n belleza de forma, f; simetría, f

**shapely** /'ʃeipli/ a bien formado; simétrico

**share** /ʃɛər/ n porción, f; parte, f; cuota, f; contribución, f; (part ownership) interés, m; (in a company) acción, f. —vt distribuir; compartir; dividir; tomar parte en. —vi participar (de); tomar parte (en). **to fall to one's s.,** tocar, corresponder. **to go shares with,** dividir con, compartir con. **to take a s. in the conversation,** tomar parte en la conversación. **paid-up s.,** com acción liberada, f. **to s. out,** repartir, distribuir

**shareholder** /'ʃɛər,houldər/ n accionista, mf

**sharer** /'ʃɛərər/ n partícipe, mf

**shark** /ʃɑrk/ n ichth tiburón, m; inf caimán, m

**sharp** /ʃɑrp/ a (of edges) afilado, cortante; (of points) punzante, puntiagudo; (of features, etc.) anguloso; (of bends, etc.) brusco; (of outlines, etc.) definido, distinto; (of pain, sound) agudo; (marked) marcado; (intense) intenso; (of winds, glance, etc.) penetrante; (of hearing) fino; (of appetite) bueno; (of showers) fuerte; (quick) rápido; (clever, etc.) vivo, listo; perspicaz; (of children) despierto, precoz; (unscrupulous) astuto, sin escrúpulos; (of criticism, remarks) mordaz; (of rebukes, sentences, etc.) severo; (of winters, etc.) riguroso; (of fighting) encarnizado; (of taste) picante; (sour) ácido; mus sostenido. —adv en punto; puntualmente. —n mus sostenido, m. **at five o'clock s.,** a las cinco en punto. **Look s.!** ¡Date prisa! **s.-edged,** afilado. **s.-eyed,** con ojos de lince; de mirada penetrante. **s.-featured,** de facciones angulosas. **s.-nosed,** de nariz puntiaguda. **s.-pointed,** puntiagudo. **s. practice,** procedimientos poco honrados, m pl. **s.-tongued,** de lengua áspera. **s. turn,** curva brusca, curva cerrada, f. **s.-witted,** de inteligencia viva, listo

**sharpen** /'ʃɑrpən/ vt (knives) afilar, amolar; (pencils, etc.) sacar punta (a); (wits, etc.) despabilar; (appetite) abrir. **This walk has sharpened my appetite,** Este paseo me ha abierto el apetito. **to s. one's claws,** afilarse las uñas

**sharper** /'ʃɑrpər/ n inf caballero de industria, timador, m; (at cards) fullero, m

**sharply** /'ʃɑrpli/ adv claramente; bruscamente; severamente; ásperamente

**sharpness** /'ʃɑrpnis/ n (of cold, etc.) intensidad, f; severidad, f; (cleverness) agudeza, perspicacia, f; (of a child) precocidad, f; (sarcasm, etc.) mordacidad, f; aspereza, f; brusquedad, f

**sharpshooter** /'ʃɑrp,ʃutər/ n franco tirador, m

**sharpsighted** /'ʃɑrp,saitid/ a de vista penetrante, listo, perspicaz

**shatter** /'ʃætər/ vt romper, quebrantar; hacer añicos; fig destrozar. **You have shattered my illusions,** Has destrozado todas mis ilusiones

**shave** /ʃeiv/ vt afeitar, rasurar; (wood, etc.) acepillar. —vi afeitarse; (of razors) afeitar. —n afeitada, f. **to have a s.,** hacerse afeitar. **to have a close s.,** inf escapar por un pelo

**shaving** /'ʃeiviŋ/ n afeitada, f; (of wood, etc.) viruta, acepilladura, f. **s.-bowl,** bacía, f. **s.-brush,** brocha de afeitar, f. **s.-glass,** espejo de afeitar, m. **s.-soap,** jabón de afeitar, m. **s.-stick,** barra de jabón de afeitar, f

**shawl** /ʃɔl/ n chal, mantón, rebozo, m

**she** /ʃi/ pers pron ella; la; (female) hembra, f; (translated by fem. ending in the case of animals, etc., e.g. she bear, osa, she cat, gata). **It is her,** Es ella. **she who is dancing,** la que baila

**sheaf** /ʃif/ n (of corn, etc.) gavilla, garba, f; (of arrows) haz, *m;* (of papers, etc.) paquete, atado, *m.* **to bind in sheaves,** agavillar

**shear** /ʃɪər/ *vt* (sheep) esquilar, trasquilar; tonsurar; cortar; (cloth) tundir

**shearer** /'ʃɪərər/ *n* (of sheep) esquilador, *m*

**shearing** /'ʃɪərɪŋ/ *n* (of sheep) esquileo, *m,* tonsura, *f;* (of cloth) tunda, *f.* **s. machine,** esquiladora, *f.* **s. season,** esquileo, *m*

**shears** /ʃɪərz/ *n pl* tijeras grandes, *f pl,* cizalla, *f*

**sheath** /ʃiθ/ *n* vaina, *f.* **s.-knife,** cuchillo de monte, *m*

**sheathe** /ʃið/ *vt* envainar; *naut* aforrar

**shed** /ʃed/ *vt* derramar; (skin, etc.) mudar; perder; (remove) quitarse, desprenderse de; (get rid of) deshacerse de. —*n* cobertizo, sotechado, *m;* cabaña, *f.* **to s. light on,** echar luz sobre, iluminar

**sheen** /ʃin/ *n* lustre, *m;* brillo, *m*

**sheep** /ʃip/ *n* oveja, *f;* carnero, *m;* ganado lanar, *m.* **He is the black s. of the family,** Es el garbanzo negro de la familia. **to cast sheep's eyes at,** lanzar miradas de carnero degollado. **s. breeder,** ganadero, *m.* **s.-dip,** desinfectante para ganado, *m.* **s.-dog,** perro de pastor, *m.* **s.-like,** ovejuno, de oveja. **s.-shearing,** esquileo, *m*

**sheepfold** /'ʃip,fould/ *n* aprisco, redil, *m*

**sheepish** /'ʃipɪʃ/ *a* tímido, vergonzoso; estúpido

**sheepishly** /'ʃipɪʃli/ *adv* tímidamente

**sheepishness** /'ʃipɪʃnɪs/ *n* timidez, cortedad, *f;* estupidez, *f*

**sheepskin** /'ʃip,skɪn/ *n* piel de carnero, *f.* **s. jacket,** zamarra, *f*

**sheer** /ʃɪər/ *a* puro; completo, absoluto; (steep) escarpado, acantilado; a pico; (of fabrics) transparente; ligero, fino. —*adv* completamente; de un golpe; (perpendicularly) a pico. **to s. off,** desviarse; largarse, marcharse

**sheet** /ʃit/ *n* (bed) sábana, *f;* (shroud) mortaja, *f;* (of paper) hoja, *f;* cuartilla, *f;* (pamphlet) folleto, *m;* (news) periódico, *m,* hoja, *f;* (of metal, etc.) lámina, plancha, *f;* (of water, etc.) extensión, *f; naut* escota, *f.* —*vt* poner sábanas en; envolver en sábanas; (a corpse) amortajar. **to be as white as a s.,** estar pálido como un muerto. **s. bend,** (knot) nudo de tejedor, *m.* **s. glass,** vidrio en lámina, *m.* **s. iron,** hierro en planchas, *m*

**sheik** /ʃik/ *n* jeque, *m*

**shekel** /'ʃekəl/ *n* (coin) siclo, *m; pl* **shekels,** dinero, *m*

**shelf** /ʃelf/ *n* estante, anaquel, *m;* (reef) banco de arena, bajío, *m;* (of rock) escalón, *m.* **to be on the s.,** *inf* quedarse para tía, quedarse para vestir imágenes

**shell** /ʃel/ *n* (of small shellfish) concha, *f;* (of tortoise) coraza, *f;* (of insects, lobsters, etc.) caparazón, *m;* (of a nut) cáscara, *f;* (of an egg) cascarón, *m;* (of peas, beans) vaina, *f;* (*com* and *mus*) concha, *f;* (of a building) casco, *m;* (outside) exterior, *m;* (empty form) apariencia, *f; mil* granada, *f.* —*vt* pelar; (nuts) descascarar; (beans, etc.) desvainar; *mil* bombardear. **to be under s.-fire,** sufrir un bombardeo. **s. shock,** neurosis de guerra, *f*

**shellfish** /'ʃel,fɪʃ/ *n* crustáceo, *m;* (as food) marisco, *m*

**shelling** /'ʃelɪŋ/ *n mil* bombardeo, *m*

**shelter** /'ʃeltər/ *n* abrigo, amparo, *m;* refugio, *m;* asilo, *m.* —*vt* dar asilo (a); abrigar; (defend) amparar, proteger; (hide) esconder. —*vi* refugiarse resguardarse; esconderse

**sheltered** /'ʃeltərd/ *a* abrigado

**sheltering** /'ʃeltərɪŋ/ *a* protector

**shelve** /ʃelv/ *vt* (books) poner en un estante; (persons) destituir; (questions, etc.) aplazar, arrinconar; proveer de estantes, *vi* (slope) inclinarse, formar declive; (of sea bed) formar escalones

**shelving** /'ʃelvɪŋ/ *a* inclinado; (of ocean bed) acantilado

**shepherd** /'ʃepərd/ *n* pastor, *m.* —*vt* guardar; guiar, conducir. **s. boy,** zagal, *m.* **shepherd's pouch,** zurrón, *m*

**shepherdess** /'ʃepərdɪs/ *n* pastora, *f*

**sherbet** /'ʃɜrbɪt/ *n* sorbete, *m*

**sheriff** /'ʃerɪf/ *n* (in U.K.) sheriff, *m;* (U.S.A.) jefe de la policía, *m*

**sherry** /'ʃeri/ *n* (vino de) jerez, *m.* **dry s.,** jerez seco, *m*

**Shetlands, the** /'ʃetləndz/ las Islas de Shetland, *f pl*

**shield** /ʃild/ *n* escudo, *m;* (round) rodela, *f; herald* escudo de armas, *m; fig* defensa, *f,* amparo, *m.* —*vt* proteger, amparar. **to s. a person,** proteger a una persona. **to s. one's eyes from the sun,** proteger los ojos del sol. **s.-bearer,** escudero, *m*

**shift** /ʃift/ *vt* mover; trasladar; quitar, librarse de; cambiar. —*vi* moverse; (of the wind) girar; cambiar. —*n* cambio, *m;* (expedient) recurso, expediente, *m;* (dodge) artificio, *m,* trampa, *f;* (of workmen) tanda, *f,* turno, *m.* **to make s.,** arreglárselas (para hacer algo); procurar (hacer algo); (manage) ir tirando. **to s. for oneself,** componérselas, arreglárselas. **to s. the scenes,** *theat* cambiar de decoración. **to s. the helm,** *naut* cambiar el timón. **to work in shifts,** trabajar por turnos

**shiftiness** /'ʃɪftɪnɪs/ *n* falta de honradez, informalidad, *f;* astucia, *f*

**shifting** /'ʃɪftɪŋ/ *a* (of light, etc.) cambiante; (of sand, etc.) movedizo; (of wind) mudable; (of moods) voluble. **s. sand,** arena movediza, *f*

**shiftless** /'ʃɪftlɪs/ *a* perezoso; sin energía, ineficaz

**shiftlessness** /'ʃɪftlɪsnɪs/ *n* pereza, *f;* falta de energía, *f*

**shifty** /'ʃɪfti/ *a* (tricky) tramposo, astuto; (dishonest) informal, falso; (of gaze) furtivo. **s.-eyed,** *a* de mirada furtiva

**Shiite** /'ʃiait/ *a* and *n* chiíta

**shilling** /'ʃɪlɪŋ/ *n* chelín, *m.* **nine shillings in the £,** nueve chelines por libra. **to cut off with a s.,** desheredar

**shilly shally** /'ʃɪli ʃæli/ *n* irresolución, vacilación, *f, vi* estar irresoluto, titubear, no saber qué hacer

**shimmer** /'ʃɪmər/ *vi* rielar; relucir. —*n* luz trémula, *f;* resplandor, *m;* viso, *m*

**shin** /ʃɪn/ *n* espinilla, *f;* (of beef) corvejón, *m.* **to s. up,** trepar

**shindy** /'ʃɪndi/ *n* suiza, reyerta, tasquera, *f.* **to kick up a s.,** armar camorra

**shine** /ʃain/ *vi* brillar; resplandecer, relucir, relumbrar. —*vt* (shoes) dar lustre (a). —*n* brillo, *m;* lustre, *m.* **in rain or s.,** en buen o mal tiempo. **to s. with happiness,** radiar felicidad. **to take the s. out of,** eclipsar

**shingle** /'ʃɪŋgəl/ *n* (pebbles) guijarros, *m pl;* cascajo, *m;* barda, *f;* (hair) pelo a la garçonne, *m;* **pl shingles,** *med* zona, *f,* herpe zóster, *m.* —*vt* (the hair) cortar a la garçonne

**shining** /'ʃainɪŋ/ *a* resplandeciente, brillante, reluciente; radiante. **s. with happiness,** radiante de felicidad. **s. example,** ejemplo notable, *m*

**shintoism** /'ʃɪntou,ɪzəm/ *n* sintoísmo, *m*

**shiny** /'ʃaini/ *a* brillante; lustroso, terso; (of trousers, etc.) reluciente; (of paper) glaseado

**ship** /ʃɪp/ *n* buque, barco, *m;* (sailing) velero, *m.* —*vt* embarcar; (oars) armar. —*vi* embarcar; (as a member of crew) embarcarse. **on board s.,** a bordo. **to s. a sea,** embarcar agua. **to take s.,** embarcar. **to s. off,** mandar. **ship's boat,** lancha, *f.* **ship's boy,** grumete, *m.* **ship's carpenter,** carpintero de ribera, *m.* **ship's company,** tripulación, *f.* **s.-breaker,** desguazador, *m.* **s.-canal,** canal de navegación, *m.* **s.-load,** cargamento, *m*

**shipbuilder** /'ʃɪp,bɪldər/ *n* constructor de buques, arquitecto naval, *m*

**shipbuilding** /'ʃɪp,bɪldɪŋ/ *n* construcción naval, *f*

**shipment** /'ʃɪpmənt/ *n* embarque, *m;* despacho por mar, *m;* (consignment) remesa, *f*

**shipowner** /'ʃɪp,ounər/ *n* naviero, *m*

**shipper** /'ʃɪpər/ *n* naviero, *m;* importador, *m;* exportador, *m*

**shipping** /'ʃɪpɪŋ/ *n* embarque, *m;* buques, barcos, *m pl;* (of a country) marina, *f.* **s. agent,** consignatario de buques, *m.* **s. company,** compañía de navegación, *f.* **s. offices,** oficinas de una compañía de navegación, *f pl*

**shipshape** /'ʃɪp,ʃeip/ *a* en buen orden; bien arreglado

**shipwreck** /'ʃɪp,rek/ *n* naufragio, *m, vt* hacer naufragar, echar a pique

**shipwrecked person** /'ʃɪp,rɛkt/ n náufrago (-ga). **to be shipwrecked,** naufragar

**shipyard** /'ʃɪp,yɑrd/ n astillero, varadero, m

**shire** /ʃaɪər/ n condado, m

**shirk** /ʃɜrk/ vt eludir, esquivar; desentenderse de. —vi faltar al deber

**shirker** /'ʃɜrkər/ n gandul (-la); persona que no cumple con su deber, f

**shirr** /ʃɜr/ vt fruncir

**shirt** /ʃɜrt/ n camisa, f. **dress s.,** camisa de pechera dura, f. **hair-s.,** cilicio, m. **in one's s.-sleeves,** en mangas de camisa. **s.-blouse,** blusa sencilla, f. **s.-collar,** cuello de camisa, m. **s. factory** or **shop,** camisería, f. **shirt-front,** pechera, f. **s.-maker,** camisero (-ra)

**shirting** /'ʃɜrtɪŋ/ n tela para camisas, f

**shiver** /'ʃɪvər/ vi temblar, tiritar; dar diente con diente; (of a boat) zozobrar. —vt (break) hacer añicos, romper; (sails) sacudir. —n temblor, estremecimiento, m; escalofrío, m; (of glass, etc.) fragmento, m, astilla, f. **You give me the shivers,** Me das escalofríos

**shivery** /'ʃɪvəri/ a tembloroso; friolero. **I feel s.,** Tengo escalofríos

**shoal** /ʃoul/ n (of fish) banco, m; gran cantidad, f; (of people) multitud, muchedumbre, f; (water) bajo fondo, m; (sand-bank) banco, bajío, m, a poco profundo. **I know shoals of people in Valencia,** Conozco a muchísima gente de Valencia

**shock** /ʃɒk/ n choque, m; elec conmoción, f; med shock, m; (med stroke) conmoción cerebral, f; (fright) sobresalto, susto, m. —vt sacudir, dar una sacudida (a); chocar; escandalizar, horrorizar. —vi chocar. **electric s.,** conmoción eléctrica, f. **She is easily shocked,** Ella se escandaliza fácilmente. **s. of hair,** mata de pelo, f. **s. absorber,** ech amortiguador, m; auto amortiguador (de los muelles), m. **s. troops,** tropas de asalto, f pl, elementos de choque, m pl

**shocking** /'ʃɒkɪŋ/ a escandaloso; repugnante, horrible; espantoso. **How s.!** ¡Qué horror! **s. bad,** malísimo

**shockingly** /'ʃɒkɪŋli/ adv horriblemente

**shod** /ʃɒd/ a calzado; (of horses) herrado

**shoddy** /'ʃɒdi/ n pacotilla, f. —a de pacotilla; espurio, falso

**shoe** /ʃu/ n zapato, m; (horse) herradura, f; (naut mech) zapata, f. —vt (horses) herrar. **I should not like to be in his shoes,** No me gustaría estar en su pellejo. **That is quite another pair of shoes,** Eso es harina de otro costal. **to cast a s.,** (of horses) desherrarse, perder una herradura. **to put on one's shoes,** ponerse los zapatos, calzarse. **to remove one's shoes,** quitarse los zapatos, descalzarse. **wooden shoes,** zuecos, m pl. **s.-buckle,** hebilla de zapato, f. **s.-lace,** cordón de zapato, m. **s.-leather,** cuero para zapatos, m; calzado, m. **s.-scraper,** limpiabarros, m, estregadera, f. **s.-shop,** zapatería, f

**shoeblack** /'ʃu,blæk/ n betún, m; (person) limpiabotas, m

**shoehorn** /'ʃu,hɔrn/ n calzador, m

**shoemaker** /'ʃu,meɪkər/ n zapatero (-ra)

**shoemaking** /'ʃu,meɪkɪŋ/ n fabricación de calzado, zapatería, f

**shoo!** /ʃu/ interj ¡fuera!; ¡zape! —vt ahuyentar

**shoot** /ʃut/ vt (throw) lanzar; precipitar; (empty) vaciar; (a rapid) salvar; (a river, etc.) echar; (an arrow, a gun, etc.) disparar; (a person, etc.) pegar un tiro (a); sports tirar; mil fusilar, pasar por las armas; (a film) hacer, impresionar. —vi lanzarse, precipitarse; (of pain) latir; (sprout) brotar; disparar; tirar; (at football) tirar a gol, chutar. **to s. a glance at,** lanzar una mirada (a). **I was shot in the foot,** Una bala me hirió en el pie. **to s. the sun,** naut tomar el sol. **to s. ahead,** tomar la delantera. **to s. at,** tirar a. **to s by,** pasar como una bala. **to s. down,** aer derribar; matar de un tiro. **to s. up,** (of children) espigarse; (of prices) subir mucho; (of cliffs, etc.) elevarse

**shoot** /ʃut/ n partida de caza, f; tiro, m; bot renuevo, retoño, m

**shooting** /'ʃutɪŋ/ n tiro, m; caza con escopeta, f; (of guns) tiroteo, m; (of an arrow) disparo, m; (of a film) rodaje, m. **to go s.,** ir a cazar con escopeta. **s.-box,**

pabellón de caza, m. **s. butts,** tiradero, m. **s. dog,** perro de caza, m. **s.-gallery,** tiro al blanco, m. **s. match,** concurso de tiro, m. **s. pain,** punzada de dolor, f. **s. party,** partida de caza, f. **s. practice,** ejercicios de tiro, m pl. **s.-range,** campo de tiro, m. **s. star,** estrella fugaz, f

**shop** /ʃɒp/ n tienda, f; (workshop) taller, m. —vi ir de compras, ir de tiendas; comprar. **to talk s.,** hablar de negocios. **s.-assistant,** dependiente (-ta). **s.-soiled,** deslucido. **s.-steward,** representante de los obreros de una fábrica o taller, m. **s. window,** escaparate, m

**shopkeeper** /'ʃɒp,kipər/ n tendero (-ra)

**shoplifter** /'ʃɒp,lɪftər/ n ladrón (-ona) de tiendas, ratero (-ra) de las tiendas

**shoplifting** /'ʃɒp,lɪftɪŋ/ n ratería en las tiendas, f

**shopper** /'ʃɒpər/ n comprador (-ra)

**shopping** /'ʃɒpɪŋ/ n compra, f; compras, f pl. **to go s.,** ir de compras. **s. basket,** cesta para compras, f. **s. center,** centro comercial, m

**shopwalker** /'ʃɒp,wɔkər/ n jefe de recepción, m

**shore** /ʃɔr/ n orilla, ribera, f; costa, f; (sands) playa, f. **off s.,** en alta mar. **on s.,** en tierra. **to come on s.,** desembarcar. **to s. up,** apuntalar, acodalar; fig apoyar

**short** /ʃɔrt/ a corto; (of persons) bajo; breve; (of temper) vivo; insuficiente; distante (de); (brusque) seco; (of money) alcanzado. —adv súbitamente; brevemente. —n (vowel) vocal breve, m; pl **shorts,** calzones cortos, m pl. **for s.,** para mayor brevedad. **for a s. time,** por poco tiempo. **in a s. time,** dentro de poco. **in s.,** en breve, en resumen, en pocas palabras. **on s. notice,** con poco tiempo de aviso. **s. of,** con la excepción de, menos. **to be s.,** faltar, ser escaso. **to be s. with someone,** tratar con sequedad (a). **to fall s. of expectations,** no cumplir las esperanzas. **to go s. of,** pasarse sin. **to grow s.,** escasear. **s.-circuit,** corto circuito, m. **s. cut,** atajo, m. **s.-haired,** pelicorto. **s.-handed,** falto de mano de obra. **s.-lived,** de vida corta; efímero, fugaz. **to be short-lived,** tener vida corta. **s.-sighted,** corto de vista. **s.-sightedness,** miopía, cortedad de vista, f. **s. story,** cuento, m. **s.-tempered,** irascible, irritable, de genio vivo. **s.-waisted,** corto de talle, m. **s.-winded,** corto de resuello; asmático

**shortage** /'ʃɔrtɪdʒ/ n falta, escasez, f; carestía, f. **water s.,** carestía de agua, f

**shortcoming** /'ʃɔrt,kʌmɪŋ/ n defecto, m; imperfección, f

**shorten** /'ʃɔrtn/ vt acortar; reducir, disminuir; abreviar. —vi acortarse

**shorthand** /'ʃɔrt,hænd/ n taquigrafía, estenografía, f. —a taquigráfico, estenográfico. **to take down in s.,** taquigrafiar. **s. writer,** estenógrafo (-fa); taquígrafo (-fa)

**shortly** /'ʃɔrtli/ adv dentro de poco, pronto; brevemente, en resumen, en pocas palabras; (curtly) bruscamente, secamente

**shortness** /'ʃɔrtnɪs/ n cortedad, f; brevedad, f; (of a person) pequeñez, f; (lack) falta, f; (of memory, sight) cortedad, f; (brusqueness) sequedad, brusquedad, f. **s. of breath,** falta de aliento, respiración difícil, f

**shot** /ʃɒt/ n perdigón, m; inf perdigones, m pl; bala, f; (firing) tiro, m; (person) tirador (-ra); (stroke, etc.) golpe, m; tirada, f; (cinema) fotograma, m. —a (of silk) tornasolado. **at one s.,** de un tiro. **like a s.,** fig como una bala. **to exchange shots,** tirotearse. **to fire a s.,** disparar un tiro. **to have a s. at,** probar suerte. **s.-gun,** escopeta, f. **s. silk,** seda tornasolada, f

**should** /ʃʊd/ v aux (expressing future) **I s. like to go to the sea,** Me gustaría ir al mar; (expressing conditional) **I s. like to see them if I could,** Me gustaría verlos si pudiera; (expressing obligation) **You s. go at once,** Debes ir en seguida; (expressing probability) **They s. arrive tomorrow,** Seguramente llegarán mañana; (expressing doubt) **If the moment s. be opportune,** Si el momento fuera oportuno. **I s. just think so!** ¡Ya lo creo! ¡No lo dudo!

**shoulder** /'ʃouldər/ n hombro, m; (of mutton) espalda, f; (of a hill) falda, f. —vt cargar al hombro, echar sobre sí; (a responsibility) cargar con, hacerse responsable para; (jostle) dar codazos (a). **s. to s.,** hombro a hombro. **S. arms!** ¡Armas al hombro! **s.-**

**blade,** omoplato, *m.* **s.-knot,** charretera, *f.* **s.-pad,** hombrera, *f.* **s.-strap,** *mil* dragona, *f;* (of a dress, etc.) tirante, *m;* (of a water carrier, etc.) correón, *m*

**shouldered** /'ʃouldərd/ *a* de hombros..., de espaldas... **round-s.,** cargado de espaldas

**shout** /ʃaut/ *vi* gritar, hablar a gritos. —*vt* gritar. —*n* grito, *m.* **shouts of applause,** aclamaciones, *f pl,* aplausos, *m pl.* **to s. from the housetops,** pregonar a los cuatro vientos. **to s. with laughter,** reírse a carcajadas. **to s. down,** silbar. **to s. out,** gritar

**shouting** /'ʃautɪŋ/ *n* gritos, *m pl,* vocerío, clamor, *m;* (applause) aclamaciones, *f pl*

**shove** /ʃʌv/ *vt* empujar; poner. —*n* empujón, *m.* **to s. along,** empujar. **to s. aside,** empujar a un lado; apartar a codazos. **to s. away,** rechazar. **to s. back,** hacer retroceder. **to s. forward,** hacer avanzar, empujar hacia adelante. **to s. off,** (a boat) echar afuera. **to s. out,** empujar hacia fuera

**shovel** /'ʃʌvəl/ *n* pala, *f.* —*vt* traspalar. **s. hat,** sombrero de teja, *m*

**show** /ʃou/ *vt* mostrar; hacer ver; (disclose) descubrir; revelar; (exhibit) exhibir; (indicate) indicar; (prove) demostrar, probar; (conduct) conducir, llevar, guiar; (explain) explicar; (oneself) presentarse. —*vi* mostrarse; verse; parecer. **to s. cause,** mostrar causa. **to s. fight,** ofrecer resistencia. **s. signs of,** dar señales de. **to s. itself,** declararse, asomarse, surgir. **to s. to the door,** acompañar a la puerta. **to s. in,** (a person) hacer entrar, introducir (en). **to s. off,** *vt* exhibir; realzar; (new clothes, etc.) lucir. —*vi* darse importancia; pavonearse. **to s. out,** (a person) acompañar a la puerta; (in anger) poner de patitas en la calle. **to s. through,** *vi* trasparentarse. —*vt* conducir por. **to s. up,** *vt* invitar a subir; (a fraud, etc.) descubrir; (a swindler) desenmascarar; (defects) revelar. —*vi* (stand out) destacarse; (be present) asomarse, asistir

**show** /ʃou/ *n* (exhibition) exposición, *f;* espectáculo, *m;* (sign) indicio, *m,* señal, *f;* (ostentation) pompa, *f,* aparato, *m,* ostentación, *f;* (appearance) apariencia, *f;* (affair) negocio, *m.* **to give the s. away,** echar los títeres a rodar. **to make a s. of,** hacer gala de. **s.-case,** escaparate, *m,* vitrina, *f.* **s. of hands,** votación por manos levantadas, *f.* **s.-room,** salón de muestras, *m*

**showdown** /'ʃou,daun/ *n* cartas boca arriba, *m*

**shower** /'ʃauər/ *n* chaparrón, chubasco, *m;* (of spray, etc.) chorro, *m;* (of stones, arrows, etc.) lluvia, *f;* (of honors) cosecha, *f,* (bridal) despedida de soltera, despedida de soltería, *f.* —*vt* derramar; rociar; mojar; llover. —*vi* chaparrear, llover. **s.-bath,** ducha, *f*

**shower cap** *n* gorro de ducha, *m*

**showery** /'ʃauəri/ *a* lluvioso

**showily** /'ʃouəli/ *adv* aparatosamente, con ostentación

**showiness** /'ʃouɪnɪs/ *n* ostentación, *f;* esplendor, *m,* magnificencia, *f*

**showman** /'ʃoumən/ *n* director de un espectáculo de feria, *m;* titiritero, *m;* pregonero, *m*

**showy** /'ʃoui/ *a* vistoso; ostentoso

**shrapnel** /'ʃræpnl/ *n* granada, *m,* granada de metralla, *f*

**shred** /ʃred/ *n* fragmento, *m;* (of cloth) jirón, *m;* brizna, *f;* *fig* pizca, *f.* —*vt* desmenuzar. **to tear in shreds,** hacer pedazos

**shrew** /ʃru/ *n* *zool* musaraña, *f;* (woman) fiera, *f*

**shrewd** /ʃrud/ *a* sagaz, perspicaz; prudente; (of the wind) penetrante; (pain) punzante. **to have a s. idea of,** tener una buena idea de. **a s. diplomat,** un fino diplomático

**shrewdly** /'ʃrudli/ *adv* sagazmente, con perspicacia; prudentemente

**shrewdness** /'ʃrudnɪs/ *n* sagacidad, perspicacia, *f;* prudencia, *f*

**shrewish** /'ʃruɪʃ/ *a* regañón

**shrewishness** /'ʃruɪʃnɪs/ *n* mal genio, *m*

**shriek** /ʃrik/ *vi* chillar, gritar. —*vt* decir a voces, gritar. —*n* chillido, *m;* grito agudo, *m.* **shrieks of laughter,** carcajadas, *f pl*

**shrieking** /'ʃrikɪŋ/ *n* gritos, chillidos, *m pl*

**shrift** /ʃrɪft/ **to give short,** enviar normala (a), enviar a paseo (a)

**shrill** /ʃrɪl/ *a* estridente, agudo

**shrillness** /'ʃrɪlnɪs/ *n* estridencia, *f*

**shrimp** /ʃrɪmp/ *n* camarón, *m,* gamba, *f,* *vi* pescar camarones

**shrine** /ʃrain/ *n* relicario, *m;* sepulcro de santo, *m;* templete, *m,* capilla, *f;* santuario, *m*

**shrink** /ʃrɪŋk/ *vi* encogerse; contraerse; disminuir, reducirse. —*vt* encoger; reducir, disminuir; desaparecer; disiparse. **I shrank from doing it,** Me repugnaba hacerlo. **to s. away from,** retroceder ante; recular ante; huir de. **to s. back,** recular (ante)

**shrinkage** /'ʃrɪŋkɪdʒ/ *n* encogimiento, *m;* contracción, *f;* reducción, disminución, *f*

**shrinking** /'ʃrɪŋkɪŋ/ *a* tímido

**shrive** /ʃraiv/ *vt* confesar

**shrivel** /'ʃrɪvəl/ *vi* avellanarse; (of persons, through old age) acartonarse, apergaminarse; (wither) marchitarse; arrugarse. —*vt* arrugar; secar, marchitar

**shroud** /ʃraud/ *n* sudario, *m,* mortaja, *f;* *Naut.* obenque, *m.* **to wrap in a s.,** amortajar

**Shrove Tuesday** /ʃrouv/ *n* martes de carnaval, *m*

**shrub** /ʃrʌb/ *n* arbusto, *m;* matajo, *m*

**shrubbery** /'ʃrʌbəri/ *n* arbustos, *m pl,* maleza, *f;* bosquecillo, *m*

**shrug** /ʃrʌg/ *vi* encogerse de hombros. —*n* encogimiento de hombros, *m*

**shrunken** /'ʃrʌŋkən/ *a* contraído; acartonado, apergaminado; seco, marchito. **shrunken head,** cabeza reducida, *f*

**shudder** /'ʃʌdər/ *vi* estremecerse; vibrar. —*n* estremecimiento, *m;* escalofrío, *m;* (of an engine, etc.) vibración, *f*

**shuffle** /'ʃʌfəl/ *vt* (the feet) arrastrar; (scrape) restregar; (cards) barajar; (papers) mezclar. —*vi* arrastrar los pies, arrastrarse; (cards) barajar; *fig* tergiversar. —*n* (of the cards) barajadura, *f; fig* evasiva, *f;* embuste, *m.* **to s. along,** andar arrastrando los pies

**shuffling** /'ʃʌflɪŋ/ *n* el arrastrar, *m,* (e.g. *the shuffling of chairs,* el arrastrar de sillas)

**shun** /ʃʌn/ *vt* evitar, rehuir, esquivar

**shunt** /ʃʌnt/ *vt* *rail* apartar; *elec* shuntar. —*vi* *rail* hacer maniobras

**shunting** /'ʃʌntɪŋ/ *n* (of trains) maniobras, *f pl*

**shut** /ʃʌt/ *vt* and *vi* cerrar. **to s. again,** volver a cerrar. **to s. down,** *vt* cerrar; (a machine) parar. —*vi* (of factories, etc.) cerrar. **to s. in,** encerrar; (surround) cercar, rodear. **to s. off,** (water, etc.) cortar; (isolate) aislar (de). **to s. out,** excluir; obstruir, impedir; negar la entrada (a). **to s. up,** *vt* cerrar; encerrar; *inf* hacer callar (a); *vi inf* callarse, cerrar la boca. **to s. oneself up,** encerrarse

**shutter** /'ʃʌtər/ *n* (window) contraventana, *f,* postigo, *m;* (of a camera) obturador, *m;* (of a fireplace) campana (de hogar), *f.* —*vt* poner contraventanas (a); cerrar los postigos de

**shuttle** /'ʃʌtl/ *n* (weaver's, and sewing-machine) lanzadera, *f,* (airplane service) puente aéreo, *m.* **s.-cock,** volante, gallito, *m*

**shy** /ʃai/ *a* (of animals) tímido, salvaje; (of persons) huraño, tímido; vergonzoso. —*vi* (of a horse) respingar; (of persons) asustarse (de). —*vt* (a ball, etc.) lanzar. —*n* (of a horse) respingo, *m;* (of a ball) lanzamiento, *m;* (try) prueba, tentativa, *f.* **to fight shy of,** procurar evitar. **to have a shy at,** probar

**shyly** /'ʃaili/ *adv* tímidamente; con vergüenza, vergonzosamente

**shyness** /'ʃainɪs/ *n* timidez, *f;* huraña, *f;* vergüenza, *f*

**Siamese** /,saiə'miz/ *a* siamés. —*n* siamés (-esa); (language) siamés, *m.* **S. cat,** gato siamés, *m*

**Siberia** /sai'bɪəriə/ Siberia, *f*

**Siberian** /sai'bɪəriən/ *a* and *n* siberiano (-na)

**sic** /sɪk/ *vt* atacar; abijar, azuzar (a dog); *adv* así (in academic prose)

**Sicilian** /sɪ'sɪlyən/ *a* and *n* siciliano (-na)

**Sicily** /'sɪsəli/ Sicilia, *f*

**sick** /sɪk/ *a* enfermo; mareado. **the s.,** los enfermos. **to be s.,** vomitar; estar enfermo. **to be s. of,** estar harto de. **to feel s.,** sentirse mareado. **to be on the s.-list,** estar enfermo. **s.-bed,** lecho de dolor, *m.* **s.-headache,** jaqueca, con náuseas, *f.* **s.-leave,** *mil* permiso por enfermedad, *m.* **s.-nurse,** enfermera, *f*

**sicken** /'sɪkən/ *vi* caer enfermo, enfermar; (feel sick) marearse; (recoil from) repugnar; (weary of) cansarse (de), aburrirse (de). —*vt* marear; dar asco (a), repugnar; cansar, aburrir. **It sickens me,** Me da asco. **He is sickening for measles,** Muestra síntomas de sarampión

**sickening** /'sɪkənɪŋ/ *a* nauseabundo; repugnante; (tedious) fastidioso

**sickle** /'sɪkəl/ *n* hoz, segadera, *f*

**sickliness** /'sɪklinɪs/ *n* falta de salud, *f;* náusea, *f;* (paleness) palidez, *f*

**sickly** /'sɪkli/ *a* enfermizo, achacoso, malucho; (of places, etc.) malsano; (pale) pálido; débil; (of a smell) nauseabundo; (mawkish) empalagoso

**sickness** /'sɪknɪs/ *n* enfermedad, *f;* mal, *m;* náusea, *f,* mareo, *m*

**side** /said/ *n* lado, *m;* (hand) mano, *f;* (of a river, etc.) orilla, *f,* margen, *m;* (of a person) costado, *m;* (of an animal) ijada, *f;* (of a hill) falda, pendiente, ladera, *f;* (of a ship) banda, *f,* costado, *m;* (aspect) aspecto, *m;* punto de vista, *m;* (party) partido, grupo, *m;* (team) equipo, *m;* (of descent) lado, *m.* —*a* lateral, de lado; oblicuo. **on all sides,** por todas partes. **on both sides,** por ambos lados. **s. by s.,** lado a lado. **the other s. of the picture,** el revés de la medalla. **to change sides,** cambiar de partido. **to pick sides,** escoger el equipo. **to put on s.,** darse tono, alzar el gallo. **to split one's sides,** desternillarse de risa, reírse a carcajadas. **to s. with,** declararse por, ponerse al lado de, tomar el partido de. **wrong s. out,** al revés. **s.-car,** sidecar, asiento lateral, *m.* **s.-chain,** *chem* cadena lateral, *f.* **s.-dish,** entremés, *m.* **s. door,** puerta lateral, *f.* **s.-face,** *a* de perfil. —*n* perfil, *m.* **s.-glance,** mirada de soslayo, *f.* **s.-issue,** cuestión secundaria, *f.* **s.-line,** negocio accesorio, *m;* ocupación secundaria, *f; rail* vía secundaria, *f.* **s.-saddle,** silla de señora, silla de montar de lado, *f.* **s.-show,** (at a fair) barraca, *f,* puesto de feria, *m;* exhibición secundaria, *f;* función secundaria, *f.* **s.-table,** trinchero, *m.* **s.-track,** *n rail* apartadero, *m.* —*vt* desviar (de), apartar (de). **s.-view,** perfil, *m.* **s.-walk,** acera, *f.* **s.-whiskers,** patillas, *f pl*

**sidelight** /'said,lait/ *n* luz lateral, *f;* (on a ship) ojo de buey, *m; fig* información incidental, *f*

**sidelong** /'said,lɔŋ/ *adv* de lado, lateralmente; (of glances) oblicuo. —*a* oblicuo

**side road** *n* camino lateral, *m*

**sideways** /'said,weiz/ *adv* oblicuamente, de lado; (edgewise) de soslayo. —*a* de soslayo

**siding** /'saidɪŋ/ *n rail* apartadero, *m*

**sidle** /'saidl/ *vi* andar (or ir) de lado. **to s. up to,** acercarse servilmente a; arrimarse (a)

**siege** /sidʒ/ *n* asedio, sitio, cerco, *m.* **to lay s. to,** poner cerco (a), sitiar, asediar cercar. **to raise a s.,** levantar un sitio

**sienna** /si'ɛnə/ *n* tierra de siena natural, *f.* **burnt s.,** tierra de siena tostada, *f*

**sieve** /sɪv/ *n* cedazo, tamiz, *m,* criba, *f, vt* tamizar, cerner, cribar

**sift** /sɪft/ *vt* (sieve) cerner, cribar; (sugar, etc.) salpicar (con); (a question) escudriñar, examinar minuciosamente

**sifting** /'sɪftɪŋ/ *n* cribado, *m;* (of a question) investigación minuciosa, *f; pl* **siftings,** cerniduras, *f pl*

**sigh** /sai/ *vi* suspirar; (of the wind) susurrar. —*n* suspiro, *m;* (of the wind) susurro, *m.* **to s. for,** suspirar por; lamentar

**sighing** /'saiɪŋ/ *n* suspiros, *m pl;* (of the wind) susurro, *m*

**sight** /sait/ *n* vista, *f;* visión, *f;* espectáculo, *m;* (fright) estantigua, *f.* —*vt* ver, divisar; (aim) apuntar. **front s.,** (of guns) alza, *f.* **short s.,** (of eyes) vista corta, *f.* **at first s.,** a primera vista. **in s.,** a la vista. **in s. of,** a vista de. **out of s.,** que no está a la vista; perdido de vista. **Out of s., out of mind,** Ojos que no ven, corazón que no siente. **to be lost to s.,** perderse de vista. **to lose s. of,** perder de vista (a). **to catch a s. of,** vislumbrar. **to come in s.,** aparecer, asomarse. **to know by s.,** conocer de vista (a). **s.-reading,** lectura a primera vista, *f*

**sightly** /'saitli/ *a* hermoso; deleitable

**sightseeing** /'sait,siɪŋ/ *n* turismo, *m.* **to go s.,** visitar los monumentos, ver los puntos de interés

**sightseer** /'sait,siər/ *n* curioso (-sa); turista, *mf*

**sign** /sain/ *n* señal, *f;* seña, *f;* indicio, *m;* (of the zo-

diac and *mus*) signo, *m;* marca, *f; eccl* símbolo, *m;* (of a shop, etc.) muestra, *f,* rótulo, *m;* (symptom) síntoma, *m.* —*vt* firmar; indicar; *eccl* persignar. **as a s. of,** en señal de. **to converse by signs,** hablar por señas. **to make the s. of the cross over,** santiguar. **to show signs (of),** dar señas (de); indicar. **s.-painter,** pintor de muestras, *m*

**signal** /'sɪgnl/ *n* señal, *f.* —*vt* señalar; hacer señas (a). —*vi* hacer señales. —*a* insigne, notable. **fog-s.,** señal de niebla, *f.* **landing s.,** *aer* señal de aterrizaje, *f.* **to give the s. for,** dar la señal para. **s.-box,** garita de señales, *f.* **s. code,** *naut* código de señales, *m*

**signaler** /'sɪgnlər/ *n* señalador, *m*

**signalize** /'sɪgnl,aiz/ *vt* señalar, distinguir

**signalman** /'sɪgnlmən/ *n rail* guardavía, *m*

**signatory** /'sɪgnə,tɔri/ *a* and *n* signatario (-ia)

**signature** /'sɪgnətʃər/ *n* firma, *f;* (*mus* and *print*) signatura, *f*

**signboard** /'sain,bɔrd/ *n* letrero, *m,* muestra, *f*

**signet** /'sɪgnɪt/ *n* sello, *m.* **s.-ring,** anillo de sello, *m*

**significance** /sɪg'nɪfɪkəns/ *n* significación, *f,* significado, *m;* importancia, *f*

**significant** /sɪg'nɪfɪkənt/ *a* significativo, significante; expresivo; importante

**significantly** /sɪg'nɪfɪkəntli/ *adv* significativamente; expresivamente

**signify** /'sɪgnə,fai/ *vt* significar; querer decir; importar. —*vi* importar, tener importancia; importar

**signpost** /'sain,poust/ *n* indicador de dirección, *m*

**Sikh** /sik/ *n* sik, *mf* (*pl* siks)

**silage** /'sailɪdʒ/ *n* forraje conservado en silo, *m*

**silence** /'sailəns/ *n* silencio, *m, interj* ¡silencio! —*vt* hacer callar, imponer silencio (a); silenciar. **to keep s.,** guardar silencio, callarse. **to pass over in s.,** pasar en silencio (por), pasar por alto de. **S. gives consent,** Quien calla otorga

**silencer** /'sailənsər/ *n* (of fire-arms) silencioso, *m; auto* silenciador, silencioso, *m*

**silent** /'sailənt/ *a* silencioso. **to become s.,** enmudecer; callar. **to remain s.,** callarse, guardar silencio; permanecer silencioso. **s. partner,** *n* socio (-ia) comanditario (-ia)

**silent film** *n* película muda, *f*

**silently** /'sailəntli/ *adv* silenciosamente, en silencio

**silhouette** /,sɪlu'et/ *n* silueta, *f.* —*vt* representar en silueta; destacar. **in s.,** en silueta. **to be silhouetted against the sky,** destacarse contra el sielo

**silica** /'sɪlɪkə/ *n* sílice, *f*

**silk** /sɪlk/ *n* seda, *f,* *a* de seda. **artificial s.,** seda artificial, *f.* **floss s.,** seda ocal, *f.* **sewing s.,** seda de coser, *f.* **twist s.,** seda cordelada, *f.* **as smooth as s.,** como una seda. **s. growing,** sericultura, *f.* **s. hat,** sombrero de copa, *m.* **s. merchandise,** sedería, *f.* **s. stocking,** media de seda, *f*

**silken** /'sɪlkən/ *a* de seda; sedoso

**silkiness** /'sɪlkinɪs/ *n* carácter sedoso, *m;* suavidad, *f*

**silk-screen process** /'sɪlk,skrin/ *n* imprenta por tamiz, imprenta serigráfica, imprenta tamigráfica, impresión con estarcido de seda, *f,* proceso tamigráfico, *m,* serigrafía, tamigrafía, *f*

**silkworm** /'sɪlk,wɜrm/ *n* gusano de seda, *m*

**silky** /'sɪlki/ *a* sedoso; (of wine) suave

**sill** /sɪl/ *n* (of a window) alféizar, antepecho, *m;* (of a door) umbral, *m*

**silliness** /'sɪlinɪs/ *n* tontería, estupidez, *f*

**silly** /'sɪli/ *a* tonto, estúpido; imbécil. —*n* tonto (-ta). **You are a s. ass,** Eres un imbécil

**silo** /'sailou/ *n* silo, *m*

**silt** /sɪlt/ *n* aluvión, *m,* sedimentación, *f.* **to s. up,** *vt* cegar (or obstruir) con aluvión. —*vi* cegarse con aluvión

**silver** /'sɪlvər/ *n* plata, *f.* —*a* de plata; argénteo; (of the voice, etc.) argentino. —*vt* platear; (mirrors) azogar; (hair) blanquear. **s. birch,** abedul, *m.* **s. fox,** zorro plateado, *m.* **s.-gry,** gris perla, *m.* **s.-haired,** de pelo entrecano. **s.-paper,** papel de estaño, *m.* **s.-plate,** *n* vajilla de plata, *f.* —*vt* platear. **s.-tongued,** de pico de oro; de voz argentina. **s. wedding,** bodas de plata, *f pl*

**silversmith** /'sɪlvər,smɪθ/ *n* platero, *m.* **silversmith's shop,** platería, *f*

**silvery** /'sɪlvəri/ *a* plateado, argentado; (of sounds) argentino

**simian** /'sɪmiən/ *a* símico

**similar** /'sɪmələr/ *a* parecido (a), semejante (a); similar; *geom* semejante. **to be s. to,** asemejarse (a), parecerse (a)

**similarity** /ˌsɪmə'lærɪti/ *n* parecido, *m*, semejanza, similitud, *f*

**similarly** /'sɪmələrli/ *adv* de un modo parecido, asimismo

**simile** /'sɪməli/ *n* símil, *m*

**simmer** /'sɪmər/ *vi* hervir a fuego lento; *fig* estar a punto de estallar. **to s. down,** *fig* moderarse poco a poco. **to s. over,** *fig* estallar

**simper** /'sɪmpər/ *vi* sonreírse bobamente

**simpering** /'sɪmpərɪŋ/ *n* sonrisilla tonta, *f*

**simperingly** /'sɪmpərɪŋli/ *adv* con sonrisa necia

**simple** /'sɪmpəl/ *a* sencillo; simple; ingenuo, inocente; crédulo; (humble) humilde; (mere) mero. **s.-hearted,** inocente, cándido, sin malicia. **s.-minded,** ingenuo; crédulo. **s.-mindedness,** ingenuidad, *f*; credulidad, *f*

**simpleton** /'sɪmpəltən/ *n* primo (-ma); papanatas, *m*, tonto (-ta)

**simplicity** /sɪm'plɪsɪti/ *n* sencillez, *f*; simplicidad, candidez, *f*

**simplifiable** /ˌsɪmplə'faiəbəl/ *a* simplificable

**simplification** /ˌsɪmpləfɪ'keɪʃən/ simplificación, *f*

**simplify** /'sɪmpləˌfai/ *vt* simplificar

**simply** /'sɪmpli/ *adv* sencillamente; simplemente, meramente; absolutamente

**simulacrum** /ˌsɪmyə'leikrəm/ *n* simulacro, *m*

**simulate** /'sɪmyəˌleit/ *vt* fingir, aparentar, simular

**simulation** /ˌsɪmyə'leiʃən/ *n* simulación, *f*, fingimiento, *m*

**simultaneous** /ˌsaiməl'teiniəs/ *a* simultáneo

**simultaneously** /ˌsaiməl'teiniəsli/ *adv* simultáneamente; al mismo tiempo (que)

**simultaneousness** /ˌsaiməl'teiniəsnɪs/ *n* simultaneidad, *f*

**sin** /sɪn/ *n* pecado, *m*, *vi* pecar; faltar (a)

**since** /sɪns/ *adv* desde entonces, desde (que). —*prep* desde. —*conjunc* desde que; ya que, puesto que. **a long time s.,** hace mucho. **not long s.,** hace poco. **How long is it s...?** ¿Cuánto tiempo hace que...? **s. then,** desde entonces

**sincere** /sɪn'sɪər/ *a* sincero

**sincerely** /sɪn'sɪərli/ *adv* sinceramente. **Yours s.,** Su afectísimo...

**sincerity** /sɪn'sɛrɪti/ *n* sinceridad, *f*

**sine** /sain/ *n* *math* seno, *m*

**sinecure** /'sainɪˌkyʊr/ *n* canonjía, sinecura, *f*, empleo de aviador (Mexican slang); *m*

**sinew** /'sɪnyu/ *n* tendón, *m*; *pl* **sinews,** nervio, *m*, fuerza, *f*

**sinewy** /'sɪnyui/ *a* (stringy) fibroso; musculoso, nervudo

**sinful** /'sɪnfəl/ *a* (of persons) pecador; (of thoughts, acts) pecaminoso

**sinfulness** /'sɪnfəlnɪs/ *n* pecado, *m*; culpabilidad, perversidad, maldad, *f*

**sing** /sɪŋ/ *vi* cantar; (of the ears) zumbar; (of wind, water) murmurar, susurrar; (of a cat) ronronear. —*vt* cantar. **to s. a child to sleep,** dormir a un niño cantando. **to s. another song,** *inf* bajar el tono. **to s. small,** hacerse el chiquito. **to s. the praises of,** hacer las alabanzas de. **to s. out,** vocear, gritar. **s.-song,** *n* canturía, *f*; concierto improvisado, *m*. —*a* monótono

**Singapore** /'sɪŋgəˌpɔr/ Singapur, *m*

**singe** /sɪndʒ/ *vt* chamuscar; (a fowl) aperdigar; (hair) quemar las puntas de los cabellos

**singer** /'sɪŋər/ *n* cantor (-ra) (professional) cantante, *mf*; (bird) ave cantora, *f*

**singing** /'sɪŋɪŋ/ *n* canto, *m*; (of the ears) zumbido, *m*. —*a* monótono. **s.-bird,** ave cantora, *f*. **s.-master,** maestro de cantar, *m*

**single** /'sɪŋgəl/ *a* único; sencillo; solo; simple; (individual) particular; individual; (unmarried) soltero. —*n* (tennis) juego sencillo, individual, *m*. **in s. file,** de reata. **to s. out,** escoger; singularizar. **s. bed,** cama de monja, *f*. **s. bedroom,** habitación individual, habitación con una sola cama, *f*. **s.-breasted,** (of

coats) recto. **s. combat,** combate singular, *m*. **s. entry,** *Com.* partida simple, *f*. **s.-handed,** de una mano; para una sola persona; sin ayuda, solo, en solitario. **s.-minded,** sin doblez, sincero de una sola idea. **s. ticket,** billete sencillo, *m*

**singleness** /'sɪŋgəlnɪs/ *n* celibato, *m*, soltería, *f*. **with s. of purpose,** con un solo objeto

**singlet** /'sɪŋglɪt/ *n* camiseta, *f*

**singly** /'sɪŋgli/ *adv* separadamente, uno a uno; a solas, solo; sin ayuda

**singular** /'sɪŋgyələr/ *a* and *n* singular, *m*

**singularity** /ˌsɪŋgyə'lærɪti/ *n* singularidad, *f*

**singularly** /'sɪŋgyələrli/ *adv* singularmente

**sinister** /'sɪnəstər/ *a* siniestro

**sink** /sɪŋk/ *vi* ir al fondo; bajar; hundirse; (of ships) irse a pique, naufragar; sumergirse; disminuir; caer (en); penetrar; (of persons, fires) morir; (of the sun, etc.) ponerse. —*vt* (a ship) echar a pique; sumergir; hundir; dejar caer; bajar; (wells) cavar; reducir, disminuir; (invest) invertir; (one's identity, etc.) tener secreto; (differences) olvidar; (engrave) grabar. **My heart sank,** Se me cayeron las alas del corazón. **He sank to his knees,** Cayó de rodillas. **He is sinking fast,** Está en las últimas. **Their words began to s. in,** Sus palabras empezaban a tener efecto (or hacer mella). **I found her sunk in thought,** La encontré ensimismada. **to s. one's voice,** bajar la voz. **to s. down on a chair,** dejarse caer en una silla. **to s. into misery,** caer en la miseria. **to s. under,** (a responsibility, etc.) estar agobiado bajo

**sink** /sɪŋk/ *n* (kitchen) fregadero, *m*; sumidero, *m*, sentina, *f*. **s. of iniquity,** sentina, *f*

**sinker** /'sɪŋkər/ *n* (engraver) grabador (-ra); (of a fishing line) plomada, *f*

**sinking** /'sɪŋkɪŋ/ *n* hundimiento, *m*; (of the sun) puesta, *f*; (of wells) cavadura, *f*; sumergimiento, *m*. **the s. of a boat,** el hundimiento de un buque. **with s. heart,** con la muerte en el alma. **s. fund,** fondo de amortización, *m*

**sinless** /'sɪnlɪs/ *a* sin pecado, inocente, puro

**sinner** /'sɪnər/ *n* pecador (-ra)

**sinuosity** /ˌsɪnyu'ɒsɪti/ *n* sinuosidad, *f*; flexibilidad, agilidad, *f*

**sinuous** /'sɪnyuəs/ *a* sinuoso, tortuoso; flexible, ágil

**sinus** /'sainəs/ *n* (anat etc.) seno, *m*

**sip** /sɪp/ *vt* sorber; (wine) saborear, paladear. —*n* sorbo, *m*

**siphon** /'saifən/ *n* sifón, *m*, *vt* sacar con sifón

**sir** /sər/ *n* señor, *m*; (British title) sir. **Dear s.,** Muy Señor mío

**sire** /sai*ə*r/ *n* (to a monarch) Señor, *m*; (father) padre, *m*; (stallion) semental, *m*. —*vt* procrear, engendrar

**siren** /'sairən/ *n* sirena, *f*. **s. suit,** mono, *m*

**sirloin** /'sərlɔin/ *n* solomillo, *m*

**sirocco** /sə'rɒkou/ *n* siroco, *m*

**sister** /'sɪstər/ *n* hermana, *f*; (before nun's christian name) Sor; (hospital) hermana del hospital, *f*; enfermera, *f*. **s. language,** lengua hermana, *f*. **s. ship,** buque gemelo, *m*. **s.-in-law,** cuñada, hermana política, *f*. **S. of Mercy,** Hermana de la Caridad, *f*

**sisterhood** /'sɪstərˌhʊd/ *n* hermandad, *f*; comunidad de monjas, *f*

**sisterly** /'sɪstərli/ *a* de hermana

**sit** /sɪt/ *vi* sentarse; estar sentado; (of birds) posarse; (of hens) empollar; (in Parliament, etc.) ser diputado; (of a committee, etc.) celebrar sesión; (on a committee, etc.) formar parte de; (function) funcionar; (of garments, food, and *fig*) sentar. **to sit a horse,** mantenerse a caballo; montar a caballo. **to sit oneself,** sentarse, tomar asiento. **to sit by,** (a person) sentarse (or estar sentado) al lado de. **to sit for** (a portrait) servir de modelo para; hacerse retratar. **to sit tight,** no moverse. **to sit down,** sentarse; (besiege) sitiar. **to sit on,** sentarse (en or sobre); (eggs) empollar; (a committee, etc.) formar parte de; (investigate) investigar; (snub) dejar aplastado (a). **to sit out,** quedarse hasta el fin (de). **to sit out a dance,** conversar un baile. **to sit up,** incorporarse en la cama; tenerse derecho; (at night) velar; (of dogs, etc.) pedir. **to sit up and take notice,** abrir los ojos. **to sit up in bed,** incorporarse en la cama. **to sit up late,** estar de pie hasta muy tarde

**sit-down strike** /'sɪt,daun/ n huelga de brazos caídos, huelga de sentados, f

**site** /sait/ n sitio, local, m; (for building) solar, m

**sitting** /'sɪtɪŋ/ n asentada, f; (of Parliament, etc.) sesión, f; (for a portrait) estadia, f; (of eggs) nidada, f. **at a s.,** de una asentada. **s.-room,** sala de estar, f

**situated** /'sɪtʃu,eitɪd/ a situado. **How is he s.?** ¿Cómo está situado? ¿Cuál es su situación?

**situation** /,sɪtʃu'eiʃən/ n situación, f; (job) empleo, m

**six** /sɪks/ a and n seis, m. **It is six o'clock,** Son las seis. **Everything is at sixes and sevens,** Todo está en desorden. **six-foot,** de seis pies. **six hundred,** seiscientos (-as)

**sixfold** /'sɪks,fould/ a séxtuplo

**sixteen** /'sɪks'tin/ a and n diez y seis, dieciséis, m. **John is s.,** Juan tiene dieciséis años

**sixteenth** /'sɪks'tinθ/ a décimosexto; (of the month) (el) diez y seis; (of monarch) diez y seis. —n dieciseisavo, m

**sixth** /sɪksθ/ a sexto; (of the month) (el) seis; (of monarchs) sexto. —n seisavo, m; sexta parte, f; mus sexta, f. **Henry the S.,** Enrique sexto. **May the s.,** el seis de mayo

**sixtieth** /'sɪkstiiθ/ a sexagésimo. —n sesentavo, m; sexagésima parte, f

**sixty** /'sɪksti/ a and n sesenta m. **John has turned s.,** Juan ha pasado los sesenta

**sizable** /'saizəbəl/ a bastante grande

**size** /saiz/ n tamaño, m; dimensión, f; (height) altura, f; (measurement) medida, f; talle, m; (in gloves, etc.) número, m; (glue) cola, f. —vt clasificar por tamaños; (glaze, etc.) encolar. **to s. up,** tomar las medidas (a).

**sizzle** /'sɪzəl/ vi chisporrotear, chirriar. —n chisporroteo, chirrido, m

**skate** /skeit/ n patín, m; ichth raya, f, vi patinar

**skater** /'skeitər/ n patinador (-ra)

**skating** /'skeitɪŋ/ n patinaje, m. **s. rink,** sala de patinar, f; pista de hielo, pista de patinar, f, patinadero, m

**skein** /skein/ n madeja, f

**skeleton** /'skɛlɪtn/ n esqueleto, m; (of a building) armadura, f; (of a literary work) esquema, m. **s. key,** ganzúa, f

**sketch** /skɛtʃ/ n croquis, apunte, m; (for a literary work) esbozo, esquema, m; (article) cuadro, artículo, m; descripción, f; theat entremés, sainete, m. —vt dibujar; esbozar, bosquejar; trazar; describir. **s.-book,** álbum de croquis, m

**sketchily** /'skɛtʃəli/ adv incompletamente

**sketching** /'skɛtʃɪŋ/ n arte de dibujar, mf. **He likes s.,** Le gusta dibujar

**sketchy** /'skɛtʃi/ a bosquejado; incompleto; escaso

**skewer** /'skyuər/ n broqueta, f, vt espetar

**ski** /ski/ n esquí, m, vi esquiar

**skid** /skɪd/ n (of a vehicle) patinazo, m, vi patinar

**skidding** /'skɪdɪŋ/ n patinaje, m

**skier** /'skiər/ n esquiador, m

**skiff** /skɪf/ n esquife, m

**skiing** /'skiɪŋ/ n patinaje sobre la nieve, m, el esquiar. **to go s.,** ir a esquiar

**skill** /skɪl/ n habilidad, f

**skilled** /skɪld/ a hábil; experto

**skilled worker** n obrero calificado, m

**skillful** /'skɪlfəl/ a hábil

**skim** /skɪm/ vt espumar; (milk) desnatar; (touch lightly) deslizarse sobre, rozar; (a book) hojear

**skimp** /skɪmp/ vt escatimar; escasear; (work) frangollar. —vi ser parsimonioso

**skimpy** /'skɪmpi/ a escaso

**skin** /skɪn/ n tez, f, cutis, m; piel, f; (of fruit) pellejo, m, piel, f; (for wine) odre, pellejo, m; (on milk) espuma, f. —vt despellejar; pelar, mondar; (graze) hacerse daño (a); inf desollar. **next to one's s.,** sobre la piel. **to s. over,** cicatrizarse. **to have a thin s.,** fig ser muy susceptible. **to save one's s.,** salvar el pellejo. **s.-deep,** superficial. **s.-tight,** escurrido, muy ajustado

**skinflint** /'skɪn,flɪnt/ n avaro (-ra)

**skinned** /skɪnd/ a de... piel

**skinny** /'skɪni/ a flaco, descarnado, magro

**skip** /skɪp/ vi retozar, brincar, saltar; saltar a la comba; (bolt) largarse, escaparse. —vt saltar; (a book) hojear; (omit) omitir; pasar por alto de. —n brinco, pequeño salto, m

**skipper** /'skɪpər/ n naut patrón, m; (inf and sports) capitán, m

**skirmish** /'skɜrmɪʃ/ vi escaramuzar. —n escaramuza, f

**skirt** /skɜrt/ n falda, f; (edge) margen, borde, m, orilla, f; (of a jacket, etc.) faldón, m —vt ladear; (hug) rodear, ceñir

**skit** /skɪt/ n sátira, f; parodia, f

**skittish** /'skɪtɪʃ/ a (of a horse) retozón; (of persons) frívolo; caprichoso

**skittle** /'skɪtl/ n bolo, m; pl **skittles,** juego de bolos, m. **s. alley,** pista de bolos, bolera, f

**skulk** /skʌlk/ vi estar en acecho; esconderse; rondar

**skull** /skʌl/ n cráneo, m; calavera, f. **s.-cap,** gorro, casquete, m; (for ecclesiastics) solideo, m

**skunk** /skʌŋk/ n zool mofeta, f, chingue, mapurite, yaguré, zorrillo, zorrino, zorro hediondo, m

**sky** /skai/ n cielo, m. **to praise to the skies,** poner en los cuernos de la luna. **s.-blue,** n azul celeste, m. —a de color azul celeste, cerúleo. **s.-high,** hasta las nubes, hasta el cielo. **s.-line,** horizonte, m. **s.-scraper,** rascacielos, m. **s.-sign,** anuncio luminoso, m

**skylight** /'skai,lait/ n claraboya, f, tragaluz, m

**slab** /slæb/ n bloque, m; losa, f, plancha, f

**slack** /slæk/ a lento; flojo; (lazy) perezoso; negligente, descuidado; com encalmado; débil. —vt ser perezoso. **the s. season,** la estación muerta. **to be s. in one's work,** ser negligente en el trabajo. **to s. off,** disminuir sus esfuerzos; dejar de trabajar

**slacken** /'slækən/ vt and vi aflojar; disminuir, reducir. **The wind slackened,** El viento amainaba, El viento aflojaba. **to s. one's efforts,** disminuir sus esfuerzos. **to s. speed,** disminuir la velocidad

**slackening** /'slækənɪŋ/ n aflojamiento, m; disminución, f

**slacker** /'slækər/ n gandul (-la)

**slackness** /'slæknɪs/ n flojedad, f; pereza, falta de energía, f; negligencia, f; com desanimación, f

**slacks** /slæks/ n pl pantalones, m pl

**slag** /slæg/ n escoria, f. **s. heap,** escorial, m

**slake** /sleik/ vt (one's thirst and lime) apagar; satisfacer

**slam** /slæm/ vt cerrar de golpe; golpear. —n (of a door) portazo, m; golpe, m; (cards) capote, m. **He went out and slammed the door,** Salió dando un portazo

**slander** /'slændər/ n calumnia, f, vt calumniar

**slanderer** /'slændərər/ n calumniador (-ra)

**slanderous** /'slændərəs/ a calumnioso

**slang** /slæŋ/ n argot, m, jerga, f, vt poner como un trapo (a), llenar de insultos

**slant** /slænt/ vi estar al sesgo; inclinarse; ser oblicuo. —vt inclinar. —n inclinación, f; oblicuidad, f. **on the s.,** inclinado. —oblicuo

**slanting** /'slæntɪŋ/ a al sesgo, inclinado; oblicuo

**slap** /slæp/ vt pegar con la mano. —n bofetada, f; palmada, f. **to s. on the back,** golpear en la espalda. **s.-dash,** (of persons) irresponsable, descuidado; (of work) chapucero, sin cuidado

**slash** /slæʃ/ vt (gash, also sleeves, etc.) acuchillar; cortar; (with a whip) dar latigazos (a). —n cuchillada, f; corte, m; latigazo, m

**slashing** /'slæʃɪŋ/ a mordaz, severo

**slat** /slæt/ n tablilla, f, vi (of sails) dar zapatazos, zapatear

**slate** /sleit/ n pizarra, f, esquisto, m; (for roofs and for writing) pizarra, f, vt (a roof) empizarrar; (censure) criticar severamente, censurar. **s.-colored,** apizarrado. **s. pencil,** pizarrín, m. **s. quarry,** pizarrería, f, pizarral, m

**slater** /'sleitər/ n pizarrero, m

**slating** /'sleitɪŋ/ n empizarrado, m; (criticism) crítica severa, censura, f; (scolding) peluca, f

**slattern** /'slætərn/ n pazpuerca, f

**slatternly** /'slætərnli/ a desgarbado, desaliñado

**slaughter** /'slɔtər/ n matanza, f; carnicería, f; —vt (animals) sacrificar, matar; matar, hacer una carnicería de. **s.-house,** matadero, m

**slaughterer** /'slɔtərər/ n jifero, carnicero, m

**Slav** /slɑv, slæv/ a and n eslavo (-va)

**slave** /sleiv/ *n* esclavo (-va). —*vi* trabajar mucho.
**white s. traffic,** trata de blancas, *f.* **s.-bangle,** esclava, *f.* **s.-driver,** capataz de esclavos, negrero, *m; fig* negrero, sayón de esclavos, *m.* **s.-trade,** trata de esclavos, *f*
**slaver** /'sleivər/ *n* negrero, *m*
**slaver** /'slævər/ *vi* babear. —*n* baba, *f*
**slavering** /'slævərɪŋ/ *a* baboso
**slavery** /'sleivəri/ *n* esclavitud, *f;* trabajo muy arduo, *m*
**slavish** /'sleivɪʃ/ *a* de esclavo; servil
**slavishly** /'sleivɪʃli/ *adv* como esclava; servilmente
**Slavonic** /slə'vɒnɪk/ *a* eslavo. —*n* (language) eslavo, *m,* lengua eslava, *f*
**slay** /slei/ *vt* matar; asesinar
**slayer** /'sleiər/ *n* matador (-ra); asesino, *mf*
**slaying** /'sleiɪŋ/ *n* matanza, *f;* asesinato, *m*
**sled** /slɛd/ *n* trineo, *m,* rastra, *f*
**sledge** /slɛdʒ/ *n* trineo, *m.* —*vi* ir en trineo. —*vt* transportar por trineo. **s.-hammer,** acotillo, *m*
**sleek** /slik/ *a* liso, lustroso; (of general appearance) pulcro, bien aseado, elegante; (of manner) obsequioso
**sleekness** /'sliknɪs/ *n* lustre, *m,* lisura, *f;* (of an animal) gordura, *f;* elegancia, *f*
**sleep** /slip/ *n* sueño, *m.* —*vi* dormir; reposar, descansar. —*vt* dormir. **a deep s.,** un sueño pesado. **He walks in his s.,** Es un sonámbulo. **to court s.,** conciliar el sueño. **to go to s.,** dormirse; entumecerse. **My foot has gone to s.,** Se me ha dormido (*or* Se me ha entumecido) el pie. **to send a person to s.,** adormecer. **to s. like a top,** dormir como un lirón. **to s. oneself sober,** dormir la mona. **to s. in,** dormir tarde; dormir en casa. **to s. off,** (a cold, etc.) curarse... durmiendo; (drunkenness) dormirla. **to s. on,** *vt* (consider) dormir sobre, consultar con la almohada. —*vi* seguir durmiendo. **to s. out,** dormir fuera de casa; dormir al aire libre
**sleeper** /'slipər/ *n* durmiente, *mf; rail* traviesa, *f;* (on a train) coche cama, *m.* **to be a bad s.,** dormir mal. **to be a good s.,** dormir bien.
**sleepily** /'slipəli/ *adv* soñolientamente
**sleepiness** /'slipinɪs/ *n* somnolencia, *f;* letargo, *m*
**sleeping** /'slipɪŋ/ *a* durmiente. —*n* el dormir. **between s. and waking,** entre duerme y vela. **s.-bag,** saco-cama, *m.* **s.-car,** coche camas, *m.* **s.-draught,** narcótico, *m.* **s. partner,** *n* socio (-ia) comanditario (-ia). **s. sickness,** enfermedad del sueño, *f*
**sleepless** /'sliplɪs/ *a* (of persons) insomne, desvelado; (unremitting) incansable; (of the sea, etc.) en perpetuo movimiento. **to spend a s. night,** pasar una noche en vela, pasar una noche toledana, pasar una noche sin dormir
**sleeplessness** /'sliplɪsnɪs/ *n* insomnio, *m*
**sleepwalker** /'slip,wɔkər/ *n* sonámbulo (-la)
**sleepwalking** /'slip,wɔkɪŋ/ *n* sonambulismo, *m*
**sleepy** /'slipi/ *a* soñoliento; letárgico. **to be s.,** tener sueño. **s.-head,** lirón, *m,* marmota, *f*
**sleet** /slit/ *n* aguanieve, cellisca, nevisca, *f, vi* caer aguanieve, cellisquear, neviscar
**sleeve** /sliv/ *n* manga, *f;* (of a hose pipe, etc.) manguera, *f; mech* manguito, *m.* **to have something up one's s.,** traer algo en la manga
**sleeved** /slivd/ *a* con mangas...; de... manga(s)
**sleeveless** /'slivlɪs/ *a* sin manga
**sleigh** /slei/ *n* trineo, *m, vi* ir en trineo
**sleight of hand** /slait/ *n* prestidigitación, *f;* juego de manos, *m*
**slender** /'slɛndər/ *a* delgado; esbelto; tenue; escaso; pequeño; ligero. **Their means are very s.,** Sus recursos son muy escasos. **It is a very s. hope,** Es una esperanza muy remota
**slenderness** /'slɛndərnɪs/ *n* delgadez, *f;* esbeltez, *f;* tenuidad, *f;* escasez, *f*
**sleuth** /sluθ/ *n* (dog) sabueso, *m; inf* detective, *m*
**slice** /slais/ *n* lonja, tajada, *f;* (of fruit) raja, *f;* (of bread, etc.) rebanada, *f;* (share) parte, porción, *f;* (for fish, etc.) pala, *f.* —*vt* cortar en tajadas, etc.; rajar; cortar
**slick** /slɪk/ *a* hábil, diestro
**slide** /slaid/ *vi* deslizarse, resbalar; (over a question) pasar por alto de; (into a habit, etc.) caer (en). —*n*
resbalón, *m;* pista de hielo, *f;* (chute) tobogán, *m;* (of a microscope) portaobjetos, *m;* (lantern) diapositiva, *f;* (for the hair) pasador, *m;* (of rock, etc.) desprendimiento, *m; mech* guía, *f.* **to let things s.,** dejar rodar la bola. **s.-rule,** regla de cálculo, *f*
**sliding** /'slaidɪŋ/ *a* resbaladizo; corredizo; movible. **s.-door,** puerta corrediza, puerta de corradera, *f.* **s.-roof,** techo corredizo, *m.* **s.-scale,** escala graduada, *f.* **s.-seat,** asiento movible, *m;* (in a rowing-boat) bancada corrediza, *f*
**slight** /slait/ *a* delgado; débil, frágil; ligero; (small) pequeño; escaso; (trivial) insignificante, poco importante. —*vt* desairar, despreciar. —*n* desaire, desprecio, *m;* falta de respeto, *f*
**slighting** /'slaitɪŋ/ *a* despreciativo, de desprecio
**slightingly** /'slaitɪŋli/ *adv* con desprecio
**slightly** /'slaitli/ *adv* ligeramente; poco. **I only know her s.,** La conozco muy poco. **s. built,** de talle delgado
**slightness** /'slaitnɪs/ *n* (slimness) delgadez, *f;* ligereza, *f;* (triviality) poca importancia, insignificancia, *f*
**slim** /slɪm/ *a* delgado; escaso. —*vi* adelgazarse. **He has very s. chances of success,** Tiene muy pocas posibilidades de conseguir el éxito
**slime** /slaim/ *n* légamo, limo, lodo, cieno, *m;* (of a snail) limazo, *m; fig* cieno, *m*
**sliminess** /'slaiminɪs/ *n* limosidad, *f;* viscosidad, *f*
**slimness** /'slɪmnɪs/ *n* delgadez, *f;* escasez, *f*
**slimy** /'slaimi/ *a* limoso, legamoso; pecinoso, viscoso; (of persons) rastrero, servil
**sling** /slɪŋ/ *vt* arrojar, lanzar; tirar con honda; (a sword, etc.) suspender; (lift) embragar; (a limb) poner en cabestrillo. —*n* (for missiles) honda, *f; Naut* balso, *m;* (for a limb) cabestrillo, *m,* charpa, *f*
**slink** /slɪŋk/ *vi* (away, off) escurrirse, escabullirse
**slip** /slɪp/ *vi* resbalar, deslizar; (stumble) resbalar, tropezar; (fall) caer; (out of place) salirse; (become untied) desatarse; (steal away) escabullirse; (glide) deslizarse; (of years) correr, pasar; (skid) patinar. —*vt* deslizar; (garments, shoes) ponerse; (dogs, cables) soltar; (an arm round, etc.) pasar; *Rail* desacoplar; (escape) escaparse de; (free oneself of) librarse de. —*n* resbalón, *m;* (skid) patinazo, *m;* (stumble) tropezón, traspié, *m;* (oversight) inadvertencia, *f;* (mistake) falta, equivocación, *f;* (moral lapse) desliz, *m;* (petticoat) combinación, *f;* (cover) funda, *f; Bot* vástago, *m; Print* galerada, *f;* (of paper) papeleta, *f; pl* **slips,** *Naut* anguilas, *f pl.* **It slipped my memory,** Se me fue de la memoria. **There's many a s. 'twixt the cup and the lip,** Del dicho al hecho hay muy gran trecho, De la mano a la boca desaparece la sopa. **to give** (someone) **the slip,** escaparse de. **You ought not to let the opportunity s.,** No debes perder la oportunidad. **to let s. a secret,** revelar un secreto. **to let s. an exclamation,** soltar (dar) una exclamación. **to s. into,** colarse en, deslizarse en. **to s. into,** colarse en, deslizarse en. **to s. into one's clothes,** vestirse rápidamente. **to s. on,** (a garment) ponerse. **to s. out,** salir a hurtadillas; escaparse; (of information) divulgarse. **s. of a boy,** mozalbete, joven imberbe, *m.* **s. of the tongue,** error de lengua, *m.* **s.-knot,** nudo corredizo, *m*
**slipcover** /'slɪp,kʌvər/ *n* cubierta, cubierta para muebles, funda, funda para muebles, *f*
**slipper** /'slɪpər/ *n* babucha, chinela, *f,* pantuflo, *m;* (heelless) chancleta, *f;* (dancing) zapatilla de baile, *f.* **s.-shaped,** achinelado
**slippered** /'slɪpərd/ *a* en zapatillas
**slipperiness** /'slɪpərinɪs/ *n* lo resbaladizo; (of persons) informalidad, *f*
**slippery** /'slɪpəri/ *a* resbaladizo; poco firme, inestable; (of persons) informal, sin escrúpulos
**slipshod** /'slɪp,ʃɒd/ *a* descuidado, negligente; poco correcto
**slipway** /'slɪp,wei/ *n* surtida, *f,* anguilas, *f pl*
**slit** /slɪt/ *vt* cortar; hender, rajar; (the throat) degollar. —*n* cortadura, *f;* resquicio, *m.* **to s. open,** abrir de un tajo
**slither** /'slɪðər/ *vi* resbalar; deslizarse
**sliver** /'slɪvər/ *n* raja, *f;* (of wood) astilla, *f;* (of cloth) tira, *f*

**slobber** /'slɒbər/ vi babear; (blubber) gimotear, n baba, f

**sloe** /slou/ n (fruit) endrina, f; (tree) endrino, m. **s.-colored,** endrino. **s.-eyed,** con ojos de mora

**slog** /slɒg/ vt golpear duramente. **to s. away,** batirse el cobre, trabajar como un negro

**slogan** /'slougən/ n grito de batalla, m; reclamo, m; frase hecha, f; mote, m

**slop** /slɒp/ n charco, m; —vi derramarse, verterse. —vt verter, derramar

**slope** /sloup/ n inclinación, f; pendiente, f; (of a mountain, etc.) falda, ladera, cuesta, f; vertiente, mf. —vi inclinarse; estar en declive; bajar (hacia). **to s. down,** declinar

**sloping** /'sloupɪŋ/ a inclinado; en declive; (of shoulders) caídos, m

**sloppy** /'slɒpi/ a casi líquido; (muddy) lodoso, lleno de barro; (of work) chapucero; (of persons) baboso, sobón. **s. sentiment,** sensiblería, f

**slot** /slɒt/ n ranura, muesca, f. **s.-machine,** máquina expendedora, f, expendedor, m; (in amusement arcades, etc.) tragaperras, m

**sloth** /slɒθ or, esp. for 2, slouθ/ n pereza, indolencia, f; zool perezoso, m

**slothful** /'slɒθfəl, 'slouθ-/ a perezoso, indolente

**slouch** /slautʃ/ n inclinación del cuerpo, f. —vi andar cabizbajo, andar arrastrando los pies. **to s. about,** vagar, golfear. **s.-hat,** sombrero gacho, m

**slough** /slʌf/ n (bog) cenagal, pantano, m, marisma, f; (of a snake) camisa, f. —vt (a skin) mudar; (prejudices, etc.) desechar

**Slovak** /'slouvak/ n eslovaco (-ca)

**Slovakian** /slou'vakiən/ a eslovaco

**sloven** /'slʌvən/ n puerco, m; (at work) chapucero, m

**Slovene** /slou'vin/ a and n esloveno (-na)

**slovenliness** /'slʌvənlinɪs/ n desaseo, desaliño, m; (carelessness) descuido, m, negligencia, f; (of work) chapucería, f

**slovenly** /'slʌvənli/ a desgarbado, desaseado; (careless) descuidado, negligente; (of work) chapucero

**slow** /slou/ a despacio; lento; (stupid) torpe; tardo; (of clocks) atrasado; (boring) aburrido; (inactive) flojo. —adv despacio, lentamente. **I was not s. to...,** No tardé en... **The clock is ten minutes s.,** El reloj lleva diez minutos de atraso. **to s. down,** aflojar el paso; ir más despacio. **s.-motion,** velocidad reducida, f. **s. train,** tren ómnibus, m. **s.-witted,** lerdo tardo

**slowcoach** /'slou,koutʃ/ n perezoso (-sa)

**"Slow Down"** «Moderar Su Velocidad»

**slow learner** n alumno de lento aprendizaje, m

**slowly** /'slouli/ adv despacio, lentamente; poco a poco

**slowness** /'slounɪs/ n lentitud, f; (delay) tardanza, f; (stupidity) torpeza, estupidez, f

**slug** /slʌg/ n babosa, f

**sluggard** /'slʌgərd/ n gandul (-la), perezoso (-a)

**sluggish** /'slʌgɪʃ/ a perezoso; (of the market) flojo; (of temperament, etc.) calmoso, flemático; (slow) lento

**sluggishness** /'slʌgɪʃnɪs/ n pereza, f; (of the market) flojedad, f; (slowness) lentitud, f

**sluice** /slus/ n esclusa, f; canal, m, acequia, f **to s. down,** lavar; echar agua sobre; (a person) dar una ducha (a), dar un baño (a). **s.-gate,** compuerta de esclusa, f; tajaderas, f pl, tablacho, m

**slum** /slʌm/ n barrio pobre, m, banda de miseria (Argentina), barriada (Peru), población (Chile), villa-miseria (Argentina), f; tugurio (Colombia), m; pl **slums,** barrios bajos, m pl

**slumber** /'slʌmbər/ vi dormir; (go to sleep) dormirse, caer dormido; (be latent) estar latente. —n sueño, m

**slump** /slʌmp/ n com baja repentina, f; fig baja, racha mala, f. —vi com bajar repentinamente. **the s.,** la crisis económica. **to s. into an armchair,** dejarse caer en un sillón

**slur** /slɜr/ vt (words) comerse sílabas o letras (de); (in writing) unir (las palabras); (mus of notes) ligar. **to cast a s. on,** difamar, manchar. **to s. over,** pasar por alto de, omitir, suprimir

**slush** /slʌʃ/ n lodo, m; agua nieve, f; (sentimentality) ñoñería, f

**slushy** /'slʌʃi/ a lodoso, fangoso

**slut** /slʌt/ n pazpuerca, marrana, f

**sly** /slai/ a astuto, taimado, socarrón; disimulado; (arch) malicioso. **on the sly,** a hurtadillas

**slyly** /'slaili/ adv astutamente; disimuladamente; (archly) maliciosamente

**slyness** /'slainɪs/ n astucia, socarronería, f; disimulo, m; malicia, f

**smack** /smæk/ n (taste) sabor, gusto, m; (tinge) dejo, m; (blow) golpe, m; (with the hand) bofetada, palmada, f; (with a whip) latigazo, m; (crack of whip) restallido, chasquido, m; (kiss) beso sonado, m; (boat) lancha de pescar, f. —vi (taste of) tener gusto de, saber a; (be tinged with) oler a. —vt (a whip) hacer restallar; (slap) pegar con la mano. **to s. one's lips over,** chuparse los dedos

**small** /smɔl/ a pequeño; menudo; menor; poco; (petty) mezquino, vulgar. —n parte estrecha, f. **a s. number,** un pequeño número. **to make a person look s.,** humillar. **to make oneself s.,** hacerse chiquito. **s.-arms,** armas portátiles, f pl. **s. change,** suelto, m. **s. craft,** embarcaciones menores, f pl. **s. fry,** pececillos, m pl; (children) gente menuda, f; gente sin importancia, f. **s. hours,** altas horas de la noche, f pl. **s.-minded,** adocenado, de cortos alcances. **s.-talk,** trivialidades, f pl, charla frívola, f

**smallish** /'smɔlɪʃ/ a bastante pequeño; más bien pequeño que grande

**smallness** /'smɔlnɪs/ n pequeñez, f; escasez, exigüidad, f

**smallpox** /'smɔl,pɒks/ n viruelas, f pl

**smart** /smɑrt/ vi picar; doler (de). —n escozor, m; dolor, m. —a severo; vivo; rápido; pronto; (competent) hábil; (clever) listo; (unscrupulous) cuco, astuto; (of personal appearance) majo; elegante, distinguido; (neat) aseado; (fashionable, etc.) de moda; de buen tono. **to s. for,** ser castigado por. **to s. under,** sufrir

**smarten** /'smɑrtn/ vt embellecer. —vi (up) ponerse elegante; mejorar. **I must go and s. myself up a little,** Tengo que arreglarme un poco

**smartly** /'smɑrtli/ adv severamente; vivamente; rápidamente; hábilmente; elegantemente

**smartness** /'smɑrtnɪs/ n viveza, f; prontitud, rapidez, f; (cleverness) despejo, m, habilidad, f; (wittiness) agudeza, f; (astuteness) cuquería, astucia, f; (of dress, etc.) elegancia, f; buen tono, m

**smash** /smæʃ/ vt romper, quebrar; (a ball, etc.) golpear; (annihilate) destruir; (an opponent) aplastar. —vi romperse, quebrarse; hacerse pedazos; (collide) chocar (con, contra); estallarse (contra); (financially) hacer bancarrota. —n rotura, f; quebrantamiento, m; estruendo, m; (financial) quiebra, ruina, f; (car, etc.) accidente, m; desastre, m, catástrofe, f **to s. to atoms,** hacer trizas. **to s. up,** hacer pedazos. **s. and grab raid,** atraco a mano armada, m

**smash hit** n éxito arrollador, éxito rotundo, m

**smattering** /'smætərɪŋ/ n conocimiento superficial, m, tintura, f, barniz, m

**smear** /smɪər/ n mancha, f; biol frotis, m. —vt embadurnar (de); manchar (con), ensuciar (con); (oneself) untarse; (blur) borrar

**smell** /smɛl/ n (sense of) olfato, m; (odor) olor, m. —vt oler. —vi oler; tener olor; (disagreeably) oler mal, tener mal olor; (stink) apestar. **How good it smells!** ¡Qué bien huele! **to s. of,** oler a. **to s. out,** husmear

**smelling** /'smɛlɪŋ/ n olfateo, m. **s.-bottle,** frasco de sales, m. **s.-salts,** sales (inglesas), f pl

**smelt** /smɛlt/ vt fundir. —n ichth eperlano, m

**smelter** /'smɛltər/ n fundidor, m

**smelting** /'smɛltɪŋ/ n fundición, f. **s. furnace,** horno de fundición, m

**smile** /smail/ vi sonreír; reírse. —vt expresar con una sonrisa. —n sonrisa, f. **Mary smiled her thanks,** María dio las gracias con una sonrisa. **smile at adversity,** ponerse buena cara a mal tiempo. **to s. at threats,** reírse de las amenazas

**smiling** /'smailɪŋ/ a sonriente, risueño

**smilingly** /'smailɪŋli/ adv sonriendo, con una sonrisa, con cara risueña

**smirch** /smɜrtʃ/ vt manchar. —n mancha, f

**smirk** /smɜrk/ vi sonreír con afectación; hacer visajes. —n sonrisa afectada, f

**smirking** /'smɜrkɪŋ/ a afectado; sonriente

**smite** /smait/ vt golpear; (kill) matar; (punish) castigar; (pain) doler; (of bright light, sounds, etc.) herir; (cause remorse) remorder. **My conscience smites me,** Tengo remordimientos de conciencia. **to be smitten by,** inf estar prendado de. **I was smitten by a desire to smoke,** Me entraron deseos de fumar

**smith** /smɪθ/ n herrero, m. **smith's hammer,** destajador, m

**smithereens** /ˌsmɪðə'rinz/ n pl añicos, m pl

**smithy** /'smɪθi, 'smɪði/ n herrería, f

**smock** /smɒk/ n blusa, f; (child's) delantal, m

**smoke** /smouk/ n humo, m. —vi humear, echar humo; (tobacco) fumar. —vt ahumar; ennegrecer; (tobacco) fumar. **smoked glasses,** gafas ahumadas, f pl. **s. helmet,** casco respiratorio, m. **s.-screen,** cortina de humo, f. **s. signal,** ahumada, f. **s.-stack,** chimenea, f

**smokeless** /'smouklɪs/ a sin humo

**smoker** /'smoukər/ n fumador (-ra)

**smoking** /'smoukɪŋ/ a humeante. —n el fumar. **"S. Prohibited,"** «Se prohibe fumar.» **non-s. compartment,** rail departamento de no fumadores, m. **s.-carriage,** rail departamento para fumadores, m. **s.-room,** fumadero, m

**smoky** /'smouki/ a humeante; lleno de humo; (black) ahumado

**smooth** /smuð/ a liso; igual; (of the skin, etc.) suave; (of water) calmo, tranquilo; (flattering, etc.) lisonjero; obsequioso; afable. —vt allanar; (hair, etc.) alisar; (paths, etc.) igualar. **to s. down,** (a person) tranquilizar, calmar. **to s. over,** (faults) exculpar. **to s. the way for,** allanar el camino para. **s.-faced,** barbilampiño, lampiño, bien afeitado, todo afeitado; fig obsequioso, untuoso. **s.-haired,** de pelo liso. **s.-spoken,** de palabras lisonjeras; obsequioso

**smoothly** /'smuðli/ adv lisamente; (of speech) afablemente; con lisonjeras. **Everything was going s.,** Todo iba viento en popa

**smoothness** /'smuðnɪs/ n igualdad, f; lisura, f; (of skin, etc.) suavidad, f; (of water) calma, tranquilidad, f; (of manner, etc.) afabilidad, f

**smother** /'smʌðər/ vt ahogar, sofocar; (a fire) apagar; (cover) envolver, cubrir

**smoulder** /'smouldər/ vi arder sin llama, arder lentamente; (of passions, etc.) arder; estar latente

**smouldering** /'smouldərɪŋ/ a que arde lentamente; fig latente

**smudge** /smʌdʒ/ vt manchar, ensuciar; (blur) borrar. —n mancha, f

**smug** /smʌg/ a satisfecho de sí mismo, pagado de sí mismo; farisaico

**smuggle** /'smʌgəl/ vt pasar de contrabando. —vi hacer contrabando

**smuggler** /'smʌglər/ n contrabandista, mf

**smuggling** /'smʌglɪŋ/ n contrabando, m

**smugly** /'smʌgli/ adv con presunción, de un aire satisfecho

**smugness** /'smʌgnɪs/ n satisfacción de sí mismo, f; fariseísmo, m

**smut** /smʌt/ n copo de hollín, m; mancha, f; (disease) tizón, m

**smutty** /'smʌti/ a tiznado; ahumado; inf verde

**snack** /snæk/ n tentempié, piscolabis, bocado, m. **to take a s.,** tomar un piscolabis

**snack bar** n merendero, m

**snaffle** /'snæfəl/ n filete, m. —vt (a horse) refrenar. **s.-bridle,** bridón, m

**snag** /snæg/ n (of a tree) tocón, m; (of a tooth) raigón, m; (problem) busilis, m; obstáculo inesperado, m

**snail** /sneil/ n caracol, m. **at a snail's pace,** a paso de tortuga

**snake** /sneik/ n serpiente, f. **s.-charmer,** encantador de serpientes, m

**snakelike** /'sneik,laik/ a de serpiente; serpentino

**snap** /snæp/ vt morder; (break) romper; (one's fin-

gers) castañetear; (a whip) chasquear; (down a lid, etc.) cerrar de golpe; (beaks, etc.) cerrar ruidosamente; photo sacar una instantánea de. —vi partirse; quebrarse; hablar bruscamente. —n (bite) mordedura, f; golpe seco, m; chasquido, m; rotura, f; (clasp) cierre, m; (of weather) temporada, f; (spirit) vigor, brío, m; photo instantánea, f. **to s. at,** procurar morder; (an invitation, etc.) aceptar gustoso. **to s. one's fingers at,** fig burlarse de. **to s. up,** coger, agarrar; (a person) cortar la palabra (a), interrumpir. **s.-fastener,** botón de presión, m

**snapdragon** /'snæp,drægən/ n dragón, m, becerra, boca de dragón, f

**snappily** /'snæpəli/ adv irritablemente

**snappishness** /'snæpɪʃnɪs/ n irritabilidad, f

**snappy** /'snæpi/ a irritable; vigoroso

**snapshot** /'snæp,ʃɒt/ n instantánea, foto, f

**snare** /snɛar/ n cepo, lazo, m, trampa, f; fig red, f. —vt coger en el lazo; fig enredar

**snarl** /snɑrl/ vi (of dogs) regañar; (cats, etc.) gruñir. —n regañamiento, m; gruñido, m

**snarling** /'snɑrlɪŋ/ n regañamiento, m; gruñidos, m pl, a gruñidor

**snatch** /snætʃ/ vt asir; agarrar; (enjoy) disfrutar; (an opportunity) tomar, aprovecharse de. —n asimiento, agarro, m; (of time) rato, m; instante, m; (of song) fragmento, m. **to make a s. at,** procurar agarrar; alargar la mano hacia. **to s. a hurried meal,** comer aprisa. **to s. away,** arrebatar, quitar; (carry off) robar. **to s. up,** coger rápidamente; coger en brazos

**sneak** /snik/ vi deslizarse (en), colarse (en); (lurk) rondar; (inform) acusar. —n mandilón, m; (accuser) acusón (-ona). **to s. off,** escabullirse, irse a hurtadillas. **s.-thief,** n garduño (-ña)

**sneaker** /'snikər/ n (shoe) zapatilla de tenis, f

**sneaking** /'snikɪŋ/ a furtivo, ruin, mezquino; secreto

**sneer** /snɪar/ vi sonreír irónicamente; burlarse, mofarse. —n sonrisa sardónica, sonrisa de desprecio, f; burla, mofa, f. **to s. at,** mofarse de, burlarse de; hablar con desprecio de

**sneering** /'snɪarɪŋ/ a mofador, burlón

**sneeringly** /'snɪarɪŋli/ adv con una sonrisa sardónica; burlonamente

**sneeze** /sniz/ vi estornudar. —n estornudo, m. **It's not to be sneezed at,** No es moco de pavo

**sniff** /snɪf/ vi respirar fuertemente; resollar. —vt oler, olfatear; aspirar. **to s. at,** oler. **to s. out,** Inf. husmear

**snigger** /'snɪgər/ vi reírse por lo bajo, reírse disimuladamente. —n risa disimulada, f

**snip** /snɪp/ vt cortar con tijeras; cortar, quitar. —n tijeretada, f; (of cloth, etc.) recorte, pedacito, m

**snipe** /snaip/ n ornith agachadiza, f. **to s. at,** Mil. pacar

**sniper** /'snaipər/ n Mil. paco, m

**snippet** /'snɪpɪt/ n pedacito, fragmento, m; (of prose, etc.) trocito, m; (of news) noticia, f

**snivel** /'snɪvəl/ vi lloriquear, gimotear

**sniveling** /'snɪvəlɪŋ/ n lloriqueo, gimoteo, m. —a llorón; mocoso

**snob** /snɒb/ n esnob, m

**snobbery** /'snɒbəri/ n snobismo, m

**snobbish** /'snɒbɪʃ/ a esnob

**snood** /snud/ n (for the hair) redecilla, f; (turkey's) moco (de pavo), m; (fishing) cendal, m

**snoop** /snup/ vi espiar; entrometerse

**snooze** /snuz/ vi dormitar, echar un sueño. —n sueñecito, m; (afternoon) siesta, f

**snore** /snɔr/ vi roncar. —n ronquido, m

**snoring** /'snɔrɪŋ/ n ronquidos, m pl

**snort** /snɔrt/ vi bufar; resoplar. —n bufido, m; resoplido, m

**snout** /snaut/ n hocico, m; (of a pig) jeta, f

**snow** /snou/ n nieve, f. —vi nevar. —vt nevar; fig inundar. **to s. under** (with), inundar con. **to be snowed up,** estar aprisionado por la nieve. **s.-blindness,** deslumbramiento causado por la nieve, m. **s.-boot,** bota para la nieve, f. **s.-bound,** aprisionado por la nieve; bloqueado por la nieve. **s.-capped,** coronado de nieve. **s.-clad,** cubierto de nieve. **s.-drift,** acumulación de nieve, f. **s.-field,** ventisquero, m. **s.-goggles,** gafas ahumadas, f pl. **s.-line,** límite de las

nieves perpetuas, *m.* **s.-man,** figura de nieve, *f.* **s.-plough,** quitanieve, *m.* **s.-shoe,** raqueta de nieve, *f.* **s.-white,** blanco como la nieve
**snowball** /'snou,bɔl/ *n* bola de nieves, *f; bot* bola de nieve, *f*
**snowdrop** /'snou,drɒp/ *n* campanilla de invierno, violeta de febrero, *f*
**snowfall** /'snou,fɔl/ *n* nevada, *f*
**snowflake** /'snou,fleik/ *n* copo de nieve, *m*
**snowstorm** /'snou,stɔrm/ *n* ventisca, *f*
**snowy** /'snoui/ *a* nevoso; de nieve
**snub** /snʌb/ *vt* repulsar; desairar, tratar con desdén. —*n* repulsa, *f,* desaire, *m;* (nose) nariz respingona, *f.* **s.-nosed,** de nariz respingona
**snuff** /snʌf/ *vt* (breathe) oler, olfatear; inhalar; (a candle) atizar, despabilar. —*n* (of a candle) moco, *m,* despabiladura, *f;* (tobacco) rapé, *m.* **to take s.,** tomar rapé. **to s. out,** extinguir. **s.-box,** caja de rapé, tabaquera, *f*
**snuffers** /'snʌfərz/ *n pl* tenacillas, despabiladeras, *f pl*
**snuffle** /'snʌfəl/ *vi* hacer ruido con la nariz; respirar fuerte; (in speaking) ganguear
**snuffling** /'snʌflɪŋ/ *a* mocoso; (of the voice) gangoso
**snug** /snʌg/ *a* caliente; cómodo; (hidden) escondido, **to have a s. income,** tener el riñón bien cubierto, ser acomodado
**snuggle** /'snʌgəl/ *vi* hacerse un ovillo; acomodarse; ponerse cómodo. **to s. up to,** arrimarse a, apretarse contra
**snugly** /'snʌgli/ *adv* cómodamente
**snugness** /'snʌgnɪs/ *n* comodidad, *f*
**so** /sou/ *adv* así; de este modo, de esta manera; por lo tanto; tanto; (before adjs. and advs. but not before **más, mejor, menos, peor,** where **tanto** is used) tan; (in the same way) del mismo modo, de igual modo; (therefore) de modo que, de manera que; (also) también; (approximately) más o menos, aproximadamente. **Is that so?** ¿De veras? **if so...,** si así es... **He has not yet done so,** no lo ha hecho todavía. **I told you so!** ¡Ya te lo dije yo! **So be it!** ¡Así sea! **so far,** hasta aquí; hasta ahora. **so forth,** etcétera. **So long!** ¡Nos vemos! **so much,** tanto. **So much the worse for them,** Tanto peor para ellos. **so to speak,** por decirlo así. **so as to,** a fin de, para. **so long as,** con tal que, a condición de que. **so on,** etcétera. **so soon as,** tan pronto como. **so that,** de suerte que, de modo que; para que; con que. **so-and-so,** *n* fulano (-na); mengano (-na). **so-called.** así llamado, supuesto. **so-so,** así-así, regular
**soak** /souk/ *vt* remojar; empapar; (skins) abrevar. —*vi* estar en remojo. —*n* remojo, *m;* (rain) diluvio, *m;* (booze) borrachera, *f.* **to s. into,** filtrar en; penetrar. **to s. through,** penetrar; filtrar **so-called,** así llamado, supuesto. **so-so,** así, regular
**soaked** /soukt/ *a* remojado. **He is s. to the skin,** Está calado hasta los huesos
**soaking** /'soukɪŋ/ *n* remojo, *m;* empapamiento, *m,*
**soap** /soup/ *n* jabón, *m.* —*vt* jabonar; (flatter) enjabonar. **a tablet of s.,** una pastilla de jabón. **soft s.,** jabón blando, *m.* **toilet s.,** jabón de tocador, jaboncillo, *m.* **s.-bubble,** burbuja de jabón, *f.* **s. dish,** jabonera, *f.* **s. factory,** jabonería, *f.* **s.-flakes,** copos de jabón, *m pl*
**soapbark tree** /'soup,bark/ *n* quillay, palo de jabón, *m*
**soap box** *n lit* caja de jabón, *f; fig* tribuna callejera, *f*
**soap opera** /'ɒpərə/ *n* radionovela (on radio), telenovela (on television), *f,* serial lacrimógeno (derogatory), *m*
**soapsuds** /'soup,sʌdz/ *n pl* jabonaduras, *f pl*
**soapy** /'soupi/ *a* cubierto de jabón; jabonoso
**soar** /sɔr/ *vi* remontarse; *fig* elevarse; (of prices, etc.) subir de golpe
**soaring** /'sɔrɪŋ/ *n* remonte, vuelo, *m; fig* aspiración, *f;* (of prices, etc.) subida repentina, *f*
**sob** /sɒb/ *vi* sollozar. —*n* sollozo, *m.* **to sob one's heart out,** llorar a lágrima viva. **to sob out,** decir sollozando, decir entre sollozos
**sobbing** /'sɒbɪŋ/ *n* sollozos, *m pl, a* sollozante
**sober** /'soubər/ *a* sobrio; moderado; (of colors) obscuro. **s.-minded,** serio; reflexivo

**sobriety** /sə'braiɪti/ *n* sobriedad, *f;* moderación, *f;* seriedad, *f;* calma, tranquilidad, *f*
**sobriquet** /'soubrɪ,kei, -,kɛt/ *n* apodo, *m*
**soccer** /'sɒkər/ *n* fútbol (Asociación), *m*
**sociability** /,soʃə'bɪlɪti/ *n* sociabilidad, *f*
**sociable** /'souʃəbəl/ *a* sociable; amistoso
**sociably** /'souʃəbli/ *adv* sociablemente; amistosamente
**social** /'souʃəl/ *a* social; sociable. —*n* reunión, velada, *f.* **s.-democrat,** *a* and *n* socialdemócrata, *mf.* **s. event,** acontecimiento social, *m.* **s. insurance,** previsión social, *f.* **s. services,** servicios sociales, *m pl.* **s. work,** asistencia social, *f*
**socialism** /'souʃə,lɪzəm/ *n* socialismo, *m*
**socialist** /'souʃəlɪst/ *a* socialista, laborista. —*n* socialista, *mf*
**socialization** /,souʃələ'zeiʃən/ *n* socialización, *f*
**socialize** /'souʃə,laiz/ *vt* socializar
**socially** /'souʃəli/ *adv* socialmente
**society** /sə'saiɪti/ *n* sociedad, *f;* (fashionable) mundo elegante, *m,* alta sociedad, *f;* compañía, *f.* **to go into s.,** (of girls) ponerse de largo; entrar en el mundo elegante. **s. hostess,** dama de sociedad, *f.* **Society for the Prevention of Cruelty to Animals,** sociedad protectora de animales, *f.* **s. news,** noticias de sociedad, *f pl*
**sociological** /,sousiə'lɒdʒɪkəl/ *a* sociológico
**sociologist** /,sousi,ɒlədʒɪst/ *n* sociólogo (-ga)
**sociology** /,sousi'ɒlədʒi/ *n* sociología, *f*
**sock** /sɒk/ *n* calcetín, *m;* (for a shoe) plantilla, *f*
**socket** /'sɒkɪt/ *n mech* encaje, cubo, ojo, *m;* (of a lamp, and *elec*) enchufe, *m;* (of the eye) órbita, cuenca, *f;* (of a tooth) alvéolo, *m;* (of a joint) fosa, *f.* **His eyes started out of their sockets,** Sus ojos estaban fuera de su órbita
**Socratic** /sə'krætɪk/ *a* socrático
**sod** /sɒd/ *n* césped, *m;* (cut) tepe, *m*
**soda** /'soudə/ *n* sosa, *f.* **caustic s.,** sosa cáustica, *f.* **s.-ash,** carbonato sódico, *m.* **s.-fountain,** aparato de aguas gaseosas, *m.* **s.-water,** sifón, *m*
**sodden** /'sɒdn̩/ *a* saturado, empapado
**sodium** /'soudiəm/ *n* sodio, *m*
**Sodomite** /'sɒdə,mait/ *n* sodomita, *mf*
**sodomy** /'sɒdəmi/ *n* sodomía, *f*
**sofa** /'soufə/ *n* sofá, *m*
**soft** /sɔft/ *a* blando; suave; muelle; (flabby) flojo; (of disposition, etc.) dulce; (effeminate) muelle, afeminado; (lenient) indulgente; (easy) fácil; (silly) tonto. **to have a s. spot for,** (a person) tener una debilidad para. **s. coal,** carbón bituminoso, *m.* **s. drink,** bebida no alcohólica, *f.* **s. felt hat,** sombrero flexible, *m.* **s. fruit,** fruta blanda, *f.* **s.-boiled,** (of eggs) pasado por agua; (of persons) inocente, ingenuo. **s.-hearted,** de buen corazón; compasivo, bondadoso. **s.-heartedness,** buen corazón, *m,* bondad, *f.* **s.-spoken,** de voz suave; que habla con dulzura, meloso. **s. water,** agua blanda, *f*
**soften** /'sɔfən/ *vt* ablandar, reblandecer; (weaken) debilitar; (mitigate) mitigar, suavizar; (the heart, etc.) enternecer. —*vi* reblandecerse; enternecerse
**softening** /'sɔfənɪŋ/ *n* reblandecimiento, *m;* (relenting) enternecimiento, *m*
**softly** /'sɔftli/ *adv* suavemente; dulcemente, tiernamente; sin ruido, silenciosamente
**softness** /'sɔftnɪs/ *n* blandura, *f;* suavidad, *f;* (sweetness, etc.) dulzura, *f;* (of character) debilidad de carácter, *f;* (silliness) necedad, estupidez, *f*
**soggy** /'sɒgi/ *a* empapado de agua; saturado
**soil** /sɔil/ *n* tierra, *f;* (country) país, *m,* tierra, *f.* —*vt* ensuciar; *Fig.* manchar. **my native s.,** mi tierra, mi patria
**soiled** /sɔild/ *a* sucio. **s. linen,** ropa sucia, *f*
**soiree** /swa'rei/ *n* velada, *f*
**sojourn** /'soudʒɜrn/ *vi* morar, residir, permanecer. —*n* residencia, permanencia, *f*
**sojourner** /'soudʒɜrnər/ *n* morador (-ra), residente, *mf*
**sol** /sɒl/ *n mus* sol, *m.* **sol-fa,** *n* solfa, *f,* solfeo, *f.* —*vt* solfear
**solace** /'sɒlɪs/ *n* consuelo, solaz, *m.* —*vt* consolar; solazar

**solar** /'soulər/ *a* solar. **s. plexus,** *anat* plexo solar, *m*.
**s. system,** sistema solar, *m*
**solder** /'sɒdər/ *n* soldadura, *f*, *vt* soldar
**soldering** /'sɒdərɪŋ/ *n* soldadura, *f*
**soldier** /'souldʒər/ *n* soldado, *m*; militar, *m*. **He
wants to be a s.,** Quiere ser militar
**soldierly** /'souldʒərli/ *a* militar; marcial
**soldiery** /'souldʒəri/ *n* soldadesca, *f*
**sole** /soul/ *n* (of a foot) planta, *f*; (of a shoe) suela, *f*;
(of a plough) cepa, *f*; *ichth* lenguado, *m*, suela, *f*.
—*vt* (shoes) solar, poner suela (a). —*a* solo, único;
exclusivo. **s. right,** exclusiva, *f*, derecho exclusivo, *m*
**solecism** /'sɒlə,sɪzəm/ *n* solecismo, *m*
**solely** /'soulli/ *adv* sólo; únicamente, puramente;
meramente
**solemn** /'sɒləm/ *a* solemne; grave; serio; (sacred) sagrado. **Why do you look so s.?** ¿Por qué estás tan
serio?
**solemnity** /sə'lɛmnɪti/ *n* solemnidad, *f*
**solemnization** /,sɒləmnə'zeɪʃən/ *n* solemnización,
celebración, *f*
**solemnize** /'sɒləm,naiz/ *vt* solemnizar
**solemnly** /'sɒləmli/ *adv* solemnemente; gravemente
**solicit** /sə'lɪsɪt/ *vt* solicitar; implorar, rogar encarecidamente
**solicitation** /sə,lɪsɪ'teɪʃən/ *n* solicitación, *f*
**solicitor** /sə'lɪsɪtər/ *n* abogado (-da)
**solicitous** /sə'lɪsɪtəs/ *a* ansioso (de), deseoso (de);
solícito, atento; (worried) preocupado
**solicitude** /sə'lɪsɪ,tud/ *n* solicitud, *f*, cuidado, *m*;
(anxiety) preocupación, *f*
**solid** /'sɒlɪd/ *a* sólido; macizo; (of persons) serio, formal; (unanimous) unánime. —*n* sólido, *m*. **a s. meal,**
una comida fuerte. **He slept for ten s. hours,** Durmió
por diez horas seguidas. **solid-colored material,** tela
lisa, *f*. **s. food,** alimentos sólidos, *m pl*. **s. geometry,**
geometría del espacio, *f*. **solid gold,** oro de ley, *m*. **s.
tire,** llanta de goma maciza, *f*
**solidarity** /,sɒlɪ'dærɪti/ *n* solidaridad, *f*
**solidification** /sə,lɪdəfɪ'keɪʃən/ *n* solidificación, *f*
**solidify** /sə'lɪdə,faɪ/ *vt* solidificar. —*vi* solidificarse;
congelarse
**solidity** /sə'lɪdɪti/ *n* solidez, *f*; unanimidad, *f*
**solidly** /'sɒlɪdli/ *adv* sólidamente
**soliloquize** /sə'lɪlə,kwaɪz/ *vi* soliloquiar, hablar a solas
**soliloquy** /sə'lɪləkwi/ *n* soliloquio, *m*
**solitaire** /'sɒlɪ,tɛər/ *n* (diamond and game) solitario,
*m*
**solitary** /'sɒlɪ,tɛri/ *a* solitario; solo, aislado, único. **He
was in s. confinement for three months,** Estuvo incomunicado durante tres meses. **There is not a s.
one,** No hay ni uno
**solitude** /'sɒlɪ,tud/ *n* soledad, *f*
**solo** /'soulou/ *n* (performance and cards) solo, *m*. **to
sing a s.,** cantar un solo. **It was his first s. flight,**
Era su primer vuelo a solas
**soloist** /'soulouɪst/ *n* solista, *mf*
**solstice** /'sɒlstɪs, 'soul-/ *n* solsticio, *m*. **summer s.,**
solsticio vernal, *m*. **winter s.,** solsticio hiemal, *m*
**solubility** /,sɒljə'bɪlɪti/ *n* solubilidad, *f*
**soluble** /'sɒlyəbəl/ *a* soluble
**solution** /sə'luʃən/ *n* solución, *f*
**solvable** /'sɒlvəbəl/ *a* que se puede resolver, soluble
**solve** /sɒlv/ *vt* resolver, hallar la solución de
**solvency** /'sɒlvənsi/ *n* solvencia, *f*
**solvent** /'sɒlvənt/ *a com* solvente; (*chem* and *fig*) disolvente. —*n* disolvente, *m*
**somatic** /sou'mætɪk/ *a* somático
**somber** /'sɒmbər/ *a* sombrío
**somberly** /'sɒmbərli/ *adv* sombríamente
**somberness** /'sɒmbərnɪs/ *n* lo sombrío; sobriedad, *f*;
melancolía, *f*
**some** /sʌm; *unstressed* səm/ *a* alguno (-a), algunos
(-as); (before a masculine sing. noun) algún; unos
(-as); un poco de, algo de; (as a partitive, often not
translated, e.g. *Give me s. wine,* Dame vino); (approximately) aproximadamente, unos (-as). —*pron*
algunos (-as), unos (-as); algo, un poco. **I should like
s. strawberries,** Me gustaría comer unas fresas. **s.
day,** algún día. **S. say yes, others no,** Algunos dicen

que sí, otros que no. **There are s. sixty people in the
garden,** Hay unas sesenta personas en el jardín
**somebody, someone** /'sʌmbɒdi; 'sʌm,wʌn/ *n* alguien, *mf*. **s. else,** otro (-a), otra persona, *f*. **S. or
other said that the book is worth reading,** No sé
quién dijo que el libro vale la pena de leerse. **to be
s.,** *inf* ser un personaje
**somehow** /'sʌm,hau/ *adv* de un modo u otro, de alguna manera. **S. I don't like them,** No sé por qué,
pero no me gustan
**somersault** /'sʌmər,sɔlt/ *n* salto mortal, *m*, *vi* dar un
salto mortal
**something** /'sʌm,θɪŋ/ *n* algo, *m*, alguna cosa, *f*.
—*adv* algún tanto. **Would you like s. else?** ¿Quiere
Vd. otra cosa? **He left s. like fifty thousand dollars,**
Dejó algo así como cincuenta mil dolares. **He has s.
to live for,** Tiene para que vivir
**sometime** /'sʌm,taɪm/ *adv* algún día, alguna vez; en
algún tiempo. —*a* ex-. **Come and see me s. soon,**
Ven a verme algún día de estos. **He will have to go
abroad s. or another,** Tarde o temprano, tiene que ir
al extranjero. **s. last month,** durante el mes pasado
**sometimes** /'sʌm,taɪmz/ *adv* algunas veces, a veces.
**s. happy, s. sad,** algunas veces feliz y otras triste, ora
feliz ora triste
**somewhat** /'sʌm,wʌt/ *adv* algo; algún tanto, un
tanto; un poco. **I am s. busy,** Estoy algo ocupado. **He
is s. of a lady-killer,** Tiene sus puntos de castigador,
Tiene algo de castigador
**somewhere** /'sʌm,wɛər/ *adv* en alguna parte. **s.
about,** por ahí. **s. else,** en otra parte
**somnambulism** /sɒm'næmbyə,lɪzəm/ *n* somnambulismo, *m*
**somnambulist** /sɒm'næmbyəlɪst/ *n* somnámbulo
(-la)
**somnolence** /'sɒmnələns/ *n* somnolencia, *f*
**somnolent** /'sɒmnələnt/ *a* soñoliento; soporífero
**son** /sʌn/ *n* hijo, *m*. **son-in-law,** yerno, hijo político,
*m*
**sonata** /sə'nɑtə/ *n* sonata, *f*
**song** /sɒŋ/ *n* canto, *m*; canción, *f*; (poem) poema, *f*,
verso, *m*. **It's nothing to make a s. about,** No es
para tanto. **to break into s.,** ponerse a cantar. **the S.
of Songs,** Cantar de los Cantares, *m*. **s.-bird,** ave ca-
nora, *f*. **s.-book,** libro de canciones, *m*. **s.-writer,**
compositor (-ra) de canciones
**sonic** /'sɒnɪk/ *a* sónico. **sonic boom,** estampido
sónico, *m*
**sonnet** /'sɒnɪt/ *n* soneto, *m*
**sonorous** /sə'nɔrəs/ *a* sonoro
**sonorousness** /sə'nɔrəsnɪs/ *n* sonoridad, *f*
**soon** /sun/ *adv* pronto; dentro de poco, luego. **as s.
as,** así que, en cuanto, luego que, no bien... **as s. as
possible,** lo antes posible, lo más pronto posible, con
la mayor antelación posible, cuanto antes. **s. after,**
poco después (de). **See you s.!** ¡Hasta pronto!
**sooner or later,** tarde o temprano. **the sooner the
better,** cuanto antes mejor. **No sooner had he left
the house, when...** Apenas hubo dejado la casa,
cuando... **Emily would sooner go to London,** Emilia
preferiría a Londres (A Emilia le gustaría más ir a
Londres)
**soot** /sʊt/ *n* hollín, *m*, *vt* cubrir de hollín
**soothe** /suð/ *vt* tranquilizar, calmar, (pain) aliviar,
mitigar
**soothing** /'suðɪŋ/ *a* calmante, tranquilizador, sosegador; (of powders, etc.) calmante
**soothingly** /'suðɪŋli/ *adv* con dulzura; suavemente;
como un consuelo
**soothsayer** /'suθ,seɪər/ *n* adivino (-na), adivinador
(-ra)
**soothsaying** /'suθ,seɪɪŋ/ *n* adivinanza, *f*
**sooty** /'sʊti/ *a* cubierto de hollín; negro como el hollín
**sop** /sɒp/ *n* sopa, *f*; (bribe) soborno, *m*
**sophism** /'sɒfɪzəm/ *n* sofisma, *m*
**sophist** /'sɒfɪst/ *n hist* sofista, *m*; (quibbler) sofista,
*mf*
**sophistic** /sə'fɪstɪk/ *a philos* sofista; (of persons, arguments) sofístico
**sophisticated** /sə'fɪstɪ,keɪtɪd/ *a* nada ingenuo; mundano; (cultured) culto

**sophistication** /sə,fɪstɪ'keɪʃən/ *n* falta de simplicidad, *f;* mundanería, *f;* cultura, *f*

**sophistry** /'sɒfəstri/ *n* sofistería, *f*

**Sophoclean** /,sɒfə'kliən/ *a* sofocleo

**soporific** /,sɒpə'rɪfɪk/ *a* soporífico

**sopping** /'sɒpɪŋ/ *a* muy mojado. **s. wet,** hecho una sopa

**soprano** /sə'prænou/ *n* (voice and part) soprano, *m;* (singer) soprano, tiple, *mf*

**sorcerer** /'sɔrsərər/ *n* encantador, mago, brujo, *m*

**sorceress** /'sɔrsərɪs/ *n* hechicera, bruja, *f*

**sorcery** /'sɔrsəri/ *n* sortilegio, *m,* hechicería, brujería, *f;* encanto, *m*

**sordid** /'sɔrdɪd/ *a* sórdido; (of motives, etc.) ruin, vil

**sordidness** /'sɔrdɪdnɪs/ *n* sordidez, *f;* (of motives, etc.) vileza, bajeza, *f*

**sordine** /'sɔrden/ *n Mus.* sordina, *f*

**sore** /sɔr/ *a* doloroso, malo; (sad) triste; (annoyed) enojado; (with need, etc.) extremo. —*n* llaga, *f;* (on horses, etc., caused by girths) matadura, *f; Fig.* herida, *f;* recuerdo doloroso, *m.* **to open an old s.,** *Fig.* renovar la herida. **running s.,** úlcera, *f.* **s. throat,** dolor de garganta, *m*

**sorely** /'sɔrli/ *adv* grandemente; muy; urgentemente. **He was s. tempted,** Tuvo grandes tentaciones

**soreness** /'sɔrnɪs/ *n* dolor, *m;* (resentment) amargura, *f,* resentimiento, *m;* (ill-feeling) rencor, *m*

**sorrel** /'sɔrəl, 'sɒr-/ *a* alazán. —*n* (horse) alazán, *m; Bot.* acedera, *f*

**sorrow** /'sɒrou/ *n* pesar, *m,* aflicción, pesadumbre, *f;* tristeza, *f.* —*vi* afligirse; entristecerse. **To my great s.,** Con gran pesar mío. **s.-stricken,** afligido, agobiado de pena

**sorrowful** /'sɒrəfəl/ *a* afligido, angustiado; triste

**sorrowfully** /'sɒrəfəli/ *adv* con pena, tristemente

**sorrowing** /'sɒrouɪŋ/ *a* afligido. —*n* aflicción, *f;* lamentación, *f*

**sort** /sɔrt/ *n* especie, *f;* clase, *f;* tipo, *m.* —*vt* separar (de); clasificar. **a s. of hat,** una especie de sombrero. **all sorts of,** toda clase de. **He is a good s.,** Es buen chico. **He is a queer s.,** Es un tipo raro. **in some s.,** hasta cierto punto. **I am out of sorts,** Estoy destemplado. **Nothing of the s.!** ¡Nada de eso!

**sorter** /'sɔrtər/ *n* oficial de correos, *m;* clasificador (-ra)

**sorting** /'sɔrtɪŋ/ *n* clasificación, *f*

**sot** /sɒt/ *n* zaque, pellejo, *m*

**sotto voce** /'sɒt'ou voutʃi/ *adv* a sovoz, en voz baja

**soul** /soul/ *n* alma, *f;* espíritu, *m;* (departed) ánima, *f;* (being) ser, *m;* (life) vida, *f;* (heart) corazón, *m.* **All Souls' Day,** Día de los Difuntos, *m.* **He is a good s.!** ¡Es un bendito! **She is a simple s.,** Ella es una alma de Dios. **without seeing a living s.,** sin ver un bicho viviente. **Upon my s.!** ¡Por mi vida! **s. in purgatory,** alma en pena, *f.* **s.-stirring,** emocionante

**soulful** /'soulfəl/ *a* sentimental, emocional; espiritual; romántico

**soulless** /'soullɪs/ *a* sin alma; mecánico

**sound** /saund/ *n* sonido, *m;* son, *m;* ruido, *m;* (strait) estrecho, *m.* —*vi* sonar; hacer ruido; resonar; (seem) parecer. —*vt* sonar; (the horn, the alarm, musical instrument) tocar; (express) expresar; proclamar; (praise) celebrar; *Naut.* hondear; *Med.* tentar; (the chest) auscultar; (try to discover) tentar, sondar; (experience) experimentar. **to the s. of,** al son de. **s.-box,** (of a gramophone) diafragma, *m.* **s.-detector,** fonolocalización de aviones, *f.* **s.-film,** película sonora, *f.* **s.-proof,** (of radio studios, etc.) aislado de todo sonido. **s.-track,** guía sonora, banda sonora, *f.* **s.-wave,** onda sonora, *f*

**sound** /saund/ *a* sano; (of a person) perspicaz; (reasonable) lógico, razonable; (of a policy, etc.) prudente; (of an argument, etc.) válido; (of an investment) seguro; (solvent) solvente; (good) bueno; (deep) profundo. —*adv* profundamente, bien

**sounding** /'saundɪŋ/ *n Naut.* sondeo, *m; pl* **soundings,** sondas, *f pl.* —*a* sonoro. **to take soundings,** sondar, echar la plomada. **s.-board,** tabla de armonía, *f*

**soundless** /'saundlɪs/ *a* sin ruido, silencioso

**soundly** /'saundli/ *adv* sanamente; juiciosamente; prudentemente; bien; (deeply) profundamente

**soundness** /'saundnɪs/ *n* (of a person) perspicacia, *f;* (of a policy, etc.) prudencia, *f;* (of an argument, etc.) validez, fuerza, *f;* (financial) solvencia, *f*

**soup** /sup/ *n* sopa, *f.* **clear s.,** consommé, *m.* **thick s.,** puré, *m.* **to be in the s.,** *Inf.* estar aviado. **s.-ladle,** cucharón, *m.* **s.-plate,** plato sopero, *m.* **s.-tureen,** sopera, *f*

**sour** /sauər/ *a* ácido, agrio; (of milk) agrio; (of persons, etc.) agrio, desabrido. —*vt* agriar. **to go s.,** volverse agrio. **S. grapes!** ¡Están verdes!

**source** /sɔrs/ *n* (of a river, etc.) nacimiento, *m;* fuente, *f;* (of infection) foco, *m.* **to know from a good s.,** saber de buena tinta

**sourly** /'sauərli/ *adv* agriamente

**sourness** /'sauərnɪs/ *n* acidez, agrura, *f;* acrimonia, *f*

**south** /sauθ/ *n* sur, *m;* mediodía, *m.* —*a* del sur. —*adv* hacia el sur. **S. African,** *a* and *n* sudafricano (-na). **S. American,** *a* and *n* sudamericano (-na). **s.-east,** *n* sudeste, *m.* —*a* del sudeste. —*adv* hacia el sudeste. **s.-easter,** viento del sudeste, *m.* **s.-easterly,** *a* del sudeste; al sudeste. —*adv* hacia el sudeste. **s.-eastern,** del sudeste. **s.-s.-east,** *n* sudsudeste, *m.* **s.-s.-west,** sudsudoeste, *m.* **s.-west,** *n* sudoeste, *m.* —*a* del sudoeste. —*adv* hacia el sudoeste. **s.-west wind,** viento sudoeste, ábrego, *m.* **s.-westerly,** *a* del sudoeste. —*adv* hacia el sudoeste. **s.-western,** del sudoeste

**South Africa** República Sudafricana, *f*

**South America** América del Sur, Sudamérica, *f*

**southerly** /'sʌðərli/ *a* del sur; hacia el sur. **The house has a s. aspect,** La casa está orientada al sur

**southern** /'sʌðərn/ *a* del sur; del mediodía; meridional. **S. Cross,** Cruz, *f,* Crucero, *m.* **s. express,** sudexpreso, *m*

**southerner** /'sʌðərnər/ *n* habitante del sur, *m*

**South Sea** Mar del Sur, Mar del Pacífico, *m*

**southward** /'sauθwərd/ *Naut.* 'sʌðərd/ *a* del sur; al sur. —*adv* hacia el sur

**souvenir** /,suvə'nɪər/ *n* recuerdo, *m*

**sovereign** /'sɒvrɪn/ *a* soberano. —*n* soberano (-na); (coin) soberano, *m*

**sovereignty** /'sɒvrɪnti/ *n* soberanía, *f*

**soviet** /'souvi,et/ *n* soviet, *m,* *a* soviético

**Soviet Union, the** la Unión Soviética, *f*

**sow** /sau/ *n* cerda, puerca, marrana, *f;* (of a wild boar) jabalina, *f;* (of iron) galápago, *m*

**sow** /sou/ *vt* sembrar; esparcir; diseminar

**sower** /'souər/ *n* sembrador (-ra)

**sowing** /'souɪŋ/ *n* sembradura, siembra, *f.* **s. machine,** sembradera, *f.*

**soya bean** /'sɔiə/ *n* soja, *f*

**spa** /spɑ/ *n* balneario, *m;* (spring) manantial mineral, *m,* caldas, *f pl*

**space** /speis/ *n* espacio, *m;* (of time) temporada, *f;* intervalo, *m;* (*Print., Mus.*) espacio, *m.* —*vt* espaciar. **blank s.,** blanco, *m.* **s.-bar,** tecla de espacios, *f,* espaciador, *m*

**spacious** /'speiʃəs/ *a* espacioso; amplio

**spaciousness** /'speiʃəsnɪs/ *n* espaciosidad, *f;* amplitud, *f*

**spade** /speid/ *n* pala, azada, *f;* (cards) espada, *f.* **to call a s. a s.,** llamar al pan pan y al vino vino, llamar a las cosas por su nombre. **s.-work,** trabajo preparatorio, *m,* labor de pala, *f*

**spaghetti** /spə'geti/ *n* fideos, macarrones, *m pl*

**Spain** /spein/ España, *f*

**span** /spæn/ *vt* medir a palmos; rodear; medir; (cross) atravesar, cruzar. —*n* palmo, *m;* espacio, *m,* duración, *f;* (of a bridge) vano, *m;* (of wing, *Aer.,* *Zool.*) envergadura, *f;* (distance) distancia, *f.* **single-s. bridge,** puente de vano único. **the brief s. of human life,** la corta duración de la vida humana

**spangle** /'spæŋgəl/ *n* lentejuela, *f;* (tinsel) oropel, *m.* —*vt* adornar con lentejuelas; sembrar (de), esparcir (de). **spangled with stars,** sembrado de estrellas

**Spaniard** /'spænyərd/ *n* español (-la). **a young S.,** un joven español

**spaniel** /'spænyəl/ *n* perro de aguas, perro sabueso español *m;* (cocker) sabueso, *m*

**Spanish** /'spænɪʃ/ *a* español. —*n* (language) español, castellano, *m.* **a S. girl,** una muchacha española. **in S. fashion,** a la española. **S. American,** *a* and *n* hispanoamericano (-na). **S. broom,** retama de olor, *f.* **S. fly,** cantárida, *f*

**Spanish America** Hispanoamérica, *f*

**spank** /spæŋk/ *vt* pegar con la mano, azotar. —*n* azotazo, *m.* **to s. along,** correr rápidamente; (of a horse) galopar

**spanking** /'spæŋkɪŋ/ *n* azotamiento, vapuleo, *m*

**spanner** /'spænər/ *n* llave inglesa, llave de tuercas, *f*

**spar** /spɑr/ *n Naut.* mastel, *m; Mineral.* espato, *m;* (boxing) boxeo, *m;* (quarrel) disputa, *f.* —*vi* boxear; (argue) disputar

**spare** /spɛər/ *a* (meager) frugal, escaso; (of persons) enjuto, flaco; (available) disponible; (extra) de repuesto. —*n* recambio, *m.* **s. part,** pieza de recambio, pieza de repuesto, *f.* **s. room,** cuarto de amigos, *m.* **s. time,** ratos de ocio, *m pl,* tiempo disponible, *m.* **s. wheel,** rueda de repuesto, *f*

**spare** /spɛər/ *vt* (expense, etc.) escatimar; ahorrar; (do without) pasarse sin; (give) dar; (a life, etc.) perdonar; (avoid) evitar; dispensar de; (grant) hacer gracia de; (time) dedicar. **I cannot s. her,** No puedo estar sin ella. **They have no money to s.,** No tienen dinero de sobra. **to be sparing of,** ser avaro de

**sparingly** /'spɛərɪŋli/ *adv* frugalmente; escasamente. **to eat s.,** comer con frugalidad

**spark** /spɑrk/ *n* chispa, *f;* (gallant) pisaverde, *m.* —*vi* chispear, echar chispas

**sparking** /'spɑrkɪŋ/ *a* chispeante. —*n* emisión de chispas, *f.* **s.-plug,** bujía de encendido, *f*

**sparkle** /'spɑrkəl/ *vi* centellear, rutilar, destellar; *Fig.* brillar; (of wines) ser espumoso. —*n* centelleo, destello, *m; Fig.* brillo, *m*

**sparkling** /'spɑrklɪŋ/ *a* rutilante, centelleante, reluciente; *Fig.* brillante, chispeante; (of wines) espumante

**sparring match** /'spɑrɪŋ/ *n* combate de boxeo amistoso, *m*

**sparrow** /'spærou/ *n* gorrión, *m.* **s.-hawk,** gavilán, esparaván, *m*

**sparse** /spɑrs/ *a* claro, ralo; esparcido

**sparsely** /'spɑrsli/ *adv* escasamente

**Sparta** /'spɑrtə/ Esparta, *f*

**Spartan** /'spɑrtn/ *a* and *n* espartano (-na)

**spasm** /'spæzəm/ *n* espasmo, *m;* ataque, *m;* acceso, *m*

**spasmodic** /spæz'mɒdɪk/ *a* espasmódico; intermitente

**spasmodically** /spæz'mɒdɪkli/ *adv* espasmódicamente

**spat** /spæt/ *n* (gaiter) polaina de tela, *f*

**spate** /speit/ *n* crecida, *f; Fig.* torrente, *m.* **in s.,** crecido

**spatter** /'spætər/ *vt* salpicar; (*Fig.* smirch) manchar. —*vi* rociar. —*n* salpicadura, *f;* rociada, *f*

**spatula** /'spætʃələ/ *n* espátula, *f*

**spawn** /spɔn/ *vt* and *vi* desovar; engendrar. —*n* huevas, *f pl,* freza, *f;* (offspring) producto, *m*

**spawning** /'spɔnɪŋ/ *n* desove, *m*

**speak** /spik/ *vi* hablar; pronunciar un discurso; (sound) sonar. —*vt* decir; (French, etc.) hablar. **She never spoke to him again,** Nunca volvió a dirigirle la palabra. **roughly speaking,** aproximadamente, más o menos. **Speaking for myself,** En cuanto a mí, Por mi parte. **without speaking,** sin decir nada, sin hablar. **to s. for,** (a person) hablar por. **to s. for itself,** hablar por sí mismo, ser evidente. **to s. one's mind,** decir lo que se piensa. **to s. of,** hablar de. **to s. out,** hablar claro; hablar alto. **to s. up for,** (a person) hablar en favor de (alguien)

**speaker** /'spikər/ *n* el, *m,* (f, la) que habla; (public) orador (-ra). **the S.,** el Presidente de la Cámara de los Comunes

**speaking** /'spikɪŋ/ *a* hablante; para hablar; elocuente, expresivo. —*n* habla, *f,* discurso, *m.* **They are not on s. terms,** No se hablan. **within s. distance,** al habla. **s.-trumpet,** portavoz, *m.* **s.-tube,** tubo acústico, *m*

**spear** /spɪər/ *n* lanza, *f;* (javelin) venablo, *m;* (harpoon) arpón, *m.* —*vt* herir con lanza, alancear; (fish) arponear. **s.-head,** punta de la lanza, *f.* **s.-thrust,** lanzada, *f*

**special** /'spɛʃəl/ *a* especial; particular; extraordinario. —*n* (train) tren extraordinario, *m.* **s. correspondent,**

corresponsal extraordinario, *m.* **s. friend,** amigo (-ga) del alma, amigo íntimo

**specialist** /'spɛʃəlɪst/ *n* especialista, *mf*

**specialization** /,spɛʃələ'zeiʃən/ *n* especialización, *f*

**specialize** /'spɛʃə,laiz/ *vt* especializar. —*vi* especializarse

**specially** /'spɛʃəli/ *adv* especialmente; particularmente; sobre todo

**specialty** /,spɛʃi'ælɪti/ *n* particularidad, *f;* especialidad, *f*

**species** /'spiʃiz, -siz/ *n* especie, *f;* raza, *f*

**specific** /spɪ'sɪfɪk/ *a* específico; explícito. —*n* específico, *m.* **s. gravity,** peso específico, *m,* densidad, *f*

**specifically** /spɪ'sɪfɪkli/ *adv* específicamente; explícitamente

**specification** /,spɛsəfɪ'keiʃən/ *n* especificación, *f*

**specify** /'spɛsə,fai/ *vt* especificar

**specimen** /'spɛsəmən/ *n* espécimen, *m;* ejemplo, *m; Inf.* tipo, *m*

**specious** /'spiʃəs/ *a* especioso

**speciousness** /'spiʃəsnɪs/ *n* plausibilidad, *f;* apariencia engañosa, *f*

**speck** /spɛk/ *n* pequeña mancha, *f;* punto, *m;* átomo, *m;* (on fruit) maca, *f*

**speckle** /'spɛkəl/ *vt* motear, manchar

**speckled** /'spɛkəld/ *a* abigarrado; con manchas

**spectacle** /'spɛktəkəl/ *n* espectáculo, *m;* escena, *f; pl* **spectacles,** gafas, *f pl,* anteojos, *m pl.* **s.-case,** cajita para las gafas, *f*

**spectacled** /'spɛktəkəld/ *a* con gafas, que lleva gafas

**spectacular** /spɛk'tækyələr/ *a* espectacular

**spectator** /'spɛkteitər/ *n* espectador (-ra)

**specter** /'spɛktər/ *n* espectro, fantasma, *m*

**spectral** /'spɛktrəl/ *a* espectral

**spectroscope** /'spɛktrə,skoup/ *n* espectroscopio, *m*

**spectrum** /'spɛktrəm/ *n Phys.* espectro, *m*

**speculate** /'spɛkyə,leit/ *vi* especular (sobre, acerca de); *Com.* especular (en)

**speculation** /,spɛkyə'leiʃən/ *n* especulación, *f*

**speculative** /'spɛkyə,leitiv/ *a* especulativo

**speculator** /'spɛkyə,leitər/ *n* especulador (-ra)

**speech** /spitʃ/ *n* habla, *f;* palabra, *f;* (idiom) lenguaje, *m;* (language) idioma, *m; Gram.* oración, *f;* (address) discurso, *m;* disertación, *f.* **part of s.,** parte de la oración, *f.* **to make a s.,** pronunciar un discurso. **s. maker,** orador (-ra)

**speechless** /'spitʃlɪs/ *a* mudo; sin habla; desconcertado, turbado

**speed** /spid/ *n* prisa, rapidez, *f;* velocidad, *f.* —*vt* dar la bienvenida (a); conceder éxito (a); (accelerate) acelerar. —*vi* darse prisa; correr a toda prisa; (of arrows) volar. **at full s.,** a toda prisa, a toda velocidad; a todo correr. **maximum s.,** velocidad máxima, *f.* **with all s.,** a toda prisa. **s. of impact,** velocidad del choque, *f.* **s.-boat,** lancha de carrera, *f.* **s.-limit,** velocidad máxima, *f,* límite de velocidad, *m*

**speedily** /'spidli/ *adv* aprisa, rápidamente; prontamente

**speediness** /'spidɪnɪs/ *n* rapidez, prisa, celeridad, *f;* prontitud, *f*

**speeding** /'spidɪŋ/ *n* exceso de velocidad, *m.* **s. up,** aceleración, *f*

**speedometer** /spi'dɒmɪtər/ *n* cuentakilómetros, *m*

**speedway** /'spid,wei/ *n* autódromo, *m,* pista de ceniza, *f*

**speedy** /'spidi/ *a* rápido; pronto

**spell** /spɛl/ *n* ensalmo, hechizo, *m;* encanto, *m;* (bout) turno, *m;* (interval) rato, *m;* temporada, *f.* —*vt* (a word) deletrear; (a word in writing) escribir; (mean) significar; (be) ser. **a s. of good weather,** una temporada de buen tiempo. **by spells,** a ratos. **to learn to s.,** aprender la ortografía. **s.-bound,** encantado, fascinado; asombrado

**spelling** /'spɛlɪŋ/ *n* deletreo, *m;* ortografía, *f.* **s.-book,** silabario, *m;* **s. mistake,** falta de ortografía, *f*

**spelling bee** *n* certamen de deletreo, *m*

**spend** /spɛnd/ *vt* gastar; (time, etc.) pasar; perder; consumir, agotar. —*vi* gastar, hacer gastos. **to s. oneself,** agotarse

**spendthrift** /'spɛnd,θrɪft/ n derrochador (-ra), manirroto (-ta). —a despilfarrado, pródigo

**spent** /spɛnt/ a agotado, rendido. **The night is far s.,** La noche está avanzada. **s. bullet,** bala fría, f

**sperm** /spɜrm/ n Biol. esperma, f; (whale) cachalote, m

**spermaceti** /,spɜrmə'sɛti/ n esperma de ballena, f

**sphere** /sfɪər/ n esfera, f. **s. of influence,** zona de influencia, f

**spherical** /'sfɛrɪkəl, 'sfɪər-/ a esférico

**sphinx** /sfɪŋks/ n esfinge, f. **s.-like,** de esfinge

**spice** /spais/ n especia, f; Fig. sabor, m; (trace) dejo, m. —vt especiar. **s. cupboard,** especiero, m

**spick and span** /'spɪk ən 'spæn/ a limpio como una patena; (brand-new) flamante; (of persons) muy compuesto

**spicy** /'spaisi/ a especiado; aromático; Fig. picante

**spider** /'spaidər/ n araña, f. **spider's web,** telaraña, f

**spidery** /'spaidəri/ a de araña; lleno de arañas. **s. writing,** letra de patas de araña, f

**spigot** /'spɪɡət/ n espiche, m

**spike** /spaik/ n punta (de hierro, etc.), f; escarpia, f; (for boots) clavo, m; Bot. espiga, f. —vt clavetear; (a cannon) clavar

**spill** /spɪl/ vt derramar. —n (fall) caída, f

**spilling** /'spɪlɪŋ/ n derramamiento, derrame, m

**spin** /spɪn/ vt hilar; (a cocoon) tejer; (a top) bailar; (a ball) tornear; (a coin) lanzar. —vi hilar; girar, bailar. —n vuelta, f; paseo, m. **to send spinning downstairs,** hacer rodar por la escalera (a). **to s. a yarn,** contar un cuento. **to s. out,** prolongar

**spinach** /'spɪnɪtʃ/ n espinaca, f

**spinal** /'spainl/ a espinal. **s. anaesthesia,** raquianestesia, f. **s. column,** columna vertebral, f

**spindle** /'spɪndl/ n huso, m; Mech. eje, m. **s.-shaped,** ahusado

**spine** /spain/ n Anat. espinazo, m, columna vertebral, f; Bot. espina, f; (of a porcupine, etc.) púa, f

**spineless** /'spainlɪs/ a Zool. invertebrado; Fig. débil

**spinet** /'spɪnɪt/ n espineta, f

**spinner** /'spɪnər/ n hilandero (-ra); máquina de hilar, f

**spinney** /'spɪni/ n arboleda, f; bosquecillo, m

**spinning** /'spɪnɪŋ/ n hilado, m; hilandería, f. **s.-machine,** máquina de hilar, f. **s.-top,** trompo, m, peonza, f. **s.-wheel,** rueca, f

**spinster** /'spɪnstər/ n soltera, f. **confirmed s.,** solterona, f

**spiny** /'spaini/ a con púas; espinoso

**spiral** /'spairəl/ a espiral; en espiral. —n espiral, f

**spirally** /'spairəli/ adv en espiral

**spire** /spaiⁱr/ n (of a church) aguja, f; espira, f

**spirit** /'spɪrɪt/ n espíritu, m; alma, f; (ghost) aparecido, fantasma, m; (outstanding person) ingenio, m, inteligencia, f; (disposition) ánimo, m; (courage) valor, espíritu, m; (for a lamp, etc.) alcohol, m. **the Holy S.,** El Espíritu Santo. **to be in high spirits,** no caber de contento, saltar de alegría. **to be in low spirits,** estar desalentado, estar deprimido. **to be full of spirits,** ser bullicioso, tener mucha energía. **to keep up one's spirits,** sostener el valor. **to s. away,** quitar secretamente, hacer desaparecer; (kidnap) secuestrar. **s.-level,** nivel de burbuja, m. **s.-stove,** cocinilla, f

**spirited** /'spɪrɪtɪd/ a animado, vigoroso; fogoso, animoso, brioso

**spiritless** /'spɪrɪtlɪs/ a sin espíritu, apático; flojo, débil; (depressed) abatido, desalentado; (cowardly) sin valor, cobarde

**spiritual** /'spɪrɪtʃuəl/ a espiritual

**spiritualism** /'spɪrɪtʃuə,lɪzəm/ n espiritismo, m; Philos. espiritualismo, m

**spiritualist** /'spɪrɪtʃuəlɪst/ n espiritista, mf; Philos. espiritualista, mf

**spiritualistic** /,spɪrɪtʃuə'lɪstɪk/ a espiritista; Philos. espiritualista, f

**spirituality** /,spɪrɪtʃu'ælɪtɪ/ ' n espiritualidad, f

**spiritually** /'spɪrɪtʃuəli/ adv espiritualmente

**spirituous** /'spɪrɪtʃuəs/ a espiritoso

**spirt** /spɜrt/ vi, vt, n. See **spurt**

**spit** /spɪt/ n (for roasting) espetón, asador, m; (sand-

bank) banco de arena, m; (of land) lengua de tierra, f; (spittle) saliva, f. **the spit of, the spit and image of, the spitting image of,** la imagen viva de, la segunda edición de, f. —vt (skewer) espetar; (saliva, etc.) escupir; (curses, etc.) vomitar. —vi escupir, expectorar; (of a cat) fufear, decir fu; (sputter) chisporrotear; (rain) lloviznar

**spite** /spait/ n malevolencia, mala voluntad, hostilidad, f; rencor, m, ojeriza, f. —vt contrariar, hacer daño (a). **He has a s. against them,** Les tiene rencor. **in s. of,** a pesar de; a despecho de

**spiteful** /'spaitfəl/ a rencoroso, malévolo

**spitefully** /'spaitfəli/ adv malévolamente; con rencor; por maldad; por despecho

**spitefulness** /'spaitfəlnɪs/ n malevolencia, f; rencor, m

**spitfire** /'spɪt,faiⁱr/ n cascarrabias, mf, furia, f

**spittle** /'spɪtl/ n saliva, f

**splash** /splæʃ/ vt salpicar (de); manchar (con). —vi derramarse, esparcirse; chapotear, chapalear. —n chapoteo, m; (of rain, etc.) chapaleteo, m; (stain or patch) mancha, f. **John was splashing about in the sea,** Juan chapoteaba en el mar. **to make a s.,** Fig. causar una sensación. **s.-board,** alero, m

**spleen** /splin/ n Anat. bazo, m; esplín, m

**splendid** /'splɛndɪd/ a espléndido; magnífico; glorioso; excelente

**splendidly** /'splɛndɪdli/ adv espléndidamente; magníficamente; excelentemente

**splendor** /'splɛndər/ n resplandor, m; magnificencia, f; (of exploits, etc.) esplendor, brillo, m

**splice** /splais/ vt (ropes, timbers) empalmar; (marry) unir, casar. —n empalme, m

**splint** /splɪnt/ n Surg. férula, f. **to put in a s.,** entablar

**splinter** /'splɪntər/ vt astillar, hacer astillas. —vi hacerse astillas

**splintery** /'splɪntəri/ a astilloso

**split** /splɪt/ vi henderse; resquebrajarse; (of seams) nacerse; abrirse; dividirse. —vt hender; partir; dividir; abrir; (the atom) escindir. —n hendedura, f; grieta, f; división, f; (in fabric) rasgón, m; (quarrel) ruptura, f. **to s. hairs,** andar en quisquillas, pararse en pelillos, sutilizar. **I have a splitting headache,** Tengo un dolor de cabeza que me trae loco. **to s. one's sides,** reírse a carcajadas, desternillarse de risa. **to s. on a rock,** estrellarse contra una roca. **to s. the difference,** partir la diferencia. **The blow s. his head open,** El golpe le abrió la cabeza. **to s. on,** Inf. delatar, denunciar

**splotch** /splɒtʃ/ n mancha, f, borrón, m

**splutter** /'splʌtər/ vi chisporrotear; (of a person) balbucir. —n chisporroteo, m. **to s. out,** decir tartamudeando

**spoil** /spɔil/ n botín, despojo, m; (of war) trofeo, m. —vt estropear; echar a perder; (diminish) mitigar; (a child) mimar; (injure) dañar; (destroy) arruinar, destruir. —vi estropearse; echarse a perder. **to be spoiling for a fight,** tener ganas de pelearse. **You have spoilt my fun,** Me has aguado la fiesta. **s.-sport,** aguafiestas, mf

**spoiled** /spɔild/ a (of a child, etc.) mimado, consentido, malacostumbrado

**spoke** /spouk/ n (of a wheel) rayo, m; (of a ladder) travesaño, peldaño, m; Naut. cabilla (de la rueda del timón), f

**spoken** /'spoukən/ a hablado. **well-s.,** bien hablado; cortés

**spokesman** /'spouksmən/ n portavoz, m. **to be s.,** llevar la palabra

**spoliation** /,spouli'eifən/ n expoliación, f; despojo, m

**sponge** /spʌndʒ/ n esponja, f; (cadger) gorrón (-ona); (cake) bizcocho, m. —vt limpiar con esponja. **to s.,** Inf. vivir de gorra. **s.-holder,** esponjera, f

**sponger** /'spʌndʒər/ n gorrón (-ona), vividor, m, sablista, mf

**sponginess** /'spʌndʒinɪs/ n esponjosidad, f

**sponging** n esponjadura, f; Inf. sablazo, m

**spongy** /'spʌndʒi/ a esponjoso

**sponsor** /'spɒnsər/ n garante, mf; valedor (-ra), patron (-na); (godfather) padrino, m; (godmother) madrina, f, (radio and TV) auspiciador, patrocinador, m

**spontaneity** /ˌspɒntəˈniːti, -ˈneɪ-/ n espontaneidad, f
**spontaneous** /spɒnˈteɪniəs/ a espontáneo. **s. combustion,** combustión espontánea, f
**spontaneously** /spɒnˈteɪniəsli/ adv espontáneamente
**spook** /spuːk/ n fantasma, espectro, m
**spool** /spuːl/ n (for thread) bobina, f, carrete, m; (in a sewing machine) canilla, f; (of a fishing rod) carrete, m
**spoon** /spuːn/ n cuchara, f. —vt sacar con cuchara. —vi (slang) besuquearse. **to s.-feed,** dar de comer con cuchara (a); tratar como a un niño (a)
**spoonful** /ˈspuːnfʊl/ n cucharada, f
**spoor** /spʊr, spɔr/ n pista, huella de animal, f; rastro, m
**sporadic** /spəˈrædɪk/ a esporádico
**spore** /spɔr/ n Bot. espora, f; Zool. germen, m
**sport** /spɔrt/ n deporte, sport, m; deportismo, m; (jest) broma, f; (game) juego, m; (plaything) juguete, m; (pastime) pasatiempo, m. —vi jugar; recrearse, divertirse. —vt llevar; ostentar, lucir. **He is a s.,** Es un buen chico. **to make s. of,** burlarse de. **sports car,** coche de deporte, m. **sports ground,** campo de recreo, m. **sports jacket,** chaqueta de deporte, americana, f. **sports shirt,** camisa corta, f
**sporting** /ˈspɔrtɪŋ/ a deportista; caballeroso. **I think there is a s. chance,** Me parece que hay una posibilidad de éxito
**sporting goods** n artículos de deporte, efectos de deportes, m pl
**sportive** /ˈspɔrtɪv/ a juguetón; bromista
**sportsman** /ˈspɔrtsmən/ n deportista, m; aficionado al sport, m; Fig. caballero, señor, m; buen chico, m
**sportsmanlike** /ˈspɔrtsmənˌlaɪk/ a de deportista; caballeroso
**sportsmanship** /ˈspɔrtsmənˌʃɪp/ n deportividad, f
**spot** /spɒt/ n mancha, f; pinta, f; (on the face, etc.) peca, f; grano, m; (place) sitio, m; lugar, m; (of liquor) trago, m; (of food) bocado, m; (of rain) gota, f. —vt manchar; motear; (recognize) reconocer; (understand) darse cuenta de, comprender. **a tender s.,** Fig. debilidad, f. **on the s.,** en el acto. **s. ball,** (billiards) pinta, f. **s. cash,** dinero contante, m
**spotless** /ˈspɒtlɪs/ a saltando de limpio; sin mancha; inmaculado; puro; virgen
**spotlight** /ˈspɒtˌlaɪt/ n luz del proyector, f; proyector, m
**spotted** /ˈspɒtɪd/ a (stained) manchado; (of animals, etc.) con manchas; (of garments, etc.) con pintas
**spotty** /ˈspɒti/ a lleno de manchas; moteado; (pimply) con granos
**spouse** /spaʊs/ n esposo, m; esposa, f
**spout** /spaʊt/ vi chorrear; Inf. hablar incesantemente. —vt arrojar; vomitar; Inf. declamar, recitar. —n (of a jug, etc.) pico, m; (for water, etc.) tubo, m, cañería, f; canalón, m; (gust) ráfaga, nube, f. **down s.,** tubo de bajada, m
**spouting** /ˈspaʊtɪŋ/ n chorreo, m; Inf. declamación, f
**Sprachgefühl** /ˈʃpraːxɡəˌfiːl/ n sentido del idioma, m
**sprain** /spreɪn/ vt dislocar, torcer. —n dislocación, f, esguince, m. **Victoria has sprained her foot,** Victoria se ha torcido el pie
**sprat** /spræt/ n sardineta, f
**sprawl** /sprɔl/ vi recostarse (en); extenderse; (of plants) trepar. **He went sprawling,** Cayó cuan largo era
**spray** /spreɪ/ n (branch) ramo, m; (of water, etc.) rocío, m; (of the sea) espuma, f; (mechanical device) pulverizador, m. —vt pulverizar; rociar; regar; (the throat) jeringar
**spread** /sprɛd/ vt tender (de); cubrir (de); poner; (stretch out) extender; (open out) desplegar; (of disease, etc.) propagar; diseminar; divulgar, difundir. —vi extenderse; propagarse; difundirse; divulgarse; (become general) generalizarse. —n extensión, f; expansión, f; propagación, f; divulgación, f; (Aer. and of birds) envergadura, f. **Carmen s. her hands to the fire,** Carmen extendió las manos al fuego. **The peacock s. his tail,** El pavo real hizo la rueda. **The dove s. its wings,** La paloma desplegó sus alas. **to s. out,** vt extender; desplegar; (scatter) esparcir, vi extenderse. **spread like wildfire,** correr como pólvora

en reguero, propagarse como un reguero de pólvora, ser un reguero de pólvora
**spreading** /ˈsprɛdɪŋ/ n (of a disease) propagación, f; (of knowledge, etc.) divulgación, f; expansión, f; extensión, f
**spreadsheet** /ˈsprɛdˌʃiːt/ n hoja de cálculo, f
**spree** /spriː/ n juerga, parranda, f; excursión, f. **to go on the s.,** ir de juerga, ir de picos pardos
**sprig** /sprɪg/ n ramita, f; (of heather, etc.) espiga, f; (scion) vástago, m
**sprightliness** /ˈspraɪtlɪnɪs/ n vivacidad, f, despejo, m; energía, f
**sprightly** /ˈspraɪtli/ a vivaracho, despierto; enérgico
**spring** /sprɪŋ/ vi saltar, brincar; (become) hacerse; (seek) buscar; (of plants, water) brotar; (of tears) arrasar, llenar; (from) originarse (en), ser causado (por); inspirarse (en). —vt (a mine) volar; (a trap) soltar. **to s. a surprise,** dar una sorpresa. **to s. a surprise on a person,** coger a la imprevista (a). **to s. at a person,** precipitarse sobre. **to s. to one's feet,** ponerse de pie de un salto. **to s. back,** saltar hacia atrás; recular; volver a su sitio. **to s. open,** abrirse súbitamente. **to s. up,** (of plants) brotar, crecer; (of difficulties, etc.) surgir, asomarse
**spring** /sprɪŋ/ n (jump) salto, brinco, m; (of water) fuente, f, manantial, m; (season) primavera, f; (of a watch, etc.) resorte, f; (of a mattress, etc.) muelle, m. —a primaveral. —vi saltar, brincar. **at one s.,** en un salto. **to give a s.,** dar un salto. **s.-board,** trampolín, m. **s.-mattress,** colchón de muelles, m. **s.-tide,** marea viva, f
**springiness** /ˈsprɪŋɪnɪs/ n elasticidad, f
**springlike** /ˈsprɪŋˌlaɪk/ a primaveral
**springtime** /ˈsprɪŋˌtaɪm/ n primavera, f
**sprinkle** /ˈsprɪŋkəl/ vt esparcir; salpicar; rociar
**sprinkling** /ˈsprɪŋklɪŋ/ n salpicadura, f; rociadura, f; pequeño número, m. **a s. of snow,** una nevada ligera
**sprint** /sprɪnt/ vi sprintar. —n sprint, m
**sprite** /spraɪt/ n trasgo, m; hada, f
**sprout** /spraʊt/ vi brotar, despuntar, retoñar, tallecer; germinar. —vt salir. —n brote, retoño, pimpollo, m; germen, m. **Brussels sprouts,** coles de Bruselas, f pl
**spruce** /spruːs/ a peripuesto, muy aseado, pulido; elegante, n Bot. pícea, f. **to s. oneself up,** arreglarse, ponerse elegante
**spruceness** /ˈspruːsnɪs/ n aseo, buen parecer, m, elegancia, f
**spry** /spraɪ/ a activo, ágil
**spur** /spɜr/ n espuela, f; aguijada, f; (of a bird) espolón, m; Bot. espuela, f; (of a mountain range) espolón, estribo, m; Fig. estímulo, m. —vt espolear, picar con la espuela; calzarse las espuelas; Fig. estimular, incitar. **on the s. of the moment,** bajo el impulso del momento
**spurious** /ˈspjʊriəs/ a espurio; falso
**spurn** /spɜrn/ vt rechazar; tratar con desprecio; menospreciar
**spurt** /spɜrt/ vi (gush) chorrear, borbotar; brotar, surgir; (in racing, etc.) hacer un esfuerzo supremo. —vt hacer chorrear; lanzar. —n (jet) chorro, m; esfuerzo supremo, m
**sputter** /ˈspʌtər/ vi chisporrotear; crepitar; (of a pen) escupir; (of a person) balbucir
**sputtering** /ˈspʌtərɪŋ/ n chisporroteo, m; crepitación, f; (of a person) balbuceo, m
**sputum** /ˈspjuːtəm/ n esputo, m
**spy** /spaɪ/ vt observar, discernir. —vi espiar, ser espía. —n espía, mf. **to spy out the land,** explorar el terreno. **to spy upon,** espiar; seguir los pasos (a). **spy-glass,** catalejo, m
**spying** /ˈspaɪɪŋ/ n espionaje, m
**squabble** /ˈskwɒbəl/ n disputa, f; riña, f. —vi pelearse; disputar
**squabbling** /ˈskwɒblɪŋ/ n riñas, querellas, f pl; disputas, f pl
**squad** /skwɒd/ n escuadra, f; pelotón, m
**squadron** /ˈskwɒdrən/ n Mil. escuadrón, m; Nav. escuadra, f; Aer. escuadrilla, f; (of persons) pelotón, m. **s.-leader,** comandante, m
**squalid** /ˈskwɒlɪd/ a escuálido; (of quarrels, etc.) sórdido, mezquino
**squall** /skwɔl/ vi berrear; chillar. —n berrido, m;

chillido, *m;* (storm) chubasco, turbión, *m;* (storm) chubasco, turbión, *m; Fig.* tormenta, tempestad, *f*

**squalor** /'skwɒlər/ *n* escualidez, *f;* sordidez, mezquindad, *f*

**squander** /'skwɒndər/ *vt* derrochar, tirar, desperdiciar; (time, etc.) malgastar

**squanderer** /'skwɒndərər/ *n* derrochador (-ra)

**squandering** /'skwɒndərɪŋ/ *n* derroche, desperdicio, dispendio, *m;* (of time, etc.) pérdida, *f,* desperdicio, *m*

**square** /skwɛər/ *n Math.* cuadrado, *m;* rectángulo, *m;* (of a chessboard) escaque, *m;* (of a draughtboard and of graph paper) casilla, *f;* (in a town) plaza, *f;* (of troops) cuadro, *m, a* cuadrado; justo; igual; (honest) honrado, formal; (unambiguous) redondo, categórico; *Math.* cuadrado. **She wore a silk s. on her head,** Llevaba un pañuelo de seda en la cabeza. **five s. feet,** cinco pies cuadrados. **nine feet s.,** nueve pies en cuadro. **on the s.,** honradamente. **a s. dance,** contradanza, *f.* **a s. meal,** una buena comida. **s. dealing,** trato limpio, *m.* **The account is s.,** La cuenta está justa. **to get s. with,** desquitarse (de), vengarse de. **s. measure,** medida de superficie, *f.* **s. root,** raíz cuadrada, *f.* **s.-shouldered,** de hombros cuadrados

**square** /skwɛər/ *vt* cuadrar; escuadrar; (arrange) arreglar; (bribe) sobornar; (reconcile) acomodar; *Math.* cuadrar. —*vi* conformarse (con), cuadrar (con). **to s. the circle,** cuadrar el círculo. **to s. one's shoulders,** enderezarse. **to s. accounts with,** saldar cuentas con. **to s. up to,** (a person) avanzar belicosamente hacia

**squarely** /'skwɛərli/ *adv* en cuadro; directamente; sin ambigüedades, rotundamente; (honestly) de buena fe, honradamente

**squareness** /'skwɛərnɪs/ *n* cuadratura, *f;* (honesty) honradez, buena fe, *f*

**squash** /skwɒʃ/ *vt* aplastar. —*vi* aplastarse; apretarse. —*n* aplastamiento, *m;* (of fruit, etc.) pulpa, *f;* (of people) agolpamiento, *m;* muchedumbre, *f;* (drink) refresco (de limón, etc.), *m,* (sport) frontón con raqueta, *m*

**squashy** /'skwɒʃi/ *a* blando y húmedo

**squat** /skwɒt/ *vi* acuclillarse, agacharse, agazaparse ponerse en cuclillas; estar en cuclillas; (on land, etc.) apropiarse sin derecho. —*a* rechoncho

**squatter** /'skwɒtər/ *n* intruso (-sa); colono usurpador, *m*

**squatter town** *n.* See **shanty town**

**squawk** /skwɔk/ *vi* graznar; lanzar gritos agudos. —*n* graznido, *m;* grito agudo, *m*

**squeak** /skwik/ *vi* (of carts, etc.) chirriar, rechinar; (of shoes) crujir; (of persons, mice, etc.) chillar; (slang) cantar. —*n* chirrido, crujido, *m;* chillido, *m.* **to have a narrow s.,** escapar por un pelo

**squeaking** /'skwikɪŋ/ *n* chirrido, rechinamiento, *m;* crujido, *m;* (of humans, mice, etc.) chillidos, *m pl*

**squeal** /skwil/ *vi* lanzar gritos agudos, chillar; (complain) quejarse; (slang) cantar. —*n* grito agudo, chillido, *m*

**squealing** /'skwilɪŋ/ *n* gritos agudos, chillidos, *m pl*

**squeamish** /'skwimɪʃ/ *a* que se marea fácilmente; mareado; (nauseated) asqueado; delicado; remilgado

**squeamishness** /'skwimɪʃnɪs/ *n* tendencia a marearse, *f;* delicadeza, *f;* remilgos, *m pl*

**squeeze** /skwiz/ *vt* apretar; estrujar; (fruit) exprimir; (extort) arrancar; (money from) sangrar. —*n* (of the hand, etc.) apretón, *m;* estrujón, *m;* (of fruit juice) algunas gotas (de). **It was a tight s. in the car,** Íbamos muy apretados en el coche. **He was in a tight s.,** Se encontraba en un aprieto. **to s. one's way through the crowd,** abrirse camino a codazos por la muchedumbre. **to s. in,** *vt* hacer sitio para. —*vi* introducirse con dificultad (en)

**squelch** /skwɛltʃ/ *vi* gorgotear, chapotear. —*vt* aplastar

**squib** /skwɪb/ *n* (firework) rapapiés, buscapiés, *m;* (lampoon) pasquinada, *f*

**squid** /skwɪd/ *n* calamar, *m*

**squint** /skwɪnt/ *n* estrabismo, *m;* mirada furtiva, *f; Inf.* vistazo, *m,* mirada, *f.* —*vi* ser bizco; bizcar. **to s. at,** mirar de soslayo. **s.-eyed,** bizco. **to be s.-eyed,** mirar contra el gobierno

**squire** /skwaɪər/ *n* escudero, *m;* hacendado, *m.* —*vt* escoltar, acompañar

**squirm** /skwɜrm/ *vi* retorcerse; (with embarrassment) no saber dónde meterse. —*n* retorcimiento, *m.* **to s. along the ground,** arrastrarse por el suelo

**squirrel** /'skwɜrəl// *n* ardilla, *f*

**squirt** /skwɜrt/ *vt* (liquids) lanzar. —*vi* chorrear, salir a chorros. —*n* chorro, *m;* (syringe) jeringa, *f*

**stab** /stæb/ *vt* apuñalar, dar de puñaladas (a); herir. —*n* puñalada, *f;* herida, *f;* (of pain, and *Fig.*) pinchzo, *m.* **a s. in the back,** una puñalada por la espalda

**stability** /stə'bɪliti/ *n* estabilidad, *f;* solidez, firmeza, *f*

**stabilize** /'steibə,laiz/ *vt* estabilizar

**stable** /'steibəl/ *a* estable; fijo, firme. —*n* cuadra, caballeriza, *f;* (for cows, etc.) establo, *m.* —*vt* poner en la cuadra; alojar. **s.-boy,** mozo de cuadra, *m*

**stack** /stæk/ *n* (of hay) niara, *f,* almiar, *m;* (heap) montón, *m;* (of rifles) pabellón, *m;* (of a chimney) cañón, *m.* —*vt Agr.* hacinar; amontonar; *Mil.* poner (las armas) en pabellón

**stacked** /stækt/ *a* (woman) abultada de pechera

**stadium** /'steidiəm/ *n* estadio, *m*

**staff** /stæf/ *n* vara, *f;* (bishop's, and *Fig.*) báculo, *m;* (pilgrim's) bordón, *m;* (pole) palo, *m;* (flagstaff) asta, *f;* (of an office, etc.) personal, *m;* (editorial) redacción, *f;* (corps) cuerpo, *m; Mil.* plana mayor, *f,* estado mayor, *m; Mus.* pentagrama, *m.* —*vt* proveer de personal. **general s.,** estado mayor general, *m.* **s. officer,** *Mil.* oficial de estado mayor, *m*

**stag** /stæg/ *n* ciervo, *m.* **s.-beetle,** ciervo volante, *m.* **s.-hunting,** caza del ciervo, *f*

**stage** /steidʒ/ *n* (for workmen) andamio, *m;* (of a microscope) portaobjetos, *m; Theat.* escena, *f,* tablas, *f pl;* teatro, *m;* (of development, etc.) etapa, *f,* fase, *f.* —*vt Theat.* escenificar, poner en escena; *Theat.* representar; (a demonstration, etc.) arreglar. **by easy stages,** poco a poco; (of a journey) a pequeñas etapas. **to come on the s.,** salir a la escena. **to go on the s.,** hacerse actor (actriz), dedicarse al teatro. **s. carpenter,** tramoyista, *m.* **s.-coach,** diligencia, *f.* **s.-craft,** arte de escribir para el teatro, *f;* arte escénica, *f.* **s.-direction,** acotación, *f.* **s.-door,** entrada de los artistas, *f.* **s.-effect,** efecto escénico, *m.* **s.-fright,** miedo al público, *m.* **s.-hand,** tramoyista, sacasillas, metesillas y sacamuertos, *m.* **s. manager,** director de escena, *m.* **s.-whisper,** aparte, *m*

**stagger** /'stægər/ *vi* tambalear; andar haciendo eses; (hesitate) titubear, vacilar. —*vt* desconcertar. —*n* titubeo, tambaleo, *m; Aer.* decalaje, *m.* **staggered working hours,** horas de trabajo escalonadas, *f pl*

**staggering** /'stægərɪŋ/ *a* tambaleante; (surprising) asombroso, sorprendente; (dreadful) espantoso. **a s. blow,** un golpe que derriba

**staging** /'steidʒɪŋ/ *n* (scaffolding) andamio, *m; Theat.* producción, *f;* representación, *f;* decorado, *m*

**stagnancy** /'stægnənsi/ *n* (of water) estancación, *f;* (inactivity) estancación, *f;* paralización, *f*

**stagnant** /'stægnənt/ *a* estancado; paralizado. **to be s.,** estar estancado. **s. water,** agua estancada, *f*

**stagnate** /'stægneit/ *vi* estancarse; estar estancado; (of persons) vegetar

**stagnation** /stæg'neiʃən/ *n* (of water) estancación, *f;* estagnación, *f;* parálisis, *f*

**staid** /steid/ *a* serio, formal, juicioso

**staidness** /'steidnɪs/ *n* seriedad, formalidad, *f*

**stain** /stein/ *vt* manchar; (dye) teñir. —*n* mancha, *f;* colorante, *m.* **without a s.,** *Fig.* sin mancha. **stained glass,** vidrio de color, *m.* **s.-remover,** quitamanchas, *m*

**stainless** /'steinlis/ *a* sin mancha; inmaculado, puro

**stair** /stɛər/ *n* escalón, peldaño, *m;* escalera, *f; pl* **stairs,** escalera, *f.* **a flight of stairs,** una escalera; un tramo de escaleras. **below stairs,** escalera abajo. **s.-carpet,** alfombra de escalera, *f.* **s.-rod,** varilla para alfombra de escalera, *f*

**staircase** /'stɛər,keis/ *n* escalera, *f.* **spiral s.,** escalera de caracol, *f*

**stake** /steik/ *n* estaca, *f;* (for plants) rodrigón, *m;* (gaming) envite, *m,* apuesta, *f;* (in an undertaking) interés, *m; pl* **stakes,** (prize) premio, *m;* (race) carrera, *f.* —*vt* estacar; (plants) rodrigar; (bet) jugar. **at s.,**

en juego; en peligro. **to be burnt at the s.,** morir en la hoguera. **to s. one's all,** jugarse el todo por el todo. **to s. a claim,** hacer una reclamación. **to s. out,** jalonar

**stalactite** /stə'læktait/ *n* estalactita, *f*

**stalagmite** /stə'lægmait/ *n* estalagmita, *f*

**stale** /steil/ *a* no fresco; (of bread, etc.) duro; seco; (of air) viciado; viejo; pasado de moda; (tired) cansado

**stalemate** /'steil,meit/ *n* (chess, checkers) tablas, *f pl; Fig.* punto muerto, *m.* **to reach a s.,** llegar a un punto muerto

**staleness** /steilnɪs/ *n* rancidez, *f;* (of bread, etc.) dureza, *f;* (of news, etc.) falta de novedad, *f*

**stalk** /stɔk/ *n Bot.* tallo, *m;* pedúnculo, *m;* (of a glass) pie, *m.* —*vi* andar majestuosamente; *Fig.* rondar. —*vt* (game) cazar al acecho; (a person) seguir los pasos (a)

**stalking horse** /'stɔkɪŋ/ *n* boezuelo, *m; Fig.* pretexto, disfraz, *m*

**stall** /stɔl/ *n* (in a stable) puesto (individual), *m;* (stable) establo, *m;* (choir) silla de coro, *f;* (in a fair, etc.) barraca, *f,* puesto, *m; Theat.* butaca, *f;* (fingerstall) dedal, *m.* —*vt* (an engine) cortar accidentalmente. —*vi Auto.* pararse de pronto; *Aer.* perder velocidad; (of a cart, etc.) atascarse. **pit s.,** *Theat.* butaca de platea, *f*

**stalling** /'stɔlɪŋ/ *n Auto.* parada accidental, *f; Aer.* pérdida de velocidad, *f.* **Stop s.!** ¡Déjate de rodeos!

**stallion** /'stælyən/ *n* semental, *m*

**stalwart** /'stɔlwərt/ *a* robusto, fornido; leal; valiente

**stalwartness** /'stɔlwərtnɪs/ *n* robustez, *f;* lealtad, *f;* valor, *m*

**stamen** /'steimən/ *n Bot.* estambre, *m*

**stamina** /'stæmənə/ *n* resistencia, *f*

**stammer** /'stæmər/ *vi* tartamudear; (hesitate in speaking) titubear, balbucir. —*n* tartamudez, *f;* titubeo, balbuceo, *m*

**stammerer** /'stæmərər/ *n* tartamudo (-da)

**stammering** /'stæmərɪŋ/ *a* tartamudo; balbuciente. —*n* tartamudeo, *m;* balbuceo, *m*

**stamp** /stæmp/ *vt* estampar; imprimir; (documents) timbrar; pegar el sello de correo (a); (characterize) sellar; (*Fig.* engrave) grabar; (coins) acuñar; (press) apisonar; (with the foot) golpear con los pies, patear; (in dancing) zapatear. —*n* (with the foot) patada, *f,* golpe con los pies, *m;* (mark, etc.) marca, *f;* (rubber, etc.) estampilla, *f;* matasellos, *m;* cuño, *m;* (for documents) póliza, *f;* timbre, *m;* (for letters) sello, *m;* (machine) punzón, *m;* mano de mortero, *f;* (*Fig.* sign) sello, *m;* (kind) temple, *m,* clase, *f.* **The events of that day are stamped on my memory,** Los acontecimientos de aquel día están grabados en mi memoria. **to s. out,** (a fire, etc.) extinguir, apagar; (resistance, etc.) vencer; destruir. **postage-s.,** sello de correos, *m.* **s.-album,** álbum de sellos, *m.* **s.-duty,** impuesto del timbre, *m.* **s.-machine,** expendedor automático de sellos de correo, *m*

**stampede** /stæm'pid/ *n* fuga precipitada, *f;* pánico, *m.* —*vi* huir precipitadamente; (of animals) salir de estampía; huir en desorden. —*vt* hacer perder la cabeza (a), sembrar el pánico entre

**stamping** /'stæmpɪŋ/ *n* selladura, *f;* (of documents) timbrado, *m;* (of fabrics, etc.) estampado, *m;* (with the feet) pataleo, *m;* (in dancing) zapateo, *m*

**stance** /stæns/ *n* posición de los pies, *f;* postura, *f*

**stanch** /stɔntʃ/ *vt* restañar

**stand** /stænd/ *vi* estar de pie; ponerse de pie, incorporarse; estar; hallarse; sostenerse; ser; ponerse; (halt) parar; (remain) permanecer, quedar. —*vt* poner; (endure) resistir; tolerar; sufrir; (entertain) convidar. **S.!** ¡Alto! **as things s.,** tal como están las cosas. **I cannot s. any more,** No puedo más. **I cannot s. him,** No le puedo ver. **Nothing stands between them and ruin,** No hay nada entre ellos y la ruina. **I stood him a drink,** Le convidé a un trago. **How do we s.?** ¿Cómo estamos? **It stands to reason that...,** Es lógico que... **Edward stands six feet,** Eduardo tiene seis pies de altura. **to s. accused of,** ser acusado de. **to s. godfather** (or **godmother**) **to,** sacar de pila (a). **to s. in need (of),** necesitar, tener necesidad (de). **to s. on end,** (of hair) ponerse de

punta, despeluzarse, **to s. one in good stead,** ser útil, ser ventajoso. **to s. one's ground,** no ceder, tenerse fuerte. **to s. to attention,** cuadrarse, permanecer en posición de firmes. **to s. well with,** tener buenas relaciones con, ser estimado de. **to s. aside,** tenerse a un lado; apartarse; (in favor of someone) retirarse. **to s. back,** quedarse atrás; recular, retroceder. **to s. by,** estar de pie cerca de; estar al lado de; estar presente (sin intervenir); ser espectador; estar preparado; (one's friends) ayudar, proteger; (a promise, etc.) atenerse (a); ser fiel (a); (a ship) mantenerse listo. **s.-by,** *n* recurso, *m.* **to s. for,** representar; simbolizar; (mean) significar; (Parliament, etc.) presentarse como candidato; (put up with) tolerar, sufrir. **to s. in,** colaborar. **to s. in with,** estar de acuerdo con, ser partidario de; compartir. **to s. off,** mantenerse a distancia. **to s. out,** (in relief, and *Fig.* of persons) destacarse; (be firm) resistir, mantenerse firme; *Naut.* gobernar más afuera. **S. out of the way!** ¡Quítate del medio! **to s. over,** (be postponed) quedar aplazado. **to s. up,** estar de pie; ponerse de pie, incorporarse; tenerse derecho. **to s. up against,** resistir; oponerse a. **to s. up for,** defender; volver por. **to s. up to,** hacer cara a

**stand** /stænd/ *n* puesto, *m;* posición, actitud, *f;* (for taxis, etc.) punto, *m;* (in a market, etc.) puesto, *m; Sports.* tribuna, *f;* (for a band) quiosco, *m;* (of a dish, etc.) pie, *m; Mech.* sostén, *m;* (opposition) resistencia, oposición, *f.* **to make a s. against,** oponerse resueltamente (a); ofrecer resistencia (a). **to take one's s.,** fundarse (en), apoyarse (en). **to take up one's s. by the fire,** ponerse cerca del fuego

**standard** /'stændərd/ *n* (flag) estandarte, *m,* bandera, *f;* (for gold, weights, etc.) marco, *m;* norma, *f;* convención, regla, *f;* (of a lamp) pie, *m;* (pole) poste, *m;* columna, *f;* (level) nivel, *m.* —*a* corriente; normal; típico; clásico. **It is a s. type,** Es un tipo corriente. **gold s.,** patrón de oro, *m.* **s. author,** autor clásico, *m.* **s. formula,** fórmula clásica, *f.* **s. of living,** nivel de vida, *m.* **s.-bearer,** abanderado, *m.* **s.-lamp,** lámpara vertical, *f*

**standardization** /,stændərdə'zeifən/ *n* (of armaments, etc.) unificación de tipos, *f;* (of dyestuffs, medicinals, etc.) control, *m,* estandarización, *f*

**standardize** /'stændər,daiz/ *vt* hacer uniforme; controlar

**standing** /'stændɪŋ/ *a* de pie, derecho; permanente, fijo; constante. —*n* posición, *f;* reputación, *f;* importancia, *f;* antigüedad, *f.* **It is a quarrel of long s.,** Es una riña antigua. **s. committee,** comisión permanente, *f.* **s. room,** sitio para estar de pie, *m.* **s. water,** agua estancada, *f.* **standoffish,** frío, etiquetero; altanero. **stand-offishness,** frialdad, *f;* altanería, *f.*

**standpoint,** punto de vista, *m*

**standstill** /'stænd,stɪl/ *n* parada, *f;* pausa, *f.* **at a s.,** parado; (of industry) paralizado

**stanza** /'stænzə/ *n* estrofa, estancia, *f*

**staple** /'steipəl/ *n* (fastener) grapa, *f;* (of wool, etc.) hebra, fibra, *f;* producto principal (de un pais), *m;* (raw material) materia prima, *f; a* principal; más importante; corriente

**stapler** /'steiplər/, (device) cosepapeles, engrapador, *m,* atrochadora (Argentina), *f*

**star** /star/ *n* (all meanings) estrella, *f;* (asterisk) asterisco, *m.* —*vt* estrellar, sembrar de estrellas; marcar con asterisco. —*vi* (Theat. cinema) presentarse como estrella, ser estrella. **stars and stripes,** las barras y las estrellas. **to be born under a lucky s.,** tener estrella. **to see stars,** ver estrellas. **s.-gazing,** observación de las estrellas, *f;* ensimismamiento, *m.* **s.-spangled,** estrellado, tachonado de estrellas, sembrado de estrellas. **s.-turn,** gran atracción, *f*

**starboard** /'starbərd/ *n Naut.* estribor, *m*

**starch** /startʃ/ *n* almidón, *m,* las harinas, *f pl,* *vt* almidonar

**starchy** /'startʃi/ *a* almidonado; (of food) feculento; *Fig.* tieso, encogido, etiquetero

**stare** /stɛər/ *vi* mirar fijamente; abrir mucho los ojos. —*n* mirada fija, *f.* **stony s.,** mirada dura, *f.* **to s. at,** (a person) clavar la mirada en; mirar de hito en hito (a). **The explanation stares one in the face,** La explicación salta a la vista (o está evidente). **to s. into**

**space,** mirar las telarañas. **to s. out of countenance,** avergonzar con la mirada

**starfish** /'star,fıʃ/ n estrella de mar, f

**staring** /'steərıŋ/ a (of colors) chillón, llamativo, encendido. **s. eyes,** ojos saltones, m pl; ojos espantados, m pl

**stark** /stark/ a rígido; Poet. poderoso; absoluto. **s. staring mad,** loco de atar. **s.-naked,** en cueros vivos, en pelota

**starless** /'starlıs/ a sin estrellas

**starlight** /'star,laıt/ n luz de las estrellas, f, a estrellado

**starry** /'starı/ a estrellado, sembrado de estrellas

**start** /start/ vi estremecerse, asustarse; saltar; (set out) salir; ponerse en camino; (of a train, a race) arrancar; ponerse en marcha; Aer. despegar; (begin) empezar; (of timbers) combarse. —vt empezar; (a car, etc.) poner en marcha; (a race) dar la señal de partida; (a hare, etc.) levantar; (cause) provocar, causar; (a discussion, etc.) abrir; iniciar. —n (fright) susto, m; (setting out) partida, salida, f; (beginning) principio, comienzo, m; (starting-point of a race) arrancadero, m; Aer. despegue, m; (advantage) ventaja, f. **at the s.,** al principio. **for a s.,** para empezar. **from s. to finish,** desde el principio hasta el fin. **She started to cry,** Se puso a llorar. **He has started his journey to Canada,** Ha empezado su viaje al Canadá. **I started up the engine,** Puse el motor en marcha. **to get a s.,** asustarse; tomar la delantera. **to give** (a person) **a s.,** asustar, dar un susto (a); dar la ventaja (a). **to give** (a person) **a s. in life,** ayudar a alguien a situarse en la vida. **to make a fresh s. (in life),** hacer vida nueva, empezar la vida de nuevo. **to s. after,** lanzarse en busca de; salir tras. **to s. back,** retroceder; emprender el viaje de regreso; marcharse. **to s. off,** salir, partir; ponerse en camino. **to s. up,** vi incorporarse bruscamente, ponerse de pie de un salto; (appear) surgir, aparecer. —vt (an engine) poner en marcha

**starter** /'startər/ n iniciador (-ra); (for a race) starter, juez de salida, m; (competitor in a race) corredor, m; (of a car, etc.) arranque, m

**starting** /'startıŋ/ n (setting out) salida, partida, f; (beginning) principio, m; (fear) estremecimiento, m; susto, m. **s.-gear,** palanca de arranque, f. **s.-handle,** manivela de arranque, f. **s.-point,** punto de partida, m; Fig. arrancadero, punto de arranque, m. **s.-post,** puesto de salida, m

**startle** /'startl/ vt asustar, sobresaltar, alarmar. **The news startled him out of his indifference,** Las noticias le hicieron salir de su indiferencia

**startling** /'startlıŋ/ a alarmante; (of dress, etc.) exagerado; (of colors) chillón

**starvation** /star'veıʃən/ n hambre, f; Med. inanición, f. **s. diet,** régimen de hambre, m. **s. wage,** ración de hambre, f

**starve** /starv/ vi morir de hambre; pasar hambre, no tener bastante que comer; no comer. —vt matar de hambre; privar de alimentos (a). **I am simply starving,** Tengo una hambre canina, Me muero de hambre. **to s. with cold,** vi morir de frío. —vt matar de frío

**starved** /starvd/ a muerto de hambre, hambriento. **s. of affection,** hambriento de cariño

**starving** /'starvıŋ/ a que muere de hambre, hambriento

**state** /steıt/ n estado, m; condición, f; (anxiety) agitación, ansiedad, f; (social) rango, m; (pomp) magnificencia, pompa, f; (government, etc.) Estado, m; nación, f. —a de Estado; de gala, de ceremonia. **the married s.,** el estado matrimonial. **s. of war,** estado de guerra. **in s.,** con gran pompa. **to lie in s.,** (of a body) estar expuesto. **s. apartments,** habitaciones de gala, f pl. **s. banquet,** comida de gala, f. **s. coach,** coche de gala, m. **s. control,** control por el Estado, m. **S. Department,** Ministerio de Estado, m. **s. education,** instrucción pública, f. **State of the Union message,** Mensaje al Congreso, m. **s. papers,** documentos de Estado, m pl

**state** /steıt/ vt decir (que), afirmar (que); (one's case, etc.) exponer; explicar; Math. proponer

**statecraft** /'steıt,kræft/ n arte de gobernar, m

**stated** /'steıtıd/ a arreglado, indicado; fijo. **the s.**

**date,** la fecha indicada. **at s. intervals,** a intervalos fijos

**statehood** /'steıthʊd/ n estadidad, f

**stateliness** /'steıtlınıs/ n dignidad, f; majestad, f

**stately** /'steıtlı/ a majestuoso; imponente; noble; digno

**statement** /'steıtmənt/ n afirmación, declaración, f; resumen, m; exposición, f; Law. deposición, f; Com. estado de cuenta, m. **to make a s.,** hacer una declaración

**stateroom** /'steıt,rum/ n sala de recepción, f; (on a ship) camarote, m

**statesman** /'steıtsmən/ n hombre de estado, m

**statesmanlike** /'steıtsmən,laık/ a de hombre de estado

**statesmanship** /'steıtsmən,ʃıp/ n arte de gobernar, m

**static** /'stætık/ a estático

**statics** /'stætıks/ n estática, f

**station** /'steıʃən/ n (place) puesto, sitio, m; (Rail. and Eccl.) estación, f; (social) posición social, f; Naut. apostadero, m; Surv. punto de marca, m. —vt estacionar, colocar, poner. **to s. oneself,** colocarse. **Stations of the Cross,** Estaciones, f pl. **s.-master,** jefe de la estación, m

**stationary** /'steıʃə,nɛri/ a estacionario; inmóvil; Astron. estacional

**stationer** /'steıʃənər/ n papelero (-ra). **stationer's shop,** papelería, f

**stationery** /'steıʃə,nɛri/ n papelería, f, efectos de escritorio, m pl; papel de escribir, m

**station wagon** n psicorre, coche camioneta, coche rural, m

**statistical** /stə'tıstıkəl/ a estadístico

**statistician** /ˌstætı'stıʃən/ n estadista, m

**statistics** /stə'tıstıks/ n estadística, f

**statuary** /'stætʃu,ɛri/ a estatuario. —n estatuaria, f; estatuas, f pl; (sculptor) estatuario, m

**statue** /'stætʃu/ n estatua, f; imagen, f

**statuesque** /ˌstætʃu'ɛsk/ a escultural

**statuette** /ˌstætʃu'ɛt/ n figurilla, f

**stature** /'stætʃər/ n estatura, f; (moral, etc.) valor, m

**status** /'steıtəs, 'stætəs/ n (Law. etc.) estado, m; posición, f; rango, m. **What is his s. as a physicist?** ¿Cómo se le considera entre los físicos? **social s.,** posición social, f; rango social, m

**statute** /'stætʃut/ n ley, f; acto legislativo, m; estatuto, m; regla, f. **s. book,** código legal, m

**statutory** /'stætʃu,tɔri/ a establecido; reglamentario; estatutario

**staunch** /stɔntʃ/ a leal, fiel; firme, constante. —vt restañar

**staunchness** /'stɔntʃnıs/ n lealtad, fidelidad, f; firmeza, f

**stave** /steıv/ n (of a barrel, etc.) duela, f; (of a ladder) peldaño, m; (stanza) estrofa, f; Mus. pentagrama, m. **to s. in,** abrir boquete en; romper a golpes; quebrar. **to s. off,** apartar, alejar; (delay) aplazar, diferir; (avoid) evitar; (thirst, etc.) dominar

**stay** /steı/ vt detener; (a judgment, etc.) suspender. —vi permanecer; quedarse; detenerse; (of weather, etc.) durar; (lodge) hospedarse, vivir. **to come to s.,** venir a ser permanente. **to s. a person's hand,** detenerle el brazo. **to s. at home,** quedarse en casa. **s.-at-home,** a casero. —n persona casera, f. **to s. the course,** terminar la carrera. **S.! Say no more!** ¡Calle! ¡No diga más! **to s. away,** ausentarse. **to s. up,** no acostarse; velar. **to s. with,** quedarse con; alojarse con; quedarse en casa de, vivir con

**stay** /steı/ n estancia, permanencia, f; residencia, f; (restraint) freno, m; Law. suspensión, f; (endurance) aguante, m, resistencia, f; Naut. estay, m; (prop) puntal, m; Fig. apoyo, soporte, m; pl **stays,** corsé, m

**stead** /stɛd/ n lugar, m. **in the s. of,** en lugar de, como substituto de. **It has stood me in good s.,** Me ha sido muy útil

**steadfast** /'stɛd,fæst/ a fijo; constante; firme; tenaz. **s. gaze,** mirada fija, f

**steadfastly** /'stɛd,fæstlı/ adv fijamente; con constancia; firmemente; tenazmente

**steadfastness** /'stɛd,fæstnıs/ n fijeza, f; constancia, f; firmeza, f; tenacidad, f

**steadily** /'stɛdli/ adv firmemente; (without stopping)

sin parar; continuamente; (assiduously) diligentemente; (uniformly) uniformemente. **Prices have gone up s.,** Los precios no han dejado de subir. **He looked at it s.,** Lo miraba sin pestañear (or fijamente)

**steadiness** /'stɛdɪnɪs/ *n* estabilidad, *f;* firmeza, *f;* constancia, *f;* (of persons) seriedad, formalidad, *f;* (of workers) diligencia, asiduidad, *f*

**steady** /'stɛdi/ *a* firme; seguro; fijo; constante; uniforme; continuo; estacionario; (of persons) serio, formal, juicioso; (of workers) diligente, asiduo. —*vt* afirmar; (persons) hacer más serio (a); (nerves, etc.) calmar, fortificar. **a s. job,** un empleo seguro. **S.!** ¡Calma!; *Naut.* ¡Seguro! **He steadied himself against the table,** Se apoyó en la mesa

**steak** /steik/ *n* tajada, *f;* biftec, *m*

**steal** /stil/ *vt* robar, hurtar; tomar. —*vi* robar, ser ladrón; (glide) deslizarse; (overwhelm) dominar, ganar insensiblemente (a). **to s. a kiss,** robar un beso. **to s. a look at,** mirar de soslayo (or de lado). **to s. away,** escurrirse, escabullirse; marcharse a hurtadillas. **to s. in,** deslizarse en, colarse en

**stealthily** /'stɛlθɪli/ *adv* a hurtadillas; a escondidas, furtivamente

**stealthiness** /'stɛlθɪnɪs/ *n* carácter furtivo, *m*

**stealthy** /'stɛlθi/ *a* furtivo; cauteloso

**steam** /stim/ *n* vapor, *m.* —*a* de vapor. —*vi* echar vapor. —*vt Cul.* cocer al vapor; (clothes) mojar; (windows, etc.) empañar. **to have the s. up,** estar bajo presión. **The windows are steamed,** Los cristales están empañados. **s.-boiler,** caldera de vapor, *f.* **s.-engine,** máquina de vapor, *f.* **s.-hammer,** maza de fragua, *f.* **s.-heat,** calefacción por vapor, *f.* **s.-roller,** *Lit.* apisonadora, *Fig.* fuerza arrolladora, *f*

**steamboat** /'stim,bout/ *n* vapor, *m*

**steamer** /'stimər/ *n Cul.* marmita al vacío, *f; Naut.* buque de vapor, *m*

**steamship** /'stim,ʃɪp/ *n* buque de vapor, piróscafo, *m*

**steamy** /'stimi/ *a* lleno de vapor

**steed** /stid/ *n* corcel, *m*

**steel** /stil/ *n* (metal, and *Poet.* sword) acero, *m;* (for sharpening) afilón, *m.* —*a* de acero; acerado. —*vt* acerar; *Fig.* endurecer. **to be made of s.,** *Fig.* ser de bronce. **He cannot s. himself to do it,** No puede persuadirse a hacerlo. **cold s.,** arma blanca, *f.* **stainless s.,** acero inoxidable, *m.* **s.-engraving,** grabado en acero, *m*

**steel mill** *n* fábrica de acero, *f*

**steep** /stip/ *a* acantilado, escarpado; precipitoso; (of stairs, etc.) empinado; (of price) exorbitante. —*vt* (soak) remojar, empapar; *Fig.* absorber; (in a subject) empaparse (en). —*n* remojo, *m.* **It's a bit s.!** *Inf.* ¡Es un poco demasiado!

**steeping** /'stipɪŋ/ *n* remojo, *m,* maceración, *f*

**steeple** /'stipəl/ *n* campanario, *m,* torre, *f;* aguja, *f*

**steeplechase** /'stipəl,tʃeis/ *n* steeplechase, *m,* carrera de obstáculos, *f*

**steepness** /'stipnɪs/ *n* carácter escarpado, *m,* lo precipitoso

**steer** /stɪr/ *vt Naut.* gobernar; (a car, etc.) conducir; *Fig.* guiar, conducir. —*vi Naut.* timonear; *Naut.* navegar; *Auto.* conducir. —*n Zool.* novillo, *m.* **to s. clear of,** evitar. **to s. one's way through the crowd,** abrirse paso entre la muchedumbre

**steerage** /'stɪərɪdʒ/ *n* gobierno, *m;* (stern) popa, *f;* (quarters) entrepuente, *m.* **to go s.,** viajar en tercera clase

**steering** /'stɪrɪŋ/ *n Naut.* gobierno, *m;* (tiller, etc.) gobernalle, timón, *m;* (of a vehicle) conducción, *f.* **s.-column,** barra de dirección, *f.* **s.-wheel,** *Auto.* volante de dirección, *m; Naut.* rueda del timón, *f*

**stellar** /'stɛlər/ *a* estelar

**stem** /stɛm/ *n* (of a tree) tronco, *m;* (of a plant) tallo, *m;* (of a glass, etc.) pie, *m;* (*Mus.* of a note) rabo, *m;* (of a pipe) tubo, *m;* (of a word) radical, *m.* —*vt* (check) contener; (the tide) ir contra; (the current) vencer; (dam) estancar. **from s. to stern,** de proa a popa

**stench** /stɛntʃ/ *n* tufo, hedor, *m,* hediondez, *f*

**stencil** /'stɛnsəl/ *n* patrón para estarcir, *m;* estarcido, *m.* —*vt* estarcir

**stenographer** /stə'nɒɡrəfər/ *n* estenógrafo (-fa), taquígrafo (-fa)

**stenography** /stə'nɒɡrəfi/ *n* estenografía, taquigrafía, *f*

**stentorian** /stɛn'tɔriən/ *a* estentóreo

**step** /stɛp/ *n* paso, *m;* (footprint) huella, *f;* (measure) medida, *f;* (of a stair, etc.) escalón, peldaño, *m,* grada, *f;* (of a ladder) peldaño, *m;* (of vehicles) estribo, *m;* (grade) escalón, *m; Mus.* intervalo, *m.* **at every s.,** a cada paso. **flight of steps,** escalera, *f;* (before a building, etc.) escalinata, *f.* **in steps,** en escalones. **to bend one's steps towards,** dirigirse hacia. **to keep in s.,** llevar el paso. **to take a s.,** dar un paso. **to take steps,** tomar medidas. **s. by s.,** paso a paso; poco a poco. **s.-dance,** baile típico, *m.* **s.-ladder,** escalera de tijera, *f*

**step** /stɛp/ *vi* dar un paso; pisar; andar. **Please s. in!** Sírvase de entrar. **Will you s. this way, please?** ¡Haga el favor de venir por aquí! **to s. aside,** ponerse a un lado; desviarse; *Fig.* retirarse (en favor de). **to s. in,** entrar; intervenir (en); (meddle) entrometerse. **He stepped into the train,** Subió al tren. **to s. on,** pisar. **to s. on board,** *Naut.* ir a bordo. **to s. out,** salir; (from a vehicle) bajar; (a dance) bailar. **He stepped out a moment ago,** Salió hace un instante

**stepbrother** /'stɛp,brʌðər/ *n* hermanastro, medio hermano, *m*

**stepchild** /'stɛp,tʃaild/ *n* hijastro (-ra)

**stepdaughter** /'stɛp,dɔtər/ *n* hijastra, *f*

**stepfather** /'stɛp,faðər/ *n* padrastro, *m*

**stepmother** /'stɛp,mʌðər/ *n* madrastra, *f*

**steppe** /stɛp/ *n* estepa, *f*

**steppingstone** /'stɛpɪŋ,stoun/ *n* pasadera, *f; Fig.* escabel, escalón, *m*

**stepsister** /'stɛp,sɪstər/ *n* hermanastra, media hermana, *f*

**stepson** /'stɛp,sʌn/ *n* hijastro, *m*

**stereotype** /'stɛriə,taip/ *n* estereotipia, *f,* clisé, *m, vt* (*Print.* and *Fig.*) estereotipar

**sterile** /'stɛrɪl/ *a* estéril; árido

**sterility** /stə'rɪlɪti/ *n* esterilidad, *f;* aridez, *f*

**sterilization** /,stɛrələ'zeifən/ *n* esterilización, *f*

**sterilize** /'stɛrə,laiz/ *vt* esterilizar

**sterilizer** /'stɛrə,laizər/ *n* esterilizador, *m*

**sterling** /'stɜrlɪŋ/ *a* esterlina *f; Fig.* genuino. **pound s.,** libra esterlina, *f*

**stern** /stɜrn/ *a* severo, austero; duro. —*n Naut.* popa, *f*

**sternly** /'stɜrnli/ *adv* con severidad, severamente, duramente

**sternness** /'stɜrnnɪs/ *n* severidad, *f;* dureza, *f*

**sternum** /'stɜrnəm/ *n Anat.* esternón, *m*

**stethoscope** /'stɛθə,skoup/ *n* estetoscopio, *m*

**stevedore** /'stivɪ,dɔr/ *n* estibador, *m*

**stew** /stu/ *vt* guisar a la cazuela, estofar; (mutton, etc.) hervir; (fruit) cocer. —*n* estofado, *m; Inf.* agitación, *f.* **to be in a s.,** *Inf.* sudar la gota gorda. **stewed fruit,** compota de frutas, *f.* **s.-pot,** cazuela, olla, *f,* puchero, *m*

**steward** /'stuərd/ *n* administrador, *m;* mayordomo, *m;* (provision) despensero, *m; Naut.* camarero, *m*

**stewardess** /'stuərdɪs/ *n Naut.* camarera, *f*

**stick** /stɪk/ *vt* clavar (en), hundir (en); (put) poner; sacar; (stamps, etc.) pegar; fijar; (endure) resistir; tolerar. —*vi* clavarse, hundirse; estar clavado; pegarse; (remain) quedar; (in the mud, etc.) atascarse, embarrancarse, (on a reef) encallarse; (in the throat, etc.) atravesarse; (stop) detenerse. **It sticks in my throat,** *Inf.* No lo puedo tragar. **Friends always s. together,** Los amigos no se abandonan. **The nickname stuck to him,** El apodo se le quedó. **to s. at,** persistir en; desistir (ante); pararse (ante); tener escrúpulos sobre. **to s. at nothing,** no tener escrúpulos. **He stuck at his work,** Siguió trabajando. **to s. down,** pegar. **to s. out,** *vi* proyectar; sobresalir. —*vt* (one's chest) inflar; (one's tongue) sacar. **His ears s. out,** Tiene las orejas salientes. **to s. to,** (one's job) no dejar; (one's plans) adherirse (a); (one's principles) ser fiel (a); (one's friends) no abandonar; (one's word, etc.) cumplir; atenerse a. **to s. up,** *vi* (of hair) erizarse, ponerse de punta; salirse. —*vt* clavar; (a notice) fijar. **to s. up for,** (a person) defender

**stick** /stɪk/ *n* estaca, *f;* (for the fire) leña, *f;* (walking-s.) bastón, *m;* (of office) vara, *f;* (of sealing-wax,

etc.) barra, *f;* palo, *m;* (baton) batuta, *f;* (of celery) tallo, *m.* **in a cleft s.,** entre la espada y la pared. **to give** (a person) **the s.,** dar palo (a)
**stickiness** /'stɪkɪnɪs/ *n* viscosidad, *f*
**sticking plaster** *n* esparadrapo, *m*
**stick-in-the-mud** /'stɪkɪnðə,mʌd/ *n* chapado a la antigua, *m*
**stickler** /'stɪklər/ *n* rigorista, *mf.* **to be a s. for etiquette,** ser etiquetero
**sticky** /'stɪki/ *a* pegajoso, viscoso; *Fig.* difícil
**stiff** /stɪf/ *a* rígido; inflexible; tieso; (of paste, etc.) espeso; (of manner) distante; (of a bow, etc.) frío; (of a person) almidonado, etiquetero; severo; (of examinations, etc.) difícil; (strong) fuerte; (of price, etc.) alto, exorbitante; (of a shirt front, etc.) duro. **s. with cold,** aterido de frío. **s. neck,** torticolis, *m.* **s.-necked,** terco, obstinad
**stiffen** /'stɪfən/ *vt* reforzar; atiesar; (paste, etc.) hacer más espeso; (*Fig.* strengthen) robustecer; (make more obstinate) hacer más tenaz. —*vi* atiesarse; endurecerse; (straighten oneself) enderezarse; (of manner) volverse menos cordial; (become firmer) robustecerse; (become more obstinate) hacerse más tenaz. **The breeze stiffened,** Refrescó el viento
**stiffly** /'stɪfli/ *adv* tiesamente; rígidamente; obstinadamente
**stiffness** /'stɪfnɪs/ *n* rigidez, *f;* tiesura, *f;* dureza, *f;* (of manner) frialdad, *f;* (obstinacy) terquedad, obstinación, *f;* (of an examination, etc.) dificultad, *f*
**stifle** /'staɪfəl/ *vt* ahogar, sofocar; apagar; suprimir
**stifling** /'staɪflɪŋ/ *a* sofocante, bochornoso
**stigma** /'stɪgmə/ *n* estigma, *m*
**stigmatize** /'stɪgmə,taɪz/ *vt* estigmatizar
**stile** /staɪl/ *n* (nearest equivalent) portilla con escalones, *f*
**stiletto** /stɪ'letou/ *n* estilete, *m*
**still** /stɪl/ *a* tranquilo; inmóvil; quedo; silencioso; (of wine) no espumoso. —*n* silencio, *m.* **in the s. of the night,** en el silencio de la noche. **Keep s.!** ¡Estate quieto! **to keep s.,** quedarse inmóvil, no moverse. **s.-birth,** nacimiento de un niño muerto, *m.* **s.-born,** nacido muerto. **s. life,** *Art.* bodegón, *m,* naturaleza muerta, *f*
**still** /stɪl/ *vt* hacer callar, acallar; calmar, tranquilizar; apaciguar; (pain) aliviar
**still** /stɪl/ *adv* todavía, aún; (nevertheless) sin embargo, no obstante; (always) siempre. **I think she s. visits them every week,** Me parece que sigue visitándoles cada semana. **s. and all,** con todo y eso. **s. more,** aún más
**still** /stɪl/ *n* alambique, *m.* **salt water s.,** adrazo, *m*
**stillness** /'stɪlnɪs/ *n* quietud, tranquilidad, *f;* silencio, *m.* **in the s. of the night,** en el silencio de la noche
**stilt** /stɪlt/ *n* zanco, *m*
**stilted** /'stɪltɪd/ *a* ampuloso, campanudo, hinchado
**stimulant** /'stɪmyələnt/ *a* and *n* estimulante, *m*
**stimulate** /'stɪmyə,leɪt/ *vt* estimular; incitar (a), excitar (a)
**stimulating** /'stɪmyə,leɪtɪŋ/ *a* estimulante; (encouraging) alentador; (inspiring) sugestivo, inspirador
**stimulation** /,stɪmyə'leɪʃən/ *n* excitación, *f;* (stimulus) estímulo, *m*
**stimulus** /'stɪmyələs/ *n* estímulo, *m; Med.* estimulante, *m;* (incentive) impulso, incentivo, *m;* acicate, aguijón, *m*
**sting** /stɪŋ/ *vt* picar, pinchar; (of snakes, etc.) morder; (of hot dishes) resquemar; (of hail, etc.) azotar; (pain) atormentar; (provoke) provocar (a), incitar (a). —*n* (*Zool.* organ) aguijón, *m; Bot.* púa, *f;* (of a scorpion) uña, *f;* (of a serpent) colmillo, *m;* (pain and wound) pinchazo, *m;* (serpent's) mordedura, *f;* (stimulus) acicate, estímulo, *m;* (torment) tormento, dolor, *m*
**stingily** /'stɪndʒəli/ *adv* avaramente, tacañamente
**stinginess** /'stɪndʒɪnɪs/ *n* tacañería, avaricia, *f*
**stinging** /'stɪŋɪŋ/ *a* picante; *Fig.* mordaz; (of blows) que duele
**stingy** /'stɪndʒi/ *a* tacaño, avaro, mezquino
**stink** /stɪŋk/ *vi* apestar, heder, oler mal. —*n* tufo, *m,* hediondez, *f*
**stinking** /'stɪŋkɪŋ/ *a* apestoso, hediondo, fétido, mal oliente

**stint** /stɪnt/ *vt* escatimar; limitar. —*n* límite, *m,* restricción, *f.* **without s.,** sin límite; sin restricción.
**stipend** /'staɪpɛnd/ *n* estipendio, salario, *m*
**stipple** /'stɪpəl/ *vt Art.* puntear. —*n* punteado, *m*
**stipulate** /'stɪpyə,leɪt/ *vi* estipular, poner como condición. —*vt* estipular, especificar. **They stipulated for a five-day week,** Pusieron como condición (*or* Estipularon) que trabajasen cinco días por semana
**stipulation** /,stɪpyə'leɪʃən/ *n* estipulación, *f;* condición, *f*
**stir** /stɜr/ *vt* agitar; revolver; (the fire) atizar; (move) mover; (emotionally) conmover, impresionar; (the imagination) estimular. —*vi* moverse. —*n* movimiento, *m;* conmoción, *f;* (bustle) bullicio, *m;* sensación, *f.* **to make a s.,** causar una sensación. **to s. one's coffee,** revolver el café. **to s. up discontent,** fomentar el descontento
**stirring** /'stɜrɪŋ/ *a* conmovedor, emocionante, impresionante; (of times, etc.) turbulento, agitado
**stirrup** /'stɜrəp, 'stɪr-/ *n* estribo, *m.* **s.-cup,** última copa, *f.* **s.-pump,** bomba de mano (para líquidos), *f*
**stitch** /stɪtʃ/ *n* (action) puntada, *f;* (result) punto, *m; Surg.* punto de sutura, *m;* (pain) punzada, *f,* pinchazo, *m.* —*vt* coser; *Surg.* suturar
**stoat** /stout/ *n* armiño, *m;* (weasel) comadreja, *f*
**stock** /stɒk/ *n* (of a tree) tronco, *m;* (of a rifle) culata, *f;* (handle) mango, *m;* (of a horse's tail) nabo, *m;* (stem for grafting etc.) injerto, *m;* (race) raza, *f;* (lineage) linaje, *m,* estirpe, *f;* (supply) provisión, *f;* reserva, *f;* (of merchandise) surtido, *m; Cul.* caldo, *m;* (collar) alzacuello, *m; Bot.* alhelí, *m;* (government) papel del estado, *m,* valores públicos, *m pl;* (financial) valores, *m pl,* (of a company) capital, *m;* (of goods) existencias, *f pl,* **stocks,** *Hist.* cepo, *m;* (of goods) existencias, *f pl,* stock, *m,* a corriente; del repertorio. **in s.** en existencia. **lives.,** ganado *m.* **rolling-s.,** *Rail.* materia móvil ferroviario, *m.* **s. phrase** frase hecha, *f.* **s. size,** talla corriente, *f.* **to lay in a s. of,** hacer provisión de, almacenar, **to stand s.-still,** quedarse completamente inmóvil, **to take s.,** *Com.* hacer inventario. **to take s. of,** inventariar; examinar, considerar. **s.-breeder,** ganadero, *m.* **s.-broker,** corredor de bolsa, bolsista, *m.* **s. exchange,** bolsa, *f.* **s.-in-hand,** *Com.* existencias, *f pl.* **s.-in-trade** (*Com.* etc.) capital, *m.* **s.-raising,** cría de ganados, ganadería, *f.* **s.-taking,** *Com.* inventario, *m*
**stock** /stɒk/ *vt* proveer (de), abastecer (de); (of shops) tener existencia de
**stockade** /stɒ'keɪd/ *n* estacada, empalizada, *f,* vt empalizar
**stocking** /'stɒkɪŋ/ *n* media, *f.* **nylon stockings,** medias de cristal (or de nilón), *f pl*
**stocky** /'stɒki/ *a* rechoncho, doblado, achaparrado
**stodgy** /'stɒdʒi/ *a* (of food) indigesto; (of style, etc.) pesado, amazacotado
**stoic** /'stouɪk/ *a* and *n* estoico (-ca)
**stoical** /'stouɪkəl/ *a* estoico
**stoicism** /'stouə,sɪzəm/ *n* estoicismo, *m*
**stoke** /stouk/ *vt* (a furnace, etc.) cargar, alimentar; (a fire) echar carbón, etc., en. **s.-hole,** cuarto de fogoneros, *m; Naut.* cámara de calderas, *f*
**stoker** /'stoukər/ *n* fogonero, *m;* (mechanical) cargador, *m*
**stole** /stoul/ *n* (*Eccl.* and of fur, etc.) estola, *f*
**stolid** /'stɒlɪd/ *a* impasible, imperturbable
**stolidity** /stə'lɪdɪti/ *n* impertubabilidad, impasibilidad, *f*
**stolidly** /'stɒlɪdli/ *adv* impertubablemente
**stomach** /'stʌmək/ *n* estómago, vientre, *m;* apetito, estómago, *m;* (courage) corazón, valor, *m.* —*vt* digerir; (tolerate) tragar, sufrir. **s.ache,** dolor de estómago, *m*
**stone** /stoun/ *n* piedra, *f;* (gem) piedra preciosa, *f;* (of cherries, etc.) hueso, *m;* (of grapes, etc.) pepita, *f; Med.* cálculo, *m.* —*a* de piedra. —*vt* apedrear; (a wall, etc.) revestir de piedra; (fruit) deshuesar. **to pave with stones,** empedrar. **to leave no s. unturned,** no dejar piedra sin remover. **within a stone's throw,** a corta distancia, a un paso. **S. Age,** edad de piedra, *f.* **s.-breaker,** cantero, picapedrero, *m.* **s.-cold,** muy frío, completamente frío **s.-deaf,** *a* completamente sordo. **s.-fruit,** fruta de hueso, *f.* **s.-**

**mason,** mazonero, albañil, *m;* picapedrero, *m.* **s.-quarry,** pedrera, cantera, *f*

**stonily** /'stounḷi/ *adv* fríamente; fijamente, sin pestañear

**stoniness** /'stouninɪs/ *n* lo pedregoso; (of hearts, etc.) dureza, *f;* (of stares, etc.) fijeza, inmovilidad, *f*

**stoning** /'stouniŋ/ *n* apedreamiento, *m,* lapidación, *f*

**stony** /'stouni/ *a* pedregoso; (of hearts, etc.) duro, insensible, empedernido; (of a stare, etc.) fijo, duro

**stool** /stul/ *n* banquillo, taburete, *m;* (feces) excremento, *m*

**stoop** /stup/ *vi* inclinarse, doblarse; encorvarse; ser cargado de espaldas; andar encorvado; (demean oneself) rebajarse (a). —*n* inclinar, doblar. —*n* inclinación, *f;* cargazón de espaldas, *f*

**stooping** /'stupiŋ/ *a* inclinado, doblado; (of shoulders) cargado

**stop** /stɒp/ *vt* (a hole) obstruir, atascar; (a leak) cegar, tapar; (a tooth) empastar; (stanch) restañar; (the traffic, etc.) parar; detener; (prevent) evitar; (discontinue) cesar (de), dejarse de; (cut off) cortar; (end) poner fin (a), acabar con; (payment) suspender. —*vi* parar; detenerse; cesar; terminar; (stay) quedarse, permanecer. **I stopped myself from saying what I thought,** Me abstuve de decir lo que pensaba, Me mordí la lengua. **They stopped the food-supply,** Cortaron las provisiones. **to s. beating about the bush,** dejarse de historias. **to s. one's ears,** *Fig.* taparse los oídos. **to s. payments,** suspender pagos

**stop** /stɒp/ *n* parada, *f;* pausa, *f;* interrupción, *f;* cesación, *f;* (of an organ) registro, *m.* **"Stop,"** (road sign) «Alto.» **full s.,** *Gram.* punto, *m.* **tram s.,** parada de tranvía, *f.* **to come to a full s.,** pararse de golpe; cesar súbitamente. **to put a s. to,** poner fin a, poner coto a, acabar con. *f pl.* **s.-watch,** cronógrafo, *m*

**stopgap** /'stɒp,gæp/ *n* (person) tapagujeros, *m;* substituto, *m*

**stoppage** /'stɒpɪdʒ/ *n* parada, *f;* cesación, *f;* suspensión, *f;* interrupción, *f;* pausa, *f;* (obstruction) impedimento, *m;* obstrucción, *f.* **s. of work,** suspensión de trabajo, *f*

**stopper** /'stɒpər/ *n* tapón, *m;* obturador, *m, vt* cerrar con tapón, taponar

**stopping** /'stɒpiŋ/ *n* parada, *f;* cesación, *f;* suspensión, *f;* (of a tooth) empaste, *m.* **without s.,** sin parar. **without s. to draw breath,** de un aliento. **s.-place,** paradero, *m;* (of buses, etc.) parada, *f.* **s. train,** tren ómnibus, *m.* **s. up,** obturación, *f*

**storage** /'stɔrɪdʒ/ *n* almacenamiento, *m;* (charge) almacenaje, *m;* (place) depósito, *m.* **cold s.,** cámara frigorífica, *f.* **s. battery,** acumulador, *m*

**store** /stɔr/ *n* provisión, *f;* abundancia, *f;* reserva, *f;* (of knowledge, etc.) tesoro, *m;* (for furniture, etc.) depósito, almacén, *m; pl* **stores,** (shop) almacenes, *m pl;* (food) provisiones, *f pl;* (Mil. etc.) pertrechos, *m pl.* —*vt* proveer; guardar, acumular; tener en reserva; (furniture, etc.) almacenar; (hold) caber en, tomar. **in s.,** en reserva; en depósito, en almacén. **to set s. by,** estimar en mucho; dar importancia a. **to set little s. by,** estimar en poco; conceder poca importancia a. **s.-room,** despensa, *f*

**storehouse** /'stɔr,haus/ *n* almacén, *m; Fig.* mina, *f,* tesoro, *m*

**storied** /'stɔrid/ *a* de...pisos. **two-s.,** de dos pisos

**stork** /stɔrk/ *n* cigüeña, *f*

**storm** /stɔrm/ *n* tempestad, tormenta, *f,* temporal, *m; Fig.* tempestad, *f; Mil.* asalto, *m.* —*vt Mil.* tomar por asalto, asaltar. —*vi* (of persons) bramar de cólera. **to take by s.,** tomar por asalto; *Fig.* cautivar, conquistar. **s. cloud,** nubarrón, *m.* **s.-signal,** señal de temporal, *f.* **s.-tossed,** *a* sacudido por la tempestad. **s. troops,** tropas de asalto, *f pl.* **s. window,** contravidriera, *f*

**stormily** /'stɔrməli/ *adv* tempestuosamente; con tormenta

**storming** /'stɔrmiŋ/ *n* (Mil. etc.) asalto, *m;* violencia, *f.* **s.-party,** pelotón de asalto, *m*

**stormy** /'stɔrmi/ *a* tempestuoso; de tormenta; (of life, etc.) borrascoso; (of meetings, etc.) tempestuoso

**story** /'stɔri/ *n* historia, *f;* cuento, *m;* anécdota, *f;* (funny) chiste, *m;* (plot) argumento, enredo, *m;* (fib) mentira, *f;* (floor) piso *m.* **It's always the same old s.,** Es siempre la misma canción (or historia). **That is**

**quite another s.,** Eso es harina de otro costal. **short s.,** cuento, *m.* **s. book,** libro de cuentos, *m.* **s. teller,** cuentista, *mf;* (fibber) mentiroso (-sa)

**stoup** /stup/ *n* copa, *f;* pila de agua bendita, *f*

**stout** /staut/ *a* fuerte; (brave) intrépido, indómito; (fat) gordo, grueso; (firm) sólido, firme; (decided) resuelto; vigoroso. —*n* (drink) cerveza negra, *f.* **s.-hearted,** valiente, intrépido

**stove** /stouv/ *n* estufa, *f;* (open, for cooking) cocina económica, *f;* (gas, etc., for cooking) cocina, *f,* fogón, *m.* **s. pipe,** tubo de la chimenea, *m*

**stow** /stou/ *vt* meter, poner; colocar; (hide) esconder; (cargo) estibar, arrimar

**stowaway** /'stouə,wei/ *n* polizón, llovido, *m, vi* embarcarse secretamente

**straddle** /'strædḷ/ *vi* (Nav. etc.) graduar el tiro. —*vt* montar a horcajadas en. **s.-legged,** patiabierto

**strafe** /streif/ *vt* bombardear concentradamente; castigar; reñir

**straggle** /'strægəl/ *vi* rezagarse; vagar en desorden; dispersarse; estar esparcido; extenderse

**straggler** /'stræglər/ *n* rezagado (-da)

**straggling** /'stræglɪŋ/ *a* disperso; esparcido

**straight** /streit/ *a* derecho; recto; (of hair) lacio; directo; (tidy) en orden; (frank) franco; (honest) honrado. —*adv* derecho; en línea recta; directamente. **Keep s. on!** ¡Siga Vd. derecho! **to go s. to the point,** dejarse de rodeos, ir al grano. **to look s. in the eyes,** mirar derecho en los ojos. **s. away,** inmediatamente, en seguida. **s. out,** sin rodeos

**straighten** /'streitṇ/ *vt* enderezar; poner derecho; poner en orden; arreglar. —*vi* ponerse derecho; enderezarse. **to s. one's face,** componer el semblante. **to s. the line,** *Mil.* rectificar el frente. **to s. out,** poner en orden; *Fig.* desenredar. **to s. oneself up,** erguirse

**straightforward** /,streit'fɔrwərd/ *a* honrado, sincero; franco; (simple) sencillo. **s. answer,** respuesta directa, *f*

**straightforwardly** /,streit'fɔrwərdli/ *adv* honradamente; francamente

**straightforwardness** /,streit'fɔrwərdnɪs/ *n* honradez, *f,* integridad, *f;* franqueza, *f;* (simplicity) sencillez, *f*

**straightness** /'streitnɪs/ *n* derechura, rectitud, *f;* (of persons) honradez, probidad, *f*

**straightway** /'streit'wei, -,wei/ *adv* al instante, inmediatamente

**strain** /strein/ *vt* estirar; forzar; esforzar; (one's eyes) quebrarse; (one's ears) aguzar (el oído); (a muscle, etc.) torcer; (a friendship) pedir demasiado a, exigir demasiado (de); (a person's patience, etc.) abusar (de); (words) tergiversar; (embrace) abrazar estrechamente (a); (filter) filtrar; *Cul.* colar. —*vi* hacer un gran esfuerzo, esforzarse (para). —*n* tirantez, *f;* tensión, *f;* (effort) esfuerzo, *m;* (sprain) torcedura, *f;* (nervous) tensión nerviosa, *f; Mech.* esfuerzo, *m;* (breed) raza, *f; Biol.* cepa, *f;* (tendency) tendencia, *f;* (heredity) herencia, *f;* rasgo, *m,* vena, *f;* (style) estilo, *m; Mus.* melodia, *f;* (of mirth, etc.) son, ruido, *m;* (poetry) poesía, *f.* **to s. a point,** hacer una excepción. **to s. after effect,** buscar demasiado el efecto

**strained** /streind/ *a* tenso; (of muscles, etc.) torcido; (of smiles, etc.) forzado. **s. relations,** *Polit.* estado de tirantez, *m*

**strainer** /'streinər/ *n* filtro, *m;* coladero, *m*

**strait** /streit/ *n* Geog. estrecho, *m.* **to be in great straits,** estar en un apuro. **s. laced,** *Fig.* de manga estrecha, *f*

**straiten** /'streitṇ/ *vt* estrechar; limitar, **in straitened circumstances,** en la necesidad

**Strait of Magellan** /mə'dʒelən/ Estrecho de Magallanes, *m*

**Straits Settlements** Establecimientos del Estrecho, *m pl*

**strand** /strænd/ *n* (shore) playa, *f;* (of a river) ribera, orilla, *f;* (of rope) cabo, ramal, *m;* (of thread, etc.) hebra, *f;* (of hair) trenza, *f.* —*vt* and *vi* (a ship) encallar, varar. **to be stranded,** hallarse abandonado; (by missing a train, etc.) quedarse colgado. **to leave stranded,** abandonar, dejar plantado (a)

**strange** /streindʒ/ *a* (unknown) desconocido; nuevo; (exotic, etc.) extraño, singular; extraordinario; raro;

exótico. **I felt very s. in a s. country,** Me sentía muy solo en un país desconocido. **He is a very s. person,** Es una persona muy rara

**strangely** /'streindʒli/ adv extrañamente, singularmente; de un modo raro

**strangeness** /'streindʒnis/ n novedad, f; singularidad, f; rareza, f

**stranger** /'streindʒər/ n desconocido (-da); (from a foreign country) extranjero (-ra); (from another region, etc.) forastero (-ra).

**strangle** /'stræŋɡəl/ vt estrangular; (a sob, etc.) ahogar

**stranglehold** /'stræŋɡəl,hould/ n collar de fuerza, m. **to have a s. (on),** tener asido por la garganta; paralizar

**strap** /stræp/ n correa, f; tirante de botas, m, vt atar con correas

**strapping** /'stræpiŋ/ a rozagante, robusto

**stratagem** /'strætədʒəm/ n estratagema, f, ardid, m

**strategic** /strə'tidʒik/ a estratégico

**strategist** /'strætidʒist/ n estratego, m

**strategy** /'strætidʒi/ n estrategia, f

**stratification** /,strætəfi'keiʃən/ n estratificación, f

**stratosphere** /'strætə,sfiər/ n estratosfera, f

**stratum** /'streitəm, 'strætəm/ n Geol. estrato, m, capa, f; (social, etc.) estrato, m

**straw** /strɔ/ n paja, f. **I don't care a s.,** No se me da un bledo. **to be not worth a s.,** no valer un ardite. **to be the last s.,** ser el colmo. **to drink through a s.,** sorber con una paja. **s. hat,** sombrero de paja, m. **s.-colored,** pajizo

**strawberry** /'strɔ,beri/ n (plant and fruit, especially small or wild) fresa, f; (large cultivated) fresón, m. **s. bed,** fresal, m. **s. ice,** helado de fresa, m

**stray** /strei/ vi errar, vagar; perderse; (from a path, etc., also Fig.) descarriarse. —n animal perdido, m; niño (-ña) sin hogar. —a descarriado, perdido; errante; (sporadic) esporádico

**stray bullet** n bala perdida, f

**streak** /strik/ n raya, f; (in wood and stone) vena, f; (of light) rayo, m; (of humor, etc.) rasgo, m. —vt rayar. **like a s. of lightning,** como un relámpago

**streaky** /'striki/ a rayado; (of bacon) entreverado

**stream** /strim/ n arroyo, riachuelo, m; río, m; (current) corriente, f; (of words, etc.) torrente, m. —vi correr, fluir; manar, brotar; (float) flotar, ondear. —vt (blood, etc.) manar, echar. **The tears streamed down Jean's cheeks,** Las lágrimas corrían por las mejillas de Juana. **s.-lined,** fuselado

**streamer** /'strimər/ n gallardete, m, serpentina, f; (on a hat, etc.) cinta colgante, f, siguemepollo, m

**stream-of-consciousness** n escritura automática, f, fluir de la conciencia, m, flujo de la subconciencia, monólogo interior, m

**street** /strit/ n calle, f. **the man in the s.,** el hombre medio. **at s. level,** a ras de suelo. **s. arab,** golfo, m. **s. cries,** gritos de vendedores ambulantes, m pl. **s. entertainer,** saltabanco, m. **s. brawl, s. fight,** algarada callejera, f. **s. fighting,** luchas en las calles, f pl. **s. musician,** músico ambulante, m. **s.-sweeper,** barrendero, m. **s.-walker,** buscona, prostituta, f

**strength** /streŋkθ, streŋθ/ n fuerza, f; (of colors, etc.) intensidad, f; (of character) firmeza (de carácter), f; (of will) resolución, decisión, f; Mil. complemento, m. **by sheer s.,** a viva fuerza. **on the s. of,** confiando en, en razón de

**strengthen** /'streŋkθən, 'stren-/ vt fortificar; consolidar; reforzar. —vi fortificarse; consolidarse; reforzarse

**strengthening** /'streŋkθəniŋ, 'stren-/ a fortificante; tonificante. —n refuerzo, m; fortificación, f; consolidación, f

**strenuous** /'strenyuəs/ a activo, enérgico; vigoroso; (arduous) arduo

**strenuously** /'strenyuəsli/ adv enérgicamente, vigorosamente

**strenuousness** /'strenyuəsnis/ n energía, f; vigor, m; (arduousness) arduidad, f

**streptococcus** /,streptə'kɒkəs/ n Med. estreptococo, m

**streptomycin** /,streptə,maisin/ n Med. estreptomicina, f

**stress** /stres/ n tensión, f; impulso, m; importancia, f, énfasis, m; Gram. acento (tónico), m; acentuación, f; Mech. esfuerzo, m. —vt acentuar; poner énfasis en, insistir en. **under s. of circumstance,** impulsado por las circunstancias. **times of s.,** tiempos turbulentos, m pl. **to lay great s. on,** insistir mucho en; dar gran importancia a

**stretch** /stretʃ/ vt (make bigger) ensanchar; (pull) estirar; (one's hand, etc.) alargar, extender; (knock down) tumbar. —vi ensancharse; dar de sí; ceder; extenderse. **to s. oneself,** estirarse, desperezarse. **to s. as far as,** llegar hasta, extenderse hasta. **to s. a point,** hacer una concesión. **to s. one's legs,** estirar las piernas

**stretch** /stretʃ/ n estirón, m; tensión, f; (of country, etc.) extensión, f; (scope) alcance, m. **by a s. of the imagination,** con un esfuerzo de imaginación. **He can sleep for hours at a s.,** Puede dormir durante horas enteras

**stretcher** /'stretʃər/ n (for gloves) ensanchador, m; dilatador, m; (for canvas) bastidor, m; (for wounded, etc.) camilla, f. **s.-bearer,** camillero, m

**strew** /stru/ vt esparcir; derramar

**stricken** /'strikən/ a (wounded) herido; (ill) enfermo; (with grief) afligido, agobiado de dolor. **s. in years,** entrado en años

**strict** /strikt/ a exacto; estricto; escrupuloso; severo

**strictly** /'striktli/ adv exactamente; estrictamente; severamente, con severidad. **s. speaking,** en rigor, en realidad

**strictness** /'striktnis/ n exactitud, f; escrupulosidad, f; rigor, m; severidad, f

**stricture** /'striktʃər/ n Fig. crítica severa, censura, f. **to pass strictures on,** criticar severamente

**stride** /straid/ vi andar a pasos largos, dar zancadas; cruzar a grandes trancos. —vt cruzar de un tranco; poner una pierna en cada lado de. —n zancada, f, paso largo, tranco, m. **to s. up and down,** dar zancadas

**strident** /'straidnt/ a estridente; (of colors) chillón

**strife** /straif/ n lucha, f, conflicto, m

**strike** /straik/ vt golpear; pegar, dar una bofetada (a); (wound) herir; (a coin) acuñar; (a light) encender; (of a snake) morder; (a blow) asestar, dar; (of ships, a rock, etc.) chocar contra; estrellarse contra; (flags) bajar, arriar; (a tent) desmontar; (camp) levantar; (come upon) llegar a; (discover) encontrar por casualidad, tropezar con; hallar, descubrir; (seem) parecer; (impress) impresionar; (of ideas) ocurrirse; (an attitude) tomar, adoptar; (of a clock) dar; (a balance) hacer; (a bargain) cerrar, llegar a; (level) nivelar; (cuttings) enraizar. —vi golpear; (of a clock) dar la hora; (of a ship) encallar; (go) ir; (penetrate) penetrar; (of a cutting) arraigar; (sound) sonar. **He struck the table with his fist,** Golpeó la mesa con el puño. **I was very much struck by the city's beauty,** La belleza de la ciudad me impresionó mucho. **The news struck fear into their hearts,** La noticia les llenó el corazón de miedo. **The clock struck three,** El reloj dio las tres. **The hour has struck,** Fig. Ha llegado la hora. **How did the house s. you?** ¿Qué te pareció la casa? **to s. a bargain,** cerrar un trato. **to s. a blow,** asestar un golpe. **to s. across country,** ir a campo traviesa. **to s. an attitude,** tomar una actitud. **to s. home,** dar en el blanco; herir; herir en lo más vivo; hacerse sentir. **to s. at,** asestar un golpe (a); acometer, embestir; atacar. **to s. down,** derribar; (of illness) acometer. **to s. off,** (a head, etc.) cortar; (a name) borrar, tachar; (print) imprimir. **to s. out,** vi asestar un golpe (a); (of a swimmer) nadar; echarse, lanzarse. —vt (a word, etc.) borrar, rayar; (begin) iniciar. **to s. through,** (cross out) rayar, tachar; (of the sun's rays, etc.) penetrar. **to s. up,** vt tocar; empezar a cantar; (a friendship) trabar. —vi empezar a tocar. **to s. up a march,** Mil. batir la marcha

**strike** /straik/ n huelga, f. —vi declararse en huelga. **go-slow s.,** turguismo, m. **lock-out s.,** huelga patronal, f. **sit-down s.,** huelga de brazos caídos, f. **to go on s.,** declararse en huelga. **s.-breaker,** esquirol, m. **s.-pay,** subsidio de huelga, m

**striker** /'straikər/ n huelguista, mf

**striking** /'straıkıŋ/ a notable, sorprendente; (impressive) impresionante; que llama la atención; llamativo

**string** /strıŋ/ n bramante, m; cuerda, f; (ribbon) cinta, f; (of beads, etc.) sarta, f; (of onions) ristra, f; (of horses, etc.) reata, f; hilera, f; (of a bridge) cable, m; (of oaths, lies) sarta, serie, f; (of beans) fibra, f. —vt encordar; (beads, etc.) ensartar; (beans) quitar las fibras (de). **He is all strung up,** Se le crispan los nervios. **the strings,** los instrumentos de cuerda. **a s. of pearls,** un collar de perlas. **for strings,** Mus. para arco. **to pull strings,** Fig. manejar los hilos. **to s. up,** (an instrument) templar; (a person) pender, ahorcar. **s. bean,** judía verde, f

**stringed** /strıŋd/ a (of musical instruments) de cuerda. **s. instrument,** instrumento de cuerda, m

**stringency** /'strındʒənsı/ n severidad, f; estrechez, f

**stringent** /'strındʒənt/ a estricto, severo

**stringy** /'strıŋı/ a fibroso; filamentoso; correoso; arrugado

**strip** /strıp/ vt desnudar; despojar (de), quitar; robar; (a cow) ordeñar hasta agotar la leche. —vi desnudarse. —n (tatter) jirón, m; tira, lista, f; (of wood) listón, m; (of earth) pedazo, m; (Geog. of land) zona, f. **to s. off,** vt quitar; (bark from a tree) descortezar; (one's clothes) despojarse de. —vi desprenderse, separarse

**stripe** /straıp/ n raya, lista, f; (Mil. etc.) galón, m; (lash) azote, m. —vt rayar. **the stripes of the tiger,** las rayas del tigre

**striped** /straıpt, 'straıpıd/ a listado, a rayas; con rayas. **s. trousers,** pantalón de corte, m

**stripling** /'strıplıŋ/ n joven imberbe, pollo, mancebo, m

**strive** /straıv/ vi esforzarse (a); pugnar (por, para); trabajar (por); (fight against) luchar contra; pelear con. **He was striving to understand,** Pugnaba por (or Se esforzaba a) comprender

**stroke** /strouk/ n (blow) golpe, m; (of the oars) golpe del remo, m, remada, f; (at billards) tacada, f; (in golf) tirada, f; (in swimming) braza, f; (of a clock) campanada, f; (of a pen) rasgo de la pluma, m; (of a brush) pincelada, f; Mech. golpe de émbolo, m; (caress) caricia con la mano, f. —vt acariciar con la mano. **on the s. of six,** al acabar de dar las seis. **to have a s.,** tener un ataque de apoplejía. **s. of genius,** rasgo de ingenio, m. **s. of good luck,** racha de buena suerte, f

**stroll** /stroul/ vi pasearse, vagar. —n vuelta, f, paseo, m. **to go for a s.,** dar una vuelta

**stroller** /'stroulər/ n paseante, mf

**strolling** /'stroulıŋ/ a errante; ambulante. **s. player,** n cómico (-ca) ambulante

**strong** /strɔŋ/ a fuerte; vigoroso; robusto; enérgico; firme; poderoso; (of colours) intenso, vivo; (of tea, coffee) cargado; Gram. fuerte. **The government took s. measures,** El gobierno tomó medidas enérgicas. **They gave very s. reasons,** Alegaron unas razones muy poderosas. **Grammar is not his s. point,** La gramática no es su punto fuerte. **The enemy is s. in numbers,** El enemigo es numéricamente fuerte. **The society is four thousand s.,** La sociedad tiene cuatro mil miembros. **s. box,** caja de caudales, f. **s. man,** hombre fuerte, m; (in a circus) hércules, m. **s.-minded,** de espíritu fuerte; independiente. **s. room,** cámara acorazada, f

**stronghold** /'strɔŋ,hould/ n fortaleza, f; refugio, m

**strongly** /'strɔŋlı/ adv vigorosamente; fuertemente; firmemente

**strop** /strɔp/ n (razor) suavizador, m, vt suavizar

**strophe** /'stroufi/ n estrofa, f

**structural** /'strʌktʃərəl/ a estructural

**structurally** /'strʌktʃərəli/ adv estructuralmente, desde el punto de vista de la estructura

**structure** /'strʌktʃər/ n estructura, f; edificio, m; construcción, f

**struggle** /'strʌgəl/ vi luchar; pelear; disputarse. —n lucha, f; combate, m; conflicto, m. **to s. to one's feet,** luchar por levantarse. **without a s.,** sin luchar

**struggling** /'strʌglıŋ/ a pobre, indigente, que lucha para vivir

**strum** /strʌm/ vt (a stringed instrument) rascar; tocar mal

**strumpet** /'strʌmpıt/ n ramera, f

**strut** /strʌt/ vi pavonearse. —vt (prop) apuntalar. —n pavonada, f; (prop) puntal, m. **to s. out,** salir de un paso majestuoso

**strychnine** /'strıknin/ n estricnina, f

**stub** /stʌb/ n (of a tree) tocón, m; (of a pencil, candle, etc.) cabo, m; pedazo, fragmento, m; (of a cigarette or cigar) colilla, f. **s.-book,** talonario, m

**stubble** /'stʌbəl/ n rastrojo, m; (beard) barba de tres días, f

**stubborn** /'stʌbərn/ a inquebrantable, tenaz; persistente; (pig-headed) terco, testarudo

**stubbornness** /'stʌbərnıs/ n tenacidad, f; terquedad, testarudez, f

**stucco** /'stʌkou/ n estuco, m, vt estucar

**stud** /stʌd/ n (of horses) caballeriza, f; (nail) tachón, m; (for collars) pasador para camisas, m. —vt tachonar; sembrar. **dress s.,** botón de la pechera, m. **s.-farm,** potrero, m

**student** /'studnt/ n estudiante, mf. —a estudiantil

**studied** /'stʌdid/ a estudiado; calculado; (of style) cerebral, reflexivo; (intentional) deliberado

**studio** /'studi,ou/ n estudio, m. **broadcasting s.,** estudio de emisión, m

**studious** /'studias/ a estudioso, aplicado; (deliberate) intencional, deliberate; (eager) solícito, ansioso

**studiously** /'studiasli/ adv estudiosamente; con intención, deliberadamente; solícitamente

**study** /'stʌdı/ n estudio, m; solicitud, f, cuidado, m; investigación, f; (room) gabinete, cuarto de trabajo, m. —vt ocuparse de, cuidar de, atender a; considerar; estudiar; examinar; (the stars) observar; (try) procurar. —vi estudiar. **in a brown s.,** en Babia. **to make a s. of,** hacer un estudio de, estudiar. **to s. for an examination,** prepararse para un examen

**stuff** /stʌf/ n substancia, materia, f; (fabric) tela, f, paño, m; (rubbish) cachivaches, m pl, cosas, f pl. —a de estofa. —vt henchir; llenar; Cul. rellenar; (with food) ahitar (de); (cram) atestar, apretar; (furniture) rehenchir; (an animal, bird) disecar; (put) meter, poner. **S. and nonsense!** ¡Patrañas! **to be poor s.,** ser de pacotilla; no valer para nada

**stuffed animal** /stʌft/ n animal disecado, m

**stuffiness** /'stʌfınıs/ n mala ventilación, f; falta de aire, f; calor, m

**stuffing** /'stʌfıŋ/ n (of furniture) rehenchimiento, m; Cul. relleno, m

**stuffy** /'stʌfi/ a mal ventilado, poco aireado, ahogado

**stultify** /'stʌltə,faı/ vt hacer inútil; invalidar; hacer ridículo

**stumble** /'stʌmbəl/ vi tropezar; dar un traspié; (in speaking) tartamudear. —n tropezón, m; traspié, m. **to s. through a speech,** pronunciar un discurso a tropezones. **to s. against,** tropezar contra. **to s. upon, across,** tropezar con; encontrar por casualidad

**stumbling block** n tropiezo, impedimento, m

**stump** /stʌmp/ n (of a tree) tocón, m; (of an arm, leg) muñón, m; (of a pencil, candle) cabo, m; (of a tooth) raigón, m; (of a cigar) colilla, f; (cricket) poste, montante, m; Art. esfumino, m; (leg) pata, f. —vt (disconcert) desconcertar; Art. esfumar; recorrer. **to s. up,** Inf. pagar

**stun** /stʌn/ vt dejar sin sentido (a); aturdir de un golpe (a); (astound) pasmar

**stunning** /'stʌnıŋ/ a aturdidor; que pasma; Inf. estupendo

**stunt** /stʌnt/ vt impedir el crecimiento de; encanijar. —n (advertising) anuncio de reclamo, m; recurso (para conseguir algo), m; proeza, f

**stunted** /'stʌntıd/ a (of trees, etc.) enano; (of children) encanijado; (of intelligence) inmaduro

**stupefaction** /,stupə'fækʃən/ n estupefacción, f; estupor, m

**stupefy** /'stupə,faı/ vt atontar, embrutecer; causar estupor (a), asombrar

**stupendous** /stu'pendəs/ a asombroso; enorme

**stupid** /'stupıd/ a (with sleep, etc.) atontado; (silly) estúpido, tonto. —n tonto (-ta)

**stupidity** /stu'pıdıti/ n estupidez, f; tontería, f

**stupor** /'stupər/ n estupor, m

**sturdiness** /'stərdınıs/ n robustez, f, vigor, m; firmeza, tenacidad, f

**sturdy** /'stɜrdi/ *a* robusto, vigoroso, fuerte; firme, tenaz

**sturgeon** /'stɜrdʒən/ *n Ichth.* esturión, *m*

**stutter** /'stʌtər/ *vi* tartamudear. —*vt* balbucir. —*n* tartamudeo, *m*

**stutterer** /'stʌtərər/ *n* tartamudo (-da)

**stuttering** /'stʌtərɪŋ/ *a* tartamudo; balbuciente. —*n* tartamudeo, *m*

**sty** /stai/ *n* (pig) pocilga, *f; Med.* orzuelo, *m*

**Stygian** /'stɪdʒiən/ *a* estigio

**style** /stail/ *n* (for etching) buril, *m; (Lit., Art., Archit.,* etc.) estilo, *m;* (fashion) moda, *f;* (model) modelo, *m;* (behavior, tone, etc.) tono, *m;* elegancia, *f;* (kind) especie, clase, *f;* (designation) tratamiento, *m; vt* llamar, nombrar. **the latest styles from Madrid,** los últimos modelos de Madrid. **He has a very individual s.,** Su estilo es muy personal. **They live in great s.,** Viven en gran lujo

**stylet** /'stailɪt/ *n* estilete, *m*

**stylish** /'stailɪʃ/ *a* elegante

**stylishness** /'stailɪʃnɪs/ *n* elegancia, *f*

**stylist** /'stailɪst/ *n* estilista, *mf*

**stylize** /'stailaiz/ *vt* estilizar

**suasion** /'sweiʒən/ *n* persuasión, *f*

**suasive** /'sweisɪv/ *a* suasorio, persuasivo

**suave** /swɑv/ *a* afable, cortés, urbano; (of wine) suave

**suavity** /'swɒvɪti/ *n* afabilidad, urbanidad, *f*

**subaltern** /sʌb'ɔltərn/ *n Mil.* subalterno, *m, a* subalterno, subordinado

**subcommittee** /'sʌbkə,mɪti/ *n* subcomisión, *f*

**subconscious** /sʌb'kɒnʃəs/ *a* subconsciente. **the s.,** la subconsciencia

**subconsciously** /sʌb'kɒnʃəsli/ *adv* subconscientemente

**subcutaneous** /,sʌbkyu'teiniəs/ *a* subcutáneo

**subdivide** /,sʌbdɪ'vaid/ *vt* subdividir. —*vi* subdividirse

**subdivision** /'sʌbdɪ,vɪʒən/ *n* subdivisión, *f*

**subdominant** /sʌb'dɒmənənt/ *n Mus.* subdominante, *f*

**subdue** /səb'du/ *vt* subyugar, sojuzgar, vencer; (one's passions) dominar; (colors, voices) suavizar; (lessen) mitigar; apagar

**subdued** /səb'dud/ *a* (of colors) apagado; (of persons) sumiso; (depressed) deprimido, melancólico. **in a s. voice,** en voz baja

**subheading** /'sʌb,hɛdɪŋ/ *n* subtítulo, *m*

**subhuman** /sʌb'hyumən/ *a* subhumano

**subject** /*n.* 'sʌbdʒɪkt; *v.* səb'dʒɛkt/ *a* sujeto; sometido (a); expuesto (a). —*n* (of a country) súbdito (-ta); sujeto, *m;* (of study) asignatura, materia, *f;* (theme) tema, *m; (Gram., Philos.)* sujeto, *m.* —*vt* subyugar; someter. **It can only be done s. to his consent,** Podrá hacerse únicamente si él lo consiente. **to change the s.,** cambiar de conversación. **to s. to criticism,** criticar (a). **s.-matter,** materia, *f;* (of a letter) contenido, *m*

**subjection** /səb'dʒɛkʃən/ *n* sujeción, *f;* sometimiento, *m.* **He was in a state of complete s.,** Estaba completamente sumiso. **to bring into s.,** subyugar

**subjective** /səb'dʒɛktɪv/ *a* subjetivo

**subjectiveness** /səb'dʒɛktɪvnɪs/ *n* subjetividad, *f*

**subjectivism** /səb'dʒɛktə,vɪzəm/ *n* subjetivismo, *m*

**subjoin** /səb'dʒɔin/ *vt* añadir, adjuntar

**subjugate** /'sʌbdʒə,geit/ *vt* subyugar, someter

**subjugation** /,sʌbdʒə'geiʃən/ *n* subyugación, *f*

**subjunctive** /səb'dʒʌŋktɪv/ *a* and *n* subjuntivo *m*

**sublet** /*v.* sʌb'lɛt; *n.* 'sʌb,lɛt/ *vt* subarrendar. —*n* subarriendo, *m*

**sublimate** /*v.* 'sʌblə,meit; *n.* -mɪt/ *vt* sublimar. —*n* sublimado, *m*

**sublimation** /,sʌblɪ'meiʃən/ *n* sublimación, *f*

**sublime** /sə'blaim/ *a* sublime; absoluto, completo; extremo. **the s.,** lo sublime

**sublimely** /sə'blaimli/ *adv* sublimemente; completamente

**submachine gun** /,sʌbmə'ʃin/ *n* pistola ametralladora, metralleta, *f,* subfusil ametrallador, *m*

**submarine** /,sʌbmə'rin/ *a* submarino. —*n*

submarino, *m.* **midget s.,** submarino enano, submarino de bolsillo, *m.* **s. chaser,** cazasubmarino, *m*

**submerge** /səb'mɜrdʒ/ *vt* sumergir; inundar. —*vi* sumergirse. **The submarine submerged,** El submarino se sumergió

**submergence** /səb'mɜrdʒəns/ *n* sumergimiento, *m,* sumersión, *f;* hundimiento, *m*

**submersible** /səb'mɜrsəbəl/ *a* sumergible

**submersion** /səb'mɜrʒən/ *n* sumersión, *f;* hundimiento, *m*

**submission** /səb'mɪʃən/ *n* sometimiento, *m;* sumisión, resignación, *f;* docilidad, *f*

**submissive** /səb'mɪsɪv/ *a* sumiso, dócil, manso

**submissively** /səb'mɪsɪvli/ *adv* sumisamente, con docilidad

**submissiveness** /səb'mɪsɪvnɪs/ *n* sumisión, docilidad, *f*

**submit** /səb'mɪt/ *vt* someterse (a); doblarse ante; (a scheme, etc.) someter; presentar; (urge) proponer. —*vi* someterse; resignarse; (surrender) rendirse, entregarse. **to s. to arbitration,** someter a arbitraje

**subnormal** /sʌb'nɔrməl/ *a* anormal

**subordinate** /*adj.,n.* sə'bɔrdnɪt; *v.* -dn,eit/ *a* subordinado; subalterno, inferior; secundario. —*n* subordinado (-da). —*vt* subordinar

**subordination** /sə,bɔrdn'eiʃən/ *n* subordinación, *f*

**suborn** /sə'bɔrn/ *vt* sobornar, cohechar

**subplot** /'sʌb,plɒt/ *n* intriga secundaria, trama secundaria, *f*

**subpoena** /sə'pinə/ *n* citación, *f, vt* citar

**subscribe** /səb'skraib/ *vt* and *vi* subscribir; (to a periodical, etc.) abonarse (a)

**subscriber** /səb'skraibər/ *n* subscriptor (-ra); abonado (-da)

**subscription** /səb'skrɪpʃən/ *n* subscripción, *f;* (to a periodical, series of concerts, etc.) abono, *m;* (to a club) cuota, *f*

**subsection** /'sʌb,sɛkʃən/ *n* subsección, *f*

**subsequent** /'sʌbsɪkwənt/ *a* subsiguiente, subsecuente; posterior. **s. to,** después de, posterior a. **s. upon,** de resultas de

**subsequently** /'sʌbsikwəntli/ *adv* más tarde; subsiguientemente; posteriormente

**subservience** /səb'sɜrviens/ *n* servilidad, *f;* utilidad, *f*

**subservient** /səb'sɜrviənt/ *a* servil; subordinado; útil

**subside** /səb'said/ *vi* (of water) bajar; (of ground) hundirse; (of foundations) asentarse; disminuir; calmarse; (be quiet) callarse. **to s. into a chair,** dejarse caer en un sillón

**subsidence** /səb'saidns/ *n* hundimiento, *m;* desplome, derrumbamiento, *m;* (of floods) bajada, *f;* (of anger, etc.) apaciguamiento, *m*

**subsidiary** /səb'sɪdi,ɛri/ *a* subsidiario

**subsidize** /'sʌbsɪ,daiz/ *vt* subvencionar

**subsidy** /'sʌbsɪdi/ *n* subvención, *f,* subsidio, *m;* prima, *f*

**subsist** /səb'sɪst/ *vi* subsistir

**subsistence** /səb'sɪstəns/ *n* subsistencia, *f*

**subsoil** /'sʌb,sɔil/ *n* subsuelo, *m*

**substance** /'sʌbstəns/ *n* substancia, *f*

**substantial** /səb'stænʃəl/ *a* substancial; sólido; importante

**substantially** /səb,stænʃəli/ *adv* substancialmente; sólidamente

**substantiate** /səb'stænʃi,eit/ *vt* establecer, verificar; justificar

**substantiation** /səb,stænʃi'eiʃən/ *n* comprobación, *f,* verificación, *f;* justificación, *f*

**substantive** /'sʌbstəntɪv/ *a* real, independiente; *Gram.* substantivo. —*n Gram.* substantivo, *m*

**substitute** /'sʌbstɪ,tut/ *n* substituto (-ta); (material) substituto, *m.* —*vt* substituir, reemplazar. **to be a s. for,** hacer las veces de

**substitution** /,sʌbstɪ'tuʃən/ *n* substitución, *f,* reemplazo, *m*

**substratum** /'sʌb,streitəm, -,stretəm/ *n* substrato, *m*

**subterfuge** /'sʌbtər,fyudʒ/ *n* subterfugio, *m;* evasiva, *f*

**subterranean** /,sʌbtə'reiniən/ *a* subterráneo

**subtitle** /'sʌb,taitl/ *n* subtítulo, *m;* (on films) guión, *m*

**subtle** /'sʌtl/ a sutil; delicado; penetrante; (crafty) astuto

**subtlety** /'sʌtlti/ n sutileza, f; delicadeza, f; (craftiness) astucia, f

**subtly** /'sʌtli/ adv sutilmente; con delicadeza

**subtract** /səb'trækt/ vt restar, substraer

**subtraction** /səb'trækʃən/ n resta, substracción, f

**suburb** /'sʌbərb/ n suburbio, m; pl **suburbs,** las afueras, f pl los arrabales, m pl

**suburban** /sə'bɜrbən/ a suburbano

**subvention** /səb'venʃən/ n subvención, f

**subversion** /səb'vɜrʒən/ n subversión, f

**subversive** /səb'vɜrsɪv/ a subversivo

**subvert** /səb'vɜrt/ vt subvertir

**subway** /'sʌb,wei/ n (passageway) pasaje subterráneo, m; (underground railway) metro (Spain, Puerto Rico), subte (Argentina), m

**succeed** /sək'sid/ vt seguir (a); suceder (a); heredar. —vi seguir (a); suceder (a); (be successful) tener éxito. **I did not s. in doing it,** No logré hacerlo. **to s. to the throne,** subir al trono

**succeeding** /sək'sidɪŋ/ a subsiguiente; futuro; consecutivo; sucesivo

**success** /sək'sɛs/ n éxito, m; triunfo, m. **to be a s.,** tener éxito. **The film was a great s.,** La película tuvo mucho éxito

**successful** /sək'sɛsfəl/ a que tiene éxito; afortunado, venturoso; próspero.

**successfully** /sək'sɛsfəli/ adv con éxito; prósperamente

**succession** /sək'sɛʃən/ n sucesión, f; (series) serie, f; (inheritance) herencia, f; (descendants) descendencia, f. **in s.,** sucesivamente

**successive** /sək'sɛsɪv/ a sucesivo

**successor** /sək'sɛsər/ n sucesor (-ra)

**succinct** /sək'sɪŋkt/ a sucinto, conciso

**succinctly** /sək'sɪŋktli/ adv sucintamente, brevemente, en pocas palabras

**succor** /'sʌkər/ vt socorrer, auxiliar. —n socorro, m, ayuda, f

**succulence** /'sʌkyələns/ n suculencia, f

**succulent** /'sʌkyələnt/ a suculento

**succumb** /sə'kʌm/ vi sucumbir; someterse, ceder

⚡**such** /sʌtʃ/ a tal; parecido, semejante; así; tanto; (before an adjective, adverb) tan. —n el, m, (f, la) que, los, m pl, (f pl, las) que; tal. **s. men,** tales hombres. **I have never seen s. magnificence,** Nunca no he visto tanta magnificencia. **s. an important man,** un hombre tan importante. **s. pictures as these,** cuadros como estos. **S. is life!** ¡Así es la vida! **science as s.,** la ciencia como tal. **s.-and-s.,** tal y tal

**suchlike** /'sʌtʃ,laik/ a parecido, semejante; de esta clase

**suck** /sʌk/ vt chupar; (the breast) mamar; sorber; (of a vacuum cleaner, etc.) aspirar. —n chupada, f; succión, f. **to s. down,** tragar. **to s. up,** aspirar; absorber

**sucker** /'sʌkər/ n Zool. ventosa, f; Bot. acodo, mugrón, m; (greenhorn) primo, m; (pig) lechón, m

**suckle** /'sʌkəl/ vt amamantar, dar el pecho (a)

**suckling pig** /'sʌklɪŋ/ n lechón, cochinillo, m

**suction** /'sʌkʃən/ n succión, f; aspiración, f. **s.-pump,** bomba aspirante, f

**Sudanese** /,sudn'iz/ a and n sudanés (-esa)

**Sudan, the** /su'dæn/ el Sudán, m

**sudden** /'sʌdn/ a súbito; (unexpected) inesperado, impensado; (of bends) brusco. **all of a s.,** de repente; súbitamente

**suddenly** /'sʌdn̩li/ adv súbitamente; de pronto, de repente

**suddenness** /'sʌdn̩nɪs/ n carácter repentino, m; (of a bend, etc.) brusquedad, f

**suds** /sʌdz/ n pl jabonaduras, f pl; espuma, f

**sue** /su/ vt Law. proceder contra, pedir en juicio; Law. demandar; (beg) suplicar. **to sue for peace,** pedir la paz

**suede** /sweid/ n ante, m. **s. glove,** guante de ante, m

**suet** /'suɪt/ n sebo, m

**Suez Canal, the** /'su'ɛz/ el Istmo de Suez, m

**suffer** /'sʌfər/ vt sufrir, padecer; pasar, experimentar; (tolerate) tolerar; (allow) permitir. —vi sufrir.

**She suffers from her environment,** es la víctima de su medio ambiente

**sufferance** /'sʌfərəns/ n tolerancia, f. **on s.,** por tolerancia

**sufferer** /'sʌfərər/ n enfermo (-ma); víctima, f

**suffering** /'sʌfərɪŋ/ n sufrimiento, padecimiento, m; dolor, m. —a sufriente

**suffice** /sə'fais/ vi ser suficiente, bastar. —vt satisfacer

**sufficiency** /sə'fɪʃənsi/ n suficiencia, f; (of money) subsistencia, f

**sufficient** /sə'fɪʃənt/ a suficiente, bastante. **to be s.,** bastar, ser suficiente

**sufficiently** /sə'fɪʃəntli/ adv suficientemente, bastante

**suffix** /'sʌfɪks/ n Gram. sufijo, m

**suffocate** /'sʌfə,keit/ vt ahogar, sofocar, asfixiar. —vi sofocarse, asfixiarse

**suffocating** /'sʌfə,keitɪŋ/ a sofocante, asfixiante

**suffocation** /,sʌfə'keiʃən/ n sofocación, asfixia, f; ahogo, m

**suffrage** /'sʌfrɪdʒ/ n sufragio, m; voto, m. **universal s.,** sufragio universal, m

**suffragette** /,sʌfrə'dʒɛt/ n sufragista, f

**suffuse** /sə'fyuz/ vt bañar, inundar, cubrir

**sugar** /'ʃugər/ n azúcar, m. —vt azucarar. **brown s.,** azúcar moreno, m. **loaf s.,** azúcar de pilón, m. **white s.,** azúcar blanco, m. **to s. the pill,** dorar la píldora. **s.-almond,** peladilla, f. **s.-basin,** azucarera, f. **s.-beet,** remolacha, f. **s.-candy,** azúcar candi, m. **s.-cane,** caña de azúcar, f. **s.-cane syrup,** miel de caña, f. **s.-paste,** alfeñique, m, alcorza, f. **s.-refinery,** fábrica de azúcar, f. **s.-tongs,** tenacillas para azúcar, f pl

**sugary** /'ʃugəri/ a azucarado; Fig. meloso, almibarado

**suggest** /səg'dʒɛst/ vt implicar; indicar, dar a entender; sugerir; (advise) aconsejar; (hint) insinuar; (evoke) evocar. **I suggested they should go to London,** Les aconsejé que fueran a Londres. **An idea suggested itself to him,** Se le ocurrió una idea

**suggestion** /səg'dʒɛstʃən/ n sugestión, f; insinuación, f

**suggestive** /səg'dʒɛstɪv/ a sugestivo; estimulante

**suicidal** /,suə'saidl̩/ a suicida. **s. tendency,** tendencia suicida, tendencia al suicidio, f

**suicide** /'suə,said/ n (act) suicidio, m; (person) suicida, mf. **to commit s.,** darse la muerte, quitarse la vida suicidarse

**suit** /sut/ n (request) petición, súplica, f; oferta de matrimonio, f; Law. pleito, m; (of clothes) traje, m; (cards) palo, m; (of cards held) serie, f, vt convenir; sentar; ir bien (a); venir bien (a); (adapt) adaptar. **S. yourself!** ¡Haz lo que quieras! **The arrangement suits me very well,** El arreglo me viene muy bien. **The climate doesn't s. me,** El clima no me sienta bien. **The color does not s. you,** El color no te va bien. **to follow s.,** seguir el ejemplo (de); (cards) jugar el mismo palo. **s.-case,** maleta, f

**suitability** /,sutə'bɪlɪti/ n conveniencia, f; aptitud, f

**suitable** /'sutəbəl/ a conveniente; apropiado; apto; a propósito. **Not s. for children,** No apto para menores. **to make s. for,** adaptar a las necesidades de

**suitably** /'sutəbli/ adv convenientemente; apropiadamente

**suite** /swit/ n (of retainers, etc.) séquito, acompañamiento, m; (of furniture, etc.) juego, m; Mus. suite, f. **private s.,** habitaciones particulares, f pl. **s. of rooms,** apartamento, m

**suitor** /'sutər/ n Law. demandante, m; pretendiente, m

**sulk** /sʌlk/ vi ponerse malhumorado, ser mohíno

**sulkiness** /'sʌlkinɪs/ n mohína, f, mal humor, m

**sulky** /'sʌlki/ a mohíno, malhumorado

**sullen** /'sʌlən/ a taciturno, hosco; malhumorado, sombrío; (of a landscape, etc.) triste, sombrío

**sullenly** /'sʌlənli/ adv taciturnamente, hoscamente

**sullenness** /'sʌlənnɪs/ n taciturnidad, hosquedad, f, mal humor, m

**sully** /'sʌli/ vt desdorar, empañar; manchar

**sulphur** /'sʌlfər/ n azufre, m

**sulphuric** /sʌl'fyʊrɪk/ a sulfúrico

**sulphurous** /'sʌlfərəs/ a sulfuroso

**sultan** /'sʌltn̩/ n sultán, m

**sultriness** /'sʌltrinɪs/ n bochorno, calor sofocante, m

**sultry** /'sʌltri/ a bochornoso, sofocante

**sum** /sʌm/ n suma, f; total, m; cantidad, f; (in arithmetic) problema (de aritmética), m. —vt sumar, calcular. **in sum,** en suma; en resumen. **to sum up,** recapitular; resumir; (a person) tomar las medidas (a)

**summarily** /sə'meərəli/ adv someramente; Law. sumariamente

**summarize** /'sʌmə,raiz/ vt resumir brevemente; compendiar

**summary** /'sʌməri/ a somero; Law. sumario. —n resumen, sumario, compendio, m. **summary records,** actas resumidas, f pl

**summer** /'sʌmər/ n verano, estío, m. **to spend the s.,** veranear. **s.-house,** cenador, m. **s.-time,** verano, m; hora de verano, f. **s. wheat,** trigo tremesino, m

**summing-up** /'sʌmɪŋ,ʌp/ n recapitulación, f

**summit** /'sʌmɪt/ n cima, cumbre, f; Fig. apogeo, m

**summitry** /'sʌmɪtri/ n diplomacia en la cumbre, f

**summon** /'sʌmən/ vt llamar, hacer venir; mandar, requerir; Law. citar. **to s. up one's courage,** cobrar ánimos

**summons** /'sʌmənz/ n llamamiento, m; Mil. intimación, f; Law. citación, f. —vt Law. citar

**sump** /sʌmp/ n (of a motor-car) pozo colector, m; Mineral. sumidero, m

**sumptuous** /'sʌmptʃuəs/ a suntuoso, lujoso, magnífico

**sumptuousness** /'sʌmptʃuəsnɪs/ n suntuosidad, magnificencia, f

**sun** /sʌn/ n sol, m. **The sun was shining,** Hacía sol, El sol brillaba. **to bask in the sun,** tomar el sol. **sunbathing,** baños de sol, m pl. **sun-blind,** toldo para el sol, m. **sun-bonnet,** capelina, f. **sun-glasses,** gafas ahumadas, f pl. **sun-helmet,** casco colonial, m. **sunspot,** Astron. mancha del sol, f; (freckle) peca, f. **sun-worship,** adoración del sol, f

**sunbeam** /'sʌn,bim/ n rayo de sol, m

**sunburn** /'sʌn,bɜrn/ n quemadura del sol, f; bronceado, m

**sunburnt** /'sʌn,bɜrnt/ a quemado por el sol; bronceado, tostado por el sol

**sundae** /'sʌndei/ n helado de frutas, m

**Sunday** /'sʌndei/ n domingo, m. **in his S. best,** en su traje dominguero, endomingado. **S. school,** escuela dominical, f

**Sunday's child** n niño nacido de pies, niño nacido un domingo, niño mimado de la fortuna

**sunder** /'sʌndər/ vt dividir en dos, hender; separar

**sundial** /'sʌn,daiəl/ n reloj de sol, reloj solar, m

**sundown** /'sʌn,daun/ n puesta del sol, f

**sundry** /'sʌndri/ a varios (-as). —n pl **sundries,** artículos diversos, m pl; Com. varios, m pl. **all and s.,** todo el mundo, todos y cada uno

**sunflower** /'sʌn,flauər/ n girasol, tornasol, m, trompeta de amor, f

**sunken** /'sʌŋkən/ a (of eyes, etc.) hundido

**sunless** /'sʌnlɪs/ a sin sol

**sun letter** n letra solar, f

**sunlight** /'sʌn,lait/ n luz del sol, f, rayos del sol, m pl. **artificial s.,** sol artificial, m. **in the s.,** al sol

**sunny** /'sʌni/ a de sol; bañado de sol; asoleado; expuesto al sol; (face) risueño; (of disposition, etc.) alegre. **to be s.,** hacer sol

**sunrise** /'sʌn,raiz/ n salida del sol, f. **from s. to sunset,** de sol a sol

**sunset** /'sʌn,sɛt/ n puesta del sol, f. **at s.,** a la caída (or puesta) del sol

**sunshade** /'sʌn,ʃeid/ n parasol, quitasol, m, sombrilla, f

**sunshine** /'sʌn,ʃain/ n luz del sol, f. **in the s.,** al sol

**sunstroke** /'sʌn,strouk/ n insolación, f

**sup** /sʌp/ vt sorber. —vi cenar. —n sorbo, m

**super** /'supər/ n (actor) comparsa, mf; (film) superproducción, f; (of a beehive) alza, f

**superabundance** /,supərə'bʌndəns/ n superabundancia, sobreabundancia, f

**superabundant** /,supərə'bʌndənt/ a superabundante, sobreabundante. **to be s.,** sobreabundar

**superannuate** /,supər'ænyu,eit/ vt (retire) jubilar

**superannuated** /,supər'ænyu,eitid/ a (retired) jubilado; (out-of-date) anticuado

**superannuation** /,supər,ænyu'eiʃən/ n (retirement and pension) jubilación, f

**superb** /su'pɜrb/ a magnífico, espléndido

**superbly** /su'pɜrbli/ adv magníficamente

**supercargo** /,supər'kargou/ n Naut. sobrecargo, m

**supercharger** /'supər,tʃardʒər/ n (Auto., Aer.) compresor, m

**supercilious** /,supər'siliəs/ a altanero, altivo, orgulloso; desdeñoso

**superciliousness** /,supər'siliəsnɪs/ n altanería, altivez, f, orgullo, m; desdén, m

**superficial** /,supər'fiʃəl/ a superficial

**superficiality** /,supər,fiʃi'æliti/ n superficialidad, f

**superficially** /,supər'fiʃəli/ adv superficialmente

**superfine** /,supər'fain/ a superfino

**superfluity** /,supər'fluiti/ n superfluidad, f

**superfluous** /su'pɜrfluəs/ a superfluo. **to be s.,** sobrar

**superfortress** /'supər,fɔrtrɪs/ n Aer. superfortaleza volante, f

**superhuman** /,supər'hyumən/ a sobrehumano

**superimpose** /,supərɪm'pouz/ vt sobreponer

**superintend** /,supərɪn'tend/ vt superentender, dirigir

**superintendent** /,supərɪn'tendənt/ n superintendente, mf; director (-ra); (school) inspector; (police) subjefe de la policía, m

**superior** /sə'pɪəriər/ a superior; (in number) mayor; (smug) desdeñoso. —n superior (-ra). **Mother S.,** (madre) superiora, f. **s. to,** superior a; encima de

**superiority** /sə,pɪəri'ɔriti/ n superioridad, f

**superlative** /sə'pɜrlətɪv/ a extremo, supremo; Gram. superlativo. —n Gram. superlativo, m

**superlatively** /sə'pɜrlətɪvli/ adv en sumo grado, superlativamente

**superman** /'supər,mæn/ n superhombre, m

**supermarket** /'supər,markɪt/ n supermercado, m

**supernatural** /,supər'nætʃərəl/ a sobrenatural

**supernumerary** /,supər'numə,rɛri/ a and n supernumerario (-ia)

**superposition** /,supərpə'zɪʃən/ n superposición, f

**superscribe** /'supər,skraib/ vt sobrescribir; poner el sobrescrito (a)

**superscription** /,supər'skrɪpʃən/ n (on letters, documents) sobrescrito, m; leyenda, f

**supersede** /,supər'sid/ vt reemplazar; suplantar

**supersensible** /,supər'sensəbəl/ a suprasensible

**superstition** /,supər'stɪʃən/ n superstición, f

**superstitious** /,supər'stɪʃəs/ a supersticioso

**supertax** /'supər,tæks/ n impuesto suplementario, m

**supervene** /,supər'vin/ vi sobrevenir

**supervise** /'supər,vaiz/ vt superentender, vigilar; dirigir

**supervision** /,supər'vɪʒən/ n superintendencia, f; dirección, f

**supervisor** /'supər,vaizər/ n superintendente, mf; inspector (-ra); director (-ra)

**supine** /a. su'pain; n. 'supain/ a supino; indolente, negligente. —n Gram. supino, m

**supper** /'sʌpər/ n cena, f. **the Last S.,** la Última Cena. **to have s.,** cenar. **s.-time,** hora de cenar, f

**supplant** /sə'plænt/ vt suplantar; usurpar; reemplazar

**supplanter** /sə'plæntər/ n suplantador (-ra)

**supple** /'sʌpəl/ a flexible; dócil, manso; (fawning) adulador, servil, lisonjero

**supplement** /'sʌpləmənt/ n suplemento, m; (of a book) apéndice, m

**supplementary** /,sʌplə'mentəri/ a suplementario; adicional

**suppleness** /'sʌpəlnɪs/ n flexibilidad, f; docilidad, f; servilidad, f

**suppliant** /'sʌpliənt/ a and n suplicante, mf

**supplicate** /'sʌpli,keit/ vt and vi suplicar

**supplication** /, s½plɪ'keiSən/ n suplicación, f; súplica, f

**supply** /sə'plai/ vt proveer (de); suministrar; proporcionar, dar; (a deficiency) suplir; (a post) llenar; (a post temporarily) reemplazar. —n suministro, surtimiento, m; provisión, f; (of electricity, etc.) suministro, m; Com. oferta, f; (person) substituto (-ta); pl **supplies,** Com. existencias, f pl; Mil. pertrechos, m pl;

víveres, *m pl,* provisiones, *f pl.* **s. and demand,** oferta y demanda, *f*

**support** /sə'pɔrt/ *vt* apoyar, sostener; mantener; (endure) soportar; (a cause) apoyar, defender; (corroborate) confirmar, vindicar. —*n* apoyo, *m;* sostén, *m;* soporte, *m.* **to speak in s. of,** defender, abogar por. **to s. oneself,** ganarse la vida, mantenerse

**supporter** /sə'pɔrtər/ *n* apoyo, *m;* defensor (-ra); partidario (-ia)

**suppose** /sə'pouz/ *vt* suponer; imaginar(se); creer. **always supposing,** dado que, en el caso de que. **Supposing he had gone out?** ¿Y si hubiera salido? **I don't s. they will go to Spain,** No creo que vayan a España. **He is supposed to be clever,** Tiene fama de listo

**supposed** /sə'pouzd, -'pouzɪd/ *a* supuesto; que se llama a sí mismo

**supposition** /ˌsʌpə'zɪʃən/ *n* suposición, hipótesis, *f*

**suppress** /sə'prɛs/ *vt* reprimir; (yawns, etc.) ahogar; contener; (heresies, rebellions, books, etc.) suprimir; (dissemble) disimular, esconder; (a heckler, etc.) hacer callar

**suppressed** /sə'prɛst/ *a* reprimido; contenido; disimulado

**suppression** /sə'prɛʃən/ *n* represión, *f;* supresión, *f;* disimulación, *f*

**suppurate** /'sʌpyə,reit/ *vi* supurar

**suppuration** /ˌsʌpyə'reiʃən/ *n* supuración, *f*

**supremacy** /sə'prɛməsi/ *n* supremacía, *f*

**supreme** /sə'prim/ *a* supremo; sumo. **with s. indifference,** con suma indiferencia. **s. court,** tribunal supremo, *m*

**surcharge** /'sɜr,tʃɑrdʒ/ *n* sobrecarga, *f*

**sure** /ʃʊr/ *a* seguro; cierto. —*adv* seguramente. **Be s. to...!** ¡Ten cuidado de...! ¡No dejes de...! **to be s.,** seguramente, sin duda; ¡claro!; (fancy!) ¡no me digas!; ¡qué sorpresa! **I am not so s. of that,** No diría yo tanto. **Come on Thursday for s.,** Venga el jueves sin falta. **It is s. to rain tomorrow,** Seguramente va a llover mañana. **to make s. of,** asegurarse de. **to be (or feel) s.,** estar seguro. **s.-footed,** de pie firme, seguro

**surely** /'ʃʊrli/ *adv* seguramente; sin duda, ciertamente; por supuesto

**sureness** /'ʃʊrnɛs/ *n* seguridad, *f;* certeza, *f*

**surety** /'ʃʊrɪti/ *n* garantía, fianza, *f;* (person) garante, *mf.* **to go s. for,** ser fiador (de), salir garante (por)

**surf** /sɜrf/ *n* resaca, *f;* rompiente, *m;* oleaje, *m.* **s.-board,** aquaplano, *m.* **s.-riding,** patinaje sobre las olas, *m*

**surface** /'sɜrfɪs/ *n* superficie, *f;* exterior, *m.* —*a* superficial. —*vi* (of a submarine) salir a la superficie. **on the s.,** en superficie

**surface mail** *n* correo por vía ordinaria, servicio ordinario, servicio per vía de superficie, *m*

**surfeit** /'sɜrfɪt/ *n* exceso, *m,* superabundancia, *f;* saciedad, *f.* —*vt* hartar; saciar

**surge** /sɜrdʒ/ *vi* (of waves) embravecerse, hincharse; (of crowds) agitarse, bullir; (of emotions) despertarse. —*n* (of sea, crowd, blood) oleada, *f;* (of anger) ola, *f.* **The blood surged into his face,** La sangre se le subió a las mejillas

**surgeon** /'sɜrdʒən/ *n* cirujano, *m;* (Nav., Mil.) médico, *m*

**surgery** /'sɜrdʒəri/ *n* cirugía, *f;* (doctor's) consultorio, *m;* (dispensary) dispensario, *m*

**surgical** /'sɜrdʒɪkəl/ *a* quirúrgico

**surliness** /'sɜrlinɪs/ *n* mal genio, *m,* taciturnidad, *f;* brusquedad, *f*

**surly** /'sɜrli/ *a* taciturno, huraño, malhumorado; brusco

**surmise** /sər'maiz/ *n* conjetura, suposición, *f.* —*vt* conjeturar; adivinar; imaginar, suponer. —*vi* hacer conjeturas

**surmount** /sər'maunt/ *vt* superar, vencer; coronar

**surname** /'sɜr,neim/ *n* apellido, *m,* *vt* denominar, nombrar

**surpass** /sər'pæs/ *vt* superar, exceder; aventajarse (a); eclipsar

**surpassing** /sər'pæsɪŋ/ *a* sin par, incomparable

**surplus** /'sɜrplʌs/ *n* exceso, sobrante, *m;* (Com. of ac-

counts) superávit, *m.* **sale of s. stock,** liquidación de saldos, *f*

**surprise** /sər'praiz, sə-/ *n* sorpresa, *f;* asombro, *m.* —*vt* sorprender; asombrar. **to s.** (someone) **in the act,** coger en el acto. **to take** (a person) **by s.,** sorprender (a). **He was surprised into admitting it,** Cogido a la imprevista, lo confesó

**surprising** /sər'praizɪŋ, sə-/ *a* sorprendente

**surrealism** /sə'riə,lɪzəm/ *n* surrealismo, *m*

**surrealist** /sə'riəlɪst/ *a* and *n* surrealista, *mf*

**surrender** /sə'rɛndər/ *vt* rendir, entregar; (goods) ceder, renunciar (a). —*vi* rendirse, entregarse; abandonarse. —*n* rendición, capitulación, *f;* entrega, *f;* (of goods) cesión, *f;* (of an insurance policy) rescate, *m.* **to s. oneself to remorse,** abandonarse (or entregarse) al remordimiento. **to s. unconditionally,** entregarse a discreción

**surreptitious** /ˌsɜrəp'tɪʃəs/ *a* subrepticio

**surreptitiously** /ˌsɜrəp'tɪʃəsli/ *adv* subrepticiamente, a hurtadillas

**surround** /sə'raund/ *vt* rodear; cercar; *Mil.* asediar, sitiar. —*n* borde, *m.* **Peter was surrounded by his friends,** Pedro estaba rodeado por sus amigos

**surrounding** /sə'raundɪŋ/ *a* (que está) alrededor de; vecino. **the s. country,** los alrededores

**surroundings** /sə'raundɪŋz/ *n pl* cercanías, *f pl,* alrededores, *m pl;* (environment) medio, *m;* (medio) ambiente, *m*

**surtax** /'sɜr,tæks/ *n* impuesto suplementario, *m*

**surveillance** /sər'veiləns/ *n* vigilancia, *f*

**survey** /*v.* sər'vei/ *vt* contemplar, mirar; (events, etc.) pasar en revista; estudiar; (land, etc.) apear; (a house, etc.) inspeccionar. —*n* vista general, *f;* inspección, *f;* (of facts, etc.) examen, *m;* estudio, *m;* (of land, etc.) apeo, *m;* (of literature, etc.) bosquejo, breve panorama, *m*

**surveying** /sər'veiɪŋ/ *n* agrimensura, *f*

**surveyor** /sər'veiər/ *n* agrimensor, *m;* (superintendent) inspector, *m;* superintendente, *m*

**survival** /sər'vaivəl/ *n* supervivencia, *f.* **s. of the fittest,** supervivencia de los más aptos, *f*

**survive** /sər'vaiv/ *vt* sobrevivir a. —*vi* sobrevivir; (of customs) subsistir, durar

**survivor** /sər'vaivər/ *n* sobreviviente, *mf*

**susceptibility** /sə,sɛptə'bɪliti/ *n* susceptibilidad, *f;* tendencia, *f; pl* **susceptibilities,** sensibilidad, *f*

**susceptible** /sə'sɛptəbəl/ *a* susceptible; impresionable; sensible; (to love) enamoradizo. **He is s. to bronchitis,** Es susceptible a la bronquitis

**suspect** /*a.,* *n.* 'sʌspɛkt; *v.* sə'spɛkt/ *a* and *n* sospechoso (-sa). —*vt* sospechar; dudar; imaginar, suponer. —*vi* tener sospechas

**suspend** /sə'spɛnd/ *vt* suspender. **suspended animation,** muerte aparente, *f*

**suspender** /sə'spɛndər/ *n* liga, *f; pl* **suspenders,** (braces) tirantes del pantalón, *m pl.* **s.-belt,** faja, *f*

**suspense** /sə'spɛns/ *n* incertidumbre, *f.* **to keep** (a person) **in s.,** dejar en la incertidumbre (a)

**suspension** /sə'spɛnʃən/ *n* suspensión, *f.* **s.-bridge,** puente colgante, *m.* **s. of payments,** suspensión de pagos, *f*

**suspicion** /sə'spɪʃən/ *n* sospecha, *f;* (touch) dejo, *m;* cantidad muy pequeña, *f.* **to be above s.,** estar por encima de toda sospecha. **to be under s.,** estar bajo sospecha. **I had no suspicions...,** No sospechaba...

**suspicious** /sə'spɪʃəs/ *a* (by nature) suspicaz; sospechoso. **to make s.,** hacer sospechar

**suspiciously** /sə'spɪʃəsli/ *adv* suspicazmente, desconfiadamente; de un modo sospechoso. **It seems s. like...,** Tiene toda la apariencia de...

**suspiciousness** /sə'spɪʃəsnɪs/ *n* carácter sospechoso, *m,* lo sospechoso; suspicacia, *f*

**sustain** /sə'stein/ *vt* sostener; mantener; sustentar; apoyar; corroborar, confirmar; (a note) prolongar. **to s. injuries,** recibir heridas

**sustenance** /'sʌstənəns/ *n* mantenimiento, *m;* sustento, *m,* alimentos, *m pl*

**suture** /'sutʃər/ *n* sutura, *f*

**svarabhakti** /ˌsfarə'bakti/ *a* esvarabático

**svelte** /svɛlt/ *a* esbelto, gentil

**swab** /swɒb/ *vt Naut.* lampacear; limpiar con lampazo; *Surg.* tamponar. —*n* lampazo, *m; Surg.* torunda, *f,* tampón, *m*

**swaddle** /'swɒdl/ *vt* envolver; (infants) fajar

**swaddling clothes** /'swɒdlɪŋ/ *n pl* pañales, *m pl.* **to be still in s. clothes,** *Fig.* estar en mantillas, estar en pañales

**swag** /swæg/ *n* botín, *m*

**swagger** /'swægər/ *vi* fanfarronear, pavonearse; darse importancia. —*n* pavoneo, *m;* aire importante, *m;* (coat) tonto, *m.* —*a* majo; de última moda

**swaggering** /'swægərɪŋ/ *a* fanfarrón, jactancioso; importante

**Swahili** /swɑ'hili/ suaili; *n* suaili, *m*

**swain** /swein/ *n* zagal, *m;* enamorado, *m;* pretendiente, amante, *m*

**swallow** /'swɒlou/ *vt* tragar, engullir. —*n* trago, *m;* sorbo, *m; Ornith.* golondrina, *f.* **to s. an insult (a story),** tragar un insulto (una historia). **to s. one's words,** retractarse. **to s. one's pride,** bajar la cerviz, humillarse. **to s. up,** tragar; absorber.

**swamp** /swɒmp/ *n* pantano, *m,* marisma, *f.* —*vt* sumergir; (a boat) echar a pique, hundir; (inundate) inundar

**swampy** /'swɒmpi/ *a* pantanoso

**swan** /swɒn/ *n* cisne, *m.* **swan's down,** plumón de cisne, *m.* **s.-song,** canto del cisne, *m*

**swank** /swæŋk/ *n* pretensiones, *f pl, vi* darse humos

**sward** /swɔrd/ *n* césped, *m,* hierba, *f*

**swarm** /swɔrm/ *n* enjambre, *m;* (of people) muchedumbre, multitud, *f;* tropel, *m.* —*vi* (of bees) enjambrar; (of other insects) pulular; (of people) hormiguear, bullir, pulular. —*vt* (climb) trepar. **to s. with,** estar infestado de

**swarthiness** /'swɔrðinɪs/ *n* tez morena, *f;* color moreno, *m*

**swarthy** /'swɔrði/ *a* moreno

**swashbuckler** /'swɒʃ,bʌklər, 'swɔʃ-/ *n* perdonavidas, matasiete, *m*

**swashbuckling** /'swɒʃ,bʌklɪŋ/ *a* matamoros, valentón, fanfarrón

**swastika** /'swɒstɪkə/ *n* esvástica, cruz gamada, *f*

**swathe** /swɒð/ *vt* envolver; fajar; (with bandages) vendar

**swathing** /'swɒðɪŋ/ *n* envoltura, *f;* (bandages) vendas, *f pl*

**sway** /swei/ *vi* balancearse; oscilar; (stagger, of persons) bambolearse; (totter, of things) tambalearse; (of carriages) cabecear; (gracefully, in walking) cimbrarse. —*vt* balancear, mecer; oscilar; hacer tambalear; (influence) influir, inclinar; (govern) regir, gobernar. —*n* balanceo, *m;* oscilación, *f;* vaivén, *m;* tambaleo, *m;* (influence) ascendiente, dominio, *m,* influencia, *f;* (rule) imperio, poder, *m.* **to hold s. over,** gobernar, regir

**swear** /swεər/ *vt* jurar; (*Law.* etc.) declarar bajo juramento. —*vi* jurar; (curse) echar pestes, blasfemar. **to s. at,** maldecir. **to s. by,** jurar por; poner fe implícita en. **to be sworn in,** prestar juramento. **to s. in,** tomar juramento (a). **to s. to,** atestiguar

**sweat** /swεt/ *n* sudor, *m; Inf.* trabajo arduo, *m.* —*vi* sudar. —*vt* sudar; hacer sudar; (workers) explotar. **by the s. of one's brow,** con el sudor de la frente, con el sudor del rostro. **s.-gland,** glándula sudorípara, *f*

**sweated** /'swεtɪd/ *a* (of persons) explotado; (of labor) mal retribuido

**sweater** /'swεtər/ *n* suéter, jersey, *m*

**sweating** /'swεtɪŋ/ *n* transpiración, *f;* (of workers) explotación, *f*

**sweaty** /'swεti/ *a* sudoroso

**Swede** /swid/ *n* sueco (-ca); (vegetable) naba, *f*

**Sweden** /'swidn/ *n* Suecia, *f*

**Swedish** /'swidɪʃ/ *a* sueco. —*n* (language) sueco, *m*

**sweep** /swip/ *vi* extenderse (por); (cleave) surcar; pasar rápidamente (por); invadir; dominar; andar majestuosamente; (with a brush) barrer. —*vt* barrer; pasar (por); (the strings of a musical instrument) rasguear; (the sea) navegar por; (mines) barrer; (the horizon, etc.) examinar; (a chimney) deshollinar; (with a brush) barrer; (remove) arrebatar; quitar; llevarse; (abolish) suprimir. **to s. along,** *vt* (of the current, crowds, etc.) arrastrar. —*vi* pasar majestuosamente;

correr rápidamente (por). **to s. aside,** apartar con la mano; abandonar; (a protest) desoír, no hacer caso de. **to s. away,** (remove) llevarse; destruir; suprimir. **to s. down,** *vt* barrer; (carry) arrastrar. —*vi* (of cliffs, etc.) bajar; (of an enemy) abalanzarse (sobre); lanzarse (por). **to s. off,** barrer; (a person) llevarse sin perder tiempo; arrebatar con violencia (a). **to be swept off one's feet,** ser arrastrado (por); perder el balance; (of emotion) ser dominado por. **to s. up,** recoger; barrer

**sweep** /swip/ *n* barredura, *f;* (of a chimney) deshollinador, *m;* (of the tide) curso, *m;* (of a scythe, etc.) golpe, *m;* (range) alcance, *m;* (fold) pliegue, *m;* (curve) curva, *f;* (of water, etc.) caudal, *m;* (of wings) envergadura, *f.* **with a s. of the arm,** con un gesto del brazo. **to make a clean s. of,** hacer tabla rasa de

**sweeping** /'swipɪŋ/ *a* completo; comprensivo; demasiado general; radical. **a s. judgment,** un juicio demasiado general. **s. change,** cambio radicale, *m pl.* **s. brush,** escoba, *f*

**sweepings** /'swipɪŋz/ *n pl* barreduras, *f pl;* residuos, *m pl;* (of society) heces, *f pl*

**sweepstake** /'swip,steik/ *n* lotería, *f*

**sweet** /swit/ *a* dulce; (of scents) oloroso, fragante; (of sounds) melodioso, dulce; (charming) encantador; amable; (pretty) bonito. —*n* bombón, *m;* golosina, *f;* (at a meal) (plato) dulce, *m;* dulzura, *f;* (beloved) amor, *m,* querido (-da). **How s. it smells!** ¡Qué buen olor tiene! **the sweets of life,** las dulzuras de la vida. **s.-pea,** guisante de olor, *m,* haba de las Indias, *f.* **s.-potato,** batata, *f.* **s.-scented,** perfumado, fragante. **s.-tempered,** amable, de carácter dulce. **s.-toothed,** goloso. **s.-william,** *Bot.* clavel de la China, clavel de ramillete, clavel de San Isidro, ramillete de Constantinopla, *m,* minutisa, *f*

**sweetbread** /'swit,brεd/ *n* lechecillas, *f pl*

**sweeten** /'switn/ *vt* azucarar; endulzar. **Cervantes sweetens one's bitter moments,** Cervantes endulza los momentos agrios

**sweetheart** /'swit,hɑrt/ *n* amante, *mf,* amado (-da); (as address) querido (-da)

**sweetish** /'switɪʃ/ *a* algo dulce

**sweetly** /'switli/ *adv* dulcemente; (of scents) olorosamente; (of sounds) melodiosamente; (of behavior, etc.) amablemente

**sweetmeat** /'swit,mit/ *n* bombón, dulce, *m*

**sweetness** /'switnɪs/ *n* dulzura, *f;* (of scents) buen olor, *m,* fragancia, *f;* (of sounds) melodía, dulzura, *f;* (of character) bondad, amabilidad, *f*

**sweet potato** *n* batata, *f,* boniato, buniato, camote, *m*

**sweet sixteen** *n* (age) los dieciséis abriles, *m pl;* (party) quinceañera (at age fifteen) *f*

**swell** /swεl/ *vi* hincharse; (of the sea) entumecerse; crecer; aumentarse. —*vt* hinchar; aumentar. —*n* (of the sea) oleada, *f,* oleaje, *m;* (of the ground) ondulación, *f;* (of sound) crescendo, *m;* (increase) aumento, *m;* (dandy) pisaverde, elegante, *m;* (important person) pájaro gordo, *m;* (at games, etc.) espada, *m.* —*a* estupendo; elegantísimo; de primera, excelente. **to suffer from swelled head,** tener humos, darse importancia. **This foot is swollen,** Este pie está hinchado (or tumefacto). **The refugees have swelled the population,** Los refugiados han aumentado la población. **eyes swollen with tears,** ojos arrasados de lágrimas. **to s. with pride,** hincharse de orgullo

**swelling** /'swεlɪŋ/ *n* hinchazón, *f; Med.* tumefacción, *f;* (bruise, etc.) chichón, *m*

**swelter** /'swεltər/ *vi* abrasarse; arder. —*n* bochorno, calor sofocante, *m*

**swerve** /swɜrv/ *vi* desviarse; apartarse (de); torcerse. —*n* desvío, *m*

**swift** /swɪft/ *a* rápido, veloz; pronto. —*adv* velozmente, rápidamente. —*n Ornith.* vencejo, *m.* **s.-flowing,** (of rivers, etc.) de corriente rápida. **s.-footed,** de pies ligeros

**swiftly** /'swɪftli/ *adv* rápidamente, velozmente

**swiftness** /'swɪftnɪs/ *n* rapidez, velocidad, *f;* prontitud, *f*

**swim** /swɪm/ *vi* nadar; flotar; (glide) deslizarse; (fill) inundarse. —*vt* (a horse) hacer nadar; pasar a nado; nadar. —*n* natación, *f.* **eyes swimming with tears,**

ojos inundados de lágrimas. **He enjoys a s.,** Le gusta nadar. **My head swims,** Se me va la cabeza. **Everything swam before my eyes,** Todo parecía bailar ante mis ojos. **to be in the s.,** formar parte (de), ser (de); (be up to date) estar al corriente. **to s. with the tide,** ir con la corriente
**swimmer** /'swɪmər/ n nadador (-ra). **He is a bad s.,** Él nada mal
**swimming** /'swɪmɪŋ/ n natación, f; (of the head) vértigo, m. **s.-bath,** piscina, f. **s.-costume,** traje de baño, m. **s.-pool,** piscina al aire libre, f
**swindle** /'swɪndl/ vt engañar, estafar; defraudar (de). —n estafa, f, timo, m; engaño, m; impostura, f
**swindler** /'swɪndlər/ n estafador (-ra), trampeador (-ra); engañador (-ra)
**swine** /swaɪn/ n cerdo, puerco, m; (person) cochino (-na). **a herd of s.,** una manada de cerdos
**swineherd** /'swaɪn,hɜrd/ n porquero, m
**swing** /swɪŋ/ vi balancearse; oscilar; (hang) colgar, pender; columpiarse; girar; dar la vuelta; (of a boat) bornear. —vt balancear; (hang) colgar; (rock) mecer; (in a swing, etc.) columpiar; hacer oscilar; (raise) subir. —n oscilación, f; vaivén, m; balanceo, m; (rhythm) ritmo, m; (seat, etc.) columpio, m; (reach) alcance, m. **The door swung open,** La puerta se abrió silenciosamente. **He swung the car round,** Dio la vuelta al auto. **He swung himself into the saddle,** Montó de un salto. **to be in full s.,** estar a toda marcha. **to go with a s.,** tener mucho éxito. **s.-bridge,** puente giratorio, m. **s.-door,** puerta giratoria, f
**swinging** /'swɪŋɪŋ/ a oscilante; pendiente; rítmico. —n balanceo, m; oscilación, f; vaivén, m; ritmo, m. **s. stride,** andar rítmico
**swinish** /'swaɪnɪʃ/ a porcuno, de cerdo; cochino, sucio
**swipe** /swaɪp/ vt golpear duro; aplastar. —n golpe fuerte, m
**swirl** /swɜrl/ vi arremolinarse. —n remolino, m
**swish** /swɪʃ/ vt (of an animal's tail) agitar, mover, menear; (of a cane) blandir; (thrash) azotar. —vi silbar; (of water) susurrar; (of a dress, etc.) crujir. —n silbo, m; (of water) susurro, murmullo, m; (of a dress, etc.) crujido, m
**Swiss** /swɪs/ a and n suizo (-za)
**switch** /swɪtʃ/ n vara, f; (riding) látigo, m; (of hair) trenza, f; Elec. interruptor, m; Rail. aguja, f; (Rail. siding) desviadero, m. —vt azotar; (a train) desviar; Elec. interrumpir; (transfer) trasladar; (of an animal, its tail) remover, mover rápidamente. **to s. off,** (Elec. and telephone) cortar; (Radio. and Auto.) desconectar. **to s. on,** conectar; (a light) poner (la luz); (a radio) encender
**switchback** /'swɪtʃ,bæk/ n subida en zigzag, f; (amusement) montañas rusas, f pl
**switchboard** /'swɪtʃ,bɔrd/ n cuadro de distribución, m
**Switzerland** /'swɪtsərlənd/ Suiza, f
**swivel** /'swɪvəl/ n torniquete, m; anillo móvil, m; pivote, m. —vi girar sobre un eje; dar una vuelta. **s.-chair,** silla giratoria, f. **s.-door,** puerta giratoria, f
**swoon** /swun/ vi desvanecerse, desmayarse. —n desmayo, desvanecimiento, m
**swoop** /swup/ vi calarse, abatirse; (of robbers, etc.) abalanzarse (sobre). —n calada, f. **at one fell s.,** de un solo golpe
**sword** /sɔrd/ n espada, f; sable, m. **to measure swords with,** cruzar espadas con. **to put to the s.,** pasar a cuchillo (a). **s.-arm,** brazo derecho, m. **s.-cut,** sablazo, m. **s.-dance,** danza de espadas, f. **s.-fish,** pez espada, pez sierra, espadarte, m, jifia, f. **s.-play,** esgrima, f; manejo de la espada, m. **s.-thrust,** golpe de espada, m; estocada, f
**swordsman** /'sɔrdzmən/ n espadachín, m; esgrimidor, m
**swordsmanship** /'sɔrdzmən,ʃɪp/ n manejo de la espada, m; esgrima, f
**sybarite** /'sɪbə,raɪt/ a and n sibarita, mf
**sybaritic** /,sɪbə'rɪtɪk/ a sibarítico, sibarita
**sycamore** /'sɪkə,mɔr/ n sicomoro, m; falso plátano, m
**sycophancy** /'sɪkəfənsi/ n servilismo, m
**sycophant** /'sɪkəfənt/ n sicofanta, m
**syllabic** /sɪ'læbɪk/ a silábico

**syllable** /'sɪləbəl/ n sílaba, f
**syllabus** /'sɪləbəs/ n programa, m; compendio, m
**syllogism** /'sɪlə,dʒɪzəm/ n silogismo, m
**sylph** /sɪlf/ n sílfide, f, silfo, m; (woman) sílfide, f; (hummingbird) colibrí, m. **s.-like,** de sílfide; como una sílfide
**sylvan** /'sɪlvən/ a selvático, silvestre; rústico
**symbiosis** /,sɪmbi'ousɪs/ n simbiosis, f
**symbol** /'sɪmbəl/ n símbolo, emblema, m; Math. símbolo, m; (of rank, etc.) insignia, f
**symbolical** /sɪm'bɒlɪkəl/ a simbólico
**symbolism** /'sɪmbə,lɪzəm/ n simbolismo, m
**symbolist** /'sɪmbəlɪst/ n simbolista, mf
**symbolize** /'sɪmbə,laɪz/ vt simbolizar
**symmetrical** /sɪ'mɛtrɪkəl/ a simétrico
**symmetry** /'sɪmɪtri/ n simetría, f
**sympathetic** /,sɪmpə'θɛtɪk/ a simpático; compasivo; (of the public, etc.) bien dispuesto. —n Anat. gran simpático, m. **s. words,** palabras de simpatía, f pl. **s. ink,** tinta simpática, f
**sympathetically** /,sɪmpə'θɛtɪkli/ adv simpáticamente; con compasión
**sympathize** /'sɪmpə,θaɪz/ vi simpatizar (con); (understand) comprender; (condole) compadecerse (de), condolerse (de); dar el pésame
**sympathizer** /'sɪmpə,θaɪzər/ n partidario (-ia)
**sympathy** /'sɪmpəθi/ n simpatía, f; compasión, f. **Paul is in s. with their aims,** Pablo está de acuerdo con sus objetos. **Please accept my s.,** (on a bereavement) Le acompaño a Vd. en su sentimiento
**symphonic** /sɪm'fɒnɪk/ a sinfónico
**symphony** /'sɪmfəni/ n sinfonía, f
**symposium** /sɪm'pouziəm/ n colección de artículos, f
**symptom** /'sɪmptəm/ n síntoma, m; señal, f, indicio, m. **to show symptoms of,** dar indicios de
**symptomatic** /,sɪmptə'mætɪk/ a sintomático
**synagogue** /'sɪnə,gɒg/ n sinagoga, f
**synchronization** /,sɪŋkrənə'zeɪʃən/ n sincronización, f
**synchronize** /'sɪŋkrə,naɪz/ vi coincidir, tener lugar simultáneamente; sincronizarse. —vt sincronizar
**synchronous** /'sɪŋkrənəs/ a sincrónico
**syncopate** /'sɪŋkə,peɪt/ vt (Gram. Mus.) sincopar
**syncopation** /,sɪŋkə'peɪʃən/ n Mus. síncopa, f
**syndical** /'sɪndɪkəl/ a sindical
**syndicalism** /'sɪndɪkə,lɪzəm/ n sindicalismo, m
**syndicalist** /'sɪndɪkəlɪst/ n sindicalista, mf
**syndicate** /n. 'sɪndɪkɪt; v. -,keɪt/ n sindicato, m, vt sindicar
**syndication** /,sɪndɪ'keɪʃən/ n sindicación, f
**synod** /'sɪnəd/ n Eccl. sínodo, m
**synonym** /'sɪnənɪm/ n sinónimo, m
**synonymous** /sɪ'nɒnəməs/ a sinónimo
**synopsis** /sɪ'nɒpsɪs/ n sinopsis, f
**synoptic** /sɪ'nɒptɪk/ a sinóptico
**syntax** /'sɪntæks/ n sintaxis, f
**synthesis** /'sɪnθəsɪs/ n síntesis, f
**synthetic** /sɪn'θɛtɪk/ a sintético
**synthetize** /'sɪnθə,taɪz/ vt sintetizar
**syphilis** /'sɪfəlɪs/ n sífilis, f
**syphilitic** /,sɪfə'lɪtɪk/ a and n sifilítico (-ca)
**Syracuse** /'sɪrə,kyus, -,kyuz/ Siracusa, f
**syren** /'saɪrən/ n. See **siren**
**Syria** /'sɪriə/ Siria, f
**Syrian** /'sɪriə/ a and n siríaco (-ca), sirio (-ia)
**syringe** /sə'rɪndʒ/ n jeringa, f, vt jeringar
**syrup** /'sɪrəp, 'sɜr-/ n jarabe, m; (for bottling fruit, etc.) almíbar, m
**syrupy** /'sɪrəpi, 'sɜr-/ a siroposo
**system** /'sɪstəm/ n sistema, m; régimen, m; método, m; (body) organismo, m. **He has no s. in his work,** No tiene método en su trabajo. **the nervous s.,** el sistema nervioso. **the feudal s.,** el feudalismo, m; sistema feudal
**systematic** /,sɪstə'mætɪk/ a sistemático, metódico
**systematically** /,sɪstə'mætɪkli/ adv sistemáticamente, metódicamente
**systematization** /,sɪstəmətə'zeɪʃən/ n sistematización, f
**systematize** /'sɪstəmə,taɪz/ vt sistematizar
**systole** /'sɪstə,li/ n Med. sístole, f

# T

**t** /ti/ n (letter) te, f. —a en T, en forma de T. **T bandage,** vendaje en T, m. **T square,** regla T, f

**tab** /tæb/ n oreja, f

**tabby** /'tæbi/ n gato romano, m; (female) gata, f; Inf. vieja chismosa, f

**tabernacle** /'tæbər,nækəl/ n tabernáculo, m; templo, m; Archit. templete, m; Eccl. custodia, f

**tabes** /'teibiz/ n Med. tabes, f

**table** /'teibəl/ n mesa, f; (food) comida, mesa, f; (of the law, weights, measures, contents, etc.) tabla, f; (of land) meseta, f; (of prices) lista, tarifa, f. —vt (parliament) poner sobre la mesa; enumerar, apuntar, hacer una lista de. **to clear the t.,** alzar (or levantar) la mesa. **to lay the t.,** cubrir (or poner) la mesa. **to have a table d'hôte meal,** tomar el menú. **to rise from the t.,** levantarse de la mesa. **to sit down at the t.,** ponerse a la mesa. **The tables are turned,** Se volvió la tortilla. **side t.,** aparador, trinchero, m. **small t.,** mesilla, f. **t. of contents,** tabla de materias, f, índice, índice de materias, índice general, m. **t.-centrepiece,** centro de mesa, m. **t.-cloth,** mantel, m. **t.-companion,** comensal, mf **t.-knife,** cuchillo de mesa, m. **t.-lamp,** quinqué, m; lampara de mesa, f. **t.-land,** meseta, f. **t.-leg,** pata de una mesa, f. **t.-linen,** mantelería, f. **t.-napkin,** servilleta, f. **t.-runner,** camino de mesa, m. **t.-spoon,** cuchara para los legumbres, f. **t.-talk,** conversación de sobremesa, f. **t.-turning,** mesas que dan vueltas, f pl. **t.-ware,** artículos para la mesa, m pl

**tableau** /tæ'blou/ n cuadro, m. **tableaux vivants,** cuadros vivos, m pl

**tablespoonful** /'teibəlspun,fʊl/ n cucharada, f

**tablet** /'tæblɪt/ n tabla, f; (with inscription) tarjeta, losa, lápida, f; Med. comprimido, m, tableta, f; (of soap, chocolate) pastilla, f. **writing t.,** taco de papel, m

**tabloid** /'tæblɔid/ n comprimido, m, pastilla, f

**taboo** /tə'bu, tæ-/ n tabú, m. —a prohibido, tabú. —vt declarar tabú, prohibir

**tabor** /'teibər/ n Mus. tamboril, tamborín, m. **t. player,** tamborilero, m

**tabouret** /,tæbə'rɛt/ n (stool) taburete, m; (for embroidery) tambor de bordar, m; Mus. tamborilete, m

**tabulate** /'tæbyə,leit/ vt resumir en tablas; hacer una lista de, catalogar

**tabulation** /,tæbyə'leiʃən/ n distribución en tablas, f

**tacit** /'tæsɪt/ a tácito

**taciturn** /'tæsɪ,tɜrn/ a taciturno, sombrío, reservado, de pocas palabras

**taciturnity** /,tæsɪ'tɜrnɪti/ n taciturnidad, f; reserva, f

**tack** /tæk/ n (nail) tachuela, puntilla, f; Sew. hilván, embaste, m; Naut. amura, f; Naut. puño de amura, m; Naut. bordada, f; Fig. cambio de política, m. —vt clavar con tachuelas; Sew. hilvanar, embastar; Fig. añadir. —vi Naut. virar; Fig. cambiar de política, adoptar un nuevo plan de acción. **t. puller,** sacabrocas, m

**tackle** /'tækəl/ n aparejo, m; maniobra, f; Naut. cuadernal, m, jarcia, f; (gear) aparejos, avíos, m pl; (football) carga, f. —vt agarrar, asir; Fig. atacar, abordar; (football) cargar; (undertake) emprender; (a problem) luchar con. **t.-block,** polea, f

**tackling** /'tæklɪŋ/ n aparejo, m, maniobra, f; Naut. cordaje, m

**tacky** /'tæki/ a pegajoso, viscoso

**tact** /tækt/ n tacto, m, discreción, diplomacia, delicadeza, f

**tactful** /'tæktfəl/ a lleno de tacto, diplomático, discreto

**tactfully** /'tæktfəli/ adv discretamente, diplomáticamente

**tactical** /'tæktɪkəl/ a táctico

**tactically** /'tæktɪkli/ adv según la táctica; del punto de vista táctico

**tactician** /tæk'tɪʃən/ n táctico, m

**tactics** /'tæktɪks/ n pl táctica, f

**tactile** /'tæktɪl/ a táctil; tangible

**tactless** /'tæktlɪs/ a que no tiene tacto, sin tacto alguno, indiscreto

**tactlessly** /'tæktlɪsli/ adv impolíticamente, indiscretamente

**tactlessness** n falta de tacto, f

**tadpole** /'tædpoul/ n renacuajo, m

**taffeta** /'tæfɪtə/ n tafetán, m

**tag** /tæg/ n herrete, m; (label) marbete, m, etiqueta, f; (of tail) punta del rabo, f; (of boot) tirador de bota, m; (game) marro, m; (rag) arrapiezo, m; (quotation) cita bien conocida, f; (of song, poem) refrán, m. **to play t.,** jugar al marro

**Tagus** /'teigəs/ el Tajo, m

**Tahiti** /tə'hiti/ Taiti, Tahiti, m

**tail** /teil/ n cola, f, rabo, m; (plait) trenza, f; (wisp of hair) mechón, m; (of a comet) cola, cabellera, f; (of a note in music) rabito, m; (of a coat) faldon, m; (of a kite) cola, f; (of the eye) rabo, m; (retinue) séquito, m, banda, f; (of an aeroplane) cola, f; (end) fin, m; (of coin) cruz, f; (line) fila, cola, f. —vt seguir de cerca, pisarle (a uno) los talones. **to t. after,** seguir de cerca. **to t. away,** disminuir; desaparecer, perderse de vista. **to t. on,** unir, juntar. **to turn t.,** volver la espalda, poner los pies en polvorosa. **with the t. between the legs,** con el rabo entre piernas. **t.-board,** (of a cart) escalera, f. **t.-coat,** frac, m. **t.-end,** extremo, m; fin, m; lo último. **t.-feather,** pena, f. **t.-fin,** aleta caudal, f; Aer. timón de dirección, m. **t.-light,** farol trasero, m. **t.-piece,** (of a violin, etc.) cola, f; Print. marmosete, culo de lámpara, m. **t. spin** Aer. barrena de cola, f. **t. wind,** viento de cola, m

**tailed** /teild/ a de rabo. **big-t.,** rabudo, de cola grande. **long-t.,** rabilargo. **short-t.,** rabicorto

**tailless** /'teilɪs/ a rabón, sin rabo

**tailor** /'teilər/ n sastre (-ra). **t.-made,** n traje sastre, m, a de hechura de sastre. **tailor's shop,** sastrería, f

**tailoring** /'teilərɪŋ/ n sastrería, f; (work) corte, m

**taint** /teint/ n corrupción, f; infección, f; (blemish) mancha, f; (tinge) dejo, m. —vt corromper, pervertir; inficionar; (meat) corromper. —vi corromperse, inficionarse; (meat) corromperse

**take** /teik/ vt tomar; (receive) aceptar; (remove) quitar; (pick up) coger; (grab) asir, agarrar; Math. restar; (carry) llevar; (a person) traer, llevar; (guide) conducir, guiar; (win) ganar; (earn) cobrar, percibir; obtener; (make prisoner) hacer prisionero, prender; (a town, etc.) tomar, rendir, conquistar; (appropriate) apoderarse de, apropiarse; (steal) robar, hurtar; (ensnare) coger, cazar con trampas; (fish) pescar, coger; (a trick, in cards) hacer (una baza); (an illness) contraer, coger; (by surprise) sorprender, coger desprevenido (a); (attract) atraer; (drink) beber; (a meal) tomar; (select) escoger; (hire) alquilar; (suppose) suponer; (use) emplear, usar; (impers., require) necesitarse, hacer falta; (purchase) comprar; (assume) adoptar, asumir; (a leap) dar (un salto); (a walk) dar (un paseo); (a look) echar (un vistazo); (measures) tomar (medidas); (the chair) presidir; (understand) comprender; (a photograph) sacar (una fotografía); (believe) creer; (consider) considerar; (a note) apuntar; (jump over) saltar; (time) tomar, emplear. **I t. size three in shoes,** Calzo el número tres. **to t. to be,** (believe) suponer; (mistake) creer equivocadamente. **to t. (a thing) badly,** tomarlo (or llevarlo) a mal. **The book took me two hours to read,** Necesité dos horas para leer el libro, Leí el libro en dos horas. **And this, I t. it, is Mary?** ¿Y supongo que ésta será María? **to be taken with,** ser entusiasta de; (of persons) estar prendado de. **to t. aback,** desconcertar, coger desprevenido (a). **to t. again,** volver a tomar; llevar otra vez; (a photograph) retratar otra vez. **to t. along,** llevar; traer. **to t. away,** quitar; llevarse. **to t. back,** devolver; (retract) retractar; (receive) recibir (algo) devuelto. **to t. down,** bajar; (a building) derribar; (machinery) desmontar; (hair) deshacerse (el cabello); (swallow) tragar; (in writing) apuntar;

(humble) quitar los humos (a), humillar. **to t. for,** creer, imaginar; (a walk, etc.) llevar a; (mistake) creer erróneamente; tomar por. **Whom do you t. me for?** ¿Por quién me tomas? **to. t. for granted (assume),** dar por descontado, dar por lecho, dar por sentado, dar por supuesto; (underestimate) no hacer caso de, tratar con indiferencia. **t. the lion's share (of),** llevarse la parte del león (de), llevarse la tajada del león (de). **t. shape,** cobrar perfiles más nítidos, estructurarse con más nitidez, ir adquiriendo consistencia, tomar forma. **t. the law into one's own hands,** tomar la justicia por la mano. **to t. from,** privar, quitar de; (subtract) restar; substraer de. **to t. in,** (believe) tragar, creer; (sail) acortar las velas; (deceive) engañar; (lead in) hacer entrar; (accept) recibir, aceptar. **to t. off,** quitar; (surgically) amputar; (one's hat, etc.) quitarse (el sombrero); (eyes) sacar; (take away) llevarse; (mimic) imitar; (ridicule) ridiculizar; (unstick) despegar; (discount) descontar. **to t. on,** emprender; aceptar; (at sports) jugar. **to t. on oneself,** encargarse de, tomar por su cuenta, asumir. **to t. out,** sacar; extraer; (remove) quitar; (outside) llevar fuera; (for a walk) llevar a paseo; (obtain) obtener, sacar; (tire) agotar, rendir. **to t. over,** tomar posesión de; asumir; (show) mostrar, conducir por. **t. the bull by the horns,** ir al toro por los cuernos. **take seriously,** tomar en serio. **to t. up,** subir; (pick up) recoger; tomar; (a challenge, etc.) aceptar; (a dress, etc.) acortar; (absorb) absorber; (of space) ocupar; (of time) ocupar, hacer perder; (buy) comprar; (adopt) dedicarse a; (arrest) arrestar, prender; (criticize) censurar, criticar; (begin) empezar; (resume) continuar

take /teik/ *vi* tomar; (be successful) tener éxito; (of vaccination, etc.) prender; (a good (bad) photograph) salir bien (mal). **to t. after,** salir a, parecerse a; (of conduct) seguir el ejemplo de; **to t. off,** salir; *Aer.* despegar. **to t. on,** *Inf.* lamentarse. **to t. to,** dedicarse a; darse a; (of persons) tomar cariño a; (grow accustomed) acostumbrarse a. **to t. up with,** hacerse amigo de

take /teik/ *n* toma, *f;* cogida, *f; Print.* tomada, *f; Theat.* taquilla, *f.* **t.-in,** engaño, *m.* **t.-off,** *Aer.* (recorrido de) despegue, *m;* caricatura, *f;* sátira, *f*

taker /ˈteikər/ *n* tomador (-ra)

taking /ˈteikɪŋ/ *n* toma, *f;* secuestro, *m, n pl* **takings,** ingresos, *m pl*; *Theat.* taquilla, entrada, *f.* —*a* atractivo, encantador; simpático; (of disease) contagioso

talc /tælk/ *n Mineral.* talco, *m*

talcum powder /ˈtælkəm/ *n* talco, polvo de talco, *m*

tale /teil/ *n* (recital) narración, historia, *f;* relato, *m;* cuento, *m;* leyenda, historia, fábula, *f;* (number) cuenta, *f,* número, *m;* (gossip) chisme, *m.* **old wives' t.,** cuento de viejas, *m.* **to tell a t.,** contar una historia. **to tell tales,** contar cuentos; revelar secretos, chismear

talebearer /ˈteilˌbɛərər/ *n* correveidile, *mf;* chismoso (-sa), soplón (-ona)

talebearing /ˈteilˌbɛarɪŋ/ *n* el chismear, *m*

talent /ˈtælənt/ *n* (coin) talento, *m;* (ability) ingenio, *m;* habilidad, *f.* **the best t. in Spain,** la flor de la cultura española

talented /ˈtæləntɪd/ *a* talentoso, ingenioso

talisman /ˈtælɪsmən/ *n* talismán, *m*

talit /ˈtalɪs, talit/ taled, *m*

talk /tɔk/ *vi* and *vt* hablar, decir. **to t. business,** hablar de negocios. **to t. for talking's sake,** hablar por hablar. **to t. French,** hablar francés. **to t. nonsense,** decir disparates. **to t. too much,** hablar demasiado; *Inf.* hablar por los codos, irse (a uno) la lengua. **to t. about,** hablar de; conversar sobre. **to t. at,** decir algo a alguien para que lo entienda otro. **Are you talking at me?** ¿Lo dices por mí? **to t. away,** seguir hablando; disipar. **to t. into,** persuadir, inducir (a). **to t. of,** hablar de; charlar sobre. **to t. on,** hablar acerca de (or sobre); (continue) seguir hablando. **to t. out of,** disuadir de. **to t. out of turn,** meterse donde no le llaman, meter la pata. **to t. over,** hablar de; discutir, considerar. **to t. round,** persuadir. **to t. to,** (address) hablar a; (consult) hablar con; (scold) reprender. **to t. to each other,** hablarse. **to t. up,** hablar claro

talk /tɔk/ *n* conversación, *f;* (informal lecture) charla, *f;* (empty words) palabras, *f pl;* (notoriety) escándalo, *m;* rumor, *m.* **There is t. of...,** Se dice que...; Se habla de que. **to give a t.,** dar una charla. **to indulge in small t.,** hablar de cosas sin importancia, hablar de naderías

talkative /ˈtɔkətɪv/ *a* locuaz, gárrulo, hablador, decidor. **to be very t.,** ser muy locuaz; *Inf.* tener mucha lengua

talkativeness /ˈtɔkətɪvnɪs/ *n* locuacidad, garrulidad, *f*

talker /ˈtɔkər/ *n* hablador (-ra), conversador (-ra); (lecturer) orador (-ra); (in a derogatory sense) fanfarrón (-ona), charlatán (-ana). **to be a good t.,** hablar bien, ser buen conversacionista

talking /ˈtɔkɪŋ/ *a* que habla, hablante; (of birds, dolls, etc.) parlero. **to give a good t. to,** dar una peluca (a). **t.-film,** película sonora, *f.* **t.-machine,** fonógrafo, *m*

tall /tɔl/ *a* alto; (of stories) exagerado. **five feet tall,** de cinco pies de altura

tallboy /ˈtɔlˌbɔi/ *n* cómoda alta, *f*

tallness /ˈtɔlnɪs/ *n* altura, *f;* estatura, talla, *f;* (of stories) lo exagerado

tallow /ˈtælou/ *n* sebo, *m.* **t. candle,** vela de sebo, *f.* **t. chandler,** velero (-ra). **t.-faced,** con cara de color de cera

tallowy /ˈtæloui/ *a* seboso

tally /ˈtæli/ *n* tarja, tara, *f;* cuenta, *f.* —*vt* llevar la cuenta (de). —*vi* estar conforme, cuadrar

Talmud /ˈtɑlmʊd/ *n* Talmud, *m*

Talmudic /talˈmʊdɪk/ *a* talmúdico

tamable /ˈteiməbəl/ *a* domable, domesticable

tambour /ˈtæmbʊr, tæmˈbʊr/ *n Mus.* tambor, *m;* (for embroidery) tambor (or bastidor) para bordar, *m*

tambourine /ˌtæmbəˈrin/ *n* pandereta, *f*

tame /teim/ *a* domesticado, manso; (spiritless) sumiso; (dull) aburrido, soso. —*vt* domar, domesticar; (curb) reprimir, gobernar, domar, suavizar. **to grow t.,** domesticarse

tameness /ˈteimnɪs/ *n* mansedumbre, *f;* sumisión, timidez, *f*

tamer /ˈteimər/ *n* domador (-ra)

taming /ˈteimɪŋ/ *n* domadura, *f.* **The T. of the Shrew,** La Fierecilla Domada

tamp /tæmp/ *vt* apisonar; (in blasting) atacar (un barreno)

tamper /ˈtæmpər/ *vi* (with) descomponer, estropear; (meddle with) meterse con; (witnesses) sobornar; (documents) falsificar

tampon /ˈtæmpɒn/ *n Surg.* tampón, tapón, *m, vt* taponar

tan /tæn/ *vt* curtir, adobar; (of sun) tostar, quemar; (slang) zurrar. —*vi* tostarse por el sol. —*n* color café claro, *m;* bronceado, cutis tostado, *m.* —*a* de color café claro

tandem /ˈtændəm/ *n* tándem, *m*

tang /tæŋ/ *n* (of sword, etc.) espiga, *f;* (flavor) fuerte sabor, *m;* (sound) retintín, *m*

tangent /ˈtændʒənt/ *a* and *n* tangente *f.* **to go off on a t.,** *Fig.* salir por la tangente

tangerine /ˌtændʒəˈrin/ *a* and *n* tangerino (-na). **t. orange,** naranja mandarina, *f*

tangible /ˈtændʒəbəl/ *a* tangible; *Fig.* real

Tangier /tænˈdʒɪər/ Tánger, *m*

tangle /ˈtæŋgəl/ *n* embrollo, enredo, nudo, *m;* (of streets) laberinto, *m; Fig.* confusión, *f.* —*vt* embrollar, enmarañar; (entangle) enredar; *Fig.* poner en confusión, complicar. —*vi* enmarañarse

tank /tæŋk/ *n* tanque, depósito (de agua, etc.), *m;* cisterna, *f;* (as a reservoir) aljibe, estanque, *m; Mil.* tanque, carro de asalto, *m*

tankard /ˈtæŋkərd/ *n* pichel, bock, *m*

tanker /ˈtæŋkər/ *n* petrolero, *m*

tanned /tænd/ *a* bronceado, quemado por el sol, dorado por el sol

tanner /ˈtænər/ *n* curtidor, *m;* (slang) medio chelín, *m.* **tanner's scraper,** descarnador, *m.* **tanner's vat,** noque, *m*

tannery /ˈtænəri/ *n* curtiduría, *f*

**tannic** /'tænɪk/ *a Chem*. tánico. **t. acid,** ácido tánico, *m*

**tannin** /'tænɪn/ *n Chem*. tanino, *m*

**tanning** /'tænɪŋ/ *n* curtido, adobamiento, *m*

**tantalize** /'tæntḷ,aiz/ *vt* tentar, atormentar, provocar

**tantalizing** /'tæntḷ,aizɪŋ/ *a* tentador, atormentador; provocativo

**tantamount** /'tæntə,maunt/ *a* equivalente, igual. **to be t. to,** ser equivalente a

**tantrum** /'tæntrəm/ *n* pataleta, rabieta, *f*, berrinche, *m*

**taoism** /'dauɪzəm/ *n* taoísmo, *m*

**taoist** /'dauɪst/ *n* taoísta, *mf*

**tap** /tæp/ *n* (blow) pequeño golpe, toque ligero, *m*; palmadita, *f*; (for drawing water, etc.) grifo, *m*, llave, *f*; (of a barrel) canilla, *f*; (brew of liquor) clase de vino, *f*; (tap-room) bar con mostrador, *m*; (tool) macho de terraja, *m*; (piece of leather on shoe) tapa, *f*; *pl* **taps,** *Mil*. toque de apagar las luces, *m*. —*vt* (strike) golpear ligeramente, dar una palmadita a; (pierce) horadar; (a barrel) decentar; *Surg*. hacer una puntura en; (trees) sangrar; *Elec*. derivar (una corriente); (of water, current) tomar; (information) descubrir; (telephone) escuchar las conversaciones telefónicas. —*vi* golpear ligeramente. **to tap at the door,** llamar suavemente a la puerta. **on tap,** en tonel. **screw-tap,** terraja, *f*. **tap-dance,** claqué, *m*. **tap-root,** raíz pivotante, *f*

**tape** /teip/ *n* (linen) cinta de hilo, *f*; (cotton) cinta de algodón, *f*; (telegraph machine) cinta de papel, *f*; (surveying) cinta para medir, *f*. **adhesive t.,** cinta adhesiva, *f*. **red t.,** balduque, *m*; *Fig*. burocracia, *f*; formulismo, *m*. **t.-machine,** telégrafo de cotizaciones, bancarias, *m*. **t.-measure,** cinta métrica, *f*

**taper** /'teipər/ *n* bujía, cerilla, *f*; *Eccl*. cirio, *m*. —*vi* ahusarse, rematar en punta. —*vt* afilar

**tapering** /'teipərɪŋ/ *a* cónico, piramidal; (of fingers) afilado

**tapestried** /'tæpəstrid/ *a* cubierto de tapices, tapizado

**tapestry** /'tæpəstri/ *n* tapiz, *m*. **t. weaver,** tapicero, *m*

**tapeworm** /'teip,wɜrm/ *n* tenia, lombriz solitaria, *f*

**tapioca** /,tæpi'oukə/ *n* tapioca, *f*

**tapir** /'teipər/ *n Zool*. danta, *f*

**tar** /tɑr/ *n* alquitrán, *m*, brea, *f*. —*vt* embrear, alquitranar. **to tar and feather,** emplumar. **coal t.,** alquitrán mineral, *m*

**tarantella** /,tærən'tɛlə/ *n* tarantela, *f*

**tarantula** /tə'ræntʃələ/ *n* tarántula, *f*

**tardily** /'tardḷi/ *adv* tardíamente; lentamente

**tardiness** /'tardinɪs/ *n* tardanza, lentitud, *f*

**tardy** /'tardi/ *a* (late) tardío; (slow) lento; (reluctant) desinclinado

**tare** /tɛər/ *n Bot*. yero, *m*; (in the Bible) cizaña, *f*; *Com*. tara, *f*; (of a vehicle) peso en vacío, *m*

**target** /'tɑrgɪt/ *n* blanco (de tiro), *m*; (shield) rodela, tarja, *f*. **t. practice,** tiro al blanco, *m*

**tariff** /'tærɪf/ *n* tarifa, *f*. **to put a t. on,** tarifar

**tarlatan** /'tarlətn/ *n* tarlatana, *f*

**tarmac** /'tarmæk/ *n* alquitranado, *m*

**tarn** /tɑrn/ *n* lago de montaña, *m*

**tarnish** /'tarnɪʃ/ *n* deslustre, *m*. —*vt* deslustrar, empañar; *Fig*. obscurecer, manchar. —*vi* deslustrarse

**tarpaulin** /tar'pɔlɪn, 'tɑrpəlɪn/ *n* alquitranado, encerado, *m*

**tarred** /tard/ *a* alquitranado, embreado

**tarring** /'tarɪŋ/ *n* embreadura, *f*

**tarry** /'tari/ *vi* tardar, detenerse

**tart** /tart/ *a* ácido, acerbo, agridulce; *Fig*. áspero. —*n* tarta, *f*; pastelillo de fruta, *m*

**tartan** /'tartn/ *n Naut*. tartana, *f*; (plaid) tartán, *m*

**tartar** /'tartər/ *n Chem*. tártaro, *m*; (in teeth) sarro, tártaro, *m*; **cream of t.,** (cremor) tártaro, *m*. **t. emetic,** tártaro emético, *m*. **Tartar,** *a* and *n* tártaro (-ra)

**Tartary** /'tartəri/ Tartaria, *f*

**tartly** /'tartli/ *adv* ásperamente, agriamente

**tartness** /'tartnɪs/ *n* acidez, *f*; *Fig*. aspereza, *f*

**task** /tæsk/ *n* tarea, labor, *f*; empresa, *f*; misión, *f*. **to take to t.,** regañar, censurar. **t.-force,** (naval or military) contingente, *m*

**taskmaster** /'tæsk,mæstər/ *n* el que señala una tarea; amo, *m*

**tassel** /'tæsəl/ *n* borla, *f*; (of corn) panoja, espiga, *f*

**taste** /teist/ *n* gusto, *m*; (flavor) sabor, *m*; (specimen) ejemplo, *m*, idea, *f*; (small quantity) un poco, muy poco; (liking) afición, inclinación, *f*; (of drink) sorbo, trago, *m*; (tinge) dejo, *m*. —*vt* (appraise) probar; gustar, percibir el gusto de; (experience) experimentar, conocer. —*vi* tener gusto, tener sabor. **a matter of t.,** cuestión de gusto. **Each to his own t.,** Entre gustos no hay disputa. **He had not tasted a bite,** No había probado bocado. **in bad (good) t.,** de mal (buen) gusto; de mal (buen) tono. **to have a t. for,** ser aficionado a, gustar de. **to t.,** *Cul*. a gusto, a sabor. **to t. of,** tener gusto de, saber a

**tasted** /'teistɪd/ *a* (in compounds) de sabor...

**tasteful** /'teistfəl/ *a* de buen gusto

**tastefully** /'teistfəli/ *adv* con buen gusto

**tastefulness** /'teistfəlnɪs/ *n* buen gusto, *m*

**tasteless** /'teistlɪs/ *a* insípido, soso, insulso; de mal gusto

**tastelessness** /'teistlɪsnɪs/ *n* insipidez, insulsez, *f*; mal gusto, *m*

**taster** /'teistər/ *n* catador, *m*; (vessel) catavino, *m*

**tasting** /'teistɪŋ/ *n* saboreo, *m*, gustación, *f*, *a* (in compounds) de sabor...

**tasty** /'teisti/ *a* apetitoso, sabroso

**tatter** /'tætər/ *n* andrajo, harapo, *m*; jirón, *m*. **to tear in tatters,** hacer jirones

**tattered** /'tætərd/ *a* andrajoso, haraposo

**tatting** /'tætɪŋ/ *n* frivolité, *m*

**tattoo** /tæ'tu/ *n* tatuaje, *m*; *Mil*. retreta, *f*; (display) parada militar, *f*. —*vt* tatuar

**tattooing** /tæ'tuɪŋ/ *n* tatuaje, *m*; tamboreo, *m*

**taunt** /tɔnt/ *n* mofa, *f*, insulto, escarnio, *m*. —*vt* insultar, atormentar. **to t. with,** echar en cara

**taunting** /'tɔntɪŋ/ *a* insultante, burlón, insolente

**tauntingly** /'tɔntɪŋli/ *adv* burlonamente, insolentemente

**Taurus** /'tɔrəs/ *n* tauro, toro, *m*

**taut** /tɔt/ *a* tieso, tirante, tenso; en regla; *Naut*. **to make t.,** tesar

**tauten** /'tɔtn/ *vt* tesar; poner tieso

**tautness** /'tɔtnɪs/ *n* tensión, *f*

**tautological** /,tɔtḷ'ɒdʒɪkəl/ *a* tautológico

**tautology** /tɔ'tɒlədʒi/ *n* tautología, *f*

**tavern** /'tævərn/ *n* taberna, *f*; (inn) mesón, *m*, posada, *f*. **t.-keeper,** tabernero, *m*

**tawdrily** /'tɔdrɪli/ *adv* llamativamente, de un modo cursi

**tawdriness** /'tɔdrinɪs/ *n* charrería, *f*

**tawdry** /'tɔdri/ *a* chillón, charro, cursi

**tawny** /'tɔni/ *a* leonado

**tax** /tæks/ *n* contribución, gabela, imposición, *f*; *Fig*. carga, *f*; *vt* imponer contribuciones (a); *Law*. tasar; *Fig*. cargar, abrumar. **to tax with,** tachar (de), acusar (de). **direct (indirect) tax,** contribución directa (indirecta), *f*. **tax-collector,** recaudador de contribuciones, *m*. **tax-free,** libre de impuestos. **tax-rate,** tarifa de impuestos, *f*, cupo, *m*. **tax-register,** lista de contribuyentes, *f*

**taxable** /'tæksəbəl/ *a* imponible, sujeto a impuestos

**taxation** /tæk'seiʃən/ *n* imposición de contribuciones (or impuestos), *f*

**tax evasion** *n* evasión tributaria, *f*

**taxi** /'tæksi/ *n* taxi, *m*. —*vi* ir en un taxi; *Aer*. correr por tierra. **t. driver,** chófer de un taxi, taxista, *m*. **t. rank, taxi stand,** parada de taxis, *f*

**taxidermist** /'tæksɪ,dɜrmɪst/ *n* taxidermista, *mf*

**taxidermy** /'tæksɪ,dɜrmi/ *n* taxidermia, *f*

**taximeter** /'tæksi,mitər/ *n* taxímetro, *m*

**taxpayer** /'tæks,peiər/ *n* contribuyente, *mf*

**taxpaying** /'tæks,peiɪŋ/ *a* tributario, que paga contribuciones

**tax reform** *n* reforma impositiva, reforma tributaria, *f*

**tea** /ti/ *n* (liquid) té, *m*; (meal) merienda, *f*. **to have tea,** tomar el té, merendar. **tea-caddy,** bote para té, *m*. **tea-chest,** caja para té, *f*. **tea-cup,** taza para té, *f*. **tea-dance,** té baile, *m*. **tea-kettle** or **tea-pot,** tetera, *f*. **tea-leaf,** hoja de té, *f*. **tea-party,** reunión para tomar el té, *f*. **tea-room,** sa-

lón de té, *m.* **tea-rose,** rosa de té, *f.* **tea-set,** juego de té, *m.* **tea-strainer,** colador de té, *m.* **tea-time,** hora de té, *f.* **tea-urn,** samovar, *m,* tetera para hacer té, *f.*
**tea-waggon,** carrito para el té, *m*
**teach** /titʃ/ *vt* (a person) enseñar, instruir; (a subject) enseñar; (to lecture on) ser profesor de; (a lesson) dar una lección (de). —*vi* (be a teacher) dedicarse a la enseñanza. **to teach at...,** desempeñor una cátedra en... **to t. a person Spanish,** enseñar el castellano a alguien. **to t. how to,** enseñar a (followed by infin.)
**teachability** /ˌtitʃəˈbɪlɪti/ *n* docilidad, *f*
**teachable** /ˈtitʃəbəl/ *a* educable; dócil
**teacher** /ˈtitʃər/ *n* preceptor, *m;* profesor, maestro, *m.*
**woman t.,** profesora, maestra, *f*
**teaching** /ˈtitʃɪŋ/ *n* enseñanza, *f;* (belief) doctrina, *f,* a docente. **t. profession,** magisterio, *m*
**teaching method** *n* método didáctico, *f*
**teak** /tik/ *n Bot.* teca, *f;* (wood) madera de teca, *f*
**team** /tim/ *n* (of horses) tiro, *m;* (of oxen, mules) par, *m,* pareja, yunta, *f; Sports.* partido, equipo, *m;* compañía, *f,* grupo, *m.* —*vt* enganchar, uncir. **t.-work,** cooperación, *f*
**teamster** /ˈtimstər/ *n* gañán, *m*
**tear** /tɪər/ *vt* rasgar; romper; lacerar; (in pieces) hacer pedazos, despedazar; (scratch) arañar; *Fig.* atormentar. **to t. asunder,** romper; desmembrar. **to t. away,** arrancar, quitar violentamente. **to t. down,** derribar, echar abajo. **to t. off,** arrancar; desgajar. **to t. oneself away,** arrancarse, desgarrarse. **to t. one's hair,** arrancarse los pelos, mesarse. **to t. open,** abrir apresuradamente. **to t. up,** hacer pedazos; (uproot) arrancar, desarraigar.
**tear** /tɛər/ *vi* rasgarse; romper; correr precipitadamente. **to t. along,** correr rápidamente (por). **to t. away,** marcharse corriendo. **to t. down,** bajar corriendo. **to t. into,** entrar corriendo en. **to t. off,** irse precipitadamente, marcharse corriendo. **to t. up,** subir corriendo; llegar corriendo; atravesar rápidamente
**tear** /tɛər/ *n* lágrima, *f;* (drop) gota, *f.* **with tears in one's eyes,** con lágrimas en los ojos. **to shed tears,** llorar, lagrimear. **to wipe away one's tears,** secarse las lágrimas. **t.-drop,** lágrima, *f.* **t.-duct,** conductor lacrimal, *m.* **t.-gas,** gas lacrimante, *m.* **t.-stained,** mojado de lágrimas
**tear** /tɛər/ *n* (rent) rasgón, *m*
**tearful** /ˈtɪərfəl/ *a* lloroso, lacrimoso
**tearfully** /ˈtɪərfəli/ *adv* con lágrimas en los ojos
**tearing** *n* rasgadura, *f,* desgarro, *m*
**tearjerker** /ˈtɪərˌdʒɜrkər/ *n* drama lacrimón, *m*
**tease** /tiz/ *vt* (card) cardar; (annoy) fastidiar, irritar, molestar; (chaff) tomar el pelo (a), embromar; (pester) importunar. —*n* bromista, *mf*
**teasel** /ˈtizəl/ *n Bot.* cardencha, *f,* *vt* cardar
**teaser** /ˈtizər/ *n* (problem) rompecabezas, *m;* (person) bromista, *mf*
**teaspoon** /ˈtiˌspun/ *n* cucharita, *f*
**teaspoonful** /ˈtispunˌfʊl/ *n* cucharadita, *f*
**teat** /tit, tɪt/ *n* pezón, *m;* (of animals) teta, *f*
**technical** /ˈtɛknɪkəl/ *a* técnico. **t. offence,** *Law.* cuasidelito, *m.* **t. school,** escuela industrial, *f*
**technicality** /ˌtɛknɪˈkælɪti/ *n* carácter técnico, *m;* tecnicismo, *m;* detalle técnico, *m*
**technician** /tɛkˈnɪʃən/ *n* técnico, *m*
**technicolor** /ˈtɛknɪˌkʌlər/ *n* tecnicolor, *m*
**technique** /tɛkˈnik/ *n* técnica, *f;* ejecución, *f;* mecanismo, *m*
**technological** /ˌtɛknəˈlɒdʒɪkəl/ *a* tecnológico
**technologist** /tɛkˈnɒlədʒɪst/ *n* tecnólogo, *m*
**technology** /tɛkˈnɒlədʒi/ *n* tecnología, *f*
**teddy bear** /ˈtɛdi/ *n* osito de trapo, *m*
**tedious** /ˈtidiəs/ *a* aburrido, tedioso, pesado
**tediously** /ˈtidiəsli/ *adv* aburridamente
**tediousness** /ˈtidiəsnɪs/ *n* aburrimiento, *m,* pesadez, *f*
**tedium** /ˈtidiəm/ *n* tedio, *m,* monotonía, *f*
**tee** /ti/ *n Sports.* meta, *f;* (golf) tee, *m;* (letter) te, *f;* cosa en forma de te, *f.* —*vt* (golf) colocar la pelota en el tee
**teem** /tim/ *vi* rebosar (de), abundar (en); pulular, hormiguear, estar lleno (de); (with rain) diluviar
**teeming** /ˈtimɪŋ/ *a* prolífico, fecundo. **t. with,** abundante en, lleno de

**teens** /tinz/ *n pl* números y años desde trece hasta diez y nueve; edad de trece a diez y nueve años de edad. **to be still in one's t.,** no haber cumplido aún los veinte
**teeter** /ˈtitər/ *vi* balancearse, columpiarse
**teethe** /tið/ *vi* endentecer, echar los dientes
**teething** /ˈtiðɪŋ/ *n* dentición, *f.* **t.-ring,** chupador, *m*
**teetotal** /tiˈtoʊtl/ *a* abstemio
**teetotalism** /tiˈtoʊtlˌɪzəm/ *n* abstinencia completa de bebidas alcohólicas, *f*
**teetotaller** /tiˌtoʊtlər/ *n* abstemio (-ia)
**teetotum** /tiˈtoʊtəm/ *n* perinola, *f*
**telecast** /ˈtɛlɪˌkæst/ *vt* teledifundir
**telecommunication** /ˌtɛlɪkəˌmyunɪˈkeɪʃən/ *n* telecomunicación, *f*
**telegram** /ˈtɛlɪˌgræm/ *n* telegrama, *m*
**telegraph** /ˈtɛlɪˌgræf/ *n* telégrafo, *m.* —*vi* telegrafiar; *Fig.* hacer señas. —*vt* telegrafiar, enviar por telégrafo. **t. line,** línea telegráfica, *f.* **t. office,** central de telégrafos, *f.* **t. pole,** poste telegráfico, *m.* **t. wire,** hilo telegráfico, *m*
**telegraphic** /ˌtɛlɪˈgræfɪk/ *a* telegráfico
**telegraphist** /təˈlɛgrəfɪst/ *n* telegrafista, *mf*
**telegraphy** /təˈlɛgrəfi/ *n* telegrafía, *f.* **wireless t.,** telegrafía sin hilos, *f*
**telemetry** /təˈlɛmɪtri/ *n* telemetría, *f*
**teleology** /ˌtɛliˈɒlədʒi/ *n* teleología, *f*
**telepathic** /ˌtɛləˈpæθɪk/ *a* telepático
**telepathy** /təˈlɛpəθi/ *n* telepatía, *f*
**telephone** /ˈtɛləˌfoʊn/ *n* teléfono, *m.* —*vi* telefonear. —*vt* telefonear, llamar por teléfono. **to be on the t.,** (speaking) estar communicando; (of subscribers) tener teléfono. **dial t.,** teléfono automático, *m.* **t. call,** comunicación telefónica, *f;* conversación telefónica, *f.* **t. call box,** teléfono público, *m.* **t. directory,** guía de teléfonos, *f.* **t. exchange,** central telefónica, *f.* **t. number,** número de teléfono, *m.* **t. operator,** telefonista, *mf.* **t. receiver,** receptor telefónico, *m.* **t. wire,** hilo telefónico, *m*
**telephonic** /ˌtɛləˈfɒnɪk/ *a* telefónico
**telephonist** /təˈlɛfənɪst/ *n* telefonista, *mf*
**telephony** /təˈlɛfəni/ *n* telefonía, *f.* **wireless t.,** telefonía sin hilos, *f*
**teleprinter** /ˈtɛləˌprɪntər/ *n* teletipo, *m*
**telescope** /ˈtɛləˌskoup/ *n* telescopio, catalejo, *m.* —*vt* enchufar. —*vi* enchufarse, meterse una cosa dentro de otra
**telescopic** /ˌtɛləˈskɒpɪk/ *a* telescópico; de enchufe
**televise** /ˈtɛləˌvaiz/ *vt* trasmitir por televisión
**television** /ˈtɛləˌvɪʒən/ *n* televisión, *f.* **on television,** por televisión. **I saw her on television,** La vi por televisión
**television series** *n* serie televisiva, *f*
**tell** /tɛl/ *vt* contar, narrar; decir; revelar; expresar; (the time, of clocks) marcar; (inform) comunicar, informar; (show) indicar, manifestar; (explain) explicar; distinguir; (order) mandar; (compute) contar. —*vi* decir; (have effect) producir efecto. **We cannot t.,** No sabemos. **Who can t.?** ¿Quién sabe? **T. that to the marines!;** Cuéntaselo a tu tía! **to t. its own tale,** hacer ver por sí mismo lo que hay. **to t. again,** volver a decir; contar otra vez. **to t. off,** regañar, reñir; (on a mission) despachar, mandar. **to t. on,** delatar. **to t. upon,** afectar
**teller** /ˈtɛlər/ *n* narrador (-ra); (of votes) escrutador (-ra) de votos; (payer) pagador; (bank) cajero (-ra), *m*
**telling** /ˈtɛlɪŋ/ *a* notable, significante. —*n* narración, *f*
**telltale** /ˈtɛlˌteil/ *n* chismoso (-sa), soplón (-ona); (informer) acusón (-ona). *Fig.* indicio, *m,* señal, *f,* a revelador
**temerity** /təˈmɛrɪti/ *n* temeridad, *f*
**temper** /ˈtɛmpər/ *n* (of metals) temple, *m;* (nature) naturaleza, *f,* carácter, *m;* espíritu, *m;* (mood) humor, *m;* (anger) mal genio, *m.* —*vt* (of metals) templar; moderar, mitigar; mezclar. —*vi* templarse. **bad (good) t.,** mal (buen) humor. **to keep one's t.,** no enojarse, no impacientarse. **to lose one's t.,** enojarse, perder la paciencia
**tempera** /ˈtɛmpərə/ *n Art.* templa, *f.* **in t.,** al temple, *m*
**temperament** /ˈtɛmpərəmənt, -prəmənt/ *n* tempera-

mento, *m;* modo de ser, natural, *m,* naturaleza, índole, *f; Mus.* temple, *m*

**temperamental** /ˌtɛmpərə'mɛntḷ, -prə'mɛn-/ *a* natural, innato; caprichoso

**temperamentally** /ˌtɛmpərə'mɛntḷi, -prə'mɛn- *adv* por naturaleza

**temperance** /'tɛmpərəns/ *n* moderación, templanza, *f;* sobriedad, abstinencia, *f*

**temperate** /'tɛmpərɪt/ *a* moderado; sobrio; (of regions) templado. **t. zone,** zona templada, *f*

**temperately** /'tɛmpərɪtli/ *adv* sobriamente

**temperateness** /'tɛmpərɪtnɪs/ *n* moderación, sobriedad, mesura, *f;* (of regions) templanza, *f*

**temperature** /'tɛmpərətʃər/ *n* temperatura, *f.* **to have a t.,** tener fiebre

**tempered** /'tɛmpərd/ *a* de humor..., de genio... **to be good (bad) t.,** ser de buen (mal) humor

**tempering** /'tɛmpərɪŋ/ *n* temperación, *f*

**tempest** /'tɛmpɪst/ *n* tempestad, borrasca, *f,* temporal, *m; Fig.* tormenta, *f*

**tempest in a teapot** borrasca en un vaso de agua, *m*

**tempestuous** /tɛm'pɛstʃuəs/ *a* tempestuoso, borrascoso; *Fig.* impetuoso, violento

**tempestuousness** /tɛm'pɛstʃuəsnɪs/ *n* lo tempestuoso; *Fig.* impetuosidad, violencia, *f*

**temple** /'tɛmpəl/ *n* templo, *m; Anat.* sien, *f*

**tempo** /'tɛmpou/ *n Mus.* tiempo, *m*

**temporal** /'tɛmpərəl/ *a* temporal; (transient) transitorio, fugaz; *Anat.* temporal. —*n Anat.* hueso temporal, *m*

**temporality** /ˌtɛmpə'rælɪti/ *n* temporalidad, *f*

**temporarily** /ˌtɛmpə'rɛərəli/ *adv* provisionalmente

**temporariness** /'tɛmpəˌrɛrɪnɪs/ *n* interinidad, *f*

**temporary** /'tɛmpəˌrɛri/ *a* provisional, interino

**temporize** /'tɛmpəˌraiz/ *vi* ganar tiempo; contemporizar

**temporizing** /'tɛmpəˌraizɪŋ/ *n* contemporización, *f, a* contemporizador

**tempt** /tɛmpt/ *vt* tentar; atraer, seducir

**temptation** /tɛmp'teifən/ *n* tentación, *f;* aliciente, atractivo, *m*

**tempter** /'tɛmptər/ *n* tentador (-ra)

**tempting** /'tɛmptɪŋ/ *a* tentador, atrayente; seductor

**ten** /tɛn/ *a* diez; (of the clock) las diez, *f pl;* (of age) diez años, *m pl, n* diez, *m;* (a round number) decena, *f;* **ten-millionth,** *a* and *n* diezmillonésimo *m.* **ten months old,** diezmesino. **ten syllable,** decasílabo. **ten thousand,** *a* and *n* diez mil *m.* **There are ten thousand soldiers,** Hay diez mil soldados. **ten-thousandth,** *a* and *n* diezmilésimo *m*

**tenable** /'tɛnəbəl/ *a* sostenible, defendible

**tenacious** /tə'neifəs/ *a* tenaz; (stubborn) porfiado, obstinaz, terco; (sticky) adhesivo. **to be t. of life,** estar muy apegado a la vida

**tenaciously** /tə'neifəsli/ *adv* tenazmente; porfiadamente

**tenacity** /tə'næsɪti/ *n* tenacidad, *f;* porfía, *f;* tesón, *m*

**tenancy** /'tɛnənsi/ *n* inquilinato, *m;* tenencia, *f*

**tenant** /'tɛnənt/ *n* arrendatario (-ia), inquilino (-na); habitante, *m;* morador (-ra)

**tench** /tɛntʃ/ *n Ichth.* tenca, *f*

**tend** /tɛnd/ *vt* cuidar, atender; guardar; vigilar. —*vi* tender; inclinarse (a), propender (a)

**tendency** /'tɛndənsi/ *n* tendencia, inclinación, propensión, *f;* proclividad, *f*

**tendentious** /tɛn'dɛnfəs/ *a* tendencioso

**tender** /'tɛndər/ *n* guardián, *m; Com.* oferta, propuesta, *f; Naut.* falúa, *f;* (of a railway engine) ténder, *m.* **legal t.,** moneda corriente, *f*

**tender** /'tɛndər/ *a* tierno; delicado; (of conscience) escrupuloso; (of a subject) espinoso; compasivo, afectuoso, sensible; muelle, blando. **t.-hearted,** compasivo, tierno de corazón

**tender** /'tɛndər/ *vt* ofrecer; dar; presentar. —*vi* hacer una oferta. **to t. condolences,** dar el pésame. **to t. one's resignation,** presentar la dimisión. **to t. thanks,** dar las gracias

**tenderly** /'tɛndərli/ *adv* tiernamente

**tenderness** /'tɛndərnɪs/ *n* ternura, *f;* sensibilidad, *f;* delicadeza, *f;* dulzura, *f;* indulgencia, *f;* compasivi-

dad, benevolencia, *f;* escrupulosidad, *f;* mimo, cariño, *m*

**tendon** /'tɛndən/ *n Anat.* tendón, *m.* **t. of Achilles,** tendón de Aquiles, *m*

**tenement** /'tɛnəmənt/ *n* casa de vecindad, *f;* vivienda, *f; Poet.* morada, *f*

**Teneriffe** /ˌtɛnə'rif/ Tenerife, *f*

**tenet** /'tɛnɪt/ *n* principio, dogma, *m,* doctrina, *f*

**tenfold** /a.'tɛn,fould; *adv.* -'fould/ *a* décuplo. —*adv* diez veces

**tennis** /'tɛnɪs/ *n* tenis, *m.* **to play t.,** jugar al tenis. **t. ball,** pelota de tenis, *f.* **t. court,** campo de tenis, *m,* cancha de tenis, pista de tenis, *f.* **tennis club,** club de tenis, *m.* **t. racket,** raqueta de tenis, *f;* **tennis shoe,** zapatilla de tenis, *f*

**tenon** /'tɛnən/ *n* espiga, *f, vt* espigar

**tenor** /'tɛnər/ *n* curso, *m;* tenor, contenido, *m; Mus.* tenor, *m;* Mus. alto, *m;* (mus. instrument) viola, *f.* —*a Mus.* de tenor

**tense** /tɛns/ *n Gram.* tiempo, *m.* —*a* tirante, estirado, tieso; tenso

**tenseness** /'tɛnsnɪs/ *n* tirantez, *f;* tensión, *f*

**tensile** /'tɛnsəl/ *a* tensor; extensible

**tension** /'tɛnfən/ *n* tensión, *f; Elec.* voltaje, *m,* tensión, *f;* (of sewing-machine) tensahílo, *m.* **state of t.,** (diplomatic) estado de tirantez, *m*

**tent** /tɛnt/ *n* tienda (de campaña), *f;* (bell) pabellón, *m; Surg.* tienda, *f.* **oxygen t.,** tienda oxígena, *f.* **to pitch tents,** armar las tiendas de campaña; acamparse. **to strike tents,** plegar tiendas. **t. fly,** toldo de tienda, *m.* **t. maker,** tendero, *m.* **t. peg,** clave que sujeta las cuerdas de una tienda, *f.* **t. pole,** mástil (or montante) de tienda, *m*

**tentacle** /'tɛntəkəl/ *n* tentáculo, *m*

**tentative** /'tɛntətɪv/ *a* tentativo, interino, provisional, de prueba, *n* tentativa, *f,* ensayo, *m*

**tentatively** /'tɛntətɪvli/ *adv* por vía de ensayo, experimentalmente

**tenth** /tɛnθ/ *a* décimo; (of monarchs) diez; (of the month) (el) diez. —*n* décimo, *m;* (part) décima parte, *f; Mus.* decena, *f*

**tenthly** /'tɛnθli/ *adv* en décimo lugar

**tenuity** /tə'nuɪti/ *n* tenuidad, *f;* sutilidad, *f;* delgadez, *f*

**tenuous** /'tɛnyuəs/ *a* tenue; sutil; delgado; fino

**tenure** /'tɛnyər/ *n* tenencia, posesión, *f;* (duration) duración, *f;* (of office) administración, *f*

**tepid** /'tɛpɪd/ *a* tibio

**tepidity** /tɛ'pɪdɪti/ *n* tibieza, *f*

**tercentenary** /ˌtɜrsɛn'tɛnəri/ *n* tercer centenario, *f*

**tercet** /'tɜrsɪt/ *n* terceto, *m*

**term** /tɜrm/ *n* (limit) límite, fin, *m;* (period) plazo, tiempo, período, *m;* (schools, universities) trimestre, *m;* (Math. Law. Logic.) término, *m;* (word) expresión, palabra, *f pl.* **terms,** (conditions) condiciones, *f pl;* (charges) precios, *m pl,* tarifa, *f;* (words) términos, *m pl,* palabras, *f pl.* —*vt* llamar, calificar. **for a t. of years,** por un plazo de años. **in plain terms,** en palabras claras. **on equal terms,** en condiciones iguales. **to be on bad (good) terms with,** estar en (or tener) malas (buenas) relaciones con. **to come to terms,** llegar a un acuerdo; hacer las paces. **What are your terms?** ¿Cuáles son sus condiciones? (price) ¿Cuáles son sus precios? **terms of sale,** condiciones de venta, *f pl*

**termagant** /'tɜrməgənt/ *n* arpía, fiera, *f*

**terminable** /'tɜrmənəbəl/ *a* terminable

**terminal** /'tɜrmənl/ *a* terminal, final; (of schools, universities) trimestre. —*n* término, *m; Elec.* borne, *m;* (schools, universities) examen de fin de trimestre, *m;* (railway) estación terminal, *f;* (Archit. and figure) término, *m; Archit.* remate, *m*

**terminate** /'tɜrmə,neit/ *vt* limitar; terminar, concluir, poner fin (a). —*vi* terminarse, concluirse (por); cesar

**termination** /ˌtɜrmə'neifən/ *n* terminación, conclusión, *f* fin, *m; Gram.* terminación, *f;* cabo, remate, *m*

**terminology** /ˌtɜrmə'nɒlədʒi/ *n* nomenclatura, terminología, *f*

**terminus** /'tɜrmənəs/ *n* (railway) estación terminal, *f;* (Archit. and figure) término, *m; Archit.* remate, *m; Myth.* Término

**termite** /'tɜrmait/ *n Ent.* termita, *m*

**term paper** *n* trabajo de examen, *m*

**terms of trade** *n* relación de los precios de intercambio, *f*

**terrace** /'terəs/ *n* terraza, *f*, *vt* terraplenar

**terraced** /'terəst/ *a* en terrazas; con terrazas

**terracotta** /ˌterə'kptə/ *n* terracota, *f*

**terrain** /tə'rein/ *n* terreno, campo, *m*, región, *f*

**terrapin** /'terəpɪn/ *n* tortuga de agua dulce, *f*

**terrestrial** /tə'restriəl/ *a* terrestre, terrenal

**terrible** /'terəbəl/ *a* terrible, pavoroso, espantoso; *Inf.* tremendo

**terribleness** /'terəbəlnɪs/ *n* terribilidad, *f*, lo horrible

**terrier** /'teriər/ *n* terrier, *m*; *Inf.* soldado del ejército territorial, *m*

**terrific** /tə'rɪfɪk/ *a* espantoso, terrible; *Inf.* atroz, tremendo

**terrify** /'terəˌfai/ *vt* aterrorizar, espantar, horrorizar

**terrifying** /'terəˌfaiɪŋ/ *a* aterrador, espantoso

**territorial** /ˌterɪ'tɔriəl/ *a* territorial. —*n* soldado del ejército territorial, *m*

**territoriality** /ˌterɪˌtɔri'ælɪti/ *n* territorialidad, *f*

**territory** /'terɪˌtɔri/ *n* región, comarca, *f*; (state) territorio, *m*; jurisdicción, *f*. **mandated territory,** territorio bajo mandato, *m pl*

**terror** /'terər/ *n* terror, pavor, espanto, *m*. **the Reign of T.,** el Reinado del Terror, *m*. **t.-stricken,** espantado, muerto de miedo

**terrorism** /'terəˌrɪzəm/ *n* terrorismo, *m*

**terrorist** /'terərɪst/ *n* terrorista, *m*

**terrorization** /ˌterərə'zeiʃən/ *n* aterramiento, *m*

**terrorize** /'terəˌraiz/ *vt* aterrorizar

**terse** /tɜrs/ *a* conciso, sucinto; seco, brusco

**tersely** /'tɜrsli/ *adv* concisamente; secamente

**terseness** /'tɜrsnɪs/ *n* concisión, *f*; brusquedad, *f*

**tertiary** /'tɜrʃi,eri, -ʃəri/ *a* tercero; *Geol.* terciario. —*n Eccl.* terciario, *m*

**tessera** /'tesərə/ *n* tesela, *f*

**test** /test/ *n* (proof) prueba, *f*; examen, *m*; investigación, *f*; (standard) criterio, *m*, piedra de toque, *f*; *Chem.* análisis, *m*; (trial) ensayo, *m*; *Zool.* concha, *f*. —*vt Chem.* ensayar, probar, poner a prueba; examinar; (eyes) graduar (la vista). **to put to the t.,** poner a prueba. **to stand the t.,** soportar la prueba. **t. match,** partido internacional de cricket, *m*. **t. meal,** *Med.* comida de prueba, *f*. **t. pilot,** *Aer.* piloto de pruebas, *m*. **t. tube,** tubo de ensayo, *m*

**testament** /'testəmənt/ *n* testamento, *m*. **the New T.,** el Nuevo Testamento, *m*. **the Old T.,** el Antiguo Testamento, *m*

**testamentary** /ˌtestə'mentəri/ *a* testamentario

**testate** /'testeit/ *a* testado

**testator** /'testeitər/ *n* testador, *m*, (**testatrix,** testadora, *f*)

**testicle** /'testɪkəl/ *n* testículo, *m*

**testification** /ˌtestɪfɪ'keiʃən/ *n* testificación, *f*

**testify** /'testəˌfai/ *vt and vi* declarar, atestar; *Law.* atestiguar, testificar, dar fe

**testily** /'testɪli/ *adv* malhumoradamente

**testimonial** /ˌtestə'mouniəl/ *n* recomendación, *f*; certificado, *m*; (tribute) homenaje, *m*

**testimony** /'testəˌmouni/ *n* testimonio, *m*, declaración, *f*; (proof) prueba, *f*. **in t. whereof,** en fe de lo cual. **to bear t.,** atestar

**testiness** /'testɪnɪs/ *n* mal humor, *m*, irritación, *f*

**testing grounds** /'testɪŋ/ *n* campo de experimentación, campo de pruebas, *m*

**testy** /'testi/ *a* enojadizo, irritable, irascible, quisquilloso

**tetanus** /'tetnəs/ *n* tétano, *m*

**tether** /'teðər/ *n* traba, atadura, maniota, *f*. —*vt* atar con una correa. **to be at the end of one's t.,** acabarse la resistencia; acabarse la paciencia

**Teuton** /'tutn/ *n* teutón (-ona)

**Teutonic** /tu'tɒnɪk/ *a* teutónico

**text** /tekst/ *n* texto, *m*; (subject) tema, *m*; (motto) lema, *m*; (of a musical composition) letra, *f*. **t.-book,** libro de texto, *m*

**textile** /'tekstail/ *a* textil, de tejer. —*n* textil, *m*, materia textil, *f*; tejido, *m*

**textual** /'tekstʃuəl/ *a* textual

**texture** /'tekstʃər/ *n* (material and *Biol.*) tejido, *m*; textura, *f*

**Thailand** /'tai,lænd/ Tailandia, *f*

**thalamus** /'θæləməs/ *n* (*Anat., Bot.*) tálamo, *m*

**Thames, the** /temz/ *n* el Támesis, *m*. **to set the T. on fire,** descubrir la pólvora

**than** /ðæn, ðen; *unstressed* ðən, ən/ *conjunc* que; (between **more, less,** or **fewer** and a number) de; (in comparisons of inequality) que, but que becomes(*a*) del (de la, de los, de las) que if the point of comparison is a noun in the principal clause, which has to be supplied mentally to fill up the ellipsis; (*b*) de lo que if there is no noun to act as a point of comparison, e.g. **He was older than I thought,** Era más viejo de lo que yo pensaba. **They have less than they deserve,** Tienen menos de lo que merecen. **They lose more money than (the money) they earn,** Pierden más dinero del que ganan. **He will meet with more opposition than he thought,** Va a encontrar más oposición de la que pensaba. **I have more books than you,** Tengo más libros que tú. **She has fewer than nine and more than five,** Ella tiene menos de nueve y más de cinco

**thank** /θæŋk/ *vt* agradecer, dar las gracias (a). **to t. for,** agradecer. **I will t. you to be more polite,** Le agradecería que fuese más cortés. **He has himself to t. for it,** Él mismo tiene la culpa de ello. **No, t. you,** No, muchas gracias. **T. goodness!** ¡Gracias a Dios!

**thank** /θæŋks/ *n* (now in pl. only, **thanks**) gracias, *f pl*. **a vote of thanks,** un voto de gracias. **Many thanks!** ¡Muchas gracias! **to return thanks,** dar las gracias. **thanks to,** merced a, debido a. **thanks to you,** gracias a tí. **t.-offering,** ofrecimiento en acción de gracias, *m*

**thankful** /'θæŋkfəl/ *a* agradecido. **I am t. to see,** Me alegro de ver, Me es grato ver

**thankfully** /'θæŋkfəli/ *adv* con gratitud, agradecido

**thankfulness** /'θæŋkfəlnɪs/ *n* agradecimiento, *m*; gratitud, *f*

**thankless** /'θæŋklɪs/ *a* ingrato; desagradecido; desagradable

**thanksgiving** /ˌθæŋks'gɪvɪŋ/ *n* acción de gracias, *f*. **t. service,** servicio de acción de gracias, *m*. **Thanksgiving ( Day),** *n* día de acción de dar gracias, día de gracias, *m*

**that** /ðæt; *unstressed* ðət/ *dem a* ese, *m*; esa, *f*; aquel, *m*; aquella, *f*, *dem. pron* ese, *m*; ésa, *f*; eso, *neut*; aquél, *m*; aquélla, *f*; aquello, *neut*; (standing for a noun) el, *m*; la, *f*; lo, *neut* **All t. there is,** Todo lo que hay. **His temperament is t. of his mother,** Su temperamento es el de su madre. **We have not come to t. yet,** Todavía no hemos llegado a ese punto. **T. is what I want to know,** Eso es lo que quiero saber. **with t.,** con eso; (thereupon) en eso. **Go t. way,** Vaya Vd. por allí; Tome Vd. aquel camino. **T. is to say...,** Es decir.... **What do you mean by t.?** ¿Qué quiere usted decir con eso? **The novel is not as bad as all t.,** La novela no es tan mala como tú piensas (*or* como dicen, etc.)

**that** /ðæt; *unstressed* ðət/ *pron rel* que, *m*; la cual, *f*; lo cual, *neut*; (of persons) a quien, *mf*; a quienes, *mf pl*; (with from) de quien, *mf*; de quienes, *mf pl*; (of place) donde. **The letter t. I sent you,** la carta que te mandé. **The box t. John put them in,** la caja en la cual los puso Juan. **The last time t. I saw her,** La última vez que la vi

**that** /ðæt; *unstressed* ðət/ *conjunc* que; (of purpose) para que; afin de que; (before infin.) para; (because) porque. **O t. he would come!** ¡Ojalá que viniese! **so t.,** para que; (before infin.) para; (as a result) de manera que; de modo que. **It is better t. he should not come,** Es mejor que no venga. **now t.,** ahora que

**thatch** /θætʃ/ *n* barda, *f*, *vt* bardar

**thaw** /θɔ/ *n* deshielo, *m*. —*vt* deshelar; derretir. —*vi* deshelarse; derretirse

**the** /*stressed* ði; *unstressed* ðə; *stressed before a consonant* ðə, *unstressed before a vowel* ði/ *def art* el, *m*; la, *f*; lo, *neut*; los, *m pl*; las, *f pl*; (before feminine sing. noun beginning with stressed a or ha) el; (untranslated between the name and number of a monarch, pope, ruler, e.g. *Charles the Tenth,* Carlos diez). —*adv* (before a comparative) cuanto, tanto más. **at the** or

**to the,** al, *m*, (also before feminine sing. noun beginning with a or ha); a la, *f*; a lo, *neut*; a los, *m pl*; a las, *f pl*. **from the** or **of the,** del, *m*, (also before feminine sing. noun beginning with stressed a or ha); de la, *f*; de lo, *neut*; de los, *m pl*; de las, *f pl*. **the one,** see **one. The sooner the better,** Cuanto antes mejor. **The room will be all the warmer,** El cuarto estará tanto más caliente

**theater** /'θiətər/ *n* teatro, *m*; (lecture) anfiteatro, *m*; (drama) teatro, *m*, obra dramática, *f*; (scene) teatro, *m*, escena, *f*. **t. attendant,** acomodador (-ra)

**theater-in-the-round** /'θiətərɪnðə'raund/ *n* teatro circular, teatro en círculo, *m*

**Theatine** /θi'ɑtɪn, ɪtɪn/ *a* and *n Eccl*. teatino *m*

**theatrical** /θi'ætrɪkəl/ *a* teatral. —*n pl* **theatricals,** funciones teatrales, *f pl*. **amateur theatricals,** función de aficionados, *f*. **t. company,** compañía de teatro, *f*. **t. costumier,** mascarero (-ra), alquilador (-ra) de disfraces. **t. manager,** empresario de teatro, *m*

**theatricality** /θi,ætrɪ'kælɪti/ *n* teatralidad, *f*

**Theban** *a* and *n* tebeo (-ea), tebano (-na)

**Thebes** /θibz/ Tebas, *f*

**thee** /ði/ *pers pron* te; (after prep.) tí. **with t.,** contigo

**theft** /θɛft/ *n* robo, hurto, *m*

**their** /ðɛər; *unstressed* ðər/ *poss a* su, *mf sing*; sus, *pl*; de ellos, *m pl*; de ellas, *f pl*. **They have t. books,** Tienen sus libros. **I have t. books,** Tengo los libros de ellos

**theirs** /ðɛərz/ *poss pron* (el) suyo, *m*; (la) suya, *f*; (los) suyos, *m pl*; (las) suyas, *f pl*; de ellos, *m pl*; de ellas, *f pl*. **These hats are t.,** Estos sombreros son los suyos

**them** /ðɛm; *unstressed* ðəm, əm/ *pers pron* ellos, *m pl*; ellas, *f pl*; (as object of a verb) los, *m pl*; las, *f pl*; (to them) les

**thematic** /θi'mætɪk/ *a* temático

**theme** /θim/ *n* tema, asunto, *m*; tesis, *f*; *Mus*. tema, motivo, *m*

**themselves** /ðəm'sɛlvz, ,ðɛm-/ *pers pron pl* ellos mismos, *m pl*; ellas mismas, *f pl*, *reflexive pron* sí; sí mismos; (with a reflexive verb) se. **They t. told me about it,** Ellos mismos me lo dijeron. **They left it for t.,** Lo dejaron para sí (mismos)

**then** /ðɛn/ *adv* (of future time) entonces; (of past time) a la sazón, en aquella época, entonces; (next, afterwards) luego, después, en seguida; (in that case) en este caso, entonces; (therefore) por consiguiente. —*a* de entonces. —*n* entonces, *m*. —*conjunc* (moreover) además; pues. **And what t.?** ¿Y qué pasó después?; ¿Y qué pasará ahora?; ¿Y qué más? **by t.,** por entonces. **now and t.,** de vez en cuando. **now... t.,** ya... ya, ora... ora. **since t.,** desde aquel tiempo; desde entonces; desde aquella ocasión. **until t.,** hasta entonces; hasta aquella época. **well t.,** bien, pues. **t. and there,** en el acto, en seguida; allí mismo

**thence** /ðɛns/ *adv* desde allí, de allí; (therefore) por eso, por esa razón, por consiguiente

**thenceforth** /,ðɛns'fɔrθ/ *adv* de allí en adelante, desde entonces

**theocracy** /θi'ɒkrəsi/ *n* teocracia, *f*

**theocratic** /,θiə'krætɪk/ *a* teocrático

**theologian** /,θiə'loudʒən/ *n* teólogo, *m*

**theological** /,θiə'lɒdʒɪkəl/ *a* teológico, teologal

**theologize** /θi'ɒlə,dʒaiz/ *vi* teologizar

**theology** /θi'ɒlədʒi/ *n* teología, *f*

**theorem** /'θiərəm/ *n* teorema, *m*

**theoretical** /,θiə'rɛtɪkəl/ *a* teórico

**theoretically** /,θiə'rɛtɪkli/ *adv* teóricamente, en teoría

**theorist** /'θiərɪst/ *n* teórico, *m*

**theorize** /'θiə,raiz/ *vi* teorizar

**theory** /'θiəri/ *n* teoría, *f*

**theosophical** /,θiə'sɒfɪkəl/ *a* teosófico

**theosophist** /θi'ɒsəfɪst/ *n* teósofo, *m*

**theosophy** /θi'ɒsəfi/ *n* teosofía, *f*

**therapeutic** /,θɛrə'pyutɪk/ *a* terapéutico. —*n* **therapeutics,** terapéutica, *f*

**therapeutist** /θɛrə'pyutɪst/ *n* terapeuta, *mf*

**therapy** /'θɛrəpi/ *suffix* terapia, *f*

**there** /ðɛər; *unstressed* ðər/ *adv* allí; ahí, allá; (at that point) en eso; (used pronominally as subject of verb) haber, e.g. T. *was once a king,* Hubo una vez un rey;

*What is t. to do here?* ¿Qué hay que hacer aquí? —*interj* ¡vaya!; (I told you so!) ¡ya ves! ¡ya te lo dije yo!; (in surprise) ¡toma! **about t.,** cerca de allí. **down t.,** allí abajo. **in t.,** allí dentro. **out t.,** allí fuera. **over t.,** ahí; allá a lo lejos. **up t.,** allí arriba. **T. came a time when...,** Llegó la hora cuando... **T. it is!** ¡Allí está! **t. is** or **t. are,** hay. **t. was** or **t. were,** había, hubo. **t. may be,** puede haber, quizás habrá. **t. must be,** tiene que haber. **t. will be,** habrá. **T., t.!** (to a child, etc.) ¡Vamos!

**thereabouts** /'ðɛər,bauts/ *adv* (near to a place) cerca de allí, por ahí, allí cerca; (approximately) aproximadamente, cerca de

**thereafter** /,ðɛər'æftər/ *adv* después, después de eso

**thereby** /,ðɛər'bai/ *adv* (near to that place) por allí cerca; (by that means) con lo cual, de este modo

**therefore** /'ðɛər,fɔr/ *adv* por lo tanto, por eso, así, por consiguiente; por esta razón

**therein** /,ðɛər'ɪn/ *adv* (inside) allí dentro; (in this, that particular) en estre, en eso, en ese particular

**thereinafter** /,ðɛərɪn'æftər/ *adv* posteriormente, más adelante

**thereupon** /'ðɛərə,pɒn/ *adv* (in consequence) por consiguiente, por lo tanto; (at that point) luego, en eso; (immediately afterwards) inmediatamente después, en seguida

**thermal** /'θɜrməl/ *a* termal. **t. springs,** aguas termales, termas, *f pl*

**thermodynamics** /,θɜrmoudai'næmɪks/ *n* termodinámica, *f*

**thermoelectric** /,θɜrmouɪ'lɛktrɪk/ *a* termoeléctrico

**thermometer** /θər'mɒmɪtər/ *n* termómetro, *m*

**Thermopylae** /θər'mɒpə,li/ Termópilas, *f*

**thermos flask** /'θɜrməs/ *n* termos, *m*

**thermostat** /'θɜrmə,stæt/ *n* termostato, *m*

**thermostatic** /,θɜrmə'stætɪk/ *a* termostático

**thesaurus** /θɪ'sɔrəs/ *n* tesoro, tesauro, *m*

**these** /ðiz/ *dem pron pl* of **this,** éstos, *m pl*; éstas, *f pl*, *dem* estos, *m pl*; estas, *f pl*. **Aren't t. your flowers?** ¿No son éstas tus flores? **T. pictures have been sold,** Estos cuadros han se han vendito

**thesis** /'θisɪs/ *n* tesis, *f*

**Thespian** /'θɛspiən/ *a* dramático

**Thessaly** /'θɛsəli/ Tesalia, *f*

**they** /ðei/ *pers pron pl* ellos, *m pl*; ellas, *f pl*; (people) se (followed by sing. verb). **T. say,** Dicen, Se dice

**thick** /θɪk/ *a* espeso; (big) grueso, (wall) grueso, (string, cord) gordo; (vapors) denso; (muddy) turbio; (dense, close) tupido apretado; (numerous) numeroso, repetido, continuo; (full of) lleno (de); (of voice) velado, indistinto; (obtuse) estúpido, lerdo; (friendly) íntimo. —*adv* densamente; continuamente, sin cesar. **three feet t.,** de tres pies de espesor. **That's a bit t.!** ¡Eso es un poco demasiado! **to be as t. as thieves,** estar unidos como los dedos de la mano. **t.-lipped,** con labios gruesos, bezudo. **t.-headed,** estúpido, lerdo. **t.-skinned,** de piel gruesa; *Zool*. paquidermo; *Fig*. sin vergüenza, insensible. **t. stroke,** (of letters) grueso, *m*

**thick** /θɪk/ *n* espesor, *m*; parte gruesa, *f*; lo más denso; (of a fight) lo más reñido; centro, *m*. **in the t. of,** en el centro (de), en medio de

**thicken** /'θɪkən/ *vt* espesar; (increase) aumentar, multiplicar; *Cul*. espesar. —*vi* espesarse; condensar; aumentar, multiplicarse; (of a mystery, etc.) complicarse; hacerse más denso; *Cul*. espesarse

**thickening** /'θɪkənɪŋ/ *n* hinchamiento, *m*; gordura, *f*; (*Cul*. and of paints) espesante, *m*

**thicket** /'θɪkɪt/ *n* matorral, soto, *m*, maleza, *f*; (grove) boscaje, *m*

**thickly** /'θɪkli/ *adv* densamente; espesamente; continuamente, sin cesar; (of speech) indistintamente

**thickness** /'θɪknɪs/ *n* espesor, *m*; grueso, *m*; densidad, *f*; (of liquids) consistencia, *f*; (layer) capa, *f*; (of speech) dificultad (en el hablar), *f*

**thickset** /'θɪk'sɛt/ *a* doblado

**thief** /θif/ *n* ladrón (-ona); (in a candle) moco de vela, *m*. **Stop t.!** ¡Ladrones! **thieves' den,** *Fig*. cueva de ladrones, *f*

**thieve** /θiv/ *vi* hurtar, robar. —*vt* robar

**thievish** /'θivɪʃ/ *a* ladrón

**thigh** /θai/ *n* muslo, *m*. **t.-bone,** fémur, *m*

**thimble** /'θimbəl/ *n* dedal, *m*

**thimbleful** /'θimbəl,fʊl/ *n* lo que cabe en un dedal; *Fig.* dedada, *f*

**thin** /θin/ *a* delgado; (lean) flaco; (small) pequeño; delicado; fino; (of air, light) tenue, sutil; (clothes) ligero; (sparse) escaso; transparente; (watery) aguado; (of wine) bautizado; (not close) claro; (of arguments) flojo. —*vt* adelgazar; aclarar; *Agr.* limpiar; reducir. —*vi* adelgazarse; afilarse; reducirse. **somewhat t.,** (of persons) delgaducho, algo flaco. **to grow t.,** enflaquecer; afilarse. **to make t.,** hacer adelgazar volver flaco. **t.-clad,** ligero de ropa; mal vestido. **t.-faced,** de cara delgada. **t.-lipped,** de labios apretados. **t.-skinned,** de piel fina; *Fig.* sensitivo, sensible

**thine** /ðain/ See **theirs.** *poss pron* (el) tuyo, *m*; (la) tuya, *f*; (los) tuyos, *m pl*; (las) tuyas, *f pl*; tu, *mf*; tus, *mf pl*; de ti. **The fault is t.,** La culpa es tuya, La culpa es de ti

**thing** /θiŋ/ *n* cosa, *f*; objeto, artículo, *m*; (affair) asunto, *m*; (contemptuous) sujeto, tipo, *m*; (creature) ser, *m*, criatura, *f*; *pl* **things,** (belongings) efectos, trastos, *m pl*; (luggage) equipaje, *m*; (clothes) trapitos, *m pl*; (circumstances) circunstancias, condiciones, *f pl*. **above all things,** ante todo, sobre todo. **a very pretty little t.,** (child) una pequeña muy mona. **as things are,** tal como están las cosas. **for one t.,** en primer lugar. **Her behavior is not quite the t.,** La conducta de ella no está bien vista. **The bad t. is that...,** Lo malo es que... **The good t. is that...,** Menos mal que...; Lo bueno es que... **No such t.!** ¡No hay tal!; ¡Nada de eso! **Poor t.!** ¡Pobrecito!; (woman) ¡Pobre mujer!; (man) ¡Pobre hombre! **to be just the t.,** venir al pelo. **with one t. and another,** entre unas cosas y otras. **I like things Spanish,** Me gusta lo español

**think** /θiŋk/ *vt* and *vi* pensar; (believe) creer; (deem) considerar, juzgar; imaginar; (suspect) sospechar; (opine) ser de opinión (que). **And to t. that...!** ¡Y pensar que...! **As you t. fit,** Como usted quiera, Como a usted le parezca bien. **He thought as much,** Se lo figuraba. **He little thought that...!** ¡Cuán lejos estaba de pensar que...! **He thinks nothing of...,** No le importa...; Desprecia..., Tiene una opinión bastante mala de.... **I don't t. so,** No lo creo. **I should t. not!** ¡Claro que no! ¡Eso sí que no! **I should t. so!** ¡Claro! ¡Ya lo creo! **It makes me t. of...,** Me hace pensar en... **One might t.,** Podría creerse... **to t. better of something,** cambiar de opinión, considerar mejor. **to t. highly ( badly) of,** tener buen (mal) concepto sobre. **to t. over carefully,** pensarlo bien, considerar detenidamente. *Inf.* consultar con la almohada. **to t. proper,** creer conveniente. **to t. to oneself,** pensar para sí (o entre sí). **to t. too much of oneself,** pensar demasiado en sí; tener demasiada buena opinión de sí mismo; tener humos. **What do you t. about it?** ¿Qué te parece? **to t. about,** (of persons) pensar en; (of things) pensar de (or sobre); meditar, considerar, reflexionar sobre. **to t. for,** pensar por. **to t. of,** pensar en; pensar de (or sobre). **What do you t. of this?** ¿Qué te parece esto? **to t. out,** idear, proyectar, hacer planes para; (a problem) resolver. **to t. over,** pensar; reflexionar sobre, meditar sobre. **I shall t. it over,** Lo pensaré.

**thinker** /'θiŋkər/ *n* pensador, *m*

**thinking** /'θiŋkiŋ/ *n* pensamiento, *m*, reflexión, meditación, *f*; juicio, *m*; opinión, *f*, parecer, *m* —*a* pensador; inteligente; racional; serio. **To my way of t.,** Según pienso yo, A mi parecer. **way of t.,** modo de pensar, *m*

**thinly** /'θinli/ *adv* delgadamente; esparcidamente; (lightly) ligeramente; poco numeroso

**thinness** /'θinnis/ *n* delgadez, *f*; (leanness) flaqueza, *f*; sutileza, tenuidad, *f*; (lack) escasez, *f*; pequeño número, *m*; poca consistencia, *f*

**third** /θɜrd/ *a* tercero (tercer before *m, sing* noun); (of monarchs) tercero; (of the month) (el) tres. —*n* tercio, *m*, tercera parte, *f*; *Mus.* tercera, *f*. **T. time lucky!** ¡A la tercera va la vencida! **t. class,** *n* tercera clase, *f*. —*a* de tercera clase. **t. party,** tercera persona, *f*. **t.-party insurance,** seguro contra tercera per-

sona, *m*. **t. person,** tercero (-ra); *Gram.* tercera persona, *f*. **t.-rate,** de tercera clase

**thirdly** /'θɜrdli/ *adv* en tercer lugar

**thirst** /θɜrst/ *n* sed, *f*; *Fig.* deseo, *m*, ansia, *f*; entusiasmo, *m*. **to satisfy one's t.,** apagar (or matar) la sed

**thirsty** /'θɜrsti/ *a* sediento. **to be t.,** tener sed. **to make t.,** dar sed.

**thirteen** /'θɜr'tin/ *a* and *n* trece *m*. **t. hundred,** *a* and *n* mil trescientos *m*

**thirteenth** /θɜr'tinθ/ *a* décimotercio; (of monarchs) trece; (of month) (el) trece, *m*, *n* décimotercio, trezavo, *m*

**thirtieth** /'θɜrtiəθ/ *a* trigésimo; (of month) (el) treinta, *m*. —*n* treintavo, *m*

**thirty** /'θɜrti/ *a* and *n* treinta, *m*. **t.-first,** treinta y uno

**this** /ðis/ *dem a* este, *m*; esta, *f*, *dem pron* éste, *m*; ésta, *f*; esto, *neut* **by t. time,** a esta hora, ya. **like t.,** de este modo, así. **T. is Wednesday,** Hoy es miércoles. **What is all t.?** ¿Qué es todo esto?

**thistle** /'θisəl/ *n* cardo, *m*. **t.-down,** papo de cardo, vilano de cardo, *m*

**thither** /'θiðər, 'ðið-/ *adv* allá, hacia allá; a ese fin. —*a* más remoto

**thong** /θɔŋ/ *n* correa, tira, *f*

**thoracic** /θɔ'ræsik/ *a* torácico

**thorax** /'θɔræks/ *n* tórax, *m*

**thorn** /θɔrn/ *n* espina, *f*; (tree) espino, *m*; *Fig.* abrojo, *m*, espina, *f*. **to be a t. in the flesh of,** ser una espina en el costado de.. **t. brake,** espinar, *m*

**thornless** /'θɔrnlis/ *a* sin espinas

**thorny** /'θɔrni/ *a* espinoso; *Fig.* difícil, arduo

**thorough** /'θɜrou/ *a* completo; perfecto; (conscientious) concienzudo; (careful) cuidadoso. **t.-bred,** (of animals) de pura raza, de casta; (of persons) bien nacido. **t.-paced,** cabal, consumado

**thoroughfare** /'θɜrə,fɛər/ *n* vía pública, *f*. **"No t.,"** «Prohibido el paso», «Calle cerrada»

**thoroughly** /'θɜrəli/ *adv* completamente; (of knowing a subject) a fondo; concienzudamente

**thoroughness** /'θɜrənis/ *n* perfección, *f*; minuciosidad, *f*

**those** /ðouz/ *dem a pl* of **that,** esos, *m pl*; esas, *f pl*; aquellos, *m pl*; aquellas, *f pl*, *dem pron* ésos, *m pl*; ésas, *f pl*; aquéllos, *m pl*; aquéllas, *f pl*; (standing for a noun) los, *m pl*; las, *f pl*. **t. who,** quienes, *mf pl*; **t. that** or **which,** los que, *m pl*; las que, *f pl*. **Your eyes are t. of your mother,** Tus ojos son los de tu madre

**thou** /ðau/ *pers pron* tú

**though** /ðou/ *conjunc* (followed by subjunc. when doubt is implied or uncertain future time) aunque, bien que; (nevertheless) sin embargo, no obstante; (in spite of) a pesar de que; (but) pero. **as t.,** como si (followed by subjunc.). **even t.,** aunque (followed by subjunc.)

**thought** /θɔt/ *n* pensamiento, *m*; meditación, reflexión, *f*. **some thoughts on...** algunas reflexiones sobre...; opinión, *f*; consideración, *f*; idea, *f*, propósito, *m*; (care) cuidado, *m*, solicitud, *f*; *Inf.* pizca, *f*. **on second thought,** después de pensarlo bien. **The t. struck him,** Se le ocurrió la idea. **to collect one's thoughts,** orientarse; informarse (de). **t.-reading,** adivinación del pensamiento, *f*. **t.-transference,** telepatía, transmisión del pensamiento, *f*

**thoughtful** /'θɔtfəl/ *a* pensativo, meditabundo; serio; especulativo; (provident) previsor; (kind) atento, solícito; cuidadoso; (anxious) inquieto, intranquilo

**thoughtfully** /'θɔtfəli/ *adv* pensativamente; seriamente; (providently) con previsión; (kindly) atentamente, solícitamente

**thoughtfulness** /'θɔtfəlnis/ *n* natural reflexivo, *m*, seriedad, *f*; (kindness) solicitud, atención, *f*; (forethought) previsión, *f*

**thoughtless** /'θɔtlis/ *a* irreflexivo; (careless) descuidado, negligente; (unkind) inconsiderado; (silly) necio, estúpido

**thoughtlessly** /'θɔtlisli/ *adv* sin pensar, irreflexivamente; negligentemente

**thoughtlessness** /'θɔtlisnis/ *n* irreflexión, *f*; descuido, *m,* negligencia, *f;* (unkindness) inconsideración, *f;* (silliness) neciedad, *f*

**thousand** /'θauzənd/ *a* mil. —*n* mil, *m;* millar, *m.* **one t.,** mil, *m.* **one t. three hundred,** *a* mil trescientos, *m pl;* mil trescientas, *f pl.* —*n* mil trescientos, *m pl.* **two ( three) t.,** dos (tres) mil. **by thousands,** por millares; por miles. **t.-fold,** mil veces más

**thousandth** /'θauzəndθ/ *a* and *n* milésimo *m*

**Thrace** /θreis/ Tracia, *f*

**thrall** /θrɔl/ *n* esclavo (-va); esclavitud, *f*

**thrash** /θræʃ/ *vt* azotar, apalear; *Agr.* trillar, desgranar; *Inf.* triunfar sobre, derrotar. —*vi Agr.* trillar el grano; arrojarse, agitarse. *Fig.* **to t. out,** ventilar

**thrashing** /'θræʃɪŋ/ *n* apaleamiento, *m,* paliza, *f; Agr.* See **threshing**

**thread** /θrɛd/ *n* hilo, *m;* (fibre) hebra, fibra, *f,* filamento, *m;* (of a screw) filete, *m; Fig.* hilo, *m, a* de hilo. —*vt* (a needle) enhebrar; (beads) ensartar; (make one's way) colarse a través de, atravesar; pasar por. **to hang by a t.,** pender de un hilo. **to lose the t. of,** *Fig.* perder el hilo de

**threadbare** /'θrɛd,bɛər/ *a* raído; muy usado; *Fig.* trivial, viejo

**threadlike** /'θrɛd,laik/ *a* como un hilo, filiforme

**threadworm** /'θrɛd,wɜrm/ *n m,* lombriz intestinal, *f*

**threat** /θrɛt/ *n* amenaza, *f*

**threaten** /'θrɛtn/ *vt* and *vi* amenazar. **to t. with,** amenazar con

**threatening** /'θrɛtnɪŋ/ *a* amenazador. —*n* amenazas, *f pl*

**threateningly** /'θrɛtnɪŋli/ *adv* con amenazas

**three** /θri/ *a* and *n* tres *m;* (of the clock) las tres, *f pl;* (of one's age) tres años, *m pl.* **t.-color process,** tricromía, *f.* **t.-colored,** tricolor. **t.-cornered,** triangular; (of hats) de tres picos, tricornio. **t.-cornered hat,** sombrero de tres picos, tricornio, *m.* **t. decker,** *Naut.* navío de tres puentes, *m;* novela larga, *f.* **t. deep,** en tres hileras. **t. hundred,** *a* and *n* trescientos *m.* **t.-hundredth,** *a* and *n* tricentésimo *m.* **t.-legged,** de tres patas. **t.-legged stool,** banqueta, *f.* **t.-per-cents,** accion al tres por ciento (3%), *f.* **t.-phase,** *Elec.* trifásico. **t.-ply,** (of yarn) triple; (of wood) de tres capas. **t.-quarter,** de tres cuartos. **t. quarters of an hour,** tres cuartos de hora, *m pl.* **t.-sided,** trilátero. **t. speed gear box,** cambio de marcha de tres velocidades, *m.* **t.-stringed,** *Mus.* de tres cuerdos. **t. thousand,** *a* tres mil, *mf pl; n* tres mil, *m*

**threefold** /'θri,fould/ *a* triple

**Three Musketeers, the** los Tres Mosqueteros

**threescore** /'θri'skɔr/ *a* and *n* sesenta, *m pl*

**threesome** /'θrisəm/ *n* partido de tres, *m*

**threnody** /'θrɛnədi/ *n* treno, *m*

**thresh** /θrɛʃ/ *vt* trillar, desgranar. —*vi* trillar el grano. **to t. out,** ventilar

**threshing** /'θrɛʃɪŋ/ *n* trilla, *f.* **t. floor,** era, *f.* **t. machine,** trilladora, *f*

**threshold** /'θrɛʃould/ *n* umbral, *m; Psychol.* limen, *m; Fig.* comienzo, principio, *m;* (entrance) entrada, *f.* **to cross the t.,** atravesar (or pisar) los umbrales

**thrice** /θrais/ *adv* tres veces

**thrift** /θrɪft/ *n* frugalidad, parsimonia, *f*

**thriftless** /'θrɪftlɪs/ *a* malgastador, manirroto

**thrifty** /'θrɪfti/ *a* frugal, económico

**thrill** /θrɪl/ *n* estremecimiento, *m;* emoción, *f.* —*vt* conmover, emocionar; penetrar. —*vi* estremecerse, emocionarse

**thriller** /'θrɪlər/ *n* libro, *m,* (or comedia, *f)* sensacional; (detective novel) novela policíaca, *f*

**thrilling** /'θrɪlɪŋ/ *a* sensacional, espeluznante; (moving) emocionante, conmovedor

**thrive** /θraiv/ *vi* prosperar, medrar; enriquecerse, tener éxito; (grow) desarrollarse, robustecerse; florecer; (of plants) acertar

**thriving** /'θraivɪŋ/ *a* próspero; floreciente; robusto, vigoroso

**throat** /θrout/ *n* garganta, *f;* orificio, *m;* (narrow entry) paso, *m.* **sore t.,** dolor de garganta, *m.* **to cut one's t.,** cortarse la garganta. **to take by the t.,** asir (or agarrar) por la garganta

**throat cancer** *n* cáncer de la garganta, *m*

**throaty** /'θrouti/ *a* indistinto, ronco

**throb** /θrɒb/ *n* latido, *m;* pulsación, *f;* vibración, *f; Fig.* estremecimiento, *m.* —*vi* palpitar, latir; vibrar

**throbbing** /'θrɒbɪŋ/ *n* pulsación, *f;* vibración, *f.* —*a* palpitante; vibrante. **t. pain,** dolor pungente, *m*

**throe** /θrou/ *n* dolor, *m,* agonía, angustia, *f.* **in the throes of,** en medio de; luchando con; en las garras de. **throes of childbirth,** dolores de parto, *m pl.* **throes of death,** agonía de la muerte, *f*

**thrombosis** /θrɒm'bousɪs/ *n Med.* trombosis, *f*

**throne** /θroun/ *n* trono, *m;* (royal power) corona, *f,* poder real, *m.* —*vt* elevar al trono. **speech from the t.,** el discurso de la corona, *m*

**throng** /θrɔŋ/ *n* muchedumbre, multitud, *f.* —*vi* apiñarse remolinarse, acudir. —*vt* atestar, llenar de bote en bote

**throstle** /'θrɒsəl/ *n Ornith.* tordo, malvís, *m*

**throttle** /'θrɒtl/ *n Mech.* regulador, *m; Auto.* estrangulador, *m; Inf.* garganta, *f.* —*vt* estrangular; *Fig.* ahogar, suprimir. **to open ( close) the t.,** abrir (cerrar) el estrangulador

**throttling** /'θrɒtlɪŋ/ *n* estrangulación, *f*

**through** /θru/ *prep* por; al través de; de un lado a otro de; por medio de; (between) entre; por causa de; gracias a. —*adv* al través; de un lado a otro; (whole) entero, todo; (from beginning to end) desde el principio hasta el fin; (to the end) hasta el fin. —*a* (of passages, etc.) que va desde... hasta...; (of trains) directo. **to look t. the window,** mirar por la ventana, asomarse a la ventana. **to be wet t.,** estar calado hasta los huesos; estar muy mojado. **to carry t.,** llevar a cabo. **to fall t.,** caer por; (fail) fracasar. **to sleep the whole night t.,** dormir durante toda la noche, dormir la noche entera. **t. and t.,** completamente. **through the length and breadth of,** a lo largo y a lo ancho de, hasta los últimos rincones de. **t. traffic,** tráfico directo, *m.* **t. train,** tren directo, *m*

**throughout** /θru'aut/ *prep* por todo; durante todo. —*adv* completamente; (from beginning to end) desde el principio hasta el fin; (everywhere) en todas partes

**throw** /θrou/ *vt* arrojar, lanzar, echar; (fire) disparar; (pottery) plasmar; (knock down) derribar; (slough) mudar (la piel); (cast off) despojarse de; (a rider) desmontar; (a glance) echar, dirigir (una mirada, etc.); (silk) torcer; (dice) echar; (light) dirigir, echar. **to t. oneself at the head of,** echarse a la cabeza de. **to t. open,** abrir de par en par; abrir. **to t. overboard,** *Naut.* echar al mar; desechar; (desert) abandonar. **to t. about,** esparcir, desparramar; derrochar. **to t. aside,** echar a un lado, desechar; abandonar, dejar. **to t. away,** tirar; desechar; (spend) malgastar, derrochar; (waste) sacrificar; (of opportunities) malograr, perder. **to t. back,** devolver; echar hacia atrás. **to t. down,** derribar, dar en el suelo con; echar abajo; (arms) rendir. **to t. down the glove,** arrojar el guante. **to t. oneself down,** tumbarse, echarse; (descend) echarse abajo. **to t. oneself down from,** arrojarse de. **to t. in,** echar dentro; (give extra) añadir; (the clutch) embragar; insertar; (a remark) hacer (una observación). **to t. off,** despojarse de; quitarse; (refuse) rechazar; sacudirse; (get rid of) despedir; (renounce) renunciar; (exhale) emitir; despedir; (verses) improvisar. **to t. on,** echar sobre; (garments) ponerse. **to t. oneself upon,** lanzarse sobre. **to t. out,** expeler; hacer salir; plantar en la calle; (utter) proferir, soltar; (one's chest) inflar. **to t. over,** (desert) abandonar, dejar. **to t. up,** (build) levantar; lanzar en el aire; (a post, etc.) renunciar (a), abandonar; vomitar

**throw** /θrou/ *n* echada, *f;* tiro, *m;* (at dice) lance, *m;* jugada, *f;* (wrestling) derribo, *m.* **within a stone's t.,** a tiro de piedra. **t.-back,** retroceso, *m; Biol.* atavismo, *m*

**thrower** /'θrouər/ *n* tirador (-ra), lanzador (-ra)

**throwing** /'θrouɪŋ/ *n* lanzamiento, *m,* lanzada, *f.* **t. the hammer,** lanzamiento del martillo, *m*

**thrum** /θrʌm/ *vt* and *vi* tocar mal; (of keyed instruments) teclear; (of stringed instruments) rascar las cuerdas (de)

**thrush** /θrʌʃ/ *n Ornith.* tordo, *m*

**thrust** /θrʌst/ *n* empujón, *m;* (with a sword) estocada, *f;* (fencing) golpe, *m;* (with a lance) bote, *m;* ataque, *m;* asalto, *m.* —*vt* empujar; (put) meter; (insert) introducir; (pierce) atravesar; (out, through, of the head, etc.) asomar. —*vi* acometer, atacar, embestir; meterse, introducirse; (intrude) entrometerse; (fencing) dar un golpe. **to t. aside,** empujar a un lado; (proposals) rechazar. **to t. back,** hacer retroceder, empujar hacia atrás; (words) tragarse; (thoughts) apartar, rechazar. **to t. down,** empujar hacia abajo; hacer bajar; *Fig.* reprimir. **to t. forward,** empujar hacia delante; hacer seguir. **to t. oneself forward,** adelantarse; *Fig.* ponerse delante de los otros, darse importancia. **to t. in,** introducir; (stick) hincar; (insert) intercalar. **to t. on,** hacer seguir; empujar sobre; (garments) ponerse rápidamente. **to t. oneself in,** introducirse; entrometerse. **to t. out,** echar fuera; hacer salir, echar; expulsar; (the tongue) sacar (la lengua); (the head, etc.) asomar. **to t. through,** atravesar; (pierce) traspasar. **to t. one's way through,** abrirse paso por. **to t. upon,** imponer, hacer aceptar

**thud** /θʌd/ *n* sonido sordo, *m*; golpe sordo, *m*

**thug** /θʌg/ *n* asesino, criminal, *m*

**thumb** /θʌm/ *n* pulgar, *m*. —*vt* hojear; ensuciar con los dedos. **under the t. of,** *Fig.* en el poder de. **t. index,** índice pulgar, *m*. **t.-mark,** huella del dedo, *f*. **t.-screw,** tornillo de orejas, *m*, **t.-stall,** dedil, *m*. **t.-tack,** chinche, *m*

**thump** /θʌmp/ *n* golpe, porrazo, *m*. —*vt* and *vi* golpear, aporrear; (the ground, of rabbits) zapatear

**thunder** /'θʌndər/ *n* trueno, *m*; (of hooves, etc.) estampido, *m*; estruendo, *m*. —*vi* tronar; retumbar; *Fig.* fulminar. —*vt* gritar en una voz de trueno, rugir. **to t. along,** avanzar como el trueno; galopar ruidosamente. **t.-clap,** trueno, *m*. **t.-cloud,** nube de tormenta, *f*, nubarrón, *m*. **t.-storm,** tronada, *f*. **t. struck,** muerto, estupefacto. **to be thunderstruck,** quedarse frío

**thunderbolt** /'θʌndər,boult/ *n* rayo, *m*

**thunderer** /'θʌndərər/ *n* fulminador, *m*. **the Thunderer,** Júpiter tonante, Júpiter tronante, *m*; el «Times» londinense, *m*

**Thuringia** /θʊ'rɪndʒiə/ Turingia, *f*

**Thursday** /'θɜːrzdei/ *n* jueves, *m*. **Holy T.,** Jueves Santo, *m*

**thus** /ðʌs/ *adv* así; de este modo; en estos términos; hasta este punto. **t. far,** hasta ahora; hasta este punto; hasta aquí. **Thus it is that...,** Así es que...

**thwack** /θwæk/ *n* golpe, *m*; *vt* golpear

**thwart** /θwɔrt/ *vt* frustrar, impedir

**thy** /ðai/ *poss a* tu, *mf*; tus, *m pl*, and *f pl*

**thyme** /taim/ *n Bot.* tomillo, *m*

**thymus** /'θaiməs/ *n Anat.* timo, *m*

**thyroid** /'θairɔid/ *a* tiroideo. **t. gland,** tiroides, *f*

**thyself** /ðai'self/ *poss pron* tu mismo, *m*; tu misma, *f*; (with prep.) tí mismo, *m*; tí misma, *f*; (in a reflexive verb) te

**tiara** /ti'ærə, -'ɑrə/ *n* tiara, *f*

**Tiberias** /tai'bɪəriəs/ Tiberíades, *f*

**Tibetan** /tɪ'betn̩/ *a* and *n* tibetano (-na); (language) tibetano, *m*

**tibia** /'tɪbiə/ *n Anat.* tibia, *f*

**tic** /tɪk/ *n* (twitch) tic nervioso, *m*

**tick** /tɪk/ *n Ent.* ácaro, *m*; (sound) tictac, *m*; (cover) funda de colchón, *f*; *Inf.* fiado, crédito, *m*; (mark) marca, *f vi* hacer tictac. —*vt* poner una marca contra. **on t.,** *Inf.* al fiado. **to t. off,** poner una marca contra; *Inf.* reñir. **to t. over,** *Auto.* andar, marchar

**ticket** /'tɪkɪt/ *n* billete, *m*; (for an entertainment) entrada, localidad, *f*; (label) etiqueta, *f*; (pawn) papeleta de empeño, *f*; (for luggage) talón, *m*; (*Polit.* U.S.A.) candidatura, *f*, *vt* marcar. **to take one's t.,** sacar el billete (for an entertainment or the entrada, *f*). **excursion t.,** billete de excursión, *m*. **return t.,** billete de ida y vuelta, *m*. **season t.,** billete de abono, *m*. **single t.,** billete sencillo, *m*. **t. agency,** (for travel) agencia de viajes, *f*; (for entertainments) agencia de teatros, *f*. **t. collector or inspector,** revisor, *m*. **t. holder,** tenedor de billete, *m*; abonado (-da). **t. office,** (railway) despacho de billetes, *m*; taquilla, *f*. **t.-of-leave,** libertad condicional, *f*. **t. punch,** sacabocados, *m*; (on tramcars) clasificador de billetes, *m*

**ticking** /'tɪkɪŋ/ *n* (sound) tictac, *m*; (cloth) cotí, *m*

**tickle** /'tɪkəl/ *vt* hacer cosquillas (a), cosquillear; irri-

tar; (gratify) halagar; (amuse) divertir. —*vi* tener cosquillas; hacer cosquillas; ser irritante

**ticklish** /'tɪklɪʃ/ *a* cosquilloso; (of persons) difícil, vidrioso; (of affairs) espinoso, delicado

**tidal** /'taidl/ *a* de marea. **t. wave,** marejada, *f*; *Fig.* ola popular, *f*

**tidbit** /'tɪd,bɪt/ *n* See **titbit**

**tiddlywinks** /'tɪdli,wɪŋks/ *n* juego de la pulga, *m*

**tide** /taid/ *n* marea, *f*; (season) tiempo, *m*, estación, *f*; (trend) corriente, *f*; (progress) curso, *m*; marcha, *f*. —*vi* (with over) vencer, superar; aguardar la ocasión. **to go against the t.,** ir contra la corriente. **to go with the t.,** seguir la corriente. **high t.,** marea alta, *f*. **low t.,** marea baja, *f*, bajamar, *m*. **neap t.,** marea muerta, *f*. **t. mark,** lengua del agua, *f*

**tideless** /'taidlɪs/ *a* sin mareas

**tidily** /'taidli/ *adv* aseadamente; en orden, metódicamente

**tidiness** /'taidnɪs/ *n* aseo, *m*; buen orden, *m*

**tidings** /'taidɪŋz/ *n pl* noticias, nuevas, *f pl*

**tidy** /'taidi/ *a* aseado; metódico, en orden; pulcro; *Inf.* considerable. —*vt* poner en orden, asear; limpiar; (oneself) arreglarse

**tie** /tai/ *n* lazo, *m*, atadura, *f*; (knot) nudo, *m*; (for the neck) corbata, *f*; *Sports.* empate, *m*; *Mus.* ligado, *m*; *Archit.* tirante, *m*; (spiritual bond) lazo, *m*; (burden) carga, responsabilidad, *f*; **tie clasp,** pisa corbata, *mf*. **tie-pin,** alfiler de corbata, *m*. **tie seller,** corbatero (-ra)

**tie** /tai/ *vt* atar; (bind) ligar; (lace) lacear; (a knot) hacer; (with a knot) anudar; (unite) unir; (*Fig.* bind) constreñir, obligar; (limit) limitar, restringir; (occupy) ocupar, entretener; (hamper) estorbar, impedir. —*vi* atarse; *Sports.* empatar. **to tie one's tie,** hacer la corbata. **to tie down,** atar a; limitar; obligar. **They tied him down to a chair,** Le ataron a una silla. **to tie together,** enlazar, ligar; unir. **to tie up,** liar, atar; (wrap) envolver; recoger; *Naut.* amarrar, atracar; (restrict) limitar, restringir; (invest) invertir

**tie-breaker** /'tai,breikər/ *n* desempate, *m*

**tier** /'tɪər/ *n* fila, hilera, *f*. **in tiers,** en gradas; (of a dress) en volantes

**tiff** /tɪf/ *n* disgusto, *m*

**tiger** /'taigər/ *n* tigre, *m*. **t.-cat,** gato (-ta) atigrado (-da). **t.-lily,** tigridia, *f*

**tigerish** /'taigərɪʃ/ *a* atigrado, de tigre; salvaje, feroz

**tight** /tait/ *a* apretado; (not leaky) hermético, impermeable; (taut) tieso, tirante; (narrow) estrecho; (trim) compacto; (of clothes) muy ajustado; (shut) bien cerrado; *Naut.* estanco; (risky) peligroso, difícil; (miserly) tacaño; (of money, goods) escaso; **to be t.-fisted,** ser una como un puño. **to hold t.,** agarrar fuerte. **t. corner,** *Fig.* aprieto, lance apretado, *m*. **t.-rope,** cuerda de volantinero, *f*. **t.-rope walker,** alambrista, *mf*; volantinero (-ra), bailarín de la cuerda floja, *m*. **t.-rope walker's pole,** balancín, *m*

**tighten** /'taitn/ *vt* estrechar, apretar; (stretch) estirar; (of saddle girths) cinchar. —*vi* estrecharse; estirarse

**tightly** /'taitli/ *adv* estrechamente

**tightness** /'taitnɪs/ *n* estrechez, *f*; tirantez, tensión, *f*; (feeling of constriction) opresión, *f*;

**tights** /taits/ *n pl* mallas, *f pl*

**tigress** /'taigrɪs/ *n* tigresa, *f*

**tile** /tail/ *n* teja, *f*; (for flooring) baldosa, losa, *f*; (ornamental) azulejo, *m*; (hat) chistera, *f*. —*vt* tejar; embaldosar. **t. floor,** enlosado, embaldosado, *m*. **t. manufacturer,** tejero, *m*. **t. works** or **yard,** tejar, *m*, (Colombia) galpón *m*

**tiler** /'tailər/ *n* solador, *m*; tejero, *m*

**till** /tɪl/ *n* (for money) cajón, *m*. —*vt Agr.* cultivar, labrar. —*prep* hasta. —*conjunc* hasta que

**tillable** /'tɪləbl/ *a* laborable

**tillage** /'tɪlɪdʒ/ *n* labranza, *f*, cultivo, *m*; tierra de labrantío, *f*

**tiller** /'tɪlər/ *n Agr.* labrador, *m*; *Bot.* mugrón, renuevo, vástago, *m*; *Naut.* caña del timón, *f*

**tilling** /'tɪlɪŋ/ *n Agr.* cultivo, laboreo, *m*

**tilt** /tɪlt/ *n* inclinación, *f*; ladeo, *m*; (fight) torneo, *m*, justa, *f*. —*vt* inclinar; ladear; (a drinking vessel) empinar. —*vi* inclinarse; ladearse; (fight) justar. **to t. against,** *Fig.* arremeter contra, atacar. **at full t.,** a todo correr. **t. hammer,** martinete de báscula, *m.* **t.-yard,** palestra, *f*

**tilting** /'tɪltɪŋ/ *n* incinación, *f;* (fighting) justas, *f pl.* —*a* inclinado

**timber** /'tɪmbər/ *n* madera de construcción, *f;* (trees) árboles de monte, *m pl;* bosque, *m;* (beam) viga, *f; Naut.* cuaderna, *f.* —*vt* enmaderar. **t. line,** límite del bosque maderable, *m.* **t. merchant,** maderero, *m.* **t. wolf,** lobo gris, *m.* **t. work,** maderaje, *m.* **t. yard,** maderería, *f,* corral de madera, *m*

**timbered** /'tɪmbərd/ *a* enmaderado; (with trees) arbolado

**timbre** /'tæmbər, 'tɪm-/ *n Mus.* timbre, *m*

**timbrel** /'tɪmbrəl/ *n Mus.* tamborete, tamboril, *m*

**time** /taɪm/ *n* (in general) tiempo, *m;* (epoch) época, edad, *f;* tiempos, *m pl;* (of the year) estación, *f;* (by the clock) hora, *f;* (lifetime) vida, *f;* (particular moment of time) momento, *m;* (occasion) sazón, ocasión, *f;* (day) día, *m;* (time allowed) plazo, *m;* (in repetition) vez, *f; Mus.* compás, *m; Mil.* paso, *m.* —*vt* ajustar al tiempo; hacer con oportunidad; (regulate) regular; calcular el tiempo que se emplea en hacer una cosa; (a blow) calcular. **all the t.,** todo el tiempo; continuamente, sin cesar. **a long t.,** mucho tiempo. **a long t. ago,** mucho tiempo ha, hace mucho tiempo. **at a t.,** a la vez, al mismo tiempo; (of period) en una época. **at any t.,** a cualquier hora; en cualquier momento; (when you like) cuando gustes. **at no t.,** jamás, nunca. **at some t.,** alguna vez; en alguna época. **at some t. or another,** un día u otro; en una u otra ocasión; en alguna época. **at that t.,** en aquella época; en la sazón; en aquel instante. **at the one t.,** de una vez. **at the present t.,** en la actualidad, al presente. **at the proper t.,** a su debido tiempo; a la hora señalada; a la hora conveniente. **at the same t.,** al mismo tiempo. **at the same t. as,** mientras, a medida que; al mismo instante que, **at times,** a veces, en ocasiones. **behind the times,** *Fig.* atrasado de noticias; pasado de moda. **behind t.,** atrasado. **by that t.,** para entonces. **every t.,** cada vez; siempre. **for some t.,** durante algún tiempo. **for some t. past,** de algún tiempo a esta parte. **for the t. being,** de momento, por ahora, por lo pronto. **from this t.,** desde hoy; desde esta fecha. **from this t. forward,** de hoy en adelante. **from t. to t.,** de vez en cuando, de cuando en cuando, de tarde en tarde. **in a month's t.,** en un mes. **in a short t.,** en breve, dentro de poco. **in good t.,** puntualmente; temprano. **in my t.,** en mis días, en mis tiempos. **in olden times,** antiguamente, en otros tiempos. **in the course of t.,** andando el tiempo, en el transcurso de los años. **in the t. of,** en la época de. **in t.,** (promptly) a tiempo; con el tiempo. **in t. to come,** en el porvenir. **It is t. to...,** Es hora de.... **many times,** frecuentemente, muchas veces. **Once upon a t.,** Érase una vez, Una vez había, Érase que érase, Érase que se era. **Since t. out of mind,** Desde tiempo inmemorial. **the last (next) t.,** la última (próxima) vez. **this t. of year,** esta estación del año. **T. hangs heavy on his hands,** El tiempo se le hace interminable. **T. flies,** El tiempo vuela. **T. will tell!** ¡El tiempo lo dirá! ¡Veremos lo que veremos! **What t. is it?** ¿Qué hora es? **The t. is...,** La hora es... **within a given t.,** dentro de un plazo dado. **to be out of t.,** estar fuera de compás. **to gain t.,** ganar tiempo. **to have a good t.,** pasarlo bien, divertirse. **to have a bad t.,** pasarlo mal; *Inf.* tener un mal cuarto de hora. **to have no t. to,** no tener tiempo para + noun or pronoun, no tener tiempo de + infinitive. **to keep t.,** guardar el compás. **to kill t.,** engañar (or entretener) el tiempo. **to mark t.,** marcar el paso; *Fig.* hacer tiempo. **to pass the t.,** pasar el rato; pasar el tiempo. **to pass the t. of day,** saludar. **to serve one's t.,** (to a trade) servir el aprendizaje; (in prison) cumplir su condena; *Mil.* hacer el servicio militar. **to take t. to,** tomar tiempo para. **to take t. by the forelock,** asir la ocasión por la melena. **to waste t.,** perder el tiempo. **t. exposure,** pose, *f.* **t. fuse,** espoleta de tiempo, espoleta graduada, *f.* **t.-honored,** tradicional, consagrado por el tiempo. **t.-keeper,** capataz, *m;* reloj, *m.* **t.-saving,** que ahorra el tiempo. **t.-server,** lameculos, *mf.* **t.-signal,** señales horarias, *f pl.* **t.-table,** horario, *m;* itinerario, programa, *m* (railway) guía de ferrocarriles, *f.* **t. to come,** porvenir, *m,* lo venidero

**timed** /taɪmd/ *a* calculado; **(ill-)** intempestivo; **(well-)** oportuno

**timeless** /'taɪmlɪs/' *a* eterno

**timeliness** /'taɪmlɪnɪs/ *n* tempestividad, oportunidad, *f*

**timely** /'taɪmli/ *a* oportuno

**timepiece** /'taɪm,pis/ *n* reloj, *m*

**time zone** *n* huso esférico, huso horario, *m*

**timid** /'tɪmɪd/ *a* tímido, asustadizo, medroso; (shy) vergonzoso

**timidity** /tɪ'mɪdɪti/ *n* timidez, *f;* vergüenza, *f*

**timing** /'taɪmɪŋ/ *n* medida del tiempo, *f; Mech.* regulación, *f;* (timetable) horario, *m*

**timorous** /'tɪmərəs/ *a* timorato, apocado, asustadizo

**timorousness** /'tɪmərəsnɪs/ *n* encogimiento, *m,* timidez, *f*

**tin** /tɪn/ *n* (metal) estaño, *m;* (container) lata, *f;* (sheet) hojalata, *f;* (money) plata, *f.* —*vt* estañar; (place in tins) envasar en lata; cubrir con hojalata, hoja de aluminio, *f.* **tin-foil,** papel de estaño, *m.* **tin hat,** casco de acero, *m.* **tin opener,** abrelatas, abridor de latas, *m.* **tin-plate,** hojalata, *f.* **tin soldier,** soldado de plomo, *m.* **tin ware,** hojalatería, *f*

**tincture** /'tɪŋktʃər/ *n* tintura, *f,* tinte, *m; Med.* tintura, *f;* (trace) dejo, *m;* (veneer) capa, *f.* —*vt* teñir, tinturar

**tinder** /'tɪndər/ *n* yesca, *f.* **t. box,** yescas, lumbres, *f pl*

**tinge** /tɪndʒ/ *n* tinte, matiz, *m; Fig.* dejo, toque, *m.* —*vt* matizar, tinturar; *Fig.* tocar

**tingle** /'tɪŋgəl/ *n* picazón, comezón, *f;* (thrill) estremecimiento, *m.* —*vi* picar; (of ears) zumbar; (thrill) estremecerse (de); vibrar

**tingling** /'tɪŋglɪŋ/ *n* picazón, *f;* (of the ears) zumbido, *m;* (thrill) estremecimiento, *m*

**tinker** /'tɪŋkər/ *n* calderero remendón, *m.* —*vt* remendar. —*vi* chafallar. **to t. with,** jugar con

**tinkle** /'tɪŋkəl/ *n* tilín, retintín, *m;* campanilleo, *m;* cencerreo, *m.* —*vi* tintinar. —*vt* hacer tintinar

**tinkling** /'tɪŋklɪŋ/ *n* retintín, tintineo, *m;* campanilleo, *m*

**tinned** /tɪnd/ *a* (of food) en lata, en conserva

**tinsel** /'tɪnsəl/ *n* oropel, *m;* (cloth) lama de oro o plata, *f,* brocadillo, *m; Fig.* oropel, *m.* —*a* de oropel; de brocadillo; *Fig.* charro. —*vt* adornar con oropel

**tinsmith** /'tɪn,smɪθ/ *n* hojalatero, estañador, *m*

**tint** /tɪnt/ *n* tinta, *f,* color, *m;* matiz, *m;* tinte, *m.* —*vt* colorar, teñir; matizar

**tinting** /'tɪntɪŋ/ *n* tintura, *f,* teñido, *m*

**tiny** /'taɪni/ *a* diminuto, minúsculo, menudo, chiquito

**tip** /tɪp/ *n* punta, *f;* cabo, *m,* extremidad, *f;* (of an umbrella, etc.) regatón, *m;* (of a lance) borne, *f;* (of a cigarette) boquilla, *f;* (of a shoe) puntera, *f;* (of a finger) yema, *f;* (for rubbish) depósito de basura, *m;* (gratuity) propina, *f;* (information) informe oportuno, *m;* (tap) golpecito, *m.* **to have on the tip of one's tongue,** tener en la punta de la lengua. **tip-cart,** volquete, *m.* **tip-up seat,** asiento plegable, *m*

**tip** /tɪp/ *vt* inclinar; volcar, voltear; (drinking vessel) empinar; poner regatón, etc. (a); *Poet.* tocar, golpear ligeramente; (reward) dar propina (a). —*vi* inclinarse; (topple) tambalearse; (reward) dar propina. **to tip the wink,** guiñar el ojo (a). **to tip off,** (liquids) echar; hacer caer; (inform) decir en secreto; informar oportunamente. **to tip over,** *vt* volcar; hacer caer. —*vi* volcarse; caer; (of a boat) zozobrar. **to tip up,** *vt* (a seat) levantar; (money) proporcionar (el dinero); (upset) volcar; hacer perder el equilibrio. —*vi* volcarse; (of a seat) levantarse; (lose the balance) perder el equilibrio

**tipple** /'tɪpəl/ *n* bebida, *f.* —*vt* beber, sorber. —*vi* empinar el codo

**tippler** /'tɪplər/ *n* borracho (-cha)

**tipsily** /'tɪpsɪli/ *adv* como borracho

**tipsiness** /'tɪpsɪnɪs/ *n* borrachera, *f*

**tipsy** /'tɪpsi/ *a* achispado, algo borracho. **to be t.,** estar entre dos luces, estar entre dos velas

**tiptoe** /'tɪp,tou/ **(on)** *adv* de puntillas; *Fig.* excitado, ansioso. **to stand on t.,** ponerse de puntillas, empinarse

**tirade** /'taɪreɪd/ *n* diatriba, *f*

**tire** /tai³r/ *n* (of a cart, etc.) llanta, *f; Auto.* neumático, *m;* (of a perambulator, etc.) rueda de goma, *f.* **balloon t.,** neumático balón, *m.* **pneumatic t.,** neumático, *m.* **slack t.,** neumático desinflado, *m.* **solid t.,** neumático macizo, *m.* **spare t.,** neumático de recambio (or de repuesto), *m.* **t. burst,** estallido de un neumático, *m.* **t. valve,** válvula de cámara (del neumático), *f*

**tire** /tai³r/ *vt* cansar, fatigar; (bore) aburrir. —*vi* cansarse, fatigarse; aburrirse. **to be tired of,** estar cansado de. **to grow tired,** empezar a cansarse. **to t. out,** rendir de cansancio

**tired** /tai³rd/ *a* cansado, fatigado. **to be sick and t. of,** estar hasta la coronilla (de), (of persons) con. **t. of,** cansado de; disgustado de

**tiredness** /'tai³rdnɪs/ *n* cansancio, *m,* fatiga, *f;* aburrimiento, *m*

**tireless** /'tai³rlɪs/ *a* infatigable, incansable

**tirelessly** /'tai³rlɪsli/ *adv* sin tregua, sin cesar

**tiresome** /'tai³rsəm/ *a* fastidioso, molesto, pesado; (dull) aburrido

**tiresomeness** /'tai³rsəmnɪs/ *n* pesadez, *f,* fastidio, *m;* tedio, aburrimiento, *m*

**tiring** /'tai³rɪŋ/ *a* fatigoso

**tissue** /'tɪʃu/ *n* (cloth) tisú, *m,* lama, *f;* (paper) pañuelito *m; Biol.* tejido, *m;* (series) serie, sarta, *f.* **t. paper,** papel de seda, *m*

**tit** /tɪt/ *n Ornith.* paro, *m.* **tit for tat,** tal para cual

**Titan** /'taitn/ *n* titán, *m*

**titanic** /tai'tænɪk/ *a* titánico

**titbit** /'tɪt,bɪt/ *n* golosina, *f*

**tithe** /taið/ *n* décima, *f;* fracción, pequeña parte, *f, vt* diezmar. **t. gatherer,** diezmero (-ra)

**titillate** /'tɪtl,eit/ *vt* titilar, estimular

**titivate** /'tɪtə,veit/ *vi* arreglarse

**title** /'taitl/ *n* título, *m;* (right) derecho, *m;* documento, *m.* **to give a t.,** intitular; ennoblecer. **t. deed,** títulos de propiedad, *m.* **t. page,** portada, *f.* **t. role,** papel principal, *m*

**titter** /'tɪtər/ *vi* reírse disimuladamente. —*n* risa disimulada, *f*

**tittle** /'tɪtl/ *n* adarme, tilde, ápice, *m*

**titular** /'tɪtʃələr/ *a* titular; nominal

**to** /tu/ *unstressed* tʊ, tə/ *prep* a; (as far as) hasta; (in the direction of) en dirección a, hacia; (with indirect object) a; (until) hasta; (compared with) en comparación con, comparado con; (against) contra; (according to) según; (as) como; (in) en; (so that, in order to, for the purpose of) para; (indicating possession) a, de; (of time by the clock) menos; (by) por; (before verbs of motion or which imply motion) a (sometimes para); (before some other verbs) de; en; (before verbs of beginning, inviting, exhorting, obliging) a; (indicating indirect object) a; (before a subjunctive or infinitive indicating future action or obligation) que. **To** is often not translated. With most Spanish infinitives no separate translation is necessary, e.g. leer, decir, to read, to speak. Some verbs are always followed by a preposition (e.g. *to begin to speak,* empezar a hablar, etc.). —*adv* (shut) cerrado. **to come to,** volver en sí. **to lie to,** *Naut.* ponerse a la capa. **to and from,** de un lado a otro. **face to face,** cara a cara. **He has been a good friend to them,** Ha sido un buen amigo para ellos. **That is new to me,** Eso es nuevo para mí. **He went to London,** Se fue a Londres. **to go to France ( Canada),** ir a Francia (al Canadá). **the road to Madrid,** la carretera de Madrid. **She kept the secret to herself,** Guardó el secreto para sí. **to go to the dentist,** ir al dentista. **We give it to them,** Se lo damos a ellos. **It belongs to me,** Pertenece a mí. **What does it matter to you?** ¿Qué te importa a tí? **I wish to see him,** Quiero verle. **They did it to help us,** Lo hicieron para ayudarnos. **I have to go to see her,** Tengo que ir a verla. **to this day,** hasta hoy, hasta el presente. **It is a quarter to six,** Son las seis menos cuarto. **to the last shilling,** hasta el último chelín. **the next to me,** el que me sigue. **closed to the public,** cerrado para el público

**toad** /toud/ *n* sapo, *m*

**toadstool** /'toud,stul/ *n* hongo, *m.* **poisonous t.,** seta venenosa, *f*

**toady** /'toudi/ *n* lameculos, *mf* adulador (-ra). —*vt* lamer el culo (a), adular

**toast** /toust/ *n Cul.* tostada, *f;* (drink) brindis, *m.* —*vt* tostar; brindar, beber a la salud de. —*vi* brindar. **buttered t.,** mantecada, *f.* **t.-rack,** portatostadas, *m*

**toaster** /'toustər/ *n* (device) tostador, *m;* (person) brindador, *m*

**toasting** /'toustɪŋ/ *n* tostadura, *f,* tueste, *m,* a de tostar. **t.-fork,** tostadera, *f*

**tobacco** /tə'bækou/ *n* tabaco, *m.* —*a* tabacalero. **black** or **cut t.,** picadura, *f.* **leaf t.,** tabaco de hoja, *m.* **mild t.,** tabaco flojo, *m.* **pipe t.,** tabaco de pipa, *m.* **plug t.,** tabaco para mascar, *m.* **strong t.,** tabaco fuerte, *m.* **Turkish t.,** tabaco turco, *m.* **Virginian t.,** tabaco rubio, *m.* **t.-pipe,** pipa (de tabaco), *f.* **t.-pipe cleaner,** escobillón para limpiar pipas, *m.* **t. plantation,** tabacal, *m.* **t. planter,** tabacalero (-ra). **t. poisoning,** tabaquismo, *m.* **t.-pouch** or **jar,** tabaquera, *f*

**tobacconist** /tə'bækənɪst/ *n* tabaquero (-ra). **tobacconist's shop,** tabaquería, *f*

**toboggan** /tə'bɒgən/ *n* tobogán, *m.* —*vi* ir en tobogán. **t. run,** pista de tobogán, *f*

**tocsin** /'tɒksɪn/ *n* rebato, *m*

**today** /tə'dei/ *adv* hoy; ahora, actualmente, al presente, hoy día. —*n* el día de hoy. **from t.,** desde hoy. **from t. forward,** de hoy en adelante

**toddle** /'tɒdl/ *vi* hacer pinos, empezar a andar; (stroll) dar una vuelta; (leave) marcharse

**toddy** /'tɒdi/ *n* ponche, *m*

**toe** /tou/ *n* dedo del pie, *m;* (cloven) pezuña, *f;* uña, *f;* (of furniture) base, *f,* pie, *m;* (of stockings, shoes) punta, *f.* **He stepped on my toe,** Me pisó el dedo del pie. **big toe,** dedo pulgar del pie, dedo gordo del pie, *m.* **little toe,** dedo pequeño del pie, *m.* **to toe the line,** ponerse en la raya; *Fig.* cumplir con su deber. **toe-cap,** puntera, *f.* **toe-dancing,** baile de puntillas, *m.* **toe-nail,** uña del dedo del pie, *f*

**toffee** /'tɔfi/ *n* caramelo, *m*

**toga** /'tougə/ *n* toga, *f*

**together** /tə'gɛðər/ *adv* junto; (uninterruptedly) sin interrupción; (in concert) simultáneamente, a la vez, al mismo tiempo; (consecutively) seguido. **t. with,** con; junto con; en compañía de; (simultaneously) a la vez que

**toil** /tɔil/ *n* labor, *f,* trabajo, *m —pl.* **toils,** lazos, *m pl; Fig.* redes, *f pl.* —*vi* trabajar, afanarse. **to t. along,** caminar penosamente (por); adelantar con dificultad. **to t. up,** subir penosamente

**toiler** /'tɔilər/ *n* trabajador (-ra)

**toilet** /'tɔilɪt/ *n* tocado, *m;* atavío, *m;* vestido, *m;* (w.c.) retrete, excusado, *m;* (for ladies) tocador, *m.* **to make one's t.,** arreglarse. **t. case,** neceser, *m.* **t.-paper,** papel higiénico, *m.* **t.-powder,** polvos de arroz, *m pl.* **t. roll,** rollo de papel higiénico, *m.* **t.-set,** juego de tocador, *m.* **t. soap,** jabón de olor, jabón de tocador, *m*

**toiling** /'tɔilɪŋ/ *n* trabajo duro, *m, a* laborioso, trabajador

**token** /'toukən/ *n* señal, muestra, *f;* prueba, *f;* (presage) síntoma, indicio, *m;* (remembrance) recuerdo, *m.* **as a t. of,** en señal de; como recuerdo de

**Tokyo** /'touki,ou/ Tokio, *m*

**tolerable** /'tɒlərəbəl/ *a* tolerable, soportable, llevadero; (fairly good) mediano, mediocre, regular

**tolerably** /'tɒlərəbli/ *adv* bastante

**tolerance** /'tɒlərəns/ *n* tolerancia, *f;* paciencia, indulgencia, *f*

**tolerant** /'tɒlərənt/ *a* tolerante; indulgente

**tolerate** /'tɒlə,reit/ *vt* tolerar, sufrir, soportar; permitir

**toleration** /,tɒlə'reiʃən/ *n* tolerancia, *f;* indulgencia, paciencia, *f.* **religious t.,** libertad de cultos, *f*

**toll** /toul/ *n* (of a bell) tañido, doble, *m;* (for passage) peaje, portazgo, *m;* (for grinding) derecho de molienda, *m.* —*vt* and *vi* doblar, tañer. **to t. the hour,** dar la hora. **t. call,** conferencia telefónica interurbana, llamada a larga distancia, *f.* **t. gate,** barrera de peaje, *f.* **t. house,** oficina de portazgos, *f*

**toll booth** *n* caseta de pago, *f*

**tolling** /'toulɪŋ/ *n* tañido, clamor (de las campanas), *m*

**Tom** /tɒm/ n Tomás, m; (cat) gato, m. **Tom, Dick and Harry,** Fulano, Zutano y Mengano

**tomahawk** /'tɒməˌhɔk/ n hacha de guerra de los indios, f

**tomato** /tə'meitou/ n tomate, jitomate, (Mexico) m. **t. plant,** tomatera, f. **t. sauce,** salsa de tomate, f

**tomb** /tum/ n tumba, f, sepulcro, m

**tombac** /'tɒmbæk/ n tombac, m, tumbaga, f

**tomboy** /'tɒmˌbɔi/ n muchachote, torbellino, m

**tombstone** /'tumˌstoun/ n piedra mortuoria, f, monumento funerario, m

**tome** /toum/ n tomo, volumen, m

**tomfoolery** /ˌtɒm'fuləri/ n necedad, tontería, f; payasada, f

**tommy gun** /'tɒmi/ n pistola automática

**tomorrow** /tə'mɔrou/ adv and n mañana, f. **a fortnight t.,** mañana en quince. **the day after t.,** pasado mañana. **t. afternoon ( morning),** mañana por la tarde (mañana). **T. is Friday,** Mañana es viernes

**ton** /tʌn/ n tonelada, f

**tonality** /tou'næliti/ n tonalidad, f

**tone** /toun/ n tono, m; (Mus. Med. Art.) tono, m; (of the voice) acento, m, entonación, f; (of musical instruments) sonido, m; (shade) matiz, m. —vt entonar; Photo. virar. **to t. down,** vt (of colors) amortiguar; Fig. suavizar, modificar. —vi (Art. Mus.) amortiguarse; Fig. suavizarse, modificarse. **to t. in with,** (of colors) vt armonizar con. —vi armonizarse, corresponder en tono o matiz. **to t. up,** vt subir de color, intensificar el color de; Med. entonar, robustecer. **t. poem,** poema sinfónico, m

**tonelessly** /'tounlisli/ adv sin tono; apáticamente

**tongs** /tɒnz/ n pl tenazas, f pl; tenacillas, f pl. **curling t.,** tenacillas para el pelo, f pl. **sugar t.,** tenacillas para azúcar, f pl

**tongue** /tʌn/ n Anat. lengua, f; (language) idioma, m, lengua, f; (speech) modo de hablar, m, habla, f; Mus. lengüeta, f; (of buckle) diente, m; (of shoe) oreja, f; (of land) lengua, f; (of a bell) badajo, m; (flame) lengua, f. **My t. ran away with me,** Inf. Se me fue la mula. **to give t.,** ladrar. **to hold one's t.,** cerrar el pico, tener la boca. **t. of fire,** lengua de fuego, f. **t. tied,** con impedimento en el habla; turbado, confuso; mudo. **t.-twister,** trabalenguas, m

**-tongued** a de voz...

**tonic** /'tɒnik/ a tónico. —n Med. tónico, reconstituyente, m; Mus. tónica, f

**tonight** /tə'nait/ adv and n esta noche

**tonnage** /'tʌnidʒ/ n tonelaje, porte, m; (duty) derecho de tonelaje, m

**tonner** /'tʌnər/ n Naut. de... toneladas

**tonsil** /'tɒnsəl/ n amígdala, f

**tonsillitis** /ˌtɒnsə'laitis/ n amigdalitis, f

**tonsure** /'tɒnʃər/ n Eccl. tonsura, f, vt tonsurar

**tonsured** /'tɒnʃərd/ a tonsurado

**too** /tu/ adv demasiado; (very) muy; también; además. **too hard,** demasiado difícil, demasiado rígido; (of persons) demasiado duro. **too much,** demasiado. **too often,** con demasiada frecuencia

**tool** /tul/ n herramienta, f; utensilio, m; instrumento, m; (person) criatura, f. —vt labrar con herramienta; (a book) estampar en seco. **t.-bag,** capacho, m. **t. box,** caja de herramientas, f

**tooling** /'tulin/ n (of books) estampación en seco, f

**toot** /tut/ n sonido de bocina, m, vi sonar una bocina

**tooth** /tuθ/ n diente, m; muela, f; (of comb) púa, f; (taste) gusto, paladar, m; (cog) diente de rueda, m; (of saw) diente, m. —vt dentar; mellar. —vi Mech. engranar. **armed to the teeth,** armado hasta los dientes. **double t.,** muela, f. **false teeth,** dentadura postiza, f. **set of teeth,** dentadura, f. **to cut one's teeth,** echar los dientes. **to have a sweet t.,** ser muy goloso. **to show one's teeth,** enseñar los dientes. **t.-brush,** cepillo para los dientes, m. **t. drawing,** extracción de un diente, f. **t.-paste,** pasta dentífrica, f

**toothache** /'tuθˌeik/ n dolor de muelas, m

**toothed** /tuθt/ a con dientes; dentado

**toothless** /'tuθlis/ a desdentado, sin dientes; (of combs) sin púas

**toothpick** /'tuθˌpik/ n mondadientes, m

**top** /tɒp/ n (summit) cima, cumbre, f; (of a tree) copa, f; (of the head) coronilla, f; (of a page) cabeza,

f; (crest) copete, m, cresta, f; (surface) superficie, f; (of a wall) coronamiento, m; (tip) punta, f; (point) ápice, m; (of a tram, bus) imperial, baca, f; (of a wave) cresta, f; (acme) auge, m; (of a class) primero (de la clase), m; (highest rank) último grado, m; (of a plant) hojas, f pl; (of a piano) cima, f; Naut. cofa, f; (head of a bed, etc.) cabeza, f; (lid) tapadera, f; (toy) trompo, peón, m; (humming) trompa, f, a más alto; máximo; (chief) principal, primero. —vt (cover) cubrir de; (cut off) desmochar; (come level with) llegar a la cima de; (rise above) elevarse por encima (de), coronar, dominar; (be superior to) exceder, aventajar; (golf) topear. **at the top,** a la cabeza; a la cumbre. **from top to bottom,** de arriba abajo. **on top of,** encima de; (besides) en adición a, además de. **to be top-dog,** ser un gallito. **to sleep like a top,** dormir como un lirón. **top boots,** botas de campaña, f pl. **top-dog,** vencedor, m; poderoso, m. **top-hat,** sombrero de copa, m. **top-heavy,** más pesado por arriba que por abajo

**topaz** /'toupæz/ n topacio, jacinto occidental, m

**topcoat** /'tɒpˌkout/ n sobretodo, gabán, m

**top floor** n piso alto, m

**topic** /'tɒpik/ n asunto, tema, m

**topical** /'tɒpikəl/ a tópico; actual

**topknot** /'tɒpˌnɒt/ n cresta, f, penacho, m; (of birds) moño, m; copete, m

**topmast** /'tɒpˌmæst/ Naut. -məst/ n mastelero, m

**topmost** /'tɒpˌmoust/ a más alto; más importante

**topographer** /tə'pɒgrəfər/ n topógrafo, m

**topographical** /ˌtɒpə'græfikəl/ a topográfico

**topography** /tə'pɒgrəfi/ n topografía, f

**topple** /'tɒpəl/ vi tambalearse, estar al punto de caer. **to t. down,** volcarse; derribarse; caer. **to t. over,** vi venirse abajo; perder el equilibrio. —vt derribar, hacer caer

**topsail** /'tɒpˌseil/ Naut. -səl/ n gavia, f

**topsy-turvy** /'tɒpsi'tɜrvi/ a desordenado. —adv en desorden, patas arriba, de arriba abajo

**toque** /touk/ n toca, f

**torch** /tɔrtʃ/ n antorcha, hacha, tea, f. **electric t.,** lamparilla eléctrica, f. **t.-bearer,** hachero, m

**torchlight** /'tɔrtʃˌlait/ n luz de antorcha, f. **by t.,** a la luz de las antorchas

**torment** /v. tɔr'mɛnt, n. 'tɔrmɛnt/ n tormento, m, angustia, f; (torture) tortura, f; suplicio, m; mortificación, f; disgusto, m. —vt atormentar, martirizar; (torture) torturar; molestar

**tormentor** /tɔr'mɛntər/ n atormentador (-ra)

**tornado** /tɔr'neidou/ n tornado, m

**torpedo** /tɔr'pidou/ n torpedo, m; Ichth. pez torpedo, m. —vt torpedear. **self-propelling t.,** torpedo automóvil, m. **t.-boat,** torpedero, m. **t.-boat destroyer,** cazatorpedero, contratorpedero, m. **t. netting,** red contra torpedos, f. **t. station,** base de torpederos, f. **t. tube,** tubo lanzatorpedos, m

**torpedoing** /tɔr'pidouin/ n torpedeamiento, torpedeo, m

**torpid** /'tɔrpid/ a aletargado, entorpecido; (of the mind) torpe, tardo, apático

**torpidity, torpor** /tɔr'piditi, 'tɔrpər/ n letargo, m; apatía, f

**torrent** /'tɔrənt/ n torrente, m

**torrential** /tɔ'rɛnʃəl/ a torrencial

**torrid** /'tɔrid/ a tórrido. **t. zone,** zona tórrida, f

**torsion** /'tɔrʃən/ n torsión, f

**torso** /'tɔrsou/ n torso, m

**tort** /tɔrt/ n Law. tuerto, m

**tortoise** /'tɔrtəs/ n tortuga, f. **t.-shell,** carey, m. —a de carey

**tortuous** /'tɔrtʃuəs/ a tortuoso

**tortuousness** /'tɔrtʃuəsnis/ n tortuosidad, f

**torture** /'tɔrtʃər/ n tortura, f, tormento, m; angustia, f. —vt torturar, dar tormento (a); martirizar

**torturer** /'tɔrtʃərər/ n atormentador (-ra)

**torturing** /'tɔrtʃərin/ a torturador, atormentador; angustioso

**toss** /tɔs/ n sacudimiento, m, sacudida, f; (of the head) movimiento (de cabeza), m; (bull fighting) cogida, f; (from a horse) caída de caballo, f. —vt echar, lanzar; agitar, sacudir; (of bulls) acornear. —vi agitarse; (of plumes, etc.) ondear; (in a boat) ba-

lancearse a la merced de las olas; jugar a cara o cruz. **to t. in a blanket,** mantear, dar una manta (a). **to t. aside,** echar a un lado; abandonar. **to t. off,** beber de un trago. **to t. up,** jugar a cara o cruz
**tot** /tɒt/ n (child) nene (-na), crío (-ía); (of drink) vaso pequeño, m. **to tot up,** sumar
**total** /'toutl/ a total; absoluto, completo, entero. —n total, m, suma, f. —vt sumar. —vi ascender (a). **t. employment,** ocupación total, f. **t. war,** guerra total, f
**totalitarian** /tou,tælɪ'tɛəriən/ a totalitario
**totality** /tou'tælɪti/ n totalidad, f
**totally** /'toutḷi/ adv totalmente, completamente
**totem** /'toutəm/ n tótem, m
**totemism** /'toutə,mɪzəm/ n totemismo, m
**totter** /'tɒtər/ vi (of persons) bambolearse; tambalear, estar a punto de caer; Fig. aproximarse a su fin
**tottering** /'tɒtərɪŋ/ a vacilante; tambaleante. —n bamboleo, m; tambaleo, m
**toucan** /'tukæn/ n Ornith. tucán, m
**touch** /tʌtʃ/ vt tocar; (brush against) rozar; (reach) alcanzar; (musical instruments) tocar; (move) emocionar, enternecer; (spur on) aguijar; (food) tomar; (affect) influir, afectar; (arouse) despertar, estimular; (equal) compararse con, igualar; (consider) tratar ligeramente (de); (money) dar un sablazo (a). —vi tocarse; imponer las manos para curar. **I have not touched a bite,** No he probado un bocado. **This touches me dearly,** Esto me toca de cerca. **to t. at,** hacer escala en, tocar en (un puerto). **to t. off,** descargar. **to t. up,** retocar; corregir. **to t. upon,** (a subject) tratar superficialmente de, tratar ligeramente de; hablar de; considerar
**touch** /tʌtʃ/ n (sense of) tacto, m; (contact) toque, contacto, m; (brushing) roce, m; (tap) golpe ligero, m; palmadita, f; (of an illness) ataque ligero, m; Mus. dedeo, m; (little) dejo, m; (test) prueba, f; toque, m; Art. toque, m, pincelada, f. **by the t.,** a tiento, m. **in t. with,** en relaciones con; en comunicación con; al corriente de. **to give the finishing t.,** dar la última pincelada; dar el último toque. **t.-line,** (football) línea de toque, línea lateral, f. **t.-me-not,** Inf. erizo, m. **t.-stone,** piedra de toque, f
**touched** /tʌtʃt/ a emocionado, conmovido
**touchiness** /'tʌtʃɪnɪs/ n susceptibilidad, f
**touching** /'tʌtʃɪŋ/ a patético, conmovedor. —prep tocante a, acerca de. —n tocamiento, m
**touchy** /'tʌtʃi/ a susceptible, quisquilloso, vidrioso
**tough** /tʌf/ a (hard) duro; vigoroso, fuerte, robusto; resistente; (of character) tenaz, firme; (of a job) difícil; espinoso. —n chulo, m
**toughen** /'tʌfən/ vt endurecer. —vi endurecerse
**toughness** /'tʌfnɪs/ n dureza, f; vigor, m, fuerza, f; resistencia, f; tenacidad, firmeza, f; dificultad, f
**Toulouse** /tʊ'luz/ Tolosa, f
**toupee** /tu'pei/ n tupé, m
**tour** /tʊr/ n viaje, m, excursión, f. —vi viajar. —vt viajar por. **circular t.,** Theat. en tour, de gira
**touring** /'tʊrɪŋ/ a de turismo. —n turismo, m; viaje, m. **t. car,** coche de turismo, m
**tourist** /'tʊrɪst/ n turista, mf; viajero (-ra). **t. agency,** agencia de turismo, f, patronato de turismo, m. **t. ticket,** billete kilométrico, m
**tournament** /'tʊrnəmənt/ n torneo, m, justa, f; (of games) concurso, m
**tourniquet** /'tɜrnɪkɪt, 'tʊr-/ n torniquete, m
**tousle** /'tauzəl, -səl/ vt despeinar; desordenar el pelo
**tout** /taut/ n buhonero, m. **to t. for,** pescar, solicitar
**tow** /tou/ n remolque, m; (rope) estopa, f. —vt (Naut. Auto.) remolcar. **on tow,** a remolque. **tow-path,** camino de sirga, m. **tow rope,** cable de remolque, m
**towage** /'touɪdʒ/ n remolque, m; (fee) derechos de remolque, m pl
**towards** /tɔrdʒ/ prep hacia, en dirección a; (of time) sobre, cerca de; (concerning) tocante a; (with persons) para, con
**towel** /'tauəl/ n toalla, f. **roller t.,** toalla continua, f. **t. rail,** toallero, m
**toweling** /'tauəlɪŋ/ n tela para toallas, f
**tower** /'tauər/ n torre, f; (fortress) fortaleza, f; (belfry) campanario, m; (large) torreón, m. —vi elevarse. **to t. above,** destacarse sobre, sobresalir; Fig. sobrepujar, superar
**towered** /'tauərd/ a torreado; de las... torres. **high t.,** de las altas torres
**towering** /'tauərɪŋ/ a elevado; dominante; orgulloso; Fig. violento, terrible
**town** /taun/ n población, f, pueblo, m; ciudad, f. **t. clerk,** secretario de ayuntamiento, m. **t. council,** concejo municipal, m. **t. councilor,** concejero municipal, m. **t. crier,** pregonero, m. **t. hall,** (casa de) ayuntamiento, casa consistorial, f. **t. house,** casa de ciudad, f. **t. planning,** urbanismo, m; reforma urbana, f. **t. wall,** muralla, f
**"Town Ahead"** «Poblado Próximo»
**townsman** /'taunzmən/ n ciudadano, m
**town worthy** n persona principal de la ciudad, f
**toxic** /'tɒksɪk/ a tóxico
**toxicological** /,tɒksɪkə'lɒdʒɪkəl/ a toxicológico
**toxicologist** /,tɒksɪ'kɒlədʒɪst/ n toxicólogo, m
**toxicology** /,tɒksɪ'kɒlədʒi/ n toxicología, f
**toxin** /'tɒksɪn/ n toxina, f
**toy** /tɔi/ n juguete, m. —vi (with) jugar con; acariciar. **toy maker,** fabricante de juguetes, m
**toyshop** /'tɔi,ʃɒp/ n juguetería, tienda de juguetes, f
**trace** /treis/ n huella, pista, f, rastro, m; vestigio, m; indicio, m, evidencia, f; (of a harness) tirante, m; (touch) dejo, m; (of fear, etc.) sombra, f. —vt trazar; (through transparent paper) calcar; seguir la pista (de); (write) escribir; (discern) distinguir; investigar; descubrir; determinar; (walk) atravesar, recorrer. **to t. back,** (of ancestry, etc.) hacer remontar (a)
**traceable** /'treisəbəl/ a que se puede trazar; atribuible
**tracer** /'treisər/ n trazador (-ra). **t. bullet,** bala luminosa, f
**tracery** /'treisəri/ n tracería, f
**trachea** /'treikiə/ n Anat. tráquea, f
**trachoma** /trə'koumə/ n Med. tracoma, f
**tracing** /'treisɪŋ/ n calco, m; trazo, m; seguimiento, m. **t.-paper,** papel de calcar, m
**track** /træk/ n huella, f, rastro, m; (for racing, etc.) pista, f; (of wheels) rodada, f; (railway) vía, f; (of a boat) estela, f; (path) senda, vereda, f; (sign) señal, evidencia, f; (course) ruta, f. —vt rastrear, seguir la pista (de); Naut. sirgar. **to t. down,** seguir y capturar. **double t.,** vía doble, f. **off the t.,** extraviado; (of a train) descarrilado; Fig. por los cerros de Úbeda. **side t.,** desviadero, m. **to keep t. of,** Inf. no perder de vista (a); seguir las fortunas de
**trackless** /'træklɪs/ a sin camino; sin huella; (of trams, etc.) sin rieles; (untrodden) no pisado
**tract** /trækt/ n tracto, m; región, f; Anat. vía, f; (written) tratado, m
**tractability** /,træktə'bɪliti/ n docilidad, f
**tractable** /'træktəbəl/ a dócil
**traction** /'trækʃən/ n tracción, f. **t.-engine,** máquina de arrastre (or de tracción), f
**tractor** /'træktər/ n máquina de arrastre, f; tractor, m
**trade** /treid/ n comercio, m; tráfico, m; negocio, m; industria, f; (calling) oficio, m, profesión, f; (dealers) comerciantes, mf pl. —vi comerciar, traficar. —vt cambiar. **to t. on,** explotar, aprovecharse de. **by t.,** de oficio, por profesión. **t.-mark,** marca de fábrica, f. **t.-name,** razón social, f. **t. price,** precio para el comerciante, m. **t. union,** sindicato, m. **T. Union Congress,** Congreso de Sindicatos, m. **t. unionism,** sistema de sindicatos obreros, m. **t.-winds,** vientos alisios, m pl
**trader** /'treidər/ n comerciante, traficante, mf; mercader, m; (boat) buque mercante, m
**tradesman** /'treidzmən/ n tendero, m. **tradesmen's entrance,** puerta de servicio, f
**trading** /'treidɪŋ/ n comercio, tráfico, m. —a mercantil, comerciante, mercante. **t. ship,** buque mercante, m. **t. station,** factoría, f
**tradition** /trə'dɪʃən/ n tradición, f
**traditional** /trə'dɪʃənl/ a tradicional; del lugar
**traditionalism** /trə'dɪʃənl,ɪzəm/ n tradicionalismo, m
**traditionalist** /trə'dɪʃənlɪst/ n tradicionalista, mf
**traditionally** /trə'dɪʃənli/ adv según la tradición, tradicionalmente

**traduce** /trə'dus/ *vt* calumniar, denigrar, vituperar

**traducer** /trə'dusər/ *n* calumniador (-ra)

**traffic** /'træfɪk/ *n* comercio, negocio, tráfico, *m;* (in transit) transporte, *m;* (in movement) circulación, *f.* —*vi* comerciar, traficar, negociar. **to cause a block in the t.,** interrumpir la circulación. **t. block,** obstrución del tráfico, *f,* atasco en la circulación, *m.* **t. indicator,** (on a car) indicador de dirección, *m.* **t. island,** refugio para peatones, salvavidas, *m.* **t. light,** disco, *m,* luz (de tráfico), *f,* semáforo, *m.* **t. roundabout,** redondel, *m*

**trafficker** /'træfɪkər/ *n* traficante, *mf*

**tragedian** /trə'dʒidiən/ *n* trágico, *m*

**tragedy** /'trædʒidi/ *n* tragedia, *f*

**tragic** /'trædʒɪk/ *a* trágico

**tragicomedy** /ˌtrædʒɪ'kɒmɪdi/ *n* tragicomedia, *f*

**tragicomic** /ˌtrædʒɪ'kɒmɪk/ *a* tragicómico

**trail** /treil/ *n* rastro, *m,* pista, huella, *f;* (path) sendero, *m;* (of a comet) cola, cabellera, *f.* —*vt* rastrear, seguir el rastro de; (drag) arrastrar; (the anchor) garrar. —*vi* arrastrar; (of plants) trepar. **on the t. of,** en busca de; siguiendo el rastro de; **put somebody on the t. of...** darle a fulano la pista de...

**trailer** /'treilər/ *n* cazador (-ra); perseguidor (-ra); *Auto.* remolque, *m;* (cinema) anuncio de próximas atracciones, *m; Bot.* talle rastrero, *m*

**train** /trein/ *n* (railway) tren, *m;* (of a dress) cola, *f;* (retinue) séquito, *m;* (procession) desfile, *m,* comitiva, *f;* (series) serie, sucesión, *f;* (of gunpowder) reguero de pólvora, *m.* **down t.,** tren descendente, *m.* **excursion t.,** tren de excursionistas, *m.* **express t.,** exprés, tren expreso, *m.* **fast t.,** rápido, *m.* **goods t.,** tren de mercancías, *m.* **mail t.,** tren correo, *m.* **next t.,** próximo tren, *m.* **passenger t.,** tren de pasajeros, *m.* **stopping t.,** tren ómnibus, *m.* **through t.,** tren directo, *m.* **up t.,** tren ascendente, *m.* **put somebody on the t. of...** darle a fulano la pista de...

**trailer** /'treilər/ *n* cazador (-ra); perseguidor (-ra); *Auto.* remolque, *m;* (cinema) anuncio de próximas atracciones, *m; Bot.* talle rastrero, *m* **t.-bearer,** paje que lleva la cola, *m;* dama de honor, *f;* (of a cardinal, etc.) caudatario, *m.* **t.-ferry,** buque transbordador, *m.* **t.-oil,** aceite de ballena, *m.* **t. service,** servicio de trenes, *m*

**train** /trein/ *vt* educar; adiestrar; enseñar; *Sports.* entrenar; (firearms) apuntar; (plants) guiar; (accustom) habituar, acostumbrar; (a horse for racing) entrenar; (circus) amaestrar. —*vi* educarse; adiestrarse; *Sports.* entrenarse

**trainer** /'treinər/ *n* (of men and racehorses) entrenador, *m;* (of performing animals) domador, *m*

**training** /'treinɪŋ/ *n* educación, *f;* enseñanza, instrucción, *f; Sports.* entrenamiento, *m.* **t.-college,** escuela normal, *f.* **t.-ship,** buque escuela, *m*

**trait** /treit/ *n* rasgo, *m,* característica, *f*

**traitor** /'treitər/ *n* traidor, *m*

**traitress** /'treitrɪs/ *n* traidora, *f*

**trajectory** /trə'dʒɛktəri/ *n* trayectoria, *f*

**tram** /træm/ *n* tranvía, *m.* —*a* tranviario. **t. conductor,** cobrador de tranvía, *m.* **t. depot,** cochera de tranvías, *f.* **t. stop,** parada de tranvía, *f*

**trammel** /'træməl/ *n* (of a horse) traba, *f; Fig.* obstáculo, estorbo, *m.* —*vt* travar; *Fig.* estorbar, impedir

**tramp** /træmp/ *n* (person) vagabundo (-da); vago (-ga); (walk) caminata, *f,* paseo largo, *m;* ruido de pasos, *m; Naut.* vapor volandero, *m.* —*vi* ir a pie; patear; vagabundear. —*vt* vagar por

**trample** /'træmpəl/ *n* pisoteo, *m;* (of feet) ruido de pasos, *m.* —*vt* pisotear, pisar, hollar. —*vi* pisar fuerte. **to t. on,** *Fig.* atropellar humillar

**trance** /træns/ *n* rapto, arrobamiento, *m; Med.* catalepsia, *f*

**tranquil** /'træŋkwɪl/ *a* tranquilo, apacible; sereno, sosegado

**tranquility** /træŋ'kwɪlɪti/ *n* tranquilidad, paz, quietud, *f;* serenidad, *f,* sosiego, *m;* calma, *f*

**tranquilize** /'træŋkwə,laɪz/ *vt* tranquilizar, sosegar, calmar

**tranquilizer** /'træŋkwə,laɪzər/ *n* calmante, *m*

**tranquilizing** /'træŋkwə,laɪzɪŋ/ *a* sosegador, tranquilizador

**trans-** *prefix* trans-. **t.-Pyrenean,** *a* traspirenaico. **to t.-ship,** trasbordar. **t.-shipment,** trasbordo, *m.* **t.-Siberian,** trasiberiano

**trans-** *prefix* trans-. **t.-Pyrenean,** *a* traspirenaico. **to t.**

**-ship,** trasbordar. **t.-shipment,** trasbordo, *m.* **t.-Siberian,** trasiberiano

**transact** /træn'sækt/ *vt* despachar, hacer. —*vi* despachar un negocio

**transaction** /træn'sækʃən/ *n* desempeño, *m;* negocio, *m;* transacción, operación, *f; pl* **transactions** (of a society) actas, *f pl*

**transatlantic** /ˌtrænsət'læntɪk/ *a* transatlántico. **t. liner,** transatlántico, *m*

**transcend** /træn'sɛnd/ *vt* exceder, superar, rebasar. —*vi* trascender

**transcendence** /træn'sɛndəns/ *n* superioridad, *f;* trascendencia, *f*

**transcendental** /ˌtrænsɛn'dɛntl̩/ *a* trascendental

**transcontinental** /ˌtrænskɒntn̩'ɛntl̩/ *a* transcontinental

**transcribe** /træn'skraɪb/ *vt* trascribir, copiar; *Mus.* trascribir, adaptar

**transcriber** /træn'skraɪbər/ *n* copiador (-ra); *Mus.* adaptador (-ra)

**transcript** /'trænskrɪpt/ *n* traslado, trasunto, *m;* (student's) certificado de estudios, certificado de materias aprobadas, *m,* constancia de estudios, copia del expediente académico, hoja de estudios, *f*

**transcription** /træn'skrɪpʃən/ *n* trascripción, copia, *f,* trasunto, *m; Mus.* trascripción, adaptación, *f,* arreglo, *m*

**transept** /'trænsɛpt/ *n Archit.* transepto, crucero, *m*

**transfer** /*v.* træns'fɜr, *n.* 'trænsfər/ *n* traslado, *m;* trasferencia, *f,* traspaso, *m; Law.* cesión, enajenación, *f;* (picture) calcomanía, *f.* —*vt* trasladar; trasferir; pasar; *Law.* enajenar, ceder; estampar; calcografiar. —*vi* trasbordarse. **deed of t.,** escritura de cesión, *f.* **t.-paper,** papel de calcar, *m*

**transferable** /træns'fɜrəbəl/ *a* trasferible

**transferee** /ˌtrænsfə'ri/ *n* cesionario (-ia)

**transference** /træns'fɜrəns/ *n* traslado, *m;* transferencia, *f; Law.* cesión, enajenación, *f*

**transferor** /træns'fɜrər/ *n* cesionista, *mf*

**transfiguration** /ˌtrænsfɪgyə'reɪʃən/ *n* trasfiguración, *f*

**transfigure** /træns'fɪgyər/ *vt* trasfigurar, trasformar

**transfix** /træns'fɪks/ *vt* traspasar; *Fig.* paralizar

**transfixion** /træns'fɪkʃən/ *n* trasfixión, *f*

**transform** /træns'fɔrm/ *vt* trasformar; convertir, cambiar. **It is completely transformed,** Está completamente trasformado

**transformation** /ˌtrænsfər'meɪʃən/ *n* trasformación, *f;* conversión, *f,* cambio, *m*

**transformative** /træns'fɔrmətɪv/ *a* trasformador

**transformer** /træns'fɔrmər/ *n Elec.* trasformador, *m*

**transfuse** /træns'fyuz/ *vt* trasfundir

**transfusion** /træns'fyuʒən/ *n* trasfusión, *f.* **blood t.,** trasfusión de sangre, *f*

**transgress** /træns'grɛs/ *vt* exceder, sobrepasar; (violate) contravenir, violar, pecar contra. —*vi* pecar

**transgression** /træns'grɛʃən/ *n* contravención, trasgresión, *f;* pecado, *m*

**transgressor** /træns'grɛsər/ *n* trasgresor (-ra), pecador (-ra)

**transient** /'trænʃənt, -ʒənt/ *a* transitorio, fugaz, pasajero; perecedero

**transiently** /'trænʃəntli, -ʒənt-/ *adv* pasajeramente

**transit** /'trænsɪt/ *n* tránsito, paso, *m;* transporte, *m; Astron.* tránsito, *m.* **in t.,** de tránsito

**transition** /træn'zɪʃən/ *n* transición, *f;* cambio, *m;* tránsito, paso, *m*

**transitional** /træn'zɪʃənl̩/ *a* de transición, transitorio

**transitive** /'trænsɪtɪv/ *a Gram.* transitivo, activo. **t. verb,** verbo transitivo, verbo activo, *m*

**transitively** /'trænsɪtɪvli/ *adv* transitivamente

**transitorily** /ˌtrænsɪ'tɔrəli/ *adv* transitoriamente; provisionalmente

**transitoriness** /'trænsɪˌtɔrinəs/ *n* brevedad, *f,* lo fugaz

**transitory** /'trænsɪˌtɔri/ *a* transitorio, fugaz, pasajero, breve

**translatable** /træns'leitəbəl/ *a* traducible

**translate** /træns'leit/ *vt* traducir; interpretar; (transfer) trasladar

**translation** /træns'leiʃən/ *n* traducción, *f;* versión, *f;* traslado, *m*

**translator** /træns'leitər/ n traductor (-ra)
**translucence** /træns'lusəns/ n traslucidez, f
**translucent** /træns'lusənt/ a traslúcido, trasparente
**transmigrate** /træns'maigreit/ vi trasmigrar
**transmigration** /ˌtrænsmai'greiʃən/ n trasmigración, f
**transmissibility** /trænsˌmısə'bıliti/ n trasmisibilidad, f
**transmissible** /træns'mısəbəl/ a trasmisible
**transmission** /træns'mıʃən/ n trasmisión, f
**transmit** /træns'mıt/ vt trasmitir; remitir, dar
**transmitter** /træns'mıtər/ n trasmisor (-ra); Radio. radiotrasmisor, m; Elec. trasmisor, m
**transmutable** /træns'myutəbəl/ a trasmutable
**transmutation** /ˌtrænsmyu'teiʃən/ n trasmutación, f
**transmute** /træns'myut/ vt trasmutar
**transoceanic** /ˌtrænsouʃi'ænık/ a transoceánico
**transom** /'trænsəm/ n travesaño, m; Naut. yugo de popa, m
**transpacific** /ˌtrænspə'sıfık/ a traspacífico
**transparency** /træns'pɛərənsi/ n trasparencia; diafanidad, f; (picture) trasparente, m
**transparent** /træns'pɛərənt/ a trasparente; diáfano; (of style) claro, limpio
**transpiration** /ˌtrænspə'reiʃən/ n traspiración, f
**transpire** /træn'spaiˀr/ vi traspirar; rezumarse; hacerse público; Inf. acontecer. —vt exhalar
**transplant** /træns'plænt/ vt trasplantar
**transplantation** /ˌtrænsplæn'teiʃən/ n trasplante, m, trasplantación, f
**transport** /v. træns'pɔrt, n. 'trænspɔrt/ n trasporte, m; Naut. navío de trasporte, m; Aer. avión de trasporte, m; (fit) acceso, paroxismo, m. —vt trasportar; (convicts) deportar; Fig. (joy) colmar; (rage) llenar
**transportable** /træns'pɔrtəbəl/ a trasportable
**transportation** /ˌtrænspər'teiʃən/ n trasporte, m; (convicts) deportación, f
**transporter** /træns,pɔrtər/ n trasportador (-ra)
**transpose** /træns'pouz/ vt trasponer; Mus. trasportar
**transposition** /ˌtrænspə'zıʃən/ n trasposición, f
**transversal** /træns'vɜrsəl/ a and n trasversal, m
**transverse** /træns'vɜrs/ a trasverso, trasversal
**transversely** /træns'vɜrsli/ adv trasversalmente
**trap** /træp/ n trampa, f; cepo, m; (net) lazo, m, red, f; (for mice, rats) ratonera, f; Mech. sifón de depósito, m; pequeño carruaje de dos ruedas, f; (door) puerta caediza, f; Theat. escotillón, m, pl **traps**, trastos, m pl; equipaje, m. —vt coger con trampa; hacer caer en el lazo; Fig. tender el lazo. —vi armar una trampa; armar lazo. **to fall into a t.,** Fig. caer en la trampa. **to pack one's traps,** liar el hato
**trapeze** /træ'piz/ n trapecio (de gimnasia), m
**trapper** /'træpər/ n cazador de animales de piel, m
**trappings** /'træpıŋz/ n pl arneses, jaeces, m pl; arreos, aderezos, m pl, galas, f pl
**trash** /træʃ/ n paja, hojarasca, f; (of sugar, etc.) bagazo, m; trastos viejos, m pl; cachivaches, m pl; (literary) paja, f
**trashy** /'træʃi/ a de ningún valor, inútil, despreciable
**traumatic** /trɔ'mætık/ a Med. traumático
**traumatism** /'trɔmə,tızəm/ n Med. traumatismo, m
**travail** /trə'veil/ n dolores de parto, m pl. —vi estar de parto; trabajar
**travel** /'trævəl/ n el viajar, viajes, m pl. —vi viajar; ver mundo; (of traffic) circular, pasar, ir. —vt viajar por; recorrer; (with number of miles) hacer. **to t. over,** viajar por; recorrer. **t. worn,** fatigado con el viaje
**travel agent** n agente de viajes, mf
**traveled** /'trævəld/ a que ha viajado, que ha visto muchas partes
**traveler** /'trævələr/ n viajero (-ra); pasajero (-ra). **commercial t.,** viajante, mf **traveler's check,** cheque de viajeros, m. **traveler's joy,** Bot. clemátide, f
**traveling** /'trævəlıŋ/ n viajes, m pl. —a viajero; para (or de) viaje; (itinerant) ambulante. **t. crane,** grúa móvil, f. **t. expenses,** gastos de viaje, m pl. **t. requisites,** objetos de viaje, m pl. **t. rug,** manta, f. **t. show,** circo ambulante, m
**traversable** /trə'vɜrsəbəl/ a atravesable, transitable, practicable
**traverse** /n., a. 'trævərs; v. trə'vɜrs/ n travesaño, m; Law. negación, f; (Mil. Archit.) través, m; (crossing)

travesía, f, a transversal. —vt atravesar, cruzar; Law. negar
**travesty** /'trævəsti/ n parodia, f, vt parodiar
**trawl** /trɔl/ vt rastrear. —vi pescar a la rastra. **t.-net,** red de arrastre, f
**trawler** /'trɔlər/ n barco barredero, m; pescador a la rastra, m
**trawling** /'trɔlıŋ/ n pesca a la rastra, f
**tray** /trei/ n bandeja, f; (of a balance) platillo, m; (in a wardrobe, etc.) cajón, m; (trough) artesa, f
**treacherous** /'trɛtʃərəs/ a traidor, falso, pérfido, fementido; (of memory) infiel; engañoso; (of ice, etc.) peligroso
**treacherously** /'trɛtʃərəsli/ adv traidoramente, a traición
**treachery** /'trɛtʃəri/ n perfidia, traición, falsedad, f
**treacle** /'trikəl/ n melado, m
**tread** /trɛd/ n pisada, f; paso, m; (of a stair) peldaño, m; (of tire) pastilla, f; (walk) andar, porte, m, vi pisar; (trample) pisotear; hollar; (oppress) oprimir. —vt hollar; (a path) abrir; recorrer; caminar por; bailar. **to t. the grapes,** pisar las uvas. **to t. the stage,** pisar las tablas. **to t. under foot,** hollar; pisotear. **to t. on,** pisar. **to t. on one's heels,** pisarle los talones a uno; seguir de cerca. **to t. out,** (a measure) bailar
**treading** /'tredıŋ/ n pisoteo, m
**treadle** /'tredl/ n pedal, m; (of a loom) cárcola, f
**treadmill** /'tred,mıl/ n molino de rueda de escalones, m; Fig. rueda, f
**treason** /'trizən/ n traición, f. **high t.,** alta traición, lesa majestad, f
**treasonable** /'trizənəbəl/ a desleal, traidor
**treasonably** /'trizənəbli/ adv traidoramente
**treasure** /'trɛʒər/ n tesoro, m; riqueza, f, caudal, m; Fig. perla, f. —vt atesorar; acumular (or guardar) riquezas; (a memory) guardar. **t. trove,** tesoro hallado, m
**treasurer** /'trɛʒərər/ n tesorero (-ra)
**treasury** /'trɛʒəri/ n tesorería, f; (government department) Ministerio de Hacienda, m; (anthology) tesoro, m. **t. bench,** banco del Gobierno, m
**treat** /trit/ n (pleasure) gusto, placer, m; (present) obsequio, m; (entertainment) fiesta, f. —vt tratar; Med. tratar, curar; (regale) obsequiar. —vi (stand host) convidar; (of) tratar de, versar sobre; (with) negociar con
**treatise** /'tritıs/ n tesis, monografía, disertación, f, tratado, m
**treatment** /'tritmənt/ n tratamiento, m; (of persons) conducta hacia, f, modo de obrar con, m; Med. tratamiento, m; (Lit., Art.) procedimiento, m, técnica, f
**treaty** /'triti/ n tratado, pacto, m; (bargain) contrato, m
**treble** /'trebəl/ n Mus. tiple, m; voz de tiple, f. —a triple; Mus. sobreagudo. —vt triplicar; vi triplicarse. **t. clef,** clave de sol, f
**trebling** /'treblıŋ/ n triplicación, f
**tree** /tri/ n árbol, m; (for shoes) horma, f; (of a saddle) arzón, m. **breadfruit t.,** árbol del pan, m. **Judas t.,** árbol de amor, m. **t. of knowledge,** árbol de la ciencia, m. **t.-covered,** arbolado. **t.-frog,** rana de San Antonio, f
**treeless** /'trilıs/ a sin árboles
**trefoil** /'trifɔil/ n trébol, trifolio, m
**trek** /trek/ vi caminar, andar
**trellis** /'trelıs/ n enrejado, m; (for plants) espaldera, f. —vt cercar con un enrejado; construir espalderas
**tremble** /'trembəl/ vi temblar; estremecerse; trepidar; vibrar; (sway) oscilar; (of flags) ondear; agitarse; ser tembloroso. **His fate trembled in the balance,** Su suerte estaba en la balanza. **to t. all over,** temblar de pies a cabeza
**trembling** /'tremblıŋ/ n temblor, m; estremecimiento, m; trepidación, f; vibración, f; (fear) agitación, ansiedad, f; temor, m. —a tembloroso; trémulo
**tremendous** /trı'mɛndəs/ a terrible, espantoso; formidable; grande; importante; Inf. tremendo; enorme
**tremendously** /trı'mɛndəsli/ adv terriblemente, Inf. enormemente
**tremor** /'tremər/ n temblor, movimiento sísmico, m; (thrill) estremecimiento, m; vibración, f

**tremulous** /'trɛmyələs/ a trémulo, tembloroso; vacilante; tímido
**tremulously** /'trɛmyələsli/ adv trémulamente; tímidamente
**tremulousness** /'trɛmyələsnɪs/ n lo tembloroso; vacilación, f; timidez, f
**trench** /trɛntʃ/ n zanja, f, foso, m; (for irrigation) acequia, f; Mil. trinchera, f. —vt hacer zanjas (en); acequiar; Mil. atrincherar. **t.-fever,** tifus exantemático, m. **t.-foot,** pie de trinchera, m. **t.-mortar,** mortero de trinchera, m
**trenchant** /'trɛntʃənt/ a mordaz
**trencher** /'trɛntʃər/ n trinchero, m
**trend** /trɛnd/ n curso, rumbo, m; Fig. tendencia, f; dirección, f. —vi Fig. tender
**trepan** /trɪ'pæn/ vt Surg. trepanar
**trepanning** /trɪ'pænɪŋ/ n Surg. trepanación, f
**trepidation** /ˌtrɛpɪ'deiʃən/ n trepidación, f
**trespass** /'trɛspəs, -pæs/ n violación de propiedad, f; ofensa, f; pecado, m; (in the Lord's Prayer) deuda, f. —vi (on land) entrar sin derecho, violar la propiedad; (upon) entrar sin permiso en; (with patience, etc.) abusar de; (against) pecar contra, infringir
**trespasser** /'trɛspəsər, -pæs-/ n violador (-ra) de la ley de propiedad. **"Trespassers will be prosecuted,"** «Entrada prohibida,» «Prohibido el paso»
**tress** /trɛs/ n (plait) trenza, f; rizo, bucle, m; pl **tresses,** cabellera, f
**trestle** /'trɛsəl/ n caballete, m; armazón, m. **trestle-table,** mesa de caballete, f
**triad** /'traiæd/ n terna, f; Mus. acorde, m
**trial** /'traiəl/ n prueba, f, ensayo, m; examen, m; (experiment) tentativa, f, experimento, f; (misfortune) desgracia, pena, f; (nuisance) molestia, f; Law. vista de una causa, f. **on t.,** a prueba; Law. en proceso. **to bring to t.,** procesar. **to stand one's t.,** ser procesado. **t. run,** marcha de ensayo, f. **t. trip,** Naut. viaje de ensayo, m
**trial and error** n tanteos, m. **by trial and error,** por tanteos.
**triangle** /'trai,æŋgəl/ n triángulo, m. **acute-angled t.,** triángulo acutángulo, m. **obtuse-angled t.,** triángulo obtusángulo, m. **right-angled t.,** triángulo rectángulo, m. **the eternal t.,** el eterno triángulo
**triangular** /trai'æŋgyələr/ a triangular, triángulo
**triangulation** /trai,æŋgyə'leiʃən/ n (in surveying) triangulación, f
**tribal** /'traibəl/ a tribal
**tribe** /traib/ n tribu, f
**tribesman** /'traibzmən/ n miembro de una tribu, m
**tribulation** /ˌtribyə'leiʃən/ n tribulación, f; pena, aflicción, desgracia, f
**tribunal** /trai'byunl/ n (seat) tribunal, m; (court) juzgado, m; (confessional) confesionario, m
**tribunate** /'tribyənit/ n tribunado, m
**tribune** /'tribyun/ n (person) tribuno, m; tribuna, f
**tribunicial** a tribúnico
**tributary** /'tribyə,tɛri/ a and n tributario m.
**tribute** /'tribyut/ n tributo, m; contribución, imposición, f
**trice** /trais/ n tris, soplo, m. **in a t.,** en un periquete, en un avemaría, en dos trancos
**tricentennial** /ˌtraisɛn'tɛniəl/ a de trescientos años; n tercer centenario, tricentenario, m
**trick** /trik/ n (swindle) estafa, f, engaño, m; (ruse) truco, m, estratagema, ardid, f; (mischief) travesura, f; burla, f; (illusion) ilusión, f; (habit) costumbre, f; (affectation) afectación, f; (jugglery) juego de manos, m; (knack) talento, m; (at cards) baza, f. —vt engañar, estafar; (with out) adornar, ataviar; (with into) inducir fraudulentamente. —vi trampear. **dirty t.,** Inf. mala pasada, perrada, f. **His memory plays him tricks,** La memoria le engaña. **to play a t. on,** gastar una broma (a). **to play tricks,** hacer travesuras. **t. riding,** acrobacia ecuestre, f
**trickery** /'trikəri/ n maullería, superchería, f; fraude, engaño, m
**trickle** /'trikəl/ n chorrito, hilo (de agua, etc.) m. —vi gotear. **to t. down,** deslizar por, correr por, escurrir por
**trickling** /'triklɪŋ/ n goteo, m; (sound) murmullo, m.

**trickster** /'trikstər/ n embustero (-ra), trampeador (-ra). **to be a t.,** ser buena maula
**tricky** /'triki/ a informal, maullero; (of things) difícil, complicado; (clever) ingenioso
**tricolor** /'trai,kʌlər/ a tricolor
**tricycle** /'traisikəl/ n triciclo, m
**tried** /traid/ a probado
**triennial** /trai'ɛniəl/ a trienal
**trifle** /'traifəl/ n (object) baratija, fruslería, f; pequeñez, tontería, bagatela, f; Culin. f; (small amount) pequeña cantidad, f, muy poco (de); (adverbially) algo. —vi entretenerse, jugar. —vt (away) malgastar. **to t. with,** jugar con
**trifler** /'traiflər/ n persona frívola, f; (with affections) seductor (-ra)
**trifling** /'traiflɪŋ/ a insignificante, sin importancia, trivial
**trigger** /'trigər/ n (of a fire-arm) gatillo, m; Mech. tirador, m
**trigonometric** /ˌtrigənə'mɛtrik/ a trigonométrico
**trigonometry** /ˌtrigə'nɒmitri/ n trigonometría, f
**trilingual** /trai'lɪŋgwəl/ a trilingüe
**trill** /tril/ n trino, m, vi trinar
**trillion** /'trilyən/ n trillón, m
**trilogy** /'trilədʒi/ n trilogía, f
**trim** /trim/ a aseado; bien arreglado; bien ajustado; elegante; bonito; (of sail) orientado. **She has a t. waist,** Inf. Tiene un talle juncal. —n orden, m; buen estado, m; buena condición, f; (toilet) atavío, m. —vt arreglar; (tidy) asear; pulir; (ornament) ornar, adornar; (adapt) ajustar, adaptar; Sew. guarnecer; (lamps) despabilar; (a fire) atizar; (hair, moustache) atusar, recortar; (trees) mondar, atusar; alisar; (sails) templar, orientar; (distribute weight in a boat) equilibrar; (of quill pens) tajar. —vi (waver) nadar entre dos aguas. **to t. oneself up,** arreglarse
**trimly** /'trimli/ adv aseadamente; lindamente
**trimmer** /'trimər/ n guarnecedor (-ra); contemporizador (-ra)
**trimming** /'trimɪŋ/ n arreglo, m; guarnición, f; (on a dress) pasamanería, f; adorno, m; Agr. poda, f; adaptación, f, ajuste, m; pl **trimmings,** accesorios, m pl
**trimness** /'trimnɪs/ n aseo, buen orden, m; buen estado, m; elegancia, lindeza, f; (slimness) esbeltez, f
**Trinidad and Tobago** /'trinidæd; tə'beigou/ Trinidad, f, y Tobago, m
**Trinidadian** /ˌtrini'deidiən/ n and a trinitario (-ria)
**Trinity** /'triniti/ n Trinidad, f
**trinket** /'triŋkit/ n joya, alhaja, f; dije, m, chuchería, baratija, f
**trinomial** /trai'noumiəl/ a Math. de tres términos. —n Math. trinomio, m
**trio** /'triou/ n trío, m
**trip** /trip/ n excursión, f; viaje, m; (slip) traspié, tropiezo, m; (in wrestling) zancadilla, f; (mistake) desliz, m. —vi (stumble) tropezar, caer; (move nimbly) andar airosamente, ir (or correr) ligeramente; (frolic) bailar, saltar; (wrestling, games) echar la zancadilla; (err) equivocarse; cometer un desliz. —vt (up) hacer caer; echar la zancadilla (a); coger en una falta; hacer desdecirse; coger en un desliz; Naut. levantar (el ancla)
**tripartite** /trai'pɑrtait/ a tripartito
**tripartition** /ˌtraipar'tiʃən/ n tripartición, f
**tripe** /traip/ n callos, m pl
**triple** /'tripəl/ a triple. —vt triplicar. —vi triplicarse
**triplet** /'triplit/ n Poet. terceto, m; Mus. tresillo, m; cada uno (una) de tres hermanos (hermanas) gemelos (-as)
**triplicate** /a. 'triplikit, v. -ˌkeit/ a triplicado. —vt triplicar
**triplication** /ˌtripli'keiʃən/ n triplicación, f
**tripod** /'traipod/ n trípode, m
**Tripoli** /'tripəli/ Trípoli, f
**tripper** /'tripər/ n turista, excursionista, mf
**trippingly** /'tripiŋli/ adv ligeramente
**triptych** /'triptik/ n tríptico, m
**trite** /trait/ a vulgar, trivial
**triteness** /'traitnɪs/ n trivialidad, vulgaridad, f

**triumph** /'traiəmf/ n triunfo, m. —vi triunfar; (over) triunfar de, vencer

**triumphal** /trai'ʌmfəl/ a triunfal. **t. arch,** arco de triunfo, m

**triumphant** /trai'ʌmfənt/ a triunfante, victorioso

**triumvirate** /trai'ʌmvərɪt/ n triunvirato, m

**trivet** /'trɪvɪt/ n trébedes, f pl, trípode, m

**trivial** /'trɪvɪəl/ a trivial, frívolo; insignificante, sin importancia

**triviality** /ˌtrɪvi'ælɪti/ n trivialidad, frivolidad, f; insignificancia, f

**trochlea** /'trɒkliə/ n Anat. tróclea, f

**trodden** /'trɒdn̩/ a trillado, batido

**troglodyte** /'trɒglə‚dait/ a and n troglodita, mf

**Trojan** /'troudʒən/ a and n troyano (-na). **the T. War,** la guerra de Troya, f

**trolley** /'trɒli/ n Elec. trole, m; (for children) carretón, m. **t.-bus,** trolebús, m. —n **trolley car** tranvía, m. **t.-pole,** trole, m

**trollop** /'trɒləp/ n tarasca, ramera, f

**trombone** /trɒm'boun/ n trombón, m. **t. player,** trombón, m

**troop** /trup/ n banda, muchedumbre, f; Theat. compañía, f; (of cavalry) escuadrón, m; pl **troops,** Mil. tropas, f pl; ejército, m. —vi ir en tropel, congregarse; (with away) marcharse en tropel, retirarse; (with out) salir en masa. **fresh troops,** tropas frescas, f pl. **storm troops,** tropas de asalto, f pl. **t.-ship,** transporte de guerra, m

**trooper** /'trupər/ n soldado de caballería, m

**trope** /troup/ n tropo, m

**trophy** /'troufi/ n trofeo, m

**tropic** /'trɒpɪk/ a and n trópico, m

**tropical** /'trɒpɪkəl/ a tropical

**tropism** /'troupɪzəm/ n tropismo, m

**trot** /trɒt/ n trote, m. —vi trotar. —vt hacer trotar. **to t. out,** Inf. sacar a relucir

**troth** /trɔθ/ n fe, f; palabra, f. **to plight one's t.,** dar palabra de matrimonio, desposarse

**trotting** /'trɒtɪŋ/ a trotón. —n trote, m

**troubadour** /'trubə‚dɔr/ n trovador, m, a trovadoresco

**trouble** /'trʌbəl/ n (grief) aflicción, angustia, f; (difficulty) dificultad, f; (effort) esfuerzo, m; pena, desgracia, f; (annoyance) disgusto, sinsabor, m; (unrest) confusión, f, disturbio, m; (illness) enfermedad, f; mal, m; (disagreement) desavenencia, f. **The t. is....,** Lo malo es; La dificultad está en que... **to be in t.,** estar afligido; estar en un apuro, estar entre la espada y la pared. **to be not worth the t.,** no valer la pena. **to stir up t.,** revolver el ajo; armar un lío. **to take the t. to,** tomarse la molestia de

**trouble** /'trʌbəl/ vt turbar; agitar; afligir, inquietar; (badger) importunar; (annoy) molestar; (cost an effort) costar trabajo (e.g., Learning Spanish did not t. him much, No le costó mucho trabajo aprender el castellano). —vi preocuparse; darse la molestia; inquietarse

**troubled** /'trʌbəld/ a agitado; inquieto; preocupado; (of life) accidentado, borrascoso. **to fish in t. waters,** pescar en agua turbia, pescar en río revuelto

**troublesome** /'trʌbəlsəm/ a dificultoso; molesto; inconveniente; importuno; fastidioso

**trough** /trɔf/ n gamella, f; (for kneading bread) artesa, f; (of the waves) seno, m; (meteorological) mínimo, m. **drinking t.,** abrevadero, m. **stone t.,** pila, f

**trounce** /trauns/ vt zurrar, apalear; Fig. fustigar

**troupe** /trup/ n compañía, f

**trousers** /'trauzərz/ n pl pantalones, m pl. **plus four t.,** pantalones de golf, m pl. **striped t.,** pantalón de corte, m. **t. pocket,** bolsillo del pantalón, m. **t. press,** prensa para pantalones, f

**trousseau** /'trusou/ n ajuar de novia, m

**trout** /traut/ n trucha, f

**trowel** /'trauəl/ n Agr. almocafre, m; (mason's) paleta, f, palustre, m

**Troy** /trɔi/ Troya, f

**troy weight** /trɔi/ n peso de joyería, m

**troy weight** n peso de joyería, m

**truant** /'truənt/ n novillero, m; haragán (-ana). —a haragán, perezoso. **to play t.,** (from school) hacer novillos; ausentarse

**truce** /trus/ n tregua, f; suspensión, cesación, f

**truck** /trʌk/ n (lorry) camión, m; carretilla de mano, f; (railway) vagón de carga, m; (intercourse) relaciones, f pl; (trash) cachivaches, m pl, cosas sin valor, f pl

**truckage** /'trʌkɪdʒ/ n camionaje, m; acarreo, m

**truckle** /'trʌkəl/ vi humillarse, no levantar los ojos. **t. bed,** carriola, f

**truculence** /'trʌkyələns/ n truculencia, agresividad, f

**truculent** /'trʌkyələnt/ a truculento, agresivo

**trudge** /trʌdʒ/ vi caminar a pie; andar con dificultad, caminar lentamente, andar trabajosamente, n caminata, f

**true** /tru/ a verdadero; real; leal, sincero; fiel; exacto; honesto; genuino; auténtico; alineado, a plomo. **That is t. of....** Es propio de.... —adv realmente; exactamente. **t.-bred,** de casta legítima. **t.-hearted,** leal, fiel, sincero

**truffle** /'trʌfəl/ n trufa, f. **to stuff with truffles,** trufar

**truism** /'truɪzəm/ n perogrullada, f

**truly** /'truli/ adv lealmente; realmente, verdaderamente; en efecto, por cierto; sinceramente, de buena fe. **Yours t.,** su seguro servidor (su s.s.)

**trump** /trʌmp/ n (cards) triunfo, m; son de la trompeta, m; Inf. gran persona, joya, f. —vt ganar con el triunfo. **to t. up,** inventar. **t.-card,** naipe de triunfo, m

**trumpery** /'trʌmpəri/ a de pacotilla; ineficaz. —n oropel, m

**trumpet** /'trʌmpɪt/ n trompeta, f. —vt trompetear; Fig. pregonar. —vi (of elephant) barritar. **ear-t.,** trompetilla (acústica), f. **speaking t.,** portavoz, m. **t. blast,** trompetazo, m. **t. shaped,** en trompeta

**trumpeter** /'trʌmpɪtər/ n trompetero, trompeta, m

**trumpeting** /'trʌmpɪtɪŋ/ n trompeteo, m; (of elephant) barrito, m

**truncate** /'trʌŋkeit/ a truncado. —vt truncar

**truncheon** /'trʌntʃən/ n porra (de goma), f; bastón de mando, m. **blow with a t.,** porrazo, m

**trundle** /'trʌndl/ vt and vi rodar

**trunk** /trʌŋk/ n (Anat. Bot.) tronco, m; (elephant's) trompa, f; (railway) línea principal, f; baúl, m; cofre, m; pl **trunks,** (Elizabethan, etc.) trusas, f pl; calzoncillos cortos, m pl. **wardrobe t.,** baúl mundo, m. **t.-call,** conferencia telefónica, f. **t.-line,** tronco, m. **t.-road,** carretera de primera clase, carretera mayor, f

**truss** /trʌs/ n Med. braguero, m; (of straw, etc.) haz, m; (of blossom) racimo, m; (framework) armazón, f. —vt atar; Cul. espetar; (a building) apuntalar

**trust** /trʌst/ n fe, confianza, f; deber, m; Law. fideicomiso, m; (credit) crédito, m; esperanza, expectación, f; Com. trust, m. —vt tener confianza en; confiar en; esperar; creer; Com. dar crédito (a). —vi confiar; Com. dar crédito. **in t.,** en confianza, en administración, en depósito. **on t.,** al fiado

**trustee** /trʌ'sti/ n guardián, m; Law. fideicomisario, depositario, consignatario, m

**trustful** /'trʌstfəl/ a confiado

**trustingly** /'trʌstɪŋli/ adv confiadamente

**trust release** n extinción de fideicomiso, f

**trustworthiness** /'trʌst‚wɜrðinɪs/ n honradez, probidad, integridad, f; (of statements) exactitud, f

**trustworthy** /'trʌst‚wɜrði/ a digno de confianza, honrado; fidedigno, seguro; exacto

**trusty** /'trʌsti/ a leal, fiel; firme, seguro

**truth** /truθ/ n verdad, f; realidad, f; exactitud, f. **the plain t.,** la pura verdad. **to tell the t.,** decir la verdad

**truthful** /'truθfəl/ a veraz; exacto, verdadero

**truthfulness** /'truθfəlnɪs/ n veracidad, f; exactitud, f

**try** /trai/ vt and vi procurar, tratar de; (test) probar, ensayar; (a case, Law.) ver (el pleito); (strain) poner a prueba; (tire) cansar, fatigar; (annoy) molestar, exasperar; (afflict) hacer sufrir, afligir; (attempt) intentar; (judge) juzgar; (the weight of) tomar a pulso; (assay) refinar. —n tentativa, f; (football) try. **try as he would....,** Por más que hizo.... **to try hard to,** hacer un gran esfuerzo para. **to try one's luck,** probar fortuna. **to try on clothes,** probarse (un vestido, etc.). **to try out,** poner a prueba, probar. **to try to,** tratar de, procurar

**trying** /'traɪɪŋ/ a molesto; fatigoso; irritante; (painful) angustioso, penoso

**tryst** /trɪst/ n cita, f; lugar de cita, m. —vt citar. —vi citarse

**tsar** /zɑr, tsɑr/ n zar, m

**tsarina** /zɑ'rinə, tsɑ-/ n zarina, f

**tsetse fly** /tset'se, 'tɪtsi/ n mosca tsetsé, f

**tub** /tʌb/ n cuba, f, artesón, m; cubeta, f. —vi bañarse. **tub thumper,** Inf. gerundio, m

**tuba** /'tubə/ n Mus. tuba, f

**tube** /tub/ n tubo, m; (railway) metro, ferrocarril subterráneo, m; tubo, m; Anat. trompa, f. **Eustachian t.,** Anat. trompa de Eustaquio, f. **Fallopian t.,** trompa de Falopio, f. **inner t.,** Auto. cámara de aire, f. **speaking t.,** tubo acústico, m. **test t.,** tubo de ensayo, m

**tuber** /'tubər/ n tubérculo, m

**tubercular** /tʊ'bɜrkyələr/ a tuberculoso

**tuberculosis** /tʊ,bɜrkyə'loʊsɪs/ n tuberculosis, f

**tuberose** /'tub,roʊz/ n nardo, m, tuberosa, f

**tubing** /'tubɪŋ/ n tubería, f

**tubular** /'tubyələr/ a tubular

**tuck** /tʌk/ n Sew. alforza, f; pliegue, m. —vt recoger; Sew. alforzar. —vi hacer alforzas. **to t. in,** (in bed) arropar; Inf. tragar. **to t. under,** poner debajo; doblar. **to t. up,** (in bed) arropar; (skirt) sofaldar; (sleeves) arremangar

**tucker** /'tʌkər/ n camisolín, m

**Tuesday** /'tuzdeɪ/ n martes, m. **Shrove T.,** martes de carnaval, m

**tuft** /tʌft/ n (bunch) manojo, m; (on the head) copete, moño, m, cresta, f; (tassel) borla, f; mechón, m

**tug** /tʌg/ n tirón, m; sacudida, f; (boat) remolcador, m. —vt tirar de; halar; sacudir. —vi tirar con fuerza. **to give a tug,** dar una sacudida. **tug of war,** Lit. lucha de la cuerda, f; Fig. estira y afloja, m sing

**tuition** /tu'ɪʃən/ n (teaching) instrucción, enseñanza, f; lecciones, f pl; (fee) cuota, f

**tulip** /'tulɪp/ n tulipán, m. **t. wood,** palo de rosa, m

**tulle** /tul/ n tul, m

**tumble** /'tʌmbəl/ n caída, f; (somersault) tumbo, m; voltereta, f. —vi caer; (acrobats) voltear, dar saltos. —vt hacer caer; desarreglar. **to t. down,** venirse abajo; caer por. **t. down,** ruinoso, destartalado. **to t. off,** caer de. **to t. out,** vt hacer salir; arrojar. —vi salir apresuradamente. **to t. over,** vt tropezar con. —vi volcarse. **to t. to,** Inf. caer en la cuenta

**tumbler** /'tʌmblər/ n (acrobat) volteador (-ra); vaso para beber, m

**tumbrel** /'tʌmbrəl/ n carreta, f

**tumefaction** /,tumə'fækʃən/ n tumefacción, f

**tumid** /'tumɪd/ a túmido, hinchado

**tumor** /'tumər/ n tumor, m

**tumult** /'tumʌlt/ n alboroto, tumulto, m; conmoción, agitación, f; confusión, f

**tumultuous** /tu'mʌltʃuəs/ a tumultuoso, alborotado; ruidoso; confuso; turbulento, violento

**tumulus** /'tumyələs/ n túmulo, m

**tun** /tun/ n tonel, m, cuba, f, vt entonelar, embarrilar

**tuna** /'tɑni/ n atún, m.

**tune** /tun/ n melodía, f; son, m; armonía, f; Fig. tono, m; Inf. suma, f. —vt Mus. afinar, templar; Radio. sintonizar; (up, an engine) ajustar (un motor). —vi (in) sintonizar el receptor; (up, Mus.) templar (afinar) los instrumentos. **in t.,** Mus. afinado, templado; Fig. armonioso; (agreement) de acuerdo, conforme. **out of t.,** Mus. desafinado, destemplado. **to be out of t.,** desentonar, discordar; Fig. no armonizar, no estar en armonía. **to go out of t.,** desafinar. **to put out of t.,** destemplar. **to change one's t.,** Inf. bajar el tono

**tuneful** /'tunfəl/ a melodioso

**tunefully** /'tunfəli/ adv melodiosamente, armoniosamente

**tunefulness** /'tunfəlnɪs/ n melodía, f

**tuneless** /'tunlɪs/ a disonante, discordante

**tuner** /'tunər/ n afinador, templador, m; Radio. sintonizador, m

**tungsten** /'tʌŋstən/ n tungsteno, m

**tunic** /'tunɪk/ n túnica, f

**tuning** /'tunɪŋ/ n afinación, f; Radio. sintonización, f. **t. fork,** diapasón normal, m. **t. key,** templador, m

**Tunis** /'tunɪs/ Túnez, m

**Tunisian** /tu'nɪʒən/ a and n tunecino (-na)

**tunnel** /'tʌnl/ n túnel, m. —vt hacer (or construir) un túnel por. —vi hacer un túnel

**tunneling** /'tʌnlɪŋ/ n construcción de túneles, f; horadación, f

**turban** /'tɜrbən/ n turbante, m

**turbid** /'tɜrbɪd/ a turbio; Fig. confuso, **to make t.,** enturbiar

**turbine** /'tɜrbɪn, -baɪn/ n turbina, f

**turbulence** /'tɜrbyələns/ n turbulencia, f; desorden, m; agitación, f

**turbulent** /'tɜrbyələnt/ a turbulento; alborotado; (stormy) borrascoso; agitado

**tureen** /tʊ'rin/ n sopera, f

**turf** /tɜrf/ n césped, m; (fuel) turba, f; (racing) carreras de caballos, f pl

**turgid** /'tɜrdʒɪd/ a turgente, hinchado; (of style) pomposo

**turgidity** /tər'dʒɪdɪti/ n turgencia, f; pomposidad, f

**Turk** /tɜrk/ n turco (-ca). **Turk's head,** (duster) deshollinador, m; Naut. cabeza de turco, f

**Turkey** /'tɜrki/ Turquía, f

**turkey** /'tɜrki/ n (cock) pavo, m; (hen) pava, f; **t. red,** rojo turco, m

**Turkish** /'tɜrkɪʃ/ a turco. —n (language) turco, idioma turco, m. **T. bath,** baño turco, m. **T. slipper,** babucha, f. **T. towel,** toalla rusa, f

**turmeric** /'tɜrmərɪk/ n cúrcuma, f. **t. paper,** papel de cúrcuma, m

**turmoil** /'tɜrmɔɪl/ n alboroto, tumulto, desorden, m

**turn** /tɜrn/ n turno, m; (twist) torcimiento, m; (bend) recodo, m, vuelta, f; (in a river) meandro, m; (in a road) viraje, m; (revolution) vuelta, revolución, f; (direction) dirección, f; (in spiral stair) espira, f; Theat. número, m; (change) cambio, m; vicisitud, f; (appearance) aspecto, m; (service) servicio, m; (nature) índole, naturaleza, f; (of phrase) giro, m, expresión, f; (walk) vuelta, f, paseo, m; (talent) talento, m. **a sharp t.,** (in a road) un viraje rápido. **at every t.,** a cada instante; en todas partes. **bad t.,** flaco servicio, m. **by turns,** por turnos. **good t.,** servicio, favor, m. **in its t.,** a su vez. **in t.,** sucesivamente. **Now it's my t.,** Ahora me toca a mí. **The affair has taken a new t.,** El asunto ha cambiado de aspecto. **turn of the century,** vuelta del siglo, f. **turn of the millenium,** vuelta del milenio, f. **t. a t.,** Cul. a la perfección. **to have a t. for,** tener talento para. **to take turns at,** alternar en. **t.-table,** (railway) plataforma, f; (of a gramophone) disco giratorio, m. **t. up,** barahúnda, conmoción, f; (of trousers) dobladillo (del pantalón), m

**turn** /tɜrn/ vt (on a lathe) tornear; (revolve) dar vueltas a, girar; (a key, door handle, etc.) torcer; (the leaves of a book) hojear; (the brain) trastornar; (a screw) enroscar; (the stomach) revolver (el estómago), marear; (go round) doblar, dar la vuelta a; (change) cambiar, mudar; (translate) traducir, verter; (dissuade) disuadir; (deflect) desviar; (apply) adaptar; (direct, move) volver; (concentrate) dirigir; concentrar; (turn over) volver del revés al derecho; (upside-down) volver lo de arriba abajo; (make) hacer, volver; (make sour) volver agrio; (transform) transformar convertir; Mil. envolver. **He has turned thirty,** Ha cumplido los treinta. **He said it without turning a hair,** Lo dijo sin pestañear. **He turned his head,** Volvió la cabeza. **They have turned the corner,** Han doblado la esquina; Fig. Han pasado la crisis. **"Please t. over,"** «A la vuelta (de la página).» m **to t. a deaf ear to,** no dar oídos a, no hacer caso de. **to t. one's hand to,** aplicarse a. **to t. to account,** sacar ventaja (de). **to t. adrift,** dejar a la merced de las olas; echar de casa, poner en la calle; abandonar. **to t. against,** causar aversión, hacer hostil. **to t. aside,** desviar. **to t. away,** despedir; rechazar; (the head, etc.) volver; desviar. **to t. back,** hacer volver; enviar de nuevo; (raise) alzar; (fold) doblar; (the clock) retrasar. **to t. down,** doblar; (gas) bajar; (a glass, etc.) poner boca abajo; (reject) rechazar; (a suitor) dar calabazas (a). **to t. from,** alejar de, desviar de. **to t. in,**

doblar hacia dentro; entregar. **to t. in one's toes,** ser patizambo. **to t. inside out,** volver al revés. **to t. into,** (enter) entrar en; (change) cambiar en, transformar en; convertir en; (translate) traducir a. **to t. off,** (dismiss) despedir; (from) desviarse de, dejar; (light) apagar; (water) cortar; *Mech.* cerrar; (disconnect) desconectar; (avoid) evitar; (refuse) rechazar. **to t. off the tap,** (water, gas) cerrar la llave (del agua, del gas). **to t. on,** (light) encender; (water, gas, etc.) abrir la llave (del agua, del gas); (steam) dar (vapor); (electric current) establecer (la corriente eléctrica); (eyes) fijar. **to t. out,** (expel) expeler, echar; (dismiss) despedir; (animals) echar al campo; (produce) producir; (dress) vestir; (equip) equipar, guarnecer; (a light) apagar. **to t. over,** (the page) volver (la hoja); (transfer) ceder, traspasar; revolver; (upset) volcar, considerar, pensar. **to t. round,** dar vuelta (a); girar; (empty) descargar. **to t. up,** levantar; apuntar; hacia arriba; (the earth) labrar, cavar; (a glass) poner boca arriba; (one's sleeves, skirt) arremangar; (fold) doblar. **to t. up one's nose at,** mirar con desprecio. **to t. upon,** atacar, volverse contra, acometer; depender de, estribar en. **to t. upside down,** volver lo de arriba abajo; revolver; revolcar

**turn** /tɜrn/ *vi* (in a lathe) tornear; (revolve) girar, dar vueltas; (depend) depender (de); torcer; volverse; dar la vuelta; girar sobre los talones; dirigirse (a, hacia); (move) mudar de posición; (deviate) desviarse (de); (be changed) convertirse (en); (become) hacerse, venir a ser; (begin) meterse (a); (take to) dedicarse a; (seek help) acudir; (change behavior) enmendarse, corregirse; (the stomach) revolver (el estómago); (go sour) agriarse, avinagrarse; (rebel) sublevarse. **He turned to the left,** Dio la vuelta a la izquierda; Torció hacia la izquierda. **My head turns,** (with giddiness) Se me va la cabeza. **to t. about,** voltearse, dar la vuelta. **to t. against,** coger aversión (a), disgustarse con; volverse hostil (a). **to t. aside,** desviarse; dejar el camino. **to t. away,** volver la cabeza; apartarse; alejarse. **to t. back,** volver atrás; volver de nuevo; retroceder; volver sobre sus pasos. **to t. down,** doblarse; reducirse. **to t. from,** alejarse de; apartarse de, huir de. **to t. in,** doblarse hacia dentro; (retire) acostarse. **to t. into,** transformarse en; convertirse en. **to t. off,** (depart from) desviarse (de); (fork) torcer, bifurcarse. **to t. out,** estar vuelto hacia fuera; (leave ome) salir de casa; (rise) levantarse (de la cama); (arrive) llegar, presentarse; (attend) asistir, acudir; (result) resultar. **to t. over,** mudar (or cambiar) de posición, revolverse; (upset) voltearse, volcarse. **to t. round,** girar; volverse; cambiar de frente; cambiar de dirección, dar la vuelta; (*Auto., Aer.*) virar; (change views) cambiar de opinión; (change sides) cambiar de partido. **to t. round and round,** dar vueltas, girar. **to t. to,** (apply to) acudir a; (begin) ponerse a; (become) convertirse en; (face) dirigirse hacia; (address) dirigirse a. **to t. up,** (crop up) surgir, aparecer; (arrive) llegar; (happen) acontecer; (be found again) volver a hallarse, reaparecer; (cards) venir; (of hats) levantar el ala; (of hair, etc.) doblarse. **His nose turns up,** Tiene la nariz respingona

**turncoat** /'tɜrn,kout/ *n* desertor (-ra), renegado (-da). **to become a t.,** volver la casaca

**turned-up** /'tɜrnd'ʌp/ *a* (of hats) con el ala levantada; (of noses) respingona

**turner** /'tɜrnər/ *n* (craftsman) tornero, torneador, *m*

**turnery** /'tɜrnəri/ *n* tornería, *f*

**turning** /'tɜrnɪŋ/ *n* (bend) vuelta, *f*; (turnery) tornería, *f*; (of milk, etc.) agrura, *f*; *pl* **turnings,** *Sew.* ensanche, *m.* **t.-point,** punto decisivo, *m*; crisis, *f*

**turnip** /'tɜrnɪp/ *n* nabo, *m.* **t. field,** nabar, *m*

**turnover** /'tɜrn,ouvər/ *n Com.* ventas, *f pl*; *Cul.* pastelillo, *m*

**turnpike** /'tɜrn,paik/ *n* barrera de portazgo, *f*

**turnstile** /'tɜrn,stail/ *n* torniquete, *m*

**turpentine** /'tɜrpən,tain/ *n* aguarrás, *m*, trementina, *f*

**turpitude** /'tɜrpɪ,tud/ *n* infamia, maldad, *f*

**turquoise** /'tɜrkɔiz, -kwɔiz/ *n* turquesa, *f*

**turret** /'tɜrɪt/ *n* torrecilla, almenilla, *f*; *Naut.* torre blindada, *f*

**turreted** /'tɜrɪtɪd/ *a* con torres, guarnecido de torres; en forma de torre

**turtle** /'tɜrtl/ *n* tortuga (dove) tórtolo (-la); (sea) tortuga de mar, *f.* **to turn t.,** voltearse patas arriba; *Naut.* zozobrar. **t. soup,** sopa de tortuga, *f*

**Tuscan** /'tʌskən/ *a and n* toscano (-na)

**Tuscany** /'tʌskəni/ Toscana, *f*

**tusk** /tʌsk/ *n* colmillo, *m*

**tussle** /'tʌsəl/ *n* lucha, *f*; agarrada, *f.* —*vi* luchar, pelear; tener una agarrada

**tutelage** /'tutlɪdʒ/ *n* tutela, *f*

**tutelar** /'tutlər/ *a* tutelar

**tutor** /'tutər/ *n* (private) ayo, *m*; profesor (-ra); (Roman law) tutor, *m*; (supervisor of studies) preceptor. —*vt* enseñar, instruir. —*vi* ser profesor, dar clases

**tutorial** /tu'tɔriəl/ *n* (university) seminario, *m*; (private) clase particular, *f*

**tutoring** /'tutɔrɪŋ/ *n* enseñanza, instrucción, *f*

**twaddle** /'twɒdl/ *n* disparates, *m pl*, tonterías, patrañas, *f pl*

**twain** /twein/ *a* and *n* dos, *m*

**twang** /twæŋ/ *n* punteado de una cuerda, *m*; (of a guitar) zumbido, *m*; (in speech) gangueo, *m.* —*vt* puntear; (las cuerdas de un instrumento) rasguear. —*vi* zumbar. **to speak with a t.,** hablar con una voz gangosa

**tweak** /twik/ *n* pellizco, *m*; sacudida, *f*, tirón, *m.* —*vt* pellizcar; sacudir, tirar

**tweed** /twid/ *n* mezcla, *f*, cheviot, *m*

**tweezers** /'twizərz/ *n pl* pinzas, tenacillas, *f pl*

**twelfth** /twelfθ/ *a* duodécimo; (of the month) (el) doce; (of monarchs) doce. —*n* duodécimo, *m*; (part) dozavo, *m*, duodécima parte, *f.* **T.-night,** Día de Reyes, *m*, Epifanía, *f*

**twelve** /twelv/ *a* and *n* doce *m*; (of age) doce años, *m pl.* **t. o'clock,** las doce; (mid-day) mediodía, *m*; (midnight) media noche, *f*, las doce de la noche. **t.-syllabled,** dodecasílabo

**twentieth** /'twentiɪθ/ *a* vigésimo; (of the month) (el) veinte; (of monarchs) veinte, *n* vigésimo, *m*; (part) vientavo, *m*, vigésima parte, *f*

**twenty** /'twenti/ *a* veinte; (of age) veinte años, *m pl*, *n* veinte, *m*; (score) veintena, *f.* **t.-first,** vigésimo primero; (of date) (el) veintiuno, *m*, (In modern Spanish the ordinals above *décimo* "tenth" are generally replaced by the cardinals, e.g. *the twenty-ninth chapter,* el capítulo veintinueve.)

**twice** /twais/ *adv* dos veces. **t. as many** or **as much,** el doble

**twiddle** /'twɪdl/ *vt* jugar con; hacer girar. —*vi* girar; vibrar. —*n* vuelta, *f.* **to t. one's thumbs,** dar vuelta a los pulgares, estar mano sobre mano

**twig** /twɪg/ *n* ramita, pequeña rama, *f*

**twilight** /'twai,lait/ *n* crepúsculo, *m*; media luz, *f.* —*a* crepuscular. **in the t.,** en el crepúsculo; en la media luz. **t. sleep,** parto sin dolor, *m*

**twin** /twɪn/ *a* gemelo, mellizo; doble. —*n* gemelo (-la), mellizo (-za); (of objects) pareja, *f*, par, *m.* **t.-engined,** bimotor. **t. screw,** (*Naut. Aer.*) de dos hélices

**twine** /twain/ *n* bramante, cordel, *m*; guita, *f.* —*vt* enroscar; (weave) tejer; (encircle) ceñir; (round, about) abrazar. —*vi* (of plants) trepar; entrelazarse; (wind) serpentear

**twinge** /twɪndʒ/ *n* punzada, *f*, dolor agudo, *m*; *Fig.* remordimiento, tormento, *m.* —*vi* causar un dolor agudo

**twining** /'twainɪŋ/ *a Bot.* trepante, voluble. **t. plant,** planta enredadera (or trepante), *f*

**twinkle** /'twɪŋkəl/ *vi* centellear, chispear, titilar; (of eyes) brillar; (of feet) moverse rápidamente, bailar. —*n* (in the eye) chispa, *f*

**twinkling** /'twɪŋklɪŋ/ *n* centelleo, *m*; titilación, *f*; (of the eye) brillo, *m*; (glimpse) vislumbre, *m*; *Fig.* instante, momento, *m.* —*a* titilante, centelleador. **in a t.,** en un dos por tres. **in the t. of an eye,** en un abrir y cerrar de ojos

**twin-tailed comet** /'twin,teild/ *n* ceratias, *m*

**twirl** /twɜrl/ *n* rotación, vuelta, *f*; pirueta, *f.* —*vi* hacer girar; voltear; torcer; (a stick, etc.) dar vueltas (a). —*vi* girar, dar vueltas; dar piruetas

**twirp** /twɜrp/ *n Inf.* renacuajo, *m*

**twist** /twɪst/ *n* (skein) mecha, *f;* trenza, *f;* (yarn) torzal, *m;* (of tobacco) rollo, *m;* (of bread) rosca de pan, *f;* (act of twisting) torcimiento, *m,* torsión, *f;* (in a road, etc.) recodo, *m,* curva, vuelta, *f;* (pull) sacudida, *f;* (contortion) regate, esguince, *m;* (in a winding stair) espira, *f;* (in ball games) efecto, *m;* (in a person's nature) peculiaridad, *f;* falta de franqueza, *f;* (to words) interpretación, *f.* —*vt* torcer; enroscar; (plait) trenzar; (wring) estrujar; (weave) tejer; (encircle) ceñir; (a stick, etc.) dar vueltas a; (of hands) crispar; (distort) interpretar mal, torcer. —*vi* torcerse; enroscarse; (wind) serpentear; dar vueltas; (coil) ensortijarse; (writhe) undular, retorcerse; (of a stair) dar vueltas

**twisted** /'twɪstɪd/ *a* torcido; (of persons) contrahecho

**twisting** /'twɪstɪŋ/ *n* torcimiento, *m;* torcedura, *f;* serpenteo, *m;* (interlacing) entrelazamiento, *m.* —*a* sinuoso, serpenteado

**twit** /twɪt/ **(with)** *vt* echar en cara

**twitch** /twɪtʃ/ *n* sacudida, *f,* tirón, *m;* (nervous) contracción nerviosa, *f.* —*vt* tirar bruscamente, quitar rápidamente; agarrar; (ears, etc.) mover; (hands) &crispar, retorcer. —*vi* crisparse; (of ears, nose) moverse

**twitching** /'twɪtʃɪŋ/ *n* sacudida, *f;* (contraction) crispamiento, *m,* contracción nerviosa, *f;* (pain) punzada, *f;* (of conscience) remordimiento, *m*

**twitter** /'twɪtər/ *n* piada, *f,* gorjeo, *m.* —*vi* piar, gorjear

**two** /tu/ *a* and *n* dos, *m;* (of the clock) (las) dos, *f pl;* (of age) dos años, *m pl.* —*a* de dos. **in two,** en dos partes. **in two's,** de dos en dos. **one or two,** uno o dos; algunos, *m pl;* algunas, *f pl.* **two against two,** dos a dos. **two by two,** de dos en dos, a pares. **Two can live as cheaply as one,** Donde come uno comen dos. **to put two and two together,** atar cabos. **two-edged,** de dos filos. **two-faced,** de dos caras; *Fig.* de dos haces. **to be two-faced,** hacer a dos caras. **two-headed,** de dos cabezas; bicéfalo. **two hundred,** *a* and *n* doscientos, *m.* **two hundredth,** *a* ducentésimo. —*n* ducentésima parte, *f;* doscientos, *m.* **two-legged,** bípedo. **two-ply,** de dos hilos. **two-seater,** *a* de dos asientos. **two-speed gear box,** cambio de marcha de dos velocidades, *m.* **two-step,** paso doble, *m.* **two of a kind,** (well-matched) tal para cual. **two-way switch,** *Elec.* interruptor de dos direcciones, *m*

**twofold** /*a.* 'tu,fould/ *adv.* -'fould/ *a* doble. —*adv* doblemente, dos veces

**twosome** /'tusəm/ *n* partido de dos, *m*

**two's words theory** *n* teoría de los dos gladios, *f*

**tying** /'taɪɪŋ/ *n* ligadura, *f;* atadura, *f*

**tympanum** /'tɪmpənəm/ *n* (*Anat., Archit.*) tímpano, *m*

**type** /taip/ *n* tipo, *m; Print.* carácter, *m,* letra de imprenta, *f,* tipo, *m.* —*vt* and *vi* escribir a máquina. **t. case,** caja de imprenta, *f.* **t. founder,** fundidor de letras de imprenta, *m.* **t. foundry,** fundición de tipos, *f.* **t.-setter,** cajista, *mf* **t.-setting,** composición tipográfica, *f*

**typewriter** /'taip,raitər/ *n* máquina de escribir, *f*

**typewriting** /'taip,raitɪŋ/ *n* mecanografía, *f, a* mecanográfico

**typewritten** /'taip,rɪtn̩/ *a* escrito a máquina

**typhoid** /'taifɔid/ *n* tifoidea, fiebre tifoidea, *f*

**typhoon** /tai'fun/ *n* tifón, *m*

**typhus** /'taifəs/ *n* tifus, tabardillo pintado, *m*

**typical** /'tɪpɪkəl/ *a* típico, característico; simbólico

**typify** /'tɪpə,fai/ *vt* simbolizar, representar; ser ejemplo de

**typist** /'taipɪst/ *n* mecanografista, *mf;* mecanógrafo (-fa)

**typographer** /tai'pɒgrəfər/ *n* tipógrafo, *f*

**typographic** /,taipə'græfɪk/ *a* tipográfico

**typography** /tai'pɒgrəfi/ *n* tipografía, *f*

**tyrannical** /tɪ'rænɪkəl/ *a* tiránico, déspótico

**tyrannization** /,tɪrənə'zeiʃən/ *n* tiranización, *f*

**tyrannize** /'tɪrə,naiz/ *vi* tiranizar

**tyranny** /'tɪrəni/ *n* tiranía, *f,* despotismo, *m*

**tyrant** /'tairənt/ *n* déspota, *m,* tirano (-na)

**Tyre** /taiər/ Tiro, *m*

**Tyrolese** /,tairə'liz/ *a* and *n* tirolés (-esa)

**Tyrol, the** /tɪ'roul/ el Tirol

**Tyrrhenian** /tɪ'riniən/ *a* tirreno

**Tyrrhenian Sea, the** el Mar Tirreno, *m*

# U

**u** /yu/ *n* (letter) u, *f.* **U-boat,** submarino, *m.* **u-shaped,** en forma de U
**ubiquitous** /yu'bɪkwɪtəs/ *a* ubicuo, omnipresente
**ubiquity** /yu'bɪkwɪti/ *n* ubicuidad, omnipresencia, *f*
**udder** /'ʌdər/ *n* ubre, teta, mama, *f*
**ugh** /ʊx, ʌg/ *interj* ¡uf!
**ugliness** /'ʌglɪnɪs/ *n* fealdad, *f;* (moral) perversidad, *f;* (of a situation) peligro, *m,* lo difícil
**ugly** /'ʌgli/ *a* feo; (morally) repugnante, asqueroso, perverso; (of a situation) peligroso, difícil; (of a wound) grave, profundo; (of a look) amenazador; *Inf.* desagradable; (of weather) borrascoso. **to make u.,** afear, hacer feo
**Ukraine** /yu'krein/ Ucrania, *f*
**Ukrainian** /yu'kreiniən/ *a* and *n* ucranio (-ia)
**ukulele** /ˌyukə'leili/ *n Mus.* ucelele, *m*
**ulcer** /'ʌlsər/ *n* úlcera, *f*
**ulcerate** /'ʌlsə,reit/ *vt* ulcerar. —*vi* ulcerarse
**ulceration** /ˌʌlsə'reiʃən/ *n* ulceración, *f*
**ulcerous** /'ʌlsərəs/ *a* ulceroso
**ulterior** /ʌl'tɪəriər/ *a* (of place) ulterior; (of time) posterior, ulterior; (of motives) interesado, oculto; **ulterior motive,** segunda intención, *f*
**ultimate** /'ʌltəmɪt/ *a* último; fundamental, esencial
**ultimately** /'ʌltəmɪtli/ *adv* por fin, al final; esencialmente
**ultimatum** /ˌʌltə'meitəm/ *n* ultimátum, *m*
**ultimo** /'ʌltəˌmou/ *adv* del mes anterior
**ultra** /'ʌltrə/ *a* exagerado, extremo. —*prefix* ultra-. **u-red,** ultrarrojo. **u.-violet,** ultravioleta
**ultramarine** /ˌʌltrəmə'rin/ *a* ultramarino. —*n* azul de ultramar, *m*
**ultramontane** /ˌʌltrəmɒn'tein/ *a* ultramontano
**ululation** /ˌʌlyə'leiʃən/ *n* ululación, *f,* ululato, *m*
**umbilical** /ʌm'bɪlɪkəl/ *a* umbilical
**umbilicus** /ʌm'bɪlɪkəs/ *n* ombligo, *m*
**umbra** /'ʌmbrə/ *n Astron.* cono de sombra, *m*
**umbrage** /'ʌmbrɪdʒ/ *n Poet.* sombra, *f;* resentimiento, enfado, *m.* **to take u.,** ofenderse, resentirse
**umbrella** /ʌm'brelə/ *n* paraguas, *m.* **u. maker,** paragüero (-ra). **u. shop,** paragüería, *f.* **u. stand,** paragüero, *m*
**umpire** /'ʌmpaiʳr/ *n Sports.* árbitro, *m; Law.* juez arbitrador, tercero en discordia, *m.* —*vt* arbitrar
**un-** *prefix* Used before adjectives, adverbs, abstract nouns, verbs and translated in Spanish by **in-, des-, nada, no, poco, sin,** as well as in other ways
**unabashed** /ˌʌnə'bæʃt/ *a* desvergonzado, descarado, insolente; (calm) sereno, sosegado
**unabashedly** /ˌʌnə'bæʃɪdli/ *adv* sin rubor
**unabated** /ˌʌnə'beitɪd/ *a* no disminuido; cabal, entero
**unabbreviated** /ˌʌnə'brivi,eitɪd/ *a* íntegro, sin abreviar
**unable** /ʌn'eibəl/ *a* incapaz, impotente; (physical defect) imposibilitado. **to be u. to,** no poder, serle a uno imposible. **to be u. to control,** no poder controlar
**unabridged** /ˌʌnə'brɪdʒd/ *a.* See **unabbreviated**
**unaccented** /ʌn'æksentɪd/ *a* sin acento
**unacceptability** /ˌʌnæk,septə'bɪlɪti/ *n* lo inaceptable
**unacceptable** /ˌʌnæk,septəbəl/ *a* inaceptable
**unaccepted** /ˌʌnæk,septɪd/ *a* rechazado, no aceptado
**unaccommodating** /ʌnə'kɒmədeitɪŋ/ *a* poco complaciente, nada servicial
**unaccompanied** /ˌʌnə'kʌmpənid/ *a* solo, sin compañía; *Mus.* sin acompañamiento
**unaccomplished** /ˌʌnə'kɒmplɪʃt/ *a* incompleto, sin terminar, inacabado; (not clever) sin talento
**unaccountability** /ˌʌnəˌkauntə'bɪlɪti/ *n* lo inexplicable; falta de responsabilidad, irresponsabilidad, *f*
**unaccountable** /ˌʌnə'kauntəbəl/ *a* inexplicable; irresponsable
**unaccountably** /ˌʌnə'kauntəbli/ *adv* inexplicablemente, extrañamente

**unaccredited** /ˌʌnæ'kredɪtɪd/ *a* no acreditado, extraoficial
**unaccustomed** /ˌʌnə'kʌstəmd/ *a* no habituado; (unusual) desacostumbrado, insólito, inusitado
**unacknowledged** /ˌʌnæk'nɒlɪdʒd/ *a* no reconocido; (of letter) sin contestación, por contestar; no correspondido, sin devolver; (of crimes, etc.) inconfeso, no declarado
**unacquainted** /ˌʌnə'kweintɪd/ *a* que no conoce; que desconoce, que ignora; no habituado. **to be u. with,** no conocer; ignorar; no estar acostumbrado a
**unadaptable** /ˌʌnə'dæptəbəl/ *a* inadaptable (also of persons)
**unadorned** /ˌʌnə'dɔrnd/ *a* sin adorno sencillo, que no tiene adornos
**unadulterated** /ˌʌnə'dʌltə,reitɪd/ *a* sin mezcla, no adulterado, natural; genuino, verdadero; puro
**unadventurous** /'ʌnæd'vɛntʃərəs/ *a* nada aventurero, que no busca aventuras, tímido; tranquilo, sin incidente
**unadvisability** /ˌʌnædˌvaizə'bɪlɪti/ *n* imprudencia, *f;* inoportunidad, *f*
**unadvisable** /ˌʌnædˌvaizə'bəl/ *a* imprudente; inoportuno, no conveniente
**unadvisedly** /ˌʌnædˌvaizɪdli/ *adv* imprudentemente
**unaffected** /ˌʌnə'fektɪd/ *a* natural, llano, sin melindres; impasible; genuino, sincero. **u. by,** no afectado por
**unaffectedly** /ˌʌnə'fektɪdli/ *adv* sin afectación
**unaffectedness** /ˌʌnə'fektɪdnɪs/ *n* naturalidad, sencillez, *f;* sinceridad, franqueza, *f*
**unaffiliated** /ˌʌnə'fɪli,eitɪd/ *a* no afiliado
**unafraid** /ˌʌnə'freid/ *a* sin temor
**unaided** *a* sin ayuda, solo a solas
**unaired** /ʌn'eərd/ *a* sin ventilar, no ventilado; húmedo, sin airear
**unalloyed** /ˌʌnə'lɔid/ *a* sin mezcla, puro
**unalterability** /ʌn,ɔltərə'bɪlɪti/ *n* lo inalterable; constancia, *f*
**unalterable** /ʌn'ɔltərəbəl/ *a* inalterable; invariable, constante
**unambiguous** /ˌʌnæm'bɪgyuəs/ *a* no ambiguo, nada dudoso, claro
**unambitious** /ˌʌnæm'bɪʃəs/ *a* sin ambición; modesto
**unamusing** /ˌʌnə'myuzɪŋ/ *a* nada divertido
**unanimity** /ˌyunə'nɪmɪti/ *n* unanimidad, *f*
**unanimous** /yu'nænəməs/ *a* unánime
**unanimously** /yu'nænəməsli/ *adv* unánimemente, por unanimidad. **carried u.,** adoptado por unanimidad
**unanswerability** /ʌn,ænsərə'bɪlɪti/ *n* imposibilidad de negar, *f;* lo irrefutable
**unanswerable** /ʌn'ænsərəbəl/ *a* incontestable, incontrovertible, incontrastable, irrefutable
**unanswered** /ʌn'ænsərd/ *a* no contestado, sin contestar; (unrequited) no correspondido
**unapparent** /ˌʌnə'pærənt/ *a* no aparente
**unappealable** /ˌʌnə'piləbəl/ *a* inapelable
**unappeasable** /ˌʌnə'pizəbəl/ *a* implacable
**unappeased** /ˌʌnə'pizd/ *a* no satisfecho; implacable
**unappetizing** /ʌn'æpɪ,taizɪŋ/ *a* no apetitoso; (unattractive) repugnante, feo
**unappreciated** /ˌʌnə'priʃi,eitɪd/ *a* desestimado, no apreciado, tenido en poco; (misunderstood) mal comprendido
**unapproachable** /ˌʌnə'proutʃəbəl/ *a* inaccesible
**unapproachableness** /ˌʌnə'proutʃəbəlnɪs/ *n* inaccesibilidad, *f*
**unappropriated** /ˌʌnə'proupri,eitɪd/ *a* no concedido; libre
**unapproved** /ˌʌnə'pruvd/ *a* sin aprobar, no aprobado
**unarm** /ʌn'ɑrm/ *vt* desarmar. —*vi* desarmarse, quitarse las armas
**unarmed** /ʌn'ɑrmd/ *a* desarmado; indefenso; (*Zool., Bot.*) inerme

**unarranged** /ˌʌnəˈreindʒd/ a no arreglado, sin clasificar; (accidental) fortuito, casual

**unartistic** /ˌʌnarˈtɪstɪk/ a no artístico

**unascertainable** /ˌʌnæsərˈteinəbəl/ a no verificable

**unashamed** /ˌʌnəˈʃeimd/ a sin vergüenza; tranquilo, sereno; insolente, descarado

**unasked** /ʌnˈæskt/ a sin pedir; no solicitado; espontáneo; (uninvited) no convidado

**unassailable** /ˌʌnəˈseiləbəl/ a inexpugnable; irrefutable; incontestable

**unassisted** /ˌʌnəˈsɪstɪd/ a. See **unaided**

**unassuming** /ˌʌnəˈsumɪŋ/ a modesto, sin pretensiones

**unattached** /ˌʌnəˈtætʃt/ a suelto; *Law.* no embargado; *Mil.* de reemplazo; independiente

**unattainable** /ˌʌnəˈteinəbəl/ a inasequible, irrealizable

**unattainableness** /ˌʌnəˈteinəbəlnɪs/ n imposibilidad de alcanzar (or realizar), f; inaccesibilidad

**unattended** /ˌʌnəˈtɛndɪd/ a solo, sin acompañamiento; (of ill person) sin tratamiento; (of entertainment, etc.) no concurrido

**unattested** /ˌʌnəˈtɛstɪd/ a sin atestación

**unattractive** /ˌʌnəˈtræktɪv/ a poco atrayente, desagradable, antipático, feo

**unattractiveness** /ˌʌnəˈtræktɪvnɪs/ n fealdad, falta de hermosura, f; lo desagradable

**unauthentic** /ˌʌnɔˈθɛntɪk/ a no auténtico, sin autenticidad; apócrifo

**unauthorized** /ʌnˈɔθəˌraizd/ a no autorizado

**unavailable** ˌ½nəˈveiləbəl/ a inaprovechable

**unavailing** /ˌʌnəˈveilɪŋ/ a inútil, vano

**unavenged** /ˌʌnəˈvɛndʒd/ a no vengado, sin castigo

**unavoidable** /ˌʌnəˈvɔidəbəl/ a inevitable, preciso, necesario. **to be u.,** no poder evitarse, no tener remedio

**unavoidableness** /ˌʌnəˈvɔidəbəlnɪs/ n inevitabilidad, necesidad, f

**unavoidably** /ˌʌnəˈvɔidəbli/ adv irremediablemente

**unaware** /ˌʌnəˈwɛər/ a ignorante; inconsciente. **to be u. of,** ignorar, desconocer; no darse cuenta de

**unawareness** /ˌʌnəˈwɛərnɪs/ n ignorancia, f, desconocimiento, m; inconsciencia, f

**unawares** /ˌʌnəˈwɛərz/ adv (by mistake) sin querer, inadvertidamente; (unprepared) de sobresalto, de improviso, inopinadamente. **He caught me u.,** Me cogió desprevenido

**unbalance** /ʌnˈbæləns/ vt desequilibrar, hacer perder el equilibrio; *Fig.* trastornar

**unbalanced** /ʌnˈbælənst/ a desequilibrado; *Fig.* trastornado; *Com.* no balanceado

**unbaptized** /ʌnˈbæptaizd/ a no bautizado, sin bautizar

**unbar** /ʌnˈbɑr/ vt desatrancar; *Fig.* abrir

**unbearable** /ʌnˈbɛərəbəl/ a intolerable, insufrible, inaguantable, inllevable, insoportable

**unbearably** /ʌnˈbɛərəbli/ adv insoportablemente

**unbeatable** /ʌnˈbitəbəl/ a inmejorable

**unbeaten** /ʌnˈbitn/ a (of paths) no frecuentado, no pisado; (of armies) no derrotado, no batido; invicto

**unbecoming** /ˌʌnbɪˈkʌmɪŋ/ a impropio, inapropiado, inconveniente; indecoroso, indigno; indecente; (of clothes) que no va bien, que sienta mal

**unbelief** /ˌʌnbɪˈlif/ n incredulidad, f

**unbelievable** /ˌʌnbɪˈlivəbəl/ a increíble

**unbelievably** /ˌʌnbɪˈlivəbli/ adv increíblemente

**unbeliever** /ˌʌnbɪˈlivər/ n incrédulo (-la), descreído (-da)

**unbeloved** /ˌʌnbɪˈlʌvd/ a no amado

**unbend** /ʌnˈbɛnd/ vt desencorvar, enderezar; entretenerse, descansar; (*Naut.* of sails) desenvergar; (*Naut.* of cables) desamarrar. —vi enderezarse; mostrarse afable

**unbending** /ʌnˈbɛndɪŋ/ a inflexible, rígido, tieso; *Fig.* inexorable, inflexible, duro, terco; (amiable) afable, jovial

**unbiased** /ʌnˈbaiəst/ a imparcial, ecuánime

**unbidden** /ʌnˈbɪdn/ a espontáneo; (uninvited) no convidado, no invitado

**unbind** /ʌnˈbaind/ vt desligar, desatar; (bandages) desvendar; (books) desencuadernar

**unbleached** /ʌnˈblitʃt/ a crudo, sin blanquear

**unblemished** /ʌnˈblɛmɪʃt/ a no manchado; (pure) sin mancha, inmaculado, puro

**unblessed** /ʌnˈblɛst/ a no bendecido, no consagrado; (accursed) maldito; (unhappy) desdichado

**unblushing** /ʌnˈblʌʃɪŋ/ a desvergonzado, insolente

**unbolt** /ʌnˈboult/ vt descerrojar, desempernar

**unborn** /ʌnˈbɔrn/ a sin nacer, no nacido todavía; venidero

**unbosom** /ʌnˈbʊzəm/ vt confesar, declarar. **to u. oneself,** abrir su pecho (a) or (con)

**unbought** /ʌnˈbɔt/ a no comprado; gratuito, libre; (not bribed) no sobornado

**unbound** /ʌnˈbaund/ a suelto, libre; (of books) en rama, no encuadernado

**unbounded** /ʌnˈbaundɪd/ a ilimitado, infinito; inmenso

**unbowed** /ʌnˈbaud/ a erguido; no encorvado; (undefeated) invicto

**unbreakable** /ʌnˈbreikəbəl/ a irrompible, inquebrantable

**unbridled** /ʌnˈbraidld/ a desenfrenado, violento; licencioso

**unbroken** /ʌnˈbroukən/ a no quebrantado, intacto, entero; continuo, incesante; no interrumpido; (of soil) virgen; (of a horse) indomado, invioldo; (of the spirit) indómito; (of a record) no batido

**unbrotherly** /ʌnˈbrʌðərli/ a poco fraternal, indigno de hermanos

**unbuckle** /ʌnˈbʌkəl/ vt deshebillar

**unburden** /ʌnˈbɜrdn/ vt descargar; aliviar. **to u. oneself,** (express one's feelings) desahogarse

**unburied** /ʌnˈbɛrid/ a insepulto

**unburnt** /ʌnˈbɜrnt/ a no quemado; incombusto

**unbusinesslike** /ʌnˈbɪznɪsˌlaik/ a informal; poco comercial, descuidado

**unbutton** /ʌnˈbʌtn/ vt desabrochar, desabotonar

**uncalled** /ʌnˈkɔld/ a no llamado, no invitado. **u.-for,** impertinente; innecesario

**uncannily** /ʌnˈkænˌji/ adv misteriosamente

**uncanniness** /ʌnˈkæninɪs/ n lo misterioso

**uncanny** /ʌnˈkæni/ a misterioso, horroroso, pavoroso

**uncared-for** /ʌnˈkɛərdˌfɔr/ a abandonado, desatendido, desamparado

**uncarpeted** /ʌnˈkɑrpɪtid/ a sin alfombra

**uncaught** /ʌnˈkɔt/ a no prendido, libre

**unceasing** /ʌnˈsisɪŋ/ a continuo, incesante, sin cesar, constante

**unceasingly** /ʌnˈsisɪŋli/ adv incesantemente, sin cesar

**uncensored** /ʌnˈsɛnsərd/ a no censurado

**unceremonious** /ˌʌnsɛrəˈmouniəs/ a sin ceremonia, familiar; descortés, brusco

**unceremoniousness** /ˌʌnsɛrəˈmouniəsnɪs/ n falta de ceremonia, familiaridad, f; incivilidad, descortesía, f

**uncertain** /ʌnˈsɜrtn/ a incierto, dudoso, inseguro; precario; (hesitant) indeciso, vacilante, irresoluto

**uncertainly** /ʌnˈsɜrtnli/ adv inciertamente

**uncertainty** /ʌnˈsɜrtnti/ n incertidumbre, duda, f; inseguridad, f; irresolución, f

**uncertificated** /ˌʌnsərˈtɪfɪˌkeitid/ a sin certificado (of teachers, etc.) sin título

**uncertified** /ʌnˈsɜrtəˌfaid/ a sin garantía; no garantizado; (of lunatics) sin certificar

**unchain** /ʌnˈtʃein/ vt desencadenar

**unchallenged** /ʌnˈtʃæləndʒd/ a incontestable

**unchangeable** /ʌnˈtʃeindʒəbəl/ a invariable, inalterable, inmutable

**unchangeableness** /ʌnˈtʃeindʒəbəlnɪs/ n invariabilidad, inalterabilidad, f

**unchanging** /ʌnˈtʃeindʒɪŋ/ a inmutable, invariable

**uncharitable** /ʌnˈtʃærəbəl/ a nada caritativo, duro; intolerante, intransigente

**uncharitableness** /ʌnˈtʃærɪtəbəlnɪs/ n falta de caridad, f; intolerancia, intransigencia

**uncharitably** /ʌnˈtʃærɪtəbli/ adv sin caridad; con intolerancia

**unchaste** /ʌnˈtʃeist/ a incasto, incontinente; deshonesto, impuro, lascivo

**unchecked** /ʌnˈtʃɛkt/ a desenfrenado; (unproved) no comprobado; *Com.* no confrontado

**unchivalrous** /ʌnˈʃɪvəlrəs/ a nada galante, nada caballeroso

**unchristened** /ʌnˈkrɪsənd/ a no bautizado, sin bautizar

**unchristian** /ʌnˈkrɪstʃən/ a (heathen) pagano; poco cristiano, indigno de un cristiano, nada caritativo

**uncircumcised** /ʌnˈsɜrkəm,saɪzd/ a incircunciso

**uncircumscribed** /ʌnˈsɜrkəm,skraɪbd/ a incircunscripto

**uncivil** /ʌnˈsɪvəl/ a descortés, incivil

**uncivilizable** /ʌnˈsɪvə,laɪzəbəl/ a reacio a la civilización

**uncivilized** /ʌnˈsɪvə,laɪzd/ a no civilizado, bárbaro, salvaje, inculto

**uncivilly** /ʌnˈsɪvəli/ adv descortésmente

**unclad** /ʌnˈklæd/ a sin vestir; desnudo

**unclasp** /ʌnˈklæsp/ vt (jewelery) desengarzar; desabrochar; (of hands) soltar, separar

**unclassifiable** /ʌnˈklæsə,faɪəbəl/ a inclasificable

**unclassified** /ʌnˈklæsə,faɪd/ a sin clasificar

**uncle** /ˈʌŋkəl/ n tío, m; (pawnbroker) prestamista, m

**unclean** /ʌnˈklin/ a sucio, puerco, inmundo; desaseado; impuro, obsceno; (ritually) poluto

**uncleanliness** /ʌnˈklɛnlɪnɪs/ n suciedad, porquería, f; desaseo, m; falta de limpieza, f

**uncleanly** /ʌnˈklɛnli/ a sucio, puerco; desaseado

**uncleanness** /ʌnˈklinnɪs/ n suciedad, f; impureza, obscenidad, inmoralidad, f

**unclench** /ʌnˈklɛntʃ/ vt (of hands) abrir

**Uncle Tom's Cabin** La Cabaña del Tío Tom

**unclouded** /ʌnˈklaʊdɪd/ a sin nubes, despejado, claro

**uncoil** /ʌnˈkɔɪl/ vt desarrollar. —vi desovillarse; (of snakes) desanillarse

**uncollected** /ˌʌnkəˈlɛktɪd/ a disperso; no cobrado; (in confusion) confuso, desordenado

**uncolored** /ʌnˈkʌlərd/ a incoloro; Fig. imparcial, objetivo, sencillo

**uncombed** /ʌnˈkoʊmd/ a despeinado, sin peinar

**uncomfortable** /ʌnˈkʌmftəbəl/ a incómodo; (anxious) intranquilo, inquieto, desasosegado, preocupado; (awkward) molesto, difícil, desagradable. **to be u.**, (people) estar incómodo; (anxious) estar preocupado; (of things) ser incómodo

**uncomfortableness** /ʌnˈkʌmfərtəbəlnɪs/ n incomodidad, f; malestar, m; intranquilidad, preocupación, f; dificultad, f; lo desagradable

**uncomfortably** /ʌnˈkʌmfərtəbli/ adv incómodamente; intranquilamente; desagradablemente

**uncomforted** /ʌnˈkʌmfərtɪd/ a desconsolado, sin consuelo

**uncommercial** /ˌʌnkəˈmɜrʃəl/ a no comercial

**uncommon** /ʌnˈkɒmən/ a poco común, extraordinario, singular, raro, extraño; infrecuente; insólito

**uncommonly** /ʌnˈkɒmənli/ adv extraordinariamente, muy; infrecuentemente, raramente

**uncommonness** /ʌnˈkɒmənnɪs/ n infrecuencia, rareza, f; singularidad, f

**uncommunicative** /ˌʌnkəˈmyunɪkətɪv/ a reservado, poco expresivo

**uncommunicativeness** /ˌʌnkəˈmyunɪkətɪvnɪs/ n reserva, f

**uncomplaining** /ˌʌnkəmˈpleɪnɪŋ/ a resignado, que no se queja

**uncomplainingly** /ˌʌnkəmˈpleɪnɪŋli/ adv con resignación

**uncompliant** /ˌʌnkəmˈplaɪant/ a sordo, inflexible

**uncomplicated** /ʌnˈkɒmplɪ,keɪtɪd/ a sencillo, sin complicaciones

**uncomplimentary** /ˌʌnkɒmpləˈmɛntəri/ a descortés, poco halagüeño, ofensivo

**uncompromising** /ʌnˈkɒmprəˌmaɪzɪŋ/ a inflexible, estricto, intolerante; irreconciliable

**unconcealed** /ˌʌnkənˈsild/ a no oculto; abierto

**unconcern** /ˌʌnkənˈsɜrn/ n indiferencia, frialdad, f, desapego, m; (lack of interest) apatía, despreocupación, f; (nonchalance) desenfado, m, frescura, f

**unconcerned** /ˌʌnkənˈsɜrnd/ a indiferente, frío, despegado; apático, despreocupado; desenfadado, fresco

**unconcernedly** /ˌʌnkənˈsɜrnɪdli/ adv con indiferencia; sin preocuparse; con desenfado

**unconditional** /ˌʌnkənˈdɪʃənl/ a incondicional, absoluto. **u. surrender**, rendición incondicional, f

**unconditionally** /ˌʌnkənˈdɪʃənli/ adv incondicionalmente; Mil. a discreción

**unconfessed** /ˌʌnkənˈfɛst/ a inconfeso

**unconfined** /ˌʌnkənˈfaɪnd/ a suelto, libre; ilimitado; sin estorbo

**unconfirmed** /ˌʌnkənˈfɜrmd/ a no confirmado; (report) sin confirmar

**uncongenial** /ˌʌnkənˈdʒinyəl/ a incompatible, antipático; desagradable, repugnante

**uncongeniality** /ˌʌnkən,dʒiniˈælɪti/ n incompatibilidad, antipatía, f; repugnancia, f; lo desagradable

**unconnected** /ˌʌnkəˈnɛktɪd/ a inconexo; Mech. desconectado; (relationship) sin parentesco; (confused) incoherente

**unconquerable** /ʌnˈkɒŋkərəbəl/ a invencible, indomable, inconquistable

**unconquered** /ʌnˈkɒŋkərd/ a no vencido

**unconscientious** /ˌʌnkɒnʃiˈɛnʃəs/ a poco concienzudo

**unconscionable** /ʌnˈkɒnʃənəbəl/ a excesivo, desmedido; sin conciencia

**unconscious** /ʌnˈkɒnʃəs/ a inconsciente; (senseless) insensible, sin sentido; espontáneo; (unaware) ignorante. **to be u. of,** ignorar; perder la consciencia de. **to become u.,** perder el sentido

**unconsciously** /ʌnˈkɒnʃəsli/ adv inconscientemente, involuntariamente

**unconsciousness** /ʌnˈkɒnʃəsnɪs/ n inconsciencia, f; (hypnosis, swoon) insensibilidad, f; (unawareness) ignorancia, falta de conocimiento, f

**unconsecrated** /ʌnˈkɒnsɪ,kreɪtɪd/ a no consagrado

**unconsidered** /ˌʌnkənˈsɪdərd/ a indeliberado; sin importancia, trivial

**unconstitutional** /ˌʌnkɒnstɪˈtuʃənl/ a anticonstitucional, inconstitucional

**unconstitutionally** /ˌʌnkɒnstɪˈtuʃənli/ adv inconstitucionalmente

**unconstrained** /ˌʌnkənˈstreɪnd/ a libre; voluntario; sin freno

**uncontaminated** /ˌʌnkənˈtæmɪ'neɪtɪd/ a incontaminado; puro, sin mancha, impoluto

**uncontested** /ˌʌnkənˈtɛstɪd/ a sin oposición

**uncontradicted** /ˌʌnkɒntrəˈdɪktɪd/ a sin contradicción; incontestable

**uncontrollable** /ˌʌnkənˈtroʊləbəl/ a irrefrenable, incontrolable, inmanejable; (temper) ingobernable, indomable

**uncontrolled** /ˌʌnkənˈtroʊld/ a libre, no controlado; desenfrenado, desgobernado

**unconventional** /ˌʌnkənˈvɛnʃənl/ n poco convencional; bohemio, excéntrico, extravagante; original

**unconventionality** /ˌʌnkən,vɛnʃəˈnælɪti/ a excentricidad, extravagancia, independencia de ideas, f; (of a design) originalidad, f

**unconversant** /ˌʌnkənˈvɜrsənt/ a poco familiar, poco versado (en)

**unconverted** /ˌʌnkənˈvɜrtɪd/ a no convertido; sin transformar

**unconvinced** /ˌʌnkənˈvɪnst/ a no convencido

**unconvincing** /ˌʌnkənˈvɪnsɪŋ/ a no convincente, poco convincente, que no me (nos, etc.) convence; frívolo

**uncooked** /ʌnˈkʊkt/ a crudo, no cocido, sin cocer

**uncork** /ʌnˈkɔrk/ vt destapar, descorchar, quitar el corcho

**uncorrected** /ˌʌnkəˈrɛktɪd/ a sin corregir, no corregido

**uncorroborated** /ˌʌnkəˈrɒbə,reɪtɪd/ a no confirmado, sin confirmar

**uncorrupted** /ˌʌnkəˈrʌptɪd/ a incorrupto; puro, no pervertido; (unbribed) no sobornado, honrado

**uncorruptible** /ˌʌnkəˈrʌptəbəl/ a incorruptible

**uncountable** /ʌnˈkaʊntəbəl/ a innumerable

**uncounted** /ʌnˈkaʊntɪd/ a no contado, sin cuenta

**uncouple** /ʌnˈkʌpəl/ vt soltar; desenganchar, desconectar

**uncouth** /ʌnˈkuθ/ a grosero, chabacano, tosco, patán

**uncouthness** /ʌnˈkuθnɪs/ n grosería, tosquedad, patanería, f

**uncover** /ʌn'kʌvər/ vt descubrir; (remove lid of) destapar; (remove coverings of) desabrigar, desarropar; (leave unprotected) desamparar; (disclose) revelar, dejar al descubierto. —vi descubrirse, quitar el sombrero

**uncovered** /ʌn'kʌvərd/ a descubierto; desnudo; sin cubierta

**uncreated** /ˌʌnkri'eitid/ a increado

**uncritical** /ʌn'kritikəl/ a sin sentido crítico, poco juicioso

**uncross** /ʌn'krɔs/ vt (of legs) descruzar

**uncrossed** /ʌn'krɔst/ a (of check) sin cruzar

**uncrowned** /ʌn'kraund/ a antes de ser coronado; sin corona

**unction** /'ʌŋkʃən/ n unción, f; untadura, f, untamiento, m; (unguent) ungüento, m; (zeal) fervor, m; (flattery) insinceridad, hipocresía, f; (relish) gusto, entusiasmo, m. **extreme u.,** extremaunción, f

**unctuous** /'ʌŋktʃuəs/ a untuoso, craso; insincero, zalamero

**uncultivable** /ʌn'kʌltəvəbəl/ a incultivable

**uncultivated** /ʌn'kʌltəˌveitid/ a inculto, yermo; (barbarous) salvaje, bárbaro; (uncultured) inculto, tosco; no cultivado

**uncultured** /ʌn'kʌltʃərd/ a inculto, iletrado

**uncurbed** /ʌn'kərbd/ a sin freno; Fig. desenfrenado

**uncurl** /ʌn'kərl/ vt desrizar vi desrizarse; desovillarse

**uncurtained** /ʌn'kərtn̩d/ a sin cortinas; con las cortinas recogidas

**uncut** /ʌn'kʌt/ a sin cortar, no cortado; (of gems) sin labrar

**undamaged** /ʌn'dæmidʒd/ a indemne, sin daño

**undated** /ʌn'deitid/ a sin fecha

**undaunted** /ʌn'dɔntid/ a intrépido, atrevido

**undeceive** /ˌʌndɪ'siv/ vt desengañar, desilusionar

**undecided** /ˌʌndɪ'saidid/ a (of question) pendiente, indeciso; dudoso; vacilante, irresoluto

**undecipherable** /ˌʌndɪ'saifərəbəl/ a indescifrable; ilegible

**undeclared** /ˌʌndɪ'kleərd/ a no declarado

**undefended** /ˌʌndɪ'fɛndid/ a indefenso

**undeferable** /ˌʌndɪ'fərəbəl/ a inaplazable

**undefiled** /ˌʌndɪ'faild/ a impoluto, incontaminado; puro

**undefinable** /ˌʌndɪ'fainəbəl/ a indefinible; inefable, vago

**undefined** /ˌʌndɪ'faind/ a indefinido; indeterminado

**undelivered** /ˌʌndɪ'livərd/ a no recibido; (speech) no pronunciado; (not sent) no enviado

**undemonstrative** /ˌʌndə'mɒnstrətiv/ a poco expresivo, reservado

**undeniable** /ˌʌndɪ'naiəbəl/ a incontestable, innegable, indudable; excelente; inequívoco, evidente

**undeniably** /ˌʌndɪ'naiəbli/ adv indudablemente

**undenominational** /ˌʌndɪˌnɒmə'neiʃənl/ a sin denominación

**undependable** /ˌʌndɪ'pɛndəbəl/ a indigno de confianza

**under** /'ʌndər/ prep debajo de; bajo; (in) en; (less than) menos de, menos que; (at the orders of) a las órdenes de, al mando de; (in less time than) en menos de; (under the weight of) bajo el peso de; (at the foot of) al abrigo de; (for less than) por menos de; (at the time of) en la época de, en tiempos de; (according to) según, conforme a, en virtud de (e.g. *under the law,* en virtud de la ley); (of monarchs) bajo (or durante) el reinado de; (of rank) inferior a; (in virtue of) en virtud de; (of age) menor de; (with penalty, pretext, etc.) so; en; a (see below for examples); (Agr. of fields) plantado de, sembrado de. **u. arms,** bajo las armas. **u. contract,** bajo contrato. **u. cover,** al abrigo de, bajo cubierto. **u. cover of,** bajo pretexto de, so color de. **u. fire,** bajo fuego. **u. oath,** bajo juramento. **u. pain of,** so pena de. **u. sail,** a la vela. **u. separate cover,** bajo cubierta separada, en sobre apartado, por separado. **u. steam,** al vapor. **u. way,** en camino; en marcha; en preparación. **to be u. an obligation,** deber favores; (to) tener obligacion de; estar obligado a

**under** /'ʌndər/ a inferior; (of rank) subalterno, subordinado; bajo, bajero. —adv debajo; abajo; más abajo; menos; (for less) para menos; (ill) mal; (insufficient) insuficiente. **to bring u.,** someter, subyugar. **to keep u.,** dominar, subyugar

**underact** /ˌʌndər'ækt/ vt hacer un papel sin fogosidad

**underarm** /'ʌndərˌɑrm/ n sobaco, m. —a sobacal; (of bowling) de debajo del brazo. **to serve u.,** sacar por debajo

**underbid** /ˌʌndər'bid/ vt ofrecer menos que

**underbred** /ˌʌndər'brɛd/ a mal criado, mal educado

**undercharge** /ˌʌndər'tʃɑrdʒ/ vt cobrar menos de lo debido

**underclothes** /'ʌndərˌklouz, -ˌklouðz/ n ropa interior, f, paños menores, m pl

**undercurrent** /'ʌndərˌkərənt/ n corriente submarina, f; Fig. tendencia oculta, f

**undercut** /'ʌndərˌkʌt/ n (of meat) filete, m

**underdeveloped** /ˌʌndərdɪ'vɛləpt/ a de desarrollo atrasado; Photo. no revelado lo suficiente

**underdog** /'ʌndərˌdɔg/ n víctima, f; débil, paciente, m. **underdogs,** los de abajo, m pl

**underdone** /'ʌndər'dʌn/ a (of meat) crudo, medio asado

**underdress** /ˌʌndər'drɛs/ vt and vi vestir(se) sin bastante elegancia

**underestimate** /ˌʌndər'ɛstəˌmeit/ vt tasar en menos; desestimar, menospreciar

**underfeed** /ˌʌndər'fid/ vt alimentar insuficientemente

**underfoot** /ˌʌndər'fut/ adv debajo de los pies, en el suelo

**undergo** /ˌʌndər'gou/ vt sufrir, padecer, pasar por. **undergo surgery,** someterse a la cirugía

**undergraduate** /ˌʌndər'grædʒuit/ n estudiante no graduado, m

**underground** /a., n. 'ʌndərˌgraund; adv. -'graund/ a subterráneo; Fig. oculto, secreto. —adv bajo tierra, debajo de la tierra; Fig. en secreto, ocultamente. —n sótano, m; metro, ferrocarril subterráneo, m

**undergrown** /ˌʌndər'groun/ a enclenque

**undergrowth** /'ʌndərˌgrouθ/ n maleza, f

**underhand** /'ʌndərˌhænd/ adv Fig. bajo mano, ocultamente, a escondidas. —a Fig. secreto, oculto

**underlie** /ˌʌndər'lai/ vt estar debajo de; servir de base a, caracterizar

**underline** /ˌʌndər'lain/ vt subrayar

**underling** /'ʌndərliŋ/ n subordinado (-da)

**underlying** /'ʌndərˌlaiiŋ/ a fundamental, básico, esencial

**undermentioned** /ˌʌndər'mɛnʃən/d a abajo citado

**undermine** /ˌʌndər'main/ vt socavar, excavar; minar, destruir poco a poco

**undermining** /ˌʌndərˌmainiŋ/ n socava, excavación, f; destrucción, f, a minador

**underneath** /ˌʌndər'niθ/ adv debajo. —prep bajo, debajo de

**undernourished** /ˌʌndər'nəriʃt/ a mal alimentado

**undernourishment** /ˌʌndər'nəriʃmənt/ n desnutrición, f

**underpaid** /ˌʌndər'peid/ a insuficientemente retribuido, mal pagado

**underpass** /'ʌndərˌpæs, -ˌpɑs/ n pasaje por debajo, m

**underpay** /ˌʌndər'pei/ vt pagar mal, remunerar (or retribuir) deficientemente

**underpayment** /ˌʌndər'peimənt/ n retribución mezquina, f; pago insuficiente, m

**underpin** /ˌʌndər'pin/ vt apuntalar, socalzar

**underpopulated** /ˌʌndər'pɒpyəˌleitid/ a con baja densidad de población

**underprivileged** /'ʌndər'privəlidʒd/ a menesteroso, pobre, necesitado

**underrate** /ˌʌndər'reit/ vt tasar en menos; tener en poco, desestimar, menospreciar

**underripe** /'ʌndərˌraip/ a verde

**undersecretary** /'ʌndərˌsɛkrəˌtɛri/ n subsecretario (-ia)

**undersell** /ˌʌndər'sɛl/ vt vender a un precio más bajo que

**underside** /'ʌndərˌsaid/ n revés, envés, m

**undersigned** /'ʌndərˌsaind/ a infrascrito, suscrito. **the u.,** el abajo firmado, el infrascrito

**undersized** /'ʌndər'saizd/ a muy pequeño, enclenque, enano

**underskirt** /'ʌndərˌskərt/ n enagua, f; refajo, m

**underslung** /'ʌndər'slʌŋ/ a Auto. con bajo centro de gravedad

**understand** /ˌʌndər'stænd/ vt comprender, entender; (know) saber; (be acquainted with) conocer; (hear) oír, tener entendido; (mean) sobrentender. —vi comprender, entender; oír, tener entendido. **to u. each other,** comprenderse. **It being understood that...,** Bien entendido que...

**understandable** /ˌʌndər'stændəbəl/ a comprensible; inteligible. **It is very u. why he does not wish to come,** Se comprende muy bien por qué no quiere venir

**understanding** /ˌʌndər'stændiŋ/ n (intelligence) entendimiento, m, inteligencia, f; (agreement) acuerdo, m; (knowledge) conocimiento, m; (wisdom) comprensión, sabiduría, f. —a inteligente; sabio; (sympathetic) comprensivo, simpático. **to come to an u.,** ponerse de acuerdo

**understandingly** /ˌʌndərstændiŋ/ adv con inteligencia; con conocimiento (de); con simpatía

**understate** /ˌʌndər'steit/ vt decir menos que, rebajar, describir sin énfasis

**understatement** /'ʌndərsteitmənt/ n moderación, f

**understudy** /'ʌndər,stʌdi/ n sobresaliente, mf. —vt sustituir

**undertake** /ˌʌndər'teik/ vt comprometerse a, encargarse de; emprender, abarcar, acometer

**undertaker** /'ʌndər,teikər/ n empresario, director de pompas fúnebres, m

**undertaking** /ˌʌndər'teikiŋ/ n empresa, tarea, f; garantía, promesa, f; (funerals) funeraria, f

**undertone** /'ʌndər,toun/ n voz baja, f; Art. color tenue (or apagado), m. **in an u.,** en voz baja

**undervalue** /ˌʌndər'vælyu/ vt tasar en menos; tener en poco, despreciar

**underwater** /'ʌndər'wɔtər/ a subacuático, submarino. **underwater flipper,** aleta de bucear

**underweight** /'ʌndər'weit/ a de bajo peso, que pesa menos de lo debido, flaco

**underworld** /'ʌndər,wɜrld/ n (hell) infierno, averno, m; (slums) hampa, f, fondos bajos de la sociedad, m pl; heces de la sociedad, f pl

**underwrite** /ˌʌndər'rait/ vt Com. asegurar contra riesgos; reasegurar; obligarse a comprar todas las acciones de una compañía no subscritas por el público, mediante un pago convenido

**underwriter** /'ʌndər,raitər/ n asegurador, m; reasegurador, m

**underwriting** /'ʌndər,raitiŋ/ n aseguro, m; reaseguro, m

**undeserved** /ˌʌndɪ'zɜrvd/ a inmerecido, no merecido

**undeserving** /ˌʌndɪ'zɜrviŋ/ a indigno, desmerecedor; que no merece

**undesirable** /ˌʌndɪ'zaiʳrəbəl/ a no deseable; nocivo, pernicioso; (unsuitable) inconveniente

**undesired** /ˌʌndɪ'zaiʳrd/ a no deseado; no solicitado, no buscado

**undesirous** /ˌʌndɪ'zaiʳrəs/ a no deseoso

**undestroyed** /ˌʌndɪ'strɔid/ a sin destruir, no destruido, intacto

**undetected** /ˌʌndɪ'tɛktɪd/ a no descubierto

**undeveloped** /ˌʌndɪ'vɛləpt/ a no desarrollado; rudimentario; inmaturo; (of a country) no explotado, virgen; Photo. no revelado; (of land) sin cultivar

**undeviating** /ʌn'divi,eitiŋ/ a directo; constante, persistente

**undigested** /ˌʌndɪ'dʒɛstɪd/ a no digerido, indigesto

**undignified** /ʌn'dɪgnə,faid/ a sin dignidad; poco serio; indecoroso

**undiluted** /ˌʌndɪ'lutɪd/ a sin diluir, puro

**undiminished** /ˌʌndɪ'mɪnɪʃt/ a no disminuido, sin disminuir, cabal, íntegro

**undimmed** /ʌn'dɪmd/ a no obscurecido, brillante

**undiplomatic** /ˌʌndɪplə'mætɪk/ a impolítico, indiscreto

**undirected** /ˌʌndɪ'rɛktɪd/ a sin dirección; (of letters) sin señas

**undiscernible** /ˌʌndɪ'sɜrnəbəl/ a imperceptible, invisible

**undiscerning** /ˌʌndɪ'sɜrnɪŋ/ a sin percepción, obtuso, sin discernimiento

**undisciplined** /ʌn'dɪsəplɪnd/ a indisciplinado

**undisclosed** /ˌʌndɪ'sklouzd/ a no revelado, secreto

**undiscouraged** /ˌʌndɪ'skɜrɪdʒd/ a animoso, sin flaquear, sin desaliento

**undiscovered** /ˌʌndɪ'skʌvərd/ a no descubierto, ignoto

**undiscriminating** /ˌʌndɪ'skrɪmə,neitiŋ/ a sin distinción; sin sentido crítico

**undisguised** /ˌʌndɪ'skaizd/ a sin disfraz; abierto, claro

**undismayed** /ˌʌndɪs'meid/ a intrépido, impávido; sin desaliento

**undisposed** /ˌʌndɪ'spouzd/ a desinclinado; (of property) no enajenado, no invertido

**undisputed** /ˌʌndɪ'spyutɪd/ a incontestable, indisputable

**undistinguishable** /ˌʌndɪ'stɪŋgwɪʃəbəl/ a indistinguible

**undistinguished** /ˌʌndɪ'stɪŋgwɪʃt/ a (of writers) poco conocido; indistinto; sin distinción

**undisturbed** /ˌʌndɪ'stɜrbd/ a sin tocar; tranquilo, sereno, impasible

**undivided** /ˌʌndɪ'vaidɪd/ a indiviso, íntegro; junto; completo, entero

**undo** /ʌn'du/ vt anular; reparar; desatar, deshacer; desasir; abrir

**undoing** /ʌn'duiŋ/ n anulación, f; (reparation) reparación, f; (opening) abrir, m; ruina, f

**undomesticated** /ˌʌndə'mɛsti,keitɪd/ a salvaje, no domesticado; poco casero

**undone** /ʌn'dʌn/ a and part sin hacer; deshecho; arruinado, perdido. **I am undone!** ¡Estoy perdido! **to come u.,** desatarse. **to leave u.,** dejar sin hacer

**undoubted** /ʌn'dautɪd/ a indudable, evidente, incontestable

**undoubtedly** /ʌn'dautɪdli/ adv sin duda

**undrained** /ʌn'dreind/ a sin drenaje

**undramatic** /ˌʌndrə'mætɪk/ a no dramático

**undreamed** /ʌn'drimd/ a no soñado. **u. of,** inopinado, no imaginado

**undress** /ʌn'drɛs/ vt desnudar, desvestir. —vi desnudarse. —n traje de casa, m; paños menores, m pl; Mil. traje de cuartel, m

**undressed** /ʌn'drɛst/ a desnudo; en paños menores; (of wounds) sin curar; Com. en rama, en bruto

**undrinkable** /ʌn'drɪŋkəbəl/ a impotable

**undue** /ʌn'du/ a excesivo, indebido; injusto; impropio; (of a bill of exchange) por vencer

**undulant** /'ʌndʒələnt/ a ondulante. **u. fever,** fiebre mediterránea, fiebre de Malta, f

**undulate** /'ʌndʒə,leit/ vi ondular, ondear

**undulating** /'ʌndʒə,leitiŋ/ a ondulante

**undulation** /ˌʌndʒə'leifən/ n ondulación, undulación, f, ondeo, m; fluctuación, f

**undulatory** /'ʌndʒələ,tɔri/ a ondulatorio, undoso

**unduly** /ʌn'duli/ adv excesivamente, demasiado, indebidamente; injustamente

**undutiful** /ʌn'dutəfəl/ a desobediente, irrespetuoso

**undutifulness** /ʌn'dutəfəlnɪs/ n desobediencia, falta de respeto, f

**undying** /ʌn'daiiŋ/ a inmortal, imperecedero; eterno

**unearned** /ʌn'ɜrnd/ a no ganado; inmerecido

**unearth** /ʌn'ɜrθ/ vt desenterrar; Fig. descubrir, sacar a luz

**unearthing** /ʌn'ɜrθiŋ/ n desenterramiento, m; Fig. descubrimiento, m, revelación, f

**unearthly** /ʌn'ɜrθli/ a sobrenatural; misterioso, aterrador, espantoso

**uneasily** /ʌn'izəli/ adv con dificultad; incómodamente; inquietamente

**uneasiness** /ʌn'izinɪs/ n malestar, m; (discomfort) incomodidad, f; (anxiety) inquietud, intranquilidad, f, desasosiego, m

**uneasy** /ʌn'izi/ a incómodo; inseguro; inquieto, intranquilo, desasosegado; aturdido, turbado. **to become u.,** inquietarse

**uneatable** /ʌn'itəbəl/ a incomible

**uneaten** /ʌn'itn/ a no comido

**uneconomical** /ˌʌnɛkə'nɒmɪkəl/ a poco económico, costoso, caro

**unedifying** /ʌn'ɛdə,faiiŋ/ a poco edificante

**unedited** /ʌn'ɛditɪd/ a inédito

**uneducated** /ʌn'ɛdʒə͵keitɪd/ a ignorante; ineducado, inculto, indocto
**unembarrassed** /͵ʌnɛm'bærəst/ a sereno, tranquilo, imperturbable; (financially) sin deudas, acomodado
**unemotional** /͵ʌnɪ'mouʃənl/ a frío, impasible
**unemployable** /͵ʌnɛm'plɔiəbəl/ a sin uso, inservible; (of persons) inútil para el trabajo
**unemployed** /͵ʌnɛm'plɔid/ a sin empleo; (out of work) sin trabajo, parado; desocupado, ocioso; inactivo. —n paro obrero, m. **the u.,** los sin trabajo, los cesantes, los desocupados
**unemployment** /͵ʌnɛm'plɔimənt/ n paro forzoso, m. **u. benefit,** subvención contra el paro obrero, f. **u. insurance,** seguro contra el paro obrero, m,
**unencumbered** /͵ʌnɛn'kʌmbərd/ a libre, independiente; (of estates) libre de gravamen; (untaxable) saneado
**unending** /ʌn'ɛndɪŋ/ a perpetuo, eterno, sin fin; inacabable, constante, continuo, incesante
**unendurable** /͵ʌnɛn'dʊrəbəl/ a insoportable, insufrible, intolerable
**unenlightened** /͵ʌnɛn'laitṇd/ a ignorante
**unenterprising** /ʌn'ɛntɜr͵praizɪŋ/ a poco emprendedor, tímido
**unenthusiastic** /͵ʌnɛn͵θuzi'æstɪk/ a sin entusiasmo, tibio
**unenviable** /ʌn'ɛnviəbəl/ a no envidiable
**unequal** /ʌn'ikwəl/ a desigual; inferior; (out of proportion) desproporcionado; injusto; insuficiente; incapaz; (of ground) escabroso. **to be u. to the task,** ser incapaz de la tarea; no tener fuerzas para la tarea
**unequalled** /ʌn'ikwəld/ a sin igual, incomparable, sin par, único
**unequally** /ʌn'ikwəli/ adv desigualmente
**unequivocal** /͵ʌnɪ'kwɪvəkəl/ a inequívoco; redondo, claro, franco
**unerring** /ʌn'ɜrɪŋ, -'ɛr-/ a infalible; seguro
**unerringly** /ʌn'ɜrɪŋli, -'ɛr- adv infaliblemente; sin equivocarse
**unessential** /͵ʌnə'sɛnʃəl/ a no esencial
**unesthetic** /͵ʌnɛs'θɛtɪk/ a antiestético
**uneven** /ʌn'ivən/ a desigual; (of roads) escabroso, quebrado; (of numbers) impar; irregular
**unevenly** /ʌn'ivənli/ adv desigualmente
**unevenness** /ʌn'ivənnɪs/ n desigualdad, f; desnivel, m, irregularidad, f. **the unevenness of the terrain,** lo desigual del terreno, lo accidentado del terreno, m
**uneventful** /͵ʌnɪ'vɛntfəl/ a sin incidentes, sin acontecimientos notables; tranquilo
**unexaggerated** /͵ʌnɪg'zædʒə͵reitɪd/ a nada exagerado
**unexamined** /͵ʌnɪg'zæmɪnd// a no examinado, sin examinar
**unexampled** /͵ʌnɪg'zæmpəld/ a sin igual, sin par
**unexceptionable** /͵ʌnɪk'sɛpʃənəbəl/ a intachable, irreprensible; correcto; impecable, perfecto
**unexhausted** /͵ʌnɪg'zɔstɪd/ a no agotado; inexhausto
**unexpected** /͵ʌnɪk'spɛktɪd/ a inesperado, imprevisto, inopinado, impensado; repentino, súbito
**unexpectedly** /͵ʌnɪk'spɛktɪdli/ adv inesperadamente; de repente
**unexpectedness** /͵ʌnɪk'spɛktɪdnɪs/ n lo inesperado
**unexpired** /͵ʌnɪk'spaiərd/ a (of bill of exchange) no vencido; (of lease) no caducado
**unexplored** /͵ʌnɪk'splɔrd/ a inexplorado
**unexpressed** /͵ʌnɪk'sprɛst/ a no expresado; tácito, sobrentendido
**unexpurgated** /ʌn'ɛkspər͵geitid/ a sin expurgar, completo
**unfading** /ʌn'feidɪŋ/ a inmarcesible, inmarchitable; eterno, inmortal
**unfailing** /ʌn'feilɪŋ/ a inagotable; inexhausto; seguro; indefectible
**unfailingly** /ʌn'feilɪŋli/ adv siempre, constantemente; sin faltar
**unfair** /ʌn'fɛər/ a injusto; vil, bajo, soez; de mala fe, engañoso; (of play) sucio
**unfairly** /ʌn'fɛərli/ adv injustamente; de mala fe
**unfairness** /ʌn'fɛərnɪs/ n injusticia, f; mala fe, f
**unfaithful** /ʌn'feiθfəl/ a infiel; desleal; inexacto, incorrecto. **to be u. to,** ser infiel a; faltar a

**unfaithfulness** /ʌn'feiθfəlnɪs/ n infidelidad, f; deslealtad, f; inexactitud, f
**unfaltering** /ʌn'fɔltərɪŋ/ a sin vacilar; resuelto, firme
**unfamiliar** /͵ʌnfə'mɪlyər/ a poco familiar; desconocido. **to be u. with,** ser ignorante de
**unfashionable** /ʌn'fæʃənəbəl/ a pasado de moda, fuera de moda; poco elegante
**unfashionableness** /ʌn'fæʃənəbəlnɪs/ n falta de elegancia, f
**unfashionably** /ʌn'fæʃənəbli/ adv contra la tendencia de la moda; sin elegancia
**unfasten** /ʌn'fæsən/ vt desatar; desabrochar, desenganchar; abrir; aflojar; soltar
**unfathomable** /ʌn'fæðəməbəl/ a insondable; impenetrable, inescrutable
**unfavorable** /ʌn'feivərəbəl/ a desfavorable, adverso, contrario
**unfavorably** /ʌn'feivərəbli/ adv desfavorablemente
**unfeathered** /ʌn'fɛðərd/ a implume, sin plumas
**unfeeling** /ʌn'filɪŋ/ a insensible, impasible, frío; duro, cruel
**unfeigned** /ʌn'feind/ a sincero, natural, verdadero
**unfenced** /ʌn'fɛnst/ a descercado, sin tapia; abierto
**unfermented** /͵ʌnfər'mɛntɪd/ a no fermentado; tibio
**unfetter** /ʌn'fɛtər/ vt desencadenar, destrabar; poner en libertad, librar
**unfilial** /ʌn'filiəl/ a poco filial, desobediente
**unfinished** /ʌn'fɪnɪʃt/ a incompleto, inacabado; sin acabar; imperfecto
**unfit** /ʌn'fit/ a incapaz; incompetente, inepto; (unsuitable) impropio; (useless) inservible, inadecuado; (unworthy) indigno; (ill) enfermo, malo. —vt inhabilitar, incapacitar. **u. for human consumption,** impropio para el consumo humano
**unfitness** /ʌn'fɪtnɪs/ n incapacidad, f; incompetencia, ineptitud, f; impropiedad, f; falta de mérito, f; falta de salud, f
**unfix** /ʌn'fɪks/ vt desprender, despegar, descomponer; soltar. **to come unfixed,** desprenderse
**unflagging** /ʌn'flægɪŋ/ a incansable, infatigable; persistente, constante
**unflattering** /ʌn'flætərɪŋ/ a poco halagüeño
**unflinching** /ʌn'flɪntʃɪŋ/ a inconmovible, resuelto, firme
**unfold** /ʌn'fould/ vt desplegar, desdoblar; tender; abrir; (plans) revelar, descubrir; contar, manifestar. —vi abrirse
**unfolding** /ʌn'fouldɪŋ/ a que se abre. —n despliegue, m; revelación, f; narración, f
**unforced** /ʌn'fɔrst/ a libre; espontáneo; fácil; natural
**unforeseen** /͵ʌnfɔr'sin/ a imprevisto, inesperado
**unforgettable** /͵ʌnfər'gɛtəbəl/ a inolvidable
**unforgivable** /͵ʌnfər'gɪvəbəl/ a inexcusable, imperdonable
**unforgiving** /͵ʌnfər'gɪvɪŋ/ a implacable, que no perdona, inexorable
**unforgotten** /͵ʌnfər'gɒtṇ/ a no olvidado
**unformed** /ʌn'fɔrmd/ a informe; rudimentario; inmaturo; (inexperienced) inexperto, sin experiencia
**unfortunate** /ʌn'fɔrtʃənɪt/ a desdichado, infortunado, desgraciado, desventurado. —n desdichado (-da); pobre, mf; (prostitute) perdida, f
**unfortunately** /ʌn'fɔrtʃənɪtli/ adv por desdicha, desgraciadamente
**unfounded** /ʌn'faundɪd/ a infundado, inmotivado, sin fundamento, injustificado
**unframed** /ʌn'freimd/ a sin marco
**unfrequented** /ʌn'frikwəntɪd/ a poco frecuentado, solitario, retirado, aislado
**unfriendliness** /ʌn'frɛndlinɪs/ n hostilidad, falta de amistad, frialdad, f; huraña, insociabilidad, f
**unfriendly** /ʌn'frɛndli/ a hostil, enemigo; (of things, events) perjudicial; huraño, insociable
**unfrock** /ʌn'frɒk/ vt degradar, exclaustrar
**unfruitful** /ʌn'frutfəl/ a estéril, infecundo; infructuoso, improductivo, vano
**unfulfilled** /͵ʌnfəl'fɪld/ a incumplido, sin cumplir; malogrado
**unfurl** /ʌn'fɜrl/ vt desplegar; Naut. izar (las velas)
**unfurnished** /ʌn'fɜrnɪʃt/ a desamueblado, sin muebles; desprovisto (de), sin

**ungainliness** /ʌn'geinlinis/ n falta de gracia, torpeza, f, desgarbo, m

**ungainly** /ʌn'geinli/ a desgarbado

**ungallant** /ʌn'gælənt/ a poco caballeroso, nada galante

**ungenerous** /ʌn'dʒɛnərəs/ a poco generoso; avaro, tacaño, mezquino; injusto

**ungentlemanly** /ʌn'dʒɛntl|mənli/ a poco caballeroso, indigno de un caballero

**unglazed** /ʌn'gleizd/ a sin vidriar; (paper) sin satinar; deslustrado

**ungloved** /ʌn'glʌvd/ a sin guante(s)

**unglue** /ʌn'glu/ vt desencolar, despegar

**ungodliness** /ʌn'gɒdlinis/ n impiedad, f

**ungodly** /ʌn'gɒdli/ a impío, irreligioso

**ungovernable** /ʌn'gʌvərnəbəl/ a ingobernable, indomable; irrefrenable

**ungraceful** /ʌn'greisfəl/ a desagraciado, desgarbado, sin gracia

**ungracious** /ʌn'greiʃəs/ a desagradable, poco cortés, desdeñoso

**ungraciousness** /ʌn'greiʃəsnis/ n descortesía, aspereza, inurbanidad, f

**ungrammatical** /ˌʌngrə'mætikəl/ a antigramatical, incorrecto

**ungrateful** /ʌn'greitfəl/ a ingrato, desagradecido; desagradable, odioso

**ungratefulness** /ʌn'greitfəlnis/ n ingratitud, f; lo desagradable

**ungrounded** /ʌn'graundid/ a infundado; sin motivo

**ungrudging** /ʌn'grʌdʒiŋ/ a no avaro, liberal; generoso, magnánimo

**ungrudgingly** /ʌn'grʌdʒiŋli/ adv de buena gana

**unguarded** /ʌn'gɑrdid/ a indefenso, sin protección; descuidado; indiscreto, imprudente; sin reflexión

**unguided** /ʌn'gaidid/ a sin guía

**unhallowed** /ʌn'hæloud/ a impío, profano

**unhampered** /ʌn'hæmpərd/ a desembarazado, libre

**unhappily** /ʌn'hæpəli/ adv desafortunadamente, por desgracia

**unhappiness** /ʌn'hæpinis/ n infelicidad, desgracia, desdicha, tristeza, f

**unhappy** /ʌn'hæpi/ a infeliz, desgraciado, desdichado, triste; (ill-fated) aciago, funesto, malhadado; (remark) inoportuno, inapropiado

**unharmed** /ʌn'harmd/ a ileso, sano y salvo; (of things) indemne, sin daño

**unharness** /ʌn'harnis/ vt desaparejar; desenganchar; desarmar

**unhealthiness** /ʌn'hɛlθinis/ n falta de salud, f; (of place) insalubridad, f

**unhealthy** /ʌn'hɛlθi/ a enfermizo; malsano, insalubre

**unheard** /ʌn'hɜrd/ a no oído; sin ser escuchado; desconocido. **u.-of,** inaudito, no imaginado

**unheeding** /ʌn'hidiŋ/ a distraído; desatento, sin prestar atención (a); descuidado

**unhelpful** /ʌn'hɛlpfəl/ a poco servicial; inútil

**unhesitating** /ʌn'hɛzi,teitiŋ/ a resuelto, decidido; pronto, inmediato

**unhesitatingly** /ʌn'hɛzi,teitiŋli/ adv sin vacilar

**unhinge** /ʌn'hindʒ/ vt desgoznar, desquiciar; (of the mind) trastornar

**unhitch** /ʌn'hitʃ/ vt desenganchar; descolgar

**unholy** /ʌn'houli/ a impío, sacrílego

**unhonored** /ʌn'ɒnərd/ a sin que se reconociese sus méritos; despreciado; (check) protestado

**unhook** /ʌn'hʊk/ vt desenganchar; desabrochar; descolgar

**unhoped-for** /ʌn'houptfɔr/ a inesperado

**unhurt** /ʌn'hɜrt/ a ileso, incólume, sano y salvo; (of things) sin daño

**unicellular** /ˌyunə'sɛlyələr/ a unicelular

**unicolored** /'yuni,kʌlərd/ a unicolor

**unicorn** /'yuni,kɔrn/ n unicornio, m

**unidentified** /ˌʌnai'dɛntə,faid/ a no reconocido, no identificado

**unification** /ˌyunəfi'keiʃən/ n unificación, f

**uniform** /'yunə,fɔrm/ a uniforme; igual, constante, invariable; homogéneo. —n uniforme, m. **in full u.,** de gran uniforme. **to make u.,** uniformar, igualar, hacer uniforme

**uniformity** /ˌyunə'fɔrmiti/ n uniformidad, igualdad, f

**uniformly** /'yunə,fɔrmli/ adv uniformemente

**unify** /'yunə,fai/ vt unificar; unir

**unilateral** /ˌyunə'lætərəl/ a unilateral

**unimaginable** /ˌʌni'mædʒənəbəl/ a inimaginable, no imaginable

**unimaginative** /ˌʌni'mædʒənətiv/ a sin imaginación

**unimpaired** /ˌʌnim'pɛərd/ a no disminuido; sin alteración; intacto, entero; sin menoscabo

**unimpeachable** /ˌʌnim'pitʃəbəl/ a irreprochable, intachable

**unimportance** /ˌʌnim'pɔrtn̩s/ n no importancia, insignificancia, trivialidad, f

**unimportant** /ˌʌnim'pɔrtn̩t/ a sin importancia, nada importante, insignificante, trivial

**unimpressive** /ˌʌnim'prɛsiv/ a poco impresionante; nada conmovedor; (of persons) insignificante

**uninflammable** /ˌʌnin'flæməbəl/ a no inflamable, incombustible

**uninfluenced** /ˌʌnin'fluənsd/ a no afectado (por), libre (de)

**uninformed** /ˌʌnin'fɔrmd/ a ignorante

**uninhabitable** /ˌʌnin'hæbitəbəl/ a inhabitable

**uninhabited** /ˌʌnin'hæbitid/ a deshabitado, inhabitado, vacío, desierto

**uninjured** /ʌn'indʒərd/ a ileso; sin daño

**uninspired** /ˌʌnin'spaiᵊrd/ a sin inspiración; pedestre, mediocre

**uninstructive** /ˌʌnin'strʌktiv/ a nada instructivo

**uninsured** /ˌʌnin'ʃʊrd/ a no asegurado

**unintelligent** /ˌʌnin'tɛlidʒənt/ a nada inteligente, corto de alcances, tonto

**unintelligibility** /ˌʌnin,tɛlidʒə'biliti/ n incomprensibilidad, f, lo ininteligible

**unintelligible** /ˌʌnin'tɛlidʒəbəl/ a ininteligible, incomprensible

**unintentional** /ˌʌnin'tɛnʃənl/ a involuntario, inadvertido

**unintentionally** /ˌʌnin'tɛnʃənli/ adv sin querer, involuntariamente

**uninterested** /ʌn'intərəstid/ a no interesado, despreocupado

**uninteresting** /ʌn'intərəstiŋ/ a sin interés, poco interesante, soso

**uninterrupted** /ˌʌnintə'rʌptid/ a ininterrumpido, sin interrupción; continuo, incesante

**uninvited** /ˌʌnin'vaitid/ a no invitado, no convidado, sin invitación; (unlooked-for) no buscado

**uninviting** /ˌʌnin'vaitiŋ/ a poco atrayente; inhospitalario

**union** /'yunyən/ n unión, f; Mech. manguito de unión, m; conexión, f; (poverty) asociación, f; (of trade) gremio de oficios, m; sindicato (obrero), m; (workhouse) asilo, m; (U.S.A.) Estados Unidos de América, m pl

**unionism** /'yunyə,nizəm/ n unionismo, m

**unionist** /'yunyənist/ n Polit. unionista, mf

**unique** /yu'nik/ a único, sin igual, sin par

**uniqueness** /yu'niknis/ n unicidad, f; lo singular

**unisexual** /ˌyunə'sɛkʃuəl/ a unisexual

**unison** /'yunəsən,/ n unisonancia, f. **in u.,** al unísono

**unit** /'yunit/ n unidad, f. **u. bookcase,** librería en secciones, f

**Unitarian** /ˌyuni'tɛəriən/ a and n unitario (-ia)

**Unitarianism** /ˌyuni'tɛəriə,nizəm/ n unitarismo, m

**unite** /yu'nait/ vt unir, juntar; combinar, incorporar; (of countries) unificar; (of energies, etc.) reunir. —vi unirse, juntarse; reunirse, concertarse; convenirse

**united** /yu'naitid/ a unido; junto. **the U. Nations,** las Naciones Unidas, f pl

**unitedly** /yu'naitidli/ adv unidamente; armoniosamente, de acuerdo

**United States of America** los Estados Unidos, m pl

**unity** /'yuniti/ n unidad, f; Math. la unidad; unión, f; conformidad, armonía, f. **the three unities,** las tres unidades

**universal** /ˌyunə'vɜrsəl/ a universal; general; común. **to make u.,** universalizar, generalizar. **u. joint,** junta universal, f; Auto. cardán, m

**universality** /ˌyunəvər'sæliti/ n universalidad, f

**universalize** /ˌyunə'vɜrsə,laiz/ vt universalizar

**universe** /'yunə,vɜrs/ n universo, m; creación, f, mundo, m

**university** /,yunə'vɜrsɪtɪ/ n universidad, f. —a universitario. **u. degree,** grado universitario, m

**unjust** /ʌn'dʒʌst/ a injusto

**unjustifiable** /ʌn,dʒʌstə'faiəbəl/ a injustificable, indisculpable, inexcusable

**unjustifiably** /ʌn,dʒʌstə'faiəbli/ adv injustificadamente, inexcusablemente

**unjustly** /ʌn'dʒʌstli/ adv injustamente, sin razón

**unkempt** /ʌn'kempt/ a despeinado; desaseado, sucio

**unkind** /ʌn'kaind/ a nada bondadoso, nada amable; poco complaciente; duro, cruel; desfavorable, nada propicio

**unkindly** /ʌn'kaindli/ adv sin bondad; con dureza, cruelmente

**unkindness** /ʌn'kaindnɪs/ n falta de bondad, f; severidad, crueldad, dureza, f, rigor, m; acto de crueldad, m

**unknowable** /ʌn'nouəbəl/ a impenetrable, incomprehensible, insondable

**unknowingly** /ʌn'nouɪŋli/ adv sin querer, involuntariamente; sin saberlo; insensiblemente

**unknown** /ʌn'noun/ a ignoto, desconocido; Math. incógnito. —n lo desconocido, misterio, m; Math. incógnita, f; (person) desconocido (-da), forastero (-ra). Math. **u. quantity,** incógnita, f

**unlabeled** /ʌn'leibəld/ a sin etiqueta

**unlace** /ʌn'leis/ vt desenlazar; desatar

**unladylike** /ʌn'leidi,laik/ a indigno (or impropio) de una dama; vulgar, ordinario, cursi

**unlamented** /,ʌnlə'mɛntɪd/ a no llorado, no lamentado

**unlatch** /ʌn'lætʃ/ vt alzar el pestillo de, abrir

**unlawful** /ʌn'lɔfəl/ a ilegal, ilícito

**unlawfulness** /ʌn'lɔfəlnɪs/ n ilegalidad, f

**unlearn** /ʌn'lɜrn/ vt olvidar, desaprender

**unleash** /ʌn'liʃ/ vt soltar

**unleavened** /ʌn'lɛvənd/ a ázimo, sin levadura

**unless** /ʌn'lɛs/ conjunc a no ser que, a menos que, como no, si no (all followed by subjunc.); salvo, excepto, con excepción de

**unlicensed** /ʌn'laisənst/ a no autorizado, sin licencia

**unlike** /ʌn'laik/ a disímil, desemejante; distinto, diferente. —prep a distinción de, a diferencia de, al contrario de. **They are quite u.,** No se parecen nada

**unlikeliness** /ʌn'laiklinɪs/ n improbabilidad, f

**unlikely** /ʌn'laikli/ a improbable, inverosímil; arriesgado

**unlikeness** /ʌn'laiknɪs/ n desemejanza, diferencia, f

**unlimited** /ʌn'lɪmɪtɪd/ a ilimitado, infinito, inmenso; sin restricción; excesivo, exagerado. **unlimited telephone,** teléfono no medido (Argentina)

**unlined** /ʌn'laind/ a no forrado, sin forro; sin rayas; (of face) sin arrugas

**unlit** /ʌn'lɪt/ a no iluminado, oscuro, sin luz

**unload** /ʌn'loud/ vt descargar; aligerar; Naut. hondear; (of shares) deshacerse de. —vi descargar

**unloading** /ʌn'loudɪŋ/ n descarga, f, descargue, m

**unlock** /ʌn'lɒk/ vt desencerrar, abrir; Fig. revelar, descubrir

**unlooked-for** /ʌn'lʊktfɔr/ a inopinado, inesperado

**unloose** /ʌn'lus/ vt desatar; soltar; poner en libertad

**unlovable** /ʌn'lʌvəbəl/ a indigno del querer; antipático, poco amable; repugnante

**unloveliness** /ʌn'lʌvlinɪs/ n falta de hermosura, fealdad, f

**unlovely** /ʌn'lʌvli/ a nada hermoso, feo; desagradable

**unluckily** /ʌn'lʌkəli/ adv desafortunadamente, por desgracia

**unluckiness** /ʌn'lʌkinɪs/ n mala suerte, f; (unsuitability) inoportunidad, f; lo nefasto, lo malo

**unlucky** /ʌn'lʌki/ a de mala suerte; desdichado, desgraciado, infeliz; (ill-omened) funesto, nefasto, fatal; inoportuno, inconveniente

**unmanageable** /ʌn'mænɪdʒəbəl/ a indomable, indócil; ingobernable, inmanejable; (unwieldy) difícil de manejar, pesado

**unmannerliness** /ʌn'mænərlinɪs/ n mala crianza, descortesía, f

**unmannerly** /ʌn'mænərli/ a mal educado, descortés

**unmarketable** /ʌn'markɪtəbəl/ a invendible

**unmarriageable** /ʌn'mærɪdʒəbəl/ a incasable

**unmarried** /ʌn'mærid/ a soltero, célibe

**unmask** /ʌn'mæsk/ vt desenmascarar; Fig. quitar la careta (a). —vi quitarse la máscara; Fig. quitarse la careta, descubrirse

**unmeaning** /ʌn'minɪŋ/ a sin sentido, vacío, sin significación

**unmelodious** /,ʌnmə'loudiəs/ a sin melodía, discorde

**unmendable** /ʌn'mɛndəbəl/ a incomponible

**unmentionable** /ʌn'mɛnʃənəbəl/ a que no se puede mencionar; indigno de mencionarse

**unmerciful** /ʌn'mɜrsifəl/ a sin piedad, sin compasión; cruel, despiadado, duro

**unmerited** /ʌn'mɛrɪtɪd/ a inmerecido, desmerecido

**unmethodical** /,ʌnmə'θɒdɪkəl/ a poco metódico

**unmindful** /ʌn'maindfəl/ a olvidadizo; desatento; negligente. **u. of,** sin pensar en, olvidando

**unmistakable** /,ʌnmɪ'steikəbəl/ a inequívoco; manifiesto, evidente, indudable

**unmistakably** /,ʌnmɪ'steikəbli/ adv indudablemente

**unmitigated** /ʌn'mɪtɪ,geitɪd/ a no mitigado; completo, absoluto; (of rogue) redomado

**unmixed** /ʌn'mɪkst/ a sin mezcla; puro, sencillo; (free) limpio

**unmoor** /ʌn'mʊr/ vt desamarrar

**unmoral** /ʌn'mɔrəl, -'mɒr-/ a amoral, no moral; sin fin didáctico

**unmounted** /ʌn'mauntɪd/ a desmontado

**unmoved** /ʌn'muvd/ a fijo; (unemotional) impasible, frío; (determined) firme, inflexible, inexorable

**unmuffle** /ʌn'mʌfəl/ vt desembozar, descubrir

**unmusical** /ʌn'myuzɪkəl/ a sin afición a la música; sin oído (para la música); inarmónico

**unnamable** /ʌn'neiməbəl/ a que no se puede nombrar, innominable

**unnatural** /ʌn'nætʃərəl/ a desnaturalizado; (of vices, etc.) contra natural; innatural; (of style) rebuscado; artificial; inhumano, cruel

**unnaturalness** /ʌn'nætʃərəlnɪs/ n lo monstruoso; lo innatural; artificialidad, f; inhumanidad, f

**unnavigable** /ʌn'nævɪgəbəl/ a innavegable, no navegable

**unnecessarily** /,ʌnnɛsə'sɛrəli/ adv inútilmente, innecesariamente, sin necesidad

**unnecessariness** /ʌn'nɛsə,serinɪs/ n inutilidad, f; superfluidad, f; lo innecesario

**unnecessary** /ʌn'nɛsə,seri/ a innecesario, superfluo, inútil

**unneighborly** /ʌn'neibərli/ a de mala vecindad, impropio de vecinos, poco servicial

**unnerve** /ʌn'nɜrv/ vt acobardar quitar el valor, desanimar

**unnoticed** /ʌn'noutɪst/ a inadvertido, no observado

**unobliging** /ʌnə'blaidʒɪŋ/ a nada servicial

**unobservable** /ʌnbə'zɜrvəbəl/ a inobservable

**unobservant** /,ʌnəb'zɜrvənt/ a inobservante

**unobserved** /,ʌnəb'zɜrvd/ a sin ser notado, desapercibido

**unobstructed** /,ʌnəb'strʌktɪd/ a no obstruido; sin obstáculos; libre

**unobtainable** /,ʌnəb'teinəbəl/ a inalcanzable, inaseíble

**unobtrusive** /,ʌnəb'trusɪv/ a discreto, modesto

**unobtrusiveness** /,ʌnəb'trusɪvnɪs/ n discreción, modestia, f

**unoccupied** /ʌn'ɒkyə,paid/ a (at leisure) desocupado, ocioso, sin ocupación; vacío, vacante, libre; (untenanted) deshabitado

**unofficial** /,ʌnə'fɪʃəl/ a no oficial

**unopened** /ʌn'oupənd/ a sin abrir, cerrado; (of exhibitions, etc.) no inaugurado

**unopposed** /,ʌnə'pouzd/ a sin oposición

**unorganized** /ʌn'ɔrgə,naizd/ a inorganizado; Biol. inorgánico

**unoriginal** /,ʌnə'rɪdʒənl/ a poco original

**unorthodox** /ʌn'ɔrθə,dɒks/ a heterodoxo

**unostentatious** /,ʌnɒstən'teiʃəs/ a sencillo, modesto, sin ostentación

**unostentatiousness** /ˌʌnɒstən'teiʃəsnɪs/ n sencillez, modestia, falta de ostentación, f

**unpack** /ʌn'pæk/ vt desempaquetar; (trunks) vaciar; (bales) desembalar. —vi desempaquetar; deshacer las maletas

**unpacking** /ʌn'pækɪŋ/ n desembalaje, m

**unpaid** /ʌn'peid/ a sin pagar, no pagado

**unpalatable** /ʌn'pælətəbəl/ a de mal sabor; desagradable

**unparalleled** /ʌn'pærə,lɛld/ a sin paralelo, sin par, sin igual

**unpardonable** /ʌn'pardnəbəl/ a imperdonable, inexcusable, irremisible

**unparliamentary** /ˌʌnparlə'mɛntəri/ a poco parliamentario

**unpatriotic** /ˌʌnpeitri'ɒtɪk/ a antipatriótico

**unpaved** /ʌn'peivd/ a sin empedrar

**unperceived** /ˌʌnpər'sivd/ a inadvertido, sin ser notado

**unperturbed** /ˌʌnpər'tɜrbd/ a impasible, sin alterarse, sereno

**unpleasant** /ʌn'plɛzənt/ a desagradable, desapacible; ofensivo; (troublesome) enfadoso, molesto

**unpleasantly** /ʌn'plɛzəntli/ adv desagradablemente

**unpleasantness** /ʌn'plɛzəntnɪs/ n lo desagradable; disgusto, sinsabor, m; (disagreement) disputa, riña, f

**unpleasing** /ʌn'plizɪŋ/ a nada placentero; desagradable, sin atractivos

**unplug** /ʌn'plʌg/ vt desenchufar

**unpoetic, unpoetical,** /ˌʌnpou'ɛtɪk; ˌʌnpou'ɛtɪkəl/ a poco poético

**unpolished** /ʌn'pɒlɪʃt/ a sin pulir, tosco, mate; Fig. inculto, cerril. **u. diamond,** diamante en bruto, m

**unpolluted** /ˌʌnpə'lutɪd/ a impoluto, incontaminado; puro, sin pervertir

**unpopular** /ʌn'pɒpyələr/ a impopular

**unpopularity** /ˌʌnpɒpyə'lærɪti/ n impopularidad, f

**unpractical** /ʌn'præktɪkəl/ a impracticable, imposible; (of persons) sin sentido práctico

**unpracticed** /ʌn'præktɪst/ a no practicado; inexperto, inhábil

**unpraiseworthy** /ʌn'preiz,wɜrði/ a inmeritorio

**unprecedented** /ʌn'prɛsɪ,dɛntɪd/ a sin precedente, inaudito

**unprejudiced** /ʌn'prɛdʒədɪst/ a sin prejuicios, imparcial

**unpremeditated** /ˌʌnpri'mɛdɪ,teitɪd/ a sin premeditación, indeliberado, impremeditado

**unprepared** /ˌʌnprɪ'pɛərd/ a sin preparación, no preparado; desprevenido; desapercibido (unready)

**unpreparedness** /ˌʌnprɪ'pɛərɪdnɪs/ n falta de preparación, imprevisión, f, desapercibimiento, m

**unprepossessing** /ˌʌnpripə'zesɪŋ/ a poco atrayente, antipático

**unpresentable** /ˌʌnprɪ'zɛntəbəl/ a impresentable

**unpretentious** /ˌʌnprɪ'tɛnʃəs/ a sin pretensiones, modesto

**unpriced** /ʌn'praist/ a sin precio

**unprincipled** /ʌn'prɪnsəpəld/ a sin consciencia, sin escrúpulos

**unprinted** /ʌn'prɪntɪd/ a sin imprimir, no impreso

**unprocurable** /ˌʌnprou'kyʊrəbəl/ a inalcanzable, inasequible

**unproductive** /ˌʌnprə'dʌktɪv/ a improductivo; infructuoso, estéril

**unproductiveness** /ˌʌnprə'dʌktɪvnɪs/ n infructuosidad, f; esterilidad, f

**unprofessional** /ˌʌnprə'fɛʃənl/ a sin profesión; contrario a la ética profesional

**unprofitable** /ʌn'prɒfɪtəbəl/ a improductivo, infructuoso; sin provecho; inútil; nada lucrativo

**unprogressive** /ˌʌnprə'grɛsɪv/ a reaccionario

**unpromising** /ʌn'prɒməsɪŋ/ a poco halagüeño

**unpronounceable** /ˌʌnprə'naunsəbəl/ a impronunciable

**unpropitious** /ˌʌnprə'pɪʃəs/ a desfavorable, nada propicio, nada halagüeño

**unprosperous** /ʌn'prɒspərəs/ a impróspero

**unprotected** /ˌʌnprə'tɛktɪd/ a sin protección; (of persons) indefenso, desvalido

**unproved** /ʌn'pruvd/ a no probado, sin demostrar

**unprovided** /ˌʌnprə'vaidɪd/ a desapercibido, desprovisto. **u. for,** sin provisión (para); sin medios de vida, desamparado

**unprovoked** /ˌʌnprə'voukt/ a no provocado, sin provocación; sin motivo

**unpublished** /ʌn'pʌblɪʃt/ a inédito, no publicado, sin publicar

**unpunctual** /ʌn'pʌŋktʃuəl/ a no puntual, retrasado

**unpunctuality** /ʌnˌpʌŋktʃu'ælɪti/ n falta de puntualidad, f, retraso, m

**unpunctually** /ʌn'pʌŋktʃuəli/ adv sin puntualidad, tarde, con retraso

**unpunishable** /ʌn'pʌnɪʃə bəl/ a no punible

**unpunished** /ʌn'pʌnɪʃt/ a impune, sin castigo

**unpurchasable** /ʌn'pɜrtʃɪsəbəl/ a que no puede comprarse

**unqualified** /ʌn'kwɒlə,faid/ a incapaz, incompetente; (with professions) sin título; (downright) incondicional, absoluto

**unquenchable** /ʌn'kwɛntʃəbəl/ a inextinguible, inapagable; insaciable

**unquestionable** /ʌn'kwɛstʃənəbəl/ a indiscutible, indudable, indubitable

**unquestionably** /ʌn'kwɛstʃənəbli/ adv indudablemente

**unquiet** /ʌn'kwaiɪt/ a inquieto, intranquilo; agitado

**unravel** /ʌn'rævəl/ vt deshilar; destejer; (a mystery, etc.) desentrañar, desembrollar, descifrar

**unraveling** /ʌn'rævəlɪŋ/ n deshiladura, f; aclaración, f

**unreadable** /ʌn'ridəbəl/ a ilegible

**unreadiness** /ʌn'rɛdinɪs/ n falta de preparación, f, desapercibimiento, m; lentitud, f

**unready** /ʌn'rɛdi/ a desapercibido, desprevenido; lento

**unreal** /ʌn'riəl/ a irreal; falso, imaginario, ilusorio; ficticio; artificial; insincero, hipócrita; ideal; incorpóreo

**unreality** /ˌʌnri'ælɪti/ n irrealidad, f; falsedad, f; artificialidad, f; lo quimérico

**unreasonable** /ʌn'rizənəbəl/ a irrazonable, irracional; disparatado, extravagante; (with price, etc.) exorbitante, excesivo

**unreasonableness** /ʌn'rizənəbəlnɪs/ n irracionalidad, f; exorbitancia, f

**unreasonably** /ʌn'rizənəbli/ adv irracionalmente

**unreasoning** /ʌn'rizənɪŋ/ a irracional; sin motivo, sin causa

**unreceipted** /ˌʌnrɪ'sitɪd/ a sin recibo

**unrecognizable** /ʌn'rɛkəg,naizəbəl/ a que no puede reconocerse; imposible de reconocer

**unrecognized** /ʌn'rɛkəg,naizd/ a no reconocido

**unreconciled** /ʌn'rɛkən,saild/ a no resignado, no reconciliado

**unrectified** /ʌn'rɛktə,faid/ a no corregido, sin rectificar

**unredeemed** /ˌʌnrɪ'dimd/ a no redimido; no mitigado; (of pledges) sin desempeñar

**unrefined** /ˌʌnrɪ'faind/ a no refinado, impuro; inculto, grosero

**unreformed** /ˌʌnrɪ'fɔrmd/ a no reformado

**unrefuted** /ˌʌnrɪ'fyutɪd/ a no refutado

**unregenerate** /ˌʌnrɪ'dʒɛnərɪt/ a no regenerado

**unregretted** /ˌʌnrɪ'grɛtɪd/ a no llorado, sin lamentar

**unrehearsed** /ˌʌnrɪ'hɜrst/ a sin preparación, Theat. sin ensayar; (extempore) improvisado

**unrelated** /ˌʌnrɪ'leitɪd/ a inconexo; (of persons) sin parentesco

**unrelenting** /ˌʌnrɪ'lɛntɪŋ/ a implacable, inflexible, inexorable

**unreliability** /ˌʌnrɪ,laiə'bɪlɪti/ n incertidumbre, f; el no poder confiar en, informalidad, inestabilidad, f

**unreliable** /ˌʌnrɪ,laiəbəl/ a incierto, dudoso, indigno de confianza; (of persons) informal

**unrelieved** /ˌʌnrɪ'livd/ a no aliviado; absoluto, completo, total

**unremitting** /ˌʌnrɪ'mitɪŋ/ a incansable

**unremunerative** /ˌʌnrɪ'myunərətɪv/ a sin remuneración, no remunerado

**unrepealed** /ˌʌnrɪ'pild/ a vigente

**unrepentant** /ˌʌnrɪ'pɛntn̩t/ a impenitente

**unrepresentative** /ˌʌnrɛprɪˈzɛntətɪv/ a poco representativo

**unrepresented** /ˌʌnrɛprɪˈzɛntɪd/ a sin representación

**unrequited** /ˌʌnrɪˈkwaitɪd/ a no correspondido

**unreserved** /ˌʌnrɪˈzɜrvd/ a no reservado; expresivo, comunicativo, expansivo, franco

**unreservedly** /ˌʌnrɪˈzɜrvɪdli/ adv sin reserva; con toda franqueza

**unresisting** /ˌʌnrɪˈzɪstɪŋ/ a sin oponer resistencia

**unresolved** /ˌʌnrɪˈzɒlvd/ a sin resolverse, vacilante; incierto, dudoso, inseguro; sin solución

**unresponsive** /ˌʌnrɪˈspɒnsɪv/ a flemático; insensible, sordo

**unresponsiveness** /ˌʌnrɪˈspɒnsɪvnɪs/ n flema, f; insensibilidad, f

**unrest** /ʌnˈrɛst/ n desasosiego, m, agitación, inquietud, f

**unrestful** /ʌnˈrɛstfəl/ a agitado, inquieto, intranquilo

**unrestrained** /ˌʌnrɪˈstreind/ a desenfrenado; ilimitado, sin límites; sin reserva

**unrestricted** /ˌʌnrɪˈstrɪktɪd/ a sin restricción; ilimitado

**unrevealed** /ˌʌnrɪˈvild/ a no revelado, por descubrir, no descubierto

**unrewarded** /ˌʌnrɪˈwɔrdɪd/ a sin premio, no recompensado

**unrighteous** /ʌnˈraitʃəs/ a injusto, malo, perverso

**unrighteousness** /ʌnˈraitʃəsnɪs/ n injusticia, f; maldad, perversidad, f

**unripe** /ʌnˈraip/ a verde, inmaturo

**unripeness** /ʌnˈraipnɪs/ n falta de madurez, f

**unrivaled** /ʌnˈraivəld/ a sin igual, sin par

**unroll** /ʌnˈroul/ vt desarrollar. —vi desarrollarse; (unfold) desplegarse (a la vista)

**unromantic** /ˌʌnrouˈmæntɪk/ a poco (or nada) romántico

**unruffled** /ʌnˈrʌfəld/ a sereno, plácido, ecuánime; no arrugado; (of hair) liso

**unruliness** /ʌnˈrulinɪs/ n turbulencia, indisciplina, f; insubordinación, rebeldía, f

**unruly** /ʌnˈruli/ a ingobernable, revoltoso; refractario, rebelde; (of hair) indomable

**unsaddle** /ʌnˈsædl/ vt desensillar; derribar (del caballo, etc.)

**unsafe** /ʌnˈseif/ a inseguro; peligroso; arriesgado; (to eat) nocivo

**unsafeness** /ʌnˈseifnɪs/ n inseguridad, f; peligro, riesgo, m

**unsaid** /ʌnˈsɛd/ a sin decir, no dicho

**unsalable** / ½nˈseiləbəl/ a invendible

**unsalaried** /ʌnˈsælərid/ a no asalariado

**unsalted** /ʌnˈsɔltɪd/ a soso, sin sal

**unsanctioned** /ʌnˈsæŋkʃənd/ a no permitido, sin sancionar

**unsanitary** /ʌnˈsænɪˌteri/ a antihigiénico

**unsatisfactoriness** /ˌʌnsætɪsˈfæktərinɪs/ n lo insatisfactorio

**unsatisfactory** /ˌʌnsætɪsˈfæktəri/ a poco (or nada) satisfactorio; no aceptable

**unsatisfied** /ʌnˈsætɪsˌfaid/ a no satisfecho; descontento; no convencido; (hungry) no harto; Com. no saldado

**unsatisfying** /ʌnˈsætɪsˌfaiŋ/ a que no satisface

**unsavoriness** /ʌnˈseivərinɪs/ n insipidez, f, mal sabor, m; lo desagradable; sordidez, suciedad, f

**unsavory** /ʌnˈseivəri/ a insípido, de mal sabor; desagradable; sórdido, sucio

**unscalable** /ˌʌnˈskeiləbəl/ a inascendible, virgen

**unscathed** /ʌnˈskeiðd/ a sin daño, ileso

**unscented** /ʌnˈsɛntɪd/ a sin perfume, sin olor, no fragante

**unscholarly** /ʌnˈskɒlərli/ a nada erudito; indigno de un erudito

**unscientific** /ˌʌnsaiənˈtɪfɪk/ a no científico

**unscrew** /ʌnˈskru/ vt destornillar. —vi destornillarse

**unscrewing** /ʌnˈskruɪŋ/ n destornillamiento, m

**unscrupulous** /ʌnˈskrupyələs/ a sin escrúpulos, poco escrupuloso, desaprensivo

**unscrupulousness** /ʌnˈskrupyələsnɪs/ n falta de escrúpulos, desaprensión, f

**unseal** /ʌnˈsil/ vt desellar, romper (or quitar) el sello (de)

**unseasonable** /ʌnˈsizənəbəl/ a intempestivo, fuera de sazón; inoportuno, inconveniente. **at an u. hour,** a una hora inconveniente, a deshora

**unseasonableness** /ʌnˈsizənəbəlnɪs/ n lo intempestivo, inoportunidad, f

**unseasonably** /ʌnˈsizənəbli/ /adv intempestivamente; a deshora; inoportunamente

**unseasoned** /ʌnˈsizənd/ a Cul. sin sazonar, soso; (wood) verde; no maduro, sin madurar

**unseat** /ʌnˈsit/ vt (from horse) tirar, echar al suelo; Polit. desituir

**unseaworthy** /ʌnˈsiˌwɜrði/ a innavegable

**unseemliness** /ʌnˈsimlinɪs/ n falta de decoro, f; indecencia, f

**unseemly** /ʌnˈsimli/ a indecoroso, indigno; indecente; impropio

**unseen** /ʌnˈsin/ a no visto, invisible; inadvertido; secreto, oculto. —n versión al libro abierto, f. **the u.,** lo invisible

**unselfish** /ʌnˈsɛlfɪʃ/ a desinteresado, abnegado, nada egoísta; generoso

**unselfishness** /ʌnˈsɛlfɪʃnɪs/ n abnegación, f; desinterés, m; generosidad, f

**unsentimental** /ʌnˌsɛntəˈmɛntḷ/ a no sentimental

**unserviceable** /ʌnˈsɜrvɪsəbəl/ a inservible, inútil, que no sirve para nada, sin utilidad

**unsettle** /ʌnˈsɛtḷ/ vt desarreglar; desorganizar; hacer inseguro; agitar, perturbar

**unsettled** /ʌnˈsɛtḷd/ a inconstante, variable; Com. pendiente, sin pagar; incierto; sin resolver; (of estates) sin solucionar

**unshackle** /ʌnˈʃækəl/ vt desencadenar

**unshakable** /ʌnˈʃeikəbəl/ a inconmovible, firme

**unshapely** /ʌnˈʃeipli/ a desproporcionado

**unshaven** /ʌnˈʃeivən/ a sin afeitar

**unsheathe** /ʌnˈʃið/ vt desenvainar, sacar

**unsheltered** /ʌnˈʃɛltərd/ a desabrigado, desamparado; no protegido, sin protección; (of places) sin abrigo, expuesto; (from) sin defensa contra

**unship** /ʌnˈʃip/ vt desembarcar; (the oars) desarmar

**unshod** /ʌnˈʃɒd/ a descalzo; (of a horse) sin herraduras

**unshorn** /ʌnˈʃɔrn/ a sin esquilar; intonso

**unshrinkable** /ʌnˈʃrɪŋkəbəl/ a que no se encoge

**unshrinking** /ʌnˈʃrɪŋkɪŋ/ a intrépido; resoluto, sin vacilar

**unsightly** /ʌnˈsaitli/ a feo, horrible, repugnante, antiestético

**unsinkable** /ʌnˈsɪŋkəbəl/ a insumergible

**unskilled** /ʌnˈskɪld/ a inexperto, inhábil, imperito, torpe

**unsmokable** /ʌnˈsmoukəbəl/ a (of tobacco) infumable

**unsociability** /ˌʌnsoufəˈbɪliti/ n insociabilidad, huraña, esquivez, f

**unsociable** /ʌnˈsoufəbəl/ a insociable, huraño, esquivo, arisco

**unsocial** /ʌnˈsoufəl/ a insocial, antisocial

**unsold** /ʌnˈsould/ a no vendido, sin vender

**unsolder** /ʌnˈsɒdər/ vt desoldar, desestañar

**unsoldierly** /ʌnˈsouldʒərli/ a indigno de un soldado; poco marcial

**unsophisticated** /ˌʌnsəˈfɪstɪˌkeitɪd/ a ingenuo, inocente, cándido

**unsought** /ʌnˈsɔt/ a no solicitado; no buscado

**unsound** /ʌnˈsaund/ a enfermo; defectuoso; (rotten) podrido; (fallacious) erróneo, poco convincente; (of persons) informal, indigno de confianza; (of religious views) heterodoxo. **of u. mind,** insano

**unsoundness** /ʌnˈsaundnɪs/ n lo defectuoso; mal estado, m; falsedad, f; informalidad, f; heterodoxia, f

**unsparing** /ʌnˈspɛərɪŋ/ a severo, implacable; generoso, pródigo

**unspeakable** /ʌnˈspikəbəl/ a indecible, inefable; que no puede mencionarse, horrible

**unspecified** /ʌnˈspɛsəˌfaid/ a no especificado

**unspoiled** /ʌnˈspɔilt/ a intacto; ileso, indemne; no corrompido; no estropeado; (of children) no mimado

**unspoken** /ʌnˈspoukən/ a no pronunciado

**unsportsmanlike** /ʌn'spɔrtsmən‚laik/ a indigno de un cazador; indigno de un deportista; nada caballeroso. **to play in an u. way,** jugar sucio

**unstable** /ʌn'steibəl/ a inestable; variable; inconstante; vacilante, irresoluto

**unstained** /ʌn'steind /a no manchado; no teñido; inmaculado, sin mancha

**unstamped** /ʌn'stæmpt/ a sin sello; no sellado

**unstatesmanlike** /ʌn'steitsmən‚laik/ a impropio (or indigno) de un hombre de estado

**unsteadiness** /ʌn'stɛdinɪs/ n inestabilidad, falta de firmeza, f; inconstancia, f

**unsteady** /ʌn'stɛdi/ a inestable, inseguro; inconstante

**unstick** /ʌn'stɪk/ vt desapegar

**unstitch** /ʌn'stɪtʃ/ vt desapuntar

**unstressed** /ʌn'strɛst/ a sin énfasis; (of syllables) sin acento

**unstudied** /ʌn'stʌdid/ a no estudiado; natural, espontáneo

**unsubstantial** /‚ʌnsəb'stænʃəl/ a insubstancial; ligero; irreal, imaginario; incorpóreo; aparente

**unsuccessful** /‚ʌnsək'sɛsfəl/ a sin éxito; infructuoso. **to be u.,** no tener éxito

**unsuccessfully** /‚ʌnsək'sɛsfəli/ adv en vano, sin éxito

**unsuitability** /‚ʌnsutə'bɪlɪti/ n impropiedad, f; inconveniencia, incongruencia, f; incapacidad, f; inoportunidad, f

**unsuitable** /ʌn'sutəbəl/ a inapropiado; inconveniente; impropio; inservible; incapaz; inoportuno

**unsung** /ʌn'sʌŋ/ a no cantado; no celebrado en verso

**unsupported** /‚ʌnsə'pɔrtid/ a sin apoyo; sin defensa; no favorecido

**unsurmountable** /‚ʌnsər'mauntəbəl/ a insuperable, infranqueable

**unsurpassable** /‚ʌnsər'pæsəbəl/ a inmejorable, insuperable

**unsurpassed** /‚ʌnsər'pæst/ a sin par

**unsuspecting** /‚ʌnsə'spɛktɪŋ/ a no suspicaz, confiado, no receloso

**unswerving** /ʌn'swɜrvɪŋ/ a directo; sin vacilar, constante

**unsymmetrical** /‚ʌnsɪ'mɛtrɪkəl/ a asimétrico

**unsympathetic** /‚ʌnsɪmpə'θɛtɪk/ a indiferente, incompasivo; antipático

**unsystematic** /‚ʌnsɪstə'mætɪk/ a sin sistema, asistemático, no metódico

**untalented** /ʌn'tæləntɪd/ a sin talento

**untamed** /ʌn'teimd/ a indomado, cerril, bravío, no domesticado; desenfrenado, violento

**unteach** /ʌn'titʃ/ vt desenseñar

**untenable** /ʌn'tɛnəbəl/ a insostenible

**untenanted** /ʌn'tɛnəntɪd/ a desalquilado, deshabitado; vacío, desierto

**unthankful** /ʌn'θæŋkfəl/ a ingrato, desagradecido

**unthinkable** /ʌn'θɪŋkəbəl/ a inconcebible; imposible

**unthinking** /ʌn'θɪŋkɪŋ/ a sin reflexión; desatento; indiscreto

**unthinkingly** /ʌn'θɪŋkɪŋli/ adv sin pensar

**unthread** /ʌn'θrɛd/ vt deshebrar

**untidily** /ʌn'taidli/ adv en desorden, sin aseo

**untidiness** /ʌn'taidinɪs/ n desorden, m; desaseo, desaliño, m; falta de pulcritud, f

**untidy** /ʌn'taidi/ a desarreglado; desaseado; abandonado; en desorden, sin concierto

**untie** /ʌn'tai/ vt desatar, desanudar; (knots) deshacer

**until** /ʌn'tɪl/ prep hasta. —conjunc hasta que. (The subjunc. is required in clauses referring to future time, e.g. No venga usted hasta que le avise yo, Don't come until I tell you. In clauses referring to past or present time the indicative is generally used, e.g. No la reconocí hasta que se volvió, I didn't recognize her until she turned round)

**untilled** /ʌn'tɪld/ a sin cultivar

**untimeliness** /ʌn'taimlinɪs/ n inoportunidad, f; lo prematuro

**untimely** /ʌn'taimli/ a inoportuno, intempestivo; prematuro

**untiring** /ʌn'taiᵊrɪŋ/ a incansable, infatigable

**unto** /'ʌntu/ unstressed -tə/ prep hacia

**untold** /ʌn'tould/ a no revelado; no narrado; sin decir, no dicho; incalculable

**untouchable** /ʌn'tʌtʃəbəl/ a que no puede tocarse, intangible; (of castes) intocable

**untouched** /ʌn'tʌtʃt/ a sin tocar; intacto, incólume

**untrained** /ʌn'treind/ a indisciplinado; inexperto; no adiestrado

**untranslatable** /‚ʌntræns'leitəbəl/ a intraducible

**untraveled** /ʌn'trævəld/ a no frecuentado; (of persons) provinciano

**untried** /ʌn'traid/ a no experimentado. **u. knight,** caballero novel, m

**untrodden** /ʌn'trɒdn̩/ a no hollado, no frecuentado; inexplorado, virgen

**untroubled** /ʌn'trʌbəld/ a tranquilo, sosegado

**untrue** /ʌn'tru/ a mentiroso, falso, engañoso; ficticio, imaginario; traidor, desleal; infiel

**untrustworthiness** /ʌn'trʌst‚wɜrðinɪs/ n incertidumbre, inseguridad, f; (of persons) informalidad, f

**untrustworthy** /ʌn'trʌst‚wɜrði/ a indigno de confianza; incierto, dudoso; desleal

**untruth** /ʌn'truθ/ n mentira, falsedad, f; ficción, f

**untruthful** /ʌn'truθfəl/ a mentiroso; falso

**untruthfulness** /ʌn'truθfəlnɪs/ n falsedad, f

**untwist** /ʌn'twist/ vt destorcer

**unused** /ʌn'yuzd/ a no empleado; /ʌn'yust/ desacostumbrado; inusitado; (postage stamp) sin sellar

**unusual** /ʌn'yuʒuəl/ a fuera de lo común, desacostumbrado; extraño, raro, peregrino, extraordinario

**unusually** /ʌn'yuʒuəli/ adv excepcionalmente; infrecuentemente

**unusualness** /ʌn'yuʒuəlnɪs/ n lo insólito; rareza, f

**unutterable** /ʌn'ʌtərəbəl/ a indecible, inexpresable

**unvarnished** /ʌn'vɑrnɪʃt/ a sin barnizar; Fig. sencillo

**unvarying** /ʌn'vɛɑriiŋ/ a invariable, constante, uniforme

**unveil** /ʌn'veil/ vt quitar el velo; (memorial) descubrir; Fig. revelar. —vi quitarse el velo; revelarse, quitarse la careta

**unventilated** /ʌn'vɛntleitid/ a sin ventilación; sin aire, ahogado; (of topics) no discutido

**unverifiable** /ʌn‚vɛrə'faiəbəl/ a que no puede verificarse

**unverified** /ʌn‚vɛrə'faid/ a sin verificar

**unvisited** /ʌn'vɪsɪtɪd/ a no visitado; no frecuentado

**unvoiced** /ʌn'vɔist/ a no expresado

**unwanted** /ʌn'wɒntɪd/ a no deseado; superfluo, de más

**unwarlike** /ʌn'wɔr‚laik/ a nada marcial, pacífico

**unwarranted** /ʌn'wɔrəntɪd/ a sin garantía; inexcusable, injustificable

**unwary** /ʌn'wɛɑri/ a incauto, imprudente

**unwashed** /ʌn'wɒʃt/ a sin lavar; sucio

**unwatched** /ʌn'wɒtʃt/ a no vigilado

**unwavering** /ʌn'weivərɪŋ/ a resuelto, firme; inexorable; (gaze) fijo

**unwaveringly** /ʌn'weivərɪŋli/ adv sin vacilar; inexorablemente

**unwearied** /ʌn'wiᵊrid/ a incansable; infatigable

**unwelcome** /ʌn'wɛlkəm/ a mal acogido; inoportuno; desagradable

**unwell** /ʌn'wɛl/ a indispuesto

**unwholesome** /ʌn'houlsəm/ a malsano, nocivo, insalubre

**unwholesomeness** /ʌn'houlsəmnɪs/ n insalubridad, f

**unwieldiness** /ʌn'wildinɪs/ n pesadez, dificultad de manejarse, f

**unwieldy** /ʌn'wildi/ a pesado, abultado, difícil de manejar

**unwilling** /ʌn'wɪlɪŋ/ a desinclinado, reluctante

**unwillingly** /ʌn'wɪlɪŋli/ adv de mala gana

**unwillingness** /ʌn'wɪlɪŋnɪs/ n falta de inclinación, repugnancia, f

**unwind** /ʌn'waind/ vt desenvolver; (thread) desdevanar, desovillar. —vi desarrollarse; desdevanarse

**unwise** /ʌn'waiz/ a imprudente, indiscreto, incauto; (lacking wisdom) tonto

**unwisely** /ʌn'waizli/ adv imprudentemente, indiscretamente

**unwitting** /ʌn'witɪŋ/ a inconsciente

**unwittingly** /ʌn'witɪŋli/ adv sin darse cuenta

**unwomanly** /ʌn'wumənli/ a poco femenino

**unwonted** /ʌn'wɒntɪd/ a insólito, inusitado

**unworkable** /ʌn'wɜrkəbəl/ a impráctico
**unworkmanlike** /ʌn'wɜrkmən,laik/ a chapucero, charanguero
**unworldly** /ʌn'wɜrldli/ a poco, mundano, espiritual
**unworn** /ʌn'wɔrn/ a sin llevar, nuevo
**unworthiness** /ʌn'wɜrðinis/ n indignidad, f
**unworthy** /ʌn'wɜrði/ a indigno
**unwounded** /ʌn'wundɪd/ a no herido, sin herida, ileso
**unwrap** /ʌn'ræp/ vt desenvolver, desempapelar
**unwritten** /ʌn'rɪtn/ a no escrito. **u. law,** ley consuetudinaria, f
**unyielding** /ʌn'yildɪŋ/ a duro, firme; (of persons) inflexible, terco, resuelto, obstinado
**unyoke** /ʌn'youk/ vt desuncir, quitar el yugo
**up** /ʌp/ adv (high) arriba, en alto; (higher) hacia arriba; (out of bed) levantado; (standing) de pie; (finished) concluido, terminado; (of time) llegado; (excited) agitado; (of sun, etc.) salido; (come or gone up) subido; (of universities) en residencia; (for discussion) bajo consideración; (abreast of) al lado, al nivel; (incapable) incapaz, incompetente; (ill) enfermo, indispuesto. **"Up,"** (on elevators) «Para subir.» (For various idiomatic uses of up after verbs, see verbs themselves.) a (in a few expressions only) ascendente. —prep en lo alto de; hacia arriba de; a lo largo de; (with country) en el interior de; (with current) contra. **to be up in arms,** sublevarse, rebelarse. **to be very hard up,** ser muy pobre, estar a la cuarta pregunta. **to drink up,** beberlo todo. **to go or come up,** subir. **to lay up,** acumular. **to speak up,** hablar en voz alta. **He has something up his sleeve,** Tiene algo en la manga. **It is all up,** Todo se acabó, Mi gozo en el pozo. **It is not up to much,** Vale muy poco; No es muy fuerte. **It is up to you,** Tú dirás, Tú harás lo que te parezca. **What is he up to?** ¿Qué está tramando? **What's up?** ¿Qué pasa? ¿Qué hay? **up and down,** adv bajando y subiendo, de arriba abajo; de un lado a otro; por todas partes. **up-and-down,** a fluctuante; (of roads) undulante (de of life) accidentado, borrascoso. **ups and downs,** vicisitudes, f pl, altibajos, m pl. **up-grade,** subida, f. **up in,** versado en, perito en. **well up in,** fuerte en. **up North,** al norte; en el norte; hacia el norte. **up there,** allí arriba, allí en lo alto. **up to,** hasta; (aware) al corriente de, informado de. **up to date,** adv hasta la fecha. **up-to-date,** a de última moda; al día. **up to now,** hasta ahora. **up train,** tren ascendente. **Up with...!** ¡Arriba! **Up you go!** (to children) ¡Upa!
**upbraid** /ʌp'breid/ vt reprender, echar en cara
**upbringing** /'ʌp,brɪŋɪŋ/ n crianza, educación, f
**upcountry** /n., a 'ʌp,kʌntri; adv. ʌp'kʌntri/ n tierra adentro, f; lo interior (de un país). —a de tierra adentro, del interior. —adv tierra adentro, hacia el interior
**update** /'ʌp,deit/ vt actualizar, poner al día
**upheaval** /ʌp'hivəl/ n solevantamiento, m; trastorno, m
**uphill** /a, adv. 'ʌp'hɪl; n. 'ʌp,hɪl/ a ascendente; penoso, fatigoso, difícil. —adv cuesta arriba, pecho arriba
**uphold** /ʌp'hould/ vt sostener, apoyar; (help) ayudar, consolar; (protect) defender; (countenance) aprobar; Law. confirmar
**upholder** /ʌp'houldər/ n sostenedor (-ra), defensor (-ra)
**upholster** /ʌp'houlstər, ə'poul-/ vt entapizar, tapizar
**upholsterer** /ʌp'houlstərər; ə'poulʒ/ n tapicero, m
**upholstery** /ʌp'houlstəri, ə'poulʒ/ n tapicería, f; (of car) almohadillado, m
**upkeep** /'ʌp,kip/ n mantenimiento, m, conservación, f
**upland** /'ʌplənd/ n tierra alta, f, a alto, elevado
**uplift** /v. ʌp'lɪft; n. 'ʌp,lɪft/ vt elevar. —n elevación, f; Inf. fervor, m
**upon** /ə'pɒn/ prep. See **on**
**upper** /'ʌpər/ a comparat superior; alto; de arriba. —n (of shoe) pala, f, Sports. **u.-cut,** golpe de abajo arriba, upper-cut, m. **U. Egypt,** Alto Egipto, m. **u. hand,** dominio, m; superioridad, ventaja, f. **u. house,** cámara alta, f; senado, m. **u. ten,** los diez primeros

**upper classes** a clases altas, capas altas, f pl
**uppermost** /'ʌpər,moust/ a más alto, más elevado; predominante, principal; más fuerte. —adv en primer lugar; en lo más alto. **to be u.,** predominar
**upright** /'ʌp,rait/ a recto, derecho; vertical; (honorable) honrado, digno, recto. —n (stanchion) mástil, soporte, palo derecho, montante, m. —adv en pie; derecho
**uprightly** /'ʌp,raitli/ adv rectamente, honradamente
**uprightness** /'ʌp,raitnis/ n rectitud, honradez, probidad, f
**uprising** /'ʌp,raizɪŋ/ n insurrección, sublevación, f
**uproar** /'ʌp,rɔr/ n alboroto, tumulto, estrépito, m, conmoción, f
**uproarious** /ʌp'rɔriəs/ a tumultuoso, estrepitoso
**uproot** /ʌp'rut/ vt desarraigar; Fig. arrancar; (destroy) extirpar
**uprooting** /ʌp'rutɪŋ/ n desarraigo, m; arranque, m; extirpación, f
**upset** /v. ʌp'sɛt; n. 'ʌp,sɛt/ vt volcar; (overthrow) derribar, echar abajo; (frustrate) contrariar; desarreglar; (distress) trastornar, turbar; (of food) hacer mal. —vi volcarse. —n vuelco, m; trastorno, m. **u. price,** tipo de subasta, m
**upsetting** /ʌp'sɛtɪŋ/ a turbante, inquietante
**upshot** /'ʌp,ʃɒt/ n resultado, m; consecuencia, f
**upside** /'ʌp,said/ n lado superior, m; parte superior, f; (of trains) andén ascendente, m. **u. down,** al revés, de arriba abajo; en desorden
**upstairs** /'ʌp'stɛərz/ adv arriba, en el piso de arriba; (with go or come) al piso de arriba
**upstanding** /ʌp'stændɪŋ/ a gallardo, guapo. **an u. young man (woman),** un buen mozo (una buena moza)
**upstart** /'ʌp,start/ n arribista, mf; advenedizo (-za), insolente, mf; presuntuoso (-sa)
**upstream** /'ʌp'strim/ a and adv contra la corriente, agua arriba, río arriba
**upturned** /'ʌp,tɜrnd/ a (of noses) respingada
**upward** /'ʌpwərd/ a ascendente, hacia arriba
**upwards** /'ʌpwərdz/ adv hacia arriba; en adelante. **u. of,** más de
**Urals, the** /'yʊrəlz/ los Urales, m pl
**uranium** /yʊ'reiniəm/ n Mineral. uranio, m
**Uranus** /'yʊrənəs, yʊ'rei-/ n Astron. Urano, m
**urban** /'ɜrbən/ a urbano, ciudadano
**urbane** /ɜr'bein/ a cortés, urbano, fino
**urbanity** /ɜr'bæniti/ n urbanidad, cortesía, finura, f
**urbanization** /,ɜrbənə'zeiʃən/ n urbanización, f
**urbanize** /'ɜrbə,naiz/ vt urbanizar
**urban renewal** n renovación urbana, renovación urbanística, f
**urchin** /'ɜrtʃin/ n galopín, granuja, pilluelo, m
**ureter** /yʊ'ritər/ n Anat. uréter, m
**urethra** /yʊ'riθrə/ n Anat. uretra, f
**urge** /ɜrdʒ/ vt empujar, impeler; incitar, estimular, azuzar, animar; pedir con urgencia, recomendar con ahínco, instar, insistir (en). —n instinto, impulso, m; deseo, m; ambición, f
**urgency** /'ɜrdʒənsi/ n urgencia, f; importancia, perentoriedad, f
**urgent** /'ɜrdʒənt/ a urgente; importante, apremiante, perentorio. **to be u.,** urgir
**urgently** /'ɜrdʒəntli/ adv urgentemente
**uric** /'yʊrik/ a úrico
**urinal** /'yʊrənl/ n orinal, urinario, m
**urinalysis** /,yʊrə'næləsis/ n análisis de orina, urinálisis, m
**urinary** /'yʊrə,nɛri/ a urinario
**urinary tract** n conducto urinario, m, vías urinarias, f pl
**urinate** /'yʊrə,neit/ vi orinar
**urine** /'yʊrin/ n orín, m
**urn** /ɜrn/ n urna, f; (for coffee) cafetera, f; (for tea) tetera, f
**Ursa** /'ʊrsə/ n Astron. osa, f. **U. Major,** osa mayor, f. **U. Minor,** osa menor, f
**urticaria** /,ɜrti'kɛəriə/ n Med. urticaria, f
**Uruguayan** /,yʊrə'gweiən/ a and n uruguayo (-ya)
**us** /ʌs/ pron nos; (with prep.) nosotros. **He came toward us,** Vino hacia nosotros

**usable** /'yuzəbəl/ a aprovechable, servible

**usage** /'yusɪdʒ/ n (handling) tratamiento, m; uso, m, costumbre, f

**use** /yus/ n uso, m; manejo, empleo, m; (custom) costumbre práctica, f; (need) necesidad, f; (usefulness) aprovechamiento, m; Law. usufructo, m. **directions for use,** direcciones para el uso, f pl, **for the use of...,** para uso de... **in use,** en uso. **out of use,** anticuado; fuera de moda. **to be of no use,** no servir; ser inútil. **to have no use for,** no tener necesidad de; Inf. tener en poco. **to make use of,** servirse de, aprovechar; Law. ejercer. **to put to use,** poner en uso, poner en servicio

**use** /yuz/ vt usar; (employ) emplear; (utilize) servirse de, utilizar; (handle) manejar; hacer uso de; (consume) gastar, consumir; (treat) tratar; practicar. **to use up,** agotar, acabar con; consumir. —vi impers acostumbrar, soler (e.g. It used to happen that..., Solía ocurrir que...). (**Used to** and the verb which follows are often translated simply by the imperfect tense of the following verb, e.g. I used to see her every day, La veía todos los días. Use of the verbs acostumbrar or soler to translate used to adds emphasis to the statement)

**used** /yuzd/ a and past part /yust/ acostumbrado, habituado; empleado; (clothes) usado; (postage stamp) sellado. **to become u. to,** acostumbrarse a

**useful** /'yusfəl/ a útil; provechoso; servicial

**usefully** /'yusfəli/ adv útilmente; con provecho

**usefulness** /'yusfəlnɪs/ n utilidad, f; valor, m

**useless** /'yuslɪs/ a inútil; vano, infructuoso. **to render u.,** inutilizar

**uselessness** /'yuslɪsnɪs/ n inutilidad, f

**user** /'yuzər/ n el, m, (f, la) que usa, comprador (-ra)

**usher** /'ʌʃər/ n ujier, m; (in a theater) acomodador (-ra). —vt introducir, anunciar; acomodar

**usual** /'yuʒuəl/ a usual, acostumbrado, habitual; normal, común. **as u.,** como siempre. **in the u. form,** Com. al usado; como de costumbre. **with their usual courtesy,** con la cortesía que les es característica

**usually** /'yuʒuəli/ adv por lo general, ordinariamente

**We u. go out on Sundays,** Acostumbramos salir los domingos

**usurer** /'yuʒərər/ n usurero (-ra)

**usurious** /yu'ʒuriəs/ a usurario

**usurp** /yu'sɜrp/ vt usurpar; asumir, arrogarse

**usurpation** /,yusər'peɪʃən/ n usurpación, f; arrogación, f

**usurper** /yu'sɜrpər/ n usurpador (-ra)

**usurping** /yu'sɜrpɪŋ/ a usurpador

**usury** /'yuʒəri/ n usura, f. **to practice u.,** usurear, dar (or tomar) a usura

**utensil** /yu'tɛnsəl/ n utensilio, instrumento, m; herramienta, f. **kitchen utensils,** batería de cocina, f

**uterine** /'yutərɪn/ a Med. uterino

**uterus** /'yutərəs/ n útero, m

**utilitarian** /yu,tɪlɪ'tɛəriən/ a utilitario

**utilitarianism** /yu,tɪlɪ'tɛəriə,nɪzəm/ n utilitarismo, m

**utility** /yu'tɪlɪti/ n utilidad, f; ventaja, f, beneficio, provecho, m. **u. goods,** artículos fabricados bajo la autorización del gobierno, m pl

**utilizable** /,yutl'aizəbəl/ a utilizable, aprovechable

**utilization** /,yutWə'zeiSən/ n empleo, aprovechamiento, m

**utilize** /'yutl,aiz/ vt utilizar, servirse de; aprovechar

**utmost** /'ʌt,moust/ a (outermost) extremo; (farthest) más remoto, más distante; (greatest) mayor, más grande. —n lo más; todo lo posible. **to do one's u.,** hacer todo lo posible, hacer todo lo que uno pueda

**utopian** /yu'toupiən/ a utópico

**utter** /'ʌtər/ a completo, total; terminate, absoluto; sumo, extremo. **He is an u. fool,** Es un tonto de capirote

**utter** /'ʌtər/ vt pronunciar, proferir, decir, hablar; (a sigh, cry, etc.) dar; (express) manifestar, expresar, explicar; (coin) poner en circulación; (a libel) publicar; (disclose) revelar, descubrir

**utterance** /'ʌtərəns/ n expresión, manifestación, f; pronunciación, f; (style) lenguaje, m

**utterly** /'ʌtərli/ adv enteramente, completamente

**uttermost** /'ʌtər,moust/ a. See **utmost**

**uvula** /'yuvyələ/ n Anat. úvula, f

**uxorious** /ʌk'sɔriəs/ a uxorio

# V

**v** /vi/ *n* (letter) ve, *f*; pieza en forma de V, *f*

**vacancy** /'veikənsi/ *n* vacío, *m;* vacancia, *f;* (mental) vacuidad, *f;* (of offices, posts) vacante, *f;* (leisure) desocupación, ociosidad, *f;* (gap, blank) vacío, *m,* laguna, *f*

**vacant** /'veikənt/ *a* vacío; despoblado, deshabitado; (free) libre; (of offices, etc.) vacante; (leisured) ocioso; (absent-minded) distraído; (vague) vago; (foolish) estúpido, estólido

**vacantly** /'veikəntli/ *adv* distraídamente; estúpidamente

**vacate** /'veikeit/ *vt* dejar vacío; (a post) dejar; (a throne) renunciar a; dejar vacante; *Mil.* evacuar; *Law.* anular, rescindir

**vacation** /vei'keiʃən/ *n* (of offices) vacante, *f;* (holiday) vacaciones, *f pl, f.* **the long v.,** las vacaciones de verano. **to be on a v.,** estar de vacaciones

**vaccinate** /'væksə,neit/ *vt* vacunar

**vaccination** /,væksə'neiʃən/ *n* vacunación, *f*

**vaccine** /væk'sin/ *n* vacuna, *f*

**vacillate** /'væsə,leit/ *vi* (sway) oscilar; (hesitate) vacilar, titubear, dudar

**vacillating** /'væsə,leitɪŋ/ *a* vacilante

**vacillation** *n* vacilación, *f*

**vacuity** /væ'kyuiti/ *n* vacuidad, *f*

**vacuous** /'vækyuəs/ *a* desocupado, ocioso; estúpido, vacío

**vacuum** /'vækyum/ *n* vacío, *m.* **v. brake,** freno al vacío, *m.* **v. cleaner,** aspirador de polvo, *m.* **v. flask,** termos, *m.* **v. pump,** bomba neumática, *f.* **vacuumshelf dryer,** secador al vacío, *m*

**vade mecum** /'vei'di mikəm, 'vɑ-/ *n* vademécum, *m*

**vagabond** /'vægə,bɒnd/ *n* vagabundo (-da); vago, *m;* (beggar) mendigo (-ga). —*a* vagabundo, errante

**vagabondage** /'vægə,bɒndɪdʒ/ *n* vagabundeo, *m,* vagancia, *f*

**vagary** /və'gɛəri, 'veigəri/ *n* (whim) capricho, antojo, *m,* extravagancia, *f;* (of the mind) divagación, *f*

**vagina** /və'dʒainə/ *n* vagina, *f*

**vaginal** /'vædʒənl/ *a* vaginal

**vagrancy** /'veigrənsi/ *n* vagancia, *f*

**vagrant** /'veigrənt/ *n* vago, *m, a* vagabundo, errante

**vague** /veig/ *a* vago; indistinto; equívoco, ambiguo; (uncertain) incierto

**vaguely** /'veigli/ *adv* vagamente

**vagueness** /'veignɪs/ *n* vaguedad, *f*

**vain** /vein/ *a* vano; (fruitless) infructuoso; (useless) inútil; (unsubstantial) fútil, insubstancial; fantástico; (empty) vacío; (worthless) despreciable; (conceited) vanidoso, presumido. **in v.,** en vano, en balde, inútilmente. **v. about,** orgulloso de

**vainglorious** /vein'glɔriəs, -'glour-/ *a* vanaglorioso

**vaingloriousness** /vein'glɔriəsnɪs/ *n* vanagloria, *f*

**vainly** /'veinli/ *adv* vanamente; inútilmente; (conceitedly) vanidosamente, con vanidad

**valance** /'væləns/ *n* cenefa, *f*

**vale** /veil/ *n* (valley) valle, *m.* —*interj* ¡adiós! —*n* (good-bye) vale, *m*

**valediction** /,vælɪ'dɪkʃən/ *n* despedida, *f;* vale, *m*

**valedictory** /,vælɪ'dɪktəri/ *a* de despedida

**Valencian** /və'lɛnʃiən/ *a* and *n* valenciano (-na)

**valency** /'veilənsi/ *n Chem.* valencia, *f*

**valet** /væ'lei, 'vælɪt/ *n* criado, *m.* **v. de chambre,** ayuda de cámara, *m*

**valetudinarian** /,vælɪ,tudn'ɛəriən/ *a* valetudinario

**Valhalla** /væl'hælə, vɑl'hɑlə/ *n* el Valhala, *m*

**valiant** /'vælyənt/ *a* valiente, esforzado, animoso, bravo

**valiantly** /'vælyəntli/ *adv* valientemente

**valid** /'vælɪd/ *a* válido, valedero; (of laws in force) vigente

**validate** /'vælɪ,deit/ *vt* validar

**validation** /,vælɪ'deiʃən/ *n* validación, *f*

**validity** /və'lɪdɪti/ *n* validez, *f*

**validly** /'vælɪdli/ *adv* válidamente

**valise** /və'lis/ *n* valija, *f,* saco de viaje, *m*

**Valkyrie** /væl'kɪəri/ *n* Valquiria, *f*

**valley** /'væli/ *n* valle, *m*

**valor** /'vælər/ *n* valor, *m,* valentía, *f*

**valorous** /'vælərəs/ *a* valoroso, esforzudo, intrépido

**valuable** /'vælyuəbəl/ *a* valioso; costoso; precioso; estimable; excelente. —*n pl* **valuables,** objetos de valor, *m pl*

**valuableness** /'vælyuəbəlnɪs/ *n* valor, *m*

**valuation** /,vælyu'eiʃən/ *n* valuación, tasación, *f;* estimación, *f*

**valuator** /'vælyu,eitər/ *n* tasador, *m*

**value** /'vælyu/ *n* valor, *m;* precio, *m;* estimación, *f;* importancia, *f;* (Gram. Mus.) valor, *m;* pl **values,** valores morales, principios, *m pl.* —*vt* tasar, valorar; estimar; apreciar; tener en mucho; hacer caso de; considerar. **to be of v.,** ser de valor

**valued** /'vælyud/ *a* apreciado, estimado; precioso

**valueless** /'vælyulɪs/ *a* sin valor; insignificante

**valuer** /'vælyuər/ *n* tasador, *m*

**valve** /vælv/ *n* (Elec., Mech., Anat.) válvula, *f;* (Bot., Zool.) valva, *f*

**valved** /vælvd/ *a* con válvulas; (in compounds) de... válvulas

**valvular** /'vælvyələr/ *a* valvular

**vamp** /væmp/ *n* (of a shoe) pala (de zapato), *f;* (patch) remiendo, *m; Mus.* acompañamiento improvisado, *m; Inf.* aventurera, *f.* —*vt* (of shoes) poner palas (a); (patch) remendar; *Mus.* improvisar un acompañamiento; (of a woman) fascinar, engatusar

**vampire** /'væmpai³r/ *n* vampiro, *m*

**van** /væn/ *n* (Mil., Nav., Fig.) vanguardia, *f;* camión, *m;* (for delivery) camión de reparto, *m;* (for furniture) conductora de muebles, *f;* (removal) carro de mudanzas, *m;* (mail) camión postal, *m;* (for bathing) caseta de baño, *f;* (for guard on trains) furgón de equipajes, *m;* (railroad car) vagón, *m*

**vandal** /'vændl/ *a* and *n* vándalo (-la); bárbaro (-ra)

**vandalism** /'vændl,ɪzəm/ *n* vandalismo, *m*

**Vandyke** /væn'daik/ *n* cuadro de Vandyke, *m.* **V. beard,** perilla, *f.* **V. collar,** cuello de encaje, *m*

**vane** /vein/ *n* (weathercock) veleta, *f;* (of a windmill) aspa, *f;* (of a propeller) paleta, *f;* (of a feather) barba, *f;* (of a surveying instrument) pínula, *f*

**vanguard** /'væn,gɑrd/ *n* vanguardia, *f.* **in the v.,** a vanguardia; *Fig.* en la vanguardia

**vanilla** /və'nilə/ *n* vainilla, *f*

**vanish** /'vænɪʃ/ *vi* desaparecer; desvanecerse; disiparse

**vanishing** /'vænɪʃɪŋ/ *n* desaparición, *f;* disipación, *f.* **v. cream,** crema desvanecedora, *f.* **v. point,** punto de la vista, *m*

**vanity** /'vænɪti/ *n* vanidad, *f.* **v. case,** polvera de bolsillo, *f*

**vanquish** /'væŋkwɪʃ/ *vt* vencer, derrotar

**vanquisher** /'væŋkwɪʃər/ *n* vencedor (-ra)

**vantage** /'væntɪdʒ, 'van-/ *n* ventaja (also in tennis), *f.* **v.-ground,** posición ventajosa, *f;* sitial de privilegio, *m*

**vapid** /'væpɪd/ *a* insípido, insulso; (of speeches, etc.) soso, aburrido, insípido

**vapidity** /və'pɪditi/ *n* insipidez, sosería, *f*

**vapor** /'veipər/ *n* vapor, *m; pl* **vapors,** (hysteria) vapores, *m pl.* —*vi* (boast) jactarse, baladronear; decir disparates. **v. bath,** baño de vapor, *m*

**vaporizable** /,veipə'raizəbəl/ *a* vaporizable

**vaporization** /,veipərə'zeiʃən/ *n* vaporización, *f*

**vaporize** /'veipə,raiz/ *vt* vaporizar. —*vi* vaporizarse

**vaporizer** /'veipə,raizər/ *n* vaporizador, *m*

**vaporous** /'veipərəs/ *a* vaporoso

**variability** /,vɛəriə'bɪliti/ *n* variabilidad, *f*

**variable** /'vɛəriəbəl/ *a* variable. —*n Math.* variable, *f*

**variably** /'vɛəriəbli/ *adv* variablemente

**variance** /'vɛəriəns/ *n* variación, *f,* cambio, *m;* desacuerdo, *m,* disensión, *f;* diferencia, contradicción, *f.* **at v.,** en desacuerdo, reñidos; hostil (a), opuesto (a); (of things) distinto (de), en contradicción (con)

**variant** /'veəriənt/ n variante, f
**variation** /ˌveəri'eifən/ n variación, f; cambio, m; variedad, f; diferencia, f; (Mus. magnetism) variación, f
**varicose** /'væriˌkous/ a varicoso
**varied success** /'veərid/ éxito vario, m
**variegate** /'veəriiˌgeit/ vt abigarrar, matizar, salpicar
**variegated** /'veəriiˌgeitid/ a abigarrado; variado; mezclado
**variegation** /ˌveəriiˈgeifən/ n abigarramiento, m; diversidad de colores, f
**variety** /vəˈraiiti/ n variedad, f; diversidad, f; (choice) surtido, m. **v. show,** función de variedades, f
**various** /'veəriəs/ a vario, diverso; diferente
**variously** /'veəriəsli/ adv diversamente
**varix** /'veəriks/ n várice, f
**varnish** /'varniʃ/ n barniz, m. —vt barnizar; (pottery) vidriar; (conceal) disimular. **copal v.,** barniz copal, m. **japan v., charol japonés, m. lacquer v.,** laca, f. **v. remover,** (for nails) quitaesmalte, m
**varnishing** /'varniʃiŋ/ n barnizado, m; (of pottery) vidriado, m
**vary** /'veəri/ vt variar; cambiar; diversificar; modificar. —vi variar; cambiar; (be different) ser distinto (de); (deviate) desviarse (de); (disagree) estar en desacuerdo, distar, estar en contradicción. **to v. directly (indirectly),** Math. variar en razón directa (inversa)
**varying** /'veəriiŋ/ a variante, cambiante, diverso
**vascular** /'væskyələr/ a vascular
**vase** /veis, veiz, vaz/ n vaso, jarrón, m; urna, f
**vaseline** /'væsəˌlin/ n vaselina, f
**vassal** /'væsəl/ n vasallo (-lla); esclavo (-va), siervo (-va). —a tributario
**vast** /væst/ a vasto, extenso; enorme; grande. —n vastedad, inmensidad, f
**vastly** /'væstli/ adv enormemente; muy; con mucho
**vastness** /'væstnis/ n vastedad, extensión, f; inmensidad, f; enormidad, f, gran tamaño, m; grandeza, f
**vat** /væt/ n cuba, tina, f; alberca, f, estanque, m. **dyeing vat,** cuba de tintorero, f. **tanning vat,** noque, m. **wine vat,** lagar, m
**Vatican** /'vætikən/ a and n Vaticano, m
**vaticinate** /vəˈtisiˌneit/ vt and vi vaticinar, profetizar
**vaticination** /vəˌtisiˈneifən/ n vaticinio, m, predicción, f
**vaudeville** /'vɔdvil/ n vodevil, m, zarzuela cómica, f
**vault** /vɔlt/ n Archit. bóveda, f; caverna, f; (for wine) bodega, cueva, f; (in a bank) cámara acorazada, f; (in a church) cripta, f; sepultura, f; (of the sky) bóveda celeste, f; (leap) salto, m; voltereta, f. —vi (jump) saltar; (with a pole) saltar con pértiga; saltar por encima de; voltear. —vt Archit. abovedar; saltar
**vaulted** /'vɔltid/ a abovedado
**vaulter** /'vɔltər/ n saltador (-ra)
**vaulting** /'vɔltiŋ/ n construcción de bóvedas, f; bóvedas, f pl; edificio abovedado, m; (jumping) salto, m. **v.-horse,** potro de madera, m
**vaunt** /vɔnt/ vi jactarse (de), hacer gala (de); triunfar (sobre). —vt ostentar, sacar a relucir; (praise) alabar. —n jactancia, f
**veal** /vil/ n ternera, f. **v.-cutlet,** chuleta de ternera, f
**vector** /'vektər/ n vector, m
**Veda** /'veidə/ n Veda, m
**veer** /viər/ vi (of the wind) girar; (of a ship) virar; Fig. cambiar (de opinión, etc.). —vt virar
**vegetable** /'vedʒtəbəl/ n vegetal, m; legumbre, f; pl **vegetables,** (green and generally cooked) verduras, f pl; (raw green) hortalizas, f pl. **v. dish,** fuente de legumbres, f. **v. garden,** huerto de legumbres, m; **v. ivory,** marfil vegetal, m. **v. kingdom,** reino vegetal, m. **v. soup,** sopa de hortelano, f
**vegetal** /'vedʒitl/ a vegetal
**vegetarian** /ˌvedʒiˈteəriən/ a and n vegetariano (-na)
**vegetarianism** /ˌvedʒiˈteəriəˌnizəm/ n vegetarianismo, m
**vegetate** /'vedʒiˌteit/ vi vegetar
**vegetation** /ˌvedʒiˈteifən/ n vegetación, f
**vehemence** /'viəməns/ n vehemencia, f; violencia, f; impetuosidad, f; pasión, f, ardor, m
**vehement** /'viəmənt/ a vehemente; violento; impetuoso; apasionado

**vehemently** /'viəməntli/ adv con vehemencia; violentamente; con impetuosidad; apasionadamente
**vehicle** /'viikəl/ n vehículo, m; (means) medio, m; instrumento, m
**vehicular** /vi'hikyələr/ a vehicular, de los vehículos; de los coches. **v. traffic,** circulación de los coches, f; los vehículos
**veil** /veil/ n velo, m; (curtain) cortina, f; (disguise) disfraz, m; (excuse) pretexto, m; (appearance) apariencia, f. —vt velar; cubrir con un velo; (hide) tapar, encubrir; (dissemble) disimular; (disguise) disfrazar. **to take the v.,** tomar el velo, profesar
**vein** /vein/ n (Anat., Bot.) vena, f; (Geol., Mineral.) veta, f, filón, m; (in wood) fibra, hebra, f; (Fig. streak) rasgo, m; (inspiration) vena, f; (mood) humor, m
**veined, veiny** /veind; 'veini/ a venoso; de venas; veteado
**velar** /'vilər/ a velar
**vellum** /'veləm/ n vitela, f
**velocity** /vəˈlɔsiti/ n velocidad, f; rapidez, f
**velodrome** /'viləˌdroum/ n velódromo, m
**velours** /vəˈlʊr/ n terciopelo, m
**velvet** /'velvit/ n terciopelo, m, a hecho de terciopelo; aterciopelado
**velveteen** /ˌvelviˈtin/ n pana, f, veludillo, m
**velvety** /'velviti/ a aterciopelado
**venal** /'vinl/ a venal
**venality** /viˈnæliti/ n venalidad, f
**vend** /vend/ vt vender
**vendor** /'vendər/ n vendedor (-ra)
**veneer** /vəˈniər/ vt chapear, taracear; (conceal) disimular, disfrazar. —n taraceado, chapeado, m; (plate) chapa, hoja para chapear, f; (Fig. gloss) barniz, m, apariencia, f
**venerability** /ˌvenərəˈbiliti/ n venerabilidad, respetabilidad, f
**venerable** /'venərəbəl/ a venerable
**venerate** /'venəˌreit/ vt venerar, reverenciar
**veneration** /ˌvenəˈreifən/ n veneración, f
**venerator** /'venəˌreitər/ n venerador (-ra)
**venereal** /vəˈniəriəl/ a venéreo. **v. disease,** enfermedad venérea, f
**Venetian** /vəˈnifən/ a and n veneciano (-na). **v. blinds,** persianas, celosías, f pl
**Venezuelan** /ˌvenəˈzweilən/ a and n venezolano (-na)
**vengeance** /'vendʒəns/ n venganza, f
**vengeful** /'vendʒfəl/ a vengativo
**venial** /'viniəl/ a venial
**veniality** /ˌviniˈæliti/ n venialidad, f
**Venice** /'venis/ Venecia, f
**venison** /'venəsən/ n venado, m
**venom** /'venəm/ n veneno, m
**venomous** /'venəməs/ a venenoso; maligno, malicioso
**venomously** /'venəməsli/ adv con malignidad, maliciosamente
**venomousness** /'venəməsnis/ n venenosidad, f; malignidad, f
**venous** /'vinəs/ a venoso
**vent** /vent/ n abertura, f; salida, f; (air-hole) respiradero, m; (in pipes) ventosa, f; (in fire-arms) oído, m; Anat. ano, m; (Fig. outlet) desahogo, m; expresión, f. —vt dejar escapar; (pierce) agujerear; (discharge) emitir, vomitar; (relieve) desahogar; expresar, dar expresión (a), dar rienda suelta (a)
**venter** /'ventər/ n Law. vientre, m
**ventilate** /'ventlˌeit/ vt ventilar; discutir
**ventilation** /ˌventlˈeifən/ n ventilación, f
**ventilator** /'ventlˌeitər/ n ventilador, m
**ventricle** /'ventrikəl/ n ventrículo, m
**ventriloquism** /venˈtriləˌkwizəm/ n ventriloquia, f
**ventriloquist** /venˈtriləkwist/ n ventrílocuo (-ua)
**venture** /'ventʃər/ n ventura, f; riesgo, m; aventura, f; especulación, f. —vt arriesgar, aventurar; (stake) jugar; (state) expresar. —vi aventurarse; (dare) atreverse, osar; permitirse. **at a v.,** a la ventura. **to v. on,** arriesgarse a; probar ventura con; lanzarse a; (a remark) permitirse. **to v. out,** atreverse a salir

**venturesome** /'vɛntʃərsəm/ *a* atrevido, audaz; (dangerous) arriesgado, peligroso

**venturesomeness** /'vɛntʃərsəmnɪs/ *n* atrevimiento, *m*, temeridad, *f*; (risk) riesgo, peligro, *m*

**Venus** /'vinəs/ *n* (planet) Venus, *m*; (woman) venus, *f*

**veracious** /və'reiʃəs/ *a* veraz, verídico; verdadero

**veracity** /və'ræsɪti/ *n* veracidad, *f*; verdad, *f*

**veranda** /və'rændə/ *n* veranda, *f*

**verb** /vɜrb/ *n* verbo, *m*. **auxiliary v.,** verbo auxiliar, *m*. **intransitive v.,** verbo intransitivo (neutro), *m*. **reflexive v.,** verbo reflexivo, *m*. **transitive v.,** verbo transitivo, *m*

**verbal** /'vɜrbəl/ *a* verbal

**verbally** /'vɜrbəli/ *adv* de palabra, verbalmente

**verbatim** /vər'beitɪm/ *a* textual. —*adv* textualmente, palabra por palabra

**verbiage** /'vɜrbiɪdʒ/ *n* verbosidad, palabrería, *f*

**verbose** /vər'bous/ *a* verboso, prolijo

**verbosity** /vər'bɒsɪti/ *n* verbosidad, *f*

**verdancy** /'vɜrdnsi/ *n* verdura, *f*, verdor, *m*

**verdant** /'vɜrdnt/ *a* verde

**verdict** /'vɜrdɪkt/ *n* Law. veredicto, fallo, *m*, sentencia, *f*; opinión, *f*, juicio, *m*. **to bring in a v.,** fallar sentencia.

**verdigris** /'vɜrdɪˌgris/ *n* cardenillo, verdín, *m*

**verdure** /'vɜrdʒər/ *n* verdura, *f*, verdor, *m*; *Fig.* lozanía, *f*

**verge** /vɜrdʒ/ *n* (wand) vara, *f*; (edge) margen, borde, *m*; (of a lake, etc.) orilla, *f*; (horizon) horizonte, *m*; *Fig.* víspera, *f*, punto, *m*. **on the v. of,** al margen de, a la orilla de. **to be on the v. of,** *Fig.* estar a punto de; estar en vísperas de

**verger** /'vɜrdʒər/ *n* macero, *m*; (in a church) pertiguero, *m*

**verifiable** /ˌvɛrə'faiəbəl/ *a* verificable

**verification** /ˌvɛrəfɪ'keiʃən/ *n* verificación, *f*

**verifier** /'vɛrəˌfaiər/ *n* verificador (-ra)

**verify** /'vɛrəˌfai/ *vt* verificar, confirmar; probar

**verily** /'vɛrəli/ *adv* de veras, en verdad

**verisimilitude** /ˌvɛrəsɪ'mɪlɪˌtud/ *n* verosimilitud, *f*

**veritable** /'vɛritəbəl/ *a* verdadero

**veritably** /'vɛritəbli/ *adv* verdaderamente

**verity** /'vɛriti/ *n* verdad, *f*

**vermicelli** /ˌvɜrmɪ'tʃɛli/ *n* fideos, *m pl*

**vermilion** /vər'mɪlyən/ *n* bermellón, *m*

**vermin** /'vɜrmɪn/ *n* bichos dañinos, *m pl*; (insects) parásitos, *m pl*

**vermouth** /vər'muθ/ *n* vermut, *m*

**vernacular** /vər'nækyələr/ *a* vernáculo; nativo; vulgar. —*n* lengua popular, *f*; lenguaje vulgar, *m*

**versatile** /'vɜrsətl/ *a* Zool. versátil; inconstante, voluble; (clever) de muchos talentos; de muchos intereses; adaptable; completo, cabal

**versatility** /ˌvɜrsə'tɪlɪti/ *n* (cleverness) muchos talentos, *m pl*; adaptabilidad, *f*

**verse** /vɜrs/ *n* verso, *m*; (stanza) estrofa, *f*; (in the Bible) versículo, *m*; (poetry) poesía, *f*, versos, *m pl*. **to make verses,** escribir versos

**versed** /vɜrst/ *a* versado, experimentado

**versicle** /'vɜrsɪkəl/ *n* versículo, *m*

**versification** /ˌvɜrsəfɪ'keiʃən/ *n* versificación, *f*

**versifier** /'vɜrsəˌfaiər/ *n* versificador (-ra)

**versify** /'vɜrsəˌfai/ *vt and vi* versificar

**version** /'vɜrʒən/ *n* versión, *f*; traducción, *f*; interpretación, *f*

**versus** /'vɜrsəs/ *prep* contra

**vertebra** /'vɜrtəbrə/ *n* vértebra, *f*

**vertebral** /'vɜrtəbrəl/ *a* vertebral

**vertebrate** /'vɜrtəbrɪt/ *n* vertebrado, *m*

**vertex** /'vɜrtɛks/ *n* (Geom., Anat.) vértice, *m*; Astron. cenit, *m*; cumbre, *f*

**vertical** /'vɜrtɪkəl/ *a* vertical

**verticality** /ˌvɜrtɪ'kælɪti/ *n* verticalidad, *f*

**vertiginous** /vər'tɪdʒənəs/ *a* vertiginoso

**vertigo** /'vɜrtɪˌgou/ *n* vértigo, *m*

**verve** /vɜrv/ *n* brío, *m*, fogosidad, *f*

**very** /'vɛri/ *a* mismo; (mere) mero; (true) verdadero; (with adjective and comparative) más grande; *Inf.* mismísimo; (complete) perfecto, completo. **The v. thought of it made him laugh,** Sólo con pensarlo se rió (*or* La mera idea le hizo reír). **this v. minute,** este mismísimo instante. **the v. day,** el mismo día

**very** /'vɛri/ *adv* muy; mucho; demasiado; (exactly) exactamente; completamente; absolutamente. **He is v. worried,** Está muy preocupado. **He is not v. well,** (i.e. rather ill) Está bastante bien. **This cloth is the v. best,** Esta tela es la mejor que hay. **I like it v. much,** Me gusta muchísimo. **He is v. much pleased,** Está muy contento. **so v. little,** tan poco; tan pequeño. **v. well,** muy bien

**vesicle** /'vɛsɪkəl/ *n* vesícula, *f*

**vesper** /'vɛspər/ *n* estrella vespertina, *f*, héspero, *m*; *pl* **vespers,** *Eccl.* vísperas, *f pl*

**vessel** /'vɛsəl/ *n* vasija, *f*, recipiente, *m*; (boat) barco, buque, *m*; (Anat., Bot.) vaso, *m*

**vest** /vɛst/ *n* camiseta, *f*; (waistcoat) chaleco, *m*. —*vt* vestir; (with authority, etc.) revestir de; (property, etc.) hacer entrega de, ceder. —*vi* tener validez; (dress) vestirse. **vested interests,** intereses creados, *m pl*. **v.-pocket,** bolsillo del chaleco, *m*. **v.-pocket camera,** cámara de bolsillo, *f*

**vestal** /'vɛstl/ *a* vestal; virgen, casto. —*n* vestal, *f*; virgen, *f*

**vestibule** /'vɛstəˌbyul/ *n* vestíbulo, *m*; (anteroom) antecámara, *f*; (of a theatre box) antepalco, *m*; Anat. vestíbulo, *m*

**vestige** /'vɛstɪdʒ/ *n* vestigio, rastro, *m*; sombra, *f*; Biol. rudimento, *m*

**vestment** /'vɛstmənt/ *n* hábito, *m*; Eccl. vestidura, *f*

**vestry** /'vɛstri/ *n* vestuario, *m*, sacristía, *f*

**vesture** /'vɛstʃər/ *n* traje, hábito, *m*, vestidura, *f*

**Vesuvius** /və'suviəs/ Vesubio, *m*

**veteran** /'vɛtərən/ *a* veterano; de los veteranos; aguerrido; anciano; experimentado. —*n* veterano (-na)

**veterinary** /'vɛtərəˌnɛri/ *a* veterinario. **v. science,** veterinaria, *f*. **v. surgeon,** veterinario, *m*

**veto** /'vitou/ *n* veto, *m*; prohibición, *f*. —*vt* poner el veto; prohibir

**vex** /vɛks/ *vt* contrariar, irritar; enojar; (make impatient) impacientar; fastidiar; (afflict) afligir, acongojar; (worry) inquietar

**vexation** /vɛk'seiʃən/ *n* contrariedad, irritación, *f*; enojo, enfado, *m*; (impatience) impaciencia, *f*; fastidio, *m*; aflicción, *f*; inquietud, *f*; disgusto, *m*

**vexatious** /vɛk'seiʃəs/ *a* irritante; enojoso, enfadoso; fastidioso, molesto

**vexatiousness** /vɛk'seiʃəsnɪs/ *n* fastidio, *m*, molestia, *f*; incomodidad, *f*; contrariedad, *f*

**vexed** /vɛkst/ *a* discutido; contencioso; (thorny) espinoso, difícil

**vexing** /'vɛksɪŋ/ *a* irritante; molesto; enfadoso

**via** /'vaiə, 'viə/ *n* vía, *f*, *prep* por, por la vía de

**viability** /ˌvaiə'bɪlɪti/ *n* viabilidad, *f*

**viable** /'vaiəbəl/ *a* viable

**viaduct** /'vaiəˌdʌkt/ *n* viaducto, *m*

**vial** /'vaiəl/ *n* frasco, *m*, ampolleta, *f*

**vibrant** /'vaibrənt/ *a* vibrante

**vibrate** /'vaibreit/ *vi* vibrar; (of machines) trepidar; oscilar. —*vt* hacer vibrar, vibrar

**vibration** /vai'breiʃən/ *n* vibración, *f*; trepidación, *f*; oscilación, *f*

**vibrator** /'vaibreitər/ *n* Elec. vibrador, *m*; Radio. oscilador, *m*

**vicar** /'vɪkər/ *n* vicario, *m*; (of a parish) cura, *m*. **v.-general,** vicario general, *m*

**vicarious** /vai'kɛəriəs/ *a* vicario; sufrido por otro; experimentado por otro

**vicariously** /vai'kɛəriəsli/ *adv* por delegación; por substitución. **I know it only vicariously,** Lo conozco sólo por referencia

**vice** /vais/ *n* vicio, *m*; defecto, *m*; (in a horse) vicio, resabio, *m*; (tool) tornillo de banco, *m*, *prefix* vice. **v.-admiral,** vicealmirante, *m*. **v.-chairman,** vicepresidente (-ta). **v.-chancellor,** vicecanciller, *m*. **v.-consul,** vice-cónsul, *m*. **v.-consulate,** vice-consulado, *m*. **v.-president,** vicepresidente (-ta)

**viceroy** /'vaisrɔi/ *n* virrey, *m*

**vice versa** /'vaisə,vɜrsə, 'vais-/ *adv* viceversa

**vicinity** /vɪ'sɪnɪti/ *n* vecindad, *f*; (nearness) cercanía, proximidad, *f*. **to be in the v. of,** estar en la vecindad de

**vicious** /'vɪʃəs/ *a* vicioso. **v. circle,** círculo vicioso, *m*
**viciousness** /'vɪʃəsnɪs/ *n* viciosidad, *f;* (in a horse) resabios, *m pl*
**vicissitude** /vɪ'sɪsɪ,tud/ *n* vicisitud, *f*
**vicissitudinous** /vɪ,sɪsɪ'tudnəs/ *a* accidentado, vicisitudinario
**victim** /'vɪktəm/ *n* víctima, *f*
**victimization** /,vɪktəmə'zeɪʃən/ *n* sacrificio, *m;* tormento, *m*
**victimize** /'vɪktə,maiz/ *vt* hacer víctima (de); sacrificar; ser víctima (de), sufrir; (cheat) estafar, engañar
**victor** /'vɪktər/ *n* víctor, vencedor, *m*
**victoria** /vɪk'tɔriə/ *n* victoria, *f*
**Victorian** /vɪk'tɔriən/ *a* victoriano
**victorious** /vɪk'tɔriəs/ *a* victorioso, triunfante. **to be v.,** triunfar, salir victorioso
**victoriously** /vɪk'tɔriəsli/ *adv* victoriosamente, triunfalmente
**victory** /'vɪktəri/ *n* victoria, *f*
**victual** /'vɪtl/ *n* vitualla, vianda, *f; pl* **victuals,** víveres, *m pl,* provisiones, *f pl.* —*vt* avituallar; abastecer. —*vi* tomar provisiones
**victualler** /'vɪtlər/ *n* abastecedor (-ra), proveedor (-ra)
**victualling** /'vɪtlɪŋ/ *n* abastecimiento, *m*
**vide** /wɪde, 'vaidi, 'videi/ *Latin imperative* véase, véanse
**videlicet** /wɪ'deɪlɪ,kɛt, vi'deləsɪt/ *adv* a saber
**video** /'vɪdi,ou/, *n* vídeo, *m*
**videotape** /'vɪdiou,teip/ *n* videograbación, videocinta, *f*
**vie** /vai/ *vi* (with) competir con; rivalizar con; (with a person for) disputar; luchar con
**Vienna** /vi'ɛnə/ Viena, *f*
**Viennese** /,viə'niz/ *a* and *n* vienés (-esa)
**view** /vyu/ *n* vista, *f;* perspectiva, *f,* panorama, *m;* (landscape) paisaje, *m;* escena, *f;* inspección, *f;* (judgment) opinión, *f,* parecer, *m;* consideración, *f;* (appearance) apariencia, *f;* aspecto, *m;* (purpose) propósito, *m,* intención, *f;* (sight) alcance de la vista, *m;* (show) exposición, *f.* —*vt* examinar; inspeccionar; (look at) mirar; (see) ver, contemplar; considerar. **in v. of,** en vista de. **in my v.,** en mi opinión, según creo yo. **on v.,** a la vista. **to keep in v.,** no perder de vista; *Fig.* no olvidar, tener presente. **to take a different v.,** pensar de un modo distinto. **to v. a house,** inspeccionar una casa. **with a v. to,** con el propósito de. **v.-finder,** enfocador, *m.* **v.-point,** punto de vista, *m*
**viewer** /'vyuər/ *n* espectador (-ra); examinador (-ra)
**viewing** /'vyuɪŋ/ *n* inspección, *f,* examen, *m*
**vigil** /'vɪdʒəl/ *n* vela, vigilia, *f; Eccl.* vigilia, *f*
**vigilance** /'vɪdʒələns/ *n* vigilancia, *f,* desvelo, *m*
**vigilant** /'vɪdʒələnt/ *a* vigilante, desvelado
**vigilantly** /'vɪdʒələntli/ *adv* vigilantemente
**vignette** /vɪn'yɛt/ *n* viñeta, *f*
**vigor** /'vɪgər/ *n* vigor, *m,* fuerza, *f*
**vigorous** /'vɪgərəs/ *a* vigoroso, enérgico, fuerte
**vigorously** /'vɪgərəsli/ *adv* con vigor
**Viking** /'vaikɪŋ/ *n* vikingo, *m*
**vile** /vail/ *a* vil; bajo; despreciable; infame; *Inf.* horrible
**vilely** /'vaili/ *adv* vilmente; *Inf.* mal, horriblemente
**vileness** /'vailns/ *n* vileza, *f;* bajeza, *f;* infamia, *f*
**vilification** /,vɪləfɪ'keiʃən/ *n* vilipendio, *m,* difamación, *f*
**vilifier** /'vɪlə,faiər/ *n* difamador (-ra)
**vilify** /'vɪlə,fai/ *vt* vilipendiar, difamar
**villa** /'vɪlə/ *n* villa, torre, casa de campo, *f;* hotel, *m*
**village** /'vɪlɪdʒ/ *n* aldea, *f,* pueblo, *m*
**villager** /'vɪlɪdʒər/ *n* aldeano (-na)
**villain** /'vɪlən/ *n Hist.* villano, *m;* malvado, *m*
**villainous** /'vɪlənəs/ *a* malvado; infame; vil
**villainously** /'vɪlənəsli/ *adv* vilmente
**villainy** /'vɪləni/ *n* vileza, infamia, maldad, *f*
**vindicate** /'vɪndɪ,keit/ *vt* vindicar, justificar; defender
**vindication** /,vɪndɪ'keiʃən/ *n* vindicación, justificación, *f;* defensa, *f*
**vindicative** /vɪn'dɪkətɪv/ *a* vindicativo, vindicador, justificativo
**vindicator** /'vɪndɪ,keitər/ *n* vindicador (-ra)
**vindictive** /vɪn'dɪktɪv/ *a* vengativo; rencoroso

**vindictively** /vɪn'dɪktɪvli/ *adv* vengativamente; rencorosamente
**vindictiveness** /vɪn'dɪktɪvnɪs/ *n* deseo de venganza, *m;* rencor, *m*
**vine** /vain/ *n* vid, parra, *f;* (twining plant) enredadera, *f.* **v.-arbor,** emparrado, *m.* **v.-branch,** sarmiento, *m.* **v.-clad,** cubierto de parras. **v.-grower,** vinicultor, *m.* **v.-growing,** vinicultura, *f.* **v.-leaf,** hoja de parra, *f.* **v.-pest,** filoxera, *f.* **v.-stock,** cepa, *f*
**vinegar** /'vɪnɪgər/ *n* vinagre, *m.* **v.-cruet,** vinagrera, *f.* **v.-sauce,** vinagreta, *f*
**vinegary** /'vɪnɪgəri/ *a* vinagroso
**vineyard** /'vɪnyərd/ *n* viña, *f,* viñedo, *m.* **v.-keeper,** viñador, *m*
**vinification** /,vɪnəfɪ'keiʃən/ *n* vinificación, *f*
**vinosity** /vai'nɒsiti/ *n* vinosidad, *f*
**vinous** /'vainəs/ *a* vinoso
**vintage** /'vɪntɪdʒ/ *n* vendimia, *f;* (of wine) cosecha (de vino), *f*
**vintner** /'vɪntnər/ *n* vinatero, *m*
**viola** /vi'oulə/ *n* (*Mus., Bot.*) viola, *f.* **v. player,** viola, *mf*
**violate** /'vaiə,leit/ *vt* (desecrate) profanar; (infringe) contravenir, infringir; (break) romper; (ravish) violar
**violation** /,vaiə'leiʃən/ *n* profanación, *f;* (infringement) contravención, *f;* (rape) violación, *f*
**violator** /'vaiə,leitər/ *n* violador (-ra); (ravisher) violador, *m*
**violence** /'vaiələns/ *n* violencia, *f*
**violent** /'vaiələnt/ *a* violento
**violently** /'vaiələntli/ *adv* con violencia
**violet** /'vaiəlit/ *n* violeta, *f.* —*a* violado, **v. color,** violeta, color violado, *m*
**violin** /,vaiə'lin/ *n* violín, *m*
**violinist** /,vaiə'linist/ *n* violinista, *mf*
**violoncellist** /,vaiələn'tʃɛlist/ *n* violoncelista, *mf*
**violoncello** /,vaiələn'tʃɛlou/ *n* violoncelo, *m*
**viper** /'vaipər/ *n* víbora, *f*
**viperish** /'vaipərɪʃ/ *a* viperino
**virago** /vɪ'rɑgou/ *n* virago, *f,*
**Virgilian** /vər'dʒɪliən/ *a* virgiliano
**virgin** /'vɜrdʒɪn/ *n* virgen, *f;* (sign of the zodiac) Virgo, *m.* —*a* virginal; (untouched) virgen. **the V.,** la Virgen. **v. soil,** tierra virgen, *f*
**virginal** /'vɜrdʒənl/ *a* virginal
**virginity** /vər'dʒɪnɪti/ *n* virginidad, *f*
**Virgo** /'vɜrgou/ *n* Virgo, *m*
**virile** /'vɪrəl/ *a* viril
**virility** /və'rɪlɪti/ *n* virilidad, *f*
**virtual** /'vɜrtʃuəl/ *a* virtual
**virtue** /'vɜrtʃu/ *n* virtud, *f*
**virtuosity** /,vɜrtʃu'ɒsiti/ *n* virtuosidad, *f*
**virtuoso** /,vɜrtʃu'ousou/ *n* virtuoso (-sa)
**virtuous** /'vɜrtʃuəs/ *a* virtuoso
**virulence** /'vɪryələns/ *n* virulencia, *f*
**virulent** /'vɪryələnt/ *a* virulento
**virulently** /'vɪryələntli/ *adv* con virulencia
**virus** /'vairəs/ *n* virus, *m*
**visa** /'vizə/ *n* visado, *m*
**visage** /'vɪzɪdʒ/ *n* cara, *f,* rostro, *m;* semblante, aspecto, *m*
**viscera** /'vɪsərə/ *n* víscera, *f*
**visceral** /'vɪsərəl/ *a* visceral
**viscid** /'vɪsɪd/ *a* viscoso
**viscosity** /vɪ'skɒsiti/ *n* viscosidad, *f*
**viscount** /'vai,kaunt/ *n* vizconde, *m*
**viscountess** /'vai,kauntɪs/ *n* vizcondesa, *f*
**viscous** /'vɪskəs/ *a* viscoso
**visé** /'vizei/ *n* visado, *m, vt* visar
**visibility** /,vɪzə'bɪlɪti/ *n* visibilidad, *f.* **poor v.,** mala visibilidad, *f*
**visible** /'vɪzəbəl/ *a* visible; aparente, evidente
**visibly** /'vɪzəbli/ *adv* visiblemente; a ojos vistas
**Visigoth** /'vɪzɪ,gɒθ/ *n* visigodo (-da)
**Visigothic** /,vɪzɪ'gɒθɪk/ *a* visigodo, visigótico
**vision** /'vɪʒən/ *n* visión, *f;* (eyesight) vista, *f.* **field of v.,** campo visual, *m*
**visionary** /'vɪʒə,nɛri/ *a* and *n* visionario (-ia)
**visit** /'vɪzɪt/ *n* visita, *f;* (inspection) inspección, *f;* (doctor's) visita de médico, *f.* —*vt* visitar; hacer una visita (a); ir a ver; inspeccionar; (frequent) frecuen-

tar; (Biblical) visitar. **to be visited by an epidemic,** sufrir una epidemia. **to go visiting,** ir de visita. **to pay a v.,** hacer una visita

**visitation** /ˌvɪzɪˈteɪʃən/ *n* visita, *f;* *Eccl.* visitación, *f;* (inspection) inspección, *f;* (punishment) castigo, *m*

**visiting** /ˈvɪzɪtɪŋ/ *a* de visita. **v. card,** tarjeta de visita, *f.* **v. card case,** tarjetero, *m.* **visiting hours,** horas de visita, *f pl*

**visitor** /ˈvɪzɪtər/ *n* visita, *f;* (official) visitador, *m*

**visor** /ˈvaizər/ *n* visera, *f*

**vista** /ˈvɪstə/ *n* vista, perspectiva, *f*

**visual** /ˈvɪʒuəl/ *a* visual. **the v. arts,** las artes visuales

**visualize** /ˈvɪʒuəˌlaiz/ *vt and vi* imaginarse, ver mentalmente

**vital** /ˈvaitl̩/ *a* vital; esencial; trascendental

**vitalism** /ˈvaitl̩ˌɪzəm/ *n* vitalismo, *m*

**vitality** /vaiˈtæliti/ *n* vitalidad, *f*

**vitalize** /ˈvaitl̩ˌaiz/ *vt* vitalizar, vivificar; reanimar

**vitals** /ˈvaitlz/ *n pl* partes vitales, *f pl;* *Fig.* entrañas, *f pl*

**vitamin** /ˈvaitəmin/ *n* vitamina, *f*

**vitiate** /ˈvɪʃiˌeit/ *vt* viciar; corromper, contaminar

**viticultural** /ˌvɪtɪˈkʌltʃərl/ *a* vitícola

**viticulture** /ˈvɪtɪˌkʌltʃər/ *n* viticultura, *f*

**vitreous** /ˈvɪtriəs/ *a* vítreo, vidrioso

**vitrification** /ˌvɪtrəfɪˈkeiʃən/ *n* vitrificación, *f*

**vitrify** /ˈvɪtrəˌfai/ *vt* vitrificar. —*vi* vitrificarse

**vitriol** /ˈvɪtriəl/ *n* vitriolo, ácido sulfúrico, *m*

**vitriolic** /ˌvɪtriˈɒlik/ *a* vitriólico

**Vitruvius** /vɪˈtruviəs/ *Vitrubio, m*

**vituperable** /vaiˈtupərəbəl/ *a* vituperable

**vituperate** /vaiˈtupəˌreit/ *vt* vituperar

**vituperation** /vaiˌtupəˈreiʃən/ *n* vituperio, *m*

**vituperative** /vaiˈtupərətiv/ *a* vituperador

**vivacious** /vɪˈveiʃəs, vai-/ *a* animado, vivaracho

**vivaciously** /vɪˈveiʃəsli, vai-/ *adv* animadamente

**vivacity** /vɪˈvæsiti, vai-/ *n* vivacidad, animación, *f*

**viva voce** /ˈvaivə ˈvousi, ˈvivə/ *a* oral. —*n* examen oral, *m*

**vivid** /ˈvɪvid/ *a* vivo; brillante; intenso; (of descriptions, etc.) gráfico

**vividly** /ˈvɪvidli/ *adv* vivamente; brillantemente

**vividness** /ˈvɪvidnis/ *n* vivacidad, *f;* intensidad, *f;* (strength) fuerza, *f*

**vivification** /ˌvɪvəfɪˈkeiʃən/ *n* vivificación, *f*

**vivify** /ˈvɪvəˌfai/ *vt* vivificar, avivar

**vivifying** /ˈvɪvəˌfaiŋ/ *a* vivificante

**vivisection** /ˌvɪvəˈsekʃən/ *n* vivisección, *f*

**vixen** /ˈvɪksən/ *n* raposa, zorra, *f;* (woman) arpía, *f*

**viz.** a saber

**vizier** /vɪˈzɪər, ˈvɪzyər/ *n* visir, *m.* **grand v.,** gran visir, *m*

**vocabulary** /vouˈkæbyəˌleri/ *n* vocabulario, *f*

**vocal** /ˈvoukəl/ *a* vocal. **v. cords,** cuerdas vocales, *f pl*

**vocalist** /ˈvoukəlist/ *n* cantante, *mf.* voz, *f*

**vocalization** /ˌvoukələˈzeiʃən/ *n* vocalización, *f*

**vocalize** /ˈvoukəˌlaiz/ *vt* vocalizar

**vocation** /vouˈkeiʃən/ *n* vocación, *f;* oficio, *m;* empleo, *m;* profesión, *f*

**vocational** /vouˈkeiʃən̩l/ *a* profesional; práctico. **vocational guidance,** guía vocacional, orientación profesional, *f.* **v. training,** instrucción práctica, *f;* enseñanza de oficio, *f*

**vociferate** /vouˈsɪfəˌreit/ *vt* gritar. —*vi* vociferar, vocear

**vociferation** /vouˌsɪfəˈreiʃən/ *n* vociferación, *f*

**vociferous** /vouˈsɪfərəs/ *a* (noisy) ruidoso; vocinglero, clamoroso

**vociferously** /vouˈsɪfərəsli/ *adv* ruidosamente; a gritos

**vodka** /ˈvɒdkə/ *n* vodca, *m*

**vogue** /voug/ *n* moda, *f.* **in v.,** en boga, de moda

**voice** /vɔis/ *n* voz, *f.* —*vt* expresar, interpretar, hacerse eco de; hablar. **in a loud v.,** en voz alta. **in a low v.,** en voz baja

**voiced** /vɔist/ *a* (in compounds) de voz...; hablado

**void** /vɔid/ *a* (empty) vacío; (vacant) vacante; deshabitado; (lacking in) privado (de), desprovisto (de); (without) sin; *Law.* inválido, nulo; sin valor. —*n* vacío, *m.* —*vt* evacuar; *Law.* anular; invalidar

**voile** /vɔil/ *n* espumilla, *f*

**volatile** /ˈvɒlətl̩/ *a* volátil; (light) ligero; (changeable) voluble, inconstante

**volatility** /ˌvɒləˈtɪliti/ *n* volatilidad, *f;* ligereza, *f;* volubilidad, *f*

**volatilization** /ˌvɒlətlə̩ˈzeiʃən/ *n* volatilización, *f*

**volatilize** /ˈvɒlətl̩ˌaiz/ *vt* volatilizar. —*vi* volatilizarse

**volcanic** /vɒlˈkænik/ *a* volcánico

**volcano** /vɒlˈkeinou/ *n* volcán, *m.* **extinct v.,** volcán extinto, *m*

**volition** /vouˈlɪʃən/ *n* volición, *f;* voluntad, *f*

**volley** /ˈvɒli/ *n* (of stones, etc.) lluvia, *f;* (of firearms) descarga, *f;* (of cannon, naval guns) andanada, *f;* *Sports.* voleo, *m;* (of words, etc.) torrente, *m;* (of applause and as a salute) salva, *f.* —*vt Sports.* volear; (abuse, etc.) dirigir. —*vi* lanzar una descarga, hacer una descarga

**volt** /voult/ *n Elec.* voltio, *m;* (of a horse and in fencing) vuelta, *f.* **v.-ampere,** voltamperio, *m*

**voltage** /ˈvoultidʒ/ *n* voltaje, *m.* **v. control,** mando del voltaje, *m*

**voltaic** /vɒlˈteiik/ *a* voltaico

**Voltairian** /voulˈteəriən/ *a* volteriano

**voltmeter** /ˈvoultˌmitər/ *n* voltímetro, *m*

**volubility** /ˌvɒlyəˈbɪliti/ *n* garrulidad, locuacidad, *f*

**voluble** /ˈvɒlyəbəl/ *a* gárrulo, locuaz

**volume** /ˈvɒlyum/ *n* (book) tomo, *m;* (amount, size, space) volumen, *m;* (of water) caudal (de río), *m;* (mass) masa, *f;* (of smoke) humareda, *f,* nubes de humo, *f pl*

**volumed** /ˈvɒlyumd/ *a* (in compounds) en... volúmenes, de... tomos

**volumetric** /ˌvɒlyəˈmetrik/ *a* volumétrico

**voluminous** /vəˈlumɪnəs/ *a* voluminoso

**voluminousness** /vəˈlumɪnəsnis/ *n* lo voluminoso

**voluntarily** /ˌvɒlənˈterəli/ *adv* voluntariamente

**voluntariness** /ˌvɒlənˈterinis/ *n* carácter voluntario, *m*

**voluntary** /ˈvɒlənˌteri/ *a* voluntario; espontáneo; libre; (charitable) benéfico; (intentional) intencional, deliberado. —*n* solo de órgano, *m*

**volunteer** /ˌvɒlənˈtɪər/ *n Mil.* voluntario (-ia). —*a* de voluntarios. —*vt* ofrecer; contribuir; expresar. —*vi* ofrecerse para hacer algo; *Mil.* alistarse, ofrecerse a servir como voluntario

**volunteering** /ˌvɒlənˈtɪəriŋ/ *n* voluntariado, *m*

**voluptuary** /vəˈlʌptʃuˌeri/ *n* voluptuoso (-sa); sibarita, *mf*

**voluptuous** /vəˈlʌptʃuəs/ *a* voluptuoso

**voluptuously** /vəˈlʌptʃuəsli/ *adv* voluptuosamente

**voluptuousness** /vəˈlʌptʃuəsnis/ *n* voluptuosidad, *f;* sensualidad, *f*

**volute** /vəˈlut/ *n Archit.* voluta, *f*

**vomit** /ˈvɒmit/ *vt and vi* vomitar; arrojar, devolver. —*n* vómito, *m*

**vomiting** /ˈvɒmitiŋ/ *n* vómito, *m*

**voodoo** /ˈvudu/ *n* vudú, *m*

**voracious** /vɔˈreiʃəs/ *a* voraz

**voracity** /vɔˈræsiti/ *n* voracidad, *f*

**vortex** /ˈvɔrteks/ *n* torbellino, *m,* vorágine, *f; Fig.* vórtice, *m*

**vortical** /ˈvɔrtikəl/ *a* vortiginoso

**votary** /ˈvoutəri/ *n* devoto (-ta), adorante, *mf;* partidario (-ia)

**vote** /vout/ *n* voto, *m;* (voting) votación, *f;* (suffrage) sufragio, *m;* (election) elección, *f.* —*vt* votar; asignar; nombrar; elegir; (consider) tener por. —*vi* votar, dar el voto. **casting v.,** voto de calidad, *m.* **to put to the v.,** poner a votación. **to v. down,** desechar, rechazar. **v. of confidence,** voto de confianza, *m.* **v. of thanks,** voto de gracias, *m*

**voter** /ˈvoutər/ *n* votante, *mf;* votador (-ra); elector (-ra)

**voting** /ˈvoutiŋ/ *n* votación, *f;* elección, *f.* —*a* de votar; electoral. **v. paper,** papeleta de votación, *f*

**votive** /ˈvoutiv/ *a* votivo. **v. offering,** exvoto, *m*

**vouch** /vautʃ/ *vi* atestiguar, afirmar; garantizar; responder (de)

**voucher** /ˈvautʃər/ *n* (guarantor) fiador (-ra); (guarantee) garantía, *f;* (receipt) recibo, *m;* (proof) prueba, *f;* documento justificativo, *m;* vale, bono, *m*

**vouchsafe** /vautʃ'seif/ vt conceder, otorgar
**vouchsafement** /vautʃ'seifmənt/ n concesión, f, otorgamiento, m
**vow** /vau/ n voto, m; promesa solemne, f. —vt hacer voto (de), hacer promesa solemne (de); jurar. **to take a vow,** hacer un voto
**vowel** /'vauəl/ n vocal, f
**voyage** /'vɔiidʒ/ n viaje (por mar), m; travesía, f. —vi viajar por mar. **Good v.!** ¡Buen viaje!, Feliz viaje!
**voyager** /'vɔiidʒər/ n viajero (-ra)
**vulcanite** /'vʌlkə,nait/ n ebonita, f
**vulcanization** /,vʌlkənə'zeiʃən/ n vulcanización, f
**vulcanize** /'vʌlkə,naiz/ vt vulcanizar
**vulgar** /'vʌlgər/ a vulgar; (ill-bred) ordinario, cursi; (in bad taste) de mal gusto; trivial; adocenado;

(coarse) grosero. —n vulgo, populacho, m. **v. fraction,** fracción común, f
**vulgarism** /'vʌlgə,rizəm/ n vulgarismo, m; vulgaridad, f
**vulgarity** /vʌl'gæriti/ n vulgaridad, f; grosería, f; mal tono, m, cursilería, f
**vulgarize** /'vʌlgə,raiz/ vt vulgarizar; popularizar
**vulgarly** /'vʌlgərli/ adv vulgarmente; comúnmente; groseramente
**Vulgate** /'vʌlgeit/ n Vulgata, f
**vulnerability** /,vʌlnərə'biiti/ n vulnerabilidad, f
**vulnerable** /'vʌlnərəbəl/ a vulnerable
**vulpine** /'vʌlpain/ a vulpino; astuto
**vulture** /'vʌltʃər/ n buitre, m
**vulva** /'vʌlvə/ n vulva, f

# W

**w** /'dʌbəl,yu/ n ve doble, f
**wabble** /'wɒbəl/ vi. See **wobble**
**wad** /wɒd/ n (of straw, etc.) atado, m; (of notes, etc.) rollo, m; (in a gun) taco, m. —vt Sew. acolchar; (furniture) emborrar; (guns) atacar; (stuff) rellenar
**wadding** /'wɒdɪŋ/ n borra, f; (lining) entretela, f; (for guns) taco, m; (stuffing) relleno, m
**waddle** /'wɒdl/ n anadeo, m, vi anadear
**waddling** /'wɒdlɪŋ/ a patojo, que anadea
**wade** /weid/ vi and vt andar (en el agua, etc.); vadear; (paddle) chapotear. **to w. in**, entrar en (el agua, etc.); Fig. meterse en. **to w. through**, (a book) leer con dificultad; estudiar detenidamente; ir por
**wader** /'weidər/ n el, m, (f, la) que vadea; (bird) ave zancuda, f; pl **waders**, botas de vadear, f pl
**wafer** /'weifər/ n (host) hostia, f; (for sealing) oblea, f; (for ices) barquillo, m
**waffle** /'wɒfəl/ n Cul. fruta de sartén, f
**waft** /wɑft/ vt llevar por el aire o encima del agua; hacer flotar; (stir) mecer; (of the wind) traer. —n (fragrance) ráfaga de olor, f
**wag** /wæg/ n (of the tail) coleada, f; movimiento, m; meneo, m; (jester) bromista, mf. —vt mover ligeramente; agitar; (of the tail) menear (la cola), colear. —vi menearse; moverse; oscilar; (of the world) ir. **And thus the world wags**, Y así va el mundo
**wage** /weidʒ/ vt emprender; sostener; hacer. **to w. war**, hacer guerra. —n pl. **wages**, salario, m
**wager** /'weidʒər/ n (bet) apuesta, f; (test) prueba, f, vt (bet) apostar; (pledge) empeñar. **to lay a w.**, hacer una apuesta
**waggish** /'wægɪʃ/ a zumbón, jocoso; cómico
**waggishness** /'wægɪʃnɪs/ n jocosidad, f
**waggle** /'wægəl/ vt menear; mover; agitar; oscilar. —vi menearse; moverse; agitarse; oscilar. —n meneo, movimiento, m; oscilación, f
**Wagnerian** /vɑg'nɪəriən/ a wagneriano
**wagon** /'wægən/ n carro, m; carreta, f; (railway) vagón, m. **w.-lit**, coche cama, m. **w.-load**, carretada, f; vagón, m
**wagoner** /'wægənər/ n carretero, m
**waif** /weif/ n niño (-ña) sin hogar; animal perdido o abandonado, m; objeto extraviado, m; objeto sin dueño, m. **waifs and strays**, niños abandonados, m pl
**wail** /weil/ n lamento, gemido, m; (complaint) queja, f. —vi lamentarse, gemir; quejarse (de). —vt lamentar, deplorar
**wailer** /'weilər/ n lamentador (-ra)
**wailing** /'weilɪŋ/ n lamentaciones, f pl, gemidos, m pl, a lamentador, gemidor
**wainscot** /'weinskət, -skɒt/ n entablado de madera, m. —vt enmaderar; poner friso de madera (a)
**waist** /weist/ n cintura, f; (blouse) blusa, f; (belt) cinturón, m; (bodice) corpiño, m; (narrowest portion) cuello, m, garganta, f; Naut. combés, m. **w.-band**, pretina, f. **w.-deep**, hasta la cintura. **w.-line**, cintura, f. **w. measurement**, medida de la cintura, f. **w.-coat**, chaleco, m. **w. strap**, trincha, f
**wait** /weit/ vi and vt esperar, aguardar; (serve) servir. **to keep waiting**, hacer esperar. **to w. at table**, servir a la mesa. **to w. on oneself**, servirse a sí mismo; cuidarse a sí mismo; hacer las cosas por sí solo. **to w. one's time**, aguardar la ocasión. **to w. for**, (until) esperar hasta que; (of persons) esperar (a), aguardar (a); (in ambush) acechar. **to w. upon**, (serve) servir (a); (visit) visitar; presentar sus respetos (a); (Fig. accompany) acompañar; (follow) seguir a
**wait** /weit/ n espera, f; (pause) pausa, f, intervalo, m; (ambush) asechanza, f; pl **waits**, coro de noche-buena, m. **to lie in w. for**, estar en acecho para
**waiter** /'weitər/ n camarero, mozo, m; (tray) bandeja, f
**waiting** /'weitɪŋ/ n espera, f. —a que espera; de espera; de servicio. **lady-in-w.**, dama de servicio, f. **w.-**

**maid**, camarera, doncella, f. **w.-room**, (of a bus station, etc.) sala de espera, f; (of an office) antesala, f
**waitress** /'weitrɪs/ n camarera, f
**waive** /weiv/ vt renunciar (a); desistir (de)
**wake** /weik/ vi estar despierto; despertarse; (watch) velar. —vt despertar; (a corpse) velar (a). —n vela, f; vigilia, f; (of a corpse) velatorio, m; (holiday) fiesta, f; (of a ship) estela, f. **in the w. of**, Naut. en la estela de; después de; seguido de
**wakeful** /'weikfəl/ a vigilante; (awake) despierto. **to be w.**, pasar la noche en vela
**wakefulness** /'weikfəlnɪs/ n vigilancia, f; (sleeplessness) insomnia, f
**waken** /'weikən/ vi despertarse. —vt despertar; (call) llamar
**waking** /'weikɪŋ/ a despierto; de vela. —n despertar, m; (watching) vela, f
**wale** /weil/ n (weal) verdugo, m, huella de azote, f, vt azotar
**Wales** /weilz/ (País de) Gales, m
**walk** /wɔk/ n (pace) paso, m; (modo de) andar, m; (journey on foot) paseo, m, vuelta, f; (long) caminata, f; (promenade) paseo, m, avenida, f; (path) senda, f; (rank) clase social, f; esfera, f; profesión, f; ocupación, f. **quick w.**, paseo rápido, m; (pace) andar rápido, m. **to go for a w.**, ir de paseo. **to take a w.**, dar un paseo (or una vuelta), pasear. **to take for a w.**, llevar a pasear, sacar a paseo. **w.-out**, (strike) huelga, f. **w.-over**, triunfo, m, (or victoria, f) fácil. **w. past**, desfile, m
**walk** /wɔk/ vi andar, caminar; ir a pie; (take a walk) pasear, dar un paseo; (of ghosts) aparecer; (behave) conducirse. —vt hacer andar; (take for a walk) sacar a paseo; andar de una parte a otra (de), recorrer; (a specified distance) hacer a pie, andar; (a horse) llevar al paso. **to w. abroad**, dar un paseo; salir. **to w. arm in arm**, ir de bracero. **to w. past**, pasar; (in procession) desfilar. **to w. quickly**, andar de prisa. **to w. slowly**, andar despacio, andar lentamente. **to w. the hospitals**, estudiar en los hospitales. **to w. the streets**, recorrer las calles; vagar por las calles. **to w. about**, pasearse; ir y venir. **to w. after**, seguir (a), ir detrás de. **to w. along**, andar por; recorrer. **to w. away**, marcharse, irse. **to w. away with**, (win) ganar, llevarse; (steal) quitar, tomar, alzarse con. **to w. back**, volver; volver a pie, regresar a pie. **to w. in**, entrar en; entrar a pie en; (walk about) pasearse en. **to w. on**, seguir andando; (step on) pisar. **to w. out**, salir. **to w. over**, andar por; llevar la victoria (a); triunfar fácilmente sobre. **to w. round**, dar la vuelta a. **to w. round and round**, dar vueltas. **to w. up**, subir andando; subir. **to w. up and down**, dar vueltas, ir y venir
**walker** /'wɔkər/ n (pedestrian) peatón, m; andador (-ra); (promenader) paseante, mf
**walking** /'wɔkɪŋ/ n el andar; (excursion on foot) paseo, m. —a andante; de andar; a pie; ambulante. **at a w. pace**, a un paso de andadura. **w. encyclopedia**, enciclopedia ambulante, f. **w. match**, marcha atlética, f. **w.-stick**, bastón, m. **w. tour**, excursión a pie, f
**Walkyrie** /'wal'kɪəri/ n valquiria, f
**wall** /wɔl/ n muro, m; (rampart) muralla, f; (Fig. and of an organ, cavity, etc.) pared, f. **partition w.**, tabique, m. **Walls have ears**, Las paredes oyen. **w. lizard**, lagartija, f. **w. map**, mapa mural, m. **w.-painting**, pintura mural, f. **w.-paper**, papel pintado, m. **w. socket**, Elec. enchufe, m
**wall** /wɔl/ vt cercar con un muro; amurallar. **to w. in**, murar. **to w. up**, tapiar, tabicar
**wallet** /'wɒlɪt/ n cartera, f; bolsa de cuero, f
**wallflower** /'wɔl,flauər/ n alhelí, m
**Walloon** /wɒ'lun/ a and n valón (-ona)
**wallop** /'wɒləp/ n golpe, m, vt tundir, zurrar
**wallow** /'wɒlou/ vi revolcarse; encenagarse; (in riches, etc.) nadar (en). —n revuelco, m

**walnut** /'wɔl,nʌt/ n (tree and wood) nogal, m; (nut) nuez de nogal, f

**walrus** /'wɔlrəs/ n morsa, f

**waltz** /wɔlts/ n vals, m, vi valsar

**wan** /wɑn/ a ojeroso, descolorido; (of the sky, etc.) pálido, sin color

**wand** /wɒnd/ n vara, f; (conductor's) batuta, f. **magic w.**, varita mágica, f

**wander** /'wɒndər/ vi errar, vagar; (deviate) extraviarse; (from the subject) desviarse del asunto; divagar; (be delirious) delirar. —vt vagar por, errar por, recorrer

**wanderer** /'wɒndərər/ n vagabundo (-da); hombre, m, (f, mujer) errante; (traveler) viajero (-ra)

**wandering** /'wɒndəriŋ/ a errante; vagabundo; nómada; (traveling) viajero; (delirious) delirante; (of thoughts, the mind) distraído; (of cells, kidneys, etc.) flotante. —n vagancia, f; viaje, m; (delirium) delirio, m; (digression) divagación, f; (of a river, etc.) meandro, m. **the w. Jew**, el judío errante

**wane** /wein/ vi (of the moon, etc.) menguar; (decrease) disminuir; (Fig. decay) decaer. —n (of the moon) menguante de la luna, f; mengua, f; disminución, f; decadencia, f

**waning** /'weiniŋ/ a menguante

**wanly** /'wanli/ adv pálidamente; Fig. tristemente

**wanness** /'wannis/ n palidez, f; Fig. tristeza, f

**want** /wɒnt/ vt (lack) carecer de, faltar; (need) necesitar, haber menester de; (require or wish) querer, desear; (demand) exigir; (ought) deber; (do without) pasarse sin. —vi hacer falta; carecer (de); (be poor) estar necesitado. **I don't w. to**, No quiero, No me da la gana. **to be wanted**, hacer falta; (called) ser llamado. **You are wanted on the telephone**, Te llaman por teléfono

**want** /wɒnt/ n (lack) falta, f; escasez, carestía, f; (need) necesidad, f; (poverty) pobreza, indigencia, f; (absence) ausencia, f; (wish) deseo, m; exigencia, f. **in w. of**, por falta de; en la ausencia de. **to be in w.**, estar en la necesidad, ser indigente

**wanted** /'wɒntid/ a se necesita; (advertisement) demanda, f. **Estelle wants me to write a letter**, Estrella quiere que escriba una carta. **What do you w. me to do?** ¿Qué quiere Vd. que haga?; ¿En qué puedo servirle? **What does Paul w.?** ¿Qué quiere Pablo?; (require) ¿Qué necesita Pablo? **He wants (needs) a holiday**, Le hacen falta unas vacaciones, Necesita unas vacaciones

**wanting** /'wɒntiŋ/ a deficiente (en); falto (de); (scarce) escaso; ausente; (in intelligence) menguado. —prep (less) menos; (without) sin. **to be w.**, faltar. **to be w. in**, carecer de

**wanton** /'wɒntn/ a (playful) juguetón; (wilful) travieso; (loose) suelto, libre; (unrestrained) desenfrenado; extravagante; excesivo; caprichoso; (disheveled) en desorden; (reckless) indiscreto; (of vegetation) lozano; (purposeless) inútil, imperdonable; frívolo; (unchaste) disoluto; lascivo. —n mujer disoluta, f; ramera, f; (child) niño (-ña) juguetón (-ona)

**wantonly** /'wɒntnli/ adv innecesariamente; sin motivo; excesivamente; lascivamente

**war** /wɑr/ n guerra, f. —a de guerra; guerrero. —vi guerrear. **at war with**, en guerra con. **cold war**, guerra tonta, f. **on a war footing**, en pie de guerra. **We are at war**, Estamos en guerra. **to be on the war-path**, Fig. Inf. buscar pendencia, tratar de armarla. **to declare war on**, declarar la guerra (a). **to make war on**, hacer la guerra (a). **war to the death**, guerra a muerte, f. **war correspondent**, corresponsal en el teatro de guerra, m. **war-cry**, alarido de guerra, grito de combate, grito de guerra m. **war-dance**, danza guerrera, f. **war horse**, caballo de batalla, m. **war loan**, empréstito de guerra, m. **war-lord**, adalid, caudillo, jefe militar, m. **war material**, pertrechos de guerra, m pl; municiones, f pl. **war memorial**, monumento a los caídos, m. **war minister**, Ministro de la Guerra, m. **war neurosis**, neurosis de guerra, f. **War Office**, Ministerio de la Guerra, m. **war plane**, avión de guerra, m. **war-ship**, barco (or buque) de guerra, m. **war-wearied**, agotado por la guerra

**warble** /'wɔrbəl/ vt and vi trinar; gorjear; murmurar. —n trino, m; gorjeo, m; murmurio, m

**ward** /wɔrd/ n protección, f; (of a minor) pupilo (-la); (of locks, keys) guarda, f; (of a city) barrio, distrito, m; (of a hospital, etc.) sala, f; (of a prison) celda, f; (fencing) guardia, f. **w.-room**, cuarto de los oficiales, m. **w. sister**, hermana de una sala de hospital, f

**ward** /wɔrd/ vt proteger, defender. **to w. off**, desviar; evitar

**warden** /'wɔrdn/ n guardián, m; director (-ra); (of a prison) alcaide, m; (of a church) mayordomo de la iglesia, m; (of a port) capitán, m

**warder** /'wɔrdər/ n (jailer) guardián, m; alabardero, guardia, m

**wardress** /'wɔrdris/ n guardiana, f

**wardrobe** /'wɔrdroub/ n guardarropa, ropero, m; (clothes) ropa, f; Theat. vestuario, m. **w. trunk**, baúl mundo, m

**ware** /wɛər/ n mercadería, f; (pottery) loza, f; pl **wares**, mercancías, f pl

**warehouse** /n. 'wɛər,haus; v. -,hauz/ n almacén, m, vt almacenar

**warehouseman** /'wɛər,hausmən/ n almacenero, m

**warfare** /'wɔr,fɛər/ n guerra, f; lucha, f; arte militar, m, or f. **chemical w.**, guerra química, f

**war head** n (of torpedo) cabeza de combate, punto de combate, f; (of missile) detonante, m

**war hero** n héroe de guerra, m

**war heroine** n heroína de guerra, f

**warily** /'wɛərəli/ adv con cautela, cautelosamente; prudentemente

**wariness** /'wɛərinis/ n cautela f; prudencia, f

**warlike** /'wɔr,laik/ a belicoso, guerrero; militar, de guerra; marcial. **war-spirit**, espíritu belicoso, m, marcialidad, f

**warm** /wɔrm/ a caliente; (lukewarm) tibio; (hot) caluroso; (affectionate) cordial, cariñoso, afectuoso; (angry) acalorado; (enthusiastic) entusiasta, ardiente; (art) cálido; (of coats, etc.) de abrigo; (fresh) fresco, reciente; Inf. adinerado. —vt calentar; Fig. encender; entusiasmar. —vi calentarse; Fig. entusiasmarse (con). **to have a w. at the fire**, calentarse al lado del fuego. **to be w.**, (of things) estar caliente; (of coats, etc.) ser de abrigo; (of the weather) hacer calor; (of people) tener calor. **to grow w.**, calentarse; (grow angry) excitarse, agitarse; (of a discussion) hacerse acalorado. **to keep w.**, conservar caliente; calentar. **to keep oneself w.**, estar caliente, no enfriarse. **to w. up**, calentar. **w.-blooded**, de sangre caliente; ardiente. **w.-hearted**, de buen corazón; generoso; afectuoso, cordial. **w.-heartedness**, buen corazón, m; generosidad, f; cordialidad, f

**warming** /'wɔrmiŋ/ n calentamiento, m; calefacción, f. —a calentador; para calentar. **w.-pan**, calentador, m

**warmly** /'wɔrmli/ adv (affectionately) cordialmente, afectuosamente; con entusiasmo; (angrily) acaloradamente. **to be w. wrapped up**, estar bien abrigado

**warmonger** /'wɔr,mʌŋgər/ n atizador de guerra, belicista, fautor de guerra, fomentador de guerra, propagador (-ra) de guerra

**warmth** /wɔrmθ/ n calor, m

**warn** /wɔrn/ vt advertir; prevenir; amonestar; (inform) avisar

**warning** /'wɔrniŋ/ n advertencia, f; aviso, m; amonestación, f; (lesson) lección, f; escarmiento, m; alarma, f. —a amonestador; de alarma. **to give w.**, prevenir, advertir; (dismiss) despedir. **to take w.**, escarmentar

**warningly** /'wɔrniŋli/ adv indicando el peligro; con alarma; con amenaza

**warp** /wɔrp/ vt torcer; combar; Naut. espiar; (the mind) pervertir. —vi torcerse; combarse, bornearse; Naut. espiarse. —n (in a fabric) urdimbre, f; (in wood) comba, f, torcimiento, m; Naut. espía, f. **w. and woof**, trama y urdimbre, f

**warping** /'wɔrpiŋ/ n (of wood) combadura, f; (weaving) urdidura, f; Naut. espía, f; (of the mind) perversión, f. **w. frame**, urdidera, f

**warrant** /'wɔrənt, 'wɒr-/ n autoridad, f; justificación, f; autorización, f; garantía, f; decreto de prisión, m; orden, f; Com. orden de pago, f; Mil. nombramiento, m; motivo, m, razón, f. —vt justificar; autorizar; garantizar, responder por; asegurar. **pay w.,** boletín de pago, m

**warrantable** /'wɔrəntəbəl/ a justificable

**warrantor** /'wɔrən,tɔr/ n garante, mf

**warranty** /'wɔrənti/ n autorización, f; justificación, f; Law. garantía, f

**warren** /'wɔrən/ n (for hunting) vedado, m; (rabbit) conejera, f; vivar, m, madriguera, f

**warrior** /'wɔriər/ n guerrero, m; soldado, m

**Warsaw** /'wɔrsɔ/ n Varsovia, f

**wart** /wɔrt/ n verruga, f

**wary** /'wɛəri/ a cauto, cauteloso; prudente

**wash** /wɒʃ/ vt lavar; (dishes) fregar; (lave) bañar; (clean) limpiar; (furrow) surcar; (wet) regar, humedecer; (with paint) dar una capa de color o de metal. —vi lavarse; lavar ropa. **Two of the crew were washed overboard,** El mar arrastró a dos de los tripulantes. **Will this material w.?** ¿Se puede lavar esta tela? ¿Es lavable esta tela? **to w.** ashore, echar a la playa. **w. away,** (remove by washing) quitar lavando; derrubiar; (water or waves) arrastrar, llevarse. **to w.** one's hands, lavarse las manos. **to look washed out,** estar ojeroso. **to w. down,** lavar; limpiar; (remove) llevarse; (accompany with drink) regar. **to w. off,** vt quitar lavando; hacer desaparecer; borrar; (of waves, etc.) llevarse; (of color) desteñir. —vi borrarse; desteñirse. **to w. up,** lavar los platos, fregar la vajilla; (cast up) desechar. **w.** one's dirty laundry in public, sacar los más sucios trapillos a la colada

**wash** /wɒʃ/ n lavadura, f, lavado, m; baño, m; (clothes) ropa para lavar, ropa sucia, f; colada, f; (of the waves) chapoteo, m; (lotion) loción, f; (coating) capa, f; (silt) aluvión, m. **w.-basin,** palangana, f; lavabo, m. **w.-board,** tabla de lavar, f. **w.-house,** lavadero, m. **w.-leather,** gamuza, badana, f. **w.-out,** fracaso, m. **w.-stand,** aguamanil, lavabo, m. **w.-tub,** cuba de lavar, f

**washable** /'wɒʃəbəl/ a lavable

**washer** /'wɒʃər/ n lavador (-ra); (washerwoman) lavandera, f; (machine) lavadora, f; Mech. arandela, f

**washerwoman** /'wɒʃər,wʊmən/ n lavandera, f

**washing** /'wɒʃɪŋ/ n lavamiento, m; ropa sucia, ropa para lavar, f; ropa limpia, f; ropa, f; (bleaching) blanqueadura, f; (toilet) abluciones, f pl; Eccl. lavatorio, m; pl **washings,** lavazas, f pl. **There is a lot of w. to be done,** Hay mucha ropa que lavar. **w.-board,** tabla de lavar, f. **w.-day,** día de colada, m. **w.-machine,** lavadora, máquina de lavar, f. **w.-soda,** carbonato sódico, m. **w.-up,** lavado de los platos, m. **w.-up machine,** fregador mecánico de platos, m

**wasp** /wɒsp/ n avispa, f. **wasp's nest,** avispero, m. **w.-waisted,** (of clothes) ceñido, muy ajustado

**waspish** /'wɒspɪʃ/ a enojadizo, irascible; malicioso; mordaz

**wastage** /'weɪstɪdʒ/ n desgaste, desperdicio, m

**waste** /weɪst/ vt desperdiciar, derrochar, malgastar; (time) perder; consumir; corroer; (devastate) asolar, devastar; echar a perder; malograr; disipar; agotar. —vi gastarse; consumirse; perderse. **to w. time,** perder el tiempo. **to w. away,** (of persons) demacrarse, consumirse

**waste** /weɪst/ n (wilderness) yermo, desierto, m; (vastness) inmensidad, vastedad, f; (loss) pérdida, f; (squandering) despilfarro, derroche, m; disminución, f; (refuse) desechos, m pl; (of cotton, etc.) borra, f; disipación, f. —a (of land) sin cultivar; yermo; inútil; desechado, de desecho; superfluo. **to lay w.,** devastar. **w. land,** yermo, m; tierras sin cultivar, f pl. **w. paper,** papel usado, papel de desecho, m. **w.-paper basket,** cesto para papeles, m. **w.-pipe,** desaguadero, tubo de desagüe, m

**wasteful** /'weɪstfəl/ a pródigo, derrochador, manirroto; antieconómico; ruinoso; inútil

**wastefully** /'weɪstfəli/ adv pródigamente; antieconómicamente; inútilmente

**wastefulness** /'weɪstfəlnɪs/ n prodigalidad, f, despil-

farro, m; pérdida, f; gasto inútil, m; falta de economía, f

**waster** /'weɪstər/ n gastador (-ra); disipador (-ra); (loafer) golfo, m

**watch** /wɒtʃ/ vi velar; mirar. —vt mirar; observar; guardar; (await) esperar; (spy upon) espiar, acechar. **to w. for,** buscar aguardar. **to w. over,** vigilar, guardar; (care for) cuidar; proteger

**watch** /wɒtʃ/ n (at night) vela, f; (wakefulness) desvelo, m; observación, vigilancia, f; (Mil. Naut.) guardia, f; (sentinel) centinela, m; (watchman) sereno, vigilante, m; (guard) ronda, f; (timepiece) reloj de bolsillo, m. **to be on the w.,** estar al acecho, estar al alerta, estar a la mira. **to keep w.,** vigilar. **dog w.,** media guardia, f. **pocket w.,** reloj de bolsillo, m. **wrist w.,** reloj de pulsera, m. **w.-case,** caja de reloj, relojera, f. **w.-chain,** cadena de reloj, leontina, f. **w.-dog,** perro guardián, m. **w.-glass,** cristal de reloj, m. **w.-making,** relojería, f. **w.-night,** noche vieja, f. **w.-spring,** muelle de reloj, m, espiral, f. **w.-tower,** vigía, atalaya, f

**watcher** /'wɒtʃər/ n observador (-ra); espectador (-ra); (at a sick bed) el, m, (f, la) que vela a un enfermo

**watchful** /'wɒtʃfəl/ a vigilante, alerto; observador; atento, cuidadoso

**watchfully** /'wɒtʃfəli/ adv vigilantemente; atentamente

**watchfulness** /'wɒtʃfəlnɪs/ n vigilancia, f; cuidado, m; desvelo, m

**watching** /'wɒtʃɪŋ/ n observación, f; (vigil) vela, f

**watchmaker** /'wɒtʃ,meɪkər/ n relojero (-ra). **watchmaker's shop,** relojería, f

**watchman** /'wɒtʃmən/ n vigilante, sereno, m; guardián, m

**watchword** /'wɒtʃ,wɜrd/ n (password) consigna, contraseña, f; (motto) lema, m

**water** /'wɔtər/ n agua, f; (tide) marea, f; (of precious stones) aguas, f pl; (urine) orina, f; (quality) calidad, clase, f. —a de agua; por agua; acuático; hidráulico. **fresh w.,** (not salt) agua dulce, f; agua fresca, f. **hard w.,** agua cruda, f. **high w.,** marea alta, f. **low w.,** marea baja, f. **of the first w.,** de primera clase, f. **running w.,** agua corriente, f. **soft w.,** agua blanda, f. **to make w.,** Naut. hacer agua; orinar. **to take the waters,** tomar las aguas. **under w.,** adv debajo del agua. —a acuático. **w.-bird,** ave acuática, f. **w. blister,** ampolla, f. **w.-boatman,** chinche de agua, f. **w.-borne,** flotante. **w.-bottle,** cantimplora, f. **w.-brash,** acedia, f. **w.-butt,** barril, m, pipa, f. **w.-carrier,** aguador (-ra). **w.-cart,** carro de regar, m. **w.-closet,** retrete, excusado, m. **w.-color,** acuarela, f. **w.-color painting,** pintura a la acuarela, f. **w.-colorist,** acuarelista, mf **w.-cooled,** enfriado por agua. **w.-cooler,** cantimplora, f. **w.-finder,** zahorí, m. **w. front,** (wharf) muelle, m; puerto, m; litoral, m. **w.-gauge,** indicador de nivel de agua, m, vara de aforar, f. **w.-glass,** vidrio soluble, silicato de sosa, m. **w. heater,** calentador de agua, m. **w.-ice,** helado, m. **w.-level,** nivel de las aguas, m. **w.-lily,** nenúfar, m, azucena de agua, f. **w.-line,** lengua de agua, f; (of a ship) línea de flotación, f. **w.-logged,** anegado en agua. **w.-main,** cañería maestra de agua, f. **w. man,** barquero, m. **w.-melon,** sandía, f. **w. mill,** aceña, f. **w.-nymph,** náyade, f. **w.-pipe,** cañería del agua, f. **w. pitcher,** jarro, m. **w. plant,** planta acuática, f. **w.-polo,** polo acuático, m. **w.-power,** fuerza hidráulica, f. **w.-rate,** cupo del consumo de agua, m. **w. snake,** culebra de agua, f. **w. softener,** generador de agua dulce, m; purificador de agua, m. **w. spaniel,** perro (-rra) de aguas. **w. sprite,** ondina, f. **w.-supply,** abastecimiento de agua, m; traída de aguas, f. **w. tank,** depósito para agua, m. **w. tower,** arca de agua, f. **w.-way,** canal, m; (of a ship) canal, río m, o vía f, navegable. **w.-wheel,** rueda hidráulica, f, azud, m; (for irrigation) aceña, f. **w. wings,** nadaderas, f pl

**water** /'wɔtər/ vt (irrigate, sprinkle) regar; (moisten) mojar; (cattle, etc.) abrevar; (wine, etc.) aguar; diluir con agua; (bathe) bañar. —vi (of animals) beber agua; (of engines, etc.) tomar agua; (of the eyes, mouth) hacerse agua. **My mouth waters,** Se me hace agua la boca

**watercourse** /'wɔtər,kɔrs/ n corriente de agua, f; cauce, m; lecho de un río, m
**watercress** /'wɔtər,krɛs/ n berro, mastuerzo, m
**watered** /'wɔtərd/ a regado, abundante en agua; (of silk) tornasolado
**watered-down** /'wɔtərd'daun/ Fig. pasado por agua
**waterfall** /'wɔtər,fɔl/ n salto de agua, m, cascada, catarata, f
**wateriness** /'wɔtərinıs/ n humedad, f; acuosidad, f
**watering** /'wɔtərıŋ/ n riego, m; irrigación, f; (of eyes) lagrimeo, m; (of cattle, etc.) el abrevar (a); Naut. aguada, f. **w.-can**, regadera, f. **w.-cart**, carro de regar, m. **w.-place**, (for animals) aguadero, m; (for cattle) abrevadero, m; (spa) balneario, m; (by the sea) playa de veraneo, f
**watermark** /'wɔtər,mɑrk/ n (in paper) filigrana, f; nivel del agua, m. —vt filigranar
**waterproof** /'wɔtər,pruf/ a impermeable; a prueba de agua. —n impermeable, m. —vt hacer impermeable, impermeabilizar
**water-repellent** /'wɔtərı,pɛlənt/ a repelente al agua
**watershed** /'wɔtər,ʃɛd/ n vertiente, f; línea divisoria de las aguas, f; (river-basin) cuenca, f
**waterspout** /'wɔtər,spaut/ n bomba marina, manga, trompa, f
**watertight** /'wɔtər,tait/ a impermeable, estanco; a prueba de agua; (of arguments, etc.) irrefutable
**watertightness** /'wɔtər,taitnıs/ n impermeabilidad, f
**waterworks** /'wɔtər,wɜrks/ n establecimiento para la distribución de las aguas, m; obras hidráulicas, f pl
**watery** /'wɔtəri/ a (wet) húmedo; acuoso; (of the sky) de lluvia; (of eyes) lagrimoso, lloroso; (sodden) mojado; (of soup, etc.) claro; insípido
**watt** /wɒt/ n vatio, m. **w. hour,** vatio hora, m. **w.-meter,** vatímetro, m
**wattage** /'wɒtıdʒ/ n vatiaje, m
**wattle** /'wɒtl/ n zarzo, m; (of turkey) barba, f; (of fish) barbilla, f
**wave** /weiv/ vi ondear; ondular; flotar; hacer señales. —vt (brandish) blandir; agitar; (the hair) ondular; ondear; hacer señales (de). **They waved goodby to him,** Le hicieron adiós con la mano; Le hicieron señas de despedida; Se despidieron de él agitando el pañuelo
**wave** /weiv/ n (of the sea) ola, f; Phys. onda, f; (in hair or a surface) ondulación, f; (movement) movimiento, m; (of anger, etc.) ráfaga, f. **long w.,** onda larga, f. **medium w.,** onda media, f. **short w.,** onda corta, f. **sound w.,** onda sonora, f. **to have one's hair waved,** hacerse ondular el pelo. **w. band,** franja undosa, escala de longitudes de onda, f. **w. crest,** cresta de la ola, cabrilla, f. **w.-length,** longitud de onda, f
**wavelet** /'weivlıt/ n pequeña ola, olita, f; (ripple) rizo (del agua), m
**wave of immigration** una imigración, f
**waver** /'weivər/ vi ondear; oscilar; (hesitate) vacilar, titubear; (totter) tambalearse; (weaken) flaquear
**waverer** /'weivərər/ n irresoluto (-ta), vacilante, m
**wavering** /'weivərıŋ/ n vacilación, irresolución, f. —a oscilante; vacilante, irresoluto; flotante
**waving** /'weivıŋ/ n ondulación, f; oscilación, f; agitación, f; movimiento, m. —a ondulante; oscilante; que se balancea
**wavy** /'weivi/ a ondulado; flotante
**wax** /wæks/ n cera, f; (cobblers') cerote, m; (in the ear) cerilla, f. —a de cera. —vt encerar. —vi crecer; hacerse; ponerse. **to wax enthusiastic,** entusiasmarse. **waxed paper,** papel encerado, m. **wax chandler,** cerero, m. **wax doll,** muñeca de cera, f. **wax modeling,** modelado en cera, m, ceroplástica, f. **wax taper,** blandón, m
**waxen** /'wæksən/ a de cera; como la cera; de color de cera
**waxing** /'wæksıŋ/ n enceramiento, m; (of the moon) crecimiento, m; aumento, m
**wax museum** n museo de cera, m
**waxwork** /'wæks,wɜrk/ n figura de cera, f
**waxy** /'wæksi/ a. See **waxen**
**way** /wei/ n camino, m; senda, f; paso, m; ruta, f; (railway, etc.) vía, f; dirección, f; rumbo, m; distancia, f; (journey) viaje, m; (sea crossing) travesía, f;

avance, progreso, m; (Naut. etc.) marcha, f; método, m; modo, m; (means) medio, m; manera, f; (habit) costumbre, f; (behavior) conducta, f, modo de obrar, m; (line of business, etc.) ramo, m; (state) estado, m, condición, f; (course) curso, m; (respect) punto de vista, m; (particular kind) género, m; (scale) escala, f. **a long way off,** a gran distancia, a lo lejos. **a short way off,** a poca distancia, no muy lejos. **by way of,** pasando por; por vía de; como; por medio de; a modo de. **by the way,** de paso; durante el viaje; durante la travesía; a propósito, entre paréntesis. **in a small way,** en pequeña escala. **in a way,** hasta cierto punto; desde cierto punto de vista. **in many ways,** de muchos modos; por muchas cosas. **in no way,** de ningún modo; nada. **in the way,** en el medio. **in the way of,** en cuanto a, respecto a; en materia de. **I went out of my way to,** Dejé el camino para; Me di la molestia de. **Is this the way to...?** ¿Es este el camino a...? **Make way!** ¡Calle! **Milky Way,** vía láctea, f. **on the way,** en camino; al paso; durante el viaje. **out of the way,** puesto a un lado; arrinconado; apartado, alejado; (imprisoned) en prisión; fuera del camino; remoto; (unusual) original. **over the way,** en frente; al otro lado (de la calle, etc.). **right of w.,** derecho de paso, m. **The ship left on its way to...,** El barco zarpó con rumbo a... **the Way of the Cross,** vía crucis, f. **This way!** ¡Por aquí!; De este modo, Así. **this way and that,** en todas direcciones, por todos lados. **"This way to...,"** «Dirección a...» A... **under way,** en camino; en marcha; en preparación. **to bar the way,** cerrar el paso. **to be in the way,** estorbar. **to be out of the way of doing,** haber perdido la costumbre de hacer (algo). **to clear the way,** abrir paso, abrir calle; Fig. preparar el terreno. **to force one's way through,** abrirse paso por. **to find a way,** encontrar un camino; Fig. encontrar medios. **to find one's way,** hallar el camino; orientarse. **to get into the way of,** contraer la costumbre de. **to get under way,** Naut. zarpar, hacerse a la vela; ponerse en marcha. **to give way,** ceder; (break) romper. **to go a long way,** ir lejos; contribuir mucho. **to have one's way,** salir con la suya. **to keep out of the way,** vt and vi esconder(se); mantener(se) alejado; mantener(se) apartado. **to lose one's way,** perder el camino; desorientarse; Fig. extraviarse. **to make one's way,** abrirse paso. **to make one's way back,** bajar. **to make one's way round,** dar la vuelta a. **to make one's way up,** subir. **to make way,** hacer lugar; hacer sitio; dar paso (a). **to pay one's way,** ganarse la vida; pagar lo que se debe. **to prepare the way for,** preparar el terreno para. **to put out of the way,** poner a un lado; apartar; (kill) matar; (imprison) poner en la cárcel; hacer cautivo (a). **to see one's way,** poder ver el camino; poder orientarse; ver el modo de hacer algo; ver cómo se puede hacer algo. **ways and means,** medios y arbitrios, m pl. **way back,** camino de regreso, m; vuelta, f. **way down,** bajada, f. **way in,** entrada, f. **way out,** salida, f. **way round,** camino alrededor, m; solución, f; modo de evitar..., m. **way through,** paso, m. **way up,** subida, f
**wayfarer** /'wei,fɛərər/ n transeúnte, mf; viajero (-ra)
**wayfaring** /'wei,fɛərıŋ/ a que va de viaje; errante, ambulante
**waylay** /'wei,lei/ vt asechar, salir al paso (de)
**wayside** /'wei,said/ n borde del camino, m. —a (of flowers) silvestre; (by the side of the road) en la carretera
**wayward** /'weiwərd/ a caprichoso; desobediente; voluntarioso; travieso; rebelde
**waywardness** /'weiwərdnıs/ n desobediencia, indocilidad, f; voluntariedad, f; travesura, f; rebeldía, f
**we** /wi/ pron nosotros, m pl; nosotras, f pl. (Usually omitted except for emphasis or for clarity.) **We are in the garden,** Estamos en el jardín. **We have come, but they are not here,** Nosotros hemos venido pero ellos no están aquí
**weak** /wik/ a débil; flojo; frágil; delicado; (insecure) inseguro; (of arguments) poco convincente; (of prices, markets, etc.) flojo, en baja. **w.-eyed,** de vista floja. **w.-kneed,** débil de rodillas; Fig. sin voluntad.

**w.-minded,** sin carácter; pusilánime; **w. spot,** debilidad, *f;* flaco, *m;* lado débil, *m;* desventaja, *f*

**weaken** /'wikən/ *vt* debilitar; (diminish) disminuir. —*vi* debilitarse; flaquear, desfallecer; (give way) ceder

**weakening** /'wikənɪŋ/ *n* debilitación, *f.* —*a* debilitante; enervante

**weaker** /'wikər/ *a compar* más débil. **the w.** **sex,** el sexo débil

**weakling** /'wiklɪŋ/ *n* ser delicado, *m,* persona débil, *f;* cobarde, *m; Inf.* alfeñique, *m*

**weakly** /'wikli/ *a* enfermizo, delicado, enclenque. —*adv* débilmente

**weakness** /'wiknɪs/ *n* debilidad, *f;* imperfección, *f*

**weal** /wil/ *n* bienestar, *m;* prosperidad, *f;* (blow) verdugo, *m*

**wealth** /wɛlθ/ *n* riqueza, *f;* abundancia, *f;* bienes, *m* *pl*

**wealthy** /'wɛlθi/ *a* rico, adinerado, acaudalado; abundante (en)

**wean** /win/ *vt* destetar, ablactar; separar (de); privar (de); enajenar el afecto de; (of ideas) desaferrar (de)

**weaning** /'winɪŋ/ *n* ablactación, *f,* destete, *m*

**weapon** /'wɛpən/ *n* arma, *f; pl* **weapons,** (*Zool.,* *Bot.*) medios de defensa, *m pl.* **steel w.,** arma blanca, *f*

**wear** /wɛər/ *n* uso, *m;* gasto, *m;* deterioro, *m;* (fashion) moda, boga, *f.* **for hard w.,** para todo uso. **for** **one's own w.,** para su propio uso. **for evening w.,** para llevar de noche. **for summer w.,** para llevar en verano. **w. and tear,** uso y desgaste, *m;* deterioro natural, *m*

**wear** /wɛər/ *vt* llevar; llevar puesto; traer; usar; (have) tener; (exhibit) mostrar; (be clad in) vestir; (waste) gastar; deteriorar; (make) hacer; (exhaust) agotar, cansar, consumir. —*vi* (last) durar; (of persons) conservar(se); (of time) correr; avanzar. **She** **wears well,** Está bien conservada. **to w. one's heart** **on one's sleeve,** tener el corazón en la mano. **to w.** **the trousers,** *Fig. Inf.* llevar los pantalones. **to w.** **well,** durar mucho. **to w. away,** *vt* gastar, roer; (rub out) borrar; consumir. —*vi* (of time) pasar lentamente, transcurrir despacio. **to w. down,** gastar; consumir; reducir; agotar las fuerzas de; destruir; (tire) fatigar. **to w. off,** *vt* destruir; borrar. —*vi* quitarse; borrarse; *Fig.* desaparecer, pasar. **to w. on,** (of time) transcurrir, correr, pasar. **to w. out,** *vt* usar; romper con el uso; consumir, acabar con; (exhaust) agotar; (tire) rendir. —*vi* usarse; romperse con el uso; consumirse

**wearable** /'wɛərəbəl/ *a* que se puede llevar

**wearer** /'wɛərər/ *n* el, *m;* (f, la) que lleva alguna cosa

**weariness** /'wɪərɪnɪs/ *n* cansancio, *m,* fatiga, lasitud, *f;* aburrimiento, *m;* aversión, repugnancia, *f*

**wearing** /'wɛərɪŋ/ *n* uso, *m;* desgaste, *m.* —*a* (tiring) agotador; cansado. **w. apparel,** ropa, *f*

**wearisome** /'wɪərɪsəm/ *a* cansado; laborioso; aburrido, tedioso, pesado

**wearisomely** /'wɪərɪsəmli/ *adv* tediosamente

**wearisomeness** /'wɪərɪsəmnɪs/ *n* cansancio, *m;* aburrimiento, tedio, hastío, *m*

**weary** /'wɪəri/ *a* cansado, fatigado; aburrido; hastiado; impaciente; tedioso, enfadoso. —*vt* cansar, fatigar; aburrir; hastiar; molestar. —*vi* cansarse, fatigarse; aburrirse. **to w. for,** anhelar, suspirar por; (miss) echar de menos (a). **to w. of,** aburrirse de; (things) impacientarse de; (people) impacientarse con

**weasel** /'wizəl/ *n* comadreja, *f*

**weather** /'wɛðər/ *n* tiempo, *m;* intemperie, *f;* (storm) tempestad, *f.* —*a Naut.* del lado del viento; de barlovento. —*vt* (of rain, etc.) desgastar; curtir; secar al aire; *Naut.* pasar a barlovento; (bear) aguantar, capear; (survive) sobrevivir a; luchar con. —*vi* curtirse a la intemperie. **Andrew is a little under the w.,** Andrés está algo destemplado; (with drink) Andrés tiene una mona, *f;* (depressed) Andrés está melancólico. **to** **be bad (good) w.,** hacer mal (buen) tiempo. **What is** **the w. like?** ¿Qué tiempo hace? ¿Cómo está el tiempo? **w.-beaten,** curtido por la intemperie. **w.** **chart,** carta meteorológica, *f.* **w. conditions,** condiciones meteorológicas, *f pl.* **w. forecast,** pronóstico del tiempo, *m.* **w.-hardened,** endurecido a la intemperie.

**w. prophet,** meteorologista, *mf* **w. report,** boletín meteorológico, *m.* **w.-worn,** gastado por la intemperie; curtido por la intemperie

**weathercock** /'wɛðər,kɒk/ *n* veleta, *f*

**weathering** /'wɛðərɪŋ/ *n* desintegración por la acción atmosférica, *f*

**weather-resistant** /'wɛðərrɪ,zɪstənt/ *a* resistente a la intemperie

**weave** /wiv/ *vt* tejer; trenzar; entrelazar; *Fig.* tejer. —*vi* tejer. —*n* tejido, *m;* textura, *f*

**weaver** /'wivər/ *n* tejedor (-ra)

**weaving** /'wivɪŋ/ *n* tejido, *m;* tejeduría, *f.* **w. ma-** **chine,** telar, *m*

**web** /wɛb/ *n* tejido, *m;* tela, *f;* (network) red, *f;* (spider's) telaraña, *f;* (of a feather) barba, *f;* (of birds, etc.) membrana interdigital, *f;* (of intrigue) red, *f;* (snarl) lazo, *m,* trampa, *f.* **web-foot,** pie palmado, *m.* **web-footed,** palmípedo.

**webbed** /wɛbd/ *a* (of feet) unido por una membrana

**wed** /wɛd/ *vt* casarse con; (join in marriage, cause to marry) casar; *Fig.* unir. —*vi* estar casado; casarse

**wedded** /'wɛdɪd/ *a* casado; matrimonial, conyugal; *Fig.* unido (a); aficionado (a), entusiasta (de), devoto (de); aferrado (a). **to be w. to one's own opinion,** estar aferrado a su propia opinión

**wedding** /'wɛdɪŋ/ *n* boda, *f,* casamiento, *m;* (with golden, etc.) bodas, *f pl;* (union) enlace, *m, a* de boda, nupcial, matrimonial, conyugal; de novios, de la novia. **golden w.,** bodas de oro, *f pl.* **silver w.,** bodas de plata, *f pl.* **w. bouquet,** ramo de la novia, *m.* **w.-breakfast,** banquete de bodas, *m.* **w.-cake,** torta de la boda, *f,* pan de la boda, *m.* **w.-day,** día de la boda, *m.* **w.-march,** marcha nupcial, *f.* **w.-present,** regalo de boda, regalo de la boda, *m.* **w.-ring,** anillo de la boda, *m.* **w. trip,** viaje de novios, *m*

**wedge** /wɛdʒ/ *n* cuña, *f;* (under a wheel) calza, alzaprima, *f; Mil.* cuña, mella, *f;* (of cheese) pedazo, *m.* —*vt* acuñar, meter cuñas; (a wheel) calzar; (fix) sujetar. **to be the thin end of the w.,** ser el principio, ser el primer paso. **to drive a w.,** *Mil.* hacer mella, practicar una cuña. **to w. oneself in,** introducirse con dificultad (en). **w.-shaped,** cuneiforme

**wedlock** /'wɛd,lɒk/ *n* matrimonio, *m*

**Wednesday** /'wɛnzdei/ *n* miércoles, *m*

**wee** /wi/ *a* pequeñito, chiquito. **a wee bit,** un poquito

**weed** /wid/ *n* mala hierba, *f;* tabaco, *m;* (cigar) cigarro, *m;* (person) madeja, *f;* (*Fig.* evil) cizaña, *f.* —*vt* carpir, desherbar, sachar, sallar, escardar; *Fig.* extirpar, arrancar. **w.-grown,** cubierto de malas hierbas. **to w. out,** extirpar; quitar

**weeder** /'widər/ *n* (person) escardador (-ra); (implement) sacho, *m*

**weeding** /'widɪŋ/ *n* (also *Fig.*) escarda, *f*

**weedy** /'widi/ *a* lleno de malas hierbas; *Fig.* raquítico

**week** /wik/ *n* semana, *f.* **in a w.,** de hoy en ocho (días); en una semana; después de una semana. **once** **a w.,** una vez por semana. **a w. ago,** hace una semana. **Michael will come a w. from today,** Miguel llegará hoy en ocho, *m,* Miguel vendrá hoy en ocho, *m.* **w.-day,** día de trabajo, día laborable, día de la semana que no sea el domingo. **on weekdays,** entre semana, *m.* **w.-end,** fin de semana, *m.* **w.-end case,** saco de noche, *m*

**weekly** /'wikli/ *a* semanal, semanario; de cada semana. —*adv* semanalmente, cada semana. —*n* semanario, *m,* revista semanal, *f*

**weep** /wip/ *vt* llorar. **to w. for,** (a person) llorar (a); (on account of) llorar por; (with happiness, etc.) llorar de. **They wept for joy,** Lloraron de alegría

**weeping** /'wipɪŋ/ *n* lloro, llanto, *m,* lágrimas, *f pl.* —*a* lloroso, que llora; (of trees) llorón. **w.-willow,** sauce llorón, *m*

**weevil** /'wivəl/ *n* gorgojo, *m*

**weigh** /wei/ *vt* pesar; (consider) considerar, ponderar, tomar en cuenta; comparar; (the anchor) levar. —*vi* pesar; ser de importancia. **to w. anchor,** zarpar, levar el ancla, hacerse a la vela. **to w. down,** pesar sobre; sobrecargar; hacer inclinarse bajo; *Fig.* agobiar. **to be weighed down,** hundirse por su propio peso; *Fig.* estar agobiado. **to w. out,** pesar. **to w.** **with,** influir (en). **w.-bridge,** báscula, *f*

**weighing** /'weiɪŋ/ n pesada, f; (weight) peso, m; (of the anchor) leva, f; (consideration) ponderación, consideración, f. **w.-machine,** báscula, f

**weight** /weit/ n peso, m; (heaviness) pesantez, f; cargo, m; (of a clock and as part of a system) pesa, f; Fig. peso, m, importancia, f. —vt cargar; (a stick) emplomar; aumentar el peso (de); poner un peso (a). **gross w.,** peso bruto, m. **heavy w.,** peso pesado, m. **light w.,** peso ligero, m. **middle w.,** peso medio, m. **net w.,** peso neto, m. **to lose w.,** adelgazar. **loss of w.,** (of a person) adelgazamiento, m. **to put on w.,** cobrar carnes, hacerse más gordo. **to put the w.,** Sports. lanzar el peso. **to throw one's w. about,** Inf. darse importancia. **to try the w. of,** sopesar. **weights and measures,** pesas y medidas, f pl. **weightlifting,** halterofilia, f

**weighty** /'weiti/ a pesado; (influential) influyente; importante, de peso; grave

**weir** /wiər/ n presa, esclusa, f; (for fish) cañal, m

**weird** /wiərd/ a misterioso, sobrenatural; fantástico; mágico; (queer) raro, extraño. **the W. Sisters,** las Parcas

**weirdly** /'wiərdli/ adv misteriosamente; fantásticamente; (queerly) de un modo raro, extrañamente

**weirdness** /'wiərdnıs/ n misterio, m; cualidad fantástica, f; lo sobrenatural; (queerness) rareza, f

**welcome** /'wɛlkəm/ a bienvenido; (pleasant) grato, agradable. —n bienvenida, f; buena acogida, f; (reception) acogida, f. —vt dar la bienvenida (a); acoger con alegría, acoger con entusiasmo; agasajar, festejar; (receive) acoger, recibir; recibir con gusto. **W.!** ¡Bienvenido! **to bid w.,** dar la bienvenida (a). **You are w.,** Estás bienvenido. **You are w. to it,** Está a su disposición

**welcoming** /'wɛlkəmıŋ/ a acogedor, cordial, amistoso

**weld** /wɛld/ vt soldar; combinar; unificar

**welder** /'wɛldər/ n soldador, m

**welding** /'wɛldıŋ/ n soldadura, f; unión, fusión, f

**welfare** /'wɛl,fɛər/ n bienestar, bien, m; (health) salud, f; prosperidad, f; intereses, m pl. **w. state,** estado benefactor, estado de beneficencia, estado socializante, m. **w. work,** obra social, f

**well** /wɛl/ a bien; bien de salud; bueno; conveniente; (advantageous) provechoso; favorable; (happy) feliz; (healed) curado; (recovered) repuesto. **I am very w.,** Estoy muy bien. **to get w.,** ponerse bien. **to make w.,** curar. **w. enough,** bastante bien

**well** /wɛl/ adv bien; (very) muy; favorablemente; convenientemente; (easily) sin dificultad. **as w.,** también. **as w. as,** tan bien como; además de. **That is all very w. but...,** Todo eso está muy bien pero... **to be w. up in,** estar versado en. **to get on w. with,** llevarse bien con algn. **Very w.!** ¡Está bien!; Muy bien. **w. and good,** bien está. **w. now,** ahora bien. **w. then,** conque; pues bien. **w.-advised,** bien aconsejado; prudente. **w.-aimed,** certero. **w.-appointed,** bien provisto; (furnished) bien amueblado. **w.-attended,** concurrido. **w.-balanced,** bien equilibrado. **w.-behaved,** bien educado; (of animals) manso. **w.-being,** bienestar, m; felicidad, f. **w.-born,** bien nacido, de buena familia. **w.-bred,** bien criado, bien educado; (of animals) de pura raza. **w.-chosen,** bien escogido. **w.-defined,** bien definido. **w.-deserved,** bien merecido. **w.-disposed,** bien dispuesto; favorable; bien intencionado. **w.-doing,** n el obrar bien; obras de caridad, f pl, a bondadoso, caritativo. **w.-done,** a bien hecho. —interj ¡bravo! **w.-educated,** instruido, culto. **w.-favored,** guapo, de buen parecer. **w.-founded,** bien fundado. **w.-groomed,** elegante. **w.-grounded,** bien fundado; bien instruido. **w.-informed,** instruido; culto, ilustrado. **w.-intentioned,** bien intencionado. **w.-known,** bien conocido, notorio. **w.-meaning,** bien intencionado. **w.-modulated,** armonioso. **w.-off,** acomodado, adinerado; feliz. **w.-read,** culto, instruido. **w.-shaped,** bien hecho; bien formado. **w.-shaped nose,** nariz perfilada, f. **w.-spent,** bien empleado. **w.-spoken,** bien hablado; bien dicho. **w.-stocked,** bien provisto. **w.-suited,** apropiado. **w.-timed,** oportuno. **w.-to-do,** acomodado, rico. **w.-wisher,** amigo (-ga). **w.-worn,** raído; (of paths) trillado

**well** /wɛl/ n pozo, m; (of a stair) caja, f; cañón de es-

calera, m; (fountain) fuente, f, manantial, m; (of a fishing boat) vivar, m; (of a ship) sentina, f. **w.-sinker,** pocero, m

**well** /wɛl/ vi chorrear, manar, brotar, fluir

**Welsh** /wɛlʃ/ a galés, de Gales. —n (language) galés, m. **the W.,** los galeses

**Welshman** /'wɛlʃmən/ n galés, m

**Welshwoman** /'wɛlʃ,wumən/ n galesa, f

**welt** /wɛlt/ n (of shoe) vira, f, cerquillo, m; (in knitting) ribete, m; (weal) verdugo, m

**Weltanschauung** /'vɛltən,ʃauəŋ/ n cosmovisión, postura de vida, f

**welter** /'wɛltər/ vi revolcarse; bañarse (en), nadar (en). —n confusión, f, tumulto, m; mezcla, f. **w.-weight,** peso welter, m

**wench** /wɛntʃ/ n mozuela, muchacha, f

**wend** /wɛnd/ vt dirigir, encaminar. —vi ir. **to w. one's way,** dirigir sus pasos, seguir su camino

**Wesleyan** /'wɛsliən/ a wesleyano, metodista. —n metodista, mf

**west** /wɛst/ n oeste, m; poniente, m; occidente, m. —a del oeste; occidental. —adv hacia el oeste, a poniente; al occidente. **W. Indian,** de las Antillas, de las Indias Occidentales. **w.-north-w.,** oesnoroeste, m. **w.-south-w.,** oessudueste, m. **w. wind,** viento del oeste, poniente, m

**westerly** /'wɛstərli/ a del oeste; hacia el oeste; occidental

**western** /'wɛstərn/ a occidental; del oeste. —n (novel) novela caballista, f; (film) película del oeste, f

**westernized** /'wɛstər,naizd/ a influido por el occidente

**westernmost** /'wɛstərn,moust/ a más al oeste

**West Indies** Indias Occidentales, f pl

**westward** /'wɛstwərd/ a que está al oeste. —adv hacia el oeste; hacia el occidente

**wet** /wɛt/ a mojado; húmedo; (rainy) lluvioso. —vt mojar; humedecer. —n (rain) lluvia, f. **"Mind the wet paint!"** «¡Cuidado, recién pintado!» **to be wet,** estar mojado; (of the weather) llover. **to get wet,** mojarse. **wet blanket,** Fig. aguafiestas, mf **wet through,** (of persons) calado, hecho una sopa. **wet-nurse,** nodriza, f

**wetness** /'wɛtnıs/ n humedad, f; (rain) lluvia, f

**wetting** /'wɛtıŋ/ n mojada, f; humectación, f; (soaking) remojo, m

**whack** /wæk/ n golpe, m; (try) tentativa, f; (portion) porción, parte, f. —vt golpear, aporrear, pegar

**whale** /weil/ n ballena, f. **sperm w.,** cachalote, m. **w.-oil,** aceite de ballena, m

**whalebone** /'weil,boun/ n barbas de ballena, f pl, ballena, f

**whaler** /'weilər/ n (man) ballenero, pescador de ballenas, m; (boat) buque ballenero, m

**whaling** /'weilıŋ/ a ballenero. —n pesca de ballenas, f. **w.-gun,** cañón arponero, m

**wharf** /wɔrf/ n muelle, embarcadero, descargadero, m, vt amarrar al muelle

**what** /wʌt/ unstressed wət/ a pron (interrogative and exclamatory) qué; cómo; (relative) que; el que, m; la que, f; lo que, neut; los que, m pl; las que, f pl; (which, interrogative) cuál, mf; cuáles, mf pl; (how many) cuantos, m pl; cuantas, f pl; (interrogative and exclamatory) cuántos, m pl; cuántas, f pl; (how much, interrogative and exclamatory) cuánto, m; cuánta, f. **And w. not,** Y qué sé yo qué más. **Make w. changes you will,** Haz los cambios que quieras. **W. confidence he had...,** La confianza que tenía... **W. is this called?** ¿Cómo se llama esto? **W. did they go there for?** ¿Por qué fueron? **W. do you take me for?** ¿Por quién me tomas? **That was not w. he said,** No fue eso lo que dijo. **to know what's w.,** saber cuántas son cinco. **You have heard the latest news, w.?** Has oído las últimas noticias, ¿verdad? **A pity!** ¡Qué lástima! **W., do you really believe it?** ¿Lo crees de veras? **W. else?** ¿Qué más? **W. for?** ¿Para qué? **what's-his-name,** fulano (-la) de tal, m. **W. ho!** ¡Hola! **W. if...?** ¿Qué será si...? **W. is the matter?** ¿Qué pasa? ¿Qué hay? **w. though...,** aun cuando...; ¿Qué importa qué? **w. with one thing, w. with another,** entre una cosa y otra. **What's more,...** Es más,...

**whatever** /wʌt'ɛvər/ a pron cuanto; todo lo que; cualquier cosa que; cualquier. **W. sacrifice is necessary,** Cualquier sacrificio que sea necesario. **W. I have is yours,** Todo lo que tenga es vuestro. **W. happens,** Venga lo que venga. **It is of no use w.,** No sirve absolutamente para nada

**wheal** /wil/ n. See weal

**wheat** /wit/ n trigo, m. —a de trigo. **summer w.,** trigo tremesino, m. **whole w.,** a de trigo entero. **w.-ear,** espiga de trigo, f. **w.-field,** trigal, m. **w.-sheaf,** gavilla de trigo, f

**wheaten** /'witn/ a de trigo; del color del trigo

**wheedle** /'widl/ vt lagotear, engatusar; (flatter) halagar; (with out) sacar con mimos

**wheedling** /'widlɪŋ/ a zalamero, mimoso; marrullero. —n lagotería, f, mimos, m pl; (flattery) halagos, m pl; marrullería, f

**wheel** /wil/ n rueda, f; (bicycle) bicicleta, f; (for steering a ship) timón, m; rueda del timón, f; (for steering a car) volante, m; (for spinning) rueca, f; (potter's) rueda de alfarero, f; (of birds) vuelo, m; (turn) vuelta, f; Mil. conversión, f. **Catherine w.,** (firework) rueda de Santa Catalina, f. **back w.,** rueda trasera, f. **front w.,** rueda delantera, f. **to break on the w.,** enrodar. **to go on wheels,** ir en ruedas; Fig. ir viento en popa. **to take the w.,** (in a ship) tomar el timón; tomar el volante. **w. of fortune,** rueda de la fortuna, f. **w.-chair,** silla de ruedas, f. **w.-house,** timonera, f. **w.-mark,** rodada, f

**wheel** /wil/ vt hacer rodar; (push) empujar; (drive) conducir; transportar; llevar; pasear; (turn) hacer girar. —vi girar; dar vueltas; ir en bicicleta. **to w. about,** cambiar de frente; volverse; cambiar de rumbo

**wheelbarrow** /'wil,bærou/ n carretilla, f

**wheeled** /wild/ a de... ruedas; con ruedas. **w. chair,** silla de ruedas, f

**wheeling** /'wilɪŋ/ n rodaje, m; Mil. conversión, f; (of birds) vuelos, m pl, vueltas, f pl. **free-w.,** rueda libre, f

**wheelwright** /'wil,rait/ n carpintero de carretas, ruedero, m

**wheeze** /wiz/ vi ser asmático, jadear, respirar fatigosamente, resollar

**wheezing** /'wizɪŋ/ n resuello, jadeo, m; respiración fatigada, f

**whelp** /wɛlp/ n cachorro (-rra). —vi and vt parir

**when** /wɛn/ unstressed wən/ adv cuando (interrogative, cuándo); (as soon as) tan pronto como, en cuanto; (meaning "and then') y luego, y entonces; (although) aunque. **I will see you w. I return,** Te veré cuando vuelva. **W. he came to see me he was already ill,** Cuando vino a verme estaba enfermo ya. **We returned a week ago, since w. I have not been out,** Volvimos hace ocho días y desde entonces no he salido. **Since w.?** ¿Desde cuándo?

**whence** /wɛns/ adv de donde (interrogative, dónde); a donde (interrogative a dónde); por donde, de que; por lo que. **W. does he come?** ¿De dónde viene? **W. comes it that?** ¿Cómo es que...?

**whenever** /wɛn'ɛvər/ adv cuando quiera que, siempre que; cada vez que, todas las veces que; cuando

**where** /wɛər/ adv pron donde (interrogative, dónde); en donde; en que (interrogative, en qué); (to where with verbs of motion) a donde (interrogative, a dónde); (from where with verbs of motion) de donde (interrogative, de dónde). **W. are you going to?** ¿A dónde va Vd.? **This is w. we get out,** (of a bus, etc.) Nos apeamos aquí

**whereabouts** /'wɛərə,bauts/ adv (interrogative) dónde; (relative) donde. —n paradero, m

**whereas** /wɛər'æz/ conjunc (inasmuch as) visto que, ya que; (although) mientras que

**whereat** /wɛər'æt/ adv por lo cual; a lo cual

**whereby** /wɛər'bai/ adv cómo; por qué; por el cual, con el cual

**wherefore** /'wɛər,fɔr/ adv (why) por qué; por lo cual. —n porqué, m

**wherein** /wɛər'ɪn/ adv en donde (interrogative, en dónde); en que (interrogative, en qué)

**whereinto** /wɛər'ɪntu/ adv en donde; dentro del cual; en lo cual

**whereof** /wɛər'ʌv/ adv de que; (whose) cuyo

**whereon** /wɛər'ɒn/ adv sobre que; en qué

**whereto** /wɛər'tu/ adv adonde; a lo que

**whereupon** /,wɛərə'pɒn/ adv dónde; sobre lo cual, con lo cual; en consecuencia de lo cual

**wherever** /wɛər'ɛvər/ adv dondequiera (que), en cualquier sitio; adondequiera (que). **Sit w. you like,** Siéntate donde te parezca bien

**wherewith** /wɛər'wiθ, -'wɪð/ adv con que (interrogative, con qué)

**wherewithal** /'wɛərwɪð,ɔl, -wɪθ-/ n lo necesario; dinero necesario, m

**whet** /wɛt/ vt (knives, etc.) afilar, amolar, aguzar; (curiosity, etc.) excitar, estimular

**whether** /'wɛðər/ conjunc si; que; sea que, ya que. **W. he will or no,** Que quiera, que no quiera. **w. or not,** si o no

**whetstone** /'wɛt,stoun/ n afiladera, amoladera, piedra de amolar, f

**whetting** /'wɛtɪŋ/ n aguzadura, amoladura, f; (of curiosity, etc.) estimulación, excitación, f

**whey** /wei/ n suero (de la leche), m

**which** /wɪtʃ/ a and pron cuál, mf; cuáles, mf pl; (interrogative, qué); el cual, m; la cual, f; lo cual, neut; los cuales, m pl; las cuales, f pl; el que, m; la que, f; lo que, neut; los que, m pl; las que, f pl; (who) quien. **all of w.,** todo lo cual, etc. **in w.,** en donde, en el que; donde. **the w.,** el cual, la cual, etc. **W. would you like?** ¿Cuál quieres? **The documents w. I have seen,** Los documentos que he visto. **W. way have we to go?** ¿Por dónde hemos de ir?

**whichever** /wɪtʃ'ɛvər/ a and pron cualquiera (que), mf; cualesquiera, mf pl; el que, m; la que, f; (of persons only) quienquiera (que), mf; quienesquiera (que), mf pl **Give me w. you like,** Dame el que quieras. **I shall take w. of you would like to come,** Me llevaré a cualquiera de Vds. que guste de venir

**whiff** /wɪf/ n (of air) soplo, m; vaho, m; fragancia, f

**while** /wail/ n rato, m; momento, m; tiempo, m. **after a w.,** al cabo de algún tiempo, después de algún tiempo. **a little w. ago,** hace poco. **all this w.,** en todo este tiempo. **at whiles,** a ratos, de vez en cuando. **between whiles,** de cuando en cuando; entre tanto. **It is worth your w. to do it,** Vale la pena de hacerse. **Mary smiled the w.,** María mientras tanto se sonreía. **once in a w.,** de vez en cuando; en ocasiones

**while** /wail/ conjunc mientras (que); al (followed by an infinitive); al mismo tiempo que; a medida que; (although) aunque; si bien. **w. I was walking down the street,** mientras andaba por la calle, al andar yo por la calle. —vt **to w.** ( away), pasar, entretener. **to w. away the time,** pasar el rato

**whim** /wɪm/ n capricho, antojo, m; manía, f; extravagancia, f; fantasía, f

**whimper** /'wɪmpər/ n quejido, sollozo, gemido, m, vi lloriquear, quejarse, sollozar, gemir

**whimpering** /'wɪmpərɪŋ/ n lloriqueo, llanto, m, a que lloriquea

**whimsical** /'wɪmzɪkəl/ a antojadizo, caprichoso; fantástico

**whimsicality** /,wɪmzɪ'kælɪti/ n capricho, m, extravagancia, f; fantasía, f

**whimsically** /'wɪmzɪkli/ adv caprichosamente; fantásticamente

**whine** /wain/ vi gimotear, lloriquear; quejarse

**whining** /'wainɪŋ/ n gimoteo, lloriqueo, m; quejumbres, f pl. —a que lloriquea; quejumbroso

**whinny** /'wɪni/ n relincho, hin, m, vi relinchar

**whip** /wɪp/ vt azotar; pegar; Cul. batir; Sew. sobrecoser; (ropes, etc.) ligar; (defeat) vencer. —vi moverse rápidamente. **to w. down,** vi bajar volando, bajar corriendo. —vt arrebatar (de). **to w. in,** entrar precipitadamente (en), penetrar apresuradamente (en). **to w. off,** cazar a latigazos, despachar a golpes; (remove) quitar rápidamente; (persons) llevar corriendo, llevar aprisa. **to w. open,** abrir rápidamente. **to w. out,** vt (draw) sacar rápidamente; (utter) saltar diciendo (que); proferir. —vi escabullirse, escaparse, salir apresuradamente. **to w. round,** volverse de repente. **to w. up,** vt (horses, etc.) avivar con el látigo;

(snatch) coger de repente agarrar; (gather) reunir. —*vi* (mount) subir corriendo

**whip** /wɪp/ *n* azote, zurriago, *m;* (riding) látigo, *m.* **blow with a w.,** latigazo, *m.* **to have the w.-hand,** mandar, tener la sartén por el mango; tener la ventaja. **w.-cord,** tralla del látigo, *f*

**whippet** /'wɪpɪt/ *n* especie de perro (-rra) lebrero (-ra)

**whipping** /'wɪpɪŋ/ *n* paliza, *f,* vapuleo, azotamiento, *m.* **w. post,** picota, *f.* **w. top,** trompo, *m,* peonza, *f*

**whirl** /wɜrl/ *n* vuelta, *f,* giro, *m;* rotación, *f; Fig.* torbellino, *m.* —*vi* girar; dar vueltas; (dance) bailar, danzar. —*vt* hacer girar; dar vueltas (a); (carry) llevar rápidamente. **to w. along,** volar (por), pasar aprisa (por); dejar atrás los vientos, correr velozmente. **to w. past,** pasar volando (por); pasar como una exhalación. **to w. through,** atravesar rápidamente, cruzar volando

**whirligig** /'wɜrlɪ,gɪg/ *n* perinola, *f;* (merry-go-round) tiovivo, *m*

**whirlpool** /'wɜrl,pul/ *n* vórtice, remolino, *m; Fig.* vorágine, *f*

**whirlwind** /'wɜrl,wɪnd/ *n* torbellino, *m,* manga de viento, *f*

**whirr** /wɜr/ *n* zumbido, *m;* (of wings) ruido (de las alas), *m.* —*vi* girar; zumbar

**whirring** /'wɜrɪŋ/ *n* zumbido, *m;* ruido, *m.* —*a* que gira; que zumba

**whisk** /wɪsk/ *n* cepillo, *m; Cul.* batidor, *m;* (movement) movimiento rápido, *m.* —*vt Cul.* batir; (wag) menear, mover rápidamente; (with off, away) quitar rápidamente; sacudirse; arrebatar; (take away a person) llevarse (a). —*vi* moverse rápidamente; andar rápidamente

**whiskered** /'wɪskərd/ *a* bigotudo

**whiskers** /'wɪskərz/ *n pl* mostacho, *m,* patillas, barbas, *f pl;* (of a feline) bigotes, *m pl*

**whisky** /'wɪs-/ *n* güisqui, *m*

**whisper** /'wɪspər/ *n* cuchicheo, *m;* (rumour) voz, *f;* (of leaves, etc.) susurro, murmullo, *m.* —*vi* and *vt* cuchichear, hablar al oído; (of leaves, etc.) susurrar; (of rumors) murmurar. **in a w.,** al oído, en un susurro

**whisperer** /'wɪspərərsol/ *n* cuchicheador (-ra); (gossip) murmurador (-ra)

**whispering** /'wɪspərɪŋ/ *n* cuchicheo, *m;* susurro, *m;* (gossip) murmurio, *m.* **w. gallery,** galería de los murmullos, *f. Inf.* sala de los secretos, *f*

**whistle** /'wɪsəl/ *n* (sound) silbido, silbo, *m;* (instrument) pito, silbato, *m; Inf.* gaznate, *m.* —*vi* and *vt* silbar. **blast on the w.,** pitido, *m.* **to w. for,** llamar silbando; *Inf.* esperar sentado, buscar en vano

**whistler** /'wɪslər/ *n* silbador (-ra)

**whistling** /'wɪslɪŋ/ *n* silbido, *m, a* silbador

**whit** /wɪt/ *n* pizca, *f,* bledo, *m.* **not a w.,** ni pizca

**white** /waɪt/ *a* blanco; pálido; puro. —*n* color blanco, blanco, *m;* (pigment) pintura blanca, *f;* (whiteness) blancura, *f;* (of egg) clara (del huevo), *f;* (person) blanco, *m.* **Elizabeth went w.,** Isabel se puso pálida. **the w.,** (billiards) la blanca. **the w. of the eye,** lo blanco del ojo. **w. ant,** hormiga blanca, termita, *f.* **w. cabbage,** repollo, *m.* **w. caps,** (of waves) cabrillas, *f pl;* (of mountains) picos blancos, *m pl.* **w. clover,** trébol blanco, *m.* **w. corpuscle,** glóbulo blanco, *m.* **w. currant,** grosella blanca, *f.* **w. elephant,** elefante (-ta) blanco (-ca). **w. ensign,** pabellón blanco, *m.* **w.-faced,** de cara pálida. **w. fish,** pescado blanco, *m.* **w. flag,** bandera blanca, *f.* **w.-haired,** de pelo blanco. **w. heat,** calor blanco, *m,* candencia, *f;* ardor, *m.* **w. horses,** cabrillas, palomas, *f pl.* **w.-hot,** incandescente. **W. House, the,** la Casa Blanca, *f.* **w. lead,** albayalde, *m.* **w. lie,** mentira inocente, mentira oficiosa, mentira piadosa, la mentirilla, *f.* **w. man,** blanco, hombre de raza blanca, *m.* **the white man's burden,** la misión sagrada de la civilización blanca, *f.* **w. meat,** carne blanca, pechuga, *f.* **w. paper,** libro blanco, *m.* **w. sauce,** salsa blanca, *f.* **w. slave,** víctima de la trata de blancas, *f.* **w. slavery,** trata de blancas, *f.* **w. sugar,** azúcar blanco, azúcar de flor, *m.* **w. woman,** mujer de raza blanca, *f*

**whiten** /'waɪtn/ *vt* blanquear. —*vi* blanquearse

**whiteness** /'waɪtnɪs/ *n* blancura, *f;* palidez, *f;* pureza, *f; Poet.* nieve, *f*

**whitening** /'waɪtnɪŋ/ *n* blanqueo, *m;* blanco de España, *m;* blanco para los zapatos, *m*

**whitewash** /'waɪt,wɒʃ/ *vt* blanquear, jalbegar, encalar; (*Fig.* of faults) disculpar, justificar

**whitewashing** /'waɪt,wɒʃɪŋ/ *n* blanqueo, *m,* encaladura, *f*

**whither** /'wɪðər/ *adv* (interrogative) adónde; (with a clause) adonde

**whithersoever** /,wɪðərsou'ɛvər/ *adv* adondequiera

**whiting** /'waɪtɪŋ/ *n* blanco de España, *m;* blanco para los zapatos, *m;* (fish) pescadilla, *f,* merlango, *m*

**whitish** /'waɪtɪʃ/ *a* blanquecino

**whitlow** /'wɪtlou/ *n* panadizo, *m*

**Whitsun** /'wɪtsən/ *a* de Pentecostés.

**Whitsunday** /'wɪt'sʌndeɪ/ *n* domingo de Pentecostés, *m*

**Whitsuntide** /'wɪtsən,taɪd/ *n* pascua de Pentecostés, *f*

**whittle** /'wɪtl/ *n* navaja, *f.* —*vt* cercenar, cortar; (sharpen) afilar, sacar punta (a); tallar; *Fig.* reducir. **to w. away, down,** *Fig.* reducir a nada

**whizz** /wɪz/ *n* silbido, zumbido, *m,* vi silbar, zumbar

**whizzing** /'wɪzɪŋ/ *n* silbido, *m, a* que zumba

**who** /hu/ *pron* (interrogative) quién, *mf;* quiénes, *mf pl;* (relative) quien, *mf;* quienes, *mf pl;* que; (in elliptical constructions the person that, etc.) el que, *m;* la que, *f;* los que, *m pl;* las que, *f pl*

**whoa** /wou/ *interj* ¡so!

**whoever** /hu'ɛvər/ *pron* quienquiera (que); cualquiera (que); quien.

**whole** /houl/ *a* (healthy) sano; (uninjured) ileso, entero; todo. —*n* todo, *m;* total, *m;* totalidad, *f;* conjunto, *m.* **on the w.,** por regla general, en general; en conjunto. **the w. week,** la semana entera, toda la semana. **w.-hearted,** sincero, genuino; entusiasta. **w.-heartedly,** de todo corazón. **w.-heartedness,** sinceridad, *f;* entusiasmo, *m.* **w. length,** *a* de cuerpo entero. **w. number,** número entero, *m*

**wholemeal** /'houl'mil/ *n* harina de trigo entero, *f, a* de trigo entero

**wholeness** /'houlnɪs/ *n* totalidad, *f;* integridad, *f;* todo, *m*

**wholesale** /'houl,seɪl/ *a Com.* al por mayor; en grueso; *Fig.* general; en masa. —*n* venta al por mayor, *f.* **w. price,** precio al por mayor, *m.* **w. trade,** comercio al por mayor, *m*

**wholesaler** /'houl,seɪlər/ *n* comerciante al por mayor, *mf* mercader de grueso, *m*

**wholesome** /'houlsəm/ *a* sano; saludable; (edifying) edificante

**wholesomeness** /'houlsəmnɪs/ *n* sanidad, *f;* lo sano; lo saludable

**wholly** /'houli/ *adv* completamente, enteramente, totalmente; integralmente; del todo

**whom** /hum/ *pron* quien, a quien, *mf;* a quienes, *mf pl;* (interrogative) a quién, *mf;* a quiénes, *mf pl;* al que, *m;* la que, *f;* a los que, *m pl;* a las que, *f pl.* **from w.,** de quien; (interrogative) de quién. **the man w. you saw,** el hombre a quien viste

**whoop** /wup, wʊp/ *n* alarido, grito, *m;* estertor de la tos ferina, *m.* —*vi* dar gritos, chillar; /hup/ (whooping-cough) toser

**whooping cough** /'hupɪŋ/ *n* tos ferina, coqueluche, *f*

**whore** /hɔr/ *n* puta, ramera, *f*

**whorl** /wɜrl/ *n* (of a shell) espira, *f; Bot.* verticilo, *m;* (of a spindle) tortera, *f*

**whorled** /wɜrld, wɔrld/ *a Bot.* verticilado; (of shells) en espira

**whose** /huz/ *pron* cuyo, *m;* cuya, *f;* cuyos, *m pl;* cuyas, *f pl;* de quien, *mf;* de quienes, *mf pl;* (interrogative) de quién, *m;* de quiénes; **W. daughter is she?** ¿De quién es ella la hija? **This is the writer w. name I always forget,** Este es el autor cuyo nombre siempre olvido

**whosoever** /,husou'ɛvər/ *pron.* See **whoever**

**why** /waɪ/ *adv* (interrogative) por qué; (on account of which) por el cual, *m;* por la cual, *f;* por lo cual, *neut;* por los cuales, *m pl;* por las cuales, *f pl;* (how) cómo. —*n* ni porqué, *m,* interj ¡qué!; ¡cómo!; ¡vaya! si. **not to know the why or wherefore,** no saber ni el porqué ni el cómo, no saber ni el qué ni el por qué. **Why! I have just come,** ¡Si no hago más de llegar! **Why not?** ¿Por qué no? ¡Cómo no!

**wick** /wɪk/ n mecha, torcida, f

**wicked** /'wɪkɪd/ a malo; malvado, perverso; pecaminoso; malicioso; (mischievous) travieso

**wickedly** /'wɪkɪdli/ adv mal; perversamente; maliciosamente

**wickedness** /'wɪkɪdnɪs/ n maldad, f; perversidad, f; pecado, m; (mischievousness) travesura, f

**wicker** /'wɪkər/ n mimbre, m, a de mimbre

**wicket** /'wɪkɪt/ n postigo, portillo, m; (half-door) media puerta, f; (at cricket) meta, f. **w.-keeper,** guardameta, m

**wide** /waid/ a ancho; (in measurements) de ancho; vasto; extenso; grande; amplio; (loose) holgado; (distant) lejos; liberal; general, comprensivo. —adv lejos; completamente. **far and w.,** por todas partes. **to be too w.,** ser muy ancho; estar muy ancho; (of garments) venir muy ancho. **two feet w.,** dos pies de ancho. **w.-awake,** muy despierto; despabilado; vigilante. **w.-eyed,** con los ojos muy abiertos; asombrado. **w.-open,** abierto de par en par

**widely** /'waidli/ adv extensamente; generalmente; (very) muy

**widen** /'waidn̩/ vt ensanchar; extender. —vi ensancharse; extenderse

**widening** /'waidn̩ɪŋ/ n ensanche, m; extensión, f

**widespread** /'waid'sprɛd/ a universal, generalizado; extenso; esparcido. **to become w.,** generalizarse

**widow** /'widou/ n viuda, f. —vt dejar viuda; dejar viudo; Fig. privar. **to be a grass w.,** estar viuda. **to become a w.,** enviudar, perder al esposo. **widow's pension,** viudedad, f. **widow's weeds,** luto de viuda, m

**widowed** /'widoud/ a viudo

**widower** /'widouər/ n viudo, m. **to become a w.,** perder a la esposa, enviudar

**widowhood** /'widou‚hʊd/ n viudez, f

**width** /widθ/ n anchura, f; (of cloth) ancho, m; (of mind) liberalismo, m. **double w.,** (cloth) doble ancho, m

**wield** /wild/ vt (a scepter) empuñar; (power, etc.) ejercer; (a pen, sword) manejar

**wife** /waif/ n esposa, mujer, f; mujer, f; comadre, f. **husband and w.,** los cónyuges, los esposos. **old wives' tale,** cuento de viejas, m. **The Merry Wives of Windsor,** Las alegres comadres de Windsor. **to take to w.,** contraer matrimonio con, tomar como esposa (a)

**wifely** /'waifli/ a de esposa, de mujer casada; de mujer de su casa; conyugal

**wig** /wɪg/ n peluca, f; (hair) cabellera, f. **top wig,** peluquín, m. **wigmaker,** peluquero, m

**wigged** /wɪgd/ a con peluca, de peluca

**wigging** /'wɪgɪŋ/ n (scolding) peluca, f

**wigwam** /'wɪgwɒm/ n tienda de indios, f

**wild** /waild/ a (of animals, men, land) salvaje; (barren) desierto, yermo; (mountainous) riscoso, montañoso; (of plants, birds) silvestre; montés; (disarranged) en desorden, desarreglado; (complete) absoluto, completo; (dissipated) disipado, vicioso; (foolish) alocado; (of the sea) bravío; (of weather, etc.) borrascoso; (mad with delight, etc.) loco; (frantic, mad) frenético, loco; (with 'talk,' etc.) extravagante; insensato, desatinado; (shy) arisco; (incoherent) inconexo, incoherente; (frightened) alarmado, espantado; (wilful) travieso, indomable. —n tierra virgen, f; desierto, m; soledad, f. **It made me w.,** (angry) Me hizo rabiar. **to run w.,** volver al estado silvestre; (of persons) llevar una vida de salvajes; volverse loco. **to shoot w.,** errar el tiro. **to spread like w. fire,** propagarse como el fuego. **w. beast,** fiera, f. **w. boar,** jabalí, m. **w. cat,** gato montés, m. **w. duck,** pato silvestre, m. **w. goat,** cabra montesa, f. **w.-goose chase,** caza infructuosa, f; empresa quimérica, f. **w. oats,** avenas locas, f pl; Fig. indiscreciones de la juventud, f pl. **to sow one's w. oats,** andarse a la flor del berro

**wilderness** /'wɪldərnɪs/ n desierto, m; yermo, páramo, despoblado, m; soledad, f; (jungle) selva, f; (maze) laberinto, m; infinidad, f

**wildly** /'waildli/ adv en un estado salvaje; sin cultivo;

(rashly) desatinadamente; sin reflexión, sin pensar; (incoherently) incoherentemente; (stupidly, of looking, etc.) tontamente; (in panic) con ojos espantados, con terror en los ojos, alarmado

**wildness** /'waildnɪs/ n salvajez, f; estado silvestre, m; naturaleza silvestre, f; (ferocity) ferocidad, f; (of the wind, sea) braveza, f; (of the wind) violencia, f; (impetuosity) impetuosidad, f; (of statements, etc.) extravagancia, f; (incoherence) incoherencia, f; (disorder) desorden, m; (wilfulness, of children) travesuras, f pl; (of the expression) gesto espantado, m

**wile** /wail/ n estratagema, f, engaño, m, ardid, f

**wilily** /'wailɪli/ adv astutamente

**wiliness** /'wailɪnɪs/ n astucia, f

**will** /wɪl/ n voluntad, f; albedrío, m; (wish) deseo, m; (pleasure) discreción, f, placer, m; (legal document) testamento, m. **against my w.,** contra mi voluntad. **at w.,** a voluntad; a gusto; a discreción. **free w.,** libre albedrío, m. **of one's own free w.,** por su propia voluntad. **iron w.,** voluntad de hierro, f. **last w. and testament,** última disposición, última voluntad, f. **to do with a w.,** hacer con toda el alma, hacer con entusiasmo. **to make one's w.,** otorgar (hacer) su testamento. **w.-power,** fuerza de voluntad, f

**will** /wɪl/ vt querer; disponer, ordenar; (bequeath) legar, dejar en testamento, mandar; (oblige) sugestionar (a una persona) para que haga algo; hipnotizar. —vi aux querer; (As a sign of the future it is not translated separately in Spanish) **I w. come tomorrow,** Vendré mañana. **John does not approve, but I w. go,** Juan no lo aprueba pero yo quiero ir. **Do what you w.,** Haga lo que a Vd. le parezca bien, Haga lo que Vd. quiera; Haga lo que haga. **Boys w. be boys,** Los niños son siempre niños. **He w. not ( won't) do it,** No lo hará; No quiere hacerlo

**willful** /'wɪlfəl/ a rebelde, voluntarioso; (of children) travieso; (of crimes, etc.) premeditado

**willfully** /'wɪlfəli/ adv voluntariosamente; intencionadamente; (of committing crimes) con premeditación

**willfulness** /'wɪlfəlnɪs/ n rebeldía, f; (obstinacy) terquedad, obstinación, f

**William the Silent** /'wɪlyəm/ Guillermo el Taciturno

**willing** /'wɪlɪŋ/ a dispuesto, inclinado; (serviceable) servicial; deseoso; espontáneo; complaciente; gustoso; (willingly) de buena gana. **to be w.,** estar dispuesto (a), querer; consentir (en)

**willingly** /'wɪlɪŋli/ adv de buena gana, con gusto

**willingness** /'wɪlɪŋnɪs/ n buena voluntad, f; deseo de servir, m; complacencia, f; (consent) consentimiento, m

**will-o'-the-wisp** /'wɪləðə'wɪsp/ n fuego fatuo, m

**willow** /'wɪlou/ n sauce, m. **weeping w.,** sauce llorón, m. **w.-pattern china,** porcelana de estilo chino, f. **w. tree,** sauce, m

**willowy** /'wɪloui/ a lleno de sauces; (slim) cimbreño, esbelto, alto y delgado

**willy nilly** /'wɪli 'nɪli/ adv de buen o mal grado, mal que bien

**wilt** /wɪlt/ vi (of plants) marchitarse, secarse; Fig. languidecer; ajarse. —vt marchitar; Fig. ajar; hacer languidecer

**wily** /'waili/ a astuto, chuzón

**wimple** /'wɪmpəl/ n toca, f

**win** /wɪn/ vt ganar; (reach) alcanzar, lograr; (a victory, etc.) llevarse; conquistar. —vi ganar; triunfar. —n triunfo, m. **to win back,** volver a ganar; recobrar

**wince** /wɪns/ vi retroceder, recular; (flinch) quejarse; (of a horse) respingar. —n respingo, m. **without wincing,** sin quejarse; estoicamente

**winch** /wɪntʃ/ n cabria, f; (handle) manubrio, m

**wind** /wɪnd/ n viento, m; aire, m; (flatulence) flatulencia, f; (breath) respiración, f; aliento, m; (idle talk) paja, f. **breath of w.,** soplo de viento, m. **following w.,** viento en popa, m. **high w.,** viento alto, viento fuerte, m. **land w.,** viento terrenal, m. **It's an ill w. that blows nobody good,** No hay mal que por bien no venga. **There is something in the w.,** Hay algo en el aire, Se trama algo. **to get w. of,** husmear. **to sail before the w.,** navegar de viento en popa. **The w. stiffened,** Refrescó el viento. **You took the w. out of his sails,** Le deshinchaste las velas. **w.-instrument,** instrumento de viento, m. **w.-proof,** a prueba del viento. **w.-swept,** expuesto a todos los vientos. **w. storm,** ventarrón, *m*

**wind** /waind/ *vi* serpentear; desfilar lentamente; torcerse. —*vt* (turn) dar vueltas (a); (a handle) manejar, mover; (a watch) dar cuerda (a); (wool, etc.) devanar, ovillar; (wrap) envolver; (of arms, embrace) rodear (con); (a horn) tocar. **to w. off,** devanar; desenrollar. **to w. round,** (wrap) envolver; (skirt) rodear; (embrace) ceñir con (los brazos); (pass by) pasar por; deslizarse por; (of snakes) enroscarse. **to w. up,** (a watch) dar cuerda (a); (thread) devanar; (conclude) concluir; *Com.* liquidar; (excite) agitar, emocionar

**windbag** /'wind,bæg/ *n* pandero, *m,* sacamuelas, *mf*

**winder** /'waindər/ *n* (person) devanador (-ra); (machine) devanadera, *f;* (of a clock) llave, *f*

**windfall** /'wind,fɔl/ *n* fruta caída del árbol, *f;* (good luck) breva, *f;* ganancia inesperada, lotería, *f*

**windiness** /'windinis/ *n* tiempo ventoso, *m;* situación expuesta a todos los vientos, *f;* (of speech) pomposidad, verbosidad, *f*

**winding** /'waindiŋ/ *a* tortuoso; (e.g., road) sinuoso; serpentino; en espiral. —*n* tortuosidad, *f;* meandro, recoveco, *m,* vuelta, curva, *f.* **w. sheet,** mortaja, *f,* sudario, *m.* **w. stair,** escalera de caracol, *f.* **w.-up,** conclusión, *f; Com.* liquidación, *f*

**windlass** /'windləs/ *n* torno, *m*

**windless** /'windlis/ *a* sin viento

**windmill** /'wind,mil/ *n* molino de viento, *m*

**window** /'windou/ *n* ventana, *f;* (of a shop) escaparate, *m;* (in a train, car, bank, etc.) ventanilla, *f;* (booking office) taquilla, *f;* (of a church) vidriera, *f.* **casement w.,** ventana, *f.* **sash w.,** ventana de guillotina, *f.* **small w.,** ventanilla, *f.* **stained glass w.,** vidriera, *f.* **to lean out of the w.,** asomarse a la ventana. **to look out of the w.,** mirar por la ventana. **w. blind,** (Venetian) persiana, *f;* transparente, *m;* (against the sun) toldo, *m.* **w.-dresser,** decorador (-ra) de escaparates, *m.* **w. frame,** marco de ventana, *m.* **w.-pane,** cristal (de ventana), *m.* **w.-shutter,** contraventana, *f.* **w.-sill,** repisa de la ventana, *f,* alféizar, *m*

**windpipe** /'wind,paip/ *n* tráquea, *f*

**windscreen** /'wind,skrin/ *n* parabrisas, guardabrisa, *m.* **w.-wiper,** limpiaparabrisas, limpiavidrios, *m*

**windward** /'windwərd/ *n* barlovento, *m.* —*a* de barlovento. —*adv* a barlovento

**windy** /'windi/ *a* ventoso; expuesto al viento; (of style) hinchado, pomposo. **It is w.,** Hace viento

**wine** /wain/ *n* vino, *m;* zumo fermentado (de algunas frutas), *m.* —*a* de vino; de vinos; para vino. **in w.,** *Cul.* en vino; (drunk) ebrio, borracho. **heavy w.,** vino fuerte, *m.* **light w.,** vino ligero, *m.* **local w.,** vino del país, *m,* **matured w.,** vino generoso, *m.* **red w.,** vino tinto, *m.* **thin w.,** vinillo, *m.* **white w.,** vino blanco, *m.* **w.-cellar,** bodega, cueva, *f.* **w.-colored,** de color de vino. **w.-cooler,** cubo para enfriar vinos, *m.* **w. country,** tierra de vino, *f.* **w. decanter,** garrafa para vino, *f.* **w.-grower,** vinicultor (-ra). **w.-growing,** *n* vinicultura, *f.* —*a* vinícola. **w. lees,** zupia, *f.* **w. merchant,** comerciante en vinos, *mf.* **w. press,** lagar, *m.* **w.-taster,** catavinos, *m.* **w. waiter,** bodeguero, *m*

**wineskin** /'wain,skin/ *n* bota, *f,* odre, pellejo, *m*

**wing** /wiŋ/ *n* (of a bird and *Zool. Archit. Aer. Mil. Bot.*) ala, *f;* (flight) vuelo, *m; Theat.* bastidor, *m; Fig.* protección, *f.* —*vt* dar alas (a); llevar sobre las alas; (wound) herir en el ala; herir en el brazo; volar por. —*vi* volar. **beating of wings,** batir de alas, aleteo, *m.* **in the wings,** *Theat.* entre bastidores. **on the w.,** al vuelo. **to clip a** ( **person's) wings,** cortar (*or* quebrar) las alas (a). **under his w.,** bajo su protección. **w.-case,** élitro (de un insecto), *m.* **w. chair,** sillón con orejas, *m.* **w.-commander,** teniente coronel de aviación, *m.* **w.-span,** (*Zool.* and *Aer.*) envergadura, *f.* **w.-spread,** extensión del ala, *f.* **w.-tip,** punta del ala, *f*

**winged** /wiŋd/ *esp. Literary* 'wiŋid/ *a* alado, con alas; (in compounds) de alas...; (swift) alado; (of style) elevado, alado

**wink** /wiŋk/ *vi* (blink) pestañear; (as a signal, etc.) guiñar; (of stars, etc.) titilar, parpadear, centellear. —*vt* guiñar (el ojo). —*n* pestañeo, *m;* guiño, *m.* **not**

**to sleep a w.,** no pegar los ojos. **to take forty winks,** echar una siesta. **to w. at,** guiñar el ojo (a); (ignore) hacer la vista gorda

**winking** /'wiŋkiŋ/ *n* (blinking) parpadeo, *m;* (as a signal) guiños, *m pl;* (of stars, etc.) titilación, *f,* pestañeo, *m.* —*a* (of stars, etc.) titilante. **like w.,** en un abrir y cerrar de ojos.

**winner** /'winər/ *n* ganador (-ra); vencedor (-ra)

**winning** /'winiŋ/ *a* ganador; vencedor; (attractive) encantador. —*n* ganancia, *f.* **w. number,** número galardonado, número premiado, número vencedor, *m.* **w.-post,** meta, *f.* **w. side,** *Sports.* equipo vencedor, *m;* (politics, etc.) partido vencedor, *m*

**winnings** /'winiŋz/ *n* ganancias, *f pl*

**winnow** /'winou/ *vt* aventar, abalear; *Fig.* separar

**winnower** /'winouər/ *n* aventador (-ra)

**winnowing** /'winouiŋ/ *n* abaleo, aventamiento, *m; Fig.* separación, *f.* **w. fork,** bieldo, *m.* **w. machine,** aventador mecánico, *m*

**winsome** /'winsəm/ *a* sandunguero; dulce, encantador

**winsomeness** /'winsəmnis/ *n* sandunga, *f;* encanto, *m,* dulzura, *f*

**winter** /'wintər/ *n* invierno, *m.* —*a* de invierno; hiemal. —*vi* pasar el invierno, invernar. —*vt* (of cattle, etc.) guardar en invierno. **in w.,** en invierno, durante el invierno. **w. clothes,** ropa de invierno, *f.* **w. palace,** palacio de invierno, *m.* **w. quarters,** invernadero, *m.* **w. season,** invierno, *m;* temporada de invierno, *f.* **w. sleep,** invernada, *f.* **w. solstice,** solsticio hiemal, *m.* **w. sports,** deportes de nieve, *m pl.* **w. wheat,** trigo de invierno, *m*

**wintry** /'wintri/ *a* de invierno; invernal; (of a smile, etc.) glacial

**wipe** /waip/ *vt* limpiar; (rub) frotar; (dry) secar; (remove) quitar. —*n* limpión, *m;* (blow) golpe de lado, *m.* **to w. one's eyes,** enjugarse las lágrimas. **to w. off, out,** limpiar; (remove) quitar; (erase) borrar; (kill) destruir completamente, exterminar; (a military force) destrozar; (a debt) cancelar

**wire** /waiᵊr/ *n* alambre, *m;* hilo metálico, *m;* telégrafo (eléctrico), *m; Inf.* telegrama, *m.* —*vt* atar con alambre; (fence) alambrar; (snare) coger con lazo de alambre; (of electrical equipment, etc.) instalar; (telegraph) telegrafiar. —*vi* (telegraph) telegrafiar. **barbed w.,** alambre espinoso, *m.* **live w.,** alambre cargado (de electricidad), *m;* (person) fuerza viva, *f.* **w.-cutters,** cortaalambres, *m pl.* **w.-entanglement,** *Mil.* alambrada, *f.* **w. fence,** alambrera, *f,* cercado de alambre, *m.* **w. gauze,** tela metálica, *f.* **w. nail,** punta de París, *f.* **w.-netting,** malla de alambre, *f;* alambrado, *m.* **w.-pulling,** influencias secretas, *f pl;* intrigas políticas, *f pl*

**wiredraw** /'waiᵊr,drɔ/ *vt* estirar (alambre), tirar (el hilo de hierro, plata, etc.); (arguments, etc.) sutilizar

**wiredrawer** /'waiᵊr,drɔər/ *n* estirador, *m*

**wiredrawing** /'waiᵊr,drɔiŋ/ *n* tirado, *m; Fig.* sutileza, *f*

**wireless** /'waiᵊrlis/ *a* sin hilos; (of a message) radiotelegráfico; por radio. —*n* telegrafía sin hilos, *f;* radiotelefonía, *f;* (telegram) radiocomunicación, *f;* (broadcasting) radio, *f.* —*vt* radiotelegrafiar. **Let's listen to the w.,** Vamos a escuchar la radio. **portable w.,** radio portátil, *f.* **w. engineer,** ingeniero radiotelegrafista, *m.* **w. enthusiast,** radioaficionado (-da). **w. licence,** permiso de radiorreceptor, *m.* **w. operator,** radiotelegrafista, *mf.* **w. room,** cuarto de telegrafía sin hilos, *m.* **w. set,** aparato de radio, *m.* **w. station,** estación de radiotelegrafía, *f;* (broadcasting) radioemisora, *f.* **w. telegraph,** telégrafo sin hilos, *m.* **w. telegraphy,** telegrafía sin hilos, radiografía, *f.* **w. telephony,** telefonía sin hilos, *f.* **w. transmission,** radioemisión, *f*

**wiretap** /'waiᵊr,tæp/ *vi* poner escucha. —*vt* poner escucha a

**wiring** /'waiᵊriŋ/ *n* instalación de alambres eléctricos, *f*

**wiry** /'waiᵊri/ *a* semejante a un alambre; (of persons) nervudo

**wisdom** /'wizdəm/ *n* sabiduría, *f;* (learning) saber, *m;* (judgment) juicio, *m.* **Book of W.,** Libro de la Sabiduría, *m.* **w.-tooth,** muela del juicio, *f*

**wise** /waiz/ *a* sabio; juicioso, prudente; (informed) enterado, noticioso. **a w. man,** un sabio. **in no w.,** de ningún modo. **the W. Men of the East,** los magos. **w. guy,** *Inf.* toro corrido, *m*
**wisely** /'waizli/ *adv* sabiamente; prudentemente, con prudencia
**wish** /wiʃ/ *n* deseo, *m*. **Best wishes for the New Year,** Los mejores deseos para el Año Nuevo. **w.-bone,** espoleta, *f*
**wish** /wiʃ/ *vt* querer; desear; ansiar; (with "good morning", etc.) dar. **I w. he were here!** ¡Ojalá que estuviera aquí! **Theresa wishes us to go,** Teresa quiere que vayamos. **I w. it had happened otherwise,** Quisiera que las cosas hubiesen pasado de otra manera. **I w. you would make less noise,** Me gustaría que hicieses menos ruido. **I only w. one thing,** Solamente deseo una cosa. **I w. you good luck,** Te deseo mucha suerte. **I wished him a merry Christmas,** Le deseé unas Pascuas muy felices, Le felicité las Pascuas. **to w. a prosperous New Year,** desear un próspero Año Nuevo. **to w. good-by,** despedirse (de). **to w. good day,** dar los buenos días. **to w. for,** desear
**wisher** /'wiʃər/ *n* el que, *m*, (*f*, la que) desea, deseador (-ra)
**wishful** /'wiʃfəl/ *a* deseoso; ansioso; ávido. **w. thinking,** ilusiones, *f pl*; optimismo injustificado, optimismo exagerado, *m*
**wisp** /wisp/ *n* mechón, *m;* jirón, *m;* trozo, pedazo, *m*
**wistaria** /wi'stɪəriə, -'stɛər-/ *n* vistaria, *f*
**wistful** /'wistfəl/ *a* ansioso; triste; patético; (envious) envidioso; (regretful) de pesar; (remorseful) de remordimiento; (thoughtful) pensativo
**wistfully** /'wistfəli/ *adv* con ansia; tristemente; patéticamente; con envidia; con pesar; con remordimiento; pensativo
**wistfulness** /'wistfəlnɪs/ *n* ansia, *f;* tristeza, *f;* (envy) envidia, *f;* (regret) pesar, *m;* (remorse) remordimiento, *m;* (thoughtfulness) lo pensativo, lo distraído
**wit** /wit/ *n* (reason) juicio, *m;* agudeza, gracia, *f,* rasgo de ingenio, *m;* ingenio, *m;* inteligencia, *f,* talento, *m;* (person) hombre de ingenio, *m;* mujer de ingenio, *f.* **my five wits,** mis cinco sentidos. **to be at one's wits' end,** no saber qué hacer. **to live by one's wits,** ser caballero de industria. **to lose one's wits,** perder el juicio
**witch** /witʃ/ *n* bruja, *f.* **witches' sabbath,** aquelarre, *m.* **w.-doctor,** hechicador, mago, *m.* **witch-hazel,** carpe, *m;* loción de carpe, *f*
**witchcraft** /'witʃ,kræft/ *n* brujería, *f;* sortilegio, encantamiento, *m*
**witchery** /'witʃəri/ *n* brujería, *f; Fig.* encanto, *m,* magia, *f*
**with** /wiθ, wið/ *prep* con; en compañia de; en casa de; (against) contra; (among) entre; en; (by) por; (towards) hacia; para con; (according to) según; (notwithstanding) a pesar de; a; (concerning) con respecto a; en el caso de. **Rose is w. Antony,** Rosa está con Antonio. **He was w. his dog,** Estaba acompañado por su perro. **He pulled at it w. both hands,** Lo tiró con las dos manos. **filled w. fear,** lleno de miedo. **to shiver w. cold,** temblarse de frío. **the girl w. golden hair,** la muchacha del pelo dorado. **They killed it w. one blow,** Lo mataron de un solo golpe. **It rests w. you to decide,** Tú tienes que decidirlo; Te toca a tí decidirlo. **to begin w.,** para empezar; *v* empezar por. **w. all speed,** a toda prisa. **to part w.,** desprenderse de; (of people) despedirse de; separarse de. **w. that...,** (at once) en esto... (disease and poverty, etc.) **are still with us,** están todavía en el mundo
**withal** /wɪð'ɔl, wɪθ-/ *adv* además; al mismo tiempo. —*prep* con
**withdraw** /wɪð'drɔ, wɪθ-/ *vt* retirar; (words) retractar; (remove) quitar, privar (de); (a legal action) apartar. —*vi* retirarse; retroceder; apartarse; irse
**withdrawal** /wɪð'drɔəl, wɪθ-/ *n* retirada, *f;* (retirement) retiro, *m;* apartamiento, *m*
**withdrawn** /wɪð'drɔn, wɪθ-/ *a* (abstracted) ensimismado, meditabundo
**wither** /'wɪðər/ *vi* marchitarse, secarse, ajarse. —*vt*

marchitar, secar, ajar; *Fig.* hacer languidecer, matar; (snub) avergonzar
**withered** /'wɪðərd/ *a* marchito, mustio; muerto; (of persons) acartonado, seco
**witheredness** /'wɪðərdnɪs/ *n* marchitez, *f;* sequedad, *f*
**withering** /'wɪðərɪŋ/ *a* que marchita; (scorching) abrasador, ardiente; (scornful) despreciativo, desdeñoso; (biting) mordaz, cáustico
**withers** /'wɪðərz/ *n* cruz, *f*
**withhold** /wɪθ'hould, wɪð-/ *vt* retener; detener; (restrain) refrenar; apartar; (refuse) negar; abstenerse de; (refuse to reveal) ocultar
**withholding** /wɪθ'houldɪŋ, wɪð-/ *n* detención, *f;* (refusal) negación, *f*
**within** /wɪð'ɪn, wɪθ-/ *adv* dentro, adentro; en el interior; en casa; *Fig.* en su interior. **He stayed w.,** Se quedó dentro. **Is Mrs. González w.?** ¿Está en casa la Sra. González?
**within** /wɪð'ɪn, wɪθ-/ *prep* dentro de; el interior de; en; entre; (within range of) al alcance de; a la distancia de; (near) cerca de; a poco de; (of time) en el espacio de, en; dentro de; (almost) por poco, casi. **He was w. an inch of being killed,** Por poco le matan. **to be w. hearing,** estar al alcance de la voz. **seen from w.,** visto desde dentro. **twice w. a fortnight,** dos veces en quince días. **w. himself,** por sus adentros, entre sí. **w. an inch of,** *Fig.* a dos dedos de. **w. a few miles of Edinburgh,** a unas millas de Edimburgo. **w. a short distance,** en una corta distancia; a poca distancia
**without** /wɪð'aut, wɪθ-/ *prep* sin; falto de; (outside) fuera de; (beyond) más allá de. —*adv* exteriormente; por fuera; hacia afuera; fuera. **It goes w. saying,** No hay que decir. **w. more ado,** sin más ni más. **w. my knowledge,** sin que yo lo supiese. **w. regard for,** sin miramentos por. **w. saying more,** sin decir más. **without batting an eyelash,** sin sobresaltos
**withstand** /wɪθ'stænd, wɪð-/ *vt* resistir, oponerse (a); soportar
**withstanding** /wɪθ'stændɪŋ, wɪð-/ *n* resistencia, oposición (a), *f*
**witless** /'wɪtlɪs/ *a* sin seso, tonto, necio
**witness** /'wɪtnɪs/ *n* (evidence) testimonio, *m;* (person) testigo, *mf;* espectador (-ra). **in w. whereof,** en fe de lo cual. **to bear w.,** atestiguar; dar testimonio. **to bring forward witnesses,** hacer testigos. **w. my hand,** en fe de lo cual, firmo. **w.-box,** puesto de los testigos, *m.* **w. for the defence,** testigo de descargo, *mf.* **w. for the prosecution,** testigo de cargo, *mf*
**witness** /'wɪtnɪs/ *vt* (show) mostrar, señalar; (see) ser testigo de, ver, presenciar; *Law.* atestiguar. —*vi* dar testimonio; servir de testigo
**witticism** /'wɪtə,sɪzəm/ *n* rasgo de ingenio, donaire, *m,* agudeza, *f*
**wittily** /'wɪtli/ *adv* ingeniosamente, donairosamente, agudamente
**wittiness** /'wɪtnɪs/ *n* viveza de ingenio, donosura, *f*
**witty** /'wɪti/ *a* salado, gracioso. **w. sally,** agudeza, *f*
**wizard** /'wɪzərd/ *n* mago, hechicero, *m*
**wizardry** /'wɪzədri/ *n* magia, *f*
**wizened** /'wɪzənd/ *a* seco, arrugado; (of persons) acartonado
**wobble** /'wɒbəl/ *vi* tambalearse, balancearse; (quiver) temblar; oscilar; *Mech.* galopar; (stagger) titubear; *Fig.* vacilar
**wobbly** /'wɒbli/ *a* que se bambolea; inestable; *Fig.* vacilante
**woe** /wou/ *n* dolor, *m;* congoja, aflicción, *f;* mal, desastre, infortunio, *m.* **Woe is me!** ¡Ay de mí! ¡Desdichado de mí!
**woebegone** /'woubɪ,gɔn/ *a* angustiado
**woeful** /'woufəl/ *a* triste; doloroso; funesto
**woefully** /'woufəli/ *adv* tristemente; dolorosamente
**wolf** /wʊlf/ *n* lobo (-ba). **a w. in sheep's clothing,** un lobo en piel de cordero. **to cry w.,** gritar «el lobo!» **to keep the w. from the door,** ponerse a cubierto del hambre. **w.-cub,** lobezno, *m.* **w.-hound,** perro lobo, *m.* **w. pack,** manada de lobos, *f*
**wolfish** /'wʊlfɪʃ/ *a* lobuno, de lobo (-ba)
**wolfram** /'wʊlfrəm, 'vɒl-/ *n* volframio, *m*
**woman** /'wʊmən/ *n* mujer, *f;* hembra, *f;* (lady-in-

waiting) dama de servicio, *f.* **a fine figure of a w.,** una real hembra. **w. doctor,** médica, *f.* **w.-hater,** misógino, *m.* **w. of the town,** mujer de la vida airada, *f.* **w. of the world,** mujer de mundo, *f*

**womanhood** /'wʊmən,hʊd/ *n* feminidad, *f;* sexo feminino, *m*

**womanish** /'wʊmənɪʃ/ *a* afeminado

**womankind** /'wʊmən,kaɪnd/ *n* el sexo femenino, las mujeres

**womanliness** /'wʊmənlɪnɪs/ *n* feminidad, *f;* carácter femenino, *m*

**womanly** /'wʊmənli/ *a* femenino, de mujer

**womb** /wum/ *n* útero, *m,* matriz, *f; Fig.* seno, *m*

**women's dormitory** /'wɪmɪnz/ *n* residencia para señoritas, *f*

**wonder** /'wʌndər/ *n* maravilla, *f;* prodigio, *m;* portento, milagro, *m;* (surprise) sorpresa, *f;* admiración, *f;* asombro, *m;* (problem) enigma, *m;* misterio, *m.* —*vi* admirarse, asombrarse, maravillarse; sorprenderse. —*vt* (ask oneself) preguntarse; desear saber. **I wondered what the answer would be,** Me preguntaba qué sería la respuesta. **It is no w. that...,** No es mucho que..., No es sorprendente que... **It is one of the wonders of the world,** Es una de las maravillas del mundo. **to work wonders,** hacer milagros. **to w. at,** asombrarse de, maravillarse de; sorprenderse de. **w.-working,** milagroso

**wonderful** /'wʌndərfəl/ *a* maravilloso; magnífico; asombroso; *Inf.* estupendo

**wonderfully** /'wʌndərfli/ *adv* maravillosamente; admirablemente

**wondering** /'wʌndərɪŋ/ *a* de asombro, sorprendido; perplejo

**wonderingly** /'wʌndərɪŋli/ *adv* con asombro

**wonderland** /'wʌndər,lænd/ *n* mundo fantástico, *m;* reino de las hadas, *m;* país de las maravillas, *m.* **"Alice in W.,"** Alicia en el país de las maravillas

**wonderment** /'wʌndərmənt/ *n.* See **wonder**

**wondrous** /'wʌndrəs/ *a* maravilloso. —*adv* extraordinariamente

**wont** /wɔnt, wount/ *n* costumbre, *f.* —*vi* soler. **as he was w.,** Como solía

**won't** /wount/. See **will not**

**wonted** /'wɔntɪd, 'woun-/ *a* sólito, acostumbrado

**woo** /wu/ *vt* galantear; hacer la corte (a), solicitar amores a; cortejar; *Fig.* solicitar; perseguir

**wood** /wʊd/ *n* bosque, *m;* madera, *f;* (for the fire, etc.) leña, *f;* (cask) barril, *m.* —*a* de madera; (of the woods) selvático. **dead w.,** ramas muertas, *f pl; Fig.* paja, *f.* **w. alcohol,** alcohol metílico, *m.* **w.-anemone,** anémona de los bosques, *f.* **w.-block floor,** entarimado, *m.* **w.-borer,** xiló-fago, *m.* **w.-carver,** tallista, *mf* **w.-carving,** talla en madera, *f.* **w.-craft,** conocimiento del campo, *m.* **w.-cut,** grabado en madera, *m.* **w.-cutter,** leñador, *m.* **w.-engraver,** grabador (-ra) en madera. **w.-engraving,** grabado al boj, *m.* **w.-fibre,** fibra de madera, *f.* **w.-louse,** cochinilla, *f.* **w.-nymph,** ninfa de los bosques, *f.* **w.-pigeon,** paloma torcaz, *f.* **w.-pile,** pila de leña, leñera, *f.* **w.-pulp,** pulpa de madera, *f.* **w.-shaving,** acepilladura, *f.* **w.-splinter,** tasquil, *m,* astilla, *f.* **w.-wind,** *Mus.* madera, *f.* **w.-worm,** carcoma, *f*

**wooded** /'wʊdɪd/ *a* provisto de árboles, plantado de árboles, arbolado

**wooden** /'wʊdn/ *a* de madera; de palo; (of smiles) mecánico; (stiff) indiferente, sin emoción; (clumsy) torpe; (of character) inflexible. **He has a w. leg,** Tiene una pata de palo. **w. beam,** madero, *m;* viga de madera, *f.* **w. bridge,** pontón, *m.* **w. galley,** *Print.* galerín, *m*

**woodland** /*n.* 'wʊd,lænd/ *a* -lənd/ *n* bosques, *m pl.* —*a* de bosque; silvestre

**woodpecker** /'wʊd,pɛkər/ *n* pájaro carpintero, picamaderos, *m*

**woodshed** /'wʊd,ʃɛd/ *n* leñera, *f*

**woodwork** /'wʊd,wɜrk/ *n* maderaje, *m;* molduras, *f pl;* carpintería, *f*

**woody** /'wʊdi/ *a* leñoso; arbolado, con árboles. **w. tissue,** tejido leñoso, *m*

**wooer** /'wuər/ *n* pretendiente, galanteador, *m*

**woof** /wʊf/ *n* trama, *f*

**wooing** /'wuɪŋ/ *n* galanteo, *m*

**wool** /wʊl/ *n* lana, *f.* —*a* de lana; lanar. **to go w.-gathering,** estar distraído. **to pull the w. over a person's eyes,** engañar como a un chino. **w.-bearing,** lanar. **w.-carding,** cardadura de lana, *f.* **w.-growing,** cría de ganado lanar, *f.* **w. merchant,** comerciante en lanas, *mf,* lanero, *m.* **w.-pack,** fardo de lana, *m.* **w. trade,** comercio de lana, *m*

**woollen** /'wʊlən/ *a* de lana; lanar. —*n* paño de lana, *m;* género de punta de lana, *m*

**woolliness** /'wʊlɪnɪs/ *n* lanosidad, *f*

**woolly** /'wʊli/ *a* lanudo, lanoso; de lana; *Bot.* velloso; (of hair) lanoso, crespo. —*n* género de punta de lana, *m;* (sweater) jersey, *m*

**word** /wɜrd/ *n* palabra, *f; Gram.* vocablo, *m; Theol.* verbo, *m;* (maxim) sentencia, *f,* dicho, *m;* (message) recado, *m;* (news) aviso, *m,* noticias, *f pl;* (*Mil.* command) voz de mando, *f;* (order) orden, *f;* (password) contraseña, *f;* (term) término, *m.* —*vt* expresar; formular; (draw up) redactar; escribir. **He was as good as his w.,** Fue hombre de palabra. **I do not know how to w. this letter,** No sé cómo redactar esta carta. **in a w.,** en una palabra; en resumidas cuentas. **by w. of mouth,** de palabra. **I give you my w. for it,** Le doy mi palabra de honor. **in other words,** en otros términos; en efecto. **the W.** ( of God), el Verbo (de Dios). **to have a w. with,** hablar con; conversar con; entablar conversación con. **to leave w.,** dejar recado. **to have words with,** tener palabras con. **to keep one's w.,** cumplir su palabra

**word index** *n* índice de vocablos, *m*

**wordiness** /'wɜrdɪnɪs/ *n* palabrería, verbosidad, *f*

**wording** /'wɜrdɪŋ/ *n* fraseología, *f;* expresión, *f;* estilo, *m;* (terms) términos, *m pl;* (drawing up) redacción, *f*

**word processing** /'wɜrd ,prɒsɛsɪŋ/ *n* tratamiento de textos, procesamiento de textos, *m*

**wordy** /'wɜrdi/ *a* verboso, prolijo

**work** /wɜrk/ *n* trabajo, *m;* (sewing) labor, *f;* (literary, artistic production and theological) obra, *f;* (behavior) acción, *f,* acto, *m;* (employment) empleo, *m;* (business affairs) negocios, *m pl; pl* **works,** obras, fortificaciones, *f, pl;* obras públicas, *f pl;* construcciones, *f pl;* (of a machine) mecanismo, *m;* motor, *m;* (factory) fábrica, *f,* taller, *m.* **w. of art,** obra de arte. **w. accident,** accidente del trabajo, *m.* **w.-bag,** bolsa de costura, *f,* saco de labor, *m.* **w.-box,** (on legs) costurero, *m;* (small) neceser de costura, *m.* **w.-people,** obreros (-as). **w.-room,** taller, *m;* (study) estudio, *m;* (for sewing) cuarto de costura, *m.* **w.-table,** banco de taller, *m;* (for writing) mesa de escribir, *f*

**work** /wɜrk/ *vi* trabajar; *Sew.* hacer labor de aguja, coser; (embroider) bordar; *Mech.* funcionar, marchar; (succeed) tener éxito; ser eficaz; (be busy) estar ocupado; (be employed) tener empleo; (of the face) demudarse, torcerse; (ferment) fermentar; (operate) obrar *vt* trabajar; operar, hacer funcionar; mover; (control) manejar; (a mine) explotar; (embroider) bordar; (wood) tallar; (a problem) resolver; calcular; (iron, etc.) labrar; (the soil) cultivar; (a ship) maniobrar; (do) hacer; (bring about) efectuar; traer consigo; producir; (agitate oneself) agitarse, emocionarse, excitarse. **to w. in repoussé,** repujar. **to w. loose,** desprenderse. **to w. one's passage,** trabajar por el pasaje. **to w. overtime,** trabajar horas extraordinarias. **to w. two ways,** ser espada de dos filos. **to w. at,** trabajar en; ocuparse en; dedicarse a. **to w. in,** *vt* introducir; insinuar. —*vi* combinarse. **to w. into,** penetrar en. **to w. off,** usar, emplear; (get rid of) deshacerse de, librarse de. **to w. on, upon,** influir en; obrar sobre; estar ocupado en. **to w. out,** *vt* calcular; resolver; (a mine, topic, etc.) agotar; (develop) elaborar, desarrollar; trazar, planear; (find) encontrar. —*vi* llegar (a); resultar; venir a ser. **to w. up,** crear; (promote) fomentar; producir; (excite) agitar, excitar; (fashion) dar forma (a), labrar; (finish) terminar

**workable** /'wɜrkəbəl/ *a* laborable; factible, practicable; (of a mine) explotable

**workableness** /'wɜrkəbəlnɪs/ *n* practicabilidad, *f*

**workaday** /'wɜrkə,dei/ *a* de todos los días; prosaico

**workbench** /'wɜrk,bɛntʃ/ *n* banco de mecánico, *f,*

banco de taller, banco de trabajo, *m*, mesa de trabajo, *f*

**workday** /'wɜrk,dei/ *n* día de trabajo, día laborable, *m*

**worker** /'wɜrkər/ *n* trabajador (-ra); (manual) obrero (-ra); (of a machine) operario (-ia). **w.-ant,** hormiga obrera, *f.* **w.-bee,** abeja obrera, *f*

**workhouse** /'wɜrk,haus/ *n* asilo, *m*

**working** /'wɜrkɪŋ/ *a* de trabajo; (of capital) de explotación; trabajador, que trabaja; obrero. —*n* trabajo, *m;* (of a machine, organism, institution) funcionamiento, *m;* explotación, *f;* (of a mine) laboreo, *m;* (of a ship) maniobra, *f;* (of metal, stone, wood) labra, *f;* operación, *f;* (result) efecto, resultado, *m;* (calculation) cálculo, *m.* **"Not w.,"** «No funciona.» **to be in w. order,** funcionar bien. **w.-class,** clase obrera, *f;* pueblo, *m.* **w.-clothes,** ropa de trabajo, *f.* **w.-day,** día de trabajo, *m.* **w.-hours,** horas de trabajo, horas hábiles, *f pl.* **w. hypothesis,** postulado, *m.* **w.-man,** obrero, *m;* trabajador, *m.* **w.-out,** elaboración, *f;* ensayo, *m.* **w.-plan,** plan de trabajo, *m.* **w.-woman,** obrera, *f;* trabajadora, *f*

**workless** /'wɜrklɪs/ *a* sin trabajo

**workman** /'wɜrkmən/ *n* obrero, *m;* (agricultural) labrador, *m*

**workmanlike** /'wɜrkmən,laik/ *a* bien hecho, bien acabado; (clever) hábil

**workmanship** /'wɜrkmən,ʃɪp/ *n* trabajo, *m;* manufactura, *f;* hechura, *f;* (cleverness) habilidad, *f*

**works** /wɜrks/ *n* fábrica, *f*

**workshop** /'wɜrk,ʃɒp/ *n* taller, *m*

**world** /wɜrld/ *n* mundo, *m.* For all the w. as if..., Exactamente como si... **to see the w.,** ver mundo. **to treat the w. as one's oyster,** ponerse el mundo por montera. **w. without end,** por los siglos de los siglos. **w.-power,** potencia mundial, gran potencia, *f.* **w.-wide,** mundial, universal

**world almanac** *n* compendio mundial, *m*

**worldliness** /'wɜrldlinɪs/ *n* mundanería, *f,* conocimiento del mundo, *m;* frivolidad, vanidad mundana, *f;* egoísmo, *m;* prudencia, *f*

**worldly** /'wɜrldli/ *a* de este mundo; mundano; humano; profano; frívolo. **to be w.-wise,** tener mucho mundo

**worm** /wɜrm/ *n* gusano, *m;* lombriz, *f;* *Chem.* serpentín, *m;* (of a screw) tornillo sinfín, *m;* (person) gusano, *m;* *Fig.* gusano roedor, remordimiento, *m.* **intestinal w.,** lombriz intestinal, *f,* gusano de la conciencia. **w.-eaten,** carcomido. **w.-hole,** picadura de gusano, lombriguera, *f.* **w.-powder,** polvos antihelmínticos, *m pl.* **w.-shaped,** vermiforme

**worm** /wɜrm/ *vt* (a dog) dar un vermífugo (a). —*vi* arrastrarse como un gusano. **to w. one's way into,** deslizarse en; *Fig.* insinuarse en, introducirse en. **to w. out,** (secrets, information) sonsacar

**wormwood** /'wɜrm,wʊd/ *n* ajenjo, *m*

**wormy** /'wɜrmi/ *a* gusanoso, lleno de gusanos

**worn** /wɔrn/ *a* (of garments) raído; estropeado; gastado; (of paths) trillado; (of the face) arrugado; cansado. **w. out,** acabado; muy usado; (tired) rendido; (exhausted) agotado

**worrier** /'wɜriər/ *n* inquietador (-ra); receloso (-sa); aprensivo (-va)

**worry** /'wɜri/ *n* preocupación, inquietud, ansiedad, *f;* problema, cuidado, *m.* —*vt* (prey) zamarrear; preocupar, inquietar; molestar; importunar. —*vi* estar ocupado, estar intranquilo, inquietarse. **Don't worry,** Pierda cuidado, No pase cuidado

**worrying** /'wɜriɪŋ/ *a* inquietante, perturbador; molesto

**worse** /wɜrs/ *a compar* peor; inferior. —*adv* peor; menos. —*n* lo peor. **so much the w.,** tanto peor. **to be w. off,** estar peor; estar en peores circunstancias; ser menos feliz. **to be the w. for wear,** ser muy usado; estar ajado; ser ya viejo. **to grow w.,** empeorarse; (of an ill person) ponerse peor. **w. and w.,** de mal en peor, peor que peor. **w. than ever,** peor que nunca

**worsen** /'wɜrsən/ *vt* agravar, hacer peor; exasperar. —*vi* agravarse, empeorarse; exasperarse

**worsening** /'wɜrsənɪŋ/ *n* agravación, *f,* empeoramiento, *m;* exasperación, *f*

**worship** /'wɜrʃɪp/ *n* culto, *m;* adoración, *f;* veneración, *f.* —*vt* adorar; reverenciar. —*vi* adorar; rezar; dar culto (a). **place of w.,** edificio de culto, *m.* **Your W.,** vuestra merced

**worshipful** /'wɜrʃɪpfəl/ *a* venerable, respetable

**worshipper** /'wɜrʃɪpər/ *n* adorador (-ra); *pl* **worshippers,** (in a church, etc.) fieles, *m pl,* congregación, *f*

**worshipping** /'wɜrʃɪpɪŋ/ *n* adoración, *f,* culto, *m*

**worst** /wɜrst/ *a* el (la, etc.) peor; más malo. —*adv* el (la, etc.) peor. —*n* el (la, etc.) peor; lo peor. —*vt* vencer, derrotar; triunfar sobre **If the w. comes to the w.,** En el peor de los casos. **The w. of it is that...,** Lo peor es que... **to have the w. of it,** salir perdiendo, llevar la peor parte

**worsted** /'wʊstɪd, 'wɜrstɪd/ *n* estambre, *m, a* de estambre

**worth** /wɜrθ/ *n* valor, *m;* precio, *m;* mérito, *m, a* (que) vale; de precio de; cuyo valor es de; equivalente a; (que) merece; digno de. **He bought six hundred pesetas w. of sweets,** Compró seiscientas pesetas de dulces. **He sang for all he was w.,** Cantó con toda su alma. **It is w. seeing,** Es digno de verse, Vale la pena de verse. **to be w.,** valer. **to be w. while,** valer la pena, merecer la pena

**worthily** /'wɜrðili/ *adv* dignamente

**worthiness** /'wɜrðinɪs/ *n* mérito, valor, *m*

**worthless** /'wɜrθlɪs/ *a* sin valor; sin mérito; inútil; malo; (of persons) vil, despreciable, indigno

**worthlessness** /'wɜrθlɪsnɪs/ *n* falta de valor, *f;* falta de mérito, *f;* inutilidad, *f;* (of persons) bajeze, vileza, *f*

**worthy** /'wɜrði/ *a* digno de respeto, benemérito, respetable; digno, merecedor; meritorio. —*n* varón ilustre, hombre célebre, *m;* héroe, *m;* (*Inf. Ironic.*) tío, *m.* **to be w. of,** ser digno de, merecer

**would** /wʊd/ *unstressed* wəd/ *preterite and subjunctive of* **will.** (indicating a conditional tense) **They w. come if...,** Vendrían si...; (indicating an imperfect tense) **Often he w. sing,** Muchas veces cantaba, **Now and then a blackbird w. whistle,** De vez en cuando silbó un mirlo; (expressing wish, desire) **What w. they?** ¿Qué quieren? **The place where I w. be,** El lugar donde quisiera estar. **W. I were at home!** ¡Ojalá que estuviese en casa! **I thought that I w. tell you,** Se me ocurrió la idea de decírselo. **It w. seem that...,** Parece ser que..., Según parece...; Se diría que... **He said that he w. never have done it,** Dijo que no lo hubiera hecho nunca. **They w. have been killed if he had not rescued them,** Habrían sido matados si él no los hubiese salvado. **He w. go,** Se empeñó en ir. **He w. not do it,** Rehusó hacerlo, Se resistió a hacerlo; No quiso hacerlo. **This w. probably be the house,** Sin duda esta sería la casa. **W. you be good enough to...,** Tenga Vd. la bondad de..., Haga el favor de...

**would-be** /'wʊdbi/ *a* supuesto; llamado; aspirante (a); en esperanza de (followed by infin.); (frustrated) frustrado, malogrado

**wound** /wund/ *n* herida, *f.* —*vt* herir; (the feelings) lastimar, lacerar. **deep w.,** herida penetrante, *f.* **the wounded,** los heridos

**wounding** /'wundɪŋ/ *n* herida, *f, a Fig.* lastimador

**wraith** /reiθ/ *n* fantasma, espectro, *m,* sombra, *f*

**wrangle** /'ræŋgəl/ *vi* discutir; altercar, disputar acaloradamente; reñir; (bargain) regatear. —*n* argumento, *m;* disputa, *f,* altercado, *m;* riña, *f*

**wrangler** /'ræŋglər/ *n* disputador (-ra); (Cambridge University) laureado en matemáticas, *m*

**wrangling** /'ræŋglɪŋ/ *n* disputas, *f pl,* altercación, *f;* (bargaining) regateo, *m*

**wrap** /ræp/ *vt* envolver; arrollar; cubrir; abrigar; (conceal) ocultar. —*n* envoltorio, *m;* abrigo, *m;* *pl* **wraps,** abrigos y mantas de viaje, *m pl.* **W. yourself up well!** ¡Abrígate bien! **to be wrapped up in,** estar envuelto en; *Fig.* estar entregado a, estar absorto en; (a person) estar embelesado con

**wrapper** /'ræpər/ *n* envoltura, *f;* embalaje, *m;* (of a newspaper) faja, *f;* (of a book) sobrecubierta, *f;* (dressing-gown) bata, *f,* salto de cama, *m*

**wrapping** /'ræpɪŋ/ *n* envoltura, cubierta, *f.* **w.-paper,** papel de envolver, *m*

**wrath** /ræθ/ *n* ira, *f*

**wrathful** /'ræθfəl/ *a* airado

**wreak** /rik/ *vt* ejecutar; (anger, etc.) descargar. **to w. one's vengeance,** vengarse

**wreath** /riθ/ *n* guirnalda, *f;* corona, *f;* trenza, *f.* **funeral w.,** corona funeraria, *f*

**wreathe** /rið/ *vt* trenzar; (entwine) entrelazar (de); (garland) coronar (de), enguirnaldar (con); (encircle) ceñir, rodear; (a face in smiles) iluminar

**wreck** /rɛk/ *n* naufragio, *m;* buque naufragado, *m;* destrucción, *f; Fig.* ruina, *f;* (remains) restos, *m pl;* (person) sombra, *f.* —*vt* hacer naufragar; destruir; *Fig.* arruinar; hacer fracasar. **I am a complete w.,** *Inf.* Estoy hecho una ruina. **to be wrecked,** irse a pique, naufragar; *Fig.* arruinarse; frustrarse

**wreckage** /'rɛkɪdʒ/ *n* naufragio, *m;* restos de naufragio, *m pl;* ruinas, *f pl;* (of a car, plane, etc.) restos, *m pl;* accidente, *m*

**wrecked** /rɛkt/ *a* naufragado

**wrecker** /'rɛkər/ *n* destructor (-ra); (of ships) raquero, *m*

**wren** /rɛn/ *n* reyezuelo, *m*

**wrench** /rɛntʃ/ *n* (jerk) arranque, *m;* (pull) tirón, *m;* (sprain) torcedura, *f;* (tool) llave, *f;* (pain) dolor, *m.* —*vt* arrancar; forzar; torcer, dislocar. **He has wrenched his arm,** Se ha torcido el brazo

**wrest** /rɛst/ *vt* arrebatar, arrancar

**wrestle** /'rɛsəl/ *vi* luchar. —*n* lucha grecorromana, *f; Fig.* lucha, *f.* **to w. with,** *Fig.* luchar con; luchar contra

**wrestler** /'rɛslər/ *n* luchador, *m*

**wrestling** /'rɛslɪŋ/ *n* lucha grecorromana, *f.* **all-in-w.,** lucha libre, *f.* **w.-match,** lucha, *f*

**wretch** /rɛtʃ/ *n* infeliz, *mf;* (ruffian) infame, *m;* (playful) picaruelo (-la). **a poor w.,** un pobre diablo

**wretched** /'rɛtʃɪd/ *a* (unhappy) infeliz, desdichado; miserable; pobre; (ill) enfermo; horrible; malo; mezquino; despreciable; lamentable

**wretchedly** /'rɛtʃɪdli/ *adv* tristemente; pobremente; muy mal; ruinmente

**wretchedness** /'rɛtʃɪdnɪs/ *n* infelicidad, desdicha, *f;* miseria, pobreza, *f;* escualidez, *f;* ruindad, *f*

**wriggle** /'rɪgəl/ *vi* agitarse, moverse; menearse; serpear, culebrear; retorcerse. —*n* See under **wriggling. to w. into,** insinuarse en, deslizarse dentro (de). **to w. out,** escaparse. **to w. out of a difficulty,** extricarse de una dificultad

**wriggling** /'rɪglɪŋ/ *n* meneo, *m;* retorcimiento, *m;* serpenteo, culebreo, *m*

**wring** /rɪŋ/ *vt* torcer; estrujar; exprimir; arrancar; (force) forzar. **to w. one's hands,** restregarse las manos. **to w. the neck of,** torcer el pescuezo (a). **to w. out,** exprimir; estrujar

**wringer** /'rɪŋər/ *n* torcedor (-ra); (for clothes) exprimidor de ropa, *m*

**wringing** /'rɪŋɪŋ/ *n* torsión, *f.* **w.-machine,** exprimidor de ropa, *m*

**wrinkle** /'rɪŋkəl/ *n* arruga, *f;* pliegue, *m; Inf.* noción, *f.* —*vt* arrugar. —*vi* arrugarse. **to w. one's brow,** (frown) fruncir el ceño; (in perplexity) arrugar la frente

**wrinkling** /'rɪŋklɪŋ/ *n* arrugamiento, *m*

**wrinkly** /'rɪŋkli/ *a* arrugado

**wrist** /rɪst/ *n* muñeca, *f.* **w.-band,** tira del puño de la camisa, *f.* **w. bandage,** pulsera, *f*

**wristlet** /'rɪstlɪt/ *n* pulsera, *f;* manguito elástico, *m.* **w. watch,** reloj de pulsera, *m*

**writ** /rɪt/ *n* escritura, *f; Law.* decreto judicial, mandamiento, *m;* orden, *f;* título ejecutorio, *m;* hábeas corpus, *m.* **Holy W.,** la Sagrada Escritura. **to issue a w.,** dar orden. **to serve a w.,** notificar una orden. **w. of privilege,** auto de excarcelación, *m*

**write** /rait/ *vt and vi* escribir; *Fig.* mostrar. **He writes a good hand,** Tiene buena letra. **I shall w. to them for a list,** Les escribiré pidiendo una lista. **to w. back,** contestar por escrito; contestar a una carta. **to w. down,** poner por escrito; anotar, apuntar; describir. **to w. for,** escribir para; escribir para pedir algo; escribir algo en vez de otra persona. **to w. off,** escribir; escribir rápidamente; cancelar. **to w. on,** seguir escribiendo; escribir sobre. **to w. out,** copiar; redactar. **to w. over again,** escribir de nuevo, escribir otra vez, volver a escribir. **to w. up,** redactar; *Com.* poner al día; (praise) escribir alabando

**writer** /'raitər/ *n* escritor (-ra); autor (-ra). **the present w.,** el que, *m,* (*f,* la que) esto escribe. **writer's cramp,** calambre del escribiente, *m*

**writhe** /raið/ *vi* retorcerse

**writhing** /'raiðɪŋ/ *n* retorsión, *f*

**writing** /'raitɪŋ/ *n* escritura, *f;* (work) escrito, *m;* inscripción, *f;* documento, *m;* (style) estilo, *m;* (hand) letra, *f;* el arte de escribir; trabajo literario, *m.* **in one's own w.,** de su propia letra. **in w.,** por escrito. **w.-case,** escribanía, *f.* **w.-desk,** escritorio, *m.* **w.-pad,** taco de papel, *m.* **w.-paper,** papel de escribir, *m.* **w.-table,** mesa de escribir, *f*

**written** /'rɪtn/ *a* escrito

**wrong** /rɒŋ/ *a* injusto; mal; equivocado, erróneo; inexacto; falso; incorrecto; desacertado; inoportuno. **It is the w. one,** No es el que hacía falta; No es el que quería. **to be in the w. place,** estar mal situado; estar mal colocado. **to be w.,** estar mal; no tener razón; (mistaken) estar equivocado; (of deeds or things) estar mal hecho; (be unjust) ser injusto; (of clocks) andar mal. **to do w.,** hacer mal; obrar mal. **to get out of bed on the w. side,** levantarse del izquierdo. **to go w.,** (of persons) descarriarse; (of affairs) ir mal; salir mal; frustrarse; (of apparatus) estropearse, no funcionar. **We have taken the w. road,** Nos hemos equivocado de camino. **You were very w. to...,** Has hecho muy mal en... **w.-headed,** terco, obstinado; disparatado. **w.-headedness,** terquedad, obstinación, *f.* **w. number,** (telephone) número errado, *m.* **w. side,** revés, *m;* lado malo, *m.* **w. side out,** al envés; al revés

**wrong** /rɒŋ/ *adv* mal; injustamente; sin razón; incorrectamente; equivocadamente; (inside out) al revés. **to get it w.,** (a sum) calcular mal; (misunderstand) comprender mal

**wrong** /rɒŋ/ *n* mal, *m;* injusticia, *f;* perjuicio, *m;* ofensa, *f,* agravio, *m;* culpa, *f;* error, *m.* **to be in the w.,** no tener razon; haber hecho mal. **to put one in the w.,** echar la culpa (a), hacer responsable mal

**wrong** /rɒŋ/ *vt* hacer mal (a); perjudicar; ser injusto con; ofender

**wrongdoer** /'rɒŋ,duər/ *n* malhechor (-ra); pecador (-ra); perverso (-sa)

**wrongdoing** /'rɒŋ,duɪŋ/ *n* maldad, maleficencia, *f;* pecado, *m;* injusticia, *f*

**wrongful** /'rɒŋfəl/ *a* injusto; perjudicial; falso

**wrongfully** /'rɒŋfəli/ *adv* injustamente; falsamente

**wrongly** /'rɒŋli/ *adv* injustamente; erróneamente, equivocadamente; perversamente; mal

**wrongness** /'rɒŋnɪs/ *n* mal, *m;* injusticia, *f;* falsedad, *f;* inexactitud, *f,* error, *m*

**wrought** /rɔt/ *a* forjado; labrado; (hammered) batido; trabajado. **w. iron,** hierro dulce, hierro forjado, *m.* **w. up,** muy excitado, muy agitado, muy nervioso

**wry** /rai/ *a* torcido; tuerto; triste; pesimista; desilusionado; irónico. **wry face,** mueca *f,* de desengaño, de ironía, de disgusto, etc. **make a wry face,** torcer el gesto. **wry neck,** *Ornith.* torcecuello, *m*

**wryly** /'raili/ *adv* tristemente; irónicamente

**Wuthering Heights** /'wʌðərɪŋ/ Cumbres borrascosas

**wye** /wai/ *n* (letter) ye, i griega, *f;* horquilla, cosa en forma de Y, *f*

# XYZ

x /ɛks/ n equis, f
x-ray /'ɛks,rei/ vt tomar una radiografía (de). **x-ray,** rayo x, m pl. **x-ray examination,** examen con rayos x, m. **x-ray photograph,** radiografía, f
xylophone /'zailə,foun/ n xilófono, m
y /wai/ n (letter) i griega, ye, f
yacht /yɒt/ n yate, m. **y. club,** club marítimo, m. **y. race,** regata de yates, f
yachting /'yɒtɪŋ/ n navegación en yate, f, paseo en yate, m
yachtsman /'yɒtsmən/ n deportista náutico, balandrista, balandrismo, m
yank /yæŋk/ n tirón, m, sacudida, f. —vt dar un tirón (a); sacar de un tirón
Yankee /'yæŋki/ a and n yanqui, mf
yap /yæp/ vi ladrar. —n ladrido, m
yapper /'yæpər/ n (yapping dog) gozque, gozquejo, m
yapping /'yæpɪŋ/ n ladridos, m pl, a que ladra
yard /yɑrd/ n (measure) yarda, f; Naut. verga, f; corral, m; (courtyard) patio, m. —vt acorralar. **goods y.,** estación de mercancías, f. **y.-arm,** penol (de la verga), m. **y.-stick,** vara de medir de una yarda, f
yarn /yɑrn/ n hilaza, f; hilo, m; (story) historia, f, cuento, m. **to spin a y.,** contar una historia
yaw /yɔ/ vi Naut. guiñar; Aer. serpentear. —n Naut. guiñada, f; Aer. serpenteo, m
yawl /yɔl/ n yola, f; bote, m
yawn /yɔn/ vi bostezar; quedarse con la boca abierta; (of chasms, etc.) abrirse. —n bostezo, m. **to stifle a y.,** ahogar un bostezo
yawning /'yɔnɪŋ/ a abierto. —n bostezos, m pl
ye /ði/ spelling pron. yi/ pers pron vos, vosotros
yea /yei/ adv en verdad, ciertamente; y aun... no sólo... sino. —n si, m
year /yiər/ n año, m; pl **years,** años, m pl, edad, f. **We are getting on in years,** Nos vamos haciendo viejos. **He is five years old,** Tiene cinco años. **all the y. round,** todo el año, el año entero. **by the y.,** al año. **every other y.,** cada dos años, un año sí y otro no. **in after years,** en años posteriores. **last y.,** el año pasado. **next y.,** el año próximo. el año que viene. **y. after y.,** año tras año. **New Y.,** Año Nuevo, m. **to see the New Y. in,** ver empezar el Año Nuevo. **New Year's Day,** día de Año Nuevo, m. **(A) Happy New Y.!** ¡Feliz Año Nuevo! **y.-book,** anuario, m
yearling calf /'yiərlɪŋ/ n becerra f
yearly /'yiərli/ a anual. —adv anualmente, cada año; una vez al año
yearn /yɜrn/ vi anhelar, suspirar (por); desear vivamente
yearning /'yɜrnɪŋ/ n sed, ansia, f; anhelo, deseo vehemente, m. —a ansioso; anhelante; (tender) tierno
yeast /yist/ n levadura, f
yell /yɛl/ vi and vt chillar; gritar. —n chillido, m; grito, m
yelling /'yɛlɪŋ/ n chillidos, m pl; gritos, m pl, gritería, f
yellow /'yɛlou/ a amarillo; (of hair) rubio; (cowardly) cobarde; (newspaper) amarillista, sensacionalista. **to turn y.,** vi ponerse amarillo; amarillear. —vt volver amarillo. **y. fever,** fiebre amarilla, f. **y.-hammer,** Ornith. emberizo, m
yellowing /'yɛlouɪŋ/ n amarilleo, m
yellowish /'yɛlouɪʃ/ a amarillento
yellowness /'yɛlounɪs/ n amarillez, f
yellow pages n páginas amarillas, páginas doradas, f pl
yelp /yɛlp/ vi gañir. —n gañido, m
yelping /'yɛlpɪŋ/ n gañidos, m pl
yen /yɛn/ n (currency) yen, m; (desire) deseovivo, m
yeoman /'youmən/ n pequeño propietario rural, m; soldado de caballería, m. **Y. of the Guard,** alabardero de la Casa Real, m
yes /yɛs/ adv sí. **Yes?** ¿De verdad? ¿Y qué pasó después? ¿Y entonces? **to say yes,** decir que sí; dar el sí.
yes-man, amenista, sacristán de amén, m
yesterday /'yɛstər,dei/ adv ayer. —n ayer, m. **the day before y.,** anteayer
yet /yɛt/ adv aún, todavía. **as yet,** hasta ahora; todavía. **He has not come yet,** No ha venido todavía. **yet again,** otra vez
yet /yɛt/ conjunc sin embargo, no obstante, con todo; pero. **The book is well written and yet I do not like it,** El libro está bien escrito, y sin embargo no me gusta
yew /yu/ n tejo, m; madera de tejo, f
Yiddish /'yɪdɪʃ/ n yídis, yídish, yídico, m; a yídico
yield /yild/ vt producir; dar; (grant) otorgar; (afford) ofrecer; (surrender) ceder. —vi producir; (submit) rendirse, someterse; (of disease) responder; (give way) flaquear, doblegarse; dar de sí; (consent) consentir (en); (to circumstances, etc.) ceder (a), sucumbir (a). —n producción, f, producto, m; Com. rédito, m; (crop) cosecha, f. **to y. to temptation,** ceder a la tentación. **to y. up,** entregar; devolver
yielding /'yildɪŋ/ a flexible; (soft) blando; dócil, sumiso; fácil; condescendiente
yogurt /'yougərt/ n yogur, m
yoke /youk/ n yugo, m; (of oxen) yunta, f; (for pails) balancín, m; (of a garment) canesú, m; Fig. férula, f, yugo, m. —vt uncir, acoplar. **to throw off the y.,** sacudir el yugo
yokel /'youkəl/ n patán, rústico, m
yolk /youk/ n (of an egg) yema, f
yonder /'yɒndər/ a aquel, m; aquella, f; aquellos, m pl; aquellas, f pl. —adv allí; allí a lo lejos
yore /yɔr/ n **in days of y.,** antaño; en otro tiempo
you /yu; unstressed yʊ, yə/ pers pron nominative (polite form) usted (Vd.), mf; ustedes (Vds.), mf pl; (familiar form) sing tu, mf; (pl) vosotros, m pl; vosotras, f pl; (one) uno, m; una, f; se (followed by 3rd pers. sing. of verb). —pers pron acc (polite form) le, m; la, f; les, m pl; las, f pl; a usted, a ustedes; (informal form) te, mf, os, mf pl; (after most prepositions) ti, mf; vosotros, m pl; vosotras, f pl. **Are you there?** (telephone) ¡Oiga! **I gave the parcel to you,** Te (os) di el paquete; Di el paquete a usted (a ustedes). **I shall wait for you in the garden,** Te (os) esperaré en el jardín; Esperaré a Vds. (a Vd.) en el jardín. **This present is for you,** Este regalo es para tí (para vosotros, para Vd. (Vds.)). **Away with you!** ¡Vete! ¡Marchaos! **Between you and me,** Entre tú y yo. **you can't eat your cake and have it too,** no hay rosa sin espinas. **You never can tell,** No se sabe nunca, Uno no sabe nunca
young /yʌŋ/ a joven; nuevo, reciente; inexperto; poco avanzado. —n cría, f; hijuelos, m pl. **y. blood,** Inf. pollo pera, m. **y. girl,** jovencita, f. **y. man** joven, m. **y. people,** jóvenes, m pl. **in his y. days,** en su juventud. **The night is y.,** La noche está poca avanzada. **to grow y. again,** rejuvenecer. **with y.** (of animals) preñada f
younger /'yʌŋgər/ a más joven; menor. **Peter is his y. brother,** Pedro es su hermano menor. **to look y.,** parecer más joven
youngish /'yʌŋgɪʃ/ a bastante joven
youngster /'yʌŋstər/ n jovencito, chico, muchacho, m; niño, m
your /yʊr, yɔr; unstressed yər/ a poss (polite form) su (pl sus), de usted (Vd.), (pl de ustedes (Vds.)); (familiar form) tu (pl vuestro). **I have y. papers,** Tengo tus (vuestros) papeles; Tengo los papeles de Vd. (or de Vds.). **How is y. mother?** ¿Cómo está su (tu) madre? **It is y. turn,** Te toca a ti, Le toca a Vd.
yours /yʊrz, yɔrz/ pron poss (polite form) (el) suyo, m; (la) suya, f; (los) suyos, m pl; (las) suyas, f pl; el, m; la, f; lo, neut; los, m pl; las, f pl; de usted (Vd.), mf sing or de ustedes (Vds.), mf pl; (familiar form) (el) tuyo, m; (la) tuya, f; (los) tuyos, m pl; (las) tuyas, f pl; (el) vuestro, m; (la) vuestra, f; (los) vuestros, m pl; (las) vuestras, f pl. **This is a picture of y.,**

(addressing one person), Este es uno de los cuadros de usted (Vd.), Este es uno de tus cuadros. **This hat is mine, it is not y.,** Este sombrero es el mío, no es el tuyo. **The horse is y.,** El caballo es tuyo (de Vd.). **Y. affectionately,** Un abrazo de tu amigo... **Y. faithfully,** Queda de Vd. su att. (atentísimo) s.s. (seguro servidor). **Y. sincerely,** Queda de Vd. su aff. (afectuoso)

**yourself** /yʊr'sɛlf, yɔr- yər-/ *pers pron* (familiar form *sing*) tú mismo, *m;* tú misma, *f;* (after a preposition) ti, *mf;* (polite form) usted (Vd.) mismo, *m;* usetd misma, *f;* *pl* **yourselves,** (familiar form) vosotros mismos, *m pl;* vosotras mismas, *f pl;* (polite form) ustedes (Vds.) mismos, *m pl;* ustedes mismas, *f pl.* **This is for y.,** Esto es para ti; Esto es para Vd.

**youth** /yuθ/ *n* juventud, *f;* (man) joven, chico, mozalbete, *m;* (collectively) jóvenes, *m pl,* juventud, *f*

**youthful** /'yuθfəl/ *a* joven, juvenil; de la juventud

**yowl** /yaul/ *n* gañido, aullido, *m.* —*vi* gañir, aullar

**Yucatan** /,yukə'tæn/ *a* yucateco

**yucca** /'yʌkə/ *n Bot.* yuca, *f*

**Yugoslav** /'yugou,slɑv/ *n* yugoeslavo (-va). —*a* yugoeslavo

**Yugoslavia** /,yugou'slaviə/ Yugoslavia, *f*

**Yukon, the** /'yukɒn/ el Yukón, *m*

**Yule** /yul/ *n* Navidad, *f.* **y.-log,** leño de Navidad, *m.* **y-tide,** Navidades, *f pl*

**z** /zi/ *n* (letter) zeda, zeta, *f*

**zeal** /zil/ *n* celo, entusiasmo, *m;* ardor, fervor, *m*

**zealot** /'zɛlət/ *n* fanático (-ca)

**zealous** /'zɛləs/ *a* celoso, entusiasta

**zealously** /'zɛləsli/ *adv* con entusiasmo

**zebra** /'zibrə/ *n* cebra, *f*

**zenith** /'zinιθ/ *n* cenit, *m; Fig.* apogeo, punto culminante, *m*

**zephyr** /'zɛfər/ *n* céfiro, *m,* brisa, *f*

**zero** /'zιɑrou/ *n* cero, *m.* **below z.,** bajo cero. **z. hour,** hora cero, *f*

**zest** /zɛst/ *n* sabor, gusto, *m;* entusiasmo, *m.* **to eat with z.,** comer con buen apetito. **to enter on with z.,** emprender con entusiasmo

**zigzag** /'zιg,zæg/ *n* zigzag, *m.* —*a* and *adv* en zigzag. —*vi* zigzaguear, hacer zigzags, serpentear; (of persons) andar haciendo eses

**Zimbabwe** /zιm'bɑbwei/ Zimbabue

**zinc** /zιηk/ *n* cinc, *m.* **z. oxide,** óxido de cinc, *m*

**Zion** /'zaiən/ *n* Sión, *m*

**Zionism** /'zaiə,nιzəm/ *n* sionismo, *m*

**Zionist** /'zaiənιst/ *n* and *a* sionista

**zip** /zιp/ *n* (of a bullet) silbido, *m; Inf.* energía, *f.* **zip fastener,** cierre de cremallera, *m*

**zip code** *n* código postal, *m*

**zipper** /'zιpər/ *n* cremallera, *f,* cierre relámpago, cierre, cerrador, *m*

**zircon** /'zɜrkɒn/ *n* circón, *m*

**zither** /'zιθər/ *n* cítara, *f*

**zodiac** /'zoudi,æk/ *n* zodiaco, *m*

**zone** /zoun/ *n* zona, *f;* faja, *f*

**zoo** /zu/ *n* jardín zoológico, *m*

**zoological** /,zouə'lɒdʒιkəl/ *a* zoológico. **Z. garden,** jardín zoológico, *m*

**zoologist** /zou'ɒlədʒιst/ *n* zoólogo, *m*

**zoology** /zou'ɒlədʒi/ *n* zoología, *f*

**zoom** /zum/ *n* zumbido, *m.* —*vi* zumbar; *Aer.* empinarse

**Zulu** /'zulu/ *a* and *n* zulú *mf*

**Zuyder Zee, the** /'zaidər 'zei, 'zi/ el Zuyderzée, *m*

# Spanish Irregular Verbs

| Infinitive | Present | Future | Preterit | Past Part. |
|---|---|---|---|---|
| andar | ando | andaré | anduve | andado |
| caber | quepo | cabré | cupe | cabido |
| caer | caigo | caeré | caí | caído |
| conducir | conduzco | conduciré | conduje | conducido |
| dar | doy | daré | di | dado |
| decir | digo | diré | dije | dicho |
| estar | estoy | estaré | estuve | estado |
| haber | he | habré | hube | habido |
| hacer | hago | haré | hice | hecho |
| ir | voy | iré | fui | ido |
| jugar | juego | jugaré | jugué | jugado |
| morir | muero | moriré | morí | muerto |
| oir | oigo | oiré | oí | oído |
| poder | puedo | podré | pude | podido |
| poner | pongo | pondré | puse | puesto |
| querer | quiero | querré | quise | querido |
| saber | sé | sabré | supe | sabido |
| salir | salgo | saldré | salí | salido |
| ser | soy | seré | fui | sido |
| tener | tengo | tendré | tuve | tenido |
| traer | traigo | traeré | traje | traído |
| valer | valgo | valdré | valí | valido |
| venir | vengo | vendré | vine | venido |
| ver | veo | veré | vi | visto |

# Las formas del verbo inglés

**1.** Se forma la 3ª persona singular del tiempo presente exactamente al igual que el plural de los sustantivos, añadiendo **-es** o **-s** a la forma sencilla según las mismas reglas, así:

| (1) | teach | pass | wish | fix | buzz | | |
|---|---|---|---|---|---|---|---|
| | teaches | passes | wishes | fixes | buzzes | | |

| (2) | place | change | judge | please | freeze | | |
|---|---|---|---|---|---|---|---|
| | places | changes | judges | pleases | freezes | | |

| (3a) | find | sell | clean | hear | love | buy | know |
|---|---|---|---|---|---|---|---|
| | finds | sells | cleans | hears | loves | buys | knows |

| (3b) | think | like | laugh | stop | hope | meet | want |
|---|---|---|---|---|---|---|---|
| | thinks | likes | laughs | stops | hopes | meets | wants |

| (4) | cry | try | dry | carry | deny | | |
|---|---|---|---|---|---|---|---|
| | cries | tries | dries | carries | denies | | |

Cinco verbos muy comunes tienen 3ª persona singular irregular:

| (5) | go | do | say | have | be |
|---|---|---|---|---|---|
| | goes | does | says | has | is |

**2.** Se forman el tiempo pasado y el participio de modo igual, añadiendo a la forma sencilla la terminación **-ed** o **-d** según las reglas que siguen:

(1)  Si la forma sencilla termina en **-d** o **-t,** se le pone **-ed** como sílaba aparte:

| end | fold | need | load | want | feast | wait | light |
|-----|------|------|------|------|-------|------|-------|
| ended | folded | needed | loaded | wanted | feasted | waited | lighted |

(2)  Si la forma sencilla termina en cualquier otra consonante, se añade también **-ed** pero sin hacer sílaba aparte:

(2a)

| bang | sail | seem | harm | earn | weigh |
|------|------|------|------|------|-------|
| banged | sailed | seemed | harmed | earned | weighed |

(2b)

| lunch | work | look | laugh | help | pass |
|-------|------|------|-------|------|------|
| lunched | worked | looked | laughed | helped | passed |

(3)  Si la forma sencilla termina en **-e,** se le pone sólo **-d:**

(3a)

| hate | taste | waste | guide | fade | trade |
|------|-------|-------|-------|------|-------|
| hated | tasted | wasted | guided | faded | traded |

(3b)

| free | judge | rule | name | dine | scare |
|------|-------|------|------|------|-------|
| freed | judged | ruled | named | dined | scared |

(3c)

| place | force | knife | like | hope | base |
|-------|-------|-------|------|------|------|
| placed | forced | knifed | liked | hoped | based |

(4)  Una **-y** final que sigue a cualquier consonante se cambia en **-ie** al añadir la **-d** del pasado/participio:

| cry | try | dry | carry | deny |
|-----|-----|-----|-------|------|
| cried | tried | dried | carried | denied |

**3.** Varios verbos muy comunes forman el tiempo pasado y el participio de manera irregular. Pertenecen a tres grupos.

(1) Los que tienen una sola forma irregular para tiempo pasado y participio, como los siguientes:

| bend | bleed | bring | build | buy | catch | creep | deal |
|------|-------|-------|-------|-----|-------|-------|------|
| bent | bled | brought | built | bought | caught | crept | dealt |

| dig | feed | feel | fight | find | flee | get | hang |
|-----|------|------|-------|------|------|-----|------|
| dug | fed | felt | fought | found | fled | got | hung |

| have | hear | hold | keep | lead | leave | lend | lose |
|------|------|------|------|------|-------|------|------|
| had | heard | held | kept | led | left | lent | lost |

| make | mean | meet | say | seek | sell | send | shine |
|------|------|------|-----|------|------|------|-------|
| made | meant | met | said | sought | sold | sent | shone |

| shoot | sit | sleep | spend | stand | strike | sweep | teach |
|-------|-----|-------|-------|-------|--------|-------|-------|
| shot | sat | slept | spent | stood | struck | swept | taught |

690

(2) Los que tienen una forma irregular para el tiempo pasado y otra forma irregular para el participio, como los siguientes:

| be | beat | become | begin | bite |
|------|--------|---------|--------|--------|
| was | beat | became | began | bit |
| been | beaten | become | begun | bitten |

| blow | break | choose | come | do |
|-------|--------|---------|-------|------|
| blew | broke | chose | came | did |
| blown | broken | chosen | come | done |

| draw | drink | drive | eat | fall |
|-------|--------|--------|-------|--------|
| drew | drank | drove | ate | fell |
| drawn | drunk | driven | eaten | fallen |

| fly | forget | freeze | give | go |
|-------|-----------|---------|-------|-------|
| flew | forgot | froze | gave | went |
| flown | forgotten | frozen | given | gone |

| grow | hide | know | ride | ring |
|-------|--------|--------|-------|-------|
| grew | hid | knew | rode | rang |
| grown | hidden | known | ridden | rung |

| rise | run | see | shake | shrink |
|-------|------|------|--------|---------|
| rose | ran | saw | shook | shrank |
| risen | run | seen | shaken | shrunk |

| sing | sink | speak | steal | swear |
|-------|-------|--------|--------|--------|
| sang | sank | spoke | stole | swore |
| sung | sunk | spoken | stolen | sworn |

| swim | tear | throw | wear | write |
|-------|-------|---------|-------|---------|
| swam | tore | threw | wore | wrote |
| swum | torn | thrown | worn | written |

(3) Los que no varían del todo, la forma sencilla funcionando también como pasado/participio; entre éstos son de mayor frecuencia:

| bet | burst | cast | cost | cut |
|-------|-------|--------|--------|-------|
| hit | hurt | let | put | quit |
| read | set | shed | shut | slit |
| spit | split | spread | thrust | wet |

691

# Numbers/Números

## Cardinal/Cardinales

| | | |
|---|---|---|
| one | 1 | uno, una |
| two | 2 | dos |
| three | 3 | tres |
| four | 4 | cuatro |
| five | 5 | cinco |
| six | 6 | seis |
| seven | 7 | siete |
| eight | 8 | ocho |
| nine | 9 | nueve |
| ten | 10 | diez |
| eleven | 11 | once |
| twelve | 12 | doce |
| thirteen | 13 | trece |
| fourteen | 14 | catorce |
| fifteen | 15 | quince |
| sixteen | 16 | dieciséis |
| seventeen | 17 | diecisiete |
| eighteen | 18 | dieciocho |
| nineteen | 19 | diecinueve |
| twenty | 20 | veinte |
| twenty-one | 21 | veinte y uno (or veintiuno) |
| twenty-two | 22 | veinte y dos (or veintidós) |
| thirty | 30 | treinta |
| thirty-one | 31 | treinta y uno |
| thirty-two | 32 | treinta y dos |
| forty | 40 | cuarenta |
| fifty | 50 | cincuenta |
| sixty | 60 | sesenta |
| seventy | 70 | setenta |
| eighty | 80 | ochenta |
| ninety | 90 | noventa |

| | | |
|---|---|---|
| one hundred | 100 | cien |
| one hundred one | 101 | ciento uno |
| one hundred two | 102 | ciento dos |
| two hundred | 200 | doscientos, -as |
| three hundred | 300 | trescientos, -as |
| four hundred | 400 | cuatrocientos, -as |
| five hundred | 500 | quinientos, -as |
| six hundred | 600 | seiscientos, -as |
| seven hundred | 700 | setecientos, -as |
| eight hundred | 800 | ochocientos, -as |
| nine hundred | 900 | novecientos, -as |
| one thousand | 1,000 | mil |
| two thousand | 2,000 | dos mil |
| one hundred thousand | 100,000 | cien mil |
| one million | 1,000,000 | un millón |
| two million | 2,000,000 | dos millones |

## Ordinal/Ordinales

| | | |
|---|---|---|
| first | 1st / 1° | primero |
| second | 2nd / 2° | segundo |
| third | 3rd / 3° | tercero |
| fourth | 4th / 4° | cuarto |
| fifth | 5th / 5° | quinto |
| sixth | 6th / 6° | sexto |
| seventh | 7th / 7° | séptimo |
| eighth | 8th / 8° | octavo |
| ninth | 9th / 9° | noveno |
| tenth | 10th / 10° | décimo |

# Days of the Week/Días de la Semana

| | | | |
|---|---|---|---|
| Sunday | domingo | Thursday | jueves |
| Monday | lunes | Friday | viernes |
| Tuesday | martes | Saturday | sábado |
| Wednesday | miércoles | | |

# Months/Meses

| | | | |
|---|---|---|---|
| January | enero | July | julio |
| February | febrero | August | agosto |
| March | marzo | September | septiembre |
| April | abril | October | octubre |
| May | mayo | November | noviembre |
| June | junio | December | diciembre |

# Weights and Measures/Pesos y Medidas

| | | | | | | |
|---|---|---|---|---|---|---|
| 1 centímetro | = | .3937 inches | 1 kilolitro | = | 264.18 gallons |
| 1 metro | = | 39.37 inches | 1 inch | = | 2.54 centímetros |
| 1 kilómetro | = | .621 mile | 1 foot | = | .305 metros |
| 1 centigramo | = | .1543 grain | 1 mile | = | 1.61 kilómetros |
| 1 gramo | = | 15.432 grains | 1 grain | = | .065 gramos |
| 1 kilogramo | = | 2.2046 pounds | 1 pound | = | .455 kilogramos |
| 1 tonelada | = | 2.204 pounds | 1 ton | = | .907 toneladas |
| 1 centilitro | = | .338 ounces | 1 ounce | = | 2.96 centilitros |
| 1 litro | = | 1.0567 quart (liquid); | 1 quart | = | 1.13 litros |
| | | .908 quart (dry) | 1 gallon | = | 4.52 litros |

# Signs/Señales

| Caution | Precaución | No smoking | Prohibido fumar |
|---|---|---|---|
| Danger | Peligro | No admittance | Entrada prohibida |
| Exit | Salida | One way | Dirección única |
| Entrance | Entrada | No entry | Dirección prohibida |
| Stop | Alto | Women | Señoras, Mujeres, Damas |
| Closed | Cerrado | Men | Señores, Hombres, Caballeros |
| Open | Abierto | Ladies' Room | El cuarto de damas |
| Slow | Despacio | Men's Room | El servicio |

# Useful Phrases/Locuciones Útiles

**Good day, Good morning.** Buenos días.
**Good afternoon.** Buenas tardes.
**Good night, Good evening.** Buenas noches.
**Hello.** ¡Hola!
**Welcome!** ¡Bienvenido!
**See you later.** Hasta luego.
**Goodbye.** ¡Adiós!
**How are you?** ¿Cómo está usted?
**I'm fine, thank you.** Estoy bien, gracias.
**I'm pleased to meet you.** Mucho gusto en conocerle.
**May I introduce** . . . Quisiera presentar . . .
**Thank you very much.** Muchas gracias.
**You're welcome.** De nada *or* No hay de qué.
**Please.** Por favor.
**Excuse me.** Con permiso.
**Good luck.** ¡Buena suerte!
**To your health.** ¡Salud!

**Please help me.** Ayúdeme, por favor.
**I don't know.** No sé.

**I don't understand.** No entiendo.
**Do you understand?** ¿Entiende usted?
**I don't speak Spanish.** No hablo español.
**Do you speak English?** ¿Habla usted inglés?
**How do you say . . . in Spanish?** ¿Cómo se dice . . . en español?
**What do you call this?** ¿Cómo se llama esto?
**Speak slowly, please.** Hable despacio, por favor.
**Please repeat.** Repita, por favor.
**I don't like it.** No me gusta.
**I am lost.** Ando perdido; Me he extraviado.

**What is your name?** ¿Cómo se llama usted?
**My name is** . . . Me llamo . . .
**I am an American.** Soy norteamericano.
**Where are you from?** ¿De dónde es usted?
**I'm from** . . . Soy de . . .

**How is the weather?** ¿Qué tiempo hace?

**It's cold (hot) today.** Hace frío (calor) hoy.

**What time is it?** ¿Qué hora es?

**How much is it?** ¿Cuánto es?

**It is too much.** Es demasiado.

**What do you wish?** ¿Qué desea usted?

**I want to buy** . . . Quiero comprar . . .

**May I see something better?** ¿Podría ver algo mejor?

**May I see something cheaper?** ¿Podría ver algo menos caro?

**It is not exactly what I want.** No es exactamente lo que quiero.

**I'm hungry.** Tengo hambre.

**I'm thirsty.** Tengo sed.

**Where is there a restaurant?** ¿Dónde hay un restaurante?

**I have a reservation.** Tengo una reservación.

**I would like** . . . Quisiera . . .; Me gustaría . . .

**Please give me** . . . Por favor, déme usted . . .

**Please bring me** . . . Por favor, tráigame usted . . .

**May I see the menu?** ¿Podría ver el menú?

**The bill, please.** La cuenta, por favor.

**Is service included in the bill?** ¿El servicio está incluido en la cuenta?

**Where is there a hotel?** ¿Dónde hay un hotel?

**Where is the post office?** ¿Dónde está el correo?

**Is there any mail for me?** ¿Hay correo para mí?

**Where can I mail this letter?** ¿Dónde puedo echar esta carta al correo?

**Take me to** . . . Lléveme a . . .

**I believe I am ill.** Creo que estoy enfermo.

**Please call a doctor.** Por favor, llame al médico.

**Please call the police.** Por favor, llame a la policía.

**I want to send a telegram.** Quiero poner un telegrama.

**As soon as possible.** Cuanto antes.

**Round trip.** Ida y vuelta.

**Please help me with my luggage.** Por favor, ayúdeme con mi equipaje.

**Where can I get a taxi?** ¿Dónde se puede encontrar un taxi?

**What is the fare to** . . . ¿Cuánto es el pasaje hasta . . . ?

**Please take me to this address.** Por favor, lléveme a esta dirección.

**Where can I change my money?** ¿Dónde puedo cambiar mi dinero?

**Where is the nearest bank?** ¿Dónde está el banco más cercano?

**Can you accept my check?** ¿Puede aceptar usted mi cheque?

**Do you accept traveler's checks?** ¿Aceptan cheques de viaje?

**What is the postage?** ¿Cuánto es el franqueo?

**Where is the nearest drugstore?** ¿Dónde está la farmacia más cercana?

**Where is the men's (women's) room?** ¿Dónde está el servicio de caballeros (de señoras)?

**Please let me off at** . . . Por favor, déjeme bajar en . . .

**Right away.** ¡Pronto!

**Help.** ¡Socorro!

**Who is it?** ¿Quién es?

**Just a minute!** ¡Un momento no más!

**Come in.** ¡Pase usted!

**Pardon me.** Dispense usted.

**Stop.** ¡Pare!

**Look out.** ¡Cuidado!

**Hurry.** ¡De prisa! *or* ¡Dése prisa!

**Go on.** ¡Siga!

**To (on, at) the right.** A la derecha.

**To (on, at) the left.** A la izquierda.

**Straight ahead.** Adelante.